Fitzhenry & Whiteside

CANADIAN THESAURUS

Fitzhenry & Whiteside

Fitzhenry & Whiteside Canadian Thesaurus

Fitzhenry and Whiteside Limited
195 Allstate Parkway
Markham, Ontario L3R 4T8

www.fitzhenry.ca godwit@fitzhenry.ca

Fitzhenry & Whiteside acknowledges with thanks the Canada Council for the Arts, the Government of Canada through its Book Publishing Industry Development Program, and the Ontario Arts Council for their support of our publishing program.

10 9 8 7 6 5 4 3 2 1

Canadian Cataloguing in Publication Data

Main entry under title:
The Fitzhenry & Whiteside Canadian Thesaurus

ISBN 1-55041-189-6 (bound) 1-55041-198-5 (pbk.)

1. English language – synonyms and antonyms. I. Chambers, Jack K. 1938- II. Title: Fitzhenry & Whiteside Canadian Thesaurus

PE1591.F48 2001 423'.1 C00-931602-7

Printed in Canada.

Cover and book design: Darrell McCalla

Fitzhenry & Whiteside

CANADIAN THESAURUS

Editorial Director: Dr. J.K. Chambers,
Professor of Linguistics, University of Toronto

Compiled by Celia Munro

Editors:
Richard Dionne
Elizabeth Ballantyne
Evan Jones

With files from:
Andrew Burns
Paul Dutton
Dagmar King
Barbara Ann Kipfer
Penny Hozy
Marie Peters
Fraser Sutherland

We thank the following specialists for reviewing the Fitzhenry & Whiteside Canadian Thesaurus:

- **Gerald Soon**
  President of the British Columbia
  Teachers' Library Association
  Librarian, Burnsview Junior Secondary School
  Surrey, British Columbia

- **Dr. Robert Myles**
  Associate Director – English Programs
  English and French Language Centre
  McGill University
  Montreal, Quebec

- **Dr. Randall Martin**
  Professor of English
  University of New Brunswick
  Fredericton, New Brunswick

- **Jo-Anne Naslund**
  Education Librarian
  University of British Columbia
  Vancouver, British Columbia

- **George Greason**
  Program Consultant, History and Social Sciences
  Ontario Ministry of Education (retired)
  Toronto, Ontario

- **Michael Stubitsch**
  Coordinator of English
  Program Department
  Scarborough Board of Education
  Toronto, Ontario

This treasure house of words
is dedicated to
Robert I. Fitzhenry
and
Bob Read

Preface

Thesaurus as Treasure House

J.K. Chambers

People who use thesauruses are usually people who love words. They are "word-struck," as the Ottawa broadcaster Robert MacNeil described himself; their feelings are "word-shaped," as the Nova Scotia novelist Ernest Buckler described his young hero in *The Mountain and the Valley*.

Of course, the love of words is not required of a thesaurus-user. Thesauruses find their niche on the reference shelves for a very practical reason. People need synonyms. If you are writing a report on a conference, you can only say "say" so many times; you owe it to yourself, as much as to your readers, to put in the occasional "affirm," "declare," "report," "suggest," or one of the 96 other possibilities you can find below in the entry for **say**. If you are stuck in your crossword puzzle on a five-letter word for "élan" that has "om" as the second and third letters, check the entry for **élan**. (Go ahead. This thesaurus will help you where others may not.) If you are struggling to think of the word that means something like "profanity," but not exactly that, look up **profanity** and discover "blasphemy," "imprecation" and "obscenity" among the 18 or so shades and nuances of profanity.

Whenever the thesaurus comes to our aid in these mundane ways, we give a little sigh of relief, a nod of approval. Those are the uses that make it a marketable commodity. Those are the reasons that justify the space it takes on your bookshelf.

But there is another reason — a deeper reason — for giving this thesaurus a nod of approval. Grasp the book in your hand, heft it to shoulder height, and realize that this block of bound paper is a treasure house of all we know or think we know about the world.

Do you consider that fanciful? Oddly enough, that was exactly what the inventor of the thesaurus had in mind for it. The word *thesaurus* means "treasure house" in Greek, and that word was carefully chosen by Peter Mark Roget (1779-1869), the original thesaurist, so that his classically-trained readers would know about the world of wonders contained between its covers.

Roget began compiling lists of related words when he was a teenaged medical student at the University of Edinburgh. He saw his word-lists as a way of demonstrating the interconnections among scientific concepts. He added to his word-lists, as time allowed, throughout a long and distinguished career as physician, professor of physiology, inventor, author and encyclopedist. When he retired from medicine in 1840, he began organizing the synonyms in earnest. *Roget's Thesaurus of English Words and Phrases* was published in 1852 when its compiler was 73 years old. In his stately introduction, he said:

> The present Work is intended to supply, with respect to the English language, a desideratum hitherto unsupplied in any language; namely, a collection of the words it contains and of the idiomatic combinations peculiar to it, arranged, not in the alphabetical order as they are in a Dictionary, but according to the *idea*s which they express.

Roget's format was to organize words under six superordinate categories: Abstract Relations, Space, Matter, Intellect, Volition, and Morality. Each of these was then further subcategorized down to what were considered the most basic groupings. Roget's model, as for so many nineteenth-century intellectual achievements, was Linnaeus's botanical taxonomy. Instead of genus and species, Roget filled the nodes of his language-tree with words and idioms. Readers were expected to wend their way through the 1,000 or more categories until they found the set of synonyms they were seeking.

Roget's first thesaurus must have been devilishly hard to use, but nevertheless, it was an enormous success. By the time Roget died at 91 he had supervised 25 further editions and printings in about 22 years. He did, in later editions, make one small concession to the users of the book by adding a short alphabetical index as a guide to the categories. The editors who succeeded him, starting with his son John Lewis Roget, added more and more entries to the alphabetical index until finally it rivalled the main body of the text in length.

Modern editors realized that most users relied on the alphabetical index to find their way through the thesaurus. Today, Roget's thematic organization has pretty well disappeared in favour of alphabetic organization, as in *Fitzhenry & Whiteside's Canadian Thesaurus*. It is not hard to guess how Roget might feel about the elimination of his themes; tracing the connections among those grand ideas was the intellectual purpose of the book, as he saw it. And he probably would not be very happy to know that his greatest single achievement and the one to which his name is indelibly attached finds its greatest use among people trying to avoid repeating the same word in their reports, or hoping to solve recalcitrant crossword clues.

Roget, in spite of himself, gave us an invention of great practical value. Exactly as he hoped, it was "a desideratum hitherto unsupplied" by anyone before him. It has turned out to be one that we can hardly do without. The fact that it is now organized like a dictionary does not, of course, make it function like a dictionary. Thesauruses are, and always have been, inside-out dictionaries. With a dictionary, you know a word and look up its meaning. With a thesaurus, you know a meaning to look up a word.

Modern thesauruses like this one also contain a great deal more than

Roget could ever have imagined. In the entry for **cancer,** besides the synonyms that Roget knew (*blight, canker, tumour*), there is a host of words he could not know: *carcinoma, malignancy, sarcoma.* The entry for **computer,** of course, limns a whole category beyond Roget's imagining. Roget would be delighted by the expansion of his thesaurus to take in modern medicine and computers. He would probably be surprised to learn that in this modern thesaurus schoolchildren can look up **urine** and giggle at its synonyms, or find **nightclub** here in all its manifestations from *supper club* to *honky-tonk*, and **gay** with a meaning quite different from the two that Roget knew.

The thesaurus proved to be too useful to be merely the repository of intellectual concepts that Roget intended. The English language is vast, and Roget's invention helps those of us who are word-struck to find our way through it.

A few other modern languages approach the vastness of English, and they too have their thesauruses. A couple of ancient languages are also vast, and so Classical Greek and Latin have thesauruses too. With the ancient languages, the making of a thesaurus is a finite task: the makers can strive to put every known word into its appropriate categories. This is not so with living languages, where new words pop up daily. It is especially not so with English, which has shown an astounding propensity to expand its vocabulary from the very beginning of its recorded history.

English has expanded by absorbing vocabulary from other languages. The first written records of the English language already include borrowed words. Alongside the native vocabulary of the Angles and Saxons, the original English-speakers, were imported words that came from the Old Norse spoken by the marauders from across the North Sea. These are homely words such as the third-person pronouns *they-them*, *Thursday* (Thor's day), and such common words as *cake*, *egg*, *die*, *fog*, *knife*, *neck*, *scowl*, and *smile*, to name a few. When languages borrow words from other languages, the borrowed words often replace the old words so that there is no increase in the vocabulary. But sometimes the borrowed words coexist with the old words with specialized meanings, and then the vocabulary increases. That happened with the Norse borrowings in a few instances, so that nowadays we have the Norse word *disk* as well as the English word *dish*, and the Norse word *skirt* as well as English *shirt.* They can be traced back to the same roots, but in English they have developed different (but clearly-related) meanings.

At the same time as the Norsemen were raiding Great Britain from the east, Christian missionaries were arriving from Ireland in the west. Along with the new religion, the missionaries introduced the Latin names for previously unknown occupations (*abbot*, *disciple*, *nun*), places (*altar*, *school*) and occasions *(Mass, Sabbath).* So while the homely vocabulary expanded with Norse loanwords, the cultural vocabulary expanded with Latin loanwords.

A century or so later, the Normans conquered England and superimposed their dialect of Norman French on English society, or at least on its higher echelons. The long-term effects of the Norman conquest were mainly linguistic, because when the English language resurfaced as the official language, after more than a century and a half as a minority language, it was essentially re-formed. Most obviously — and most relevant for thesaurus-users — the English vocabulary had increased with hundreds of Norman words for government (*authority, council, decree, liberty, treasurer*), education (*geometry, grammar, logic, study*), medicine (*anatomy, physician, surgeon*), style (*cape, dress, satin, veil*), and every other cultural category. Sometimes the Norman word replaced the English one *(prince* for *atheling, marriage* for *troth)* but sometimes both were retained. To this day, whenever both the Norman word and the English word survive, the Norman one is always the more socially refined, as in *pork* compared to *pig*, *flesh* to *meat, petticoat* to *slip, amorous* to *loving, virtue* to *goodness.*

In the age of exploration inaugurated by Christopher Columbus, the islanders of England had a natural sea-faring advantage. They became colonists around the globe, and everywhere they settled they planted the English language. In keeping with the expansive spirit of the language, the colonists simply adopted the local words for any new objects, no matter how exotic the words sounded.

Something similar is happening today in our increasingly cosmopolitan communities. Instead of the English language spreading into places where other languages are spoken, the people who speak those other languages are spreading into English-speaking regions. The result is much the same: the English vocabulary continually absorbs new words.

As a result, the sources of our modern English vocabulary are truly astounding. Of course, we seldom give them a thought. We might recognize the Italian-ness of our musical terms (*aria, finale, opera, piano, prima donna*, and many others), but we are less conscious of the Dutch origins of painting terms such as *easel, landscape* and *sketch.* Canadians might be aware of the native American source of words like *caribou, chocolate, moccasin, potato, raccoon, skunk*, and *toboggan*, but we are less likely to recognize the Malay source of *amuck* (as in *run amuck*), *gingham, gong*, and *ketchup*, or the Polynesian source of *taboo* and *tattoo*, or the Hindi source of *jungle* and *shampoo.*

Our English vocabulary boasts denser connections than the most complex DNA molecule. Our native word *hunt* has been challenged by French loanwords not once but twice — first by *catch* from Norman and then by *chase* from standard French — and has survived, but so of course have its challengers, with different meanings. We can accuse someone of being *pusillanimous* or of being *narrow-minded*, and, although they mean exactly the same thing, the Latin-based word outclasses the Anglo-Saxon one, giving us a kind of luxurious insult. For meat grilled on a skewer we have no fewer than three words: *brochette* from French, *shishkebab* from Turkish and *souvlaki* from Greek. We can talk about *epiphanies* (from Classical Greek), *manifestations* (from Latin) or *showings* (from Old English). We may have *foes* or *enemies* or *adversaries* or *opponents* — a chain of words with roots in Old English, Old French, Biblical Latin and Classical Latin, respectively, though every link in the chain is English.

Such diversity is a wonderful thing. And it helps to have a guide to it, as Roget knew, not only, of course, for solving the clue in the crossword puzzle, important though that is, but also to see the assemblage of words in one place, to feel its diversity as Roget hoped we would, to wonder at its democracy. And here in the *Canadian Thesaurus* is our Canadian vocabulary where it belongs, with *concessions* and *sideroads* in the entry for **road** and *jambusters* with the rest of the **desserts** and *Sasquatches* and *wendigoes* among the **monsters**.

The *Fitzhenry & Whiteside Canadian Thesaurus* owes its existence to the vision and hard work of Robert I. Fitzhenry, who recently retired as president of the publishing company he co-founded. Bob Fitzhenry has been an estimable patron of Canadian English research for many years. In the 1970s, he took the initiative for producing a worthy Canadian general-purpose dictionary. First, he secured the rights to *Funk & Wagnalls College Dictionary*, a truly excellent American dictionary that was being discontinued in the United States, and then he recruited Walter S. Avis (1919-79), the senior lexicographer in the country, to Canadianize it. The first edition of *Funk & Wagnalls Canadian College Dictionary* was published in 1978, and it went through further Canadianizations in editions published in 1980, 1982, 1986 and 1989. It received good reviews and attracted a loyal crowd of users who swear by it to this day. Among all his other accomplishments as a publisher, Bob may be proudest of his dictionary.

I was flattered when Bob asked me to act as a consultant on the successive editions of the dictionary. I was prouder still to head Bob's advisory board in the 1980s when he decided to make a more aggressive effort at developing Canadian English reference materials. This *Thesaurus* is one result of that effort.

Sponsoring studies on Canadian English as Bob has done for so many years is a relatively self-effacing activity with modest dividends for a publisher. Neither his profile nor his profit margin makes Bob do it. It goes deeper than that. Bob Fitzhenry is word-struck, and always has been. His feelings are word-shaped. He published these books because he wants to read them. Those of us who are also word-struck are in his debt.

Introduction

A good thesaurus is designed to help you find the word you want, where and when you want it. People who put thesauruses together usually approach the matter by two different methods.

The first takes its cue from the Englishman, Peter Mark Roget (1779-1869), who developed a system of classifying words that, in one incarnation or another, is still widely used today. And because *Roget's* — like *Webster's* — is not in copyright, you will often see the name in thesaurus titles. Interestingly, Roget was a physician and scientist, not a linguist or lexicographer. His goal was to classify under headings and subheadings everything known about the universe and its contents. It is understandable, but ironic, that Roget's system, brilliant intellectual achievement that it was, evolved into a wordbook and not a worldbook. We look to Roget's classifications today not so much to understand the world as to find our way among words. His scheme has stood the test of time remarkably well, but it does have drawbacks, primarily a severe learning curve. Using a Roget's thesaurus requires frequent recourse to an index which, albeit comprehensive, is long, cumbersome and time-consuming. A typical index in a Roget's thesaurus occupies at least one-third of the total length of the thesaurus.

The alternative to numbering conceptual headings and subheadings in a thesaurus is to arrange keywords in alphabetical order. This type of arrangement, however, has its own drawbacks, primarily because it looks *barebones* in comparison to the richness and variety of the Roget's scheme. Alphabetically arranged thesauruses usually include only common and not proper nouns, and they tend to overemphasize general words and abstractions. You may find boldfaced keywords like **ability** or **vexation** with lots of synonyms placed below each, but you will be given only the barest pointers to what's implied by **boat** or **mammal**. Then, too, alphabetical thesauruses typically provide little insight into the contexts in which words are used.

No thesaurus is a substitute for a good dictionary and no thesaurus can be expected to provide pronunciations, syllabications, definitions, etymologies, and usage notes. But a good thesaurus — by displaying a wealth of synonyms — does what it does better than a dictionary.

This first, fully Canadian thesaurus built from scratch is formatted alphabetically because we believe such a layout is easier to use. Each entry contains a wide range of synonyms, many typically not found in other alphabetically arranged thesauruses.

We all know the English language contains few if any pure synonyms — words that may be readily substituted without any loss in meaning or connotation. Every word, particularly in context, usually suggests a marginal difference at least in meaning and emphasis.

The goal of this thesaurus is to give you as much scope as possible so you can make an informed word choice from several possibilities. The list of related words under each keyword recognizes the fact that people use a thesaurus for different reasons. Perhaps you may wish to find a word that means roughly the same thing as the one you look up.

happiness *n.* **1.** blessedness, bliss, buoyancy, cheeriness, contentment, delight, ecstasy, effervescence, elation, enchantment, enjoyment, euphoria, exhilaration, exuberance, gaiety, gladness, glee, good cheer *or* humour *or* spirits, hilarity, hopefulness, joy, jubilation, laughter, lightheartedness, mirth, paradise, pleasure, rejoicing, satisfaction, vivacity, well-being *Antonyms:* depression, distress, grief, misery, sorrow **2.** aptness, felicity, good fortune *or* luck, opportuneness, propitiousness, relevance

At other times, however, you may need a word that means the exact opposite. Our listings are designed to accomodate such a demand. This thesaurus provides a list of synonyms as well as, wherever feasible, a list of possible antonyms at the end of the entry.

The list of synonyms provided shows a wide semantic range. Note that sometimes we believe it is useful to distinguish clusters of words whose general import is markedly different, or clusters worth isolating for some other reason. Such clustered groups are numbered, with that group whose meaning is most commonly sought placed first.

walk *n.* **1.** constitutional, hike, jaunt, march, parade, perambulation, peregrination, portage, promenade, ramble, saunter, stroll, tour, traipse, tramp, walkabout *Nonformal:* sashay, schlep **2.** gait, pace, step, stride, tread **3.** aisle, alley, avenue, boardwalk, boulevard, bricks, by-path, byway, carrying place, catwalk, close, course, court, crossing, esplanade, footpath, footway, gangway, lane, mall, passage, path, pathway, pavement, pier, platform, Plus-15 *(Calgary)*, promenade, road, route, sidewalk, street, track, trail **3.** area, arena, bailiwick, course, domain, dominion, field, province, sphere, terrain, territory *Nonformal:* beat, turf **4.** calling, career, discipline, line, métier, profession, trade, vocation, walk of life – *v.* **1.** advance, amble, go, hike, jog, knock about, march, meander, mince, pace, parade, patrol, perambulate, plod, prance, promenade, rove, run, sashay, shuffle, slog, stalk, step, stride, stroll, strut, tour, traipse, tramp, traverse, tread, trek, trudge, wander *Antonyms:* idle, rest, sit **2.** accompany, chaperone, escort, exercise, guide, lead, protect, shepherd, tail **3.** abandon, break away *or* out, decamp, depart, desert, egress, exit, flee, forsake, leave, quit, retire, terminate *Nonformal:* scram, skedaddle, take a powder **4.** protest, rebel, revolt, shut down, stop or stop work, strike, walk out

The above example expresses the fact that the first sense of the noun **walk** ("I took a *walk* around the block") is the most common, followed by other senses exemplified in sentences, such as, "We swept the leaves off the *walk*," and, "University graduates follow different *walks* in their professional careers." Notice that, as in a dictionary, we include different parts of speech under the same keyword whenever the spelling is identical. Should the keyword be spelled differently, however, no matter what part of speech, we list it separately. Thus **labour** *n.* is followed by a separate entry for **laboured** *adj.* and for **labourer** *n.*

Sometimes you are not seeking a synonym or a related word at all: you want, instead, an implied subdivision or subset of a word. This is often the case when one looks for a specific noun. Perhaps you are thinking of a type of amphibian, but do not have the word at your fingertips. Under the keyword **amphibian** you will find:

amphibian *n.* cold-blooded vertebrate *Kinds of amphibians:* bullfrog, fire salamander, frog, grass frog, leopard frog, midwife toad, newt, polliwog, salamander, spring peeper, tadpole, toad, tree frog

In addition to the "*Kinds of...*" label, you will also find such list headings as "*Common...*," "*Types of...*," "*Parts of...*," "*Varieties of...*," and "*Groupings of...*," which refer to broad categories or divisions.

plant *n.* **1.** flower, greenery, plant kingdom, plant life, vegetable kingdom, verdure *Groupings of plants:* annual, aquatic, aromatic, berry, biennial, bulb, bush, cacti, evergreen, flora, flowering, fruit, garden flower, grain, grass, grasslike, gymnosperm, hardwood, heath, herbaceous, herbs, hothouse, insectivorous, ivy, legume, liverwort, marsh, medicinal, mosses, nut tree, perennial, plankton, reed, seaweed, sedge, shrub, softwood, tree, tuber, vegetable, vine, water, weed, wildflower *Immature plant*: cutting, seed, seedling, shoot, slip, sprout **2.** assembly line, Dickensian workhouse *(Nonformal)*, establishment, factory, foundry, industry, manufactory, mill, premises, shop, sweatshop, workshop, yard **3.** apparatus, appliances, buildings, devices, equipment, machinery, means, tools, workings **4.** artifice, chicanery, con *(Nonformal)*, deceit, deception, dodge, duplicity, fraud, hoax, swindle, trap, trick, wile **5.** agent, imposter, informant, informer, mole, operative, sleuth, source, spy, undercover agent *Nonformal:* narc, snitch, snoop, tipster – *v.* **1.** bury, cover, disseminate, grow, implant, raise, scatter, seed, sow, stock, transplant **2.** deposit, fix, imbed, insert, institute, lodge, park, position, root, set, settle, station *Nonformal:* plop, plunk **3.** build, erect, establish, found, install, institute, originate, launch **4.** hit, label, land, punch, strike *Nonformal:* sock, suck

These and any lists like them supplied in this thesaurus are not meant to be comprehensive, much less all-inclusive. However, they do provide a wide and varied range of possibilities.

To help you discriminate further between and among words, we sometimes provide an italicized label within each keyword entry, often in brackets following a word. These explanatory or usage labels are given to words that might appear odd, ambiguous, or confusing when read as part of a list, or simply to words that require further explication.

mania *n.* addiction, cacoethes, compulsion, craving, craze, delirium, desire, enthusiasm, fad, fancy, fascination, fetish, fixation, frenzy, furor, hangup, hysteria, *idée fixe (French)*, infatuation, insanity, lunacy, madness, obsession, passion, preoccupation, rage, urge *Kinds of mania:* Anglomania *(England)*, Beatlemania *(The Beatles)*, bibliomania *(Books)*, egomania *(Oneself)*, Francomania *or* Gallomania *(France)*, graphomania *(Writing)*, kleptomania *(Stealing)*, monomania *(One subject)*, mythomania *(Lies)*, necromania *(Death)*, nymphomania *(Female lust)*, satyromania *(Male lust)*, theomania *(God)*, Trudeaumania *(Pierre Trudeau)*, zoomania *(Animals)*

When the same label occurs more than once, it becomes an alphabetized heading for a list. The most common and important of which is *Nonformal.* Although words so labelled may be very common, not to mention colourful and idiomatic, they are often used outside formal or polite speech — in dictionaries they often bear such usage labels as *Slang*, *Informal*, *Colloq.* (Colloquial), *Dial.* (Dialect), *Offensive*, *Vulgar* and *Fig.* (Figurative). While we don't strive to achieve the precision or refinement in our usage, field, and locality labels that dictionaries do, we *do* identify words to help alert you to the fact that they should be used with more than ordinary care in some contexts. Here's an example.

dapper *adj.* chic, classy, dashing, jaunty, natty, neat, nifty, rakish, sharp, showy, smart, spruce, stylish, swank, swanky, trim, well-dressed, well-groomed *Nonformal:* dressed to the nines, posh, ragged out, ritzy, snazzy, spiffy *Antonyms:* dishevelled, frowzy, ill-groomed, rumpled

We have also identified those tricky words that are often confused and/or mistakenly used: *affect* and *effect*, *cite* and *sight*, *principal* and *principle*, and so on. These words and dozens of others have been designated as *Commonly misused* and are listed at the conclusion of each appropriate entry — just one more feature to help users best select the words they want.

Because this is the first authentically Canadian thesaurus, we take special pride in including specifically Canadian words, although we do not label them as Canadianisms, since the entire thesaurus is, in fact, Canadian. Words specific to other countries or languages are tagged: *British*, *U.S.*, *French*, etc. The salient fact is that you will find here Canadian words not found in any other thesaurus. Among the synonyms for **benefit**, for example, are *baby bonus*, and *pogey*. Some other examples: **dump** (*nuisance grounds*), **fish** (*capelin, Digby chicken, goldeye, Solomon Gundy*), **gulch** (*coulee, dry wash*), **monster** (*Sasquatch, wendigo*), **pastry** (*butter tart*), **road** (*autoroute, concession road, corduroy road, ice road*), **store** (*depanneur, groceteria*).

Entries like those for **parliament, party, region** and **province**, are especially rich in Canadian words.

province *n.* **1.** borough, country, demesne, district, division, neighbourhood, parish, precinct, quarter, region, state, territory, ward, zone *Canadian provinces and territories:* Alberta, British Columbia, Manitoba, New Brunswick, Newfoundland, Northwest Territories, Nova Scotia, Nunavut, Ontario, Prince Edward Island, Quebec, Saskatchewan, Yukon *Names for residents of Canadian provinces and territories:* Albertan, British Columbian, Inuit, Labradorian, Manitoban, New Brunswicker, Newfoundlander, Northerner, Nova Scotian, Nunavummiut, Ontarian, Prince Edward Islander, Quebecker, Québécois, Saskatchewaner, Yukoner *Nonformal names for residents of Canadian provinces and territories:* Bluenose *(Nova Scotian)*, herring choker *(New Brunswicker)*, Habitant, *(Québécois)*, Spud Islander *(P.E.I.) Newfoundland:* livyer, Newfie, Newfoundlander *Nonformal names for Canadian provinces:* Breadbasket *(Saskatchewan)*, Canada's Ocean Playground *(Nova Scotia)*, Keystone Province *(Manitoba)*, La Belle Province *(Quebec)*, Picture Province *(New Brunswick)*, the Rock *(Newfoundland)*, Upper Canada *(Ontario)*, Wild Rose Country *(Alberta) British Columbia:* Left Coast, Lotusland *Prince Edward Island:* Abegweit, Million Acre Farm, Minago, the Island **2.** arena, *arrondissement (French)*, bailiwick, beat *(Nonformal)*, billet, charge, concern, department, jurisdiction, orbit, place, sphere, station **3.** business, calling, discipline, employment, field, forte, job, metier, office, profession, role, speciality, trade

As you seek the word you want, this book will lead you into a world of identity, similarity, and antithesis. We believe that when you emerge, you'll have the word you want and need. We also hope your quest will be **enjoyable** — agreeable, amusing, delectable, delicious, delightful, entertaining, fun…

ABBREVIATIONS USED IN THIS BOOK

adj.	adjective
adv.	adverb
conj.	conjunction
fem.	feminine
interj.	interjection
masc.	masculine
n.	noun
pl.	plural
prep.	preposition
pron.	pronoun
v.	verb

abandon *n.* **1.** carelessness, heedlessness, recklessness *Antonyms:* caution, safety **2.** dissipation, licentiousness, profligacy, wantonness – *v.* abdicate, back *or* bail *or* bow out, desert, discontinue, disown, ditch, drop, dump, leave *or* leave behind, let go, quit, reject, relinquish, renounce, run away, scuttle, ship out, surrender, walk out on *Antonyms:* adopt, defend, hold, keep, maintain, support, take, uphold

abashed *adj.* ashamed, bewildered, bugged, chagrined, confounded, confused, crushed, discombobulated, disconcerted, embarrassed, fazed, humbled, humiliated, mortified, rattled, shy, taken aback *Antonyms:* at ease, bold, composed, confident

abate *v.* **1.** decline, decrease, diminish, dwindle, ebb, lessen, let up, recede, subside, taper off, wane *Antonyms:* boost, escalate, increase, magnify **2.** allay, assuage, lessen, mitigate, moderate, mollify, quell, reduce, subdue, temper *Antonyms:* amplify, augment, enhance

abbreviation *n.* abridgement, abstract, clipping, compendium, condensation, contraction, digest, outline, précis, reduction, shortening, sketch, summary, syllabus, synopsis

abdicate *v.* abandon, cede, drop, forgo, leave, quit, relinquish, renounce, resign, retire, surrender, vacate, waive, withdraw, yield *Antonyms:* seize, take *Commonly misused:* **abrogate, arrogate**

abdominal *adj.* belly, duodenal, gastric, intestinal, stomach, ventral, visceral *Abdominal regions:* epigastric, hypogastric, left hypochondrium, left iliac, left lumbar, right hypochondrium, right iliac, right lumbar, umbilical

abduct *v.* carry off, grab, kidnap, remove, seize, shanghai, snatch, spirit away

aberrant *adj.* abnormal, atypical, deviant, different, nonstandard, odd, peculiar, unusual, weird *Nonformal:* mental, psycho, wacko *Antonyms:* average, common, commonplace, normal

abet *v.* advocate, aid, assist, back, condone, egg on *(Nonformal)*, encourage, endorse, goad, incite, instigate, prod, promote, provoke, sanction, spur, support, urge *Antonyms:* discourage, dissuade, frustrate, impede

abeyance *n.* adjournment, arrest, cold storage *(Nonformal)*, deferral, discontinuance, dormancy, inactivity, intermission, recess, remission, suspension

abhor *v.* abominate, despise, detest, dislike, execrate, hate, loathe, scorn, shun *Antonyms:* admire, cherish, delight in, love, relish

abide *v.* **1.** dwell, inhabit, live, lodge, nest, reside, room, settle, squat, stay *Antonyms:* roam, wander **2.** allow, endure, subsist, tolerate *Antonyms:* cast off, rebel

abiding *adj.* constant, continuing, enduring, eternal, everlasting, lasting, permanent, persistent, persisting, steadfast, steady *Antonyms:* brief, ephemeral, fleeting, momentary, transitory

ability *n.* adeptness, adroitness, aptitude, bent, capability, cleverness, command, craft, deftness, dexterity, expertise, expertness, facility, faculty, finesse, flair, genius, gift, handiness, ingenuity, knack, know-how, mastery, proficiency, qualification, skilfulness, skill, strength, talent, understanding *Nonformal:* savvy, the goods, the stuff *Antonyms:* inability, incapability, incapacity, incompetence, ineptness, powerlessness

abject *adj.* base, contemptible, degraded, dejected, deplorable, dishonourable, fawning, forlorn, grovelling, hangdog *(Nonformal)*, hopeless, low, miserable, servile, submissive, worthless *Antonyms:* dignified, distinguished, elevated, exalted, grand

ablaze *adj.* **1.** afire, aflame, alight, blazing, burning, fiery, flaming, flaring, ignited, lighted *Antonyms:* colourless, dark, pale, pallid **2.** ardent, emotional, enthusiastic, fervid, spirited, zealous *Antonyms:* bored, dull, uncommitted

able *adj.* accomplished, adept, adroit, artful, bright, brilliant, capable, clever, competent, cunning, deft, dexterous, easy, effective, efficient, equal to, equipped, expert, fitted, gifted, good at *or* with, ingenious, intelligent, knowing, masterful, masterly, powerful, practiced, prepared, proficient, qualified, ready, sharp, skilful, skilled, smart, strong in *or* at, talented, trained *Antonyms:* amateurish, inadequate, incapable, incompetent, ineffective, inefficient, inept, mediocre, unfit, unskilful, weak

able-bodied *adj.* capable, firm, fit, hale, hardy, healthy, hearty, lusty, powerful, robust, stout, strapping, strong, sturdy, vigorous *Antonyms:* ailing, debilitated, sickly, tender, weak

abnegation *n.* abandonment, abstinence, denial, forbearance, refusal, relinquishment, rejection, renunciation, sacrifice, self-denial, temperance *Antonyms:* indulgence, surrender

abnormal *adj.* aberrant, anomalous, atypical, bizarre, curious, deviant, deviate, different, divergent, eccentric, exceptional, extraordinary, irregular, odd, off-base, peculiar, preternatural, queer, strange, uncommon, unexpected, unnatural, unusual, weird *Nonformal:* funny, screwy, wacky *Antonyms:* conventional, familiar, ordinary, usual

abnormality *n.* aberration, anomaly, deformity, deviance, deviation, difference, eccentricity, exception, extraordinariness, irregularity, oddity, peculiarity, singularity, strangeness, uncommonness, unnaturalness, unusualness

aboard *adj.* consigned, embarked, en route, loaded, on, on board, travelling

abode *n.* address, base, *casa (Italian & Spanish)*, domicile, dwelling *or* dwelling place, fireside, habitat, hearth, home, homestead, house, household, housing, living quarters, lodging, place *or* place of residence, residence, roof over one's head, sanctuary *Nonformal:* digs, hangout, pad, roost

abolish *v.* abate, abrogate, annihilate, annul, cancel, dissolve, eliminate, end, eradicate, erase, expunge, extinguish, extirpate, finish, inhibit, invalidate, negate, nix *(Nonformal)*, nullify, obliterate, overthrow, overturn, prohibit, quash, repeal, repudiate, rescind, revoke, scrub, set aside, squelch, stamp out, suppress, terminate, vacate, wipe out *Antonyms:* authorize, continue, create, enact, establish, found, introduce, revive, sustain

abolition *n.* abolishment, annihilation, annulment, cancellation, destruction, dissolution, elimination, end, ending, eradication, extirpation, invalidation, negation, nullification, obliteration, overthrow, overturning, quashing, repeal, repudiation, rescinding, rescindment, subversion, suppression, termination, voiding *Antonyms:* continuance, creation, introduction, revision

abominable *adj.* abhorrent, atrocious, awful, base, beastly, contemptible, cursed, despicable, detestable, disgusting, foul, grim, hateful, heinous, hellish, horrible, loathsome, nauseating, odious, offensive, repellent, reprehensible, repugnant, repulsive, revolting, rotten, terrible, vile, wretched *Antonyms:* admirable, charming, commendable, delightful, pleasing, satisfactory

abomination *n.* **1.** anathema, crime, curse, evil, horror, offence, plague, shame, torment, wrongdoing **2.** animosity, aversion, enmity, hatred, hostility, loathing, repugnance

aboriginal *adj.* ancient, earliest, endemic, first, indigenous, native, original, primordial *Antonyms:* immigrant, migrant, peregrine – *n.* autochthon, indigene, local, native

abort *v.* arrest, break off, call off, cancel, check, drop, end, fail, halt, interrupt, lay off, nullify, quit, scratch, scrub, terminate *Antonym:* complete, finish

abortion *n.* **1.** dilatation and curettage *or* D&C, expulsion, miscarriage, premature delivery, termination **2.** blunder, defeat, failure, fiasco, misadventure *Antonyms:* success, triumph, victory **3.** deformity, malformation, miscreation, monstrosity

abortive *adj.* failed, fruitless, futile, ineffective, ineffectual, miscarried, unavailing, unproductive, unsuccessful, useless, vain *Antonyms:* triumphant, victorious

abound *v.* be plentiful, crawl with, crowd, flourish, flow, infest, overflow, proliferate, swarm, swell, teem, thrive *Antonyms:* lack, need, want

about *adv.* **1.** around, back, backward, in reverse, reverse, round **2.** almost, approximately, in general, near, nearly, roughly – *prep.* **1.** around, encircling, round, surrounding, through, throughout **2.** adjacent, beside, near, nearby **3.** as concerns, as regards, concerned with, concerning, connected with, dealing with, pertaining to, referring to, regarding, relative to, respecting, touching, with respect to

above *prep.* **1.** beyond, exceeding, greater than, higher than, larger than, over and above **2.** aloft, atop, beyond, high, higher, on high, over, overhead, raised, superior, upon *Antonyms:* below, beneath, under, underneath

aboveboard *adj.* candid, forthright, frank, honest, open, straight, straightforward, true, trustworthy, truthful, up-front *(Nonformal)*, veracious *Antonyms:* clandestine, deceitful, dishonest, secret – *adv.* candidly, frankly, honestly, openly, overtly, truly, truthfully

abrasion *n.* attrition, chafing, friction, grating, grinding, kneading, rasping, rub, rubbing, scouring, scraping, scratch, scuff, wear, wearing

abrasive *adj.* **1.** cutting, erosive, grinding, rough, scratchy, scuffing, wearing **2.** biting, caustic, cutting, galling, hurtful, irritating, sharp, spiky, unpleasant *Antonyms:* smooth, soft, tender – *n.* emery board, emery cloth, file, pumice, sandpaper, scour pad, steel wool

abreast *adj.* acquainted, *au courant (French)*, contemporary, familiar, informed, in touch, knowledgeable, up, up-to-date, up to speed *(Nonformal)*, versed *Antonyms:* outmoded, out of date – *adv.* alongside, beside, equal, in line, level, next to, off, opposite *Antonyms:* afar, away, out of line

abridgement *n.* abbreviation, abstract, brief, compendium, condensation, contraction, cutting, digest, outline, précis, reduction, shortening, summary, synopsis *Antonyms:* addition, augmentation, increase

abroad *adj.* at large, away, elsewhere, out and about *(Nonformal)*, overseas, touring, travelling

abrogate *v.* abate, abolish, annul, cancel, dissolve, end, finish off, invalidate, negate, nix *(Nonformal)*, nullify, quash, reject, repeal, retract, revoke, scrub, undo, vacate, void *Commonly misused:* **abdicate**, **arrogate**

abrupt *adj.* **1.** blunt, brief, brusque, crusty, curt, direct, gruff, impetuous, impolite, rude, short, snappy, snippy, uncivil, ungracious *Antonyms:* easy, leisurely, slow, thoughtful **2.** hasty, hurried, precipitous, quick, rushing, sudden, surprising, unanticipated, unexpected, unforeseen *Antonyms:* anticipated, awaited, due, expected, foreseen, promised

abscond *v.* bolt, break, disappear, escape, flee, leave, make away *or* off, make scarce, pull out, quit, run away, skip out, slip away, sneak away, steal away, take off *Nonformal:* duck out, go AWOL, scram, skedaddle, split, take a powder, vamoose *Antonyms:* come, emerge, remain, return, stay

absence *n.* **1.** absenteeism, nonappearance, nonattendance, truancy *Nonformal:* hooky, no-show **2.** dearth, deficiency, drought, inadequacy, insufficiency, lack, need, omission, privation, unavailability, void, want *Antonyms:* abundance, surplus

absent *adj.* **1.** astray, away, AWOL *(Nonformal)*, elsewhere, gone, off *or* out, removed, vanished **2.** bare, blank, deficient, devoid, hollow, lacking, minus, missing, omitted, vacant, wanting

absenteeism *n.* absence, defection, desertion, nonattendance, skipping, truancy

absent-minded *adj.* absorbed, abstracted, bemused, daydreaming, distracted, dreaming, dreamy, engrossed, faraway, forgetful, heedless, inattentive, lost, oblivious, preoccupied, remote, removed, unaware, unconscious, unthinking, withdrawn *Nonformal:* mooning, out to lunch, pipe dreaming, spacey, woolgathering *Antonyms:* alert, awake, observant, vigilant

absolute *adj.* **1.** altogether, categorical, certain, complete, conclusive, consummate, decisive, definite, downright, entire, final, full, infallible, out-and-out, outright, perfect, pure, sheer, supreme, thorough, thoroughgoing, total, unabridged, unadulterated, unalloyed, unconditional, undeniable, undiluted, unequivocal, unlimited, unmitigated, unmixed, unqualified, unquestionable, unreserved, unrestricted, utter, whole, without limit *Antonyms:* haphazard, incomplete, partial, sketchy **2.** absolutist, authoritarian, autocratic, dictatorial, sovereign, totalitarian, tyrannical

absolutely *adv.* actually, categorically, certainly, conclusively, decidedly, decisively, definitely, doubtless, exactly, positively, precisely, really, surely, truly, unquestionably *Antonyms:* conditionally, erratically, probably, reasonably, somewhat

absolutism *n.* absolute monarchy, autarchy, autocracy, czarism, despotism, dictatorship, iron rule, Stalinism, totalitarianism, tyranny

absolve *v.* acquit, clear, discharge, exculpate, exempt, exonerate, forgive, free, let go, liberate, loose, pardon, release, relieve, set free, spare, vindicate *Antonyms:* accuse, blame, charge, condemn, denounce, pass sentence on, reproach

absorb *v.* **1.** blot, consume, devour, drink, imbibe, ingest, soak up, sop up, sponge up, suck in, swallow, take in *Antonyms:* disperse, dissipate, exude **2.** assimilate, comprehend, digest, follow, get, grasp, incorporate, learn, sense, subsume, take in, understand **3.** captivate, concern, consume, employ, engage, engross, fascinate, fill, hold, immerse, involve, monopolize, obsess, preoccupy, rivet **4.** block, dampen, intercept, muffle

absorbent *adj.* permeable, porous, receptive, retentive, spongy *Antonyms:* imperious, watertight

absorbing *adj.* arresting, captivating, consuming, engrossing, enthralling, exciting, fascinating, gripping, interesting, intriguing, monopolizing, preoccupying, riveting, spellbinding *Antonyms:* boring, dreary, dull, monotonous, tedious, tiresome

absorption *n.* **1.** assimilation, consumption, digestion, imbibing, incorporation, ingestion, intake, osmosis, penetration, saturation, taking in **2.** captivation, fascination, intentness, preoccupation

abstain *v.* abjure, abnegate, avoid, cease, constrain, curb, decline, deny oneself, do without, eschew, evade, fast, forbear, forgo, give up, hold back, pass up, quit, refrain, refuse, renounce, shun, spurn, starve, withhold *Antonyms:* abandon oneself, give in, indulge, partake, permit, yield

abstemious *adj.* abstinent, austere, frugal, moderate, restraining, self-denying, sober, sparing, temperate *Antonyms:* greedy, intemperate, self-indulgent

abstinence *n.* abnegation, asceticism, avoidance, celibacy, chastity, forbearance, moderation, refraining, renunciation, self-control, self-denial, self-restraint, sobriety, temperance *Antonyms:* abandon, gluttony, wantonness

abstract *adj.* abstruse, complex, conceptual, deep, hypothetical, ideal, indefinite, intellectual, philosophical, recondite, theoretical, transcendental, unreal *Antonyms:* actual, concrete, definite, factual, material, real, specific – *n.* abridgment, brief, compendium, condensation, digest, outline, précis, résumé, summary, synopsis – *v.* **1.** abbreviate, abridge, condense, digest, distill, outline, shorten, summarize *Antonyms:* combine, complete, increase, unite **2.** detach, disconnect, disengage, dissociate, extract, isolate, part, remove, separate, steal, take away, withdraw *Antonyms:* add, combine, inject, restore

abstracted *adj.* bemused, bewildered, distracted, heedless, oblivious, preoccupied, thoughtless *Nonformal:* on cloud nine, spaced out *Antonyms:* alert, attentive, thoughtful, wide-awake

abstraction *n.* absorption, aloofness, consideration, contemplation, detachment, musing, pensiveness, pondering, preoccupation, reflection, remoteness, reverie, ruminating, thinking

abstruse *adj.* complex, complicated, cryptic, deep, difficult, enigmatic, esoteric, heavy, hidden, incomprehensible, intricate, involved, mysterious, obscure, profound, puzzling, recondite, subtle, unfathomable, vague *Antonyms:* apparent, clear, conspicuous, evident, perceptible, transparent, unsubtle *Commonly misused:* **obtuse**

absurd *adj.* crazy, foolish, idiotic, ill-advised, illogical, inane, incongruous, irrational, laughable, ludicrous, nonsensical, preposterous, ridiculous, senseless, silly, unreasonable *Nonformal:* daffy, dippy, dizzy, flaky, kooky, loony, nutty, screwy, wacky *Antonyms:* logical, prudent, rational, reasonable

absurdity *n.* craziness, farce, folly, foolishness, idiocy, illogicality, improbability, inanity, incongruity, insanity, irrationality, ludicrousness, *reductio ad absurdum (Latin)*, ridiculousness, senselessness, silliness, stupidity, unreasonableness *Antonyms:* consistency, sensibility, truism

abundance *n.* affluence, ampleness, bounty, copiousness, fortune, opulence, plenitude, plenty, profusion, prosperity, riches, wealth *Antonyms:* dearth, deficiency, lack, scarcity

abundant *adj.* abounding, ample, bounteous, bountiful, copious, full, generous, heavy, lavish, luxuriant, overflowing, plenteous, plentiful, plenty, profuse, rich, teeming *Nonformal:* awash in, lousy *or* rife with, rolling in *Antonyms:* deficient, inadequate, sparse

abuse *n.* **1.** corruption, crime, debasement, delinquency, desecration, exploitation, harm, hurt, impairment, injury, injustice, maltreatment, misapplication, misconduct, misdeed, mishandling, mismanagement, misuse, offence, violation, wrongdoing *Antonyms:* honesty, integrity, truth **2.** belittlement, blame, castigation, censure, curse, defamation, derision, insult, invective, reproach, revilement, scolding, slander, swearing, tirade, upbraiding, vilification, vituperation *Antonyms:* acclaim, commendation, compliment, praise, respect – *v.* **1.** corrupt, damage, defile, desecrate, ill-treat, impair, injure, maltreat, mar, mishandle, mistreat, molest, oppress, pervert, rough up, spoil, victimize, violate *Antonyms:* care for, nurture, protect, tend **2.** badmouth, belittle, berate, castigate, cut down, decry, defame, dig, harangue, insult, kick around *(Nonformal)*, minimize, nag, offend, oppress, persecute, reproach, revile, scold, slander, trash, upbraid *Nonformal:* bash, dump on, slam, slap, smear *Antonyms:* applaud, eulogize, extol, vindicate **3.** dissipate, exhaust, exploit, impose on, misemploy, mishandle, misuse, overburden, overtax, overwork, spoil, squander, taint, waste, wrong *Antonyms:* cherish, conserve, protect, shield, sustain

abusive *adj.* censorious, contumelious, defamatory, derisive, disparaging, insolent, insulting, invective, libellous, maligning, mean, offensive, reproachful, reviling, rude, sarcastic, scathing, scolding, scurrilous, sharp-tongued, slanderous, upbraiding, vilifying *Antonyms:* approving, complimentary, flattering, laudatory, praising

abut *v.* **1.** adjoin, border on, butt against, join, neighbour, touch, verge upon **2.** bestraddle, bestride, rest on

abysmal *adj.* bottomless, deep, extreme, fathomless, plumbless, prodigious

abyss *n.* chasm, crevasse, depth, fissure, gorge, gulf, hole, pit, void *Antonyms:* peak, pinnacle, summit, zenith

academic *adj.* **1.** bookish, erudite, intellectual, learned, pedantic, scholarly, scholastic, studious *Antonyms:* everyday, illiterate, untutored **2.** abstract, conjectural, hypothetical, philosophical, speculative, theoretical – *n.* academician, bluestocking, don, fellow, lecturer, master, professor, pupil, scholar, scholastic, student, teacher, tutor

academy *n.* college, institute, school, think-tank *(Nonformal) Kinds of academy*: boarding school, collegiate institute, elementary school, finishing school, high school, institute, institution, middle school, military school, prep school, public school, secondary school, seminary, separate school

accede *v.* **1.** accept, acquiesce, admit, agree, comply, concede, consent, endorse, grant, submit, subscribe, yield **2.** assume, attain, come to, inherit, succeed *Antonyms:* challenge, demur, object *Commonly misused:* **exceed**

accelerate *v.* advance, drive, expedite, fire up, hasten, hurry, impel, make tracks *(Nonformal)*, quicken, rev *or* speed up, speed, spur, step up *Antonyms:* brake, decelerate, delay, hinder, impede, plod, stop

acceleration *n.* dispatch, expedition, hastening, hurrying, quickening, speeding up, stepping up

accent *n.* **1.** articulation, beat, cadence, emphasis, enunciation, inflection, intonation, metre, modulation, pitch, pronunciation, rhythm, stroke, timbre, tone **2.** diacritical mark *Kinds of accent mark: cedilla (French & Spanish), tilde (Spanish & Portuguese), umlaut (German) French:* aigu, circonflexe, grave **3.** emphasis, importance, significance, stress, weight – *v.* accentuate, emphasize, highlight, stress, underline, underscore

accept *v.* **1.** acquire, get, receive, secure, welcome *Antonyms:* decline, lose, reject **2.** affirm, agree *or* subscribe to, approve, authorize, embrace, endorse, espouse, involve, take on *Nonformal:* get behind, go for, okay, root for, rubber stamp *Antonyms:* deny, refuse, spurn **3.** admit, allow, consent, grant, incorporate *Commonly misused:* **except**

acceptable *adj.* adequate, admissible, all right, average, common, decent, fair, passing, pleasing, respectable, satisfactory, standard, sufficient, tolerable, welcome *Nonformal:* A-OK, copesetic, okay *Antonyms:* unacceptable, unsatisfactory, unsuitable

acceptance *n.* acknowledgment, admission, agreement, approval, assent, belief, compliance, consent, yes *Nonformal:* go-ahead, green light, nod, okay *Antonyms:* refusal, rejection

accepted *adj.* accustomed, acknowledged, agreed, allowed, approved, authorized, card-carrying, chosen, confirmed, conventional, credited, current, customary, endorsed, established, legitimate, normal, orthodox, popular, preferred, received, recognized, regular, sanctioned, standard, straight, time-honoured, touted, universal, usual, welcomed *Nonformal:* kosher, legit *Antonyms:* abnormal, irregular, unconventional, unorthodox, weird

access *n.* **1.** admission, admittance, entry, ingress, key, open door *Antonyms:* hindrance, interference **2.** approach, avenue, course, door, entrance, passage, path, road, route, way **3.** connection, contact, password – *v.* attain, enter, gain admission *or* entry, go into, reach

accessible *adj.* approachable, attainable, available, convenient, employable, exposed, gettable *(Nonformal)*, handy, near, obtainable, open, operative, possible, practicable, public, reachable, ready, susceptible, unrestricted, usable *Antonyms:* hidden, inaccessible, secreted, unapproachable, unavailable, unobtainable, unreachable

accession *n.* attainment, inauguration, induction, succession, taking on *or* over

accessory *adj.* ancillary, adjunct, auxiliary, subordinate, subsidiary *Antonyms:* first, foremost, primary – *n.* **1.** abettor, accomplice, aide, assistant, associate, co-conspirator, colleague, confederate, conspirator, helper, partner *Antonyms:* adversary, antagonist, rival **2.** accent, accoutrement, addition, adjunct, adornment, appendage, appendix, appointment, appurtenance, attachment, complement, component, decoration, extension, extra, fitting, frill, ornament, supplement, trim, trimming *Kinds of fashion accessories:* aigrette, aiguilette, *asayib (Middle East)*, belt, bollo tie, bow tie, broach, bustle, chaps, cravat, cuff-links, cummerbund, epaulet, fichu, *gamsbart (Austria)*, garter, gloves, hat, headdress, jewellery, *kola (Afghanistan)*, *obi (Japanese)*, *paillette (Scandinavia)*, purse, sash, scarf, shoes, *soyate (Mexico)*, spats, spurs, tie, *tzute (Guatemala)*, *vainag (Baltic)*

accident *n.* **1.** blow, calamity, casualty, collision, crackup, disaster, event, misadventure, misfortune, mishap, smash *Nonformal:* fender-bender, pile-up **2.** adventure, chance, circumstance, fate, fluke, fortune, happening, happenstance, luck, occurrence, turn *Antonyms:* intention, law, predesign

accidental *adj.* adventitious, casual, chance, coincidental, contingent, fluky, fortuitous, inadvertent, incidental, random, serendipitous, uncalculated, unexpected, unforeseen, unintended, unintentional, unplanned *Antonyms:* calculated, designed, intended, planned

acclaim *n.* applause, approbation, celebration, cheering, clapping, commendation, exaltation, honour, plaudits, praise, recognition *Nonformal*: kudos, raves *Antonyms:* bad press, brickbats, censure – *v.* acknowledge, applaud, approve, assent, hail, praise, vote in, welcome

acclamation *n.* **1.** adulation, applause, approval, cheering, endorsement, honour, jubilation, laudation, plaudits, tribute *Antonyms:* contempt, derision, scorn **2.** ballotless, by popular opinion, unanimous consent, unopposed, without opposition

acclimatize *v.* accommodate, accustom, adapt, adjust, harden, inure, season, toughen

accolade *n.* approval, award, badge, decoration, distinction, honour, kudos *(Nonformal)*, laurel, praise, recognition

accommodate *v.* **1.** aid, arrange, assist, avail, benefit, comfort, favour, help, indulge, oblige, provide, serve, supply, support *Antonyms:* aggravate, exacerbate, hinder **2.** accord, accustom, adapt, adjust, agree, attune, comply, conform, coordinate, correspond, fit, harmonize, integrate, modify, reconcile, settle, tailor *Antonyms:* conflict, contend **3.** board, contain, entertain, furnish, harbour, hold, house, put up, receive, rent, shelter, supply, take in, welcome

accommodating *adj.* considerate, cooperative, friendly, helpful, hospitable, kind, neighbourly, obliging, user-friendly, willing *Antonyms:* disobliging, inconsiderate, rude, uncooperative

accommodation *n.* **1.** adaptation, adjustment, compromise, modification, reconciliation, settlement *Antonyms:* controversy, dissension, quarrel **2.** assistance, benefit, consideration, courtesy, favour, generosity, hospitality, kindness, patronage, willingness **3.** aid, amenity, appliance, appurtenance, convenience, facility, service

accommodations *n. pl.* apartment, arrangements, bed, board, home, hostel, hotel, house, housing, lodging, motel, quarters, residence, roof, rooms, shelter *Nonformal:* crib, digs, pad

accompaniment *n.* **1.** background, backing, backup, harmony, part **2.** addition, extra, supplement, support

accompany *v.* **1.** associate with, attend, bear *or* bear company, bring, chaperone, conduct, consort *or* consort with, escort, go along *or* with, keep company, show about *or* around, squire, take out, usher *Nonformal:* hang out with, shadow, stick to, tag along **2.** add, appear with, append, be connected, coexist, coincide, complete, follow, go together, occur with, supplement

accomplice *n.* abettor, accessory, aide, ally, assistant, associate, buddy, co-conspirator, collaborator, colleague, confederate, conspirator, henchman, insider, partner

accomplish *v.* **1.** achieve, act *or* act out, actualize, arrange, arrive *or* arrive at, attain, bring about *or* off, carry off *or* out, come through, construct, determine, discharge, do, do justice to, effect, effectuate, enact, engineer, erect, establish, execute, fix, form, fulfill, gain, get, make, make concrete *or* good *or* happen, manage, materialize, move, perform, prevail, produce, pull off, put over, realize, resolve, rig, settle, sort out, succeed, thrash out, triumph, win, work *or* work out *Nonformal:* get there, make *or* nail it, pull off, rack up *Antonyms:* fail, fall short, forsake, give up, miscarry **2.** cap, carry through, clinch, close, complete, conclude, consummate, crown, end, finish, perfect, seal, secure, settle, sew up *(Nonformal)*, terminate, wind up

accomplished *adj.* **1.** able, adept, brainy, cultivated, expert, gifted, masterly, polished, practiced, proficient, sharp, skilful, skilled, talented *Nonformal:* savvy, with it *Antonyms:* amateurish, incapable, incompetent **2.** achieved, consummated, done, finished, fulfilled, perfected, realized, terminated

accomplishment *n.* **1.** achievement, attainment, carrying out, completion, conclusion, consummation, coup, culmination, doing, effecting, effort, end, enforcement, execution, exploit, feat, finalization, fruition, fulfillment, hat trick *(Hockey)*, performance, production, realization, stroke, success, triumph *Antonyms:* collapse, failure, fiasco, flop *(Nonformal)* **2.** ability, art, capability, finish, proficiency, skill, talent

accordingly *adv.* appropriately, consequently, correspondingly, duly, equally, ergo, hence, in consequence, properly, proportionately, respectively, subsequently, suitably, then, therefore, thus

account *n.* **1.** annal, bulletin, chronicle, detail, explanation, history, narration, narrative, play by play *(Nonformal)*, recital, report, story, take, tale, version **2.** basis, cause, ground, grounds, interest, justification, motive, rationale, reason, regard **3.** amount due, balance, bill, books, charge, debt, finances, inventory, invoice, ledger, obligation, reckoning, record, register, report, score, statement, tab, tally, total

accountant *n.* actuary, analyst, auditor, bookkeeper, CA, calculator, cashier, CGA, clerk, comptroller, CPA, examiner, public accountant, teller *Nonformal:* bean counter, pencil pusher

accretion *n.* accumulation, augmentation, buildup, increase, raise, rise *Antonyms:* attrition, erosion, reduction

accrue *v.* accumulate, amass, build up, collect, enlarge, gather, grow, increase *Antonyms:* dissipate, dwindle, squander, wane

accumulate *v.* **1.** acquire, agglomerate, amalgamate, assemble, cache, collect, compile, concentrate, gather, heap, hoard, incorporate, lump, mass, pile, stockpile, store, unite *Antonyms:* disperse, disseminate, dissipate, scatter **2.** accrue, augment, expand, extend, gain, grow, increase, multiply, procure, profit, rise, snowball, swell, wax

accumulation *n.* addition, agglomeration, aggregation, augmentation, buildup, collection, conglomeration, gathering, growth, heap, hoarding, mass, pile, quantity, stack, stock, store, trove

accuracy *n.* accurateness, certainty, closeness, correctness, definitiveness, exactitude, faultlessness, meticulousness, preciseness, precision, sharpness, veracity *Antonyms:* carelessness, imprecision, incorrectness

accurate *adj.* actual, authentic, authoritative, careful, certain, complete, conclusive, correct, definite, detailed, discriminating, distinct, exact, explicit, factual, faithful, faultless, flawless, genuine, irrefutable, just, methodical, meticulous, on the money *(Nonformal)*, perfect, precise, punctilious, right, scientific, scrupulous, specific, strict, total, true, truthful, unerring, undeniable, undisputed, unimpeachable, unmistakable, unquestionable, valid, veracious *Antonyms:* defective, faulty, imperfect, inexact

accusation *n.* admonishment, admonition, allegation, arraignment, attribution, blame, censure, charge, chiding, citation, complaint, criticism, denunciation, detention, gripe, impeachment, imputation, incrimination, indictment, insinuation, recrimination, rebuke, reprimand, reproach, reproof, writ *Nonformal:* beef, blast, flak, knock, rap

accuse *v.* **1.** allege, attack, attribute, betray, blame, censure, cite, denounce, hold accountable, impeach, implicate, impugn, impute, incriminate, inculpate, indict, involve, litigate, lodge a complaint, reprehend, reproach, sue *Nonformal:* blow the whistle, brand, finger, pin on *Antonyms:* absolve, defend, deny, vindicate **2.** apprehend, arraign, arrest, charge, prosecute, summon

accustomed *adj.* acclimatized, acquainted, adapted, confirmed, disciplined, familiar, familiarized, given to, habituated, inured, prepared, seasoned, trained *Antonyms:* foreign, unfamiliar, unused

ace *adj.* champion, crackerjack *(Nonformal)*, matchless, outstanding, superb *Antonyms:* average, mediocre, run-of-the-mill *(Nonformal)* – *n.* **1.** champion, crack shot, master, star, virtuoso, wizard *Antonyms:* amateur, beginner, dilettante, novice **2.** aviator, flier, flyboy *(Nonformal)*, pilot

acerbity *n.* acidity, astringency, bitterness, ill temper, irritability, mordancy, rancour, sharpness, sourness, tartness

ache *n.* anguish, hurt, misery, pain, pang, pounding, smarting, soreness, spasm, suffering, throb, throbbing – *v.* **1.** hurt, pain, pound, smart, suffer, throb, twinge **2.** crave, desire, hanker, languish, long, pine, want, yearn

achieve *v.* accomplish, actualize, amass, arrive, arrive at, attain, bring about *or* off, carry off *or* out *or* through, clean up, clinch, close, come through, compass, complete, conclude, consummate, crown, do, earn, effect, effectuate, enact, end, execute, finish, follow through, fulfill, gain, gain advantage, get, get done, impress, land, make, make it, make out, manage, obtain, procure, produce, pull off, put across *or* over, put away, reach, realize, reap, resolve, score, seal, secure, see through, settle, snag, solve, succeed, thrive, triumph, win, wind up, work out, wrap up *Nonformal:* knock off, mop up, nail, notch, polish off, rack up, sew up *Antonyms:* botch, bungle, fail, founder

achievement *n.* accomplishment, actualization, arrival, attainment, award, breakthrough, completion, conquest, consummation, coup, culmination, distinction, eminence, encompassment, exploit, feat, fruition, fulfillment, gaining, illustriousness, implementation, landmark, laurels, mastery, materialization, maturation, merit, milepost, milestone, payoff, performance, performing, preeminence, procurement, prominence, rank, realization, reaping, renown, reputation, repute, satisfaction, securing, succeeding, success, superiority, triumph, victory, winning, worth *Antonyms:* breakdown, crash, defeat, failure, loss

acid *adj.* acerbic, acidulous, acrid, biting, bitter, caustic, corrosive, piquant, pungent, sharp, tart, vinegary *Antonyms:* benign, bland, gentle, mild, pleasant, saccharine, sweet – *n.* acidity, hydracid, oxyacid *Antonyms:* alkali, neutralizer

acidulous *adj.* bitter, dry, piquant, sharp, sour, tart *Antonyms:* sugary, sweet

acknowledge *v.* **1.** accede, accept, acquiesce, admit, agree, approve, attest *or* defer to, confess, grant, notice, subscribe *Antonyms:* deny, disavow, repudiate **2.** address, answer, greet, hail, recognize, salute *Antonyms:* ignore, snub **3.** certify, endorse, ratify, support, uphold *Antonyms:* disregard, reject, renounce

acknowledged *adv.* accepted, accredited, admitted, answered, approved, conceded, confessed, declared, professed, recognized *Antonyms:* cast off, discarded, pretended

acknowledgment *n.* **1.** acceptance, acquiescence, admission, affirmation, allowance, assent, assertion, avowal, compliance, concession, concurrence, confession, confirmation, corroboration, declaration, profession, ratification, realization, recognition *Antonyms:* refutation, rejection **2.** acclamation, answer, apology, applause, appreciation, bestowal, cookie *(Nonformal)*, credit, gift, gratitude, greeting, guarantee, hailing, letter, nod, notice, reaction, reference, receipt, reply, response, return, salute, statement, support, thanks

acme *n.* apogee, climax, peak, pinnacle, summit, zenith *Antonyms:* nadir, perigee, valley

acolyte *n.* aide, assistant, attendant, follower, helper

acquaint *v.* accustom, advise, brief, divulge, enlighten, familiarize, fill in, inform, introduce, let know, make familiar, notify, present, reveal, tell, warn *Antonyms:* ignore, obfuscate

acquaintance *n.* **1.** conversance, familiarity, grasp, intimacy, ken, knowledge, relationship, understanding *Antonyms:* ignorance, unfamiliarity **2.** associate, colleague, companion, contact, friend, neighbour *Antonyms:* alien, stranger

acquiescence *n.* acceptance, approval, assent, compliance, concurrence, conformity, consent, giving in, obedience, resignation, submission, submissiveness, yielding *Antonyms:* belligerence, pugnacity

acquire *v.* access, achieve, adopt, amass, annex, appropriate, arrogate, assume, attain, bring in, buy, buy out *or* up, catch, collect, come by, commandeer, confiscate, draw, earn, expropriate, find, gain, gather, get, grab, have, induce, inherit, land, obtain, pick up, procure, purchase, receive, secure, steal, take, take over *or* possession of, usurp, win *Nonformal:* cop, corral, hijack, liberate, lock up, rack up, scare up, score, snag *Antonyms:* forfeit, forgo, give up, lose, relinquish, renounce, surrender, waive

acquisition *n.* accretion, achievement, acquirement, acquiring, attainment, gain, possession, prize, procurement, property, purchase, retrieval *Antonyms:* donation, dispersal, loss, sale

acquisitive *adj.* avaricious, covetous, demanding, grabbing, grasping, greedy, predatory, rapacious *Antonyms:* eleemosynary, generous, liberal

acquit *v.* **1.** act, bear, behave, carry, comport, conduct, perform **2.** absolve, clear, discharge, excuse, exonerate, free, let go, let off, liberate, release, relieve, vindicate *Antonyms:* condemn, convict, find guilty

acquittal *n.* absolution, amnesty, clearance, deliverance, discharge, dismissal, exemption, exoneration, liberation, pardon, release, relief, reprieve, vindication *Antonyms:* conviction, indictment

acrid *adj.* acid, astringent, biting, caustic, cutting, harsh, mordant, nasty, pungent, sarcastic, sharp, stinging, trenchant, vitriolic *Antonyms:* balmy, restful, sweet

acrimonious *adj.* acerbic, angry, astringent, bellicose, belligerent, bitter, churlish, crabby, cranky, cross, cutting, irascible, irate, nasty, peevish, rancorous, sarcastic, sharp, spiteful, testy *Antonyms:* benign, forgiving, good-tempered, tranquil

acrimony *n.* animosity, antipathy, asperity, astringency, bitterness, ill will, irascibility, malice, peevishness, rancour, rudeness, sarcasm, spite, unkindness *Antonyms:* amity, friendliness, friendship, good will, peacefulness, tranquility, warmth

acrobat *n.* aerialist, athlete, balancer, contortionist, dancer, funambulist, gymnast, stunt man *or* woman, tumbler

across *adj.* athwart, crosswise, oblique, traverse – *prep.* beyond, opposite, over, past

act *n.* **1.** accomplishment, achievement, action, deed, doing, execution, exploit, feat, move, operation, performance, step, undertaking **2.** amendment, announcement, bill, clause, code, commitment, decree, document, edict, enactment, judgment, law, measure, order, ordinance, resolution, statute, verdict, writ **3.** bit, curtain, epilogue, gag, introduction, number, performance, piece, prologue, routine, scene, show, schtick *(Nonformal)*, sketch, spot, stunt **4.** affectation, attitude, dissimulation, façade, fake, false front, feint, pose, posture, pretense, put-on, sham, simulation, stance – *v.* **1.** accomplish, achieve, appear, behave, bring out, carry on *or* out, comport, conduct, enact, execute, function, go about, operate, perform, perpetrate, practice, strike, take on, take steps, undertake, work **2.** burlesque, characterize, dramatize, emote, entertain, feign, ham *(Nonformal)*, impersonate, mime, mimic, mug, parody, perform, personify, play, playact, portray, pretend, rehearse, represent, role-play, simulate, star, stooge, strut

acting *adj.* adjutant, alternate, assistant, assuming, delegated, deputy, interim, provisional, substitute, surrogate, temporary *Latin:* ad interim, pro tempore – *n.* characterization, depiction, dramatics, dramatization, enactment, entertainment, histrionics, imitation, impersonation, mimicry, pantomime, performance, playing, portrayal, posturing, pretense, pretending, recreation, rendition, showing off, simulation, stage-craft, theatre, theatricals

action *n.* **1.** accomplishment, achievement, act, activity, animation, business, commission, commotion, dealings, deed, doing, effort, enterprise, execution, exercise, exertion, exploit, feat, force, functioning, handiwork, happening, manoeuvre, motion, move, movement, operation, performance, procedure, process, reaction, response, step, stroke, thrust, transaction, undertaking, work, working **2.** battle, combat, conflict, contest, encounter, engagement, fight, fray, skirmish, warfare **3.** case, cause, claim, lawsuit, litigation, proceeding, prosecution, suit

activate *v.* arouse, energize, impel, incite, initiate, mobilize, motivate, move, prompt, propel, rouse, start, stimulate, stir, trigger *Antonyms:* arrest, halt, impede

active *adj.* **1.** aggressive, agile, alert, animated, assiduous, bold, bustling, busy, chipper, daring, dashing, determined, dexterous, diligent, dynamic, eager, energetic, enterprising, enthusiastic, eventful, fireball *(Nonformal)*, forceful, forcible, hardworking, industrious, intense, inventive, involved, keen, lively, persevering, purposeful, ready, resolute, sharp, sprightly, spry, zealous *Antonyms:* disinterested, indolent, lazy, sluggish, torpid, unconcerned **2.** alive, at work, brisk, flowing, functioning, going, in force, in play, in process, mobile, moving, operating, operative, progressive, rolling, running, shifting, working *Antonyms:* dormant, idle, inactive, inert

activity *n.* act, action, animation, avocation, bustle, commotion, deed, endeavour, enterprise, entertainment, exercise, exertion, game, hobby, interest, job, labour, motion, movement, occupation, pastime, project, pursuit, task, to-do *(Nonformal)*, undertaking, venture, work *Antonyms:* inertia, languor, lassitude

actor *n.* entertainer, performer, player, thespian, trouper *Kinds of actor:* amateur, bit player, character, clown, comedian, extra, headliner, impersonator, ingénue, lead, leading man *or* woman, mime, mimic, movie *or* television star, mummer, pantomimist, stand-in, star, straight man *or* woman, understudy, ventriloquist, villain, walk-on

actual *adj.* **1.** authentic, categorical, certain, concrete, confirmed, definite, factual, genuine, indisputable, real, realistic, substantive, tangible, true, truthful, undeniable, unquestionable, verified *Antonyms:* fictitious, hypothetical, probable, spectral, supposed, theoretical, unreal, untrue **2.** current, exact, existing, existent, extant, live, living, original, prevailing

actuality *n.* achievement, actualization, fact, materialization, reality, substance, truth

actually *adv.* absolutely, *de facto (Latin)*, genuinely, indeed, in fact, in reality, in truth, literally, really, tangibly, truly, veritably

acumen *n.* acuity, astuteness, awareness, brains, brilliance, cleverness, comprehension, cunning, discrimination, farsightedness, grasp, guile, ingenuity, insight, intellect, intelligence, intuition, judgment, keenness, perception, percipience, perspicacity, refinement, sagacity, sensitivity, sharpness, shrewdness, smartness, smarts *(Nonformal)*, understanding, vision, wisdom, wit

acute *adj.* **1.** critical, crucial, dangerous, decisive, desperate, dire, essential, grave, important, serious, sudden, urgent, vital *Antonyms:* irrelevant, meaningless, nonessential **2.** agonizing, cutting, distressing, excruciating, fierce, intense, keen, overpowering, overwhelming, piercing, poignant, powerful, racking, severe, sharp, shooting, stabbing, violent *Antonyms:* gentle, mild, soft **3.** astute, bright, canny, clever, discerning, discriminating, exquisite, incisive, ingenious, insightful, intense, intuitive, judicious, keen, observant, penetrating, perceptive, perspicacious, piercing, quick-witted, sensitive, smart, subtle *Antonyms:* dense, dim, obtuse, slow, stupid **4.** peaked, piked, pointed, sharp, sharpened, spiked *Antonyms:* blunt, dull

adage *n.* aphorism, apothegm, axiom, byword, dictum, epigram, maxim, motto, precept, proverb, saw, saying

adamant *adj.* determined, die-hard, firm, fixed, flinty, hard-nosed *(Nonformal)*, immovable, inflexible, insistent, intransigent, obdurate, relentless, resolute, rigid, set, stalwart, stubborn, tough, unbending, unbreakable, unrelenting, unshakable, unyielding *Antonyms:* compliant, docile, easygoing, flexible, lax, pliant, tractable, yielding

adapt *v.* acclimate, accommodate, adjust, alter, change, comply, conform, fashion, fit, harmonize, make, match, modify, qualify, readjust, reconcile, remodel, revise, shape, square, suit, tailor *Commonly misused:* **adopt**

adaptable *adj.* **1.** adjustable, alterable, changeable, compliant, conformable, elastic, flexible, fluctuating, malleable, movable, multifaceted, pliant, reversible, shifting, variable, versatile *Antonyms:* inflexible, rigid **2.** able, adroit, fluid, handy, mercurial, quicksilver, resourceful

adaptation *n.* adjustment, adoption, alteration, condensation, conversion, modification, refitting, remodeling, reworking, transformation, variation

add *v.* **1.** admit, affix, annex, append, augment, build up, charge up, continue, hitch on, hook on, include, increase, inject, insert, instill, interject, interpolate, interpose, introduce, intrude, join together, put in *Nonformal:* fill in, throw in, toss aboard, work in *Antonyms:* deduct, diminish, lessen, reduce, remove, subtract, take away *or* from **2.** calculate, compute, count, enumerate, figure, reckon, sum up, tabulate, tally, total

added *adj.* additional, augmented, bonus, boosted, enlarged, expanded, extra, increased, supplementary, surplus

addict *n.* aficionado, devotee, enthusiast, fan *or* fanatic, follower, habitué *Nonformal:* buff, crackhead, hound, fiend, junkie, nut

addicted *adj.* habituated, hooked, inclined, obsessed, predisposed, prone, strung out *(Nonformal)*

addiction *n.* bent, craving, dependence, devotion, enslavement, fixation, habit, illness, madness, monkey *(Nonformal)*, obsession, problem, sickness

addition *n.* **1.** accessory, accompaniment, accoutrement, addendum, additive, adjunct, aggrandizement, annex, annexation, appendage, appendix, appurtenance, attachment, augmentation, auxiliary, bonus, codicil, complement, concomitant, continuation, dividend, embellishment, enhancement, enlargement, enrichment, expansion, extension, extra, gain, increase, increment, reinforcement, rider, supplement *Antonyms:* deduction, diminution, lessening, reduction, removal, subtraction **2.** calculation, computation, counting, reckoning, summation, tabulation, totalling

additional *adj.* added, appended, auxiliary, bonus, extra, farther, further, increased, more, other, over-and-above, renewed, supplementary

additionally *adv.* again, also, as well, beyond, besides, excessively, farther, further, in addition, moreover, over, to boot *(Nonformal)*, too

additive *n.* add-on, addition, enhancement, extra, preservative, substitute *Kinds of additive:* agar, alum, aspartame, carrageenin, chemical, collagen, gum arabic, mineral, octane, pectin, protein, saccharin, salt, sulfate, vitamin

address *n.* **1.** abode, domicile, dwelling, home, house, location, number, residence, street, whereabouts **2.** appellation, designation, heading, honour, moniker *(Nonformal)*, name, term, title **3.** discourse, dissertation, harangue, homily, oration, sermon, speech, spiel *(Nonformal)*, talk, tirade **4.** ability, adroitness, bearing, behaviour, dexterity, dispatch, manner, polish, savoir-faire, skilfulness, tact – *v.* **1.** approach, buttonhole *(Nonformal)*, call, discuss, hail, speak *or* speak to, talk to **2.** dispatch, forward, inscribe, label, mark, postmark, remit, route, send, ship, transmit

adept *adj.* able, accomplished, adroit, capable, deft, dexterous, expert, masterful, masterly, practiced, proficient, quick, sharp, skilful, skilled, slick, smooth, versed *Nonformal:* crackerjack, hot at *or* with, hotshot *Antonyms:* amateurish, awkward, clumsy, inept, unskilled – *n.* connoisseur, craftsperson, expert, master, old hand, veteran, virtuoso

adequacy *n.* amplitude, capacity, enough, plenty, profusion, *quantum sufficit (Latin)*, sufficiency *Antonyms:* dearth, inadequacy, lack

adequate *adj.* acceptable, all right, comfortable, commensurate, enough, equal, passable, requisite, satisfactory, sufficient, suitable, tolerable *Antonyms:* deficient, inadequate, insufficient, lacking

adequately *adv.* acceptably, decently, enough, fairly well, fittingly, modestly, pleasantly enough, presentably, satisfactorily, sufficiently

adhere *v.* attach, cement, cling, fasten, fix, glue, hold fast, paste, stick, unite

adhesive *adj.* clingy, gelatinous, gooey, gummed, holding, mucilaginous, sticking, sticky, tenacious – *n.* cement, glue, gum, paste, plaster, tape, wax

adjacent *adj.* abutting, adjoining, beside, bordering, close, close by, contiguous, near, neighbouring, next door, next to, touching *Antonyms:* distant, far away, remote, separated

adjoining *adj.* bordering, connecting, contiguous, interconnecting, joined, joining, juxtaposed, near, neighbouring, touching, verging *Antonyms:* disconnecting, divergent, separate

adjourn *v.* bench *(Nonformal)*, defer, delay, discontinue, hold off, hold over, hold up, postpone, put off, recess, restrain, shelve, stay, stop, suspend *Antonyms:* assemble, convene, gather

adjournment *n.* break, deferment, deferral, discontinuation, intermission, interruption, pause, postponement, prorogation, recess, stay, suspension

adjudicate *v.* arbitrate, decide, determine, judge, mediate, referee, settle, umpire

adjunct *adj.* assistant, auxiliary, reserve, secondary, supplementary – *n.* accessory, addendum, addition, appendage, appurtenance, associate, auxiliary, complement, subordinate, supplement *Antonyms:* core, heart

adjust *v.* **1.** arrange, clarify, conclude, conform, coordinate, doctor *(Nonformal)*, fine tune, fix up, grade, modify, organize, regulate, sort, standardize, straighten, tune **2.** acclimatize, accommodate, acculturate, accustom, adapt, alter, compose, conform, fit, fix, grow used to, habituate, harmonize, reconcile, rectify, remodel, settle, suit, tailor, transculturate *Antonyms:* contradict, oppose, rebel, reject, repudiate

adjustment *n.* **1.** allotment, benefit, compensation, pay, payment, reimbursement, remuneration, share, stake **2.** accommodation, compromise, reconciliation, resolution, settlement **3.** alteration, change, conversion, modification, variation **4.** alignment, calibration, correction, fine-tuning, tweak

adjutant *n.* aide, aide-de-camp, assistant, auxiliary, helper

administer *v.* apply, apportion, authorize, contribute, deal, deliver, disburse, dispense, distribute, dole, extend, furnish, give, impose, issue, manage, measure, mete out, offer, portion, proffer, provide, regulate, serve, supply, tender

administration *n.* affairs, agency, authority, bureau, cabinet, charge, command, control, direction, enforcement, execution, executive, executives, governing body, government, guidance, handling, headquarters, jurisdiction, legislation, management, ministry, officers, officials, organization, oversight, policy, power *or* powers, regulation, rule, superintendence, supervision *Nonformal:* brass *or* top brass, front office

administrative *adj.* authoritative, bureaucratic, central, commanding, controlling, deciding, decision-making, departmental, directing, directorial, executive, governing, governmental, in charge *or* control, jurisdictional, legislative, managerial, official, organizational, policy-making, presiding, regulatory, ruling, superintending, supervising

administrator *n.* ambassador, authority, boss, CEO, CFO, cabinet minister, captain, chairperson, chief, commander, consul, controller, dean, director, executive, general manager, governor, head, leader, manager, master, mayor, minister, official, organizer, overseer, premier, president, prime minister, reeve, superintendent, supervisor *Nonformal:* big brother, exec, head honcho

admirable *adj.* choice, commendable, deserving, estimable, excellent, exquisite, fine, good, greatest, laudable, meritorious, praiseworthy, respected, solid, super, superior, valuable, worthy *Antonyms:* bad, mediocre, poor, unrespectable, worthless

admiration *n.* adoration, affection, appreciation, approval, deference, delight, esteem, estimation, favour, fondness, glorification, homage, honour, idolatry, idolization, liking, love, praise, recognition, regard, respect, reverence, veneration, wonder, worship *Antonyms:* disgust, distaste, repugnance

admire *v.* adore, applaud, appreciate, approve, cherish, commend, credit, delight in, esteem, extol, fancy, glorify, hail, honour, idolize, laud, marvel at, praise, prize, rate highly, respect, revere, treasure, value, venerate, wonder at, worship *Antonyms:* condemn, deride, despise, scorn, spurn

admissible *adj.* acceptable, allowable, allowed, applicable, appropriate, fair, fitting, just, justifiable, lawful, legal, legitimate, likely, logical, okay *(Nonformal)*, passable, permissible, permitted, pertinent, possible, probable, proper, rational, reasonable, relevant, right, suitable, tolerable, tolerated, warranted, worthy *Antonyms:* disallowed, inadmissible, intolerable, unacceptable

admission *n.* **1.** acknowledgment, admittance, affidavit, affirmation, allowance, assent, assertion, attestation, avowal, certification, concession, confession, confirmation, declaration, deposition, designation, disclosure, divulgence, profession, recognition, revelation, statement, testimonial, testimony **2.** entrance, entrée, ingress, reception

admit *v.* **1.** accept, bless, entertain, give access, grant, initiate, introduce, let in, permit, receive, take in *Antonyms:* deny, exclude, prohibit, reject **2.** accede, accord, acknowledge, acquiesce, adopt, affirm, agree, allow, approve, avow, bare, come clean *(Nonformal)*, communicate, concede, concur, confess, confide, confirm, consent, credit, declare, disclose, divulge, explain, grant, indicate, open up, own, proclaim, profess, recite, recognize, relate, reveal, subscribe to, suggest, talk, tell, tolerate, uncover, unveil, yield *Antonyms:* dismiss, expel, forbid

admonish *v.* **1.** alert, caution, check, counsel, exhort, forewarn, urge, warn **2.** berate, call down, censure, chide, enjoin, rebuke, reprimand, reproof, reprove, scold, sit on, speak *or* talk to, upbraid *Nonformal*: rap, tell off *Antonyms:* applaud, commend, congratulate, laud, praise

adolescence *n.* minority, pre-adulthood, pubescence, teen, youth, youthfulness *Antonyms:* infancy, old age, seniority

adolescent *adj.* boyish, girlish, immature, juvenile, pre-adult, pubescent, puerile, teen, teenage, young, youthful – *n.* juvenile, kid, minor, pre-adult, teen, teenager, youngster, youth *Nonformal:* punk, teeny-bopper

adopt *v.* **1.** accept, affirm, appropriate, approve, assent, choose, embrace, endorse, espouse, opt, pick, ratify, select, take on *or* over **2.** assume responsibility for, care for, foster, harbour, protect *Antonyms:* abandon, disavow, disclaim, disown, repudiate, spurn *Commonly misused:* **adapt**

adoption *n.* acceptance, approbation, appropriation, approval, assumption, confirmation, embrace, enactment, endorsement, espousal, fostering, ratification

adorable *adj.* appealing, attractive, charming, cuddly, cute, darling, delectable, delightful, dishy *(Nonformal)*, fetching, heavenly, luscious, pleasant, pleasing, pretty, sexy, suave *Antonyms:* despicable, displeasing, unlovable

adoration *n.* admiration, ardour, attachment, devotion, esteem, estimation, exaltation, glorification, honour, idolization, infatuation, love, passion, reverence, veneration, weakness, worshipping, yen *Nonformal*: crush, shine *Antonyms:* contempt, disinterest, hatred

adore *v.* cherish, dote on, esteem, exalt, glorify, honour, idolize, love, prize, revere, treasure, venerate, worship *Antonyms:* abhor, abominate, despise, detest, execrate

adorn *v.* array, beautify, bedeck, deck, decorate, doll *or* dress up, embellish, emblazon, embroider, enhance, enrich, garnish, gussy *or* spruce up *(Nonformal)*, ornament, prettify, prink, trim *Antonyms:* despoil, divest, strip

adornment *n.* accessory, decoration, doodad *(Nonformal)*, fandangle, embellishment, enhancement, frill, frippery, ornament, ornamentation, trimming

adrift *adj.* afloat, aimless, astray, caught in the doldrums, drifting, floating, goalless, loose, lost at sea, off course, purposeless, wandering *Antonyms:* focused, purposeful, rooted, sailing along,

adroit *adj.* able, adept, apt, artful, clean, clever, crack, cunning, deft, dexterous, expert, foxy, good at *or* in, handy, ingenious, masterful, neat, nifty, nimble, proficient, quick-witted, sharp, skilful, skilled, slick, smart at *Nonformal*: crackerjack, savvy *Antonyms:* awkward, blundering, bungling, clumsy, ham-fisted, inept

adulation *n.* **1.** acclaim, applause, approbation, commendation, praise, worship **2.** blandishment, flattery, fawning, sycophancy *Antonyms:* calumniation, censure, condemnation

adult *adj.* developed, elder, fully grown, grown, grown-up, mature, of age, ripe, ripened, senior *Antonyms:* babyish, childish, infantile – *n.* man, old-timer *(Nonformal)*, veteran, woman

adulterate *v.* abase, alloy, amalgamate, cheapen, contaminate, corrupt, cut, debase, defile, degrade, denature, depreciate, deteriorate, devalue, diminish, doctor *(Nonformal)*, impair, infiltrate, load, mix, pervert, plant, pollute, reduce, shave, spike, spoil, taint, thin, vitiate, water down, worsen

adulterous *adj.* cheating, double-crossing, extracurricular, fast, illicit, immoral, promiscuous, two-timing *(Nonformal)*

adultery *n.* affair, cheating, cuckoldry, infidelity *Nonformal:* fling, hanky-panky, musical beds, playing *or* fooling around

advance *adj.* ahead, beforehand, earlier, early, first, foremost, forward, in front, leading, – *n.* **1.** advancement, amelioration, betterment, boost, breakthrough, development, enrichment, furtherance, gain, growth, headway, improvement, increase, progress, progression, promotion, rise, upgrade **2.** approach, move, overture, proposal, proposition, suggestion **3.** allowance, credit, deposit, down payment, front money, hike, increase, loan, prepayment, retainer, stake – *v.* **1.** accelerate, achieve, bring forward, conquer, drive, elevate, forge *or* forge ahead, gain ground, go forward *or* places, hasten, launch, move forward *or* on, proceed, progress, promote, propel, send forward, speed, step forward *Antonyms:* regress, set back, withdraw **2.** boost, develop, elevate, enlarge, grow, improve, increase, magnify, multiply, pan out, prosper, raise, thrive, upgrade, uplift *Antonyms:* decrease, diminish, lessen, retard **3.** adduce, allege, benefit, boost, encourage, foster, further, introduce, offer, plug, present, proffer, promote, propose, push, put forward, serve, set forth, submit, suggest, urge *Nonformal:* ballyhoo, hype *Antonyms:* hold back, impede, retreat **4.** credit, furnish, lend, loan, pay, provide

advanced *adj.* **1.** ahead, avant-garde, breakthrough, cutting-edge, excellent, exceptional, extreme, first, foremost, forward, improved, leading, liberal, perfected, precocious, progressive, radical, refined *Antonyms:* backward, behind, retarded, undeveloped **2.** aged, along in years, ancient, latter, old, venerable

advancement *n.* advance, amelioration, betterment, elevation, gain, headway, improvement, march, progress, progression, rise, upgrading *Antonyms:* reversal, setback

advantage *n.* **1.** aid, ascendancy, asset, assistance, benefit, blessing, comfort, convenience, influence, profit, resources **2.** boon, break, choice, edge, favour, hold **3.** authority, dominance, edge, eminence, leg-up *(Nonformal)*, mastery, position, preeminence, start, superiority *Antonyms:* curse, disadvantage, drawback, handicap, hindrance

advantageous *adj.* beneficial, convenient, expedient, favourable, helpful, opportune, profitable, propitious, rewarding, useful, valuable, well-sited, well-situated, worthwhile *Antonyms:* detrimental, unfavourable, unfortunate, useless *Commonly Misused:* **adventitious**

advent *n.* appearance, approach, arrival, beginning, coming, entrance, occurrence, onset, rearing, visitation

adventitious *adj.* **1.** accidental, casual, chance, fortuitous, incidental, serendipitous, unexpected **2.** extraneous, foreign, nonessential, superfluous *Antonyms:* inherent, intrinsic, innate *Commonly misused:* **advantageous**

adventure *n.* chance, endangerment, enterprise, experience, exploit, feat, happening, hazard, incident, jeopardy, peril, risk, speculation, trip, undertaking, venture

adventurer *n.* buccaneer, coureur de bois *(Historical)*, daredevil, entrepreneur, explorer, fortune-hunter, gambler, globetrotter, hero, heroine, knight, mercenary, opportunist, pioneer, pirate, risk-taker, rogue, romantic, soldier of fortune, speculator, swashbuckler, traveller, venturer, voyager, wanderer *Antonyms:* bore, couch potato *(Nonformal)*, homebody

adventurous *adj.* **1.** audacious, bold, brave, courageous, daredevil, enterprising, headstrong, intrepid, rash, reckless, risk-taking, venturesome, venturous *Antonyms:* careful, circumspect, prudent, tentative, wary **2.** chancy *(Nonformal)*, dangerous, foolhardy, hazardous, rash, risky

adversary *n.* antagonist, attacker, contestant, enemy, foe, match, opponent, opposite camp, rival *Antonyms:* accomplice, ally, collaborator, colleague, confederate

adverse *adj.* **1.** antithetical, at odds, confrontational, dissenting, inimical, opposing, ornery, reluctant, repugnant, unfriendly, unwilling **2.** detrimental, disadvantageous, inopportune, negative, noxious, unfavourable, unfortunate, unlucky *Antonyms:* advantageous, beneficial, fortunate, helpful, lucky *Commonly misused:* **averse**

adversity *n.* affliction, bad break *or* luck, blight, calamity, catastrophe, contretemps, difficulty, dire straits, distress, hardship, hard times, misery, misfortune, mishap, reverse, sorrow, suffering, trial, trouble *Antonyms:* boon, felicity, prosperity, success, well-being

advertise *v.* **1.** blazon, boost, build up, draw attention to, endorse, exhibit, expose, flaunt, flourish, herald, pitch, proclaim, promote, promulgate, publicize, push, reveal, sponsor, tout *Nonformal:* ballyhoo, drum *or* drum up, hang out one's shingle, hype, plug, puff up **2.** announce, communicate, declare, disclose, display, divulge, inform, make known, show

advertisement *n.* announcement, banner, bill, circular, classified ad, commercial, endorsement, flyer, literature, notice, pixel board, propaganda, publication, publicity, want ad *Nonformal:* infomercial, plug, spam

advertising *n.* announcement, billing, blurb, brochure, exhibition, exposition, flyer, marketing, notice, pitch, posting, proclamation, promo *or* promotion, publicity, public relations, spread *Nonformal*: hoopla, hype, plug, screamer, spam

advice *n.* **1.** aid, consultation, counsel, direction, encouragement, exhortation, forewarning, guidance, help, input, instruction, judgment, lesson, opinion, persuasion, proposal, recommendation, suggestion, view, word **2.** admonition, caution, dissuasion, tip, warning *Commonly misused:* **advise**

advisable *adj.* appropriate, apt, commendable, desirable, expedient, fit, fitting, judicious, politic, prudent, recommended, seemly, sensible, sound, suggested, suitable *Antonyms:* ill-advised, impolitic, improper

advise *v.* **1.** acquaint, apprise, break *or* fill in, clue *or* clue in, inform, keep posted, make known, notify, post, report, tell, tip off, update **2.** admonish, advocate, caution, charge, counsel, direct, dissuade, encourage, enjoin, exhort, guide, instruct, level with, point out, prepare, prompt, recommend, steer *(Nonformal)*, suggest, urge, warn *Commonly misused:* **advice**

advisor *n.* agent, aide, authority, coach, confidant, consultant, counsel, counsellor, expert, guide, helper, instructor, judge, mentor, partner, right-hand man *or* woman *(Nonformal)*, teacher, tutor

advisory *adj.* consultative, counselling, guiding, helping, monitorial, recommending, regulatory, synodal

advocate *n.* **1.** admirer, apostle, attorney, backer, campaigner, champion, counsel, defender, exponent, lawyer, lobbyist, partisan, pleader, promoter, proponent, proposer, protagonist, publicist, speaker, spokesperson, supporter, upholder *Antonyms:* adversary, opponent **2.** agent, arbitrator, go-between, intermediary, negotiator, representative – *v.* advance, argue for, associate with, back, bless, bolster, boost, campaign for, champion, encourage, endorse, espouse, favour, fight for, go for *or* with, hold with, justify, press for, promote, propose, push, put forward, recommend, represent, root for, speak for, stick by, stump *or* thump for, support, urge *Antonyms:* contradict, oppose, resist, speak against, take issue with *Commonly misused:* **surrogate**

aegis *n.* auspices, guardianship, patronage, protection, sponsorship

aerial *adj.* **1.** aeolian, airy, celestial, chimerical, ethereal, exalted, gaseous, heavenly, imaginary, insubstantial, intangible, lofty, olympian **2.** airborne, flying, volitant, winged – *n.* antenna, mast, rabbit ears *(Nonformal)*, tower

aesthetic *adj.* **1.** artistic, beautiful, elegant, exquisite, graceful, tasteful, well-composed **2.** discriminating, fastidious, polished, refined **3.** empathetic, impressionable, perceptive, sensitive *Commonly misused:* **ascetic**

afar *adv.* abroad, at a distance, away, distantly, far-off, over there, remotely, yonder

affable *adj.* amiable, approachable, benevolent, civil, congenial, cordial, courteous, easygoing, friendly, genial, gentle, good-humoured, good-natured, gracious, kindly, mild, pleasant, sociable, warm *Antonyms:* brusque, cold, distant, haughty, rude, standoffish

affair *n.* **1.** activity, assignment, avocation, calling, case, circumstance, concern, duty, employment, episode, event, happening, incident, interest, job, mission, obligation, occupation, occurrence, office function, proceeding, profession, project, province, pursuit, question, realm, responsibility, subject, task, topic, transaction, undertaking **2.** intimacy, intrigue, liaison, love, relationship, rendezvous, romance *Nonformal:* fling, fooling *or* sleeping around

affect *v.* **1.** act on, apply to, concern, impinge, induce, interest, involve, pertain to, prevail **2.** act, assume, bluff, contrive, counterfeit, fake, feign, imitate, pretend, put on, sham, simulate **3.** alter, change, disturb, influence, inspire, impress, modify, move, overcome, stir, sway, touch, transform, upset

affectation *n.* airs, appearance, artificiality, dandyism, display, façade, false front, front, guise, imitation, insincerity, mannerism, pose, pretense, pretentiousness, sham, show, simulation *Commonly misused:* **affection**

affected *adj.* **1.** altered, changed, concerned, distressed, excited, grieved, impressed, influenced, moved, overwhelmed, overwrought, stimulated, stirred, swayed, sympathetic, tender, torn, touched, transformed, troubled, upset, wracked *Antonyms:* unconcerned, unharmed, untouched **2.** artificial, assumed, awkward, camp, conceited, contrived, counterfeit, fake, false, feigned, grandiose, imitated, insincere, melodramatic, ostentatious, overdone, pompous, precious, put-on, self-conscious, shallow, sham, simulated, spurious, stiff, stilted, studied, superficial, theatrical, unnatural *Nonformal:* hammy, high-falutin, phoney, schmaltzy *Antonyms:* authentic, genuine, natural, real **3.** attacked, harmed, hurt, injured, seized, struck

affection *n.* **1.** ardour, attachment, care, closeness, devotion, endearment, feeling, fondness, friendliness, friendship, inclination, kindness, liking, love, passion, regard, sentiment, solicitude, tenderness, warmth *Nonformal:* puppy love, shine, soft spot, weakness *Antonyms:* disinterest, distaste, enmity, dislike, loathing, repugnance, revulsion **2.** inclination, penchant, predilection, predisposition, propensity, tendency *Commonly misused:* **affectation**

affectionate *adj.* **1.** dear, devoted, doting, fond, loving, partial, warm **2.** amiable, caring, friendly, kind-hearted, soft-hearted, sweet *Antonyms:* cold, cool, glacial, indifferent, stony, undemonstrative, unfeeling

affidavit *n.* affirmation, certificate, declaration, deposition, oath, *procès-verbal (French)*, sworn statement, testimony

affiliate *n.* arm, branch, offshoot, organization, partner, subsidiary – *v.* ally, annex, associate, band together, combine, connect, join, link, pair up, relate, team, tie up, unite *Nonformal:* come aboard, go partners, hook up *Antonyms:* divide, separate, split up

affiliation *n.* **1.** alignment, alliance, association, coalition, combination, confederation, conjunction, connection, fusion, integration, partnership, tie-in **2.** brotherhood, denomination, fraternity, friendship, persuasion, sect, sisterhood, sorority **3.** circle, club, company, fellowship, society

affinity *n.* **1.** alikeness, alliance, analogy, association, closeness, connection, consanguinity, correspondence, kinship, likeness, relationship, resemblance, semblance, similarity, similitude *Antonyms:* difference, disparity, dissimilarity **2.** affection, attraction, compatibility, inclination, leaning, liking, partiality, proclivity, propensity, rapport, sympathy *Nonformal:* good vibes, thing, weakness *Antonyms:* abhorrence, animosity, aversion, dislike, hostility

affirm *v.* **1.** allege, assert, aver, avow, declare, endorse, profess, pronounce, witness **2.** attest, authenticate, bear out, certify, confirm, corroborate, countersign, ratify, swear *or* swear to, testify to, vouch *or* vouch for *Antonyms:* deny, disallow, refute, reject, renounce, repudiate, rescind

affirmation *n.* affidavit, assertion, attestation, avowal, certification, confirmation, declaration, oath, pronouncement, ratification, statement, sworn statement, testimony *Nonformal:* green light, okay *Antonym:* denial, veto

affirmative *adj.* **1.** acquiescent, agreeable, consenting, corroborative, emphatic, *en* *rapport (French)*, supportive **2.** approving, blessing, sanctioning, validating, warranting – n. a go *(Nonformal)*, a positive thumbs-up, assent, aye, yea, yes

affix *v.* **1.** add, annex, append, attach, bind, fasten, glue, hitch on, join, paste, rivet, stick, tack on, tag on *Antonyms:* detach, disconnect, remove, separate, split, take off, unfasten, unglue **2.** attribute to, credit with, pin on

afflict *v.* agonize, annoy, beset, bother, burden, distress, grieve, harass, hurt, oppress, pain, pester, plague, press, smite, strike, torment, torture, trouble, try, vex, worry, wound *Antonyms:* abate, alleviate, mitigate, relieve *Commonly misused:* **inflict**

affliction *n.* adversity, anguish, calamity, depression, difficulty, disease, disorder, distress, grief, hardship, heavy load *(Nonformal)*, hurt, illness, infirmity, misery, misfortune, ordeal, pain, plague, plight, scourge, sorrow, suffering, torment, trial, tribulation, trouble, woe *Antonyms:* health, robustness, well-being

affluent *adj.* **1.** moneyed, opulent, prosperous, rich, upper-class, upscale, uptown, wealthy, well-off, well-to-do *Nonformal:* flush, loaded, well-heeled *Antonyms:* destitute, impoverished, penniless, poor **2.** abounding, abundant, copious, full, plenteous, rife *Antonyms:* rare, scarce, sparse *Commonly misused:* **effluent**

afford *v.* **1.** allow, bear, incur, manage, spare, stand, support, sustain **2.** bestow, furnish, generate, give, grant, impart, offer, provide, render, supply, yield

affront *n.* aspersion, derision, humiliation, indignity, insult, offence, provocation, putdown *(Nonformal)*, ridicule, slap in the face, slight – *v.* confront, flout, impugn, insult, malign, offend, outrage, provoke, slur, snub

aficionado *n.* buff, collector, connoisseur, enthusiast, expert, fan, patron, specialist

afraid *adj.* abashed, aghast, alarmed, anxious, apprehensive, aroused, averse, blanched, cowardly, cowed, daunted, discouraged, disheartened, dismayed, distressed, disturbed, fainthearted, fearful, frightened, frozen, horrified, intimidated, nervous, panic-stricken, petrified, rattled, reluctant, scared, shocked, startled, stunned, terrified, timid, upset, worried *Antonyms:* audacious, bold, fearless

after *adv.* consequently, next, subsequently – *prep.* as a result of, because of, consequent to, following, in pursuit of, in the style of, later, modelled on, on account of, owing to, since, subsequent to, whereupon *Antonyms:* before, previous to

aftermath *n.* aftereffect, afterglow, consequence, effect, eventuality, issue, outcome, payoff *(Nonformal)*, remainder, repercussion, result, sequel, upshot, wake

afternoon *n.* **1.** cocktail hour, p.m., post meridian, sundown, *Nonformal:* arsenic hour, over the yardarm **2.** closing part, middle years, twilight, waning years

afterthought *n.* reconsideration, reflection, retrospection, review, second thought

afterward *adv.* after, eventually, following, later, next, soon, subsequently, then, thereafter, ultimately

again *adv.* **1.** afresh, anew, another time, encore, freshly, in response, in return, newly, once more, over, recurrently, repeatedly **2.** *au contraire (French)*, conversely, moreover, notwithstanding, on the other hand

against *prep.* **1.** at odds with, contrary to, in disagreement with, opposite to, versus **2.** athwart, face-to-face with, in contact with, leaning upon, pressing, *vis-à-vis (French)*

age *n.* **1.** adolescence, change of life, childhood, climacteric, development, grand climacteric, infancy, majority, manhood, maturity, menopause, middle age, old age, prime of life, prepubescence, pubescence, ripe old age, salad days *(Nonformal)*, seniority, stage, teen years, womanhood, youth **2.** caducity, decline of life, deterioration, dotage, elderliness, senescence, senility **3.** aeon, duration, epoch, era, generation, lifetime, period, span – *v.* **1.** grow, grow old *or* up, mature, mellow, ripen, season **2.** decline, deteriorate, fail, get along, have had one's day, have seen better days, show one's years, weather, wear

aged *adj.* **1.** ancient, antiquated, elderly, grey-headed, hoary, long-lived, old, used, venerable, vintage, worn-out **2.** full-grown, mature, mellowed, seasoned, tempered

agency *n.* **1.** auspices, influence, instrument, intercession, intervention, means, mechanism, medium, organ, power, vehicle **2.** bureau, firm, office, organization

agenda *n.* calendar, card, diary, docket, itinerary, lineup, list, plan, program, schedule, timetable

agent *n.* **1.** author, cause, channel, factor, force, funnel, instrument, means, medium, organ, power, prime mover, vehicle **2.** abettor, advocate, assignee, broker, delegate, deputy, emissary, envoy, executor, factotum, functionary, go-between, middleperson, negotiator, operative, promoter, representative, salesman, saleswoman, steward, substitute, surrogate

aggrandize *v.* acclaim, applaud, augment, boost, commend, dignify, distinguish, enlarge, exaggerate, expand, extend, glorify, heighten, honour, increase, intensify, jump, magnify, multiply, parlay, praise, promote *Nonformal:* ballyhoo, beef up, hike, hype *Antonyms:* belittle, disparage, downgrade

aggravate *v.* **1.** annoy, bother, exasperate, gall, irritate, peeve, pester, pique, provoke, rouse, vex *Nonformal:* bug, dog, get *or* get to, grate, hack, irk, nag, needle, nettle, pick on **2.** add insult to, complicate, deepen, enhance, exacerbate, exaggerate, heighten, increase, inflame, intensify, magnify, mount, rise, worsen *Antonyms:* alleviate, assuage, calm, placate, reconcile *Commonly misused:* **aggregate**

aggravation *n.* **1.** affliction, annoyance, bother, difficulty, distress, exasperation, hassle, irritant, irritation, pain, provocation, teasing, vexation, worry *Nonformal:* botheration, headache, pain in the neck, pet peeve **2.** amplifying, exacerbation, exaggeration, heightening, increase, inflammation, intensification, magnification

aggregate *adj.* amassed, assembled, total, whole – *n.* **1.** all, body, entirety, sum, whole *Nonformal:* the lot, the works, whole shebang **2.** accumulation, agglomeration, assemblage, bulk, collection, combination, conglomerate, conglomeration, gross, mass, mixture, pile, quantity, sum, totality – *v.* accumulate, amass, assemble, collect, combine, heap, mix, number, pile, sum, total *Commonly misused:* **aggravate**

aggression *n.* **1.** assault, attack, encroachment, fight, foray, incursion, initiative, invasion, offence, onslaught, push, raid, sortie **2.** antagonism, belligerence, combativeness, contentiousness, hostility, pugnacity, truculence, warmongering

aggressive *adj.* **1.** assailing, attacking, belligerent, combative, contentious, disruptive, disturbing, encroaching, hawkish, hostile, intrusive, offensive, provocative, quarrelsome, scrappy, threatening, warlike **2.** assertive, bold, domineering, forceful, insistent, in your face *(Nonformal)*, pugnacious, pushy, vigorous *Antonyms:* mild, quiet, retiring, submissive

aggressor *n.* adversary, attacker, belligerent, instigator, invader

aggrieved *adj.* **1.** afflicted, distressed, disturbed, grieving, harmed, injured, pained, saddened, unhappy, worried **2.** ill-used, mistreated, persecuted, wronged *Antonyms:* assisted, championed, defended

aghast *adj.* **1.** agape, agog, amazed, appalled, astonished, astounded, awestruck, confounded, dumfounded, overwhelmed, stunned, surprised, thunderstruck **2.** afraid, alarmed, anxious, dismayed, frightened, horrified, petrified, shocked, startled, terrified

agile *adj.* **1.** athletic, energetic, fleet, limber, lithe, quick, rapid, sportive, sprightly, supple, vigorous, winged, zippy *Antonyms:* awkward, clumsy, lumbering, slow, ungainly **2.** acute, alert, brisk, bustling, deft, dexterous, keen, lively, nimble, on the ball *(Nonformal)*, prompt, sharp, smart, spry

agility *n.* **1.** adroitness, coordination, dexterity, fleetness, lightness, nimbleness, proficiency, suppleness **2.** acuteness, alertness, cleverness, liveliness, promptness, quickness, readiness, sharpness

aging *v.* **1.** maturing, mellowing, ripening, seasoning, settling down, tempering **2.** declining, getting on, slumping, waning, wasting away, wearing out

agitate *v.* **1.** beat, churn, convulse, disturb, rouse, ruffle, shake, stir, toss **2.** alarm, argue, arouse, craze, disconcert, dispute, disquiet, disturb, excite, foment, fluster, incite, inflame, perturb, stir, trouble, unhinge, unnerve, upset, worry *Nonformal:* egg on, spook *Antonyms:* appease, calm, mollify **3.** campaign, canvass, debate, lobby, muckrake, press for

agitator *n.* **1.** advocate, agent, champion, demagogue, disrupter, dissident, disturber, firebrand, inciter, instigator, malcontent, mover, muckraker, partisan, propagandist, provocateur, provoker, pusher, rabble-rouser, radical, rebel, reformer, revisionist, revolutionary, ringleader, troublemaker, zealot *Antonyms:* conciliator, pacifist, peacemaker **2.** eggbeater, blender, mixer, vibrator, whisk

agnostic *n.* doubter, freethinker, nonbeliever, sceptic *Antonyms:* believer, zealot

ago *adj.* bygone, departed, gone, over, past – *adv.* erstwhile, formerly, heretofore, of old, since

agog *adj.* **1.** alert, avid, curious, eager, enthusiastic, expectant, keen *Antonyms:* apathetic, indifferent, nonchalant **2.** astounded, awestruck, dumfounded, flabbergasted, open-eyed, wide-eyed

agonize *v.* afflict, distress, disturb, grapple with, labour, pour over, squirm, strain, strive, struggle, suffer, torment, torture, try, worry, wrestle, writhe

agonizing *adj.* disturbing, excruciating, extreme, harrowing, heart-rending, gut-wrenching, intense, painful, racking, struggling, suffering, tortuous *Antonyms:* at ease, comfortable, content

agony *n.* affliction, anguish, distress, misery, pangs, passion, suffering, throes, torment, torture, woe, wretchedness *Antonyms:* ecstasy, passion, rapture

agree *v.* **1.** accede, accept, acquiesce, assent, come around, concede, consent, go along, yield **2.** accommodate, accord, adapt, adopt, coincide, concur, conform, harmonize, match, meet, parallel, synchronize *Antonyms:* contradict, differ **3.** affirm, approve, authorize, back, bless, boost, certify, embrace, endorse, favour, okay *(Nonformal)*, permit, sanction, support, undersign, underwrite **4.** acknowledge, admit, confirm, recognize *Antonyms:* dispute, dissent, refute

agreeable *adj.* **1.** acquiescent, affirmative, affirming, amenable, approving, complying, concurring, confirming, congenial, consenting, corroborative, endorsing, favourable, in accord, positive, ratifying, responsive, supporting, sympathetic, tractable, well-disposed, willing, yielding *Antonyms:* converse, negative, unsympathetic **2.** acceptable, delectable, delightful, enjoyable, fair, fine, gratifying, palatable, pleasant, pleasing, pleasurable, welcome *Nonformal:* dandy, hunky-dory, swell *Antonyms:* disagreeable, displeasing, offensive, unlikeable, unpleasant **3.** appropriate, befitting, compatible, consistent, fitting, proper *Antonyms:* inappropriate, unacceptable, unfit

agreeably *adv.* affably, affirmatively, amiably, amicably, appropriately, benevolently, charmingly, cheerfully, convivially, favourably, genially, good-naturedly, graciously, happily, kindly, obligingly, peacefully, pleasingly, politely, satisfactorily, sympathetically, well, willingly, wonderfully *Antonyms:* downheartedly, grudgingly, grumpily

agreement *n.* **1.** acceding, acceptance, accession, accommodation, accord, accordance, acknowledging, acknowledgment, acquiescence, affinity, affirmation, amenability, amity, approbation, approval, assent, assenting, blessing, common view, concert, concurrence, congruity, consensus, consent, correspondence, deal, endorsement, engagement, entente, harmony, rapport, tractability, unanimity, unison, unity *Nonformal:* good vibes *or* vibrations, green light, nod, okay, say-so *Antonyms:* altercation, division, strife **2.** arrangement, bargain, bond, charter, code, compact, concord, concordance, constitution, contract, convention, conveyance, covenant, deal, handshake *(Nonformal)*, indenture, licence, mediation, pact, protocol, settlement, treaty, understanding **3.** conformity, congruence, likeness, resemblance, similarity, symmetry *Antonyms:* disparity, incongruity

agricultural *adj.* agrarian, farming, gardening, horticultural, ranch, rural, rustic

agriculture *n.* agribusiness, agrobiology, agrology, agronomics, agronomy, animal husbandry, cultivation, culture, farming, horticulture, hydroponics, sharecropping, subsistence farming, tillage, truck farming

aground *adj.* beached, bottomed out, disabled, foundered, grounded, marooned, reefed, shipwrecked, stranded, swamped, wrecked *Nonformal:* high-and-dry, left in the lurch, on the rocks *Antonyms:* adrift, afloat, at sea, buoyant

ahead *adv.* **1.** afore, betimes, earlier, in advance **2.** before, in front, leading **3.** along, forth, forward, on, onward

aid *n.* **1.** assistance, comfort, gift, hand, ministration, reinforcement, relief, remedy, rescue, succour, support, treatment *Antonym:* hindrance **2.** advisor, angel, backer, benefactor, patron, Good Samaritan, underwriter **3.** allowance, benefit, contribution, fellowship, gift, handout, patronage, stipend, subsidy, support – *v.* **1.** accommodate, alleviate, assist, bail out, chip in, cooperate, lend a hand to, lighten, oblige, relieve *Antonyms:* hinder, impede, obstruct, oppose, thwart **2.** back, encourage, stand by, subsidize, support, sustain **3.** console, mitigate, salve, solace, soothe, succour

aide *n.* adjutant, aide-de-camp, assistant, attendant, deputy, girl *or* man Friday, gofer *(Nonformal)*, helper, right-hand person, steward, supporter

ail *v.* **1.** ache, burn, hurt, irritate, suffer, throb, torment, wince **2.** bother, languish, pine, waste away, weaken, worry *Antonyms:* bloom, convalesce, enliven, refresh, rejuvenate, thrive

ailing *adj.* bedridden, below par, debilitated, diseased, down, feeble, ill, indisposed, infirm, run-down, sick, sickly, unwell, weak *Nonformal:* laid-up, out of commission, rocky, under the weather *Antonyms:* blooming, healthy, salubrious

ailment *n.* bug, complaint, condition, disease, disorder, illness, infection, infirmity, malady, sickness, syndrome

aim *n.* **1.** ambition, aspiration, destination, determination, goal, hope, intention, purpose, thesis **2.** angle, course, direction, slant, tendency – *v.* **1.** direct, fix on, focus, head for, point at *or* to, sight, steer, target, train, zero in on, zoom in on **2.** conspire to, desire, endeavour, have in mind, intend, mean, plan, propose, resolve

aimless *adj.* accidental, blind, capricious, careless, casual, chance, desultory, drifting, erratic, fanciful, fickle, flighty, frivolous, goalless, haphazard, heedless, pointless, purposeless, rambling, random, shiftless, stray, undirected, unguided, unpredictable, wandering, wayward *Antonyms:* deliberate, purposeful, resolute

air *n.* **1.** ambience, appearance, atmosphere, attitude, aura, bearing, carriage, demeanour, deportment, feel, feeling, flavour, impression, look, manner, mien, mood, presence, property, quality, semblance, style, tone **2.** blast, breath, breeze, draft, ozone *(Nonformal)*, ventilation, wind, zephyr **3.** lay, melody, song, strain, theme, tune **4.** airspace, atmosphere, heavens, oxygen, sky, stratosphere – *adj.* aeronautical *Kinds of air or aeronautical sports:* ballooning, flying, gliding, hang-gliding, parachuting, parasailing, sky-diving – *v.* **1.** broadcast, disseminate, disperse, publish **2.** aerate, air-condition, circulate, cool, expel, expose, fan, freshen, open, oxygenate, purify, refresh, ventilate

aircraft *n.* airplane, plane *Common aircraft:* amphibian, autogyro, bush plane, Concorde, dirigible, flying boat, helicopter *or* chopper, Hercules, hot-air balloon, hydroplane, jet *or* jet plane, passenger plane, propeller *or* prop plane, rocket ship, rotor, rotorplane, seaplane, shuttle, skiplane, space shuttle, supersonic jet, trainer, turbojet, VTOL, Zeppelin *Nonformal:* blimp, buster *Common Canadian aircraft:* Avro Arrow *(Historical)*, Beaver, Buffalo, bush plane, Canadair CL-28 Argus, Canadair CL-215, Caribou, CF-18, Chinook, Dash 8, fire bomber, Otter, Twin Otter

airplane *n.* air bus, aircraft, airliner, flying machine, plane *Parts of an airplane:* aileron, black box, cargo bay, cockpit, flaps, flight deck, fuel tank, elevator, galley, landing gear, nose wheel, rudder, tail fin, wings *See also:* **aircraft**

airport *n.* aerodrome, airfield, airstrip, hangar, helipad, heliport, home plate *(Nonformal)*, installation, landing field *or* strip, runway, strip *Major Canadian Airports:* Calgary Intl., Edmonton Intl., Fredericton, Gander, Halifax Intl., Lester B. Pearson Intl. *(Toronto)*, Moncton, Ottawa Intl., Prince George, Québec, Regina, Saint John, Thunder Bay, Vancouver Intl., Victoria Intl., Winnipeg Intl. *Montréal:* Dorval, Mirabel

airs *n.* affectation, affectedness, arrogance, false front, haughtiness, hauteur, mannerism, ostentation, pomposity, pose, pretense, pretentiousness, put-on, show, snootiness *(Nonformal)*, superciliousness

airship *n.* balloon, blimp *(Nonformal)*, dirigible, Zeppelin

airtight *adj.* **1.** closed, hermetically sealed, impenetrable, impervious, sealed, shut, snug, vacuum **2.** certain, incontestable, indisputable, irrefutable, unassailable

airy *adj.* **1.** aerial, blowy, breezy, drafty, exposed, fluttering, fresh, gaseous, gusty, light, open, out-of-doors, pneumatic, spacious, uncluttered, vaporous, ventilated, well-ventilated, windy *Antonyms:* stale, stuffy, suffocating **2.** animated, blithe, bouncy, buoyant, cheerful, cheery, effervescent, fanciful, flippant, frolicsome, gay, graceful, happy, high-spirited, jaunty, light, light-hearted, lively, merry, sprightly, whimsical *Antonyms:* gloomy, glum, melancholy, morose **3.** dainty, delicate, diaphanous, flimsy, fragile, frail, light, rare, rarefied, thin, vaporous, volatile, weightless **4.** ethereal, illusory, imaginary, immaterial, intangible, tenuous, visionary

aisle *n.* alley, corridor, gangway, hallway, opening, passage, passageway, path, walk, way

ajar *adj.* **1.** open, unclosed, unlatched, unshut **2.** incongruous, discordant, out of whack *(Nonformal)*

akin *adj.* affiliated, allied, analogous, comparable, consanguine, corresponding, kindred, parallel, related, similar *Antonyms:* disparate, divergent, foreign

alacrity *n.* alertness, avidity, briskness, cheerfulness, dispatch, eagerness, ebullience, enthusiasm, fervour, gaiety, get up and go *(Nonformal)*, liveliness, quickness, readiness, sprightliness, willingness, zeal *Antonyms:* apathy, ennui, lethargy, reluctance, unwillingness

à la mode *adj.* chic, fashionable, in *(Nonformal)*, in vogue, stylish *French:* au courant, dernier cri, soignée

alarm *n.* **1.** anxiety, apprehension, cold feet *(Nonformal)*, consternation, dismay, distress, dread, fear, fright, horror, nervousness, panic, scare, strain, stress, tension, trepidation, uneasiness, upset *Antonyms:* calm, composure, sangfroid, serenity **2.** alert, call, caution, cry, flap, flash, forewarning, scream, shout, signal, summons, tip, trumpet, warning *Kinds of alarm:* beacon, bell, bugle call, DEW Line, early warning, foghorn, gong, horn, klaxon, mayday, searchlight, siren, SOS, squeal, tocsin, whistle – *v.* **1.** amaze, astonish, chill, daunt, dismay, distress, frighten, make jump, panic, scare, startle, surprise, terrify, unnerve, upset *Nonformal:* scare silly *or* stiff, spook *Antonyms:* assure, calm, reassure **2.** call to arms, rouse, signal, warn

alarmist *n.* Cassandra, doomsayer, pessimist, scaremonger, worrywart *(Nonformal)*

album *n.* **1.** anthology, collection, holder, miscellany, notebook, omnibus, portfolio, register, scrapbook **2.** compact disc *or* CD,

LP, record, soundtrack, vinyl, wax *(Nonformal)*

alchemy *n.* black magic, chemistry, sorcery, transformation, voodoo, witchcraft, wizardry

alcohol *n.* **1.** aqua vitae, bung-your-eye *(Newfoundland)*, drink, grog, intoxicant, liquor, spirits *Nonformal:* booze, firewater, hard stuff, hooch, moonshine, rotgut, sauce **2.** ethanol, fuel, methanol

alcoholic *adj.* brewed, distilled, fermented, hard, inebriant, inebriating, intoxicating, spirituous – *n.* chronic drinker, dipsomaniac, drunkard *Nonformal:* barfly, boozehound, lush, otis, rubby, shako, wino

alcove *n.* **1.** anteroom, bay, bower, carrel, compartment, corner, cubbyhole, cubicle, niche, nook, recess, stall, study **2.** a room of one's own, bower, haven, hideaway, sanctum

alert *adj.* active, attentive, bright, cagey, careful, circumspect, clever, heedful, keen, observant, on guard, perceptive, quick, ready, sharp, spirited, streetwise, vigilant, wary, watchful *Nonformal:* bright-eyed and bushy-tailed, heads-up, jazzed, wide-awake *Antonyms:* careless, heedless, languid, oblivious – *n.* admonition, alarm, buzzer, flap, high sign, hue and cry, mayday, sign, signal, siren, SOS, tipoff, warning – *v.* **1.** alarm, cry havoc, flag, forewarn, inform, notify, signal, sound the alarm, warn **2.** confide, let in on, tip *or* tip off

alias *adv.* also called, otherwise – *n.* assumed name, name, nickname, pen name, pseudonym, sobriquet, stage name *French:* nom de guerre, nom de plume *Nonformal:* AKA, handle, moniker

alibi *n.* account, affirmation, answer, assertion, assurance, avowal, cover, declaration, defence, excuse, explanation, justification, plea, pretext, proof, reason, statement, vindication *Nonformal:* cock and bull story, song and dance *Commonly misused:* **excuse**

alien *adj.* **1.** exotic, foreign, otherworldly, strange, unusual **2.** contradictory, contrary, dissimilar, extraneous, extrinsic, inappropriate, incongruous, separate *Antonyms:* affiliated, akin, like, pertinent, relevant – *n.* **1.** extraterrestrial, visitor from outer space *Nonformal:* E.T., FOB, furriner, Martian, the Greys, the Whites, Xenomorph **2.** foreigner, immigrant, incomer, interloper, intruder, invader, migrant, newcomer, outsider, refugee, settler, squatter, stranger, visitor *Antonyms:* citizen, compatriot, indigene

alienate *v.* come between, divide, divorce, estrange, marginalize, part, separate, turn away, turn off *Antonyms:* bring together, fascinate, harmonize

alienation *n.* breach, breaking off, coolness, division, divorce, estrangement, indifference, remoteness, rupture, separation, unfriendliness, variance, withdrawal *Antonyms:* affection, allegiance, attachment

alight *adj.* ablaze, aflame, aglow, burning, conflagrant, fiery, illuminated, in flames, lucent, luminous, lustrous, resplendent *Antonyms:* lacklustre, lifeless, sombre – *v.* **1.** dismount, get off, unmount **2.** land, perch, settle *Antonyms:* launch, set forth

align *v.* **1.** affiliate, agree, ally, associate, cooperate, enlist, join **2.** adjust, arrange, calibrate, coordinate, even, fix, line up, make parallel, order, range, regulate, straighten *Antonyms:* misalign, scramble

alike *adj.* akin, allied, analogous, approximate, associated, cognate, comparable, concurrent, correspondent, corresponding, double, duplicate, equal, equivalent, facsimile, identical, kindred, like, matching, mated, parallel, related, resembling, same, selfsame, similar, uniform *Antonyms:* different, dissimilar, diverse, separate, unlike – *adv.* analogously, comparably, comparatively, consonantly, correspondingly, equally, equivalently, evenly, identically, in common, likewise, similarly, uniformly *Antonyms:* differently, distinctly, unequally

alimentary *adj.* comestible, dietary, digestible, nourishing, nutritional, nutritious, peptic, salubrious, sustaining, wholesome

alimony *n.* divorce settlement, keep, living, maintenance, provision, sustenance, upkeep

alive *adj.* **1.** animate, awake, breathing, cognizant, conscious, corporeal, dynamic, existent, existing, extant, functioning, growing, incarnate, knowing, live, living, mortal, operative, palpable, running, subsisting, viable, vital, working *Antonyms:* dead, deceased, departed, inanimate, inoperative **2.** active, alert, animated, breezy, brisk, bustling, cheerful, dynamic, eager, effervescent, energetic, lively, quick, ready, spirited, sprightly, spry, stirring, vigorous, vital, vivacious, zestful *Antonyms:* apathetic, dull, inactive, lifeless, spiritless **3.** abundant, crammed, infested, overflowing, replete, rife, teeming **4.** fresh, in memory, recollected, revered, unforgotten

alkaline *adj.* alkali, antacid, basic, chemical, neutralizing, salty, soluble

all *adj.* any, bar none, complete, each, entire, every, every single, exhaustive, total, whole *Antonyms:* none, not a soul, nothing – *adv.* **1.** altogether, completely, entirely, exactly, fully, just, purely, quite, totally, utterly, wholly **2.** alone, exclusively, nothing but, only, solely – *n.* **1.** aggregate, everything, mass, sum total, totality, whole **2.** macrocosm, universe, world *Nonformal:* jackpot, whole enchilada *or* kit and caboodle *or* shebang *or* shooting match

allay *v.* **1.** appease, assuage, calm, conciliate, curb, ease, lull, mollify, pacify, placate, propitiate, quell, reassure, soothe *Antonyms:* arouse, disturb, incite, stir up **2.** content, gratify, quench, satiate, satisfy, slake

allegation *n.* accusation, assertion, avowal, blame, charge, claim, denunciation, deposition, statement

allege *v.* **1.** adduce, advance, affirm, assert, avow, bear witness, charge, cite, declare, insist, lay charges, maintain, put forward *Antonyms:* deny, disavow, gainsay, repudiate **2.** claim, imply, impute, insinuate

alleged *adj.* **1.** announced, asserted, declared, described, stated **2.** dubious, ostensible, pretended, professed, purported, questionable, so-called, supposed, suspect, suspicious *Antonyms:* actual, real, true

allegorical *adj.* connotative, emblematic, figurative, illustrative, metaphorical, symbolic, symbolizing, typifying

allegory *n.* **1.** fable, figuration, moral, myth, parable, story, symbol, symbolism, symbolization, tale, typification **2.** analogy, metaphor, simile

allergy *n.* allergic disorder, anaphylaxis, hypersensitivity, susceptibility *Allergic reactions:* asthma, cold sore, conjunctivitis, crawling skin, eczema, hives, itchy eyes, runny nose, sneezing, wheezing

alleviate *v.* allay, appease, assuage, calm, cushion, deaden, diminish, ease, lessen, lighten, mitigate, moderate, mollify, pacify, reduce, release, relieve, soften, solace, temper *Antonyms:* inflame, provoke

alley *n.* alleyway, back street, blind-alley, cul-de-sac, footpath, lane, passage, passageway, path, pathway, walkway

alliance *n.* **1.** affiliation, affinity, association, band, bloc, cartel, coalition, coherence, collaboration, collective, collusion, combination, combine, conclave, consortium, confederacy, confederation, conglomerate, cooperative, faction, federation, fusion, guild, league, organization, partnership, pool, union *Antonyms:* dissociation, disunion, division, schism, severance **2.** betrothal, connubiality, consanguinity, engagement, kinship, marriage, matrimony, tie, union, wedlock **3.** agreement, compact, concord, covenant, pact, treaty

allied *adj.* affiliated, associated, bound, cognate, combined, confederate, connected, correlated, homogeneous, joint, kindred, linked, married, related, unified, united, wed

allot *v.* administer, allocate, allow, apportion, appropriate, assign, budget, cut, deal, designate, dispense, distribute, divide, divvy, dole, dole out, earmark, give, measure, mete, parcel, portion, ration, share, slice up

allotment *n.* allocation, allowance, appropriation, concession, cut, end, grant, lot, measure, part, piece, plot, portion, quota, ration, share, slice, split

allow *v.* **1.** allocate, allot, apportion, assign, award, bestow, dispense, dole out, endow, give, grant, lot, mete, provide *Antonyms:* deny, forbid, refuse **2.** accord, accredit, acknowledge, acquiesce, admit, approve, assent, authorize, avow, bear, brook, certify, commission, comply with, concede, confess, consent, empower, endorse, endure, favour, grant permission, hold with, indulge, let, license, live with, oblige, pass, permit, put up with, recognize, release, sanction, stand, suffer, support, tolerate, warrant, yield *Antonyms:* ban, forbid, prohibit, refuse **3.** keep in mind, make provision for, take into consideration

allowance *n.* **1.** adaptation, adjustment, admission, advantage, concession, dispensation, licence, sanction, toleration **2.** allocation, allotment, amount, annuity, apportionment, bequest, commission, contribution, endowment, gift, honorarium, inheritance, interest, legacy, pay, pension, ration, remittance, remuneration, salary, share, stipend, subsidy, wage **3.** concession, cut, deduction, discount, rebate, reduction

alloy *n.* amalgam, blend, combination, composite, compound, fusion, hybrid, mix, mixture, reduction *Common alloys:* brass, bronze, carbon steel, cast iron, chrome, coin nickel, Damascus steel, graphite steel, permalloy, pewter, pinchbeck, solder, stainless steel, sterling silver, white gold, wrought iron – *v.* amalgamate, blend, combine, compound, fuse, mix, synthesize

allude *v.* **1.** hint, imply, insinuate, intimate, refer, suggest **2.** cite, mention, point to *Antonyms:* disregard, ignore, miss *Commonly misused:* **elude**

allure *n.* appeal, attraction, charisma, charm, enchantment, enticement, glamour, lure, magnetism, seductiveness, temptation – *v.* attract, bait, beguile, bewitch, cajole, captivate, charm, coax, come on, decoy, draw, enchant, entice, entrap, fascinate, hook, induce, inveigle, lead on, magnetize, persuade, pull, seduce, tantalize, tempt, vamp, wile, win over *Antonyms:* disgust, nauseate, sicken, revolt

allusion *n.* charge, citation, connotation, denotation, hint, implication, indication, inference, innuendo, insinuation, intimation, mention, quotation, reference, remark, statement, suggestion *Commonly misused:* **illusion**

ally *n.* accessory, accomplice, associate, collaborator, colleague, compatriot, comrade in arms, confederate, confrere, co-worker, friend, helper, partner *Antonyms:* adversary, antagonist, enemy, foe, rival – *v.* band together, collaborate, combine, join with, link, partner with, stand together, team up with

almanac *n.* annual, calendar, chronicle, journal, record, register, registry, yearbook

almighty *adj.* absolute, all-knowing, all-powerful, all-seeing, boundless, celestial, controlling, divine, enduring, eternal, everlasting, godlike, godly, hallowed, heavenly, immortal, infinite, invincible, limitless, mighty, omnipotent, omnipresent, omniscient, supreme *Antonyms:* feeble, insignificant, paltry, powerless, weak – *adv.* exceedingly, excessively, munificently

almost *adv.* about, about to, all but, approximately, around, bordering on, close to, close upon, essentially, in effect, just about, most, much, nearly, near to, nigh, not quite, practically, pretty much, pretty near, relatively, roughly, substantially, virtually, well-nigh

aloft *adv.* above, high, in the air, on high, over, straight up, topside, up *Antonyms:* below, down, low

alone *adj.* **1.** companionless, detached, discrete, individual, isolated, lone, one, only, separate, separated, single, singular, sole, solitary, solo, unaccompanied, unaided, unassisted, unattached, unattended, unique *Antonyms:* coupled, grouped **2.** abandoned, bereft, derelict, desolate, forlorn, forsaken **3.** incomparable, matchless, peerless, unequalled, unique, unmatched, unparalleled, unrivaled, unsurpassed *Antonyms:* equalled, surpassed – *adv.* independently, once, singlehandedly, singly, solely

Antonyms: accompanied, assisted, jointly, together

along *adv.* **1.** ahead, forth, forward, on, onward **2.** consistent with, during, in keeping with, in the course of **3.** adjacent, next to, on one side – *prep.* beside, by, on the edge of, through

alongside *prep.* apace with, beside, by, close, close by, equal with, next to, parallel to *or* with

aloof *adj.* **1.** above, apart, casual, chilly, cold, cool, detached, distant, forbidding, haughty, offish, remote, standoffish, stuck up *(Nonformal)*, supercilious, unapproachable, unconcerned, unresponsive, unsympathetic *Antonyms:* friendly, gregarious, neighbourly, sociable **2.** alone, insular, reserved, reticent, secluded, shy, solitary, withdrawn – *adv.* arm's-length, at a distance

aloud *adv.* audibly, clearly, distinctly, fortissimo, intelligibly, loudly, lustily, noisily, out loud, plainly, resoundingly, vociferously *Antonyms:* inaudibly, noiselessly, quietly, silently, soundlessly

alphabet *n.* ABCs, characters, fundamentals, hieroglyphics, ideographs, letters, morphemes, rudiments, rune, script, semaphore, signs, symbols, writing system *Some alphabets:* Arabic, Braile, Cyrillic, German, Greek, Hebrew, International Phonetic *or* I.P.A., manual, Morse, Phoenician, Roman

alphabetical *adj.* abecedarian, consecutive, graded, ideographic, indexed, logical, ordered, progressive, sequential

alphabetize *v.* arrange, categorize, classify, codify, index, order, systematize

alpine *adj.* aerial, elevated, high, high-reaching, lofty, mountainous, mountaintop, snow-capped, soaring, towering

already *adv.* at present, before, before now, by now, by then, earlier, even now, formerly, heretofore, just now, now, once, previously, then

also *adv.* additionally, again, along, along with, as well, besides, conjointly, further, furthermore, including, likewise, more, moreover, plus, still, to boot *(Nonformal)*, together with, too

altar *n.* chancel table, communion table, pedestal, font, sanctum, shrine, tabernacle *Commonly misused:* **alter**

alter *v.* adapt, adjust, amend, change, conform, convert, develop into, diversify, fashion, fine tune, fit, fix, make different, metamorphize, metamorphose, modify, mutate, position, recast, reconcile, reconstruct, refashion, reform, remodel, renovate, reshape, revamp, revise, shape, shift, square, suit, tailor, tailor-make, transform, transmute, turn, vary *Nonformal:* doctor, fiddle with, fudge, morph *Commonly misused:* **altar**

alteration *n.* **1.** adaptation, adjustment, amendment, conversion, correction, deviation, difference, divergence, editing, modification, mutation, readjustment, reformation, remodeling, reshaping, revision, shift, switch, transformation, transmutation, vicissitude **2.** change, exchange, shuffle, substitution, transition, transposition

altercation *n.* **1.** argument, bickering, conflict, controversy, disagreement, dispute, falling-out, quarrel, set-to, spat, squabbling, tiff, words, wrangle *Nonformal:* beef, blowup, rumble **2.** battle, brannigan, brawl, brush, combat, contest, donnybrook, dust up *(Nonformal)*, fight, fracas, fray, mêlée, row, rumpus, run-in

altered *adj.* adjusted, changed, converted, corrected, diversified, doctored *(Nonformal)*, modified, redone, refitted, remodelled, renovated, reshaped, revised, transformed, updated

alternate *adj.* alternating, every other, every second, intermittent, periodic, recurrent, recurring, rotating – *n.* backup, call up, double, equivalent, fill-in, proxy, replacement, second, stand-in, substitute, surrogate, understudy – *v.* equivocate, fluctuate, go to and fro, interchange, oscillate, platoon, see-saw, shilly-shally, substitute, transpose, vacillate, waver *Commonly misused:* **alternative**

alternative *adj.* different, other, substitute, surrogate – *n.* backup, choice, opportunity, option, other, pick, preference, recourse, selection, substitute *Commonly misused:* **alternate**

altitude *n.* **1.** distance, elevation, height, peak, summit **2.** eminence, loftiness, rank, stature

altogether *adv.* **1.** absolutely, completely, fully, perfectly, quite, thoroughly, totally, unconditionally, utterly, well, wholly *Antonyms:* halfway, incompletely, partially, somewhat **2.** all in all, all told, bodily, collectively, conjointly, *en bloc (French)*, en masse, in all, *in toto (Latin)*, whole **3.** by and large, all things considered

altruistic *adj.* benevolent, big-hearted, bountiful, charitable, considerate, generous, good, humanitarian, kind, open-handed, magnanimous, philanthropic, selfless, self-sacrificing, unselfish *Antonyms:* greedy, mean, miserly, self-centred

alumni *n. pl.* college *or* university graduates, graduands, graduates, old grad *(Nonformal)*, postgraduates

always *adv.* **1.** consistently, constantly, continually, invariably, regularly, repeatedly, unceasingly, without exception **2.** eternally, ever, everlasting, evermore, forever, forevermore, for keeps, *in perpetuum (Latin)*, perpetually *Antonyms:* infrequently, never, rarely, scarcely, seldom

amalgam *n.* admixture, alloy, amalgamation, blend, combination, composite, compound, fusion, hodgepodge, mishmash, mixture *Nonformal:* combo, soup, stew

amalgamate *v.* alloy, blend, combine, come together, compound, consolidate, fuse, incorporate, integrate, interfuse, intermix, join *or* join together, meld, merge, mingle, network, tie in, unite *Antonyms:* disunite, divide, part, separate, split

amass *v.* accumulate, aggregate, assemble, collect, compile, garner, gather, heap, hoard, make, pile, squirrel away *(Nonformal)*, stockpile, store *Antonyms:* spend, squander

amateur *n.* apprentice, beginner, dabbler, dilettante, layperson, learner, neophyte, nonprofessional, novice, probationer, recruit *Nonformal:* bush leaguer, greenhorn, hopeful *Antonyms:* expert, professional, veteran

amatory *adj.* admiring, affectionate, amorous, ardent, attracted, coquettish, desirous, erotic, fervent, flirtatious, languishing, lovesick, loving, passionate, rapturous, wooing, yearning

amaze *v.* affect, alarm, astonish, astound, awe, bewilder, confound, daze, dumfound, electrify, flabbergast, impress, marvel, move, perplex, shock, stagger, startle, strike, stun, stupefy, surprise, touch *Nonformal:* blow away, bowl down *or* over, floor

amazement *n.* admiration, astonishment, awe, bewilderment, perplexity, shock, stupefaction, surprise, wonder, wonderment *Nonformal:* show-stopper, something else, stunner

ambassador *n.* **1.** agent, attaché, diplomat, emissary, envoy, representative *Kinds of ambassador:* agent-general, consul, consul-general, high commissioner, minister, nuncio, plenipotentiary **2.** go-between, harbinger, intermediary, messenger

ambience *n.* atmosphere, aura, character, flavour, milieu, mood *Nonformal:* vibes, vibrations

ambiguity *n.* abstruseness, ambivalence, double-entendre, double meaning, doubt, doubtfulness, dubiousness, duplicity, enigma, equivocation, inconclusiveness, indefiniteness, obscurity, uncertainty, unclearness, vagueness *Antonyms:* clarity, explicitness, simplicity

ambiguous *adj.* circuitous, cryptic, dubious, enigmatic, inconclusive, indeterminate, misleading, mystifying, obscure, paradoxical, problematical, puzzling, questionable, tenebrous, two-faced, uncertain, unclear, undecipherable, unintelligible, vague *Antonyms:* clear, definite, simple

ambition *n.* **1.** appetite, craving, desire, drive, eagerness, energy, enterprise, enthusiasm, hankering, hunger, initiative, keenness, longing, passion, push, resolve, striving, thirst, yearning, zeal *Antonyms:* lackadaisicalness, lethargy **2.** aim, aspiration, dream, goal, hope, ideal, intent, objective, plan, purpose, *raison d'être (French)*, target, wish

ambitious *adj.* **1.** aggressive, ardent, aspiring, avid, climbing, designing, desirous, determined, driven, driving, eager, earnest, energetic, enterprising, enthusiastic, goal-oriented, high-reaching, hopeful, hungry, industrious, longing, power-loving, purposeful, pushy, resourceful, self-starting, sharp, striving, thirsty, zealous *Antonyms:* apathetic, inert, languid, lethargic, unaspiring **2.** arduous, bold, challenging, demanding, difficult, effortful, elaborate, energetic, exacting, formidable, grandiose, hard, impressive, lofty, severe, strenuous, visionary *Antonyms:* easy, modest, simple

ambivalence *n.* ambiguity, capriciousness, confusion, contradiction, doubt, equivocation, fluctuation, hesitation, inconclusiveness, inconsistency, indecision, indecisiveness, mixed feelings, oscillation, uncertainty, unsettledness, vacillation *Nonformal:* blowing hot and cold, waffling *Antonyms:* conviction, definiteness, sureness, unalterability

amble *v.* dawdle, drift, loiter, meander, ramble, saunter, stroll, toddle, traipse, walk, wander *Nonformal:* mosey, sashay *Antonyms:* hustle, run, rush, sprint

ambrosia *n.* choice morsel, essence, honey, manna, nectar

ambulatory *adj.* itinerant, mobile, moving, nomadic, on foot, perambulatory, peripatetic, roving, strolling, vagabond, walking *Antonyms:* fixed, stationary

ambush *n.* blind, cover, hiding place, retreat, sneak *or* surprise attack, trap – *v.* bushwack, fall upon, lie in wait for, strike, surprise, sweep down upon, take unawares, trap

ameliorate *v.* alleviate, amend, assuage, better, ease, fix, help, improve, lighten, mitigate, rectify, reform, remedy, set right, upgrade *Antonyms:* aggravate, exacerbate, intensify

amen *adv.* exactly, truly, verily – *interj.* agreed, don't I know it, exactly, *finito (Italian)*, hear hear *(British)*, *inshalla (Arabic)*, right on, so be it, so it is, so shall it be, that's all *or* it, yes *French:* c'est bien, c'est ça, c'est la vie, mais oui, naturellement

amenable *adj.* **1.** acquiescent, adaptable, agreeable, biddable, compliant, cooperative, docile, easygoing, manageable, obedient, open, pliable, responsive, tractable, willing *Antonyms:* inflexible, mulish, obdurate, obstinate, stubborn **2.** accountable, answerable, liable, responsible

amend *v.* adjust, alter, change, correct, edit, enhance, fix, help, improve, mend, modify, recast, rectify, reform, remedy, repair, revise, right, square

amendment *n.* addendum, adjunct, alteration, amelioration, attachment, change, clause, codicil, correction, enhancement, modification, proviso, rectification, reform, reformation, repair, revision, rider, supplement

amends *n. pl.* acknowledgement, apology, atonement, compensation, expiation, indemnity, propitiation, *quid pro quo (Latin)*, quittance, recompense, redress, reparation, requital, restitution, restoration, satisfaction

amenity *n.* **1.** affability, agreeableness, amiability, attractiveness, charity, charm, cordiality, courtesy, delightfulness, geniality, gentility, gratefulness, kindness, mildness, pleasantness, politeness, refinement *Antonyms:* bad manners, discourtesy, impoliteness, incivility, rudeness **2.** advantage, betterment, comfort, convenience, enhancement, enrichment, excellence, extravagance, facility, frill, luxury, merit, pleasantry, quality, service

amiable *adj.* affable, agreeable, breezy, buddy-buddy *(Nonformal)*, charming, cheerful, delightful, easy, easygoing, engaging, genial, good-humoured, good-natured, gracious, kind, kindly, lenient, lovable, mellow, mild, obliging, pleasant, pleasing, responsive, sociable, sweet-tempered, unreserved, warm, warmhearted, winning, winsome *Antonyms:* antagonistic, hostile, loathsome *Commonly misused:* **amicable**

amicable *adj.* accessible, accordant, brotherly, civil, cordial, courteous, courtly, cozy, friendly, harmonious, neighbourly, peaceable, peaceful, polite, sympathetic, understanding *Antonyms:* antagonistic, bellicose, belligerent, disagreeable *Commonly misused:* **amiable**

amid *prep.* amidst, among, amongst, between, during, in the middle of, mid, surrounded by, throughout

amiss *adj.* bad, confused, crooked, defective, erring, erroneous, fallacious, false, faulty, flawed, imperfect, improper, inaccurate, inappropriate, incorrect, mistaken, unsuitable, wrong *Antonyms:* accurate, appropriate, correct, proper, suitable – *adv.* badly, defectively, erroneously, faultily, improperly, inappropriately, incorrectly, mistakenly, unfavourably, unsuitably, wrongly *Antonyms:* correctly, properly, suitably

amity *n.* accord, benevolence, civility, cordiality, entente, fellowship, fraternity, friendliness, friendship, harmony, kindliness, neighbourliness, sorority, understanding *Antonyms:* acrimony, discord, hostility

ammunition *n.* **1.** ammo *(Nonformal)*, armament, iron rations, matériel, munitions *Kinds of ammunition:* ball, belt, bomb, buckshot, bullet, cannonball, cartridge, charge, explosive, fuse, grenade, gunpowder, missile, napalm, powder, rocket, shell, shot, shrapnel, torpedo, words **2.** goods, materials, resources

amnesty *n.* absolution, dispensation, forgiveness, grace, immunity, *non prosequitur (Latin)*, overlooking, pardon, reprieve *Antonyms:* confinement, detainment

amock *adv.* berserk, crazily, destructively, ferociously, frenziedly, insanely, madly, maniacally, murderously, out of control, savagely, violently, wildly *Antonyms:* circumspectly, judiciously

among *prep.* amid, amidst, between, betwixt, encompassed by, mid, surrounded by, with

amoral *adj.* **1.** abandoned, free-living, intemperate, lax, licentious, loose, uninhibited, unrestrained *Antonyms:* chaste, modest, temperate **2.** crooked, devious, dishonest, shameless, unethical, unscrupulous *Antonyms:* ethical, upstanding, virtuous *Commonly misused:* **immoral**

amorous *adj.* affectionate, amatory, ardent, attached, doting, enamoured, fond, impassioned, infatuated, in love, lovesick, loving, lustful, passionate, romantic *Nonformal:* hot and heavy, sweet for *or* on *Antonyms:* aloof, cold, distant, standoffish

amorphous *adj.* **1.** baggy, characterless, formless, indeterminate, irregular, nebulous, shapeless, unformed, unstructured *Antonyms:* definite, distinct, regular, shaped, structured **2.** hazy, ill-defined, indefinite, obscure, vague *Antonyms:* particular, specific

amount *n.* **1.** aggregate, all, body, bulk, bundle, effect, entirety, expanse, extent, magnitude, mass, matter, measure, pile, portion, quantity, result, substance, sum, supply, the lot, total, volume, whole **2.** cost, damage *(Nonformal)*, expense, price

amour *n.* affair, *affaire de coeur (French)*, entanglement, fling, flirtation, hanky-panky *(Nonformal)*, liaison, love, love affair, passion, romance *Antonyms:* enmity, hatred, indifference

amphetamine *n.* stimulant *Nonformal:* bennies, coast to coasts, crank, crystal, dexies, hearts, jelly beans, meth, pep pills, purple hearts, speed, uppers

amphibian *n.* cold-blooded vertebrate *Kinds of amphibians:* bullfrog, fire salamander, frog, grass frog, leopard frog, midwife toad, newt, polliwog, salamander, spring peeper, tadpole, toad, tree frog

ample *adj.* abounding, abundant, bounteous, bountiful, broad, capacious, commodious, copious, expansive, extensive, full, gazillion *(Nonformal)*, generous, lavish, liberal, more than enough, plenteous, plentiful, plenty, profuse, rich, roomy, spacious, substantial, unrestricted, vast, voluminous *Antonyms:* inadequate, meagre, restricted, skimpy

amplification *n.* **1.** addition, augmentation, boost, buildup, expansion, heightening, increase, lengthening, raising, strengthening, stretching, widening **2.** deepening, development, elaboration, enlargement, intensification, magnification, supplementing

amplifier *n.* ear trumpet, hearing aid, megaphone, microphone, public address system *or* P.A. *Nonformal:* amp, squawk box

amplify *v.* **1.** add, augment, boost, elaborate, expand, extend, flesh out, heighten, hike up *(Nonformal)*, increase, inflate, intensify, lengthen, pad, pyramid, raise, strengthen, stretch, swell, widen *Antonyms:* abbreviate, compress, condense, decrease, simplify **2.** deepen, develop, enlarge, magnify, supplement

amply *adv.* abundantly, acceptably, adequately, appropriately, bountifully, capaciously, completely, copiously, extensively, fittingly, generously, greatly, lavishly, liberally, plenteously, plentifully, profusely, properly, richly, right, satisfactorily, substantially, sufficiently, suitably, thoroughly *Antonyms:* insufficiently, poorly, scantily, thinly

amputate *v.* cut away *or* off, decapitate, dismember, excise, lop off, remove, separate, sever, truncate *Antonyms:* attach, bond, hitch, join, weld

amuse *v.* **1.** charm, cheer, delight, enlighten, enliven, grab, gratify, interest, please, regale, tickle *Nonformal:* crack up, knock dead, slay, wow *Antonyms:* bore, jade, tire, wear **2.** distract, divert, entertain, relax

amusement *n.* **1.** beguilement, cheer, delight, distraction, diversion, enjoyment, fun, gladdening, glee, gratification, hilarity, laughter, merriment, mirth, pleasure, regalement *Antonyms:* boredom, displeasure, monotony, sadness, tedium **2.** entertainment, festivity, fête, game, hoopla, pastime, picnic, play, recreation, sport, whoopee *Nonformal:* ball, field day, high time, laughs **3.** adventure, caper, escapade, jaunt, journey, lark, spree

amusing *adj.* agreeable, camp, charming, cheerful, cheering, comical, delightful, diverting, droll, enchanting, engaging, enjoyable, entertaining, fun, funny, gladdening, gratifying, humorous, interesting, jocular, joshing, laughable, lively, merry, pleasant, pleasing, witty *Antonyms:* boring, dead, flat, stale, tiresome

anachronism *n.* antique, archaism, dinosaur, fossil, misplacement, solecism

analgesic *adj.* alleviative, anesthetic, emollient – *n.* anodyne, depressant, narcotic, opiate, painkiller, sedative, soporific, tranquilizer

analogous *adj.* akin, alike, comparable, consonant, convertible, correspondent, corresponding, equivalent, homologous, interchangeable, kindred, like, parallel, related, resembling, undifferentiated, uniform *Antonyms:* contrasting, different, disparate, unlike

analogy *n.* affinity, alikeness, comparison, correlation, correspondence, equivalence, likeness, metaphor, parallel, relation, resemblance, semblance, similarity, simile, similitude

analysis *n.* **1.** appraisal, assessment, breakdown, categorization, commentary, criticism, critique, deconstruction, dissection, editorial, estimation, evaluation, examination, explication, finding, inquiry, interpretation, investigation, judgment, opinion, outline, reasoning, report, scrutiny, search, stratification, study, summary, theorization **2.** dream interpretation, psychoanalysis

analyst *n.* **1.** commentator, examiner, inquisitor, investigator, ombudsperson, pollster, questioner *Nonformal:* bean counter, number cruncher **2.** alienist, doctor, psychiatrist, psychoanalyst, psychologist, psychotherapist, therapist *Nonformal:* guru, shrink

analytical *adj.* cogent, diagnostic, dissecting, examining, explanatory, inquiring, interpretive, investigative, judicious, logical, organized, perceptive, precise, questioning, rational, scientific, searching, solid, sound, studious, testing, thorough, valid *Antonyms:* impetuous, rash, spontaneous

analyze *v.* appraise, assay, assess, break down, check, compute, consider, construe, demonstrate, determine, dissect, divide, estimate, evaluate, examine, experiment, gauge, inspect, interpret, investigate, judge, measure, parse, prove, rate, read, rehash, resolve, sample, scrutinize, separate, set, size, study, survey, taste, test, try, try on, valuate, value, weigh *Nonformal:* chew over, confab, get down to brass tacks, kick around *Antonyms:* extemporize, synthesize

anarchist *n.* agitator, iconoclast, insurgent, insurrectionist, malcontent, mutineer, nihilist, rebel, revolutionary, sans-culotte, subversive, terrorist

anarchy *n.* chaos, confusion, disorder, disorganization, lawlessness, mayhem, mob rule, nihilism, rebellion, revolution, riot, sedition, tumult, turmoil *Antonyms:* control, law, order, rule

anathema *n.* **1.** ban, censure, condemnation, curse, damnation, denouncement, denunciation, excommunication, imprecation, malediction, proscription, reprobation, reproof, taboo *Antonyms:* approval, blessing **2.** abomination, bane, detestation, enemy, pariah

anatomy *n.* **1.** build, composition, conformation, figure, form, frame, framework, makeup, physique, shape, structure **2.** analysis, dismemberment, dissection, division, investigation, morphology, vivisection

ancestor *n.* antecedent, family, forebear, forefather, founder, grandparent, parent, precursor, predecessor, procreator, progenitor *Antonyms:* contemporary, offspring

ancestral *adj.* affiliated, congenital, consanguine, familial, genealogical, hereditary, inborn, inherited, innate, lineal, maternal, parental, paternal, totemic, tribal

ancestry *n.* antecedent, breeding, derivation, descent, extraction, forebear, forerunner, genealogy, genesis, heritage, history, kindred, line, lineage, origin, parentage, precursor, progenitor, race, source, stock

anchor *n.* base, fastener, mainstay, mooring, rock *(Nonformal)*, security, support *Kinds of anchor:* fluke, grapnel, mushroom, patent – *v.* attach, berth, dock, fasten, fix, hold, hook, moor, secure, stay, tie, tie up

ancient *adj.* **1.** aged, age-old, hoary, superannuated, timeworn, wizened, wrinkled *Antonyms:* infantile, new-fledged, unweaned **2.** antique, enduring, grey, immemorial, long-lasting, old, prehistoric, primeval, venerable **3.** archaic, obsolescent, obsolete, out-moded, retired – *n.* antediluvian, elder, Methuselah, primordial

ancillary *adj.* accessory, accompanying, additional, adjunct, appurtenant, attending, contributory, extraneous, incidental, satellite, secondary, subordinate, subservient, subsidiary, supplementary *Antonyms:* cardinal, chief, main, major, premier

and *conj.* added to, along with, also, as well as, furthermore, including, moreover, plus, together with

androgynous *adj.* bisexual, epicene, gynandromorphic, hermaphroditic, intersexual, synthesis *Antonyms:* feminine, masculine

android *n.* automaton, cyborg, droid, mechanical person, robot

anecdote *n.* account, chronicle, incident, narration, narrative, recital, relation, reminiscence, saga, sketch, story, tale *Nonformal:* fish story, old chestnut, yarn

anemic *adj.* bloodless, chalky, feeble, frail, infirm, insipid, lacklustre, languid, pale, pallid, sallow, sickly, wan, watery, weak *Antonyms:* florid, vigorous, zesty

anesthesia *n.* dullness, lack of feeling, narcosis, numbness, paralysis, sleep, unconsciousness

anesthetic *n.* analgesic, gas, hypnosis, opiate, painkiller, sleep-inducer, soporific, spinal epidural *Kinds of anesthetic:* local *or* topical *or* general, chloroform, ether, laughing gas *(Nonformal),* nitrous oxide, novocaine, sodium pentothal

anew *adv.* again, another time, encore, fresh, from scratch, lately, new, newly, once again, once more, over, over again, recently

angel *n.* **1.** archangel, celestial being, cherub, divine messenger, guardian, heavenly being, holy being, seraph, spirit, spiritual being, supernatural being *Names of angels:* Abaddon, Abdizuel, Abraxas, Adriel, Amnediel, Anael, Anixiel, Anpiel, Apollyon, Ardifiel, Ariel, Asasiel, Asmodeus, Atliel, Azael, Azariel, Barbiel, Belial, Cassiel, Dardiel, Dirachiel, Enediel, Ergediel, Gabriel, Geniel, Hamaliel, Hanael, Huratapel, Israfil, Jahoel, Jazeriel, Lucifer, Mastema, Metatron, Michael, Miel, Neciel, Phanuel, Rachiel, Raguel, Rahab, Ramiel, Raphael, Sachiel, Samael, Sandalphon, Schliel, Seraphiel, Uriel, Zechariah *Antonyms:* demon, devil, fiend **2.** backer, benefactor, contributor, fairy godmother, philanthropist, supporter

angelic *adj.* adorable, beatific, beneficent, celestial, darling, devout, divine, entrancing, godly, good, heavenly, holy, innocent, kind, lovely, newborn, pious, pure, righteous, saintly, self-sacrificing, virtuous *Antonyms:* blasphemous, devilish, diabolic, iniquitous, profane

anger *n.* acerbity, acrimony, animosity, antagonism, asperity, choler, disapprobation, displeasure, distemper, enmity, fury, ill temper, ire, outburst, outrage, rage, tantrum, umbrage, wrath *Nonformal:* boiling point, cat fit, conniption, conniption fit, dander, slow burn, snit *Antonyms:* amiability, elation, glee, goodwill, satisfaction – *v.* enrage, excite, fire up, flare up, get mad, ignite, incense, inflame, infuriate, insult, irk, lash into, madden, nettle, offend, outrage, peeve, pique, rage, rankle, rave, rile, roil, rouse, tick off, upset, vex *Nonformal:* blow up, boil *or* boil over, breathe fire, burn, burn up, flip, foam *or* froth at the mouth, get one's dander up, get steamed up, raise one's hackles, see red, whip up, work up *Antonyms:* assuage, calm, gratify, placate, soothe

angle *n.* **1.** bend, corner, crevice, crook, divergence, dogleg, elbow, flare, flexure, fork, incline, intersection, knee, nook, notch, point, slant, turn, turning, twist, Y-crotch **2.** aim, approach, aspect, bias, direction, hand, intention, outlook, perspective, plan, position, purpose, side, slant, standpoint, viewpoint – *v.* **1.** cast, ensnare, fish, jig, plunk, spin, trawl, troll **2.** aim for, contrive, gerrymander, hatch, intrigue, jockey, plan, plot, take care of

Anglicanism *n.* Church of England *Kinds of Anglicanism:* Anglo-Catholicism, Broad Church, High Church, Low Church

angry *adj.* acrimonious, affronted, aggrieved, antagonized, ardent, aroused, bad-tempered, choleric, convulsed, cross, displeased, dissatisfied, enraged, exacerbated, explosive, fractious, fuming, furious, heated, ill-tempered, incensed, inflamed, infuriated, irate, mad, maddened, outraged, put out, quick-tempered, raging, riled, sore, splenetic, stormy, vexed, wrathful *Nonformal:* beside oneself, boiling, bugged, burned up, hopping mad, hot, hotheaded, hot-tempered, pissed off, steamed *or* steamed up, ticked off, worked up *Antonyms:* amiable, calm, friendly, gratified, loving

angst *n.* anxiety, disquietude, dread, perturbation, *Weltschmerz (German)*

anguish *n.* affliction, agony, distress, compunction, grief, heartache, heartbreak, hurt, misery, pain, pang, remorse, sorrow, suffering, throe, torment, woe, wretchedness *Antonyms:* ecstasy, felicity, jubilation – *v.* bemoan, suffer, wail, wring one's hands *Antonyms:* celebrate, rejoice

angular *adj.* **1.** awkward, bony, gangling, gaunt, lanky, lean, rangy, scrawny, sharp, skinny, spare, thin *Antonyms:* buxom, corpulent **2.** bent, bifurcate, cornered, crooked, crossed, forked, intersectional, jagged, oblique, sharp-cornered, skewed, slanted, staggered *Antonyms:* direct, linear, uncurved

animal *adj.* beastlike, beastly, bestial, bodily, brutish, carnal, corporeal, earthy, feral, fleshly, mammalian, muscular, natural, physical, sensual, untamed, wild – *n.* animal kingdom, beast, being, creature, fauna, living thing *Nonformal:* critter, varmint *Animal Collectives:* bed *(Eel, oyster)*, bevy *(Quail)*, charm *(Finch)*, clowder *(Cat)*, colony *(Ant, beaver)*, company *(Parrot)*, covey *(Partridge, quail)*, crash *(Rhinoceros)*, cry *(Hound)*, exaltation *(Lark)*, flight *(Bird, butterfly)*, flock *(Bird, duck, sheep)*, gaggle *(Goose)*, gang *(Elk)*, herd *(Cow, elephant, horse)*, kennel *(Dog)*, knot *(Toad)*, leap *(Leopard)*, litter *(Kitten, pig, puppy)*, murder *(Crow)*, murmuration *(Starling)*, pack *(Dog, wolf)*, pair *(Horse, ox)*, parliament *(Owl)*, plague *(Locust)*, pod *(Whale)*, pride *(Lion)*, school *(Fish, porpoise)*, skein *(Goose)*, skulk *(Fox)*, sloth *(Bear)*, team *(Horse, ox)*, train *(Camel)*, troop *(Gorilla)*, unkindness *(Raven)*, watch *(Nightingale)*, yoke *(Ox)* *Groupings of animals:* amphibian, bird, carnivore, domestic animal, echinoderm, herbivore, invertebrate, insect, insectivore, mammal, pet, reptile, rodent, sponge, vertebrate, wild *Kinds of animal sound:* bark, barking, bawl, bay, bell, bellow, birdcall, bleat, bray, call, caterwaul, cry, grunt, howl, low, mating call *or* cry, meow, moo, neigh, nicker, oink, roar, scream, screech, snarl, snort, squall, squeak, squeal, stridulation, ululation, whicker, whine, whinny, yawp, yelp, yip, yowl *Kinds of animal sports:* barrel racing, bronco busting, bullfighting, bullriding, calf roping, camel racing, chuckwagon racing, cockfighting, dog racing, dressage, horseback riding, horse racing, polo, pony trekking, riding, rodeo, roping, show jumping, steeplechase, steer roping, steer wrestling, trail riding *Kinds of domestic animal food:* bird seed, grain, grass, hay, kibbles, mash, saltlick, scratch, seed, silage, swill *Kinds of young animals:* calf, chick, colt, cub, duckling, fawn, fledgling, foal, kitten, lamb, litter, piglet, polliwog, pullet, pup, tadpole, whelp

animate *adj.* active, alert, alive, animated, breathing, dynamic, energized, gay, happy, live, lively, moving, spirited, viable, vital, vivacious *Antonyms:* drowsy, dull, lethargic – *v.* activate, arouse, cheer, embolden, encourage, energize, enliven, exalt, excite, fire, gladden, hearten, impel, incite, inform, inspire, inspirit, instigate, invigorate, kindle, liven, move, quicken, revive, rouse, spark, spur, stimulate, stir, urge, vitalize *Antonyms:* check, curb, deter, dull, inhibit

animated *adj.* alert, ardent, blissful, brisk, buoyant, *caloroso (Italian)*, dynamic, ebullient, elated, energetic, energized, enthusiastic, excited, fervent, full of piss and vinegar *(Nonformal)*, gay, happy, lively, passionate, peppy, quick, snappy, spirited, sprightly, vibrant, vigorous, vital, vitalized, vivacious, vivid, zealous, zestful *Antonyms:* apathetic, dejected, inactive, lethargic, passive

animation *n.* action, ardour, bounce, *brio (Italian)*, briskness, buoyancy, dash, dynamism, ebullience, élan, elation, energy, enthusiasm, esprit, excitement, exhilaration, fervour, gaiety, glow, gusto, high spirits, life, liveliness, passion, pep, sparkle, spirit, verve, vibrancy, vigour, vim, vitality, vivacity, zeal, zest, zestfulness, zing

anime *n.* animation, cartoon, comic book *or* strip, graphic novel, Japanese animation *Japanese:* manga, shojo story

animosity *n.* acrimony, animus, antagonism, antipathy, aversion, bad blood, bitterness, contention, displeasure, enmity, hate, hatred, hostility, ill will, malevolence, malice, rancour, resentment, spleen, virulence *Antonyms:* amity, friendship, goodwill, harmony, sympathy

animus *n.* **1.** antipathy, hard feelings, hostility, malice, rancour *Antonyms:* amity, good will, sympathy **2.** aim, aspiration, intention, objective, purpose **3.** mind, soul, spirit, will

annals *n. pl.* account, archives, chronicles, chronology, daybook, diary, history, journal, memorial, record, register, yearbook

annex *n.* **1.** addendum, adjunct, appendix, arm, attachment, postscript, subsidiary, supplement **2.** addition, extension, wing – *v.* add, adjoin, adopt, affix, append, appropriate, associate, attach, connect, fasten, hitch on *or* up, hook up, join, link, seize, take on *or* over, unite *Nonformal:* slap *or* tack *or* tag on, tag *Antonyms:* detach, disconnect, disengage, separate, unfasten

annexation *n.* addition, appropriation, augmentation, concomitance, enlargement, expansion, incorporation, merger, takeover, usurpation *Antonyms:* detachment, severance

annihilate *v.* annul, butcher, cancel, decimate, demolish, dissipate, efface, eradicate, erase, exterminate, extirpate, finish, massacre, purge, put to the sword, rout, rub out, slaughter, slay, trounce, vanquish, wipe out, wreck *Nonformal:* do in, wipe the floor with *Antonyms:* rebuild, rejuvenate, revive

anniversary *n.* commemoration, feast, festival, occasion, remembrance, rite *Kinds of wedding anniversary:* paper *(1st)*, cotton *(2nd)*, leather *(3rd)*, flowers *or* fruit *(4th)*, wood *(5th)*, iron *(6th)*, wool *(7th)*, bronze *(8th)*, pottery *(9th)*, tin *(10th)*, steel *(11th)*, linen *(12th)*, lace *(13th)*, ivory *(14th)*, crystal *(15th)*, china *(20th)*, silver *(25th)*, pearl *(30th)*, coral *(35th)*, ruby *(40th)*, sapphire *(45th)*, gold *(50th)*, emerald *(55th)*, diamond *(60th)*

annotate *v.* commentate, construe, criticize, define, elucidate, explain, expound, footnote, gloss, highlight, illustrate, interpret, mark up, note, remark

annotation *n.* comment, commentary, citation, definition, elucidation, endnote, exegesis, explanation, explication, footnote, gloss, illustration, interpretation

announce *v.* advertise, blazon, broadcast, communicate, declaim, declare, disclose, disseminate, divulge, give out, herald, impart, issue, make known, make public, pass the word, proclaim, promulgate, propound, publicize, publish, release, report, reveal, spread around, state, tell, trumpet *Antonyms:* bury, cover up, hide, suppress, withhold

announcement *n.* advertisement, advice, brief, broadcast, broadsheet, bulletin, communication, communiqué, disclosure, edict, expression, flyer, message, news, notice, notification, posting, prediction, press release, proclamation, promulgation, publication, report, revelation, statement

announcer *n.* anchorperson, broadcaster, commentator, communicator, deejay *or* disc jockey *or* DJ, emcee, harbinger, host, master of ceremonies *or* MC, newscaster, play-by-play person, reporter, ringmaster, telecaster, the voice *(Nonformal)*, veejay

annoy *v.* badger, bother, bug, chafe, chivvy, curdle, exasperate, get to, harass, hassle, incense, inflame, infuriate, irk, nag, pester, pick on, provoke, tease, torment, vex *Nonformal:* drive bananas, get in one's face *Antonyms:* disregard, ignore, pay no heed to

annoyed *adj.* aggravated, irritated, offended, put off *or* out, riled, roiled, soured, vexed *Nonformal:* cheesed off, fit to be tied, frosted, miffed *Antonyms:* composed, equitable, stoical

annual *adj.* anniversary, every year, once a year, year-end, yearlong, yearly – *n.* almanac, periodical, serial, yearbook, yearly

annul *v.* abolish, abrogate, annihilate, call off, cancel, countermand, delete, discharge, dissolve, erase, invalidate, negate, neutralize, nullify, quash, recall, repeal, rescind, retract, reverse, revoke, undo, void, wipe out *Antonyms:* reinstate, restore

annulment *n.* abolition, abrogation, breakup, cancellation, discharge, dissolution, erasure, invalidation, negation, neutralization, nullification, reconveyance, renouncement, repeal, rescinder, retraction, reversal, revocation *Antonyms:* rebirth, renaissance, renewal, resumption

anoint *v.* **1.** bless, consecrate, crown, dedicate, enthrone, hallow, ordain, sanctify **2.** daub, dress, pomade, salve, smear, wax

anomalous *adj.* **1.** atypical, bizarre, discordant, eccentric, exceptional, foreign, incongruous, inconsistent, irregular, mismatched, odd, out of place, peculiar, preternatural, queer, quirky, rare, strange, unnatural, unrepresentative, untypical, unusual *Antonyms:* ordinary, regular, usual **2.** deviant, divergent, errant, straying, wayward

anomaly *n.* aberration, abnormality, curiosity, departure, deviation, eccentricity, exception, freak, incongruity, inconsistency, irregularity, museum piece, nonconformity, oddity, peculiarity, rarity *Nonformal:* fish out of water, oddball, queer duck *Antonyms:* average, commonplace, garden-variety, normal, standard

anonymous *adj.* incognito, nameless, pseudonymous, secret, unacknowledged, unclaimed, uncredited, undisclosed, unidentified, unknown, unnamed, unsigned, unspecified *Antonyms:* accredited, credited, identified, named

answer *n.* **1.** acknowledgment, comeback, comment, confirmation, countercharge, counterclaim, defence, denial, disclosure, echo, feedback, guff *(Nonformal)*, justification, observation, parting shot, plea, reaction, rebuttal, reciprocation, refutation, rejoinder, repartee, reply, reposit, response, retort, return, riposte *Antonyms:* inquiry, interrogation, query, question **2.** elucidation, explanation, interpretation, key, reason, resolution, solution – *v.* **1.** acknowledge, correspond, echo, reply, respond, retort, return *Nonformal:* lip, sass, shoot back *Antonyms:* ask, inquire, query, question **2.** come back at, confound, contradict, defend, deny, refute, uphold **3.** clear up, explain, figure *or* sort *or* work out

answerable *adj.* **1.** accountable, bound, chargeable, compelled, constrained, liable, obligated, responsible, subject **2.** disprovable, rebuttable, refutable

antagonism *n.* **1.** animosity, antipathy, antithesis, clash, conflict, contention, contrariness, enmity, friction, hatred, hostility, rancour *Antonyms:* love, passion, tenderness **2.** disagreement, discord, dissension, opposition, resistance

antagonist *n.* adversary, competitor, contender, enemy, foe, match, opponent, opposer, problem, rival, villain *Antonyms:* confederate, helpmate, partner

antagonize *v.* alienate, anger, annoy, counteract, estrange, harangue, harass, insult, irritate, offend, oppose, repel *Antonyms:* appease, mollify, pacify, placate, soothe

antecedent *adj.* anterior, earlier, foregoing, former, past, preceding, precursory, previous, prior *Antonyms:* after, coming, ensuing, following – *n.* ancestry, cause, descent, determinant, extraction, forebears, genealogy, predecessor, progenitor, reason, stock

antedate *v.* **1.** back date, forerun, occur earlier, precede, predate **2.** hasten, precipitate, rush

antediluvian *adj.* **1.** aged, age-old, anachronistic, ancient, antiquated, antique, archaic, hoary, obsolete, old, old-fashioned, out-of-date, primeval, primitive, primordial, superannuated, venerable **2.** barbaric, coarse, crude, primitive, rudimentary, uncivilized, unpolished *Antonyms:* debonair, sophisticated

antenna *n.* aerial, ear, feeler, rabbit ears *(Nonformal)*, receiver, sensor, sky wire, spike, tower, wire

anterior *adj.* antecedent, beginning, foregoing, former, past, precedent, preceding, previous, prior *Antonyms:* after, posterior

anthem *n.* canticle, chant, chorus, evensong, hymn, melody, motet, song

anthropology *n.* culture, folklore, sociology *Kinds of anthropology:* applied, archaeology, ethnology, linguistic, physical, theoretical

antibiotic *n.* growth-arresting *or* growth-destroying microorganism *Kinds of antibiotic:* ampicillin, penicillin, streptomycin, sulfa drug, sulfonamide, tetracycline

anticipate *v.* **1.** assume, await, conjecture, expect, figure, forecast, foresee, foretaste, foretell, hope *or* look *or* wait for, plan on, predict, prognosticate, prophesy, see, suppose, visualize, wait **2.** forestall, intercept, preempt, prevent **3.** consider, daydream, envisage, imagine, think about

anticipation *n.* apprehension, awareness, foreboding, foreseeing, foresight, foretaste, forethought, guess, hunch, inkling, intuition, notion, preconception, premonition, prescience, presentiment, prior knowledge, readiness, realization, sneaking suspicion

anticlimax *n.* decline, deflation, descent, disappointment, drop, letdown, slump *Antonyms:* climax, culmination, height, peak, zenith

antics *n. pl.* capers, escapades, frolic, hijinks, jokes, larks, monkey business, monkey-shines *(Nonformal)*, romp, shenanigans, tomfoolery, tricks

antidote *n.* antacid, antitoxin, antivenin, buffer, corrective, counteractant, counteragent, countermeasure, counterstep, cure, medicine, negator, neutralizer, nullifier, preventive, remedy, serum, treatment

antiquated *adj.* aged, ancient, antique, archaic, dated, obsolescent, old, old-fashioned, old hat, outdated, outmoded, out-of-date, outworn, passé *Antonyms:* contemporary, conventional, fashionable, stylish

antique *adj.* antiquarian, archaic, obsolete, old-fashioned, outdated, venerable, vintage *Antonyms:* modern, novel, recent – *n.* antiquity, artifact, heirloom, museum piece *(Nonformal), objet d'art (French)*, rarity, relic

antiquity *n.* **1.** classical times, former age, long ago, of yore, old age, olden days, past, venerableness **2.** anachronism, artifacts, dinosaur *(Nonformal)*, fossil, relic **3.** ancientness, caducity, hoariness, old age, oldness

antiseptic *adj.* aseptic, germ-free, pure, sterile, uncontaminated *Antonyms:* impure, infected, polluted, septic – *n.* antitoxin, bactericide, barbicide, cleanser, detergent, disinfectant, fumigant, germicide, preventative, prophylactic, purifier, sterilizer *Kinds of antiseptic*: alcohol, carbolic acid, hydrogen peroxide, merbromin *or* Mercurochrome, tincture of iodine

antisocial *adj.* alienated, ascetic, austere, cynical, introverted, misanthropic, nonparticipating, reclusive, remote, reserved, retiring, solitary, standoffish, uncommunicative, unfriendly, withdrawn *Antonyms:* companionable, friendly, gregarious, philanthropic

antithesis *n.* antonym, contradiction, contrary, contrast, converse, counter, flip side *(Nonformal)*, inverse, nemesis, opposite, other side, reverse *Antonyms:* analogy, equivalent, match, peer, twin

antitoxin *n.* antibiotic, antibody, antidote, antiseptic, antiserum, antivenin, counteractant, counter-agent, inoculation, medicine, neutralizer, preventive, serum, sterilizer, vaccine

anxiety *n.* angst, apprehension, concern, disquiet, distress, doubt, dread, foreboding, fretfulness, fuss, misery, misgiving, mistrust, nervousness, panic, shakes, shivers, stage fright, suffering, suspense, sweat, trouble, uncertainty, unease, watchfulness, *Weltschmerz (German)*, worry *Nonformal:* cold sweat, creeps, fidgits, heebie-jeebies, jitters, pins and needles, willies *Antonyms:* aplomb, assurance, confidence, relief, security

anxious *adj.* **1.** afraid, apprehensive, careful, choked, clutched, concerned, disquieted, distressed, disturbed, dreading, fearful, fidgety, fretful, jumpy, nervous, overwrought, restless, scared, shaky, spooked, taut, troubled, uneasy, unquiet, uptight, wired, worried *Nonformal:* antsy, in a sweat, jittery, on tenterhooks, sweating bullets, unglued, with baited breath *Antonyms:* calm, collected, confident, cool, nonchalant **2.** aghast, agog, ardent, avid, breathless, desirous, eager, enthusiastic, expectant, fervent, hyper, impatient, intent, itching, keen, thirsty, yearning, zealous *Antonyms:* averse, disinclined, hesitant, loath, reluctant

any *adj.* either, every, one and all, solitary, some, whatever, whichever, whichsoever – *adv.* at all, to some extent – *n.* anybody, anyone, anything, aught, everybody, everyone, some, somebody, someone

anybody *n.* all, anyone, everybody, everyone, masses, people, person, public, anywho *(Nonformal)*

anyhow *adv.* **1.** about, any way, around, by any means, randomly **2.** however, nevertheless, notwithstanding, regardless **3.** at random, heedlessly, negligently, recklessly, without thinking

anyone *n.* all, anybody, any person, everybody, everyone, *le premier venu (French)*, masses, one, public

anyway *adv.* anyhow, ever, however, nevertheless, nonetheless, once, regardless

apart *adv.* **1.** afar, alone, aloof, aside, away, by itself, cut off, disconnectedly, distantly, distinctly, exclusively, freely, independently, individually, isolated, privately, separately, singly, solo, to itself **2.** asunder, in half, in pieces, in two

apartment *n.* **1.** accommodation, bachelor, chambers *or* rooms *(British)*, flat, living quarters, lodging, rental *Kinds of apartment:* bedsitter *or* bedsit *(British)*, cold-water flat, co-op, condominium *or* condo, duplex, fiveplex, fourplex, garden apartment, granny flat, loft, maid's quarters, penthouse, railroad flat, studio, suite, tenement, walk-up *French:* appartement, maisonette *Nonformal:* digs, pad **2.** building, complex, low-rise, high-rise

apathetic *adj.* **1.** aloof, callous, cold, cool, detached, disinterested, emotionless, flat, impassive, indifferent, passive, removed, stolid, torpid, uncaring, unconcerned, unfeeling, unmoved, unresponsive, untouched, withdrawn *Antonyms:* caring, committed, concerned, responsive **2.** bovine, dilatory, inert, lackadaisical, laid-back *(Nonformal)*, languid, lethargic, listless, loath, reluctant, slack, spiritless *Antonyms:* active, bothered, enthusiastic

apathy *n.* **1.** aloofness, coolness, detachment, disinterest, dispassion, disregard, dullness, emotionlessness, indifference, inertness, lassitude, lethargy, listlessness, numbness, passiveness, passivity, sluggishness *Antonyms:* anxiety, concern, emotion, enthusiasm, interest **2.** despondency, hopelessness, melancholy, resignation, *Weltschmerz (German)*, withdrawal

ape *n.* monkey, old world primate *Kinds of ape:* baboon, chimpanzee, gibbon, gorilla, macaque, orangutang, rhesus, spider monkey – *v.* affect, burlesque, caricature, copy, counterfeit, echo, emulate, imitate, impersonate, mimic, mirror, mock, parody, parrot, simulate

aperture *n.* cavity, chink, cleft, crack, cranny, eyelet, fissure, gap, hatch, hole, interstice, nook, opening, orifice, porthole, window

apex *n.* acme, apogee, cap, climax, crown, culmination, highest, highlight, peak, pinnacle, point, summit, vertex, zenith *Antonyms:* bottom, low, nadir

aphorism *n.* adage, apothegm, axiom, epigram, maxim, moral, *mot juste (French)*, motto, precept, proverb, rule, saw, saying, shibboleth, truism

apiece *adv.* a pop *(Nonformal)*, a side, each, for each, individually, per, respectively, separately, severally, singly, to each *Antonyms:* all together, collectively, en masse, overall, together

aplomb *n.* assurance, composure, confidence, equanimity, poise, sang-froid, savoir-faire *Antonyms:* befuddlement, confusion, discomfiture, embarrassment

apocalyptic *adj.* augural, foreboding, foreshadowing, foretokening, inauspicious, ominous, portentous, prophetic, revolutionary *Commonly misused:* **apocryphal**

apocryphal *adj.* bogus, debatable, doubtful, dubious, false, fictitious, heretical, make-believe, questionable, spurious, unauthenticated *Antonyms:* authenticated, doubtless, proven *Commonly misused:* **apocalyptic**

apogee *n.* **1.** brink, frontier, outer edge, vertex **2.** apex, climax, crest, tip

apologetic *adj.* atoning, attritional, compunctious, conciliatory, contrite, defensive, deferent, expiatory, explanatory, penitent, propitiatory, regretful, remorseful, repentant, rueful, self-effacing, self-incriminating, sorry, supplicating *Antonyms:* belligerent, flagrant, remorseless, unrepentant

apologize *v.* **1.** admit guilt, ask forgiveness *or* pardon, atone, clear *or* excuse oneself, concede, confess, explain, make amends *or* reparations, plead, purge, retract, square, withdraw **2.** bolster, defend, support **3.** excuse, justify, mitigate, vindicate

apology *n.* **1.** acknowledgment, admission, amends, atonement, concession, confession, expiation, *mea culpa (Latin)*, redress, regret, reparation, penitence **2.** defence, excuse, explanation, extenuation, justification, mitigation, plea, vindication

apoplexy *n.* brain hemorrhage, seizure, stroke, thrombosis, unconsciousness

apostate *adj.* disloyal, faithless, lapsed – *n.* backslider, blasphemer, defector, deserter, dissenter, heretic, nonconformist, recanter, recidivist, renegade, repudiator, traitor, turncoat

apostle *n.* advocate, champion, companion, converter, evangelist, follower, messenger, missionary, pioneer, preacher, propagandist, proponent, proselytizer, witness *Antonyms:* dissident, infidel

appall *v.* alarm, amaze, awe, confound, daunt, disconcert, dishearten, dismay, faze, frighten, gross out *(Nonformal)*, horrify, insult, intimidate, outrage, petrify, scare, shake, shock, terrify, throw, unnerve

appalling *adj.* alarming, astounding, awful, daunting, disheartening, dismaying, fearful, formidable, frightening, frightful, ghastly, grim, harrowing, horrid, horrific, horrifying, insufferable, intimidating, loathsome, petrifying, repelling, shocking, terrible, terrifying, unnerving *Antonyms:* comforting, consoling, encouraging, heartening, reassuring

apparatus *n.* **1.** accoutrement, appliance, contraption, device, equipment, furnishings, gadget, gear, implement, machine, machinery, means, mechanism, outfit, paraphernalia, stuff, tackle, tools, utensils *Nonformal:* doodad, doohickey, gizmo, whangdoodle, whatchamacallit, widget **2.** bureaucracy, hierarchy, network, organization, setup, structure, system

apparel *n.* attire, clothing, dress, garb, garments, raiment, vestment, wear *Nonformal:* duds, get up, glad rags

apparent *adj.* **1.** blatant, clear, conspicuous, distinct, evident, lucid, manifest, obvious, overt, palpable, perceptible, plain, potent, public, striking *Antonyms:* ambiguous, dubious, hazy, shrouded **2.** credible, deceptive, delusive, likely, ostensible, outward, plausible, possible, probable, seeming, superficial, supposed

apparently *adv.* **1.** clearly, conspicuously, indubitably, manifestly, obviously, openly, overtly, palpably, patently, perceptibly, plainly, tangibly **2.** allegedly, as if *or* though, evidently, intuitively, most likely, ostensibly, outwardly, plausibly, possibly, probably, professedly, reasonably, reputably, seemingly, supposedly *Antonyms:* improbably, unlikely

apparition *n.* bogeyman, chimera, delusion, *doppelgänger (German)*, ghost, hallucination, haunt, hobgoblin, illusion, manifestation, phantom, presence, spectre, spirit, spook *(Nonformal)*, sprite, vision, will o' the wisp, wraith

appeal *n.* **1.** allure, attraction, attractiveness, beauty, charm, engagingness, fascination, glamour, interestingness, pleasingness, power, seductiveness *Antonym:* repulsiveness **2.** beseechment, *cri du coeur (French)*, entreaty, invocation, petition, plea, prayer, request, supplication – *v.* **1.** appeal to, beg, beseech, call *or* call upon, entreat, implore, importune, petition, plead, pray, seek, solicit, supplicate, urge **2.** allure, attract, beguile, captivate, charm, enchant, engage, entice, fascinate, interest, intrigue, invite, please, tantalize, tempt *Antonyms:* alienate, bore, repulse, revolt

appear *v.* **1.** arise, arrive, attend, begin, check *or* clock in, come, come across *or* in *or* into *or* on *or* upon, come to light, crop up, drop in, encounter, enter, get in, loom, make it, materialize, occur, pop in *or* up, present, punch *or* weigh in, roll in *or* out, show *or* turn up, surface, take place *Nonformal:* blow in, breeze in, make the scene *Antonyms:* disappear, dissolve, vanish **2.** clarify, elucidate, emerge, exhibit, manifest *Antonyms:* disguise, hide, obfuscate **3.** create, develop, invent, perform, play **4.** imitate, look like, mimic, resemble, seem, simulate **5.** enter, present oneself, spring forth, take part

appearance *n.* **1.** aura, façade, front, guise, idea, illusion, impression, mirage, pretense, reflection, semblance, spectre, vision, window dressing *Antonyms:* essence, interior, reality **2.** air, aspect, attitude, bearing, carriage, characteristic, countenance, demeanour, deportment, dress, fashion, feature, form, image, looks, manner, mien, pose, presence, semblance, shape, stamp, visage **3.** actualization, advent, appearing, arrival, debut, display, emergence, entrance, exhibition, introduction, manifestation, materialization, presence, representation, unveiling *Antonyms:* retirement, withdrawal

appease *v.* allay, alleviate, assuage, blunt, conciliate, content, diffuse, ease, gratify, lessen, lull, meet halfway, mitigate, mollify, pacify, patch things up *(Nonformal)*, placate, propitiate, quell, quench, quiet, satisfy, slake, soothe, subdue, sweeten, yield *Antonyms:* aggravate, antagonize, arouse, discompose, provoke

appeasement *n.* accommodation, acquiescence, adjustment, alleviation, assuagement, compromise, concession, conciliation, easing, lessening, lulling, mitigation, moderation, olive branch, pacification, peace offering, placation, quieting, reconciliation, reparation, restoration, satisfaction, settlement, softening, solace, soothing *Antonyms:* goad, provocation

append *v.* add, adjoin, affix, annex, attach, conjoin, fasten, fix, supplement *Nonformal:* tack *or* tag on *Antonyms:* detach, disconnect, disengage, remove, separate

appendage *n.* **1.** accessory, addendum, addition, adjunct, annex, appendix, appurtenance, attachment, auxiliary, extremity, limb, member, projection, protuberance, suffix, supplement *Antonyms:* centre, core, marrow, nucleus **2.** assistant, attendant, factotum, henchperson, satellite, subordinate, sycophant, vassal *Nonformal:* flunky, goon, sidekick *Antonyms:* kingpin, overlord, principal, sovereign

appendix *n.* addendum, addition, attachment, codicil, extension, extra, index, notes, postscript, rider, supplement, table

appertain *v.* apply, bear, belong, connect, pertain, refer, relate

appetite *n.* craving, demand, fondness, greed, hankering, hunger, inclination, itch, liking, longing, lust, passion, penchant, proclivity, propensity, taste, thirst, urge, voracity, weakness, willingness, yearning, yen, zest *Antonyms:* abhorrence, aversion, dislike, repugnance, revulsion

appetizer *n.* antipasto, apéritif, canapé, crudité, finger food, hors d'oeuvre, pâté, snack, spread, tapas, taste, tidbit **2.** come-on, foretaste, lure, prelude, preview, sample, teaser

appetizing *adj.* ambrosian, appealing, delectable, delicious, divine, flavoursome, good-tasting, luscious, mouth-watering, palatable, piquant, savoury, seductive, succulent, sweetened, tantalizing, tasty, tempting, toothsome *Nonformal:* delish, scrumptious, yummy *Antonyms:* distasteful, nauseating, unappetizing, unsavoury

applaud *v.* acclaim, approve, boost, cheer, clap, commend, compliment, encourage, eulogize, extol, exult, glorify, hail, laud, magnify, pay homage to, plug, praise, raise the rafters *(Nonformal)*, rave, recommend, root, salute *Antonyms:* boo, condemn, criticize, decry, deride

applause *n.* acclamation, accolade, approbation, approval, cheering, cheers, clapping, commendation, curtain call, eulogy, hand, hand-clapping, hurrah, huzzah, ovation, panegyric, plaudits, praise, rooting, round, triumph *Antonyms:* derision, hiss, silence

apple *n.* fruit *Kinds of apple:* Baldwin, Bishop's pippin, Bourassa, crabapple, Delicious, Empire, Fameuse, Golden Delicious, Granny Smith, Gravenstein, Ida Red, Jonathan, Macintosh, Macoun, northern spy, pippin, Rome, Royal Gala, russet, snow, Spartan, Wealthy, Winesap

appliance *n.* apparatus, device, gadget, implement, instrument, machine, mechanism, tool *Kinds of kitchen appliance:* blender, breadmaker, broiler, can-opener, churn, coffee grinder *or* mill, Cuisinart *(Trademark)*, dishwasher, eggbeater, espresso machine, food mill, food processor, freezer, fridge *(Nonformal)*, ice cream maker, juicer, meat grinder, microwave oven, refrigerator, stove, toaster, toaster oven, waffle iron

applicable *adj.* appropriate, apropos, apt, befitting, fitting, germane, material, meet, pertinent, relevant, suitable, suited *Nonformal:* kosher, legit, on target, on the nose *Antonyms:* inapplicable, irrelevant, wrong

applicant *n.* candidate, claimant, contestant, hopeful, job hunter, petitioner, postulant, seeker, suitor, supplicant

application *n.* **1.** attention, attentiveness, commitment, concentration, dedication, deliberation, diligence, effort, engrossment, perseverance, persistence, resolution, study, work, zeal *Antonyms:* absent-mindedness, abstraction, indolence, laziness, sloth **2.** employment, exercise, function, operation, play, practice, program, purpose, use, utilization **3.** bearing, pertinence, purpose, relevance, significance **4.** entreaty, inquiry, petition, plea, request **5.** balm, dressing, emollient, formulation, lotion, ointment, plaster, poultice, remedial agent, salve, unguent **6.** software *Kinds of computer application:* accounting, communications, computer-aided design *or* CAD, crime, database, desktop publishing, games, graphics, language processing, programming, project management, robotics, spreadsheet, utility, word processing

applied *adj.* empirical, functional, practical, used, utilized *Antonyms:* abstract, pure, theoretical

apply *v.* **1.** address, bend, buckle *or* knuckle down *(Nonformal)*, commit, concentrate, dedicate, devote, direct, give, persevere, study, try, work *Antonyms:* abandon, neglect **2.** affect, allude, appertain, bear upon, be pertinent, concern, connect, fit, involve, pertain, refer, regard, relate, suit, touch **3.** administer, affix, anoint, bestow, cover, fasten, join, lay on, place, put on, rub, smear, spread, touch **4.** appeal, audition, call upon, enlist, implore, seek, solicit, try for **5.** assign, avail, employ, engage, execute, exercise, exploit, handle, implement, practice, utilize

appoint *v.* **1.** assign, call, choose, commission, delegate, designate, direct, install, name, nominate, ordain, select *Antonyms:* discharge, dismiss, fire **2.** arm, equip, fit, fit out, furnish, gear, outfit, provide, rig, supply, turn out *Antonyms:* dismantle, divest, strip

appointment *n.* **1.** arrangement, assembly, assignation, audience, conclave, conference, congress, consultation, convention, date, encounter, engagement, gathering, get-together, gig *(Nonformal)*, interview, invitation, meeting, parley, rally, rendezvous, reunion, session, showdown, talk, tryst **2.** approval, authorization, commissioning, deputation, designation, installation, naming, nomination, ordination, plum *(Nonformal)*, promotion, responsibility, selection **3.** appointee, assignment, candidate, delegate, employment, job, nominee, office, office-holder, place, place-holder, post, representative, situation, station, work

appointments *n.* accoutrements, appurtenances, belongings, bits and pieces *(British)*, chattels, equipages, fitting, fixture, furnishing *or* furnishings, gear, harness, munition, outfit, paraphernalia, personal effects, trappings *Nonformal:* kit, rig, stuff

apportion *v.* accord, administer, allocate, allot, assign, bestow, cut, dispense, distribute, divide, divvy *(Nonformal)*, give, lot, measure, mete, parcel, part, partition, prorate, ration, share, slice, split *Antonyms:* amass, hoard, stockpile

appraisal *n.* assessment, calculation, determination, estimate, estimation, evaluation, inspection, judgment, opinion, pricing, rating, reckoning, survey, valuation

appraise *v.* ascertain, assay, assess, audit, calculate, discover, estimate, evaluate, examine, eye, figure, gauge, inspect, price, rate, scrutinize, size, survey, valuate, value *Nonformal:* ballpark, check out, guesstimate, size up, take one's measure *Commonly misused:* **apprise**

appreciable *adj.* apparent, ascertainable, clear-cut, considerable, definite, detectable, discernible, distinguishable, estimable, evident, goodly, good-sized, healthy, large, manifest, marked, measurable, noticeable, obvious, perceivable, perceptible, ponderable, pronounced, recognizable, sensible, significant, sizable, substantial, tangible, visible *Antonyms:* imperceptible, indiscernible, small, trivial, unsubstantial

appreciate *v.* **1.** acknowledge, apprehend, comprehend, fathom, grasp, know, perceive, read, realize, recognize, understand *Nonformal:* catch the drift, savvy *Antonyms:* misunderstand, underrate **2.** enhance, fortify, gain, grow, improve, increase, inflate, intensify, rise *Antonyms:* deflate, depreciate, devaluate, fall **3.** admire, adore, applaud, cherish, enjoy, esteem, extol, flip over *(Nonformal)*, honour, like, love, praise, prize, rate highly, regard, relish, respect, savour, treasure, value, venerate *Antonyms:* belittle, disdain, disparage, scorn **4.** be grateful, be thankful for, never forget, thank

appreciation *n.* **1.** admiration, affection, attraction, awareness, empathy, enjoyment, esteem, grasp, high regard, knowledge, liking, love, perception, realization, regard, relish, respect, sensitivity, sympathy, understanding **2.** enhancement, gain, growth, improvement, increase, inflation, rise *Antonyms:* decline, depreciation, devaluation, fall **3.** acknowledgment, commendation, gratefulness, gratitude, gratuity, indebtedness, obligation, *pourboire (French)*, raise, recognition, testimonial, thankfulness, thanks, tip, tribute *Antonyms:* ingratitude, thanklessness, ungratefulness

appreciative *adj.* **1.** admiring, affectionate, beholden, considerate, cordial, enthusiastic, friendly, generous, kindly, magnanimous, pleased, receptive, responsive, satisfied, supportive, sympathetic *Antonyms:* callous, hard-hearted **2.** alive, *au fait (French)*, aware, cognizant, conscious, enlightened, keen, knowledgeable, mindful, perceptive, recognizing, regardful, respectful, responsive, sensitive, understanding *Antonyms:* blind, ignorant, unaware

apprehend *v.* **1.** absorb, accept, appreciate, believe, comprehend, conceive, digest, fathom, foresee, grasp, have, imagine, know, perceive, read, realize, recognize, sense, think, understand *Nonformal:* catch, get *or* get the picture *Antonyms:* misapprehend, miss, misunderstand **2.** arrest, capture, grab, seize, take in, take prisoner *Nonformal:* bag, bust, collar, nab, nail *Antonyms:* discharge, let go, liberate, release, set free

apprehension *n.* **1.** alarm, apprehensiveness, concern, disquiet, doubt, dread, fear, foreboding, misgiving, mistrust, premonition, presentiment, suspicion, the willies *(Nonformal)*, trepidation, uneasiness, worry *Antonyms:* assurance, composure, serenity **2.** awareness, comprehension, grasp, idea, intellect, intelligence, judgment, ken, knowledge, perception, perspicacity, realization, thought, understanding *Antonyms:* incomprehension, mystery **3.** arrest, bust *(Nonformal)*, capture, detention, seizure, taking *Antonyms:* amnesty, liberation, release

apprehensive *adj.* afraid, alarmed, concerned, disquieted, doubtful, fearful, fretful, jumpy, mistrustful, shaky, suspicious, timorous, troubled, uncertain, uneasy, uptight, worried *Nonformal:* in a dither, jittery, spooked *Antonyms:* assured, at ease, confident, nonchalant, unafraid

apprentice *n.* amateur, beginner, freshman, learner, neophyte, newcomer, novice, novitiate, probationer, pupil, rookie, starter, student, tyro *Antonyms:* expert, journeyperson, veteran, wizard

apprise *v.* acquaint, advise, announce, brief, enlighten, inform, notify, tell, warn *Nonformal:* bring up to speed, place in the picture, tip off *Antonyms:* screen, shield *Commonly misused:* **appraise**

approach *n.* **1.** access, avenue, coming, conflux, convergence, entrance, gate, landing, nearing, passage, path, road, way *Antonyms:* departure, exit **2.** attitude, concept, course, idea, manner, means, method, mode, *modus operandi (Latin)*, plan, procedure, program, style, system, technique, way **3.** attempt, bid, feeler, gesture, offer, overture, proposition, tender, wrinkle *(Nonformal)* – *v.* **1.** advance toward, approximate, belly up to *(Nonformal)*, border, close in, come at, converge, creep up on, draw near, gain on, inch toward, loom up, move toward, near, progress toward, verge upon *Antonyms:* break camp, recede, take leave **2.** accost, address, advise, annoy, appeal to, apply to, beseech, brace, call, challenge, confer, confront, consult, entice, entreat, face, greet, hail, introduce, make advances, make an overture, propose, proposition, request, solicit, speak *or* talk to *Nonformal:* buttonhole, sound out, take aside **3.** begin, commence, embark, get rolling, set about, start, undertake

approachable *adj.* accessible, affable, agreeable, congenial, cordial, friendly, open, receptive, sociable *Antonyms:* aloof, cool, distant, harsh, unfriendly

approbation *n.* admiration, approval, consent, endorsement, esteem, favour, go-ahead, high regard, permission, praise, recognition, sanction, support *Nonformal:* okay, the nod *Antonyms:* censure, condemnation, disapproval, disfavour, stricture

appropriate *adj.* adapted, applicable, apropos, apt, becoming, befitting, belonging, congruous, convenient, correct, deserved, desired, due, fit, fitting, germane, good, just, opportune, pertinent, proper, relevant, right, rightful, seemly, suitable, timely, true, useful, well-suited, well-timed *Antonyms:* improper, inappropriate, incorrect – *v.* annex, borrow, confiscate, embezzle, grab, hijack, liberate, lift, misappropriate, pilfer, pocket, secure, snatch, steal, take over, usurp *Nonformal:* filch, swipe, take the five finger discount

appropriation *n.* **1.** allocation, allotment, allowance, apportionment, assignment, budgeting, concession, donation, earmarking, endowment, funding, gift, giving, grant, provision, sponsorship, stipend, subsidy **2.** confiscation, expropriation, grab, seizure, take-in *(Nonformal)*, takeover, usurpation

approval *n.* acclaim, admiration, applause, appreciation, approbation, authorization, backing, blessing, certification, commendation, concurrence, consent, esteem, favour, imprimatur, leave, licence, liking, permission, praise, regard, respect, sanction, support, valediction *Nonformal:* go ahead, green light, okay, stroking *Antonyms:* dislike, disparagement, displeasure, dissatisfaction, objection

approve *v.* accept, acclaim, admire, advocate, aid, applaud, appreciate, approbate, authenticate, back, champion, commend, condone, confirm, endorse, esteem, favour, get behind, hold with, like, praise, ratify, regard highly, respect, sanction, smile on, support, uphold *Nonformal:* go for, okay, rubber stamp *Antonyms:* condemn, disapprove, object to, veto

approximate *adj.* bordering, circa, close, comparative, estimated, guessed, imprecise, inexact, near, neighbouring, proximate, relative, rough, surmised *Nonformal:* ballpark, guesstimate *Antonyms:* accurate, definite, exact, precise, specific – *v.* estimate, extrapolate, interpolate, reach, reckon, resemble, take a stab at *(Nonformal)*

approximately *adv.* about, almost, around, carefully, closely, comparatively, generally, jointly, loosely, meticulously, more or less, nearly, relatively, roughly, scrupulously, similarly, strictly, upwards of, very close to

apropos *adj.* applicable, appropriate, appurtenant, apt, befitting, belonging, correct, fit, fitting, germane, material, opportune, pertinent, proper, related, relevant, right, right on, seemly, suitable *Antonyms:* out of character, unsuitable – *adv.* appropriately, aptly, opportunely, pertinently, relevantly, suitably, timely

apt *adj.* **1.** able, adept, astute, bright, clever, expert, gifted, ingenious, intelligent, learned, prompt, ready, sharp, skilled, skilful, smart, talented, teachable *Nonformal:* nobody's fool, sharp as a whip *Antonyms:* awkward, clumsy, incompetent, inept, maladroit **2.** disposed, given, inclined, liable, likely, prone, ready, tending **3.** applicable, appropriate, apropos, befitting, correct, fitting, germane, on the mark *(Nonformal)*, pertinent, proper, relevant, seemly, suitable

Antonyms: ill-fitted, ill-suited, improper, irrelevant

aptitude *n.* ability, bent, capability, capacity, cleverness, competence, disposition, faculty, flair, gift, giftedness, inclination, intelligence, knack, leaning, proficiency, propensity, quickness, talent *Nonformal:* right stuff, savvy, smarts

aquatic *adj.* amphibian, amphibious, floating, marine, maritime, oceanic, pelagic, sea, swimming, water, watery *Kinds of aquatic or water sports:* barefooting, boating, body surfing, canoeing, diving, dragon boat racing, fishing, kayaking, parasailing, pool volleyball, rafting, rowing, sailboarding, sailing, scuba diving, snorkelling, surfing, synchronized swimming, water polo, water skiing, windsurfing, yachting

aqueduct *n.* canal, channel, chute, conduit, course, culvert, duct, flume, gully, gutter, pipeline, sewer, water passage, waterworks

aquiline *adj.* aduncous, beaked, crooked, eagle-like, hooked, prominent, protruding, Roman

arable *adj.* cultivable, fecund, fertile, plantable, plowable, productive, rural, tillable *Antonyms:* arid, inhospitable, waste

arbiter *n.* adjudicator, autocrat, despot, go-between, intermediary, judge, last word *(Nonformal)*, mediator, moderator, referee, ultimate authority, umpire *Commonly misused:* **arbitrator**

arbitrary *adj.* **1.** absolute, autocratic, bossy, despotic, dictatorial, dogmatic, domineering, flat out *(Nonformal)*, high-handed, imperious, magisterial, overbearing, peremptory, tyrannical, tyrannous **2.** approximate, capricious, chance, erratic, fanciful, frivolous, inconsistent, irrational, irresponsible, offhand, optional, random, subjective, superficial, unaccountable, unscientific, wayward, whimsical, wilful *Antonyms:* logical, objective, rational, reasonable, sensible

arbitrate *v.* adjudicate, conciliate, decide, determine, intervene, judge, mediate, meet halfway, negotiate, pass judgment, placate, reconcile, referee, settle, smooth, umpire

arbitration *n.* adjudication, adjustment, agreement, compromise, determination, judgment, mediation, settlement

arbitrator *n.* adjudicator, fixer, judge, mediator, middleperson, referee, umpire *Commonly misused:* **arbiter**

arboreal *adj.* arboreous, arborescent, coniferous, deciduous, dendroid, shrublike, treelike, woody

arc *n.* arch, bend, bow, crescent, curvature, curve, half-moon, parabola, round

arcade *n.* **1.** archway, breezeway, cloister, colonnade, gallery, loggia, pergola, peristyle, portico **2.** mall, market, plaza, shops, stalls

arcane *adj.* cryptic, enigmatic, esoteric, hidden, impenetrable, mysterious, mystic, occult, otherworldly, recondite, secret, shrouded, unaccountable, unknowable *Antonyms:* humdrum, obvious, pedestrian

arch *adj.* **1.** artful, coy, frolicsome, knowing, mischievous, pert, playful, roguish, saucy, waggish **2.** accomplished, champion, chief, consummate, expert, finished, first, foremost, greatest, head, highest, leading, main, major, master, preeminent, premier, primary, principal, superior, top **3.** deceitful, scheming, sly, tricky, wily – *n.* archway, bend, bow, bridge, camber, curvature, curve, dome, hump, semicircle, span, vault – *v.* **1.** bestraddle, bridge, span **2.** bend, bow, curve, sweep *Kinds of arch:* elliptical, equilateral, rampant, rounded, segmental

archaeologist *n.* classicist, culturist, excavator, paleontologist, prehistorian, scientist

archaeology *n.* antiquarianism, classicism, paleohistory, paleontology, prehistory

archaic *adj.* antediluvian, antiquated, antique, discontinued, hackneyed, obsolete, old-fashioned, outmoded, out-of-date, quaint *Antonyms:* modern, new, novel

archetype *n.* classic, example, exemplar, first principle, ideal, magnum opus, masterpiece, masterwork, model, monomyth, paradigm, pattern, precept, prototype, standard

architect *n.* artist, builder, constructor, creator, designer, draftsperson, engineer, inventor, maker, master builder, mastermind, originator, planner, strategist, tactician *Kinds of architect:* civil, domestic, industrial, landscape, urban planner

architecture *n.* **1.** arrangement, building, composition, constitution, construction, edifice, fabric, framework, makeup, style **2.** architectural design, building design, construction, planning, structure *Kinds and styles of architecture:* academic, art deco, art modern, arts and crafts, baroque, Bauhaus, beaux arts, brutalism, Byzantine, Chateau, classical, college, colonial, contemporary, domestic, ecclesiastical, Edwardian, Egyptian, Elizabethan, 50's contemporary, functionalist, Georgian, Gothic, Greco-Roman, Greek, Greek Revival, hard, hi-tech, industrial, Islamic, Italianate, Mayan, Mestizo, modern, museum, neoclassical, New England, Palladian, Prairie, Queen Anne, Regency, Renaissance, rococo, Roman, Romanesque, Second Empire, Spanish Colonial, Tudor, Utopian, Victorian Gothic, Victory housing, Wright School

archive *n.* **1.** annals, archives, chronicle, collection, document, excerpt, extract, file, memorabilia, paper, public papers, records, register, roll, writing **2.** caché, collection, depository, library, museum, office, registry, repertory, repository, stock, storage, storehouse, treasury, vault

archway *n.* arcade, curved opening, entrance, gateway, passage, threshold

arctic *adj.* **1.** boreal, northern, polar **2.** chilly, freezing, frigid, frozen, gelid, glacial, icy, nippy, very cold **3.** aloof, cool, dispassionate, distant, heartless, unresponsive

ardent *adj.* agog, avid, blazing, brilliant, burning, consuming, desirous, eager, enthusiastic, fervent, fervid, fierce, fiery, hot-headed, hungry, impassioned, intense, keen, lovey-dovey *(Nonformal),* lusty, passionate, rich, spirited, strong, thirsty, vehement, volatile, warm, white hot, zealous *Antonyms:* apathetic, cool, frigid, impassive, lukewarm

ardour *n.* avidity, devotion, eagerness, earnestness, ebullience, enthusiasm, feeling, fervour, fierceness, fire, gusto, heat, intensity, keenness, oomph *(Nonformal),* passion, rapture, spirit, vehemence, verve, warmth, white heat, zeal, zest

arduous *adj.* backbreaking, burdensome, difficult, emphatic, exacting, exhausting, fierce, forceful, formidable, gruelling, harsh, heavy, laborious, mighty, onerous, painful, powerful, punishing, rigorous, severe, sharp, steep, taxing, tiring, troublesome, trying, uphill, wearying *Antonyms:* easy, effortless, facile, simple

area *n.* breadth, compass, distance, expanse, extent, field, operation, range, scope, size, space, sphere, stretch, width **2.** *arrondissement (French),* court, district, land, locale, neighbourhood, parcel, patch, plot, precinct, province, quarter, region, square, terrain, territory, tract, zone *Nonformal:* beat, hood, neck of the woods, turf *Kinds of area measurements:* acre, arpent, centare, concession, hectare, section, square foot *or* inch *or* kilometre *or* metre *or* mile

arena *n.* **1.** amphitheatre, boards, bowl, circus, coliseum, course, diamond, field, forum, gardens, ground, gym, gymnasium, hippodrome, ice, pad, park, pit, platform, ring, rink, square, stadium, stage **2.** domain, expertise, forte, métier, province

argue *v.* **1.** agitate, assert, aver, claim, contend, defend, hold, maintain **2.** challenge, charge, combat, confound, confute, contest, contradict, controvert, counter, criticize, defy, deny, dicker, differ, dispute, fall out, go at, haggle, have out, hold, jump, jump on, lay *or* light into, litigate, quarrel, tangle with *Nonformal:* bump heads, cross swords, lock horns **3.** cavil, debate, disagree, hash over, have words, nitpick, oppose, persuade, plead, question, rebut, refute, remonstrate, take issue, talk back, thrash out, toss around *Nonformal:* face-off, kick around **4.** convince, demonstrate, dissuade, elucidate, explain, expostulate, reason, talk into *or* out of

argument *n.* **1.** assertion, asseveration, avowal, brouhaha, case, claim, conflict, confrontation, contention, contest, controversy, debate, defence, dialectic, difference, disagreement, discord, discordance, discussion, dispute, dissension, dissent, dissidence, donnybrook, embroilment, falling-out, fracas, fray, friction, imbroglio, plea, quarrel, rift, row, run-in, set-to, shouting match, spat, tiff, tussle, wrangle *Nonformal:* beef, blowup, dust-up, face-off, flap, rhubarb, ruckus, rumpus *Antonyms:* accord, agreement, concurrence, rebuttal, refutation **2.** abstract, demonstration, grounds, polemic, proof, rationale, reason, rebuttal, refutation, summary, syllabus **3.** gist, subject matter, thesis, topic

argumentative *adj.* belligerent, cantankerous, chippy, combative, contentious, contrary, controversial, cranky, disputatious, irascible, litigious, opinionated, ornery, pugnacious, quarrelsome *Nonformal:* salty, scrappy, spiky *Antonyms:* accommodating, amenable, compliant, conciliatory, obliging

arid *adj.* **1.** barren, bone-dry, desert, desiccant, dry, dusty, moistureless, parched, thirsty, waterless, withered *Antonyms:* lush, rich, verdant, wet **2.** bare, boring, colourless, depleted, desolate, destitute, drab, dreary, dull, flat, impoverished, infertile, insipid, lacklustre, lifeless, spiritless, sterile, tedious, unanimated, uninspired, uninteresting, vapid, wearisome *Antonyms:* exciting, lively, spirited, stimulating, vivacious

arise *v.* **1.** ascend, climb, go up, jump, levitate, loom, mount, move upward, rise, soar, stand, tower **2.** appear, begin, commence, crop up *(Nonformal)*, derive, emanate, emerge, ensue, flow, follow, happen, head, issue, occur, originate, proceed, result, rise, spring, spring forth, start **3.** awaken, get up, turn out *Nonformal:* hit the deck, pile out, rise and shine

aristocracy *n.* elite, gentility, gentry, high society, nobility, noblesse, peerage, privileged, society, upper class *or* crust *French:* beau monde, haute monde *Antonyms:* commoners, hoi polloi, lower classes, masses, vassalage

aristocrat *n.* blue-blood, chevalier, count, duke, earl, grandee, lady, lord, marquis, nobleperson, patrician, peer, seigneur, viscount *Nonformal:* silk stocking, swell

aristocratic *adj.* blue-blooded, courtly, dignified, elegant, elite, fine, haughty, noble, patrician, polished, privileged, refined, snobbish, thoroughbred, upper-class, well-born, well-bred, well-heeled *Antonyms:* common, plebian, proletarian

arithmetic *n.* addition, algorithm, calculation, computation, division, estimation, figuring, multiplication, number, reckoning, subtraction, sums

arm *n.* **1.** bough, branch, fin, flipper, handle, hook, limb, member, projection, wing **2.** branch, brook, channel, creek, estuary, firth, inlet, rivulet, sound, strait, stream, subdivision, tributary – *v. accoutre (French)*, appoint, array, deck, equip, fortify, furnish, gear, gird, guard, issue, load, load up, mobilize, outfit, pack, prepare, prime, protect, provide, ready, rig, strengthen, supply, tote

armada *n.* argosy, escadrille, fleet, flotilla, force, navy, squadron, task force

armament *n.* ammunition, arms, artillery, cannon, defence, gun, hardware, heat *(Nonformal)*, *matériel (French)*, means of defence, missilery, munition, nuclear weapon, ordnance, protection, security, war equipment, weapon, weaponry

armistice *n.* agreement, cease-fire, cooling-off period, discontinuance, hiatus, lull, peace, stand down, suspension, treaty, truce

armour *n.* bulletproof vest, carapace, chain mail, covering, guard, mail, panoply, plate, protection, security, sheath, shell, shield *Pieces of armour:* anime, breastplate, backplate, culet, rump-guard, fauld, gorget, harness, helmet, pauldrons, sallet, tassets, visor

armoury *n.* ammunition depository *or* depot, arsenal, cache, depot, factory, headquarters, *magasin (French)*, magazine, plant, repository, storehouse, warehouse

arms *n.* **1.** accoutrements, armaments, artillery, equipment, firearms, gear, guns, munitions, weaponry, weapons **2.** blazonry, coat, crest, emblem, ensign, escutcheon, heraldry, insignia, shield, signet

army *n.* **1.** array, cloud, company, crowd, division, flock, group, horde, host, legion, mob, multitude, outfit, pack, regiment, scores, swarm, throng, unit **2.** armada, armed force, armoured division, army base, battalion, battery, battle group, brigade, Canadian Forces, column, combat team, command, company, corps, detail, division, fleet, flight, flotilla, forces, garrison, group, militia, navy, patrol unit, platoon, regiment, regular army, reserve, soldiers, soldiery, squad, squadron, standing army, station, task force, troops, wing *Former Canadian Armed Forces:* Canadian Army, Royal Canadian Air Force, Royal Canadian Army, Royal Canadian Navy *Groupings of army units:* artillery, cavalry, infantry, medical corps, ordnance, signals

aroma *n.* **1.** balm, bouquet, fragrance, incense, odour, perfume, redolence, scent, smell, spice **2.** aura, character, essence, flavour, hallmark, nature, taste, tone, trait

aromatic *adj.* ambrosial, balmy, fragrant, odoriferous, perfumed, pungent, redolent, savoury, scented, spicy, sweet, sweet-smelling *Antonyms:* acrid, fetid, foul, rank, stinking

around *adv.* **1.** encircling, enclosing, encompassing, enveloping, hedging, ring, surrounding **2.** about town, here and there, out and about **3.** accessible, attainable, available, obtainable, reachable **4.** close to, near, neighbouring, roughly – *prep.* **1.** all over, encompassing, enveloping, surrounding, throughout **2.** circa, close to, in the vicinity of, near, nearby

arouse *v.* agitate, alarm, alert, animate, awaken, call, challenge, electrify, enliven, entice, evoke, excite, foment, foster, galvanize, goad, incite, inflame, instigate, kindle, move, provoke, rally, rouse, send, spark, spur, stimulate, stir, summon, thrill, touch off, waken, warm, whet, whip *or* work up *Nonformal:* egg on, hype *or* psyche up *Antonyms:* bore, exhaust, tire, wear out

arraign *v.* **1.** accuse, blame, charge, denounce, impeach, incriminate, indict, pin on *(Nonformal)*, prosecute, summon **2.** call to account, censure, impugn, reprehend, stigmatize, upbraid

arrange *v.* **1.** align, allocate, allot, allow, appoint, apportion, appropriate, array, assemble, assign, catalogue, categorize, class, classify, collect, file, grade, hierarchize, line up, marshal, order, organize, pigeonhole, prepare, put in order, rank, sort, systemize **2.** fix *(Nonformal)*, plan, prepare, schedule, set up **3.** accommodate, bring *or* come to terms, deal, get together, handle, settle, straighten *or* work out **4.** adapt, compose, conduct, orchestrate, set to music, transcribe, transpose **5.** call, conduct, convene, summon

arrangement *n.* **1.** alignment, allocation, array, categorization, classification, codification, combination, design, distribution, form, grouping, line-up, method, order, organization, pattern, rank, sequence, structure, system **2.** adjustment, agreement, compact, compromise, deal, layout, organization, package, plan, preparation, provision, schedule, settlement, setup, terms, understanding **3.** adaptation, chart, composition, instrumentation, interpretation, lead sheet, orchestration, score, version

array *n.* **1.** arrangement, batch, body, bunch, bundle, clump, cluster, collection, congregation, design, display, exhibition, formation, host, lineup, lot, multitude, order, parade, pattern, set, show, supply, throng **2.** apparel, finery, guise, raiment *Nonformal:* get-up, glad rags, threads, togs – *v.* align, amass, arrange, display, exhibit, form, group, line-up, marshal, organize, parade, range, set, show

arrears *n. pl.* back payment, balance due, debit, debt, deficit, liability, moneys behind *or* owed, obligation

arrest *n.* **1.** apprehension, captivity, capture, confinement, constraint, detention, imprisonment, incarceration, jailing, protective custody, snare, snatch *Nonformal:* bust, collar, grab *Antonyms:* dismissal, release **2.** blockage, cessation, check, delay, end, halt, hindrance, inhibition, interruption, obstruction, prevention, restraint, stall, stay, stop, stoppage, suppression, suspension – *v.* **1.** apprehend, capture, catch, detain, get, imprison, incarcerate, jail, round up, seize, snatch, tag, take prisoner *Nonformal:* bag, book, bust, collar, grab, hook, nab, pull *or* run in *Antonyms:* free, release **2.** absorb, attract, catch, engage, engross, fascinate, grip, hold **3.** block, check, curb, delay, drop, end, freeze, halt, hinder, hold, inhibit, interrupt, obstruct, prevent, restrain, restrict, retard, shut down, stall, stay, stop, suppress *Antonyms:* accelerate, excite, promote

arresting *adj.* attracting, conspicuous, engaging, engrossing, eye-catching, fascinating, gripping, noteworthy, remarkable, striking *Antonyms:* nondescript, prosaic

arrival *n.* **1.** accession, advent, alighting, appearance, approach, coming, debarkation, entrance, influx, ingress, landing *Antonyms:* disappearance, leave-taking **2.** attainment, consummation, fulfillment, realization, completion *Antonyms:* abdication, resignation

arrive *v.* **1.** access, advance, alight, anchor, appear, attain, come, come ashore, come to *or* down *or* in, debark, descend upon, detrain, disembark, dismount, dock, draw near, drop anchor, enter, gain ingress, make land, moor, put down *or* in, reach, rendezvous, show, show up, sign in, tie up, touch down, turn up *Nonformal:* blow *or* breeze *or* buzz *or* check *or* clock in, bob up, drop *or* edge in, fall in *or* by, get in *or* to *or* inside *or* down, hit, hit town, land, pop in *or* up, pull *or* punch *or* ring *or* roll in, splash down *Antonyms:* depart, exit, leave, weigh anchor, withdraw **2.** advance, claw one's way up, cut a swath, flourish, progress, prosper, thrive

arrogance *n.* airs, aloofness, audacity, bluster, braggadocio, brazenness, cheek, cockiness, conceit, disdain, effrontery, gall, haughtiness, hauteur, high-handedness, hubris, imperiousness, impudence, loftiness, nerve, overconfidence, pomposity, presumption, pride, snobbishness, swagger, temerity, vanity *Nonformal:* chutzpah, moxie *Antonyms:* bashfulness, humility, modesty, shyness, timidity

arrogant *adj.* ambitious, autocratic, bossy, cavalier, cocky, conceited, contemptuous, contumelious, disdainful, domineering, egocentric, grandiose, haughty, immodest, imperious, lofty, lordly, magisterial, patronizing, pompous, presumptuous, pretentious, pushy, scornful, self-important, snobbish, supercilious, superior, vainglorious *Nonformal:* high-and-mighty, high-falutin, hoity-toity, puffed up, snooty *Antonyms:* humble, modest, polite, servile, shy

arrogate *v.* **1.** appropriate, assume, commandeer, confiscate, demand, expropriate, help oneself to, preempt, presume, seize, usurp **2.** ascribe, attribute, betray *(Nonformal)*, finger, impute, incriminate, point out *Commonly Misused:* **abdicate, abrogate**

arsenal *n.* armoury, cache, depository, depot, *magasin (French)*, magazine, munitions dump, plant, repository, stock, stockpile, store, storehouse, weapons supply

arson *n.* burning, combustion, firing, incendiarism, pyromania, torching

art *n.* **1.** adroitness, aptitude, artistry, craft, craftsmanship, creativity, dexterity, expertise, facility, imagination, ingenuity, inventiveness, knack, know-how, knowledge, mastery, method, profession, savvy *(Nonformal)*, skill, talent, trade, virtuosity **2.** abstraction, carving, creation, description, design, illustration, imitation, modeling, moulding, oeuvre, painting, portrayal, representation, sculpting, shaping, simulation, sketching, symbolization, work *Art equipment*: air brush, art paper, brush, canvas, chalk, charcoal, crayon, drawing paper, drawing pencil, drier, easel, fixative, maulstick, medium, paint, paint-box, paintbrush, palette, palette knife, pastel, pencil, pigment, sketchbook, sketchpad, spatula, spray gun, varnish, water-colour *Kinds of visual art:* animation, architecture, arts and crafts, *beaux arts (French)*, carving, ceramics, cinematography, commercial, costume design, drawing, engraving, etching, fashion/design, film, fine, folk, furniture design, glass blowing, graphic, interior design, jewellery design, landscaping, photography, pottery, printmaking, representative, sculpture, sketching, textile design, video, visual *Visual art groups, movements, and styles:* abstract expressionism, academic, Art Deco, Art Nouveau, Barbizon, baroque, Bauhaus, Beaver Hall Hill Group *(Montreal)*, Bolognese, Byzantine, Canadian, Chinese, conceptual, cubist, Dada, Der Blaue Reiter, De Stijl, Die Brücke, Flemish, Florentine, German expressionist, Group of Seven, Hellenic, impressionism, Inuit, Lombard, Mannerist, minimalism, modern, Mogul, op art, Paduan, Painters Eleven, Persian, plein-air, pointillistic, pop art, post-impressionism, postmodernism, Pre-Raphaelite, Raphaelite, rococo, Roman, Romantic, Sienese, Surrealism *See also:* **artwork, painting 3.** artfulness, artifice, astuteness, canniness, craftiness, cunning, deceit, duplicity, guile, slyness, trickery, wiliness

artery *n.* **1.** avenue, boulevard, channel, conduit, corridor, course, highway, line, passage, pathway, road, route, sewer, thoroughfare, track, tube, way **2.** aorta, blood vessel, carotid, pulmonary artery, red pipe *(Nonformal)*, vein

artful *adj.* adept, adroit, clever, crafty, deft, designing, dexterous, foxy *(Nonformal)*, ingenious, masterly, proficient, resourceful, scheming, sharp, shrewd, skilful, slick, sly, smart, smooth, tricky, wily *Antonyms:* clumsy, unskilled, untalented

arthritis *n.* gout, joint inflammation *or* stiffening, rheumatism *Types of arthritis:* Behçet's syndrome, colitic, osteoarthritis, psoriatic, Reiter's syndrome, rheumatoid

article *n.* **1.** commodity, object, piece, product, unit, ware **2.** analysis, column, commentary, composition, editorial, discourse, dissertation, essay, exposition, memoir, monograph, opus, piece, position paper, report, review, sketch, survey, thesis, think piece *(Nonformal)*, tract, treatise, write-up **3.** auxiliary word *Kinds of grammatical article:* definite, determinative, indefinite, postdeterminative **4.** exclusive, feature, lead, news piece *or* item, story **5.** chapter, clause, detail, item, paragraph, part, point, provision, section – *v.* **1.** apprentice, bind over, indenture, obligate **2.** catalogue, focus, itemize, organize, set forth, specify

articulate *adj.* **1.** clear, clear-cut, coherent, comprehensible, definite, distinct, easy to understand, eloquent, expressive, fathomable, flowing, fluent, glib, graceful, intelligible, lucid, meaningful, silver-tongued, understandable, well-spoken *Antonyms:* faltering, incoherent, mumbled, poorly-spoken **2.** conjoined, connected, hinged, joined – *v.* **1.** enunciate, express, mouth, pronounce, say, sound off, speak, state, talk, utter, verbalize, vocalize, voice **2.** clarify, come out with, explicate, illuminate **3.** connect, couple, fit together, hinge, integrate, join, link

articulation *n.* **1.** delivery, diction, emphasis, enunciation, expression, intonation, modulation, pronunciation, saying, speaking, statement, utterance, verbalization, vocalization, voicing **2.** connection, coupling, hinge, joining, joint, junction, juncture, unification, union, yoking

artifact *n.* **1.** antique, antiquity, fossil, object, relic, remains, remanant, vestige **2.** artwork, craft, creation, handiwork, object, product

artifice *n.* **1.** contrivance, device, dodge, feint, gambit, gimmick, hoax, machination, manoeuvre, play, ploy, ruse, sleight, strategy, subterfuge, tactic, wile **2.** adroitness, artfulness, chicanery, craftiness, deception, dishonesty, duplicity, guile, imposture, scheming, shrewdness, slyness, trickery, wiliness *Antonyms:* artlessness, naiveté, sincerity

artificer *n.* artist, builder, craftsperson, creator, Daedalus, designer, inventor, manufacturer, originator, parent

artificial *adj.* **1.** affected, bogus *(Nonformal)*, contrived, counterfeit, false, feigned, forced, hollow, insincere, laboured, mannered, pretended, simulated, spurious, theatrical, unnatural *Antonyms:* genuine, heartfelt, sincere **2.** ersatz, fabricated, faked, imitation, man-made, manufactured, phoney, plastic, sham, synthetic, unreal *Antonyms:* authentic, bona fide, legitimate

artillery *n.* anti-aircraft guns, armament, arms, battery, bazooka, canons, canonry, gunnery, guns, munitions, ordnance, weapons, weaponry *Nonformal:* AAs, big guns, rainmakers

artisan *n.* artificer, craftsperson, creator, expert, journeyman, maker, skilled worker *Historical*: manufacturer, master, mechanic

artist *n.* architect, author, carver, ceramicist, chef, cinematographer, composer, creator, dancer, director, drafter, fashion designer, filmmaker, glass-blower, inventor, maestro, master, musician, originator, painter, performer, photographer, player, playwright, poet, potter, sculptor, thespian, writer, virtuoso *French:* artiste, auteur, cordon bleu

artistic *adj.* **1.** aesthetic, artful, harmonious, grand style, ornamental, well-composed *Nonformal:* artsy-craftsy, arty, long-haired **2.** accomplished, authoritative, brave, brilliant, creative, imaginative, inventive, masterful, skilful, talented, virtuoso **3.** elegant, polished, refined, sensitive *Antonyms:* boorish, clumsy

artistry *n.* ability, art, creativity, dexterity, finesse, flair, genius, knack, mastery, style, talent, touch, virtuosity

artless *adj.* candid, direct, genuine, guileless, honest, ingenuous, innocent, naive, natural, open, outright, plain, pure, simple, sincere, straight, straightforward, true, trusting, unadorned, unaffected, uncontrived, unpretentious, unsophisticated *Antonyms:* conniving, crafty, cunning, designing

artwork *n.* composition, creation, *kunst (German)*, magnum opus, masterpiece, museum piece, work of art *French:* chef d'oeuvre, objet d'art

as *adv.* along these lines, correspondingly, equally, in this way, on the lines of, thus, to illustrate, to prove the point, to the degree that, to the same extent – *conj.* because, for instance, however, inasmuch as, in view of the fact that, *parce que (French)*, seeing that, since

ascend *v.* arise, clamber *or* float up, climb, gain altitude, levitate, lift off, mount, rocket, scale, shoot up, soar, surge, tower *Antonyms:* fall, plunge, sink

ascendancy *n.* authority, command, control, dominance, domination, dominion, leg up *(Nonformal)*, mastery, power, predominance, prevalence, reign, rule, sovereignty, superiority, supremacy, sway, upper hand *Antonyms:* inferiority, servility, subjection, subordination, weakness

ascent *n.* **1.** ascension, climbing, escalation, going up, lift, mounting, rising, scaling, soaring **2.** acclivity, grade, gradient, incline, ramp, rise, slope **3.** advancement, boost, gain, hike, increase, promotion, raise *Antonyms:* demotion, descent, downfall, drop, setback

ascertain *v.* check, confirm, detect, determine, discover, ensure, establish, fix, identify, learn, peg, read, see, settle, size, tell, uncover, verify, *Nonformal:* check out, eyeball, get down cold, size up *Antonyms:* lose sight of, overlook

ascetic *adj.* abstemious, abstinent, austere, harsh, rigid, rigorous, self-denying, severe, stern, strict *Antonyms:* hedonistic, epicurean – *n.* abstainer, anchorite, celibate, hermit, monk, nun, puritan, recluse, Spartan, stoic *Antonyms:* gourmand, pleasure seeker *Commonly misused:* **aesthetic**

asceticism *n.* abstinence, abstemiousness, austerity, eschewal, fasting, flagellation, frugality, hair shirt *(Nonformal)*, monasticism, mortification, mysticism, penitence, puritanism, self-control, self-denial *Commonly misused:* **aestheticism**

ascribe *v.* accredit, assign, attribute, chalk up to, charge, credit, hang on, impute, refer, reference, set down

ashamed *adj.* abashed, apologetic, chagrined, conscience-stricken, contrite, crestfallen, debased, demeaned, discomfited, disconcerted, distraught, distressed, embarrassed, flustered, guilty, hesitant, humbled, mortified, penitent, regretful, remorseful, repentant, shamed, shamefaced, sheepish, sorry *Antonyms:* gratified, honoured, pleased

ashen *adj.* **1.** anemic, faint, grey, pallid, pasty, sallow, toneless, white **2.** aghast, horror-struck, scared to death, terrified, terror-ridden, white as a sheet

ashes *n.* **1.** charcoal, cinders, embers, soot **2.** fragments, remains, residue, ruins

ashore *adv.* aground, beached, on land *or* shore, shorewards

aside *adv.* abreast, afar, alone, alongside, apart, away, away from, near, nearby, privately, separately

asinine *adj.* crass, cretinous, dense, dull, dumb, foolish, headlong, inane, moronic, puerile, reckless, short-sighted, silly, stupid *Nonformal:* blockheaded, crackbrained *Antonyms:* prudent, thoughtful, well-advised

ask *v.* **1.** catechize, cross-examine, examine, inquire, interrogate, investigate, postulate, probe, query, question, quiz *Nonformal:* grill, pop the question *Antonyms:* answer, reply, respond **2.** appeal, apply, beg, beseech, hustle, implore, plead, solicit *Nonformal:* cadge, hit up, sponge, urge **3.** demand, order, need, require, requisition, want **4.** beckon, call upon, invite, request, seek, summon

askance *adv.* crookedly, disapprovingly, distrustfully, doubtfully, dubiously, enviously, evasively, indirectly, jealously, mistrustfully, obliquely

askew *adj.* awry, bent, buckled, crooked, curved, knotted, lopsided, oblique, off-centre, slanted, slanting, topsy-turvy, turned, twisted *Antonyms:* aligned, even, straight, true

asleep *adj.* **1.** comatose, dozing, hibernating, napping, oblivious, resting, sleeping, slumbering, somnolent, unconscious *Nonformal:* catchin' some zzz's, conked, crashed, flaked *or* sacked *or* zonked out, snoozing *Antonyms:* awake, out and about **2.** dormant, inert, quiescent, unawakened *Antonyms:* functional, lively **3.** blind, ignorant, unaware, unprepared *Antonyms:* chary, vigilant, watchful

aspect *n.* **1.** air, angle, appearance, attitude, bearing, carriage, countenance, demeanour, deportment, detail, direction, expression, face, facet, feature, form, gimmick, guise, hand, image, item, lay, lie, look, manner, mien, phase, position, regard, semblance, side, situation, slant, switch, twist, view **2.** outlook, perspective, prospect, scene, vista

asperity *n.* acerbity, acrimony, astringency, bitterness, causticity, churlishness, crabbiness, crossness, difficulty, disagreeableness, harshness, irascibility, irritability, malice, moroseness, peevishness, rancour, roughness, sharpness, snappishness, sullenness, tartness, waspishness *Antonyms:* courtesy, gallantry, suaveness, urbanity

asphyxiate *v.* choke, garrote, smother, stifle, strangle, suffocate, throttle *Antonyms:* aerate, open up, oxygenate

aspiration *n.* **1.** aim, ambition, craving, desire, direction, dream, eagerness, endeavour, goal, hope, inclination, longing, object, objective, passion, pursuit, push, resolve, urge, vocation, wish, work, yearning **2.** breathing, inhalation, inspiration, respiration

aspire *v.* aim, covet, crave, desire, dream, hanker, hope, long, plan toward, pursue, seek, shoot for, strive, struggle, try, want, wish, yearn

aspiring *adj.* ambitious, avid, eager, endeavouring, enthusiastic, expectant, hopeful, hungry, impassioned, lofty, longing, striving, wishful, zealous *Nonformal:* eager beaver, on the make, wannabe *Antonyms:* hidebound, plodding

ass *n.* **1.** beast of burden, burro, donkey, jack, jennet, jenny, mule, pack animal **2.** dolt, dunce, fool, idiot, imbecile, lummox, nincompoop *Nonformal:* dingbat, hoser, jerk, turkey **3.** buttocks *Nonformal:* arse, backside, behind, bottom, bum, butt, caboose, can, derriere, fanny, gluteus maximus, keister, moon, rear, rump, tush

assail *v.* **1.** assault, attack, besiege, blitz, bombard, fall upon, launch out against, lay hands on, light into, pounce upon, rush **2.** blister, castigate, censure, criticize, flay, harangue, lambaste, rebuke, skin alive, trash, vilify, take to task, work over *Antonyms:* congratulate, hail

assailant *n.* **1.** abuser, assaulter, attacker *Nonformal:* goon, hitman, mugger, trigger man **2.** adversary, antagonist, combatant, enemy, foe, villain

assassin *n.* bravo, cutthroat, eliminator, enforcer, executioner, gunman, killer, liquidator, murderer, shootist, slayer, trigger person *Nonformal:* butcher, hatchet person, hitperson

assassinate *v.* burn, destroy, eliminate, execute, impugn, kill, liquidate, murder, neutralize, slaughter, slay *Nonformal:* bump *or* kiss *or* knock off, do in, rub *or* take *or* wipe out, waste

assault *n.* aggression, attack, barrage, battery, blitz *or* blitzkrieg, encroachment, fighting, foray, fusillade, incursion, intrusion, invasion, offence, offensive, onslaught, push, raid, rampage, rape, seizure, storm, storming, usurpation, violation *Antonyms:* defence, protection, resistance – *v.* **1.** batter, beat, buffet, *coup de main (French)*, hammer, hit, maul, molest, pummel, rape, terrorize **2.** attack, blitz, charge, fall upon, launch out against, pound, rush, storm

assay *n.* analysis, appraisal, assessment, determination, estimation, evaluation, examination, inspection, investigation, measurement, rating, survey, test, trial, valuation – *v.* **1.** analyze, appraise, assess, break down, check out, consider, evaluate, gauge, measure, size up *(Nonformal)*, test, titrate, weigh **2.** attempt, make an effort, tackle, take on, undertake

assemblage *n.* **1.** aggregation, association, collection, company, congregation, convergence, crowd, flock, gathering, group, host, multitude, swarm, throng **2.** assortment, conglomeration, miscellany, potpourri **3.** collage, decoupage, mosaic

assemble *v.* **1.** accumulate, agglomerate, amass, codify, collect, compile, corral, group, lump *Nonformal:* flock to, scare up **2.** connect, construct, contrive, create, design, erect, fabricate, fashion, fit, form, join, model, piece *or* put together, set up, shape, unite, weld **3.** bring *or* come together, congregate, convene, gather, huddle, marshal, meet, mobilize, muster, organize, rally, reunite, round up, summon *Antonyms:* adjourn, disband, disperse, divide, scatter

assembly *n.* **1.** accumulation, aggregation, assemblage, association, audience, band, body, bunch, cluster, collection, company, composition, conclave, confab *(Nonformal)*, conference, congregation, congress, convocation, council, crew, crowd, drove, faction, flock, gathering, get-together, group, huddle, mass, meeting, multitude, rally, scrum, sit-in, synod, throng, turnout **2.** adjustment, attachment, building, collection, construction, erection, fabrication, joining, manufacture, setup, welding **3.** levee, party, reception, salon, soiree

assent *n.* acquiescence, agreement, authorization, concession, concurrence, permission, sanction, submission – *v.* acquiesce, adopt, agree, cave in, consent, credit, embrace, espouse, knuckle under, shake on, subscribe, surrender, yield *Antonyms:* deny, protest, refuse, reject, spurn

assert *v.* acknowledge, advance, affirm, allege, argue for, attest, aver, avouch, avow, champion, cite, claim, contend, declare, defend, hold, insist, lay down, maintain, make plain, own, proclaim, profess, pronounce, propound, put forward, say, speak out *or* up, stand by, state, stress, swear support, uphold, warrant *Nonformal:* butt in, shoot off one's mouth, sound off, take a stand *Antonyms:* deny, disavow, disclaim, refute

assertion *n.* affirmation, allegation, announcement, attestation, avowal, contention, declaration, dictum, guarantee, insistence, pronouncement, report, statement *Nonformal:* say-so, two cents' worth

assertive *adj.* absolute, aggressive, assured, brash, certain, confident, decided, decisive, demanding, dogmatic, domineering, driving, emphatic, firm, forceful, forward, in your face *(Nonformal)*, insistent, militant, overbearing, positive, pushy, strong-willed, sure *Antonyms:* bashful, hesitant, insecure, meek, timid

assess *v.* **1.** charge, collect, cost, demand, exact, extort, fix, gather, impose, levy, mark down *or* up, price, raise, rate, reduce, set, summon, tax, value **2.** consider, estimate, evaluate, measure, ponder, think about

assessment *n.* appraisal, charge, computation, determination, estimate, estimation, evaluation, fee, judgment, levy, rate, rating, reckoning, review, tariff, tax, valuation

asset *n.* advantage, benefit, blessing, boon, boost, credit, distinction, edge, help, resource, selling point, service, talent, treasure *Antonyms:* debit, disadvantage, handicap

assets *n. pl.* bankroll, belongings, capital, credit, effects, equity, estate, funds, goods, holdings, nest egg, net worth, possessions, resources, riches, stake, stash, valuables, wealth *Antonyms:* debits, debts, liabilities, obligations

assiduous *adj.* **1.** attentive, devoted, diligent, eager, industrious, scrupulous, steady, studious, zealous *Antonyms:* careless, inattentive, negligent **2.** indefatigable, laborious, persevering, persistent, tireless, unflagging, unremitting, untiring *Antonyms:* idle, lazy, slack, slothful

assign *v.* **1.** allocate, allot, apportion, classify, commit, consign, deal, delegate, detail, determine, dish out, dispense, distribute, divide, dole, earmark, establish, give, grant, hand out *or* over, mete, pigeonhole, prescribe, relegate, specify **2.** appoint, ascribe, attach, authorize, charge, credit, designate, indicate, stipulate

assignation *n.* affair, appointment, date, engagement, illicit meeting, indiscretion, rendezvous, secret meeting, tryst

assignment *n.* **1.** allocation, allotment, apportionment, attribution, commission, consignment, designation, distribution, position, post, stint **2.** chore, duty, homework, job, lesson, mission, practice, responsibility, task **3.** appointment, authorization, grant, transference

assimilate *v.* **1.** comprehend, digest, familiarize, grasp, incorporate, ingest, learn, sense, soak up, take in *or* up, understand **2.** acclimatize, accommodate, acculturate, accustom, adapt, adjust, blend in, conform, fit, homogenize, match, mingle, parallel, standardize, transculturate *Nonformal:* go native, hit the beach *Antonyms:* alienate, exile, ostracize

assist *n.* aid, boost, collaboration, furtherance, hand, support – *v.* abet, aid, back, befriend, benefit, boost, expedite, facilitate, further, give a lift to, help, pave the way, push, reinforce, relieve, stand by, support, sustain, work for *Nonformal:* hype, plug, root for *Antonyms:* frustrate, handicap, impede, obstruct, run interference

assistance *n.* abetment, aid, backing, benefit, boost, collaboration, comfort, compensation, cooperation, facilitation, furtherance, hand, help, helping hand, lift, reinforcement, relief, service, support, sustenance *Types of assistance:* alms, baby bonus *(Historical)*, employment insurance *or* EI, Family Benefits, financial, grant, scholarship, student loan, welfare, Worker's Compensation *Nonformal:* the dole, pogey *Antonyms:* hindrance, obstruction, opposition, resistance

assistant *n.* abettor, accessory, accomplice, adherent, adjunct, agent, aide, ally, appointee, apprentice, associate, attendant, auxiliary, backup, butler, caddy, collaborator, colleague, confederate, *confrère (French)*, cooperator, deputy, follower, girl *or* man Friday, help, helper, helpmate *or* helpmeet, mate, partner, representative, second, servant, subordinate, supporter *Antonyms:* antagonist, enemy, nemesis

associate *n.* affiliate, ally, cohort, collaborator, colleague, companion, compatriot, comrade, confederate, consort, cooperator, co-worker, crony, friend, helper, mate, pal, partner, peer, sidekick *(Nonformal)* *Antonyms:* adversary, competitor, opponent, rival – *v.* **1.** accompany, amalgamate, befriend, come together, consort, fraternize, get together, go partners with, hobnob, join, mix, pool, team up, work with *Nonformal*: in cahoots with, hang around, hang out, **2.** affiliate, blend, bracket, combine, conjoin, connect, correlate, couple, group, identify, join, league, link, lump together, mix, pair, relate, unite, yoke *Antonyms:* detach, disconnect, dissociate, distance, isolate

association *n.* **1.** affiliation, allegiance, alliance, band, bloc, brotherhood, bunch, circle, clan, clique, club, coalition, combine, company, confederation, congress, consortium, cooperative, corporation, crew, crowd, family, federation, fellowship, fraternity, gang, group, guild, league, lodge, mob, order, organization, outfit, partnership, party, pool, ring, sisterhood, society, sorority, syndicate, tribe, troupe, union, *verein (German) Nonformal:* hookup, machine, ratpack **2.** acquaintance, acquaintanceship, camaraderie, companionship, comradeship, cooperation, fellowship, fraternization, friendship, relationship **3.** bond, combination, concatenation, concomitance, concordance, correlation, *esprit de corps (French)*, identification, impression, joining, juxtaposition, linkage, linking, mental link, mixture, pairing, relation, tie, union

assort *v.* alphabetize, analyze, arrange, catalogue, categorize, codify, file, grade, group, index, methodize, number, order, pigeonhole, rate, screen, sift, systemize, tabulate *Antonyms:* disarrange, disorder, disorganize

assorted *adj.* **1.** diverse, heterogeneous, manifold, mingled, miscellaneous, motley, multifarious, sundry, variegated, various **2.** arranged, classified, coordinated, gathered, grouped, harmonized, matched, selected

assortment *n.* collection, conglomeration, farrago, gallimaufry, goulash, grouping, hash, hodgepodge, medley, mélange, miscellany, mishmash, mixed bag *(Nonformal)*, mixture, mosaic, motley, olio, potpourri, salmagundi, variety

assuage *v.* allay, alleviate, appease, calm, comfort, compose, conciliate, console, cool, cool off *or* out, ease, lessen, lighten, lull, mitigate, moderate, mollify, pacify, placate, propitiate, quench, quiet, relieve, satisfy, soften, soothe, sweeten, temper, tranquilize *Nonformal:* chill, make nice *Antonyms:* aggravate, augment, enkindle, inflame

assume *v.* **1.** believe, conclude, conjecture, dare say, deduce, fancy, guess, hypothesize, imagine, infer, opine, posit, postulate, reckon, suppose, surmise, suspect **2.** accept, attempt, attend to, embark *or* enter, upon, embrace, engage in, seize, set about, shoulder, take on *or* up, turn to, undertake, venture **3.** act, adopt, affect, bluff, counterfeit, don, exchange, fake, feign, imitate, impersonate, mimic, pretend, sham, simulate **4.** annex, commandeer, hijack, pre-empt, seize, snatch, take command *or* over *or* the helm

assumed *adj.* **1.** accepted, allowed, believed, conjectured, given, presumed, presupposed, supposed, surmised, tacit, understood *Antonyms:* explicit, known, stated **2.** affected, artificial, bogus, counterfeit, fake, false, feigned, fictitious, imitation, phoney *(Nonformal)*, pretended, pseudo, put-on, sham, simulated, so-called, spurious *Antonyms:* actual, authentic, natural, positive, real

assumption *n.* **1.** axiom, belief, conjecture, deduction, dogma, expectation, guess, hunch, hypothesis, inference, premise, presumption, presupposition, supposition, surmise, theorem, theory, understanding *Nonformal:* shot in the dark, sneaking suspicion **2.** arrogation, expropriation, pre-emption, seizure, takeover, usurpation **3.** arrogance, braggadocio, brazenness, conceit, contemptuousness, disdainfulness, effrontery, hubris, imperiousness, impertinence, insolence, nerve, presumption, pretension *Nonformal:* chutzpah, moxie **4.** ascension, deification, elevation, exaltation

assurance *n.* **1.** aplomb, arrogance, assuredness, audacity, boldness, bravery, certainty, certitude, confidence, conviction, courage, effrontery, equanimity, faith, firmness, intrepidness, mettle, pluck, poise, positiveness, presumption, security, self-confidence, self-reliance, sureness, trust *Antonyms:* diffidence, distrust, doubt, insecurity **2.** affirmation, assertion, declaration, guarantee, insurance, oath, pledge, promise, support, vow, warrant, warranty, word

assure *v.* **1.** clinch, complete, confirm, consummate, declare, ensure, establish, guarantee, make sure, seal, secure, set *Nonformal:* bet on, cinch, lock, nail down, put on ice **2.** buck *or* brace up *(Nonformal)*, comfort, convince, encourage, hearten, inspire, persuade, put one's mind at rest, reassure, relieve, satisfy, soothe **3.** affirm, attest, certify, confirm, depose, inform, pledge, swear, tell, testify, vouch for, vow, warrant

assured *adj.* **1.** absolute, categorical, certain, clear, clear-cut, clinched, confirmed, correct, decided, definite, definitive, dependable, ensured, evident, exact, explicit, express, fixed, guaranteed, indubitable, in the bag *(Nonformal)*, irrefutable, obvious, patent, plain, positive, pronounced, resolved, sealed, secure, set, settled, specific, stated, straightforward, sure, unambiguous, undisputed, undoubted, unequivocal *Antonyms:* ambiguous, doubtful, indefinite, uncertain, unsure **2.** assertive, audacious, balanced, collected, composed, confident, imperturbable, poised, sanguine, secure, self-assured, self-confident, self-possessed, sure, unflappable, unhesitating, urbane *Antonyms:* bashful, hesitant, retiring, self-effacing, timid

astonish *v.* amaze, astound, bewilder, boggle, confound, daze, dumfound, overwhelm, shock, startle, stun, stupefy, surprise, take aback *Nonformal:* blow away, bowl *or* knock over, flabbergast, floor, wow

astonishing *adj.* amazing, astounding, bewildering, breathtaking, extraordinary, impressive, marvellous, miraculous, spectacular, staggering, startling, striking, stunning, stupefying, stupendous, surprising, unbelievable, wonderful, wondrous *Antonyms:* anticipated, boring, expected, mundane

astonishment *n.* amazement, awe, bewilderment, confusion, consternation, perplexity, shock, stupefaction, surprise, wonder, wonderment

astound *v.* amaze, appall, astonish, bedazzle, bewilder, confound, confuse, daze, dumfound, electrify, flummox, nonplus, overwhelm, shock, stagger, startle, stun, stupefy, surprise, take aback *Nonformal:* blow away, bowl over, boggle the mind, flabbergast, gobsmack *Antonyms:* bore, jade

astral *adj.* celestial, ghostly, heaven-like, heavenly, immaterial, sidereal, spectral, starlike, star-shaped, stellar

astray *adj. & adv.* aberrant, abroad, adrift, afield, amiss, at large, awry, faulty, lost, off-course, roaming, straying, vanished, wandering

astride *adj. & adv.* across, astraddle, piggyback, sitting on, straddling

astringent *adj.* **1.** acrid, acerbic, bitter, caustic, penetrating, pungent, piercing, sharp, tart, trenchant **2.** harsh, hurtful, severe, spiteful, stern, styptic, testy, vitriolic

astrologer *n.* astromancer, diviner, predictor, seer, soothsayer

astronaut *n.* aviator, cosmonaut, moonman *(Nonformal)*, pilot, rocketeer, space explorer, spaceman, spacewoman

astronomy *n.* astrochemistry, astrometry, astrophysics, celestial mechanics, meteoritics, solar physics

astute *adj.* acute, adroit, brainy, bright, calculating, candid, canny, clever, cogent, crafty, designing, discerning, discriminating, eagle-eyed, foxy, insightful, intelligent, keen, knowing, Machiavellian, perceptive, perspicacious, quick, sagacious, savvy *(Nonformal)*, sharp, shrewd, sly, trenchant *Antonyms:* dull, naive, slow

asunder *adj.* broken, cleft, detached, disconnected, disjointed, disjunct, disunited, separated from, severed, torn – *adv.* apart, disjoined, divided, in half, piecemeal, rent, separated, split, to bits *or* smithereens

asylum *n.* **1.** ashram, cover, den, harbour, haven, hideaway, hideout, hole, hospice, ivory tower, refuge, retreat, room of one's own, safe house, safety, sanctuary, sanctum, security, shelter **2.** Bedlam, mental hospital *or* institution, sanatorium *Nonformal:* funny farm, loony bin, madhouse, nuthouse **3.** almshouse, debtor's prison, home, orphanage, poorhouse

asymmetry *n.* disparity, disproportion, distortion, imbalance, incompatibility, incongruity, irregularity, unevenness *Antonyms:* harmoniousness, uniformity

at *prep.* according to, attending, by, by way of, close to, dependent upon, during the course *or* lapse of, engaged *or* occupied in, from, having reference to, in, in contact with, in pursuit *or* quest of, in the condition of, in the direction of, in the position *or* state of, near, on, out of, present in, on the stroke of, through, to the extent of, towards, upon, upon the point of, viewed from, within the limits of

atelier *n.* craft shop, gallery, garret, library, parlour, studio, workroom, workshop

atheism *n.* apostasy, disbelief, dissent, doubt, impiety, irreligion, nihilism, nonbelief, scepticism, unbelief *Antonyms:* belief, faith

atheistic *adj.* agnostic, disbelieving, free thinking, impious, irreligious, nihilistic, sceptical, unbelieving, ungodly

athlete *n.* amateur, challenger, competitor, contender, contestant, games player, jock *(Nonformal)*, jockey, Olympian, player, professional, runner, sport, sportsman, sportswoman, track star

athletic *adj.* **1.** able-bodied, acrobatic, active, agile, competitive, energetic, fit, sturdy, vigorous *Antonyms:* awkward, clumsy, flat-footed, ungainly **2.** brawny, burly, husky, muscular, powerful, robust, sinewy, stalwart, strapping, strong *Antonyms:* delicate, feeble, fragile, frail

athletics *n. pl.* contest, drill, events, exercises, games, practice, races, recreation, sports, workout *Selected athletic competitions:* Arctic Winter Games, Commonwealth Games, Highland Games, Jeux de francophonie, Olympic Games, Pan American Games, Paralympics, Special Olympics

atmosphere *n.* **1.** air, ambience, aura, background, character, climate, colour, conditions, element, environment, essence, feel, feeling, flavour, gist, habitat, impression, influences, intention, meaning, medium, milieu, mood, place, property, purpose, quality, scene, semblance, sense, setting, spirit, substance, surroundings, temper, tenor, timbre, tone, vibrations **2.** aerosphere, air, heavens, sky *Kinds of atmospheric layer:* boundary layer, exosphere, ionosphere, lower atmosphere, magnetosphere, mesosphere, outer atmosphere, ozone layer, stratosphere, thermosphere, upper atmosphere, Van Allen belt

atom *n.* **1.** bit, crumb, dot, fragment, grain, iota, jot, mite, modicum, morsel, particle, scintilla, scrap, shred, smidgen, snippet, speck, trace, whit **2.** atomic particle, electron, elementary particle, ion, lepton, meson, muon, neutrino, parton, proton, quark, shell *Kinds of atoms:* acceptor, asymmetric carbon, discrete, excited, hot, impurity, isobar, isotopic, labeled, neutral, normal, nuclear isomer, radical, radioactive, recoil, stripped

atomic *adj.* **1.** diminutive, fragmentary, granular, infinitesimal, microscopic, minute, tiny **2.** atom-powered, fissionable, fusible, nuclear, thermonuclear

atone *v.* accommodate, answer, apologize, appease, balance, compensate, compose, conciliate, correct, counterbalance, countervail, expiate, make amends *or* peace *or* reparation, mend, offset, outweigh, pacify, pay, propitiate, recompense, reconcile, redeem, redress, repair, requite, settle, square with, suffer for *Nonformal:* make up, pay one's dues, take one's medicine

atonement *n.* amends, compensation, conciliation, expiation, payment, penance, propitiation, recompense, redemption, redress, reparation, restitution, satisfaction

atrocious *adj.* **1.** abominable, appalling, awful, bad, barbaric, beastly, criminal, cruel, deplorable, desperate, detestable, diabolical, disgusting, dreadful, execrable, fiendish, foul, flagrant, gross, harsh, heinous, horrible, horrid, horrifying, loathsome, lousy *(Nonformal)*, monstrous, nasty, nefarious, noisome, offensive, outrageous, reprehensible, repulsive, rotten, scandalous, shocking, sickening, terrible, unspeakable, vile, villainous, wicked *Antonyms:* admirable, benevolent, generous, kind **2.** boorish, campy, cheap, coarse, crude, indecent, obscene, tasteless, tawdry, vulgar

atrocity *n.* abomination, barbarity, brutality, crime, cruelness, cruelty, enormity, evil, fiendishness, heinousness, horror, infamy, inhumanity, monstrosity, monstrousness, nefariousness, offence, offensiveness, outrage, ruthlessness, savagery, viciousness, villainousness, villainy, wickedness, wrong *Antonyms:* gentility, humanity

atrophy *n.* decline, degeneration, deterioration, diminution, disintegration, downgrade, emaciation, deteriorate, withering – *v.* decay, fall *or* waste *or* wither away, shrivel

attach *v.* **1.** add, adhere, affix, annex, append, bind, connect, couple, fasten, fix, hitch, hook, join, link, rivet, secure, stick, tack on, tie, unite *Nonformal:* make fast, slap *or* tag on *Antonyms:* detach, disconnect, dissociate, separate **2.** commandeer, confiscate, impress, seize, take over

attachment *n.* **1.** accessory, addendum, addition, adjunct, appendage, augmentation, codicil, insert, postscript, rider **2.** affection, devotion, fidelity, fondness, friendship, liking, love, loyalty, partiality, possessiveness, regard, tenderness *Nonformal:* crush, shine, yen *Antonyms:* animosity, antipathy, aversion, distaste, hostility **3.** bond, connection, fastening, link, linkage **4.** appropriation, garnishment, seizure **5.** assignment, posting, secondment

attack *n.* **1.** advance, aggression, assault, barrage, blitz, blitzkrieg, charge, counterattack, counteroffensive, *coup de main (French)*, drive, offence, offensive, onrush, onset, onslaught, outbreak, raid, sally, skirmish, sortie, storm, strike, thrust, volley *Antonyms:* retreat, withdrawal **2.** assault, molestation, rape, violation **3.** abuse, aggression, belligerence, blame, censure, combativeness, criticism, denigration, denunciation, diatribe, slander, tirade, tongue-lashing *(Nonformal)*, verbal assault, vilification *Antonyms:* defence, support, vindication **4.** ailment, bout, breakdown, convulsion, disease, disorder, dysfunction, fit, illness, paroxysm, seizure, spasm, spell **5.** approach, business, method, procedure, process – *v.* **1.** assail, assault, bash, bat, berate, beset, besiege, blast, blitz, blockade, bomb, bombard, bushwhack, charge, combat, descend *or* pounce *or* spring on, fall upon, fight, fly at, harass, harm, harry, hit, hold up, hurt, impugn, invade, jump, kick, lambaste, lay *or* light *or* rip into, loot, malign, maraud, molest, mug, overrun, pillage, pirate, plunder, prey, punch, raid, ransack, rape, revile, rush, sack, scramble, seize, set upon, slam, slap around, smash, stab, stomp, storm, strafe, strike, take *or* take on, terrorize, torpedo, victimize, vilify, violate, wallop, waylay *Nonformal:* go for, jump on, knock cold, trash, waste, work over *Antonyms:* defend, guard, protect, support, sustain **2.** launch into, set to, tackle, take up, tear into, turn to, work *Nonformal:* buckle down, deal with, dive into, plunge into

attain *v.* accomplish, achieve, earn, fulfill, get, make it, reach, realize, secure, succeed, walk off with, win *Nonformal:* get one's hands on, make good, snag

attainable *adj.* accessible, accomplishable, achievable, at hand, available, feasible, likely, obtainable, possible, potential, practicable, probable, procurable, reachable, realistic, realisable, securable, within reach, within the realm of, workable *Nonformal:* no problem *or* sweat, piece of cake *Antonyms:* impossible, improbable

attempt *n.* aim, assay, bid, challenge, chance, dare, effort, endeavour, enterprise, essay, exertion, experiment, gamble, hazard, one's all *or* best, opportunity, provocation, reconnaissance, sally, sortie, striving, struggle, trial, try *or* tryout, turn, undertaking, venture, work – *v.* aim, aim *or* bid for, chance, commit oneself to, endeavour, engage in, enter upon, essay, go for *or* into, have a fling at *(Nonformal)*, hazard, initiate, pursue, push, risk, scheme, set out, shoot at *or* for, solicit, strive, struggle, tackle, take on, take a crack at, test, try, try out, undertake, venture, work *or* work through *Antonyms:* abandon, desert, forgo

attend *v.* **1.** appear, be present at *or* there, drop in, frequent, go to, haunt, pop up, show, sit in on, take in, turn up, visit **2.** assist, care for, doctor, do for, look after, mind, minister to, nurse, serve, shepherd, succour, tend, wait upon, watch, work for **3.** catch, concentrate on, devote oneself to, follow, hear, harken, heed, listen, mark, mind, monitor, notice, observe, pay attention to, regard, see to, take notice of, watch *Antonyms:* disregard, ignore, neglect **4.** accompany, chaperone, concern oneself with, escort, follow, go with, guard, serve, usher, wait upon

attendance *n.* **1.** assemblage, assembly, audience, box office, congregation, crowd, draw, gallery, gate, gathering, house, observers, onlookers, patrons, public, spectators, turnout, witnesses **2.** company, court, entourage, escort, following, retinue, suite, train

attendant *adj.* accessory, accompanying, ancillary, associated, coincident, concomitant, consequent, incidental, related – *n.* **1.** acolyte, aide, assistant, *au paire (French)*, auxiliary, batman, butler, caddy, chaperone, companion, custodian, domestic, doorman, equerry, escort, footman, guide, helper, housekeeper, lackey, lady-in-waiting, locker room aide, maid, major-domo, nurse, orderly, page, pump jockey *(Nonformal)*, retainer, seneschal, servant, server, steward, stewardess, understudy, usher, valet, waiter **2.** gallant, knight errant, Lochinvar

attention *interj.* hark, heads up, hear ye, hello, listen, look, look sharp, stop, watch out, yo – *n.* **1.** absorption, acuity, acuteness, application, awareness, concentration, concern, consciousness, consideration, contemplation, deliberation, diligence, immersion, industry, ministration, observation, readiness, recognition, regard, scrutiny, study, thought, thoughtfulness, wakefulness *Antonyms:* carelessness, disregard, thoughtlessness **2.** amenity, care, civility, compliment, consideration, courtesy, deference, gallantry, mindfulness, politeness, respect, service

attentive *adj.* **1.** alert, awake, aware, circumspect, concentrating, heedful, listening, mindful, observant, preoccupied, solicitous, vigilant, wary, watchful, wide awake *Antonyms:* absent-minded, careless, remiss **2.** chivalrous, civil, concerned, conscientious, courteous, gallant, polite, solicitous *Antonyms:* aloof, indifferent, neglectful, negligent **3.** drawn in, enthralled, fascinated, hooked, immersed, intent, interested

attenuate *v.* **1.** abate, contract, deflate, dilute, dissipate, draw out, lessen, mitigate, rarefy, reduce, sap, shrink *Antonyms:* amplify, distend, expand, increase, inflate **2.** cripple, debilitate, disable, enfeeble, impair, weaken *Commonly misused:* **extenuate**

attest *v.* adjure, affirm, announce, argue, assert, authenticate, bear out *or* witness, certify, confirm, corroborate, declare, demonstrate, exhibit, give evidence, prove, ratify, show, substantiate, support, sustain, swear, testify, uphold, verify, vouch, witness *Antonyms:* contradict, deny, disprove, gainsay, refute

attic *n.* dormer, garret, *grenier (French)*, hayloft, loft, storeroom

attire *n.* apparel, clothing, costume, raiment, robes, vestment *Nonformal:* duds, get-up, threads – *v.* adorn, clothe, drape, dress, garb *Nonformal:* deck out, doll *or* spruce up, outfit

attitude *n.* **1.** air, approach, bent, bias, disposition, inclination, leaning, mental state, mindset, opinion, outlook, perspective, position, predisposition, prejudice, proclivity, sensibility, sentiment, slant *(Nonformal)*, temper **2.** aspect, bearing, carriage, countenance, demeanour, deportment, manner, mien, pose, position, posture, presentation, stance, stand

attorney *n.* advocate, barrister, counsel, counsellor, lawyer, pleader, solicitor *Nonformal:* ambulance chaser, legal beagle *or* eagle, mouthpiece

attract *v.* allure, appeal to, bait, beckon, beguile, bewitch, bring, captivate, charm, court, draw in, enchant, endear, engage, enthral, entice, fascinate, induce, interest, intrigue, inveigle, invite, lure, magnetize, pull, score, seduce, send, solicit, spellbind, steer, tempt *Nonformal:* grab, hook, mousetrap, slay, wow *Antonyms:* affront, insult, offend, outrage

attraction *n.* **1.** affinity, allure, appeal, attractiveness, bait, captivation, charm, chemistry, draw, enchantment, endearment, enticement, fascination, inclination, interest, invitation, lure, magnetism, pull, seduction, solicitation, sympathy, teaser, temptation *Antonyms:* nauseation, rejection, repulsion **2.** centre ring, event, feature, headliner, main event, production, show

attractive *adj.* aesthetic, agreeable, alluring, appealing, arresting, artistic, attractive, beautiful, bewitching, captivating, charming, comely, cute, darling, delicate, delightful, elegant, enchanting, engaging, enthralling, enticing, fair, fascinating, fetching, fine, glamorous, good-looking, gorgeous, graceful, handsome, inviting, lovely, photogenic, pleasant, pleasing, prepossessing, pretty, sexy, striking, stunning, tasteful, winning *Antonyms:* offensive, repulsive, ugly, unpleasant

attribute *n.* aspect, character, characteristic, facet, feature, idiosyncrasy, indication, mark, note, particularity, peculiarity, point, property, quality, quirk, sign, speciality, symbol, token, trait, virtue – *v.* account for, accredit, allocate, allot, apply, ascribe, assign, associate, attach, connect, credit, designate, fix upon, hang *or* pin on, hold responsible, impute, name, place, refer

attrition *n.* abrasion, atrophy, attenuation, badgering, chafing, corrosion, debilitation, depreciation, disintegration, erosion, grinding *or* wearing down, persecution, plaguing, rasping, rubbing, thinning, weakening, wear *Antonyms:* accretion, growth, increase

attune *v.* acclimatize, accommodate, accustom, adapt, adjust, balance, compensate, conform, coordinate, counterbalance, familiarize, harmonize, integrate, proportion, reconcile, regulate, temper *Antonyms:* clash, dispute, wrangle

atypical *adj.* abnormal, anomalous, deviant, different, divergent, eccentric, exceptional, irregular, nonconforming, odd, peculiar, strange, unrepresentative, unusual, weird *Antonyms:* conventional, run-of-the-mill

auburn *n.* brown *Shades of auburn:* burnt sienna, chestnut, copper, hazel, henna, nut, reddish-brown, russet, rust, tawny, titian

auction *n.* bidding, e-bay *(Trademark)*, estate *or* garage sale, haggling, sale, tag sale – *v.* auctioneer, barter, peddle, put on the block, sell, trade

audacious *adj.* bold, brash, brazen, fearless, foolhardy, forward, impudent, intrepid, rash, reckless, saucy, shameless, unabashed, undaunted, valiant, venturesome *Antonyms:* circumspect, cowardly, judicious, pusillanimous, wary

audacity *n.* adventurousness, boldness, bravery, cheek, courage, daring, dauntlessness, effrontery, fearlessness, nerve, panache, pluck, presumption, rashness, recklessness, resoluteness *Nonformal:* chutzpah, guts, moxie *Antonyms:* cravenness, timorousness, weak-heartedness

audible *adj.* aural, clear, detectable, discernible, distinct, hearable, heard, loud, perceptible, plain, resounding, within earshot *Antonyms:* faint, inaudible, indistinct, low

audience *n.* **1.** audition, conference, consideration, consultation, conversation, discussion, hearing, interview, meeting, reception, tryout *(Nonformal)* **2.** admirers, aficionados, assemblage, assembly, congregation, crowd, devotees, fans, following, gallery, gathering, house, listeners, market, onlookers, patrons, playgoers, public, railbirds *(Nonformal)*, spectators, theatregoers, turnout, viewers, witnesses

audit *n.* analysis, check, examination, inquiry, inspection, inventory, investigation, probe, report, review, scrutiny, survey, verification, view – *v.* analyze, check, examine, go over, inspect, investigate, review, scrutinize, verify

audition *n.* bench test, dry run, examination, hearing, performance, preliminary, qualifying examination, trial, test, tryout *(Nonformal)*

auditor *n.* accountant, actuary, analyst, authenticator, bookkeeper, examiner, inspector

auditorium *n.* amphitheatre, arena, assembly *or* concert *or* music *or* reception hall, barn, hall, movie *or* opera house, playhouse, theatre

augment *v.* add to, amplify, boost, build, compound, develop, enhance, enlarge, expand, extend, grow, heighten, improve, increase, inflate, intensify, magnify, mount, multiply, progress, raise, reinforce, strengthen, supplement, swell *Nonformal:* beef up, embroider, flesh out *Antonyms:* contract, curtail, decrease, diminish, shrink

augmentation *n.* accession, addition, amplification, boost, development, en hancement, enlargement, enrichment, expansion, extension, growth, heightening, improvement, increase, inflation, intensification, magnification, raise, reinforcement, strengthening, supplement

augur *n.* diviner, forecaster, fortuneteller, harbinger, herald, oracle, predictor, prognosticator, prophet, seer, soothsayer – *v.* bespeak, bode, figure out, forecast, foreshadow, foretell, harbinger, herald, portend, predict, presage, prognosticate, promise, prophesy, read, signify, soothsay *Nonformal:* have a hunch, psyche out

augury *n.* boding, divination, forecast, forerunner, foretoken, forewarning, harbinger, herald, mark, omen, portent, precursor, prediction, presage, prophecy, sign, soothsaying, token, warning

august *adj.* baronial, brilliant, dignified, eminent, exalted, glorious, grandiose, highfalutin *(Nonformal)*, high-minded, high-ranking, honourable, imposing, impressive, kingly, lofty, lordly, magnificent, majestic, monumental, noble, princely, regal, resplendent, stately, venerable

aura *n.* air, ambience, appearance, aspect, atmosphere, bearing, character, charm, enchantment, essence, fascination, feel, flavour, form, glamour, guise, image, mien, mood, property, quality, resemblance, scent, semblance, similarity, similitude, stamp, style, suggestion, tinge, tone, veneer

aureole *n.* effulgence, glory, halo, luminescence, radiance, ring of light

auspices *n. pl.* aegis, authority, backing, care, charge, control, direction, favour, guidance, influence, patronage, protection, sponsorship, supervision, support

auspicious *adj.* advantageous, bright, encouraging, favourable, felicitous, fortunate, golden, happy, hopeful, lucky, opportune, promising, propitious, prosperous, rosy, timely, well-timed *Antonyms:* discouraging, ominous, star-crossed, unfortunate, unlucky

austere *adj.* **1.** bald, bare, bare-bones, barren, bleak, clean, cold, plain, primitive, rustic, severe, simple, spare, Spartan, stark, subdued, unadorned, unembellished *Antonyms:* comfortable, exuberant, lush, luxurious, warm **2.** ascetic, chaste, dour, earnest, exacting, forbidding, formal, frugal, grim, grave, hard, harsh, inexorable, inflexible, obdurate, penny-pinching *(Nonformal)*, puritanical, rigid, rigorous, self-disciplined, severe, sober, solemn, sombre, stern, stiff, strait-laced, strict, stringent, unrelenting *Antonyms:* comfortable, flexible, indulgent, loose, permissive

austerity *n.* **1.** abstinence, acerbity, asceticism, asperity, astringency, chastity, continence, economy, exactingness, exactness, formality, frugality, grimness, hardness, harshness, inclemency, inflexibility, obduracy, prudence, puritanism, refraining, rigidity, rigour, self-denial, self-discipline, seriousness, severity, sobriety, solemnity, sternness, stiffness, stoicism, strictness, stringency **2.** baldness, barrenness, grimness, plainness, primitiveness, simplicity, spareness, starkness, unpretentiousness

authentic *adj.* **1.** dependable, faithful, reliable, true, trustworthy, veritable *Antonyms:* divergent, unfaithful **2.** accredited, authorized, genuine, legitimate, original, real, pure, valid *Nonformal:* A-OK, grassroots, honest-to-goodness, legit, simon-pure *Antonyms:* counterfeit, fake, fraudulent, synthetic

authentication *n.* accredition, attestion, authorization, bearing out, certification, confirmation, corroboratation, endorsement, guarantee, justification, provenance, substantiation, validation, verification, vouchsafement, warrant

author *n.* **1.** architect, begetter, beginner, composer, creator, designer, instigator, maker, originator, parent, prime mover, producer **2.** anthologist, bard, biographer, columnist, comedian, commentator, correspondent, critic, dramatist, essayist, ghostwriter, historian, journalist, lexicographer, narrator, novelist, playwright, poet, producer, publicist, reporter, reviewer, screenwriter, scribe, speechwriter, storyteller, writer *Nonformal:* ink slinger, word slinger, wordsmith – *v.* commit to paper, create, design, jot down, pen, scrawl, write *Nonformal:* bang out, dash off, knock out, scriven

authoritarian *adj.* absolute, authoritative, autocratic, despotic, dictatorial, disciplinarian, doctrinaire, dogmatic, domineering, harsh, imperious, magisterial, rigid, severe, strict, totalitarian, tyrannical, unyielding *Antonyms:* democratic, flexible, indulgent, lenient, liberal – *n.* autocrat, despot, dictator, disciplinarian, tyrant *Commonly misused:* **authoritative**

authoritative *adj.* **1.** accurate, authentic, canonical, decisive, masterly, prestigious, proven, recognized, reliable, scholarly, sound, superior, trustworthy, validated, verified, weighty *Antonyms:* ambiguous, equivocal, misleading **2.** arbitrary, commanding, controlling, despotic, doctrinaire, dogmatic, domineering, governing, imperious, magisterial, tyrannical *Antonyms:* humble, subservient, timid, weak *Commonly misused:* **authoritarian**

authoritatively *adv.* commandingly, domineeringly, imperatively, with magesty, officially, powerfully, potently, weightily

authority *n.* **1.** ascendancy, command, control, dominion, *droit (French)*, mastery, power, right, upper *or* whip hand **2.** authorization, jurisdiction, licence, mandate, permission, power of attorney **3.** confidence, consequence, importance, personal influence, prestige, prominence, respect, stature, sway **4.** adjudicator, arbiter, arbitrator, boss, judge, lawmaker **5.** advisor, cognescenti, colour comentator, expert, master, professional, pundit, scholar, specialist **6.** administration, commission, regulatory body **7.** precedent, precept, principle

authorize *v.* accede, accept, accord, accredit, acknowledge, acquiesce, admit, affirm, agree, agree to, allow, appoint, approve, assent, attest, back, back up, be behind, bequeath, bestow, bless, bring about, certify, champion, charge, commend, commission, confer, confirm, consent, constitute, countenance, delegate, effect, empower, enable, enact, encourage, endorse, endow, entitle, entrust, establish, furnish, give authority to, give leave, grant, impose, induct, initiate, install, invest, legislate, let, license, maintain, make, mandate, name, nominate, oblige, okay *(Nonformal)*, ordain, order, parcel out, pass, permit, place, praise, privilege, put through, qualify, ratify, recommend, relegate, require, rubber-stamp, sanction, select, support, underwrite, uphold, validate, vest, vote in, vouch for, vouchsafe, warrant, yield *Antonyms:* exclude, forbid, outlaw, preclude, prohibit

authorship *n.* composition, creation, literary art, source, writing *Kinds of authorship:* biography writing, book writing, creative writing, criticism, essay writing, expository writing, feature writing, journalism, libretto writing, magazine writing, novel writing, playwriting, poetry, screenplay-writing, short story writing, songwriting, technical writing, verse writing

autistic *adj.* catatonic, numb, remote, self-absorbed *or* -contained *or* -interested, uncommunicative, unresponsive, unsociable

autocracy *n.* absolutism, czarism, despotism, dictatorship, monarchy, oligarchy, oppression, satrapy, totalitarian government, tyranny *Antonyms:* democracy, republic, self-government

autocratic *adj.* absolute, all-powerful, arbitrary, bossy *(Nonformal)*, despotic, dictatorial, domineering, driving, imperious, peremptory, tyrannical

autograph *n.* endorsement, handwriting, inscription, John Hancock *(U.S.)*, seal, signature, token, writing – *v.* endorse, engross, handwrite, ink, inscribe, pen, seal, sign, undersign

automated *adj.* automatic, computerized, electrical, electronic, mechanical, mechanized, motorized, programmed, robotic

automatic *adj.* **1.** assured, certain, habitual, impulsive, inevitable, instinctive, instinctual, intuitive, knee-jerk *(Nonformal)*, mechanical, natural, necessary, reflex, routine, unavoidable, unconscious, unforced, unintentional, unthinking *Antonyms:* conscious, deliberate, intentional, voluntary **2.** automated, electric, electronic, mechanical, mechanized, motorized, robotic, self-moving, self-regulating, self-starting

automation *n.* computerization, industrialization, mechanization *Commonly misused:* **automaton**

automaton *n.* android, cyborg, machine, mechanical person, pawn, puppet, robot, self-functioning machine *Nonformal:* droid, mech *Commonly misused:* **automation**

automobile *n.* auto, car, motorized vehicle, motor vehicle *Nonformal:* banger, Bennett buggy *(Historical)*, boat, buggy, clunker, crate, heap, jalopy, junker, lemon, wagon, wheels, wreck *Historical Canadian automobiles:* Bricklin, Buick McLaughlin, Galt, LeRoy, Russell, Thomas, Tudhope *Kinds of automobile or motor vehicle:* ATV *or* all terrain vehicle, brougham, cabriolet, compact, convertible, coupe, four-by-four *or* 4x4, hardtop, hatchback, jeep, limousine *or* limo, minivan, motorcar, phaeton, race *or* racing car, recreation vehicle *or* RV, roadster, runabout, sedan, sports car, station wagon, stock car, stretch limousine *or* limo, subcompact, sports utility vehicle *or* SUV, taxi, touring car, turbo, two-door, van *Kinds of automobile racing:* Cart, drag, Formula A, Formula G, Formula One, grand touring car *or* GT, Indy, stock car *Popular automobile manufacturers:* Alfa Romeo, Bentley, BMW, Chevrolet, Chrysler, Citroen, Ferrari, Fiat, Ford, General Motors *or* GM, Honda, Hyundai, Isuzu, Lada, Lamborghini, Land Rover, Mazda, Mercedes, Mitsubishi, Nissan, Peugeot, Renault, Rolls Royce, Saab, Saturn, Suburu, Suzuki, Toyota, Volkswagon, Volvo

autonomous *adj.* free, independent, self-determining *or* -governing *or* -ruling, sovereign *Antonyms:* colonial, dependent, puppet, satellite, subjugated

autonomy *n.* freedom, independence, liberty, self-determination, self-government, self-rule, sovereignty *Antonyms:* dependency, foreign rule, occupation

autumn *n.* fall, harvest time, Indian summer, September equinox

auxiliary *adj.* abetting, accessory, adjuvant, ancillary, appurtenant, backup, complementary, contributory, extra, reserve, secondary, spare, subordinate, subservient, subsidiary, supplementary, supporting *Antonyms:* cardinal, essential, leading, main, principal

avail *n.* account, advantage, applicability, appropriateness, fitness, service, use, usefulness – *v.* **1.** aid, assist, benefit, profit, take advantage of, use **2.** answer, fulfill *or* meet the need, profit, satisfy, serve, suffice, work

available *adj.* accessible, achievable, applicable, at hand, attainable, convenient, feasible, free, handy, obtainable, on hand, prepared, procurable, purchasable, reachable, ready, realizable, securable, serviceable, usable, vacant *Nonformal:* on deck *or* tap, up for grabs *Antonyms:* busy, engaged, in use, occupied

avalanche *n.* barrage, deluge, landslide, mass, snowslide, torrent *Types of avalanche:* hard slab, soft slab, soft snow, wet snow

avant-garde *adj.* Bohemian, counter-cultural, *dernier cri (French)*, experimental, innovative, liberal, new, pioneering, progressive, radical, revolutionary, unconventional, unorthodox, vanguard *Nonformal:* bizarre, cutting *or* leading edge, state-of-the-art, way-out *Antonyms:* conservative, conventional, traditional

avarice *n.* close-fistedness, covetousness, frugality, greed, greediness, miserliness, parsimony, penny-pinching *(Nonformal)*, penuriousness, stinginess, thrift *Antonyms:* benevolence, generosity, unselfishness

avenge *v.* exact vengeance, get even, pay back, punish, redress, repay, requite, retaliate, revenge, square accounts *(Nonformal)*, vindicate

avenue *n.* access, *allée (French)*, alley, approach, boulevard, channel, circle, concourse, course, drive, entrance, entry, exit, highroad, mall, outlet, parkway, passage, pathway, promenade, road, route, street, terrace, thoroughfare, way

average *adj.* common, commonplace, customary, everyday, fair, familiar, general, hackneyed, humdrum, intermediate, mainstream, median, mediocre, medium, middle, middling, moderate, normal, ordinary, passable, regular, run-of-the-mill, standard, tolerable, typical, undistinguished, unexceptional, usual *Nonformal:* boilerplate, garden-variety, nowhere, so-so, vanilla, white bread *Antonyms:* abnormal, different, remarkable, special, unusual – *n.* mean, median, medium, middle, midpoint, norm, normal, par, rule, standard, typical, usual – *v.* balance, equate, even out, figure, reckon

averse *adj.* afraid, antagonistic, balky, contrary, disinclined, indisposed, inimical, loath, opposed, perverse, reluctant, unfavourable, unwilling *Antonyms:* agreeable, amenable, eager, inclined, keen *Commonly misused:* **adverse**

aversion *n.* abhorrence, anathema, antipathy, distaste, dread, fear, horror, ill will, odium, reluctance, repugnance *Antonyms:* flair, partiality, penchant, predilection, propensity

avert *v.* avoid, deflect, deter, fend *or* stave *or* ward off, foil, forestall, frustrate, halt, look away, preclude, prevent, rule out, shove aside, shunt, thwart, turn, turn aside *or* away

aviary *n.* birdcage, birdhouse, coop, cot, dovecot, perch, pigeon loft, roost

aviation *n.* aerodynamics, aeronautics, air travel, flight, navigation, piloting

aviator *n.* aeronaut, airman, airwoman, bush pilot, flier, navigator, pilot *Nonformal:* barnstormer, flyboy, throttle jockey, topgun

avocation *n.* amusement, calling, diversion, hobby, line of business, occupation, pastime, recreation, side interest, sideline, vocation *Nonformal:* bag, schtick

avoid *v.* abstain, avert, bypass, circumlocute, circumvent, deflect, desist, ditch, divert, dodge, elude, escape, eschew, evade, fend off, flee, keep clear, lay low, recoil, shake, shirk, shun, shy, sidestep, skip, skirt, slip out on, stay away, stay out, steer clear of, turn aside, ward off, withdraw *Nonformal:* deke, dipsy-doodle, give the cold shoulder *Antonyms:* confront, face, find, invite, solicit

avoidance *n.* abstention, delay, departure, dodge, elusion, escape, flight, forbearance, nonparticipation, parry, passive resistance, prevention, recession, recoil, restraint, retreat, run-around, self-restraint, shirking, shunning

avow *v.* acknowledge, admit, affirm, allow, assert, assure, aver, concede, confess, declare, maintain, proclaim, profess, state, swear

await *v.* anticipate, be contingent on, cool one's heels *or* jets *(Nonformal)*, expect, watch for

awake *adj.* alive, aroused, attentive, aware, circumspect, conscious, knowing, observant, on guard, roused, vigilant, watchful *Antonyms:* asleep, inattentive, sleeping, somnolent, unaware – *v.* **1.** arise, become aware, get *or* wake up, hit the deck *(Nonformal)*, revive, stir, wake *Antonyms:* die out, extinguish **2.** arouse, incite, kindle, provoke, rouse, stimulate

awaken *v.* activate, alert, animate, arouse, call forth, enliven, excite, fan, galvanize, incite, kindle, provoke, quicken, rally, revive, rouse, stimulate, wake, whet *Antonyms:* bore, check, frustrate, subdue

awakening *n.* **1.** activation, animating, arousal, birth, enlivening, genesis, incitement, kindling, provocation, stimulation, waking **2.** rebirth, renaissance, renascence, renewal, revival

award *n.* accolade, allotment, bestowal, citation, conferral, decoration, decree, distinction, donation, endowment, gift, grant, hall of fame election, honour, Nobel Prize, plaque, prize, trophy *Kinds of award: Canadian:* bp Nichol Chapbook, Canada Council, Christie, Cross of Valour, Dora Mavor Moore, East Coast Music, Gelber Prize, Gemini, Genie, Giller Prize, Golden Reel, Governor-General's, Griffin Poetry Prize, Jessie, Juno, Lionel, Medal of Bravery, Molson Prize, Order of Military Merit, Prix Athanase-David, Prix Gilles-Corbeil, Prix Trillium, Star of Courage, Stephen Leacock, Trillium Book *British and Commonwealth:* Booker Prize, Distinguished Flying Cross *(Air Force)*, Distinguished Service Cross *(Navy)*, Distinguished Service Order, Knight of the Garter, Victoria Cross *U.S.:* Academy Award *or* Oscar, Emmy, Grammy, National Book Award, Pulitzer Prize, Tony *See also:* **decoration, medal** – *v.* accord, allocate, allot, apportion, assign, bestow, confer, donate, endow, gift, grant, hand out, present, reward

aware *adj.* acquainted, alert, alive, appraised, appreciative, apprehensive, apprised, attentive, *au courant (French)*, awake, cognizant, conscious, enlightened, familiar, grounded, heedful, informed, knowing, knowledgeable, mindful, on to, perceptive, receptive, sensible, sentient, sharp *Nonformal:* cool, into, on the beam, plugged into, savvy, tuned in, up on, wise, wise to, with it *Antonyms:* ignorant, oblivious, unaware

awareness *n.* acquaintanceship, alertness, aliveness, appreciation, apprehension, attention, cognizance, comprehension, consciousness, discernment, enlightenment, experience, familiarity, information, knowledge, mindfulness, perception, percipience, perspicaciousness, realization, recognition, sagacity, sentience, sensibility, understanding

away *adj.* abroad, absent, distant, elsewhere, gone, lacking, not here *or* present *or* there, omitted, out, remote – *adv.* afar, apart, aside, beyond, distantly, elsewhere, far away *or* off, farther, further, not present, out and about *(Nonformal)*, remote, yonder

awe *n.* admiration, apprehension, astonishment, consternation, dread, esteem, fear, fright, regard, respect, reverence, shock, stupefaction, terror, veneration, wonder, wonderment, worship *Antonyms:* contempt, disdain, insolence, scorn – *v.* alarm, amaze, appal, astonish, daunt, dazzle, frighten, grandstand, horrify, impress, intimidate, scare, startle, strike, stun, stupefy, terrify *Nonformal:* blow away, cow, flabbergast, showboat *Antonyms:* disenchant, disillusion

awesome *adj.* alarming, amazing, awe-inspiring, beautiful, breathtaking, daunting, dreadful, exalted, fearsome, formidable, frantic, frightening, grand, horrifying, imposing, impressive, intimidating, magnificent, majestic, moving, overwhelming, striking, stunning, stupefying, stupendous, terrifying, unforgettable, wonderful *Nonformal:* clean outta sight, far-out, hairy, mind-blowing

awful *adj.* abominable, alarming, appalling, atrocious, bad, deplorable, depressing, dire, distressing, dreadful, fearful, frightful, ghastly, gruesome, harrowing, hideous, horrendous, horrible, nasty *(Nonformal)*, negative, offensive, raunchy, repulsive, shocking, terrible, tough, unpleasant, unsightly *Antonyms:* amazing, excellent, fabulous, wonderful

awfully *adv.* **1.** badly, clumsily, disgracefully, disreputably, dreadfully, excessively, extremely, inadequately, incompletely, poorly, reprehensibly, shoddily, terribly, unforgivably, unpleasantly, wickedly, wretchedly **2.** dearly, greatly, hugely, immensely, indeed, much, profoundly, quite, truly, very

awkward *adj.* **1.** amateurish, blundering, bungling, churlish, clumsy, gauche, gawky, graceless, indelicate, inelegant, inept, maladroit, stiff, stumbling, uncoordinated, ungraceful *Nonformal:* all thumbs, butterfingers, klutzy *Antonyms:* adept, adroit, graceful, skilful **2.** compromising, degrading, embarrassing, uncomfortable, unusual *Nonformal:* loaded, sticky, touchy *Antonyms:* pleasant, satisfactory **3.** dangerous, difficult, hazardous, painful, precarious, prickly, risky, thorny, troublesome, trying *Antonyms:* convenient, easy **4.** bulky, cumbersome, inconvenient, massive, ungainly, unmanageable

awkwardness *n.* amateurishness, artlessness, clumsiness, coarseness, crudeness, difficulty, discomfort, embarrassment, gawkiness, gracelessness, inability, incompetence, inconvenience, inelegance, ineptitude, inexpertness, maladroitness, rudeness, stickiness, tactlessness, trouble, ungainliness, unpleasantness, untimeliness *Antonyms:* agility, grace, skill

awning *n.* canopy, covering, door cover, marquee, protection, shade, shelter, sunshade, tarpaulin, tent

awry *adj.* afield, asymmetrical, bent, catawampus *(Nonformal)*, cockeyed, crooked, curved, lopsided, ludicrous, off-course, slanting, turned, zigzag – *adv.* amiss, askance, askew, astray, crookedly, off the mark

axe *n.* blade, chopper *Kinds of axes:* adze, battle-axe, broad-axe, camp, cruiser's, double-bit, fireman's, half, hatchet, Hudson Bay, ice, pickax, single-bit, tomahawk, utility – *v.* chop, cut, fell, hew, trim

axiom *n.* adage, aphorism, dictum, law, maxim, moral, postulate, precept, principle, proverb, saying, theorem, truism, truth

axiomatic *adj.* absolute, accepted, assumed, certain, fundamental, given, obvious, presupposed, self-evident, understood, unquestioned

axis *n.* axle, hinge, pin, pivot, pole, rod, shaft, shank, spindle, stalk, stem, support, turning point

axle *n.* arbour, axis, gudgeon, mandrel, pin, pivot, pole, rod, shaft, spindle, stalk, stem, support

azure *adj.* blue, cerulean, cobalt-blue, deep-blue, lapis lazuli, sky-blue, sky-coloured, ultramarine – *n.* blueness, cyan, empyrean, firmament, heaven, hyaline, lividness

babble *n.* burble, clamour, drivel, gab, gabble, gibberish, gossip, idle talk, jabbering, jargon, murmur, muttering, prattle, tattling – *v.* blab, blubber, blurt, cackle, chat, chatter, gibber, go on, gossip, gush, jabber, mumble, mutter, patter, prate, prattle, rant, rave, squeal, talk foolishly, talk incoherently, tattle, trivialize *Nonformal:* gas, run off at the mouth, run on *Antonyms:* articulate, lecture, sermonize

baby *n.* **1.** babe, bairn *(Scottish)*, bundle, child, infant, kid, newborn, papoose, suckling, toddler, tot, youngster **2.** coward, crybaby, sissy *(Nonformal)*, sook *(Maritimes)*, weakling – *v.* cater to, cherish, coddle, cosset, cuddle, dote on, foster, humour, indulge, mollycoddle, nurse, overindulge, pamper, pet, serve, spoil *Antonyms:* abuse, mistreat

bacchanalia *n.* bash, carouse, debauch, jollification, orgy, revelry, saturnalia *Nonformal:* drunkfest, hot time, love-in, tear

bachelor *n.* **1.** single, single *or* unmarried man, stag *(Nonformal)* **2.** boulevardier, Casanova, Don Juan, ladies' man, playboy, rake, womanizer *Nonformal:* lady-killer, lover boy, skirt-chaser, swinger

back *adj.* **1.** aft, after, astern, back of, behind, end, final, following, hind, hindmost, posterior, rear, tail *Antonyms:* advance, fore, front **2.** delayed, earlier, elapsed, former, overdue, past, previous – *n.* aft, back end, backside, end, extremity, far end, hindquarter, posterior, rear, reverse, stern, tail, tail end, tailpiece – *v.* **1.** abet, abide by, advocate, ally, assist, champion, countenance, encourage, endorse, favour, finance, sanction, second, sponsor, stake, subsidize, support, sustain, underwrite, uphold *Nonformal:* bankroll, boost, grubstake, side with, stand behind, stick by *Antonyms:* attack, combat, hinder, thwart, undermine, weaken **2.** drive *or* fall back, recede, regress, repel, repulse, retract, retreat, reverse, withdraw *Antonyms:* move forward, push

backbone *n.* **1.** spine, support, vertebra, vertebral column **2.** character, courage, determination, firmness, fortitude, grit, guts *(Nonformal)*, heart, intestinal fortitude, mettle, moral fibre, nerve, pluck, resolution, resolve, spunk, stamina, steadfastness, tenacity, toughness, will power *Antonyms:* cowardice, timidity

backer *n.* advocate, ally, angel, benefactor, champion, endorser, fairy godmother *(Nonformal)*, patron, promoter, protagonist, sponsor, staker, supporter, underwriter, well-wisher *Antonyms:* adversary, antagonist, opponent

backfire *v.* backlash, boomerang, bounce back, disappoint, explode, fail, flop *(Nonformal)*, miscarry, rebound, recoil, ricochet, spring back

background *n.* accomplishments, attainment, backdrop, breeding, capacity, circumstances, context, credentials, culture, education, environment, experience, framework, grounding, history, preparation, qualifications, rearing, training, upbringing *Antonyms:* centre stage, foreground

backing *n.* accompaniment, adherence, advocacy, aegis, aid, assistance, championing, encouragement, endorsement, funds, grant, help, patronage, reinforcement, sanction, sponsorship, subsidy, support *Antonyms:* detriment, sabotage, subversion

backlash *n.* backfire, boomerang, kick *(Nonformal)*, reaction, recoil, repercussion, response, retaliation

backlog *n.* accumulation, excess, hoard, inventory, pile-up, quantity, reserve, resources, stock, stockpile, store, supply

backward *adj.* **1.** arrested, behind, below par, challenged, delayed, dense, dull, inverted, late, rearward, regressive, retrograde, slow, sluggish, subnormal, underdeveloped, undeveloped *Antonyms:* advanced, forward **2.** afraid, averse, bashful, demure, diffident, disinclined, hesitant, humble, indisposed, modest, reluctant, reserved, retiring, shy, tardy, timid, unwilling, wavering *Antonyms:* bold, brash, eager, forward, willing **3.** astern, back, behind, inverted, rear, rearward, reverse *Antonyms:* forward, frontward

backwash *n.* aftermath, repercussion, result, track, trail, wake, wash

backwoods *n.* back country, brush, bush, forest, frontier, hinterland, interior, outback, rural area, timberland, wilderness, woodland *Nonformal:* back forty, boondocks, sticks *Antonyms:* big time, city, downtown, main street

backyard *n.* acreage, courtyard, garden, grass, home, lawn, terrace, turf *(Nonformal)*, yard

bacteria *n. pl.* germs, microbes, monera, pathogens *(Taxonomy)*, prokaryote *Groupings of bacteria: Bacilli:* Bacillus proteus, Bacillus subtilis, Clostridium sporogenes, Salmonella typhi *Cocci:* Diplococcus, Sarcina, Staphylococcus, Streptococcus *Spirilla:* Spirillum undulum, Spirochetes, Thiospirillum, Vibrio comma *Kinds of bacteria:* blue-green algae, endospore-forming, lactic acid, mycoplasmas, spirochetes

bad *adj.* **1.** abominable, amiss, atrocious, awful, base, beastly, corrupt, criminal, defective, deficient, delinquent, dreadful, evil, immoral, iniquitous, mean, nefarious, odious, raunchy, reprobate, sinful, sleazy, vicious, vile, villainous, wicked *Nonformal:* crummy, lousy *Antonyms:* agreeable, beneficial, ethical, fine, first-rate, good, moral, proper, righteous, virtuous **2.** badly made, careless, cheap, poor, shoddy, unacceptable **3.** ailing, diseased, ill, pained, sick, unwell *Antonyms:* healthful, wholesome **4.** damaging, dangerous, deleterious, detrimental, disastrous, distressing, grave, harmful, harsh, hurtful, injurious, intense, painful, ruinous, serious, severe, terrible, unhealthy **5.** adverse, disagreeable, discouraged, discouraging, displeasing, distressing, gloomy, grim, melancholy, troubled, troubling, unfavourable, unfortunate, unhappy, unpleasant **6.** decayed, gamy, high, mouldy, off, putrid, rancid, rotten, sour, spoiled *Antonyms:* fresh, new, ripe **7.** disobedient, ill-behaved, misbehaving, mischievous, naughty, unruly, wrong *Antonyms:* docile, good, obedient – *n.* abomination, atrocity, evil, infamy, iniquity, wickedness *Antonyms:* benefaction, good deed

badge *n.* brand, chevron, crest, device, emblem, ID *(Nonformal)*, identification, insignia, mark, marker, medallion, motto, pin, ribbon, sceptre, shield, sign, stamp, symbol, token

badly *adv.* **1.** abominably, awkwardly, blunderingly, carelessly, clumsily, crudely, defectively, erroneously, faultily, haphazardly, imperfectly, inadequately, incompetently, ineffectively, ineptly, maladroitly, negligently, poorly, stupidly, unfavourably, unfortunately, unskilfully, unsuccessfully, weakly, wrongly *Antonyms:* ably, competently, correctly, properly, satisfactorily **2.** criminally, immorally, improperly, naughtily, shamefully, unethically, wickedly *Antonyms:* ethically, morally, properly, righteously, rightly **3.** acutely, deeply, desperately, exceedingly, extremely, gravely, greatly, hard, intensely, painfully, roughly, seriously, severely *Antonyms:* easily, lightly, trivially

baffle *v.* **1.** addle, amaze, astound, befuddle, bewilder, blank, boggle, confound, confuse, daze, disconcert, dumfound, elude, faze, floor, mix up, muddle, mystify, nonplus, perplex, puzzle, rattle, stump, stun, throw *Antonyms:* clarify, clear up, elucidate, explain **2.** beat, block, check, circumvent, dash, defeat, disappoint, foil, frustrate, hinder, impede, obstruct, prevent, ruin, thwart, upset *Antonyms:* assist, encourage, support

bag *n.* **1.** case, container, gear, sack *Kinds of bag:* attaché, backpack, briefcase, carryall, carry-on, duffel, grub-bag, gunnysack, handbag, holdall, kitbag, knapsack, laundry, pack, pocket, pocketbook, purse, rucksack, saddlebag, satchel, suitcase, tote **2.** business, calling, concern, interest, thing – *v.* **1.** balloon, billow, bulge, swell **2.** droop, flap, flop, hang, lop, sag

baggage *n.* **1.** accoutrements, bags, belongings, caboodle *(Nonformal)*, carry-on, effects, equipment, gear, kit, luggage, paraphernalia, parcels, suitcases, tote, tote bag, trappings, trunk **2.** emotional problem, psychosis *Nonformal:* hang-up, history

baggy *adj.* billowing, bulging, drooping, flabby, flaccid, floppy, ill-fitting, loose, oversize, roomy, sagging, slack, unshapely *Antonyms:* close, close-fitting, constricted, snug, tight

bail *n.* assurance, bond, collateral, guarantee, money, pledge, recognizance, security, surety, warranty – *v.* **1.** ladle, remove, scoop, spoon, withdraw **2.** abet, aid, assist, free, redeem, rescue, save **3.** abandon, desert, flee *Nonformal:* cop out, pack it in, parachute *Antonyms:* remain, stay, stick it out

bait *n.* attraction, bribe, carrot *(Nonformal)*, come-on, enticement, fly, inducement, lure, seducement, snare, temptation, trap – *v.* **1.** anger, annoy, badger, bother, gall, harass, heckle, hound, irk, irritate, nag, needle, persecute, provoke, tease, torment **2.** allure, attract, bedevil, beguile, draw, entice, fascinate, lure, seduce, tempt

balance *n.* **1.** account, difference, dividend, excess, extra, profit, remainder, remnants, residue, rest, surplus **2.** aplomb, calmness, composure, equanimity, imperturbability, level-headedness, poise, self-control, stability, steadfastness, steadiness **3.** antithesis, ballast, compensation, counteraction, counterbalance, counterpoise, equilibrium, equity, equivalence, evenness, stabilizer, stasis, symmetry, tension *Antonyms:* disproportion, instability, shakiness, uncertainty **4.** accord, affinity, agreement, conformity, congruity, correspondence, equality, harmony, level, match, neutral, par, parallel, parity, proportion, resemblance, similarity, similitude, uniformity, unity – *v.* **1.** compare, consider, deliberate, estimate, evaluate, weigh the odds *(Nonformal)* **2.** adjust, audit, ballast, calculate, compute, count, enumerate, equate, estimate, figure, harmonize, reconcile, settle, square, stabilize, sum up, tally

balanced *adj.* **1.** counterbalanced, equalized, equitable, equivalent, even, fair, offset, proportional, stable, symmetrical, uniform *Antonyms:* biased, distorted, jaundiced, lopsided, weighted **2.** calm, harmonious, poised *Antonyms:* bipolar, chaotic, renegade, unchecked, wild **3.** confirmed, settled, validated

balcony *n.* balustrade, box, catwalk, deck, gallery, *lanai (Hawaiian)*, mezzanine, platform, porch, portico, stoop, terrace, veranda, widow's walk *Nonformal:* greys, peanut gallery, the gods

bald *adj.* **1.** bare, depilated, glabrous, hairless, naked, shaven, smooth, stark, uncovered *Antonyms:* furry, grizzly, hirsute, shaggy **2.** barren, bleak, exposed, impoverished, meagre, scanty, stark *Antonyms:* fecund, fertile, lush, rich **3.** blunt, candid, downright, frank, from the hip *(Nonformal)*, plain-spoken *Antonyms:* circuitous, evasive, introverted, prevaricating

baleful *adj.* calamitous, deadly, destructive, detrimental, evil, harmful, hurtful, injurious, malevolent, malignant, menacing, nefarious, noxious, odious, ominous, pernicious, ruinous, sinister, threatening, venomous, vindictive, woeful *Antonyms:* benevolent, benign, friendly, good, healthy

balk *v.* **1.** baffle, bar, beat, circumvent, counteract, cramp, dash, defeat, demur, disappoint, disconcert, elude, foil, forestall, frustrate, hinder, obstruct, prevent, stall, stop, thwart *Antonyms:* abet, aid, assist, help, sustain **2.** check, flinch, pull up, quail, recoil, spring back, shy away

balky *adj.* averse, chippy, contrary, hesitant, immovable, indisposed, inflexible, intractable, negative, nervous, obstinate, ornery, perverse, reluctant, reticent, stubborn, unbending, uncooperative, unmanageable, unpredictable, unruly

ball *n.* **1.** cannonshot, drop, globe, marble, orb, pearl, pellet, pigskin *(Football)*, pill *(Baseball)*, projectile, round, sphere, spheroid **2.** dance, fandango, festivity, fete, formal, gala, jamboree, prom, quadrille, saraband *Nonformal:* blast, shindig **3.** frolic, fun, good time, riot

ballad *n.* carol, *chanson (French)*, chant, ditty, epic, folk song, lay, narrative verse, ode, oral tradition, poem, serenade, song, tune

ballast *n.* balance, balancer, counterbalance, counterweight, equalizer, stabilizer, support, weight

balloon *n.* airship, blimp *(Nonformal)*, dirigible, zeppelin – *v.* billow, bloat, blow up, bulge, dilate, distend, enlarge, expand, inflate, puff out, swell *Antonyms:* collapse, deflate, puncture, shrink

ballot *n.* choice, election, franchise, lot, plebiscite, poll, referendum, selection, slate, ticket, vote

balm *n.* alleviation, analgesic, assuagement, comfort, consolation, curative, easement, emollient, formula, lotion, mitigation, ointment, palliative, pomade, poultice, refreshment, remedy, restorative, salve, solace, soother, substance, unction, unguent *Antonyms:* abrasive, acid, caustic, irritant, vitriol

balmy *adj.* **1.** fair, mild, pacific, pleasant, summery, temperate, tranquil *Antonyms:* arid, harsh, rough, stormy **2.** absurd, crazy, daft, deranged, foolish, harebrained, idiotic, insane, mentally incompetent, *non compos mentis (Latin)*, preposterous, silly, stupid *Nonformal:* bananas, barmy, cracked, loony, loopy, nuts, nutty, potty, squirrely, wacky *Antonyms:* lucid, ponderous, reasoned, thoughtful

bamboozle *v.* baffle, befuddle, bilk, confound, confuse, deceive, defraud, delude, dupe, fool, hoax, hoodwink, mystify, perplex, puzzle, stump, swindle, trick *Nonformal:* con, flimflam, grift, rip-off, sucker

ban *n.* banishment, bar, blackball, blacklist, boycott, censorship, embargo, injunction, interdiction, limitation, no-no *(Nonformal)*, prohibition, proscription, refusal, restriction, stoppage, suppression, taboo *Antonyms:* authorization, legalization, permission – *v.* avoid, banish, bar, blackball, blacklist, boycott, count out, debar *or* disbar, disallow, disregard, eliminate, embargo, except, exclude, exempt, expel, forbid, omit, ostracize, outlaw, preclude, prohibit, proscribe, refuse, reject, remonstrate, repudiate, rule out, snub, spurn, stifle, strike, suspend, veto *Antonyms:* allow, approve, permit, sanction

banal *adj.* bland, clichéd, cliché-ridden, common *or* commonplace, conventional, corny, dull, everyday, flat, hackneyed, humdrum, insipid, ordinary, overdone, pedestrian, prosaic, sentimental, square, stale, stereotyped, stock, tired, trite, unimaginative, uninspired, unoriginal, vapid, watery *Nonformal:* hokey, old hat, pablum *Antonyms:* distinctive, fresh, imaginative, interesting, original

banality *n.* bromide, buzz word, catch phrase, cliché, familiar tune, platitude, saw, saying, sentimentality, triviality, truism *Nonformal:* chestnut, old saw *Antonyms:* innovation, novelty

band *n.* **1.** assembly, association, bevy, bloc, body, bunch, cadre, clique, club, cluster, collection, company, corps, coterie, covey, crew, faction, gang, gathering, group, horde, menagerie, outfit, party, society, team **2.** combo, ensemble *or* jazz ensemble, musical group, orchestra, pop *or* rhythm & blues *or* rock group, symphony, travelling minstrels, troupe **3.** bandeau, belt, binding, chain, circle, circuit, cord, elastic, harness, hoop, ligature, line, link, manacle, ribbon, ring, rope, sash, scarf, shackle, stay, strap, string, strip, tape, tie, truss – *v.* **1.** affiliate, ally, amalgamate, combine, consolidate, gather, group, league, merge, team, unite **2.** brand, identify, mark *Antonyms:* cleave, disperse, disunite, segregate

bandage *n.* cast, compress, dressing, gauze, plaster, poultice – *v.* bind, cover, dress, swathe, truss

bandit *n.* brigand, crook, desperado, gangster, gunman, hacker, highwayman, hijacker, hooligan, invader, marauder, mobster, outlaw, pillager, pirate, plunderer, racketeer, raider, renegade, robber, ronin, thief, villain *Antonyms:* Mountie, sheriff, the law

bane *n.* affliction, blight, burden, curse, despair, destruction, downfall, misery, nuisance, pest, plague, poison, ruination, scourge, torment, trial, tribulation, trouble, undoing, venom, woe *Antonyms:* amelioration, benefit, relief

bang *n.* **1.** blast, boom, burst, clang, clap, clash, crack, detonation, discharge, explosion, noise, peal, pop, report, roar, roll, rumble, salvo, shot, sound, thud, thump, thunder, thunderclap, wham **2.** bash, beat, belt, blow, bump, clatter, collision, crash, hit, pounding, rap, slam, smack, thump, whack – *v.* **1.** boom, burst, clang, detonate, drum, explode, peal, rattle, sound, thump, thunder **2.** bash, bat, batter, belt, box, bump, collide, crack, cuff, hammer, hit, knock, pummel, punch, smack, smash, sock, strike, wallop, whack

banish *v.* alienate, ban, cast out, deport, discard, discharge, dislodge, dismiss, dispel, drive away, eject, eliminate, eradicate, evict, exclude, exile, expatriate, expel, extradite, isolate, ostracize, oust, outlaw, proscribe, relegate, remove, sequester, shun, transport *Antonyms:* accept, admit, embrace, receive, welcome

bank *n.* **1.** cay, cliff, coast, edge, embankment, ground, lakefront, lakeshore, ledge, levee, moraine, mound, oceanfront, riverfront, riverside, seabank, sea front, shallow, shoal, shore, waterfront *Canadian ocean banks:* Banquereau, Belle Isle, Browns, Funk Island, George's Grand, Hamilton, Harrison, Makkovik, Nain, Sable Island, Saglek **2.** armory, cache, *caisse populaire (Quebec)*, coffer, commercial *or* counting house, credit union, depository, depot, fund, institution, investment firm, lending *or* savings institution, repository, reserve, safe, savings, stock, storehouse, treasury, trust company, vault, warehouse **3.** array, line, rank, row, sequence, series, succession, tier **4.** draw, kitty, pile, pot, reserve – *v.* **1.** accumulate, amass, collect, deposit, hoard, invest, lay away, save, speculate, stash, stockpile *Nonformal:* salt or sock or squirrel away *Antonyms:* spend, squander, throw away **2.** bend, camber, cant, incline, lean, pitch, slant, slope, tilt *Antonyms:* straighten, unbend **3.** damp, damp off, dampen, extinguish, reduce to embers, turn down

bankroll *n.* cash, money, nestegg, roll, savings *Nonformal:* blunt, bundle, loot, stash, wad – *v.* back, capitalize, finance, fund, pay for, provide capital or money for, sponsor, stake, support

bankrupt *adj.* belly up *(Nonformal)*, broke, destitute, exhausted, failed, impoverished, indebted, insolvent, ruined, spent *Antonyms:* flush, prosperous, wealthy – *v.* beggar, break, cripple, crush, destroy, exhaust, impoverish, pauperize, ruin

bankruptcy *n.* Chapter 11, default, destitution, disaster, failure, indebtedness, indigence, insolvency, liquidation, loss, nonpayment, penury, privation, receivership, ruin *Antonyms:* prosperity, solvency, wealth

banner *adj.* exceptional, extraordinary, great, stellar *Antonyms:* disastrous, horrible – *n.* advertisement, announcement, colours, emblem, ensign, flag, headline, pennant, standard, streamer

banter *n.* badinage, chaffing, chitchat, derision, exchange, fun, gossip, jeering, jesting, joking, joshing, kidding, mockery, play, raillery, repartee, ribbing, ridicule, teasing – *v.* chaff, deride, fool, fun, jeer, jest, jive, joke, josh, kid, mock, rag, razz *(Nonformal)*, ridicule, taunt, tease

baptism *n.* ablution, anointing, baptismal, christening, confirmation, consecration, dedication, immersion, initiation, introduction, purification, rebirth, rite, ritual, sanctification, sprinkling

baptize *v.* admit, anoint, christen, cleanse, dip, immerse, initiate, introduce, name, purify, regenerate, sanctify, sprinkle

bar *n.* **1.** barricade, barrier, blank wall, block, clog, deterrent, encumbrance, fence, hindrance, hurdle, impediment, logjam, obstacle, obstruction, pale, rail, railing, restraint, roadblock, snag, stanchion, stop, stumbling block, traverse, wall *Antonyms:* aid, benefit, opening **2.** after-hours club, alehouse, beer garden, beer *or* corner joint, beer parlour, beverage room, brasserie, cabaret, cocktail lounge, hotel, nightclub, pub, public house, rathskeller, saloon, speakeasy, taproom, tavern *Nonformal:* blind pig, dive, watering hole **3.** batten, crossbar, crosspiece, I-beam, lever, paling, pole, rail, rod, shaft, spar, spoke, stake, stick, strip, stripe **4.** attorneys, barristers, counsellors, judiciary, jurists, lawyers, legal fraternity, legal system, solicitors – *v.* **1.** barricade, block, blockade, bolt, caulk, close, dam, dike, fasten, fence, jam, latch, lock, plug, seal, secure, wall **2.** ban, boycott, circumvent, condemn, debar, deny, disallow, discountenance, discourage, eliminate, enjoin, except, exclude, exile, forbid, freeze out *(Nonformal)*, frustrate, hinder, interdict, interfere, keep out, limit, obstruct, ostracize, outlaw, override, preclude, prevent, prohibit, refuse, reject, restrain, rule out, segregate, shut out, stop, suspend *Antonyms:* accept, allow, open, permit, welcome

barb *n.* **1.** arrow, bristle, dart, point, prickle, prong, quill, shaft, spike, spur, thistle, thorn **2.** affront, comment, criticism, cut, dig, gibe, insult, needle, rebuff, sarcasm, scoff, sneer *Antonyms:* acclaim, compliment, tribute

barbarian *adj.* barbarous, boorish, brutal, coarse, crude, cruel, inhuman, lowbrow *(Nonformal)*, merciless, primitive, rough, rude, savage, uncivil, uncouth, uncultivated, unsophisticated, untamed, vulgar, wild *Antonyms:* civilized, cultured, genteel, refined – *n.* beast, bigot, boor, brute, cannibal, ignoramus, lout, monster, philistine, rascal, ruffian, savage, thug, troglodyte, underling, vandal, vulgarian, yahoo *(Nonformal) Antonyms:* gentleman, lady

barbaric *adj.* barbarian, barbarous, boorish, brutal, coarse, cruel, fierce, graceless, inhuman, lowbrow *(Nonformal)*, primitive, rough, rude, savage, tasteless, uncivilized, uncouth, vulgar, wild *Antonyms:* cultivated, humane, refined, sophisticated

barbarism *n.* **1.** atrocity, barbarity, brutality, cruelty, inhumanity, savagery **2.** corruption, impropriety, malapropism, misusage, misuse, solecism, spoonerism, vulgarism

barbecue *n.* **1.** brazier, broiler, charcoal grill, fireplace, gas grill, grill, hibachi, roaster, rotisserie **2.** BBQ, clambake, cookout, dinner, party, picnic, supper, weeny roast *(Nonformal)* – *v.* broil, charcoal, fry, grill, sear, smoke

barber *n.* beautician, coiffeur *(Masc.)*, coiffeuse *(Fem.)*, cosmetician, esthetician, haircutter, hairdresser, hair stylist

bare *adj.* **1.** arid, bald, barren, blank, bleak, clear, denuded, desert, desolate, divested, empty, exposed, glabrous, in the altogether *(Nonformal)*, lacking, mean, naked, nude, open, peeled, scanty, shorn, stark, stripped, unclad, unclothed, uncovered, undressed, unfurnished, vacant, vacuous, void, wanting *Antonyms:* clad, concealed, covered, dressed, protected **2.** ascetic, austere, basic, essential, hard, literal, meagre, mean, mere, modest, plain, scant, severe, sheer, simple, spare, spartan, stark *Antonyms:* bedecked, embellished, luxurious, ornate – *v.* disclose, divulge, exhibit, expose, publish, reveal, show, uncover, unroll, unveil *Antonyms:* cover, hide

barefoot *adj.* **1.** discalceate, discalced, shoeless, unshod *Antonyms:* booted, shod **2.** burdenless, carefree, careless, unencumbered, fancy free, *sans souci (French)*, unfettered

barely *adv.* **1.** almost, by the skin of one's teeth *(Nonformal)*, hardly, just, not quite, only just, scantily, scarcely **2.** baldly, openly, nakedly, plainly

bareness *n.* **1.** dishabille, nakedness, nudity, starkness, unadornment, unclothed state, undress **2.** austereness, bleakness, desolateness, plainness, starkness

bargain *n.* **1.** agreement, arrangement, bond, business, compact, contract, convention, covenant, deal, engagement, negotiation, pact, pledge, promise, stipulation, transaction, treaty, understanding **2.** budget price, buy, deal, discount, good buy *or* deal *or* value, low price, markdown, reduction, sale, value *Nonformal:* bargoon, giveaway, steal – *v.* agree, arrange, barter, buy, compromise, confer, contract, deal, dicker, drive *or* strike a bargain, haggle, hammer *or* work out a deal *(Nonformal)*, negotiate, promise, sell, stipulate, trade, traffic, transact

bark *n.* **1.** carapace, case, casement, casing, coat, cortex, hide, husk, peeling, pelt, rind, shell, skin **2.** bay, growl, grunt, howl, roar, snarl, woof, yap, yelp, yip – *v.* bay, cry, howl, snap, snarl, woof, yap, yelp, yip

barn *n.* cowbarn, cowhouse, cowshed, *étable (French)*, granary *(British)*, grange, shed, silo, stable, stall

barracks *n.* army camp, billet, bivouac, camp, cantonment, caserne, dormitory, encampment, garrison, quarters

barrage *n.* assault, battery, blast, bombardment, broadside, burst, cannonade, crossfire, discharge, fire, fusillade, gunfire, hail, onslaught, plethora, profusion, rain, salvo, shelling, shower, storm, stream, surge, torrent, volley

barrel *n.* cask, container, drum, firkin, hogshead, keg, tub, vat, vessel – *v.* careen, make tracks *(Nonformal)*, pile into, speed, storm, zoom

barren *adj.* **1.** arid, childless, depleted, desert, desolate, dry, effete, fallow, impotent, impoverished, infertile, parched, sparse, sterile, unfertile, unfruitful, unproductive, waste *Antonyms:* fecund, fruitful, lush, productive **2.** dull, flat, fruitless, futile, lacklustre, profitless, stale, unprofitable, unrewarding, useless *Antonyms:* interesting, profitable, rich, useful **3.** blank, empty, hollow, vacant

barricade *n.* bar, barrier, blank wall, block, blockade, fence, fort, obstruction, palisade, roadblock, stockade, wall – *v.* bar, block, blockade, defend, fortify, obstruct, shut in

barrier *n.* **1.** bar, check, difficulty, encumbrance, handicap, hindrance, hurdle, impediment, limit, limitation, obstacle, restraint, restriction, stumbling block **2.** barricade, blockade, boom, bound, boundary, confines, curtain, ditch, enclosure, fence, fortification, gully, hurdle, impediment, logjam, moat, obstruction, pale, palisade, railing, rampart, roadblock, stop, trench, wall

barter *v.* bargain, deal, exchange, horse-trade, swap, trade, truck

base *adj.* abject, abominable, cheap, coarse, contemptible, corrupt, despicable, dishonorable, disreputable, foul, grovelling, humble, ignoble, immoral, indelicate, knavish, lowly, mean, menial, paltry, scandalous, servile, shameful, shoddy, sleazy, sordid, sorry, squalid, trashy, unworthy, vile, vulgar, worthless, wretched *Antonyms:* admirable, good, honest, moral, noble – *n.* **1.** basis, bed, bedrock, bottom, foot, footing, foundation, ground, groundwork, infrastructure, lowest point, nadir, rest, rock, root, seat, seating, substratum, substructure, support, underpinning *Antonyms:* apex, crown, peak, summit, top **2.** anchor *(Nonformal)*, authority, basis, core, essence, evidence, foundation, fundamental, heart, infrastructure, key, origin, root, source **3.** camp, Canadian Forces Base *or* CFB, centre, depot, garrison, headquarters, home, port, site, station, terminal – *v.* build on, construct, depend, derive, establish, found, ground, hinge, locate, predicate, prop, rest, station, stay

baseball *n.* ball *(Nonformal)*, organized baseball *Baseball equipment:* ball, bases, bat, batting gloves, catcher's mask, glove, helmet, home plate, mitt, mound, rosin bag, rubber, shinguards, spikes *Baseball leagues:* A, AA, AAA, American, Collegiate, Instructional, Little, National *Canadian major league baseball teams:* Montreal Expos, Toronto Blue Jays *Positions in baseball and designated number:* batboy, catcher *(1)*, centrefield *(8)*, coaches, first base *(3)*, left field *(7)*, manager, pitcher *(2)*, right field *(9)*, second base *(4)*, shortstop *(6)*, third base *(5)*, umpire *Scoring and procedure in baseball:* at bat, balk, ball, batter up, bean ball, box score, brushback, designated hitter, double, double play, double switch, error, extra innings, fly-out, force *or* forced out, foul ball, foul-out, full count, grand slam, ground-out, ground rule double, hit batsman *or* batter, hit for the cycle, home run *or* dinger, inning, line-out, on deck, passed ball, perfect game, pick-off, pitch, pitch-out, pop fly, retire the side, run, single, stolen base, strike, strike-out, strike zone, tag *or* tag out, the count, the score, triple, walk *or* base on balls, wild pitch

baseless *adj.* bottomless, flimsy, groundless, reasonless, spurious, unconfirmed, uncorroborated, unfounded, ungrounded, unjustifiable, unjustified, unsubstantiated, unsupported, untenable, unwarranted, without merit *Antonyms:* authenticated, confirmed, proven, substantiated

bashful *adj.* abashed, backward, blushing, chary, confused, constrained, coy, demure, diffident, embarrassed, humble, modest, overmodest, reserved, reticent, retiring, self-conscious, self-effacing, shrinking, shy, silent, timid, unassertive *Antonyms:* aggressive, arrogant, bold, brash, conceited

basic *adj.* bottom line, capital, central, chief, elemental, elementary, essential, indispensable, inherent, intrinsic, key, main, necessary, primary, primitive, principal, radical, underlying, vital *Nonformal:* meat-and-potatoes, nitty-gritty *Antonyms:* ancillary, minor, peripheral, secondary, supporting

basically *adv.* essentially, firstly, fundamentally, in essence, inherently, in substance, intrinsically, mostly, primarily

basics *n.* ABC's, brass tacks *(Nonformal)*, core, essentials, fundamentals, grassroots, hard facts, practicalities, rudiments, three R's

basin *n.* **1.** bowl, ewer, pan, pot, sink, tub, vessel **2.** bay, coulee, crater, depression, hollow, sinkhole

basis *n.* base, bed, bottom, foot, footing, foundation, ground, grounds, groundwork, reason, rest, resting place, seat, substructure, support

bask *v.* gloat, laze, lie in, loll, lounge, relax, revel *or* rejoice in, sun, sunbathe, tan, toast, wallow, warm

basket *n.* bassinet, bin, box, bushel, case, container, cradle, crate, creel, hamper, pannier, tote, wicker basket

basketball *n.* b-ball, hoops, round ball *Basketball equipment:* backboard, basketball, court, hoop, net, running shoes *Basketball Leagues:* National Basketball Association *or* NBA, National Collegiate Athletic Association *or* NCAA *Canadian Basketball teams:* Toronto Raptors, Vancouver Grizzlies *Positions in basketball:* centre, left forward, left guard, point guard, power forward, right forward, right guard, shooting guard, small forward *Scoring and procedure in basketball:* assist, bank shot, basket *or* field goal, blocking, charging, dead ball, double dribble, dribbling, force-out, foul *or* infraction, foul out, foul shot, free throw, game, goaltending, hacking, half, hook, jump ball, jumper, jump shot, lay-up, overtime, overtime period, palming, pass, personal foul, quarter, rebound, scoop shot, score, shot, shot clock, sky hook, technical foul, three-point play, three-pointer, throw-in, travelling, turnover *Nonformal:* air ball, alley-oop, bucket, dunk, slam dunk, swish

bass *adj.* deep, heavy, phat *(Nonformal)*, resonant, sepulchral – *n.* baritone, basso, basso profundo, bull fiddle, guitar, gutbucket *(Nonformal) Antonyms:* soprano, tenor, treble

bastard *adj.* **1.** baseborn, false, fatherless, illegitimate, impure, natural, out-of-wedlock **2.** bogus, counterfeit, ersatz, fake, false, pseudo, spurious *Antonyms:* accepted, legitimate – *n.* love child, moonlight child *(Newfoundland)*, natural child

baste *v.* **1.** drip, grease, lard, moisten, slather **2.** catch, fasten, sew, stitch, tack **3.** beat, lambaste, pound, trounce

bastion *n.* barbican, blockhouse, bulwark, citadel, defence, fortification, fortress, keep, mainstay, parapet, prop, protection, rock, stronghold, support, tower

bat *n.* **1.** chiroptera, *fledermaus (German)*, flying mammal, nocturnal creature **2.** belt, crack, knock, slam, smack, strike, swat, thump, thwack, whack – *v.* **1.** bang, belt, bop, crack, hit, lob, loft, rap, slam, smack, sock, strike, swat, thump, thwack, wallop, whack **2.** blink, flicker, wink

batch *n.* accumulation, aggregation, amount, array, assemblage, assortment, bunch, bundle, clump, cluster, clutch, collection, crowd, group, lot, pack, parcel, quantity, set, shipment, volume

bath *n.* ablution, cleansing, dip, dousing, gargle, lavation, scrubbing, shower, soak, soaking, soaping, sponging, tub, wash, washing

bathe *v.* clean, douche, drench, launder, rinse, scrub, soak, wash

bathos *n.* **1.** cloyishness, mushiness, sentimentality *Nonformal:* schmaltz, sugary-sweetness **2.** anticlimax, descent, letdown

bathroom *n.* bath, head, ladies' *or* men's room, lavatory, outbuilding, outhouse, powder room, privy, rest room, toilet, washroom, water closet *or* WC, women's room *Nonformal:* can, crapper, gent's, john, loo

baton *n.* bat, billyclub, club, cudgel, mace, nightstick, priest *(Nonformal)*, rod, staff, stick, truncheon, wand

battalion *n.* brigade, contingent, division, force, horde, host, legion, multitude, phalanx, throng, unit

batten *v.* board up, clamp *or* nail down, cover, fasten, fix, secure, strip, tie, tighten

batter *n.* **1.** concoction, covering, dough, mix, mixture, mush, preparation **2.** batsman, hitter, slugger – *v.* assault, bash, beat, break, bruise, buffet, clobber, crush, drub, hurt, injure, lash, pelt, pound, pummel, punch out, punish, ruin, shatter, smash, strike, thrash, trounce, wallop, wreck

battery *n.* **1.** abuse, assault, attack, beating, mayhem, mugging, thumping, violence **2.** array, batch, body, bunch, bundle, chain, cluster, group, series, set **3.** electrical cell *Kinds of electrical battery:* accumulator, alkaline, atomic, cell, dry, fuel cell, lead-acid, Leyden jar, mercury, nickel-cadmium, solar, storage, voltaic, wet cell **4.** artillery, cannon, cannonry, gunnery unit, guns, weapons

battle *n.* action, assault, attack, barrage, battle royal, blitz, bout, brawl, campaign, clash, combat, conflict, confrontation, contention, contest, crusade, dispute, donnybrook, duel, encounter, fight, foray, hostility, joust, onslaught, row, rumble, showdown, skirmish, sortie, strife, struggle, tussle, war, warfare *Antonyms:* accord, armistice, entente, peace, truce – *v.* agitate, argue, batter, beat, brawl, clamour, clash, combat, contend, contest, crusade, dispute, encounter, feud, fight, massacre, pommel, skirmish, slaughter, struggle, tug, war, wrestle

battlefield *n.* arena, battleground, combat zone, field, front, front line, war area *Canadian Battlefields:* Batoche, Beaver Dam, Châteauguay, Crysler's Farm, Cut Knife Hill, Duck Lake, Fort Beauséjour, Fort Chambly, Fort Frontenac, Fort Niagara, Frenchman's Butte, Loon Lake, Moraviantown, Plains of Abraham, Put-In-Bay, Queenston Heights, Red River, Restigouche, Ridgeway, Saint-Charles, Saint-Denis, Saint-Eustache, Ste. Foy, Stony Creek

bawdy *adj.* blue *(Nonformal)*, cheap, coarse, dirty, earthy, erotic, gross, indecent, indecorous, indelicate, lascivious, lecherous, lewd, libidinous, licentious, lustful, obscene, pornographic, ribald, risqué, rude, salacious, suggestive, vulgar *Antonyms:* chaste, decent, modest, moral, upright

bay *n.* **1.** anchorage, arm, back harbour, basin, bayou, bight, cove, estuary, fiord, firth, gulf, harbour, inlet, lagoon, loch, mouth, narrows, sound, strait, water **2.** bark, bellow, clamour, cry, growl, howl, wail, yelp **3.** alcove, bow window, compartment, niche, nook, opening, oriel, picture window, recess – *v.* bark, bellow, cry, howl, yap, yelp

bazaar *n.* agora, exchange, flea market, garage sale, market, marketplace, rummage *or* yard sale

be *v.* **1.** befall, come about, happen, occur, take place, transpire **2.** abide, act, be alive, breathe, continue, endure, exist, go on, have being, have place, hold, inhabit, last, live, move, obtain, persist, prevail, remain, rest, stand, stay, subsist, survive *Antonyms:* die, expire, pass away

beach *n.* coast, margin, oceanfront, *plage (French)*, *playa (Spanish)*, sea front, seashore, seaside, shore, shoreline, *spiaggia (Italian)*, strand, waterfront, waters' edge – *v.* run aground *or* ashore, maroon, scuttle, strand, wreck

beached *adj.* abandoned, aground, ashore, deserted, grounded, marooned, stranded, washed up

beacon *n.* alarm, alert, beam, bonfire, buoy, flare, flirrup *(Newfoundland)*, guidepost, lamp, lantern, light, lighthouse, lodestar, radar, rocket, sign, warning signal, watchtower

bead *n.* ball, blob, bubble, dab, dot, driblet, drop, droplet, globule, grain, particle, pellet, pill, shot, speck

beads *n. pl.* choker, necklace, pearls, pendant, rosary, wampum

beam *n.* **1.** beacon, emission, finger, flicker, foxfire, glare, gleam, glimmer, glint, glitter, glow, laser, light, ray, shaft, shimmer, shoot, sparkle, stream, twinkle **2.** balance, bar, board, girder, joist, piece, rafter, support, timber, truss *Kinds of beam:* I plate girder, wide flange – *v.* broadcast, disseminate, emit, give off, give out, glare, glow, radiate, send, transmit, yield

beaming *adj.* animated, cheerful, genial, grinning, happy, joyful, radiant, shining, smiling, sparkling, sunny *Antonyms:* glowering, morose, sullen, surly

bean *n.* legume *Kinds of bean:* adsuki, black, broad, butter, chickpea, coffee, fava, garbanzo, green, haricot, kidney, lentil, lima, mung, navy, northern, pink, pinto, red, scarlet runner, soya, string, wax, white

bear *n.* bruin, ursus *Kinds of bear:* black, brown, cub, grizzly, Kodiak, nanook, panda, polar, spirit *(Aboriginal)* – *v.* **1.** endure, have, hold, maintain, possess, roll with the punches *(Nonformal)*, shoulder, suffer, support, sustain, tolerate, uphold, weather, withstand *Antonyms:* abandon, drop, give in, quit, relinquish, yield **2.** beget, breed, bring forth, create, develop, engender, form, fructify, generate, invent, make, produce, propagate, provide, reproduce **3.** bring, buck, carry, convey, deliver, ferry, fetch, lug, move, pack, take, tote, transfer, transport

bearable *adj.* acceptable, admissible, allowable, endurable, livable, manageable, satisfactory, sufferable, supportable, sustainable, tolerable *Antonyms:* insufferable, intolerable, oppressive, unendurable

beard *n.* barb, bristles, brush, five-o'clock shadow *(Nonformal)*, fuzz, hair, muttonchops, prickle, stubble, whiskers *Kinds of beard:* Abe Lincoln, chin whiskers, full, Fu Manchu, goatee, Imperial, Van Dyke – *v.* brazen out, challenge, confront, defy, face, stand up to

bearded *adj.* bristly, bushy, goateed, hairy, hirsute, shaggy, stubbled, stubbly, unshaven, whiskered

bearer *n.* **1.** agent, carrier, conveyor, courier, emissary, messenger, mule *(Nonformal)*, porter, redcap, runner, transporter **2.** beneficiary, cashier, collector, consignee, payee

bearing *n.* **1.** application, connection, import, meaning, pertinence, reference, relation, relevance, significance, weight *Antonyms:* inconsequence, irrelevance, non sequitur **2.** air, aspect, attitude, behaviour, carriage, conduct, demeanour, display, front, look, manner, mien, poise, pose **3.** aim, alignment, course, direction, heading, orientation, tack **4.** axis, caster, fulcrum, pivot, swivel **5.** braving, brooking, sustaining, tolerating

beast *n.* **1.** animal, creature, mammal *Nonformal:* beastie, critter, varmint **2.** barbarian, brute, hellcat, monster, savage

beastly *adj.* abominable, animal, awful, barbarous, base, bestial, boorish, brutal, brutish, carnal, coarse, cruel, degraded, depraved, disgusting, feral, foul, gluttonous, gross, inhuman, irrational, loathsome, low, mean, monstrous, nasty, obscene, offensive, repulsive, rotten, sadistic, savage, terrible, unclean, unpleasant, vile, vulgar *Antonyms:* agreeable, fine, good, humane, sensitive

beat *adj.* exhausted, fatigued, tired, wearied, weary, worn-out – *n.* **1.** hit, lash, punch, shake, slap, strike, swing, thump **2.** b.p.m. *(Nonformal)*, cadence, flow, flutter, meter, oscillation, palpitation, pulsation, pulse, rhythm, throb, thump **3.** assignment, circuit, course, district, neighbourhood, orbit, path, patrol, precinct, responsibility, rounds, route, run, tour – *v.* **1.** bang, bash, bat, batter, belt, box, break, bruise, buffet, cane, clout, club, crush, flagellate, flail, flog, hammer, hit, knead, knock, lash, lick, mash, maul, pelt, pound, punish, ram, rap, slap, slug, smack, spank, stir, strike, swat, thrash, thump, thwack, trounce, wallop, whale, whip **2.** flicker, flop, flutter, jounce, palpitate, pulse, ripple, throb, tremble, vibrate, writhe **3.** *blanchir (French)*, defeat, eclipse, edge out *(Nonformal)*, outdo, outstrip, overwhelm, pulverize, pummel, shellac, smite, surpass, trounce, vanquish *Antonyms:* fail, lose, surrender **4.** fashion, forge, form, hammer, model, shape, work **5.** aerate, stir, whip, whisk

beaten *adj.* **1.** bested, conquered, cowed, crushed, defeated, frustrated, humbled, licked, mastered, overpowered, overthrown, overwhelmed, routed, thwarted, trounced, vanquished, worsted **2.** aerated, blended, bubbly, churned, creamy, foamy, frothy, mixed, stirred, whipped, whisked **3.** forged, formed, hammered, milled, pounded, rolled, shaped, stamped, tamped, tramped, worked **4.** drawn, fatigued, footsore, haggard, hollow-eyed, saddlesore *Antonyms:* energized, refreshed

beatification *n.* deification, elevation, enchantment, exultation, felicity, glorification, intoxication, rapture

beatnik *n.* beat, Bohemian, dropout *Nonformal:* deadbeat, deadhead, flower child, hippie, hipster, longhair

beau *n.* **1.** admirer, beloved, boyfriend, escort, fiancé, flame, inamorato, love, lover, main squeeze *(Nonformal)*, paramour, squire, steady, suitor, swain, sweetheart, true love **2.** Beau Brummell, blade, clotheshorse, coxcomb, dandy, fashion plate, fop, fribble, popinjay, swell *(Nonformal)*

beautiful *adj.* aesthetic, alluring, appealing, artful, artistic, attractive, awesome, beauteous, becoming, *bella (Italian)*, bewitching, blooming, breathtaking, captivating, charming, comely, cosmetic, dazzling, decorative, divine, dramatic, elegant, enchanting, exciting, exquisite, fair, fine, good-looking, gorgeous, graceful, grand, handsome, harmonious, heart-stirring, ideal, inspiring, lovely, magnificent, marvellous, moving, musical, ornamental, photogenic, picturesque, pleasing, pretty, radiant, ravishing, refined, satisfying, statuesque, stimulating, stunning, stylish, sublime, tasteful, thrilling, winsome *French:* beau, belle *Nonformal:* bonny, dishy *Antonyms:* frightful, hideous, odious, repulsive, unattractive

beautifully *adv.* alluringly, appealingly, attractively, charmingly, delightfully, divinely, elegantly, entrancingly, excellently, exquisitely, gorgeously, gracefully, handsomely, ideally, magnificently, pleasingly, splendidly, tastefully, wonderfully *Antonyms:* grotesquely, horribly, wretchedly

beautify *v.* adorn, bedeck, burnish, deck out, decorate, doll *or* dress *or* make up, embellish, enhance, festoon, garnish, gild, glamorize, grace, groom, improve, ornament, preen, prettify, smooth, sort, tease, untangle *Nonformal:* gussy *or* spiff *or* spruce up *Antonyms:* disfigure, mar, soil

beauty *n.* **1.** allure, attraction, bloom, brightness, charm, class, comeliness, elegance, exquisiteness, fairness, glamour, glory, good looks, gorgeousness, handsomeness, loveliness, lustre, magnificence, majesty, pageantry, pulchritude, radiance, resplendence, richness, splendour, sumptuousness *Antonyms:* detraction, disadvantage, flaw, ugliness, unseemliness **2.** belle, charmer, dream, enchantress, femme fatale, goddess, knockout, lovely, ornament, seductress, siren, Venus, vision *Nonformal:* beaut, cat's pyjamas, corker, crackerjack, dandy, dilly, doozy, eyeful, good-looker, humdinger, knockout, looker, stunner *Antonyms:* dowd, frump **3.** advantage, appeal, attractiveness, benefit, salient *or* selling *or* strong point, strength

becalm *v.* calm, deprive of wind, lull, soothe, stall, still, strand *Antonyms:* freshen, stir, whip up

because *prep.* as, being, considering, due to, inasmuch as, in that, on account of, owing to, since, through, whereas *Antonyms:* although, despite

beckon *v.* **1.** bid, call, call forth *or* out, coax, entice, gesture, invite, summon **2.** bait, beguile, charm, lure, tease, tempt, tickle one's fancy *(Nonformal) Antonyms:* cast off, repel

become *v.* **1.** evolve, change into, convert, develop into, emerge as, grow into, incline, mature, metamorphose, morph *(Nonformal)*, shift, turn into *or* out **2.** behoove, enhance, fit, flatter, suit *Antonyms:* detract, take away

becoming *adj.* attractive, beautiful, befitting, chic, comely, compatible, coordinated, correct, decorous, enhancing, fair, fit, fitting, flattering, in keeping, neat, nice, presentable, pretty, proper, seemly, suitable, tasteful, well-chosen *Antonyms:* improper, out of line, ugly, unsuitable

bed *n.* **1.** area, border, frame, garden, ground, piece, plot, row, strip **2.** bedstead, furniture *Kinds of bed:* bassinet, bedroll, berth, box spring, bunk, cot, couch, cradle, crib, davenport, divan, double, foldaway, folding, full-size, futon, gurney, hammock, hospital, king-size, mattress, Murphy *(Trademark)*, pallet, platform, poster, queen-size, rollaway, single, stretcher, tatami mat, truckle, trundle, twin, waterbed **3.** basis, bedrock, bottom, footing, foundation, ground, groundwork, platform, rest, seat, substratum **4.** deposit, load, seam, vein – *v.* **1.** ground, implant, inlay, insert, plant **2.** entice, seduce, sleep with

bedazzle *v.* astound, bewilder, blind, captivate, charm, confuse, daze, dazzle, dumfound, enchant, enthrall, impress, overwhelm, stagger, stun

bedding *n.* bedclothes, bedspread, blankets, comforter, counterpane, covers, duvet, eiderdown, pillowcases, quilt, sheets

bedevil *v.* **1.** harangue, harass, hector, hound, pester, provoke, torment, torture **2.** befuddle, bewitch, confound, discombobulate, entice, hex, hypnotize, mesmerize, muddle, puzzle, rattle **3.** ensnare, entangle, hamper, trip up

bedlam *n.* chaos, clamour, commotion, confusion, din, disquiet, disquietude, furor, hubbub, madhouse, maelstrom, noise, pandemonium, racket, shambles, tumult, turmoil, uproar *Antonyms:* order, peace, tranquility

bedraggled *adj.* dishevelled, dirty, messy, scruffy, sloppy, slovenly, unclean, unkempt *Antonyms:* elegant, spiffy *(Nonformal)*

beef *n.* **1.** cattle, flesh, steak *Common cuts of beef:* brisket, chuck, flank, loin, plate, rib, round, rump, shank, sirloin, short rib *Beef foods:* extract, boiled, bouillon, bully, chipped, corned, dried, ground round, hamburger, jerky, Kobe, pastrami, prime rib, roast, salt, smoked, stewing, suet, tea **2.** argument, bellyache, complaint, grievance, gripe, protest – *v.* bitch, complain, crab, gripe, grouse, grumble, protest, squawk, whine, yammer *Antonyms:* accept, applaud, commend

beefy *adj.* burly, corpulent, fat, fleshy, massive, muscular, portly, powerful, stalwart, stocky, strapping *Antonyms:* lithe, slender, wiry

beer *n.* fermented brew *Kinds of beer:* ale, amber brew, bitter, bock, brown cream ale, dark, home brew, ice, lager, light, malt, malt liquor, mead, pilsner, porter, pulque, red, spruce, stout, strong, wheat, weiss *Nonformal:* barley sandwich, bottle, brewski, cold one, frosty, suds, wobbly pop

befall *v.* betide, break, come off, develop, ensue, gel, happen, materialize, occur, take place, transpire

befitting *adj.* appropriate, apt, *comme il faut (French)*, conforming, correct, decent, decorous, fit, fitting, germane, just, pertinent, proper, right, seemly, suitable *Antonyms:* improper, inappropriate, irrelevant, unfit, wrong

before *adv.* ahead, back, before present, earlier, fore, former, formerly, forward, gone, gone by, heretofore, in advance, in front, past, previous, previously, since, sooner *Antonyms:* after, behind, later – *prep.* ahead of, ante, antecedent to, earlier than, ere, in advance of, in front of, preceding, previous to, prior to, since, subsequent to

beforehand *adv.* ahead, already, ante, antecedently, before, before now, earlier, early, fore, in advance, in anticipation, in the past, previous, previously, sooner *Antonyms:* belatedly, afterwards

befriend *v.* advise, aid, assist, benefit, encourage, enhance, favour, help, shake hands with, side with, socialize with, stand by, support, sustain, uphold, welcome *Nonformal:* take a shine to, take up with

beg *v.* ask, beseech, demand, entreat, hustle, implore, panhandle, plead, solicit, supplicate *Nonformal:* mooch, sponge

beget *v.* afford, breed, bring, bring about, cause, create, effect, engender, father, generate, get, mother, multiply, occasion, procreate, produce, propagate, reproduce, result in, sire *Antonyms:* abort, cancel, nullify

beggar *n.* bum, cadger, deadbeat, dependent, destitute, freeloader, hobo, indigent, mendicant, moocher, panhandler, pauper, scrounger, street person, supplicant, tramp, vagabond, vagrant *Nonformal:* rubby, sponge

begin *v.* activate, actualize, appear, arise, break ground, bring about, bud, cause, come forth, commence, create, derive from, effect, emanate, embark on, emerge, enter, establish, found, generate, germinate, get cracking *(Nonformal)*, happen, inaugurate, induce, initiate, instigate, institute, introduce, issue forth, launch, lead, make, motivate, occur, originate, prepare, proceed from, produce, result from, rise, spring, sprout, start, trigger, undertake *Antonyms:* cease, complete, end, finish, stop, terminate

beginner *n.* **1.** amateur, apprentice, fledgling, freshman, greenhorn *(Nonformal)*, learner, neophyte, newcomer, novice, novitiate, probationer, recruit, starter, student, trainee *Antonyms:* authority, expert, master, professional, veteran **2.** initiator, instigator, prime mover, source

beginning *adj.* inaugural, initial, primeval, rudimentary – *n.* antecedent, basis, birth, commencement, conception, creation, dawn, embryo, formation, fount, genesis, inauguration, inception, induction, infancy, initiation, introduction, onset, opening, origin, preface, preliminary, prelude, preparation, prologue, propagation, provenance, root, rudiment, source, start, stem, threshold *Antonyms:* closing, completion, ending, finish, termination

begrudge *v.* be jealous *or* reluctant, covet, envy, grudge, resent, turn green *(Nonformal) Antonyms:* celebrate, rejoice, take pleasure in

beguile *v.* **1.** amuse, attract, charm, cheer, delight, distract, divert, engross, entertain, entice, interest, occupy *Nonformal:* tickle, tickle pink **2.** betray, bluff, cheat, deceive, delude, double-cross, dupe, finesse, fool, hoodwink, jockey, lure, manipulate, mislead, seduce, take in, trick *Nonformal:* bamboozle, con, diddle, flimflam, scam, string along, suck in *Antonyms:* alert, enlighten, put right

behave *v.* **1.** be civil *or* nice *or* orderly, obey *Nonformal:* shape up, tow the line **2.** comport, conduct, control, manage, react

behaviour *n.* action, air, aspect, attitude, bearing, carriage, comportment, conduct, decorum, demeanour, deportment, etiquette, form, manner, manners, mien, poise, presence, style, tact, tone, turn, way, ways

behead *v.* axe, chop, cut, cut down, decapitate, execute, fell, guillotine, head, hew, lop off

behest *n.* bidding, charge, command, decree, demand, dictate, direction, expressed desire, injunction, instruction, mandate, order, request, wish, word *Commonly misused:* **bequest**

behind *adv.* **1.** after, afterwards, following, next, subsequently, trailing **2.** backward, behindhand, behind schedule *or* time, belated, delayed, dilatory, in arrears, laggard, late, off the pace, overdue, slow, sluggish, tardy – *n.* back, backside, bottom, butt, buttocks, *derrière (French),* gluteus maximus, haunches, hind end, hindquarters, posterior, rear, rump, seat, tail *Nonformal:* arse, ass, bum, caboose, duff, fanny, keister, tush – *prep.* **1.** backing, following, for, in agreement, subsequent to, supporting **2.** causing, initiating, instigating, responsible for

behold *v.* discern, espy, eye, eyeball, note, notice, observe, perceive, peruse, regard, scan, see, spot, spy, survey, view, watch, witness *Antonyms:* ignore, pass by

beholden *adj.* bound, grateful, indebted, obligated, obliged, owing, responsible, thankful *Antonyms:* thankless, ungrateful

beige *adj. & n.* brown, buff, camel, caramel, champagne, cinnamon, coffee, cream, ecru, fawn, khaki, mushroom, neutral, oatmeal, sand, tan – *adj.* boring, conservative, drab, dull, straitlaced

being *n.* **1.** character, entity, essence, individuality, marrow, nature, personality, quintessence, self, soul, spirit, substance, texture **2.** animal, beast, body, conscious entity, creature, entity, human, human being, individual, living thing, man, mortal, organism, person, personage, soul, woman **3.** existence, life, reality

belabour *v.* abuse, assail, badger, batter, berate, buffet, castigate, drub, flay, flog, thrash *Nonformal:* beat to death, work over *Antonyms:* compliment, praise *Commonly misused:* **beleaguer**

belated *adj.* delayed, late, long-delayed, long-in-coming, overdue, remiss, slow, tardy *Antonyms:* prompt, timely

belch *n.* burp, gas, hiccup – *v.* burp, discharge, disgorge, emit, erupt, give off, gush, hiccup, repeat, vent, vomit

beleaguer *v.* assail, beset, besiege, block, bombard, corral, hem in, hurry, surround *Antonyms:* dismiss, free, release, set free *Commonly misused:* **belabour**

belfry *n.* bell tower, campanile, carillon, cupola, dome, head, minaret, spire, steeple, tower, turret

belie *v.* **1.** confute, contradict, controvert, deny, disaffirm, disagree, disprove, gainsay, negate, oppose, repudiate *Antonyms:* acknowledge, attest to, support **2.** colour, conceal, deceive, disguise, distort, falsify, garble, gloss over, hide, mislead, misrepresent, pervert, trump up, twist, warp

belief *n.* acceptance, acknowledgment, admission, adoption, affirmation, assurance, attitude, axiom, basis, bias, certitude, code, concept, conception, conjecture, conviction, credence, credo, creed, doctrine, estimation, faith, foundation, gospel, grounds, hope, hypothesis, idea, ideal, ideology, inference, interpretation, intuition, keystone, knowledge, maxim, mindset, opinion, outlook, persuasion, position, precept, premise, profession, rationale, rule, school, sentiment, stance, stand, standpoint, supposition, sureness, teaching, tenet, theory, thesis, thinking, thought, trust, understanding, view, viewpoint *Antonyms:* distrust, doubt, dubiety, incredulity, scepticism

believable *adj.* aboveboard, authentic, conceivable, convincing, credible, imaginable, impressive, likely, persuasive, plausible, possible, presumable, presumptive, probable, rational, reasonable, reliable, satisfying, straight, supposable, tenable, tried, trustworthy, trusty, unquestionable *Antonyms:* dubious, implausible, questionable, unacceptable

believe *v.* accept, affirm, assume, be observant *or* pious, conclude, consider, countenance, credit, deduce, deem, esteem, expect, favour, feel, figure, find, gather, have faith, hold, hypothesize, imagine, infer, intuit, judge, know, maintain, posit, postulate, presume, presuppose, rate, reckon, recognize, regard, rely, see, sense, suppose, take, think, trust, understand, view, visualize *Nonformal:* bet on, buy, have a hunch, swallow *Antonyms:* distrust, doubt, know, question

believer *n.* adherent, churchgoer, communicant, convert, devotee, disciple, doctrinaire, dogmatist, follower, proselyte, religious person, theist, zealot *Antonyms:* agnostic, atheist, heretic, nihilist

belittle *v.* abuse, attack, calumniate, censure, condemn, criticize, decry, defame, denigrate, deplore, deprecate, depreciate, deride, detract, diminish, discount, discredit, disfavour, disparage, downgrade, downplay, expostulate, fault, humble, lament, lower, malign, minimize, revile, ridicule, run *or* shoot *or* tear down, scoff at, scorn, slander, slight, traduce, underestimate, underrate, undervalue *Nonformal:* knock, pan, roast *Antonyms:* elevate, exalt, magnify, praise, vaunt

bell *n.* instrument *Kinds of bell:* alarm, Angelus, breakfast, carillon, chime, church, clock chime, cowbell, death *or* passing, dinner, doorbell, door chime, fire, gong, hand, harness, Sanctus, school, sheep, signal, sleigh, telephone, tintinnabulum, tocsin, triangle

bellicose *adj.* **1.** aggressive, antagonistic, combative, hawkish, livid, militant, provocative, pugnacious, rabid, volcanic, warlike, warmongering *Antonyms:* dovelike, peaceful **2.** cantankerous, cranky, fractious, irritable, petulant, short-fused, testy *Antonyms:* congenial, compliant, docile, friendly

belligerent *adj.* aggressive, antagonistic, ardent, argumentative, battling, bellicose, bitchy, cantankerous, combative, contentious, fierce, fighting, hostile, hot-tempered, militant, obstinate, pugilistic, quarrelsome, scrappy, truculent, warlike *Nonformal:* flip, in-your-face, ornery *Antonyms:* amicable, benign, conciliatory, harmonious, nonviolent

bellwether *n.* augur, forerunner, harbinger, herald, precursor, predecessor, prophet, sign, vanguard, warning

belly *n.* gut, navel, ponch, pot, stomach *Nonformal:* Molson muscle, spare tire – *v.* balloon, bloat, distend, expand, swell *Antonyms:* dwindle, shrivel, wither

belong *v.* **1.** apply, associate, be akin, bear, befit, concern, correlate, correspond, fit, go with, harmonize, pertain, relate, reside, suit, touch, vest *Antonyms:* alienate, exclude **2.** affiliate, fit in, hang around *or* run with, owe allegiance *or* support

belonging *n.* acceptance, affinity, association, attachment, fellowship, inclusion, kinship, loyalty, relevance, security, unity *Antonyms:* alienation, estrangement

belongings *n. pl.* accoutrements, appurtenances, assets, bits and pieces *(British)*, chattels, effects, gear, goods, paraphernalia, personal property, possessions, property, stuff *(Nonformal)*

beloved *adj.* admired, adored, cared for, cherished, darling, dear, dearest, endeared, esteemed, favourite, hallowed, highly regarded *or* valued, idolized, loved, popular, precious, prized, respected, revered, sweet, treasured, venerated, well-liked, worshiped *Antonyms:* disparaged, vilified – *n.* darling, dear, dearest, idol, inamorato, love, lover, significant other, sweetheart, treasure, true love

below *adj.* earthbound, earthly, mortal, mundane, terrene, terrestrial *Antonyms:* celestial, transcendent – *adv.* below ground, submerged, underground, underlying – *prep.* beneath, inferior to, less than, lower than, subordinate to, subservient to, under, underneath, unworthy of

belt *n.* **1.** band, cummerbund, girdle, sash, strap, string, waistband **2.** area, district, land, layer, meridian, region, stretch, swath, territory, tract, zone – *v.* **1.** bash, bat, biff, blast, blow, bop, clobber, hit, slam, slug, smack, smash, sock, strap, switch, wallop, whip **2.** band, bind, encircle, encompass, envision, strap, surround

bemoan *v.* bay, bewail, complain, deplore, greet *(Scottish)*, grieve *or* weep for, lament, mourn, pine for, regret, rue, sop *Antonyms:* celebrate, make merry, rejoice

bemused *adj.* abstracted, dazed, engrossed, oblivious, preoccupied, stupefied *Nonformal:* head in the clouds, on cloud nine, tipsy, under the influence, woolgathering *Antonyms:* alert, attentive, lucid, sober

bench *n.* **1.** bank, bleacher, chair, lawn seat, pew, seat, settee **2.** board, console, counter, desk, easel, ledge, shelf, table, trestle, workbench, work table **3.** court, courtroom, judiciary, judges, magistrate, the bar, tribunal – *v.* penalize, make one, ride the pine *(Nonformal)*, sideline, suspend, take out of play

benchmark *n.* criterion, gauge, goal, indicator, measure, reference, standard, touchstone, yardstick

bend *n.* angle, arc, bow, corner, crook, curvature, curve, deflection, deviation, flexure, hook, lean, loop, round, sag, shift, tack, tilt, turn, twist – *v.* **1.** angle away *or* off, arch, bow, buckle, camber, capitulate, careen, circle, contort, crimp, crinkle, crook, crouch, curl, curve, deflect, deform, detour, double, flex, incline, lean, loop, round, spiral, stoop, swerve, tilt, turn, twist, veer, verge, warp, waver, yaw **2.** bring to terms, change, compel, direct, mould, overwhelm, persuade, pervert, shape, subdue, submit, sway, vanquish, yield *Antonyms:* free up, loosen, unchain

beneath *adv.* below deck *or* ground, subterraneously, underground, underneath – *prep.* below, inferior to, less than, lower than, subject to, subordinate to, under, underneath, unworthy of

benediction *n.* beatitude, benedicite, blessing, consecration, favour, grace, gratitude, invocation, *Kaddish (Judaism)*, praise, prayer, sanctification, thanks, thanksgiving *Antonyms:* damnation, excommunication

benefactor *n.* aid, angel, assistant, backer, contributor, donor, humanitarian, patron, philanthropist, promoter, protector, sponsor, subsidizer, sugar daddy *(Nonformal)*, supporter *Commonly misused:* **beneficiary**

beneficence *n.* **1.** altruism, brotherly *or* sisterly love, chivalry, humanitarianism **2.** alms, donation, largesse, munificence, offertory, succour *Antonym:* parsimony *Commonly misused:* **benevolence**

beneficial *adj.* advantageous, benign, constructive, favourable, favouring, good, healing, healthful, helpful, invigorating, profitable, propitious, restorative, salubrious, salutary, serviceable, towardly, useful, valuable, wholesome, worthy *Antonyms:* detrimental, harmful, pernicious, toxic

beneficiary *n.* charity case, grantee, heir, heiress, inheritor, legatee, payee, pensioner, possessor, receiver, recipient, survivor *Commonly misused:* **benefactor**

benefit *n.* **1.** account, advantage, asset, assistance, avail, betterment, favour, gain, good, profit, prosperity, use, worth **2.** aid, blessing, extras, free lunch *(Nonformal)*, godsend, grant, help, perk, subvention, welfare *Government:* baby bonus, Employment Insurance *or* EI, pension, pogey *(Nonformal)*, old age pension, veterans' allowance **3.** ball, bazaar, charitable affair, charity performance, concert, dance, event, exhibition, fair, fete, raffle – *v.* advance, aid, ameliorate, assist, avail, better, build, contribute to, favour, further, help, improve, profit, promote, relieve, serve, succour, work for *Antonyms:* damage, deprive, harm, impair

benevolence *n.* amity, charity, clemency, compassion, empathy, feeling, friendliness, friendship, generosity, goodness, good will, humanity, kindheartedness, kindness, sympathy *Antonyms:* ill will, malevolence, selfishness *Commonly misused:* **beneficence**

benevolent *adj.* **1.** altruistic, big-hearted, bountiful, caring, chivalrous, compassionate, considerate, generous, helpful, humane, humanitarian, kind, kindhearted, liberal, magnanimous, philanthropic, tenderhearted, warmhearted, well-disposed *Antonyms:* malignant, vicious **2.** charitable, not-for-profit, eleemosynary *Antonyms:* greedy, miserly, self-serving

benign *adj.* **1.** amiable, compassionate, complaisant, compliant, friendly, generous, genial, gentle, good, good-hearted, gracious, kind, kindly, merciful, obliging, sympathetic, yielding **2.** advantageous, auspicious, beneficent, bright, charitable, encouraging, favourable, fortunate, good, lucky, merciful, propitious, salutary *Antonyms:* harsh, hateful, malicious, severe **3.** curable, harmless, limited, nonrecurring, remediable, slight *Antonyms:* inoperable, malignant, terminal **4.** balmy, favourable, gentle, mild, pleasant, refreshing, temperate, warm *Antonyms:* biting, icy, terrible

bent *adj.* **1.** angled, arched, bowed, contorted, crooked, curved, curvilinear, drooping, droopy, hooked, humped, hunched, inclined, limp, looped, round, rounded, sinuous, slouchy, slumped, stooped, twined, twisted, warped, wilted *Antonyms:* aligned, erect, even, straight, true **2.** bound, decided, determined, disposed, inclined, intent, leaning, predisposed, resolute, set – *n.* ability, aim, aptitude, disposition, facility, faculty, flair, forte, genius, gift, inclination, knack, mindset, penchant, predilection, predisposition, preference, proclivity, propensity, set, tack, talent, tendency, weakness for *Nonformal:* bag, druthers, groove, head, nose for, thing *or* thing for

bequeath *v.* bestow, commit, divvy up *(Nonformal)*, endow, entrust, give, grant, hand down *or* on, impart, leave to, pass on, transmit, will

bequest *n.* bequeathment, bestowal, device, dower, endowment, estate, gift, heritage, inheritance, legacy, settlement, testament, trust *Commonly misused:* **behest**

berate *v.* belittle, chastise, chide, defame, denigrate, harangue, make fun of, rebuke, revile, scold, scorn, skivver *(P.E.I.)*, upbraid *Nonformal:* chew out, do a hatchet job on, growl, light into, read out, scorch *Antonyms:* compliment, extol, recommend

bereavement *n.* deprivation, distress, grief, loss, misery, misfortune, mourning, sorrow, tribulation, woe

bereft *adj.* **1.** bereaved, fatherless *or* motherless, lacking, minus, orphaned, parentless, without **2.** deprived *or* devoid *or* robbed of, destitute, dispossessed, fleeced, impoverished, in want of, indigent, needy, out-of-pocket, poverty-stricken, shorn, wanting,

berm *n.* barrier, hillock, ledge, mound, shelf, shoulder, slope

berry *n.* fruit, hip, kernel, seed *Kinds of berry:* bakeapple, bearberry, bilberry, blackberry, black raspberry, blueberry, boysenberry, brambleberry, candleberry, capillaire *(Newfoundland)*, cloudberry, cranberry, dewberry, dogberry *(Atlantic provinces)*, elderberry, gooseberry, ground cherry, huckleberry, juniper, lingonberry, loganberry, mulberry, pigeon berry, raspberry, saskatoon, soapolallie, squawberry, strawberry, teaberry, whortleberry

berserk *adj.* frantic, frenzied, insane, mad, maniacal, out-of-control *(Nonformal)*, rabid, raging, raving, violent, wild *Antonyms:* calm, lucid, normal, sane

berth *n.* **1.** anchorage, bed, bedroom, billet, bunk, compartment, cot, dock, hammock, haven, harbour, jetty, levee, mooring, pier, port, quay, slip, wharf **2.** appointment, capacity, connection, employment, job, living, office, place, post, profession, responsibility, situation, spot, tenure – *v.* billet, bunk, cast anchor, lodge, moor, occupy, stay, tied up *Antonyms:* depart, launch, set sail

beseech *v.* appeal, beg, entreat, go on one's knees, implore, importune, petition, plead, pray, solicit, supplicate

beset *adj.* chivvied, harried, hounded, infested, lousy *or* plagued with, tormented – *v.* assail, attack, bedevil, beleaguer, besiege, dog, entangle, harass, hassle, henpeck, invade, nag, overrun, perplex, pester, plague, storm, strike, surround

beside *prep.* abreast, adjacent, adjoining, alongside, aside, bordering, by, close, close upon, connected with, contiguous, in juxtaposition, near, nearby, neck-and-neck, neighbouring, next to, nigh, opposite, overlooking, round, verging on *or* with *Antonyms:* afar, distant, removed *Commonly misused:* **besides**

besides *adv.* added to, additionally, along with, and don't forget, apart from, aside from, as well, beyond, conjointly, else, exceeding, extra, further, furthermore, likewise, moreover, more than, not counting, other than, otherwise, plus, secondly, supplementarily, together with, too – *prep.* apart, but, except, excluding, other than, outside of, save, without *Commonly misused:* **beside**

besiege *v.* **1.** assail, beleaguer, beset, buttonhole, pester, plague, nag *Nonformal:* bug, come at from all sides, hound, work over **2.** attack, crowd, encircle, encompass, hem in, lay seige to, shut in, surround, trap

besmirch *v.* asperse, calumniate, defame, defile, impugn, malign, slander, slur, soil, stain, sully, vilify *Nonformal:* bad mouth, dis, drag through the mud, slam

besmirched *adj.* befouled, blemished, dishonoured, fouled, soiled, stained, sullied, tainted, tarnished *Antonyms:* honourable, impeccable, simon pure

besotted *adj.* **1.** drunk, inebriate, tipsy, under the influence *Nonformal:* hammered, jiggered, loaded, potted **2.** befuddled, brainless, fatuous, foolish, idiotic, stupid **3.** fixated, hung up on, infatuated, obsessed, possessed *Antonyms:* apathetic, dispassionate, indifferent

best *adj.* **1.** champion, crack, excellent, first, greatest, highest, incomparable, inimitable, matchless, outstanding, peerless, sterling, superlative, supreme, unequalled **2.** capital, choicest, finest, most advantageous *or* desireable *or* fitting, optimum, paramount, preferred, premium, primo *(Nonformal)*, terrific **3.** chief, biggest, greater, largest, most of **4.** leading, most likely, prime – *adv.* advantageously, attractively, creditably, excellently, extremely, gloriously, greatly, honourably, illustriously, magnanimously, most deeply, most fortunately, most fully, most highly, most sincerely – *n.* choice, cream, elite, favourite, finest, first flower, gem, model, nonpareil, paragon, pick, prime, prize, select, top – *v.* conquer, defeat, lick *(Nonformal)*, outclass, overcome, trounce, vanquish

bestial *adj.* **1.** barbarous, brutish, feral, instinctual, primitive, savage *Antonyms:* civilized, humane **2.** base, debauched, depraved, gross, immoral, lascivious, lewd, obscene, raunchy *Antonyms:* demure, pious, wholesome

bestow *v.* accord, apportion, award, bequeath, cede, commit, confer, donate, endow, entrust, favour, gift, give, grant, hand out, impart, lavish, offer, present, vouchsafe *Antonyms:* acquire, earn, net, obtain, secure

bet *n.* ante, chance, cover, dice, gamble, game, hazard, long shot, odds, play, pledge, raffle, risk, speculation, stake, sure thing *(Nonformal)*, sweepstakes, venture, wager *Kinds of horse racing bet:* box, daily double, exactor, on the nose *(Nonformal)*, place, quinella, rolling pick three, show, super seven, triactor, trifecta, win, win four – *v.* ante up, dice, gamble, game, hazard, risk, set, speculate, take a flyer *(Nonformal)*, toss up, trust, venture, wager

bête noire *n.* adversary, antagonist, bane, bugaboo, bugbear, devil, enemy, foe, nemesis, pain, pest, thorn in the side

betray *v.* **1.** abandon, break trust, commit treason, cross, deceive, double-cross, forsake, inform on, jilt, let down, mislead, sell out, turn in, turn informer, two-time *Antonyms:* champion, stand behind **2.** blurt out, disclose, divulge, evince, give away, inform, lay bare, make known, reveal, tell, uncover, unmask *Nonformal:* blow the whistle on, finger, fink, knife, rat, sing, snitch, squeal, tattle *Antonyms:* keep faith, remain silent

betrayal *n.* **1.** chicanery, deception, dishonesty, disloyalty, double-cross *or* -dealing, duplicity, falseness, giveaway, letdown, sellout, treachery, treason, trickery, unfaithfulness *Antonyms:* allegiance, devotion, fealty **2.** disclosure, divulgence, revelation *Nonformal:* ratting, singing, snitching, squealing *Antonyms:* guarding, preserving, safeguarding

betroth *v.* become engaged, bind, commit, contract, engage, jump the broom *(Nonformal)*, plight, promise, troth, vow

betrothal *n.* betrothing, covenant, engagement, espousal, handfast, promise, troth, vow *Antonyms:* annulment, divorce

better *adj.* **1.** best, bigger, exceeding, excellent, finer, greater, higher quality, larger, largest, longer, more, more select *or* useful *or* valuable, preferred, preponderant, prominent, superior, weightier, worthier *Antonyms:* inferior, shoddy **2.** fitter, healthier, improved, improving, mending, progressing, recovered, recovering, stronger, well *Antonyms:* unhealthy, worse – *adv.* excellently, more advantageously *or* attractively *or* competently *or* completely, *or* effectively *or* thoroughly, preferably *Nonformal*: fine, great *Antonyms:* inferior, lesser, substandard – *v.* advance, ameliorate, amend, correct, enhance, exceed, forward, further, help, improve, mend, mitigate, outshine, outstrip, promote, raise, rectify, refine, reform, revamp, spruce up, surpass, top, transcend *Antonyms:* depress, devaluate, impoverish, lessen, worsen

betterment *n.* advancement, amelioration, edification, improvement, progress, prosperity, upgrading *Antonyms:* impoverishment, recession, relapse

between *prep.* amid, amidst, among, at intervals, betwixt, bounded by, centrally located, enclosed by, halfway, in, inserted, mid, middle, midway, separating, surrounded by

bevel *adj.* canted, oblique, slanted, sloped – *n.* diagonal, slope, tilt – *v.* angle, cant, cut, flute, mitre, slant

beverage *n.* cooler, draft, drink, drinkable, home brew, libation, liquid, liquid refreshment, liquor, pop, potable, potation, soda, stimulant, swill, thirst quencher

bevy *n.* assembly, band, bunch, cluster, collection, company, covey, crew, crowd, flock, gaggle, galaxy, gathering, party, phalanx, swarm, throng, troupe

bewail *v.* bemoan, cry, deplore, grieve for, lament, moan, mourn, regret, repent, rue, wail, weep over *Nonformal:* eat one's heart out, sing the blues *Antonyms:* celebrate, revel

beware *v.* attend, avoid, be careful *or* cautious *or* wary, guard, guard against, heed, keep an eye peeled *(Nonformal)*, mind, shun, take care, watch out

bewilder *v.* addle, baffle, befuddle, bemuse, bother, confound, confuse, daze, disconcert, disorient, distract, dumfound, fluster, mix up, muddle, mystify, paralyze, perplex, puzzle, rattle, stump, stun, stupefy, throw off, upset *Nonformal*: boggle, buffalo, discombobulate, floor, flummox, mess with one's head, psych out, shake, snow

bewildered *adj.* agog, astounded, awed, awestruck, baffled, confused, dazed, disconcerted, dizzy, dumfounded, flabbergasted, giddy, muddled, mystified, nonplused, perplexed, puzzled, rattled, speechless, startled, stunned, stupefied, surprised, thrown, thunderstruck, uncertain, unglued *Nonformal:* bowled over, floored *Antonyms:* unfazed, unflappable, unruffled

bewitch *v.* **1.** allure, attract, beguile, captivate, capture, charm, control, dazzle, draw, enchant, enrapture, enthral, entrance, fascinate, hex, hypnotize, send, slay, spell, spellbind, tantalize, tickle pink *(Nonformal) Antonyms:* exasperate, irritate, vex **2.** bedevil, demonize, hagride, hex, jinx, obsess, plague, possess, put the whammy on *(Nonformal)*, witch

bewitched *adj.* captivated, charmed, enamoured, enchanted, enraptured, entranced, fascinated, hooked, mesmerized, possessed, spellbound, transformed *Nonformal:* moonstruck, starry-eyed *Antonyms:* disgusted, repulsed

bewitchment *n.* enchantment, entrancement, obsession, possession, witchery

beyond *adv.* down the road, further on, over there – *prep.* above, across, after, ahead, apart from, away from, before, behind, besides, clear of, farther, free of, further, hyper, moreover, more remote, outside, over, past, remote, superior to, without, yonder

bias *n.* **1.** attitude, bent, bigotry, discrimination, disposition, favouritism, inequity, intolerance, jaundice, leaning, mind-set, one-sidedness, partiality, predilection, predisposition, prejudice, proclivity, proneness, standpoint, swerving, tendency, tilt, 'tude *(Nonformal)*, turn, viewpoint *Antonyms:* equality, fairness, impartiality, neutrality, objectivity **2.** angle, cant, cross, fabric, inclination, slant – *v.* distort, favour, incline, influence, prejudice, slant, sway, twist, warp, weight

bible *n.* authority, guidebook, handbook, manual, pharmacopoeia, primer, text

Bible *n.* God's word, Holy Bible, Holy Scripture, Sacred Canon, Scripture, testament, text, the Book of Books, the Good Book, the Scriptures, the Word of God *Books of the Apocrypha:* Baruch, Bel and the Dragon, Ecclesiasticus, Esdras, Esther, Judith, Maccabees, Sinach, Susanna, The Letter of Jeremiah, The Prayer of Azariah and the Song of the Three Young Men, The Prayer of Manasseh, Tobit, Wisdom *Books of the Bible:* Acts, Amos, Chronicles, Colossians, Corinthians, Daniel, Deuteronomy, Ecclesiastes, Ephesians, Esther, Exodus, Ezekiel, Ezra, Galatians, Genesis, Habakkuk, Haggai, Hebrews, Hosea, Isaiah, James, Jeremiah, Job, Joel, John, Jonah, Joshua, Jude, Judges, Kings, Lamentations, Leviticus, Luke, Malachi, Mark, Matthew, Micah, Nahum, Nehemiah, Numbers, Obadiah, Peter, Philemon, Philippians, Proverbs, Psalms, Revelation, Romans, Ruth, Samuel, Song of Solomon, Thessalonians, Timothy, Titus, Zechariah, Zephaniah *Divisions of the Bible:* Acts of the Apostles, Apocalypse, Apocrypha, Epistles, Gospels, New Testament, Old Testament, Pentateuch, Revelation, the Prophets *Kinds of Christian Bible:* Authorized *or* King James Version, Douay, Jerusalem, New English, Septuagint, Vulgate

bibliography *n.* list of works, works cited *Kinds of bibliography:* annotated, annual, bibliography of bibliographies, compendium, critical, national, period, subject, trade

bicker *v.* argue, brawl, cavil, disagree, dispute, fall out, fight, hassle, pick at, quarrel, quibble, row, scrap, scrape, spar, spat, squabble, wrangle *Antonyms:* accord, acquiesce, assent, cooperate, harmonize

bicycle *n.* bike, cycle, moped, mountain bike, racer, scooter, tandem, two-wheeler, vehicle, velocipede, wheels – *v.* bike, exercise, pedal, travel, trip, wheel

bid *n.* ante, declaration, feeler, invitation, offer, pass, proffer, proposal, proposition, request, submission, summons, tender – *v.* **1.** make a pitch, offer, present, proffer, propose, render, submit, tender, venture **2.** call, charge, conjecture, greet, say, summon, tell, wish

bide *v.* abide, attend, await, continue, dwell, linger, live, remain, reside, stay, wait, watch for *Nonformal:* hang around *or* in *or* out, sit tight, stick around *Antonyms:* flee, leave, spirit away, vanish

big *adj.* **1.** ample, bulky, burly, buxom, capacious, commodious, considerable, copious, elephantine, enormous, extensive, fat, full, gargantuan, gigantic, heavyweight, hefty, huge, hulking, humongous *(Nonformal)*, husky, immense, jumbo, king-sized, large, mammoth, massive, monster, monstrous, opulent, oversized, ponderous, prodigious, roomy, rotund, sizable, spacious, strapping, substantial, titanic, vast, voluminous, walloping, whopping *Antonyms:* diminutive, insignificant, little, miniature **2.** consequential, considerable, eminent, heavy-duty, heavyweight, important, influential, leading, main, material, meaningful, momentous, paramount, powerful, prime, principal, prominent, serious, significant, substantial, super, valuable, weighty *Antonyms:* humble, insignificant, minor, modest, unknown **3.** awash, brimming, crowded, full, loaded, overflowing, packed, swarming, teeming **4.** carrying, heavy, laden, pregnant

bigot *n.* anti-Semite, diehard, dogmatist, extremist, fanatic, monomaniac, persecutor, racist, redneck *(Nonformal)*, sectarian, segregationist, sexist, xenophobe, zealot

bigoted *adj.* biased, closed-minded, intolerant, irrational, jaundiced, narrow-minded, one-sided, opinionated, overzealous, partisan, prejudiced, racist, sectarian, sexist, slanted *Antonyms:* broad-minded, tolerant, unprejudiced

bigwig *n.* ace, captain, celebrity, chief, heavyweight, king, mogul, nabob, rajah, star, top brass, tycoon *Nonformal:* big cheese *or* shot, head honcho, high mucky-muck

bilingual *n. bilingue (French & Italian), bilingüe (Spanish),* fluent in two languages, linguist, polyglot, *zweisprachig (German)*

bilious *adj.* **1.** acrimonious, acerbic, bitter, choleric, crotchety, irascible, sour, testy *Antonyms:* benign, innocuous **2.** gippy tummy *(Nonformal),* ill, nauseated, nauseous, queasy, sick, sick to one's stomach

bilk *v.* beat, cheat, circumvent, deceive, defraud, fleece, foil, rook, swindle, trick *Nonformal:* bamboozle, con, grift, scam, soak

bill *n.* **1.** account, *addition (French),* charge, check, chit, *conto (Italian),* debt, invoice, note, *rechnung (German),* reckoning, score, statement, tab, tally *Nonformal:* damage, IOU **2.** bank note, buck *(Nonformal),* currency, dollar, money **3.** act, draft, legislation, measure, projected law, proposal, proposed act **4.** advertisement, agenda, bulletin, card, catalogue, flyer, handbill, handout, inventory, leaflet, list, listing, notice, placard, playbill, poster, program, roster, schedule, syllabus **5.** beak, mandible, nose, proboscis, snout – *v.* **1.** charge, invoice, send the account, tabulate **2.** advertise, announce, book, post, promote

billet *n.* accommodation, barracks, berth, bivouac, housing, lodgings, quarters – *v.* accommodate, bank, bunk in *(Nonformal),* harbour, lodge, put up, quarter, shelter, stable

billow *n.* breaker, crest, mass, roller, surge, swell, tide, wave – *v.* balloon, belly, bloat, bounce, bulge, heave, pitch, puff up, ripple, rock, roll, surge, swell, toss, undulate, wave *Antonyms:* calm, deflate

billowy *adj.* bouncing, bouncy, bulgy, falling, flowing, heaving, puffy, rippled, rippling, rising, rolling, surging, swelling, swirling, swollen, undulating, waving, wavy *Antonyms:* flat, pacific, smooth

bin *n.* basket, box, chest, crate, crib, cupboard, hamper, hold, hutch, locker, receptacle, repository, tote

bind *n.* box, crunch, difficulty, dilemma, hot water, nuisance, predicament, quandary, squeeze, sticky *or* tight situation, tight spot *Nonformal:* lose-lose *or* no-win situation, pickle – *v.* **1.** adhere, attach, chain, cinch, clamp, connect, encase, fasten, fetter, fix, glue, hitch, lace, lash, manacle, moor, paste, pin, pinion, rope, shackle, strap, swathe, tack on, tether, tie, tie up, truss, unite, wrap, yoke *Nonformal:* hook on *or* up *Antonyms:* free, loosen, undo, unfasten, untie **2.** compel, confine, constrain, detain, engage, enslave, force, hamper, hinder, hogtie, indenture, lock up, necessitate, obligate, oblige, prescribe, require, restrain, restrict, yoke

binding *adj.* compulsory, conclusive, imperative, incumbent, irrevocable, mandatory, necessary, obligatory, permanent, required, unalterable *Antonyms:* discretionary, optional, unforced – *n.* adhesive, bandage, bond, chain, fastener, rope, shackle, strap, tape, tether, tie, wrapper

binge *n.* affair, bender, blind, bout, carousal, debauch, drunk, fling, jag, orgy, revel, spree, time *Nonformal:* hoot, tear, toot, wind'em up – *v.* gorge, overeat, overindulge, pig out *(Nonformal)*

biography *n.* account, annals, autobiography, chronicle, curriculum vitae *or* CV, diary, herstory *(Nonformal),* history, journal, lifestory, memoir, profile, recollection, résumé

bird *n.* birdlife, chick, fledgling, flock *(pl.),* fowl *Groupings of birds:* birds of prey, cage, fish-eating, fruit-eating, game, insect-eating, land, migratory, passerine songbirds, poultry, seabird, shorebird, songbird, wader, waterfowl *Nonformal:* birdie, feathered folk, fowls of the air *Kinds of birds:* albatross, auk, bittern, blackbird, blue grouse, bunting, bustard, buzzard, Canada goose, Canada jay *or* gray jay, canary, cardinal, chickadee, chicken, condor, coot, cormorant, crane, crow, cuckoo, dodo, dotterel *(Newfoundland),* duck, eagle, egret, emu, finch, flamingo, flicker, flycatcher,

Franklin's grouse, Franklin's gull, fulmar, godwit, goose, grackle, great blue heron, grebe, grouse, gull, hawk, heron, hoopoe, hornbill, Hudsonian chickadee, Hudsonian curlew, hummingbird, jay, junco, kestrel, killdeer, kingbird, kingfisher, kittiwake, kiwi, lark, linnet, loggerhead shrike, loon, lovebird, magpie, mockingbird, Mother Cary's chicken *(Nonformal)*, mousebird, murr, myna, nighthawk, nightingale, nightjar, oriole, ortolan, osprey, ostrich, owl, parrot, peewit, pelican, penguin, petrel, pigeon, pine grosbeak, plover, prairie chicken, quail, rail, raven, red-tailed hawk, red-winged blackbird, rhea, rock ptarmigan, Ross's goose, rough-legged hawk, sacred ibis, sandpiper, sapsucker, secretary bird, sharp-tailed grouse, shrike, snow bunting *or* snowbird, snow goose, snowy owl, sparrow, spruce goose *or* fool hen, starling, stork, swallow, swan, swift, tanager, tern, thrasher, thrush, tinamou, toucan, trogon, turkey, turtledove, vulture, warbler, whippoorwill, whiskyjack, whooping crane, wood duck, woodpecker, wren *Immature birds:* chick, fledgling, nestling *Kinds of bird sound:* cackle, call, carol, chatter, cheep, chirp, chirr, chirrup, chitter, cluck, cock-a-doodle-doo, coo, crow, drum, gabble, gobble, honk, hoot, peep, pipe, quack, roll, sing, trill, tweet, twit, twitter, warble, whistle *Provincial & Territorial Birds:* Atlantic puffin *(Newfoundland)*, black-capped chickadee *(New Brunswick)*, blue jay *(P.E.I.)*, great gray owl *(Manitoba)*, great horned owl *(Alberta)*, gyrfalcon *(Northwest Territories)*, loon *(Ontario)*, osprey *(Nova Scotia)*, raven *(Yukon)*, snowy owl *(Quebec)*, Stellar's jay *(B.C.)* western sharp-tailed grouse *(Saskatchewan)*

birth *n.* **1.** bearing, beginning, birthing, blessed event, childbearing, childbirth, creation, delivery, labour, naissance, nativity, parturition, travail **2.** ancestry, background, breeding, derivation, descent, extraction, forebears, genealogy, heritage, legacy, line, lineage, nobility, parentage, pedigree, station, stock, strain **3.** beginning, commencement, dawn, dawning, emergence, fountainhead, genesis, onset, opening, origin, outset, rise, source, start *Antonyms:* death, demise, end, extinction, passing

biscuit *n.* bannock, cookie, cracker, fortune cookie, hardtack, saltine, scone, ship-tack, wafer

bisect *v.* bifurcate, cleave, cross, dichotomize, divide, halve, separate, sever, split *Antonyms:* fuse, join, unite, weld

bit *n.* **1.** atom, chunk, crumb, dab, dash, division, dollop, dose, droplet, excerpt, flake, fraction, fragment, grain, iota, jot, modicum, morsel, parcel, part, particle, piece, pinch, portion, sample, scintilla, scrap, section, segment, shard, share, shaving, shred, slice, sliver, smattering, smidgen, smithereen, snippet, speck, sprinkling, taste, trace, trickle, trifle **2.** blink of an eye, flash, instant, jiffy, minute, moment, period, sec *(Nonformal)*, second

bitch *n.* **1.** beef *(Nonformal)*, complaint, critique, grievance, gripe, peeve **2.** female canine *or* dog **3.** harpy, harridan, shrew, termagant, virago, witch – *v.* carp, criticize, gripe, grouse, nag, protest *Nonformal:* bellyache, squawk *Antonyms:* compliment, praise

bite *n.* **1.** itch, laceration, nip, pain, pinch, prick, puncture, sting, wound *Nonformal:* chaw, chomp **2.** edge, kick *(Nonformal)*, piquancy, punch, pungency, spice **3.** bit, morsel, taste – *v.* chew, clamp, crunch, crush, cut, eat, gnaw, grip, hold, lacerate, masticate, munch, nibble, nip, pierce, pinch, puncture, rend, ruminate, seize, sever, snap, taste, tooth *Nonformal:* champ, chaw, chomp, sink one's teeth into

biting *adj.* bitter, blighting, caustic, cold, cutting, freezing, harsh, incisive, ironic, nipping, penetrating, piercing, pungent, raw, sarcastic, scathing, severe, sharp, stinging, tart, trenchant, vitriolic *Antonyms:* benign, bland, weak

bitter *adj.* **1.** acrimonious, antagonistic, begrudging, crabby, embittered, estranged, fierce, galling, hateful, hostile, morose, mordent, rancorous, repugnant, resentful, sardonic, sore, splenetic, stinging, sullen, tragic, venomous, virulent, vitriolic *Antonyms:* appreciative, balmy, friendly, gentle, happy **2.** acerbic, acid, acrid, astringent, harsh, nasty, pungent, sour, tart, unsweetened, vinegary *Antonyms:* mild, sugary, sweet

bitterness *n.* **1.** acrimoniousness, agony, anguish, asperity, distress, grievousness, harshness, hostility, mordancy, pain, painfulness, sarcasm, venom, virulence *Antonyms:* cheerfulness, gaiety, joy, vivaciousness **2.** acidity, astringency, piquancy, pungency, sharpness, sourness, tartness

bizarre *adj.* abnormal, camp, comical, curious, eccentric, extraordinary, fantastic, freakish, grotesque, ludicrous, odd, offbeat, peculiar, queer, ridiculous, singular, unusual, weird, wild *Nonformal:* kooky, oddball, off-the-wall, squirrely, way out *Antonyms:* common, conventional, normal, traditional

black *adj.* **1.** *Black shades:* charcoal, coal, ebon, ebony, jet, moonless, murky, nocturnal, obsidian, onyx, overcast, pitch-dark, raven, sable, slate, sombre, sooty *Antonyms:* bright, white **2.** atrocious, bleak, dark, depressing, depressive, dismal, dispiriting, distressing, doleful, dreary, foreboding, funereal, gloomy, hopeless, horrible, mournful, ominous, oppressive, sad, sinister, sombre, sullen, threatening *Antonyms:* amicable, bright, cheerful, good, happy **3.** bad, black-hearted, diabolical, evil, foul, iniquitous, mean, nefarious, odious, villainous, wicked *Antonyms:* angelic, good, heavenly, pure

blacklist *n.* ban, blackball, boycott, censor, condemn, expel, ostracize, outlaw, proscribe, reject, spurn, stigmatize *Antonyms:* aid, enlist, hire, support

blackmail *n.* bribe, bribery, extortion, hush money, payoff *(Nonformal)*, protection money, ransom, tribute – *v.* bleed, bribe, coerce, compel, demand, exact, extort, force, ransom, squeeze, threaten *Nonformal:* milk, shakedown

blackout *n.* **1.** ban, censorship, cover-up, curtain, repression, smoke screen, veil of secrecy **2.** catalepsy, coma, faint, oblivion, passing out, senselessness, somnolence, swoon, unconsciousness

blade *n.* cutlass, dagger, dirk, edge, épée, kirpan, knife, lancet, machete, rapier, scimitar, shank, stiletto, switchblade, sword, ulu

blame *n.* accusation, arraignment, attack, attribution, castigation, censure, charge, complaint, condemnation, criticism, culpability, denunciation, deprecation, diatribe, disapprobation, disapproval, disfavour, disparagement, fault, guilt, impeachment, implication, imputation, incrimination, inculcation, indictment, invective, liability, obloquy, onus, rap *(Nonformal)*, rebuke, recrimination, remonstrance, reprimand, reproach, reprobation, reproof, repudiation, responsibility, slur, stricture *Antonyms:* absolution, commendation, credit, exoneration, tribute – *v.* accuse, admonish, ascribe, attribute, berate, castigate, censure, charge, chide, condemn, criticize, denounce, disapprove, expostulate, find fault, hold accountable *or* responsible, indict, knock, lambaste, object to, objurgate, protest, rail, rebuke, recriminate, remonstrate, reprehend, reproach, reprove, scold, take to task, tax, upbraid, vituperate *Nonformal:* blast, blister, finger, give hell, go after, have at, jump on, kick, lay into, lay out, rake over the coals, rap, rip into, roast, saddle, scorch, skin, sound off, tongue-lash, trash, work over *Antonyms:* acquit, clear, praise, vindicate

blameless *adj.* above suspicion, clean, clear, exemplary, faultless, guilt-free, guiltless, immaculate, impeccable, inculpable, innocent, irreproachable, perfect, pure, righteous, unblemished, unimpeachable, unsullied, upright, virtuous *Antonyms:* at fault, culpable, guilty, responsible

blanch *v.* **1.** fear, flinch, pale, recoil, shrink, start, wince **2.** bleach, boil, poach, simmer, whiten, whitewash

bland *adj.* banal, benign, boring, dull, flat, flavourless, humdrum, insipid, mild, monotonous, nothing, tame, tasteless, tedious, unexciting, uninspiring, uninteresting, vapid, watery, weak *Nonformal:* blah, ho-hum, pablum, plain vanilla, wishy-washy *Antonyms:* distinctive, exciting, inspiring, memorable, stimulating

blandish *v.* cajole, coax, compliment, flatter, wheedle *Nonformal:* apple-polish, blarney, palaver, soft soap, sweet talk *Antonyms:* abuse, criticize, curse

blank *adj.* **1.** deadpan, dull, empty, expressionless, hollow, immobile, impassive, inane, inexpressive, inscrutable, lifeless, masklike, noncommittal, poker-faced, stiff, stupid, unexpressive, unreadable, vacuous, vague *Antonyms:* alert, completed, expressive, lively, valuable **2.** bare, clean, clear, fresh, new, pale, plain, spotless, unfilled, unmarked, untouched, unused, vacant, virgin, void, white – *n.* emptiness, gap, nothingness, space, *tabula rasa (Latin)*, vacancy, vacuum, void *Antonyms:* fullness, repletion, surfeit

blanket *adj.* absolute, across-the-board, all-embracing, all-inclusive, comprehensive, overall, pandemic, powerful, sweeping, unconditional, wide-ranging *Antonyms:* limited, narrow, specific – *n.* carpet, coating, cover, covering, coverlet, envelope, film, layer, mat, sheath, strip, wrapper *Kinds of blanket:* afghan, Chilkat, comforter, coverlet, duvet, eiderdown, fleece, Hudson's Bay, Mackinaw, point, quilt, rug, sheet, throw – *v.* bury, cloud, coat, conceal, cover, eclipse, envelop, hide, mask, obscure, overcast, overlay, overspread, suppress, surround *Antonyms:* expose, illuminate, uncover, unveil

blare *v.* bellow, blast, boom, bray, clamour, clang, honk, hoot, peal, resound, roar, scream, shout, shriek, sound out, toot, trumpet *Antonyms:* muffle, silence, turn down

blarney *n.* cajolery, coaxing, compliments, flattery, honey *or* silvery-tongued words, ingratiation *Nonformal:* baloney, flummery, foam, froth, oil, soft soap, sweet talk *Antonyms:* authenticity, genuineness, sincerity

blasé *adj.* apathetic, bored, cloyed, cool, disenchanted, glutted, indifferent, jaded, lukewarm, mellow, nonchalant, offhand, uncaring, unconcerned, unexcited, uninterested, unmoved, weary, world-weary *Antonyms:* affected, caring, enthusiastic

blasphemous *adj.* cursing, disrespectful, godless, impious, insulting, irreligious, irreverent, obscene, profane, sacrilegious, swearing *Antonyms:* devout, godly, pious, religious, reverential

blasphemy *n.* abuse, desecration, execration, heresy, impiety, impiousness, imprecation, indignity, irreverence, profanity, sacrilege, scoffing, swearing

blast *n.* **1.** blow, gale, gridley grinder *(P.E.I.)*, hurricane, squall, storm, strong wind, tempest, wind **2.** bang, blare, blow, burst, clang, clap, crack, din, explosion, honk, peal, roar, scream, shoot, slam, smash, sound, trumpet, wail **3.** ball *(Nonformal)*, good time, party – *v.* **1.** blare, honk, peel, resound, roar, scream, shriek, toot **2.** blow up, bomb, burst, dynamite, explode, level, shell, torpedo

blatant *adj.* barefaced, brassy, conspicuous, egregious, flagrant, flashy, flaunting, garish, gaudy, glaring, loud, naked, obvious, obnoxious, ostentatious, outright, overt, plain, prominent, pronounced, screaming, shameless, showy, unabashed, unblushing *Antonyms:* demure, dignified, elegant, hidden, tasteful

blaze *n.* bonfire, combustion, conflagration, fire, flame, forest fire, fury, inferno, pyre, wildfire – *v.* burn, dazzle, erupt, flare, glitter, glow, shine, sparkle *Antonyms:* extinguish, fade away

bleach *v.* blanch, decolourize, etiolate, lighten, peroxide, wash out, whiten, whitewash *Antonyms:* darken, dye, soil, stain

bleak *adj.* **1.** black, cheerless, comfortless, dark, depressing, discouraging, disheartening, dismal, drear, dreary, funereal, gloomy, grim, hard, harsh, hopeless, joyless, lonely, melancholy, oppressive, sad, sombre, uninviting, unpromising *Antonyms:* cheerful, cozy, encouraging, promising **2.** austere, bare, barren, bombed-out, burned, clear-cut, cleared, deforested, desolate, empty, exposed, open, scorched, windswept *Antonyms:* protected, sheltered, verdant **3.** biting, bitter, cold, cutting, raw

bleed *v.* **1.** drain, exude, flow, gush, hemorrhage, leak, leech, ooze, phlebotomize, run, seep, shed, spurt, trickle, weep *Antonyms:*

cauterize, staunch, stem, stop **2.** blackmail, confiscate, deplete, drain, extort, extract, fleece, impoverish, leech, milk *(Nonformal)*, overcharge, squeeze, steal **3.** ache, agonize, feel for, grieve, pity, suffer, sympathize

blemish *n.* **1.** abscess, acne, beal, bedsore, birthmark, boil, bruise, bunion, canker, carbuncle, chancre, cold sore, corn, discolouration, disfigurement, fistula, freckle, gumboil, lesion, lump, mole, papula, papule, piles, pimple, pock, polyp, pustule, scar, sore, swelling, ulcer, ulceration, wart, welt *Nonformal:* hickey, zit **2.** blot, blotch, brand, defect, deformity, fault, flaw, imperfection, mark, patch, scratch, smudge, speck, spot, stain, stigma, taint – *v.* damage, harm, injure, soil, stain, sully, tarnish

blend *n.* alloy, amalgam, brew, combination, combo *(Nonformal)*, composite, compound, concoction, fusion, mix, mixed bag, mixture, synthesis, union – *v.* amalgamate, arrange, coalesce, combine, commingle, complement, compound, dissolve, fit, fuse, go with, harmonize, integrate, intermix, marry, meld, mix, scramble, stir, suit, synthesize, toss, unify, unite

bless *v.* absolve, anoint, baptize, beatify, bestow, canonize, celebrate, commend, confirm, consecrate, cross, dedicate, endow, enshrine, exalt, extol, favour, glorify, grace, grant, hallow, honour, laud, magnify, make holy, offer benediction, ordain, praise, pray for, pronounce holy, sacrifice, sanctify, sign, sprinkle, thank *Antonyms:* accuse, anathematize, damn, excommunicate

blessed *adj.* **1.** awarded, bequested, blest, charmed, endowed, favoured, fortunate, furnished, granted, lucky **2.** adored, beatified, consecrated, divine, enthroned, exalted, glorified, hallowed, holy, reborn, redeemed, religious, resurrected, revered, rewarded, sacred, sacrosanct, sanctified, saved, spiritual *Antonyms:* cursed, damned, reviled **3.** blissful, glad, happy, joyful, joyous, jubilant

blessing *n.* **1.** absolution, baptism, benediction, commendation, consecration, dedication, divine sanction, grace, invocation, sanctification, thanks, thanksgiving, unction *Antonyms:* condemnation, curse, malediction **2.** advantage, asset, benefit, boon, bounty, break, favour, fortune, gain, gift, godsend, good, good luck, help, kindness, lucky break, miracle, profit, service, stroke of luck, windfall *Antonyms:* deprivation, disadvantage, drawback **3.** acquiescence, approval, consent, good wishes, permission, sanction

blight *n.* adversity, affliction, bane, canker, contamination, corruption, curse, decay, devastation, disease, evil, eyesore, fungus, infestation, mildew, pest, pestilence, pollution, rot, scourge, sight, withering, woe – *v.* annihilate, crush, damage, dash, decay, injure, mar, ruin, shrivel, spoil, taint, trash, wreck *Antonyms:* build, construct, patch

blind *adj.* **1.** eyeless, purblind, sightless, visually handicapped *or* impaired **2.** dense, heedless, imperceptive, inattentive, inconsiderate, myopic, nearsighted, obtuse, one-track, shortsighted, single-minded, thick, unaware **3.** careless, hasty, impetuous, indiscriminate, random, rash, reckless, uncontrolled **4.** ignorant, implacable, irrational, knee jerk *(Nonformal)*, mindless, senseless, unreasoning **5.** concealed, disguised, hidden, obscured, unmarked **6.** barred, blocked, closed-off, dead-end, impassable – *adv.* by the seat of one's pants *(Nonformal)*, instinctually, unaided, without help – *n.* **1.** cover, curtain, drape, mask, screen, shade, window shade, vertical **2.** ambush, camouflage, hideaway, hiding place, trap **3.** deception, decoy, dodge, pretext, red herring, ruse, smokescreen, subterfuge, trick – *v.* **1.** blindfold, gouge *or* put out one's eyes **2.** bedazzle, daze, dazzle, overwhelm, stun, stupefy **3.** deceive, disguise, hoodwink, obfuscate, obscure, pull the wool over one's eyes *(Nonformal)*

blink *v.* **1.** bat, bat the eyes, flicker, flutter, glimpse, peek, peep, peer, squint, wink **2.** flash, glimmer, glisten, glitter, shimmer, sparkle, twinkle *Antonyms:* dull, fade **3.** cringe, flinch, pull back, quail, recoil, wince *Antonyms:* brazen, confront, face

bliss *n.* **1.** beatitude, blessedness, ecstasy, euphoria, felicity, gladness, happiness, joy, rapture *Antonyms:* anguish, despair, distress, grief, heartbreak **2.** Avalon, Eden, Elysium, Elysian Fields, heaven, nirvana, Olympus, paradise, Pearly Gates, Promised Land, utopia, Valhalla *Antonyms:* bedlam, damnation, Hades, Hell

blissful *adj.* beatific, cool, delighted, delightful, dreamy, ecstatic, elated, enchanted, enraptured, euphoric, floating, flying, gleeful, happy, heavenly, joyful, joyous *Nonformal:* high, spaced out, trippy, walking on air *Antonyms:* dejected, depressed, miserable

blister *n.* abscess, boil, bubble, burn, canker, carbuncle, chancre, cyst, pimple, pustule, sore, swelling, ulcer, wale, weal, welt – *v.* **1.** castigate, criticize, denounce, flay, skin alive *(Nonformal)* **2.** peel, scorch, sear, singe

blithe *adj.* animated, carefree, cheerful, cheery, chirpy, gay, gleeful, happy, in good spirits, jaunty, jocund, jolly, jovial, joyful, jubilant, lighthearted, merry, mirthful, sprightly, sunny, tickled pink *(Nonformal)*, vivacious, winsome *Antonyms:* dejected, depressed, gloomy, morose, sad, unhappy

blizzard *n.* Alberta clipper, blast, gale, precipitation, snow devil, snowfall, snowstorm, squall, tempest, *tempête de neige (French)*, whiteout

bloat *v.* balloon, belly, billow, blow up, dilate, distend, enlarge, expand, inflate, swell *Antonyms:* contract, deflate, shrink, shrivel, wither, wrinkle

bloated *adj.* ballooning, bulging, corpulent, distended, flatulent, inflated, pompous, swollen, turgid

bloc *n.* alliance, association, caucus, clique, club, coalition, combination, contingent, cooperative, coterie, faction, federation, group, league, machine, party, union

block *n.* **1.** bar, brick, cake, chunk, cube, hunk *(Nonformal)*, ingot, loaf, lump, mass, section, segment, slab, slice, solid, square **2.** barrier, blockage, bottleneck, clog, hindrance, impediment, jam, logjam, obstruction, roadblock, snag, stop, stopgap, stoppage, wall **3.** instrument *Kinds of blocks and pulleys:* dock, gin, snatch, square-cheeked, tackle, triple-sheave **4.** area, community, neighbourhood, precinct, square, street, township *Nonformal:* 'hood, stompin' ground – *v.* **1.** arrest, bar, barricade, beat off, blockade, brake, check, choke, clog, close, close out, counter, curb, dam, deter, filibuster, halt, hinder, hold up, impede, intercept, interfere, obstruct, occlude, parry, prevent, stall, stop, stop up, stymie, tackle, thwart *Nonformal:* snooker, stonewall *Antonyms:* advance, foster, further, promote, push **2.** delineate, demarcate, lay *or* map *or* rough *or* work out, outline, plan, practice, run through, sketch **3.** prohibit, silence, smother, squelch, stifle, suppress, veto

blockade *n.* besiegement, embargo, encirclement, shutdown – *v.* beleaguer, besiege, cordon *or* cut off, encircle, hem in, surround

blockhead *n. Nonformal:* ass, chowderhead, chucklehead, dimwit, dogburger, dolt, doofus, dope, knucklehead, mallethead, meathead, mullethead, numbskull, twit

blonde *adj.* albino, blond *(Masc.)*, fair, fair-haired, light-haired, pale, washed-out *Blonde shades:* ash, bleached, bottle, champagne, flaxen, ginger, golden, honey, peroxide, platinum, sandy, straw, strawberry, tow-head

blood *n.* **1.** gore, hemoglobin, plasma, vital fluid **2.** ancestry, birth, consanguinity, descendants, descent, extraction, family, kindred, kinship, line, lineage, origin, pedigree, relations, stock **3.** dandy, gallant, rake, swell, toff *(British)*, young gentleman *Antonyms:* bastard, beggar, mudlark, peasant

bloodless *adj.* **1.** anemic, ashen, pale, pallid, pasty, whey-faced, white as a ghost *Antonyms:* rosy, ruddy, wholesome **2.** cold, coldhearted, heartless, insensitive, pitiless, ruthless, uncaring *Antonyms:* caring, compassionate, loving **3.** diplomatic, nonviolent, without opposition, unopposed *Antonyms:* bloody, savage, violent **4.** apathetic, feeble, frail, lifeless, listless, sluggish, weak, without vigour *or* strength *Antonyms:* passionate, pulsating, vibrant

bloodshed *n.* butchery, carnage, decimation, destruction, execution, homicide, killing, massacre, murder, pogrom, slaughter, war

bloody *adj.* **1.** barbarous, bloodthirsty, brutal, cruel, cutthroat, ferocious, fierce, gory, grim, hard-fought, heavy, murderous, sanguinary, savage **2.** cursed, damned, detestable, revolting *Antonyms:* blessed, revered, sanctified

bloom *n.* **1.** blossom, efflorescence, flower, flowering, wildflower *Antonyms:* decay, thorn **2.** beauty, charm, elegance, glow, radiance – *v.* blossom, burgeon, burst, burst forth, flourish, flower, grow, thrive *Antonyms:* decline, droop, fade, fail, languish, perish

blossom *n.* bloom, blossoming, bud, floret, flower, posy – *v.* bloom, bud, develop, evolve, flourish, flower, grow, mature, open up *or* out, progress, prosper, succeed, thrive, unfold, unfurl *Antonyms:* die, wither

blot *n.* blemish, blotch, discoloration, eyesore, mar, smear, smirch, smudge, splotch, spot, stain, stigma – *v.* **1.** bespatter, dirty, discolour, disfigure, disgrace, mark, smudge, smut, soil, spoil, spot, stain, sully, tarnish **2.** absorb, dry, soak up, take up

blouse *n.* upper-body garment *Kinds of blouse:* bodice, button-down, pullover, shell, shirt, slipover, top, t-shirt, turtleneck, v-neck

blow *n.* **1.** bang, bash, bat, belt, bop, box, bump, crack, hit, jab, jar, jolt, kick, knock, poke, pound, punch, rap, sallywinder *(Nonformal)*, shock, slam, slap, slug, smack, smash, sock, strike, swat, swing, swipe, thump, thwack, uppercut, wallop, whack **2.** affliction, calamity, casualty, catastrophe, come *or* letdown, debacle, disappointment, disaster, frustration, jolt, misadventure, misfortune, mishap, reverse, setback, shock, tragedy, upset, vexation **3.** blast, draft, flurry, gale, gust, hurricane, puff, squall, strong breeze, tempest, typhoon, wind – *v.* **1.** breathe, exhale, expel, puff **2.** blast, sound, toot, whistle **3.** blow *or* burn out, burst, explode, pop

bludgeon *n.* baton, billyclub, blackjack, club, cudgel, nightstick, sap – *v.* beat, clobber, club, pound, pummel

blue *adj. & n. Blue shades:* aquamarine, azure, cyan, cerulean, cobalt, hyacinth, indigo, navy, reflex, royal, sapphire, sky, teal, turquoise, ultramarine – *adj.* **1.** crestfallen, dejected, depressed, despondent, dismal, dispirited, down in the mouth *or* dumps *(Nonformal)*, downcast, downhearted, gloomy, glum, low, melancholy, sad, unhappy, woebegone *Antonyms:* cheerful, elated, happy, sunny **2.** bawdy, dirty, indecent, lewd, naughty, obscene, off-colour, pornographic, risqué, salty, shady, smutty, spicy, suggestive, vulgar, wicked *Antonyms:* decent, respectable

blueprint *n.* blues *(Nonformal)*, diagram, draft, outline, plan, proof, prototype, representation, schedule, vandyke

blues *n.* dejection, depression, despondency, doldrums, dumps, gloom, gloominess, glumness, low spirits, melancholy, mournfulness, sadness, unhappiness *Antonyms:* ecstacy, joy, rapture **2.** music, R & B *(Nonformal)*, soul *See also:* **music**

bluff *adj.* blunt, blustery, brief, brusque, candid, crusty, direct, downright, earthy, forthright, frank, gruff, hearty, honest, honourable, open, plain-spoken, rough, straightforward *Antonyms:* delicate, diplomatic, discreet, sensitive, tactful – *n.* **1.** bank, cliff, crag, escarpment, headland, hill, mountain, palisade, peak, precipice, promontory, ridge, rock **2.** brush, copse, clump of trees, scrub, thicket, wood **3.** boast, braggadocio, bravado, deception, delusion, façade, fake, false colours *or* front, feint, fraud, front, lie, pretense, pretext, ruse, sham, show, stall, trick – *v.* bamboozle, beguile, betray, counterfeit, deceive, defraud, delude, double-cross, fake, feign, fool, hoodwink, humbug, juggle, lie, mislead, pretend, put on, simulate, trick *Nonformal:* bull, con, hornswaggle, psych out, sham

blunder *n.* bungle, error, fall, fault, *faux pas* (*French*), gaffe, goof, impropriety, inaccuracy, indiscretion, lapse, misstep, mistake, oversight, slip, solecism, stumble, trip *Nonformal:* blooper, boner, boo-boo, flub, fluff, no-no *Antonyms:* accuracy, achievement, correctness, perfection, success – *v.* be at fault *or* in error, blow it *(Nonformal)*, botch, bumble, bungle, flounder, goof, make a mistake, muff, slip up, stagger, stumble

blunt *adj.* **1.** abrupt, barefaced, brief, brusque, candid, curt, explicit, forthright, frank, gruff, impolite, matter-of-fact, outspoken, pithy, plain-spoken, short, straightforward, tactless, uncivil, unpolished *Antonyms:* courteous, diplomatic, tactful **2.** dull, edgeless, obtuse, round, rounded, unsharpened *Antonyms:* acute, keen, sharp – *v.* anesthetize, dampen, deaden, desensitize, dull, mollify, numb, sap, soften, water down (*Nonformal*), weaken

blur *n.* **1.** blot, blotch, smear, smudge, splotch **2.** cloud, confusion, fog, haze – *v.* becloud, bedim, befog, blear, blind, cloud, darken, daze, dim, fog, mask, muddy, obfuscate, obscure, shade, smear *Antonyms:* brighten, clean, clear, illuminate

blush *n.* bloom, colour, colouring, flush, glow, pink tinge, reddening, redness, rosiness, ruddiness – *v.* colour, crimson, flush, glow, mantle, pink, redden, rouge, turn red *or* scarlet *Antonyms:* blanch, drain, fade, pale, whiten

bluster *n.* bluff, boasting, boisterousness, bombast, braggadocio, bragging, bravado, bullying, rage, showboat *(Nonformal)*, swagger, swaggering – *v.* boast, brag, brazen, browbeat, bully, domineer, gloat, grandstand, hector, intimidate, rant, rave, strut, swagger *Nonformal:* bulldoze, cow, crow, roar, roister, show off, storm, talk big *Antonyms:* cower, grovel, shrink, wince

blusterer *n.* boaster, braggart, bully *Nonformal:* big mouth, blowhard, know-it-all, smartass, windbag

board *n.* **1.** lumber, plank, wood *Kinds of board:* batten, clapboard, lath, panel, paneling, plywood, shake, sheathing, sheet, shingle, siding, slab, slat, stovewood, timbering, timberwork, two-by-four, weather **2.** cabinet, committee, council, diet, directorate, executive, forum, trustees, synod **3.** accommodations, fare, lodgings, meal, rations – *v.* **1.** catch, climb on, embark, enter, entrain, get on, mount **2.** accommodate, bed, billet, care for, feed, harbour, house, lodge, provide, put up, quarter, room

boast *n.* avowal, bluster, bravado, crow, exaggeration, gasconade, grandiloquence, heroics, joy, pretension, pride, treasure, vaunt – *v.* acclaim, advertise, blow out of proportion *or* up, bluster, brag, brandish, celebrate, claim, declaim, display, enlarge, exaggerate, exhibit, expose, exult, flash, flatter oneself, flaunt, flourish, gloat, glory, heighten, herald, hold forth, laud, magnify, orate, overstate, parade, pontificate, praise, prate, preen, pride oneself, promote, puff, ramble, rant, relish, revel *or* revel in, show off, spout, swagger, tout, triumph, trumpet, vaunt, yell *Nonformal:* ballyhoo, blow one's own horn, talk big *Antonyms:* animadvert, cover up, depreciate, disavow, disclaim

boastful *adj.* arrogant, bombastic, cocky, conceited, crowing, egotistic, exultant, loudmouth, pompous, pretentious, puffed-up, self-aggrandizing *or* -applauding, snooty (*Nonformal*), strutting, swaggering, vainglorious, vaunting *Antonyms:* deprecating, humble, modest, self-effacing, unassuming

boat *n.* craft, ship, tub, vehicle, vessel *Kinds of boat:* ark, barge, bark, cabin cruiser, canal, caboteur, canoe, catamaran, Chebucto, cruiser, dinghy, dory, dragger, ferry, Garden Island schooner, goelette, gondola, highliner, houseboat, Hudson's Bay, hydrofoil, iceboat, icebreaker, junk, ketch, lake, launch, lifeboat, Mackinaw, motorboat, ocean liner, one-lunger *(Nonformal)*, packet, pleasure, pointer, powerboat, punt, raft, sailboat, salt-banker, scallop dragger, schooner, scow, shell, skiff, sloop, speedboat, steamboat, sturgeon-head, supertanker, whaleboat, yacht, York *Atlantic Provinces:* Cape Islander, strait *French:* bateau, canot-du-maître *Newfoundland:* bully, rodney *North:* kaiak *or* kayak, komatik, umiak *See also:* **ship** – *v.* **1.** cruise, paddle, punt, putter, row, sail, scull, navigate, steam, travel **2.** barge, ferry, float, raft, ship

boating *n.* canoeing, cruising, drifting, paddling, rowing, sailing, sculling, trawling, yachting

bode *v.* auger, forebode, foreshadow, foretell, forewarn, portend, predict, presage, prophesy

bodily *adj.* animal, carnal, corporal, corporeal, fleshly, human, material, mortal, natural, normal, organic, physical, sensual, somatic, substantial, tangible *Antonyms:* ethereal, intangible, spiritual

body *n.* **1.** anatomy, build, constitution, figure, form, frame, physique, shape, torso, trunk **2.** being, creature, human, individual, mortal, party, person, personage **3.** assembly, basis, bulk, chassis, core, crux, essence, frame, gist, hull, main part, pith, skeleton, staple, substance, substructure, sum, total, trunk, whole **4.** array, batch, bevy, bloc, bunch, bundle, clump, cluster, corpus, crowd, group, horde, lot, majority, mass, mob, multitude, party, set, throng **5.** cadaver, carcass, corpse, dearly departed, deceased, loved one, remains, stiff *(Nonformal)* **6.** consistency, fabric, richness, strength, substance, tangibility, texture

bog *n.* caribou bog (*Atlantic Provinces*), fen, lowland, marsh, marshland, moors, morass, muskeg, peat, quagmire, quaking bog, slough, sump, swamp, wetland

bogus *adj.* artificial, counterfeit, ersatz, fake, false, fictitious, forged, fraudulent, pretended, simulated, spurious *Nonformal:* phoney, pseudo, sham *Antonyms:* actual, authentic, real, true

bohemian *adj.* artsy, *outré (French)*, avant-garde, eccentric, hip *(Nonformal)*, off-beat, unorthodox – *n.* beatnik, deadhead, maverick, nonconformist

boil *n.* abscess, blister, carbuncle, furuncle, proud flesh *(Nonformal)*, pustule, sore, tumour, ulcer – *v.* bubble, coddle, cook, heat, parboil, poach, simmer, steam, steep, stew

boiling *adj.* **1.** baking, blistering, broiling, burning, fiery, hot, red-hot, roasting, scalding, scorching, sizzling, torrid, tropical, warm **2.** angry, enraged, fuming, indignant, infuriated, over the edge *(Nonformal)*, seething, turbulent

boisterous *adj.* clamorous, effervescent, energetic, loud, mischievous, noisy, rambunctious, raucous, riotous, roisterous, rollicking, rough, rowdy, rude, stormy, tempestuous, unrestrained, unruly, uproarious, vociferous, wild *Antonyms:* calm, demure, peaceful, quiet, restrained

bold *adj.* **1.** adventurous, audacious, brave, courageous, dauntless, enterprising, fearless, gallant, game, heroic, intrepid, plucky, resolute, smart, spunky, unafraid, undaunted, valiant *Antonyms:* cowardly, fainthearted, meek, modest, timid, unabashed **2.** blatant, brash, brazen, cocksure, disrespectful, familiar, forward, fresh, impertinent, nervy, pert, presumptuous, pushy, sassy, saucy *Nonformal*: cheeky, lippy, smartalecky *Antonyms:* conservative, dull, retiring, shy **3.** bright, clear, colourful, eye-catching, flashy, lively, loud, prominent, pronounced, showy, vivid *Antonyms:* pale, restrained, soft

boldness *n.* arrogance, audacity, brass, brazenness, carelessness, cheek *(Nonformal)*, contempt, defiance, disrespect, effrontery, gall, guff, heedlessness, impertinence, impudence, insolence, insubordination, offensiveness, presumption, rashness, recklessness *Antonyms:* diffidence, meekness, modesty, shyness

bolster *n.* cushion, pad, prop – *v.* aid, assist, bear up, boost, brace, bulwark, buoy, buttress, carry, comfort, confirm, cradle, cushion, encourage, help, maintain, reinforce, stay, strengthen, support, sustain, uphold *Nonformal:* brace, buck *or* hold up *Antonyms:* hinder, weaken

bolt *n.* **1.** bar, catch, coupling, deadbolt, fastener, key, latch, lock, nut, padlock, peg, pin, pipe, rivet, rod, screw, skewer, sliding bar, spike, stake, staple, stud *Kinds of bolt:* carriage, eye, hook, stove, toggle, U-bolt **2.** cylinder, length, package, roll, spindle, spiral **3.** flash, fulmination, lightning, streak, thunderbolt – *v.* **1.** abscond, bound, cut loose, cut out, dash, desert, ditch, drop out, escape, flee, fly, jump, leap, make off, opt out, run, scamper, scoot, skip, take flight, take off *Nonformal:* hightail *or* hotfoot it, skedaddle **2.** fasten, latch, lock, secure **3.** devour, gobble, gulp, lay in

bomb *n.* **1.** charge, explosive, explosive device, weapon *Kinds of bomb:* atomic, Cobalt (*Medicine*), fireball, grenade, hydrogen, mine, missile, nuclear, pipe, plastic, projectile, rocket, shell, smart, torpedo **2.** bust, failure, flop, turkey *(Nonformal)* – *v.* **1.** blitz, bombard, let 'em have it *(Nonformal)*, pound, shell, throw a bomb at, torpedo **2.** fail, fall flat, flop, *Nonformal:* crash and burn, lay an egg *Antonyms:* succeed, triumph

bombard *v.* assail, assault, attack, barrage, batter, beset, besiege, blast, blitz, bomb, cannonade, charge, descend upon, harass, hound, launch, open fire, pester, shell, storm, strafe, strike, surge

bombastic *adj.* declamatory, flowery, fustian, grandiloquent, histrionic, inflated, ostentatious, overblown, pompous, ranting, rhapsodic, rhetorical, sonorous, swollen, turgid, verbose, windy, wordy *Nonformal:* big-talking, high-flown

bona fide *adj.* authentic, genuine, legitimate, real, tried-and-true *Nonformal:* for real, kosher, legit, the real thing *Antonyms:* artificial, counterfeit, fake, spurious

bond *n.* **1.** affiliation, affinity, association, attachment, connection, friendship, hookup, interrelationship, liaison, link, marriage, network, obligation, relation, relationship, tie, union **2.** agreement, bargain, certificate, collateral, compact, contract, convention, covenant, debenture, guarantee, guaranty, indenture, obligation, pact, pledge, promise, security, transaction, warrant, warranty, word *Antonyms:* denial, disclaimer, repudiation **3.** binding, cord, fastener, fastening, fetter, ligament, linkage, restraint, rope, shackle, tie – *v.* bind, cohere, connect, fasten, fix, fuse, glue, gum, interlock, paste, unite *Antonyms:* detach, disintegrate, dissolve, separate

bondage *n.* captivity, chains, confinement, enslavement, imprisonment, indentureship, oppression, restraint, serfdom, servitude, slavery, subjection, subjugation, thralldom

bone *n.* **1.** calcified *or* ossified *or* skeletal material *Kinds of human skeletal bone:* anvil *(Ear)*, astragalus *(Ankle)*, backbone *(Spine)*, cannon, carpal *or* metacarpal *(Fingers)*, cheekbone, clavicle, coccyx *(Rump)*, collarbone, femur *(Thighbone)*, funny *(Nonformal)*, hallux, hipbone, humerus, ilium, mandible *(Jawbone)*, mastoid, nasal, occipital, ossicle, parietal, patella *(Kneecap)*, pelvis, radius, rib, sacrum, scapula, sesamoid, shinbone, shoulder blade, stapes, sternum, stirrup, talus, tarsel *or* metatarsel, temporal, tibia, ulna, vertebra, wristbone **2.** ivory, tusk, whalebone

bonspiel *n.* championship, competition, curling tournament, round robin, showdown, spiels *(Nonformal)*, tournament

bonus *n.* award, benefit, bounty, commission, compensation, dividend, donation, extra, fringe benefit, gift, grant, gratuity, handout, honorarium, inducement, largesse, pay, premium, present, prize, recompense, reward, special compensation, tip *Nonformal:* golden hello *or* parachute, goody, gravy, perk, plus *Antonyms:* forfeiture, penalty

bon vivant *n.* epicure, gourmand, gourmet, hedonist, pleasure-seeker, voluptuary *Antonyms:* abstainer, ascetic, puritan

book *n.* opus, production, title, tome, volume, work *Generic kinds of book:* adventure, album, annual, anthology, atlas, autobiography, bestseller, bible, biography, book with legs *(Nonformal)*, booklet, brochure, catalogue, children's, coffee-table, colouring, comic, compendium, confession, cook, copybook, day, diary, dictionary, encyclopedia, essays, fairy tale collection, fantasy, fiction, glossary, graphic novel, handbook, hardcover, illustrated, journal, lexicon, manual, memoir, nonfiction, notebook, novel, omnibus, page-turner, picaresque, picture, pocket, portfolio, potboiler, prayer, primer, psalm, psalter, reader, record, reference, report, reprint, rhyming dictionary, romance, schoolbook, sketchbook, songbook, speller, storybook, textbook, thesaurus, tract, trade, treasury, treatise, wordbook, yearbook, young adult *German:* *bildungsroman, kunstleroman* *Holy books:* Avesta *(Zoroastrianism)*, Bible*(Christianity)*, Book of Mormon *(Mormonism)*, Guru Granth Sahib *(Sikhism)*, Hebrew Bible, Kitab-i-Aqdas *(Baha'i)*, Koran *(Islamic)*, Talmud, Tao Te Ching *(Taoism)*, Torah *(Judaism)* *Buddhism:* Pali Scriptures, Tripitaka *Hinduism:* Ghita, Mahabharata, Puranas, Ramayana, Upanishads, Vedas *Jainism:* Anuyoga, Siddhanta *Physical kinds of book:* bound volume, casebound, cased, cloth, hardbound, leather-bound, limp-bound, paperback, soft-cover *Sizes of book:* elephant folio, folio, miniature, octavo *or* 8vo, octodecimo *or* eighteenmo *or* 18mo, quarto *or* 4to, sextodecimo *or* sixteenmo *or* 16mo, twelvemo *or* 12mo – *v.* **1.** accuse, arrest, charge, press charges, read the rights to **2.** charter, engage, enroll, enter, hire, line up, order, organize, pencil in, procure, program, register, reserve, schedule, set up *Antonyms:* cancel, void, withdraw

bookish *adj.* **1.** erudite, informed, knowledgeable, lettered, learned, literary, long-hair *(Nonformal)*, scholarly, well-read **2.** academic, theoretical **3.** dry, dull, finicky, narrow, nerdy *(Nonformal)*, pedantic, pettifogging, punctilious, rigid, stuffy, tedious

boom *n.* **1.** bang, cannonade, explosion, report, reverberation, roar, rumble, thunder **2.** advance, boost, development, expansion, explosion, gain, growth, improvement, increase, inflation, jump, prosperity, prosperousness, push, rush, spurt, upsurge, upswing *Antonyms:* collapse, crash, decline, downturn, failure, recession, slump **3.** beam, chain, pole, spar – *v.* appreciate, boost, develop, enhance, expand, flourish, gain, grow, increase, intensify, prosper, rise, spurt, succeed, swell, thrive, vaunt *Antonyms:* decrease, devalue, minimize

boomerang *v.* backfire, backlash, bounce back, come back, kick back, react, rebound, recoil, return, reverse, ricochet

boon *n.* **1.** godsend, piece of luck, stroke of fortune, windfall **2.** aid, benefit, blessing, dispensation, favour, gift, good deed, help, kindness, offering, present, reward, service – *adj.* bosom, close, convivial, favourite, intimate, lifelong

boor *n.* buffoon, bumpkin, clod, lout, oaf, philistine *Nonformal:* clodhopper galoot, hayseed, hobbledehoy, klutz, lummox, yahoo

boorish *adj.* awkward, bad-mannered, barbaric, bearish, cantankerous, churlish, clumsy, coarse, crude, gross, gruff, ill-mannered, impolite, loud, loutish, low-bred, lubberly, oafish, ornery, provincial, rough, rude, rustic, swinish, ugly, uncivilized, uncouth, uncultured, uneducated, unpolished, vulgar *Antonyms:* cultured, genteel, polite, refined

boost *n.* **1.** addition, advance, breakthrough, expansion, hike, hoist, improvement, increase, increment, jump, lift, push, raise, rise, shove, step-up, thrust, upgrade *Antonyms:* decline, decrease, deterioration, fall, reduction, setback **2.** aid, assistance, backup, charge, encouragement, hand, handout, help, helping hand, lift, pick-me-up *(Nonformal)*, praise, promotion, refresher, support – *v.* **1.** advance, assist, elevate, encourage, extol, foster, heighten, hoist, improve, inspire, lift, plug (*Nonformal*), praise, promote, push, raise, support, sustain, thrust, uplift, upraise *Antonyms:* condemn, cut, decrease, hinder, pare, reduce **2.** add, amplify, augment, beef up (*Nonformal*), charge, develop, enlarge, expand, extend, heighten, hike, increase, jack up, jump, magnify, multiply, raise *Antonyms:* decrease, devalue, diminish, lower

boot *n.* *chaussure (French)*, footwear *Kinds of boot:* arctic, billy, cowboy, calk *or* drive *or* Larigan's *or* Lumberman's rubbers, cossacks, desert, galoshes, gumboots, hip-waders, ice-creepers, jackboots *North:* kamilt, mukluks, overshoes, riding, rubbers, sprogs, steel-toed, waders *Trademarks:* Dr. Marten's, Wellingtons– *v.* bounce, drive, drop-kick, eject, give the old heave-ho *(Nonformal)*, kick, kick out, knock, oust, punt, shove, turf *See also:* **shoe**

booth *n.* carrel, closet, compartment, corner, counter, cubbyhole, cubicle, dispensary, display, enclosure, hutch, kiosk, nook, pew, stall, stand

border *n.* **1.** boundary, bounds, brim, brink, circumference, confines, edge, end, extremity, 49th parallel (*Canada-U.S.*), fringe, fringe land, frontier, limit, line, lip, margin, pale, perimeter, periphery, rim, threshold, verge **2.** cuff, edging, flounce, hem, ruffle, skirt, trim – *v.* abut, adjoin, bind, communicate, conjoin, contour, define, delineate, edge, encircle, enclose, flank, frame, fringe, hem, join, line, march, margin, mark off, neighbour, outline, rim, set off, side, skirt, surround, touch, trim, verge

borderline *adj.* ambiguous, ambivalent, doubtful, either way, equivocal, indecisive, indefinite, inexact, marginal, open, problematic, uncertain, unclear, undecided, unsettled *Nonformal:* iffy, on the bubble *Antonyms:* definite, exact

bore *n.* bother, dull person, nuisance pest *Nonformal:* bummer, creep, deadhead, downer, drag, drip, grind, Hypnos, nag, pain, Somnos, stuffed shirt, wet blanket, yawn – *v.* **1.** annoy, bother, discomfort, drag, exhaust, fatigue, irk, irritate, jade, pall, pester, tax, tire, trouble, turn off, vex, wear, wear out, weary *Antonyms:* amuse, divert, engross, fascinate, stimulate **2.** auger, burrow, drill, gouge, mine, penetrate, perforate, pierce, punch, puncture, ream, root, sink, tunnel

boredom *n.* apathy, detachment, disgust, disinterest, doldrums, dullness, ennui, fatigue, flatness, indifference, jadedness, lassitude, listlessness, lethargy, monotony, sameness, tedium, weariness *Nonformal:* the blahs, cabin fever, MEGO (my eyes glaze over), *Antonyms:* amusement, entertainment, excitement, interest, stimulation

boring *adj.* bland, humdrum, monotonous, tedious, tiresome, vapid *Nonformal:* a yawn, dead, dry as dust, dull as dishwater, ho-hum, nothing to write home about *Antonyms:* appealing, barn-burning *(Nonformal)*, exciting, interesting

borrow *v.* acquire, adopt, appropriate, assume, beg, bite, bum, cadge, hire, negotiate, obtain, pawn, pirate, pledge, rent, simulate, take, tap *Nonformal:* liberate, mooch, sponge, touch *Antonyms:* advance, give, lend, loan, provide, return, supply

bosom *adj.* best, cherished, closest, dear, faithful, intimate, near and dear – *n.* **1.** breast, bust, chest **2.** centre, core, heart, soul

boss *n.* brass, chief, director, employer, executive, foreman, leader, manager, overseer, owner, president, taskmaster *Nonformal:* big cheese, head honcho – *v.* administrate, command, control, direct, dominate, domineer, manage, oversee, preside, run, steer, supervise

bossy *adj.* demanding, despotic, dictatorial, domineering, high-handed, insistent, overbearing, overruling, pushy, severe, tyrannical *Antonyms:* diffident, retiring, shy

botany *n.* horticulture, natural history, phytobiology, phytology, plant biology *or* science *Botany fields:* agriculture, agrobiology, agronomy, algology, aquaculture *or* aquiculture, bacteriology, botanical histochemistry, bryology, dendrology, ethnobotany, floriculture, forestry, fungology, genetics, gnotobiology, histology, horticulture, hydroponics, mycology, olericulture, paleobotany, palynology, phycology, phytochemistry, phytogeography, phytography, phytopathology, phytotomy, plant morphology, plant physiology, pomology

bother *n.* **1.** annoyance, drag, handicap, headache, imposition, inconvenience, nuisance, pain, pest, trial, trouble, worry *Nonformal:* bitch, hassle **2.** ado, commotion, dither, fuss, hubbub, to-do – *v.* **1.** annoy, disconcert, exasperate, harass, hector, hound, perplex, perturb, pester, ruffle, tease, try, vex *Nonformal:* bug, flummox *Antonyms:* aid, assist, facilitate, further, help **2.** concern, discommode, distress, fret, put to the trouble, trouble, upset

bothersome *adj.* aggravating, annoying, awkward, burdensome, complicated, delicate, difficult, disquieting, distressing, disturbing, embarrassing, exasperating, galling, heavy, inconvenient, inopportune, intricate, irritating, knotty, labyrinthine, oppressive, painful, perplexing, perturbing, problematical, provoking, puzzling, sensitive, taxing, thorny, ticklish, tiresome, tricky, troublesome, unsettling, untimely, upsetting, worrying *Antonyms:* beneficial, convenient, helpful, useful

bottle *n.* container, vessel *Kinds of bottle:* canteen, carafe, carboy, cruet, decanter, demijohn, ewer, flagon, flask, jar, jeroboam, jug, litre, magnum, Methuselah, urn, vial *Nonformal:* forty-pounder, mickey, Texas mickey– *v.* bottle up, cage, confine, contain, cork, curb, encapsulate, hem, jar, package, pen, pin, suppress

bottleneck *n.* blockage, congestion, constriction, clog, deterrent, hindrance, impediment, logjam, restriction, snag, stoppage, traffic jam

bottom *adj.* **1.** base, nadir, nethermost, primary, rock-bottom, the pits *(Nonformal)*, underlying, undermost *Antonyms:* higher, top, upper – *n.* basis, bed, bedrock, cause, core, depths, essence, floor, foot, footing, foundation, ground, groundwork, quintessence, seat, soul, source, substance, substratum, support, underneath, underside *Antonyms:* cover, height, lid, peak, summit **2.** behind, butt, buttocks, *derrière (French)*, posterior, rump, seat, tail *Nonformal:* bum, caboose, can, cheeks, duff, fanny, keister, tush

bottomless *adj.* abyssal, boundless, deep, endless, inexhaustible, infinite, limitless, unending, unfathomable, unlimited *Antonyms:* ephemeral, shallow, superficial, surface

bough *n.* branch, extension, limb, runner, shoot, sprig, switch, tendril, twig

bouillon *n.* beef *or* chicken *or* vegetable stock, broth, consommé, soup, stock

boulevard *n.* artery, avenue, centre strip, concourse, drag *(Nonformal)*, highway, passage, path, road, street, strip, thoroughfare, track, way

bounce *n.* animation, dynamism, ebullience, energy, exuberance, get up and go, liveliness, pep, rebound, spring, verve, vigour, vitality, vivacity, zip *(Nonformal)* – *v.* **1.** backlash, boomerang, bump, carom *(Billiards)*, glance off, hurdle, jump, leap, rebound, recoil, ricochet, snap back, spring back, vault **2.** eject, oust, reject, throw *or* turf out *(Nonformal)*, toss

bound *adj.* **1.** apprenticed, beholden, contracted, duty-bound, enslaved, fettered, indentured, obliged, pledged, promised, *Antonyms:* at large, free, unencumbered **2.** coerced, compelled, constrained, driven, forced, impelled, obligated, required, urged **3.** certain, destined, doomed, fated, firm, mandated, sure **4.** bandaged, chained, fast, restrained, secured, tied, wrapped, yoked **5.** bent, determined, driven, intent, resolved, under compulsion – *n.* boundary, confine, edge, end, environs, extremity, fringe, limit, limitation, line, margin, pale, periphery, precinct, purlieu, rim, verge – *v.* **1.** circumscribe, confine, define, delimit, demarcate, determine, encircle, enclose, hem in, limit, mark, measure, restrain, restrict, surround, terminate **2.** bounce, hurdle, jump, leap, pounce, spring, vault

boundary *n.* ambit, barrier, beginning, border, borderline, bounds, brink, circumference, confines, demarcation, edge, environs, extent, extremity, frame, frontier, horizon, limit, limits, line, margin, mark, outer limits, outline, pale, perimeter, periphery, precinct, radius, rim, terminal

bounded *adj.* belted, bordered, circumscribed, compassed, confined, contiguous, defined, edged, encircled, enclosed, encompassed, enveloped, fenced, flanked, fringed, girdled, hedged, limited, restricted, rimmed, ringed, surrounded, walled *Antonyms:* endless, forever, unlimited

boundless *adj.* abysmal, bottomless, deep, endless, extreme, great, immeasurable, immense, incalculable, indefinite, inexhaustible, infinite, limitless, measureless, profound, tremendous, unbounded, unconfined, unending, unfathomable, unlimited, untold, vast, wide open *Antonyms:* calculable, confined, limited, restricted

bountiful *adj.* abundant, ample, bounteous, copious, cornucopian, exuberant, generous, lavish, liberal, luxuriant, magnanimous, munificent, plenteous, plentiful, plenty, profuse, prolific *Antonyms:* paltry, penurious, scanty

bouquet *n.* **1.** boutonniere, buttonhole, corsage, flowers, garland, lei, nosegay, posy, spray, wreath **2.** aroma, aura, balm, essence, fragrance, incense, odour, perfume, redolence, savour, scent, smell, spice

bourgeois *adj.* **1.** commonplace, conventional, middlebrow *Antonyms:* avant-garde, chic **2.** materialistic, mercantile, monied, propertied – *n.* capitalist, merchant, middle class, tradesperson

bout *n.* **1.** battle, boxing match, competition, contest, encounter, engagement, fight, fistfight, match, prize fight, pugilistic contest, sparring, round, struggle *Nonformal:* mill, set-to **2.** at bat, inning, period, season, spell, turn **3.** bender, binge, course, run, session, spree, stint, stretch, tear (*Nonformal*), tour, turn

bovine *adj.* cowlike, enduring, even-tempered, impassive, imperturbable, phlegmatic, placid, ruminative, slow-moving, stalwart, steady, stoic, stolid, wooden *Antonyms:* animated, ebullient, mercurial

bow *n.* **1.** bend, bending, bob, curvature, curve, genuflection, inclination, round, turn **2.** boat front, bowsprit, fore *or* forepart, head, nose, prow, stem – *v.* **1.** accept, acquiesce, bend, capitulate, cave in, comply, concede, defer, give in, kowtow, relent, salaam, submit, succumb, surrender, yield **2.** arch, bend, bob, crook, curtsey, curve, dip, droop, duck, genuflect, hunch, incline, nod, stoop

bowdlerize *v.* blue–pencil, censor, clean up, edit, expunge, expurgate, omit, strike out

bowels *n. pl.* belly, core, deep, depths, entrails, guts, heart, hold, innards, insides, interior, intestines, penetralia, recesses, viscera, vitals

bower *n.* alcove, arbour, boudoir, chamber, gazebo, grotto, haven, recess, retreat, sanctuary

bowl *n.* **1.** basin, casserole, container, crater, crock, deep dish, dish, hollow, jar, knock, pitcher, plate, pot, saucer, strike, tureen, urn, vessel **2.** amphitheatre, arena, coliseum, stadium – *v.* fling, hurl, pitch, revolve, roll, rotate, spin, throw, toss, trundle, whirl

bowling *n.* bowls *Kinds of bowling:* bocce, candlepin, five-pin, lawn, tenpin *or* tenpins *Scoring and procedure in bowling:* ace, approach, curve ball, delivery, foul line, frame, gutter ball, handicap, hook ball, miss, perfect game, pocket, score, spare, split, straight ball, strike

box *n.* bin, carton, case, casket, chest, coffer, container, crate, hutch, pack, package, portmanteau, receptacle, trunk – *v.* **1.** buffet, clout, cuff, duke, hit, hook, pummel, punch, scrap, slap, slug, sock, strike, wallop, whack, whomp **2.** bottle up, confine, corral, crate, encase, pack, package, pen, shut in, wrap

boxer *n.* champion, contender, fighter, prizefighter, pugilist, scrapper *Nonformal:* champ, palooka, pug, slugger

boxing *n.* bareknuckle fighting, fisticuffs, manly art of self-defence, prizefighting, pugilism, sparring *Nonformal:* slugfest, the fight game *Kinds of boxing fouls:* backhanding, biting, butting, clutching, elbowing, heeling, hitting below the belt, hitting downed opponent, hitting with open glove, holding, kneeing, pivot blow, rabbit punch, rope-a-dope *(Nonformal)*, thumbing *Kinds of boxing punches:* body blow, bolo, chop, combination, counter-punch, cross, haymaker, hook, jab, kidney, knockout, left or lefthander *or* hook, one-two, rabbit, roundhouse, sidewinder, sneak, sucker, solarplexus, straight, swing, uppercut *Nonformal:* kayo, K.O., T.K.O *Kinds of boxing weight divisions:* bantamweight, cruiserweight, featherweight, flyweight, heavyweight, junior lightweight, light flyweight, light heavyweight, light middleweight, lightweight, light welterweight, middleweight, super bantamweight, superheavyweight, welterweight

boy *n.* child, *garçon (French)*, junior, lad, laddie, manchild, master, schoolfellow, sprig, stripling, whippersnapper, youngster, youth *Nonformal:* little shaver, small fry, sprout

boycott *n.* embargo, interdiction, prohibition – *v.* blackball, blacklist, eschew, pass up, picket, proscribe, refrain from, shun, shut out, snub, stay away from *Antonyms:* befriend, cater to, court, spend time with

boyfriend *n.* admirer, beau, companion, date, escort, inamorato, lover, paramour, suitor, swain, sweetheart, true love, wooer, young man *Nonformal:* crush, flame, gentleman caller *or* friend, guy, heartthrob, main man *or* squeeze, man, significant other, squeeze, steady

boyhood *n.* adolescence, childhood, halcyon days, heyday, puerility, salad days *(Nonformal)*, young manhood, youth *Antonyms:* adulthood, manhood

brace *n.* arm, bearing, block, bolster, bracket, buttress, cantilever, lever, prop, rafter, reinforcement, rib, shore, splice, stanchion, stave, stay, strut, support, truss, vice – *v.* bandage, bind, bolster, buck up *(Nonformal)*, buttress, fasten, fortify, gird, hold up, prepare, prop, ready, reinforce, shore up, steady, strap, strengthen, support, tie, tighten, uphold *Antonyms:* abandon, detach, disconnect, leave hanging *(Nonformal)*

bracelet *n.* anklet, armlet, bangle, charm bracelet, jewellery, ornament, trinket *Nonformal:* handcuff, manacle

bracer *n.* refresher, reviver *Nonformal:* hair of the dog, just what the doctor ordered, nip of the creature, pick-me-up

bracket *n.* area, category, class, division, grade, level, order, parenthesis, rank, section, set, stratum – *v.* **1.** angle iron, brace, buttress, prop, support **2.** couple, link, pair, parenthesize, yoke

brackish *adj.* bilge, bitter, briny, distasteful, saline, saltish, salty, stale *Antonyms:* fresh, sweet

bracing *adj.* animating, brisk, chilly, cool, crisp, energizing, exhilarating, fortifying, fresh, invigorating, lively, quickening, refreshing, restorative, reviving, rousing, stimulating, stimulative, tonic, vigorous *Antonyms:* debilitating, draining, exhausting, sapping, soporific, taxing, tiring

brag *adj.* boast, crow, flaunt, hyperbolize, prate, swagger, swash *Nonformal:* beat the drum, blow *or* toot one's own horn, pat oneself on the back, shovel

braggart *n.* blusterer, boaster, braggadocio, maw-mouth, *(Newfoundland)*, showoff, swaggerer, trumpeter *Nonformal:* big talker, blowhard, grandstander, hotshot, know-it-all, peacock, showboat, windbag

braid *n.* cornrow, pigtail, queue, wreath – *v.* entwine, interlace, intertwine, interweave, lace, mesh, pigtail, plait, ravel, twine, twist, weave

brains *n.* acuity, genius, head, intellect, intelligence, mastermind, mentality, perspicacity, sagacity, sapience, wisdom, wit *Nonformal:* grey cells *or* matter, smarts

brainstorm *n.* brainwave, caprice, flash, inspiration, notion, revelation, whim – *v.* pool ideas, group think, have a think tank

brainwash *v.* condition, convince, disinform, hypnotize, inculcate, indoctrinate, influence, instill, mesmerize, persuade, proselytize, teach *Antonyms:* deprogram, disabuse

brake *n.* **1.** anchor, brakepad, constraint, control, curb, damper, deterrent, discouragement, flap, hindrance, hurdle, obstacle, rein, restraint, retarding device, stop **2.** bush, copse, thicket – *v.* bar, block, dam, decelerate, halt, hamper, hinder, impede, moderate, obstruct, reduce, slacken, slow, slow down, stop *Antonyms:* accelerate, burn rubber *(Nonformal)*, speed up

bramble *n.* brier, burr, bush, gorse, hedge, nettle, prickly shrub, thistle, thorn

branch *n.* **1.** arm, bough, extension, fork, growth, limb, offshoot, shoot, spray, sucker, tendril, tributary **2.** affiliate, branch office *or* plant, chapter, division, local, lodge, offshoot, organ, post, satellite, wing – *v.* bifurcate, divide, fork, spread, stem

brand *n.* **1.** cast, character, class, description, grade, kind, make, quality, sort, species, type, variety **2.** colophon, emblem, hallmark, heraldry, imprint, label, logo, logotype, mark, marker, monogram, name, sign, stamp, symbol, trademark, trade name – *v.* **1.** categorize, compartmentalize, identify, label, mark, name, personalize, pigeonhole, stigmatize **2.** besmirch, defame, impugn, libel, scorch, sear, sully

brandish *v.* display, disport, exhibit, expose, flash, flaunt, parade, raise, shake, show, show off, sport, swing, threaten, trot out, warn, wield

brass *n.* **1.** metal alloy **2.** horn *Brass wind instruments:* alpenhorn, althorn *or* alto horn, bugle, clarion, cornet, English horn, flugelhorn, French horn, hunting horn, mellophone, sackbut, slide trombone, sousaphone, trombone, trumpet, tuba, valve trombone *See also:* **instrument, woodwind** **3.** audacity, brazenness, effrontery, gall, impudence, impulsiveness, insolence, nerve *Nonformal:* chutzpah, moxie

brat *n.* cub, *enfant terrible (French),* juvenile delinquent, kid, hooligan, pismire, rascal, terror, unruly child, urchin, whippersnapper, youngster *Nonformal:* punk, puppy, scamp

bravado *n.* bluster, boastfulness, bombast, braggadocio, bragging, grandiosity, pretension, self-aggrandizement *or* -glorification, swaggering *Nonformal:* big talk, hot air, machismo *Antonyms:* meekness, shyness, unpretentiousness

brave *adj.* adventuresome, adventurous, assured, audacious, bold, chivalrous, confident, courageous, daring, dashing, dauntless, defiant, determined, fearless, fire-eating *(Nonformal),* fresh, gallant, game, gritty, gutsy, hardy, heroic, indomitable, intrepid, lionhearted, mettlesome, nervy, plucky, resolute, sanguine, sassy, skookum tumtum *(Pacific Coast),* spirited, spunky, stalwart, steadfast, stout-hearted, strong, tenacious, unafraid, undaunted, undeterred, unflinching, valiant, valorous, venturesome *Antonyms:* afraid, cowardly, craven, fearful, frightened, scared, shrinking, timid – *v.* bear, beard, brook, challenge, confront, court, dare, defy, endure, face, risk, stand tall, suffer, support, take on, venture, withstand *Antonyms:* give in, retreat, surrender

bravery *n.* audacity, backbone, boldness, chivalry, courage, courageousness, daring, dauntlessness, derring-do, fearlessness, fight, fortitude, gallantry, grit, hardiness, heart, heroism, intestinal fortitude, intrepidity, mettle, nerve, pluck, prowess, resolution, spirit, spunk, starch, stomach, strength, tenacity, valiance, valour *Nonformal:* balls, guts, moxie, right stuff *Antonyms:* cowardice, faintheartedness, fearfulness, fright, timidity

bravura *adj.* audacious, brilliant, daring, dashing, dramatic, virtuoso *Antonyms:* common, inferior, regular – *n.* audacity, daring, éclat, wizardry

brawl *n.* altercation, argument, battle royal, brannigan, broil, clash, disorder, dispute, donnybrook, feud, fight, fracas, fray, free-for-all, fuss, hassle, imbroglio, mêlée, punch-up, quarrel, riot, row, ruckus, scrap, scuffle, squabble, tumult, uproar, wrangle *Nonformal*: dust up, rhubarb *Antonyms:* accord, agreement, cease-fire, entente, peace, truce – *v.* argue, battle, bicker, dispute, fight, quarrel, roughhouse, row, rumble, scrap, scuffle, spat, squabble, tiff, trade punches, tussle, wrangle, wrestle

brawn *n.* clout, energy, flesh, might, muscles, power, punch, sinew, strength, vigour

brawny *adj.* able-bodied, athletic, beefy *(Nonformal),* bulky, burly, fleshy, hardy, hefty, Herculean, husky, muscular, powerful, robust, sinewy, strapping, sturdy, tough, vital *Antonyms:* frail, scrawny, skinny, thin, weak

bray *n.* blare, blast, bleat, cry, honk, neigh, whinny – *v.* announce, bawl, cry, hoot, sound off, trumpet

brazen *adj.* brash, brassy, coppery, impertinent, impudent, loudmouthed, metallic, shameless *Nonformal:* cheeky, cocky, nervy, hot-shot, in your face *Antonyms:* demure, meek, modest, quiet

breach *n.* **1.** contravention, dereliction, disobedience, disregard, fracture, infraction, infringement, neglect, noncompliance, nonobservance, offence, transgression, trespass, violation *Antonyms:* compliance, fulfillment, honour **2.** alienation, break, difference, discord, disharmony, dissension, disunity, division, estrangement, fissure, fracture, quarrel, rent, rift, rupture, schism, secession, separation, severance, split, variance, withdrawal *Antonyms:* cohesion, confederation, union **3.** aperture, break, chasm, chip, cleft, crack, discontinuity, fissure, gap, hole, opening, rent, rift, rupture, slit, split – *v.* break open, burst, bust *(Nonformal)*, cave in, cleave, crack, fracture, rend asunder, rupture

bread *n.* aliment, comestibles, diet, fare, feed, food, grub (*Nonformal*), nourishment, nutriment, provisions, staff *or* stuff of life, sustenance, victuals *Kinds of bread:* anadama, bagel, banana, baguette, bialy, biscuit, black, bran muffin, breadcrumbs, breadstick, brioche, brown, bun, cake, challah, chapati, cornbread, cream cracker, croissant, crouton, egg, English muffin, French, garlic, graham cracker *or* wafer, hamburger *or* hot dog bun, hardtack, hush puppy, Italian, johnny cake, malt, matzo, melba toast, muffin, naan, nut, oatcake, onion bun, papadum, pita, poori, popover, pretzel, pumpernickel, raisin, roll, rusk, rye, saltine, semolina, seven-grain, ship biscuit, soda cracker, soda, sourdough, Texas toast, tortilla, unleavened, wafer, water biscuit, whole-grain, wholewheat, Wonder bread *(Trademark)*, zwieback

breadth *n.* amplitude, area, broadness, comprehensiveness, diameter, dimension, expanse, extensiveness, extent, fullness, gamut, greatness, inclusiveness, largeness, latitude, magnitude, measure, orbit, range, reach, scale, scope, size, space, span, spread, stretch, sweep, vastness, wideness, width

break *n.* **1.** breach, cleft, crack, division, eye, fracture, gap, gash, hole, opening, rent, rift, rupture, schism, split, tear *Antonyms:* connection, seal, union **2.** adjournment, breather, breathing space, caesura, continuance, cutoff, halt, hiatus, interlude, intermission, interruption, interval, layoff, letup, lull, pause, recess, respite, rest, suspension, ten *(Nonformal)*, time off *or* out **3.** alienation, altercation, breach, change, clash, difference, dispute, divergence, estrangement, fight, misunderstanding, rift, rupture, schism, separation, split, trouble **4.** accident, advantage, chance, favourable circumstance, fortune, good luck, luck, occasion, opening, opportunity, shot *(Nonformal)* – *v.* **1.** annihilate, burst, bust, cleave, collapse, come apart, crack, crack up *or* open, crash, crumble, crush, damage, dash, decay, decompose, demolish, destroy, deteriorate, disable, disintegrate, disunite, divide, explode, fracture, fragment, pile up, powder, pulverize, rear end, rend, rive, ruin, rupture, sever, shatter, sideswipe, slam, smash, snap, splinter, split, squash, torpedo, total, trash, wallop, wreck *Antonyms:* fix, mend, repair **2.** diminish, lessen, lighten, moderate, reduce, weaken **3.** bankrupt, confound, cow, demoralize, demote, dispirit, downgrade, enervate, enfeeble, humiliate, impair, impoverish, incapacitate, subdue, undermine, weaken **4.** breach, contravene, disobey, disregard, infringe, offend, renege, transgress, violate *Antonyms:* adhere to, conform, follow, obey, observe **5.** abandon, abscond, clear *or* let out, cut, dash, discontinue, escape, flee, fly, get *or* run away, give up, interrupt, stop, suspend

breakable *adj.* brittle, crisp, crumbly, delicate, flimsy, fracturable, fragile, frail, ramshackle, shatterable, splintery, vitreous, weak *Antonyms:* indestructible, lasting, resistant

breakaway *adj.* mutinous, rebellious, seditious, separatist – *n.* breakout, escape, jailbreak – *v.* avoid, bolt, clear, escape, extricate, go in alone, run for it, shake off, split the defence *(Hockey) Nonformal:* fly the coop, steer clear

breakdown *n.* **1.** blown fuse *(Nonformal)*, collapse, crackup, disintegration, disruption, failure, mishap, stoppage **2.** account, analysis, categorization, classification, diagnosis, dissection, itemization, list

breaker *n.* bore, foam, froth, growler, roller, spray, spume, tidal wave, wave

breakfast *n.* American Plan, bacon & eggs,

brekkie *(Nonformal)*, cereal, continental breakfast, English breakfast, meal, oatmeal, porridge *French:* déjeuner à la fourchette, petit déjeuner

breakthrough *n.* advance, boost, development, discovery, find, finding, gain, improvement, increase, invention, leap, leap of the imagination, progress, quantum leap, rise, step forward

breakup *n.* cleavage, crackup, disintegration, dispersal, dissolution, divorce, ending, fissure, parting, rift, secession, separation, split, splitting, termination *Antonyms:* convergence, marriage, union

breakwater *n.* barrier, bulwark, embankment, headland, jetty, pier, promontory, rampart, reef, sandspit, seawall, wharf

breast *n.* **1.** bosom, chest, mammary gland, nipple, pap, teat **2.** centre, conscience, heart, soul

breath *n.* **1.** animation, breathing, exhalation, expiration, gasp, gulp, inhalation, inspiration, insufflation, respiration, wheeze **2.** break, breather, instant, moment, pause, respite, rest, second, space **3.** dash, hint, murmur, shade, soupçon, streak, suggestion, suspicion, touch, trace, undertone, whiff, whisper

breathe *v.* **1.** aspirate, blow, buzz, choke, chuff, cough, distend, drag, draw *or* draw in, exhale, expire, fan, fill, gasp, gulp, heave, hiss, huff, inflate, inhale, pant, puff, pull at *or* on, rasp, respire, scent, sibilate, sigh, smoke, sniff, sniffle, snore, snort, suck, swell, throb, wheeze, whiff, whisper, whistle, whoop, wind **2.** articulate, confide, express, inform, mention, say, tell, utter, voice, whisper **3.** imbue, impart, infuse, inject, inspire, instill

breathless *adj.* **1.** asthmatic, blown, choking, exhausted, gasping, gulping, out-of-breath, panting, short-winded, spent, stertorous, wheezing, winded **2.** agog, anxious, astounded, avid, eager, excited, flabbergasted, open-mouthed, thunderstruck

breed *n.* brand, character, class, extraction, family, genus, ilk, kind, line, lineage, lot, nature, pedigree, progeny, race, sort, species, stamp, stock, strain, stripe, type, variety – *v.* bear, beget, bring about, bring forth, cause, create, deliver, engender, father, generate, give birth, give rise, hatch, impregnate, induce, make, multiply, originate, procreate, produce, propagate, reproduce, sire

breeder *n.* **1.** animal raiser, cattleworker, kennel, rancher, shepherd, stocker, stud **2.** atomic reactor, furnace, nuclear pile, nuclear reactor, reactor

breeding *n.* ancestry, civility, conduct, courtesy, cultivation, culture, deportment, development, gentility, grace, lineage, manners, polish, raising, rearing, refinement, schooling, training, upbringing, urbanity

breeze *n.* **1.** air, chinook, current, draft, flurry, gust, light wind, puff, waft, whiff, wind, zephyr **2.** simplicity *Nonformal:* bird, cakewalk, cat's paw, cinch, duck soup, piece of cake, snap

breezy *adj.* **1.** blowing, blowy, blusterous, blustery, drafty, fresh, gusty, squally, windy **2.** airy, blithe, buoyant, carefree, casual, cheerful, debonair, easy, easygoing, informal, light, lighthearted, relaxed, sunny, unconstrained *Antonyms:* depressed, mournful, sad, serious

brethren *n.* brothers, congregation, flock, fold, followers, fraternity, laity, parish, people

brevet *n.* brief, charge, commission, concession, document, exequatur, grant, licence, mandate, trust, warrant

brevity *n.* briefness, conciseness, curtness, economy, incisiveness, pithiness, pointedness, shortness, succinctness, terseness *Antonyms:* long-windedness, prolixity, redundancy, verbosity, wordiness

brew *n.* **1.** beer, beverage, broth, distillation, drink, fermentation, infusion, liquor, mixture, preparation **2.** blend, compound, concoction, hash, hodgepodge, melange, miscellany, mishmash, potpourri – *v.* **1.** boil, cook, infuse, mull, soak, steep, stew **2.** breed, concoct, contrive, develop, devise, excite, foment, form, gather, hatch, mull, plan, plot, project, scheme, start

bribe *n.* bait, blackmail, enticement, fee, gift, graft, gratuity, incentive, inducement, influence peddling, payoff, perquisite, price, protection, remuneration, reward, sweetener, take, tip *Nonformal:* election goody, hush money, kickback, payola – *v.* corrupt, entice, influence, lure, tamper, tempt, tip *Nonformal:* buy off, fix, get to, grease *or* oil a palm

brick *n.* adobe, block, cement, clay, clinker, firebrick, paving-stone, unit – *v.* cover, enclose, stone, tile, slate, wall up

bridal *adj.* conjugal, connubial, marital, marriage, matrimonial, nuptial, wedding

bridge *n.* arch, branch, catwalk, connection, extension, gangplank, link, overpass, scaffold, span, trestle, viaduct *Kinds of bridge:* cantilever, covered, drawbridge, footbridge, ice, overpass, pontoon, railroad, Roman, rope, skywalk, suspension, toll, trestle, truss, viaduct, walkway, wooden – *v.* arch over, attach, bind, branch, connect, couple, cross, extend, go over, join, link, reach, span, traverse, unite *Antonyms:* cleave, divide, sever, split

bridgehead *n.* advance position, beachhead, front-line, outpost, spearhead, stronghold, vanguard

bridle *n.* check, control, curb, deterrent, halter, harness, headstall, leash, rein, restraint, shackle, trammel – *v.* **1.** check, constrain, control, curb, govern, hold back, inhibit, master, moderate, repress, restrain, subdue, suppress, withhold **2.** capture, harness, hitch up

brief *adj.* **1.** casual, ephemeral, evanescent, fast, flashing, fleeting, hasty, impermanent, instantaneous, limited, meteoric, momentary, passing, quick, rapid, short-lived, short-term, speedy, sudden, swift, temporary, transient, transitory *Antonyms:* circuitous, detailed, diffuse, lengthy, protracted **2.** abrupt, blunt, brusque, curt, laconic, succinct, terse **3.** cursory, curtailed, skimpy, slight, small – *n.* abridgment, abstract, condensation, digest, outline, précis, sketch, summary, synopsis – *v.* advise, apprise, enlighten, epitomize, explain, fill in, inform, initiate, instruct, orient, prepare, prime, recapitulate, summarize, update *Nonformal:* bring up to speed, provide the lowdown

briefcase *n.* attaché case, baggage, carrier, case, folder, laptop, notebook, portfolio, satchel

briefing *n.* conference, directions, discussion, guidance, information, informing, initiation, instruction, meeting, priming, rundown, update

briefly *adv.* concisely, crisply, curtly, fleetingly, for a short while, in a nutshell *(Nonformal)*, in short, momentarily, succinctly, tersely *Antonyms:* at great length, long-windedly

brigade *n.* army, band, body, company, contingent, corps, crew, detachment, division, fleet, force, group, organization, outfit, party, platoon, squad, squadron, team, troop, unit, wing

bright *adj.* **1.** ablaze, aglow, alight, auroral, beaming, blatant, blazing, blinding, brazen, burnished, clear, coloured, colourful, dazzling, effulgent, flaming, flashing, flashy, glaring, gleaming, glistening, glittering, glitzy (*Nonformal*), glorious, glossy, glowing, gorgeous, illuminated, incandescent, intense, light, luminous, lustrous, moonlit, phosphorescent, polished, radiant, resplendent, scintillating, shimmering, shining, shiny, showy, slick, sparkling, sunny, vivid *Antonyms:* cloudy, dark, dim, gloomy, overcast **2.** animated, cheerful, gay, genial, glad, happy, jolly, jovial, joyful, joyous, keen, lighthearted, lively, merry, optimistic, spirited, sprightly, vivacious **3.** auspicious, cheering, encouraging, excellent, favourable, golden, good, hopeful, optimistic, promising, propitious, rosy **4.** acute, advanced, alert, astute, aware, brainy, brilliant, clear-headed, clever, discerning, ingenious, intelligent, inventive, keen, knowing, perspicacious, precocious, quick, quick-witted, sharp, smart *Antonyms:* dim-witted, dull, dumb, idiotic, simple **5.** clement, cloudless, fair, favourable, limpid, mild, pleasant, sunny, unclouded

brighten *v.* **1.** buff up, burnish, gleam, light up, polish, shine *Antonyms:* blacken, overshadow, shadow **2.** buoy *or* cheer up, clear up, encourage, enliven, gladden, hearten, improve, look up, make happy *Antonyms:* darken, depress, sadden

brilliance *n.* **1.** charisma, excellence, glory, grandeur, lustre, majesty, preeminence, radiance, resplendence, splendour, sumptuousness **2.** brightness, clarity, colourfulness, richness, vividness **3.** agility, cleverness, nimbleness, quick-wittedness

brilliant *adj.* **1.** celebrated, eminent, excellent, exceptional, famous, glorious, illustrious, magnificent, outstanding, splendid, superb *Antonyms:* average, everyday, garden-variety, ordinary, unexceptional **2.** accomplished, acute, astute, brainy, bright, clever, discerning, expert, genius, gifted, ingenious, intellectual, intelligent, inventive, knowing, knowledgeable, masterly, penetrating, profound, quick, quick-witted, sharp, smart, talented, virtuoso *Antonyms:* dim-witted, mediocre, slow, untalented

brim *n.* border, brink, edge, fringe, ledge, lip, rim, top, verge

brimming *adj.* awash, brimful, chock-full, crammed, crowded, filled, flooded, flush, full, jammed, loaded, overabounding, overfilled, overflowing, overfull, packed, running over, stuffed, teeming *Antonyms:* barren, dry, empty

brindled *adj.* barred, dappled, freckled, marbled, mottled, speckled, spotted, stippled, streaked, striped, tabby, tawny, variegated

brine *n.* **1.** alkali, ocean, saline solution, salt *or* sea water **2.** embalming fluid, formaldehyde, monosodium glutamate, myrrh, pickle, pickling solution, preservative, salt, vinegar

bring *v.* **1.** draw, earn, fetch, gain, get, gross, make, net, pay, produce, profit, realize, return, sell for, total, yield **2.** bear, carry, convey, deliver, fetch, gather, go for, import, retrieve, transfer, transport, usher *Nonformal:* lug, tote, truck **3.** cause, compel, induce, tempt **4.** call for, entail, involve, require **5.** do to, inflict, visit upon, wreak

brink *n.* border, boundary, brim, cuff, edge, fringe, frontier, limit, lip, margin, perimeter, periphery, rim, skirt, threshold, verge

brisk *adj.* **1.** active, adroit, agile, alert, animated, bustling, busy, energetic, fast, lively, nimble, quick, speedy, sprightly, spry, vigorous *Antonyms:* heavy, lazy, lethargic, slow **2.** biting, bracing, chilly, crisp, exhilarating, fresh, invigorating, keen, nippy, refreshing, sharp, snappy, stimulating

bristle *n.* barb, coarse hair, hackle, spike, spine, stubble, thorn, whisker – *v.* **1.** rise *or* stick up, stand on end **2.** annoy, bother, hatchel, heckle, irritate, rankle, rub the wrong way *(Nonformal)*, ruffle

brittle *adj.* breakable, crisp, crumbling, delicate, fragile, frail, frangible, friable, papery, rigid, shatterable, skin and bones *(Nonformal)*, weak, wizened *Antonyms:* durable, strong, sturdy

broach *v.* **1.** begin, crack, decant, open, pierce, puncture, start, tap, uncork **2.** advance, approach, bring up, hint, interject, introduce, mention, move, offer, raise, speak *or* talk of, suggest, touch on

broad *adj.* **1.** extended, outstretched, sweeping, unlimited, wide, widespread **2.** ample, capacious, expansive, generous, immense, large, roomy, spacious, voluminous **3.** clear, obvious, open, plain **4.** comprehensive, deep, encyclopedic, extensive, far-ranging *or* reaching, important, inclusive, momentous, pandemic, significant, ubiquitous, universal *Antonyms:* close, confined, limited, restricted, specific

broadcast *n.* air time, program, radiocast, show, simulcast, telecast, transmission, webcast *(Nonformal)* – *v.* advertise, announce, beam, blazon, circulate, communicate, declare, disseminate, distribute, post, proclaim, promulgate, publicize, publish, relay, report, send out, spread, telecast, telegraph, telephone, televise, transmit *Antonyms:* conceal, disguise, hide, mask

broadcasting *n.* airing, air time, announcing, auditioning, informing, newscasting, performing, posting, radio, reporting, telecasting, television, transmission, transmitting

broaden *v.* augment, develop, enlarge, expand, extend, fatten, grow, increase, open up, spread, stretch, supplement, swell, widen *Antonyms:* circumscribe, constrain, diminish, narrow, reduce, restrict, simplify

broad-minded *adj.* advanced, catholic, cosmopolitan, flexible, freethinking, liberal, open, open-minded, permissive, progressive, receptive, responsive, tolerant, unbiased, wide *Antonyms:* bigoted, closed-minded, dogmatic, inflexible, pettifogging, prejudiced, puritanical

broadside *n.* **1.** assault, attack, barrage, battery, cannonade, discharge, fusillade, mad minute *(Nonformal)*, salvo, volley **2.** broadsheet, circular, handbill, leaflet, tabloid

brochure *n.* advertisement, booklet, circular, document, flyer, folder, handbill, leaflet, pamphlet

broil *n.* altercation, brawl, contest, dispute, dust-up *(Nonformal)*, quarrel, spat, squabble, struggle, turmoil, wrangle – *v.* bake, barbecue, burn, cook, fry, griddle, grill, heat, melt, roast, scorch, sear, toast, warm

broke *adj.* bankrupt, bereft, busted *(Nonformal)*, cleaned out, deficient, depleted, destitute, dirt poor, drained, empty, exhausted, failed, flat, foreclosed, hard up, impecunious, impoverished, in debt *or* receivership *or* want, indebted, indigent, insolvent, moneyless, needy, penniless, penurious, pinched, poor, poverty-stricken, ruined, strapped, stripped, totalled, undone, wanting, wiped out, without *Antonyms:* affluent, comfortable, prosperous, rich, wealthy

broken *adj.* **1.** damaged, defective, disabled, faulty, in disrepair, inoperative, not functioning *or* working *Nonformal:* busted, down, haywire *Antonyms:* complete, mint, undamaged **2.** disjointed, fractured, fragmented, halting, hesitant, hesitating, imperfect, incoherent, in pieces, mangled, mutilated, mumbled, muttered, stammering, stuttering, unintelligible, weak *Antonyms:* eloquent, flowing, fluid, smooth **3.** beaten, browbeaten, crippled, crushed, defeated, demolished, demoralized, destroyed, humbled, oppressed, overpowered, routed, shattered, smashed, subdued, vanquished **4.** deteriorated, exhausted, infirm, injured, rundown, spent, worn out **5.** disconnected, discontinuous, disturbed, erratic, fragmentary, incomplete, intermittent, interrupted, irregular, spasmodic, spastic, veering **6.** bankrupt, finished, ruined **7.** domesticated, disciplined, indoctrinated, initiated, schooled, tamed, trained

brokenhearted *adj.* aching, crestfallen, crushed, desolate, despairing, despondent, devastated, disappointed, disconsolate, grief-stricken, grieved, heartbroken, heartsick, inconsolable, miserable, mournful, prostrated, sorrowful, wretched

broker *n.* agent, dealer, go-between, intermediary, intermediate, mediator, middleman *Kinds of broker:* curb, diamond, discount, floor trader, grain, insurance, land, market maker, mortgage, pawn, real estate, ship, stock, stockjobber

bromide *n.* aphorism, banality, chestnut *(Nonformal)*, cliché, expression, hackneyed expression, inanity, maxim, old saw *or* tune, platitude, triteness, truism

bronze *adj.* chestnut, copper-coloured, golden, henna, metallic-brown, reddish-brown, roan, rust-coloured, sorrel, terra cotta – *n.* **1.** glyph, sculpture, sculptured piece, statue, work of art **2.** alloy, copper/tin alloy, metal, ore

brood *n.* breed, chicks, cluster, clutch, descendants, family, flock, infants, issue, litter, offspring, posterity, progeny, young – *v.* agonize, bleed, chafe inwardly, consider, deliberate, despond, dwell upon, fret, gloom, grieve, lament, languish, meditate, mope, mull over, muse, ponder, reflect, ruminate, sigh, speculate, sulk, think about, think upon, worry

brook *n.* beck, branch, burn, creek, rill, river, rivulet, run, runnel, stream, streamlet, watercourse – *v.* accept, bear, beard, endure, hold out, suffer, tolerate, weather, withstand

broom *n.* sweeper *Kinds of broom:* besom, birch, carpet sweeper, cornbroom, curling, feather duster, floor brush, mop, stable, whisk

broth *n.* bouillon, consommé, decoction, potage, purée, soup, stock

brothel *n.* bawdy house, bordello, whorehouse *Nonformal:* cathouse, red-light district, dude ranch

brother *n.* associate, chum, colleague, companion, comrade, confrère, fellow, frater, mate, pal, partner, peer *Nonformal:* bro', bub, bud, buddy, homeboy

brotherhood *n.* **1.** amity, camaraderie, companionship, consanguinity, equality, family, family connection, fellowship, filiation, friendliness, friendship, intimacy, kinship, race, relationship **2.** affiliation, alliance, association, clan, clique, club, community, comradeship, coterie, fraternity, guild, league, order, secret society, sect, society, union

brotherly *adj.* benevolent, charitable, compassionate, comradely, cordial, friendly, generous, intimate, kindly, neighbourly, personal, philanthropic, solicitous, sympathetic, understanding

brow *n.* **1.** aspect, bearing, countenance, crown, face, forehead, ridge, visage **2.** border, brim, brink, crest, rim, summit, tip, verge

browbeat *v.* badger, bludgeon, bluster, bulldoze, bully, castigate, coerce, cow, domineer, dragoon, frighten, harass, hector, intimidate, nag, oppress, overbear, threaten, tyrannize

brown *adj. & n.* colour *Brown shades:* amber, auburn, bay, beige, brick, bronze, buff, burnt sienna, chestnut, chocolate, cinnamon, cocoa, coffee, copper, ecru, fawn, ginger, hazel, henna, khaki, mahogany, nutbrown, ochre, puce, reddish-brown, reddish-tan, russet, rust, sepia, snuff- coloured, sorrel, tan, tawny, terra cotta, toast, umber

browse *v.* check over, dip into, examine, flip *or* leap through, glance at, inspect loosely, look, peruse, read, rifle through, scan, skim, skip through *Antonyms:* analyse, examine, scrutinize, study

bruise *n.* abrasion, black-and-blue mark, black eye, black mark, blemish, contusion, discoloration, injury, mark, swelling, wound – *v.* batter, beat, black, blacken, blemish, contuse, damage, dent, injure, mar, mark, pound, wound

brunette *adj.* brown, brunet (*Masc.*), dark, pigmented, tanned, tawny

brunt *n.* burden, force, impact, pressure, shock, strain, stress, thrust, violence

brush *n.* **1.** clash, conflict, confrontation, encounter, fight, fracas, run-in, scrap, set-to, skirmish, tap, touch, tussle **2.** bracken, brushwood, bushes, chaparral, copse, cover, gorse, grove, hedge, scrub, shrubbery, thicket, undergrowth, wood **3.** sweeper *Kinds of brush:* currycomb, hairbrush, lint brush, polisher, toothbrush, whisk – *v.* caress, comb, contact, flick, glance, graze, kiss, scrape, shave, skim, smooth, stroke, sweep, tickle, touch

brusque *adj.* bluff, blunt, crusty, curt, laconic, pithy, plain-spoken, rude, short, terse *Antonyms:* chatty, loquacious

brutal *adj.* barbaric, beastly, brutish, callous, carnal, coarse, cold-blooded, crude, fierce, grim, inhumane, remorseless, rough, rude, sadistic, savage, swinish, unfeeling, unrelenting, vicious *Antonyms:* civilized, gentle, humane

brutality *n.* atrocity, barbarism, bloodlust, callousness, cruelty, ferocity, mercilessness, savagery, viciousness, violence *Antonyms:* benevolence, charity, empathy, sympathy

brutally *adv.* barbarously, cold-bloodedly, diabolically, fiercely, mercilessly, murderously, ruthlessly, viciously *Antonyms:* compassionately, gently, softly, with feeling

brute *adj.* animal, bestial, bodily, carnal, physical, strong – *n.* animal, barbarian, beast, cannibal, churl, creature, degenerate, devil, fiend, lout, monster, ogre, ruffian, sadist, savage, scamp, swine

bubble *n.* droplet, effervescence, fizz, foam, froth, globule – *v.* boil, burble, churn, eddy, effervesce, fizz, foam, froth, gurgle, issue, percolate, ripple, simmer, smoulder, spume, trickle, well

buck *n.* **1.** male, stag *Kinds of buck:* antelope, deer, goat, rabbit, ram **2.** blade, dandy, ladies' man, man about town, playboy, young man **3.** dollar, greenback *(U.S.)*, loonie, *Nonformal:* dead president, smacker – *v.* contend, contest, oppose, resist

bucket *n.* barrel, basin, billycan, can, cask, container, pail, scuttle, tin, vessel

buckle *n.* catch, clamp, clasp, clip, fastener, fastening, harness, hasp – *v.* bend, bulge, collapse, contort, crumple, distort, fold *or* fold in, twist, warp, yield

bucolic *adj.* agrarian, pastoral, provincial, rural *Antonyms:* city, metropolitan, urban – *n.* farmer, hayseed, herder, rancher, rube *(Nonformal)*, rustic, shepherd

bud *n.* bloom, blossom, embryo, nucleus, shoot, sprout – *v.* burgeon, burst, develop, emerge, grow, shoot forth *or* up, sprout

Buddhism *n.* Buddhist religion *Kinds of Buddhism:* Ch'an, Chen Yen, Ching-t'u, Jodo, Mahayana, Nichiren, Shin, Shingon, Soka Gakkai, Tendai, Theravada *or* Hinayana, T'ien-t'ai, Vajarayana, Zen

budding *adj.* beginning, blossoming, burgeoning, bursting forth, developing, embryonic, fledgling, flowering, fresh, germinating, growing, incipient, maturing, nascent, opening, promising, sprouting

buddy *n.* **1.** associate, best friend, chum, colleague, companion, comrade, confidant, co-worker, crony, fellow, friend, intimate, mate, pal, peer *Nonformal:* chief, guy, sidekick **2.** bud *(Nonformal)*, fellow, man, man in the street, stranger

budge *v.* bend, change, change position, convince, dislodge, give way, inch, influence, move, persuade, propel, push, roll, shift, stir, yield *Antonyms:* remain firm, stand fast, stay resolute

budget *n.* account, allowance, cash flow, estimate, finances, funds, means, planned disbursement, spending plan, statement – *v.* apportion, calculate, estimate, plan, predict, ration

buff *adj. & n. Buff colours:* blonde, light brown, nude, ochre, sand, straw, tan, tawny, yellow-brown, yellowish – *n.* aficionado, collector, devotee, enthusiast, expert, zealot – *v.* burnish, polish, shine

buffalo *n.* ungulate *Kinds of buffalo:* beefalo, bison, Cape Buffalo, water buffalo, wisent – *v.* baffle, confuse, stump *Nonformal:* flummox, hornswoggle

buffer *n.* **1.** barrier, border, breakwater, defense, dike, embankment, intermediary, levee, partition, safeguard, screen, shield, windbreak **2.** absorber, bulwark, bumper, cushion, fender, shock absorber

buffet *n.* **1.** café, cafeteria, lunch counter *or* wagon, snack bar, table **2.** counter, serving table, sideboard **3.** all you can eat *(Nonformal)*, array of food, salad bar, smörgåsbord, spread – *v.* batter, beat, blow, box, bump, clobber, cuff, flail, force, hit, jolt, knock, pound, pummel, push, rap, shove, slap, smack, smash against, spank, strike, thrash, thump, wallop

buffoon *n.* antic, clown, comedian, comic, fool, harlequin, jester, joker, merry-andrew, prankster, wag, zany

bug *n.* **1.** fly, hemiptera, heteroptera, homoptera, insect *Nonformal:* buggy, cootie, creepy crawly *Bug features:* abdomin, antennae, eyes, leg, piercers, rostrum, stink gland, suckers, wings *Selected bugs:* aphid, back swimmer *or* water boatman, bedbug, beetle, black fly, blowfly, capsid, cicada, cricket, damselfly, deer-fly, dragonfly, earwig, flea, flower-bug, froghopper, grasshopper, greenfly, jumping plant lice, lantern fly, Junebug, leaf, leafhopper, mayfly *or* ephemerid, mealy, midge, mite, mosquito, moth, plant, plant hopper, pond skater, potato beetle, praying mantis, saucer, scale insect, shieldbug, spittlebug, squash, termite, treehopper, tsetse fly, water scorpion, water strider, weevil, whitefly, wireworm, woodborer **2.** cold, disease, flu, germ, illness, infection, influenza, pneumonia **3.** eavesdropping device, microphone, tap, wire, wiretap – *v.* **1.** aggravate, agitate, annoy, badger, bedevil, bother, harass, hector, infuriate, irk, irritate, madden, provoke, rankle, taunt, tease, torment *Antonyms:* calm, comfort, soothe **2.** eavesdrop, listen, listen in, overhear, spy, tap, wiretap

bugle *n.* coronet, horn, tooter, trumpet – *v.* call for, signal, summon

build *n.* body, conformation, constitution, figure, form, frame, habit, physique, shape, size, structure – *v.* **1.** assemble, carpenter, compose, construct, create, engineer, erect, fabricate, fashion, forge, form, frame, institute, invent, make, manufacture, mould, organize, produce, raise, rear, synthesize, write *Nonformal:* knock together, slap *or* throw together *Antonyms:* demolish, destroy, dismantle, dynamite, raze, tear down, weaken **2.** develop, establish, formulate, found, inaugurate, initiate, mount, originate, start **3.** accelerate, aggrandize, amplify, augment, boost, compound, enlarge, escalate, expand, extend, heighten, improve, increase, intensify, magnify, multiply, strengthen, swell, wax *Antonyms:* decline, decrease, dilute, dismantle, end, finish, mount **4.** contrive, model, pound, reconstruct, shape **5.** comprise, constitute, embody

builder *n.* architect, artisan, carpenter, constructor, contractor, craftsperson, engineer, erector, fabricator, generator, inventor, maker, manufacturer, mason, programmer

building *n.* architecture, construction, domicile, dwelling, edifice, erection, framework, hall, home, house, hut, pile, superstructure, tower *Building materials:* adobe, board and batten, brick, bricks and mortar, cement, concrete, corrugated steel, flagstone, flooring, glass, ice, lath and plaster, masonry, paving, plaster, quarry tile, reinforced concrete, roofing, shingles, snow, steel, sticks and stones, stone, stonework, straw, tarpaper, tile, veneer, wattle and daub, wood

buildup *n.* accretion, accumulation, development, enlargement, escalation, expansion, gain, growth, heap, increase, load, mass, stack, stockpile, store *Antonyms:* decrease, drop-off, reduction, shrinkage

built-in *adj.* **1.** congenital, deep-seated, essential, implicit, inborn, included, incorporated, ingrained, inherent, innate, inseparable, integral, intrinsic *Antonyms:* accessory, add-on, adjunct, corollary **2.** custom, fitted, made-to-order

bulb *n.* ball, bunch, corn, globe, head, knob, nodule, nub, protuberance, swelling, tube

bulge *n.* blob, bump, bunching-up, dilation, distention, growth, hump, jut, lump, nodule, outgrowth, projection, prominence, protrusion, protuberance, swelling, tuberosity, tumefaction *Antonyms:* crater, dent, depression, hollow, pit, trough – *v.* balloon, bloat, bug out *(Nonformal)*, dilate, distend, enlarge, expand, jut, overhang, pouch, project, protrude, swell

bulk *n.* **1.** body, lion's share *(Nonformal)*, main part, majority, mass, plurality, principal *Antonyms:* minority, minor share **2.** aggregate, amount, amplitude, bigness, dimensions, extent, immensity, largeness, magnitude, mass, quantity, quantum, size, substance, total, totality, volume, weight

bulkhead *n.* **1.** barrier, *cloison (French)*, dividing wall, panel, partition **2.** doorway, hatch, hatchway

bulky *adj.* **1.** big, colossal, cumbersome, enormous, gross, heavy, hefty, huge, hulking, immense, large, long, mammoth, massive, monumental, substantial, unmanageable, unwieldy, voluminous, weighty *Antonyms:* manageable, neat, slim, small, tidy **2.** beefy *(Nonformal)*, corpulent, stout, sturdy, thickset

bulldoze *v.* **1.** bludgeon, bluster, browbeat, bully, coerce, cow, dragoon, harass, hector, intimidate **2.** plow through *or* under, raze, run over *or* through

bullet *n.* ammo, ammunition, ball, BB, bolt, cap, cartridge, dose, lead, missile, munition, pellet, projectile, rocket, shell, shot, slug

bulletin *n.* account, announcement, break, calendar, communication, communiqué, dispatch, flash, handout, item, message, news, news flash, notice, notification, posting, program, publication, release, report, scoop, spot report, statement, storm warning, warning *Nonformal:* skinny, off the wire

bullion *n.* bar, currency, gold *or* silver coin, ingot, plate, precious metals

bully *n.* blusterer, harasser, heckler, intimidator, oppressor, persecutor, ruffian, thug, tormenter, tough – *v.* browbeat, coerce, cow, domineer, dragoon, enforce, harass, hector, intimidate, menace, oppress, overbear, persecute, terrorize, threaten, torment, tyrannize *Nonformal:* lean on, push around, ride roughshod over, shake down, strong-arm

bulwark *n.* anchor, barrier, bastion, buttress, casement, citadel, defence, embankment, fort, fortification, fortress, guard, mainstay, protection, rampart, safeguard, security, stronghold, support, wall

bum *n.* **1.** bag lady, beggar, derelict, drifter, floater, hobo, street urchin, tramp, transient, vagabond, vagrant **2.** backside, buttocks, *derrière (French) Nonformal:* arse, caboose, duff, fanny

bumbling *adj.* awkward, blundering, clumsy, fumbling, gauche, gawky, ham-handed *(Nonformal),* ungainly

bump *n.* **1.** bang, blow, collision, crash, hit, impact, jolt, knock, punch, slam, slap, sock, thud, wallop, whack **2.** gnarl, hump, knot, lump, node, nodule, protuberance, swelling – *v.* **1.** bang, bounce, box, buck, bunt, butt, carom, clap, clatter, collide, crack, crash, hit, jab, jar, jerk, jolt, jostle, jounce, knock, pat, plop, plunk, poke, pound, punch, rap, rattle, slam, slap, smack, strike, thump, thwack **2.** budge, challenge, demote, dislodge, dismiss, displace, move, shift **3.** grind, gyrate, jerk, jolt **4.** assassinate, eliminate, kill, knock off *(Nonformal),* remove

bumptious *adj.* aggressive, arrogant, boastful, brash, brassy, brazen, cheeky *(Nonformal),* forward, insolent, obtrusive, overbearing, pushy, self-assertive *Antonyms:* modest, unpretentious

bun *n.* pastry, roll *Kinds of buns:* bagel, calabrese, chelsea, cinnamon, croissant, cruller, dinner, Danish, doughnut, éclair, hamburger, honey, hot dog, kaiser, muffin, onion, poppy seed, scone, sesame seed, seven-grain, sticky, sweet

bunch *n.* assortment, band, batch, bevy, bouquet, bundle, clump, cluster, collection, flock, gathering, group, heap, host, number, pack, parcel, party, quantity, sheaf, spray, stack, swarm, thicket, tussock – *v.* agglomerate, amass, assemble, bundle, cluster, collect, congregate, cram, crowd, flock, gather, group, huddle *Antonyms:* break up, disperse, dissipate, scatter

bundle *n.* accumulation, assortment, bag, bale, box, bunch, carton, clump, cluster, collection, group, kit 'n' koboodle *(Nonformal),* lot, mass, pack, package, packet, parcel, pile, quantity, roll, stack, wad – *v.* accumulate, bale, bind, clothe, collect, fasten, pack, package, tie, truss, wrap

bungle *v.* blunder, botch, bumble, confuse, distort, err, flounder, flub, fluff, fudge, fumble, mess, miscalculate, misconstrue, mishandle, misjudge, mismanage, mistake, muddle, ruin, spoil, stumble, wreck *Nonformal:* bollix, goof *or* gum *or* louse up, mess *or* screw up, muff *Antonyms:* accomplish, achieve, carry off, effect, triumph

bungler *n.* blockhead, blunderer, botcher, dolt, dunce, fool, fumbler, idiot, incompetent, loser, spoiler *Nonformal:* bonehead, clod, clumsy oaf, duffer, klutz, stumblebum

bunk *n.* **1.** bed, berth, cot, hammock, hay, kip, pallet, sack **2.** empty talk, foolishness, nonsense, poppycock, silliness, tommyrot *(Nonformal)* – *v.* bed down, hit the hay *(Nonformal),* sleep, turn in

bunker *n.* **1.** bin, box, bulwark, chest, coffer, enclosure, footlocker, fortification, locker, safe, shelter, strong box, treasury **2.** mound, obstacle, sand trap, sandy hollow

bunkum *n.* balderdash, froth, nonsense *Nonformal:* claptrap, crap, garbage, horsefeathers, humbug *Antonyms:* coherence, sense, sobriety

bunt *v.* advance, butt, move, prod, propel, push, shove, tap, thrust

buoy *n.* beacon, float, guide, marker, navigational aid *or* marker, signal *Kinds of buoy:* bell, breeches, can, gas-lighted, junction, spar, whistling, wreck – *v.* bolster, boost, cheer, cheer up, encourage, hearten, keep afloat, lift, prop, raise, support, sustain, uphold *Antonyms:* depress, dishearten, dispirit

buoyancy *n.* **1.** animation, bounce, cheerfulness, cheeriness, ebullience, effervescence, exuberance, gaiety, good humour, happiness, high spirits, jollity, lightness, liveliness, pep, spiritedness, zing *(Nonformal)* **2.** airiness, ethereality, floatability, levity, lightness, weightlessness

buoyant *adj.* **1.** animated, blithe, breezy, bright, carefree, cheerful, debonair, effervescent, elastic, expansive, happy, jaunty, jovial, joyful, lighthearted, lively, peppy, resilient, sunny, vivacious *Antonyms:* gloomy, heavy, hopeless, morose **2.** afloat, airy, bouncy, floatable, floating, light, resilient, unsinkable, weightless

burden *n.* **1.** accountability, anxiety, care, charge, concern, onus, responsibility, tax **2.** affliction, albatross *(Nonformal)*, deadweight, encumbrance, grievance, hardship, hinderance, millstone, strain, stress, trial, tribulation, trouble, weight **3.** cargo, goods, load, quantity, work **4.** carrying, portage, transport, vessel – *v.* **1.** afflict, bother, choke, clog, cram, crowd, crush, encumber, hamper, handicap, hinder, impede, load, oppress, overload, overwhelm, press, tax, trouble, try, vex, weigh on *or* with, worry **2.** charge with, entrust, tax *Nonformal:* dump on, saddle with

burdensome *adj.* arduous, cumbersome, herculean, laborious, onerous, oppressive, ponderous, strenuous, tough *Nonformal:* headachy, heavy

bureau *n.* **1.** chest, chest of drawers *Kinds of bureau:* chiffonier, commode, desk, dresser, highboy, sideboard, wardrobe, writing desk **2.** agency, branch, department, division, office

bureaucracy *n.* administration, authority, civil service, directorate, establishment, government, management, ministry, officialdom, officials, power, rule, system *Nonformal:* city hall, red tape, rug-ranking

burgeon *v.* bloom, blossom, bud, develop, flourish, germinate, grow, intensify, multiply, proliferate, sprout

burglar *n.* bandit, housebreaker, pilferer, prowler, robber, stealer, thief *Nonformal:* cat burglar, lockpick, raccoon, safecracker, second-story man

burglary *n.* break-in, caper, crime, filching, heist, housebreaking, larceny, pilferage, prowl, robbery, safecracking, stealing, theft, thieving

burial *n.* entombment, exequy, funeral, inhumation, interment, last rites, obsequies, sepulture

burlesque *adj.* comic, farcical, ironical, ludicrous, mock, mocking, parodic, satirical – *n.* caricature, farce, hootchy-kootchy show *(Nonformal)*, lampoon, lampoonery, mock, mockery, parody, pastiche, peep show, revue, satire, send-up, sham, show, skin show, spoof, strip, takeoff, travesty

burly *adj.* able-bodied, athletic, beefy, big, brawny, bruising, bulky, hefty, hulking, husky, muscular, portly, powerful, stocky, stout, strapping, strong, sturdy, thickset *Nonformal:* buff, hunky, pumped *Antonyms:* lean, lithe, scrawny

burn *n.* **1.** brand, injury, lesion, scald, scorch, trauma, wound *Degrees of burn:* first *(redness)*, second *(blistering)*, third *(charring of tissue, destruction of skin)* **2.** affront, derision, insult, lampoon, slander, slight – *v.* **1.** broil, cauterize, char, combust, cook, roast, scald, scorch, sear, singe, sizzle, smoke, smoulder, toast, torch **2.** explode, fire, flame, flare up, ignite, kindle, set ablaze *or* afire *or* aflame *or* alight, spark **3.** beam, blaze, flare, flash, flicker, glare, gleam, glow, illuminate, light, torch **4.** distress, heckle, insult, irritate, pain, scorn, slander, wound

burning *adj.* **1.** afire, aflame, alight, blazing, blistering, broiling, conflagrant, enkindled, fiery, flaming, flaring, gleaming, glowing, heated, hot, ignited, illuminated, incandescent, in flames, kindled, on fire, oxidizing, red hot, scorching, searing, sizzling, smoking, smouldering, torrid, white-hot *Antonyms:* cool, cooling, mild, numbing **2.** aglow, desirous, enraptured, fervent, impassioned, impetuous, zealous **3.** acrid, biting, caustic, irritating, painful, sharp, smarting, stinging, tingling **4.** acute, compelling, critical, crucial, dire, essential, exigent, imperative, important, importunate, instant, pressing, significant, urgent, vital *Antonyms:* insignificant, secondary, trivial

burnish *v.* buff *or* rub up, dress, furbish, gloss, polish, shine, wax *Antonyms:* dull, tarnish

burrow *n.* couch, den, dugout, foxhole, hole, hovel, lair, retreat, shelter, tunnel, warren – *v.* delve, dig, excavate, hollow *or* scoop out, mine, tunnel, undermine

burst *n.* acceleration, boost, burst of speed, gust, race, surge, spurt – *v* **1.** blow up, explode, open, rupture, shatter, split **2.** discharge, eject, emerge, gush, jet, vomit

bury *v.* **1.** entomb, inter, plant, put away, sink *Antonyms:* dig up, discover, expose, find, unearth **2.** cache, conceal, cover up, hide, screen, secrete, shroud, stash **3.** deluge, embed, engulf, ensconce, flood, implant, overwhelm, submerge, swamp **4.** forget, put out of mind, repress **5.** catch up, engross, occupy

bus *n.* conveyance, transit, transportation, vehicle *Kinds of bus:* commuter, double-decker, jitney, minibus, omnibus, red rocket *(Toronto)*, school, tour, streetcar, weed *(Nonformal)* – *v.* carry, coach, commute, convey, drive, haul, transport, truck

bush *n.* **1.** bramble, briar, kudzu, plant, shrub, shrubbery, vine **2.** back country, backwoods, brush, forest, hedge, hinterland, jungle, plant, scrub, scrubland, shrubs, thicket, wild, woodland

bushwhacker *n.* **1.** frontiersman, frontierswoman, pioneer, settler, trailblazer **2.** guerrilla, Maquis, partisan, rebel, resistance

bushy *adj.* bristling, fluffy, fringed, full, furry, fuzzy, hairy, heavy, hirsute, leafy, luxuriant, prickly, rough, rumpled, shaggy, stiff, thick, tufted, unkempt, unruly, wiry, woolly *Antonyms:* bald, glabrous, hairless

busily *adv.* ardently, assiduously, carefully, diligently, eagerly, earnestly, energetically, expeditiously, fervently, indefatigably, industriously, laboriously, painstakingly, purposefully, restlessly, strenuously, studiously, unremittingly, vigorously, zealously *Antonyms:* indifferently, lazily

business *n.* **1.** affairs, commerce, company, concern, corporation, enterprise, establishment, firm, house, industry, institution, market, organization, outfit, partnership, plant, syndicate, venture, works **2.** calling, career, craft, employment, field, function, game, line, livelihood, métier, occupation, profession, pursuit, specialty, trade, undertaking, vocation, work *Nonformal:* bag, racket **3.** affair, assignment, duty, function, interest, lookout, responsibility, task **4.** issue, matter, personal, point at hand, problem, topic **5.** amount of commerce, free enterprise, trade, volume **6.** approach, practice, procedure, usage

businesslike *adj.* accomplished, careful, correct, diligent, direct, disciplined, earnest, effective, efficient, enterprising, expeditious, hardworking, impersonal, industrious, methodical, orderly, practical, professional, regular, routine, serious, skilful, systematic, thorough, workaday *Antonyms:* careless, disorderly, disorganized, inefficient, sloppy

businessperson *n.* businessman, businesswoman, capitalist, dealer, employer, entrepreneur, executive, financier, franchiser, industrialist, manager, merchant, organization man *or* woman, professional, shopkeeper, tycoon

bust *n.* **1.** apprehension, arrest, capture, detention, nab, pickup, raid, seizure **2.** bronze head, head and shoulders, likeness, model, portrait, sculpture, statue **3.** bosom, breasts, chest, cleavage **4.** depression, hard times, recession, slowdown, slump – *v.* **1.** break, fail, fold up, go bankrupt, ruin **2.** apprehend, arrest, collar, detain, nab, raid, run in

bustle *n.* activity, ado, agitation, clamour, commotion, do, excitement, flurry, furore, fuss, hubbub, rumpus, stir, to-do, tumult, turmoil, uproar, whirl, whirlwind *Antonyms:* inaction, quiet, stillness – *v.* dash, flit, flutter, hasten, hurry, hustle, move quickly, run, rush, scamper, scramble, scurry, scuttle, stir, tear, whirl *Antonyms:* idle, laze, lie around, loaf, rest

busy *adj.* **1.** active, assiduous, diligent, employed, energetic, engrossed, hectic, hustling, industrious, lively, on assignment, overloaded, persevering, slaving, strenuous, tireless, working *Nonformal:* buzzing, humming, snowed, swamped *Antonyms:* idle, inactive, indolent, unoccupied **2.** engaged, in conference, occupied, unavailable **3.** inquisitive, interfering, meddlesome, nosy **4.** excessive, flowery, fussy, muddled, overdone, over-the-top *(Nonformal),* rococo – *v.* absorb, devote, engage, occupy, tax, work at *Nonformal:* plug away at, take up

busybody *n.* chatterbox, eavesdropper, fussbudget, gossip, intermeddler, intriguer, intruder, meddler, pry, scandalmonger, shook *(P.E.I.),* snoop, snooper, tattletale, troublemaker *Nonformal:* buttinsky, kibitzer, rubberneck, yenta

but *adv.* exclusively, inclusively, only, purely, solely – *conj.* except, however, nevertheless, notwithstanding, on the contrary – *prep.* bar, barring, except, save, with the exception of

butcher *n. boucher (French), carnicero (Spanish), fleischer (German), macellaio (Italian),* meat merchant *or* purveyor *or* vendor – *v.* **1.** annihilate, assassinate, demolish, destroy, execute, exterminate, kill, massacre, murder, slaughter, slay, terminate **2.** carve, chop, cut, destroy, dress, mince, slice, split, trim **3.** botch, bungle, ruin, wreck *Nonformal:* make a hash of, play havoc with, screw up

butler *n.* chamberlain, head servant, house boy, major-domo, man, manservant, seneschal, servant, steward, valet

butt *n.* **1.** base, bottom, edge, end, extremity, foot, shaft, stock, stump, tail, tip **2.** chump, dupe, fool, joke, laughingstock, sport, subject, sucker, target, victim *Nonformal:* clay pigeon, easy mark, fall guy, goat, mark, sap, setup, sitting duck **3.** buttock, *derrière (French) Nonformal;* ass, behind, bum, caboose, duff, gluteus maximus, tush – *v.* bang, batter, buck, buffet, bump, collide, hook, jab, knock, punch, push, ram, smack, strike

butte *n.* bank, embankment, foothills, hill, hillock, mound, terrace

butter *n.* clarified butter, dairy product, lubricant – *v.* **1.** besmear, coat, dab, grease, slap on, smear, spread **2.** flatter, praise, soft-soap, soften up

butterflies *n.* cold sweat, fear, heebie-jeebies *(Nonformal),* jitters, nerves, nervousness, shakes, stage fright, trepidation

buttocks *n.* backside, butt, croup *(Equestrian),* gluteus maximus, haunches, hindquarters, posterior, rump, seat, tail *Nonformal:* arse, bum, caboose, can, cheeks, fanny, keister, tush

button *n.* **1.** buckle, clasp, fastener, stud **2.** dial, knob, switch, tuner – *v.* buckle, close, fasten, hook, latch, rivet, seal, secure, snap, shut

buttonhole *v.* cajole, detain, importune, press, pressure, push, take by the lapel, urge, wheedle

buttress *n.* abutment, brace, column, cornerstone, mainstay, pier, pillar, prop, reinforcement, shore, stanchion, stay, strut, support – *v.* back *or* beef up, bolster, brace, buildup, bulwark, carry, jazz up *(Nonformal),* prop, reinforce, shore, strengthen, support, sustain, uphold

buxom *adj.* bosomy, busty, curvaceous, full-bosomed, hearty, plump, robust, stacked *(Nonformal),* voluptuous *Antonyms:* slender, svelte, thin

buy *n.* acquisition, bargain, deal, find, investment, purchase, value – *v.* **1.** acquire, bargain *or* barter *or* contract *or* pay for, get, invest, obtain, procure, purchase, redeem, score (*Nonformal*), secure, take *Antonyms:* auction, barter, retail, sell, vend **2.** bribe, corrupt, ransom, suborn, tamper *Nonformal:* fix, grease palm, have, land, lubricate, reach, redeem, sop, square

buzz *n.* **1.** drone, fizz, fizzle, hiss, hum, murmur, purr, ring, ringing, sibilation, whir, whisper **2.** charge, high, rush, tingle, thrill **3.** chitchat, rumour, scandal, scuttlebutt (*Nonformal*) – *v.* broadcast, gossip, palaver, spread rumours

by *adv.* aside, at hand, beyond, close, handy, in reach, near, over, past – *prep.* **1.** along, alongside, beside, close to, near, nearby, next to, nigh, over, past, round, via **2.** along with, by means *or* way of, on, over, through, with

bygone *adj.* anachronistic, ancient, antiquated, archaic, belated, dated, dead, defunct, departed, erstwhile, extinct, forgotten, former, gone, in oblivion, late, of old, olden, old-fashioned, old-time, one-time, out-of-date, past, previous, sometime, vanished *Antonyms:* coming, current, future, prospective

bylaw *n.* act, bill, canon, enactment, law, legislation, ruling, statute

bypass *n.* alternate route, detour, roundabout – *v.* avoid, circumnavigate, circumvent, deke (*Nonformal*), detour, deviate from, ignore, neglect, omit, sidestep, skirt *Antonyms:* connect, converge, join, link, meet

bystander *n.* eyewitness, gaper, innocent, looker-on, observer, onlooker, passerby, railbird (*P.E.I.*), spectator, viewer, watcher, witness

byword *n.* adage, aphorism, axiom, catchphrase, catchword, dictum, epithet, maxim, motto, precept, proverb, saw, saying, shibboleth, slogan, standing joke (*Nonformal*)

Byzantine *n.* calculating, complicated, cunning, elaborate, guileful, intricate, labyrinthian *or* labyrinthine, Machiavellian, perplexing, shrewd

cab *n.* calèche, car, carriage, hack, hackney, hansom, jitney, surrey, taxi, taxicab

cabal *n.* **1.** band, clique, coalition, confederacy, coterie, crew, enclave, faction, gang, junta, league, ring, set, union **2.** connivance, conspiracy, design, intrigue, plot, racket, scheme

cabaret *n.* bar, bistro, café, disco, discothèque, nightclub, supper club, tavern *Nonformal:* dive, watering hole

cabin *n. cabane à sucre (Quebec),* camboose, camp, chalet, cottage, home, house, hovel, hut, lodge, quarters, room, shack, shanty, shed, stateroom

cabinet *n.* **1.** cupboard, depository, repository *Kinds of cabinet:* armoire, bookcase, breakfront, buffet, bureau, carrel, chest, chest of drawers, chiffonier, china, closet, clothes chest, commode, console, credenza, display case, dresser, escritoire, filing, hamper, highboy, hope chest, hutch, kitchen, liquor, locker, safe, secretary, shelf, tool, trunk, vanity, wardrobe, writing desk **2.** administration, administrators, advisors, assembly, bureaucracy, committee, council, councilors, department heads, executives, governing body, government, ministry, privy council **3.** atelier, den, private chamber *or* room, sanctum, scriptorium

cable *n.* **1.** chain, cord, cordage, guy, line, rope, strand, wire **2.** cablegram, e-mail, fax, message, news, telegram, telegraph, wire

cache *n.* **1.** accumulation, assets, fund, hoard, reserve, stake, stockpile, store, supplies, supply, treasure, treasury, wealth *Nonformal:* kitty, nest egg, stash **2.** hiding place, repository, storehouse, vault – *v.* accumulate, bury, conceal, cover, hide, lay away, maintain, park, put away, save, secrete, squirrel away, stash, store *Commonly misused:* **cachet**

cachet *n.* **1.** design, label, seal, slogan, stamp, trademark **2.** characteristic, distinction, distinguishing feature *or* mark, idiosyncrasy *Commonly misused:* **cache**

cackle *n.* **1.** chortling, chuckling, clacking, clucking, crowing, snigger, tittering **2.** babble, chatter, chit-chat *(Nonformal),* drivel, idle *or* small talk, maundering, prating, rambling – *v.* **1.** chortle, chuckle, clack, click, cluck, crow, giggle, quack, snicker, titter, twitter **2.** babble, bandy, be loquacious *or* talkative, blather, chatter, chitter-chatter *(Nonformal),* gab, gossip, jabber, prate, prattle, tattle, twaddle

cacophonous *adj.* discordant, dissonant, grating, harsh, inharmonious, jangly *(Nonformal),* jarring, noisy, raucous, shrill, strident, unmusical *Antonyms:* melodious, peaceful, restful, smooth, soothing

cacophony *n.* caterwauling, clamour, disharmony, dissonance, noise, pandemonium, stridency, turbulence *Antonyms:* harmony, order, unity

cad *n.* knave, rake, rapscallion, rascal, rogue, scoundrel, sleeveen *(Newfoundland) Nonformal:* bastard, bounder, creep, cur, heel, jerk, louse, rat, rotter, stinker, worm *Antonyms:* aristocrat, gentleman

cadaverous *adj.* ashen, bloodless, corpselike, deathlike, deathly, emaciated, ghostly, haggard, hollow-eyed, pale, pallid, sallow, sick, skeletal, spectral, thin, wan, wasted *Antonyms:* healthy, high-coloured, lively, plump

cadence *n.* **1.** accent, inflection, intonation, lilt, modulation, timbre **2.** beat, count, measure, meter, pulse, rhythm, swing, tempo

cadenza *n.* bravura, flourish, improvisation, interpolation, ornamentation, solo, virtuoso performance

cadre *n.* **1.** force, key group, officers, organization, personnel, staff **2.** core, framework, infrastructure, nucleus

Caesar *n.* absolute ruler, autocrat, czar, despot, emperor, kaiser, khan, king, master, pendragon, pharaoh, potentate, rajah, ruler, sachem, sagamore, satrap, shah, sheik, shogun, tycoon, tyrant

café *n.* bistro, cabaret, cafeteria, canteen, coffee bar *or* house *or* shop, diner, green room, lunchroom, *patisserie (French)*, restaurant, snack bar, tearoom

cage *n.* box, cell, corral, crate, dungeon, enclosure, fold, pen, pound, prison – *v.* close *or* fence *or* shut in, confine, enclose, hold, impound, imprison, incarcerate, jail, lock up, pen, restrain, trap *Antonyms:* free, let loose, manumit

cajole *v.* blandish, coax, deceive, delude, dupe, entice, entrap, flatter, get around, induce, influence, inveigle, jolly, lure, seduce, soften, tempt, urge, wheedle, work on *Nonformal:* bootlick, brown-nose, butter *or* butter up, con, snow, soft-soap, stroke, sweet-talk *Antonyms:* bully, coerce, force

cake *n.* **1.** baked sweet *Kinds of cake:* angel food, Banbury tart, bangbelly, bannock *(Scotland)*, Battenberg, Bible, Bundt, cheese, chocolate, coffee, cupcake, devil's food, fruitcake, genoise, gingerbread, honey, jelly roll, kuchen, layer, marble, *mille feuille (Quebec)*, pancake, pound, Sachertorte, sally lunn, savarin, short, sinnel, spice, sponge, stollen, teacake, torte, upside down, wedding, white, yellow **2.** bar, block, brick, floe, loaf, slab – *v.* coagulate, congeal, solidify, thicken

calamitous *adj.* adverse, afflictive, blighting, cataclysmic, catastrophic, deadly, deplorable, devastating, dire, disastrous, fatal, grievous, harmful, heartbreaking, lamentable, regrettable, ruinous, tragic, unfavourable, unfortunate, woeful *Antonyms:* advantageous, beneficial, favourable, fortunate, helpful

calamity *n.* **1.** cataclysm, catastrophe, collapse, disaster, downfall, misfortune, mishap, reverse, ruin, woe *Nonformal:* unholy mess, Waterloo *Antonyms:* benefit, blessing, good fortune **2.** adversity, affliction, distress, hardship, tragedy, trial, tribulation, wretchedness

calculable *adj.* **1.** accountable, ascertainable, computable, countable, estimable, foreseeable, measurable, predictable *Antonyms:* immeasurable, inestimable, unfathomable **2.** dependable, reliable, stable, steady, trustworthy

calculate *v.* **1.** add, adjust, cast, cipher, compute, count, determine, divide, enumerate, figure, keep tab, measure, multiply, number, rate, reckon, size up, subtract, sum, take off, tally, total, tote *(Nonformal)*, value, weigh, work out **2.** anticipate, appraise, assume, estimate, forecast, gauge, guess, judge, suppose **3.** aim, design, plan, plot, predetermine, premeditate

calculated *adj.* considered, deliberate, intended, intentional, planned, premeditated, purposeful, wilful *Antonyms:* hasty, hurried, impulsive, spontaneous, unintentional

calculating *adj.* **1.** artful, canny, contriving, counting, crafty, cunning, designing, devious, discreet, figuring, guarded, guileful, judgmental, Machiavellian, manipulative, politic, scheming, sharp, shrewd, sly, wary, wily *Antonyms:* direct, guileless, honest, sincere, undesigning **2.** careful, cautious, chary, circumspect, considerate, gingerly, intelligent, premeditative

calculation *n.* **1.** answer, computation, estimate, estimation, forecast, prediction, prognosis, prognostication, reckoning, result, total, totalling **2.** caution, circumspection, deliberation, forethought, planning, precaution *Antonyms:* abandon, impulsiveness, spontaneity

calculator *n.* adding machine *Kinds of calculator:* abacus, analog computer, counter, digital computer, pari-mutuel machine, pocket, rule, slide rule, totalizer

calendar *n.* agenda, almanac, annals, book of hours, bulletin, chronology, daybook, diary, docket, journal, list, log, logbook, program, record, register, schedule, timetable *Kinds of calendars:* Chinese, Church, ecclesiastical, Gregorian, Hebrew *or* Jewish, Hindu, Julian, Muslim, Republican *or* Revolutionary, Roman

calibrate *v.* adjust, correct, determine, fine tune, fit, graduate, measure, phase, regulate, taper, titrate

calibre *n.* **1.** bore, capacity, class, diameter, gauge, grade, length, measure, quality, weight **2.** ability, capability, character, constitution, dignity, distinction, endowment, essence, faculty, force, gifts, merit, nature, power, quality, stature, strength, talent, value, virtue, worth, worthiness

call *n.* **1.** cry, hail, hello, screech, shout, whoop, yell *Nonformal:* holler, yawp **2.** bleat, bray, coo, hoot, howl, neigh **3.** alarm, alert, bell, signal, SOS, warning **4.** command, invitation, notice, summons **5.** basis, grounds, option, reason **6.** claim, onus, responsibility **7.** bent, drive, urging, vocation **8.** appointment, exchange of cards *or* pleasantries, stop, visit – *v.* **1.** accost, address, cry out, hail **2.** chatter, chirp, chirrup, coo, pipe, sound, trill, tweet, twitter, whistle **3.** appeal to, invoke, proclaim, pronounce *Antonyms:* reject, renounce **4.** arouse, awake, excite, incite, stir up *Antonyms:* assuage, calm, ease **5.** entice, imitate, lure, persuade, seduce **6.** challenge, charge, demand, exact **7.** assemble, bring together, convene, convoke, muster, summon *Antonyms:* demobilize, muster-out, release **8.** christen, designate, dub, identify, label, name, style, term, title **9.** approximate, augur, consider, estimate, evaluate, guesstimate *(Nonformal)*, predict, prophesy, reason, reckon **10.** communicate with, telephone *Nonformal:* buzz, phone, ring, ring up **11.** begin, bring to action, commence, initiate, open, start **12.** announce, declare, judge, pronounce **13.** arrest, end, finish, stop, suspend, terminate

calligraphy *n.* chirography, fist *(Nonformal)*, graphology, handwriting, longhand, penmanship, scrawl, script, writing

calling *n.* art, business, career, craft, employment, life's work, line, métier, mission, occupation, profession, province, pursuit, racket, trade, vocation, work *Nonformal:* bag, cup of tea

callous *adj.* apathetic, cold, hard, hard-boiled *(Nonformal)*, hard-nosed, hardened, heartless, indifferent, obdurate, thick-skinned, uncaring, unfeeling, unrepentant *Antonyms:* compassionate, sensitive, sympathetic *Commonly misused:* **callow**

callow *adj.* guileless, immature, inexperienced, jejune, juvenile, naive, puerile, raw, unfledged, unsophisticated, untrained, untried, young *Nonformal:* green, wet behind the ears, not up to snuff *Commonly misused:* **callous**

calm *adj.* **1.** inactive, motionless, neutral, quiescent, quiet, still *Antonyms:* agitated, blustery, boiling, disturbed, stormy **2.** gentle, halcyon, laid-back *(Nonformal)*, peaceable, serene *Antonyms:* belligerent, bombastic, moody, tempestuous, uneasy **3.** clear- *or* cool-headed, collected, composed, imperturbable, levelheaded, patient, self-possessed, steady, unflappable, unruffled *Antonyms:* discomposed, disconcerted, emotional, nervous, theatrical – *n.* **1.** eye, hush, lull, quiet, quietude **2.** felicity, harmoniousness, peace, peacefulness, tranquility – *v.* appease, assuage, compose, manage, minister to, pacify, placate, relax, still, tranquilize *Nonformal:* get a grip, hold on, rein in, simmer *or* tone down

camaraderie *n.* brotherhood, companionship, comradeship, confraternity, conviviality, fellowship, fraternization, friendship, good-fellowship, gregariousness, sisterhood, sociability, sorority, togetherness *Antonyms:* bad blood, civil war, estrangement, separation

camel *n.* beast of burden, ruminant, ship of the desert *(Nonformal) Kinds of camel:* Arabian *or* dromedary *(One-hump)*, Bactrian *(Two-hump)*

cameo *n.* **1.** bit part, brief *or* guest appearance, vignette, walk-on role **2.** gem, medallion, miniature, portrait

camera *n.* photographic apparatus *Common cameras:* box, cinematograph, digital, disposable, instant, miniature, movie, pinhole, single-lens reflex, space, 3-D, twin-lens reflex, videocam, vitascope *Trademark:* Canon, Hasselblad, Kodak, Konica, Leica, Minolta, Nikon, Olympus, Pentax, Polaroid, Zeiss

camouflage *n.* **1.** blind, cloak, concealment, cover, deceptive marking, disguise, fake, guise, masking, paint, protective colouring *or* coloration, screen, shade, shroud, veil *Nonformal:* red herring, smoke screen **2.** deceit, false front, front, mask, masquerade, mimicry, persona – *v.* beard *(Nonformal)*, cloak, conceal, cover up, deceive, disguise, dissemble, dissimulate, dress up, hide, mask, obfuscate, obscure, screen, veil *Antonyms:* bare, expose, reveal, uncover, unmask

camp *adj.* affected, artificial, avant-garde, contemporary, current, far-out, futuristic, mannered, ostentatious, posturing – *n.* **1.** bivouac, encampment, outdoor site, tent *Kinds of camp:* army, boot, bush, camboose, campground, campsite, caravansary, cottage, day, detention, fish, hobo jungle *(Nonformal)*, hockey, hunt, lean-to, lodge, log cabin, logging, outpost, overnight, shack, shanty, sugar, summer, tepee, training **2.** association, caucus, group, party, sect – *v.* **1.** bivouac, encamp, pitch camp *or* one's tent, rough it, tent **2.** park *(Nonformal)*, perch, remain, settle, squat, stay

campaign *n.* attack, crusade, drive, expedition, fight, movement, offensive, operation, push, rush, warfare – *v.* agitate, canvass, contend, contest, crusade, electioneer, lobby, solicit votes, tour *Nonformal:* barnstorm, grandstand, main street, politick, press the flesh, stump, whistle-stop

camper *n.* **1.** backpacker, explorer, hiker, scout, tenant, tourist, vacationer, wanderer **2.** bus, caravan, conveyance, hardtop, motor home, recreational vehicle, RV, tent trailer, trailer, truck, van, vehicle, Winnebago *(Trademark)*

camping *n.* anchoring, bivouacking, mooring, parking, resting, sleeping out, squatting *(Nonformal)*, staying, tenting, vacationing

campus *n.* academe, academia, college, college grounds, commons, quadrangle *or* quad *(Nonformal)*, school grounds, track, university, yard

can *n.* bucket, canister, container, package, receptacle, tin, vessel – *v.* **1.** bottle, jar, keep, preserve, put up **2.** dismiss, fire, let go, make redundant, release, terminate

Canadian *n.* Canadien, Canadienne, habitant *(Historical) Nonformal:* Canuck, Canajun, Canayen, hoser

canal *n.* aqueduct, channel, conduit, course, ditch, duct, estuary, firth, sluice, trench, water, watercourse, waterway

canary *adj.* amber, gold, lemon, ochre, saffron, yellow – *n.* **1.** bird, finch, songbird **2.** informer, informant, *Nonformal:* fink, rat, snitch, squealer, tattletale

cancel *v.* **1.** annul, blue-line, delete, discard, efface, eliminate, erase, expunge, neutralize, nullify, obliterate, purge, strike out, void, wipe out **2.** efface, mark, stamp, validate **3.** back out, break, postpone, take a rain check *(Nonformal)*, withdraw **4.** compensate, countermand, make up for, reimburse

cancellation *n.* **1.** abandonment, abolition, abrogation, annulment, calling off, deferment, deletion, dissolution, dissolving, elimination, ending, neutralization, nullification, overruling, postponement, quashing, recall, repeal, repudiation, reversal, reversing, revoking, termination, undoing, withdrawal

cancer *n.* **1.** carcinoma, cyst, disease, growth, glioma, leukemia, lymphoma, malignancy, malignant tumour, melanoma, metastasis, neuroblastoma, sarcoma, tumour **2.** blight, canker, curse, evil, pestilence, plague, poison, rot, sickness

candid *adj.* **1.** aboveboard, authentic, blunt, forthright, frank, free, genuine, guileless, honest, informal, ingenuous, open, outspoken, sincere, straightforward, truthful, unequivocal, unstudied, up front *(Nonformal)* *Antonyms:* designing, diplomatic, wily **2.** off the cuff *(Nonformal)*, impromptu, spontaneous, unplanned, unrehearsed **3.** fair, impartial, just, objective, scrupulous, unbiased *Antonyms:* biased, corrupt

candidate *n.* applicant, aspirant, claimant, competitor, contender, contestant, entrant, hopeful, nominee, office seeker, petitioner, possibility, runner, seeker *Nonformal:* favourite *or* fortunate son, parachute candidate, presser of flesh, stalking horse, wannabe *Antonyms:* spin doctor, supporter, voter

candle *n.* flambeau, flame, flare, rush *or* tallow *or* votive light, taper, torch, wax

candour *n.* **1.** artlessness, directness, explicitness, forthrightness, frankness, guilelessness, honesty, ingenuousness, openness, outspokenness, probity, simplicity, sincerity, straightforwardness, truthfulness, uprightness, veracity *Antonyms:* cunning, deceit, intrigue **2.** fairness, impartiality, objectivity, unequivocalness *Antonyms:* bias, corruption, prejudice

candy *n.* bonbon, confectionary, *confit (French)*, sweet, sweetmeat *Kinds of candy:* almond bark, blackball, brittle, butterscotch, candy cane, caramel, chocolate, chocolate bar, cinnamon heart, cotton candy, fudge, gumdrop, gummy, halvah, jawbreaker, jelly bean, jujube, lemon drop, licorice, lollipop, marzipan, mint, molasses, nougat, peanut brittle, penuche, peppermint, praline, rock, saltwater taffy, sucker *(Nonformal)*, taffy, toffee, Turkish delight, wine gum – *v.* glaze, sugarcoat, sweeten

cane *n.* **1.** alpenstock, crook, crutch, cudgel, shillelagh *(Irish)*, staff, stick, walking stick **2.** reed, rush, shoot, stalk, stem – *v.* beat, flail, horsewhip, lash, rap, slap, smite, strike, thrash *Nonformal:* lace, whale

canine *adj.* doggish, dog-like, fox-like, foxy, lupine, wolfish, wolf-like, vulpine – *n.* dog *Nonformal:* mutt, pooch, pup, puppy

canker *n.* **1.** abscess, blister, boil, carbunkle, infection, inflammation, lesion, sore, ulcer **2.** bane, blight, curse, poison, scourge, woe – *v.* decay, deteriorate, fester, rot, ulcerate

cannibal *n.* anthropophagite, barbarian, fiend, flesh-eater, headhunter, man-eater, monster, ogre, wendigo

cannon *n.* **1.** anti-aircraft gun, armament, artillery, field gun, firearm, gun, howitzer, mortar *Nonformal:* ack-ack, caps, Big Bertha, rainmaker **2.** cylinder, sheathing, sleeve – *v.* blast, blitz, bombard, cannonball, discharge, fire away at, open fire, shell, shoot *Commonly misused:* **canon**

cannonball *n.* ammunition, ball, bullet, mortar, round, shell, shot, shrapnel – *v.* **1.** dive, jump, plunge **2.** attack, bomb, cannonade, fire upon *See also:* **cannon**

canny *adj.* **1.** astute, cagey, careful, cautious, circumspect, discreet, judicious, knowing, perspicacious, prudent, sagacious, sharp, shrewd, smart, wary, wise **2.** able, acute, adroit, artful, clever, dexterous, ingenious, nimble-witted, quick, quick-witted, skilful, street-smart *(Nonformal)*, streetwise *Antonyms:* bumbling, inept, obtuse, unskilled **3.** cheap, economical, frugal, parsimonious, thrifty, tight-fisted

canoe *n.* boat *Kinds of canoe:* aluminum, birch-bark, dugout, fiberglass, kayak, kevlar, Montreal, northern, outrigger, parchment, Peterborough, pirogue, war

canon *n.* **1.** body of laws *or* rules, command, declaration, decree, dictate, doctrine, dogma, edict, law, lore, maxim, order, ordinance, principle, regulation, rule, statute, tenet **2.** body of work, life's work, literary output, recognized works **3.** sacred books *or* teachings *or* words *or* writings **4.** benchmark, criterion, standard *Commonly misused:* **cannon**

canonize *v.* beatify, bless, consecrate, dedicate, deify, enshrine, exalt, glorify, idolize, love, saint, sanctify, sanction, worship *Antonyms:* damn, defile, sully

canopy *n.* **1.** awning, cover, marquee, overhang, panoply, parachute, porte-cochère, umbrella **2.** shade, shadow, sunshade

cant *n.* **1.** angle, inclination, slope, tilt **2.** argot, business-speak, buzz *or* catchwords, jargon, phrase, shoptalk, stock, truism **3.** deceit, hypocrisy, insincerity, lip service *(Nonformal)*, piety, sanctimony – *v.* angle, bevel, careen, grade, heel, incline, lean, list, recline, rise, slant, slope, tilt, tip

cantata *n.* aria, canticle, chorus, drama, oratorio, recitation

canteen *n.* **1.** *casse-croûte (Quebec)*, coffee truck, concession stand, kitchen, lunch counter, mobile kitchen, snack bar, snack *or* tuck shop **2.** bottle, flask, jug, mickey, wineskin

canvas *n.* **1.** backdrop, cloth, duck, fabric, fly, sail, sailcloth, tarp, tarpaulin, tenting **2.** artwork, painting, picture, piece, work *Commonly misused:* **canvass**

canvass *n.* poll, query, questioning, solicitation – *v.* **1.** campaign, consult, electioneer, poll, seek, solicit, survey **2.** analyze, apply, argue, check, check over, debate, discuss, examine, investigate, review, study *Commonly misused:* **canvas**

canyon *n.* chasm, coulee, divide, gap, glen, gorge, gulch, gulf, gully, ravine, valley

cap *n.* hat, headgear, head wear *Kinds of cap:* baseball, beanie, dunce, jester's, juliet, liberty, nightcap, porter's, service, skullcap, stocking, tuque, watch, yarmulke – *v.* beat, better, complete, consummate, cover, crown, eclipse, exceed, excel, outdo, outstrip, surpass, top, transcend *See also:* **hat**

capability *n.* **1.** ability, adequacy, aptitude, art, capacity, competence, craft, cunning, effectiveness, efficacy, efficiency, facility, faculty, means, might, potency, potential, power, proficiency, qualification, skill, wherewithal *Antonyms:* inability, incompetence, inefficiency, ineptitude **2.** endurance, fortitude, guts *(Nonformal)*, perseverance, stamina, strength, tolerance

capable *adj.* able, accomplished, adapted, adept, adequate, apt, *au fait (French)*, clever, competent, deft, dynamite *(Nonformal)*, efficient, experienced, fitted, gifted, intelligent, masterly, professional, proficient, proper, qualified, skilful, suited, talented, vet *(Nonformal)*, veteran *Antonyms:* incompetent, ineffective, inept, unqualified, unskilled

capacious *adj.* abundant, ample, broad, comfortable, commodious, comprehensive, expansive, extensive, generous, liberal, plentiful, roomy, sizable, spacious, substantial, vast, voluminous, wide *Antonyms:* confined, constricted, cramped, restricted, tight

capacity *n.* **1.** adequacy, aptness, bent, brains, calibre, capability, competency, faculty, forte, gift, intelligence, knack, qualification, readiness, skill, talent **2.** accommodation, bulk, contents, dimensions, expanse, extent, holding ability, mass, measure, proportions, quantity, room, scope, size, space, spread, sufficiency, sweep, volume *Antonyms:* dearth, deficiency, lack, shortage, vacuity **3.** character, office, place, position, role, situation **4.** amplitude, magnitude, output, range, reach, velocity

cape *n.* **1.** finger, head, headland, jetty, peninsula, point, promontory, spit **2.** cloak, mantle, poncho, shawl

caper *n.* antic, escapade, gambol, jest, joke, lark, mischief, practical joke, prank, revel, rollick, shenanigan, sport, stunt, tomfoolery, trick *Nonformal:* gag, hijinks, monkeyshine, rib – *v.* bounce, bound, cavort, dance, frisk, frolic, gambol, hop, jump, leap, let loose, play, rollick, romp, skip, spring *Nonformal:* cut loose, raise hell

capital *adj.* basic, cardinal, central, chief, controlling, dominant, essential, first, foremost, fundamental, leading, main, major, most important, number one, outstanding, overruling, paramount, predominant, preeminent, primary, prime, principal, prominent, significant, underlying, vital – *n.* **1.** assets, cash, estate, finances, fortune, funds, gold, interests, investment, kitty, means, money, nest egg *(Nonformal)*, principal, property, resources, stake, stock, treasure, wealth **2.** city, metropolis, municipality, principal city, seat of government *Canadian capitals:* Charlottetown *(P.E.I.)*, Edmonton *(Alberta)*, Fredericton *(New Brunswick)*, Halifax *(Nova Scotia)*, Iqaluit *(Nunavut Territory)*, Ottawa, Ontario *(Federal Capital)*, Quebec City *(Quebec)*, Regina *(Saskatchewan)*, St. John's *(Newfoundland)*, Toronto *(Ontario)*, Victoria *(British Columbia)*, Whitehorse *(Yukon)*, Winnipeg *(Manitoba)*, Yellowknife *(Northwest Territories)* *Commonly misused:* **capitol**

capitalism *n.* free enterprise, laissez-faire, liberal economy, private enterprise, private ownership, privatization, reinvestment

capitalist *n.* banker, entrepreneur, financier, investor, moneyman, owner, robber baron *(Nonformal)*, tycoon

capitalize *v.* **1.** benefit, cash in, exploit, gain, obtain, profit, realize, reap **2.** back, finance, found, fund, subsidize, underwrite

capitol *n.* U.S. legislative building, U.S. legislature, U.S. statehouse *Commonly misused:* **capital**

capitulate *v.* acquiesce, bow, buckle under, cave *or* give in, cede, come to terms, concede, defer, fold, give in, quit, relent, submit, succumb, surrender, yield *Antonyms:* beat, conquer, crush, defeat, vanquish

capitulation *n.* accedence, concession, giving in *or* up, knuckling under, relenting, resignation, submission, succumbing, surrender, yielding

caprice *n.* brain wave *(Nonformal)*, crotchet, eccentricity, fancy, humour, idiosyncrasy, impulse, notion, oddity, peculiarity, quirk, vagary, whim, whimsy

capricious *adj.* changeable, fanciful, fickle, flighty, impulsive, mercurial, moody, quicksilver, variable, volatile, wavering, wayward, whimsical *Nonformal:* helter-skelter, shilly-shallying *Antonyms:* even, regular, steady

capsize *v.* flip, invert, keel *or* tip *or* turn over, roll, turn turtle *(Nonformal)*, upset

capsule *adj.* abbreviated, abridged, canned *(Nonformal)*, condensed, edited, epitomized, pocket, shortened, summarized, tabloid – *n.* cap, dose, lozenge, pastille, pellet, pill, tablet

captain *n.* authority, boss, chief, chieftain, commander, director, guide, head, leader, lord, master, officer, operator, owner, pilot, skipper – *v.* command, govern, lead, pilot, skipper, steer, take command

caption *n.* explanation, header, heading, inscription, reference, outline, subtitle

captivate *v.* allure, attract, beguile, bewitch, charm, dazzle, delight, draw in, enamour, enchant, enrapture, enslave, ensnare, entertain, enthrall, entrance, fascinate, gratify, grip, hold, hook, hypnotize, infatuate, inflame, intrigue, lure, magnetize, mesmerize, please, seduce, spellbind, take, vamp *(Nonformal)*, wile, win *Antonyms:* frighten, repel, repulse

captive *adj.* **1.** arrested, behind bars, bound, caged, confined, enslaved, fettered, imprisoned, incarcerated, incommunicado, in custody, jailed, locked *or* penned up, restricted, subjugated **2.** beguiled, bewitched, charmed, delighted, enchanted, enraptured, enslaved, enthralled, fascinated, hypnotized, infatuated – *n.* convict, detainee, hostage, internee, prisoner, slave, victim

captivity *n.* bondage, confinement, constraint, custody, detention, enslavement, impoundment, imprisonment, incarceration, internment, jail, servitude, slavery, subjection, vassalage *Antonyms:* emancipation, freedom, liberation, manumission

capture *n.* **1.** abduction, acquisition, apprehension, appropriation, arrest, ensnarement, grab *(Nonformal)*, holding, imprisonment, securement, seizure, trapping *Nonformal:* bag, bust, collar **2.** booty, catch, loot, prey, prize, swag, victim – *v.* **1.** abduct, apprehend, arrest, catch, clutch, collar, corner, corral, detain, embroil, enmesh, ensnare, entangle, entice, entrap, get, grab, hold, hook, inveigle, lasso, lure, mislead, pick up, pinch, pull in, round up, run in, seduce, seize, snare, snatch, take,

take captive *or* prisoner, tempt, trap, trick *Nonformal:* bag, bust, nab, nail, reel *or* rope in *Antonyms:* release, set free, turn loose **2.** conquer, ensnare, overcome, overpower, overwhelm, trap, vanquish, victimize **3.** acquire, obtain, procure, secure, win

car *n.* auto, automobile, flivver, limousine, motor vehicle, transportation, vehicle *Nonformal:* Bennett buggy *(Historical)*, buggy, heap, hot rod, jalopy, wheels, wreck *See also:* **automobile**

caravan *n.* **1.** band, cavalcade, company, convoy, cortege, expedition, procession, retinue, travellers, troop **2.** convoy, motorcade, safari, train, wagon train **3.** bus, camper, R.V., van, Winnebago *(Trademark)*

carcass *n.* **1.** body, cadaver, corpse, dead body, remains, roadkill **2.** chassis, corpus, frame, framework, hulk, ruins, shell, skeleton, wreck

card *n.* **1.** badge, billet, check, docket, identification, label, paper, pass, voucher **2.** devil's picturebook *(P.E.I.)*, playing card *Card groupings:* ace, bower, clubs, deck, deuce *or* two, diamonds, eight, eight-spot, face card, five, five-spot, four, four-spot, hearts, jack, joker, king, knave, lady, nine, nine-spot, pack, queen, seven, seven-spot, six, six-spot, spades, suit, ten, ten-spot, three, three-spot, trey *Card games:* 21, auction bridge, auction 45s, baccarat, bezique, blackjack, canasta, casino, contract bridge, crazy eights, cribbage, draw poker, écarté, euchre, fifty-two pick-up, fish, floater, gin rummy, hearts, ombre, pinochle, piquet, poker, rummy 500, skat, solitaire, stud poker, three-card monte, war, whist **3.** agenda, calendar, poster, program, schedule, sheet, ticket, timetable **4.** buffoon, character, comic, humorist, jester, joker, prankster, stooge *(Nonformal)*, wag, wisecracker, wit

cardinal *adj.* **1.** basic, central, chief, essential, first, foremost, fundamental, greatest, highest, important, indispensable, key, leading, main, overriding, overruling, paramount, pivotal, preeminent, primary, prime, principal, ruling, vital *Antonyms:* dispensable, secondary, subordinate, unessential **2.** carmine, crimson, red, scarlet, vermillion

cardiovascular *adj.* heart, vascular *Cardiovascular ailments:* angina *or* angina pectoris, arrhythmia, cardiac *or* myocardial infarction, cardiac arrest, congenital heart disease, congestive heart failure, coronary, coronary thrombosis, heart attack *or* condition, heart failure *or* disease, high blood pressure, hypertension, tachycardia, vascular disease

care *n.* **1.** attention, carefulness, caution, circumspection, conscientiousness, consideration, diligence, discrimination, effort, fastidiousness, forethought, meticulousness, pains, precaution, prudence, regard, solicitude, TLC *(Nonformal)*, vigilance, watchfulness *Antonyms:* carelessness, inattention, indifference, neglect **2.** aegis, charge, control, custody, direction, guardianship, keeping, management, ministration, protection, safekeeping, stewardship, superintendence, supervision, trust, tutelage, wardship **3.** angst, anxiety, concern, disquiet, unease, worry *Antonyms:* calm, ease, insouciance – *v.* **1.** admire, adore, desire, dote on, embrace, fancy, harbour, hold dear, honour, like, love, prize, regard highly, revere, treasure, value, venerate, want, worship *Antonyms:* discard, disown, reject **2.** attend, comfort, consider, cosset, encourage, foster, look after, mind, minister, mother, nourish, nurse, nurture, protect, support, sustain, take pains, tend, wait on, watch *or* watch over *Antonyms:* abandon, desert, neglect

careen *v.* bend, cant, deviate, diverge, heel, incline, keel *or* turn over, lean, list, lurch, pitch, sheer, shift, slant, slope, sway, swerve, tend, tilt, tip, veer

career *n.* business, calling, course, employment, field, job, life's work, line, livelihood, occupation, profession, pursuit, specialty, vocation, work *Nonformal:* dodge, game

carefree *adj.* airy, at ease, blithe, breezy, buoyant, calm, careless, cheerful, cheery, cool, easy, easygoing, happy, happy-go-lucky, insouciant, jaunty, jovial, laid-back *(Nonformal)*, lighthearted, radiant, relaxed, secure, sunny, trouble-free, untroubled *Antonyms:* blue, cheerless, dejected, desolate, melancholy

careful *adj.* **1.** anal retentive *(Nonformal)*, assiduous, choosy, conscientious, fastidious, exact, exacting, finicky, fussy, industrious, keen, meticulous, painstaking, particular, persnickety, picky, precise, rigorous, self-disciplined, strict, sedulous, thorough, *Antonyms:* hasty, lazy, slapdash **2.** alert, apprehensive, attentive, aware, cagey, cautious, chary, calculating, discreet, guarded, mindful, observant, on guard, proper, prudent, thoughtful, vigilant, wakeful, wary, watchful *Antonyms:* careless, inattentive, neglectful

carefully *adv.* advisedly, anxiously, attentively, cautiously, concernedly, conscientiously, consciously, correctly, deliberately, delicately, discreetly, exactly, faithfully, fastidiously, fully, gingerly, guardedly, heedfully, intentionally, laboriously, meticulously, particularly, providently, prudently, regardfully, reliably, scrupulously, solicitously, thoughtfully, vigilantly, warily, watchfully *Antonyms:* carelessly, heedlessly, thoughtlessly

careless *adj.* **1.** absent-minded, abstracted, dreamy, flighty, forgetful, inattentive, irrational, mindless, thoughtless, unmindful, unthinking *Antonyms:* attentive, careful, cautious **2.** breezy, casual, cavalier, devil-may-care *(Nonformal)*, easygoing, fanciful, free, madcap, nonchalant, wanton, wild *Antonyms:* anxious, concerned **3.** brash, disregardful, half-assed *(Nonformal)*, half-hearted, haphazard, harebrained, hasty, heedless, ill-advised, ill-considered, impetuous, improvident, imprudent, impulsive, inaccurate, inadvertent, incautious, inconsiderate, indifferent, indiscreet, inexact, irresponsible, lazy, neglectful, negligent, offhand, rash, reckless, remiss, slack, slapdash, slipshod, sloppy, unceremonious, unreliable, untidy *Antonyms:* alert, wary, watchful

caress *n.* cuddle, embrace, endearment, feel, hug, kiss, pat, pet, rub, snuggle, squeeze, stroke, touch – *v.* cosset, cuddle, dandle, finger *(Nonformal)*, fondle, massage, nestle, nuzzle, pat, pet, rub, stroke, touch

careworn *adj.* **1.** drooping, exhausted, faint, fatigued, flagging, footsore, haggard, overworked, spent, taxed, tired, toilworn, weakened, weary, worn *Nonformal:* down and out, tuckered out, wiped **2.** depressed, dispirited, forlorn, heavy-laden, melancholy, oppressed, sorrowful, sorry

cargo *n.* baggage, burden, consignment, contents, freight, goods, haul, lading, load, merchandise, payload, shipload, shipment, tonnage

caricature *n.* burlesque, cartoon, drawing, farce, lampoon, mockery, parody, pasquinade, sardonic portrait *or* representation, satire, sketch, spoof, squib, take-off, travesty – *v.* ape, burlesque, deride, exaggerate, imitate, lampoon, laugh at, make fun of, mimic, mock, parody, ridicule, satirize, stultify

carnage *n.* annihilation, bloodbath, bloodshed, butchery, decimation, ethnic cleansing, extermination, genocide, homicide, killing, liquidation, manslaughter, massacre, mass destruction *or* extermination, murder, slaughter, slaying, warfare

carnal *adj.* **1.** animal, bodily, earthly, fleshly, physical, sensuous, worldly *Antonyms:* metaphysical, spiritual, transcendent **2.** erotic, lascivious, lecherous, lewd, libidinous, licentious, lustful, orgiastic, prurient, salacious, sensual, sexual, sexy

carnival *n.* bacchanal, ceilidh, celebration, circus, exhibition, fair, *fasching (German)*, festival, fête, fiesta, gala, jamboree, jubilee, jump-up, levee, Mardi Gras, masque, Oktoberfest, orgy, party, revelry, side show, street fair *Nonformal:* carny, ex

carnivore *n.* cannibal, flesh-eater, meat-eater *Antonyms:* herbivore, vegan, vegetarian

carnivorous *adj.* flesh-eating, man-eating, predatory, rapacious, voracious

carol *n.* anthem, ballad, canticle, canzonet, chorus, Christmas song, ditty, hymn, madrigal, melody, noël, song, strain, tune

carouse *v.* drink, frolic, imbibe, make merry, play, quaff, revel, riot, roister, spree, wassail *Nonformal:* booze, party, raise Cain

carpenter *n.* artisan, builder, cabinetmaker, craftsperson, joiner, labourer, woodworker

carpet *n.* carpeting, covering, matting, rug, tapestry *Kinds of carpet & rug:* area, Aubusson, Axminster, bearskin, Bokhara, broadloom, Brussels, Caucasian, flokati, hooked mat, Indian, Indo-Tabriz, Kirman, Navaho, Oriental, Persian, pile, prayer, rag, runner, scatter, shag, steamer, Tabriz, throw, Turkish, Turkoman, wall-to-wall, Wilton

carriage *n.* **1.** transport vehicle *Kinds of carriage:* barouche, brougham, buggy, cabriolet, calèche, coach, gig, hackney, jig, jitney, perch, phaeton, four wheeler, surrey, tillbury, trap, victoria, *voiture (French)* **2.** conveyance, delivery, freight, movement, portage, shipment, transit, transport, transportation **3.** appearance, aspect, bearing, cast, comportment, demeanour, deportment, manner, mien, posture, presence, stance

carrier *n.* **1.** cargo handler, carter, conveyer, courier, hauler, mailperson, runner, shipper, taxi, transporter, trucker, wagoner **2.** disease-carrier, transmitter, vector *Nonformal:* germbag, patient zero, Typhoid Mary

carry *v.* **1.** bring, cart, convey, ferry, fetch, freight, haul, heft, hoist, lift, move, portage, relay, shift, transfer, transmit, transplant, truck **2.** accept, assume, burden oneself, shoulder, take on *or* up **3.** deal *or* traffic in, handle, have, hold, keep, maintain, possess, sell, shelve, stock, supply **4.** behave, comport, conduct, govern, hold **5.** adopt, capture, gain, pass, ratify, succeed, triumph, win, win over **6.** imply, indicate, involve, motivate, move, signal, urge **7.** continue, extend, range, reach, stretch out to **8.** bear, produce, sustain, yield **9.** confirm, corroborate, endorse, support

cart *n.* wagon *Kinds of cart:* barrow, dogcart, dolly, dray, go-cart, gurney, handcart, jigger *(P.E.I.)*, lunch, pushcart, Red River, rickshaw, tumbrel, two-wheeler, wheelbarrow *See also:* **wagon** – *v.* carry off, haul away, remove, transport, truck

carte blanche *n.* blank cheque, free hand *or* scope, immunity, unrestricted authority

carton *n.* bin, box, case, casket, chest, container, crate, pack, package – *v.* box *or* package *or* wrap up, pack, seal

cartoon *n.* **1.** animation, caricature, comic book, comics, comic strip, funnies, funny pictures, lampoon, *manga (Japanese)*, panel, takeoff *Nonformal:* anime, toon **2.** depiction, diagram, drawing, painting, sketch – *v.* caricature, draw, illustrate, portrait, sketch

cartoonist *n.* animator, artist, caricaturist, comic *or* sketch artist

cartridge *n.* **1.** ammunition, ball, bullet, canister, cap, case shot, grenade, magazine, projectile, shell **2.** capsule, case, casing, cassette, container, cylinder, reservoir

carve *v.* **1.** butcher, cleave, cut, dissect, hack, hew, rough-hew, slash, slaughter, slice, trim **2.** chip, chisel, fashion, form, incise, make, model, pattern, sculpt, shape, shave, tool, whittle

cascade *n.* avalanche, cataract, chute, deluge, falls, flood, fountain, outpouring, rapids, sault, shower, spout, torrent, watercourse, waterfall – *v.* descend, disgorge, fall, flood, gush, overflow, pitch, plunge, pour, run, spew, spill, surge

case *n.* **1.** baggage, basket, bin, box, cabinet, caddy, carton, coffer, container, covering, crate, drawer, envelope, folder, holder, jacket, receptacle, safe, scabbard, suitcase, tote, tray, trunk, wallet **2.** action, argument, claim, court action *or* matter, dispute, lawsuit, litigation, petition, proceedings, process, suit **3.** circumstance, event, fact, incident, situation, set of facts, state, state of affairs **4.** crisis, dilemma, predicament, problem, quandary, question **5.** episode, experience, happening, instance, occurrence **6.** argument, evidence, position, proof, rationale, reasons **7.** relationship *Kinds of grammatical case:* ablative, accusative, dative, genitive, locative, nominative, objective, possessive, prepositional, vocative **8.** frame, integument, sheath, shell, wrapper, wrapping **9.** bunch, number, pair, selection, set – *v.* **1.** crate, encase, pack, parcel up, sheathe, wrap **2.** check *or* scout out, examine, explore, investigate, reconnoiter, scout, survey

cash *n.* **1.** available funds, banknote, buck, bullion, coin, currency, dollars, funds, legal tender, liquid *or* ready assets, note, payment, resources, riches, wherewithal *Nonformal:* buck, almighty dollar, cash money, chicken feed, dough, kitty, loot, mad money, moolah, peanuts, savings, wampum *Small amounts of cash:* change, mad *or* pin *or* pocket money, petty cash, small change, spending money **2.** cash box *or* register, float, petty cash, reserve, till, treasury – *v.* **1.** break, change, exchange, honour **2.** liquidate, pay, payout, redeem, turn in

cashier *n.* accountant, banker, bursar, clerk, collector, paymaster, purser, receiver, teller, treasurer – *v.* discard, discharge, dismiss, displace, expel, fire, remove *Nonformal:* axe, boot, bounce, sack

casino *n.* betting house *or* parlour *or* shop, clubhouse, gambling den, gaming room, parlour club, pool hall, saloon, track

cask *n.* barrel, container, drum, firkin, hogshead, keg, kilderkin, puncheon, receptacle, tierce, tub, vat, vessel

casket *n.* bin, box, carton, case, chest, coffer, coffin, container, jewel box, receptacle, sarcophagus

cast *n.* **1.** ejection, flip, fling, heave, hurl, launch, lob, pitch, projection, propulsion, sling, throw, thrust, toss **2.** copy, duplicate, embodiment, facsimile, figure, form, mould, plaster, replica, sculpture, shape, template **3.** actors, artists, body, characters, company, crew, *dramatis personae (Latin)*, ensemble, list, parts, personae, players, repertory company, roles, troupe **4.** air, bent, bias, complexion, countenance, disposition, hue, humour, inclination, mien, mood, shade, temperament, tendency, tinge, tint, tone, trait, visage **5.** conjecture, destiny, divination, fate, forecast, fortune, lot, portion, prediction, prophecy **6.** bandage, brace, dressing, protector, wrap – *v.* **1.** bang, chuck, chunk, direct, drive, drop, fling, heave, hurl, launch, lob, pitch, sling, throw, thrust, toss, whip *Antonyms:* catch, receive **2.** allot, appoint, assign, choose, decide upon, designate, detail, distribute, give out, name, nominate, peg, pick, select **3.** arrange, come up with, continue, contrive, design, devise, hatch, scheme **4.** chart, estimate, forecast, foretell, project **5.** add, add up, calculate, count, determine, number, reckon, sum, tally, total **6.** fashion, form, model, mould, shape **7.** exoviate, lose, moult, shed, shuck, throw off *Antonyms:* assume, grow into, put on **8.** deposit, direct, scatter, splatter, spray, spread, sprinkle, strew *Antonyms:* assemble, collate, collect **9.** denounce, dismiss, reject, throw aside **10.** *Nautical:* fall off, put about, tack, turn, veer **11.** bend, go off kilter, turn, twist, warp

castaway *adj.* **1.** abandoned, derelict, discarded, forsaken, rejected, second-hand, sloughed off, thrown away, unwanted **2.** adrift, grounded, marooned, stranded, stuck – *n.* **1.** beggar, derelict, hobo, homeless person, itinerant, nomad, panhandler, rover, scavenger, tramp, urchin, vagabond, vagrant, waif, wanderer **2.** excommunicate, exile, expatriate, non-person, outcast, outlaw, pariah, political refugee, stray **3.** castoff, discard, hand-me-down *(Nonformal)*, secondhand **4.** factory reject, irregular, reject, x-out

caste *n.* class, degree, estate, grade, lineage, order, position, race, rank, social order, sphere, standing, station, status, stratum, system

castigate *v.* berate, censure, chasten, chastise, correct, criticize, discipline, excoriate, flog, lambaste, lash, penalize, punish, rail, rebuke, reprimand, thrash, upbraid *Nonformal:* chew out, dress down, tongue-lash *Antonyms:* commend, extol, praise *Commonly misused:* **denigrate**

castle *n.* alcazar, château, citadel, donjon, fortress, hold, keep, mansion, palace, *schloss (German)*, stronghold, tower, villa

castrate *v.* alter, change, cripple, cut, desex, emasculate, fix, geld, mutilate, neuter, spay, sterilize

casual *adj.* **1.** accidental, adventitious, chance, fluky, fortuitous, haphazard, impromptu, impulsive, infrequent, random, serendipitous, spontaneous, unexpected, unintentional, unplanned *Antonyms:* arranged, deliberate, expected, intentional **2.** contract, incidental, intermittent, irregular, occasional, part-time, seasonal, temporary *Antonyms:* fixed, permanent, steady **3.** blasé, easygoing, folksy, homey, informal, insouciant, mellow, nonchalant, unconcerned, unfussy *Antonyms:* ceremonial, dressy, formal

casualty *n.* **1.** accident, blow, calamity, catastrophe, chance, debacle, disaster, misadventure, misfortune, mishap **2.** fatality, the dead, the injured, killed, lost, missing, prey, sufferer, victim, wounded

casuistry *n.* chicanery, deception, deceptiveness, delusion, equivocation, evasion, fallacy, lie, sophistry, speciousness, trick

cat *n. chat (French)*, feline, grimalkin, kitty, malkin, mouser, puss, pussy *Domestic cats:* alley, barn, Burmese, calico, ginger, Himalayan, house, Maine coon, Manx, Persian, short-haired, Siamese, tabby, tortoise shell *Wild cats:* bobcat, cheetah, cougar, jaguar, leopard, lion, lynx, mountain lion, ocelot, panther, puma, tiger, wildcat

cataclysm *n.* apocalypse, calamity, catastrophe, disaster, disturbance, flood, inundation, misadventure, overflow, tragedy, unholy mess *(Nonformal)*, upheaval, woe

catalogue *n.* archive, bibliography, brief, bulletin, calendar, chronicle, classification, compendium, concordance, directory, document, draft, gazetteer, index, inventory, list, magazine, record, register, roll, roster, schedule, specification, syllabus, synopsis – *v.* alphabetize, categorize, classify, code, document, file, index, inventory, list, sort *Nonformal:* button down, peg, pigeonhole

catalyst *n.* agitator, dynamo *(Nonformal)*, enzyme, goad, impetus, impulse, incentive, incitement, motivation, provocation, radical stimulus, spur, synergist

catapult *n.* arbalest, ballista, crossbow, mortar, sling, slingshot, trebuchet – *v.* fling, hurl, let rip *(Nonformal)*, shoot, sling

catastrophe *n.* **1.** adversity, affliction, apocalypse, calamity, cataclysm, crash, debacle, disaster, emergency, fiasco, havoc, misadventure, misery, misfortune, reverse, tragedy, trial, trouble, upheaval, wreck *Nonformal:* bad news, the big one, the end, the worst **2.** conclusion, curtains *(Nonformal)*, dénouement, revelation

catch *n.* **1.** bolt, buckle, clamp, clasp, clip, fastener, hasp, hook, latch, snap **2.** condition, conundrum, crux, deception, decoy, drawback, hitch, obstacle, proviso, snag, take, trap, trick *Antonyms:* advantage, benefit, boon, reward – *v.* **1.** catch in the act, come across *or* upon, detect, discover, encounter, run across, stumble into *or* upon, surprise **2.** apprehend, arrest, capture, collar, come up with, entrap, get, grab, handle, lasso, pick up, secure, siege, smoke out, snare, stop, take captive *or* into custody, trap *Nonformal:* bag, bust, nab, nail, snag **3.** accost, grip, hold, lay, retain **4.** absorb, acquire, apprehend, arrive at, assimilate, comprehend, contract, detect, digest, ensnare, fathom, follow, grasp, perceive, realize, recognize, understand *Nonformal:* get the drift, savvy, see daylight *Antonyms:* confuse, misunderstand **5.** check, hold back, reconsider, restrain, think twice **6.** captivate, charm, enchant, tantalize, win **7.** attend, experience, see, take in, view, visit, watch **8.** explode, ignite, kindle, take fire

catching *adj.* **1.** communicable, contagious, dangerous, endemic, epidemic, infectious, noxious, pandemic, transferable, transmittable **2.** alluring, appealing, attractive, captivating, charming, enchanting, fetching, gripping, inviting, provocative, seductive, spellbinding, winsome

catchword *n.* buzzword, byword, catch phrase, cliché, code word, in-word, maxim, motto, password, pet expression, refrain, shibboleth, slogan, watchword

catchy *adj.* addictive, captivating, fetching, haunting, melodious, memorable, popular, tantalizing, tuneful *Antonyms:* banal, mundane

catechism *n.* creed *or* religious creed, doctrine, dogma, education, instruction, manual, outline

catechize *v.* **1.** cross-examine, drill, examine, grill *(Nonformal)*, interrogate, question **2.** discipline, edify, educate, indoctrinate, instruct, school, teach, tutor

categorical *adj.* absolute, certain, clear-cut, definitive, direct, downright, emphatic, explicit, express, forthright, positive, specific, straight-out, sure, unambiguous *Antonyms:* conditional, uncertain, vague

categorize *v.* access, class, classify, codify, group, identify, peg, pigeonhole, size up, sort, stereotype, typecast

category *n.* class, classification, department, division, grade, group, grouping, header, heading, kind, league, level, list, order, pigeonhole, position, rank, section, sort, type

cater *v.* **1.** furnish, help, outfit, procure, provide, provision, purvey, supply **2.** baby, coddle, gratify, humour, indulge, minister to, pamper, pander to, spoil

caterwaul *v.* **1.** bark, cry, howl, meow, mew, scream, screech, shriek, squall, squeal, wail, whimper, whine, yap, yell, yelp **2.** argue, bicker, carry on, debate, dispute, quibble

catharsis *n.* ablution, abreaction, cleansing, expurgation, lustration, psychocatharsis, purgation, purging, purification

cathedral *n.* basilica, church, holy place, minster, sanctuary, temple

catholic *adj.* all-embracing, comprehensive, cosmic, cosmopolitan, ecumenical, extensive, general, generic, global, inclusive, liberal, open-minded, tolerant, universal, whole, wide, worldly, worldwide *Antonyms:* exclusive, narrow-minded, parochial, sectarian

cattle *n.* **1.** bovine, cow, kine, livestock, stock *Groupings of cattle:* beef, dairy, milch, milk, dual-purpose *Kinds of cattle:* Aberdeen, Angus, Ayrshire, Beefmaster, Blonde D'Aquitaine, Brahma, Canadian, Chianina, Galloway, Gelbvieb, Guernsey, Hays Converter, heifer *(immature)*, Hereford, Highland, Holstein, Jersey, Limousin, longhorn, Marie Anjou, Meuse-Rhine-Yssel, Piedmontese, Pinzgauer, Red Angus, Saler, Santa Gertrudis, shorthorn, Simmental, Swiss Brown, Tarentaise, Texas longhorn, Welsh Black *Nonformal:* dogie, moo cow **2.** commonality, followers, herd, hoi polloi, masses, multitudes, sheep

catty *adj.* backbiting, bitchy, ill-natured, malicious, mean, nasty, rancorous, spiteful, venomous, vicious *Antonyms:* benevolent, charitable, compassionate, generous, kind

caucus *n.* assembly, conclave, conference, convention, council, gathering, get-together, legislature, meeting, political committee, session

cause *n.* **1.** aim, determinant, goal, ground, ideal, justification, motive, object, principle, question, rationale, reason, stimulus, tenet **2.** antecedent, derivation, driving force *or* force, genesis, instigator, originator, root, wellspring **3.** action, case, legal brief, suit – *v.* **1.** bring about, effect, found, initiate, institute, occasion, originate, start **2.** coerce, compel, constrain, dragoon, force, induce, make, order, press, push, strong-arm **3.** incite, influence, inspire, move, persuade, prompt, provoke

caustic *adj.* **1.** abrasive, acid, acrid, acrimonious, astringent, biting, bitter, burning, corroding, corrosive, erosive, harsh, mordant, pungent, sour, tart, vitriolic **2.** abusive, berating, contemptuous, cruel, cynical, denouncing, derisive, double-edged, insulting, ironic, mean, mocking, sarcastic, sardonic, satirical, scornful, taunting, teasing, uncharitable, unkind **3.** abrupt, angry, blunt, brusque, discourteous, edgy, graceless, gruff, hostile, ill-tempered, impolite, irascible, moody, peevish, petulant, rude, short, surly, testy, touchy, unmannerly, waspish *Antonyms:* civil, courteous, polite, refined

caution *n.* **1.** acumen, alertness, attention, canniness, care, carefulness, circumspection, concern, considerateness, counsel, deliberation, diplomacy, discreetness, discretion, discrimination, foresight, forethought, forewarning, good sense, heed, judiciousness, perspicacity, providence, prudence, sense, shrewdness, solicitude, tact, thoughtfulness, vigilance, watchfulness, wisdom *Antonyms:* carelessness, daring, imprudence, rashness, recklessness **2.** admonition, advice, caveat, injunction, notice, observation, premonition, warning – *v.* admonish, advise, alert, exhort, flag, forewarn, tip, urge, warn *Nonformal:* red flag, tip off

cautious *adj.* alert, attentive, cagey, calculating, canny, careful, chary, circumspect, considerate, constrained, dainty, deliberate, delicate, diplomatic, discreet, discriminating, fastidious, frugal, gingerly, guarded, heedful, hesitant, inhibited, judicious, leery, particular, politic, provident, prudent, punctilious, pussyfooting *(Nonformal)*, reluctant, restrained, safe, sagacious, scrupulous, searching, squeamish, suspicious, tentative, timid, uneasy, vigilant, wary, watchful *Antonyms:* careless, foolhardy, impetuous, madcap, rash

cavalcade *n.* array, column, company of horsemen, convoy, drill, march-past, motorcade, parade, procession, review, spectacle, train, troop, unit

cavalier *adj.* **1.** arrogant, condescending, curt, disdainful, haughty, high-and-mighty, insolent, lofty, lordly, overbearing, proud, scornful, supercilious, superior *Antonyms:* deferential, humble, modest, polite **2.** blasé, careless, crass, devil-may-care, flip, indifferent, nonchalant, off-hand, *pacocurante (Italian)* – *n.* beau, *caballero (Spanish)*, *chevalier (French)*, escort, esquire, gallant, gentleman, horse soldier, hussar, knight, man about town

cavalry *n.* army, dragoons, horse, horsemen, horse soldiers, hussars, lancers, mounted men *or* rifles *or* troops, rangers, squadron, troops, uhlans *Antonyms:* foot soldier, infantryman

cave *n.* catacomb, cavern, cavity, crypt, den, dugout, grotto, hole, hollow, lair, rock shelter, tunnel, underground chamber – *v.* abdicate, accede, capitulate, collapse, concede, forsake, give in, submit, surrender, yield, yield the field

caveat *n.* admonition, alarm, caution, forewarning, information, monition, notice, notification, sign, warning

cavernous *adj.* **1.** abysmal, broad, chambered, commodious, deep-set, gaping, hollow, hollowed out, huge, roomy, spacious, sunken, vast, wide, yawning *Antonyms:* narrow, shallow, slim **2.** alveolate, perforated, porous, sievelike

cavity *n.* crater, dent, depression, excavation, gap, hole, hollow, pit, pocket, sinus, socket, vacuity, void, vug

cavort *v.* caper, carry on, cut loose, dance, fool around, frisk, frolic, gambol, play, prance, revel, rollick, romp, roughhouse, sport *Nonformal:* horse *or* monkey around

cay *n.* atoll, bar, coastal island, islet, key, reef, sandbank, sandbar

cease *v.* back *or* break off, close, conclude, culminate, desist, die, discontinue, drop, end, fail, finish, halt, intermit, leave off, quit, refrain, stay, stop, surcease, terminate *Nonformal:* call it a day, fold up, pack it in, shut down, wind up *Antonyms:* begin, commence, continue, initiate, start

ceaseless *adj.* ad infinitum *or* nauseam, amaranthine, constant, continual, continuous, endless, eternal, everlasting, forever, incessant, indefatigable, interminable, never-ending, nonstop, perennial, perpetual, unceasing, unending, uninterrupted, unremitting, untiring *Antonyms:* broken, erratic, intermittent, irregular, sporadic

cede *v.* **1.** abandon, abdicate, accord, allow, capitulate, concede, drop, fold, give in *or* up, relinquish, renounce, resign, surrender, waive, yield *Antonyms:* fight, keep, retain **2.** bequeath, convey, deed, grant, hand over, part with, transfer

ceiling *n.* **1.** canopy, cover, covering, lid, roof *or* roofing, top, topside, upper side, vaulting *Kinds of ceiling:* cathedral, dropped, skylight, tin, vaulted **2.** altitude, atmosphere, cloud cover, height **3.** boundary, glass ceiling *(Nonformal)*, limit, peak, pinnacle, upper limit

celebrate *v.* **1.** cheer, drink to, fête, frolic, party, rejoice, revel **2.** commend, congratulate, extol, glorify, honour, laud, praise, make much of *(Nonformal)* **3.** ballyhoo, broadcast, eulogize, proclaim, publicize, spread the word, trumpet **4.** commemorate, consecrate, dedicate, mark, memorialize, solemnize **5.** hold, observe, participate, perform

celebrated *adj.* acclaimed, distinguished, eminent, famed, famous, glorious, great, high-powered *(Nonformal)*, illustrious, immortal, important, large, laureate, lionized, notable, outstanding, popular, preeminent, prominent, renowned, revered, storied, well-known *Antonyms:* forgotten, insignificant, obscure, unknown

celebration *n.* **1.** anniversary, bacchanalia, birthday, ceilidh, centennial, ceremony, charivari, commemoration, entertainment, feast *or* feast day, festival, festivity, fête, fiesta, frolic, gala, graduation, holiday, initiation, jubilee, levee, merrymaking, observance, party, remembrance, revel, rite, ritual, sacrament, soirée, spree, tribute, triumph, wake, wedding *Nonformal:* bash, blast, blowout, do, hoopla, rave, shindig, whoop-de-doo, wingding **2.** elation, exultation, glee, jollity, joy, joyousness, jubilation, merriment, rejoicing

celebrity *n.* **1.** dignitary, famous figure *or* person, figure, hero, immortal, luminary, magnate, movie star, notable, personage, personality, rock star, superstar, worthy *Nonformal:* celeb, glitterati, lion, name *Antonyms:* has-been, nobody, unknown **2.** distinction, *éclat (French)*, eminence, fame, glory, honour, notability, notoriety, popularity, preeminence, prestige, prominence, renown, reputation, repute, stardom *Antonyms:* insignificance, nonentity, obscurity

celerity *n.* alacrity, briskness, dispatch, expedition, fleetness, haste, hurry, hustle, promptness, quickness, rapidity, speediness, swiftness *Antonyms:* inertia, lethargy, slowness

celestial *adj.* angelic, astral, beatific, blessed, cosmic, divine, Elysian, eternal, ethereal, godlike, hallowed, heavenly, holy, immortal, otherworldly, spiritual, sublime, supernatural, transcendental *Antonyms:* carnal, earthly, mundane, terrestrial

celibacy *n.* abstinence, chastity, continence, monasticism, purity, singleness, virginity, virtue *Antonyms:* debauchery, lechery, licentiousness, promiscuity

cell *n.* **1.** fundamental structural unit *Kinds of cell:* amoeba, gamete, germ, ovum, sperm, spore *Parts of a cell:* centriole, chloroplast, chromatin, cytoplasm, endoplasmic reticulum, Golgi complex *or* vesicle, lamella, lysosome, microfibrils, microtubules, microvilli, mitochondrion, nuclear envelope, nuclear pore, nucleolus, pinocytotic vesicle, plasma membrane, reticulum, tonoplast, vacuole **2.** cage, dungeon, hold, keep, lockup, pen **3.** apartment, booth, chamber, cloister, closet, compartment, cubicle, room of one's own, sanctum, vault **4.** body, branch, coterie, division, sect

cellar *n.* basement, bomb shelter, bunker, crypt, dungeon, pantry, storage room, sub-basement, underground, vault *Kinds of cellar:* cantina, coal, cold, potato, root, storm, tornado, wine

cement *n.* adhesive, binder, bond, concrete, glue, grout, lime, mortar, plaster, sealant – *v.* attach, bind, bond, cohere, fasten, fuse, glue, join, paste, solder, unite, weld *Commonly misused:* **concrete**

cemetery *n.* burial ground *or* place, catacomb, crypt, grave, graveyard, mausoleum, mortuary, necropolis, ossuary, potter's field, sepulchre, tomb, vault *Nonformal:* bone orchard, boneyard

censor *n.* critic, censor board, editor, inspector, regulator, reviewer – *v.* abridge, amend, ban, blacklist, black *or* bleep out *(Nonformal)*, blue-pencil, bowdlerize, conceal, control, cork, cut, delete, edit, examine, excise, expurgate, forbid, muzzle, repress, restrain, restrict, sanitize, squelch, strike out, suppress *Antonyms:* allow, release, sanction *Commonly misused:* **censure**

censorious *adj.* accusatory, captious, carping, caviling, chiding, complaining, condemnatory, condemning, critical, deprecatory, disapproving, disparaging, faultfinding, hypercritical, reproaching, severe *Antonyms:* approving, complimentary, laudatory

censorship *n.* ban, blackout, bowdlerization, control, cutting, editing, expurgation, forbiddance, forbidding, hushing up, restriction, stifling, suppression

censure *n.* admonition, blame, castigation, condemnation, criticism, disapproval, dressing down, rebuke, remonstrance, reprimand, reproach, reproof, stricture *Antonyms:* approval, commendation, compliment, encouragement – *v.* abuse, admonish, attack, berate, blame, castigate, chastise, chide, condemn, denounce, deprecate, discipline, rebuke, remonstrate, reprimand, reproach, reprove, upbraid *Antonyms:* applaud, commend, laud *Commonly misused:* **censor**

census *n.* **1.** listing, returns, statement, statistics, Statistics Canada *or* StatsCan *(Nonformal)* **2.** count, demographics, enumeration, head count, poll, population, tabulation, tally

central *adj.* basic, cardinal, centre, chief, core, dominant, essential, fundamental, important, key, leading, main, master, outstanding, overriding, paramount, pivotal, predominant, primary, prime, principal, salient, significant *Antonyms:* corollary, outer, peripheral, subordinate, subsidiary

centralize *v.* accumulate, amalgamate, assemble, coalesce, concentrate, condense, consolidate, converge, draw together, focus, gather, incorporate, integrate, organize, unify *Antonyms:* decentralize, expand, separate, spread out

centre *adj.* central, equidistant, inside, interior, mean, median, middle *Antonym:* outer, peripheral – *n.* **1.** axis, core, crux, essence, focal point, focus, gist, heart, nub, nucleus, pivot, root, seat, source *Antonyms:* border, fringe, perimeter **2.** central business district *or* CBD, city centre, depot, downtown, meeting place, metropolis – *v.* **1.** align, centralize, focalize *Antonyms:* divert, skew **2.** concentrate, converge, focus, hone in, intensify *Antonyms:* blur, distract **3.** assemble, bring *or* join together, consolidate, gather, unite *Antonyms:* disseminate, scatter

centrifugal *adj.* diffusive, divergent, diverging, eccentric, efferent, outward, radial, radiating, spiral, spreading

ceramics *n. pl.* agate ware, basalt-ware, bisque, china, clay pots, crackleware, crockery, crocks, delftware, della Robbia ware, dishes, earthenware, eggshell porcelain, enamel, faience, fiestaware, ironstone, jasperware, lustreware, majolica, mosaic, porcelain, pottery, Queens ware, raku, spatter ware, sponge-ware, stoneware, terra cotta *Ceramic terms:* armature, baffle, bat, bench wheel, bisquit, casting, chuck, chum, coil, fettle, fire, flashing, glaze, grout, jigger, jolly, kiln, knead, lustre, luting, pug, rib, slip, slurry, spall, throw

cereal *n.* **1.** breakfast food *Kinds of cereal:* congee *(Chinese)*, corn flakes, cornmeal mush, granola, grits, gruel, muesli, multigrain, oatmeal, porridge, toasties *(Nonformal)*, puffed rice, rolled oats **2.** barley, bran, buckwheat, corn, grain, maize, meal, oats, rice, rye, wheat

cerebral *adj.* analytic, bookish, brainy, intellectual, literary, literate, mental, noetic, rational, reasoning, thinking, thoughtful, versed *Nonformal:* egghead, highbrow *Antonyms:* emotional, instinctual, intuitive

ceremonial *adj.* august, imposing, liturgical, lofty, mannered, ritualistic, solemn, stately, studied, stylized *Antonyms:* casual, conventional, informal, relaxed, simple *Commonly misused:* **ceremonious**

ceremonious *adj.* civil, conventional, courteous, courtly, decorous, deferential, dignified, exact, formal, majestic, meticulous, precise, proper, punctilious, seemly, solemn, stately *Antonyms:* casual, informal, relaxed *Commonly misused:* **ceremonial**

ceremony *n.* **1.** anniversary, bar *or* bat mitzvah, celebration, event, function, happening *(Nonformal)*, observance, occasion, pageant, party, potlatch, rite, rite of passage, ritual, service **2.** courtesy, decorum, etiquette, form, formalism, liturgy, nicety, politeness, pomp, propriety, protocol **3.** exercise, formality, function, manner

certain *adj.* **1.** clear, convinced, decided, determined, firm, precise, pronounced **2.**

absolute, beyond doubt *or* question, certified, guaranteed, incontrovertible, indisputable, irrefutable, unequivocal, unmistakable **3.** assured, destined, fated, fixed, inescapable, inevitable, infallible, predestined **4.** consistent, dependable, faithful, reliable, steadfast, true, trustworthy, unerring, unfailing, unflagging

certainly *adv.* absolutely, admittedly, assuredly, clearly, conclusively, decidedly, definitely, determinedly, distinctly, doubtless, *exactement (French)*, exactly, explicitly, indeed, indubitably, inevitably, inexorably, irrefutably, manifestly, obviously, palpably, patently, plainly, positively, precisely, really, strongly, surely, truly, undeniably, undoubtedly, unequivocally, unmistakably, unquestionably, without fail *Antonyms:* hesitantly, possibly *Commonly misused:* **certainty**

certainty *n.* **1.** assurance, authoritativeness, belief, certitude, conviction, credence, definiteness, firmness, staunchness, steadiness, sureness surety, trust *Antonyms:* conjecture, doubt, indecision, qualm **2.** fact *or* documented *or* known fact, reality, sure thing *(Nonformal)*, truth, verity *Commonly misused:* **certainly**

certificate *n.* authority, authorization, credential, identification *Kinds of certificate:* affidavit, deed, degree, deposit, deposition, diploma, guarantee, licence, ownership, passport, registration, registry, safe-conduct, stock, teaching, ticket, title, visa, voucher, warranty

certification *n.* **1.** accreditation, authorization, basis, credentials, deed, degree, diploma, entitlement, licence, mandate, official document, order, ordinance, paper, pass, passport, permission, permit, qualification, recognition, recommendation, references, regulation, right, safe-conduct, sanction, substantiation, testament, testimonial, title, validation, visa, voucher, warrant, warranty **2.** authentication, confirmation, corroboration, documentation, guarantee, proof, support, verification

certify *v.* approve, attest, authenticate, aver, avow, bear out, confirm, corroborate, declare, endorse, guarantee, justify, notarize, notify, profess, prove, reassure, sanction, state, substantiate, support, swear, testify, uphold, validate, verify, vindicate, vouch, witness *Antonyms:* debunk, decertify, disprove

cessation *n.* abeyance, arrest, break, breather *(Nonformal)*, close, conclusion, cut-off, discontinuance, end, ending, finish, freeze, halt, hiatus, intermission, interruption, interval, layoff, pause, recess, remission, respite, rest, standstill, stay, stop, stoppage, suspension, termination, time-out *Antonyms:* commencement, continuation, resumption

chafe *v.* **1.** anger, annoy, bother, exasperate, fret, fume, gall, grate, harass, incense, inflame, irk, irritate, offend, provoke, rage, rub, ruffle, vex, worry *Antonyms:* alleviate, appease, calm, placate, soothe **2.** abrade, corrode, damage, erode, excoriate, graze, hurt, impair, inflame, peel, rasp, rub, scrape, scratch, skin, wear *Antonyms:* assuage, ease, soothe *Commonly misused:* **chaff**

chaff *n.* **1.** crust, debris, dregs, husks, pod, refuse, remains, rubbish, shell, waste **2.** banter, frivolity, fun, humour, jocularity, jocundity, joshing *(Nonformal)*, kidding, mocking, raillery, witticism – *v.* deride, jeer, joke, jolly, mock, poke fun at, ridicule, scoff, taunt *Nonformal:* josh, kid, rag, razz, rib *Commonly misused:* **chafe**

chagrin *n.* discomfiture, disgruntlement, dismay, embarrassment, frustration, humiliation, ill-humour, irritation, mortification, peevishness, vexation – *v.* abash, annoy, confuse, crush, discomfit, discompose, disconcert, disgrace, dismay, displease, disquiet, dissatisfy, embarrass, humiliate, irk, irritate, mortify, perturb, shame, upset, vex

chain *n.* **1.** bond, cable, fastener, fob, leash, line, link, tape *(Surveying)*, tie **2.** continuity, order, progression, row, sequence, string, succession, train **3.** association, conglomerate, group, series, syndicate – *v.* **1.** bind, confine, fasten, fetter, handcuff, manacle, restrain, shackle, tether, tie up, trammel *Antonyms:* free, liberate, release, unfetter **2.** bind, couple, join, link, marry, yoke *Antonyms:* part, separate

chair *n.* **1.** perch *(Nonformal)*, seat, testing place *Kinds of chair:* Adirondack, armchair, banquette, barber's, Barcelona, basket, Bath, beanbag, bench, camp, captain's, card, chaise longue, Chippendale, club, deck, desk, dining, director's, Eames, easy, ergonomic, fanback, folding, highchair, Laurentian *or* Muskoka, lounge, Morris, office, orthopedic, parlour, pew, pottychair, prie-dieu, reclining, rickshaw, rocking, sedan, settle, sling, swing, throne, wicker, Windsor, wing **2.** authority, captain, CEO, chairman, chairperson, chairwoman, director, helm, leader, master, president, principal, professorship, throne – *v.* conduct, facilitate, govern, moderate, oversee, preside over, regulate, supervise

chairperson *n.* chair, chairman *or* woman, convener, facilitator, head, head honcho *(Nonformal)*, leader, president, speaker

challenge *n.* **1.** call to arms, dare, defiance, demand, invitation to fight, provocation, threat, ultimatum **2.** allegation, claim, complaint, contradiction, dispute, grievance, inquiry, objection, protest, reproof **3.** effort, enterprise, exertion, obstacle, risk, struggle, test, trial, undertaking, venture – *v.* **1.** beard, compete, confront, cross, dare, defy, face off, fight, throw down the gauntlet **2.** contradict, dispute, doubt, investigate, object to, query, question *Antonyms:* acquiesce, agree, allow, concur, consent **3.** accost, block, confront, stop, waylay **4.** arouse, excite, invigorate, spur, stimulate, utilize **5.** overload, strain, tax, test, try **6.** arouse, call up *or* upon, demand, invite, summon *or* summon to battle

chamber *n.* **1.** antechamber, apartment, bedchamber, bedroom, berth, boudoir, cabin, cell, compartment, cubicle, enclosure, flat, lodging, office, parlour, room, salon, studio, suite **2.** assembly, congress, council, legislature, organization, representatives, synod

champion *adj.* best, capital, chief, choice, distinguished, excellent, first, greatest, illustrious, outstanding, peerless, premier, prime, principal, prize-winning, splendid, super, superior, top-notch, tops *(Nonformal)*, unbeaten, undefeated, world-class – *n.* **1.** advocate, ally, angel, backer, benefactor, endorser, exponent, guardian, patron, proponent, supporter, sympathizer **2.** champ *(Nonformal)*, conqueror, defender, hero, heroine, master, medalist, nonpareil, paladin, partisan, protector, titleholder, upholder, vanquisher, victor, warrior, white knight, winner – *v.* advocate, back, defend, espouse, fight for, promote, support, uphold

championship *n.* competition winner, crown, state of supremacy, triumph, victory *Kinds of sports championship: Baseball:* All-Star Game, American League Pennant, National League pennant, World Series *Basketball:* National Basketball Association *or* NBA, NCAA March Madness Playoffs *Boxing:* International Boxing Federation *or* IBF, World Boxing Association *or* WBA, World Boxing Council *or* WBC *Curling:* Brier, Scott Tournament of Hearts, Silver Broom *Football:* College Bowl, Grey Cup, Super Bowl, Vanier Cup *Golf:* Australian Masters, British Open, Canadian Open, Ladies' Professional Golfers Association of America *or* LPGA, Masters, President's Cup, Professional Golfers' Association of America *or* PGA, Ryder Cup, U.S. Open, U.S. Women's Open, Walker Cup *Hockey:* Allan Cup, All-Star Game, Canada Cup, Centennial Cup, Memorial Cup, National Hockey League *or* NHL, Olympic Games, Spengler Cup, Stanley Cup, World Cup *Horse Racing:* Canadian Triple Crown *(Breeders' Stakes, Prince of Wales, Queen's Plate)*, Triple Crown *(Belmont, Kentucky Derby, Preakness) Skiing:* Alpine Combined, Biathlon, Downhill, Nordic Combined, Olympic Games, World Championship Slalom, World Cup *Soccer:* European Cup, World Cup *Tennis:* Australian Open, British Open *or* Wimbledon, Canadian Open, Davis Cup, French Open, Olympic Games, U.S. Open

chance *adj.* accidental, adventitious, casual, contingent, fluky, fortuitous, fortunate, happy, inadvertent, incidental, lucky, odd, offhand, random, serendipitous, unforeseeable, unforeseen, unintentional, unplanned *Antonyms:* arranged, deliberate, designed, expected – *n.* **1.** break *or* lucky break, fortune, kismet, long shot, luck, luck of the draw, providence **2.** accident, fluke, happenstance, serendipity **3.** likelihood, lot, opportunity, possibility, probability, prospect **4.** bet, gamble, hazard, risk, speculation, stake, try, venture, wager – *v.* **1.** bet, hazard, risk, speculate, stake, take a flyer *(Nonformal)* **2.** befall, betide, come about, happen, hit *or* light upon, occur, transpire

chancellor *n.* chief, chief secretary, judge, judicial officer, official, minister of state, provost, university head

change *n.* **1.** adaptation, alteration, conversion, departure, divergence, modification, reconstruction, renewal, transformation, transition **2.** alternate, changeover, exchange, replacement, substitution, swap, switch, trade, transfer **3.** diversity, variance, variation, variety **4.** evolution, metamorphosis, mutation, phase, realignment, shift, transformation **5.** coins, copper, dimes, loonies, nickels, pennies, pocket money, quarters, silver, toonies – *v.* **1.** alter, doctor, influence, jockey, manipulate, modify, switch, tamper with, **2.** exchange, interchange, replace, trade **3.** adapt, convert, morph *(Nonformal)*, reorganize, replace, reshape, restyle, revamp, shift, transfer, transfigure, transmogrify, transmute

changeable *adj.* **1.** capricious, chameleonlike, fickle, inconstant, indecisive, mercurial, unpredictable *Antonyms:* constant, dependable, steadfast **2.** alterable, convertible, modifiable, transformable, transmutable *Antonyms:* immutable, permanent, set **3.** diversified, multi-faceted, variegated

channel *n.* **1.** agency, agent, avenue, course, instrument, means, medium, ministry, organ, route, vehicle, way **2.** aqueduct, arroyo, artery, canal, conduit, ditch, duct, furrow, groove, gully, gutter, narrows, pipe, reach, run, river, route, sewer, strait, trench, trough, tunnel, watercourse **3.** approach, inlet, neck, passage, pathway, raceway, runway, seaway, sluice, smye, tideway, waterway – *v.* **1.** carry, conduct, convey, direct, funnel, guide, pipe, route, send, siphon, transmit, transport **2.** burrow, carve, furrow, groove, hollow out

chant *n.* **1.** canon, carol, chorus, hymn, lilt, melody, plainsong, psalm, refrain, singing, song, tune **2.** incantation, intonation, invocation, litany – *v.* carol, chorus, croon, descant, drone, harmonize, intone, recite, repeat, shout, sing, trill, vocalize, warble

chaos *n.* anarchy, bedlam, cacophony, confusion, disarray, disorder, disorganization, free-for-all, hitherie-hie *(P.E.I.)*, lawlessness, mayhem, misrule, muddle, pandemonium, snarl, tumult, turmoil, unruliness *Nonformal:* hubbub, rat's nest *Antonyms:* law and order, orderliness, organization

chaperone *n.* babysitter, bodyguard, companion, duenna, escort, gooseberry *(P.E.I.)*, governess, guardian, nanny, supervisor – *v.* accompany, escort, preside *or* watch over, shepherd

chaplain *n.* clergyman, cleric, curé, minister, padre, *papa (Greek Orthodox)*, pastor, preacher, priest, rabbi, reverend, vicar

chapter *n.* **1.** affiliate, branch, conclave, council, fraternity, lodge, offshoot, society, sorority, troop **2.** clause, division, part, section, subdivision, topic, unit *Antonyms:* entirety, totality, whole **3.** eon, age, cycle, episode, epoch, era, period, phase, span, stretch

character *n.* **1.** appearance, aspect, attribute, cast, constitution, courage, disposition, ethos, grain, habits, honour, humour, individuality, integrity, intelligence, kind, makeup, mettle, mind, mood, moral turpitude, mystique, nature, personality, quality, rectitude, sense, set, shape, singularity, speciality, spirit, strength, style, temper, temperament, trait, type, uprightness, vein **2.** fame, name, place, position, rank, record, reference, report, reputation, repute, standing, station, status **3.** crank, customer, eccentric, figure, oddball, oddity, odd person, original, personage, personality, weirdo *(Nonformal)* **4.** cipher, device, emblem, figure, hieroglyph, letter, logo, mark, monogram, number, numeral, rune, sign, symbol, type **5.** impersonation, part, person, persona, personification, portrayal, role

characteristic *adj.* **1.** diagnostic, differentiating, discriminative, distinctive, distinguishing, emblematic, indicative, individual, individualistic, individualizing, local, marked, original, particular, peculiar, proper, regular, representative, singular, special, specific, symbolic, typical, unique **2.** essential, exclusive, idiosyncratic, inborn, inbred, ingrained, inherent, innate, native, normal, personal, private – *n.* aspect, attribute, badge, bearing, bent, calibre, cast, character, component, distinction, earmark, essence, feature, flavour, idiosyncrasy, particularity, peculiarity, point, property, quality, quirk, specialty, streak, stripe, style, thumbprint, trademark, trait

characterize *v.* brand, constitute, define, delineate, describe, designate, differentiate, discriminate, distinguish, identify, indicate, inform, mark, peg, personalize, pigeonhole, portray, represent, signalize, stamp, symbolize, typecast, typify

charade *n.* deception, disguise, façade, fake, farce, make-believe, mimicry, pantomime, pretense, pretension, put-on, travesty, trick *Antonyms:* reality, truth

charge *n.* **1.** amount, assessment, bill, cost, demurrage, expense, fare, fee, liability, price, price tag, rate, toll, value, worth *Nonformal:* bad news, damage, exposure **2.** accusation, allegation, blame, complaint, impeachment, imputation, indictment, information *(Legal)*, summons **3.** assault, attack, blitz, forward march, onslaught, sally, storming **4.** admonition, bidding, command, demand, direction, exhortation, injunction, instruction, request **5.** congregation, dependent, flock, protégé, responsibility, ward **6.** administration, care, chaperonage, control, custody, direction, fostering, guardianship, guidance, husbandry, keeping, management, superintendence, supervision, trust, tutelage **7.** calling, commitment, duty, incumbency, living, obligation, office, promise, word **8.** capacity, complement, extent, limit, load, magnitude, payload, potency, power, range, scope, size, volume **9.** albatross, burden, encumbrance, handicap, liability, millstone **10.** account, credit, invoice, statement, tab, tick *(Nonformal)* **11.** dynamite, explosive, TNT – *v.* **1.** ask, bill, demand, exact, invoice, levy, price, require, sell for **2.** book, buy on credit, chalk up *(Nonformal)*, debit, run up **3.** accuse, arraign, blame, denounce, impute, indict, put on report **4.** decree, direct, enjoin, exhort, instruct, order, require, warn **5.** electrify, energize, excite, galvanize, ignite, invigorate, refuel, renew, stir up **6.** activate, arm, fill, infuse, load up, prime **7.** assault, attack, descend *or* set upon, overrun, ram, storm, **8.** encumber, handicap, overburden, tax, weigh down

charisma *n.* allure, animal magnetism, appeal, charm, chemistry, dazzle, fascination, flash, glamour, magnetism, pizazz *(Nonformal)*, power, star quality, witchery

charitable *adj.* **1.** accommodating, altruistic, beneficent, benevolent, bountiful, clement, considerate, favourable, generous, gracious, humane, humanitarian, kind, liberal, magnanimous, merciful, philanthropic *Antonyms:* close-fisted, mean, stingy, unkind **2.** all heart *(Nonformal)*, big-hearted, broad-minded, easy, forbearing, forgiving, indulgent, sympathetic, thoughtful, tolerant, understanding *Antonyms:* adamant, cold-hearted, implacable

charity *n.* **1.** affection, altruism, amity, benevolence, bountifulness, bounty, generosity, goodness, good will, grace, humaneness, humanity, indulgence, kindness, lenity, love, magnanimity, mercy, philanthropy *Antonyms:* hatred, ill will, intolerance, malice **2.** clemency, compassion, fellow feeling, forgiveness, lenience, soft-heartedness *Antonyms:* brutal, merciless, pitiless, ruthless **3.** alms, assistance, beneficence, contribution, donation, endowment, fund, gift, grant, handout, largesse, offering, patronage

charlatan *n.* cheat, deceiver, fake, fraud, grifter, hypocrite, impostor, mountebank, pretender, quack, swindler, trickster *Nonformal:* four-flusher, phoney, snake oil salesman

charm *n.* **1.** allure, appeal, attraction, beauty, charisma, delightfulness, desirability, enchantment, fascination, glamour, grace, lure, magic, magnetism, pizazz *(Nonformal)*, sorcery, spell, star quality **2.** amulet, fetish, talisman *Kinds of charm:* four-leaf clover, good-luck, hex sign, hoodoo, horseshoe, keepsake, love, lucky piece, magic potion *or* spell, mascot, memento, rabbit's foot, scarab, voodoo, wishbone – *v.* **1.** attract, captivate, delight, enrapture, enthrall, fascinate, inveigle, please, tickle, transport, turn on *(Nonformal)*, vamp, win, win over **2.** beguile, bewitch, enchant, hypnotize, mesmerize

charming *adj.* absorbing, amiable, appealing, attractive, bewitching, captivating, charismatic, delectable, delightful, desirable, elegant, engaging, entrancing, eye-catching, fascinating, fetching, glamorous, graceful, inviting, irresistible, likeable, lovable, lovely, magnetic, pleasing, ravishing, seductive, tantalizing, tempting, titillating, winsome *Antonyms:* disgusting, frightful, repulsive

chart *n.* blueprint, chronicle, diagram, graph, guide, map, outline, plan, plot, rough draft, schematic, scheme, sketch, table, tabulation – *v.* arrange, blueprint, cast, delineate, design, devise, direct, draft, graph, guide, lay out, limn, map, outline, pilot, plan, plot, project, shape, sketch, steer

charter *adj.* founding, original, pioneer, prime – *n.* **1.** agreement, bond, compact, concession, contract, covenant, deed, document, indenture, Magna Carta, permit **2.** concession, franchise, immunity, lease, licence, permit, prerogative, privilege, right, title – *v.* **1.** engage, hire, lease, rent **2.** authorize, establish, found, legalize, sanction

chase *n.* game, hunt, prey, quarry, sport – *v.* charge, check *or* follow up, follow, go after, hound, hunt, locate, pursue, run after *or* down, track *or* track down

chasm *n.* **1.** abyss, arroyo, breach, canyon, cleavage, cleft, crater, crevasse, fissure, flume, gorge, gulch, gulf, hole, hollow, opening, pit, ravine, rent **2.** blank, break, gap, interruption, schism, void

chaste *adj.* **1.** austere, celibate, immaculate, innocent, monogamous, moral, pure, restrained, spotless, stainless, uncontaminated, unstained, unsullied, virginal, virtuous, wholesome *Antonyms:* debauched, depraved, impure, lascivious, wanton **2.** clean, elegant, natural, plain, refined, simple, unadorned, unaffected, unpretentious *Antonyms:* florid, purple *(Nonformal)*, turgid

chasten *v.* **1.** admonish, berate, castigate, correct, discipline, dramatize, humble, humiliate, mitigate, rebuke, reprimand, reproach, reprove, tongue-lash *(Nonformal)*, upbraid *Antonyms:* commend, congratulate, praise **2.** moderate, restrain, soften, subdue, tame, temper **3.** boil down *or* off, clean, cleanse, decontaminate, filter, purify, refine, sanitize, wash *Antonyms:* adulterate, pollute, soil

chastise *v.* beat, discipline, flog, lash, punish, read *(P.E.I.)*, rebuke, reprimand, scourge, spank, strap, thrash, wallop, whip *Antonyms:* caress, cuddle, embrace, fondle

chastity *n.* **1.** celibacy, chasteness, cleanness, decency, devotion, honour, innocence, integrity, maidenhood, modesty, monogamy, morality, purity, singleness, sinlessness, temperance, uprightness, virginity, virtue *Antonyms:* debauchery, immorality, lewdness, licentiousness, profligacy **2.** abstinence, continence, forbearance, restraint *Antonyms:* indulgence, intemperance

chat *n.* conversation, discussion, exchange, interchange, small talk – *v.* babble, gossip, interface, palaver, prattle, speak, talk *Nonformal:* chew the fat, gab, shoot the breeze

château *n.* **1.** country estate, hall, manor house, mansion, palace, villa, vineyard estate, winery **2.** *castillo (Spanish)*, castle, citadel, fortress, stronghold

chatelaine *n.* dame, lady, matron, mistress *or* lady of the house

chattel *n.* **1.** affects, belongings, possession, property **2.** serf, servant, slave

chatter *n. & v.* babble, blab, blabber, blather, chat, gabble, gibber, gossip, jabber, natter, palaver, prate, prattle, rattle *Nonformal:* drool, gab, gas, jaw, yak *or* yackety-yack, yammer

chatty *adj.* **1.** conversational, effusive, fast-talking, flip, fluent, gabby, garrulous, glib, gossipy, gregarious, gushing, loquacious, prattling, spontaneous, talkative, verbose, vocal, voluble, windy, wordy *Nonformal:* barkative *(P.E.I.)*, flap-jawed, gassy, loose-lipped, loose-tongued *Antonyms:* quiet, reserved, reticent, silent **2.** easy, engaging, familiar, friendly, informal *Antonyms:* formal, structured, terse

chauffeur *n.* bus *or* cab *or* limousine *or* taxi driver, cabby *(Nonformal)*, coachman *or* coachwoman, driver, motorperson, teamster, wagoner, whip – *v.* drive, ferry, motor, transport

chauvinism *n.* bigotry, ethnocentricity, jingoism, machismo, nationalism, partisanship, patriotism, racism, sexism, vainglory

cheap *adj.* **1.** bargain *or* bargain-basement, buy, cut-price, cut-rate, economical, half-priced, inexpensive, low-cost *or* priced, marked down, on sale, reduced, sale, slashed, thrifty, utility *Antonyms:* costly, dear, expensive **2.** bogus, common, inferior, junky, ordinary, paltry, poor, ratty, rubbishy, second-rate, shabby, sordid, sorry, tatty, tawdry *Nonformal:* cheesy, crappy, cruddy *Antonyms:* crafted, pedigreed, valuable, well-made **3.** abject, base, beggarly, contemptible, despicable, dirty, dishonest, low, mean, nasty, scurvy, vile, vulgar *Antonyms:* admirable, decent, good, honourable, virtuous **4.** avaricious, frugal, parsimonious, penny-wise, stingy, thrifty, tight *or* tightfisted *Antonyms:* charitable, generous

cheapen *v.* **1.** adulterate, belittle, corrupt, damage, debase, degrade, demean, depreciate, devalue, diminish, discredit, disparage, minimize *Antonyms:* enhance, improve, raise **2.** downgrade, drop, mark down, reduce, slash, undervalue

cheat *n.* **1.** charlatan, confidence trickster, conniver, crook, deceiver, decoy, defrauder, double-crosser, double-dealer, fake, hypocrite, impostor, knave, pretender, quack, rascal, rogue, swindler, trickster *Nonformal:* grifter, shark **2.** artifice, chicanery, coverup, deceit, deception, dirty trick, dodge, double-dealing, fake, fix, frame, fraud, hoax, hustle, racket, sham, swindle, trickery *Nonformal:* bamboozlement, con, fast one, flim-flam, hanky-panky, rip-off, shady deal, snow job, sting – *v.* **1.** beat, beguile, bilk, cross, deceive, defraud, delude, double-cross *or* deal, dupe, finagle, fleece, fudge, hoodwink, mean-price *(P.E.I.)*, mislead, rig, rope in, sucker, swindle, take, trick, victimize *Nonformal:* bamboozle, bleed, con, milk, stack the deck, step out on, two-time **2.** baffle, defeat, deprive, elude, escape, foil, frustrate, prevent, thwart *Nonformal:* hose, shaft, stiff

check *n.* **1.** analysis, authentication, confirmation, corroboration, due diligence, inquiry, inspection, investigation, perusal, review, scrutiny, verification **2.** bottleneck, brake, constraint, control, curb, damper, delay, hindrance, impediment, inhibition, limitation, obstruction **3.** cross, dot, indication, mark, sign, slip, tally, tick **4.** disappointment, frustration, rebuff, reversal, reverse, setback **5.** backcheck, bodycheck, crosscheck, forecheck, hipcheck, hit, pokecheck, slam *(Nonformal)* – *v.* **1.** arrest, bar, block, choke *or* choke off, close, counteract, cut short, foil, halt, interrupt, limit, neutralize, preclude, rein in, repress, snub, squelch, stay, stop, suppress, thwart *Antonyms:* activate, foster, incite, instigate **2.** authenticate, check out, corroborate, delve into, examine, explore, inquire, inspect, investigate, look, observe, peek, peruse, probe, reconnoitre, research, scrutinize, study, substantiate, test, validate **3.** baffle, delay, detain, discourage, frustrate, hinder, hold, impede, inhibit, obstruct, pause, retard, slacken, slow, stymie *Antonyms:* encourage, facilitate, stimulate **4.** block, bodycheck, crunch, hit, press, punish, shadow, sock *(Nonformal)*

checked *adj.* **1.** kaleidoscopic, mosaic, motley, mutable, parquet, patchwork, patterned, plaid, quilted, spotted, tartan, tessellate, variegated **2.** blocked, controlled, curbed, fettered, inhibited, restrained, *Antonyms:* free, liberated, unhampered **3.** brought to a close, concluded, ended, finished, stopped, terminated

cheer *n.* **1.** acclamation, approbation, approval, cry, encouragement, hoorah, hooray, hurray, huzza, ovation, plaudits, roar *Antonyms:* censure, condemnation, disapprobation **2.** delight, gladness, happiness, heartiness, joy, revelry – *v.* **1.** animate, brace *or* buck up, brighten, buoy, comfort, console, elate, elevate, embolden, encourage, enliven, exhilarate, gladden, hearten, help, incite, perk up, please, solace, strengthen, uplift *Antonyms:* darken, depress, discourage, sadden **2.** acclaim, applaud, clap, encourage, hail, hurrah, rise to, salute, support, yell *Nonformal:* egg on, plug, root for *Antonyms:* boo, heckle, hiss, razz *(Nonformal)*

cheerful *adj.* animated, blithe, bouncy, bright, bucked *(Nonformal)*, buoyant, cheery, chipper, chirpy, effervescent, enthusiastic, glad, good-humoured *or* natured, happy, hearty, high, hilarious, hopeful, jaunty, jolly, joyful, lighthearted, lively, merry, optimistic, perky, pleasant, roseate, rosy, snappy, sparkling, sprightly, sunny, upbeat, vivacious *Antonyms:* cheerless, dejected, depressed, dismal, gloomy

cheerfulness *n.* animation, buoyancy, cheeriness, delight, exuberance, gaiety, geniality, glee, happiness, hilarity, hopefulness, jauntiness, jocundity, joy, joyousness, lightheartedness, merriment, mirth, optimism *Antonyms:* gloominess, sadness, sullenness

cheering *adj.* auspicious, bright, comforting, encouraging, happy, heartening, hopeful, pleasant, promising, propitious

cheerless *adj.* **1.** abandoned, austere, barren, black, bleak, comfortless, dark, dejected, depressing, deserted, desolate, dingy, dismal, dispiriting, dolorous, drab, dreary, dull, empty, forlorn, funereal, gloomy, grim, jarring, lightless, lonely, melancholic, murky, oppressive, sombre, sorrowful, sullen, sunless, uncomfortable, unhappy, uninviting, wintry, woeful *Antonyms:* exciting, lovely, wonderful **2.** aching, afflicted, crushed, dejected, depressed, despairing, despondent, disconsolate, down, downcast, downhearted, glum, grave, grief-stricken, grieving, heartbroken, heartsick, heartsore, joyless, lamenting, melancholy, miserable, mourning, sad, saddened, saturnine, serious, sorrowful, tragic, weeping, woeful *Antonyms:* cheery, elated, happy, jolly

cheese *n.* pressed curd *Kinds of cheese:* American, Asiago, Bel Paese, blue, Boursin, brick, Brie, caciocavallo, Caerphilly, Camembert, cheddar, cheese food, Cheshire, chèvre, colby, cottage, cream, Danish blue, Derby, Edam, Emmenthal, farmer's, feta, fontina, Gjetost, Gloucester, goat, Gorgonzola, Gouda, Gruyère, Havarti, jack, Jarlsberg, Lancashire, Leicester, Liederkranz, Limburger, Liptauer, marble, Monterey Jack, mozzarella, muenster, Oka, Parmesan, Pecorino, Pont L'Évèque, Port-Salud, pot, processed, provolone, rat, red Windsor, ricotta, Romano, Roquefort, saganaki, sapsago, smoked, Stilton, Swiss, Tilsit, Vacherin, Wensleydale

chef *n.* baker, *chef de cuisine (French)*, confectioner, cook, culinarian, food preparer, gastronome, gourmet, head chef *or* cook, line cook, pastry chef, short-order cook, sous chef *Nonformal:* cookie, hash slinger

chemical *adj.* alchemical, analytical, artificial, compound, drug, ersatz, synthesized, synthetic, synthetical *Chemical elements:* Actinium *(Ac)*, Aluminum *(Al)*, Americium *(Am)*, Argon *(Ar)*, Arsenic *(As)*, Astatine *(At)*, Barium *(Ba)*, Berkelium *(Bk)*, Beryllium *(Be)*, Bismuth *(Bi)*, Boron *(B)*, Bromine *(Br)*, Cadmium *(Cd)*, Calcium *(Ca)*, Californium *(Cf)*, Carbon *(C)*, Cerium *(Ce)*, Cesium *(Cs)*, Chlorine *(Cl)*, Chromium *(Cr)*, Cobalt *(Co)*, Copper *(Cu)*, Curium *(Cm)*, Dysprosium *(Dy)*, Einsteinium *(Es)*, Erbium *(Er)*, Europium *(Eu)*, Fermium *(Fm)*, Fluorine *(F)*, Francium *(Fr)*, Gadolinium *(Gd)*, Gallium *(Ga)*, Germanium *(Ge)*, Gold *(Au)*, Hafnium *(Hf)*, Helium *(He)*, Holmium *(Ho)*, Hydrogen *(H)*, Indium *(In)*, Iodine *(I)*, Iridium *(Ir)*, Iron *(Fe)*, Krypton *(Kr)*, Lanthanum *(La)*, Lawrencium *(Lw)*, Lead *(Pb)*, Lithium *(Li)*, Lutetium *(Lu)*, Magnesium *(Mg)*, Manganese *(Mn)*, Mendelevium *(Md)*, Mercury *(Hg)*, Molybdenum *(Mo)*, Neodymium *(Nd)*, Neon *(Ne)*, Neptunium *(Np)*, Nickel *(Ni)*, Niobium *(Nb)*, Nitrogen *(N)*, Nobelium *(No)*, Osmium *(Os)*, Oxygen *(O)*, Palladium *(Pd)*, Phosphorus *(P)*, Platinum *(Pt)*, Plutonium *(Pu)*, Polonium *(Po)*, Potassium *(K)*, Praseodymium *(Pr)*, Promethium *(Pm)*, Protactinium *(Pa)*, Radium *(Ra)*, Radon *(Rn)*, Rhenium *(Re)*, Rhodium *(Rh)*,

Rubidium *(Rb)*, Ruthenium *(Ru)*, Samarium *(Sm)*, Scandium *(Sc)*, Selenium *(Se)*, Silicon *(Sl)*, Silver *(Ag)*, Sodium *(Na)*, Strontium *(Sr)*, Sulfur *(S)*, Tantalum *(Ta)*, Technetium *(Tc)*, Tellurium *(Te)*, Terbium *(Tb)*, Thallium *(Tl)*, Thorium *(Th)*, Thulium *(Tm)*, Tin *(Sn)*, Titanium *(Ti)*, Tungsten *(W)*, Uranium *(U)*, Vanadium *(V)*, Xenon *(Xe)*, Ytterbium *(Yb)*, Yttrium *(Y)*, Zinc *(Zn)*, Zirconium *(Zr)* *Chemical processes:* acetification, acidification, alkinization, carbonation, catalysis, chlorination, copolymerization, electrolysis, fermentation, hydration, hydrogenation, isomerization, nitration, oxidation, phospherization, polymerization, reduction, saturization, sulphation, sulphatization, sulphonation

chemistry *n.* **1.** chemical analysis *or* study, chemical processes, scientific discipline **2.** affinity, attraction, draw, enchantment, gravitation, interest, magnetism, pull, spark *(Nonformal)*

cheque *n.* **1.** bank draft, commercial paper, draft, promissory note, slip *Kinds of cheque:* alimony, baby bonus, banker's, blank, bounced, cashier's, certified, employment, insurance, lottery, not sufficient funds *or* NSF, pension, post-dated, settlement, teller's, traveller's, treasury, welfare **2.** bill, charge, chit, receipt, tab

cherish *v.* **1.** adore, dote on, esteem, fancy, hold dear, idolize, love, revere, venerate *Antonyms:* abhor, despise, hate, loathe **2.** aid, care for, coddle, cradle, cultivate, defend, feed, foster, guard, harbour, nourish, nurse, nurture, preserve, shelter, succour, support, sustain *Antonyms:* abuse, neglect

cherry *adj.* blooming, blushing, bright red, cerise, claret, crimson, dark red, red, reddish, rosy, ruddy

chess *n.* game, hobby, pastime *Chess pieces:* bishop, king, knight, pawn, queen, rook *or* castle

chest *n.* **1.** bosom, breast, bust, front, pectoral *or* pecs, sternum, thorax, torso, upper trunk **2.** bin, box, bureau, cabinet, case, chiffonier, closet, commode, crib, cupboard, dresser, locker, receptacle, sea chest, strongbox, treasury, trunk, vault, wardrobe

chew *v.* **1.** bite, champ, chomp, consume, crunch, devour, dispatch, eat, feast upon, gnaw, grind, gulp, gum, masticate, munch, nibble, rend **2.** consider, deliberate, meditate, ponder, ruminate, turn over *(Nonformal)*, weigh

chic *adj.* current, dapper, dashing, elegant, exclusive, faddish, fashionable, modern, modish, natty, sharp, smart, stylish, swank, trendy, voguish *Nonformal:* chichi, classy, hip, last word, mod *Antonyms:* inelegant, old-fashioned, passé, unfashionable

chicanery *n.* artifice, cheating, deception, deviousness, dishonesty, double-crossing *or* -dealing, duplicity, fraud, gambit, machination, ploy, ruse, sophistry, subterfuge, trickery, underhandedness *Nonformal:* dirty pool, guile, hanky-panky *Antonyms:* forthrightness, honesty, truth

chicken *n.* **1.** barnyard fowl, cock, hen, poultry, rooster *Nonformal:* biddy, clucker, *Groupings of chicken:* broiler, capon, cockerel, free range, fryer, layer, pullet, roaster, stewing fowl *or* hen *Breeds of chicken:* bantam, black Brahma, black Minorca, Cochin, Cornish hen, leghorn, Minorca, Orpington, Plymouth Rock, Rhode Island Red, Wyandotte *Parts of chicken:* back, beak, breast, feet, gizzard, heart, leg, liver, neck, wing **2.** coward *Nonformal:* fraidy- *or* scaredy-cat, milquetoast, mouse, sissy, wimp, wuss, yellow-belly

chide *v.* admonish, berate, blame, call down, castigate, censure, chew out *(Nonformal)*, condemn, criticize, find fault, lecture, rebuke, reprehend, reprimand, reproach, reprove, scold, upbraid *Antonyms:* approve, boost, extol, honour, laud

chief *adj.* **1.** arch, capital, cardinal, central, champion, controlling, first, foremost, grand, head, highest, key, leading, main, major, master, paramount, potent, predominant, preeminent, premier, primal, primary, prime, principal, ruling, star, stellar, superior, supreme, uppermost, vital *Antonyms:* least, minor, subordinate, subsidiary **2.** consequential, crucial, essential, important, momentous, outstanding, significant, telling, weighty – *n.* captain, commander, head, master, president, sachem, sagamore, superior *Nonformal:* head muckety-muck, mugwump

chiefly *adv.* above all, especially, essentially, importantly, in general, largely, mainly, mostly, overall, predominantly, primarily, principally, usually

child *n.* adolescent, babe, baby, *bairn (Scottish)*, bambino, descendant, *grommet (Newfoundland)*, infant, issue, juvenile, neonate, newborn, offspring, preteen, progeny, teenager, toddler, tot, urchin, young, youngster, youth *Nonformal:* ankle-biter, kid, rug rat, teenybopper, tyke

childbirth *n. accouchement (French)*, birth, blessed event, childbearing, childbed, confinement, delivery, labour, lying-in, nativity, parturiency, parturition, procreation, propagation, reproduction, travail

childhood *n.* adolescence, babyhood, boyhood, girlhood, immaturity, infancy, minority, puberty, teens, youth

childish *adj.* babyish, foolish, immature, infantile, infant-like, juvenile, petty, puerile, silly, unsophisticated, weak *Antonyms:* adult, grown-up, mature, sensible

childlike *adj.* artless, believing, credulous, forthright, frank, guileless, ingenuous, innocent, naive, natural, open, simple, spontaneous, trustful, trusting, unaffected, unfeigned, wonderful, wondrous *Antonyms:* cynical, jaded, wordly

children *n.* brood, daughters, descendants, family, fruit, get, heirs, issue, kids *(Nonformal)*, little ones, offspring, progeny, seed, sons, spawn, whelp, young people, youth

chill *adj.* **1.** arctic, breezy, cold, frigid, nippy, penetrating **2.** aloof, apathetic, cold, cool, distant, impassive, indifferent, reticent, standoffish, unfriendly, unsociable – *n.* **1.** bite, coldness, coolness, crispness, frigidity, gelidity, iciness, nip, rawness, sharpness **2.** cold, fever, flu, grippe, influenza, pneumonia, shakes, shivers, sniffles – *v.* **1.** air condition, benumb, cool, freeze, ice *or* put on ice *(Nonformal)*, refrigerate *Antonyms:* heat *or* warm up, melt, thaw, toast **2.** check, depress, discourage, dishearten, dispirit

chilly *adj.* **1.** brisk, cold, cool, cutting, frigid, frosty, nippy, penetrating, shivering **2.** aloof, detached, reserved, stony, unfriendly, unresponsive, unsympathetic, withdrawn *Antonym:* amiable, warm, welcoming

chime *n.* angelus, bells, carillon, glockenspiel, gong, tocsin, triangle, wind chime – *v.* **1.** announce, bring, clang, peal, resound, reverberate, ring, ring in, sound, toll, usher **2.** blend, complement, enhance, harmonize, mesh, synchronize

chimera *n.* daydream, delusion, dream, fabrication, fancy, fantasy, figment, hallucination, illusion, nightmare, phantom, pipe dream, spectre *Antonyms:* reality, truth

chimney *n.* chimney pot, fireplace, flue, funnel, pipe, smokeshaft, smokestack, stack, stovepipe, vent

china *n.* coffee *or* tea service, crockery, dishes, dishware, tableware *China manufacturers:* Aynsley, Clare, Coalport, Dansk, Denby, Hutschenreuther, Lenox, Limoges, Meissen, Mikasa, Minton, Rosenthal, Royal Albert, Royal Copenhagen, Royal Crown Derby, Royal Doulton, Royal Worcester, Thomas, Wedgewood

chintzy *adj.* brightly coloured, cheap, flimsy, flowery, garish, gaudy, kitsch, loud, ostentatious, shoddy, tacky, tawdry *Antonyms:* classy, elegant, plain

chip *n.* **1.** bit, fragment, shard, shaving **2.** crack, defect, fault, flaw, imperfection **3.** coin, counter, disc, marker, slug, token **4.** circuit element, integrated circuit, silicon crystal – *v.* break off, chop, cut, notch, shape, whittle

chipper *adj.* alert, animate, animated, bright, brisk, gay, happy, keen, lively, spirited, sprightly, vivacious *Antonyms:* despondent, glum, sad, unhappy

chirp *v.* call, chip, chirrup, lilt, peep, pipe, purl, quaver, roll, sing, sound, trill, tweet, twitter, warble

chisel *n.* blade, edge, gouge, knife, tool – *v.* carve, cut, hew, incise, reduce, roughcast, sculpt, shape

chivalry *n.* courage, courtesy, courtliness, devotion, fairness, fidelity, fortitude, gallantry, gentlemanliness, knighthood, politeness, stalwartness, valiance, valour *Antonyms:* boorishness, cowardice, cruelty, dishonour, rudeness

chloroform *n.* anaesthetic, analgesic, drug, narcotic, opiate, painkiller, solvent – *v.* anaesthetize, deaden, desensitize, dope *(Nonformal)*, drug, knock out, sedate, tranquilize

choice *adj.* best, elect, excellent, exclusive, grade A, preeminent, prime, prize, rare, select, superior, supreme, top, top rank *Nonformal:* A-1, top drawer, tops *Antonyms:* inferior, ordinary, poor, shoddy – *n.* **1.** decision, election, finding, judgment, nomination, pick, selection, vote **2.** alternative, equivalent, option, other, substitute, surrogate **3.** desire, favourite, pleasure, predilection, preference, taste

choke *v.* **1.** asphyxiate, bunk, constrict, garrote, gasp, gibbet, noose, rasp, squeeze, strangle *or* strangulate, throttle, wring **2.** bar, block, clog, close, congest, dam, obstruct **3.** check, control, curb, inhibit, muzzle, suppress *Nonformal:* clench, grip, shorten up **4.** blanket, consume, destroy, envelop, overload, overwhelm, wrap

choleric *adj.* acerbic, bad-tempered, bitter, brusque, churlish, crabbed, crabby, cranky, cross, crusty, easily provoked, edgy, fiery, fractious, grouchy, gruff, ill-humoured, impolite, irascible, irritable, peevish, peppery, petulant, quick-tempered, rancorous, rude, short-tempered, snappish, surly, testy, thin-skinned, touchy, volatile, wrathful

choose *v.* **1.** accept, adopt, appoint, call for, cast, commit, co-opt, decide on, designate, determine, discriminate between, elect, embrace, espouse, favour, judge, make a choice *or* decision, name, opt for, pick, prefer, see fit to, select, set aside, settle upon, single out, slot, tab, take, want, weigh, will *Antonyms:* decline, dismiss, exclude, leave, reject **2.** crave, desire, fancy, wish, yearn **3.** cull, glean, separate, sort, winnow

choosy *adj.* demanding, discriminating, eclectic, exacting, fastidious, finicky, fussy, over-particular, particular, picky, select, selective *Antonyms:* easy to please, indiscriminate

chop *n.* **1.** bite, bop, buffet, cutting blow *or* stroke, hit, smack, wallop, whack **2.** *côtelette (French)*, cutlet, flank, piece of meat – *v.* **1.** cut, hack, notch, slash, whack **2.** axe, cleave, divide, fell, gash, grind, hackle, hew, lacerate, lop, mangle, mutilate, sever, shear, slice, smite, split, truncate **3.** cut up, dice, fragment, hash, mince **4.** shift, vacillate, veer

choppy *adj.* bumpy, inclement, jolting, ripply, rough, undulating, uneven, unstable, violent, wavering, wavy, wild *Antonyms:* calm, smooth, windless

choral *adj.* choir, hymnal, liturgical, operatic, psalmic, sacred, singing, vocal *Kinds of choral music:* anthem, cantata, choral fantasy, chorale, hymn, mass, motet, oratorio, psalm

chord *n.* **1.** musical note, tones combination *Kinds of chords:* arpeggio, augmented, diminished, dominant, fifth, guitar *or* organ *or* piano chord, major, minor, seventh, tonic, triad, truncated **2.** concern, echo, emotion, empathy, fellow feeling, involvement, pathos, response, sympathy, vibes *(Nonformal)* **3.** diagonal, line *or* straight line, perpendicular, secant, tangent, transversal, vector *Commonly misused:* **cord**

chore *n.* **1.** assignment, *devoir (French)*, effort, errand, housework, job, routine, scutwork *(Nonformal)*, stint, task, workout *Antonyms:* joy, pleasure **2.** burden, duty, grind, obligation, responsibility, trial, tribulation

chorus *n.* **1.** choir, chorale, choral society, choristers, ensemble, glee club, singers, vocalists, voices **2.** burden, chant, chorale, melody, motif, recurrent stanza *or* verse, refrain, response, ritornello, song, strain, theme, tune, utterance, verse **3.** accord, concert, concord, consonance, harmony, mantra, unison *Antonyms:* cacophony, discordance, dissonance

chosen *adj.* adopted, called, conscripted, designated, destined, elected, exclusive, named, pegged, picked, popular, preferred, tabbed *Antonyms:* ignored, neglected, overlooked – *n.* best, choice, *crème de la crème (French),* elect, premier, select

christen *v.* anoint, baptize, bless, dedicate, denominate, designate, dub, entitle, immerse, inaugurate, launch, name, term, title

Christianity *n.* Christendom *Groupings of Christianity:* Amish, Anabaptist, Anglican, Baptist, Calvinist, Christian Science, Congregational, Doukhabour, Eastern *or* Orthodox, Episcopalian, Fundamentalist, Jehovah's Witness, Lutheran, Methodist, Mennonite, Mormon, Pentecostal, Presbyterian, Protestant, Puritan, Quaker, Roman Catholic, Seventh-Day Adventist, Scientology, Shaker, Society of Friends, Unification Church, United Church, Unitarian, Wesleyan

chronic *adj.* **1.** basic, deep-rooted, established, ingrained, intrinsic, lasting, permanent, perpetual, rooted *Antonyms:* petty, superficial, trifling **2.** constant, continual, incessant, lingering, perennial, persistent, prolonged, protracted, sustained, unabating, unrelenting *Antonyms:* infrequent, occasional, once in a while **3.** confirmed, habitual, hard-nosed, hardened, incurable, incorrigible, inveterate, recidivist, recurrent, repeating *Antonyms:* correctable, reclaimable, redeemable, worth saving

chronicle *n.* account, annals, chronology, date book, daytimer, diary, Hansard, herstory, history, journal, log, memoir, narration, narrative, register, report, story, timetable – *v.* enter, narrate, note, preserve, put on record, record, recount, register, relate, report, set *or* take down, tell

chronological *adj.* consecutive, ordered, organized, progressive, sequential, serial *Antonyms:* haphazard, intermittent, irregular

chubby *adj.* **1.** ample, big, buxom, chunky, corpulent, fat, fatty, flabby, fleshy, full-figured, hefty, overweight, plump, podgy, portly, pudgy, roly-poly, rotund, round, squat, stout, stubby, well-fed *Nonformal:* pleasingly plump, tubby, zaftig *Antonyms:* lean, skinny, slender

chuck *v.* **1.** cast, fling, flip, heave, hurl, let fly, pitch, shy, sling, throw, toss, wing *(Nonformal)* **2.** abandon, desert, discard, dump, jettison, scrap, shed, slough, throw away *or* out **3.** cashier, eject, evict, expel, *Nonformal:* boot, kick out, turf *or* turf out **4.** caress, dab, pat, tap, tweak

chuckle *n.* chortle, fun time *(Nonformal),* giggle, grin, laugh, laughter, merriment, mirth, suppressed laughter – *v.* laugh, make merry, snicker, snigger, titter

chum *n.* *ami (French),* associate, blood brother, bosom buddy, close friend, companion, comrade, confrère, crony, friend, mate, pal, playmate, sidekick *(Nonformal)* – *v.* ally, associate, pal *or* hang around with *(Nonformal)*

chummy *adj.* affectionate, buddy-buddy, close, confidential, constant, cozy, devoted, familiar, friendly, intimate, thick *Antonyms:* antagonistic, hostile, rancorous

chunk *n.* **1.** block, clod, dollop, glob, hunk, lump, nugget, part, piece, portion, slab **2.** array, group, heap, mass, mound, wad

chunky *adj.* **1.** beefy, chubby, dumpy, fat, fleshy, heavy-set, plump, rotund, stocky, stout, thickset *Antonyms:* narrow, slim, svelte, thin **2.** bulky, cumbersome, large, oversize

church *n.* **1.** abbey, basilica, bethel, building, cathedral, chapel, *duomo (Italian),* mission, mosque, oratory, place of worship, sanctuary, shrine, synagogue, tabernacle, temple **2.** apostolic church, body of Christ, Children of God *or* light, Christendom, Church of Christ, communion, evensong, liturgy, mass, novena, public worship, religious services, vespers, vigils **3.** affiliation, body, chapter, congregation, connection, creed, cult, denomination, doctrine, faction, faith, gathering, holy order, order, papacy, parish, persuasion, rabbinate, religion, sacred calling, schism, sect, society, the cloth, the ministry, the priesthood

churlish *adj.* **1.** bad-tempered, brusque, cantankerous, caustic, crabby, crusty *(Nonformal)*, difficult, disagreeable, fractious, grouchy, gruff, grumpy, ill-humoured, intractable, irascible, irritable, mean, ornery, querulous, sour, surly, unruly, vitriolic *Antonyms:* amiable, even-tempered, patient **2.** boorish, crisp, loutish, uncivilized, unmannered, vulgar

churn *v.* agitate, beat, jolt, mix up, rile *or* stir *or* whip up, seethe, stoke, swirl *Antonyms:* calm, soothe

chute *n.* **1.** aqueduct, channel, course, conduit, coulee, culvert, eavestrough, gulch, gutter, incline, runway, shaft, slide, trough **2.** cataract, fall, flume, rapids, sault, waterfall **3.** cage, cell, hopper, pen

cigar *n. Nonformal:* seegar, stogie *Kinds of cigar:* Cheroot, Churchill, cigarillo, corona, Cuban, culebra, Havana, lonsdale, panatela, robusto

cigarette *n. Nonformal:* butt, cancer stick, cig, coffin nail, fag, gasper, smoke *Kinds of cigarette:* Canadian, Egyptian, English, filter, king-size, lite, menthol, Russian, Turkish, U.S.

cinch *n.* **1.** band, belt, girdle, girth, strap **2.** sure thing *Nonformal:* bird, breeze, child's play, duck soup, in the bag, picnic, piece of cake, pushover, shoo-in, snap

cinema *n.* cine, film, motion pictures, movies, movie house *or* palace *or* theatre, moving pictures, photoplay, pictures, picture show, playhouse, screening, show, show hall *(P.E.I.) Nonformal:* big screen, flic *or* flicks, silver screen, talkies *See also:* **film**

cipher – *n.* **1.** code, cryptogram, encoded *or* secret message **2.** answer, explanation, key, password, solution **3.** deadwood, nonentity, person of no value *Nonformal:* empty suit, nobody, nothing **4.** goose egg, *nada (Spanish)*, nothing, zero *Nonformal:* diddly-squat, zilch, zip **5.** autograph, mark, monogram, seal, signature *Nonformal:* John Henry, X – *v.* **1.** calculate, count, decipher, decode, estimate, figure, figure out, reckon, resolve, solve, unravel **2.** disguise, encipher, encrypt, hide, safeguard

circa *prep.* about, approximately, around, close to, near, nearby, roughly *Antonyms:* exactly, precisely

circle *n.* **1.** aureole, band, belt, circlet, corona, crown, disc, equator, garland, halo, hoop, ring, rondelle, wheel, wreath **2.** assembly, associates, cabal, camp, clan, clique, club, companions, company, comrades, coterie, coven, covey, crew, cronies, crowd, fellowship, fraternity, friends, gang, group, insiders, intimates, lodge, party, set, society, sorority **3.** circumference, domain, field, jurisdiction, perimeter, province, range, realm, region, scope, sphere, zone **4.** full turn, path, orbit, revolution, 360 degrees **5.** circuit, cycle, lap, revolution, series, set **6.** gallery, loggia, mezzanine, porch, veranda – *v.* **1.** encircle, enclose, encompass, envelop, gird, girdle, hem in, loop, mill round, ring *or* ring around, roll, surround **2.** gyrate, pirouette, pivot, revolve, rotate, spiral

circuit *n.* **1.** course, lap, loop, orbit, path, rote, run, track, trail **2.** beat, itinerary, progression, rounds, routine, sequence **3.** boundary, bounds, circumference, limits, outer edge, periphery, rim

circuitous *adj.* Byzantine, complicated, convoluted, indirect, labyrinthine, meandering, oblique, rambling, roundabout, serpentine, tortuous *Antonyms:* direct, straightforward, undeviating, unswerving

circular *adj.* **1.** ecliptic, hooped, oblique, oval, ring-shaped, round *or* rounded, spherical **2.** devious, indirect, roundabout **3.** common, general, public, universal – *n.* advertisement, booklet, brochure, handbill, handout, insert, leaflet, literature, notice, pamphlet, publication, statement

circulate *v.* **1.** circle, come full circle, encircle, move *or* pass around, orbit, return, revolve, rotate **2.** fraternize, mingle, mix, move *or* pass through, perambulate, peregrinate, travel **3.** course, diffuse, disperse, drift, flow, issue, meander, permeate, radiate **4.** advertise, broadcast, disseminate, distribute, exchange, interchange, post, promulgate, propagate, publicize, publish, report, spread *Antonyms:* censor, silence, suppress

circulation *n.* **1.** circuit, gyration, motion, pirouette, revolution, rotation, round, turn, whirl **2.** current, flow, flux, passage, stream **3.** audience, broadcast, demographic, dissemination, distribution, market, public, reach, spread, subscription, transmission **4.** coin, currency, exchange, legal tender, medium, money, paper money, specie

circumference *n.* border, boundary, bounds, circuit, compass, edge, extremity, fringe, girth, limit, margin, outline, perimeter, periphery, rim, verge *Antonyms:* centre, core, middle

circumlocution *n.* avoidance, diffuseness, discursiveness, euphemism, evasion, indirectness, periphrasis, pleonasm, prolixity, redundancy, tautology, wordiness *Antonyms:* conciseness, directness, preciseness

circumscribe *v.* **1.** define, delimit, delineate, demarcate, designate, determine, fix, mark off, outline, set limits **2.** bind, circumvent, confine, encircle, enclose, encompass, ground, hinder, hamper, hem in, hinder, limit, quarantine, restrain, restrict, surround, trammel *Antonyms:* free, liberate, unfetter

circumstance *n.* **1.** action, concomitant, condition, determinant, factor, influence, qualification **2.** accident, case, crisis, episode, event, happening, incident, instance, occasion, occurrence, place, scenario, scene, situation **3.** clause, component, detail, element, fact, feature, item, matter, particular, specific **4.** ceremony, display, fanfare, formality, pageant, pomp, ritual, show

circumstances *n. pl.* affairs, assets, capital, chances, class, degree, financial status, footing, income, lot, means, position, property, prospects, prosperity, rank, rating, resources, situation, standing, state, station, status, straits, vicissitudes, worldly goods, worth

circumstantial *adj.* **1.** conjectural, inconclusive, hearsay, indirect, inferential, irrelevant, peripheral, secondary, third party, unessential, unimportant *Antonyms:* primary, significant **2.** accidental, adventitious, coincidental, concomitant, conditional, dependent, fortuitous, incidental, provisional, serendipitous **3.** detailed, exact, explicit, minute, particular, pointed, specific *Antonyms:* sweeping, vague

circumvent *v.* **1.** avoid, bypass, escape, evade, foil, shun, sidestep, skirt *Nonformal:* deke out , fight shy of, take off *Antonyms:* confront, face **2.** befool, deceive, fool, hoodwink, outfox, outjockey, outmanoeuvre, outsmart, outwit, trick *Nonformal:* hornswaggle, rook **3.** besiege, blockade, circumscribe, compass, entrap, envelop, gird, ring, skirt, surround

circus *n.* **1.** bazaar, big top, carnival, entertainment, exhibition, fair, festival, hippodrome, ring, rodeo, show, spectacle **2.** band, Cirque du Soleil *(Trademark)*, company, performers, troupe **3.** anarchy, bedlam, chaos, donnybrook, free-for-all, madhouse, mayhem, pandemonium *Nonformal:* hullaballoo, shindy

citadel *n.* bastion, blockhouse, bulwark, castle, fastness, fort, fortification, fortress, keep, manor, rampart, redoubt, stronghold, tower

citation *n.* **1.** example, excerpt, extract, illustration, passage, quotation, reference, saying, source **2.** award, commendation, laudation, mention, panegyric, praise, reward, salutation, tribute *Antonyms:* censure, deprecation **3.** bidding, charge, subpoena, summons **4.** calculation, enumeration, reckoning, recounting, summation

cite *v.* **1.** adduce, allege, allude to, document, enumerate, evidence, excerpt, exemplify, extract, illustrate, indicate, mention, name, note, number, offer, point out, present, quote, recite, recount, repeat, specify, tell **2.** arraign, call, command, name, order, summon, subpoena *Commonly misused:* **sight, site**

citizen *n.* aboriginal, burgher, civilian, commoner, denizen, dweller, householder, inhabitant, landed immigrant, indigene, national, native, occupant, resident, taxpayer, townsperson, villager, voter *Antonyms:* alien, foreigner

city *n.* borough, burg, central business district *or* CBD, conurbation, downtown, greater metropolitan area, megacity, megalopolis, metropolis, municipality, urban complex *or* corridor, *ville (French) Names for city residents:* Calgarian, Charlottetowner, Edmontonian, Frederictoner, Haligonian, Hamiltonian, Montrealer, Moose Javian, Ottawan, Reginan, Saskatooner, St. Johnner, Torontonian, Vancouverite, Victorian, Winnipegger *Nonformal:* corner boy *(St. John's)*, Hambletonian *(Hamilton)*, hogtowner *(Toronto) Some nonformal names for Canadian cities:* Buckle of the Wheat Belt *(Winnipeg)*, Cradle of Confederation *(Charlottetown)*, Edmonchuck *(Edmonton)*, Foothill City *(Calgary)*, Steel Town *(Hamilton)*, *Toronto:* Hog Town, the Queen City

civic *adj.* municipal, patriotic, political, public, public-spirited, social *Commonly misused:* **civil**

civil *adj.* **1.** accommodating, affable, civilized, *comme il faut (French)*, cordial, courteous, courtly, couth, cultivated, decorous, diplomatic, formal, genteel, gracious, kind, mannerly, polished, polite, refined, suave, urbane, well-bred, well-mannered *Antonyms:* bumptious, discourteous, ill-mannered, rude **2.** communal, general, governmental, lay, official, non-criminal, political, secular *Antonyms:* ecclesiastical, military **3.** domestic, internal, home-grown, local, neighbourhood **4.** calm, careful, collected, level-headed, placid, rational *Commonly misused:* **civic**

civilian *adj.* nonmilitant, nonmilitary, pacifist, private, volunteer – *n.* citizen, civvie *(Nonformal))*, nonbelligerent, noncombatant

civilization *n.* **1.** acculturation, advancement, cultivation, culture, development, edification, education, enlightenment, illumination, progress, refinement, socialization, sophistication, transculturation **2.** community, culture, customs, ethos, habits, laws, mores, nation, people, populace, population, society, values *Antonyms:* barbarism, bestiality, savagery **3.** city, development, downtown, town, urban core *Nonformal:* big smoke, Portage and Main *Antonyms:* back country, frontier, outback, wilderness

civilize *v.* **1.** acculturate, broaden, bring up to snuff *(Nonformal)*, edify, enlighten, polish, refine, sophisticate **2.** break in, domesticate, gentle, instruct, tame, teach, train, tutor

cladding *n.* clapboard, coat *or* outer coat, curtain, exterior, façade, face, plating board, siding, skin, superstructure, surface, veneer, wall

claim *n.* **1.** birthright, domain, due, entitlement, equity, estate, interest, ownership, right, title **2.** allegation, assertion, call, case, complaint, demand, statement, suit **3.** entreaty, petition, plea, request **4.** dominion, holding, jurisdiction, land, possession, stake – *v.* **1.** acquire, appropriate, commandeer, demand, expropriate, requisition **2.** assert, avow, declare, hold, maintain, proclaim **3.** beg, deserve, entreat, require, summon

clairvoyance *n.* acumen, chiromancy, discernment, divination, extrasensory perception *or* ESP, feeling, foreknowledge, insight, intuition, omen, perception, precognition, premonition, sapience, second sight, sixth sense, telepathy

clairvoyant *adj.* clear-sighted, discerning, extrasensory, farseeing, farsighted, fey, judicious, intuitive, long-sighted, oracular, penetrating, perceptive, prescient, prophetic, psionic *(Nonformal)*, psychic, second-sighted, sibylline, spiritualistic, telepathic, visionary – *n.* augur, chiromancer, diviner, fortuneteller, medium, oracle, palm reader, prophet, psychic, seer, sibyl, soothsayer, telepathist, visionary

clammy *adj.* damp, dank, drizzly, foggy, misty, moist, mouldy, muggy, perspiring, slimy, soggy, sticky, sweating, sweaty, wet *Antonyms:* arid, dry

clamour *n.* **1.** babel, ballyhoo, cacophony, caterwauling, din, discordance, hoo-ha *(Nonformal)*, outcry, racket, shout, vociferation *Antonyms:* hush, quietude, silence, stillness **2.** bedlam, brouhaha, commotion, fracas, free-for-all, hubbub *(Nonformal)*, pandemonium, ruckus, tumult, uproar

Antonyms: peacefulness, repose, serenity, tranquility – *v.* **1.** bellow, cry, holler, howl, roar, screech, shout, trumpet *Nonformal:* raise Cain, squawk, yammer **2.** compel, demand, hound, importune, insist upon, oblige, press *or* push for *Antonyms:* abandon, reject, renounce, walk away from

clamp *n.* **1.** bear hug *or* hug, clench, clinch, embrace, grip, half nelson, hammerlock, hold, lock **2.** catch, clasp, fastener, press, snap, vice – *v.* **1.** brace, clinch, fix, grapple, immobilize, make fast, secure, squeeze, strengthen, support

clan *n.* ancestry, association, background, band, brood, brotherhood, bunch, clique, coterie, coven, covey, faction, family, fraternity, gang, group, house, ilk, insiders, kindred, kinfolk, lineage, sect, set, sisterhood, society, sorority, stock, strain, tribe

clandestine *adj.* **1.** closet, concealed, confidential, covert, hidden, private, secret, stealthy, undercover *Nonformal:* cloak-and-dagger, hush-hush *Antonyms:* conspicuous, obvious, open, overt, up-front **2.** artful, fraudulent, furtive, illegitimate, illicit, sly, surreptitious, underhand

clannish *adj.* akin, alike, cliquish, close, exclusive, familial, family, kindred, insular, narrow, related, reserved, sectarian, selective, unfriendly, unreceptive *Antonyms:* generic, open, universal

clap *n.* **1.** bang, blast, burst, crack, crash, discharge, peal **2.** hit, pat, slap, strike, thrust, wallop, whack – *v.* **1.** acclaim, applaud, approve, cheer, extol, laud, praise **2.** bang, buffet, cuff, pat, slap, smite, strike, thwack, whack **3.** dash, fling, force, pitch, slam, toss

clarification *n.* definition, description, elucidation, explanation, explication, exposition, illumination, interpretation, resolution, simplification, solution, unravelment, vivification *Antonyms:* befuddlement, bewilderment, obfuscation, perplexity

clarify *v.* **1.** clear up, decipher, describe, elucidate, explain, explicate, illuminate, interpret, make clear, reiterate, restate **2.** distill, extract, filter, purify, refine, strain

clarion *adj.* **1.** acute, blaring, earsplitting, loud, penetrating, resounding, sharp, shrill, strident, trumpeting, unmistakable **2.** clear, definite, distinct, exact, resonant, ringing, sweet, true – n. bell, klaxon, signal, tocsin, trumpet, warning

clarity *n.* accessibility, accuracy, acuity, brightness, brilliance, certainty, clearness, comprehensibility, directness, distinctness, exactness, explicity, lucidness, obviousness, openness, palpability, plainness, preciseness, precision, purity *Antonyms:* cloudiness, complication, haziness, obfuscation, obscurity

clash *n.* **1.** antagonism, antipathy, argument, bad blood, collision, conflict, confrontation, disagreement, discord, dispute, dissension, enmity, friction, hostility, ill will, opposition, quarrel, strife, struggle, tussle *Antonyms:* accord, happiness, harmony **2.** altercation, battle, brannigan, brawl, donnybrook, fight, fracas, fray, row, run-in, scrimmage, set-to, showdown, skirmish, spat, squabble, tiff *Nonformal:* dust-up, scrap **3.** clamour, clang, clank, clatter, din, noise, racket, tumult, uproar – *v.* argue, battle, brawl, bump *or* crash *or* run *or* smash into, butt *or* butt heads, combat, come to blows, conflict, contend, differ, disagree, do battle, duel, encounter, engage, feud, fight, grapple, jar, jolt, jostle, joust, meet, quarrel, row, scuffle, struggle, tussle, war, wrangle *Nonformal:* cross swords, face off, raise Cain

clasp *n.* **1.** broach, buckle, catch, clamp, clip, fastener, fastening, hasp, hook, pin, safety pin, snap **2.** bear hug *or* hug, clinch, embrace, grip, squeeze – *v.* **1.** clinch, clutch, embrace, enfold, grab, grasp, grip, hold, hug, press, seize, snatch, squeeze **2.** bolt, buckle, clamp, clip, connect, fasten, grapple, latch, link, pin, secure

class *adj.* A-1 *(Nonformal)*, authoritative, esteemable, first-rate, professional, well-done – *adv.* admirably, elegantly, exquisitely, faultlessly, flawlessly, matchlessly, perfectly, superbly, with panache *or* style – *n.* **1.** charm, dash, élan, elegance, flair, grace, chutzpah *(Nonformal)*, panache, pizzazz, polish, sophistication, style, urbanity **2.** ancestry, background, birth, breeding, caste, clan, derivation, descent, description, estate, extraction, family, genealogy, genre, genus, hierarchy, ilk, lineage, origin, pedigree, stock **3.** branch, body, category, colloquium, course, company, denomination, department, division, company, grade, group, form, kind, school, sect, section, segment, seminar, tutorial **4.** calibre, designation, league, level, position, rank, sphere, standing, stratum, stripe, tier **5.** calibre, character, determination *Nonformal:* backbone, smarts, stuff – *v.* account, allot, analyze, appraise, assess, assign, assort, brand, catalogue, categorize, classify, codify, consider, designate, discriminate, evaluate, gauge, grade, group, identify, judge, mark, pigeonhole, rank, rate, score, sift, sort, weigh up

classic *adj.* **1.** ageless, archetypal, authoritative, best, capital, champion, consummate, definitive, distinguished, excellent, exemplary, famous, finest, first-rate, noteworthy, outstanding, paramount, perfect, prime, quintessential, superior, time-honoured, timeless, time-tested, top, universal, well-known *Antonyms:* ephemeral, fleeting, inferior, poor, second-rate **2.** basic, characteristic, familiar, normal, prototypical, standard, traditional, true-to-form, typical – *n.* **1.** *chef d'oeuvre (French)*, definitive work, magnum opus, masterpiece, nonpareil, **2.** model, paradigm, prototype, standard *Commonly misused:* **classical**

classical *adj.* **1.** austere, balanced, elegant, formal, harmonious, polished, pure, refined, restrained, simple, symmetrical, tasteful, understated, well-proportioned **2.** ancient, Attic, Augustan, canonical, colonial, epic, Grecian, Greek, Hellenic, heroic, Homeric, humanistic, Latin, Roman, vintage **3.** literary, serious *Nonformal:* highbrow, highfalutin, long-haired *Commonly misused:* **classic**

classification *n.* allocation, analysis, apportionment, arrangement, assignment, assortment, branch, cataloguing, categorization, category, class, codification, consignment, coordination, denomination, departmentalization, designation, disposition, division, genre, gradation, grade, grading, grouping, order, ordering, organization, pigeonholing, placement, positioning, range, rank, section, sizing, sort, sorting, taxonomy, type

classify *v.* alphabetize, analyze, appraise, arrange, assess, assort, brand, breakdown, catalogue, categorize, codify, collocate, correlate, dispose, divide, docket, evaluate, file, grade, group, identify, index, label, match, name, number, order, organize, peg, pigeonhole, range, rank, rate, regiment, segregate, size, sort, systematize, tabulate, tag, type *Antonyms:* disarrange, discompose, jumble, scramble, shuffle

classy *adj.* chic, dashing, deluxe, elegant, elite, exclusive, fancy, fashionable, high-class, impressive, modish, noble, select, stylish, superior *Nonformal:* sharp, snazzy, swank *or* swanky, tony *Antonyms:* blowzy, droll, slatternly, slovenly, tacky

clatter *n.* **1.** clamour, noise, racket, rattle, shattering *Antonyms:* calm, serenity, silence **2.** commotion, pandemonium, raucousness, ruckus, rumpus, uproar **3.** babble, cackle, chatter, chitchat, gibberish, gossip, idle talk, jabber, palaver, prattle, talk, tattle – *v.* **1.** bang, clang, clash, crash, resound, reverberate, shatter **2.** babble, chatter, jabber, prattle, yammer **3.** stomp, thump about, traipse, tramp *(Nonformal)* *Antonyms* creep, skulk, slink, tiptoe

clause *n.* amendment, article, bill, codicil, condition, detail, fine print, heading, item, paragraph, passage, provision, proviso, qualification, requirement, rider, section, sentence, specification, stipulation, subsection, ultimatum

claw *n.* barb, clapper, crook, grapnel, grappler, hook, manus, nail, nipper, paw, pincer, retractile, spur, talon, tentacle – *v.* **1.** dig, gouge, graze, hurt, lacerate, mangle, maul, open, rip, scrabble, scrape, scratch, slash, tear **2.** clutch, grab, grasp, hook, lay hold of, seize, snatch **3.** recoup, recover, regain, retrieve, take *or* win back

clay *n.* **1.** alumina/silica conglomerate *Kinds of clay:* adobe, Albany, ball, bentonite, Blackbird, earthenware, fire, gumbo, kaolin, loam, loess, secondary, shale, short, slip, stoneware, terra cotta **2.** earth, mire, muck, mud, soil

clean *adj.* **1.** cleansed, decontaminated, dirt-free, disinfected, spic-and-span, tidy, unsoiled *Antonyms:* dirty, filthy, stained, tarnished **2.** chaste, immaculate, innocent, pristine, pure, unadulterated, unpolluted, untainted, vestal, virgin *Antonyms:* corrupted, debased, depraved **3.** beneficial, healthful, hygienic, wholesome *Antonyms:* deleterious, injurious, pernicious, toxic **4.** even, neat, orderly, precise, regular, sharp, smart, smooth, straight, streamlined, symmetrical, trim, well-defined *Antonyms:* asymmetrical, irregular, jagged **5.** accomplished, adroit, dexterous, errorless, fair, flawless, handy, legal, perfect, polished, skilful, within bounds, without foul *or* mishap *Anto-nyms:* bumbling, gauche, maladroit **6.** alive, fresh, natural, vibrant *Antonyms:* fetid, rancid, rotten, stinking **7.** on the wagon *(Nonformal)*, purged, recovered, sober, straight **8.** camera-ready, final, legible, readable *Antonyms:* annotated, blue-penciled, marked up – *adv.* absolutely, completely, conclusively, decisively, definitely, thoroughly, totally – *v.* **1.** bathe, brush, burnish, dust, launder, mop, polish, rinse, scour, scrub, shampoo, shower, sterilize, tidy up, vacuum, wash *Antonyms:* besmirch, dirty, muddy, smudge, soil **2.** cashier, clear *or* force *or* throw out, dismiss, drive away, expel, fire, terminate **3.** debone, dress, eviscerate, fillet, gut, trim

clean-cut *adj.* **1.** categorical, chiselled, clear, definite, definitive, etched, explicit, express, outlined, sharp, specific, well-defined *Antonyms:* ambiguous, blurry, indefinite, messy, vague **2.** clean-shaven, neat, snappy *(Nonformal)*, tidy, well-groomed, wholesome

cleanse *v.* decontaminate, disinfect, expurgate, fumigate, launder, purge, purify, refine, restore, rinse, sanitize, scour, scrub, sterilize, wash *Antonyms:* befoul, defile, desecrate, pollute, sully

cleanser *n.* abrasive, antiseptic, bleach, cathartic, deodorant, detergent, disinfectant, fumigant, lather, polish, purgative, purifier, soap

clear *adj.* **1.** bright, calm, cloudless, fair, fine, halcyon, light, pleasant, serene, shining, sunny, unclouded *Antonyms:* cloudy, foggy, hazy, misty, overcast **2.** crystal *or* crystalline, diaphanous, glassy, gossamer, pellucid, pure, see-through, thin, translucent, transparent *Antonyms:* dark, dull, opaque **3.** apparent, audible, coherent, conceivable, conspicuous, definite, distinct, explicit, incontrovertible, intelligible, legible, lucid, manifest, obvious, open-and-shut *(Nonformal)*, palpable, patent, perceptible, plain, precise, pronounced, recognizable, sharp, simple, spelled out, straightforward, unambiguous, uncomplicated, understandable, unequivocal, unmistakable, unquestionable *Antonyms:* ambiguous, doubtful, indistinct, obscured, unrecognizable **4.** absolved, blameless, clean, discharged, dismissed, exonerated, guiltless, innocent, not guilty, unblemished, untarnished, untroubled *Antonyms:* culpable, guilty, sin-ridden **5.** bare, empty, exposed, free, open, unhampered, unhindered, unimpeded, unlimited, unobstructed, vacant, wide *Antonyms:* blocked, encumbered, fettered – *v.* **1.** clarify, define, elucidate, explain, fine up *(P.E.I.)*, illuminate, interpret, make plain, shed light on *Antonyms:* confuse, garble, mystify **2.** clean, filter, purge, purify, refine, sanitize, strain, wipe away **3.** break, brighten, lighten *Antonyms:* rain, storm **4.** bus, eliminate, empty, remove, rid, strip, take away *Antonyms:* add, augment, prepare, set **5.** absolve, acquit, emancipate, exculpate, exonerate, let go *or* off *(Nonformal)*, liberate *Antonyms:* condemn, convict, sentence **6.** acquire, earn, gain, glean, harvest, haul, net, profit, realize, reap, win *Antonyms:* deplete, lose, squander, waste **7.** accede, admit, allow, approve, assent, authorize, certify, consent, endorse, entitle, grant, license, pass, permit, ratify, sanction, stamp *Antonyms:* ban, forbid, nullify, veto **8.** get past, hurdle, jump, leap *or* pass over, surmount, vault *Antonyms:* balk, freeze, hesitate, refuse, stop **9.** discharge, pay *or* pay off, satisfy, settle **10.** climb out of *(Nonformal)*, detach, dislodge, extract, extricate, free, loose *Antonyms:* enmesh, ensnare, entangle, entrap

clearance *n.* **1.** dispossession, eviction, expulsion, ouster, removed, separation **2.** allowance, aperture, elbowroom, gap, headroom, headway, leeway, margin, opening, passage, space **3.** approval, authorization, papers, passage, permission, sanction **4.** closeout, fire sale, markdown, reduction, sale

clear-cut *adj.* **1.** absolute, apparent, appreciable, barefaced, categorical, certain, clear, comprehensible, conspicuous, definite, detailed, discernible, distinct, evident, exact, explicit, express, fixed, graphic, intelligible, lucid, manifest, obvious, palpable, patent, perceptible, perspicuous, plain, positive, precise, salient, sharp, sure, unambiguous, unconditional, undeniable, understandable, unequivocal, unmistakable, unqualified, vivid, well-defined *Antonyms:* ambiguous, obscure, vague **2.** bald, denuded, flat, harvested, logged, moonscaped *(B.C.)*, raped, scarred, stripped – *v.* demolish, denude, devastate, fell, harvest, log, raze, strip

clearing *n.* **1.** field, glade, grassy knoll, grove, meadow, open space **2.** barracks, bush settlement, encampment

clearly *adv.* **1.** beyond question, certainly, emphatically, explicitly, incontrovertibly, indubitably, patently, undeniably, undoubtedly *Antonyms:* ambiguously, open to question, vaguely **2.** in plain sight, noticeably, obviously, openly, patently, visibly *Antonyms:* clandestinely, covertly, secretly, underhandedly

cleavage *n.* **1.** break, chasm, cleft, divide, division, fracture, gap, hole, opening, partition, rift, rupture, schism, separation, split *Antonyms:* connection, unification, unity **2.** boobs *(Nonformal)*, bosom, breasts

cleave *v.* **1.** break, chop, crack, fracture, hack, halve, hew, open, part, partition, penetrate, rend, sever, slice, sunder *Antonyms:* connect, join, marry, unite **2.** abide *or* stand by, adhere, cling, connect, fuse, join, link, marry, merge, remain faithful, unite, wed *Antonyms:* divide, divorce, separate

cleft *adj.* cloven, cracked, crenelated, divergent, divided, parted, rent, riven, ruptured, separated, split, sundered – *n.* aperture, arroyo, breach, break, chasm, chink, cleavage, crack, cranny, crevice, division, fissure, fracture, gap, gorge, gulch, fork, indentation, opening, ravine, rent, rift, schism, slit

clemency *n.* **1.** compassion, consideration, forbearance, forgiveness, kindness, leniency, magnanimity, mercy, pardon, tolerance *Antonyms:* hard-heartedness, harshness, implacability, pitilessness, severity **2.** calmness, gentleness, mildness, moderation, patience, pleasantness, temperance *Antonyms:* tempestuousness, turbulence

clement *adj.* **1.** benevolent, charitable, considerate, forgiving, humane, indulgent, kindhearted, lenient, merciful, pardoning, patient, soft-hearted, sympathetic, tender *Antonyms:* harsh, malicious, ruthless, scolding, vengeful **2.** balmy, clear, fair, fine, halcyon, peaceful, still, warm *Antonyms:* freezing, frigid, icy, stormy

clench *n.* clamp, firm hold, grapple, grasp, grip, hammerlock, hold, iron *or* steel grip, Shawinigan handshake *(Nonformal)*, stranglehold – *v.* **1.** clasp, clutch, constrict, grab, grasp, grip, hold, seize **2.** bolt, brace, gird, hook, lock, nail, rivet, screw **3.** gnash, grind, grit

clergy *n.* canonry, cardinalate, clerics, conclave, deaconry, ecclesiastics, first estate, holy order, ministry, pastorate, prelacy, priesthood, rabbinate, sacerdotalism, the cloth *Antonyms:* laity, lay-persons

cleric *n.* abbé, archbishop, bishop, cardinal, cassock, chaplain, churchman, churchwoman, curate, curé, dean, divine, ecclesiastic, elder, evangelist, father, minister, missionary, monsignor, padré, *papa (Greek Orthodox)*, parson, pastor, pontiff, preacher, priest, rabbi, rector, reverend, shepherd, theologian, vicar *Nonformal:* bible thumper, blackcoat, saddle-bag preacher, sermonizer *Antonyms:* layman, laywoman, parishioner

clerical *adj.* **1.** administrative, paper-pushing, secretarial, stenographic, subordinate, white-collar **2.** apostolic, canonical, churchy, ecclesiastic, episcopal, holy, monastic, papal, pastoral, pontifical, priestly, rabbinical, sacerdotal, sacred, theological

clerk *n.* agent, assistant, recorder, recordkeeper, transcriber *Kinds of clerk:* actuary, auditor, billing, bookkeeper, cashier, checkout, counterperson, court, duty, file, gate, law, legal secretary, municipal, notary, office, payroll, polling, retail, production, receptionist, registrar, sales, stenographer, teller, transcriber

clever *adj.* **1.** acute, brainy, capable, competent, gifted, intelligent, keen, nimble, quick *or* quick-witted, smart, talented *Nonformal:* on the ball, savvy, smart as a whip *Antonyms:* dull-witted, dumb **2.** astute, discerning, foxy, knowing, sagacious, shrewd *Nonformal:* cagey, canny *Antonyms:* artless, guileless, naive **3.** brilliant, cosmopolitan, fluid *(Nonformal)*, glib, ingenious, inventive, masterful, original, polished, suave, urbane, well-versed, witty *Antonyms:* ill-contrived, ramshackle, shoddy, shy, slipshod **4.** able, adept, adroit, dexterous, handy, nimble, proficient, skilful, sprightly *Antonyms:* clumsy, inept

cliché *n.* banality, buzzword, hackneyed *or* trite expression, inanity, old maxim, platitude, saw, stereotype, triviality, truism *Nonformal:* bromide, familiar tune, old chestnut, potboiler *Antonyms:* gem, novelty, original

click *n. & v.* bang, beat, clack, clank, clap, clink, cluck, crack, jangle, jingle, rattle, snap, sound, strike, tap, tick – *v.* communicate, connect, correlate, get along, harmonize, hit it off *(Nonformal)*, like, relate, succeed, transmit

client *n.* **1.** buyer, consumer, customer, *habitué (French)*, patient, patron, purchaser, regular, subscriber **2.** apprentice, dependent, disciple, follower, protégé, pupil

clientele *n.* audience, business, consumers, custom, customers, dependents, fans, market, patrons, public, regulars, shoppers, subscribers, theatregoers, ticket holders

cliff *n.* bluff, crag, escarpment, face, ledge, overhang, precipice, promontory, scar, scarp, sheer wall, tor

climactic *adj.* acute, consequential, critical, crucial, decisive, desperate, dire, heightened, important, intensive, momentous, paramount, peak, pivotal, pressing, significant, urgent

climate *n.* **1.** clime, conditions, forecast, humidity, latitude, temperature, weather **2.** air, ambience, atmosphere, aura, background, condition, disposition, environment, feeling, medium, milieu, mood, spirit, surroundings, temper, tendency, tone, trend, vibes *(Nonformal)*, **3.** district, environs, locality, neighbourhood, province, region, zone

climax *n.* **1.** acme, apex, apogee, capstone, crest, crowning point, culmination, dénouement, extremity, glory, height, heyday, highlight, high spot, intensification, limit, maximum, meridian, orgasm, payoff, peak, pinnacle, pitch, summit, tiptop, top, utmost, zenith **2.** break point, crisis, critical juncture, crossroads, crunch, crux, head, turning point, zero hour – *v.* accomplish, achieve, cap, conclude, crown, culminate, end, finish, fulfill, peak, please, satisfy, succeed, terminate, top, tower *Commonly misused:* **crescendo**

climb *n.* **1.** ascension, hike, mount, trek *Antonyms:* descent, glissade **2.** advancement, growth, progression, promotion *Antonyms:* regression, reversal, setback **3.** aiguille, bluff, cliff, crag, elevation, face, grade, hill, mountain, peak, precipice, ridge, spire, summit, tower, wall **4.** course, game trail, path, route, track – *v.* **1.** ascend, clamber up, mount, scale *Climbing styles: acheval (French)*, aid *or* artificial *or* nailing, alpine, andinismo, avue *or* flight *or* on sight, big wall, bouldering, capsule, choss *(Nonformal)*, clean, cliffing, crack, Euro style *or* sport, face, free, friction *or* smear, hangdogging, high altitude *or* expedition, ice, oxygenless, pink paint, red point, roped solo, simu, waterfall *Climbing equipment:* abseil device, aider *(etrier)*, anchor, ascender *(jumar)*, avalanche cord, belay device, bollard, bolt, chaulk, chock, cliffhanger, clinometer, comming device, corabiner, crampon, harness, hook, kermantle, ice axe *or piolet (French)*, nut, piton, probe, prusik, rivet, rope **2.** escalate, increase, rise, swell, wax *Antonyms:* decline, decrease, diminish, plummet, wane **3.** improve, make headway, move ahead *or* forward, proceed, rise up *Antonyms:* fall back, retrogress, worsen

clinch *v.* **1.** clamp, grip, hold, rivet, tack **2.** assure, cap, cinch, clasp, clutch, conclude, confirm, decide, determine, finish, grab, grapple, grasp, seal, secure, seize, set, settle, sew up *(Nonformal)*, sign, snatch, verify **3.** cuddle, embrace, hug, snuggle

cling *v.* **1.** adhere, entangle, stick, surround, wind around *Antonyms:* billow, drift, ripple **2.** clutch, embrace, grasp, grip, hang onto, hold *or* hold fast, hug *Antonyms:* break apart, detach, let go, loosen, release **3.** cherish, cleave to, hold dear, idolize, love *Antonyms:* eschew, reject, renounce

clinic *n.* **1.** dispensary, doctor's office, hospital, infirmary, medical centre, sick bay, surgery *(British)* **2.** class, conference, course, instruction, lesson, round, schooling, tutorial

clinical *adj.* **1.** analytic, antiseptic, cold, detached, disinterested, dispassionate, emotionless, impersonal, objective, sanitized, scientific, unemotional **2.** bare, functional, utilitarian

clink *n.* **1.** chinking, ding, dinging, ringing **2.** cell, detention, jail *or* jailhouse, lock-up, penitentiary *Nonformal:* can, hoosegow, joint, lockdown, slammer, stick – *v.* bang, chink, clang, jangle, jingle, ring, sound, tingle, tinkle

clip *n.* **1.** clamp, clasp, connector, fastener, hook, pin **2.** cartridge, canister, magazine, round **3.** abbreviation, section, segment, selection, sequence, snippet, teaser **4.** bale, bundle, package, parcel – *v.* **1.** cut, mow, shave, shear, strip, trim **2.** abridge, compress, condense, crop, curtail, cut, reduce, shorten, truncate **3.** blow, box, clout, cuff, cut, knock, punch, smack, smite, sock, take, thump, wallop, whack **4.** amble, breeze *or* sail *or* tear along, dash, fly, hasten, race, run, rush, speed, sprint *Antonyms:* crawl, slow, stop **5.** clamp, connect, fasten, hold, hook, join, pin, tie, unite

clique *n.* bevy, circle, clan, club, coterie, faction, fraternity, gang, in-group, knot, pack, ring, sect, set, sorority *Nonformal:* bunch, crew, crowd, mob, old-boy *or* old-girl network, outfit

cloak *n.* **1.** overgarment *Kinds of cloak:* academic gown *or* hood *or* robe, blanket, burnoose, cape, capote, cardinal, cassock, djellaba, domino, duster, frock, gaberdine, judge's gown *or* robe, kaftan, kimono, kirtle, mantilla, mantle, mantua, master's gown, military cloak, monk's robe, opera cape *or* cloak, pelisse, plaid, poncho, robe, ruana, serape, shawl, shroud, slicker, smock, soutane, stole, tabard, toga, tunic, wraparound, wrapper *North:* anorak, atigi, parka **2.** artifice, feint, masquerade, subterfuge – *v.* **1.** adorn, array, blanket, clothe, coat, cover, display, drape, dress, enswathe, envelop, hang, model, sheathe, swaddle, wrap **2.** camouflage, cloud, conceal, disguise, dissemble, eclipse, evade, hide, mask, obscure, screen, shroud, veil *Antonyms:* reveal, uncover, unmask

clobber *v.* **1.** beat, belt, drub, hit, jab, lick *(Nonformal)*, maul, prod, slam, slug, smash, thrash, trim, wallop, whack, whip **2.** annihilate, defeat, quash, trounce, vanquish

clock *n.* alarm, chronograph, chronometer, digital watch, hourglass, pendulum, stopwatch, sundial, timekeeper, timepiece, timer, watch *Nonformal:* devil's mill, tattler, ticker, tick-tock – *v.* gauge, measure, record, test, time

clog *n.* **1.** block, blockage, fill, impediment, jam, obstruction, overcrowding, snag, stuffing **2.** bottleneck, deterrent, drag, hindrance, hitch – *v.* **1.** block, choke, close, plug, seal, steal, stop **2.** curb, delay, detain, fetter, frustrate, hamper, hinder, hobble, impede, shackle, slow, tie up, trammel *Antonyms:* encourage, foster, permit

cloister *n.* **1.** abbey, cell, chapter house, convent, friary, hermitage, house, lamasery, monastery, nunnery, priory, religious community **2.** arcade, colonnade, corridor, entrance, gallery, hall, hallway, lobby, loggia, passageway, pergola, portico, walkway **3.** bower, ivory tower, retreat, sanctuary, sanctum, seclusion – *v.* confine, enclose, isolate, lock *or* seal in, segregate, separate, sequester, shut off

cloistered *adj.* hermitic, insulated, isolated, protected, reclusive, retired, secluded, sequestered, sheltered, shielded, withdrawn *Antonyms:* exposed, open, unguarded, unprotected, vulnerable

clone *n.* copy, counterpart, doppelgänger *(German)*, double, duplicate, duplication, facsimile, replica, reproduction, rip-off *(Nonformal)*, twin – *v.* copy, ditto, duplicate, photocopy, replicate, scan, trace, transcribe, transfer, Xerox *(Trademark)*

close *adj.* **1.** abutting, adjacent, adjoining, at hand, convenient, hard by, near *or* nearby, near-at-hand, neighbouring, proximate **2.** compact, concentrated, congested, crowded, dense, jam-packed *(Nonformal)*, tight, tight-knit *Antonyms:* barren, commodious, empty, sparse **3.** airless, heavy, humid, muggy, musty, oppressive, stifling, stuffy, suffocating *Antonyms:* airy, breezy, fresh, well-ventilated **4.** approximate, faithful, recognizable, similar *Nonformal:* in the ballpark, warm, within spitting distance *Antonyms:* different, disparate, incongruous, unalike **5.** acute, conscientious, exact, exacting, focussed, intense, literal, precise, rigorous, scrupulous, strict, stringent, thorough *Antonyms:* cursory, fleeting, perfunctory, superficial **6.** confidential, covert, hidden, hush-hush, on the q.t. *(Nonformal)*, private, quiet, unknown *Antonyms:* conspicuous, obvious, open, overt **7.** abreast, even, hard fought, neck and neck, photo finish, well contested, well-matched *Nonformal:* by a hair *or* whisker, close shave **8.** beloved, dear, devoted, inseparable, intimate, loyal *Nonformal:* buddy-buddy, thick, tight *Antonyms:* aloof, at odds, estranged, unfriendly **9.** cheap, economical, frugal, miserly, skinflint, stingy, thrifty, tight-fisted *Antonyms:* liberal, openhanded, profligate **10.** buzz *(Nonformal)*, military, short – *adv.* a little short of, almost, a look and a half *(P.E.I.)*, nearly, stone's throw, verging on – *n.* **1.** adjournment, cessation, closure, completion, conclusion, culmination, end, finale, finish, sign-off, swan song *(Nonformal)*, termination, wind-up *Antonyms:* beginning, birth **2.** *British:* courtyard, entryway, laneway, opening – *v.* **1.** bolt, fasten, latch, padlock, secure, shut, shutter *Antonyms:* open, unlock **2.** block, caulk, dam, fill, obstruct, plug, seal *or* stop up **3.** assemble, coalesce, come together, fuse, join, meet, merge, unite *Antonyms:* break, disperse, scatter, separate **4.** cease, discontinue, end, fold up, halt, shut down, stop, wind *or* wrap up *Nonformal:* put a lid on, shutter *Antonyms:* commence, establish, initiate **5.** enclose, enfold, enwrap, shut in *Antonyms:* loose, release, set free **6.** clutch, grapple, lock horns, seize **7.** agree, assent, clinch, compact, consummate, contract, sign *Nonformal:* button down, sew up **8.** achieve, end up, finish, play out

closed *adj.* **1.** concluded, decided, ended, final, finished, over, resolved, settled, terminated **2.** barred, barricaded, dead end, inaccessible, off limits, sealed, shut **3.** confidential, exclusive, gated, guarded, locked, private, restricted **4.** independent, self-contained, self-sufficient, self-sustaining **5.** bankrupt, chapter 11, failed, gone fishing *(Nonformal)*, insolvent, ruined, shut

close-mouthed *adj.* buttoned *or* clammed up, close- *or* tight-lipped, concise, evasive, laconic, mute, quiet, reserved, reticent, silent, taciturn, terse, uncommunicative *Antonyms:* chatty, open, outspoken

closet *adj.* clandestine, concealed, covert, discreet, hushed, latent, personal, private, secret, stealthy, under wraps *(Nonformal)*, undiscovered, veiled *Antonyms:* obvious, overt, public – *n.* bin, buffet, cabinet, cedar *or* storage chest, chamber, clothes room, cold storage, container, depository, locker, pantry, receptacle, recess, repository, room, safe, sideboard, storage, vault, walk-in, wardrobe – *v.* cage, cloak, cloister, conceal, confine, hide, pen, put *or* store away, seclude, sequester, veil, withdraw

closure *n.* **1.** block, bolt, bung, cap, cork, fastener, latch, lid, lock, obstruction, occlusion, padlock, plug, seal, stop, stopper, tampon, tap **2.** completion, cloture, conclusion, consummation, culmination, ending, fulfillment, realization, resolution, termination *Antonyms:* beginning, commencement, suspense

clot *n.* blob, block, clump, cluster, coagulation, conglutination, embolism *or* embolus, gob, lump, occlusion, thrombus – *v.* coagulate, coalesce, congeal, gel, obstruct, set, thicken

cloth *n.* **1.** bolt, dry goods, fabric, material, shroud, synthetics, textiles *Kinds of cloth:* broadcloth, corduroy, cotton, denim, felt, flannel, fleece, lace, linen, nylon, organza, polyester, rayon, satin, silk, suede, taffeta, terry cloth, toile, tulle, velour, velvet, wool *Trademark:* Gortex, Orlon **2.** dish rag, J-Cloth *(Trademark)*, rag, sponge, towel

clothe *v.* array, attire, bundle up, clad, cloak, coat, costume, cover, deck, decorate, don, drape, draw on, dress, endue, enwrap, equip, exhibit, fit, garb, gear, gown, invest, mantle, outfit, robe, shroud, slip on, suit up, swaddle, turn out, vest, wear, wrap *Nonformal:* rig, tog *Antonyms:* disrobe, expose, strip, undress

clothing *n.* apparel, appearance, array, attire, costume, covering, dress, ensemble, fashion, finery, garb, garment, outfit, raiment, regalia, toggery, wardrobe, wear *Nonformal:* duds, get-up, glad rags, hand-me-downs, threads, weeds *Groupings of clothing:* black tie, couturier, designer, evening, formal, leisure, office, off-the-rack, *prêt à porter (French)*, ready-to-wear, semi-formal, sportswear, uniform, wash-and-wear, working *Kinds of clothing accessories:* bath ware, belt, blouse, bodysuit, braces, cap, cloak, coat, dress, hat, jacket, jumper, overalls, pants, pinafore, scarf, separates, shirt, shoes, shorts, skirt, slacks, socks, stockings, suit, suspenders, sweater, swimsuit, t-shirt, tie, trousers, underclothes, underwear, vest

cloud *n.* **1.** fog, haze, mist, murk, nebula, platform of the gods *(Nonformal)*, scud, smog, smoke, steam, vapour *Cloud families:* high *(*20,000 feet plus*)*, low *(*surface-6500 feet*)*, middle *(*6500-20,000 feet*)*, vertical displacement *(*1600-20,000 feet*)* *Kinds of cloud:* altocumulus, altostratus, cirrocumulus, cirrostratus, cirrus, cumulonimbus, cumulus, nimbostratus, stratocumulus, stratus **2.** blues, depression, despair, despondency, doldrums, funk *(Nonformal)*, gloomy *or* troubled state, grief, melancholy, sadness, sorrow, suffering, woe *Antonyms:* buoyancy, cheerfulness, high spirits **3.** army, congregation, group, horde, host, legion, mass, multitude, plethora, swarm, throng **4.** camouflage, cover, screen, shadow, veil **5.** blemish, blur, defect, flaw, fault, imperfection, mar, smudge, stain, stigma, tarnish – *v.* **1.** befog, blind, blur, darken, dim, eclipse, envelop, fog, gloom, mist, overcast, overshadow, shade, shadow, shroud, veil *Antonyms:* brighten, clarify, illuminate, uncover **2.** baffle, complicate, confound, confuse, disorient, embarrass, flummox *(Nonformal)*, fluster, muddle, mystify, obscure, perturb **3.** brand, mark, slur, stigmatize, sully, tarnish

cloudy *adj.* **1.** chill, dull, grey, hazy, leaden, misty, overcast, sunless *Antonyms:* bright, sunny **2.** ambiguous, blurred, confused, indefinite, indistinct, muddy, murky, mysterious, nebulous, obscure, unclear, unknown, vague *Antonyms:* comprehended, determined, known, understood **3.** doubtful, questionable, suspect, suspicious *Antonyms:* accepted, approved, celebrated, recognized, vouched for **4.** dark, glowering, saturnine, sombre, sullen *Antonyms:* blithe, cheery, happy

clout *n.* **1.** authority, eminence, esteem, influence, might, power, prestige, pull, standing, sway, weight – *v.* box, clobber, concuss, cuff, daze, hit, homer, pound, smack, strike, thump, thwack, wallop *Nonformal:* kayo, nail **2.** grand slam, hit, line drive *Nonformal:* blast, frozen rope, rocket, shot, two- *or* three-bagger

clown *n.* antic, buffoon, comedian, comic, fool, funnyman, gawmoge *(Nonformal)*, harlequin, humorist, jester, joker, madcap, merry-andrew, merrymaker, mime, mummer, pierrot, prankster, punch, quipster, wag, wit, zany *Nonformal:* card, cutup, life of the party, wisecracker – *v.* act crazy, fool, frolic, have fun, jest, joke, kid around, play, tease *Antonyms:* sweat, toil, work

cloying *n.* **1.** rich *or* sweet, sugar-coated, sugary, syrupy *Nonformal:* gooey, sticky **2.** mawkish, saccharin, sentimental *Nonformal:* gushy, mushy, schmaltzy, soppy

club *n.* **1.** bat, baton, billy, blackjack, bludgeon, cosh, cudgel, hammer, mace, mallet, nightstick, stick, swatter, truncheon *Some Common clubs and lodges:* biker, boys and girls, bridge, chess, country, curling, fitness, golf and country, Grand Orange Lodge, gun, health, hockey, Knights of Columbus, Lions, Rotary, Royal Canadian Legion, seniors, skating, ski, social **2.** alliance, association, brotherhood, bunch, circle, clan, clique, company, coterie, crew, diet, faction, fellowship, fraternity, gang, guild, league, lodge, mob, order, organization, outfit, ring, set, society, sorority, union **3.** clubhouse, facility, hangout, joint, lodge, meeting room, stomping ground *(Nonformal)* – *v.* **1.** bash, baste, batter, beat, bludgeon, clobber, clout, cosh, cudgel, hammer, hit, pound, pummel, strike, whack **2.** band together, collect, combine, consolidate, merge, pool, unite

clue *n.* cue, evidence, giveaway *(Nonformal)*, hint, indication, inkling, intimation, key, lead, pointer, scent, sign, spoor, suggestion, suspicion, tip, tipoff, trace, track, trail, vestige – *v.* acquaint, advise, apprise, bring up to speed *(Nonformal)*, fill in, hint, indicate, inform, intimate, notify, post, suggest, tell, warn

clump *n.* **1.** batch, bundle, cluster, colony, copse, group, knot, mound, thicket, wad **2.** blob, chunk, hunk, lump, mass, nugget **3.** plunk *(Nonformal)*, thud, thump – *v.* **1.** barge, bumble, clatter, galumph, hobble, limp, lumber, plod, scuff, stamp, stomp, stump, thud, thump, tramp *Antonyms:* creep, prowl, skulk, slither, tiptoe **2.** amass, assemble, collect, combine, compile, gather, group, join, pile, stack, stook, throw together, unite *Antonyms:* disperse, divide, scatter

clumsy *adj.* **1.** awkward, boorish, gauche, gawky, jerky, stumbling, uncoordinated, ungainly, ungraceful **2.** bungling, inept, inexperienced, without skill *Nonformal:* ham-fisted, klutzy *Antonyms:* adept, competent, dexterous, proficient **3.** blundering, embarrassing, ill-conceived, inopportune, maladroit, painful, tactless, thoughtless *Antonyms:* diplomatic, polished, smooth **4.** bulky, cumbersome, hefty, unmanageable, unwieldy

cluster *n.* band, bevy, body, bunch, clutch, collection, covey, crew, gathering, group, pack, party, school, set – *v.* accumulate, aggregate, assemble, associate, bundle, bunch, bunch up, crowd around, cumulate, flock, gather *Antonyms:* divide, scatter, separate

clutch *n.* **1.** clamp, clasp, clench, clinch, grasp, grip, hold **2.** crisis, crucial moment, crunch, crux, emergency, exigency, extremity, pinch, push, strait **3.** bevy, brood, nest, number – *v.* capture, catch, clench, cling to, collar, ensnare, grab, grapple, grasp, grip, hold, hook, nab, seize, snare, snatch, take

clutches *n.* command, control, custody, dominance, dominion, grasp, grip, keep, keeping, possession, power, sway

clutter *n.* **1.** bedlam, chaos, confusion, derangement, disarray, disorder, farrago, hodgepodge, huddle, jumble, litter, medley, mess, motley, muddle, pandemonium, shuffle, tumble, untidiness *Antonyms:* neatness, order, organization **2.** chattering, interference, static – *v.* crowd, dirty, disarray, jam-pack, jumble, litter, muddle, rummage, scatter, scramble, snarl, strew *Antonyms:* arrange, straighten, tidy

coach *n.* **1.** advisor, conductor, director, drillmaster, educator, guru, gym teacher, instructor, manager, mentor, supervisor, teacher, trainer, tutor **2.** bus, calèche, car, carriage, chaise, four-wheeler, phaeton, stage, train, tram, vehicle – *v.* drill, educate, guide, instruct, lead, oversee, prepare, prime, prompt, ready, school, teach, train, tutor *Antonyms:* discourage, disparage, suppress

coagulate *v.* clot, compact, concentrate, condense, consolidate, curdle, gel, gelatinize, harden, scab, set, solidify, thicken *Antonyms:* dissolve, liquefy, melt, thin

coal *adj.* black, dark brown, ebony, jet – *n.* **1.** anthracite, bitumen, black diamonds, briquette, carbon, charcoal, cinder, coke, fuel, lignite **2.** ash, cinder, clinker, ember

coalesce *v.* amalgamate, blend, cleave, cohere, combine, commingle, connect, consolidate, fuse, incorporate, integrate, join, link, merge, mix, unite, wed *Antonyms:* divide, part, rend, sever

coarse *adj.* **1.** bristly, bumpy, calloused, chapped, coarse-grained, craggy, grainy, granular, harsh, jagged, lumpy, particulate, prickly, rough, rugged, sandy, scratchy, uneven, unpolished *Antonyms:* fine-grained, polished, smooth **2.** callow, crude, grassroots, green, homespun, native, natural, primitive, raw, rough, rough-hewn, rudimentary, rustic, uncultivated, undeveloped, unfiltered, unfinished, unpasteurized, unprocessed, unrefined, virginal *Antonyms:* civilized, experienced, knowledgeable, savvy **3.** base, blue, boorish, brutish, cheap, common, crass, dirty, earthy, filthy, foul, gross, gruff, immodest, improper, inelegant, loudmouthed, loutish, low, mean, nasty, obscene, off-colour, offensive, raunchy, raw, scatological, tacky, uncivil, uncouth, vulgar *Antonyms:* genteel, modest *Commonly misused:* **course**

coarseness *n.* **1.** bad manners, bawdiness, crudeness, earthiness, gaucherie, indelicacy, lack of breeding, misconduct, poor taste, ribaldry, roughness, rowdyism, rudeness, smuttiness, vulgarity **2.** bristliness, itchiness, prickliness, roughness, shagginess *Antonyms:* polish, smoothness, softness

coast *n.* bank, beach, coastline, littoral, seaboard, seacoast, seaside, shore, shoreline, strand, strip – *v.* cruise, drift, float, freewheel, get by, glide, sail, skate, slide, taxi, waft

coat *n.* **1.** coating, covering, crust, enamel, finish, glaze, gloss, lacquer, lamination, layer, overlay, painting, plaster, priming, tinge, varnish, wash, whitewash **2.** outerwear, overgarment *Kinds of coat:* anorak, blanket, blazer, blouse, bodycoat, bolero, bomber jacket, capote, capuchin, car, chesterfield, cutaway, denim jacket, dinner jacket, doublet, down jacket, dress, duffel, Eton jacket, fur, hockey jacket, Hudson's Bay, jerkin, jumper, loden, Mackinaw, Mao jacket, mess jacket, morning, Nehru jacket, oilskin, overcoat, parka, peacoat, pelisse, poncho, Prince Albert, raincoat, reefer, sealskin, shooting jacket, slicker, sports jacket, tabard, tail coat, tails, topcoat, trench, tuxedo, ulster, watch, windbreaker *Trademark*: Burberry, London Fog **3.** bark, epidermis, fell, finish, fleece, fur, hair, hide, husk, integument, jacket, leather, membrane, peel, pelage, pellicle, pelt, rind, scale, shell, skin, slough, wool – *v.* apply, cover, crust, enamel, foil, glaze, incrust, laminate, layer, paint, plaster, plate, smear, spread, stain, surface, urethane, varnish

coating *n.* batter, blanket, bloom, coat, covering, crust, dusting, encrustation, film, finish, glaze, lamination, layer, membrane, paint, patina, sheet, skin, varnish, veneer

coax *v.* **1.** argue into, beguile, blandish, cajole, entice, flatter, hook, induce, inveigle, lure, persuade, pester, plague, press, prevail upon, soothe, sweet-talk, talk into, tease, tempt, urge, wheedle, wile, worm *Nonformal:* arm-twist, con *Antonyms:* browbeat, bully, coerce, intimidate, threaten **2.** devise, engineer, guide, influence, lead, manipulate, manoeuvre, mastermind, shape, steer **3.** garner, glean, obtain, pry loose *(Nonformal)*

cobble *v.* fabricate, fashion, fix, forge, invent, make, make do, mend, patch up, repair

cocaine *n.* anesthetic, drug, narcotic, street drug *Nonformal:* blow, C, charlie, coke, crack, dust, lines, nose candy, snow, white

cock *n.* **1.** chanticleer, cockerel, drake, gander, gobbler *(Nonformal)*, male bird *or* chicken *or* fowl, rooster **2.** buddy, chum, confrère, crony, fellow, friend, mate, old friend, pal, sidekick *(Nonformal)* **3.** absurdity, balderdash, drivel, nonsense, rubbish *Nonformal:* baloney, bull, crock, hokum, malarkey **4.** faucet, nozzle, spigot, tap, valve **5.** champion, dean, head, hero, kingpin, leader, paladin **6.** bellwether, indicator, weathercock, weather vane – *v.* **1.** aim, position, ready, set, tilt **2.** bristle, perk up, raise, rise, set, stack, stand, stand up *or* upright, stiffen up, tilt, tip

cockeyed *adj.* **1.** cross-eyed, squinting, strabismal, walleyed **2.** angled, askew, aslant, awry, crooked, distorted, irregular, skewed, slanted, sloped, sloping, tilted, twisted, warped **3.** asinine, faulty, foolish, inane, mistaken, outlandish, ridiculous, wrong *Nonformal:* cockamamie, insane, nonsensical, senseless

cocktail *n.* highball, long drink, mixed drink, punch, stirrup cup *Kinds of cocktail:* B-52, Black Russian, Bloody Caesar *or* Mary, brandy Alexander, brown cow, callibogus *(Newfoundland)*, Cape Cod, crantini, Cuba libre, daiquiri, greyhound, Harvey Wallbanger, hot buttered rum, hot toddy,

Irish coffee, Long Island Ice Tea, Manhattan, margarita, martini, mint julep, Moscow mule, old-fashioned, orange blossom, Pimm's cup, piña colada, pink lady, planter's punch, rickey, Rob Roy, rum and cola, rusty nail, rye and ginger, scotch and soda, screwdriver, Singapore sling, sloe gin fizz, Spanish coffee, spritzer, stinger, toddy, Tom and Jerry, Tom Collins, vodka paralyzer, vodka tonic, whisky sour, white lady, White Russian, wine cooler, zombie

cocoon *n.* **1.** aurelia, casing, chrysalis, encasement, larva, pupa **2.** barrier, defence, enclosure, protection, protective covering, shield – *v.* cushion, encase, enclose, envelop, insulate, pad, protect, swaddle, swathe, wrap *Antonyms:* bare, expose, strip, unfasten, unfurl

coddle *v.* **1.** baby, cosset, dote on, favour, humour, indulge, mollycoddle, pamper, please, spoil *Antonyms:* ignore, ill-treat, neglect **2.** boil, brew, cook, poach, simmer, steam

code *n.* **1.** body of law, corpus juris, statute book *Kinds of legal code:* civil, constitutional, federal, Justinian, municipal, Napoleonic, penal, provincial **2.** canon, command direction, directive, instruction, language, program, regulation, rule, standard, system **3.** convention, ethics, ethos, maxim, morality, morals, precept, value system **4.** character, cipher, cryptograph, letter, script, symbol – *v.* encode, encrypt, scramble

codify *v.* arrange, catalogue, classify, document, enumerate, formalize, normalize, organize, perpetuate, preserve, record, regularize, set in order, standardize, systematize *Antonyms:* destroy, disorder, lose

coerce *v.* **1.** compel, drive, force, impel, lean *or* put the squeeze on *(Nonformal)*, press, pressurize, prevail upon *Antonyms:* discourage, dissuade, hamper, hinder **2.** beat down, browbeat, bulldoze, control, cow, dominate, domineer, dragoon, intimidate, menace, oblige, railroad, strong-arm *(Nonformal)*, terrorize, threaten, trample, tyrannize *Antonyms:* beg, blandish, cajole, inveigle, plead

coercion *n.* **1.** browbeating, bullying, compulsion, constraint, domination, duress, extortion, force, forcible *or* moral *or* physical restraint, intimidation, menace, pressure, threat of violence **2.** dictatorship, government by force, military *or* police state, totalitarianism, tyranny

coexist *v.* accommodate, cooperate, get along *(Nonformal)*, go hand in hand with, help, interact, live alongside, share, support, support one another, synergize, tolerate

coexistence *n.* accord, agreement, concurrence, mutual, nonaggression, noninterference, harmoniousness, parallelism, simultaneity, symbiosis, synchronimity, toleration *Antonyms:* discord, enmity

coffee *n.* **1.** beverage, *café (French)*, drink *Nonformal:* brew, ink, java, joe, mud *Kinds of coffee:* Arabica, Blue Mountain, *café au lait (French)*, *caffe latte (Italian)*, cappuccino, Colombian, decaffeinated, Ethiopian, Greek, Hawaiian, espresso, French roast, Java, Latte, Mocha, Mochaccino, Turkish **2.** colour, pigment *Coffee shades:* brown, burnt sienna, creamy brown, tan

coffer *n.* box, caddy, case, casket, caisson, chest, locker, moneychest, repository, safe, strongbox, treasure chest, treasury, trousseau, war chest

coffin *n.* box, burial case, casket, catafalque, kist *(British)*, mummy case, pall, pine box, sarcophagus *Nonformal:* dead man's *or* wooden overcoat

cog *n.* **1.** cogwheel, differential, flywheel, gear, prong, ratchet, sprocket, tine, tooth, transmission, wheel **2.** aid, assistant, intern, junior, small fish *or* fry, subordinate, underling **3.** cheat, chicanery, deception, fabrication, falsehood, fib, hoax, prevarication, trickery – *v.* cheat, deceive, load the dice, rig, swindle *Nonformal:* con, flimflam

cogency *n.* bearing, conviction, effectiveness, force, pertinence, power, punch, relevance, sagacity, strength, validity, weight *Antonyms:* impotence, ineffectiveness

cogent *adj.* apt, authoritative, clear, compelling, conclusive, convincing, fitting, forceful, germane, influential, justified, meaningful, on the mark *(Nonformal)*, persuasive, pertinent, potent, powerful, relevant, sagacious, significant, telling, valid, weighty, well-grounded, wise *Antonyms:* discursive, impotent, meandering, trifling, weak

cogitate *v.* conceive, concentrate, consider, contemplate, deliberate, focus, meditate, mull over, muse, ponder, reason, reflect, review, ruminate, speculate, study, think, think about *Nonformal:* brainstorm, chew on, stew over

cogitation *n.* consideration, contemplation, deliberation, meditation, musing, reflection, rumination, speculation, thought *Antonyms:* impulse, intuition, whim

cognate *adj.* **1.** agnate, connatural, consanguineous, kindred, related **2.** affiliated, akin, alike, allied, analogous, associated, connected, corresponding, fraternal, like, same, similar, sororal *Antonyms:* alien, dissimilar, foreign, strange – *n.* blood, brother, clan, family, house, kin, kindred, kinsman, people, relation, relative, sister, tribe

cognition *n.* **1.** acknowledgment, apprehension, comprehension, consciousness, discernment, heed, intelligence, knowledge, observance, observation, perception, perspicacity, reasoning, recognition, understanding, wisdom **2.** acknowledgment, acumen, awareness, keenness of mind, ken, wisdom

cognizant *adj.* acquainted *or* conversant with, aware, conscious, conversant, familiar, grounded, informed, knowing, knowledgeable, mindful, observant, perceptive, posted, privy to, schooled, sensible, sentient, tuned in, versed *Nonformal:* clued in, in the loop, on to, wise to *Antonyms:* misinformed, unacquainted, unaware, unknowledgeable

cohabit *v.* conjugate, couple, live common-law, live *or* room together, partner up *Nonformal:* shack up, share digs, split the rent

coherence *n.* **1.** clarity, comprehensibility, consistency, intelligibility, lucidity, rationality, understandability *Antonyms:* confusion, incoherence, irrationality **2.** adherence, attachment, bond, cohesion, conjunction, connection, union

coherent *adj.* **1.** clear, comprehensible, identifiable, intelligible, lucid, meaningful, rational, understandable **2.** consistent, logical, orderly, organized, reasoned, sound, systematic *Antonyms:* confusing, disjointed, illogical, inconsistent, rambling **3.** adhering, attached, clinging, connected, inseparable, inseverable, joined

cohort *n.* **1.** accomplice, adherent, aide, ally, assistant, associate, chum, colleague, companion, company, comrade, confederate, confrère, consort, contingent, crony, disciple, fellow, follower, friend, hand, henchman, legion, mate, partisan, partner, regiment, satellite, sidekick *(Nonformal)*, supporter **2.** brigade, company, crew, entourage, gang, group, legion, regiment, team

coiffure *n.* bob, comb-out, cut, haircut, hairdo *or* hairstyle, permanent, wave *Nonformal:* coif, do, perm, updo

coil *n.* **1.** braid, bundle, circle, convolution, corkscrew, curl, curlicue, gyration, helix, lap, loop, mound, pile, plait, ring, roll, scroll, shock, spiral, tendril, turn, twine, twirl, twist, whorl, wind **2.** difficulty, imbroglio, mess, pickle, problem, situation – *v.* convolute, corkscrew, curl, entwine, fold, heap, intertwine, loop, pile, rotate, scroll, slack, snake around *(Nonformal)*, spiral, turn, twine, twist, wind, wrap around, writhe

coin *n.* cash, change, coinage, currency, gold, legal tender, money, silver, small change *Kinds of Canadian coin:* copper *or* penny, dime *or* ten-cent piece, fifty-cent piece, nickel *or* five-cent piece, loonie *or* dollar coin, quarter *or* twenty-five-cent piece, toonie *or* two-dollar coin *Historical:* Brock copper, Gloriam Regni, Halifax currency, leather dollar – *v.* **1.** brainstorm *(Nonformal)*, come up with, compose, conceive, contrive, create, design, fabricate, forge, formulate, invent, make up, manufacture, mould, name, originate, spark, trump up **2.** issue, mint, produce, stamp

coincide *v.* **1.** agree, coexist, correspond, jibe, match, occur simultaneously, synchronize **2.** concur, go along with, harmonize, mesh *Antonyms:* differ, disagree, diverge, part, separate

coincidence *n.* **1.** accident, chance, fate, fluke, fortuity *or* fortuna, happening, happenstance, luck, serendipity **2.** agreement, concomitance, correspondence, harmony, parallelism, rapport, synchronicity, unison

coincidental *adj.* by chance, casual, circumstantial, fortuitous, haphazard, inadvertent, incidental, random, unintentional, unplanned *Antonyms:* calculated, deliberate, intentional, planned, prearranged

cold *adj.* **1.** arctic, biting, bitter, blasting, bracing, brisk, chill, chilly, crisp, cutting, freezing, frigid, frosty, gelid, glacial, ice-cold, icy, inclement, intense, keen, nippy, numbing, penetrating, piercing, raw, severe, sharp, stinging *Antonyms:* balmy, gentle, sunny, tropical **2.** chattering, chilled, chilled to the bone, covered with goose-bumps, frozen solid, have the shakes *(Nonformal)*, hypothermal, shaking, shivering, shuddering *Antonyms:* boiling, hot, overheated, warm **3.** aloof, apathetic, distant, indifferent, phlegmatic, remote, stony, undemonstrative, unresponsive *Antonyms:* caring, committed, dedicated, nurturing, supportive **4.** desolate, harsh, inhospitable, joyless, stark *Antonyms:* comfortable, cozy, hospitable, welcoming **5.** clinical, detached, dispassionate, impartial, impersonal, objective *Antonyms:* idiosyncratic, partisan, prejudiced, subjective, whimsical **6.** cool, lukewarm, reserved, restrained, unenthusiastic *Antonyms:* emotional, enthusiastic, frenzied, passionate **7.** dead, deceased, defunct, out, unconscious *Nonformal:* dead to the world, gone, passed out, stiff, taking a dirt nap, toast **8.** dry, matter-of-fact, prosaic, sober, workaday *Antonyms:* curious, extraordinary, irregular, unusual **9.** faded, faint, not fresh, old, spoiled, stale, weak *Antonyms:* clear, new, recent, sharp **10.** mistaken, off-base *or* -target, on the wrong track, out in left field **11.** at one's mercy, cornered, in a tight fix, on the spot, over a barrel, trapped – *adv.* **1.** absolutely, completely, entirely, thoroughly, with certainty, without a doubt **2.** ad-lib *(Nonformal)*, extemporaneously, on sight, unrehearsed, without preparation **3.** precipitously, suddenly, without notice *or* warning – *n.* **1.** chill, draft, freeze, deep freeze, frost, refrigeration, wintertime **2.** bug, chills, fever, flu, goosebumps, infection, influenza, *la grippe (French)*, rheum, runny nose, shakes, shivers, sniffles, virus

coliseum *n.* agora, amphitheatre, arena, bowl, exhibition hall, forum, hippodrome, open-air theatre, stadium, sports hall *or* stadium, theatre

collaborate *v.* **1.** coauthor, come together, concord, concur, cooperate, co-produce, fraternize, fuse, get together, go partners *(Nonformal)*, interface, join forces, join *or* team *or* work together, link *or* team up, participate, unite, work with **2.** be in cahoots with *(Nonformal)*, collude, conspire, intrigue

collaborator *n.* **1.** assistant, associate, cohort, colleague, confederate, co-worker, fellow traveller *(Nonformal)*, fraternizer, ghostwriter, helper, partner, teammate, team player **2.** quisling, stooge *(Nonformal)*, traitor

collapse *n.* **1.** avalanche, catastrophe, cave-in, disaster, failure, rupture, washout **2.** bankruptcy, crash, debacle, downfall, fiasco, insolvency, ruin, ruination, undoing **3.** breakdown, crackup, exhaustion, faint, swoon – *v.* **1.** break, buckle, cave in, conk out *(Nonformal)*, crumble, disintegrate, fail, fall apart *or* down *or* in pieces, give in *or* out *or* way, rupture, shatter, topple *Antonyms:* build up, buttress, prop, reinforce, support **2.** break down, faint, founder, keel over *(Nonformal)*, pass out, swoon, take sick **3.** come to nothing, fall through, nosedive, peter out *(Nonformal)*, subside *Antonyms:* forge ahead, prevail, triumph **4.** close down, close the doors, deflate, downsize, fold down, restructure, retool, telescope, wind *or* wrap up *Antonyms:* burgeon, flourish, grow, prosper, thrive

collar *n.* **1.** neckwear *Kinds of collar:* butterfly, choker, clerical, dickey, dog, Eton, fichu, flea, frill, high, jabot, mock turtle, neckband, ruff, turtleneck, Vandyke **2.**

anchorage *(Newfoundland)*, berth, moorage – *v.* **1.** accost, detain, waylay *Nonformal:* buttonhole, lay hold of **2.** apprehend, arrest, capture, nab *(Nonformal)*

collate *v.* arrange, assemble, bracket, categorize, collect, compare, crosscheck, gather, group, match, order, relate, sort

collateral *adj.* **1.** bordering, parallel, side-by-side **2.** accompanying, associated, attendant, coexistent, concomitant, concurrent, connected **3.** confirming, contributory, corroborative, supporting **4.** accessory, additional, satellite, secondary, subordinate, supplementary – *n.* bond, guarantee, pledge, promise, security, surety

colleague *n.* aide, ally, assistant, associate, auxiliary, buddy, chummy *(Newfoundland)*, coadjutor, cohort, collaborator, companion, comrade, confederate, confrère, co-worker, crony, fellow, friend, helper, pal, partner, sidekick *(Nonformal)*, teammate, workmate *Antonyms:* adversary, foe, opponent, rival

collect *adj. & adv.* C.O.D., payable upon receipt, reverse-charge – *n.* invocation, prayer, worship – *v.* **1.** accumulate, acquire, compile, obtain, put together, raise **2.** amass, save, stash, stockpile, store up, stow away *Antonyms:* run through, squander, waste **3.** come together, congregate, converge, huddle up, muster *Antonyms:* break up, disperse, dissipate **4.** carry *or* take away, fetch, gather up, pick up, pull in, receive, round up, take in **5.** compose, corral, get one's act together, rally, recover, regroup, settle **6.** conclude, glean, infer, reason

collected *adj.* composed, confident, poised, self-possessed, serene, unruffled *Nonformal:* cool, unflappable *Antonyms:* distraught, frantic

collection *n.* **1.** accumulation, amassing, assembling, compilation, gathering, hoard **2.** body, canon, corpus, holdings, inventory, stock, treasury **3.** anthology, assemblage, festschrift, garland, omnibus **4.** assortment, gallimaufry, hodgepodge, jumble, medley, miscellany, variety **5.** assembly, company, congregation, crowd, group, swarm, throng **6.** contribution, donation, offering, offertory, tithe **7.** disposal, pickup, relocation, removal **8.** heap, mass, mound, pile

collective *adj.* aggregate, assembled, collated, combined, common, compiled, composite, concentrated, concerted, concurrent, conjoint, consolidated, cooperative, corporate, cumulative, gathered, grouped, joint, massed, mutual, shared, united *Antonyms:* divided, individual, singular, solitary – *n.* aggregate, body, combine, commune, cooperative, co-op, enterprise, gathering, grassroots organization, group, kibbutz, organization, party, union

collector *n.* acquisitor, connoisseur, enthusiast, gatherer, hoarder, hunter, specialist *Nonformal:* buff, fan, pack rat *Kinds of collector:* antiquarian *(antiques)*, audiofile *(records)*, bibliofile *(books)*, cartophile *(cards)*, herpetologist *(reptiles and amphibians)*, horologist *(watches and clocks)*, lepidopterist *(butterflies)*, numismatist *(coins)*, philatelist *(stamps)*

college *n.* **1.** academy, alma mater, institute, institution, lyceum, seminary, university *Kinds of college:* affiliated community, Frontier College, Khaki College *(Historical)*, polytechnical, services, technical *Quebec:* CEGEP, classical, séminaire **2.** department, discipline, faculty, school **3.** academia, campus, halls of ivy *(Nonformal)* **4.** community, company, congregation, league *See also:* **school**

collide *v.* **1.** bang *or* crash *or* plow *or* smash into, bump, hit, jolt, meet head-on, ram, sideswipe, strike **2.** battle, clash, combat, differ, disagree, dispute, feud, fight, haggle, joust, object, oppose, quarrel, spar, spat, squabble, struggle, tangle, tiff, war, wrangle *Antonyms:* agree, cooperate, harmonize

collision *n.* **1.** accident, car crash, contact, crash, destruction, impact, pileup, sideswipe, slam, smash, wreck *Nonformal:* fender-bender, head-on, rear-ender, **2.** battle, clash, conflict, disagreement, discord, dissension, donnybrook, quarrel, spat *Antonyms:* affinity, agreement, support, unity

colloquial *adj.* casual, common, conversational, demotic, dialectal, everyday, familiar, idiomatic, informal, popular, street, vernacular *Antonyms:* formal, Queen's English

colloquy *n.* conference, conversation, dialogue, discourse, discussion, forum, huddle, interchange, powwow

collusion *n.* cabal, chicanery, complicity, confidence game *or* trick, connivance, conspiracy, deceit, dodge, game, graft, intrigue, plot, racket, scam, scheme, swindle *Nonformal:* con game, double-cross, flim-flam

colonial *adj.* branch, dependent, provincial, subject, territorial – *n.* **1.** colonist, emigrant, habitant, homesteader, immigrant, loyalist, pioneer, settler **2.** hayseed, hick, provincial, rustic, yokel *Nonformal:* greenhorn, rube

colonization *n.* **1.** establishment, foundation, installation, peopling, settlement **2.** conquest, domination, subjugation, subordination

colonnade *n.* arcade, breezeway, cloister, columniation, covered walk, gallery, loggia, peripteros, peristyle, piazza, porch, portico, veranda

colony *n.* **1.** block, borough, community, district, hamlet, homestead, neighbourhood, precinct, region, section, settlement, town, turf, village, ward **2.** dependency, outpost, protectorate, satellite, territory **3.** flock, group, herd, pack, school

colossal *adj.* **1.** Brobdingnagian, enormous, gargantuan, giant, gigantic, huge, humongous *(Nonformal)*, immense, mammoth, monstrous, titanic *Antonyms:* infinitesimal, minuscule, tiny **2.** awesome, beyond belief, excessive, inordinate, monumental, prodigious, staggering, towering

colour *adj.* additional, analytical, background, descriptive, elaborative, embellishing – *n.* **1.** light, light rays *Categories of colour:* achromatic *(blacks, greys, whites)*, chromatic colour spectrum *or* wheel *(blues, greens, indigos, reds, violets, yellows) Groupings and properties of colours:* cold, complementary, cool, full, gloss, halftone, intensity, iridescence, luminosity, monochromatic, polychromatic, prismatic, semigloss, tertiary, tint, warm *Primary colours:* blue, red, yellow *Secondary colours:* green, orange, purple **2.** dye *or* dyestuff, paint, pigment, stain, tincture **3.** bloom, blush, flush, hue, ruddiness, tinge **4.** cast, complexion, pigmentation, skin shade **5.** ambience, atmosphere, aura, flavour, milieu, sense of place **6.** animation, emphasis, force, intensity, life, liveliness, resonance, strength, timbre, vigour, vivacity, vividness **7.** breed, character, ilk, kind, make, sort, stripe, variety **8.** appearance, aspect, demeanor, effect, outward semblance, show **9.** badge, banner, emblem, flag, insignia, medal – *v.* **1.** breathe, distort, dress up, exaggerate, imbue, instill, misconstrue, overstate, point, stretch, temper, twist **2.** blush, burn, cloak, crimson, disguise, flush, mask, pretext, redden, suffuse

colourful *adj.* **1.** bright, chromatic, flashy, florid, gaudy, gay, graphic, intense, jazzy, kaleidoscopic, lively, loud, motley, prismatic, psychedelic, rainbow, rich, showy, splashy, variegated *Antonyms:* colourless, dark, dreary, faded, pale **2.** animated, arresting, brilliant, interesting, picturesque, stimulating, vibrant, vivid *Antonyms:* boring, conventional, dull, monotonous **3.** eccentric, flaky, idiosyncratic, odd, peculiar, quirky, unusual

colourless *adj.* **1.** achromatic, bleached, hueless, uncoloured, washed out, white, without tone *Antonyms:* flushed, glowing, healthy, robust, ruddy **2.** anemic, ashen, bloodless, characterless, drab, dreary, dull, faded, flat, insipid, lacklustre, lifeless, pale, pallid, pasty, prosaic, sallow, sickly, tame, uninteresting, vacuous, vapid, wan, waxen *Antonyms:* animated, exciting, unusual

column *n.* **1.** caryatid, obelisk, mast, pier, pilaster, pillar, post, pylon, spar, spine, spire, stalagmite, stalk, standard, totem pole, upright *Parts of a column:* architrave, astragal, base, capital, cornice, frieze, shaft *Styles of column:* Corinthian, Doric, engaged, fluted, Ionic **2.** cadre, company, corps, division, file, formation, group, legion, line, procession, queue, row, section, series, squad, string, team, train, unit **3.** article, commentary, essay, feature, op-ed piece, opinion, piece, viewpoint

coma *n.* blackout, catatonia, insensibility, swoon, syncope, torpor, unconsciousness

comatose *adj.* **1.** cataleptic, catatonic, drugged, insensible, otiose, out, out cold, prostrate *(Nonformal)*, senseless, soporose, torpid, unconscious *Antonyms:* awake, aware, conscious **2.** dopey *(Nonformal)*, drowsy, lethargic, phlegmatic, sleepy *Antonyms:* alert, energetic

comb *n.* **1.** currycomb, grooming device, pick, rake, toothed strip **2.** crest, feather, plume, ridge, spine – *v.* **1.** arrange, brush, curry, disentangle, fix, groom, smooth, straighten, tidy, unsnarl, untangle **2.** beat the bushes *(Nonformal)*, forage, hunt, scour, search, search out, seek **3.** inspect, investigate, probe, rummage, sift through, screen, scrutinize

combat *n.* **1.** battle, brawl, conflict, contest, dispute, duel, encounter, engagement, fight, fray, skirmish, sortie *Kinds of personal combat sports:* arm *or* wrist wrestling, boxing, fencing, Greco-Roman wrestling, jousting, judo, jujitsu, karate, kick boxing, kung-fu, martial arts, stick fighting, sumo wrestling, tae kwon do, wrestling *Antonyms:* agreement, armistice, peace, surrender, truce **2.** fighting, hostilities, military operation *or* theatre, war, warfare, wartime – *v.* **1.** buck, clash, contest, defy, dispute, do battle, fight, go up against, grapple, oppose, take on, take the field, wage war **2.** contend, fight off, impede, obstruct, oppose, resist, struggle

combatant *adj.* belligerent, pugnacious, ready to fight – *n.* aggressor, assailant, competitor, contender, contestant, enemy, fighter, foe, gladiator, knight, militarist, participant, person-at-arms, plaintiff, pugilist, rival, soldier, warrior

combative *adj.* aggressive, antagonistic, bellicose, belligerent, cantankerous, contentious, fractious, hawkish, hostile, inimical, militant, ornery, pugnacious, quarrelsome, scrappy, trigger-happy *(Nonformal)*, warlike *Antonyms:* harmonious, pacifist, peaceful

combination *n.* **1.** amalgamation, blending, composite, compound, homogeny, synthesis, unification, union **2.** affiliation, alliance, association, bloc, cabal, cartel, circle, clique, club, coalition, combine, confederacy, confederation, conjunction, connection, consolidation, consortium, conspiracy, coterie, federation, gang, guild, hansa, hookup *(Nonformal)*, league, merger, partnership, party, pool, ring, set, syndicate, trust, unification, union **3.** blend, hodgepodge, jumble, medley, mélange, miscellany, mishmash, mix, mixture, mosaic, olio, patchwork, potpourri, stew **4.** line, order, sequence, succession

combine *n.* aggregate, array, collection, consortium, gang, group, ring – *v.* **1.** ally, amalgamate, band together, bind, blend, bracket, bunch up, coalesce, commingle, cooperate, couple, fuse, get together, incorporate, intermix, join, join forces, link up, marry, merge, mix, pool, tack *or* tag on, team *or* tie up with, unionize, unite, wed *Antonyms:* detach, dissociate, dissolve, divide, part **2.** assemble, compose, connect, put together, synthesize, throw together

combustible *adj.* **1.** burnable, combustive, easily ignited, explosive, fiery, flammable, ignitable, incendiary, inflammable *Antonyms:* noncombustible, non-flammable, soaking wet *(Nonformal)* **2.** anxious, edgy, excited, high-strung, hot-headed, peppery, volatile *Antonyms:* calm, even-tempered, serene

combustion *n.* agitation, blaze, burning, conflagration, disturbance, explosion, fire, flame, ignition, kindling, oxidization, pyrolysis, thermogenesis, tumult

come *v.* **1.** approach, bear down on, close *or* fall in, draw near, move hither *or* to *or* towards **2.** appear, arrive, breeze *or* burst in, buzz in *(Nonformal)*, check *or* clock in, drop by, hit town, punch *or* roll *or* sign in, show up **3.** befall, conclude, end up, fare, happen, occur, proceed, prove *or* work out, result, take place, transpire **4.** cover, extend, go, range, reach, travel **5.** derive, emanate, emerge, ensue, flow, follow, issue, spring forth, stem **6.** advance, emerge, move into view, step forward

comeback *n.* **1.** answer, gibe, lip *(Nonformal)*, rejoinder, repartee, reply, response, retaliation, retort, riposte **2.** improvement, rally, rebound, recovery, resurgence, return, revival, victory, win

comedian *n.* actor, clown, comic, entertainer, *farceur (French)*, funnyman, funnywoman, humorist, jester, joker, jokester, prankster, quipster, stand-up comic, wag, wit, zany *Nonformal:* cutup, wisecracker

comedown *n.* blow, collapse, comeuppance, crash, decline, defeat, disappointment, downfall, failure, flop, letdown, reverse, setback *Antonyms:* ascent, promotion, success

comedy *n.* drollery, facetiousness, fun, hilarity, humour, jesting, joking, laughs *(Nonformal)*, levity, wit *Kinds of comedy:* black, burlesque, camp, caricature, *commedia dell'arte (Italian)*, domestic, drawing-room, errors, farce, harlequinade, impersonation, lampoon, low, madcap, manners, musical, pantomime, parody, romantic, satire, screwball, sentimental, situation comedy (sit-com), slapstick, stand-up, vaudeville *Antonyms:* adversity, catastrophe, drama, humiliation, tragedy

comely *adj.* **1.** agreeable, alluring, appealing, attractive, beauteous, beautiful, becoming, blooming, bonny, exquisite, fair, fetching, fine, glowing, good-looking, handsome, lovely, pleasing, pretty, pulchritudinous, radiant, sightly, whistle bait *(Nonformal) Antonyms:* homely, plain, ugly **2.** cultivated, decent, decorous, dignified, fitting, formal, mannerly, moral, personable, polished, polite, prim, punctilious, refined, respectful, sedate, suitable, urbane *Antonyms:* disrespectful, pert, rude, tasteless

comet *n.* celestial body, meteor, meteorite, orb *Names of comets:* Bennett's, Biela's, Giacobini-Zinner, Encke's, Hale-Bopp, Halley's, Kohoutek's, Meier's, Van den Bergh's, West's

comfort *adj.* alleviating, assuasive, easing, mitigating, palliative, relieving, remedial, rest, soothing – *n.* **1.** aid, balm, commiseration, consolation, help, mollifying *or* placating *or* soothing words, reassurance, relief, solace, succour, sympathy *Antonyms:* annoyance, irritant, nuisance, torment **2.** cheer, contentment, ease, enjoyment, gratification, peace, pleasure, relaxation, repose, satisfaction, serenity, tranquility, well-being *Antonyms:* anxiousness, discontent, distress, restlessness, unease **3.** accoutrement, indulgence, luxury, richness, sumptuousness *Antonyms:* barrenness, emptiness, poverty, starkness – *v.* **1.** allay, alleviate, ameliorate, assuage, calm, console, ease, lull, quiet, relieve, soothe *Antonyms:* aggravate, agitate, bother, intensify, irk **2.** aid, assist, bolster *or* brace up, buttress, encourage, hearten, restore, support, sustain *Antonyms:* ruin, sabotage, sap, subvert, undermine

comfortable *adj.* **1.** accepting, at ease, content, pleased, quiescent, satisfied, serene *Antonyms:* at odds, disapproving, unhappy **2.** casual, homey, livable, loose-fitting, relaxed, snug, unpretentious, workaday *Antonyms:* black *or* white tie, ceremonial, formal, ritual **3.** affluent, easy, in the lap of luxury, moneyed, prosperous, rich, well-off *or* -to-do, well-situated *or* -fixed *Nonformal:* loaded, on easy street *Antonyms:* destitute, hardscrabble, impecunious, impoverished, indigent

comic *adj.* droll, funny, hilarious, humorous, ridiculous, silly – *n.* **1.** cartoon, comic *or* funny *or* picture book, comic strip, graphic novel, magazine, *manga (Japanese)*, sequential art *Nonformal:* funnies, strip **2.** clown, comedian, jester, joker, prankster, satirist, stand-up comedian *or* comic, wit

comical *adj.* absurd, amusing, camp, entertaining, facetious, farcical, funny, humorous, jocular, joking, joshing, laughable, ludicrous, priceless, ridiculous, sidesplitting, waggish, witty *Nonformal:* loony, nutty, wacky *Antonyms:* dramatic, sad, serious, unamusing

coming *adj.* **1.** advancing, anticipated, approaching, at hand, close, converging, drawing near, due, en route, eventual, expected, fated, foreseen, forthcoming, getting near, immediate, imminent, impending, incipient, near, nearing, next, nigh, on the horizon, predestined, preparing, prospective, subsequent *Antonyms:* departing, going, leaving, retreating **2.** aspiring, deserving, developing, emerging, enterprising, future, in the ascendant, promising, rising, up-and-coming *Antonyms:* commonplace, lacklustre, mediocre, run-of-the-mill – *n.* accession, advent, appearance, approach, arrival, entrance, landing

command *n.* **1.** authority, charge, control, dominance, dominion, government, jurisdiction, leadership, mastership, mastery, might, power, prerogative, regulation, right, rule, ruling, say-so *(Nonformal)*, sovereignty, supremacy, sway, will **2.** behest, bidding, call, charge, decree, demand, dictate, direction, edict, fiat, imperative, instruction, law, mandate, order, ordinance, proclamation, requisition, rule, summons, ultimatum, warrant, will, word, writ **3.** comprehension, grasp, knowledge, skill, understanding – *v.* **1.** appoint, assign, authorize, bid, call upon, charge, decree, demand, direct, enjoin, give the order, instruct, invite, order, require **2.** administer, boss, conquer, control, govern, guide, lead, power, preside over, rule, supervise, wield **3.** compel, exact, force, insist upon, requisition **4.** cap, crown, dominate, dwarf, eclipse, overlook, overshadow, top, tower over, transcend

commander *n.* administrator, admiral, boss, captain, chief, commandant, commissioned officer, czar, director, field marshall, general, head, high priest, king, leader, lord, manager, *maréchal (French)*, master, president, ruler, ship's captain *or* officer, shogun, skipper *Nonformal:* big cheese, head honcho, higher-up, kingpin, top banana *or* brass *or* dog

commandeer *v.* **1.** attach, confiscate, expropriate, garnishee, impound, seize, sequester, take over **2.** abduct, draft, impress, kidnap, press, shanghai

commanding *adj.* **1.** august, authoritative, autocratic, demanding, forceful, imperious, imposing, masterful, noble, peremptory, potent, powerful, self-assured, self-confident *Antonyms:* retiring, shrinking, shy, submissive, timid **2.** administrating, controlling, directing, governing, heading, leading, managing, mandating, ruling, supervising **3.** awesome, expansive, extensive, far-reaching *or* sighted, impressive, majestic, wide

commemorate *v.* acclaim, admire, celebrate, eulogize, exalt, extol, glorify, honour, immortalize, laud, memorialize, pay tribute to, perpetuate, praise, remember, salute, sanctify, sing the praises of, solemnize *Antonyms:* criticize, deride, forget, lambaste

commemoration *n.* **1.** celebration, ceremony, festivity, holiday **2.** anniversary, celebration, festschrift, funeral, homage, honour, memorial service, remembrance, salute, tribute, wake **3.** gravestone, historical marker, marker, plaque, relic, stone

commemorative *adj.* celebratory, ceremonial, honouring, memorial, observing, remembering, solemn

commence *v.* begin, break ground, dive in *(Nonformal)*, embark on, enter into *or* upon, establish, inaugurate, initiate, instigate, launch, open, originate, pioneer, set about *or* in motion, start, turn on *Antonyms:* cease, complete, conclude, desist

commend *v.* **1.** accredit, advocate, boost, bring to one's attention, build up, endorse, promote, put in a good word for, introduce, recommend, speak well *or* highly of, support, vouch for *Antonyms:* eschew, forswear, renounce, repudiate **2.** bestow, commit, consign, entrust, invest, put in one's care, trust **3.** acclaim, applaud, celebrate, extol, hail, laud, lionize, praise *Antonyms:* defame, denigrate, impugn, malign **4.** greet, present regards *or* respect, remember, salute, say hello

commendable *adj.* admirable, creditable, deserving, estimable, excellent, exemplary, laudable, meritorious, praiseworthy, principled, respectable, sterling, worthy *Antonyms:* disgraceful, ignominious

commendation *n.* **1.** acclaim, acclamation, advocacy, approbation, approval, credit, endorsement, good opinion *or* word, honour, kudos, laurels, panegyric, praise, promotion, recommendation, reference, sanction, tribute **2.** badge, certificate, medal, plaque, ribbon, trophy

commensurate *adj.* **1.** balanced, coextensive, concordant, concurring, consistent, corresponding, equal, equivalent, even, harmonious, matching, parallel, on the same plane, synchronous *Antonyms:* disparate, incompatible, unequal **2.** adequate, appropriate, competent, enough, fitting, in keeping, okay *(Nonformal)*, proportionate *Antonyms:* deficient, inadequate, wanting

comment *n.* **1.** annotation, criticism, critique, elucidation, footnote, interpolation, marginalia, note, review **2.** answer, aside, comeback, crack, observation, opinion, pronouncement, reaction, remark, reply, response, statement – *v.* **1.** address, declare, expound, interject, mention, observe, opine, reflect, remark, say, speak, speak to, touch upon **2.** clarify, explain, illuminate, illustrate, interpret

commentary *n.* **1.** analysis, breakdown, colour, critical treatment, criticism, critique, discourse, editorial, elucidation, explanation, explanatory *or* illustrative notes, observation, remark, review, study, write-up *(Nonformal)* **2.** annotation, exegesis, explication, footnote, gloss, scholia

commentator *n.* analyst, annotator, broadcaster, columnist, correspondent, critic, expositor, interpreter, observer, pundit, reporter, reviewer, sportscaster, writer

commerce *n.* **1.** business, buying and selling, commercialism, dealings, exchange, marketing, merchandising, selling, trade, traffic, transaction, truck *(Nonformal)* **2.** association, colloquy, communication, communion, congress, connection, conversation, dialogue, discussion, fellowship, interchange, intercourse, interface, interlocution, parley

commercial *adj.* **1.** business, entrepreneurial, marketable, mercantile, profitable, profit-making, saleable, trading, wholesaling **2.** avaricious, greedy, materialistic, mercenary, rapacious – *n.* ad *or* advertisement, broadcast, informercial *Nonformal:* pitch *or* sales pitch, plug, spot

commercialize *v.* capitalize, cash in on *(Nonformal)*, make money, make profitable *or* saleable, market, realize, sell

commingle *v.* admix, amalgamate, blend, combine, compound, fuse, integrate, intermingle, intermix, join, merge, mingle, mix, unite *Antonyms:* divide, separate, sever

commiserate *v.* ache, comfort, console, empathize, feel, feel for, pity, soothe, sympathize

commission *n.* **1.** agency, appointed *or* legislated body, assembly, board, board of inquiry, cabinet, committee, council, delegation, legation **2.** assignment, business, business at hand, charge, command, direction, duty, errand, obligation, task **3.** authority, certificate *or* certification, charter, decree, degree, diploma, edict, licence, papers, permit, writ **4.** allotment, compensation, fee, pay, remuneration, share *Nonformal:* cut, piece of the action **5.** accomplishment, act, deed, enactment, execution, performance – *v.* **1.** accredit, appoint, assign, authorize, decree, delegate, empower, enact, license **2.** book, contract for, finance, order, purchase, requisition, underwrite **3.** anoint, baptize, christen, consecrate, dedicate, inaugurate, launch, name **4.** bestow, commit, consign, deliver, entrust, fit out, fix up, make ready, provision, supply

commit *v.* **1.** accomplish, achieve, act, carry out, complete, do, effectuate, enact, execute, perform, perpetrate, pull, pull off, wreak **2.** allocate, allot, bestow, charge, commend, confide, consign, convey, delegate, deliver, deposit, devote, dispatch, entrust, give, grant, hand over, invest, leave to, preserve, refer, rely upon, send, submit, transfer *Antonyms:* receive, release, withhold **3.** assure, attest, certify, guarantee, insure, pledge, promise, swear, vouch, vow *Antonyms:* disavow, disclaim, forswear, renounce, repudiate **4.** bind, confine, hospitalize, ice *(Nonformal)*, imprison, incarcerate, institutionalize, place in detention, put away, take into custody **5.** conclude, determine, make up one's mind, resolve, settle, take a stand *Antonyms:* dither, equivocate, prevaricate, waffle

commitment *n.* **1.** assignment *or* business to attend to, duty, engagement, obligation, responsibility, undertaking, work **2.** assurance, covenant, guarantee, pledge, promise, vow, warrant, word **3.** confinement, custody, detention, hospitalization, incarceration, institutionalization, internment, mittimus *(Legal)*, remand *Antonyms:* emancipation, freedom, release **4.** ardour, dedication, devotion, enthusiasm, fervency, passion, sincerity, spirit, vehemence, zeal *Antonyms:* indifference, sang-froid, selfishness

committee *n.* advisory board, body, body of persons, consultants, delegation, detail, group, jury, panel, task force

commodious *adj.* abundant, ample, big, capacious, comfortable, expansive, extensive, great, large, loose, plenty, roomy, spacious, vast, wide *Antonyms:* pinched, restrictive, small, tight

commodity *n.* article of trade, asset, belonging, chattel, goods, item, line, material, merchandise, produce, product, property, resource, staple, stock, ware

common *adj.* **1.** accepted, accustomed, conventional, correct, customary, expected, familiar, standard, traditional, usual *Antonyms:* aberrant, abnormal, deviant, perverse **2.** acknowledged, established, general, known *or* well-known, prevailing, understood, universal, widespread *Antonyms:* exclusive, hermetic, hidden, limited, obscure **3.** average, colloquial, demotic, garden variety, everyday *or* workaday, humdrum, nondescript, ordinary, plain, regular, simple, unexceptional, vernacular *Antonyms:* bizarre, eccentric, esoteric, fantastic, outlandish **4.** collective, communal, joint, mutual, shared *Antonyms:* distinct, individual, lone, solitary **5.** base, cheap, coarse, ignoble, ill-bred, low, mean, tawdry **6.** chronic, confirmed, habitual, hardened, inveterate, recurrent **7.** dime-a-dozen, hackneyed, overused, pedestrian, schmaltzy, stale, stereotypical, trite, well-trodden **8.** civic, municipal, public – *n.* campus, green, village green, greenspace, park, quadrangle, square

commonplace *adj.* characterless, clichéd, colourless, hackneyed, humdrum, mediocre, middling, mundane, ordinary, pedestrian, prosaic, sober, stereotyped, tame, threadbare, trite, unexceptional, uninteresting, unnoteworthy *Nonformal:* boilerplate, run-of-the-mill *Antonyms:* exciting, extraordinary, interesting, strange, unusual – *n.* **1.** adage, axiom, maxim, notable passage *or* extract, truism **2.** banality, bromide, cliché, convention, familiarity, old chestnut, platitude

commonsense *adj.* astute, cool *(Nonformal)*, discerning, down-to-earth, judicious, levelheaded, matter-of-fact, practical, pragmatic, prudent, rational, realistic, reasonable, sane, sensible, shrewd, sound *Antonyms:* daft, foolish, impractical, irrational, unreasonable

commotion *n.* **1.** agitation, bedlam, bustle, clamour, clatter, confusion, disturbance, dither, furore, fuss, outcry, pandemonium, racket, rumpus, stir, tumult *Nonformal:* big stink, bother, brouhaha, flap, foofaraw, hoo-ha, to-do **2.** brawl, donnybrook, fight, fisticuffs *(Nonformal)*, imbroglio, mêlée, row, rumble **3.** insurgence, insurrection, mutiny, rebellion, revolt, riot, uprising

communal *adj.* civic, collective, common, community, cooperative, general, joint, mutual, neighbourhood, shared *Antonyms:* exclusive, individual, personal, private, single

commune *n.* **1.** bloc, collective, commonality, cooperative, co-op, family, kibbutz **2.** municipality, neighbourhood, town, township, village – *v.* **1.** confer, confide, converse, discourse, discuss, have a word with, negotiate, parley **2.** contemplate, mediate, muse, ponder, reflect, relate to

communicable *adj.* **1.** catching, contagious, contractible, infectious, pandemic, pestilential, transferable, transmittable *Antonyms:* isolated, nontransferable

communicate *v.* **1.** acquaint, advertise, advise, announce, apprise, blurt out, bring out *or* up, broadcast, come out with, convey, disclose, divulge, enlighten, give notice *or* word to, inform, lay open, make known, mention, notify, pass along, proclaim, publicize, publish, put about *or* forth *or* out, relate, report, set forth *or* out, speak, state, tell, verbalize, vocalize *Antonyms:* censor, inhibit, muzzle, silence, withhold **2.** hint, impart, imply, intimate, reveal, signify, suggest *Antonyms:* cloak, conceal, hide, mask **3.** infect, infest, pass on to, spread, transfer, transmit **4.** bestow, confer, deliver, grant, offer, proffer *Antonyms:* hang onto, keep, retain **5.** be in touch with, call, connect with, chat, contract, correspond, deal with, dial, e-mail, exchange views, fax, get in touch with, have commerce *or* intercourse with, interact, interchange, interface, network, phone, reach, ring up, touch base, write *Nonformal:* confab, gab, get on the horn

communication *adj.* language, linguistic, speaking, speech, verbal – *n.* **1.** announcement, articulation, disclosure, discussion, dissemination, exchange, interchange, intercourse, publication, traffic, transference, transmission **2.** contents, data, information, tidings *Nonformal:* goods, info, lowdown, poop, scoop, skinny **3.** announcement, brief, bulletin, code, communiqué, directive, dispatch, e-mail, facsimile, fax, flyer, handbill, letter, memo *or* memorandum, message, missive, note, statement, story **4.** channel, conduit, course, line *or* line of connection, path

communications *n.* broadcasting, information, journalism, magazines, media, news, *newspapers*, PR *(Nonformal)*, press, print, publicity, public relations, radio, television, webcasting

communicative *adj.* **1.** barkative *(P.E.I.)*, chatty, conversational, effusive, expansive, gabby, garrulous, gushing, loquacious, outgoing, talkative, voluble *Antonyms:* quiet, reserved, reticent, secretive, taciturn, tight-lipped **2.** candid, forthcoming, frank, gregarious, open, straightforward, unreserved **3.** enlightening, good to know, informative, instructive, revealing

communion *n.* **1.** accord, affinity, agreement, association, closeness, close relationship, cooperation, fellowship, friendship, harmony, intercourse, intimacy, rapport, sharing, sympathy, synergy, togetherness, unity **2.** bread and wine, the Body of Christ, the breaking of bread, the Eucharist

Communism *n.* Bolshevism, collective *or* public *or* state ownership, collectivism, social democracy, socialism, state socialism *Kinds of Communism:* Fourierism, Maoism, Marxism, Marxist-Leninism, Sovietism, Trotskyism

Communist *adj. & n.* Bolshevik, Bolshevist, collectivist, communalist, Fourierist, leftist, Leninist, Marxist, socialist, Trotskyite *Nonformal:* bolshie, commie, lefty, pinko, Red

community *n.* **1.** centre, city, colony, commune, crossroads, district, hamlet, locality, metropolis, neighbourhood, outport, settlement, territory, town, turf *(Nonformal)*, village, *ville (French)* **2.** association, band, body politic, brotherhood, citizenry, clan, class, cloister, commonwealth, company, constituency, coterie, class, family, federation, folk, general public, guild, league, lodge, nation, people, populace, public, residents, sisterhood, social class, society, state, totemic *or* totemistic group, tribe **3.** co-tenancy, joint ownership *or* possession, partnership **4.** accord, affinity, agreement, amity, commonality, fellowship, harmony, homogeneity, identity, kinship, likeness, sameness, semblance, similarity, unity

commute *v.* **1.** carpool, drive, shuttle, take the train, taxi, transit *Nonformal:* bus *or* hoof *or* subway it, ride the red rocket *(Toronto)*, straphang **2.** curtail, decrease, diminish, lighten, reduce, shorten **3.** adjust, alter, exchange, modify, substitute

compact *adj.* **1.** bunched, chock-full, close-knit, congested, crammed, crowded, dense, fine-grained, packed *or* pressed tightly together, snug, solid, stuffed, tight **2.** brief, concise, condensed, cryptic, laconic, pithy, short, succinct, terse, to the point *Nonformal:* boiled down, in a nutshell, short and sweet *Antonyms:* garrulous, prolix, rambling **3.** bantam, capsule, diminutive, pocket, pocket-sized, portable, short, small-scale, transportable, trim *Antonyms:* commodious, full-size, large, sprawling – *n.* **1.** agreement, bargain, concordance, covenant, entente, handshake, pact **2.** makeup *or* powder case, vanity – *v.* amalgamate, bind, cement, compress, concentrate, condense, consolidate, pack together, press closely, squeeze together *Antonyms:* disperse, loosen, separate

companion *n.* **1.** accomplice, ally, amigo, associate, buddy, chum, colleague, comrade, confederate, confrère, consort, co-worker, crony, fellow, friend, playmate, twin *Nonformal:* pal, roomie, sidekick **2.** aide, assistant, attendant, au pair, chaperon, duenna, escort, nanny, nurse, tutor, underling **3.** guidebook, tour *or* handbook, travel guide *Trademarks:* Baedeker, Blue Guide, Fodor's, Lonely Planet, Michelin, Rough Guide **4.** counterpart, match, mate, partner, twin – *v.* accompany, chaperone, escort, hang with *(Nonformal)*, pilot, shepherd, squire, steer, usher

companionable *adj.* affable, agreeable, amicable, congenial, convivial, cordial, cozy, familiar, friendly, genial, good-natured, gregarious, intimate, neighbourly, sociable, social *Nonformal:* clubby, tight *Antonyms:* aloof, reclusive, taciturn

companionship *n.* amity, camaraderie, comradeship, conviviality, fellowship, fraternity, fraternization, friendship, harmony, togetherness

company *n.* **1.** assemblage, bloc, body, caucus, cavalcade, congregation, congress, contingent, crowd, group, host, multitude **2.** alliance, assembly, circle, clique, faction, gathering, guild, league, society, The 100 *(Historical)*, union **3.** celebrants, guest list, guests, merrymakers, party-goers, visitors **4.** companionship, fellowship, friendship, presence, *Antonyms:* loneliness, solitude **5.** business, concern, conglomerate, corporation, enterprise, establishment, firm, house, institution **6.** affiliates, associates, cohorts, co-workers, partners **7.** actors, cast, chorus, dramatis personae, ensemble, performers, troupe **8.** battery, detachment, patrol, platoon, section, squad, troop **9.** crew, messmates, sailors, team, unit

comparable *adj.* **1.** affined, akin, alike, allied, analogous, cognate, corresponding, equivalent, fitting, harmonious, kindred, like, near, parallel, proportionate, related, resembling, similar, symmetrical *Antonyms:* different, dissimilar, divergent, unequal **2.** commensurate, identical, tantamount, the same as, uniform

comparative *adj.* **1.** analogous, approaching, approximate, connected, correlative, corresponding, equivalent, in proportion, like, matching, near, parallel, proximate, related, similar, vying *Antonyms:* dissimilar, distinct, diverse, incongruous, unrelated **2.** contingent, estimated, guesstimate, hypothetical, not absolute, provisional, qualified, relative

compare *v.* **1.** balance, contrast, differentiate, discern, equate, juxtapose, liken, link, measure, set *or* stack against, verify, weigh **2.** associate *or* identify with, correspond, look like, resemble, take after **3.** analyze, consider, contemplate, examine, inspect, mull over, observe, scrutinize, sort out, study

comparison *n.* **1.** apposition, contrast, differentiation, juxtaposition, opposition, segregation, separation, weighing **2.** analysis, appraisal, assessment, consideration, estimate, judgment, measurement, opposition, review, testing **3.** agreement, association, connection, correlation, correspondence, kinship, likeness, match, parallel, relation, resemblance, similarity, similitude **4.** allegory, analogy, illustration, metaphor, simile, similitude

compartment *n.* alcove, bay, berth, booth, carrel, cell, chamber, corner, cubbyhole, cubicle, department, division, niche, nook, part, piece, pigeonhole, place, portion, section, slot, stall, subdivision

compass *n.* **1.** ambit, area, circuit, district, domain, expanse, extent, field, purview, radius, realm, sphere, stretch, sweep **2.** detector, direction finder, Global Positioning System *or* GPS, guide, gyrocompass, loran, magnetic guide, navigation device, needle, range, ratio direction finder *or* RDF, reach, scale, shoran, spectrum **3.** border, bound, boundary, bounds, circumference, girth, limit, perimeter, periphery, rim – *v.* **1.** circle, circuit, circumambulate, revolve, rotate **2.** contain, cordon, corral, encircle, enclose, encompass, ensphere, envelop, environ, girdle, surround **3.** apprehend, comprehend, discern, fathom, grasp, perceive, realize, seize, understand **4.** accomplish, achieve, attain, consummate, do, enact, execute, fulfill, gain, make, perform, produce, pull off *(Nonformal)*, reach, realize, succeed **5.** cabal, concoct, conspire, design, devise, frame, hatch, machinate, plan, plot, scheme

compassion *n.* benevolence, charity, clemency, commiseration, condolence, consideration, empathy, feeling, grace, heart, humanity, kindness, lenity, magnanimity, mercy, pity, ruth, soft-heartedness, softness, sympathy, tenderness, understanding *Antonyms:* apathy, cold-heartedness, disinterest, indifference

compassionate *adj.* benevolent, caring, charitable, concerned, considerate, forbearing, gracious, humane, indulgent, kind-hearted, kindly, lenient, merciful, pitying, responsive, soft-hearted, sympathetic, tender, tender-hearted, understanding, warm, warmhearted *Antonyms:* callous, heartless, inhumane, pitiless, uncaring

compatible *adj.* **1.** agreeable, congenial, cooperative, fitting, in sync *(Nonformal)*, like-minded, reconcilable, simpatico, suitable, sympathetic, well-matched, well-suited *Antonyms:* antagonistic, at odds, incompatible **2.** accordant, concordant, conforming, congruent, consistent, consonant, correspondent, harmonious, in keeping, synchronized, undeviating *Antonyms:* contradictory, divergent, inconsistent **3.** adaptable, analogous, comparable, like, matching, parallel, related, similar *Antonyms:* different, opposite

compel *v.* **1.** bulldoze *(Nonformal)*, coerce, cooperate, demand, dragoon, enforce, enjoin, exact, force, impel, induce, insist, intimidate, make, necessitate, oblige, pressure, railroad, squeeze, urge *Antonyms:* hinder, prevent, restrain **2.** conquer, defeat, overpower, overrun, overthrow, overwhelm, rout, squash, vanquish **3.** drive, guide, herd, hustle, move, press, propel, push, shepherd

compelling *adj.* **1.** animating, arousing, engaging, enthralling, exciting, galvanizing, inspiring, motivating, moving, provoking, rousing, seductive, spellbinding, stimulating, stirring, touching *Antonyms:* boring, dull, soporific **2.** cogent, conclusive, convincing, effective, efficacious, forceful, incontrovertible, influential, persuasive, pointed, powerful, telling, weighty *Antonyms:* ineffective, unsuccessful, vain **3.** acute, burning, critical, crucial, imperative, important, life-and-death, pressing, unavoidable, urgent *Antonyms:* insignificant, petty, trivial

compendious *adj.* abridged, brief, close, compact, concise, condensed, contracted, digested, direct, epigrammatic, laconic, short, succinct, summarized, summary, synoptic, terse *Antonyms:* lengthy, prolix, sweeping

compendium *n.* **1.** addition, anthology, collection, compilation, garland, omnibus, selected works, selection **2.** abridgement, abstract, capsulization, digest, précis, syllabus

compensate *v.* **1.** cover, indemnify, pay, pay back *or* up, recompense, refund, reimburse, remunerate, repay, requite, satisfy, shell out **2.** atone, make amends *or* good, redress, repair **3.** balance, cancel out, counteract, counterbalance, counterpoise, countervail, equalize, negate, neutralize, nullify, offset, set off, stabilize **4.** avenge, better, get even, retaliate, seek justice, square accounts, strike back, wreak vengeance

compensation *n.* **1.** allowance, benefit, bonus, commission, dispensation, earnings, fee, honorarium, income, net, pay, payment, pittance, profit, recompense, remittance, remuneration, reward, royalty, salary, stipend, take, take-home, tip, wages **2.** adjustment, cost, coverage, damage, defrayal, fine, indemnity, penalty, premium, recompense, reimbursement, repayment, satisfaction, settlement **3.** amends, atonement, blood money, redress, reparation, restitution **4.** reciprocation, reprisal, retaliation, revenge, vendetta, vengeance **5.** balance, counterbalance, equivalent, neutralization, nullification, offsetting, symmetry

compete *v.* attempt, bandy, battle, bid, challenge, clash, confront, contend, contest, dispute, face off, fence, fight, go for, grapple, have at, joust, lock horns *(Nonformal)*, match, meet, oppose, oppugn, pit against, play, rival, spar, strive, struggle, take on, tangle with, trade, try, tug, tussle, vie, wrestle *Antonyms:* cooperate, harmonize, support

competence *n.* **1.** ability, adequacy, capability, capacity, competency, expertise, fitness, know-how, makings, means, might, proficiency, qualification, skill, suitability, wherewithal *Nonformal:* goods, moxie, savvy *Antonyms:* inability, incompetence, inefficiency **2.** adequacy, capital, earnings, fortune, funds, income, jointure, living standard, means, moolah *(Nonformal)*, sufficiency, wealth **3.** allowance, authority, jurisdiction, power

competent *adj.* **1.** able, accomplished, adapted, *au fait (French)*, capable, clever, complete, conversant, dexterous, educated, efficient, endowed, knowledgeable, masterly, polished, proficient, qualified, skilled, trained, versed *Nonformal:* dynamite, savvy *Antonyms:* incompetent, unqualified, unskilled **2.** accredited, approved, authorized, carded *(Nonformal)*, certified, established, sanctioned **3.** adequate, appropriate, fair, fit, good, middling, okay *(Nonformal)*, passing, proper, satisfactory, sufficient, suitable *Antonyms:* insufficient, unsuitable, wrong **4.** coherent, *compos mentis (Latin)*, lucid, responsible, sane, sound

competition *n.* **1.** bee, bonspiel, bout, candidacy, championship, clash, contention, contest, duel, encounter, engagement, event, face-off, fight, game, joust, match, meeting, pairing off, penalty shot, playdown, race, rivalry, round robin, run, show, strife, striving, struggle, tournament, trial, tug-of-war *Nonformal:* gunfight, horserace, sudden death **2.** adversary, antagonist, challenger, contender, contestant, enemy, nemesis, opponent, opposition, rival *Antonyms:* ally, associate, partner

competitive *adj.* aggressive, ambitious, antagonistic, belligerent, combative, contentious, cutthroat, dog-eat-dog *(Nonformal)*, enterprising, hawkish, opposing, rival, vying *Antonyms:* apathetic, cooperative, unaspiring

competitor *n.* adversary, aspirant, candidate, challenger, contestant, dark horse *(Nonformal)*, disputant, entrant, foe, match, opponent, opposition, rival, vier

compilation *n.* accumulation, aggregation, album, anthology, assemblage, assortment, collected *or* selected works, collection, compendium, Festschrift, garnering, gathering, greatest hits *(Nonformal)*, incorporation, miscellanea, miscellany, omnibus, scrapbook, selection, suite, symposium, treasury

compile *v.* accumulate, amass, anthologize, arrange, assemble, collate, collect, concentrate, congregate, consolidate, edit, garner, gather, glean, group, marshal, muster, organize, select, unite *Antonyms:* diffuse, disassemble, disperse, scatter

complacent *adj.* **1.** arrogant, cocky, conceited, confident, contented, egotistic, gratified, pleased, pretentious, proud, satisfied, self-assured, self-righteous, self-satisfied, smug, vain *Antonyms:* gracious, humble, self-effacing **2.** calm, collected, comfortable, composed, content, easygoing, impassive, settled *Antonyms:* agitated, anxious, excited *Commonly misused:* **complaisant**

complain *v.* bemoan, carp, caterwaul, cavil, criticize, denounce, deplore, deprecate, disagree, disapprove, execrate, fight, find fault, fret, fuss, gainsay, grieve, gripe, groan, grouch, grumble, inveigh, lament, moan, mumble, murmur, mutter, nag, object, oppose, protest, remonstrate, reproach, resist, scold, sigh, snivel, spurn, squawk, wail, whine *Nonformal:* beef, bitch, crab, grouse, kick, kvetch, tsk-tsk *or* tut-tut *Antonyms:* accept, approve, praise

complaint *n.* **1.** annoyance, cavil, clamour, criticism, disagreement, dissatisfaction, faultfinding, grumbling, jeremiad, lament, moan, objection, protest, protestation, remonstrance, reproach, trouble, wail, whine *Nonformal:* beef, bitch, squawk **2.** accusation, action, charge, claim, grievance, indictment, suit **3.** affliction, ailment, condition, disease, disorder, illness, indisposition, infirmity, malady, sickness, syndrome, trouble

complaisance *n.* acquiescence, agreeableness, amiability, compliance, considerateness, courtesy, couth, decorum, deference, flexibility, friendliness, geniality, grace, graciousness, kindness, politeness, respect, sociability *Antonyms:* churlishness, disrespect, rudeness

complaisant *adj.* accommodating, agreeable, amiable, compliant, conciliatory, courteous, deferential, easy, easygoing, friendly, generous, good-natured, good-tempered, indulgent, lenient, mild, obliging, polite, solicitous, submissive, yielding *Antonyms:* churlish, obstinate, perverse *Commonly misused:* **complacent**

complement *n.* **1.** completion, consummation, enhancement, enrichment, finishing touch, last piece, rounding off **2.** accompaniment, addition, adjunct, background, companion, correlate, counterpart, equivalent, fellow, match, pendant, remainder, supplement, twin **3.** aggregate, all, allowance, balance, capacity, company, crew, entirety, outfit, quota, team, total – *v.* **1.** accomplish, achieve, clinch, close, complete, conclude, consummate, crown, fill, finish, fulfill, perfect, round *or* top off **2.** add, append, augment, boost, enhance, supplement, supply *Commonly misused:* **compliment**

complementary *adj.* **1.** analogous, companion, complemental, correlative, correspondent, equivalent, integral, interconnected, interdependent, interrelated, matched, mated, mutual, paired, parallel, reciprocal, twin *Antonyms:* contradictory, different, incompatible, incongruous **2.** closing, completing, culminating, finishing, fulfilling *Commonly misused:* **complimentary**

complete *adj.* **1.** accomplished, achieved, capped, compassed, concluded, consummated, determined, done, effected, ended, executed, exhausted, *finis (French)*, *finito (Italian)*, home free *(Nonformal)*, realized *Antonyms:* fragmentary, partial **2.** exact, excellent, exemplary, exhaustive, faultless, flawless, ideal, optimal, perfect, pure, supreme, thorough, undiminished, undivided *Antonyms:* deficient, incomplete **3.** absolute, all, entire, full, gross, intact, integral, plenary, replete, total, unabbreviated, unabridged, uncut, whole *Antonyms:* deficient, incomplete **4.** all-out, categorical, full-blown, full-fledged, full-scale, maximum, outright, tutti, unmitigated, utter – *v.* **1.** accomplish, achieve, act, actualize, administer, answer, bring about *or* off, carry through, close, complete, conclude, consummate, crown, discharge, dispatch, do, effect, enact, execute, fill, finalize, finish, fulfill, implement, make, meet, produce, realize, render, satisfy, settle, sign off, terminate, transact *Nonformal:* get there, knock *or* pull off, make it, sew *or* wind *or* wrap up *Antonyms:* begin, commence, initiate, start **2.** better, enhance, enrich, heighten, improve, magnify, polish, reinforce, sharpen *Commonly misused:* **replete**

completely *adv.* absolutely, all, altogether, comprehensively, consummately, effectively, *en masse (French)*, entirely, exclusively, extensively, finally, fully, fundamentally, in all *or* entirety *or* toto, outright, painstakingly, perfectly, quite, really, reservedly, roundly, solely, solidly, thoroughly, totally, ultimately, unanimously, unconditionally, unequivocally, uniquely, utterly, well, wholly, without exception *or* reservation

complex *adj.* **1.** circuitous, complicated, confused, convoluted, difficult, discursive, entangled, hi-tech *(Nonformal)*, intricate, involved, knotty, rambling, snarled, sophisticated, tangled, technical, tortuous, unfathomable, winding *Antonyms:* clear, easy, elementary, obvious, simple, uncomplicated **2.** bewildering, cryptic, enigmatic, hidden, indecipherable, inscrutable, labyrinthine, muddled, obscure, paradoxical, perplexing, puzzling **3.** assembled, blended, combined, composite, fused, meshed, mixed, multiple, synthesized – *n.* **1.** aggregate, composite, compound, conglomerate, ecosystem, group, network, organization, scheme, structure, syndrome, synthesis, system, totality, whole **2.** anxiety, delusion, fear, fetish, fixation, hang-up *(Nonformal)*, *idée fixe (French)*, insanity, mania, neurosis, obsession, phobia, preoccupation, repression

complexion *n.* **1.** aspect, attitude, cast, character, demeanour, disposition, guise, humour, individuality, kind, light, look, makeup, nature, personality, posture, quality, semblance, stamp, style, temperament, type, visage **2.** appearance, countenance, flush, front, glow, hue, looks, mug *(Nonfor-*

mal), natural colour, pigmentation, skin, skin colour *or* colouring *or* tone, texture, tinge, tint, visage

complexity *n.* **1.** convolution, density, detail, intricacy, involution, involvement, machination, minutiae, multifacedness, multifariousness, multiplicity, technical detail **2.** conundrum, difficulty, dilemma, knot, labyrinth, maze, paradox, puzzle, quandary

complicated *adj.* **1.** arduous, Byzantine, circuitous, complex, confused, convoluted, difficult, elaborate, entangled, hard, high-tech *(Nonformal)*, intricate, involved, knotty, labyrinthine, perplexing, problematic, profound, puzzling, riddling, sophisticated, tangled, tortuous, troublesome *Antonyms:* clear, easy, simple, uncomplicated, uninvolved, user-friendly **2.** compounded, interlaced, mingled, miscellaneous, mixed, multifarious, multiple, variegated, various

complication *n.* **1.** complexity, dilemma, imbroglio, intricacy, labyrinth, paradox, problem, puzzle, riddle *Nonformal:* rat's nest, snake pit *Antonyms:* breeze, child's play, sinecure **2.** catch, development, difficulty, drawback, hindrance, hurdle, obstacle *Nonformal:* glitch, hitch, snag

complicity *n.* **1.** abetment, agreement, collaboration, collusion, connivance, conspiracy, cooperation, implication, intrigue, involvement, partnership *Antonyms:* ignorance, innocence **2.** complexity, convolution, difficulty, Gordian knot, intricacy, maze, morass, quagmire

compliment *n.* **1.** admiration, adulation, applause, approval, commendation, congratulations, endorsement, eulogy, flattery, good word, honour, kudos, laudation, praise, sanction, tribute, veneration *Antonyms:* criticism, disparagement, insult, reproach **2.** best wishes, greetings, regards, respects, salutations **3.** bouquet, gift, gratuity, lagniappe, *pourboire (French)*, present, tip – *v.* adulate, applaud, celebrate, commend, congratulate, endorse, eulogize, exalt, extol, hail, honour, laud, praise, recommend, salute, sanction, toast *Antonyms:* condemn, decry, reprehend *Commonly misused:* **complement**

complimentary *adj.* **1.** adulatory, appreciative, approving, commendatory, congratulatory, flattering, highly favourable, honouring, laudatory, panegyrical, well-wishing *Antonyms:* abusive, critical, disparaging, faultfinding, insulting, unflattering **2.** free, gratis, hand-out, no charge, on-the-house, voluntary *Nonformal:* comp, freebie *Commonly misused:* **complementary**

comply *v.* **1.** adhere, conform, heed, obey, observe, respect *Nonformal:* play ball, toe the line *Antonyms:* disobey, disregard, reject **2.** accede, acquiesce, agree, assent, consent, relent, submit, yield *Nonformal:* cave in, cry uncle, fold *Antonyms:* defy, oppose, resist

component *adj.* composing, constituent, formative, fractional, partial, sectional – *n.* byte, constituent, element, factor, feature, ingredient, item, member, part, piece, section, segment, unit

compose *v.* **1.** be part of, comprise, consist of, constitute, form, make up **2.** construct, fabricate, fashion, forge, make, manufacture, mould, produce, put together **3.** author, coin, conceive, create, design, devise, invent, knock off *(Nonformal)*, orchestrate, originate, pen, scribble, script, write **4.** calm, collect, console, contain, control, pacify, placate, quiet, soothe, still **5.** align, arrange, group, organize, place, position, set, situate **6.** adjust, conciliate, reconcile, resolve, settle *Commonly misused:* **comprise**

composer *n.* arranger, author, balladeer, lyricist, maestro, minstrel, musician, musicographer, melodist, orchestrator, scorer, scribe, songsmith, songwriter, symphonist, tone poet, troubadour, tunesmith, writer

composite *adj.* blended, combined, complex, compound, conglomerate, mixed, synthesized *Antonyms:* homogenous, single, uniform – *n.* admixture, agglomerate, aggregate, amalgam, blend, combination, combo *(Nonformal)*, compound, fusion, integration, intermixture, medley, mix, mixture, pastiche, synthesis, union

composition *n.* **1.** amalgamation, assembly, combination, commingling, compounding, integration, synthesis, union **2.** admixture, alloy, amalgam, compound, concoction, mixture, mosaic, patchwork **3.** brainchild *(Nonformal)*, creation, opus, work, writing *Kinds of composition:* article, concerto, dissertation, drama, melody, music, novel, play, poetry, prose, rhapsody, romance, score, screenplay, short story, song, study, symphony, thesis, verse **4.** essay, exercise, exposition, school work **5.** adjustment, agreement, bargain, compromise, deal, settlement

compost *n.* **1.** admixture, blend, composition, compound, dressing, gallimaufry, hodgepodge, material, medley, mix, mixture, mosaic, potpourri **2.** fertilizer, humus, manure, mulch, ordure, pile, zoo poo *(Trademark)*

composure *n.* assurance, calm, control, cool-headedness, dispassion, equanimity, equilibrium, even temper, imperturbability, levelheadedness, nonchalance, poise, polish, quiescence, sang-froid, sedateness, self-assurance, serenity, stability, stillness *Antonyms:* agitation, excitability, impatience, nervousness

compound *adj.* blended, complex, diverse, hybrid, integrated, manifold, mixed, multifarious, multiple, varied – *n.* **1.** admixture, aggregate, amalgam, amalgamation, blend, combination, combo *(Nonformal)*, composite, conglomerate, fusion, goolash, medley, mishmash, mixture, soup, stew, synthesis, union **2.** base camp, complex, courtyard, enclosure, estate, headquarters, property, quadrangle, square, yard – *v.* **1.** amalgamate, blend, combine, commingle, fuse, mingle, mix, synthesize, unite *Antonyms:* divide, separate **2.** aggravate, complicate, exacerbate, heighten, increase, intensify, magnify *Antonyms:* lessen, minimize, mitigate **3.** agree, bargain, compromise, reconcile, settle, shake down *(Nonformal)*

comprehend *v.* **1.** absorb, appreciate, assimilate, conceive, discern, envision, fathom, know, perceive, see, understand *Nonformal:* capiche, catch, click, get, grasp **2.** constitute, contain, embrace, encompass, hold, include, take in *Antonyms:* misapprehend, misconstrue, misinterpret, mistake, pervert

comprehensible *adj.* articulate, clear, coherent, explicit, intelligible, legible, logical, lucid, manifest, obvious, plain, straightforward, unambiguous, understandable, user-friendly *Antonyms:* ambiguous, confused, incomprehensible, paradoxical *Commonly misused:* **comprehensive**

comprehension *n.* **1.** apprehension, awareness, capacity, cognizance, conception, discernment, grasp, intelligence, judgment, knowledge, perception, realization, sense, understanding *Antonyms:* incomprehension, misapprehension, unawareness **2.** area, department, extent, field, jurisdiction, knowledge, limits, reach, realm, scope, sphere **3.** compass, comprisal, comprehensiveness, containment, coverage, inclusion, span

comprehensive *adj.* **1.** absolute, all-embracing, all-inclusive, blanket, broad, catholic, compendious, complete, definitive, encyclopedic, exhaustive, expansive, extensive, far-reaching, full, global, inclusive, in depth, overall, sweeping, thorough, umbrella, wall-to-wall, whole, wide, widespread *Antonyms:* incomplete, limited, narrow, restricted, specific **2.** aware, cognitive, discerning, intelligent, mental, rational, reasoning, thinking *Commonly misused:* **comprehensible**

compress *n.* application, bandage, cloth, dressing, pad, plaster, pledget, poultice – *v.* **1.** compact, cram, crowd, jam, pack, press, squeeze, wedge **2.** abbreviate, abridge, boil down, clarify, concentrate, condense, reduce, set, solidify, summarize, thicken, zip

comprise *v.* amount to, compass, comprehend, consist of, constitute, contain, cover, embody, embrace, enclose, encompass, hold, include, incorporate, involve, make up, span, take in *Commonly misused:* **compose**

compromise *n.* **1.** accommodation, adjustment, agreement, appeasement, arrangement, cease-fire, compact, concession, deal, détente, give and take, pact, settlement, trade-off truce, understanding **2.** balance, golden mean, happy medium, means, *mezzo termine (Italian)*, middle course *or* ground – *v.* **1.** adjust, agree, arbitrate, bargain, concede, conciliate, give in, make concession, modify, negotiate, settle, strike balance, trade off *Nonformal:* go fifty-fifty *or* 50/50, meet halfway, split the difference *Antonyms:* argue, contest, differ, disagree **2.** blight, discredit, dishonour, endanger, expose, hazard, imperil, jeopardize, mar, prejudice, risk, spoil, undermine, weaken *Antonyms:* boost, enhance, support

compulsion *n.* **1.** coercion, constraint, duress, obligation, pressure, provocation **2.** hang up *(Nonformal)*, irresistible, necessity, overwhelming impulse, strong desire, tendency *or* urge

compulsive *adj.* **1.** compelling, forceful, gripping, irrestible, rousing *Nonformal:* blistering, page-turner, un-put-downable **2.** addictive, anal-retentive *(Nonformal)*, fetishistic, incorrigible, involuntary, irrational, obsessive, overfastidious, overwhelming, urgent

compulsory *adj.* **1.** basic, binding, *de rigueur (French)*, dictated, imperative, inescapable, mandatory, a must *(Nonformal)*, necessary, obligatory, required, requisite *Antonyms:* discretionary, optional, voluntary **2.** authoritative, coercive, constraining, controlling, dominating, forced, imposed, strong-arm *(Nonformal)*

compunction *n.* conscience, contrition, guilt, misgiving, pang, penitence, pity, qualm, regret, remorse, repentance, rue, second thought, self-reproach, shame, sorrow *Antonyms:* callousness, defiance

computation *n.* **1.** adding, addition, appraisal, appreciation, calculation, calibration, casting, ciphering, computing, counting, data processing, enumeration, estimation, evaluation, figuring, gauging, measurement, numeration, reckoning, summation, totalling **2.** amount, bottom line *(Nonformal)*, count, number, quantity, score, tally, total

compute *v.* add, appraise, calculate, calibrate, cipher, count, count heads, enumerate, estimate, evaluate, figure, gauge, measure, rate, sum, tally, total, weigh

computer *n.* **1.** electronic data processor, hardware *Kinds of computer:* analog, clone, data processor, laptop, mainframe, microcomputer, minicomputer, palmtop, personal computer *or* PC, pocket, supercomputer *Parts of a computer:* BIOS (Basic Input/Output/System), cache, chips, circuitry, hard drive, monitor *or* video terminal, motherboard, port, power supply, random access memory *or* RAM, read-only memory *or* ROM, read-write head, sound card, system chassis *Computer devices or peripherals:* CD ROM drive, keyboard, light pen, modem, mouse, optical character recognition or OCR, printer, scanner **2.** accountant, actuary, bean counter *(Nonformal)*, bookkeeper, calculator, estimator, figurer, mathematician, statistician

comrade *n.* ally, associate, bosom buddy, buddy, chum, colleague, companion, compatriot, confidante, crony, fellow, friend, mate, pal, partner, sidekick *(Nonformal)*, *tovarisch (Russian) Antonyms:* enemy, foe, rival

con *adv.* against, at odds *or* variance, in opposition – *n.* **1.** argument, nay, negative, no, opposition **2.** disadvantage, downside, drawback, flip side, trouble **3.** bluff, cheat, crime, deception, double-cross, dupe, fraud, hoax, graft, grift, swindle, trick **4.** convict, criminal, felon, lifer *(Nonformal)*, jailbird – *v.* **1.** bilk, cajole, cheat, coax, deceive, defraud, double-cross, dupe, fool, hoax, hoodwink, inveigle, mislead, rook, swindle, trick *Nonformal:* bamboozle, flimflam, hornswoggle, rip off, take **2.** cram *(Nonformal)*, examine, inculcate, ingrain, learn, master, memorize, peruse, scrutinize, study **3.** direct, drive, guide, navigate, pilot, steer

concave *adj.* cupped, curved, depressed, dimpled, dipped, excavated, hollow, indented, scooped, sinking, sunken *Antonyms:* bulging, convex, swollen *Commonly misused:* **convex**

conceal *v.* burrow, bury, cache, camouflage, cloak, cloud, couch, cover, cover up, curtain, disguise, dissemble, enshroud, harbour, hide, hole up, keep dark *or* secret, mask, obscure, plant, screen, secrete, shelter, shroud, stow, tuck away, veil, wrap *Antonyms:* disclose, divulge, expose, reveal, unmask

concealed *adj.* **1.** buried, cached, camouflaged, covered up, enshrouded, guarded, hidden, masked, obscured, screened, secret, shrouded, stashed, under cover *or* wraps, unseen, veiled **2.** clandestine, covert, hugger-mugger *(Nonformal)*, hushed-up, private, secret

concealment *n.* **1.** blanket, blind, camouflage, cover-up, deception, disguise, evasion, feint, masking, prevarication, smokescreen, subterfuge **2.** bolt-hole, hideaway, hiding place, priest's hole *(Historical)*, secret room *Nonformal:* laundromat, skunk works

concede *v.* **1.** accede, accept, acknowledge, acquiesce, admit, agree, allow, assent, come around, defer to, give in *or* up *or* way, go along with, knuckle under, permit, recognize surrender, vouchsafe, yield **2.** bequeath, deliver, give, grant, release, tender, transfer

conceit *n.* **1.** arrogance, egotism, hubris, narcissism, pomposity, pride, self-admiration, self-exaltation, self-importance, self-love, smugness, swagger, vainglory, vanity *Antonyms:* diffidence, humility, modesty **2.** caprice, dream, pipe dream, quirk, whim **3.** comparison, expression, literary technique, metaphor, trope, wordplay **4.** creativity, fancy, imagination, inventiveness, lateral thinking **5.** apprehension, conception, conviction, idea, notion, opinion, sentiment, thought

conceited *adj.* arrogant, big-headed, boastful, bragging, egotistical, proud, rodomontade, self-important, smug, vain, vainglorious *Nonformal:* big-talking, puffed-up *Antonyms:* humble, modest, unassuming

conceivable *adj.* believable, comprehensible, credible, imaginable, knowable, perceivable, plausible, possible, reasonable, tenable, thinkable, understandable *Antonyms:* unfathomable, unthinkable, out of this world *(Nonformal)*

conceive *v.* **1.** come up with *(Nonformal)*, concoct, conjure *or* dream up, create, design, develop, devise, envision, fabricate, fancy, fashion, formulate, imagine, manufacture, plan, plot, realize, visualize **2.** comprehend, grasp, ponder, understand *Nonformal:* capiche, get **3.** believe, consider, judge, maintain, recognize, see, suppose, think, view **4.** become pregnant, beget, create, procreate

concentrate *v.* **1.** attend, brood, contemplate, examine, focus, meditate, scrutinize, study, think *Nonformal:* buckle *or* knuckle down, hone in **2.** boil *or* pare down, clarify, condense, distill, filtrate, intensify, purify, rarefy, reduce, refine, thicken **3.** assemble, bunch, cluster, converge, crowd, gather, huddle, localize, swarm *Antonyms:* diffuse, disperse

concentration *adj.* death, detention, extermination, holding, internment, labour, work – *n.* **1.** absorption, application, attention, contemplation, deliberation, engrossment, examination, focus, involvement, meditation, mindfulness, musing, reflection, rumination, scrutiny, sedulity, single-mindedness, study, thought **2.** accumulation, aggregation, amassing, assembly, cluster, collection, congregation, convergence, flock, group, herd, mass, mob, party, unity *Antonyms:* diffusion, dispersion, scattering **3.** coagulation, compression, concretion, condensation, distillation, intensification, purification, strengthening, thickening

concept *n.* belief, conviction, idea, impression, notion, opinion, presumption, sense, supposition, surmise, theory, thought, view

conception *n.* **1.** apprehension, belief, conceit, conviction, hypothesis, idea, interpretation, notion, perception, philosophy, theory, thought, view **2.** comprehension, consideration, deliberation, meditation, musing, philosophizing, speculation, thinking **3.** beginning, commencement, dawn, genesis, launch, opening, start **4.** conceiving, fertilization, germination, impregnation, insemination

concern *n.* **1.** attention, care, heedfulness, interest, solicitude, thoughtfulness **2.** anxiety, disquietude, distress, stress, trepidation, trouble, unease, worry **3.** affair, department, dominion, duty, expertise, field, jurisdiction, responsibility **4.** business, company, enterprise, firm, organization, partnership **5.** applicability, association, bearing, connection, pertinence, regard, relation, relevance – *v.* **1.** appertain *or* apply to, bear on *or* upon, depend upon, pertain *or* refer to, regard, relate to **2.** devote, engage, interest, involve, occupy, turn on *(Nonformal)* **3.** bother, disconcert, disquiet, distress, disturb, irritate, perturb, trouble, upset, vex, worry *Nonformal:* bug, eat away at, ride, stress out

concerned *adj.* **1.** attentive, caring, mindful, solicitous, thoughtful **2.** implicated, interested, involved, mixed with, privy to *Antonyms:* aloof, detached, disinterested **3.** anxious, bothered, distressed, disturbed, perturbed, stressed, troubled, uneasy, upset, uptight *(Nonformal)*, worried, worried sick *Antonyms:* calm, carefree, untroubled

concert *n.* **1.** ensemble, musical, musicale, performance, recital, show *Kinds of concert:* band, bandshell, bluegrass, classical, chamber, folk, jazz, philharmonic, popular *or* pop *or* pops, rap, rock, symphony *Nonformal:* gig, promenade, prom **2.** accord, agreement, consensus, concord, concordance, unanimity *Antonyms:* discord, disunity, friction **3.** collaboration, cooperation, fellowship, fraternity, give-and-take, solidarity, teamwork, togetherness – *v.* **1.** ally, combine, cooperate, harmonize, league, merge, unite *Nonformal:* hook up, join forces **2.** cabal, collaborate, complot, plot **3.** arrange, contrive, design, devise, plan, schedule, sort out

concerted *adj.* **1.** agreed upon, collaborative, combined, cooperative, coordinated, joint, mutual, planned, prearranged, premeditated, united *Antonyms:* separate, uncontrived, uncooperative, unplanned **2.** committed, decided, determined, devoted, earnest, resolute, serious, sincere, wholehearted

concession *n.* **1.** accommodation, adjustment, allowance, compromise, modification, trade-off **2.** acknowledgment, capitulation, conceding, surrender, yielding **3.** authority, leave, licence, permission, right, sanction **4.** booth, business, casse-croûte, franchise, kiosk, operation, stand **5.** exception, exemption, privilege, immunity **6.** area, block, jurisdiction, subdivision, surveyed land **7.** catch *(Nonformal)*, condition, proviso, qualification, restriction, stipulation

concierge *n.* caretaker, custodian, doorkeeper, guardian, ostiary, porter

conciliate *v.* **1.** appease, assuage, bring around, dulcify, mollify, pacify, placate, soothe *Antonyms:* aggravate, intensify **2.** arbitrate, intervene, mediate, negotiate **3.** heal, make peace *or* up, iron *or* sort out, patch up, reconcile, reunite *Antonyms:* divide, estrange, separate

conciliatory *adj.* appeasing, assuaging, forgiving, irenic, mollifying, peaceable, placating, quieting, soothing

concise *adj.* **1.** abbreviated, abridged, compact, compressed, condensed, short **2.** brief, curt, laconic, pithy, succinct, terse *Antonyms:* diffuse, garrulous, rambling

conclave *n.* **1.** assembly, conference, gathering, mating, powwow *(Nonformal)* **2.** *concilium (Latin)*, conventicle, council, presbytery, synod *Commonly misused:* **enclave**

conclude *v.* **1.** cease, close, complete, desist, end, finish, halt, stop, terminate, wind *or* wrap up *Antonyms:* begin, commence, start **2.** accomplish, bring about, clinch, consummate, effect, effectuate, resolve, settle **3.** adjudge, decide, deduce, derive, draw, figure, gather, glean, infer, intuit, judge, presume, ratiocinate, reason, suppose, surmise, think **4.** choose, elect, decide, determine, elect, settle on

conclusion *n.* **1.** cessation, close, closure, completion, dénouement, end, finish, stop, termination, windup **2.** afterward, coda, epilogue, finale, summary, synopsis, wrap-up **3.** aftereffect, aftermath, consequence, effect, issue, outcome, repercussion, result, upshot, **4.** calculation, deduction, estimation, evaluation, inference, judgment, surmisal **5.** conviction, decision, decree, determination, finding, pronouncement, ruling, sentence, verdict **6.** agreement, arrangement, bargain, compact, contract, deal, pact, settlement

conclusive *adj.* absolute, all out, clear, clinching, convincing, deciding, definite, flat-out *(Nonformal)*, incontrovertible, indisputable, irrefutable, irrevocable, resolving, settling, unambiguous, unconditional, undeniable, unmistakable, unquestionable *Antonyms:* contestable, disputable, doubtful, questionable, vague

concoct *v.* **1.** brew, compose, compound, make, mix, prepare, throw together *(Nonformal)* **2.** contrive, cook *or* dream up *(Nonformal)*, fabricate, hatch, imagine, invent, originate, think up

concoction *n.* **1.** blend, brew, combination, compound, mixture, preparation, product **2.** contrivance, creation, design, fabrication, invention, plot, ploy, scheme

concomitant *adj.* **1.** accessory, accompanying, adjuvant, affiliate, ancillary, associate, associative, attendant, auxiliary, conjoined, connected, corollary, jointed, linked **2.** coeval, coexistent, collateral, concurrent, coterminous, in tempo *or* time, parallel, simultaneous, synchronous, synergistic – *n.* **1.** accessory, adjunct, appendage, attendant, corollary **2.** coeval, coexistent, colleague, contemporary, parallel, peer **3.** coincidence, simultaneity, synchronicity **4.** by-product, consequence, effect, offshoot, result, side effect

concord *n.* **1.** accord, agreement, concert, concordance, harmony, unison, unity *Antonyms:* clash, discord, dissonance **2.** affinity, amity, fraternity, friendship, good will, peace, rapport *Antonyms:* conflict, estrangement, strife **3.** cartel, concordat, convention, *entente cordiale (French)*, treaty

concourse *n.* **1.** assembly, conference, confluence, conflux, convergence, gathering, meeting, mobilization, rally **2.** cluster, crowd, crush *(Nonformal)*, gang, horde, mob, multitude, press, swarm, throng **3.** area, mall, passageway, plaza, shopping area, space, station, terminal, waiting room **4.** boulevard, esplanade, thoroughfare

concrete *adj.* **1.** caked, calcified, cemented, compact, compressed, congealed, dried, firm, hardened, petrified, set, solid, solidified, strong, unyielding **2.** actual, bodily, corporeal, earthly, material, objective, physical, positive, real, substantial *Antonyms:* abstract, immaterial, theoretical **3.** accurate, detailed, distinct, exact, explicit, factual, precise, specific *Antonyms:* general, vague – *n.* **1.** building material, cement, ferroconcrete, pavement – *v.* cake, clot, coagulate, coalesce, concretize, congeal, consolidate, harden, set, solidify, thicken *Commonly misused:* **cement**

concur *v.* **1.** accede, agree, approve, consent, uphold **2.** band *or* pull together, conform, cooperate, harmonize, join, league, synergize **3.** coexist, coincide, parallel, synchronize **4.** come together, connect, converge, intersect, meet

concurrent *adj.* **1.** accordant, affirmative, agreeing, concordant, conforming, harmonious, like-minded, positive **2.** allied, collaborating, conjunctive, cooperating, joined, leagued, synergistic, united **3.** coincidental, collateral, in sync *(Nonformal)*, parallel, synchronous **4.** convergent, intersecting, meeting, merging

concussion *n.* **1.** brain bruise, bump, goose egg *(Nonformal)*, head injury, hit, shock, trauma **2.** buffeting, collision, crash, jar, jolt, jostle, shake, smash *Commonly misused:* **contusion**

condemn *v.* **1.** blacklist, blame, castigate, censure, criticize, denounce, deprecate, disparage, reprehend, reproach, vilify *Nonformal:* knock, rap, skin alive, tar and feather *Antonyms:* commend, praise **2.** convict, doom, find guilty, punish, sentence *Nonformal:* put away, send up **3.** ban, banish, blackball, boycott, censor, disallow, forbid, interdict, prohibit *Antonyms:* allow, condone, legalize

condemnation *n.* **1.** aspersion, censure, criticism, denouncement, deprecation, rebuke, reproach, reprobation, reproof, stricture, vilification, vituperation *Antonyms:* approval, endorsement, praise **2.** ban, blacklisting, excommunication, exile, outlawing, prohibition, proscription

condensation *n.* **1.** compaction, compression, concentration, consolidation, contraction, essence, reduction, shortening, shrinking **2.** abridgment, abstract, brief, digest, epitome, précis, sketch, summary, synopsis **3.** buildup, dew, distillation, evaporation, moisture, perspiration, precipitate, precipitation, rainfall **4.** amalgamation, blending, convergence, fusion, merging

condense *v.* **1.** compress, concentrate, consolidate, contract, decrease, downsize, retrench, shrink **2.** abbreviate, abridge, chop *(Nonformal)*, edit, encapsulate, reduce, shorten, summarize **3.** alter, change, harden, liquidize, melt, precipitate, solidify

condescend *v.* **1.** bend, descend, humble, humour, lower, patronize, stoop, talk down to, tolerate **2.** accommodate, accord, comply, concede, deign, grant, submit, vouchsafe, yield

condescending *adj.* arrogant, complaisant, disdainful, egotistical, haughty, humiliating, lofty, lordly, patronizing, presumptuous, snobbish, supercilious, superior *Nonformal:* high-hat, snooty

condescension *n.* airs *(Nonformal)*, disdain, gall, haughtiness, loftiness, lordliness, patronization, snobbery, superciliousness, superiority, toleration *Antonyms:* humility, modesty, self-effacement

condiment *n.* dressing, flavouring, sauce, seasoning, spice *Kinds of condiment: ajvar (Adriatic)*, anchovy paste, chutney, cornichon, horseradish, hot sauce, *kejapmanis (Indonesian)*, ketchup, *mam tom (Asian)*, maple syrup, mayonnaise, mustard, *nampla (Thai)*, *nuoc mam (Vietnamese)*, olive oil, piccalilli, pepper sauce, pepper, pickle, preserves, relish, salsa, salt, soya *or* steak sauce, tamari, tartar sauce, vinegar, *wasabi (Japanese)*, Worcestershire Sauce *Trademark:* HP, Tabasco *See also:* **sauce**

condition *n.* **1.** fettle, fitness, health, repair, shape, state **2.** abnormality, affection, ailment, complaint, disease, ill, illness, infirmity, malady, problem, syndrome, trouble, weakness **3.** contingency, essential, must, necessity, precondition, prerequisite, requirement **4.** clause, limitation, qualification, restriction, stipulation *Nonformal:* catch, small print, string **5.** class, echelon, grade, level, status, stratum – *v.* **1.** control, decide, determine **2.** limit, qualify, restrict, specify, stipulate **3.** coach, practice, tone up, train, work out **4.** accustom, equip, harden, inure, prepare, toughen

conditional *adj.* contingent, dependent, provisional, qualified, relative, reliant *or* relying, stipulatory, subject to, tentative, uncertain *Antonyms:* absolute, categorical, unrestricted

condolence *n.* comfort, commiseration, compassion, consolation, pity, regard, solace, sympathy

condom *n.* birth control device, contraceptive, prophylactic *Nonformal:* French letter, glove, night cap, party hat, rubber, safe

condominium *n.* apartment, cooperative duplex, flat, high-rise, tenement, town house *Nonformal:* condo, co-op

condone *v.* allow, excuse, forget, forgive, ignore, let pass, okay *(Nonformal)*, overlook, pardon, pass over, remit *Antonyms:* censure, condemn, denounce, disapprove, punish

conducive *adj.* advantageous, contributive, favourable, helpful, instrumental, productive, promoting, serviceable, supportive, tending, useful *Antonyms:* adverse, inimical, unfavourable

conduct *n.* **1.** actions, attitude, bearing, behaviour, deportment, manners, posture **2.** administration, care, control, direction, execution, guidance, handling, leadership, management, regulation, rule, superintendence, supervision – *v.* **1.** accompany, escort, guide, lead, pilot, shepherd, steer, usher **2.** administer, chair, command, control, direct, govern, handle, head, manage, orchestrate, oversee, preside, regulate, rule, run **3.** act, bear, behave, carry on **4.** carry, channel, convey, impel, move, transmit

conductor *n.* administrator, boss, captain, chief, director, engineer, head, leader, maestro, president, skipper, supervisor *Kinds of musical conductor:* band leader *or* master, choirmaster, concertmaster, Kapellmeister, music director, orchestra leader

conduit *n.* conductor, course *Kinds of conduit:* aqueduct, cable, canal, channel, culvert, duct, eavestrough, flume, gully, gutter, main, passage, pipe, pipeline, race, sewer, spout, trough, tube, watercourse

confection *n.* **1.** bar, bonbon, cake, candy, cookie, dainty, jam, pastry, square, sweet, treat *(Nonformal)* **2.** composition, compound, drug, electuary, elixir, medicine, mixture, production, syrup

confederacy *n.* **1.** affiliation, alliance, association, coalition, compact, confederation, federation, government, league, partnership, union **2.** cabal, complicity, complot, conspiracy, intrigue, scheming **3.** *Confederate states:* Arkansas, Alabama, Florida, Georgia, Louisiana, Mississippi, North Carolina, South Carolina, Tennessee, Texas, Virginia

confederate *adj.* allied, amalgamated, associated, federated, leagued, unionized – *n.* **1.** ally, associate, colleague, comrade, conspirator, fellow, fellow traveller, partner, rebel **2.** abettor, accessory, accomplice, co-conspirator, collaborator, conspirator

confederation *n.* affiliation, alliance, association, coalition, commonwealth, confederacy, consolidation, dominion, federation, fusion, hookup *(Nonformal)*, interdependence, league, merger, partnership, unification, union, unity *Dates of confederation:* Alberta *(September 1, 1905)*, British Columbia *(July 20, 1871)*, Manitoba *(July 15, 1870)*, New Brunswick *(July 1, 1867)*, Newfoundland *(March 31, 1949)*, Northwest Territories *(July 15, 1870)*, Nova Scotia *(July 1, 1867)*, Nunavut *(April 1, 1999)*, Ontario *(July 1, 1867)*, P.E.I. *(July 1, 1873)*, Quebec *(July 1, 1867)*, Saskatchewan *(September 1, 1905)*, Yukon Territory *(July 13, 1898)*

confer *v.* **1.** accord, allot, award, bestow, donate, give, grant, honour, lay on, present, provide, vouchsafe **2.** confab *(Nonformal)*, converse, debate, deliberate, discuss, meet, negotiate, talk

conference *n.* **1.** confabulation, consultation, conversation, debate, dialogue, discussion, exchange, forum, huddle, interchange, interview, meeting, palaver, talk **2.** assembly, convention, gathering, groupthink *(Nonformal)*, seminar, symposium, trade-show **3.** association, chapter, club, collective, conclave, guild, incumbency, league, organization, society, union **4.** congregation, diocese, parish, presbytery, synod **5.** awarding, bestowal, conferment, donation, giving, presentation

confess *v.* **1.** admit, blurt out, confide, declare, disclose, profess, reveal *Nonformal:* come clean, leak, own up, rat, snitch, squeal **2.** acknowledge, affirm, assert, attest, concede, grant *Antonyms:* deny, disavow, repudiate

confession *n.* **1.** acknowledgment, admission, admittance, disclosure, divulgence, exposure, proclamation, revelation, statement, utterance *Antonyms:* concealment, denial, disavowal **2.** affirmation, assertion, avowal, declaration, profession **3.** belief, church, doctrine, faith, school, system, tenet

confidante *n.* adviser, alter ego, buddy, chum, companion, comrade, confidant *(Masc.)*, crony, familiar, friend, intimate, mate, pal *Nonformal:* amigo, bosom buddy *Commonly misused:* **confident**

confide *v.* **1.** admit, confess, disclose, divulge, impart, reveal, tell, whisper *Nonformal:* spill to, unload on **2.** bestow, charge, commend, commit, consign, delegate, entrust, present, relegate, trust

confidence *n.* **1.** assurance, belief, dependence, expectation, faith, hope, reliance, trust **2.** courage, fearlessness, mettle, moxie *(Nonformal)*, nerve, pluck, self-assurance, spirit, tenacity, verve **3.** arrogance, audacity, boldness, effrontery, impudence, insolence, presumption *Nonformal:* brass, chutzpah, gall

confident *adj.* **1.** audacious, bold, brave, cocky, courageous, dauntless, fearless, intrepid, nervy *(Nonformal)*, presumptuous, unafraid, undaunted, valiant **2.** assured, certain, convinced, expectant, high, hopeful, positive, secure, sure, trusting, upbeat *Antonyms:* doubtful, dubious, tentative **3.** composed, level-headed, poised, self-assured, self-possessed, self-reliant *Commonly misused:* **confidante**

confidential *adj.* **1.** arcane, classified, closet, covert, hushed, hush-hush *(Nonformal)*, inside, intimate, personal, private, privileged, privy, secret, top-secret *Antonyms:* common, public, well-known **2.** attached, bosom, close, dear, faithful, familiar, intimate, reliable, trustworthy *Nonformal:* buddy-buddy, thick, tight

confidentially *adv.* covertly, *entre nous (French)*, in confidence, in secret, personally, privately, *sub rosa (Latin)*

configuration *n.* arrangement, cast, composition, conformation, contour, deployment, disposition, figure, form, outline, positioning, setup, shape, structure, topology

confine *v.* **1.** bar, detain, enslave, immure, imprison, incarcerate, intern, jail, quarantine *Antonyms:* free, emancipate, liberate **2.** bind, bound, circumscribe, constrain, cool, cork, cramp, curb, delimit, demarcate, enclose, fix, girdle, hinder, limit, repress, restrain, restrict, shorten

confined *adj.* bottled up, bound, circumscribed, compassed, cooped up, cramped, detained, enclosed, grounded, hampered, immured, imprisoned, incarcerated, indisposed, jailed, laid up, limited, locked up, restrained, restricted, sealed up, shut in *Antonyms:* liberated, released, unfettered

confinement *n.* **1.** bondage, circumscription, constraint, control, custody, detention, enclosure, imprisonment, incarceration, limitation, narrowness, quarantine, restraint, restriction **2.** accouchement, childbed, childbirth, delivery, expectancy, labour, lying-in, parturition, pregnancy, travail

confines *n.pl.* border, boundary, bound, circumference, compass, dimension, edge, extent, frontier, limit, margin, periphery, precinct, range, reach, region, scope, stretch, sweep

confirm *v.* **1.** authenticate, bless, certify, corroborate, endorse, ensure, justify, prove, ratify, sanction, subscribe, substantiate, support, uphold, validate, verify, vouch, warrant, witness *Antonyms:* contradict, contravene, disprove, refute **2.** assure, buttress, clinch, establish, fix, fortify, invigorate, reinforce, settle, strengthen

confirmation *n.* **1.** acceptance, agreement, approval, assent, attestation, authentication, backing, corroboration, endorsement, establishment, ratification, reinforcement, sanction, support, validation **2.** clincher *(Nonformal)*, evidence, proof, testimony, witness

confirmed *adj.* **1.** accepted, accustomed, entrenched, established, factual, fixed, guaranteed, habituated, hardened, ingrained, inured, long-established, proven, ratified, rooted, seasoned, settled, staid, true, valid *Antonyms:* denied, uncommitted, unconfirmed **2.** chronic, deep-rooted, deep-seated, dyed-in-the-wool *(Nonformal)*, habitual, inveterate

confiscate *v.* annex, appropriate, assume, commandeer, expropriate, grab, hijack, impound, liberate *(Nonformal)*, rob, seize, sequester, steal, take *or* take over, usurp *Antonyms:* release, return, restore

conflagration *n.* blaze, bonfire, burning, fire, flame, holocaust, inferno, wildfire

conflict *n.* **1.** altercation, argument, battle, clash, collision, competition, contest, controversy, disagreement, dispute, donnybrook, engagement, fight, fracas, fuss, quarrel, row, run-in, rupture, scene, spat, split, struggle, trouble, war, wrangle *Nonformal:* hassle, rhubarb, ruckus *Antonyms:* accord, harmony, peace, treaty, truce **2.** animosity, antagonism, antipathy, bickering, contention, difference, discord, discordance, dissension, dissidence, disunity, division, enmity, friction, hostility, incompatibility, incongruity, opposition, strife, variance – *v.* brawl, clash, collide, combat, contend, contest, contrast, differ, disagree, disturb, fight, interfere, oppose, scrap, slug, strive, struggle, tangle *Antonyms:* agree, coincide, harmonize, reconcile

conflicting *adj.* **1.** ambivalent, antipodal, antithetical, contradictory, contrary, converse, counter, diametric, differing, discrepant, dissonant, fluctuating, incompatible, incongruous, inconsistent, inflexible, irreconcilable, irresolute, opposite, paradoxical, polar, reverse, unappeasable, uncompromising *Antonyms:* agreeing, compatible, congruous, harmonious, synchronized **2.** antagonistic, argumentative, clashing, discordant, hostile, opposed, oppositional

confluence *n.* **1.** coming together, convergence, junction, union *Antonyms:* bifurcation, divergence, fork, separation **2.** assembly, concourse, congregation, crowd, gathering, meeting, rally

conform *v.* **1.** adapt, adjust, agree, correspond, dovetail, fit, harmonize, jibe *(Nonformal),* match, reconcile, square, tailor **2.** acknowledge, assimilate, comply, follow, obey, observe, respect, yield

conformable *adj.* **1.** adapted, agreeable, amenable, applicable, appropriate, befitting, comparable, congrous, consistent, fitting, harmonious *Antonyms:* disparate, mismatched **2.** like, matching, resembling, similar **3.** compliant, docile, dutiful, flexible, obedient, submissive, tractable, yielding *Antonyms:* difficult, intransigent, stubborn

conformation *n.* **1.** anatomy, arrangement, build, cast, configuration, figure, form, formation, framework, outline, shape, structure **2.** agreement, balance, correspondence, harmony, proportion, symmetry, uniformity **3.** assimilation, compliance, conformity, obedience, observance

conformity *n.* **1.** acquiescence, adherence, compliance, obedience, observance, orthodoxy, submission **2.** affinity, agreement, allegiance, coherence, congruity, consistency, consonance, correspondence, harmony, homogeneity, resemblance, similarity

confound *v.* **1.** amaze, astonish, astound, baffle, bewilder, discomfit, dumfound, flabbergast, mystify, nonplus, perplex, puzzle, rattle, surprise, throw off *Antonyms:* clear up, ease, pacify, relieve **2.** blur, confuse, intermingle, mingle, mix up, transpose **3.** curse, damn, denounce, execrate, fulminate, hex, jinx, maledict

confront *v.* **1.** beard, brave, challenge, counter, defy, encounter, face, meet, oppose, rebuke, resist, tackle *(Nonformal) Antonyms:* avoid, dodge, evade **2.** compare, contrast, counterpoise, pit against

confrontation *n.* **1.** battle, conflict, contest, crisis, dispute, donnybrook, duel, encounter, face-off, fight, match, meeting, set-to, showdown, strife **2.** challenge, dare, defiance, opposition, provocation, threat

confuse *v.* **1.** addle, amaze, astonish, baffle, befuddle, bewilder, confound, disconnect, disorient, disturb, fluster, mystify, nonplus, perplex, perturb, puzzle, stupefy, unsettle *Nonformal:* flummox, rattle, rumple, stagger, stump **2.** disarray, jumble, mistake, muddle, transpose **3.** blend, blur, interchange, intermingle, lump together *(Nonformal),* mingle, mix up, obscure *Antonyms:* differentiate, separate

confused *adj.* **1.** addled, astonished, baffled, bewildered, blurry, cockeyed, dazed, discombobulated, dishevelled, disoriented, flummoxed *(Nonformal),* mystified, perplexed, perturbed, puzzled, rattled, unglued, unsettled, upended, upset *Antonyms:* aware, enlightened, informed **2.** ambiguous, disjointed, incomprehensible, inexplicable, knotty, labyrinthine, misleading, obscure **3.** chaotic, disordered, higgledy-piggledy *(Nonformal),* jumbled, lawless, messy, mixed-up, tangled, topsy-turvy, uncontrolled *Antonyms:* arranged, neat, orderly, tidy

confusion *n.* **1.** agitation, bewilderment, consternation, daze, discombobulation, distraction, disturbance, fluster, perplexity, unrest *Nonformal:* dither, lather **2.** anarchy, bedlam, chaos, disorder, havoc, hubbub, mêlée, pandemonium, upheaval *Nonformal:* hawey-cawey, higgledy-piggledy, hugger-mugger, state **3.** disorganization, disarray, jumble, mess, mixup, muddle

confute *v.* confound, contradict, controvert, defeat, demolish, dismay, disprove, expose, invalidate, negate, overturn, rebuke, rebut, refute, silence, subvert, upset, vanquish *Antonyms:* confirm, prove

congeal *v.* coagulate, compress, concentrate, condense, crystallize, freeze, gel, glaciate, harden, jellify, solidify, thicken *Antonyms:* liquefy, soften, thin

congenial *adj.* affable, agreeable, bonny *(Scottish)*, clubby *(Nonformal)*, companionable, compatible, complaisant, congruous, consistent, convivial, cooperative, cordial, delightful, favourable, fit, friendly, genial, good-humoured, gracious, harmonious, jovial, kindly, kindred, pleasant, pleasing, sociable, sympathetic, well-suited *Antonyms:* caustic, offensive, rude, vitriolic

congenital *adj.* cognate, complete, constitutional, inborn, inbred, indigenous, inherent, innate, intrinsic, inveterate, latent, native, natural

congested *adj.* accumulated, blocked, choked, clogged, crammed, crowded, filled, gorged, gridlocked, inundated, jammed, mobbed, obstructed, occluded, overcrowded, overfilled, overflowing, packed, plugged, stopped, stoppered, stuffed, stuffed-up, teeming *Nonformal:* chock-full, jam-packed *Antonyms:* clear, empty, free, unimpeded, unobstructed

congestion *n.* accumulation, blockage, bottleneck, clogging, crowding, excess, jam, mass, overcrowding, overpopulation, plethora, profusion, surfeit, surplus

conglomerate *adj.* **1.** amassed, assorted, blended, clustered, composite, gathered, heterogeneous, indiscriminate, miscellaneous, mixed, motley, multifarious, variegated – *n.* accumulation, agglomeration, aggregate, aggregation, amassment, assortment, collection, combination, composite, hoard, mass, medley, miscellany, potpourri, trove **2.** business, cartel, company, corporation, firm, house, monopoly, partnership, syndicate, trust – *v.* accumulate, amass, blend, clump, cohere, collect, compile, garner, gather, glean, hoard

congratulate *v.* acclaim, acknowledge, applaud, bless, boost, compliment, extol, felicitate, hail *(Nonformal)*, laud, praise, rejoice with, salute, stroke, toast *Antonyms:* commiserate, condemn, condole, deride

congratulations *n. pl.* applause, best wishes, compliments, felicitations, kudos, praise, regards, salutations

congregate *v.* assemble, besiege, bunch up, collect, concentrate, convene, converge, flock, gather, group, mass, meet, muster, pack, rally, rendezvous, round up, swarm, teem, throng *Antonyms:* dispel, disperse, dissipate, separate

congregation *n.* assemblage, assembly, audience, bloc, body, brethren, caucus, churchgoers, clan, collection, company, congress, coterie, crew, crowd, disciples, fellowship, flock *(Nonformal)*, following, gathering, group, hoard, host, laity, mob, multitude, parishioners, public, throng, turnout

congress *n.* **1.** assembly, association, caucus, chamber, club, committee, conference, convention, council, delegation, encounter, fraternity, government, guild, league, legislative body, legislature, meeting, order, parliament, representatives, senate, society, the house, union **2.** coitus, copulation, fornication, sexual intercourse

congruent *adj.* agreeable, coinciding, compatible, concurring, conforming, consistent, corresponding, harmonious, identical overlapping, synchronous

congruous *adj.* **1.** accordant, agreeing, compatible, concordant, congruent, consistent, consonant, corresponding, harmonious, homogeneous, matching, parallel, sympathetic **2.** appropriate, apropos, apt becoming, expedient, fitting, proper, seemly, suitable

conjectural *adj.* academic, assumed, figured, hypothetical, putative, speculative, supposed, surmised, suspected, theoretical

conjecture *n.* assumption, conclusion guess, hunch, hypothesis, inference inkling, intuition, notion, opinion, presumption, speculation, stab, supposition suspicion, theory, view *Nonformal:* guesstimate, take *Antonyms:* fact, proof, reality – *v.* assume, believe, divine, estimate, feel figure, guess, guesstimate *(Nonformal)* hypothesize, imagine, infer, judge, predict presume, pretend, reckon, speculate, suppose, surmise, suspect, theorize, think

conjugal *adj.* bridal, connubial, marital, married, matrimonial, nuptial, spousal, wedded *Antonyms:* separate, single

conjunction *n.* **1.** affiliation, agreement, alliance, amalgamation, association, cahoots *(Nonformal)*, collusion, combination, concourse, connection, hookup, joining, linking, merger, partnership, symbiosis, synergy, tandem, unification, union *Antonyms:* isolation, seclusion **2.** coincidence, concomitance, concurrence, congruency, contemporariness, parallelism, simultaneity, synchronism, unison

conjure *v.* **1.** adjure, appeal, beckon, beseech, call upon, enjoin, implore, pray, summon, supplicate **2.** bewitch, charm, divine, enchant, entrance, fascinate, hex, invoke, raise

connect *v.* **1.** affix, attach, bracket, combine, conjoin, correlate, couple, fasten, fuse, hitch *or* hook on, interface, join, link, marry, meld, splice, tie, unite, wed, yoke *Antonyms:* detach, divide, sever, split **2.** affiliate, ally, amalgamate, associate, bond, come together, converge, incorporate, meet, merge, network *(Nonformal) Antonyms:* diverge, part **3.** adjoin, border on, contact, meet, touch **4.** agree, communicate, correlate, equate, identify, jibe *(Nonformal)*, relate *Antonyms:* contrast, differ

connected *adj.* **1.** affiliated, akin, allied, applicable, coherent, joined, linked, pertinent, related, shared, similar **2.** associated, banded, bracketed, combined, consecutive, continuous, coupled, joined, linked, matched, mated, related, undivided, united **3.** important, influential, networked, plugged-in *Antonyms:* insulated, isolated

connection *n.* **1.** attachment, combination, coupling, fastening, joining, juncture, link, marriage, network, tie, union **2.** bond, bracket, buckle, elbow, fuse, joint, seam, splice, yoke, zipper **3.** agreement, coherence, congruity, consistency, continuity, correlation, correspondence, harmony, interrelation, logic, relationship, relevance **4.** affiliation, alliance, association, incorporation, partnership, sect **5.** business, commerce, communication, dealings, intercourse, negotiation **6.** contact, go-between, intermediary, middleman *or* middlewoman **7.** blood, folk, family, house, kin, relation

connive *v.* **1.** angle, collude, conspire, contrive, cook up *(Nonformal)*, devise, finagle, frame, hatch, intrigue, machinate, operate, plot, promote, scheme, wrangle **2.** abet, accept, allow, concur, condone, encourage, forgive, ignore, neglect, overlook, remit

connoisseur *n.* aesthete, aficionado, authority, buff, cognoscente, critic, devotee, dilettante, epicure, expert, fanatic *or* fan, freak *(Nonformal)*, gourmet, judge, maven, savant, specialist *Antonyms:* amateur, beginner, dabbler, novice

connotation *n.* allusion, association, colouring, denotation, hint, implication, inference, intention, intimation, nuance, sense, significance, suggestion, undertone

connote *v.* attest, betoken, designate, evidence, express, hint at, imply, import, indicate, insinuate, intimate, mean, purport, signify, suggest *Commonly misused:* **denote**

connubial *adj.* conjugal, marital, married, matrimonial, nuptial, spousal, wedded

conquer *v.* **1.** beat, defeat, lick *(Nonformal)*, master, overcome, overrun, overthrow, subdue, triumph, trounce, vanquish **2.** achieve, acquire, appropriate, claim, gain, seize, take, usurp

conqueror *n.* champion, conquistador, hero, lord, master, subduer, subjugator, vanquisher, victor, winner *Antonyms:* loser, vanquished

conquest *n.* **1.** acquisition, annexation, appropriation, captive, clean sweep *(Nonformal)*, coup, defeat, domination, invasion, mastery, occupation, overthrow, subjugation, takeover, triumph, usurpation, victory, win **2.** booty, catch, haul, loot, perks, plunder, prize, swag *(Nonformal)*, take **3.** desire, enchantment, enthrallment, fancy, object, pleasure, seduction

consanguinity *n.* **1.** affiliation, affinity, agnate, ancestry, blood, brotherhood, cognate, connection, family, family tie, filiation, genealogy, heritage, kin, kinship, lineage, race, relation, sisterhood **2.** affinity, attraction, bond, connection, empathy, intimacy, sympathy

conscience *n.* **1.** awareness, censor, inner voice, knowledge, mind, psyche, thought **2.** compunction, conduct, discrimination, duty, ethics, forethought, grace, integrity, morals, principles, scruples

conscientious *adj.* **1.** accommodating, civil, considerate, courteous, devoted, dutiful, ethical, faithful, gallant, gracious, high-minded, high-principled, honest, honourable, incorruptible, just, moral, pious, principled, right, scrupulous, straightforward, true, upright, virtuous *Antonyms:* amoral, corrupt, insidious **2.** attentive, careful, diligent, fastidious, hard-working, heedful, meticulous, painstaking, punctilious, punctual, reliable, responsible, solicitous, thorough, thoughtful *Antonyms:* careless, negligent, remiss, slack, unreliable

conscious *adj.* **1.** affected, calculated, contemplated, deliberate, designed, intentional, meant, premeditated, purposeful, rational, responsible, self-conscious, studied, willful *Antonyms:* accidental, uncalculated, unintended **2.** acquainted, alert, apprised, assured, attentive, awake, aware, certain, cognizant, conversant, discerning, informed, keen, knowing, mindful, noticing, observing, reasoning, recognizing, responsive, sentient, understanding, vigilant, watchful *Antonyms:* insensible, oblivious, unaware, unconscious **3.** appreciated, felt, perceived, sensed

consciousness *n.* **1.** alertness, apprehension, awareness, cognition, sensibility, sentience, thought **2.** belief, conviction, feeling, knowledge, realization, recognition, regard, sense, understanding

conscript *n.* draftee, enlister, inductee, private, recruit – *v.* call up, draft, enlist, impress, induct, mobilize, recruit

consecrate *v.* **1.** anoint, apotheosize, beatify, bless, canonize, exalt, glorify, hallow, honour, ordain, regard, revere, sanctify, venerate **2.** dedicate, devote, pledge, promise, reserve

consecutive *adj.* attendant, chronological, connected, constant, continuous, ensuing, following, linear, logical, numerical, progressive, running, sequential, serial, subsequent, succeeding, successive, uninterrupted

consensus *n.* accord, agreement, approval, concord, concurrence, conformity, correspondence, general opinion, harmony, unanimity, unity *Antonyms:* disagreement, discord

consent *n.* **1.** acquiescence, allowance, approval, assent, authorization, blessing, *carte blanche (French)*, permission, permit, sanction, sufferance, understanding *Nonformal:* blank check, go-ahead, green light, okay *Antonyms:* denial, forbiddance **2.** accord, compliance, concord, concurrence, conformity, harmony, unity *Antonyms:* contention, dissonance – *v.* accede, accord, agree, allow, assent, comply, concede, concur, grant, let, permit, vouchsafe *Antonyms:* ban, disallow, prohibit

consequence *n.* **1.** aftermath, bottom line, Catch-22, conclusion, effect, end, event, fallout, follow-up, issue, outcome, outgrowth, reaction, repercussion, result, sequel, spin-off, upshot, wake **2.** authority, distinction, eminence, fame, importance, notability, position, prestige, rank, renown, reputation, repute, standing, stature, status **3.** account, concern, exigency, interest, magnitude, moment, note, pith, portent, significance, value, weight

consequent *adj.* **1.** consistent, ensuing, following, resultant, resulting, sequential, subsequent, successive **2.** deductible, logical, necessary, obvious, predictable, rational, reasonable

consequential *adj.* **1.** big, considerable, eventful, far-reaching, grave, important, influential, material, meaningful, momentous, notable, potent, prominent, serious, significant, stupendous, substantial, weighty *Antonyms:* trivial, unimportant **2.** aggrandized, egocentric, big-headed *(Nonformal)*, pompous, preening, pretentious, proud, self-important, vainglorious, vaunting *Antonyms:* humble, modest, unassuming

conservation *n.* attention, care, conservancy, control, defence, ecology, environmentalism, governing, guarding, husbandry, maintenance, forest management, perpetuation, preservation, protection, safeguarding, safekeeping, safety, saving, security, shielding, support, upholding, ward *Antonyms:* destruction, neglect, waste

conservative *adj.* cautious, constant, controlled, conventional, firm, guarded, illiberal, inflexible, moderate, old-fashioned, old-guard, old-line, orthodox, reactionary, restrained, right-wing, safe, stable, staid, steady, traditional *Antonyms:* imaginative, innovative, liberal, progressive, radical – *n.* moderate, conserver, conventionalist, old guard, preserver, rightist, right-winger, tory, traditionalist *Antonyms:* agitator, innovator, progressive, radical, revolutionary

conserve *v.* husband, maintain, preserve, protect, recycle, safeguard, save, shield *Antonyms:* spoil, squander

consider *v.* **1.** chew over *(Nonformal)*, contemplate, deliberate, examine, interpret, judge, meditate, mull over, muse, ponder, reason, ruminate, scrutinize, speculate, study, think about *or* out *or* over, weigh *Antonyms:* disregard, ignore, neglect **2.** account, believe, conclude, count, deem, look at *or* upon, reckon, regard **3.** accede, acknowledge, admit, allow for, concede, grant, heed, provide for, take into account **4.** acclaim, celebrate, honour, praise, recognize, value

considerable *adj.* **1.** abundant, ample, appreciable, astronomical, big, bountiful, comfortable, extensive, great, hefty, huge, large, lavish, plentiful, sizable, substantial, weighty **2.** consequential, distinguished, famous, important, influential, illustrious, important, major, marked, powerful, significant *Antonyms:* inconsequential, insignificant, unremarkable

considerate *adj.* amiable, attentive, charitable, compassionate, generous, giving, gracious, indulgent, kind, thoughtful *Antonyms:* careless, self-centered, greedy

consideration *n.* **1.** application, attention, cogitation, concentration, contemplation, deliberation, discussion, examination, forethought, inspection, notice, observation, reflection, regard, review, rumination, scrutiny, study, thought **2.** conclusion, decision, estimation, evaluation, judgment, opinion, verdict, view **3.** attentiveness, awareness, concern, considerateness, courtesy, esteem, estimation, favour, friendliness, heed, heedfulness, indulgence, kindness, mercy, mindfulness, regard, solicitude, sympathy, tact, thoughtfulness *Antonyms:* contempt, disregard **4.** admiration, esteem, high regard, praise, respect *Antonyms:* censure, condemnation **5.** consequence, gravity, importance, magnitude, significance, substance, value, weight *Antonyms:* irrelevance, insignificance **6.** commission, fee, gratuity, payment, percentage, perquisite, recompense, remuneration, reward, salary, tip, wage

consign *v.* **1.** appoint, assign, authorize, commend, commission, commit, confide, delegate, deposit, entrust, give, relegate, remit, transmit **2.** convey, deliver, dispatch, forward, hand over, issue, route, send, ship, transfer

consignment *n.* **1.** assignment, commission, committal, delegation, delivery, dispatch, distribution, entrustment, relegation, transferral **2.** baggage, cargo, contents, freight, goods, load, luggage, payload, product, shipment, wares

consistency *n.* **1.** accord, agreement, coherence, cohesion, compatibility, conformability, congruity, consonance, constancy, evenness, fealty, harmony, homogeneity, regularity, similarity, stability, steadfastness, steadiness, suitability, symmetry, uniformity, union, unity **2.** compactness, composition, density, firmness, hardness, make-up, porousness, quality, stickiness, texture, thickness, viscosity

consistent *adj.* **1.** constant, dependable, devoted, equable, even, expected, homogeneous, invariable, loyal, persistent, rational, regular, same, steady, true, unchanging, unfailing, uniform, unvarying *Antonyms:* changing, erratic, irregular **2.** accordant, agreeable, coherent, compatible, conforming, congruous, consonant, harmonious, like, logical, matching, sympathetic

Antonyms: contradictory, contrary, discordant, inconsistent, inharmonious

consolation *n.* alleviation, calming, cheer, comfort, compassion, condolence, ease, encouragement, help, mitigation, mollification, pity, relief, solace, succour, support, sympathy *Antonyms:* aggravation, irritation

console *n.* bracket, cabinet, dash *or* dashboard, shelving unit, sideboard – *v.* assuage, buck up *(Nonformal)*, calm, cheer, comfort, condole, encourage, gladden, hearten, lift, reassure, relieve, solace, soothe, sympathize *Antonyms:* aggravate, distress, sadden, torment

consolidate *v.* **1.** amalgamate, amass, band, bind, blend, combine, compact, compound, concentrate, condense, connect, develop, federate, fuse, incorporate, join, league, mass, merge, mix, pool, telescope *(Nonformal)*, unify, unite *Antonyms:* disintegrate, dissipate, undermine, weaken **2.** bolster, buttress, cement, fortify, harden, reinforce, secure, set, solidify, stabilize, strengthen

consolidation *n.* alliance, amalgamation, association, attachment, coalition, combination, compression, concentration, concert, federation, fortification, fusion, incorporation, integration, merger, reinforcement, solidification, strengthening, unification *Antonyms:* disintegration, dissolution

consonance *n.* **1.** accord, agreement, concord, conformity, congruence, congruity, consistency, correspondence, suitableness, unity *Antonyms:* discord, incongruity **2.** alliteration, assonance, chorus, diapason, harmony, melody, music, repetition, rhyme, sound, tune *Antonyms:* cacophony, dissonance

consonant *adj.* **1.** accordant, agreeing, akin, alike, analogous, blending, coincident, comparable, compatible, concordant, congenial, congruous, consistent, correspondent, corresponding, harmonious, like, parallel, similar, suitable, sympathetic, uniform **2.** melodious, pleasant, resonant, sweet, symphonic, tuneful

consort *n.* **1.** amigo, associate, ally, chum, companion, comrade, confrere, crony, fellow, friend, helpmate **2.** husband, mate, pal, partner, spouse, wife – *v.* **1.** accompany, associate, attend, befriend, chum together, fraternize, join, mingle, socialize *Nonformal:* pal *or* run with **2.** agree, arrange, blend, chime, cohere, correspond, fit together, harmonize, jibe *(Nonformal)*, mesh, synchronize, synthesize, tally, unite

consortium *n.* association, bloc, body, coalition, compact, company, concern, coterie, fellowship, group, guild, hanse, interest, league, power alliance, set union

conspicuous *adj.* **1.** apparent, appreciable, clear, discernible, distinct, easily seen, evident, manifest, noticeable, obvious, patent, perceptible, plain, simply there *(Nonformal)*, visible *Antonyms:* concealed, hidden, imperceptible, obscure **2.** arresting, blatant, flagrant, flashy, garish, glaring, gross, loud, notorious, outlandish, showy, splashy, striking *Nonformal:* glitzy, in yer face, jazzy *Antonyms:* modest, understated

conspiracy *n.* **1.** connivance, countermine, counterplot, fix, game, intrigue, machination, plot, scheme, sedition, stratagem, subterfuge, treachery, trick **2.** cabal, clique, collusion, combination, confederacy, faction, junta, league, ring, society

conspire *v.* **1.** conduce, connive, contrive, cook up *(Nonformal)*, devise, hatch, intrigue, machinate, manoeuvre, operate, plot, promote, scheme, wangle **2.** collaborate, collude, combine, concur, confederate, cooperate, fuse, join, league, merge

constancy *n.* **1.** adherence, allegiance, ardour, attachment, certainty, dependability, devotedness, devotion, doggedness, faithfulness, fidelity, fixedness, honesty, loyalty, perseverance, staunchness, steadfastness, steadiness, surety, tenacity, trustworthiness, truthfulness, zeal *Antonyms:* fickleness, infidelity, unfaithfulness **2.** immutability, monotony, permanence, regularity, stability, unchangeableness, uniformity *Antonyms:* instability, variety

constant *adj.* **1.** ceaseless, chronic, continual, continuous, endless, enduring, eternal, everlasting, firm, fixed, habitual, immutable, incessant, interminable, invariable, lasting, nonstop, permanent, perpetual, persistent, relentless, stable, steadfast, steady, sustained, unalterable, unbroken, unending, uninterrupted, unrelenting, unremitting *Antonyms:* changeable, deviating, intermittent **2.** abiding, allegiant, attached, dependable, determined, devoted, dogged, faithful, fast, loyal, persevering, resolute, staunch, true, trustworthy, trusty, unfailing, unflagging, unwavering *Antonyms:* inconstant, unfaithful **3.** consistent, homogeneous, monolithic, monotonous, regular, standard, symmetrical, unchanging, uniform, unvarying *Antonyms:* irregular, variable

consternation *n.* alarm, amazement, anxiety, awe, bewilderment, confusion, dismay, distress, dread, fear, fright, funk *(Nonformal)*, horror, muddle, panic, perplexity, scare, shock, stupefaction, terror, trepidation, wonder *Antonyms:* calm, cool *(Nonformal)*

constituency *n.* **1.** body politic, citizenry, electorate, electors, folk, grassroots, membership, nation, people, population, public, supporters, voters, voting public **2.** district, dual riding *(Historical)*, municipality, pocket, borough, precinct, province, riding, system, voting area, ward

constituent *adj.* **1.** basic, component, elemental, essential, formative, fundamental, integral, primary **2.** deciding, electing, electoral, enfranchised, voting – *n.* **1.** bit, component, element, essential, factor, fraction, fundamental, ingredient, makings, material, part, piece, portion, principle, unit **2.** balloter, citizen, elector, taxpayer, voter

constitute *v.* **1.** complete, compose, compound, comprise, embody, fill, integrate **2.** build, commission, construct, create, develop, establish, fabricate, fix, form, found, institute, make **3.** appoint, delegate, depute, elect, empower, inaugurate, install, name, nominate, ordain, sanction *Antonyms:* remove, topple **4.** authorize, decree, enact, enforce, impose, legalize, legislate, pass

constitution *n.* **1.** cast, character, composition, condition, disposition, essence, habit, humour, mentality, mettle, mood, nature, personality, spirit, temper, temperament **2.** architecture, build, composition, construction, content, design, form, frame, habit, health, make-up, physique, structure, vitality **3.** body of laws, canon, charter, code, composition, *corpus juris (Latin)*, custom, law, legislation, principles *Canadian Constitutions:* Act of Union, BNA Act, Constitutional Act, Quebec Act, Royal Proclamation of 1763 *Constitutional concepts:* Deux Nations, distinct society, founding nation, founding people, French fact, notwithstanding clause, sovereignty-association, special status, triple-E Senate **4.** appointment, creation, establishment, formation, foundation, organization

constitutional *adj.* **1.** basic, built-in, congenital, deep-seated, elementary, essential, fundamental, inborn, inbred, ingrained, inherent, innate, intrinsic, natural, organic, vital **2.** aboveboard, approved, chartered, democratic, ensured, judicial, lawful, legal, legitimate, licit, protected, sanctioned, statutory, valid, vested *Antonyms:* criminal, illicit **3.** beneficial, good, healthful, healthy, salubrious, wholesome *Antonyms:* noxious, pernicious – *n.* airing, exercise, hike, perambulation, ramble, saunter, stroll, walk

constrain *v.* **1.** bar, check, confine, constrict, curb, deny, deprive, disallow, hold back, hold down, impede, inhibit, repress, restrain, stifle, withhold **2.** bind, bridle, chain, confine, hem in, hog-tie *(Nonformal)*, hold, immure, imprison, incarcerate, inter, jail *Antonyms:* free, manumit **3.** browbeat, bully, coerce, compel, drive, force, induce, intimidate, impel, make, necessitate, oblige, pressure, urge *Nonformal:* bulldoze, railroad

constraint *n.* **1.** coercion, compulsion, duress, force, pressure, repression *Antonyms:* emancipation, freedom, liberty **2.** arrest, confinement, detainment, imprisonment, incarceration *Antonyms:* leave, release **3.** block, bond, fetter, handcuff, ligature, manacles, rope, tie, yoke **4.** check, confinement, cramp, curb, damper, deterrent, encumbrance, hindrance, impediment, limitation, restraint, restriction **5.** bashfulness, diffidence, embarrassment, hang-up *(Nonformal)*, humility, inhibition, modesty, reservation, reserve, restraint, shyness, timidity

constrict *v.* **1.** bind, block, confine, cramp, curb, impede, restrain, restrict, retard, thwart *Antonyms:* free, loosen **2.** choke, clench, squeeze, strangle, strangulate **3.** attenuate, compress, concentrate, condense, contract, draw together, limit, narrow, pinch, shrink, tauten, tighten

constriction *n.* **1.** arresting, binding, choking, compression, narrowing, reduction, squeezing, stranglehold, tightening **2.** blockage, bottleneck, check, constraint, curb, hampering, hindrance, impediment, limitation, obstruction, resistance, restraint, restriction **3.** contraction, cramp, pressure, stenosis, strangulation, stricture, tightness

construct *n.* creation, fabrication, formulation, framework, ideology, invention, model, paradigm, theory – *v.* **1.** assemble, build, compound, constitute, create, engineer, erect, fabricate, fashion, forge, form, found, frame, invent, make, manufacture, organize, produce, put together, put up, raise, rear, set up, shape, structure, throw together *(Nonformal) Antonyms:* bulldoze, demolish, dismantle, level, raze **2.** compose, design, devise, dream up, formulate, imagine

construction *n.* **1.** architecture, arrangement, assembly, building, composition, configuration, elevation, erection, fabrication, formation, organization, shaping, structure *Kinds of construction:* bricklaying, bridge, cabinetmaking, dam, earthmoving, excavation, finishing, foundation, framing, heavy, highway, home, hypothetical, masonry, modular, plumbing, post-and-beam, remodeling, roofing, timber framing, tunnel, wattle-and-daub, wiring, wood-frame **2.** aspect, composition, constitution, fashion, form, look, make, meaning, shape, style **3.** exegesis, explanation, interpretation, opinion, reading, rendering, rendition, translation, version *Nonformal:* spin, take

constructive *adj.* **1.** advantageous, beneficial, effective, expedient, helpful, positive, practical, productive, useful, valuable *Antonyms:* destructive, ineffective, negative, useless **2.** architectural, building, constructional, edificial, structural **3.** assumed, connoted, implicit, implied, inferred, insinuated, meant, presumed, understood

construe *v.* **1.** analyze, decipher, deconstruct, deduce, define, explain, explicate, expound, infer, interpret, parse, read, render, spell out, take, translate, understand *Antonyms:* convolute, muddy

consul *n.* agent, ambassador, delegate, emissary, envoy, lawyer, legate, magistrate, nuncio, plenipotentiary, officer, representative *Commonly misused:* **council, counsel**

consult *v.* **1.** ask, inquire, query, quiz **2.** compare, confer, debate, deliberate, discuss, meet, talk

consultation *n.* **1.** appointment, confab *(Nonformal),* conference, council, deliberation, dialogue, discussion, examination, hearing, interview, meeting, parley, preliminary discussion, session, sitting **2.** advice, guidance, instruction, recommendation, second opinion

consume *v.* **1.** drink, devour, down, eat, eat up, feed, gorge, gulp, guzzle, ingest, nibble, put away *or* down, swallow, swill *Nonformal:* inhale, polish off, scarf, wolf **2.** annihilate, burn, demolish, destroy, devastate, extinguish, finish, overwhelm, ravage, raze, ruin, wreck *Antonyms:* conserve, protect **3.** deplete, dissipate, exhaust, expend, spend, squander, waste, wear out *Antonyms:* bank, save **4.** absorb, captivate, charm, concern, engage, engross, fascinate, fixate, hypnotize, mesmerize, monopolize, obsess, occupy, preoccupy, rivet

consummate *adj.* absolute, best, brilliant, complete, crowning, extraordinary, faultless, finished, flawless, gifted, ideal, impeccable, inimitable, matchless, peerless, perfect, polished, superlative, supreme, topnotch, transcendent, ultimate, unsurpassable, virtuoso, whole – *v.* accomplish, achieve, attain, cap, carry out, complete, crown, execute, fulfill, perfect, produce, realize

consumption *n.* **1.** conflagration, demolition, destruction, devastation, loss, razing, ruin, waste *Antonyms:* construction, rebuilding **2.** drinking, eating, feeding, ingestion, replenishment, repletion, satiety, surfeit *Nonformal:* guzzling, scarfing **3.** amount, decrease, depletion, diminution, expenditure, quantity, rate, use, utilization **4.** affliction, disease, illness, malady, phthisis, progressive emaciation, pulmonary sickness, tuberculosis *or* TB, white plague

contact *adj.* bodily, close, corporeal, corporal, physical, touching – *n.* **1.** closeness, contiguity, contingence, impact, impingement, junction, juxtaposition, nearness, propinquity, proximity, relation, touching, union **2.** commerce, communication, conversation, correspondence, dealings, interaction, interchange, social exchange *or* intercourse, touch **3.** acquaintance, connection, go-between, informant, insider *(Nonformal)*, middleman *or* woman, source, spokesperson – *v.* **1.** approach, call, communicate, e-mail, fax, interact, interface, network, notify, phone, relate, ring up, speak *or* talk to, telephone, touch base, visit, write **2.** abrade, collide, converge, encounter, impinge, meet, scrape *Antonyms:* diverge, separate **3.** affect, influence, impress, reach, stir, sway *Commonly misused:* **contract**

contagion *n.* **1.** circulation, communication, contact, dissemination, spread, transfer, transmission **2.** disease, epidemic, illness, infection, pestilence, plague, virus **3.** adulteration, bane, contamination, corruption, perversion, pollution

contagious *adj.* **1.** catching, communicable, epidemic, infectious, pandemic, spreading, transferable, transmissible, transmittable **2.** deadly, fatal, harmful, mortal, noxious, pestilential, poisonous *Antonyms:* salubrious, wholesome

contain *v.* **1.** bottle up, cover, enclose, encompass, hold **2.** accommodate, carry, comprise, consist of, embody, embrace, entail, equal, include, incorporate, involve **3.** bind, circumscribe, confine, encircle, girdle, hem in, surround **4.** arrest, check, control, curb, govern, harness, limit, quash, quell, rein, repress, restrain, restrict, smother, stifle, stop *Antonyms:* allow, free, liberate

container *n.* holder, receptacle, repository *Kinds of container:* bag, barrel, basin, basket, beaker, bin, bottle, bowl, box, bucket, caddy, cage, caisson, can, canister, canteen, carafe, carton, case, cask, casket, cauldron, chamber, chest, churn, cistern, cookie jar, cradle, crate, crock, cupboard, ewer, firkin, flask, glass, hamper, hogshead, humidor, hutch, jar, jigger, jug, keg, kettle, kist *(Scottish)*, knapsack, mug, pail, pan, pipeline, pot, pouch, purse, reliquary, sack, scuttle, stein, tank, tankard, tote, tub, vase, vat, vessel, vial

contaminate *v.* **1.** dirty, foul, infect, pollute, soil, spoil, stain, taint *Antonyms:* clean, decontaminate, disinfect, purify, sanitize **2.** adulterate, corrupt, debase, defile, deprave, desecrate, harm, injure, pervert, profane, sully, tarnish, violate *Antonyms:* honour, respect

contamination *n.* **1.** decay, disease, dirtying, foulness, germ, impurity, infection, offal, pestilence, poisoning, radiation, spoilage, taint, toxin, virus *Antonyms:* decontamination, sanitization, sterilization **2.** adulteration, corruption, defilement, degradation, filth, moral decay, perversion, violation

contemplate *v.* **1.** brood, cogitate, consider, deliberate, examine, meditate, mull over, muse, percolate, ponder, reflect, ruminate, size up, study, take in, think about *or* over, weigh *Nonformal:* chew, kick around **2.** aim, anticipate, conspire, design, envisage, expect, foresee, intend, mean, perpend, plan, plot, propose, scheme, speculate **3.** eyeball *(Nonformal)*, gaze upon, look *or* stare at, observe, perceive, see

contemplation *n.* **1.** cogitation, consideration, deliberation, examination, inspection, meditation, musing, observation, pondering, prayer, reflection, reverie, rumination, scrutiny, study, survey, thought **2.** aim, anticipation, aspiration, design, expectation, goal, intention, plan, purpose, speculation

contemplative *adj.* abstracted, brooding, cogitative, intent, introspective, lost, meditative, musing, pensive, pondering, ponderous, rapt, reflecting, reflective, ruminative, speculative, thinking, thoughtful *Antonyms:* alert, heedful, mindful

contemporary *adj.* **1.** accompanying, associated, attendant, coeval, coexistent, co-existing, coincident, concomitant, concurrent, connected, contemporaneous, existing, linked, related, simultaneous, synchronous *Antonyms:* preceding, succeeding **2.** current, existent, extant, modern, new, present, present-day, recent, topical *Antonyms:* obsolete, old-fashioned, out-of-date, passé, vintage **3.** abreast, hot, latest, now, ultramodern, up-to-date, up-to-the-minute *French:* à la mode, au courant *Nonformal:* hip, just out, mod, newfangled – *n.* associate, colleague, equal, peer *Antonyms:* predecessor, successor, subordinate

contempt *n.* **1.** antipathy, aversion, condescension, defiance, derision, disdain, disregard, disrespect, distaste, hatred, humiliation, impudence, indignity, loathing, malice, mockery, neglect, repugnance, ridicule, scorn, slight, snobbery *Antonyms:* admiration, esteem, honour, respect **2.** disfavour, disgrace, dishonour, disrepute, ignominy, shame,

contemptible *adj.* abhorrent, abject, abominable, bad, base, cheap, currish, degenerate, despicable, detestable, dirty, disgusting, hateful, ignominious, inferior, mean, scrofulous, shameful, sordid, sorry, vile, worthless, wretched *Nonformal:* lousy, lowdown *Antonyms:* admirable, honourable, laudable, praiseworthy *Commonly misused:* **contemptuous**

contemptuous *adj.* arrogant, cavalier, condescending, contumelious, cynical, derisive, disdainful, dismissive, disrespectful, haughty, insolent, insulting, scornful, sneering, snobbish, supercilious *Antonyms:* civil, courteous, gracious, humble, polite *Commonly misused:* **contemptible**

contend *v.* **1.** challenge, compete, contest, play for, strive, vie *Antonyms:* capitulate, surrender **2.** argue, bicker, debate, dispute, quarrel, remonstrate *Antonyms:* concede, yield **3.** battle, brawl, clash, duel, fight, scrap, spar, struggle, tussle *Antonyms:* flee, retreat **4.** affirm, assert, aver, claim, maintain

content *adj.* **1.** at ease, comfortable, fulfilled, finished, full, glad, gratified, happy, replete, sated, satiated, satisfied, smug, tranquil **2.** accepting, agreeable, appeased, assenting, complacent, consenting, resigned, submissive *Antonyms:* arrogant, rebellious, recalcitrant – *n.* **1.** body, components, composition, constitution, entrails, essence, gist, guts, heart, idea, ingredients, insides, matter, meaning, meat *(Nonformal),* significance, subject, subject matter, substance, text **2.** amount, capacity, compass, distance, extent, hold, length, magnitude, quantity, size, volume **3.** comfort, ease, gratification, happiness, peace, peace of mind, pleasure, satisfaction, serenity *Antonyms:* anxiety, sorrow – *v.* appease, captivate, charm, delight, enrapture, gladden, gratify, humour, indulge, mollify, pamper, placate, please, reconcile, satisfy, suffice, thrill, tickle *(Nonformal)* *Antonyms:* aggravate, anger

contented *adj.* **1.** at ease *or* home *or* peace *or* rest, carefree, cheerful, comfortable, glad, happy, pleased, relaxed, serene, thankful *Antonyms:* annoyed, anxious, troubled **2.** complacent, gratified, mollified, placated, satisfied *Antonyms:* disgruntled, dissatisfied

contention *n.* **1.** altercation, argument, battle, competition, conflict, contest, controversy, difference, discord, dispute, dissension, disunity, enmity, feud, fight, fray, hostility, quarrel, rivalry, scrap, scuffle, set-to, skirmish, squabble, strife, struggle, war, wrangle *Nonformal:* beef, hassle, run in, scene, scrap *Antonyms:* accord, concord, harmony **2.** allegation, assertion, belief, charge, claim, hypothesis, opinion, philosophy, position, theory, thought, view, viewpoint

contentious *adj.* aggressive, bellicose, captious, fractious, hawkish, litigious, peevish, petulant, pugnacious, ornery, refractory, surly, warlike *Antonyms:* accommodating, cooperative, hospitable

contentment *n.* comfort, complacency, composure, ease, equanimity, fulfillment, gladness, gratification, happiness, peace, pleasure, repletion, satisfaction, serenity, well-being *Antonyms:* discomfort, displeasure, uneasiness, unhappiness

contents *n. pl.* capacity, cargo, chapters, constituents, details, divisions, elements, entrails, essence, filling, freight, furnishing, ingredients, inventory, lading, load, packing, parts, shipment, stuffing, sum *Nonformal:* guts, innards, nub, what's inside

contest *n.* **1.** action, altercation, battle, brawl, brush, combat, conflict, controversy, discord, dispute, domestic encounter, engagement, fight, fray, rivalry, row, rumple, rumpus, run-in, scrap, set-to, skirmish, strife, struggle, tug-of-war *(Nonformal) Antonyms:* accord, harmony, peace **2.** argument, debate, exchange, heated discussion, meeting, war of words **3.** bonspiel, challenge, competition, face-off, match, meet, playoff, round robin, show-down, tip-off, tournament – *v.* **1.** attempt, challenge, compete, contend, rival, strive, struggle, take on, vie **2.** argue, bicker, defend, dispute, quarrel, question *Antonyms:* back off, concede **3.** attack, battle, brawl, conflict, donnybrook, duel, dust-up *(Nonformal)*, feud, fight, row, scrap, strike, wrangle

contestant *n.* **1.** aspirant, candidate, competitor, contender, contestee, entrant, hopeful, participant, player, team member, wannabe winner *(Nonformal)* **2.** adversary, antagonist, challenger, combatant, disputant, litigant, rival

context *n.* ambience, atmosphere, backdrop, background, circumstances, climate, conditions, element, environment, framework, locale, location, meaning, medium, milieu, *mise en scène (French)*, place, qualifying factor, relation, scene, setting, situation, space, sphere, surroundings

contiguous *adj.* **1.** abutting, adhering, adjacent, adjoining, bordering, cleaving, close, conterminous, fused, juxtapositional, linked, meeting, near, nearing, neighbouring next, next to, touching *Antonyms:* detached, distant, far-flung, independent, separated

continent *adj.* **1.** abstentious, abstinent, acetic, austere, moderate, refraining restrained, self-restrained, teetotalling, temperate *Antonyms:* excessive, indulgent, profligate, reckless **2.** celibate, chaste, inhibited, unsullied, vestal, virginal *Antonyms:* libidinous, licentious, wanton – *n.* continental landform, landmass, mainland *Names of continents and land masses:* Africa, Antarctica, Asia and Europe *or* Eurasia, Australia, North America, South America

continental *adj.* **1.** broad, capacious, expansive, extensive, gigantic, huge, immense, large, massive, sizable, sweeping, vast, voluminous, wide *Antonyms:* limited, narrow, small, tight **2.** civilized, cosmopolitan, cultivated, European, highbrow, intellectual, refined, sophisticated, suave, urbane *Antonyms:* parochial, provincial

contingency *adj.* alternate, back-up, bad-out *(Nonformal)*, emergency, substitute – *n.* **1.** accident, chance, possibility, uncertainty **2.** crisis, emergency, exigency, happening, incident, occasion, predicament, quandary, strait, turning point **3.** adjunct, incidental, insignificance, nonessential, sideline, subsidiary, triviality

contingent *adj.* **1.** liable, likely, possible, probable, uncertain, unforeseeable, unpredictable **2.** accidental, adventitious, casual, chance, fluky, fortuitous, haphazard, random, serendipitous *Antonyms:* certain, inevitable, necessary **3.** conditional, dependent, provisional, relative, subject to, waiting for – *n.* **1.** allotment, batch, bunch, cut, division, part, portion, quota, share **2.** assembly, body, company, coterie, delegation, entourage, followers, group, mission, party, posse, quota, section, set, troop

continual *adj.* **1.** ceaseless, constant, continuous, endless, enduring, eternal, everlasting, incessant, infinite, interminable, limitless, looped, perpetual, prolonged, relentless, running, steady, timeless, unbroken, unending, unlimited, untold *Antonyms:* ceasing, erratic, intermittent, irregular, spasmodic **2.** frequent, habitual, inveterate, perennial, persistent, recurrent, regular, repeat *Commonly misused:* **continuous**

continuance *n.* **1.** continuation, elongation, extension, lengthening, protraction, spreading **2.** adjournment, hiatus, postponement **3.** endurance, lingering, longevity, maintenance, permanence, perseverance, persistence, survival **4.** constancy, duration, length, period, run, spell, stretch, term, time

continuation *n.* **1.** preservation, progression, propagation, protraction, recommencement, renewal, restart, resumption, return succession **2.** extension, extrapolation, lengthening, prolongation, protraction, stretching **3.** addendum, addition, adjunct, afterthought, appendix, epilogue, installment, postscript, PS, sequel, supplement

continue *v.* **1.** abide, endure, keep, linger, maintain, outlive, perpetuate, persevere, persist, pursue, remain, survive, sustain *Antonyms:* leave, surrender **2.** advance, carry forward *or* on, drive, forge ahead, go on, keep going, march along, proceed, progress *Antonyms:* quit, retreat **3.** begin again *or* over, pick up, recommence, reestablish, renew, reopen, restart, restore, resume, return to **4.** extend, lengthen, prolong, reach, spread, stretch *Antonyms:* limit, narrow, restrict

continuity *n.* **1.** continuum, durability, endurance, perpetuity, survival **2.** chain, coherence, connection, flow, linkage, order, progression, sequence, succession, train, unity **3.** constancy, consistency, homogeneity, monotony, sameness, uniformity

continuous *adj.* **1.** ceaseless, constant, incessant, infinite, monotonous, never-ending, nonstop, ongoing, perpetual, recurrent, repetitive, steady, unbroken, unceasing, unfaltering, uninterrupted *Antonyms:* broken, irregular **2.** consecutive, joined, linked, orderly, sequential, tight, unified *Commonly misued:* **continual**

contort *v.* **1.** bend, curve, disfigure, gnarl, knot, misshape, turn, twist, warp, wind, wrench, writhe **2.** bias, brutalize, colour, corrupt, deform, distort, misconstrue, pervert, skew, slant, strain

contortion *n.* **1.** asymmetry, convolution, crookedness, disfigurement, deformity, distortion, inequality, malformation **2.** gnarl, kink, knot, twist, warp, wrinkle

contour *n.* composition, configuration, curve, delineation, form, lineament, line, outline, profile, relief, shape, silhouette – *v.* **1.** construct, fashion, form, mold, shape **2.** delineate, demarcate, draw, limn, outline, profile, trace

contraband *adj.* banned, black-market, bootlegged, excluded, forbidden, illegal, illicit, prohibited, proscribed, smuggled, unauthorized, unlawful – *n.* **1.** black marketing, bootlegging, gunrunning, piracy, poaching, racketeering, rumrunning, smuggling, trafficking, violation **2.** bootleg, smuggled goods, swag *(Nonformal) Common contraband:* aliens, arms, exotic animals, jewels, liquor, narcotics, recordings, rum, software, tobacco

contraceptive *n.* birth control device, guard, preventative measure, prophylactic, safeguard *Common contraceptive:* abstinence, birth control pill, condom *or* French letter *or* prophylactic *or* rubber, contraceptive foam, diaphragm, intrauterine device *or* IUD, morning-after pill, oral contraceptive, rhythm method, spermicidal jelly, sponge, the pill *(Nonformal)*

contract *n.* **1.** agreement, arrangement, bargain, bond, commission, commitment, compact, concordat, convention, covenant, deal, deposition, engagement, gentleman's agreement *(Nonformal)*, guarantee, handshake, indenture, obligation, pact, paper, pledge, promise, proof, record, settlement, treaty, understanding, undertaking, vow **2.** association, betrothal, marriage, matrimony, union, wedlock – *v.* **1.** acquire, break out, catch, come down with *(Nonformal)*, develop, get, incur, sink, succumb to, weaken *Antonyms:* avert, avoid, escape, ward off **2.** accept, adjust, agree, arrange, assent, assume, bargain, bound, buy into, clinch, close, come to terms, commit, consent, covenant, engage, enter into, indenture, initial, negotiate, obligate, pact, pledge, promise, settle, sign, stipulate, swear to, undertake *Nonformal:* hammer out, ink *Antonyms:* decline, disagree, refuse, turn down **3.** abbreviate, abridge, compress, condense, confine, constrict, curtail, cut, decrease, deflate, diminish, downsize, dwindle, lessen, narrow, reduce, remit, shorten, shrink, shrivel, slash, tighten, trim, truncate *Antonyms:* augment, expand, widen **4.** affiance, betroth, espouse, marry, wed *Antonyms:* divorce, separate **5.** crease, crinkle, furrow, pucker, purse, wrinkle *Commonly misused:* **contact**

contraction *n.* **1.** compression, condensing, constriction, cramping, curtailment, decrease, diminishing, dwindling, lessening, receding, recession, reduction, restriction, shortening, shrinkage, shrinking, shrivelling, squeezing, subtraction, tightening *Antonyms:* expansion, growth, swelling **2.** abbreviation, abridgement, abstract, digest, epitome, précis, synopsis

contradictory *adj.* **1.** anti *(Nonformal)*, antithetical, conflicting, contrary, counteractive, discrepant, incompatible, incongruous, irreconcilable, nullifying, opposing, opposite, paradoxical, polar, reverse **2.** antagonistic, argumentative, confrontational, controversial, disputatious, negative, polemic

contraption *n.* apparatus, artifice, contrivance, creation, device, gadget, implement, invention, machine, tool, utensil *Nonformal:* doohickey, gizmo, thingamajig, whirligig

contrary *adj.* **1.** adamant, antagonistic, balky, contumacious, headstrong, hostile, inimitable, mulish, negative, obstinate, ornery, perverse, recalcitrant, restive, stubborn, uncooperative, unfriendly, unruly, willful *Antonyms:* accommodating, agreeable, cooperative **2.** antithesis, antithetical, clashing, conflicting, contradictory, converse, counter, discordant, incongruous, inconsistent, inverse, opposite, reverse *Antonyms:* consistent, lucid **3.** adverse, calamitous, detrimental, disadvantageous, incommodious, opposed, unfavourable *Antonyms:* auspicious, expedient

contrast *n.* **1.** balancing, comparison, differentiation, examination, juxtaposition, weighing **2.** contradiction, difference, distinction, divergence, diversity, incompatibility, inconsistency, opposition, variation **3.** brightness, clarity, colour, lucidity, sharpness, tone, weight – *v.* **1.** analyze, collate, compare **2.** differentiate, discriminate, distinguish, diverge, off-set, oppose, vary *Antonyms:* homogenize, merge

contravene *v.* **1.** breach, break, combat, conflict with, defy, disobey, encroach, infringe, obstruct, transgress, trespass, violate *Antonyms:* abide, comply, obey **2.** belie, contradict, disaffirm, dispute, impugn, negate, oppose, refute, repudiate *Antonyms:* advocate, support

contribute *v.* **1.** accord, add *or* add to, advance, afford, aid, assist, augment, bestow, chip in *(Nonformal)*, commit, cooperate, enrich, fortify, furnish, give, help, present, proffer, promote, provide, reinforce, sacrifice, share, sponsor, strengthen, subscribe, subsidize, supply, support, uphold *Antonyms:* disregard, ignore, neglect **2.** bequeath, bequest, confer, dispense, donate, endow, grant,

contribution *n.* **1.** addition, augmentation, improvement, increase, input, offering, present, subscription, supplement **2.** alms, benefaction, beneficence, bestowal, boon, charity, donation, gift, grant, handout, largesse, Peter's pence, subsidy **3.** argument, article, copy, editorial, insert, letter, story, text **4.** assessment, custom, duty, impost, levy, tariff, tax

contrite *adj.* apologetic, begging, chastened, compunctious, conscience-stricken, humble, on one's keens *(Nonformal)*, penitent, regretful, remorseful, repentant, sorrowful, sorry, tearful *Antonyms:* proud, satisfied, smug

contrition *n.* attrition, compunction, contriteness, humiliation, penance, penitence, regret, remorse, repentance, rue, self-reproach, shame, sorrow

contrivance *n.* **1.** apparatus, appliance, contraption, creation, device, engine, equipment, gadget, gear, gimmick, implement, instrument, invention, machine, mechanism, Rube Goldberg contraption, tool, utensil **2.** angle, artifice, conspiracy, design, fabrication, intrigue, plan, plot, project, ruse, scheme, stratagem, trick, twist **3.** adaptability, creativity, imagination, ingenuity, originality, resourcefulness

contrive *v.* brew *(Nonformal)*, coin, concoct, construct, create, design, devise, dream up, engineer, fabricate, fashion, forge, form, formulate, frame, hatch, imagine, invent, improvise, make, machinate, manage, manipulate, manufacture, plan, plot, program, rig, scheme, throw together, trump up *Nonformal:* cook up, finagle, wangle, whip up

control *n.* **1.** ascendancy, authority, charge, command, dictate, direction, discipline, domination, dominion, government, guidance, management, mastership, mastery, might, power, regulation, rule, superintendence, supervision, supremacy, sway, wheel *Nonformal:* clout, driver's seat, inside track, upper hand **2.** break, bridle, chain, check, curb, deterrent, governor, harness, inhibitor, leash, limitation, muzzle, repression, restriction, tether, yoke **3.** button, dial, high/low, joystick, knob, on/off, regulator, remote, switch, zapper *(Nonformal)* – *v.* **1.** dictate, discipline, dominate, domineer, exploit, hold face *(Nonformal)*, hold serve, master, predominate, reign, rule, subjugate, tame, vanquish, whip **2.** advise, administer, boss, chaperone, command, conduct, direct, discipline, employ, govern, guide, handle, head, hold the purse strings *(Nonformal)*, instruct, lead, maintain, manage, manipulate, mastermind, order, oversee, pilot, regulate, run, steer, superintend, supervise, wield **3.** adjust, box in *(Nonformal)*, bridle, check, collect, constrain, contain, harness, limit, moderate, prevent, quell, repress, restrain, yoke **4.** check, confirm, corroborate, establish, prove, rectify, substantiate, test, verify

controversial *adj.* **1.** arguable, contestable, controvertible, debatable, disputable, doubtful, dubious, litigious, moot, polemical, problematic, questionable, suspect, uncertain, under question *or* scrutiny, unsettled *Antonyms:* accepted, decided, settled **2.** contentious, disputatious, explosive, hot *(Nonformal)*, incendiary, inflammatory, loaded *(Nonformal)*, provocative, scandalous, touchy

controversy *n.* altercation, argument, conflict, contention, contradiction, debate, difference, disagreement, discrepancy, dispute, dissension, fuss, gainsaying, hot potato *(Nonformal)*, opposition, polemic, quarrel, row, scene, scrap, squabble, strife, tiff, variance *Antonyms:* agreement, concession

contumacious *adj.* contemptuous, dissentious, disobedient, insubordinate, intractable, rebellious, recalcitrant, refractory, seditious, stubborn *Antonyms:* acquiescent, amenable, malleable

contusion *n.* bang, black eye *or* shiner *(Nonformal)*, bruise, bump, injury, knock, swelling, wound *Commonly misused:* **concussion**

conundrum *n.* anagram, difficulty, enigma, mystery, paradox, poser, problem, puzzle, question, rebus, riddle

convalescent *adj.* **1.** healing, mending, rallying, recovering, recuperating, rehabilitating, restored, strengthening **2.** curative, recuperative, rehabilitative, remedial, reparative, restitutive, restorative *Antonyms:* debilitating, draining, enervating – *n.* case, invalid, patient, sufferer, valetudinarian, victim

convene *v.* **1.** call, convoke, enlist, marshall, muster, send for, summon *Nonformal:* corral, round up **2.** assemble, collect, congregate, form, gather, meet, rally, unite *Antonyms:* adjourn, disperse, dissolve, scatter

convenience *n.* **1.** accessibility, expedience, handiness, opportuneness, serviceability, suitability, timeliness, usefulness, utility **2.** accommodation, advantage, assistance, benefit, comfort, ease, enjoyment, means, relief, satisfaction, support **3.** accessory, aid, amenity, appliance, comforts, facility, luxury, service, time-saver **4.** avail, choosing, disposal, leisure, pace, time

convenient *adj.* **1.** advantageous, aiding, appropriate, assisting, beneficial, commodious, conducive, contributive, favourable, helpful, opportune, seasonable, serviceable, suitable, suited, timely *Antonyms:* damaging, detrimental **2.** accessible, adaptable, at hand, available, close, handy, nearby, ready, time-saving, useful, within reach *Antonyms:* inaccessible, troublesome, worthless **3.** understandable, user-friendly, well-planned *Antonyms:* confusing, difficult

convent *n.* abbey, cloister, monastery, nunnery, order, priory, religious community *or* house, retreat, sanctuary, sisterhood

convention *n.* **1.** assembly, conclave, conference, congress, convocation, discussion, meeting, powwow, rally **2.** cartel, council, delegation, group, guild, lodge, sect, society, union **3.** code, custom, decorum, etiquette, fashion, form, formality, habit, law, mores, practice, propriety, protocol, rule, standard, tradition **4.** accord, compact, constitution, contract, deal, pact, settlement, treaty

conventional *adj.* **1.** accepted, approved, common, current, customary, orthodox, practiced, popular, standard, traditional, wide-spread **2.** banal, formulaic, hackneyed, parochial, prosaic, routine, run-of-the-mill, stereotypical, trite, unoriginal *Nonformal:* humdrum, lame *Antonyms:* avant-garde, cutting-edge, novel **3.** bourgeois, conforming, conservative, moderate, narrow, puritanical, rigid, sober, square *(Nonformal)*, straight, strait-laced *Antonyms:* eccentric, radical, revolutionary **4.** authorized, binding, contracted, defined, legal, negotiated, sanctioned, stipulated

converge *v.* assemble, close in, combine, concentrate, concur, draw together, focus, gather, intersect, join, meet, merge, mingle, rally, swarm, unite *Antonyms:* diverge, scatter, separate

conversant *adj.* acquainted, aware, cognizant, comprehending, conscious, educated, experienced, familiar, informed, knowing, learned, privy, proficient, sensible, skilled, versed, well-informed *Nonformal:* in the loop, plugged in, up to speed *Antonyms:* ignorant, naive, uninformed

conversation *n.* banter, chat, chatter, chitchat, communication, dialogue, discourse, discussion, exchange, intercourse, meeting, palaver, parley, speech, talk, *tête-à-tête (French) Nonformal:* confab, hot stove, rap *or* rap session

converse *adj.* antithetical, contradictory, contrary, counter, different, opposite, reversed, transposed – *n.* **1.** communication, conversation, dialogue, exchange, talk **2.** antithesis, flip side *(Nonformal)*, inverse, mirror image, obverse, opposite, reverse – *v.* chat, commune, communicate, confer, connect, discuss, exchange, interface, parley, speak, talk *Nonformal:* gab, rap, schmooze, shoot the breeze

convert *n.* believer, born again, disciple, follower, neophyte, novice, novitiate, proselyte *Antonyms:* apostate, dissenter – *v.* **1.** become, metamorphize, mutate, regenerate, transform, transmogrify **2.** alter, change, make over, modify, morph *(Nonformal)*, rearrange, rebuild, refurbish, remodel, restore *Antonyms:* conserve, maintain, preserve **3.** accommodate, adapt, adjust, bend, develop, evolve *Antonyms:* stagnate, vegetate **4.** bias, brainwash, bring around, convince, influence, mould, persuade, program, sway, win over **5.** exchange, redeem, return **6.** baptize, introduce, proselytize, reclaim, redeem, reform, save

convertible *adj.* adaptable, alterable, changeable, exchangeable, interchangeable, mutable, transferable *Antonyms:* fixed, homeostatic, intransigent, rigid – *n.* **1.** automobile, car, roadster *Nonformal:* ragtop, soft-top **2.** recliner, sofa-bed, studio couch

convex *adj.* arched, bent, bowed, bulged, curving, gibbous, protuberant, raised, rounded *Antonyms:* concave, cupped, hollowed, sunken *Commonly misused:* **concave**

convey *v.* **1.** bear, carry, drag, ferry, move, portage, pull, shoulder, tote, transport, truck *Nonformal:* lug, schlep **2.** channel, conduct, funnel, siphon **3.** exchange, grant, pass on, send, transfer, transmit **4.** communicate, dispatch, express, impart, tell **5.** conduct, escort, guide, lead

conveyance *n.* **1.** movement, portage, transfer, transport **2.** transportation *Common human conveyances:* airplane, automobile, boat, buggy, bus, cab, calèche, canoe, car, carriage, cart, coach, ferry, hansom, helicopter, jitney, kayak, litter, rickshaw, rig, shank's mare *(Nonformal)*, ship, sleigh, snowmobile, streetcar, subway, surrey, train, tram, trolley, truck, van, wagon **3.** communication, electronic data interchange *(E.D.I.)*, exchange, interchange, transfer, transference, transmission

convict *n.* captive, criminal, culprit, felon, malefactor, prisoner, repeat offender, transgressor *Nonformal:* con, jailbird – *v.* condemn, declare *or* find *or* pronounce guilty, imprison, judge, sentence *Nonformal:* put away, send up, throw the book at *Antonyms:* absolve, acquit, clear

conviction *n.* **1.** belief, creed, doctrine, ethic, faith, outlook, persuasion, philosophy, position, principle, religion, tenet, view **2.** condemnation, fall, judgment, punishment, sentence, unfavourable verdict *Antonyms:* acquittal, exoneration, pardon

convince *v.* assure, brainwash, bring around, demonstrate, induce, persuade, prevail upon, prove, satisfy, sell, sway, turn, win over

convincing *adj.* acceptable, authoritative, believable, cogent, conclusive, credible, dependable, impressive, incontrovertible, moving, persuasive, powerful, rational, reasonable, reliable, satisfactory, satisfying, solid, sound, swaying, telling, valid *Antonyms:* dubious, far-fetched, implausible, inconclusive, incredible

convivial *adj.* affable, amiable, cheerful, entertaining, festive, friendly, fun-loving, gay, genial, gregarious, hearty, hospitable, jocund, jolly, jovial, lively, merry, mirthful, pleasant, sociable, vivacious *Antonyms:* depressing, dreary, sombre

convocation *n.* **1.** ceremony, commencement, graduation, promotion, rite, ritual **2.** assembly, conclave, concourse, conference, congregation, congress, convention, council, diet, get-together, levee, meeting, synod, turnout *Nonformal:* confab, meet **3.** amassing, calling, gathering, marshalling, mustering, summoning

convolution *n.* **1.** circumlocution, complexity, entanglement, intricacy, involution, Gordian knot, knottiness, mess, perplexity, sinuousness, tanglement, tortuousness *Antonyms:* plainness, simplicity **2.** circumvolution, coil, contortion, curlicue, flexing, gyration, helix, loop, snaking, spiral, swirl, twist, undulation, winding

convoy *n.* armada, armed guard, assemblage, cavalcade, contingent, cortège, fleet, flotilla, fur brigade *(Historical)*, group, line, procession, train – *v.* accompany, attend, conduct, chaperone, escort, guard, protect, usher

convulsion *n.* **1.** attack, conniption *(Nonformal)*, epilepsy, fit, grand mal, paroxysm, petit mal, seizure, spasm, throw **2.** agitation, anarchy, bedlam, chaos, clamour, commotion, dissidence, disturbance, ferment, fulmination, pandemonium, rebellion, revolution, riot, social unrest, tumult, upheaval, uprising *Antonyms:* harmony, peace **3.** cataclysm, disaster, earthquake, rocking, shake, shift, shock, trembling, turbulence

cook *n.* baker, chef, food preparer, gourmet, line cook, mess sergeant *Nonformal:* cookie, hash slinger *Cooking methods:* barbecue, broiler, camp stove, convection oven, cookstove, crock pot, dutch oven, fryer, griddle, gridiron, grill, hibachi, hot-plate, microwave oven, Mongolian pepper pot, oven, pressure cooker, range, roaster, rotisserie, saucepan, slow cooker, smoker, spit, steamer, stove, tandoor, toaster, toaster oven, waffle iron, wok – *v.* bake, barbecue, blanch, boil, braise, broil, brown, coddle, deep fry, fricassee, fry, griddle, grill, heat, melt, microwave, pan-fry, parboil, poach, prepare, pressure-cook, roast, sauté, scald, sear, simmer, sizzle, smoke, steam, steep, stew, stir-fry, toast

cool *adj.* **1.** air-conditioned, arctic, biting, chilling, chilly, cold, coldish, coolish, frigid, frosty, gelid, icy, nippy, refreshing, refrigerated, shivery, snappy, wintry *Antonyms:* hot, tepid, warm **2.** assured, blasé, calm, collected, composed, cool-headed, deliberate, imperturbable, level-headed, philosophical, phlegmatic, placid, relaxed, self-controlled, self-possessed, serene, stolid, tranquil, unemotional, unexcited, unflappable, unruffled *Nonformal:* easygoing, laid-back, together *Antonyms:* edgy, excitable, nervous **3.** aloof, antisocial, detached, disdainful, dismissive, dispassionate, distant, haughty, impassive, indifferent, inhospitable, nonchalant, remote, rude, snobby, standoffish, unapproachable, uncommunicative, unfeeling, unfriendly, unresponsive *Nonformal:* high-and-mighty, snooty *Antonyms:* gregarious, outgoing, receptive, sociable **4.** excellent, great, neat, stupendous, swell *Nonformal:* fab, gear, groovy, hip, magic, peachy-keen – *n.* **1.** assurance, balance, calmness, composure, confidence, cool-headedness, countenance, equanimity, equilibrium, nerve, nonchalance, poise, sang-froid, serenity, tranquility **2.** coldness, freshness, frigidity, frostiness, nip, rawness – *v.* **1.** air-condition, air-cool, chill, freeze, frost, ice, lose heat, reduce, refrigerate *Antonyms:* heat, warm **2.** abate, allay, assuage, calm, compose, contain, control, dampen, lessen, mitigate, moderate, mollify, pacify, quiet, reduce, rein, repress, restrain, suppress, temper *Antonyms:* agitate, excite, trouble

coop *n.* box, cage, enclosure, henhouse, pen, pound – *v.* confine, detain, enclose, hold, house

cooperate *v.* abet, advance, agree, aid, assist, back, collaborate, combine, comply with, concur, conduce, conspire, contribute, coordinate, forward, further, help, interact, join, league, participate, partner, pitch in, pool resources, share, side with, stick together, succour, take part, team up, unite, uphold, work together *Nonformal:* come forward, twin *Antonyms:* fight, hamper, impede, obstruct, thwart

cooperation *n.* **1.** agreement, aid, assistance, cahoots *(Nonformal)*, collaboration, combined *or* concerted effort, concurrence, conspiracy, fusion, give-and-take, harmony, help, helpfulness, participation, partisanship, partnership, reciprocity, service, symbiosis, synergy, teamwork, togetherness, unity *Antonyms:* discord, dissension, hindrance, opposition, rivalry **2.** alliance, association, benefit, coalition, combination, confederacy, consortium, co-op, family, federation, pool, team, union *Antonyms:* free agent, independent

cooperative *adj.* **1.** collaborative, collective, collegial, collusive, combined, common, concerted, concurrent, coordinated, harmonious, in league, interdependent, joint, linked, participating, shared, symbiotic, synergistic, unified, united, uniting *Antonyms:* autonomous, unallied **2.** accommodating, assisting, companionable, helpful, reciprocal, responsive, sociable, supportive *Antonyms:* antagonistic, competitive – *n.* alliance, co-housing, combine, commune, community, confederation, co-op, pool *See also:* **cooperation**

coordinate *adj.* alike, correlative, equal, equalized, equivalent, like, parallel, similar, tantamount *Antonyms:* contrasting, disparate, incongruous – *n.* **1.** associate, colleague, confrere, partner, peer **2.** analogue, complement, correspondent, counterpart, equal, likeness, match, similarity, twin – *v.* **1.** balance, even, harmonize, level, match, smooth, square *(Nonformal)* **2.** adjust, alphabetize, arrange, categorize, classify, correlate, integrate, methodize, organize, proportion, regulate, systematize, tabulate **3.** agree, combine, conform, harmonize, join, link, pool, pull together, reciprocate, reconcile, relate, synchronize, team up *Antonyms:* segregate, separate

coordination *n.* **1.** ability, agility, athleticism, deftness, dexterity, finesse, fluidity, grace, skill, timing *Antonyms:* clumsiness, ineptitude **2.** accord, agreement, collaboration, concert, cooperation, harmony, interaction, togetherness *Antonyms:* dissension, separation

cope *v.* **1.** come through, endure, make do, manage, survive, weather *Nonformal:* eke *or* scratch out, get by, live with, stay afloat *Antonyms:* collapse, crumble, fail **2.** adapt, adjust, confront, contend, deal *or* grapple with, face, handle

copious *adj.* **1.** abundant, alive *or* thick with, ample, aplenty, bounteous, bountiful, extensive, generous, great, heavy, large, lavish, liberal, overflowing, plenteous, plentiful, plenty, plethoric, prodigal, replete, rich **2.** diffuse, loquacious, prolix, verbose, wordy *Antonyms:* concise, terse

copulate *v.* breed, conjugate, couple, fornicate, have sex, know, make love, mate, procreate, sleep together *or* with *Nonformal:* bang, boff, do it, fool around, get busy, make-out, screw, shag

copy *interj.* are you with me, *comprende (Spanish)*, get it, understand *Nonformal:* capiche, 10-4 – *n.* **1.** carbon copy, double, duplicate, emulation, facsimile, fax, paraphrase, pattern, photocopy, replication, reproduction, scan, stat, transcription *Trademark:* photostat, Xerox **2.** clone, fake, forgery, imitation, knock off *(Nonformal)*, plagiarism, replica, sham **3.** article, book, draft, edition, issue, manuscript, matter, piece, printed *or* written matter, specimen, story, version, volume **4.** focus, issue, material, news item, story, subject *or* subject matter, substance, topic – *v.* **1.** clone, double, duplicate, fax, pattern, photocopy, photostat, replicate, reproduce, scan, trace, transcribe, Xerox *(Trademark)* **2.** counterfeit, pirate, plagiarize, rip-off, simulate, steal **3.** ape, echo, emulate, follow, imitate, impersonate, make like *(Nonformal)*, mimic, mirror, model, parody, parrot, repeat *Antonyms:* create, initiate, originate

copyright *adj.* licensed, proprietary, protected, secure *Antonyms:* accessible, in the public domain – *n.* licence, patent, registration, trademark – *v.* control, document, patent, protect, register, safeguard, trademark

coquet *v.* flirt, operate, philander, seduce, tantalize, tease, toy, trifle, vamp

coquette *n.* flirt, operator, strumpet, tease *Nonformal:* gold digger, hotsie potatsie, mantrap

cord *n.* **1.** bond, cable, connection, cordage, fibre, lanyard, line, link, piping, rein, rope, shaganappi *(Cree)*, strand, string, tendon, tie, twine, wire **2.** chain, check, curb, fetter, noose, prohibition, restraint – *v.* **1.** bind, bundle, fasten, package, secure, string-up, tie **2.** load, pile, stack, stockpile, store *Commonly misused:* **chord**

cordial *adj.* **1.** affable, agreeable, amicable, cheerful, companionable, congenial, earnest, friendly, genial, gracious, neighbourly, polite, respectful, responsive, sincere, sociable, social, sympathetic, tender, warm, welcoming, wholehearted *Antonyms:* aloof, cold, distant, formal **2.** bracing, invigorating, refreshing, restorative, stimulating, uplifting *Antonyms:* enervating, exhausting – *n.* bracer, cocktail, drink, liqueur, refreshment, restorative, reviver, tonic *Nonformal:* hair of the dog, pick-me-up

cordiality *n.* affability, agreeableness, amenity, amiability, earnestness, feeling, fellow, friendliness, generosity, geniality, gratefulness, heartiness, mutuality, pleasantness, responsiveness, sincerity, sympathy, understanding, warmth, wholeheartedness *Antonyms:* belligerence, hostility, pugnacity

cordon *n.* **1.** adornment, braid, cord, *cordon bleu (French)*, decoration, distinction, embellishment, honour, insignia, ornament, riband, ribbon, sash **2.** barricade, barrier, chain, *cordon sanitaire (French)*, delineation, demarcation, enclosure, line, perimeter, picket line, ring, row, stationary line – *v.* barricade, enclose, guard, isolate, partition, protect, quarantine, safeguard, separate

core *n.* **1.** essence, focus, gist, heart, kernel, main idea, marrow, meat, nucleus, pith, root, spirit, substance, thrust, upshot *Nonformal:* bottom line, nitty-gritty, nub, nuts and bolts *Antonyms:* façade, immateriality, irrelevancy, shell, surface **2.** centre, guts *(Nonformal)*, inside, interior, middle *Antonyms:* cladding, epidermis, exterior, outside

cork *n.* plug, spigot, stopcock, stopper, stopple, top, valve – *v.* **1.** bottle *or* close *or* stop up, confine, contain, plug, retain, seal **2.** quash, quell, repress, smother, stifle, suppress, swallow

corn *n.* **1.** cereal, fodder, grain, maize *Kinds of corn:* feed, golden bantam, green, Indian, peaches and cream, popping, yellow *Parts of corn:* cob, ears, husk, kernel, stalk, tassel **2.** callosity, callous, thickening **3.** banality, bromide, chestnut, old joke, platitude, saw, truism

corner *n.* **1.** angle, bend, branch, crook, crotch, *cul-de-sac (French)*, dogleg, fork, veer **2.** crossing, crossroads, intersection, joint, junction **3.** deadlock, difficulty, dilemma, distress, fix, hole, impasse, impediment, jam, knot, plight, predicament, scrape, stalemate *Nonformal:* box, pickle, tight spot **4.** edge, margin, recess, rim **5.** cranny, hide-out, retreat, secret place **6.** area, district, place, region, section *Nonformal:* neck of the woods, turf – *v.* **1.** catch, frustrate, foil, trap, tree *(Nonformal)* **2.**

appropriate, buy up, control, dominate, monopolize, own, tie up

cornucopia *n.* abundance, avalanche, bonanza, copiousness, horn of plenty, mother lode, myriad, outpouring, plenty, plethora, profusion, ton *Antonyms:* insufficiency, lack, meagreness

corny *adj.* **1.** banal, clichéd, commonplace, contrived, dull, feeble, hackneyed, shopworn, stale, stereotyped, stock, trite *Nonformal:* cornball, goofy, hokey *Antonyms:* original, unique **2.** maudlin, mawkish, melodramatic, overdone, sentimental, unsophisticated *Nonformal:* cheesy, hammed up, Hollywood, sappy

corollary *adj.* adjunct, associated, related, sideline, supplementary – *n.* **1.** aftereffect, consequence, culmination, effect, end, product, result, sequel, spin-off *(Nonformal)*, upshot **2.** conclusion, deduction, induction, inference, ratiocination, reasoning

coronation *n.* accession, ascension, ceremony, consecration, crowning, empowerment, enthronement, inauguration, installation, investiture *Antonyms:* abdication, usurpation

corporal *adj.* anatomical, bodily, carnal, fleshly, human, material, physical, sensual, somatic – *n.* noncom *(Nonformal)*, noncommissioned *or* petty officer, soldier *Commonly misused:* **corporeal**

corporation *n.* **1.** association, business, company, conglomerate, crown corporation, enterprise, legal entity, organization, partnership **2.** advisors, assembly, board, cabinet, chamber, committee, congregation, congress, council, diet, directorate, directors, executive, governing body, jury, ministry, outfit, panel, parliament, ring, senate, society, syndicate, synod, trustees

corporeal *adj.* **1.** bodily, earthly, human, mortal, physical, somatic *Antonyms:* ethereal, spiritual, translucent **2.** manifest, material, objective, palpable, perceptive, physical, sensible, somatic, substantial, tangible *Commonly misused:* **corporal**

corps *n. pl.* **1.** brigade, company, crew, detachment, division, outfit, regiment, squad, squadron, trained group, troop, unit **2.** band, body, crew, crowd, gang, mob, party, team, throng *Commonly misused:* **corpse**

corpse *n.* body, bones, cadaver, carcass, carrion, *corpus delicti (Latin)*, dead body *or* person, deceased, decedent, mortal, remains, skeleton, stiff *(Nonformal) Commonly misused:* **corps**

corpulent *adj.* fat, beefy, bulky, burly, fleshy, full-figured, heavy, hefty, large, obese, overblown, overweight, plump, plus-sized, portly, robust, roly-poly, rotund, stout, tubby *(Nonformal)*, well-padded *Antonyms:* emaciated, gaunt, scrawny, thin

corpus *n.* **1.** body, collection, canon, compilation, entirety, *oeuvre (French)*, text, whole **2.** assets, capital, principal **3.** anatomy, skeleton, structure

corral *n.* enclosure, fold, paddock, pen, pound – *v.* bring together, capture, contain, drive, enclose, fence *or* gather in, herd, round up, shepherd *Nonformal:* buttonhole, coop up

correct *adj.* **1.** accurate, actual, equitable, exact, factual, faithful, faultless, flawless, impeccable, legitimate, meticulous, perfect, precise, right, unmistaken *Nonformal:* bang on, for sure, on target, on the money *Antonyms:* false, fallacious, wrong **2.** acceptable, appropriate, becoming, conforming, conventional, customary, decent, decorous, diplomatic, fitting, nice, normal, orthodox, prevailing, proper, punctilious, routine, seemly, standard, suitable, traditional *Antonyms:* improper, inappropriate, schlocky *(Nonformal)*, unsuitable – *v.* **1.** admonish, castigate, censure, chasten, chastise, chide, criticize, discipline, penalize, punish, reform, reprimand, reprove *Antonyms:* compliment, excuse, humour, indulge, praise **2.** alter, ameliorate, amend, better, change, cure, debug, edit, emend, fix, help, improve, mend, polish, rectify, redress, remedy, review, revise, right, upgrade *Nonformal:* shape up, straighten out *Antonyms:* damage, harm, impair, ruin, spoil **3.** cancel, compensate, counteract, counterbalance, neutralize, offset

correction *n.* **1.** admonition, castigation, chastisement, discipline, dressing-down *(Nonformal)*, punishment, reformation, reproof **2.** adjustment, alteration, amelioration, amendment, change, editing, fixing, improvement, mending, modification, rectification, reexamination, remodeling, repair, revising, righting

corrective *adj.* **1.** antidotal, counteracting, curative, healing, palliative, restorative, therapeutic **2.** disciplinary, punitive, reformatory, remedial

correctly *adv.* **1.** accurately, meticulously, perfectly, precisely, right, scrupulously, well *Antonyms:* carelessly, erroneously, inaccurately **2.** befittingly, decently, decorously, fitly, fittingly, justly, nicely, properly, rightly, with style

correctness *n.* **1.** appropriateness, aptness, fitness, good breeding, rightness, seemliness, suitability **2.** civility, decency, decorousness, decorum, etiquette, properness, propriety *Antonyms:* bad taste, impropriety **3.** accuracy, definiteness, definitiveness, exactitude, exactness, faultlessness, fidelity, integrity, preciseness, precision, regularity, truth *Antonyms:* dishonesty, falseness

correlate *adj.* analogous, interchangeable, parallel, reciprocal, similar – *n.* analogue, complement, correlative, correspondence, counterpart, likeness, match, parallel, pendant, reciprocal, twin – *v.* compare, connect, correspond, equate, parallel, relate, tie in

correlation *n.* **1.** analogy, commonality, comparison, connection, correspondence, equivalence, match, parallel, similitude **2.** interaction, interchange, interconnection, interdependence, interrelationship, mutuality, reciprocity, relationship

correspond *v.* **1.** communicate, drop a line *(Nonformal)*, e-mail, exchange letters *or* views, pen, reply, respond, send word, write **2.** accord, agree, confirm, dovetail, fit, match, meet, relate, pertain, touch *or* verge on **3.** compare, complement, correlate, equal, harmonize, mirror, reciprocate, resemble

correspondence *n.* **1.** card, communication, e-mail, epistle, letters, messages, post, writing **2.** analogy, comparability, comparison, correlation, equivalence, likeness, parallelism, relation, resemblance, similarity **3.** accord, agreement, balance, coherence, concordance, concurrence, conformity, congruity, consistency, consonance, fitness, form, harmony, integration, order, proportion, regularity, suitability, symmetry, uniformity

corridor *n.* **1.** aisle, alley, breezeway, gerbil tube *(Nonformal)*, lane, passageway, walkway **2.** channel, isthmus, narrows, strip **3.** arcade, entrance hall, entranceway, entryway, foyer, gallery, hall, hallway

corroborate *v.* certify, check out, confirm, double check, endorse, prove, strengthen, substantiate, support, validate, verify *Antonyms:* contradict, disprove, negate, refute

corrode *v.* **1.** crumble, decay, deteriorate, eat away, erode, oxidize, rot, rust, waste *or* wear away **2.** corrupt, degenerate, destroy, gnaw, harm, hurt, impair, injure, ravage, raze, ruin

corrosive *adj.* **1.** acerbic, acrid, consuming, corroding, erosive, wasting, wearing *Antonyms:* healing, restorative, soothing **2.** acrimonious, biting, caustic, cutting, incisive, mordant, sarcastic, scathing **3.** bad, corruptive, crippling, destructive, impairing, noxious, ruinous, weakening

corrugated *adj.* channeled, creased, crinkled, crumpled, fluted, folded, furrowed, grooved, irregular, puckered, ridged, rough, wrinkled *Antonyms:* even, flat, level, smooth

corrupt *adj.* **1.** bent *(Nonformal)*, criminal, crooked, deceitful, dishonest, double-dealing, fraudulent, shady, underhanded, unethical, unprincipled, untrustworthy **2.** distorted, falsified, skewed *Nonformal:* doctored, fudged **3.** base, debauched, defiled, degenerate, depraved, miscreant, perfidious, perverted, reprobate, treacherous, twisted, vicious, vile **4.** contaminated, decomposed, infected, polluted, putrid, rotten, tainted – *v.* **1.** abase, abuse, cheapen, debase, demoralize, deprave, destroy, pervert, ruin, spoil, sully, vitiate **2.** blackmail, bribe, coax, fix, grease, mulct, oil, pay off **3.** adulterate, befoul, blemish, blight, contaminate, infect, poison, pollute, soil, stain, taint **4.** falsify, lie, misrepresent, skew *Nonformal:* doctor, fudge **5.** crumble, decay, deteriorate, oxidize, perforate, putrefy, rust

corruption *n.* **1.** bribery, criminality, crookedness, dishonesty, double-dealing, extortion, fraud, fraudulence, knavery, malfeasance, payoff, payola, profiteering, shadiness *Antonyms:* integrity, virtue **2.** adulteration, chicanery, distortion, falsification, lying, manipulation, misrepresentation *Antonyms:* truthfulness, veracity **3.** baseness, befoulment, contamination, debasement, debauchery, decadence, defilement, degeneration, depravity, iniquity, turpitude, venality, vice, vileness *Antonyms:* chastity, morality, purity **4.** decay, decomposition, infection, perforation, poisoning, pollution, putrescence, putrification, rot

cortege *n.* cavalcade, column, dead march, entourage, funeral procession, procession, retinue, train

cosmetic *adj.* **1.** plastic, shallow, superficial, surface **2.** ameliorating, beautifying, improving, uplifting

cosmetics *n.* beauty aids, *geschmuck (German)*, make-up, toiletries *Nonformal:* paint, putty, war paint *Kinds of cosmetics:* astringent, base, blush, cleanser, cold cream, concealer, eye liner, eyeshadow, foundation, liner, lipstick, mascara, moisturizer, nail polish, perfume, powder, rouge, toner

cosmic *adj.* **1.** global, huge, immense, infinite, limitless, measureless, universal, vast, worldwide *Antonyms:* infinitesimal, miniscule, minute **2.** astral, astrological, astrophysical, atomic, celestial, empyrean, heavenly, otherworldly, planetary **3.** aligned, harmonious, neat, orderly, predictable, sequential, tidy *Antonyms:* chaotic, confused, helter-skelter

cosmopolitan *adj.* **1.** catholic, ecumenical, global, metropolitan, multicultural, pandemic, public, universal, worldwide *Antonyms:* limited, narrow **2.** cultivated, cultured, polished, smooth, sophisticated, street-smart *(Nonformal)*, urbane, well-travelled, worldly-wise *Antonyms:* hidebound, parochial – *n.* globetrotter, jet-setter, sophisticate, world citizen *or* traveller

cosmos *n.* **1.** all creation, galaxy, heavens macrocosm, universe, world **2.** entity, organism, system, unit **3.** alignment, balance, harmony, order, organization, structure, symmetry

cosset *v.* baby, cherish, coddle, indulge, nurture, pamper, pet *Antonyms:* abuse, mistreat, neglect

cost *n.* **1.** amount, bottom dollar *or* line, charge, disbursement, dues, expenditure, expense, figure, outlay, out of pocket expense, payment, price, setback, tab, tariff, value, worth *Nonformal:* damage, price tag, ticket **2.** damage, deprivation, detriment, exposure *(Nonformal)*, forfeit, harm, hurt, injury, loss, penalty, risk, sacrifice, suffering – *v.* **1.** amount to, bring in, fetch, incur, realize, sell for, set-back *(Nonformal)*, yield **2.** appraise, assess, budget, estimate, price, tally, value

costly *adj.* **1.** dear, excessive, exorbitant, expensive, extortionate, extravagant, high-priced, premium, unreasonable *Nonformal:* pricey, steep, stiff *Antonyms:* cheap, economical, fair, reasonable **2.** cherished, inestimable, invaluable, precious, priceless, prized **3.** choice, elegant, excellent, exquisite, gorgeous, rare, *recherché (French)*, splendid *Antonyms:* tasteless, tawdry, vulgar

costume *n.* apparel, clothes, clothing, dress, ensemble, fashion, garb, gear, habit, outfit, raiment, uniform, vestment, wardrobe *Nonformal:* getup, rig

coterie *n.* bunch, circle, clan, clique, club, coalition, crew, crowd, faction, federation, fellowship, fraternity, gang, group, guild, lodge, order, organization, pack, rat pack *(Nonformal)*, sect, set, society, sorority, union

cottage *n.* boathouse, bungalow, cabana, cabin, camp, chalet, cot, croft *(Scottish)*, hunt camp, hut, lodge, shack, shanty, summer *or* vacation home, the lake *(Nonformal)*, villa

cottager *n.* city slicker *(Nonformal)*, summer folk, tourist, vacationer, weekender

couch *n.* chaise lounge, chesterfield, davenport, day bed, dias, divan, loveseat, ottoman, settee, sofa – *v.* **1.** express, formulate, frame, imply, phrase, set forth, suggest, utter, word **2.** ambush, hide, lurk, prowl, skulk **3.** bend, bow, crouch, lower, squat, stoop **4.** lounge, recline, repose, rest, stretch out

cough *n.* cold, croup, expulsion, hack, hem, whoop – *v.* bark, choke, expectorate, gasp, hack, hawk, hem, spit up, whoop

council *n.* **1.** administration, advisory board, cabinet, chamber, committee, congress, diet, directorate, governing body, ministry, panel, parliament, soviet, syndicate, synod *Nonformal:* brain trust, kitchen cabinet **2.** assembly, commission, conclave, conference, convention, convocation, forum, inquisition, tribunal **3.** conferring, consultation, debate, deliberation, discussion *Commonly misused:* **consul, counsel**

counsel *n.* **1.** advice, consideration, consultation, deliberation, direction, guidance, instruction, opinion, recommendation, suggestion, tip off *(Nonformal)*, warning **2.** adviser, advocate, attorney, barrister, counselor, lawyer, legal adviser, representative, solicitor **3.** aim, ambition, aspiration, desire, direction, goal, intent, intention, motive, objective, plan, purpose, target – *v.* advise, advocate, caution, direct, enjoin, exhort, guide, inform, instruct, prescribe, prompt, recommend, suggest, teach, urge, warn *Nonformal:* huddle, kibitz, steer *Commonly misused:* **consul, council**

counsellor *n.* **1.** advisor, advocate, attorney, consultant, counsel, pleader, representative, solicitor *Nonformal:* legal eagle, mouthpiece **2.** coach, guide, instructor, mentor, psychiatrist, psychologist, teacher

count *n.* **1.** calculation, computation, enumeration, numeration, reckoning, result, sum **2.** census, number, outcome, poll, result, total, whole **3.** baron, duke, earl, lord, marquis, noble, nobility, peer, *Graf (German)*, royal, viscount – *v.* **1.** add up, calculate, cast, cipher, compute, estimate, figure, quantify, reckon, score, sum, tabulate, tally, tote *or* tote up, total **2.** enumerate, inventory, list, name, tick off **3.** consider, deem, esteem, hold, impute, judge, look *or* look upon, mean, rate, regard, signify, think **4.** include, number among, take note **5.** carry weight, cut ice *(Nonformal)*, have importance, import, matter, tell, value, weigh **6.** anticipate, depend, expect, hang *or* hinge upon, hope, need, presume

countenance *n.* **1.** air, appearance, aura, demeanour, expression, looks, mien, semblance **2.** complexion, face, features, form, looks, visage **3.** assurance, calmness, composure, confidence, cool *(Nonformal)*, equilibrium, placidity, poise, sang-froid, self-control, serenity, tranquility **4.** approval, authorization, backing, blessing, encouragement, endorsement, patronage, sanction, support – *v.* abet, allow, authorize, back, condone, encourage, endorse, foster, permit, sanction, stomach *(Nonformal)*, support, tolerate

counter *adj.* adverse, against, antagonistic, antipodal, antithetical, clashing, conflicting, contradictory, contrary, contrasting, counteractive, different, dissimilar, opposed, opposite, reverse *Antonyms:* parallel, similar – *adv.* against, against the current *or* grain *or* tide, contrarily, contrariwise, conversely, in opposition, oppositely, poles apart *(Nonformal)* – *n.* **1.** antithesis, contrary, contrast, flip-side *(Nonformal)*, mirror-image, opposite, reverse **2.** answer, comeback, rebuttal, retaliation, retort **3.** bar, bench, buffet, display shelf *or* table, ledge, mantle, showcase, table, workbench **4.** chip, marker, ticket, token **5.** accountant, actuary, bean counter *(Nonformal)*, calculator, enumerator, mathematician, reckoner, tabulator – *v.* **1.** antagonize, challenge, clash, conflict, confute, contradict, contravene, counteract, cross, disagree, offset, oppose, oppugn *Antonyms:* accept, surrender, yield **2.** answer, meet, play off, reply, respond, retaliate, retort, return, riposte **3.** circumvent, defend, fend *or* ward off, foil, frustrate, hinder, obstruct, parry, rebuff, repel, repulse, resist, retaliate, thwart

counteract *v.* buck *(Nonformal)*, check, contradict, contravene, countervail, cross, defeat, foil, frustrate, hinder, invalidate, negate, neutralize, offset, oppose, oppugn, prevent, resist, thwart, undo

counterbalance *n.* **1.** balance, counterforce, equilibrium, equalizer, neutralizer, offset, weight **2.** antagonism, clash, cross current, friction, opposition, resistance – *v.* balance, compensate, correct, counteract, counterpoise, neutralize, offset, right, stabilize

counterfeit *adj.* **1.** artificial, bogus, copied, ersatz, fake, false, forged, fraudulent, imitation, mock, pirate, plagiarized, pseudo, sham, spurious, synthetic **2.** affected, assumed, feigned, fictitious, pretended, simulated – *n.* **1.** carbon copy, dummy, facsimile, fake, imitation, knock-off, phoney *(Nonformal)*, reproduction, simulacrum **2.** deception, fraud, hoax, imposture, sham **3.** bad *or* rubber cheque, base coin, forgery, funny money *(Nonformal)* – *v.* **1.** clone, copy, forge, imitate *Nonformal:* knock *or* rip off **2.** ape, bluff, fabricate, fake, feign, impersonate, mimic, pretend, simulate

countermand *v.* **1.** annul, cancel, invalidate, nullify, override, repeal, rescind, reverse, revoke, veto *Antonyms:* reinforce, sustain, uphold **2.** recall, recant, retract, take back

counterpart *n.* **1.** copy, duplicate, effigy, look-a-like, replica, reproduction *Nonformal:* dead ringer, spitting-image **2.** analogue, complement, coordinate, correlate, correspondent, parallel **3.** bosom buddy, colleague, companion, equal, fellow, friend, pal, peer, mate *Nonformal:* alter ego, sidekick

countless *adj.* endless, immeasurable, incalculable, infinite, innumerable, limitless, many, multitudinous, myriad, plethora, stacks, untold *Nonformal:* mucho, umpteen *Antonyms:* finite, limited, restricted

country *adj.* **1.** agrarian, agricultural, backhome, bucolic, pastoral, rural, sylvan, woodsy **2.** folk, homespun, plain, rustic, simple, unadorned, unpolished, unrefined – *n.* **1.** commonwealth, community, dominion, geopolitical entity, kingdom, land, nation, nation-state, realm, region, soil, sovereign, state, terrain, territory **2.** citizenry, citizens, electorate, grassroots, inhabitants, people, populace, public, society, voters

countryman *n.* **1.** citizen, compadre, compatriot, fellow citizen, kinsman, landsman, pilgrim *(Nonformal)* **2.** autochthon, indigene, inhabitant, local, native **3.** agriculturist, backwoodsman, farmer, husbandman, *paisano (Spanish)*, peasant, rancher, rustic, swain *Nonformal:* bumpkin, cornpone, hayseed, hick, hillbilly, rube, yokel

countryside *n.* agricultural region, arable land, farm country, farmland, foothills, grassland, grazing country, highlands, lowlands, moors, pasture, plains, prairies, rural district, savanna *or* savannah, steppes, uplands, veldt, woodland *Nonformal:* boondocks *or* boonies, neck of the woods, outback, the sticks

county *n.* borough, burgh, canton, constituency, district, division, parish, quarter, shire, territory, township

coup *n.* **1.** *coup d'état (French)*, insurgence, mutiny, overthrow, quiet revolution, rebellion, revolt, revolution, seizure, takeover, uprising **2.** accomplishment, achievement, *coup de main (French)*, exploit, feat, masterstroke, stratagem, stroke of genius, tour de force, triumph, victory

coup de grace *n.* crowning *or* finishing touch, doom, end, mortal stroke *Nonformal:* clincher, crusher, kayo, knock-out blow, the kill

couple *n.* **1.** duo, mates, partners, twosome **2.** both, brace, couplet, deuce, duet, dyad match, pair, span, team, twins, two **3.** coupler, harness, link, yoke – *v.* **1.** attach, cohere, combine, connect, fuse, hook up, join, link, merge, unite, yoke *Antonyms:* cleave, divide **2.** marry, wed *Nonformal:* get hitched, tie the knot *Antonyms:*

divorce, separate **3.** copulate, fornicate, have sex, mate

coupon *n.* advertisement, bounce back *(Nonformal)*, certificate, credit slip, discount, ration *or* redemption slip, token, voucher

courage *n.* adventurousness, backbone, boldness, bravery, daring, dauntlessness, élan, fearlessness, fortitude, gallantry, gameness, gimp *(P.E.I.)*, grit, heroism, intestinal fortitude, intrepidity, mettle, nerve, pluck, resolution, skookum tumtum *(Pacific Coast)*, spirit, spunk, temerity, toughness, valour, venturesomeness *Nonformal:* guts, moxie *Antonyms:* cowardice, fear, fright, timidity

courier *n.* **1.** bicycle courier, carrier, delivery service, dispatcher, messenger, mule *(Nonformal)*, postal service *or* worker, runner **2.** agent, attaché, diplomat, emissary, envoy

course *n.* **1.** class, lecture, lesson, seminar, session, tutorial **2.** curriculum, program, speciality, subject **3.** advance, development, evolution, furtherance, progression **4.** duration, phase, period, span, stretch *(Nonformal)*, term **5.** beat *(Nonformal)*, direction, flow, path, route, trajectory, way **6.** chain, cycle, sequence, series, succession, train **7.** action, drill *(Nonformal)*, manner, methodology, *modus operandi (Latin)*, plan, policy, principles, procedure, routine, scheme, system **8.** portion, serving *Kinds of dining course:* aperitif, appetizer, canapés, dessert, entrée, main course, *plat du jour (French)*, salad, savoury, soup, starter, *tapas (Spanish) Italian:* antipasto, primi, secondi **9.** downs, golf course, greens and fairways, links, range **10.** circuit, oval, racetrack, raceway, track **11.** band, belt, layer, level, stratum, tier – *v.* **1.** chase, follow, hound, hunt, pursue, stalk, tail, track **2.** bolt, dart, dash, hasten, race, run, scamper, surge **3.** cover, cross, flow, proceed, progress, travel, traverse, wind *Commonly misused:* **coarse**

court *n.* **1.** attendants, cortège, entourage, escort, retainers, retinue, train **2.** basketball *or* squash court, playing area *Tennis:* clay, grass **3.** bar, bench, court of appeal, judiciary, kangaroo court *(Nonformal)*, session *Kinds of Canadian court:* appellate, county, district, King's *or* Queen's Bench, provincial, Federal, Small Claims, Supreme **4.** close, courtyard, enclosure, patio, *piazza (Italian)*, plaza, quadrangle, square **5.** attention, deference, flattery, homage **6.** courtship, gallantry, pursuit, wining and dining *(Nonformal)*, wooing **7.** assembly, board of directors, council, diet, legislative body, officials, synod **8.** castle, chateau, estate, manor house, palace, *palazzo (Italian)*, villa – *v.* **1.** adore, blandish, cajole, fawn over, flatter, pander **2.** captivate, charm, date, serenade, woo **3.** attract, entice, inspire, invite, solicit, tempt

courteous *adj.* affable, chivalrous, civil, companionable, congenial, considerate, cordial, deferential, friendly, gallant, gracious, obliging, polite, respectful, solicitous, tactful, thoughtful, urbane *Antonyms:* ornery, rude, ungracious

courtesy *n.* **1.** attentiveness, chivalry, consideration, courtliness, culture, diplomacy, gallantry, graciousness, manners, polish, politeness, propriety, refinement, respect, social graces, tact, thoughtfulness, *Antonyms:* boorishness, churlishness, discourtesy, impertinence, rudeness **2.** bow, curtsy, genuflection, handshake, nod, reception, regards, salutation, welcome

courtly *adj.* **1.** ceremonious, chivalrous, civilized, cultured, debonair, decorous, dignified, elegant, formal, gallant, polished, polite, pompous, proper, refined, respectful, suave, studied, urbane **2.** fawning, honey-tongued, mealy-mouthed, obsequious, sycophantic, unctuous, wheedling

courtship *n.* dalliance, dating, engagement, love, lovemaking, pursuit, romance, serenading, suit, wooing

couturier *n.* designer, dress maker, fashion house, *modiste (French)*, salon, seamstress, stylist

cove *n.* **1.** anchorage, bay, bayou, bight, channel, estuary, firth, fjord, harbour, inlet, recess, refuge, retreat, sound **2.** cave, cavern, cavity, combe, grotto, hideaway, hollow, niche, nook, recess

covenant *n.* **1.** agreement, bargain, bond, compact, concordant, contract, deal, deed, indenture, treaty, warrant **2.** oath, pledge, promise, vow, word – *v.* avow, contract, promise, swear

cover *n.* **1.** awning, canopy, canvas, ceiling, dome, parasol, roof, tarp *or* tarpaulin, tent, umbrella **2.** case, envelope, lid, sheathe, top, wrapper **3.** bedspread, blanket, coverlet, duvet, eiderdown, quilt, sheet **4.** camouflage, disguise, façade, front, guise, mask, smokescreen *(Nonformal)* **5.** bolt-hole *(Nonformal)*, haven, hideaway, lair, refuge, retreat, room of one's own, sanctuary **6.** cloak, curtain, mantle, shield, veil – *v.* **1.** house, protect, screen, shelter, shield, shade **2.** accoutre, bundle up *(Nonformal)*, clothe, enwrap, invest, outfit, swaddle *Antonyms:* bare, divest, strip **3.** befog, bury, cache, cloud, conceal, hide, obscure *Antonyms:* expose, reveal, unearth **4.** blanket, carpet, coat, envelop, overlay **5.** allow for, contain, deal with, encompass, include **6.** cross, journey *or* pass over, range, span, track, travel, traverse **7.** broadcast, describe, detail, follow, investigate, narrate, recount, relate, report, write up **8.** relieve, replace, stand in for, substitute, understudy **9.** bulwark, defend, guard, reinforce, safeguard **10.** coat, paint, slobber on, smear, spread over, varnish

covert *adj.* **1.** backstairs, clandestine, furtive, hush-hush *(Nonformal)*, mysterious, private, secret, *sub-rosa (Latin)*, surreptitious, ulterior, under wraps, unsuspected *Antonyms:* blatant, obvious, open **2.** camouflaged, cloaked, concealed, disguised, hidden, incognito, masked, obscured, shrouded, undercover, veiled *Antonyms:* clear, evident, overt – *n.* **1.** camouflage, cover, mask, screen, shield, shroud **2.** haven, hiding place, protection, refuge, resort, retreat, sanctuary, shelter

covertly *adv.* clandestinely, furtively, privately, secretly, slyly, stealthily, surreptitiously, undercover, underhandedly *Nonformal:* hush-hush, on the q.t., under the table *Antonyms:* boldly, obviously

covet *v.* begrudge, crave, desire, envy, fancy, grudge, hunger *or* lust after, pine, resent, want, wish, yearn *Antonyms:* forswear, reject, renounce, scorn

covetous *adj.* **1.** begrudging, envious, green-eyed, jealous, resentful **2.** avaricious, burning, craving, desirous, greedy, lustful, rapacious, thirsty, voracious, wanting

covey *n.* bevy, cluster, clutch, company, drove, flight, flock, gaggle, group, herd, horde, pack, shoal, school, set, swarm

cow *n.* bovine, heifer *Nonformal:* Bessy, Elsie, milker – *v.* appall, browbeat, buffalo, daunt, disconcert, dismay, faze, intimidate, rattle *Antonyms:* calm, hearten, placate, support

coward *n.* craven, dastard, deserter *Nonformal:* baby, chicken, milksop, mouse, sissy *Antonyms:* lion-heart, paladin, warrior

cowardly *adj.* afraid, anxious, apprehensive, cowering, craven, fainthearted, fearful, frightened, gutless, nervous, panicky, pusillanimous, recreant, shrinking, soft, spineless, timid, timorous, weak-kneed *Nonformal:* lily-livered, yellow *Antonyms:* bold, brave, dauntless, intrepid

cower *v.* cringe, crouch, draw back, hide, quail, recoil, shrink, tremble, wince *Antonyms:* challenge, flourish, swagger

coxswain *n.* boatman *or* -woman, boatswain, guide, helmsperson, master, pilot, sailor *Nonformal:* cox, jack tar

coy *adj.* **1.** bashful, demure, diffident, hesitant, modest, proper, quiet, retiring, self-effacing, shy, timid, unassertive *Antonyms:* bold, brash, impudent **2.** coquettish, flirtatious, philandering, playful, seductive, sportive, teasing

cozy *adj.* comfortable, convenient, familiar, homey, intimate, safe, secure, settled in, snug, warm *Nonformal:* comfy, cushy *Antonyms:* distressing, godforsaken, uncomfortable

crabby *adj.* cantankerous, choleric, cross, crotchety, crusty, gloomy, grouchy, huffy, ill-tempered, ornery, peevish, saturnine, short, snippy, sour, splenetic, sulky, surly *Antonyms:* affable, cordial, happy

crack *adj.* able, ace, best, expert, first-class, first-rate, masterly, proficient, skilful, stupendous, superior, talented *Antonyms:* all thumbs, awkward – *n.* **1.** bang, blast, boom, burst, crash, explosion, noise, pop, smash, snap, sound, splintering, splitting **2.** break, chip, chink, fissure, fracture, rent, rift, rupture, split **3.** bash, belt, blow, buffet, clap, clip, clout, cuff, shot, slam, slap, smack, stab, stroke, thump, thwack, wallop, whack, wham **4.** aperture, gap, interval, interstice, opening, space **5.** comeback, dig, gag, insult, jest, jibe, joke, remark, return, wisecrack, witticism **6.** attempt, go *(Nonformal)*, round, turn, try **7.** flash, instant, jiffy, moment, sec *(Nonformal)*, second **8.** burglar, cat burglar, crook, purloiner, robber, stealer, thief **9.** ace, champion, maestro, master, prodigy, top gun *(Nonformal)*, virtuoso, wizard **10.** blemish, defect, deficiency, fault, flaw, foible, imperfection, shortcoming, wart – *v.* **1.** break, burst, chip, cleave, fracture, rupture, separate, snap **2.** bang, blast, boom, clap, crash, pop, thunder **3.** bash, buffet, clip, clout, cuff, hit, slap, thumb, whack, wallop **4.** derange, explode, go to pieces *Nonformal:* come apart *or* undone, flip out, have a fit, lose it **5.** break into, decipher, decode, figure *or* work out, hack, open, solve, unravel **6.** break down, collapse, fail **7.** destroy, harm, hurt, impair, injure, mar, ruin, spoil **8.** jest, joke, quip, wisecrack *Nonformal:* josh, kid

cradle *n.* **1.** basket, bassinet, bed, carrycot *(British)*, cot, crib, hamper, incubator, pannier, trundle bed **2.** basis, beginning, commencement, fountainhead, genesis, origin, root, source, wellspring **3.** birthplace, fatherland, homecountry *or* homeland, motherland, native soil **4.** brace, platform, scaffolding, support – *v.* cherish, coddle, harbour, hold, lull, nestle, nourish, nurse, nurture, protect, rock, shield, soothe, support, tend, watch over *Antonyms:* abandon, desert, neglect

craft *n.* **1.** aircraft, airplane, barge, boat, module, plane, probe, ship, shuttle, spacecraft, vehicle, vessel, watercraft **2.** art, business, calling, career, discipline, employment, handicraft, line, métier, occupation, profession, pursuit, trade, vocation, work **3.** bric-a-brac, creation, folk-art, handiwork, knickknack, product **4.** ability, adeptness, adroitness, aptitude, art, artistry, cleverness, competence, dexterity, expertise, expertness, flair, ingenuity, knack, know-how, proficiency, skill, technique, workmanship **5.** artfulness, artifice, cageyness, contrivance, craftiness, cunning, deceit, duplicity, foxiness, guile, ruse, shrewdness, slyness, stratagem, strategy, subterfuge, trickery, wiliness – *v.* build, create, design, fashion, produce, sculpt, shape

craftsman *n.* artisan, artist, craftsperson, craftswoman, journeyman, machinist, maker, manufacturer, master, mechanic, skilled person *or* worker, smith, specialist, technician

crafty *adj.* artful, cagey, calculating, canny, clever, cunning, deceitful, designing, devious, disingenuous, duplicitous, foxy, insidious, manipulative, scheming, shrewd, slick, slippery, sly, smooth, streetwise *(Nonformal)*, subtle, treacherous, tricky, wily *Antonyms:* foursquare, upright, virtuous

craggy *adj.* angular, broken, harsh, jagged, precipitous, rocky, rough, rugged, scabrous, stony, uneven *Antonyms:* fluid, glassy, sleek

cram *v.* **1.** prepare, prime, ready, research, review, study *Nonformal:* bone-up, hit the books **2.** compact, compress, crowd, crush, fill, force, jam *or* jam-pack *(Nonformal)*, overcrowd, overfill, press, ram in, squeeze, wedge **3.** gobble, shovel, stuff *Nonformal:* choke back, wolf *or* work down

cramp *n.* **1.** ache, charley horse *(Nonformal)*, contraction, convulsion, crick, pain, pang, spasm, stitch, twinge **2.** block, check, glitch *(Nonformal)*, hindrance, impediment, obstruction, restriction – *v.* **1.** check, circumscribe, confine, constrain, encumber, hamper, hamstring, handicap, hinder, impede, inhibit, limit, obstruct, restrain, restrict, shackle, stymie, thwart *Antonyms:* boost, enhance, goad, prod **2.** bind, clamp, clasp, fasten, secure, tie, tighten

cramped *adj.* **1.** closed *or* hemmed in, congested, crowded, incommodious, overcrowded, packed, squeezed, tight *Nonformal:* chock-a-block, jam-packed *Antonyms:*

large, open, spacious, uncrowded **2.** circumscribed, handicapped, hindered, oppressed, smothered, stifled

crane *n.* **1.** bird, bittern, cormorant, egret, great blue heron, heron **2.** capstan, derrick, gantry, hoist, lift, pulley, tackle, winch – *v.* extend, lift, gawk *(Nonformal)*, reach, stretch out

crank *n.* **1.** arm, crankshaft, handle, lever, shaft **2.** character, crackpot, eccentric, fanatic, nonconformist, outsider, zealot **3.** faultfinder, griper, grouch, grumbler, malcontent, pettifogger, whiner *Nonformal:* bellyacher, sorehead **4.** caprice, conceit, fancy, notion, passing fancy, quirk, whim, whimsy – *v.* **1.** move, reel, rotate, spin, turn, twist, wind **2.** power *or* rev up, start, turn on, turn over

cranky *adj.* **1.** bad-humoured, bearish, bitchy, cantankerous, choleric, crabby, crotchety, disagreeable, grouchy, grumpy, ill-humoured, irascible, irritable, mean, ornery, peevish, quarrelsome, quick-tempered, ratty *(Nonformal)*, snappish, sullen, surly, testy, tetchy, ugly *Antonyms:* amiable, cheerful, sunny **2.** anomalous, bizarre, capricious, eccentric, freakish, odd, peculiar, queer, quirky, strange, weird *Nonformal:* freaky, kinky **3.** jittery, loose, rickety, shaky, tottering, unreliable, unsafe, unsound

cranny *n.* breach, chink, cleft, crack, crevice, fissure, gap, groove, hole, interstice, niche, nook, notch, opening, recess, rift

crap *n.* **1.** baloney, bull, foolishness, hot air, hogwash, malarkey, nonsense *Nonformal:* flapdoddle, hooey, jack, tripe **2.** garbage, junk, refuse, rubbish, trash, waste **3.** excrement *Nonformal:* do, doggy-do, doodle, poop, road apple, turd

crash *n.* **1.** accident, bump, collision, concussion, crackup, crunch, impact, jar, jolt, sideswipe, smash, smash-up, wreck *Nonformal:* fender-bender, rear-ender **2.** bang, blast, boom, burst, clang, clap, clash, clatter, crack, din, peal, racket, slam, sound, thunder, thunderclap, wham **3.** bankruptcy, collapse, failure, insolvency, misfortune, ruin, slump, washout *(Nonformal)* **4.** abend, break- *or* shut-down, freeze-up, function *or* hard disk failure, meltdown *(Nonformal)*, system failure – *v.* **1.** break, destroy, fracture, rend, shatter, smash **2.** descend, disrupt, ditch, dive, fall, hurtle, overturn, pitch, plummet, plunge, topple, tumble, upset **3.** bump, collide, crack up, knock, meet, plow *or* smash into **4.** collapse, fall through *or* flat, freeze, halt, seize up, suspend, fail *Nonformal:* bite the dust, buy the farm, die **5.** barge in, break in upon, gatecrash, intrude, invade, trespass **6.** boom, clatter, roar, thunder **7.** languish, recline, retire, sleep, sprawl *Nonformal:* hit the hay *or* sack, slumber **8.** capitulate, lose, stumble, yield *Nonformal:* choke, throw in the hat *or* towel

crass *adj.* boorish, coarse, indelicate, inelegant, insensitive, rude, shameless, stupid, thoughtless, uncouth, unthinking, vulgar, witless *Nonformal:* hardcore, in your face *Antonyms:* politic, prudent, suave

crate *n.* box, carton, case, chest, footlocker, hamper, locker, packing *or* shipping case – *v.* box *or* box up, case, package, parcel, protect, stow, wrap

crater *n.* abyss, cavity, depression, dip, divot, hole, hollow, pit, slough

crave *v.* **1.** covet, desire, dream about *(Nonformal)*, hunger, long, pine, want, yearn *Antonyms:* dislike, reject, spurn **2.** ask, beg, beseech, entreat, implore, petition, plead, request, solicit, supplicate

craven *adj.* base, cowardly, fearful, gutless, pusillanimous, scared, timid, weak *Nonformal:* lily-livered, weak-kneed, wimpy *Antonyms:* daring, high-spirited, venturesome – *n.* coward, dastard, poltroon, recreant *Nonformal:* baby, chicken, scaredy-cat, wuss *Antonyms:* gallant, hero, heroine, lion-heart

craving *n.* appetite, desire, hankering, hunger, hurting, itch, longing, lust, need, passion, the munchies *(Nonformal)*, thirst, urge, yearning, yen *Antonyms:* disinterest, dislike, loathing

crawl *n.* sidle, slink, slow motion, snail's pace *(Nonformal)* – *v.* **1.** creep, meander, mosey *(Nonformal)*, poke *or* worm along, saunter, shuffle, take it slow **2.** crouch, hug the earth, lie low *or* supine, squat **3.** fawn, flatter, grovel, kowtow, cater *or* pander to, toady *Nonformal:* back-scratch, bootlick, suck up to **4.** abound, flood, infest, overflow, swarm, teem **5.** feel creepy, get the heebie-jeebies *(Nonformal)*, prickle, tingle

craze *n.* **1.** enthusiasm, fad, fashion, infatuation, in-thing *(Nonformal)*, kick, mania, mode, novelty, passion, preoccupation, rage, trend, vogue **2.** breakdown, crack-up *(Nonformal)*, derangement, insanity, mental disorder **3.** blemish, chap, check, chink, crack, flaw, fracture, gash, imperfection, slit, split – *v.* **1.** bewilder, confuse, dement, derange, distract, enrage, frenzy, infatuate, inflame, madden, unbalance, unhinge **2.** blemish, break, check, chip, crack, dilapidate, fracture, impair, injure, mar, rip, spoil

crazy *adj.* **1.** berserk, cracked, crazed, daft, delirious, demented, deranged, erratic, frenzied, idiotic, insane, lunatic, mad, maniacal, *non compos mentis (Latin)*, strange, touched, unbalanced, unhinged *Nonformal:* ape, balmy, bananas, barmy, batty, bonkers, cuckoo, dippy, flaky, flipped, flipped out, freaked out, fruity, haywire, kooky, looney, mental, moonstruck, nuts, nutty, potty, psycho, raving, screwball, unglued, unzipped, wacky *Antonyms:* rational, reasonable, sane, sensible **2.** asinine, foolish, goofy, idiotic, ill-conceived, impracticable, imprudent, inappropriate, irresponsible, nonsensical, preposterous, puerile, ridiculous, senseless, silly, unrealistic *Nonformal:* half-baked, harebrained, haywire, wonky **3.** absurd, bizarre, eccentric, fantastic, inexplicable, ludicrous, odd, outrageous, peculiar, weird **4.** ardent, devoted, eager, enamoured, fanatical, infatuated, keen, mad about, passionate, smitten, wild, zealous *Antonyms:* cool, indifferent, uncaring, uninterested **5.** dilapidated, precarious, rickety, run-down, tottery, unsound

cream *adj.* creamy, eggshell, glaucous, ivory, off-white, vanilla – *n.* **1.** balm, cosmetic, emollient, emulsion, essence, jelly, liniment, lotion, lubricant, moisturizer, oil, ointment, paste, pomade, salve, unction, unguent **2.** best, crème-de-la-crème, choice, elect, elite, favourite, finest, flower, nonesuch, nonpareil, optimum, pick, pride, prime, prize, quintessence, select, top – *v.* **1.** beat up, churn, emulsify, foam, froth, lather, spume, thicken, whip, whisk **2.** remove, scoop up, skim, take off **3.** beat, clobber, defeat, overcome, overwhelm, shellac *(Nonformal)*, vanquish

creamy *adj.* buttery, milky, rich, smooth, soft, thick, velvety

crease *n.* **1.** corrugation, fold, furrow, groove, overlap, pleat, pucker, ridge, ruck, tuck, wrinkle **2.** *Hockey:* goal line, net, protected area – *v.* **1.** cockle, corrugate, crimp, crinkle, crumple, dog-ear *(Nonformal)*, double up, fold, plait, pucker, ridge, ruck up, rumple, wrinkle **2.** brush, graze, kiss, scrape, skin, touch

create *v.* **1.** actualize, build, compose, construct, craft, erect, fabricate, fashion, forge, form, knock together, make, manufacture, mix, produce, set up, shape *Antonyms:* annihilate, demolish, destroy **2.** author, brainstorm *(Nonformal)*, coin, concoct, contrive, design, develop, devise, dream up, establish, formulate, hatch, imagine, initiate, institute, invent, launch, make up, organize, originate, plan, program, start **3.** beget, engender, father, mother, parent, procreate, rear, sire, spawn **4.** cause, effect, elicit, generate, occasion, provoke **5.** appoint, designate, install, instate, invest, name, nominate, ordain

creation *n.* **1.** construction, establishment, fabrication, formation, making, production **2.** achievement, concept, concoction, handiwork, idea, invention, piece *Nonformal:* baby, brainchild **3.** beginning, birth, foundation, genesis, inception, origin, start **4.** generation, nascence, procreation, siring

creative *adj.* **1.** abstract, adroit, artistic, artsy *(Nonformal)*, clever, conceptual, gifted, imaginative, ingenious, innovative, inspired, intelligent, inventive, original, resourceful, talented, visionary *Antonyms:* dim-witted, dull **2.** fecund, fertile, pregnant, productive, prolific, rich, thriving

creator *n.* **1.** architect, artist, author, composer, designer, founder, generator, initiator, inventor, maker, mastermind, originator, producer **2.** Allah, Ancient of Days, Brahma,

Glooscap, God, Great Spirit, Raven, The Almighty, Turtle, Yahweh *See also:* **God**

creature *n.* **1.** being, body, entity, fellow, individual, man, mortal, person, personage, soul, woman *Antonyms:* apparition, nonentity, wraith **2.** animal, bandersnatch, creation, earthling, living thing, lower animal, organism *Nonformal:* critter, varmint **3.** dependent, flunkey, inferior, minion, puppet, subject, subordinate, sycophant, underling *(Nonformal)*

credence *n.* **1.** belief, certainty, confidence, faith, reliance, trust *Antonyms:* doubt, scepticism, uncertainty **2.** accreditation, assurance, endorsement, recommendation

credential *n.* authorization, voucher, warrant *Types of credential:* birth certificate, citizenship papers, deed, degree, diploma, driver's licence, health card, marriage licence, passport, social insurance number *or* SIN, visa

credibility *n.* **1.** believability, plausibility, solidness, soundness, validity, veracity **2.** honesty, integrity, rectitude, reliability, trustworthiness,

credible *adj.* **1.** believable, conceivable, imaginable, likely, logical, plausible, possible, probable, rational, reasonable, satisfying, seeming, solid, sound, supposable, tenable, valid, well-founded, worthy *Antonyms:* doubtful, implausible, incredible, questionable **2.** aboveboard, creditable, dependable, honest, reliable, sincere, straight, trustworthy, trusty, up-front, *Commonly misused:* **creditable, credulous**

credit *n.* **1.** belief, certainty, dependence, faith, reliance, trust *Nonformal:* stock, store **2.** distinction, good name, influence, reputation, repute, position, prestige, standing, status **3.** honesty, integrity, reliability, trustworthiness **4.** advantage, benefit, blessing, bonus, boon, improvement **5.** acclaim, approval, attention, commendation, kudos, recognition, thanks, tribute **6.** accreditation, acknowledgment, ascription, attribution, citation, reference, signature **7.** assets, balance, wealth **8.** debenture, extension, installment plan, lien, loan, mortgage, tab *(Nonformal)* – *v.* **1.** accredit, ascribe, assign, attribute, charge, defer, lay, refer **2.** esteem, honour, recognize, respect, thank *Antonyms:* disgrace, dishonour, neglect

creditable *adj.* admirable, august, commendable, deserving, esteemed, estimable, excellent, exemplary, fine, impressive, laudable, marked, meritorious, notable, outstanding, praiseworthy, renowned, reputable, respected, signal, venerable, wonderful, worthy *Antonyms:* blameworthy, horrible, lousy, shameful, *Commonly misused:* **credible**

credit card *n.* charge *or* debit card, plastic *(Nonformal) Trademarks:* American Express, ATM card, Diner's Club, En Route, Interac, MasterCard, VISA

credulous *adj.* accepting, believing, confiding, easy *(Nonformal)*, green, gullible, naive, simple, superstitious, trusting, uncritical, unquestioning, unsophisticated, unsuspecting, unsuspicious, unwary, wide-eyed *Antonyms:* cynical, incredulous, sceptical, suspecting, wary *Commonly misused:* **credible**

creed *n.* **1.** belief *or* belief system, canon, conviction, credenda, credo, denomination, doctrine, dogma, ethics, faith, gospel, ideology, morals, persuasion, philosophy, principles, religion, school, tenet, theology, world view **2.** affirmation, confession of faith, declaration

creek *n.* **1.** brook, brooklet, burn, channel, course, crick *(Nonformal)*, ditch, firth, race, rill, river, rivulet, run, runnel, spring, stream, streamlet, tributary, watercourse **2.** bay, cove, estuary, firth, fjord, inlet

creep *n.* cur, lowlife, pervert, swine *Nonformal:* bastard, goof, jerk, louse, stinker, weirdo – *v.* **1.** crawl, drag, idle, inch along, move slowly, trudge, worm, wriggle *Antonyms:* flounce, sashay, swagger **2.** prowl, skulk, slink, slither, tiptoe *Nonformal:* gumshoe, pussyfoot **3.** cower, cringe, flinch, grovel, kowtow, quail **4.** glide, shift, slide, slip

creepy *adj.* **1.** awful, direful, disgusting, dreadful, frightening, ghoulish, gruesome, horrible, horrific, macabre, menacing, nasty, nightmarish, ominous, sinister, terrifying, threatening, unpleasant *Antonyms:* bewitching, captivating, enchanting **2.** disquieting, disturbing, eerie, hair-raising *(Nonformal)*, scary, spooky, uncanny, unsettling, weird

crescendo *n.* amplification, din, expansion, fullness, increase, intensification, magnification, surge, swell – *v.* balloon, boom, broaden, develop, distend, enlarge, expand, extend, increase, intensify, mount, resound, rise, surge, swell, thunder, widen *Antonyms:* contract, decrease, ebb *Commonly misused:* **climax**

crescent *adj.* **1.** bowed, bow-shaped, concave, convex, curved, semicircular **2.** burgeoning, growing, increasing, waxing – *n.* **1.** bow, concave, convex, curve, scythe, semicircle, sickle **2.** crescent moon, demilune, half-moon, moon **3.** avenue, boulevard, circle, drive, lane, place, road, row, street

crest *n.* **1.** badge, bearings, charge, device, emblem, insignia, regalia, symbol **2.** caruncle, cockscomb, comb, crown, feather, mane, panache, plume, tassel, tuft **3.** hogback, projection, protuberance, ridge, spine **4.** acme, apex, highest point, peak, pinnacle, summit, zenith *Antonyms:* base, bottom, foot **5.** cap, crown, headpiece, helmet – *v.* cap, crown, culminate, peak, tower, top off

crevasse *n.* abyss, breach, chasm, cleft, crack, fissure, gorge, gully, opening, ravine, rift, rupture, trench

crew *n.* **1.** company, congregation, corps, outfit, squad, staff, team, troop, troupe, workers **2.** assemblage, band, body, clique, crowd, faction, gang, group, party, posse

crib *n.* **1.** bassinet, bed, carrycot *(British)*, cot, cradle, manger **2.** booth, cage, coop, stall **3.** barrel, bin, box, compartment, rack, trough **4.** cabin, cottage, house, hovel, hut, shanty **5.** chamber, closet, corner, cubbyhole, nook, room **6.** aid, key, legend, study notes, translation *Nonformal:* cheat-sheet, pony **7.** appropriation, grab, imitation, lifting, passing off, piracy, plagiarism, theft – *v.* **1.** filch, imitate, lift, pilfer, pirate, plagiarize, purloin, snatch, steal *Nonformal:* liberate, pinch **2.** cloister, closet, confine, coop up, enclose, hold, impound, restrain **3.** bolster, brace, buttress, prop, reinforce, support

crick *n.* **1.** ache, charley horse *(Nonformal)*, cramp, kink, pain, stiffness, stitch, twinge, wrench **2.** brook, brooklet, channel, creek, rill, river, rivulet, stream, streamlet, watercourse

crime *n.* **1.** abomination, atrocity, breach, break, corruption, criminality, delinquency, dereliction, felony, illegality, infraction, infringement, lawlessness, malfeasance, misconduct, misdeed, misdemeanour, offence, sin, transgression, trespass, unlawful act, vice, villainy, violation, wickedness, wrong *Antonyms:* benefaction, good deed, service **2.** crying shame *(Nonformal)*, disgrace, injustice, outrage, shame

criminal *adj.* **1.** crooked, felonious, illegal, illicit, lawless, scandalous, shady, unlawful, *Antonyms:* commendable, honest, honourable, lawful, legal **2.** corrupt, immoral, iniquitous, nefarious, unscrupulous, vicious, villainous, wicked, wrong **3.** at fault, blameworthy, condemnable, culpable, indicatable, peccant *Antonyms:* commendable, innocent, praiseworthy **4.** exorbitant, extortionate, overpriced, unconscionable – *n.* crook, culprit, delinquent, desperado, drug dealer, felon, fugitive, gangster, hoodlum, jailbird *or* yardbird *(Nonformal)*, lawbreaker, malefactor, mobster, murderer, offender, outlaw, racketeer, sinner, smuggler, thief, transgressor, trespasser, wrongdoer *Antonyms:* paragon, pillar of society, saint

crimp *n.* **1.** cockle, corrugation, crease, crinkle, crumple, curl, flute, fold, furrow, gather, groove, pleat, pucker, ridge, ruck, rumple, wave, wrinkle **2.** abductor, cheat, con, kidnapper, prowler, rustler, swindler, thief – *v.* **1.** coil, crease, crinkle, crumple, curl, fold, friz, furrow, gash, pleat, ruck, screw, scrunch, set, swirl, undulate, wave, wrinkle *Antonyms:* iron, smooth, straighten **2.** arrest, bottleneck, check, cramp, encumber, frustrate, hamper, hinder, impede, inhibit, obstruct, restrict, stop, thwart **3.** abduct, carry off, kidnap, spirit away *(Nonformal)*

cringe *v.* **1.** cower, draw back, flinch, quail, quiver, recoil, tremble, winch *Antonyms:* brave, challenge, face **2.** bootlick *(Nonformal)*, court, fawn, flatter, kowtow, grovel, slaver, toady

crinkle *v.* **1.** coil, crackle, crease, crimp, crumple, curl, fold, pucker, ruck, ruffle, rumple, scallop, scrunch, twist, wreath, wrinkle *Antonyms:* spread, stretch, unfurl **2.** rustle, sibilate, swish, whisper *Antonyms:* bang, crash, stomp

cripple *v.* attenuate, damage, debilitate, destroy, disable, hamstring, hinder, hobble, hurt, immobilize, impair, incapacitate, injure, lame, maim, paralyze, prostrate, ruin, sideline *(Nonformal)*, spoil, stifle, undermine, weaken *Antonyms:* aid, assist, expedite, facilitate, further

crisis *n.* **1.** calamity, catastrophe, dilemma, dire straits, disaster, emergency, extremity, imbroglio, impasse, mess, perplexity, pinch, plight, predicament, pressure situation, strait, trauma, trial, trouble, urgency *Nonformal:* crunch, pickle, stew *Antonyms:* ease, peace, quiet **2.** climax, corner, crossroad, crux, culmination, juncture

crisp *adj.* **1.** brittle, crumbly, crusty, dry, short *Antonyms:* limp, soft, soggy **2.** crispy, crunchy, firm, fresh, green, plump, ripe *Antonyms:* mushy, spoiled **3.** bracing, brisk, chilly, clear, cloudless, fresh, invigorating, refreshing, stimulating *Antonyms:* balmy, humid, scorching **4.** abrupt, biting, blunt, brief, brusque, concise, curt, incisive, penetrating, pithy, short, succinct, tart, terse **5.** clean, neat, slick *(Nonformal)*, smart, spruce, tidy, trim, well-groomed, well-kept *Antonyms:* crumpled, ruffled, wrinkled **6.** animated, fascinating, interesting, lively, provocative, spirited, stimulating, vigorous *Antonyms:* dull, enervating, lifeless **7.** crimped, crispate, curly, frizzy, rippled, wavy *Antonyms:* flat, straight, uncurled

criterion *n.* barometer, benchmark, example, foundation, gauge, law, measure, model, paradigm, pattern, precedent, principle, proof, prototype, rule, standard, test, touchstone, yardstick

critic *n.* **1.** columnist, commentator, essayist, writer **2.** analyzer, authority, connoisseur, evaluator, expert, interpreter, judge, master, pundit **3.** attacker, belittler, blamer, censor, censurer, complainer, defamer, detractor, disputer, doubter, faultfinder, knocker, nit-picker *(Nonformal) Antonyms:* advocate, backer, proponent

critical *adj.* **1.** acute, all-important, conclusive, consequential, crucial, decisive, high-priority, important, integral, momentous, pivotal, pressing, serious, significant, strategic, urgent, vital, weighty *Antonyms:* insignificant, irrelevant, trivial **2.** dangerous, desperate, dire, grave, hazardous, perilous, precarious, risky **3.** belittling, captious, carping, cavilling, censorious, condemning, cutting, derogatory, disapproving, discriminating, disparaging, faultfinding, nit-picking *(Nonformal) Antonyms:* appreciative, approving, complimentary, permissive **4.** analytical, astute, conscientious, detailed, exact, judicial, meticulous, penetrating, perceptive, precise, scientific, scrupulous **5.** annotative, clarifying, editorial, explanatory, explicative, scholastic

criticism *n.* **1.** appraisal, assessment, evaluation, interpretation, judgment, observation **2.** article, commentary, critique, editorial, review, story, write-up *Nonformal:* blurb, piece **3.** aspersion, censure, condemnation, denunciation, disapproval, disparagement, opposition, stricture *Nonformal:* bad press, blast, flak, hit, knock, pan, put down, rap, slam *Antonyms:* honour, kudos, praise **4.** carping, cavilling, faultfinding, nit-picking *(Nonformal)*, pettifogging, quibbling **5.** analysis, deconstruction, examination, exegesis, exposition, interpretation, reading, study

criticize *v.* **1.** belittle, carp, cavil, censure, clapper-claw *(P.E.I.)*, pettifog *Nonformal:* bad-mouth, knock, nit-pick, pan, trash *Antonyms:* commend, extol, laud **2.** analyze, appraise, assess, critique, evaluate, examine, judge, probe, review, scrutinize, study

croak *v.* **1.** caw, gasp, grunt, quack, squawk, wheeze **2.** depart, die, expire, kick the bucket *(Nonformal)*, pass away, perish **3.** complain, doom, forebode, gripe *(Nonformal)*, growl, grumble, moan, portend, warn, yammer

crony *n.* acquaintance, associate, bosom *or* good buddy, chum, colleague, companion, comrade, confidant, confrere, friend, intimate, mate, pal, sidekick *(Nonformal)* *Antonyms:* adversary, foe, rival

crook *n.* **1.** angle, bend, bow, curve, fold, hook, kink, turn, twist **2.** cheat, criminal, filcher, knave, pilferer, purloiner, racketeer, robber, rogue, scoundrel, swindler, thief, villain – *v.* angle, bend, bow, curve, fork, hook, meander, snake, wind, zigzag *Antonyms:* straighten, uncoil

crooked *adj.* **1.** bent, bowed, contorted, distorted, gnarled, misshapen, twisted, warped **2.** circuitous, curved, deviating, hooked, kinky, meandering, oblique, rambling, serpentine, snaky, spiral, twisting, winding **3.** asymmetric, awry, cockeyed, irregular, topsided, skewed, slanted, tilted, topsy-turvey, uneven **4.** corrupt, crafty, criminal, deceitful, devious, dishonest, dishonourable, dubious, evil, fraudulent, illegal, lying, nefarious, questionable, ruthless, shady, shifty, treacherous, underhand, unlawful, unprincipled, unscrupulous, untruthful *Antonyms:* ethical, fair, lawful, upright

crop *n.* **1.** annual production, cash crop fruit, gleaming, growth, harvest, output, produce, reaping, vintage, yield **2.** assortment, batch, clump, cluster, collection, crowd, gathering, group **3.** bullwhip, lash, whip **4.** elflock, head of hair, mop, shock, thatch, tress – *v.* **1.** chop, clip, cut, detach, hew, mow, pare, pluck, prune, reduce, shave, shear, shorten, skive, slash, snip, top, truncate **2.** cultivate, farm, gleam, grow, pick, raise, ranch, reap, rear

cross *adj.* **1.** angry, cantankerous, captious, cavilling, choleric, churlish, crabby, cranky, crotchety, crusty, disagreeable, faultfinding, fractious, fretful, grouchy, grumpy, ill-humoured, ill-tempered, impatient, irascible, irritable, peevish, pettish, petulant, put out, querulous, quick-tempered, short, snappy, splenetic, surly, testy, tetchy, touchy, vexed, waspish *Antonyms:* congenial, delighted, pleasant **2.** crosswise, diagonal, oblique, transverse **3.** adverse, contrary, opposed, oppositional *Nonformal:* anti, at loggerheads **4.** give-and-take, joint, mutual, reciprocal **5.** blended, composite, intermingled, melded, mixed – *adv.* **1.** adversely, at odds *or* variance, contrarily, counter, in opposition **2.** crossways, decussately, obliquely, transversely – *n.* **1.** crosier, crucifix, crux, emblem, icon, insignia, rood, staff, symbol *Kinds of cross:* Ansate, Celtic, crosslet, Cross of Lorraine, fleury, fourchée, Greek, Jerusalem, Latin, Maltese, Papal, St. Andrew's, St. George's, Tau **2.** affliction, burden, heartache, misery, misfortune, sorrow, suffering, trial, tribulation, trouble, weight, woe *Antonyms:* ecstasy, joy, pleasure **3.** bridge, convergence, crossing, crossroad, crosswalk, intersection, junction **4.** block, difficulty, frustration, hindrance, impediment, thwarting **5.** amalgamation, blend, hybrid, meld, mixture – *v.* **1.** cut, navigate, pass over, sail, span, traverse, voyage **2.** bisect, bridge, converge, crisscross, crosscut, divide, extend over, intersect, meet, overpass **3.** betray, block, bollix *(Nonformal)*, deny, double-cross, flummox, foil, foul up, frustrate, hinder, impede, interfere, obstruct, oppose, resist, stump, stymie, thwart **4.** braid, intertwine, lace, link, pleat, weave **5.** blend, crossbreed, cross-fertilize, cross-pollinate, hybridize, interbreed, mingle, mix

crossroads *n.* **1.** crisis, critical point, juncture, moment of truth, point of decision, rub, Rubicon, turning point **2.** gathering *or* meeting place, hamlet, hub, village, whistle stop *(Nonformal)* **3.** convergence, crossing, interchange, intersection, junction

crosswise *adv.* **1.** across, aslant, athwart, crisscross, cross, crossways, diagonally, horizontally, longways, over, perpendicularly, sideways, transversely, vertically **2.** against, at odds, contradictorily, in opposition, versus

crotchety *adj.* **1.** awkward, bad-tempered, bearish, cantankerous, contrary, crabby, cranky, cross, crusty, curmudgeonly, difficult, disagreeable, fractious, grumpy, irritable, obstinate, obstreperous, ornery, peevish, surly, testy, waspish, waspy *Antonyms:* calm, composed, collected, cool **2.** capricious, changeable, eccentric, erratic, flighty *(Nonformal)*, mercurial, odd, peculiar, perverse, queer, strange *Antonyms:* conventional, staid, traditional

crouch *v.* **1.** bend *or* bend down, bow, dip, duck, huddle, hunch, hunker down, kneel, squat, stoop, stoop low *Antonyms:* leap up, spring, vault **2.** bootlick, cower, cringe, fawn, pander to, wait upon, wince

crow *n.* bird, jackdaw, oscine, raven, rook – *v.* **1.** boast, brag, exult, flaunt, gasconade, gloat, parade, posture, trumpet, vaunt *Antonyms:* deprecate, downplay, minimize **2.** babble, burble, coo, gurgle, murmur

crowd *n.* **1.** army, drove, flood, great unwashed *(Nonformal)*, herd, horde, legion, mass, mob, multitude, pack, people, rabble, swarm, throng **2.** clique, club, company, coterie, crew, faction, gang, group, party, posse **3.** array, assortment, bunch, cluster, collection, hoard, set, stockpile, supply **4.** attendants, audience, fans, house, spectators, turnout, viewers – *v.* **1.** congest, compress, cram, fill, pack, squeeze, stuff **2.** crush, elbow, jostle, push, shove, squash **3.** cluster, congregate, convene, forgather, gather, huddle, throng **4.** coerce, compel, constrain, demand, oblige, pressure, railroad

crowded *adj.* **1.** awash, brimming, congested, crammed, dense, full, huddled, jammed, loaded, massed, mobbed, overflowing, packed, populous, swarming, teeming, tight, thronged, *Nonformal:* chockablock, wall-to-wall *Antonyms:* deserted, desolate, empty, lonely, roomy, sparse

crown *n.* **1.** circlet, coronal, coronet, diadem, headband, headdress, tiara **2.** crowned head, emperor, empress, king, monarch, monarchy, potentate, queen, royalty, ruler, sovereign, supreme ruler, throne **3.** award, garland, honour, kudos, laurels, prize, top prize, trophy, victory, wreath **4.** acme, apex, apogee, cap, climax, head, meridian, peak, pinnacle, spire, summit, top *Antonyms:* base, bottom, nadir **5.** brow, head, skull *Nonformal:* noggin, tuque **6.** cap, hat, headdress, headpiece, helmet **7.** banner, bearings, emblem, heraldic device, regalia, sceptre, stardust, symbol – *v.* **1.** adorn, decorate, dignify, empower, festoon, honour, inaugurate, induct **2.** cap, climax, complete, consummate, crest, finish, fulfill, perfect, round off, surmount, terminate, top, top off **3.** biff *(Nonformal)*, box, cuff, hit, knock, punch, smite, strike

crowning *adj.* climactic, consummate, culminating, excellent, final, paramount, pinnacle, supreme, ultimate *Antonyms:* initial, introductory, seminal

crucial *adj.* **1.** central, climactic, compelling, deciding, decisive, essential, high-priority, imperative, important, insistent, key *(Nonformal)*, momentous, necessary, pivotal, pressing, searching, showdown, vital *Antonyms:* irrelevant, peripheral, secondary **2.** acute, critical, desperate, dire, grave, perilous, serious, severe, urgent, touchy *(Nonformal)*

crucify *v.* **1.** execute, hang, kill, martyr, persecute, sacrifice **2.** abuse, harangue, harrow, hound, mortify, punish, rack, stock, torment, torture, vilify *Nonformal:* nail, pan, slam **3.** beat, crush, defeat, trounce, vanquish *Nonformal:* clobber, crush, cream, shellac

crude *adj.* **1.** natural, pure, raw, unprocessed, unrefined **2.** coarse, homespun, primitive, rough-hewn, rudimentary, rustic, simple, unfinished *Antonyms:* high-tech, refined **3.** amateur, callow, green, immature, unripe, unskilled, untangled, untaught, untrained *Antonyms:* polished, professional **4.** blunt, boorish, crass, indelicate, rude, thoughtless, uncouth *Antonyms:* gallant, suave, urbane **5.** base, bawdy, indecent, lewd, obscene, offensive, vulgar *Antonyms:* chaste, pure, tasteful **6.** apparent, bare, blatant, exposed, glaring, naked, outright, overt, plain, undisguised *Antonyms:* concealed, hidden

cruel *adj.* **1.** atrocious, barbarous, bestial, bitter, bloodthirsty, brutal, degenerate, demoniac, depraved, evil, ferocious, fierce, hateful, hellish, inhuman, malevolent, monstrous, pernicious, ruthless, sadistic, sinful, spiteful, unnatural, unrelenting, vengeful, vicious, wicked **2.** callous, cold-blooded, excruciating, flinty, hard, hardhearted, harsh, heartless, inhumane, merciless, painful, pitiless, relentless, stony-hearted, tyrannical, uncaring, unfeeling, unkind *Antonyms:* benevolent, compassionate, humane, kind, merciful

cruelty *n.* **1.** animality, barbarity, bestiality, bloodthirstiness, brutality, depravity, ferocity, fiendishness, fierceness, inhumanity, malice, malignity, murderousness, persecution, rancour, ruthlessness, sadism, savagery, spite, torture, truculence, viciousness, wickedness **2.** callousness, coldness, despotism, hardheartedness, harshness, heartlessness, insensibility, insensitiveness, mercilessness, unkindness *Antonyms:* benevolence, humaneness, mercy

cruise *n.* boat trip, crossing, expedition, jaunt, journey, sail, sea trip, voyage – *v.* **1.** coast, sail, travel, vacation, voyage, yacht **2.** drift, prowl, meander, range, wander **3.** hustle, lure, pander, solicit

cruiser *n.* **1.** boat, cabin cruiser, man-of-war, motorboat, vessel, yacht **2.** automobile, car, police *or* squad car, vehicle

crumb *n.* atom, bit, dab, dash, grain, iota, jot, mite, morsel, ounce, particle, pinch, shred, sliver, smidgen, snippet, soupçon, speck

crumble *v.* break, crush, disintegrate, grind, mash, pound, powder, pulverize, shatter, smash, split, sprinkle, squish

crumbly *adj.* breakable, brittle, crisp, crunchy, fragile, frail, friable, oxidized, powdery, shivery, short, soft, worn *Antonyms:* hard, solid, unbreakable

crummy *adj.* **1.** cheap, contemptible, inferior, junky, rubbishy, shabby, shoddy, trashy, useless, valueless, worthless *Antonyms:* choice, fine, supreme **2.** bad, crappy *(Nonformal)*, ill, lousy, miserable, pathetic, sick, unwell, wretched

crumple *v.* **1.** crease, crimp, crinkle, crush, fold, furrow, pucker, ruck, ruffle, rumple, scrunch, wrinkle **2.** break down, buckle, cave in, collapse, fall, give way, yield

crunch *n.* **1.** crackle, pop, snap **2.** crisis, critical point, crux, deadline, difficulty, emergency, problem, test, trial, trouble, wire *(Nonformal)* – *v.* **1.** bite, champ, chew, chomp, gnaw, grind, masticate, munch **2.** crush, pulverize, shatter, smash

crusade *n.* campaign, demonstration, drive, expedition, holy war, jihad, march, movement, push – *v.* **1.** attack, battle, combat, fight, push, war **2.** campaign, canvass, disseminate, lobby, preach, promulgate, proselytize, pump *(Nonformal)*, spread the word

crush *n.* **1.** crowd, drove, gathering, horde, huddle, jam, multitude, press, throng **2.** desire, flame, infatuation, love affair, passion, puppy love *(Nonformal)* – *v.* **1.** bruise, compress, extract, mash, press, squash, squeeze **2.** beat, break, crumble, crunch, pound, powder, pulverize, smash, triturate **3.** conquer, defeat, overcome, overpower, overwhelm, quell, subdue, vanquish **4.** crowd, jam, push, shove **5.** chagrin, deride, disgrace, dismay, embarrass, humble, humiliate, mortify, reduce, ridicule, shame

crushed *adj.* **1.** annihilated, beaten, debased, destroyed, disgraced, humiliated, racked, ravaged, razed, reduced, ruined, savaged, wrecked **2.** flattened, ground, hammered, milled, paved, pounded, pulverized, steamrollered

crust *n.* bark, coat, coating, covering, encrustation, film, hull, husk, layer, outside, rind, scab, shell, skin, surface

crustacean arthropod *Common crustacean:* barnacle, crab, crawdad, crayfish, lobster, prawn, shrimp, sowbug

crusty *adj.* **1.** brittle, crisp, hard, short, well-baked, well-done *Antonyms:* pliant, soft, supple **2.** abrupt, bluff, blunt, brief, brusque, cantankerous, captious, choleric, crabby, cranky, cross, curt, dour, gruff, harsh, ill-humoured, irascible, irritable, peevish, prickly, sarcastic, scornful, short-tempered, snappish *(Nonformal)*, snarling, snippety, snippy, splenetic, surly, testy, touchy *Antonyms:* diplomatic, good-natured, mirthful

crux *n.* **1.** bottom line, core, essence, gist, heart, kernel, matter, meaning, meat, nitty-gritty *(Nonformal)*, nub, pith, point, purport, substance **2.** bafflement, Catch-22, conundrum, difficulty, dilemma, enigma, mystery, perplexity, problem, puzzle, riddle *Nonformal:* brain-teaser, catch **3.** crosier, cross, crucifix, icon, rood, staff, symbol

cry *n.* **1.** bark, bawl, bellow, caterwaul, cheer, clamour, crow, exclamation, expletive, fuss, holler, hoot, howl, hullabaloo, hurrah, outcry, roar, ruckus, scream, screech, shout, shriek, squall, squawk, squeak, uproar, vociferation, wail, whine, whistle, whoop, yammer, yawp, yell, yelling, yelp *Antonyms:* drone, mumble, murmur **2.** bawling, bewailing, distress, grieving, keening, lament, mourning, pain, snivelling, sobbing, sorrow, tears, wailing, weeping, whimpering, woe **3.** battle cry, byword, catchphrase, catchword, motto, shibboleth, signal, slogan **4.** advertising, exposure, hue and cry, publicity *Nonformal:* ballyhoo, buzz, plug **5.** appeal, demand, entreaty, imploration, petition, plea, request, solicitation, supplication – *v.* **1.** bark, bay, bellow, blaze, chatter, cheer, crow, holler, howl, roar, scream, screech, shout, shriek, squawk, thunder, whinny, whistle, whoop, yell, yelp **2.** bawl, bemoan, bewail, break down, caterwaul, complain, deplore, grieve, groan, keen, lament, mewl, moan, mourn, regret, shed tears, sniff, snivel, sob, sorrow, ululate, wail, weep, whimper, whine, yammer, yowl *Nonformal:* blubber, boohoo, choke *or* crack up *Antonyms:* chortle, chuckle, giggle, laugh **3.** appeal, ask, demand, entreat, implore, obsecrate, plead, pray, request, solicit **4.** advertise, blazon, broadcast, herald, proclaim, promote, promulgate, trumpet

crypt *n.* burial, catacomb, cavity, grave, grotto, mausoleum, sepulchre, tomb, vault

cryptic *adj.* **1.** abstruse, ambiguous, elliptical, enigmatic, equivocal, evasive, incomprehensible, murky, mystifying, opaque, puzzling, unclear, vague *Antonyms:* explicit, lucid, trenchant **2.** apocryphal, arcane, cabalistic, dark, Delphic, esoteric, hidden, inexplicable, mysterious, mystical, occult, recondite, secret, secretive, veiled

crystal *adj.* clear, limpid, lucid, luminous, pellucid, transparent – *n.* **1.** glass, glassware, tableware **2.** gem, mineral, precious stone, quartz, rock, stone

crystallize *v.* **1.** coalesce, come together, form, materialize, take shape *Antonyms:* dissipate, dissolve, unravel **2.** freeze, harden, set, solidify

cubicle *n.* booth, carrel, cell, closet, compartment, niche, nook, room, stall, workstation

cuddle *n. & v.* caress, clasp, cosset, embrace, hold, huddle, hug, nestle, nuzzle, pet, snuggle, touch *Antonyms:* cuff, needle, prod

cudgel *n.* bat, billy club, blackjack, bludgeon, cane, club, mace, nightstick, rod, shill, stick, switch, truncheon – *v.* beat, buffet, clobber, club, cuff, pound, pummel, shellac *(Nonformal)*, trounce

cue *n.* **1.** catchword, fillip, goad, nod, prompt, reminder, sign, signal, stimulus **2.** hint, lead, suggestion, tip off **3.** disposition, frame *or* state of mind, humour, mind, mood, spirit, temper – *v.* indicate, nod, prompt, remind, signal *Commonly misused:* **queue**

cuff *n.* **1.** beating, belt, biff, box, buffet, chop, clip, clout, hit, knock, punch, slap, smack, thump, wallop, whack **2.** bond, bracelet *(Nonformal)*, fetter, handcuff, manacle – *v.* **1.** bat, beat, belt, biff, box, buffet, clap, clobber, clout, hit, knock, pummel, punch, slap, smack, smite, spank, thump, whack *Antonyms:* coddle, fondle, pet **2.** arrest, chain, fetter, manacle, tether

cull *v.* **1.** choose, discriminate, elect, extract, pick out, pluck, prefer, select, sift, single out, thin, winnow **2.** accumulate, amass, collect, extract, garner, gather, glean *Antonyms:* disseminate, sow, spread

culminate *v.* cap, climax, conclude, crown, end, finish, peak, top off *Antonyms:* begin, commence, initiate

culmination *n.* **1.** apex, apogee, height, limit, maximum, peak, perfection, pinnacle, summit, top, zenith *Nonformal:* capper, crowning touch *Antonyms:* base, low point, nadir **2.** climax, completion, conclusion, consummation, denouement, finale, finish, punch line *Antonyms:* dawn, genesis, preface

culpable *adj.* accountable, answerable, at fault, blamable, blameworthy, censurable, guilty, impeachable, indictable, liable, peccant, responsible *Antonyms:* guiltless, innocent

culprit *n.* convict, criminal, delinquent, felon, fugitive, guilty party, jailbird, malefactor, miscreant, perpetrator, offender, rascal, reprobate, sinner, transgressor, wrongdoer *Nonformal:* con, perp, yardbird

cult *n.* **1.** belief, creed, faith, ideology, order, party, religion, school, sect **2.** admirers, band, believers, devotees, disciples, fan club *(Nonformal)*, followers **3.** craze, idolization, devotion, reverence, veneration, worship, zealotry

cultivate *v.* **1.** breed, crop, develop, farm, garden, harvest, manage, plant, propagate, raise, tend **2.** amend, dress, fertilize, plow, till **3.** advance, aid, back, encourage, forward, foster, help, patronize, promote *Antonyms:* hinder, impede **4.** civilize, develop, discipline, educate, improve, instruct, learn, polish, refine, study, teach, train **5.** attend, court, curry favour, pursue, woo

cultivation *n.* **1.** breeding, civility, culture, delicacy, gentility, grooming, manners, polish, refinement, sophistication, taste **2.** edification, education, enlightenment, learning, letters, schooling **3.** advancement, advocacy, encouragement, enhancement, furtherance, improvement, nurture, patronage, progress, promotion, support **4.** agribusiness, agriculture, agronomy, aquaculture, development, farming, gardening, horticulture, husbandry, planting, plowing, tilling, work

culture *n.* **1.** civilization, convention, customs, ethos, folklore, folkways, life style, mores, society **2.** accomplishment, Cancult *(Nonformal)*, education, enlightenment, erudition, experience, high culture, learning, letters, scholarship, schooling, sophistication, training **3.** class, courtesy, elegance, finish, gentility, good breeding, grace, manners, polish, refinement, style, taste **4.** agriculture, breeding, cultivation, dressing, farming, harrowing, hoeing, husbandry, pruning, hoeing, tilling – *v.* fertilize, furrow, garden, manure, plow, till, work

cultured *adj.* **1.** civilized, cultivated, genteel, high-class, polished, refined, sophisticated, travelled, up-to-date, urbane, well-bred *French:* au courant, distingué *Antonyms:* common, inelegant, uncultivated, unrefined, vulgar **2.** accomplished, advanced, *cum laude (Latin)*, enlightened, erudite, high-brow, informed, intellectual, knowledgeable, learned, lettered, literary, scholarly, versed **3.** bred, created, farmed, grown, raised, reared

culvert *n.* canal, channel, conduit, ditch, drain, duct, gutter, pipe, sewer, storm sewer, trough, watercourse *Antonyms:* blockage, dam, stop

cumbersome *adj.* **1.** awkward, bulky, clumsy, heavy, hefty, incommodious, leaden, unmanageable, weighty *Antonyms:* compact, convenient, handy, serviceable, wieldy **2.** burdensome, onerous, oppressive, ponderous, suffocating, tiresome, troublesome, vexatious

cumulative *adj.* **1.** accumulative, aggregate, amassed, collective, heaped **2.** accruing, advancing, growing, heightening, increasing, intensifying, magnifying, multiplying

cunning *adj.* **1.** artful, cagey, calculating, canny, crafty, devious, foxy, guileful, intelligent, keen, knowing, Machiavellian, sharp, shifty, shrewd, slick, slippery, sly, streetwise *(Nonformal)*, subtle, tricky, wary, wily *Antonyms:* artless, ethical, frank **2.** able, adroit, astute, clever, creative, deft, dexterous, ingenious, skilful **3.** adorable, amusing, appealing, cute, sweet, winsome – *n.* **1.** craftiness, deceit, duplicity, guile, stealth, subtlety, trickery, underhandedness, wile **2.** acumen, aptitude, cleverness, deftness, dexterity, flair, genius, ingenuity, inventiveness, knack, resourcefulness, skill, talent **3.** destiny, fate, fortune, karma, kismet, lot **4.** basin, cavity, concavity, depression, hole, hollow, pit

cup *n.* **1.** beaker, bowl, can, chalice, container, demitasse, dish, glass, goblet, mug, sleeve, tankard, tumbler **2.** award, first prize, prize, reward, trophy, top honours

cupboard *n.* armoire, buffet, cabinet, closet, corner cabinet, cubbyhole, locker, pantry, repository, sideboard, storeroom

cupidity *n.* acquisitiveness, appetite, avarice, covetousness, desire, eagerness, greed, hankering, hungering, longing, rapaciousness, rapacity, selfishness, yearning *Antonyms:* generosity, liberality, munificence

curable *adj.* correctable, fixable, improvable, reparable, restorable, treatable *Antonyms:* incurable, terminal

curate *n.* chaplain, clergyman, clergywoman, cleric, minister, padre, parish priest, person of the cloth, preacher, reverend *French:* abbé, curé

curative *adj.* alleviative, beneficial, corrective, curing, healing, healthful, health-giving, invigorating, medicinal, recuperative, remedying, restorative, salutary, therapeutic, tonic, wholesome *Antonyms:* deleterious, pernicious, poisonous – *n.* cure, fixer, pick-me-up *(Nonformal)*, panacea, remedy, tonic

curator *n.* caretaker, custodian, guardian, keeper, manager, overseer, protector, shepherd, steward, superintendent, warden

curb *n.* **1.** brake, bridle, check, control, deterrent, harness, hindrance, limitation, rein, restraint, restriction **2.** border, curbstone, edge, gutter, ledge, margin, sidewalk **3.** barricade, barrier, fence, palisade, railing, wall – *v.* bridle, check, constrain, contain, control, cork up, curtail, inhibit, rein in, repress, restrain, subdue, suppress, tie, withhold *Antonyms:* indulge, oblige, satisfy

curdle *v.* clabber, coagulate, congeal, curd, ferment, go off *(Nonformal)*, spoil, sour, thicken

cure *n.* **1.** aid, alleviation, antidote, assistance, corrective, counteractive, counteragent, countermeasure, drug, elixir, fix *or* quick fix *(Nonformal)*, help, medication, medicine, panacea, remedy, restorative, therapeutic **2.** healing, recovery, reparation, treatment **3.** drying, pickling, preservation, salting, smoking – *v.* **1.** alleviate, better, correct, doctor *(Nonformal)*, dose, dress, ease, heal, help, improve, medicate, mend, minister to, nurse, rehabilitate, relieve, restore, right, shake *(Nonformal)*, treat *Antonyms:* devitalize, enervate, sicken **2.** rectify, redress, remedy **3.** age, cook, dry, keep, mature, pickle, preserve, salt, season, smoke

curiosity *n.* **1.** anomaly, hobby-horse *(Nonformal)*, idiosyncrasy, marvel, oddity, phenomenon, queerness, wonder **2.** bibelot, conversation piece, curio, knickknack, *objet d'art (French)*, peculiar *or* singular object, trinket **3.** inquisitiveness, interest, investigation, questioning, research, scouting, searching, study **4.** interference, intrusiveness, kibitzing *(Nonformal)*, meddling, nosiness, officiousness, snooping

curious *adj.* **1.** analytical, examining, inquiring, inquisitive, inspecting, interested, investigative, questioning, scrutinizing, searching *Antonyms:* indifferent, uninquisitive, uninterested **2.** impertinent, interfering, intrusive, meddlesome, meddling, nosy, peeping, prurient, prying **3.** exotic, extraordinary, mysterious, novel, peculiar, quaint, rare, remarkable, singular, unconventional, unexpected, unique *Antonyms:* common, everyday, familiar, ordinary **4.** bizarre, odd, puzzling, queer, strange, unorthodox, unusual, weird

curl *n.* **1.** coil, crimp, curlicue, friz, kink, loop, ringlet, twist, wave **2.** curvature, meandering, spiral, swirl, turning, whorl, winding – *v.* **1.** coil, corkscrew, crimp, entwine, friz, kink, loop, twine, twirl, twist, wave, wind, wreath **2.** curve, meander, snake, spiral, turn, zig-zag

curling *n.* ice game *or* sport, little rocks *(Children)*, roarin' game *(Newfoundland)* *Curling equipment:* broom, brush, granite, gripper, hack, hammer, handle, house, ice, lid, pebble, rink, rock, sheet, slider, stone, sweep, twelve- *or* eight- *or* four-foot circle *Positions in curling:* lead, second, skip, spare, vice *or* vice skip *Curling termi-*

nology: back line, hack weight, blank ends, burning the rock, button, button weight, come-around, delivery, downweight, draw *or* guard weight, ends, guard, hog line, in- *or* out-turn, jet ice, mixed curling, push *or* slide delivery, take-out weight, t-line, t-line weight, upweight

currency *n.* **1.** bill, cash, coinage, coins, legal tender, money, wad, *wampum (Native Peoples)*, York currency *(Historical) Nonformal:* dough, jack **2.** acceptance, circulation, *dernier cri (French)*, fashion, popularity, prevalence, renown, run, vogue

current *adj.* **1.** extant, happening, immediate, in progress, now, present **2.** contemporary, fashionable, modern, new, trendy, up-to-date *Nonformal:* hip, mud, with it **3.** afoot, circulating, reported, rumoured, topical, widely-known *Nonformal:* going-around, in the air **4.** accepted, common, customary, ordinary, popular, prevalent, standard, typical, widespread – *n.* **1.** coarse, flow, flux, jet, motion, river, rush, tide, undertow **2.** breeze, draft, drift, inclination, inflow, jet stream, movement, tendency, trend, wind **3.** conduction, electricity, juice *(Nonformal) Kinds of electrical current:* absorption, active, alternating current *or* AC, convection, direct current *or* DC, displacement, galvanic, induction, low-frequency, high-frequency, multiphase, magnetizing, oscillating, reactive, voltaic

curriculum *n.* course of study, education, major, minor, reading list, study, subject

curry *n.* dip, flavouring, powder, relish, sauce, spice, stew – *v.* **1.** brush, clean, comb, groom, hose *or* rub down, scrub, tend, wash **2.** beat, belt, clobber, clout *(Nonformal)*, hit, pummel, punch, strike, thrash

curse *n.* **1.** anathema, blasphemy, cursing, damning, execration, expletive, fulmination, imprecation, malediction, oath, objuration, obloquy, obscenity, profanation, profanity, sacrilege, swear word, vilification *Nonformal:* four-letter word, fuddle-duddle **2.** bane, burden, cross, evil, misfortune, plague, scourge, torment, tribulation, trouble, vexation **3.** *cantrip (Scottish)*, charm, conjuration, enchantment, evil eye *(Nonformal)*, incantation, invocation, jinx, magic spell, malediction, sorcery, witchery – *v.* **1.** anathematize, blaspheme, cuss *(Nonformal)*, damn, swear *Antonyms:* bless, consecrate, honour **2.** afflict, blight, burden, doom, plague, scourge, torment, trouble, vex *Antonyms:* ameliorate, better, improve **3.** bewitch, enchant, hex, jinx, spook *(Nonformal)*

cursed *adj.* **1.** abominable, atrocious, damnable, detestable, devilish, disgusting, evil, execrable, fiendish, hateful, heinous, infamous, infernal, loathsome, odious, pernicious, pestilential, vile **2.** accursed, bedeviled, blighted, damned, doomed, ill-fated, ill-starred, ruined, star-crossed, unfortunate, woebegone, wretched *Antonyms:* fortunate, happy, providential

cursory *adj.* brief, careless, casual, desultory, fast, haphazard, hasty, hurried, offhand, passing, perfunctory, quick, random, rapid, shallow, short, sketchy, slapdash, slight, sloppy, speedy, summary, superficial, swift, uncritical *Antonyms:* detailed, rigorous, thorough

curt *adj.* **1.** brief, concise, laconic, pithy, short, succinct, summary, terse *Antonyms:* circumlocutory, effusive, loquacious **2.** abrupt, blunt, brusque, churlish, gruff, imperious, offhand, sharp, snappish, snippy, tart, unceremonious, uncivil, ungracious *Antonyms:* diplomatic, gracious, suave

curtail *v.* abbreviate, abridge, circumscribe, cut short, edit, lessen, limit, reduce, shorten, slash, trim, truncate *Antonyms:* append, attach, extend

curtain *n.* **1.** backdrop, covering *Kinds of curtain and drape:* blind, decoration, drape, drapery, film, fire screen, hanging, jalousie, panel, partition, *portière (French)*, purdah, rag, roller, roll up shade, roman shade, screen, shade, shield, shroud, shutter, tapestry, valance, veil, venetian blind **2.** barrier, bulwark, divider, fence, partition, screen, wall **3.** death, destruction, end, extinction, final moment, finale, obliteration, ruin – *v.* blind, close, conceal, cover, hide, shade, shut off, veil *Antonyms:* exhibit, expose, uncover

curvaceous *adj.* bosomy, buxom, comely, curvy, full-figured, pleasing, rounded, sexy, shapely, statuesque, voluptuous, well-proportioned *Antonyms:* slender, twiggy, waiflike, willowy

curve *n.* **1.** arc, arch, bend, bow, camber, chord, circle, circuit, concavity, contour, crook, curlicue, deflection, ellipse, flexure, hairpin, half-moon, helix, horseshoe, hyperbola, incurvation, loop, meniscus, ogee, parabola, rondure, round, swerve, trajectory, turn, whorl **2.** distribution, grading system, ranking – *v.* arc, arch, bow, buckle, bulge, coil, crook, crumple, curl, deviate, gyrate, hook, inflect, loop, snake, spiral, stoop, swerve, turn, twist, veer, wind, wreath

curved *adj.* arched, bent, bowed, circular, crooked, curly, curvilinear, elliptical, looped, round, serpentine, sigmoid, sinuous, snaky, sweeping, swirly, turned, twisted, twisting, wreathed *Antonyms:* linear, straight, unbent

cushion *n.* **1.** bolster, headrest, mat, pad, pillow **2.** buffer, bumper, fender, mud guard, shock absorber – *v.* **1.** buttress, defend, prop up, protect, screen, shield, support, veil **2.** buffer, dampen, lessen, mitigate, moderate, modify, mollify

custodian *n.* **1.** chatelaine, curator, guardian, keeper, majordomo, protector, seneschal, sentinel, steward, warden, watch **2.** caretaker, cleaner, janitor, super *(Nonformal)*, superintendent

custody *n.* aegis, auspices, care, charge, control, guardianship, keeping, management, possession, protection, safekeeping, supervision, trusteeship, tutelage, ward, wardship

custom *adj.* custom-made, individual, made-to-order, personal, unique – *n.* **1.** convention, manner, method, policy, practice, observance, tradition, usage, way, wont **2.** habit, knee-jerk action *(Nonformal)*, routine, second nature, unconsciousness **3.** business, clientele, market, patronage, prospect, trade **4.** dues, rates, tariff, tax duty **5.** *cens et rentes (Historical)*, rent, service, tribute, tithe, token

customary *adj.* common, established, familiar, habitual, natural, normal, ordinary, traditional, typical, usual *Antonyms:* abnormal, exceptional, unusual

customer *n.* buyer, client, consumer, end-user, patron, purchaser, regular, shopper, user

cut *adj.* **1.** carved, cleft, divided, rent, separated, severed, split, sundered **2.** damaged, hurt, impaired, injured, lacerated, mutilated, slashed, slit, wounded **3.** dredged, furrowed, grooved, incised, indented, scored **4.** cheap, discount, half-price, marked down, on sale, pared, reduced, remaindered **5.** adulterated, attenuated, diluted, rarefied, thinned, thinned out, watered-down **6.** abbreviated, abridged, brief, clipped, concise, condensed, contracted, crisp, edited, elliptic, laconic, pruned, shortened, succinct, terse, truncated – *n.* **1.** hacking, lacerating, penetrating, piercing, puncturing, severing, slashing, wounding **2.** cleft, flesh wound, gash, incision, injury, laceration, opening, slash, wound **3.** abridgement, deletion, excision, omission, outtake, piece, portion, section, segment **4.** canal, channel, dredge line, furrow, passage, path, swath **5.** beeline *(Nonformal)*, bypass, detour, route, short-cut, straight-line **6.** abuse, affront, indignity, insult, rebuff, rejection, slight, snub **7.** arrangement, fashion, form, look, style – *v.* **1.** gash, gouge, lacerate, penetrate, pierce, prick, puncture, slash, stab **2.** cleave, dissect, divide, saw off, segment, separate, sever, skive, sunder **3.** amputate, detach, dismember, guillotine, hack off, limb, part, quarter, remove **4.** dice, julienne, pare, slice **5.** burrow, dig, dredge, excavate, hollow, mine, shovel **6.** clip, chop, dock, prune, shave, shear, sickle, snip, trim **7.** axe, chainsaw, clear-cut, fell, hew, lumber, moonscape *(B.C.)*, raze **8.** birch, flagellate, flog, lash, strike, switch, whip **9.** afflict, aggrieve, anguish, hurt, injure, pain, torment, wound *Antonyms:* alleviate, comfort, soothe **10.** affront, avoid, ignore, insult, ostracize, rebuff, reject, slight, snub *Nonformal:* brush off, cold shoulder **11.** call in sick, play hooky *Nonformal:* ditch, skip **12.** bisect, cross, divide, intersect **13.** abbreviate, abridge, blue pencil, condense, contract, edict, excise, pare down, purge, reduce, shorten, truncate **14.** collect, draw, garner, glean, harvest, reap, yield **15.** attenuate, break *or* water down, dilute, doctor *(Nonformal)*, temper, thin, weaken *Antonyms:* bolster, concentrate, fortify, strengthen **16.** act, do, perform, play, present **17.** check, curb, desist, discontinue, end, finish, stop, terminate **18.** shift, swerve, tack, turn, veer

cute *adj.* **1.** attractive, bonny, charming, comely, cuddly, dainty, dreamy *(Nonformal)*, handsome, lovely, pretty **2.** artful, clever, crafty, cunning, sly, tricky, wily *Antonyms:* artless, simple, straightforward

cutlery *n.* flatware, silverware *Kinds of cutlery:* carving fork, carving knife, chopsticks, dessert fork, dessert spoon, dinner fork, fish knife, fork, knife, ladle, oyster fork, spoon

cutoff *n.* **1.** branch, fork, off-ramp, pass, shortcut, turn **2.** expiration date, limit, termination

cutting *adj.* **1.** acid, acrimonious, barbed, biting, bitter, caustic, hateful, hurtful, malicious, nasty, penetrating, piercing, pointed, probing, raw, sarcastic, sardonic, scathing, severe, sharp, stinging, trenchant, wounding *Antonyms:* kind, mollifying, soothing **2.** axing, cleaving, felling, severing, shearing *Kinds of cutting tool:* adze, alpenstock, axe, chainsaw, chisel, cleaver, clipper, edger, graver, hatchet, knife, lancet, lawn mower, machete, paper cutter, pickaxe, pipe cutter, pruner, razor, router, saw, scalpel, scissors, scythe, shears, sickle, stylus, wire cutter

cybernetics *n.* artificial intelligence *or* AI, autonetics, bionetics, computer science, organic programming, robotics, servomechanics

cycle *n.* **1.** course, orbit, pattern, phase, rotation, run, *samsara (Buddhism)*, sequence, track **2.** aeon, age, epoch, era, millennium, period, span, stretch **3.** bicycle, bike, monocycle, moped, motorcycle, mountain bike, scooter, tricycle, trike, unicycle – *v.* **1.** reappear, recur, repeat, return **2.** circle, complete, evolve, orbit, pass, revolver **3.** bike, peddle, pump, ride, roll, travel

cyclone *n.* gale, hurricane, monsoon, storm, tempest, tornado, twister *(Nonformal)*, typhoon, vortex, waterspout, whirlwind, windstorm

cylinder *n.* barrel, bobbin, cask, chamber, container, cork, drum, keg, puncheon, reel, roll, roller, scroll case, spindle, spool, tube

cynic *n.* carper, caviler, disbeliever, doubter, killjoy, mocker, pessimist, scoffer, sceptic, sneerer *Nonformal:* doubting Thomas, downer, wet blanket *Antonyms:* cheerleader, Dr. Pangloss, optimist

cynical *adj.* contemptuous, critical, distrusting, doubtful, mocking, pessimistic, sarcastic, scoffing, scornful, sceptical, sneering, suspicious, unbelieving, wry *Antonyms:* hopeful, roseate, trusting

cynosure *n.* **1.** centre of attraction, focal point, focus, magnet, prime focus, tourist attraction *Nonformal:* hot spot, lightening rod **2.** beacon, buoy, guide, guiding light, lighthouse, lodestar, Northstar, Polaris, polstar, signpost

cyst *n.* beal, blister, growth, pouch, sore, tumour, wen *Kinds of cyst:* developmental, hydatid, retention

czar *n.* **1.** autocrat, caesar, despot, dictator, emperor, kaiser, khan, king, mogul, nabob, rajah, ruler, satrap, viceroy **2.** boss, chief, decision-maker, leader *Nonformal:* big cheese, head honcho, top brass

dab *n.* bit, drop, fleck, flick, pat, peck, smudge, speck, spot, stroke, touch *Nonformal:* dollop, smidgen

dabble *v.* dally, dip into, flirt *or* trifle with, patchky *(Yiddish)*, play, tinker, trifle *Nonformal:* dilly-dally, fiddle with, fool *or* monkey around, lollygag

dabbler *n.* amateur, beginner, dilettante, hobbyist, layman, laywoman, nonprofessional, novice, scribbler, tinkerer

daft *adj.* absurd, asinine, crazy, daffy, demented, deranged, dopey, foolish, idiotic, inane, insane, lunatic, mad, ridiculous, silly, simple, stupid, touched, unbalanced, unhinged, unsound, witless *Nonformal:* cracked, crackers, nuts, nutty, screwy, wacky

dagger *n.* knife, shiv *(Nonformal) Kinds of dagger:* ba chan shuang dao *(Chinese)*, bodkin, dirk, kirpan *(Sikh)*, kris *(Malaysian)*, poniard, short sword, skean, stiletto, stylet *Japanese:* hishi, kozuka, tanto, yoroitoshi – *v.* jab, knife, perforate, pierce, shiv *(Nonformal)*, skewer, stab, stick

daily *adj.* circadian, common, commonplace, constant, cyclic, day-to-day, diurnal, everyday, often, once daily, ordinary, periodic, quotidian, regular, routine

dainty *adj.* **1.** attractive, charming, comely, cute, darling, delightful, fair, graceful, petite, pleasing, pretty *Antonyms:* clumsy, inelegant, unsightly, vulgar **2.** airy, delicate, diaphanous, ethereal, exquisite, fine, fragile, lacy, light, refined, soft, subtle *Antonyms:* coarse, crude, heavy **3.** choice, delectable, delicious, savory, select, sweet, tasteful, tasty, tender, yummy *(Nonformal) Antonyms:* horrible, unappetizing

dairy *adj.* milk *Kinds of dairy food:* bonnyclabber, butter, buttermilk, cheese, clabber, cream, *crème fraiche (French)*, curds, eggnog, goat's milk, half-and-half, heavy cream, ice cream, light cream, milk, quark, sour cream, sweet butter, whey, whipping cream, yogurt

dalliance *n.* **1.** dabbling, dawdling, delay, delaying, frittering, idling, loafing, loitering, playing, procrastination, trifling **2.** amorous play, caresses, carrying on, coquetry, fling, flirtation, flirting, fondling, fooling around *(Nonformal)*, frolick, love affair, relationship, seduction, toying

dally *v.* dawdle, delay, hang about, idle, lag, linger, loiter, procrastinate, putter, tarry, trail, trifle with, waste time, while away *Nonformal:* dilly-dally, futz around, lollygag *Antonyms:* hasten, hurry, push on

dam *n.* aboideau, bank, barrage, barrier, beaver dam, dike, ditch, embankment, gate, hindrance, levee, logjam, milldam, obstruction, sluicegate, wall – *v.* bar, barricade, block, check, choke, clog, close, confine, halt, hinder, hold back, impede, obstruct, plug, restrain, restrict, slow, stop up, suppress

damage *n.* **1.** accident, blemish, blow, breakage, bruise, casualty, catastrophe, contusion, destruction, devastation, disturbance, harm, injury, knockout, marring, mishap, mutilation, ravage, ruin, ruination, waste, wound, wreckage *Antonyms:* improvement, profit, reparation **2.** adulteration, contamination, corruption, debasement, deterioration, pollution, spoilage **3.** adversity, affliction, deprivation, evil, hardship, mischief, outrage, reverse, suffering **4.** depreciation, detriment, endangerment, exposure, hurt, liability, risk, vulnerability

– *v.* **1.** abuse, batter, blight, break, burn, contuse, corrupt, crack, cripple, deface, disfigure, disintegrate, harm, hurt, impair, incapacitate, injure, lacerate, maim, maltreat, mangle, mar, mutilate, ravage, rot, ruin, rust, scathe, scorch, scratch, smash, split, stab, stain, tarnish, tear, vandalize, vitiate, weaken, wound, wreck, wrong *Antonyms:* better, fix, improve, mend, repair **2.** contaminate, corrode, defile, dirty, infect, pollute, spoil, tamper with, undermine

damaged *adj.* beat-up, bent, blemished, broken, bruised, busted, contused, flawed, fouled up, gone, hobbled, hurt, impaired, imperfect, injured, marred, run down, spoiled *Nonformal:* cooked, had it, kaput, messed *or* mucked up, no go, screwed up, shot

damages *n.* compensation, cost, dues, expenses, fine, forfeiture, indemnity, payment, penalty, price, reimbursement, reparation, sconce *(British)*

damaging *adj.* bad, defamatory, detrimental, evil, harmful, hurtful, injurious, libellous, noxious, prejudicial, ruinous, slanderous *Antonyms:* advantageous, favourable

dame *n.* aristocrat, baroness, blue blood, countess, dowager, gentlewoman, grande dame, lady, lady of the chamber, marchioness, marquise, matriarch, matron, noblewoman

damn *v.* **1.** abuse, attack, blaspheme, blast, castigate, censure, condemn, confound, convict, criticize, curse, denounce, excoriate, execrate, fulminate against, imprecate, inveigle, objurgate, penalize, punish, revile *Nonformal:* darn, pan, slag, slam *Antonyms:* acclaim, compliment, extol, laud, praise **2.** ban, banish, cast out, excommunicate, expel, outlaw, proscribe, sentence

damnable *adj.* abhorrent, abominable, depraved, despicable, detestable, dratted *(Nonformal)*, execrable, hateful, horrible, infamous, maleficent, nefarious, odious, offensive, outrageous, wicked *Antonyms:* admirable, commendable, exemplary, fine, worthy *Commonly misused:* **damned**

damned *adj.* accursed, blamed, blighted, confounded, cursed, doomed, ill-fated, infamous, lousy *(Nonformal)*, ruined, star-crossed, unhappy, unwelcome – *adv.* altogether, awfully, extremely, terribly, very *Commonly misused:* **damnable**

damp *adj.* clammy, dank, dewy, drenched, dripping, drizzly, foggy, humid, misty, moist, muggy, saturated, soaked, soaking, sodden, soggy, sopping, steamy, sticky, vaporous, waterlogged, watery, wet *Antonyms:* arid, dry, parched – *n.* dankness, dew, fog, humidity, mist, moisture, mugginess, perspiration, sogginess, vapour, wateriness, wetness *Antonyms:* aridity, aridness, dryness

dampen *v.* **1.** bedew, douse, humidify, hydrate, irrigate, lubricate, mist, moisten, rinse, soak, spray, sprinkle, water, wet **2.** bridle, check, chill, constrain, cool, curb, dash, deaden, depress, diminish, discourage, dismay, dispirit, dull, impede, inhibit, muffle, restrain, restrict, stifle *Antonyms:* excite, inspire, motivate

damper *n.* **1.** barrier, check, flue, gate, plate **2.** difficulty, discouragement, drag, encumbrance, gloom, hindrance, hitch, impediment, inhibition, knot, obstacle, obstruction, pall, restraint, restriction, setback, stay *Antonyms:* encouragement, inspiration **3.** kill-joy *Nonformal:* crybaby, moaner, skeleton at the banquet, wet blanket

dance *n.* boogie *(Nonformal)*, rhythmic gyration *Kinds of dance:* ballet, ballroom, baton, belly, bird, break, Buffalo, Charleston, chicken, clog, conga, disco, experimental, fancy shawl, flamenco, folk, foxtrot, Ghost, highland, Horse, hula, interpretive, jazz, jig, jitterbug, jive, lambada, line-dancing, macarena, *maxixe (Brazilian)*, *mazurka (Polish)*, modern, Morris *(English)*, one-step, polka, quadrille, Rabbit, Red River jig, reel, rhumba, round, samba, saraband, shimmy, skank, slam, square, stomp, strathspey, Sun, sword, tango, tap, twist, two-step, victory *or* endzone *(Football)*, waltz, War, Wolf *Kinds of dance events:* ball, ballet, barn, cotillion, formal, frolic, hoe-down, hop, masked ball *or* masquerade, mixer, powwow *(Aboriginal)*, promenade, record hop, round, shindig, social, sock hop – *v.* gyrate, hop, jig, jitter, jive, promenade, rattle, reel, rock, roll, shake, skip, spin, step, strut, sway, swing, tap, waltz, whirl *Nonformal:* boogie, cut a rug, get down, shake one's booty

dancer *n.* expressionist *Kinds of dancer:* aerobic, ballet, belly, clog, exotic, flamenco, folk, highland, hula, interpretive, jazz, line, modern, step, stripper, stripteaser, tap, topless

dancing *adj.* **1.** flickering, flitting, shimmering, sparkling, twirling *Antonyms:* steady, unwavering **2.** grooving, lively, moving, prancing, shaking, swaying

dandle *v.* amuse, caress, cosset, cradle, cuddle, fondle, love, nuzzle, rock

dandy *adj.* **1.** dapper, foppish, jaunty, natty, sharp, snazzy, spruce, swanky *Antonyms:* casual, sloppy **2.** excellent, fine, first-rate, great, super, superb, swell *(Nonformal)*, terrific *Antonyms:* appalling, awful, dreadful, terrible – *n.* **1.** Beau Brummel, blade, buck, clotheshorse, coxcomb, dude, fashion plate, fop, gallant, peacock, popinjay, sharp dresser, spark, swell *Antonyms:* bum, hobo, slob **2.** beauty, fine thing, gem, nonpareil *Nonformal:* beaut, killer *Antonyms:* dud, lemon

danger *n.* crisis, emergency, endangerment, exigency, hazard, jeopardy, menace, peril, pitfall, precariousness, predicament, risk, threat, uncertainty, vulnerability *Nonformal:* hot water, loose cannon, thin ice

dangerous *adj.* **1.** alarming, bad, chancy, critical, delicate, dicey *(Nonformal)*, erratic, explosive, faulty, formidable, hazardous, menacing, nasty, perilous, precarious, risky, serious, shaky, slippery, threatening, treacherous, tricky, uncertain, unreliable, unsound, unstable, unsteady, untrustworthy **2.** deadly, fatal, lethal, mortal, terminal, unhealthy *Antonyms:* innocuous, wholesome **3.** exposed, insecure, out on a limb *(Nonformal)*, unprotected, unsafe, unshielded, vulnerable, weak *Antonyms:* harmless, protected, safe, secure

dangerously *adv.* carelessly, critically, daringly, desperately, harmfully, hazardously, perilously, precariously, recklessly, seriously

dangle *v.* **1.** brandish, entice, flaunt, flourish, lure, tantalize, tease **2.** droop, hang, suspend, sway, swing, trail **3.** hover, linger, loom, wait

dangling *adj.* disconnected, drooping, hanging, loose, pendent, swaying, swinging, trailing *Antonyms:* gathered, tight, secure

dank *adj.* chilly, clammy, close, damp, dripping, humid, mildewy, moist, muggy, slimy, soggy, steamy, sticky, wet *Antonyms:* arid, dehydrated, dry

dapper *adj.* chic, classy, dashing, jaunty, natty, neat, nifty, rakish, sharp, showy, smart, spruce, stylish, swank, swanky, trim, well-dressed, well-groomed *Nonformal:* dressed to the nines, posh, ragged out, ritzy, snazzy, spiffy *Antonyms:* dishevelled, frowzy, ill-groomed, rumpled

dappled *adj.* Appaloosa, brindle, calico, flecked, freckled, motley, mottled, multicolour, multihued, parti-coloured, piebald, speckled, spotted, stippled, varicoloured, variegated

dare *v.* **1.** beard, brave, court, defy, disregard, oppose, threaten, withstand *Antonyms:* fear, submit **2.** challenge, confront, provoke, taunt, test

daredevil *adj.* adventurous, audacious, bold, brash, brave, breakneck, daring, dauntless, death-defying, fearless, foolhardy, harebrained, heedless, impetuous, imprudent, impulsive, intrepid, madcap, nervy, precipitate, rash, reckless, unafraid, venturesome, wild *Nonformal:* gutsy, kamikaze *Antonyms:* careful, cautious, chary, unexciting – *n.* adventurer, braveheart, desperado, exhibitionist, hotspur, madcap, showoff, stuntperson *Nonformal:* devil-may-care, Evel Kneival, hellion, wildcat

daring *adj.* adventurous, audacious, bold, brassy, brave, cheeky, cocky, courageous, fearless, foolhardy, forward, game, gritty, gutsy *(Nonformal)*, gutty, impulsive, intrepid, plucky, rash, reckless, salty, smart, spunky, venturesome *Antonyms:* anxious, careful, cautious, fearful, wary

dark *adj.* **1.** clouded, cloudy, darkened, dim, dingy, drab, dull, dusky, foggy, lightless, misty, murky, overcast, pitch-black, pitch-dark, shaded, shadowy, shady, sombre, sunless, tenebrous, unlit *Antonyms:* bright, sunny **2.** black, charcoal, coal, jet, slate, sooty *Antonyms:* light, white **3.** brunet *(Masc.)*, brunette *(Fem.)*, ebony, sable, tan *Antonyms:* blonde, fair, light, towheaded **4.** bleak, blue, cheerless, dismal, doleful, drab, foreboding, gloomy, grim, hopeless, joyless, morbid, morose, mournful, ominous, sombre, unpropitious *Antonyms:* happy, glorious, pleasant **5.** abstruse, anagogic, arcane, cabalistic, complicated, concealed, cryptic, deep, Delphian, enigmatic, esoteric, hidden, indistinct, intricate, knotty, mysterious, mystic, mystifying, nebulous, obscure, occult, opaque, puzzling, recondite, secret **6.** atrocious, bad, corrupt, damnable, evil, foul, hellish, horrible, immoral, infernal, nefarious, satanic, sinful, sinister, vile, wicked **7.** benighted, dull, ignorant, unenlightened, unread *Antonyms:* erudite, learned – *n.* **1.** darkness, dimness, dullness, dusk, duskiness, evening, murk, night, nightfall, overcast, shade, shadows, twilight **2.** concealment, denseness, inscrutability, mystery, seclusion, secrecy **3.** incomprehension, ignorance, unawareness, unfamiliarity, vagueness *Antonyms:* comprehension, knowledge

darken *v.* **1.** adumbrate, blacken, cloud over *or* up, dim, fog, grey, haze, make dark, overcast, overshadow, screen, shade, shadow, shelter, shield *Antonyms:* brighten, clear up **2.** depress, discourage, dispirit, pall, sadden, upset *Antonyms:* cheer, gladden **3.** bewilder, confuse, muddle, obfuscate, obscure, veil *Antonyms:* clear, enlighten

darkness *n.* **1.** adumbration, blackness, blackout, brownout, cloudiness, cover, dark, darkness, dimness, dullness, dusk, duskiness, eclipse, gloom, gloominess, murk, murkiness, nightfall, penumbra, pitch darkness, semi-darkness, shade, shadow, shelter, twilight *Antonyms:* brightness, dazzle, light **2.** blindness, denseness, ignorance, incomprehension, isolation *Antonyms:* realization, understanding **3.** curse, depravity, evil, malevolence, turpitude, vice, villainy, wickedness **4.** covertness, obscurity, secrecy, stealth *Antonyms:* clarity, openness

dart *n.* **1.** arrow, blow dart, javelin, missile, stinger, weapon **2.** fold, pleat, tuck – *v.* bound, career, cast, dash, flash, flit, hurtle, move quickly, pitch, propel, race away, run, rush, scamper, scoot, scurry, sprint *Antonyms:* amble, meander, saunter

dash *n.* **1.** bit, drop, flavour, grain, hint, lick, little, part, pinch, scattering, seasoning, smack, *soupçon (French)*, sprinkle, sprinkling, squirt, streak, suggestion, suspicion, taste, tincture, tinge, touch, trace, trifle **2.** race, run, sortie, sprint, spurt **3.** animation, brio, élan, energy, esprit, flair, flourish, force, impressiveness, intensity, life, might, panache, power, spirit, strength, style, vehemence, verve, vigour, vim, vivacity – *v.* **1.** bolt, bound, careen, charge, chase, dart, flee, fly, gallop, hasten, hurry, race, run, rush, scamper, scoot, scurry, shoot, speed, spring, sprint, tear *Antonyms:* crawl, dawdle, walk **2.** baffle, balk, beat, blight, circumvent, confound, crash, dampen, defeat, destroy, discourage, end, foil, frustrate, nip, ruin, shatter, smash, splinter, thwart **3.** bludgeon, cast, cudgel, fling, hit, hurl, hurtle, shiver, slam, sling, splash, splatter, throw

dashing *adj.* adventurous, animated, bold, chic, dapper, debonair, elegant, exuberant, fashionable, fearless, flamboyant, gallant, jaunty, keen, lively, modish, showy, smart, spirited, sporty, stylish, swashbuckling *Antonyms:* boring, dreary, dull, lacklustre

dastardly *adj.* **1.** afraid, chicken-livered *(Nonformal)*, cowardly, cowering, craven, faint-hearted, frightened, pusillanimous, recreant, shy, skittish, timid, timorous *Antonyms:* brave, courageous, gallant, intrepid, plucky **2.** abject, atrocious, base, deceitful, despicable, low, mean, shameful, skulking, sneaky, underhanded, vile *Antonyms:* honourable, noble

data *n. pl.* abstracts, bytes, compilations, conclusions, details, documents, dope *(Nonformal)*, dossier, evidence, experiments, facts, figures, goods, information, input, knowledge, materials, measurements, memoranda, reports, results, score, statistics *or* stats

date *n.* **1.** age, century, course, day, duration, epoch, era, generation, hour, juncture, moment, period, quarter, reign, span, spell, stage, term, time, year **2.** appointment, assignation, call, engagement, interview, meeting, rendezvous, tryst, visit **3.** boyfriend, companion, consort, escort, friend, girlfriend, mate, partner – *v.* **1.** antedate, assign, determine, exist from, fix, isolate, mark, measure, record, register **2.** associate with, attend, consort with, escort, go together *or* with, keep company, run with, see, take out **3.** age, antiquate, obsolesce, outdate

dated *adj.* antiquated, archaic, *démodé (French)*, obsolescent, obsolete, old-fashioned, out, outdated, outmoded, passé, past, unfashionable, untrendy, worn, yesterday's news *(Nonformal) Antonyms:* chic, cool, current, hip, trendy

daughter *n.* child, descendant, heiress, issue, offspring, step-daughter

daunt *v.* alarm, appal, baffle, browbeat, bully, consternate, cow, deter, discourage, dishearten, dismay, dispirit, foil, frighten, horrify, intimidate, put off, scare, shake, subdue, terrify, thwart *Antonyms:* egg on *(Nonformal)*, incite, inspire

dauntless *adj.* bold, brave, courageous, daring, fearless, gallant, game, heroic, intrepid, lionhearted, resolute, unafraid, unconquerable, unflinching, valiant, valorous *Antonyms:* craven, timorous

dawdle *v.* amble, delay, drag, fritter away, idle, lag, laze, loaf, loiter, loll, lounge, meander, perambulate, procrastinate, put off, saunter, stay, stroll, tarry, toy, trail, trifle, wait, waste time *Nonformal:* dilly-dally, goof off, hang about *or* out, mosey *Antonyms:* fly, hasten, hurry, rush

dawn *n.* **1.** aurora, bright, cockcrow, daybreak, daylight, early bright, first blush *or* light, light, morn, morning, sunrise, sunup **2.** advent, awakening, beginning, birth, commencement, dawning, foundation, genesis, onset, origin, outset, rise, source, start, unfolding – *v.* appear, begin, develop, emerge, glimmer, initiate, lighten, loom, open, originate, rise, show, start, unfold *Antonyms:* fall, perish, set

day *n.* **1.** age, ascendancy, cycle, epoch, era, generation, period, prime, term, time **2.** astronomical day, dawn-to-dark, daylight, daytime, diurnal course, light, nautical day, sidereal day, sunlight, sunrise-to-sunset, sunshine, twenty-four hours, working day

daybreak *n.* break of day, crack of dawn, dawn, first light, morn, morning, sunrise, sunup *Antonyms:* evening, twilight, sundown, sunset

day-care *n.* baby sitter *or* sitter, childcare, day nursery, junior kindergarten, kindergarten, nursery school, playschool, preschool

daydream *n.* dream, fancy, fantasy, fond hope, imagination, imagining, notion, pipe dream, reverie, vision, wish *Nonformal:* fool's paradise, la-la land, woolgathering – *v.* conceive, dream, envision, fancy, fantasize, hallucinate, imagine, muse, speculate *Nonformal:* moon, pipe dream, stargaze

daylight *n.* **1.** daytime, light, light of day, luminosity, sunbeam, sunshine *Antonyms:* darkness, shadow **2.** clarity, clearness, comprehension, full knowledge, full view, intelligibility, lucidity, openness, perspicuity, public attention, publicity, understanding *Antonyms:* muddle, obscurity

daytime *n.* day, daylight, light, noonday, sunshine *Antonyms:* darkness, nighttime

daze *n.* fog, stupour, trance – *v.* addle, amaze, astonish, astound, befuddle, bewilder, confound, confuse, dazzle, disorder, distract, flabbergast *(Nonformal)*, fuddle, mix up, muddle, mystify, overwhelm, paralyze, perplex, petrify, puzzle, shock, stagger, startle, stun, stupefy, surprise

dazzle *n.* **1.** brilliance, flash, glare, glitter, radiance, sparkle **2.** dash, flamboyance, magnificence, panache, splendour, wonder

– *v.* addle, amaze, astonish, astound, awe, bedazzle, blind, boggle, dumfound, impress, overawe, overpower, overwhelm, puzzle, stagger, stun, stupefy *Nonformal:* blow one's mind, flabbergast *Antonyms:* bore, dull

deactivate *v.* close off, cut, decommission, end, finish, kill, shut down, switch *or* turn off, terminate *Antonyms:* activate, boot, energize, flip on, start, switch on

dead *adj.* **1.** at rest, cadaverous, deceased, departed, expired, martyred, no more, passed away *or* on, perished *Nonformal:* cold, gone, rubbed *or* snuffed out **2.** asleep, beat, breathless, bushed, catatonic, exhausted, inanimate, inert, insensible, moribund, oblivious, pooped, spent, tired, torpid, unconscious, worn out *Nonformal:* out, out cold, tuckered out, whacked *or* wiped out **3.** arid, empty, lost, sterile, useless **4.** concluded, done, done for, extinguished, *hors de combat (French)*, finished, played out, terminated, zapped *(Nonformal)* **5.** bygone *or* gone, dead and buried *(Nonformal)*, defunct, extinct, former, late, obsolete, passé **6.** cold, impassive, indifferent, inhuman, numb, soulless, spiritless, unemotional, unsympathetic *Antonyms:* compassionate, feeling, warm **7.** broken, damaged, disabled, down, inoperative, kaput *(Nonformal)*, out of order, ruined **8.** dull, flat, lacklustre, lustreless, matte *Antonyms:* burnished, glossy **9.** dampened, deadened, muffled, muted, subdued, suppressed *Antonyms:* sharp, shrill **10.** absolute, complete, sheer, total, unmitigated **11.** accurate, exact, flawless, perfect, true, unerring *Antonyms:* missed, off, wide – *adv.* absolutely, as the crow flies, directly, in a straight line, precisely, straight ahead, true – *n.* **1.** body, cadaver, carcass, corpse, *corpus delicti (Latin)*, deceased, dearly departed, decedent, departed, late lamented, remains, stiff *(Nonformal)* **2.** ancestors, forefathers, forbear, precursor, predecessor

deaden *v.* **1.** abate, alleviate, benumb, blunt, chloroform, cushion, dampen, depress, desensitize, dim, diminish, dope *(Nonformal)*, dull, exhaust, freeze, knock out, lay out, lessen, numb, reduce, retard, slow, soften, stun, suppress *Antonyms:* arouse, electrify, rile, stimulate **2.** drown, hush, muffle, mute, quiet, repress, smother, stifle **3.** check, deprive, destroy, devitalize, frustrate, impair, incapacitate, injure, paralyze, suck the life out of *(Nonformal)*, unnerve, weaken

deadhead *n.* **1.** debris, driftwood, floating log, flotsam, jetsam, snag **2.** freeloader, free-rider, gatecrasher, sponger **3.** beatnik, Bohemian, drop-out, flower-child, hippie, peacenik

deadline *n.* critical *or* decisive moment, drop-dead date *(Nonformal)*, due date, moment of truth, target date, time limit, ultimatum, zero hour

deadlock *n.* Catch-22, cessation, checkmate, dead end, dead heat, dilemma, draw, full stop, gridlock, halt, impasse, Mexican standoff, square, stalemate, standoff, standstill, tie *Nonformal:* box, pickle

deadly *adj.* **1.** awful, catastrophic, dangerous, death-dealing, destructive, detrimental, dire, extreme, fatal, grave, harmful, hazardous, implacable, incurable, lethal, life-threatening, malignant, mortal, noxious, pestilent, poisonous, terminal **2.** bloodthirsty, brutal, cruel, fierce, homicidal, maniacal, merciless, murderous, remorseless, ruthless, savage, unrelenting, violent **3.** accurate, on target, precise, skilled, unerring

deadpan *adj.* blank, empty, expressionless, hollow, immobile, impassive, inexpressive, inscrutable, mask-like, nonchalant, poker-faced, straight-faced, unrevealing, vacant, vacuous *Antonyms:* expressive, telltale

deadwood *n.* baggage, circumlocution, clutter, detritus, excess, garbage, junk, pleonasm, redundancy, refuse, superfluity, surplus, tautology, wastage, waste

deaf *adj.* **1.** deafened, hard of hearing, stone deaf, unhearing **2.** bullheaded, headstrong, intractable, obstinate, perverse, strong-willed, stubborn, unmoveable, unwavering **3.** heedless, indifferent, insensitive, oblivious, regardless, unresponsive

deafening *adj.* blaring, booming, clamorous, clangurous, crashing, ear-piercing, earsplitting, earthshaking, fortissimo, headsplitting, jarring, piercing, resounding, shrill, thunderous, window-rattling *Antonyms:* hushed, inaudible, low-pitched, quiet, silent

deal *n.* **1.** accord, agreement, appointment, arrangement, bargain, compromise, conception, contract, negotiation, pact, pledge, prearrangement, transaction, understanding **2.** chance, game, hand, opportunity, round – *v.* **1.** administer, allot, apportion, assign, bestow, deliver, disburse, dish out, dispense, disperse, disseminate, distribute, divide, divvy, dole out, drop, give, hand out, impart, measure, mete out, partake, participate, render, reward, share **2.** bargain, barter, negotiate, swap, talk, trade, transact

dealer *n.* agent, broker, bursar, businessperson, dispenser, jobber, marketer, merchandiser, merchant, owner, retailer, salesperson, supplier, trader, tradesperson, trafficker, vendor, wheeler-dealer *(Nonformal)*, wholesaler

dean *n.* **1.** chief, elder, first, head, leader, officer, paragon, president, principal, provost, ranking *or* senior member, registrar, senior, university head *Kinds of academic dean:* arts, engineering, graduate studies, humanities, medicine, pharmacy, residence, science **2.** clergyman, clergywoman, cleric, curate, ecclesiastic, minister, pastor, priest, rector, vicar

dear *adj.* **1.** costly, expensive, high-priced, overpriced, pricey, rich, steep, stiff, valuable *Antonyms:* cheap, inexpensive **2.** beloved, cherished, close, darling, endeared, esteemed, familiar, favourite, honoured, intimate, loved, precious, prized, respected, treasured *Antonyms:* disliked, hated – *n.* beloved, darling, favourite, honey, jewel, love, loved one, lover, partner, precious, sweetheart, treasure, true love

dearly *adv.* affectionately, closely, devotedly, familiarly, fondly, greatly, intimately, lovingly, preciously, tenderly, yearningly

dearth *n.* absence, deficiency, exiguousness, impoverishment, inadequacy, infrequency, insufficiency, lack, meagreness, need, paucity, poverty, privation, scantiness, scarcity, shortage, sparsity, want *Antonyms:* abundance, plethora, presence

death *n.* afterlife, annihilation, biological death, brain death, casualty, cessation, clinical death, decease, demise, departure, dissolution, downfall, dying, end, ending, end *or* cessation of life, eradication, eternal rest, exit, expiration, extermination, extinction, fatality, finish, grave, journey's end, loss, mortality, necrosis, oblivion, parting, passing away, release, rest, shades *or* shadow, sleep, termination, winterkill *Nonformal:* curtains, end of the line *or* road, eternal rest, last muster, the big sleep, the Long Traverse *Antonyms:* beginning, birth, emergence, genesis, origin *Personifications and symbols of death:* Acheron, Angel of Death, Azrael, Black Death, death's-head, Grim Reaper, Jordan, Jordan's bank, Pale Horse, river of death, skull and crossbones, Stygian shore, Thanatos

deathly *adj.* cadaverous, corpse-like, deathlike, dreadful, gaunt, ghastly, grim, haggard, horrible, macabre, pale, pallid, wan, wasted

debacle *n.* breakdown, catastrophe, collapse, crackup, crash, defeat, devastation, disaster, dissolution, downfall, drubbing, failure, fiasco, overthrow, reversal, rout, ruin, ruination, trouncing, washout, waste of time *(Nonformal)*

debase *v.* **1.** abase, belittle, besmirch, blacken, blemish, cheapen, debauch, defile, degrade, demean, deprave, deprecate, depreciate, deride, desecrate, devalue, discredit, disgrace, dishonour, disparage, disrespect, drag down, humiliate, impair, level, lower, minimize, mortify, reduce, shame, undermine, vitiate *Antonyms:* elevate, enhance, improve, refine, uplift **2.** adulterate, bastardize, contaminate, corrupt, dilute, dirty, doctor *(Nonformal)*, foul, mar, mix, muddy, pervert, pollute, smear, smudge, soil, spoil, stain, sully, taint, tarnish, thin, weaken *Antonyms:* cleanse, purify

debatable *adj.* arguable, borderline, contestable, controversial, disputable, doubtful, dubious, iffy *(Nonformal)*, moot, polemical, problematic, questionable, uncertain, undecided, unsettled *Antonyms:* accepted, incontrovertible, irreproachable

debate *n.* **1.** altercation, argument, argumentation, controversy, dialectic, disagreement, discord, discussion, disputation, dispute, dissension, logomachy, polemic **2.** competition, contention, contest, match, opposition, showdown, struggle, wrangle **3.** analysis, cogitation, consideration, contemplation, deliberation, examination, meditation, reflection, review, scrutiny, study, thought – *v.* **1.** altercate, argue, bandy, contend, contest, differ, disagree, discuss, dispute, dissent, moot, oppose, question, spar, wrangle *Antonyms:* agree, harmonize, settle **2.** cogitate, consider, contemplate, deliberate, examine, meditate, mull over, ponder, rationalize, reason, reflect, revolve, ruminate, think over *or* through, scrutinize, study, weigh *Antonyms:* disregard, ignore, neglect, overlook

debauch *v.* **1.** abuse, bastardize, befoul, brutalize, corrupt, debase, defile, demoralize, deprave, mar, pervert, pollute, profane, ravish, ruin, soil, subvert, sully, taint, tarnish, violate, warp **2.** entice, inveigle, lead astray, lure, seduce, tempt **3.** carouse, dissipate, make merry, party, revel, roister, wassail *Nonformal:* party hardy, live fast

debauched *adj.* abandoned, corrupt, debased, defiled, degenerate, degraded, depraved, dissipated, dissolute, fast, immoral, intemperate, lascivious, lewd, licentious, orgiastic, profligate, reprobate, unrestrained, violated, wanton, wicked *Antonyms:* abstemious, chaste, pure

debauchery *n.* carousal, depravity, dissoluteness, drunkenness, excess, fast living *(Nonformal)*, immorality, indulgence, infidelity, intemperance, lasciviousness, lechery, lewdness, libertinism, licentiousness, lust, orgy, overindulgence, profligacy, revelry, saturnalia, seduction, self-indulgence, wantonness *Antonyms:* moderation, morality, restraint

debilitate *v.* atrophy, blunt, castrate, cripple, deplete, deprive, disable, drain, emasculate, enervate, enfeeble, eviscerate, exhaust, fatigue, harm, hurt, impair, incapacitate, injure, mar, prostrate, sap, spoil, tire, undermine, weaken, wear *Antonyms:* animate, energize, enliven, stimulate, vitalize

debility *n.* atrophy, caducity, decrepitude, disease, enervation, enfeeblement, exhaustion, faintness, fatigue, feebleness, frailty, impotence, impuissance, incapacity, infirmity, languor, lassitude, malaise, neurasthenia, prostration, senility, sickliness, spiritlessness, weakness, weariness

debit *n.* charge, cost, debt, disbursement, expenditure, expense, loss, reduction, withdrawal *Antonyms:* addition, asset, credit, deposit, increase – *v.* charge, deduct, lower, reduce, subtract

debonair *adj.* affable, blithe, breezy, buoyant, casual, charming, cheerful, courteous, dapper, dashing, elegant, gallant, gay, happy, jaunty, jocund, pleasant, refined, slick *(Nonformal)*, smooth, sprightly, suave, urbane *Antonyms:* awkward, bumbling, clumsy

debris *n.* bits, crap *(Nonformal)*, detritus, dregs, driftwood, dross, flotsam, fragments, garbage, jetsam, junk, leftovers, litter, mess, odds and ends, offal, pieces, refuse, remains, rubbish, rubble, ruins, shards, slag, slash, trash, waste, wreckage

debt *n.* accountability, arrears, bill, check, chit, claim, debit, deficit, dire straits, dues, hock *(Nonformal)*, incumbrance, IOU, liability, money owed, mortgage, obligation, promissory note, tab, voucher

debunk *v.* deflate, demystify, deride, discover, disparage, disprove, expose, lampoon, mock, puncture, roast, ridicule, send *or* show up, uncloak, unmask *Antonyms:* back, support, uphold

debut *n.* beginning, coming out, commencement, first public appearance, first step, inauguration, initiation, introduction, launch, opener, premiere, presentation – *v.* begin, commence, embark upon, enter into, launch, open, take up *Antonyms:* cancel, conclude, finish, terminate

decadence *n.* **1.** corruption, debasement, degeneracy, degeneration, degradation, dissipation, dissolution, evil, perversion, self-indulgence **2.** decay, decline, deterioration, downfall, downgrade, regression

decadent *adj.* corrupt, debased, debauched, decaying, declining, degenerate, degraded, depraved, dissolute, effete, gone to hell *(Nonformal)*, immoral, moribund, rotten, self-indulgent, tainted, wanton, wicked *Antonyms:* decent, ethical, moral, principled, virtuous

decal *n.* bumper *or* window sticker, label, permit, print, sign, sticker

decamp *v.* abscond, bolt, break camp, depart, desert, disappear, elope, escape, evacuate, flee, fly, leave, light out, make tracks, march, move off *or* on, run away *or* off, shove off, skip, slink *or* slip away, sneak off, steal away, strike the tents, take flight, take off, vacate *Nonformal:* cut and run, cut out, go AWOL, hightail it, mosey, scram, skedaddle, split, take a moonlight flight, vamoose *Antonyms:* homestead, occupy, squat

decanter *n.* beaker, bottle, carafe, caster, cruet, ewer, jug, pitcher, stoppered bottle, vessel

decapitate *v.* axe, behead, bring to the block, chop off, decollate, execute, guillotine, lop off, top, truncate

decay *n.* **1.** atrophy, caries, blight, decomposition, gangrene, mortification, perishing, putrefaction, putrescence, rot, rust, spoilage, wasting, withering *Antonyms:* growth, repair **2.** collapse, corrosion, corruption, decadence, degeneracy, depreciation, deterioration, dilapidation, disintegration, disrepair, dissolution – *v.* **1.** atrophy, blight, corrode, curdle, decompose, deteriorate, disintegrate, dissolve, dwindle, fade, fail, fester, go bad, lessen, mildew, mortify, mould, moulder, perish, putrefy, rot, rot away, rust away, sap, shrivel, sicken, sink, slump, suppurate, turn, wane, waste away, weaken *Antonyms:* flourish, flower, grow **2.** collapse, corrupt, crumble, decline, defile, degenerate, depreciate, pollute, spoil

decayed *adj.* **1.** bad, corroded, decomposed, gangrenous, moulded, perished, putrid, rank, rotted, rotten, spoiled, wasted, withered **2.** contaminated, corrupted, debased, neglected, polluted, ruined, undermined

deceased *adj.* collapsed, concluded, demised, departed, destroyed, dead, ended, exhausted, expended, expired, exterminated, extinguished, finished, killed, lifeless, passed away, perished, succumbed, terminated, vanished, yielded *Nonformal:* bought it, cashed in, checked out, croaked, popped off

deceit *n.* artifice, blind, cheating, chicanery, craft, craftiness, cunning, deceitfulness, deception, dishonesty, duplicity, fake, falseness, feint, fraud, fraudulence, guile, hoax, hocus-pocus, hypocrisy, imposture, misrepresentation, pretense, ruse, sellout, sham, slyness, stratagem, subterfuge, swindle, treachery, trick, trickery, underhandedness *Nonformal:* con, dirty dealing *or* pool *or* trick *or* work, flimflam, monkey-business, whitewash *Antonyms:* candour, frankness, honesty, sincerity, truthfulness

deceitful *adj.* artful, beguiling, bent *(Nonformal)*, clandestine, counterfeit, crafty, cunning, deceiving, deceptive, delusive, delusory, designing, dishonest, disingenuous, double-dealing, duplicitous, fallacious, false, foxy, fraudulent, furtive, guileful, hypocritical, illusory, indirect, insidious, insincere, knavish, lying, mendacious, misleading, roguish, scheming, sham, shifty, slick, sly, sneaky, subtle, treacherous, tricky, two-faced, underhanded, untrustworthy, untruthful, wily *Antonyms:* candid, straightforward, truthful

deceive *v.* beguile, betray, bilk, cheat, circumvent, cross up, defraud, delude, disappoint, double-cross, dupe, ensnare, entrap, fake, falsify, fool, hoax, hoodwink, juke *(P.E.I.)*, lead on, misinform, mislead, outfox, outmanoeuvre, outwit, rob, swindle, take, trick *Nonformal:* bamboozle, con, doctor, hoke up, scam, shaft, string along, sucker, two-time

decelerate *v.* brake, check, ease *or* loosen up, delay, gear down, hang back, reduce speed, restrain, retard, slow down *or* up, throttle *or* wind down *Antonyms:* accelerate, hasten, speed up, spur

decency *n.* appropriateness, ceremoniousness, civility, conventionality, correctness, courtesy, decorum, dignity, fittingness, honesty, propriety, respectability, righteousness, seemliness, virtue *Antonyms:* indecency, rudeness, vulgarity

decent *adj.* **1.** accommodating, agreeable, becoming, befitting, comely, *comme il faut (French)*, compliant, correct, courteous, decorous, delicate, genteel, good-natured, gracious, fit, fitting, friendly, good, helpful, honest, honourable, kind, kindly, mannerly, nice, noble, obliging, polite, presentable, proper, recognized, reputable, reserved, respectable, right, seemly, standard, suitable, thoughtful, trustworthy, upright, warm, worthy *Antonyms:* discourteous, unsuitable **2.** chaste, clean, ethical, immaculate, moderate, moral, prudent, pure, spotless, stainless, straight, unblemished, undefiled, untarnished, virtuous **3.** acceptable, adequate, all right, ample, comfortable, competent, fair, good, good enough, middling, moderately good, okay *(Nonformal)*, passable, presentable, reasonable, satisfactory, sufficient, suitable, tolerable

decentralize *v.* break apart *or* up, disperse, distribute, detach, devolve, divide, farm out *(Nonformal)*, individualize, localize, separate, split, spread, subdivide, weaken *(Politics) Antonyms:* coalesce, concentrate, consolidate, converge, merge

deception *n.* artifice, beguilement, betrayal, blarney, bluff, catch, cheat, confidence game, cover-up, craftiness, cunning, deceit, decoy, disinformation, dodge, double-dealing, duplicity, equivocation, falsehood, fraud, gimmick, guile, hoax, hypocrisy, illusion, lie, lying, mendacity, pretence, pretext, ruse, sham, stratagem, subterfuge, swindle, trick, trickery, wile *Nonformal:* con, fast shuffle, flim-flam, hogwash, malarkey, snow job, racket, rip-off, scam, sting, whitewash *Antonyms:* candour, fidelity, frankness, truthfulness

deceptive *adj.* ambiguous, beguiling, crafty, cunning, deceitful, deceiving, delusive, delusory, designing, dishonest, disingenuous, fake, fallacious, false, feigned, fishy *(Nonformal)*, foxy, fraudulent, illusory, indirect, insidious, insincere, knavish, lying, misleading, mock, roguish, scheming, seeming, shifty, slick, slippery, sly, sneaky, snide, specious, spurious, treacherous, tricky, two-faced, underhanded, unreliable, wily *Antonyms:* aboveboard, honest, on the level, straightforward

decide *v.* **1.** ascertain, commit, conclude, decree, determine, figure, find, opt, resolve, rule, settle, specify, stipulate, surmise **2.** arbitrate, arrange, dictate, direct, impose, judge, mediate **3.** appoint, assign, choose, dedicate, designate, elect, foreordain, ordain, select, vote

decided *adj.* **1.** absolute, assured, categorical, certain, clear, clear-cut, clinched, definite, determined, distinct, established, explicit, express, fated, firm, fixed, indisputable, inflexible, nailed, positive, pronounced, resolved, settled, sure, undeniable, undisputed, unhesitating, unmistakable, unquestionable *Antonyms:* dubious, hesitant, irresolute, undetermined, weak **2.** decisive, emphatic, earnest, forceful, obstinate, purposeful, resolute, strong-willed *Antonyms:* reluctant, timid

deciding *adj.* **1.** cardinal, chief, critical, crucial, essential, important, influential, necessary, pivotal, prime, principal, vital *Antonyms:* immaterial, irrelevant, nonessential **2.** clinching, conclusive, decisive, definitive, determining, final, settling *Antonyms:* confusing, obscure, unsure

decimate *v.* annihilate, butcher, destroy, exterminate, massacre, reduce, ruin, slash, slaughter, truncate

decipher *v.* construe, crack, decode, decrypt, deduce, disentangle, explain, figure *or* make out, interpret, read, render, reveal, solve, translate, understand, unravel, untangle, work out *Antonyms:* code, encipher, encrypt

decision *n.* **1.** accord, adjudication, award, benchmark, landmark, call, compromise, determination, end, finding, judgment, outcome, precedent, pronouncement, result, ruling, sentence, settlement, verdict **2.** choice, inclination, intention, mind, objective, preference, purpose, resolution, selection, understanding, volition, will

decisive *adj.* **1.** absolute, assertive, assured, categorical, certain, conclusive, decided, definite, definitive, imperative, positive, resolute, resolved, set, unmistakable **2.** determined, firm, forceful, intent, powerful, strong-minded, unwavering *Antonyms:* fluctuating, hesitating, uncertain, vacillating *Commonly misused:* **derisive**

deck *n.* **1.** balcony, dais, layer, platform, *pont (French)*, porch, portico, stoop, terrace, tier, topside *(Nonformal)*, veranda **2.** floor, ground, surface, *terra firma (Latin)* **3.** pack, cards *or* playing cards, suit – *v.* **1.** accoutre, adorn, array, attire, beautify, bedeck, clothe, decorate, doll *or* dress up, dress, embellish, festoon, garland, garnish, grace, gussy up *(Nonformal)*, ornament, prettify, primp, slick, spiff, trim **2.** fell, flatten, floor, knock down *or* out, kayo *(Nonformal)*, level

declaim *v.* **1.** hold forth, lecture, pronounce, recite, sermonize, soliloquize *Nonformal:* soapbox, speechify, spiel **2.** condemn, decry, denounce, harangue, spout-off (N*onformal) Commonly Misused:* **proclaim**

declaration *n.* **1.** acknowledgment, admission, affirmation, assertion, confirmation, dissemination, position, profession **2.** announcement, broadcast, bulletin, document, mission statement, notification, proclamation, pronouncement, report **3.** deposition, oath, *procès-verbal (French)*, plea, statement, testimony

declare *v.* **1.** acknowledge, admit, affirm, allege, announce, assert, asseverate, attest, aver, avow, bring up, certify, cite, claim, convey, maintain, notify, proclaim, profess, pronounce, propound, purport, put forward, say, speak out *or* up, spout, state, swear, tell, testify, trumpet **2.** disclose, make known, prove, reveal

declared *adj.* acknowledged, admitted, affirmed, announced, asserted, asseverated, attested, averred, avowed, certified, cited, claimed, conveyed, disclosed, known, owned up to *(Nonformal)*, proclaimed, professed, pronounced, propounded, revealed, stated, sworn, testified to, vouched for

decline *n.* **1.** abatement, backsliding, decay, declivity, decrease, depreciation, depression, devaluation, diminution, descent, dip, downgrade, downswing, downtrend, downturn, drop-off, ebb, lapse, loss, lowering, recession, reduction, sag, slide, slip, slump, subsidence, wane, weakening *Antonyms:* improvement, rise, upswing **2.** downward angle, cant, drop, grade, inclination, incline, pitch, slant, slope **3.** dotage, enfeeblement, regression, senility – *v.* **1.** abate, atrophy, decay, decrease, descend, diminish, dip, drop, fade *or* fade away, fail, fall, languish, lessen, lower, melt away, recede, return, revert, run down, sag, set, settle, shrink, sink, slide, slip, slope, slump, wane, weaken *Nonformal:* bottom out, go downhill, hit rock bottom *or* the skids, take a nose dive, take a turn for the worse *Antonyms:* flourish, increase, peak, rise, thrive **2.** abjure, abstain, avoid, balk, bypass, demur, deny, desist, dismiss, forbear, forgo, gainsay, not buy *(Nonformal)*, pass, refrain, refuse, reject, renounce, repudiate, send regrets, snub, spurn, turn down *Antonyms:* accept, adopt, approve, consent, participate

declining *adj.* decaying, decreasing, degenerating, deteriorating, drooping, dropping, ebbing, failing, falling, lapsing, lessening, receding, sagging, shrinking, sinking, slipping, slumping, waning, weakening *Antonyms:* energetic, expanding, healthy, multiplying, vigorous

decommission *v.* discharge, dismiss, fire, lay off, let go, muster out, release, remove *Antonyms:* appoint, authorize, commission, hire

decompose *v.* **1.** crumble, decay, disintegrate, mortify, putrefy, rot, spoil **2.** break down, deconstruct, dissect, distill, reduce, separate

decomposition *n.* **1.** caries, decay, disintegration, gangrene, mortification, putrefaction, putrescence, rot **2.** atomization, distillation, hydrolysis, minimization, separation

decompress *v.* **1.** diminish, ease, release, relieve, remove pressure, unzip *(Nonformal)* **2.** reconstitute, recover, restore, *Antonyms:* compact, compress, reduce

decontaminate *v.* clean, cleanse, delouse, disinfect, fumigate, neutralize, pasteurize, purge, purify, refine, sanitize, sterilize *Antonyms:* contaminate, infect, pollute

décor *n.* adornment, arrangement, colour scheme, decoration, furnishings, furniture, interior design, presentation, ornamentation, scenic decoration

decorate *v.* **1.** adorn, beautify, bedeck, brighten, colour, embellish, enhance, festoon, finish, furbish, garnish, gild, illuminate, jazz *or* spruce up *(Nonformal)*, ornament, paint, perfect, renovate, trim **2.** anoint, award, bestow, celebrate, cite, confer, honour, laureate

decoration *n.* **1.** adornment, beautification, beautifying, bedecking, designing, embellishment, enhancement, enrichment, festooning, garnishing, illumination, improvement, jazz, ornamentation, trimming *Kinds of decoration:* appliqué, bauble, braid, colour, curlicue, design, doodad, filigree, finery, flounce, flourish, foofaraw, fretwork, frill, frippery, furbelow, garnish, gewgaw, gilt, gimcrack, gingerbread, inlay, lace, ornament, marquetry, parquetry, ribbon, scroll, sequin, spangle, tattoo, tinsel, trimming, wreath **2.** accolade, award, badge, citation, colours, cross, distinction, emblem, garter, laurels, medal, order, ribbon, star *Canadian decorations:* Cross of Valour, Medal of Bravery, Order of Canada, Star of Courage *See also:* **awards, medals**

decorative *adj.* baroque, elaborate, embellished, flamboyant, florid, gilt, ornamented, ornate, rococo *Antonyms:* austere, bare, plain, severe, Spartan

decorous *adj.* **1.** appropriate, becoming, befitting, comely, *comme il faut (French)*, correct, fit, fitting, meet, proper, right, seasonable, seemly, suitable **2.** ceremonial, ceremonious, civilized, conforming, conventional, deferential, demure, dignified, elegant, formal, good, mannerly, nice, polite, prim, punctilious, refined, respectable, staid *Antonyms:* brazen, inappropriate, raucous, rowdy, undignified

decorum *n.* **1.** breeding, ceremony, courtesy, decency, deportment, dignity, etiquette, gentility, grace, graciousness, manners, politeness, *politesse (French)*, propriety, protocol, punctilio, respectability, sedateness, social grace, tact, taste *Antonyms:* churlishness, impoliteness, tactlessness, vulgarity **2.** appropriateness, becomingness, conformity, congruity, correctness, seemliness, suitability, suitableness

decoy *n.* **1.** camouflage, deception, ensnarement, enticement, inducement, pretense, snare, temptation, trap, trick **2.** *agent provocateur (French)*, bait, blind, by-bidder, lure, plant, red herring – *v.* allure, bait, deceive, delude, ensnare, entice, entrap, inveigle, lure, mislead, rope in, seduce, steer, tempt, trap *Nonformal:* chum, con, sucker

decrease *n.* **1.** attrition, decline, downturn, drop, erosion, expenditure, falling off, loss, recession **2.** compression, condensation, constriction, contraction, curtailment, cut, cutback, diminishing, dwindling, ebb, reduction, relief, shortening, shrinkage, subsidence, waning *Antonyms:* expansion, extension, growth **3.** abatement, alleviation, lessening, mitigation, slackening – *v.* **1.** abate, collapse, contract, crumble, decline, degenerate, descend, deteriorate, die away *or* down, die *or* peter out, diminish, dissipate, drop, dwindle, ease, ebb, erode, evaporate, fade, fall off, lessen, let up, lower, lull, moderate, recede, settle, shrink, shrivel, sink, slacken, slow down, slump, subside, taper, wane, waste, weaken, wear, wither *Antonyms:* augment, enlarge, expand, extend, increase **2.** compress, concentrate, condense, constrict, curb, curtail, deplete, downsize, narrow *or* pare down, quell, quiet, reduce, restrain, roll back

decree *n.* act, announcement, charge, command, commandment, declaration, dictum, directive, edict, enactment, judgment, law, mandate, order, ordinance, proclamation, pronouncement, regulation, rule, ruling, statute, the word *(Nonformal)* – *v.* adjudge, appoint, command, direct, enjoin, establish, instruct, legalize, legislate, mandate, ordain, order, pronounce

decrepit *adj.* **1.** battered, bedraggled, broken-down, creaky, debilitated, deteriorated, dilapidated, flimsy, fragile, insubstantial, ramshackle, rickety, run-down, seedy, shabby, shaking, tacky, threadbare, tottering, tumbledown, unsound, used, weather-beaten, worn-out **2.** aged, antiquated, doddering, enfeebled, frail, haggard, incapacitated, infirm, tired, wasted, weak, wizened, worn *Antonyms:* dynamic, energetic, spry, strong, vigorous

decry *v.* belittle, censure, condemn, denounce, deprecate, discredit, disparage, jeer *or* sneer at, vilify *Nonformal:* badmouth, knock *or* put down, slam, trash

dedicate *v.* **1.** allot, apportion, assign, commit, obligate, relegate **2.** anoint, bless, consecrate, enshrine, hallow, praise, sanctify, set apart *Antonyms:* defame, desecrate, dishonour, profane **3.** address, inscribe, sign **4.** commit, devote, offer, pledge, promise **5.** open, reveal, unveil

dedicated *adj.* **1.** devoted, enthusiastic, hardworking, loyal, purposeful, single- minded, sworn, wholehearted, zealous *Antonyms:* apathetic, indifferent, nonchalant, uncaring **2.** bound, committed, engaged, obligated, obliged, pledged, promised

dedication *n.* **1.** adherence, allegiance, commitment, devotedness, devotion, faith, faithfulness, fidelity, loyalty, resolution, selflessness, single-mindedness, wholeheartedness, zeal *Antonyms:* apathy, coolness, indifference, torpor **2.** award, benefaction, bestowal, donation, endowment, gift, inscription, largesse, offering, presentation, token **3.** benediction, genuflection, homage, honour, oblation, praise, prayer, regard, supplication, worship **4.** faith, holiness, morality, obedience, piety, reverence, veneration, virtue **5.** celebration, ceremony, function, observance, rite, ritual, service

deduce *v.* analyze, arrive at, conceive, conclude, deem, derive, determine, draw, elicit, extract, figure, follow, gather, glean, imagine, infer, judge, presume, reach, reason, receive, reckon, suppose, take, trace, understand, work out

deducible *adj.* a priori, deductive, derivable, inferable, inferential, knowable, provable, reasoned, traceable, understandable

deduct *v.* abstract, decrease, diminish, discount, draw back, lessen, rebate, reduce, remove, subtract, take, take away *or* off, withdraw *Nonformal:* cut back, knock *or* lop off, roll back *Antonyms:* enhance, enlarge, increase

deduction *n.* **1.** abatement, allowance, credit, cut, decrease, decrement, depreciation, diminution, discount, dockage, excision, rebate, reduction, removal, subtraction, waning, withdrawal, write-off **2.** answer, assumption, attainment, conclusion, consequence, contemplation, corollary, deliberation, finding, inference, judgment, meditation, musing, opinion, presumption, reasoning, reflection, result, rumination, speculation, thought, understanding

deed *n.* **1.** achievement, accomplishment, exploit, feat, reality **2.** act, action, commission, doing, enterprise, manoeuvre, performance, stunt, undertaking **3.** agreement, bond, certificate, charter, compact, contract, conveyance, covenant, document, lease, papers *(Nonformal)*, proof, record, security, title, transaction, transfer, warranty – *v.* bequeath, bestow, cede, confer, pass over, transfer

deem *v.* allow, appraise, assume, believe, calculate, conceive, conjecture, consider, esteem, estimate, feel, guess, hold, imagine, judge, know, presume, reckon, regard, sense, set store by *(Nonformal)*, suppose, surmise, suspect, think, understand, view

deep *adj.* **1.** bottomless, broad, far-reaching, fathomless, great, infinite, mighty, spacious, subterranean, vast, wide *Antonyms:* confined, shallow, small, tiny **2.** ardent, critical, earnest, grave, heartfelt, important, keen, philosophical, piercing, poignant, pressing, profound, serious, vital *Antonyms:* cosmetic, insubstantial, petty, superficial, trivial **3.** baritone, full-toned, hollow, low, resonant, reverberating, resounding, rich, sepulchral, sonorous *Antonyms:* high-pitched, shrill **4.** acute, arcane, astute, complex, knowing, learned, penetrating, sagacious, sapient, wise *Antonyms:* callow, naive **5.** abstruse, cryptic, hidden, mysterious, obscure, recondite, secret *Antonyms:* apparent, blatant, obvious, open, overt **6.** absorbed, engaged, engrossed, lost in, rapt **7.** artful, cagey, canny, designing, Machiavellian *Antonyms:* candid, credulous, straightforward – *adv.* at the limits, beyond one's depth, far along, over one's head – *n.* **1.** body of water, ocean, sea **2.** abyss, bottomlessness, bowels, cavity, chasm, depths, hell, nether world, pit, the infinite *(Nonformal)*

deepen *v.* **1.** broaden, dig, dig out, dredge, enlarge, excavate, expand, extend, hollow, scoop *or* scrape out **2.** aggravate, develop, enhance, heighten, increase, intensify, magnify, reinforce, strengthen *Antonyms:* assuage, mitigate

deeply *adv.* acutely, affectingly, completely, feelingly, genuinely, gravely, intensely, mournfully, movingly, passionately, profoundly, sadly, seriously, severely, surely, thoroughly *Antonyms:* lightly, partially, slightly, superficially

deface *v.* **1.** blemish, damage, deform, demolish, destroy, disfigure, distort, harm, impair, injure, mangle, mar, misshape, mutilate, offend, scratch, spoil, sully, tarnish, trash, vandalize, wreck *Antonyms:* mend, repair, restore **2.** cancel, eliminate, eradicate, expunge, obliterate, remove

de facto *adj.* accepted, actual, existent, existing, extant, recognized *Antonyms:* illusionary, spectral – *adv.* actually, in actuality, in effect *or* fact *or* reality

defamation *n.* aspersion, belittlement, calumny, character assassination, denigration, deprecation, detraction, disparagement, imputation, libel, lie, obloquy, opprobrium, slander, slur, smear, traducement, vilification *Nonformal:* backbiting, backstabbing, black eye, brickbat, cheap shot, hit, knock, low blow, mud, rap, slam, trash talk

defamatory *adj.* abusive, calumnious, derogatory, injurious, insulting, libellous, maligning, offensive, slanderous, traducing, vituperative

defame *v.* accuse, assail, besmirch, blacken, blemish, brand, censure, criticize, curse, cut up, damn, decry, defile, denigrate, denounce, deprecate, derogate, devalue, discredit, disfavour, disprove, execrate, falsify, humble, humiliate, imprecate, impugn, insinuate, insult, libel, malign, misrepresent, muckrake, reproach, revile, slander, slur, smear, stain, stigmatize, sully, taint, tarnish, vilify, vituperate *Nonformal:* badmouth, dis, slag, trash *Antonyms:* applaud, extol, laud, praise

default *n.* **1.** delinquency, dereliction, disregard, failure, fault, forfeiture, lapse, miss, neglect, negligence, non-payment, non-remittance, shortcoming **2.** automatic choice *or* option *or* selection, predefined course, preset value – *v.* **1.** bilk, dodge, evade, fail, let slide *or* slip, neglect, shirk, skip, stiff *(Nonformal)* **2.** concede, forfeit, lose, yield

defeat *n.* **1.** annihilation, conquest, destruction, loss, mastery, overthrow, rout, subjugation, slaughter, upset **2.** beating, lambasting, thrashing, thumping, trouncing, whipping *Nonformal:* licking, whupping **3.** bafflement, blow, check, debacle, disappointment, disillusionment, downfall, failure, fall, frustration, letdown, rebuff, reversal, reverse, thwarting – *v.* **1.** annihilate, beat down, break, conquer, cripple, crush, decimate, drub, extinguish, master, neutralize, nullify, obliterate, overpower, overturn, overwhelm, poleaxe, put down, quash, quell, reduce, repress, repulse, rout, ruin, slaughter, smash, subdue, suppress, trounce, vanquish *Nonformal:* butcher, clobber, kayo *or* KO, lick, pound, shellac, trash, wallop **2.** baffle, balk, checkmate, confound, frustrate, humble, impede, outwit, set back, thwart, undermine *Nonformal:* flummox, torpedo, smoke, snooker **3.** beat, best, better, exceed, excel, outclass, outdo, outrun, outshine, outstrip, overcome, prevail, surpass, surmount, top, transcend, triumph *Nonformal:* blow away, cream, lather

defeatist *adj.* depressing, discouraging, gloomy, hopeless, naysaying, negative, pessimistic *Antonyms:* faithful, hopeful, Panglossian – *n.* doomster, gloom merchant *(Nonformal)*, naysayer, negativist, pessimist, quitter, submitter, yielder *Antonyms:* optimist, Pollyanna

defecate *v.* evacuate, excrete, pass stool, void feces *Nonformal:* crap, dump, poop

defect *n.* **1.** deficiency, drawback, failing, fault, foible, imperfection, infirmity, shortcoming, weakness **2.** blemish, blotch, deformity, discolouration, flaw, glitch, gremlin *(Nonformal)*, knot, mark, marring, scar, scratch, speck, spot, stain – *v.* abandon, abscond, back out, break faith, depart, desert, forsake, leave, pull out, quit, reject, renounce, sell out, tergiversate, withdraw *Antonyms:* cooperate, enlist, join

defection *n.* abandonment, alienation, dereliction, desertion, disaffection, divorce, estrangement, forsaking, parting, rebellion, rejection, repudiation, revolt, secession, separation, withdrawal *Antonyms:* confederation, marriage, union

defective *adj.* abnormal, amiss, broken, damaged, deficient, faulty, flawed, impaired, imperfect, inadequate, incomplete, injured, insufficient, lacking, short, sick, unfinished, unhealthy, unsound, wanting *Antonyms:* adequate, intact, normal, whole, working

defence *n.* **1.** alibi, answer, apology, argument, excuse, exoneration, explanation, extenuation, justification, plea, rationalization, rejoinder, reply, response, retort, return, vindication **2.** protection, reassurance, safety, sanctuary, security, strength **3.** bulwark, casement, citadel, cover, fort, fortress, garrison, guard, rampart, screen, self-protection, shelter, shield

defenceless *adj.* declawed, exposed, helpless, liable, naked, open, powerless, unarmed, unguarded, unprotected, vulnerable, weak *Antonyms:* guarded, protected, safe and sound, secure

defend *v.* **1.** avert, beat off, block, check, contain, contest, control, cover, curb, deflect, deter, fend off, fight back, foil, frustrate, garrison, guard, hedge, maintain, oppose, parry, preserve, prevent, protect, rebuff, repel, repulse, resist, safeguard, save, secure, shelter, shield, stave off, stonewall, stop, stymie, thwart, ward off, watch over *Antonyms:* cower, quit, submit, yield **2.** advocate, aid, apologize for, argue, assert, back, champion, endorse, espouse, explain, justify, maintain, plead, rationalize, recommend, second, stand by, support, sustain, uphold, vindicate, voice, warrant *Antonyms:* hurt, injure, offend

defendant *n.* appellant, correspondent, defence, litigant, oppositionist, respondent, the accused *Antonyms:* accuser, applicant, claimant, plaintiff, prosecutor

defensible *adj.* defendable, excusable, fit, justifiable, logical, pardonable, permissible, plausible, proper, rational, tenable, valid, vindicable, warrantable

defensive *adj.* **1.** alert, attentive, careful, cautious, chary, circumspect, guarded, heedful, observant, vigilant, wary, watchful *Antonyms:* careless, heedless, nonchalant **2.** belligerent, confrontational, hypersensitive, sensitive, sore, tetchy, thin-skinned, touchy **3.** averting, defending, foiling, forestalling, prepared, preventive, protective, safeguarding

defer *v.* **1.** accede, accommodate, acquiesce, adapt, adjust, admit, agree, assent, bow, buckle, capitulate, cave, comply, concede, cringe, give in, knuckle under, obey, submit, succumb, yield **2.** adjourn, block, cool it *(Nonformal)*, delay, detain, extend, hinder, hold up, impede, intermit, lay over, lengthen, postpone, procrastinate, prolong, protract, put off, remit, retard, set aside, shelve, slow, stall, stay, suspend, table, waive

deference *n.* **1.** acquiescence, capitulation, complaisance, compliance, condescension, docility, obedience, submission, yielding *Antonyms:* disobedience, insubordination, noncompliance, nonobservance, revolt **2.** attention, civility, consideration, courtesy, esteem, homage, honour, obeisance, politeness, regard, respect, reverence, thoughtfulness, veneration *Antonyms:* contempt, discourtesy, dishonour, impertinence, irreverence *Commonly misused:* **difference**

deferential *adj.* **1.** civil, considerate, courteous, disarming, ingratiating, polite, regardful, respectful **2.** acquiescent, complaisant, dutiful, obedient, obsequious, servile, submissive, subservient, sycophantic

deferment *n.* adjournment, cessation, deferral, delay, hold, interruption, moratorium, pause, postponement, putting off, recess, stay, suspension

defiance *n.* antagonism, challenge, combativeness, confrontation, disobedience, disregard, insubordination, insurgency, intransigence, mutiny, noncompliance, opposition, rebellion, rebelliousness, recalcitrance, resistance, revolt, sedition *Antonyms:* acquiescence, compliance, obedience, submission, subservience

defiant *adj.* adamant, aggressive, antagonistic, bellicose, belligerent, challenging, contumacious, disobedient, disregardful, headstrong, insolent, insubmissive, insubordinate, mulish, mutinous, obstinate, provocative, pugnacious, rebellious, recalcitrant, recusant, refractory, resistant, scornful, stubborn, truculent, unruly, unyielding *Antonyms:* craven, obedient, respectful, submissive

deficiency *n.* **1.** absence, dearth, deficit, dereliction, failure, inadequacy, insufficiency, lack, loss, need, neglect, paucity, privation, scarcity, shortage, shortcoming, want, weakness *Antonyms:* abundance, adequacy, sufficiency, surfeit **2.** defect, drawback, fault, flaw, imperfection

deficient *adj.* **1.** amiss, damaged, defective, faulty, flawed, impaired, inadequate, inferior, insufficient, lacking, meagre, rare, scanty, scarce, short, shy, sketchy, skimpy, unsatisfactory, wanting, weak *Antonyms:* adequate, satisfactory, sufficient **2.** fragmentary, incomplete, limited, part, partial *Antonyms:* complete, finished, full

deficit *n.* accounts payable, arrears, bills, debt, default, deficiency, difference, dues, indebtedness, insufficiency, red numbers *(Nonformal)*, shortage, shortfall

defile *v.* **1.** abuse, besmirch, debase, deflower, degrade, desecrate, disgrace, dishonour, molest, profane, rape, ravish, shame, sully, violate *Antonyms:* honour, protect **2.** adulterate, contaminate, corrupt, dirty, discolour, pollute, smear, soil, stain, taint, tarnish, trash, vitiate *Antonyms:* clean, improve, sanitize

defiled *adj.* **1.** besmirched, desecrated, dishonoured, profaned, ravished, violated **2.** corrupted, dirty, impure, polluted, spoilt, tainted, unclean *Antonyms:* clean, immaculate, pristine, uncontaminated

define *v.* **1.** clarify, construe, describe, detail, determine, elucidate, establish, explain, expound, flesh out, formalize, illustrate, interpret, point out, specify, spell out, translate **2.** assign, characterize, denominate, denote, designate, distinguish, entitle, exemplify, label, name **3.** border, bound, circumscribe, compass, confine, delimit, delineate, demarcate, edge, encircle, enclose, encompass, envelop, fence *or* wall in, fix, flank, gird, girdle, limit, mark out, outline, rim, set, stake out, surround, verge

definite *adj.* **1.** absolute, accurate, assured, authentic, beyond doubt *or* question, bona fide, certain, clear, clear-cut, conclusive, concrete, convinced, decided, dependable, direct, distinguishable, downright, evident, express, factual, forthright, genuine, graphic, guaranteed, incontestable, incontrovertible, indisputable, indubitable, irrefutable, manifest, obvious, palpable, patent, perfect, plain, positive, pronounced, proven, reliable, self-evident, sharp, straightforward, sure, true, undeniable, undoubted, unequivocal, unimpeachable, unmistakable, unquestionable, vivid, well-founded *Antonyms:* equivocal, uncertain, unknown **2.** categorical, clearly defined, definitive, determined, distinct, established, exact, explicit, firm, fixed, particular, precise, set, specific, well-defined, well-marked *Antonyms:* obscure, unclear, vague

definition *n.* **1.** answer, clarification, description, elucidation, explanation, gloss, illustration, interpretation, rationale **2.** analogue, annotation, characterization, denotation, determination, diagnosis, formalization, key, representation, synonym, terminology, translation **3.** border, boundary, bounds, contour, frame, limit, line, outline, rim, shape **4.** clarity, distinctiveness, image, lucidity, perceptibility, sharpness, view

definitive *adj.* **1.** absolute, categorical, clear-cut, definite, downright, explicit, express, plain, precise, specific **2.** concluding, decisive, final, last, settling, terminal, ultimate, unalterable **3.** accurate, authoritative, best, complete, exhaustive, reliable

deflate *v.* **1.** chasten, dash, debunk, disconcert, disgrace, dispirit, embarrass, humble, humiliate, mortify, knock *or* put *or* take down, shame, shoot down *(Nonformal)*, squash **2.** collapse, depress, exhaust, release, shrink

deflect *v.* avert, bounce *or* glance off, deviate, divert, parry, ricochet, shy, skid, slue, swerve, turn, turn aside, veer, whirl

deformed *adj.* abnormal, askew, awry, bent, blemished, bowed, buckled, contorted, crooked, curved, damaged, disfigured, disjointed, distorted, gnarled, ill-made, impaired, irregular, knotted, lame, maimed, malformed, mangled, marred, misconceived, misshapen, twisted, warped

deformity *n.* aberration, abnormality, asymmetry, contortion, crookedness, damage, defect, disfigurement, distortion, injury, irregularity, malformation, warp

defraud *v.* beguile, bilk, cheat, deceive, delude, dupe, embezzle, swindle, take, trick, victimize *Nonformal:* bamboozle, fleece, hose, shaft

defray *v.* amortize, clear, cover, discharge, foot *(Nonformal)*, honour, liquidate, pay for, satisfy, settle, square

deft *adj.* able, adept, adroit, agile, apt, clever, crackerjack *(Nonformal)*, dexterous, expert, fleet, fluid, handy, ingenious, neat, nimble, proficient, prompt, quick, ready, skilful, skilled *Antonyms:* awkward, bumbling, clumsy, maladroit

defunct *adj.* **1.** cold, dead, deceased, departed, done, exhausted, expired, extinct, gone, inanimate, inoperative, invalid, kaput *(Nonformal)*, late, lifeless, lost, nonexistent, vanished *Antonyms:* active, functional, live, working **2.** anachronistic, bygone, obsolete, useless

defy *v.* **1.** beard, brave, brook, endure, resist, stomach, suffer, survive, thwart, tolerate, weather, withstand **2.** challenge, confront, dare, face, oppose, question, square off, test **3.** disregard, flout, ignore, neglect, overlook, slight, spurn

degeneracy *n.* **1.** abasement, corruption, debauchery, decadence, degradation, depravity, dissoluteness, evil, immorality, iniquity, meanness, sin, viciousness **2.** atrophy, decay, decline, decrease, deterioration, disintegration, retrogression

degenerate *adj.* base, corrupt, debased, debauched, decadent, decayed, degenerated, degraded, demeaned, depraved, deteriorated, diseased, dissolute, effete, failing, fallen, immoral, infamous, low, mean, miscreant, nefarious, overripe, perverted, retrogressive, rotten, sinking, unhealthy, vicious, villainous, wicked, worsening – *n.* **1.** deviate, miscreant, offender, pervert, reprobate **2.** bag lady, beggar, bum, derelict, ne'er-do-well, street person, vagrant – *v.* backslide, corrode, decay, decline, decrease, descend, deteriorate, disintegrate, lapse, regress, revert, sink, slip, worsen

degradation *n.* **1.** abasement, debasement, decline, demotion, deterioration, downgrading, mortification, reduction **2.** decadence, degeneracy, degeneration, depravity, discredit, disgrace, dishonour, evil, humiliation, ignominy, perversion, shame *Antonyms:* amelioration, edification, enlightenment

degrade *v.* **1.** abase, belittle, break, bump, cast down, cheapen, corrupt, debase, debauch, declass, decry, degenerate, demean, demote, depose, deprave, derogate, deteriorate, detract, disbar, discredit, disgrace, dishonour, disparage, humble, humiliate, impair, injure, pan, pervert, put down, rule out, shame, sink, take *or* tear down, vitiate *Nonformal:* bust, run down, shoot down, slam *Antonyms:* dignify, elevate, ennoble, improve, promote **2.** cut, diminish, doctor *(Nonformal)*, water, weaken *Antonyms:* fortify, increase, intensify

degree *n.* **1.** amount, amplitude, compass, dimension, expanse, gauge, intensity, level, limit, magnitude, measure, pitch, potency, rate, scope, severity, shade, size, space **2.** development, division, gradation, interval, line, mark, notch, order, period, plane, ratio, rung, scale, stage, stair, step, stint, term **3.** class, dignity, position, rank, standing, station, status **4.** academic distinction *or* honour, approbation, approval, credentials, distinction, eminence, honour, recognition, sheepskin *Common academic degrees:* Bachelor of Arts *or* BA, Bachelor of Commerce *or* BCom, Bachelor of Education *or* BEd, Bachelor of Laws *or* LLB, Bachelor of Science *or* BSc, Doctor of Dental Medicine *or* DMD, Doctor of Divinity *or* DD, Doctor of Laws *or* LLD, Doctor of Medicine *or* MD, Doctor of Philosophy *or* PhD, Master in Business Administration *or* MBA, Master of Arts *or* MA, Master of Library Science *or* MLS, Master of Science *or* MSc

dehydrate *v.* **1.** bake, desiccate, dry, dry out *or* up, evaporate, parch **2.** age, cure, preserve, salt, smoke, sun dry

deify *v.* adore, apotheosize, consecrate, elevate, ennoble, enthrone, exalt, extol, glorify, idealize, idolize, immortalize, praise, venerate, worship

deign *v.* **1.** accept, agree, allow, assure, consent, grant, guarantee, permit, vouchsafe **2.** condescend, humble, lower oneself, patronize, stoop

deity *n.* celestial, celestial being, creator, divine being, divinity, god, goddess, godhead, idol, immortal, man upstairs *(Nonformal)*, supreme being *See also:* **god**

dejected *adj.* abject, black, bleak, blue, cheerless, clouded, crestfallen, dampened, depressed, despondent, disconsolate, discouraged, disheartened, dismal, dispirited, doleful, downcast, downhearted, drooping, gloomy, glum, hurting, inconsolable, low, low-spirited, melancholy, miserable, morose, sad, sagging, spiritless, woebegone, wretched *Antonyms:* blithe, cheerful, encouraged, happy, lighthearted

deke *n.* deception, decoy, escape, evasion, feint, head fake, manoeuvre, move, ploy, ruse, Savardian spinorama *(Nonformal)*, tactic – *v.* avoid, dipsy-doodle *(Nonformal)*, dodge, duck, elude, evade, shift, sidestep, swerve

delay *n.* **1.** adjournment, downtime, interruption, interval, moratorium, postponement, reprieve, stay, stop, suspension *Antonyms:* acceleration, advance, hurry **2.** bottleneck, detention, hindrance, holdup, impediment, obstruction, setback, snag, stall, tie-up **3.** dawdling, loitering, tarrying *Nonformal:* dilly-dallying, lollygagging – *v.* **1.** defer, hold, lay over, postpone, prolong, protract, put off, shelve, stay, stop, suspend **2.** arrest, bar, block, check, choke, clog, curb, hamper, impede, inhibit, interfere, keep, obstruct, procrastinate, restrict, retard, stall *Antonyms:* expedite, facilitate **3.** dawdle, drag, hold over, lag, linger, loiter, prevent, slacken, tarry, temporize *Antonyms:* accelerate, hasten, quicken, rush

delectable *adj.* ambrosial, appetizing, delicate, delicious, delightful, divine, enjoyable, enticing, exquisite, heavenly, palatable, pleasant, pleasurable, satisfying, savoury, scrumptious, tasty, toothsome, yummy *(Nonformal) Antonyms:* awful, disagreeable, disgusting, horrid, nasty

delegate *n.* agent, alternative, ambassador, appointee, commissioner, congressman, congresswoman, consul, councillor, deputy, emissary, envoy, front, legate, magistrate, member, minister, nominee, nuncio, ombudsperson, plenipotentiary, premier, proxy, reeve, regent, rep, replacement, representative, senator, spokesperson, stand-in, substitute, surrogate, trustee, vicar *Nonformal:* mouthpiece, people's choice – *v.* accredit, appoint, assign, authorize, cast, charge, choose, commission, constitute, depute, deputize, designate, elect, empower, entrust, invest, license, mandate, name, nominate, ordain, select, swear in, warrant

delegation *n.* **1.** appointment, assignment, authorization, charge, consignment, deputation, election, mandate, nomination, relegation, trust **2.** board, committee, contingent, envoy, gathering, legation, mission, organization, representatives, Royal Commission

delete *v.* alter, annul, blue-pencil, cancel, clean, crop, cut, drop, edit, efface, eliminate, erase, exclude, expunge, gut, obliterate, omit, remove, rub out, snip, squash, strike out, wipe out *Antonyms:* add, append, augment

deleterious *adj.* bad, baneful, calamitous, cancerous, damaging, deadly, destroying, destructive, detrimental, dire, harmful, hazardous, hurtful, injurious, nocuous, noxious, pernicious, prejudicial, ruinous, toxic, vicious, wicked *Antonyms:* ameliorative, helpful, innocuous, wholesome

deliberate *adj.* **1.** advised, aforethought, calculated, cold-blooded, conscious, considered, cut-and-dried *(Nonformal)*, designed, express, fixed, intended, intentional, judged, meticulous, planned, pondered, prearranged, predetermined, premeditated, projected, purposeful, reasoned, schemed, studious, thought-out, voluntary, weighed, willful *Antonyms:* accidental, inadvertent, unconscious, unintended **2.** careful, cautious, leery, prudent, shrewd, wary **3.** dilatory, leisurely, relaxed, slow, steady, unhurried *Antonyms:* hasty, impetuous – *v.* **1.** brood, cerebrate, cogitate, concentrate, consider, contemplate, examine, focus, inspect, meditate, mull over, muse, ponder, premeditate, reflect, review, ruminate, scrutinize, study, think *or* think over, weigh **2.** argue, bargain, confer, consult, debate, demonstrate, discuss, huddle, meet, negotiate, parley, powwow, reason, talk

deliberately *adv.* advisedly, by design, calculatingly, consciously, determinedly, freely, independently, intentionally, knowingly, on purpose, pointedly, purposely, purposively, resolutely, studiously, voluntarily, willfully, wittingly

deliberation *n.* **1.** brooding, cerebration, concentration, consideration, contemplation, examination, excogitation, focus, inspection, introspection, meditation, mulling over, musing, pondering, premeditation, reflection, review, rumination, scrutiny, study, thought, thoughtfulness, weighing **2.** calculation, design, determination, intention, purpose, purposefulness, resolve, volition, willfulness **3.** advisement, argument, conference, consultation, debate, dialogue, discussion, reasoning **4.** care, carefulness, caution, chariness, circumspection, deliberateness, discretion, evenness, firmness, forethought, guardedness, methodicalness, meticulousness, orderliness, prudence, scrupulousness, slowness, solidness, stability, steadiness, sureness, thoroughness, vigilance, wariness, watchfulness *Antonyms:* heedlessness, indifference

delicacy *n.* **1.** airiness, daintiness, elegance, etherealness, exquisiteness, fineness, slenderness, smoothness, softness, subtlety, tenderness, tenuity, translucency, transparency **2.** brittleness, feebleness, flimsiness, fragility, frailness, susceptibility *Antonyms:* resilience, sturdiness, toughness **3.** art, caution, craft, diplomacy, discretion, political correctness, refinement, sensitivity, subtlety, tact, wile **4.** agility, coordination, dexterity, ease, expertise, facility, finesse, grace, nimbleness, skill *Nonformal:* savvy, the touch *Antonyms:* awkwardness, clumsiness **5.** ambrosia, dainty, delight, dessert, choice morsel, food, goody *(Nonformal)*, indulgence, morsel, sweet, tidbit, treat

delicate *adj.* **1.** aerial, dainty, delightful, elegant, ethereal, exquisite, faint, filmy, fine-grained, finespun, gauzy, gossamer, mild, muted, pale, select, soft, subdued, subtle *Antonyms:* crude, rough, unrefined **2.** appealing, delectable, delicious, delightful, flavourful, fragrant, pleasing, savoury, tasty *Antonyms:* overpowering, pungent, strong **3.** ailing, debilitated, decrepit, feeble, flimsy, fracturable, fragile, frail, frangible, infirm, sick, sickly, slender, slight, susceptible, tender, unhealthy, weak *Antonyms:* healthy, strong **4.** adept, careful, cautious, deft, discreet, discriminating, expert, fastidious, finicky, fussy, gentle, graceful, persnickety, precise, proficient, scrupulous, skilled, tactful *Antonyms:* bumbling, inept, puzzled **5.** compassionate, concerned, feeling, gentle-souled, responsive, sensitive, sympathetic, tender *Antonyms:* callous, cold-blooded, cruel **6.** critical, difficult, hair-trigger *(Nonformal)*, mercurial, precarious, sensitive, touchy, tricky, uncertain, unpredictable, volatile *Antonyms:* calm, even, steady **7.** fine, minor, minute, negligible, slight, small *Antonyms:* glaring, obvious

delicately *adv.* carefully, cautiously, daintily, deftly, elegantly, exquisitely, fastidiously, finely, gracefully, sensitively, skilfully, softly, subtly, tactfully

delicious *adj.* adorable, ambrosial, appetizing, choice, delectable, delightful, enjoyable, exquisite, good, gratifying, heavenly, luscious, mellow, mouth-watering, piquant, pleasant, pleasing, rare, rich, savoury, scrumptious, spicy, sweet, tasteful, tasty, tempting, toothsome, well-prepared, well-seasoned, yummy *(Nonformal) Antonyms:* disagreeable, gross, putrid, unpleasant

delight *n.* contentment, ecstasy, enchantment, enjoyment, felicity, fruition, gladness, glee, gratification, happiness, hilarity, joy, mirth, pleasure, rapture, satisfaction, transport *Antonyms:* horror, sadness, sorrow – *v.* allure, amuse, attract, charm, cheer, content, divert, enchant, enrapture, entertain, exult, fascinate, gladden, gratify, please, pleasure, rejoice, satisfy, send, thrill *Nonformal:* knock dead *or* out, slay *Antonyms:* disgust, distress, gall, irk, vex

delighted *adj. aux anges (French)*, captivated, charmed, ecstatic, elated, enchanted, entranced, excited, fulfilled, gladdened, gratified, happy, joyous, jubilant, overjoyed, over the moon, pleasantly surprised, pleased, thrilled

delightful *adj.* adorable, agreeable, alluring, amusing, attractive, beautiful, brilliant, captivating, charming, cheery, clever, congenial, delicious, enchanting, engaging, enjoyable, entertaining, fair, fascinating, gratifying, heavenly, luscious, pleasant, pleasing, rapturous, ravishing, refreshing, satisfying, scrumptious *(Nonformal)*, thrilling *Antonyms:* awful, nasty, unpleasant

delineate *v.* **1.** chart, depict, design, draft, draw, engrave, etch, figure, image, line, map, outline, paint, pen, portray, profile, sketch, trace **2.** define, describe, discuss, narrate, read, report, state, talk out

delinquency *n.* **1.** crime, fault, misbehaviour, misconduct, misdeed, misdemeanour, offence, wrongdoing **2.** default, dereliction, disregard, failure, lapse, negligence, remissness

delinquent *adj.* **1.** behind, careless, defaulting, derelict, lax, neglectful, negligent, overdue, procrastinating, remiss, slack, tardy **2.** blameworthy, culpable, guilty, irresponsible, offending, reprehensible – *n.* **1.** debtor, defaulter, derelict **2.** criminal, culprit, desperado, felon, greaser *(Nonformal)*, hoodlum, juvenile delinquent, lawbreaker, malefactor, miscreant, offender, outlaw, sinner, wrongdoer, young offender

delirious *adj.* **1.** aberrant, babbling, bewildered, carried away, confused, crazed, crazy, demented, deranged, deviant, disarranged, disordered, distracted, disturbed, dizzy, hallucinatory, imbalanced, incoherent, insane, irrational, lunatic, mad, maniac, maniacal, manic, overexcited, overwrought, rabid, rambling, ranting, raving, unhinged, unreasonable, unsettled, wandering *Nonformal:* dingy, flipped, psycho, unglued, wigged out *Antonyms:* calm, coherent, lucid, rational, sensible **2.** beside oneself, delighted, ecstatic, elated, happy, joyous, jubilant, overjoyed, transported *Antonyms:* cheerless, sad, unhappy

delirium *n.* deliriousness, delirium tremens, dementia, derangement, exhaustion psychosis, frenzy, furore, fury, hallucination, hysteria, incoherence, insanity, lunacy, madness, mania, passion, rage, ranting, raving, restlessness *Nonformal terms for delirium tremens:* blue devils, purple monkeys *or* pink elephants, the DTs, the horrors, the screaming meemies, the shakes

deliver *v.* **1.** bring, carry, cart, convey, courier, discharge, distribute, e-mail, fax, give, hand-carry, hand over, pass, provide, remit, supply, transfer, transport **2.** heave, hurl, pitch, throw, toss *Nonformal:* whip, wing **3.** address, announce, broach, communicate, declare, express, impart, lecture, present, proclaim, pronounce, publish, read, say, soapbox *(Nonformal)*, state, tell, utter, vent, voice **4.** abandon, cede, commit, grant, relinquish, resign, surrender, transfer, yield **5.** acquit, discharge, emancipate, free, liberate, loose, ransom, redeem, release, rescue, save, set free **6.** bear, bring forth, drop, give birth *or* life, issue, produce

deliverance *n.* **1.** absolution, acquittance, amnesty, armistice, emancipation, escape, extrication, freedom, liberation, manumission, pardon, ransom, redemption, release, rescue, salvation, truce *Antonyms:* constraint, imprisonment, incarceration **2.** declaration, elocution, expression, interpretation, lecture, opinion, oration, pronouncement, speech, statement, talk

delivery *n.* **1.** commitment, consignment, conveyance, dispatch, distribution, drop, freighting, giving *or* handing over, mailing, portage, post, rendering, rendition, shipment, surrender, transfer, transferral, transmission **2.** amnesty, deliverance, emancipation, escape, freeing, liberation, pardon, release, rescue **3.** accent, articulation, diction, elocution, emphasis, enunciation, flow, inflection, intonation, modulation, pronunciation, speech, tone, utterance **4.** accouchement, bearing, birth, bringing forth, caesarean, childbearing, childbirth, confinement, labour, lying-in, parturition, travail **5.** pitch, throw, toss *See also:* **pitch**

dell *n.* coulee, dale, dingle, gap, glen, gorge, hollow, pass, ravine, vale, valley

delude *v.* beguile, betray, bluff, cheat, deceive, double-cross, dupe, elude, evade, fool, frustrate, hoax, hoodwink, misguide, mislead, take in, trick *Nonformal:* con, snow

deluge *n.* avalanche, barrage, cataclysm, cataract, downpour, drencher, flood, flux, inundation, overflowing, overrunning, pour, rush, shower, spate, torrent – *v.* **1.** douse, drench, drown, engulf, flood, flush, gush, overflow, overrun, pour, stream, submerge, teem **2.** bewilder, crowd, crush, exhaust, glut, inundate, overcrowd, overload, oversupply, overwhelm, smother, swamp *Nonformal:* bury, snow under

delusion *n.* **1.** fallacy, misbelief, misconception, mistake, self-deception **2.** apparition, fantasy, figment, hallucination, illusion, mirage, vision **3.** artifice, chicanery, duplicity, fraud, knavery, machination, ploy, subterfuge

delusive *adj.* **1.** beguiling, deceiving, deceptive, deluding, false, misleading, spurious **2.** apparent, chimerical, fanciful, illusory, imaginary, seeming, visionary

deluxe *adj.* **1.** choice, classy, costly, elegant, excellent, exclusive, grand, luxurious, opulent, palatial, plush, rich, select, special, splendid, sumptuous, superior *Nonformal:* five-star, gear, grade A, posh, top-notch *Antonyms:* impoverished, poor, squalid **2.** dear, exorbitant, pricey, steep *Antonyms:* cheap, economical

delve *v.* analyze, burrow, dig, examine, ferret out, inquire, investigate, probe, research, rummage, search, seek, sift, unearth

demagogue *n.* agitator, fanatic, firebrand, fomenter, haranguer, hothead *(Nonformal)*, incendiary, inciter, inflamer, instigator, leader, rabble-rouser, radical, rebel, revolutionary, troublemaker

demand *n.* **1.** charge, claim, command, insistence, order, stipulation **2.** application, bidding, call, desire, entreaty, imploration, importunity, petition, plea, request, requisition, supplication **3.** inquiry, necessity, need, requirement, want – *v.* **1.** ask, inquire, solicit **2.** call, challenge, charge, claim, command, compel, dictate, enjoin, exact, extort, impose, insist, invoke, necessitate, oblige, order, requisition, rule, summon **3.** extract, force, harass, hound **4.** need, require, want

demanding *adj.* **1.** backbreaking, challenging, onerous, taxing, tough, trying, wearing *Antonyms:* easy, facile, painless, simple, uncomplicated **2.** bothersome, captious, cavilling, dictatorial, difficult, exigent, imperious, insistent, querulous, stringent **3.** compelling, critical, essential, urgent, vital

demarcate *v.* define, delimit, delineate, determine, draw boundaries, fix, mark *Antonyms:* blur, obscure

demarcation *n.* **1.** border, bound, boundary, confine, delimitation, enclosure, fence line, limit, margin, terminus **2.** differentiation, distinction, division, separation, split

dematerialize *v.* disappear, disintegrate, dissolve, evanesce, evaporate, fade *or* rust away, vanish *Antonyms:* appear, manifest, materialize, take form *or* shape

demean *v.* abase, abash, belittle, crush, debase, decry, deflate, degrade, demote, depose, depreciate, devalue, diminish, discredit, disgrace, dishonour, humble, humiliate, mortify, put down, reduce, shame, vitiate *Antonyms:* dignify, elevate, glorify, honour

demeanour *n.* air, appearance, aura, bearing, behaviour, carriage, comportment, composure, conduct, countenance, deportment, expression, manner, mien, physiognomy, presence, style, visage

demented *adj.* crazed, crazy, daft, delirious, deranged, distracted, distraught, foolish, frenzied, hysterical, idiotic, insane, lunatic, mad, maniacal, psychopathic, psychotic, schizoid, unbalanced, unhinged, unsound *Nonformal:* bananas, bonkers, flipped *or* wigged out, nuts, psycho, unglued *Antonyms:* lucid, normal, rational, reasonable, sensible

demerit *n.* **1.** deduction, demerit point, fine, minus, penalty, point taken off *Antonyms:* credit, reward, value **2.** breach, error, misconduct, misdemeanour, offence, transgression, violation

demilitarize *v.* civilize, deactivate, decamp, demobilize, disarm, disband, evacuate, muster out, neutralize

demise *n.* annihilation, collapse, death, decease, departure, downfall, end, ending, expiration, extinction, failure, fall, fate, passing, ruin, silence, termination – *v.* bequeath, convey, pass, transfer, transmit, will

demobilize *v.* deactivate, demilitarize, disarm, disband, dismiss, lay down arms, muster out *Antonyms:* activate, arm, mobilize, muster

democracy *n.* commonwealth, constitutional government, egalitarianism, equalitarianism, equality, freedom, parliamentary government, representative government, republicanism, self-government, suffrage, the vote *(Nonformal) Antonyms:* dictatorship, oligarcy, totalitarianism

democratic *adj.* chosen, common, communal, constitutional, egalitarian, electoral, equal, free, libertarian, orderly, popular, populist, representative, republican, self-governing, self-ruling, voting *Antonyms:* authoritarian, monarchical

demolish *v.* annihilate, blow-up, bomb, bulldoze, burst, consume, crush, destroy, devastate, devour, dismantle, flatten, level, obliterate, overthrow, pulverize, raze, ruin, smash, take out, thrust, total, trash, wreck *Antonyms:* build, construct, repair, restore, strengthen

demon *n.* **1.** archfiend, daimon, devil, evil *or* malignant spirit, fiend, ghoul, goblin, imp, kelpie, incubus, malevolence, succubus, wendigo *Japanese:* kappa, kitsune *Judaism:* dybbuk, Lilith, shedim **2.** beast, brute, hellion, hellkite, maniac, monster, rascal, rogue **3.** doer, dynamo, man *or* woman of action, performer, powerhouse, type A personality, workhorse *Nonformal:* eager-beaver, go-getter

demonic *adj.* **1.** crazed, demoniac, demoniacal, devilish, diabolic, diabolical, evil, fiendish, hellish, impious, insane, mad, maniacal, renegade, satanic, serpentine, violent, wicked **2.** aroused, determined, enthused, fired-up *(Nonformal)*, frenetic, frenzied, inspired, possessed

demonstrable *adj.* **1.** ascertainable, attestable, axiomatic, certain, conclusive, evident, incontrovertible, indubitable, irrefutable, obvious, positive, provable, self-evident, unmistakable, verifiable **2.** affective, emotional, expressive, feeling, graphic, illustrative, open, revealing, vivid

demonstrate *v.* **1.** define, describe, detail, edify, educate, elaborate, explain, inform, spell out, teach **2.** ascertain, authenticate, confirm, debunk, determine, establish, evidence, evince, prove, test, try, validate **3.** advertise, display, exhibit, feature, manifest, show, showcase **4.** join forces, march *or* march on, picket, protest, rally, remonstrate, sit in, strike, take action, walk out

demonstration *n.* **1.** affirmation, authentication, confirmation, evidence, proof, validation, verification **2.** display, example, exhibition, exposition, performance, production, showing **3.** analysis, assessment, dry run, experiment, test, tryout **4.** expression, manifestation, show, symbol, token **5.** march, parade, picket, protest, rally, show of force, sit-in, walkout

demonstrative *adj.* **1.** affectionate, candid, communicative, effusive, emotional, expressive, gushing, loving, open, outgoing, outspoken, profuse, tender, unconstrained, unreserved, unrestrained, warmhearted *Antonyms:* aloof, cool, contained, distant **2.** descriptive, elucidatory, explanatory, expository, expressive, illustrative, indicative, informative, instructive **3.** certain, conclusive, convincing, definite, final, showing, validating

demoralize *v.* **1.** chill, cripple, cut off at the knees *(Nonformal)*, dampen, daunt, debilitate, deject, depress, disconcert, discourage, dishearten, disparage, dispirit, embarrass, enfeeble, muddle, nonplus, rattle, sap, shake, undermine, unglue, unnerve, unsettle, upset, weaken *Antonyms:* encourage, inspire, support

demote *v.* break, bump, bust *(Nonformal)*, declass, degrade, demerit, dismiss, downgrade, knock off, lower, reduce *Antonyms:* advance, elevate, promote, raise, upgrade

demotic *adj.* colloquial, common, everyday, popular, simplified, unpretentious, vernacular, vulgar *Antonyms:* elevated, pompous

demur *n.* **1.** compunction, criticism, disapproval, dissent, doubt, grievance, misgiving, mistrust, objection, protest, qualm, reluctance, remonstrance, scepticism, scruple, unwillingness *Antonyms:* accession, agreement, compliance **2.** delay, dodge, demurral, hesitation – *v.* **1.** balk, dodge, duck, hesitate, pause, vacillate, waffle, waver **2.** cavil, challenge, contest, disagree, disapprove, dispute, dissent, doubt, object, oppose, protest, question, refuse, remonstrate, resist, take exception *Antonyms:* accede, agree, comply *Commonly misused:* **demure**

demure *adj.* **1.** bashful, blushing, coy, modest, prim, proper, shy, timid, unassertive, unassuming *Antonyms:* brash, brazen, forward, impudent, shameless **2.** close, discreet, grave, reserved, reticent, retiring, sedate, serious, silent, sober, solemn *Commonly misused:* **demur**

demystify *v.* clarify, clear up, debunk, decipher, decode, disentangle, elucidate, enlighten, explain, explicate, expose, illuminate, lay open, resolve, reveal, simplify, solve, unravel, untangle, unveil *Antonyms:* confuse, muddle, obscure

den *n.* **1.** atelier, cloister, family room, haunt, hideaway, hideout, hole, library, playroom, recreation *or* rumpus room, refuge, retreat, sanctuary, sanctum, scriptorium, snuggery, studio, study, workshop **2.** burrow, cave, cavern, cubbyhole, lair, lodge, nest, shelter

denial *n.* **1.** disavowal, gainsay, refutation, repudiation *Antonyms:* acknowledgment, admission **2.** disapproval, dissent, nonacceptance, rebuff, rebuttal, refusal, rejection, renunciation *Antonyms:* acceptance, approval, welcoming **3.** cancellation, nay, negation, nullification, prohibition, thumbs down *(Nonformal)*, turndown, veto, void

denigrate *v.* belittle, besmirch, blacken, calumniate, decry, defame, disparage, impugn, libel, malign, revile, scandalize, traduce, vilify *Nonformal:* bad-mouth, blister, dis, knock, roast *Antonyms:* acclaim, admire, cheer, compliment, extol

denizen *n.* **1.** citizen, dweller, habitant, inhabitant, local, national, native, resident, resider, subject **2.** habitué, patron, regular

denomination *n.* **1.** belief, church, communion, connection, creed, cult, group, persuasion, religion, school, sect *Religious denominations:* Adventist, Amish, Anglican, Bahai, Baptist, Buddhist, Christian Reformed, Confucian, Dukhobor, Evangelical, Greek Orthodox, Hindu, Hutterite, Islamic, Jehovah's Witness, Latter-Day Saint, Lutheran, Mennonite, Methodist, Moravian Brethren, Mormon, Pentecostal, Presbyterian, Quaker, Roman Catholic, Russian Orthodox, Salvation Army, Shaker, Sikh, Sufi, Taoist, Ukrainian Catholic, Unitarian, United Church *Judaism:* Conservative, Orthodox, Reform **2.** appellation, brand, classification, concept, designation, flag, grade, identification, label, name, size, style, tab, tag, term, title, unit, value *Nonformal:* handle, moniker **3.** body, category, class, genus, group, ilk, kind, measure, species, variety

denote *v.* **1.** characterize, distinguish, earmark, exemplify, indicate, mark, note, point out, represent, show, signify, stand for, symbolize, typify **2.** allude, denominate, designate, express, imply, import, intimate, mean, name *Commonly misused:* **connote**

dénouement *n.* close, completion, conclusion, consequence, consummation, culmination, effect, end, final act, finale, finish, outcome, punch line, resolution, result, solution, termination *Antonyms:* beginning, commencement, opening, start

denounce *v.* **1.** attack, blacklist, boycott, brand, castigate, censure, criticize, decry, excoriate, expose, impeach, impugn, inveigh against, ostracize, proscribe, rebuke, reprehend, reprimand, reproach, reprobate, reprove, revile, scold, smear, stigmatize, threaten, upbraid, vilify, vituperate **2.** accuse, arraign, blame, charge, condemn, finger *(Nonformal)*, implicate, incriminate, indict, name, prosecute

dense *adj.* **1.** close, compact, compressed, condensed, crammed, crowded, jam-packed, massed, solid, thick, thickset *Antonyms:* scattered, sparse, thin, transparent **2.** doltish, dull, dumb, half-witted, ignorant, obtuse, phlegmatic, simple, slow *or* slow-witted, sluggish, stupid, torpid *Antonyms:* alert, bright, clever, intelligent, quick

density *n.* **1.** closeness, compactness, concretion, consistency, crowdedness, denseness, heaviness, mass, solidity, substantiality, thickness, weight **2.** blockheadedness, dullness, foolishness, obtuseness, slow-wittedness, sluggishness, stupidity, vacuity *Antonyms:* cleverness, quickness, swiftness

dent *n.* cavity, concavity, crater, crenelle, depression, ding, dip, furrow, hollow, impression, indentation, nick, notch, pit, trough – *v.* chip, crush, depress, dig, dimple, furrow, gouge, hollow, imprint, indent, mark, nick, notch, perforate, pit, press *or* push in, ridge, scrape, scratch

denunciation *n.* **1.** castigation, censure, condemnation, criticism, cursing, damning, denouncement, disapproval, fulmination, invective, obloquy, reprehension, reprobation, stigmatization, vituperation, warning **2.** accusation, arraignment, blame, charge, incrimination, indictment

deny *v.* **1.** abjure, confute, contradict, disagree, disprove, dispute, negate, nullify, rebut, refute *Antonyms:* admit, affirm, agree, concede, recognize **2.** hold, keep, maintain, repress, withhold *Antonyms:* release, relinquish **3.** ban, bar, decline, disallow, eschew, exclude, lock out, oppose, prohibit, rebuff, refuse, reject, repel, turn away *or* down *Antonyms:* accept, give entry **4.** disavow, discard, disclaim, disown, forsake, repudiate, snub, spurn *Antonyms:* acknowledge, embrace

deodorant *n.* absorbent, air freshener, antiperspirant, deodorizer, disinfectant, fumigant, pit-juice *(Nonformal)*, roll-on

deodorize *v.* aerate, air out, cleanse, disinfect, freshen, fumigate, perfume, purify, refresh, sanitize, sweeten, ventilate

depart *v.* **1.** abandon, abdicate, decamp, desert, disappear, escape, exit, forsake, go away, go forth, leave, march out, migrate, move on *or* out, part, quit, secede, split, vacate, vanish, withdraw *Nonformal:* hit the trail, scram *Antonyms:* arrive, remain, stay, turn up **2.** break, deviate, digress, dissent, diverge, stray, swerve, turn aside, vary, veer, wander **3.** croak *(Nonformal)*, decease, die, expire, pass away *or* on, perish

departed *adj.* **1.** gone, left, migrated, moved away *or* on, vacated, vanished, withdrawn **2.** dead, deceased, expired, late, lifeless, passed away

department *n.* administration, agency, annex, area, arm, *arrondissement (French)*, assignment, avocation, bailiwick, beat, branch, bureau, cabinet, chapter, circuit, class, concession, constituency, detachment, district, division, domain, dominion, duty, extension, field, function, jurisdiction, ministry, niche, office, precinct, province, quarter, realm, region, responsibility, section, sector, slot, specialty, spot, station, subdivision, subsidiary, unit, ward, wing

departure *n.* **1.** abandonment, decampment, departing, desertion, dispersion embarkation, escape, evacuation, exit exodus, flight, getaway, going, leave-taking, leaving, migration, recession, retreat, separation, stampede, vanishing act *(Nonformal)*, withdrawal *Antonyms:* advent, arrival, coming, entrance, return **2.** aberration, branching off *or* out, declination, deflection, deviation, difference, digression, divergence, diversion, innovation, novelty, shift, straying, variance, variation, veering **3.** death, demise, end, expiration, farewell, finish, passing

dependable *adj.* always there, certain, constant, faithful, honest, loyal, reliable, responsible, secure, stable, staunch, steadfast, steady, sure, tried, true, trustworthy, unfailing *Nonformal:* rock solid, true blue *Antonyms:* irresponsible, unreliable, unstable, untrustworthy

dependence *n.* **1.** association, attachment, band, bond, connection, linkage, relationship, tie **2.** assurance, belief, confidence, dependency, faith, hope, reliance, trust **3.** helplessness, inability, ineptitude, powerlessness, vulnerability, weakness *Antonyms:* independence, self-reliance **4.** abjection, servility, subjection, submission, subordination, subservience **5.** addiction, devotion, habit, need, problem, requirement, substance abuse, urge, yoke *Nonformal:* monkey, security blanket

dependent *adj.* **1.** defenceless, helpless, humble, indigent, needful, vulnerable, weak **2.** ancillary, conditional, contingent, controlled, determined by, inferior, lesser, reliant, secondary, subject to, subordinate, supported, sustained **3.** associated, attached, clinging, dangling, hanging – *n.* charge, child, hanger-on, minor, the needy, recipient, vassal, youth

depict *v.* characterize, delineate, describe, draw, illustrate, interpret, outline, paint, picture, portray, relate, render, report, represent, sketch, state

depiction *n.* description, drawing, illustration, image, interpretation, outline, painting, picture, portrayal, rendering, rendition, representation, sketch

deplete *v.* **1.** consume, decrease, diminish, drain, dry up, enervate, exhaust, finish, milk, sap, suck, undermine, use up, waste, weaken *Antonyms:* invigorate, refresh, vitalize **2.** bankrupt, bleed, draw, empty, evacuate, expend, impoverish, lessen, reduce, spend, squander *Antonyms:* augment, enhance, expand, fill, increase

depleted *adj.* **1.** bleary, collapsed, consumed, devitalized, devoid, drained, effete, enervated, exhausted, lessened, sapped, used, vacant, washed out, wasted, weakened, worn *Antonyms:* dynamic, energetic **2.** bankrupt, bare, bereft, blank, decreased, destitute, emptied, gone, impoverished, reduced, spent

deplorable *adj.* awful, blameworthy, calamitous, dire, dirty, disastrous, disgraceful, dishonourable, disreputable, distressing, dolorous, dreadful, execrable, faulty, grievous, grim, heartbreaking, heart-rending, horrifying, intolerable, lamentable, miserable, overwhelming, pitiable, poor, regrettable, reprehensible, rotten, sad, scandalous, sickening, terrible, tragic, unfortunate, unsatisfactory, woeful, wretched *Antonyms:* admirable, excellent, fantastic, laudable, superb

deplore *v.* bemoan, bewail, complain, kvetch *(Nonformal)*, lament, moan, mourn, regret, repent, rue, wail *Antonyms:* exult, rejoice

deploy *v.* **1.** apply, employ, exercise, use, utilize **2.** arrange, expand, extend, fan out, form, front, open, position, redistribute, set up, unfold

deport *v.* **1.** banish, cast out, dismiss, displace, exile, expatriate, expel, extradite, oust, relegate, ship out, transport **2.** act, bear, behave, carry, conduct, demean

deportation *n.* banishment, displacement, eviction, exile, expatriation, expulsion, extradition, relegation, removal, transportation

depose *v.* **1.** bounce, cashier, chuck *(Nonformal)*, demote, dethrone, dismiss, downgrade, eject, impeach, oust, overthrow, throw out, topple, unseat, upset **2.** attest, asseverate, declare, give oath, state, swear, testify

deposit *n.* **1.** installment, pledge, reservation, retainer, savings, security, stake, warranty **2.** accumulation, alluvium, diluvium, dregs, drift, grounds, lees, precipitate, sediment, settlings, silt, slag **3.** armoury, arsenal, bank, safe, store, vault, warehouse – *v.* **1.** accumulate, amass, bank, collect, entrust, garner, hoard, invest, keep, put aside, save, store **2.** arrange, park, place, plant, position, put, situate, stash, stow

deposition *n.* **1.** affidavit, affirmation, allegation, announcement, attestation, declaration, evidence, sworn statement, testimony, transcript, truth **2.** booting *(Nonformal)*, dethroning, discharge, dismissal, displacement, ousting, removal **3.** allocation, arrangement, deposit, distribution

depository *n.* arsenal, bank, base, box, cache, chest, collection, depot, garage, magazine, repertory, repository, safe, station, storage, store, storehouse, storeroom, terminus, vault, warehouse

depot *n.* **1.** cache, depository, drop-off point, dump, repository, storage place, store, storehouse, storeroom, warehouse **2.** bus *or* railway station, station house, stop, terminal, terminus

deprave *v.* bastardize, contaminate, corrupt, debase, degrade, demoralize, pervert, pollute, ruin, subvert, sully, vitiate, warp

depraved *adj.* abandoned, base, corrupted, debased, debauched, degenerate, degraded, dirty, dirty-minded, dissolute, evil, filthy, immoral, infamous, lascivious, lewd, licentious, low, mean, miscreant, nefarious, odious, perverted, profligate, rotten, ruined, shameless, sinful, unnatural, vicious, vile, villainous, wanton, warped, wicked *Nonformal:* kinky, twisted *Antonyms:* chaste, decent, proper, pure, wholesome *Commonly misused:* **deprived**

depravity *n.* abandonment, baseness, contamination, corruption, criminality, debasement, debauchery, degeneracy, degradation, depravation, evil, immorality, iniquity, perversion, profligacy, sinfulness, vice, viciousness, wickedness

deprecate *v.* **1.** abuse, belittle, degrade, denigrate, deplore, deride, disparage, malign, put down, traduce **2.** condemn, denounce, expostulate, plead *or* protest against, reject, remonstrate *Antonyms:* approve, commend *Commonly misused:* **depreciate**

deprecatory *adj.* **1.** belittling, chastising, chiding, condemnatory, criticizing, deflating, deriding, derogative, derogatory, detracting, devaluating, diminishing, disparaging, minimizing, underestimating, underrating *Antonyms:* esteeming, inflating **2.** self-conscious, self-doubting, self-effacing, unassuming *Antonyms:* bold, brazen, proud **3.** apologetic, regretful, remorseful, rueful, saddened, sorry

depreciate *v.* **1.** cancel, cheapen, cut, decrease, deflate, depress, devaluate, downgrade, drop, lessen, lower, mark down, reduce, soften, underrate, undervalue *Antonyms:* augment, enhance, expand, increase, rise **2.** belittle, decry, denigrate, devalue, diminish, discredit, disparage, disregard, minimize, slight, undervalue *Antonyms:* extol, laud, praise *Commonly misused:* **deprecate**

depreciation *n.* **1.** cheapening, decline, decrease, deflation, depression, devaluation, drop, fall, falling off, lessening, lowering, recession, reduction, sag, shrinkage, slump, wane *Antonyms:* appreciation, increase *or* rise in value, maximization **2.** belittlement, diminution, discrediting, disparagement, minimization, mockery, slight, underestimation

depredation *n.* crime, desecration, despoiling, destruction, devastation, laying waste, looting, marauding, pillage, piracy, plunder, ransacking, ravaging, robbery, sacking

depress *v.* **1.** deject, discourage, dishearten, dismay, dispirit, distress, oppress, sadden, trouble, try *Antonyms:* cheer, elevate, gladden, uplift **2.** afflict, debilitate, drain, dull, enervate, exhaust, reduce, sap, slow, weaken, weary *Antonyms:* energize, invigorate, vitalize **3.** abase, cheapen, lower, reduce *Antonyms:* increase, raise **4.** flatten, level, lower, press *or* push down, settle, sink, squash

depressant *n.* calmative, downer *(Nonformal)*, opiate, relaxant, sleeping pill, soporific, tranquilizer *Kinds of depressant:* alcohol, amobarbital atropine, barbitone, barbitor, barbituric acid, belladonna, bromide, carbromal, chloral hydrate, codeine, diazepam, flurazepam, halazepam, heroin, laudanum, meperidine, methadone, methaqualone, morphine, pentobarbital, phenobarbital, reserpine *Trademark:* Quaalude, Valium

depressed *adj.* **1.** blue, crestfallen, dejected, despondent, disconsolate, discouraged, dispirited, down, downcast, downhearted, glum, hurting, low, low-spirited, melancholy, morose, neurasthenic, pessimistic, sad, sorrowful, unhappy, woebegone *Antonyms:* buoyant, happy, jubilant, optimistic **2.** alienated, destitute, disadvantaged, distressed, humble, impoverished, low, marginalized, mean, needy, poor, poverty-stricken, underprivileged, unfortunate **3.** deflated, depreciated, devalued, slumped, stagnant, weakened **4.** concave, hollow, indented, recessed, set back, sunken **5.** flattened, flush, level, pushed down, smooth, splay

depressing *adj.* black, bleak, discouraging, disheartening, dismal, dispiriting, dreary, funereal, gloomy, heartbreaking, hopeless, joyless, melancholy, mournful, oppressive, sad, sombre, upsetting *Antonyms:* cheery, joyful, uplifting

depression *n.* **1.** bleakness, blues, cheerlessness, dejection, depressive psychosis, desolation, despair, desperation, despondency, discouragement, dispiritedness, distress, dolefulness, downheartedness, dreariness, gloom, gloominess, heavy-heartedness, lowness, melancholia, misery, sadness, sorrow, unhappiness, worry, wretchedness *Nonformal:* dumps, jim-jams **2.** bad *or* hard times, bust, crash, crisis, decline, deflation, Dirty *or* Hungry Thirties *(Historical)*, downturn, drop, failure, inactivity, panic, recession, slump, stagnation, unemployment **3.** basin, bowl, cavity, concavity, crater, dent, dimple, dip, excavation, hole, hollow, impression, indentation, pit, pocket, pockmark, scoop, sink, sinkhole, slough *(Prairies)*, valley

deprivation *n.* **1.** deficiency, destitution, disadvantage, disenfranchisement, distress, hardship, impoverishment, marginalization, neediness, paucity, poverty, privation, shortage, victimization, want **2.** blockade *or* blockage *(Military)*, denial, deprival, embargo, hold, prohibition, punishment, refusal, retention, sanction, withholding **3.** debarment, disbarment, disentitlement, divestment, expulsion, ousting, removal, stripping, toppling

deprive *v.* **1.** deny, prohibit, refuse, withhold *Antonyms:* give, offer, share **2.** denude, disinherit, dispossess, divest, dock, expropriate, remove, rob, seize, skim, stiff *(Nonformal)*, strip, take away

deprived *adj.* **1.** destitute, disadvantaged, disenfranchised, impecunious, needy, poor, underprivileged *Antonyms:* fortunate, privileged, well-off **2.** lacking, limited, short, wanting *Antonyms:* flush, full, replete **3.** bare, bereft, dispossessed, naked, shorn, stripped, without *Commonly misused:* **depraved**

depth *n.* **1.** abyss, base, bottom, declination, deepness, drop, fissure, lowness, pit, substratum *Antonyms:* apex, apogee, crown, summit, zenith **2.** acumen, astuteness, discernment, insight, intellect, intelligence, keenness, penetration, profoundness, profundity, sagacity, sense, sharpness, weightiness, wisdom *Antonyms:* inanity, shallowness, superficiality **3.** consequence, import, importance, influence, measure, seriousness, solemnity, strength, value **4.** degree, extent, intensity, level, measurement, pitch, state

deputize *v.* appoint, assign, authorize, charge, commission, consign, delegate, designate, empower, enable, entrust, name, nominate, ordain, pass on, relegate

deputy *adj.* appointed, assistant, associate, designated, elected, ordained, subordinate – *n.* agent, alternate, ambassador, appointee, assistant, bureaucrat, commissioner, consul, delegate, diplomat, emissary, envoy, factor, functionary, go-between, intermediary, lieutenant, mediator, messenger, minister, negotiator, operative, provost, proxy, representative, spokesperson, stand-in, substitute, surrogate, understudy, vicegerent, viceroy *Nonformal:* backup, pinch-hitter, sidekick

derange *v.* **1.** confound, confuse, disarray, discombobulate *(Nonformal)*, disorder, disorganize, disturb, muddle, ruffle, unbalance *Antonyms:* arrange, order **2.** craze, dement, discommode, discompose, disconcert, distract, excite, fluster, madden, perplex, unhinge, unsettle, upset *Antonyms:* assuage, calm

deranged *adj.* **1.** berserk, crazed, crazy, delirious, demented, disconcerted, distracted, frantic, frenzied, insane, irrational, lunatic, mad, maddened, maniacal, perplexed, unbalanced, unhinged, unsettled, unsound *Nonformal:* bananas, cracked, flipped, flipped out, loco, loony, nuts, unglued *Antonyms:* calm, lucid, normal, sound **2.** disorganized, jumbled, messed *or* screwed up *(Nonformal)*, muddled, untidy

derelict *adj.* **1.** behind, careless, delinquent, dilatory, disregardful, heedless, irresponsible, lax, neglectful, negligent, remiss, slack, tardy, undependable, unreliable, untrustworthy **2.** abandoned, castoff, deserted, desolate, discarded, forsaken, neglected, relinquished, solitary **3.** decrepit, dilapidated, dingy, faded, ramshackle, ruined, rundown, seedy, threadbare, tumbledown, weathered – *n.* **1.** beachcomber, bum *(Nonformal)*, hobo, loafer, ne'er-do-well, outcast, scavenger, street-person, vagabond, vagrant **2.** debtor, defaulter, delinquent, dodger, evader, shirker, slacker

dereliction *n.* **1.** carelessness, default, delay, delinquency, dilatoriness, disregard, evasion, failure, fault, forgetfulness, heedlessness, improvidence, imprudence, inattentiveness, incautiousness, indiscretion, inexactness, infraction, laxity, looseness, neglect, neglectfulness, negligence, nonperformance, omission, oversight, remissness, shoddiness, shortcoming, tardiness, transgression, violation, wrongdoing *Antonyms:* care, diligence, punctuality, thoroughness **2.** idleness, indolence, laziness, lethargy, shiftlessness, slackness, sloppiness, sloth, slovenliness **3.** abandonment, apostasy, defection, desertion, disavowal, dissidence, faithlessness, forsaking, heresy, nonobservance, recreance, rejection, relinquishment, renunciation

deride *v.* chaff, detract, disdain, disparage, flout, gibe, insult, jeer, kid, knock, laugh at, mock, put down, reproach, rib, ridicule, scoff, scorn, sneer, taunt, twit *Nonformal:* burn, dis, dump on, pan, roast, slag, slam

derision *n.* contempt, detraction, disdain, disrespect, insult, jeer, jibe, lampoon, mockery, parody, pasquinade, poke, quip, raillery, ridicule, sarcasm, satire, scoffing, scorn, slight, slur, sneering, spurn, taunt, travesty *Nonformal:* Bronx cheer, cheek, dig, lip, roast, rub, sass *Antonyms:* acclaim, accolade, approval, cheer, praise

derisive *adj.* cocky, contemptuous, derisory, disdainful, fresh, impudent, insulting, jeering, mocking, nervy, ridiculing, rude, sarcastic, sassy, saucy, scoffing, scornful, smart, taunting *Nonformal:* cheeky, flip, lippy, smart-alecky, smart-ass *Commonly misused:* **decisive**

derivation *n.* **1.** ancestry, beginning, descent, extraction, genealogy, genesis, lineage, provenance, wellspring **2.** basis, etymology, foundation, history, origin, root, source

derivative *adj.* **1.** acquired, developed, drawn, obtained, received, retrieved **2.** consequential, emanating, ensuing, following, resultant **3.** after, aped, copied, fashioned, imitated, mimicked, mirrored, parroted, replicated **4.** conventional, hackneyed, trite, unimaginative, uninventive, unoriginal – *n.* branch, by-product, descendant, offshoot, outgrowth, produce, result, spawn, spin-off

derive *v.* **1.** amass, attain, bring forth, collect, cull, draw, extract, gain, garner, gather, get, glean, harvest, net, obtain, procure, reap, receive, secure, winnow **2.** arrive at, conclude, decide, deduce, deem, determine, infer, judge, presume, reason, reckon, suppose, surmise **3.** arise, come, descend, emanate, emerge, evolve, flow from, issue, hail, originate, proceed, result, spring *or* stem from

derogatory *adj.* belittling, calumnious, censorious, contumelious, critical, cutting, defamatory, degrading, demeaning, deprecatory, detracting, disdainful, dishonouring, disparaging, faultfinding, humiliating, injurious, malevolent, malicious, maligning, minimizing, offensive, reproachful, sarcastic, scornful, slanderous, unfavourable, vilifying *Antonyms:* complimentary, flattering, fulsome, laudatory

descend *v.* **1.** cascade, dip, dive, drop, fall, nose-dive, plummet, plunge, sink, slide *Antonyms:* ascend, climb, mount, scale, soar **2.** abase, condescend, crouch, degenerate, humble, lower oneself, sink, stoop **3.** decline, deteriorate, founder *Nonformal:* crash, hit rock bottom *or* the skids **4.** alight, arrive, deplane, disembark, land **5.** derive, emanate, issue, result, spring, stem from

descendant *n.* brood, child, children, heir, issue, kin, offshoot, offspring, posterity, product, progeny, scion, seed, spin-off

descent *n.* **1.** dive, drop, fall, nose dive, plummet, plunge, tumble *Nonformal:* belly flop, header **2.** crumbling, decay, decline, deterioration, disintegration, downfall, lapse, setback, slump **3.** declension, declivity, gradient, hill, incline, jump, leap, pitch, sag, slant, slope **4.** ancestry, blood, derivation, extraction, family, family tree, genealogy, heredity, lineage, origin, parentage, pedigree, relationship, strain

describe *v.* **1.** call, characterize, communicate, connote, define, delineate, denote, depict, detail, distinguish, elucidate, evidence, exemplify, explain, express, illuminate, impart, imply, indicate, insinuate, interpret, label, mark, name, narrate, peg, prove, recount, report, show, signify, specify, state, tell, term **2.** draw, frame, illustrate, image, outline, paint, picture, portray, sketch, symbolize

description *n.* **1.** account, blueprint, characterization, delineation, depiction, explanation, illustration, picture, record, representation, view **2.** brand, breed, category, character, class, classification, genre, genus, ilk, kind, nature, order, sort, species, stripe, type, variety

descriptive *adj.* definitive, depictive, detailed, eloquent, elucidative, explanatory, explicative, expository, expressive, graphic, identifying, illustrative, indicative, pictorial, picturesque, revealing, vivid

desecrate *v.* abuse, blaspheme, contaminate, defile, devastate, dishonour, pervert, pillage, pollute, profane, ravage, violate *Antonyms:* esteem, glorify, prize, respect, value

desecration *n.* abuse, blasphemy, debasement, defilement, impiety, irreverence, profanity, sacrilege, violation

desensitize *v.* acclimatize, blunt, callous, deaden, dull, habituate, harden, inure, numb, season, stiffen, toughen

desert *adj.* arid, bare, barren, desolate, dry, infertile, lonely, solitary, uncultivated, uninhabited, unproductive, waste, wild – *n.* arid region, badlands, barren, barren land, flats, sand dunes, wasteland, wilderness, wilds – *v.* abandon, abscond, bail out, betray, check out, decamp, defect, depart, ditch, drop out, escape, flee, forsake, go AWOL, leave, opt out, quit, relinquish, renounce, resign, strand, vacate, walk *Antonyms:* aid, help, remain

deserted *adj.* **1.** abandoned, bereft, cast-off, derelict, forlorn, forsaken, marooned, neglected, relinquished, stranded **2.** bare, barren, desolate, empty, godforsaken, isolated, lonely, lorn, solitary, uninhabited, unoccupied, vacant

deserter *n.* absconder, betrayer, criminal, defector, delinquent, derelict, escapee, escaper, fugitive, lawbreaker, refugee, renegade, shirker, slacker, traitor, truant, turncoat

desertion *n.* abandonment, absconding, avoidance, backsliding, betrayal, defection, departure, dereliction, disaffection, disavowal, divorce, escape, evasion, flight, forsaking, leaving, relinquishment, renunciation, repudiation, retirement, retreat, secession, separation, truancy, withdrawal

deserve *v.* demand, earn, gain, get, justify, merit, rate, warrant

deserving *adj.* admirable, commendable, due, estimable, fitting, laudable, merited, meritorious, needy, praiseworthy, rightful, worthy *Antonyms:* undeserving, unworthy

desiccate *v.* dehydrate, dry, evaporate, exsiccate, parch *Antonyms:* dampen, hydrate, moisten, wet

design *n.* **1.** arrangement, blueprint, chart, composition, conception, configuration, construction, delineation, depiction, diagram, drawing, form, illustration, layout, makeup, model, motif, organization, outline, pattern, picture, plan, prototype, scheme, shape, sketch, study, style, treatment **2.** aim, deliberation, end, enterprise, game, game plan, goal, intention, machination, meaning, notion, object, objective, pitch, plan, plot, point, project, proposition, purport, recipe, scenario, schema, scheme, setup, target, thinking, thought, trick, undertaking, view, will – *v.* accomplish, achieve, aim, arrange, blueprint, cast, chart, compose, conceive, construct, contemplate, contrive, cook up *(Nonformal)*, create, delineate, describe, devise, draft, draw, effect, execute, fabricate, fashion, form, frame, intend, invent, make, mean, mind, plan, prepare, project, propose, purpose, scheme, sketch, set apart, tailor, think up, trace

designate *v.* allocate, allot, appoint, apportion, assign, authorize, call, characterize, charge, choose, commission, connote, constitute, delegate, depute, deputize, dictate, dub, earmark, elect, entitle, favour, finger, indicate, label, make, mark, mete, name, nominate, opt, peg, pick, point out *or* to, prefer, select, set apart *or* aside, show, single out, slot, specify, stipulate, style, symbolize, tab, tag, term, title

designation *n.* **1.** appellation, class, classification, denomination, description, distinction, epithet, genre, identification, indication, label, make, mark, moniker *(Nonformal)*, name, naming, species, specification, style, title **2.** appointment, choice, delegation, election, nomination, recognition, selection

designedly *adv.* advisedly, calculatedly, deliberately, intentionally, knowingly, on purpose, purposely, willfully

designer *n.* **1.** architect, artificer, artist author, craftsperson, creator, decorator delineator, deviser, draftsperson, fashioner founder, illustrator, inventor, originator painter, producer, programmer, stylist **2** conniver, conspirator, contriver, fox *(Nonformal)*, generator, intriguer, mastermind planner, plotter, schemer

designing *adj.* artful, conniving, conspiring, crafty, crooked, cunning, devious Machiavellian, plotting, scheming, shrewd sly, tricky, wily

desirable *adj.* **1.** acceptable, advantageous advisable, agreeable, beneficial, covetable eligible, enviable, expedient, good, grateful gratifying, helpful, pleasing, preferable profitable, useful, welcome, worthwhile *Antonyms:* disagreeable, distasteful, unacceptable, unpopular **2.** adorable, alluring attractive, charming, drop-dead beautiful *(Nonformal)*, fascinating, fetching, gorgeous, seductive, sexy

desire *n.* ambition, appetite, ardour, aspiration, attraction, compulsion, covetousness craving, devotion, drive, eagerness, Eros fancy, fascination, fervour, fondness, frenzy, greed, hankering, hunger, impetus impulse, incentive, inclination, infatuation liking, longing, love, lust, mania, motive need, passion, predilection, proclivity, relish, thirst, urge, want, weakness, will, wish yearning, yen – *v.* ache, aim, aspire, brood chafe, choose, cotton to, covet, crave dream, drool, enthuse, fancy, gush, hanker hunger *or* itch *or* long for, like, long, lust need, pine, rave, require, rhapsodize, thirst *or* yearn *or* yen for, want, wish

desist *v.* abandon, abstain, avoid, break off cease, discontinue, end, forbear, halt pause, quit, refrain, relinquish, resign, stop surcease, suspend, yield

desk *n.* escritoire, writing surface *Kinds of desks:* carrel, computer, door, kneehole lectern, pulpit, roll-top, *secrétaire (French)* secretary, writing, table

desolate *adj.* **1.** abandoned, bare, barren bereft, derelict, empty, forsaken, lonely lonesome, unfrequented, uninhabited unoccupied, unused, vacant *Antonyms* frequented, full, occupied **2.** black, bleak, blue, cheerless, comfortless, dejected, depressed, depressing, despondent, disconsolate, dismal, dolorous, downcast, dreary, forlorn, funereal, gloomy, hurting, inconsolable, joyless, melancholy, miserable, sombre, sorrowful, tragic, wretched *Antonyms:* cheerful, happy, joyous, lighthearted

desolation *n.* **1.** bareness, barrenness, bleakness, desert, desolateness, isolation, solitariness, solitude, waste, wilderness, wildness **2.** annihilation, destruction, devastation, dissolution, extinction, ruin, ruination, wreckage **3.** anguish, dejection, despair, distress, gloom, gloominess, loneliness, melancholy, misery, sadness, unhappiness, woe, wretchedness

despair *n.* anguish, dashed hopes, dejection, depression, desperation, despondency, discouragement, disheartenment, ennui, forlornness, gloom, hopelessness, melancholy, misery, ordeal, pain, sorrow, trial, tribulation, *Weltschmerz (German)*, wretchedness – *v.* abandon hope, drop, give up, lose faith *or* heart *or* hope *or* meaning, relinquish, renounce, resign, surrender, yield

despairing *adj.* anxious, blue, brokenhearted, dejected, depressed, despondent, disconsolate, downcast, forlorn, hopeless, inconsolable, melancholy, miserable, oppressed, pessimistic, sad, suicidal, upset, wretched

desperado *n.* bandit, convict, criminal, cutthroat, fugitive, gangster, gunman, hoodlum, lawbreaker, mugger, outlaw, ruffian, thug, tough

desperate *adj.* **1.** atrocious, audacious, dangerous, daring, death-defying, foolhardy, hasty, headlong, headstrong, impetuous, incautious, madcap, precipitate, rash, reckless, risky, scandalous **2.** despairing, despondent, downcast, forlorn, futile, gone, hard up *(Nonformal)*, hopeless, inconsolable, irrecoverable, irretrievable, useless, vain, wretched **3.** acute, critical, crucial, dire, drastic, extreme, fierce, furious, grave, great, intense, terrible, urgent, vehement, vicious, violent

desperately *adv.* **1.** carelessly, dangerously, dramatically, gravely, harmfully, like mad *(Nonformal)*, perilously, seriously, severely **2.** appallingly, badly, fearfully, frightfully, hopelessly, shockingly

desperation *n.* **1.** agony, anguish, anxiety, concern, dejection, depression, desolation, despair, despondency, discomfort, distraction, distress, fear, gloom, grief, heartache, hopelessness, melancholy, misery, pain, sorrow, torture, trouble, unhappiness, worry **2.** acuteness, crisis, emergency, gravity, immediacy, pressure of necessity, real need, urgency

despicable *adj.* abject, awful, base, beastly, cheap, contemptible, detestable, dirty, disgraceful, disreputable, hateful, ignominious, loathsome, low, mean, pitiful, reprehensible, scrofulous, scurvy, shameful, sleazy, slimy, sordid, vile, worthless, wretched *Antonyms:* admirable, honest, moral, noble, virtuous

despise *v.* abhor, abominate, contemn, deride, detest, disdain, disregard, eschew, execrate, flout, hate, loathe, put down, reject, renounce, repudiate, revile, run down, scorn, shun, slight, snub, spurn, trash *(Nonformal)*, undervalue *Antonyms:* admire, adore, cherish, esteem

despoil *v.* depredate, deprive, desecrate, desolate, destroy, devastate, dispossess, maraud, pillage, plunder, raid, rape, ravage, rifle, rob, sack, spoil, steal, strip, waste, wreak havoc, wreck

despondent *adj.* beside oneself, blue, dejected, depressed, despairing, disconsolate, discouraged, disheartened, dispirited, doleful, down, down in the dumps *(Nonformal)*, downcast, downhearted, forlorn, gloomy, glum, grieving, hopeless, low, melancholy, miserable, morose, mournful, sad, sorrowful, woebegone, wretched *Antonyms:* buoyant, cheerful, hopeful, glad, optimistic

despot *n.* autocrat, czar, dictator, monocrat, oppressor, satrap, tyrant *Nonformal:* mobocrat, slave driver

dessert *n.* sweet *Kinds of dessert:* apple pandowdy, baked Alaska, baklava, banana split, Bavarian cream, blancmange, blueberry grunt *(Nova Scotia)*, bombe, Boston cream pie, bread pudding, brown betty, cake, cassata, Charlotte russe, cobbler, compote, crème brûlé, crème caramel, crêpe suzette, custard, doughnut, duff, flan, floating island, flummery, frappé, frozen custard, frozen yogurt, fruit cup, gelato, glacé, granita, *halvah (Turkish)*, ice cream, Indian pudding, jambuster *(Winnipeg)*, Joe Louis *(Trademark)*, marrons glacés, meringue, millefeuille, mousse, mud pie, Nanaimo bar, parfait, Peach Melba, pudding, pumpkin pie, rice pudding, Sacher torte, sherbet, snow pudding, sorbet, soufflé, strawberry shortcake, strudel, sundae, tiramisu, trifle, vacherin, zabaglione *See also:* **doughnut, pastry, pie**

destabilize *v.* keel *or* knock over, unbalance, unhinge, unsettle, upset *Antonyms:* balance, sustain, prop, settle

destination *n.* aim, ambition, course, design, end, goal, harbour, intention, landing-place, object, objective, purpose, resting-place, station, target, terminal, terminus

destined *adj.* appointed, assigned, booked, bound, brewing, certain, chosen, closed, coming, compelled, compulsory, condemned, consigned, delegated, designated, determined, directed, doomed, foreordained, forthcoming, inescapable, inevitable, intended, looming, meant, ordained, overhanging, predestined, predetermined, prepared, sealed, scheduled, settled, slated, specified, stated, unavoidable

destiny *n.* afterlife, break *or* breaks, certainty, circumstance, conclusion, design, expectation, fate, fortune, future, inevitability, intention, karma, kismet, lot, luck, predestination, predetermination, prospect, serendipity, one's stars *(Nonformal)*

destitute *adj.* **1.** badly off, bankrupt, bereft, broke, cleaned out, deficient, deprived, devoid, distressed, drained, empty, hard up, impecunious, impoverished, indigent, insolvent, lacking, moneyless, needy, overdrawn, pauperized, penniless, penurious, pinched, poor, poverty-stricken, ruined, short, stone broke, wanting *Nonformal:* busted, dead *or* flat broke, dirt poor, seedy, strapped *Antonyms:* affluent, flush, opulent, rich, wealthy **2.** abandoned, defenceless, exposed, forsaken, helpless, naked, unprotected, unprovided, unsupplied, vulnerable *Antonyms:* guarded, protected

destroy *v.* abolish, abrogate, annihilate, annul, assassinate, beat, butcher, consume, crush, damage, decimate, deface, defeat, demolish, desecrate, desolate, despoil, devastate, dismantle, dispatch, dissolve, do away with, douse, efface, eliminate, end, eradicate, erase, excise, execute, exhaust, expunge, exterminate, extirpate, finish, kill, level, liquidate, massacre, murder, negate, nullify, obliterate, overturn, pillage, plunder, pull down, pulverize, ravage, raze, ruin, sabotage, sack, shatter, slaughter, slay, squash, squelch, stifle, subdue, suppress, torpedo, uproot, vitiate, wipe out, wreck *Nonformal:* axe, nuke, total, trash, waste *Antonyms:* build, create, manufacture, shape

destruction *n.* abolition, annihilation, bane, collapse, crackup, crash, crashing, crushing, damage, debacle, debris, demolition, devastation, disruption, dissolution, elimination, end, eradication, extermination, extinction, havoc, liquidation, litter, loss, massacre, mess, murder, obliteration, overthrow, pileup, ravaging, ruin, sacking, shipwreck, slaughter, slaying, subversion, undoing, wreck, wreckage *Antonyms:* conservation, creation, preservation

destructive *adj.* adverse, antagonistic, awful, baneful, barbarous, bloodthirsty, calamitous, cancerous, cankerous, catastrophic, corrosive, cutthroat, damaging, dangerous, deadly, deleterious, derogatory, detrimental, devastating, dire, disastrous, discrediting, distressing, dreadful, erosive, evil, fatal, fearful, harmful, hazardous, hurtful, injurious, intense, internecine, lethal, mortal, murderous, noxious, offensive, perilous, pernicious, pestilent, risky, ruinous, severe, treacherous, troublesome, ugly, wicked *Antonyms:* ameliorative, beneficial, constructive, helpful

desultory *adj.* aimless, arbitrary, capricious, chance, changeable, chaotic, digressive, disconnected, discursive, disorderly, errant, erratic, fitful, haphazard, inconsistent, inconstant, irregular, purposeless, rambling, random, roving, shifting, slapdash, spasmodic, unconnected, unmethodical, unsteady, unsystematic, wandering, willy-nilly *(Nonformal) Antonyms:* consistent, dedicated, diligent, steady

detach *v.* **1.** abstract, alienate, cut off, disaffiliate, disassemble, disassociate, disconnect, disengage, disentangle, disjoin, dismount, dissociate, disunite, divide, divorce, free, isolate, loose, loosen, part, remove, segregate, separate, sever, sunder, take apart, tear off, uncouple, unfasten, unhitch, withdraw *Antonyms:* attach, bind, connect, fasten, fetter **2.** dispatch, forward, move, send, ship out

detached *adj.* **1.** alienated, alone, apart, disconnected, discrete, disjoined, divided, free, freestanding, isolated, loose, loosened, marginalized, removed, separate, severed, single, unconnected *Antonyms:* bound, combined, connected, fastened **2.** abstract, aloof, apathetic, casual, cool, disinterested, dispassionate, distant, impartial, impersonal, indifferent, neutral, nonchalant, objective, remote, removed, reserved, unbiased, uncommitted, unconcerned, uncurious, uninvolved, unprejudiced, withdrawn *Antonyms:* biased, concerned, interested, involved, partisan

detachment *n.* **1.** aloofness, coolness, dreaminess, impartiality, incuriosity, indifference, neutrality, nonpartisanship, objectivity, preoccupation, remoteness, unconcern *Antonyms:* bias, influence, interest, worry **2.** army, body, detail, force, organization, party, patrol, special force, squad, task force, troop, unit **3.** disconnection, disengagement, disjoining, dissolution, disunion, divergence, division, divorce, partition, rupture, separation, severing, split-up *Antonyms:* confederacy, marriage, merger, union

detail *n.* **1.** aspect, component, design, element, fact, factor, feature, fine point, fraction, item, minor point, minutia, nicety, part, particular, peculiarity, point, portion, specific, specification, structure, technicality, trait, triviality *Antonyms:* aggregate, mass, sum, total **2.** exactness, fidelity, fussiness, meticulousness, rigour, scrupulousness, thoroughness *Antonyms:* carelessness, heedlessness, sloppiness **3.** army detail, assignment, body, detachment, duty, fatigue, force, group, organization, party, squad, troop – *v.* analyze, catalogue, communicate, delineate, depict, describe, designate, elaborate, embellish, enumerate, epitomize, exhibit, itemize, lay out, make clear, narrate, outline, particularize, portray, produce, recapitulate, recite, recount, rehearse, relate, report, reveal, set forth, show, specialize, specify, spell out, stipulate, summarize, tell, uncover

detailed *adj.* accurate, complete, complex, comprehensive, copious, definitive, developed, elaborate, exact, exhaustive, fine, inclusive, intricate, involved, itemized, meticulous, minute, narrow, nice, particular, precise, specific, thorough *Antonyms:* brief, compact, pithy, sketchy

detain *v.* apprehend, arrest, bog down, check, confine, constrain, curb, delay, hinder, hold, hold back, hold up, impede, inhibit, intern, keep, keep back, reserve, restrain, retain, retard, withhold *Antonyms:* free, liberate, release, unfetter

detect *v.* ascertain, disclose, discover, distinguish, encounter, espy, expose, find, identify, note, notice, observe, perceive, recognize, reveal, see, smoke out, spot, turn up, uncover, unearth, unmask

detection *n.* apprehension, disclosure, discovery, exposé, exposure, ferreting out, find, revelation, tracking down, uncovering, unearthing, unmasking

detective *n.* agent, analyst, constable, informer, investigator, plainclothes officer, police officer, private investigator, reporter, sergeant, spy *Nonformal:* dick, gumshoe, private eye, sleuth

detention *n.* apprehension, arrest, bust, confinement, custody, detainment, impediment, imprisonment, incarceration, internment, jail, jailing, keeping, quarantine, restraint, retention, withholding *Antonyms:* acquittal, emancipation, freedom, liberation, release

deter *v.* avert, block, caution, chill, dampen, daunt, discourage, dissuade, divert, forestall, frighten, hinder, hobble, impede, inhibit, obstruct, obviate, preclude, prevent, prohibit, restrain, rule *or* shut out, stop, turn off *Antonyms:* encourage, foster, support

detergent *n.* abstergent, cathartic, cleaner, cleaning agent, cleanser, detersive, purgative, purifier, soap, solvent

deteriorate *v.* adulterate, corrode, corrupt, crumble, debase, debilitate, decay, decline, decompose, degenerate, degrade, deprave, depreciate, descend, disintegrate, ebb, fade, fail, fall apart, flag, go, impair, injure, languish, lapse, lessen, lower, pervert, regress, retrograde, retrogress, rot, sink, skid, slide, spoil, undermine, vitiate, weaken, wear away, worsen *Nonformal:* downhill, lose it *Antonyms:* advance, convalesce, get better, improve, recover

deterioration *n.* abasement, adulteration, atrophy, corrosion, crumbling, debasement, decadence, decay, declension, declination, decline, decomposition, degeneration, degradation, depreciation, descent, devaluation, dilapidation, disintegration, dislocation, disrepair, downfall, downgrade, downturn, drop, fall, lapse, lessening, perversion, retrogression, rotting, ruin, slump, spoiling, vitiation, worsening *Antonyms:* amelioration, elevation, improvement, restoration

determination *n.* **1.** assurance, backbone, boldness, bravery, certainty, certitude, constancy, conviction, dauntlessness, decision, dedication, doggedness, dogmatism, firmness, fortitude, grit, independence, obstinacy, perseverance, persistence, purpose, purposefulness, resoluteness, resolution, resolve, steadfastness, stubbornness, tenacity, will power *Antonyms:* doubt, hesitation, indecision, vacillation **2.** conclusion, judgment, opinion, resolution, result, settlement, solution, verdict *Antonyms:* deadlock, stalemate, standstill **3.** aim, design, desire, direction, goal, intention, objective, purpose, will **4.** disclosure, discovery, revelation, unearthing

determine *v.* **1.** arbitrate, ascertain, certify, check, demonstrate, detect, discover, divine, establish, figure, hear, learn, see, tell, verify, work out *Antonyms:* ignore, neglect, overlook **2.** clinch, complete, conclude, decide, dispose, end, finish, halt, nail *or* pin down *(Nonformal)*, resolve, rule, settle, terminate, wind *or* wrap up **3.** actuate, bias, direct, incline, induce, influence, move, persuade, predispose, regulate, shape

determined *adj.* bent, decided, decisive, dogged, driven, earnest, firm, fixed, hell-bent for leather *(Nonformal)*, intent, obstinate, pat, persevering, persistent, purposeful, resolute, resolved, serious, settled, single-minded, steadfast, strong-minded, strong-willed, stubborn, tenacious, unhesitating *Antonyms:* disinterested, happy-go-lucky, indifferent, lax, unconcerned

deterrent *n.* barricade, bridle, check, curb, defence, discouragement, hindrance, impediment, leach, obstacle, preventative, rein, restraint, shackle

detest *v.* abhor, abominate, despise, dislike, execrate, hate, loathe, repudiate, scorn, spurn *Antonyms:* adore, cherish, love, relish

detestable *adj.* abhorred, abhorrent, abominable, accursed, atrocious, awful, despicable, disgusting, execrable, gross, hateable, heinous, horrid, loathsome, monstrous, obnoxious, odious, offensive, outrageous, repugnant, repulsive, revolting, rotten, shocking, sleazy, slimy, sorry, vile *Nonformal:* godawful, lousy, lowdown *Antonyms:* bewitching, charming, enchanting, irresistible

dethrone *v.* depose, disenthrone, dismiss, displace, impeach, oust, remove, topple, uncrown, unseat, unthrone

detonate *v.* bang, blast, blow up, bomb, bombard, burst, destroy, discharge, explode, fulminate, ignite, light, mushroom *(Nonformal)*, napalm, raid, rake, set off, shell, strafe, torpedo

detour *n.* alternate route, back road, branch, bypass, byroad, circuitous route, circumnavigation, circumvention, course, deviation, divergence, diversion, fork, roundabout way, secondary highway, service road, substitute, temporary route – *v.*

change course, deflect, redirect, reroute, shortstop *(Nonformal)*, turn aside

detract *v.* **1.** belittle, blister, cheapen, decrease, decry, depreciate, derogate, devaluate, diminish, discount, discredit, disesteem, lessen, lower, minimize, mudsling, pan, reduce, subtract, underrate, undervalue, withdraw *Nonformal:* knock, laugh at, put down, run *or* shoot down *Antonyms:* augment, enhance, reinforce, strengthen **2.** avert, deflect, distract, disturb, diverge, divert *Commonly misused:* **distract**

detraction *n.* abuse, aspersion, belittlement, calumny, damage, defamation, denigration, deprecation, disparagement, harm, hurt, injury, injustice, innuendo, insinuation, libel, lie, minimization, obloquy, pejorative, rap, revilement, ridicule, scandal, scurrility, slander, smear campaign *(Nonformal)*, tale, traducement, vilification, vituperation, wrong

detriment *n.* bane, damage, disability, disadvantage, drawback, handicap, harm, hindrance, hurt, impairment, injury, loss, prejudice, spoiling *Antonyms:* aid, assistance, help

detrimental *adj.* adverse, bad, baleful, damaging, deleterious, destructive, disadvantageous, disturbing, evil, harmful, hurtful, ill, inimical, injurious, mischievous, negative, nocuous, pernicious, prejudicial, unfavourable *Antonyms:* advantageous, beneficial, efficacious, helpful, salutary

devastate *v.* **1.** demolish, desolate, despoil, destroy, devour, level, loot, pillage, plunder, raid, ravage, raze, ruin, sack, smash, spoil, waste, wreck *Nonformal:* total, trash, **2.** confound, crush, humiliate, mortify, overwhelm, vanquish

devastation *n.* confusion, demolition, desolation, destruction, havoc, loss, pillage, plunder, reduction, rubble, ruin, ruination, waste

develop *v.* **1.** deepen, edify, enrich, evolve, flourish, grow up, improve, mature, mellow, ripen *Antonyms:* regress, worsen **2.** amplify, augment, broaden, cultivate, dilate, enlarge, extend, grow, heighten, intensify, lengthen, spread, stretch, widen *Antonyms:* shrink, stunt **3.** actualize, advance, beautify, build up, establish, exploit, finish, progress, prosper, reach, realize, thrive *Antonyms:* destroy, inhibit, ruin, stifle **4.** define, elaborate, explain, magnify, perfect, polish, promote, refine, strengthen, unfold, unfurl, work out

development *n.* **1.** addition, advancement, augmentation, boost, elaboration, enlargement, evolution, evolving, expansion, flowering, growth, improvement, increase, maturation, maturity, perfecting, progression, ripening, spreading, unfolding *Antonyms:* declension, recession, retardation, retrogression **2.** circumstance, event, eventuality, happening, incident, issue, materialization, occurrence, outcome, phenomenon, result, situation, upshot

deviant *adj.* abnormal, anomalous, atypical, different, divergent, freaky, irregular, off-key, perverse, preternatural, queer, twisted, unrepresentative, untypical, wayward *Nonformal:* bent, kinky *Antonyms:* conventional, normal, orthodox, straight, straightforward – *n.* **1.** dissenter, eccentric, heretic, miscreant, misfit, nonconformist *Nonformal:* freak, oddball **2.** debauchee, degenerate, lecher, molester, offender, pervert, sex fiend, sexual predator, voyeur

deviate *v.* **1.** angle *or* bear *or* edge off, break pattern, drift, err, stray, swerve, turn, turn aside, veer, wander **2.** contrast, deflect, depart, depart from, differ, digress, divagate, diverge, vary *Antonyms:* adhere, conform, correspond

deviation *n.* aberration, alteration, anomaly, breach, change, deflection, departure, detour, difference, digression, discrepancy, disparity, divergence, diversion, fluctuation, inconsistency, irregularity, modification, shift, turning, variance, variation

device *n.* **1.** accessory, apparatus, contraption, contrivance, creation, equipment, gadget, implement, instrument, invention, machine, mechanism, tackle, tool, utensil *Nonformal:* doohickey, gizmo, thingamajig, whatchamacallit **2.** artifice, clever move, craft, craftiness, cunningness, design, dodge, evasion, expedient, fake, feint, finesse, gambit, game, gimmick, improvisation, machination, manoeuvre, method, pattern, plan, plot, ploy, project, proposition, purpose, racket, ruse, scheme, shenanigan *(Nonformal)*, shift, stratagem, strategy, stunt, subterfuge, trap, trick, wile **3.** badge, crest, design, emblem, figure, insignia, logo, motif, motto, pattern, sign, slogan, symbol, token

devil *n.* demon, *diablo (Spanish)*, evil spirit, fiend, *Teufel (German)*, Adversary, Angel of Death, Apollyon, Asmodeus, Astaroth, Author *or* Father of Evil, Azazel, Beelzebub, Belial, Belphegor, *Eblis (Muslim)*, Evil Incarnate, Evil One, fallen angel, Father of Lies, His Satanic Majesty, Lucifer, Mammon, Mastema, Mephistopheles, Prince of Darkness, Satan, serpent, Tempter, Wicked One *Nonformal:* Old Harry, Old Ned, Old Nick, the Deuce, the Dickens

devilish *adj.* accursed, atrocious, bad, brutish, cloven-hoofed, cursed, damnable, demonic, detestable, diabolic, diabolical, evil, execrable, fiendish, hellish, infernal, iniquitous, Mephistophelian, nefarious, satanic, villainous, wicked *Antonyms:* angelic, godly, saintly

deviltry *n.* diablerie, diabolicalness, diabolism, evil, fiendishness, heinousness, hellishness, iniquity, knavery, malevolence, maliciousness, mischief, monkeybusiness *(Nonformal)*, nefariousness, rascality, roguery, sinfulness, sorcery, transgression, turpitude, vice, viciousness, villainy, wickedness, witchcraft *Antonyms:* goodness, moral excellence, virtue

devious *adj.* **1.** artful, crafty, deceitful, dishonest, dishonourable, duplicitous, errant, evasive, foxy, fraudulent, insincere, scheming, shady, shifty, shrewd, sly, surreptitious, tricky, underhanded, wily *Antonyms:* candid, forthright, honest, straightforward **2.** aberrant, irregular, meandering, rambling, straying, swerving, wandering, winding, writhing *Antonyms:* linear, straight, true

devise *v.* arrange, blueprint, brainstorm, cast, chart, conceive, concoct, construct, contrive, craft, create, design, discover, forge, form, formulate, frame, hatch, imagine, improvise, invent, machinate, make *or* think up, mastermind, plan, plot, prepare project, scheme, shape, spark, work ou *Nonformal:* dream *or* whip up, throv together

devoid *adj.* bare, barren, bereft, blank, deficient, denuded, destitute, empty, impoverished, innocent, lacking, needing, unprovided, vacant, vacuous, void, wanting, withou *Antonyms:* abounding, flush, full, replete

devote *v.* allot, apply, apportion, assign bestow, bless, commit, confide, consecrate consign, dedicate, donate, enshrine entrust, give, pledge, present, reserve, sanctify, vow

devoted *adj.* adherent, affectionate, ardent caring, committed, concerned, consecrated, constant, dear, dedicated, devout, doting, dutiful, faithful, fond, loyal, staunch steadfast, true, zealous *Antonyms:* disloyal, inconstant, indifferent, unfaithful

devotee *n.* adherent, admirer, aficionado amateur, believer, booster, disciple, enthusiast, fanatic, fancier, follower, habitué lover, promoter, supporter, votary *Nonformal:* fan, groupie, hanger-on, stage doo Johnnie *Antonyms:* critic, detractor

devotion *n.* **1.** adherence, adoration affection, allegiance, ardour, attachment commitment, constancy, dedication, deference, devotedness, devoutness, earnestness, enthusiasm, faithfulness, fervour fondness, intensity, love, loyalty, passion reverence, sanctity, zeal *Antonyms:* disregard, neglect, thoughtlessness **2.** communion, consecration, observance, piety praise, prayer, service, spirituality, thanksgiving, worship

devour *v.* **1.** absorb, bolt, consume, cram drink in, eat, enjoy, feast *or* feed on, gobble, gorge, go through, gulp, inhale, relish swallow, take, take in *Nonformal:* chow down, polish off, scarf, wolf **2.** annihilate atrophy, cripple, destroy, enfeeble, exhaust emaciate, impair, waste

devout *adj.* adherent, adoring, ardent, deep devoted, earnest, faithful, fervent, fervid genuine, heartfelt, holy, intense, orthodox passionate, pious, prayerful, profound, reli gious, reverent, serious, sincere, venerating, worshipping, zealous *Antonyms:* impious, indifferent, passive

dew *n.* condensation, dampness, droplets, fog, moisture, perspiration, steam, water, wet, wetness *Antonyms:* aridity, dehydration, dryness

dewy *adj.* **1.** damp, hydrated, moist, steamy, watery, wet **2.** budding, fresh, gentle, ingenuous, invigorating, new, pristine, refreshing, soft, tender, unblemished, undeveloped, vernal, youthful

dexterity *n.* ability, adroitness, aptitude, aptness, art, artistry, cleverness, craft, cunning, deftness, effortlessness, expertise, expertness, facility, finesse, handiness, ingenuity, knack, know-how, mastery, neatness, nimbleness, proficiency, readiness, skill, smoothness *Antonyms:* clumsiness, inability, incompetence, ineptitude

dexterous *adj.* able, active, adept, adroit, agile, apt, artful, clever, deft, expert, facile, handy, ingenious, masterly, neat, nimble, nimble-fingered, proficient, prompt, quick, skilful, skilled, slick, smooth *Nonformal:* crack, crackerjack, savvy *Antonyms:* awkward, clumsy, gauche

diabolic *adj.* atrocious, cruel, demonic, devilish, evil, fiendish, hellish, impious, infernal, Mephistophelean, monstrous, nasty, nefarious, satanic, serpentine, shocking, unpleasant, vile, villainous, wicked *Antonyms:* benevolent, gentle, good, kind

diagnose *v.* analyze, determine, distinguish, examine, identify, interpret, investigate, pinpoint, place, pronounce, recognize, spot, study, test

diagnosis *n.* analysis, diagnostics, conclusion, examination, identification, interpretation, investigation, opinion, prediction, prognostication, pronouncement, prophecy, scrutiny, summary

diagnostic *adj.* analytic, examining, identifying, investigatory, scrutinizing *Kinds of diagnostic examination:* biopsy, blood count, blood pressure, blood test, colonoscopy, electrocardiography, electroencephalography, mammography, Pap test *or* smear, urinalysis *Kinds of diagnostic picture or graph:* computer-assisted tomography *or* CAT scan, electrocardiogram *or* ECG *or* EKG, electroencephalogram *or* EEG, encephagraph, encephalogram, magnetic resonance image *or* MRI, MR scan, position emission tomography *or* PET scan, radiogram, radiograph, ultrasound, X-ray

diagonal *adj.* askew, bevelled, biased, crossed, inclining, kitty-cornered, oblique, skewed, slanted, transverse

diagonally *adv.* at an angle, aslant, cornerways, crossways, crosswise, kitty-corner, obliquely, slantways

diagram *n.* blueprint, chart, description, design, draft, drawing, figure, floor plan, game plan, illustration, layout, outline, plan, representation, sketch

dialect *n.* accent, argot, colloquialism, folk speech, idiom, jargon, *joual (Quebec)*, localism, patois, provincialism, regionalism, slang, tongue, vernacular

dialectic *adj.* analytic, argumentative, controversial, logical, persuasive, polemical, rational, rationalistic – *n.* argumentation, contention, debate, deduction, discussion, disputation, logic, persuasion, polemic, reasoning

dialogue *n.* address, article, chat, colloquy, communication, confabulation, conference, conversation, converse, discourse, discussion, dissertation, essay, exchange of views, homily, interchange, lecture, oration, parley, remarks, repartee, rhetoric, script, sermon, speech, talk, thesis, treatise, verbalization *Nonformal:* confab, get-together, huddle, spiel

diameter *n.* bore, breadth, broadness, calibre, length, measurement, thickness, width

diametrical *adj.* absolute, antipodal, antithetical, complete, conflicting, contrary, contrasting, counter, extreme, opposed, opposite *Antonyms:* related, similar

diamond *n.* carbon crystal, gem, mineral *Nonformal:* ring, rock *Kinds of diamond* *cut:* brilliant, briolette, double rose, Kohinoor, Marquise, Regent *or* Pitt, rose

diaphanous *adj.* chiffon, clear, delicate, filmy, fine, flimsy, gauzy, gossamer, light, limpid, see-through, sheer, thin, translucent, transparent *Antonyms:* cloudy, dark, murky, turbid

diary *n.* account, agenda, appointment book, chronicle, daily record, daybook, engagement book, journal, log, minutes, notebook, record, summary

diatribe *n.* abuse, castigation, criticism, denunciation, disputation, harangue, invective, jeremiad, objection, onslaught, philippic, revilement, screed, stricture, tirade, vituperation

dictate *n.* behest, bidding, command, decree, dictum, edict, fiat, injunction, law, mandate, order, precept, principle, requirement, rule, statute, word – *v.* **1.** bid, charge, command, control, decree, direct, enjoin, guide, impose, instruct, manage, ordain, order, prescribe, pronounce, rule **2.** account, compose, deliver, draft, emit, formulate, interview, orate, read, record, say, speak, talk, transmit, utter, verbalize

dictator *n.* absolutist, autocrat, caesar, chief, commander, czar, despot, disciplinarian, leader, lord, magnate, martinet, master, mogul, oligarch, oppressor, overlord, padshah, ringleader, ruler, satrap, slave driver *(Nonformal)*, sultan, taskmaster, tyrant

dictatorial *adj.* absolute, arbitrary, authoritarian, authoritative, autocratic, bossy, despotic, domineering, imperious, lordly, oppressive, overbearing, totalitarian, tyrannical *Antonyms:* democratic, egalitarian, suppliant, tolerant

dictatorship *n.* absolute rule, absolutism, authoritarianism, autocracy, coercion, despotism, fascism, monocracy, totalitarianism, tyranny, unlimited rule *Antonyms:* democracy, parliamentarianism

diction *n.* **1.** rhetoric, usage, vocabulary, wordage, words, word-usage **2.** articulation, delivery, elocution, eloquence, enunciation, expression, fluency, inflection, intonation, language, lingo, locution, oratory, parlance, phraseology, phrasing, pronunciation, rhetoric, speech, verbalism, verbiage, wording

dictionary *n.* lexicon, reference, wordbook *Kinds of dictionary:* bilingual, biographical, children's, college, desk, dialect, etymological, foreign-language, gazetteer, geographical, glossary, philosophy, psychology, rhyming, school, science, slang, standard, thesaurus, unabridged, usage

dictum *n.* **1.** assertion, command, declaration, decree, dictate, edict, fiat, order, pronouncement **2.** adage, aphorism, axiom, maxim, moral, motto, precept, proverb, rule, saw, saying, truism

didactic *adj.* academic, advisory, edifying, educational, enlightening, exhortative, expository, homiletic, instructive, moralizing, pedagogic, pedantic, preachy, preceptive, sermonizing

die *v.* **1.** decease, demise, depart, disappear, drop dead, end, expire, fall, finish, pass away, perish, succumb, vanish *Nonformal:* bite the dust, buy the farm, check *or* conk out, croak, dirt map, flatline, kick the bucket, meet one's maker **2.** abate, break down, cease, crumble, decay, decline, deteriorate, dilapidate, diminish, droop, dwindle, ease off, ebb, evanesce, fade, fade away *or* out, fail, halt, lapse, let up, lose power, melt away, pass, recede, retrograde, rot, run down, run low *or* out, sink, slacken, stop, subside, wane, weaken, wear away, wilt, wither *Nonformal:* fizzle, peter out *Antonyms:* flourish, grow, wax

diet *n.* **1.** daily bread, drink, eats, edibles, fare, food, nourishment, provisions, rations, snack, sustenance, viands, victuals, vittles *(Nonformal)* **2.** abstinence, calorie counting, fast, regimen, restriction, starvation, weight-loss, weight-reduction *Kinds of diet:* balanced, diabetic, high-calorie, high-vitamin, liquid, low-calorie, low-carbohydrate, low-fat, low-salt, low-sodium, macrobiotic, reducing, soft, vegetarian **3.** assembly, body, board, chamber, commission, congress, council, court, legislature, parliament, provincial *or* national assembly, regulatory body, session – *v.* abstain, count calories, fast, go without, lose weight, reduce, slim, weight-watch *Antonyms:* binge, feast, gormandize

differ *v.* bicker, clash, conflict, contend, contradict, debate, demur, depart from, deviate, disagree, dispute, dissent, diverge, divide, fight, fall out, object, oppose, quarrel, reverse, squabble, take exception *or* issue, vary *Nonformal:* bump heads, lock horns *Antonyms:* accord, acquiesce, agree, coincide, harmonize

difference *n.* **1.** contrast, deviation, discrepancy, dissimilarity, divergence, incongruity, inconsistency, inequality **2.** alteration, change, departure, modification, transformation, variation **3.** differentia *(Latin)*, exception, foible, idiosyncrasy, oddity, peculiarity, quirk, singularity, specialness, uniqueness **4.** gradation, nuance, shade, subtlety, tinge, trace **5.** balance, deficit, excess, leftover, remainder, residue, rest, shortfall, surplus **6.** altercation, argument, clash, controversy, disagreement, discord, dispute, dissidence, falling out, parting of ways, quarrel, rupture, schism, spat, squabble, tiff *Nonformal:* blowup, run-in, words **7.** bone of contention, cause, issue, matter, problem, question **8.** adjudication, choice, decision, determination, discrimination, distinction, judgment *Commonly misused:* **deference**

different *adj.* **1.** at odds, conflicting, contradictory, contrary, contrasting, deviating, differing, discordant, discrepant, disparate, dissimilar, dissonant, divergent, diverse, incompatible, incongruous, inconsistent, irreconcilable, mismatched, opposing, opposite, separate, unequal, unlike, unrelated, varied *Antonyms:* identical, similar, uniform **2.** altered, changed, made over, modified, re-engineered, retooled, re-vamped, transmogrified **3.** distinct, distinctive, eccentric, irregular, outstanding, particular, peculiar, quirky, strange, unique, unusual, variant *Antonyms:* normal, standard **4.** assorted, miscellaneous, mixed, motley, multifarious, sundry, various

differentiate *v.* characterize, choose, contrast, demarcate, discern, discriminate, distinguish, indicate, separate, set apart, sever, sort, split hairs *(Nonformal)*, understand

differently *adv.* abnormally, alternatively, antithetically, contrarily, discordantly, disparately, dissimilarly, distinctively, divergently, diversely, incompatibly, incongruously, individually, negatively, otherwise, separately, uniquely, variously *Antonyms:* concordantly, similarly

difficult *adj.* **1.** abstract, abstruse, arduous, baffling, bewildering, challenging, complex, complicated, confounding, confusing, cumbersome, dark, deep, demanding, enigmatic, entangled, esoteric, exacting, exhausting, fatiguing, formidable, gruelling, hard, hidden, inexplicable, intricate, involved, irksome, knotty, laborious, labyrinthine, mysterious, mystical, mystifying, obscure, onerous, oppressive, paradoxical, perplexing, pressing, problematic, profound, puzzling, rigorous, severe, stressful, subtle, tangled, taxing, thorny, ticklish, tough, tricky, trying, unclear, unfathomable, unintelligible, vexing, wearisome, weighty *Nonformal:* backbreaking, heavy sledding, high maintenance, sticky *Antonyms:* light, manageable, obvious, straightforward, uncomplicated **2.** bloody-minded *(Nonformal)*, boorish, fractious, intractable, obdurate, obstinate, obstreperous, pigheaded, prickly, recalcitrant, refractory, rigid, stubborn, tiresome, troublesome, unmanageable *Antonyms:* accommodating, amenable, cooperative, pleasant

difficulty *n.* ado, adversity, aggravation, alarm, anxiety, awkwardness, block, bother, bottleneck, catch, check, complexity, complication, concern, conundrum, crisis, deadlock, delay, dilemma, discomfiture, disquiet, distress, disturbance, drawback, embarrassment, fear, frustration, grievance, hardship, hitch, holdup, imbroglio, impasse, impediment, interference, interruption, irritation, knot, mess, muddle, nuisance, obstacle, obstruction, perplexity, predicament, pressure, problem, provocation, puzzle, quagmire, quandary, setback, snag, strain, struggle, stumbling block, tribulation, trouble, turmoil, undoing, unease, vexation, vicissitude, weight, worry *Nonformal:* botheration, bug, downside, fix, hassle, kettle of fish, pickle, stew, tight spot

diffidence *n.* bashfulness, constraint, doubt, fear, hesitancy, hesitation, humility, insecurity, meekness, modesty, reluctance, reserve, self-consciousness, self-doubt, sheepishness, shyness, timidity, timidness *Antonyms:* assurance, boldness, courage, self-confidence

diffident *adj.* bashful, chary, constrained, coy, demure, distrustful, doubtful, flinching, hesitant, humble, insecure, meek, modest, reluctant, reserved, retiring, self-conscious, self-effacing, sheepish, shrinking, shy, suspicious, timid, timorous, unassertive, unassuming, unobtrusive, unsure, withdrawn *Antonyms:* abrasive, in your face *(Nonformal)*, obnoxious, pompous

diffuse *adj.* **1.** bumbling, circumlocutory, copious, diffusive, digressive, discursive, exuberant, lavish, lengthy, long, long-winded, loose, loquacious, meandering, profuse, prolix, rambling, redundant, vague, verbose, waffling, windy, wordy *Antonyms:* apposite, brief, concentrated, succinct, terse **2.** catholic, circulated, dispersed, disseminated, distributed, expanded, extended, general, propagated, radiated, scattered, separated, spread out, strewn, universal, widespread — *v.* broadcast, circulate, disperse, disseminate, distribute, permeate, pour, publish, spread, radiate, scatter, sow

diffusion *n.* **1.** broadcast, circulation, dispersal, dispersion, dissemination, dissipation, distribution, expansion, propaganda, propagation, scattering, spread **2.** loquaciousness, prolixity, verbiage, verbosity, wordiness

dig *n.* criticism, comment, put down, remark *Nonformal:* flak, jab, poke, shot, snarky comment, zinger – *v.* **1.** bore, burrow, channel, clean, deepen, dredge, drill, entrench, excavate, furrow, hoe, hollow, mine, penetrate, pierce, rout, scoop out, shovel, till, tunnel, undermine **2.** drive, gouge, jab, jog, nudge, plunge, poke, prod, punch, ram, sink, stab, stick, thrust **3.** analyze, delve into, discover, exhume, expose, extract, extricate, inquire, investigate, look into, probe, research, retrieve, root, search, sift, study, uncover, unearth

digest *n.* abridgement, abstract, brief, compendium, compilation, condensation, précis, sketch, summary, survey, synopsis – *v.* **1.** absorb, consume, dissolve, eat, incorporate, swallow, take **2.** analyze, assimilate, consider, contemplate, deliberate, grasp, master, meditate, ponder, study, take in, think about *or* over, understand **3.** abide, bear, brook, endure, stand, stomach, suffer, swallow, tolerate, undergo

digestion *n.* **1.** absorption, assimilation, conversion, eupepsia, incorporation, ingestion *Antonyms:* dyspepsia, indigestion **2.** cognizance, comprehension, grasp, integration, mastery, understanding

digging *n.* burrowing, delving, excavating, furrowing, tunnelling, unearthing *Kinds of digging tool:* auger, backhoe, dibble, hoe, mattock, pickaxe, piton, plough, shovel, spade

digit *n.* **1.** appendage, claw, extremity, feeler, finger, phalange, toe **2.** figure, integer, notation, number, numeral, symbol, whole number

dignified *adj.* aristocratic, august, classic, classical, courtly, cultured, decorous, distinguished, elegant, eminent, exalted, extravagant, formal, gentlemanly, grand, grave, high-flown, honourable, imperial, imposing, kingly, ladylike, lofty, lordly, magisterial, noble, ornate, pompous, pretentious, princely, proud, queenly, regal, reserved, respected, solemn, sombre, stately, sublime, superior, upright *Antonyms:* crass, inelegant, unbecoming, undignified, vulgar

dignify *v.* adorn, advance, aggrandize, distinguish, elevate, ennoble, exalt, glorify, grace, honour, magnify, praise, prefer, promote, raise *Antonyms:* deride, jeer, scorn

dignity *n.* character, consequence, courtliness, culture, decency, decorum, distinction, elevation, eminence, ethics, etiquette, excellence, glory, grace, grandeur, gravity, greatness, hauteur, honour, importance, loftiness, majesty, merit, nobleness, poise, prestige, propriety, quality, rank, regard, renown, respectability, seemliness, self-respect, significance, solemnity, standing, state, stateliness, station, stature, status, sublimity, virtue, worth

digress *v.* depart, deviate, diverge, meander, ramble, roam, stray, swerve, wander

digression *n.* aside, circumlocution, departure, detour, deviation, divergence, diversion, *divertissement (French)*, drifting, embellishment, excursion, improvisation, sidetrip, variation

dike *n.* aboideau, bank, barrier, breakwater, bulwark, dam, ditch, earthwork, embankment, floodgate, gutter, levee, moat, obstruction, ridge, trench, wall, waterway

dilapidated *adj.* battered, broken-down, damaged, decayed, decrepit, dishevelled, impaired, marred, neglected, old, ramshackle, ratty, rickety, ruined, rundown, seedy, shabby, threadbare, tumbledown, uncared for, unkempt, weatherbeaten, well used, worn, worn-out *Nonformal:* beat-up, dog-eared *Antonyms:* new, repaired, restored, shiny

dilate *v.* amplify, augment, broaden, develop, distend, enlarge, expand, expatiate, expound, extend, increase, inflate, lengthen, prolong, protract, stretch, swell, widen *Antonyms:* compress, constrict, contract, narrow, shrink

dilatory *adj.* dallying, delaying, laggard, late, lax, lazy, lethargical, lingering, loitering, neglectful, negligent, procrastinating, remiss, slack, slow, sluggish, tardy, tarrying, time-wasting, unhurried *Antonyms:* prompt, punctual

dilemma *n.* bind, Catch-22, corner, crisis, difficulty, embarrassment, fix, hole, impasse, jam, mess, mire, perplexity, plight, predicament, problem, puzzle, quandary, spot, strait *Nonformal:* between a rock and a hard place, box, pickle, the lady or the tiger

dilettante *n.* aesthete, amateur, connoisseur, dabbler, hobbiest, nonprofessional, trifler

diligence *n.* **1.** activity, alertness, application, assiduity, assiduousness, attention, attentiveness, briskness, care, carefulness, commitment, constancy, earnestness, exertion, heedfulness, industry, intensity, intent, intentness, perseverance, rigour, vigour **2.** carriage, coach, conveyance, stagecoach

diligent *adj.* active, assiduous, attentive, busy, careful, conscientious, constant, determined, dogged, dutiful, earnest, fastidious, hardworking, indefatigable, industrious, laborious, painstaking, persevering, persistent, studious, tireless, zealous *Antonyms:* careless, dilatory, inconstant, indifferent, lazy

dilute *v.* adulterate, alter, attenuate, cut, decrease, deliquesce, denature, diffuse, diminish, doctor *(Nonformal)*, irrigate, lessen, liquefy, mitigate, mix, moderate, modify, qualify, reduce, shave, temper, thin, water, weaken *Antonyms:* concentrate, condense, focus, fortify, intensify

diluted *adj.* adulterated, cut, impaired, impoverished, light, reduced, thinned, watered down, watery, weak, weakened *Nonformal:* doctored, wishy-washy

dim *adj.* **1.** blurred, cloudy, dark, darkish, dingy, dreary, dusk, faded, faint, flat, grey, indistinct, lacklustre, lightless, matte, monotonous, murky, muted, obscured, overcast, pale, poorly lit, shadowy, tarnished, unclear *Antonyms:* bright, clear, cloudless, fair **2.** dense, doltish, dull, dumb, obtuse, slow, stupid, thick, torpid, unintelligent, weak-minded **3.** depressing, disapproving, discouraging, gloomy, sceptical, sombre, suspicious, unfavourable, unpromising – *v.* becloud, blur, cloud, darken, dull, eclipse, fade, fog, haze, muddy, obfuscate, obscure, pale

dimension *n.* **1.** ambit, amplitude, area, breadth, bulk, capacity, depth, extent, height, length, magnitude, measure, measurement, proportion, range, reach, scale, scope, size, thickness, volume, width **2.** aspect, facet, factor, issue, phase, side

diminish *v.* **1.** abate, abbreviate, abridge, alleviate, atrophy, attenuate, contract, crop, curtail, cut, decay, decline, decrease, dilute, dim, drain, drop, dwindle, ebb, erode, fade, impair, lessen, lighten, lower, mitigate, moderate, narrow, recede, reduce, shrink, shrivel, slacken, subside, taper, temper, truncate, wane, weaken, wither *Antonyms:* amplify, enhance, enlarge, heighten, increase **2.** abuse, belittle, decry, demean, depreciate, detract from, devalue, minimize, put down *Nonformal:* badmouth, dump on, write off

diminutive *adj.* bantam, dwarfed, Lilliputian, little, micro, miniature, minute, petite, small, tiny, undersized, wee *Nonformal:* itsy-bitsy, pint-sized, teeny *Antonyms:* big, colossal, enormous, giant

din *n.* boisterousness, brouhaha, buzz, cacophony, clamour, clangour, clash, clatter, commotion, confusion, crash, dissonance, jangle, outcry, pandemonium, percussion, racket, row, shout, sound, stridency, tumult, uproar *Antonyms:* quiet, silence, tranquility

dine *v.* banquet, break bread, breakfast, consume, eat, feast, feed, fête, gluttonize, gorge, gourmandize, lunch, *manger (French)*, sup, tuck in *Nonformal:* pig out, stuff one's face *Antonyms:* fast, starve

diner *n.* bistro, booth, cafe, cafeteria, canteen, coffee shop, concession, dining car, fast-food outlet, greasy spoon *(Nonformal)*, grill, lunch counter, lunchroom, lunch wagon, quick-lunch, restaurant, roadhouse, sandwich shop, snack bar

dingy *adj.* cheerless, colourless, dark, dim, dirty, discoloured, dismal, drab, dreary, dull, faded, gloomy, grimy, grubby, grungy *(Nonformal)*, hazy, leaden, lacklustre, muddy, murky, obscure, rundown, seedy, shabby, shadowy, smeared, smoggy, soiled, sooty, tenebrous, worn *Antonyms:* bright, cheerful, glittering, luminous, radiant

dinner *n.* **1.** din-din *(Nonformal)*, nourishment, potluck, meal, repast, spread, supper **2.** banquet, feast, fête, party, roast

dinosaur *n.* extinct reptile, ornithischia, saurischia *Kinds of dinosaur:* Acrocanthosaur, Albertosaur, Allosaur, Ankylosaur, Apatosaur, Argentinosaur, Brachiosaur, Brontosaur, Camarasaur, Champsosaur, Compsognathus, Daspletosaur, Deinonychus, Dilophosaur, Diplodocus, Dromiceiomimus, Dryosaur, Edmontosaur, Eoraptor, Hadrosaur, Hypacrosaur, Hypsilophodont, Iguanodontid, Kentrosaur, Lambeosaur, Maiasaur, Ornithomimid, Orodromeus, Pachycephalosaur, Parasaurolophus, Plateosaur, Protoceratops, Saltasaur, Saurolophus, Seismosaur, Stegoceras, Stegosaur, Supersaur, Titanosaur, Triceratops, Troodon, Tyrannosaur, Tyrannosaurus Rex, Ultrasaur, Utahraptor, Velociraptor

dip *n.* **1.** basin, concavity, decline, declivity, depression, descent, downswing, downtrend, drop, fall, fall-off, hole, hollow, incline, lowering, pitch, sag, sink, sinkhole, slip, slope, slump **2.** concoction, mixture, preparation, sauce *Kinds of dip:* baba ghanouj, blue cheese, cheese, chip, clam, fondue, hummus, French onion, guacamole, oil, salsa, shrimp, sour cream and onion, spinach, tahini, tapenade, tzatziki **3.** bath, dive, douche, drenching, dunking, immersion, plunge, skinny dip *(Nonformal)*, soak, soaking, submersion, swim – *v.* **1.** bend, decline, descend, disappear, droop, fade, fall, lower, nose-dive, plummet, plunge, recede, sag, sink, skew, skid, slant, slip, slope, slump, spiral, subside, swoop, tilt, tumble, veer **2.** bail, bucket, decant, dish, draft off, draw *or* draw out, dredge, handle, ladle, lift, offer, reach into, scoop, shovel, spoon, strain **3.** baptize, bathe, douse, drench, immerse, irrigate, moisten, plunge, put in, rinse, soak, steep, submerge, submerse, wash, water, wet

diploma *n.* authority, award, certificate, charter, commission, confirmation, credentials, degree, document, honour, parchment, recognition, sheepskin, voucher

diplomacy *n.* **1.** adroitness, delicacy, discernment, discretion, grace, prudence, skill, sophistication, tact **2.** foreign affairs, international relations, negotiations, statesmanship *Kinds of diplomacy:* appeasement, balance of power, brinkmanship, colonialism, containment, détente, deterrence, dollar, entente, expansionism, imperialism, isolationism, manifest destiny, mercantilism, militarism, neocolonialism, neutralism, peaceful coexistence, peace offensive, protectionism *Nonformal:* good-neighbour policy, gunboat diplomacy, open-door policy, shuttle diplomacy

diplomat *n.* agent, agent-general, ambassador, attaché, *chargé d'affaires (French)*, chef de mission, conciliator, consul, embassy, emissary, envoy, go-between, high commissioner, intermediary, legate, mediator, minister, moderator, negotiator, nuncio, plenipotentiary, statesman, stateswoman

diplomatic *adj.* **1.** adept, civil, courteous, delicate, discreet, discerning, judicious, perspicacious, poised, polite, politic, prudent, sensitive, strategic, suave, subtle, tactful, thoughtful, urbane *Antonyms:* impolitic, indelicate, insensitive, rude, tactless **2.** ambassadorial, consular, governmental, ministerial, political

dire *adj.* **1.** alarming, appalling, awful, calamitous, catastrophic, deplorable, depressing, disastrous, dismal, dreadful, fateful, fearful, frightful, gloomy, grievous, grim, heartbreaking, horrible, horrid, immoderate, inauspicious, lamentable, ominous, oppressing, portentous, regrettable, ruinous, shocking, terrible, unfortunate, unpropitious *Antonyms:* beneficial, good, helpful **2.** acute, desperate, drastic, emergency, extreme, imperative, pressing, urgent *Antonyms:* gradual, secondary

direct *adj.* **1.** blunt, candid, direct, downright, explicit, express, forthright, frank, honest, outspoken, plain, primary, sincere, straight, unconcealed, undisguised, unreserved *Antonyms:* ambiguous, devious, sly, subtle **2.** continuous, lineal, linear, shortest, straight, through, true, unbroken, undeviating, uninterrupted, unswerving *Antonyms:* circuitous, crooked – *v.* **1.** administer, advise, aim, boss, charge, command, conduct, control, dictate, dominate, escort, govern, guide, handle, head, head up, influence, instruct, lead, manage, mastermind, operate, order, oversee, pilot, point, present, preside over, regulate, rule, set, shepherd, show, steer, superintend, supervise, target, teach, tell **2.** address, designate, inscribe, label, mail, mark, route, send

direction *n.* **1.** aim, angle, aspect, bearing, bent, bias, course, current, drift, end, inclination, objective, orientation, outlook, path, range, road, route, slant, standpoint, tack, tendency, tenor, track, trajectory, trend, way **2.** administration, charge, command, control, directive, government, guidance, guidelines, leadership, management, ministration, regulation, supervision **3.** advice, advisement, instruction, prescription, recommendation, specification, tip **4.** assignment, briefing, notification, plan, orders, summons

directive *n.* charge, command, communication, decree, dictate, edict, mandate, message, notice, order, ordinance, ruling, ukase, word

directly *adv.* **1.** candidly, face-to-face, honestly, literally, openly, plainly, pointblank, straightforwardly, truthfully, unequivocally **2.** at once, first off, forthwith, hastily, immediately, instantaneously, instantly, presently, promptly, pronto *(Nonformal)*, quickly, right away, shortly, soon, speedily, straightaway

director *n.* administrator, chair, chief, conductor, controller, executive, executive officer, governor, head, key player, kingpin *(Nonformal)*, leader, manager, organizer, overseer, president, principal, supervisor

directory *n.* index, listing *Kinds of directory:* almanac, atlas, Baedeker, business, city, gazetteer, guidebook, handbook, phone book *(Nonformal)*, reference book, register, roadbook, roster, telephone book, white pages, yellow pages

dirge *n.* chant, cry, elegy, funeral song, hymn, jeremiad, keen, lament, march, monody, requiem, song, threnody

dirt *n.* **1.** dust, earth, loam, mud, soil **2.** adulteration, blemish, blight, blot, blur, contamination, corruption, debris, defilement, dregs, dross, excrement, film, filth, foreign matter, foulness, garbage, grime, grit, impurity, infection, leavings, litter, lumps, mire, muck, offal, pollution, powder, refuse, remains, residue, rottenness, rubbish, rubble, sand, scraps, sediment, slime, slop, smear, smudge, soiling, soot, spoilage, stain, sweepings, swill, waste *Nonformal:* crud, gook, gunk, scuzz **3.** gossip, information, knowledge, news, scoop, story, word *Nonformal:* dope, lowdown **4.** immorality, indecency, obscenity, pornography, smut

dirty *adj.* **1.** besmirched, contaminated, corrupt, decayed, defiled, dingy, discoloured, dusty, faded, fetid, filthy, foul, fouled, greasy, grimy, grubby, impure, messy, mucky, muddy, murky, polluted, scruffy, scummy, smeared, smudged, soiled, sooty, spattered, spotted, stained, sullied, tainted, unclean, unhygienic, unsanitary, unwashed *Nonformal:* grungy, icky, yucky *Antonyms:* clean, pure, sanitized **2.** contemptible, despicable, low, mean, nasty, scrofulous, vile *Antonyms:* friendly, kind, nice **3.** blue *(Nonformal)*, coarse, immoral, impure, lascivious, lewd, licentious, obscene, pornographic, ribald, risqué, salacious, scatological, smutty, sordid, vulgar *Antonyms:* moral, reputable, restrained, upright – *v.* **1.** bedaub, befoul, begrime, besmirch, blacken, blemish, blotch, contaminate, darken, dim, discolour, encrust, foul, grime, mar, mark, muddy, pollute, rot, rust, smear, smirch, smudge, smutch, soil, spoil, spot, stain, taint, tar, tarnish *Antonyms:* clean, sanitize, sterilize, tidy **2.** bastardize, blot, corrupt, damage, debase, decay, defame, defile, pervert, sully *Antonyms:* glorify, honour

disability *n.* affliction, ailment, ataxia, complaint, defect, detriment, disablement, disadvantage, disorder, disqualification, drawback, enervation, enfeeblement, feebleness, handicap, impairment, impotency, inability, incapacity, incompetency, infirmity, injury, lack, malady, palsy, paralysis, weakness

disable *v.* batter, debilitate, cripple, disarm, hamstring, handicap, hurt, immobilize, impair, incapacitate, mangle, neutralize, paralyze, ruin, sabotage, shatter, spoil, take out, undermine, weaken, wreck *Nonformal:* clip one's wings, hog-tie

disabled *adj.* broken down, challenged, hamstrung, handicapped, helpless, hurt, impotent, incapacitated, infirm, laid up, maimed, mangled, out of service, paralyzed, paraplegic, quadraplegic, sidelined, silenced, stalled, unable, weakened, wounded, wrecked *Antonyms:* able-bodied, fit, hale, healthy

disadvantage *n.* burden, damage, defect, detriment, difficulty, disservice, drawback, fault, flaw, handicap, hardship, hindrance, impediment, injury, liability, limitation, loss, minus, nuisance, obstacle, prejudice, problem, snag, stumbling block, weakness *Antonyms:* advantage, benefit, convenience, help, profit

disadvantaged *adj.* alienated, boxed in, cornered, deprived, destitute, discriminated against, disenfranchised, downtrodden, forgotten, handicapped, hard up, impoverished, locked out, marginalized, needy, poor, struggling, underprivileged, victimized, vulnerable *Antonyms:* endowed, powerful, rich

disadvantageous *adj.* adverse, contrary, damaging, deleterious, detrimental, embarrassing, harmful, ill-timed, inconvenient, inopportune, prejudicial, unfavourable, unhelpful, unprofitable *Antonyms:* beneficial, expedient, favourable, profitable

disaffect *v.* agitate, alienate, antagonize, discompose, disquiet, disturb, disunite, divide, estrange, repel, upset, wean *Antonyms:* attract, allure, entice

disaffected *adj.* alienated, antagonistic, discontented, disloyal, dissatisfied, estranged, hostile, mutinous, rebellious, revolutionary, seditious, unfriendly *Antonyms:* agreeable, friendly, supportive

disaffection *n.* alienation, animosity, antagonism, aversion, breach, disagreement, discontent, disloyalty, estrangement, hatred, hostility, repugnance, resentment, unfriendliness

disagree *v.* **1.** break with, contend, differ, dispute, dissent, diverge, part company, sever relations, take issue, think differently **2.** argue, bicker, cross swords, fall out, feud, fight, lace *or* rip into *(Nonformal)*, quarrel **3.** buck *(Nonformal)*, clash, conflict, contradict, contravene, fail to conform, fly in the face of, run counter to **4.** bother, disturb, nauseate, offend, sicken, trouble

disagreeable *adj.* annoying, awful, bad, bad-tempered, bellicose, brusque, cantankerous, churlish, contentious, contrary, cross, difficult, disgusting, disobliging, displeasing, disputatious, distasteful, distressing, grouchy, ill-natured, irritable, nasty, obnoxious, offensive, peevish, pettish, petulant, querulous, repellent, repugnant, repulsive, rotten, rude, snappy, sour, surly, ugly, unappetizing, unfriendly, ungracious, unhappy, uninviting, unlikeable, unpalatable, unpleasant, upsetting, waspish, whiny, woeful *Antonyms:* agreeable, congenial, delightful, friendly, pleasant

disagreement *n.* altercation, animosity, antagonism, argument, beef, bickering, breach, break, clash, conflict, contention, contest, controversy, debate, difference, discord, dissent, diversity, division, falling out, fight, friction, hostility, incompatibility, incongruity, inconsistency, misunderstanding, opposition, quarrel, schism, spat, split, squabble, strife, wrangle *Antonyms:* accord, agreement, correspondence, harmony, unity

disallow *v.* ban, bar, cancel, censor, deny, disavow, disclaim, dismiss, embargo, exclude, forbid, kill, nix *(Nonformal)*, prohibit, proscribe, rebuff, refuse, reject, repudiate, veto, withhold *Antonyms:* authorize, grant, permit, sanction

disappear *v.* **1.** dissipate, dissolve, ebb, erode, evanesce, evaporate, fade, melt away, recede, sink, vanish *Antonyms:* appear, materialize, reappear **2.** abscond, escape, flee, fly, leave, retreat, take flight, vacate, vamoose *(Nonformal)*, withdraw **3.** depart, die, exit, pass, pass away, perish

disappearance *n.* departure, desertion, disappearing act, disintegration, dispersal, dissipation, dissolution, ebbing, escape, evanescence, evaporation, exit, exodus, extinction, extirpation, fading, loss, melting, receding, removal, vanishing, withdrawal

disappoint *v.* **1.** disenchant, disillusion, dismay, dissatisfy, fail, put out *(Nonformal)* **2.** balk, block, circumvent, deceive, defeat, foil, frustrate, hinder, thwart **3.** abandon, desert, forsake *Nonformal:* leave in the lurch, stand up

disappointed *adj.* **1.** blue, cheerless, crestfallen, dejected, depressed, despondent, disconsolate, discouraged, disheartened, disillusioned, dispirited, distressed, down, downcast, heartbroken, inconsolable, low, morose, sad, saddened, shattered **2.** baffled, blocked, checked, contravened, defeated, foiled, frustrated, let down, outsmarted, shot down *(Nonformal)* **3.** angry, annoyed, disgruntled, displeased, dissatisfied, irked, sour, unhappy, upset *Nonformal:* in a blue funk, ticked off

disappointment *n.* **1.** blow, defeat, comedown, failure, fiasco, letdown, setback *Nonformal:* bummer, bust, calamity, disaster, fizzle, non-event, washout **2.** chagrin, despondency, discouragement, distress, pain, regret, sadness, sorrow, time of troubles

disapproval *n.* censure, condemnation, criticism, denunciation, deprecation, disfavour, dislike, displeasure, objection, opprobrium, remonstration, reproach, reproof, stricture, vitriol *Antonyms:* acceptance, assent, reception

disapprove *v.* blackball, blame, censure, chastise, condemn, criticize, damn, decry, denounce, deplore, deprecate, detract, disagree, disallow, discountenance, discourage, disesteem, disfavour, dislike, dismiss, expostulate, forbid, frown upon, fulminate, look down on, object, oppose, refuse, reject, remonstrate, reprehend, reprobate, reprove, spurn, veto *Nonformal:* knock, nix, pan *Antonyms:* applaud, approve, commend, compliment, endorse

disarm *v.* **1.** cripple, debilitate, disable, incapacitate, paralyze, put out of action, subdue, weaken **2.** deactivate, de-escalate, defuse, demilitarize, demobilize, disband, invalidate, neutralize, strip, unarm, **3.** allure, attract, befriend, bewitch, captivate, charm, coax, conciliate, convince, enchant, entice, fascinate, ingratiate, mollify, pacify, persuade, seduce, set at ease, win over *Antonyms:* alarm, antagonize, challenge

disarmament *n.* arms limitation *or* reduction, conquest, de-escalation, demilitarization, demobilization, disablement, disqualification, neutralization, occupation, pacification, paralyzation, reduction

disarming *adj.* charming, convincing, deferential, enticing, ingratiating, insinuating, inveigling, irresistible, likeable, persuasive, seductive, winning *Antonyms:* bellicose, combative, pugnacious

disarray *n.* chaos, clutter, confusion, disarrangement, discomposure, disharmony, dishevelment, disorder, disorganization, farrago, holy *or* unholy mess *(Nonformal)*, jumble, mess, muddle, shambles, snarl, tangle, unruliness, untidiness *Antonyms:* arrangement, harmony, method, neatness, system – *v.* crease, dishevel, muss up, rumple, tumble, upset, wrinkle

disassemble *v.* break apart *or* up, disperse, dissipate, scatter, separate, take apart, take to pieces *Antonyms:* gather, unify, unite

disassociate *v.* abstract, alienate, cleave, detach, disband, disengage, disperse, disrupt, divide, excuse, isolate, recuse, remove *or* sever oneself, resign, secede, splinter, *Antonyms:* associate, confederate, unite

disaster *n.* accident, adversity, affliction, bale, bane, blight, blow, calamity, cataclysm, catastrophe, collapse, collision, crash, debacle, defeat, depression, emergency, exigency, failure, fall, famine, flood, grief, hard luck, harm, hazard, holocaust, misadventure, mischance, misfortune, mishap, nightmare, reverse, ruin, ruination, setback, slip, stroke, tragedy, undoing, upset, woe, wreck *Nonformal:* bomb, bust, flop, holy *or* unholy mess, washout

disastrous *adj.* adverse, appalling, black, calamitous, cataclysmic, catastrophic, deplorable, destructive, detrimental, devastating, dire, dreadful, fatal, harmful, heavy-duty *(Nonformal)*, horrendous, ill-fated, luckless, pitiable, ruinous, severe, terrible, tragic, unfortunate, unpropitious, wretched *Antonyms:* auspicious, beneficial, lucky

disavow *v.* abjure, cast off, contradict, deny, disallow, disclaim, disown, forswear, gainsay, impugn, negate, refuse, reject, repudiate, take back, unsay *Nonformal:* wash one's hands of, weasel out

disband *v.* break up, close, demobilize, dismiss, disperse, dissipate, dissolve, distribute, fold, muster out, release, retire, scatter, send home, separate, strew *Nonformal:* demob, mothball *Antonyms:* organize, unite

disbelief *n.* atheism, agnosticism, distrust, doubt, incredulity, mistrust, nihilism, rejection, scepticism *Antonyms:* belief, credence, credulity, faith, trust

disbelieve *v.* discount, discredit, distrust, doubt, eschew, mistrust, question, reject, repudiate, scorn, suspect, wonder about

disbelieving *adj.* ain't buying *(Nonformal)*, cagey, cynical, doubting, incredulous, leery, mistrustful, questioning, sceptical, suspicious, unbelieving

disburse *v.* ante-up, contribute, deal, defray, dispense, disseminate, distribute, divide, divvy, dole out, expend, fork out, give, outlay, partition, pay off *or* out, spend, use *Nonformal:* foot the bill, shell out *Commonly misused:* **disperse**

disbursement *n.* cost, expenditure, expense, outgoing, outlay, payment, spending

disc *n.* **1.** coin, circle, discus, face, orb, plate, platter, ring, roundel, sabot **2.** disk *Kinds of computer disc:* CD-ROM, compact *or* CD, Digital Versatile Disk *or* DVD *(Trademark)*, diskette, double-sided, floppy, high density, laser, magnetic, mini CD, 3 1/4 *or* 5 1/2 inch floppy, record, zip

discard *n.* disposable, extra, hand-me-down, reject, remnant, throwaway – *v.* abandon, abdicate, abjure, banish, cancel, cashier, cast aside, chuck, desert, dismiss, dispatch, dispense, dispose, ditch, divorce, drop, eject, eliminate, expel, forsake, jettison, junk, off-load, oust, reject, relinquish, remove, renounce, repeal, repudiate, scrap, shed, throw overboard, toss, weed, write off *Nonformal:* deep-six, give the old heave-ho, kiss goodbye *or* off *Antonyms:* keep, reserve, retain, save

discern *v.* **1.** apprehend, ascertain, behold, comprehend, detect, determine, divine, espy, focus, get the picture *(Nonformal)*, judge, know, note, notice, observe, perceive, read, recognize, remark, see, take in, view **2.** differentiate, discriminate, distinguish, make out, separate, spot *Antonyms:* confuse, mix up, muddle

discernible *adj.* apparent, appreciable, audible, clear, detectable, distinct, noticeable, obvious, palpable, perceivable, perceptible, plain, recognizable, tangible, visible

discerning *adj.* acute, astute, bright, brilliant, clear-sighted, clever, critical, discriminating, ingenious, insightful, intelligent, judicious, keen, knowing, knowledgeable, penetrating, perceptive, percipient, perspicacious, quick, sagacious, sage, sensitive, sharp, shrewd, subtle, wise *Antonyms:* dull-witted, slow, stupid

discharge *n.* **1.** barrage, blast, burst, cannonade, detonation, explosion, fire, fusillade, report, salvo, shot, shower, volley **2.** defecation, ejaculation, ejection, elimination, emission, emptying, flow, outflow, outpouring, pus, secretion, seepage, separation, sperm, vent, unburdening, unloading, voiding **3.** acquittal, clearance, exoneration, freedom, liberation, pardon, parole, release, relief, remittance **4.** annulment, dismissal, firing, separation, termination *Nonformal:* axe, bounce, pink slip, the boot, walking papers – *v.* **1.** bleed, disembogue, dispense, ejaculate, eject, emanate, emit, empty, evacuate, excrete, exhale, expectorate, expel, exude, flush, give off, gush, issue, leak, ooze, purge, radiate, regurgitate, release, run, secrete, shed, spew, spill out, spout, spurt, unload, vent, void, vomit **2.** burst, detonate, erupt, explode, fire, go off, shoot **3.** dismiss, eliminate, expel, lay off, let go, liquidate, oust, relieve *Nonformal:* bust, sack, send packing, show the gate **4.** disengage, emancipate, free, liberate, loosen, manumit, pardon, unchain **5.** honour, meet, pay, pay up, satisfy, settle, square **6.** abrogate, absolve, acquit, annul, cancel, clear, dissolve, exonerate, invalidate

disciple *n.* acolyte, adherent, apostle, attendant, believer, catechumen, cohort, convert, devotee, enthusiast, fanatic, follower, henchman, learner, neophyte, partisan, proselyte, pupil, satellite, student, supporter, votary, witness, zealot *Nonformal:* booster, fan, groupie, junkie, sidekick, wannabe

disciplinarian *n.* authoritarian, bully, despot, drill sergeant, enforcer, formulist, martinet, master, slave driver, stickler, taskmaster, teacher, trainer, tyrant

discipline *n.* **1.** conduct, control, cultivation, development, drilling, education, inculcation, indoctrination, obedience, orderliness, practice, preparation, restraint, self-control, training, will **2.** castigation, chastisement, comeuppance, correction, penalty, punishment, scourge, the rod *(Nonformal)* **3.** area, branch, course, curriculum, expertise, field, interest, major, profession, specialty, subject – *v.* **1.** break in, control, curb, direct, drill, educate, form, instruct, manage, restrain, school, shape, socialize, supervise, take in hand, teach, train **2.** castigate, chastise, chew or ream out *(Nonformal)*, correct, penalize, punish, reprimand

disclaim *v.* abandon, abnegate, contradict, decline, deny, disavow, discard, disown, forswear, gainsay, minimize, negate, recant, refuse, reject, renounce, repudiate, retract, revoke, spurn, traverse *Antonyms:* accept, affirm, receive

disclose *v.* acknowledge, admit, bare, betray, broadcast, circulate, confess, display, divulge, exhibit, expose, impart, inform, leak, make known, open, post, publish, relate, reveal, show, spill, tell, uncover, unfurl, utter *Nonformal:* rat, squeal *Antonyms:* conceal, cover, hide, mask, veil

disclosure *n.* acknowledgment, admission, advertisement, announcement, betrayal, broadcast, bulletin, confession, declaration, discovery, divulgence, enlightenment, exposure, leak, news release, posting, publication, revelation, tip, tipoff, uncovering

discoloration *n.* blanching, bleaching, dimming, fading, paling, waning, whitening

discolour *v.* begrime, blot, defile, dim, dirty, dull, fade, fox, mar, mark, rust, smear, soil, stain, streak, sully, tar, tarnish, tinge, wash out

discomfit *v.* **1.** defeat, frustrate, hamper, hinder, impede, rout, upset, vanquish **2.** abash, baffle, confuse, discompose, disconcert, disorder, disturb, embarrass, perturb

discomfiture *n.* abashment, anxiety, bafflement, bother, chagrin, confusion, defeat, demoralization, disconcertion, disgrace, embarrassment, frustration, humiliation, irritation, shame, upset, vexation *Antonyms:* attainment, pride, success

discomfort *n.* ache, annoyance, displeasure, disquietude, distress, embarrassment, hurt, illness, irritant, irritation, malaise, neuralgia, nuisance, pain, soreness, trouble, uneasiness, unpleasantness, upset, vexation *Antonyms:* comfort, ease, reassurance, solace – *v.* annoy, bother, burden, discommode, disconcert, distress, disturb, fluster, inconvenience, irk, irritate, trouble, upset, vex *Antonyms:* comfort, ease, help

disconcert *v.* abash, baffle, balk, bewilder, confound, confuse, demoralize, disarrange, discombobulate *(Nonformal)*, discomfit, discommode, discompose, discountenance, disturb, embarrass, faze, fluster, frustrate, hinder, impede, nonplus, perplex, perturb, puzzle, rattle, ruffle, trouble, unbalance, undo, unsettle, upset, worry *Antonyms:* aid, assist, calm, settle, soothe

disconcerted *adj.* annoyed, bewildered, confused, distracted, disturbed, embarrassed, fazed, flustered, nonplused, perturbed, rattled, ruffled, shaken, thrown, troubled, unglued, unsettled, upset *Nonformal:* all shook up, psyched out, unglued

disconnect *v.* break, break off, cut, detach, disassociate, disengage, dissever, divide, drop, hang up, part, separate, sever, sign off, terminate, uncouple

disconnected *adj.* **1.** broken, detached, disjointed, interrupted, loose, out of service, separated, severed, unhinged **2.** bumbling, confused, disordered, garbled, illogical, incoherent, irrational, irregular, jumbled, mixed-up, muddled, rambling, uncoordinated, unintelligible, wandering *Antonyms:* lucid, rational, reasonable

disconsolate *adj.* **1.** crestfallen, crushed, depressed, despairing, destroyed, discouraged, distressed, doleful, down, downcast, downhearted, grief-stricken, heartbroken, hurting, inconsolable, miserable, neurasthenic, sad, sorrowful, unhappy, woeful, *Antonyms:* glad, happy, joyful **2.** cheerless, cold, comfortless, dark, dejected, desolate, drear, dreary, forlorn, funereal, gloomy, hopeless, melancholy, sombre, wretched

discontent *n.* boredom, depression, discontentment, displeasure, dissatisfaction, ennui, envy, fretfulness, pessimism, regret, restlessness, uneasiness, unhappiness, vexation, *Weltschmerz (German)*, world-weariness *Antonyms:* comfort, contentment, gratification, satisfaction

discontented *adj.* blue, chafed, complaining, crabby, disaffected, discontented, disgruntled, displeased, dissatisfied, disturbed, down in the mouth *(Nonformal)*, exasperated, fretful, griping, kvetching, malcontent, miserable, perturbed, petulant, picky, querulous, restless, testy, unhappy, upset, vexed, weary, world-weary *Antonyms:* cheerful, content, happy, pleased, satisfied

discontinuance *n.* adjournment, ceasefire, cessation, close, closing, discontinuation, disjunction, end, ending, finish, intermission, respite, separation, stop, stoppage, suspension, termination

discontinue *v.* abandon, break off, cease, close, desist, disconnect, disjoin, drop, end, finish, give up, halt, interpose, interrupt, intervene, kill, knock *or* leave off, part, pause, prevent, quit, refrain from, scrub, separate, stop, surcease, suspend, terminate *Nonformal:* bag it, blow off

discontinuous *adj.* alternating, broken, choppy, desultory, disconnected, disjointed, disordered, erratic, incoherent, intermittent, interrupted, irregular, muddled, punctuated, spasmodic, undulatory, unorganized, variable, wavy *Antonyms:* constant, incessant, regular, steady

discord *n.* **1.** animosity, antagonism, clash, conflict, contention, disagreement, dissension, division, falling-out, friction, hostility, run-in, strife, wrangling *Antonyms:* accord, peace, tranquility **2.** babel, cacophony, clangour, din, disharmony, dissonance, harshness, jangle, noise, racket, rumpus, sour note, tumult *Antonyms:* harmony, melody

discount *n.* allowance, concession, cut, cut rate, decrease, deduction, depreciation, exemption, markdown, rebate, reduction, refund, rollback, sale, subtraction – *v.* **1.** curtail, cut, decrease, deduct, diminish, exempt, mark down, reduce, refund, slash, strike *or* take off *Antonyms:* increase, raise **2.** belittle, depreciate, disdain, dismiss, dispute, doubt, malign, mistrust, reject, repudiate, scoff at **3.** disregard, ignore, minimize, neglect, omit, overlook, pass over, slight, snub, waive

discountenance *v.* **1.** abash, agitate, alarm, contradict, confound, confuse, discombobulate *(Nonformal)*, discomfit, disconcert, disquiet, distress, embarrass, mortify, perturb, shame, trouble, upset *Antonyms:* allay, appease, calm, soothe **2.** boycott, condemn, disapprove, discourage, disfavour, oppose, punish, rebuff, refuse, reject, resist, scorn, slight, snub *Antonyms:* endorse, sanction, support

discourage *v.* **1.** bother, cloud, dampen, dash, daunt, demoralize, depress, dishearten, dismay, disparage, dispirit, distress, frighten, intimidate, irk, oppress, sadden, vex *Nonformal:* cast down, cow *Antonyms:* embolden, hearten **2.** blunt, cool, curb, deter, disincline, dissuade, divert, frustrate, hinder, hold back *or* off, impede, inhibit, interfere, keep back, obstruct, prevent, prohibit, quell, rein in, repress, restrain, scare, sidetrack, squelch, stifle, unnerve *Antonyms:* abet, encourage, urge **3.** advise *or* warn against, condemn, disapprove, disfavour, forbid, oppose, scorn, slight, spurn *Antonyms:* condone, countenance, welcome

discouraged *adj.* blue, crestfallen, dashed, daunted, depressed, disheartened, dismayed, dispirited, down, downbeat, downcast, finished, glum, pessimistic, sad, shot to pieces *(Nonformal) Antonyms:* heartened, hopeful, optimistic

discouraging *adj.* awkward, black, bleak, cool, daunting, depressing, disheartening, dispiriting, frustrating, not helpful, inopportune, off-putting, oppressive, unfavourable, unpropitious, upsetting *Antonyms:* encouraging, refreshing, welcome

discourse *n.* **1.** address, chat, confab *(Nonformal)*, conference, conversation, dialogue, forum, lecture, lesson, newsgroup *(Computer)*, palaver, speech, parlay, talk **2.** diatribe, dissertation, essay, harangue, homily, oration, philippic, sermon, treatise – *v.* argue, comment, confer, consult, converse, debate, deliberate, develop, discuss, dispute, elaborate, enlarge, expand, explain, expound, lecture, modulate, orate, perorate, remark, sermonize, talk, voice *Nonformal:* chew over, kick around

discourteous *adj.* abrupt, bad-mannered, boorish, brusque, crisp, curmudgeonly, gruff, ill-mannered, impertinent, impolite, impudent, inconsiderate, insolent, rude, surly, uncivil, uncouth, ungracious, unmannerly *Antonyms:* civil, courteous, gracious, polite, well-mannered

discover *v.* **1.** ascertain, catch, come *or* happen upon, descry, determine, discern, distinguish, encounter, espy, explore, fathom, find, glimpse, hear, identify, learn, locate, notice, realize, recognize, see, sense, spot, stumble across, surprise, trip over **2.** crack, decipher, decode, decrypt, detect, disclose, elicit, expose, reveal, solve, suss out *(Nonformal)*, uncover, unearth, unmask **3.** coin, conceive, concoct, contrive, design, devise, dream *or* think up, fabricate, innovate, introduce, invent, originate, pioneer

discovery *n.* **1.** breakthrough, find, innovation, invention, serendipity, strike, treasure, trove **2.** detection, disclosure, excavation, exposure, finding, learning, locating, recognition, sensing, sighting

discredit *n.* **1.** aspersion, blame, disfavour, disgrace, dishonour, disparagement, disrepute, distress, ignobility, ignominy, ill repute, rejection, shame, smirch, stain, stigma, suspicion, taint **2.** denial, disbelief, doubt, incredulity, question, scepticism – *v.* **1.** blame, censure, defame, degrade, destroy, detract, disfavour, disgrace, dishonour, disparage, frown upon, reproach, ruin, slander, slur, smear, tear down, vilify *Nonformal:* mudsling, slag, trash *Antonyms:* applaud, commend, honour, laud, praise **2.** challenge, debunk, disbelieve, disprove, dispute, doubt, explode, expose, mistrust, question, reject, show up

discreet *adj.* alert, attentive, cagey, careful, cautious, chary, circumspect, considerate, controlled, diplomatic, discerning, discriminating, evasive, guarded, intelligent, judicious, noncommital, observant, politic, prudent, reasonable, reserved, restrained, safe, sagacious, secretive, strategic, tactful, thoughtful, vigilant, wary, watchful, wise, worldly-wise *Antonyms:* incautious, overt, rash, unwise *Commonly misused:* **discrete**

discrepancy *n.* **1.** ambiguity, conflict, contrast, difference, disagreement, disparity, dissimilitude, dissonance, divergence, error, incongruity, inconsistency, split, variance *Antonyms:* agreement, compatibility, conformity **2.** bone of contention, conflict, point at issue, problem, question under discussion

discrepant *adj.* clashing, conflicting, contradictory, contrary, different, discordant, dissonant, divergent, incompatible, incongruous, inharmonious, jarring, out of whack *(Nonformal)*, paradoxical, poles apart, varying *Antonyms:* cogent, congruent, consistent

discrete *adj.* detached, different, diffuse, disconnected, discontinuous, disjunctive, distinct, independent, individual, isolated, separate, singular, sporadic, stray, unassociated, unattached *Antonyms:* combined, connected, linked, merged, united *Commonly misused:* **discreet**

discretionary *adj.* at one's choice or will, elective, nonobligatory, open, optional, self-determined, unforced, unrestricted, voluntary *Antonyms:* mandatory, restricted

discriminate *v.* differentiate, distinguish, divide, isolate, judge, perceive, prejudge, segregate, separate, set apart, single out, victimize

discriminating *adj.* **1.** acute, astute, careful, critical, cultivated, discerning, exacting, fastidious, finicky, fussy, judicious, keen, particular, picky, precise, prudent, refined, select, selective, sensitive, tasteful, wise *Nonformal:* choosy, persnickety *Antonyms:* desultory, random, unselective **2.** characteristic, differential, distinctive, distinguishing, idiosyncratic, individual, peculiar *Antonyms:* common, general, widespread

discrimination *n.* **1.** acumen, acuteness, astuteness, decision, discernment, judgment, penetration, perception, percipience, perspicacity, preference, refinement, sagacity, sense, shrewdness, subtlety, taste, understanding **2.** clearness, difference, differentiation, distinction, separation **3.** bias, bigotry, chauvinism, glass ceiling *(Nonformal)*, prejudice, racism, sexism

discursive *adj.* **1.** bumbling, circuitous, circumlocutory, diffuse, digressive, drifting, episodic, long-winded, meandering, prolix, rambling, roundabout, roving, straggling, straying, turgid, verbose, wandering, windy, wordy *Antonyms:* coherent, direct, methodical, succinct **2.** analytical, conceptual, deductive, dialectical, inductive, inferential, intellectual, logical, rational, reasoned *Antonyms:* impulsive, intuitive, sensory

discuss *v.* argue, arrange, bargain, brainstorm, chat, comment on, confabulate, confer, consider, consult, contend, contest, converse, criticize, deal, debate, deliberate, discourse, examine, explain, interpret, interrogate, interview, manipulate, negotiate, question, reason, regard, respect, review, speak, study, tackle, talk, think, treat, weigh *Nonformal:* chew the fat, gab, jaw, knock around, post, yammer, yap

discussion *n.* analysis, calculation, chat, chatter, cogitation, colloquy, communication, confabulation, conference, consideration, consultation, contention, controversy, conversation, converse, debate, deliberation, dialogue, discourse, disputation, dispute, examination, exchange, forum, meeting, palaver, parley, rebuttal, reflection, review, seminar, speculation, study, talk, *tête-à-tête (French) Nonformal:* confab, groupthink, huddle, rap session, thread

disdain *n.* antipathy, arrogance, aversion, contempt, contumely, defiance, derision, dislike, disparagement, disregard, hate, hatred, haughtiness, hauteur, indifference, insolence, loftiness, pride, ridicule, scorn, sneering, snobbishness, superciliousness – *v.* abhor, belittle, contemn, deride, despise, disparage, disregard, hate, ignore, misprize, reject, scorn, slight, sneer at, spurn, undervalue *Nonformal:* pooh-pooh, put down

disdainful *adj.* aloof, arrogant, averse, cavalier, conceited, contemptuous, cool, derisive, despising, egotistical, haughty, indifferent, insolent, overbearing, proud, rejecting, scornful, sneering, supercilious, superior *Nonformal:* hoity-toity, snooty, uppity *Antonyms:* accepting, humble, respectful

disease *n.* ache, affection, affliction, ailment, attack, blight, complaint, condition, contagion, contamination, convulsion, defect, disorder, endemic, epidemic, fever, fit, hemorrhage, illness, infection, infirmity, inflammation, malady, misery, plague, seizure, sickness, syndrome, unhealthiness, upset, virus *Nonformal:* bug, dose, what's going around *Groupings of disease:* acute condition, allergy, autoimmune, bacterial, blood, bone, cardiovascular, childhood *or* pediatric, chronic fatigue syndrome, circulatory, collagen, congenital, connective-tissue, degenerative, digestive, endemic, endocrine, epidemic, flesh-eating, functional, fungus *or* fungal gastric *or* stomach, gastrointestinal, genetic, glandular, hepatic *or* liver, hereditary, intestinal, joint, kidney *or* renal, malignant, muscular, neurological, occupational, ophthalmic, organic, pandemic, parasitic, psychogenic *or* psychosomatic, pulmonary, respiratory, sexually-transmitted *or* STD, skin, urinogenital, venereal *or* VD, viral *or* virus, wasting *Kinds of animal disease:* anthrax, Bang's Disease *or* brucellosis, blackleg, blackwater fever, bloody flux, broken wind, distemper, foot-and-mouth, heaves, loco, mad cow, malignant catarrh, mange, myxomatosis, rabies, rinderpest, scabies, sheep rot, splenic fever, staggers, swine dysentery

diseased *adj.* **1.** afflicted, ailing, contagious, debilitated, drained, endemic, enervated, epidemic, feeble, ill, indisposed, infected, infirm, rundown, sick, sickly, unhealthy, unwell, valetudinarian **2.** deranged, disturbed, morbid, pathological, psychotic, schizoid, unsound **3.** contaminated, corrupt, poisoned, riddled with graft, sullied, tainted

disembark *v.* alight, anchor, deplane, descend, detrain, dismount, land, leave, moor, unload *Antonyms:* climb aboard, embark,

disembowel *v.* cut open *or* out, draw, eviscerate, fillet, gut

disenchanted *adj.* **1.** been there done that *(Nonformal)*, blasé, cynical, demystified, disillusioned, enlightened, sophisticated, worldy-wise *Antonyms:* credulous, faithful, gullible, spellbound **2.** averse, crestfallen, crushed, dashed, disaffected, disappointed, discontented, disgruntled, disinclined, dissatisfied, let down *Antonyms:* hopeful, optimistic, wishful

disengage *v.* **1.** break away *or* off, break the connection, cut loose, detach, disconnect, divide, emancipate, free, hang up, leave flat *(Nonformal)*, liberate, part, pull back, release, retreat, ring off, separate, set free, sever, shake, uncouple, undo, unfasten, untie, withdraw *Antonyms:* couple, hitch, marry **2.** alienate, disassociate, dissociate, divorce, hide away, isolate, opt out, retire, segregate, veg out *(Nonformal)*

disentangle *v.* **1.** detach, disencumber, extricate, free, get out from under, unfold, unravel, unsnarl, untangle, untie, unwind *Antonyms:* braid, pleat, tie **2.** analyze, clarify, clear up, crack *(Nonformal)*, decipher, decode, dissect, elucidate, explicate, illuminate, solve, sort out, uncover

disfavour *n.* aversion, discredit, dishonour, dislike, displeasure, disregard, disrepute, disrespect, distaste, distrust, mistrust, shame, unpopularity *Antonyms:* credit, honour, popularity – *v.* abhor, challenge, conflict, disapprove, dislike, hate, loathe, object to, oppose, reject, scorn, snub *Antonyms:* accept, like, relish

disfigure *v.* blemish, blotch, brand, bruise, contuse, damage, deface, defile, deform, destroy, distort, gouge, hurt, injure, maim, mangle, mar, mutilate, scar, slash, trash *(Nonformal) Antonyms:* beautify, burnish, embellish, restore

disgorge *v.* **1.** belch, burst forth, eject, empty, expel, heave, jettison, regurgitate, spew, spit out, spout, spurt, throw up, vomit *Nonformal:* barf, blow chunks, puke, toss one's cookies, upchuck **2.** abandon, cast away, cast off, cede, discharge, forgo, give back *or* up, let go, release, relinquish, renounce, sacrifice, surrender, yield *Nonformal:* cough up, fork over, kiss goodbye

disgrace *n.* **1.** abasement, contempt, degradation, derision, disfavour, dishonour, disrepute, disrespect, humiliation, ignominy, infamy, obloquy, odium, opprobrium, reproach, scandal, scorn, shame, slander *Antonyms:* esteem, favour, grace **2.** black eye, blackguard, blemish, blot, bounder, cad, embarrassment, family skeleton, fool, reprobate, remittance man *(Historical)*, slur, spectacle, spot, stain, stigma, stooge, taint *Antonyms:* credit, honour, leading light, nonpareil, paragon – *v.* abase, besmirch, blacken, debase, defame, defile, degrade, deride, disfavour, dishonour, disparage, disregard, disrespect, humiliate, libel, lose face, mock, reproach, ridicule, shame, slander, slur, snub, stain, stigmatize, sully, taint, tarnish *Antonyms:* raise, uplift

disgraceful *adj.* contemptible, degrading, detestable, dishonourable, disreputable, embarrassing, flagrant, humiliating, ignoble, ignominious, improper, indecent, infamous, libelous, low, mean, mortifying, notorious, offensive, opprobrious, scandalous, shabby, shady, shameful, shameless, shocking, unrespectable, unworthy

disgruntled *adj.* annoyed, bad-tempered, bellyaching *(Nonformal)*, cantankerous, crabby, cranky, critical, crotchety, disappointed, discontented, disenchanted, displeased, dissatisfied, fractious, grouchy, grousing, grumpy, irascible, irritated, out of sorts, owly *(P.E.I.)*, peevish, petulant, splenetic, sulky, sullen, testy, unhappy, vexed *Antonyms:* contented, happy, satisfied

disguise *n.* **1.** alteration, beard, camouflage, costume, cover-up, dark glasses, domino, false face *or* front, guise, harlequin, mask, masquerade, pseudonym, veil, wig **2.** counterfeit, deceit, deception, fake, illusion, misrepresentation, pretense, semblance, subterfuge, trompe l'oeil, window dressing **3.** blind, concealment, facade, front, screen, shroud – *v.* adjust, alter, assume, belie, camouflage, change, cloak, colour, conceal, counterfeit, deceive, dissemble, distort, falsify, feign, front, fudge, hide, mask, masquerade, misrepresent, misstate, muffle, obfuscate, obscure, put on an act, pretend, shroud, touch up, twist, varnish, veil, warp, whitewash *Antonyms:* expose, reveal, unveil

disguised *adj.* **1.** camouflaged, clandestine, covert, incognito, masked, screened, undercover *Antonyms:* conspicuous, out in the open, public **2.** drunk, tipsy *Nonformal:* far gone, loaded, pie-eyed

disgust *n.* abhorrence, abomination, antipathy, aversion, detestation, dislike, distaste, hatred, loathing, nausea, objection, repugnance, repulsion, revulsion, sickness *Antonyms:* admiration, love, pleasure, satisfaction – *v.* abominate, bother, disenchant, displease, disturb, gross out *(Nonformal)*, insult, irk, nauseate, offend, outrage, pall, pique, repel, repulse, revolt, shock, sicken, turn one's stomach, upset *Antonyms:* delight, impress, please

disgusted *adj.* appalled, displeased, dissatisfied, nauseated, offended, queasy, repelled, repulsed, scandalized, shocked, sickened, squeamish, unhappy, upset, weary *Nonformal:* fed up, grossed out, turned off *Antonyms:* attracted, besotted, bewitched, mesmerized

disgusting *adj.* awful, beastly, creepy, detestable, distasteful, foul, frightful, ghastly, gross, gruesome, hateful, hideous, horrid, loathsome, lousy *(Nonformal)*, macabre, monstrous, nasty, nauseating, objectionable, obnoxious, odious, offensive, outrageous, repellent, repugnant, repulsive, revolting, rotten, scandalous, shameless, shocking, sickening, vile, vulgar *Antonyms:* adorable, charming, pleasing, winsome

dish *n.* **1.** container, receptacle, vessel *Kinds of serving dish:* bowl, breadbasket, casserole, coffee cup, coffeepot, compote, cookie jar, creamer, cruet, cup, decanter, demitasse, dessert, dinner, eggcup, finger bowl, gratin, gravy boat, jar, jug, noggin, pitcher, plate, platter, porringer, punch bowl, salad bowl, salt cellar, salver, saucer, soup bowl, sugar bowl, teapot, tea service, Thermos *(Trademark)*, tray, tureen, wine basket **2.** course, fare, food, helping, meal, recipe, serving **3.** *Nonformal:* defeat, do for, fix, make short work of, put the kibosh on, shoot down – *v.* **1.** dip, ladle, pour, scoop, serve, spoon **2.** cave in, concave, dent, depress, dig, dint, gouge, hollow, pit, pockmark, scoop

disharmony *n.* **1.** clash, conflict, contention, difference, disagreement, dissension, divergence, enmity, friction, incompatibility, opposition, strife, tension, variance *Antonyms:* accord, agreement, concord **2.** chaos, confusion, din, disarray, disorder, mess, muddle *Antonyms:* melody, order, proportion **3.** cacophony, caterwauling, clangour, discord, dissonance, farrago, imbalance, incoherence, stridency **4.** asymmetry, disproportion, distortion, lopsidedness, skewness

dishearten *v.* aggrieve, crush, dampen, darken, dash, daunt, deject, demoralize, depress, deter, discourage, dismay, disparage, dispirit, distress, humble, humiliate, oppress, ruin, sadden *Antonyms:* encourage, hearten, lift, rally

dishevelled *adj.* beat-up, bedraggled, blowzy, chaotic, dirty, disarranged, disarrayed, disordered, frowzy, grubby, ill-kempt, messed-up, messy, ruffled, rumpled, slatternly, slipshod, sloppy, slovenly, tousled, uncombed, unkempt, untidy, wrinkled *Nonformal:* mussy, scuzzy *Antonyms:* chic, dapper, neat, smart

dishonest *adj.* **1.** backbiting, bent, cheating, corrupt, crafty, crooked, cunning, designing, disreputable, faithless, false, falsehearted, guileful, hoodwinking, insincere, lying, mendacious, misleading, perfidious, roguish, shady, shifty, sinister, slippery, swindling, traitorous, treacherous, tricky, underhanded, unfair, unprincipled, unscrupulous, untrustworthy, untruthful, wily *Nonformal:* double-crossing, double-dealing, not kosher, on the pad *or* the take, two-faced, two-timing *Antonyms:* honest, honourable, law-abiding, lawful, principled **2.** bogus, counterfeit, fraudulent, phony, spurious *Antonyms:* genuine, real

dishonesty *n.* artifice, bunk, cheating, chicanery, corruption, craft, criminality, cunning, deceit, duplicity, faithlessness, falsehood, falsity, fraud, fraudulence, graft, guile, improbity, infamy, infidelity, insidiousness, knavery, knavishness, lie, lying, mendacity, perfidy, slyness, stealing, swindle, treachery, trickiness, unscrupulousness, villainy, wiliness *Nonformal:* dirty tricks, double-dealing *Antonyms:* integrity, straightforwardness, veracity

dishonour *n.* **1.** abuse, affront, degradation, discourtesy, discredit, disfavour, disgrace, disrepute, disrespect, humiliation, ignominy, indignity, infamy, insult, mortification, obloquy, offense, opprobrium, outrage, public disgrace, reproach, scandal, shame, slight *Antonyms:* integrity, rectitude, respect **2.** default, nonpayment, nonremittance – *v.* **1.** abase, blacken, blot, corrupt, debase, debauch, defame, defile, degrade, discredit, disgrace, insult, shame, sully, taint, tarnish *Antonyms:* esteem, exalt, respect, revere, worship **2.** default, disoblige, ignore, neglect, refuse to pay, run out on, shirk

dishonourable *adj.* base, contemptible, corrupt, disgraceful, false-hearted, ignoble, low, offensive, perfidious, scandalous, shabby, shady, shameful, shameless, shocking, sordid, unconscionable, unethical, unprincipled, unsavoury, unscrupulous *Antonyms:* acceptable, just, proper, true

disinclination *n.* aversion, balkiness, dislike, displeasure, distaste, hesitance, lack of sympathy, objection, opposition, recalcitrance, reluctance, repugnance, repulsion, resistance, reticence, unwillingness *Antonyms:* appeal, attraction

disinfect *v.* bleach, clean, cleanse, decontaminate, deodorize, filter, fumigate, purge, purify, refine, sanitize, scour, sterilize, wash *Antonyms:* contaminate, defile, poison, pollute, taint

disingenuous *adj.* artful, beguiling, crafty, cunning, deceitful, deceptive, designing, dishonest, duplicitous, fallacious, false, feigned, foxy, guileful, insidious, insincere, mealy-mouthed, playing all the angles, shifty, sly, sophistic, specious, tricky, two-faced *(Nonformal)*, unctuous, underhanded, unfair, wily *Antonyms:* frank, simple, sincere

disintegrate *v.* break *or* come apart, crumble, decay, decline, decompose, degenerate, dilapidate, disband, disconnect, dismantle, disorganize, disperse, dissipate, erode, evanesce, obliterate, pulverize, reduce, rot, rust *or* weather away, separate, sever, shatter, splinter, spoil, wither, worsen *Antonyms:* adhere, join, unite

disinterested *adj.* **1.** aloof, casual, detached, incurious, indifferent, remote, unconcerned, uninvolved, withdrawn **2.** dispassionate, impartial, impersonal, neutral, objective, selfless, unbiased, unselfish, no axe to grind *Antonyms:* biased, concerned, partial, prejudiced, selfish *Commonly misused:* **uninterested**

disjointed *adj. 1.* asunder, broken apart, cut up, disconnected, divided, in pieces, vivisected **2.** dislocated, displaced, loose, off-line, out of whack *(Nonformal)* **3.** aimless, bumbling, confused, incoherent, rambling **4.** episodic, fitful, intermittent, irregular, sporadic

dislike *n.* abhorrence, abomination, animosity, animus, antagonism, antipathy, aversion, detestation, disapproval, disdain, disfavour, disgust, disinclination, displeasure, dissatisfaction, distaste, dread, enmity, hate, hatred, hostility, indisposition, loathing, objection, offence, opposition, prejudice, rancour, repugnance, repulsion, scorn *Antonyms:* admiration, attraction, delight – *v.* abhor, abominate, condemn, despise, detest, disapprove, disfavour, dislike, eschew, execrate, hate, loathe, mind, mislike, object to, resent, scorn, shrink from, shun, take a dim view of *Antonyms:* esteem, favour

dislocate *v.* **1.** break, detach, disconnect, disengage, disjoint, disunite, divide, separate, sever, splinter, unhinge **2.** confuse, dishevel, disorder, displace, disrupt, disturb, jumble, misplace, mix up, move, remove, shift, ship, transfer, upset

dislocated *adj.* confused, disoriented, displaced, lost, misplaced *Nonformal:* fish out of water, out of one's head, out of whack, over one's head, right church wrong pew *Antonyms:* in the right place, on target

dislocation *n.* **1.** break, disarticulation, disconnection, disengagement **2.** confusion, disarray, discontinuity, disorder, disorganization, displacement, disruption, disturbance, misplacement

dislodge *v.* **1.** depose, disgorge, displace, dispossess, disturb, eject, evict, force *or* kick out, move, oust, turn out, uproot *Nonformal:* bump, sack **2.** break *or* pry *or* tear loose, dig out, disengage, extricate, free, loosen, pry loose, release

disloyal *adj.* cheating, disobedient, faithless, false, inconstant, mutinous, perfidious, rebellious, recreant, seditious, traitorous, treacherous, treasonable, unfaithful, untrue, untrustworthy *Nonformal:* double-crossing, two-faced *Antonyms:* constant, dependable, dutiful, true, trustworthy

disloyalty *n.* bad faith, betrayal, deceitfulness, disobedience, dissension, double-dealing *(Nonformal)*, duplicity, falseness, inconstancy, infidelity, mutiny, perfidy, rebellion, revolt, sedition, treachery, treason, unfaithfulness

dismal *adj.* **1.** black, cheerless, cloudy, dark, depressing, desolate, dim, dingy, discouraging, disheartening, dispiriting, gloomy, overcast, sombre, tenebrous *Antonyms:* bright, sunny **2.** bleak, blue, depressed, despondent, disagreeable, dispirited, dolorous, downcast, downhearted, forlorn, funereal, joyless, melancholy, miserable, mournful, sad, sorrowful *Nonformal:* down in the mouth, hurting *Antonyms:* cheery, glad, happy, joyful **3.** catastrophic, dire, ghastly, ill-fated, inauspicious, terrible, troublesome, unfortunate, unlucky **4.** boring, colourless, dreary, flat, heavy, insipid, leaden, lifeless, monotonous, pedestrian, spiritless, stale, tedious, uninteresting, wearying *Antonyms:* invigorating, lively, stimulating

dismantle *v.* break down, demolish, destroy, disassemble, dismember, level, raze, ruin, strike, strip, take apart, undo, wreck

dismay *n.* **1.** agitation, anxiety, apprehension, consternation, distress, dread, fear, horror, panic, trepidation, upset *Nonformal:* cold feet, fear and tremblings, funk **2.** blues, chagrin, disappointment, discouragement, disheartenment, disillusionment *Nonformal:* blue devils, mopes – *v.* **1.** abash, agitate, alarm, appall, bother, disconcert, disquiet, distress, disturb, horrify, rattle, scare, shake, take aback, unhinge, unnerve **2.** awe, daunt, depress, disappoint, discourage, dishearten, disillusion, dispirit, embarrass

dismember *v.* **1.** amputate, cripple, cut apart, disjoint, dislocate, dissect, maim, mutilate, rend, sever, sunder, vivisect **2.** dismantle, divide, part, partition, section

dismiss *v.* **1.** defrock, demote, discharge, downsize, drum out, expel, fire, lay off, let go, oust, retire, send away *or* packing, show out, terminate *Nonformal:* bounce, can, sack, send to the showers **2.** disband, dispense, disperse, dissolve, free, let go *or* out, release, set free **3.** banish, cast aside, discard, dispel, disregard, drive out, drop, forget, get rid of, relinquish, set aside, shelve *Nonformal:* brush *or* kiss off, ditch, flush, lose, shake **4.** deride, discount, discredit, mock, overlook, reject, repudiate, scoff, scorn

dismissal *n.* adjournment, banishment, deportation, deposal, discharge, displacement, downsizing, eviction, exile, expulsion, freedom, freeing, furlough, notice, ousting, release, removal, suspension, termination *Nonformal:* bum's rush, marching orders, pink slip, the boot

dismount *v.* **1.** alight, debark, deplane, descend, detrain, disembark, get down, throw off **2.** demolish, detach, disassemble, disengage, dislodge, dismantle, remove, separate, tear down

disobedience *n.* back talk, challenge, cheek, confrontation, contrariness, defiance, dereliction, effrontery, infraction, insubordination, intractableness, lip *(Nonformal)*, misbehaviour, mutiny, noncompliance, opposition, recalcitrance, revolt, riot, sedition, transgression, violation *Antonyms:* complaisance, obligingness, submission

disobedient *adj.* audacious, challenging, contrary, contumacious, defiant, delinquent, disloyal, disorderly, fractious, headstrong, heedless, impulsive, insubordinate, mutinous, naughty, obstinate, obstreperous, opposing, quarrelsome, rebellious, recalcitrant, reckless, refractory, resisting, riotous, saucy, stubborn, truculent, ungovernable, unmanageable, unruly, unwilling, wayward *Antonyms:* compliant, dutiful, obedient, submissive

disobey *v.* challenge, contravene, defy, deny, disregard, ignore, infringe, misbehave, mutiny, object, oppose, overstep, rebel, resist, revolt, riot, shirk, transgress, violate *Nonformal:* fly in the face of, thumb one's nose

disoblige *v.* affront, annoy, bother, displease, disturb, dissatisfy, incommode, inconvenience, insult, offend, outrage, slight, trouble, vex *Antonyms:* accommodate, aid, assist

disobliging *adj.* annoying, contrary, disagreeable, discourteous, hostile, ill-disposed, rude, unaccommodating, uncongenial, unpleasant, unsympathetic *Antonyms:* helpful, serviceable

disorder *n.* **1.** clutter, confusion, derangement, disarray, disorganization, gallimaufrey, irregularity, jumble, mess, shambles, tangle, untidiness *Nonformal:* holy mess, hugger-mugger, mishmash **2.** anarchy, brannigan, breach of the peace, brouhaha, disruption, donnybrook, disruption, fracas, fray, free-for-all, hubbub, hullabaloo, kerfuffle *(Nonformal)*, melee, pandemonium, riot, rumpus, tumult, turmoil, unruliness **3.** affliction, ailment, complaint, disease, illness, infirmity, malady, sickness, upset – *v.* clutter, confound, confuse, disarrange, discompose, dishevel, disjoint, dislocate, disorganize, disrupt, disturb, embrangle, jumble, mess *or* mix up, muddle, rummage, rumple, scatter, shuffle, snarl, tangle, tumble, unsettle, upset *Nonformal:* bollix up, make a shambles of, muss, throw a wrench in

disordered *adj.* **1.** chaotic, confused, disarranged, discombobulated *(Nonformal)*, disconnected, disjointed, dislocated, disorganized, displaced, catawampus, incoherent, jumbled, mislaid, muddled, ruffled, rumpled, shifted, shuffled, snarled, stirred up, tangled, topsy-turvey, tossed, tousled, tumbled, unregulated, unsettled, untidy *Antonyms:* clean, regulated, tidy **2.** deranged, disturbed, insane, mentally ill, neurotic, paranoid, phobic, psychoneurotic, psychotic, schizoid

disorderly *adj.* **1.** chaotic, cluttered, confused, dislocated, disorganized, haphazard, helter-skelter, heterogeneous, indiscriminate, irregular, jumbled, messed *or* mixed up, messy, scattered, scrambled, slovenly, tumultuous, uncombed, undisciplined, unkempt, unmethodical, unrestrained, unsystematic, untidy *Antonyms:* arranged, neat, organized, tidy **2.** boisterous, disobedient, disruptive, drunk, fractious, intemperate, lawless, noisy, obstreperous, on a tear *(Nonformal)*, out-of-line, raucous, rebellious, riotous, rough-and-tumble, rowdy, stormy, turbulent, uncontrollable, ungovernable, unlawful, unmanageable, unruly, wayward

disorganization *n.* chaos, confusion, derangement, disarray, disjointedness, disorder, disruption, incoherence, unconnectedness *Nonformal:* foul-up, holy *or* unholy mess, hubble-bubble, rat's nest, snafu **2.** breakup, dissolution, disunion, wrapping up, winding down

disorganized *adj.* chaotic, confused, disordered, disorderly, haphazard, jumbled, messed up, mixed up, muddled, shuffled, undisciplined, unmethodical, unsystematic *Nonformal:* mussy, screwed up, unglued, unscrewed, unzipped

disoriented *adj.* addled, adrift, astray, baffled, bewildered, confused, disconcerted, flustered, lost, mixed up, perplexed, rattled, scattered, unbalanced, unhinged, unsettled, unstable *Nonformal:* discombobulated, off, out to lunch, punch drunk

disown *v.* abandon, abnegate, cast off *or* out, cut off, deny, disallow, disavow, disclaim, forswear, reject, renounce, repudiate, retract, throw out

disparage *v.* abuse, bad-mouth, belittle, criticize, decry, defame, degrade, deject, demoralize, denigrate, deprecate, depreciate, deride, detract, discourage, discredit, disdain, dismiss, insult, malign, minimize, pan, reduce, ridicule, scorch, scorn, slam, slander, smear, traduce, underestimate, underrate, undervalue, vilify *Nonformal:* dis, rap, roast, run down, slice up

disparagement *n.* aspersion, backbiting, belittlement, blame, calumny, censure, condemnation, contempt, contumely, criticism, debasement, degradation, denunciation, depreciation, derision, derogation, detraction, discredit, disdain, disrespect, lie, prejudice, reproach, ridicule, scandal, scorn, slander *Antonyms:* exaltation, glorification, praise

disparity *n.* difference, disagreement, discrepancy, disproportion, dissimilitude, distinction, divergence, imbalance, incongruity, inequality, unlikeness, variation *Antonyms:* balance, equality, parallelism

dispassionate *adj.* abstract, aloof, calm, collected, composed, cool, deadpan, detached, disinterested, fair, impartial, impersonal, imperturbable, judicial, just, matter-of-fact, moderate, neutral, nonchalant, nondiscriminatory, objective, open-minded, phlegmatic, self-possessed, sober, temperate, unbiased, unemotional, unexcitable, unexcited, unfeeling, unflappable, uninvolved, unmoved, unprejudiced, unruffled *Antonyms:* concerned, interested, involved

dispatch *n.* **1.** account, bulletin, communication, communiqué, document, instruction, item, letter, message, missive, news, piece, posting, report **2.** celerity, expedition, haste, hurry, hustle, precipitateness, promptness, quickness, rapidity, speed, speediness, swiftness – *v.* **1.** conclude, consume, devour, dispose of, finish, polish off **2.** assassinate, butcher, cut *or* mow down, destroy, eliminate, execute, fell, finish, hew, kill, level, massacre, murder, raze, slaughter, slay, take out **3.** accelerate, address, consign, express, forward, hand-carry, hasten, hurry, issue, remit, route, run, send, ship, speed, transmit

dispel *v.* allay, banish, cancel, chase away, disband, dismiss, disperse, dissipate, drive away, eject, eliminate, expel, oust, repel, rout, scatter

dispensable *adj.* **1.** disposable, excessive, expendable, extra, gratuitous, incidental, minor, needless, nonessential, redundant, removable, superfluous, throwaway, trivial, unimportant, unnecessary, useless *Antonyms:* crucial, essential, important, necessary, vital **2.** administered, allocated, apportionable, apportioned, distributable, distributed, divisible, rationed

dispensation *n.* **1.** allocation, allotment, appointment, apportionment, award, bestowal, conferment, consignment, courtesy, disbursement, distribution, dole, endowment, indulgence, kindness, part, portion, quota, service, share **2.** amnesty, exception, exemption, immunity, licence, permission, privilege, quittance, release, relief, remission, reprieve **3.** administration, direction, implementation, management, operation, order, regulation, scheme, stewardship, superintendence, system **4.** arrangement, divine function, ordering, providence, way of life *or* thought

dispense *v.* **1.** administer, allocate, allot, apportion, assign, deal out, disburse, distribute, divide, furnish, give, hand over, measure, mete out, partition, portion, prepare, prorate, share, supply *Nonformal:* come across with, divvy, dole *or* fork out **2.** absolve, discharge, except, exempt, excuse, exonerate, let off, pardon, release, relieve, reprieve, spare *Commonly misused:* **disperse**

disperse *v.* **1.** break up, radiate, scatter, scramble *(Nonformal)*, separate, spread out, strew, take off in all directions *Antonyms:* assemble, collect, gather, muster, pool **2.** disband, dismiss, dispel, dissipate **3.** broadcast, circulate, disseminate, distribute, post *(Nonformal)*, send *Antonyms:* herd, secrete *Commonly misused:* **disburse, dispense**

dispirited *adj.* blue, crestfallen, dejected, depressed, despondent, disconsolate, discouraged, disheartened, down, downcast, downhearted, glum, low, melancholy, morose, sad, spiritless, woebegone *Antonyms:* animated, buoyant, high-spirited

displace *v.* **1.** crowd *or* move out, derange, disarrange, disestablish, dislodge, evict, exile, relocate, remove, resettle, transfer, uproot **2.** bump *(Nonformal)*, oust, overthrow, replace, supercede, supplant, take over, take the place of, unseat **3.** boot *or* throw *or* turn out, cashier, discharge, eject, expel, fire, sack *(Nonformal)*

display *n.* **1.** advertisement, demonstration, exhibition, exposition, posting, presentation, show, staging **2.** arrangement, array, assembly, assortment, collection, grouping, selection **3.** airing, disclosure, divulgence, exposure, manifestation, revelation **4.** fanfare, flourish, ostentation, pageant, panorama, parade, scene, show, spectacle *Nonformal:* showboat, splash – *v.* **1.** demonstrate, depict, exhibit, illustrate, indicate, manifest, picture, portray, present, represent, set out, show, trot out *(Nonformal)* **2.** advertise, boast, brandish, emblazen, flaunt, feature, flash, flourish, grandstand, hot-dog *(Nonformal)*, market, model, parade, perform, showcase, show off, strut **3.** bare, betray, disclose, divulge, reveal, uncover, unfurl, unmask, unveil

displease *v.* aggravate, anger, annoy, antagonize, bother, chagrin, curdle, disappoint, discontent, disgruntle, disgust, disoblige, dissatisfy, enrage, exasperate, fret, frustrate, gall, hurt, incense, irk, irritate, nettle, nick, offend, perplex, pique, provoke, repel, revolt, rile, roil, turn off *(Nonformal)*, upset, vex, worry *Antonyms:* delight, entertain, titillate

displeasure *n.* anger, annoyance, chagrin, disapprobation, disapproval, discontent, disgruntlement, dislike, dissatisfaction, dudgeon, indignation, ire, irritation, offence, resentment, umbrage, unhappiness, vexation, wrath *Antonyms:* approval, endorsement, satisfaction

disposable *adj.* **1.** accessible, at or to hand, available, liquid, obtainable, usable *Antonyms:* inaccessible, locked away, unavailable, unobtainable **2.** biodegradable, consumable, expendable, non-returnable, throwaway *Antonyms:* durable, recyclable, returnable, reusable

disposal *n.* **1.** apportionment, arrangement, array, assignment, deployment, distribution, formation, grouping, organization, placement, positioning **2.** administration, command, direction, dispensation, government, management, power **3.** assignment, consignment, conveyance, release, relinquishment, transference, transmittal **4.** dumping, elimination, removal, riddence

dispose *v.* **1.** condition, direct, incline, induce, inure, influence, lead, position, precondition, prepare, prime, prompt, tend **2.** arrange, distribute, group, line *or* set up, marshal, order, organize, place, position, range, situate **3.** attend *or* see to, conclude, finalize, finish up, put in order, put to rights, settle, sort out **4.** call the tune *(Nonformal)*, control, determine, govern, manage, oversee, shepherd **5.** auction, bestow, convey, give away, liquidate, make over, part with, sell, transfer **6.** cast away, chuck, discard, dismiss, fire, jettison, junk, toss, unload *Nonformal:* bounce, deep-six **7.** consume, devour, eat, finish *Nonformal:* demolish, gulp *or* wolf down, kill, polish off, put away

disposed *adj.* aligned, apt, biased, favourable, fixed, game *(Nonformal)*, given, inclined, liable, likely, partial, predisposed, prone, ready, subject, willing

disposition *n.* **1.** being, cast, character, complexion, constitution, emotion, frame of mind, humour, identity, individuality, makeup, mentality, mind-set, nature, outlook, personality, predisposition, readiness, spirit, stamp, temper, temperament, type **2.** bent, bias, habit, inclination, leaning, mood, penchant, predilection, proclivity, proneness, propensity, tendency **3.** adjustment, arrangement, classification, control, decision, deployment, direction, disposal, distribution, grouping, management, marshalling, order, ordering, organization, placement, plan, regulation, sequence **4.** adjustment, determination, management, settlement **5.** bequest, conveyance, sale, transfer **6.** authority, dispensation, liberty, power

dispossess *v.* **1.** commandeer, confiscate, deprive, despoil, disinherit, distrain, divest, expropriate, extort, impound, pillage, plunder, remove, rob, seize, strip, wrest *Antonyms:* entitle, give, grant **2.** banish, demote, deport, depose, dethrone, dislodge, dismiss, disown, displace, drive out, excommunicate, eject, evict, exclude, exile, expel, ostracize, oust, outlaw, supplant, unfrock, unhouse, unseat, usurp *Nonformal:* bump, send packing

disproportion *n.* asymmetry, crookedness, difference, discrepancy, disharmony, disparity, imbalance, inadequacy, incongruity, inequality, lopsidedness, unevenness *Antonyms:* balance, congruity, harmony, symmetry

disproportionate *adj.* asymmetric, disagreeing, discordant, discrepant, excessive, inordinate, irregular, lopsided, off-balance, out of whack *(Nonformal)*, overbalanced, unbalanced, unequal, uneven, unsymmetrical

disprove *v.* belie, challenge, confute, contradict, contravene, controvert, debunk, deny, discredit, expose, impugn, invalidate, negate, overthrow, overturn, puncture, rebut, refute, throw out, traverse, weaken *Nonformal:* explode, shoot *or* tear down *Antonyms:* ascertain, confirm, evince, substantiate, verify

disputable *adj.* arguable, controversial, debatable, doubtful, dubious, moot, problematic, questionable, uncertain *Antonyms:* irrefutable, undeniable

disputatious *adj.* argumentative, cantankerous, captious, caviling, contentious, controversial, litigious, polemical, pugnacious, quarrelsome

dispute *n.* altercation, argument, brawl, broil, clash, conflict, contestation, controversy, debate, difference, disagreement, discord, discussion, disputation, dissension, disturbance, donnybrook, feud, fracas, friction, imbroglio, litigation, quarrel, row, rumpus, rupture, scrimmage, spat, squabble, strife, tiff, wrangle *Nonformal:* hassle, shouting match *Antonyms:* agreement, concession, concurrence – *v.* argue, brawl, challenge, clash, contest, contradict, disagree, doubt, impugn, quarrel, question, squabble, wrangle

disqualification *n.* debarment, disenablement, disenfranchisement, disentitlement, elimination, exclusion, incapacitation, ineligibility, penalty, red card, removal, stricture, suspension

disqualify *v.* **1.** ban, bar, blackball, defrock, disfranchise, except, exclude, foul out, invalidate, penalize, preclude, prohibit, punish, rule out, suspend **2.** disable, impair, incapacitate, incur damage, knock out, lame, neutralize, paralyze, weaken

disquiet *n.* alarm, angst, anxiety, butterflies *(Nonformal)*, foreboding, impatience, perturbation, restlessness, trepidation, worry – *v.* agitate, alarm, bother, concern, discomfort, discompose, distress, disturb, fluster, harass, place on edge *or* tenterhooks, ruffle, shake, stir trouble, unnerve, upset, worry

disregard *n.* **1.** contempt, disdain, lack of respect, scorn **2.** apathy, carelessness, coldness, detachment, disinterest, indifference, lack of interest *or* involvement, neglect, negligence – *v.* **1.** belittle, condemn, despise, discount, disparage, make light of, marginalize, minimalize, sneeze at *(Nonformal)*, trivialize, think nothing of, underrate **2.** brush aside *or* off, cut, look right through, rebuff, scorn, slight, snub *Nonformal:* cold-shoulder, freeze, give the go-by **3.** gloss *or* pass over, ignore, neglect, overlook, take no notice of, turn a blind eye *Nonformal:* let slide, pay no mind, tune out, wink at

disrepair *adj.* down, out of commission *Nonformal:* busted, kaput, on the fritz – *n.* abandon, collapse, damage, decay, decline, decrepitude, deterioration, dilapidation, disintegration, neglect, rot, ruination

disreputable *adj.* **1.** base, contemptible, corrupt, despicable, disgraceful, dishonourable, dissolute, ignominious, infamous, libidinous, licentious, notorious, questionable, scandalous, scrofulous, scurvy, shady, shameful, shoddy, sordid, unsavoury, unscrupulous, vicious, vile *Antonyms:* decent, reputable, respectable, upright, worthy **2.** abject, beggarly, cheap, dingy, dirty, grimy, lowly, meagre, pitiable, shabby, soiled, sorry

disrepute *n.* discredit, disesteem, disfavour, disgrace, dishonour, ignobility, ill repute, infamy, ingloriousness, shadow, shame, sleaze factor *(Nonformal)*, stigma

disrespect *n.* boorishness, brashness, brazenness, cheek, churlishness, cloddishness, coarseness, crudeness, discourtesy, disregard, effrontery, flippancy, impertinence, impoliteness, impudence, incivility, insolence, irreverence, loutishness, pertness, rudeness, sauciness, surliness, tactlessness, tartness, uncouthness, ungraciousness, vulgarity *Nonformal:* lip, mouth, sass *Antonyms:* civility, courtesy, manners, modesty, respect – *v.* demean, dishonour, disparage, embarrass, insult, mock, shame *Nonformal:* dis, sass, talk trash

disrobe *v.* bare, denude, dismantle, divest, peel, remove, shed, strip, strip down, take off, unclothe, undress *Nonformal:* doff, peel, shuck *Antonyms:* clothe, dress

disrupt *v.* **1.** agitate, clutter, complicate, confound, confuse, derange, disorder, disturb, embroil, interfere, intrude, jumble, litter, misplace, muddle, perturb, provoke, scatter, scramble, shake, shuffle, throw off, unsettle, upset *Nonformal:* discombobulate, psych out **2.** arrest, break up, bring to a halt, interrupt, obstruct, stop *Antonyms:* assist, expedite, facilitate **3.** breach, break, destroy, disband, disintegrate, fracture, rupture, shatter, spoil

disruptive *adj.* agitating, balky, confusing, difficult, distracting, disturbing, misbehaving, obstreperous, out-of-order, provocative, rowdy, troublemaking, troublesome, unruly, unsettling, upsetting *Antonyms:* cooperative, docile, obedient, smooth

dissatisfaction *n.* **1.** alienation, anger, annoyance, bitterness, disapproval, displeasure, distaste, exasperation, frustration, irritation, vexation, wormwood *Antonyms:* enjoyment, gratification, joy, pleasure **2.** anxiety, discomfort, discontent, dismay, disquiet, distress, uneasiness *Antonyms:* acceptance, contentment, trust **3.** boredom, ennui, lassitude, listlessness, restlessness

dissatisfied *adj.* **1.** angry, annoyed, bothered, complaining, crabby, discontented, disgruntled, displeased, envious, fretting, frustrated, griping, grumbling, grumpy, irked, jaundiced, jealous, malcontent, offended, querulous, sulky, sullen, vexed *Nonformal:* in a snit, ticked off *Antonyms:* contented, pleased, satisfied **2.** disappointed, dolorous, ill-at-ease, let down, long-faced, morose, sorry, unappeased, unfulfilled

dissect *v.* **1.** carve, cleave, cut, disjoint, dismember, dissever, divide, hew, lay open, part, quarter, rend, rive, section, separate, sever, slice **2.** analyze, anatomize, dichotomize, evaluate, examine, explore, inspect, investigate, research, resolve, scrutinize, sort, study, unpack, weigh

dissection *n.* **1.** autopsy, post-mortem, vivisection **2.** analysis, breakdown, examination, inspection, investigation, probe, scrutiny, study

dissemble *v.* **1.** affect, counterfeit, dissimulate, fake it *(Nonformal)*, falsify, feign, pretend **2.** camouflage, cloak, conceal, cover up, disguise, hide, mask, shroud, whitewash

disseminate *v.* **1.** advertise, announce, blazon, broadcast, circulate, post, proclaim, promulgate, publicize, publish **2.** diffuse, disperse, dissipate, distribute, propagate, radiate, scatter, sow, spread, strew

dissemination *n.* broadcasting, circulation, diffusion, emission, distribution, posting, promulgation, propagation, publication, publishing, spreading, telling

dissent *n.* **1.** argument, conflict, contention, disagreement, heresy, nonagreement, objection, opposition, protest, refusal, resistance, spat, split, strife *Antonyms:* accord, agreement, assent, concurrence **2.** aberration, deviation, difference, divergence, exception, nonconformity, variance – *v.* **1.** argue, contradict, differ, disagree, fulminate, object, oppose, protest *Antonyms:* agree, allow, assent, concur **2.** balk, break with, buck, decline, demur, disallow, divide, refuse, resist

dissertation *n.* address, commentary, critique, discourse, disquisition, essay, exposition, monograph, position paper, study, thesis, tract, treatise

disservice *n.* bad *or* ill turn, detriment, disfavour, harm, hurt, ill, injury, injustice, unkindness, wrong

dissidence *n.* disaccord, disagreement, disharmony, dispute, dissension, dissent, rupture, schism, strife

dissident *n.* activist, agitator, dissenter, heretic, nonbeliever, nonconformist, political activist, protester, rebel, recusant, revolutionary, sectary, separatist, subversive

dissimilarity *n.* contrast, difference, discord, discordance, discrepancy, disparity, dissemblance, distance, divergence, diversity, incomparability, inconsistency, otherness, separation, variance

dissipate *v.* **1.** disappear, dispel, disperse, dissolve, evanesce, evaporate, scatter, vanish **2.** cast away, consume, deplete, expend, fritter, misspend, misuse, spend, squander, throw away, trifle, use up, waste, waste away *Nonformal:* blow, diddle, frivol, go *or* run through **3.** carouse, debauch, overindulge, philander, swing *(Nonformal)*

dissipated *adj.* **1.** burnt out, consumed, destroyed, exhausted, scattered, spent, squandered, used *or* washed up, wasted *Nonformal:* blown, played out **2.** abandoned, corrupt, debauched, dissolute, intemperate, profligate, rakish, self-indulgent, wicked

dissipation *n.* **1.** diffusion, disappearance, disintegration, dispersion, dissemination, dissolution, distribution, evanescence, scattering, vanishing **2.** abandon, debauchery, drunkenness, excess, hedonism, indulgence, intemperance, lechery, prodigality, profligacy, squandering, wantonness, waste *Nonformal:* freeliving, high living

dissociate *v.* **1.** alienate, detach, disconnect, disengage, distance, divide, divorce, estrange, isolate, secede, seclude, segregate, separate **2.** break apart *or* up, demobilize, disband, disperse, scatter

dissociation *n.* alienation, break, detachment, disconnection, disengagement, distancing, division, divorce, estrangement, isolation, retirement, seclusion, segregation, separation, severance *Antonyms:* confederation, marriage, union

dissolute *adj.* abandoned, corrupt, debauched, degenerate, dissipated, evil, fast, high living *(Nonformal)*, immoral, lascivious, lax, lewd, libertine, licentious, loose, profligate, rakish, reprobate, slack, swift, unprincipled, vicious, wanton, wayward, wicked, wild *Antonyms:* chaste, moral, upright, virtuous

dissolution *n.* **1.** annulment, breakdown, cancellation, collapse, conclusion, disintegration, divorce, foundering, liquidation, separation, split, termination *Antonyms:* beginning, creation, dawning, foundation, renewal **2.** adjournment, departure, dismissal, dispersal *Antonyms:* assembly, convergence, gathering, mobilization, mustering **3.** death, demise, end, expiration

dissolve *v.* **1.** blend, fuse, liquefy, meld, melt, thaw *Antonyms:* congeal, crystallize, solidify **2.** close, end, shut down, terminate, wind *or* wrap up *Antonyms:* begin, initiate, introduce, launch **3.** break down, collapse, crumble, disintegrate *Nonformal:* fall apart, lose it *Antonyms:* harden, strengthen **4.** abolish, abrogate, annul, cancel, invalidate, rescind, revoke, set aside *Antonyms:* authorize, certify, endorse, sanction **5.** demobilize, disband, dismiss, dispel, disperse, release *Antonyms:* collect, convene, convoke, summon **6.** disappear, dwindle, fade, dematerialize, evanesce, evaporate, vanish *Antonyms:* appear, emerge, materialize

dissonance *n.* **1.** cacophony, din, discord, discordance, harsh *or* jangling *or* jarring noise, sour note, tonal incongruity *Antonyms:* harmony, melody, music **2.** clash, conflict, contradiction, controversy, difference, discrepancy, disparity, division, incongruity, inconsistency, variance *Antonyms:* agreement, cooperation, unity

dissonant *adj.* **1.** atonal, cacophonous, discordant, grating, harsh, inharmonious, jangly, jarring, tuneless, unmelodious *Antonyms:* melodic, tuneful **2.** anomalous, conflicting, differing, difficult, hostile, incongruous, inconsistent, raucous

dissuade *v.* advise, caution, counsel, coax, convince, derail, deter, discourage, disincline, divert, hinder, lean on, prevent *Nonformal:* faze, put off *Antonyms:* encourage, persuade, rouse, sway

distance *n.* **1.** amplitude, area, breadth, expanse, extension, extent, gap, interval, kilometrage, length, mileage, orbit, purview, radius, range, reach, scope, size, sky, space, span, spread, stretch, way **2.** horizon, outskirts, provinces, remove *Nonformal:* boondocks, over yonder, sticks **3.** aloofness, coldness, coolness, detachment, remoteness, reserve, restraint, reticence, standoffishness, stiffness, unapproachability – *v.* **1.** excel, outdo, outpace, outrun, outstrip, pass **2.** alienate, detach, disengage, dissociate, estrange, move away, remove *or* separate from, segregate, withdraw

distant *adj.* **1.** abroad, away, extreme, far-flung, far-off, faraway, farther, farthest, further, furthest, inaccessible, isolated, outermost, outlying, out-of-the-way, removed, secluded, upalong *(Newfoundland)*, uttermost *Antonyms:* adjacent, adjoining, handy, nearby **2.** aloof, ceremonious, chilly, cold, cool, formal, haughty, proud, reserved, standoffish, stiff, unapproachable, uncompanionable, unfriendly, unsociable *Nonformal:* offish, stuck up *Antonyms:* close, friendly, intimate, warm **3.** doubtful, improbable, questionable, remote, slight, unlikely *Antonyms:* expected, likely, odds-on **4.** absent-minded, abstracted, musing, out to lunch *(Nonformal)*, reflective *Antonyms:* alert, attentive, focused, intent **5.** disappearing, faint, hazy, indistinct, vague *Antonyms:* dominant, unforgettable, vivid

distaste *n.* abhorrence, antipathy, aversion, detestation, disgust, dislike, displeasure, dissatisfaction, hatred, hostility, loathing, repugnance, repulsion, revulsion – *v.* **1.** abhor, abominate, detest, dislike, disrelish, hate, loathe **2.** disappoint, discontent, disgruntle, displease, dissatisfy

distasteful *adj.* abominable, bitter, detestable, disagreeable, dislikeable, displeasing, gross, hateful, loathsome, nauseous, objectionable, obnoxious, odious, offensive, painful, repellent, repugnant, savourless, sickening, unappetizing, undesirable, uninviting, unpalatable, unpleasant, unsavoury *Nonformal:* skunky, yucky *Antonyms:* agreeable, charming, enjoyable, pleasing, pleasurable

distend *v.* balloon, balloon out *(Nonformal)*, bloat, bulge, dilate, distort, enlarge, expand, increase, inflate, lengthen, stretch out, swell *Antonyms:* constrict, construct, narrow

distill *v.* **1.** boil down, brew, clarify, concentrate, draw out, evaporate, express, extract, filter, fractionate, gasify, press, purify, refine, squeeze, strain, sublimate, vaporize **2.** condense, encapsulate, summarize, synopsize, trim **3.** drip, dribble, exude, leach, leak, percolate, seep, sweat, trickle, weep

distinct *adj.* **1.** different, idiosyncratic, individual, offbeat *(Nonformal)*, singular, unconventional, unlike, unique, unusual *Antonyms:* commonplace, mundane, pedestrian **2.** detached, discrete, disparate, poles apart *(Nonformal)*, separate, unconnected, unrelated **3.** clear, enunciated, intelligible, loud and clear, lucid, perceptible, plain, sharp *Antonyms:* ambiguous, nebulous, vague **4.** decisive, definite, undeniable, unequivocal, unmistakable, unquestionable *Antonyms:* ambivalent, fluctuating, indecisive, wavering

distinction *n.* **1.** acumen, discernment, discrimination, insight, judgment, perception, perspicacity, sagacity, sensitivity **2.** difference, fine point, hidden ingredient, nicety, nuance, soupçon, subtlety **3.** attribute, characteristic, feature, mark, property, trait **4.** acclaim, eminence, excellence, glory, honour, merit, renown, respect **5.** award, badge, medal, note, symbol, title

distinctive *adj.* abnormal, atypical, characteristic, delineating, determining, different, excellent, exemplifying, extraordinary, idiosyncratic, individual, outstanding, peculiar, rare, uncommon, unique, unusual *Nonformal:* cool, offbeat *Antonyms:* dull, everyday, normal, regular, usual

distinguish *v.* **1.** delimit, demarcate, differentiate, discriminate, mark, point out, separate **2.** decide, determine, evaluate, judge, rule, weigh **3.** characterize, define, describe, exemplify, typify **4.** detect, discover, espy, eyeball *(Nonformal)*, note, notice, perceive, spot **5.** acclaim, beatify, canonize, dignify, elevate, glorify, honour, lionize

distinguished *adj.* **1.** acclaimed, aristocratic, brilliant, conspicuous, especial, extraordinary, famed, famous, foremost, glorious, marked, memorable, notable, noteworthy, preeminent, prominent, remarkable, signal, superior, talked about *or* of, well-known *Antonyms:* common, inelegant, inferior **2.** celebrated, esteemed, great, highly regarded, honoured, illustrious, noble, nonpareil, peerless, renowned, reputable, venerable

distort *v.* **1.** alter, belie, bias, change, colour, deceive, deform, deviate, disfigure, fake, falsify, fudge, garble, lie, misconstrue, misinterpret, misrepresent, pervert, skew, slant, whitewash *Nonformal:* doctor, scam **2.** angle, bend, buckle, contort, curve, gnarl, knot, mangle, muddle, twist, wrench, writhe

distortion *n.* **1.** bias, colouring, exaggeration, falsification, lie, misinterpretation, misrepresentation, perversion, slant, spin *(Nonformal)*, story *Antonyms:* clarification, truth **2.** bend, contortion, crookedness, defect, deformity, flaw, kink, twist, warp **3.** feedback, fuzz, hum, noise *or* white noise, overdrive, phase, rumble, snow, static, timbre

distract *v.* **1.** abstract, amuse, divert, entertain, occupy, sidetrack **2.** addle, befuddle, bewilder, confound, confuse, disconcert, fluster, mislead, perplex, puzzle, stall, throw off **3.** agitate, craze, derange, disturb, harass, madden, torment, trouble, unbalance, unhinge *Antonyms:* calm, placate, soothe *Commonly misused:* **detract**

distracted *adj.* **1.** abstracted, blind, brooding, engrossed, heedless, inattentive, insensible, lost, musing, oblivious, pensive, perplexed, ponderous, preoccupied, reflective, ruminative, thoughtful, unaware *Antonyms:* alert, attentive, heedful, watchful **2.** addled, bewildered, bothered, confounded, confused, disconcerted, flustered, puzzled, vexed **3.** agitated, crazed, delirious, deranged, distraught, excited, feverish, frantic, frenzied, insane, irrational, mad, overwrought, raving, ravening, troubled, wild, worked up *(Nonformal) Antonyms:* rational, sane, sober

distraught *adj.* **1.** agitated, anxious, bothered, distracted, distressed, flustered, frantic, harassed, hysterical, nonplused, overwrought, rattled, thrown, tormented, upset, worried **2.** confused, crazy, demented, deranged, insane, mad *Nonformal:* nuts, raving, unglued, wild

distress *n.* **1.** agony, anguish, anxiety, grief, heartache, heartbreak, misery, pain, sadness, sorrow, suffering, torment, unhappiness, woe *Antonyms:* contentment, happiness, joy, satisfaction **2.** danger, extreme need, jeopardy, peril, risk, trouble *Antonyms:* safety, security **3.** adversity, destitution, hardship, indigence, misfortune, poverty, privation, tribulation, trial, want, wretchedness *Antonyms:* abundance, bounty, comfort, extravagance, luxury – *v.* **1.** afflict, bother, harass, harry, hector, vex *Nonformal:* bug, discombobulate, dog, hassle, pick on, ride *Antonyms:* calm, compose, conciliate, pacify, soothe **2.** debilitate, drain, exhaust, fatigue, tax, wear out *Nonformal:* do in, sap *Antonyms:* enliven, invigorate, kindle, revitalize

distressed *adj.* **1.** afflicted, agitated, anxious, bothered, concerned, disconsolate, distracted, distraught, exercised, fidgety, harassed, hyper, inconsolable, jittery, peeved, perturbed, saddened, tormented, troubled, unsettled, upset, uptight, worried, wretched *Antonyms:* peaceful, placid, tranquil **2.** badly off *(Nonformal)*, destitute, down and out, impoverished, penniless, penurious, poor, poverty-stricken, straitened *Antonyms:* rich, wealthy, well-to-do

distribute *v.* **1.** apportion, assign, bestow, convey, deal, dispense, dispose, give, hand *or* mete *or* parcel out, ration *Nonformal:* divvy up, shell out *Antonyms:* conserve, hoard, keep, withhold **2.** broadcast, circulate, disseminate, publicize, publish *Antonyms:* ban, censor, retract **3.** bestrew, scatter, sow, sprinkle, throw, toss *Antonyms:* assemble, collect, gather **4.** arrange, categorize, classify, group, order, systematize

distribution *n.* **1.** delivery, handling, logistics, traffic, transportation **2.** allocation, assignment, disbursement, dissemination **3.** arrangement, array, deployment, dispersement, placement **4.** frequency, incidence, prevalence

district *n.* area, *arrondissement (French)*, *barrio (Spanish)*, borough, commune, community, department, locale, locality, neighbourhood, parcel, parish, precinct, quarter, region, section, sector, territory, turf, vicinity, ward *City districts:* annex, business district, Chinatown, city centre, docks, downtown, electoral, ghetto, inner city, Little Italy, midtown, residential, shanty-town, shopping, slum, suburbia, suburbs, uptown, urban centre *or* core, waterfront *Nonformal:* concrete jungle, mean streets, red-light district, skid row, tenderloin *Canadian Urban Districts:* Africville *(Halifax historical)*, Astro Hill *(Iqaluit)*, Bastion Square *(Victoria)*, Gastown *(Vancouver)*, Kwanlin Dun Village *(Whitehorse)*, Lower Town *(Quebec City)*, Market Square *(Saint John)*, Old Strathcona *(Edmonton)*, Old Charlottetown *(Charlottetown)*, Range Lake *(Yellowknife)*, Signal Hill *(St. John's)*, The Forks *(Winnipeg)*, Wascana Centre *(Regina)*, *Calgary:* Eau Claire, Marda Loop *Montreal:* Balconville, Old Montreal *or* Vieux

Montréal *Ottawa:* Byward Market, Lower Town, Parliament Hill *Toronto:* Annex, Bay Street, Cabbagetown, Forest Hill, Kensington Market, Rosedale

distrust *n.* cynicism, disbelief, doubt, misgiving, qualm, question, scepticism, suspicion, wariness *Antonyms:* confidence, faith, reliance, trust – *v.* disbelieve, discredit, dislike, doubt, mistrust, question, shy away *(Nonformal)*, suspect *Antonyms:* believe, depend, trust

distrustful *adj.* apprehensive, cagey *(Nonformal)*, cautious, chary, dubious, fearful, guarded, jealous, leery, sceptical, uneasy, uptight, wary *Antonyms:* certain, credulous, gullible, sure

disturb *v.* **1.** disarrange, dislocate, disorder, disorganize, displace, distort, foul up, interfere, jumble, muddle, shift, move, tamper with **2.** annoy, exasperate, hound, interrupt, irk, nettle, pester, pique, plague, provoke, rile, ruffle, vex *Nonformal:* bug, get to *Antonyms:* amuse, divert, gratify **3.** baffle, confound, confuse, discompose, disconcert, dismay, disquiet, shock, startle, upset *Nonformal:* flummox, rattle *Antonyms:* convince, reassure, satisfy **4.** agitate, shake *Nonformal:* fire up, make waves, rock the boat

disturbance *n.* **1.** chaos, confusion, disarray, disruption, pandemonium, upheaval *Antonyms:* calm, order, serenity, tranquility **2.** brawl, fracas, insurrection, rebellion, riot, rumble *Nonformal:* brouhaha, dust-up, slugfest *Antonyms:* amity, camaraderie, friendliness **3.** cacophony, commotion, racket, to-do *(Nonformal)*, tumult, uproar *Antonyms:* quietude, silence, stillness **4.** bother, hassle *(Nonformal)*, headache, inconvenience, intrusion, irritation, nuisance *Antonyms:* bliss, comfort, delight, pleasure **5.** bewilderment, confusion, distraction, perturbation, puzzle, upset, worry *Antonyms:* assurance, certainty, conviction **6.** active weather, cyclone, hurricane, low pressure, storm, twister

disturbed *adj.* **1.** agitated, apprehensive, concerned, uneasy, worried *Nonformal:* nervy, panicked, wired *Antonyms:* calm, composed, tranquil **2.** bewildered, confused, disoriented, flustered, shaken, unsettled, upset **3.** annoyed, bothered, harried, irritated, miffed, piqued, pissed off *(Nonformal)* **4.** insane, mentally ill, neurasthenic, neurotic, *non compos mentis (Latin)*, psychopathic, psychotic, unbalanced *Nonformal:* bonkers, mixed-up

ditch *n.* canal, channel, dike, drain, entrenchment, excavation, gully, gutter, moat, sluice, trench, trough, watercourse, waterway – *v.* **1.** abandon, cashier, chuck, desert, discard, dispose of, drop, dump, forsake, jettison, junk, leave, reject, scrap, throw away **2.** crash, crash land, derail, sideswipe, splashdown *(Nonformal)* **3.** cut, dike, furrow, groove, gully, rut, slot, trench **4.** drain, extract, pump off **5.** dodge, elude, evade, lose, shake off

dither *n.* agitation, anxiety, bother, bustle, dread, excitement, flap, fluster, flutter, fret, fuss, nervousness, panic, pother, twitter *Nonformal:* stew, tizzy – *v.* falter, hover, hesitate, oscillate, swither, teeter, vacillate, waver *Nonformal:* faff about, shilly-shally *Antonyms:* bear down, concentrate, decide

dive *n.* **1.** jump, plunge, submergence *Kinds of dive:* backflip, belly-flop, cannonball, cliff, full gainer, jackknife, pike, swallow, swan **2.** descent, fall, freefall, header, leap, lunge, nose dive **3.** brothel, club, den of iniquity, dump, fleapit, flophouse, hell hole, hole, lair – *v.* **1.** descend, dodge, duck, jump, leap, lunge, lurch, nose-dive, plummet, plunge, splash, submerge **2.** dart, dash, dip, drop, fall, pitch, spring, swoop, whisk

diverge *v.* **1.** bend, bevel, bifurcate, branch out, disseminate, dissipate, emanate, fork, oblique, radiate, scatter, slant, spread out, stem **2.** deviate, differ, digress, disagree, divide, part, separate, shift, split, stand apart, stray, vary, veer

divergence *n.* **1.** alteration, branch, detour, digression, division, off-shoot, parting *Antonyms:* coalescence, fusion, union **2.** change, deflection, departure, deviation, difference, disparity, dissimilarity, shift, varying

divergent *adj.* **1.** conflicting, contrary, differing, dissenting, opposing, poles apart

(Nonformal) Antonyms: assenting, congruent, harmonious, unanimous **2.** aberrant, bumbling, rambling, straggling, wandering, wayward *Antonyms:* direct, linear, straightforward **3.** branching, divisive, centrifugal, fanlike, furcate, radiant *Antonyms:* centripetal, concurrent, convergent

diverse *adj.* assorted, checkered, contrasting, different, disparate, dissimilar, mixed, motley, multifarious, several, sundry, unalike, unlike, varied

diversify *v.* **1.** counterbalance, distribute, divide, hedge, partition **2.** branch out, broaden, expand, extend, off-shoot, spread out, thin, variegate *Antonyms:* downsize, retract, retrench **3.** alter, change, modify, retool, transform

diversion *n.* **1.** amusement, beguilement, delight, disport, distraction, divertissement, enjoyment, entertainment, frivolity, fun, game, levity, pastime, play, pleasure, recreation, sport *Antonyms:* drudgery, monotony **2.** alteration, alternate route, bypass, change, detour, deviation, digression, shift, variation *Antonyms:* core, heart, mainline **3.** blind, deke, feint, machination, manoeuvre, stratagem, tactic

diversity *n.* **1.** assortment, conglomeration, cross-section, heterogeneity, hodgepodge, medley, melange, mixture, multiplicity, potpourri, range, selection, variety *Antonyms:* monotony, recurrence, repetition **2.** contrast, difference, discrepancy, disparateness, dissimilarity, fluctuation, incongruity, nonconformity *Antonyms:* compatibility, congruence, homogeneity

divert *v.* **1.** alter, avert, deflect, detach, detour, discourage, disengage, dissuade, lead astray, redirect, sidetrack, swerve, switch, turn aside, veer *Antonyms:* captivate, draw, lure, persuade **2.** amuse, beguile, delight, entertain, gladden, gratify, make happy, please, regale *Nonformal:* tickle, wow *Antonyms:* anger, annoy, irritate, pique

divest *v.* **1.** dump, lose, sell off, unload *Nonformal:* deep-six, ditch, 86 **2.** deprive, dispense, free, purge, relieve, rid **3.** cast off, dismantle, doff, free, peel, shuck *(Nonformal)*, strip, take off, unclothe, undress

divide *n.* border, boundary, demarcation, end, gulf, limit, partition – *v.* **1.** allocate, allot, apportion, deal, dish out, disseminate, distribute, hand *or* mete out, measure, parcel, portion, ration, share *Nonformal:* divvy, shell out *Antonyms:* conserve, hoard, hold, retain, save **2.** branch, break up, divaricate, diverge, fork, furcate, split, turn **3.** cut *or* split off, detach, divorce, isolate, part, partition, segregate, separate *Antonyms:* congregate, merge, unite **4.** bisect, break, carve, chop, cleave, cut, quarter, sever, slice *Antonyms:* connect, fuse, meld, weld **5.** arrange, assign, categorize, classify, file, order, sort **6.** alienate, disunite, estrange, pit *or* set against, set apart *Antonyms:* harmonize, solidify, synergize, unify **7.** calculate, compute, figure, reckon, work out

dividend *n.* **1.** payout, profit share, return, share **2.** benefit, bonus, cut, gain, plum, premium, reward

divine *adj.* **1.** all-powerful, almighty, angelic, beatific, blissful, celestial, cosmic, eternal, exalted, glorious, godlike, hallowed, heavenly, holy, immaculate, magnificent, mystical, omniscient, perfect, religious, sacred, sacrosanct, spiritual, sublime, supreme, transcendental, unearthly *Antonyms:* base, inglorious, misbegotten **2.** fantastic, stunning, superb, unbelievable, wonderful *Antonyms:* awful, forgettable, unprintable, wretched – *n.* chaplain, churchman, churchwoman, clergyman, clergywoman, cleric, divinity student, ecclesiastic, father, guru, minister, padre, parson, pastor, preacher, priest, rabbi, rector, reverend, theologian, vicar – *v.* anticipate, apprehend, conjecture, deduce, discern, forebode, foresee, foretell, guess, infer, intuit, perceive, predict, prognosticate, prophesy, see, suppose, surmise, suspect, visualize

divinity *n.* **1.** celestial, deity, divine nature, genius, god, goddess, godhead, godliness, guardian spirit, higher power, holiness, sanctity, spirit **2.** religion, theology, theosophy

division *n.* **1.** affiliate, associate, branch, caucus, chapter, compartment, concession, department, district, faction, lodge, member, off-shoot, post, sect, section, sector, splinter group, subdivision, wing **2.** arrangement, cataloguing, categorization, category, class, family, grading, grouping, order, ordering, rank, set, sorting, taxonomy **3.** border, boundary, demarcation, fence, limit, line, margin, partition, wall **4.** army, battalion, battery, brigade, company, corps, detachment, fleet, flotilla, garrison, legion, marines, navy forces, platoon, regiment, service, squad, squadron, task force, troop, unit **5.** allotment, apportionment, bisection, bit, cut, cutting, degree, distribution, divvy *(Nonformal)*, fraction, fragment, measurement, part, piece, portion, portioning, scale, segment, share, sharing, slice, split, splitting **6.** breach, break-up, conflict, difficulty, disagreement, disharmony, dispute, dissection, dissidence, divorce, estrangement, feud, rupture, separation, split, trouble

divorce *n.* breakup, dissolution, disunion, estrangement, parting, partition, separation, severance, split – *v.* annul, break up, detach, disconnect, dissociate, dissolve, disunite, divide, estrange, leave, nullify, part, separate, sever, split up *Antonyms:* espouse, join, marry, wed

divulge *v.* admit, confess, declare, disclose, expose, impart, leak, open *or* own up, proclaim, publish, reveal, tell *Nonformal:* cough *or* fess up, fink, go public, squeal *Antonyms:* hold back, keep secret, smother, stifle

dizzy *adj.* addled, befuddled, bemused, bewildered, blinded, confused, dazed, dazzled, faint, giddy, groggy, hazy, light, light-headed, muddled, off balance, reeling, shaky, staggering, swimming, tipsy, unsteady, vertiginous, weak-kneed, whirling *Nonformal:* gaga, punch-drunk, punchy, slap-happy, wobbly, woozy

do *n.* **1.** affair, celebration, event, festival, fête, function, gala, gathering, levee, occasion, soiree, wingding *(Nonformal)* **2.** blow-dry, bouffant, coif, cut, hairdo, hairstyle, updo – *v.* **1.** accomplish, achieve, attain, bring about, carry through, close, compass, complete, conclude, consummate, deal with, discharge, effectuate, execute, finish, finish off, implement, perfect, pull off *(Nonformal)*, realize, transact, work **2.** compose, concoct, contrive, create, develop, effect, fabricate, generate, improvise, invent, make up, originate, prepare, present, produce, see to, translate, undertake **3.** answer, avail, benefit, fulfill, hold, make the grade *(Nonformal)*, muster, pass, qualify, satisfy, serve, stand up, suffice, suit **4.** act, ape, copy, enact, imitate, impersonate, masquerade, mime, mimic, perform, play, pose **5.** behave, comport, conduct, handle, manage, proceed **6.** course, cover, cruise, journey, perambulate, ramble, range, reach, roam, scour, scout, sightsee, tour, track, travel, traverse, vacation, voyage, wander

docile *adj.* accommodating, acquiescent, adaptable, agreeable, amenable, biddable, compliant, ductile, easy, gentle, governable, handleable, humble, manageable, meek, mild, obedient, obliging, pliable, pliant, quiet, resigned, submissive, tame, teachable, tractable, usable, willing, yielding *Antonyms:* difficult, intractable, obstreperous, troublesome

dock *n.* **1.** berth, embankment, jetty, landing, levee, lock, marina, moorage, pier, quay, slip, stage *(Newfoundland)*, waterfront, wharf **2.** box, enclosure, platform – *v.* **1.** anchor, arrive, cast ashore, land, moor, park, tie up **2.** bob, clip, crop, cut off, decrease, deduct, excise, extract, mow, nip, prune, reduce, shave, shear, shorten, subtract *Antonyms:* add, augment, enhance, increase

docket *n.* **1.** agenda, calendar, card, program, schedule, ticket, timetable **2.** annotation, dossier, entry, file, marginalia, marginal note, memo, notation, note, papers, record, register **3.** label, list, seal, stamp, sticker, tag, tally, ticket – *v.* bill, book, catalogue, enroll, enter, file, index, list, log, note, poll, program, record, schedule, slate, tabulate

doctor *n.* **1.** Doctor of Medicine *or* MD, expert, healer, intern, medic, medicine man *or* woman, medico, physician, practitioner *Kinds of doctor or medical practitioner:* anesthesiologist, cardiologist, chiropractor, coroner, dentist, dermatologist, family doctor, endocrinologist, general practitioner *or* GP, medical examiner, gynecologist, internist, neurologist, obstetrician, oncologist, ophthalmologist, optometrist, orthopedist, osteopath, pathologist, pediatrician, proctologist, psychiatrist, specialist, surgeon, veterinarian *Nonformal:* bones, croaker, doc, quack, sawbones, vet **2.** academic, educator, fellow, instructor, lecturer, man *or* woman of letters, PhD, professor, teacher – *v.* **1.** administer, attend, fix, medicate, mend, overhaul, patch up, rebuild, recondition, reconstruct, repair, supply, treat **2.** adulterate, alter, contaminate, corrupt, fake, falsify, load, manipulate *Nonformal:* cook, fix

doctrinaire *adj.* **1.** authoritative, biased, by-the-book, dogmatic, inflexible, insistent, magisterial, one-sided, pedantic, pertinacious, pigheaded, prejudiced, rigid **2.** hypothetical, impractical, speculative, theoretical, unrealistic

doctrine *n.* attitude, axiom, belief, canon, conviction, credo, creed, dogma, faith, ideology, maxim, opinion, position, precept, principle, religion, tenet, theory, universal law, unwritten rule

document *n.* **1.** authorization, certificate, chit, credentials, deed, diploma, dossier, evidence, form, instrument, proof, receipt, record, testimony, ticket, voucher, warrant, writ **2.** book, bumf *(Nonformal)*, composition, copy, diary, draft, edition, file, letter, literature, manuscript *or* MS., matter, paper, parchment, piece, reading material, script, scroll, version, work, writing – *v.* **1.** adduce, affirm, authenticate, bolster, certify, confirm, corroborate, fortify, instance, reinforce, strengthen, substantiate, verify *Antonyms:* discredit, disprove, invalidate **2.** annotate, cite, footnote, itemize, name, note, particularize, quote, reference, report

doddering *adj.* decrepit, faltering, feeble, infirm, senile, shaky, shambling, tottering, trembling, unsteady, weak *Antonyms:* hale, stalwart, sturdy, vigorous

dodge *n.* **1.** chicanery, contrivance, deception, device, feint, fraud, machination, ploy, ruse, scheme, stratagem, subterfuge, trick, wile **2.** avoidance, escape, evasion, go-by *(Nonformal)* – *v.* **1.** avoid, bob and weave, dance around, dart, deke, dipsy-doodle *(Nonformal)*, duck, fend off, jouk *(P.E.I.)*, slip, swerve, twist away, veer *Antonyms:* assail, attack, tackle **2.** bolt, decamp, elude, escape, evade, leave, lose, split *Nonformal:* ditch, run *or* shake off, skip out *Antonyms:* beard, confront, face **3.** circumlocate, deceive, equivocate, fudge, hedge, parry, prevaricate, shuffle, skirt *Nonformal:* quibble, weasel, work around *Antonyms:* acknowledge, admit, confer

dog *adv.* absolutely, altogether, completely, plumb *(Nonformal)*, thoroughly, totally, unconditionally, utterly, very, wholly – *n.* **1.** bitch, canine, *canis familiaris (Latin)*, cross, crossbreed, hound, man's best friend, mix *or* mixed breed, mongrel, pack dog, pooch, pup *or* puppy, stray *Nonformal:* bowwow, doggy, fido, flea bag, flea hotel, halfbreed, heel, Heinz 57, mutt, puppy-dog *Groupings of dog:* guard, hound, miniature, non-sporting breed, pointer, retriever, sheep, show, spaniel, sporting, terrier, working *Kinds of dog:* Afghan, Airedale, Basenji, Basset *or* Basset Hound, Beagle, Bloodhound, Borzoi, Boston bull, Brittany spaniel, Bulldog, Bullmastiff, Bull Terrier, Chihuahua, Chow *or* Chow Chow, Cocker Spaniel, Collie, Dachshund, Dalmatian, Doberman Pinscher, Foxhound, Fox Terrier, German Shepherd, Golden Retriever, Great Dane, Greyhound, Husky, Irish Setter, Jack Russell Terrier, Kerry Blue Terrier, Komondor, Labrador Retriever, Lhasa Apso, Malamute, Newfoundland, Nova Scotia Duck Tolling Retriever, Pekingese, Pit Bull, Miniature *or* Standard poodle, Pug, Puli, Rottweiler, Saint Bernard, Saluki, Samoyed, Schipperke, Schnauzer, Scottish Terrier, Seeing-Eye *(Trademark)*, Setter, Springer Spaniel, Toy, Water Spaniel, Weimaraner, West Highland Terrier, Whippet, Wolfhound, Yorkshire Terrier **2.** blackguard, cad, coward, cur, good-for-nothing, ne'er-do-well, riffraff, scoundrel, scum, villain, wretch *Nonformal:* bum, heel, rotter, stinker **3.** dud, fiasco, nonstarter, poor show *Nonformal:* bomb, turkey – *v.* bother, chase, haunt, hound, plague, pursue, shadow, tag, tail, track, trail, trouble, worry

dogged *adj.* **1.** assiduous, constant, determined, do-or-die, earnest, firm, fixed, indefatigable, indomitable, intent, persevering, persistent, plucky, purposeful, relentless, resistant, resolute, set, single-minded, staunch, steadfast, steady, tenacious, unbending, unfaltering, unflagging, unflinching, unhesitating, untiring, unwavering, unyielding, wilful *Antonyms:* erratic, fickle, fitful, frivolous **2.** bull- *or* pigheaded, inflexible, intractable, intransigent, mulish, obdurate, obstinate, pertinacious, stubborn, unmoveable *Antonyms:* doubtful, half-hearted, hesitant, unsteady

dogma *n.* axiom, belief, conviction, credo, creed, doctrine, faith, ideology, maxim, philosophy, precept, principle, tenet

dogmatic *adj.* **1.** authoritative, canonical, categorical, definite, determined, doctrinaire, *ex cathedra (Latin)*, formal, magisterial, unequivocal, unqualified **2.** assertive, despotic, dictatorial, domineering, emphatic, imperious, intolerant, obdurate, one-sided, opinionated, overbearing, tyrannical

doldrums *n.* **1.** apathy, blues, boredom, depression, discontent, dullness, ennui, indifference, inertia, lassitude, letdown, listlessness, melancholy, sadness, slump, stagnation, tedium, torpor *Nonformal:* blahs, blue funk, dumps, funk **2.** calm, lull, quiet, stillness, tranquility, windlessness

dole *n.* **1.** allocation, allowance, apportionment, charitable gift, donation, employment insurance *or* EI, grant, handout, parcel, pogey *(Nonformal)*, portion, quota, share **2.** affliction, agony, anguish, desolation, grief, heartache, misery, mourning, sorrow, woe – *v.* administer, allocate, allot, apportion, bestow, confer, dispense, disperse, disseminate, distribute, divide, divvy *(Nonformal)*, donate, give *or* hand *or* mete out, heap, issue, lavish, ration

doleful *adj.* **1.** crestfallen, dejected, depressed, discontent, dismal, dispirited, dolorous, downcast, downhearted, forlorn, gloomy, grieving, lamentable, melancholy, rueful, sad, sombre, sorrowful, woeful *Antonyms:* glad, joyous, merry **2.** cheerless, depressing, dire, dreary, grim, pitiable, sordid, uninviting, wretched *Antonyms:* luxurious, opulent, sumptuous

doll *n.* **1.** baby, dolly, effigy, figure, figurine, manikin, mannequin, marionette, model, moppet, poppet *(Nonformal)*, stuffed animal, toy **2.** charmer, gem, jewel, nonpareil, *persona grata (Latin)*, posy *(P.E.I.)*, sweetheart *Nonformal:* babe, crackerjack, luv, sweet – *v.* adorn, bedeck, deck out, dress *or* gussy up, embellish, prettify

dollar *n.* bank note, bill, currency, folding money, legal tender, loonie *or* dollar coin, money, note, toonie *or* two-dollar coin *Historical:* Diefendollar, leather dollar *Nonformal:* bread, buck, cash, dead presidents *(U.S.)*, dough, green, moolah

dolorous *adj.* **1.** anguished, cheerless, depressed, discontent, melancholy, miserable, unhappy, woeful, wretched *Antonyms:* cheerful, joyous, rejoicing **2.** deplorable, dire, distressing, grievous, harrowing, heart-rending, lamentable, lugubrious, mournful, painful, regrettable, sorrowful

dolour *n.* agony, anguish, discontent, distress, grief, heartache, heartbreak, misery, pain, sadness, sorrow, suffering, upset, *Weltschmerz (German)*

domain *n.* **1.** bailiwick, beat, dominion, empire, estate, kingdom, land, neighbourhood, orbit, palatinate, precinct, province, realm, region, sphere, terrain, territory, walk, world, zone *Nonformal:* hood, stomping ground, turf **2.** calling, concern, department, discipline, field, field of expertise, occupation, slot, speciality **3.** address, home, site, Website

dome *n.* **1.** arch, bubble, bulge, covering, cupola, roof, rotunda, span, top, vault **2.** acme, apex, crown, summit, zenith **3.** head, pate *Nonformal:* bean, block, noggin, noodle, sconce

domestic *adj.* **1.** community, home-grown, homemade, indigenous, inland, internal, local, national, native **2.** home, home-centred, homey, household, residential, stay-at-home **3.** broke *(Nonformal)*, civilized, familiarized, housetrained, tame, trained *Antonyms:* feral, natural, wild – *n.* abigail, au pair, butler, chambermaid, char *or* charwoman, chauffeur, cleaner, cook, daily maid, houseboy, housekeeper, maid, manservant, major domo, nanny, nursemaid, servant, valet *Nonformal:* help, live-in, skivvy

domesticate *v.* acclimatize, accustom, break, breed, civilize, familiarize, naturalize, raise, subdue, tame, teach, train

domicile *n.* abode, accommodation, apartment, castle, condominium, co-op, dwelling, habitat, habitation, home, house, legal residence, lodgings, mansion, residence, settlement *Nonformal:* digs, roost – *v.* abide, berth, bunk, dwell, harbour, house, inhabit, live, lodge, provide shelter, quarter, reside, stay

dominant *adj.* **1.** bold, commanding, conspicuous, distinguished, exceptional, imposing, lofty, majestic, monumental, noticeable, paramount, preeminent, prominent, striking, towering, unmistakable *Antonyms:* insignificant, insubstantial, minor, unnoticeable **2.** established, extensive, general, main, popular, preponderant, prevalent, prevailing, widespread *Antonyms:* avant-garde, fringe, non-conformist, unorthodox **3.** ascendant, controlling, governing, master, reigning, ruling, sovereign *Antonyms:* impotent, powerless, subject, subordinate, subservient **4.** first, leading, number-one, numero-uno *(Nonformal)*, premier, primary, principal, winning *Antonyms:* last-place, losing, runner-up

dominate *v.* **1.** browbeat, bully, hector, intimidate, overbear *Nonformal:* bulldoze, henpeck, hound, ride **2.** conquer, crush, master, oppress, overpower, subdue, subjugate, subordinate, tyrannize **3.** boss, call the shots *(Nonformal)*, command, control, dictate, monopolize, reign, rule **4.** dwarf, eclipse, loom *or* tower over, minimize, overlie, overshadow

domination *n.* **1.** ascendancy, authority, command, control, influence, jurisdiction, masterdom, power, rule, sovereignty, superiority, supremacy, sway **2.** dictatorship, oppression, repression, subjection, subordination, suppression, terrorism, tyranny

domineering *adj.* arrogant, assertive, authoritarian, autocratic, bossy, despotic, dictatorial, directing, imperious, magisterial, overbearing, peremptory, tyrannical *Nonformal:* high-handed, iron-handed, pushy *Antonyms:* meek, obsequious, servile, shy, submissive

dominion *n.* **1.** bailiwick, country, domain, kingdom, nation, province, realm, region, satrapy, sphere, state, territory *Nonformal:* neck of the woods, turf **2.** authority, command, control, jurisdiction, power, sovereignty, sway

donate *v.* accord, award, bequeath, bestow, confer, contribute, furnish, give, give away, grant, offer, present, provide, subsidize, supply, yield *Nonformal:* kick in, pass the hat *Antonyms:* keep, repossess, retain

donation *n.* aid, alms, assistance, baksheesh, benefaction, bequest, boon, charity, contribution, dole, endowment, gift, grant, gratuity, handout, help, helping hand, largesse, offering, philanthropy, present, presentation

done *adj.* **1.** accomplished, all over, brought about, compassed, completed, concluded, consummated, contrived, effected, ended, executed, finished, fixed, fulfilled, over, perfected, performed, realized, rendered, set, succeeded, terminated, through, wrought *Nonformal:* downed, finito, wrapped *Antonyms:* aborted, incomplete, partial **2.** all in, depleted, drained, emptied out, exhausted, spent, tired, used up *Nonformal:* burned *or* tuckered out, bushed, shot, whacked *Antonyms:* energetic, fresh, zesty **3.** baked, boiled, broiled, cooked, heated, prepared, ready, warmed *Antonyms:* half-baked, raw, uncooked **4.** correct, polite, proper, right, socially acceptable, tactful *Antonyms:* gauche, indelicate, vulgar **5.** refurbished, renovated, revamped *Nonformal:* dolled *or* fixed up, gussied *or* spiffed *or* spruced up

donkey *n.* **1.** ass, beast of burden, burro, hinny, jack, jackass, jennet, jenny, mule, onager **2.** dullard, dunce, fool, idiot, nincompoop, simpleton

donnybrook *n.* affray, brawl, chaos, commotion, fight, fisticuffs, fracas, fray, free-for-all, hubbub, melee, pandemonium, row, ruckus, rumpus, scuffle, set-to, skirmish, tumult, turmoil, tussle *Nonformal:* dust-up, hellery, slugfest,

donor *n.* almsgiver, altruist, angel, backer, benefactor, bestower, contributor, donator, giver, grantor, patron, philanthropist, subscriber, underwriter *Nonformal:* fairy godmother, lady *or* lord bountiful *Antonyms:* beneficiary, inheritor, receiver, recipient

doom *n.* **1.** destiny, fate, ill fortune, lot, misfortune, wheel of fortune **2.** annihilation, calamity, death, downfall, extermination, extirpation, Grim Reaper, holocaust, kiss of death, ruin **3.** Apocalypse, Armageddon, cataclysm, curtains, end of the world, Last Judgment, sword of Damocles – *v.* **1.** banish, censure, condemn, damn, ostracize, sentence **2.** bind, destine, predetermine, set

doomed *adj.* **1.** bound, foreordained, hopeless, ill-fated, ill-omened, luckless, predestined, predetermined, preordained **2.** condemned, cursed, damned, fated **3.** cut down, destroyed, overthrown, ruined, sunk, unfortunate, wrecked

door *n.* doorway, entrance, entranceway, entry, exit, opening, portal, threshold *Kinds and parts of door:* casement, Dutch, folding, French, front, gate, hatch, jalousie, jamb, lintel, louvre, sash, screen, sliding, trapdoor

dope *adj.* amazing, cool, excellent, great, outstanding *Nonformal:* fab, gear, right on – *n.* **1.** downer, drug, illegal substance, medication, marijuana, narcotic, preparation, sedative, stimulant, substance, upper *Nonformal:* grass, Mary Jane, pot, reefer, weed **2.** information, news, score, story, tip *Nonformal:* dirt, scoop **3.** creep, drip, dullard, dumbbell, dummy, fool, jerk, klutz, loser, nerd, simpleton **4.** additive, backing, emulsion, fuel, fuel additive, gell, goop *(Nonformal)*, grease, lubricant – *v.* **1.** administer, adulterate, alter, anesthetize, apply, doctor, dose, drug, mainline *(Nonformal)*, medicate, narcotize **2.** calculate, cipher, compute, crack, decipher, decode, estimate, figure *or* work out, reckon, resolve, solve *See also:* **drugs**

dopey *adj.* **1.** comatose, confused, dazed, dense, dumb, exhausted, heavy, inert, languid, lethargic, senseless, slow, sluggish, thick, tired, torpid *Nonformal:* groggy, pepless, punchy, punch drunk **2.** foolish, idiotic, inane, ridiculous, silly, simple, stupid

dormant *adj.* **1.** asleep, comatose, hibernating, lethargic, sleeping, sluggish, slumbering *Antonyms:* active, alert, aroused, awake, conscious **2.** between jobs, down, inactive, inert, inoperative, latent, out of work, passive, quiescent

dose *n.* amount, dosage, dram, draught, fill, lot, measure, measurement, portion, potion, prescription, quantity, share, shot, spoonful *Nonformal:* fix, hit, slug – *v.* **1.** administer, anoint, apply, bestow, inject, medicate, minister, treat **2.** adulterate, blend, dilute, doctor *(Nonformal)*, fix *Commonly misused:* **douse**

dossier *n.* brief, curriculum vitae *or* CV, document, file *or* life file, papers, passport, printed matter, rap sheet, record, transcript, visa

dot *n.* **1.** dab, fleck, mark, notation, period, pinprick, speck, spot **2.** character, particle, pixel, point **3.** atom, crumb, dash, drop, droplet, fraction, grain, iota, jot, miniscule amount, minute, modicum, smidgen, soupçon – *v.* **1.** mark, note, punctuate **2.** dapple, freckle, mottle, spatter, speck, speckle, spot, sprinkle, stipple, variegate **3.** bestrew, disseminate, distribute, intersperse, pepper, scatter, spread

dotage *n.* advanced age, decrepitude, feebleness of mind, imbecility, infirmity, old age, second childhood, senility, weakness

doting *adj.* **1.** adoring, affectionate, besotted, devoted, extravagant, fascinated, fatuous, fond, foolish, indulgent, lovesick, loving, serving, silly, simple, struck **2.** decaying, decrepit, doddering, fading, feebleminded, infirm, senile, waning, wasting

double *adj.* **1.** duplicate, matched, recurrent, repeated, replicate *Antonyms:* distinct, individual, singular, unique **2.** binate, coupled, in pairs, married, paired, two combined *or* together *Antonyms:* lone, separate, sole, solitary **3.** bi-cameral, binary, bi-partisan, diploid, double-barreled, dual, dualistic, duple, two, twofold, two-ply *Antonyms:* one, single **4.** deceitful, duplistic, Janus-like, perfidious, two-faced *Antonyms:* genuine, honest, open – *adv.* **1.** encore, in addition to, twice, two times **2.** in tandem, pair-by-pair, two-by-two – *n.* **1.** extra, increase, more, seconds, twice as much, twofer *(Nonformal)* **2.** clone, copy, duplicate, match, mate, replica, twin *Nonformal:* dead ringer, lookalike, spitting image **3.** alternate, back up, counterpart, fill-in, pinch-hitter *or* -runner, second, stand-in, stunt-double, substitute, understudy *Antonyms:* lead, main, primary, star **4.** apparition, *doppelgänger (German)*, evil twin, ghost, nemesis, shadow-self, spectre, wraith **5.** ground-rule double, hit, linedrive, two-bagger *or* baser **6.** bet, bid, call, challenge – *v.* **1.** augment, duplicate, enlarge, germinate, grow, increase, magnify, multiply, repeat, supplement *Antonyms:* decrease, diminish, halve, wane **2.** act, function, perform, serve, work **3.** circumvent, dodge, elude, escape, evade, return, shake *or* shuck off *(Nonformal)* **4.** circle, circumnavigate, get *or* sail around, skirt **5.** bend, fold, tuck up, turn in **6.** bunch up, clench, close, gather, knot *Antonyms:* flex, release **7.** divvy up, go halves, share, split, subdivide **8.** couple, link, pair, team, yoke **9.** advance, drive, hit, move along *or* forward, propel

double-cross *n.* betrayal, deceit, treachery *Nonformal:* dirty trick, sellout – *v.* betray, cheat, deceive, defect, defraud, hoodwink, mislead, swindle, take in, trick *Nonformal:* con, rip-off, two-time

doubt *n.* **1.** hesitancy, indecision, irresolution, uncertainty, undecidedness, vacillation, wavering *Antonyms:* decisiveness, determination, firmness, resolution **2.** apprehension, difficulty, dilemma, disbelief, disquiet, incredulity, qualm, quandary, scruples, scepticism, suspicion *Antonyms:* acceptance, belief, credibility **3.** ambiguity, confusion, unpredictability *Antonyms:* order, predictability, regularity – *v.* **1.** disbelieve, distrust, mistrust, suspect, wonder *or* worry about **2.** equivocate, falter, hesitate *Nonformal:* shilly-shally, waffle *Antonyms:* commit, join **3.** challenge, demur, dispute, object, query, question, reject *Antonyms:* accept, approve, welcome

doubter *n.* agnostic, cynic, disbeliever, Doubting Thomas *(Nonformal)*, nonbeliever, questioner, sceptic, unbeliever *Antonyms:* disciple, fanatic, follower, zealot

doubtful *adj.* **1.** apocryphal, equivocal, faltering, hesitant, indecisive, sceptical, uncertain, unconvinced, undecided, unsettled, unsure, vacillating, wavering *Antonyms:* certain, positive, resolute, sure **2.** ambiguous, clouded, difficult, indefinite, indeterminate, indistinct, obscure, vague *Antonyms:* clear, lucid, unclouded **3.** dubious, improbable, questionable, suspect, suspicious, unbelievable, untrustworthy

doubtless *adv.* **1.** absolutely, assuredly, certainly, clearly, easily, for sure, indisputably, indubitably, of course, positively, precisely, surely, truly, unquestionably **2.** apparently, charming likely *(P.E.I.)*, most likely, ostensibly, presumably, supposedly

doughnut *n.* cake, doughboy, fritter, *krapfen (German)*, *pet-de-nonne (French)*, sinker *(Nonformal)* *Kinds of doughnut:* apple fritter, banana cream, Bavarian *or* Boston cream, Beaver Tail, beignet, bismarck, blueberry fritter, Canadian maple, cherry, chocolate, cinnamon twist, cruller, Dutchie, glazed, Hawaiian, jambuster, jelly, lemon, old-fashioned, peanut crunch, raised, raspberry, sour cream, spiced apple, strawberry, sugar, toasted coconut, twister

dour *adj.* **1.** austere, crabbed, forbidding, grim, harsh, ill-tempered, sour, stark, stern, surly *Antonyms:* refreshing, seductive, winsome **2.** difficult, intractable, obstinate, stubborn, troublesome, unyielding *Antonyms:* biddable, flexible, pliable *Commonly misused:* **dower**

douse *v.* **1.** dip, drench, duck, dunk, flush *or* flush out, hose down, wash *or* water down, immerse, plunge, rinse, saturate, shower, slop, slosh, souse, spray, submerge, wet **2.** blow *or* put out, close, extinguish, smother, snuff *or* snuff out **3.** haul down, lower, reef, take down *or* in **4.** doff, remove, shed, take off *Commonly misused:* **dose**

dovetail *n.* intersection, joint, mortise, tenon – *v.* agree, balance, coincide, conform, correspond, equal, fasten, fit, fit together, harmonize, interact, interlock, jibe, join, link, match, mortise, square, synchronize, unite *Antonyms:* disconnect, separate

dowdy *adj.* dingy, drab, dull, frowzy, frumpy, homely, old-fashioned, outdated, outmoded, out-of-date, plain, rundown, shabby, unfashionable *Antonyms:* chic, fashionable, neat, smart, trim

dower *n.* allowance, annuity, dowry, estate, heritage, inheritance, legacy, maintenance, pension, property, provision, settlement, trust, widow's portion – *v.* bestow, endow, provide *Commonly misused:* **dour**

down *adj.* **1.** crestfallen, dejected, depressed, disheartened, discontent, dispirited, downcast, melancholy, miserable, morose, sad, unhappy *Antonyms:* happy, high, up **2.** declining, declivitous, descending, downhill, downward, drooping, dropping, falling, sinking *Antonyms:* inclining, rising, upward **3.** cash, deposit, earnest **4.** broken, crippled, disabled, inactive, incapacitated, inoperative, malfunctioning, on the fritz *(Nonformal)*, out of action *or* commission, suppressed, unavailable *Antonyms:* functioning, operating, working **5.** beneath, flat, level, lower, under, underneath **6.** below par, indisposed, laid up, sick, under the weather, unwell *Antonyms:* healthy, well **7.** below, downhill, downgrade, downstairs, downstream, north *(Newfoundland)*, south **8.** cheaper, less expensive, on sale, reduced **9.** behind, in the red, lagging, losing, low, out by **10.** closed, defunct, out of business, padlocked, shuttered, shut tight **11.** hip, informed, into *or* with it, involved, knowledgeable – *adv.* **1.** at once, immediately, in advance, instantly, on the table, up-front, without delay **2.** all over, completely, everywhere, fully, totally **3.** formally, for posterity *or* the record, in writing, on paper – *n.* **1.** collapse, crash, decline, descent, downward spiral, droop, falling off, plunge, reversal of fortune, sag, setback, sink **2.** brae, butte, dune, fell, foothills, heath, hillock, moor, moorland, pastureland, savannah, steppe, veldt **3.** eider, feathers, floss, flue, fluff, fluffiness, fur, fuzz, pinfeather, plumage, thistledown **4.** action, carry, move, play – *v.* **1.** bolt, consume, eat, devour, drink, gobble, gulp, ingest, quaff, stuff, swallow *Nonformal:* guzzle, put away, wolf, wolf down **2.** chop *or* cut down, drop, fell, hew *or* knock down, lay low, level, precipitate, raze, topple *Nonformal:* deck, floor

downcast *adj.* blue, crestfallen, daunted, dejected, disappointed, discontent, discouraged, disheartened, glum, melancholy, unhappy *Nonformal:* bummed out, hangdog *Antonyms:* cheerful, elated, joyful, optimistic

downfall *n.* **1.** bankruptcy, breakdown, collapse, disgrace, failure, fall, ruination, undoing **2.** blunder, error, folly, misstep, mistake, oversight, wrong move **3.** blizzard, cascade, cloudburst, deluge, descent, downpour, flood, rain, soaker, sod-soaker *(Nonformal)*, spate, storm, thunderstorm, torrent

downgrade *adv.* below, down, downhill, downward – *n.* decline, declivity, decrease, descent, dip, inclination, pitch, slope – *v.* **1.** decrease, demerit, demote, depreciate, detract from, devalue, humble, lower, mark down, reduce, write off *Nonformal:* bump, bust *Antonyms:* advance, elevate, enhance, improve, promote **2.** decry, defame, degrade, denigrate, deprecate, disparage, revile, run down *Antonyms:* acclaim, extol, laud, praise

downplay *v.* de-emphasize, minimize, restrain, suppress, tone down, underplay, underrate, weaken *Antonyms:* emphasize, highlight, stress, underscore

downright *adj.* **1.** absolute, blatant, out-and-out, plain, thorough, thorough-going, total, unmitigated, utter, wholesale *Nonformal:* flat-out, rank **2.** blunt, forthright, frank, free-speaking, no-nonsense, open, straightforward, up-front – *adv.* evidently, incontestably, obviously, positively, undeniably, unequivocably, unmistakably

down-to-earth *adj.* common-sense, matter-of-fact, plain-spoken, practical, pragmatic, rational, realistic, sane, sensible, unsentimental *Antonyms:* baroque, extravagant, fantastic, far-fetched

downtown *n.* asphalt *or* concrete jungle, business *or* metropolitan *or* urban centre, central business district *or* CBD, *centre-ville (French)*, city centre *or* district, core, downstreet *(P.E.I.)*, inner city *Antonyms:* outskirts, suburbs

downtrodden *adj.* abused, alienated, disenfranchised, destitute, exploited, have-not, marginalized, oppressed, persecuted, subjugated, suppressed, tyrannized, victimized

downy *adj.* cozy, feathery, fleecy, fluffy, fuzzy, light, silky, soft, velvety

dowry *n.* dot, endowment, estate, gift, goods, marriage gift *or* portion *or* settlement, money, tocher *(British)*

doze *n.* catnap, drowse, nap, shut-eye, siesta, sleep, slumber *Nonformal:* forty winks, snooze – *v.* catnap, drift off, drowse, nap, nod, nod off, rest, sleep, sleep lightly, slumber *Nonformal:* flake out, kip, saw logs

draft *adj.* **1.** haulage, hauling, towing, transport **2.** outline, overview, preliminary, proposed, tentative, working **3.** from the cask, on tap, unpasteurized – *n.* **1.** blueprint, initial *or* unedited version, preliminary plan, rough, sketch, working paper **2.** air current, blast, blow, breath, breeze, gust, puff, simoom, sirocco, stepmother's breath *(P.E.I.)*, stream, updraft, waft, wind, zephyr **3.** bank draft, bill, bond, cheque, coupon, debenture, IOU *(Nonformal)*, money order, order, promissory note, warrant **4.** call-up, conscription, greetings *(Nonformal)*, levy, lottery **5.** capsule, dose, portion, potion, preparation, spoonful, tablet *Nonformal:* fix, hit **6.** bracer, drink, intoxication, libation, nip, quaff, sip, snap *(P.E.I.)*, swig *Nonformal:* jigger, pull, slurp, spot, tot **7.** baggage, burden, cargo, freight, haul, lading, load, luggage **8.** damper, flueplate, regulator – *v.* **1.** block out, compose, design, devise, draw *or* dream up, fabricate, fashion, formulate, frame, map *or* plot out, outline, rough, shape, sketch **2.** call *or* sign up, conscript, dragoon, impress, induct, press **3.** acquire, choose, nominate, pick, recruit, select, sign on

drag *n.* **1.** aggravation, annoyance, bad situation, bore, bother, burden, damper, imposition, irritant, nuisance, pain *Nonformal:* bummer, downer, wet blanket **2.** bottleneck, delay, encumbrance, friction, hangup *(Nonformal)*, hindrance, holdup, hook, impediment, problem, resistance, retardation, snag *Antonyms:* aid, boon, expedient, help **3.** avenue, road, street, strip, thoroughfare **4.** favour, influence, power, pull *Nonformal:* clout, grease **5.** odour, scent, signal, smell, track, trail **6.** buggy, carriage, cart, coach, four-wheeler, stagecoach, wagon **7.** challenge, competition, dash, race, sprint – *v.* **1.** haul, heave, move, pull, tow, tug, transport, yank *Nonformal:* lug, schlep, truck **2.** dredge, hunt, search, seek, sweep, trawl, troll **3.** crawl, creep, dally, dawdle, delay, inch, lag, limp along, linger, loiter, poke, shuffle, straggle, trail behind *Antonyms:* hurry, race, rush **4.** bully, coerce, drive into, persuade, prevail upon, strong-arm *Nonformal:* bulldoze, dragoon **5.** carry on, continue, extend, prolong, protract, spin out, stretch, sustain *Antonyms:* compress, curtail, shave, truncate

drain *n.* **1.** cesspool, channel, conduit, culvert, ditch, duct, outlet, pipe, sewer, sink, sluice, trench, watercourse **2.** consumption, demand, depletion, dissipation, drag, expenditure, levy, outflow – *v.* **1.** broach, carry *or* draw off, empty, extract, pump out, remove, siphon, sluice, tap, withdraw *Antonyms:* fill, load, pack, recharge, replenish **2.** discharge, flow out, leak, ooze, percolate, run off, seep, trickle *Antonyms:* block, clog, detain, obstruct **3.** bankrupt, exhaust, impoverish, sap, strain, tax, use up, waste *Antonyms:* enhance, enrich, improve, increase, magnify

drained *adj.* beat, bedraggled, bleary-eyed, burnt out, exhausted, far-gone, fatigued, spent, tired, used-up, washed-out, weary, worn *Nonformal:* at the wall, dead, hacked, pooped

drama *n.* **1.** play, screenplay, theatre, stage, stage play *Kinds of drama:* academic, agitprop, amateur, avant-garde, boulevard, bourgeois, Broadway, burlesque, celebratory, chronicle, closet, cup-and-saucer, dinner, domestic, Elizabethan, experimental, fringe, Grand Guignol, guerrilla, improvisation *or* improv, Jacobean, *Kabuki (Japanese)*, kitchen sink, legitimate stage, little theatre, masque, melodrama, miracle play, morality play, musical, music hall, national theatre, off Broadway, opera, pantomime, passion play, professional, propaganda play, revue, romance, shadowplay, Shakespearean, showcase, sketch, skit, street, summer stock, theatre of cruelty, theatre of the absurd, tragedy *or* tragic drama, tragicomedy, variety show, vaudeville, *wên and wu (Chinese)*, Yiddish Theatre **2.** affectation, Cheltenham tragedy *(British)*, histrionics, spectacle, theatrics **3.** absurdity, bathos, conflict, horror, humour, pathos, ridiculousness, sublimity, suffering, suspense *See also:* **comedy**

dramatic *adj.* affecting, breathtaking, cogent, electrifying, emotional, exciting, expressive, farcical, impressive, melodramatic, moving, powerful, sensational, startling, striking, sudden, suspenseful, tense, theatrical, thrilling, touching, vivid *Antonyms:* boring, languid, poor

dramatist *n.* dramaturge, librettist, playwright, screenwriter, scriptwriter *Nonformal:* ghostwriter, script doctor, scrivener *See also:* **playwright**

dramatize *v.* **1.** amplify, burlesque, emote, exaggerate, ham it up *(Nonformal)*, melodramatize, overact, overstate, playact, play up **2.** adapt, mount, present, produce, put on, stage

drape *n.* blind, cloak, cover, curtain, mantle, shade, veil – *v.* **1.** adorn, array, attire, bedeck, cascade, cloak, cover, deck, dress, embellish, enrobe, enshroud, enswathe, envelop, enwrap, garb, sheathe, shroud, swaddle, swag, swathe, swing, veil, wrap **2.** arrange, dangle, droop, drop, loop over, suspend **3.** lean on, lounge, recline, sprawl

drapery *n.* arras, backdrop, covering, curtains, drapes, drop, hanging, ornamental fabric, screen, tapestry

drastic *adj.* desperate, draconian, effective, emphatic, extensive, extreme, far-reaching, forceful, harsh, powerful, radical, severe, violent, striking *Antonyms:* effete, futile, ineffectual

draw *n.* **1.** dead heat, deadlock, photo finish *(Nonformal)*, saw-off, stalemate, standoff, tie **2.** bingo, fundraiser, gamble, game of chance, lottery *or* lotto, raffle **3.** allure, appeal, attraction, chemistry, lure, magnetism, seduction **4.** canyon, gulch, gully, ravine, rift, valley **5.** move, play, round, turn – *v.* **1.** carry, convey, drag, haul, move, pull, schlep *(Nonformal)*, tow, tug, yank **2.** caricature, delineate, depict, duplicate, etch, paint, pencil, picture, portray, profile, replicate, reproduce, show **3.** craft, design, dream up, frame, invent, make up, outline, plan, plot, produce **4.** acquire, earn, gain, garner, get, obtain, rake in, reap, secure, win *Antonyms:* forfeit, give up, lose, squander **5.** allure, attract, beguile, bewitch, captivate, charm, enchant, entice, fascinate, lure, seduce *Antonyms:* rebuff, repel, repulse, revolt **6.** call forth, distill, elicit, evoke, extract, infuse, remove, steep, take out, yield *Antonyms:* put back, return **7.** conclude, construe, deduce, derive, determine **8.** contract, heal, mend, shrink **9.** apply, put into practice, use, utilize **10.** close, do up, fasten, pull tight, seal, secure, shut, shutter **11** breathe, inhale, inspire, suck in, take *Nonformal:* drag, puff, pull **12.** free, go *or* reach for, loose, release, take in hand, unfasten, unsheathe, wield **13.** cut up *or* apart, disembowel, dismember, eviscerate, gut, remove the entrails **14.** contract, fuse, heal, knit, meld, mend, shrink **15.** bleed, cup, drain, empty, lance, take away

drawback *n.* **1.** defect, deficiency, disability, disadvantage, failing, fault, flaw, fly in the ointment *(Nonformal)*, handicap, imperfection, liability, shortcoming, weakness *Antonyms:* advantage, asset, benefit, plus **2.** barrier, catch, check, hindrance, hitch, hurdle, impediment, inconvenience, nuisance, obstacle, snag, stumbling-block *Antonyms:* asset, expediency, utility

drawing *n.* **1.** art, design, diagram, illustration, image, interpretation, picture, representation *Kinds of drawing:* caricature, cartoon, commercial, computer-assisted *or* CAD, doodle, line, mechanical, sequential, site plan, sketch, still life, storyboard, thumbnail sketch, tracing, trompe l'oeil, working *Types of drawing : Pictorial:* isometric, oblique, perspective *Technical:* auxiliary view, developmental transition, orthographic projection, revolution, section *Drawing concepts:* action, calligraphic, contained form, contour, crosshatch, gestural *Drawing media:* airbrush, black chalk, blade, charcoal, computer, Conté, graphite, grease pencil, pen, pencil **2.** copy, facsimile, likeness, portrait, replica, silhouette **3.** game of chance, lottery, lotto, sweepstakes *Nonformal:* numbers, sweeps, the big one **4.** extraction, pulling, removal, uprooting, withdrawal

drawn *adj.* enervated, exhausted, fatigued, fraught, haggard, hollow-eyed, peaked, sapped, strained, stressed, taut, tense, tired, worn *Antonyms:* energized, hale, hearty, refreshed, robust

dread *adj.* awesome, dire, fearsome, fell, hideous, horrifying, monstrous, terrible – *n.* alarm, apprehension, angst, anxiety, awe, disquiet, fear, foreboding, perturbation, queasiness, trepidation *Nonformal:* creeps, heebie-jeebies, jitters *Antonyms:* anticipation, assurance, confidence, hope – *v.* cringe at, dislike, distrust, fear, hate, shrink from, worry *Antonyms:* appreciate, enjoy, love

dreadful *adj.* **1.** abhorrent, abominable, appalling, atrocious, awful, beastly, calamitous, disgusting, distressing, ghastly, frightful, grievous, grim, heinous, horrendous, horrific, repugnant, loathsome, shameful, shocking, terrifying, tragic *Antonyms:* cheerful, happy, hilarious, joyful, thrilling **2.** disagreeable, dirty, distasteful, mean, offensive, rancid, rotten, slatternly, slovenly, stinking, uninviting, unpleasant *Antonyms:* cozy, homey, pleasant, welcoming **3.** awe-inspiring, awesome, august, commanding, formidable, imposing, majestic, monumental, reverenced, towering, wondrous *Antonyms:* diminutive, Lilliputian, infinitesimal, miniscule

dream *adj.* champion, first-rate, ideal, matchless, model, peerless, perfect, unique – *n.* **1.** chimera, daydream, delusion, fantasy, ghost, make-believe, mirage, nightmare, phantasmagoria, spectre, trance, vision, wraith **2.** abstraction, bemusement, introspection, musing, navel-gazing, reverie *Nonformal:* brown study, cloud nine **3.** aim, ambition, aspiration, desire, expectation, goal, hope, mark, wish **4.** concoction, design, idea, plan, proposal, scheme, strategy **5.** beauty, perfection *Nonformal:* babe, dish, doll, hunk – *v.* **1.** conceive, conjure *or* cook up, create, devise, envision, fantasize, hatch, imagine, make *or* think up, originate, picture, suppose, visualize **2.** aspire, burn, crave, desire, fancy, hanker, long, pine, rhapsodize, wish, yearn **3.** daydream, doodle, fritter away, idle, while away, stargaze

dreamy *adj.* **1.** astral, elusive, ethereal, gossamer, illusory, immaterial, incorporeal, intangible, misty, mythical, shadowy, vague, vaporous *Antonyms:* concrete, explicit, solid, tangible **2.** abstracted, fanciful, introspective, impractical, musing, pensive, poetic, preoccupied, otherworldly, quixotic, utopian, whimsical *Antonyms:* down-to-earth, practical, pragmatic, realistic **3.** balmy, calming, drowsy, lulling, pacific, soft, somnolent, soothing, soporific *Antonyms:* boisterous, clamorous, loud, rowdy, turbulent

dreary *adj.* **1.** black, bleak, depressing, dismal, dispiriting, doleful, downcast, forlorn, funereal, gloomy, joyless, lonely, melancholy, mournful, sad, sorrowful, wretched *Antonyms:* bright, cheerful, happy, joyful **2.** boring, colourless, drab, dull, everyday, humdrum, lifeless, monotonous, pedestrian, tedious, uneventful *Antonyms:* outlandish, outré, sensational, spectacular

dredge *v.* **1.** bring *or* drag up, clean out, dig, empty, remove, scalp, scoop, scour, shovel **2.** disclose, exhume, raise, reveal, uncover, unearth **3.** batter, coat, cover, dust, glaze, paint, sprinkle

dregs *n.* **1.** debris, deposit, detritus, dross, flotsam and jetsam, garbage, grounds, lees, leftovers, offal, refuse, remainder, remnant, residue, rubbish, scourings, sediment, settlings, trash **2.** riffraff, scum *Nonformal:* deadbeats, losers, rabble, washouts

drench *v.* deluge, dip, douse, drown, dunk, flood, imbrue, immerse, inundate, pour, saturate, soak, sop, souse, steep, submerge, teem, wet *Antonyms:* desiccate, dry, evaporate

dress *adj.* formal, Sunday *or* Sunday-best *Nonformal:* best, best bib and tucker, goto-meeting – *n.* **1.** frock, garment, gown *Kinds of dress:* chemise, cheong-sam, cocktail, crinoline, dirndl, farthingale, gown, granny, hoop, house, jumper, kirtle, mantua, micromini *or* mini, Mother Hubbard, muumuu, overskirt, paintdress, pinafore, sack, sari, sarong, sheath, shift, shirt, shirtwaist, strapless, tank, tent, tea gown **2.** apparel, array, attire, clothes, clothing, costume, ensemble, garb, gear, guise, habiliment, habit, outfit, rags, robe, suit, threads, toga, uniform, vestment, wardrobe *Nonformal:* civvies, duds, fatigues, foofaraw, getup, khakis, mufti, rig, togs, toggery, zoot suit **3.** accoutrements, black *or* white tie, caparison, dinner dress, evening gown, finery, formal wear, full regalia, glad rags, splendour, tails, tux, tuxedo *Nonformal:* blues, monkey *or* penguin suit, whites **4.** appearance, coat, covering, crust, feathers, guise, mantle, plumage, shell, skin, trappings – *v.* **1.** clothe, deck *or* fit *or* turn out, garb, outfit, put on, slip into, suit *or* tog up **2.** adorn, bedeck, decorate, embellish, furbish, garnish, spruce up, trick out *(Nonformal)*, trim **3.** bandage, bind, care for, medicate, minister to, set, swathe, tend, tie up **4.** brush, comb, curry, groom, prune, smooth, trim *Nonformal:* do, do up **5.** clean, finish, make ready, prepare, stuff **6.** cultivate, fertilize, plow, scuffle *(P.E.I.)*, till, work **7.** align, arrange, line up, put in order, straighten

dressing *n.* **1.** adhesive tape, application, Band-Aid *(Trademark)*, bandage, collodion *(Historical)*, compress, plaster, poultice, tourniquet **2.** condiment, marinade, sauce, spread, stuffing *Kinds of salad dressing:* balsamic, blue cheese, Caesar, Catalina, creamy cucumber, French, Italian, oil & vinegar, ranch, Thousand Island, vinaigrette *See also:* **condiment** **3.** compost, fertilizer, manure, muck **4.** bawling-out, censure, rebuke, scolding, stricture

dressy *adj.* chic, classy, dressed up, elaborate, elegant, extravagant, fancy, fashionable, formal, high-flown, ornate *Nonformal:* gussied up, highfalutin, ritzy

dribble *v.* **1.** dreep *(P.E.I.)*, drip, drizzle, leak, ooze, seep, spurt, squirt, trickle, weep **2.** advance, boot, bounce, drive, hit, kick, move, propel, tap, touch **3.** drivel, drool, salivate, slobber, snivel

drift *n.* **1.** implication, import, intent, meaning, significance, substance, tenor, thrust **2.** bearing, bent, course, direction, inclination, orientation, propensity, route, tendency, trend **3.** bank, clump, deposit, dune, heap, mass, mound, pile **4.** current, flow, force, wind – *v.* **1.** amble, circumnavigate, digress, meander, peregrinate, rove, stray, wander *Nonformal:* freewheel, mosey **2.** coast, float, fly, ride, sail, soar, waft **3.** do nothing, laze, lie around, loaf, lounge, take it easy *Nonformal:* bum around, lollygag, veg **4.** bank up, cover, mound, pile

drill *n.* **1.** conditioning, discipline, exercise, instruction, lesson, manoeuvres, marching, practice, preparation, procedure, repetition, routine, run-through, training, tryout, workout **2.** drilling tool *Kinds of drill or bit:* auger, awl, bodkin, bore, borer, centre, concrete, corkscrew, countersink, flat, jackhammer, metal, pick, punch, rivet gun, twist, wood – *v.* **1.** accustom, discipline, exercise, habituate, hone, instruct, practice, rehearse, school, teach, train **2.** auger, bore, dig, penetrate, perforate, pierce, prick, probe, puncture, screw, sink in **3.** catapult, fire, hit, launch, propel, punch, shoot

drink *n.* **1.** beverage, libation, liquid *or* liquid refreshment, potable, potation, potion, refreshment, thirst quencher **2.** cup, draft, dram, glass, horn *(P.E.I.)*, portion, shot, sip, swallow, swig, taste *Nonformal:* bracer, finger, hair of the dog, jigger, pick-me-up, slug, snap, snifter, spot, tot **3.** alcohol, *alcool (French)*, aperitif, beer, brew, callibogus, caribou *(Quebec)*, chaser, cocktail, high winer *(Historical)*, intoxicant, liquor, moonshine, moosemilk, nightcap, pint, poteen *(Irish)*, spirits *Nonformal:* booze, brewski, cold one, firewater, hard stuff, hooch, sauce **4.** ocean, sea, water *Nonformal:* briny deep, the blue *or* depths **5.** alcoholism, dipsomania, drunkenness, inebriation, intoxication – *v.* **1.** carouse, consume, down, drain, gulp, imbibe, indulge, lap, partake, quaff, sip, slop, slosh, slurp, swallow, wet one's whistle *Nonformal:* belt down, bolt, hit the sauce, inhale, kill, knock back, put away, swell, swig, tank up, tipple, toss *or* toss back, wash down **2.** cheer, honour, pay homage to, pledge, salute, toast **3.** absorb, draw *or* take in, gobble *or* soak up, ingest, receive

drinker *n.* alcoholic, dipsomaniac, guzzler, imbiber, inebriate, rubby, rummy, shako *(P.E.I.)*, sot, tippler *Nonformal:* boozehound, boozer, drunk, lush, soak, souse, wino *Antonyms:* abstainer, nondrinker, teetotaler

drip *n.* **1.** bead, drop, droplet, globule **2.** dribble, drizzle, leakage, light rain, rivulet, trickle **3.** drip-feed, drop by drop, intravenous-feed **4.** annoyance, bore, loser, nuisance, pain *Nonformal:* jerk, kill-joy, milksop, pill – *v.* dreep, dribble, drizzle, drop, exude, leak, ooze, percolate, plop, seep, splash, sprinkle, trickle, weep

drive *interj.* beat it, burn rubber, floor it, frappe la rue *(Nonformal)*, hit the road, let's go, step on it – *n.* **1.** airing, excursion, expedition, hitch, jaunt, journey, junket, outing, ride, run, tour, trip *Nonformal:* spin, turn, whirl **2.** ambition, desire, determination, energy, enthusiasm, force, impetus, motivation, motive, power, punch, spirit, spunk, steam, urge, vigour, vim *Nonformal:* get-up-and-go, guts, gumption, hustle, moxie, pep **3.** action, advance, appeal, campaign, cause, crusade, effort, enterprise, initiative, push, surge **4.** avenue, boulevard, byway, driveway, lane, parkway, private road, roadway, scenic route, street **5.** disk drive, floppy drive, hard drive – *v.* **1.** chauffeur, conduct, control, convey, guide, handle, herd, manage, manoeuvre, move, operate, pilot, propel, run, shepherd, steer, transport **2.** actuate, arouse, encourage, incite, induce, inspire, instigate, launch, mobilize, motivate, push, set in motion, stimulate **3.** labour, overwork, tax, toil **4.** coerce, compel, constrain, force, goad, oblige, press, prod, provoke, railroad, spur *Nonformal:* dragoon, lean on, squeeze **5.** beat, hammer, hit, knock, nail, plunge, punch, ram, sink, smite, sock, strike, thrust, thump, thwack, wham, whack **6.** cast out, expel, fend *or* hold *or* ward off, repel, repulse **7.** cruise, roll by, sail, tootle, wheel *Nonformal:* bike, motor, tool

drivel *n.* blather, claptrap, eyewash, gibberish, jabber, mumbo-jumbo, nonsense, rubbish, tripe, twaddle *Nonformal:* bunk, bunkum, codswallop, fandango, gobbledygook, hogwash, hooey, hot air, malarky, poppycock, pseudospeak, rot – *v.* babble, blabber, chitter-chatter, gas, palaver, prate, rant, rattle

driver *n.* **1.** motorist *Kinds of driver:* bus, cab *or* cabbie, car jockey, chauffeur, coachperson, drover, engineer, parking attendant *or* valet, race car, tractor, truck **2.** controller, engineer, operator, regulator **3.** buckaroo, cowboy, cowpuncher, gaucho, muleskinner, vaquero **4.** big stick *(Nonformal)*, club, one metal *or* wood

driving *adj.* active, compelling, dynamic, energetic, enterprising, forceful, galvanic, impellent, intense, lively, powerful, rapid, sweeping, urging, vigorous, violent *Antonyms:* ineffective, spasmodic, static, weak

drizzle *n.* dribble, drip, drop, mist, rain, Scotch mist, shower, spitting, spray, sprinkling – *v.* mist, mizzle, pour, rain, spatter, spit, sprinkle

droll *adj.* absurd, amusing, camp, clownish, comical, crack-up, diverting, entertaining, funny, humorous, jocular, laughable, ludicrous, quaint, ridiculous, waggish, whimsical *Antonyms:* austere, humourless, serious

drool *v.* dribble, drip, drivel, froth, ooze, run, salivate, slaver, slobber, spit, water

droop *v.* **1.** bend down *or* over, dangle, drape, loll, nod, sag, sink, slack, slouch, slump, suspend **2.** decline, fade, fail, falter, flag, give in, languish, lose heart, mope *(Nonformal)*, weaken, wilt, wither *Antonyms:* hearten, refresh, rejuvenate

droopy *adj.* bent, flabby, flaccid, floppy, languid, languorous, lassitudinous, limp, nodding, pendulous, sagging, saggy, slouchy, stooped, wilting *Antonyms:* ramrod, rigid, stiff, upright

drop *n.* **1.** ball, bead, bobble, droplet, globule, peal, tear *or* teardrop **2.** dab, dash, dot, iota, jot, molecule, nip, particle, pat, pinch, speck, splash, taste, touch, trace, trickle *Nonformal:* smidgen, tad **3.** descent, dive, fall, plunge, tumble **4.** abyss, bluff, cliff, declivity, falling away *or* off, precipice **5.** cut, decline, decrease, depreciation, diminution, dip, downturn, lessening, lowering, reduction, sag, slide, slump **6.** collapse, deterioration, disintegration, worsening – *v.* **1.** dive *or* nosedive, fall, plummet, plunge, swoop, tumble **2.** abort, cancel, cut, deep-six *(Nonformal)*, discharge, discontinue, ditch, dump, eliminate, fire, forgo, forsake, jilt, omit, renounce, sack *(Nonformal)*, terminate *Antonyms:* add, enlist, hire, induct **3.** abandon, desert, forfeit, give up, let go, lose, relinquish, surrender **4.** decline, decrease, depress, descend, diminish, dip, dwindle, lower, slacken, slide, slump, taper off *Antonyms:* develop, elevate, grow, increase **5.** collapse, die, faint, keel over, swoon **6.** bodycheck, bring *or* take down, fell, floor, shoot, strike, tackle, topple **7.** deliver, deposit, leave, let out, set down **8.** break, destroy, ruin, shatter, smash **9.** bear, bring forth, give birth, spawn, whelp **10.** blunder, bobble, botch, bumble, bungle, fumble, muff, release **11.** dribble, drip, percolate, run, seep, trickle **12.** crouch, duck, hunker down *(Nonformal)*, kneel, lie low, plop, squat **13.** bump *(Nonformal)*, demote, depose, downgrade, displace, dispossess, oust *Antonyms:* advance, ascend, climb

drought *n.* **1.** aridness, dehydration, desiccation, dryness, dry spell *Antonyms:* deluge, flood, soaking **2.** barrenness, dearth, deficiency, insufficiency, lack, need, paucity, scarcity, shortage, want *Antonyms:* abundance, multitude, plethora, profusion

drove *n.* aggregation, assemblage, bevy, body, brood, bunch, collection, colony, company, covey, crowd, crush, flight, flock, gaggle, gathering, group, herd, horde, host, litter, mob, multitude, pack, pride, rabble, school, scrum, shoal, swarm, throng

drown *v.* **1.** asphyxiate, die, expire, go down *or* under, sink **2.** bury, cover, deluge, drench, engulf, flood, inundate, saturate, sink, soak, souse, submerge, swamp **3.** alleviate, deaden, extinguish, kill, lessen, muffle, mute, obliterate, palliate, relieve, silence, stifle, wipe out *Antonyms:* amplify, enhance, magnify

drowsy *adj.* **1.** dozy, groggy, half-asleep, heavy-eyed, nodding, yawning *Antonyms:* alert, awake, attentive **2.** dreamy, hypnotic, lulling, restful, soothing, soporific *Antonyms:* bellowing, clamorous, noisy **3.** comatose, dazed, heavy, inactive, languid, lethargic, listless, sluggish, torpid *Antonyms:* energetic, lively, spirited, vigorous

drudge *n.* attendant, char, factotum, flunky, footman, hand labourer, lackey, lickspittle, menial, plodder, roustabout, servant, slave, worker, workhorse – *v.* grind, labour, moil, slave, sweat, toil, work *Nonformal:* grind and dig, slog *Antonyms:* lounge, relax, rest

drudgery *n.* chore, labour, slog, struggle, sweat, toil, work *Nonformal:* elbow grease, grind, gruntwork, KP

drug *n.* **1.** medication, medicine, physic, pill, prescription, remedy *Groupings of drug:* designer, ethical, generic, nonprescription, nonproprietary, over-the-counter, prescription, proprietary **2.** dope *(Nonformal)*, narcotic, street-drug *Kinds of street-drug:* amphetamine, barbiturate, cocaine, crack *or* crack cocaine, dimethyltryptamine *or* DMT, hallucinogen, hashish *or* hash, heroin, lysergic acid diethylamide *or* LSD, marijuana, mescaline, methylenedioxymethamphetamine *or* MDMA, mushrooms, opium, peyote, psychedelic *Nonformal:* acid, angel dust, benny, blow, blue, coke, dope, downer, E, ecstasy, grass, H, horse, jolly vegetables *or* shrooms, junk, Mary Jane, nose candy, pep pill, pot, red, smack, snow, speed, speedball, upper, weed – *v.* **1.** dope up *(Nonformal)*, dose, medicate, treat **2.** anesthetize, benumb, deaden, desensitize, sedate

drugstore *n.* apothecary, chemist's *or* chemist's shop *(British)*, dispensary, pharmacy

drum *n.* **1.** *Nonformal:* kit, percussion instrument, skins *Kinds of drum:* bass, bongo, conga, kettledrum, kick, side, snare, steel, tabla, tambour, tenor, tom-tom, tympani, war **2.** barrel, carboy, cask, container, cylinder, firkin, vat, vessel **3.** beat, knocking, rhythm, sound, tapping, thumping – *v.* **1.** beat, boom, hammer, pound, rap, tap, throb, thrum, thump, thunder **2.** catechize, drill, drive home, hammer at, inculcate, indoctrinate, reiterate, teach, train

drunk *adj.* **1.** crapulent, impaired, inebriated, intoxicated, merry, muddled, soused, tipsy *Nonformal:* boozed up, canned, crocked, half in the bag, hammered, high, hosed, jiggered, juiced, loaded, oiled, pie-eyed, plastered, potted, ripped, sloshed, soaked, stewed, stoned, tanked, three sheets to the wind, tight, totalled, wasted, zonked **2.** breathless, carried-away, ecstatic, elated, enraptured, exuberant, fervent, impassioned, transported *Nonformal:* fired-up, full of oneself – *n.* **1.** alcoholic, carouser, dipsomaniac, drinker, drunkard, inebriate *Nonformal:* alchy, boozehound, boozer, guzzler, lush, rummy, soak, sot, souse, sponge, wino **2.** bender, binge *(Nonformal)*, carousal, hellbender, jag, party, revelry, spree, wassail

dry *adj.* **1.** arid, baked, barren, depleted, desert, desiccated, drained, dried up, dusty, evaporated, exhausted, impoverished, juiceless, moistureless, rainless, shrivelled, stale, torrid, waterless *Antonyms:* damp, humid, moist, soggy, wet **2.** athirst, dehydrated, parched, thirsty **3.** apathetic, blah *(Nonformal)*, boring, bromidic, draggy, dreary, insipid, monotonous, phlegmatic, plain, simple, tedious, tiresome, trite, uninteresting, wearisome *Antonyms:* entertaining, interesting, lively **4.** deadpan, droll, ironic, low-key, restrained, sarcastic, subtle **5.** cold, drab, lifeless, sombre, stiff, undemonstrative, uninspiring **6.** on-the-wagon *(Nonformal)*, sober, straight, temperate **7.** abstemious, abstinent, non-alcoholic, prohibitionary, teetotal – *v.* **1.** bake, dehydrate, deplete, desiccate, evaporate, parch, scorch, shrivel, wilt, wither *Antonyms:* lubricate, moisten, wet **2.** blot, dehumidify, drain, sponge, swab, wipe up **3.** cure, jerk, preserve, salt, season, smoke

dual *adj.* binary, coupled, double, double-header, duplicate, dyadic, geminate, matched, paired, twin, two, twofold

dub *n.* copy, duplicate, recording, remix, replication, reproduction, sample, version – *v.* **1.** bestow, confer, designate, entitle, knight, term, title **2.** baptize, call, christen, denominate, nickname, name, tag **3.** beat, drum, knock, pound, rap, tap **4.** alter, change, copy, edit, mix, record, remix, sample, tape

dubious *adj.* **1.** arguable, contestable, debatable, disputable, doubtful, dubitable, moot, questionable *Antonyms:* incontrovertible, irrefutable, undeniable **2.** ambiguous, equivocal, hazy, imprecise, obscure, unclear, vague **3.** chancy, iffy *(Nonformal)*, improbable, risky, uncertain, unlikely, unpredictable, unsure *Antonyms:* destined, firm, fixed **4.** fishy *(Nonformal)*, shady, suspect, suspicious, untrustworthy *Antonyms:* reliable, sound, trustworthy **5.** hesitant, indecisive, leery, mistrustful, unconvinced, unsettled, wary *Antonyms:* confident, convinced, positive

duck *n.* **1.** drake, gamefowl, waterfowl *Some kinds of duck:* black, bufflehead, canvasback, eider, gadwall, goldeneye, harlequin, mallard, merganser, old squaw, pintail, redhead, ring-necked, ruddy, scaup, scoter, shoveler, whistling, widgeon, wood *Tribes of duck:* dabbling, diving, freckled, perching, sea, shelduck, steamer, stifftail **2.** dip, dunk *(Nonformal)*, immersion, plunge, submersion – *v.* **1.** dip, douse, dunk *(Nonformal)*, immerse, plunge, sink, submerge **2.** bob, hit the deck *or* dirt *(Nonformal)*, hunch down, lower, stoop **3.** avoid, dodge, elude, evade, sidestep, swerve **4.** get out of *(Nonformal)*, escape, eschew, shirk, shun, skirt

duct *n.* aqueduct, canal, channel, conduit, course, funnel, passage, pipe, sluice, tube, vent, vessel

ductile *adj.* **1.** adaptable, flexible, malleable, mouldable, pliable, pliant, responsive, supple, tensile, tractable *Antonyms:* inflexible, rigid, stiff **2.** biddable, compliant, docile, manageable, nonresisting, submitting, willing, yielding *Antonyms:* incorrigible, strong-willed, stubborn

due *adj.* **1.** chargeable, collectable, in arrears, outstanding, overdue, owed, owing, unpaid **2.** appropriate, apt, deserved, earned, fitting, just, justified, merited, proper, rightful, suitable, warranted **3.** adequate, ample, enough, substantial, sufficient **4.** anticipated, awaited, billed, coming, expected, promised, scheduled, slated **5.** ascribable, assignable, attributable, derivative, traceable – *adv.* dead on, directly, exactly, straight, undeviatingly, unswervingly – *n.* birthright, desserts, entitlement, prerogative, privilege

duel *n. affaire d'honneur (French)*, contest, face-off, fight, grudge match, pistols *(Historical)*, shoot-out, showdown, sword fight – *v.* combat, contend, feud, fight, quarrel, scuffle, war

dues *n. pl.* charge, contribution, custom, duty, exaction, expense, fee, levy, price, rates, tithe, toll, tribute

dugout *n.* bench *(Baseball)*, bomb shelter, bunker, cave, den, ditch, excavation, foxhole, hole, lair, shelter, trench

dulcet *adj.* euphonious, golden, harmonious, honeyed, lilting, lyrical, mellifluous, melodious, mollifying, musical, pleasant, pleasing, sonorous, soothing, sweet, tuneful *Antonyms:* discordant, harsh, shrill

dull *adj.* **1.** bovine, dense, dim-witted, feeble-minded, simple, slow, stupid, thickheaded, unintelligent *Antonyms:* bright, clever, intelligent **2.** inactive, inert, lifeless, listless, passionless, sluggish, spiritless, stagnant, stony, torpid, unexciting, unresponsive, wooden **3.** blunt, edgeless, rounded, unsharpened *Antonyms:* pointed, rigid, sharp **4.** bland, boring, bromidic, characterless, everyday, hackneyed, insipid, monotonous, ordinary, pedestrian, prosaic, routine, run-of-the-mill *(Nonformal)*, tedious, tired, trite **5.** bleak, cheerless, cloudy, dismal, dreary, gloomy, grey **6.** dampened, muffled, muted, *sordo (Italian)* **7.** blah *(Nonformal)*, colourless, dingy, drab, faded, faint, lacklustre, lustreless, muddy, vanilla, washed-out, weak – *v.* **1** bring *or* let down, dampen, deject, depress, discourage, dishearten, dispirit *Nonformal:* spoil the party, wet the bed **2.** anesthetize, blunt, ease, lessen, moderate, palliate

duly *adv.* **1.** accordingly, appropriately, befittingly, correctly, deservedly, properly, rightfully, suitably **2.** as scheduled, on the dot, on time, precisely, promptly, punctually

dumb *adj.* **1.** aphonic, inarticulate, mum, mute, nonverbal, nonvocal, pantomimic, signing **2.** awestruck, dumfounded, speechless, tongue-tied, wordless **3.** laconic, quiet, reserved, silent, taciturn, uncommunicative **4.** dense, doltish, dull, dunderheaded, foolish, simple-minded, slow, stupid, unintelligent

dumfounded *adj.* aghast, amazed, astonished, astounded, bewildered, confounded, confused, dismayed, dumb, nonplussed, overcome, overwhelmed, puzzled, shocked, speechless, staggered, startled, stunned, surprised, taken aback, thrown, thunderstruck *Nonformal:* bamboozled, blown away, bowled over, buffaloed, flabbergasted, floored

dummy *adj.* **1.** counterfeit, fake, placebo, sham, spurious **2.** mum, mute, silent, speechless, unspoken, wordless – *n.* **1.** crash test dummy, effigy, figure, figurehead, mannequin, model, puppet **2.** copy, imitation, sample, sham **3.** dolt, dullard, dunderhead, hoser *(Nonformal)*, numbskull, simpleton

dump *n.* **1.** dumping ground, dunghill, garbage lot, junk pile, junkyard, midden *or* kitchen midden *(Historical)*, nuisance grounds, refuse heap, rubbish pile, tip *(British)* **2.** crib, hole, hole-in-the-wall, hovel, rathole, shack, slum *Nonformal:* dive, pigsty **3.** armoury, arsenal, cache, depository, depot, magazine, storehouse – *v.* **1.** cast off, discard, reject, scrap, throw away, toss *Nonformal:* chuck, ditch **2.** clean, empty, purge, remove, unpack **3.** divest, flood the market, sell, sell off, unload **4.** move, remove, send, transfer **5.** descend, dive, drop, fall, nosedive, plunge

dun *adj.* beige, brown, drab, dusky, ecru, fulvous, greyish-brown, khaki, leaden, muddy, sallow, sooty, swarthy, tawny, umber – *v.* bother, bug *(Nonformal)*, call, demand, harass, harangue, harry, importune, nag, pester, plague, press, push

dunce *n.* ass, dimwit, fool, half-wit, idiot, ignoramus, imbecile, oaf, simpleton *Nonformal:* birdbrain, blockhead, bonehead, chucklehead, dope, dunderhead, hoser, jackass, lamebrain, lightweight, nincompoop, nitwit, scatterbrain

dungeon *n.* cage, cell, confinement, custody, donjon, enclosure, hold, jail, keep, lockup, oubliette, prison, stronghold *Nonformal:* hoosegow, slammer, the hole

dunk *v.* dip, douse, duck, immerse, saturate, soak, sop, souse, submerge, submerse, wet

duo *n.* brace, couple, doublet, duet, dyad, pair, twosome

dupe *n.* easy mark, fall guy, fool, mark, pigeon, pushover, sap, simpleton, victim *Nonformal:* fish, patsy, sitting duck, sucker – *v.* baffle, beguile, betray, cheat, circumvent, deceive, defraud, delude, double-cross, fool, hoax, hoodwink, mislead, rook, shaft, swindle, trick, victimize *Nonformal:* bamboozle, con, hornswoggle, rip off, screw

duplicate *adj.* **1.** alike, cloned, corresponding, homogeneous, identical, indistinguishable, matching, same, twin **2.** binary, doubled, dual, geminate, replicated, reproduced, twofold – *n.* **1.** clone, counterpart, dead ringer *(Nonformal)*, ditto, double, shadow self, spitting image, twin **2.** dub, copy, repetition, replica, reproduction, sample, scan *Antonyms:* model, original, prototype – *v.* **1.** dub, copy, imitate, mimeograph, photocopy, recreate, replicate, reproduce, sample **2.** double, geminate, halve, increase **3.** ditto *(Nonformal)*, do *or* say again, recapitulate, redo, reiterate, repeat

duplicity *n.* artifice, betrayal, chicanery, cunning, deceit, deception, dishonesty, dissemblance, double-dealing, duality, faithlessness, falsehood, fraud, hypocrisy, treachery *Nonformal:* dirty-dealing, two-timing *Antonyms:* candour, honesty, straightforwardness

durability *n.* backbone, continuance, endurance, lastingness, longevity, persistence, resistance, shelf life, stability, sturdiness, toughness *Nonformal:* intestinal fortitude, moxie, starch, staying power

durable *adj.* **1.** constant, endless, enduring, fixed, immutable, lasting, long-lasting, permanent *Antonyms:* ephemeral, passing, temporary **2.** hard as nails *(Nonformal)*, imperishable, long-lasting, persistent, reliable, resistant, stable, stalwart, strong, sturdy, tough

duration *n.* continuation, continuity, endurance, epoch, era, extent, half-life, length, life, period, perpetuation, run, shelf life, span, spell, stretch, term, tide, time

duress *n.* **1.** arm-twisting, bulldozing *(Nonformal)*, coercion, compulsion, constraint, enforcement, entrapment, extortion, force, pressure, threat **2.** bondage, confinement, custody, detention, imprisonment, incarceration, internment, irons, jailing, lock-and-key *(Nonformal)*

during *prep.* all along, amid, as, concurrently, meanwhile, mid, midst, throughout, while, whilst, the while

dusk *adj.* cloudy, crepuscular, dark, day's end, dim, muddy, murky, shadowy, shady – *n.* **1.** early evening, evening, evensong, eventide, night, nightfall, sundown, sunset, twilight *Antonyms:* daybreak, morning, sunrise **2.** dark, dimness, gloom, grey, obscurity, shade, shadow

dusky *adj.* **1.** cloudy, dim, dull, gloomy, grey, hazy, overcast, shadowy, shady *Antonyms:* bright, sunny **2.** dark-hued, olive-skinned, swarthy *Antonyms:* fair, light, pale

dust *n.* **1.** air particles, ashes, cinders, flakes, grit, lint, soot **2.** dirt, earth, land, mud, sand, soil **3.** dregs, garbage, junk, refuse, rubbish, trash **4.** ado, brouhaha, chaos, commotion, confusion, fracas, hubbub, stir, tumult, turmoil, uproar *Nonformal:* ruckus, rumpus – *v.* **1.** cover, dredge, powder, scatter, sift, spray, spread **2.** brush, clean, polish, spruce, sweep, tidy, wipe **3.** beat, defeat, outdo, overpower, vanquish *Nonformal:* clobber, trounce, whup **4.** annihilate, destroy, devastate, exterminate, extirpate, kill, massacre, murder, obliterate, slay

dusty *adj.* **1.** chalky, crumbly, granular, powdery, sandy **2.** dirty, grubby, sooty, unclean, unswept, untouched **3.** boring, bromidic, dry, dull, humdrum, stale, tedious, uninteresting, vapid, wearisome **4.** antiquated, mossbacked, mouldy, old, out-of-the-loop *(Nonformal)*

dutiful *adj.* acquiescent, compliant, conscientious, deferential, devoted, doting, faithful, filial, obedient, punctilious, regardful, reliable, respectful, submissive *Antonyms:* disobedient, disrespectful, insubordinate, remiss, uncaring

duty *n.* **1.** burden, commitment, engagement, incumbency, obligation, onus, responsibility **2.** assignment, function, job, mission, role, service, task **3.** charge, custom, fee, levy, tariff, tax, tithe, toll

dwarf *adj.* bantam, diminutive, Lilliputian, little, miniature, peewee, petite, small, tiny, undersized *Nonformal:* micromini, pint-sized, pocket – *n.* elf, gnome, goblin, halfling, imp, leprechaun, sprite *Nonformal:* pipsqueak, squirt – *v.* diminish, dominate, minimize, overshadow, tower over

dwell *v.* **1.** abide, bed, bunk, domicile, establish oneself, exist, homestead, inhabit, live, locate, lodge, nest, occupy, rent, reside, room, roost, settle, squat, stay, tenant **2.** continue, linger, loiter, remain, stay, tarry

dwelling *n.* abode, apartment, castle, den, domicile, habitat, home, house, lair, lodging, quarters, residence, room, space *Nonformal:* crib, digs, pad *Kinds of native dwelling:* hogan, igloo, longhouse, tepee, tupik, wickiup, wigwam *or* wikuom

dwindle *v.* **1.** abate, die out, diminish, disappear, ebb, evanesce, fade, lessen, peter out *(Nonformal)*, subside, taper off, vanish, wane **2.** decline, degenerate, deteriorate, fall, flag, go downhill *(Nonformal)*, weaken, wither

dye *n.* colour, colour agent, colourant, dyestuff, pigment, stain, tincture, tinge, tint – *v.* colour, henna, highlight, rinse, shade, streak, tint, touch up

dying *adj.* closing, declining, disappearing, disintegrating, doomed, ebbing, ending, evanescent, expiring, extinguishing, fading, failing, final, fleeting, floundering, last, moribund, mortal, setting, sinking, sliding downhill, terminal, weakening, vanishing, withering *Nonformal:* checking out, flatlining, last ditch *or* gasp

dynamic *adj.* **1.** active, aggressive, changing, charged, compelling, driving, effective, electric, energetic, enterprising, forceful, forcible, high-powered, influential, intense, lively, lusty, magnetic, potent, powerful, productive, progressive, vehement, vigorous, vital, vitalizing *Nonformal:* ballsy, go-getting, peppy, zippy *Antonyms:* apathetic, inactive, listless, sluggish, torpid **2.** driving, electrifying, galvanizing, impelling, kinetic, propulsive – *n.* energizer, motivator

dynamics *n. pl.* **1.** energetics, kinetics *Kinds and branches of dynamics:* aerodynamics, astrodynamics, barodynamics, biodynamics, electrodynamics, fluid dynamics, geodynamics, hydrodynamics, kinesiology, photodynamics, pneumodynamics, thermodynamics **2.** drive, engine, forces, influences, motivators, motor, pull **3.** chemistry, communication, connection, interaction, interfere, interplay, link, synergy

dynasty *n.* crown, hegemony, house, kingship, line, lineage, monarchy, queenship, regime, regnancy, reign, ruling house, suzerainty

eager *adj.* agog, ambitious, ardent, athirst, avid, breathless, craving, desiring, desirous, earnest, enthusiastic, impatient, impulsive, intent, keen, restless, self-starting, thirsty, zealous *Nonformal:* gung-ho, hot-to-trot, hungry, itchy *Antonyms:* apathetic, blasé, impassive, nonchalant

eagerness *n.* alacrity, animation, anticipation, anxiousness, ardour, dash, élan, enthusiasm, excitement, fervour, greediness, gusto, hunger, impatience, impetuosity, intentness, longing, vehemence, voraciousness, yearning, zeal, zest, zing *(Nonformal) Antonyms:* indifference, indolence, lethargy

eagle *n.* bird of prey, raptor *Kinds of eagle:* African fish, American *or* bald eagle, black, black-breasted, Bonelli's, booted, crested serpent, golden, harpy, imperial, Indian black, little, martial, monkey-eating, snake, tawny, Verreaux's, wedge-tailed, white-bellied sea

eagle-eyed *adj.* acute, alert, discerning, far-seeing, far-sighted, hawk-eyed, keen, penetrating, perspicacious, quick, raptorial, sharp, sharp-eyed, vigilant *Antonyms:* blind, oblivious, unobservant

ear *n.* **1.** auditory apparatus, hearing organ *Parts of the ear:* auditory nerve, cochlea, ear canal, eardrum *or* tympanic membrane, Eustachian tube, external ear, incus, internal ear, labyrinth, lobe, malleus, middle ear *or* tympanum, ossicle, outer ear, semicircular canals, stapes *or* stirrup **2.** attention, concentration, consideration, discrimination, heed, notice, observance, perception, sensitivity, thought

early *adj.* **1.** beginning, first, inaugural, initial, introductory, original, primary **2.** former, older, previous, prior **3.** ancient, antediluvian, antique, classical, old, prehistoric, primeval, primitive **4.** advanced, premature, unexpected, unseasonable, untimely – *adv.* **1.** prematurely, unexpectedly, unseasonably, untimely **2.** beforehand, earlier, formerly, heretofore, hither to, previously **3.** directly, expeditiously, immediate, instantly, promptly, quickly, shortly, speedy *Antonyms:* drawn-out, prolonged

earmark *n.* attribute, characteristic, distinction, feature, hallmark, marking, peculiarity, quality, signature, stamp, token, trait – *v.* **1.** bookmark, designate, fold over, label, mark out, name, slot, tab, tag **2.** hold back, reserve, set aside *Antonyms:* squander, use, waste

earn *v.* **1.** acquire, attain, bring home *or* in, clear, collect, come by, draw, gather, get, gross, net, obtain, procure, profit, pull, receive, score, secure *Nonformal:* bag, snag *Antonyms:* beg, borrow, steal **2.** merit, rate, reap, warrant, win

earnest *adj.* **1.** ambitious, ardent, fervid, impassioned, intent, keen, zealous *Antonyms:* apathetic, cool, indifferent **2.** genuine, heartfelt, honest, real, sincere, thoughtful, unfeigned *Antonyms:* false, fraudulent, hollow **3.** grave, important, serious, significant *Antonyms:* frivolous, trifling, trivial – *n.* assurance, bond, down payment, guaranty, insurance, payment, pledge, security

earnestness *n.* attentiveness, concentration, deliberation, determination, devotion, diligence, doggedness, firmness, gravity, intensity, meaning, perseverance, persistence, purposefulness, resolution, seriousness, sincerity, sobriety, solemnity, tenacity *Antonyms:* duplicity, emptiness, fickleness, insincerity, shallowness

earnings *n. pl.* balance, cash, cheque *or* paycheque, gain, gate, income, money, money earned, net, pay, pay packet, proceeds, profit, receipts, remuneration, return, revenue, reward, royalty, salary, stipend, take, wages *Nonformal:* bottom line, pay-off, take-home

earth *n.* **1.** biosphere, Gaia, geosphere, globe, mother earth, *mundo (Spanish)*, *mondo (Italian)*, planet, *seismos (Greek)*, sphere, temporal orb, terra firma, *welt (German)*, world **2.** alluvium, clay, compost, dirt, fill, gravel, ground, humus, loam, muck, mud, sod, soil, subsoil, topsoil, turf **3.** countryside, ground, land, landscape, terrain **4.** humanity, humankind, mankind, people **5.** burrow, den, hiding place, hole, lair, refuge

earthbound *adj.* **1.** common sense, down-to-earth, matter-of-fact, practical, pragmatic, sensible, sober **2.** corporeal, mundane, tellurian, terrestrial *Antonyms:* alien, extraterrestrial, spiritual

earthly *adj.* **1.** carnal, corporeal, fleshly, human, material, mortal, mundane, physical, practical, secular, temporal, terrene, worldly *Antonyms:* ethereal, heavenly, immaterial, spiritual **2.** conceivable, feasible, imaginable, likely, plausible, possible *Commonly misused:* **earthy**

earthquake *n.* cataclysm, convulsion, earth tremor, movement, quake, seismic wave, shake, shock, the big one *(Nonformal)*, undulation, upheaval

earthy *adj.* **1.** artless, down-to-earth, easygoing, folksy, homely, natural, plain, pragmatic, rustic, simple, unsophisticated *Antonyms:* debonair, suave, urbane **2.** crude, off-colour, raunchy, ribald, rough, tough, sensual, uninhibited, unrefined, vulgar *Commonly misused:* **earthly**

ease *n.* **1.** ability, adroitness, capability, command, deftness, dexterity, efficiency, effortlessness, expertise, facility, familiarity, flair, fluency, knack, proficiency, readiness, skilfulness *Antonyms:* clumsiness, difficulty, effort, hardship **2.** aplomb, casualness, composure, finesse, grace, informality, ingenuousness, insouciance, naturalness, nonchalance, poise, self-possession, smoothness, unaffectedness *Antonyms:* awkwardness, constraint, gaucherie **3.** affluence, comfort, contentment, enjoyment, gratification, happiness, idleness, leisure, luxury, prosperity, relaxation, repose, rest, restfulness, satisfaction, security, serenity, tranquility *Antonyms:* impoverishment, insecurity, trouble, worry – *v.* **1.** alleviate, ameliorate, appease, assuage, calm, comfort, ebb, lighten, mitigate, moderate, pacify, placate, quiet, slacken, soften, soothe, tranquilize *Antonyms:* exacerbate, irritate, torment **2.** assist, clear, expedite, facilitate, further, help, improve, promote, simplify *Antonyms:* hinder, retard, thwart **3.** edge into, escort, guide, inch, manoeuvre, move, pilot, slide, slip, squeeze, steer, usher **4.** free up, loosen, relax, unbend, unclench, unwind *Antonyms:* harden, stiffen, tense up

easily *adv.* **1.** calmly, comfortably, competently, completely, conveniently, coolly, dexterously, efficiently, effortlessly, evenly, facilely, fluently, freely, handily, lightly, plainly, quickly, rapidly, readily, regularly, simply, smoothly, steadily, surely, well, with ease *Nonformal:* hands down, like nothing, no sweat, swimmingly *Antonyms:* arduously, difficulty, painstakingly **2.** absolutely, actually, assuredly, certainly, clearly, decidedly, definitely, doubtlessly, indeed, indisputably, indubitably, no doubt, plainly, positively, really, surely, truly, undeniably, undoubtedly, unquestionably, without doubt *Antonyms:* arguably, debatably, suspiciously

east *adj.* down, eastern, eastward – *adv.* downriver, easterly – *n.* Atlantic provinces, eastern seaboard, Maritimes *or* Maritime provinces, Middle Atlantic states *Eastern Canadian Provinces*: New Brunswick, Newfoundland, Nova Scotia, Ontario, Prince Edward Island, Quebec

easy *adj.* **1.** accessible, basic, clear, effortless, elementary, facile, light, manageable, obvious, painless, plain, simple, slight, smooth, straightforward, uncomplicated, undemanding, uninvolved *Nonformal:* cinch, hassle-free, no-brainer, no problem *or* sweat *Antonyms:* arduous, complex, hard, **2.** accommodating, affable, amenable, amiable, at ease, benign, biddable, carefree, comfortable, compassionate, contented, diplomatic, easygoing, flexible, good-humoured, gregarious, indulgent, kindly, lenient, merciful, natural, open, pleasant, polite, relaxed, sociable, sympathetic, tolerant, unaffected, unpretentious, untroubled *Antonyms:* demanding, harsh, inflexible, onerous, strict, unyielding **3.** deliberate, gentle, lax, leisurely, measured, slow, unhurried *Antonyms:* accelerated, blazing, fast, hurried **4.** credulous, persuadable, yielding **5.** affluent, independent, rich, self-reliant, wealthy, well-off *Nonformal:* fat, loaded

easygoing *adj.* **1.** amenable, carefree, complaisant, even-tempered, flexible, informal, insouciant, lenient, mild, moderate, nonchalant, obliging, patient, permissive, *sans souci (French)*, tolerant, unconcerned, uncritical, undemanding *Antonyms:* anxious, fussy, irritated, tense, uptight **2.** breezy, calm, casual, leisurely, placid, relaxed, slow, tranquil, unhurried *Antonyms:* chaotic, frantic, wild

eat *v.* **1.** bite, break bread, breakfast, chew, chomp, consume, devour, dine, feast, feed, glut, gnaw, gobble, gorge, gourmandize, graze, ingest, lunch, masticate, munch, nibble, nourish, partake of, slurp, snack, sup, swallow, taste *Nonformal:* do lunch, nosh, polish off, scarf down **2.** abrade, corrode, destroy, erode, ravage, rust, waste, wear away

eavesdrop *v.* listen *or* listen in, meddle, monitor, overhear, pry, snoop, spy, wiretap *Nonformal:* bug, tap, wire

ebb *n.* **1.** ebb *or* low tide, refluence, reflux **2.** decay, decline, deterioration, downturn, slump, waning, weakening – *v.* **1.** abate, go out, recede, retreat, subside *Antonyms:* flood, surge, swell **2.** decay, decline, deteriorate, dwindle, fade, fail, peter out *(Nonformal)*, sink, taper off, waste away, weaken, wind down *Antonyms:* activate, revive, revitalize

ebony *adj.* black, charcoal, coal, crow, dark, ink, jet, night, obsidian, pitch, raven, sable, soot, tar

ebullience *n.* animation, bounce, buoyancy, effervescence, effusiveness, elation, enthusiasm, excitement, exhilaration, exuberance, high spirits, liveliness, verve, vitality, vivaciousness, zest *Antonyms:* apathy, calm, restfulness

eccentric *adj.* bizarre, capricious, cockeyed, curious, different, erratic, freak, freakish, funny, idiosyncratic, individualist, irregular, odd, offbeat, off-centre, outlandish, peculiar, quaint, queer, quirky, quizzical, singular, strange, uncommon, unconventional, unnatural, unorthodox, unusual, weird *Nonformal:* batty, far out, flaky, funky, goony, kooky, screwball, screwy, way out, wacky *Antonyms:* commonplace, conventional, ordinary, regular, typical – *n.* character, maverick, nonconformist, odd person, original *Nonformal:* case, crackpot, freak, fruitcake, kook, loony, nut, oddball, rare bird, strange duck, weirdo, wacko

eccentricity *n.* **1.** aberration, anomaly, deviation, irregularity, nonconformity, oddity, oddness, outlandishness, queerness, singularity, strangeness, unconventionality, unusualness, waywardness, weirdness *Antonyms:* commonality, conformity, regularity **2.** character trait, foible, idiosyncrasy, kink, mannerism, peculiarity, quirk

ecclesiastical *adj.* apostolic, churchly *(Nonformal)*, clerical, divine, holy, ministerial, nonsecular, pantheistical, pastoral, priestly, religious, sacerdotal, sacred, spiritual, tabernacular

echelon *n.* **1.** class, degree, grade, level, place, position, rank, tier **2.** file, line, queue, row, string

echo *n.* **1.** recurrence, reiteration, repercussion, repetition, resonance, reverberation **2.** duplication, imitation, likeness, reflection, replica, reproduction *Antonyms:* original, prototype, standard **3.** answer, chorus, refrain, response – *v.* **1.** resonate, resound, return, ring, vibrate **2.** ape *(Nonformal)*, copy, emulate, imitate, mimic, parrot, simulate *Antonyms:* compose, create, invent, originate **3.** agree with, follow suit, second, stand behind, support *Antonyms:* contest, oppose, veto

eclectic *adj.* broad, catholic, comprehensive, diverse, general, heterogeneous, inclusive, liberal, mixed, multicultural, multifarious, pluralistic, universal, varied, well-rounded *Antonyms:* exclusive, narrow, select

eclipse *n.* concealment, darkening, dimming, extinction, obliteration, overshadowing, shading, shadow, shadowing, shroud – *v.* **1.** adumbrate, black *or* blot out, cloud, conceal, cover, darken, dim, erase, obfuscate, obscure, overshadow, shadow, shroud, veil *Antonyms:* display, expose, illuminate, show, uncover, unveil **2.** dwarf, exceed, excel, outdo, outshine, overrun, surmount, surpass, transcend *Antonyms:* fail, fall short, miscarry, underachieve, underperform

ecology *n.* bionomics, biota, ecosystem, environment, flora and fauna, natural habitat, nature *Kinds of ecological cycle:* carbon, life, nitrogen, oxygen *Types of ecological consumer:* first-order, second-order, third-order

economic *adj.* **1.** budgetary, business, commercial, financial, fiscal, material, mercantile, monetary, moneymaking, pecuniary, profitable, profit-making, remunerative, trade, viable **2.** bread-and-butter, practical, prudent, useful, utilitarian

economical *adj.* **1.** canny, careful, chary, frugal, modest, parsimonious, penny-wise, prudent, saving, skimping, sparing, thrifty, tight *Antonyms:* immoderate, lavish, wasteful **2.** affordable, cheap, cost-effective, inexpensive, low-priced, marked-down, money-saving, on sale, reasonable *Antonyms:* exorbitant, expensive, overpriced **3.** efficient, mean *(Nonformal)*, practical, streamlined, timesaving, work-saving *Antonyms:* nonproductive, outdated, wasteful

economize *v.* conserve, cut back *or* corners, husband, manage, pinch pennies, sacrifice, save, scrimp, skimp, spare *Antonyms:* spend, splurge, squander, waste

economy *n.* **1.** care, caution, frugality, husbandry, restraint, retrenchment, saving scrimping, skimping, thrift, thriftiness **2** curtailment, cutback, layoff, reduction rollback, shrinkage **3.** Gross National Product *or* GNP, Gross Domestic Product *or* GDP, national income, production and distribution, stability, wealth

ecosystem *n.* biosphere, biota, community, ecology, ecosphere, ecozone, environment, flora and fauna, life cycle, natural habitat, physical environment, web

ecstasy *n.* beatitude, bliss, delight, delirium, ebullience, elation, enchantment euphoria, exaltation, fervour, frenzy, happiness, heaven, inspiration, intoxication, paradise, rapture, rhapsody, seventh heaven transport *Antonyms:* agony, anguish, distress, suffering

ecstatic *adj.* blissful, delirious, elated enraptured, euphoric, frenzied, happy, joyful, mad, overjoyed, rapturous, thrilled transported, wild *Nonformal:* floating, flying high, high, over the moon, tickled pink *Antonyms:* downhearted, grief-stricken miserable, sorrowful, unhappy

ecumenical *adj.* general, global, international, pandemic, planetary, ubiquitous universal, widespread, worldwide *Antonyms:* confined, limited, local

eddy *n.* backcurrent, backwash, Charybdis countercurrent, counterflow, counterflux maelstrom, vortex, whirlpool – *v.* revolve rotate, spin, swirl, turn, whirl

Eden *n.* Avalon, bliss, Canaan, City of God cloud cuckoo land, Elysium, garden, Garden of Irem *(Islam)*, happy hunting grounds Heaven, Land of Beulah, Land of the Leal *(Scotland)*, paradise, Promised Land Shangri-La, Valhalla *(Norse)*

edge *n.* **1.** border, bound, boundary, brim brink, butt, circumference, curb, dividing line, extremity, frame, fringe, frontier, limit line, lip, margin, outline, perimeter, periphery, rim, ring, side, threshold, tip, verge *Antonyms:* centre, core, heart **2.** advantage ascendancy, dominance, head start, lead superiority, upper hand **3.** anger, bitterness harshness, sharpness, trenchancy, vehemence, vitriol **4.** avant-garde, forefront, vanguard – *v.* **1.** bind, border, bound, fringe, margin, outline, rim, skirt, surround, trim, verge **2.** hone, sharpen, strop, whet *Antonyms:* blunt, dull, soften **3.** creep, crawl, inch, sidestep, sidle, slink *Antonyms:* hurry, race, rush

edgy *adj.* anxious, excitable, high-strung, impatient, irritable, nervous, tense, testy *Antonyms:* calm, peaceful, placid

edible *adj.* digestible, eatable, fit, flavourful, good, nourishing, palatable, savoury, succulent, tasty, wholesome, yummy *(Nonformal) Antonyms:* dyspeptic, indigestible, inedible, rancid

edict *n.* act, canon, command, commandment, decree, dictate, dictum, directive, enactment, fiat, injunction, judgment, law, mandate, manifesto, order, ordinance, precept, proclamation, prohibition, pronouncement, regulation, rule, ruling, statute, ukase, writ

edification *n.* benefit, education, enlightenment, intellectual *or* moral guidance, moral improvement, progress, uplifting

edifice *n.* building, construction, monument, skyscraper, structure, temple, tower

edit *v.* **1.** adapt, alter, amend, annotate, check, condense, copy-edit, correct, cut down, emend, fine-tune, modify, proof, read, rephrase, restyle, revise, rework, rewrite, style, tighten, touch-up, trim, verify **2.** arrange, assemble, collect, compile, prepare, put together, select **3.** bowdlerize, blue-pencil, censor, clean-up, delete, doctor *(Nonformal)*, excise, expunge, expurgate

edition *n.* copy, impression, imprint, installment, issue, number, printing, print run, program, publication, reissue, release, reprint, version, volume

editorial *n.* argument, article, column, essay, op-ed *or* opinion piece, polemic, policy *or* position statement, statement, think piece

educate *v.* acculturate, acquaint, brief, coach, cultivate, develop, discipline, drill, edify, enlighten, establish, exercise, form, ground, help, improve, indoctrinate, inform, instruct, lead, nurture, prime, school, set, teach, train, transculturate, tutor

educated *adj.* **1.** brainwashed *(Nonformal)*, instructed, prepared, schooled, shaped, taught, trained, tutored *Antonyms:* illiterate, uneducated, unschooled **2.** accomplished, bright, civilized, cultivated, developed, enlightened, enriched, erudite, experienced, expert, finished, informed, knowledgeable, learned, lettered, literate, mannered, polished, scholarly, skilled, smart, urbane, well-read *Antonyms:* barbaric, uncivilized, vulgar, well-informed

education *n.* **1.** apprenticeship, betterment, brainwashing, catechism, coaching, courses, direction, discipline, drilling, drills, edification, enhancement, enlightenment, exercise, guidance, illumination, improvement, indoctrination, instruction, learning, lessons, pedagogy, preparation, propagandism, reading, readying, refinement, research, scholarship, schooling, seasoning, study, teaching, training, tuition, tutelage, upbringing **2.** background, basics, capacity, cultivation, erudition, foundation, grounding, information, intelligence, know-how, knowledge, literacy, principles, rearing, science, skills, wherewithal, wisdom

educe *v.* **1.** bring out, derive, draw forth, elicit, evoke, extract, summon **2.** arrive at, conclude, deduce, develop, infer, reason, surmise

eerie *adj.* awesome, bizarre, creepy, fantastic, fearful, frightening, ghostly, mysterious, scary *(Nonformal)*, spectral, spooky, strange, supernatural, uncanny, unearthly, upsetting, weird *Antonyms:* banal, commonplace, everyday

efface *v.* **1.** cancel, eradicate, erase, expunge, remove, rub *or* wipe out **2.** destroy, disintegrate, obliterate, zap *(Nonformal)*

effect *n.* **1.** aftermath, bottom line *(Nonformal)*, by-product, consequence, end, fruit, outcome, reaction, repercussion, result, upshot **2.** efficacy, force, impact, influence, potency, power, validity, weight *Nonformal:* clout, punch **3.** drift, implication, intent, meaning, objective, purpose, significance, tenor **4.** accomplishment, attainment, consummation, execution, fulfillment, realization – *v.* accomplish, achieve, bring about, cause, consummate, produce *Commonly misused:* **affect**

effective *adj.* **1.** adequate, capable, competent, efficient, functional, handy, productive, serviceable, useful *Antonyms:* counterproductive, ineffectual, useless **2.** active, functioning, operational, valid, working *Antonyms:* defunct, invalid, null, void **3.** cogent, compelling, dynamic, emphatic, energetic, forceful, impressive, moving, potent, powerful, striking, trenchant *Antonyms:* frivolous, superficial, trivial **4.** able, available, capable, fit, ready *Commonly misused:* **affective**

effects *n. pl.* baggage, belongings, chattel, furnishings, goods, merchandise, movables, personal property, possessions, trappings

effectual *adj.* **1.** conclusive, deciding, decisive, effecting, effective, efficacious, efficient, functional, sufficient *Antonyms:* fruitless, futile, inoperative **2.** authoritative, binding, lawful, legal, legitimate, official, orthodox, sanctioned, statutory, warranted *Antonyms:* deviant, irregular, unofficial

effeminate *adj.* female, feminine, girlish, unmanly, womanish, womanlike, womanly *Antonyms:* manly, masculine *Commonly misused:* **effete**

effervescence *n.* **1.** animation, buoyancy, ebullience, enthusiasm, excitedness, excitement, exhilaration, exuberance, gaiety, happiness, joy, liveliness, sparkle, vim, vitality, vivacity *Antonyms:* blandness, dullness, lassitude **2.** bubbling, fizziness, fizzle, foam, gas

effervescent *adj.* animated, bouncy, bubbly, buoyant, ebullient, enthusiastic, excited, exhilarated, exuberant, gleeful, happy, high-spirited, hilarious, irrepressible, jolly, joyous, lively, merry, mirthful, sprightly, vital, vivacious *Antonyms:* boring, bovine, flat, insipid, lacklustre

effete *adj.* barren, drained, enervated, enfeebled, exhausted, feeble, ineffectual, soft, spent, unproductive, weak *Antonyms:* energetic, energized, vital *Commonly misused:* **effeminate**

efficiency *n.* ability, adaptability, adeptness, adequacy, capability, capableness, competence, competency, deftness, economy, efficacy, effectiveness, expertise, facility, faculty, know-how, productiveness, productivity, proficiency, prowess, readiness, resourcefulness, skill, strength, suitability, talent, thoroughness, utility *Antonyms:* incompetency, ineptitude

efficient *adj.* **1.** able, accomplished, adapted, adept, adroit, apt, businesslike, capable, competent, conducive, deft, effectual, efficacious, effective, experienced, expert, fitted, practiced, productive, proficient, qualified, ready, skilled, successful, systematic, useful, valuable, well-organized *Antonyms:* disorganized, incompetent, inept, slipshod, sloppy **2.** cost-effective, energy-efficient, environmentally friendly, green *(Nonformal)*, labour-saving, money-saving, time-saving **3.** careful, economical, frugal, prudent, restrained, thrifty *Antonyms:* excessive, unrestrained, wasteful *Commonly misused:* **effective**

effigy *n.* clone, dummy, figure, icon, idol, image, likeness, model, picture, portrait, puppet, representation, sculpture, statue

effluent *adj.* discharged, emanating, emitted – *n.* **1.** effluvium, pollutant, sewage, waste **2.** discharge, effluence, efflux, emanation, emission, exhalation, flow, outflow *Commonly misused:* **affluent**

effort *n.* **1.** application, battle, energy, exertion, force, labour, strain, struggle, toil, trouble, work *Nonformal:* elbow grease, push, sweat *Antonyms:* indolence, inertia, passivity, sloth **2.** attempt, endeavour, essay, try, venture *Nonformal:* crack, fling, go, shot, stab **3.** accomplishment, achievement, attainment, deed, exploit, feat

effortless *adj.* **1.** easy, facile, light, offhand, painless, simple, uncomplicated, unde manding, worry-free *Nonformal:* child's play, duck soup, no-brainer, no problem *or* sweat *Antonyms:* demanding, difficult, formidable, hard, onerous **2.** flowing, fluid, graceful, natural, running, smooth, unforced, unrestrained *Antonyms:* checked, gaited, mannered, wooden

effrontery *n.* audacity, boldness, brazenness, gall, impudence, insolence, nerve, presumption, shamelessness, temerity *Nonformal:* balls, brass, cheek, mouth *Commonly misused:* **affrontery**

effulgent *adj.* alight, beaming, bright, brilliant, incandescent, radiant, resplendent, shimmering, shining *Antonyms:* dim, dull, lacklustre

effusion *n.* **1.** discharge, effluence, effluvium, efflux, emanation, emission, escape, issue, ooze, outpouring, pouring, release, seepage, secretion, spew, spill, stream **2.** garrulousness, loquaciousness, verbosity, volubility, wordiness

effusive *adj.* demonstrative, ebullient, enthusiastic, expansive, extravagant, exuberant, gabby *(Nonformal)*, gushing, lavish, long-winded, overflowing, profuse, talkative, unconstrained, unreserved, unrestrained, verbose, windy, wordy *Antonyms:* concise, laconic, succinct, terse

egg *n.* **1.** cell, embryo, ovum, reproductive body, roe, seed **2.** cackleberry *(Nonformal) Kinds of egg dishes:* baked, boiled, buttered, caviar, coddled, devilled, eggs benedict, fried, omelette, over easy, pickled, poached, quiche, salad, Scotch, scrambled, shirred, soufflé, stuffed, sunnyside up – *v.* encourage, goad, incite, instigate, persuade, prod, push, urge

ego *n.* **1.** character, identity, individuality, personality, self **2.** assurance, conceit, egocentricity, egoism, egomania, egotism, haughtiness, megalomania, narcissism, presumption, pride, self-admiration, self-absorption, self-admiration, self-importance, self-interest, selfishness, self-pride, self-regard, self-worship, smugness, vainglory, vanity

egocentric *adj.* self-absorbed, self-centred, self-concerned, self-indulgent, self-interested, selfish, self-loving, self-serving

egotistical *adj.* affected, arrogant, boastful, bragging, conceited, haughty, inflated, megalomanical, narcissistic, pompous, presumptuous, proud, puffed up, self-admiring, self-important, snobbish, stuck-up *(Nonformal)*, supercilious, swollen, vain, vainglorious *Antonyms:* deferential, humble, modest, unassuming

egregious *adj.* appalling, atrocious, audacious, deplorable, disgraceful, extreme, flagrant, glaring, grievous, gross, infamous, insufferable, intolerable, monstrous, outrageous, preposterous, rank, scandalous, shocking, stark *Antonyms:* acceptable, decent, tolerable

eh *interj.* **1.** are you with me, capiche, catch my drift, comprehend, get it, know what I mean, okay, right, understand, yes **2.** again, louder, once more, say what, what

eject *v.* **1.** banish, cast out, debar, disbar, discharge, dislodge, dismiss, displace, dispossess, eliminate, evict, expel, fire, oust, sack, throw out *or* overboard, turn out *Nonformal:* bounce, bump, can, chuck, ditch, dump, send packing **2.** disgorge, emit, erupt, extrude, spew, spout, vomit

elaborate *adj.* **1.** Borgesian, complex, complicated, detailed, developed, difficult, exact, extensive, intricate, involved, laboured, labyrinthine, painstaking, skilful, sophisticated, studied, thorough **2.** busy, decorated, embellished, extravagant, fancy, garnished, highly-wrought, luxurious, many-faceted, ornamented, ornate, ostentatious, perfected, refined, showy *Antonyms:* basic, minimal, modest, plain, simple – *v.* **1.** clarify, comment, develop, devise, discuss, enlarge, expand, expatiate, explain, expound, flesh out, interpret, particularize, specify, treat, unfold, work out *Antonyms:* condense, simplify, streamline **2.** amplify, bedeck, decorate, embellish, enhance, garnish, ornament, polish, refine *Antonyms:* denude, strip

élan *n.* animation, ardour, bounce, brio, briskness, buoyancy, dash, esprit, excitement, flair, flourish, impetuosity, impetus, life, oomph *(Nonformal)*, panache, snap, spirit, spontaneity, style, verve, vigour, vim, vivacity, wholeheartedness, zest *Antonyms:* indolence, languor, lassitude, lethargy

elapse *v.* disappear, evanesce, expire, flow, go, lapse, pass *or* pass away, run out, slip by, transpire, vanish

elastic *adj.* **1.** ductile, extendible, flexible, limber, lithe, pliable, pliant, recuperative, resilient, rubberlike, rubbery, springy, stretchable, supple, tolerant *Antonyms:* fixed, rigid, rusted-solid **2.** adaptable, adjustable, complaisant, easy, giving, malleable, mouldable, plastic, yielding *Antonyms:* firm, obdurate, resolute, set **3.** animated, bouncy, buoyant, ebullient, effervescent, lively, spirited, sprightly

elate *v.* charm, cheer, delight, enchant, enrapture, exhilarate, gladden, hearten, please, satisfy, thrill, transport *Antonyms:* depress, sadden, shame, vex

elated *adj.* animated, aroused, blissful, content, delighted, ecstatic, euphoric, excited, exhilarated, gay, gleeful, happy, joyful, jubilant, overjoyed, pleased, proud, roused, transported, very happy *Nonformal:* flying, high, in heaven, turned-on *Antonyms:* blue, discontent, down, sad

elation *n.* bliss, buoyancy, contentedness, delight, ecstasy, enthusiasm, euphoria, excitement, exhilaration, exultation, gaiety, glee, happiness, high spirits, intoxication, joy, jubilation, pleasure, rapture, triumph *Nonformal:* buzz, charge, kick *Antonyms:* depression, sadness, unhappiness

elbow *n.* bend, corner, curve, dog leg, joint, turn – *v.* bulldoze, bump, crowd, hustle, jostle, knock, nudge, press, push, shoulder, shove

elder *adj.* **1.** earlier, firstborn, former, older, preceding, prior, senior *Antonyms:* junior, younger **2.** chief, dominant, foremost, primary, principal, ranking, superior – *n.* **1.** ancient, cailleach *(P.E.I.)*, centenarian, grande dame, grandfather, grandmother, octogenarian, older adult *or* person, old man *or* lady *or* woman, senior *or* senior citizen, septuagenarian, sexagenarian *Nonformal:* dad, fogey, geezer, golden-ager, granny, oldster, old-timer, pop *Antonyms:* babe, child, neonate, youngster **2.** ancestor, forebear, forefather, predecessor, progenitor **3.** advisor, chief, counselor, dean, guru, leader, matriarch, patriarch, sage, sensei, shaman

elderly *adj.* aged, aging, ancient, antiquated, declining, decrepit, hoary, old, retired, senescent, senior, superannuated, tired, venerable *Antonyms:* blooming, blossoming, fresh, young, youthful

elect *adj.* **1.** choice, chosen, elite, first-rate, prime, select **2.** designate, next-in-office, presumptive, prospective, to-be – *v.* **1.** acclaim, appoint, ballot, check off, designate, name, nominate, place in office, single out, vote for *Antonyms:* expel, impeach, oust, recall **2.** choose, conclude, decide, determine, opt for, resolve, settle *Antonyms:* abjure, recant, renounce

election *n.* choosing, decision, determination, judgment, nomination, option, poll, preference, selection, voting *Kinds of election:* acclamation, by-election, democratic, federal, general, mayoral, municipal, national, plebiscite, presidential, primary *(U.S.)*, provincial, referendum, state *Nonformal:* Harvard-Yale game *(U.S.)*, horse race, toss-up

elective *adj.* **1.** constituent, discretionary, optional, selective, voluntary *Antonyms:* compulsory, obligatory, necessary **2.** chosen, elected, hand-picked, selected, voted in *Antonyms:* bequeathed, divinely sanctioned, inherited

electorate *n.* citizenry, enfranchised, grass roots, people, poll, populace, voters, voting population

electric *adj.* **1.** AC, charged, DC, energized, productive, voltaic **2.** dynamic, exciting, magnetic, powerful, rousing, stimulating, stirring, tense, thrilling

electricity *n.* current, electromagnetism, hydro *or* hydroelectricity, ignition, light, magnetism, power, service, spark, utility, voltage *Kinds of electrical sciences:* elec trical engineering, electrodynamics, electrokinetics, electromechanics, electrometallurgy, electronics, electrophysics, electrostatics, magnetometery, thermionics

electrify *v.* amaze, animate, astonish, astound, charge, disturb, energize, enthuse, excite, fire, galvanize, invigorate, jar, jolt, magnetize, power, provoke, rouse, shock, startle, stimulate, stir, strike, stun, thrill, wow *(Nonformal) Antonyms:* bore, fatigue, tire

electron *n.* beta *or* cathode *or* elementary particle, negatron *Kinds of electron:* bonding, bound, conduction, excess, free, nuclear, orbital, peripheral, photoelectron, positive, primary, recoil, secondary, spinning, surface-bound, valence, wandering

electronics *n. pl.* radio electronics, radionics *Kinds of electronic circuits:* amplifier, flip-flop, gate *or* logic gate, shunt, trigger, tuned

elegance *n.* breeding, charm, chic, class, courtliness, cultivation, culture, delicacy, dignity, discernment, distinction, felicity, gentility, good taste, grace, gracefulness, hauteur, opulence, polish, propriety, refinement, sophistication, style, tastefulness *Antonyms:* crudeness, tackiness, vulgarity

elegant *adj.* **1.** august, beautiful, chic, delicate, exquisite, fancy, fashionable, fine, grand, handsome, impeccable, luxurious, majestic, opulent, ornamented, ornate, sumptuous, tasteful **2.** affected, aristocratic, cultivated, cultured, debonair, dignified, genteel, graceful, gracious, polished, refined, suave, urbane, well-bred *Antonyms:* awkward, boorish, bumbling, inelegant, ungraceful **3.** appropriate, choice, classic, clever, effective, ingenious, simple, smart, timely *Antonyms:* improper, inappropriate, unsuitable

elegy *n.* commemoration, coronach, dirge, epicedium, funeral song, Kaddish, keening, lament, meditation, monody, plaint, requiem, song of mourning *Commonly misused:* **eulogy**

element *n.* **1.** aspect, basis, bit, component, constituent, detail, essential, factor, feature, fundamental, ingredient, item, material, matter, part, particular, piece, portion, principle, section, subdivision, unit **2.** atomic *or* chemical *or* periodic element, mass, material, matter, stuff, substance *The Four Elements:* air, earth, fire, water *Groupings of elements:* metallic, nonmetallic *See also:* **chemical** **3.** domain, environment, field, habitat, habitation, locale, medium, milieu, sphere **4.** category, crowd, culture, family, group, people, race, society

elementary *adj.* **1.** basic, beginning, essential, foundational, fundamental, general, initial, introductory, original, preliminary, primary, rudimentary *Antonyms:* advanced, progressive **2.** clear, easy, facile, simple, simplified, straightforward, uncomplicated *Antonyms:* complex, difficult, hard

elephantine *adj.* awkward, bulky, bumbling, clumsy, cumbersome, enormous, heavy, hulking, lumbering, mammoth, ponderous, ungainly, unwieldy, weighty *Antonyms:* dainty, minute, precise, small

elevate *v.* **1.** boost, build up, erect, heighten, hike up, hoist, jack, levitate, lift up, pump, raise, rear, take up, tilt, uphold, uplift, upraise **2.** advance, appoint, further, promote, upgrade **3.** aggrandize, dignify, ennoble, exalt, glorify, honour *Antonyms:* belittle, demean, malign, slander, slur **4.** augment, enhance, increase, swell *Antonyms:* diminish, lessen **5.** animate, brighten, cheer, elate, excite, exhilarate, hearten, inspire, lift, rouse **6.** civilize, cultivate, edify, educate, enlighten, raise one's awareness *or* consciousness, raise up

elevated *adj.* **1.** aerial, high, high-rise, hoisted, jacked, lifted, raised, raised up, tall, towering, upheaved, uplifted, upraised **2.** dignified, eminent, formal, grand, high-minded, important, majestic, serious, solemn, stately, sublime *Antonyms:* humble, lowly, modest, simple **3.** animated, bright, cheerful, elated, exhilarated, happy, pleased

elevation *n.* **1.** acclivity, altitude, ascent, height, hill, hoist, horst, mesa, mountain, peak, platform, rise, roof, summit, top, uplift **2.** advance, advancement, aggrandizement, boost, magnification, promotion, raise *Antonyms:* decline, demotion, fall **3.** apotheosis, ennoblement, exaltation, exaltedness, glory, grandeur, loftiness, magnificence, majesty, splendour, sublimity

elf *n.* mischief-maker, nuisance, puck, terror *(Nonformal)*, trickster, troublemaker *Kinds of elf:* brownie, fairy, goblin, imp, leprechaun, pixie, sprite *See also:* **fairy**

elicit *v.* bring forth *or* out, call forth, cause, derive, draw out, educe, evince, evoke, exact, extort, extract, fetch, milk, obtain, shake, squeeze, wrest, wring out *Antonyms:* gag, restrain, silence, stifle *Commonly misused:* **illicit, solicit**

eligible *adj.* **1.** acceptable, appropriate, capable, desirable, elective, employable, equal to, fit, licensed, likely, preferable, proper, qualified, satisfactory, seemly, suitable, suited, trained, usable, worthy *Antonyms:* inappropriate, ineligible, unqualified, unsuited **2.** available, looking *(Nonformal)*, marriageable, single, unmarried

eliminate *v.* **1.** annihilate, cancel, delete, destroy, dispense with, dispose of, eject, eradicate, erase, expel, expunge, exterminate, liquidate, obliterate, phase *or* rub out, stamp *or* strike out, take *or* wipe out, terminate, throw out, waste *Antonyms:* accept, add, include, incorporate **2.** discard, disregard, drop, exclude, ignore, omit, reject, rule out, set aside *Antonyms:* consider, note, watch **3.** beat, break, check, defeat, disqualify, invalidate, oust, remove, slay, vanquish *Antonyms:* forfeit, lose, yield

elimination *n.* abolishment, abrogation, annihilation, cancellation, banishment, debarment, deletion, discharge, eradication, eviction, excision, expulsion, expurgation, extirpation, exile, proscription, purge, removal, rubbing out, suspension, termination *Antonyms:* addition, augmentation, incorporation

elite *adj.* best, choice, crack, exclusive, first-class, pick, selected, super, topflight, topnotch, upper-class, world-class – *n.* aristocracy, choice, cognoscenti, establishment, gentry, high class, high life, high society, jet set, main line, money, nobility, quality, select, society, upper class *Nonformal:* beautiful people, blue blood, carriage trade, crème de la crème, glitterati, haute monde, horsey set, in-crowd, silk stocking, smart set *Antonyms:* dregs, rabble, riffraff

elliptical *adj.* **1.** egg-shaped, ellipsoidal, oblong, oval, ovoid **2.** abbreviated, abridged, concentrated, concise, condensed, edited, shortened, terse

elocution *n.* articulation, declamation, delivery, diction, eloquence, enunciation, expression, locution, oratory, phrasing, pronunciation, public speaking, rhetoric, speech, utterance, voice culture, voice production

elongate *v.* draw out, extend, fill, lengthen, make longer, pad, prolong, protract, spin out, stretch *Antonyms:* abridge, compress, curtail, shrink

elope *v.* abscond, decamp, disappear, escape, flee, go secretly, marry privately *or* secretly, run away, steal away

eloquence *n.* **1.** articulation, delivery, diction, facility, fluency, loquacity, oration, rhetoric, style, wit **2.** expressiveness, force, mellifluousness, passion, persuasiveness, spirit, volubility, vigour, vivacity

eloquent *adj.* **1.** articulate, convincing, effective, emotional, fluent, impassioned, incisive, moving, passionate, persuasive, poignant, spirited, stirring, touching **2.** evocative, expressive, indicative, meaningful, revealing, significant, suggestive, vivid

elucidate *v.* annotate, clarify, clear *or* clear up, decode, demonstrate, enlighten, enunciate, exemplify, explain, explicate, expound, gloss, illuminate, illustrate, interpret, prove, reveal, unfold *Antonyms:* becloud, bewilder, confuse, obfuscate

elude *v.* **1.** avoid, bilk, circumvent, ditch, dodge, duck, escape, evade, jump, lose, outdistance, outrun, shake off, shirk, sidestep **2.** baffle, confound, deceive, foil, frustrate, outwit, puzzle, stump, throw off, thwart, trick *Commonly misused:* **allude**

elusive *adj.* ambiguous, baffling, cagey, deceitful, deceptive, ephemeral, equivocal evanescent, evasive, fleeting, fugitive, illusory, imponderable, indefinable, insubstantial, intangible, misleading, puzzling, shifty, slippery, subtle, transitory, tricky, unspecific, volatile *Commonly misused:* **allusive**

emaciated *adj.* angular, anorexic, atrophied, attenuated, bony, cadaverous, consumptive, famished, gaunt, haggard, lank, lean, meagre, reduced, scrawny, skeletal, skin-and-bones *(Nonformal)*, skinny, spare, thin, undernourished, underweight, wan, wasted, wizened *Antonyms:* chubby, corpulent, obese

e-mail *n.* electronic communication *or* mail, network mail *Kinds of e-mail:* flame, listserve, newsgroup, spam, usenet *Antonyms:* courier, postal system, snail mail *(Nonformal)*

emanate *v.* come forth *or* from, exude, flow, give off, issue, originate, pour *or* send forth, spring, stream, stem from, well

emanation *n.* discharge, drainage, effluence, effluent, effusion, emergence, emission, flowing, gush, issuing, leakage, oozing, outflow, outpour, proceeding, radiation, spring

emancipate *v.* deliver, discharge, disenthrall, enfranchise, free, liberate, loose, manumit, release, set free, unbind, unchain, unfetter, unshackle *Antonyms:* bind, capture, enslave

emasculate *v.* alter, castrate, cripple, debilitate, deprive, devitalize, enervate, fix *(Nonformal)*, geld, impoverish, mutilate, neuter, paralyze, sap, soften, tire, unman, unnerve, weaken *Antonyms:* energize, excite, strengthen, vitalize

embalm *v.* conserve, enshrine, freeze, immortalize, lay out, mummify, prepare, preserve, process, shroud, store, treasure, wrap

embankment *n.* balustrade, bank, barrier, bulwark, breakwater, bridge, causeway, dam, dike, dune, earthwork, jetty, levee, mound, palisade, pier, quay, rampart, support, terrace, wall, wharf

embargo *n.* ban, barrier, block, check, economic sanction, hindrance, impediment, prevention, prohibition, proscription, restraint, restriction, stoppage, trade sanction *Antonyms:* free trade, laissez-faire, unfettered flow of goods – *v.* ban, bar, check, choke, hinder, impede, inhibit, interdict, prohibit, restrain, restrict, sanction, starve, stifle, stop *Antonyms:* allow, free, liberate, permit

embark *v.* **1.** board, enplane, enter, entrain, get under way, launch, leave, sail, set out, set sail, take off, weigh anchor **2.** begin, commence, initiate, originate, undertake

embarrass *v.* abash, bewilder, bother, confuse, discomfort, discompose, disconcert, distract, distress, disturb, dumfound, faze, fluster, mortify, nonplus, perplex, perturb, plague, puzzle, rattle, shame, stun, tease, upset *Nonformal:* bug, discombobulate

embarrassment *n.* **1.** awkwardness, chagrin, discomfort, discomposure, dismay, humiliation, self-consciousness, shame *Antonyms:* comfort, composure, ease **2.** blemish, blot, known incident, mark, spot, stain, stigma **3.** abomination, boob *(Nonformal)*, disgrace, hindrance, irritation, laughing stock, nuisance, spectacle **4.** difficulty, mess, predicament, problem, sticky situation *(Nonformal)*, trouble

embassy *n.* consulate, delegation, diplomatic presence, emissary, envoy, legation, ministry, mission, representation

embattled *adj.* **1.** battling, beset, besieged, clashing, embroiled, fighting, hostile, scrapping, struggling, warring **2.** armed, arrayed, battle-ready, braced, buttressed, equipped, fitted out, fortified, outfitted, prepared, strengthened

embed *v.* bury, deposit, dig in, drive in, enclose, fasten, fix, implant, inject, inlay, insert, install, lodge, place, plant, press, put into, root, set, sink, stick *or* stuff in *Antonyms:* dislodge, loosen, uproot

embellish *v.* **1.** array, beautify, bedeck, colour, deck, decorate, emblaze, embroider, enhance, enrich, festoon, garnish, gussy *or* spruce up *(Nonformal)*, ornament, paint, trim *Antonyms:* divest, simplify, strip bare **2.** colour, distort, exaggerate, expand, fabricate, inflate, magnify, stretch the truth

embellishment *n.* addition, adornment, attachment, beautification, colouring, decoration, elaboration, embroidering, enhancement, enrichment, exaggeration, extra, fanciness, frill, garnish, ornamentation, ostentation *Nonformal:* doodad, froufrou, razzle-dazzle

embezzle *v.* abscond, defraud, extort, filch, loot, misappropriate, pilfer, purloin, skim, steal, swindle, thieve *Nonformal:* bamboozle, lift, pinch, scam, swipe

embezzlement *n.* extortion, filching, fraud, larceny, misappropriation, pilferage, pilfering, purloining, skimming, stealing, theft, thievery *Nonformal:* dirty dealing, white-collar crime

embitter *v.* aggravate, alienate, anger, annoy, antagonize, bother, disaffect, disgust, disillusion, exacerbate, exasperate, irritate, poison, rankle, sour, upset *Antonyms:* appease, mollify, please

embittered *adj.* acrimonious, annoyed, astringent, bothered, cantankerous, corrosive, crabby, cranky, crotchety, irascible, irritated, rancorous, scorned, sour, vitriolic *Antonyms:* affable, friendly, gregarious, sociable

emblem *n.* badge, banner, brand, coat of arms, colophon, colours, crest, design, device, flag, figure, hallmark, identification, image, impress, impression, insignia, logo, mark, marker, medal, monogram, motif, motto, pennant, regalia, representation, sceptre, seal, sign, signet, standard, symbol, token, totem, trademark

embody *v.* **1.** epitomize, evince, exemplify, illustrate, personify, represent, symbolize, typify **2.** collect, combine, comprehend, comprise, embrace, encompass, hold, include, incorporate, involve **3.** amalgamate, assimilate, blend, bring together, consolidate, fuse, integrate, merge, organize, unify

emboss *v.* adorn, beautify, bedeck, boss *(Nonformal)*, carve, chase, cover, decorate, engrave, ornament, raise, ridge, tool

embrace *n.* bear hug, clasp, clutch, cuddle, grasp, grip, hold, hug, snatch, squeeze – *v.* **1.** clasp, clinch, cling, clutch, couple, cradle, cuddle, encircle, enfold, entwine, envelop, fold, fondle, glom onto *(Nonformal)*, grab, grasp, grip, hold tight, hug, lock, nuzzle, press, seize, snuggle, squeeze, wrap *Antonyms:* disengage, unclasp, unclutch **2.** accept, accommodate, admit, adopt, advocate, assume, join, receive, welcome *Antonyms:* reject, spurn **3.** comprise, contain, hold, include, incorporate, subsume, take in

embroider *v.* **1.** aggrandize, amplify, colour, dramatize, elaborate, embellish, enhance, enlarge, exaggerate, expand, falsify, heighten, magnify, overdo, overembellish, overemphasize, overestimate, overstate, pad, romanticize *Antonyms:* distill, edit, pare down, prune **2.** beautify, bedeck, braid, cross-stitch, deck, decorate, garnish, ornament, pattern, quilt, stitch, weave

embroidery *n.* adornment, decoration, needlework *Kinds of cloth embroidery:* appliqué, arabesque, bargello, brocade, crewel, crochet, cross-stitch, decoration, gros point, lace, needlepoint, petit point, quilting, sampler, stitching, tapestry, tracery

embroil *v.* cause trouble, complicate, compromise, confound, confuse, derange, disorder, disturb, disunite, encumber, enmesh, ensnare, entangle, implicate, incriminate, involve, mire, muddle, perplex, snarl, tangle, trouble *Antonyms:* clear up, explicate, extricate, free, untangle

embryonic *adj.* beginning, budding, developing, elementary, fetal, gestational, immature, inaugural, inchoate, incipient, initial, introductory, opening, prefatory, primary, primordial, rudimentary *Antonyms:* advanced, developed, mature, perfected

emcee *n.* commentator, *compère (British)*, director, host *or* hostess, leader, master of ceremonies *or* M.C. – *v.* chair, direct, host, introduce, present, preside over

emend *v.* alter, better, correct, edit, improve,

polish, rectify, retouch, revise, right, touch up *Commonly misused:* **amend**

emerge *v.* **1.** appear, arise, come forth, dawn, egress, materialize, rise, spring up, surface *Antonyms:* disappear, recede, submerge, wane, withdraw **2.** come to light, develop, evolve, grow, proceed, turn up, unfold

emergency *adj.* backup, contingency, escape, reserve, safety, spare – *n.* accident, bind, clutch, crisis, crunch, danger, difficulty, distress, exigency, extremity, imbroglio, meltdown, misadventure, necessity, pass, plight, predicament, pressure, quandary, scrape, situation, squeeze, strait, tension, trouble, turning point, urgency *Nonformal:* fix, hole, hot water

emergent *adj.* appearing, budding, coming, developing, efflorescent, emanating, forthcoming, issuing, new, resulting, rising *Antonyms:* diminishing, disappearing, outgoing, regressing, retreating

emigrant *n.* alien, colonist, displaced person, émigré, evacuee, exile, expatriate, foreigner, fugitive, migrant, migrator, outcast, pilgrim, refugee, traveller, wanderer *Commonly misused:* **immigrant**

emigrate *v.* escape, flee, leave, migrate, move *or* move abroad, transmigrate, travel *Commonly misused:* **immigrate**

eminence *n.* **1.** authority, celebrity, credit, dignity, distinction, esteem, fame, glory, greatness, honour, illustriousness, importance, influence, loftiness, note, power, preeminence, prestige, prominence, rank, renown, repute, significance, standing, superiority **2.** altitude, elevation, height, high ground, highland, hill, peak, prominence, promontory, raise, rise, summit, upland

eminent *adj.* august, celebrated, conspicuous, distinguished, dominant, elevated, esteemed, exalted, famed, famous, grand, high-ranking, illustrious, important, lofty, notable, noteworthy, outstanding, paramount, preeminent, prestigious, prominent, renowned, star, superior, superstar, well-known *Nonformal:* big-league, big-name, big-time *Antonyms:* anonymous, lowly, minor, ordinary, unsung *Commonly misused:* **imminent**

eminently *adv.* conspicuously, exceedingly, exceptionally, extremely, greatly, highly, notably, outstandingly, prominently, remarkably, strikingly, surpassingly *Antonyms:* inconspicuously, unexceptionally, unprominently

emission *n.* broadcast, diffusion, discharge, ejaculation, ejection, emanation, exhalation, issue, radiation, transmission, utterance, venting

emit *v.* belch, discharge, ejaculate, emanate, erupt, excrete, expel, exude, issue, leak, let out, ooze, reek, say, shoot, spit, spurt, squirt

emotion *n.* affect, affection, concern, desire, drive, ecstasy, elation, empathy, excitement, feeling, fervour, inspiration, passion, reaction, responsiveness, satisfaction, sensation, sensibility, sentiment

emotional *adj.* **1.** ardent, demonstrative, disturbed, emotive, enthusiastic, fanatical, feeling, fervent, fervid, fiery, heated, histrionic, hot-blooded, hysterical, impetuous, impulsive, irrational, overwrought, passionate, responsive, roused, spontaneous, susceptible, tender, warm, zealous *Antonyms:* apathetic, cold, detached, insensitive, unmoved **2.** affecting, disturbing, exciting, heartbreaking, moving, pathetic, poignant, sentimental, stirring, tear-jerking, thrilling, touching

emotionless *adj.* blank, cold, cold-blooded, detached, dispassionate, distant, flat, frigid, heartless, immovable, impassive, impersonal, indifferent, matter-of-fact, nonemotional, remote, reserved, toneless, undemonstrative, unemotional, unfeeling, unimpassioned *Nonformal:* dead, deadpan, poker-faced *Antonyms:* responsive, sensitive

emperor *n.* Caesar, czar, empress, ethnarch, imperator, khan, king, leader, maharaja, mikado, monarch, Negus, overlord, padishah, raja, regent, rex, ruler, shah, shogun, sovereign, sultan

emphasis *n.* **1.** consequence, importance, moment, priority, prominence, significance **2.** force, intensity, power, strength, weight **3.** accent, accentuation, attention, beat, focus, sharpness, stress

emphasize *v.* accent, accentuate, bold, build up, call attention to, dramatize, enlarge, feature, headline, highlight, italicize, magnify, mark *or* play up, point out *or* up, punctuate, spotlight, stress, underline, underscore *Nonformal:* drive home, drum, hammer, pound *Antonyms:* hide, minimize, veil

emphatic *adj.* absolute, affirmative, assertive, assured, categorical, certain, confident, decided, definite, definitive, determined, direct, distinct, dogmatic, earnest, explicit, forceful, hard-hitting, insistent, marked, momentous, pointed, positive, powerful, pronounced, significant, sure, telling, unmistakable *Antonyms:* hesitant, tame, tentative

empire *n.* **1.** commonwealth, domain, dominion, federation, kingdom, jurisdiction, people, realm, regency, regimen, region, sovereignty, state, territory, union **2.** authority, command, control, government, power, rule, sway

empirical *adj.* demonstrable, empiric, experiential, factual, knowable, observable, observed, practical, provable, real, seen, undeniable

employ *n.* business, calling, job, occupation, service, work – *v.* **1.** appoint, charter, commission, contract, engage, enlist, enrol, hire, obtain, pay, procure, reserve, retain, secure, sign up, take on *Antonyms:* disengage, fire, terminate **2.** adopt, apply, make use of, ply, try, use, utilize, wield

employed *adj.* active, busy, contracted, engaged, gainfully employed, hired, placed, labouring, occupied, on duty, on the payroll, operating, plugging away *(Nonformal)*, signed, working *Antonyms:* idle, jobless, retired

employee *n.* agent, apprentice, assistant, associate, attendant, blue collar, clerk, cog, colleague, company man, hand, help, labourer, member, operator, pink collar, representative, salesperson, servant, staff member, wage-earner, white collar, worker *Nonformal:* desk jockey, joe punchclock *or* sixpack, slave, staffer, working-class stiff

employer *n.* boss, capitalist, CEO, chief, company, corporation, director, entrepreneur, executive, foreman, forewoman, front office, head, lord, management, manager, manufacturer, master, organization, overseer, owner, policy maker, superintendent, supervisor, taskmaster *Nonformal:* big cheese, head honcho, kingpin

employment *n.* **1.** assignment, avocation, business, calling, commission, contract, employ, engagement, enlistment, enrolment, exercise, field, job, metier, occupation, office, position, post, profession, pursuit, racket, situation, trade, vocation, work **2.** adoption, appliance, application, disposition, exercise, exertion, exploitation, handling, operation, play, practice, service, usage, use, utilization, working

emporium *n.* bazaar, bodega, boutique, corner store, department store, establishment, entrepôt, general store, groceteria, *magasin (French)*, mall, market, mart, open market, shop, store, trading centre *or* post

empower *v.* **1.** appoint, approve, authorize, capacitate, certify, charter, commission, deputize, enfranchise, entitle, entrust, equip, instruct, legalize, license, ordain, school, strengthen, validate, warrant *Antonyms:* disenfranchise, repress, weaken **2.** educate, enable, endow, outfit, permit, teach

empress *n.* czarina, emperor, ethnarch, maharani, monarch, queen, regent, regina, ruler, sovereign, sultana

emptiness *n.* **1.** barrenness, black hole, blankness, chasm, desolation, destitution, gap, hollowness, vacancy, vacuity, vacuum, void, waste, wasteland **2.** desire, hunger, lack, longing, need, starvation, want **3.** banality, foolishness, frivolity, inanity, insincerity, senselessness, silliness, stupidity, triviality, vapidity, worthlessness

empty *adj.* **1.** abandoned, bare, barren, blank, clear, dead, deflated, depleted, desert, deserted, desolate, despoiled, destitute, devoid, dry, evacuated, exhausted, forsaken, godforsaken, lacking, stark, unfurnished, uninhabited, unoccupied, vacant, vacated, vacuous, void *Antonyms:* full, inhabited, occupied **2.** aimless, banal, fatuous, flat, frivolous, fruitless, futile, hollow, idle, inane, ineffective, insincere, insipid, meaningless, nugatory, otiose, paltry, petty, purposeless, senseless, silly, trivial, unsatisfactory, unsubstantial, vain, valueless, vapid, worthless *Antonyms:* meaningful, purposeful, significant **3.** desirous, famished, hungry, longing, needy, ravenous, starving, unfed, unfilled, wanting *Antonyms:* full, satisfied, stuffed – *v.* **1.** decant, deplete, discharge, disgorge, drain, dump, eject, exhaust, expel, gut, leak, purge, release, remove, tap, unburden, unload, vacate, void *Antonyms:* cram, fill, pack, replenish, stock **2.** clear out, decamp, egress, evacuate, exit, go, leave

empty-headed *adj.* brainless, featherbrained, flighty, harebrained, ignorant, know-nothing, scatterbrained, silly, skittish, stupid, uneducated, unschooled, untaught, vacant, vacuous *Antonyms:* brainy, educated, insightful, intelligent, smart

emulate *v.* **1.** ape, copy, echo, follow *or* follow suit, imitate, mimic, mirror, model *or* pattern after, parallel, parrot, replicate, simulate, take after **2.** compare to, compete with, equal, match, rival, vie with

enable *v.* allow, accredit, approve, arm, authorize, capacitate, commission, empower, endow, facilitate, implement, invest, legalize, let, license, outfit, permit, prepare, qualify, ready, sanction, validate, warrant *Antonyms:* bar, block, hinder, impede, obstruct

enact *v.* **1.** approve, authorize, decree, legalize, legislate, ordain, pass, prescribe, proclaim, pronounce, ratify, rule, sanction, validate **2.** act, create, impersonate, mime, mimic, mirror, personify, ploy, portray, represent

enactment *n.* **1.** acting, depiction, execution, impersonation, performance, personification, playing, portrayal, representation **2.** approval, by-law, creed, direction, governance, law, legislation, mandate, ratification, regulation, statute

enamel *n. & v.* coat, finish, glaze, gloss, inlay, japan, lacquer, overlay, polish, shine, varnish, veneer

enamour *v.* allure, attract, bewitch, captivate, charm, draw, enchant, endear, enrapture, enthrall, entice, entrance, fascinate, grab, infatuate, please, vamp

enamoured *adj.* adoring, amorous, attracted, besotted, bewildered, bewitched, bothered, captivated, charmed, desirous, devoted, enchanted, enraptured, enthralled, entranced, fascinated, fond, hooked, infatuated, in love, moonstruck, smitten, swept, taken *Nonformal:* crazy over, floored, gaga, gone, stuck on, wild about *Antonyms:* disenchanted, disgusted, repelled, repulsed, revolted

encampment *n.* bivouac, camp, campground, campsite, settlement, tent site

enchant *v.* **1.** allure, attract, beguile, bewitch, captivate, charm, enamour, enrapture, enthrall, entice, entrance, fascinate, hex, hypnotize, magnetize, mesmerize, send *(Nonformal)*, spellbind **2.** amuse, delight, please, thrill, titillate *Antonyms:* annoy, irritate, upset

enchanting *adj.* agreeable, alluring, appealing, attractive, beguiling, bewitching, captivating, charming, delightful, endearing, engaging, enrapturing, enthralling, entrancing, exciting, fascinating, glamorous, intriguing, irresistible, prepossessing, ravishing, seductive, winning, winsome *Antonyms:* repulsive, revolting, ugly, unattractive

enchantress *n.* bewitcher, diviner, magician, seer, siren, sorceress, witch *Renowned Enchantresses:* Baba Yaga, Circe, Lady of the Lake, Morgan le Fay, Lorelei, Medea, Nimue, Sycorax, Titania, Viviane

encircle *v.* cincture, circle, circuit, circumscribe, compass, cover, enclose, encompass, enfold, envelop, environ, gird in, girdle, halo, hem in, invest, ring, surround, wreath

enclave *n.* district, enclosed territory, enclosure, ghetto, neighbourhood, precinct, quarter, quadrangle, territory, yard

enclose *v.* **1.** blockade, block off, bound, box up, cage, circle, circumscribe, close in, confine, coop, corral, curtain, cover, encase, encircle, enshroud, environ, fence *or* fence off, hedge *or* hem in, immure, impound, imprison, intern, jail, limit, lock in *or* up, pen, rail off, restrict, set apart, shut *or* pen in, surround, veil, wall in, wrap *Antonyms:* free, liberate, release, unpen **2.** contain, encompass, hold, include, incorporate **3.** add, adjoin, affix, append, attach, insert

enclosure *n.* **1.** arena, asylum, aviary, cage, cell, close, coop, corral, court, courtyard, enclave, garden, ghetto, hutch, jail, park, patch, pen, plot, pound, precinct, prison, quadrangle, stadium, stockade, sty, vault, yard, zone **2.** barrier, blockade, boundary, fence, hedge, limit, obstacle, partition, wall

encompass *v.* **1.** comprehend, comprise, contain, cover, embody, embrace, have, hold, house, include, incorporate, involve, subsume **2.** circle, circumscribe, compass, encircle, enclose, envelop, environ, gird, girdle, hem in, ring, surround

encore *interj.* again, *bene (Italian)*, *bis (French)*, bravo, fantastic, hurrah, once more, over, splendid, three cheers, well-done *Antonyms:* boo, hiss, yikes – *n.* reappearance, repeat, repeat performance, repetition, replay, reprise, return

encounter *n.* **1.** brush, contact, convergence, glance, meeting, passing **2.** clash, collision, combat, conflict, contention, contest, dispute, engagement, run-in, skirmish – *v.* **1.** alight upon, come across *or* upon, confront, detect, espy, experience, face, find, happen on, meet, run across *or* into, suffer, sustain, turn up **2.** affront, battle, clash with, collide, combat, conflict, confront, contend, cross swords *(Nonformal)*, do battle, engage, face, fight, grapple, meet, strive, struggle

encourage *v.* **1.** aid, animate, assist, bolster, boost, brace, buoy, cheer, comfort, countenance, egg on, embolden, energize, enliven, excite, exhilarate, fortify, foster, hearten, help, improve, incite, inspire, instigate, praise, prevail, rally, reassure, refresh, relieve, revitalize, solace, spur, stimulate, stir, strengthen, succour, support, sustain *Antonyms:* discourage, dishearten, scare **2.** abet, advance, advocate, approve, back, develop, endorse, favour, forward, further, promote, reinforce, second, subsidize, uphold *Antonyms:* deter, prevent, thwart, undermine

encouragement *n.* advance, advocacy, aid, assistance, backing, boost, cheer, comfort, confidence, consolation, faith, favour, help, helpfulness, hope, incitement, inspiration, reassurance, relief, solace, stimulus, succour, support, trust, urging *Antonyms:* discouragement, dismay, hindrance, interference

encroach *v.* advance, entrench, impinge, infringe, interfere, interpose, intervene, intrude, invade, make inroads, meddle, overstep, trench, trespass, usurp, violate *Nonformal:* barge *or* butt in, elbow *or* worm in

encumber *v.* **1.** burden, drown *(Nonformal)*, load down, oppress, overtask, overtax, saddle, tax, weigh down, weight *Antonyms:* relieve, unburden **2.** block, bridle, choke, clog, constrain, cramp, cripple, crowd, fetter, hamper, hamstring, handicap, hinder, impede, obstruct, restrain, retard, strain, trammel, trouble, vex

encyclopedic *adj.* all-embracing, all-encompassing, all-inclusive, broad, capacious, complete, comprehensive, eclectic, exhaustive, extensive, thorough, universal, vast, wide-ranging, widespread *Antonyms:* limited, myopic, narrow, specific

end *n.* **1.** adjournment, attainment, cessation, close, closing, closure, conclusion, curtain, discontinuance, ending, execution, expiration, expiry, finish, retirement, sign-off, stop, termination *Antonyms:* beginning, birth, commencement, inception, start **2.** accomplishment, achievement, consequence, consummation, culmination, dénouement, determination, finale, fulfillment, outcome, perfection, realization, resolution, result, solution, upshot, windup, wrap-up **3.** borderline, bound, boundary, confine, cusp, edge, extent, extreme, extremity, foot, head, heel, limit, limitation, nib, point, pole, stub, stump, terminal, terminus **4.** aim, aspiration, concept, design, drift, goal, intent, intention, issue, mark, object, objective, point, purpose, reason, target **5.** annihilation, apocalypse, Armageddon, calamity, catastrophe, destruction, disaster, doom, upheaval **6.** bit, butt, fragment, leftover, part, particle, piece, portion, remainder, remnant, residue, scrap, share, side, stub – *v.* **1.** abolish, abort, break off, call off, cease, close, close out, dispose of, drop, finish, halt, kill, shut down, stop, switch off, terminate *Antonyms:* begin, commence, initiate, launch start **2.** complete, conclude, consummate, crown, culminate, determine, resolve, settle, sew up **3.** die, discontinue, expire, lapse, leave, pass away, quit, relinquish

endanger *v.* compromise, expose, hazard, imperil, jeopardize, menace, risk, threaten *Antonyms:* defend, guard, preserve

endearing *adj.* adorable, charming, dear, delightful, enchanting, engaging, lovable, sweet, treasured, valued, wonderful

endearment *n.* **1.** affection, affinity, attachment, chemistry *(Nonformal)*, closeness, fondness, kinship, tie, togetherness, warmth **2.** caress, cuddle, fondle, hug, kiss, nuzzle, peck, pet, snuggle *Nonformal:* smooch, sweet nothings *or* talk

endeavour *n.* action, attempt, effort, exercise, exertion, labour, task, toil, trouble, try, work – *v.* attempt, essay, exert oneself, struggle, strive, tackle, take a crack at *(Nonformal)*, travail, try, undertake

ending *n.* cessation, close, closing, closure, completion, conclusion, consummation, culmination, dénouement, desistance, dissolution, end, epilogue, expiration, finale, finish, omega, outcome, resolution, solution, summation, swan song *(Nonformal)*, termination, terminus, wind-up *Antonyms:* beginning, birth, creation, opening

endless *adj.* **1.** boundless, ceaseless, constant, continual, countless, incalculable, infinite, limitless, numberless, unlimited, untold *Antonyms:* fathomable, specific **2.** deathless, enduring, eternal, everlasting, immortal, lasting, long-suffering, permanent, perpetual, timeless, unceasing, undying *Antonyms:* ephemeral, fleeting, short-lived, temporary, transient

endocrine *adj.* gland, glandular *Kinds of endocrine disease:* diabetes, endocrinism, goitre, hyperglycemia, hyperthyroidism, hypoglycemia, hypothyroidism

endorse *v.* **1.** authenticate, autograph, cosign, countersign, notarize, okay *(Nonformal)*, ratify, rubber-stamp, sign, subscribe, superscribe, undersign, underwrite *Antonyms:* cancel, veto **2.** adopt, advocate, back, buttress, champion, encourage, support, uphold *Antonyms:* challenge, refute, repudiate

endow *v.* accord, award, back, bequeath, bestow, confer, contribute, donate, empower, enable, enhance, enrich, favour, finance, fund, furnish, grant, invest, provide, sponsor, subscribe, subsidize, supply, support

endowment *n.* **1.** bequest, bestowal, bounty, dispensation, donation, fund, funding, gift, grant, gratuity, honorarium, income, inheritance, largesse, legacy, pension, property, provision, revenue, stake, stipend, subsidy, trust **2.** ability, aptitude, attribute, capability, capacity, faculty, flair, genius, power, qualification, quality, skill, talent

endurance *n.* **1.** continuation, continuity, durability, duration, immutability, lastingness, longevity, permanence, stability, timelessness *Antonyms:* ephemerality, fixed shelf-life, limitation **2.** fortitude, grit, mettle, patience, perseverance, persistence, resistance, resolution, stamina, sufferance, suffering, tenaciousness, tenacity, tolerance, toleration *Nonformal:* guts, legs, wind

endure *v.* **1.** acquiesce, bear, brave, brook, experience, face, go through, slave, stand, stomach, suffer, swallow, take, tolerate, undergo, weather, withstand **2.** abide, continue, hang on, last, persevere, persist, remain, stay, survive *Antonyms:* depart, disappear, leave *Commonly misused:* **inure**

enemy *n.* adversary, antagonist, archenemy, assailant, attacker, bad guy *(Nonformal)*, competitor, detractor, disputant, foe, nemesis, opponent, opposition, rival, villain *Antonyms:* ally, colleague, friend

energetic *adj.* aggressive, animated, brisk, charged, dynamic, enterprising, enthusiastic, forceful, forcible, high-powered, indefatigable, industrious, keen, kinetic, lively, mettlesome, spirited, strenuous, strong, tireless, vigorous, vivacious, zealous *Nonformal:* bright-eyed, electric, gung-ho, pumped, switched-on *Antonyms:* inactive, lazy, lifeless, torpid, weak

energize *v.* activate, animate, electrify, enliven, excite, fortify, inspire, invigorate, liven up, motivate, pep *or* pump up *(Nonformal)*, prime, quicken, reinforce, stimulate, strengthen, sustain, trigger, turn on, vitalize *Antonyms:* drain, fatigue, sap *(Nonformal)*, weaken

energy *n.* **1.** animation, application, ardour, dash, drive, dynamism, effectiveness, efficiency, élan, endurance, enterprise, exertion, fire, forcefulness, fortitude, initiative, intensity, life, liveliness, might, pluck, potency, puissance, sparkle, spirit, spontaneity, stamina, strength, toughness, vehemence, verve, vim, vitality, vivacity, zeal, zest *Nonformal:* bang, get-up-and-go, ginger, go, juice, kick, moxie, muscle, pep, pizazz, punch, sizzle, steam, zing, zip **2.** action, activity, dynamics, electricity, force, friction, heat, hydro, motion, movement, power, propulsion, thrust, work

enervated *adj.* debilitated, deteriorated, devitalized, enfeebled, exhausted, fatigued, feeble, incapacitated, lackadaisical, languid, languishing, languorous, limp, listless, prostrate, rundown, sapped, spent, spiritless, tired, undermined, unnerved, weak, weakened, worn out *Nonformal:* burnt, done in, toast, washed out

enfant terrible *n.* brute, delinquent, deviant, devilkin, elf, imp, mischief-maker, rascal, terror, troublemaker *Nonformal:* hoodlum, hooligan, punk, ruffian, scalawag

enfeeble *v.* attenuate, blunt, cripple, debilitate, deplete, devitalize, diminish, disable, exhaust, fatigue, incapacitate, sap, undermine, unhinge, unnerve, weaken, wear out *Antonyms:* energize, strengthen

enfold *v.* clasp, clinch, clutch, cover, drape, embrace, encase, encircle, enclose, encompass, engulf, enshroud, envelop, enwrap, fold, girdle, hold, hug, press, shroud, surround, swathe, wrap

enforce *v.* administer, apply, bully, coerce, commandeer, compel, constrain, demand, dictate, discharge, dragoon, effect, emphasize, exact, execute, exert, fulfill, impel, implement, impose, insist on, invoke, make, necessitate, oblige, press, reinforce, strong-arm *(Nonformal)*

enforcement *n.* administration, application, carrying out, coercion, compulsion, constraint, duress, enforcing, execution, insistence, necessitation, obligation, prescription, pressure, reinforcement, requirement

enfranchise *v.* **1.** authorize, empower, license, naturalize, qualify *Antonyms:* alienate, disempower, disenfranchise, marginalize **2.** affranchise, deliver, discharge, disengage, emancipate, free, liberate, manumit, release, unbind, unfetter, unshackle *Antonyms:* enslave, fetter, intern

engage *v.* **1.** absorb, arrest, attract, bewitch, captivate, charm, enchant, engross, enthrall, fascinate, interest, preoccupy **2.** affiance, agree, betroth, bind, commit, obligate, pledge, troth, promise, undertake, vow **3.** attach, connect, dovetail, fasten, hook, interact, interconnect, interlace, interlock, join, joint, knot, latch, lock, mesh, tie up **4.** contract, employ, hire, occupy, reserve, secure, sign **5.** enter into, involve, launch into, partake, participate, tackle, take on, take part in

engaged *adj.* **1.** absorbed, at work, busy, connected, employed, engrossed, immersed, intent, interested, involved, occupied, operating, performing, practicing, preoccupied, signed, tied up, unavailable, working, wrapped up *Antonyms:* available, free, uncommitted **2.** affianced, betrothed, committed, going steady, intended, pledged, plighted, promised, spoken for *Nonformal:* hitched, pinned *Antonyms:* single unattached **3.** battling, conflicting, disputing, fighting, quarreling, scuffling, squabbling, warring

engagement *n.* **1.** assurance, betrothal, bond, commitment, contract, espousal, oath, pact, pledge, promise, troth, vow **2.** action, battle, combat, conflict, confrontation, contest, encounter, fight, fray, skirmish **3.** appointment, arrangement, assignation, booking, date, get-together, gig, invitation, meet, meeting, party, reservation, tryst, visit

engaging *adj.* agreeable, alluring, appealing, attractive, bewitching, captivating, charming, delightful, drawing, enchanting, endearing, enticing, entrancing, fascinating, fetching, interesting, intriguing, inviting, likeable, lovable, magnetic, pleasing, winning, winsome *Antonyms:* disagreeable, offensive, unattractive, unpleasant

engender *v.* create, develop, excite, father, foment, generate, incite, induce, instigate, make, mother, muster, originate, precipitate, procreate, produce, propagate, sire, spawn

engine *n.* **1.** cylinder, dynamo, fan, generator, motor, piston, powerhouse, power plant, power source, power train, transformer *Kinds of engine:* Coaker *(Newfoundland)*, internal combustion, diesel, four-stroke, jet, make-and-break, marine, pneumatic, rotary, rubber band, steam, two-strike, turbine **2.** agent, apparatus, appliance, contrivance, device, implement, instrument, means, mechanism, tool

engineer *n.* architect, builder, contriver, designer, deviser, inventor, manager, originator, planner, schemer, surveyor, techie *(Nonformal) Kinds of engineer:* aerospace, agricultural, chemical, civil, communications, electrical, electronics, geological, highway, hydraulic, marine, mechanical, metallurgical, mining, petroleum, sanitary – *v.* arrange, cause, concoct, contrive, control, create, devise, direct, effect, machinate, manage, manoeuvre, manipulate, mastermind, negotiate, operate, originate, plan, plant, plot, rig, scheme, superintend, work *Nonformal*: doctor, finagle, scam

engrave *v.* carve, chisel, crosshatch, cut, embed, etch, impress, imprint, inscribe, intaglio, lithograph, mezzotint, ornament, print, scratch, stipple

engraving *n.* carving, cut, impression, relief *Kinds of engraving:* aquatint, block, chalcography, copperplate engraving, drypoint, etching, intaglio, line engraving, linocut, mezzotint, photoengraving, rotogravure, steel engraving, woodcut

engross *v.* absorb, arrest, attract, bewitch, busy, captivate, consume, engage, engulf, enthrall, fascinate, fill, grip, hold, immerse, involve, monopolize, occupy, preoccupy, take up *Antonyms:* bore, distract

engrossed *adj.* absorbed, assiduous, attentive, busy, captivated, caught up, consumed, deep, engaged, enraptured, enthralled, fascinated, gripped, hooked, hung up, immersed, intent, into, intrigued, lost, occupied, preoccupied, rapt, riveted, submerged, tied *or* wrapped up, transported, turned on

engrossing *adj.* absorbing, all-consuming, captivating, compelling, consuming, enthralling, exciting, fascinating, gripping, interesting, intriguing, obsessing, preoccupying, riveting, stimulating *Antonyms:* offensive, repulsive

engulf *v.* bury, consume, deluge, drown, encompass, envelop, flood, immerse, inundate, overflow, overrun, overwhelm, plunge, submerge, swallow up, swamp

enhance *v.* adorn, aggrandize, amplify, augment, beautify, boost, compliment, elevate, embellish, embroider, enlarge, exaggerate, exalt, heighten, improve, increase, intensify, lift, magnify, modify, modulate, pad, raise, reinforce, strengthen, swell, upgrade *Antonyms:* debase, decrease, diminish, minimize, reduce

enhancement *n.* aggrandizement, amplification, augmentation, beatification, betterment, edification, elaboration, elevation, embellishment, enrichment, heightening, improvement, intensification, magnification, modification, strengthening *Antonyms:* attenuation, depreciation, reduction

enigma *n.* ambiguity, arcanum, brain teaser, closed *or* sealed book, conundrum, labyrinth, maze, mystery, obscurity, perplexity, problem, puzzle, quandary, question, riddle, secret

enigmatic *adj.* ambiguous, Borgesian, cryptic, Delphian, enigmatical, incomprehensible, indecipherable, inexplicable, inscrutable, labyrinthine, mysterious, mystifying, obscure, perplexing, puzzling, secret, sphinxlike, unfathomable, unintelligible *Antonyms:* clear, comprehensible, simple, straightforward, uncomplicated

enjoin *v.* **1.** adjure, admonish, advise, appoint, bid, call upon, caution, charge, command, counsel, decree, demand, dictate, direct, forewarn, impose, instruct, ordain, order, prescribe, require, rule, tell, urge, warn **2.** ban, bar, deny, disallow, forbid, inhibit, outlaw, prohibit, restrain *Antonyms:* allow, authorize, condone

enjoy *v.* **1.** appreciate, delight *or* revel in, fancy, have fun, like, love, relish, savour *Nonformal:* cotton to, eat up, flip for *or* over *Antonyms:* abhor, despise, detest, dislike, hate **2.** benefit from, have, hold, maintain, make use of, own, profit from, retain, use, utilize

enjoyable *adj.* agreeable, amusing, delectable, delicious, delightful, entertaining, fun, genial, gratifying, groovy *(Nonformal)*, likeable, pleasant, pleasing, pleasurable, preferable, satisfying, welcome *Antonyms:* despicable, hateful, loathsome, obnoxious, unsavoury

enjoyment *n.* advantage, amusement, benefit, contentment, delectation, delight, diversion, entertainment, fun, gratification, happiness, indulgence, joy, luxury, pleasure, relish, satisfaction, thrill

enlarge *v.* add to, aggrandize, amplify, augment, blow up, boost, broaden, build, bulk, develop, diffuse, dilate, distend, elaborate, elongate, embroider, exaggerate, expand, extend, grow, heighten, increase, inflate, lengthen, magnify, multiply, pad, raise, spread, stretch, swell, widen *Nonformal:* jack up, snowball *Antonyms:* abbreviate, compress, decrease, shorten, truncate

enlargement *n.* addition, amplification, augmentation, blow-up, elongation, expansion, extension, growth, increase, inflation, magnification, spread *Antonyms:* lessening, reduction, shrinkage

enlightened *adj.* aware, broad-minded, civilized, cultivated, educated, illuminated, informed, instructed, knowledgeable, learned, literate, open-minded, reasonable, refined, schooled, sharp, smart, sophisticated, taught *Nonformal*: savvy, plugged in, tuned in *Antonyms:* ignorant, narrow-minded, unaware, uneducated

enlightenment *n.* **1.** awareness, broad-mindedness, civilization, comprehension, cultivation, erudition, insight, knowledge, literacy, raised consciousness, sophistication, understanding, wisdom *Antonyms:* blindness, darkness, ignorance **2.** edification, education, instruction, learning, schooling, teaching, training, tutelage, uplifting

enlist *v.* **1.** admit, appoint, assign, conscribe, conscript, draft, employ, engage, gather, hire, impress, incorporate, induct, initiate, inscribe, levy, mobilize, muster, obtain, place, procure, recruit, reserve, secure *Nonformal:* call up, hitch, take on *Antonyms:* discharge, fire, lay off, pass over, reject **2.** enrol, join, join up, register, serve, sign on *or* up, volunteer

enliven *v.* animate, brighten, buoy, cheer, entertain, excite, exhilarate, galvanize, gladden, hearten, inspire, invigorate, quicken, refresh, rejuvenate, renew, restore, rouse, spark, stimulate, vitalize *Antonyms:* chill, dampen, deaden, repress, subdue

enmesh *v.* capture, catch, embroil, ensnare, entangle, entrap, hook, implicate, incriminate, involve, net, snare, snarl, tangle, trammel, trap *Antonyms:* absolve, free, release

enmity *n.* acrimony, animosity, antagonism, antipathy, aversion, bad blood, bitterness, bitter resentment, disgust, dislike, hate, hatred, hostility, ill will, loathing, malevolence, malice, malignancy, rancour, spite, spleen, unfriendliness, venom *Antonyms:* affection, amity, friendship, geniality, love

ennui *n.* boredom, depression, discontent, dolefulness, gloom, langour, listlessness, melancholy, sadness, sluggishness, tedium, the blues *(Nonformal)*, weariness, *Weltschmerz (German)*

enormity *n.* **1.** abomination, atrociousness, atrocity, depravity, disgrace, evil, flagrancy, grossness, heinousness, horribleness, horror, monstrosity, monstrousness, nefariousness, outrageousness, rankness, turpitude, viciousness, vileness, villainy, wickedness **2.** bulk, capacity, greatness, hugeness, immensity, largness, massiveness, size, vastness

enormous *adj.* colossal, excessive, extensive, gargantuan, gigantic, gross, huge, immense, king-size, large, mammoth, massive, monstrous, mountainous, prodigious, stupendous, titanic, tremendous, vast *Nonformal:* humongous, jumbo *Antonyms:* diminutive, dwarf, infinitesimal, insignificant, Lilliputian

enough *adj.* acceptable, adequate, ample, bounteous, bountiful, comfortable, competent, complete, decent, full, plentiful, plenty, replete, satisfactory, sufficient, sufficing, suitable – *adv.* **1.** abundantly, acceptably, adequately, admissibly, amply, commensurately, decently, proportionately, quite, reasonably, satisfactorily, sufficiently, very **2.** averagely, barely, fairly, moderately, passably, tolerably – *n.* abundance, adequacy, ampleness, ample supply, plenty

enrage *v.* agitate, anger, annoy, fire up, ignite, incense, inflame, infuriate, irk, irritate, madden, nettle, outrage, piss *or* tick off *(Nonformal)*, prod, provoke, rile, roil, upset, vex, work up *Antonyms:* mollify, pacify, please, soothe

enrapture *v.* allure, attract, beguile, bewitch, captivate, charm, delight, draw, elate, enamour, enchant, enthrall, entrance, fascinate, please, send, spellbind, transport *Nonformal:* knock out, slay, wow

enrich *v.* **1.** advance, ameliorate, better, build, civilize, cultivate, develop, elevate, enhance, enlighten, hike, improve, raise, refine, upgrade, uplift *Antonyms:* defile, degrade, worsen **2.** adorn, aggrandize, beautify, decorate, embellish, grace, jazz up *(Nonformal)*, ornament **3.** augment, endow, increase one's wealth, pad, make rich, richen, supplement

enrichment *n.* **1.** adornment, beautification, decoration, elaboration, embellishment, fix up, refinement **2.** advancement, amelioration, betterment, consciousness raising, development, edification, education, elevation, enhancement, enlightenment, improvement, upgrading, uplifting

enrol *v.* **1.** engage, enlist, enter, join, join up, matriculate, muster, recruit, serve, sign on *or* up, subscribe, take on *Antonyms:* delist, drop *or* drop out, reject **2.** book, catalogue, chronicle, document, enter, file, inscribe, insert, list, mark, note, record, register, schedule, slate

enrolment *n.* **1.** acceptance, accession, admission, conscription, enlistment, entrance, entry, induction, matriculation, recruitment, registration **2.** number, sign up rate, size, student body, students, subscription, total, turn out

en route *adv.* in motion, in progress, in transit, on the road *or* way, on track, underway, *unterwegs (German)*

ensconce *v.* **1.** fix, install, lodge, nestle, seat, secure, settle *Antonyms:* dislodge, disturb, uninstall **2.** bury, cache, conceal, cover, hide, protect, secrete, shelter, shield, stash *Antonyms:* exhume, reveal, uncover, unearth

ensemble *n.* **1.** aggregate, assemblage, cast, collection, composite, entirety, gathering, group, organization, set, sum, total, totality, whole *Kinds of musical ensemble:* band, chamber orchestra, choir, chorus, combo *(Nonformal)*, duet, duo, nonet, octet, orchestra, orchestral, quartet, quintet, section, septet, sextet, trio **2.** apparel, attire, clothing, costume, disguise, garb, guise, outfit

enshrine *v.* bless, cherish, consecrate, dedicate, exalt, hallow, hold sacred, preserve, revere, sanctify, treasure *Antonyms:* curse, desecrate

enshroud *v.* bury, blanket, cloak, conceal, cover, disguise, dress, ensconce, envelop, hide, mask, obscure, shroud, surround, veil, wrap *Antonyms:* expose, reveal, uncover

ensign *n.* badge, banner, colours, device, emblem, flag, insignia, mark, pennant, pennon, sign, standard, streamer, symbol

enslave *v.* bind, capture, chain, control, deprive, dominate, fetter, hold, imprison, indenture, oppress, restrain, restrict, secure, shackle, subject, suppress, tether, tie, yoke *Antonyms:* emancipate, free, liberate

ensue *v.* arise, attend, befall, derive, develop, emanate, eventuate, follow, happen, issue, occur, proceed, result, stem from, succeed, transpire

ensuing *adj.* after, coming, consequential, following, later, next, posterior, preceding, resultant, subsequent, subsequential *Antonyms:* antecedent, before, earlier, preceding, prior

ensure *v.* arrange, assure, certify, cinch *(Nonformal)*, clinch, confirm, establish, guarantee, guard, protect, provide, safeguard, secure, warrant *Commonly misused:* **insure**

entail *v.* call for, command, demand, encompass, impose, involve, necessitate, need, occasion, require, take

entangle *v.* **1.** catch, enmesh, ensnare, entrap, fetter, hamper, hinder, impede, knot, snag, snare, snarl, tangle, twist **2.** embarrass, embroil, hook, implicate, involve, trap **3.** bewilder, complicate, confuse, dishevel, muddle, perplex, puzzle, ravel, unsettle *Antonyms:* clarify, resolve, simplify

entanglement *n.* **1.** complexity, complication, confusion, difficulty, embarrassment, imbroglio, intricacy, jumble, knot, mesh, mess, mix-up, muddle, problem, predicament, snare, tangle, tie-up, trap **2.** affair, association, cobweb, entrapment, implication, intrigue, involvement, network, web

enter *v.* **1.** access, appear, arrive, burst *or* come *or* drop in, gain entrance, go *or* stroll *or* walk in, infiltrate, intrude, invade, trespass *Antonyms:* depart, egress, exit, go, leave **2.** begin, commence, commit oneself, embark, enlist, enrol, join, participate in, set about, sign on *or* up, start upon, subscribe *Antonyms:* resign, retire, withdraw **3.** document, inscribe, introduce, list, log, note, post, record, register, set down, take down, write down **4.** drive *or* wedge in, inject, insert, pierce, penetrate, probe

enterprise *n.* **1.** action, activity, adventure, affair, attempt, campaign, cause, concern, crusade, deal, deed, effort, endeavour, engagement, exploit, performance, plan, program, project, pursuit, scheme, striving, task, undertaking, venture **2.** alacrity, ambition, audacity, boldness, courage, daring, dash, drive, eagerness, energy, enthusiasm, force, foresight, hustle, initiative, inventiveness, pluck, readiness, resourcefulness, self-reliance, spirit, venturesomeness, vigour, zeal *Nonformal*: get-up-and-go, grit, gumption *Antonyms:* indolence, inertia, passivity **3.** business, company, corporation, establishment, firm, house, industry, manufactory, occupation, operation, outfit, plant, process, shop, trade, work

enterprising *adj.* active, adventurous, aggressive, alert, ambitious, aspiring, audacious, bold, brisk, busy, daring, dashing, diligent, driving, eager, energetic, enthusiastic, hardworking, hustling, industrious, intrepid, keen, lively, plucky, progressive, ready, resourceful, self-starting, spirited, stirring, up-and-coming, venturesome, vigorous, zealous *Nonformal:* peppy, zippy *Antonyms:* cautious, conservative, indolent, lazy, timid

entertain *v.* **1.** amuse, beguile, captivate, charm, cheer, delight, distract, divert, elate, enthrall, gladden, gratify, humour, indulge, inspire, interest, please, recreate, regale, satisfy, stimulate **2.** comfort, dine, feed, host, lodge, quarter, receive, treat, welcome, wine **3.** cogitate on, consider, contemplate, deliberate, hold, mull *or* muse over, ponder, think about *or* over, weigh **4.** cary, cherish, foster, harbour, keep, maintain, preserve

entertaining *adj.* absorbing, affecting, amusing, captivating, charming, clever, compelling, delightful, diverting, droll, enchanting, engaging, engrossing, enjoyable, enthralling, enticing, entrancing, exciting, fascinating, fun, funny, humorous, impressive, inspiring, lively, moving, pleasant, poignant, provocative, rousing, sidesplitting *(Nonformal)*, stimulating, stirring, striking, thrilling, witty *Antonyms:* boring, dull, humdrum, tedious, unamusing

entertainment *n.* **1.** amusement, cheer, delight, distraction, diversion, divertissement, enjoyment, frolic, fun, gaiety, merriment, merrymaking, pleasure, relaxation, relief, revelry, satisfaction, surprise, treat *Nonformal:* high time, laughs **2.** ball, celebration, concert, engagement, feast, fête, film, game, leisure activity, movie, party, pastime, picnic, play, recreation, show, social, sport, spree, television, theatre *Nonformal:* bash, blow-out, gig, shindig

enthrall *v.* **1.** absorb, beguile, bewitch, captivate, charm, enchant, engage, enrapture, entrance, fascinate, grab, grip, hook, hypnotize, intrigue, mesmerize, preoccupy, rivet, spellbind *Antonyms:* disgust, repel, repulse **2.** bind, chain, control, dominate, enslave, fetter, master, oppress, subdue, subject, subjugate, yoke

enthusiasm *n.* **1.** appetite, ardour, avidity, conviction, devotion, drive, eagerness, fanaticism, fervour, intensity, interest, keenness, mania, passion, punch, relish, vehemence, vigour, zest **2.** bounce, brio, élan, energy, feeling, fire, gusto, snap, sparkle, spirit, verve, vim, vitality, vivacity, zeal *Nonformal:* get-up-and-go, pep, zip **3.** delight, ecstasy, elation, excitement, exhilaration, happiness, joy, rapture, satisfaction, transport

enthusiast *n.* addict, admirer, aficionado, believer, buff, devotee, fanatic, follower, habitué, lover, optimist, participant, partisan, rooter, supporter, votary, worshipper, zealot *Nonformal:* fan, keener, maniac

enthusiastic *adj.* animated, ardent, athirst, avid, buoyant, devoted, eager, earnest, ebullient, effervescent, elated, excited, exhilarated, exuberant, fanatical, fascinated, fervent, fervid, forceful, high-spirited, intent, interested, irrepressible, keen, lively, obsessed, passionate, rhapsodic, spirited, tantalized, thrilled, vehement, vigorous, vivacious, voracious, wholehearted, willing, zealous, zestful *Nonformal:* chipper, gung ho, hot to trot *Antonyms:* apathetic, blasé, bored, indifferent, nonchalant

entice *v.* allure, attract, bait, beguile, cajole, coax, decoy, draw, enchant, entrap, flatter, inveigle, lead on, lure, persuade, prevail on, seduce, tempt, tole, turn on, wheedle

enticement *n.* allurement, attraction, bait, blandishment, cajolery, carrot *(Nonformal)*, coaxing, come-on, decoy, inducement, inveiglement, lure, promise, seduction, snare, sweetener, temptation, trap *Antonyms:* detraction, discouragement, hindrance

entire *adj.* **1.** absolute, all, complete, consolidated, continuous, full, gross, integral, integrated, outright, plenary, thorough, total, whole *Antonyms:* discontinuous, disjointed, partial **2.** intact, perfect, sound, unbroken, undamaged, undiminished, undivided, unified, unimpaired, uninjured, unmarked, unmarred, untouched *Antonyms:* broken, fractured, shattered **3.** nonrestrictive, unconfined, unlimited, unmitigated, unqualified, unreserved, unrestricted

entirety *n.* absoluteness, aggregate, all, collectiveness, completeness, comprehensiveness, ensemble, everything, fullness, intactness, integrality, integrity, oneness, perfection, plenitude, sum, the works *(Nonformal)*, total, totality, unity, universality, whole, wholeness *Antonyms:* incompleteness, part, piece, section

entitle *v.* **1.** allow, authorize, empower, enable, enfranchise, give right, license, permit, qualify, sanction, warrant **2.** baptize, call, characterize, christen, denominate, designate, dub, knight, label, name, term, title

entity *n.* **1.** article, body, creature, individual, material, matter, object, organism, thing **2.** actuality, being, existence, occurrence, presence, reality **3.** essence, nature, quintessence, sense, spirit, substance

entourage *n.* **1.** associates, attendants, companions, company, cortège, court, courtiers, escort, followers, following, hangers-on *(Nonformal)*, retainers, retinue, staff, suite, sycophants, toadies, train **2.** element, environment, milieu, *mise en scène (French)*, place, setting, surroundings

entrance *n.* **1.** admission, admittance, entreé, importation, incoming, ingoing, invasion, outset, penetration, progress *Antonyms:* departure, egress, exit, exodus **2.** arrival, beginning, commencement, debut, inception, introduction, start **3.** enlistment, enrolment, matriculation, registration, sign-up **4.** access, avenue, channel, inlet, opening, passage, path, port, roadway *Kinds of entrance:* archway, belvedere, breezeway, corridor, door, doorway, entryway, foyer, gate, gateway, hall, hallway, lobby, passageway, porch, portal, portico, propylaeum, staircase, threshold, turnstile, vestibule, wicket – *v.* bedazzle, beguile, bewitch, charm, enchant, fascinate, seduce, tantalize

entrant *n.* **1.** aspirant, candidate, competitor, contestant, entry, participant, player, rival **2.** apprentice, beginner, convert, neophyte, newcomer, novice, petitioner, probationer

entrap *v.* allure, beguile, catch, deceive, ensnare, entice, hook, inveigle, invite, seduce, snag, snare, tantalize, tempt, trick

entreat *v.* adjure, ask, beg, beseech, conjure, implore, importune, invoke, pester, petition, plead, pray, press, request, supplicate, urge, wheedle

entreaty *n.* appeal, application, imprecation, petition, plea, prayer, request, solicitation, suit, supplication

entrée *n.* **1.** access, admission, admittance, entrance, ingress, introduction, penetration **2.** appetizer *(Quebec)*, course *or* main course, dinner, food, lunch, meal, plate, serving

entrench *v.* **1.** anchor, embed, ensconce, establish, fix, ground, implant, infix, ingrain, install, lodge, plant, root, seat, set, settle **2.** bolster, buttress, dig in, fortify, protect, reinforce, strengthen

entrepreneur *n.* backer, businessman, businessperson, businesswoman, capitalist, gambler, financier, impresario, industrialist, magnate, manager, organizer, producer, promoter, risk taker, robber baron, tycoon *(Nonformal)*

entropy *n.* corruption, decay, decline, decomposition, degeneration, degradation, lessening, loss, rot, weakening

entrust *v.* allocate, allot, assign, authorize, commend, consign, delegate, hand over, invest, relegate, rely on

entry *n.* **1.** access, admission, admittance, approach, avenue, door, doorway, entrance, entrée, gate, hall, inlet, introduction, opening, passage, passageway, portal threshold *Antonyms:* egress, exit, leave, withdrawal *See also:* **entrance** **2.** account, item, listing, log, memo, memorandum, minute, note, record, registration, report **3.** candidate, competitor, contestant, entrant, participant, player

entwine *v.* braid, coil, corkscrew, curl, embrace, encircle, enmesh, entangle, interlace, interplait, intertwine, knit, lace, plait, spiral, surround, twine, twist, weave, wind, wreath

enumerate *v.* add up, calculate, compute, count, detail, figure, identify, inventory, itemize, keep tabs, list, number, reckon, sum, tally, total

enunciate *v.* **1.** articulate, deliver, express, intone, modulate, phonate, say, show, speak, utter, vocalize, voice *Antonyms:* mutter, mumble, stammer, stutter **2.** advance, affirm, announce, broadcast, declare, lay down, outline, postulate, proclaim, promulgate, pronounce, propound, state, submit

envelop *v.* **1.** cover, drape, embrace, encase, enfold, engulf, enshroud, enwrap, invest, overlay, overspread, sheathe, shroud, swaddle, swathe, wrap *Antonyms:* reveal, strip, uncover, unwrap **2.** cloak, conceal, hide, obscure, protect, screen, secrete, shield, veil **3.** blanket, cage, circumscribe, contain, coop, corral, encircle, enclose, encompass, fence, gird, girdle, guard, hem, immure, pen, protect, surround

envelope *n.* bag, bladder, box, case, casing, coat, coating, container, cover, covering, enclosure, hide, jacket, pocket, pouch, receptacle, sac, sheath, shell, skin, vesicle, wrapper

enviable *adj.* covetable, desirable, desired, excellent, favoured, fortunate, good, lucky, much admired, privileged, superior, welcome *Antonyms:* painful, thankless

envious *adj.* coveting, covetous, desiring, desirous, grasping, green-eyed *(Nonformal)*, jealous, longing, resentful, yearning

environment *n.* **1.** ecology, ecosphere, ecosystem, ecozone, natural world, nature, physical world **2.** ambiance, atmosphere, aura, background, domain, element, encompassment, environs, habitat, locale, medium, milieu, *mise en scène (French)*, neighbourhood, precincts, scene, surroundings, terrain, territory, turf, vicinity *Nonformal:* beat, stomping ground, turf **3.** circumstance, context, contrition, mood, state, situation

environmentalist *n.* biologist, conservationist, ecologist, naturalist, preservationist *Nonformal:* greenie, tree hugger

environs *n. pl.* boundary, confine, district, fringes, limits, locality, neighbourhood, purlieu, surroundings, territory, turf *(Nonformal)*, vicinity

envision *v.* anticipate, behold, conceive, conceptualize, contemplate, envisage, externalize, fancy, foresee, grasp, imagine, predict, realize, regard, see, survey, think up, view, visualize

envoy *n.* agent, ambassador, attaché, bearer, carrier, *chargé d'affaires (French)*, consul, courier, delegate, deputy, diplomat, emissary, intermediary, medium, messenger, minister, nuncio, plenipotentiary, representative, vicar

envy *n.* **1.** anger, disaffection, discontent, green-eyed monster *(Nonformal)*, grudging, invidiousness, jealousy, malice, prejudice, rancour, resentment, rivalry, spite, spleen *Antonyms:* contentedness, happiness, satisfaction **2.** ache, covetousness, craving, desire, longing, lust, thrust, want, yearning – *v.* **1.** begrudge, grudge, loath, resent **2.** covet, crave, desire, hanker, hunger, long for, lust after, pine, thirst, want, yearn

enzyme *n.* biological catalyst, organic catalyst *Kinds of enzymes:* amylase, bromelain, cellulose, chymotrypsin, lactase, lipase, pancreatin, papain, pepsin, proteolytic, rennin, trypsin

ephemeral *adj.* brief, evanescent, fast, fleeting, impermanent, momentary, passing, short-lived, temporary, transitory *Antonyms:* fast-frozen, stable, timeless

epic *adj.* **1.** dramatic, exalted, fantastic, grandiose, heroic, impressive, larger than life, majestic, mythic, noble, poetic, sublime **2.** colossal, enormous, great, immense, lengthy, monumental, titanic, vast – *n.* account, adventure, history, legend, myth, narrative, legend, saga, story, tale

epicure *n.* aesthete, *bon vivant (French)*, connoisseur, gastronome, glutton, gourmand, gourmet, hedonist, pleasure-seeker, sensualist, sybarite

epicurean *adj.* gluttonous, hedonistic, libertine, luxury-loving, pleasure-seeking, self-indulgent, sensual, sensuous, sybaritic *Antonyms:* ascetic, austere, humble, modest – *n.* connoisseur, epicure, gastronome, glutton, gourmand, gourmet, sybarite, voluptuary

epidemic *adj.* all-encompassing, far-reaching, general, pandemic, sweeping, universal, wide-ranging – *n.* disease, contagion, outbreak, pestilence, plague, scourge, upsurge, wave

epigram *n.* aphorism, apothegm, *bon mot (French)*, gloss, joke, notice, observation, pithy saying, point, quip, remark, witticism

epilogue *n.* afterword, conclusion, ending, finale, follow-up, peroration, postscript, summation, wrap-up *(Nonformal) Antonyms:* foreword, introduction, preamble, prelude, prologue

epiphany *n.* **1.** apprehension, awareness, clarification, cognizance, comprehension, enlightenment, insight, inspiration, perception, realization, recognition, revelation **2.** embodiment, manifestation, materialization

episode *n.* **1.** adventure, affair, circumstance, event, experience, happening, incident, occurrence **2.** chapter, installment, part, passage, scene, section

episodic *adj.* **1.** anecdotal, broken, choppy, intermittent, interrupted, irregular, occasional, segmented, sporadic **2.** aimless, circumlocutory, desultory, digressive, rambling, wandering

epistle *n. billet doux (French),* card, communication, Dear John *(Nonformal),* dispatch, e-mail, invite, letter, line, memo, message, missive, note, postcard, thank-you

epitaph *n.* commemoration, elegy, eulogy, *hic jacet (Latin),* inscription, legend, memorial, monument, remembrance, saying, sentiment *Commonly misued:* **epithet**

epithet *n.* appellation, description, designation, name, nickname, sobriquet, tag, title *Commonly misued:* **epitaph**

epitome *n.* **1.** archetype, classic, climax, culmination, embodiment, example, representation, symbol **2.** abbreviation, abridgment, abstract, brief, compendium, condensation, conspectus, contraction, digest, précis, recapitulation, résumé, summary, syllabus, synopsis

epitomize *v.* **1.** embody, exemplify, depict, reflect, represent, symbolize **2.** abridge, capsulize, compress, concentrate, condense, digest, encapsulate, summarize

equal *adj.* alike, at par, balanced, commensurate, comparable, corresponding, equivalent, homogeneous, homologous, identical, like, matching, parallel, proportionate, same, uniform *Antonyms:* different, disproportionate, dissimilar, diverse, inequitable – *n.* brother, coequal, companion, compeer, competitor, complement, copy, counterpart, double, duplicate, equivalent, fellow, like, likeness, match, mate, parallel, peer, rival, twin – *v.* agree, approach, compare, correspond, emulate, equalize, homogenize, homologize, level, match, meet, parallel, reach, rival, tie, touch

equality *n.* **1.** equity, equivalence, fairness fair play, impartiality, justice, parity, rightness *Antonyms:* bias, discrimination, prejudice **2.** balance, correspondence, equitableness, equilibrium, evenness, parallelism, sameness, similarity, uniformity

equalize *v.* balance, equal, even, homogenize, homologize, level, match, parallel, rival, smooth, square, standardize, unify

equally *adv.* at the same time, in the same fashion *or* manner *or* way, on equal terms, on the same footing, to an equal degree *or* extent

equanimity *n.* calm, composure, ease, equability, levelheadedness, placidity, poise, sang-froid, self-possession, serenity, steadiness, tranquility *Antonyms:* agitation, disquiet, panic, perturbation

equate *v.* agree, assimilate, associate, balance, compare, correspond to *or* with, equalize, even, homogenize, level, liken, match, offset, pair, parallel, relate, square tally

equestrian *adj.* equine, hoofed, horselike, ungulate – *n.* horseperson, rider *Kinds of horseback rider:* cavalier, chevalier, circus rider, cossack, cowboy, dressage rider, D.Q. *(Nonformal),* eventer, gaucho, horse guard, horse soldier, hunter-jumper, hussar, jockey, knight, Mountie, Olympic, rancher, rodeo, stunt rider, vaquero

equip *v.* accoutre, adorn, appoint, arm, array, attire, deck, decorate, dress, endow, furnish, gear, implement, man, outfit, prepare, provide, qualify, ready, rig, stake, stock, supply *Antonyms:* denude, divest, strip

equipment *n.* accessory, accompaniment, accoutrement, apparatus, appliance, appurtenance, article, attachment, belonging, contraption, device, effect, facilities, fitting, fixture, furnishing, gadget, gear, goods, impediment, implement, kit, line, machinery, miscellaneous, outfit, pack, paraphernalia, provision, rig, setup, stock, stuff, supplies, tackle, tools, trapping, utensil *See* *also:* **baseball, football, golf, hockey, skiing, soccer**

equitable *adj.* candid, decent, dispassionate, ethical, fair, honest, impartial, just, moral, objective, proper, proportionate, reasonable, rightful, square, unbiased, unprejudiced *Antonyms:* inequitable, unfair, unjust, unreasonable

equity *n.* **1.** equitableness, evenhandedness, fairness, fair play, honesty, impartiality, integrity, justness, reasonableness, righteousness, square deal, uprightness *Antonyms:* bias, discrimination, injustice, prejudice, unfairness **2.** capital, investment, money, outlay, property

equivalence *n.* agreement, alikeness, conformity, correlation, evenness, homogeneity, interchangeability, likeness, match, par, parallel, parity, sameness, similarity

equivalent *adj.* agnate, akin, alike, analogous, comparable, copy, corresponding, duplicate, equal, even, homogenous, interchangeable, like, same, similar, synonymous, tantamount *Antonyms:* different, dissimilar, incomparable, unequal – *n.* correspondent, counterpart, equal, like, parallel, peer, substitute, twin

equivocal *adj.* ambiguous, ambivalent, borderline, clouded, doubtful, dubious, evasive, fishy *(Nonformal)*, hazy, indefinite, indeterminate, indistinct, misleading, oblique, obscure, problematic, puzzling, questionable, suspect, suspicious, tenebrous, uncertain, unclear, undecided, unintelligible, vague *Antonyms:* absolute, certain, evident, manifest

equivocate *v.* avoid, cavil, dodge, elude, escape, eschew, evade, fence, fudge, lie, palter, parry, pettifog, prevaricate, quibble, shuffle, sidestep, stonewall, waffle *Nonformal:* dipsy-doodle, weasel

equivocation *n.* ambiguity, avoidance, colouring, cover, deceit, deception, deceptiveness, distortion, double meaning, duplicity, evasion, fib, lie, misrepresentation, prevarication, quibbling, shuffling, speciousness, spuriousness *Antonyms:* candour, forthrightness, honesty, straightforwardness

era *n.* aeon, age, cycle, date, day, epoch, generation, period, stage, term, time *Geological eras:* Archeozoic, Cenozoic, Mesozoic, Paleozoic, Precambrian, Proterozoic

eradicate *v.* abolish, annihilate, demolish, destroy, eliminate, erase, expunge, exterminate, extinguish, extirpate, liquidate, obliterate, purge, raze, remove, root out, rub out, scratch, squash, stamp out, total, trash, uproot, wipe out

erase *v.* abolish, annul, blue pencil, cancel, clean, cut, delete, dispatch, eliminate, eradicate, excise, expunge, launder, negate, nullify, obliterate, purge, remove, stamp out, strike, wipe clean, withdraw *Antonyms:* add, mark, print, record, restore

erect *adj.* elevated, perpendicular, raised, rigid, standing, stiff, straight, straight up, upright, upstanding, vertical – *v.* assemble, build, compose, construct, create, effect, engineer, establish, fabricate, fashion, fix, forge, frame, hoist, make, manufacture, pitch, place, plant, produce, put up, raise, rear, set up, shape, station, *Antonyms:* demolish, destroy, dismantle, raze, tear down

erode *v.* abrade, consume, corrode, crumble, decay, decompose, destroy, deteriorate, disintegrate, eat, erode, gnaw, obliterate, rot, rub, rust, scrape, waste, wear

erosion *n.* abrasion, consumption, corrosion, decrease, destruction, deterioration, disintegration, wear *Antonyms:* augmentation, construction, development, growth

erotic *adj.* amatory, amorous, aphrodisiac, bawdy, blue *(Nonformal)*, carnal, dirty, earthy, erogenous, fleshly, impassioned, improper, lascivious, lecherous, lewd, obscene, raw, restricted, risqué, romantic, rousing, salacious, seductive, sensual, sexy, smutty, spicy, steamy, stimulating, suggestive, titillating, voluptuous *Antonyms:* chaste, prudish, restrained, Victorian *Commonly misused:* **exotic**

err *v.* **1.** blunder, boggle, fail, fault, flub, fluff, fumble, miscalculate, misjudge, mistake, muff, offend *Nonformal:* bollix, screw up **2.** deviate, fall, lapse, misbehave, sin, stray, transgress, trespass, trip, wander

errand *n.* appointment, assignment, charge, chore, commission, duty, job, message, mission, performance, task, trip

erratic *adj.* **1.** aberrant, abnormal, anomalous, arbitrary, bizarre, capricious, changeable, eccentric, fitful, flaky *(Nonformal)*, idiosyncratic, inconsistent, irregular, mercurial, spasmodic, uncertain, unpredictable, unreliable, unstable, unsteady, variable, volatile *Antonyms:* constant, dependable, regular, stable **2.** meandering, nomadic, stray, undirected, wandering, wayward

erroneous *adj.* aberrant, amiss, askew, awry, defective, deviant, errant, erring, fallacious, fallible, false, faulty, inaccurate, incorrect, invalid, misguided, mistaken, off, offending, shifting, sinning, specious, spurious, stray, unreliable, unsound, untrue, wayward, wrong *Antonyms:* accurate, correct, factual, flawless, precise

error *n.* **1.** blunder, deviation, erratum, failure, fault, *faux pas (French)*, flaw, gaffe, glitch, goof, impropriety, miscalculation, misdeed, misplay, miss, misstep, mistake, offence, omission, oversight, solecism, stumble, trip, wrong, wrongdoing **2.** fallacy, falsehood, falsity, inaccuracy, incongruity, misapprehension, misbelief, misconception, untruth **3.** indiscretion, lapse, peccadillo, sin, slight, slip, transgression

ersatz *adj.* artificial, bogus, copied, counterfeit, fake, false, imitation, manufactured, phoney *(Nonformal)*, pretend, sham, simulated, spurious, substitute, synthetic *Antonyms:* authentic, genuine, natural, real

erstwhile *adj.* bygone, former, late, old, once, one-time, past, preceding, previous, recent

erudite *adj.* academic, cultivated, cultured, educated, intellectual, knowledgeable, learned, lettered, literate, savvy *(Nonformal)*, scholarly, scholastic, studious, well-educated, well-read *Antonyms:* ignorant, uneducated, uninformed, untaught

erudition *n.* bookishness, brains, cultivation, culture, education, enlightenment, knowledge, learnedness, learning, letters, literacy, savvy *(Nonformal)*, scholarship schooling, studiousness

erupt *v.* belch, burst, detonate, discharge eject, eruct, explode, gush, hurl, jet, rupture, spew, spit, spout, vent, vomit *Antonyms:* hold, retain, subside

escalate *v.* amplify, ascend, broaden, climb enlarge, expand, extend, grow, heighten increase, intensify, magnify, mount, raise rise, scale, step up, widen *Antonyms:* abate, decrease, diminish, drop

escapade *n.* adventure, antic, caper, fling, folly, frolic, gag, hijinks, lark, merrymaking, mischief, monkeyshines *(Nonformal)*, prank, roguery, rollick, romp, scrape, shenanigan, spree, stunt, trick, trouble

escape *n.* **1.** break, departure, desertion, elopement, flight, freedom, getaway, hegira, leave, release, slip, withdrawal *Nonformal:* lam, spring **2.** avoidance, bypassing, circumvention, dodging, ducking, eschewal, evasion, sidestepping **3.** drain, dripping, effusion, flow, leakage, seepage – *v.* **1.** abscond, alight, bail *or* break *or* get out, begone, bolt, break, circumvent, decamp, depart, desert, dodge, duck, elope, elude, evacuate, evade, flee, fly, go, leave, quit, retreat, run, shirk, skip, shun, slip, vacate, withdraw *Nonformal*: scram, split, vamoose **2.** burst, drain, drip, emit, extricate, exude, give off, leak, ooze, seep **3.** disappear, evanesce, fade, vanish

escarpment *n.* bluff, cliff, drop, palisade, precipice, ridge, slope

eschew *v.* abandon, abjure, abstain, avoid, bilk, duck, elude, escape, evade, forbear, forgo, give up, refrain, renounce, sacrifice, shun

escort *n.* **1.** accompaniment, attendant, bodyguard, chaperone, companion, company, consort, date, guard, guide, partner, protection, protector **2.** convoy, cortège, entourage, retinue – *v.* accompany, attend, bear, bring, carry, chaperon, conduct, convoy, direct, guard, guide, lead, partner, pilot, protect, shepherd, show, squire, steer, usher

esoteric *adj.* abstruse, arcane, cryptic, deep, difficult, heavy, hermetic, hidden, inner, inscrutable, mysterious, mystical, obscure, private, profound, recondite, secret *Antonyms:* clear, obvious, plain, prosaic, simple

ESP *n.* clairvoyance, divination, extrasensory perception, intuition, psychokinesis, second sight, sixth sense, telekinesis, telepathy

especial *adj.* **1.** chief, distinguished, exceptional, extraordinary, marked, notable, noteworthy, outstanding, paramount, preeminent, supreme, surpassing, unique, unusual *Antonyms:* common, everyday, usual **2.** certain, express, particular, personal, principal, singular, special, specific

especially *adv.* abnormally, above all, chiefly, conspicuously, exceptionally, expressly, extraordinarily, mainly, markedly, notably, peculiarly, principally, singularly, specifically, strikingly, supremely, uncommonly, uniquely, unusually

espionage *n.* detective work, covert operations, intelligence, intrigue, private investigations, spying, subterfuge, reconnaissance, surveillance, undercover work

esplanade *n.* arcade, boardwalk, lane, mall, parade, path, promenade, run, sidewalk, strand, stretch, walk, wind

espouse *v.* **1.** advance, advocate, adopt, back, champion, defend, embrace, support, uphold *Antonyms:* abandon, desert, reject **2.** attach, betroth, give *or* take in matrimony, join, marry, unite, wed

essay *n.* **1.** article, composition, discourse, discussion, dissertation, explication, exposition, manuscript, paper, piece, position paper, study, theme, thesis, tract, treatise **2.** effort, endeavour, exertion, labour, struggle, travail, try, undertaking

essence *n.* **1.** backbone, base, basis, condition, core, crux, essential, fibre, form, fundamentals, germ, gist, grain, heart, kernel, lifeblood, marrow, meat, mood, nature, nub, nucleus, personality, pith, point, principle, quiddity, quintessence, reality, root, significance, soul, spirit, stuff, substance **2.** aspect, attribute, element, quality, timbre **3.** balm, being, character, cologne, concentrate, constitution, distillate, distillation, effusion, extract, fragrance, liquor, perfume, potion, property, scent, spirits, tincture

essential *adj.* **1.** basic, capital, cardinal, chief, crucial, elementary, foremost, imperative, indispensable, key, main, necessary, needed, needful, non-negotiable, prerequisite, primary, prime, principal, quintessential, required, requisite, underlying, vital *Antonyms:* dispensable, incidental, secondary, superfluous, unnecessary **2.** constitutional, deep-seated, inborn, inbred, inherent, innate, intrinsic – *n.* **1.** condition, fundamental, necessity, precondition, prerequisite, quintessence, requirement, requisite *Nonformal:* brass tacks, must, nitty-gritty *Antonyms:* nonessential, subordinate **2.** constituent, element, essence, factor, ingredient, part, principle, rudiment, vital part

establish *v.* **1.** entrench, fix, ground, implant, land, lodge, moor, place, plant, put, rivet, root, secure, settle, stabilize, station **2.** base, build, constitute, create, erect, form, found, introduce, install, institute, make, originate, set up, start **3.** authenticate, demonstrate, prove, show, substantiate, validate, verify **4.** ascertain, certify, confirm, corroborate, deduce, determine, discover, figure out, formulate, learn, solve **5.** authorize, decree, enact, legislate, ordain, prescribe, ratify

establishment *n.* **1.** business, company, concern, corporation, enterprise, factory, firm, house, organization, outfit, plant, shop, system, workplace **2.** creation, enactment, endowment, formation, formulation, foundation, founding, inauguration, installation, institution, setting up **3.** authority, established order, ruling class *Nonformal:* Château Clique, Family Compact, old guard, the man, the system

estate *n.* **1.** castle, château, country home, country place, court, demesne, domain, dominion, farm, freehold, grounds, holding, land, manor, mansion, palace, palatial residence, parcel, plantation, ranch, residence, rural seat, stately home, territory, villa **2.** bracket, caste, category, class, classification, condition, echelon, footing, grade, level, lot, order, place, position, quality, rank, shape, situation, sphere, standing, state, station, stratum, status **3.** assets, belongings, bequest, capital, chattel, effects, endowment, fortune, goods, inheritance, possessions

esteem *n.* adoration, appreciation, favour, high opinion *or* regard, homage, honour, respect, worship *Antonyms:* disdain, hate, scorn – *v.* admire, appreciate, cherish, consider, hold dear, honour, idolize, like, love, prize, rate, regard, respect, revere, treasure, value, venerate, worship

estimable *adj.* admirable, admired, commendable, decent, deserving, esteem-ed, good, honourable, laudable, meritorious, noble, praiseworthy, respected, valued, venerable, worthy *Antonyms:* disreputable, ridiculous, scorned, undeserving

estimate *n.* appraisal, assessment, calculation, conclusion, conjecture, estimation, evaluation, gauging, guess, impression, interpretation, judgment, measure, opinion, projection, reckoning, stock, survey, valuation – *v.* **1.** believe, conjecture, consider, determine, foretell, guess, predict, prophesy, regard, surmise, think **2.** appraise, assay, assess, classify, compute, deduce, evaluate, figure, enumerate, gauge, judge, measure, rank, rate, value, weigh

estimation *n.* **1.** appraisal, assessment belief, consideration, estimate, evaluation, guess, impression, judgment, opinion, reckoning, valuation, view **2.** admiration, appreciation, credit, esteem, favour, regard, respect

estrange *v.* **1.** dissociate, disunite, divide, divorce, leave, part, rupture, separate, sever, split, sunder, withdraw *Antonyms:* marry, merge, unite **2.** alienate, antagonize, disaffect, embitter, marginalize, offend

estrangement *n.* alienation, breach, breakup, disassociation, disunity, division, divorce, leaving, parting, removal, schism, separation, split, withdrawal *Antonyms:* convergence, marriage, union

estuary *n.* basin, bay, creek, fjord, firth, inlet, river mouth, tidal basin

et cetera *adv.* and more of the same, and others, and so forth *or* on, and the rest, etc., et al

etch *v.* carve, corrode, cut, define, delineate, depict, eat into, engrave, erode, execute, furrow, grave, impress, imprint, incise, inscribe, portray, represent, set forth, stamp

etching *n.* carving, engraving, impression, imprint, inscription, mezzotint, old master, photoengraving, print, reproduction, transfer

eternal *adj.* **1.** abiding, ageless, always, boundless, ceaseless, constant, continual, continuous, endless, enduring, everlasting, immortal, immutable, incessant, indefinite, infinite, lasting, never-ending, perennial, permanent, perpetual, persistent, timeless, unbroken, unceasing, undying, unending, unremitting *Antonyms:* ephemeral, finite, fleeting, mortal, transitory **2.** boring, deadly *(Nonformal)*, exhausting, monotonous, relentless, repetitive, soporific, tedious, tiring, wearying

eternally *adv.* always, continually, endlessly, ever, evermore, forever, forevermore, for keeps *(Nonformal)*, in perpetuity, now and forever, perpetually

eternity *n.* afterlife, agelessness, endlessness, eon, forever, immortality, infiniteness, infinity, perpetuity, timelessness *Antonyms:* ephemeral, transience

ethereal *adj.* **1.** dainty, delicate, exquisite, filmy, fine, flimsy, gossamer, tenuous **2.** airy, ghostly, intangible, unsubstantial, vaporous **3.** celestial, divine, heavenly, lofty, spiritual, unearthly

ethical *adj.* clean, conscientious, correct, decent, elevated, equitable, fair, fitting, good, high-principled, honest, honourable, humane, just, law-abiding, moral, noble, principled, proper, respectable, righteous, upright, upstanding, virtuous *Antonyms:* crooked, dishonourable, immoral, improper, unjust

ethics *n. pl.* beliefs, conduct, conscience, criteria, ethos, honour, ideals, morality, morals, mores, nature, normative structure, norms, practice, principles, standards, values

ethnic *adj.* **1.** cultural, indigenous, local, national, native, racial, traditional, tribal **2.** exotic, foreign, immigrant, international, migrant **3.** different, distinct, distinctive, unique

etiquette *n.* code *or* rules of conduct, custom, formalities, manners, norms, politeness, social code *or* graces

eulogize *v.* acclaim, applaud, bless, celebrate, commend, compliment, exalt, extol, flatter, glorify, hymn, laud, magnify, pay homage, praise, sing praises

eulogy *n.* acclaim, acclamation, accolade, adulation, applause, citation, commendation, compliment, encomium, exaltation, Festschrift, glorification, laudation, panegyric, plaudit, praise, salutation, tribute *Commonly misused:* **elegy**

euphemism *n.* adumbration, circumlocution, delicacy, mitigation, nicety, substitution, sugar coating *Nonformal:* pc term, weasel word

euphoria *n.* bliss, buoyancy, ecstasy, elation, exhilaration, exultation, frenzy, glee, happiness, high spirits, intoxication, joy, jubilation, madness, rapture *Antonyms:* depression, despair, despondency, gloom

euthanasia *n.* doctor assisted suicide, easy *or* painless death, happy release, mercy killing

evacuate *v.* **1.** abandon, bail out, clear, decamp, depart, desert, empty, flee, leave, pack up, pull out, quit, vacate, withdraw *Antonyms:* remain, stay **2.** discharge, displace, eject, exile, expel, force out, oust, remove *Antonyms:* admit, welcome

evade *v.* avoid, bypass, circumvent, deceive, deke, ditch, dodge, duck, elude, equivocate, escape, eschew, flee, fly, parry, prevaricate, shift, shirk, shuffle, shun *Antonyms:* brave, confront, face

evaluate *v.* appraise, assess, calculate, class, classify, estimate, gauge, grade, guesstimate *(Nonformal)*, judge, peg, rank, rate, read, reckon, size up, value, weigh

evaluation *n.* analysis, appraisal, appraisement, assessment, calculation, decision, estimate, estimation, examination, interpretation, judgment, opinion, rating, stock

evanesce *v.* disappear, disintegrate, dissipate, dissolve, dwindle, evaporate, fade, leave, melt, pass, peter out *(Nonformal)*, vanish *Antonyms:* abide, remain, stay

evangelical *adj.* bible-thumping *(Nonformal)*, biblical, crusading, heaven-struck, inspired, proselytizing, scriptural, zealous – *n.* believer, born-again, Christian, devotee, proselyte

evangelist *n.* catechist, crusader, faith healer, God botherer *(Nonformal)*, minister of the Gospel, missionary, person of God, preacher, preacher of repentance, proselytizer, reformer, revivalist

evaporate *v.* **1.** dehumidify, dehydrate, desiccate, dispel, disperse, dissipate, dissolve, dry, dry up, melt, parch, vaporize **2.** depart, disappear, evanesce, fade away, leave, pass, vanish

evaporation *n.* dehydration, desiccation, dispersal, dissipation, dissolution, drying, melting, vaporization

evasion *n.* avoidance, circumvention, dodging, equivocation, escape, excuse, lie, manoeuvre, prevarication, shirking, shuffling, stonewall tactic, subterfuge, trickery

evasive *adj.* cagey, cunning, deceitful, devious, dissembling, elusive, equivocating, indirect, intangible, lying, mendacious, misleading, nebulous, prevaricating, quicksilver, shifty, shuffling, slippery, sly, tricky, unclear, vague *Antonyms:* candid, direct, frank, honest, open

even *adj.* **1.** alike, at par, balanced, commensurate, comparable, coterminous, equal, equivalent, fifty-fifty, flat, flush, homogenous, horizontal, level, like, matching, parallel, plumb, proportional, proportionate, right, same, similar, square, true, uniform, well-balanced **2.** consistent, constant, continual, continuous, direct, flowing, regular, smooth, steady, systematic, unbroken, undeviating, uniform, uninterrupted, unvaried, unvarying *Antonyms:* choppy, episodic, erratic **3.** calm, composed, cool, equable, even-tempered, imperturbable, peaceful, placid, serene, stable, tranquil, unexcitable, unruffled *Antonyms:* agitated, excitable, quick-tempered, volcanic **4.** disinterested, dispassionate, equitable, fair, impartial, just, unbiased, unprejudiced *Antonyms:* biased, partial, unequal – *adv.* actually, all the same, although, at that moment, indeed, in fact, just, nevertheless, still, yet – *v.* balance, ballast, equal, flush, level, match, plane, smooth, square, stabilize, steady

evening *n.* close, dark, decline, dim, dusk, duskiness, eve, eventide, late afternoon, nightfall, shank of the day *(Nonformal)*, sundown, sunset, twilight *Antonyms:* dawn, morning

evenness *n.* flatness, horizontalness, levelness, rectilinearity, regularity, symmetry, uniformity

event *n.* **1.** accident, act, action, adventure, affair, business, case, circumstance, deed, episode, experience, happening, incident, matter, mishap, occasion, occurrence, phenomenon, predicament, proceeding, situation **2.** aftereffect, aftermath, conclusion, consequence, end, eventuality, happenstance, issue, offshoot, outcome, outgrowth, product, regatta, result, round robin, sequel, solution, upshot **3.** bonspiel, bout, competition, contest, game, match, meet, performance, playoff, showdown, tournament **4.** ball, box *or* church social, ceilidh, celebration, ceremony, conceit, festival, fête, function, gathering, jamboree, parade, party, show, soiree

eventful *adj.* **1.** consequential, critical, crucial, decisive, fateful, historic, important, memorable, momentous, notable, noteworthy, outstanding, remarkable, signal, significant, watershed *Antonyms:* commonplace, dull, ordinary, trivial **2.** active, busy, exciting, lively, thrilling *Nonformal:* bang-bang, best of times, worst of times

eventuality *n.* **1.** aftereffect, aftermath, backlash, consequence, effect, event, happening, issue, outcome, possibility, probability, result, sequel, upshot **2.** chance, likelihood, possibility, potential, probability, prospect

eventually *adv.* finally, in conclusion, in the end, in the long run, in time, one day, sooner or later, subsequently, ultimately

evergreen *adj.* coniferous *Kinds of coniferous trees:* arborvitae, cedar, cypress, fir, hemlock, juniper, larch, pine, spruce, yew *See also:* **tree**

everlasting *adj.* abiding, boundless, ceaseless, constant, continuous, deathless, endless, enduring, eternal, immortal, imperishable, incessant, indestructible, infinite, interminable, lasting, never-ending, permanent, perpetual, timeless, unceasing, unending, uninterrupted *Antonyms:* brief, ephemeral, fleeting, passing, temporary

everyday *adj.* **1.** commonplace, conventional, customary, familiar, frequent, habitual, mainstream, mundane, normal, ordinary, plain, regular, routine, stock, unexceptional, unimaginative, unremarkable, usual, workaday *Nonformal:* garden variety, run-of-the-mill *Antonyms:* extraordinary, special, unusual **2.** circadian, daily, diurnal, per diem, quotidian

everyone *pron.* all, all and sundry, anybody, each one, each person, everybody, the whole

everything *n.* aggregate, all *or* all things, entirety, gross, lot, mass, quantity, sum, total, universe, whole, whole lot *or* shebang *(Nonformal)*

everywhere *adv.* all over, every corner *or* place, extensively, far and wide, from sea to sea, from top to bottom, here and there, the world over, throughout, ubiquitously, universally, wall to wall

evict *v.* dislodge, dismiss, dispossess, eject, expel, force out, oust, remove, shut out, throw out, turn out *Nonformal:* bounce, chuck, give the boot *or* heave-ho, send packing, turf *Antonyms:* admit, invite, lodge, receive, welcome

eviction *n.* clearance, dislodgement, dispossession, ejection, evacuation, expulsion, ouster, removal *Nonformal:* the boot *or* toss, walking papers

evidence *n.* affirmation, attestation, averment, clue, confirmation, corroboration, data, declaration, demonstration, deposition, documentation, indication, manifestation, mark, proof, sign, smoking gun *(Nonformal)*, substantiation, testament, testimonial, testimony, witness – *v.* attest, bespeak, betoken, confirm, demonstrate, denote, designate, display, evince, exhibit, expose, illustrate, indicate, manifest, mark, proclaim, prove, reveal, show, signify, testify to, witness

evident *adj.* apparent, axiomatic, barefaced, clear *or* crystal clear, clear-cut, comprehensible, conspicuous, distinct, factual, incontestable, incontrovertible, indisputable, logical, manifest, noticeable, obvious, palpable, patent, perceptible, plain, straightforward, tangible, understandable, unmistakable, visible *Antonyms:* ambiguous, concealed, doubtful, hidden, obscure

evidently *adv.* **1.** apparently, likely, ostensibly, outwardly, probably, professedly, seemingly **2.** clearly, doubtlessly, incontestably, incontrovertibly, indisputably, manifestly, obviously, officially, patently, plainly, undoubtedly, unmistakably, without question

evil *adj.* **1.** bad, base, beastly, corrupt, damnable, depraved, execrable, foul, hateful, heinous, hideous, immoral, iniquitous, loathsome, maleficent, malevolent, malicious, malignant, nefarious, obscene, offensive, pernicious, rancorous, reprobate, repugnant, repulsive, revolting, sinful, spiteful, ugly, unpleasant, unpropitious, vicious, vile, villainous, wicked, wrathful *Antonyms:* benevolent, fortunate, kind, prelapsarian, rightful **2.** calamitous, deadly, destructive, disastrous, fatal, harmful, injurious, lethal, mortal, poisonous – *adv.* awfully, badly, balefully, corruptly, criminally, cruelly, malevolently, offensively, wickedly – *n.* **1.** baseness, corruption, crime, criminality, debauchery, depravity, deviltry, diabolism, hatred, heinousness, immorality, impiety, indecency, knavery, malevolence, meanness, mischief, obscenity, outrage, perversity, turpitude, vice, viciousness, vileness, villainy, wickedness, wrong *Antonyms:* fortune, good, purity **2.** affliction, blow, calamity, catastrophe, curse, disaster, harm, hurt, ill, injury, misery, misfortune, pain, ruin, sin, sorrow, suffering

eviscerate *v.* clean, cut, dissect, disembowel, draw, fillet, gut, vivisect

evocative *adj.* arousing, calling, exciting, provoking, reminiscent, rousing, stimulating, stirring, striking, suggestive

evoke *v.* arouse, awaken, call, call forth, conjure, educe, elicit, evince, excite, extract, incant, kindle, provoke, raise, rally, recall, revive, rouse, stimulate, stir up, summon, waken *Commonly misused:* **invoke**

evolution *n.* change, development, enlargement, evolvement, expansion, flowering, formation, growth, increase, maturation, metamorphosis, movement, natural process, progress, progression, transformation, unfolding

evolve *v.* **1.** advance, change, develop, emerge, enlarge, expand, flower, grow, improve, increase, mature, open, progress, ripen, unfold *Antonyms:* decline, ebb, revert, regress **2.** construct, devise, elaborate, excogitate, plan, produce, put together, work out

exacerbate *v.* aggravate, annoy, bother, embitter, enrage, exasperate, excite, heighten, increase, inflame, infuriate, intensify, irritate, madden, nettle, provoke, upset, vex, worsen *Nonformal:* heat up, press one's buttons *Antonyms:* calm, mitigate, mollify

exact *adj.* **1.** careful, conscientious, demanding, exacting, fussy, heedful, methodical, meticulous, painstaking, particular, punctilious, punctual, rigorous, scrupulous, severe, strict *Antonyms:* careless, imprecise, loose, rough **2.** accurate, clear, clear-cut, correct, definite, distinct, explicit, faithful, identical, literal, orderly, perfect, precise, right, specific, true, unequivocal, unerring, verbatim – *v.* command, compel, demand, force, insist, obtain, procure, request, require

exacting *adj.* **1.** careful, critical, demanding, exigent, fastidious, finicky, fussy, hard, harsh, hypercritical, imperious, particular, picky, precise, rigid, rigorous, severe, strict, stringent, tough, unsparing *Nonformal:* nitpicking, persnickety *Antonyms:* easy, effortless, simple, undemanding **2.** burdensome, difficult, exhausting, grievous, heavy, onerous, painstaking, taxing, trying

exactly *adv.* absolutely, accurately, carefully, completely, correctly, definitely, explicitly, expressly, faithfully, faultlessly, indeed, literally, methodically, positively, precisely, right, rigorously, scrupulously, specifically, square, strictly, totally, truly, truthfully, unerringly

exactness *n.* accuracy, carefulness, conformity, correctness, definiteness, faultlessness, orderliness, precision, promptitude, regularity, rigour, rigorousness, scrupulousness, standardization, strictness, truth, unequivocalness, veracity *Antonyms:* imprecision, inaccuracy, incorrectness

exaggerate *v.* amplify, boast, boost, brag, build up, colour, distort, embroider, enlarge, exalt, expand, fabricate, falsify, fudge, heighten, hike, hyperbolize, inflate, intensify, magnify, overdo, overdraw, overemphasize, overestimate, overstate, pad, play up, puff, romanticize, stretch

exaggerated *adj.* amplified, distorted, embellished, embroidered, exalted, excessive, extravagant, fabulous, fantastic, far-fetched, hyperbolic, inflated, magnified, melodramatic, overblown, overdone, overstated, overwrought, preposterous, steep, strained, stylized, unrealistic *Nonformal:* hammy, too much *Antonyms:* accurate, correct, downplayed, down-to-earth, realistic

exaggeration *n.* amplification, boast, caricature, colouring, elaboration, embroidery, enlargement, excess, extravagance, fancy, fantasy, hyperbole, inflation, magnification, overemphasis, overestimation, overstatement, pretension, romance, stretch, stretching *Nonformal:* fish story, hogwash, jazz, tall story, whopper, yarn *Antonyms:* restraint, truth, understatement

exalt *v.* **1.** acclaim, advance, aggrandize, applaud, bless, boost, build up, commend, dignify, distinguish, elevate, ennoble, extol, glorify, honour, idolize, laud, magnify, praise, promote, raise, revere, sublime, upgrade, worship *Antonyms:* belittle, debase, denigrate, humiliate, shame **2.** delight, elate, endear, gladden, please, satisfy, send *Commonly misused:* **exult**

exaltation *n.* **1.** animation, bliss, delectation, delight, ecstasy, elation, elevation, euphoria, excitement, exhilaration, inspiration, intoxication, joy, joyousness, jubilation, rapture, stimulation **2.** acclaim, acclamation, applause, blessing, homage, honour, laudation, plaudit, praise, reverence, tribute, worship **3.** advancement, aggrandizement, ennoblement, glorification, magnification, promotion, upgrading, uplifting **4.** dignity, eminence, glory, loftiness, majesty, nobility, sublimity

exalted *adj.* august, dignified, elevated, eminent, first, grand, high, highest, high-minded, high-ranking, honourable, honoured, ideal, illustrious, imposing, inflated, leading, lofty, magnificent, noble, outstanding, praised, prestigious, proud, sublime, superb, superior, top-ranking *Antonyms:* contemptible, degraded, ignoble, lowly, scrofulous

examination *n.* audit, autopsy, biopsy, checkup, diagnosis, dissection, exam, exploration, inquest, inquiry, inspection, interrogation, investigation, observation, postmortem, probe, questioning, review, scan, scrutiny, search, study, survey, test

examine *v.* analyze, appraise, ascertain, audit, case *(Nonformal)*, check, compare, confirm, consider, count, criticize, explore, eye, inquire, inspect, interrogate, investigate, look into, monitor, note, observe, oversee, probe, question, quiz, read, research, review, scan, scout, screen, scrutinize, search, sift, study, survey, test, try, verify, view, watch, weigh

example *n.* **1.** case, copy, illustration, indication, instance, occurrence, representation, sign, token **2.** fragment, part, piece, portion, sample, specimen **3.** archetype, embodiment, epitome, essence, ideal, model, mould, paradigm, paragon, pattern, precedent, prototype, quintessence, representative, standard, symbol **4.** *étude (French),* exercise, formula, lesson, problem, puzzle

exasperation *n.* aggravation, anger, annoyance, bother, exacerbation, ire, irritant, nuisance, passion, pique, plague, provocation, vexation *Antonyms:* comfort, contentment, happiness, pleasure, satisfaction

excavate *v.* blast, burrow, cut, delve, dig, dig up, dynamite, empty, exhume, gouge, grub, hollow, mine, quarry, remove, scoop, shovel, trench, tunnel, uncover, unearth

excavation *n.* **1.** archaeological *or* dig site, burrow, cavity, cut, dig, ditch, dugout, hole, hollow, mine, quarry, trench, trough, tunnel, unearthing **2.** digging, mining, scooping, shoveling

exceed *v.* beat, best, better, cap, eclipse, excel, go beyond, outdistance, outdo, outreach, outshine, outstrip, overtake, surmount, surpass, top, transcend *Commonly misused:* **accede**

exceedingly *adv.* awfully, enormously, especially, exceptionally, excessively, extraordinarily, extremely, greatly, highly, hugely, immoderately, inordinately, powerfully, really, remarkably, strikingly, superlatively, terribly, unusually, vastly, very

excel *v.* beat, better, cap, eclipse, exceed, improve upon, make it, outclass, outdo, outrival, pass, predominate, surmount, surpass, top, transcend, wax *Nonformal:* come through, shine *Antonyms:* fail, fall short, lose

excellence *n.* character, class, distinction, eminence, fineness, goodness, grade A *(Nonformal),* greatness, merit, perfection, preeminence, purity, quality, superiority, supremacy, virtue, worth *Antonyms:* failing, imperfection, sin, vice

excellent *adj.* accomplished, admirable, attractive, capital, certified, champion, choice, choicest, cool *(Nonformal),* desirable, exceptional, exemplary, exquisite, finest, first, first-class, first-rate, great, high, incomparable, invaluable, magnificent, meritorious, notable, noted, outstanding, premium, priceless, prime, select, skookum *(Pacific Coast),* striking, superb, superior, superlative, wonderful, world-class *Antonyms:* dreadful, imperfect, inferior

except *prep.* apart from, barring, besides, but, excluding, other than, omitting, rejecting, rule out, save – *v.* ban, bar, disallow, eliminate, exclude, exempt, leave out, omit, pass over, reject, rule out, snub *Commonly misused:* **accept**

exception *n.* **1.** exclusion, excusing, exemption, neglect, noninclusion, omission, rejection, repudiation, reservation **2.** anomaly, departure, deviation, difference, eccentricity, freak, inconsistency, irregularity, nonconformity, oddity, peculiarity, quirk **3.** aversion, complaint, criticism, objection, protest

exceptional *adj.* **1.** aberrant, abnormal, anomalous, atypical, deviant, inconsistent, infrequent, irregular, peculiar, rare, scarce, strange, uncommon, unique, unprecedented, unusual *Antonyms:* common, mediocre, ordinary, typical, usual **2.** awesome, excellent, extraordinary, fantastic, fine, first-class, first-rate, marvellous, outstanding, phenomenal, premium, remarkable, singular, striking, special, splash *(Nonformal),* striking, superior, wonderful, world-class *Antonyms:* average, awful, bad, inferior

excerpt *n.* citation, extract, fragment, line, paragraph, part, passage, piece, portion, quotation, quote, section, selection, sentence – *v.* choose, cite, cull, cut, extract, glean, pick, pick out, quote, select, single out

excess *n.* **1.** affluence, exorbitance, fat, glut, inundation, overabundance, overdose, overflow, overkill, overload, overrun, oversupply, plenty, plethora, profusion, redundancy, superabundance, surfeit, surplus, waste *Antonyms:* dearth, deficiency, insufficiency, lack, shortage **2.** bacchanalia, debauchery, dissipation, dissoluteness, extravagance, extreme, immoderacy, immoderation, indulgence, inordinateness, intemperance, overindulgence, prodigality, saturnalia, self-indulgence, spree **3.** balance, by-product, gain, leavings, leftover, profit, remainder, residue *Antonyms:* loss, shortcoming

excessive *adj.* **1.** boundless, disproportionate, dizzying, enormous, exorbitant, extravagant, extreme, inordinate, limitless, needless, overkill, plethoric, sky-high, superabundant, superfluous, unbounded, undue, unmeasurable *Antonyms:* limited, meagre, restricted **2.** abandoned, Dionysian, immoderate, indulgent, intemperate, over-the-top *(Nonformal)*, profligate, unbridled, unrestrained *Antonyms:* reserved, temperate

exchange *n.* **1.** barter, deal, interchange, swap, trade, traffic, transaction **2.** commutation, conversion, shift, substitution, shuffle, switch, transference, transposition **3.** Bay Street *(Nonformal)*, commercial house, e-commerce, market, network, stock exchange **4.** chat, communication, conversation, correspondence, dialogue, discourse, meeting, talk – *v.* **1.** bargain, barter, interchange, swap, trade, transact **2.** convert, metamorphose, rearrange, replace, return, shift, shuffle, substitute, switch, transfer, transform **3.** bandy, communicate, correspond, reciprocate, respond, retort, speak

excise *n.* customs, duty, levy, surcharge, tariff, tax, toll – *v.* abridge, amputate, bowdlerize, censor, cut out, delete, eradicate, erase, exorcise, expunge, extract, gut, remove, scratch out, slash, trim, truncate

excitable *adj.* edgy, emotional, fidgety, fiery, galvanic, high-strung, hysterical, impatient, impetuous, impulsive, inflammable, irascible, mercurial, moody, nervous, neurotic, passionate, peevish, quick, rash, reckless, restless, sensitive, short-fused, susceptible, temperamental, testy, touchy, uncontrolled, uneasy, vehement, violent, volatile, volcanic *Antonyms:* calm, even-tempered, imperturbable, placid, unruffled

excite *v.* **1.** arouse, awake, elicit, evoke, jar, jolt, kindle, spark, stimulate, stir **2.** agitate, anger, annoy, awaken, bother, chafe, disturb, foment, goad, incite, inflame, infuriate, irritate, madden, provoke, rouse, stir up, work up *Antonyms:* quell, quiet **3.** animate, delight, electrify, encourage, exhilarate, galvanize, inspire, move, quicken *Antonyms:* bore, lull, tire

excited *adj.* **1.** agitated, animated, aroused, awakened, charged, emotional, feverish, frantic, heated, hyper, hysterical, impassioned, moved, nervous, overwrought, passionate, roused, stimulated, stirred *Antonyms:* bored, depressed, jaded **2.** anxious, ardent, delighted, eager, earnest, enthusiastic, fervent, fervid, inspired, keen **3.** angry, disturbed, exasperated, fuming, furious, incensed, inflamed, piqued, pissed *(Nonformal)*, provoked, riled, vexed, wild *Antonyms:* calm, cool, relaxed

excitement *n.* **1.** activity, ado, agitation, animation, bother, commotion, confusion, disturbance, drama, fuss, hubbub, hullabaloo, hysteria, melodrama, movement **2.** discomposure, dither, furor, excitation, ferment, fever, flurry, frenzy, heat, passion, stimulation, tumult, urge, turmoil **3.** action, adventure, elation, emotion, enthusiasm, intoxication, thrill

exciting *adj.* animating, appealing, arousing, arresting, astonishing, bracing, breathtaking, dramatic, electrifying, exhilarating, hectic, impelling, intoxicating, intriguing, lively, moving, overwhelming, provocative, racy, riveting, rousing, sensational, stimulating, stirring, thrilling, titillating, uproarious, wild *Nonformal:* rip-roaring, spine-tingling *Antonyms:* boring, dreary, dull, monotonous, uninteresting

exclaim *v.* announce, assert, call *or* cry out, broadcast, declare, interject, proclaim, promulgate, publish, shout, shout out, utter, voice, yell *Nonformal:* bellow, blurt, burst out, holler, roar

exclude *v.* **1.** abolish, ban, bar, blackball, blacklist, block, boycott, debar, deter, disallow, embargo, evict, exclude, forbid, interdict, obstruct, ostracize, prevent, prohibit, proscribe, refuse, reject, revoke, shut out, sideline, suspend, veto, void **2.** bounce *(Nonformal)*, dismiss, eject, expel, oust, remove, throw out **3.** disregard, forget, ignore, leave out, neglect, omit, rule out, skip *Antonyms:* accept, admit, include *Commonly misused:* **preclude**

exclusion *n.* **1.** barring, blockade, boycott, debarment, debarring, eviction, forbiddance, interdiction, lockout, omission, ostracism, oversight, preclusion, prevention, prohibition, proscription, refusal, rejection, repudiation, suspension, veto *Antonyms:* adoption, inclusion, receipt **2.** alienation, discharge, dismissal, elimination, embargo, excommunication, expulsion, removal, segregation, separation

exclusive *adj.* **1.** individual, particular, selective, single, sole **2.** circumscribed, closed, distinctive, insular, original, peculiar, private, privileged, prohibitive, restricted, segregated, snobbish, snooty *(Nonformal)*, special, unique, upscale *Antonyms:* open, public, unrestricted, shared **3.** absolute, complete, entire, total, undivided

exclusively *adv.* alone, completely, entirely, only, particularly, singularly, solely, wholly

excommunicate *v.* ban, banish, cast out, curse, denounce, disconnect, dismiss, eject, exclude, expel, oust, proscribe, remove, separate

excoriate *v.* **1.** attack, berate, blister, castigate, censure, chastise, condemn, criticize, denounce, flay, lambaste, lash, rebuke, reproach, reprove, revile, scold, upbraid, vilify *Nonformal:* burn, dis **2.** chafe, debark, flail, husk, pare, peel, skin, strip, tear

excrement *n.* defecation, droppings, dung, excreta, feces, manure, stool *Nonformal:* ca-ca, crap, do, doggy-do, doodle, poop, road apple, turd

excrete *v.* defecate, discharge, eliminate, emanate, emit, expel, issue, ooze, perspire, secrete, sweat, urinate, void

excruciating *adj.* acute, agonizing, burning, consuming, exquisite, gruelling, harrowing, *in extremis (Latin)*, insufferable, intense, painful, piercing, racking, rending, searing, severe, sharp, shooting, stabbing, tearing, tormenting, torturous, unbearable, unendurable

exculpate *v.* absolve, acquit, clear, condone, declare *or* pronounce not guilty, deliver, discharge, dismiss, excuse, exonerate, forgive, free, let off, pardon, prove innocent, release, remit, reprieve, right *Antonyms:* arraign, charge, indict

excursion *n.* constitutional, cruise, day trip, expedition, jaunt, journey, junket, outing, picnic, pleasure trip, ramble, road trip, safari, tour, trek, trip, vacation, walk, wandering *Commonly misused:* **expedition**

excusable *adj.* allowable, defensible, exculpatory, explainable, fair, forgivable, justifiable, minor, pardonable, passable, permissible, plausible, reasonable, remittable, reprievable, tenable, trivial, understandable, venial, warrantable, within limits *Antonyms:* indefensible, inexcusable, unallowable, unforgivable

excuse *n.* alibi, apology, cover, cover-up, defence, evasion, expedient, explanation, grounds, justification, mitigation, plea, pretext, rationalization, reason, story, vindication, whitewash *Nonformal:* cop-out, song – *v.* **1.** absolve, acquit, clear, exculpate, exempt, exonerate, forgive, grant amnesty, pardon, relieve, remit, reprieve, shrive, spare *Antonyms:* accuse, arraign, blame, censure, chastise **2.** accept, condone, indulge, overlook, tolerate **3.** apologize for, cover, defend, explain, extenuate, justify, mitigate, rationalize **4.** discharge, dismiss, free, liberate, release

execrable *adj.* **1.** abhorrent, abominable, accursed, atrocious, confounded, cursed, despicable, detestable, disgusting, hateful, heinous, horrible, horrific, loathsome, low, monstrous, obnoxious, odious, offensive, repulsive, revolting, sickening, wretched *Antonyms:* acceptable, agreeable, attractive **2.** appalling, bad, inferior, poor, shoddy, terrible, unacceptable

execrate *v.* **1.** anathematize, berate, censure, condemn, curse, damn, denounce, excoriate, imprecate, objurgate, reprehend **2.** abhor, abominate, despise, detest, hate, loathe, revile

execration *n.* **1.** blasphemy, condemnation, curse, cursing, cussing, damnation, denunciation, excoriation, imprecation, malediction, profanity, vilification **2.** abhorrence, abomination, contempt, detestation, hatred, loathing, revilement

execute *v.* **1.** assassinate, eliminate, finish, kill, knock off *(Nonformal)*, liquidate, murder, purge, put to death, slay **2.** accomplish, achieve, administer, fulfill, perform, tackle, take on, work

execution *n.* **1.** accomplishment, achievement, administration, carrying out, completion, consummation, delivery, discharge, effect, enactment, enforcement, fulfillment, implementation, operation, performance, prosecution, realization **2.** capital punishment, death penalty, legal *or* judicial murder **3.** delivery, expression, manner, method, performance, rendering, style, touch

executive *adj.* administrative, corporate, financial, head, influential, official, organizational, powerful, rational, regulatory – *n.* administration, administrator, baron, businessman, CEO, CFO, chief, CO, commander, director, governor, head, higher-up *(Nonformal)*, industrialist, key player, kingpin, leader, management, manager, officer, policy makers, president, supervisor, top, tycoon, VP *Antonyms:* aid, assistant, underling

exemplary *adj.* **1.** admirable, commendable, estimable, excellent, honourable, laudable, meritorious, model, praiseworthy, righteous, virtuous, worthy **2.** characteristic, classic, ideal, quintessential, representative, typical

exemplify *v.* **1.** clarify, demonstrate, depict, display, elucidate, enlighten, evidence, exhibit, illuminate, illustrate, instance, show **2.** emblematize, embody, epitomize, manifest, mirror, personify, represent, symbolize, typify

exempt *adj.* absolved, clear, cleared, discharged, excepted, excluded, excused, freed, immune, liberated, outside, pardoned, released, scot-free, spared, unaccountable, unbound, unchecked, unrestrained, unrestricted, unshackled *Antonyms:* answerable, chargeable, liable, responsible, suable – *v.* absolve, clear, discharge, except, excuse, exonerate, free, grant immunity, let off, liberate, release, relieve, spare

exemption *n.* absolution, allowance, discharge, dispensation, exception, exoneration, freedom, grandfather clause, immunity, pardon, privilege, release

exercise *n.* **1.** act, action, activity, effort, exertion, motion, movement, toil **2.** application, discharge, employment, implementation, occupation, operation, performance, use, utilization **3.** exercise program *or* routine, practice, training, workout *Kinds of physical exercise:* aerobics, calisthenics, cross-training, gymnastics, isometrics, jogging, parcourse, place running, power walking, push-up, running, skipping, sit-up, stair climbing, stretching, swimming, tai chi, toe-touch, walking, weightlifting, yoga **4.** chore, étude, discipline, drill, homework, problem, task – *v.* **1.** condition, cultivate, develop, discipline, drill, foster, groom, habituate, hone, improve, practice, prepare, rehearse, set, sharpen, strain, teach, test, train, work out **2.** apply, employ, enjoy, execute, exert, exploit, handle, manoeuvre, ply, operate, use, utilize, wield

exert *v.* apply, dig, employ, endeavour, essay, exercise, expend, labour, plug, push, strain, strive, struggle, toil, use, utilize, wield, work

exertion *n.* action, activity, application, attempt, effort, employment, endeavour, exercise, industry, labour, pains, strain, striving, struggle, toil, work

exhale *v.* breathe, breathe out, discharge, eject, emanate, emit, evaporate, expel, give off, issue, let out, vaporize

exhaust *n.* discharge, emission, exhalation, flow, gas, pollution, outflow, steam, wash, waste – *v.* **1.** bankrupt, consume, deplete, devour, drain, dry up, eat up, empty, finish, impoverish, spend, squander, strain, suck dry, use up, weary **2.** burn out, debilitate, enervate, enfeeble, expend, fag, fatigue, flay, overdo, overexert, overextend, overfatigue, overwork, poop *(Nonformal)*, prostrate, sap, tire, tucker, weaken, wear out, weary **3.** discharge, emit, give off, leak

exhausted *adj.* **1.** bleary, effete, limp, sapped, spent, tired, used up, wasted, weak, wearied, worn out *Nonformal:* beat, burnt out, bushed, dead, dog-tired, done in, played out, pooped, shot, toast, washed up *Antonyms:* active, animated, invigorated, refreshed **2.** all gone, bankrupt, bare, consumed, depleted, dissipated, done, drained, dry, empty, expended, finished, gone, squandered, void *Antonyms:* conserved, kept, preserved

exhausting *adj.* arduous, back-breaking, debilitating, depleting, difficult, draining, enervating, enfeebling, fatiguing, gruelling, killer *(Nonformal)*, laborious, strenuous, taxing, tiring, weakening, wearisome *Antonyms:* invigorating, refreshing, revitalizing *Commonly misused:* **exhaustive**

exhaustion *n.* **1.** collapse, debilitation, expenditure, fatigue, lassitude, prostration, tiredness, weariness **2.** deprivation, dispossession, divestment, loss

exhaustive *adj.* all-embracing, all-encompassing, all-inclusive, all-out, complete, comprehensive, encyclopedic, extensive, far-reaching, full-blown, full-scale, in-depth, intensive, out-and-out, profound, radical, sweeping, thorough, thoroughgoing, total, whole-hog *(Nonformal)* *Antonyms:* cursory, desultory, perfunctory, sketchy, superficial *Commonly misused:* **exhausting**

exhibit *n.* display, exhibition, exposition, illustration, model, performance, presentation, show, viewing – *v.* advertise, air, brandish, demonstrate, disclose, display, evidence, evince, expose, express, feature, flash, flaunt, illustrate, indicate, make plain, manifest, mark, offer, parade, present, proclaim, reveal, roll out, show, showcase, show off, wave about

exhibition *n.* carnival, demonstration, display, exhibit, expo *or* exposition, fair, pageant, performance, presentation, representation, show, spectacle, stampede *Large Canadian exhibitions:* Calgary Stampede, Canadian National Exhibition *or* C.N.E. *(Toronto)*, Pacific National Exhibition *or* P.N.E. *(Vancouver)*

exhilarate *v.* animate, boost, buoy, cheer, delight, elate, enliven, exalt, excite, gladden, inspire, inspirit, invigorate, pep *or* perk *or* pick up, quicken, rejoice, stimulate, thrill, uplift, vitalize *Antonyms:* deject, depress, dispirit, sadden

exhilarating *adj.* breathtaking, electric, elevating, enlivening, exalting, exciting, gladdening, inspiring, intoxicating, invigorating, quickening, rousing, spine-tingling *(Nonformal)*, stimulating, stirring, thrilling, tonic, uplifting, vitalizing

exhilaration *n.* animation, cheerfulness, delight, elation, elevation, euphoria, exaltation, excitement, gaiety, galvanization, gladness, gleefulness, happiness, hilarity, inspiration, invigoration, joyfulness, liveliness, mirth, stimulation, uplift, uproar, vitalization, vivacity *Antonyms:* dejection, depression, despondency, gloom, misery

exhort *v.* advise, appeal, argue for, beseech, bid, call upon, caution, counsel, encourage, enjoin, entreat, goad, insist, persuade, plead, pressure, prompt, propel, spur, stimulate, urge, warn

exhortation *n.* admonition, advice, beseeching, bidding, caution, counsel, entreaty, goading, lecture, persuasion, plea, sermon, warning

exhume *v.* bring to light, dig up, disclose, disentomb, disinter, excavate, resurrect, reveal, uncover, unearth *Antonyms:* bury, entomb, inter

exigency *n.* acuteness, crisis, crossroad, crucible, difficulty, dilemma, distress, emergency, extremity, fix *(Nonformal)*, hardship, jam, juncture, pinch, plight, predicament, problem, quandary, situation, urgency

exigent *adj.* **1.** acute, burning, clamorous, constraining, critical, crucial, crying, imperative, importunate, insistent, pressing, threatening, urgent *Antonyms:* unnecessary, irrelevant, secondary **2.** burdensome, demanding, difficult, exacting, grievous, hard, oppressive, rigorous, severe, stringent, weighty *Antonyms:* easy, light, undemanding, unexacting

exile *n.* **1.** banishment, deportation, diaspora, dispersion, expatriation, expulsion, extradition, migration, ostracism, proscription, separation **2.** deportee, displaced person, émigré, expatriate, expellee, fugitive, nonperson, outcast, outlaw, pilgrim, refugee – *v.* alienate, banish, cast out, deport, displace, drive out, eject, evacuate, expatriate, expel, extradite, ostracize, oust, relegate

exist *v.* abide, be, breathe, continue, endure, happen, last, live, love, move, occur, prevail, remain, stand, stay, subsist, survive, think *Antonyms:* die, disappear, pass away, perish, vanish

existence *n.* **1.** actuality, animation, being, breath, continuance, continuation, duration, endurance, entity, essence, life, permanence, presence, reality, something, subsistence, survival, world **2.** affairs, daily life *or* routine, economy, environment, individuality, lifestyle, method, mode, style, way *Nonformal:* real world, rat race

exit *n.* **1.** *adieu (French)*, departure, evacuation, exodus, farewell, going, goodbye, leave-taking, leaving, retirement, retreat, withdrawal **2.** close, death, demise, expiry **3.** avenue, door, egress, fire escape, gate, hole, opening, outlet, passage out, turnoff – *v.* bid farewell, go, leave, move out, quit, retire, retreat, say goodbye, sign off, split *(Nonformal)*, withdraw *Antonyms:* arrive, enter, make an entrance

exodus *n.* departure, diaspora, emigration, evacuation, exiting, flight, leaving, migration, retirement, retreat, withdrawal

exonerate *v.* absolve, acquit, discharge, dismiss, excuse, exempt, free, justify, liberate, pardon, release, relieve, remit, vindicate

exorbitant *adj.* extravagant, dear, exacting, excessive, expensive, extortionate, extravagant, extreme, high, highway robbery *(Nonformal)*, immoderate, inordinate, outrageous, pricey, prohibitive, shocking, steep, stiff, towering, undue, unreasonable, unwarranted *Antonyms:* cheap, fair, moderate, reasonable

exorcise *v.* cast out, demystify, discharge, dispel, drive out, expel, free of demons, scare out

exotic *adj.* alien, alluring, bizarre, colourful, curious, different, extraordinary, extrinsic, fascinating, foreign, imported, mysterious, outside, rare, romantic, strange, striking, unfamiliar, unusual, way out *(Nonformal) Antonyms:* conventional, familiar, ordinary, pedestrian, plain *Commonly misused:* **erotic**

expand *v.* **1.** amplify, augment, bloat, blow up, bolster, broaden, bulk up, diffuse, dilate, distend, enlarge, extend, fan out, fill out, grow, heighten, increase, inflate, lengthen, magnify, mount, multiply, open up, pad, protract, puff up, spread, stretch, swell, thicken, unfold, unfurl, unravel, upsurge, widen *Nonformal:* beef up, hike, mushroom, slap on *Antonyms:* abbreviate, contract, decrease, reduce, shorten **2.** clarify, define, detail, develop, elaborate, embellish, explicate, explain, flesh out, illuminate, illustrate, treat

expanse *n.* acreage, area, breadth, continuum, field, prairie, space, span, spectrum, spread, stretch, sweep, tract, vista

expansion *n.* **1.** addition, amplification, augmentation, dilation, distension, enlargement, extension, increase, inflation, magnification, swelling **2.** development, evolution, growth, maturation, unfolding

expansive *adj.* **1.** all-embracing, ample, big, broad, commodious, comprehensive, exhaustive, expanding, extensive, far-reaching, great, inclusive, large, thorough, voluminous, wide, wide-ranging, widespread *Antonyms:* bordered, limited, restricted **2.** affable, communicative, demonstrative, extroverted, free, friendly, garrulous, generous, genial, gregarious, gushy *(Nonformal)*, loquacious, open, outgoing, sociable, talkative, unconstrained, uninhibited, unrepressed, unreserved, unrestrained, unsuppressed, warm *Antonyms:* inhibited, reticent, shy **3.** elastic, flexible, rubbery, springy, stretchable, stretching

expatriate *n.* departer, deportee, displaced person, emigrant, émigré, evacuee, exile, expellee, migrant, outcast, refugee – *v.* banish, deport, displace, exile, expel, ostracize, oust, proscribe, relegate, transport

expect *v.* **1.** anticipate, assume, attend, await, bargain for, believe, calculate, conjecture, contemplate, divine, envisage, feel, figure, forecast, foresee, foretell, gather, hope, imagine, look, owe, predict, presume, presuppose, sense, suppose, surmise, suspect, trust, understand **2.** demand, desire, insist, require, want, wish

expectant *adj.* **1.** anticipating, alert, anxious, apprehensive, awaiting, believing, breathless, eager, expecting, hopeful, on tenterhooks, prepared, reliant, trusting, vigilant, waiting, watchful **2.** blessed, expecting, pregnant, with child

expectation *n.* **1.** anticipation, apprehension, expectancy, suspense, wait **2.** chance, likelihood, outlook, possibility, probability, prospect **3.** assurance, belief, confidence, fear, forecast, hope, intention, notion, prediction, promise, reliance, supposition

expediency *n.* **1.** appropriateness, aptness, convenience, desirability, effectiveness, efficiency, expedience, fitness, judiciousness, opportuneness, pragmatism, properness, propitiousness, propriety, prudence, rightness, suitability, timeliness, usefulness, utility **2.** advantage, benefit, gain, helpfulness, profitableness, value, worth

expedient *adj.* advantageous, advisable, appropriate, beneficial, convenient, desirable, effective, feasible, fit, fitting, helpful, judicious, meet, opportune, politic, practicable, practical, pragmatic, profitable, proper, prudent, seasonable, suitable, tactical, timely, useful, wise, worthwhile *Antonyms:* detrimental, harmful, inappropriate, unwise, wrong *Commonly misused:* **expeditious**

expedite *v.* **1.** accelerate, administer, advance, assist, direct, facilitate, hasten, hurry, launch, precipitate, press, promote, quicken, rush, speed, urge *Nonformal:* fast track, railroad, shoot through *Antonyms:* block, curb, delay, obstruct, restrict **2.** consign, deliver, dispatch, forward, give, issue, post, remit, send, transmit

expedition *n.* **1.** campaign, caravan, cruise, crusade, enterprise, excursion, exploration, jaunt, journey, junket, mission, outing, patrol, peregrination, quest, safari, tour, travel, trek, trip, undertaking, voyage **2.** band, crew, force, gathering, group, party, posse, squad, team *Commonly misused:* **excursion**

expeditious *adj.* active, breakneck, brisk, diligent, effective, efficient, fast, fleet, hasty, immediate, instant, nimble, prompt, punctual, quick, rapid, ready, speedy, swift *Antonyms:* dilatory, lackadaisical, laggard *Commonly misused:* **expedient**

expel *v.* **1.** ban, banish, bar, blackball, cast out, chase out, deport, discharge, dismiss, displace, dispossess, drive out, eject, eliminate, evict, exclude, exile, expatriate, fire, kick *or* throw out, oust, proscribe, suspend, turn out *Nonformal:* boot, bounce, bump, can, drum out, send packing *Antonyms:* admit, receive, welcome **2.** belch, defecate, discharge, disgorge, ejaculate, emit, empty, eruct, erupt, evacuate, excrete, exude, pass, remove, spew, upchuck *(Nonformal)*, void, vomit

expend *v.* consume, disburse, dispense, dissipate, exhaust, finish, give, go through, pay *or* shell out, spend, spring for, squander, use up *Nonformal:* blow, splurge *Antonyms:* retain, save, store

expendable *adj.* dispensable, disposable, excess, nonessential, redundant, replaceable, spendable, superfluous, unimportant *Antonyms:* crucial, essential, indispensable, necessary, vital

expense *n.* amount, application, assessment, bottom line, budget, capital, charge, consumption, cost, debit, debt, disbursement, expenditure, figure, investment, liability, loan, mortgage, obligation, outlay, output, overhead, payment, payoff, payroll, price, rate, risk, spending, surcharge, tariff, toll, upkeep

expensive *adj.* costly, dear, excessive, exorbitant, high-priced, immoderate, inordinate, overpriced, pricey, prohibitive, rich, steep, stiff *Nonformal:* big-ticket, highway robbery, sky-high *Antonyms:* bargain, budget, cheap, reasonable

experience *n.* **1.** acquaintance, apprenticeship, background, contact, education, exposure, familiarity, hands-on knowledge, involvement, participation, practicality, reality, training **2.** ability, knowledge, maturity, perspicacity, seasoning, skill, sophistication, understanding, wisdom, worldliness **3.** action, activity, adventure, affair, buzz *(Nonformal)*, encounter, episode, event, happening, incident, occurrence, ordeal, test, trial, trip – *v.* apprehend, behold, encounter, endure, face, feel, go through, have, know, live through, meet, participate in, sample, sense, suffer, sustain, taste, try, undergo

experienced *adj.* accomplished, accustomed, adept, capable, competent, deft, expert, familiar, instructed, knowing, knowledgeable, master, mature, practiced, professional, qualified, rounded, seasoned, skilled, sophisticated, tested, trained, tried, versed, veteran, weathered, well-versed, wise, worldly *Antonyms:* apprentice, green, new, raw

experiment *n.* attempt, enterprise, essay, examination, exercise, experimentation, investigation, measure, observation, operation, procedure, research, scrutiny, search, study, test, trial, trial run, try, undertaking, verification – *v.* analyze, diagnose, examine, explore, investigate, practice with, probe, sample, scrutinize, speculate, study, test, try, venture, verify

experimental *adj.* **1.** advanced, avant-garde, cutting-edge, new, novel **2.** developmental, empirical, experiential, exploratory, test, trial, trial-and-error **3.** pilot, preliminary, preparatory, probationary, provisional, speculative, tentative, theoretical, unproved, untested *Antonyms:* judged, proven, tested

expert *adj.* able, adept, adroit, apt, clever, crack, crafty, deft, dexterous, experienced, facile, handy, knowledgeable, masterly, practiced, professional, proficient, qualified, savvy *(Nonformal)*, schooled, skilful, skilled, trained, virtuoso *Antonyms:* amateurish, bumbling, clumsy, incompetent, untrained – *n.* ace, artist, authority, connoisseur, crackerjack *(Nonformal)*, doyen, guru, journeyman, master, maven, professional, specialist, virtuoso, wizard, wunderkind *(Nonformal) Antonyms:* amateur, apprentice, student

expertise *n.* ability, adroitness, aptitude, aptness, cleverness, command, competence, craft, cunning, deftness, dexterity, expertness, facility, fluidity, ingeniousness, judgment, knowledge, makings, mastery, proficiency, prowess, readiness, savvy *(Nonformal)*, sharpness, skill *Antonyms:* amateurishness, ignorance, inability, ineptness, unproficiency

expiate *v.* appease, atone for, compensate, correct, make amends, rectify, redeem, redress, remedy, square things *(Nonformal)*

expiration *n.* close, death, decease, demise, departure, dying, end, expiry, finish, passing, termination *Antonyms:* beginning, birth, renewal, start

expire *v.* **1.** cease, conclude, depart, die, end, pass away, perish, quit, stop, terminate *Nonformal:* croak, meet one's maker **2.** breathe out, emit, exhale, expel

explain *v.* **1.** analyze, annotate, clarify, clear up, construe, decipher, define, delineate, demonstrate, describe, develop, disclose, elaborate, elucidate, expand, expound, extend, illuminate, rationalize, reveal, simplify, solve, spell out, translate, unfold, unravel, untangle *Antonyms:* confuse, obfuscate, obscure **2.** acquaint, advise, brief, counsel, edify, educate, enlighten, guide, indoctrinate, inform, preach, teach, tell, train, update

explanation *n.* **1.** account, breakdown, brief, clarification, elucidation, exegesis, interpretation, rendition, translation **2.** answer, apology, confession, cover, defence, excuse, gloss, story **3.** details, evidence, history, information, narrative, proof, report, significance, statement **4.** cause, justification, rationale, reason,

explanatory *adj.* allegorical, analytical, annotative, critical, declarative, demonstrative, descriptive, diagrammatic, discursive, elucidative, enlightening, exegetic, exegetical, explicative, expositional, expository, graphic, guiding, hermeneutic, illuminative, illustrative, informative, instructive, interpretive, summary, supplementary

expletive *n.* **1.** curse, cuss word *(Nonformal)*, exclamation, interjection, oath, profanity, swearing, swear word *Antonyms:* benediction, blessing, consecration **2.** augmentation, fat, filler, fluff, frills, gingerbread, padding, redundancy, superfluidity

explicate *v.* clarify, clear up, construe, demonstrate, develop, elaborate, elucidate, enlarge upon, expand, expatiate, explain, expound, illustrate, interpret, untangle

explicit *adj.* absolute, categorical, certain, clear, definite, direct, exact, express, frank, open, patent, plain, precise, specific, stated, straightforward, unambiguous, unequivocal, unqualified, unreserved *Antonyms:* ambiguous, cryptic, obscure, vague *Commonly misused:* **implicit**

explode *v.* **1.** backfire, blast, blow, blow up, bomb, burst, damage, demolish, detonate, discharge, disintegrate, dynamite, erupt, fire, fly open, go off, happen, obliterate, pop *(Nonformal)*, puncture, rupture, shatter, shell, shoot, splinter, thunder **2.** debunk, disclaim, discredit, disprove, refute, show up, sink *(Nonformal)*, undermine *Antonyms:* approve, endorse, support **3.** develop, expand, extend, grow, increase, launch, mushroom, spread, sweep *Commonly misused:* **implode**

exploit *n.* act, adventure, deed, enterprise, feat, performance – *v.* abuse, capitalize on, defraud, employ, fleece, impose upon, manipulate, mine, misuse, play, play on, profit by *or* from, take advantage, use, utilize, work *Nonformal:* bleed, milk, skin, soak

exploration *n.* analysis, examination, expedition, inquiry, inspection, investigation, probe, reconnaissance, research, scrutiny, search, study, survey

explore *v.* **1.** hunt, reconnoitre, roam, scout, search, seek, tour, travel, traverse, trek, wander **2.** analyze, burrow, delve *or* dig *or* inquire into, examine, inspect, investigate, probe, prospect, question, research, scrutinize, sift, survey, test

explosion *n.* **1.** bang, barrage, blast, blowout, bombardment, burst, combustion, concussion, crack, detonation, discharge, dynamiting, firing, flare, fulmination, fusillade, ignition, illumination, percussion, pyrotechnics, rockets, sally, salvo, tear, volley **2.** eruption, outbreak, outburst, shower, spurt, storm **3.** blowup, display, tantrum, throe, venting **4.** burgeoning, escalation, expansion, increase, mushrooming, spread

explosive *adj.* **1.** charged, consequential, controversial, passionate, sensitive, stormy, touchy, violent, volcanic *Nonformal:* hot, live *Antonyms:* dead *(Nonformal)*, meaningless **2.** combustible, dangerous, hazardous, inflammable, perilous, unstable, volatile *Antonyms:* inert, safe – *n.* ammunition, bomb, booby-trap, charge, detonator, dynamite, fireworks, grenade, gunpowder, mine, missile, munition, nitroglycerin, powder, propellant, shell, shot, TNT

exponent *n.* advocate, backer, booster, champion, defender, demonstrator, expositor, expounder, partisan, promoter, propagandist, proponent, protagonist, second, spokesman, spokeswoman, supporter, upholder *Antonyms:* adversary, detractor, opponent

export *n.* commodity, good, merchandise, produce, ware – *v.* consign, convey, freight, haul, move, send out, rail, ship, smuggle, trade, transfer, transport, truck

expose *v.* **1.** endanger, hazard, imperil, jeopardize, lay *or* leave open, make liable *or* vulnerable, risk *Antonyms:* protect, shelter, shield **2.** bare, debunk, disclose, divulge, lay bare, make known, manifest, publish, report, reveal, show, uncover, unfold, unmask, unveil *Antonyms:* conceal, hide, mask, screen **3.** advertise, air, brandish, broadcast, display, exhibit, feature, flaunt, market, parade, present, promote

exposé *n.* disclosure, divulgence, documentary, exposition, exposure, inside story, interpretation, revelation, scandal, unmasking, truth, uncovering

exposed *adj.* **1.** apparent, bare, clear, denuded, disclosed, discovered, displayed, divulged, dug up, evident, exhibited, for show, found out, laid bare, made public, manifest, naked, peeled, revealed, shown, stripped, unconcealed, uncovered, unmasked, unsealed, unveiled, visible *Antonyms:* concealed, covered, hidden, screened **2.** in danger *or* peril, liable, open, prone, sensitive, subject, susceptible, threatened, unprotected, unsheltered, vulnerable

exposition *n.* **1.** account, analysis, annotation, article, comment, commentary, composition, critique, delineation, description, details, discourse, discussion, dissertation, editorial, elucidation, essay, explanation, explication, exposé, expounding, history, illustration, interpretation, monograph, paper, piece, report, review, statement, story, text, theme, thesis, tract, treatise, treatment **2.** bazaar, circus, demonstration, display, exhibition, expo, fair, market, mart, pageant, presentation, production, show, showing, stampede

expostulate *v.* argue, dissuade, object, oppose, plead *or* reason with, point out, protest, remonstrate, urge, warm

exposure *n.* **1.** bareness, nakedness, nudity **2.** liability, susceptibility, vulnerability **3.** acknowledgment, airing, confession, disclosure, display, divulgence, exhibition, exposé, introduction, manifestation, presentation, revelation, uncovering, unmasking, unveiling *Antonyms:* concealment, covering, hiding **4.** advertisement, promotion, publicity, spotlight *Nonformal:* hype, press

expound *v.* **1.** declare, hold *or* set forth, say, state **2.** clarify, describe, elucidate, explain, explicate, flesh *or* spell out, illustrate, interpret

express *adj.* **1.** categorical, certain, clear, clear-cut, deliberate, frank, pointed, unmistakable **2.** definite, distinct, exclusive, particular, precise, singular, specific **3.** accurate, correct, direct, exact, identical, literal, precise **4.** accelerated, direct, fast, high-speed, prompt, quick, rapid, speedy, swift – *v.* **1.** articulate, assert, comment, communicate, construe, convey, declare, delineate, denote, depict, describe, disclose, discourse, divulge, elucidate, enunciate, exhibit, explain, expound, illustrate, indicate, insinuate, intimate, phrase, present, proclaim, pronounce, reveal, say, show, signify, speak, spell, state, suggest, talk, tell, testify, verbalize, voice **2.** distill, extract, force *or* press out, juice, squeeze

expression *n.* **1.** announcement, articulation, assertion, commentary, communication, declaration, definition, delivery, diction, elucidation, emphasis, explanation, interpretation, intonation, locution, mention, narration, pronouncement, remark, rendition, statement, utterance, verbalization, voicing, wording **2.** air, appearance, aspect, cast, character, countenance, face, feature, grimace, grin, look, mien, pout, simper, smile, smirk, sneer, visage **3.** indication, representation, sign, symbol, symbolization, token **4.** adage, aphorism, apothegm, euphemism, maxim, phrase, precept, proverb, saw, saying

expressionless *adj.* blank, dull, empty, impassive, inexpressive, inscrutable, lacklustre, stupid, unemotional, unexpressive, unrevealing, vacant, vacuous, wooden *Nonformal:* deadpan, poker-faced, stone-faced

expressive *adj.* **1.** articulate, communicative, demonstrative, eloquent, **2.** allusive, descriptive, illustrative, indicative, meaningful, pregnant, representative, revelatory, significant, suggestive, symbolic, telling **3.** artistic, dramatic, emotional, forcible, intense, meaningful, moving, passionate, pathetic, poignant, powerful, responsive, significant, spirited, stimulating, stirring, striking, strong, sympathetic, tender, thoughtful, touching, vivid, warm *Antonyms:* blank, cold, dull, empty, vacuous

expressly *adv.* absolutely, categorically, certainly, clearly, decidedly, definitely, distinctly, doubtlessly, easily, explicitly, finally, intentionally, manifestly, obviously, on purpose, outright, particularly, plainly, pointedly, positively, precisely, purposely, specially, specifically, surely, undeniably, unmistakably, unquestionably, without fail

Antonyms: equivocally, implicitly, indefinitely, indirectly, vaguely

expressway *n.* freeway, highway, interstate *(U.S.)*, overpass, parkway, road, toll road, superhighway, turnpike

expropriate *v.* annex, appropriate, assume, commandeer, confiscate, impound, impress, requisition, seize, sequester, take over

expulsion *n.* banishing, boot *(Nonformal)*, debarment, deportment, discharge, dislodgment, dismissal, displacement, dispossession, ejection, eviction, exclusion, exile, expatriation, extrusion, firing, ostracism, ouster, proscription, purge, relegation, removal, separation, suspension

expunge *v.* abolish, annihilate, annul, cancel, cut, delete, destroy, discard, eradicate, erase, exclude, exterminate, extinguish, extirpate, gut, kill, obliterate, raze, scrub, take out, wipe out *Antonyms:* add, append, include

exquisite *adj.* **1.** beautiful, elegant, excellent, flawless, impeccable, incomparable, matchless, outstanding, peerless, perfect, precious, rare, striking, superior **2.** admirable, consummate, deft, meticulous, precise, skilful **3.** cultivated, discriminating, fastidious, fine, refined, sensitive **4.** acute, extreme, intense, keen, overpowering, overwhelming, severe

extant *adj.* actual, alive, contemporary, current, existent, existing, in existence, living, present, real, remaining, subsisting, surviving, undestroyed

extemporaneous *adj.* ad-lib, automatic, casual, expedient, extempore, free, immediate, impromptu, improvised, impulsive, informal, made-up, makeshift, offhand, on-the-spot, spontaneous, unplanned, unprepared, unrehearsed, unstudied *Antonyms:* planned, premeditated, prepared, rehearsed

extemporize *v.* ad-lib, devise, fabricate, fake, improvise, invent, jerry-rig *Nonformal:* do offhand, knock *or* toss off, make up, wing it *Antonyms:* meditate, prepare, study

extend *v.* **1.** amplify, augment, broaden, dilate, elongate, enlarge, expand, heighten, increase, lengthen, magnify, multiply, widen **2.** open, spread out, straighten, stretch, unfold, unfurl, unroll **3.** branch, extrude, jut, project, protrude, reach, span **4.** add to, carry on, continue, develop, drag out, enhance, pad, prolong, protract, supplement *Antonyms:* abbreviate, abridge, condense, contract, shorten **5.** bestow, donate, give, grant, impart, offer, present, proffer, put forth *Antonyms:* recall, recant, withdraw

extension *n.* **1.** addendum, addition, adjunct, supplement **2.** amplification, appendage, augmentation, broadening, development, dilatation, enlargement, expansion, increase, lengthening, production, spreading out, stretching, widening **3.** extent, purview, reach, scope, span, spread, stretch, sweep **4.** allowance, continuation, deferment, drawing out, elongation, prolongation, protraction, time **5.** annex, appendix, arm, block, branch, bulge, ell, projection, protrusion, protuberance, section, segment, set, side, unit, wing

extensive *adj.* **1.** big, boundless, broad, capacious, commodious, expanded, full-scale, huge, immense, indefinite, infinite, large-scale, limitless, long, roomy, sizable, spacious, wide *Antonyms:* confined, constricted, limited, restricted, tight **2.** all-embracing, all-inclusive, complete, comprehensive, exhaustive, major, sweeping, thorough, voluminous **3.** common, commonplace, far-reaching, lengthy, pervasive, prevalent, wide-ranging, widespread

extent *n.* amount, area, bounds, breadth, bulk, capacity, command, compass, degree, dimension, distance, duration, expanse, gamut, grasp, intensity, latitude, leeway, length, limit, magnitude, mass, matter, measure, orbit, proportion, quantity, radius, range, reach, scope, size, space, span, sphere, spread, stretch, sweep, territory, time, tract, vicinity, vista, volume, wideness, width

extenuating *adj.* **1.** defencible, excusable, justifiable, legitimate, warrantable **2.** diminishing, lessening, mitigating, moderating, palliating, qualifying, reducing, whitewashing

exterior *adj.* external, extraneous, extrinsic, foreign, marginal, outdoor, outer, outermost, outlying, outside, outward, peripheral, superficial, surface *Antonyms:* inherent, inside, interior, intrinsic – *n.* **1.** coating, cover, covering, exoskeleton, external, façade, finish, outside, polish, rind, shell, skim, surface, visible part **2.** appearance, aspect, demeanour, deportment, disposition, face, mien, physiognomy

exterminate *v.* abolish, annihilate, blow away *(Nonformal)*, bomb, burn, cancel, destroy, eliminate, eradicate, erase, execute, extinguish, extirpate, kill, liquidate, massacre, murder, nullify, obliterate, raze, slaughter, slay, take *or* wipe out

external *adj.* **1.** apparent, exterior, extraneous, extrinsic, outer, outermost, outside, outward, peripheral, superficial, surface, visible *Antonyms:* inherent, inner, inside, interior **2.** alien, distant, foreign, international *Antonyms:* domestic, internal

extinct *adj.* **1.** cold, defunct, ended, extinguished, gone, inactive, inanimate, quenched, quiescent, quiet, still **2.** dead, deceased, departed, eliminated, exterminated, extirpated, fallen, late, lifeless, lost, passed, terminated, vanished *Antonyms:* living, surviving, thriving

extinguish *v.* abolish, annihilate, blow *or* put out, choke, destroy, douse, drown, eliminate, end, eradicate, erase, expunge, exterminate, kill, obliterate, quench, smother, snuff *or* stamp out, stifle, suffocate, trample

extol *v.* acclaim, applaud, bless, boost, celebrate, commemorate, commend, elegize, eulogize, exalt, glorify, hymn, laud, magnify, praise, push, rave, root, stroke

extort *v.* blackmail, bully, cheat, coerce, demand, elicit, hold up, obtain, wrench, wrest *Nonformal:* bleed, fleece, gouge, milk, pinch, soak, squeeze, sting, swindle, wring

extortion *n.* blackmail, cheating, coercion, compulsion, demand, exaction, force, fraud, oppression, payoff, pressure, protection, racket, shakedown *(Nonformal)*

extra *adj.* **1.** additional, backup, excess, further, leftover, more, reserve, spare, superfluous, supplemental, supplementary, surplus *Antonyms:* fewer, less **2.** above, better, extraordinary, great, improved, new, over, special *Antonyms:* inferior, lower, smaller – *adv.* considerably, especially, exceptionally, extraordinarily, particularly, rarely, remarkably, uncommon, unusually – *n.* accessory, addendum, addition, adjunct, appendage, appurtenance, attachment, bonus, extension, option, perk *(Nonformal)*, perquisite, supplement *Antonyms:* deduction, mulct, penalty

extract *n.* **1.** abstract, citation, clipping, cutting, excerpt, passage, quotation, selection **2.** blood, concentrate, condensation, decoction, distillate, distillation, essence, juice, liquor, sap – *v.* **1.** abridge, abstract, choose, cite, condense, copy, cut out, excerpt, glean, quote, select **2.** bring forth, bring *or* draw *or* eke out, cull, derive, distill, elicit, evoke, exact, extricate, garner, gather, obtain, pick, pluck, pry, reap, remove, separate, squeeze, tear, uproot, withdraw, wrest, wring

extraction *n.* **1.** ancestry, background, birth, blood, derivation, descent, family, lineage, origin, parentage, pedigree, race, stock **2.** abstraction, distillation, drawing, elicitation, evocation, extrication, milking, pulling, removal, separation, squeezing, uprooting, withdrawal, wrenching, wresting

extradite *v.* deliver, deport, give up, release, send away, ship out, surrender, transport, yield

extraneous *adj.* **1.** additional, adventitious, extra, extrinsic, foreign, impertinent, inapplicable, inapposite, inappropriate, irrelevant, marginal, needless, peripheral, pointless, redundant, superfluous, supplementary, unconnected, unessential, unnecessary, unneeded, unrelated, unsuitable, useless *Antonyms:* germane, pertinent, related, relevant **2.** alien, exotic, external, foreign, imported, non-domestic, strange *Antonyms:* domestic, internal, native

extraordinary *adj.* amazing, bizarre, curious, exceptional, inconceivable, incredible, outstanding, peculiar, phenomenal, rare, remarkable, special, strange, stupendous, surprising, terrific, uncommon, unimaginable, unique, unprecedented, unthinkable, unusual, weird, wonderful *Antonyms:* customary, everyday, ordinary, unremarkable, usual

extrapolate *v.* conclude, conjecture, estimate, guess, hypothesize, infer, predict, project, speculate, suppose, surmise

extraterrestrial *adj.* alien, extramundane, otherworldly, unearthly – *n.* alien, E.T., other worlders *Nonformal:* bug-eyed monsters, little green men, Martian, saucer people, spaceman, the greys, the whites, universals, visitors

extravagance *n.* absurdity, excess, exorbitance, expenditures, folly, improvidence, indulgence, intemperance, lavishness, luxury, outrageousness, overindulgence, overspending, profligacy, profusion, recklessness, squander, waste, wastefulness

extravagant *adj.* **1.** excessive, extreme, immoderate, improvident, imprudent, indulgent, lavish, profligate, reckless, unrestrained, wasteful *Antonyms:* conservative, sparing, thrifty **2.** dramatic, elaborate, fanciful, fancy, fantastic, flamboyant, flashy, foolish, garish, gaudy, grandiose, ludicrous, ornate, ostentatious, pretentious, showy, spectacular, theatrical **3.** costly, exorbitant, expensive, extortionate, overpriced, pricey *(Nonformal)*, prohibitive

extravaganza *n.* celebration, display, divertissement, gala, halftime show, musical, pageant, production, show, spectacle, spectacular

extreme *adj.* **1.** deepest, farthest, greatest, highest, longest, maximum, topmost, utmost **2.** endmost, finishing, furthest, last, outermost, remote, terminal **3.** acute, desperate, drastic, exceptional, extraordinary, great, intense, radical, remarkable, serious, severe, sheer, supreme, ultimate, uncommon, unusual, utter **4.** critical, dangerous, dire, final, hazardous, mortal, perilous **5.** absolute, complete, exacting, inflexible, strict, uncompromising **6.** excessive, extravagant, flagrant, immoderate, over-the-top, wild *Antonyms:* inhibited, repressed, restrained – *n.* **1.** apex, crown, head, extremity, maximum, pinnacle, summit, tip, top, ultimate, verge, zenith *Antonyms:* base, bottom, nadir **2.** boundary, end, extent, finish, limits, range, terminus **3.** excess, exorbitance, intemperance, extravagance *Antonyms:* moderation, restraint

extremely *adv.* acutely, awfully, drastically, exceedingly, exceptionally, excessively, exorbitantly, extraordinarily, greatly, highly, hugely, immensely, immoderately, inordinately, intensely, markedly, notably, overly, overmuch, quite, radically, remarkably, severely, strikingly, surpassingly, terribly, terrifically, totally, uncommonly, unduly, utterly, very, violently *Antonyms:* insignificantly, little, moderately, temperately

extremist *n.* agitator, devotee, fanatic, radical, reactionary, revolutionary, terrorist, ultra *or* ultraist, zealot

extremity *n.* **1.** acme, apex, apogee, border, bound, boundary, brim, brink, climax, depth, edge, end, excess, extreme, extremes, frontier, height, limit, margin, nadir, pinnacle, pole, rim, terminus, tip, top, ultimate, verge, zenith **2.** appendage, backside, digit, finger, flipper, foot, hand, head, leg, limb, posterior, toe **3.** adversity, crisis, crucible, danger, difficulty, distress, misfortune, need, poverty, severity, suffering, want

extricate *v.* clear, detach, differentiate, disencumber, disengage, disentangle, extract, free, liberate, loose, release, relieve, remove, separate, spring *(Nonformal)*, withdraw

extrinsic *adj.* **1.** exterior, external, extraneous, outer, outside, outward **2.** alien, exotic, foreign, imported *Commonly misused:* **intrinsic** **3.** superficial, superfluous, trivial, unessential, unimportant

extroverted *adj.* amicable, friendly, gregarious, loquacious, loud, obnoxious, outgoing, sociable, talkative, vocal

extrude *v.* **1.** branch, extend, jet *or* jut *or* stick out, project, protrude, reach, spread, thrust **2.** eject, expel, extract, force *or* push *or* thrust out, press, squeeze

exuberance *n.* **1.** abandon, animation, ardour, bounce, buoyancy, cheerfulness, eagerness, ebullience, effervescence, energy, enthusiasm, excitement, exhilaration, fervour, high spirits, juice, life, liveliness, passion, verve, vigour, vim, vitality, zest, zip *(Nonformal) Antonyms:* depression, despair, lethargy **2.** abundance, affluence, copiousness, effusiveness, exaggeration, excessiveness, lavishness, luxuriance, plenitude, plenty, profusion, richness, superabundance, superfluity

exuberant *adj.* **1.** animated, ardent, bouncy, brash, bubbling, buoyant, eager, ebullient, effervescent, elated, energetic, enthusiastic, excited, exhilarated, frolicsome, high-spirited, lively, passionate, sparkling, sprightly, vigorous, vivacious *Antonyms:* apathetic, dull, lifeless, subdued, unenthusiastic **2.** abundant, affluent, copious, effusive, exaggerated, excessive, fertile, fulsome, lavish, lush, luxuriant, opulent, overflowing, plenteous, plentiful, prodigal, profuse, prolific, rampant, rich, riotous, superabundant, superfluous, teeming

exude *v.* **1.** bleed, discharge, emanate, emit, issue, leak, ooze, secrete, trickle **2.** display, exhibit, give forth, give off, manifest, radiate, show

exult *v.* celebrate, cheer, elate, jubilate, make merry, gladden, glory, praise, rejoice *Commonly misused:* **exalt**

exultant *adj.* delighted, ecstatic, elated, exulting, happy, high, joyous, jubilant, overjoyed, pleased, rejoicing, revelling, transported, triumphant, victorious *Nonformal:* blown away, wowed

eye *n.* **1.** eyeball, peeper *(Nonformal)*, sight organ *Parts of the eye:* aqueous chamber, choroid, conjunctiva sac, cornea, inferior rectus muscles, iris, lens, lower eyelids, optic nerve, pupil, retina, sclera, superior rectus muscles, upper eyelids **2.** gaze, glance, look, observation, scrutiny, sight, view **3.** belief, conviction, discernment, discrimination, estimation, feeling, interpretation, judgment, mind, opinion, perception, perspective, recognition, regard, viewpoint *Nonformal:* spin, take **4.** centre, core, focal point, heart, hub, middle – *v.* check out, consider, contemplate, examine, gape, gaze *or* glance *or* look *or* stare at, inspect, leer, observe *or* regard closely, ogle, peruse, scan, scrutinize, size up, study, survey, take in, view, watch *Nonformal:* eyeball, rubberneck

eyeglasses *n. pl.* glasses, spectacles *Kinds of eyeglasses:* aviator, bifocals, cat, dark, goggles, granny glasses, lorgnette, mirrored, monocle, pincenez, polarized, progressives, safety, sunglasses, trifocals *Nonformal:* shades, specs

eyewitness *n.* beholder, bystander, observer, onlooker, spectator, viewer, witness

fable *n.* **1.** *akhyana (Indian),* allegory, axiom, fantasy, fiction, legend, moral, myth, parable, romance, saga, story, tale *Nonformal:* megillah, yarn *Antonyms:* fact, maxim, truism, truth **2.** fairy tale, falsehood, fib, figment of the imagination, lie, *Nonformal:* claptrap, cock-and-bull story, fish story, hogwash, old chestnut *or* wive's tale, tall story, urban legend, whopper

fabled *adj.* **1.** fabulous, famed, famous, incredible, legendary, mythical, reputed *Antonyms:* concrete, fundamental, pragmatic **2.** concocted, fanciful, fictitious, invented, make-believe, mythological, storied, supposed

fabric *n.* **1.** cloth, covering, fibre, material, stuff, textile *Kinds of natural fabric:* alpaca, Angora, baize, balbriggan, batik, bombazine, bouclé, broadcloth, brocade, buckram, bunting, burlap, calico, cambric, Canadian grey *(Historical),* cashmere, cheesecloth, chiffon, chine, chintz, corduroy, cotton, crepe, cretonne, crinoline, damask, denim, dimity, Donegal tweed, drill, duck, duffel, dungaree, felt, flannel, flannelette, fleece, foulard, gabardine, gingham, gossamer, gunny, haircloth, Harris tweed *(Trademark),* herringbone, hessian, homespun, horsehair, jacquard, jersey, khaki, knit, lace, lamé, lawn, linen, lisle, loden, mackinaw, mackintosh, madras, mat, melton, merino, mesh, mohair, moiré, mousseline, muslin, nankeen, oilcloth, organdy, organza, organzine, oxford, paisley, percale, plaid, plush, poplin, ratiné, raw silk, sackcloth, satin, sateen, seersucker, serge, shantung, sharkskin, silk, stroud, suede, swansdown, tartan, terry cloth, tiffany, toile, towelling, tricot, tulle, tweed, twill, velour, velvet, vicuña, voile, whipcord, wool, worsted *Kinds of synthetic fabric:* acetate, acrylic, double-knit, permanent press, nylon, polyester, leatherette, polypropylene, polyvinyl chloride *or* PVC, rayon, spandex, vinyl, wash-and-wear *Trademarks:* Banlon, Fortrel, Gore-Tex, Lastex, Lurex, Lycra, Orlon, Ultrasuede **2.** craftsmanship, feel, grade, grain, nap, pile, quality, texture, weave, workmanship **3.** building, constitution, configuration, construction, foundation, framework, infrastructure, make-up, organization, stamp, structure

fabricate *v.* **1.** assemble, build, cobble together *or* up, compile, compose, construct, create, erect, fashion, form, formulate, frame, join, make, manufacture, organize, piece together, produce, shape, turn out, whip up *Antonyms:* destroy, dismantle, take apart **2.** concoct, contrive, counterfeit, devise, fake, falsify, feign, fib, forge, fudge, invent, lie, make up, misrepresent, pretend, prevaricate, trump up *Antonyms:* authenticate, certify, validate

fabrication *n.* **1.** assembly, building, construction, creation, erection, manufacture, product, production **2.** concoction, deceit, deception, fable, fake, falsehood, fib, fiction, figment, forgery, invention, lie, myth, smoke, story, untruth *Nonformal:* line, song and dance, yarn

fabulous *adj.* **1**. amazing, astonishing, astounding, awesome, breathtaking, extravagant, fantastic, first-class, great, immense, inconceivable, incredible, marvellous, outrageous, phenomenal, prodigious, remarkable, spectacular, striking, super, superb, terrific, unbelievable, unreal, wonderful *Nonformal:* cool, outtasight, primo, super-duper *Antonyms:* mundane, ordinary, typical **2**. chimerical, concocted, eidetic, fabled, fabricated, feigned, fictitious, hypothetical, invented, legendary, made-up, make-believe, mythic, mythical, storied *Antonyms:* bona fide, certified, verified

façade *n.* **1.** appearance, colour, disguise, face, false front, frontage, guise, illusion, look, mask, masquerade, persona, pretense, shell, semblance, sham, show, window dressing *(Nonformal)* **2.** cladding, exostructure, exterior, facing, front, surface *Kinds of façade:* board and batten, brick, clapboard, glass, ivy, masonry, siding, steel, stone, stucco, veneer, wood

face *n.* **1.** air, appearance, aspect, cast, countenance, demeanor, display, expression, exterior, facet, finish, front, frontage, frontispiece, guise, look, mien, physiognomy, presentation, profile, semblance, show, silhouette, simulacrum, surface, top, visage **2.** audacity, boldness, brass, bravado, effrontery, gall, impudence, nerve *Nonformal:* chutzpah, moxie **3.** authority, dignity, honour, image, prestige, reputation, self-respect, social position, standing, status **4.** camouflage, cover, disguise, façade, mask, pretense **5.** cliff, escarpment, palisade, wall – *v.* **1.** bear, bite the bullet *(Nonformal)*, brave, brook, confront, countenance, deal *or* grapple with, encounter, endure, experience, look at *or* on, meet, resist, stand, stomach, submit, suffer, sustain, tolerate, withstand **2.** cognate, contemplate, eye, observe, realize, ruminate, think about **3.** coat, cover, dress, paint, plaster, polish

faceoff *n.* challenge, competition, heat, match race, showdown – *v.* battle, beard, compete, confront, duel *Nonformal:* go toe-to-toe, butt heads, lock horns, meet eyeball to eyeball, throw down the gauntlet

facet *n.* **1.** angle, appearance, aspect, face, feature, front, phase, plane, side, slant, surface, twist *(Nonformal)* **2.** carving, cut, design, detail, marking, point

facetious *adj.* amusing, blithe, clever, comic, comical, droll, dry, fanciful, farcical, flippant, funny, humorous, ironic, irreverent, jesting, jocular, joshing, kidding, laughable, merry, playful, ridiculous, sarcastic, satirical, smart, tongue- in-cheek, waggish, wisecracking, witty *Antonyms:* earnest, sedate, serious, sober

facile *adj.* **1.** apparent, easy, effortless, obvious, simple, superficial, uncomplicated *Nonformal:* a breeze, child's play, turkey shoot **2.** accomplished, adept, adroit, articulate, deft, dexterous, fluent, glib, hasty, light, practiced, skilful, smooth *Antonyms:* awkward, clumsy, maladroit, unskilled **3.** affable, agreeable, cooperative, easygoing, pliant, tractable, yielding *Antonyms:* immoveable, inflexible, rigid

facilitate *v.* abet, advance, aid, assuage, assist, back, ease, expedite, forward, foster, further, help, mitigate, promote, relieve, simplify, smooth, support, walk through *Nonformal:* grease the wheels, run interference *Antonyms:* delay, encumber, hamper, impede, obstruct

facilitator *n.* agent, aid, assistant, chair, discussion leader, emcee *(Nonformal)*, expediter, framer, helper, implement, implementer, instrument, medium, moderator, organizer, planner, producer, tool, vehicle

facility *n.* ability, aptitude, bent, competence, dexterity, efficiency, expertness, fluency, knack, leaning, poise, proficiency, propensity, quickness, readiness, skill, skilfulness, talent *Antonyms:* ignorance, incompetence, ineptitude

facilities *n.* **1.** accommodations, apparatus, appliances, area, building, complex, edifice, equipment, establishment, materials, means, plant, shop, system, tools, workplace **2.** ability, acquiescence, capacity, complaisance, compliance, pliancy, potential, suppleness, tractability *Antonyms:* rigidity, stiffness, stubbornness **3.** head, john *(Nonformal)*, ladies' or men's room, lavatory, loo *(British)*, toilet, washrooms

facsimile *n.* carbon copy, clone, copy, copycat, double, duplicate, fax, likeness, look-alike, miniature, mirror, photocopy, print, replica, replication, reproduction, scan, transcript, twin, Xerox *(Trademark)* *Nonformal:* dead ringer, ditto, knock-off, spitting image

fact *n.* **1.** actuality, authenticity, basis, certainty, certitude, *fait accompli (French)*, manifestation, matter, reality, substantiation, truth, verity *Antonyms:* conjecture, delusion, fancy, fiction, invention **2.** act, action, circumstance, deed, episode, event, evidence, feature, happening, occurrence, phenomenon, proceeding, transaction **3.** data, datum, detail, information, item, particular, specific, statistic, stat *(Nonformal)*, trifle

faction *n.* **1.** band, bloc, bunch, cabal, cadre, caucus, cell, circle, clan, clique, club, coalition, combine, combo, conclave, confederacy, contingent, coterie, crew, crowd, enclave, group, insiders, junta, offshoot, outfit, partnership, party, pressure group, sect, sector, set, splinter group, team, unit, wing **2.** conflict, disagreement, discord, disharmony, dissension, disunity, division, friction, rebellion, sedition, strife, schism *Antonyms:* affinity, cooperation, harmony

factious *adj.* alienated, belligerent, conflicting, contentious, contumacious, disaffected, disputatious, divisive, fighting, hostile, insubordinate, insurgent, insurrectionary, litigious, malcontent, mutinous, partisan, quarrelsome, rebellious, rival, sectarian, seditious, troublemaking, tumultuous, turbulent, warring *Antonyms:* allegiant, devoted, loyal, pledged *Commonly misused:* **factitious, fractious**

factitious *adj.* affected, artificial, assumed, counterfeit, fabricated, feigned, insincere, invented, mock, premeditated, spurious *Antonyms:* spontaneous, unrestrained *Commonly misused:* **factious**

factor *n.* **1.** catalyst, cause, circumstance, consideration, determinant, influence, means **2.** aspect, cog, component, constituent, element, ingredient, instrument, item, part, part and parcel *(Nonformal)*, portion **3.** agent, aid, bailiff, bankroll, businessperson, commission merchant, consignor, doer, financier, medium, middleperson, proxy, seneschal, steward

factory *n.* assembly *or* production line, business establishment, foundry, mill, manufacturer, manufactory, plant, shop, sweatshop, works, workshop

factotum *n.* general labourer *or* contractor, girl *or* man Friday, handyman, jack-of-all-trades, production assistant, summer student *Nonformal:* gofer, temp

factual *adj.* absolute, accurate, actual, authentic, bona fide, card-carrying, certain, circumstantial, close, correct, credible, descriptive, detailed, exact, faithful, genuine, hard, legitimate, literal, objective, obvious, positive, precise, real, specific, sure-enough *(Nonformal)*, true, unadorned, unbiased, undoubted, unquestionable, valid, veritable *Antonyms:* embellished, fanciful, fictitious, unreal

faculty *n.* **1.** ability, adroitness, aptitude, aptness, bent, capability, capacity, cleverness, dexterity, facility, flair, forte, genius, gift, instinct, intelligence, knack, leaning, penchant, power, proclivity, propensity, property, quality, skill, strength, strong point, talent *Nonformal:* nose, right stuff *Antonyms:* failing, inability, shortcoming, weakness **2.** advisors, department, fellows, instructors, lecturers, members, mentors, pedagogues, personnel, professors *or* profs *(Nonformal)*, researchers, scholars, staff, teachers, tutors, workers

fad *n.* amusement, caprice, conceit, craze, cry, custom, *dernier cri (French)*, fancy, fashion, frivolity, hobby, humour, innovation, mania, mode, passing fancy, passion, quirk, rage, style, trend, vagary, vogue *Nonformal:* fool notion, kick, latest word, newest wrinkle, in thing

fade *v.* **1.** abate, decline, deteriorate, die out, diminish, disappear, disperse, dissipate, dissolve, droop, dwindle, enervate, evanesce, evaporate, flag, languish, lessen, rust away, sink, slack off, taper, tire, vanish, wane, waste away, weaken, wilt, wither *Antonyms:* flourish, prosper, thrive **2.** blanch, bleach, dim, discolour, dull, etiolate, grow dim, lose brightness *or* colour *or* lustre, neutralize, pale, tarnish, tone down, wash out, whiten *Antonyms:* brighten, illuminate, irradiate

faded *adj.* ashen, bleached, dim, dingy, discoloured, dull, etiolated, lustreless, pale, pallid, shabby, shopworn, tattered, threadbare, tired, used, wan, washed out, wasted, worn *Antonyms:* bright, colourful, radiant

fail *v.* **1.** backslide, break down, decline, disappoint, fall, fizzle, flop, flounder, fold, lose, miscarry, miss, slip *Nonformal:* bomb, crash and burn, explode, fall flat *or* short, miss the grade *Antonyms:* accomplish, achieve, deliver, succeed **2.** break, bust, close, crash, default, dishonour, end, fall insolvent, finish, fold, founder, go bankrupt *or* broke *or* under, lose money, terminate *Nonformal:* go belly up, hit the skids, run into the ground *Antonyms:* bloom, flourish, grow, prosper **3.** abandon, abort, back out, desert, discount, disregard, fault, forget, forsake, ignore, neglect, omit, overlook, pass, slight *Antonyms:* complete, finish, fulfill, realize **4.** deteriorate, dissipate, fade, dwindle, languish, lose strength, sicken, wane, weaken, wither

failing *adj.* declining, defeated, deficient, ebbing, faint, falling, feeble, inadequate, insufficient, scant, scanty, scarce, short, shy, unavailing, unsuccessful, wanting, weakening – *n.* defect, deficiency, drawback, error, failure, fault, flaw, frailty, imperfection, infirmity, peccadillo, shortcoming, vice, weakness *Antonyms:* advantage, asset, métier, specialty, strength

failure *n.* **1.** botch, bust, defeat, loss, misadventure, miscarriage, washout, wreck *Nonformal:* flopperoo, shellacking *Antonyms:* success, triumph, victory **2.** bankruptcy, collapse, fiasco, insolvency, loss, write-off *Antonyms:* prosperity, wealth **3.** breakdown, deficiency, deterioration, inadequacy, meltdown **4.** defaulter, derelict, disappointment, dud, fainéant, flop, incompetent, loser, underachiever *Nonformal:* also-ran, bum, good-for-nothing, lemon, slider

faint *adj.* **1.** breathless, delicate, dizzy, enervated, exhausted, faltering, fatigued, feeble, fragile, light-headed, pale, weak, woozy *(Nonformal) Antonyms:* energetic, hale, hearty **2.** deadened, distant, far-off, half-heard, hushed, imperceptible, inaudible, indistinct, light, low, muffled, murmuring, muted, muttering, quiet, scarcely-heard, slight, soft, thin, whispered *Antonyms:* bright, clear, loud, thunderous **3.** afraid, cowardly, fearful, frightened, intimidated, nervous, terrified, tenuous, timid, timorous *Antonyms:* brash, brave, courageous, lion-hearted – *n.* blackout, collapse, coma, dizziness, insensibility, knockout, stupor, swoon, unconscious, vertigo – *v.* black *or* pass out, collapse, drop, fade, fall, keel over, languish, succumb, swoon, weaken

fainthearted *adj.* afraid, cowardly, craven, dismayed, fearful, frightened, intimidated, nervous, pusillanimous, scared, terrified, timid, timorous, upset *Antonyms:* bold, brave, dauntless, intrepid, valiant

fair *adj.* **1.** equal, evenhanded, honourable, impartial, just, lawful, legitimate, neutral, nonpartisan, objective, reasonable, square, straight, unbiased, unprejudiced *Antonyms:* bigoted, discriminatory, one-sided **2.** blanched, bleached, blond, blonde, creamy, fair-haired, fair-skinned, flaxen-haired, light, pale, pearly, silvery, snowy, tow-haired, tow-headed, whitish **3.** adequate, average, common, commonplace, decent, indifferent, mediocre, medium, moderate, okay *(Nonformal)*, ordinary, passable, reasonable, respectable, satisfactory, tolerable, usual **4.** balmy, bright, calm, clear, clement, dry, favourable, fine, mild, placid, pleasant, sunny, tranquil, unclouded **5.** attractive, beautiful, charming, comely, graceful, handsome, pretty, winsome *Antonyms:* homely, ugly, unsightly – *n.* bazaar, carnival, celebration, centennial, display, exhibit, exhibition, exposition, fall fair, festival, fête, gala, market, observance, occasion, pageant, show, spectacle

fair-haired *adj.* **1.** adored, cherished, choice, chosen, favourite, pet, precious, preferred, prized, selected, treasured **2.** blond, blonde, creamy, flaxen, light

fairly *adv.* **1.** deservedly, equitably, honestly, honourably, impartially, justly, objectively, properly, reasonably **2.** adequately, enough, kind of, moderately, pretty well, quite, rather, reasonably, somewhat, tolerably

fairness *n.* candour, charity, civility, consideration, courtesy, decency, duty, equitableness, equity, fair-mindedness, fair play, good faith, goodness, honesty, honour, humanity, impartiality, integrity, justice, moderation, open-mindedness, propriety, rationality, reasonableness, righteousness, rightfulness, rightness, seemliness, suitability, tolerance, truth, uprightness, veracity

fairy *n.* demon, familiar, genius, spirit *Kinds of fairy:* bogey, brownie, bugbear, dwarf, elf, fay, genie, gnome, goblin, gremlin, imp, kelpie, kobold, leprechaun, mermaid, nix, nymph, peri, pixie, Puck, Redcap, siren, sprite, sylph, Tinker Bell, wight

fairy tale *n.* allegory, cock-and-bull-story, exaggeration, fable, fantasy, fib, fiction, invention, myth, narration, narrative, parable, romance, saw, story, tale *Nonformal:* tall tale, yarn

faith *n.* **1.** assurance, certainty, confidence, conviction, credence, dependence, stock, store, sureness, trust, truth *Antonyms:* doubt, rejection, scepticism **2.** belief, canon, church, communion, confession, credo, creed, denomination, doctrine, dogma, doxy, gospel, orthodoxy, persuasion, piety, piousness, principle, profession, religion, revelation, teaching, tenet, theism, theology, worship *Antonyms:* agnosticism, atheism, denial **3.** allegiance, commitment, dedication, faithfulness, fealty, fidelity, loyalty,

faithful *adj.* **1.** conscientious, constant, dependable, devoted, devout, dutiful, earnest, honest, honourable, incorruptible, loving, loyal, obedient, pious, reliable, religious, resolute, reverent, sincere, staunch, stalwart, steadfast, trustworthy, unswerving, unwavering, upright *Antonyms:* disloyal, fickle, traitorous **2.** accurate, authentic, exact, genuine, literal, precise, strict, true, truthful, uncompromising, veracious *Antonyms:* fake, false, fictionalized, romanticized

faithless **1.** *adj.* capricious, changeable, corruptible, deceitful, dishonest, disloyal, disobedient, dubious, false, insincere, perfidious, recidivous, traitorous, treacherous, unfaithful, unreliable, untrue, untrustworthy, untruthful, wavering, wicked *Nonformal:* double-dealing, two-timing **2.** agnostic, atheistic, cynical, doubtful, godless, infidel, nonbelieving, sceptical *Antonyms:* devout, pious, religious

fake *adj.* affected, artificial, assumed, bastard, bogus, concocted, counterfeit, fabricated, false, fictitious, forged, fraudulent, imitation, invented, make-believe, mock, pretended, pseudo *(Nonformal)*, reproduced, simulated, spurious *Antonyms:* actual, authentic, bona fide, genuine, legitimate – *n.* bluff, copy, counterfeit, deception, fabrication, forgery, fraud, hoax, imitation, imposter, pretense, reproduction, sham, sleight, swindle *Nonformal:* moose quack *or* pasture, phoney, plant, scam, spoof *Antonyms:* genuine article, real thing, truth – *v.* **1.** act, bluff, cheat, copy, counterfeit, disguise, fabricate, feign, forge, pretend, sham, simulate **2.** ad-lib, extemporize, improvise, invent, wing it *(Nonformal)*

fall *n.* **1.** descent, dip, dive, drop, freefall, nose dive, plunge, slip, spill, tumble *Nonformal:* belly-flop, header, wipe out **2.** decline, declivity, grade, hill, pitch, slant, slope *Antonyms:* ascent, climb, rise **3.** abasement, cut, decrease, degradation, deterioration, diminution, downgrade, ebb, lessening, lowering, recession, reduction, sag, slump **4.** breakdown, collapse, death, defeat, destruction, disaster, downfall, failure, loss, ruin, submission, surrender, Waterloo **5.** autumn, harvest *or* harvest time, Indian summer **6.** err, fault, *felix culpa (Latin)*, fortunate fall, lapse, sin, transgression – *v.* **1.** cascade, come-a-cropper *(Nonformal)*, crash, descend, dip, dive, flop, nose-dive, plummet, plunge, sink, slip, stumble, topple, totter, trip, tumble **2.** bend, capitulate, cave *(Nonformal)*, collapse, defer, give in, go under, kneel, lower, prostrate, settle, stoop, submit, succumb, surrender, yield **3.** decline, decrease, depreciate, die, diminish, drag, dwindle, ebb, fade, lessen, perish, recede, resign, slump, subside, wane **4.** arise, befall, chance, come about, evolve, happen, occur, take place **5.** be suspended, dangle, drape, droop, hang **6.** come, flow, go, move, pass, proceed **7.** drop *or* fall away, slant, slope, tilt

fallacious *adj.* beguiling, deceptive, deluding, delusive, erroneous, false, fraudulent, illogical, illusory, incorrect, invalid, irrational, misleading, mistaken, sophistic, spurious, unfounded, ungrounded, unreasonable, unsound, untenable, untrue, wrong *Nonformal:* bum, off, phoney, way off *Antonyms:* authentic, correct, genuine, right, true

fallacy *n.* casuistry, delusion, error, faulty reasoning, flaw, heresy, illogicalness, illusion, inconsistency, incorrectness, invalidity, misapprehension, miscalculation, misconception, misinterpretation, mistake, mistaken belief, non sequitur, paralogism, sophism, sophistry, speciousness, unsoundness, untruth *Antonyms:* accuracy, fact, reality, truth

fallen *adj.* **1.** corrupted, decayed, disgraced, erring, impure, lapsed, postlapsarian, prodigal, ruined, spotted, wanton, wayward *Antonyms:* innocent, pure **2.** brought down, collapsed, conquered, defeated, overthrown, undone, vanquished **3.** dead, deceased, killed, lost, mortal, perished, slain, slaughtered

fallible *adj.* careless, errant, error-prone, human, imperfect, mortal, open to error *or* question, uncertain, unreliable, untrustworthy, weak *Antonyms:* faultless, impeccable, perfect, sound

fallout *n.* aftereffect, aftermath, aftershock, backlash, by-product, conclusion, consequence, debris, outcome, reaction, repercussion, result, trail, wake

fallow *adj.* dormant, idle, inactive, inert, neglected, quiescent, resting, slack, undeveloped, unplanted, unprepared, unproductive, unseeded, unsown, untilled, unused, vacant, virgin *Antonyms:* fertile, flourishing, thriving, verdant

false *adj.* **1.** apocryphal, casuistic, distorted, erroneous, fallacious, fanciful, fictitious, illusive, imaginary, inaccurate, incorrect, inexact, invalid, misrepresentative, mistaken, sophistical, specious, unfounded, untruthful, wrong *Antonyms:* correct, exact, true **2.** adulterated, artificial, bastard, bogus, contrived, copied, counterfeit, ersatz, fabricated, fake, feigned, forged, fraudulent, hollow, imitation, made-up, make-believe, manufactured, mock, ostensible, pretend, seeming, sham, so-called, *soi-disant (French)*, spurious, substitute, synthetic, trumped up, unreal, unsound, untrue *Nonformal:* phoney, pseudo *Antonyms:* authentic, genuine, true, valid **3.** beguiling, corrupt, crooked, cunning, deceitful, deceiving, deceptive, devious, dishonest, dishonourable, duplicitous, faithless, false-hearted, hypocritical, insincere, lying, mendacious, misleading, perjured, roguish, traitorous, treacherous, underhanded, unfaithful, untrustworthy, wicked *Nonformal:* double-dealing, shady, sharp, two-faced *Antonyms*: devoted, faithful, loyal, sincere, trustworthy

falsehood *n.* canard, cover-up, deceit, deception, dishonesty, distortion, equivocation, fable, fabrication, fallacy, falseness, falsity, fiction, figment, fraud, fraudulence, hoax, infidelity, lie, mendacity, perfidy, pretense, prevarication, sham, story, untruthfulness *Nonformal:* fish story, line, tall tale, whopper, yarn *Antonyms:* actuality, axiom, fact, truth

falsely *adv.* basely, crookedly, deceitfully, dishonestly, dishonourably, disloyally, faithlessly, knavishly, maliciously, roguishly, traitorously, treacherously, unscrupulously

falsify *v.* **1.** adulterate, alter, belie, change, contort, contradict, counterfeit, deceive, distort, dress up, embroider, exaggerate, fake, frame, fudge, gloss, lie, misquote, misrepresent, pervert, prevaricate, tamper with, trump up, twist, warp *Nonformal:* cook, doctor, pencil-whip, salt **2.** contravene, debunk, deride, disprove, invalidate, rebut, refute

falter *n.* hesitation, pause, quaver, stammer, stutter, uncertainty – *v.* **1.** demur, hang back, hem and haw *(Nonformal)*, hesitate, lose courage, pause, reconsider, vacillate, waver *Antonyms:* sign up, step forward, volunteer **2.** lurch, stagger, stumble, teeter, wobble *Antonyms:* prance, step lively, stride **3.** come a-cropper *(Nonformal)*, deteriorate, die, fade, fall back, flounder, give way, lose momentum, weaken *Nonformal:* drop the ball, fluff *Antonyms:* advance, move forward, progress

fame *n.* acclaim, acclamation, acknowledgment, celebrity, credit, distinction, *éclat (French)*, elevation, eminence, esteem, estimation, exaltation, favour, glory, greatness, heyday, honour, illustriousness, immortality, laurels, lustre, note, notoriety, popularity, preeminence, prominence, public regard, rank, recognition, regard, renown, reputation, repute, splendour, standing, stardom, superiority *Nonformal:* drawing power, everyone's fifteen minutes *Antonyms:* disgrace, disrepute, ignominy, infamy, obscurity

familial *adj.* ancestral, congenital, connate, connected, genealogical, genetic, hereditary, inherited, innate, intrinsic, kindred, lineal, maternal, matriarchal, paternal *Antonyms:* alien, extrinsic, foreign

familiar *adj.* **1.** abreast, acquainted, apprised, *au courant (French)*, aware, briefed, cognizant, conscious, conversant, informed, knowledgeable, mindful, up-to-date *Nonformal:* clued-in, in the know, plugged in, savvy, up to speed *Antonyms:* benighted, ignorant, unaware **2.** accepted, accustomed, average, common, commonplace, conventional, current, customary, demotic, established, everyday, frequent, general, generic, habitual, household, known, mundane, natural, normal, ordinary, pedestrian, perennial, popular, prevalent, public, quotidian, recognizable, regular, repeated, routine, settled, solid, standard, steady, stock, traditional, typical, unexceptional, unremarkable, usual, vernacular, well-known, workaday *Antonyms:* bizarre, outlandish, uncommon, unusual **3.** a pro *(Nonformal)*, *au fait (French)*, experienced, practiced, skilled **4.** affable, amicable, comfortable, cordial, cozy, easy, free-and-easy, friendly, genial, gregarious, homey, neighbourly, open, relaxed, sociable *Nonformal:* chummy, thick, tight *Antonyms:* aloof, cold, detached, distant , officious, recherché, unorthodox **5.** arrogant, bold, forward, informal, insolent, obnoxious, unconstrained *Nonformal:* brassy, cheeky, in your face – *n.* **1.** demon, fairy, ghost, goblin, gremlin, imp, pet, servant, spirit, sprite **2.** best friend, bro *(Nonformal)*, buddy, chum, guardian angel, intimate *See also:* **fairy**

familiarity *n.* **1.** awareness, cognition, comprehension, experience, feel, grasp, know-how, knowledge, sense, understanding *Antonyms:* ignorance, inexperience **2.** acquaintance, closeness, ease, fellowship, freedom, friendliness, friendship, gregariousness, informality, intimacy, naturalness, openness, sociability, unceremoniousness **3.** boldness, cheekiness, forwardness, impertinence, impudence, insolence, liberty, undue presumption *or* license *Antonyms:* constraint, decorum, distance, formality

familiarize *v.* acclimatize, accustom, acquaint, adapt, coach, condition, enlighten, habituate, inform, instruct, inure, learn, orientate, prime, school, season, train, use

family *n.* **1.** ancestors, ancestry, birth, blood, brethren, brood, children, clan, descendants, descent, dynasty, extraction, folk, forebears, forefathers, genealogy, generations, house, household, ilk, inheritance, in-laws, issue, kin, kindred, kinship, line, lineage, menage, network, offspring, parentage, paternity, pedigree, people, progenitors, progeny, relations, relatives, siblings, tribe **2.** branch, category, class, designation, division, genre, genus, group, grouping, kind, section, species, subdivision

famine *n.* dearth, destitution, drought, hunger, lack, misery, need, paucity, poverty, scarcity, shortage, sorrow, starvation, want

famished *adj.* appetitive, empty, hollow, hungering, hungry, ravenous, starved, starving, voracious *Nonformal:* peckish, wolfish *Antonyms:* full, sated, satiated

famous *adj.* acclaimed, applauded, august, brilliant, celebrated, conspicuous, distinguished, elevated, eminent, excellent, extraordinary, foremost, honoured, illustrious, imposing, influential, leading, lionized, memorable, much-publicized, notable, noted, noteworthy, notorious, outstanding, peerless, popular, powerful, preeminent, prominent, recognized, remarkable, renowned, reputable, signal, well-known *Nonformal:* big-time, star *Antonyms:* forgotten, obscure, unexceptional

fan *n.* **1.** addict, adherent, admirer, aficionado, amateur, devotee, enthusiast, fanatic, follower, frequenter, lover, patron, rooter, supporter, zealot *Nonformal:* buff, deadhead, freak, groupie **2.** air conditioner, blower, palm leaf, propeller, vane, ventilator, windmill – *v.* **1.** aerate, air-condition, air-cool, blow, cool, refresh, ruffle, stir, ventilate, winnow **2.** expand, expose, flare, layout, open up, shuffle, spread, whip through **3.** arouse, excite, exhort, incite, stir up, urge **4.** fail, miss, strike out *Nonformal:* draw a blank, drop the ball, whiff

fanatic *n.* activist, addict, devotee, enthusiast, extremist, fiend, fool, maniac, militant, radical, ultraist, visionary, zealot *Nonformal:* demon, freak, keener

fanatical *adj.* **1.** burning, devoted, enthusiastic, extreme, fervent, feverish, fiery, frenetic, frenzied, heated, hotheaded, hysterical, immoderate, infatuated, monomanical, obsessed, overzealous, passionate, rabid, zealous *Antonyms:* aloof, cool, detached, disinterested **2.** biased, bigoted, dogmatic, intolerant, narrow gauge *(Nonformal)*, narrow-minded, opinionated, partisan, prejudiced, single-minded, xenophobic **3.** hardcore, headstrong, intransigent, incorrigible, obstinate, stubborn, uncompromising, unreasonable,

fanaticism *n.* **1.** bias, bigotry, hatred, intolerance, prejudice, rage, single-mindedness **2.** dedication, devotion, extremism, frenzy, infatuation, madness, mania, obsessiveness, overenthusiasm, passion, zealotry

fanciful *adj.* **1.** chimerical, dreamlike, fairy-tale, fantastic, fictional, fictitious, illusory, imaginary, imagined, mythical, unreal, unsubstantial **2.** absurd, bizarre, capricious, curious, eccentric, extravagant, fabulous, grotesque, imaginative, incredible, preposterous, whimsical *Antonyms:* conventional, ordinary, pedestrian **3.** imaginative, innovative, inventive, new, original, quixotic, romantic, unheard of, visionary

fancy *adj.* adorned, baroque, beautiful, bedecked, complicated, decorated, decorative, deluxe, elaborate, elegant, embellished, extravagant, florid, frilly, gaudy, intricate, lavish, ornamental, ornamented, ornate, ostentatious, resplendent, rich, rococo, showy, special, spiffy *(Nonformal)*, sumptuous, unusual *Antonyms:* modest, paltry, plain, simple, unadorned, understated – *n.* **1.** chimera, daydream, dream, fantasy, fata morgana, figment, hallucination, illusion, imagination, mirage, reverie, vision **2.** caprice, extravagance, impulse, inclination, liking, notion, pleasure, whim, yen *Antonyms:* aversion, disinclination, dislike – *v.* **1.** believe, conceive, conjecture, create, dream up, envisage, envision, fantasize, imagine, picture, realize, think up, visualize **2.** conjecture, expect, figure, guess, presume, reckon, suppose, surmise, think **3.** crave, covet, desire, hanker, lean toward, like, love, pine for, prefer, want, yearn *Antonyms:* abhor, dislike, hate, loathe

fanfare *n.* bustle, cheering, commotion, demonstration, display, flourish, fuss, parade, pomp, show, trumpeting *Nonformal:* ballyhoo, hoopla, hype, whoop-de-do

fantasize *v.* daydream, dream, envision, hallucinate, imagine, play with the idea, project oneself, star gaze, speculate, visualize, wonder about *Nonformal:* blue sky, muse, pipe dream, trip out, woolgather

fantastic *adj.* **1.** absurd, bizarre, capricious, exaggerated, extravagant, fanciful, freakish, grotesque, illusory, imaginary, impractical, impulsive, irrational, ludicrous, odd, phantasmagoric, quaint, ridiculous, strange, whimsical *Nonformal:* flaky, off the wall *Antonyms:* factual, mundane, normal, ordinary, realistic **2.** beyond belief, brilliant, excellent, generous, good, great, incredible, marvelous, splendid, wonderful *Nonformal:* cool, gear, splendiferous **3.** enormous, extreme, massive, monstrous, monumental, overwhelming, prodigious, stupendous, towering, tremendous

fantasy *n.* **1.** apparition, appearance, chimera, delusion, dream, fabrication, fancy, fata morgana, fool's paradise, hallucination, illusion, image, imagination, invention, mirage, pipe dream, reverie, trip *(Nonformal)*, vagary, vision *Antonyms:* fact, reality, verity **2.** fantasia *(Music)*, legend, myth, romance, story, tale, theme

far *adj.* afar, distant, faraway, far-flung, far-off, far-out, far-removed, farther, further, good ways, outlying, out-of-the-way, remote, removed, to hell and gone *(Nonformal) Antonyms:* adjacent, adjoining, bordering, close, near – *adv.* **1.** considerably, decidedly, extremely, greatly, incomparably, much, notably, quite, significantly, somewhat, truly, very, very much **2.** a good *or* long way off, far off, not there, off, wide, wide of the mark

faraway *adj.* **1.** distant, far, far-flung, far-off, far-removed, outlying, remote, removed, upcountry *Nonformal:* off island, out and about **2.** absent-minded, absorbed, abstracted, detached, distracted, inattentive, lost, oblivious, preoccupied **3.** barely perceptible, faint, indistinct, muted

farce *n.* **1.** broad comedy, burlesque, camp, caricature, comedy, *commedia dell'arte (Italian)*, exaggeration, parody, satire, skit, slapstick, theatre of the absurd, travesty **2.** absurdity, buffoonery, horseplay, joke, ludicrousness, mockery, nonsense, play, ridiculousness, sham *Antonyms:* ceremony, pomp, solemnity *See also:* **comedy, drama**

farcical *adj.* absurd, amusing, campy, comic, comical, derisory, diverting, droll, funny, laughable, ludicrous, nonsensical, outrageous, preposterous, ridiculous, risible, slapstick, stupid, theatrical

fare *n.* **1.** admission, charge, check, expense, pass, payment, price, tariff, ticket, token, toll **2.** customer, passenger, rider, traveller **3.** diet, consumables, eatables, food, meal, menu, provision, rations, table d'hôte, victuals – *v.* accomplish, act, conduct oneself, do, get along *or* on, handle, happen, make out, perform, proceed, result, turn out

farewell *adj.* closing, concluding, departing, final *or* last leaving, parting, resignation, summary – *interj. aloha (Hawaiian), auf wiedersehen (German)*, best wishes *or* my best, bon voyage, *do widzenia (Polish), farväl (Swedish)*, God be with you *or* goodbye, God speed you *or* Godspeed, *hamba kahle (Zulu)*, peace be with you, *Sayonara (Japanese), shalom (Hebrew), vaarwel (Dutch) French: à bien tôt, adieu, au revoir, bon voyage Italian: arrivederci, ciao Spanish: adios, hasta la vista or mañana Nonformal:* ba-bye, catch you later, I'm history, next time, *salut (Quebec)*, see you, so long, taut sails, ta-ta *(British)*, ta-ta for now *or* T.T.F.N., toodle-tee-doo – *n.* **1.** departure, goodbye, leave-taking, parting, salutation, send off **2.** final curtain *or* round, finish, last call *or* harrah, swan song, validiction

far-fetched *adj.* bizarre, doubtful, dubious, fantastic, forced, illogical, implausible, improbable, inconsequential, incredible, laboured, preposterous, remote, strained, strange, unbelievable, unconvincing, unlikely, unnatural, unrealistic *Nonformal:* fishy, hard-to-take, hokey *Antonyms:* acceptable, credible, plausible, probable

farm *n.* acreage, belt, claim, croft, estate, farmstead, field, grassland, holding, homestead, land, manor, meadow, nursery, orchard, pasture, patch, ranch, soil, station, steading, territory, tract, vineyard *Historical:* bush farm, ribbon farm, seigniory – *v.* **1.** crop, cultivate, dress, garden, graze, grow, harrow, harvest, homestead, husband, landscape, look after, plant, plow, produce crops, raise, ranch, reap, run, seed, share crop, sow, superintend, tend, till, work **2.** contract, job out, lease, let, rent, subcontract

farmer *n.* agriculturalist, agronomist, bucolic, crofter, cropper, cultivator, depot farmer *(Historical)*, fruit-grower, gardener, gleaner, grazer, grower, habitant, harvester, homesteader, horticulturist, planter, plowman, producer, rancher, ranchman, rustic, sharecropper, stockperson, yeoman *Nonformal:* plow jockey, stubble-jumper

farming *n.* agriculture, agronomy, aquaculture, breeding, crop-raising, cultivation, culture, feeding, fertilizing, gardening, gleaning, grazing, growing, harvesting, homesteading, husbandry, hydroponics, landscaping, managing, ranching, reaping, seeding, sharecropping, soil culture, threshing, tillage

far-out *adj.* avant-garde, bizarre, creative, daring, experimental, exploratory, extreme, imaginative, innovative, new, novel, original, outré, progressive, radical, uncommon, unique, unorthodox *Nonformal:* off the wall, wacky, wired *Antonyms:* banal, common, traditional

farrago *n.* conglomerate, gallimaufry, hash, helter-skelter, hodgepodge, jumble, medley, melange, melting pot, mishmash, mixture, muddle, potpourri, salmagundi *Nonformal:* olla-podrida, unholy mess

far-reaching *adj.* broad, consequential, considerable, epochal, eventful, extensive, influential, loaded *(Nonformal)*, momentous, portentous, significant, substantial, transcendental, universal, weighty *Antonyms:* insignificant, paltry, trivial

farsighted *adj.* **1.** farseeing, hypermetropic *Antonyms:* blind, myopic, nearsighted, shortsighted **2.** acute, canny, cautious, clairvoyant, discerning, judicious, level-headed, perceptive, politic, prescient, provident, prudent, sagacious, sage, shrewd, visionary, well-balanced, wise

farther *adj.* inaccessible, off and beyond, out *or* over there, over yonder – *adv.* away, beyond, distantly, faraway, far-off, further, longer, remotely, yonder

farthest *adj.* farthermost, furthest, last, lattermost, outermost, outmost, remotest, to hell and gone *(Nonformal)*, ultimate, utmost

fascinate *v.* absorb, allure, animate, arouse, attract, awe, beguile, captivate, charm, delight, draw, enamour, enchant, engross, enrapture, enslave, ensnare, enthral, entice, excite, hook *(Nonformal)*, hypnotize, infatuate, intoxicate, intrigue, invite, kindle, lure, mesmerize, obsess, rivet, seduce, spellbind, stimulate, stir, tantalize, tempt, thrill, titillate, transfix *Antonyms:* alienate, disenchant, disgust, nauseate, repel, repulse

fascinated *adj. aux anges (French)*, bedazzled, dazzled, smitten, transported *Nonformal:* driven out of one's mind, turned on, wowed *Antonyms:* detached, indifferent, uninterested *See also:* **fascinate**

fascinating *adj.* addictive, alluring, bewitching, captivating, charming, compelling, delectable, enchanting, engaging, engrossing, enticing, glamorous, gripping, interesting, intriguing, irresistible, page-turning *(Nonformal)*, ravishing, riveting, seductive, siren, spellbinding *Antonyms:* annoying, boring, bothersome, insufferable, tedious, tiresome

fascination *n.* **1.** allurement, animal magnetism, captivation, enthrallment, enticement, obsession **2.** charm, enchantment, magic, piquancy, power, sorcery, spell, trance, witchcraft

fascism *n.* absolutism, autocracy, despotism, dictatorship, military *or* police state, one-party system, totalitarianism, tyranny

fashion *n.* **1.** air, attitude, behaviour, convention, custom, demeanour, deportment, formula, habit, manner, method, mien, mode, *modus operandi (Latin)*, mores, observance, order, pattern, practice, precedent, prevalence, procedure, style, system, technique, tendency, tone, usage, way, wont **2.** craze, *dernier cri (French)*, fad, furor, look, taste, trend, vogue *Nonformal:* bandwagon, in thing, last word, latest, newest-wrinkle, rage – *v.* **1.** build, construct, create, cut, design, devise, dream up, erect, fabricate, forge, form, frame, make, manufacture, model, mould, plan, plot, produce, sculpt *Nonformal:* knock *or* throw together, pump *or* turn out **2.** accommodate, adapt, adjust, fit, shape, suit, tailor, work

fashionable *adj.* **1.** contemporary, current, faddish, favoured, in style *or* vogue, modern, modish, new, newfangled, popular, prevailing, trendy, upscale, up-to-date, up-to-the-minute, well-liked *Nonformal:* chichi, hot, in, last word, latest, latest thing, mod, now, with it *Antonyms:* dated, frumpy, obsolete, outmoded, unpopular **2.** chic, dashing, rakish, smart, stylish, swank, swish – *n.* clotheshorse, fashion victim, man-about-town, slave to fashion, smart set *(Nonformal)*, trendsetter *French:* mondain, mondaine

fashioned *adj.* assembled, cobbled together, crafted, created, fixed, forged, formed, framed, made, modeled, moulded, sculpted, shaped, tailored

fast *adj.* **1.** accelerated, breakneck, brisk, dashing, expeditious, flashing, fleeting, flying, hasty, hurried, mercurial, quick, racing, rapid, speedy, swift, winged *Nonformal:* chop chop, snappy, wham-bam *Antonyms:* dilatory, leisurely, plodding, slow **2.** agile, adept, adroit, astute, bright, clever, ingenious, nimble, quick-witted, sharp *Antonyms:* backward, slow-witted, vacuous **3.** firm, impregnable, permanent, secure, stable, tight *Antonyms:* feeble, tenuous, unstable, wobbly **4.** close, constant, faithful, staunch, steadfast *Antonyms:* intermittent, on again off again, rocky *(Nonformal)* **5.** bawdy, debauched, easy, flirtatious, lascivious, lecherous, lewd, licentious, loose, lustful, promiscuous, rakish, salacious, wanton – *adv.* **1.** expeditiously, flat-out, hastily, hurriedly, instanter, now, posthaste, promptly, quickly, rapidly, speedily, *subito (Italian)*, swiftly, this minute, *tout de suite (French) Nonformal:* double-quick, lickety-split, pronto *Antonyms:* gingerly, idly, leisurely, slowly **2.** deeply, firmly, fixedly, securely, solidly, soundly, steadfastly, tightly – *n.* abstention, abstinence, cleansing, diet, fasting, purification, Ramadan – *v.* abstain, deny oneself, diet, famish, forbear, go hungry, refrain, starve

fasten *v.* **1.** affix, anchor, belt, bind, bolt, bond, brace, catch, cement, chain, close, connect, couple, fix, glue, grip, hold, hook, join, link, mortise, nail, rivet, screw, secure, set, solder, stick, tack on, tie, truss, unite, weld *Antonyms:* free, loosen, sever **2.** adhere, attach, cleave, clench, cling, glom onto *(Nonformal)*, hitch, hold *or* latch onto, moor, tag **3.** direct, orient, steer, watch *Nonformal:* eye, eyeball, goggle, oogle, rubberneck **4.** ascribe, associate with, attribute, blame, chalk up to, impute, lay on

fastening *n.* affixing, attachment, fixing *Some kinds of fastening devices:* bar, bolt, brace, buckle, button, catch, chain, clamp, clasp, clincher, clip, dowel, handcuffs, hasp, hook, hook and eye, latch, lock, nail, padlock, peg, pin, rivet, rope, screw, snap, spike, staple, tack, tether, Velcro *(Trademark)*, vise, yoke, zipper

fastidious *adj.* captious, careful, choosy, critical, dainty, delicate, demanding, difficult, discriminating, exacting, finicky, fussy, hypercritical, meticulous, overdelicate, overnice, particular, persnickety, pettifogging, picky, punctilious, refined, squeamish, stickling *Nonformal:* fuss pot, nitpicking, too too nice *Antonyms:* careless, casual, easygoing, lenient, slack

fat *adj.* avoir dupois, beefy, big, brawny, broad, bulging, bulky, burly, chunky, corpulent, distended, dumpy, elephantine, fleshy, gargantuan, heavy, heavyset, hefty, husky, inflated, large, meaty, obese, oversize, overweight, paunchy, plump, portly, potbellied, pudgy, rotund, solid, stout, stubby, swollen, thickset, *zaftig (German) Nonformal:* butterball, jelly-belly, roly-poly, tubby *Antonyms:* angular, bony, lean, scrawny, thin

fatty *adj.* **1.** adipose, buttery, cholesterol-laden, greasy, lardaceous, laden with lard, oily, rich **2.** affluent, cushy, high-paying, lucrative, profitable, prosperous, remunerative *Antonyms:* unprofitable, unrewarding **3.** abundant, fertile, flourishing, fructuous, fruitful, good, plentiful, productive, prolific, thriving *Antonyms:* barren, lean, poor – *n.* **1.** blubber, cellulite, corpulence, fatness, flab, obesity, paunch, surfeit, surplus, tissue **2.** cooking material *Kinds of fat:* bacon, butter, chicken, cocoa butter, drippings, *ghee (Indian)*, goose, lard, margarine, oil, *schmaltz (Yiddish)*, shortening, suet, tallow **3.** abundance, bounty, fecundity, richness, wealth

fatal *adj.* **1.** calamitous, castastrophic, cataclysmic, deadly, destructive, final, killing, lethal, malignant, mortal, pernicious, ruinous, terminal, toxic *Antonyms:* benign, harmless, innocuous **2.** decisive, determining, unlucky, zero *(Nonformal)* **3.** critical, destined, fateful, foreordained, inevitable, inescapable, predestined,

fatality *n.* **1.** accident, calamity, catastrophe, disaster, death, incident, killing, misadventure, murder **2.** body, casualty, dead person, loss, victim

fate *n.* **1.** destiny, divine will, foreordainment, fortuna, fortune, karma, kismet, luck, predestination, providence, stars *(Nonformal)* **2.** afterworld, future, hereafter *Nonformal:* great beyond, last stop **3.** circumstance, consequence, course, determination, lot, outcome, resolution, result, way **4.** death, destruction, disaster, doom, end, undoing **5.** bête-noir, doppleganger, nemesis, opposite number

fateful *adj.* **1.** acute, conclusive, critical, crucial, decisive, eventful, important, momentous, ominous, portentous, significant *Antonyms:* inconsequential, insignificant, nugatory, ordinary, unimportant **2.** apocalyptic, calamitous, catastrophic, deadly, fatal, lethal, mortal

father *n.* **1.** ancestor, begetter, forebear, padre, papa, parent, pater, patriarch, procreator, progenitor, sire *Nonformal:* dad, old man, pa, pop **2.** clergyman, cleric, confessor, curé, ecclesiastic, minister, parson, pastor, preacher, priest, prophet **3.** creator, establisher, founder, nation builder, originator, signer – *v.* beget, breed, create, engender, establish, found, generate, institute, invent, make, originate, parent, procreate, produce, sire, spawn

fatherland *n.* birthplace, cradle, home, homeland, mother country, motherland, native land *or* soil *or* old country *(Nonformal)*

fatherly *adj.* affectionate, benevolent, benign, caring, forbearing, indulgent, kind, kindly, nurturing, obliging, paternal, protective, shielding, supportive *Antonyms:* cold, harsh, malevolent, tyrannical

fathom *n.* 1.829 meters, six feet, span of two arms outstretched – *v.* **1.** absorb, appreciate, assimilate, catch, comprehend, conceive, digest, follow, grasp, interpret, investigate, puzzle out, realize, solve, take in, understand **2.** ascertain, determine, gauge, measure, measurement, plumb, probe, read, reckon, sound, take

fatigue *n.* burnout, debility, dullness, enervation, ennui, exhaustion, faintness, feebleness, heaviness, hebetude, languor, lassitude, lethargy, listlessness, overtiredness, tiredness, weakness, weariness *Antonyms:* alertness, animation, energy, vigour, zest – *v.* exhaust, tire, tucker *or* wear out, weary *Nonformal:* do in, poop

fatigued *adj.* all in, beat, bedraggled, burned out, done in, droopy, dropping, exhausted, fagged, footsore, jaded, languid, languorous, listless, overtired, prostrate, spent, tired, wasted, weary, worn-out *Nonformal:* bushed, dead, dead-tired, dog-tired, finished, running on empty, whacked, zonked

fatness *n.* breadth, bulkiness, corpulence, flab, fleshiness, girth, heaviness, largeness, obesity, plumpness, portliness, size, stoutness, weight

fatten *v.* **1.** add to, augment, build up, broaden, enrich, expand, fertilize, increase, thicken, widen **2.** bloat, cram, distend, feed, fill, force feed, nourish, overfeed, plump, round out, spread, stuff, swell *Antonyms:* diet, starve

fatty *adj.* blubbery, cholesterol-filled, chubby, fat, greasy, gristly, lardy, loaded with calories, marbled, oily, oleaginous, rich, suety

fatuity *n.* absurdity, asininity, foolishness, idiocy, illogicalness, inanity, mindlessness, nonsense, silliness, smug, stupidity, vacuity, vapidity, witlessness *Antonyms:* profundity, sagacity, soundness

fatuous *adj.* asinine, brainless, dense, dull, foolish, idiotic, imbecile, inane, ludicrous, mindless, moronic, puerile, sappy, silly, simple, stupid, vacuous, witless *Antonyms:* stern, weighty, wise

faucet *n.* cock, fixture, nuzzle, pump, spigot, spout, stopcock, tap, valve

fault *n.* **1.** blemish, blot, bug *(Nonformal)*, defect, error, failing, flaw, foible, gremlin, imperfection, mar, rip, shortcoming, stain, tear, typo **2.** blunder, delinquency, faux pas, gaffe, impropriety, inaccuracy, indiscretion, lapse, malfeasance, misconduct, misdeed, mistake, offence, oversight, peccadillo, sin, slip, slip-up, solecism, transgression, trespass, vice, violation, weakness, wrong, wrongdoing **3.** accountability, answerability, blame, culpability, liability, responsibility **4.** break, chink, cleft, crack, crevice, division, fissure – *v.* blame, call to account, censure, criticize, find fault with, finger point *(Nonformal)*, hold accountable *or* responsible, impugn, inculpate

faultfinding *adj.* captious, carping, caviling, complaining, crabby, cranky, critical, discontented, fussy, grumbling, hypercritical, nagging, niggling, Pecksniffian, pettifogging, picky, querulous, quibbling, trenchant *Nonformal:* beefing, bellyaching, griping, nitpicky *Antonyms:* appreciative, approving, laudatory, uncritical

faultless *adj.* **1.** blameless, guiltless, innocent, irreproachable, pure, sinless, spotless, stainless, unblemished, unmarked, unsullied, whole *Antonyms:* blameworthy, culpable, criminal, guilty, sinful **2.** exquisite, flawless, ideal, immaculate, impeccable, on target, perfect, pristine, supreme, textbook *(Nonformal)*

faulty *adj.* **1.** bad, erroneous, fallacious, flawed, impaired, imperfect, improper, inaccurate, incorrect, inexact, tainted, unfit, unreliable, unsound, unsteady, warped, wonky *(Nonformal)*, wrong *Antonyms:* flawless, impeccable, perfect **2.** blemished, botched, broken, damaged, defective, malfunctioning, marked, marred, seconds *(Nonformal)*

faux pas *n.* bad move, blunder, botch, breach of etiquette, bungle, error, false step, gaffe, indiscretion, misstep, mistake, offence, slip, stumble, social blunder, solecism *Nonformal:* blooper, flub, goof

favour *n.* **1.** aid, assistance, backing, beau geste, benefit, boon, cooperation, courtesy, dispensation, gesture, good turn *or* will, help, indulgence, kindness, largesse, *mitzvah (Hebrew)*, service, support *Antonyms:* disfavour, disservice, wrong **2.** admiration, approbation, consideration, esteem, friendliness, good account *or* opinion, grace, liking, regard, respect, **3.** approval, allowance, assent, benediction, blessing, encouragement, gracious consent, leave, kind permission **4.** bonboniere, compliment, gift, momento, present, remembrance, token, trinket **5.** aegis, championship, patronage, protection, sponsorship **6.** advantage, edge, lead, upperhand – *v.* **1.** abet, accommodate, advance, approve, aid, assist, back, champion, encourage, further, help, facilitate, oblige, sanction, support *Antonyms:* disapprove, inconvenience, oppose, thwart **2.** accept, advocate, choose, elect, endorse, opt for, patronize, pick, promote, side with, single out **3.** appreciate, be pro, fancy, lean toward, like, prefer, respect, smile on, value **4.** correspond, echo, look like, mirror, resemble, take after **5.** baby, care for, coddle, indulge, pamper, spare, spoil

favourable *adj.* **1.** advantageous, assisting, beneficial, convenient, gratifying, helpful, seasonable, timely, useful, welcome, well-timed *Antonyms:* deterring, inauspicious, obstructing, unhelpful **2.** auspicious, fortunate, hopeful, lucky, opportune, promising, propitious, providential **3.** affirmative, agreeable, approbative, commendatory, complimentary, encouraging, enthusiastic, good, inclined, laudatory, predisposed, positive, prosperous *Antonyms:* disagreeable, disapproving, ill-disposed **4.** amicable, benevolent, benign, clement, friendly, kind, pleasant, pleasing, reassuring, sympathetic, understanding, well-disposed

favourably *adv.* **1.** agreeably, amiably, approvingly, cordially, courteously, enthusiastically, fairly, generously, genially, graciously, heartily, helpfully, kindly, positively, receptively, willingly *Antonyms:* malevolently, menacingly, threateningly **2.** advantageously, auspiciously, conveniently, fortunately, happily, opportunely, profitably, prosperously, satisfyingly, successfully, swimmingly, well *Antonyms:* lucklessly, unfortunately, unpropitiously

favoured *adj.* **1.** best-liked, blessed, chosen, fair-haired, lucky, pet *(Nonformal)*, popular, preferred, well-liked **2.** advantaged, dominant, elite, privileged, prosperous, recommended, selected

favourite *adj.* admired, adored, beloved, best-loved, cherished, choice, darling, dear, dearest, desired, esteemed, favoured, liked, pet, popular, precious, preferred, prized, revered, treasured, wished-for *Antonyms:* discarded, forsaken, neglected, rejected – *n.* **1.** beloved, darling, dear, favourite daughter *or* son, ideal, idol, jewel, love, *persona grata (Latin)*, teacher's pet *(Nonformal)*, treasure, **2.** choice, front-runner, number one, person to beat, shoo-in *(Nonformal)*

favouritism *n.* bias, discrimination, inclination, inequity, nepotism, one-sidedness, partiality, partisanship, preference, preferential treatment, unfairness *Antonyms:* equality, fairness, neutrality, objectivity

fawn *n.* **1.** Bambi, buck, doe, young deer **2.** beige, brown, dun, ecru, grey-brown, light-brown, moleskin, sun-kissed, tan, taupe – *v.* abase, bow, cajole, cater to, curry favour, defer, flatter, grovel, ingratiate, kneel, kowtow, pander, scrape, stroke, submit, toady, truckle *Nonformal:* apple-polish, butter up

fawning *adj.* abject, bootlicking *(Nonformal)*, bowing, compliant, cowering, crawling, cringing, deferential, flattering, humble, ingratiating, kowtowing, prostrate, scraping, servile, spineless, submissive, subservient *Antonyms:* haughty, indifferent, rebellious – *n.* blandishment, bowing and scraping, honeyed phrases *or* words, obsequiousness, sweet talk, sycophancy, toadyism

fear *n.* agitation, alarm, angst, anxiety, apprehension, concern, cowardice, despair, dismay, distress, doubt, dread, faintheartedness, foreboding, fright, horror, misgiving, panic, phobia, presentiment, qualm, suspicion, terror, timidity, trepidation, unease, worry *Nonformal:* creeps, heebie-jeebies, jitters *Antonyms:* aplomb, confidence, courage – *v.* **1.** blanch, cower, cringe, crouch, dread, falter, flinch, lose courage, quail, quaver, quiver, recoil, shrink from, shudder, tremble **2.** beware, distrust, fret over, mistrust, suspect, worry about

fearful *adj.* **1.** appalling, atrocious, awful, baleful, dire, distressing, dreadful, eerie, frightful, ghastly, ghoulish, grisly, gruesome, hideous, horrendous, horrible, horrifying, lurid, macabre, monstrous, morbid, shocking, sinister, strange, terrible, unspeakable, upsetting **2.** afraid, aghast, alarmed, cowardly, diffident, disturbed, fainthearted, frightened, intimidated, phobic, running scared, shaky, sheepish, shrinking, skittish, spineless, timid, weak-kneed *Nonformal:* in a sweat, jittery, lily-livered *Antonyms:* bold, brave, gallant, intrepid, valiant **3.** agitated, anxious, apprehensive, disquieted, hesitant, nervous, panicky, tense, uneasy, worried *Nonformal:* hung up, uptight **4.** august, awe-inspiring, astounding, formidable, imposing, impressive, overwhelming, respected, revered, reverential, sublime **5.** excessive, extreme, formidable, outrageous, overindulgent

feasible *adj.* **1.** achievable, attainable, doable, likely, performable, practicable, probable, profitable, realizable, reasonable, viable, worthwhile *Antonyms:* impossible, impracticable, untenable, unworkable **2.** appropriate, beneficial, expedient, fit, fitting, okay *(Nonformal)*, suitable, **3.** believable, conceivable, imaginable, possible sounds good *(Nonformal)*

feast *n.* bacchanalia, banquet, barbecue buffet, celebration, dinner, entertainment festivity, fête, fiesta, gala, luau, meal, merrymaking, picnic, potlatch *(Native Peoples)*, reception, refreshment, repast, saturnalia, smörgåsbord, spread, treat *Nonformal:* blowout, scoff – *v.* banquet carouse, celebrate, eat, entertain, gorge indulge, overindulge, party, quaff, refresh regale, relish, revel, stuff, treat, wassail wine and dine

feat *n.* **1.** accomplishment, achievement, act attainment, deed, enterprise, exploit, *fait accompli (French)*, undertaking **2.** manoeuvre, move, performance, stunt, trick

feather *n.* aigrette, calamus, covert, crest down, fin, fluff, fringe, panache, penna pinion, plumage, plume, pompon, quill, tuft

feathery *adj.* **1.** downy, feathered, fluffy light, pennate, soft, tufted **2.** airy, ethereal gossamer, insubstantial, lightweight, slight thin, weightless, wispy *Antonyms:* substantial, thick, weighty

feature *n.* **1.** aspect, attribute, characteristic, component, constituent, detail, element, facet, factor, ingredient, item, property, quality, trait, virtue **2.** attraction draw, blue plate, highlight, sale, special specialty, trademark **3.** documentary, film motion picture, movie, presentation *See also:* **film** **4.** article, column, comment commentary, editorial, item, piece, report story – *v.* **1.** accentuate, emphasize, give prominence, highlight, mark, show, spotlight, stress, underline, underscore **2** advance, advertise, display, exhibit, promote **3.** appear, headline, include, present star

features *n. pl.* appearance, characteristics countenance, face, lineaments, looks, mug *(Nonformal)*, physiognomy, visage

febrile *adj.* delirious, fevered, feverish fiery, flushed, hot, inflamed, pyretic

feces *n.* discharge, dreck, droppings, dung, excrement, excretion, guano, manure, ordure, stool, waste *Nonformal:* caca, cow plops, doo-doo, number two, poop, road apples

feckless *adj.* **1.** enervated, feeble, ineffective, ineffectual, lethargic, limp, listless, sapped *(Nonformal)*, useless, weak *Antonyms:* energized, vigorous **2.** careless, heedless, incautious, irresponsible, reckless, wild *Antonyms:* careful, deliberate

fecund *adj.* **1.** fertile, fructiferous, fruitful, generating, productive, prolific, propagating, reproducing, rich, spawning, teeming *Antonyms:* barren, destitute, effete, void **2.** artistic, creative, imaginative, innovative, inspired, inventive,

federal *adj.* **1.** bureaucratic, Crown, executive, governmental, internal, jurisdictional, legal, national, official, parliamentary, political, sovereign **2.** central, common, communal, general, public, universal **3.** confederated, federated, joined, merged, solidified, united **4.** authoritative, legal, official, sanctioned

federation *n.* alliance, amalgamation, association, brotherhood, coalition, combination, confederacy, league, nation, organization, partnership, sisterhood, syndicate, syndication, union

fee *n.* bill, charge, commission, compensation, cost, cut, emolument, expense, honorarium, pay, payment, percentage, piece, price, recompense, remuneration, reward, salary, share, slice, stipend, take, wage

feeble *adj.* **1.** delicate, flimsy, fragile, frail, shaky, weak **2.** debilitated, decrepit, emasculated, enervated, enfeebled, exhausted, impotent, infirm, powerless, weakened *Nonformal:* out of gas, woozy *Antonyms:* ardent, hearty, robust **3.** inadequate, ineffectual, insubstantial, lame, pathetic, pitiful, poor, slight, tenuous, thin **4.** faint, indistinct, light, low, quiet, soft

feeble-minded *adj.* doddering, dumb, imbecilic, senile, senseless, simple-minded, slow, stupid *Nonformal:* dimwitted, empty upstairs, numbskull, weak in the upper storey

feebleness *n.* **1.** debility, decrepitude, enervation, etiolation, exhaustion, languor, lassitude, malaise, senility, sickliness, unhealthiness *Antonyms:* vibrancy, vitality **2.** delicacy, flimsiness, frailness, frailty, infirmity, infirmness, weakness **3.** helplessness, impotence, inability, inadequacy, incapacity, incompetence, ineffectiveness, ineffectualness, insignificance, insufficiency, lameness

feed *n.* **1.** edibles, fodder, food, foodstuff, forage, meal, pasturage, pasture, provender, victuals, vittles *(Nonformal) Kinds of animal feed:* alfalfa, barley, bran, clover, corn, flaxseed, grain, grass, hay, millet, oats, sorghum, timothy, wheat **2.** broadcast, program, signal, transmission – *v.* **1.** fuel, give, nourish, provide, serve, supply, sustain **2.** foster, furnish, maintain, provision, stock **3.** eat, dine, fatten, feast, gorge, gratify, regale **4.** augment, bolster, encourage, nurture, strengthen, support

feedback *n.* **1.** answer, commentary, criticism, critique, reaction, reply, response **2.** distortion, hum, interference, noise *or* white noise, static – *v.* distort, flange, hum, overdrive, phase

feel *n.* **1.** air, ambience, atmosphere, aura, character, feeling, finish, milieu, nature, quality, semblance, sensation, sense, spirit, surface, tactility, texture, vibes *(Nonformal)* **2.** ability, adroitness, cleverness, deftness, knack, know-how, perception, touch, understanding – *v.* **1.** caress, contact, examine, explore, finger, fondle, frisk, grope, massage, palpate, paw, pinch, press, squeeze, stroke, tickle, touch **2.** acknowledge, appreciate, comprehend, discern, notice, observe, perceive, sense, sympathize, understand **3.** believe, consider, have a hunch *or* inkling, judge, opine, suppose, suspect, think **4.** encounter, experience, know, meet, receive, suffer, undergo

feeling *adj.* emotional, human, sensitive, sentient, warm *or* warm-blooded – *n.* **1.** awareness, capacity, faculty, instinct, palpability, perception, sentience, touch, understanding **2.** effect, impression, palpitation, prickle, quiver, sensation, sense, tingle, vibration **3.** affection, attitude, emotion, fondness, reaction, response, sentiment **4.** appreciation, care, compassion, concern, empathy, pathos, pity, sympathy, tenderness, warmth **5.** ability, aptitude, deftness, astuteness, skill, talent **6.** ardour, fervour, intensity, passion, responsiveness, rush *(Nonformal)*, sensitivity, sensuality, spirit, zeal **7.** assessment, belief, hunch, judgment, opinion, outlook, spin, take, view

feign *v.* **1.** act, assume, bluff, deceive, deke *(Nonformal)*, fake, pretend, sham, simulate **2.** concoct, create, devise, dissemble, fabricate, falsify, invent, lie **3.** copy, counterfeit, duplicate, forge, imitate, reproduce

feigned *adj.* artificial, counterfeit, fabricated, fake, false, fictitious, imitation, insincere, pretended, put-on, sham, simulated, spurious *Nonformal:* knock-off, phoney *Antonyms:* authentic, bona fide, genuine, pure, real

feint *n.* artifice, bait, blind, bluff, cheat, deceit, decoy, deke *(Nonformal)*, diversion, dodge, fake, hoax, hoodwinking, make-believe, play, ploy, pretense, pretension, pretext, red herring, ruse, sham, straw man, trick, wile

feisty *adj.* argumentative, courageous, dauntless, defiant, fiery, frisky, hot-tempered, peppery, plucky, quick-tempered, spirited, spunky, untamed, wild *Antonyms:* quiet, shy, tame, timid

felicitous *adj.* agreeable, applicable, appropriate, apropos, apt, effective, fit, fitting, germane, inspired, just, meet, neat, opportune, pat, pertinent, propitious, relevant, seasonable, suitable, well-timed *Antonyms:* ill-timed, inappropriate, irrelevant, malapropos

felicity *n.* **1.** bliss, congruity, decorousness, delight, ecstasy, enjoyment, elegance, good fortune, happiness, joy, luck, pleasure, prosperity, rapture *Antonyms:* poverty, sadness, sorrow **2.** appropriateness, congruity, effectiveness, expedience, pertinence, satisfaction, suitability

feline *adj.* artful, canny, cat-like, crafty, cunning, furtive, leonine, sleek, sly, sinuous, sneaky, stealthy, subtle, tricky, wily – *n.* cat, kitten, kitty, lion, lynx, ocelot, pussy *(Nonformal)*, tiger *See also:* **cat**

fell *adj.* callous, cruel, ferocious, fierce, inhuman, merciless, nefarious, pernicious, pitiless, ruthless, savage, sinister, truculent, vicious, vitriolic – *n.* **1.** down, hill, hillock, moor, ridge, swell **2.** coat, fleece, fur, hide, jacket, pelt – *v.* **1.** chop down, cut, down, drop, gash, ground, hack, hew, level, lop, prostrate, raze, sever **2.** dash, flatten, floor, knock out, strike down, topple

fellow *adj.* affiliated, akin, allied, associated, connected, joint, kindred, like, related, similar, united *Antonyms:* separated, divided, estranged, hostile – *n.* **1.** acquaintance, ally, affiliate, associate, compadre, compañero, comrade, colleague, companion, co-worker, crony, equal, friend, gentleman, mate, peer, scion, sidekick *(Nonformal) Antonyms:* antagonist, adversary, enemy, nemesis, rival **2.** amigo, bloke, boy, bro' *(Nonformal)*, brother, buddy, chap, chum, guy, human, individual, lad, male, man, person, young whippersnapper

fellowship *n.* **1.** alliance, association, brotherhood, club, company, fraternity, guild, league, order, sisterhood, society, sorority **2.** acquaintance, affability, amity, camaraderie, communion, companionship, comradeship, conviviality, familiarity, friendliness, intimacy, kindliness, sociability, togetherness

felon *n.* convict, criminal, delinquent, lawbreaker, loser, malefactor, offender, outlaw *Nonformal:* con, lifer

female *adj.* feminine, gynecomorphous, gynocentric, she, womanlike, womanly *Nonformal:* skirt, tomato – *n.* bitch *(canine)*, doe, gal *(Nonformal)*, girl, woman *Equine:* filly, mare *Female forms of address:* lady, madam *or* ma'am, *memsahib (Hindu)*, Miss, Mistress, Mrs., Ms. *French:* madame *or* Mme, mademoiselle *or* Mlle, mesdames *or* Mmes *(Plural) German:* Frau, Fraülein *Italian:* signora, signorina *Portuguese:* dona, senhora *Spanish:* doña, señora, señorita

feminine *adj.* distaff, effeminate, female, girlish, kittenish *(Nonformal)*, ladylike, womanly

fen *n.* bog, fenland, lowland, marsh, morass

muskeg, quagmire, slough, swamp, wetland

fence *n.* **1.** backstop, balustrade, bar, barricade, barrier, block, dike, line, paling, palisade, rampart, roadblock, stockade, wall *Kinds of fence:* barbed-wire, board, brush, deer, chain-link, hedge, net, outfield, picket, post, rail, railing, screen, sheep, snake, snow, stake, stone, sunk, weir, wooden, zigzag **2.** cover, guard, safeguard, safety screen, stop **3.** dealer, go-between, launderer, receiver of stolen goods, runner, swagsman *(Nonformal),* trafficker – *v.* **1.** bulwark, cage, circumscribe, coop up, corral, demarcate, encircle, enclose, pen, surround, wall in **2.** divide, exclude, keep out, restrict, segregate, separate **3.** dodge, duck, equivocate, evade, sidestep *Nonformal:* hem and haw, pussyfoot around **4.** contend, duel, joust, tilt, thrust and parry *Fencing terms:* button, corps à corps, counterriposte, doigté, engarde, épé, fleche, foil, hit, lunge, parry, piste, repêchage, riposte, saber, sentiment du fer, touché

fend *v.* **1.** avert, avoid, defend, deflect, hold *or* stave *or* ward off, guard, parry, protect, rebuff, reject, repel, repulse, resist, shield, spurn **2.** get along *or* by, grub along *(Nonformal),* make do *or* ends meet, squeak by, subsist, survive

feral *adj.* **1.** savage, uncultivated, undomesticated, untamed, wild *Antonyms:* docile, domesticated, safe, tame **2.** beastly, bestial, brutish, cruel, deadly, deathly, fell, ferocious, fierce, frenzied, furious, inhuman, rapacious, ruthless, violent

ferment *n.* **1.** agitation, anxiety, brouhaha, discontent, excitement, fervour, frenzy, fuss, imbroglio, tempest, trouble, turmoil, tumult, unrest, uproar, upswell *Antonyms:* peace, serenity, tranquility **2.** bacteria, enzyme, leaven, mould, pepsin, yeast – *v.* **1.** brew, bubble, churn, effervesce, fester, fizz, foam, froth, leaven, ripen, simmer, smoulder, work **2.** agitate, arouse, excite, foment, inflame, provoke, stir-up *Antonyms:* assuage, calm, soothe, unruffle

ferocious *adj.* **1.** barbaric, bloodthirsty, brutal, brutish, cruel, fierce, lupine, merciless, murderous, pitiless, predatory, rapacious, relentless, ruthless, savage, vehement, violent, voracious, wild *Antonyms:* calm, docile, gentle **2.** acute, extreme, flaming, grave, intense, poignant, sharp, vivid *Antonyms:* blunt, dull, mild, tepid

ferret *n.* ermine, polecat, predacious carnivore, stoat, weasel – *v.* drive *or* flush out, exhume, investigate, hunt, probe, pry, search *or* sniff out, unearth *Antonyms:* conceal, cover, veil

ferry *n.* barge, conveyance, craft, ferryboat, packet – *v.* bear, boat, carry, chauffeur, convey, deliver, fare, lug, run, send, ship, shuttle, taxi, tote, transport

fertile *adj.* **1.** abundant, arable, bountiful, fecund, fruitful, lush, plentiful, producing, prolific, rich, teeming, yielding **2.** bearing, gravid, pregnant, reproductive, spawning *Antonyms:* barren, sterile **3.** creative, fructuous, generative, inventive, potent, productive

fertility *n.* **1.** abundance, copiousness, fecundity, gravidity, plentifulness **2.** creativeness, fruitfulness, generative capacity, productivity, resourcefulness *Antonyms:* barrenness, sterility

fertilize *v.* **1.** compost, enrich, feed, fructify, generate, germinate, mulch, pollinate **2.** fecundate, knock up *(Nonformal)* impregnate, inseminate, procreate, propagate

fertilizer *n.* enriching material *Kinds of fertilizer*: bone meal, chemical, compost, dung, guano, humus, manure, mulch, nitrate, peat moss, potash, top dressing

fervent *adj.* **1.** animated, ardent, eager, ecstatic, emotional, energetic, enthusiastic, excited, fervid, gung ho *(Nonformal),* hearty, heated, impassioned, intense, passionate, perfervid, responsive, tender, vehement, zealous *Antonyms:* apathetic, detached, unfeeling **2.** blazing, burning, fiery, glowing, hot, warm *Antonyms:* cold, frigid, icy

fervour *n.* ardency, ardour, eagerness, earnestness, enthusiasm, excitement, fervency, fire, heartiness, heat, intensity, love, oomph *(Nonformal),* passion, response, vehemence, warmth, zeal *Antonyms:* aloofness, cold-heartedness, indifference

fester *v.* **1.** boil, burn, dwell, fret, rage, seethe, smoulder, steam, stew, worry **2.** blister, canker, chafe, decay, peel, suppurate, ulcerate

festival *n.* anniversary, banquet, carnival, celebration, *champêtre (Quebec)*, feast, fête, gala, get-together, holiday, jubilee, occasion, party, revelry, social, wassail *Nonformal:* bash, blowout, jump-up *See also:* **holiday**

festive *adj.* amusing, celebrative, convivial, cordial, delightful, entertaining, fun, gay, genial, hearty, hospitable, jolly, joyful, joyous, jubilant, merry, sportive, social *Antonyms:* dour, funereal, gloomy, morbid

festivity *n.* amusement, anniversary, ball, banquet, bazaar, carnival, celebration, clambake, commemoration, dance, entertainment, fair, feast, festival, fête, field day, fiesta, fun, function, gaiety, gala, get-together, jubilee, merrymaking, party, pleasure, potlatch, prom, revel, revelry, treat *Nonformal:* barn burner, bash, blowout, do, hoopla, old home week, rave, shindig, wingding

fetch *v.* **1.** bear, bring back *or* in, convey, deliver, get *or* go get, retrieve *Nonformal:* russell up, schlep, truck **2.** draw, earn, elicit, produce, render, supply, yield

fetching *adj.* alluring, attractive, beautiful, captivating, charming, cute, enchanting, enticing, handsome, pleasing, provocative, striking, winsome *Antonyms:* repellent, repulsive, ugly

fête *n.* barbecue, bazaar, carnival, celebration, dinner, fair, feast day, festival, garden party, holiday, holy day, kitchen racket *(Newfoundland)*, merrymaking, party, revelry – *v.* celebrate, dine, entertain, feast, honour, lionize, regale, treat

fetid *adj.* disgusting, foul, fusty, gamy, gross, malodorous, mephitic, mouldy, noxious, offensive, putrid, rancid, rank, reeking, repugnant, repulsive, revolting, rotten, smelly, stinking, stinky, strong *Antonyms:* aromatic, fragrant

fetish *n.* **1.** attraction, bias, craze, fixation, leaning, mania, obsession, penchant, predilection, propensity, thing *(Nonformal)* **2.** amulet, charm, horseshoe, ornament, rabbit's foot, scarab, talisman, token

fetter *v.* bind, chain, check, confine, cuff, curb, hamper, hamstring, handcuff, hinder, hobble, hog-tie, hold, leash, manacle, put in irons, repress, restrain, restrict, shackle, tie, trammel *Antonyms:* emancipate, free, loosen, untie

fetters *n. pl.* ball and chain, bindings, bondage, bonds, chains, cuffs, irons, manacles, obstruction, restraint, shackles

feud *n.* bad blood *(Nonformal)*, brawl, combat, conflict, contention, contest, discord, dispute, dissension, enmity, estrangement, falling out, fight, grudge, hostility, quarrel, rivalry, row, run-in, squabble, strife, vendetta *Antonyms:* accord, congeniality, cooperation, fellowship, harmony – *v.* bicker, brawl, clash, contend, disagree, duel, war, wrangle *Antonyms:* agree, assent, cooperate, harmonize

fever *n.* **1.** chill, delirium, flush, heat, pyrexia, temperature *Nonformal:* sweat, the shakes **2.** agitation, ecstasy, excitement, ferment, fervour, frenzy, passion, restlessness, unrest

feverish *adj.* **1.** burning up, febrile, fevered, flushed, hot, pyretic, warm **2.** agitated, distracted, excited, fervid, frantic, frenetic, frenzied, furious, heated, hectic, high-strung, impatient, inflamed, nervous, obsessive, overwrought, passionate, restless, uneasy, worked up in a dither *(Nonformal)* *Antonyms:* calm, cool, tranquil

few *adj.* exiguous, inconsiderable, insignificant, meagre, negligible, not many, nugatory, scant, sporadic *Antonyms:* abundant, bounteous, plentiful – *pron.* a couple or, handful, not many, some

fiancée *n.* affianced, engaged person, fiancé *(Masc.)*, future, husband-to-be, intended, lover, prospective spouse, significant other, steady, wife- to-be

fiasco *n.* abortion, blunder, bobble, bomb, botch-up, breakdown, catastrophe, debacle, disaster, embarrassment, error, failure, farce, flop, mess, miscarriage, ruin, wash-out *Antonyms:* accomplishment, achievement, feat, success

iat *n.* authorization, command, decree, dictate, dictum, droit, edict, endorsement, mandate, order, ordinance, proclamation, sanction, warrant

ib *n.* cock-and-bull story, fabrication, falsehood, falsity, fiction, invention, lie, prevarication, story, tale, tall tale, untruth, white lie, yarn *Antonyms:* actuality, reality, truth – *v.* equivocate, fabricate, falsify, invent, lie, manufacture, palter, prevaricate, tell tales

ibre *n.* **1.** cord, filament, hair, nap, pile, shred, strand, string, strip, tendril, thread, vein, warp, web, weft **2.** backbone, character, decency, integrity, probity, spine, strength, substance

ibrous *adj.* coarse, hairy, pulpy, ropy, sinewy, stalky, stringy, threadlike, veined, wiry, woody

ickle *adj.* **1.** capricious, changeable, changing, erratic, flighty, fluctuating, impetuous, impulsive, inconstant, irresolute, mercurial, moonish, mutable, quicksilver, shifting, transitory, unfixed, unreliable, unstable, wavering, whimsical, vacillating *Antonyms:* constant, fixed, loyal, steadfast **2.** fast and loose, fly-by-night, shifty, tricky, undependable

iction *n.* **1.** anecdote, book, cliff-hanger, drama, fable, legend, literature, myth, narrative, novel, potboiler *(Nonformal)*, romance, story, tale **2.** canard, fabrication, falsehood, fib, figment of the imagination, improvisation, invention, lie, prevarication *Nonformal:* cock-and-bull story, old wive's tale *See also:* **novel**

ictitious *adj.* apocryphal, artificial, assumed, bogus, chimerical, concocted, counterfeit, created, deceptive, ersatz, fabricated, fake, false, feigned, fictional, illusory, imagined, invented, made-up, make-believe, mock, mythical, sham, simulated, synthetic, trumped-up, untrue *Nonformal:* cooked-up, phoney *Antonyms:* authentic, genuine, legitimate, real, true

fiddle *n.* instrument *or* stringed instrument, viol, viola, violin – *v.* dabble, fidget, fribble, fool *or* monkey around, fuss, idle, mess *or* muck about, play, potter, putter, tamper, tinker, toy, trifle

fidelity *n.* **1.** allegiance, attachment, constancy, dependability, devotion, faith, faithfulness, fealty, integrity, loyalty, piety, reliability, staunchness, steadfastness, trustworthiness *Antonyms:* disloyalty, faithlessness, perfidy, treachery **2.** accuracy, adherence, adhesion, closeness, conformity, correspondence, exactitude, exactness, naturalism, preciseness, precision, realism, scrupulousness

fidget *v.* chafe, doodle, fiddle, fret, fuss, jiggle, jitter *(Nonformal)*, play, squirm, stir, toss, trifle, twiddle, worry

fidgety *adj.* anxious, apprehensive, high-strung, hyper, impatient, jerky, jumpy, nervous, restive, restless, spooked, squirrely, uneasy, worrisome *Nonformal:* antsy, jittery, edgy, twitchy, wired

field *n.* **1.** acreage, cropland, demesne, enclosure, farmland, glebe, grassland, ground, land, lea, meadow, moorland, pasture, patch, plot, ranchland, steppe, terrain, territory, tillage, tract, *veld (South Africa)*, vineyard **2.** amphitheatre, athletic arena, circuit, course, court, diamond, fairground, golf course, green, gridiron, grounds, park, playground, playing area, racecourse, racetrack, range, rink, stadium, track, turf **3.** area, bailiwick, circle, domain, dominion, environment, jurisdiction, orbit, precinct, province, purview, range, reach, region, scope, sweep, territory, walk **4.** department, division, office, part, section **5.** activity, avocation, calling, discipline, job, métier, occupation, specialty, vocation, work **6.** balance, crowd, host, pack, remainder, rest, swarm – *v.* catch, defend, deflect, handle, pick-up, protect, receive, retrieve, screen

fiend *n.* **1.** barbarian, beast, brute, degenerate, demon, devil, monster, ogre, savage **2.** addict, aficionado, devotee, enthusiast, fan, fanatic, freak *(Nonformal)*, monomaniac, zealot

fiendish *adj.* **1.** accursed, atrocious, baleful, barbaric, barbarous, bloodthirsty, cruel, damnable, demonic, demoniacal, devilish, diabolical, dire, evil, feral, ferocious, ghoulish, hellborn, hellish, hideous, horrid, infernal, inhuman, inhumane, malicious, monstrous, odious, satanic, sinister, venomous, vicious *Antonyms:* benign, heavenly, kind **2.** brutal, demanding, difficult, exacting, harsh, merciless, perilous, rigourous, ruthless, unrelenting, unyielding *Antonyms:* easy, piece of cake *(Nonformal)*

fierce *adj.* **1.** angry, animal, awful, barbarous, bloodthirsty, brutal, brutish, cruel, cutthroat, dangerous, enraged, fell, feral, ferocious, frightening, furious, horrible, howling, infuriated, malevolent, menacing, murderous, powerful, primitive, raging, raving, relentless, savage, stormy, terrible, threatening, truculent, tumultuous, uncontrollable, untamed, venomous, vicious, violent, wild *Antonyms:* affectionate, calm, civilized, docile, peaceful **2.** fiery, intense, passionate, strong, tempestuous, vehement *Antonyms:* bland, disinterested, dispassionate

fiercely *adv.* **1.** angrily, awfully, brutally, ferociously, frighteningly, horribly, malevolently, menacingly, passionately, riotously, roughly, savagely, severely, terribly, threateningly, tigerishly, turbulently, uncontrollably, venomously, viciously, violently *Antonyms:* peacefully, softly, soothingly **2.** forcefully, forcibly, frantically, frenziedly, furiously, hard, impetuously, irresistibly, madly, tempestuously, vehemently, wildly

fiery *adj.* **1.** ablaze, afire, aflame, alight, blazing, burning, combustible, conflagrant, flaming, flaring, glowing, heated, hot, ignited, inflamed, red-hot **2.** choleric, fervid, feverish, fierce, hotheaded, hot-tempered, impassioned, impetuous, impulsive, irascible, irritable, passionate, peppery, perfervid, unrestrained, vehement, violent *Antonyms:* aloof, cool, indifferent

fight *n.* action, affray, aggression, altercation, argument, assault, attack, battle, belligerence, bloodshed, blowup, bout, brannigan, brawl, brush, clash, combat, combativeness, conflict, confrontation, contention, contest, controversy, disagreement, dispute, dissension, donnybrook, duel, encounter, engagement, exchange, feud, fisticuffs, flap, fracas, fray, free-for-all, fuss, hostility, joust, match, mêlée, pugnacity, quarrel, riot, round, row, scrap, scrimmage, scuffle, skirmish, spat, strife, struggle, tif tussle, vendetta, war, warfare, wranglin *Nonformal:* dustup, rhubarb, ruckus, rumble, rumpus, set-to *Antonyms:* civility, cooperation, harmony – *v.* assault, attack, bandy, battle, bicker, box, brawl, challenge, clash, contend, cross swords *(Nonformal)*, dispute, duel, encounter, exchange blows, feud, grapple, joust, oppose, quarrel, scrap, scuffle, skirmish, spar, strive, struggle, tif tussle, war, wrangle

fighter *n.* **1.** aggressor, antagonist, assailan boxer, cavalier, champion, combatant, competitor, contender, contestant, counterrevolutionary, disputant, duelist, enforcer, gladiator, goon *(Hockey)*, guerrilla, hooligan, janissary, knight, mercenary, militant, palooka *(Nonformal)*, prizefighter, pugilis revolutionary, rival, slugger, soldier, warric **2.** attack plane, interceptor, jet, warplane

fighting *adj.* **1.** aggressive, angry, argumentative, battle-ready, bellicose, belligeren combative, contentious, disputatious, ferocious, hawkish, hostile, militant, pugnacious, quarrelsome, scrappy, truculen warlike, *Antonyms:* appeasing, conciliatory, pacifying, placating **2.** battling, brawing, combating, jousting, scrapping, skirmishing, sparring, struggling, tilting, wrestling – *n.* battle, engagemen exchange of fire, hostilities, skirmish, war

figment *n.* chimera, creation, daydream, dream, fable, fabrication, fiction, hallucination, illusion, improvisation, invention, nightmare

figurative *adj.* allegorical, denotative, descriptive, emblematical, fanciful, illustrative, metaphorical, pictorial, representative, symbolic *Antonyms:* accurate, exac factual, literal

figure *n.* **1.** bust, cast, composition, depiction, doll, drawing, effigy, figurine, illustr

tion, image, likeness, model, mould, piece, portrait, representation, sculpture, sketch, statue, waxwork **2.** anatomy, appearance, attitude, body, build, carriage, cast, chassis *(Nonformal)*, form, frame, mass, physique, pose, posture, proportions, shape, silhouette, torso **3.** character, device, emblem, euphemism, expression, figure of speech, motif, ornament, symbol, trope, turn **4.** amount, cipher, cost, digit, integer, number, numeral, price, quotation, rate, sum, terms, total, value, worth **5.** celebrity, dignitary, force, leader, notable, personage, personality, presence, somebody *Nonformal:* big name, glitterati, star **6.** decoration, design, diagram, embellishment, pattern – *v.* **1.** add, calculate, cipher, compute, count, enumerate, estimate, number, reckon, sum, tally, tot up, total, tote, work out **2.** conceive, dream up, envision, imagine, picture, visualize **3.** chart, contour, delineate, depict, design, draft, draw, picture, represent **4.** believe, conjecture, decipher, opine, reason, reckon, suppose, surmise

figurehead *n.* **1.** nominal *or* titular head, puppet *Nonformal:* dummy, front man, mouthpiece, nonentity, stooge, straw boss *or* man **2.** carving, figure, ornament

filament *n.* cable, cord, fibre, hair, ligature, line, rope, strand, string, suture, thread, twine, web, wire

filch *v.* embezzle, liberate, palm, pilfer, pinch, purloin, rob, scrounge, sneak, snipe, steal, take, thieve *Nonformal:* bag, boost, lift, nip, rip off, snitch, swipe

file *n.* **1.** column, echelon, line, list, order, parade, queue, rank, row, string, tier, troop **2.** cookie, docket, documents, dossier, folder, information, record **3.** box, cabinet, compartment, drawer, envelope, repository **4.** abrasive, corundum, emery board, rasp – *v.* **1.** alphabetize, arrange, catalogue, categorize, classify, docket, document, index, list, order, pigeonhole, place, record, register, save, slot, tabulate **2.** apply, deposit, dispatch, enter, post, put *or* send *or* turn in, submit **3.** grind, hone, pumice, sand, scrape, sharpen, smooth, whet

filial *adj.* affectionately, daughterlike, childlike, demonstrative, devoted, dutiful, fond, loyal, respectful, sonlike *Antonyms:* alienated, disrespectful, estranged

filibuster *n.* **1.** delay, hindrance, obstruction, opposition, postponement, procrastination, stonewalling **2.** adventurer, buccaneer, corsair, freebooter, guerrilla, mercenary, pirate, raider – *v.* block, declaim, delay, harangue, hinder, obstruct, orate, postpone, prevent, speechify *(Nonformal)*

filigree *adj.* delicate, elaborate, elegant, exquisite, fanciful, fine, lacy, ornate, sheer, silken – *n.* fretwork, interlace, lace, lattice *or* lattice work, netting, ornamentation, ornateness, scrollwork, wirework

fill *n.* clean fill, debris, dirt, earth, filler, garbage, gravel, padding, refuse, rubbish, rubble, soil, stone, stuffing – *v.* **1.** brim, bulge, cram, glut, gorge, heap, jam-pack *(Nonformal)*, laden, load, pack, puff *or* pump up, stuff, surfeit, swell, tank up, top off **2.** furnish, impregnate, inflate, provide, replenish, supply, stock **3.** congest, crowd, occupy, permeate, pervade, saturate, suffuse, take up **4.** clog, close, cork, plug, stop up, top **5.** conform to, fulfill, meet, satisfy

filling *adj.* fulfilling, satiating, satisfying, surfeiting – *n.* cartridge, centre, contents, dressing, filler, innards, insides, packing, padding, stuffing, wadding

film *n.* **1.** cinema, flick *(Nonformal)*, footage, motion *or* moving picture, movie, picture show, rushes, talkie *(Historical)* *Film Terms:* big close up *or* BCU, blue screen, closeup, cut, dailies, day for night, dissolve, dolly, fade-in, fade-out, honey wagon, hot seat, jump cut, long shot, loosen, master, move, pan, outtake, rushes, take, tighten, wrap, zoom in *or* out *Kinds of film:* action, adventure, animated, arthouse, avant-garde, black and white, black comedy, B movie, cartoon, *cinema verité (French)*, cult, colour, comedy, crime drama, docudrama, documentary, drama, educational, feature, film noir, foreign, French New Wave, homage, horror, made-for-TV, murder mystery *or* mystery, musical, neo-realism, pornography, realism, romance, romantic comedy, samurai, satire, science fiction, screwball comedy, short, silent, slapstick, slasher, snuff, sound, spaghetti western, surrealist, suspense, thriller, tragedy, underground, western *Nonformal:* chop socky, dramedy, mockumentary, porn, slice and dice, talkie **2.** blur, cloud, coat, coating, covering, dusting, gauze, haze, haziness, layer, membrane, mist, mistiness, nebula, opacity, scum, sheet, skin, tissue, transparency, veil, web – *v.* do a take, document, photograph, roll, shoot, video, videotape

filmy *adj.* **1.** chiffon, clear, diaphanous, fine, fine-grained, gauzy, light, see-through, sheer, transparent **2.** blurred, blurry, cloudy, dim, hazy, membranous, milky, misty, opalescent, opaque, pearly

filter *n.* cheesecloth, colander, gauze, membrane, mesh, purifier, refiner, refinery, sieve, sifter, strainer, weeping tile – *v.* **1.** clarify, clean, distill, drain, filtrate, osmose, percolate, purify, refine, screen, separate, sieve, sift, strain, winnow **2.** effuse, escape, exude, leak, ooze, seep, vent

filth *n.* **1.** crud, dirt, dregs, dung, excrement, feces, filthiness, foulness, garbage, grime, impurity, muck, nastiness, offal, pollution, putrefaction, refuse, sewage, silt, slime, slop, sludge, slush, trash, uncleanness **2.** corruption, contamination, obscenity, pornography, profanity, rottenness, rudeness, smut

filthy *adj.* **1.** begrimed, dirty, dishevelled, foul, grimy, gross, grubby, impure, miry, mucky, muddy, polluted, putrid, repulsive, revolting, scummy, slimy, sloppy, smoky, sooty, squalid, unclean, unkempt, unwashed, verminous, vile *Nonformal:* cruddy, grotty, grungy, scuzzy *Antonyms:* clean, spotless, sterile **2.** base, bawdy, blue *(Nonformal)*, coarse, contemptible, corrupt, depraved, despicable, dirty-minded, foul-mouthed, indecent, lascivious, lewd, licentious, loathsome, low, nasty, obscene, offensive, pornographic, profane, scatological, sleazy, smutty, suggestive, vulgar

finagle *v.* cheat, connive, conspire, defraud, dupe, fleece, hoax, intrigue, manoeuvre, plot against, swindle, trick, victimize *Nonformal:* bamboozle, con, flim-flam, scam

final *adj.* **1.** closing, concluding, crowning, ending, finishing, hindmost, lag, last, last-minute, latest, latter, terminating, ultimate *Antonyms:* first, initial, introductory, opening **2.** absolute, conclusive, decided, decisive, definite, definitive, determinative, immutable, incontrovertible, irrefutable, irrevocable, settled, unanswerable, unappealable *Antonyms:* changeable, revocable, repealable

finale *n.* cessation, climax, close, conclusion, culmination, curtain, dénouement, end, ending, epilogue, finish, last act, peroration, summation, swan song *(Nonformal)*, windup *Antonyms:* commencement, introduction, opening, preamble, prologue

finalize *v.* clinch, complete, conclude, end, finish off *or* up, ink *(Nonformal)*, perfect, resolve, seal, terminate, wrap up *Antonyms:* commence, continue, initiate, prolong, protract

finality *n.* certitude, completeness, conclusiveness, decisiveness, entirety, finish, immutability, inevitableness, irrevocability, resolution, settlement, totality, unavoidability, wholeness

finally *adv.* **1.** after all, already, at last *or* length, belatedly, despite delay, eventually, in conclusion *or* the end, lastly, someday, sometime, subsequently, ultimately **2.** assuredly, certainly, completely, conclusively, decisively, determinately, inescapably, inexorably, irrevocably, permanently, undoubtedly

finance *n.* account, banking, business, commerce, economy, financial *or* fiscal affairs, finances, financial world, investment, money management *or* matters *Nonformal:* Bay Street, big bucks, Wall Street – *v.* aid, assist, back, bankroll *(Nonformal)*, capitalize, fund, produce *(Theatrical)*, sponsor, support, stake

finances *n. pl.* affairs, affluence, assets, backing, budget, capital, cash, estate, fortune, funds, holdings, income, kitty *(Nonformal)*, means, money, nest egg, possessions, property, purse, reserves, resources, revenue, riches, savings, securities, situation, stake, substance, wealth

financial *adj.* banking, budgetary, business, commercial, economic, fiscal, monetary, money, pecuniary *Financial Terms:* ASE, bear market *(Falling)*, bond, bull market *(Rising)*, buyback, buy long, buy on margin, call, commodities, compounded, convertible, debenture, dividend, Dow Jones, equity, fixed rate, forward exchange, front end loader, future, index, initial public offering *or* IPO, insider buyout, insider trading, interest, junk bonds, leveraged buyout *or* LBO, merger, money market, mutual funds, NASDAQ, NYSE, option, poison pill, pot, price/earnings ratio, raider, return, scorched earth, securities, sell off, sell short, shark, standard and poor, stock, take over, take private, TSE, variable rate, VSE, white knight, yield

financier *n.* backer, banker, broker, businessperson, capitalist, entrepreneur, financial expert, fundraiser, investor, lender, Maecenas, merchant, moneylender, moneyman, operator, patron, philanthropist, speculator, sponsor, staker, stockbroker, supporter, tycoon, venture capitalist *Nonformal:* angel, bankroll, grubstaker, meal ticket, the city, the money

financing *n.* allowance, backing, expenditure, expense, expenses, funding, grant, loan, money, outlay, payment, remittance, sponsorship, stake, stipend, support

find *n.* acquisition, asset, bargain, bargoon *(Nonformal)*, boon, catch, discovery, gem, godsend, good buy, jewel, treasure, windfall – *v.* arrive at, attain, catch sight of, chance upon, come across, come up with, discover, encounter, gain, hit *or* light *or* stumble into *or* upon, learn, locate, meet, reach, recover, spot, track down, turn up, uncover, unearth *Antonyms:* lose, mislay, misplace

finding *n.* **1.** bonanza, breakthrough, discovery, jackpot, strike **2.** conclusion, decision, decree, judgment, outcome, pronouncement, recommendation, result, sentence, verdict

fine *adj.* **1.** admirable, choice, excellent, exceptional, expensive, exquisite, first-rate, great, outstanding, ripping *(British)*, superior, very good **2.** doing well, getting along, good, holding one's own, recovering *Nonformal:* a-okay, cool, copesetic, hunky-dory, not too shabby, solid, tickety-boo **3.** dainty, delicate, diaphanous, ethereal, filmy, fine-drawn, fine-grained, fine-spun, fragile, frail, gauzy, gossamer, light, lightweight, sheer, thin, threadlike **4.** inconsequential, microscopic, minute, small, teeny, tiny, undetectable, very small **5.** appreciative, discerning, discriminating, educated, insightful, intuitive, perceptive, trained **6.** affected, elegant, fastidious, meticulous, polished **7.** alluring, attractive, beautiful, fine-looking, handsome, striking **8.** balmy, bright, clear, clement, cloudless, dry, fair, pleasant, splendid, sunny **9.** clarified, clean, clear, pure, sterling, unadulterated *Antonyms:* dirty, mixed, muddy **10.** ambiguous, insubstantial, precarious, ropy *(Nonformal)*, slender, tenuous, precarious **11.** acute, keen, razor-edged, sharp, well-honed – *interj.* agree, okay *(Nonformal)*, right, right on, so be it, yes – *n.* adjustment, amends, assessment, damages, fee, forfeit, penalty, punishment, reparation, sum, wergeld – *v.* dock, exact, extort, levy, penalize, punish, seize, tax, wrest, wring

finery *n.* adornment, clothes, frills, frippery, gaudery, ornamentation, splendour, trappings *Nonformal:* best bib and tucker, gladrags, Sunday best

fine-spun *adj.* delicate, diaphanous, flimsy, gauzy, gossamer, lacy, nice, refined, sheer, thin, translucent *Antonyms:* dense, heavy, opaque, thick

finesse *n.* acumen, adeptness, adroitness, artfulness, cleverness, competence, craftiness, cunning, dash, diplomacy, discretion, feint, gamesmanship, guile, know-how, panache, polish, quickness, *savoir-faire (French)*, savvy *(Nonformal)*, skill, sophistication, subtlety, tact, verve, wile *Antonyms:* awkwardness, clumsiness, ungainliness – *v.* cheat, contrive, evade, finagle, handle, jockey, manoeuvre, manipulate, operate, stickhandle *(Nonformal)*, trick, work, work around

finger *n.* appendage, claw, digit, feeler, phalange *or* phalanx – *v.* **1.** feel, fiddle with, grope, handle, manipulate, maul, meddle, palpate, paw, play *or* toy with, thumb, touch **2.** accuse, betray, blame, charge, condemn, identify, impugn, point at *Nonformal:* rat, sing, snitch, squeal

finicky *adj.* choosy, critical, difficult, exacting, fastidious, fussy, hard to please, hypercritical, nitpicking, particular, pettifogging, persnickety, picky, scrupulous, stickling *Antonyms:* accepting, complacent, easygoing

finish *n.* **1.** close, conclusion, end, finale, last stage *or* stop, stop, termination, wrap-up **2.** accomplishment, achievement, attainment, completion, culmination, execution, fulfillment, realization *Antonyms:* beginning, birth, commencement, genesis **3.** coating, covering, glaze, lacquer, polish, varnish, wax **4.** glossiness, grain, lustre, patina, shine, smoothness, surface, texture **5.** appearance, beauty, cultivation, elegance, grace, refinement – *v.* **1.** cease, close, desist, end, halt, terminate, shut down, stop *Antonyms:* begin, commence, start **2.** accomplish, achieve, cap, climax, clinch, complete, conclude, culminate, finalize, fulfill, implement, perfect, wind *or* wrap up **3.** consume, deplete, desiccate, devour, drain, drink, eat, empty, exhaust, expend, spend, squander, use up *Antonyms:* conserve, preserve, replenish **4.** coat, glaze, lacquer, polish, refine, sand, smooth, stain, treat, varnish, veneer, wax **5.** annihilate, assassinate, best, defeat, destroy, dispatch, execute, exterminate, extirpate, kill, liquidate, murder, overcome, sanitize *(Nonformal)*, slaughter, slay, wipe out

finished *adj.* **1.** ceased, completed, concluded, done, ended, closed, executed, finalized, fulfilled, realized, resolved, settled, stopped, terminated, through, worked out *Nonformal:* ancient history, on ice, yesterday's news **2.** cultivated, cultured, elegant, impeccable, perfected, polished, refined, suave, urbane **3.** accomplished, consummate, deft, expert, flawless, masterful, practised, professional, proficient, skillful *Antonyms:* amateurish, unskilled **4.** cashed-in, gone, wiped-out *Nonformal:* kaput, pfft, toast, totalled

finite *adj.* bound, bounded, circumscribed, confined, definable, demarcated, determinate, exact, fixed, limited, precise, restricted, specific *Antonyms:* boundless, endless, eternal, infinite, limitless

fire *n.* **1.** blaze, bonfire, brightness, burning, campfire, charring, combustion, conflagration, embers, flame, flare, glow, hearth, heat, inferno, pyrolysis, scorching, searing, sparks, tinder, wildfire **2.** animation, ardour, brio, dash, drive, eagerness, energy, enthusiasm, excitement, exhilaration, fervour, gusto, impetuosity, intensity, passion, spirit, verve, vigour, vim, vivacity, zeal – *v.* **1.** animate, arouse, drive, electrify, enliven, enthuse, exalt, excite, galvanize, heighten, impassion, incite, inflame, inform, inspire, intensify, intoxicate, irritate, provoke, quicken, rouse, stir, thrill **2.** banish, cancel, defrock, depose, dethrone, discard, discharge, dismiss, dispense, downsize, drop, eject, eliminate, expel, impeach, let go, make redundant, oust, relieve, remove, replace, retire, supersede, supplant, terminate, unseat *Nonformal:* axe, boot, bounce, bump, can, give the gate, kick out, pink slip, sack, send packing, uninstall

firefighter *n.* fire-eater, fireman, smoke eater, smoke jumper *Firefighting terms* backdraft, bean pot, blow up, bucket brigade, cover, extinguisher, firebreak, fire drill, fire engine *or* truck, hot spot, hydrant, inferno, mop up, 96, pumper, sprinkler system, stand pipe, water bombing, water tower

fireproof *adj.* fire-resistant, flame-retardant, incombustible, nonflammable, unburnable

fireside *adj.* amiable, casual, easy, folksy, friendly, genial, informal, laid-back, low key, natural, neighbourly, nonformal *Antonyms*: ceremonious, formal, pompous – *n.* abode, chimney corner, domicile, dwelling, fender, fire, fireplace, habitation, hearth, hearthside, hearthstroke, home, hug, ingle, inglenook

fireworks *n.* pyrotechnics *Kinds of fireworks:* bomb, burning schoolhouse, candlebomb, cannon cracker, cap, Catherine wheel, cherry bomb, cracker, firecracker, fizgig, flare, flowerpot, pinwheel, rocket, Roman candle, serpent, skyrocket, snake, sparkler, squib, torpedo, whiz-bang

firm *adj.* **1.** close-grained, compact, compressed, concentrated, concrete, condensed, congealed, dense, hard, hardened, heavy, impenetrable, impermeable, impervious, inflexible, petrified, resistant, solid, solidified, stiff, thick, tough, unyielding *Antonyms:* flexible, malleable, pliant **2.** anchored, bolted, bound, braced, cemented, durable, embedded, entrenched, fastened, fixed, immobile, motionless, riveted, rooted, screwed in, secure, secured, set, settled, soldered, stable, stationary, steady, sturdy, taut, tight, unalterable, unmoving, unshakable **3.** controlled, disciplined, resolute, strict, unwavering **4.** abiding, adamant, consistent, constant, determined, enduring, hard-nosed, immutable, obstinate, persistent, refractory, rigid, staunch, steadfast, stubborn, tenacious, true *Antonyms:* changeable, fickle, mercurial **5.** hardy, robust, strong, substantial, vigorous – *n.* association, business, company, concern, conglomerate, corporation, enterprise, house, incorporation, multinational, organization, outfit, partnership, syndicate

firmly *adv.* adamantly, constantly, determinedly, doggedly, durably, fast, fixedly, hard, immovably, inflexibly, intently, motionlessly, obdurately, obstinately, persistently, pertinaciously, purposefully, resolutely, rigidly, securely, solid, solidly, soundly, steadily, stiffly, strongly, stubbornly, tenaciously, thoroughly, tight, tightly, unflinchingly, unwaveringly, with perseverance *Antonyms:* erratically, variably, waveringly

firmness *n.* **1.** compactness, density, durability, fixedness, hardiness, hardness, impenetrability, impermeability, imperviousness, resistance, rigidity, ruggedness, solidity, soundness, stability, steadiness, stiffness, strength, sturdiness, substantiality, tautness, tension, tightness, toughness *Antonyms:* frailty, levity, softness **2.** constancy, determination, doggedness, fidelity, immutability, loyalty, obstinacy, permanence, persistence, purposefulness, resoluteness, resolution, resolve, stamina, staunchness, steadfastness, strength, stubbornness, tenacity *Antonyms:* adaptability, changeability, fickleness, weakness **3.** dogmatism, fundamentalism, orthodoxy, purism, strictness, traditionalism

first *adj.* **1.** basic, cardinal, elementary, key, inaugural, initial, introductory, primary, rudimentary, virgin *Antonyms:* following, last, secondary **2.** beginning, earliest, early, opening, primal, primeval, primitive, primordial, *sub initio (Latin)* **3.** aboriginal, native, original, primigenial, primogenitary **4.** best, chief, eminent, first-class, foremost, greatest, leading, main, number one, numero uno *(Nonformal)*, preeminent, premier, principal – *adv.* beforehand, firstly, initially

First Peoples *n.* aboriginal, aborigine, First Nations, Native Peoples, original *Legal Designations:* non-status Indian, non-treaty Indian, status Indian, treaty Indian *First Peoples' language groupings:* Algonquian, Athapaskan, Inuit-Aleut, Haida, Tlingit, Iroquoian, Ktunaxa Kinbasket, Salishan, Siouan, Tsimshian, Wakashan *First Peoples' culture regions:* Arctic, Great Plains, Northeast, Northwest Coast, Plateau, Subarctic *See also:* **organization**

first-rate *adj.* accomplished, ace, capital, choice, excellent, expert, extraordinary, fine, first-class, humdinging *(Nonformal)*, masterful, nonpareil, outstanding, remarkable, stellar, sterling, superlative, wonderful *Antonyms:* lacking, incommensurate, inferior, mediocre

fiscal *adj.* capital, cash, economic, financial, monetary, money, pecuniary

fish *n.* *ichthys (Greek)*, pisces, *poisson (French) Groupings of fish:* demersal, freshwater, pelagic, saltwater *Kinds of fish:* alewife, anchovy, angelfish, angler, Arctic char, Atlantic salmon, Aurora trout, barbel, barracuda, bass *or* rock bass, blackfish, bloater, bluefish, bonefish, bonito, bowfin, brisling, *brochet (French)*, brook trout, burbot, butterfish, candlefish *or* oolichan, capelin, carp, catfish, characin, chinook *or* chum *or* coho salmon, chub, cisco, cod *or* codfish, crappie, croaker, dace, darter, dogfish, Dolly Varden trout, dorado, doré, eel, flounder, flying, gar, gaspereau, goatfish, goby, goldeye, goldfish, goosefish, grouper, gunnel, guppy, haddock, hagfish, hake, halibut, herring, jackfish, killifish, lancelet, lake trout *or* touladi, lamprey, lingcod, livebearers, lookdown, lungfish, mackerel, madtom, man-of-war, manta, marlin, menhaden, minnow, monkfish, mooneye, mullet, mummichog, muskellunge *or* muskie, northern cod, northern pike, ocean perch *or* redfish, orange roughy, ouananiche, paddlefish, parrot, perch, piccanan, pickerel, pike, pipefish, piranha, plaice, pollack, pompano, porgy, puffer, quillback, rainbow trout *or* steel-head, ray, redhorse, red snapper, sailfish, salmon, sand tiger, sardine, sawfish, scad, scorpionfish, sculpin, scup, sea horse, shad, shark, shiner, Siamese fighting, silver hake, silverside, skate, smelt, sockeye salmon, sole, splake, sprat, stickleback, stingray, striped bass, sturgeon, sucker, sunfish, swordfish, tarpon, tautog, tetra, tilefish, togue, tomcod, trout, tullibee, tuna, turbot, tyee, viperfish, wahoo, walleye, weakfish, whitebait, whiting, Winnipeg goldeye, wrass, wrymouth, yellowtail *Cured or prepared fish:* caviar, ceviche, Digby chicken, finnan haddie, kippers, lox, pickled herring, smoked mackerel *or* salmon, Solomon Gundy, *taramasalata (Greek)* – *v.* angle, bait, bob, extract, extricate, jig, net, produce, pull out, seine, trawl, troll

fishy *adj.* cagey, dishonest, doubtful, dubious, embellished, embroidered, far-fetched, improbable, questionable, shady, slippery, tricky, unlikely *Antonyms:* credible, factual, gospel, literal, truthful

fission *n.* break, cleaving, disjuncture, division, parting, rupture, scission, separation, severance – *v.* atomize, bisect, break, cleave, disintegrate, divide, fragment, part, separate, shatter, smash, splinter, split

fissure *n.* abyss, break, cavity, chasm, chink, cleft, cranny, crevice, cut, fault, fracture, furrow, groove, hole, interspace, narrows, notch, rent, riff, rupture, scission, split – *v.* bisect, break, cleave, crack, divide, divorce, part, separate, split

fist *n.* **1.** hand, paw *Nonformal:* duke, fin, knuckle sandwich, mitt **2.** calligraphy, conditional, penmanship, writing style

fit *adj.* **1.** adapted, adjusted, conditonal, equipped, prepared, prepped, primed, ready, suitable, suited, trained, treated **2.** acceptable, appropriate, apt, decorous, deserving, due, fair, fitting, justifiable, proper, right, rightful **3.** able, adequate, capable, competent, decent, eligible, qualified, well-suited, worthy **4.** able-bodied, buff *(Nonformal)* hale, healthy, robust, sound, toned, trim, well, wholesome *Antonyms:* flabby, unfit, unhealthy – *n.* attack, bout, burst, conniption *(Nonformal)*, convulsion, frenzy, outbreak, paroxysm, rush, seizure *or* epileptic seizure, spasm, spell, stroke, tantrum, throe, turn, twitch – *v.* **1.** agree, belong, blend, click, complement, dovetail, harmonize, interlock, join, match, relate, suit **2.** accommodate, adapt, adjust, alter, arrange, change, modify **3.** accoutre, arm, equip, furnish, kit out *(Nonformal)*, outfit, prepare, provide, ready, rig

fitful *adj.* broken, capricious, changeable, erratic, fickle, flickering, fluctuating, haphazard, hit-or-miss, intermittent, interrupted, irregular, restless, shifting, spasmodic, sporadic, uneasy, unstable, variable *Antonyms:* constant, orderly, predictable, uniform

fitness *n.* **1.** condition, fettle, health, physical conditioning *or* fitness, repair, robustness, shape, strength, tone, trim, vigour *Kind of fitness:* aerobic, anaerobic, cardio-respiratory, cardiovascular, muscle conditioning **2.** adequacy, admissibility, appropriateness, aptitude, competence, eligibility, expediency, preparedness, qualification, readiness, suitability **3.** accommodation, accordance, adaptation, agreeableness, applicability, assimilation, compatibility, correspondence, harmony, seasonableness **4.** congeniality, decency, decorum, order, propriety, seemliness, rightness

fitted *adj.* **1.** adapted, assimilated, compatible, made, matched, shaped, suited, tailored, tailor-made **2.** accoutred, appointed, armed, decked out *(Nonformal)*, equipped, furnished, implemented, outfitted, provided, supplied

fitting *adj.* appropriate, apt, correct, decent, deserved, felicitous, fit, fortunate, meet, merited, opportune, pertinent, proper, relevant, right, seemly, suitable, warranted *Antonyms:* improper, inappropriate, unfortunate

fix *n.* **1.** box, corner, difficulty, dilemma, embarrassment, hole, mess, plight, predicament, quandary, scrape, spot, state *Nonformal:* jam, muddle, pickle, stew **2.** dose, hit, injection, score, shot, sip, slug **3.** bearing, location, place, position – *v.* **1.** adjust, amend, correct, debug, emend, mend, overhaul, patch, rebuild, recondition, reconstruct, regulate, repair, restore, revamp, revise, sort *Antonyms:* break, destroy, shatter, wreck **2.** affix, anchor, attach, bind, catch, cement, congeal, connect, couple, embed, entrench, fasten, glue, graft, harden, implant, ingrain, install, instill, link, lodge, make firm, moor, nail, pin, place, plant, position, rivet, root, secure, set, settle, solidify, stabilize, stay put, steady, tie **3.** concentrate, direct, focus on, level at, obsess over **4.** arrange, conclude, coordinate, decide, define, determine, dispose, establish, organize, plan, prepare, resolve, set, settle, set up, solve, work out **5.** bribe, buy, buy off, corrupt, fiddle, frame, influence, manoeuvre, manipulate, prearrange, predesign, preplan, rig, tamper with *Nonformal:* doctor, fudge, lubricate **6.** avenge, get *(Nonformal)*, get even *or* revenge, hurt, injure, punish, revenge, take retribution *Antonyms:* absolve, forgive, pardon

fixation *n.* attachment, block, complex, craze, enthusiasm, fascination, fetish, hangup *(Nonformal)*, hysteria, *idée fixe (French)*, infatuation, lunacy, madness, mania, obsession, preoccupation

fixed *adj.* **1.** anchored, attached, fastened, firm, hitched, immobile, immovable, nailed, rooted, secure, still *Antonyms:* mobile, moving, shaky **2.** abiding, certain, changeless, definite, enduring, established, inalterable, permanent, resolute, rigid, rock solid *(Nonformal)*, set, settled, solid, stable, stationary, steadfast, stubborn, sure, tenacious, unalterable, unbending, unchanging, undeviating *Antonyms:* pliant, unsure **3.** focused, intent, locked, narrow, steady, unfaltering, unwavering **4.** all done, arranged, confirmed, decided, planned, prearranged, resolved, set up, taken care of **5.** going, in order, mended, put right, rebuilt, repaired, sorted out, whole, working *Antonyms:* broken, destroyed, wrecked **6.** castrated, emasculated, gelded, neutered, spayed

fizz *n.* bubbles, bubbling, carbonation, effervescence, foam, gas, hiss, sibilation, sparkle, spumescence – *v.* bubble, effervesce, fizzle, froth, hiss, seethe, sibilate, sparkle, sputter

fizzle *n.* **1.** collapse, comedown, disappointment, failure, fiasco, flop *(Nonformal)*, letdown, setback **2.** bubbles, carbonation, effervescence, fizz, hiss, sparkle – *v.* **1.** abort, burn out, collapse, crash and burn *(Nonformal)*, die, exhaust, fail, fall through, fold, misfire, tire, weaken **2.** bubble, fizz, froth, hiss, sparkle, sputter

flabbergast *v.* abash, amaze, astonish, astound, confound, daze, disconcert, dumfound, make speechless, nonplus, overcome, overwhelm, shock, stagger, stun, surprise, upset *Nonformal:* blow away, bowl over, throw, gobsmack

flabby *adj.* baggy, doughy, drooping, fat, flaccid, floppy, gone to seed *(Nonformal)*, hanging, lax, limp, loose, pendulous, sagging, slack, sloppy, soft, toneless, unfit, weak *Antonyms:* firm, hard, strong, taut, tense

flaccid *adj.* debilitated, drooping, emasculated, enervated, enfeebled, flabby, flimsy, infirm, lax, limp, loose, nerveless, pendulous, sapped, slack, soft, weak, weakened *Antonyms:* firm, taut, toned, tumescent, turgid

flag *n.* banner, bunting, colours, ensign, guidon, national flag, pennant, standard, streamer *Historical Canadian flags:* Canadian Red Ensign, fleur-de-lys, Royal Union, St. George's cross – *v.* **1.** gesture, hail, indicate, motion, salute, signal, warn, wave **2.** decline, deteriorate, die, droop, ebb, fade, fail, faint, fall, fall off, languish, sag, sink, slump, succumb, wane, weaken, wilt

flagellation *n.* beating, flogging, hair shirt, lashing, masochism, punishment, scourging, strapping, whipping

flagrant *adj.* atrocious, awful, barefaced, blatant, bold, brazen, conspicuous, disgraceful, dreadful, egregious, flaunting, glaring, gross, heinous, horrifying, immodest, in your face *(Nonformal)*, monstrous, notorious, offensive, outrageous, rank, scandalous, shameless, shocking, striking, wicked *Antonyms:* benevolent, charitable, good-hearted, kind

flail *n.* ball and chain, medieval weapon, threshing tool – *v.* **1.** beat, buffet, flog, horsewhip, lash, strike, thrash, thresh **2.** oscillate, sway, swing, undulate, wave

flair *n.* **1.** ability, accomplishment, aptitude, aptness, bent, dexterity, faculty, feel, forte, genius, gift, knack, mastery, proclivity, talent, turn **2.** chic, dash, elegance, glamour, panache, presence, style, taste, verve, zip *Nonformal:* pizzazz, shine, splash

flak *n.* abuse, admonitions, animadversion, aspersions, bad press, castigation, censure, chastisement, complaint, criticism, disapproval, disapprobation, imputation, reprehension, reproach, reproof, strictures, vituperation *Antonyms:* applause, approval, kudos, praise

flake *n.* **1.** lamina, layer, membrane, peel, pellicle, scab, scale, scurf, section, shaving, skin, slice, sliver, stratum **2.** dilettante, dolt, dunce, eccentric, fool, nincompoop, ninny *Nonformal:* airhead, ditz, dope, hoser – *v.* exfoliate, peel, scab, scale

flaky *adj.* **1.** ditzy *(Nonformal)*, dopey, eccentric, egocentric, erratic, foolish, idiosyncratic, irresponsible, whimsical, unreliable *Antonyms:* grave, serious, sober **2.** cracked, dry, flocculent, furfuraceous, lentiginous, powdery, scabby, scaly, squamous *Antonyms:* oily, satiny, smooth

flamboyant *adj.* baroque, brilliant, colourful, dazzling, exciting, extravagant, flaming, flashy, florid, gaudy, luscious, luxuriant, ornate, ostentatious, overelaborate, peacockish, pretentious, purple, resplendent, rococo, showy, splashy, sporty, swank, swashbuckling, theatrical *Nonformal:* gassy, jazzy *Antonyms:* modest, plain, simple

flame *n.* **1.** blaze, brightness, fire, flash, flicker, glare, gleam, glimmer, glint, glow, light, luminosity, lustre, shimmer, sparkle **2.** ardour, devotedness, devotion, enthusiasm, fervency, feverishness, fire, intensity, passion, warmth *Antonyms:* aloofness, frostiness, indifference **3.** admirer, adorer, beau, beloved, darling, gallant, heartthrob, heart's desire, inamorata, inamorato, lover, paramour, sweetheart, true love

flaming *adj.* **1.** ablaze, afire, aflame, alight, blazing, burning, fiery, ignited, in flames, raging **2.** animated, ardent, aroused, eager, enthusiastic, fervent, frenzied, hot, intense, passionate, stimulated *Antonyms:* cold, cool, dispassionate, indifferent **3.** barefaced, blatant, brazen, conspicuous, evident, flagrant, flaunting, inveterate, notorious, obvious, overt

flange *n.* brim, border, edge, lip, ridge, rim, skirt, splay – *v.* alter, distort, phase shift, vary

flap *n.* **1.** accessory, adjunct, appendage, apron, cover, drop, extension, fold, hanging, lapel, lobe, overlap, pendant, skirt, tab, wing **2.** ado, crisis, crux, emergency, excitement, frenzy, kerfuffle *(Nonformal)*, predicament, stir – *v.* agitate, beat, flail, flop, flutter, shake, swing, thrash, vibrate, wave

flare *n.* **1.** alarm, beacon, direction, flame, flirrup *(Newfoundland)*, guide, light, rocket, signal, torch, warning **2.** amplification, broadening, dilation, enlargement, expansion, extension, increase, swelling *Antonyms:* compression, contraction, decrease – *v.* **1.** blaze, boil over, burn, burn up, dazzle, erupt, explode, gleam, glitter, glimmer, radiate, sparkle **2.** broaden, dilate, expand, extend, grow, increase, splay, spread, widen *Antonyms:* diminish, recede, retract

flare-up *n.* blast, blowout, blowup, burst, eruption, explosion, flash, gush, hot spot, outburst, rush, spew, torrent *Antonyms:* calm, tranquility, peacefulness

flash *adj.* **1.** abrupt, breakneck, express, immediate, instantaneous, precipitate, prompt, quick, rapid, speedy, sudden, swift **2.** blatant, flagrant, flashy, gaudy, ostentatious, outlandish, sporty, vulgar – *n.* **1.** beam, bedazzlement, blaze, brilliance, burst, cannonball, coruscation, dazzle, flame, flare, flicker, glare, gleam, glimmer, glint, glisten, glitter, glow, illumination, incandescence, lightning, phosphorescence, ray, shimmer, shine, spark, streak, stream, twinkling **2.** crack, impulse, instant, minute, moment, second, streak, stroke, tick, twinkle, wink *Nonformal:* blue streak, jiffy *Antonyms:* eons, eternity, forever **3.** blatancy, display, flagrance, flamboyance, gaudiness, parade, pretentiousness, showiness, spectacle **4.** article, brief, broadcast, bulletin, communication, dispatch, newscast, news clip *or* report, story **5.** ace, genius, magician, master, talent, virtuoso, wizard, *wunderkind (German) Nonformal:* crackerjack, star, whiz – *v.* **1.** bedazzle, blaze, coruscate, dazzle, flame, flare, flicker, gleam, glimmer, glint, glitter, glow, light, phosphoresce, radiate, reflect, shine, spark, sparkle, twinkle **2.** bolt, dart, dash, flit, fly, race, scoot *(Nonformal)*, shoot, speed, spring, streak, sweep, whistle, zoom **3.** brandish, expose, flaunt, flourish, parade, present, reveal, show off **4.** cable, communicate, e-mail, fax, send, telegram, telegraph, wire

flashback *n.* **1.** memory, recall, recollection, remembrance, reminiscence, retrospection, reverberation, review *Antonyms:* forgetfulness, oblivion **2.** delusion, dream, hallucination, illusion *or* optical illusion, trip

flashy *adj.* blatant, brazen, catchpenny, cheap, flamboyant, flaunting, florid, garish, gaudy, glaring, glittering, glittery, glitzy, jazzy, loud, meretricious, ornate, ostentatious, showy, snazzy, sparkling, tacky, tasteless, tawdry, tinsel, vulgar *Nonformal:* all hat and no cattle, Hollywood *Antonyms:* downbeat, modest, natural, plain, unaffected

flask *n.* beaker, bottle, canteen, carafe, chalice, container, crock, crystal, decanter, demijohn, ewer, flagon, glass, goblet, gourd, horn, jar, jug, thermos, tumbler, urn, vial, water bottle

flat *adj.* **1.** even, flush, horizontal, level, regular, smooth, straight, unbroken **2.** collapsed, dead, fallen, outstretched, prone, prostrate, reclining, splay, supine **3.** deflated, empty, low, shallow **4.** bankrupt, broke, impecunious, impoverished, penniless, pinched, poor, skint *(British)*, strapped, tapped out *Nonformal:* busted, hard-up **5.** absolute, categorical, conclusive, definite, definitive, explicit, express, final, fixed, positive, total, unconditional, unequivocal, unmitigated, unqualified, utter **6.** firm, fixed, stable, steady, uniform, unvarying **7.** banal, boring, colourless, dull, dim, drab, inane, innocuous, insipid, jejune, lacklustre, lifeless, monotonous, muted, off, prosaic, spiritless, tedious, uninteresting *Nonformal:* blah, ho hum *Antonyms:* bubbly, effervescent, exciting **8.** flavourless, stale, tasteless, unpalatable, unsavoury, unseasoned, watery – *n.* **1.** apartment, condo, co-op, crash pad *(Nonformal)*, joint, lodging, pad, rental, room, rooms, suite, tenement, walk-up **2.** horizontal, level, plane, smooth **3.** flatland, plain, prairie, savannah

flatland *n.* champaign, grassland, heath, lowland, moor, plain, pampas, plateau, prairie, savannah, steppe, tableland, tundra, veldt

flatten *v.* **1.** fell, floor, level, hit, knock *or* lay out, prostrate, punch, subdue, take down, trample *Nonformal:* kayo, plaster **2.** compress, crush, deflate, depress, smooth, smoothen *(Nonformal)*, spread out, squash, straighten

flatter *v.* **1.** adulate, beguile, blandish, blarney, bootlick, build up, cajole, charm, court, exalt, fawn, glorify, grovel, humour, inveigle, kowtow, laud, massage, praise, puff, toady *Nonformal:* brownnose, butter *or* sweeten up, slobber over, snow, stroke, sweet-talk *Antonyms:* criticize, belittle, demean **2.** adorn, beautify, complement, embellish, enhance, fit, grace, perfect, set off, suit *Antonyms:* detract, diminish, undermine, undo

flattering *adj.* **1.** admiring, adulatory, blandishing, cajoling, eulogizing **2.** fawning, mealy-mouthed, obsequious, oily, panegyrical, servile, smarmy *(Nonformal)*, sycophantic, unctuous, wheedling **3.** agreeable, attractive, beautiful, becoming, complimentary, enhancing, lovely *Antonyms:* diminishing, unattractive

flattery *n.* **1.** adulation, applause, blandishment, blarney, cajolery, compliments, plaudits **2.** flummery, fulsomeness, obsequiousness, sycophancy, unctuousness *Nonformal:* apple polishing, bootlicking, hokum, puffery, soft-soap, sweet talk

flatulence *n.* **1.** *blähung (German)*, fart *(Nonformal)*, *flatuosité (French)*, gas, wind **2.** babble, boasting, crap *(Nonformal)*, empty talk, idle chatter, hot air, rodomontade, twaddle

flatulent *adj.* bloated, bombastic, inflated, long-winded, oratorical, overblown, pompous, pretentious, prolix, superficial, swollen, tedious, tumescent, turgid, windy, wordy *Antonyms:* concise, pithy, terse

flaunt *v.* advertise, air, boast, brandish, broadcast, declare, disclose, display, disport, divulge, exhibit, expose, flash, flourish, grandstand, hotdog *(Nonformal)*, parade, proclaim, reveal, showcase, show off, sport, streak, vaunt *Antonyms:* conceal, hide, veil *Commonly misused:* **flout**

flavour *n.* **1.** acidity, aroma, astringency, bitterness, flavouring, hotness, piquancy, pungency, relish, saltiness, savour, seasoning, smack, sourness, spiciness, sweetness, tang, tartness, taste, twang, vim, zest, zing **2.** aspect, characteristic, essence, nature, quality, spirit, soul, touch – *v.* ginger, impart, infuse, lace, pepper, salt, season, spice

flavouring *n.* additive, condiment, essence, extract, herb, quintessence, relish, seasoning, spice, zest

flavourful *adj.* appetizing, delectable, delicious, mouthwatering, palpable, piquant, sapid, savoury, spicy, tasty, yummy *(Nonformal) Antonyms:* bland, dull, flat, tasteless

flavourless *adj.* bland, boring, dull, flat, insipid, mild, mushy, overdone, stale, tasteless, vapid, watered-down *Antonyms:* delicious, mouthwatering, spicy

flaw *n.* **1.** blemish, defect, deficiency, deformity, demerit, disfigurement, failing, fallibility, fault, foible, imperfection, inadequacy, incompleteness, infirmity, insufficiency, pitfall, problem, shortcoming, weakness **2.** break, crack, fissure, rent, tear – *v.* blemish, deface, deform, disfigure, distort, mar, mark, scar, sully, taint, tarnish

flawless *adj.* absolute complete, faultless, immaculate, impeccable, intact, irreproachable, perfect, spotless, thorough, unblemished, unmarred, whole

flaxen *adj.* aureate, auric, blond, buff, buff-yellow, flax-coloured, gold, golden, pale yellow, straw, straw-coloured, yellow

flay *v.* **1.** attack, berate, castigate, clapperclaw *(P.E.I.)*, criticize, disparage, execrate, lambaste, revile, ridicule, roast, scathe, upbraid *Antonyms:* applaud, eulogize, extol, laud, praise **2.** beat, cane, excoriate, flog, lash, peel, pommel, skin, strip, switch, whip

fleck *n.* bit, dot, mark, patch, piece, pinpoint, speck, speckle, spot, streak, stripe – *v.* dapple, dot, dust, mark, mottle, speckle, spot, stipple, streak, variegate

fledgling *n.* amateur, apprentice, baby, beginner, debutante, greenhorn, infant, minor, neophyte, novice, rookie, recruit, sapling, stripling, tenderfoot, youngster, young 'un *Antonyms:* expert, journeyman, old hand, veteran

flee *v.* abscond, break away, decamp, depart, desert, disappear, elude, escape, evade, get *or* get away, jump, leave, retreat, run, run away, scamper, scram, skip, split, take flight *or* off, vanish *Nonformal:* make tracks, scoot, skedaddle, vamoose *Antonyms:* abide, remain, stay

fleece *n.* coat, coating, down, feathers, fluff, fur, fuzz, hair, nap, pile, plume, wool – *v.* cheat, defraud, divest, gouge, hose, mean-price *(P.E.I.)*, overcharge, rip off, rob, rook, soak, steal, stick, swindle, take *Nonformal:* bleed, con, milk, sting

fleecy *adj.* downy, fluffy, hairy, hirsute, shaggy, soft, woolly *Antonyms:* bald, glabrous, smooth

fleet *adj.* agile, brisk, expeditious, fast, flying, hasty, lively, mercurial, meteoric, nimble, quick, rapid, speedy, swift, winged – *n.* armada, boats, flotilla, formation, line, naval force, navy, sea power, ships, squadron, vessels, warships

fleeting *adj.* brief, ephemeral, flash in the pan *(Nonformal)*, momentary, passing, transient, transitory, temporary, short-lived, vanishing *Antonyms:* endless, enduring, eternal, everlasting, perpetual

flesh *n.* **1.** body, brawn, corpuscles, fat, fatness, meat, muscle, plasm, plasma, protoplasm, pulp, skin, tissue *Antonyms:* bones, ossicles, skeleton **2.** Homo sapiens, humanity, humankind, human nature, human race, living creatures, mankind, people, race, world **3.** blood, brother, child, cousin, family, ilk, kindred, kinfolk, relation, relative, sister *Antonyms:* alien, stranger, foreigner

fleshly *adj.* **1.** bodily, corporal, corporeal, earthly, human, material, mundane, physical, secular, somatic, terrestrial, worldly *Antonyms:* ethereal, metaphysical, spiritual **2.** animal, animalistic, carnal, desiring, erotic, lascivious, lecherous, lewd, lustful, profane, sensuous, voluptuous *Antonyms:* chaste, modest, pure

fleshy *adj.* ample, beefy, brawny, chubby, chunky, corpulent, fat, heavy, hefty, meaty, obese, overweight, plump, portly, pudgy, Rubenesque, stout, voluptuous, *zaftig (German) Nonformal:* tubby, well-padded *Antonyms:* angular, lanky, lithe, slender, thin, willowy

flex *v.* **1.** contract, exert, strain, stretch, tighten, utilize, work **2.** angle, bend, crook, curve, draw out, extend, move, ply, spring

flexibility *n.* adaptability, adjustability, affability, bendiness *(Nonformal)*, compliance, docility, elasticity, extensibility, give, limberness, litheness, plasticity, pliancy, springiness, tractability *Antonyms:* fixity, rigidity, tautness, tightness

flexible *adj.* **1.** adaptable, adjustable, bendable, malleable, mouldable, pliable, pliant, switch hitting, variable *Antonyms:* fixed, rigid, stiff, **2.** acquiescent, amenable, complaisant, compliant, open to suggestion, tractable, yielding *Antonyms:* difficult, stubborn, unyielding **3.** adroit, agile, deft, dextrous, limber, lithe, nimble, prehensile

flicker *n.* beam, flare, flash, gleam, glimmer, ray, spark – *v.* blaze, blink, burn, flare, flash, glance, gleam, glimmer, glint, glitter, glow, quaver, quiver, scintillate, shimmer, sparkle, twinkle, vibrate, waver

flight *n.* **1.** aerial navigation, aeronautics, aviation, flying, gliding, mounting, navigation, soaring, takeoff, trajectory, winging **2.** journey, migration, movement, passage, trip *Nonformal:* hop, jump **3.** break, breakout, departure, escape, exit, exodus, fleeing, getaway, retreat **4.** aircraft, airplane, connection, plane, transportation

flighty *adj.* capricious, changeable, crazy, dizzy, empty-headed, fickle, flaky *(Nonformal)*, flip, frivolous, giddy, impetuous, impulsive, inconstant, irresponsible, light-headed, lively, mercurial, scatterbrained, silly, thoughtless, unstable, vacillating, volatile, wavering, whimsical, wild *Antonyms:* grounded, pondering, serious, thoughtful, wise

flimflam *n* **1** confidence game, deception, fraud, hoax, humbug, pretense, swindle, trickery *Nonformal:* bamboozlement, con game, rip-off, scam, sting **2.** babble, baloney, foolishness, nonsense *Nonformal:* bunk, crap, malarkey, garbage, twaddle

flimsy *adj.* **1.** chiffon, delicate, diaphanous, fragile, gauzy, gossamer, insubstantial, light, papery, sheer, slight, thin, transparent *Antonyms:* heavy, opaque, thick **2.** fallacious, groundless, illogical, implausible, improbable, inadequate, inept, lame, not persuasive, poor, puerile, slapdash, superficial, thin, transparent, trifling, trivial, unreasonable, unsubstantial, weak, without grounds *Antonyms:* documented, irrefutable, serious, substantial **3.** cheap, cheesy *(Nonformal)*, decrepit, defective, feeble, frail, meagre, rickety, rocky, shaky, sleazy, slight, unsound, weak, wobbly *Antonyms:* durable, robust, strong

flinch *n.* balk, blink, cringe, crouch, dodge, duck, recoil, retreat, swerve, wince – *v.* balk, blink, cringe, crouch, dodge, duck, evade, quail, recede, recoil, retreat, shirk, shrink back, shudder, shun, start, swerve, wince *Antonyms:* brave, counter, face, resist

fling *n.* **1.** chuck, firing, heave, hurl, launching, lob, peg, pitch, shot, slinging, throw, toss **2.** affair, extramarital affair, rendezvous, romance, threesome, tryst **3.** bender *(Nonformal)*, binge, celebration, fun, indulgence, orgy, party, rampage, splurge, spree, swing **4.** assay, attempt, crack, effort, gamble, go, trial, try, venture *Nonformal:* stab, whirl – *v.* cast, catapult, chuck, dump, fire, heave, hurl, jerk, launch, let fly *or* loose, lob, peg, pitch, precipitate, propel, send, shy, sling, throw, toss

flip *adj.* flippant, glib, impertinent, pert, saucy – *n.* **1.** collapse, fall, overturn, reversal, roll, somersault, tumble, upset **2.** crack, flick, flop, flounce, snap – *v.* **1.** flick, hit, switch, throw, toss **2.** reverse, roll *or* turn over, somersault, tumble **3.** flip out, freak *Nonformal:* go nuts, hit the roof, lose it

flippancy *n.* backtalk, cheek, cheekiness, cockiness, disrespect, freshness, gall, impertinence, impudence, irreverence, mischievousness, rudeness, sass *(Nonformal)*, sauciness, waggishness *Antonyms:* awe, respect, reverence, seriousness

flippant *adj.* bold as brass *(Nonformal)*, chatty, cheeky, cocky, frivolous, glib, gossipy, impertinent, impudent, insolent, irreverent, lippy, nervy, off-hand, pert, playful, rude, sassy, saucy, superficial, talkative *Antonyms:* gracious, polite, respectful, serious

flirt *n.* coquette, heartbreaker, hussy, philanderer, playboy, seducer, vamp, wanton – *v.* banter, dally, entice, lead on, philander, pick up, proposition, seduce, sport, tantalize, tease, toy, trifle, vamp, wanton, woo *Nonformal:* bat the eyes, that up, come on, fool around with, hit on, string along

flirtation *n* affair, amour, brief encounter, come on *(Nonformal)*, coquetry, courtship, coyness, dalliance, encounter, entanglement, intrigue, liaison, philandering, romance, sport, trifling, tryst *Antonyms:* marriage, matrimony, wedlock

flirtatious *adj.* alluring, amorous, come-hither *(Nonformal)*, coquettish, coy, dallying, enticing, seductive, sensual, sloe-eyed, sportive, tantalizing, teasing

flit *v.* beat, dance, dart, flap, flash, flicker, float, flutter, fly, hop, hover, skim, zoom *Nonformal:* scoot, scud

float *n.* bobber, buoy, cork, life jacket, life preserver, lifesaver, pontoon, raft – *v.* **1** bob, buoy, rest, swim, waft *Antonyms* drown, sink, submerge **2.** dance, fly, glide, hang, hover, sail, skim, slide, slip **3.** drift, meander, ramble, roam, straggle, wander **4.** begin, commence, initiate, instigate, kick off, launch, start, undertake **5.** bear along, bolster, brace, reinforce, strengthen, support, uphold **6.** broadcast, circulate, disperse, disseminate, distribute, issue, proclaim, put forward, spread

floater *n.* **1.** beachcomber, drifter, hobo, nomad, part-time *or* transient worker, rambler, roamer, rolling stone, rover, sun-downer, vagabond, wanderer **2.** balloter, elector, proxy, repeater, nonpartisan *or* repeat voter **3.** cadaver, corpse, dead body, stiff

flocculent *adj.* cottony, downy, fleecy, floccose, fluffy, hairy, lanate, lanated, soft, woolly

flock *n.* army, assembly, bevy, collection, colony, company, congregation, coterie, crowd, drove, gathering, group, herd, host, legion, mass, multitude, throng *See also* **animal** – *v.* collect, congregate, converge, crowd, gather, group, herd, huddle, mass, throng, troop

flog *v.* beat, belt, cane, flagellate, flay, hide, hit, larrup, lash, paddle, pummel, strap, strike, tan, thrash, trounce, whip

flood *n.* **1.** alluvion, cataract, deluge, downpour, drencher, freshet, inundation, overflow, pour, spate, torrent *Prince Edward Island:* blueberry run, gullywasher, sod soaker **2.** bore, current, drift, flow, flux, outpouring, rush, stream, surge, tide, wave **3.** abundance, bounty, copiousness, cornucopia, excess, glut, multitude, plenty, profusion, superabundance, surplus – *v.* bring over, choke, cover, deluge, drown, engulf, fill, flow, glut, gush, immerse, inundate, overflow, oversupply, overwhelm, pour over, rush, saturate, stream, submerge, surge, swamp, swarm, sweep

floor *n.* **1.** bed, boards, bottom, carpet, deck, flooring, footing, foundation, ground, landing, mat, nadir, surface, terrace, underlay **2.** layer, level, stage, storey, tier **3.** arena, canvas, dais, forum, pit, platform, podium, pulpit, rostrum, stage – *v.* **1.** beat, defeat, fell, finish, flatten, knock down *or* out, level, overcome, overthrow, vanquish **2.** amaze, astonish, awe, baffle, bewilder, confound, disconcert, dumfound, flummox, nonplus, perplex, stump

flop *n.* **1.** bomb, bust, debacle, disaster, dud, failure, fiasco, lemon, loser, miscarriage, washout *Antonyms:* hit, success, triumph **2.** bang, bump, clash, flap, knock, noise, thud, thwack, whack, whomp, whop **3.** dive, fall, plunge, spill *(Nonformal)*, stumble, tumble – *v.* **1.** collapse, droop, drop, flap, flounder, flutter, hang, jerk, lop, sag, sink, slump, stagger, teeter, topple, toss, tumble **2.** bomb, close, fail, fall flat *or* short, fold, founder, miscarry, misfire, wash out *Antonyms:* flourish, prosper, succeed

floppy *adj.* baggy, dangling, droopy, flabby, flaccid, flapping, hanging, loose, sagging *Antonyms:* firm, taunt, tight, straight

floral *adj.* blooming, blossoming, florescent, floriate, floricultural, florid, flowered, flowering, flowery, garden, horticultural, in bloom *or* flower

florid *adj.* **1.** flush, flushed, glowing, high-coloured, robust, rosy, rosy-cheeked, ruddy, sanguine *Antonyms:* anemic, dull, pale, pasty, wan **2.** adorned, baroque, bombastic, decorated, embellished, embroidered, fancy, festooned, flowery, grandiloquent, high-flown, lush, luxuriant, ornate, overloaded, purple *Antonyms:* concise, pithy, plain

flounce *n.* **1.** edging, flange, frill, fringe, furbelow, ornament, ruffle, skirt, trimming, valance **2.** careen, flounder, lurch, jerk, pitch, plunge, reel, stagger, stumble, sway, swing, totter, tumble – *v.* **1.** bounce, fling, jerk, prance, sashay *(Nonformal)*, spring, storm, strut, toss **2.** double, fold, gather, pleat, ply, tuck **3.** careen, flounder, lurch, pitch, plunge, stagger, totter, tumble

flounder *n.* careen, fall, lurch, plunge, pratfall, stagger, struggle, stumble, sway, totter, tumble – *v.* blow, blunder, bumble, careen, err, fall, falter, fluff, fumble, lumber, lurch, mess up *(Nonformal)*, muddle, shuffle, slip, stagger, stammer, struggle, stumble, swing, thrash, tilt, toil, topple, toss, totter, trip, tumble, wallow, waver, welter, wobble *Commonly misused:* **founder**

flour *n.* meal *Kinds of flour and meal:* barley, bleached, blue cornmeal, buckwheat, bulgur, cornmeal, couscous, enriched, farina, gluten, grits, groats, hominy, kasha, oat bran, pastry, peanut, rice, semolina, soy flour, unbleached, white, wheat germ, whole-wheat – *v.* **1.** coat, cover, dust, powder, sprinkle **2.** break up, grind, pulverize, sift

flourish *n.* **1.** adornment, decoration, device, embellishment, embroidery, floweriness, frill, ornament, trimming **2.** cadenza, fanfare, flight, improvisation, riff, roulade, run **3.** blazon, brandishing, display, showing, wave – *v.* **1.** burgeon, develop, expand, flower, grow, increase, multiply, prosper, succeed, thrive *Antonyms:* decline, dwindle, fade, shrink, wane **2.** brandish, display, flaunt, swing, wave, wield

flourishing *adj.* blooming, burgeoning, doing well, exuberant, going strong, growing, lush, luxuriant, productive, prospering, prosperous, rampant, rich, robust, successful, thriving, vigorous *Nonformal:* mushrooming, roaring

flout *n.* aspersion, indignity, insult, irreverence, jeer, jest, mock, mockery, putdown, ridicule, scoff, taunt *Nonformal:* crack, slam, dig – *v.* affront, defy, deride, disdain, disobey, disregard, gibe, gird, ignore, insult, jeer, laugh at, malign, mock, outrage, repudiate, ridicule, scoff, scorn, slight, sneer, spurn, taunt *Antonyms:* esteem, honour, regard, respect, revere *Commonly misused:* **flaunt**

flow *n.* **1.** advance, career, course, current, drift, flowing, flux, movement, onrush, passage, progress, progression, reflux, river, run, rush, sequence, spout, spurt, strain, tide, trajectory, trend **2.** abundance, avalanche, deluge, effusion, flood, gush, issue, oozing, outflow, overflow, plethora, profusion, shower, spate, strain **3.** balance, clarity, continuity, ease, elegance, eloquence, facility, felicity, finish, fluency, glide, grace, harmony, lucidity, polish, proportion, rhythm, smoothness – *v.* **1.** circulate, coast, drift, glide, go, move, proceed, roll, run, sweep, travel **2.** cascade, gush, issue, pour, stream, trickle

flower *n.* **1.** annual, bloom, blossom, bud, cluster, perennial, posy, spike *Kinds of flowers:* acacia, African violet, amaranth, anemone, arbutus, arnica, artichoke, asphodel, aspidistra, aster, azalea, baby's breath, baby-blue-eyes, bachelor button, begonia, betony, black-eyed Susan, bleeding heart, bluebell, brown-eyed Susan, buttercup, cactus, calla lily, camellia, campanula, Canada anemone, Canada dogwood, Canada lily, Canada thistle, candytuft, carnation, cattail, century plant, chrysanthemum, clematis, coreopsis, cornflower, cosmos, cowslip, crocus, cyclamen, daffodil, dahlia, daisy, dandelion, delphinium, dogwood, duckweed, edelweiss, fairy-slipper, foxglove, frangipani, freesia, fuchsia, gardenia, geranium, gladiolus, harebell, hawkweed, heather, hibiscus, hyacinth, hydrangea, impatiens, Indian paintbrush, Indian pipe, indigo, iris, jack-in-the-pulpit, jonquil, lady's mantle, lady's slipper, larkspur, lavender, lilac, lily, lily of the valley, lobelia, lotus, love-lies-bleeding, lungwort, lupine, magnolia, mallow, marguerite, marigold, marsh mallow, mayflower, moccasin flower, mock orange, monkshood, morning glory, narcissus, nasturtium, oleander, orchid, pansy, passionflower, pennyroyal, peony, petunia, pink, poinsettia, poppy, prickly pear, primrose, Queen Anne's lace, ragwort, ranunculus, rhododendron, rose, safflower, salmon flower, snapdragon, snowball, snowdrop, spirea, stinking willie, sunflower, sweet pea, sweet alyssum, sweet william, tiger lily, tulip, Venus flytrap, viburnum, violet, wallflower, water lily, wild mustard, yarrow, yucca, zinnia *Provincial flowers:* arctic poppy *(Nunavut)*, dogwood *(British Columbia)*, fireweed *(Yukon)*, lady's slipper *(Prince Edward Island)*, mayflower *(Nova Scotia)*, mountain avens *(Northwest Territories)*, pitcher plant *(Newfoundland)*, prairie crocus *(Manitoba)*, purple violet *(New Brunswick)*, western red lily *(Saskatchewan)*, white garden lily *or* Madonna lily *(Quebec)*, white trillium *(Ontario)*, wild rose *(Alberta)* **2.** best, choice, cream, elite fat, height, pick, pride, prime, prize, top **3** adornment, decoration, device, embellishment, floral design, flourish, ornament ornamentation, rosette – *v.* blossom, bloom blow, burgeon, effloresce, evolve, flourish mature, open, prosper, thrive, unfold

flowery *adj.* **1**. blooming, blossoming, blossomy, botanic, dendritic, efflorescent, floral, flower-patterned, flowered, fragrant herbaceous, sylvan, verdant **2**. aureate baroque, bombastic, decorative, elaborate embellished, figurative, florid, grandiloquent, high-flown, histrionic, inflated, ornamented, ornate, overwrought, purple rhetorical, rococo, showy, turgid *Antonyms:* concise, laconic, pithy, succinct terse

flowing *adj.* **1.** cursive, effortless, free graceful, rolling, smooth, sweeping **2.** fluid harmonious, regular, streaming, unbroken uninterrupted **3.** full, healthy, lustrous manageable, profuse, rich, rippling, shiny *Antonyms:* damaged, dry, unhealthy

fluctuate *v.* alternate, change, equivocate oscillate, shift, shilly-shally *(Nonformal)* undulate, vacillate, vary, vibrate, waffle waver, wobble *Antonyms:* abide, persist stay

fluctuating *adj.* alternating, ambivalent capricious, changeable, changing, fickle inconstant, irregular, irresolute, mercurial mutable, on the fence *(Nonformal)*, oscillating, swaying, uncertain, uncommitted undulating, vacillating, wavering *Antonyms:* constant, stable, unmoving, unshakable

fluency *n.* articulateness, capability, command, control, diplomacy, ease, eloquence expressiveness, facility, flow, readiness smoothness, urbanity *Antonyms:* awkwardness, gaucherie, heavy-handedness maladroitness

fluent *adj.* articulate, cohesive, comprehensive, connected, conversant, easy, effortless, eloquent, facile, flowing, fluid, mellifluous, silver-tongued, smooth, streaming, up to speed *(Nonformal)*, verbose, well-spoken, well-versed, well-written *Antonyms* incoherent, mute, out of touch, taciturn, uncommunicative

fluffy *adj.* **1.** downy, feather-like, feathery, fleecy, flossy, furry, gossamer, linty, silky, soft *Antonyms:* hard, inflexible, rigid **2.** airy, delicate, ethereal, frothy, light, lightweight, smooth, weightless **3.** empty, entertaining, frivolous, Hollywood *(Nonformal)*, light-hearted, shallow, superficial, unprofound, vacuous

fluid *adj.* **1.** aqueous, changeable, flowing, liquefied, liquid, melted, molten, running, runny, watery *Antonyms:* firm, fixed, hard, solid **2.** easy, eloquent, fluent, glib, graceful, smooth – *n.* beverage, broth, drink, juice, liquid, liquor, solution

fluke *n.* **1.** accident, bad luck, blessing, chance, fortuity, fortune, hap *(Nonformal)*, happenstance, luck, lucky break, quirk, serendipity, windfall **2.** arrowhead, barb, dart, harpoon, head, tip

flummox *v.* amaze, astonish, baffle, bamboozle *(Nonformal)*, befuddle, bewilder, boggle, confound, confuse, disconcert, floor, fluster, mystify, perplex, perturb, puzzle, rattle, stump, stymie, throw off *Antonyms:* assuage, calm, mollify, placate, soothe

flunky *n.* footman, lackey, manservant, menial, puppet, sycophant, toady, underling, varlet, yes-man *Nonformal:* gofer, stooge

flurry *n.* **1.** ado, burst, bustle, commotion, excitement, flap, flutter, furor, stew, stir, to-do, tumult, turmoil, whirl **2.** dusting, gust, gusting rain, snow, snow shower, snowfall, snowsquall, squall, whirlwind, wind – *v.* agitate, bewilder, bother, confuse, discombobulate *(Nonformal)*, discompose, disconcert, disquiet, distract, disturb, excite, fluster, frustrate, hurry, perplex, perturb, provoke, rattle, ruffle, unsettle, upset

flush *adj.* **1.** aligned, centred, direct, even, exact, flat, head-on, horizontal, level, plane, precise, smooth, square, straight, tight, true *Antonyms*: craggy, irregular, rough **2.** abundant, affluent, full, generous, opulent, overflowing, profuse, prosperous, rich, wealthy, well-off, well-to-do *Nonformal:* loaded, ready for bear *Antonyms*: broke, poor, underprivileged **3.** blushing, flushed, hardy, hale, healthy, hearty, lively, pink, pink cheeked, robust, rosy, rosy-cheeked, ruddy, rugged, spirited, strong, sturdy, vigorous, vital – *n.* **1.** bloom, blush, colour, freshness, glow, redness, rosiness **2.** delight, elation, euphoria, joy, rush *(Nonformal)*, tingle **3.** card *or* full suit, hand, royal flush, straight flush **4.** febricity, fever, feverishness, fire, heat, hectic flush, illness, sickness, virus, warmth **5.** clean, cleaning, flushing, irrigation, scouring, scrub, scrubbing, wash – *v.* **1.** blush, colour, crimson, excite, flame, glow, mantle, redden, rose, rouge, shine *Antonyms*: blanch, pale **2.** cleanse, drench, flood, hose, purge, remove, rinse, swab, wash, wet **3.** drive out, expel, expose, reveal **4.** align, even-up, level, make even

flushed *adj.* **1.** blushing, burning, crimson, febrile, feverish, hot, red, rosy, ruddy, sanguine, sweaty, warm *Antonyms:* cold, pale, pallid, wan **2.** animated, aroused, enthused, excited, glowing, high, impassioned, inspired *Antonyms:* fatigued, indifferent, tired

fluster *n.* agitation, commotion, disturbance, dither, flurry, flutter, perturbation, state, turmoil, upset *Nonformal:* flap, stew, tizzy – *v.* addle, agitate, bewilder, bother, confuse, craze, disquiet, disturb, excite, fouster *(P.E.I.)*, muddle, nonplus, perplex, perturb, puzzle, rattle, ruffle, stir up, unhinge, upset, work up *Nonformal:* discombobulate, spook *Antonyms*: calm, mollify, placate, soothe

flutter *n.* **1.** activity, ado, agitation, bustle, commotion, disorder, frenzy, hubbub, nervous excitement, sensation, squall, stir, storm, tempest, tizzy *(Nonformal)*, tumult, upset **2.** beat, beating, flap, flapping, flicker, flit, motion, movement, palpitation, pitapat, throb – *v.* **1.** agitate, bat, beat, dance, drift, flap, flicker, flit, flop, fluctuate, hover, oscillate, quaver, quiver, swing, throb, vibrate, wave, wiggle, wobble **2.** bafflement, befuddlement, bewilderment, confusion, dither, fluster, **3.** baffle, bother, confound, confuse, discombobulate *(Nonformal)*, fluster, nonplus, perplex, trouble, worry

flux *n.* **1.** course, discharge, ebb, flood, flow, gush, outflow, surge **2.** change, fluctuation, instability, movement, transition, turmoil, uncertainty, unrest **3.** diarrhea, dysentery, green apple quick step *(P.E.I.)*, run-outs and walk-ins *(Nonformal)*, scours

fly *adj. British:* alert, clever, sapient, up to snuff *(Nonformal)* – *n.* **1.** bug, critter *(Nonformal)*, insect *Kinds of fly:* black, blowfly, caddis, chalcid, cluster, cranefly, deerfly, dragonfly, firefly, horsefly, housefly, moose, mosquito, tsetse **2.** cover, flap, overlap, overlayer, tent flap *or* fly **3.** button fly, zipper – *v.* **1.** aviate, buzz, circle, climb, dive, drift, glide, hover, jet, land, manoeuvre, pilot, remain aloft, scud, soar, speed, swoop, take flight, take off, travel, wing **2.** abscond, avoid, break, disappear, elope, escape, flee, withdraw *Nonformal:* beat it, skedaddle, vamoose **3.** bolt, dart, dash, glide, hurdle, hurry, hustle, race, run, rush, scoot, shoot, speed, sprint

fly-by-night *adj.* **1.** brief, ephemeral, fleeting, impermanent, short-lived, transitory *Antonyms:* constant, enduring, long-living **2.** crooked, discreditable, dishonest, disreputable, dubious, Jack Nasty *(Nonformal)*, shady, undependable, unreliable, untrustworthy *Antonyms:* establish, dependable, honest, reputable

flyer *n.* **1.** ace, airman, aviator, barnstormer, bombardier, co-pilot, flier, navigator, pilot, skyperson *Nonformal:* flyboy, jet jockey, top gun **2.** advertisement, broadsheet, handbill, handout, leaflet **3.** gamble, jump, leap, risk, shot in the dark *(Nonformal)*

flying *adj.* **1.** aerial, aeronautical, airborne, avian, floating, gliding, hovering, soaring, swooping, winged **2.** expeditious, hasty, hurried, hurrying, in and out *(Nonformal)*, prompt, quick, rushed, speeding, speedy, swift

foam *n.* bubbles, fluff, froth, head, lather, spray, spume, suds, surf – *v.* aerate, boil, bubble, burble, effervesce, fizz, froth, gurgle, hiss, lather, seethe, simmer, sparkle

foamy *adj.* boiling, bubbling, bubbly, carbonated, ebullient, effervescent, fizzy, foaming, frothy, lathery, light, seething, simmering, sudsy, yeasty *Antonyms*: flat, leaden, heavy

focus *n.* **1.** attractor, centre, convergence, cynosure, epicenter, focal point, ground zero, hypocentre **2.** crux, essence, gist, heart, hub, kernel, locus, marrow, meat, nerve centre, nub *(Nonformal)*, nucleus, pith, seat – *v.* adjust, aim, centre, centralize, concentrate, contract, converge, fixate, key on, look at, pinpoint, rivet, sharpen, spotlight, zero *or* zoom in

fodder *n.* edibles, feed, food, foodstuff, forage, nourishment, provender, rations, silage, stock, sustenance, victuals

foe *n.* adversary, antagonist, challenger, enemy, match, opponent, rival *Antonyms:* ally, comrade, partner

fog *n.* **1.** cloud, condensation, haze, mist, pea soup *(Nonformal)* **2.** befuddlement, blindness, confusion, daze, maze, obscurity, perplexity, stupor, trance, vagueness – *v.* addle, becloud, befuddle, bewilder, blind, blur, cloud, confuse, eclipse, muddle, muddy, mystify, obfuscate, obscure, perplex, puzzle *Antonyms:* clarify, explicate, illuminate

fogey *n.* anachronism, antique, conservative, crone, fossil, relic, square *Nonformal:* fuddy-duddy, geezer, stick-in-the-mud

foggy *adj.* **1.** blurred, cloudy, dark, dim, filmy, fuzzy, grey, hazy, indistinct, misty, murky, nebulous, obscure, shadowy, unclear, vague, vaporous *Antonyms*: clear, distinct, precise **2.** addled, befuddled, bewildered, confused, dim-witted, dull, muddled, perplexed, vacuous *Nonformal:* dizzy, dopey, fuzzy, puzzled

foible *n.* blemish, defect, eccentricity, failing, fault, frailty, idiosyncrasy, imperfection, infirmity, oddity, peculiarity, quirk, shortcoming, vice, weakness

foil *n.* **1.** antithesis, complement, contrast, counter, offset, opposite, reverse **2.** balking, check, defeat, destruction, frustration, hindrance, prevention, upset **3.** adornment, background, coat, coating, covering, layer, leaf, ornamentation, setting, sheet **4.** arms, blade, guard, instrument, steel, sword, weapon, weaponry – *v.* baffle, balk, buffalo *(Nonformal)*, check, circumvent, counter, cramp, curb, dash, defeat, disappoint, dodge, elude, frustrate, hinder, nullify, outsmart, outwit, prevent, quash, rattle, restrain, shake, stop, stymie, thwart *Antonyms*: encourage, foster, further, promote, support

fold *n.* **1.** bend, circumvolution, corrugation, crease, crimp, crinkle, doubling, flexure, furrow, gather, groove, hem, knife-edge, lapel, layer, overlap, pleat, ply, pucker, ridge, ruck, ruffle, rumple, shirring, smocking, tuck, turn, wrinkle **2.** arena, confine, coop, enclosure, pen, yard **3.** assembly, congregation, flock, laity, parish, parishioners – *v.* **1.** bend, corrugate, crease, crimp, crisp, crumple, curl, dog-ear, double, furrow, gather, groove, hem, intertwine, lap, overlap, overlay, plait, pleat, pucker, purse, replicate, ridge, ruck, ruffle, tuck, turn over *or* under, wrinkle *Antonyms*: flatten, iron, plain, smooth, straighten **2.** break, close, collapse, crash, fail, give in *or* over *or* up, shut down, throw down one's cards, yield *Nonformal:* bust, cash it in, go under *Antonyms:* prosper, succeed, thrive

folder *n.* binder, case, dossier, Duo-Tang *(Trademark)*, envelope, file, pocket, portfolio, sheath, wrapper

foliage *n.* flora, frondescence, greenery, growth, herbage, leafage, leaves, local vegetation, verdure

folk *adj.* communal, customary, country, homespun, homey, rustic, traditional – *n.* body politic, clan, community, confederation, culture *or* ethnic group, family, household, ilk, inhabitants, kin, kindred, kinfolk, kith and kin, lineage, masses, menage, nation, nationality, parents *(Nonformal)*, people, population, proletariat, public, race, relations, settlement, society, stock, tribe

folklore *n.* ancient beliefs *or* practice *or* wisdom, custom, fable, legends, lore, myth, mythology, oral history *or* record, sagas, sayings, stories, superstitions, traditions

follow *interj.* capeesh *(Nonformal)*, comprehend, copy, get, heed, note, understand *Antonyms:* misinterpret, misunderstand – *v.* **1.** come after *or* from *or* next, ensue, proceed *or* spring from, replace, result, succeed, supersede, supplant *Antonyms*: antecede, lead, precede, preface **2.** chase, give chase, go after, hound, hunt, pursue, run after *or* down, search, seek, shadow, stalk, stick to, tag along, tail, tailgate *(Nonformal)*, track, trail *Antonyms:* abandon, elude, escape **3.** abide by, accord, adhere *or* agree to, adopt, comply, conform, cultivate, emulate, follow suit, harmonize, hold fast, imitate, keep, keep faith, match, mimic, mirror, obey, observe, practice, regard, scrutinize, study, support, take after, watch *Antonyms:* disobey, elude, forsake, ignore, renounce

follower *n.* adherent, advocate, apostle, attendant, backer, believer, convert, devotee, disciple, fan, imitator, member, minion, participant, partisan, patron, promoter, proselyte, protégé, pupil, pursuer, representative, servant, supporter, sycophant, votary, worshipper, zealot *Nonformal:* groupie, lamb *Antonyms:* leader, maverick, radical, revolutionary

following *adj.* after, attendant, back, coming, coming next, consecutive, consequent, consequential, ensuing, later, latter, next, next in line, posterior, resulting, sequacious, sequent, sequential, subsequent, successive, then, trailing *Antonyms*: aforementioned, antecedent, preceding – *n.* adherents, attendants, audience, backers, believers, circle, cortege, disciples, entourage, fans, patrons, public, retinue, supporters

folly *n.* absurdity, craziness, daftness, foolhardiness, foolishness, idiocy, imbecility, imprudence, inanity, indiscretion, irrationality, lunacy, madness, nonsense, preposterousness, rashness, recklessness, senselessness, triviality, vice *Antonyms:* judgment, moderation, sanity, sense, wisdom

foment *v.* abet, agitate, arouse, brew, encourage, excite, foster, goad, incite, instigate, promote, provoke, raise, spur, stimulate, whip up *(Nonformal) Antonyms:* calm, mollify, placate, subdue

fomentation *n.* **1.** agitation, awakening, incitement, inducement, inflammation, prompting, provocation, rabble-rousing, urging *Antonyms:* appeasement, mitigation, relief **2.** collodion *(Historical)*, lotion, plaster, poultice, salve, treatment

fomenter *n.* abettor, agitator, demagogue, hatemonger, inciter, instigator, rabble-rouser, warmonger

fond *adj.* adoring, affectionate, amorous, besotted, caring, devoted, doting, enamoured, indulgent, keen on, liking, loving, partial, predisposed, responsive, romantic, sentimental, sympathetic, tender, warm *Nonformal:* crazy about *or* for *or* over *Antonyms:* aloof, averse, disinterested, indifferent

fondle *v.* caress, clutch, coddle, cosset, cuddle, embrace, feel, grab, grope, hug, love, neck, nestle, nuzzle, pat, paw, pet, snuggle, stroke, touch *Nonformal:* cop a feel, goose

fondness *n.* affection, attachment, devotion, fancy, kindness, liking, love, partiality, penchant, predilection, preference, soft spot *(Nonformal)*, susceptibility, taste, tenderness, weakness *Antonyms:* antagonism, antipathy, aversion, contempt, dislike, enmity, hatred, loathing, repulsion

food *n.* ambrosia, bread, bread and butter, cuisine, edibles, diet, fare, feed, food and drink, foodstuff, larder, meal, menu, muckamuck *(Pacific Coast)*, nourishment, provender, rations, comestibles, spread, sustenance, tucker *(Australian)*, viands, victuals *Nonformal:* chow, eats, fixings, grub, scarf *or* scoff, tuck, vittles

fool *n.* **1.** ass, buffoon, clod, dolt, dummy, dunce, half-wit, idiot, ignoramus, innocent, laughing stock, ninny, nitwit, numskull, oaf, ownshook *(Newfoundland)*, simpleton *Nonformal:* birdbrain, blockhead, buggerlugs *(Atlantic Provinces)*, dimwit, dunderhead, imbecile, jackass, lamebrain, nincompoop, pushover, sap, stooge, sucker, twit **2.** clown, comic, harlequin, jester, joker **3.** butt, easy mark *(Nonformal)*, mark, victim – *v.* bluff, cheat, deceive, delude, dupe, fox, hoax, juke, lead on, mislead, outfox, pretend, take in, trick *Nonformal*: bamboozle, con, flim-flam, hornswaggle, scam, snow

fooled *adj.* deceived, deluded, duped, hosed, misled, outfoxed, sucked in, tricked *Nonformal:* bamboozled, conned, flim-flammed, snow-jobbed

foolery *n.* amusement, antics, buffoonery, caper, childishness, clownery, deviltry, escapade, farce, festivity, fling, folly, frolic, gambol, games, harlequinade, hijinks, horseplay, lark, larking, mirth, play, pleasure, tomfoolery, tricks, sport

foolhardy *adj.* adventuresome, audacious, bold, breakneck, daring, devil-may-care *(Nonformal)*, harebrained, headstrong, hell-bent, impetuous, imprudent, irresponsible, madcap, precipitate, rash, reckless, venturesome *Antonyms:* cautious, circumspect, prudent, shrewd, watchful

foolish *adj.* absurd, asinine, brainless, crazy, daffy, daft, doltish, feebleminded, half-witted, harebrained, idiotic, ill-advised, imbecilic, irrational, ludicrous, lunatic, mad, nonsensical, preposterous, ridiculous, senseless, silly, stupid, unintelligent, unwise, witless, zany *Nonformal:* cockamamie, dippy, half-baked, kooky, loony, nutty, wacky *Antonyms:* cautious, clever, intelligent, prudent, wary

foolishly *adv.* absurdly, idiotically, ill-advisedly, imprudently, incautiously, indiscreetly, mistakenly, stupidly, unwisely without thought, working on hormones *Antonyms*: prudently, sagaciously, thoughtfully, wisely

foolishness *n.* **1.** buffoonery, carryings-on, clownishness, craziness, irresponsibility, jest, joke, joshing, mischief, mockery, nonsense, rubbish, silliness, stupidity, tricks, twaddle *Nonformal:* claptrap, horsefeathers **2.** absurdity, idiocy, insanity, insensibility, irrationality, ludicrousness, lunacy, senselessness, witlessness

foolproof *adj.* airtight, assured, certain, fail-safe, firm, guaranteed, impregnable, incontestable, infallible, in the can *(Nonformal)*, invincible, inviolable, invulnerable, sound, solid, sure, trouble-free, unbeatable *Antonyms:* faulty, risky, unreliable, vulnerable

foot *n.* **1.** extremity, heel, hoof, paw, sole, toe, tootsy *(Nonformal)* **2.** base, bottom, footing, foundation, lowest point, nadir, substratum, substructure, support – *v.* **1.** clog, dance, perambulate, plod, skip, step, stroll, walk *Nonformal:* hoof, prance **2.** finance, fund, pay, spend, splurge *Nonformal:* bankroll, shell out

football *n.* ball, game, gridiron, pigskin, sport *Groupings of football:* Australian rules, Canadian, rugby, soccer, U.S. *Kinds of football equipment:* ball *or* pigskin, cleats, face mask, helmet, mouth guard, pads, uniform *Kinds of football formation and pass patterns:* buttonhook, crossing pattern, cut back, down and out, drop kick, fade away, fake-out, flare *or* swing pass, fly, grind it out, hand-off, hook pattern, huddle, in the red zone, keeper, man-to-man defence, nickel, option, rollout, run and shoot offence, screen pass, shotgun offence, sideline pass, single zone coverage, slant-in pattern, sweep, the short game, wedge *or* flying wedge, west coast offence, wing, zone defence *Kinds of positions in football:* cornerback, flanker, fullback, guard, halfback, import player, kick returner, linebacker *(Middle, Strongside, Weakside)*, lineman, nose tackle, placekicker, punter, quarterback, rover, rush end, safety, slot, split end, tackle, tailback, tight end *Kinds of scoring and procedure in football:* catch, conversion, down, end zone, field goal, first down, fumble, gain, goalposts, half *or* half-time, kickoff return, loss, overtime, pass, point, possession, punt, quarter, quick kick, rouge, safety, second down, snap, tackle, touchdown, yardage

footing *n.* **1.** capacity, character, condition, grade, place, position, rank, relations, relationship, situation, standing, state, station, status, terms **2.** basement, base, bedrock, bottom, caisson, establishment, foot, foundation, ground, infrastructure, installation, seat, settlement, support, underpinning, understructure

footloose *adj.* at large, autonomous, available, detached, emancipated, fancy free, free, freewheeling, independent, liberated, loose, on the loose *(Nonformal)*, self-determined, single, unattached, unencumbered, unhampered, unimpeded *Antonyms:* bridled, confined, hampered, obstructed, restained

footnote *n.* annotation, bibliography, citation, commentary, documentation, end notes, explanation, explication, exegesis, gloss, marginalia, notation, note, reference

footprint *n.* **1.** dint, fossil print, impression, imprint, pad, pawmark, pawprint, print, pug, pugmark, spoor, track, trail, tread **2.** area, dominion, location, occupied space, reach, requirement, size

fop *n.* beau, cavalier, coxcomb, dandy, dude, flash, gallant, popinjay, silkstocking *(Historical)*, sport *Nonformal:* blade, clotheshorse, fashion plate, jack-a-dandy, peacock, snappy dresser, toff

forage *n.* edibles, fodder, food, grub *(Nonformal)*, victuals – *v.* cast about, comb, dig, explore, grub, hunt, pilfer, plunder, raid, rake, ransack, rummage, scour, search, seek

foray *n.* excursion, incursion, invasion, irruption, looting, marauding, pillaging, plunder, mission, raid, sally, sortie, thrust, venture – *v.* assault, attack, invade, loot, pillage, plunder, raid, sack, steal

forbear *v.* **1.** abstain, avoid, break off, bridle, cease, curb, decline, desist, eschew, forgo, go easy, hold back, inhibit, keep from, omit, pause, refrain, resist, restrain, shun, stay, stop, withhold *Antonyms:* imbibe, indulge, partake **2.** abide, bear, endure, forgive, have pity on, pardon, persevere, reprieve, sacrifice, spare, tolerate, wait

forbearance *n.* abstinence, avoidance, endurance, fortitude, moderation, patience, refraining, resignation, resistance, restraint, self-control, temperance *Antonyms:* anger, impetuosity, indulgence, intolerance, shortness

forbearing *adj.* benevolent, charitable, clement, considerate, easy, forgiving, gentle, humane, humanitarian, indulgent, long-suffering, merciful, mild, moderate, patient, thoughtful, tolerant *Antonyms*: harsh, intolerant, malevolent, merciless

forbid *v.* ban, banish, block, cancel, censor, debar, declare illegal, deny, deprive, disallow, enjoin, exclude, forestall, freeze, halt, hinder, hold up, impede, inhibit, interdict, nix *(Nonformal)*, obstruct, oppose, outlaw, prevent, prohibit, proscribe, restrict, rule out, stop, stymie, veto *Antonyms:* authorize, endorse, grant, permit, sanction

forbidden *adj.* banned, closed, contraband, off limits, outlawed, prohibited, proscribed, refused, taboo, *verboten (German)*, vetoed

forbidding *adj.* daunting, disagreeable, dour, farouche *(French)*, frightening, grim, hostile, menacing, odious, offensive, off-putting, ominous, repellent, repulsive, sinister, threatening, tough, unapproachable, unfriendly, unpleasant *Antonyms:* approachable, attractive, benign, congenial, safe, welcoming

force *n.* **1.** ability, capability, clout, determination, drive, dynamism, effectiveness, effect, energy, enterprise, fury, horsepower, impact, impetus, influence, intensity, momentum, potency, power, pull, punch, push, reaction, repercussion, resistance, speed, spirit, strength, stress, tension, velocity, vigour *Nonformal:* bite, kick, what it takes **2.** authority, coercion, compulsion, domination, duress, fierceness, forcefulness, intimidation, might, pressure, puissance, tyranny, vehemence, violence *Antonyms:* leniency, softness **3.** cogency, conviction, efficiency, reasonableness, soundness, substantiality, validity, weight **4.** bevy, body, crew, employees, gang, help, personnel, retinue, staff, troop – *v.* **1.** break in *or* open, burst, bust *or* crack open, jimmy, propel, push, thrust, twist, wrench, wrest **2.** burden, cause, charge, coerce, command, compel, convince, demand, dragoon, enforce, exact, impel, impose, insist, motivate, necessitate, obligate, oblige, occasion, order, press, pressure, propel, require, seduce, spark, stimulate, strongarm, urge, wrest

forced *adj.* **1.** coerced, compelled, compulsory, conscripted, constrained, enforced, grudging, inflexible, mandatory, obligatory, peremptory, rigid, unwilling *Antonyms:* elective, flexible, voluntary **2.** affected, artificial, contrived, insincere, laboured, stiff, strained, unnatural *Antonyms:* easy, natural, simple

forceful *adj.* cogent, compelling, convincing, dominant, dynamic, effective, electric, energetic, forcible, gutsy, persuasive, pithy, potent, powerful, stringent, strong, telling, vehement, vigorous, virile, weighty *Nonformal:* powerhouse, take charge, type A *Antonyms:* exhausted, faint, feeble, powerless, weak

forcible *adj.* **1.** active, assertive, cogent, compelling, effective, efficient, energetic, intense, persuasive, potent, strong, telling, vigorous, weighty *Antonyms:* feeble, frail, weak **2.** aggressive, coercive, drastic, fierce, mighty, militant, powerful, rough, tough *(Nonformal)*, vehement

fore *adj.* anterior, antecedent, anticipatory, earlier, first, forehand, former, front, preceding, previous, prior, old, olden – *interj.* beware, caution, heads up, look out, out of the way – *n.* bow, face, foredeck, forefront, foremost, forepart, front, head, prow, stem

forebode *v.* augur, betoken, bode, divine, forecast, foresee, foreshadow, foretell, foretoken, forewarn, indicate, omen, portend, predict, presage, promise, warn

foreboding *adj.* **1.** anxious, apprehensive, bothered, concerned, disquieting, fearful, perturbing, troubling, uneasy, worried **2.** inauspicious, ill-fated, ill-omened, ominous, portentous, precautionary, premonitory, warning **3.** dark, dire, dreary, evil, gloomy, intimidating, menacing, sinister, threatening, unpromising – *n.* **1.** angst, anxiety, apprehension, apprehensiveness, chill, dread, funny feeling *(Nonformal)*, misgiving **2.** augury, foreshadowing, foretoken, forewarning, portent, prediction, premonition, presage, prophecy, warning

forecast *n.* **1.** augury, cast, conjecture, divination, foreknowledge, foreseeing, foresight, foretelling, forethought, foretoken, precognition, prediction, prescience, prophecy **2.** budget, calculation, estimate, extrapolation, guess, interpretation, outlook, plan, planning, prognosis, prognostication, projection – *v.* anticipate, augur, calculate, conclude, conjecture, demonstrate, determine, divine, estimate, figure, foresee, foretell, gather, gauge, guess, infer, plan, portend, predetermine, predict, presage, prognosticate, prophesy, reason, soothsay, surmise

forefather *n.* ancestor, antecedent, author, begetter, father, forebear, forerunner, founder, kinsman, originator, parent, paterfamilias, patriarch, precursor, predecessor, procreator, progenitor, relative, sire *Antonyms*: children, descendent, progeny

forefront *n.* beginning, centre, cutting edge, focus, fore, foreground, front, lead, leading edge, limelight, prominence, vanguard *Antonyms*: margin, periphery, sideline

foregoing *adj.* above, aforementioned, aforesaid, antecedent, former, past, precedent, preceding, previous, prior *Antonyms*: future, pending, prospective

foregone *adj.* **1.** anticipated, certain, expected, foreseen, in-evitable, predetermined, predicted *Antonyms:* incomplete, uncertain, unfinished **2.** finished, happened, occurred, past

foreign *adj.* **1.** abroad, external, imported, international, out of province, outside, overseas, trans-oceanic *Nonformal:* across the pond, off-island *Antonyms*: indigenous, internal, local, native **2.** alien, different, exotic, strange, uncharacteristic, unfamiliar, unknown, weird *Antonyms:* banal, everyday, normal **3.** extra, extraneous, incompatible, incongruous, inconsistent, irrelevant, superfluous, unrelated

foreigner *n.* alien, emigrant, émigré, immigrant, newcomer, outlander, outsider, peregrine, pilgrim, stranger, tramontane, visitor *Antonyms*: autochthon, indigene, native

foreman *n.* boss, bossman, floor walker, gaffer *(British)*, headman, lead hand, manager, overseer, superintendent, supervisor, taskmaster, top dog *(Nonformal)*

foremost *adj.* champion, chief, first, fore, front, head, headmost, highest, inaugural, initial, leading, most important, number one, numero uno *(Nonformal)*, paramount, preeminent, premier, primary, prime, principal, supreme, top

foreordain *v.* bespeak, consecrate, destine, doom, earmark, fate, foretell, prearrange, predestine, predetermine, predict, preordain

forerunner *n.* **1.** advance man, advertisement, announcement, augury, foreshadow, foretoken, forewarning, harbinger, herald, indication, omen, portent, premonition, presage, preview, sign, token, vanguard, warning **2.** ancestor, antecedent, antecessor, forefather, founder, lead, original, precursor, predecessor, progenitor

foresee *v.* anticipate, apprehend, discern, divine, envisage, espy, expect, forebode, forecast, foreknow, foretell, perceive, predict, presage, prognosticate, prophesy, visualize

foreshadow *v.* augur, betoken, bode, forebode, foretell, hint, imply, indicate, omen, portend, predict, prefigure, presage, prophesy, shadow, signal, suggest

foresight *n.* awareness, circumspection, clairvoyance, discernment, discretion, foreknowledge, forethought, insight, perception, planning, precognition, preconception, premeditation, preparedness, prescience, providence, prudence, sagacity *Antonyms:* carelessness, hindsight, imprudence, neglect

forest *n.* backwoods, bluff, brake, bush, clump, copse, drunken forest *(Northern)*, grove, growth, jungle, park woodland, rainforest, shelter, spinney *(British)*, stand, taiga, thicket, timberland, trees, weald, wildwood, wood, woodlot, woods *Canadian forest regions:* Acadian, Boreal, Coast, Columbia, Deciduous, Great Lakes-St. Lawrence, Montane, Subalpine

forestall *v* **1.** avert, avoid, block, divert, frustrate, hinder, intercept, obviate, preclude, prevent, promote, thwart *Antonyms:* forward, foster, promote **2.** anticipate, envision, expect, foreglimpse, foresee, foretaste, predict, presume

forestry *n.* arboriculture, dendrology, forestation, forest management, silviculture, tree-planting

foretell *v.* announce, anticipate, apprehend, augur, betoken, bode, call, call it *(Nonfor-*

mal), declare, disclose, divine, figure out, forebode, forecast, foreknow, foreshadow, forewarn, portend, predict, prefigure, presage, proclaim, prognosticate, prophesy, read, reveal, signify, soothsay, tell, warn

forethought *n.* anticipation, caution, discretion, farsightedness, foresight, judgment, precaution, premeditation, preparedness, prudence, sense *Antonyms:* carelessness, impulsiveness, neglect

forever *adv.* always, endurably, endlessly, eternally, ever, everlastingly, forevermore, for good *or* keeps *or* life, infinitely, in perpetuity, interminably, lastingly, permanently, perpetually, 'till death do us part *(Nonformal) Antonyms*: briefly, fleetingly, temporarily

forewarn *v.* admonish, advise, alarm, alert, caution, dissuade, flag *(Nonformal)*, forebode, portend, tip off

foreword *n.* introduction, preamble, preface, preliminary, prelude, prologue *Antonyms:* addendum, afterword, appendix, epilogue

forfeit *n.* amercement, cost, damage, detriment, divestment, expense, fine, forfeiture, injury, loss, mulct, penalty, sacrifice, sconce *(British)* – *v.* cede, default, give up, lose, relinquish, renounce, sacrifice, surrender, walk away from, yield *Antonyms:* keep, maintain, retain

forfeiture *n.* amercement, charge, compensation, cost, denial, expense, fee, fine, forfeit, loss, mulct, non-restoration, penalty, penalization, punishment, sacrifice, sequestration, surrender *Antonyms:* acquisition, gain, profit, retention

forge *n.* blacksmith, foundry, furnace, hearth, ironworks, metalworks, smelter, smithy, smithery – *v.* **1.** beat, cast, design, fabricate, fashion, form, hammer out, make, mold, produce, shape **2.** coin, concoct, copy, counterfeit, duplicate, fake, falsify, feign, hoke up *(Nonformal)*, imitate, pirate, reproduce, trace, transcribe, trump up **3.** advance, move, pioneer, plod, press onward, proceed, progress, trudge

forgery *n.* carbon copy, cheat, copy, counterfeit, fabrication, fake, falsification, fraudulence, imitation, look-alike, phoney *(Nonformal)*, plagiarism, sham

forget *v.* **1.** cease *or* fail to remember, disremember, misrecollect *Nonformal:* blow, draw a blank, fluff **2.** leave behind *or* out *or* undone, neglect, omit **3.** discount, dismiss, disregard, let be, lose interest, overlook, pass over, take no notice of, think nc more of *(Nonformal)*, write off

forgetful *adj.* absent-minded, abstracted amnesic, bemused, careless, distracted dreamy, heedless, inattentive, lax, moony neglectful, negligent, oblivious, preoccu pied, slack, unmindful, woolgathering *Anto nyms:* attentive, careful, mindful, retentive

forgetfulness *n.* absent-mindedness Alzheimers disease, blackout, blank, brai fade *(Nonformal)*, carelessness, heedless ness, inattention, memory block *or* lapse oblivion, obliviousness, repression, shor memory, woolgathering *Antonyms*: atten tiveness, mindfulness, remembrance

forgive *v.* absolve, acquit, allow for, clea commute, condone, exculpate, excuse exempt, exonerate, extenuate, forbear, fo get, let pass, make allowance, overloo pardon, relent, reprieve, wink at *(Nonfo mal) Antonyms:* blame, censure, charg condemn, reproach

forgiveness *n.* absolution, acquitta amnesty, clemency, dispensation, exoner tion, grace, immunity, impunity, indemnit lenience, mercy, overlooking, pardon, pit reprieve, respite, vindication *Antonym* accusation, blame, charge, punishmen recrimination

forgo *v.* abandon, abdicate, abjure, abstai cede, desist, eschew, forbear, forsake, gi up, go without, leave out, pass, qu refrain, relinquish, renounce, resign, resis sacrifice, surrender, swear off, wai *Antonyms*: enjoy, partake

forgotten *adj.* buried, bygone, erased, gon lapsed, lost, obliterated, omitted, pas repressed *Antonyms*: recalled, recollecte remembered, retained

fork *n.* **1.** implement, tool, utensil *Kinds of fork:* barley, hay, manure, silage, spading, table, tuning **2.** angle, bend, bifurcation, branching, corner, crossroads, crotch, crutch, division, elbow, furcation, intersection, junction, limb, prong, scission, separation, split, turn – *v.* **1.** angle, bifurcate, branch, branch off *or* out, diverge, divide, part, separate, split **2.** convey, fling, give, heave, lift, lob, shovel, throw, toss, transfer

forked *adj.* angled, bifurcated, branching, dichotomous, divided, halved, ramified, separated, split

forlorn *adj.* **1.** abandoned, alone, deserted, destitute, forgotten, forsaken, friendless, godforsaken, homeless, lost, solitary, poor **2.** bereft, blue, cheerless, comfortless, depressed, desolate, despairing, desperate, despondent, destroyed, disconsolate, helpless, hopeless, inconsolable, lonely, lonesome, melancholy, miserable, neurasthenic, pathetic, pitiful, tragic, unhappy, woebegone, wretched *Antonyms:* cheerful, hopeful, uplifted

form *n.* **1.** cast, configuration, conformation, construction, contour, cut, design, die, embodiment, formation, model, mould, outline, pattern, plan, profile, scheme, skeleton, structure, style, system **2.** character, class, description, grade, kind, make, manifestation, manner, method, mode, practice, rank, semblance, sort, species, stamp, style, system, type, variation **3.** anatomy, appearance, being, body, build, condition, fettle, figure, fitness, frame, health, object, outline, person, physique, shape, silhouette **4.** arrangement, format, framework, harmony, order, orderliness, organization, placement, proportion, symmetry **5.** behaviour, canon, ceremony, conduct, convention, custom, decorum, etiquette, fashion, formality, habit, law, manner, method, mode, practice, precept, procedure, proceeding, process, propriety, protocol, regulation, rite, ritual, rule, setup, usage, way **6.** application, blank, chart, data sheet, document, letter, paper, questionnaire, sheet – *v.* **1.** acquire, appear, arise, condense, crystallize, develop, grow, harden, materialize, mature, rise, take shape **2.** arrange, assemble, bring about, build, cast, complete, conceive, construct, contrive, create, cultivate, cut, design, develop, devise, erect, establish, fabricate, fashion, finish, fix, found, frame, invent, make, manufacture, model, mould, organize, outline, pattern, plan, plot, produce, project, set, shape, structure, trace, turn out **3.** act as, compose, comprise, constitute, figure in, make up, serve as

formal *adj.* **1.** affected, aloof, ceremonious, correct, decorous, distant, exact, methodical, nominal, polite, precise, prim, punctilious, reserved, seemly, sententious, starched, stately, stiff, stilted, straight, stuffy, unbending *Antonyms:* casual, easygoing, informal, relaxed **2.** approved, binding, confirmed, established, explicit, lawful, legal, official, prescribed, *pro forma (Latin)*, proper, regulated *Antonyms:* criminal, improper, unlawful **3.** arranged, designed, harmonious, orderly, stylized, symmetrical, uniform, well-proportioned – *n.* celebration, ceremony, commencement, convocation, do *(Nonformal)*, function, gala, graduation, inauguration, party, soiree, ritual

formality *n.* **1.** ceremoniousness, conventionalism, correctness, decorum, dignity, etiquette, formalness, pomp, pomp and circumstance, propriety, solemnity, stiffness, stiltedness, weight **2.** ceremony, convention, custom, form, liturgy, procedure, protocol, rite, ritual, rubric, rule, tradition

format *n.* appearance, arrangement, blueprint, composition, contour, design, dimensions, form, frame, framework, layout, model, order, organization, outline, pattern, plan, protocol *(Computer)*, scheme, shape, size, structure, style

formation *n.* appearance, architecture, arrangement, build, compilation, composition, configuration, construction, creation, design, development, establishment, fabrication, grouping, layout, manufacturing, order, production, shapable, structure

formative *adj.* determinative, developmental, fledgling, impressionable, influenceable, malleable, pliant, shapable, susceptible

former *adj.* above, aforementioned, aforesaid, ancient, antecedent, anterior, bygone, ci-devant, departed, earlier, erstwhile, first, foregoing, late, long ago *or* gone, of yore, old, old- time, once, one-time, past, preceding, previous, sometime *Antonyms:* coming, ensuing, following, latter, subsequent

formerly *adv.* already, anciently, away back, back, back when, before, before now, earlier, eons ago, erstwhile, heretofore, lately, long ago, once, previously

formidable *adj.* **1.** arduous, backbreaking, challenging, difficult, exhausting, hard, intimidating, laborious, onerous, overpowering, overwhelming, rough, strenuous, toilsome, uphill *Antonyms:* easy, encouraging, heartening, pleasant **2.** awesome, Brobdingnagian, colossal, gigantic, huge, impressive, indomitable, mammoth, massive *Antonyms:* Lilliputian, miniscule, peanut, picayune, shrimp

formless *adj.* amorphous, baggy, chaotic, diffuse, disorganized, incoherent, indefinite, indeterminate, indistinct, nebulous, obscure, orderless, shapeless, undefined, unformed, unorganized *Antonyms*: definite, outlined, shaped

formula *n.* algorithm, axiom, blueprint, canon, cliché, code, creed, custom, direction, method, *modus operandi (Latin)*, prescription, password, procedure, protocol, recipe, rite, ritual, rule, shibboleth, specifications, theorem, tradition, way

formulate *v.* articulate, codify, coin, compose, concoct, contrive, cook up, couch, define, detail, develop, devise, draft, draw *or* dream up, evolve, express, forge, frame, hatch, invent, make, make up, map out, originate, particularize, phrase, plan, prepare, say, set down, specify, state, systematize, vamp, work *or* write out

forsake *v.* abandon, abdicate, cast off, desert, discard, disclaim, disown, divorce, forgo, forswear, jettison, jilt, leave, quit, relinquish, renounce, repudiate, resign, set aside, spurn, surrender, throw over *Antonyms*: endure, remain, support, tolerate

forsaken *adj.* abandoned, banished, cast off *or* out, derelict, deserted, desolate, destitute, discarded, disowned, forlorn, ignored, isolated, jilted, left behind, marooned, ostracized, outcast, scorned, thrown over *Antonyms*: backed, nurtured, supported, sustained

forswear *v.* abandon, abjure, deny, disavow, disclaim, disown, drop, forgo, forsake, give up, recall, recant, reject, renege, renounce, repudiate, retract, take back, withdraw

fort *n.* blockhouse, camp, castle, citadel, fortification, fortress, garrison, keep, outpost, post, redoubt, station, stronghold

forte *adj.* blaring, booming, deafening, ear-splitting, forceful, fortissimo, intense, loud, piercing, resounding, stentorian, thunderous – *adv.* loudly, noisily, resoundingly ringingly – *n.* ability, ableness, aptitude competence, effectiveness, efficiency, eminency, faculty, gift, medium, métier, specialty, strength, strong point, talent *Nonformal:* bag, long *or* strong suit, thing

forthcoming *adj.* **1.** anticipated, approaching, at hand, awaited, coming, destined due to be published, expected, fated, imminent, impending, inescapable, inevitable looming, nearing, oncoming, pending, predestined, prospective, resulting, upcoming **2.** fabricated, formed, invented, made, prepared, produced, ready **3.** accessible approachable, available, obtainable, open – *n.* advance, advent, appearance, approach arising, arrival, emergence, imminence manifestation, materialization

forthright *adj.* aboveboard, bald, blunt candid, categorical, direct, forward, frank honest, open, outspoken, plain, plain-spoken, real, simple, sincere, straight, straightforward, undisguised, up-front *Antonyms* dishonest, furtive, secret, sneaky, underhanded – *adv.* directly, downright, straight ahead, undeviatingly

forthwith *adv.* abruptly, at once, away directly, immediately, instantly, now, quickly, straightaway, suddenly, this instant, without delay

fortification *n.* barricade, barrier, bastion battlement, block, blockhouse, breastwork buffer, bulwark, bunker, castle, citadel crenelation, defence, enclosure, entrench ment, fort, fortress, garrison, keep, outpost, protection, rampart, reinforcement, stockade, stronghold, support, tower, trench, wall

fortify *v.* **1.** brace, build up, bulwark, buttress, consolidate, entrench, garrison, gird, prepare, protect, ready, reinforce, secure, shore up, strengthen, support, sustain *Antonyms:* debilitate, impair, reduce, weaken **2.** cheer, embolden, encourage, energize, enliven, hearten, invigorate, rally, reassure, refresh, renew, restore, rouse, stir *Antonyms:* demoralize, depress, dishearten

fortitude *n.* backbone, boldness, bravery, constancy, dauntlessness, determination, endurance, fearlessness, firmness, grit, hardihood, heart, mettle, nerve, patience, perseverance, pluck, resilience, resoluteness, spirit, spunk, stamina, staying power, stoutheartedness, strength, tenacity, valour *Nonformal:* bottled *or* dutch courage, guts, starch, stomach *Antonyms*: feebleness, timidity, weakness

fortress *n.* alcazar, bastion, castle, citadel, fort, fortification, hold, keep, martello *or* martello tower, post, safehold, stronghold

fortuitous *adj.* accidental, casual, chance, contingent, felicitous, fluky, fortunate, haphazard, hit or miss *(Nonformal)*, inadvertent, lucky, providential, serendipitous, unforeseen, unpremeditated

fortuity *n.* accident, adventitiousness, casualty, chance, coincidence, contingence, fortune, flukiness, good luck, hap, happenstance, luck, serendipity, vicissitudes

fortunate *adj.* **1.** auspicious, convenient, encouraging, felicitous, fortuitous, hopeful, lucky, opportune, promising, providential, timely, triumphant, victorious *Nonformal:* hot, on a roll *Antonyms:* hapless, ill-fated, star-crossed, unlucky, wretched **2.** advantageous, affluent, blessed, charmed, favoured, flourishing, golden, happy, healthy, profitable, prosperous, rosy, successful, thriving, wealthy, well-off, well-to-do

fortunately *adv.* auspiciously, favourably, happily, luckily, opportunely, prosperously, providentially, satisfyingly, seasonably, successfully, swimmingly *(Nonformal)*, well

fortune *n.* **1.** affluence, capital, estate, inheritance, opulence, portion, possessions, property, prosperity, resources, riches, substance, treasure, wealth, wherewithal, worth *Antonyms:* destitution, hardship, indigence, penury, poverty **2.** accident, break, chance, circumstances, destiny, expectation, fate, fluke, good medicine *(Native Peoples)*, karma, kismet, life, luck, lucky break *or* hit, providence, shot, stab, success

fortuneteller *n.* advisor, astronomer, augur, channeller, chiromancer, clairvoyant, crystal-ball gazer, diviner, medium, mind reader, mitt reader *(Nonformal)*, necromancer, oracle, palm *or* tarot *or* tea-leaf reader, predictor, prophet, seer, soothsayer, spiritualist

forum *n.* **1.** assembly, colloquy, debate, exchange of views, meeting, symposium **2.** bench, board, court, curia, tribunal **3.** agora, arena, market, meeting place, plazza, public square, *rialto (Italian)*, square

forward *adj.* **1.** anterior, bow, facial, first, fore, foremost, front, head, leading, ventral **2.** advanced, avant-garde, civilized, cultured, cutting *or* leading edge, industrialized, progressive, technological, well-developed *Antonyms:* backward, behind, regressive **3.** aggressive, assuming, audacious, barefaced, bold, brash, brazen, cheeky, confident, familiar, fresh, impertinent, impudent, nervy, overassertive, overweening, pert, precocious, presuming, presumptuous, pushy, rude, sassy, self-assertive, smart, smart-alecky *(Nonformal)*, uppity, wise *Antonyms:* diffident, modest, shy – *adv.* ahead, antecedently, beforehand, fore, forth, frontward, in advance, onward *Antonyms:* afterward, backward – *v.* **1.** address, consign, deliver, dispatch, e-mail, express, freight, post, remit, route, send, ship, transmit, transport **2.** advance, aid, assist, back, champion, encourage, expedite, favour, foster, further, hasten, help, promote, serve, speed, support, uphold *Antonyms:* bar, block, hinder, uphold

forward-looking *adj.* advanced, avant-garde, contemporary, dynamic, futuristic, mod *(Nonformal)*, modern, modish, perceptive, ultramodern, up-to-the-minute *Antonyms:* antiquated, old-fashioned, stale, passé

fossil *n.* **1.** deposit, evidence, impression, petrifaction, reconstruction, relic, remains, skeleton, specimen, trace **2.** ancient, antique *Nonformal:* mossback, old fogey, old-timer

fossilized *adj.* **1.** ancient, antediluvian, antiquated, antique, archaic, dated, dilapidated, extinct, fuddy-duddy *(Nonformal)*, fusty, medieval, moth-eaten, musty, obsolete, old, old-fangled, old-fashioned, old-fogyish, old-world, out-of-date, outworn, passé, prehistoric, primitive, stale, stodgy, superannuated, timeworn *Antonyms:* avant-garde, fresh, hip, modish, new **2.** calcified, hardened, indurated, lithified, petrified, stiffened

foster *v.* advance, aid, back, champion, cherish, cultivate, encourage, facilitate, feed, forward, further, harbour, nourish, nurture, promote, rear, serve, stimulate, support, sustain, train, uphold *Antonyms:* combat, curb, curtail, inhibit, oppose

foul *adj.* **1.** base, corrupt, crooked, dishonest, fraudulent, inequitable, not cricket *(Nonformal)*, notorious, shady, underhanded, unfair, unjust, unscrupulous, vicious, wicked *Antonyms:* admirable, fair, respectable **2.** abhorrent, contaminated, detestable, dirty, disgusting, fetid, filthy, hateful, heinous, horrid, impure, loathsome, mucky, nasty, nauseating, polluted, putrid, rancid, rank, repellent, revolting, rotten, squalid, stinking, sullied, tainted, unclean *Antonyms:* attractive, clear, fresh, spotless **3.** abusive, blasphemous, blue, coarse, foul-mouthed, gross, indecent, low, obscene, offensive, profane, raunchy, rude, scatological, scurrilous, smutty, vulgar *Antonyms:* chaste, decent, modest, pure **4.** adverse, cloudy, disagreeable, gloomy, inclement, rainy, stormy, tempestuous, unfavourable, unpleasant, wet **5.** blocked, caught, entangled, hindered, impeded, obstructed, stopped – *n.* breach of conduct, infraction, infringement, misconduct, out of bounds *or* play, penalty, unfairness, violation *Antonyms:* fair play, legal play – *v.* befoul, begrime, besmear, besmirch, block, choke, clog, contaminate, defile, desecrate, dirty, discolour, entangle, pollute, smear, smudge, snarl, soil, spot, stain, sully, taint, tarnish *Antonyms:* cleanse, clear, purge, purify, sanitize

foul-mouthed *adj.* abusive, blasphemous crude, cursing, course, dirty, filthy, foul foul-tongued, lewd, obscene, offensive profane, Rabelaisian, raw, risque, rude scatological, vituperative, vulgar

found *adj.* **1.** discovered, detected exhumed, located, uncovered, unearthed **2** all in, included, part of the package – *v.* **1** begin, build, commence, constitute, con struct, create, endow, erect, establish, fash ion, father, fix, form, get going, ground inaugurate, initiate, institute, launch, orga nize, originate, plant, raise, rear, rest, rin in, root, settle, stay, support, sustain **2.** cas melt, model, mould, sculpt, solder, weld

foundation *n.* **1.** ballast, base, bed bedrock, bottom, caisson, footing, grounc work, hardpan, infrastructure, stability, sul stratum, substructure, support, underpi ning, understructure **2.** bequeathal, don tion, endorsement, endowment, fund, gif settlement **3.** establishment, institutio organization **4.** assumption, basis, essenc gist, grounds, hypothesis, nitty-gritt premise, root, warrant *Nonformal:* ABC bottom line, nub **5.** beginning, commenc ment, creation, dawn, onset, launch, origi start **6.** base, beauty product, cosmetic cream, make-up, moisturizer, powder

founder *n.* architect, author, creator, disco erer, establisher, founding member, instig tor, inventor, organizer, originator, prir mover, producer *Founders of religions ar sects:* Buddha *or* Gautama Buddha *(Bu dhism)*, Charles and John Wesley *(Metho ism)*, Confucius *or* Kung Fu-tzu *(Conf cianism)*, Emanuel Swedenborg *(Chur of the New Jerusalem)*, Jesus Chri *(Christianity)*, John Calvin *(Calvinism* Joseph Smith *(Mormon Church)*, Lao-t *(Taoism)*, Mahavira *or* Vardhamana *or* Ji *(Jainism)*, Martin Luther *(Lutheranism* Mary Baker Eddy *(Christian Science* Menno Simons *(Mennonitism)*, Mirza A Muhammad of Shiraz *or* the Bab *(Babism*

Muhammad *(Islam)*, Nanak *(Sikhism)*, Zoroaster *or* Zarathustra *(Zoroastrianism)* – *v.* **1.** become waterlogged, capsize, go under, keel over, sink, submerge **2.** cave in, collapse, crash and burn *(Nonformal)*, crumble, fail, fall **3.** brakedown, limp, pull up lame, sprawl, stagger, stumble *Commonly Misused:* **flounder**

foundling *n.* castaway, guttersnipe, mudlark, orphan, outcast, stray, waif, wastrel, urchin

fountain *n.* **1.** geyser, gush, jet, spray, spring, waterworks, well **2.** cause, font, inception, mainspring, origin, root, source, wellspring **3.** basin, chamber, hold, receptacle, reservoir, supply

fountainhead *n.* agent, author, beginning, birth, causation, creator, derivation, generator, genesis, headwater, inception, origin, originator, prime mover, provenance, rise, source, springhead, wellspring

foxy *adj.* **1.** artful, crafty, cunning, deceitful, devious, dishonest, furtive, guileful, insidious, shrewd, sly, subtle, tricky, wily **2.** alluring, attractive, desirable, hot *(Nonformal)*, sexy, voluptuous **3.** defective, faulty, flawed, soiled, tainted, tarnished **3.** auburn, henna, reddish-brown, roan, rufous, russet, rust

foyer *n.* antechamber, anteroom, entrance, entry, front room, hall, lobby, reception, vestibule

fracas *n.* affray, altercation, battle, battle royal, bickering, brannigan, brawl, dispute, disturbance, donnybrook, feud, fight, fray, mêlée, mixup, quarrel, riot, row, run-in, scrimmage, scuffle, squabble, trouble, tumult, uproar, words *Nonformal:* free-for-all, rhubarb, ruckus, rumpus, set-to

fractional *adj.* **1.** apportioned, fragmentary, incomplete, parceled, part, partial, piecemeal, sectional, segmented **2.** few, insignificant, little, meagre, microscopic, negligible, picayune, puny, slight, small, tiny, trivial

fractious *adj.* **1.** bitchy, captious, crabby, cross, fretful, grouchy, huffy, irritable, mean, ornery, owly, peevish, pettish, petulant, querulous, scrappy, snappish, testy, thin-skinned, touchy *Antonyms:* agreeable, amiable, biddable, charming **2.** disorderly, headstrong, intractable, rebellious, recalcitrant, refractory, uncompliant, undisciplined, unmanageable, unruly, wayward, wild *Antonyms:* affable, docile, tractable *Commonly misused:* **factious**

fracture *n.* breach, break, cleavage, cleft, crack, fissure, fragmentation, gap, opening, rent, rift, rupture, schism, severance, split, wound – *v.* break, cleave, crack, dislocate, fragment, open, rend, rupture, separate, sever, split *Antonyms*: join, link, unite

fragile *adj.* breakable, brittle, crisp, crumbly, dainty, decrepit, delicate, feeble, fine, flimsy, fracturable, frail, frangible, friable, infirm, insubstantial, shivery, slight, unsound, weak *Antonyms:* durable, elastic, flexible, sturdy, tough

fragment *n.* atom, bit, bite, chip, chunk, crumb, cut, end, fraction, grain, hunk, iota, jot, lump, morsel, part, particle, piece, portion, remnant, scrap, share, shred, slice, sliver, smithereen *(Nonformal) Antonyms*: aggregate, entirety, total, whole

fragrance *n.* aroma, aura, balm, bouquet, incense, odour, perfume, redolence, scent, smell, spice

fragrant *adj.* ambrosial, aromatic, delectable, delicious, delightful, flowery, fruity, musky, nice-smelling, odiferous, odorous, perfumed, redolent, savoury, scented, spicy, sweet, sweet-scented, sweet-smelling *Antonyms:* fetid, malodorous, reeking

frail *adj.* **1.** ailing, debilitated, feeble, ill, infirm, rocky, shaky, sickly, thin, unhealthy, unsound, unwell, valetudinary, weak *Antonyms:* hale, healthy, hearty **2.** breakable, brittle, crisp, crumbly, delicate, flimsy, fracturable, fragile, frangible, insubstantial, slender, slight, tender, tenuous, wispy *Antonyms:* invulnerable, sound, strong **3.** irresolute, spineless, temptable, vulnerable, weak-willed *Nonformal:* poor fish, weak sister, wishy-washy *Antonyms:* resolute, steadfast, undeviating

frailty *n.* **1.** daintiness, debility, decrepitude, delicacy, feebleness, flimsiness, infirmity, susceptibility, weakness *Antonyms:* fortitude, health, might, strength **2.** blemish, defect, deficiency, error, failing, fault, flaw, foible, imperfection, shortcoming, vice, weak point *Antonyms:* advantage, asset, strength

frame *n.* **1.** anatomy, body-type, build, figure, form, physique, shape **2.** border, case, casement, casing, edge, framing, fringe, margin **3.** architecture, arrangement, configuration, conformation, composition, framework, network, organization, outline, pattern, plan, structure, system, topology **4.** backing, exoskeleton, foundation, groundwork, infrastructure, mount, mounting, scaffolding, shell, skeleton, substructure, support, underframe **5.** exposure, film, picture, shot, take – *v.* **1.** compose, conceive, concoct, contrive, design, devise, draft, draw, dream up, form, formulate, invent, make, map out, outline, plan, prepare, shape, sketch, write **2.** articulate, couch, express, phrase, put forth, say, speak, state, utter **3.** accuse, cheat, deceive, fix, prearrange, recriminate, rig, scheme against, set-up, trap, victimize **4.** border, bound, edge, trim

framework *n.* **1.** bare bones, core, foundation, frame, groundwork, outline, plan, schema, scheme, shell, skeleton, structure, topology **2.** arena, basis, paradigm, perspective, point of view, position, situation

franchise *n.* **1.** authorization, authority, ballot, charter, grant, licence, permission, prerogative, privilege, right, suffrage, vote, warrant, warranty **2.** business, chain, concession, shop, store, restaurant **3.** discharge, exemption, immunity, release

frank *adj.* aboveboard, apparent, artless, barefaced, blunt, bold, brazen, candid, direct, downright, familiar, flat-out *(Nonformal)*, forthright, free, guileless, heart-to-heart, honest, ingenuous, matter-of-fact, natural, open, outright, outspoken, plain, plain-spoken, real, sincere, straight, straightforward, transparent, truthful, unconcealed, undisguised, uninhibited, unreserved, unrestricted, up front, upright *Antonyms:* crafty, cunning, indirect, reserved – *n.* correspondence, letter, mail, message, parcel, postage stamp, postmark, signature, stamp

frankly *adv.* bluntly, candidly, dead level *(Nonformal)*, directly, freely, honestly, in truth, openly, plainly, straight, without reserve

frantic *adj.* agitated, crazy, delirious, deranged, distraught, distressed, frenzied, hyper, insane, keyed *or* worked up, overwrought, rabid, violent *Nonformal:* foaming at the mouth, in a tizzy, unzipped, wild, worked up *Antonyms:* calm, composed, poised

fraternal *adj.* associated, brotherly, clannish, congenial, familial, friendly, intimate, kind *Antonyms*: alien, estranged, malevolent, malicious

fraternity *n.* **1.** affiliation, association, brotherhood, camaraderie, companionship, comradeship, fellowship, kinship, sisterhood, sorority *Antonyms*: animosity, enmity, estrangement, hostility **2.** circle, clan, club, company, guild, house, league, letter society, order, organization, set, society, union

fraternize *v.* associate, chum with, concur, consort, cooperate, hang out, hobnob, join, keep company, league, loosen *or* open up, mingle, mix, pal around, run with, socialize, unite, warm up *Antonyms*: alienate, antagonize, estrange, oppose

fraud *n.* **1.** artifice, blackmail, chicanery, craft, deceit, deception, duplicity, extortion, fraudulence, graft, guile, hoax, hustle, imposture, lie, misrepresentation, racket, sham, swindling, treachery, trickery *Nonformal:* bamboozlement, con, double-dealing, hocus-pocus, scam, snow job, sting **2.** charlatan, cheat, confidence trickster, counterfeiter, deceiver, embezzler, fake, imposter, liar, quack, rapscallion, scamp, scoundrel *Nonformal:* grifter, phoney, pseud *or* pseudo

fraudulent *adj.* **1.** counterfeit, false, forged, phoney *(Nonformal)*, sham, spurious **2.** crafty, criminal, crooked, deceitful, deceptive, devious, dishonest, dishonourable, dirty-dealing *(Nonformal)*, duplicitous, knavish, swindling, treacherous, tricky *Antonyms:* genuine, honest, lawful principled, trustworthy

fraught *adj.* abounding, attended, bristling, charged, filled, full, heavy, laden, replete, weighted *Antonyms*: bereft, depleted, empty, lacking

fray *n.* battle, brawl, clash, combat, conflict, contest, disturbance, donnybrook, fight, fracas, mêlée, quarrel, riot, row, ruckus, rumpus, scuffle, set-to, uproar – *v.* **1.** chafe, come apart, erode, frazzle, ravel, shred, tatter, tear, unravel, wear **2.** addle, agitate, aggravate, bewilder, bother, confuse, discomfit, discompose, disconcert, disturb, fluster, gall, irk, muddle, peeve, perturb, rankle, ruffle, unnerve, unsettle, vex *Antonyms*: calm, pacify, placate, soothe **3.** argue, attack, bicker, challenge, contest, dispute, fight, quarrel, row

freak *n.* **1.** aberration, abnormality, anomaly, curiosity, irregularity, malformation, monstrosity, mutation, oddity, rarity **2.** addict, afficionado, buff, devotee, fan *or* fanatic, follower, zealot *Nonformal:* fiend, groupie, nut **3.** caprice, conceit, crank, crochet, fancy, notion, passing fad, quirk, whim **4.** character, eccentric, individual, maverick, misfit, nonconformist, original *Nonformal:* loony, nutbar, oddball, weirdo **5.** accident, chance event, fluke, fortuity, happenstance, luck, serendipity – *v.* **1.** breakdown, fall apart *Nonformal:* blow a fuse *or* gasket, crack, flip, freak out, go mad, lose it, wig out *Antonyms:* calm down, relax **2.** dream, envision, fantasize, flashback, hallucinate, imagine, trip *or* trip out *(Nonformal)*

freakish *adj.* **1.** aberrant, abnormal, bizarre, crazy, fantastic, far-out, freaky, odd, outlandish, *outre (French)*, preternatural, strange, unconventional, unusual, weird, whimsical *Antonyms:* natural, ordinary, typical **2.** anomalous, arbitrary, capricious, erratic, extraordinary, random, singular

free *adj.* **1.** complimentary, costless, courtesy, donated, for nothing, gratis, gratuitous, honorary, unasked-for, unpaid, voluntary, without charge *Antonyms:* costly, expensive, pricey **2.** available, clear, disengaged, empty, extra, idle, loose, not busy, spare, unclogged, unemployed, unengaged, uninhabited, unoccupied, unused, vacant *Antonyms:* blocked, busy, secured, tied up **3.** at liberty, single, unattached, unblocked, unfettered, unhampered, unimpeded, unmarried, unrestrained, unrestricted **4.** emancipated, enfranchised, freed, liberated, manumitted, permitted, released, unbound *Antonyms:* captive, detained, incarcerated **5.** autonomous, democratic, independent, self-directing, self-governing, self-ruling, separate, sovereign, *sui juris (Latin)*, unconstrained **6.** accessible, approachable, candid, casual, communicative, easy, familiar, fancy-free, footloose, free-spirited, informal, light-hearted, outspoken, plain-spoken, relaxed, talkative, unconventional, unguarded *Antonyms:* aloof, burdened, ceremonious, tied-down **7.** big-hearted, bountiful, charitable, eager, generous, giving, handsome, hospitable, lavish, liberal, munificent, open-handed, unsparing, willing *Antonyms:* stingy, tight, ungenerous – *v.* **1.** absolve, acquit, bail out, deliver, discharge, dismiss, emancipate, extricate, let go, liberate, loosen, manumit, pardon, parole, release, relieve, rescue, save, set free, spring, turn loose, unbind, unchain, undo, unfetter, unleash, untie *Antonyms:* confine, imprison, incarcerate, limit, restrict **2.** cast off, clear, cut loose, discharge, disencumber, disengage, disentangle, extricate, relieve, rid, unburden, unload

freedom *n.* **1.** abandon, boldness, candour, directness, ease, facility, familiarity, forthrightness, forwardness, frankness, impertinence, informality, openness, overfamiliarity, presumption, readiness, spontaneity *Antonyms:* caution, inhibition, wariness **2.** carte blanche, elbowroom, facility, flexibility, free rein, latitude, leeway, leisure, licence, margin, opportunity, prerogative, privilege, range, scope *Antonyms:* dispensation, limitation, prohibition, restriction **3.** abolition, deliverance, delivery, discharge, emancipation, exemption, immunity, liberation, liberty, manumission, parole, probation, release *Antonyms:* bondage, captivity, dependence **4.** autonomy, democracy, franchise, independence, representative government, self-determination, self-government, sovereignty

free-for-all *n.* battle, brawl, broil, brouhaha, commotion, disturbance, donnybrook, embroilment, fight, fracas, fray, hubbub, mêlée, racket, riot, row, slugfest *(Nonformal)*, tumult, turmoil, uproar

freely *adv.* **1.** artlessly, candidly, easily, effortlessly, fancy-free *(Nonformal)*, frankly, loosely, naturally, openly, plainly, spontaneously, unhindered, unreservedly **2.** amply, bountifully, considerably, copiously, extravagently, handsomely, lavishly, liberally **3.** at will, independently, readily, voluntarily, willingly

free-thinking *adj.* broad-minded, impartial, latitudinarian, liberal, liberal-minded, liberalistic, open, open-minded, progressive, receptive, tolerant, unbiased, unconventional *Antonyms:* close-minded, conforming, conservative – *n.* catholicism, broad-mindedness, liberalism, openness, receptivity, tolerance

freeze *n.* **1.** arctic frost, cold, cold front, deep freeze, frost, snap, winter **2.** discontinuation, embargo, halt, moratorium, prohibition, recall, restriction, shutdown, standstill, stoppage, suspension – *v.* **1.** chill, congeal, glaciate, harden, ice over *or* up, lose heat, nip, pierce, quiver, refrigerate, shiver, stiffen *Antonyms:* boil, cook, heat, melt **2.** anesthetize, benumb, blunt, deaden, desensitize, drug, medicate, numb, paralyze **3.** arrest, block, brake, check, curb, discourage, fix, halt, hinder, immobilize, inhibit, prohibit, quash, repress, restrain, retain, squelch, stop **4.** frighten, petrify, scare, spook, startle, strike dumb, stun, stupefy, terrify

freezing *adj.* arctic, biting, bitter, chilled, chilly, cold, cutting, frigid, frost-bound, frosty, gelid, glacial, icy, nippy, numbing, penetrating, polar, raw, shivery, snappy, wintry *Antonyms*: hot, warm, sweltering

freight *n.* bales, ballast, bulk, burden, carriage, consignment, contents, conveyance, encumbrance, haul, lading, load, merchandise, pack, packages, shipment, shipping, tonnage, transportation, wares, weight – *v.* carry, convey, load, mail, pack *or* pack up, schlep *(Nonformal)*, send, ship, transport

frenetic *adj.* delirious, demented, distraught, excited, fanatical, frantic, frenzied, hectic, hyperactive, insane, mad, maniacal, obsessive, overwrought, rabid, wild *Nonformal:* hyped up, hyper, wired *Antonyms* disinterested, languid, slow

frenzied *adj.* berserk, convulsive, delirious distracted, distraught, excited, feverish frantic, frenetic, hysterical, mad, maniacal nuts *(Nonformal)*, uncontrolled *Antonyms:* calm, peaceful, soothing

frenzy *n.* agitation, confusion, convulsion craze, delirium, excitement, ferment, fever fit, furor, fury, fuss, hysteria, lather, lunacy madness, mania, paroxysm, turbulence turmoil *Nonformal:* conniption, flap, foofaraw *Antonyms:* calm, collectedness composure, sanity – *v.* craze, dement, drive crazy *or* insane, enrage, excite, incense infuriate, madden *Nonformal:* unhinge work up

frequency *n.* **1.** abundance, commonness frequentness, persistence, prevalence recurrence, regularity, repetition, repetitiveness **2.** band, oscillation, pattern, radio wave, resonance, rhythm, vibration, wave *or* wavelength

frequent *adj.* constant, continual, customary, general, habitual, numerous, often, perpetual, persistent, recurrent, repeated, successive, ubiquitous, usual *Antonyms:* few infrequent, occasional, rare – *v.* attend regularly, drop in, hang about, haunt, hit infest, overrun, patronize, revisit, visit

frequently *adv.* commonly, habitually intermittently, many times, much, often ordinarily, periodically, regularly, repeatedly, successively *Antonyms:* hardly ever infrequently, rarely

fresh *adj.* **1.** brand-new, current, different latest, modern, new, new-fangled, novel original, recent, freshing, revolutionary unconventional, unusual, up-to-date *Nonformal:* now, the latest, this seasons **2.** clean, clear, dewy, gleaming, glistening natural, pristine, pure, sparkling, uncontaminated, unpolluted, unprocessed, untainted, untouched, virginal *Antonyms:* grungy polluted, processed **3.** bracing, brisk, cool crisp, invigorating, quick, sharp, stimulating *Antonyms:* dull, misty, stale **4.** bright colourful, graphic, lifelike, picturesque stimulating, true-to-life, vivid **5.** active, alert, blooming, bouncing, chipper, energetic, glowing, hale, hardy, healthy, invigorating, keen, like new, lively, perky, refreshed, rested, restored, relaxed, rosy, ruddy, shining, sprightly, spry, stimulated, vigourous, vital, wholesome, young, youthful *Antonyms:* exhausted, old, weary **6.** crude, green, immature, inexperienced, raw, sophomoric, unfledged, unseasoned, untrained **7.** brash, brazen, cheeky, forward, importunate, impudent, pert, precocious, rude, saucy *Antonyms*: cautious, wary **8.** additional, extra, further, more, supplementary

freshen *v.* **1.** air, clean, cleanse, purify, refresh, spruce up, sweeten, ventilate **2.** activate, enliven, invigorate, restore, revitalize, revive, rouse,

freshness *n.* **1.** bloom, brightness, cleanness, clearness, dew, dewiness, glow, shine, sparkle, vigour *Antonyms*: mustiness, staleness **2.** callowness, greenness, inexperience, rawness, youthfulness *Antonyms*: age, experience, jadedness **3.** inventiveness, newness, novelty, originality

fret *n.* **1.** ache, agitation, aggravation, annoyance, bother, irritant, irritation, nervousness, uneasiness *Nonformal:* hassle, lather, tizzy **2.** adornment, arabesque, band, border, filigree, grille, lattice, network, ornamentation, ridge, scrollwork, trellis – *v.* ache, agonize, brood, complain, fester, fume, huff, mope, rankle, stew *(Nonformal)*, suffer, worry

fretful *adj.* aggravated, anxious, bothered, captious, cranky, distressed, irritated, peevish, pestered, restless, testy, touchy, troubled, uneasy, worried, worrisome *Antonyms*: calm, contented, pleased

friable *adj.* brittle, chalky, crisp, crispy, crumbly, powdery, pulverizable, triturable *Antonyms:* firm, hard, solid

friar *n.* abbé, abbot, ascetic, brother, curé, mendicant, monastic, monk, prior, *religieux (French)*, religious

friction *n.* **1.** abrasion, agitation, chafing, erosion, filing, fretting, grating, grinding, irritation, rasping, resistance, rubbing, scraping, traction, wearing away **2.** animosity, antagonism, bickering, conflict, discontent, discord, dissension, hatred, hostility, incompatibility, interference, opposition, resentment, rivalry, strife, trouble, wrangling *Nonformal:* bad blood, flak

friend *n.* accomplice, acquaintance, adherent, advocate, ally, alter ego, *ami (French)*, amigo, associate, backer, brother, buddy, chum, chummy *(Newfoundland)*, classmate, cohort, colleague, compadre, companion, compatriot, comrade, confidant, confrere, crony, familiar, fellow, intimate, mate, pal, partner, patron, playmate, roommate, schoolmate, sister, soul mate, supporter, *tovarisch (Russian)*, well-wisher *Nonformal:* boon companion, bosom buddy, good bud, sidekick *Antonyms:* adversary, antagonist, competitor, enemy, foe

friendless *adj.* abandoned, alienated, alone, deserted, estranged, forlorn, forsaken, isolated, lonely, lonesome, ostracized, shunned, solitary, unattached *Antonyms*: mated, paired, popular

friendliness *n.* affability, amiability, amity, camaraderie, companionability, congeniality, conviviality, cordiality, friendship, geniality, good will, kindliness, kindness, neighbourliness, sociability, warmth *Antonyms*: discourtesy, incivility, rudeness

friendly *adj.* affable, affectionate, amiable, amicable, attentive, beneficial, benevolent, chummy, close, confiding, convivial, cordial, familiar, fond, fraternal, genial, good, helpful, intimate, kind, kindly, loving, loyal, neighbourly, outgoing, peaceable, receptive, sociable, welcoming, well-disposed *Nonformal:* right neighbourly, thick *Antonyms:* antagonistic, belligerent, contentious, sinister, unfriendly

friendship *n.* **1.** accord, acquaintanceship, alliance, amity, association, benevolence, brotherhood, coalition, companionship, friendliness, good will, harmony, sisterhood, solidarity, union *Antonyms:* animosity, antagonism, antipathy, aversion, strife **2.** affection, affinity, amiability, attachment, bond, closeness, connection, consonance, empathy, esteem, familiarity, fondness, intimacy, love, partiality, rapport, regard, sociability, understanding

fright *n.* **1.** alarm, apprehension, consternation, dismay, dread, fear, horror, panic, quaking, scare, shiver, shock, terror, trepidation *Antonyms:* boldness, bravery, courage, pluck **2.** blot, disaster, disaster area, dump, eyesore, horror, mess, monstrosity, spectacle *Nonformal:* sight, ugly-duckling

frighten *v.* **1.** agitate, alarm, appall, astound, awe, browbeat, chill, cow, daunt, deter, discomfort, dishearten, dismay, disquiet, horrify, panic, perturb, petrify, repel, scare, scare stiff, shock, spook, startle, unhinge, unnerve, upset *Antonyms:* assuage, calm, hearten, reassure, soothe **2.** bulldoze, bully, extort, initiate, lean on, terrorize, tyrannize

frightened *adj.* abashed, afraid, alarmed, cowed, dismayed, fearful, frozen, jittery, jumpy, nervous, paralyzed, petrified, scared, shaky, shivery, spooked, startled, terrified, terror-stricken, unnerved, upset *Nonformal:* scared witless, struck dumb, weak-kneed, yellow-bellied *Antonyms:* brave, lion-hearted, plucky

frightful *adj.* **1.** alarming, appalling, atrocious, awesome, awful, bad, calamitous, dangerous, daunting, dismaying, dreadful, fearful, ghastly, grim, grisly, gruesome, harrowing, hellish, hideous, horrendous, horrible, horrifying, macabre, nasty, paralyzing, petrifying, repellent, scary, shocking, spooky, terrible, terrifying, unnerving, unpleasant, unspeakable, vile, wicked *Antonyms:* attractive, calming, moderate, pleasant, soothing **2.** disagreeable, distressing, excessive, offensive, outrageous, over the top *(Nonformal)*, rude, upsetting, wicked *Antonyms:* formal, prim, proper

frigid *adj.* **1.** arctic, chilly, cold, freezing, frost-bound, frozen, gelid, glacial, ice-cold, icy, refrigerated, snappy, wintry *Antonyms:* hot, stifling, sweltering, warm **2.** aloof, austere, cold-hearted, cool, emotionless, flinty, forbidding, frosty, indifferent, lifeless, passionless, repellent, rigid, soulless, stiff, unapproachable, unbending, unfeeling, unloving, unresponsive *Antonyms:* cordial, friendly, hospitable, impassioned, responsive

frigidity *n.* abstinence, aloofness, apathy, austerity, chill, dispassion, iciness, impassivity, lifelessness, remoteness, unresponsiveness *Antonyms:* feeling, responsiveness, stimulation, warmth

frill *n.* amenity, bell and whistle, extravagance, flounce, frippery, furbelow, fuss, galloon, gathering, gingerbread, lace, luxury, nice touch, ornament, ruffle, superfluity, tuck *Nonformal:* decoration, fandangle, gewgaw, gimcrack *Antonyms:* essential, necessity, requirement

fringe *adj.* alternative, avant-garde, marginal, on the edge, peripheral – *n.* binding, border, borderline, brim, brink, edge, fringe land, hem, margin, outskirts, perimeter, periphery, trimming, verge – *v.* border, edge, enclose, skirt, surround, trim

fripperies *n.* **1.** accessories, adornments, baubles, decoration, finery, flamboyance, flashiness, frills, garnish, gaudery, knickknacks, ornateness, ostentation, pompousness, showiness, trifles, trinkets, trumpery *Nonformal:* gegaws, grimcracks *Antonyms:* essentials, fundamentals, simplicities **2.** chit-chat, diplomatic niceties, pleasantries, slaver, small talk, sweet nothings

frisk *v.* **1.** check, inspect, run over, search, shake down *(Nonformal)* **2.** bounce, caper, cavort, dance, frolic, gambol, hop, jump, lark, leap, play, prance, rejoice, rollick, romp, skip, sport, trip

frisky *adj.* active, bouncy, coltish, frolicsome, gamesome, gay, happy, high-spirited, kittenish, larkish, lively, peppy, playful, rollicking, romping, spirited, sportive, wicked, zippy *Antonyms:* demure, lacklustre, pensive, sedate, wooden

frivolity *n.* **1.** coquettishness, dalliance, dallying, flightiness, flippancy, flirting, folly, fribble, frippery, frivolousness, fun, gaiety, game, giddiness, jest, levity, lightheartedness, lightness, nonsense, play, silliness, sport, toying, trifling, triviality, whimsicality, whimsy *Antonyms:* earnestness, gravity, humourlessness, importance, soberness **2.**

childishness, puerility, shallowness, superficiality

frivolous *adj.* **1.** dizzy, empty-headed, facetious, featherbrained, flighty, flip, flippant, giddy, light-minded, playful, scatterbrained, shallow, sportive, teasing, tongue-in-cheek, unimportant, whimsical *Antonyms:* earnest, practical, responsible **2.** foolish, frothy, idiotic, idle, ill-considered, impractical, juvenile, light, minor, paltry, petty, pointless, senseless, superficial, trivial, two-bit *(Nonformal)*,*Antonyms:* important, significant, weighty

frolic *n.* **1.** antic, drollery, escapade, fun, gambol, game, hijinks, joke, joviality, lark, play, prank, romp, shenanigan, skylarking, sport, spree, tomfoolery, trick **2.** amusement, celebration, gaiety, jollification, merriment, revel – *v.* caper, carouse, cavort, fool around, frisk, gambol, kick up one's heels, lark, let loose, make merry, play, prance, rejoice, revel, riot, rollick, sport, spree *Nonformal:* hack around, raise hell

frolicsome *adj.* coltish, frisky, gamesome, gay, gleeful, happy, hilarious, impish, jocular, jovial, kittenish, lively, merry, mischievous, playful, roguish, rollicking, sportive, sprightly *Antonyms*: serious, somber, staid

front *adj.* ahead, anterior, beginning, facing, first, fore, foremost, forward, frontal, head, headmost, lead, leading – *n.* **1.** avant-garde, cutting *or* leading edge, forefront, forerunner, front-runner, leader, pioneer, vanguard **2.** beak, beginning, bow, breast, chest, face, fore, foreground, forehead, frontpiece, mug *(Nonformal)*, nose, proscenium, visage **3.** battlefront, frontier, line, no man's land, scene of action, van, vanguard **4.** air, appearance, bearing, carriage, countenance, demeanour, display, expression, exterior, manner, mien, persona **5.** cover up, disguise, façade, pretext, put-on, show, surface, window dressing *(Nonformal)* **6.** army, coalition, force, group, militia, movement **7.** cold *or* storm *or* warm front, turbulence, weather **8.** alliance, association, coalition, group, federation, league – *v.* **1.** affront, beard, brave, challenge, confront, dare, defy, face, meet head-on, oppose, resist **2.** camouflage, cloak, conceal, cover for, deceive, disguise, mask, shroud, veil

frontier *n.* **1.** borderline, bound, boundary, confines, edge, fringe land, limit, perimeter, verge **2.** backcountry, backwoods, bush, countryside, hinterland, outback, outskirts

frosh *n.* apprentice, beginner, first-year student, freshman, learner, neophyte, newcomer, novice, novitiate, rookie, tenderfoot, yearling

frost *n.* blight, cold, dip, drop, freeze, frostburn, Jack Frost *(Nonformal) Kinds of frost:* black, frost bump, frost-ferns, frost heave, hoarfrost, killing, permafrost, rime, silver, white, winterkill – *v.* **1.** cover, decorate, glaze, top **2.** bite, chill, freeze, grizzle, refrigerate, silver, sleet, whiten **3.** assassinate, dispatch, erase, finish off, kill, liquidate, murder, silence, slay

frosty *adj.* **1.** chilly, cold, cool, frigid, frozen, gelid, glacial, ice-capped, icy, nippy, rimy, shivery, wintry *Antonyms:* balmy, hot, humid, warm **2.** discouraging, hostile, icy, steely, uncivil, unfriendly, unwelcoming *Antonyms:* genial, receptive, warm

froth *n.* **1.** bubbles, effervescence, fizz, foam, head, lather, spray, spume, suds, yeast **2.** emptiness, fluff, frippery, pulp, shallowness, superficiality, trifles, triviality, trumpery *Antonyms:* gravity, importance, value, weight – *v.* aerate, agitate, beat, blend, bubble, foam, lather, mix, spume, whip, whisk

frothy *adj.* **1.** bubbling, fizzy, foaming, foamy, soapy, sudsy **2.** airy, flimsy, frivolous, inconsequential, insignificant, insubstantial, light, shallow, superficial, trifling, trivial, vain, windy *Antonyms:* important, substantial, weighty

frown *n.* glower, grimace, long face, scowl, wince *Antonyms:* grin, smile, smirk – *v.* cloud up, glare, gloom, glower, grimace, pout, scowl, sulk

frowzy *adj.* blowzy, careless, dishevelled, disordered, disorderly, frumpish, frumpy, grubby, loose, rumpled, scraggly, scruffy, shabby, shoddy, slack, slatternly, slipshod, sloppy, slovenly, tousled, unkempt, unsightly, untidy *Antonyms:* neat, orderly, smart, tidy, trim

frozen *adj.* **1.** arctic, chilled, cold, frigid, frore *(Historical)*, frosted, icebound, ice-cold, ice-covered, iced, icy, numb **2.** fixed, immortal, pegged, permanent, petrified, rooted, solidified, stiff, stock-still, stopped, stuck, suspended **3.** aloof, cold-blooded, cold-hearted, dispassionate, heartless, impassive, unemotional, unfeeling, unresponsive *Antonyms:* ardent, passionate, sensitive

frugal *adj.* **1.** abstinent, chary, conserving, economical, economizing, miserly, parsimonious, penurious, prudent, saving, scrimping, self-controlled, self-sacrificing, skimping, sparing, stingy, temperate, thrifty, tight-fisted *Antonyms:* extravagant, wasteful **2.** bare bones, cheap, exiguous, inexpensive, low-priced, meagre, scanty, slight, spare *Antonyms:* exorbitant, lavish

frugality *n.* care, cautiousness, conservation, economy, husbandry, miserliness, moderation, parsimony, penny-pinching ways, penuriousness, prudence, saving, scrimping, stinginess, thrift *Antonyms:* extravagance, lavishness, prodigality, wastefulness

fruit *n.* **1.** berry, crop, grain, growth, harvest, nut, pome, produce, result, yield *Kinds of fruit:* apple, banana, black currant, breadfruit, cantalope, cherry, citron, clementine, coconut, crabapple, currant, date, durian, fig, granadilla, grape, grapefruit, greengage, guava, jackfruit, jujube, kiwi, kumquat, lemon, lime, loquat, mango, medlar, melon, nectarine, olive, orange, papaya, passion, pawpaw, peach, pear, persimmon, pineapple, plantain, plum, pomegranate, pomelo, prune, quince, sapodilla, soursop, starfruit, tamarillo, tamarind, tangelo, tangerine, tomato, watermelon **2.** advantage, benefit, consequence, effect, gain, outcome, pay, profit, result, return, reward

fruitful *adj.* **1.** abounding, abundant, copious, plenteous, plentiful, profuse, prolific **2.** advantageous, beneficial, conducive, effective, gainful, profitable, rewarding, successful, useful, well-spent, worthwhile *Antonyms:* futile, pointless, useless **3.** blossoming, fecund, fertile, flourishing, fructiferous, productive, propagating, reproducing, rich, spawning *Antonyms:* barren, fruitless, infertile

fruition *n.* achievement, actualization, attainment, completion, fulfillment, enjoyment, gratification, materialization, maturity, realization, ripening, satisfaction, success *Antonyms:* deterioration, failure, frustration

fruitless *adj.* **1.** barren, bootless, empty, infertile, sterile, unfruitful, unproductive, *Antonyms:* abundant, fecund, fertile, fruitful **2.** abortive, futile, gainless, idle, ineffective, ineffectual, in vain, pointless, profitless, unavailable, unavailing, unprofitable, unsuccessful, useless, vain *Antonyms:* effective, useful

frustrate *v.* annul, arrest, baffle, balk, bar, beat, betray, bilk, block, break, cancel, check, circumvent, conquer, counter, counteract, cramp, crimp, dash, defeat, depress, disappoint, discourage, dishearten, foil, forbid, forestall, forsake, halt, hinder, impede, inhibit, neutralize, nullify, obstruct, prevent, renege, repudiate, retract, revert, stump, stymie, thwart *Antonyms:* encourage, endorse, further, promote, stimulate

frustrated *adj.* balked, checkmated, crabbed, cramped, defeated, disappointed, discontented, discouraged, disheartened, embittered, foiled, irked, resentful, stonewalled, stymied, thwarted, unsated *Antonyms:* aided, fulfilled, furthered

frustration *n.* annoyance, blockage, chagrin, circumvention, defeat, disappointment, dissatisfaction, failure, grievance, hindrance, impediment, irritation, letdown, obstruction, resentment, thwarting, vexation *Nonformal:* bitter pill, bummer, downer, drag, the old one-two *Antonyms:* achievement, advancement, fulfillment, gain

fry *n.* child, fledgling, infant, kid *(Nonformal)*, young – *v.* brown, burn *(Nonformal)*, cook, deep-fry, French-fry, fricassee, grill, pan-fry, sauté, sear, singe, sizzle

fuddled *adj.* bemused, bewildered, confused, dazed, drunk, frustrated, groggy, inebriated, intoxicated, muddled, nonplused, perplexed, punch-drunk, punchy, puzzled, tipsy, upset *Antonyms:* alert, clear-minded, sober

fudge *n.* balderdash, bunk, humbug, nonsense, psychobabble, rubbish, twaddle *Nonformal:* bull, crap, gobbledygook, hogwash, malarkey – *v.* change, colour, cook up, doctor *(Nonformal)*, embellish, embroider, equivocate, evade, exaggerate, fake, falsify, magnify, manipulate, misrepresent, overstate, pad, skew, slant, twist

fuel *n.* ammunition, combustible, electricity, energy, fodder, food, gas, juice *(Nonformal)*, material, means, nourishment, propellant *Kinds of fuel:* benzine, coal, gasoline, kerosene, oil, paraffin, peat, petroleum, whale oil, wood – *v.* charge, encourage, energize, fan, feed, fill *or* gas *or* tank up, fire, incite, inflame, nourish, recharge, service, supply, sustain *Antonyms:* dampen, neglect, put out, starve

fugitive *adj.* **1.** ephemeral, erratic, fleeting, fly-by-night, impermanent, momentary, passing, short-lived, temporary, transient, transitory, volatile, wandering *Antonyms:* direct, permanent **2.** at large, avoiding, AWOL, escaped, evasive, fleeing, loose, on the lam, runaway, wanted – *n.* deserter, dodger, escapee, exile, outcast, outlaw, refugee, runaway, truant

fulfilled *adj.* comfortable, contented, delighted, euphoric, gratified, happy, pleased, sated, satisfied *Antonyms:* disappointed, dissatisfied, unhappy – *v.* accomplished, achieved, actualized, attained, carried out, completed, concluded, consummated, crowned, dispatched, effected, executed, finished, matured, obtained, perfected, performed, reached, realized *Antonyms:* aborted, failed, neglected

fulfillment *n.* accomplishment, achievement, attainment, completion, consummation, end, implementation, perfection, realization, satisfaction, success *Antonyms:* block, failure, frustration, obstacle

full *adj.* **1.** abounding, abundant, adequate, ample, awash, big, bounteous, brimming, burdened, bursting, copious, crammed, crowded, extravagant, filled, generous, imbued, jam-packed, laden, lavish, loaded, packed, padded, plentiful, plenteous, replete, satisfied, saturated, standing room only *or* SRO, stocked, sufficient, suffused, surfeited, teeming, voluminous, weighted *Nonformal:* chock-full, running over *Antonyms:* blank, devoid, empty, faint, limited **2.** all-inclusive, broad, catholic, circumstantial, complete, comprehensive, definitive, detailed, entire, exhaustive, extensive, intact, integral, itemized, maximum, particularized, perfect, plenary, thorough, unabridged, uncut, unedited, unlimited, whole *Antonyms:* abridged, incomplete, partial **3.** booming, clear, deep, distinct, loud, resonant, rich, rounded, stentorian, throaty **4.** glutted, gorged, jaded, sated, satiate, stuffed *Antonyms:* hungry, unsatisfied, wanting – *adv.* absolutely, completely, directly, extremely, fully, head-on, perfectly, right, straight, undeviatingly, unequivocally, very

full-bodied *adj.* concentrated, fruity, full-flavoured, heady, heavy, mellow, potent, redolent, rich, robust, strong, well-endowed, well-matured *Antonyms:* lame, watered-down, weak

full-grown *adj.* adult, developed, full-blown, full-fledged, grown, grown-up, marriageable, mature, nubile, of age, prime, ready, ripe, ripened *Antonyms:* green, immature, undeveloped

fullness *n.* **1.** abundance, adequateness, ampleness, amplitude, copiousness, fill, glut, plenitude, plenty, plenum, profusion, repletion, sufficiency, surfeit, totality, wealth *Antonyms:* emptiness, paucity, scarcity, want **2.** breadth, broadness, completeness, completion, comprehensiveness, entirety, extensiveness, satisfaction, scope, vastness, wideness **3.** congestion, dilation, roundness, satiation, satiety, saturation, swelling, tumescence, voluptuousness

full-scale *adj.* all-encompassing, all-out, broad-based, complete, comprehensive, exhaustive, extensive, full-blown, in-depth, major, sweeping, thorough, total, unlimited, wide-ranging *Antonyms:* fractional, half-hearted, partial

fully *adv.* **1.** absolutely, adequately, altogether, completely, comprehensively, downright, entirely, outright, perfectly, positively, quite, royally, satisfactorily, thoroughly, totally, utterly, well *Nonformal:* all the way, from soup to nuts **2.** abundantly, amply, enough, plentifully, sufficiently,

fulminate *v.* **1.** berate, bluster, castigate, censure, condemn, criticize, curse, declaim, denounce, fume, intimidate, inveigh against, menace, protest, rage, rail, swear at, upbraid, vilify, vituperate *Antonyms:* extol, laud, praise **2.** blast, blow up, detonate, discharge, explode, thunder

fulmination *n.* **1.** condemnation, curse, denunciation, diatribe, intimidation, invective, obloquy, outburst, reprobation, tirade, warning *Antonyms:* applause, kudos, praise **2.** blast, detonation, discharge, eruption, explosion

fulsome *adj.* adulatory, bombastic, buttery, cloying, excessive, fawning, glib, grandiloquent, gross, high-flown, inordinate, insincere, nauseating, offensive, oily, overdone, saccharine, sickening, slick, smarmy *(British)*, smooth, suave, sycophantic, unctuous *Antonyms:* down-to-earth, genuine, sincere

fumble *v.* blunder, botch, bumble, bungle, confound, drop, err, flounder, flub, fluff, misdirect, misemploy, mishandle, misjudge, mismanage, mistreat, muff, mumble, ruin, spoil, stumble *Nonformal:* bollix, goof, screw up

fume *n.* effluvium, emanation, exhalation, exhaust, gas, miasma, mist, odour, pollution, reek, smell, smog, smoke, steam, trace, vapour, whiff – *v.* **1.** anger, boil, ferment, fester, fret, madden, rage, rant, seethe, simmer, sizzle, smoulder, storm **2.** discharge, emit, exhaust, reek, smoke, steam, vapour

fumigate *v.* air, clean, cleanse, debug *(Nonformal)*, deodorize, disinfect, purify, sanitize, sterilize

fun *adj.* amusing, boisterous, convivial, delightful, diverting, enjoyable, entertaining, good, happy, lively, merry, pleasant, witty – *n.* a break, absurdity, amusement, antics, buffoonery, celebration, cheer, clowning, distraction, diversion, enjoyment, entertainment, escapade, festivity, foolery, frolic, gaiety, gambol, game, holiday, horseplay, jesting, jocularity, joke, jollity, joy, junket, laughter, merriment, merrymaking, mirth, nonsense, pastime, picnic, play, playfulness, pleasure, recreation, rejoicing, relaxation, romp, romping, solace, sport, tomfoolery, treat *Nonformal:* ball, field day, riot *Antonyms:* chore, drudgery, work

function *n.* **1.** action, activity, behaviour, business, capacity, charge, concern, duty, employment, exercise, faculty, goal, job, mark, mission, object, objective, occupation, office, operation, part, post, power, province, purpose, responsibility, role, service, situation, target, task, use, utility, work **2.** affair, celebration, gathering, get-together, levee, meeting, occasion, party, reception *Nonformal:* do, shindig, wingding – *v.* act, behave, go, officiate, operate, perform, run, serve, work

functional *adj.* active, effective, effectual, functioning, handy, occupational, operational, operative, practicable, practical, running, serviceable, useful, utilitarian, working

functionary *n.* administrator, apparatchik, bureaucrat, civil *or* public servant, commissar, official, office holder, plenipotentiary *Nonformal:* buck passer, paper shuffler, space cadet, talking head

fund *n.* capital, endowment, foundation, hoard, inventory, kitty, money, nest egg, pile, pool, repository, reserve, reservoir, savings, source, stock, store, storehouse, supply, treasury, trust – *v.* back, endow, finance, invest in, maintain, patronize, pay for, sponsor, subsidize, support *Nonformal:* bankroll, chip in, dish out

fundamental *adj.* axiomatic, basic, cardinal, central, constitutional, crucial, elemental, elementary, essential, first, foundational, grassroots, indispensable, integral, intrinsic, key, major, necessary, organic, original, paramount, primary, prime, primitive, primordial, principal, requisite, root, rudimentary, significant, structural, supporting, sustaining, underlying, vital *Non-*

formal: meat-and-potatoes, nitty-gritty *Antonyms:* incidental, lesser, secondary, subsidiary, superfluous

fundamentals *n. pl.* axioms, basics, components, constituents, cornerstone, crux, elements, essentials, factors, foundation, principles, roots, rudiments, rules, theorems *Nonformal:* ABCs, brass tacks

funds *n. pl.* affluence, assets, award, backing, bankroll, budget, capital, cash, coffers, collateral, currency, dough *(Nonformal)*, earnings, finance, fluid assets, gift, means, money, possessions, prize, proceeds, profits, property, purse, reserve, resources, revenue, reward, savings, securities, stakes, store, wealth, wherewithal, winnings

funeral *n.* burial, ceremony, cremation, entombment, interment, last rites, mourning period, obsequies, requiem, sepulture, services, solemnities, wake

funereal *adj.* black, bleak, dark, deathlike, depressing, depressive, dirgelike, dismal, doleful, dreary, elegiac, gloomy, grave, grim, lamenting, melancholy, mournful, sad, sepulchral, serious, solemn *Antonyms:* bright, celebratory, cheerful, uplifting

fungus *n.* parasitic plant *Groupings of fungus:* ascomycetous, basidiomycetous, deuteromycetous, sac fungi *Kinds of fungus:* aspergillus, athlete's foot, boletus, bracket, bread mould, cup, deathcap, gill, jelly, lichen, mildew, morel, mould, mushroom, penicillium, psilocybe, puffball, ringworm, smut, stinkhorn, toadstool, truffle, verticillium, yeast

funk *n.* **1.** bathos, blues, dejection, depression, despair, despondency, doldrums, downcast attitude, downheartedness, dumps, heartache, low-spirits, malaise, melancholy, misery, mopes, pathos, weariness *Antonyms:* cheer, high-spirits, lightheartedness, merriment, mirth **2.** alarm, consternation, dread, fright, horror, panic, qualm, terror, timidity, trepidation **3.** malodour, mustiness, odour, reek, smell, stench, stink **4.** blues, jazz, rhythm and blues *or* R & B, soul

funky *adj.* bluesy, down-to-earth, earthy, excellent, fashionable, simple, stylish, trendy, unpretentious *Nonformal:* cool, dope, fab, gear, groovy, hep, hip, with it

funnel *n.* **1.** chimney, flue, shaft *or* smokeshaft, stack, stovepipe, tube **2.** cone, instrument, siphon, tool, utensil – *v.* carry, channel, conduct, convey, direct, filter, move, pass, pipe, pour, siphon, transmit, transport

funny *adj.* **1.** amusing, blithe, capricious, clever, comic, diverting, droll, entertaining, facetious, gay, good-humoured, hilarious, humorous, hysterical, jocose, jocular, joking, jolly, laughable, ludicrous, merry, mirthful, playful, priceless, ridiculous, riotous, silly, slapstick, waggish, whimsical, witty *Antonyms:* grave, melancholy, serious, solemn, stern **2.** absurd, bizarre, curious, different, eccentric, extravagant, fanciful, fantastic, far-fetched, fictional, foolish, hallucinatory, implausible, incredible, mysterious, nonsensical, odd, outlandish, peculiar, perplexing, preposterous, puzzling, queer, strange, unbelievable, unlikely, unreal, unusual, weird *Antonyms:* ordinary, regular, typical, usual

fur *n.* coat, covering, down, fell, fleece, fluff, fuzz, hair, hide, pelt, wool

furbish *v.* brighten, buff, burnish, clean, fix up, glaze, gloss, improve, polish, recondition, refurbish, rehabilitate, renew, renovate, restore, rub, shine, smooth, spruce up

furious *adj.* **1.** blustering, blustery, concentrated, excessive, extreme, flaming, intense, intensified, rough, savage, stormy, tempestuous, terrible, tumultuous, turbulent, unrestrained, violent, wild *Antonyms:* calm, dispassionate, impassive, mild **2.** angry, crazed, demented, enraged, fierce, frantic, frenetic, frenzied, fuming, incensed, infuriated, insane, irrational, livid, mad, maddened, maniac, rabid, raging, unreasonable, wrathful *Nonformal:* beside oneself, boiling, browned off, fit to be tied, hopping mad, smoking, steamed *Antonyms:* pleased, serene, tranquil

furnace *n.* boiler, crematorium, forge, heater, heating system, hell *(Nonformal)*, incinerator, inferno, kiln, oil burner, oven, smithy, stove

furnish *v.* **1.** accoutre, arm, array, clothe, decorate, equip, fit, outfit, provision, rig, turn out **2.** afford, appoint, bestow, deliver, endow, grant, hand over, inform, offer, present, provide, supply

furniture *n.* appliances, appurtenance, chattel, equipment, furnishings *Kinds of furniture*: bed, bookcase, buffet, bureau, cabinet, chair, chest, chesterfield, commode, couch, counter, davenport, desk, dresser, file *or* filing cabinet, highboy, sideboard, sofa, stool, table *Styles and periods of furniture:* Adam, Adirondack, Art Deco, Art Nouveau, Baroque, Bauhaus, Biedermeirer, Byzantine, Chinoiserie, Chippendale, Colonial, Cotswold School, De Stijl, Directoire, Duncan Phyfe, Egyptian, Empire, French Provincial, Georgian, Hepplewhite, Italian Renaissance, Jacobean, Louis XIII, Louis XIV, Louis XV, Louis XVI, Mission, Modern, Neoclassical, Palladian, Queen Anne, Restoration, Rococo, Scandinavian, Shaker, Sheraton, Spanish Renaissance, Stuart, Tudor, Venetian, Victorian, William and Mary

furor *n.* **1.** ado, brouhaha, commotion, disturbance, fuss, gusto, hullabaloo, outcry, tempest, tumult, uproar **2.** enthusiasm, fever, fire, fit, passion, rapture, zeal *Antonyms:* aloofness, calm, detachment, indifference **3.** craze, frenzy, fury, hysteria, insanity, mania, tantrum

furrowed *adj.* bevelled, channeled, creased, crinkled, crumpled, corrugated, fluted, grooved, incised, indented, knitted, pleated, ruffled, rumpled, scored, scratched, wrinkled *Antonyms:* ironed, smooth, straightened

further *adj.* additional, advanced, distant, extra, farther, fresh, supplementary – *v.* advance, aid, assist, ballyhoo, champion, contribute, encourage, engender, facilitate, foster, generate, hasten, plug, promote, propagate, push, serve, succour, support *Antonyms:* foil, frustrate, hinder, impede

furtherance *n.* **1.** advancement, advocacy, aid, backing, boosting, championing, fostering, help, promotion, service, support *Antonyms:* hindrance, impediment, obstacle **2.** advance, development, evolution, furthering, headway, growth, improvement, progress, progression

furtive *adj.* artful, cautious, clandestine, cloaked, conspiratorial, covert, crafty, cunning, disguised, elusive, evasive, foxy, guileful, hidden, hush-hush *(Nonformal)*, insidious, masked, scheming, secretive, shifty, skulking, slinking, sly, sneaky, sub-rosa, surreptitious, tricky, undercover, underhand, wily *Antonyms:* candid, honest, open, undisguised

fury *n.* acerbity, acrimony, anger, asperity, bluster, ferocity, fierceness, force, frenzy, furor, impetuosity, indignation, intensity, ire, rabidity, rage, rampancy, savagery, severity, tempestuousness, turbulence, vehemence, violence, wrath *Nonformal:* blowup, boiling point, conniption, rise, stew, storm *Antonyms:* apathy, dispassion, indifference, neutrality

fuse *n.* **1.** charge, detonator, explosive, load **2.** circuit breaker, guard, safeguard, shield – *v.* amalgamate, blend, cement, coalesce, combine, commingle, integrate, intermix, join, meld, merge, mingle, smelt, solder, unite, weld *Antonyms:* diffuse, dispense, dissipate, scatter, separate

fusion *n.* alloy, amalgam, amalgamation, blend, blending, coalescence, commingling, compound, integration, intermixture, junction, melding, merging, mixture, synthesis, union, uniting, welding

fussy *adj.* anal *(Nonformal)*, careful, choosy, conscientious, dainty, difficult, discriminating, exact, exacting, fastidious, finicky, meticulous, nitpicky, painstaking, particular, pettifogging, persnickety, picky, punctilious, scrupulous, squeamish, stickling *Antonyms:* careless, easygoing, laidback *(Nonformal)*

fustian *adj.* affected, bombastic, flowery, grandiloquent, inflated, orotund, overstated, pompous, purple, sesquipedalian, swollen, tumescent, tumid, turgescent, turgid, windy *Antonyms:* concise, pithy, plain, simple – *n.* affectation, bombast, bragging, bravado, circumlocution, flatulence, grandiosity, jargon, magniloquence, overstatement, pomposity, turgidity, verbiage

futile *adj.* abortive, barren, delusive, empty, exhausted, forlorn, fruitless, hollow, hopeless, idle, impractical, ineffective, ineffectual, insufficient, nugatory, otiose, trifling, unproductive, unprofitable, unsatisfactory, unsuccessful, useless, vain, worthless *Antonyms:* constructive, effective, fruitful, useful, worthwhile

future *adj.* anticipated, coming, desired, determined, emergent, eventual, fated, forthcoming, hereafter, hoped-for, imminent, later, planned, predicted, probable, projected, prospective *Nonformal:* down the pike, from here in – *n.* by-and-by, destiny, eventuality, fate, karma, *mañana (Spanish)*, tomorrow

fuzz *n.* beggar's velvet *(Nonformal)*, down, dustball, fibre, floss, fluff, fur, hair, lint, nap, particles, pile

fuzzy *adj.* **1.** down-covered, downy, flossy, fluffy, frizzy, furry, hairy, linty, napped, woolly **2.** bleary, blurred, dim, distorted, faint, foggy, hazy, ill-defined, indefinite, indistinct, misty, murky, obscure, shadowy, unclear, vague *Antonyms:* clear, detailed, precise

gab *n.* babble, blarney, causerie, chatter, chitchat, conversation, gossip, jabber, patter, prattle, small talk – *v.* babble, blab, blather, buzz, chat, chatter, gibber, gossip, jabber, jaw, palaver, prate, prattle *Nonformal:* chew the fat, rap, shoot the breeze, yammer, yap

gad *v.* cruise, gallivant, jaunt, knock about, maunder, meander, ramble, range, roam, rove, stray, traipse, wander

gadget *n.* apparatus, appliance, contraption, contrivance, device, gimmick, implement, instrument, invention, machine, mechanism, object, thing, tool, utensil *Nonformal:* doodad, gizmo, jobbie, thingamabob, thingamajig, whatchamacallit, whatsit, widget

gaff *n.* harpoon, hook *or* iron hook, peavey, spar, spur – *v.* cheat, deceive, swindle, trick *Nonformal:* bamboozle, con, snow

gaffe *n.* blooper, blunder, indiscretion, malapropism, mistake, slip, solecism *French:* faux pas, gaucherie *Nonformal:* clanger, boner, booboo, howler

gag *n.* caper, crack, drollery, facetiousness, foolery, hoax, horseplay, jest, joke, practical joke, prank, pun, quip, ruse, trick, wile, wisecrack, witticism *Nonformal:* monkeyshine, shenanigan – *v.* **1.** censure, constrain, cork, curb, deaden, inhibit, muffle, mute, muzzle, obstruct, quash, quell, quiet, repress, restrain, shut down *or* up, silence, smother, squash, squelch, stifle, still, stop, suffocate, suppress, throttle **2.** choke, cough, gasp, heave, retch, spit up, whoop

gaggle *n.* agglomeration, assemblage, assortment, bunch, cluster, congregation, flock, group, host, multitude, pack, swarm, throng, troupe – *v.* cackle, caw, clack, cluck, gabble, gobble, squawk

gaiety *n.* **1.** animation, blitheness, cheer, elation, entertainment, exhilaration, festivity, fun, geniality, gladness, glee, happiness, hilarity, jollity, lightheartedness, liveliness, merriment, mirth, pleasantness, revelry, sport, sprightliness, vivacity, whoopee *(Nonformal) Antonyms:* despondency, gloom, jim-jams, melancholy, misery, sadness **2.** brightness, brilliance, colour, intensity, radiance, richness, show, sparkle, vividness

gaily *adv.* blithely, brightly, brilliantly, cheerfully, colourfully, flamboyantly, gleefully, happily, joyfully, laughingly, lightheartedly, merrily, sparklingly, spiritedly, vivaciously *Antonyms:* dismally, morosely, sadly, unhappily

gain *n.* **1.** boom, crescendo, enlargement, expansion, growth, headway, improvement, increase, inflation, rise, upturn *Nonformal:* boost, buildup, hike *Antonyms:* decline, downturn, recession, reversal **2.** acquisition, addition, annexation, attainment **3.** advantage, avail, benefit, blessing, boon, plus **4.** bottom line, earnings, gravy *(Nonformal)*, gross, income, net, payoff, percentage, pickings, proceeds, profit, receipts, remuneration, return, reward, spoils, take, wages, winnings, yield *Antonyms:* debt, forfeiture, loss, sacrifice **5.** achievement, triumph, victory, win *Antonyms:* defeat, failure **6.** first down, forward motion, ground, yardage – *v.* **1.** acquire, annex, attain, bring in, capture, collect, come by *or* into, earn, gather, glean, harvest, obtain, procure, reap, secure, seize *Nonformal:* bag, clean *or* rack up, clear, land, score *Antonyms:* lose, yield **2.** boost, build up, crescendo, enlarge, expand, fatten, flourish, gather, grow, increase, intensify, mount, multiply, proliferate, shoot up, snowball, spread *Nonformal:* beef *or* jack up, skyrocket *Antonyms:* ebb, fade away, peter out, wane **3.** advance, go *or* move forward, improve, make headway *or* strides, progress, rally, recuperate *Antonyms:* sicken, sink, relapse, vanquish **4.** approach, arrive, catch up, draw near, overhaul, overtake, reach **5.** accomplish, carry off, consummate, succeed, triumph, win *Antonyms:* choke, fail, falter

gainsay *v.* call *(Nonformal)*, challenge, contest, contradict, contravene, deny, disagree, disclaim, disprove, dispute, fight, impugn, negate, oppose, question, refute, repudiate, resist *Antonyms:* back, confirm, support

gait *n.* amble, canter, gallop, march, motion, pace, run, step, stride, tread, trot, walk

gala *adj.* **1.** celebratory, convivial, entertaining, festal, festive, gay, gleeful, good-time, high-spirited, hilarious, jolly, jovial, joyful, joyous, lively, merry, mirthful, rollicking, romping, spirited *Antonyms:* elegiac, funereal, grave, mournful, sombre **2.** black-tie, ceremonial, colourful, dramatic, dress-up, flashy, formal, glamorous, glittering, gorgeous, grand, magnificent, majestic, opulent, showy, solemn, spectacular, splendid, star-studded, stately, stellar, sumptuous, theatrical, white-tie – *n.* anniversary, ball, bash, benefit, carnival, celebration, ceremony, charity event, extravaganza, festival, festivity, fête, fundraiser, happening, jubilee, levee, occasion, pageant, party *Nonformal:* shindig, wingding

galactic *adj.* **1.** astronomical, celestial, cosmic, heavenly, intergalactic, out of this world *(Nonformal)*, starry, stellar, universal **2.** colossal, enormous, epic, gargantuan, gigantic, huge, immeasurable, immense, vast *Antonyms:* confined, limited, small

gale *n.* Alberta pipeline, blast, blow, burst, chinook, cyclone, gridley grinder *(P.E.I.)*, hurricane, mistral, mosser *(Maritimes)*, nor'wester, outburst, snow-eater, squall, storm, tempest, tornado, typhoon, wind, windstorm *Beaufort gale classifications:* moderate *(51-61 km/hr)*, fresh *(62-74 km/hr)*, strong *(75-88 km/hr)*, whole *(89-101 km/hr)*

gall *n.* **1.** acrimony, animosity, antipathy, bad blood, bile, bitterness, enmity, hostility, ill humour, malice, rancour, resentment, spite, spleen, venom **2.** audacity, boldness, brashness, brass, brazenness, cool, effrontery, impudence, insolence, nerve, presumption, sauciness, temerity *Nonformal:* balls, cheek, chutzpah, crust, face, front, guts, moxie **3.** abrasion, canker, graze, raw *or* sore spot, scrape, sore, ulcer, wound – *v.* **1.** aggravate, distress, exacerbate, incense, inflame, irritate, pain, rankle, vex **2.** abrade, chafe, fray, gnaw *or* grind away at, grate, rasp, rub, scrape

gallant *adj.* **1.** adventurous, bold, brave, courageous, daring, dashing, dauntless, doughty, fearless, game, great-hearted, gritty, gutsy *(Nonformal)*, heroic, high-spirited, honourable, intrepid, lion-hearted, noble, plucky, resolute, staunch, stouthearted, unafraid, unbowed, undaunted, unstinting, valiant, valorous *Antonyms:* afraid, cowardly, craven, fearful, ignoble **2.** attentive, chivalrous, considerate, courteous, courtly, deferential, gentlemanly, gracious, kindly, magnanimous, mannerly, obliging, polite, suave, thoughtful, urbane, well-bred *Antonyms:* churlish, discourteous, ill-mannered, rude **3.** august, dignified, elegant, imperial, lofty, magnificent, majestic, noble, princely, regal, splendid, stately – *n.* **1.** admirer, adorer, beau, beloved, betrothed, boyfriend, cicisbeo, date, escort, fiancé, lover, paramour, partner, pursuer, squire, suitor, swain, sweetheart *Nonformal:* Casanova, Romeo **2.** adventurer, caballero, cavalier, champion, dandy, daredevil, gay blade, hero, knight, paladin, stalwart *Nonformal:* dude, stud, swell

gallantry *n.* **1.** ceremony, chivalry, consideration, courtesy, courtliness, decorum, graciousness, kindliness, magnanimity, mannerliness, politeness, propriety, refinement, respect, tact, uprightness, thoughtfulness *Antonyms:* disrespect, effrontery, rudeness **2.** audacity, backbone, boldness, bravery, courage, daring, dauntlessness, dedication, determination, devotion, endurance, fearlessness, fidelity, fortitude, grit, heart, heroism, indomitability, intrepidity, mettle, nerve, pluck, reliability, resoluteness, spirit, stalwartness, steadfastness, stout-heartedness, tenacity, valour *Nonformal:* gumption, guts, moxie *Antonyms:* cowardliness, irresolution, timidity **3.** blandishment, cajolery, courtship, lovemaking, romance, wooing *Nonformal:* sweet-nothings, sweet-talk, wining and dining

gallery *n.* **1.** auction hall *or* room, exhibition area *or* hall, display area *or* room, museum, salon, showroom **2.** balcony, loggia, patio, porch, veranda **3.** bleachers, elevated seats, stands *Nonformal:* cheap seats, gods, peanut gallery, rafters **4.** audience, masses, onlookers, public, rail-birds *(Maritimes)*, spectators *Nonformal:* hoi polloi, plebes, riffraff **5.** adit, arcade, cloister, course, passage, promenade, tunnel, underground passage

gallimaufry *n.* confusion, goulash, gumbo, hash, hodgepodge, jumble, medley, mishmash, mixture, salmagundi

galling *adj.* aggravating, annoying, bitter, bothersome, exasperating, grievous, humiliating, irritating, nettlesome, painful, plaguing, provoking, upsetting, vexatious, vexing *Antonyms:* calming, palliative, soothing

gallivant *v.* cruise, flit, gad about, jaunt, meander, ramble, range, roam, rove, stray, traipse, wander *Nonformal:* hit the road, knock *or* trot around

gallop *n.* exercise, gait *or* leaping gait, race, ride, spin *(Nonformal)* – *v.* bolt, canter, career, dart, dash, hasten, hurdle, hurry, lope, pace, race, run, speed, sprint, stride, take off, trot, work

galore *adv.* abundantly, aplenty, considerably, copiously, everywhere, in abundance *or* great numbers *or* profusion, more than enough *or* one needs *Antonyms:* scarcely, somewhat

galvanize *v.* animate, arouse, awaken, electrify, energize, excite, fire up, inspire, invigorate, jolt, motivate, move, provoke, shock, spur, startle, stimulate, stir, thrill, vitalize, waken *Nonformal:* turn on, zap *Antonyms:* depress, dull, enervate, immobilize

gambit *n.* **1.** artifice, design, device, manoeuvre, plan, play, plot, ploy, risk, ruse, stratagem, trick *Nonformal:* flier, long-shot, shot in the dark **2.** beginning, first step, initiation, introduction, launch, opening move, start

gamble *n.* bet, chance, lottery, outside chance, parlay, punt, raffle, risk, speculation, stab, uncertainty, venture, wager *Nonformal:* long shot, toss-up – *v.* **1.** back, bet, brave, challenge, chance, dare, defy, face, game, put up, risk, set, speculate, stake, venture, wager **2.** endanger, expose, hazard, imperil, jeopardize

gambling *n.* action, betting, card playing, games of chance, gaming, play, punting, speculation, the rackets, wagering *Gambling events and games:* baccarat, beano, bingo, blackjack *or* twenty-one, bridge, Caribbean stud poker, chemin de fer, cock fighting, craps, dice, dog *or* horse racing, faro, keno, liar, lottery, lotto, monte, numbers, off-track betting *or* OTB, pinochle, poker, rouge et noir, roulette, Russian roulette, slot machine, stook, wheel of fortune

gambol *v.* bound, caper, cavort, frolic, hop, jump, leap, play, prance, romp, skip, spring, tumble

game *adj.* **1.** agreeable, amenable, anxious, diligent, eager, enthusiastic, ready, waiting, willing, zealous **2.** courageous, feisty, heroic, intrepid, plucky, resolute, spirited, tenacious, tough – *n.* **1.** bonspiel, bout, championship, competition, contest, diversion, duel, encounter, entertainment, event, faceoff, meet, play, round, recreation, showdown, sport *Children's games:* blindman's bluff, british bulldog, five-hundred-up, follow-the-leader, fox and geese, hide-and-seek, hopscotch, house, jacks, kick-the-can, marbles, Marco Polo, murderball, musical chairs, peekaboo, pin-the-tail-on-the-donkey, post office, red light/green light, red rover, round base *(Maritimes)*, Simon says, skipping rope, spin the bottle, tether ball, tiddlywinks **2.** calling, craft, life's work, line, métier, occupation, profession, specialty, trade, vocation *Nonformal:* bag, racket, thing **3.** animal life, fish, fowl, government beef

(Prairies), kill, prey, quarry, Queen's mutton, wild animals, wildlife, wild meat *Kinds of wild game:* bear, buffalo, caribou, deer, duck, grouse, hare, moose, partridge, pheasant, rabbit, venison, wild boar, wild turkey *See also:* **fish 4.** design, device, dodge, hoax, plan, plot, ploy, prank, scheme, stratagem, strategy, tactic, trick

gamut *n.* compass, extent, field, range, run, scale, scope, series, spectrum, sweep

gang *n.* assemblage, association, band, bunch, cabal, circle, clan, clique, club, company, coterie, crew, crowd, gathering, group, horde, knot, lot, mob, organization, outfit, pack, party, ring, squad, syndicate, team, triad, tribe, troop, troupe, unit, workers *Nonformal:* rat pack, zoo – *v.* band *or* come together, congregate, form, gather, join forces, link up, swarm, unite

gangster *n.* capo, crime boss, criminal, crook, dealer, desperado, extortionist, freebooter, godfather, gunman, hoodlum, hooligan, larcenist, malefactor, mobster, pusher, racketeer, ruffian, thug, tough, *yakuza (Japanese) Nonformal:* banger, goon, hood, mafioso, moll, mug, plug-ugly, punk

gap *n.* **1.** aperture, cavity, chink, cleft, crack, cranny, crevice, fault, fissure, fracture, hole, interstice, mouth, notch, opening, orifice, **2.** abyss, arroyo, canyon, chasm, gorge, gulch, gully, pass, passageway, ravine, trench, valley **3.** blankness, emptiness, hollow, nothing, space, vacancy, vacuum, void **4.** contrast, difference, discrepancy, disparity, dissimilarity, dissonance, divergence, inconsistency, rift **5.** abatement, break, delay, disruption, hiatus, interruption, interval, lull, pause, postponement, recess, rest, suspension **6.** absence, deficiency, lack, need, shortage, shortfall, wanting

gape *v.* **1.** beam, bore, eye, eyeball, focus, gawk, glare, look, ogle, peer, rubberneck *(Nonformal)*, stare, take in **2.** divide, open, part, yawn, yawp *(Nonformal)*

gaping *adj.* broad, cavernous, expansive, great, open, vast, wide, yawning *Antonyms:* closed, narrow, shut, small, tiny

garage *n.* **1.** building, carport, parkade, parking space, storage **2.** body shop, gas station, mechanic shop, panel beater *(British)*, service centre – *v.* cover, house, preserve, protect, shelter, shield, store, winter

garb *n.* accoutrement, apparel, array, attire, clothes, clothing, costume, covering, dress, garments, habiliments, habit, livery, outfit, rags, raiment, robe, suit, uniform, vestments, wardrobe, wear *Nonformal:* duds, gear, rags *or* glad rags, regalia, threads, toggery, togs, weeds – *v.* clad, clothe, cover, deck *or* deck out, drape, dress, fit, garment, invest, robe, suit up, turn out *Nonformal:* rig up, tog

garbage *n.* **1.** castoffs, debris, detritus, dreck *(Nonformal)*, dregs, dross, junk, leftovers, litter, muck, offal, refuse, remains, residue, rubbish, rubble, scrapings, scraps, scum, sewage, slag, slop, sweepings, swill, trash, waste **2.** absurdity, balderdash, foolishness, incongruity, irrationality, malarkey, meaninglessness, nonsense, preposterousness, ridiculousness, senselessness *Nonformal:* bafflegab, baloney, bovine skedaddle, bull, doublespeak, gobbledygook, jabberjack, poppycock, tommyrot

garble *v.* **1.** befuddle, bungle, confound, confuse, disorder, jumble, mismanage, mix up, muddle, screw up *(Nonformal)* **2.** change, colour, distort, doctor *(Nonformal)*, falsify, fudge, misinform, misquote, misrepresent, misstate, mutilate, pervert, skew, slant, tamper with, twist, warp

garden *n.* bed, conservatory, enclosure, field, *jardin (French)*, nursery, oasis, patch, plot, terrace *Kinds of garden:* annual, arbour, arboretum, backyard, botanical, bower, espalier, flower, greenhouse, hedge, hedgerow, herb, hothouse, lawn, market, orchard, *parterre (French)*, path, patio, perennial, pergola, pool, quad *(Nonformal)*, rock, topiary, vegetable, water, wilderness, wildflower, yard – *v.* cultivate, farm, grow, plant, prune, raise, scuffle *(Historical)*, till, weed, work

gargantuan *adj.* big, Brobdingnagian, colossal, elephantine, enormous, giant, gigantic, huge, immense, large, leviathan, mammoth, massive, monstrous, monumental, mountainous, prodigious, titanic, towering, tremendous, vast, whopping *Nonformal:* humongous, super-duper *Antonyms:* meagre, miniature, paltry, puny, tiny

garish *adj.* baroque, blatant, brassy, brazen, cheap, crude, flashy, gaudy, glaring, loud, meretricious, ornate, ostentatious, overdone, raffish, showy, tasteless, tawdry, tinsel, trashy, vulgar *Nonformal:* chintzy, screaming *Antonyms:* elegant, plain, simple, understated

garland *n.* **1.** bay, chaplet, coronet, crown, festoon, halo, headband, laurels, lei, token, wreath **2.** accumulation, anthology, assemblage, collection, compendium, compilation, digest, treasury – *v.* adorn, bedeck, crown, deck, dignify, endow, ennoble, honour

garments *n. pl.* apparel, array, attire, clothes, clothing, costume, cover, covering, disguise, guise, habiliments, habit, livery, outfit, raiment, suit, uniform, vestments, wardrobe, wear *Nonformal:* duds, garb, gear, get-up, rags, threads, toggery

garner *v.* accumulate, amass, assemble, collect, cull, cumulate, deposit, gather, glean, harvest, hoard, husband, put away, reap, reserve, save, stockpile, store *or* store up, treasure *Antonyms:* squander, use up, waste

garnish *n.* addition, adornment, attachment, bells and whistles *(Nonformal)*, decoration, dressing, embellishment, enhancement, improvement, ornament, ornamentation, trimming – *v.* add, adorn, beautify, bedeck, deck, decorate, dress *or* fix up, embellish, enhance, grace, improve, trim *Antonyms:* denude, spoil, strip

garrison *n.* **1.** battery, brigade, cadre, corps, detachment, division, escadrille, guard, military force, militia, picket, platoon, regiment, soldiery, squadron, troops, unit **2.** barracks, bivouac, blockhouse, camp, citadel, command, fort, fortification, fortress, post, station, stronghold *French:* caserne, cordon sanitaire – *v.* **1.** defend, fortify, guard, hold, preserve, protect **2.** bivouac, camp, dwell, inhabit, man, occupy **3.** place, position, post, station

garrulous *adj.* barkative *(P.E.I.)*, glib, long-winded, loquacious, rambling, talkative, verbose, voluble, wordy *Nonformal:* chatty, flap-jawed *Antonyms:* close-mouthed, concise, reticent, succinct, terse

gas *n.* **1.** combustible fuel, energy, fossil fuel, gasoline **2.** air, cloud, evaporation, exhaust, fog, fume, miasma, smoke, steam *Groupings of gas:* fluid, inert, noble, rare **3.** belch, burp, discharge, emanation, emission, fart *(Nonformal)*, flatulence, release, wind **4.** blather, fancy talk, long-windedness, loquaciousness, verbosity, wordiness *Nonformal:* cockalorum, hot air, jazz, twaddle, yadda yadda yadda **5.** amusement, diversion, excitement, festivity, frolic, fun, gaiety, merrymaking, recreation, revelry, sport *Nonformal:* blast, buzz, howl, kick, riot – *v.* **1.** disinfect, exterminate, fumigate, kill, poison, spray, sterilize **2.** discharge, dissipate, emanate, emit, fume, give off, pass, release, send forth, spread **3.** anesthetize, benumb, deaden, desensitize, freeze *(Nonformal)*, paralyze, render unconscious, stupefy **4.** accelerate, quicken, speed up *Nonformal:* burn rubber, floor *or* gun *or* punch it, squeal off

gash *n.* cleft, cut, furrow, gouge, groove, incision, laceration, mark, nip, slice, slit, split, wound – *v.* carve, cleave, cut, gouge, incise, injure, knife, lance, nip, notch, rend, score, slash, slit, tear

gasp *n.* breath, gulp, heave, snort, whoop – *v.* choke, gulp, pant, puff, struggle, wheeze

gate *n.* **1.** access, door, entrance, entry, gateway, hatch, ingress, opening, portal, threshold, turnstile **2.** aboiteau, floodgate, lock, sluicegate, valve, weir **3.** bar, barricade, barrier, roadblock **4.** box office earnings, gross, proceeds, receipts, take *(Nonformal)* **5.** audience, crowd, head count, house, paid attendance **6.** dismissal *Nonformal:* boot, heave-ho, walking papers – *v.* confine, constrain, detain, pen, restrain, restrict, stop *Antonyms:* free, open, release

gateway *n.* arch, doorway, enclosure, entrance, exit, hatchway, opening, passage, portal

gather *n.* crease, fold, kink, pleat, ruffle, wrinkle – *v.* **1.** accumulate, amass, collect, hoard, lay *or* rake in, put together, stash away, stock *or* store up **2.** assemble, band *or* come *or* get together, cluster, congregate, convene, convoke, foregather, huddle, marshall, meet, merge, mobilize, muster, rally, summon **3.** bring in, cut, glean, harvest, husband, pick, reap, sow **4.** choose, codify, collect, compile, cull, pick, select, systematize **5.** burgeon, expand, flourish, grow, increase, swell **6.** conclude, deduce, extract, infer, reason, reckon, suppose, surmise, suspect, think, understand **7.** clasp, enfold, grasp, hold, hug, squeeze **8.** contract, crease, crinkle, crumple, fold, furrow, knit, pucker, ruffle, wrinkle

gathering *adj.* approaching, building, imminent, impending, looming, rising, threatening – *n.* **1.** collection, company, congregation, crowd, flock, group, host, multitude, pack, troop **2.** assembly, conclave, conference, convention, meeting **3.** coffee klatch, function, get-together, levee, party, powwow, social, soirée *Nonformal:* do, hoodang, kitchen party, shindig

gauche *adj.* **1.** awkward, bungling, clumsy, coltish, uncoordinated, ungainly, ungraceful *Antonyms:* adroit, deft, graceful **2.** base, boorish, brutish, coarse, crass, crude, ill-mannered, rude, tactless, uncouth, vulgar *Antonyms:* elegant, gracious, polished, tasteful

gaudy *adj.* blatant, brazen, bright, cheap, flashy, flaunting, florid, garish, gimcrack, glaring, loud, meretricious, obnoxious, obtrusive, ostentatious, overdone, pretentious, raffish, showy, splashy, tasteless, tawdry, too too much *(Nonformal)*, vulgar *Antonyms:* colourless, dull, modest, refined, sedate

gauge *n.* **1.** bore, calibre, capacity, degree, depth, diameter, dimension, draft, height, magnitude, proportion, scope, size, span, thickness, width **2.** bar, barometer, benchmark, criterion, guide, indicator, measure, meter, model, norm, paradigm, pattern, rule, scale, standard, test, touchstone, yardstick – *v.* appraise, assay, calculate, calibrate, classify, determine, estimate, evaluate, figure, grade, guess, judge, measure, peg, quantify, rate, reckon, size, tally, weigh

gaunt *adj.* **1.** angular, bony, cadaverous, drawn, emaciated, haggard, hollow-cheeked, lanky, lean, rawboned, scraggy, scrawny, skeletal, skinny, spare, thin, wasted, wiry *Antonyms:* chubby, healthy, plump, robust, stout **2.** bare, bleak, desolate, destitute, dreary, forlorn, gloomy, grim, harsh, lonely

gauzy *adj.* diaphanous, ethereal, fine-spun, flimsy, gossamer, light, revealing, see-through, sheer, silken, thin, translucent, transparent *Antonyms:* coarse, heavy, opaque

gawk *v.* gaze, goggle, leer, look, marvel, ogle, peer, stare *Nonformal:* rubberneck, yawp *Antonyms:* ignore, overlook, pass by

gawky *adj.* awkward, clownish, clumsy, gauche, lanky, loutish, lumbering, maladroit, uncouth, ungainly *Nonformal:* klutzy, with two left feet *Antonyms:* graceful, well-coordinated

gay *adj.* **1.** homoerotic, homophile, homosexual, lesbian, same-sex **2.** animated, blithe, bouncy, carefree, cheery, chipper, confident, convivial, devil-may-care *(Nonformal)*, festive, frivolous, frolicsome, fun-loving, glad, gleeful, happy, insouciant, jaunty, jolly, joyful, keen, lighthearted, lively, merry, mirthful, spirited, sporty, sprightly, sunny, vivacious *Antonyms:* cheerless, grave, sedate, serious, sombre **3.** brilliant, colourful, flamboyant, flashy, garish, gaudy, intense, ornamental, rich, showy, vivid *Antonyms:* colourless, drab, dull, funereal

gaze *n.* glance, glimpse, leer, once-over *(Nonformal)*, stare – *v.* eye, gape, gawk, goggle, inspect, look, observe, ogle, peek at, peep, peer, regard, scrutinize, size up, stare, survey, take in, view, watch *Nonformal:* gawk, moon over

gazette *n.* daily, journal, newspaper, newssheet, paper, periodical, publication, rag *(Nonformal)*, the news

gear *n.* **1.** cog *or* cogwheel, flywheel, gearbox, gearcase, gearing, gearshift, inner workings, machinery, mechanism, pinion, sprocket, train, transmission, wheel, wheelworks *Kinds of gear:* annular, bevel, elliptical, spur, spur and crown, square **2.** apparatus, equipment, implements, instruments, kit, rig, setup *(Nonformal)*, supplies, tools, utensils **3.** apparel, clothing, garments, outfit, wear *Nonformal:* duds, get-up, ready-mades **4.** baggage, belongings, effects, fittings, fixtures, furnishings, luggage, paraphernalia, possessions, trappings *Nonformal:* bits and pieces, kit and caboodle, stuff, things **5.** cordage, rig *or* rigging, ropework, ship's ropes, tack, tackle – *v.* appoint, arm, equip, fit up *or* out, furnish, outfit, provision, rig *or* rig out, turn out

gelatinous *adj.* coagulated, gelled, gluey, glutinous, gummy, jellied, mucilaginous, sticky, thick, viscid, viscous *Antonyms:* liquid, runny, watery

geld *v.* **1.** castrate, emasculate, neuter, remove, spay *Nonformal:* deball, fix **2.** debilitate, deplete, deprive, devitalize, enervate, enfeeble, strip, weaken

gem *n.* **1.** bauble, bijou, diamond, jewel, jewellery, ornament, pearl, prize, rock, stone, treasure, trinket **2.** marvel, perfection, *rara avis (Latin)*, stroke of genius, wonder **3.** dear, nonpareil, paragon, sweetheart *Nonformal:* aces, sweetie, the greatest, tops

gemstone *n.* jewel, precious *or* semi-precious stone *Kinds of gemstone:* agate, alexandrite, amber, amethyst, aquamarine, beryl, bloodstone, cairngorm, carbuncle, cat's eye, chalcedony, citrine, cornelian, diamond, emerald, fire opal, garnet, jade, jasper, jet, lapis lazuli, malachite, moonstone, olivine, onyx, opal, peridot, rose quartz, ruby, sapphire, sardonyx, spinel, tiger's eye, topaz, tourmaline, turquoise, zircon

gender *n.* category, classification, condition, difference, kind, quality, sex, sort

genealogy *n.* ancestry, background, bloodline, breeding, derivation, descent, extraction, family tree, history, lineage, parentage, pedigree, record of descent, roots, stock, strain, studbook

general *adj.* **1.** across-the-board, all-around, blanket, broad, catholic, comprehensive, ecumenical, encyclopedic, extensive, far-reaching, global, inclusive, indiscriminate, overall, panoramic, sweeping, total, ubiquitous, unconfined, universal, unlimited, unrestricted, wholesale, wide *or* widespread, worldwide **2.** accepted, accustomed, common, conventional, customary, everyday, familiar, generic, normal, ordinary, prevalent, regular, routine, run-of-the-mill, typical, usual *Antonyms:* particular, specific, unusual **3.** approximate, ill-defined, imprecise, inaccurate, indefinite, indistinct, inexact, loose, nebulous, speculative, vague *Antonyms:* accurate, definite, precise **4.** assorted, composite, diversified, heterogeneous, hodgepodge, miscellaneous, mixed, mixed bag *(Nonformal)* **5.** collaborative, collective, combined, communal, concerted, cooperative, joint, linked, mutual, unified, united – *n.* brigadier, brass *(Nonformal)*, chief of staff, commander, commander-in-chief, field marshal, officer, generalissimo, military leader, supreme commander

generalization *n.* **1.** abstraction, assumption, conclusion, hypothesis, idea, observation, postulation, summary, summing up, synthesis, theory **2.** broad statement, convenience, expedient, generality, oversimplification, simplification, whitewash

generally *adv.* **1.** approximately, roughly, roundly **2.** all in all, all things considered, by and large, chiefly, mainly, mostly **3.** almost always, customarily, most often, normally, regularly, routinely, typically, usually *Antonyms:* hardly, never, rarely

generate *v.* **1.** bring about, cause, create, develop, devise, effect, form, found, give rise *or* birth to, hatch, initiate, institute, introduce, occasion, originate, precipitate, produce *Antonyms:* annihilate, destroy, extinguish, terminate **2.** bear, beget, engender, father, mother, multiply, parent, propagate, reproduce, sire, spawn

generation *n.* **1.** age, day *(Nonformal)*, era, lifespan, lifetime, thirty years **2.** age group, coevals, contemporaries, peers **3.** descendants, issue, offspring, progeny **4.** bearing, begetting, breeding, genesis, multiplying, procreation, production, propagation, reproduction, spawning **5.** creation, development, formation, hatching, invention, making, manufacturing, originality, originating, production, shaping

generic *adj.* **1.** all-encompassing, blanket, comprehensive, general, sweeping, universal, wide-ranging *Antonyms:* individual, unique **2.** collective, common, mutual, shared **3.** indefinite, no-name *(Nonformal)*, non-specific, undefined, unlabelled, unmarked *Antonyms:* focused, limited, specific

generosity *n.* **1.** altruism, beneficence, benevolence, *caritas (Latin)*, charity, largesse, liberality, munificence, openhandedness, philanthropy **2.** bigheartedness, concern, heart, hospitality, kindness, magnanimity, sympathy, tenderheartedness, warmth

generous *adj.* **1.** altruistic, beneficent, benevolent, charitable, chivalrous, considerate, giving, good, helpful, high-minded, honest, honourable, hospitable, just, kind, kindhearted, lofty, philanthropic, thoughtful *Antonyms:* mean, misanthropic, selfish **2.** bountiful, easy, free, gracious, liberal, magnanimous, munificent, openhanded, unsparing, unstinting *Antonyms:* cheap, miserly, parsimonious, tight-fisted **3.** abundant, big, bounteous, full, handsome, large, lavish, overflowing, plentiful, prodigal, rich *Antonyms:* meagre, small, tiny **4.** fecund, fertile, lush, luxuriant, productive *Antonyms:* barren, fallow

genesis *n.* **1.** beginning, birth, commencement, creation, dawn, formation, inception, propagation, rise, start *Antonyms:* apocalypse, completion, conclusion, end, finish **2.** cradle, fountainhead, origin, root, seed, source, spring, wellspring

genetic *adj.* **1.** hereditary, inherited, innate, Mendelian, transferred **2.** biochemical, cellular, chromosomal, deoeyribonucleic, genotypic, helical, molecular, protein-based, ribonucleic

genial *adj.* affable, agreeable, amiable, blithe, buoyant, cheerful, cheery, congenial, cordial, easygoing, enlivening, friendly, glad, good-natured, hearty, high, jolly, jovial, joyous, kind, kindly, merry, neighbourly, nice, pleasant, sociable, sunny, upbeat, uplifting, warmhearted *Nonformal:* chipper, perky *Antonyms:* discourteous, frigid, rude, sullen, ungracious

geniality *n.* affability, amenity, amiability, cheerfulness, cheeriness, conviviality, cordiality, friendliness, gayness, generosity, graciousness, heartiness, joy, joyousness, kindness, niceness, pleasantness, sunniness, warmth *Antonyms:* cheerlessness, coldness, hostility, rancour

genitals *n. pl.* crotch, genitalia, penis, phallus, pubic region, reproductive *or* sex organs, testicles, vagina *Nonformal:* family jewels, naughty bits, package, private parts

genius *n.* **1.** ability, accomplishment, acumen, acuteness, aptitude, aptness, astuteness, bent, brains, brilliance, capability, capacity, creativity, discernment, endowment, faculty, flair, foresight, gift, grasp, imagination, inclination, ingenuity, inspiration, intellect, intelligence, inventiveness, knack, originality, propensity, prowess, reach, sagacity, skill, talent, understanding, vision, wisdom *Antonyms:* ignorance, ineptitude, stupidity **2.** expert, gifted person, maestro, master, mastermind, mental giant, prodigy, savant, virtuoso, *wunderkind (German) Nonformal:* ace, conduit, crackerjack *Antonyms:* dunce, fool, idiot, simpleton **3.** characteristic, essence, ethos, gist, humour, ilk, nature, spirit, temperament, trait, type

genocide *n.* annihilation, carnage, decimation, elimination, eradication, ethnic cleansing, extermination, Holocaust, killing, mass murder, massacre, purge, slaughter

genre *n.* brand, category, character, class, classification, fashion, form, genus, group, kind, quality, school, sort, species, style, type *Classical literary genres:* comedy, epic, history, satire, tragedy

genteel *adj.* **1.** aristocratic, civil, cultured, elegant, fashionable, formal, graceful, high-class, mannerly, noble, polished, polite, refined, respectable, sophisticated, stylish, tony *(Nonformal)*, urbane, well-bred, well-mannered *Antonyms:* obnoxious, rude, vulgar **2.** overrefined, pretentious *Nonformal:* la-di-da, posh, toffee-nosed

gentility *n.* **1.** courtesy, culture, decorum, elegance, etiquette, polish, politeness, propriety, refinement, respectability, sophistication, urbanity *Antonyms:* boorishness, coarseness, grossness, indelicacy, vulgarity **2.** aristocracy, blueblood, elect, elite, gentry, leisure class, nobility, ruling class, upper crust *(Nonformal)*

gentle *adj.* **1.** affable, agreeable, amiable, considerate, easy, genial, humane, kindly, lenient, merciful, patient, pleasant, pleasing, soft, softhearted, sweet-tempered, sympathetic, temperate, tender *Antonyms:* fell, fierce, harsh, heartless **2.** benign, biddable, docile, domesticated, laid back *(Nonformal)*, manageable, meek, mellow, placid, pliable, tame *Antonyms:* savage, violent, wild **3.** balmy, bland, calm, gradual, halcyon, light, low, mild, pacific, peaceful, quiet, serene, slight, smooth, tranquil, untroubled **4.** chivalrous, courteous, courtly, cultured, elegant, gallant, genteel, gracious, polished, polite, refined

gentlemanly *adj.* civil, courteous, cultivated, debonair, decent, kind, polite, sophisticated, suave, thoughtful, well-mannered

gentry *n.* aristocracy, blueblood, elite, gentlefolk, nobility, noblesse, patriciate, select few, the leisure *or* privileged *or* ruling class, upperclass

genuine *adj.* **1.** candid, earnest, frank, heartfelt, honest, natural, open, sincere, unaffected, undesigning, unfeigned, upfront *Antonyms:* affected, artificial, bogus, false, insincere **2.** absolute, accurate, actual, authentic, authenticated, bona fide, certain, certified, existent, factual, legitimate, literal, official, original, precise, proven, pure, real, sound, sterling, tested, true, trustworthy, undoubted, unquestionable, valid *Nonformal:* honest-to-goodness, legit *Antonyms:* counterfeit, fake, unreal

genus *n.* branch, category, class, classification, denomination, description, designation, division, family, genre, ilk, kind, kingdom, nature, phylum, school, sort, species, type, variety

geography *n.* area, geographics, geomorphology, geophysics, global positioning, landscape, layout, location, physical features, physiography, terrain, topography

geriatric *adj.* aged, aging, ancient, antiquated, decrepit, elderly, gerontological, greyhaired, hoary, nostologic, old, senescent, superannuated, wizened

germ *n.* **1.** bacterium, disease, microbe, microorganism, parasite, pathogen, plague, virus *Nonformal:* bug, cootie **2.** beginning, bud, cause, egg, embryo, genesis, head, inception, nucleus, origin, root, seed, source, start

germane *adj.* applicable, appropriate, apropos, apt, connected, fitting, material, opportune, pertinent, proper, related, relevant, right on *(Nonformal)*, suitable *Antonyms:* extraneous, foreign, immaterial, inappropriate, unrelated

germinate *v.* bud, develop, flourish, generate, grow, live, shoot, sprout, swell, take root, thrive

gestation *n.* **1.** fecundation, gravidity, incubation, parturiency, pregnancy, reproduction **2.** development, evolution, growth, maturation

gesture *n.* action, body language, bow, curtsy, dumb show, expression, genuflection, gesticulation, indication, intimation, motion, movement, nod, pantomime, posture, salute, shrug, sign, signal, sign language, wave, wink *Nonformal:* body English, finger, Salmon Arm salute – *v.* act out, flag, gesticulate, indicate, mime, motion, pantomime, sign, signal

get *n.* breed, brood, children, family, issue, litter, offspring, progeny, spawn *Nonformal:* kids, young'uns– *v.* **1.** acquire, annex, capture, gain, glean, grab, grasp, obtain, procure, secure, seize, take *Nonformal:* bag, rack up, score, snag **2.** bring in, clear, earn, fetch, make, merit, net, receive, warrant **3.** buy, purchase, redeem **4.** catch, contract, fall, get sick, succumb *Antonyms:* cure, heal, mend **5.** capiche *(Nonformal)*, comprehend, follow, know, learn, master, realize, understand **6.** discern, follow, hear, note, observe, overhear, perceive **7.** adjust, arrange, cook, fix, manage, prepare **8.**

beget, breed, father, generate, impregnate, procreate, produce, propagate, sire **9.** affect, allure, amuse, arouse, bend, captivate, carry, compel, convince, coax, dispose, draw, effect, elicit, entertain, entice, excite, gratify, impress, induce, influence, inspire, motivate, move, predispose, prompt, provoke, satisfy, stimulate, stir, strike, sway, touch, urge, win over **10.** arrive, come, disembark, hit town *(Nonformal)*, land, pull in, turn up **11.** fool *Nonformal:* flummox, hornswaggle, snow, take

getaway *n.* **1.** breakout, decampment, departure, escape, flight, lam *(Nonformal)*, slip **2.** amusement, frolic, hiatus, holiday, R&R *(Nonformal)*, relaxation, respite, rest, road trip, romp, sabbatical, vacation **3.** cabin, camp, cottage, haven, hideaway, resort, retreat

get-together *n.* barn dance, box *or* church *or* pie social, celebration, coffee klatch, dinner party, function, gathering, kitchen party, party, powwow, reunion, social, soiree *Nonformal:* do, hoedown, meet, shindig

get-up *n.* **1.** appearance, arrangement, composition, fashion, format, look, mode, organization, style, vogue **2.** ambition, drive, dynamism, enterprise, gimp *(Maritimes)*, go, gumption *(Nonformal)*, hustle, initiative, push, spunk **3.** apparel, attire, clothes, clothing, costume, dress, garb, garment, outfit, trappings, wardrobe *Nonformal:* duds, toggery

ghastly *adj.* **1.** appalling, dire, dreadful, fiendish, frightening, ghoulish, grisly, gruesome, hideous, horrendous, horrible, horrid, macabre, nightmarish, shocking, terrifying, unearthly **2.** ashen, cadaverous, colourless, corpse-like, deathlike, drawn, faint, haggard, lurid, pale, wan, worn **3.** brutal, contemptible, deplorable, despicable, disgusting, frightful, godawful *(Nonformal)*, loathsome, offensive, terrible, unpleasant, wretched

ghetto *n.* district, enclave, 'hood *(Nonformal)*, neighbourhood, quarter, section, slum, ward

ghost *n.* **1.** apparition, daimon, demon, ethereal being, eudemon, familiar, fetch, haunt, phantasm, phantom, poltergeist, revenant, soul, spectre, spirit, spook, vision, wraith **2.** glimmer, hint, shade, shadow, suggestion, trace **3.** author, grub *(Nonformal)*, hack, substitute, writer

ghostly *adj.* **1.** astral, eerie, ghostlike, haunted, illusory, incorporeal, insubstantial, otherworldly, phantasmal, scary, shadowy, spectral, spooky, supernatural, unearthly, wraithlike *Antonyms:* corporeal, earthly, material, natural **2.** drawn, gaunt, ghastly, hollow-eyed, lurid, pale, sickly, skeletal, wan

ghoulish *adj.* **1.** creepy, eerie, hair-raising, scary, spooky *(Nonformal)*, uncanny, weird **2.** abominable, accursed, barbaric, barbarous, beastly, bloodthirsty, brutal, brutish, cold-blooded, contemptible, cruel, damnable, disgusting, execrable, feral, ferocious, heartless, grisly, gruesome, hideous, horrendous, horrible, horrid, inhuman, macabre, merciless, monstrous, morbid, pitiless, ruthless, sadistic, savage, vicious, vile, wretched

giant *adj.* **1.** astronomic, Brobdingnagian, colossal, enormous, huge, hulking, king-size, large, mammoth, massive, mighty, titanic, vast, whopping *Nonformal:* humongous, jumbo, mega *Antonyms:* little, small, tiny **2.** distinctive, dominant, eminent, fabled, famed, great, immortal, influential, legendary, noteworthy, preeminent, remarkable, seminal – *n.* Atlas, behemoth, colossus, Goliath, leviathan, titan, whale

gibberish *n.* abracadabra, babble, blather, chatter, claptrap, double-talk, drivel, gabble, jabber, jargon, nonsense, palaver, prattle, twaddle *Nonformal:* bafflegab, balderdash, baloney, bull, bunkum, gobbledygook, hokum, jazz, jive, malarkey, mumbo jumbo, scat

giddy *adj.* **1.** brainless, capricious, changeable, empty-headed, erratic, featherbrained, fickle, flighty, frivolous, harebrained, heedless, impulsive, inconstant, punchy, scatterbrained, silly, slaphappy *(Nonformal)*, thoughtless, vacillating, whimsical, wild *Antonyms:* earnest, resolute, serious **2.** dizzy, lightheaded, reeling, rotating, unbalanced, unsteady, weak-kneed, whirling, woozy

gift *n.* **1.** ability, accomplishment, aptitude, attribute, bent, capability, capacity, faculty, flair, forte, genius, head, instinct, knack, power, propensity, skill, specialty, talent **2.** allowance, alms, award, baksheesh, benefaction, bequest, bestowal, blessing, bonus, boon, bounty, contribution, courtesy, dispensation, donation, endowment, favour, goody *(Nonformal)*, grant, gratuity, handout, honorarium, largesse, legacy, offering, potlatch, present, presentation, remembrance, reward, souvenir, token

gifted *adj.* able, accomplished, adroit, brilliant, clever, deft, endowed, expert, ingenious, intelligent, masterly, phenomenal, skilled, smart, talented *Nonformal:* swift, top notch *Antonyms:* amateurish, lost, untalented

gig *n.* assignment, booking, concert, employment, engagement, job, performance, position, show, stint

gigantic *adj.* Brobdingnagian, colossal, elephantine, enormous, gargantuan, giant, gross, herculean, huge, immense, large, leviathan, mammoth, massive, monstrous, prodigious, stupendous, titanic, tremendous, vast, whopping *Nonformal:* humongous, jumbo, monster *Antonyms:* diminutive, insignificant, little, miniature, puny

giggle *n. & v.* cackle, chortle, chuckle, guffaw, ha-ha *(Nonformal)*, laugh, snicker, snigger, titter, twitter

gigolo *n.* **1.** companion, fancyman *(Nonformal)*, paid escort, prostitute **2.** Casanova, gallant, ladies' man, Lothario, paramour, playboy, rake, swinger *(Nonformal)*, libertine, womanizer

gild *v.* **1.** adorn, beautify, bedeck, brighten, coat, decorate, embellish, embroider, enhance, enrich, garnish, glitter, gloss, grace, gussy *or* spruce up *(Nonformal)*, ornament, overlay, tinsel, varnish **2.** camouflage, gloss *or* paint over, sugar-coat, whitewash *(Nonformal)*

gimmick *n.* **1.** artifice, catch, deceit, dodge, fake, feint, gambit, game, hitch, manoeuvre, means, method, ploy, ruse, scheme, secret, stratagem, stunt, trick, wile **2.** aid, apparatus, contraption, contrivance device, doohickey *(Nonformal)*, gadget instrument, novelty, tool

ginger *adj.* beige, cinnamon, reddish-brown, russet, tan, tawny – *n.* animation energy, liveliness, mettle, pep, piquancy spice, spirit, spunk, zest *Nonformal:* pizzazz, zip – *v.* electrify, energize, enliven invigorate, kick *or* pep *or* perk *or* pump up rouse, spice, stimulate *Antonyms:* bore dampen, enervate

gingerly *adj.* careful, cautious, chary, circumspect, hesitant, reluctant, wary – *adv.* carefully, cautiously, daintily, delicately, fastidiously, guardedly, hesitantly, reluctantly safely, squeamishly, timidly, warily *Antonyms:* boldly, carelessly, confidently, rashly

gird *v.* **1.** band, belt, bind, circle, enfold, fasten, girdle, ring **2.** circumscribe, encircle enclose, encompass, environ, hem in, pen surround **3.** bolster, brace, buttress, fortify reinforce, secure, steel, strengthen, support **4.** accoutre, arrange, clothe, endow, equip fit, fix, furnish, gear, outfit, prep, prepare ready, rig **5.** abuse, gibe, goad, jeer, mock ridicule, taunt, trash, vilify *Nonformal.* razz, tear down

girdle *n.* **1.** brace, corset, foundation strays, support, undergarment **2.** band belt, cord, cummerbund, obi, sash, ribbon **3.** border, circumference, compass, edge limit, perimeter, skirt – *v.* **1.** band, belt bind, brace, cinch, fasten, tie **2.** circle encircle, enclose, encompass, enwrap, gird ring, surround

girl *n.* **1.** colleen *(Irish)*, demoiselle, *Fräulein (German)*, *jeune fille (French)*, lass, mademoiselle, maiden, miss, ms., nymphet, *senorita (Spanish)*, she, sheila *(Australia)*, tom boy, wench, young lady *or* woman, youth *Nonformal:* filly, kid missy, Rita, she lad **2.** abigail, assistant, au pair, handmaiden, maid, maidservant, secretary, servant, typist **3.** beloved, finacée lady love, significant

girth *n.* **1.** ambit, border, circumference, compass, diameter, outline, perimeter, radius, rim, zone **2.** band, bellyband, belt, fastener, girdle, sash, strap **3.** bulk, middle pot, stomach, tummy *(Nonformal)*, waist, waistline

gist *n.* basis, bottom line, core, drift, essence, heart, idea, marrow, matter, meaning, meat, nucleus, pith, point, sense, significance, spirit, straight goods, stuff, subject, substance, theme, thrust, topic, upshot *Nonformal:* nitty-gritty, short and sweet

give *v.* **1.** administer, assign, bestow, consign, contribute, deal, dole out, donate, furnish, grant, hand over, offer, part with, present, proffer, provide, supply, transfer, vouchsafe *Antonyms:* hold, receive, take **2.** air out, communicate, confer, deliver, dispense, express, impart, issue, read, say, tell, utter **3.** back *or* break down, bend, buckle, cede, concede, consent, crumble, knuckle under, relent, relinquish, soften, surrender, yield *Nonformal:* cave, cry uncle *Antonyms:* brave, endure, hold out **4.** compress, flatten, go elastic, spring, squish, stretch **5.** break, collapse, crumple, crush, fall, go down or under, tumble **6.** cause, emit, generate, produce, radiate, throw off **7.** display, execute, exhibit, feature, perform, play, put on, show, stage

given *adj.* **1.** accepted, accorded, admitted, allowed, conceded, concurred, recognized, understood, vouchsafed **2.** arranged, fixed, set, specified, stated, stipulated **3.** awarded, bestowed, conferred, contributed, donated, granted, presented **4.** addicted, apt, disposed, inclined, likely, predisposed, prone, wont

glacial *adj.* **1.** arctic, biting, bitter, chilly, cold, cool, freezing, frosty, frozen, gelid, icy, nippy, piercing, polar, raw, wintry *Antonyms:* balmy, hot, warm **2.** aloof, distant, emotionless, frigid, inaccessible, indifferent, remote, reserved, standoffish, unapproachable, unemotional, withdrawn **3.** antagonistic, antithetical, hostile, inimical, unfriendly *Antonyms:* cheery, cordial, friendly **4.** deliberate, gradual, measured, ponderous, slow, turtle-like, unhurried *Antonyms:* fast, speedy, swift

glacier *n.* glacial mass, glaciation, iceberg, icecap, ice dike *or* field *Types of Glacier:* continental, piedmont, valley

glad *adj.* **1.** beaming, delighted, charmed, contented, elated, gratified, happy, joyful, overjoyed, pleased, satisfied, thrilled, tickled *(Nonformal) Antonyms:* devastated, sorrowful, unhappy **2.** animated, bright, cheerful, cheering, delightful, gay, genial, gladsome, gleeful, jovial, joyous, jubilant, light-hearted, merry *Antonyms:* depressing, displeasing, melancholy

gladly *adv.* blissfully, blithely, cheerfully, cheerily, contentedly, delightedly, ecstatically, enthusiastically, freely, gaily, genially, gleefully, gratefully, happily, heartily, joyfully, lovingly, merrily, passionately, pleasurably, readily, warmly, willingly, with pleasure *or* relish, zealously *Antonyms:* dolefully, grudgingly, reluctantly, unwillingly

gladness *n.* animation, blitheness, cheer, delight, felicity, gaiety, glee, happiness, high spirits, hilarity, jollity, joy, joyousness, levity, mirth, pleasure, thankfulness *Antonyms:* moroseness, sadness

glamorous *adj.* alluring, attractive, beautiful, bewitching, captivating, charismatic, charming, dazzling, enchanting, entrancing, fascinating, glittering, gorgeous, lovely, radiant, ravishing, seductive, smart, stylish *Nonformal:* glammy, glitzy, ritzy, with sizzle, swanky *Antonyms:* colourless, dull, unexciting

glamour *n.* **1.** allure, appeal, attraction, beauty, charisma, charm, draw, elegance, magnetism, panache, seduction, sophistication, style, suaveness, urbanity, vitality *Nonformal:* glitz, razzle-dazzle, swank **2.** bewitchment, enchantment, magic, occult, witchcraft, witchery, wizardry

glance *n.* **1.** blink, eye, eyeball, flash, fleeting look, gander, gaze, glimpse, look, peek, peep, peer, perusal, quick look, sight, slant, squint, view *Nonformal:* look-see, once-over **2.** coruscation, flash, gleam, glimmer, glint, glisten, reflection, shimmer, sparkle, twinkle – *v.* **1.** browse, eye, flash, gaze, glimpse, lamp *(Nonformal)*, look, peek, peep, peer, take in, view **2.** dip into, flip *or* leaf *or* rifle *or* skim through, peruse, scan **3.** bounce, brush, careen, carom, contact, deflect, graze, kiss, rebound, ricochet, shave, sideswipe, skim, skip, slide **4.**

coruscate, flash, gleam, glimmer, glint, glisten, glitter, reflect, shimmer, shine, touch, twinkle

glare *n.* **1.** blaze, brilliance, flame, flare, glow, light, reflection, snowblink, snowshine **2.** dirty look, evil eye, frown, glower, scowl *Nonformal:* hairy eyeball, look daggers **3.** blatancy, dazzle, display, flashiness, glitter, showiness, vulgarity – *v.* **1.** beam, blaze, blind, blur, daze, dazzle, flame, flare, glow, radiate, shine **2.** bore, fix, frown, gape, gawk, glower, menace, peer, pierce, scowl, stare

glaring *adj.* **1.** audacious, blatant, capital, conspicuous, crying, egregious, evident, excessive, extreme, flagrant, manifest, noticeable, obtrusive, obvious, open, outrageous, outré, outstanding, overt, patent, visible *Antonyms:* concealed, hidden, obscure **2.** cheap, flashy, garish, gaudy, loud, ostentatious, showy, tacky *(Nonformal)*, tawdry **3.** blinding, bright, brilliant, dazzling, flaming, harsh, intense, strong, vivid

glass *n.* **1.** container, stemware, vessel *Kinds of drinking glass:* beer mug, claret, cocktail, flagon, flute, goblet, highball, hock, hollow-stemmed, jigger, juice, liqueur, margarita, martini, mug, old-fashioned, parfait, pilsner, pony, punch cup, rock, schooner, seidel, sherbet, sherry, shotglass, sleeve, snifter, stein, tall, tankard, tumbler, water, wineglass, yard **2.** looking glass, mirror, pane, window

glasses *n. pl.* bifocals, eyeglasses, frames, goggles, lorgnette, monocles, peepers, pince-nez, reading glasses, spectacles, sunglasses, trifocals *Nonformal:* cat glasses, grannies, shades, specs

glassy *adj.* **1.** blank, cold, dazed, dull, empty, expressionless, fixed, lifeless, vacant, vacuous, wooden **2.** burnished, clear, glazed, icy, polished, shiny, sleek, slick, slippery, smooth, transparent, vitreous

glaze *n.* coat, enamel, film, finish, glint, gloss, haze, lacquer, lustre, patina, polish, sheen, shine, varnish – *v.* buff, burnish, coat, cover, enamel, furbish, gloss, lacquer, overlay, polish, rub, shine, varnish

gleam *n.* **1.** glimmer, glow, ray, sparkle, twinkle **2.** hint, indication, inkling, shadow, trace – *v.* beam, burn, coruscate, flare, flash, glint, radiate *See also:* **glimmer**

glean *v.* **1.** accumulate, amass, collect, garner, gather, harvest, pick, reap, select, sift, tassel, winnow **2.** ascertain, conclude, deduce, discover, extract, find out, learn, scope out *(Nonformal)*

glee *n.* **1.** blitheness, cheerfulness, delight, elation, enjoyment, exhilaration, exuberance, exultation, fun, gaiety, gladness, happiness, hilarity, jocularity, jollity, joyfulness, joyousness, liveliness, merriment, mirth, pleasure, sprightliness, triumph, verve *Antonyms:* depression, gloom, melancholy, misery, sadness **2.** composition, music, number, piece, score

gleeful *adj.* delighted, elated, exalted, exuberant, exultant, frolicsome, gay, gratified, happy, hilarious, jovial, joyful, jubilant, lighthearted, merry, mirthful, overjoyed, pleased, triumphant *Antonyms:* blue, dejected, down

glib *adj.* **1.** artful, devious, fast-talking, ingratiating, insincere, oily, slick, slippery, smooth, smooth-talking, suave, unctuous *Antonyms:* genuine, real, sincere **2.** chatty, effusive, fluid, gabby, garrulous, long-winded, loquacious, prolix, talkative, verbose *Antonyms:* concise, succinct, terse

glide *n.* flit, flow, fly, glissade, sail, slide, slither, soar, sweep – *v.* **1.** coast, drift, float, flow, fly, roll, sail, scud, skate, skip, slither, soar, stream, waft, wing **2.** advance, elapse, move, pass *or* slip by, roll on, progress, slide, travel

glimmer *n.* **1.** flicker, glance, gleam, glint, glow, ray, scintillation, shimmer, sparkle, twinkle **2.** idea, notion, perception, shadow, smatter, suggestion, suspicion, whisper – *v.* flicker, glisten, glitter, glow, scintillate, shimmer, shine, sparkle, twinkle *See also:* **gleam, glitter**

glimpse *n.* **1.** eye, flash, glance, impression, look, look-see *(Nonformal)*, peek, peep, pike, quick look, sight, sighting, squint, view **2.** glimmer, hint, inkling, intimation, suggestion, suspicion, trace, vague idea *or* notion – *v.* descry, espy, eye, find, look, see, sight, spot, spy, view

glint *n.* **1.** blaze, flare, flash, glaze, gleam, glitter, gloss, glow, lustre, patina, radiance, reflection, sheen, shimmer, shine, sparkle **2.** glimpse, impression, look, look-see *(Nonformal)*, peak, peep, quick look, side-glance – *v.* **1.** flash, gleam, glisten, glitter, glow, radiate, reflect, shimmer, shine, sparkle **2.** dart, dash, flit, fly, hasten, hurry, race, rush, scamper, scoot, scramble, scud, scurry, scuttle, skip, speed, tear, zoom *Antonyms:* crawl, creep, lumber, stroll

glisten *n.* brightness, reflection, rippling, sheen, shimmer *Antonyms:* dullness, gloom – *v.* dance, glow, light up, radiate, twinkle *See also:* **shine, twinkle**

glitter *n.* brilliance, display, flashiness, glamour, magnificence, sparkle, splendour, tinsel *Nonformal:* glitz, razzmattazz, razzle-dazzle – *v.* glint, scintillate, shimmer, shine, sparkle *See also:* **glisten**

gloat *v.* boast, brag, crow, delight in, exult, horse-laugh *(Nonformal)*, rejoice, strut, swagger, triumph, vaunt

glob *n.* blob, chunk, clod, clump, drop, globule, lump, mass, piece, slab, wad *Nonformal:* gob, hunk

global *adj.* **1.** all-encompassing, all-inclusive, all-out, broad, catholic, complete, comprehensive, encyclopedic, exhaustive, extensive, far-reaching, full-fledged, full-scale, general, intercontinental, international, pandemic, sweeping, thorough, total, ubiquitous, unbounded, universal, unlimited, vast, wide-ranging, world, worldwide *Antonyms:* circumscribed, confined, limited **2.** circular, cylindrical, egg-shaped, elliptical, globate, globose, globular, orbicular, oval, ovate, ovoid, rotund, round, spherical

globe *n.* **1.** ball, orb, round, sphere, spheroid **2.** biosphere, creation, earth, four corners, Gaia, geosphere, *mundo (Spanish)*, planet, spaceship Earth, terra firma, world

globetrotter *n.* cosmopolite, drifter, exile, man without a country, peregrinator, peripatetic, pilgrim, rambler, rover, sightseer, tourist, traveller, trekker, voyager, voyageur, wanderer, wayfarer *Nonformal:* jetsetter, rolling stone, tripster

gloom *n.* **1.** angst, anguish, chagrin, cheerlessness, dejection, depression, desolation, despair, despondency, discouragement, dispirit, distress, doldrums, dolour, downheartedness, dread, dullness, dumps, foreboding, grief, heaviness, heavy-heartedness, malaise, melancholia, misery, morbidity, mourning, neurasthenia, pessimism, sadness, sorrow, unhappiness, woe *Nonformal:* blue funk, catatonia *Antonyms:* cheerfulness, happiness, joy, radiance **2.** blackness, darkness, dusk, murkiness, shade, shadow *Antonyms:* brightness, light, sun **3.** buss *(Maritimes)*, frown, mope, pout, sulk, umbrage – *v.* **1.** bedim, blacken, cloud, darken, dim, eclipse, murk, overcast, shade, shadow, threaten **2.** ache, agonize, brood, depress, dishearten, droop, frown, languish, lose heart, mope, pout, sadden, sink, sulk

gloomy *adj.* **1.** blue, broody, cheerless, crabby, crestfallen, dejected, depressed, despondent, disconsolate, dispirited, dour, down, downcast, downhearted, forlorn, funereal, glum, joyless, low, melancholy, mirthless, miserable, moody, moping, morose, mournful, oppressed, pessimistic, sad, saturnine, solemn, sulky, sullen, surly, unhappy, weary, woebegone *Antonyms:* blithe, cheerful, jolly, merry **2.** bad, bleak, cold, comfortless, dark, depressing, desolate, discouraging, disheartening, dismal, dispiriting, drab, dreary, dull, dusky, oppressive, overcast, sombre *Antonyms:* bright, brilliant, light, radiant, sunny

glorification *n.* adoration, aggrandizement, canonization, celebration, deification, elevation, exaltation, laudation, lionization, praise, reverence, sanctification, veneration, worship

glorify *v.* **1.** acclaim, adore, apotheosize, beatify, bless, boost, build up, canonize, celebrate, commend, deify, dignify, distinguish, elevate, enhance, ennoble, enshrine, eulogize, exalt, extol, honour, idolize, immortalize, laud, lift up, lionize, magnify, panegyrize, praise, raise, revere, sanctify, venerate, wax poetic about, worship *Antonyms:* condemn, debase, defile, dishonour, humiliate **2.** boast, colour, embellish, exaggerate, glamorize, idealize, inflate, romanticize *Nonformal:* ballyhoo, build *or* pump up, oversell

glorious *adj.* **1.** august, celebrated, distinguished, divine, elevated, eminent, esteemed, exalted, famed, famous, grand, great, heroic, honoured, illustrious, immortal, legendary, majestic, memorable, mythic, noble, notable, noted, preeminent, renowned, time-honoured, venerable, well-known *Antonyms:* commonplace, humdrum, minor, ordinary, trivial, workday **2.** beautiful, bright, brilliant, dazzling, delightful, enjoyable, excellent, fine, gorgeous, gratifying, heavenly, magnificent, marvellous, pleasurable, radiant, remarkable, resplendent, shining, splendid, sublime, superb, triumphant, wonderful *Antonyms:* dreary, dull, gloomy, unpleasant

glory *n.* **1.** celebrity, dignity, distinction, éclat, eminence, esteem, fame, grandeur, greatness, honour, illustriousness, importance, majesty, nobility, notability, preeminence, prestige, prominence, renown, repute, stardom *Antonyms:* insignificance, lowliness, unimportance **2.** apex, crown, height, heyday, peak, prosperity, top, triumph, watermark **3.** radiance, resplendence, splendour, sublimity **4.** acclaim, accolades, adoration, aggrandizement, devotion, exaltation, glorification, homage, kudos, laudation, magnification, praise, reverence, tribute, veneration, worship *Antonyms:* criticism, disdain, indifference **5.** bliss, heaven, hereafter, kingdom come, paradise **6.** aura, circle, gloria, halo, nimbus, ring – *v.* **1.** bask, delight, exalt, joy, jubilate, rejoice, revel, triumph, wallow **2.** bluster, boast, brag, gasconade, rodomontade, swagger, vaunt

gloss *n.* **1.** annotation, comment, commentary, definition, elucidation, explanation, footnote, interpretation, marginalia, note, translation **2.** brightness, burnish, finish, glaze, lustre, polish, sheen, shine, varnish *Antonyms:* darkness, dullness, muddiness **3.** appearance, cosmetics, deceit, deception, delusion, disguise, façade, false front, pretext, semblance, sham *(Nonformal)*, show, smokescreen, trick – *v.* **1.** annotate, comment, construe, define, elucidate, explain, explicate, interpret, translate **2.** belie, camouflage, conceal, cover up, deceive, disguise, falsify, hide, mask, misrepresent, rationalize, smooth over, sugarcoat, veil *Nonformal:* doctor, whitewash **3.** buff, burnish, glaze, lacquer, polish, shine, smooth, varnish

glossary *n.* definitions, directory, index, key, lexicon, listing, reference, terminology, thesaurus, vocabulary, wordbook, wordlist

glossy *adj.* **1.** bright, brilliant, burnished, glassy, glazed, glistening, lustrous, polished, reflective, satiny, shiny, silky, sleek, slick *Antonyms:* drab, dull, matte **2.** cosmetic, deceiving, illusory, misleading, shallow, specious, superficial, trivial – *n.* image, picture, print, photograph, reproduction, shot, snapshot, still

glove *n.* cestus, covering, finger mitten, gauntlet, mitt, mitten, muff

glow *n.* **1.** aura, beam, brightness, brilliance, effulgence, flash, gleam, glimmer, glint, glisten, glitter, glitz *(Nonformal)*, light, luminosity, lustre, pizzazz, radiance, ray, sheen, shimmer, shine, sparkle, tinsel **2.** bloom, fettle, fitness, flush, health, robustness, rosiness, ruddiness, sanguineness, vigour, vitality, well-being **3.** animation, ardour, *brio (Italian)*, élan, emotion, enthusiasm, excitement, heat, life, mettle, passion, spirit, vitality, vivacity, warmth, zest **4.** a high, drunkenness, happiness, inebriation, intoxication, tipsiness – *v.* **1.** brighten, burn, flame, flare, gleam, glimmer, glisten, glitter, incandesce, light, radiate, shine, sparkle **2.** beam, bloom, blush, flush, mantle, redden, tingle

glowing *adj.* **1.** aglow, beaming, bright, burning, flaming, flickering, illuminated, incandescent, lambent, luminous, phosphorescent, radiant, shining, sparkling, suffused **2.** brilliant, intense, resplendent, splendid, vibrant, vivacious, vivid **3.** ecstatic, glad, happy, joyful, pleased, tickled **4.** flushed, hale, healthy, hearty, robust, ruddy, sanguine **5.** ardent, complimentary, enthusiastic, favourable, fervid, flattering, impassioned, keen, laudatory, passionate, rave *(Nonformal)*, rhapsodic, starry-eyed, zealous

glue *n.* adhesive, cement, epoxy, gum, mucilage, paste, plaster *Nonformal:* glop, stickum – *v.* adhere, affix, attach, cement, connect, fasten, gum, paste, plaster, stick, unite

glum *adj.* blue, cynical, dejected, depressed, dispirited, gloomy, melancholy, miserable, moody, morose, neurasthenic, pessimistic, sad, sullen, unhappy, woebegone *Nonformal:* crumpled, down-in-the-dumps, down-in-the-mouth *Antonyms:* ecstatic, elated, sunny

glut *n.* excess, overabundance, oversupply, plenitude, saturation, superabundance, superfluity, surfeit, surplus, too much *Antonyms:* dearth, lack, paucity, scarcity – *v.* **1.** burden, clog, congest, cram, deluge, flood, inundate, load, overload, overstock, oversupply, overwhelm, saturate, swamp **2.** cloy, devour, feast, fill, gorge, overfeed, overindulge, pack, pall, sate, satiate, stuff, surfeit

glutinous *adj.* adhesive, cohesive, gooey *(Nonformal)*, gummy, mucilaginous, sticky, tacky, viscid, viscous

glutton *n.* gourmand, hefty eater, overeater, trencherman *Nonformal:* crammer, gobbler, greedygut, hog, pig, stuffer

gluttonous *adj.* acquisitive, craving, devouring, excessive, gormandizing, grasping, greedy, hungry, insatiable, intemperate, open-mouthed, overindulgent, rapacious, ravenous, unquenchable

gluttony *n.* excess, excessiveness, gourmandizing, greed, hunger, insatiability, intemperance, overeating, overindulgence, voracity, wantonness *Antonyms:* restraint, temperance

gnarled *adj.* **1.** bent, bumpy, burled, contorted, crooked, distorted, knobby, knotted, misshapen, nodular, protruding, twisted *Antonyms:* sleek, straight, unblemished **2.** calloused, corrugated, craggy, hard, leathery, rough, rugged, tough, weather-beaten, worn, wrinkled *Antonyms:* silky, smooth, soft

gnaw *v.* **1.** bite, chomp, chow down *(Nonformal)*, eat, gnash, masticate, munch, nibble, ruminate **2.** afflict, chafe, distress, disturb, fester, gall, grate, harrow, haunt, oppress, pain, pester, plague, rankle, torment, torture, trouble, wear down, weigh on, worry, vex

gnome *n.* **1.** dwarf, elf, fairy, goblin, hobgoblin, imp, sprite, troll **2.** adage, aphorism, chestnut *(Nonformal)*, cliché, epigram, maxim, platitude, proverb, saw, saying, truism

go *interj.* begone, escape, exit, get out, leave, run *Nonformal:* amscray, beat it, scram, vamoose – *n.* **1.** ambition, drive, élan, energy, enterprise, forcefulness, hustle, initiative, spirit, vigour, vivacity, zip *Nonformal:* chutzpah, get-up-and-go, gumption, moxie, oomph **2.** attempt, chance, effort, shot, spell, stab, stretch, try, turn, undertaking *Nonformal:* crack, whack, whirl **3.** agreement, bargain, contract, deal, dicker, negotiation, trade – *v.* **1.** advance, approach, cruise, fare, flow, journey, move, near, pass, pass along, proceed, progress, stream, travel, venture **2.** decamp, depart, escape, exit, flee, fly, leave, push off, quit, retire, run away, take flight, take off, withdraw *Nonformal:* beat it, lam, make tracks, motor, scram, skedaddle, split, vamoose **3.** act, function, operate, perform, run, serve, work **4.** cover, encompass, extend, spread, stretch, sweep **5.** cease, collapse, disappear, elapse, end, evanesce, expire, fail, give way, happen, lapse, pass *or* pass away, perish, proceed, succumb, transpire, vanish, yield **6.** agree, aid, compliment, contribute, fit, foster, further, harmonize, help, suit **7.** bear up, endure, forbear, last, stand, stomach, suffer, tolerate, weather

goad *n.* **1.** catalyst, compulsion, desire, drive, impetus, impulse, impulsion, incentive, incitation, incitement, motivation, pressure, stimulant, stimulation, stimulus, urge **2.** lash, prod, prong, spur, whip – *v.* animate, annoy, arouse, bully, coerce, drive, encourage, excite, exhort, force, harass, hound, impel, incite, inspirit, instigate, irritate, key up, lash, move, press, prick, prod, prompt, propel, provoke, push, spark, spur, stimulate, sting, tease, thrust, trigger, turn on, urge, whip, work up, worry *Nonformal:* egg on, fire up, needle

go-ahead *n.* approval, authorization, blessing, clearance, confirmation, consent, endorsement, imprimatur, leave, liberty, licence, permission, sanction *Nonformal:* green light, nod, okay, thumbs up

goal *n.* aim, ambition, aspiration, design, desire, destination, direction, dream, end, hope, intent, intention, limit, mark, motive, notion, object, objective, plan, point, purpose, scheme, target, wish

go-between *n.* **1.** agent, broker, connection, contact, dealer, distributor, fence, intermediary, interpreter, middleman, middlewoman, representative, spokesperson *Nonformal:* front, mouthpiece **2.** arbitrator, conciliator, judge, mediator, moderator, negotiator, ombudsperson, peacemaker, referee

gobble *v.* **1.** bolt, consume, cram, devour, eat, glut, gulp, guzzle, ingest, raven, stuff, swallow *Nonformal:* chow *or* wolf down, inhale, shovel in **2.** acquire, assume, grab, grapple, grasp, seize, take

goblin *n.* bocan *(P.E.I.)*, bogeyman, brownie, elf, fairy, gnome, gremlin, hobgoblin, imp, jinker *(Newfoundland)*, kelpie, kobold, leprechaun, ouphe, peri, puck, sprite, troll

God *n.* Absolute *or* Ultimate Being, Adonai, Allah, Almighty, Ancient of Days, Creator, Elohim, Father, Giver of Life, Holy One *or* Spirit, Jah, Yahweh, Jehovah, Lord, Maker, Man Upstairs *(Nonformal)*, Power, Prime Mover, Providence, Shaper, Waheguru

god *n.* deity, demigod, *deva (Hindu)*, divine ruler, idol, spirit, theocrat, totem *Egyptian gods:* Anubis, Bes, Geb, Horus, Khem, Min, Neph, Nephthys, Osiris, Ptah, Ra *or* Amen-Ra, Sebek, Serapis, Set, Shu, Thoth *Greek gods:* Aeolus, Apollo, Apollon, Ares, Asclepius, Comus, Cronos, Dionysus, Eros, Hades, Helios, Hephaestus, Heracles, Hermes, Hymen, Hypnus, Momus, Morpheus, Pan, Plutus, Poseidon, Priapus, Prometheus, Thanatos, Zepherus, Zeus *Hindu gods:* Agni, Brahma, Ganesha, Indra, Kama, Krishna, Kubera, Mahakala, Rahu, Rama, Rudra, Shiva, Surya, Vayu, Vishnu, Yama *Japanese gods:* Bishamon, Daikoku, Ebisu, Hachiman, Hotei, Izanagi, Jizo, Jurojin, Koshin, Raiden, Susano-o *Mesopotamian gods:* Adad, Anum, Asallukhi, Ashur, Attis, Baal, Dagan, Dumuzi, Enki, Enlil, Marduk, Nabu, Nannar, Nergal, Ninurta, Shamash, Utu *Native North American gods:* Chakekenapok, Chipiapoos, Coyote, Earth *or* Great Mother, Glooscap, Great Spirit, Manitou, Mesakkummikokwi, Nanabozo, Napi, Raven, Sila, Silap Inua, Sun Father, Tarquiup Inua, Thunderbird, Tirawa, Tornarsuk, Wabosso, Water Serpent, Wathatotaro, Wihio *Native South American gods:* Huitzilopochtli, Ometecuhtli, Quetzalcoatl, Sinteotl, Tlaloc, Tonatiyu, Ueueteotl, Xipe, Xochipilli *Roman gods:* Aesculapius, Bacchus, Cupid, Dis, Faunus, Hercules, Hyperion, Janus, Jupiter, Liber, Mars, Mercury, Mithras, Mors, Neptune, Orcus, Picus, Pluto, Saturn, Sol, Somnus, Uranus, Vulcan *Scandinavian gods:* Balder, Bor, Bori, Bragi, Frey, Heimdall, Höder, Hoenir, Loki, Magni, Mimir, Modi, Njord, Odin, Thor, Tyr

goddess *n.* dryad, female deity, Fury, Muse, nymph *Egyptian goddesses:* Bast, Hathor, Ishtar, Isis, Nut *Greek goddesses:* Aphrodite, Artemis, Athena, Demeter, Eos, Eris, Gaea, Hebe, Hecate, Hera, Hestia, Hygeia, Iris, Nephthys, Mnemosyne, Nemesis, Nike, Nyx, Persephone, Psyche, Rhea, Selene, Themis *Hindu goddesses:* Devi, Durga, Kali, Lakshmi, Parvati, Radha, Sakti, Sarasvati, Sita, Tara *Japanese goddesses:* Amaterasu, Benten, Inari, Izanami, Kwannon *Mesopotamian goddesses:* Astarte, Ereshkigal, Inanna, Nisaba *Native North American goddesses:* Arnquagssaq, Changing Woman, Corn Mother, Kadlu, Nerrivik Nuliajuk, Sedna *Native South American goddesses:* Chalchihuitlicue, Coatlicue Xilonen *Roman goddesses:* Aurora, Bellona, Ceres, Cybele, Diana, Flora, Juno Luna, Minerva, Nox, Ops, Pomona, Proserpina, Psyche, Salus, Venus, Vesta *Scandinavian goddesses:* Freya, Frigg, Hela

godforsaken *adj.* **1.** abandoned, bleak deserted, desolate, dismal, dreary, forlorn gloomy, lonely, neglected, out-of-the-way remote **2.** corrupt, depraved, evil, godless vile, wicked, wretched

godless *adj.* **1.** agnostic, atheistic, blasphemous, graceless, heathen, impious, infidel irreligious, nonreligious, profane, secular, ungodly, unholy, unreligous, unrighteous, worldly **2.** debased, depraved, malevolent, unclean, unprincipled

godliness *n.* holiness, piousness, purity, religiosity, reverence, righteousness, saintliness, sanctity, spirituality

godly *adj.* **1.** angelic, celestial, divine, holy, pious, saintly, virtuous **2.** born-again, devout, god-fearing, Jesus-loving, prayerful, religious, revering, righteous, worshipful, zealous

godsend *n.* advantage, benediction, benefit, blessing, boon, gift, good, gravy *(Nonformal)*, manna, saviour, windfall

gofer *n.* aide, assistant, attendant, employee, errand boy *or* girl, fetcher, lacky, helper, right-hand man *or* woman, subordinate, worker *Nonformal:* mule, stepnfetchit

goggle *n.* gaze, glad eye, inspection, leer, look, stare – *v.* bulge, eye, gape, gawk, gaze, glare, leer, ogle, peep, regard, scrutinize, squint, stare, view *Nonformal:* check out, eyeball

golden *adj.* **1.** blond, blonde, caramel, flaxen, gold, honeyed, sandy, straw, tan, tawny, wheat, yellow **2.** auspicious, blissful, bright, fortunate, happy, heavenly, lucky, prime, superb **3.** affluent, halcyon, prosperous, rich, thriving, wealthy **4.** brilliant, excellent, exceptional, fantastic, fine, perfect, thriving **5.** cherished, dear, invaluable, precious, priceless, prized, sterling, treasured, valuable, worthy

golf *n.* game, links, round, sport *Golf course terms:* 18 holes, 9 holes, apron, back nine, bunker, collar, course, cup, dogleg, executive course, fairway, flag *or* flagstick, fringe, front nine, green, hazard, hole, lip, marker, obstruction, out of bounds *or* o.b., par-3 course, par-3, par-4, par-5, pin, putting green, rough, sand trap, tee, water hazard *Kinds of golf equipment:* ball, ball scoop, brassie, club, driver, glove, golf cart, iron, long iron, mashie, metal wood, mid-iron, niblick, putter, short iron, spoon, tee, wedge, wood *Scoring in golf:* albatross, birdie, bogey, double bogey, eagle, handicap, hole-in-one *or* ace, mulligan *or* mully, over *or* under par, par, penalty, round *Kinds of shot:* approach, blast, chili dip, chip, cut, dead aim, draw, drive, duck hook, duff, fade, fat, flier, head lift, hook, knife, lag, lob, long iron, pitch, pop-up, provisional, pull, punch, push, putt, run-up, sand, shank, slice, stubby, tee, thin, top, water, worm burner

gone *adj.* **1.** absent, departed, moved away, split *(Nonformal)*, withdrawn **2.** astray, long lost, mislaid, misplaced, missing, vanished **3.** consumed, depleted, dissipated, dried-up *(Nonformal)*, ended, finished, no more, over, past, spent, taken *or* used up, wasted **4.** dead, deceased, defunct, extinct, flat line, inanimate, lifeless, passed away *Nonformal:* belly up, dead meat **5.** burnt-out, dizzy, dog-weary, drained, enervated, exhausted, faint, feeble, tired, weak *Nonformal:* bagged, beat, tuckered **6.** hopeless, irretrievable, lost, ruined, undone, unsalvageable *Nonformal:* crashed and burned, kaput **7.** aux anges, ecstatic, enamoured, enraptured, infatuated, in love, obsessed, transported *Nonformal:* gaga, tickled

good *adj.* **1.** blameless, ethical, exemplary, godly, guiltless, honest, honourable, innocent, irreproachable, lily-white, moral, pious, proper, pure, religious, righteous, spotless, uncorrupted, unsullied, upstanding, virginal, virtuous, worthy *Nonformal:* scrumptious, yummy *Antonyms:* corrupt, fallen, sinful **2.** agreeable, conforming, dutiful, loyal, obedient, respectful, tractable, well-behaved *Antonyms:* defiant, naughty, wild **3.** affectionate, benevolent, caring, charitable, compassionate, decent, gracious, humane, kind, kind-hearted, loving, merciful, nice, obliging, open-handed, solicitous, sympathetic, tender, warm *Antonyms:* harsh, mean, strict **4.** able, accomplished, ace *(Nonformal)*, adept, admirable, adroit, commendable, efficient, estimable, expert, gifted, laudable, model, praiseworthy, proficient, qualified, skilful, suitable, talented *Antonyms:* incompetent, maladroit, unable **5.** amazing, attractive, beautiful, choice, comely, fair, fancy, fetching, fine, gorgeous, great, pretty, smashing *(Nonformal)* **6.** capital, excellent, fantastic, grand *Nonformal:* beaut *or* beauty, gear, hunky-dory, rip-roaring **7.** best, bosom, cherished, close, dear, familiar, intimate **8.** approving, auspicious, benign, favourable, fortunate, promising, propitious *Antonyms:* ill, inauspicious, unfavourable **9.** beneficial, flavourful, fresh, health-preserving, life-giving, palatable, pleasing, satisfying, tasty, unspoiled, wholesome **10.** advantageous, appropriate, fitting, helpful, just, needed, positive, right, salutary, sound, superior, valid, valuable, welcome **11.** adequate, ample, bountiful, enough, generous, lavish, liberal, plenty, sizeable, substantial, sufficient, tons *(Nonformal) Antonyms:* insufficient, meagre, miserly **12.** balmy, clear, clear-skied, clement, halcyon, pleasant, sunny, warm *Antonyms:* cloudy, dirty *(Newfoundland)*, stormy, tempestuous **13.** authentic, bona fide, genuine, orthodox, real, strict, true-blue *(Nonformal)*, trustworthy, valid *Antonyms:* counterfeit, fake, fraudulent – *n.* **1.** advantage, asset, blessing, boon, favour, gain, helpfulness, serviceability, use, usefulness, utility, value, worth **2.** avail, benefit, interest, profit, welfare, well-being **3.** dignity, excellence, ideal, merit, morality, rectitude, righteousness, virtue *See also:* **goods**

goodbye *interj.* adieu, bye, cheerio, ciao, farewell, it's been real, see you later, so long *Nonformal:* ta-ta, tootle-loo, thanks for the memories – *n.* farewell, leave-taking, parting, send-off, swan song

good-for-nothing *adj.* feckless, idle, indolent, irresponsible, lazy, lethargic, pepless, shiftless, slothful, useless, worthless – *n.* black sheep, deadbeat, idler, loafer, ne'er-do-well, prodigal, remittance man, scamp, slouch, wastrel, wretch *Nonformal:* bum, hoser, loser, no-good, slacker, slider

good-hearted *adj.* agreeable, altruistic, benevolent, brotherly, caring, charitable, clement, congenial, considerate, cordial, decent, generous, gentle, good-tempered, gracious, humane, humanitarian, indulgent, kind, kind-natured, lenient, liberal, loving, material, merciful, mild, munificent, obliging, philanthropic, sisterly, soft-hearted, sweet-natured, tender, thoughtful, virtuous, warm, well-intentioned, well-meaning, *Antonyms:* mean, misanthropic, selfish

good-humoured *adj.* accommodating, affable, amiable, blithe, buoyant, cheerful, genial, happy, jocund, merry, pleasant, smiling, sociable, social, sunny, warm *Antonyms:* depressed, morose, sullen

goodness *n.* **1.** character, decency, excellence, ethicality, grace, honesty, honour, integrity, morality, rectitude, righteousness, superiority, uprightness, virtue *Antonyms:* corruption, evil, immorality, wickedness **2.** beneficence, benevolence, generosity, good will, mercy, philanthropy *Antonyms:* miserliness, stinginess **3.** friendliness, geniality, goodheartedness, graciousness, humaneness, kindheartedness, kindliness, kindness, obligingness, willingness *Antonyms:* antagonism, hostility, misanthropy **4.** essence, heart, quality, soul, spirit, strength **5.** benefit, healthfulness, nutritiousness, salubrity, value, wholesomeness, worth *Antonyms:* noxiousness, toxicity

goods *n. pl.* **1.** appurtenances, belongings, cargo, chattels, effects, equipment, freight, furnishings, furniture, gear, material, merchandise, paraphernalia, possessions, produce, property, stock, trappings, wares *Nonformal:* bit and pieces, movables, stuff, things **2.** ability, aptitude, capability, competence, faculty, flair, ingenuity, proficiency, skill, talent

good will *n.* **1.** altruism, benevolence, charity, goodness, heart, humanitarianism, humanity, kindheartedness, kindness, philanthropy **2.** acquiescence, cordiality, favourableness, friendliness, readiness, willingness, zeal **3.** esteem, good name, intangible assets, notoriety, rep *(Nonformal)*, reputation, repute, status

gooey *adj.* adhesive, gluey, glutinous, gummy, mucilaginous, mucky, soft, sticky, tacky, viscous

gore *n.* **1.** bloodshed, butchery, carnage, killing, massacre, slaughter **2.** blood, guts, ichon, life fluid **3.** godet, gusset, inlay, insert – *v.* disembowel, gouge, gut, hook, horn, impale, injure, jab, penetrate, perforate, pierce, prick, puncture, shish kebab *(Nonformal)*, skewer, spear, stab, wound

gorge *n.* **1.** abyss, basin, canyon, coulee, couloir, crater, crevasse, dale, dell, ditch, gulch, gully, hollow, passageway, ravine valley **2.** bar, barrier, block, blockade, impasse, impediment, obstruction, stoppage – *v.* banquet, cram, devour, eat, feast, feed, glut, gormandize, guzzle, overindulge, stuff, surfeit *Nonformal:* gobble, scoff, tie on the feedbag

gorgeous *adj.* amazing, arresting, attractive, beautiful, bonny, brilliant, comely, commanding, compelling, dazzling, delightful, distinguished, dreamy *(Nonformal)*, electrifying, elegant, exquisite, eye-catching, fair, fascinating, fetching, fine, good-looking, handsome, impressive, lovely, magnificent, memorable, noticeable, pleasing, pretty, prominent, ravishing, remarkable, resplendent, sensational, showy, spectacular, striking, stunning, sublime, superb, unusual, wonderful *Antonyms:* cheap, dull, homely, plain, shoddy

gormandize *v.* cram, devour, feast, gluttonize, gorge, gulp, inhale *(Nonformal)*, stuff

gory *adj.* **1.** brutal, disgusting, grisly, gross, grotesque, gruesome, horrible, macabre, offensive, upsetting, violent **2.** bleeding, blood-soaked, bloodstained, bloody, sanguine

gospel *n.* **1.** credo, creed, doctrine, guide, principle, truth, verity, way **2.** evangel, glad tidings, good news, sacred word, teachings, word of God *New Testament Gospels:* John, Luke, Mark, Matthew

gossamer *adj.* airy, delicate, diaphanous, filmy, fine, flimsy, gauzy, light, sheer, silky, transparent, unsubstantial, wispy *Antonyms:* coarse, heavy, thick – *n.* line, silk, thread, web

gossip *n.* **1.** banter, chatter, chitchat, idle *or* small talk, palaver *Nonformal:* buzz, scuttlebutt, verbal diarrhea, word on the street **2.** calumny, defamation, rumour, scandal, slander *Nonformal:* dirt, dirty linen **3.** busybody, meddler, rumourmonger, scandalmonger, snoop, talebearer *Prince Edward Island:* shook, snool *Nonformal:* bigmouth, blabbermouth, flibbertigibbet, snitch, tattletale – *v.* **1.** natter, prattle *Nonformal:* run off at the mouth, shoot the breeze, shmooze **2.** badmouth, defame, malign, slander, smear, spread rumours, sully **3.** blab, break confidence *or* trust, report, tattle, tell secrets *Nonformal:* snitch, spill the beans, squeal

gothic *adj.* **1.** eerie, frightful, horrifying, macabre, spooky, supernatural **2.** bizarre, eccentric, grotesque, inexplicable, outlandish, unaccountable, weird **3.** ancient, antiquated, medieval, old-fashioned, outmoded *Antonyms:* cutting-edge, modern, newfangled **4.** barbarous, boorish, coarse, rough, rude, savage, uncivilized, uncouth, uncultivated, vulgar *Antonyms:* civilized, polite, refined

gouge *n.* blade, chisel, cutting tool, knife, scraper – *v.* **1.** chisel, cut, gorge, poke, scoop, scrape, shave, whittle **2.** cheat, defraud, extort, overcharge, price-gouge, profiteer, swindle *Nonformal:* mean price, soak

gourmet *adj.* **1.** aesthetic, fancy, gastronomical, refined **2.** delicious, delightful, enjoyable, tasty, wonderful – *n.* cognascenti, connoisseur, critic, educator, epicure, food lover, gastronome, gastronomist, sophisticated palate

govern *v.* **1.** administer, captain, chair, command, conduct, control, dictate, direct, dominate, execute, guide, handle, head, hold dominion *or* office *or* sway, lead, manage, master, operate, order, oversee, pilot, regulate, reign, rule, run, steer, superintend, supervise **2.** influence, shape, shepherd, sway **3.** affect, conclude, decide, determine, manipulate, prejudice, resolve **4.** check, curb, inhibit, limit, modify, restrain, subdue, tame

governess *n.* babysitter, chaperon, duenna, instructor, maid, mentor, nanny, teacher, tutor

government *n.* **1.** administration, bureaucracy, executive, management, ministry, Ottawa *(Nonformal)*, parliament, political community, politics *Components of Canadian government:* Cabinet, Departments, Executive, Federal Court, Governor General, House of Commons, Judiciary, Legislature, Prime Minister, Prime Minister's Office, Privy Council, Senate, Sovereign,

Supreme Court, Supreme Territorial Courts, Treasury Board *Levels of government:* aboriginal, federal, municipal, national, provincial, self-government, territorial **2.** authority, command, control, direction, discipline, domination, dominion, governance, guidance, influence, jurisdiction, law, power, predominance, presidency, regency, regime, regimentation, regulation, reign, rule, sovereignty, superintendence, supervision, supremacy, sway

governor *n.* **1.** administrator, boss, captain, chief, commander, director, executive, head, head honcho *(Nonformal)*, intendant, leader, manager, overseer, presiding officer, ruler, superintendent, supervisor **2.** brake, curb, limiter, regulator, stifler, stopper

gown *n.* **1.** ballgown, costume, dress, evening dress, garment, negligée, nightgown, wrap **2.** academic *or* clerical *or* official *or* professional garb, apparel, chlamys, cloak, habit, raiment, robe, surgical apron, toga, uniform, vestment – *v.* adorn, cloak, clothe, cover, drape, dress, invest, wrap

grab *v.* **1.** catch, clutch, collar, corral, grapple, grasp, grip, hook, land, latch, pluck, snatch *Nonformal:* bag, glom, nab, snap up **2.** annex, appropriate, assume, capture, claim, conquer, expropriate, gain, seize, subsume, take *or* take over, usurp

grace *n.* **1.** benevolence, charity, compassion, forbearance, forgiveness, generosity, goodness, good will, kindness, love, mercy, tenderness *Antonyms:* antipathy, harshness, ill will **2.** allure, attractiveness, beauty, charm, comeliness, delightfulness, loveliness, pleasantness **3.** adroitness, breeding, cultivation, decency, decorum, dignity, ease, elegance, etiquette, finesse, finish, fluidity, gracefulness, manners, poise, polish, savoir-faire, smoothness, style, urbanity *Antonyms:* boorishness, clumsiness, inelegance, vulgarity **4.** benediction, blessing, invocation, petition, prayer, thanks, thanksgiving **5.** benefaction, clemency, consideration, dispensation, extension, favour, grant, indulgence, leniency, pardon, quarter, reprieve *Antonyms:* censure, penalty, reprimand – *v.* **1.** adorn, beautify, bedeck, deck, decorate, embellish, enhance, enrich, garnish, ornament **2.** crown, dignify, distinguish, elevate, favour, glorify, honour *Antonyms:* desecrate, dishonour, insult, ruin, spoil

graceful *adj.* **1.** adroit, agile, controlled, deft, dexterous, elastic, flowing, nimble, pliant, poised, practiced, rhythmic, skilled, smooth, springy *Antonyms:* awkward, clumsy, gauche, gawky **2.** limber, lissome, lithe, shapely, statuesque, supple, willowy **3.** aesthetic, artistic, beautiful, becoming, charming, dainty, decorative, delicate, elegant, exquisite, fair, fine, harmonious, lovely, natural, neat, pleasing, pretty, refined, seemly, symmetrical, tasteful *Antonyms:* tacky, tawdry, vulgar

graceless *adj.* **1.** awkward, blundering, bumbling, bungling, clumsy, gauche, gawky, inelegant, klutzy *(Nonformal)*, lumbering, maladroit, muddling, stumbling, tactless **2.** coarse, crass, crude, foul-mouthed, gross, profane, rude, vulgar

gracious *adj.* **1.** affable, charitable, civil, compassionate, courteous, forthcoming, friendly, genial, giving, hospitable, indulgent, kind, merciful, obliging, polite, tender *Antonyms:* curt, ornery, snide, surly **2.** cultivated, elegant, refined, sophisticated, stately, upscale, uptown *(Nonformal)*, urbane *Antonyms:* coarse, crude, mean – *interj. Nonformal:* by Jesus, egad, gadzooks, golly, golly gee, gosh, heavens to Betsy, holy jumpin', I'll be, lands, Lordy, my my, my stars, shiver me timbers, snakes alive, yikes

gradation *n.* **1.** arrangement, array, band, calibration, classification, grouping, measurement, ordering, progression, rank, scale, sequence, series, spectrum, succession **2.** degree, difference, distinction, divergence, grade, level, mark, notch, nuance, place, point, position, shade, stage, step, value, variation

grade *n.* **1.** acclivity, ascent, cant, climb, declivity, descent, downgrade, elevation, embankment, gradient, group, hill, incline, lean, pitch, plane, ramp, rise, slant, slope, tangent, tilt, upgrade **2.** category, class, classification, division, order, standard **3.** calibre, degree, echelon, gradation, letter, level, mark, notch, percentage, place, position, rank, stage, step, tier – *v.* **1.** arrange, brand, classify, evaluate, group, order, rank, rate, sort, value **2.** bulldoze, lay gravel *or* stone, level, plough, resurface, scrape, smooth, steamroll

gradient *adj.* descending, falling, rising, sloping – *n.* acclivity, angle, bank, declivity, grade, hill, inclination, incline, pitch, rise, slope

gradual *adj.* **1.** crab-like, creeping, deliberate, glacial, leisurely, measured, ponderous, slow, unhurried *Antonyms:* immediate, instantaneous, overnight **2.** bit-by-bit, continuous, incremental, piecemeal, progressive, regular, steady, step-by-step, successive *Antonyms:* arbitrary, haphazard, random **3.** even, gentle, moderate *Antonyms:* abrupt, steep, sudden

gradually *adv.* **1.** by degrees, constantly, continuously, increasingly, piecemeal, progressively, regularly, sequentially, serially, steadily, successively **2.** deliberately, leisurely, slowly **3.** evenly, gently, imperceptibly, moderately, unhurriedly

graduate *n.* alumna, alumnus, bachelor, certificate *or* degree holder, collegian, doctor, grad *(Nonformal)*, graduand, grantee, master, product, recipient, scholar, student – *v.* **1.** complete, deserve, earn, finish, merit **2.** ascend, evolve, improve, increase, move ahead, promote, rise, step up **3.** adjust, calibrate, caliper, divide into, mark, measure out, rule off, set

graft *n.* bootle, booty, bribe, filthy lucre *(Nonformal)*, profit, share, spoils, take – *v.* affix, attach, implant, insert, join, plant, propagate, splice, transplant

grain *n.* **1.** cereal plant, kernel, seed *Kinds of grain:* barley, buckwheat, cereal, corn *(British)*, durum wheat, flax, maize, millet, oats, oilseed, quinoa, rice, rye, triticale, wheat *See also:* **wheat** **2.** current, direction, fibre, pattern, striation, surface, texture, tooth, weave, weft **3.** atom, bit, crumb, dash, dot, fragment, granule, iota, jot, mite, modicum, molecule, morsel, particle, pinch, scintilla, speck, tidbit, tittle, touch, trace, trifle, whit **4.** character, constitution, disposition, fortitude, grit, mettle, moral fibre, pluck, spirit, temperament – *v.* bray, crush, flour, granulate, grind, mill, pebble, pound, powder, process, pulverize, thrash

grammar *n.* ABCs *(Nonformal)*, diction, language, linguistic structure, morphology, parsing, rules of language, sentence structure, speech *Grammar systems:* etymology, orthography, phonology, prosody, semantics, syntax

grand *adj.* **1.** august, dignified, elevated, exalted, glorious, grave, illustrious, important, imposing, impressive, influential, lofty, lordly, magnificent, majestic, mighty, monumental, noble, princely, regal, serious, significant, solemn, splendid, stately, striking, sublime, weighty *Antonyms:* base, common, everyday, insignificant, minor, trivial **2.** chief, head, highest, leading, main, preeminent, principal, supreme **3.** haughty, ostentatious, pompous, pretentious, showy *Antonyms:* humble, modest, simple **4.** ambitious, big, brave, enterprising, grandiose, large, risky **5.** all-encompassing, comprehensive, general, inclusive, sweeping *Antonyms:* limited, specific **6.** excellent, fine, first-class *or* first-rate, great, marvellous, outstanding, sterling, stupendous, superb, terrific, wonderful *Nonformal:* five-star, smashing *Antonyms:* dreadful, horrific **7.** classy, gorgeous, luxurious, opulent, palatial, rich, sumptuous *Nonformal:* posh, ritzy

grandeur *n.* **1.** gravity, importance, influence, significance, solemnity, weight **2.** augustness, celebrity, dignity, distinction, elevation, eminence, fame, glory, grandiosity, loftiness, magnificence, majesty, nobility, preeminence, stateliness, sublimity **3.** beauty, brilliance, fineness, handsomeness, impressiveness, luxuriousness, opulence, richness, splendour, sumptuousness, transcendency *Antonyms:* shabbiness, wretchedness **4.** ceremony, glitter, pomp, showiness, theatrics **5.** amplitude, breadth, expansiveness, extent, greatness, immensity, vastness

grandiloquent *adj.* bombastic, flatulent, flowery, high-flown, inflated, magniloquent, overblown, pompous, pretentious, purple, rhetorical, swollen, turgid *Antonyms:* pithy, temperate, understated

grandiose *adj.* affected, bombastic, extravagant, flamboyant, lofty, ostentatious, pompous, pretentious, showy, splashy, theatrical *Antonyms:* humble, modest, simple, small, unpretentious

grant *n.* **1.** allotment, assistance, award, benefaction, bequest, boon, bounty, charity, contribution, donation, endowment, gift, gratuity, handout, honourarium, stipend, subsidy **2.** admission, allowance, authorization, concession, consent, liberty, licence, privledge, sanction, warrant – *v.* **1.** allocate, allot, award, bestow, cede, give, impart, permit, present, yield **2.** accede to, accord, acknowledge, admit, agree to, allow, assign, concede

granule *n.* crumb, grain, kernel, mite, particle, pellet, seed, smidgen *(Nonformal)*, speck

grape *n.* berry, vine fruit *Common varieties of grape:* Cabernet Sauvignon, Carignar, Chardonnay, Concord, Grenache, Merlot, Pinefura, Pinot Noir, Riesling, Rkatsiteli, Sauvignon Blanc, Sémillon, Shiraz, Trebbiano *General Varieties:* blanc *(White)*, gris *(Red-pink)*, jaune *(Yellow)*, noir *(Black)*, rose *(Pink)*, rouge *(Red)*, vert *(Green)*

graph *n.* aid, chart, diagram, embellishment, representation, tool *Kinds of graph:* area, bar, column, line, pie, radar, scatter

graphic *adj.* **1.** clear, cogent, colourful, compelling, concrete, convincing, definite, descriptive, distinct, explicit, expressive, lively, lucid, precise, realistic, specific, striking, telling, unequivocal, vivid *Antonyms:* imprecise, vague, woolly **2.** delineated, depicted, descriptive, diagrammatic, engraved, etched, iconographic, illustrated, illustrative, outlined, painted, photographic, pictorial, pictured, portrayed, representational, sketched, traced, visible, visual

graphics *n. pl.* graphic arts, printmaking *Kinds of graphics:* block prints, computer, engraving, etching, lithography, silkscreen printing, silverpoint, stained glass, woodcuts

grapple *v.* **1.** catch, clutch, grab, grasp, grip, hold, hook, seize **2.** attack, battle, combat, confront, encounter, engage, face, fight, scuffle, struggle, tussle, wrestle

grasp *n.* **1.** cinch, clamp, clasp, clench, clinch, embrace, ensnare, glom onto *(Nonformal)*, hold, hug **2.** comprehension, knowledge, mastery, understanding **3.** care, control, domination, government, hand, hold, jurisdiction, ownership, possession – *v.* **1.** comprehend, envisage, fathom, follow, know, learn, master, perceive, pick up, realize, see, take in, understand **2.** accept, acknowledge, appreciate, recognize **3.** apprehend, bag *(Nonformal)*, catch, clasp, clinch, clutch, collar, embrace, enclose, grab, grapple, grip, hold, hook, palm, seize, snatch, take *Antonyms:* free, let go, release

grasping *adj.* acquisitive, avaricious, grabby *(Nonformal)*, greedy, predatory, rapacious, usurious, voracious *Antonyms:* altruistic, generous, giving

grass *n.* greenery, ground cover, herbage, lawn, yard *Kinds of grass:* alfalfa, bamboo, beach, bent, Bermuda, bluegrass, buffalo, bunch, Canada bluegrass, clover, fescue, hay, lemon, marsh hay, red clover, rice, rye, sedge, silage, sparrow, wild oats, wild rice

grassland *n.* downs, grazing land, greenbelt, meadow, park, parkette, parkland, pasturage, pasture, plain, prairie, range, savannah, steppe, veldt

grassroots *adj.* **1.** bottom-up, communal, democratic, everyday, folk, local, native, neighbourhood, ordinary, popular, rural **2.** basic, common-sense, down-to-earth, earthy, fundamental, practical, sensible, simple, sound – *n.* **1.** body politic, citizenry, community, electorate, middle *or* working class people, public, rank and file, taxpayers, the people, voters **2.** basis, foundation, fountainhead, home, origin, wellspring

grate *n.* **1.** bars, framework, lattice, screen, slats, trellis **2.** fireside, hearth, inglenook – *v.* **1.** abrade, bark, erode, file, grind, rasp, rub, scrape, shred, strip, tear, wear **2.** aggravate, annoy, harass, irk, irritate, nettle, rankle, roil *Nonformal:* hassle, tick-off *Antonyms:* calm, quiet, settle **3.** creak, scratch, scroop, shrill, squeak

grateful *adj.* **1.** appreciative, indebted, much obliged, thankful *Antonyms:* disregardful, heedless **2.** agreeable, delightful, happy, pleasant, pleasing, soothing, welcome *Antonyms:* miserable, odious, undesired

gratification *n.* delight, enjoyment, fulfillment, happiness, indulgence, kicks *(Nonformal)*, joy, pleasure, recompense, relish, reward, satisfaction *Antonyms:* disappointment, pain, sadness, sorrow

gratify *v.* appease, content, delight, enchant, favour, fulfill, hit the spot *(Nonformal)*, humour, indulge, oblige, please, requite, satisfy *Antonyms:* disappoint, offend, pain, sadden

grating *adj.* **1.** annoying, bothersome, disagreeable, displeasing, irksome, irritating, offensive, unpleasant, vexatious *Antonyms:* agreeable, calming, pleasant **2.** discordant, grinding, harsh-sounding, hoarse, jarring, rasping, scraping, shrill, squeaky, strident, stridulous *Antonyms:* dulcet, mellifluous, melodic, musical, soft – *n.* bars, cover, grate, lattice, partition, screen, slats

gratitude *n.* acknowledgment, appreciation, appreciativeness, gratefulness, indebtedness, obligation, praise, recognition, requital, responsiveness, thankfulness, thanksgiving

gratuitous *adj.* **1.** baseless, causeless, groundless, indefensible, needless, nonessential, out of the blue *(Nonformal)*, reasonless, supererogatory, superfluous, uncalled-for, unfounded, unjustified, unmerited, unnecessary, unprovoked, unsupportable, unwarranted *Antonyms:* deserved, earned, expected, justifiable **2.** complimentary, free, gifted, gratis, no charge, token

gratuity *n.* benefaction, bonus, boon, bounty, contribution, donation, fringe benefit, gift, largesse, offering, perk, perquisite, *pourboire (French)*, present, recompense, reward, salve, sweetener, tip, token

grave *adj.* **1.** acute, consequential, critical, crucial, dire, exigent, heavy, important, major, momentous, pressing, serious, severe, significant, urgent, vital, weighty *Antonyms:* minor, trifling, trivial **2.** dangerous, deadly, destructive, grievous, hazardous, life or death, ominous, perilous, threatening **3.** dignified, dour, earnest, grim, leaden, no-nonsense, sedate, serious, sober, solemn, staid, strictly business *(Nonformal)*, unsmiling *Antonyms:* facetious, foolish, frivolous **4.** dull, funereal, long-faced, muted, quiet, sarcophagus, sombre, subdued *Antonyms:* celebratory, effervescent, jocular – *n.* burial, catacomb, crypt, mausoleum, ossuary, resting place, sepulchre, shrine, tomb, vault

gravelly *adj.* **1.** broken, bumpy, open-metal *(New Zealand)*, pebbly, rocky, rough, stony, unpaved **2.** croaking, harsh, hoarse, rasping, throaty, whisky *(Nonformal) Antonyms:* silky, smooth

graveyard *n.* bone factory *(Nonformal)*, burial ground, cemetery, charnel house, God's acre, memorial park, necropolis

gravitate *v.* **1.** draw *or* drift *or* head *or* lean *or* move *or* swing toward, point, turn **2.** decline, descend, drop, fall, lower, sink

gravity *n.* **1.** force, gravitation, heaviness, pull, pressure, weight **2.** consequence, importance, momentousness, significance, solemnity, weightiness *Antonyms:* insignificance, irrelevance **3.** acuteness, concern, exigency, seriousness, severity, urgency **4.** dignity, reserve, sedateness, sobriety, solemnity

graze *v.* **1.** eat, feed, forage, nourish, pasture **2.** bounce *or* brush off, contact, deflect, glance, reflect, skim, skip, touch **3.** abrade, blemish, cut, injure, mar, score, scrape, wound

grease *n.* bacon fat, butter, drippings, fat, lard, lubrication, oil, ointment, tallow, unction – *v.* anoint, butter, daub, dress, lard, lubricate, oil, slick, smear

greasy *adj.* **1.** fatty, greased, lubricated, oily, salved, slick, slimy, slithery, smeared, swabbed **2.** flattering, slippery, smarmy *(Nonformal)*, smooth, sneaky, unctuous

great *adj.* **1.** abundant, ample, big, bulky, colossal, considerable, enormous, excessive, extended, extensive, fat, gigantic, huge, husky, immense, jumbo *(Nonformal)*, large, lengthy, long, mammoth, oversize, prodigious, prolonged, pronounced, protracted, stupendous, titanic, towering, tremendous, vast, voluminous *Antonyms:* diminutive, meagre, small, tiny **2.** adept, consummate, deft, exceptional, expert, fine, first-rate, gifted, masterly, proficient, skilled, wonderful *Nonformal:* crack, major-league *Antonyms:* incompetent, unqualified, unskilled **3.** admirable, best, dynamite, excellent, fine, impressive, marvellous, outstanding, perfect, positive, remarkable, superlative, terrific, transcendent *Nonformal:* dynamite, number one *Antonyms:* bad, base, disgusting, horrible **4.** august, capital, chief, commanding, grand, heroic, honourable, lofty, lordly, noble, paramount, primary, princely, regal, royal, stately, sublime, superior *Antonyms:* ignoble, inconsequential, inferior **5.** celebrated, distinguished, eminent, exalted, famed, famous, glorious, highly-regarded, illustrious, leading, notable, noted, noteworthy, prominent, renowned, star **6.** basic, cardinal, essential, important, main, major, needed, principal, required, significant, singular, vital

greatly *adv.* abundantly, considerably, conspicuously, eminently, emphatically, enormously, exceedingly, exceptionally, extremely, famously, highly, hugely, immeasurably, immensely, incalculably, incomparably, incredibly, infinitely, inimitably, intensely, largely, markedly, mightily, most, much, notably, powerfully, remarkably, strikingly, superlatively, supremely, surpassingly, tremendously, vastly, very much *or* well

greatness *n.* **1.** abundance, amplitude, bulk, enormity, largeness, length, magnitude, mass, prodigiousness, size, smallness, vastness, weight *Antonyms:* littleness, narrowness **2.** celebrity, distinction, glory, illustriousness, note, place, position, prominence, renown, stature **3.** altruism, benevolence, generosity, idealism, liberality, magnanimity, morality *Antonyms:* avarice, parsimoniousness, prejudice **4.** brawn, energy, might, potency, power, strength *Antonyms:* impotence, weakness **5.** consequence, importance, merit, significance, weightiness **6.** dignity, eminence, grandeur, loftiness, majesty, nobility, stateliness, sublimity

greed *n.* acquisitiveness, avarice, covetousness, craving, desire, eagerness, excess, graspingness, hunger, indulgence, insatiability, longing, mammon, ravenousness, selfishness, voracity *Antonyms:* altruism, benevolence, generosity, munificence

greedy *adj.* **1.** avaricious, avid, covetous, desirous, eager, grasping, impatient, rapacious *Antonyms:* content, happy, satisfied **2.** craving, gluttonous, hungry, insatiate, voracious *Antonyms:* full, gratified, satisfied, surfeited **3.** close, close-fisted, grudging, miserly, parsimonious, penny-pinching, penurious, selfish, stingy, tight-fisted *Antonyms:* altruistic, benevolent, generous

green *adj.* **1.** fecund, flourishing, lush, luxuriant, verdant, vibrant, vigorous, vital *Antonyms:* desiccated, parched, withered **2.** immature, incomplete, unripe, unseasoned *Antonyms:* developed, mature, ready, vine-ripened **3.** amateur, apprentice, inexperienced, juvenile, new, novice, sophomoric, unfledged *Antonyms:* experienced, polished **4.** artless, credulous, gullible, ingenuous, innocent, naive, simple, unsophisticated *Antonyms:* knowing, sharp, wily **5.** hungover, pale, queasy, seasick, sickly, unhealthy, wan, woozy *Antonyms:* fit, hale, hardy **6.** all-natural, fresh, raw, unadulterated, unprocessed, untreated **7.** conservationist, ecological, environmental, preserving – *n.* **1.** blue-yellow, colour *Green shades:* apple, aquamarine, chartreuse, emerald, hunter, forest, grass, jade, kelly, lime, malachite, moss, olive, pea-green, pine, sage, sea, spinach, verdigris, viridian, willow-green **2.** common, garden, grass, greenbelt, greenlawn, lea, meadow, park, parkette, pasture, plot, space, steppe, turf, valley, veldt, yard **3.** fibre, legume, plant, salad, vegetable *Nonformal:* rabbit food, veggies **4.** hole, putting surface, short grass *Nonformal:* dance floor, inside the flag, table

greenery *n.* **1.** foliage, foliation, herbage, leafage, leaves, plants, vegetation, verdure **2.** arbour, gazebo, greenhouse, hothouse, solarium

greet *v.* **1.** accost, acknowledge, address, approach, attend, bow, call to, compliment, curtsy, embrace, exchange, flag, hail, herald, meet, nod, pay respects, receive, recognize, salute, say hello, shake hands, usher in, welcome, whistle **2.** bewail, cry, mourn, weep

greeting *n.* **1.** embrace, hail, handshake, hello, howdydoo *(Nonformal)*, hug, kiss, reception, recognition, regards, salaam, salutation, salute, welcome **2.** card, e-mail, epistle, fax, letter, message, note, postcard

gregarious *adj.* affable, clubby *(Nonformal)*, companionable, convivial, cordial, extroverted, friendly, fun, outgoing, sociable, social *Antonyms:* antisocial, misanthropic, reserved, solitary, standoffish, withdrawn

grey *adj.* cloudy, dark, dismal, gloomy, miserable, overcast, sombre – *n.* colour, *gris (French) Grey shades:* ash, cement, cloud, dove, heather, oyster, peppery-grey, pewter, silver, slate, smoke

grief *n.* **1.** affliction, agony, anguish, bemoaning, bereavement, bewailing, dejection, depression, desolation, despair, despondency, discomfort, disquiet, distress, dolour, gloom, heartache, heartbreak, infelicity, lamentation, malaise, melancholy, misery, mortification, mournfulness, mourning, pain, regret, remorse, rue, sadness, sorrow, suffering, torture, trial, tribulation, trouble, *tsures (Yiddish)*, unhappiness, upset, woe, worry *Antonyms:* cheer, delight, happiness, joy, jubilation **2.** annoyance, bother, grievance, harassment, hassle *(Nonformal)*, problem, vexation,

grievance *n.* **1.** allegation, charge, complaint, gripe, jeremiad, objection, problem, *Nonformal:* beef, bellyache, stink **2.** affliction, injury, injustice, wrong **3.** distress, grief, hardship, misery, pain, resentment sorrow, trial, tribulation, trouble, unhappiness

grieve *v.* **1.** ache, bemoan, bewail, cry, deplore, keen, lament, mourn, regret, rue, sorrow, suffer, wail, weep **2.** distress, inflict, injure, pain, sadden, slight, trouble, upset *Antonyms:* cheer, comfort, console, ease, gladden

grievous *adj.* **1.** appalling, atrocious, deplorable, earthshattering, egregious, flagrant, glaring, grave, heavy, heinous, intolerable, monstrous, offensive, outrageous, serious, shameful, villainous *Antonyms:* benign, light, trivial **2.** dire, dismal, disquieting, distressing, disturbing, dreadful, heart-rending, lamentable, mournful, pathetic, pitiful, sad, sorrowful, tragic, upsetting *Antonyms:* heart-warming, uplifting **3.** afflicting, agonizing, calamitous, damaging, harmful, hurtful, injurious, oppressive, taxing, tough, troublesome, unbearable, wounding *Antonyms:* healing, palliative, soothing

grill *v.* **1.** barbecue, broil, cook, griddle, rotisserie **2.** cross-examine, drill, interrogate, interview, query, question **3.** abuse, blast, harass, harry, hector, lambaste, punish, ream out *(Nonformal)*, reprimand, scold, skivver *(Maritimes)*

grim *adj.* **1.** cruel, ferocious, formidable, hardhearted, ruthless, truculent, vicious *Antonyms:* kind, lenient, sympathetic **2.** deleterious, destructive, fatal, fierce, harmful, mortal, savage *Antonyms:* beneficial, benign, healthful **3.** intractable, merciless, relentless, severe, uncompromising, unsparing, unyielding *Antonyms:* coldhearted, compassionate, humane, merciful **4.** dreadful, frightful, ghastly, grisly, hideous, horrible, repellent, terrifying *Antonyms:* charming, delightful, lovely **5.** agonizing, arduous, harrowing, joyless, painful, pleasureless, tortuous, wretched *Antonyms:* delightful, easy, simple **6.** morose, sad, scowling, sombre, sour, surly, unhappy *Antonyms:* happy, joyous, jubilant **7.** bleak, dark, foreboding, funeral, gloomy, ominous, sinister, threatening *Antonyms:* auspicious, bright, propitious, sunny

grimace *n.* frown, moue, mug, scowl, smirk, sneer, wry face – *v.* contort, deform, distort, frown, mouth, mug, scowl, sneer

grime *n.* clobber *(Maritimes)*, crud *(Nonformal)*, dirt, dust, filth, mire, mud, rust, scum, slime, smut, soot – *v.* befoul, contaminate, dirty, mess up, muddy, stain, sully, tarnish

grimy *adj.* begrimed, besmirched, cruddy *(Nonformal)*, dingy, dirty, filthy, foul, grubby, grungy, messy, mucky, nasty, smeared, soiled, sooty, sordid, squalid, unclean *Antonyms:* clean, glittering, sparkling

grind *n.* **1.** chore, drudgery, employment, industry, job, labour, moil, rat race *(Nonformal)*, routine, struggle, sweat, task, toil, treadmill, work, workload **2.** clangour, jangle, rasp, scrape, scratch, screech, twang **3.** disintegration, filing, grating, milling, pounding, pulverizing, rasping, sanding, scraping, stoning, whetting – *v.* **1.** abrade, chew, crush, file, grate, pulverize, scrape, wear down **2.** hone, polish, sand, sharpen, taper, whet **3.** harass, hound, irritate, oppress, pain, plague, tax, torment, torture **4.** endeavour, exert oneself, labour, sweat, toil, try, work **5.** apply oneself, learn, master, memorize, study *Nonformal:* hit the books, pull an all-nighter

grip *n.* **1.** brace, cinch, clamp, clasp, clench, clutch, embrace, fastening, grapple, grasp, handshake, hold, hook, purchase, snatch **2.** authority, control, custody, direction, domination, influence, management, mastery, possession, power, rule, subjection, supervision, sway, thumb *(Nonformal)* **3.** acumen, comprehension, handle, ken, knowledge, perception, understanding *Nonformal:* know-how, savvy **4.** backpack, bag, knapsack, purse, suitcase, valise **5.** gaffer, gofer *(Nonformal)*, handyman *or* handywoman, key grip, sceneman *or* scenewoman, stagehand – *v.* **1.** clasp, clutch, glom *(Nonformal)*, grasp, hold, seize, snag, snatch, take **2.** capture, delight, engross, enthral, entrance, fascinate, hold, hypnotize, interest, involve, mesmerize, rivet, spellbind

gripe *n.* affliction, complaint, concern, criticism, grievance, grumble, lament, objection, problem, worry *Nonformal:* beef, headache – *v.* **1.** complain, disapprove, groan, grouch, grumble, moan, mutter, protest, whimper, whine *Nonformal:* beef, bellyache, bitch, carp, crab, grouse, yammer **2.** anger, annoy, bother, disturb, irritate, nag, pain, vex **3.** ache, afflict, cramp, hurt, pinch, press, squeeze

gripping *adj.* compelling, exciting, fascinating, fixating, fixing, holding, hypnotizing, interesting, involving, mesmerizing, obsessing, page-turning, riveting, spellbinding *Antonyms:* burning, dull, soporific

grisly *adj.* **1.** appalling, awful, chilling, disgusting, dreadful, eerie, frightful, ghastly, gory, grim, gross, grotesque, gruesome, hideous, horrible, horrific, horrifying, lurid, macabre, nauseating, shocking, sick, sickening, terrible *Antonyms:* agreeable, attractive, charming, innocuous, pleasant **2.** dangerous, dire, forbidding, foreboding, intimidating, menacing, ominous, sinister, threatening, scary *(Nonformal)*, terrifying, terrorizing *Antonyms:* benign, harmless, safe

grit *n.* **1.** coarseness, grain, gravel, particles, powder, pumice, sand, sandstone, soot, stone **2.** backbone, bravery, courage, determination, endurance, fearlessness, fortitude, intrepidity, marrow, mettle, nerve, perseverance, pluck, spirit, stamina, temerity, valour, will power *Nonformal:* chutzpah, guts, moxie, spunk, starch *Antonyms:* fear, hesitation, timidity

gritty *adj.* **1.** abrasive, crumbly, grainy, granular, gravelly, lumpy, rough, sandy, scratchy, stony *Antonyms:* creamy, smooth, velvety **2.** courageous, dauntless, determined, dogged, flinty, game, plucky, relentless, single-minded, spirited, staunch, stouthearted, tenacious, tough, unfaltering *Nonformal:* ballsy, feisty, gutsy, nervy *Antonyms:* reserved, shy, timid

groan *n.* complaint, cry, fuss, gripe, grievance, grouse, grumble, grunt, moan, objection, sigh, whine *Nonformal:* beef, kvetch – *v.* bemoan, complain, cry, fret, lament, moan, object, whine, worry

grocery *n.* convenience *or* corner store, greengrocer, groceteria, market, merchant store, supermarket, superstore

groggy *adj.* **1.** befuddled, dazed, dizzy, exhausted, foggy, fuzzy, half-asleep, hazy, muddled, out of it *(Nonformal)*, punch drunk, puzzled, sleepy, staggering, stunned, stupefied, tired *Antonyms:* aware, clear, lucid **2.** drunk, giddy, inebriated, intoxicated, punchy, reeling, woozy *Nonformal:* boozed, disguised, doped, high, hopped up loaded, pie-eyed, plastered, slap-happy *Antonyms:* clean, sober, straight

groom *n.* **1.** benedict, bridegroom, fiancé, husband, spouse, suitor **2.** equestrian, hostler, stablehand – *v.* **1.** brush, clean, curry, dress, neaten, preen, pretty *or* gussy up *(Nonformal)*, prim, primp, refresh, tend, tidy **2.** initiate, prep, prepare, prime, ready, shape, show one the ropes *(Nonformal)*, touch, train

groove *n.* **1.** canal, channel, corrugation, crease, depression, ditch, flute, furrow, gouge, hollow, incision, indentation, notch, rabbet, rut, score, slit, slot, sluice, trench, valley **2.** conduct, custom, habit, manner, pace, rote, routine, tradition, way **3.** beat, feel, flow, pattern, pulse, rhythm, tempo

groovy *adj.* **1.** amusing, enjoyable, entertaining, excellent, exciting, fun, great, hilarious *Nonformal:* crazy, far out, kooky, wild **2.** danceable, flowing, funky, melodic, rhythmic *Nonformal:* cool, phat, trippy **3.** chi-chi, current, fashionable, in vogue, modern, popular, stylish, trendy *Nonformal:* hip, hot, swank, tony, with it

grope *n.* contact, feel, impingement, infringement, squeeze, touch, trespass, unwanted advance, violation – *v.* **1.** cast about, explore, feel for, flounder, fumble, pry, root, rummage, search, seek **2.** examine, fondle, grab, handle, molest, squeeze *Nonformal:* cop a feel, goose

gross *adj.* **1.** aggregate, all, before returns, entire, pre-tax, pre-expense, outright, total, whole *Antonyms:* net, partial, take-home **2.** arrent, awful, blatant, egregious, flagrant, heinous, outrageous, rank, shameful, shocking **3.** absolute, capital, complete, downright, excessive, exorbitant, extreme, glaring, immoderate, inordinate, manifest, obvious, out-and-out *(Nonformal)*, unmitigated, unqualified, utter **4.** boorish, carnal, coarse, corporeal, crass, crude, fleshly, foul, ignorant, improper, impure, indecent, indelicate, inelegant, insensitive, lewd, low-minded, obscene, offensive, rank, raunchy, raw, ribald, rough, rude, scatological, smutty, tasteless, uncouth, unseemly, vulgar, yukky *(Nonformal)* *Antonyms:* cultivated, decent, delicate, proper, refined **5.** big, bulky, corpulent, dense, fat, fleshy, great, heavy, hulking, large, massive, obese, overweight, portly, stout, thick, unwieldy, weighty – *n.* aggregate, all, bulk, entirety, mass, sum, total, total, totality, whole, whole enchilada *or* shebang *(Nonformal)* – *v.* bag *(Nonformal)*, bring *or* reel in, clear, earn, get, make, profit, realize, receive, take, yield

grotesque *adj.* aberrant, abnormal, absurd, bizarre, deformed, distorted, eerie, extravagant, fanciful, fantastic, flamboyant, freakish, incongruous, ludicrous, malformed, misshapen, monstrous, odd, outlandish, perverted, preposterous, queer, ridiculous, strange, surreal, ugly, uncanny, unnatural, weird *Antonyms:* average, everyday, natural, normal, realistic

grotto *n.* **1.** burrow, catacomb, cave, cavern, cavity, cove, hollow, nook, recess **2.** alcove, asylum, corner, cover, cubbyhole, haven, hermitage, hideaway, mew, niche, refuge, resort, retreat, sanctuary, shelter

grouch *n.* bear, complainer, crank, curmudgeon, faultfinder, grumbler, malcontent, whiner *Nonformal:* grump, sorehead, sourpuss, wet blanket – *v.* complain, fret, fuss, gripe, groan, grumble, mope, mutter, sulk *Nonformal:* belly-ache, bitch, grouse

grouchy *adj.* argumentative, cantankerous, complaining, cranky, cross, crusty, discontented, grumbling, grumpy, ill-tempered, irascible, irritable, owly *(P.E.I.)*, peevish, petulant, querulous, snappy, sulky, surly, testy *Nonformal:* chippy, pissy *Antonyms:* even-tempered, good-humoured, gracious

ground *n.* **1.** dirt, dust, earth, field, land, loam, sand, sod, soil, terra firma, terrain, turf **2.** fodder *(Nonformal)*, grist, matter, subject, theme, topic **3.** basis, cause, foundation, motive, occasion, rationale, reason, source – *v.* **1.** beach, dock, floor, land, strand **2.** educate, enlighten, groom, illuminate, initiate, shape, teach, train, tutor **3.** bar, circumscribe, confine, detain, hog-tie *(Nonformal)*, limit, prevent, prohibit, restrict, tether, tie

groundless *adj.* bankrupt, baseless, cockamamie *(Nonformal)*, empty, false, flimsy, gratuitous, illogical, illusory, imaginary, off-base, unfounded, unjustified, unproven, unsupported, untrue, unwarranted *Antonyms:* justified, logical, proven, reasonable, substantiated, supported

grounds *n. pl.* **1.** area, common, country, demesne, district, domain, environs, estate, fields, gardens, habitat, holding, land, lot, premises, property, real estate, realm, sphere, terrace, terrain, territory, tract, yard, zone **2.** base, basis, brass tacks *(Nonformal)*, cause, determinant, footing, foundation, motive, premise, proof, rationale, reason, root, seat, underpinning **3.** deposit, dregs, grout, leavings, lees, precipitate, precipitation, residue, sediment, settlings, slag

groundwork *n.* **1.** base, basis, caisson, footing, foundation, root, support **2.** ABC's *(Nonformal)*, background, conditioning, elementals, essentials, footwork, fundamentals, preliminaries, preparation, research

group *n.* **1.** accumulation, amount, assortment, batch, bunch, bundle, cluster, collection, combination, few, host, lot, number, quantity, total, sum **2.** affiliation, alliance, army, assemblage, assembly, association, auxiliary, band, bloc, body, branch, cartel, cast, circle, clan, class, clique, club, colony, community, company, conglomerate, congregation, corps, coterie, covey, crew, crowd, division, drove, faction, fellowship, fleet, gang, gathering, herd, league, lodge, mob, order, organization, pack, party, platoon, regiment, ring, school, scrum, sect, set, society, squad, swarm, syndicate, team, union, unit *See also:* **First Peoples** – *v.* **1.** assemble, associate, bunch, cluster, collect, congregate, consort, corral, crowd, fraternize, gather, huddle, link, muster, order, organize **2.** arrange, assort, bracket, categorize, class, classify, file, range, rank, sort, systematize

grouse *n.* bird, fowl, game – *v.* carp, carry on, caterwaul, complain, fret, fume, fuss, gripe, grouch, grumble, lament, moan, mutter, whimper, whine, yammer *Nonformal:* bellyache, bitch, kvetch

grovel *v.* **1.** beg, cater to, court, fawn, humble oneself, implore, kowtow, prostrate, toady, wheedle *Nonformal:* apple-polish bootlick, brown-nose, crawl, kiss ass *Antonyms:* defy, rebel, upset **2.** bask or delight *or* indulge in, flounder, revel, wallow, welter

grovelling *adj.* **1.** acquiescent, brown-nosing *(Nonformal)*, cowering, crawling creeping, deferential, fawning, humble kowtowing, obsequious, prostrate, servile slouching, spineless, submissive, sycophantic, toadying, unassertive *Antonyms:* disdainful, haughty, proud **2.** base, dirty grody *(Nonformal)*, gross, low, mean shabby, sordid, vile, wretched *Antonyms* elevated, grand, lofty

grow *v.* **1.** abound, advance, age, amplify augment, build, burgeon, develop, enlarge evolve, expand, extend, flourish, gain, get bigger *or* taller, heighten, increase, mature mount, multiply, ripen, shoot, spring up stretch, swell, thrive, wax *Antonyms* decline, diminish, dwindle, shrink, wane **2** arise, become, burst forth, derive, emanate germinate, originate, rise, spring, sprout **3** breed, crop, cultivate, farm, garden, plant propagate, raise, rear

growl *n.* **1.** complaint, grumble, a show of one's teeth, snarl, utterance, warning **2** boom, reverberation, roar, rumble, sound thunder – *v.* **1.** beef, bellyache *(Nonformal)*, complain, fret, fuss, gripe, grumble snarl **2.** boom, echo, murmur, reverberate roar, roll, rumble

growth *n.* **1.** addition, advance, amplification, augmentation, boom, broadening crescendo, enlargement, expansion, gain increase, magnification, multiplication, proliferation, prosperity, ripening, rise, stretching, sprouting, surge, unfolding, waxing widening **2.** advancement, cultivation, betterment, change, development, evolution learning, maturation, progress, uplifting **3** cancer, cyst, lump, malignancy, mole, neoplasm, sarcoma, swelling, tuber, tumour **4** bulge, bump, burl, knot, outgrowth **5** beginning, genesis, origin, root, source

grub *n.* **1.** comestibles, edibles, feed, fodder, food, nourishment, provisions rations, sustenance, viands, victuals *Nonformal:* chow, eats, muckamuck, nosh, vittles

2. beetle, bug, creepy-crawly *(Nonformal)*, larva, maggot – *v.* **1.** drudge, grind, labour, moil, plod, slave, slog, sweat, toil, work **2.** burrow, comb, delve, dig, forage, hunt, root, rummage, scour, search

rubby *adj.* dingy, dirty, filthy, foul, grimy, infested, mangy, messy, muddy, scuzzy *(Nonformal)*, shabby, shoddy, slatternly, sloppy, slovenly, soiled, sooty, squalid, ungroomed, unkempt, unwashed *Antonyms:* bathed, clean, disinfected, sanitized, tidy, washed

rudge *n.* animosity, animus, antipathy, aversion, bad blood, bitterness, dislike, enmity, envy, hate, ill will, jealousy, malice, peeve, pique, rancour, resentment, spitefulness *Antonyms:* appreciation, goodwill, liking, thankfulness – *v.* begrudge, covet, envy, mind, resent *Antonyms:* applaud, celebrate, welcome

ruelling *adj.* arduous, backbreaking, brutal, challenging, crushing, demanding, difficult, exacting, excruciating, exhausting, fatiguing, fierce, hard, harsh, herculean, laborious, nightmarish *(Nonformal)*, racking, severe, strenuous, taxing, torturous, troublesome, trying, wearying *Antonyms:* easy, enjoyable, pleasant, undemanding

ruesome *adj.* abominable, alarming, appalling, awful, chilling, creepy, eerie, fearful, frightful, ghastly, grim, grisly, gross, hair-raising, hideous, horrendous, horrible, horrid, horrifying, loathsome, lurid, macabre, monstrous, morbid, nightmarish, offensive, repugnant, repulsive, shocking, sick, terrible *Antonyms:* appealing, benign, cheerful, pleasant, sweet

ruff *adj.* **1.** cracked, croaking, croaky, grating, guttural, harsh, hoarse, husky, low, rasping, throaty, whisky *(Nonformal) Antonyms:* mellifluous, pleasant, sweet **2.** abrupt, blunt, brusque, cantankerous, churlish, crisp, crusty, curmudgeonly, curt, grouchy, insensitive, irritable, pointed, rough, rude, sharp, short, surly, tactless, testy, truculent *Nonformal:* grumpy, snippy *Antonyms:* civil, courteous, diplomatic

rumble *n.* **1.** carp, complaint, grievance, gripe, objection, protest *Nonformal:* bellyache, grouse, squawk, yammer **2.** echo, growl, growling, reverberation, roar, roll, rumble, thunder – *v.* **1.** bark, complain, mutter, object, whine **2.** bitch *(Nonformal)*, cavil, growl, grunt, gurgle, mumble, murmur, protest, roar, rumble

grumpy *adj.* bad-tempered, cantankerous, crabby, cranky, cross, crotchety, discontented, dour, grouchy, ill-tempered, irascible, irritable, moody, peckish *(British)*, peevish, prickly, quarrelsome, short-tempered, snippy *(Nonformal)*, sore, sour, sulky, sullen, surly, testy *Antonyms:* cheerful, happy, pleasant

guarantee *n.* **1.** agreement, assurance, certainty, charter, contract, covenant, handshake *(Nonformal)*, oath, pledge, promise, testament, vow, warrant, warranty, word **2.** bond, certificate, collateral, money, security, surety – *v.* affirm, answer for, assure, attest, back, certify, confirm, endorse, ensure, get *or* stand behind, insure, maintain, pledge, promise, protect, reassure, secure, support, swear, underwrite, vouch for, warrant

guaranteed *adj.* affirmed, approved, ascertained, assured, attested, backed, bonded, certain, certified, confirmed, endorsed, insured, pledged, plighted, protected, sealed, secured, sure, sure-fire, vested, warranted

guard *n.* **1.** attentiveness, care, carefulness, caution, guardedness, heed, prudence, vigilance, wariness, watchfulness **2.** armour, armament, buffer, bulwark, cowcatcher, defence, fortification, Palladium, protection, rampart, safeguard, screen, shield, stronghold **3.** beefeater *(British)*, bodyguard, bouncer, chaperon, convoy, custodian, duenna, escort, guardian, guardsman, jailer, keeper, pastillion, protector, sentinel, sentry, soldier, warden, warder, watchman – *v.* babysit, care for, chaperon, check, cover, defend, ensure, fend for, keep, look after, lookout for, maintain, mother, mind, observe, oversee, patrol, police, preserve, protect, ride shotgun, safeguard, save, screen, secure, shelter, shepherd, shield, supervise, sustain, tend, watch *Antonyms:* disregard, ignore, neglect

guarded *adj.* **1.** cagey, calculating, careful, cautious, chary, circumspect, diplomatic, discreet, gingerly, leery, noncommittal, prudent, reserved, restrained, reticent, safe, suspicious, vigilant, wary, watchful *Antonyms:* careless, heedless, hell-bent, reckless **2.** attended, controlled, defended, protected, safeguarded, shielded, supervised, tended, watched over *Antonyms:* ignored, neglected, overlooked

guardian *n.* attendant, babysitter, champion, conservationist, custodian, defender, escort, guard, keeper, nurse, officer, overseer, park warden, patrol, preserver, protector, safeguard, sentinel, shepherd, sitter, sponsor, superintendent, supervisor, trustee, vigilante, watchdog

guerrilla *adj.* camouflaged, jungle, military – *n.* combatant, counterrevolutionary, freedom fighter, insurgent, irregular, mercenary, partisan, rebel, resistance, revolutionary, saboteur, subversive, terrorist

guess *n.* assumption, belief, conclusion, conjecture, deduction, estimate, feeling, guesswork, hunch, hypothesis, inference, judgment, notion, opinion, postulation, prediction, presumption, reckoning, sneaking suspicion, speculation, supposition, surmisal, suspicion, theory, thesis, view *Nonformal:* ballpark figure, guesstimate, shot, stab *Antonyms:* certainty, fact – *v.* believe, calculate, chance, conjecture, deduce, deem, divine, estimate, fancy, fathom, figure, guesstimate *(Nonformal)*, hazard, hypothesize, imagine, infer, judge, opine, pick, predict, pretend, reason, reckon, select, speculate, suppose, surmise, suspect, theorize, think, venture

guest *adj.* celebrated, eminent, invited, outside, prestigious, prominent, special, stand-in, substitute – *n.* billeter, boarder, caller, commensal, companion, company, customer, fellow, frequenter, inmate *(Nonformal)*, lodger, mate, out-of-towner, patron, recipient, renter, roomer, sharer, sojourner, tenant, transient, visitant, visitor

guidance *n.* **1.** advice, auspices, counsel, counselling, direction, government, leadership, management, navigation, supervision, **2.** conduct, control, conveyance, help instruction, teaching, tutelage

guide *n.* **1.** attendant, captain, chaperon cicerone, conductor, coyote *(Nonformal)* director, escort, leader, pilot, *Sherpa (Tibetan)*, tour guide, usher **2.** advisor exemplar, example, guru, ideal, inspiration lead, master, mentor, model, paradigm pathfinder, pioneer, prototype, rock *(Nonformal)*, role model, standard, trailblazer **3.** beacon, clue, cynosure, fixed point landmark, lodestar, marker, north star point, pointer, sign, signal, signpost **4.** Baedeker, bible, catalogue, compendium directory, enchiridion, guidebook, handbook, information, instructions, key, manual, map, *vade mecum (Latin)* – *v.* **1.** captain, conduct, convoy, direct, lead, manoeuvre, marshal, navigate, route, show, steer **2.** accompany, attend, chaperone, escort shepherd, superintend, supervise **3.** control, govern, handle, influence, manage manipulate, mastermind, oversee, regulate sway **4.** advise, counsel, educate, groom inform, initiate, instruct, train, tutor

guideline *n.* **1.** bench mark, criterion cynosure, format, gauge, guide, index instruction, key, marker, maxim, measure pointer, prescription, reference point, regulation, rule, specification, standard, touchstone, yardstick **2.** borderline, boundary chalk *(Nonformal)*, confine, limit, margin outline, perimeter

guild *n.* association, brotherhood, club company, congregation, corporation, federation, fellowship, fraternity, group, hanse, league, lodge, order, organization, profession, sisterhood, society, sorority, trade league *or* union, union

guile *n.* artfulness, artifice, chicanery, cleverness, craftiness, cunning, deceit, deception, dirty dealing *(Nonformal)*, dishonesty, duplicity, knavery, ruse, shrewdness, slyness, treachery, trickery, wiliness *Antonyms:* candour, frankness, honesty, sincerity, truthfulness

guileless *adj.* aboveboard, artless, candid forthright, foursquare, frank, genuine, honest, innocent, naive, natural, open, simple sincere, straightforward, truthful, unaffect ed, unguarded, unsophisticated, unstudied *Antonyms:* affected, deceitful, designing, Machiavellian

guilt *n.* **1.** answerability, blameworthiness, censureability, culpability, liability, onus, responsibility, suability *Antonyms:* blamelessness, honour, innocence, virtue **2.** contrition, disgrace, embarrassment, guiltiness, penitence, regret, remorse, self-condemnation, shame **3.** crime, criminality, delinquency, dereliction, dishonour, error, failing, fault, indiscretion, iniquity, lapse, malfeasance, misbehaviour, misconduct, misstep, sin, slip, transgression, wrong

guiltless *adj.* blameless, chaste, clean, clear, crimeless, exemplary, faultless, good, immaculate, inculpable, innocent, irreproachable, pure, sinless, unsullied, untainted, untarnished, virtuous *Antonyms:* culpable, guilty, responsible

guilty *adj.* **1.** accusable, at fault, blameworthy, caught red-handed *(Nonformal)*, censurable, chargeable, criminal, culpable, delinquent, erring, fallen, felonious, liable, offending, responsible, wicked, wrong *Antonyms:* blameless, innocent, righteous, virtuous **2.** blamed, censured, condemned, convicted, damned, doomed, impeached, judged, proscribed, sentenced **3.** abashed, ashamed, compunctious, conscience-stricken, contrite, hangdog, regretful, remorseful, repentant, shamefaced, sheepish, sorry, uneasy *Antonyms:* brazen, belligerent, contentious

guise *n.* air, appearance, aspect, behaviour, cloak, demeanour, disguise, façade, face, front, mask, mien, persona, posture, pretence, role, semblance, show

guitar *n.* axe *(Nonformal)*, instrument *Kinds of guitar and plucked stringed instrument:* acoustic, balalaika, banjo, bass, bazouki, classical, concert, Dobro, double bass, electric, fretless, Hawaiian, lap *or* pedal steel, lute, mandolin, semi-acoustic, sitar, Spanish, steel, tenor guitar, 12-string, ukulele *Trademark guitars:* Charvel, Epiphone, Fender, Gibson, Gretsch, Guild, Ibanez, Les Paul, Rickenbacker, Seagull, Stratocaster, Takamine, Telecaster, Vox, Washburn *See also:* **instrument**

gulch *n.* basin, crevice, ditch, fissure, gorge, gully, gut *(British Columbia)*, passage, passageway, ravine, valley *Prairies:* coulee, dry wash, wadi

gulf *n.* **1.** abyss, break, canyon, chasm, cleft, crack, gorge, gulch, gully, opening, pit **2.** disparity, division, estrangement, gap, inequality, rift, schism, separation, space **3.** basin, bay, cove, firth, harbour, lagoon, loch, sound

gullible *adj.* believing, credulous, easy, green *(Nonformal)*, innocent, naive, trusting, unsuspecting, wide-eyed *Antonyms:* cynical, jaded, suspicious, worldly

gully *n.* canyon, channel, ditch, gorge, gulch, ravine, valley

gulp *n.* chug, draught, gasp, mouthful, swallow, swig – *v.* **1.** belt, bolt, choke down, consume, cram, devour, dispatch, dispose, drink, eat, gobble, guzzle, imbibe, pour, quaff, slop, slosh, stuff, swallow, swig, swill, take in, wolf *or* wolf down *Nonformal:* chug-a-lug, inhale, knock back, scarf down, toss down *or* off **2.** bridle, gasp, hold back, muzzle, smother, stifle, strangle, suppress

gum *n.* **1.** adhesive, cement, elastic, epoxy, glue, mucilage, paste, pine gum, pitch, resin, rubber, tar **2.** bubblegum, chewing gum, stick *(Nonformal)* – *v.* adhere, attach, connect, fix, glue, paste, plaster, stick

gumption *n.* **1.** ambition, courage, daring, drive, élan, energy, enterprise, hustle, initiative, nerve, pluck, spirit, verve, zeal *Nonformal:* chutzpah, get-up-and-go, guts, jam, moxie, spunk, zip **2.** acumen, astuteness, brains, cleverness, common sense, cunning, guile, intelligence, shrewdness, slyness, subtlety, wisdom *Nonformal:* savvy, smarts

gun *n.* **1.** cannon, firearm, pistol, machine gun, revolver, rifle, shotgun, weapon *Nonformal:* piece, Saturday night special **2.** detonation, discharge, ejection, gunfire, salute, shot, signal **3.** artillery man *or* woman, assassin, gunman, gunwoman, gunner, hired gun, marksman, markswoman, mercenary, rifleman, riflewoman, sharpshooter, shooter, sniper – *v.* **1.** assassinate, damage, fell, fire on, injure, harm, hit, hurt, kill, liquidate, murder, shoot, wound *Nonformal:* bump off, hit **2.** hunt, pursue, seek, track

guru *n.* advisor, authority, guide, guiding light, inspiration, kahuna, leader, maharishi, master, mentor, priest, rabbi, sage, sensei, swami, teacher, tutor, wiseperson

gush *n.* **1.** blast, cascade, deluge, flood, flow, flux, jet, pouring, rush, spate, spray, stream, surge, tide, torrent, wall, wave **2.** Cheltenham tragedy *(British)*, effusion, emotionalism, eruption, excess, fit, histrionics, outburst, outpouring, profusiveness *Antonyms:* calm, indifference, repression – *v.* **1.** cascade, course, flood, flow, flush, issue, jet, overflow, pour, run, rush, stream, surge, swamp, swell, teem, tide *Antonyms:* dribble, drip, trickle **2.** effervesce, emote, enthuse, exaggerate, rhapsodize, sentimentalize *Nonformal:* ooze, rave, slobber

gushy *adj.* demonstrative, effusive, emotional, gushy, maudlin, mawkish, melodramatic, sentimental *Nonformal:* chintzy, Hollywood, mushy, sappy

gust *n.* blast, blow, breeze, burst, eruption, explosion, fit, flurry, gale, outburst, puff, rush, squall, storm, surge, wind

gusto *n.* **1.** ardour, brio, delight, élan, emotion, enthusiasm, exhilaration, feeling, fervour, heart, passion, verve, zeal **2.** appetite, appreciation, delectation, enjoyment, liking, palate, pleasure, preference, relish, savour, taste, zest

gut *adj.* **1.** basic, emotional, fundamental, immediate, innate, instinctive, intuitive, involuntary, knee-jerk, natural, reflexive, spontaneous, uncalculated, unconscious, unthinking, visceral **2.** breezy, cushy *(Nonformal)*, easy, painless, simple, straightforward, uncomplicated – *n.* **1.** abdomen, belly, bowel, bulge, entrails, innards, intestine, midriff, paunch, stomach, viscera *Nonformal:* beerbelly, breadbasket, Molson muscle, pot, tummy **2.** dell, gorge, gully, isthmus, narrows, passage, passageway, ravine, strait – *v.* **1.** clean, disembowel, draw, empty, eviscerate **2.** clean out, loot, plunder, ransack, ravage, sack, strip

gutless *adj.* abject, afraid, cowardly craven, fainthearted, fearful, feeble, irresolute, spineless, submissive, timid, weak *Nonformal:* chicken, lily-livered, sucky, yellow *Antonyms:* bold, determined, intrepid, resolute

guts *n.* **1.** backbone, courage, fearlessness, fortitude, grit, heart, kick, mettle, pith, pluck, spirit, stamina, vigour, zeal, zest *Nonformal:* cheek, chutzpah, feistiness, jam, moxie, spunk, zip **2.** arrogance, gall, impudence, impertinence **3.** elements, essence, gist, matter, meat, nitty-gritty *(Nonformal)*, nub, nucleus **4.** components, contents, core, ingredients, innards, insides, organs, workings

gutsy *adj.* bodacious, bold, courageous, daring, fearless, heroic, intrepid, lionhearted, plucky, spirited, strong *Nonformal:* feisty, spunky *Antonyms:* afraid, shy, timid

gutter *n.* canal, channel, ditch, eavestrough, furrow, groove, sewer, trench, trough, watercourse

guttural *adj.* deep, glottal, gravelly, growling, gruff, harsh, hoarse, husky, inarticulate, low, rasping, rough, sepulchral, thick, throaty, whisky-voiced

guy *n.* bloke, chap, fellow, *gars (French)*, gentleman, lad, male, man, youth *Nonformal:* ace, big guy, bonhomme, boss, buddy, captain, cat, chief, dad, dude, fella, friend, governor *(British)*, homey, Jack, Joe, Mac, mate, pal

guzzle *v.* bolt, consume, devour, drain, drink, empty, gulp, quaff, swig *Nonformal:* chug, inhale, knock back, swill

gymnasium *n.* amphitheatre, arena, athletic club, bath, coliseum, exercise room, fitness centre, gym, health club, hippodrome, pit, recreation centre, ring, rink, school, spa, stadium, theatre

gymnastics *n. pl.* acrobatic exercise *Kinds of gymnastics:* balance beam, balls, floor exercises, hoops, horizontal bar, parallel bars, pommel horse, power vaulting, rhythmics, ribbons, rings, trampoline, tumbling, vaulting

gyrate *v.* circle, circulate, pirouette, revolve, rotate, spin, spiral, turn, twirl, whirl

habit *n.* **1.** bent, bias, constitution, convention, custom, disposition, gravitation, groove, habitude, hangup *(Nonformal)*, impulsion, inclination, mannerism, pattern, penchant, persuasion, practice, proclivity, proneness, propensity, quirk, routine, rule, rut, set, style, susceptibility, tendency, usage, use, way, weakness, wont **2.** addiction, compulsion, dependence, desire, fixation, need, obsession **3.** apparel, array, articles, attire, clothes, clothing, costume, dress, fashion, garb, outfit, raiment, robe, suit, uniform, vesture

habitable *adj.* comfortable, homey, inhabitable, livable, occupiable, residential, tenantable *Antonyms*: barren, desolate, uncomfortable, unlivable

habitat *n.* **1.** abode, accommodations, address, apartment, berth, domicile, dwelling, habitation, haunt, haven, hearth, home, homestead, house, locale, locality, lodging, occupancy, quarters, range, residence, residency, roost, settlement, site, surroundings, territory, turf *Nonformal:* 'hood, neck of the woods **2.** biosphere, ecosphere, ecosystem, ecozone, element, environment, microcosm, terrain

habitual *adj.* **1.** accepted, accustomed, automatic, common, constant, conventional, customary, disciplined, familiar, fixed, frequent, ingrained, mechanical, methodical, natural, normal, ordinary, perfunctory, practiced, regular, repeated, rooted, routine, standard, steady, traditional, usual *Antonyms:* abnormal, exceptional, extraordinary, infrequent, strange, unusual **2.** chronic, compulsive, confirmed, established, hardened, inveterate, persistent

habituate *v.* acclimatize, accommodate, acculturate, accustom, adjust, break in, condition, discipline, familiarize, harden, inure, transculturate

hack *adj.* banal, common, commonplace, hackneyed, stereotyped, threadbare, trite, unoriginal, worn-out *Antonyms:* fresh, original, seminal – *n.* **1.** cut, dent, gash, incision, notch, slice, split **2.** brougham, buggy, cab, calèche, carriage, coach, hackney, hansom, jitney, rickshaw, taxi, transport **3.** drudge, ghostwriter, penny-a-liner, scribbler, scrivener, writer-for-hire **4.** cart *or* draft *or* dray *or* hired *or* plow horse, mount, nag, riding *or* saddle horse, Rocinante, workhorse **5.** cough, expulsion, heave, spasm, sputter, whoop – *v.* **1.** axe, butcher, chop, cut, destroy, dice, hew, mangle, notch, score, scythe, sever, slash, slice, trim, truncate **2.** cough, gasp, heave, sputter, whoop

hacker *n.* **1.** computer programmer, cyberpunk *(Nonformal)*, intruder, operator, software specialist, systems engineer, technician **2.** duffer, golfer, Mr. *or* Ms. Mulligan *(Nonformal)*, weekend golfer

hackneyed *adj.* banal, clichéd, common, everyday, old, outdated, overused, overworked, pedestrian, quotidian, stale, stereotyped, stock, threadbare, timeworn, tired, trite, unoriginal, worn-out *Nonformal:* hokey, old hat *Antonyms:* imaginative, new, novel, striking, unusual

hag *n.* beldame, fishwife, harpy, harridan, sorceress, virago, witch *Nonformal:* battle ax, old bat

haggard *adj.* **1.** ashen, cadaverous, careworn, drawn, emaciated, exhausted, faded, fagged, fatigued, gaunt, ghastly, hollow-cheeked, hollow-eyed, pale, pallid, scraggy, shrunken, skeletal, spare, starved, tired, wan, wasted, weak, weakened, wearied, worn, worn-down, wrinkled *Antonyms:* energetic, hale, robust, vigorous, youthful **2.** crazed, frenetic, hysterical, insane, wild, wild-eyed

haggle *v.* argue, bargain, barter, bicker, cavil, chaffer, deal, dispute, mean-price *(P.E.I.)*, quarrel, quibble, squabble, wrangle *Nonformal:* beat down, dicker, horse-trade

hail *n.* **1.** greeting, halloo *(Nonformal)*, nod, salute, tip of the hat, welcome, wink **2.** barrage, bombardment, broadside, salvo, storm, volley **3.** hailstones, hailstorm, ice, lumps, pelting, rain, shower, sleet, torrent – *v.* **1.** barrage, batter, bombard, buffet, pelt, pour, rain, shower, storm, volley **2.** accost, acknowledge, address, call, flag, flag down, greet, hello, recognize, salute, shout, signal, sing out, wave, welcome, yell *Nonformal:* holler, whistle down or up **3.** be *or* come from, begin, derive, emanate, evolve, issue, originate, spring, stem, trace one's roots to **4.** acclaim, applaud, cheer, commend, compliment, exalt, glorify, honour, praise, recommend, root for *Antonyms:* boo, condemn, hiss, insult, jeer

hair *n.* **1.** cilium, feeler, fibril, fibre, filament, strand *Kinds of hair:* beard, bristle, brush, coat, cowlick, crop, eyebrow, eyelash, fleece, fringe, frizette, fur, fuzz, lint, locks, mane, ruff, shock, sideburn, thatch, toupée, tresses, tuft, whiskers, wig, wool *Nonformal:* chop *or* mutton chop, mop **2.** fraction, hairbreadth, instant, narrow margin, nose, nostril, smidgen, split second, trifle, whisker *(Nonformal)*

haircut *n.* coiffure, cut, do *(Nonformal)*, hairdo, style *Kinds of haircut*: afro, beehive, blunt cut, bob, bouffant, braid, brush-cut, bun, buzz, Caesar, chignon, corn row, crewcut, dreadlocks, ducktail, feather cut, flattop, fuzz cut, hockey hair *(Nonformal)*, mohawk, mushroom, natural, pageboy, permanent, pigtails, pixie, ponytail, punk, razor cut, ringlets, shag, spike, streaked, surf cut, updo, wet look

hairdresser *n.* barber, haircutter, hair stylist *French:* coiffeur, coiffeuse, friseur

hairless *adj.* bald, bald-headed, beardless, clean-shaven, depilated, glabrous, shaved, shaven, smooth, smooth-faced, tonsured

hair-raising *adj.* alarming, breathtaking, creepy, exciting, frightening, horrifying, scary, shocking, spine-tingling, terrifying, thrilling, unnerving, upsetting

hairsplitting *adj.* anal *(Nonformal)*, captious, critical, exacting, fastidious, finicky, fussy, meticulous, nit-picking, particular, persnickety, pettifogging, petty, precise, quibbling *Antonyms:* lax, negligent, unconcerned

hairy *adj.* **1.** bearded, bristly, bushy, downy, fleecy, fluffy, furry, fuzzy, hirsute, rough, shaggy, stubbly, tufted, unshaven, unshorn, whiskered, woolly *Antonyms:* bald, depilated, glabrous, shaven, tonsured **2.** bloodcurdling, dangerous, difficult, frightening, frightful, hair-raising, intimidating, life-threatening, menacing, scary, shocking, unnerving *Antonyms:* bland, boring, dull

halcyon *adj.* calm, carefree, casual, easy, favourable, golden, happy, leisurely, pacific, peaceful, placid, quiet, reposeful, restful, serene, tranquil, trouble-free, worry-free *Antonyms:* blustery, stormy, tempestuous, troubled, tumultuous

hale *adj.* able-bodied, blooming, fit, flourishing, healthy, hearty, robust, sound, strapping, strong, vigorous, well, wholesome *Nonformal:* alive and kicking, in the pink *Antonyms:* ailing, frail, infirm, sickly

half *adj.* bisected, divided, fifty-fifty *or* 50/50, fractional, halved, incomplete, limited, moderate, partial *Nonformal:* even-steven, halfsies *Antonyms:* complete, entire, total, whole – *adv.* **1.** halfway, incompletely, partially, partly, somewhat, to a degree **2.** closely, nearly, to a considerable extent – *n.* **1.** bisection, division, equal share, fraction, hemisphere, part, period, piece, portion, section **2.** counterpart, match, mate, one of a pair

halfhearted *adj.* apathetic, careless, cool, cursory, indifferent, irresolute, lackadaisical, lacklustre, listless, lukewarm, passive, perfunctory, spiritless, tame, tepid, unenthusiastic, uninterested *Antonyms:* ambitious, avid, concerned, excited, zealous

halfway *adj.* **1.** central, centre, equidistant, intermediate, median, mid, middle, midpoint, midway **2.** fractional, fragmentary, imperfect, incomplete, partial – *adv.* **1.** comparatively, compromisingly, conciliatorily, in part, medially, middling, midway, nearly, partially, partly **2.** betwixt and between *(Nonformal)*, imperfectly, insufficiently, moderately, unsatisfactorily

hall *n.* **1.** breezeway, corridor, connecting passage, gallery, passageway **2.** entranceway, entry, foyer, lobby, vestibule **3.** amphitheatre, arena, armoury, assembly room, auditorium, ballroom, banquet, church, community centre, concert *or* dance *or* recital *or* symphony *or* town hall, gymnasium, lyceum, refectory,

hallmark *n.* authentication, badge, brand, certification, characteristic, device, emblem, endorsement, indication, indicator, insignia, mark, ratification, seal, sign, signet, spoor, stamp, sure *or* telltale sign, symbol, trademark

hallowed *adj.* anointed, beatified, blessed, consecrated, dedicated, divine, enshrined, holy, honoured, inviolable, revered, sacred, sacrosanct, sanctified *Antonyms:* damned, excommunicated

hallucinate *v.* daydream, envision, fantasize, imagine, see, trip out *(Nonformal)*, visualize

hallucination *n.* **1.** apparition, chimera, daydream, dream, eidolon, fantasy, illusion, image, mirage, nightmare, perception, phantasm, phantasmagoria, phantom, pipe dream, vision *Nonformal:* pink elephant, purple monkey, trip **2.** confused state, delusion, disorientation, false notion, self-deception

halo *n.* **1.** ambiance, aura, aurora, brilliance dignity, gleam, glory, grandeur, holiness, illustriousness, lustre, magnificence, majesty, nimbus, quality, radiance, resplendence, solemnity, splendour **2.** aureole, corona, crown, ring

halt *n.* arrest, break, cease-fire, close, cutoff, end, freeze *(Nonformal)*, hiatus, impasse, intermission, interruption, interval, layoff, letup, pause, standstill, stop, stoppage, termination – *v.* brake, cease, check, curb, desist, deter, drop anchor, end, frustrate, hamper, hesitate, hold back, impede, intermit, interrupt, linger, obstruct, pause, prevent, pull up, put a stop to, quit, rest, stall, stay, stem, stop, suppress, suspend, terminate, vanquish, wait *Antonyms:* begin, commence, continue, resume

halter *n.* **1.** bridle, harness, headstall, headgear, leash, rein, restraint, rope, thong, trammel **2.** bowstring, garrote, hangman's knot *or* noose *or* rope, hemp, noose, rope

halting *adj.* awkward, broken, bumbling, choppy, clumsy, faltering, gauche, hesitant, imperfect, indecisive, inept, irresolute, laboured, lumbering, lurching, maladroit, slow, stammering, stumbling, stuttering, uncertain, vacillating, wavering *Antonyms:* flowing, fluent, smooth

halve *v.* **1.** bisect, cut in two, dichotomize, divide, divide *or* share equally, go Dutch *(Nonformal)*, lessen, sever, split, take away **2.** draw, even, match, split, tie *(Golf)*

ham *n.* **1.** cured pork, *jambon (French)* *Kinds of ham:* Black Forest, Danish, home-cured, honey glaze, old-fashioned, picnic, prosciutto, salted, Serrano, Smithfield, smoked, Virginia, Westphalian **2.** actor, buffoon, clown, fool *Nonformal:* grandstander, showoff – *v.* clown, exaggerate, hot-dog, showboat *(Nonformal)*

hamlet *n.* community, corners, crossroads, parish, rural neighbourhood, settlement, small town, village, wick

hammer *n.* implement, instrument, tool *Kinds of hammer:* ballpeen, battering ram, blacksmith's, bricklayer's, claw, jackhammer, mallet, peen, punch, rawhide, riveting, rubber, shoemaker's, sledgehammer, straighthammer, tack, tinner's – *v.* **1.** bang, bash, batter, beat, bodycheck, drive, hit, knock, nail, pound, pummel, punch, slug, smash, strike, tap, whack **2.** fabricate, fashion, flatten, form, make, mold, shape, **3.** accomplish, bring about or to pass, com plete, produce, resolve **4.** keep at *or* on, persevere, persist, plug away *or* along **5.** brainwash, drill into, inculcate, indoctrinate **6.** crush, defeat, humiliate, vanquish *Nonformal:* clobber, drub, paste, thrash, trounce, whomp

hamper *n.* basket, bassinet, bin, creel, laundry basket, pannier, storage – *v.* baffle, balk, bar, bind, block, check, clog, cramp, curb, discomfit, encumber, entangle, fetter, foil, frustrate, get in the way, hamstring, hinder, hog-tie, impede, inhibit, obstruct, prevent, restrain, restrict, retard, shackle, stymie, thwart, tie *Nonformal:* cramp one's style, get in the way *Antonyms:* aid, assist, facilitate

hand *adj.* handcrafted, hand-done, handmade – *n.* **1.** digits, extremity, fingers, grappler, grasp, grip, manual extremity, palm *Nonformal:* duke, fist, ham, meathook, mitt, paw **2.** agency, aid, assistance, direction, help, influence, intervention, part, participation, relief, share, succour, support **3.** applause, clap, ovation, round of applause, thunderous reception **4.** calligraphy, chirography, handwriting, longhand, penmanship, script **5.** aide, artificer, artisan, assistant, associate, craftsperson, employee, farm-hand, handyman *or* handywoman, helper, hired hand, hireling, jack, labourer, man, menial, operative, redneck *(Nonformal)*, woman, worker, workingman, workingwoman **6.** ability, art, artistry, craftsmanship, knack, manner, mark, skill **7.** auspices, authority, care, charge, command, control, custody, dominion, guidance, hold, jurisdiction, keeping, management, possession, power, stewardship, supervision – *v.* **1.** convey, deliver, furnish, give, hand-deliver, hand over, offer, pass, present, provide, reach, transfer, transmit, turn over, yield **2.** aid, assist, conduct, guide, help, lead, minister to

handbag *n.* bag, briefcase, carryall, clutch, fannypack, grip, pocketbook, portmanteau, purse, reticule, satchel, shoulder bag, tote, valise, wallet

handbook *n.* Baedeker, bill book, cookbook, field guide, how-to book, instruction book, manual, notebook, operator's guide, pocketbook, repair manual, travel guide, *vade mecum (Latin)*

handcuff *n.* bracelet, cuff, darbies *(British)*, fetter, shackle, tie – *v.* **1.** arrest, fetter, manacle, shackle **2.** frustrate, hamper, hinder, impede, inhibit, thwart

handful *n.* **1.** minimum, modicum, scant amount, scattering, small number *or* quantity, smattering, sprinkling, thimbleful, wee bit *(Nonformal)* **2.** brat, hellion, holy terror *(Nonformal)*, imp, menace, nuisance, pest, rapscallion, scamp, terror, troublemaker *Antonyms:* angel, cherub, teacher's pet

handicap *n.* **1.** affliction, baggage *(Nonformal)*, barrier, block, burden, detriment, disability, disadvantage, drawback, encumbrance, equalizer, hangup, hindrance, impairment, impediment, limitation, load, millstone, obstacle, restriction, shortcoming, stumbling block *Antonyms:* asset, benefit, boon **2.** advantage, edge, favour, head start, lead, upper hand – *v.* burden, cripple, disadvantage, encumber, hamper, hamstring, hinder, hog-tie *(Nonformal)*, hold back, impede, limit, restrict, retard, sideline, take out *Antonyms:* aid, benefit, boost, help

handicraft *n.* **1.** art, craft, design, expertise, skill, workmanship **2.** job, life's work, occupation, office, profession, shop, trade, vocation, work **3.** art, commodity, knickknack, product

handiness *n.* **1.** accessibility, availability, closeness, convenience, immediacy, nearness, practicality, proximity **2.** ability, adroitness, aptitude, artistry, capability, cleverness, craft, deftness, dexterity, efficiency, expertise, facility, know-how, motor skill, proficiency *Antonyms:* clumsiness, awkwardness, ineptitude

handiwork *n.* achievement, artifact, craft, creation, design, handicraft, handwork, invention, piece, product, production, result, work

handle *n.* **1.** arm, crank, grip, handgrip, hilt, holder, knob, shaft, stem, stock, tiller **2.** designation, flag, label, moniker *(Nonformal)*, name, office, rubric, tag, title – *v.* **1.** examine, feel, finger, fondle, grasp, hold, manipulate, maul, operate, palpate, paw *(Nonformal)*, pick up, poke, test, thumb, touch, try **2.** carry, deal *or* traffic in, market, offer, retail, sell, stock, trade **3.** behave, conduct, perform, react, treat **4.** control, direct, manage, operate, run

hand-me-down *adj.* cast-off, inherited, passed on, pre-owned, reach-me-down *(Nonformal)*, recycled, secondhand, used, worn

handout *n.* **1.** alms, benevolence, charity, dole, donation, gift, largesse, offering, share, share-out **2.** advertisement, bulletin, coupon, flyer, giveaway, handbill, junk mail, news, pamphlet, pass, promo, promotional literature

handsome *adj.* **1.** attractive, beautiful, becoming, clean-cut, comely, dapper, elegant, fair, fine, good-looking, gorgeous, hunky *(Nonformal)*, impressive, lovely, slick, smart, well-dressed, well-proportioned *Antonyms:* frightening, scary, ugly, unattractive **2.** abundant, ample, bounteous, bountiful, considerable, extensive, full, generous, gracious, large, lavish, liberal, magnanimous, munificent, openhanded, plentiful, princely, sizable, unsparing *Antonyms:* meagre, mean, miserly, ungenerous

handsomely *adv.* abundantly, amply, bountifully, generously, liberally, magnanimously, munificently, nobly, plentifully, richly

hand-to-mouth *adj.* beggarly, impoverished, improvident, meagre, mean, paycheque-to-paycheque, poor, scant, shabby *Antonyms:* flush, opulent, superfluous

handwriting *n.* calligraphy, chirography, hand, hieroglyphics, longhand, mark, penmanship, scrawl, scribble, script, scriving, style, writing *Nonformal:* chicken scratch, fist

handy *adj.* **1.** able, adaptable, adept, adroit, clever, deft, dexterous, expert, fit, ingenious, nimble, proficient, ready, skilled, skillful *Antonyms:* awkward, clumsy, incompetent, inept **2.** accessible, adjacent, at *or* to hand, available, close, close-at-hand, close by, convenient, easy, functional, helpful, manageable, near, near-at-hand, nearby, on hand, practical, profitable, ready, serviceable, useful, within reach *Antonyms:* inaccessible, inconvenient, unavailable

handyman *n.* factotum, general contracto[r] *or* labourer, jack, jack-of-all-trades, od[d] jobber, repairman, repairwoman, superintendent

hang *v.* **1.** attach, fasten, fix, hinge, hitc[h], hold, support, suspend, swing, tie **2.** execute, gibbet, hoist, kill, lynch *Nonforma[l]:* scrag, top **3.** bend, bow, dangle, dip, droo[p], flag, incline, loll, sag, slump, wave, wilt **4** adorn, bedeck, cover, deck, decorate, drape, embellish, enhance, ornament **5** await, be contingent on, depend, pend, re[st] on, revolve around **6.** cleave to, clenc[h], cling, grasp, hold on **7.** float, hover, loo[m], menace, threaten

hangar *n.* airdock, dock, garage, housin[g], roundhouse, shed, shelter, workshop

hanging *adj.* **1.** dangling, drooping, flagging, flapping, flopping, floppy, loose, pendent, pendulous, suspended, swinging, unattached, unsupported **2.** fence-sittin[g] *(Nonformal)*, undecided, unresolved, unsettled, wavering **3.** beetling, extending, jutting, overhanging, projecting, protrudin[g] – *n.* **1.** execution, gibbeting, killing, lynching *Nonformal:* mob justice, necktie socia[l] **2.** adornment, artwork, covering, curtain, drapery, embellishment, ornamentation, painting, picture, rug, tapestry, wallpaper

hangout *n.* bar, club, gathering *or* meetin[g] place, locale, local spot, resort, scene *Nonformal:* joint, stomping ground

hangover *n.* alcohol poisoning, crapulence, headache, katzenjammer *Nonformal:* cotton tongue, a doozy, big head, bottl[e] fatigue, morning after, the shakes, whisk[y] flu

hangup *n.* block, complex, difficulty, fear, fixation, inhibition, obsession, phobia, problem, kink, vexation *Nonformal:* baggage, thing

hankering *n.* ache, craving, desire, hunge[r], itch, longing, pining, thirst, urge, want, weakness, wish, yearning, yen, zazzle *(Nonformal)*

hanky-panky *n.* **1.** adultery, affair, dalliance, flirtation, love affair, romance *Nonformal:* fling, fooling around, lollygagging **2.** chicanery, deceit, foolery, trickery *Nonformal:* hocus-pocus, hokey-pokey, monkey business, mumbo-jumbo, shenanigans

haphazard *adj.* **1.** accidental, aimless, casual, chance, desultory, erratic, fluke, incidental, offhand, purposeless, random, spontaneous, sporadic, sudden, unconscious, unconsidered, uncoordinated, unexpected *Antonyms:* arranged, planned, preset, programmed **2.** careless, disorderly, disorganized, higgledy-piggledy, indiscriminate, irregular, loose, reckless, slapdash, slapped *or* thrown together, slipshod, unorganized, unplanned, willy-nilly *Antonyms:* careful, ordered, rehearsed, structured, systematic

hapless *adj.* cursed, damned, ill-fated, luckless, miserable, star-crossed, unfortunate, unhappy, unlucky, woeful, wretched *Antonyms:* blessed, charmed, felicitous, fortunate, lucky

happen *adv.* chances are, likely, maybe, perhaps – *v.* **1.** appear, arise, arrive, become of, befall, betide, come about *or* after *or* down, crop up, develop, ensue, fall, follow, go on, issue, materialize, occur, pass, present itself, proceed, result, take place, transpire, turn out **2.** chance upon, discover, encounter, find, light *or* luck upon, meet, stumble across *or* on *Antonyms:* dodge, miss, sidestep

happening *n.* accident, adventure, affair, case, chance, circumstance, episode, event, experience, gathering, incident, milestone, occasion, occurrence, phenomenon, proceeding, scene, show, spectacle *Antonyms:* nonevent, yawn *(Nonformal)*

happenstance *n.* accident, chance, circumstance, coincidence, fate, fluke, serendipity, stroke of luck, synchronicity

happily *adv.* **1.** agreeably, blissfully, cheerfully, delightedly, enthusiastically, felicitously, freely, gaily, gladly, gleefully, gracefully, heartily, hilariously, joyfully, laughingly, lightheartedly, lovingly, merrily, playfully, pleasantly, sincerely, smilingly, swimmingly, warmly, willingly *Antonyms:* angrily, bitterly, resentfully **2.** ably, aptly, auspiciously, deftly, diplomatically, propitiously, providentially, skillfully, tactfully

happiness *n.* **1.** blessedness, bliss, buoyancy, cheeriness, contentment, delight, ecstasy, effervescence, elation, enchantment, enjoyment, euphoria, exhilaration, exuberance, gaiety, gladness, glee, good cheer *or* humour *or* spirits, hilarity, hopefulness, joy, jubilation, laughter, lightheartedness, mirth, paradise, pleasure, rejoicing, satisfaction, vivacity, well-being *Antonyms:* depression, distress, grief, misery, sorrow **2.** aptness, felicity, good fortune *or* luck, opportuneness, propitiousness, relevance

happy *adj.* **1.** advantageous, appropriate, apt, auspicious, befitting, convenient, correct, enviable, favourable, felicitous, fitting, fortunate, just, lucky, nice, opportune, proper, propitious, providential, right, successful, suitable, well-timed *Antonyms:* star-crossed, unfortunate, unlucky **2.** *aux anges (French)*, blessed, blissful, blithe, captivated, cheerful, contented, delighted, ecstatic, elated, enraptured, exultant, glad, gleeful, gratified, joyful, joyous, jubilant, laughing, light, mirthful, overjoyed, peaceful, playful, pleased, rapturous, satisfied, sparkling, sunny, thrilled *Nonformal:* chipper, flying high, in seventh heaven, over the moon, tickled pink, walking on air *Antonyms:* despondent, displeased, gloomy, miserable, sad **3.** chance, flukey, incidental, serendipitous, unintentional, unwitting

happy-go-lucky *adj.* blithe, carefree, casual, cheerful, desultory, devil-may-care, easygoing, free and easy, insouciant, lighthearted, nonchalant, slaphappy *(Nonformal)*, trusting, unconcerned, unencumbered, waggish *Antonyms:* cheerless, dolorous, gloomy, morose, serious

harangue *n.* address, admonition, blast, bombast, declamation, diatribe, discourse, exhortation, homily, jeremiad, lecture, oration, outpouring, philippic, reproof, rodomontade, sermon, speech, spiel *(Nonformal)*, tirade – *v.* declaim, drone on, exhort, filibuster, hold forth, lecture, orate, preach, rant, rave, reprimand, reproach, reproof, sermonize *P.E.I.:* read, skivver

harass *v.* aggravate, agitate, annoy, arouse, attack, badger, bait, bedevil, beleaguer, besiege, bother, chevy, confuse, cross, discomfit, distress, encumber, exasperate, fret, frustrate, gall, hamper, harry, impede, irritate, peeve, provoke, siege, tantalize, taunt, tease, torment, try, unsettle, upset, vex *Nonformal:* bug, burn, chew out, dog, dress down, hassle, hound, needle, ride

harbinger *n.* augury, forerunner, foretoken, herald, indicator, messenger, omen, portent, precursor, presage, sign, signal

harbour *n.* **1.** anchorage, bay, bight, breakwater, cove, dock, firth, gulf, inlet, jetty, landing, mooring, storage, wharf **2.** asylum, cover, haven, port, refuge, retreat, rock *(Nonformal)*, sanctuary, sanctum, security, shelter, solace – *v.* **1.** accommodate, board, conceal, defend, guard, hide, house, protect, provide refuge, put up, quarter, safeguard, screen, shelter, shield **2.** believe, cherish, consider, entertain, foster, hold, maintain, nurse, nurture, regard

hard *adj.* **1.** arduous, backbreaking, brutal, burdensome, complicated, demanding, difficult, exhausting, fatiguing, formidable, harrowing, heavy, involved, irksome, laborious, onerous, painful, rigorous, rough, rugged, sapping, sticky, stiff, strenuous, taxing, thorny, tiring, tough, troublesome, trying, uphill, wearing *Antonyms:* easy, effortless, facile, simple, straightforward, uncomplicated **2.** adamantine, compact, compressed, concentrated, consolidated, dense, firm, hardened, impenetrable, indurate, inflexible, iron, packed, rigid, rock-like, rocky, set, solid, stiff, stony, thick, unyielding *Antonyms:* flexible, fluid, malleable, soft **3.** austere, bitter, bleak, callous, cold, cold-blooded, cruel, disagreeable, dour, exacting, grim, harsh, hostile, intemperate, pitiless, ruthless, severe, stern, strict, stringent, unfeeling, unjust, unkind, unpleasant, unsparing, unsympathetic *Antonyms:* amiable, friendly, humane, kind, pleasant **4.** absolute, actual, bare, bottom line, definite, down-to-earth, genuine, indisputable, plain, positive, practical, pragmatic, realistic, sure, true, undeniable, unvarnished, verified **5.** ardent, assiduous, avid, diligent, eager, energetic, enterprising, fervent, industrious, intense, passionate, persevering, persistent, relentless, resolute, spirited, steady, unremitting, unwavering, willing, zealous *Antonyms:* indifferent, lazy, phlegmatic **6.** alcoholic, boozy *(Nonformal)*, fortified, numbing, spiked, spirituous, strong **7.** dogged, hardheaded, headstrong, intractable, mulish, obdurate, obstinate, ornery, pertinacious, strong-willed, stubborn, surly, unmanageable, unreasonable *Antonyms:* amenable, compliant, docile, tractable – *adv.* arduously, assiduously, determinedly, doggedly, exhaustingly, gruelingly, industriously, intensely, intently, laboriously, painstakingly, steadily, strenuously, vigorously *Antonyms:* easily, gently, lazily, lightly, softly, weakly

hard-core *adj.* **1.** dedicated, determined, devoted, diehard, dyed-in-the-wool *(Nonformal)*, enthusiastic, extreme, faithful, fanatical, incorrigible, inflexible, intransigent, irreclaimable, obstinate, recidivous, resolute, rigid, staunch, steadfast, stubborn, uncompromising, unyielding *Antonyms:* giving, submissive, yielding **2.** aggressive, angry, fast, loud, pounding, rhythmic

harden *v.* **1.** acclimatize, accustom, adapt, adjust, callous, case-harden, conform, deaden, desensitize, discipline, dull, embitter, habituate, inure, roughen, season, steel, stiffen, strengthen, teach, train **2.** cement, compact, congeal, firm up, freeze, gel, iceup, lock in, solidify, stabilize

hardened *adj.* **1.** cast in stone, concrete, firm, fixed, fossilized, frozen, hard, steely **2.** battle-scarred, experienced, inured, seasoned, tempered, tested, toughened, veteran **3.** callous, flinty, implacable, indifferent, inflexible, obdurate, pitiless, remorseless, unrelenting, unyielding **4.** chronic, habitual, impenitent, incorrigible, inveterate, recidivous, repeat, reprobate

hard-fisted *adj.* **1.** avaricious, close-fisted, mean, miserly, penny-pinching, penurious, stingy, tightfisted, ungenerous *Nonformal:* chintzy, skinflint *Antonyms:* extravagant, generous, prodigal **2.** absolute, autocratic, cruel, despotic, hardhanded, hardhearted, harsh, implacable, merciless, oppressive, pitiless, ruthless, severe, tyrannical, vicious *Antonyms:* democratic, liberal, propitious

hardheaded *adj.* **1.** bullheaded, hard, hardnosed, headstrong, intractable, mulish, obstinate, pertinacious, perverse, pigheaded, resolute, stubborn, tough, unsentimental, unyielding *Antonyms:* approachable, open **2.** astute, cool, levelheaded, Machiavellian, practical, pragmatic, rational, realistic, shrewd *Antonyms:* idealistic, impractical, sentimental, unrealistic

hardhearted *adj.* brutish, callous, cold, cold-blooded, cruel, hard, hard-boiled *(Nonformal),* heartless, implacable, indifferent, inhuman, insensitive, intolerant, merciless, obdurate, pitiless, stony, uncaring, uncompassionate, unemotional, unfeeling, unkind, unsympathetic *Antonyms:* empathetic, forgiving, sympathetic, warmhearted

hard-hitting *adj.* captious, censorious, critical, cutting, exacting, forceful, incisive, on the mark *(Nonformal),* penetrating, trenchant, uncompromising *Antonyms:* conciliatory, gentle, sparing, weak

hardly *adv.* barely, comparatively, faintly, gradually, imperceptibly, inconceivably, infrequently, little, only just, perceptibly, rarely, scarcely, seldom, slightly, sparsely, sporadically *Antonyms:* amply, appreciably, certainly, fully

hard-nosed *adj.* **1.** inflexible, intractable, relentless, rigid, stubborn, unyielding *Antonyms:* amenable, flexible, open-minded **2.** all-business, bottom-line, businesslike, commercial, efficient, ruthless

hardship *n.* adversity, affliction, burden, calamity, catastrophe, curse, danger, difficulty, disaster, discomfort, distress, drudgery, fatigue, grief, grievance, hazard, heartache, injury, labour, mischance, misery, misfortune, need, oppression, peril, persecution, privation, reversal, rigour, sorrow, suffering, tragedy, travail, trial, tribulation, vicissitude, worry *Nonformal:* hard knocks, tough break *Antonyms:* blessing, comfort, help, prosperity, relief

hardware *n.* **1.** accoutrement, appliance, appurtenances, conveniences, fastener, fitting, fixtures, implements, ironware, kitchenware, metalware, paraphernalia, plumbing, tool, utensils *Kinds of hardware and equipment:* adaptor, angle brace, angle bracket, bearing, bit, blowtorch, bolt, brace, bracket, bushing, cable, caster, catch, chain, chuck, clamp, clip, coil spring, collar, corner brace, cotter, coupler, coupling, crank, dolly, elbow, expansion bolt, eyebolt, flange, funnel, gaff, gasket, glue gun, grease gun, grommet, guide, hammer, hasp, hinge, hook, hook and eye, hose, jack, joint, ladder, latch, machine bolt, mop, mortar, nail, nut, oil can, padlock, paintbrush, paint roller, paint tray, pipe, plate, plug, plunger, pull, punch, ring, ringbolt, rivet, rod, rubber washer, saw, sawhorse, scaffold, screw, screwdriver, shovel, slide, soldering iron, spike, spring, stanchion, standard, stay, stud, switch, swivel, tack, toggle bolt, tool kit, toolbox, U-bolt, valve, vise, washer, welder, wing bolt, workbench **2.** armament, arms, equipment, gear, material, munitions, weapons **3.** component, computer system, digital equipment, electronics, guts *(Nonformal),* peripheral device *Kinds of computer hardware:* central processing unit *or* CPU, disk *or* hard drive, input *or* output port, joystick, keyboard, microphone, modem, monitor, motherboard, mouse, printer, scanner

hardy *adj.* **1.** able, able-bodied, brawny, burly, fit, hale, hefty, muscular, physically fit, powerful, resourceful, robust, rugged, seasoned, solid, sound, stout, strong, sturdy, substantial, tenacious, tough, toughened, unflagging, vigorous *Antonyms:* delicate, feeble, fragile, sickly, weak **2.** bold, brave, courageous, daring, devil-may-care, fearless, foolhardy, intrepid, lionhearted, rash *Antonyms:* cowardly, craven, dastardly

harebrained *adj.* absurd, asinine, careless, crazy, dizzy, empty-headed, fatuous, featherbrained, flighty, foolish, frivolous, giddy, heedless, idiotic, improvident, inane, irresponsible, mindless, preposterous, rash, reckless, scatterbrained, silly, stupid, unstable, unthinking *Nonformal:* barmy, half-baked, loony *Antonyms:* calculated, farsighted, prudent

harlequin *adj.* checkered, brightly coloured, diamond-patterned, motley, multi-coloured, parti-coloured, spangled, sparkling, variegated – *n.* buffoon, clown, fool, jester, merry-andrew, pantaloon, pantomimist, stooge

harm *n.* **1.** accident, damage, fall, hurt, ill, impairment, infliction, injury, loss, marring, misfortune, ravage, ruin, ruination, violence *Antonyms:* convalescence, healing, improvement, reparation **2.** abuse, deleteriousness, detriment, disservice, evil, foul play, grievance, immorality, mischief, misuse, noxiousness, outrage, perniciousness, sabotage, sin, sinfulness, transgression, vandalism, vice, wickedness, wrong *Antonyms:* justice, rectitude, righteousness – *v.* **1.** beat, bruise, cripple, crush, damage, hurt, impair, injure, maim, mangle, mess up, molest, mutilate, nick, scrape, spoil, stab, total *(Nonformal)*, trample, traumatize, vandalize, wound, wreck *Antonyms:* aid, alleviate, better **2.** abuse, blemish, cast aspersions on, defame, disparage, ill-treat, maltreat, mar, misuse, outrage, prejudice, ruin, sabotage, shatter, shock, slander, smear, sully, tarnish, traduce, undermine, wrong *Antonyms:* help, honour, support

harmful *adj.* adverse, bad, baleful, baneful, calamitous, catastrophic, corrosive, corrupting, crippling, damaging, deleterious, detrimental, dire, disastrous, dreadful, hurtful, incendiary, injurious, malicious, malignant, menacing, murderous, noxious, painful, pernicious, pestilential, ruinous, septic, sinister, subversive, toxic, unhealthy, virulent *Antonyms:* beneficial, good, healthy, helpful, safe

harmless *adj.* benign, gentle, ineffectual, innocent, innocuous, inoffensive, manageable, nontoxic, painless, powerless, reliable, safe, simple, sound, sure *Antonyms:* dangerous, destructive, poisonous, unhealthy

harmonious *adj.* **1.** barbershop *(Nonformal)*, chiming, concordant, consonant, dulcet, euphonious, harmonic, harmonizing, mellifluous, melodic, melodious, musical, sonorous, sweet-sounding, tuneful *Antonyms:* discordant, dissonant, grating, harsh **2.** adaptive, agreeable, amicable, balanced, compatible, congenial, congruous, coordinated, cordial, correspondent, fraternal, friendly, like, matching, peaceful, similar, symmetrical, sympathetic, sympatico *Antonyms:* contrasting, divergent, incompatible, incongruous, inconsistent

harmonize *v.* accord, adapt, adjust, agree, arrange, attune, be in tune with, blend, chime with, cohere, combine, compose, cooperate, coordinate, correlate, correspond, integrate, line up with, match, orchestrate, proportion, reconcile, relate, set, suit, synthesize, tally, unify, unite

harmony *n.* **1.** accord, affinity, agreement, amicability, amity, compatibility, concord, concurrence, conformity, consistency, cooperation, correspondence, empathy, friendship, good will, kinship, like-mindedness, peace, rapport, tranquility, unanimity, understanding, unity *Antonyms:* antagonism, conflict, disagreement, hostility, opposition **2.** arrangement, blend, blending, carol, chime, chord, chorus, composition, concert, consonance, consonancy, diapason, euphony, harmonics, mellifluousness, melodiousness, melody, music, overtone, polyphony, richness, symphony, tune, tunefulness *Antonyms:* cacophony, discordance, dissonance

harness *n.* **1.** attachment, equipage, framework, gear, halter, restraint **2.** double *or* single harness *Horse harness gear:* backstrap, bellyband *or* breeching strap, bit, blinder, breech stay, browband *or* front piece, chain *or* curb bit, check rein, cropper, crown piece, hip strap, martingale, nosepiece, pole chain, runner, saddle, swingletree *or* whiffletree, throatlatch, traces – *v.* **1.** collar, couple, hitch up, marry, rig up, saddle, yoke *Antonyms:* uncouple, unhitch, unyoke **2.** apply, bridle, channel, control, curb, direct, employ, exploit, manage, mobilize, muzzle, rein, render useful, restrain, utilize

harpoon *n.* barb, spear *or* spear gun, trident, weapon – *v.* capture, catch, hook, jacklight, kill, pierce, puncture, spear, strike, take

harridan *n.* crone, fury, grimalkin, hag, harpy, harrier, *macheshefeh (Yiddish)*, nag, shrew, termagant, virago, vixen, witch *Nonformal:* battle-axe, blister, fishwife, old biddy *or* crone *or* meany, twister

harried *adj.* **1.** agitated, annoyed, badgered, beleagured, bothered, browbeaten, chafed, discomforted, harassed, hectored, nagged, pestered, racked, tormented, troubled, vexed, worried *Antonyms:* calm, collected, composed, unruffled **2.** bombed, defeated, destroyed, invaded, looted, pillaged, plundered, punished, raided, ravaged, ruined, shelled, strafed, wasted

harrow *v.* **1.** break clod *or* land, cultivate, develop, dig, furrow, hoe, level, plow, till **2.** disquiet, distress, disturb, harry, hector, lacerate, pain, perturb, rattle, torment, trouble, unnerve, vex *Antonyms:* assuage, comfort, console

harrowing *adj.* agonizing, alarming, chilling, dangerous, distressing, disturbing, excruciating, frightening, nerve-racking, terrifying, torturous, traumatic *Antonyms:* comforting, consoling, reassuring

harsh *adj.* **1.** cacophonous, caterwauling, disagreeable, discordant, disturbing, flat, glaring, grating, hoarse, incompatible, jagged, jangling, jarring, noisy, offensive, off-key, rasping, raucous, repugnant, screeching, shrill, strident, tuneless, uneven, unmusical, unpleasant *Antonyms:* harmonious, mellifluous, soothing, sweet **2.** abusive, brutal, coarse, comfortless, crude, cruel, cussed *(Nonformal)*, discourteous, dour, grim, gruff, hairy, hard, mean, nasty, pitiless, punitive, relentless, rough, rude, ruthless, severe, stern, stringent, tough, uncivil, unfeeling, ungracious, unkind, unrelenting, wicked *Antonyms:* agreeable, gentle, kind **3.** austere, bare, barren, bleak, craggy, dreary, frozen, icy, rocky, snow *or* wind swept, stark, unforgiving, waste *Antonyms:* fecund, fertile, lush, tropical **4.** acrid, astringent, bitter, cutting, sharp, sour *Antonyms:* mild, sugary, sweet

harvest *n.* **1.** cash-crop, crop, fruit, fruition, growth, Lammas, produce, return, year's work, yield **2.** accomplishment, consequence, effect, fulfillment, gain, outcome, remains, result, reward, spoils, winnings – *v.* **1.** accumulate, acquire, amass, collect, garner, gather, get, glean, hoard, mow, pick, pluck, reap, receive, store, strip, tassel **2.** butcher, cull, kill, remove, slaughter, slay, take *(Nonformal)*

has-been *n.* ex-celebrity, former star, nobody *Nonformal:* bum, burn-out, fading light, falling star, history, washout, yesterday's news

hash *n.* assortment, clutter, confusion, farrago, gallimaufry, hodgepodge, jumble, medley, melange, mess, miscellany, mishmash, mixed bag, mix-up, muddle, patchwork, shambles *Nonformal:* dog's breakfast, slumgullion – *v.* **1.** chop, cut, dice, grind, mince, shred, slice **2.** botch, bungle, confuse, foozle, fumble, mar, mess *or* screw up *(Nonformal)*, ruin, spoil, wreck *Antonyms:* accomplish, fix, mend **3.** argue, chew the fat *(Nonformal)*, debate, discuss, reckon, resolve, review, talk

hassle *n.* altercation, argument, bickering, clamour, commotion, difficulty, disagreement, dispute, fight, hubbub, inconvenience, problem, quarrel, row, squabble, struggle, trial, trouble, tumult, turmoil, tussle, uproar, wrangle *Nonformal:* beef, rhubarb – *v.* annoy, badger, bother, disturb, harass, harry, hector, nag, persecute, pester, torment, upset, *utz (Yiddish)*, vex, worry *Nonformal:* bug, ride

haste *n.* **1.** alacrity, briskness, bustle, celerity, dispatch, drive, fleetness, hurry, hustle, nimbleness, promptness, quickness, rapidity, rush, scramble, scurry, scuttle, speed, swiftness, urgency, velocity *Antonyms:* delay, deliberation **2.** heedlessness, impetuousness, rashness, recklessness *Antonyms:* care, wariness

hasten *v.* **1.** bolt, bound, bustle, dash, flee, fly, gallop, hurry, hustle, leap, race, run, rush, scamper, scurry, speed, sprint, spurt, tear *Nonformal:* beat it, burn rubber, dart off, make tracks, put the pedal to the metal, scoot, skedaddle *Antonyms:* crawl, creep, dawdle **2.** accelerate, expedite, facilitate, goad, impel, motivate, precipitate, propel, push forward, quicken, urge *Antonyms:* delay, hold back, retard

hastily *adv.* **1.** agilely, apace, double-quick, expeditiously, fast, hurriedly, lickety-split *(Nonformal)*, nimbly, posthaste, precipitately, precipitously, promptly, quickly, rapidly, speedily, straightaway, suddenly, swiftly *Antonyms:* leisurely, lethargically, slowly **2.** carelessly, heedlessly, impetuously, impulsively, rashly, recklessly *Antonyms:* carefully, considerately

hasty *adj.* **1.** abrupt, breakneck, brisk, expeditious, fast, fleet, hurried, precipitous, prompt, quick, rapid, rushed, snappy *(Nonformal)*, speedy, sudden, swift, urgent *Antonyms:* dilatory, languorous **2.** brash, heedless, impatient, impetuous, impulsive, mindless, rash, reckless, thoughtless *Antonyms:* cautious, prudent, wary **3.** brief, cursory, haphazard, impromptu, off the cuff *(Nonformal)*, passing, perfunctory, slapdash, split-second, superficial *Antonyms:* careful, considerate, critical, measured

hat *n.* cap, *chapeau (French)*, headdress, headgear, head wear, lid *(Nonformal) Types of hat:* astrakhan, balaclava, Balmoral, bearskin, beaver, beret, boater, bonnet, bowler, busby, Christy, cloche, coolie, coonskin, cowboy, deerstalker, derby, fedora, fez, fur, Glengarry, hard, Homburg, kepi, mob, mortarboard, opera, peaked, pith helmet, Panama, pillbox, porkpie, sailor, shako, silk, slouch, snap brim, sombrero, sou'wester, stovepipe, straw, sun, tam, tarboosh, ten-gallon, top, topper *(Nonformal)*, topi, tricorne, trilby, tuque, Tyrolean, winter carnival *Trademark:* Stetson, Tilley *See also:* **cap**

hatch *n.* **1.** door, escape way, hatchway, opening, outlet, porthole, trap door **2.** cap, cover, lid, top – *v.* **1.** brainstorm, brood, concoct, contrive, create, design, devise, dream up, formulate, induce, invent, machinate, occasion, originate, plan, plot, prepare, project, scheme, set, think *or* work up *Nonformal:* cook *or* trump *or* whip up, spin, throw together **2.** bear, breed, bring forth, cause, conceive, engender, father, generate, give birth, incubate, mother, parent, procreate, produce, sire, spawn

hate *n.* animosity, aversion, disgust, enmity, execration, hatred, hostility, ill will, loathing, malevolence, odium, rancour, repugnance, venom *Antonyms:* affection, love, fondness – *v.* abhor, abominate, curse, detest, despise, disapprove, disdain, loathe, recoil from, scorn, shudder at *Antonyms:* admire, cherish, fancy, treasure

hateful *adj.* abhorrent, abominable, accursed, awful, blasted, confounded, cursed, damnable, damned, despicable, detestable, disgusting, evil, execrable, forbidding, foul, gross, heinous, horrid, infamous, invidious, loathsome, malevolent, malign, mean, nasty, nefarious, obnoxious, odious, offensive, ornery, repellent, repugnant, repulsive, resentful, revolting, spiteful, undesirable, vicious, vile *Nonformal:* bloody, cussed, pestiferous *Antonyms:* attractive, desirable, friendly, lovable

hatred *n.* abhorrence, abomination, acrimony, animosity, antagonism, antipathy, aversion, bitterness, coldness, contempt, detestation, disfavour, disgust, dislike, displeasure, distaste, enmity, execration, horror, hostility, ill will, loathing, malice, prejudice, rancour, repugnance, repulsion, revulsion, venom *Antonyms:* affection, amity, attachment, fondness, love

haughty *adj.* arrogant, cavalier, conceited, condescending, contemptuous, disdainful, imperious, inflated, insolent, overbearing, patronizing, pompous, presumptuous, proud, self-important, snobbish, supercilious *Nonformal:* highhanded, snooty, stiffnecked, stuck-up *Antonyms:* meek, mild, obsequious, self-effacing

haul *n.* booty, burden, cargo, catch, find, freight, gain, goods, harvest, lading, load, loot, payload, spoils, takings, yield *Nonformal:* swag, take – *v.* **1.** drag, heave, jerk, lug, pull, remove, tug, wrench, yank **2.** bring, carry, cart, convey, fetch, float, freight, hike, move, portage, ship, take in tow, tote, tow, trail, transport, truck

haunt *n.* abode, bar, clubhouse, den, dwelling, gathering place, habitat, hangout, headquarters, locality, meeting place, purlieu, range, rendezvous, resort, retreat, site, social club *Nonformal:* local, stomping ground, watering hole – *v.* **1.** agitate, agonize, annoy, bedevil, beset, besiege, craze, frighten, harass, harrow, hound, intrude, madden, manifest, obsess, pester, plague, possess, prey on, scare, spook, terrify, terrorize, torment, trouble, vex, worry **2.** dwell, frequent, habituate, hang about *or* around, hover, inhabit, linger, loiter, patronize, permeate, pervade, reappear, return, rise, spirit, visit

haunted *adj.* **1.** accursed, bedeviled, eerie, fiendish, ghost-ridden, nightmarish, possessed, spooked *(Nonformal)* **2.** fixated, obsessed, pained, tormented, troubled, vexed, world-weary, worried

haunting *adj.* enduring, incessant, indelible, lasting, memorable, persistent, recurring, tormenting, unforgettable

hauteur *n.* airs, arrogance, conceit, contempt, disdain, haughtiness, hubris, imperiousness, insolence, pompousness, pretentiousness, pride, scorn, self-importance, superciliousness, toploftiness *(Nonformal)*, vanity *Antonyms:* humbleness, humility, meekness, modesty

have *v.* **1.** control, corner, keep, occupy, own, possess, retain, sit on *(Nonformal)* **2.** acquire, annex, consume, gain, get, glom onto *(Nonformal)*, incorporate, obtain, procure, receive, subsume, take, take in **3.** count, enjoy, include, number, rank **4.** be exposed to, benefit, experience, feel, undergo, utilize **5.** accept, admit, cherish, consider, cultivate, embrace, entertain, foster, harbour, maintain, nurse **6.** comprehend, get the picture *(Nonformal)*, know, master, understand **7.** be afflicted *or* stricken, catch, come down with, contract, suffer from **8.** arrange, carry out, do, execute, hold, organize, plan, set up **9.** bear, bring forth, deliver, drop, give birth, issue, spawn **10.** allow, bid, brook, cause, demand, direct, effectuate, enjoin, make, tolerate **11.** beat, best, defeat, prevail, secure, triumph, win **12.** cheat, dupe, fix *(Nonformal)*, fool, outfox, outsmart, swindle, take in **13.** attack, battle, challenge, debate, duel, fight

haven *n.* **1.** a room of one's own, asylum, happy place *(Nonformal)*, hermitage, inner sanctum, oasis, refuge, retreat, safety, sanctuary, sanctum sanctorum, shelter, solace **2.** anchorage, cover, harbour, port

havoc *n.* calamity, cataclysm, catastrophe, chaos, desolation, destruction, devastation, disorder, disruption, mayhem, mêlée, ravage, ruination, shambles, wreck, wreckage *Antonyms:* order, organization, peacefulness, preservation, quiet

hawk *n.* accipitrine, bird of prey, raptor *Kinds of hawk:* buzzard, caracara, chicken, condor, Cooper's, eagle, falcon, fish, gerfalcon *or* gyrfalcon, goshawk, harrier, kestrel, kite, marsh, osprey, red-tailed, rough-legged, sharp-shinned, sparrow, vulture – *v.* distribute, huckster, peddle, push, sell, vend

hazard *n.* **1.** danger, menace, obstacle, peril, threat *Antonyms:* protection, safety **2.** accident, chance, contingency, fortuitousness, luck – *v.* **1.** attempt, broach, take, tender, try, venture, volunteer, **2.** dare, endanger, gamble, imperil, jeopardize, risk *Antonyms:* safeguard, shelter

hazardous *adj.* **1.** dangerous, difficult, perilous, risky, threatening, unsafe **2.** chancy, insecure, precarious, shaky, uncertain, unpredictable, unreliable

haze *n.* **1.** cloud, film, fog, fume, ground clouds, haziness, miasma, mist, murk, smog, smokiness, soup *(Nonformal)*, steam, vapour **2.** confusion, dimness, indistinctness, obscurity, obtuseness, vagueness *Antonyms:* clarity, succinctness – *v.* abuse, bother, harass, humiliate, initiate, razz *(Nonformal)*, screech-in *(Newfoundland)*

hazy *adj.* **1.** bleared, bleary, blurred, blurry, clouded, cloudy, dim, faint, foggy, misty, murky, smoggy, soupy *(Nonformal)*, vaporous, veiled *Antonyms:* bright, clear, light, sunny **2.** confused, fuzzy, ill-defined, indefinite, muddled, nebulous, obscure, uncertain, unclear, unintelligible, unsound, vague *Antonyms:* lucid, rational, well-defined

head *adj.* **1.** first, fore, foremost, front, premier, prime, principal, topmost *Antonyms:* base, end, trailing **2.** champion, chief, guiding, influential, leading, superior *Antonyms:* inferior, minor, subordinate – *n.* **1.** apex, apogee, brain, cranium, cusp, height, point, skull, spike, top, zenith *Nonformal:* attic, bean, belfry, dome, grey matter, lid, noggin, noodle, pate **2.** admiral, alpha female *or* male, authority, boss, captain, centre, CEO, CFO, chairman, chief, decision maker, director, general, general manager, headmaster, headmistress, leader, manager, managing director, person in charge, president, prime minister, producer, ringleader, supervisor *Nonformal:* brains, king fish, quarterback, top dog **3.** ability, acuteness, apprehension, aptitude, aptness, bent, brains, capacity, cleverness, common sense, discernment, faculty, flair, genius, gift, intellect, intelligence, judgment, knack, mentality, mind, perception, rationality, sanity, smarts *(Nonformal),* talent, thought, turn, understanding, wisdom, wits **4.** beginning, fountainhead, genesis, headwater, origin, source, spring, start, wellspring **5.** breakwater, cape, crest, headland, jetty, peak, pinnacle, point, promontory, spit, summit **6.** avant-garde, cutting *or* leading edge, forefront, pioneer, trailblazer, vanguard **7.** boiling *or* turning point, climax, crisis, critical juncture, crossroads, culmination, foam, froth **8.** banner, header, headline, title **9.** branch, category, discipline, domain, sphere, subject, theme, topic **10.** being, body, individual, number, person, soul, specimen **11.** bunch, cluster, group, selection **12.** bathroom, loo *(British),* outhouse, toilet, washroom *Nonformal:* can, crapper, john, pisser, privy – *v.* **1.** captain, chair, command, control, direct, govern, guide, lead, manage, oversee, pilot, preside, regulate, run, skipper **2.** course, move, navigate, point, shift, steer, swerve, turn, veer

headache *n.* **1.** hangover, hemicrania, migraine, splitting headache *Nonformal:* a doozy, monster, throbber **2.** bother, irritation, nuisance, pain, pest, trouble, vexation *Nonformal:* drag, hassle, pain in the ass

headfirst *adv.* **1.** forcefully, hastily, precipitately, quickly, swiftly **2.** carelessly, rashly, recklessly, thoughtlessly, with abandon

headlong *adj.* **1.** brash, breakneck, dangerous, daredevil, daring, foolhardy, impetuous, impulsive, inconsiderate, rash, reckless, thoughtless **2.** abrupt, hasty, hurried, precipitous, rushing, sudden, tempestuous – *adv.* headfirst, impetuously, impulsively, rashly, recklessly, spontaneously, wildly

headstrong *adj.* bullheaded, contrary, determined, hard-core, hard-nosed, hard-shell *(Nonformal),* inflexible, intractable, mulish, obstinate, pigheaded, refractory, rigid, self-willed, strong-minded, stubborn, uncontrollable, ungovernable, unruly, unyielding *Antonyms:* impressionable, manageable, pliant

headway *n.* advance, advancement, anabasis, forward movement, ground, improvement, increase, incursion, progression, promotion *Antonyms:* recession, regression, retreat

heady *adj.* **1.** dizzying, exciting, exhilarating, inebriating, intoxicating, overwhelming, potent, powerful, provocative, stimulating, strong, thrilling **2.** headstrong, intransigent, mulish, obstinate, rash, reckless, refractory, stubborn, unyielding

heal *v.* **1.** alleviate, cure, doctor, dress, fix, medicate, mend, minister to, patch up, physic, rebuild, reconcile, remedy, repair, restore, resuscitate, revive, salve, set, settle, soothe, treat *Antonyms:* aggravate, harm, hurt, inflame, injure **2.** convalesce, get well, improve, recover, recuperate, rehabilitate, rejuvenate, renew

healing *adj.* assuaging, comforting, corrective, curative, curing, gentle, improving, lenitive, medicinal, mitigative, palliative, recovering, recuperating, remedial, restorative, restoring, soothing, therapeutic

health *adj.* constitutional, good-for-you, healthy, hygienic, nutritious, restorative, salubrious, salutary, wholesome – *n.* **1.** complexion, condition, constitution, fettle, fitness, form, physique, shape, soundness, state, well-being *Antonyms:* disease, illness, sickness **2.** bloom, energy, haleness, hardihood, hardiness, healthiness, heartiness, robustness, stamina, strength, top form, vigour, wellness, wholeness

healthy *adj.* **1.** able-bodied, active, all right, blooming, burgeoning, disease-free, fit, flourishing, fresh, hale, hardy, hearty, lively, normal, physically fit, robust, sound, strong, sturdy, unimpaired, vigorous, virile, well, whole *Nonformal:* bright-eyed, chipper, pink, rosy-cheeked *Antonyms:* ailing, debilitated, delicate, sickly, weak **2.** advantageous, aiding, beneficial, benign, bracing, cathartic, clean, constitutional, corrective, desirable, energy-giving, fresh, healing, healthful, health-giving, helpful, hygienic, invigorating, nourishing, nutritive, restorative, salubrious, salutary, sanitary, satisfactory, stimulating, sustaining, unadulterated, unpolluted, wholesome *Antonyms:* baleful, harmful, poisonous, sickening

heap *n.* **1.** accumulation, aggregation, amassment, assemblage, bunch, bundle, clump, cluster, collection, concentration, pile, stack, stockpile, store, sum, total, whole **2.** abundance, bounty, great deal, hoard, mound, mountain, ocean, plenitude, plethora, profusion, quantity, score *Nonformal:* gobs, scads, tons *Antonyms:* iota, scrap, trifle – *v.* **1.** accumulate, add, amass, arrange, augment, bank, bunch, collect, concentrate, deposit, dump, fill, gather, group, hoard, increase, load, lump, mass, mound, pack, pile, stack, stockpile, store, swell **2.** bestow, donate, give, lavish, pour, present, rain, shower

hear *v.* apprehend, catch, comprehend, detect, eavesdrop, get, heed, listen, make out, overhear, perceive, pick up, strain, take in

hearing *n.* **1.** auditory range, detection, earshot, extent, faculty, hearing distance, range, reach **2.** ear, faculty, listening, perception, recording, sense, sound **3.** audience, audit, conference, congress, consultation, council, discussion, inquiry, interview, investigation, meeting, negotiation, presentation, reception **4.** audition, chance, opportunity, review, test, trial, tryout *Nonformal:* crack, shot, whack

hearsay *n.* gossip, idle talk, report, rumour, story, street news, tale, talk, tittle-tattle *Nonformal:* buzz, dirt, grapevine, leak, scoop, scuttlebutt, word

heart *n.* **1.** auricle, muscle, organ, vascular organ, ventricle *Nonformal:* pumper, ticker **2.** base, bosom, centre, core, crux, essence, gist, hub, kernel, middle, nub, nucleus, pith, quick, quintessence, root, seat, soul, *tum-tum (Pacific Coast) Nonformal:* bottom line, nitty-gritty **3.** affection, altruism, benevolence, charity, compassion, emotion, empathy, goodness, humaneness, kindness, love, pathos, sensibility, sensitivity, softspot *(Nonformal)*, sympathy, tenderness **4.** boldness, bravery, courage, dash, dauntlessness, élan, energy, enthusiasm, fortitude, gallantry, mettle, resolution, resolve, soul, spirit, verve, vivacity, will *Nonformal:* chutzpah, gumption, guts, moxie, pluck, spunk **5.** character, disposition, emotion, feeling, mindset, mood, nature, sentiment, state, temperament

heartbreak *n.* affliction, agony, anguish, bale, bitterness, desolation, despair, devastation, distress, grief, heartache, misery, pain, regret, remorse, rue, sorrow, suffering, torment, torture, tragedy, woe

heartbroken *adj.* crushed, cut up *(Nonformal)*, depressed, desolate, despondent, destroyed, dispirited, dolorous, gloomy, glum, grieved, hopeless, lachrymose, melancholy, morose, spiritless, sullen, undone, woebegone

hearten *v.* animate, arouse, assure, buoy, cheer, console, embolden, encourage, energize, incite, inspire, motivate, rally, reassure, rouse, stimulate, stir, strengthen, uplift *Antonyms:* depress, discourage, disillusion

heartfelt *adj.* ardent, authentic, bona fide, deep-felt, devout, earnest, fervent, genuine, hearty, honest, profound, sincere, true, unfeigned, warm, wholehearted *Antonyms:* false, fraudulent, frivolous, insincere

heartless *adj.* **1.** adamant, brutal, calculating, callous, cold, cold-blooded, cold-hearted, cruel, hard, hardhearted, harsh, inhuman, inhumane, insensitive, merciless, obdurate, pitiless, ruthless, savage, thick-skinned, uncaring, uncompassionate, unemotional, unfeeling, unkind, unsympathetic *Antonyms:* benevolent, generous, merciful, sensitive **2.** base, cowardly, craven, feeble, gutless *(Nonformal)*, spineless

heart-rending *adj.* affecting, depressing, distressing, grievous, harrowing, heartbreaking, moving, lamentable, painful, pathetic, piteous, pitiful, poignant, sad, touching, tragic

heartthrob *n.* idol, infatuation, passion *Nonformal:* babe, dreamboat, flame, god, goddess, hunk, looker, pin-up, stud

heartwarming *adj.* cheering, encouraging, gladdening, gratifying, inspiring, moving, pleasing, poignant, rewarding, satisfying, uplifting *Antonyms:* shattering, tragic, upsetting

hearty *adj.* **1.** affable, ardent, cheerful, cheery, cordial, deep-felt, enthusiastic, frank, friendly, generous, genial, genuine, glad, glowing, good, honest, impassioned, intense, jolly, jovial, neighbourly, unreserved, unrestrained, warm *Antonyms:* cool, fake, impassive **2.** active, animated, energetic, exuberant, hale, hardy, healthy, robust, solid, sound, strong, vigorous, well *Antonyms:* delicate, feeble, frail, weak **3.** ample, filling, invigorating, nourishing, satisfying, substantial

heat *n.* **1.** fever, fieriness, heat wave, hotness, hot spell, hot weather, sultriness, swelter, temperature, tepidity, torridity, warmth **2.** combustion, conduction, convection, energy, friction, incandescence, pyrolysis, radiation, thermal radiation **3.** abandon, ardour, ecstasy, emotion, eruption, explosion, feeling, fervour, fit, frenzy, fury, intensity, outbreak, outburst, passion, rapture, spasm, spirit, vehemence, violence, zeal **4.** appetite, desire, estrus, itch, longing, lust, sexual desire **5.** playdown, playoff, preliminary, quarters, race, semi, showdown, trial – *v.* **1.** blaze, boil, broil, burn, chafe, char, cook, enkindle, fire, flame, fry, incinerate, inflame, kindle, melt, reheat, roast, scald, scorch, sear, seethe, singe, smelt, swelter, thaw, toast, warm, warm up **2.** arouse, excite, foment, impassion, incense, incite, move, pique, rouse, stimulate, stir, stir up *Antonyms:* cool, curb, dampen

heated *adj.* **1.** boiling, cooked, hot, microwaved, reheated, warmed **2.** angry, animated, ardent, bitter, emotional, fervent, fierce, furious, intense, irate, lively, passionate, raging, red-hot, spirited, stormy, tempestuous, vehement, zealous, zestful

heathen *adj.* **1.** agnostic, atheistic, barbarian, godless, heretical, idolatrous, infidel, irreligious, pagan **2.** barbarian, Philistine, primitive, savage, uncivilized, uncultivated – *n.* agnostic, atheist, disbeliever, dissenter, freethinker, Gentile, heretic, iconoclast, infidel, non-believer, pagan, unbeliever

heave *n.* **1.** breaker, expansion, rise, surge, swell, undulation, wave **2.** break, crack, fault, fissure, fracture – *v.* **1.** chuck, fling, hurl, launch, lob, peg, pitch, sling, throw, toss **2.** elevate, heft, hoist, lift, pull, raise, strain, tug **3.** billow, bulge, popple, rise, surge, swell **4.** breathe, disgorge, exhale, regurgitate, sigh, utter **5.** keck, retch, throw up, vomit *Nonformal:* hurl, puke, ralph, upchuck

heaven *n.* **1.** afterlife, eternity, glory, hereafter, life after death, paradise *Designations of heaven:* Abraham's bosom, Avalon, Celestial *or* Holy City, Elysian Fields, Elysium, God's kingdom, Island of the Blessed, kingdom of glory *or* God *or* heaven, Land of the Leal *(Scottish)*, Olympus, Pure Land, *Qualiparmiut (Inuit)*, sweet-scented Rohutu *(Caribbean)*, the city of God, the Promised Land, *Tir-nan-Og (Irish)*, *Vaikuntha (Hindu)*, Valhalla, Zion *Nonformal:* happy hunting grounds, kingdom come, pearly gates, St. Peter's house **2.** cosmos, empyrean, ether, firmament, sky **3.** Beulah Land, bliss, cloudland, cloud-cuckoo-land *(Nonformal)*, dreamland, ecstasy, Eden, enchantment, enlightenment, felicity, happiness, *moksha (Hindu)*, nirvana, paradise, perfection, rapture, seventh heaven, utopia

heavenly *adj.* alluring, ambrosial, angelic, beautiful, blessed, blissful, celestial, cosmic, delicious, divine, enchanting, exquisite, glorious, godly, grand, great, holy, ideal, otherworldly, paradisaic, paradisiacal, rapturous, ravishing, sublime, superb, sweet, wonderful *Nonformal:* outta sight, scrumptious, splendiferous, to die for *Antonyms:* grim, hellish, horrible, mundane, vile

heavy *adj.* **1.** beefy, big, built, bulky, chunky, corpulent, fat, fleshy, full-figured, hefty, *gros (French)*, immense, large, massive, obese, overweight, portly, stout, thick, top-heavy *Antonyms:* slim, svelte, willowy **2.** awkward, burdensome, clumsy, cumbersome, elephantine, hulking, lumbering, ponderous, unwieldy Nonformal: clunky, lead-footed *Antonyms:* agile, graceful, light-footed, nimble **3.** abundant, ample, bounteous, copious, overflowing, plentiful, profuse, teeming **4.** authoritative, consequential, grave, important, pressing, serious, significant, substantial **5.** abstruse, deep, meaningful, penetrating, profound, rich, sagacious *Antonyms:* lightweight, shallow, simple **6.** arduous, complex, complicated, crushing, dangerous, difficult, formidable, grinding, hard, labour-intensive, mighty, onerous, Sisyphean, strenuous, tedious, tortuous, troublesome, vexatious, weighty *Antonyms:* easy, fascile, simple **7.** close, cloudy, hot, humid, leaden, oppressive, overcast, stifling, sultry *Antonyms:* breezy, cool, fresh **8.** apathetic, crestfallen, dejected, depressed, despondent, disconsolate, downcast, gloomy, glum, indifferent, lackadaisical, listless, melancholic, morose, pensive, sad, sombre, sorrowful, sullen *Antonyms:* happy, light-hearted, sunny **9.** drowsy, dull, exhausted, fatigued, nodding, sleepy, sluggish, snoozy *(Nonformal)*, tired, torpid **10.** gravid, laden, loaded, parturient, portentous, pregnant *Antonyms:* barren, fallow, infertile

heavy-handed *adj.* **1.** authoritarian, autocratic, boorish, cruel, dogmatic, domineering, excessive, harsh, insensitive, oppressive, overbearing, stern, strict, tactless **2.** awkward, bumbling, bungling, clumsy, fumbling, graceless, inept, maladroit *Nonformal:* all-thumbs, ham-fisted, ham-handed

heavy-hearted *adj.* cheerless, crestfallen, dejected, depressed, despondent, forlorn, gloomy, glum, heartsick, melancholy, morose, sad, sullen, woebegone, wretched *Nonformal:* cut up, down *Antonyms:* buoyant, cheerful, ecstatic, elated

heckle *v.* badger, bait, boo, bother, bully, deride, discomfit, disconcert, disrupt, disturb, embarrass, faze, hound, interrupt, jeer, mock, needle, pester, plague, rattle, ridicule, shout at, taunt, tease, torment, worry *Nonformal:* hassle, razz, ride

hectic *adj.* **1.** animated, boisterous, chaotic, confused, crazy, disordered, excited, exciting, fervid, flurrying, flustering, frantic, frenetic, frenzied, furious, heated, mad, restless, riotous, tumultuous, turbulent, unsettled, wild *Antonyms:* calm, peaceful, relaxing, tranquil **2.** burning, fevered, feverish, flaming, hot

hector *n.* **1.** bully, goon *(Nonformal)*, hoodlum, hooligan, rough, ruffian, thug, tough **2.** braggart, fanfaron, hot dog *(Nonformal)*, maw-mouth *(Newfoundland)*, swashbuckler – *v.* annoy, bother, bully, coerce, compel, force, harass, hassle *(Nonformal)*, intimidate, menace, plague, provoke, rant, tease, torment, torture

hedge *n.* **1.** barrier, bush, enclosure, fence, hedgerow, screen, shrubbery, thicket, wall **2.** boxed bet, caution, insurance, protection, safeguard, safety valve – *v.* **1.** block, border, cage, circumscribe, confine, coop, corral, edge, enclose, fence, girdle, hem in, hinder, immure, obstruct, pen, ring, siege, surround *Antonyms:* free, open **2.** avoid, deke, dodge, duck, equivocate, evade, prevaricate, pussyfoot, shuck *(Nonformal)*, shuffle, sidestep, waffle *Antonyms:* confront, face, meet, pursue, seek out **3.** back up, defend, fortify, insure, offset, play safe, protect, restrict, safeguard

hedonist *n. bon vivant (French)*, debauchee, epicurean, glutton, gourmand, libertine, pleasure seeker, profligate, rake, roué, sensualist, sybarite, thrill-seeker, voluptuary *Antonyms:* abstainer, ascetic, Platonist, puritan

heed *n.* application, attention, care, carefulness, caution, cognizance, concentration, concern, consideration, deliberation, interest, notice, observance, observation, regard, respect, study, thought, watchfulness – *v.* attend, care, catch, consider, follow, hark, harken, hear, keep tabs, listen, mark, mind, note, obey, observe, pay attention, pick up, regard, see, spot, watch, watch out *or* over

heedful *adj.* attentive, careful, cautious, chary, circumspect, considerate, mindful, observant, prudent, tuned in *(Nonformal)*, vigilant, wary

heedless *adj.* careless, daydreaming, disregardful, forgetful, goofing off *(Nonformal)*, impetuous, imprudent, inadvertent, inattentive, incautious, neglectful, negligent, oblivious, rash, reckless, sloppy, thoughtless, uncaring, unmindful, unobservant, unthinking, unwary *Antonyms:* aware, careful, cautious, observant, watchful

heel *n.* **1.** calcaneus, foot, hock, hoof **2.** blackguard, cad, cur, rapscallion, rascal, rogue, scamp, scoundrel, sleeveen *(Newfoundland)*, swine, villain *Nonformal:* creep, jerk, rat **3.** back, behind, crust, heelpiece, rear, remainder, remnant, stern, tail *or* tail end – *v.* **1.** careen, keel, lean, list, lurch, shift, tilt, tip, veer **2.** follow, pursue, shadow, tail, track, trail **3.** equip, fund, furnish, gear, give, outfit, provide, rig, subsidize, supply, support

hefty *adj.* **1.** ample, awkward, beefy, big, brawny, bulky, burly, colossal, cumbersome, extensive, fat, heavy, hulking, husky, large, large-scale, major, massive, ponderous, sizable, substantial, thumping *(Nonformal)*, tremendous, unwieldy, weighty *Antonyms:* light, little, minute **2.** forceful, muscular, powerful, robust, strapping, strong, sturdy, vigorous *Antonyms:* feeble, lanky, weak

hegemony *n.* authority, command, control, domination, influence, jurisdiction, leadership, mastership, power, primacy, rule, supremacy, sway

height *n.* **1.** altitude, elevation, measurement, size, stature, tallness **2.** acme, apex, apogee, crest, crown, high point, peak, pinnacle, summit, top, ultimate, zenith *Antonyms:* base, bottom, nadir **3.** dignity, eminence, exaltation, glory, grandeur, loftiness, primacy, sublimity, supremacy **4.** climax, crisis, crowning point, culmination, end, heyday, limit, maximum, *ne plus ultra (Latin) Antonyms:* insignificance, triviality

heighten *v.* aggrandize, amplify, augment, elevate, enhance, enrich, exaggerate, glorify, increase, intensify, raise, sharpen, soup up *(Nonformal)*, strengthen, uplift

heinous *adj.* abhorrent, abominable, atrocious, base, contemptible, deplorable, disgusting, evil, foul, hideous, ignoble, loathsome, monstrous, nefarious, odious, offensive, repugnant, repulsive, shocking, sickening, ugly, unspeakable, vile, wicked *Nonformal:* god-awful, gross

heir *n.* beneficiary, *dauphin (French)*, descendant, grantee, heir apparent, heiress, inheritor, legatee, successor

hell *n.* **1.** abyss, inferno, limbo, perdition, Sam Hill *(Nonformal)*, underworld *Designations of hell:* Acheron, *Adliparmiut (Inuit)*, Gehenna, Hades, *Hel (Norse)*, Pandemonium, Sheol, Tartarus, *Yoma (Japanese)* **2.** affliction, agony, chaos, curse, excruciation, misery, nightmare *(Nonformal)*, ordeal, suffering, torment, torture, trial, wretchedness **3.** castigation, censure, punishment, scolding, upbraiding

hell-bent *adj.* dead-set, determined, dogged, eager, indomitable, obstinate, persistent, relentless, resolute, stubborn, tenacious

hellish *adj.* **1.** barbaric, beastly, brutal, cruel, diabolical, ferocious, fiendish, infernal, inhuman, inhumane, Mephistophelian, sadistic, satanic, savage, sinister **2.** abominable, accursed, hateful, horrid, loathsome, miserable **3.** arduous, dire, gruelling, intense, nightmarish, upsetting

helm *n.* command, control, leadership, reins, rudder, rule, throne, wheel – *v.* direct, guide, lead, manage, pilot, run, skipper, steer

help *n.* **1.** assistance, backing, championship, cooperation, promotion, support **2.** aid, hand, rescue, saving, succour **3.** amelioration, appeasement, care, comfort, consideration, mitigation, palliation, relief, remedy, solace, sympathy **4.** advice, counsel, direction, guidance, instruction, tip, two cents *(Nonformal)* **5.** aid, alms, boon, charity, contribution, donation, gift, money, remittance, stipend, subsidy, sustenance, upkeep, welfare **6.** avail, service, use, utility **7.** aide, assistant, co-worker, crew, employee, farm hand, hand, helper, hireling, labourer, worker *Nonformal:* lackey, stooge, temp, tool – *v.* **1.** abet, accommodate, advocate, aid, assist, back, befriend, bolster, boost, collaborate, cooperate, encourage, endorse, further, intercede, open doors, patronize, plug, promote, push, sanction, serve, stand by, stimulate, sustain, uphold, work for *Nonformal:* ballyhoo, go to bat for, hype *Antonyms:* bar, discourage, hinder, impede, obstruct **2.** alleviate, ameliorate, amend, attend, better, cure, doctor, ease, facilitate, heal, improve, meliorate, mitigate, nourish, palliate, relieve, remedy, restore, revive, treat **3.** bail out, bankroll, finance, fund, pay, subsidize **4.** avoid, contain, escape, eschew, forbear, resist, stop

helper *n.* abettor, aide, ally, assistant, associate, benefactor, caddy, cohort, collaborator, co-worker, mate, partner, right-hand man *(Nonformal)*, Samaritan, second, supporter

helpful *adj.* **1.** advantageous, applicable, beneficial, bettering, conducive, constructive, effectual, favourable, fortunate, instrumental, productive, profitable, serendipitous, significant, timely, useful *Antonyms:* baneful, destructive, harmful **2.** accommodating, benevolent, caring, cooperative, kind, neighbourly, supportive, sympathetic

helping *n.* allowance, course, dollop, meal, plateful, portion, ration, scoop, serving, share

helpless *adj.* **1.** abandoned, debilitated, declawed, defenceless, dependent, destitute, disabled, feeble, forlorn, forsaken, impotent, incapable, incompetent, inefficient, infirm, invalid, newborn, over a barrel *(Nonformal)*, paralyzed, powerless, tapped-out, unable, unprotected, vulnerable, weak *Antonyms:* able, capable, competent, strong, sturdy **2.** at sea, baffled, buffaloed *(Nonformal)*, confused, muddled, mystified, stymied

helter-skelter *adj.* chaotic, confused, cursory, disordered, disorganized, haphazard, hasty, hitherie-hie *(P.E.I.)*, hit-or-miss, hurried, jumbled, muddled, perfunctory, random, slapdash, topsy-turvy *Nonformal:* catawampus, havey-cavey *Antonyms:* clear, intelligible, obvious – *adv.* carelessly, chaotically, confusingly, haphazardly, hastily, headlong, higgledy-piggledy *(Nonformal)*, indiscriminately, pell-mell, rashly, wildly – *n.* commotion, confusion, disorder, hubbub, jumble, kerfuffle *(Nonformal)*, ruckus

hem *interj.* ahem, cough, hesitation, interruption, pause, throat-clearing – *n.* border, brim, brink, edge, edging, fringe, margin, perimeter, periphery, rim, selvage, skirting, trimming, verge – *v.* **1.** bound, cage, circle, circumscribe, close in, confine, corral, define, edge, encircle, enclose, encompass, envelop, fence, girdle, pen, restrict, ring, shut in, surround **2.** dodge, evade, falter, fudge, haw, hesitate, prevaricate, pussyfoot, stammer

herald *n.* **1.** adviser, announcer, bearer, courier, crier, messenger, outrider, prophet, reporter, runner **2.** forerunner, harbinger, indicator, omen, precursor, sign, signal, token – *v.* advertise, announce, ballyhoo *(Nonformal)*, broadcast, declare, indicate, portend, proclaim, publicize, tell, tout, trumpet, usher in

heraldry *n.* **1.** armoury, badge, bar, baton, blazonry, coat of arms, crest, cross, emblazonry, emblem, ensign, escutcheon, hatchment, insignia, regalia, shield, symbol **2.** ceremony, display, formality, grandeur, pageantry, parade, pomp, ritual, solemnity, spectacle, splendour

herb *n.* flora, grass, herbage, pasture, vegetation *Kinds of herbs:* angelica, basil, bay leaf, bee balm *or* bergamot, belladonna, betony, borage, *bouquet garni (French)*, calendula, camomile, catnip, chervil, chicory, chive, cilantro, coleus, coriander, cow parsnip, cumin, dill, dittany, fennel, horehound, hyssop, lavender, lemon balm *or* verbena, licorice, lovage, mace, mandrake, mint, nightshade, oregano, parsley, patchouli, pennyroyal, peppermint, rosemary, rue, sage, sapphire, savory, sorrel, spearmint, St. John's Wort, sweet cicely *or* woodruff, tansy, tarragon, teasel, thyme, watercress, wintergreen, wormwood, wort *See also:* **spice**

herculean *adj.* **1.** colossal, gigantic, huge, massive, mighty, powerful, robust, sinewy, strapping, strong, vigorous **2.** arduous, backbreaking, crushing, difficult, exhausting, formidable, gruelling, hellish, laborious, onerous, strenuous, toilsome, tough, wearing *Nonformal:* brutal, nightmarish

herd *n.* assemblage, bevy, brood, clan, collection, covey, crowd, crush, drove, flight, flock, gaggle, gathering, group, hoi polloi, horde, lot, mass, mob, multitude, nest, pack, populace, press, rabble, school, scrum, swarm, throng – *v.* **1.** assemble, associate, bunch, collect, congregate, flock, gather, huddle, muster, rally **2.** corral, drive, force, goad, guide, lead, poke, round up, run, shepherd, spur

hereafter *adv.* eventually, following, hence *or* henceforth, in future *or* time, later, thereafter – *n.* **1.** afterlife, afterworld, Avalon, beyond, death, destiny, Elysian Fields, heaven, hell, nether world, next life, underworld, Valhalla **2.** by-and-by, future *or* future existence, life-to-be

hereditary *adj.* **1.** ancestral, bequeathed, genealogical, handed down, inherited, lineal, passed down *or* on, traditional, willed **2.** congenital, genetic, inborn, inbred, inheritable, transmitted

heredity *n.* ancestry, blood, characteristics, chromosomes, construction, DNA, genes, genetic makeup, genetics, inheritance, line, lineage, Mendelism, RNA, traits

heresy *n.* agnosticism, atheism, blasphemy, disbelief, dissidence, heterodoxy, iconoclasm, nonconformity, paganism, profanity, revisionism, schism, sectarianism, secularism, scepticism, unorthodoxy

heretic *n.* abjurer, apostate, backslider, deviationist, dissenter, dissident, freethinker, Gentile, heathen, heresiarch, iconoclast, infidel, nonconformist, pagan, recreant, recusant, renegade, renouncer, revisionist, schismatic, sectarian, separatist, sceptic

heritage *n.* **1.** ancestry, background, convention, culture, custom, tradition **2.** bequest, birthright, dowry, endowment, estate, heirloom, heirship, inheritance, legacy, lot, patrimony, portion, right, share *See also:* **site**

hermit *n.* anchorite, ascetic, eremite, lone wolf *(Nonformal)*, loner, monk, recluse, solitary, solitudinarian, troglodyte

hermitage *n.* **1.** abbey, cloister, convent, friary, monastery, nunnery, priory **2.** asylum, haven, hideaway, refuge, resort, retreat, sanctuary, shelter

hero *n.* **1.** acme, apotheosis, demigod, exemplar, gallant, god, goddess, heroine, icon, idol, knight, martyr, mentor, nonpareil, paragon, role-model, saint, saviour, superhero *Antonyms:* bad influence, evil star, hoodlum, punk **2.** champ, champion, cup holder, master, victor, winner *Nonformal:* numero uno, top dog **3.** celebrity, diva, headliner, lead, sports star, star **4.** character, leading man, leading role, male lead, principal, protagonist *Antonyms:* antagonist, enemy, stooge, villain

heroic *adj.* **1.** bold, brave, chivalrous, courageous, daring, dauntless, doughty, eminent, fearless, gallant, intrepid, lionhearted, noble, resolute, steadfast, stouthearted, undaunted, unflinching, valiant, valorous *Nonformal:* ballsy, gutsy **2.** classic, dignified, elevated, epic, grand, Homeric, legendary, mythological **3.** dramatic, enormous, exaggerated, extravagant, grandiose, high-flown, huge, high-flown, larger than life, titanic

heroin *n.* diacetylmorphine, narcotic *Nonformal:* big H, crack, crank, crap, H, horse, jones, junk, smack

heroism *n.* boldness, bravery, chivalry, courage, courageousness, daring, dauntlessness, fearlessness, fortitude, gallantry, glory, grit, intrepidity, nobility, pluck, prowess, spirit, strength, valour *Antonyms:* cowardice, cravenness

hesitant *adj.* afraid, averse, dawdling, delaying, diffident, dilatory, disinclined, doubtful, doubting, faltering, halfhearted, halting, hanging back, indecisive, irresolute, reluctant, sceptical, shy, tentative, uncertain, unsure, unwilling, vacillating, wavering *Nonformal:* on the fence, shaky *Antonyms:* confident, definite, determined, eager, enthusiastic

hesitate *v.* balk, dally, debate, defer, delay, demur, dither, doubt, equivocate, falter, flounder, fluctuate, hang *or* pull back, hedge, hover, pause, ponder, procrastinate, pussyfoot, seesaw, shift, shrink, shy away, stammer, stop, straddle, stumble, stutter, swerve, tergiversate, think about *or* twice, vacillate, waffle, wait, waver, weigh *Nonformal:* double clutch, shilly-shally *Antonyms:* continue, decide, settle

hesitation *n.* averseness, dawdling, delaying, demurral, doubt, dubiety, equivocation, faltering, fluctuation, fumbling, hesitancy, indecisiveness, irresolution, misgiving, pause, procrastination, qualm, reluctance, scepticism, stumbling, stuttering, uncertainty, vacillation, waiting, wavering *Antonyms:* certainty, resolution, tenacity, zeal

heterodox *adj.* dissenting, divergent, doubting, freethinking, heretical, iconoclastic, recusant, sceptical, unbelieving, unconventional, unorthodox *Antonyms:* conforming, loyal

heterogeneous *adj.* assorted, composite, conglomerate, contrary, different, discordant, disparate, dissimilar, diverse, diversified, incongruous, kaleidoscopic, miscellaneous, mingled, mixed, mongrel, mosaic, motley, multifarious, opposed, polymorphic, unlike, varied, variegated, various *Antonyms:* alike, homogeneous, identical, similar, uniform

hew *v.* **1.** axe, carve, chisel, chop *or* cut down, cut out, divide, fashion, fell, form, hack, lop, model, mould, prune, saw, sculpt, sever, shape, split, whittle **2.** adhere, conform, follow, heed, mind, obey, observe

hex *n.* **1.** bewitchment, cantrip, charm, conjuration, curse, jinx, *maleficio (Italian)*, sorcery, spell *Nonformal:* evil eye, whammy **2.** enchantress, sorcerer, sorceress, warlock, witch, wizard – *v.* bewitch, cast a spell, charm, curse, enchant, jinx, spook

heyday *n.* bloom, blossom, crowning point, culmination, exuberance, flowering, glory, halcyon period, peak, pinnacle, prime, salad days, summit, zenith

hiatus *n.* **1.** aperture, blank, breach, break, chasm, cleft, gap, interim, interruption, interval, lacuna, lapse, opening, recess, rift, space **2.** holiday, March *or* spring break, reading week, time-off, vacation

hibernate *v.* hide, hole up *(Nonformal)*, lie dormant *or* torpid, retire, sleep, slumber, vegetate, winter, withdraw

hidden *adj.* **1.** buried, clandestine, cloaked, concealed, covered, covert, disguised, eclipsed, imperceptible, incognito, indiscernible, invisible, latent, masked, recondite, secret, undercover, undetected, unseen, veiled, withheld *Antonyms:* exposed, revealed, uncovered, visible **2.** abstruse, arcane, clouded, cryptic, dark, esoteric, mysterious, mystical, obscure, shadowy, shrouded *Antonyms:* apparent, clear, evident, plain

hide *n.* dried barkers *(Nonformal)*, fell, husk, pelt, robe, skin – *v.* **1.** bury, cache, camouflage, cloak, conceal, cover, ensconce, harbour, hold back, mask, salt *or* stow away, screen, secrete, shelter, shield, stash, suppress, veil *Nonformal:* plant, squirrel **2.** disappear, go underground, lie low *(Nonformal)*, take cover, vanish **3.** beat, flog, hit, injure, lash, pummel, punch, punish, spank, whip, whop *(Nonformal)*, wound

hideaway *n.* cottage, den, hermitage, hideout, hidey-hole *(Nonformal)*, hiding place, lair, priest's hole, refuge, retreat, sanctuary, sanctum, secret place, shelter

hideous *adj.* abominable, appalling, awful, beastly, detestable, disgusting, dreadful, flagrant, foul, frightful, ghastly, grim, grisly, gross, grotesque, gruesome, hateful, heinous, horrendous, horrible, horrid, loathsome, macabre, monstrous, morbid, nasty, odious, offensive, repellent, repugnant, repulsive, revolting, shocking, sickening, terrible, terrifying, ugly, unsightly *Antonyms:* appealing, beautiful, captivating, entrancing, pleasant

hierarchical *adj.* arranged, calibrated, categorized, classed, classified, gradational, graded, ordered, pegged, pigeonholed, placed, ranked, spectral, structured

hierarchy *n.* **1.** caste, class *or* economic *or* social structure, degree, gradation, grade, grading, grouping, pecking order, place, position, rank, segregation, separation, slot, station **2.** apparat, bureaucracy, clericalism, elect, elite, hierocracy, matriarchy, officialdom, patriarchy, politburo, prelacy, ruling body, the establishment, theocracy, upper class

higgledy-piggledy *adj.* all over the place, chaotic, confused, disordered, disorganized, haphazard, heedless, hit-or-miss, irregular, jumbled, muddled, random, topsy-turvy, unorganized, unsystematic *Antonyms:* orderly, organized, regular, systematic – *adv.* carelessly, hastily, headlong, helter-skelter, hurriedly, pell-mell, rashly, recklessly, wildly *Antonyms:* carefully, cautiously, meticulously, neatly, precisely – *n.* anarchy, bedlam, chaos, confusion, disorder, jumble, madhouse, mess, muddle, pandemonium, salmagundi, turmoil *Antonyms:* calm, neatness, order, organization, tidiness

high *adj.* **1.** arch, capital, chief, consequential, crucial, distinguished, eminent, essential, exalted, extreme, grand, grave, important, influential, leading, necessary, noble, powerful, prominent, ruling, serious, significant, superior *Antonyms:* average, common, inconsequential, low, menial **2.** costly, dear, excessive, exorbitant, expensive, extraordinary, extravagant, extreme, high-priced, lavish, luxurious, overpriced, precious, rich, sharp, special, steep, stiff, too much **3.** aerial, alpine, cathedral, elevated, great, high-reaching, high-rise, hovering, kissing the clouds, lofty, soaring, tall, towering *Nonformal:* sky-high, sky-scraping *Antonyms:* dwarfed, low, short, stunted **4.** boisterous, bouncy, cheerful, elated, excited, exhilarated, exuberant, happy, hyped *(Nonformal)*, joyful, lighthearted, merry *Antonyms:* angry, dejected, gloomy, sad **5.** delirious, doped, drugged, drunk, euphoric, inebriated, intoxicated, tipsy *Nonformal:* flipping, flying, hammered, loaded, loved up, over the edge, potted, psyched, spaced out, stoned, tripping, wasted, zonked **6.** acute, high-pitched, loud, penetrating, piercing, piping, sharp, shrill, soprano, strident, treble *Antonyms:* deep, low, resonant **7.** arrogant, condescending, disdainful, full of oneself, haughty, hoity-toity, hubristic, pompous, pretentious, proud, snobbish, supercilious, superior *Nonformal:* snooty, stuck up **8.** by-the-book, conservative, excessive, extreme, orthodox, strict, traditional **9.** gamy, malodorous, nasty, off, overripe, ripe, rotten, smelly, stinking, strong, tainted – *adv.* **1.** above, aloft, on high, overhead, upwards **2.** excessively, immoderately, in excess, prodigally, unreservedly, without restraint – *n.* **1.** acme, altitude, apex, elevation, height, peak, rise, summit, the roof, top, zenith **2.** ebullience, ecstasy, elation, euphoria, exhilaration, long strange trip *(Nonformal)*, transport *Antonyms:* bummer, downer, skids

highborn *adj.* aristocratic, blue-blooded, genteel, gentle, highbred, noble, old school *(Nonformal)*, patrician, pedigreed, purebred, silk-stocking, thoroughbred, upper class, well connected *Antonyms:* plebeian, proletarian, untouchable, working-class

highbrow *adj.* bookish, brainy, cerebral, cultivated, deep, erudite, intellectual, ivory-towered, learned, philosophical, profound, scholarly, serious, theoretical *Nonformal:* blue-stocking, long-haired, stuffy *Antonyms:* boorish, lowbrow, vulgar – *n.* aesthetic, intellectual, mastermind, philosopher, scholar, thinker

high-class *adj.* classy, *crème de la crème (French)*, deluxe, elite, exclusive, first-rate, five-star, high-quality, luxurious, outstanding, premier, stellar, super, superior, tiptop, top-flight, upper-class, world-class *Nonformal:* posh, snooty, stuck-up *Antonyms:* boorish, shoddy, vulgar

high-flown *adj.* affected, arrogant, bloated, bombastic, conceited, condescending, disdainful, egotistical, elaborate, extravagant, flagrant, flamboyant, flashy, flaunting, florid, flowery, flowing, grand, grandiose, inflated, lofty, magniloquent, orotund, ostentatious, pompous, pretentious, purple, self-aggrandizing, sententious, snobbish, strutting, stuffy, supercilious, swollen, turgid, vain, vaunting *Antonyms:* down-to-earth, moderate, modest

highland *n.* foothill, God's country *(Nonformal)*, hill *or* hilly country, mountains, plateau, promontory, rolling country, tableland, upland *or* uplands

highlight *n.* apex, apogee, climax, feature, focal point, focus, height, peak, watershed, zenith – *v.* accent, accentuate, emphasize, feature, play up, point *or* single out, punctuate, spotlight, stress, underline

highly *adv.* decidedly, deeply, eminently, exceedingly, exceptionally, extraordinarily extremely, greatly, hugely, immensely, much, muchly, notably, plenty, profoundly, really, remarkably, strikingly, supremely, surpassingly, terrifically, tremendously, vastly, very, well *Nonformal:* awfully, mighty, terribly

high-minded *adj.* aboveboard, beyond reproach, clean, conscientious, decent, elevated, ethical, fair, foursquare, good, honest, honourable, idealistic, magnanimous, moral, noble, principled, pure, reputable, righteous, sincere, sterling, straight, true-minded, truthful, uncorrupt, upright, virtuous, worthy

high-strung *adj.* agitated, anxious, demanding, edgy, excitable, hyperactive, impatient, intolerant, irascible, irritable, jittery, jumpy, moody, nervous, neurotic, oversensitive, peevish, restless, skittish, temperamental, tense, uneasy, wrought up *Nonformal:* prickly, wired *Antonyms:* calm, collected, placid

highway *n.* artery, autobahn, autoroute, avenue, boulevard, expressway, four-lane, freeway, inter-provincial, interstate, motorway, parking lot *(Nonformal)*, parkway, path, pike, road, roadway, skyway, street, superhighway, thoroughfare, throughway *or* thruway, toll road *or* route, track, Trans-Canada, turnpike

highwayman *n.* bandit, brigand, freebooter, highway robber, hijacker, mugger, outlaw, pirate, robber, ronin *Nonformal:* blackleg, footpad, hold-up man, road agent, stick-up man

hijack *v.* coerce, commandeer, compel, dragoon, heist, kidnap, seize, take over *Nonformal:* shanghai, skyjack

hijinks *n. pl.* capers, festivities, frolic, fun, horseplay, joking, merrymaking, mirth, pranks, roughhousing *(Nonformal)*, silliness, stunts

hike *n.* **1.** constitutional, excursion, exploration, jaunt, journey, march, perambulation, ramble, stroll, trek, trip, walk, walkabout **2.** addition, augmentation, enlargement, increase, inflation, rise *Antonyms:* decrease, reduction – *v.* **1.** advance, boost, increase, jack, jump, lift, pull up, put up, raise, upgrade **2.** backpack, climb, explore, hoof *(Nonformal)*, ramble, rove, stroll, stump, tour, traipse, tramp, travel, trek, tromp, walk

hilarious *adj.* amusing, comical, convivial, entertaining, exhilarating, funny, gleeful, happy, humorous, jocular, jolly, jovial, joyous, laughable, lively, merry, mirthful, riotous, rollicking, uproarious, witty *Nonformal:* gut-busting, hysterical, priceless *Antonyms:* dull, offensive, sad, serious

hill *n.* ascent, bank, bluff, *brae (Scottish)*, butte, cliff, climb, cradle-hill *(Maritimes)*, demoiselle *(Prairies)*, down *(British)*, drumlin, dune, elevation, esker, fell, foothill, gradient, headland, highland, hillock, hilltop, hummock, hump, incline, knoll, kopje *(Afrikaans)*, mogul, moraine, mound, pile, prominence, promontory, ridge, rise, rising ground, slope, summit, till, tor, upland, uprising

hillock *n.* barrow, hill, hummock, hump, knap, knoll, mound, swell

hind *adj.* back, backward, behind, dorsal, hindmost, posterior, rear, rump, tail *Antonyms:* anterior, front, ventral

hinder *v.* arrest, balk, bar, block, bottleneck, burden, check, choke, clog, counteract, cramp, crimp, cripple, curb, debar, delay, deter, encumber, fetter, frustrate, hamper, hamstring, handicap, hog-tie, hold back, hold up, impede, inhibit, interfere, muzzle, prevent, prohibit, resist, retard, stonewall, stymie, thwart, trammel *Antonyms:* accelerate, advance, benefit, encourage, expedite

hindrance *n.* albatross, bar, barrier, catch, crimp, delay, deterrent, drag, drawback, encumbrance, excess baggage *(Nonformal)*, handicap, impediment, interference, intervention, jam, limitation, millstone, obstacle, obstruction, restraint, restriction, snag, stoppage, stumbling block, trammel, yoke *Antonyms:* asset, benefit, boost, support

Hinduism *n.* faith, religion, sanatana dharma *Major Hindu festivals:* Bandhan,

Divali, Durga Puja *or* Navaratri Raksha, Dussehra, Holi, Janmashtami, Rama Naumi, Ratha Yatra, Sarasvati Puja, Shivaratri

hinge *n.* axis, ball-and-socket, butt, elbow, hook, joint, juncture, knee, link, pin, pivot, spring, swivel *Kinds of hinge:* blind, butt, gate, H-hinge, link, plate, spring, strap, T-hinge – *v.* depend, hang, pend, pivot, rest, revolve around, stand *or* swing *or* turn on, turn

hint *n.* **1.** advice, allusion, clue, communication, connotation, gesture, glimmer, help, idea, implication, impression, indication, inference, information, inkling, innuendo, insinuation, intimation, lead, leak, mention, mote, notice, nudge, observation, omen, pointer, prompt, reference, reminder, scent, shadow, sign, suggestion, suspicion, symptom, tip, trace, warning, whiff, whisper, wink **2.** dash, shred, smack, smattering, snippet, soupçon, sprinkling, taste, tint, touch, vestige – *v.* acquaint, advise, allude to, broach, expose, foreshadow, impart, imply, indicate, infer, insinuate, intimate, leak, mention, prompt, recall, remind, shadow, signify, suggest, tip off, whisper, wink

hinterland *n.* back *or* bear *or* bush *or* cottage *or* cow *or* game *or* moose country, backwoods, borderland, bush, bushveld *(South African)*, forest, frontier, outback *(Australian)*, outpost, the back of beyond, uninhabited region, virgin land *or* territory, wasteland, wilderness, wilds, wild west, woods *Nonformal:* back forty, back of beyond, boondocks, boonies, the sticks

hip *adj.* **1.** avant-garde, cosmopolitan, cutting-edge, fashionable, sophisticated, stylish, trendy *Nonformal:* cool, funky, groovy, in **2.** aware, cognizant, conscious, informed, knowledgeable, observant, perceptive, sharp, worldly *Nonformal:* clued *or* tuned in, hep, savvy, up to speed, with it – *n.* ball-and-socket, connection, haunch, joint, juncture, pelvis, unison

hippie *n.* beatnik, bohemian, dropout, flower child, free spirit, nonconformist *Nonformal:* Deadhead, freak, hipster, longhair, pothead, weirdo

hire *n.* charge, compensation, cost, damage *(Nonformal)*, fee, payment, price, rental – *v.* **1.** appoint, authorize, book, bring in, carry, commission, contract, delegate, draft, employ, empower, engage, enlist, exploit, give work, obtain, pick, place, procure, promise, put on, retain, secure, select, sign on *or* up, take on, truck with *(Nonformal)*, use, utilize **2.** charter, lease, let, occupy, rent, sublease, sublet

hiss *n.* **1.** boo, catcall, condemnation, derision, disapproval, jeer, mockery, sneer, taunt *Nonformal:* Bronx cheer, raspberry **2.** buzz, hissing, sibilance, sibilation, whisper – *v.* **1.** boo, catcall, condemn, damn, decry, deride, give the bird *(Nonformal)*, heckle, hoot, jeer, mock, revile, ridicule, scoff, shout down, taunt *Antonyms:* applaud, approve, cheer, praise **2.** sibilate, sizzle, wheeze, whistle

historic *adj.* celebrated, consequential, extraordinary, famous, important, legendary, memorable, momentous, mythical, notable, outstanding, red-letter, remarkable, significant, well- known *Antonyms:* everyday, forgotten, ordinary, unknown

historical *adj.* **1.** ancient, antique, archival, classical, dusty, mouldy, old, past, traditional, yellowed **2.** actual, attested, authentic, chronicled, chronological, commemorated, demonstrable, documented, empirical, factual, objective, real, recorded, verifiable **3.** famous, far-reaching, important, memorable, momentous, notable, noteworthy, significant

history *n.* **1.** account, adventures, annals, autobiography, biography, chronicle, diary, epic, experiences, fortunes, genealogy, herstory, life, life story, memoirs, narration, narrative, recapitulation, recital, record, report, saga, version **2.** antiquity, bygone *or* bygones, foretime, auld lang syne, long ago, olden days *(Nonformal)*, past, yesterday, yesteryear, yore

histrionic *adj.* **1.** affected, artificial, bogus, false, forced, insincere, mannered, overdone, sensational *Nonformal:* corny, fake, hammy, phoney *Antonyms:* authentic, genuine, sincere, veritable **2.** dramatic, dramaturgical, Hollywood *(Nonformal)*, melodramatic, overacted, overplayed, theatrical

hit *n.* **1.** belt, blow, box, chop, clip, cuff, fisticuff, knock, lick, one-two, poke, punch, slap, smack, spank, tap, uppercut, wallop *Nonformal:* going over, haymaker, roundhouse, sallywinder, skite **2.** accomplishment, felicity, fortunate event, lucky break, phenom *(Nonformal)*, record breaker, sensation, show-stopper, success, triumph, victory, win **3.** collision, crash, fender-bender *(Nonformal)*, head-on, impact, smash-up **4.** dose, injection, portion, shot *Nonformal:* bang, drag, fix, toke **5.** comeback, criticism, cut, jibe, retort, riposte, sarcasm, witticism *Nonformal:* dis, rap, slam – *v.* **1.** bang, bash, bat, batter, beat, belt, biff, brain, buffet, bump, clobber, club, crack, cudgel, cuff, ding, flog, hammer, hook, jab, kick, knock out, lace, lambaste, nail, pelt, pop, pound, punch, rap, render senseless *or* unconscious, slap, smack, sock, strike, swat, tap, thrash, thump, thwack, uppercut, wallop, whack *Nonformal:* bean, boff, bonk, deck, dust, kayo *or* KO, pepper, ream, tan **2.** bump, butt, clash, collide, crash, jostle, knock *or* run into, meet, rear-end, scrape, sideswipe, smash **3.** achieve, detect, discover, find, notice, stumble upon, uncover, unearth **4.** accord, befit, coincide, correspond, fit, suit, tally **5.** affect, agitate, impinge on, influence, move, perturb, stir, touch, trouble

hitch *n.* **1.** block, catch, checkmate, crimp, crux, delay, difficulty, drag, encumbrance, frustration, glitch, halt, hindrance, hurdle, impediment, obstacle, SNAFU *(Nonformal)*, snag, stumbling block, trouble, upset **2.** gait, halt, hobble, limp, lurch **3.** jerk, pluck, pull, tug, tweak, twitch, wrench, yank **4.** duration, period, span, tenure, time **5.** knot, loop, noose, rope *(Nonformal)* **6.** lift, ride *Nonformal:* boost, leg up– *v.* **1.** attach, chain, connect, couple, fasten, harness, hook, join, lash, marry, moor, strap, tether, tie, unite, wed, yoke *Antonyms:* free, loose, loosen, release, untie **2.** falter, flounder, hobble, limp, lurch, move, stagger, walk

hitchhike *v.* case a ride, hitch *Nonformal:* long arm, thumb

hoard *n.* abundance, accumulation, agglomeration, aggregation, amassment, backlog, cache, collection, conglomeration, cumulation, funds, heap, inventory, mass, nest egg, pile, reserve, reservoir, riches, stash, stock, stockpile, store, supply, tons *(Nonformal)*, treasure, wealth *Antonyms:* dispersal, distribution, scattering – *v.* accumulate, acquire, amass, bogart *(Nonformal)*, cache, collect, deposit, garner, gather, give out, put by, save, salt *or* squirrel *or* stow away, stash, stockpile, store *Antonyms:* dispense, disseminate, distribute, scatter

hoarse *adj.* cracked, croaking, croupy, deep, discordant, grating, gravelly, growling, gruff, guttural, harsh, husky, jarring, low, ragged, raspy, raucous, rough, scratching, throaty, whispering *Antonyms:* harmonious, mellifluous, smooth

hoary *adj.* **1.** aged, ancient, antiquated, antique, dated, elderly, geriatric, old, venerable *Antonyms:* modern, new, up-to-date, youthful **2.** frosty, grey, greyed, grizzled, grizzly, silvery, snowy, white, whitened, wizened

hoax *n.* cheat, deceit, deception, fabrication, fake, falsification, fraud, gimmick, joke, lie, prank, racket, ruse, set-up, spoof, swindle, trick *Nonformal:* cock-and-bull story, con *or* con game, scam, sting, whopper – *v.* bluff, deceive, delude, dupe, fool, frame, hoodwink, rook, swindle, take in, trick *Nonformal:* bamboozle, con, fleece, flim-flam, hornswoggle, set up, sting

hobble *n.* **1.** gait, hitch, limp, shuffle, stagger, stumble, waddle **2.** chain, fetter, link, rein, restriction, ring, rope, shackle, strap, string, tether **3.** bind, blight, difficulty, embarrassment, fix, mess, predicament, scrape, spot, strait *Nonformal:* hot water, pickle, sticky situation *or* wicket – *v.* **1.** chain, confine, cripple, disable, fetter, frustrate, hamper, hamstring, hog-tie, impede, lame, maim, manacle, obstruct, restrict, shackle, tie, trammel *Antonyms:* free, loosen, unbind **2.** falter, hitch, limp, lurch, stumble, totter *Antonyms:* glide, race

hobby *n.* amusement, art, avocation, bag *(Nonformal)*, craft, craze, distraction, diversion, divertissement, fad, fancy, fun, game, interest, leisure activity *or* pursuit, obsession, occupation, pastime, pursuit, relaxation, sideline, specialty, sport, weakness, whim, whimsy

hobnob *v.* associate, chum, consort, fraternize, mingle, mix, network, rub elbows, socialize *Nonformal:* hang around *or* out, pal *or* run with, schmooze

hockey *n.* shinny, the game *Hockey equipment:* blocker *or* waffle *(Nonformal)*, catcher *or* mitt, chest protector, elbow pads, face-guard, gloves, goalie pads, helmet, jock and protective cup, mask, mouthguard, neck protector, pants, puck *or rondelle (French)*, shin pads, shoulder pads, skates, socks, stick, suspenders, tape *Kinds of hockey:* ball, bandy, field, floor, foot, ice, knob *or* table, pick-up, pond, ringette, road *or* street, sponge *Kinds of ice hockey check:* backcheck, boarding, bodycheck, cross-check, forecheck, hip, poke, stick, sweep *Parts of the arena:* bench, blueline, boards, clock, concession stand, crease, dressing room, faceoff circles, glass, goal line, gondola, hash marks, net, organ, penalty box, posts, press box, redline, stands, timekeeper's box, vendor *Positions in hockey:* centre, goalie *or* goaltender *or* netminder, left defence, left wing, right defence, right wing *Scoring and procedure in ice hockey: à but (French)*, assist, block, check, deke, drop pass, first period, goal, head deke, intermission, overtime, pass, penalty, penalty shot, save, score, second period, shot, stickhandling, sudden-death overtime, third period *Hockey trophies:* Jack Adams, Allan Cup, Lady Byng, Calder, Canada Cup, King Clancy, Hart, Bill Jennings, Bill Masterton, Memorial Cup, Norris, Lester Patrick, Lester B. Pearson, President's Cup, Maurice "Rocket" Richard, Art Ross, Frank J. Selke, Conn Smythe, Spengler, Stanley Cup, Vezina

hocus-pocus *n.* **1.** abracadabra, cant, cantrip, chant, charm, conjuring, gibberish, gobbledygook, hex, incantation, jargon, magic, mumbo-jumbo, nonsense, razzle-dazzle, witchery, wizardry **2.** artifice, cheating, chicanery, deceit, deception, delusion, feint, flim-flam *(Nonformal)*, fraud, hoax, humbug, juggling, legerdemain, mummery, razzmatazz, swindle, trick, trickery – *v.* cheat, deceive, delude, dupe, fake, fool, fraud, hoodwink, lie, swindle, trick *Nonformal:* bamboozle, snake

hodgepodge *n.* array, assortment, collection, combination, farrago, gallimaufry, hash, jumble, medley, melange, mess, miscellany, mishmash, mixed bag, mixture, patchwork, potpourri, salmagundi, stew

hoe *n.* rake, scraper, scuffle, spade, trowel *Kinds of hoe:* backhoe, draw, garden, grub, mortar, rub, scuffle, Warren, weeding – *v.* cultivate, dig, dress, garden, harrow, rake, scrape, spade, till, weed

hogwash *n.* **1.** dregs, garbage, leavings, leftovers, refuse, residue, slop, swill, waste **2.** babble, double-talk, doublespeak, foam, froth, gas, gibberish, moonshine, nonsense, psycho-babble, tripe, wind *Nonformal:* baloney, beans, cock, crap, crock, hokum, malarkey *Antonyms:* fact, reality, reason, seriousness, truth

hoist *n.* boost, crane, hoyer, jack, lift – *v.* boost, crane, elevate, erect, heave, jack, lift, pick up, raise, rear, take up, uphold, uplift

hold *n.* **1.** bear hug, clamp, clasp, clinch, clutch, embrace, grasp, grip, handle, hug, purchase, seizure, support **2.** allure, attraction, authority, charisma, charm, clout *(Nonformal)*, command, control, domination, effect, enchantment, force, influence, leverage, magnetism, mastery, possession, power, pull, sway, tenure **3.** bunker, cell, confinement, custody, hole, lockup, prison, slammer *(Nonformal)*, tank **4.** bastion, citadel, defence, donjon, foothold, fortification, keep, safehold, stronghold **5.** cellar, compartment, depository, locker, receptacle, repository, reservoir, store, storehouse, storeroom – *v.* **1.** adhere, bear, cherish, clasp, cleave, clinch, cling, clutch, embrace, foster, grab, grasp, grip, harbour, hug, keep, nurture, seize **2.** bolster, brace, buttress, endure, fix, maintain, reinforce, remain, pin down *(Nonformal)*, prop, stabilize, steady, support, sustain **3.** absorb, engross, enthrall, fascinate, grab, mesmerize, monopolize, obsess, preoccupy, spellbind, transfix **4.** accommodate, comprehend, comprise, contain, encompass, environ, extend, include, reach, surround, take in **5.** arrest, bridle, check, confine, constrain, control, detain, enclose, govern, immure, impound, inhibit, repress, restrain, stifle, subdue, suppress, withhold **6.** believe, consider, count, deem, esteem, estimate, fancy, judge, reckon, regard, think of

holdup *n.* **1.** burglary, hijack, mugging, robbery, stealing, theft *Nonformal:* heist, hustle, stick-up **2.** block, delay, gridlock, hindrance, jam, obstruction, roadblock, setback, slowdown, snag, stay, stop, traffic jam

hole *n.* **1.** cavity, cup, dip, dugout, excavation, hollow, indentation, pit, pocket, recess, scoop **2.** burrow, cavern, den, lair, **3.** aperture, breach, break, chink, cleft, corner, cut, gash, opening, orifice, perforation, puncture, rent, split, tangle, tear, vent, window **4.** box, difficulty, dilemma, emergency, fix, imbroglio, impasse, jam, mess, pickle *(Nonformal)*, plight, predicament, quandary, scrape, spot **5.** crib, dive, dump, hole-in-the-wall, hovel, joint, pigsty, rathole, slum, sty **6.** bug *(Nonformal)*, defect, deficiency, fallibility, flaw, inconsistency, non sequitur, unsoundness, weakness **7.** cell, cellar, compartment, dungeon, hold, oubliette, priest's hole, prison **8.** cubbyhole, niche, pigeonhole, slot, storage space

holiday *n.* anniversary, break, busman's holiday, celebration, feast, festival, festivity, fête, fiesta, gala, getaway, holy day, leave, liberty, long weekend, mental health day *(Nonformal)*, recess, red-letter day, respite, saint's day, time off, vacation *Holidays observed in Canada:* April Fool's Day, Arbor Day, Boxing Day, British Columbia Day, Canada Day, Civic holiday, Confederation Day, Discovery Day *(Yukon)*, Dominion Day, Family Day *(Alberta)*, Father's Day, Fête national *or* St. Jean Baptiste Day *(Quebec)*, Flag Day, Halloween, Heritage Day, Iroquois Midwinter Ceremony, Kwanza, Labour Day, Lobster Carnival *(Nova Scotia)*, March break *or* reading week, Martin Luther King Day, Mother's Day, Natal Day *(Nova Scotia and P.E.I.)*, New Brunswick Day, New Year's Day, Queen's Birthday *(B.C. and Newfoundland)*, Remembrance Day, Simcoe Day *(Ontario)*, Thanksgiving Day, Veteran's Day, Victoria Day, Weedless Wednesday *Newfoundland:* Discovery Day, Memorial Day, Regatta Day *Buddhist holidays:* Asalha, Assayuja, Birth of the Buddha, Birth *or* Death *or* Enlightenment of Kuan Yin *or* Kwannon, Buddha's Enlightenment, Cho-khor *or* Lhabab Duchen, Esala Perahera *(Sri Lankan)*, Ho Khao Slak *(Laotian)*, Kathina, Kattika, Losar *(Tibetan)*, Magha Puja, Monlam Chenmo, New Year Festival, Obon *(Japanese)*, Vesakha *Chinese holidays:* Ching Ming Festival, Chong Jiu Festival, Double Seventh, Dragon Boat Festival, Hungry Ghosts Festival, Kitchen God, Lantern Festival, Mid-Autumn Festival, Monkey's Festival, New Year, Ta Chiu *Christian holidays:* Advent, All Saints' Day, Annunciation, Ascension, Ash Wednesday, Assumption, Christmas, Christmas Eve, Corpus Christi, Easter, Easter Monday, Eastern Orthodox Easter, Epiphany, Good Friday, Lent, Martinmas, Palm Sunday, Pancake *or* Shrove Tuesday, Pentecost, St. Patrick's Day, St. Valentine's Day, Twelfth Night *Hindu holidays:* Bassant Panchami, Bhai Dooj, Diwali, Dussehra, Ganesh Chaturti, Holi, Janmashtami, Meenakshi, Naga Panchami, Rama Naumi, Ratha Yatra, Shivaratri, Teej *Islamic holidays:* Ashura, Dhu-l-Hijja, Eid-ul-Adha, Eid-ul-Fitr, Lailat ul Qadr, Maulid al Nabi, Muharram, Ramadan *Jain holidays:* Birth *or* Enlightenment of Mahavira, Paryushana *Jewish holidays:* Hannukah, Passover, Purim, Rosh Hashanah, Shavuot, Simhat Torah, Sukkot, Tisha be-Av, Tu Bishvat, Yom Kippur *Shinto holidays:* Cherry Blossom Festival, Matsuri, New Year's Day *Sikh holidays:* Baisakhi, Diwali, Guru Nanak's Birthday, Hola Mohalla, Martyrdom of Guru Arjan Dev – *v.* go away, soujourn, travel, vacation *Nonformal:* book off, cottage

holiness *n.* blessedness, consecration, devotion, devoutness, divineness, divinity, faith, godliness, goodness, grace, humility, inviolability, piety, purity, religiousness, reverence, righteousness, sacredness, saintliness, sanctity, sinlessness, spirituality, unction, virtuousness, worship

hollow *adj.* **1.** cavernous, empty, unfilled, vacant, void *Antonyms:* absolutely, completely, totally **2.** concave, cup-shaped, curved, excavated, indented, pitted **3.** deep-set, depressed, emaciated, fallen, gaunt, sunken **4.** fruitless, futile, meaningless, nugatory, otiose, pointless, pyrrhic, senseless, specious, useless, vain, worthless *Antonyms:* fruitful, meaningful, worthwhile **5.** artificial, deceitful, false, flimsy, hypocritical, insincere, weak *Antonyms:* genuine, heartfelt, solid **6.** deep, dull, echoing, flat, ghostly, low, muffled, muted, resonant, resounding, reverberant, ringing, roaring, rumbling, sepulchral, sonorous, thunderous, toneless, vibrant, vibrating – *n.* **1.** basin, bottom, bowl, cave, cavern, cavity, chamber, channel, crater, dent, depression, dimple, dip, dish, hole, indentation, kettle, pit, pocket, sag, scoop, sinkhole, slough *(Prairies)*, socket, vacuity, valley, void **2.** cleft, groove, notch, trough, – *v.* channel, dent, dig, ditch, empty, excavate, furrow, gorge, groove, indent, notch, pit, rabbet, remove, rut, scoop, shovel, trench

holocaust *n.* **1.** annihilation, butchery, carnage, crimes against humanity, destruction, devastation, ethnic cleansing, extermination, extinction, extirpation, genocide, hate crimes, killing, massacre, mass murder, pogrom, slaughter **2.** conflagration, fire, flames, inferno

holy *adj.* **1.** almighty, angelic, beatific, celestial, consecrated, divine, glorified, glorious, godlike, godly, hallowed, heavenly, immortal, infinite, limitless, omnipotent, omniscient, revered, sacred, sacrosanct, sainted, saintlike, saintly, sanctified, seraphic, venerable, venerated **2.** believing, blessed, chaste, clean, dedicated, devoted, devotional, devout, faithful, god-fearing, humble, immaculate, innocent, just, moral, perfect, pious, prayerful, pure, religious, reverent, righteous, spiritual, spotless, undefiled, unworldly, virtuous *Antonyms:* blasphemous, corrupt, desecrated, immoral, sacrilegious

homage *n.* admiration, adoration, adulation, allegiance, awe, deference, devotion, duty, esteem, faithfulness, fealty, fidelity, genuflection, honour, kneeling, laurels, loyalty, obeisance, praise, prayer, respect, reverence, service, tribute, worship *Antonyms:* contempt, disdain, scorn

home *adj.* **1.** domestic, domiciliary, family, household, inland, internal, natal, national, original, residential **2.** directed, effective, exact, influential, penetrating, piercing, pointed, powerful, weighty – *n.* abode, address, asylum, base, birthplace, country, cradle, domicile, dwelling, element, fatherland, habitat, habitation, haven, hearth, homeland, house, living quarters, lodging, motherland, nation, place, residence, retreat, roost, sanctuary, shelter, trailer, villa *Nonformal:* digs, nest, pad, stomping ground, stoop, turf

homebred *adj.* **1.** domestic, handmade, homemade, indigenous, local, native, neighbourhood, neimish *(Yiddish)*, self-taught *Antonyms:* alien, foreign, exported **2.** coarse, common, folksy, naive, primitive, provincial, rough, rural, rustic, unpolished, unrefined, unsophisticated *Antonyms:* sophisticated, suave, urbane **3.** corn *(Nonformal)*, home-brewed, moonshine

homeless *adj.* abandoned, banished, deported, derelict, desolate, destitute, disinherited, displaced, dispossessed, down and out, estranged, exiled, forsaken, houseless, itinerant, on the bum *or* skids *(Nonformal)*, out on the street, outcast, stray, uncared-for, unhoused, unsettled, vagabond, vagrant, wandering, without a roof over one's head

homely *adj.* **1.** basic, comfortable, comfy *(Nonformal)*, common, congenial, cozy, domestic, easy, everyday, familiar, folksy, friendly, homespun, humble, informal, intimate, modest, natural, ordinary, plain, rustic, simple, snug, unaffected, unassuming, unpretentious *Antonyms:* elaborate, elegant, grand, ostentatious **2.** ill-favoured, not much for looks, plain, plain-looking, ugly, unappealing, unattractive *Antonyms:* attractive, comely, pleasing, pretty

Homeric *adj.* colossal, epic, grand, heroic, imposing, impressive, lofty, magnificent, majestic, mighty, monumental, poetic, titanic, towering *Antonyms:* common, everyday, ignoble, ordinary

homicide *n.* assassination, bump off *(Nonformal)*, carnage, death, first- *or* second- *or* third-degree murder, foul play, hit, killing, manslaughter, murder, negligent homicide, serial murder, slaying, vehicular

homily *n.* discourse, dissertation, essay, fable, heart-to-heart *(Nonformal)*, instruction, lecture, lesson, reproof, sermon, talk, treatise

homogeneous *adj.* akin, alike, analogous, cognate, comparable, consistent, corresponding, equivalent, homologous, identical, kindred, like, matched, parallel, related, similar, uniform, unvarying *Antonyms:* different, disparate, diverse, unlike, varying

homosexuality *n.* gayness, homoeroticism, homosexualism, lesbianism, same sex relationship, sapphism

honest *adj.* aboveboard, authentic, bona fide, candid, conscientious, decent, direct, equitable, ethical, fair, forthright, frank, genuine, high-minded, honourable, impartial, ingenuous, just, law-abiding, level, open, outright, plain, principled, proper, real, reliable, reputable, scrupulous, sincere, square, sterling, straight, straightforward, true, trustworthy, trusty, truthful, undisguised, unfeigned, up front, upright, upstanding, veracious, virtuous *Nonformal:* A-OK, for real, kosher, legit, like it is, on the level, pukka, twenty-four-carat, true-blue, up-front, WYSIWYG *Antonyms:* corrupt, counterfeit, crooked, false, unreliable

honesty *n.* bluntness, candidness, candour, equity, evenhandedness, fairness, faithfulness, fidelity, frankness, genuineness, goodness, honour, impeccability, incorruptibility, integrity, justness, loyalty, morality, openness, outspokenness, plainness, principle, probity, rectitude, scrupulousness, sincerity, straightforwardness, straightness, trustworthiness, truthfulness, uprightness, veracity, virtue *Antonyms:* chicanery, duplicity, insincerity, mendacity, trickery

honour *n.* **1.** acclaim, accolade, adoration, adulation, aggrandizement, apotheosis, approbation, attention, award, celebration, compliment, confidence, consideration, credit, decoration, deference, dignity, distinction, elevation, esteem, exaltation, fame, favour, glorification, glory, greatness, high standing, homage, laud, laurels, lionization, notice, popularity, praise, prestige, privilege, rank, recognition, renown, reputation, repute, respect, reverence, tribute, trust, veneration, worship *Antonyms:* condemnation, contempt, degradation **2.** character, courage, decency, fairness, goodness, honesty, innocence, integrity, modesty, morals, principles, purity, rectitude, righteousness, truthfulness, virtue *Antonyms:* disgrace, dishonesty – *v.* **1.** acclaim, admire, adore, aggrandize, appreciate, celebrate, commemorate, commend, compliment, decorate, dignify, distinguish, ennoble, erect, esteem, exalt, glorify, hallow, keep, laud, lionize, magnify, observe, praise, prize, recognize, respect, revere, sanctify, value, venerate, worship *Antonyms:* condemn, defame, insult, offend, scorn **2.** discharge, pay off *or* up, redeem, satisfy, settle, square

honourable *adj.* **1.** aboveboard, creditable, equitable, estimable, ethical, fair, high-minded, honest, just, moral, principled, proper, reputable, respectable, right, righteous, true, trustworthy, trusty, uncorrupted, virtuous, worthy *Nonformal:* level, true blue *Antonyms:* corrupt, deceitful, shady **2.** acclaimed, admired, celebrated, dignified, distinguished, eminent, great, illustrious, noble, prestigious, prominent, renowned, venerable

hoodlum *n.* bruiser, criminal, crook, desperado, gangster, gunman, hooligan, juvenile delinquent, mobster, mugger, punk, rowdy, ruffian, thug, vandal *Nonformal:* goon, hood, tough

hoodwink *v.* **1.** befool, blindfold, cheat, deceive, defraud, delude, dupe, fleece, fool, gull, hoax, impose, inveigle, mislead, swindle, trick *Nonformal:* bamboozle, con, flimflam, hornswoggle, scam, take **2.** camouflage, cloak, conceal, cover up, disguise, hide, screen, veil

hook *n.* **1.** angle, arc, bend, corner, crochet, crook, curvature, curve, swerve, turn, twist **2.** bait, barb, fishgig, fishhook, fly, jig, lure, pickerel rig, plug, snare, spinner **3.** catch, clasp, fastener, hasp, hinge, hook and eye, link, lock, peg **4.** anchor, mooring, mudhook *(Nonformal)* – *v.* **1.** bend, curve, loop, turn, veer **2.** attach, clasp, clip, close, fasten, link, secure, tie **3.** bag, catch, ensnare, grapple, land, lasso, snag, snare, sniggle, spear, take in, trap *Nonformal:* nab, nail, snake **4.** captivate, charm, convince, enchant, enthrall, sway, win over *Nonformal:* fish in, wangle

hooked *adj.* angular, aquiline, bent, bowed, coined, crooked, curved, flexed, looped – *v.*

1. beguiled, bewitched, charmed, enamoured, enchanted, fixated, infatuated, obsessed, smitten *Nonformal:* crazy about, gone, hung up **2.** addicted, dependent, enslaved, strung out, using *(Nonformal)*

hoop *n.* band, belt, circlet, cincture, girdle, loop, net, rim, ring – *v.* circle, encircle, enclose, encompass, envelop, girdle, surround

hoot *n.* **1.** call, cry, howl, noise, shout, toot, whistle, whoop, yell *Nonformal:* holler, yamp, yowl **2.** amusement, fun, good time, hilarity, lark, laugh, levity, mirth, play, sport *Nonformal:* ball, gas, picnic **3.** boo, catcall, hiss, insult, jeer, mockery, outcry, raillery, taunt *Nonformal:* Bronx cheer, razz – *v.* **1.** call, cry, holler *(Nonformal)*, howl, shout, whistle, whoop, yell **2.** deride, gibe, hiss, insult, mock, ridicule, taunt, tease *Antonyms:* cheer on, laud, praise

hop *n.* **1.** bounce, bound, hippety-hop *(Nonformal)*, jump, leap, pounce, skip, spring, vault **2.** affair, ball, dance, do, mixer, party, social, sock hop, soiree *Nonformal:* clog fest, hoedown, shindig, wingding **3.** escape, flight, getaway, jaunt, run, spin, trip, vacation – *v.* **1.** board, bounce, bound, clear, fly, jet, journey, jump, leap, pounce, skip, spring, travel, vault **2.** dance, foot, prance *Nonformal:* boogie, get down, hoof

hope *n.* **1.** ambition, anticipation, aspiration, daydream, desire, dream, expectation, fantasy, goal, heart's desire, longing, pipe dream *(Nonformal)*, want, wish, yearning **2.** belief, bright side *(Nonformal)*, buoyancy, chance, confidence, conviction, faith, fortune, optimism, possibility, promise, prospect, potential, reward, trust – *v.* anticipate, contemplate, desire, expect, hang in *(Nonformal)*, long, presume, trust, wait for, want, wish, yearn *Antonyms:* despair, doubt, dread

hopeful *adj.* **1.** anticipating, blithe, buoyant, calm, comfortable, content, eager, elated, emboldened, enthusiastic, expectant, expecting, faithful, forward-looking, high, hoping, inspirited, lighthearted, optimistic, reassured, satisfied, trustful, trusting, unflagging, upbeat *(Nonformal) Antonyms:* distrusting, doubtful, pessimistic **2.** advantageous, arousing, auspicious, beneficial, bright, cheerful, cheering, conducive, elating, encouraging, exciting, expeditious, fair, favourable, fine, fit, flattering, fortunate, good, gracious, halcyon, heartening, inspiring, pleasant, probable, promising, propitious, providential, reassuring, roseate, rosy, suitable, sunny, timely, uplifting, well-timed *Antonyms:* discouraging, disheartening, unpromising **3.** assured, confident, sanguine, serene – *n.* aspirant, candidate, minor-leaguer *(Sports)*, optimist, up and comer, wannabe *(Nonformal)*, youngster

hopeless *adj.* **1.** cynical, dejected, demoralized, despairing, despondent, disconsolate, downhearted, forlorn, helpless, incurable, pessimistic, sad, sunk, tragic, unavailing, unfortunate, woebegone *Antonyms:* cheerful, encouraged, optimistic **2.** bad, desperate, futile, impossible, irredeemable, irreparable, irrevocable, lost, pointless, useless *Nonformal:* bust, gone **3.** incapable, incompetent, inefficient, inept, inexpert, unable, unfit, ungifted, unskilled, untalented *Nonformal:* a disaster, all thumbs *Antonyms:* able, deft, dexterous, gifted

horde *n.* band, crew, crowd, crush, drove, everybody, gang, gathering, host, mob, multitude, press, push, swarm, throng, turnout

horizon *n.* **1.** border, boundary, bounds, compass, extent, limit, perspective, prospect, purview, range, reach, realm, scope, sphere, stretch **2.** background, distance, skyline, vanishing point, view, vista

horizontal *adj.* even, flat, flush, level, parallel, plane, smooth, straight *Antonyms:* erect, upright, vertical

horn *n.* **1.** antler, cornu, feeler, nub, point, pommel, projection, spike, tentacle, tuft, tusk **2.** brass, brass *or* musical instrument, wind instrument *Kinds of horn:* alpenhorn, basset, bassoon, bugle, clarinet, clarion, cornet, English, euphonium, flugelhorn, French, helicon, saxophone, sousaphone, trombone, trumpet, tuba *See also:* **instrument** **3.** alarm, foghorn, honker, hooter, klaxon, noisemaker **4.** conch, cornucopia, funnel, horn of plenty – *v.* **1.** gore, impale, injure, pierce, shishkebob *(Nonformal)*, skewer, spear, stab, stick, transfix, tusk, wound **2.** barge *or* break in, crash *(Nonformal)*, crowd in on, enter, gatecrash, infringe, intrude, trespass

horny *adj.* **1.** antlered, bony, calloused, conical, cornute, gnarled, hard, hardened, horned, thick, tough, tufted, tusked **2.** ardent, aroused, burning, carnal, excited, fervent, hot, lascivious, lecherous, libidinous, lustful, passionate, randy, ready *Nonformal:* fired-up, hot and bothered, hot-to-trot, ready for bear, turned on, wound-up

horrendous *adj.* appalling, awful, dreadful, earthshattering, frightful, ghastly, gory, hideous, horrible, horrid, horrific, repellent, repulsive, revolting, scary, shocking, terrible *Antonyms:* agreeable, attractive, pleasant, pleasing

horrible *adj.* **1.** abhorrent, abominable, appalling, awful, bad, beastly, cruel, detestable, disgusting, eerie, execrable, fearful, frightening, grim, grisly, gruesome, heinous, hideous, horrendous, horrid, loathsome, lurid, mean, nasty, offensive, repulsive, revolting, scandalous, scary, shameful, terrifying *Antonyms:* appealing, attractive, charming, delightful, lovely **2.** deplorable, disagreeable, ill-mannered, obnoxious, ugly, uncouth, unpleasant, vulgar *Nonformal:* lousy, stinking

horrid *adj.* abominable, alarming, awful, chilling, deplorable, disagreeable, disgusting, dreadful, frightening, hair-raising, harrowing, hideous, horrendous, horrible, nasty, nerve-wracking, objectionable, obnoxious, obscene, odious, offensive, repugnant, repulsive, revolting, shocking, terrible, terrifying, terrorizing, unpleasant, yucky *(Nonformal)*

horrify *v.* alarm, daunt, disgust, dismay, frighten, intimidate, paralyze, petrify, scare, shake, shock, sicken, spook *(Nonformal)*, startle, stupefy, terrify, terrorize, unnerve *Antonyms:* comfort, delight, enchant, hearten, soothe

horror *n.* **1.** abhorrence, detestation, disgust, dislike, dismay, hate, hatred, loathing, repugnance, revulsion *Antonyms:* affinity, attraction, delight **2.** alarm, apprehension, chill, dread, fear, fright, panic, terror, trepidation **3.** abomination, blot, disgrace, eyesore, mess, monstrosity, sight **4.** chiller, frightshow, ghost-story, monster chiller *(Nonformal)*, monster movie, screamer, slasher film

hors d'oeuvre *n.* antipasto, *apéritif (French)*, appetizer, canapé, crudités, bar food, dim sum, finger food, foreplay, foretaste, *mezes (Greek)*, munchies *(Nonformal)*, paté, smörgåsbord, snack, starter, tapas, tidbit

horse *n.* **1.** colt, equine, filly, foal, gelding, hack, mare, stallion, stud, yearling *Nonformal:* nag, pony *Kinds of horse:* Akhal-Teke, all-purpose, Andalusian, Appaloosa, Arabian, Bashkir Curly, Belgian, bronco, buckskin, Canadian, cayuse, Chickasaw, Chincoteague pony, Clydesdale, Connemara pony, draft, Galiceno, Gotland, Hackney pony, Haflinger, Hanoverian, Hungarian, jennet, Lipizzan, Miniature, Morab, Morgan, mule, mustang, Newfoundland pony, Norwegian Fjord, paint, Palomino, Paso Fino, Percheron, pinto, Przewalski's, quarter horse, Sable Island pony, saddlebred, Shetland pony, Shire, Suffolk, Tennessee walking horse, Thorcheron, Trakehner, Welara *or* Welsh pony *Prairies:* bichon, colt *Kinds of horse racing:* flat, harness, hurdler *(Nonformal)*, pacing, point-to-point, steeplechase, thoroughbred *Kinds of race horse:* also-ran, favourite *or* odds-on favourite, mudder, pace, quarter horse, standardbred, thoroughbred, three-year-old, trots *(Nonformal)*, two-year-old **2.** clotheshorse, fashion victim, jack a dandy, sawhorse, trestle, trestle table – *v.* banter, fool, frolic, jest, joke, misbehave, play, ridicule, romp, roughhouse *(Nonformal)*, skylark, trifle

horseplay *n.* antics, buffoonery, capers, clowning, devilry, deviltry, fooling, fun, hijinks, mischief, pranks, puckishness, romping, rough-and-tumble, skylarking *Nonformal:* hellery, monkey business, roughhousing

hortatory *adj.* advisory, didactic, educational, encouraging, exhortative, inspiring, lecturing, motivating, persuasive, preaching, pressuring, reassuring, uplifting, urging

Antonyms: discouraging, disheartening, dispiriting, dissuading, hindering

horticulture *n.* agriculture, arboriculture, cultivating one's garden, floriculture, flower growing, gardening, landscape architecture, landscaping, turf culture

hoser *n.* blockhead, dolt, dope, lout, moron *Nonformal:* boob, buggerlugs, chucklehead, dunderhead, goof, goofball, goon, meathead, mullethead, nincompoop, numbskull, nutbar, rubberhead, sap, schmuck

hosiery *n.* footwear, legwear *Kinds of hosiery:* argyles, athletic, barn sock, bobbysocks, booties, dress sheers, duffel, fishnet *or* garter *or* sheer *or* silk stockings, gaiters, knee-highs, knee-socks, leggings, long johns, lumberman's sock, moccasin, nylons, oversock, pantyhose, stockings, sweat *or* tube socks, tights

hospice *n.* boarding house, guest home, hospital, hostel, hostelry, inn, lodging, *pension (French)*, monastery, nursing home, palliative care centre, resort, resting home, retreat, shelter

hospitable *adj.* accessible, accommodating, amenable, amicable, bountiful, charitable, companionable, convivial, cooperative, cordial, courteous, friendly, generous, genial, gracious, gregarious, kind, liberal, magnanimous, neighbourly, open, open-minded, receptive, responsive, sociable, welcoming *Antonyms:* intolerant, unapproachable, unreceptive

hospital *n.* clinic, extended care, facility, *hospitale (Italian)*, *hôtel-Dieu (French)*, infirmary, *krankenhaus (German)*, lazaretto, medical centre *or* institution, mental health centre, sanatorium

hospitality *n.* accommodation, affability, amiability, cheer *or* good cheer, comradeship, consideration, conviviality, cordiality, fellowship, friendliness, generosity, geniality, heartiness, neighbourliness, obligingness, open-handedness, openness, sociability, warmth, welcome

host *n.* **1.** army, array, crowd, drove, flock, gathering, group, horde, legion, multitude, myriad, score, swarm, throng **2.** anchorman, anchorperson, anchorwoman, announcer, chair, emcee, entertainer, hostess, innkeeper, landlord, madam, manager, master of ceremonies, moderator, owner, presenter, proprietor, schmooseoisie *(Nonformal)*, toastmaster, usher **3.** bread, communion, eucharist, loaf, wafer – *v.* **1.** announce, begin, chair, do the honours, introduce, present, usher **2.** accommodate, attend *or* cater to, entertain, house, put up *(Nonformal)*, receive, treat

hostile *adj.* **1.** antagonistic, argumentative, bellicose, belligerent, chippy *(Nonformal)*, contentious, disapproving, ill-disposed, inhospitable, inimical, malevolent, malignant, mean, militant, pugnacious, rancorous, ready for a fight, scrappy, snarly, surly, unfriendly, unkind, unpleasant, viperous, virulent, vitriolic *Antonyms:* agreeable, amiable, cordial, peaceful **2.** aggressive, brutal, combative, fierce, hawkish, illegal, insurgent, military, mortal, savage, violent

hostility *n.* **1.** abhorrence, animosity, animus, antagonism, antipathy, aversion, belligerence, bitterness, detestation, disaffection, enmity, estrangement, grudge, hatred, ill will, inimicality, malevolence, malice, meanness, opposition, rancour, resentment, spite, spleen, unfriendliness, venom, virulence *Nonformal:* bad blood *or* vibes, warpath *Antonyms:* agreement, amity, good will, sympathy **2.** aggression, bellicosity, combat, exchange of fire, fighting, resistance, scrapping, strife, violence, war *Antonyms:* accord, calm, peace

hot *adj.* **1.** baking, blazing, blistering, boiling, broiling, burning, conflagrant, febrile, fevered, feverish, feverous, flaming, heated, humid, igneous, parching, piping, red, roasting, scalding, scorching, searing, sizzling, smoking, steaming, stuffy, summery, sweating, sweltering, torrid, tropic, tropical, white *Antonyms:* chilly, cold, cool, freezing, frigid, frosty, icy **2.** angry, animated, ardent, contentious, excited, fervent, fervid, fierce, fiery, fighting mad, furious, ill-tempered, impassioned, impetuous, indignant, inflamed, intense, irascible, irate, mad, murderous, passionate, raging, seething, stormy, touchy, vehement, violent

Antonyms: apathetic, calm, indifferent, mild, moderate **3.** gingery, nippy, piquant, pungent, racy, sharp, spicy, strong, zestful, zesty, zippy **4.** aroused, carnal, erotic, exotic *(Nonformal)*, horny, lascivious, lewd, libidinous, lustful, passionate, prurient, racy, salacious, sensual, sexual, sexy, steamy, sultry, X-rated **5.** favoured, in demand *or* vogue, just out, latest, new, novel, popular, recent, sought-after, super *Nonformal:* fantabulous, groovy, nifty, peachy *Antonyms:* old hat *(Nonformal)*, out-of-date, stale, trite, unpopular **6.** attracted, desirous, disposed toward, eager, enamoured, enthusiastic, interested, predisposed *Nonformal:* big on, gaga over, nuts *or* wild about **7.** ambiguous, contentious, contested, controversial, debated, disputatious, embattled, explosive, in dispute, litigious, loaded, moot, polemical, touchy, under fire *or* seige, unresolved, volcanic **8.** able, capital, champion, choice, dexterous, excellent, lucky, prime, on the ball *(Nonformal)*, skilled, sound, splendid, stellar, stunning, unsurpassed **9.** active, bustling, busy, crowded, exciting, lively, swinging *Nonformal:* hopping, jumping, talk of the town **10.** fenced, illegal, looted, pilfered, purloined, snatched, stolen, taken

hot-blooded *adj.* adventuresome, amorous, ardent, bold, carnal, daring, eager, emotional, erotic, excitable, excited, fervent, intense, passionate, sensual, sexual, spirited, steamy, temperamental, virile, zealous *Antonyms:* cool, dispassionate, indifferent, prudent

hotel *n.* **1.** accommodation, *auberge (French)*, bed and breakfast *or* B & B, boarding *or* rooming house, hospice, hostel, inn, kip *(Nonformal)*, lodge, lodging, motel, motor hotel, motor inn, porterhouse *(Historical)*, public house, resort *Nonformal:* dump, fleapit, flophouse **2.** bar, beer parlour, beverage room, draft house, gin-mill, lounge, roadhouse, taproom, tavern

hotheaded *adj.* edgy, explosive, feisty, fierce, fiery, furious, hot-tempered, impetuous, impulsive, mercurial, passionate, quick-tempered, rash, reckless, stormy, tempestuous, uneven, unpredictable, unstable, violent, volcanic *Antonyms:* chary, even-tempered, laid-back, prudent

hound *n.* **1.** bird dog, canine, dog, hunting dog, pup, whelp *Nonformal:* mutt, pooch *Kinds of hound:* Afghan, basset, beagle, bloodhound, boarhound, coonhound, dachshund, elkhound, foxhound, greyhound, staghound, whippet, wolfhound *See also:* **dog 2.** fox, rake, rat *(Nonformal)*, scoundrel, villain **3.** addict, aficionado, cognoscente, connoisseur, fan, fanatic, follower, nut *(Nonformal)*, zealot – *v.* aggravate, annoy, browbeat, bulldog, bully, chase, follow, goad, harass, haunt, hunt, incite, irk, irritate, nag, nettle, persecute, pester, prod, provoke, pursue, stalk, tail, torment, trail, urge, vex

house *n.* **1.** abode, building, bungalow, castle, domicile, duplex, dwelling, edifice, habitat, home, homestead, hooch *(Nonformal)*, household, mansion, quarters, residence, shelter **2.** ancestry, clan, family, family tree, folk, ilk, kin, kindred, lineage, people, relations, relatives, root, stock, tribe **3.** amphitheatre, audience, auditorium, building, church, concert hall, hall, synagogue, temple **4.** assembly, congregation, gathering, group, listeners, parish, spectators **5.** business, company, corporation, establishment, firm, institution, publisher **6.** commons, congress, government, legislative body, legislature, parliament, senate **7.** bordello, brothel, cat house *(Nonformal)*, whorehouse – *v.* accommodate, board, contain, cover, foster, harbour, keep, lodge, possess, protect, put up, sheathe, shelter, shield, store, take in, tend

housebroken *adj.* compliant, continent, domesticated, manageable, obedient, submissive, tame *or* tamed, trained *Antonyms:* feral, wild

household *adj.* **1.** comfortable, domestic, home, home-like, homey, nondescript, ordinary, plain, residential, simple **2.** common, commonplace, current, familiar, notorious, popular, prevailing, public, recognized, stock, regular, ubiquitous, usual, well-known – *n.* brood, family, folks, hearth, hearthside, home, homestead, house, menage, people, unit

housekeeper *n.* cleaning lady, domestic help, employee, family manager, help, homemaker, househusband, housewife, maid, major-domo, seneschal, servant, staff, stay-at-home spouse, steward

housework *n.* bed-making, chores, cleaning, cooking, dishes, domestic arts *or* science, drudgery *(Nonformal)*, dusting, home economics, homemaking, home management, househusbandry, housekeeping, housewifery, ironing, laundering, mopping, polishing, sewing, stewardship, sweeping, vacuuming, washing

housing *n.* **1.** abode, accommodation, apartment, condominium, cover, digs *(Nonformal)*, domicile, dwelling, habitation, home, house, lodgings, place, quarters, residence, roof, shelter **2.** carapace, casing, cover, envelope, frame, jacket, sheath, storage, structure **3.** adornment, blanket, caparison, coat, horse *or* saddle blanket, horsecloth, magazine, ornament, saddlecloth, trapping

hovel *n.* cabin, crib, den, hut, lean-to, shack, shanty, shed, stall, sty, warren *Nonformal:* dive, dump, fleapit, hole, hole-in-the-wall, pigsty *Antonyms:* castle, mansion, palace

hover *v.* **1.** dance, drift, flicker, flit, float, flutter, fly, hang, levitate, poise, soar, suspend **2.** dilly-dally, falter, hang back, linger, loiter, pause, wait, watch, waver **3.** brew, brood, loom, lurk, menace, threaten, wait nearby

howl *n.* bay, bellow, clamour, cry, groan, hoot, outcry, roar, scream, shriek, ululation, wail, yelp, yowl – *v.* bark, bawl, bellow, blubber, caterwaul, clamour, cry, groan, growl, hoot, keen, lament, moan, roar, scream, shout, shriek, ululate, wail, weep, whimper, whine, yell, yelp, yip

hub *n.* axis, centre, core, focal point, focus, heart, middle, nerve centre, nucleus, pivot, polestar, seat

hubbub *n.* bedlam, brouhaha, buzz, clamour, commotion, confusion, din, disorder, disturbance, fuss, hullabaloo, megillah *(Yiddish)*, noise, pandemonium, racket, riot, stir, tumult, turmoil, uproar, whirl *Nonformal:* ruckus, rumpus, to-do

hubris *n.* arrogance, cockiness, conceit, disdain, egocentricity, egotism, haughtiness, narcissism, pride, self-importance, self-love, smugness, vainglory, vanity *Nonformal:* puffery, swelled-headedness *Antonyms:* diffidence, humility, modesty

huckster *n.* **1.** dealer, haggler, hawker, peddler, pitch person *(Nonformal)*, salesperson, tinker, vendor **2.** bunk artist, cheat, confidence trickster, deceiver, hustler, liar, swindler *Nonformal:* con, grifter, phoney, snake oil salesman, used car salesman

huddle *n.* **1.** assemblage, assortment, brainstorming session, bull session *(Nonformal)*, chat, cluster, confab, conference, consultation, crowd, discussion, flock, gaggle, gathering, group, grouping, herd, meeting, palaver, parley, powwow, scrimmage, scrum, tête-à-tête, throng **2.** chaos, disarray, disorder, gallimaufry, heap, hodgepodge, hugger-mugger *(Nonformal)*, jumble, medley, mess, mix, mishmash, muddle, tangle – *v.* assemble, brainstorm, cluster, cogitate, congregate, converge, crowd, flock, gather, group, mass, mobilize, nestle, rally, throng

hue *n.* attribute, cast, colour, complexion, dye, hint, shade, tincture, tinge, tint, tone, touch, variety

huff *n.* anger, annoyance, dudgeon, irritation, offence, passion, perturbation, pique, rage, snit *(Nonformal)*, state, temper, tiff, umbrage – *v.* **1.** blow, breathe, exhale, puff, wheeze, whiff **2.** aggravate, anger, annoy, bully, displease, hector, intimidate, irk, irritate, nettle, offend, pique, provoke, rile, roil, vex *Nonformal:* miff, peeve **3.** brood, fret, grouch, stew *(Nonformal)*, sulk

huffy *adj.* cloudy, crabby, crisp, crusty, irascible, irritable, moody, mopey, moping, offended, on one's high horse, ornery, owly, peevish, petulant, prickly, sensitive, shirty *(British)*, short-tempered, snappish, sulky, sullen, testy, touchy, vexed *Nonformal:* miffed, peeved *Antonyms:* cheerful, good-humoured, sunny

hug *n.* bear hug *(Nonformal)*, caress, clasp, clinch, embrace, grasp, snuggle, squeeze – *v.*

cherish, cling, cradle, cuddle, enfold, envelop, grip, harbour, hold, keep close, lock, nestle, seize, snuggle, squeeze

huge *adj.* big, bulky, colossal, elephantine, enormous, extensive, gargantuan, generous, giant, gigantic, great, gross, immeasurable, immense, jumbo, king-sized, large, lusty, magnificent, mammoth, massive, mighty, monstrous, monumental, mountainous, oversize, planetary, prodigious, stupendous, titanic, towering, tremendous, vast *Nonformal:* honking, humongous, supercolossal, whopping *Antonyms:* insignificant, microscopic, minute, paltry, small

hulk *n.* **1.** blob, body, bulk, chunk, clod, clump, hunk, lump, mass **2.** frame, hull, remains, ruins, shambles, shell, skeleton, wreck

hulking *adj.* awkward, big, bulky, clumsy, clunky *(Nonformal)*, colossal, elephantine, lumpish, massive, oafish, ponderous *Antonyms:* diminutive, little, wee

hull *n.* **1.** bark, calyx, capsule, casing, covering, husk, pod, sheath, shell **2.** argosy, boat, liner, ship, vessel – *v.* husk, pare, peel, shear, shuck, skin, uncover

hullabaloo *n.* ado, commotion, foofaraw, frenzy, furor, fuss, hubbub, katzenjammer, noise, outcry, stir, uproar *Nonformal:* big stink, hellery, kerfuffle, ruckus, rumpus, to-do

hum *n.* **1.** buzz, buzzing, droning, mumble, murmur, pulsation, purring, vibration, whizzing **2.** activity, bustle, busyness, commotion, hustle, stir – *v.* **1.** coo *(Nonformal)*, croon, drone, hem, muffle, mumble, murmur, mutter, sing, whisper **2.** babble, bustle, buzz, purr, stir, thrum, whir, whiz

human *adj.* anthropological, anthropomorphic, bipedal, civilized, fallible, fleshly, hominid, humanistic, mortal, personal, vulnerable – *n.* adult, being, body, boy, carbon unit *(Nonformal)*, character, child, girl, hominid, head, Homo sapien, human being, individual, man, mortal, person, personage, quick, soul, woman

humane *adj.* altruistic, benevolent, broad-minded, charitable, civilized, clement, compassionate, considerate, forgiving, generous, genial, gentle, gracious, helpful, humanitarian, indulgent, kind, kindhearted, kindly, lenient, magnanimous, merciful, mild, open-minded, philanthropic, sympathetic, tender, understanding, unselfish, warmhearted *Antonyms:* barbarous, beastly, brutal, devilish, inhuman

humanitarian *adj.* altruistic, beneficent, charitable, compassionate, eleemosynary, generous, giving, good, idealistic, philanthropic, princely, public-spirited – *n.* altruist, benefactor, helper, patron, philanthropist *Nonformal:* bleeding-heart, boy scout, do-gooder, Good Samaritan *or* Scout

humanity *n.* **1.** beings, everyman, Homo sapiens, human race, humans, mankind, people, persons, womankind **2.** fallibility, frailty, human nature, mortality, weakness **3.** altruism, benevolence, *caritas (Latin)*, charity, compassion, empathy, fellowship, fraternity, goodwill, grace, humanitarianism, kindness, love, philanthropy, solidarity, sorority, sympathy, tolerance *Antonyms:* misanthropy, self-centeredness, selfishness

humble *adj.* **1.** common, commonplace, humdrum, inglorious, insignificant, little, lowly, mean, modest, ordinary, plebeian, poor, proletarian, shabby, simple, small, trivial, unassuming, underprivileged, undistinguished, unimportant, unpretentious, unrefined *Antonyms:* extravagant, outrageous **2.** bashful, deferential, demure, diffident, docile, hesitant, meek, mild, modest, obliging, polite, reserved, respectful, retiring, reverential, self-effacing, shy, simple, soft-spoken, submissive, subservient, tentative, timid, timorous, tractable, unobtrusive, unostentatious – *v.* abase, abash, break, bring *or* cast down, chagrin, chasten, confound, crush, debase, deflate, degrade, demean, demote, deny, discomfit, embarrass, hide, humiliate, lower, mortify, overcome, reduce, shame, silence, sink, snub, subdue *Antonyms:* elevate, exalt, glorify, magnify, raise

humbug *n.* **1.** bluff, chicanery, confidence game, deceit, deception, falsehood, fraud, hoax, lie, swindle *Nonformal:* con, flimflam, phoney **2.** canard, charlatan, cheater, deceiver, impostor, liar, quack, quacksalver, swindler, trickster **3.** balderdash, drivel, empty talk, gammon, hocus-pocus, hogwash, nonsense, rant, rubbish, trash *Nonformal:* baloney, bull, hot air, hype, malarkey – *v.* bluff, deceive, dupe, gull, hoax, outsmart, string along, trick *Nonformal:* bamboozle, scam

humdrum *adj.* boring, bromidic, common, commonplace, dime-a-dozen, done-to-death, dreary, dull, everyday, garden variety, hackneyed, monotonous, mundane, prosaic, quotidian, routine, run of the mill, tedious, trite, unimaginative, vanilla *(Nonformal)*, wearisome – *n.* bore, drag, dullard, dullness, monotony, repetition, sameness, tedium

humid *adj.* **1.** clammy, damp, dank, moist, mucky, muggy, oozy, perspiring, sodden, soggy, steamy, sticky, stifling, stuffy, sultry, sweaty, sweltering, vaporous, warm, watery, wet *Antonyms:* arid, desert, dessicated, dry **2.** close, dense, heavy, intense, oppressive, overcast, severe, unbearable

humidity *n.* **1.** clamminess, dampness, dankness, dew, dewiness, evaporation, liquid, moisture, mugginess, perspiration, sogginess, steam, steaminess, stickiness, sultriness, sweatiness, swelter, vaporization, wet, wetness **2.** density, heaviness, intensity, oppressiveness, severity, thickness, viscosity

humiliate *v.* blister, browbeat, chagrin, chasten, conquer, crush, debase, degrade, demean, deny, discountenance, disgrace, dishonour, embarrass, hurt, knock *or* take *or* tear down, lower, mortify, overwhelm, pan, shame, smear, subdue, suppress, vanquish, wither *Antonyms:* elevate, honour, magnify

humiliation *n.* comedown, comeuppance, debasement, deflation, discomposure, disconcertion, disgrace, embarrassment, humbling, indignity, injury, mortification, putdown *(Nonformal)*, shame *Antonyms:* elevation, honour, pride

humility *n.* bashfulness, demureness, diffidence, docility, fawning, humbleness, meekness, modesty, mortification, obedience, obsequiousness, passiveness, reserve, resignation, reverence, self-abasement, self-abnegation, servility, shyness, subjection, submissiveness, subservience, supplication, timidity, timorousness, unobtrusiveness, unpretentiousness *Antonyms:* arrogance, conceit, pomposity, presumption, vanity

humorous *adj.* amusing, camp, campy, clever, comic, comical, droll, entertaining, facetious, farcical, funny, hilarious, jocose, jocular, joshing, laughable, ludicrous, merry, playful, ribald, waggish, whimsical, witty *Nonformal:* a scream, priceless *Antonyms:* earnest, grave, serious, sober, solemn

humorist *n.* buffoon, caricaturist, cartoonist, clown, comedian, funnyman, joker, jokester, parodist, quipster, satirist, standup, wag, wisecracker, wit, zany *Nonformal:* cutup, gagster, take-off artist

humour *n.* **1.** amusement, badinage, banter, comedy, drollery, facetiousness, flippancy, fun, funniness, gaiety, high spirits, jest, jesting, jocularity, joking, kidding, levity, lightness, playfulness, pleasantry, wisecrack, wit, witticism *Antonyms:* grief, melancholy, sadness, solemnity, sorrow **2.** bent, bias, caprice, character, complexion, conceit, crotchet, disposition, fancy, idiosyncrasy, makeup, mind, mood, nature, notion, personality, propensity, quirk, spirit, temper, temperament, tone, vagary, vein, whim – *v.* accommodate, amuse, baby, condescend, cosset, favour, flatter, gladden, gratify, indulge, mollify, pamper, placate, please, satisfy, spoil *Antonyms:* challenge, oppose, rebel against

hump *n.* bulge, bump, convexity, drumlin, dune, elevation, eminence, hill, hummock, knob, knurl, mound, projection, prominence, protrusion, protuberance, swelling – *v.* carry, convey, drag, elevate, hoist, jack, lift, portage, raise, schlep *(Nonformal)*, support, transport

hunch *n.* **1.** clue, feeling, foreboding, gut sense *(Nonformal)*, idea, impression, inkling, intuition, notion, premonition, presentiment, sensation, suspicion **2.** bulge, hump, hunk, lump, mass, mound, pile, protuberance – *v.* arch, bend, crouch, curve, hump, hunker down *(Nonformal)*, stoop

hunger *n.* **1.** ache, appetite, craving, desire, greed, hankering, itch, longing, lust, mania, notion, penchant, ravenousness, sweet-tooth, thirst, vacancy, void, voracity, want, yearning, yen **2.** food deprivation, famine, starvation – *v.* ache, crave, desire, itch, long, pine, thirst, want, yearn

hungry *adj.* **1.** avaricious, avid, covetous, craving, desirous, eager, famished, hankering, hoggish, keen, needing, rapacious, ravenous, starving, unfilled, unsatisfied, voracious, wanting, yearning **2.** barren, desolate, destitute, fallow, impoverished, infertile, needy, poor, starved

hunk *n.* **1.** block, chunk, clod, glob *(Nonformal)*, lump, mass, piece, rasher, serving, wad **2.** Adonis, heartthrob, macho-man, male specimen, pin-up *or* poster boy *Nonformal:* babe, dreamboat, he-man, looker, pin-up, stud

hunt *n.* chase, coursing, exploration, field sport, forage, pursuit, quest, race, raid, shoot, sport, trailing – *v.* **1.** chase, go after, follow, hound, kill, prowl, pursue, run down, shadow, shoot, stalk, trace, track, trail **2.** cast about, delve, drag, examine, ferret out, fish *or* look for, forage, investigate, nose around, probe, quest, scour, search, seek, sift through

hurdle *n.* blockade, catch, complication, difficulty, handicap, hazard, hindrance, hitch, impediment, obstacle, obstruction, snag, stumbling block – *v.* bound, clear, hop, jump, leap, skip, spring, vault *Commonly misused:* **hurtle**

hurl *n.* flip, lob, pass, peg *(Nonformal)*, pitch, sling, throw, toss – *v.* **1.** bung, cast, chuck, chunk, discharge, fire, fling, gun, heave, launch, let fly, pitch, project, propel, send, sling, throw, toss **2.** beulah *(P.E.I.)*, keck, retch, throw up, vomit *Nonformal:* blow chunks, puke, upchuck

hurricane *n.* blow *(Nonformal)*, cyclone, gale, monsoon, storm, tempest, tornado, tropical cyclone *or* storm, twister, typhoon, whirlwind, windstorm

hurried *adj.* cursory, expeditious, fast, flying, hard-pressed, hasty, last-minute, off the cuff, pressed, prompt, pushed, quick, rash, rushed, slapdash, snap *(Nonformal)*, speedy, sudden, urgent *Antonyms:* considered, dilatory, leisured, relaxed, slow

hurry *interj.* get going, move it, now, this instant *Nonformal:* chop-chop, get cracking, shake a leg, stir your stumps – *n.* celerity, commotion, dispatch, drive, expedition, expeditiousness, flurry, haste, precipitation, promptitude, quickness, rush, rustle, speediness, swiftness, urgency *Antonyms:* calmness, slowness – *v.* accelerate, bestir, breeze, bustle, dash, expedite, fleet, fly, hasten, hustle, jog, make haste *or* time, prod, quicken, race, rip, rocket, run, rush, scoot, scurry, speed, urge, whirl, whisk, whiz *Nonformal:* make tracks, zip *Antonyms:* crawl, creep, dawdle, delay

hurt *adj.* **1.** battered, bruised, contused, cut, damaged, disfigured, harmed, hit, impaired, injured, lacerated, marred, mauled, scraped, scratched, sore, wounded *Antonyms:* fresh, healed, healthy, repaired **2.** aching, aggrieved, agonized, distressed, disturbed, heartbroken, indignant, offended, pained, piqued, resentful, sad, scarred, stricken, struck, suffering, tortured, upset, woebegone *Nonformal:* miffed, peeved, shook-up *Antonyms:* calm, debonair, happy, upbeat – *n.* **1.** ache, bruise, damage, detriment, disadvantage, disaster, discomfort, distress, gash, harm, impairment, injury, loss, mark, misfortune, nick, pain, pang, ruin, scratch, sore, soreness, suffering, wound *Nonformal:* booboo, downer, ouch *Antonyms:* elation, joy, pleasure **2.** abuse, defamation, disservice, ill-treatment, maltreatment, oppression, outrage, persecution, prejudice, punishment, scandal, slander, tyranny – *v.* **1.** abuse, afflict, aggrieve, ail, belt, bite, blemish, bruise, burn, chafe, cripple, damage, disable, distress, flail, flog, grieve, harm, impair, injure, kick, lacerate, lambaste, lash, maltreat, mar, maul, pain, pierce, pinch, pommel, punch, puncture, punish, rough up, slap, slug, spoil, squeeze, sting, tear, torment, torture, trouble, violate, whack, work over, wound *Antonyms:* alleviate, benefit, compensate, help **2.** ache, agonize, anguish, bleed, cry, despair, grieve, lament, smart, sorrow, suffer, throb, weep

hurtful *adj.* cruel, cutting, damaging, detrimental, harmful, inimical, injurious, malicious, mean, mortal, nasty, noxious, poisonous, spiteful, unhealthy, unkind, upsetting, wicked, wounding *Antonyms:* complimentary, kind, laudatory, soothing

hurtle *v.* **1.** charge, fly, jump, lunge, plunge, push, race, rush *or* rush headlong, scoot, scramble, shoot, speed, spurt, tear **2.** bump, clash, collide, dash *or* run into, meet, strike *Commonly misused:* **hurdle**

husband *n.* benedict, bridegroom, groom, helpmate, man, married man, mate, mister, partner, spouse *Nonformal:* better *or* other half, hubby, old man – *v.* bank, conserve, economize, hoard, manage, preserve, put away, reserve, save *or* save up, scrimp, skimp *Antonyms:* consume, spend, waste

husbandry *n.* **1.** agrarianism, agriculture, agronomy, cultivation, farming, ranching, sharecropping, tilling **2.** conservation, direction, economy, frugality, management, providence, prudence, stewardship, thrift *Antonyms:* lavishness, overspending, prodigality

hush *n.* calm, lull, peace, peacefulness, quiet, quietude, silence, stillness, tranquility – *v.* allay, assuage, calm, choke, gag, muffle, mute, muzzle, pacify, quiet, quieten, shush, shut up, silence, soothe, stifle, still, stop, suppress

hush-hush *adj.* censored, clandestine, classified, confidential, covert, furtive, hidden, on the q.t. *(Nonformal)*, personal, private, quiet, restricted, secret, top-secret

husk *n.* bark, capsule, case, casing, chaff, coat, carapace, covering, hull, jacket, pod, rind, sheath, shell, shuck, skin

husky *adj.* **1.** beefy, big, brawny, burly, gigantic, hefty, herculean, mighty, muscular, powerful, rugged, stalwart, stocky, stout, strapping, strong, sturdy, thickset, well-built *Antonyms:* puny, slim, small, thin, weak **2.** croaking, croaky, deep, growling, gruff, guttural, harsh, hoarse, loud, rasping, raucous, rough, throaty *Antonyms:* high-pitched, shrill

hustle *n.* activity, ambitiousness, bustle, dash, drive, energy, enterprise, enthusiasm, go, haste, initiative, push, pushiness, spirit , zip *Nonformal:* get-up-and-go, gumption, spunk – *v.* **1.** bustle, fly, hasten, hotfoot *(Nonformal)*, hurry, impel, jog, press, race, rush, speed *Antonyms:* dally, dawdle, procrastinate **2.** cajole, coax, coerce, elbow, force, jostle, push, rush, shove, thrust **3.** cheat, deceive, fleece, gull, mean price *(P.E.I.)*, swindle *Nonformal:* con, sucker, take **4.** dance, disco, spin, sway, swing, twirl, wiggle *Nonformal:* boogie, get down, groove, jive

hustler *n.* **1.** bawd, entrepreneur, panderer, pimp, procurer *or* procuress, solicitor **2.** escort, gigolo, harlot, hooker, prostitute, streetwalker, whore *Nonformal:* chippy, moll, tart

hut *n.* booth, bungalow, cabin, chalet, *chantier (Quebec)*, cottage, crib, den, dugout, hooch *(Nonformal)*, house, hovel, hutch, kiosk, lean-to, lodge, quinzhee, refuge, shack, shanty, shed, shelter, summer house, *wickiup (Algonquian) Kinds of hut:* cabana, *cabane à sucre (Quebec)*, camboose, fishing *or* ice, gatehouse, outhouse, pavilion, porter's lodge, Nissen *or* Quonset *(Trademark)*, school bus *or* warming, sentry box, sod, starter's *(Golf)*, sugarshack, tollbooth *See also:* **dwelling**

hybrid *adj.* amalgamated, combined, compounded, heterogeneous, mixed, mongrel, multifaceted, recombinant *(Genetics)*, varied – *n.* amalgam, combination, composite, compound, cross, mixture, motley, pastiche, potpourrie *Nonformal:* Heinz 57, mutt

hydraulics *n.* fluid dynamics, fluidics, hydrodynamics, hydrokinetics, hydromechanics, hydrostatics

hydro *n.* charge, current, electricity, energy, hydroelectricity, lights *(Nonformal)*, power, water energy *or* power

hygienic *adj.* aseptic, clean, deodorized, disinfected, germ-free, pure, purified, sanitary, sterile, wholesome *Antonyms:* contaminated, dirty, infected

hymn *n.* anthem, sacred song *Kinds of hymn:* alleluia, canticle, carol, chant, chorale, descant, dirge, evensong, Gloria, gospel, gospel shout, laud, litany, ode, oratorio, psalm, requiem

hype *n.* advertising, blurb, buildup, media frenzy, promotion, publicity, puffery *Nonformal:* ballyhoo, plug, promo, razzmatazz – *v.* advertise, encourage, plug *(Nonformal)*, promote, publicize, sell, support, tour

hyperactive *adj.* active, attention deficient, busy, crazed, frantic, frenetic, frenzied, hectic, indefatigable, impulsive, overactive, wild *Nonformal:* crazy, hyper

hyperbole *n.* amplification, braggadocio, colouring, distortion, embellishment, embroidering, enlargement, exaggeration, magnification, overstatement, trope *Nonformal:* hype, puff

hypercritical *adj.* captious, carping, caviling, exacting, faultfinding, finicky, fussy, meticulous, overcritical, overfastidious, persnickety, priggish, quibbling *Antonyms:* blasé, tolerant, uncritical *Commonly misused:* **hypocritical**

hypnotic *adj.* **1.** anesthetic, narcotic, opiate, sleep-inducing, sleepy, somnolent, soporific, trance-inducing **2.** alluring, arresting, bewitching, captivating, charming, enchanting, engaging, engrossing, enthralling, fascinating, intriguing, irresistible, magnetic, mesmerizing, riveting, spellbinding – *n.* anesthetic, calmative, downer *(Nonformal)*, drug, medicine, narcotic, opiate, sedative, soporific, tranquilizer

hypnotize *v.* **1.** captivate, catch, charm, engross, enthrall, entrance, fascinate, induce, mesmerize, spellbind, stupefy **2.** anesthetize, drug, make drowsy *or* sleepy, narcotize, soothe

hypochondriac *adj.* **1.** anxious, atrabilious, fearing, health-conscious, health-obsessed, neurotic, obsessed, paranoid, phobic *(Nonformal)*, psychosomatic **2.** dejected, depressed, despondent, melancholy, neurasthenic, sad, unhappy – *n.* killjoy, pessimist, worrier, worrywart *(Nonformal)*

hypocrisy *n.* affectation, bad faith, bigotry, deceit, deceitfulness, deception, dishonesty, double-dealing, duplicity, fraud, insincerity, lip-service *(Nonformal)*, pharisaism, pretense, sanctimony, sham, speciousness *Antonyms:* honesty, sincerity, truthfulness

hypocrite *n.* charlatan, deceiver, dissembler, fraud, liar, pretender, quack *Nonformal:* four-flusher, phoney, sham, two-face

hypocritical *adj.* artificial, assuming, deceitful, deceptive, dissembling, double-dealing, duplicitous, false, feigning, fraudulent, insincere, pretentious, sanctimonious, self-righteous, slippery, smooth- tongued, specious, spurious, two-faced *(Nonformal)* *Commonly misused:* **hypercritical**

hypothesis *n.* assumption, axiom, basis, belief, claim, conclusion, conjecture, deduction, derivation, explanation, ground, guess, guesstimate *(Nonformal)*, inference, interpretation, opinion, position, postulate, premise, rationale, suggestion, supposition, theorem, theory, thesis

hypothesize *v.* assume, claim, conjecture, deduce, guess, infer, postulate, presume, speculate, surmise, suspect, theorize, think

hypothetical *adj.* conditional, conjectural, contestable, debatable, dialectical, disputable, doubtful, guessed, indefinite, postulated, putative, questionable, speculative, supposed, theoretical *Antonyms:* actual, confirmed, true

hysteria *n.* agitation, craze *or* craziness, delirium, excitement, feverishness, frenzy, hysterics, madness, mania, nervousness, panic, upset

hysterical *adj.* **1.** agitated, berserk, carried away, convulsive, crazed, crazy, delirious, distracted, distraught, emotional, excited, frantic, frenzied, fuming, furious, impassioned, incensed, mad, manic, neurotic, overwrought, panic-stricken, passionate, possessed, rabid, raging, rampant, raving, seething, uncontrollable, unnerved, unrestrainable, vehement, wild *Nonformal:* ballistic, flipped out *Antonyms:* calm, composed, poised **2.** absurd, amusing, comical, droll, farcical, funny, hilarious, laughable, ludicrous, ridiculous, uproarious *Nonformal:* gut-busting, knee-slapping, side-splitting

ice *n.* **1.** crystal, frozen water *Kinds of ice:* anchor, ballicatter, balliclumper, black, blue board, clumpet, cubed, drift, dry, false, field, floe, glacial, glare, glare-crust, glaze, glib, growler *(Atlantic provinces)*, hailstone, hoarfrost, iceberg, icicle, lolly, pack, pancake, permafrost, pingo, raft, rime, rotten, running, shell, sleet, slob, slur, slurry, slush, top, winter *Ice groupings:* atmospheric, coastal, ground, iceberg, mountain, polar plateau, sea **2.** gelato, *glace (French)*, ice cream, sherbet, sorbet **3.** diamonds, jewelry, loot, rocks *(Nonformal)* – *v.* **1.** chill, cool, freeze, frost, glaze, refrigerate **2.** clinch, close, complete, finish, ink *(Nonformal)* **3.** assassinate, destroy, finish off, kill, murder **4.** *Hockey:* dump, get rid of, shoot

icon *n.* carving, idol, image, likeness, painting, picture, representation, semblance, sign, statue, symbol

iconoclast *n.* **1.** critic, denouncer, destroyer, dissident, faultfinder, opponent, questioner, radical **2.** agnostic, atheist, heretic, impious person, infidel, nonbeliever, sceptic, unbeliever *Antonyms:* devotee, supporter

iconoclastic *adj.* critical, denunciatory, dissident, heretical, impious, radical, rebellious, sceptical, subversive *Antonyms:* believing, devoted, trustful, uncritical, unquestioning

icy *adj.* **1.** biting, bitter, chilly, cold, freezing, frigid, frost-bound, frosty, frozen, gelid, glacial, iced, polar, raw, refrigerated, rimy, sleeted, wintery *Antonyms:* blistering, boiling, hot, sizzling **2.** cool, dangerous, distant, forbidding, glaring, hateful, hostile, steely, uneasy, unfriendly, unwelcoming, waxy *Antonyms:* cordial, friendly, gracious, warm **3.** glazed, glibbey *(P.E.I.)*, slick, slippery

idea *n.* **1.** abstraction, brain child, concept, conceptualization, flash *(Nonformal)*, hypothesis, image, impression, notion, perception, revelation, solution, thought, vision **2.** attitude, belief, conviction, doctrine, mindset, point-of-view, opinion, sense, take, twist **3.** aim, design, game *or* master plan, plan, program, scenario, strategy *Nonformal:* angle, gimmick, slant **4.** caprice, fancy, fleeting thought, frivolity, impulse, trifle, whim **5.** awareness, clue, gleam, hint, hunch, indication, inkling, sneaking suspicion, suggestion **6.** emotion, feeling, inspiration, instinct, sentiment **7.** consequence, drift, intention, meaning, objective, purpose, reason, significance **8.** core, gist, heart, issue, keynote, message, phrase, point, seed, subject, theme, thesis, topic

ideal *adj.* **1.** archetypal, classic, consummate, desired, excellent, exemplary, flawless, impeccable, model, noble, paradigmatic, perfect, quintessential, satisfactory, untainted *Nonformal:* blue ribbon, tops **2.** abstract, chimerical, conceptual, fictitious, grandiose, hypothetical, idealized, illusory, imaginary, musing, quixotic, romantic, speculative, theoretical, unreal, unworkable, unworldly, utopian, visionary *Antonyms:* actual, factual, mundane, ordinary, real – *n.* **1.** apotheosis, archetype, beauty, best, champ, champion, *chef d'oeuvre (French)*, cream, epitome, gem, jewel, masterpiece, *ne plus ultra (Latin)*, nonpareil, original, paradigm, paragon, perfection, quintessence, shining example **2.** aim, goal, guiding light, inspiration, motive, purpose **3.** exemplar, precedent, prototype, pattern, specimen, standard, type **4.** belief, doctrine, dogma, maxim, morals, principle, standard, values

idealist *n.* **1.** Don Quixote, dreamer, escapist, ivory-towered, optimist, romancer, romantic *Nonformal:* Pollyanna, spinner, stargazer **2.** perfectionist, philosopher, theorizer, Utopian, visionary

idealistic *adj.* impractical, optimistic, perfectionistic, quixotic, romantic, starry-eyed, unrealistic, utopian *Antonyms:* down-to-earth, dystopian, pragmatic

identical *adj.* alike, carbon copy, congruous, corresponding, double, duplicate, equal, equivalent, exact, indistinguishable, interchangeable, like, matching, same, selfsame, twin, very same *Antonyms:* different, disparate, distinct, diverse, unlike

identifiable *adj.* appreciable, ascertainable, clear, detectable, discernible, distinguishable, known, nameable, observable, obvious, perceptible, recognizable, unmistakable

identification *n.* **1.** ID *Types of identification:* badge, birth certificate, DNA print, driver's licence, fingerprint, health card, identity card, initials, label, letter of introduction, monogram, passport, personal identity number *or* PIN, serial number, signature, social insurance number, student card *Nonformal:* dog tag, logo, papers, shield **2.** appellation, christening, classification, denomination, designation, discovery, indication, naming, specification **3.** empathy, fellow feeling *(Nonformal)*, likening, pathos, sympathy, synthesis

identify *v.* **1.** designate, label, term *Nonformal:* peg, tab, tag **2.** distinguish, espy, perceive, recognize, single out, spot, spy *Nonformal:* catch sight of, finger, make out **3.** characterize, connote, exemplify, mark, signify **4.** blend, fuse, join, make one, merge, unite **5.** discover, hone in on *(Nonformal)*, pick out *or* up, pinpoint, place

identity *n.* **1.** character, distinctiveness, existence, individuality, integrity, name, parentage, particularity, personality, self, selfhood, singleness, singularity, status, uniqueness **2.** accord, agreement, coherence, congruity, correspondence, empathy, equality, equivalence, likeness, oneness, rapport, resemblance, sameness, semblance, similarity, similitude, uniformity, unity

ideology *n.* **1.** beliefs, canon, credo, creed, dogma, ethos, ideas, philosophy, principles, teachings, tenets, view, world view **2.** fantasy, foresight, image, speculation, vision

idiocy *n.* craziness, fatuity, fatuousness, foolishness, giddiness, imbecility, inanity, insanity, irrationality, lunacy, madness, nonsense, rattleheadedness, recklessness, screwiness, senselessness, silliness, stupidity, tomfoolery *Antonyms:* acumen, rationality, sanity, sense, wisdom

idiom *n.* argot, brogue, cant, colloquialism, dialect, expression, idiosyncrasy, jargon, language, lingo, localism, parlance, patois, phrase, provincialism, style, talk, tongue, usage, vernacular, word *Nonformal:* jive, street talk

idiosyncrasy *n.* affectation, character traits, distinction, eccentricity, feature, habit, mannerism, oddity, peculiarity, quirk, singularity, style, temperament, trait, trick *Nonformal:* bit, schtick

idiosyncratic *adj.* **1.** characteristic, distinctive, indicative, individual, singular, symbolize *Antonyms:* common, conforming, general, regular, typical **2.** eccentric, fey, freakish, kooky *(Nonformal)*, *meshuga (Yiddish)*, odd, peculiar, strange

idiot *n.* dimwit, dunce, fool, half-wit, ignoramus, imbecile, lunatic, moron, nincompoop, nitwit, simpleton, stupid one, twit *Nonformal:* ass, blockhead, boob, dork, meathead, noodle, yo-yo, yutz *Antonyms:* brain, genius, intellectual, maestro, mastermind

idiotic *adj.* asinine, cockeyed, crazy, daft, dull, dumb, fatuous, foolhardy, foolish, half-witted, illogical, imbecilic, inane, insane, lunatic, moonstruck, moronic, nutty, senseless, silly, slow, stupid, thick-witted, unintelligent, vacuous *Nonformal:* bananas, batty, ding-a-ling, harebrained, squirrely *Antonyms:* brilliant, intelligent, learned, sensible, thoughtful

idle *adj.* **1.** asleep, at rest, dead, inert, indolent, lackadaisical, lazy, lethargic, motionless, passive, quiet, shiftless, slack, sleepy, slothful, sluggish, stationary, still, supine *Antonyms:* busy, energetic **2.** jobless, laid-off, leisured, off, out of action *or* work, unemployed, unoccupied, vegetating *Nonformal:* furloughed, on the beach, resting *Antonyms:* employed, energetic, occupied, working **3.** abandoned, barren, closed down, deserted, dusty, empty, fallow, inactive, moth-balled, on the shelf, retired, rusty, shelved, untouched, unused, vacant **4.** abortive, frivolous, fruitless, futile, groundless, hollow, ineffective, insignificant, irrelevant, pointless, rambling, superficial, trivial, unavailing, unhelpful, unnecessary, unproductive, unsuccessful, useless, vain, worthless *Antonyms:* fruitful, profitable, useful, worthwhile – *v.* crawl, decelerate, fritter *or* waste *or* while away, hold back, inch along, slack off, stagnate *Nonformal:* bum *or* fool around, goof off, mosey, poke along, toddle

idleness *n.* inaction, inactivity, lassitude, laziness, lethargy, sloth, sluggishness, torpor, unemployment

idler *n.* dawdler, lazybones, loafer, loiterer, lounger, malingerer, slouch, sluggard, wastrel *Nonformal:* bum, couch potato, do-nothing, goldbricker, good-for-nothing, goof-off, slacker, slider, sloth, slugabed

idol *n.* **1.** beloved, celebrity, darling, dear, desire, favourite, goddess, hero, inamorata, jewel *Nonformal:* pet, pin-up, pop hero, superstar, true-love, vision **2.** effigy, fetish, golden calf, icon, image, joss, statue

idolatrous *adj.* **1.** adoring, adulating, awestruck, devoted, reverential, worshipful **2.** fervent, infatuated, rabid, zealous *Antonyms:* critical, vilificatory

idolatry *n.* adoration, adulation, apotheosis, blind infatuation, deification, exaltation, glorification, hero worship, paganism

idolize *v.* admire, adore, adulate, canonize, cherish, deify, dote on, exalt, fall for *(Nonformal)*, glorify, love, revere, venerate, worship *Antonyms:* defame, deride, mock

idyllic *adj.* arcadian, blissful, bucolic, charming, ecologic, halcyon, heavenly, ideal, idealized, pastoral, peaceful, perfect, picturesque, pleasant, pleasing, poetic, romantic, rustic, unspoiled *Antonyms:* baroque, disagreeable, garish, ostentatious, unpleasant

ignite *v.* **1.** burn, catch fire, combust, fire, flare up, inflame, kindle, light, set alight *or* fire to, touch off *Antonyms:* douse, drench, put out, smother **2.** animate, arouse, awaken, electrify, excite, inspire, rally, stimulate, stir *Antonyms:* assuage, calm, ease

ignoble *adj.* **1.** contemptible, corrupt, craven, dastardly, degraded, disgraceful, dishonourable, ignominious, lewd, mean, petty, rotten, shameful, sneaky, sordid, vile, wretched *Antonyms:* gallant, honourable, noble **2.** abject, base, baseborn, coarse, common, humble, inferior, lowly, low *or* poor quality, menial, ordinary, plain, plebeian, servile, simple

ignominious *adj.* **1.** abject, despicable, disgraceful, dishonourable, disreputable, ignoble, indecorous, scrofulous, shameful, sorry, undignified *Antonyms:* credible, honourable, reputable, worthy **2.** humiliating, mortifying, scandalous, shocking, upsetting

ignominy *n.* contempt, discredit, disgrace, dishonour, humiliation, infamy, mortification, obloquy, odium, opprobrium, perfidy, reproach, shame, stigma *Antonyms:* credit, honour, repute

ignoramus *n.* *dummkopf (German)*, fool, idiot, simpleton *Nonformal:* blockhead, knucklehead, dunce, know-nothing *Antonyms:* intellectual, scholar

ignorance *n.* bewilderment, empty-headedness, half-knowledge, illiteracy, incapacity, incomprehension, inexperience, innocence, insensitivity, obtuseness, shallowness, simplicity, unawareness, unfamiliarity, unintelligence, vagueness *Antonyms:* comprehension, enlightenment, insight, knowledge, wisdom

ignorant *adj.* **1.** illiterate, uneducated, unenlightened, unlettered, unread, unschooled, untaught, untrained, untutored **2.** benighted, inexperienced, innocent, misinformed, naive, oblivious, obtuse, unaware, unconscious, uninformed, uninitiated, unknowledgeable, unwitting *Antonyms:* astute, aware, cognizant **3.** dumb, foolish, idiotic, silly, stupid *Antonyms:* brilliant, sagacious, wise

ignore *v.* **1.** avoid, brush aside, evade, pass by *or* over, pay no attention, reject, repudiate, shove away, slight, spurn *Nonformal:* cold shoulder, cut, cut dead, freeze, *Antonyms*: accept, acknowledge, welcome **2.** defy, disobey, flout *Nonformal:* fly in the face *or* teeth of, pooh-pooh *Antonyms:* abide by, follow, obey **3.** let slip, lose track of, neglect, omit, overlook *Antonyms:* care for, cherish, nourish **4.** blink *or* wink at, condone, discount, disregard, swallow, turn a blind eye *or* deaf ear to *Nonformal:* live with, tune out *Antonyms:* heed, listen to, note

ilk *n.* breed, cast, character, class, description, family, gender, genre, kind, like, make, sort, style, type, variety

ill *adj.* **1.** afflicted, ailing, awful, bedridden, below par, bilious, diseased, dizzy, feverish, nauseous, out of sorts, queasy, rickety, rotten, run down, seedy, sick, terrible *Nonformal:* down, in a bad way, laid low *or* up, off one's feed, rocky, woozy *Antonyms:* hale, hearty, well **2.** delicate, frail, infirm, mediocre, middling, poor, unsound, unstable *Antonyms:* firm, sound, strong **3.** adverse, disturbing, unfavourable, unkind, unlucky, unpromising, unwholesome *Antonyms:* beneficial, fortunate, lucky, propitious **4.** antagonistic, bitter, cruel, harmful, harsh, hostile, hurtful, malicious, noxious, spiteful, unfriendly *Antonyms:* caring, friendly, nurturing **5.** degenerate, disreputable, evil, immoral, iniquitous, sinister, unsavoury, villainous *Antonyms:* moral, pious, righteous **6.** improper, inappropriate, incorrect, unseemly, wrong *Antonyms:* correct, decorous, polite, proper **7.** ill-prepared, unproficient, unready, unsettled, untrained *Antonyms:* ready, set, trained – *adv.* **1.** amiss, badly, cruelly, disastrously, fell, not well, unkindly, wickedly **2.** barely, hardly, only just, scarcely, with difficulty **3.** awkwardly, falsely, imperfectly, imprecisely, improperly, unsuitably – *n.* **1.** disaster, discomfort, distress, harm, hurt, injury, misery, misfortune, tragedy, trouble, unhappiness woe **2.** cruelty, evil, injustice, insult, mischief, sin, transgression, wickedness wrong-doing **3.** infirmity, malady, sickness

ill-advised *adj.* botched, brash, foolhardy, foolish, harebrained, hotheaded, ill-considered, ill-judged, impolitic, imprudent, inappropriate, incautious, inconsiderate, indiscreet, injudicious, misguided, precipitate, rash, reckless, short-sighted, thoughtless, unseemly, unwise, wrong *Nonformal.* half-baked, half-cocked *Antonyms:* appropriate, judicious, seemly, sensible

ill-at-ease *adj.* anxious, awkward, disturbed, edgy, faltering, hesitant, nervous, restless, self-conscious, tense, uncomfortable, uneasy, unsure *Nonformal:* on tenterhooks, walking on eggs *Antonyms:* comfortable, quiet, relaxed, settled, sure

ill-bred *adj.* base, brutish, boorish, churlish, coarse, crass, crude, gross, hoidenish, insensitive, uncouth, uncivilized, unkempt unrefined, vulgar *Antonyms:* cultivated, refined, suave, urbane, well-bred

ill-defined *adj.* blurred, dim, fuzzy, indistinct, nebulous, poorly stated, shadowy, unclear, vague, woolly *Antonyms:* apparent, distinct, evident, manifest, obvious

ill-disposed *adj.* averse, belligerent, contrary, hostile, inimical, opposed, uncooperative, unfriendly, unwelcoming *Antonyms.* cooperative, friendly, obliging, welcoming

illegal *adj.* actionable, banned, black-market, bootleg, contraband, criminal, crooked, felonious, forbidden, illegitimate, illicit, lawless, outlawed, prohibited, proscribed, taboo, unauthorized, unconstitutional, unlawful, unlicensed, unofficial, unwarranted, violating, wrongful *Nonformal:* out of bounds *or* line, shady, under the table, wildcat *Antonyms:* lawful, legal, licit, permissible

illegible *adj.* faint, hieroglyphic, incomprehensible, indecipherable, indistinct, obscure, scrawled, unclear, undecipherable, unintelligible, unreadable *Antonyms:* clear, legible, plain, readable

illegitimate *adj.* **1.** contraband, illegal, illicit, invalid, unauthorized, unconstitutional, unlawful, unsanctioned, without papers *Nonformal:* shady, under the counter *or* table *Antonyms:* lawful, legal, legitimate, sanctioned **2.** bastard, by-blow, merry-begotten *(Newfoundland)*, misbegotten, natural

ill-fated *adj.* blighted, catastrophic, cursed, destroyed, disastrous, doomed, hapless, ill-omened, ill-starred, luckless, ruined, star-crossed, unfortunate, unhappy, unlucky *Antonyms:* auspicious, blessed, fortunate

ill-founded *adj.* baseless, empty, groundless, idle, unjustified, unproven, unreliable, unsubstantiated, unsupported, without merit *Antonyms:* justified, proven, reliable, supported

ill-humoured *adj.* acrimonious, bad-tempered, chippy, crabby, cross, disagreeable, grumpy, impatient, irascible, irritable, moody, morose, ornery, out of sorts, owly *(P.E.I.)*, petulant, sharp, snappy, sullen, surly, tart, testy, touchy, waspish *Antonyms:* affable, agreeable, amiable, delightful, pleasant

illicit *adj.* adulterous, black-market, bootleg, clandestine, contraband, criminal, felonious, forbidden, illegal, illegitimate, improper, lawless, prohibited, unauthorized, unlawful, unlicensed, wildcat, wrong, wrongful *Nonformal:* afterhours, off-limits *Antonyms:* lawful, legal, legitimate, permissible, proper *Commonly misused:* **elicit**

illiterate *adj.* ignorant, uneducated, unlettered, unread, unschooled, untaught *Antonyms:* cultured, educated, lettered, literate, taught

ill-kept *adj.* dirty, disheveled, disorderly, disorganized, filthy, messy, slatternly, sloppy, slovenly, unkempt *Antonyms:* clean, organized, spotless

ill-mannered *adj.* crass, discourteous, disrespectful, impertinent, impolite, insolent, loud, loudmouthed, offensive, rude, uncivil, ungallant, ungracious, vulgar *Antonyms:* civil, courteous, mannerly, polite, respectful

ill-natured *adj.* bad-tempered, cantankerous, caustic, choleric, churlish, cross, cussed *(Nonformal)*, disagreeable, ill-tempered, malevolent, malicious, mean, nasty, ornery, peevish, perverse, petulant, spiteful, sulky, sullen, surly, unfriendly, unkind, unpleasant *Antonyms:* cheerful, friendly, good-natured, kind

illness *n.* affliction, ailment, attack, bug *(Nonformal)*, complaint, confinement, disability, disease, disorder, failing *or* poor health, infirmity, malady, malaise, prostration, relapse, seizure, sickness *Antonyms:* health, soundness, wellbeing

illogical *adj.* absurd, crazy, fallacious, false, faulty, groundless, hollow, implausible, incongruous, inconsistent, incorrect, invalid, irrational, irrelevant, mad, meaningless, preposterous, senseless, specious, spurious, unproved, unreasonable, unscientific, unsound, untenable *Nonformal:* cockamamie, cockeyed, nutty, off the wall, screwy *Antonyms:* coherent, rational, sound, valid

ill-proportioned *adj.* askew, crooked, distorted, irregular, lopsided, misshapen, out of whack *(Nonformal)*, skewed, twisted, unbalanced, wry *Antonyms:* balanced, proportionate, symmetrical

illuminate *v.* **1.** brighten, flash, irradiate, light, lighten, light up, kindle, shine on, throw light on *Antonyms:* blacken, opaque, shadow **2.** clarify, edify, elucidate, enlighten, explain, explicate, expound, interpret, shed light on, spell out *Antonyms:* baffle, confound, mystify, obfuscate **3.** define, demonstrate, disclose, exhibit, feature, highlight, manifest, reveal, spotlight *Antonyms:* camouflage, conceal, cover, hide, shroud **4.** decorate, embellish, enamel, gild, gloss

illumination *n.* **1.** beam of light, brightness, brilliance, flame, flash, gleam, incandescence, light, lumination, luminescence, radiance, ray, shining light, sun **2.** awareness, cognizance, dawning, elucidation, enlightenment, insight, *moksha (Hindu)*, perception, revelation, understanding **3.**

adornment, decoration, embellishment, ornamentation

illusion *n.* **1.** deceit, delusion, legerdemain, sleight of hand, smoke and mirrors *(Nonformal)*, trick, trickery **2.** fallacy, false impression, misconception, misjudgment, mistake **3.** apparition, fantasy, hallucination, image, invention, mirage, phantom, phenomenon, semblance, spectre, will-o'-the-wisp *Commonly misused:* **allusion**

illusionist *n.* conjuror, magician, Merlin, performer, prestidigitator, sorceress, spellcaster, trickster, wizard

illusory *adj.* all in the mind, apparent, blue-sky *(Nonformal)*, chimerical, deceptive, false, fanciful, fantastic, fictional, hallucinatory, illusive, imaginary, seeming, unreal, visionary, whimsical *Antonyms:* authentic, bona fide, genuine, true-to-life

illustrate *v.* **1.** adorn, decorate, depict, describe, draw, embellish, engrave, illuminate, ornament, paint, pencil, picture, portray, show, sketch **2.** document, embody, epitomize, exemplify, personify, represent, typify **3.** clarify, elucidate, explain, explicate, fill in the gaps, make plain, shed light on

illustration *n.* **1.** artwork, caricature, cartoon, chart, depiction, diagram, draft, drawing, engraving, etching, figure, image, likeness, painting, photograph, portrait, print, sketch, vignette **2.** case, case in point, example, for instance *(Nonformal)*, model, object lesson, sample, specimen **3.** clarification, clearing up *(Nonformal)*, elucidation, explanation, explication

illustrative *adj.* allegorical, corroborative, descriptive, emblematic, exemplary, exemplifying, explanatory, explicatory, illuminative, indicative, interpretive, metaphoric, representative, symbolic, typical

illustrious *adj.* brilliant, celebrated, distinguished, eminent, exalted, famed, famous, glorious, great, legendary, lofty, notable, noted, preeminent, prominent, renowned, signal, splendid, star, stellar, superstar, venerable *Nonformal*: big league, heavy, name *Antonyms:* humble, infamous, lowly, meek, obscure

image *n.* **1.** bust, caricature, drawing, expression, figure, icon, illustration, painting, photograph, picture, portrait, representation, sculpture, sketch, statue, tableau, totem **2.** concept, construct, idea, impression, notion, perception, sense, thought, view, visualization **3.** alter ego, carbon copy, clone, dead ringer *(Nonformal)*, *doppelgänger (German)*, double, duplicate, effigy, fellow, likeness, mate, replica, reproduction, shadow-self **4.** appearance, aspect, form, guise, likeness, semblance, shape **5** character, face, honour, reputation, public perception *or* persona, reputation, standing, stature **6.** embodiment, epitome, example, incarnation, model, symbol, type, typical **7** figure of speech, metaphor, simile, sublimation **8.** apparition, eidolon, ghost, phantom, poltergeist, presence, reflection – *v.* **1** copy, delineate, describe, illustrate, portray, recreate, reproduce, symbolize, trace **2** call *or* dream up, envision, imagine, picture, think out, see, visualize

imagery *n.* **1.** description, figure of speech, figurative language, metaphor, simile, sublimation, trope **2.** fancy, impression, mental picture, notion, thought, visualization

imaginable *adj.* believable, conceivable, credible, likely, plausible, possible, supposable, thinkable *Antonyms:* impossible, inconceivable, incredible, unlikely

imaginary *adj.* chimerical, dream-like, dreamt, fabricated, fabulous, fanciful, far-fetched, fictitious, hypothetical, illusive, intangible, invented, legendary, make-believe, mystical, nonexistent, oneiric, pretend, quixotic, surreal, trumped up *(Nonformal)*, unreal, visionary *Antonyms:* genuine, proven, tangible *Commonly misused:* **imaginative**

imagination *n.* **1.** creative power, creativity, ingenuity, inspiration, inventiveness, mental agility, originality, resourcefulness **2.** dream, fantasy, mind's eye, vision

imaginative *adj.* **1.** artistic, clever, creative, far-sighted, fertile, ingenious, inspired, inventive, off-beat, original, poetic, productive, surrealistic, visionary *Antonyms:* common, threadbare, trite **2** absurd, fanciful, fantastic, incredible unreal, unsubstantial *Commonly misused:* **imaginary**

imagine *v.* brainstorm, conceive, conceptualize, conjure *or* cook *or* dream *or* make up, create, devise, dream, envision, fantasize, invent, perceive, picture, pretend, realize, think of *or* up, visualize **2.** apprehend, assume, believe, conjecture, deduce, deem, estimate, expect, figure, gather, guess, infer, judge, opine, presume, reckon, suppose, surmise, suspect, think

imbalance *n.* **1.** disproportion, distortion, lopsidedness, top-heaviness, unevenness **2.** bias, disparity, inequality, partiality, unfairness *Antonyms:* equality, fairness, symmetry

imbecile *adj.* **1.** backward, crazy, deranged, dimwitted, dull, feeble-minded, half-witted, hare-brained, moronic, simpleminded, slow, stupid, thick, witless *Antonyms:* intelligent, sensible, smart **2.** addlepated, asinine, fatuous, foolish, idiotic, ludicrous, silly – *n.* ass, bungler, dimwit, dolt, fool, half-wit, idiot, lamebrain, moron, nincompoop, nitwit, simpleton *Nonformal:* birdbrain, dingbat, dope, goof

imbibe *v.* **1.** consume, drink, quaff, swallow, swill *Nonformal:* booze, chug, grog, guzzle, knock back, nip **2.** absorb, acquire, assimilate, digest, gain, gather, get, ingest, inhale, learn, memorize, osmose, receive, retain, soak up, take in, understand

imbroglio *n.* altercation, argument, bickering, brawl, complication, confusion, dispute, embarrassment, entanglement, falling-out, fight, mess, misunderstanding, muddle, pickle, plight, predicament, quandary, quarrel, row, run-in, spat, squabble, tangle *Nonformal:* can of worms, how-to-do, kettle of fish, rat's nest, rhubarb, run-in, soap opera *Antonyms:* agreement, harmony, peace

mbue *v.* **1.** brainwash *(Nonformal)*, impregnate, inculcate, indoctrinate, infuse, inoculate, inspire, permeate, pervade, suffuse **2.** bathe, colour, drench, dye, saturate, soak, steep, tinge, tint, wet

mitate *v.* **1.** act *or* do *or* make like, ape *(Nonformal)*, copy, echo, emulate, follow, model *or* pattern after, parrot **2.** burlesque, caricature, impersonate, mimic, mock, parody, satirize, take-off *Nonformal:* send up, spoof **3.** clone, counterfeit, derive from, forge, match, plagiarize, replicate, reproduce *Nonformal:* crib, knock-off, pirate, steal

imitation *adj.* artificial, fake, faux, manmade, pretend, sham *Nonformal:* bogus, ersatz, mock, phoney, plastic, pseudo – *n.* **1.** clone, copy, duplication, facsimile, forgery, likeness, parallel, replica, reproduction, rip off *(Nonformal)* **2.** impersonation, impression, mimicry, parody, pastiche, spoof, travesty

imitative *adj.* **1.** copied, copycat, counterfeit, derivative, fake, false, faux, forged, mimic, mock, phoney *(Nonformal)*, plagiarized, pretend, reflective, secondhand, sham, simulated, spurious, unoriginal *Antonyms:* bona fide, original, real, unique **2.** echoic, emulative, mimetic, onomatopoeic, representative, similar, simulative, virtual

immaculate *adj.* **1.** clean, decent, dirt-free, sanitized, spotless, spic-and-span *Antonyms:* dirty, filthy, muddy **2.** above reproach, faultless, flawless, impeccable, perfect, stainless, unsullied, unvarnished **3.** chaste, guiltless, holy, innocent, pristine, saintly, sinless, uncorrupted, undefiled, virtuous

immaterial *adj.* **1.** extraneous, incidental, inconsequential, insignificant, irrelevant, meaningless, minor, of no consequence, paltry, petty, piddling *(Nonformal)*, trifling, trivial, unimportant, unnecessary, unneeded *Antonyms:* crucial, essential, germane, important, relevant **2.** aerial, airy, disembodied, ethereal, ghostly, impalpable, incorporeal, insubstantial, intangible, metaphysical, phantom, spectral, spiritual, unearthly *Antonyms:* corporeal, earthly, physical, real, tangible

immature *adj.* **1.** callow, developing, fresh, green, inexperienced, naive, prepubescent, pre-teen, tender, underage, unseasoned *Antonyms:* experienced, mature, of age **2.** crude, embryonic, half-baked, imperfect, inchoate, premature, rudimentary, undeveloped, unformed *Antonyms:* finished, perfected, prepared **3.** adolescent, babyish, childish, infantile, jejune, juvenile, puerile, shallow, sophomoric *Antonyms:* adult, manipulative, sagacious, shrewd

immeasurable *adj.* bottomless, boundless, countless, endless, extensive, great, illimitable, immense, incalculable, indeterminate, inestimable, inexhaustible, infinite, limitless, measureless, teeming, unlimited, vast *Nonformal:* gazillion, umpteen *Antonyms:* calculable, circumscribed, computable, enumerable

immediacy *n.* **1.** imminence, instancy, instantaneousness, promptitude, promptness, simultaneity, spontaneity, swiftness **2.** accessibility, availability, closeness, intimacy, nearness, presence, propinquity, proximity

immediate *adj.* **1.** early, fast, hasty, instant, instantaneous, prompt, quick, rapid, speedy, swift **2.** contemporary, current, extent, latest, live, modern, now, on-line, on hand, present, present day, recent, today, up-to-date, up-to-the-minute **3.** gut *(Nonformal)*, intuitive, involuntary, knee-jerk, reflex, spontaneous, unconscious, unrehearsed, visceral **4.** compelling, critical, exigent, important, pressing, urgent, vital **5.** abutting, adjacent, adjoining, bordering, contiguous, nearby, neighbouring, next, nextdoor, nigh, proximate, snug **6.** basic, close, close ranking, direct, intimate, intrinsic, private **7.** actual, categorical, clear, direct, explicit, honest, obvious, straightforward, unequivocal, unreserved **8.** linear, shortest, straight, unbroken, unhesitating, uninterrupted

immediately *adv.* **1.** ASAP, at once, double time, forthwith, instantaneously, instanter, instantly, now, promptly, pronto, rapidly, right away *or* now, *schnell (German)*, stat, straight away *or* off, this instant *or* minute, unhesitatingly, urgently, without delay *or* hesitation *Nonformal:* in a jiffy, lickety-split, like a bat out of hell, like new, PDQ, pretty darn quick, toot-sweet **2.** anon, forthwith, henceforth, hereupon, presently, shortly, soon, soon afterward, summarily, thereupon, when convenient

immemorial *adj.* age-old, ancient, old a[s] the hills *(Nonformal)*, back beyond memo[ry], forever, long ago, longstanding, of yor[e], old, olden, primeval, traditional, venerabl[e] *Antonyms:* current, new, recent, updated

immense *adj.* **1.** boundless, endless, exten[sive], great, immeasurable, infinite, inter[minable], limitless, measureless, unbound[ed], vast *Antonyms:* little, microscopic[,] minute, small **2.** Brobdingnagian, colossal[,] elephantine, enormous, gargantuan, giant[,] gigantic, gross, huge, humongous *(Nonformal)*, jumbo, king-size, large, massive[,] mighty, monstrous, monumental, prodi[gious], stupendous, titanic, tremendou[s] *Antonyms:* diminutive, miniature, tiny **3** amazing, excellent, first-rate, outstanding[,] superb, unbelievable, wonderful *Nonformal:* bonzer, major league

immerse *v.* **1.** bathe, dip, douse, drench[,] drown, duck, dunk, imbrue, plunge, satu[rate], sink, slop, soak, souse, sprinkle[,] steep, submerge, submerse, waterlog **2** absorb, bury, busy, engage, engross, inter[est], involve, occupy **3.** baptize, christen[,] cleanse, purify

immersed *adj.* **1.** absorbed, bound up[,] buried, busy, consumed, deep, drawn o[r] sucked in *(Nonformal)*, engaged[,] engrossed, intent, involved, mesmerized[,] occupied, preoccupied, rapt, spellbound[,] taken *or* tied *or* wrapped up *Antonyms*[:] detached, indifferent, uninvolved **2** drenched, soaked, soaking, sopping, water[logged], wet **3.** drowned, submerged, sunk[,] sunken, underwater

immigrant *n.* alien, colonist, foreigne[r,] landed immigrant, migrant, naturalized cit[izen], newcomer, non-native, permanent res[ident], pioneer, settler *Commonly misused* **emigrant**

immigrate *v.* arrive, colonize, migrat[e,] move, resettle, settle *Commonly misused* **emigrate**

imminent *adj.* approaching, at hand, clos[e,] coming, expected, fast-approaching, fort[h]coming, gathering, immediate, impending[,] in prospect *or* sight *or* store *or* view, in th[e] wind *(Nonformal)*, likely, looming, nea[r] ing, nigh, possible, probable, threatening *Antonyms:* remote, removed, unlikely *Commonly misused:* **eminent**

immobile *adj.* **1.** at rest, horizontal, idle, motionless, resting, sleeping, slumped, stagnant, static, stationary, still *Antonyms:* active, mobile, vigorous **2.** anchored, fixed, frozen, immobilized, immovable, nailed down, permanent, riveted, rooted, stable, unmovable *Antonyms:* pliant, portable

immobilize *v.* **1.** cripple, disable, fell, paralyze, stun *Nonformal:* down, fix, take out **2.** anchor, moor, secure, settle, stabilize **3.** confine, freeze, halt, restrain, retain, stop *Antonyms:* free, loose, release

immoderate *adj.* enormous, exaggerated, excessive, exorbitant, extravagant, extreme, inordinate, intemperate, overindulgent, prodigious, profligate, steep, too much, unbalanced, unbridled, unconscionable, uncontrolled, undue, unjustified, unreasonable, unrestrained, unwarranted *Antonyms:* controlled, judicious, moderate, restrained, temperate

immodest *adj.* **1.** bawdy, blue *(Nonformal)*, coarse, depraved, forward, gross, immoral, improper, indecent, indelicate, lascivious, licentious, lewd, obscene, revealing, risqué, rude, shameless, titillating, unchaste *Antonyms:* clean, family-oriented, upstanding **2.** arrogant, boasting, bold, brash, brazen, cock-sure, conceited, fresh, impudent, pushy, saucy, self-assertive, self-assured, shameful *Antonyms:* bashful, humble, reserved, shy

immoral *adj.* **1.** bad, corrupt, cruel, disgraceful, dishonest, evil, iniquitous, unacceptable, unethical, unprincipled, unscrupulous, villainous, wicked, wrong *Antonyms:* ethical, honourable, righteous, virtuous **2.** debauched, lewd, licentious, obscene, perverted, salacious, wanton *Antonyms:* chaste, pure, virginal *Commonly misused:* **amoral**

immorality *n.* **1.** baseness, corruption, depravity, dissoluteness, evil-mindedness, miscreancy, moral delinquency, turpitude, ungodliness, vileness, villainy, vulgarity **2.** lasciviousness, lecherousness, lewdness, obscenity, prurience, whorishness *Antonyms:* abstemiousness, abstinence, celibacy, forbearance **3.** evil, iniquity, sin, transgression, wickedness, wrong

immortal *adj.* **1.** abiding, ceaseless, constant, death-defying *(Nonformal)*, deathless, endless, enduring, eternal, evergreen, everlasting, imperishable, indestructible, never-ceasing, never-ending, perennial, permanent, perpetual, timeless, undying, unfading *Antonyms:* ephemeral, fleeting, passing, temporary, transitory **2.** celebrated, classic, eminent, enshrined, fabled, famous, heroic, illustrious, laureate, legendary, memorable, paragon, preeminent, storied **3.** blessed, divine, glorious, godly, holy, sacred, supreme, transcendent – *n.* celebrity, deity, demigod, demigoddess, divinity, god, goddess, legend, mythical being, star, superstar

immortalize *v.* **1.** apotheosize, canonize, deify, eternalize, perpetuate, preserve, sustain **2.** celebrate, commemorate, exalt, glorify, honour, lionize, memorialize, solemnize, tribute

immovable *adj.* **1.** at a standstill, constant, frozen, motionless, stable, static, steady, unalterable, unchanging *Antonyms:* flexible, fluid **2.** fast, firm, fixed, rooted, secure, set, solid, stationary, stuck *Antonyms:* mobile, portable **3.** adamant, die-hard, hard-nosed *(Nonformal)*, inflexible, intransigent, mulish, resolute, rigid, steadfast, stubborn, uncompromising, unshakable, unwavering, unyielding *Antonyms:* adaptable, impressionable, yielding

immune *adj.* **1.** clear, inoculated, protected, resistant, safe, vaccinated *Antonyms:* exposed, prone, susceptible **2.** defended, fortified, hardened, impervious, invulnerable, unaffected, untouched *Antonyms:* defenceless, powerless, vulnerable **3.** absolved, excused, exempt, free, spared *Antonyms:* answerable, culpable, liable

immunity *n.* **1.** barrier, buffer, defense, fortification, protection, inoculation, resistance, safety, screen, shield, wall **2.** amnesty, exclusion, exemption, freedom, release *Commonly misused:* **impunity**

immunize *v.* defend, fortify, inject, inoculate, insure against, protect, safeguard, vaccinate

immure *v.* cage, cloister, closet, confine, corral, detain, enclose, girdle, imprison, incarcerate, intern, jail, lock up, pen, pound, retain, seclude *Antonyms:* free, release *Commonly misused:* **inure**

immutable *adj.* constant, enduring, fixed, invariable, permanent, perpetual, steadfast, unalterable, unchangeable, unvarying *Antonyms:* capricious, fickle, perfidious

imp *n.* **1.** brownie, demon, devil, elf, fairy, fiend, gnome, gremlin, kobold, scut *(P.E.I.)*, sprite, troll **2.** brat, *enfant terrible (French)*, gamin, hellion, menace, nuisance, pismire *(P.E.I.)*, prankster, rascal, scamp, trickster, urchin *Nonformal:* holy terror, live-wire, wild child

impact *n.* **1.** consequences, effect, influence, mark, meaning, repercussion, significance, thrust, weight **2.** bang, blow, bounce, buffet, bump, clash, collision, concussion, contact, crash, hit, jar, jolt, knock, meeting, pound, punch, quake, ram, rap, shock, slap, smash, stroke, thump, wallop **3.** energy, force, impetus, momentum, power, propulsion, shock – *v.* compress, cram, crowd, drive, fill, pack, press, ram, squeeze, stuff, wedge in

impair *v.* attenuate, blemish, cheapen, cripple, damage, debilitate, devalue, diminish, harm, hurt, injure, lessen, mar, reduce, spoil, tarnish, total *(Nonformal)*, undermine, vitiate, weaken *Antonyms:* better, enhance, improve, strengthen

impaired *adj.* **1.** drunk, hampered, inebriated, intoxicated, unsound, wasted *Nonformal:* blowing over, hammered, in one's cups, loaded, over the limit, plastered, smashed **2.** broken, damaged, defective, faulty, flawed, harmed, hurt, imperfect, injured, malfunctioning, marred, spoiled, unsound *Nonformal:* busted, had it, kaput, on the blink, toast, totalled

impale *v.* harpoon, jab, lance, perforate, pierce, puncture, run through, shishkebab *(Nonformal)*, skewer, spear, spike, stab, stick, transfix

impalpable *adj.* **1.** airy, disembodied, ethe real, immaterial, indiscernible, intangibl insubstantial *Antonyms:* corporeal, tang ble **2.** fine, imperceptible, infinitesima minute *Antonyms:* observable, obvious

impart *v.* **1.** admit, announce, blurt *(Non formal)*, break, communicate, convey, di close, discover, divulge, expose, heral inform, intimate, mention, relate, revea suggest, tell, transmit *Antonyms:* concea deny, suppress **2.** afford, allow, assig award, bestow, cede, confer, conve donate, give, grant, offer, present, rende yield *Antonyms:* deprive, remove, tak away, withhold

impartial *adj.* detached, disinterested, di passionate, equitable, evenhanded, fai fair-minded, just, level, mugwumpian *(Non formal)*, neutral, nonpartisan, objectiv open-minded, unbiased, uninvolved, unpre udiced *Antonyms:* biased, bigoted, infl enced

impartiality *n.* detachment, disinterest, di passion, equity, fairness, lack of bias, leve headedness, neutrality, nonpartisanshi objectivity, open-mindedness *Antonym* bias, favouritism, partiality

impassable *adj.* barricaded, blocke impenetrable, impervious, obstructe unnavigable, washed-out *Antonyms:* clea open, passable *Commonly misuse* **impassible**

impasse *n.* blind alley, box, Catch-2 checkmate, corner, cul-de-sac, dead en deadlock, dilemma, jam, Mexican stando *(Nonformal)*, mire, morass, pause, pligh pocket, predicament, point nonplu quandary, stalemate, standoff, standsti *Nonformal:* fix, hole

impassible *adj.* **1.** cold, dispassionat hardhearted, heartless, insensitive, steel unemotional, unfeeling, unresponsi *Antonyms:* loving, passionate, warm immune, impregnable, indestructibl invincible, invulnerable, untouchable Co monly *misused:* **impassable**

impassioned *adj.* animated, arden aroused, burning, emotional, enthusiasti excited, fervent, fierce, fiery, glowing, heated, inspired, intense, melodramatic, moving, powerful, rousing, stirring, vehement, vivid, worked up, zealous *Nonformal:* riled up, steamed *Antonyms:* apathetic, impassive, indifferent, objective, pedestrian

impassive *adj.* **1.** aloof, apathetic, callous, cold, dry, emotionless, hardened, heartless, incurious, indifferent, inexpressive, matter-of-fact, nonchalant, passionless, phlegmatic, poker-faced *(Nonformal)*, reserved, reticent, self-contained, spiritless, stoic, taciturn, unconcerned, unemotional, unexcitable, unfeeling, unflappable, unmoved, wooden *Antonyms:* moved, responsive, warm **2.** calm, collected, composed, coolheaded, level, pacific, peaceful, placid, poised, quiet, sedate, serene, unruffled, together *(Nonformal)*, tranquil *Antonyms:* dizzy, excited, giddy **3.** blind *or* immune to, impervious, inanimate, insensate, insensible, lifeless, unconscious

impatience *n.* **1.** agitation, anxiety, brusqueness, edginess, fitfulness, fretfulness, irritability, nervousness, restlessness **2.** eagerness, enthusiasm, hastiness, impetuosity, itchiness, keenness, yearning, zest

impatient *adj.* **1.** abrupt, curt, restless, restive, skittish, snappy, waspish *Nonformal:* antsy, fidgety, jittery, short-fused, squirmish *Antonyms:* blasé, nonchalant, unconcerned **2.** eager, headlong, hotheaded, impulsive, rash *Nonformal:* gung-ho, hopped up, hot to trot, rarin' to go *Antonyms:* cautious, chary, guarded, reluctant **3.** careless, cursory, fast, headless, hurried, quick, unconsidered *Antonyms:* deliberate, intense, studied

impeach *v.* **1.** accuse, arraign, censure, charge, incriminate, indict, prefer charges *Antonyms:* acquit, clear, release **2.** challenge, criticize, denounce, disparage, query, question, reprimand *Antonyms:* champion, promote, support

impeccable *adj.* **1.** absolute, exact, exquisite, faultless, flawless, immaculate, perfect, precise, unerring *Nonformal:* on target, tiptop *Antonyms:* defective, deficient, faulty, flawed **2.** blameless, chaste, guiltless, impeccant, innocent, irreproachable, pure, saintly, sinless, stainless, unblemished, unerring, unimpeachable, unsullied, virtuous *Antonyms:* blameworthy, corrupt, sinful

impecunious *adj.* destitute, impoverished, indigent, insolvent, mendicant, needy, penniless, pinched, poor, poverty-stricken *Nonformal:* broke, skint, strapped *Antonyms:* affluent, prosperous, rich, wealthy

impede *v.* bar, brake, check, clog, close *or* cut off, curb, delay, deter, discomfit, disrupt, freeze, hamper, handicap, hinder, interfere, obstruct, restrain, retard, stonewall, stop, stymie, thwart *Nonformal:* cramp, hang *or* hold up *Antonyms:* advance, assist, further, help, promote

impediment *n.* **1.** bar, barrier, block, blockage, bottleneck, Catch-22, catch, chain, check, cramp, curb, dead weight, delay, deterrent, drag, drawback, encumbrance, hazard, hindrance, hitch, hurdle, millstone, objection, obstacle, obstruction, restriction, road block, rub, setback, shackle, snag, stoppage, stricture, stumbling block, wall *Nonformal*: baggage, glitch *Antonyms:* benefit, encouragement, relief, support **2.** defect, detriment, difficulty, disadvantage, fault, flaw, handicap

impel *v.* **1.** drive, exhort, force, goad, incite, inspire, instigate, lean on, motivate, prompt, stimulate, urge, whip *Nonformal:* railroad, ramrod, squeeze *Antonyms:* blunt, discourage, prohibit, smother **2.** actuate, get going, prod, propel, push, shove, spur *Antonyms:* arrest, check, curb, hold back, restrain

impending *adj.* anticipated, brewing, coming, forthcoming, gathering, hovering, imminent, in the cards *or* offing, looming, lurking, menacing, nearing, ominous, on the horizon, threatening, waiting *Antonyms:* distant, receding, retreating

impenetrable *adj.* **1.** airtight, bulletproof, close, dark, deep, dense, hermetic, locked up tight, puncture proof, sealed away, watertight *Antonyms:* accessible, available, open **2.** abstruse, beyond comprehension, inscrutable, recondite, undecipherable, unfathomable, unintelligible *Antonyms:* clear-cut, intelligible, lucid, unambiguous **3.** callous, close-minded, hardened, inflexible, intransigent, obdurate, stubborn, thick-skinned *Antonyms:* accepting, forbearing, lenient, tolerant

impenitent *adj.* callous, defiant, hard, incorrigible, inured, miscreant, reprobate, shameless, unfeeling, unrepentant, without remorse *Antonyms:* chastened, humbled, merciful, repentant

imperative *adj.* **1.** acute, burning, clamorous, compulsory, critical, crucial, essential, exigent, immediate, important, importunate, inescapable, insistent, life and death *(Nonformal)*, mandatory, necessary, obligatory, pressing, urgent, vital *Antonyms:* avoidable, nonessential, optional, unnecessary **2.** aggressive, authoritative, bidding, commanding, dictatorial, dogmatic, domineering, imperial, imperious, magisterial, peremptory – *n.* **1.** bidding, command, dictate, mandate, order, prescription **2.** charge, dire necessity, duty, exigency, liability, obligation, onus, responsibility, say-so, urgency

imperceptible *adj.* **1.** ephemeral, evanescent, faint, fine, gradual, inconspicuous, infinitesimal, microscopic, minute, slight, small, tiny, undetectable, unnoticeable, wee *(Nonformal) Antonyms:* hulking, immense, mammoth **2.** impalpable, imponderable, intangible, invisible, unknowable, vague *Antonyms:* actual, concrete, material

imperceptive *adj.* blind, dim, dull, insensible, oblivious, obtuse, purblind, slow, thick *(Nonformal)*, unconscious

imperfect *adj.* **1.** blemished, broken, damaged, defective, disfigured, flawed, faulty, impaired, injured, inoperative, kaput *(Nonformal)*, marred, unsound *Antonyms:* flawless, perfect, pristine **2.** crude, deficient, immature, inchoate, incomplete, inexact, limited, partial, patchy, rough, rudimentary, sketchy, undeveloped, unfinished *Antonyms:* absolute, complete, whole **3.** below *or* sub par, indifferent, lacking, lousy, mediocre, middling, so-so, wanting *Nonformal:* Mickey Mouse, piss-poor

imperfection *n.* **1.** deficiency, drawback, foible, inadequacy, liability, limitation, peccadillo, shortcoming, vice, weakness, weak point **2.** blemish, crack, defect, deformity, fault, flaw, rent, run, scratch, stain, taint

imperial *adj.* **1.** kingly, majestic, noble, queenly, regal, royal, sovereign *Antonyms:* inferior, proletarian, subaltern **2.** august, dignified, exalted, grand, imposing, lofty, lordly, magnificent, purple, splendid *Antonyms:* mean, nondescript, prosaic, ribald **3.** absolute, authoritative, chief, commanding, governing, magisterial, paramount, predominant, ruling, supreme *Commonly misused:* **imperious**

imperialism *n.* **1.** acquisitiveness, colonialism, empire-building, expansionism, exploitation, foreign policy **2.** grandeur, greatness, impressiveness, loftiness, magnificence, majesty, pomp, regalness

imperil *v.* chance, compromise, endanger, expose, gamble, hazard, jeopardize, put in danger, risk *or* tempt fate *Antonyms:* guard, protect, secure

imperious *adj.* **1.** arbitrary, arrogant, bossy, commanding, despotic, dictatorial, domineering, exacting, haughty, magisterial, overbearing, peremptory, tyrannical *Nonformal:* high and mighty, pushy, whip-cracking *Antonyms:* abject, fawning, obsequious, subservient **2.** acute, critical, dire, imperative, important, necessary, pressing, urgent, vital *Antonyms:* inconsequential, trifling *Commonly misused:* **imperial**

imperishable *adj.* adamantine, enduring, everlasting, eternal, evergreen *(Nonformal)*, immortal, indestructible, perennial, permanent, perpetual, unalterable, unbreakable, undying, unfading *Antonyms:* evanescent, fading, mortal, transient

impermanent *adj.* brief, disappearing, ephemeral, evanescent, fleeting, fly-by-night *(Nonformal)*, inconstant, mortal, mutable, passing, permutable, short-lived, temporary, transient, transitory *Antonyms:* eternal, fixed, lasting, permanent

impermeable *adj.* **1.** closed, hermetic, impassable, impenetrable, impervious, leakproof, non-porous, resistant, sealed, waterproof *Antonyms:* absorbent, porous

2. close, compact, dense, jungly, solid, thick, tight

impersonal *adj.* **1.** detached, disinterested, dispassionate, equal, fair, impartial, neutral, objective, straight, unbiased, uncoloured, unprejudiced **2.** bureaucratic, businesslike, by-the-book, cool, emotionless, formal, indifferent, matter-of-fact, official, remote, stiff, wooden *Antonyms:* friendly, intimate, outgoing, personal, warm

impersonate *v.* act, act out, ape, copy, enact, imitate, masquerade, mimic, mirror, portray, pose, pretend, represent *Nonformal:* do, monkey, parrot

impertinence *n.* **1.** audacity, boldness, brass, brazenness, cheek, disrespect, effrontery, forwardness, gall, incivility, insolence, nerve, pertness, presumption, rudeness *Nonformal:* backtalk, chutzpah, gumption, lip, moxie, sass, sauce *Antonyms:* politeness, respect, reverence **2.** absurdity, disjunction, inappropriateness, immateriality, irrelevance, non sequitur, unconnectedness

impertinent *adj.* **1.** bold, brazen, cheeky, discourteous, disrespectful, forward, fresh, ill-mannered, impudent, out-of-line, presumptuous, rude, unmannerly *Nonformal:* brassy, mouthy, nervy *Antonyms:* courteous, demur, polite **2.** inappropriate, irrelevant, ludicrous, trivial, unconnected, unrelated

imperturbable *adj.* assured, calm, collected, complacent, composed, cool, nerveless, nonchalant, sedate, self-possessed, steely, stoical, thick-skinned, tranquil, unaffected, undisturbed, unexcitable, unflappable, unmoved, unruffled, untouched *Antonyms:* edgy, excitable, nervous

impervious *adj.* **1.** airtight, bulletproof, fireproof, hermetic, impenetrable, impermeable, inaccessible, sealed, tight, unpenetrable, watertight *Antonyms:* accessible, open, permeable **2.** callous, closed to, immune, insensitive, steely, thick-skinned, unaffected, unapproachable, unfeeling, unreceptive

impetuous *adj.* **1.** abrupt, headstrong, impulsive, madcap, precipitate, rash, spontaneous, spur-of-the-moment, unbridled, unexpected, unplanned, unrestrained, unthinking *Antonyms:* cautious, prudent, wary **2.** breakneck, forceful, furious, hasty, headlong, rushing, speedy, sudden, swift *Antonyms:* meandering, mild, slow

impetus *adj.* **1.** energy, force, impulse, momentum, power, pressure, push, spur **2.** catalyst, goad, incentive, motivation, stimulus, urge

impiety *n.* **1.** blasphemy, corruption, fall, iniquity, irreverence, profanity, sacrilege, sinfulness, transgression, ungodliness, wickedness **2.** affrontery, cheek, derision, disrespect, impertinence, insolence, jeering, mockery, ridicule

impinge *v.* **1.** encroach, horn in *(Nonformal)*, infringe, interfere, intrude, invade, obtrude, trespass, violate **2.** bang, buffet, bump, butt, clash, collide, hit, knock, jolt, push, shove

impious *adj.* **1.** agnostic, apostate, atheistic, blasphemous, defiling, desecrating, diabolic, godless, iniquitous, irreligious, profane, sacrilegious, sinful, ungodly, unhallowed, unrighteous, wicked *Antonyms:* devout, godly, holy, religious, reverent **2.** bold, brash, contemptuous, disdainful, disobedient, disrespectful, impolite, insolent, irreverent, rude, scornful, uncivil, wayward

impish *adj.* annoying, devilish, elfin, gamine, mischievous, naughty, playful, prankish, puckish, sportive, undisciplined, unruly, wayward *Antonyms:* behaved, demure, modest, sedate, staid

implacable *adj.* adamant, firm, grim, hard, inexorable, inflexible, intractable, iron-fisted, merciless, pitiless, rancorous, relentless, remorseless, rigid, steely, unappeasable, unbending, uncompromising, unflinching, unforgiving, unrelenting, unyielding, vindictive *Antonyms:* appeasable, flexible, lenient

implant *v.* **1.** attach, connect, embed, fix, graft, infix, inseminate, plant, root, sow, transplant **2.** brainwash *(Nonformal)*, inculcate, indoctrinate, influence, infuse, inoculate, instill, teach

implausible *adj.* doubtful, dubious, far-fetched, impossible, improbable, inconceivable, incredible, problematic, puzzling, suspect, unbelievable, unconvincing, unimaginable, unlikely, unreasonable, unsubstantial, weak *Nonformal:* crazy, far out, fishy, over-the-top *Antonyms:* feasible, likely, possible

implement *n.* agent, apparatus, appliance, contraption, device, equipment, gadget, machine, means, tool, utensil – *v.* **1.** actualize, bring about, carry out, enable, enforce, execute, invoke, perform, phase in *(Nonformal) Antonyms:* delay, hamper, hinder, impede **2.** accomplish, achieve, discharge, complete, effect, fulfill, perfect, realize, satisfy **3.** add to, augment, beef up *(Nonformal)*, furnish, increase, reinforce, subsidize, supplement *Antonyms:* diminish, remove, subtract from

implicate *v.* **1.** accuse, associate, blame, charge, cite, connect, embroil, ensnare, entangle, incriminate, inculpate, involve, link, mire, name *Nonformal:* finger, pin *Antonyms:* acquit, dissociate, eliminate, exclude, exculpate **2.** allude to, connote, hint, imply, impose, impute, indicate, insinuate, intimate, mean, signify, suggest **3.** connect, entangle, intertwine, join, tangle, twist

implication *n.* **1.** accusation, assumption, connotation, hint, hypothesis, incrimination, indication, inference, innuendo, intimation, suggestion, undertone **2.** association, connection, entanglement, involvement **3.** aftermath, conclusion, consequence, effect, meaning, outcome, ramification, result, significance

implicit *adj.* **1.** contained, implied, inferred, inherent, latent, tacit, understood, unspoken *Antonyms:* declared, explicit, expressed, obvious, patent **2.** absolute, categorical, certain, complete, definite, entire, total, unqualified, unquestionable, unshakable, virtual, wholehearted *Commonly misused:* **explicit**

implied *adj.* alluded to, assumed, connoted, figured, foreshadowed, hidden, hinted, implicit, indicated, indirect, inferential, inferred, inherent, insinuated, intended, latent, meant, signified, suggested, symbolized, tacit, undeclared, underlying, understood, unexpressed, unsaid, unspoken

implode *v.* burst inward, cave in, collapse, disintegrate, fall in, shatter *Commonly misused:* **explode**

implore *v.* appeal, beg, beseech, entreat, importune, petition, plead, pray, request, solicit, supplicate, urge *Antonyms:* demand, force, order

imply *v.* **1.** allude to, hint, insinuate, intimate, suggest **2.** betoken, connote, denote, designate, evidence, implicate, import, indicate, intend, mean, refer, signify, suggest **3.** entail, include, involve, point to, presuppose, suppose *Commonly misused:* **infer**

impolite *adj.* abrupt, bad-mannered, boorish, churlish, coarse, crass, discourteous, gauche, ill-behaved, indelicate, insolent, loutish, rough, rude, tactless, uncivil, uncouth, ungracious, unrefined *Antonyms:* civil, courteous, mannerly

impolitic *adj.* brash, careless, hasty, ill-advised, ill-judged, imprudent, inadvisable, inconsiderate, indiscreet, inexpedient, injudicious, maladroit, misguided, rash, short-sighted, stupid, undiplomatic, untimely, unwise *Antonyms:* diplomatic, expedient, judicious

import *n.* **1.** bearing, connotation, design, gist, heart, implication, intention, meaning, message, nub, objective, point, purport **2.** emphasis, importance, magnitude, significance, stress, thrust, value, weight, worth **3.** commodity, foreign goods, importation, merchandise, trade **4.** athlete, gamer *(Nonformal)*, player, ringer – *v.* bring *or* fly in, carry, introduce, move, ship, train, transfer, transport

importance *n.* **1.** accent, concern, consequence, emphasis, force, gravity, import interest, momentousness, point, precedence, priority, seriousness, significance stress, substance, urgency, usefulness value, weightiness **2.** authority, distinction eminence, esteem, fame, greatness, mark, notability, note, power, prestige, prominence, rank, reputation, salience, standing, stature, status, worth **3.** affectation, conceit, braggadocio, ego, fanfaronade, ostentation, pomposity, pretentiousness, self-importance, vanity

mportant *adj.* **1.** authoritative, chief, exceptional, leading, outstanding, remarkable, superior, topnotch *Nonformal:* front page, heavy, major league **2.** distinguished, eminent, esteemed, high-level, high-powered, illustrious, memorable, noteworthy, preeminent, prestigious, prominent *Antonyms:* inconsequential, insignificant, trifling **3.** considerable, determining, far-reaching, influential, marked, meaningful, momentous, portentous, relevant, salient, seminal, significant, weighty *Antonyms:* immaterial, nugatory, trivial **4.** critical, crucial, necessary, pressing, primary, signal, urgent, vital **5.** conceited, boastful, egotistical, haughty, inflated, pompous, rodomontade, vainglorious

mported *adj.* **1.** choice, exotic, flown-in, rare, shipped-in, transported **2.** added, alien, extraneous, foreign, introduced

mportunate *adj.* **1.** burning, clamorous, crying, demanding, earnest, insistent, pressing, solicitous, urgent *Antonyms:* relaxed, undemanding **2.** constant, determined, dogged, persevering, persistent, stubborn, unrelenting **3.** annoying, harassing, insistent, pestering, troublesome, vexatious, vexing

mportune *v.* **1.** ask, beg, beset, besiege, blandish, cajole, call upon, coax, demand, entreat, goad, insist, inveigle, motivate, nudge, pray, pressure, request, solicit, spur, supplicate, urge **2.** annoy, badger, bug *(Nonformal)*, harass, hound, nag, pester, plague, vex

mpose *v.* **1.** appoint, charge, command, compel, decree, demand, dictate, enforce, enjoin, establish, exact, fix, levy, oblige, order, prescribe, require, set **2.** annoy, bother, burden, encroach, encumber, foist, horn in *(Nonformal)*, inconvenience, inflict, infringe, intrude, obtrude, pester, presume, saddle, trouble **3.** cheat, deceive, double-cross, dupe, exploit, hoax, hoodwink, misuse, trick *Nonformal:* hornswoggle, palm off

imposing *adj.* august, awe-inspiring, big, commanding, dignified, grandiose, imperial, impressive, magnificent, majestic, massive, monumental, overwhelming, regal, stately, stirring, striking, towering *Antonyms:* insignificant, mean, modest, ordinary, poor

imposition *n.* **1.** charge, demand, duty, exaction, levy, order, request, tax, tithe, weight **2.** bother, drag *(Nonformal)*, burden, encroachment, infliction, infringement, intrusion, invasion, obtrusion, vexation **3.** artifice, cheat, craftiness, deception, feint, fraud, illusion, stratagem, trickery *Nonformal:* con, hocus-pocus

impossible *adj.* **1.** futile, hopeless, impassable, inaccessible, inexecutable, insurmountable, irreparable, unattainable, unfeasible, unworkable, useless, vain *Nonformal:* dead, no-go, no-way, no-win *Antonyms:* likely, plausible, probable **2.** absurd, crazy, inconceivable, incongruous, intolerable, ludicrous, objectionable, offensive, outrageous, preposterous, ridiculous, too much, unacceptable, undesirable, ungovernable, unreasonable, wacky *(Nonformal) Antonyms:* conceivable, logical, reasonable, valid **3.** annoying, difficult, exasperating, infuriating, irritating, tiring, upsetting

impostor *n.* actor, beguiler, bluffer, charlatan, cheat, deceiver, empiric, fake, fraud, hypocrite, imitator, impersonator, masquerader, mimic, mountebank, pretender, quack, sham, trickster *Nonformal:* con artist, four-flusher, grifter, phoney, scammer *Antonyms:* genuine article, real thing

imposture *n.* artifice, cheat, counterfeit, deception, fabrication, feint, forgery, fraud, hoax, illusion, imitation, impersonation, masquerade, ploy, pretense, quackery, ruse, scam *(Nonformal)*, sham, spoof, stratagem, swindle, trick, wile

impotence *n.* **1.** disability, feebleness, helplessness, impuissance, paralysis, powerlessness, weakness *Antonyms:* strength, virility **2.** inability, inadequacy, incompetence, ineffectiveness, inefficiency, ineptness *Antonyms:* accomplishment, force, productivity **3.** barrenness, childlessness, infertility, sterility

impotent *adj.* **1.** crippled, disabled, enfeebled, feeble, frail, incapacitated, infirm, paralyzed, powerless, prostrate, weak *Antonyms:* powerful, strong, vital **2.** bumbling, bungling, incompetent, ineffective, ineffectual, inept, unproductive *Antonyms:* able, capable, competent **3.** barren, infecund, infertile, shooting blanks *(Nonformal)*

impound *v.* **1.** cage, confine, enclose, incarcerate, immure, imprison, jail, pen, sequester *Antonyms:* free, manumit, release **2.** appropriate, claim, commandeer, confiscate, seize

impoverish *v.* **1.** bankrupt, beggar, break, ruin **2.** consume, deplete, despoil, diminish, drain, exhaust, reduce, strip, use up, wipe out *(Nonformal) Antonyms:* develop, enrich, enhance

impoverished *adj.* **1.** bankrupt, beggared, broke, destitute, disadvantaged, flat, impecunious, indigent, insolvent, needy, penniless, penurious, poor, poverty-stricken, ruined, scrimshanked *(P.E.I.)*, skint *(British)*, underprivileged *Nonformal:* dirt poor, down-and-out, have-not, on the rim, stone-broke, tapped out *Antonyms:* affluent, rich, wealthy, well-off **2.** barren, depleted, done *(Nonformal)*, drained, empty, exhausted, infecund, infertile, reduced, spent *Antonyms:* fertile, fruitful, lush

impracticable *adj.* **1.** difficult, impossible, unachievable, unattainable, unfeasible, unworkable, useless **2.** doctrinaire, impractical, inapplicable, inoperative, ivory tower, theoretical, unserviceable *Nonformal:* airy-fairy, blue sky *Antonyms:* applied, working

impractical *adj.* **1.** abstract, chimerical, idealistic, illogical, quixotic, romantic, speculative, theoretical, unrealistic, useless, visionary *Nonformal:* starry-eyed, wild *Antonyms:* down-to-earth, logical, grounded, sensible, viable **2.** impossible, improbable, inapplicable, inoperable, nonfunctional, unusable, unworkable *Antonyms:* serviceable, utilitarian, usable **3.** non-starter, not feasible *or* viable, unattainable, unsound, unwise *Antonyms:* probable, realistic, wise

imprecise *adj.* ambiguous, approximate, blurred, estimated, equivocal, extrapolated, guessed, hazy, ill-defined, indefinite, inexact, loose, off, rough, rounded, vague, woolly *Nonformal:* ballpark, fuzzy, guesstimate *Antonyms:* accurate, definite, exact

impregnable *adj.* **1.** defended, fortified, indestructible, invincible, invulnerable, secure, strong, unassailable, unconquerable *Antonyms:* exposed, insecure, open, vulnerable **2.** immovable, resistant, shatterproof, stubborn, unshakable, unyielding *Antonyms:* flexible, pliant, weak

impregnate *v.* **1.** fertilize, implant, inseminate, knock up *(Nonformal)*, produce, reproduce **2.** charge, drench, leaven, overflow, permeate, pervade, saturate, steep, suffuse **3.** brainwash, condition, fill, imbue, impress, inculcate, indoctrinate, infix, infuse, inoculate, instill, program

impress *n.* **1.** character, impression, imprint, indentation, mark, print, seal, stamp **2.** characteristic, distinction, earmark, hallmark, sign – *v.* **1.** affect, arouse, awe, electrify, enforce, establish, excite, faze, fill, fix, galvanize, influence, inspire, motivate, move, provoke, stimulate, stir, strike, sway, thrill, touch *Nonformal:* blow away, grab **2.** imbue, inculcate, inoculate, instill, register **3.** dent, emboss, engrave, etch, form, imprint, indent, inscribe, mark, press, print, stamp

impression *n.* **1.** consequence, effect, fallout, impact, reaction, response, result **2.** belief, conviction, feeling, hunch, hypothesis, inkling, intuition, notion, opinion, remembrance, theory, thought **3.** dent, depression, dint, fingerprint, footprint, hollow, hoofmark, imprint, indentation, mark, pawprint, sign, spoor, stamp, trace, track, vestige **4.** brand, cast, design, form, matrix, mould, outline, pattern **5.** burlesque, caricature, imitation, impersonation, parody, pastiche, pretense, takeoff, travesty

impressionable *adj.* affected, amenable, biddable, feeling, gullible, influenceable, ingenuous, open, perceptive, persuadable, plastic, receptive, responsive, sensible, sensitive, suggestible, susceptible, swayable, vulnerable *Antonyms:* hardened, insensitive, jaded, unresponsive

impressive *adj.* affecting, arresting, awe-inspiring, dramatic, effective, exciting, extraordinary, forcible, grand, imposing, influential, inspiring, intense, majestic, massive, monumental, moving, noble, remarkable, rousing, splendid, stirring, striking, superb, thrilling, touching, towering, vital *Nonformal:* far out, mind-blowing, snazzy, swell *Antonyms:* ordinary, uninspiring, weak

imprint *n.* **1.** characteristic, dent, design, emblem, footprint, hoofmark, impression, indentation, mark, seal, sign, signature, stamp, trace, trademark **2.** banner, heading, imprimatur, masthead, name – *v.* **1.** dent, engrave, etch, mark, stamp **2.** establish, fix, impress, inculcate, ingrain, inject, inscribe, instill

imprison *v.* **1.** cage, confine, constrain, coop, detain, fence in, immure, incarcerate, intern, jail, lock up, pen, restrain, restrict, *Nonformal:* send down *or* up, send upriver *Antonyms:* free, release

improbability *n.* implausibility, impossibility, uncertainty, unlikelihood *Nonformal:* fat *or* small chance, long shot *Antonyms:* certainty, likelihood

improbable *adj.* doubtful, dubious, fanciful, far-fetched, flimsy, implausible, inconceivable, off the wall *(Nonformal)*, questionable, remote, slim, unbelievable, unexpected, unlikely, unreasonable, weak *Nonformal:* hundred-to-one, iffy *Antonyms:* convincing, plausible, probable

improbity *n.* chicanery, corruptness, crookedness, deceit, depravity, dishonesty, falseness, shadiness *(Nonformal)*, unscrupulousness, wickedness, villainy, wrongdoing

impromptu *adj.* ad lib, dashed off, extempore, improvised, offhand, spontaneous, unpremeditated, unprepared, unrehearsed, unscripted, unstudied *Nonformal:* jam, pickup, spur-of-the-moment, tossed out – *adv. à l'improviste (French)*, from the hip, off the cuff *(Nonformal)*, offhand, on sight, unthinkingly – *n. Musical:* appoggiatura, cadenza, grace note, improvisation, interpolation, melisma, ornament, riff, run, vamp

improper *adj.* **1.** ill-adapted, ill-advised, ill-timed, impolitic, inadvisable, inappropriate, inapt, indecent, indecorous, indelicate, inexpedient, infelicitous, inopportune, maladroit, malapropos, not done, out of place, tactless, tasteless, unbecoming, unbefitting, uncouth, undignified, unfit, unseemly, unsuitable, unwarranted, vulgar, wrong *Nonformal:* at odds, bad form *Antonyms:* courtly, deferential, fitting, gracious, judicious, politic **2.** amiss, erroneous, false, faulty, inaccurate, incorrect, mistaken, off-base *(Nonformal)*, wrong *Antonyms:* accurate, right, true **3.** discordant, discrepant, incongruous, inharmonious, irregular, odd, unconventional, unusual

impropriety *n.* **1.** bad taste, barbarism, coarseness, immodesty, impudence, indecency, indelicacy, rudeness, tastelessness, tackiness *(Nonformal)*, unseemliness, vulgarity *Antonyms:* decorum, delicacy, suitability **2.** blooper, blunder, embarrassment, *faux pas (French)*, gaffe, goof, gross effort, malapropism, misdeed, misstep, misdemeanour, mistake, slip, solecism

improve *v.* **1.** ameliorate, amend, better, correct, edit, perfect, polish, rectify, refine, reform, revamp, revise, school, sharpen, tutor *Antonyms:* damage, harm, impair **2.** augment, boost, elevate, enhance, heighten, increase, lift, progress, promote, raise, soup up *(Nonformal)*, update, upgrade *Antonyms:* degrade, mar, spoil **3.** bounce back *(Nonformal)*, convalesce, gain, heal, mend, rally, recover, recuperate, strengthen

improvement *n.* **1.** addition, advancement, augmentation, cultivation, elevation, enhancement, enrichment, furtherance, gain, growth, increase, progress, promotion, retrofit, rise **2.** amelioration, amendment, change, correction, development, rectification, renovation, revision, upgrade **3.** convalescence, healing, rallying, recovery, recuperation, upturn

improvident *adj.* **1.** careless, heedless, incautious, negligent, reckless, short-sighted, thoughtless *Antonyms:* careful, cautious, wary **2.** extravagant, imprudent, lavish, prodigal, spendthrift, squandering, wasteful *Antonyms:* economical, temperate, thrifty

improvisation *n.* ad lib, cadenza, embellishment, extemporization, impulse, instant creation, jam

improvise *v.* **1.** ad lib, dash off, extemporize, fake, make do *Nonformal:* fill in, knock *or* toss off, play it by ear, wing it **2.** brainstorm, concoct, contrive, cook *or* dream *or* trump *or* whip up *(Nonformal)* create, devise, hatch, invent, jury-rig, knock off, throw off

improvised *adj.* **1.** ad lib, extemporaneous, impromptu, last minute, made-up, off the cuff *(Nonformal)*, spur-of-the-moment *Antonyms:* planned, rehearsed, studied **2.** cobbled together, jerimandered, jerry-built, jury-rigged, makeshift, quick fix, slapdash, temporary

imprudent *adj.* brash, careless, foolhardy, foolish, hasty, heedless, ill-considered, ill-judged, impetuous, impolitic, inadvisable, incautious, inconsiderate, indiscreet, inexpedient, irresponsible, rash, reckless, thoughtless, unthinking, unwise *Antonyms:* careful, considerate, discreet, responsible, wise

impudence *n.* audacity, backtalk, boldness, brazenness, defiance, disrespect, effrontery, impertinence, incivility, insolence, nerve, presumption, rudeness, sauciness, shamelessness *Nonformal:* lip, sass *Antonyms:* modesty, politeness, respect

impudent *adj.* audacious, bold, brazen, cheeky, cocky, disrespectful, feisty, forward, fresh, immodest, impertinent, insolent, presumptuous, rude, saucy *Nonformal:* in one's face, out-of-line *Antonyms:* deferential, polite, respectful

impugn *v.* assail, attack, cast aspersions upon, challenge, contradict, contravene, criticize, cross, deny, dispute, gainsay, inveigh against, knock, negate, oppose, question, rap, resist, tar, traduce *Nonfo mal:* bad mouth, dis, flay, run down, slar trash *Commonly misused:* **impute**

impulse *n.* **1.** bent, caprice, desire, driv fancy, feeling, flash, inclination, instinc libido, mind, notion, passion, reactio reflex, response, thought, urge, whim, wis **2.** beat, catalyst, drive, force, impetu impulsion, momentum, pressure, propu sion, push, rush, stimulus, stroke, surg thrust, vibration

impulsive *adj.* **1.** capricious, careles changeable, devil-may-care *(Nonformal* fickle, flighty, hasty, headlong, heedles impetuous, imprudent, inconsiderat instinctive, intuitive, involuntary, kne jerk, mercurial, quick, rash, reactionar reckless, reflex, spontaneous, sudde thoughtless, unconscious, unpremeditate unprompted, whimsical *Antonyms:* car ful, cautious, conscious, deliberat planned **2.** driving, dynamic, forcefu impelling, influential, moving, powerfu propelling, thrusting

impunity *n.* absolution, amnesty, dispens tion, exemption, indemnity, pardo reprieve, security *Commonly misuse* **immunity**

impure *adj.* **1.** carnal, coarse, corrup debased, degenerate, erotic, evil, immodes immoral, indecent, kinky *(Nonformal)*, la civious, lewd, libidinous, licentious, lov obscene, perverted, sexual, smutty, sinfu unchaste, wanton, wicked *Antonyms* moral, platonic, righteous, saintly, virgin **2.** base, contaminated, defiled, desecrate dirty, filthy, foul, gross, grubby, infecte polluted, squalid, sullied, tainted, unrefine unwholesome, vile, vitiated *Antonym* clean, immaculate, spotless, undefilec unpasteurized, unsullied **3.** admixed, adu terated, alloyed, altered, diluted, doctore *(Nonformal)*, mixed, watered-down **4.** di allowed, forbidden, unclean, unhallowec untouchable *Antonyms:* blessed, holy

impurity *n.* **1.** contaminant, corruptior defilement, dirt, filth, foreign matter, pollu tant *Antonyms:* cleanliness, purity, whole someness **2.** bawdiness, carnality, coarse ness, crudeness, degeneration, degrada tion, depravity, evilness, kink, lasciviousness, lewdness, libertinism, licentiousness, looseness, obscenity, perversion, profligacy, salacity, sinfulness, vitiation, vulgarity *Antonyms:* chastity, gentility, innocence, virginity

impute *v.* **1.** accredit, adduce, ascribe, assign, attribute, credit **2.** accuse, allege, blame, brand, censure, charge, cite, imply, indict, pin on *(Nonformal)*, stigmatize *Commonly misused:* **impugn**

in *adj.* **1.** inbound, inner, internal, inward **2.** esoteric, exclusive, limited, private, reserved, restricted, secret **3.** chic, faddish, fashionable, liked, modish, popular, stylish, trendy, ultra-modern, voguish *Nonformal:* cool, funky, groovy, hip, now – *adv.* inside, inside of, internally, inward, inwardly, therein, thereinto, within – *n.* clout, connection, influence, pull, sway – *prep.* **1.** according to, affected by, attired, engaged at, into, occupied by, sporting, wearing, within **2.** amid, among, in the midst of, on the inside of, surrounded by **3.** during, in the time of, throughout, while

inability *n.* **1.** failure, inadequacy, inaptitude, incapability, incompetence, ineffectiveness, inefficiency, ineptitude, lack, shortcoming, unfitness *Antonyms:* capability, competence, talent **2.** frailty, helplessness, impotence, ineffectualness, infirmity, powerlessness, weakness *Antonyms:* power, strength, virility

inaccessible *adj.* **1.** away, beyond *or* out of reach, distant, elusive, far, faraway, godforsaken, remote, unapproachable, unreachable **2.** impassable, impervious, insurmountable, unattainable, unavailable, unobtainable, unrealizable, well protected

inaccuracy *n.* **1.** blunder, botch, defect, distortion, erroneousness, error, fault, imprecision, inexactitude, miscalculation, misjudgment, misrepresentation, mistake, misunderstanding, oversight, slip, solecism, typo *(Nonformal) Antonyms:* accuracy, correctness **2.** fallacy, falsity, non sequitur, Sophism, wrong

inaccurate *adj.* careless, defective, erroneous, fallacious, false, faulty, imperfect, incorrect, inexact, mistaken, off, specious, unsound, untrue, vague, wrong *Nonformal:* off-base, wide *Antonyms:* accurate, correct, exact, precise, reliable

inaction *n.* dormancy, entropy, idleness, immobility, inactivity, inertia, motionlessness, rest, stagnation, stasis, torpor, vegetation *Antonyms:* activity, vitality, vivacity

inactive *adj.* **1.** abeyant, dormant, down, idle, inoperative, latent, moth-balled *(Nonformal) Antonyms:* chugging along, operative, running **2.** enervated, indolent, lazy, lethargic, limp, slack, sleepy, slothful, somnolent, tired, torpid *Antonyms:* energetic, vigorous, wired **3.** disengaged, jobless, on the street, resting, unemployed, unoccupied *Antonyms:* busy, *geschäftig (German)*, working **4.** immobile, inert, motionless, sedentary, stable, static, still *Antonyms:* fluid, in play, peripatetic **5.** calm, hushed, pacific, passive, peaceful, placid, quiescent, quiet, serene, tranquil *Antonyms:* cacaphonous, crazy, hectic, loud

inadequacy *n.* **1.** blemish, defect, drawback, failing, fault, flaw, foible, imperfection, shortcoming, weakness *Antonyms:* completeness, perfection, wholeness **2.** dearth, deficiency, deficit, incompleteness, insufficiency, lack, paucity, poverty, scantiness, shortage, shortfall, skimpiness *Antonyms:* lavishness, liberality, plethora **3.** inability, incompetence, ineffectualness, ineptitude, lack of capacity, unfitness, unsuitableness *Antonyms:* ability, deftness, knack, skill **4.** inferiority, mediocrity, nonstarter, unacceptableness

inadequate *adj.* **1.** base, damaged, defective, faulty, flawed, imperfect, incomplete, junky, low-grade, mediocre, second-rate, unacceptable, weak *Nonformal:* bush league, lousy, not up to par *or* scratch, shabby *Antonyms:* complete, great, perfect, satisfactory, top notch **2.** bare, deficient, depleted, inconsiderable, insubstantial, lacking, low, meagre, mean, poor, scanty, short, shy, skimpy, small, sparse, thin *Antonyms:* ample, substantial, sufficient **3.** incapable, incompetent, ineffective, inept, lame, maladroit, over-matched, second-rate, unable, unfit, unproductive, unqualified, unskilful, unskilled

inadmissible *adj.* banned, disallowed, exceptionable, heresay, immaterial, improper, inappropriate, irrelevant, not allowed, objectionable, prohibited, unacceptable, unallowable, unfit, unsuitable

inadvertent *adj.* accidental, automatic, involuntary, careless, heedless, knee-jerk, negligent, off the cuff *(Nonformal)*, spontaneous, thoughtless, unintentional, unplanned, unpremeditated, unthinking, unwitting *Antonyms:* cautious, conscious, prudent, thoughtful, voluntary

inadvisable *adj.* foolish, harebrained, ill-advised, impolitic, imprudent, inappropriate, indiscreet, injudicious, pointless, rash, undesirable, unsuitable, unwise

inalienable *adj.* absolute, basic, essential, fundamental, inherent, intrinsic, inviolable, nonnegotiable, nontransferable, sacrosanct, unassailable, unquestionable, untransferable

inane *adj.* **1.** asinine, daft, dull, empty-headed, fatuous, foolish, futile, harebrained, ludicrous, mindless, pointless, puerile, ridiculous, senseless, silly, stupid, unintelligent, vacant, vain, vapid, witless, worthless *Nonformal:* ditzy, thick, wacky *Antonyms:* clever, essential, sensible, significant, smart, worthwhile **2.** bankrupt, blank, empty, hollow, illogical, meaningless, vacuous, void *Antonyms:* meaningful, profound, weighty

inanimate *adj.* **1.** cold, dead, defunct, extinct, lifeless, inorganic, insentient *Antonyms:* alive, breathing, living **2.** apathetic, idle, inactive, inert, inoperative, motionless, spiritless, still, torpid **3.** catatonic, comatose, unconscious *Antonyms:* active, lively, peppy

inanity *n.* **1.** absurdity, asininity, dullness, empty-headedness, fatuity, foolishness, frivolity, futility, ineffectiveness, insipidness, jejunity, meaninglessness, pointlessness, silliness, stupidity, uselessness, worthlessness **2.** emptiness, hollowness, nothingness, triviality, vacancy, vacuity, vacuum, void

inappeasable *adj.* **1.** adamant, firm, hard-hearted, heartless, implacable, pitiless, relentless, rigid, steely, unrelenting, unfo giving, without pity **2.** avaricious, greed hungry, insatiable, rapacious, unquench able, voracious

inapplicable *adj.* **1.** extraneous, foreig immaterial, impertinent, inapposite, irrele vant, off-base *(Nonformal)*, superfluou *Antonyms:* necessary, pertinent, relevant **2** at odds *(Nonformal)*, inappropriate, inap incompatible, incongruous, inconsisten mismatched, unfit, unsuitable *Antonyms* exact, on the mark, point-device

inappropriate *adj.* **1.** bad form, badl timed, foolish, ill-adapted, ill-suited, impo lite, importune, improper, imprudent inauspicious, incongruous, incorrect, indis creet, inept, irrelevant, malapropos, no applicable, not right, off-base, off-colou *(Nonformal)*, out of line, politically inco rect, rude, tasteless, unbecoming, undeco rous, unfitting, unseasonable, unseeml unsuitable, untimely, vulgar *Antonyms* courteous, efficient, felicitous, fitting, ge teel, germane, tasteful, urbane

inapt *adj.* awkward, bumbling, bungling clumsy, gauche, graceless, hopeless ill-adapted, incompetent, inept, inexperi enced, inexpert, ill-fitted, improper, inappro priate, incongruous, infelicitous, lumbering maladroit, slow, stupid, unable, unfit ungainly, unhandy, unskilled, unsuited untimely *Nonformal:* all thumbs, Clouseau esque, clunky *Antonyms:* able, dextrous skilful *Commonly misused:* **inept**

inarticulate *adj.* **1.** dumb, mute, silent speechless, unspoken, unuttered, un voiced, voiceless, wordless **2.** awkward faltering, halting, hesitant, inaudible, inco herent, incomprehensible, indistinct, mean dering, muffled, mumbled, mumbling obscure, stammering, tongue-tied, unclear unintelligible, unpolished, vague

inattentive *adj.* absent-minded, careless distracted, dreaming, faraway, negligent oblivious, preoccupied, removed, scatter brained, thoughtless, unheeding, unmind ful, unobservant, unthinking *Nonformal* mooning, out-to-lunch, spaced-out *Antonyms:* aware, considerate, observant, vigi lant

ıaudible *adj.* faint, hushed, imperceptible, indistinct, low, muffled, mumbled, muted, noiseless, quiet, silent, soundless, still *Antonyms:* clamorous, clear, loud, noisy

ıaugurate *v.* **1.** begin, coin, commence, effectuate, establish, found, initiate, introduce, institute, invent, originate, set up, usher in **2.** anoint, appoint, assign, elect, induct, install, instate, invest, name, ordain, place **3.** celebrate, dedicate, kick off *(Nonformal)*, launch, open

ıauspicious *adj.* bad, baneful, dire, discouraging, doomed, fateful, foreboding, ill-omened, menacing, ominous, portentous, sinister, star-crossed, threatening, unfavourable, unfortunate, unlucky, unpromising, unpropitious *Antonyms:* felicitous, providential, rosy

ıbred *adj.* congenital, constitutional, deep-seated, hereditary, inborn, indigenous, indwelling, inherent, inherited, innate, native, natural *Antonyms:* acquired, cultivated, fostered

ıcalculable *adj.* **1.** beyond belief, boundless, countless, enormous, immense, incomprehensible, inestimable, infinite, innumerable, limitless, measureless, numberless, uncountable, unfathomable, untold, vast **2.** changeable, dicey, equivocal, erratic, random, too numerous to count, uncertain, unforeseen, unpredictable, variable *Antonyms:* fixed, reliable, verifiable

ıcandescent *adj.* **1.** ablaze, aglow, burning, fiery, flaming, flaring, glowing, intense, vivid **2.** bright, burnished, coruscating, dazzling, fulgent, gleaming, glittering, glossy, illuminating, irradiant, lambent, lucent, phosphorescent, radiant, resplendent, scintillating, shining, sparkling, sunny **3.** adroit, alert, aware, brainy *(Nonformal)*, bright, brilliant, cerebral, deft, gifted, intelligent, keen, nimble-witted, perceptive, quick-witted, sharp, smart

ıcantation *n.* abracadabra, bewitchment, black magic, cantrip, chant, charm, conjuration, conjuring, curse, enchantment, formula, hex, hocus-pocus, hoodoo, hymn, invocation, jinker *(Newfoundland)*, jinx, magic, mumbo-jumbo, necromancy, open sesame *(Nonformal)*, rune, sorcery, spell, voodoo, witchcraft, wizardry

incapable *adj.* **1.** all thumbs, bumbling, bungling, clumsy, inadequate, incompetent, ineffective, inept, inexperienced, inexpert, insufficient, out of one's league, unable, unequipped, unskilled, unsuited *Antonyms:* adroit, capable, expert **2.** feeble, helpless, impotent, insane, not of sound mind, *non compose mentis (Latin)*, out of one's head *(Nonformal)*, powerless, unfit, weak *Antonyms:* competent, empowered, hale, ready **3.** banned, barred, disenfranchised, disentitled, disqualified, ineligible, unqualified **4.** drunk, had too much, impaired, over the legal limit *Nonformal:* loaded, pickled, pissed, sloshed, soused

incapacitate *v.* **1.** cripple, damage, disable, disarm, hinder, hobbled, hurt, immobilize, lame, maim, paralyze, prostrate, undermine, weaken *Nonformal:* clip, goon, hamstring, hog-tie *Antonyms:* aid, facilitate, help **2.** bar, disentitle, disqualify, invalidate, prevent

incarcerate *adj.* captive, imprisoned, interned, jailed – *v.* cage, commit, confine, constrain, coop up, detain, hold, impound, imprison, intern, jail, keep captive, lock in *or* up, remand, restrain, restrict, take prisoner *Nonformal:* book, nab, put away, send down *or* up the river *Antonyms:* free, let go, release

incarnate *adj.* **1.** as big as life, corporeal, for real, in the flesh, living **2.** characterized, embodied, exemplified, incapsulated, manifested, personified, represented, typified – *v.* concretize, corporealize, embody, manifest, materialize, personify, reflect, reify, represent, typify

incautious *adj.* brazen, careless, devil-may-care, hasty, headlong, headstrong, heedless, ill-advised, improvident, imprudent, impulsive, indiscreet, negligent, rash, reckless, thoughtless, unthinking, unwary *Antonyms:* prudent, thoughtful, wary

incendiary *adj.* **1.** combustible, explosive, flammable, ignitable, volatile **2.** controversial, damaging, dangerous, inflammatory, provocative, rabble-rousing, seditious, subversive, treacherous, troublesome – *n.* **1.** arsonist, fire-bomber, fire-starter, pyromaniac *Nonformal:* firebug, pyro, torch **2.** agitator, demagogue, inciter, insurgent, rabble-rouser, rebel, revolutionary

incense *n.* aroma, balm, bouquet, essence, fragrance, odour, perfume, redolence, scent, spice – *v.* anger, displease, embitter, enrage, exasperate, fire up *(Nonformal)*, gall, inflame, pique, provoke, rankle, roil, ruffle, vex

incensed *adj.* angry, enraged, exasperated, fuming, furious, infuriated, irate, livid, maddened, miffed, outraged, white-hot, wrathful *Nonformal:* apoplectic, ballistic, cheesed-off, hopping mad, spitting bullets, steamed

incentive *adj.* attractive, convincing, incisive, inducing, inviting, luring, motivating, persuading, provocative, tempting – *n.* allurement, bait, determinant, drive, encouragement, enticement, impetus, incitement, inducement, influence, inspiration, instigation, lure, motivation, motive, perk, persuasion, provocation, rationale, reason, spur, stimulant, stimulus, temptation, urge *Nonformal:* carrot, come-on, plus *Antonyms:* deterrent, discouragement, negative

inception *n.* beginning, birth, commencement, dawn, fountain, genesis, inauguration, initiation, origin, outset, provenance, rise, root, source, start, wellspring *Antonyms:* completion, conclusion, end, finish, termination

incessant *adj. ad infinitum or nauseum (Latin)*, ceaseless, constant, continual, habitual, non-stop, never-ending, ongoing, perpetual, recurrent, relentless, repetitious, unbroken, unremitting *Antonyms:* intermittent, occasional, periodic, rare

inchoate *adj.* **1.** chaotic, confused, disconnected, disorderly, formless, incondite, incoherent, muddled, rambling *Nonformal:* catawampus, higgledy-piggledy **2.** beginning, commencing, developing, early, elementary, embryonic, germinal, incipient, primitive, rudimentary *Antonyms:* completed, developed, terminal

incident *adj.* **1.** appertaining, applicabl apropos, attending, germane, material, pe tinent, related, relevant **2.** accessory appurtenant, attendant, circumstantia contingent, dependent, provisional, sub sidiary, supplementary – *n.* **1.** action, chap ter, circumstance, episode, event, happen ing, milestone, occasion, occurrence *Non formal:* business, goings-on, thing **2.** affai calamity, commotion, confrontation, con tretemps, crisis, difficulty, disaster, distur bance, emergency, encounter, flare-up imbroglio, scene, trouble **3.** incidental minor detail, minutia, trifle

incidental *adj.* **1.** accidental, adventitious casual, chance, coincidental, fluky *(Nonfor mal)*, odd, random, unexpected, unforesee *Antonyms:* designed, planned, predicted **2** accessory, accompanying, adjunctive, ancil lary, attendant, circumstantial, conditiona contingent, related **3.** minor, nonessential secondary, subordinate, superfluous *Anto nyms:* essential, important, vital

incinerate *v.* annihilate, burn, char, cre mate, destroy, ignite, kindle, roast, scorch torch

incipient *adj.* appearing, beginning, com mencing, developing, elementary, embryon ic, forming, fundamental, growing, incep tive, inchoate, initial, introductory, nascent originating, ruing, starting

incision *n.* **1.** carving, chiselling, cleft crack, cut, engraving, fissure, furrow, gash gouge, groove, mark, nick, notch, scissure score, scratch, slit, split **2.** acumen, deci siveness, effectiveness, force, incisiveness intelligence, keenness, penetration, percep tion, power, smarts *(Nonformal)*, vigour

incisive *adj.* **1.** acute, bright, clever, insightful, intelligent, keen, penetrating, perspicacious, piercing, profound, sharp, trenchant, wise *Antonyms:* dense, dull, superficial, vague, woolly **2.** acerbic, acid, biting, caustic, crisp, cutting, mordant, sar castic, sardonic, satirical, scathing, severe slashing, tart, terse *Antonyms:* diplomatic soothing, suave

incite *v.* activate, agitate, animate, arouse, coax, drive, egg on *(Nonformal)*, encourage, excite, exhort, foment, further, goad, impel, induce, inflame, influence, inspire, instigate, motivate, persuade, promote, prompt, provoke, rouse, set off, stimulate, stir *or* whip up, sway, tempt, trigger, urge, whet *Antonyms:* dampen, deter, discourage

inclement *adj.* **1.** brutal, cold, dirty *(Nonformal)*, duckish *(Newfoundland)*, foul, hard, intemperate, nasty, raw, rough, rugged, stormy, tempestuous, violent, wintry *Antonyms:* balmy, halcyon, warm **2.** cruel, hard-hearted, harsh, merciless, pitiless, ruthless, severe, steely, unkind, unsympathetic *Antonyms:* clement, soft, yielding

inclination *n.* **1.** affection, appetite, attachment, attraction, bent, bias, desire, disposition, fancy, fondness, hankering, impulse, leaning, liking, mind, movement, partiality, penchant, pleasure, predilection, predisposition, preference, prejudice, proclivity, proneness, propensity, stomach, susceptibility, taste, tendency, trend, turn, whim, wish *Nonformal:* soft spot, thing *Antonyms:* antipathy, aversion, disinclination, dislike, revulsion **2.** acclivity, angle, bank, bend, cant, declivity, deviation, downgrade, grade, gradient, hill, incline, lean, list, pitch, ramp, slant, slope, tilt

incline *n.* acclivity, ascent, cant, descent, dip, grade, gradient, hill, inclination, leaning, plane, ramp, rise, slant, slope, tilt – *v.* **1.** aim, bend, bevel, cant, cock, deviate, diverge, heel, lay, list, recline, skew, slant, slope, tend, tilt, tip, train, turn, veer, yaw **2.** agree, acquiesce, go along *(Nonformal)*, join **3.** gravitate toward, lean, point, tend **4.** bias, bring round, convince, dispose, induce, influence, lure, persuade, predispose, prejudice, sway, touch, win over **5.** bow, curtsy, lower, nod, stoop

inclined *adj.* **1.** agreeable, apt, content, disposed, eager, enthusiastic, moved, partial, predisposed, prone, ready, willing **2.** bent, careening, falling, leaning, lilting, rising, slanted, sloping

include *v.* **1.** comprehend, comprise, consist of, constitute, contain, cover, embody, encircle, enclose, encompass, entail, hold, imply, suggest **2.** accommodate, add, admit, allow for, append, assimilate, build in, combine, count, enter, have, implicate, incorporate, insert, involve, subsume *Antonyms:* eliminate, exclude, leave out, omit

inclusive *adj.* across-the-board, all-around, all-encompassing, blanket, broad, compendious, catholic, comprehensive, encompassing, encyclopedic, full, general, global, overall, sweeping, unrestricted, whole *Antonyms:* confined, exclusive, limited, narrow, restricted

incognito *adj.* anonymous, bearded, camouflaged, clandestine, cloaked, concealed, disguised, hidden, hugger-mugger, masked, obscure, secretive, *sub rosa (Latin)*, unidentifiable, unknown, unrecognizable *Antonyms:* open, plain, recognizable – *adv.* confidentially, discreetly, mysteriously, privately, undercover – *n.* alias, concealment, cover, disguise, mask, nom de plume, pseudonym

incognizant *adj.* heedless, ignorant, innocent, unaware, unconscious, unconversant, unenlightened, uninformed, unknowledgeable, unmindful *Antonyms:* aware, conscious, knowing

incoherent *adj.* **1.** confused, disconnected, discontinuous, disjointed, disordered, illogical, jumbled, loose, muddled, puzzling, unconnected *Antonyms:* coherent, connected, intelligible, logical, rational **2.** babbling, inarticulate, incomprehensible, indistinct, indistinguishable, muffled, mumbling, muttering, rambling, stammering, unintelligible, wandering **3.** at odds, clashing, contradictory, contrary, discordant, incompatible, inconsistent, inharmonious, opposing

income *n.* assets, avails, benefits, cash, cash flow, commission, compensation, dividends, earnings, gains, gross, honorarium, interest, investments, livelihood, means, net, pay, payoff, proceeds, profit, receipts, returns, revenue, royalty, salary, wage *Nonformal:* bacon, cash cow, pickings, take

incommensurate *adj.* **1.** apples and oranges *(Nonformal)*, different, disproportionate, dissimilar, incongruous, inconsistent, inequitable, irreconcilable, unequal **2.** inadequate, incomplete, insubstantial, insufficient, meagre, paltry, wanting

incommodious *adj.* **1.** cramped, small, tight, tiny, uncomfortable *Antonyms:* large, roomy, spacious **2.** annoying, disturbing, encroaching, inconvenient, troubling

incomparable *adj.* **1.** excellent, exceptional, inimitable, matchless, paramount, peerless, perfect, preeminent, singular, sovereign, superior, supreme, surpassing, superlative, transcendent, ultimate, unequalled, unmatched, unparalleled, unrivaled, unsurpassable **2.** disproportionate, dissimilar, incommensurate, inconsistent, mismatched, unlike, unrelated

incompatibility *n.* **1.** antagonism, bad blood *(Nonformal)*, conflict, discord, dispute, dissension, enmity, hostility, uncongeniality *Antonyms:* harmony, rapport **2.** discrepancy, disparity, dissimilitude, dissonance, incongruity, inconsistency, irreconcilability, variance

incompatible *adj.* **1.** antagonistic, antipathetic, clashing, conflicting, contrary, counter, disagreeing, discordant, disparate, factious, irreconcilable, inimical, jarring, opposite, poles apart *(Nonformal)*, uncongenial, unfriendly, warring *Antonyms:* compatible, congenial **2.** inappropriate, incongruous, mismatched, unbecoming, unfitting, unsuited *Antonyms:* alike, appropriate, consistent, suitable

incompetence *n.* failure, futility, inability, inadequacy, ineffectualness, ineffectiveness, ineptitude, inferiority, insufficiency, unpreparedness, uselessness *Antonyms:* ability, competence, fitness

incompetent *adj.* amateur, amateurish, awkward, bumbling, bungling, clumsy, floundering, gauche, hopeless, inadequate, incapable, ineffectual, inefficient, inept, inexperienced, inexpert, insufficient, maladroit, unadapted, unequipped, unqualified, unskilful, unskilled, useless *Nonformal:* bush league, Clouseau-esque *Antonyms:* able, capable, expert, fit, proficient – *n.* bungler, clod, lout, lubber, oaf *Nonformal:* duffer, klutz, puzzler, struggler

incomplete *adj.* **1.** deficient, fractional, fragmentary, imperfect, insufficient, lacking, limited, part, partial, short, sketchy, wanting *Antonyms:* entire, total, whole **2.** callow, crude, defective, immature, inchoate, incondite, rough, rude, rudimentary, unaccomplished, unconsummated, under construction, undeveloped, unfinished *Antonyms:* consummate, developed, refined

incomprehensible *adj.* abstract, abstruse, arcane, baffling, cryptic, enigmatic, esoteric, impenetrable, inconceivable, intricate, mysterious, mystifying, obscure, perplexing, puzzling, recondite, unclear, unfathomable, unimaginable, unintelligible *Nonformal:* heavy, mind-boggling, tricky *Antonyms:* apparent, clear, conceivable, evident, intelligible *Commonly misused:* **incomprehensive**

incomprehensive *adj.* circumscribed, confined, exclusive, insular, limited, localized, narrow, restricted, specialized, specific *Antonyms:* all-encompassing, broad, global *Commonly misused:* **incomprehensible**

inconceivable *adj.* extraordinary, fantastic, implausible, impossible, improbable, incomprehensible, incredible, ludicrous, mind-boggling, preposterous, strange, unbelievable, unimaginable, unlikely, unthinkable *Nonformal:* tall, way out there *Antonyms:* believable, likely, possible, reasonable

inconclusive *adj.* ambiguous, circumstantial, deficient, evidence-shy, incomplete, indecisive, indeterminate, ineffective, lacking, moot, open, speculative, uncertain, unconvincing, undecided, undetermined, unfinished, unproven, unresolved, unsatisfactory, unsettled, unsubstantiated, weak *Nonformal:* the jury's still out, up in the air *Antonyms:* absolute, categorical, positive

incongruous *adj.* **1.** absurd, alien, bizarre, foreign, improper, inappropriate, out of place, unsuitable, unsuited *Antonyms:* becoming, expected, proper **2.** at odds, disparate, irregular, lopsided, mismatched, nonconforming, unbalanced, unequal, uneven, unrelated *Antonyms:* balanced, equal, parallel **3.** conflicting, contradictory, discordant, divergent, incompatible, inharmonious, world's apart *(Nonformal)* *Antonyms:* compatible, harmonious

inconsequential *adj.* **1.** cosmetic, exiguous, immaterial, inconsiderable, insignificant, light, marginal, measly, minor, negligible, superficial, trifling, trivial, unimportant, worthless *Nonformal:* dinky, nothing, small potatoes, small-time, two-bit **2.** contradictory, faulty, flawed, illogical, inconclusive, inconsistent, irrational, paradoxical, paralogical, unconnected – *n.* bagatelle, inconsequence, insignificance, nothing *(Nonformal)*, technicality, trifling, triviality

inconsiderable *adj.* catchpenny, expendable, immaterial, inconsequential, insignificant, microscopic, minute, negligible, paltry, picayune, piddling, slight, tiny, unimportant *Antonyms:* important, weighty, serious

inconsiderate *adj.* **1.** bad mannered, boorish, discourteous, impolite, indelicate, indiscreet, insensitive, intolerant, rude, self-centred, selfish, sharp, short, tactless, thoughtless, unceremonious, uncharitable, ungracious, unkind, unthinking *Antonyms:* attentive, considerate, gracious, kind **2.** brash, careless, hasty, headstrong, impolitic, impudent, impulsive, incautious, reckless

inconsistent *adj.* **1.** contradictory, illogical, incongruent, irregular, oxymoronic, paradoxical *Antonyms:* coherent, logical, rational **2.** capricious, changeable, erratic, fickle, inconstant, lubricious, mercurial, temperamental, unpredictable, unstable, unsteady, variable *Antonyms:* fixed, rooted, steadfast **3.** at odds, at variance, clashing, conflicting, contrary, discordant, discrepant, dissonant, incompatible, inharmonious, irreconcilable, warring *Antonyms:* compatible, cooperative, kindred

inconsolable *adj.* brokenhearted, comfortless, cut-up *(Nonformal)*, dejected, depressed, desolate, despairing, disconsolate, discouraged, distressed, heartbroken, heartsick, melancholy, neurasthenic, sad, stricken, woebegone *Antonyms:* carefree, joyous, jubilant

inconspicuous *adj.* camouflaged, concealed, dim, faint, hidden, indistinct, low-key, low-profile, modest, muted, ordinary, plain, quiet, retiring, shy, soft-pedaled, subtle, unassuming, unnoticeable, unobtrusive *Antonyms:* patent, plain, obvious, visible

inconstant *adj.* **1.** capricious, changeable, erratic, fickle, flighty, impulsive, inconsistent, indecisive, irregular, mercurial, moody, mutable, quicksilver, restless, turbulent, uncertain, unsettled, unstable, unsteady, volatile, wavering *Nonformal:* waffling, wishy-washy *Antonyms:* dependable, predictable, steady **2.** false, loose, unfaithful *Nonformal:* playing around, stepping out, two-timing

incontestable *adj.* absolute, certain, *de facto (Latin)*, evident, factual, immutable, incontrovertible, indisputable, irrefragable, obvious, patent, proven, real, unquestionable, unassailable, undeniable *Nonformal:* clear as day, surefire *Antonyms:* debatable, moot, theoretical

incontinent *adj.* **1.** abandoned, Babylonian, bacchanal, debauched, Dionysian, lascivious, lewd, libertine, libidinous, prodigal, profligate, promiscuous, wanton, wayward, wild **2.** excessive, immoderate, intemperate, loose, rampant, unbridled, unchecked, uncontrollable, unrestrained *Antonyms:* controlled, moderate, restrained **3.** bed-wetting, diuretic, enuritic, weak-bladdered

inconvenience *n.* annoyance, bother, botheration, burden, difficulty, discommodity, disruption, disturbance, drawback, fuss, headache *(Nonformal)*, hindrance, imposition, impediment, inopportunity, intrusion, nuisance, obstacle, pain, problem, trouble, untimeliness, vexation – *v.* annoy, beset, bother, burden, disrupt, disturb, harass, hassle *(Nonformal)*, hinder, incommode, intrude, irritate, perturb, pester, plague, trouble

inconvenient *adj.* annoying, awkward, bothersome, cumbersome, difficult, disadvantageous, disturbing, incommodious, inopportune, problematic, tiresome, troublesome, unseasonable, vexatious *Antonyms:* easy, helpful, refreshing

incorporate *adj.* **1.** associated, blended, combined, compound, conglomerate, consolidated, fused, integrated, joined, merged, mixed, united **2.** immaterial, incorporeal, otherworldly, spiritual, transcendent – *v.* **1.** amalgamate, blend, coalesce, combine, connect, consolidate, form, fuse, join, link, marry, meld, merge, mix, pool, unite, yoke **2.** admit, confederate, conglomerate, form, legitimize, share power **3.** absorb, add, assimilate, build into, inject, integrate, subsume, welcome, work in **4.** comprise, contain, encompass, include, take in **5.** characterize, corporealize, embody, personify, typify

incorporeal *adj.* **1.** astral, ethereal, ghostlike, otherworldly, phantasmal, spectral, spiritual, supernatural, transcendent *Antonyms:* earthly, fleshy, real **2.** bodiless, disembodied, immaterial, impalpable, incorporate, insubstantial, intangible, nonphysical, shadowy *Antonyms:* concrete, material, physical

incorrect *adj.* **1.** cockeyed *(Nonformal)*, distorted, erroneous, fallacious, false, faulty, flawed, illogical, imprecise, inaccurate, twisted, unsound, wrong *Antonyms:* legitimate, right, true **2.** amiss, improper, indecent, offensive, out-of-line *(Nonformal)*, rude, unacceptable, unbecoming, unfitting, unsuitable, vulgar

incorrigible *adj.* **1.** hardened, impenitent, irreclaimable, unreformable, unrepentant, unteachable, vile **2.** confirmed, deep-seated, dyed-in-the-wool *(Nonformal)*, habitual, incurable, indelible, ineradicable, inveterate, recidivist **3.** beyond remedy, hopeless, irrecoverable, kaput *(Nonformal)*, lost, ruined, uncorrectable, unremediable, unsalvageable – *n.* criminal, miscreant, villain *Nonformal:* diehard, lost cause, mule

incorruptible *adj.* **1.** above suspicion, honest, honourable, innocent, just, loyal, moral, reliable, straight, trustworthy, upright *Antonyms:* base, decrepit, evil **2.** immortal, imperishable, indestructible, inextinguishable, invincible, invulnerable, undefeatable *Antonyms:* mortal, transient

increase *n.* **1.** accumulation, addition, augmentation, boost, flood, gush, hike, increment, multiplication, raise, rise, surge, upsurge **2.** burgeoning, development, elaboration, enlargement, expansion, extension, growth, inflation, proliferation, protraction, spread, spreading *or* stretching out, swell, swelling, waxing **3.** amplification, elevation, escalation, exacerbation, exaggeration, heightening, intensification, magnification, maximization, worsening – *v.* **1.** amplify, broaden, deepen, enlarge, escalate, expand, grow, heighten, inflate, intensify, lengthen, magnify, progress, spread, snowball, thicken, widen *Antonyms:* diminish, downsize, shorten, shrink **2.** beget, breed, engender, generate, multiply, procreate, proliferate, reproduce, sprout, swarm, swell, teem **3.** advance, augment, boost, build up, develop, enhance, further, raise, reinforce, sharpen, strengthen *Antonyms:* curtail, cut off, destroy

incredible *adj.* **1.** amazing, astonishing, astounding, awe-inspiring, extraordinary, fabulous, great, marvellous, miraculous, prodigious, remarkable, sensational, stupendous, unreal, wonderful *Nonformal:* beautiful, far-out, humdinging *Antonyms:* common, garden-variety, usual **2.** absurd, dubious, far-fetched, flimsy, implausible, impossible, improbable, inconceivable, ludicrous, outlandish, preposterous, questionable, ridiculous, suspect, thin, unbelievable, unimaginable, untenable, unthinkable *Nonformal:* cockamamie, fishy, phoney *Antonyms:* believable, credible, probable *Commonly misused:* **incredulous**

incredulity *n.* caution, cynicism, disbelief, distrust, doubt, guardedness, jadedness, scepticism, suspicion, unbelief, wariness *Antonyms:* belief, innocence, naiveté, trust

incredulous *adj.* disbelieving, distrustful, doubtful, doubting, dubious, guarded, hesitant, mistrustful, questioning, quizzical, sceptical, sophisticated, suspect, suspicious, unbelieving, uncertain, unconvinced, undupable, unsatisfied, wary *Antonyms:* gullible, innocent, naive *Commonly misused:* **incredible**

increment *n.* accession, accretion, accrual, addition, advancement, augmentation, enlargement, escalation, gain, growth, increase, profit, raise, rise, step-up, supplement *Antonyms:* decrease, loss, reduction

incriminate *v.* **1.** allege, ascribe, blame, censure, implicate, inculpate, involve *Nonformal:* finger, frame, rat, snitch, whistleblow **2.** accuse, arraign, book *(Nonformal)*, charge, impeach, impute, indict *Antonyms:* acquit, free, release

incubus *n.* **1.** affliction, anxiety, burden, cross, millstone, oppression, sorrow, stress, weight **2.** cacodemon, demon, evil spirit, fiend, ghost, spectre, succubus, wraith **3.** dream, nightmare, night terror, phantasmagoria

inculcate *v.* beat *or* hammer into, brainwash, communicate, educate, impart, implant, impress, indoctrinate, instill, instruct, plant, program, proselytize, school, teach, train *Antonyms:* deprogram, estrange, wean

inculpable *adj.* aboveboard, blameless, guiltless, innocent, level, moral, pure, spotless, stainless, unimpeachable, upright, virtuous *Antonyms:* at fault, censurable, guilty, immoral

incumbent *adj.* **1.** binding, compulsory, mandatory, necessary, obligatory, required, requisite *Antonyms:* non-binding, unnecessary, voluntary **2.** conditional, contingent, dependent, leaning, resting – *n.* civil servant, functionary, lame duck *(Nonformal)*, mayor, member of legislative assembly *or* MLA, member of parliament *or* MP, member of provincial parliament *or* MPP, minister, office-holder, officer, official, president, prime minister, public official *or* servant

incur *v.* acquire, bring upon, catch, contract, draw, earn, gain, get, induce, invite, obtain, provoke, welcome

incurable *adj.* beyond hope, deadly, fatal, had it *(Nonformal)*, hopeless, impossible, inoperable, irreparable, mortal, serious, terminal, unchangeable, unrecoverable *Antonyms:* recoverable, reversible

incurious *adj.* apathetic, blasé, bored, careless, disinterested, dispassionate, heedless, inattentive, indifferent, nonchalant, unconcerned, uninterested, uninvolved *Antonyms:* interested, keen, passionate

indebted *adj.* **1.** accountable, bound, chargeable, duty-bound, honour-bound, hooked, in the red, liable, obligated, owe, owing, responsible *Antonyms:* clear, debt-free, unobliged **2.** appreciative, beholden, grateful, obliged, thankful

indecency *n.* **1.** bawdiness, foulness, grossness, impurity, lasciviousness, lewdness, licentiousness, obscenity, outrageousness, ribaldry, smuttiness, vileness *Antonyms:* chastity, purity, wholesomeness **2.** coarseness, immodesty, impropriety, inappropriateness, indecorum, indelicacy, indiscreetness, inelegance, uncouthness, vulgarity *Antonyms:* decorum, delicacy, modesty, propriety

indecent *adj.* **1.** coarse, crude, dirty, filthy, foul, foulmouthed, impure, lascivious, lewd, licentious, obscene, offensive, pornographic, raunchy, raw, rough, salacious, scatological, shameless, smutty, vile, X-rated *Nonformal:* adult, blue *Antonyms:* clean, pure, respectable **2.** gross, ill-bred, immodest, improper, indecorous, indelicate, tasteless, unseemly, vulgar *Antonyms:* decorous, seemly, tasteful

indecipherable *adj.* crabbed, cryptic, illegible, incoherent, indistinguishable, unclear, unintelligible, unreadable *Antonyms:* clear, legible, understandable

indecisive *adj.* **1.** changeable, doubtful, faltering, fickle, halting, hesitant, irresolute, on the fence, tentative, uncertain, unclear, unstable, vacillating, variable, wavering *Nonformal*: ditzy, flaky, pussyfooting, wishy-washy *Antonyms:* certain, decided, determined, resolute, unhesitating **2.** inconclusive, indeterminate, open, unascertained, uncorroborated, undecided, undetermined, unfinished, unproved, unsettled, up-in-the-air *(Nonformal)*, vague

indecorous *adj.* **1.** boorish, churlish, coarse, crass, crude, ill-bred, ill-mannered, improper, inappropriate, loutish, out-of-place, unbecoming, uncivil, unseemly **2.** discreditable, disgraceful, lewd, loose, indecent, obnoxious, obscene, offensive, raunchy *(Nonformal)*, ribald, shameful, suggestive, vulgar *Antonyms:* chaste, decent, modest **3.** indelicate, politically incorrect, tasteless, thoughtless, uncalled for, undue, unfitting *Nonformal:* out-of-line, tacky *Antonyms:* appropriate, fitting, suave

indeed *adv.* **1.** assuredly, certainly, clearly, decidedly, demonstrably, noticeably, obviously, positively, surely, unequivocally, unmistakably, visibly, without a doubt **2.** actually, in fact *or* reality, really, truly, verily **3.** above all, chiefly, for the most part, mainly, mostly, particularly, predominately, primarily, principally – *interj.* **1.** *Nonformal:* fancy that, for crying out loud, gadzooks, holy mackerel, I'll be, I'll be jiggered, my my, my stars, my word, what in the world **2.** aye, by all means, exactly, *mais oui (French)*, naturally, of course, positively, precisely, right, right you are, yes, yes indeedy, you got it

indefatigable *adj.* determined, diligent, energetic, hard-working, industrious, inexhaustible, invincible, patient, persevering, persistent, relentless, steadfast, tireless, unfaltering, unflagging, untiring, unwavering, vigorous *Nonformal:* bound and determined, iron-clad *Antonyms:* drooping, flagging, tiring

indefensible *adj.* **1.** bad, inexcusable, insupportable, objectionable, unacceptable, unconscionable, unforgivable, unjustifiable, unpardonable, untenable, unwarrantable, wrong *Antonyms:* supportable, tenable **2.** defenceless, exposed, helpless, insecure, open, unarmed, unfortified, unprotected, vincible, vulnerable

indefinable *adj.* blurry, dim, fuzzy, hazy, impalpable, indescribable, indiscernible, indistinct, ineffable, inexplicable, nebulous, obscure, unclear, vague, veiled *Antonyms:* clear, obvious, palpable

indefinite *adj.* **1.** ambiguous, doubtful, equivocal, evasive, nebulous, uncertain, unclear, unsettled, unsure, vague *Antonyms:* decided, fixed, settled **2.** broad, general, indeterminate, inexact, infinite, limitless, loose, non-specific, undefined, unlimited *Antonyms:* defined, exact, precise

indelible *adj.* **1.** constant, deep-felt, enduring, fixed, haunting, ingrained, unforgettable **2.** colourfast, fast-dyed, indestructible, irrevocable, lasting, permanent, unfading *Antonyms:* erasable, removable, temporary

indelicate *adj.* **1.** coarse, gross, inconsiderate, indecorous, obnoxious, tactless, tasteless, unbecoming, uncouth, unfeeling, unseemly, untactful *Antonyms:* considerate, proper, thoughtful **2.** base, blue *(Nonformal)*, brutish, crude, earthy, improper, indecent, lascivious, lewd, licentious, obscene, risqué, rude, suggestive, vulgar, wanton *Antonyms:* chaste, clean, wholesome

indemnify *v.* **1.** atone, compensate, pay, recompense, redress, refund, reimburse, remit, remunerate, repay, requite, satisfy, square, tender **2.** guarantee, insure, protect, safeguard, secure, underwrite

indemnity *n.* **1.** atonement, compensation, redress, reimbursement, remuneration, reparation, restitution, satisfaction **2.** assurance, guarantee, insurance, protection, protectorship, safety, security, warranty **3.** amnesty, exemption, exoneration, freedom, grace, immunity, impunity, pardon, reprieve, requital

indent *n.* **1.** cut, dent, depression, dimple, dint, furrow, groove, hollow, impression, indentation, notch, pock, recess **2.** agreement, claim, commitment, compact, contract, covenant, deal, indenture, obligation, pledge **3.** demand, exchange, exportation, order, petition, request, requisition, trade **4.** indentation, margin, space, tab – *v.* **1.** bash, bevel, dent, depress, dint, gash, hollow, impress, incise, jag, mark, nick, notch, pit, rabbet, rut, scallop, score, serrate **2.** apprentice, article, bind, contract, employ, intern, work for **3.** ask for, demand, order, request, requisition, summon **4.** cut, detach, divide, rip, separate, sever, shred, tear

indenture *n.* **1.** bond, certificate, compact, contract, covenant, deal, deed, document, lease, obligation, stipulation, written guarantee **2.** cut, dent, depression, indentation, notch, recess **3.** account, enumeration, inventory, itinerary, list, record, repertory, schedule, table, tally – *v.* **1.** apprentice, article, bind, contract, employ, hire, intern **2.** cut, gash, indent, notch, pit, recess, scar, score, serrate

independence *n.* **1.** decolonization, emancipation, freedom, home-rule, liberation, liberty, manumission, nationhood, political autonomy, release, self-determination, self-government, self-rule, separation, sovereignty **2.** disconnectedness, dissociation, individuality, singularity, uniqueness **3.** impartiality, mugwumpery *(Nonformal)*, neutrality, nonpartisanship, objectivity **4.** aplomb, autonomy, self-assurance, self-confidence, self-reliance, self-sufficiency *Nonformal:* moxie, spunk **5.** affluence, comfort, ease, easy street *(Nonformal)*, financial freedom, money, prosperity, riches, wealth, wherewithal

independent *adj.* **1.** autarchic, decolonized, emancipated, free, liberated, self-determining, self-governing, self-ruling, sovereign, unconstrained, uncontrolled, unregimented **2.** indie *(Nonformal)*, individual, separate, single, unaffiliated, unattached, unconnected, unique, unrelated **3.** impartial, neutral, noncommitted, nonpartisan, objective, unaligned, uninvolved **4.** self-contained, self-sufficient, self-supporting, self-reliant, stand-alone, unaided **5.** fancy-free *(Nonformal)*, free-spirited, free-willed, individualistic, uncommitted **6.** affluent, flush, loaded *(Nonformal)*, monied, rich, wealthy, well-off – *n.* free-agent, freelancer, individual, neutral party, nonpartisan *Nonformal:* do-it-yourselfer, mugwump

indescribable *adj.* arcane, complex, indefinable, ineffable, inexpressible, obscure, subtle, unexplainable, unspeakable, unutterable *Nonformal:* baffling, mind-blowing *Antonyms:* clear, obvious, simple

indestructible *adj.* abiding, durable, enduring, everlasting, immutable, imperishable, indelible, inextinguishable, inextirpable, invincible, lasting, nonperishable, permanent, perpetual, tough, unalterable, unbreakable, unchangeable, unfading *Nonformal:* heavy-duty, industrial-strength, ironclad, rock-solid *Antonyms:* breakable, perishable, resilient

indeterminate *adj.* **1.** ambiguous, equivocal, frail, inconclusive, moot, open, questionable, uncertain, undecided, undetermined, unfixed, unsettled, weak *Antonyms:* certain, conclusive, fixed, stipulated **2.** general, imprecise, indefinite, indistinct, inexact, unclassified, undefined, unknown, unspecified, vague *Antonyms:* definite, exact *Commonly misused:* **interminable**

index *n.* **1.** bibliography, catalogue, census, digest, directory, guide, inventory, list, system, table, table of contents **2.** appendage, extremity, forefinger, index finger, phalanx **3.** characteristic, clue, hint, indication, mark, sign, signal, token **4.** dial, gauge, guide, indicator, map, needle, rule – *v.* **1.** alphabetize, arrange, catalogue, docket, file, list, order, record, tabulate **2.** betoken, denote, evince, hint, imply, indicate, mark, point at, signal, token **3.** augment, bolster, boost, increase, inflate, raise

indicate *v.* **1.** augur, betoken, connote, denote, evince, foreshadow, hint, imply, mean, signify, suggest, symbolize **2.** designate, divulge, finger *(Nonformal)*, name, peg, pinpoint, point out *or* to, reveal, show, sign, specify, testify **3.** announce, assert, bespeak, declare, express, say, state

indication *n.* **1.** auspice, clue, evidence, explanation, foreshadowing, grounds, hint, inkling, intimation, manifestation, omen, portent, presentation, proof, reminder, symptom, vestige, warning **2.** flash, expression, gesture, glimmer, nod, note, sign, signal, token, wink **3.** amount, degree, measurement, number, quantity, sum, volume

indicative *adj.* adumbrative, characteristic, connotative, demonstrative, designative, emblematic, expressive, suggestive, symbolic, symptomatic

indicator *n.* **1.** arrow, barometer, blinker, buoy, compass, curser, gauge, guide, guidepost, instrument, inukshuk, lobstick, marker, measurement, milestone, needle, pointer, signal, signpost, speedometer, thermometer, weathervane, windsock **2.** bellwether, characteristic, earmark, emblem, hallmark, idiosyncrasy, peculiarity, sign, symptom, telltale sign, tip-off *(Nonformal)*, token

indict *v.* accuse, arraign, censure, charge, incriminate, denounce, impeach, impute, incriminate, prosecute, summon, try *Nonformal:* book, finger *Antonyms:* acquit, exculpate, exonerate

indifference *n.* **1.** aloofness, apathy, coolness, disregard, halfheartedness, impassivity, insouciance, laissez-faire, passivity, stoicism, unresponsiveness *Antonyms:* ardour, passion, zeal **2.** immateriality, inconsequence, insignificance, irrelevance, triviality, unimportance *Antonyms:* importance, significance **3.** blandness, commonness, conventionality, dullness, inferiority, mediocrity, moderateness

indifferent *adj.* **1.** apathetic, cold, distant, incurious, uncaring, unconcerned, uninterested *Antonyms:* ardent, avid, incensed **2.** careless, half-hearted, lukewarm, tepid *Nonformal:* crappy, half-assed, lousy, middling **3.** business-like, clinical, detached, disinterested, dispassionate, even-handed, fair-minded, just, impartial, neutral, nonpartisan, objective, rational, unbiased *Antonyms:* emotionally-involved, prejudiced, subjective **4.** expendable, immaterial, inconsequential, irrelevant, low-priority, minor, piddling, slight, trifling, trivial, two-bit *(Nonformal)*, unessential, unimportant, unrequired *Antonyms:* crucial, necessary, pivotal **5.** acceptable, adequate, fair, mediocre, medium, moderate, not bad, ordinary, passable, unimpressive, unnoteworthy *Nonformal:* humdrum, okay, run-of-the-mill, vanilla *Antonyms:* crackerjack, fantastic, stellar

indigenous *adj.* **1.** aboriginal, autochthonous, domestic, endemic, first, local, native, natural, original *Antonyms:* alien, displaced, foreign **2.** congenital, genetic, inborn, inbred, inherent, inherited, innate, immigrant

indigestion *n.* acid indigestion, acidosis, dyspepsia, gas, tummy ache *(Nonformal)*, heartburn, nausea, pain, upset

indigent *adj.* broke, destitute, disadvantaged, down-and-out, impecunious, impoverished, mendicant, needy, penniless, pinched, poor, poverty-stricken *Nonformal:* hard-up, skint, strapped *Antonyms:* affluent, loaded, privileged, wealthy – *n.* beggar, hobo, pauper, homeless *or* street person, vagabond *Nonformal:* bum, deadbeat, have-not, panhandler, squeegee kid

indignant *adj.* angry, annoyed, disgrun-tled, displeased, exasperated, fuming, furious, heated, huffy, incensed, irate, livid, mad, miffed, peeved, piqued, provoked, resentful, riled, scornful, upset, wrathful *Nonformal:* apoplectic, boiling, browned *or* ticked off, burned, seeing red, sore, steamed *Antonyms:* content, happy, pleased

indignation *n.* anger, displeasure, exasperation, fury, huff, ire, miff, outrage, passion, pique, rage, resentment, scorn, umbrage, wrath *Nonformal:* boiling point, slow burn, stew *Antonyms:* comfort, enjoyment, gladness

indignity *n.* abuse, affront, discourtesy, dishonour, disrespect, embarrassment, grievance, humiliation, injury, injustice, insult, obloquy, opprobrium, outrage, put-down, reproach, slander, slap in the face *(Nonformal)*, slight, slur, snub, taunt *Antonyms:* elevation, honour, praise

indirect *adj.* **1.** aimless, bent, circuitous, circular, circumlocutory, complicated, crooked, diagonal, digressive, erratic, fluctuating, irregular, jagged, long, meandering, oscillating, rambling, roundabout, round the barn *(Nonformal)*, serpentine, sinuous, snaking, tortuous, twisted, twisting, undulating, wandering, winding, zigzag *Antonyms:* clear-cut, direct, straight, undeviating, uninterrupted **2.** backhand, covert, crafty, cunning, devious, evasive, furtive, huggermugger *(Nonformal)*, Machiavellian, shifty, sidelong, sly, surreptitious, tricky, underhanded, unsavoury *Antonyms:* flagrant, obvious, straightforward **3.** accidental, circumstantial, collateral, incidental, secondary, subordinate

indiscernible *adj.* **1.** hazy, hidden, impalpable, imperceptible, indistinct, nebulous, subtle, unapparent *Antonyms:* clear, obvious, visible **2.** atomic, infinitesimal, invisible, microscopic, minuscule, minute, slight, tiny, wee *(Nonformal) Antonyms:* huge, large, massive

indiscreet *adj.* bad form *(Nonformal)*, careless, foolish, heedless, ill-advised, impolitic, imprudent, incautious, obvious, overt, rash, reckless, tactless, thoughtless undiplomatic, unwise *Antonyms:* careful, subtle, tactful

ndiscretion *n.* **1.** affair, blunder, breach of etiquette, bungle, clanger *(Nonformal)*, error, faux pas, gaffe, lapse, misdeed, misstep, mistake, peccadillo, slip, solecism, transgression **2.** carelessness, discourtesy, disservice, folly, foolishness, imprudence, inconsiderateness, insensitivity, rashness, tactlessness, thoughtlessness *Antonyms:* decorum, manners, tact

ndiscriminate *adj.* **1.** careless, casual, confused, erratic, haphazard, irregular, promiscuous, random, uncritical, unmethodical *Nonformal:* slapdash, without rhyme or reason *Antonyms:* deliberate, intentional, planned, purposeful **2.** broad, extensive, general, sweeping, wholesale, wide-ranging *Antonyms:* bounded, circumscribed, restrained **3.** chaotic, higgledy-piggledy *(Nonformal)*, jumbled, mixed, motley, scrambled, thrown-together *Antonyms:* neat, ordered, tidy

ndispensable *adj.* **1.** basic, bottom-line *(Nonformal)*, cardinal, central, crucial, essential, focal, fundamental, imperative, important, key, necessary, paramount, pivotal, substantive, vital *Antonyms:* nonessential, superfluous, unnecessary **2.** binding, certain, compulsory, inescapable, inevitable, mandatory, obligatory, requisite, unavoidable – *n.* essential, necessity, obligation, requirement

ndisposed *adj.* **1.** ailing, below par, confined, feverish, ill, infirm, sick, sickly, unwell *Nonformal:* laid up, poorly, under-the-weather *Antonyms:* fine, fit, hardy, healthy, well **2.** averse, disinclined, grudging, hesitant, loath, opposed, reluctant, resistant, unwilling *Antonyms:* affable, agreeable, cooperative

ndisputable *adj.* **1.** apparent, evident, manifest, patent, plain, positive, real *Nonformal:* crystal-clear, open-and-shut *Antonyms:* ambiguous, conjectural, speculative **2.** absolute, accurate, certain, conclusive, decisive, double-checked *(Nonformal)*, fixed, incontestable, irrefutable, sure, unassailable, undeniable, unquestionable *Antonyms:* controversial, dubious, moot

indistinct *adj.* **1.** barely discernible, bleary, blurred, confusing, dark, din, faint, faraway, fuzzy, garbled, hard to distinguish *or* hear *or* identify *or* see *or* smell, hazy, inaudible, incoherent, misty, muffled, out of focus, shadowy, unintelligible *Antonyms:* clear, lucid, perceivable, plain as day *(Nonformal)*, vivid **2.** ambiguous, ambivalent, doubtful, indefinite, inexact, not defined, obscure, uncertain, undetermined, vague *Nonformal:* confirmed, decided, fixed, resolved

indistinguishable *adj.* **1.** alike, coinciding, corresponding, duplicate, equivalent, identical, like, matched, same, selfsame, similar, synonymous, twin *Antonyms:* different, singular, unique **2.** hard to make out *(Nonformal)*, imperceptible, indefinite, invisible, shrouded, unclear, vague *Antonyms:* clear-cut, manifest, obvious

individual *adj.* **1.** alone, apart, insular, isolated, lone, only, separate, single, sole, solitary, solo *Antonyms:* collective, composite, public **2.** distinct, idiosyncratic, original, particular, personal, peculiar, singular, special, specific, unique, unusual *Antonyms:* common, general, generic – *n.* **1.** being, body, child, creature, entity, head, human, man, number, person, self, single, soul, unit, woman *Antonyms:* gang, group **2.** eccentric, exception, free-spirit, maverick, nonconformist *Nonformal:* cowboy, oddball, one-of-a-kind, rare bird *Antonyms:* clone, conventionalist

individualistic *adj.* **1.** free-thinking, original, rare, special, unique, uncommon unconventional, unorthodox *Nonformal:* offbeat, off the wall, outside the box *or* lines *Antonyms:* conventional, orthodox, traditional **2.** distinctive, distinguishing, exclusive, idiosyncratic, inherent, inner, intimate, intrinsic, personal, private *Antonyms:* common, general, public, shared **3.** bourgeois, capitalist, laissez-faire, private-enterprise *Antonyms:* communist, left-wing, socialist

individuality *n.* **1.** character, complexion, crotchet, disposition, eccentricity, ego, essence, habit, humour, identity, idiosyncrasy, make-up, manner, mark, nature, oddity, particularity, peculiarity, personality, quality, quirk, rarity, singularity, temper, temperament, trait, uniqueness, way *Antonyms:* consanguinity, sameness, similarity **2.** independence, individualism, nonconformity, originality, radicalism, separateness, separatism *Antonyms:* conformity, nationality, traditionalism, unity

indoctrinate *v.* brainwash, convince, drill, imbue, implant, inculcate, influence, instill, instruct, plant, program *(Nonformal)*, proselytize, school, teach, train

indolence *n.* hebetude, idleness, inaction, inertia, languor, lassitude, laziness, lethargy, listlessness, stupor, torpor *Antonyms:* action, energy, industriousness, verve

indolent *adj.* couch-bound, draggy, fainéant, idle, inactive, inert, lackadaisical, languid, lazy, lethargic, listless, resting, slack, slothful, slow, sluggish, torpid, vegging *(Nonformal) Antonyms:* alert, assiduous, busy, lively, vigorous

indomitable *adj.* **1.** brave, courageous, determined, dogged, fearless, intrepid, obstinate, persevering, persistent, resolute, sedulous, staunch, steadfast, stubborn, tenacious, tireless, unflinching, unstoppable, willful *Antonyms:* faltering, weak, yielding **2.** insurmountable, invincible, invulnerable, unassailable, unbeatable *Antonyms:* exposed, open to attack, vulnerable **3.** defiant, intractable, rebellious, refractory, unconquerable, uncontrollable, unyielding, rebellious *Antonyms:* biddable, pliant, submissive, yielding

indubitably *adj.* absolutely, certainly, evidently, explicitly, expressly, incontestably, incontrovertibly, indisputably, irrefragably, manifestly, obviously, patently, positively *Nonformal:* crystal-clear, open-and-shut *Antonyms:* arguably, debatably, moot

induce *v.* **1.** cajole, compel, convince, impel, incite, influence, inveigle, lead, lure, motivate, move, persuade, press, prompt, seduce, sway, urge, wheedle *Nonformal:* soft-soap, steamroll, sweet-talk *Antonyms:* curb, dissuade, hinder **2.** bring around, cause, contrive, effect, elicit, engender, evoke, generate, get, instigate, make, obtain, occasion, procure, produce **3.** conclude, deduce, determine, gather, glean, reach, reason *Commonly misused:* **deduce**

inducement *n.* allure, attraction, bait, bribe, coaxing, encouragement, goading, incentive, incitement, influence, lure, motivation, persuasion, prodding, provocation, reward, stimulation, stimulus, temptation, urging *Nonformal:* carrot, come-on, moolah, selling-point, sweetener, what-for

induct *v.* **1.** conscript, draft, enlist, enrol, impress, press, recruit, sign on *or* up *Antonyms:* demobilize, discharge, release **2.** anoint, consecrate, enthrone, inaugurate, initiate, install, instate, introduce, invest, ordain, place, screech in *(Newfoundland)*, swear in, take office

induction *n.* **1.** admission, consecration, entrance, inauguration, initiation, installation, investiture, ordination, swearing in **2.** conscription, draft, enrolment, impressment, levy, recruitment, registration, selection, summons **3.** analysis, conjecture, generalization, inference, judgment, rationalization, reasoning **4.** exhibition, offering, presentation, production, proficiency

indulge *v.* **1.** baby, coddle, cosset, delight, favour, foster, gratify, mollycoddle, nourish, please, regale, satisfy, spoil, treat *Antonyms:* abuse, chastise, harm **2.** allow, cater, entertain, humour, pander, yield *Antonyms:* forbid, prohibit **3.** bask *or* revel *or* roll in, enjoy, frolic, live well, luxuriate, rollick, wallow *Nonformal:* live it up, put on the Ritz

indulgence *n.* **1.** babying, coddling, favouring, humouring, kid-glove treatment, lenience, obliging, pandering, placating, pleasing, serving, spoiling **2.** excess, extravagance, hedonism, immoderation, permissiveness, profligacy, self-indulgence *Antonyms:* abstinence, forbearance **3.** contentment, enjoyment, fulfillment, gratification, relief, satiety, satisfaction **4.** courtesy, favour, good will, gratuity, kindness, privilege, service **5.** allowance, extension, grant, licence, permission, prolongation, time

indulgent *adj.* **1.** charitable, clement, compassionate, considerate, easy, forbearing, gentle, giving, gratifying, humane, kind, kindly, lax, lenient, merciful, mild, obliging, pacific, permissive, sympathetic, tender, tolerant *Nonformal:* big, soft *Antonyms:* austere, demanding, harsh, stern, strict **2.** excessive, extravagant, hedonistic, immoderate, intemperate, profligate, self-gratifying

industrial *adj.* **1.** blue-collar, business, commercial, factory, manufacturing, occupational, professional, smoke-stack *(Nonformal)*, trade *Antonyms:* domestic, residential **2.** efficient, industrialized, mechanized, processed, productive, streamlined **3.** durable, functional, heavy-duty *(Nonformal)*, long-lasting, powerful, resistant, shatterproof, strong, tough

industrious *adj.* active, assiduous, busy, diligent, dynamic, eager, energetic, hardworking, involved, persevering, persistent, productive, purposeful, spirited, steady, tireless, zealous *Antonyms:* idle, indolent, lackadaisical, lazy, shiftless

industry *n.* **1.** assembly, creation, construction, development, fabrication, manufacturing, production **2.** business, commerce, market, trade, traffic **3.** branch, field, line, métier, job, sector, vocation **4.** activity, application, assiduity, attention, care, determination, diligence, effort, enterprise, intentness, labour, pains, patience, perseverance, persistence, toil, vigour, work

inebriate *adj.* dazed, drunk, intoxicated, *Nonformal:* bombed, loaded, pie-eyed, soused, stoned, tight, wasted – *n.* alcoholic, dipsomaniac, drinker, drunk, drunkard, problem drinker *Nonformal:* alky, boozehound, boozer, juicer, lush, otis, rubby, sot, souse, wino – *v.* **1.** befuddle, besot, drink, intoxicate, stupefy *Nonformal:* booze, get loaded, souse, pickle oneself **2.** animate, arouse, energize, excite, exhilarate, inspire, invigorate, pep up, stimulate

inebriated *adj.* drunk, high, intoxicated, merry, tipsy *Nonformal:* blind *or* punch *or* rip-roaring drunk, blotto, bombed, boozy, loaded, pickled, plastered, polluted, ripped, smashed, stewed, stiff, stinking, stoned, tanked up, three sheets to the wind, tight

inedible *adj.* **1.** disgusting, fetid, foul, gross, putrid, revolting, rotten, unappetizing *Nonformal:* gone, off, skunky, yucky **2.** deadly, harmful, lethal, noxious, poisonous, tainted, unwholesome

ineffable *adj.* beyond words, indefinable, inexpressible, noncommunicable, unnameable, unspeakable, unutterable *Antonyms:* describable, discussible, utterable

ineffective *adj.* **1.** abortive, barren, bootless, counterproductive, fatuous, futile, inoperative, nugatory, null, sterile, unavailing, unfruitful, unproductive, unprofitable, unsuccessful, vain, void, worthless *Antonyms:* fertile, fruitful, productive **2.** bumbling, feckless, feeble, impotent, inadequate, incompetent, indecisive, ineffectual, inefficient, inept, inferior, innocuous, limited, powerless, unskilful, useless *Antonyms:* efficacious, effective, forceful

ineffectual *adj.* **1.** for naught, fruitless, gainless, pointless, sterile, unproductive, unrewarding, unsuccessful, vain **2.** artless, awkward, bumbling, bungling, feeble, impotent, inept, inept, incompetent, ineffective, inefficient, powerless, unable, unskilled *Nonformal:* lame, lightweight, spineless, wimpy

inefficient *adj.* **1.** careless, disorganized, extravagant, improvident, loose, prodigal, remiss, slack, slipshod, sloppy, slovenly, wasteful *Antonyms:* controlled, meticulous, organized **2.** clumsy, faulty, feeble, incapable, ineffective, ineffectual, inefficacious, inexpert, unfit, unprepared, unqualified, unskilled, untrained, weak, wussy *(Nonformal) Antonyms:* able, capable, competent

inelegant *adj.* **1.** awkward, clumsy, gauche, graceless, stiff, ungainly, ungraceful, wooden *Nonformal:* clunky, stone-handed **2.** abrasive, coarse, crass, crude, indelicate, loutish, obnoxious, rough, rude, uncouth, uncultivated, unpolished, unrefined, vulgar *Antonyms:* considerate, smooth, urbane

ineligible *adj.* inappropriate, not up to snuff *(Nonformal)*, prohibited, ruled out, unacceptable, uncertified, unfit, unqualified, unsuitable, unwelcome

inept *adj.* **1.** artless, awkward, bungling, clumsy, gauche, graceless, halting, ill-timed, incapable, incompetent, inexperienced, unskilled, wooden *Nonformal:* all thumbs, Clouseau-esque, ham-handed *Antonyms:* able, adroit, deft, talented **2.** absurd, foolish, daft, impolitic, improper, inane, inappropriate, infelicitous, malapropos, pointless, ridiculous, thoughtless, undue, unfit, unseasonable, unseemly, unsuitable *Antonyms:* felicitous, realistic, suitable *Commonly misused:* **inapt**

ineptitude *n.* **1.** awkwardness, clumsiness, crassness, gaucheness, inability, inadequacy, inaptitude, incapability, incapacity, incompetence, inexpertness, inferiority *Antonyms:* aptitude, deftness, skill **2.** absurdity, asininity, fatuity, foolishness, folly, inanity, irrelevance, stupidity, uselessness

inequality *n.* **1.** asperity, bias, discrimination, injustice, one-sidedness, partiality, prejudice, unfairness *Antonyms:* equity, impartiality **2.** contrast, difference, disparity, disproportion, dissimilarity, diversity, incongruity, irregularity, unevenness, variation *Antonyms:* homogeneity, similarity

inequity *n.* abuse, bias, bigotry, discrimination, foul play, grievance, injustice, maltreatment, partiality, prejudice, unfairness, wrongdoing *Commonly misused:* **iniquity**

inert *adj.* **1.** apathetic, dull, idle, indolent, languid, lazy, leaden, listless, otiose, phlegmatic, sedentary, sleepy, slothful, sluggish, somnolent *Nonformal:* dopey, pepless, pooped **2.** immobile, inactive, inanimate, motionless, quiescent, quiet, stagnant, stationary, still, unmoving **3.** asleep, dormant, oblivious, senseless, slumbering, somnolent, supine, unconscious *Nonformal:* comatose, flaked-out, out cold *Antonyms:* alert, awake, up

inertia *n.* **1.** apathy, drowsiness, dullness, fainéance, idleness, indolence, languor, lassitude, laziness, lethargy, listlessness, passivity, sloth, sluggishness, torpor, unresponsiveness, vegetation *(Nonformal) Antonyms:* activity, animation, spunk, verve, vigour **2.** immobility, inactivity, lifelessness, paralysis, stasis, stillness *Antonyms:* liveliness, energy, vitality

inescapable *adj.* certain, destined, fated, fixed, ineluctable, inevitable, inexorable, irrevocable, necessary, relentless, sure, unalterable, unavoidable, unpreventible, unstoppable

inestimable *adj.* **1.** boundless, immeasurable, immense, incalculable, infinite, manifold, prodigious, unfathomable, unlimited, untold, vast, voluminous *Antonyms:* insignificant, miniature, minuscule **2.** dear, invaluable, precious, priceless, valuable *Antonyms:* frivolous, petty, trifling

inevitable *adj.* assured, binding, certain, compulsory, decided, decreed, destined, determined, doomed, fated, fixed, foreordained, imminent, ineluctable, inescapable, karmic, necessary, obligatory, ordained, pat, prescribed, settled, sure, unalterable, unavoidable, undeniable, unpreventible *Antonyms:* avoidable, escapable, preventable, uncertain – *n.* certainty, destiny, fate, karma, kismet, obligation, surety

inexact *adj.* **1.** erroneous, fallacious, false, imperfect, inaccurate, incorrect, off-base *(Nonformal)*, wrong *Antonyms:* exact, perfect, right **2.** approximate, ballpark *(Nonformal)*, fuzzy, general, ill-defined, imprecise, indefinite, indeterminate, indistinct, lax, loose, muddled, vague, woolly *Antonyms:* concise, definite, precise

inexcusable *adj.* blameworthy, censurable, impermissible, indefensible, inexpiable, intolerable, outrageous, reprehensible, terrible, unforgivable, unjustifiable, unpardonable, untenable, unwarrantable, vile, without merit, wrong *Antonyms:* understandable, valid, warranted

inexorable *adj.* **1.** cruel, hard, harsh, immovable, implacable, ineluctable, inflexible, ironclad, merciless, obdurate, obstinate, pitiless, remorseless, resolute, rigid, severe, unappeasable, unbending, uncompromising, unmovable, unyielding *Antonyms:* flexible, lenient, sensitive, soft **2.** adamant, bound, determined, dogged, relentless, single-minded, stubborn, unalterable, unflagging, unrelenting

inexpedient *adj.* bad, counterproductive, detrimental, foolhardy, foolish, ill-advised, impolitic, impractical, imprudent, inadvisable, inane, inopportune, malapropos, rash, self-defeating, silly, unsuitable, untimely, untoward, unwise, wrong *Antonyms:* right, seasonable, timely

inexpensive *adj.* **1.** budget, cheap, economical, modest, low-priced, reasonable, thrifty *Antonyms:* costly, dear, exorbitant, expensive, pricey **2.** bargain, cut-rate, half-price, lowcost, marked down, on sale, reduced *Nonformal:* dirt cheap, real buy, steal

inexperienced *adj.* amateur, bumbling, callow, fresh, green, ignorant, immature, inept, inexpert, innocent, new, raw, rookie, sophomoric, unaccustomed, unconversant, unfamiliar, unschooled, unseasoned, unskilled, unsophisticated, untrained, untried, unversed, unworldly, verdant, virgin, young *Antonyms:* familiar, practiced, qualified

inexplicable *adj.* baffling, bizarre, enigmatic, fantastic, incomprehensible, indecipherable, indescribable, mind-boggling *(Nonformal)*, miraculous, mysterious, mystifying, obscure, odd, peculiar, puzzling, strange, unaccountable, undefinable, unexplainable, unfathomable, unintelligible, unsolvable, unusual *Antonyms:* clear, explicit, routine

inexpressive *adj.* bland, blank, deadpan, dull, emotionless, empty, flat, glassy, impassive, inanimate, inscrutable, lifeless, poker-faced, rigid, stolid, stony, inanimate, vacant, vacuous, void, wooden

inextinguishable *adj.* **1.** deathless, enduring, eternal, everlasting, immortal, imperishable, indestructible, inexhaustible, invincible, lasting, permanent, undying, unquenchable, unstoppable **2.** effervescent, irrepressible, ungovernable, unrestrainable

infallible *adj.* **1.** accurate, correct, exact, faultless, flawless, impeccable, perfect, point-device, right **2.** all-knowing, all-powerful, beyond reproach, god-like, irreproachable, omnipotent, omniscient, unerring **3.** certain, dependable, foolproof, incontrovertible, positive, sound, sure, surefire *(Nonformal)*, unerring, unfailing *Antonyms:* dubious, uncertain, unreliable, unsure

infamous *adj.* abominable, atrocious, bad, base, contemptible, corrupt, degenerate, despicable, detestable, disgraceful, dishonourable, disreputable, egregious, evil, foul, hateful, heinous, horrific, ignominious, ill-famed, iniquitous, loathsome, miscreant, monstrous, nefarious, notorious, odious, offensive, outrageous, perverse, questionable, rotten, scandalous, shady, shameful, shocking, sorry, vicious, vile, villainous, wicked *Antonyms:* honourable, noble, reputable, virtuous

infamy *n.* abomination, atrocity, disapprobation, discredit, disesteem, disgrace, dishonour, disrepute, enormity, evil, ignominy, immorality, impropriety, notoriety, notoriousness, opprobrium, outrageousness, scandal, shame, stigma, villainy, wickedness

infancy *n.* **1.** babyhood, childhood, the cradle *or* crib, youth *Antonyms:* adulthood, caducity, golden-years **2.** beginning, birth, commencement, creation, dawn, early days, emergence, establishment, foundation, genesis, inception, origins, outset, start, square-one *(Nonformal)*

infant *adj.* **1.** babyish, childish, childlike, immature, incomplete, infantile, naive, nascent, tender, unfledged, unripe **2.** developing, early, emergent, formative, growing, incipient, initial, introducing, nascent, new – *n.* **1.** babe, baby, child, neonate, newborn, papoose, suckling, toddler, tot *Nonformal:* bambino, kid, whippersnapper **2.** beginner, fledgling, frosh *(Nonformal)*, greenhorn, ingenue, neophyte, novice, rookie, tenderfoot

infantry *n.* army, commandos, foot soldiers, forces, ground troops, men-at-arms, military, soldiers, troops *Nonformal:* cannon fodder, grunts, rank and file

infatuate *n.* afficionado, buff *(Nonformal)*, devotee, enthusiast, fan, fanatic, lover, zealot – *v.* beguile, besot, capture, charm, enchant, ensnare, fascinate, hypnotize, lure, mesmerize, seduce, snare, stultify, tantalize

infatuated *adj. aux anges (French),* beguiled, besotted, bewitched, captivated, carried away, charmed, enamoured, enchanted, enraptured, enthralled, fascinated, foolish, hypnotized, inflamed, intoxicated, lovesick, love-struck, obsessed, seduced, silly, smitten, spellbound, stuck on *Nonformal:* crazy *or* mad *or* wild about, head-over-heels, hooked, hung up *Antonyms:* disenchanted, indifferent, jaded

infect *v.* **1.** contaminate, corrupt, disease, pervert, poison, pollute, spoil, stain, sully, taint *Antonyms:* clean, disinfect, sterilize **2.** affect, imbue, induce, influence, infuse, inject, inoculate, inspire

infection *n.* **1.** bacteria, blight, bug *(Nonformal),* contagion, disease, epidemic, germs, illness, malaise, sickness, sepsis, septicemia, virus **2.** contamination, corruption, impurity, poison, pollution, septicity **3.** excitation, excitement, exhilaration, fire, influence, infusion, inspiration

infectious *adj.* **1.** catching, communicable, contagious, epidemic, spreading, transferable, transmittable, virulent **2.** contaminating, corrupting, diseased, noxious, pestilential, poisoning, polluting

infelicitous *adj.* **1.** crestfallen, depressed, dispirited, doleful, down, forlorn, melancholic, miserable, morose, sad, unhappy, woeful *Antonyms:* buoyant, happy, joyful **2.** gauche, ill-chosen, inappropriate, inconsistent, inopportune, irrelevant, malapropos, poor, premature, unfavourable, unfortunate, unpropitious, unseasonable, unsuitable, untimely

infelicity *n.* **1.** adversity, bane, blight, curse, depression, desolation, despondency, gloom, hard times, hardship, ill wind, melancholy, misfortune, neurasthenia, sadness, suffering, trial, tribulation, unhappiness, woe, wretchedness *Antonyms:* glee, joy, serendipity **2.** awkwardness, incongruity, inexpedience, unfitness, untimeliness

infer *v.* **1.** arrive at, ascertain, assume, believe, conclude, conjecture, construe, deduce, derive, figure, figure out, gather, glean, guess, induce, interpret, intuit, judge, presume, presuppose, read into, rea son, reckon, speculate, suppose, surmise suspect, think, understand *Nonforma* dope out, thunk **2.** allude, hint, imply, ind cate, intimate, suggest *Commonly mis used:* **imply**

inference *n.* **1.** assumption, belief, conclu sion, conjecture, corollary, estimation guess, impression, opinion, supposition suspicion, theory, thought, understanding view **2.** deduction, induction, logic, ratioci nation, reasoning **3.** allusion, hint, implica tion, intimation, suggestion

inferior *adj.* **1.** base, *déclassé (French),* imperfect, junk, low-grade, mean, paltry poor, second-class, second-rate, shoddy sleazy, sorry, substandard, tawdry, wretche *Nonformal:* bush-league, cheesy, crappy scuzzy *Antonyms:* excellent, fine, first-clas **2.** average, common, indifferent, mediocre middling, ordinary, passable, run-of-the-mil standard *Nonformal:* garden-variety, so-so *Antonyms:* fantastic, outstanding, stellar **3** assistant, entry-level, junior, menial, mino secondary *Nonformal:* bottom-rung, sec ond-string, small-time **4.** below, lesser lower, nether, poorer, under, worse – *n* assistant, employee, flunky, helper, hired hand, junior, minion, second-fiddle *(Non formal),* servant, subordinate, underling

inferiority *n.* **1.** deficiency, imperfection inadequacy, lack, mediocrity, shortcoming worthlessness **2.** baseness, humbleness lowliness, servility, subordination, sub servience, unimportance

infernal *adj.* **1.** accursed, baleful, blamed blasted, confounded, cruel, cursed, cussed *(Nonformal),* damnable, dire, execrable iniquitous, malevolent, malicious, mon strous, odious, sinister, wicked *Antonyms* blessed, glorious, pure **2.** damned, demon ic, devilish, diabolical, fiendish, hell-born hellish, Mephistophelian, satanic *Anto nyms:* angelic, celestial, glorious, heavenly seraphic

infertile *adj.* **1.** depleted, drained, dud *(Nonformal),* exhausted, impoverished unfruitful *Antonyms:* fruitful, generative productive **2.** barren, childless, impotent nonproductive, sterile

infest *v.* **1.** abound, crowd, fill, flock, flood, overrun, overwhelm, pack, press, swarm, swell, teem, throng **2.** assail, harass, harry, infect, invade, penetrate, pester, plague

infested *adj.* **1.** alive, beset, inundated, overrun, pervaded, swarming, teeming, thronging **2.** crawling, dirty, flea-ridden, grubby, lousy, pedicular, plagued, ravaged, verminous

infidel *adj.* doubtful, faithless, freethinking, heretical, iconoclastic, nonbelieving, pagan, sceptical – *n.* atheist, disbeliever, doubting Thomas *(Nonformal)*, free-thinker, giaour, heathen, heresiarch, heretic, iconoclast, pagan, sceptic, unbeliever

infidelity *n.* **1.** adultery, affair, bad faith, betrayal, cheating, disloyalty, duplicity, faithlessness, falsity, inconstancy, lewdness, perfidy, treacherousness, treason, unfaithfulness *Nonformal:* hanky-panky, two-timing **2.** atheism, heresy, iconoclasm, nonbelief, paganism, scepticism

infiltrate *v.* **1.** absorb, imbue, percolate, permeate, saturate, seep in, soak up **2.** assimilate, creep into, encroach, entrench, filter through, infringe, insert oneself, insinuate, intrude, invade, penetrate, pervade, slip *or* sneak in, trespass

infiltrator *n.* intelligence agent, intruder, mole, narc *(Nonformal)*, operative, saboteur, secret agent, seditionary, snoop, spy, subversive, subverter, undercover agent

infinite *adj.* **1.** boundless, constant, continual, endless, enduring, eternal, everlasting, forever, incessant, interminable, never-ending, perpetual, unbounded, vast, wide *Antonyms:* circumscribed, restricted **2.** bottomless, countless, immeasurable, incalculable, inestimable, inexhaustible, innumerable, limitless, measureless, myriad, numberless, plumbless, uncounted, untold *Nonformal:* gazillion, umpteen *Antonyms:* bounded, enumerative, fathomable, measurable **3.** absolute, all-embracing, all-encompassing, all-knowing, complete, omnipotent, omniscient, perfect, supreme, total *Antonyms:* limited, partial

infinitesimal *adj.* **1.** atomic, insignificant, little, microscopic, miniature, minuscule, minute, small, tiny, wee *Antonyms:* enormous, great, huge, large, vast **2.** imperceptible, inappreciable, inconsiderable, negligible, unnoticeable *Antonyms:* considerable, noticeable, significant

infinity *n.* **1.** boundlessness, endlessness, immensity, limitlessness, vastness **2.** beyond, continuum, eternity, everlasting, forever, immortality, perpetuity, space, time, universe

infirm *adj.* **1.** ailing, anemic, debilitated, delicate, doddering, enfeebled, failing, faint, faltering, fragile, frail, ill, laid low *(Nonformal)*, lame, rocky, shaky, sick, unsound, valetudinarian, weak, wobbly *Antonyms:* healthy, hearty, robust, sturdy, vigorous **2.** aimless, changeable, inconstant, irresolute, mercurial, purposeless, quicksilver, undecided, unstable, vacillating, wavering *Antonyms:* determined, firm, stolid

infirmity *n.* **1.** affliction, ailment, bug, disease, disorder, dose, ill-health, malady, malaise, sickness *Antonyms:* hardiness, health, vigour **2.** caducity, debility, decay, feebleness, frailty, senility, sickliness, vulnerability, weakness *Antonyms:* soundness, stability, strength **3.** defect, deficiency, failing, fault, foible, imperfection, shortcoming

inflame *v.* **1.** aggravate, agitate, anger, arouse, charge-up, embitter, enrage, exacerbate, exasperate, fan, foment, frenzy, fuel, galvanize, impassion, incense, incite, provoke **2.** fire, heat, ignite, kindle, light, pyrolyze, torch

inflammable *adj.* **1.** burnable, combustible, flammable, hazardous, ignitable, incendiary **2.** arousable, bellicose, cantankerous, edgy, excitable, hot-blooded, hotheaded, irritable, ornery, short-fused, short-tempered, tempestuous, volatile, volcanic *Antonyms:* cool, easygoing, level-headed

inflammation *n.* **1.** abscess, burning, disease, gout, heat, infection, rash, sepsis, sore, soreness, swelling, tenderness **2.** blaze, burning, combustion, conflagration, fire **3.** agitation, arousal, excitation, fomentation, impassioning, incitement, instigation, provocation, rabble-rousing *Antonyms:* appeasement, mitigation, pacification **4.** anger, dander *(Nonformal)*, fury, ire, outburst, rage, temper, wrath *Antonyms:* contentment, humour, joy

inflammatory *adj.* **1.** anarchic, angering, arousing, controversial, demagogic, exciting, explosive, fiery, incendiary, inspiring, insurgent, intemperate, motivating, passionate, provocative, rabble-rousing, rebellious, revolutionary, riotous, seditious, spirited *Antonyms:* appeasing, dispassionate, pacifying **2.** bloated, diseased, distended, infected, puffy, raw, red, stretched, swollen

inflate *v.* **1.** aerate, amplify, balloon, bloat, blow up, dilate, distend, enlarge, expand, fill, increase, magnify, raise, spread out, stretch, swell, widen *Antonyms:* collapse, compress, contract, shrink **2.** aggrandize, augment, boast, boost, build *or* puff up, colour, exaggerate, flesh out, hyperbolize, maximize, overestimate *Antonyms:* deflate, diminish, lessen

inflated *adj.* **1.** amplified, augmented, bloated, dilated, distended, enlarged, extended, filled, stretched, swollen, tumescent *Antonyms:* flat, skinny, thin **2.** aureate, bombastic, diffuse, exaggerated, flatulent, flowery, fustian, grandiloquent, high-flown, ostentatious, overblown, overdeveloped, prolix, purple, rhetorical, showy, turgid, verbose, windy, wordy *Antonyms:* ascetic, simple, terse, unadorned **3.** elevated, hiked-up, increased, magnified, marked up, overestimated, padded, surcharged, tax-added *Antonyms:* lowered, marked down, reduced

inflation *n.* **1.** bloating, distension, enlargement, expansion, extension, puffiness, tumescence **2.** cost increase, escalation, hike, increase, rise, soaring costs *or* prices *Antonyms:* lowering, reduction **3.** affectation, bombast, exaggeration, excess, flatulence, grandiloquence, hyperbole, stretch, turgidity

inflection *n.* **1.** accent, articulation, change, emphasis, enunciation, intonation, modulation, pitch, pronunciation, sound, timbre, tonality, tone, variation **2.** arch, bend, bow, curve, flexion

inflexible *adj.* **1.** frozen, hard, hardened, immovable, immutable, inelastic, iron, nonflexible, rigid, set, taut, unadaptable, unbending *Antonyms:* elastic, pliant, supple **2.** adamant, determined, dogged, firm, fixed, implacable, indomitable, inexorable, intractable, obdurate, obstinate, pertinacious, relentless, resolute, rigorous, single-minded, staunch, steadfast, steely, stiff, strict, stringent, stubborn, unchangeable, uncompromising, unrelenting, unyielding *Antonyms:* compliant, obedient, yielding

inflict *v.* administer, apply, cause, command, deal out, deliver, dish out *(Nonformal)*, dispense, exact, force, impose, levy, punish, require, subject, visit, wreak *Commonly misused:* **afflict**

inflorescence *n.* **1.** bloom, blossoming, flourishing, flowering **2.** cluster, flower arrangement *Kinds of inflorescence: Compound racemose:* compound spike, compound umbel, panicle *Cymose:* compound cyme, scorpioid cyme, simple cyme, simple terminal flower *Simple racemose:* catkin, corymb, head, raceme, spike, umbel

influence *n.* **1.** access, ascendancy, agency, authority, character, charisma, clout *(Nonformal)*, command, connections, control, direction, dominion, esteem, fame, force, guidance, hold, leadership, leverage, magnetism, mark, mastery, money, monopoly, network, power, predominance, pressure, prestige, prominence, reputation, rule, supremacy weight *Nonformal:* drag, grease, in, pull **2.** consequence, effect, impact, importance, imprint, repercussion, significance – *v.* **1.** act upon, affect, alter, bias, brainwash, bribe, change, compel, control, form, impel, impact on, impress, incite, induce, manipulate, modify, move, persuade, predispose, prejudice, prevail, prompt, pull strings *(Nonformal)*, rouse, rule, seduce, sell, shape, sway, urge **2.** command, direct, guide, govern, lead, manage, regulate, steer

influential *adj.* **1.** eminent, famous, important, instrumental, potent, powerful, preeminent, prominent, significant, strong, substantial, well-known *Antonyms:* impotent, trivial, weak **2.** authoritative, cogent, controlling, decisive, determinative, dominant, effective, efficacious, governing, guiding, impressive, inspiring, leading, managing, meaningful, momentous, moving, persuasive, productive, successful, touching, useful, valid, weighty

influx *n.* **1.** arrival, convergence, immigration, flow, incursion, inflow, inundation, invasion, penetration, rush **2.** delta, discharge, mouth, river's end, watershed

inform *v.* **1.** acquaint, advise, brief, caution, clue, communicate, disclose, edify, educate, endow, enlighten, explain, familiarize, illuminate, inspire, instruct, notify, post, relate, teach, update **2.** betray, blab, leak, tattle, tell, tip, tip off *Nonformal:* rat, sing, snitch, squeal

informal *adj.* **1.** breezy, casual, congenial, easy, easygoing, folksy, frank, intimate, laid-back *(Nonformal)*, loose, mellow, natural, offhand, open, relaxed, simple, spontaneous, straightforward, unaffected, unrestrained, unstudied *Antonyms:* formal, rigid, stuffy **2.** background, off the record, unceremonious, unconventional, unofficial, unorthodox, unsanctioned *Antonyms:* conventional, customary, procedural **3.** colloquial, demotic, everyday, familiar, ordinary, popular, rustic, vernacular *Antonyms:* standardized, stylized

informant *n.* accuser, advisor, announcer, betrayer, denouncer, double-crosser, informer, messenger, notifier, reporter, source, spy, talebearer, tattler, tattletail, witness *Nonformal:* blab, blabbermouth, deep throat, narc, rat, ratfink, snitch, squealer, stool pigeon, tipster, weasel, whistle-blower

information *n.* **1.** advice, clue, confidence, counsel, data, dossier, facts, lore, material, message, network, news, notification, report, score, tip, word *Nonformal:* dirt, dope, earful, info, lowdown, poop, scoop, score, the goods, the latest, what's what, whole story **2.** enlightenment, erudition, illumination, intellect, intelligence, knowledge, sagacity, wisdom **3.** instruction, learning, orientation, teaching

informative *adj.* advisory, communicative, descriptive, edifying, educational, enlightening, explanatory, helpful, illuminating, instructive, of interest, revealing, rewarding, significant, worthwhile *Antonyms:* cryptic, reticent, secretive

informed *adj.* abreast, acquainted, *au courant (French)*, briefed, conversant, cognizant, educated, enlightened, erudite, expert, familiar, in the know, knowledgeable, learned, posted, primed, reliable, travelled, up-to-date, versant, versed, well-read, wise *Nonformal:* fly, hip, savvy, street-smart, up-to-speed *Antonyms:* foolish, ignorant, unknowledgeable

infraction *n.* breach, contravention, crime, delinquency, error, fault, *faux pas (French)*, infringement, lapse, offence, sin, slip, transgression, trespass, violation

infrequent *adj.* **1.** irregular, isolated, limited, occasional, odd, rare, scant, scanty, scattered, seldom, spasmodic, sporadic, stray, uncommon, unusual *Antonyms:* common, customary, everyday, frequent **2.** few, meagre, scarce, sparse *Antonyms:* many, multiple, numerous

infringe *v.* breach, break, chisel in *(Nonformal)*, contravene, disobey, encroach, entrench, impose, intrude, invade, lift, meddle, presume, steal, transgress, trespass, usurp, violate *Antonyms:* conform, heed, obey

infringement *n.* contravention, encroachment, imposition, infraction, invasion, noncompliance, nonconformance, nonobservance, transgression, trespass, violation

infuriate *v.* aggravate, agitate, anger, annoy, bother, enrage, exasperate, frustrate, incense, irritate, madden, pique, provoke, rile, upset, vex *Antonyms:* mollify, pacify, soothe

infuriated *adj.* aggravated, angry, annoyed, enraged, exasperated, frustrated, furious, galled, incensed, irate, mad, provoked, raging, roused, thunderous, thwarted, upset, vexed *Nonformal:* boiling, flaming, hopping, hot, jumping *Antonyms:* calm, gratified, pleased

infuse *v.* **1.** brainwash, drill, implant, inculcate, indoctrinate, inoculate, instill, instruct, introduce, leaven, osmose, permeate, saturate, teach **2.** animate, arouse, charge, inspire, invigorate, motivate, move *Antonyms:* bore, chagrin **3.** baptize, bathe, dip, drown, plunge, steep, waterlog

infusion *n.* **1.** brainwashing, education, indoctrination, inoculation, instruction, teaching **2.** brew, concoction, distillation, extract, tea **3.** baptism, bath, drenching, saturation, soaker *(Nonformal)*

ingenious *adj.* **1.** able, adaptive, artistic, bright, brilliant, canny, clever, crafty, creative, cunning, Daedalian, fertile, gifted, imaginative, innovative, intelligent, inventive, original, resourceful, shrewd *Antonyms:* artless, unimaginative, unoriginal **2.** adroit, deft, dexterous, masterly, skilful *Commonly misused:* **ingenuous**

ingenuity *n.* **1.** canniness, cleverness, cunning, shrewdness, slyness, subtleness, wittiness **2.** adeptness, creativity, dexterity, faculty, genius, imagination, inspiration, inventiveness, originality, proficiency, readiness, resourcefulness, skill, talent **3.** creation, design, device, feat, invention, product

ingenuous *adj.* **1.** artless, childlike, guileless, innocent, naive, plain, simple, trustful, trusting, unschooled, unsophisticated, unstudied *Nonformal:* green, square, wet behind the ears *Antonyms:* artful, sophisticated, worldly **2.** candid, frank, honest, natural, open, outspoken, sincere, straightforward, undisguised, unreserved, up-front *Antonyms:* crafty, devious, insincere, sly *Commonly misused:* **ingenious**

ingest *v.* absorb, consume, devour, gulp, imbibe, swallow, take *or* tuck in *Nonformal:* down, inhale, put away, scarf, wolf *Antonyms:* disgorge, void, vomit

inglorious *adj.* **1.** contemptible, disgraceful, dishonourable, disreputable, ignominious, odious, shameful, unbecoming, unseemly *Antonyms:* graceful, honourable, respected **2.** anonymous, forgotten, humble, modest, nameless, obscure, unknown, unsung, untouted *Antonyms:* famous, illustrious, renowned

ingrained *adj.* **1.** built-in, chronic, confirmed, congenital, constitutional, deep-rooted, deep-seated, fixed, fundamental, hereditary, inborn, inbred, indelible, inherent, innate, inveterate, permanent, rooted, thorough **2.** dyed, implanted, impressed, infused, injected, instilled

ingratiate *v.* attract, blandish, cajole, captivate, charm, crawl, fawn, flatter, grovel, kowtow, toady, truckle, wheedle *Nonformal:* apple-polish, bootlick, brownnose, shmooze

ingratiating *adj.* attractive, charming, deferential, disarming, fawning, flattering, obsequious, saccharine, servile, silky, smarmy *(Nonformal)*, sycophantic, toadying, unctuous

ingratitude *n.* lack of appreciation *or* thanks, neglect, omission, thanklessness, ungratefulness *Antonyms:* graciousness, recognition, thanks

ingredient *n.* additive, byte, component, constituent, element, factor, fixing, fundamental, integral, part, piece, property, unit, variable

ingress *n.* **1.** aperture, approach, archway, avenue, boulevard, course, drive, entrance, entryway, expressway, gap, gateway, hallway, inlet, lane, mouth, opening, pass, path, road, route, street, threshold, way **2.** access, admission, admittance, entrée, passage

inhabit *v.* abide, berth, bunk, dwell, homestead, live, locate, lodge, move in *or* into, occupy, people, populate, possess, reside, settle, sojourn, squat, stay, tenant *Nonformal:* doss down, nest, perch, roost

inhabitant *n.* aborigine, addressee, citizen, colonist, denizen, dweller, habitant, indigene, lessee, local, native, occupant, renter, resident, roomer, squatter, tenant

inhabited *adj.* colonized, developed, lived in, occupied, peopled, populated, settled *Antonyms:* abandoned, barren, deserted, lonely, pristine, vacant

inhale *v.* breathe, drag, draw in, gasp, inspire, insufflate, puff, pull, respire, smell, sniff, snort *(Nonformal)*, suck in *Antonyms:* exhale, expire

inharmonious *adj.* **1.** cacophonous, clashing, discordant, dissonant, grating, harsh, incompatible, inconsonant, jarring, off key, raucous, strident, tuneless *Antonyms:* harmonic, melodic, sweet, tuneful **2.** antagonistic, colliding, conflicting, contradictory, contrary, differing, disagreeable, discrepant, divergent, feuding, opposed, variant *Antonyms:* agreeable, compatible, united

inherent *adj.* **1.** built-in, congenital, deep-rooted, deep-seated, fixed, hereditary, inalienable, inborn, inbred, indigenous, ingrained, inherited, innate, internal, inward, latent, natal, native, natural, original *Antonyms:* alien, extraneous, imposed **2.** basic, characteristic, constitutional, distinctive, elementary, essential, fundamental, implicit, indispensable, integrated, intrinsic

inherit *v.* **1.** come into, fall heir to, gain, get, obtain, receive **2.** accede, assume, fall into *(Nonformal)*, succeed, take over **3.** acquire, adopt, derive, incorporate, take on

inheritance *n.* **1.** bequest, birthright, gain, gift, heritage, legacy, patrimony, primogeniture, right **2.** estate, fortune, heirloom, land, portion, possessions, share, windfall **3.** aftermath, fallout, historical baggage, history, legacy, past

inhibit *v.* **1.** arrest, avert, bar, bit, check, constrain, cramp, curb, discourage, frustrate, hinder, hold back *or* down, impede, obstruct, repress, restrain, sandbag, stop, stymie, suppress, ward off, withhold *Nonformal:* hog-tie, phase *Antonyms:* abet, encourage, further, support **2.** enjoin, forbid, outlaw, prevent, prohibit, restrict, taboo *Antonyms:* allow, legitimatize, permit

inhibited *adj.* cold, constrained, frigid, frustrated, guarded, repressed, reserved, reticent, self-conscious, shy, subdued, undemonstrative, unresponsive, withdrawn *Nonformal:* anal-retentive, uptight *Antonyms:* free, outgoing, relaxed, spontaneous

inhibition *n.* **1.** bar, barrier, blockage, check, embargo, hindrance, hobble, interference, obstacle, prevention, prohibition, restraint, restriction, shackle **2.** embarrassment, reserve, reticence, self-consciousness, shyness, sublimation, suppression

inhospitable *adj.* **1.** brusque, cold, cool, hostile, inimical, rude, short, sour, uncongenial, unfavourable, unfriendly, unkind, unreceptive, unsociable *Antonyms:* amicable, generous, genial, gracious, sociable **2.** austere, barren, bleak, comfortless, frozen, harsh, Spartan, uncompromising, unforgiving

inhuman *adj.* animal, bestial, cold-blooded, cruel, fell, feral, ferocious, mean, merciless, monstrous, pitiless, rapacious, ruthless, sadistic, savage, wild *Antonyms:* compassionate, feeling, humane, sympathetic

inhumanity *n.* **1.** barbarism, brutalism, malevolence, ruthlessness, savagery, viciousness *Antonyms:* kindness, mercy, sympathy **2.** atrocity, crime against humanity, ethnic cleansing, outrage

inimical *adj.* **1.** adverse, antagonistic, antipathetic, contrary, disaffected, hostile, ill, ill-disposed, opposite, pernicious, repugnant, unfavourable, vitriolic *Antonyms:* amicable, congenial, favourable, friendly **2.** dangerous, destructive, harmful, hurtful, injurious, noxious, unfriendly

inimitable *adj.* incomparable, matchless, nonpareil, peerless, perfect, one of a kind, suis generis, supreme, unequalled, unique, unparalleled, unrivaled

iniquity *n.* **1.** abomination, baseness, evil, heinousness, hideousness, immorality, infamy, villainy, wickedness **2.** crime, foul deed, injustice, misdeed, offence, sin, transgression, violation, violation of justice, wrong, wrongdoing *Commonly misused:* **inequity**

initial *adj.* antecedent, basic, beginning, commencing, earliest, early, elementary, embryonic, first, foremost, headmost, inaugural, incipient, infant, introductory, leading, nascent, opening, original, pioneer, primary, seminal *Antonyms:* closing, concluding, ending, final, last – *n.* identification, mark, monogram, sign, signature, symbol

Nonformal: John Hancock, X – *v.* approve, endorse, enter, inscribe, mark, sign, undersign, verify, witness

initiate *n.* acolyte, apprentice, beginner, convert, neophyte, newcomer, novice, novitiate, starter, tyro *Nonformal:* greenhorn, new guy, rookie – *v.* **1.** begin, commence, inaugurate, install, institute, introduce, launch, originate, pioneer, set up, start, trigger, usher in *Nonformal:* cook *or* dream up, kickoff **2.** brief, coach, edify, enlighten, familiarize, indoctrinate, inform, instruct, introduce, teach, train **3.** accept, admit, induct, receive *Commonly misused:* **instigate**

initiation *n.* **1.** admission, enrollment, entrance, inception, induction, installation, passage, rite of passage **2.** ceremony, delivery, doctrine, formality, investiture, program, ritual **3.** beginning, commencement, debut, foreword, inauguration, introduction, launch, preface, preliminaries, start

initiative *n.* **1.** ambition, drive, dynamism, eagerness, energy, enterprise, enthusiasm, inventiveness, leadership, mettle, originality, punch, push, resourcefulness, spunk, vigour *Nonformal:* get-up-and-go, gumption, moxie **2.** action, beginning, commencement, entering, first step, lead, push, spearhead, start, thrust, wedge

inject *v.* **1.** imbue, immunize, implant, impregnate, include, infuse, inoculate, insert, instill, introduce, put in, vaccinate *Nonformal:* mainline, shoot up **2.** add, butt *or* horn in *(Nonformal)*, contribute, interject, interrupt

injection *n.* **1.** booster, needle, shot *Nonformal:* dose, hypo, fix, jab *Kinds of injection:* enema, hypodermic, inoculation, intracardiac, intradermal, intramuscular, intraspinal, intrathecal, intravenous, percutaneous, vaccination, vaccine *Methods of injection:* cutaneous, subcutaneous **2.** addition, infusion, insertion, insinuation, intrusion

injudicious *adj.* foolhardy, foolish, hasty, heedless, ill-advised, impolitic, imprudent, incautious, indiscreet, inexpedient, rash, silly, thoughtless, unwise *Antonyms:* cautious, considerate, polite, prudent, wise

injunction *n.* **1.** admonition, behest, bidding, charge, command, commandment, court *or* restraining order, decree, demand, dictate, dictum, direction, embargo, exhortation, *fatwa (Islamic)*, instruction, mandate, order, precept, ruling, warning, word, writ **2.** banning, curbing, disallowing, prohibition, stifling, stopping

injure *v.* **1.** blight, break, contort, cripple, damage, deface, deform, destroy, disable, disfigure, distort, foul, harm, hurt, impair, mangle, mar, ruin, spoil, tarnish, undermine, weaken, wound *Nonformal:* bang *or* bung *or* rough up *Antonyms:* heal, remedy, repair **2.** abuse, affront, blacken, distress, grieve, insult, maltreat, mistreat, offend, oppress, pain, persecute, pique, torment, wrong

injurious *adj.* **1.** adverse, bad, corrupting, damaging, dangerous, deadly, deleterious, destructive, detrimental, disadvantageous, evil, harmful, hurtful, nocuous, noxious, pernicious, poisonous, ruinous, unhealthy, vitriolic *Antonyms:* healing, helpful, palliative **2.** abusive, defamatory, iniquitous, insulting, libelous, mischievous, offensive, prejudicial, seditious, slanderous, undermining, unjust, wrongful *Antonyms:* encouraging, promotional

injury *n.* **1.** affliction, agony, damage, detriment, discomfiture, distress, grievance, harm, hurt, ill, impairment, loss, misery, ruin, sore, suffering **2.** abrasion, bite, break, bruise, burn, cramp, cut, fracture, gash, laceration, lesion, mutilation, scar, scratch, shock, sprain, swelling, trauma, welt **3.** abuse, affront, evil, indignity, injustice, insult, libel, mischief, outrage, slander, tort, wrong

injustice *n.* **1.** abuse, betrayal, bias, discrimination, grievance, inequality, inequity, iniquity, malfeasance, maltreatment, miscarriage of justice, negligence, oppression, outrage, partiality, prejudice, treachery, unfairness, underhandedness, unlawfulness, villainy *Nonformal:* dirty dealings, dirty pool, low blow, sellout *Antonyms:* equality, fairness, impartiality, rectitude **2.** breach, crime, damage, encroachment, foul play, infraction, infringement, malpractice, offence, transgression, trespass, violation, wrong, wrongdoing

inkling *n.* **1.** glimmering, hint, indication, intimation, soupçon, suggestion, suspicion, whisper **2.** clue, conception, idea, notion

inky *adj.* **1.** black, ebon, ebony, jet, pitch black, pithy, raven, sable **2.** begrimed, blackened, fuliginous, ink-stained, smoky, smudged, sooty

inlaid *adj.* checkered, enameled, laid, lined, mosaic, ornamented, studded, tiled, veneered, worked

inland *adj.* **1.** domestic, internal, interior, Maritime, national, provincial **2.** backwoods, inshore, upcountry, upriver – *n.* back forty *(Nonformal)*, backcountry, bush, highcountry, hinterland, scrub, woods

inlet *n.* **1.** angle *(Newfoundland)*, armlet, basin, bay, bayou, bight, cove, creek, delta, estuary, firth, fjord, gulf, harbour, narrows, reach, saltchuck *(Pacific coast)*, sea, slough, sound, strait, stream **2.** canal, channel, culvert, entrance, mouth, opening, passage

inn *n.* accommodation, *auberge (French)*, bed and breakfast *or* B & B, boarding house, coaching house, flophouse *(Nonformal)*, hospice, hostel, hostelry, hotel, house, *kahn (Persian)*, lodge, motel, motor hotel *or* inn *or* lodge, pension, public house, resort, roadhouse, saloon *(Historical)*, stopping house, sojourn, tavern, youth hostel

innate *adj.* **1.** congenital, deep-seated, hereditary, inborn, inbred, indigenous, ingrained, inherent, inherited, instinctive, intrinsic, native, natural, normal *Antonyms:* accidental, affected, incidental, learned, nurtured **2.** basic, constitutional, elemental, essential, fundamental, primary, rudimentary **3.** automatic, direct, immediate, intuitive, knee jerk, reflex, reflexive, unconscious

inner *adj.* **1.** central, inside, interior, intestinal, inward, middle, nuclear *Antonyms:* exterior, external, outer **2.** domestic, inland, inshore, internal, local, national, provincial **3.** emotional, introspective, mental, sentimental, spiritual, subjective, visceral **4.** cryptic, esoteric, hidden, intimate, obscure, personal, private, privileged, secret *Antonyms:* clear, exposed, obvious, visible

innkeeper *n.* host, hostess, hotelier, hotelkeeper, inn-holder, innkeep, keeper, landlord, landlady, mine host *(Nonformal)*, proprietor, publican

innocence *n.* **1.** freshness, ignorance, inexperience, naiveté, purity, simplicity, unawareness, unfamiliarity, virginity *Antonyms:* cunning, guile, wiliness, worldliness **2.** blamelessness, clear conscience, guiltlessness, impeccability, righteousness, sinlessness, uprightness *Antonyms:* corruption, guilt, impurity **3.** benignity, harmlessness, innocuousness, inoffensiveness

innocent *adj.* **1.** chaste, fresh, good, honest, immaculate, pristine, pure, righteous, sinless, upright, untainted, virtuous, wide-eyed *Nonformal:* lily-white, pure as the driven snow *Antonyms:* immoral, sinful, wicked **2.** above suspicion, blameless, clean, clear, crimeless, exemplary, faultless, guilt-free, guiltless, irreproachable, spotless, unblemished, upstanding *Antonyms:* criminal, culpable, guilty **3.** benign, harmless, innocuous, inoffensive, mild, unoffending *Antonyms:* dangerous, lethal, mortal, noxious **4.** artless, childlike, credulous, guileless, gullible, ingenuous, naive, simple, slow, unsophisticated, well-intentioned, wide-eyed *Nonformal:* green, wet behind the ears *Antonyms:* Machiavellian, sophistic, sophisticated, worldly **5.** accepted, approved, lawful, legal, legitimate *Antonyms:* contraband, illicit, proscribed **6.** bereft, lacking, short, shy, wanting – *n.* angel, babe, baby, child, dove, infant, ingénue, neonate, simpleton, soul

innocuous *adj.* **1.** harmless, nonpoisonous, non-threatening, painless, safe *Antonyms:* dangerous, lethal, toxic **2.** benign, bland, flat, innocent, inoffensive, insipid, mild, unoffending *Antonyms:* obnoxious, offensive, upsetting

innovation *n.* **1.** concoction, contrivance, creation, device, fabrication, gimmick, invention, novelty *Nonformal:* contraption, gadget, gizmo, newest wrinkle, snake oil, thingamajig, thingamabob **2.** advance, alteration, breakout, change, departure, deviation, modification, revision, upgrade **3.** bridge forward, divergence, imaginative *or* technological leap, progression, stepping stone

innovate *v.* **1.** author, compose, concoct, construct, craft, create, design, draft, initiate, invent, originate, parent, produce, spawn **2.** alter, change, leap *or* vault forward, modernize, modify, move *or* step ahead, recast, redirect, revamp, revolutionize, transform, update, upgrade **3.** advance, climb, proceed, progress, strive

innuendo *n.* **1.** allusion, aside, hint, intimation, obliquity, overtone, reference, suggestion, whisper **2.** aspersion, calumny, defamation, implication, insinuation, slander, slur

innumerable *adj.* beyond measure, countless, fathomless, incalculable, indeterminate, infinite, many, multitudinous, myriad, no end to, numberless, numerous, plumbless, uncountable, unnumbered, untold *Nonformal:* bazillion, way too many *Antonyms:* calculable, computable, finite, limited, numbered

inoculate *v.* **1.** immunize, inject, protect, vaccinate **2.** brainwash, implant, impregnate, indoctrinate, infuse, inject, instill

inoffensive *adj.* **1.** friendly, harmless, humble, innocent, innocuous, middle-of-the-road, mild, neutral, peaceable, pleasant, quiet, retiring, safe, unobjectionable *Nonformal:* vanilla, white bread *Antonyms:* abrasive, dangerous, destructive, irritating, malicious, provocative, threatening

inoperative *adj.* **1.** broken, defective, destroyed, frozen, not working, out-of-order, ruined, seized, stalled, unserviceable, wrecked *Nonformal:* busted, froze up, kaput, moth-balled, on-the-fritz **2.** ineffective, ineffectual, nugatory, unproductive, useless, worthless *Antonyms:* efficient, productive, useful

inopportune *adj.* **1.** ill-timed, inconvenient, mistimed, unseasonable, untimely *Antonyms:* convenient, timely **2.** disadvantageous, ill-chosen, inappropriate, inauspicious, malapropos, unfavourable, unfortunate, unlucky, unpropitious, unsuitable *Antonyms:* appropriate, auspicious, favourable

inordinate *adj.* **1.** disproportionate, dizzying *(Nonformal)*, excessive, exorbitant, extortionate, extravagant, extreme, gratuitous, immoderate, outrageous, superfluous, towering, unconscionable, undue, unmeasurable, unwarranted *Antonyms:* acceptable, moderate, reasonable **2.** intemperate, irrational, overindulgent, uncurbed, unrestrained, wanton *Antonyms:* controlled, regulated, temperate **3.** chaotic, disorderly, eccentric, erratic, irregular, orderless, unconventional

input *n.* **1.** code, data, file, information, language, material, programs, supply **2.** contribution, idea, notion, offering, say, two cents worth *(Nonformal)*, word – *v.* code, download, enter, feed, key *or* type in, load, process, save, store

inquest *n.* **1.** audit, discussion, examination, exploration, inquiry, inquisition, inspection, investigation, probe, questioning **2.** board, body, committee, jury, panel

inquietude *n.* agitation, anxiety, apprehension, concern, disquiet, distress, dread, fear, heebie-jeebies *(Nonformal)*, nervousness, restlessness, solicitude, trepidation, uneasiness, worry *Antonyms:* aplomb, balance, composure, peace

inquire *v.* **1.** ask, catechize, cross-examine, grill *(Nonformal)*, interrogate, pry, query, question, quiz, request information, solicit **2.** analyze, examine, explore, forage, inspect, investigate, look into, probe, prospect, scrutinize, search, seek, sift, study, unearth *Nonformal:* feel at *or* out, nose *or* poke around, sift about

inquiring *adj.* analytical, curious, delving, doubtful, examining, heuristic, inquisitive, interested, interrogative, investigative, outward-looking, probing, prying, questioning, quizzical, searching, Socratic, speculative, studious, suspicious, wondering

inquiry *n.* **1.** analysis, audit, check, cross-examination, examination, exploration, hearing, inquest, inquisition, interrogation, investigation, poll, probe, pursuit, quest, research, scrutiny, search, study, survey, trial *Nonformal:* feeler, fishing expedition, grilling, third degree **2.** poser, query, question, quiz, request, stumper *(Nonformal)*

inquisition *n.* grilling, inquest, inquiry, interrogation, investigation, kangaroo court, questioning, Star Chamber *(Historical)*, tribunal, witch hunt *(Nonformal)*

inquisitive *adj.* **1.** analytical, challenging, curious, eager, interested, investigative, probing, questioning, scrutinizing, searching, sifting, speculative *Antonyms:* indifferent, unconcerned, uninterested **2.** forward, intrusive, meddlesome, meddling, nosy, prying, snooping *Nonformal:* rubbernecked, snoopy

inroad *n.* **1.** attack, encroachment, foray, impingement, incursion, intrusion, invasion, launch, offensive, onslaught, raid, spearhead, transgression, trespass, violation **2.** advance, bound, leap, progress, stride

insane *adj.* **1.** crazed, crazy, delusional, demented, deranged, irrational, lunatic, mad, maniacal, paranoid, psychotic, rabid, raging, raving, unbalanced, unhinged, unsettled, unsound *Nonformal:* balmy, barmy, bats, batty, bonkers, certifiable, cracked, crackers, cuckoo, daffy, dotty, flipped, freaked-out, goofy, haywire, loco, loony, loopy, mad as a hatter, not all there, nuts, nutty, psycho, round the bend, screwy, stark-raving mad, unglued *Antonyms:* healthy, logical, lucid, rational, sound **2.** bizarre, eccentric, foolish, frenzied, harebrained, idiotic, preposterous, senseless, witless *Antonyms:* practical, reasonable, sensible **3.** dangerous, dreadful, frightening, menacing, ominous, scary, sinister, terrifying, threatening, upsetting, wild *Antonyms:* benign, innocuous, safe

insanitary *adj.* contaminated, dirty, disease-ridden, feculent, filthy, germ-infested, impure, infected, infested, noxious, polluted, spoiled, sullied, threatening, turgid, unclean, unhealthy, unhygenic, vermin-ridden, vitiated *Antonyms:* clean, sterile, uncontaminated

insanity *n.* **1.** aberration, craziness, daftness, delirium, delusion, dementia, derangement, frenzy, hallucination, hysteria, lunacy, madness, mania, mental illness, phobia, possession *Technical terms for insanity:* character disorder, delusional, emotional disorder, maladjustment, manic-depressive psychosis, mental disorder, mental illness, neurosis, paranoia, personality disorder, psychoneurosis, psychopathy, psychosis, schizophrenia *Antonyms:* logic, lucidity, mental health, rationality, reason **2.** absurdity, folly, foolishness, irrationality, senselessness, silliness, stupidity *Antonyms:* practicality, pragmatism, sense

insatiable *adj.* gluttonous, greedy, hungry, inappeasable, intemperate, quenchless, rapacious, ravenous, unrelenting, voracious *Antonyms:* limited, quenchable, temperate

inscribe *v.* **1.** carve, cut, engrave, engross, etch, impress, imprint, list, mark, print, record, scribe, write **2.** catalogue, enlist, enrol, enter, record, register, subscribe **3.** ascribe, autograph, dedicate, name, sign

inscription *n.* **1.** calligraphy, penmanship, penwork, script, writing *Nonformal:* fist, hand **2.** engraving, epigraph, epitaph, memorial, memento **3.** autograph, dedication, entry, message, notation, quotation, saying

inscrutable *adj.* abstruse, ambiguous, arcane, cabalistic, cryptic, difficult, enigmatic, esoteric, hidden, impenetrable, incomprehensible, inexplicable, mysterious, mystic, obscure, occult, secret, sphinx-like, unaccountable, unexplainable, unfathomable, unintelligible, unknowable, unreadable *Antonyms:* clear, evident, lucid, understandable

insect *n.* **1.** arthropod, bug, creepy-crawly *(Nonformal) Groupings of insects:* lepidoptera, winged, wingless *Immature insects:* caterpillar, larva, nymph, pupa *Common insects:* alderfly, ant, aphid, arachnid, bedbug, bee, beetle, black fly, blowfly, bluebottle, body louse, boll weevil, booklouse, bristletail, butterfly, caddis fly, carpet beetle, centipede, chafer, chigger, cicada, cockroach, cricket, damsel fly, darning needle, deer fly, dobson fly, dragonfly, earwig, firefly, flea, fly, grasshopper, gypsy moth, horsefly, housefly, June bug, katydid, lacewing, ladybug, leafhopper, locust, louse, louse fly, maggot, mantid, maple borer, May fly, mite, moosefly, mosquito, moth, mud dauber, plant louse, potato bug, praying mantis, sawfly, scale insect, scorpion, sheep tick, silverfish, snakefly, spider, springtail, stonefly, stink bug, sucking louse, termite, thrips, tick, tsetse fly, walking stick, wasp, water bug, weevil, wood tick **2.** annoyance, bother, irritation, nuisance *Nonformal:* creep, louse, pain-in-the-butt

insecure *adj.* **1.** afraid, anxious, apprehensive, choked, diffident, fearful, hesitant, jumpy, questioning, shaky, touchy, troubled, uncertain, unconfident, unpoised, unsure, uptight *(Nonformal)*, worried *Antonyms:* assured, certain, confident, decisive **2.** dangerous, exposed, hazardous, jeopardous, perilous, susceptible, unguarded, unprotected, unsafe, vulnerable **3.** brittle, crumbly, flimsy, fragile, jerrybuilt, jury-rigged, rickety, shaky, unstable *Antonyms:* firm, solid, sound

insecurity *n.* **1.** danger, dodginess, dubiousness, exposure, frailty, imperilment, hazard, jeopardy, peril, precariousness, risk, susceptibility, vulnerability, weakness *Antonyms:* safety, security, strength **2.** anxiety, concern, doubt, fear, leeriness, misgiving, reservation, self-consciousness, shyness, timidity, uncertainty, wariness, worry *Antonyms:* assurance, certainty, confidence

insensible *adj.* **1.** anesthetized, catatonic, comatose, deadened, frozen, hypothermic, insensate, numb, out *(Nonformal)*, senseless, torpid, unconscious *Antonyms:* aware, cognizant, conscious **2.** apathetic, callous, cold-hearted, detached, hard, impassive, impervious, indifferent, indurate, insensitive, thick-skinned, tough, unfeeling *Antonyms:* feeling, humane, sympathetic **3.** gradual, imperceptible, inappreciable, slight, unrecognizable, vague *Antonyms:* obvious, palpable, salient **4.** blind, blinkered, ignorant, incognizant, unaware *Antonyms:* circumspect, heedful, wary **5.** absurd, brainless, dumb, foolish, illogical, irrational, senseless, stupid

insensitive *adj.* **1.** brutish, callous, cruel emotionless, hard-hearted, merciless, uncompassionate, unemotional, unkind, unmovable, unsympathetic *Antonyms:* benevolent, feeling, humane **2.** cold, deadened, frozen, inanimate, insensible, numb, sensationless, stiff, unfeeling, unresponsive *Antonyms:* awake, aware, sensitive **3.** immune, impervious, insusceptible, nonallergic, nonreactive

inseparable *adj.* attached, conjoined, connected, entwined, inalienable, indivisible, integral, integrated, intertwined, interwoven, joined at the hip *(Nonformal)*, married, secure, tied up, unified, united, whole

insert *n.* addition, entry, inclusion, insertion, intrusion *Kinds of insert:* ad, advertisement, amendment, clause, codicil, copy, flyer, handout, illustration, introduction key, pamphlet, subscription card, supplement – *v.* add, admit, cut and paste, drag *or* drop in, embed, enter, infuse, inject, inlay instill, intrude, place, put in, set, shoehorn *(Nonformal)*, work in *Antonyms:* blue-pencil, delete, remove

inside *adj.* **1.** central, inner, interior, inward, middle *Antonyms:* exterior, external peripheral **2.** classified, closet, confidential, esoteric, exclusive, internal, limited, private, restricted, secret *Nonformal:* hush-hush, imprisoned *Antonyms:* communal, public – *adv.* **1.** in-house, indoors, within **2.** basically, centrally, deeply, internally, intrinsically, inwardly *Antonyms:* externally, superficially

insides *n.* **1.** bowels, contents, filling, giblets, guts, entrails, innards, intestines, lining, organs, stomach, stuffing *(Nonformal)*, viscera **2.** bosom, breast, core, essence, heart, heartstrings, inner being, soul, spirit **3.** centre, interior, middle, recesses **4.** chips, circuits, components, constituents, dynamo, engine, ingredients, markings, mechanism, parts, pieces, workings

insidious *adj.* **1.** artful, crafty, cunning, deceitful, deceptive, Machiavellian, masterful, perfidious, shifty, sinister, sly, smooth, sneaky, stealthy, treacherous, subtle, underhanded, wily *Antonyms:* forthright, honest, open, sincere **2.** gradual, imperceptible, progressive, slight, slow and painful *Commonly misused:* **invidious**

insight *n.* acumen, appreciation, astuteness, awareness, clairvoyance, comprehension, discernment, divination, foresight, intuition, judgment, keenness, observation, penetration, perception, perspicacity, sagacity, shrewdness, sixth sense, understanding, vision, wisdom *Antonyms:* blindness, obtuseness

insightful *adj.* acute, astute, aware, clairvoyant, discerning, farsighted, incisive, intelligent, intuitive, keen, knowing, observant, penetrating, perceptive, sage, keen, shrewd, visionary, wise *Antonyms:* dull, senseless, unobservant

insignia *n.* badge, brassard, crest, decoration, emblem, hallmark, logo *(Nonformal)*, mark, regalia, sign, symbol, trademark *Kinds of ecclesiastical insignia:* cardinal's hat, crook, crosier, cross, keys, mitre, papal tiara, pastoral staff, ring, triple crown *Kinds of military insignia:* bar, chevron, eagle, epaulet, hash mark *(Nonformal)*, patch, pip, service stripe, shoulder patch, star, stripe *Kinds of royal insignia:* coronet, crown, diadem, ermine, feathers, great *or* privy seal, heraldic pall, orb, regalia, robe of state, rod, sceptre, seal, signet, tiara

insignificance *n.* **1.** inconsequence, irrelevance, meaninglessness, naught, negligibility, nothing, paltriness, triviality, unimportance, worthlessness *Antonyms:* consequence, importance, relevance **2.** littleness, meagreness, pettiness, puniness, smallness, slightness, tininess, trifle *Antonyms:* bigness, hugeness, largeness **3.** bagatelle, bauble, cipher, trifle, zero *Nonformal:* drip, flea, pushover, small potatoes

insignificant *adj.* **1.** immaterial, irrelevant, lesser, meaningless, minor, negligible, nondescript, nonessential, pointless, secondary, senseless, trifling, trivial, unimportant, worthless *Nonformal:* bush *or* minor league, Mickey-Mouse, penny ante, pissant *Antonyms:* consequential, essential, main, primary, vital **2.** inappreciable, light, lightweight, little, meagre, minimal, minuscule, paltry, petty, puny, scanty, small, small-fry *(Nonformal)*, small-time, unsubstantial, worthless *Antonyms:* considerable, large, sizable **3.** forgotten, inglorious, undignified, undistinguished, unknown, unrenowned, unstable, unsung *Antonyms:* esteemed, popular, timeless

insincere *adj.* counterfeit, deceitful, deceptive, devious, dishonest, disingenuous, dissembling, double-dealing, duplicitous, fake, false, feigning, hypocritical, mendacious, perfidious, shifty, unfaithful, untruthful *Nonformal:* phoney, two-faced *Antonyms:* direct, earnest, genuine, honest, truthful

insinuate *v.* **1.** allude, ascribe, connote, hint, imply, impute, indicate, intimate, mention, purport, refer, signify, suggest **2.** edge *or* work in, foist, infiltrate, infuse, inject, insert, instill, interject, introduce *Nonformal:* parachute, shoehorn

insinuation *n.* **1.** accusation, aspersion, clue, hint, implication, innuendo, intimidation, slur, suggestion **2.** entrance, infiltration, infusion, instillation, interjection, introduction, intrusion, placement

insipid *adj.* **1.** anemic, banal, characterless, colourless, drab, dull, feeble, flat, innocuous, jejune, lifeless, limp, mild, prosaic, spiritless, tedious, trite, vapid, watered-down, watery, weak, wishy-washy *(Nonformal) Antonyms:* engaging, exciting, lively, spirited, stimulating **2.** bland, flavourless, stale, tasteless, unappetizing, unpalatable, unsavoury, *Antonyms:* appetizing, piquant, pungent

insist *v.* **1.** advocate, ask, badger, beg, catechize, demand, entreat, exhort, expect, impel, implore, importune, order, press, request, require, urge **2.** affirm, assert, aver, claim, contend, hold, maintain, uphold **3.** dwell on, emphasize, harp, persist, remain, repeat, stress, underline, underscore

insistent *adj.* **1.** assiduous, bull-dogged *(Nonformal)*, commanding, demanding, diligent, dogged, exacting, forceful, mulish, obstinate, persevering, persistent, steadfast, stubborn, tenacious, unrelenting, unyielding **2.** compelling, critical, crucial, imperative, pressing, urgent

insobriety *n.* alcoholism, drunkenness, inebriation, intemperance, intoxication, sottedness

insolence *n.* **1.** arrogance, boldness, disrespectfulness, effrontery, impertinence, impudence, insubordination, rudeness, sass, sauce, sauciness *Nonformal:* backtalk, cheek, guff, jaw, lip, mouth *Antonyms:* civility, courtesy, deference, respect **2.** derision, insult, invective, jeer, slight, slur, taunt *Nonformal:* cheap shot, low blow, poke

insolent *adj.* brazen, contemptuous, disrespectful, impertinent, impudent, insubordinate, insulting, overbearing, pert, rude, saucy, supercilious, uncivil *Nonformal:* in your face, smart-aleky *Antonyms:* civil, courteous, deferential, respectful, submissive

insoluble *adj.* **1.** cryptic, impenetrable, indecipherable, inexplicable, mysterious, mystifying, obscure, unaccountable, unexplainable, unfathomable *Antonyms:* clear-cut, penetrable, solvable **2.** baffling, confounding, difficult, hard, mind-boggling, puzzling, taxing, unresolvable, unsolvable **3.** frozen, indissolvable, rock-hard, solid

insolvent *adj.* bankrupt, defaulting, failed, foundering, penniless, poverty-stricken, ruined, sunken, suspended, wiped out, wrecked *Nonformal:* belly up, broke, bust *Antonyms:* lucrative, profitable, successful

insomnia *n.* restlessness, sleep disorder, sleeplessness, tossing and turning, wakefulness

insouciance *n.* blitheness, breeziness, buoyancy, caprice, carefreeness, carelessness, casualness, indifference, laxity, lightness, nonchalance, oblivion, unconcern, whimsy *Antonyms:* care, concern, worry

insouciant *adj.* airy, breezy, bubbly, buoyant, capricious, carefree, careless, casual, easygoing, flighty, gay, gleeful, happy-go-lucky, heedless, jaunty, lackadaisical, lighthearted, nonchalant, sunny, unconcerned, untroubled, unworried *Antonyms:* anxious, harried, vexed

inspect *v.* check, comb through, examine, eyeball *(Nonformal)*, investigate, observe, peruse, reconnoitre, scan, scrutinize, search, study, survey, view

inspection *n.* audit, check, checkup, examination, inquest, probe, review, scan, scrutiny, search, surveillance, survey, testing *Nonformal:* look-see, once-over

inspector *n.* **1.** assessor, censor, checker, critic, detective, evaluator, examiner, investigator, ombudsperson, overseer, scrutineer, scrutinizer, superintendent, supervisor **2.** constable, officer, police officer, private investigator *or* P.I. *Nonformal:* badge, cop, dick, flatfoot, gumshoe, sleuth

inspiration *n.* **1.** breath, energy, enthusiasm, force, purpose, reason, spirit, vigour **2.** encouragement, guiding light, influence, motivation, muse, stimulus **3.** art, artistic *or* creative *or* poetic impulse, genius, idea, insight, notion, thought **4.** arousal, awakening, enlightenment, *moksha (Hindu)*, revelation

inspire *v.* **1.** affect, animate, arouse, awaken, enliven, enrapture, exalt, excite, exhilarate, galvanize, hearten, ignite, imbue, inflame, invigorate, spark, spur, stimulate, stir, strike, touch *Antonyms:* depress, discourage, dispirit **2.** boost, carry, direct, encourage, guide, impress, influence, inform, infuse, instill, move, persuade, sway **3.** bring about, cause, effect, generate **4.** breathe, draw air, inhale, pull, suck

inspired *adj.* **1.** animated, aroused, awakened, bestirred, exhilarated, heartened, inspirited, possessed, soaring, stimulated, stirred, wonderstruck **2.** brilliant, creative, gifted, heaven-sent, imaginative, one-of-a-kind, original, sterling, talented, unique, wonderful

instability *n.* **1.** disquiet, fitfulness, fluctuation, frailty, imbalance, impermanence, infirmity, inquietude, insecurity, irregularity, precariousness, shakiness, transience, uncertainty, vacillation, variability, volatility, wavering, weakness *Antonyms:* balance, permanence, steadiness, strength **2.** capriciousness, changeability, fickleness, flightiness, immaturity, irresolution, mutability, restlessness, unpredictability, unreliability, unsteadiness *Antonyms:* constancy, dependability, predictability

install *v.* **1.** add, attach, build in, connect, fix, furnish, lay, line, lodge, place, position, set up, station **2.** crown, ensconce, establish, inaugurate, induct, instate, institute, introduce, invest, plant **3.** locate, occupy, perch, rest, roost, sit

installation *n.* **1.** device, equipment, establishment, furnishing, lighting, machinery, power, system, wiring **2.** display, exhibit, opening, showing **3.** accession, coronation, establishment, inauguration, induction, installment, investiture, investment, launching, ordination, placing, positioning **4.** base, camp, CFB, fortification, post, station

installment *n.* **1.** down payment, minimum, percentage, piece, portion, sum **2.** chapter, division, edition, episode, issue, number, serial, supplement **3.** device, facility, installation, structure, system

instance *n.* detail, element, example, exemplification, frame, illustration, occasion, occurrence, part, piece, precedent, proceeding, proof, reason, representation, sample, section, situation, specimen, step

instant *adj.* **1.** direct, fast, immediate, instantaneous, prompt, quick, rapid, speedy, swift **2.** burning, consuming, critical, crucial, needed, pressing, urgent, vital – *adv.* at once, directly, forthwith, immediately, instantly, now, promptly, right away, stat, *statim (Latin)*, without delay *Nonformal:* in a snap, on the double **3.** pre-cooked, prepared, processed, ready-made, ready-to-serve – *n.* breath, heartbeat, minute, second, trice, twinkling *Nonformal:* flash, jiff, jiffy, sec, two shakes

instantly *adv.* at once, directly, first off, forthwith, immediately, instantaneously, now, right now, spontaneously, this minute, without delay *Nonformal:* pronto, yesterday

instead *adv.* alternately, alternatively, in lieu, other *or* rather than, preferably

instigate *v.* abet, actuate, encourage, fire, foment, goad, impel, incite, inflame, influence, inspire, kindle, move, needle, persuade, plan, plot, prompt, provoke, raise, rouse, scheme, set on, spur, start, stimulate, stir up, suggest, taunt, torment, urge, whip *or* work up *Nonformal:* make waves, steam up *Antonyms:* discourage, repress, restrain, stop *Commonly misused:* **initiate**

instill *v.* **1.** imbue, impart, implant, impregnate, impress, infuse, inject, inoculate, inseminate, insert, interject, transfer, transfuse **2.** brainwash, inculcate, indoctrinate, introduce, program, propagandize, teach

instinct *n.* **1.** feeling, hunch, idea, impulse, inclination, intuition, notion, predisposition, proclivity, sense, sentiment, sixth sense, tendency **2.** aptitude, bent, faculty, flair, gift, knack, nose *(Nonformal)*, talent

instinctive *adj.* **1.** congenital, habitual, inherent, innate, intuitive, natural, normal, second-nature, visceral *Antonyms:* acquired, developed, learned **2.** automatic, impulsive, instinctual, involuntary, knee-jerk *(Nonformal)*, mechanical, reflex, spontaneous, unconscious, unprompted, unthinking *Antonyms:* calculated, premeditated, voluntary

institute *n.* **1.** association, body, company, conservatory, convention, corporation, establishment, group, guild, lodge, membership, organization, parish, society **2.** academy, college, gymnasium, laboratory, library, *lycée (French)*, lyceum, research *or* training centre, school, seminary, university **3.** custom, decree, doctrine, dogma, edict, habit, law, maxim, ordinance, practice, precedent, precept, principle, regulation, rule, statute, tenet, tradition – *v.* **1.** begin, commence, inaugurate, induct, initiate, introduce, launch, organize, start **2.** create, establish, found, install, invent, originate, pioneer, set up

institution *n.* **1.** academy, college, foundation, lyceum, school, university **2.** asylum, bedlam, convalescent home, hospice, hospital, institution, *krankenhaus (German)*, lunatic asylum, prison, sanitarium *Nonformal:* funny farm, loony bin, madhouse, nuthouse **3.** convention, custom, habit, practice, principle, system, tradition **4.** business, corporation, establishment, firm, foundation, government, group, house, parliament **5.** fixture, icon, national treasure, paradigm, symbol **6.** building, commencement, creation, development, erection, founding, incorporation, launch

institutional *adj.* **1.** businesslike, bureaucratic, clinical, cold, detached, faceless, formal **2.** accepted, conventional, established, orthodox, practiced **3.** austere, bland, drab, dreary, dull, monotonous, sterile, uniform *Antonyms:* exciting, scrumptious, stimulating

instruct *v.* **1.** catechize, coach, counsel, discipline, drill, edify, educate, guide, lead, pilot, school, teach, train, tutor **2.** command, demand, direct, manage, marshal, order, organize, prescribe, regulate **3.** acquaint, apprise, disclose, enlighten, inform, impart, notify

instruction *n.* **1.** command, demand, direction, directive, injunction, mandate, order, plan, ruling **2.** apprenticeship, coaching, direction, discipline, drilling, edification, education, enlightenment, erudition, grounding, guidance, information, learning, preparation, schooling, teaching, training, tuition, tutelage **3.** decree, dictum, dogma, edict, model, precept, principle, rule, tenet

instructive *adj.* cautionary, didactic, edifying, educational, enlightening, helpful, illuminating, informative, revealing

instructor *n.* advisor, coach, demonstrator, educator, exponent, guide, guru, lecturer, master, mentor, pedagogue, prof *(Nonformal)*, professor, pundit, schoolmaster, sensei, *swami (Hindu)*, teacher, trainer, tutor

instrument *n.* **1.** apparatus, appliance, contraption, contrivance, device, gauge, implement, machinery, mechanism, tackle, tool, utensil *Kinds of musical instrument:* accordion, bagpipes, balalaika, banjo, bass, bassoon, bazouki, bell, bongo, brass, castanet, clarinet, concertina, conga, cello, drum, fiddle, flageolet, flute, French horn, glockenspiel, gong, guitar, hammered dulcimer, harmonica, horn, jaw's *or* jew's harp, jingle *or* sleigh bells, kazoo, kettledrum, keyboards, maracas, melodeon, mouth organ, oboe, ocarina, organ, pedal steel, pennywhistle, piano, piccolo, sampler, saxophone, sitar, synthesizer, tabla, tambourine, theorbo *(Historical)*, triangle, trombone, trumpet, tuba, turn-table, timpani, viola, violin, voice, whistle, xylophone, zanzithophone *Japanese:* koto, samisen *See also:* **guitar, piano** **2.** agency, agent, channel, factor, force, means, mechanism, medium, organ, vehicle **3.** cat's paw, dupe, goon, henchman, lackey, minion, pawn, stooge, toady, underling

instrumental *adj.* **1.** critical, crucial, decisive, effective, essential, key, meaningful, pivotal, relevant **2.** conducive, contributory, efficacious, helpful, important, influential, serviceable, useful, valuable

insubordinate *adj.* contumacious, defiant, disobedient, disorderly, insurgent, intractable, lawless, mutinous, rebellious, recalcitrant, refractory, seditious, subversive, turbulent, uncooperative, undisciplined, uneasy *Antonyms:* compliant, obedient, subservient, tame – *n.* agitator, dissenter, dissident, insurgent, mutineer, nonconformist, protester, punk *(Nonformal)*, rabble-rouser, rebel, resister, revolutionary

insubordination *n.* defiance, disobedience, disorder, dissent, dissidence, insurgence, insurrection, lawlessness, mutiny, rebellion, recalcitrance, resistance, revolt, revolution, riot, sedition, strike, unruliness *Antonyms:* deference, docility, obedience, submission

insubstantial *adj.* **1.** aerial, airy, chimerical, ephemeral, false, fanciful, illusory, imaginary, immaterial, incorporeal, intangible, metaphysical, unreal *Antonyms:* corporeal, real, tangible **2.** flimsy, fragile, slender, slight, thin, weak *Antonyms:* heavy, solid, thick

insufferable *adj.* detestable, distressing, dreadful, excruciating, harrowing, horrible, impossible, intolerable, outrageous, painful, unacceptable, unbearable, unendurable, unenjoyable, unpleasant *Antonyms:* delightful, engaging, entertaining

insufficient *adj.* **1.** bereft, devoid, dry, impoverished, inadequate, lacking, meagre, scanty, scarce, short, skimpy, thin, wanting *Antonyms:* ample, enough, plentiful **2.** deficient, failing, faulty, half-baked *(Nonformal)*, imperfect, incapable, incompetent, incomplete, unfinished, unqualified, unsatisfactory, weak *Antonyms:* adequate, competent, strong

insular *adj.* **1.** hidebound, inward-looking, myopic, narrow-minded, parochial, provincial, small-town *(Nonformal) Antonyms:* cosmopolitan, worldly **2.** cloistered, garrisoned, hermetic, isolated, remote, protected, secluded, separated **3.** circumscribed, encircled, surrounded

insulate *v.* **1.** coat, cushion, line, protect, tape, treat, wrap **2.** cocoon, cotton wool *(Nonformal)*, garrison, isolate, keep apart, quarantine, seclude, segregate, separate, sequester, shield

insulation *n.* baffle, buffer, cushioning, fibreglass, foam, lining, muffler, padding, protection, cold *or* heat *or* sound proofing, stuffing

insult *n.* **1.** abuse, affront, aspersion, blasphemy, despite, indignity, injury, invective, libel, offence, outrage, provocation, shame, slur, snub, travesty, unpleasantry, vexation, vilification, vituperation, wrong *Nonformal:* black eye, brickbat, dirty deed, slam, slap in the face *Antonyms:* compliment, flattery, homage, service **2.** comeback, cut, derision, discourtesy, jab, jest, joke, mockery, scoffing, scorn, slight, swipe, taunt *Nonformal:* cheap shot, dis, put-down, raspberry, zinger **3.** contempt, disdainfulness, disrespect, ignominy, impertinence, impudence, insolence, opprobrium, rudeness, superciliousness *Antonyms:* benevolence, honour, kindness – *v.* abuse, anger, annoy, belittle, burlesque, caricature, condemn, criticize, curse, debase, decry, degrade, deride, detract, dishonour, disparage, displease, flout, gird, humiliate, injure, irritate, jeer, jest, lampoon, leer, libel, mock, offend, outrage, pan, pique, provoke, revile, ridicule, satirize, scoff, scorn, slam, slander, slight, sneer, snub, swipe, taunt, vex *Nonformal:* blister, blow off, cut up, dis, dump, dump on, kick, laugh at, put down *Antonyms:* flatter, please, praise

insulting *adj.* abrasive, abusive, contemptuous, cutting, degrading, disparaging, foul-mouthed, insolent, offensive, rude, scornful, slanderous, smart-alecky *(Nonformal)*, taunting, uncouth, vitriolic *Antonyms:* complimentary, kind, respectful

insupportable *adj.* full of holes *(Nonformal)*, groundless, illogical, implausible, intolerable, irrational, slight, unacceptable, undefendable, unjustifiable, untenable, weak *Antonyms:* flawless, solid, strong

insuppressible *adj.* **1.** incorrigible, irrepressible, obstreperous, uncontrollable, unruly, unstoppable **2.** aggressive, boisterous, energetic, enthusiastic, indefatigable, in your face *(Nonformal)*, obnoxious, spirited, vigorous

insurance *n.* assurance, backing, binder, coverage, guarantee, indemnity, pogey *(Nonformal)*, protection, provision, safeguard, security, support, surety, underwriting, warranty

insure *v.* cover, ensure, guarantee, hedge one's bet, indemnify, lay off, protect, safeguard, secure, shield, underwrite, warrant

insurgent *adj.* conflagrant, disobedient, factious, insubordinate, rebellious, riotous, seditious, unruly – *n.* agitator, anarchist, demonstrator, dissident, insurrectionist, malcontent, mutineer, radical, rebel, resister, revolutionary, revolutionist, rioter, seditionist

insurmountable *adj.* hopeless, impassable, impossible, impregnable, inaccessible, indomitable, insuperable, invincible, overwhelming, unbeatable, unconquerable *Antonyms:* achievable, doable, surpassable

insurrection *n.* coup, disorder, insurgence, mutiny, rebellion, resistance, revolt, revolution, riot, sedition, uprising

intact *adj.* **1.** complete, entire, indiscrete, perfect, together, total, whole *Antonyms:* fragmented, partial **2.** flawless, pristine, sound, unblemished, unbroken, uncut, undamaged, undefiled, unharmed, unhurt, unimpaired, uninjured, unmarred, unscathed, untouched, virgin *Antonyms:* broken, disfigured, fractured

intangible *adj.* **1.** disembodied, ethereal, immaterial, impalpable, incorporeal, unreal, unsubstantial, untouchable **2.** abstract, imponderable, indefinite, indeterminate, uncertain, undefined, vague

integral *adj.* **1.** basic, constituent, core, elemental, essential, fundamental, important, indispensable, instrumental, intrinsic, necessary, part and parcel *(Nonformal)*, requisite *Antonyms:* extraneous, gratuitous **2.** complete, entire, full, intact, perfect, unbroken, undivided, whole *Antonyms:* partial, segmented, separated

integrate *v.* **1.** accommodate, amalgamate, arrange, assimilate, associate, blend, coalesce, combine, conform, conjoin, consolidate, coordinate, fuse, harmonize, incorporate, interface, intermix, join, knit, link, meld, merge, mesh, mix, reconcile, synthesize, systematize, unite *Antonyms:* divide, segregate, separate **2.** complete, conclude, finish, perfect, unify, unite

integrated *adj.* **1.** amalgamated, blended, combined, fused, harmonized, incorporated, interjoined, knit, merged, meshed, united *Antonyms:* dispersed, divided, separated **2.** acculturated, assimilated, cosmopolitan, desegregated, mixed, multicultural, transculturated *Antonyms:* exclusive, isolated, segregated

integrity *n.* **1.** candour, forthrightness, goodness, honesty, honour, purity, rectitude, righteousness, sincerity, uprightness, virtue *Antonyms:* corruption, deceit, duplicity **2.** absoluteness, coherence, cohesion, completeness, entireness, perfection, soundness, stability, totality, unity, wholeness *Antonyms:* disjunction, division, fraction

intellect *n.* **1.** cognition, comprehension, consciousness, grasp, head, intuition, judgment, perception, percipience, rationality, reason, sense, thought, understanding **2.** ability, aptitude, creativity, erudition, insight, intelligence, mentality, mind, skill, sophistication, talent, wit *Nonformal:* brains, right stuff, savvy **3.** genius, intellectual, master, mover and shaker *(Nonformal)*, philosopher, scholar, sophist

intellectual *adj.* **1.** bookish, brainy, brilliant, creative, critical, erudite, high-flown, informed, intelligent, inventive, learned, ponderous, scholarly, smart, studious, thoughtful, trenchant *Nonformal:* highfalutin, longhaired, pointy-headed **2.** abstract, cerebral, conscious, mental, metaphysical, objective, philosophical, poetic, psychological, rational, sophisticated **3.** challenging, demanding, engaging, exacting, rigorous – *n.* academic, academician, genius, mastermind, philosopher, pundit, scholar, sophist, *swami (Hindu)*, thinker, wizard *Nonformal:* brain, egghead, Einstein

intelligence *n.* **1.** acuity, acumen, adaptability, agility, alertness, aptitude, brainpower, brains, brightness, brilliance, cleverness, discernment, I.Q., judgment, luminosity, quickness, sagacity, skill, smarts *(Nonformal)*, wit *Antonyms:* dullness, ignorance, stupidity **2.** capacity, comprehension, intellect, mentality, mind, perception, reason, understanding **3.** advice, clue, data, disclosure, facts, findings, information, knowledge, leak, news, notice, notification, report, rumour, tidings, word *Nonformal*: inside story, lowdown, picture, poop, skinny, tipoff

intelligent *adj.* **1.** able, acute, apt, astute, brainy, bright, brilliant, calculating, capable, clever, discerning, enlightened, exceptional, highbrow *(Nonformal)*, imaginative, ingenious, inquiring, instructed, inventive, keen, knowing, knowledgeable, penetrating, perceptive, perspicacious, profound, quick, quick-witted, rational, ready, reasonable, resourceful, sagacious, sage, sharp, smart, thinking, understanding, well-informed, wise, witty *Antonyms:* dull, foolish, ignorant, obtuse, slow **2.** alert, alive, aware, comprehending, conscious, lucid, sound

intelligentsia *n. pl.* academe, cognoscenti, cultural *or* political elite, illuminati, intellectuals, literati, masterminds

intelligible *adj.* accessible, apprehensible, audible, clear, comprehensible, discernible, distinct, fathomable, graspable, knowable, lucid, luminous, obvious, open, plain, readable, unambiguous, understandable, unequivocal, unmistakable, visible *Antonyms:* confused, foggy, garbled, hazy, obscure

intelligibility *n.* clarity, clearness, comprehensibility, distinctness, lucidity, orderliness, precision, readability *Antonyms:* confusion, disarray, disorder

intemperate *adj.* **1.** excessive, extravagant, gluttonous, heedless, immoderate, out-of-control, passionate, profligate, reckless, unbalanced, uncontrollable, unhinged, unrestrained, wild **2.** alcoholic, bleary-eyed, drunk, drunken, high, intoxicated, liquored, sotted, tipsy, wasted *Nonformal:* boozed, hammered, jiggered, loaded, loose, painless, potted, primed, sloshed, stoned, tight **3.** freezing, icy, inclement, severe, snowy, stormy, tempestuous, wicked *(Nonformal) Antonyms:* calm, pacific, tropic

intend *v.* **1.** aim, appoint, aspire, attempt, connote, decree, dedicate, design, determine, devote, endeavour, essay, expect, figure on, hope, ordain, plan, plot, propose, reckon on, reserve, resolve, scheme, spell, strive, think, try **2.** denote, designate, express, import, indicate, mean, signify

intended *adj.* **1.** calculated, contracted, designed, planned, prearranged, proposed, scheduled **2.** destined, expected, future, possible, predestined, predetermined, prospective – *n.* betrothed, fiancé, fiancée, husband-to-be, the one *(Nonformal)*, wife-to-be

intense *adj.* **1.** acute, agonizing, biting, bitter, burning, consuming, cutting, exceptional, excessive, exquisite, extraordinary, extreme, fierce, forceful, great, overpowering, strong *Antonyms:* mild, moderate, slight **2.** ardent, diligent, eager, energetic, hard, keen, strenuous *Antonyms:* easy, gentle, relaxed **3.** deep, earnest, emotional, fervent, fervid, impassioned, piercing, profound **4.** concentrated, fortified, full, intensified, powerful, pungent *Antonyms:* diluted, weak

intensify *v.* **1.** aggravate, exacerbate, fuel, inflame, rouse, whet *Antonyms:* calm, mitigate, placate **2.** accentuate, aggrandize, augment, boost, build up, concentrate, emphasize, exaggerate, heighten, increase, magnify, raise, redouble, reinforce, rise, strengthen, stress *Nonformal:* beef up, spike *Antonyms:* decrease, dilute, weaken **3.** accelerate, deepen, escalate, hasten, quicken, step *or* speed up *Antonyms:* check, curb, slow **4.** brighten, enhance, jazz up *(Nonformal)*, lighten, sharpen *Antonyms:* cloud, muddy

intensity *n.* **1.** acuteness, brightness, clarity, concentration, deepness, degree, depth, emphasis, extremity, fierceness, force, ferociousness, ferocity, fury, magnitude, potency, power, severity, sharpness, strength, violence **2.** ardour, determination, drive, energy, fire, keenness, rigour, will **3.** earnestness, emotion, excitement, feeling, fervency, passion, warmth

intensive *adj.* **1.** complete, comprehensive, exhaustive, in-depth, thorough, thoroughgoing *Antonyms:* shallow, superficial, wanting **2.** demanding, difficult, hard, herculean, laborious, rigorous, severe *Antonyms:* easy, simple **3.** accelerated, concentrated, condensed, fast, quick, sped up *Antonyms:* dilatory, laggard, slow

intent *adj.* **1.** absorbed, alert, attentive, concentrating, deep, engaged, engrossed, immersed, industrious, intense, occupied, rapt, riveted, watchful *Antonyms:* disregardful, heedless, negligent **2.** bent, bound, committed, decided, decisive, determined, eager, earnest, enthusiastic, firm, fixed, hell-bent *(Nonformal)*, resolute, resolved, steadfast, steady, unwavering *Antonyms:* hesitant, indecisive, undetermined – *n.* **1.** aim, animus, design, desire, end, goal, intention, object, objective, plan, purport, purpose, scheme, score, target, understanding, volition, will, wish **2.** drift, idea, meaning, nub, point, significance

intention *n.* **1.** aim, bottom line, design, game plan, goal, motive, objective, plan, point **2.** import, meaning, purpose, sense, significance *See also:* **intent**

intentional *adj.* calculated, considered, deliberate, designed, intended, meant, planned, prearranged, premeditated, purposeful, studied, unforced, volitional, voluntary, willful, willing, witting *Antonyms:* accidental, forced, inadvertent, unplanned

intently *adv.* assiduously, attentively, closely, fixedly, hard, heedfully, keenly, purposefully, raptly, searchingly, sharply, steadily, watchfully

interact *v.* collaborate, combine, communicate, connect, contact, cooperate, interface, interplay, join, merge, mesh, network, relate, socialize, touch, touch base, work together

intercede *v.* **1.** barge *or* nose *or* step in, interject, interpose, intervene, intrude **2.** advocate, arbitrate, mediate, negotiate **3.** argue, beg, persuade, petition, plead, speak

intercept *v.* **1.** detain, grab, grasp, nab *(Nonformal)*, seize, snatch **2.** catch, contact, encounter, join, meet, receive **3.** arrest, block, check, curb, cut off, delay, hinder, impede, interfere, interrupt, obstruct, prevent, stifle, stonewall, stop **4.** ambush, assault, bushwack, jump *(Nonformal)*, mug

interchange *n.* **1.** alternation, exchange, replacement, shift, substitution, switch, variation **2.** barter, exchange, giving-and-taking, reciprocation, trade **3.** back and forth *(Nonformal)*, colloquy, conversation, debate, discussion, tête-à-tête, thrust and parry **4.** crossroads, hamlet, intersection, junction, off-ramp, on-ramp, whistle stop – *v.* **1.** alternate, commute, swap, substitute, transpose **2.** connect, discuss, interact, interface, network, relate, share ideas *or* thoughts

interchangeable *adj.* alike, compatible, correspondent, equal, equivalent, exchangeable, identical, like, mutual, reciprocal, same, selfsame, similar, synonymous, transposable *Antonyms:* different, diverse, incongruous

intercourse *n.* **1.** carnal knowledge, coitus, congress, copulation, fornication, intimacy, sex, sexual relations *Nonformal:* action, nookie, shagging **2.** association, communication, communion, connection, contact, converse, correspondence, give-and-take, interchange, intercommunication, mesh, team play, teamwork **3.** commerce, dealings, networking, trade, traffic, transactions, truck

interdict *n.* **1.** ban, disallowance, edict, forbiddance, injunction, law **2.** anathema, condemnation, curse, damnation, excommunication – *v.* bar, hinder, embargo, forbid, outlaw, prohibit, proscribe *Antonyms:* allow, permit, sanction

interest *n.* **1.** affection, ardour, attentiveness, attraction, concern, curiosity, enthusiasm, excitement, passion, regard, relevance, sympathy *Antonyms:* indifference, neglect **2.** bearing, consequence, gravity, import, importance, merit, note, pertinence, priority, relevance, significance, weight **3.** advantage, avail, benefit, bonus, gain, good, profit, prosperity, service, use, welfare, well-being, worth **4.** charge, cost, premium, price, rate, value **5.** accrual, dividend, earnings, payback, profit, return, yield **6.** claim, commitment, equity, holding, investment, involvement, part, participation, piece, portion, role, share, stake *Nonformal:* bit, bite, chunk, cut, slice **7.** business, job, line of work, motivation, occupation, work *Nonformal:* bag, beat, cup of tea, thing **8.** advocacy, backing, championship, connection, favour, sponsorship *Nonformal:* inside track, pull **9.** camp, community, faction, group, issue, lobby, party, persuasion, point of view, sect, side, view **10.** affairs, business matters, concerns, operation, undertakings – *v.* **1.** amuse, appeal to, arouse, attract, divert, engage, engross, entertain, enthrall, excite, fascinate, grab, hook, intrigue, kindle, move, pique, please, snare, tantalize, tempt, titillate, touch *Antonyms:* bore, repel, tire, weary **2.** affect, apply *or* pertain *or* relate to, concern, involve **3.** engage, ensnare, influence, introduce, lure, sway, win over

interested *adj.* **1.** absorbed, affected, attracted, curious, drawn, engrossed, enticed, fascinated, intrigued, lured, moved, obsessed, occupied, roused, stimulated, stirred, struck, touched *Antonyms:* bored, lethargic, tired **2.** committed, concerned, entrenched, implicated, involved, staked *(Nonformal)*, vested **3.** biased, partial, partisan, predisposed *Antonyms:* detached, fair

interesting *adj.* **1.** absorbing, affecting, alluring, amusing, appealing, arresting, attractive, captivating, compelling, curious, enchanting, engaging, engrossing, entertaining, enthralling, entrancing, fascinating, gripping, intriguing, inviting, magnetic, prepossessing, provocative, riveting, stimulating, stirring, striking, thought-provoking, *Antonyms:* boring, dull, offensive, repulsive, tedious **2.** beautiful, delightful, elegant, exceptional, exotic, fine, impressive, lovely, pleasing, pleasurable, readable, refreshing, unusual, winning

interfere *v.* **1.** frustrate, hamper, handicap, hinder, impede, inhibit, jam *(Nonformal)*, obstruct, prevent, stop, suspend, thwart, trammel **2.** butt *or* nose in *(Nonformal)*, incommode, interlope, interpose, intervene, intrude, meddle, obtrude, pry, tamper, trouble **3.** butt heads, clash, collide, conflict, disagree, fight

interference *n.* **1.** block, constraint, curb, delay, difficulty, disruption, frustration, hindrance, holdup, impediment, obstruction, snag, trouble, wall *Football and hockey terms:* call, flag clipping, foul, illegal block *or* check *or* conduct *or* manoeuvre *or* play *or* tactic, penalty, pick-play, violation **2.** atmospherics, distortion, disturbance, noise, phasing, static, white noise, wow and flutter **3.** butting *or* nosing in, encroachment, interloping, intervention, intrusion, invasion, meddling, prying, trespassing

interim *adj.* **1.** momentary, passing, *pro tempore (Latin)*, provisional, temporary, tentative, transitory *Antonyms*: established, fixed, permanent **2.** acting, deputy, intervening, makeshift, stopgap, supply – *n.* breach, break, breather *(Nonformal)*, cease-fire, gap, hiatus, interlude, intermission, interregnum, interruption, interval, layoff, letup, lull, meantime, meanwhile, pause, recess, stop, time-out, truce, wait

interior *adj.* **1.** central, inner, inside, internal, inward *Antonyms:* external, outer, outside **2.** inland, inshore, upcountry, upisland, upriver, upstream *Antonyms:* Atlantic, maritime, Pacific, seaside **3.** civil, domestic, home, in-house, local, provincial, national *Antonyms:* foreign, offshore **4.** hidden, innermost, intimate, personal, private, remote, secret *Antonyms:* communal, popular, public – *n.* **1.** inner region *or* space, insides, middle, midst, recesses *Antonyms:* exterior, outside, surface **2.** bowels, contents, innards, pulp, stomach, viscera, vitals *Antonyms*: cover, epidermis, skin **3.** bosom, core, crux, essence, heart, inner self, soul, marrow, seed **4.** backcountry, bush, heartland, hinterland, lakeland, midland, nether regions, outback *(Australia)*, upcountry, woods

interjection *n.* **1.** infusion, injection, insertion, interpolation, interposition, intrusion **2.** comment, cry, ejaculation, epithet, exclamation, remark, shout, utterance, yell

interlace *v.* **1.** blend, crisscross, intertwine, interweave, mesh, spin, twill, twine, twist, weave, wind together *Antonyms:* undo, unravel **2.** interject, interlard, intersperse, pepper, punctuate, scatter, sprinkle **3.** alternate, diversify, flip, interlock, substitute, switch, vary

interlocution *n.* chat, colloquy, conference, conversation, dialogue, discourse, discussion, exchange, palaver, talk

interloper *n.* alien, intruder, meddler, trespasser, poacher, uninvited guest, unwanted visitor *Nonformal:* buttinsky, gate-crasher

interlude *n.* break, breather *(Nonformal)*, continuance *(Law)*, delay, gap, halt, hiatus, idyll, interim, intermission, interregnum, interruption, interval, lull, meantime, meanwhile, parenthesis, pause, recess, respite, rest, spell, stop, stoppage, wait

intermediary *adj.* **1.** bisecting, dividing, intermediate, medial, middling **2.** arbitrating, chairing, counselling, intervening, mediating, moderating – *n.* **1.** broker, catalyst, delegate, emissary, entrepreneur, fixer, go-between, interceder, intermediate, mediator, middleperson, moderator, negotiator, referee **2.** agent, instrument, means, medium, vehicle

intermediate *adj.* average, between, central, centre, common, compromising, halfway, in-between, intermediary, interposed, intervening, mean, medial, median, mediocre, medium, mid, middle, middling, midway, moderate, move, neutral, transitional – *v.* adjudicate, arbitrate, chair, conciliate, counsel, hear, mediate, mitigate, negotiate, referee

interminable *adj.* **1.** boundless, ceaseless, constant, continuous, endless, eternal, everlasting, immeasurable, incessant, infinite, limitless, long, looped, never-ending, permanent, perpetual, protracted, recurrent, timeless, unceasing, uninterrupted, unlimited *Antonyms:* bounded, finite, limited, restricted **2.** battological, boring, dragging, dull, exhausting, fatiguing, humdrum, long-winded, monotonous, tedious, tiresome, wearisome *Antonyms:* exciting, varied *Commonly misused:* **indeterminate**

intermingle *v.* amalgamate, associate, blend, combine, come together, commingle, fuse, interlace, intermix, interweave, join, merge, mesh, mix, pool *Antonyms:* disperse, dissipate, scatter

intermission *n.* abeyance, adjournment, break, breather *(Nonformal)*, cessation, continuance, dormancy, interim, interlude, interregnum, interruption, interval, layoff, lull, parenthesis, pause, quiescence, recess, respite, rest, stop, stoppage, suspension, time, time-out, wait *Antonym:* continuance, resumption

intermittent *adj.* alternate, broken, fitful, infrequent, interrupted, irregular, occasional, on-again off-again *(Nonformal)*, on and off, pausing, periodic, shifting, spasmodic, sporadic *Antonyms:* continuous, regular, steady

intern *n.* **1.** apprentice, graduate *or* medical student, student, teaching fellow, trainee **2.** summer student, unpaid worker, volunteer – *v.* confine, detain, hold, impound, imprison, incarcerate, lock up, move

internal *adj.* **1.** in-house, inner, inside, interior, visceral, within *Antonyms:* external, outside **2.** congenital, inborn, inbred, ingrained, inherent, innate, intrinsic **3.** emotional, essential, innermost, personal, subjective **4.** centralized, civil, continental, domestic, federal, inland, inshore, national, provincial, up-island, upriver *Antonyms:* away *(P.E.I.)*, foreign, offshore

international *adj.* **1.** global, intercontinental, multinational, Pan-Am, universal, worldwide **2.** continental *(European)*, cosmopolitan, jet-setting *(Nonformal)*, travelled, worldly

Internet *n.* ARPANET, BITNET, cyberspace, electronic communication, e-mail, global village, Gopher, information superhighway, intranet, matrix *(Nonformal)*, net, NSFnet, telnet, Usenet, World Wide Web *or* WWW

interplay *n.* exchange, give-and-take, interaction, integration, meshing, networking, reciprocation, reciprocity, social transaction, teamwork, volleying – *v.* communicate, cooperate, dovetail, interact, reciprocate, transact

interpolation *n.* **1.** addition, appendage, aside, foreword, insertion, intercalation, interjection, interruption, introduction **2.** falsification, manipulation, obfuscation, reinterpretation *Nonformal:* doctoring, fixing

interpose *v.* **1.** insert, interject, introduce, slip *or* stick in **2.** barge *or* nose in, interfere, interlope, interrupt, intrude, meddle **3.** adjudicate, go between, intercede, intervene, mediate, step in

interpret *v.* **1.** annotate, clarify, comment, construe, define, delineate, elucidate, explain, explicate, expound, gloss, simplify, translate **2.** analyze, decipher, decode, describe, diagnose, figure out, gather, judge, read, see, solve, take, understand, view **3.** act, depict, illustrate, impersonate, perform, picture, show, stage

interpretation *n.* **1.** clarification, editing, elucidation, emendation, exegesis, explanation, explication **2.** analysis, conception, definition, diagnostics, reading, solution, spin *(Nonformal)*, take, translation, understanding, view **3.** drift, gist, heart, import, meaning, message **4.** demonstration, depiction, illustration, performance, portrayal, presentation

interpreter *n.* analyst, annotator, commentator, critic, cryptographer, demonstrator, editor, explicator, guide, lexicographer, spokesperson, stenographer, transcriber, translator

interrogate *v.* ask, catechize, cross-examine, debrief, examine, inquire, interview, investigate, probe, query, question, quiz, test *Nonformal:* grill, pump

interrogation *n.* **1.** catechism, cross-examination, examination, grilling *(Nonformal),* inquisition, interpellation, questioning **2.** demand, inquiry, query, question, quiz

interrupt *n.* command, communication, instruction, notification *(Computer),* signal – *v.* **1.** arrest, cut off *or* short, delay, disturb, halt, hinder, hold up, impede, obstruct, prevent, sever, stay, stop, suspend **2.** barge *or* break *or* burst *or* nose in, bother, come between, edge in, infringe, inject, interject, intervene, meddle

interruption *n.* **1.** abeyance, adjournment, arrest, blackout, break, cessation, continuance *(Law),* crash *(Computer),* cutoff, delay, discontinuance, disruption, dissolution, dormancy, halt, hiatus, intermission, interval, lull, outage, pause, stop, stoppage, suspension *Antonyms:* continuation, continuity, succession **2.** bar, blockage, disturbance, hindrance, impediment, obstacle **3.** breach, disconnection, disunion, division, rift, rupture, separation, severance, split

intersect *v.* **1.** bisect, crosscut, cut, divide, separate, traverse **2.** converge, crisscross, cross, intercross, join, meet, touch

intersection *n.* **1.** circle, cloverleaf, corner, crossing, crossroads, crosswalk, crossway, interchange, junction, *rondelle (French),* rotary, roundabout *(British)* **2.** cross-section, intercrossing, juncture, meeting, nexus, web

intersperse *v.* bestrew, diffuse, disseminate, distribute, diversify, infuse, interfuse, interlard, intermix, pepper, permeate, scatter, spread, sprinkle

intertwine *v.* bind, braid, connect, convolute, crisscross, cross, entwine, interknit, interlace, interweave, link, mesh, tangle, twist, weave

interval *n.* **1.** adjournment, breathing space, continuance *(Nonformal),* delay, downtime, hiatus, holiday, interim, interlude, intermission, interregnum, interruption, layover, lull, pause, playtime *(Nonformal),* recess, respite, rest, spell, time, time-out, wait **2.** breach, break, cleavage, distance, fissure, gap, opening, separation, space **3.** degree, note, octave, step, tone *Kinds of musical interval:* second, third, fourth, fifth, seventh

intervene *v.* **1.** barge *or* horn *or* butt in, interfere, interrupt, intrude, meddle **2.** come between, divide, interpose, separate, sever **3.** adjudicate, arbitrate, bargain, intercede, judge, mediate, negotiate, reconcile, referee, settle, step in **3.** befall, betide, happen, occur, take place, transpire

intervention *n.* **1.** adjudication, agency, arbitration, intercession, interposition, mediation, negotiation, peacemaking **2.** interference, interruption, intrusion, meddling, obtrusion **3.** break, hiatus, intermission, lull, rest, stoppage

interview *n.* **1.** audience, conference, consultation, dialogue, discourse, hearing, media scrum, meeting, press conference, Q and A *(Nonformal),* session, talk **2.** evaluation, examination, oral defence, query, questioning, quiz, screening, test, triage – *v.* evaluate, examine, interrogate, pump *(Nonformal),* question, quiz, sound out, talk to, test

intestinal *adj.* abdominal, bowel, celiac, duodenal, enteric, gastric, gut, inner, inside, interior, internal, inward, stomach, visceral

intestine *n.* bowel, canal, chitterling, entrails *Parts of the intestine:* appendix, ascending colon, cecum, colon, descending colon, duodenum, ileum, jejunum, large intestine, rectum, small intestine, traverse colon

intimacy *n.* affection, affinity, closeness, communion, confidence, confidentiality, endearment, familiarity, feeling, friendship, love, sex, sexual intercourse, understanding, warmth *Antonyms:* alienation, coldness, detachment, remoteness

intimate *adj.* **1.** deep, elemental, essential, ingrained, inherent, innate, innermost, personal, private, privy, profound **2.** direct, experiential, first-hand, first-person, immediate, particular *Antonyms:* distant, faraway, hearsay, remote **3.** affectionate, bosom, cherished, chummy, close, clubby, confidential, cozy, dear, dearest, devoted, faithful, fast, fond, friendly, loving, near, nearest, snug, warm *Nonformal:* comfy, thick **4.** amorous, carnal, erotic, fleshly, libidinous, passionate, sexual – *n.* acquaintance, amigo, associate, bosom buddy, brother, buddy, chum, chummy *(Newfoundland)*, close friend, companion, comrade, confidant, confidante, crony, familiar, family, fiancé, fiancée, friend, lover, mate, pal, sister – *v.* allude, assert, connote, hint, impart, imply, infer, insinuate, leak *(Nonformal)*, suggest, tip off

intimately *adv.* **1.** closely, confidentially, in confidence, personally, privately, secretly *Antonyms:* coldly, distantly **2.** amorously, carnally, erotically, passionately, sexually **3.** affectionately, dearly, fondly, lovingly, tenderly, warmly **4.** completely, fully, fundamentally, in detail, thoroughly, totally

intimation *n.* **1.** allusion, clue, cue, hint, implication, indication, inkling, innuendo, insinuation, notion, shadow, strain, streak, suggestion, suspicion, tinge, tip, trace, wind **2.** communication, declaration, notice, reminder, warning

intimidate *v.* **1.** alarm, daunt, frighten, panic, scare, spook *(Nonformal)*, startle, terrify, unnerve, upset **2.** badger, bait, bludgeon, browbeat, buffalo, bully, coerce, compel, cow, dragoon, force, hassle *(Nonformal)*, hound, oblige, ride, ruffle, strong-arm, terrorize, threaten

intimidation *n.* arm-twisting *(Nonformal)*, bullying, coercion, fear, force, full court press, pressure, terror, terrorization, threat, threatening, tyranny

intolerable *adj.* **1.** excruciating, impossible, insufferable, insupportable, odious, offensive, painful, tedious, tiresome, unacceptable, unbearable, undesirable, unendurable, unlikeable **2.** excessive, extreme, inordinate, unreasonable

intolerance *n.* **1.** ageism, anti-semitism, bigotry, chauvinism, discrimination, dogmatism, fanaticism, jingoism, lookism *(Nonformal)*, narrow-mindedness, prejudice, racism, sexism, xenophobia *Antonyms:* liberality, patience, understanding **2.** inability, incapacity, inflexibility, stubbornness, unwillingness, vulnerability

intolerant *adj.* **1.** biased, chauvinistic, extremist, illiberal, jaundiced, narrow-minded, small-minded, uncharitable, unwilling *Antonyms:* broad-minded, charitable, fair, lenient, magnanimous **2.** allergic, at risk, averse, endangered, unable to handle **3.** contemptuous, dictatorial, disdainful, dogmatic, fractious, impatient, indignant, inflexible, irate, irritable *Antonyms:* dispassionate, patient, understanding

intonation *n.* accent, cadence, colour, frequency, inflection, melody, mode, modulation, pitch, timbre, tone, voicing

intoxicated *adj.* **1.** drunk, drunken, impaired, inebriated, tipsy *Nonformal:* blotto, bombed, castaway, crocked, high, juiced, lit, loaded, looped, oiled, pickled, pie-eyed, plastered, polluted, primed, ripped, shot, sloppy, sloshed, smashed, stewed, stinking, stoned, tanked, tight, wasted **2.** absorbed, affected, captivated, carried away, delirious, dizzy, ecstatic, elated, engrossed, enraptured, euphoric, excited, exhilarated, galvanized, happy, infatuated, interested, moonstruck *(Nonformal)*, piqued, quickened, rapt, stimulated, transported, turned on *Antonyms:* bored, indifferent, repelled, repulsed

intoxicating *adj.* **1.** alluring, exciting, exhilarating, eye-popping *(Nonformal)*, happy, heady, inspiring, provocative, rousing, seductive, stimulating, stirring, tantalizing, thrilling *Antonyms:* nauseating, odious, sickening **2.** alcoholic, fermented, fortified, hard, strong *Nonformal:* boozy, spiked

intoxication *n.* **1.** alcoholism, befuddlement, bibulousness, dipsomania, drunkenness, inebriation, intemperance, tippling, tipsiness *Nonformal:* boozing, guzzling, hard *or* heavy drinking, hitting the bottle **2.** delirium, elation, excitement, exhilaration, fervour, happiness, high *(Nonformal)*, interest, stimulation

intractable *adj.* balky, headstrong, incorrigible, mulish, obstinate, opposed, pig-headed, rowdy, stubborn, uncooperative, unmanageable, unruly, wilful *Antonyms:* amenable, biddable, docile, pliable, willing *Commonly misused:* **intransigent**

intransigent *adj.* adamant, hang tough *(Nonformal)*, immovable, inflexible, obdurate, rigid, tenacious, tough, uncompromising, unbending, unyielding *Antonyms:* acquiescent, compliant, compromising *Commonly misused:* **intractable**

intrepid *adj.* audacious, bold, brave, courageous, daring, dauntless, fearless, gallant, heroic, lionhearted, resolute, spirited, stalwart, unafraid, unflinching *Nonformal:* bodacious, game *Antonyms:* cowardly, craven, timid

intricacy *n.* complexity, convolution, detail, difficulty, elaborateness, enigma, involvement, knottiness, perplexity, puzzlement, snag, web *Antonyms:* clarity, order, simplicity

intricate *adj.* **1.** baroque, Byzantine, complex, complicated, convoluted, elaborate, entangled, fancy, high-tech, involved, knotty, rococo, sophisticated, tricky *Antonyms:* plain, simple, unadorned **2.** bewildering, confusing, difficult, enigmatic, hard, labyrinthine, maze-like, perplexing, puzzling, tortuous *Antonyms:* clear, easy, obvious, painless

intrigue *n.* **1.** artifice, chicanery, conspiracy, contrivance, craft, deal, design, dodge, double-dealing, fix, frame, frame-up *(Nonformal)*, fraud, game, graft, knavery, machination, manipulation, plan, plot, ruse, scheme, stratagem, subterfuge, trickery, wile **2.** affair, amour, attachment, fling, flirtation, hanky-panky *(Nonformal)*, indiscretion, infatuation, interlude, intimacy, liaison, rendezvous, romance, tryst – *v.* **1.** angle, connive, conspire, contrive, devise, finagle *(Nonformal)*, frame, machinate, manoeuvre, operate, plan, plot, promote, scheme, wangle **2.** appeal, attract, bait, beguile, bewitch, captivate, charm, delight, draw, enchant, entertain, excite, fascinate, grab, hook, interest, pique, please, pull, rivet, send, tickle, titillate

intrinsic *adj.* authentic, basic, built-in, central, congenital, constitutional, deep-seated, elemental, essential, fundamental, genuine, hereditary, honest, inborn, inbred, indispensible, indwelling, inherent, inmost, innate, intimate, legitimate, native, natural, original, requisite, true, underlying *Antonyms:* acquired, added, artificial, extraneous, extrinsic, false, incidental, illegitimate, spurious

introduce *v.* **1.** acquaint, meet, present, shake hands **2.** announce, broach, forward, herald, offer, promote, propose, submit, suggest, unveil **3.** begin, commence, enter, establish, found, initiate, lead off, open, originate, plant, preface, start **4.** familiarize, inform, instruct, teach **5.** imbue, implant, infuse, inject, insert, instill *Antonyms:* cut out, remove, withdraw

introduction *n.* **1.** awakening, beginning, birth, commencement, debut, inception, institution, launch, start *Antonyms:* conclusion, death, termination **2.** baptism, inauguration, induction, initiation, installation **3.** acquaintance, admission, admittance, entrance, entry, familiarization, meeting, presentation **4.** foreword, lead-in, preamble, preface, preliminaries, prelims *(Nonformal)*, prelude, primer, prologue, opening, overtone *Antonyms:* afterward, epilogue, finale **5.** establishment, implantation, importation, infusion, injection, insertion

introductory *adj.* basic, beginning, early, elementary, first, inaugural, inductive, initial, opening, precursory, prefatory, preliminary, primary, rudimentary, seminal, starting *Antonyms:* closing, concluding, final, last, terminating

introspection *n.* contemplation, deep thought, introversion, meditation, reflection, rumination, scrutiny, self-analysis, self-communion, self-examination, self-reflection, soul-searching

introspective *adj.* brooding, contemplative, introverted, inward-looking, meditative, melancholy, museful, pensive, ponderous, self-absorbed, thoughtful

introverted *adj.* bashful, introspective, quiet, reserved, shy, timid, wallflowerish *(Nonformal)*, withdrawn *Antonyms:* gregarious, loud, obnoxious, outgoing

intrude *v.* barge *or* break *or* butt in, bother, encroach, gatecrash *(Nonformal)*, infringe, interfere, interject, interlope, interrupt, intervene, invade, meddle, obtrude, overstep, pester, tamper, trespass

intruder *n.* **1.** burglar, criminal, infiltrator, invader, marauder, pirate, prowler, raider, thief, trespasser **2.** busybody, gatecrasher, interloper, interrupter, *kibitzer (Yiddish)*, meddler, muckraker, nuisance, paparazzi, reporter *Nonformal:* buttinsky, nosey parker, snoop

intrusion *n.* **1.** breach, crime, encroachment, infraction, inroads, interference, invasion, transgression, trespass, usurpation, violation **2.** bother, interruption, irritant, nuisance, pain, trouble **3.** break and enter, burglary, cat burglary, home invasion, illegal entry, prowling, robbery, theft

intrusive *adj.* annoying, bothersome, forward, impertinent, importunate, interfering, interruptive, invasive, meddlesome, nosy, obtrusive, officious, prying, pushy, snoopy, unwelcome

intuition *n.* **1.** apprehension, awareness, discernment, knowledge, perception, understanding **2.** clairvoyance, divination, foresight, presentiment, sixth sense, vision **3.** feeling, hunch, indication, inkling, intimation, omen, premonition, sensation, sense, suggestion, suspicion

intuitive *adj.* **1.** automatic, direct, immediate, impulsive, inherent, innate, instinctive, involuntary, natural, reflex, spontaneous, surrealistic, untaught, unconscious, visceral *Antonyms:* deliberate, intentional **2.** apprehensive, aware, comprehending, farsighted, knowing, mindful, perceptive, percipient, understanding

intumescence *n.* **1.** amplification, bloating, broadening, dilation, distention, expansion, inflation, swelling, tumefaction, turgescence, widening **2.** bulge, goiter, growth, projection, protrusion, protuberance, swelling

inundate *v.* deluge, drown, dunk, engulf, flood, glut, immerse, overflow, overrun, overwhelm, submerge, waterlog *Nonformal:* snow, swamp

inundation *n.* **1.** blizzard, deluge, downpour, flood, gullywasher *(P.E.I.)*, storm, tidal wave, tsunami **2.** excess, glut, overflow, plenty, superabundance, superfluity, surplus

inure *v.* accustom, adapt, adjust, condition, desensitize, familiarize, habituate, harden, season, strengthen, teach, temper, toughen *Commonly misused:* **endure, immure**

invade *v.* **1.** attack, assail, assault, breach, descend upon, maraud, muscle in *(Nonformal)*, occupy, penetrate, permeate, pillage, plunder, raid, ravage, storm, trespass, violate **2.** fill, flood, overrun, overwhelm, rush, swarm **3.** examine, finger *(Nonformal)*, penetrate, poke, probe, prod **4.** encroach, infringe, interfere, interpose, interrupt, intervene, meddle, transgress, trespass

invalid *adj.* **1.** counterfeit, expired, false, falsified, fudged, illegal, illegitimate, null, spurious, unlawful, useless, void *Antonyms:* aboveboard, clean, legal **2.** bad, baseless, defective, deficient, erroneous, faulty, flawed, groundless, illogical, inaccurate, incorrect, nugatory, specious, unfounded, unsound, wrong *Antonyms:* flawless, sound, verifiable **3.** bedridden, chronically ill, diseased, enervated, feeble, hobbled, ill, peaky *(Nonformal)*, run-down, sick, wasted, weak – *n.* convalescent, dotard, infirm, patient, shut-in, valetudinarian

invalidate *v.* **1.** abolish, abrogate, annihilate, annul, cancel, counteract, counterbalance, discredit, disprove, disqualify, negate, neutralize, nullify, offset, overrule, overthrow, quash, refute, revoke, undo, void *Nonformal:* nix, not, x out *Antonyms:* authorize, certify, ratify, sanction **2.** cripple, disable, hamstring *(Nonformal)*, hobble, ruin, undermine, weaken *Antonyms:* aid, assist, empower, energize

invaluable *adj.* **1.** exceptional, inestimable, irreplaceable, matchless, precious, priceless, prized, treasured, valuable *Antonyms:* cheap, paltry, without merit, worthless **2.** central, core, essential, fundamental, indispensible, instrumental, integral, requisite, vital *Antonyms:* replaceable, superfluous

invariable *adj.* changeless, consistent, constant, fixed, immovable, immutable, inalterable, inflexible, monotonous, perpetual, regular, reliable, rigid, set, static, unchangeable, unchanging, unfailing, unfaltering, unrelieved, unvarying, unwavering *Antonyms:* capricious, changeable, irregular, mercurial

invasion *n.* **1.** aggression, assault, attack, blitzkrieg, drive, foray, forward march, incursion, initiative, launch, offensive, onslaught, penetration, push, raid, rush, sally, sortie, storming, strike, thrust **2.** breach, crime, encroachment, infringement, inroad, intrusion, overstepping, transgression, trespass, usurpation, violation **3.** colonization, conquest, foreign domination *or* rule, imperialism, occupation

invective *adj.* abusive, calumnious, castigating, caustic, censorious, critical, defamatory, insulting, offensive, slanderous, vitriolic – *n.* abuse, accusation, berating, blame, blasphemy, castigation, condemnation, denunciation, diatribe, jeremiad, reproach, revilement, sarcasm, scurrility, tirade, tongue-lashing *(Nonformal)*, vilification, vitriol, vituperation

inveigh *v.* censure, complain, criticize, defame, denounce, flay, protest, rail against, remonstrate, reproach, vituperate *Nonformal:* blast, dis, lace into, pepper, roast, skin alive, slam *Antonyms:* compliment, honour, praise *Commonly misused:* **inveigle**

inveigle *v.* allure, beguile, cajole, charm, coax, deceive, draw, entice, flatter, influence, jolly, lead on, lure, manipulate, manoeuvre, persuade, seduce, stroke, tempt, urge, wheedle, work on *Nonformal:* con, snow, suck in, sweet talk *Commonly misused:* **inveigh**

invent *v.* **1.** author, coin, compose, conceive, contrive, create, design, devise, discover, dope out *(Nonformal)*, fashion, forge, form, formulate, frame, hatch, initiate, issue, make, mint, mould, originate, plan, produce, project, think up **2.** concoct, conjure up, cook up *(Nonformal)*, equivocate, fabricate, fake, falsify, feign, fib, improvise, lie, make up, manufacture, misrepresent, misstate, pretend, prevaricate

invention *n.* **1.** construction, creation, discovery, design, fabrication, innovation **2.** apparatus, concoction, contrivance, device, gadget *Nonformal:* brain child, contraption, gimmick, gizmo, thingamajig **3.** adaptability, creativity, foresight, genius, ingenuity, inspiration, originality, resourcefulness **4.** deceit, fake, falsehood, fancy, fantasy, fib, fiction, figment, forgery, lie, prevarication, sham, untruth *Nonformal:* fish story, tall-tale, yarn *Antonyms:* reality, truism, truth

inventive *adj.* **1.** adaptive, artistic, clever, constructive, creative, formative, gifted, imaginative, ingenious, innovative, inspired, original, quick, resourceful, sharp *Antonyms:* imitative, pedestrian, trite, unimaginative, uninspired **2.** fabulous, fanciful, fantastic, fictitious, imaginary, mythical *Nonformal:* stretched, tall

inventory *n.* **1.** commodities, fund, hoard, produce, reserve, reservoir, stacks, stock, stockpile, store, supply *Inventory movement:* FIFO, FILO, JIT, KAN BAN **2.** account, backlog, catalogue, file, index, itemization, list, portfolio, record, register, roll, roster, schedule, stock book, summary, table **3.** census, count, enumeration, itemization, listing, stocktaking, tallying

inverse *adj.* **1.** antithetical, backward, bizarro *(Nonformal)*, opposite, reversed, transposed **2.** belly *or* bottom up, capsized, flipped, inside-out, inverted, overturned, tipped, topsy-turvy, up-ended, upset, upside-down – *n.* contrary, flipside, mirror image, opposite, reverse

invert *v.* **1.** capsize, flip, keel, kick *or* push *or* shove over, overturn, tip, up-end, upset, upturn **2.** flip, flip-flop, reverse, transpose

3. adjust, alter, change, convert, modify, transform

invertebrate *n.* arthropods, spineless animal *Invertebrate groupings:* arachnids, ascidian, coelenterates, crustacean, echinoderm, insects, molluscs, myriapods, nematodes, planarian, protists, protozoans, worms, sponges

invest *v.* **1.** allocate, allot, commit, contribute, disburse, expend, lay *or* put out, put in, spend **2.** buy into, chance, gamble, hazard, plunge, punt *(British)*, risk, speculate, swing *(Nonformal)*, venture **3.** advance, back, bankroll, buoy, capitalize, equip, fund, furnish, grubstake *(Nonformal)*, outfit, rig out, subsidize, support, underwrite **4.** buy, payout, procure, purchase **5.** anoint, crown, elect, inaugurate, install, instate, place, seat *Antonyms:* depose, topple, unseat **6.** approve, authorize, commission, confer, empower, enable, entrust, grant, sanction *Antonyms:* deny, disapprove, refuse **7.** bedeck, clothe, dress, enshroud, robe, swaddle, tog *(Nonformal)*, wrap *Antonyms:* denude, undress **8.** adore, celebrate, dignify, exalt, glorify, honour, praise, venerate *Antonyms:* castigate, defame, vilify **9.** besiege, circle, circumscribe, enclose, envelop, hem in, surround

investigate *v.* analyze, audit, case, check, comb, consider, delve into, dig around, discuss, examine, explore, hunt, inquire, inspect, interrogate, meddle, peruse, poke into, probe, prospect, pry, question, read up on, research, review, scan, scope out, scout, scrutinize, search, sift, skim, spy, study, wiretap

investigation *n.* analysis, background check, case, check, examination, exploration, inquest, inquisition, inspection, observation, probe, quest, research, review, scrutiny, search, sounding, study, survey *Nonformal*: fishing expedition, gander

investigator *n.* agent, analyst, auditor, checker, DEA man *(U.S.)*, detective, examiner, G-man, inquirer, inspector, ombudsperson, officer, operative, police, private detective, researcher, sleuth, spy, tester *Nonformal:* cop, dick, gumshoe, hound, P.I., private eye

investment *n.* **1.** capitalism, commerce, finance, investiture, purchase, risk, speculation, venture **2.** ante *(Nonformal)*, assets, capital, cash, funds, goods, land, material, money, property, savings, stake *Kinds of Canadian investment vehicles:* common *or* preferred stock, debenture, GIC, mutual fund, RESP, RRIF, RRSP, savings bond, term deposit **3.** contribution, endowment, grant, settlement, subsidy

inveterate *adj.* **1.** chronic, confirmed, habitual, hard-core, hardened, incorrigible, incurable, obstinate, permanent, stubborn, unyielding **2.** abiding, accustomed, continuing, customary, deep-rooted, deep-seated, enduring, entrenched, established, fixed, ingrained, long-lasting, long-lived, longstanding, perennial, perpetual, traditional, venerable *Antonyms:* fresh, new, untried

invidious *adj.* **1.** abominable, detestable, hateful, obnoxious, odious, offensive, repugnant, vilifying *Antonyms:* benevolent, generous, gratifying, pleasant **2.** calumnious, defamatory, discriminatory, libelous, malicious, prejudicial, scandalous, slanderous *Antonyms:* decent, fair, just **3.** begrudging, envious, jealous, resentful *Commonly misused:* **insidious**

invigorate *v.* activate, animate, arouse, energize, enliven, excite, exhilarate, fortify, freshen, galvanize, inspire, quicken, refresh, reinforce, rejuvenate, renew, restore, revitalize, rouse, stimulate, strengthen, vitalize *Nonformal:* pep up, put some spunk into it *Antonyms:* bore, dull, enervate, fatigue

invigorating *adj.* bracing, brisk, charged, energizing, exhilarating, fresh, healthful, lively, quickening, refreshing, rejuvenating, restorative, revitalizing, salubrious, stimulating, tonic, uplifting, vitalizing, zesty *Antonyms:* deadly, noxious, pernicious, unhealthy

invincible *adj.* bulletproof *(Nonformal)*, impassable, impregnable, indestructible, indomitable, infallible, insuperable, inviolable, invulnerable, powerful, strong, unassailable, unbeatable, unconquerable, unsurmountable, untouchable *Antonyms:* beatable, defenceless, powerless, weak

inviolable *adj.* **1.** blessed, consecrated, hallowed, holy, incorruptible, sacred, sacrosanct, sanctified, ultramontane, unbreakable, untouchable, venerated *Antonyms:* evil, profane, vile **2.** impregnable, indestructible, insuperable, invincible, secure, unassailable, unconquerable *Antonyms:* beaten, defeated, humbled, humiliated

invisible *adj.* **1.** impalpable, indetectable, indiscernible, intangible, unseeable *Antonyms:* observable, plain, visible, visual **2.** faint, imperceptible, infinitesimal, microscopic, miniscule, minute, subtle, trace, unnoticeable *Antonyms:* enormous, gargantuan, large **3.** camouflaged, concealed, backstage, behind the curtain, disguised, hidden, masked, obscured, out of sight, screened, unseen, veiled *Antonyms:* front and centre, obvious, overt, patent, prominent

invitation *n.* **1.** appeal, bid, bidding, call, challenge, invite, petition, proffering, prompting, proposal, proposition, request, solicitation, summons, supplication, urge **2.** call, card, e-mail, epistle, fax, letter, note **3.** allurement, attraction, come-on *(Nonformal)*, encouragement, enticement, inducement, lure, overture, provocation, temptation

invite *n. See* **invitation** – *v.* **1.** appeal, ask, beg, bid, call, command, entreat, petition, request, solicit, summon *Antonyms:* snub, spurn **2.** allure, attract, captivate, charm, court, countenance, draw, encourage, entice, excite, interest, inveigle, lead, lure, provoke, stimulate, tempt, welcome, woo *(Nonformal) Antonyms:* repulse, scare, terrify, upset **3.** bring on *or* out, conjure up, evoke, invoke

inviting *adj.* agreeable, alluring, appealing, attractive, beguiling, bewitching, captivating, charming, delightful, encouraging, engaging, enticing, fascinating, intriguing, magnetic, pleasing, seductive, tempting, warm, welcoming, winning, winsome *Antonyms:* disagreeable, offensive, repulsive, unpleasant

nvoke *v.* **1.** appeal to, ask *or* beg for, beseech, call upon, entreat, implore, importune, petition, pray, solicit, supplicate *Antonyms:* curse, damn, defy **2.** adduce, apply, cite, declare employ, execute, implement, initiate, put to use, refer *or* report to, use *Antonyms:* disregard, ignore, overlook, rescind **3.** awaken, call forth *or* up, conjure, invite, rouse, summon *Antonyms:* dismiss, loose, release, send away *Commonly misused:* **evoke**

involuntary *adj.* **1.** automatic, blind, conditioned, habitual, impulsive, instinctual, intuitive, knee-jerk, reflex, spontaneous, uncalculated, unconscious, unintentional, unpremeditated, unprompted, unthinking, unwitting *Antonyms:* calculated, deliberate, planned, purposeful **2.** coercive, compulsory, enforced, forced, mandatory, obligatory *Antonyms:* by choice, elective, volunteer

involve *v.* **1.** betoken, comprise, consist of, constitute, demand, embody, encompass, entail, imply, include, incorporate, necessitate, mean, presuppose, represent, require, take in **2.** affect, change, concern, impact on, influence, interest, touch, transform **3.** absorb, charm, engross, envelop, grip, obsess, occupy, preoccupy, wrap up **4.** bring into, embroil, enmesh, implicate, incriminate, point to *Nonformal:* finger, number **5.** complicate, compound, convolute, intertwine, perplex

involved *adj.* **1.** Borgesian, complex, complicated, confusing, convoluted, elaborate, Gordian, high-tech, intricate, knotty, labyrinthine, maze-like, muddled, rat's nest *(Nonformal)*, sophisticated, tangled, winding *Antonyms:* easy, elementary, simple, simplified **2.** absorbed, affected, busy, committed, concerned, employed, engaged, immersed in, interested, knee deep *(Nonformal)*, occupied, participating, submerged **3.** caught, embarrassed, embroiled, enmeshed, entangled, implicated, incriminated **4.** dating, engaged, going around with, seeing someone, taken

involvement *n.* **1.** association, commitment, dedication, employment, engagement, interest, occupation, participation, responsibility **2.** absorption, concentration, engrossment, fixation, immersion, obsession, preoccupation, submersion **3.** complexity, confusion, difficulty, entanglement, imbroglio, intricacy, labyrinth, maze, problem, puzzle

invulnerable *adj.* bombproof, bulletproof, impenetrable, impregnable, indestructible, insurmountable, invincible, protected, safe, secure, sound, strong, unassailable, unconquerable, tenable *Antonyms:* defenceless, exposed, unprotected

inward *adj.* **1.** inmost, inner, innermost, inside, interior, internal *Antonyms:* exterior, external, outer **2.** emotional, intellectual, introspective, philosophical, spiritual, subjective, visceral **3.** entering, inbound, incoming, infiltrating, inflowing, ingoing, penetrating *Antonyms:* outbound, outgoing, outward **4.** backcountry, backforty *(Nonformal)*, backwoods, inland, inshore, upcountry, upriver **5.** constitutional, implicit, ingrained, inherent, intrinsic – *adv.* centrally, deeply, inside, internally, inwardly

iota *n.* atom, bit, crumb, grain, hint, jot, mite, molecule, particle, puckle *(P.E.I.)*, scintilla, scrap, speck, sliver, soupçon, trace, whit *Nonformal:* smidgen, tinker's damn

irascible *adj.* angry, bad-tempered, bellicose, cantankerous, chippy, choleric, crabby, cranky, cross, edgy, fractious, hasty, hot-tempered, huffy, ill-natured, irritable, peppery, petulant, prickly, quick-tempered, snappish, testy, touchy, volcanic *Antonyms:* casual, pacific, placid, relaxed

irate *adj.* angered, angry, annoyed, cross, enraged, exasperated, fuming, furious, incensed, indignant, infuriated, ireful, livid, mad, nettled, piqued, provoked, raging, riled, upset, vexed, wrathful *Nonformal:* fit to be tied, rabid *Antonyms:* calm, gentle, moderate

ire *n.* acerbity, acrimony, anger, choler, dudgeon, fury, gall, indignation, passion, rage, temper, wrath *Antonyms:* equanimity, serenity

irenic *adj.* appeasing, calming, conciliatory, dovish *(Nonformal)*, gentle, halcyon, mild, mitigating, mollifying, pacific, pacifistic, peaceable, peace-loving, placating, propitiatory, reconciliatory, soothing *Antonyms* disconcerting, inflammatory, upsetting

iridescent *adj.* colourful, gleaming, glistening, kaleidoscopic, lustrous, many coloured, multi-coloured, nacreous opalescent, pearly, polychromatic, prismatic, rainbow-coloured, rainbow-like shimmering

irk *v.* **1.** aggravate, anger, annoy, bother, disturb, exasperate, fret, gall, harass, hecto incense, irritate, miff, nettle, peeve, piqu provoke, rile, ruffle, trouble, upset, ve *Nonformal:* bug, eat, grate on one's nerves hassle, put out, rasp, stick in one's craw tick off **2.** abrade, bore, drag on, fatigue tire to death, wear out, weary

irksome *adj.* aggravating, annoying, bothersome, distressing, disturbing, galling harassing, hectoring, irritating, pesk *(Nonformal)*, pestering, oppressive, tiresome, troublesome, trying, upsetting, vexing, wearisome, worrying *Antonyms:* moll fying, placating, pleasing

iron *adj.* **1.** durable, firm, hard, hardy, inde fatigable, mighty, potent, preserving, rigi robust, rock solid *(Nonformal)*, stalwar steadfast, strong, sturdy, tireless, unbreakable, vigorous, virile *Antonyms:* brittle fragile, weak **2.** adamant, callous, crue fell, grim, hard-hearted, harsh, heartless inexorable, intestinal fortitude *(Nonformal)*, merciless, obdurate, pitiless, severe steely, stern, stony, strict, stringent, tough unfeeling, unyielding *Antonyms:* benevolent, kind, nice – *n.* **1.** cast *or* pig *o* wrought iron, hematite, magnetite, meta steel **2.** energy, endurance, force, fortitude hardiness, might, potency, power, stamina strength, toughness, vigour, vitality **3** chains, fetters, handcuffs, manacles, shackles, trammels **4.** cannon, gun, pistol revolver, rifle, shotgun, weapon – *v.* ho press, press, smooth, steam, straighten

ironic *adj.* **1.** bewildering, contradictory double-edged, figurative, paradoxical, puzzling, surprising, unexpected **2.** acid, bi ing, caustic, cynical, dry, humorous, mocking, penetrating, sarcastic, sardonic, trenchant, witty, wry

irony *n.* **1.** contradiction, double entendre, illogicality, incongruity, paradox **2.** cynicism, derision, humour, mockery, parody, sarcasm, satire, scorn, wit

irradiate *v.* **1.** brighten, diffuse, glow, glisten, illuminate, illumine, light up, radiate *Antonyms:* cloud, darken **2.** educate, enlighten, explain, explicate, expose, guide, illustrate, inform, teach, throw light on **3.** bath, flood, permeate, saturate, shine, spread over, suffuse **4.** radiate, x-ray *Nonformal:* blast, zap

irrational *adj.* **1.** aberrant, disconnected, disjointed, erratic, extravagant, illogical, incoherent, inconceivable, invalid, over the edge *(Nonformal)*, unreasonable, unsound *Antonyms:* clear, logical, orderly, patterned **2.** absurd, asinine, brainless, crazy, delirious, demented, foolish, injudicious, insane, ludicrous, mad, mindless, nonsensical, preposterous, raving, ridiculous, senseless, silly, unstable, unthinking *Nonformal:* addlepated, cockamamie, flaky, iffy *Antonyms:* sagacious, sensible, wise

irrationality *n.* **1.** craziness, dementia, feeble-mindness, insanity, lunacy, madness, senility, unreasonableness, unsoundness *Antonyms:* capability, lucidity, sanity **2.** absurdity, folly, idiocy, inanity, illogicality, kookiness *(Nonformal)*, nonsense, ridiculousness, silliness *Antonyms:* intelligence, prudence, sobriety

irreconcilable *adj.* **1.** hardline, hostile, implacable, inimical, intransigent, rancorous, unforgiving, unyielding, vengeful, vindictive **2.** clashing, conflicting, diametrically opposed, divergent, incompatible, incongruous, inconsistent, opposed – *n.* die-hard, immovable object, intransigent *Nonformal:* bitter-ender, last-ditcher

irrecoverable *adj.* gone, beyond hope, irreclaimable, irredeemable, irremediable, irreparable, irretrievable, lost, unsalvagable, unsaveable *Antonyms:* salvageable

irrefutable *adj.* absolute, beyond question, certain, conclusive, given, incontestable, incontrovertible, indisputable, proven, self-evident, sure as shootin' *(Nonformal)*, unarguable, unassailable, undeniable, unquestionable

irregular *adj.* **1.** capricious, changeable, erratic, fickle, fitful, fluctuating, inconstant, mercurial, shifting, uncertain, unpredictable, unreliable, unstable, unsteady, variable, volatile, wavering *Antonyms:* continual, incessant, rhythmic **2.** aberrant, abnormal, anomalous, atypical, deviant, different, divergent, eccentric, exceptional, improper, odd, peculiar, queer, quirky, singular, unconventional, unusual *Antonyms:* congruent, matching, symmetrical, uniform **3.** arbitrary, herky-jerky *(Nonformal)*, indiscriminate, jerky, nonuniform, patchy, random, sporadic, uneven *Antonyms:* conventional, methodical, formal, systematic **4.** blemished, damaged, flawed, imperfect, marked, misshaped, soiled **5.** all over the map *(Nonformal)*, disorderly, improper, uncouth, unmannered, unruly, vulgar – *n.* **1.** casual, freelancer, hireling, independent, mercenary, outside help, scab *(Nonformal)*, temp **2.** discard, imperfect, reject, second, throwaway

irregularity *n.* **1.** asymmetry, crookedness, jaggedness, lumpiness, patchiness, raggedness, roughness, unevenness *Antonyms:* congruity, symmetry, synchronicity **2.** aberration, abnormality, anomaly, breach, deviation, oddity, peculiarity, singularity, unconventionality, unorthodoxy **3.** blemish, flaw, imperfection, mark, rip, spot, tear **4.** confusion, disorderliness, disorganization, fluctuation, inconsistency, randomness, uncertainty, unsteadiness

irregularly *adv.* disconnectedly, erratically, fitfully, haphazardly, infrequently, intermittently, occasionally, off and on *(Nonformal)*, periodically, slapdash, spasmodically, sporadically, uncommonly, unevenly

irrelevant *adj.* extraneous, foreign, immaterial, inapplicable, inappropriate, inapt, inconsequent, inconsequential, insignificant, pointless, remote, unconnected, unimportant, unnecessary, unrelated *Antonyms:* applicable, essential, pertinent

irreligious *adj.* **1.** atheistic, disbelieving, godless, heathen, infidel, sceptical *Antonyms:* believing, faithful, devout **2.** heretical, impious, profane, sacrilegious, secular, sinful, ungodly, vile, wicked

irremediable *adj.* **1.** deadly, fatal, finished, hopeless, incorrigible, incurable, inoperable, irredeemable, irreparable, lost, mortal, ruined, terminal, unsaveable *Nonformal:* sunk, undone *Antonyms:* fixable, treatable

irremovable *adj.* anchored, fast, firm, fixed, frozen, immovable, ingrained, permanent, riveted, rooted, solid, stuck, unchangeable *Antonyms:* conveyable, transferable

irreplaceable *adj.* essential, indispensible, instrumental, integral, invaluable, one-of-a-kind, precious, priceless, rare, unique, valuable, vital *Antonyms:* expendable, useless, worthless

irrepressible *adj.* **1.** blithe, bright, bubbling, buoyant, cheerful, ebullient, effervescent, enthusiastic, exuberant, high, hopeful, optimistic, rhapsodical, vivacious *Antonyms:* depressed, melancholy, neurasthenic, unhappy **2.** boisterous, insurgent, rebellious, tumultuous, unconstrained, uncontrollable, unmanageable, unquenchable, unrestrained, unruly, unstoppable, wild *Antonyms:* civil, orderly, pliant

irreproachable *adj.* blameless, exemplary, faultless, good, guiltless, high-principled, honest, impeccable, inculpable, innocent, inviolate, perfect, pure, righteous, squeaky-clean *(Nonformal)*, sterling, unimpeachable, upright, upstanding, virtuous *Antonyms:* disgraceful, reprehensible, sinful

irresistible *adj.* **1.** alluring, beautiful, charming, enchanting, fascinating, glamorous, lovable, ravishing, scrumptious, seductive, stunning, tempting, traffic-stopping *(Nonformal) Antonyms:* disgusting, repulsive, scary **2.** beckoning, compelling, inescapable, magnetic, overpowering, overwhelming, potent, powerful, predestined, unavoidable **3.** indomitable, insuperable, invincible, unconquerable, unsubduable *Antonyms:* defenceless, vulnerable, weak

irresolute *adj.* ambivalent, capricious, changing, doubting, faltering, fickle, fitful, fluctuating, halting, hesitant, hesitating, indecisive, infirm, shaky, tentative, tremulous, uncertain, undecided, unsettled, unstable, unsteady, vacillating, wavering, weak *Nonformal:* wishy-washy, wobbly *Antonyms:* firm, fixed, stable, steady

irresponsible *adj.* carefree, derelict, dilatory, flighty, harebrained, heedless, immature, lackadaisical, laggard, lawless, lazy, negligent, rash, reckless, scatterbrained, shiftless, thoughtless, unreliable, untrustworthy *Nonformal:* devil-may-care, harum-scarum *Antonyms:* careful, dependable, responsible, reliable, thoughtful

irretrievable *adj.* beyond repair, hopeless, irremediable, irreversible, lost, nonreversible, overwritten, unrecoverable, unsalvageable *Nonformal:* finished, gone

irreverence *n.* **1.** derision, discourtesy, disdain, disparagement, disrespect, flippancy, impertinence, impudence, insolence, insult, mockery, ridicule, sassiness *Nonformal:* cheek, lip, sauce **2.** blasphemy, desecration, godlessness, heresy, impiety, profanity, sacrilege, sinfulness *Antonyms:* grace, praise, reverence

irrevocable *adj.* binding, changeless, conclusive, established, fixed, immutable, indelible, irretrievable, irreversible, mandatory, permanent, unalterable, unchangeable, unrepealable, unrevocable *Nonformal:* carved-in-stone, hard-and-fast, ironclad *Antonyms:* alterable, mutable, protean, retractable, reversible

irrigate *v.* dampen, deluge, drench, drown, flood, freshen, invigorate, moisten, refresh, revitalize, saturate, soak, sprinkle, wash, water, waterlog, wet *Antonyms:* dehydrate, desiccate, dry

irritable *adj.* **1.** annoyed, bearish, bitchy, bristly, brooding, cantankerous, captious, carping, choleric, complaining, contentious, crabby, cranky, cross, crotchety, difficult, disputatious, dissatisfied, dyspeptic, exasperated, fiery, fractious, fretful, fretting, gloomy, grouchy, grumbling, grumpy, ill-humoured, irascible, moody, ornery, peevish, petulant, prickly, querulous, resentful, short-tempered, snappish, snappy, surly, testy, tetchy, touchy, waspish *Antonyms:* agreeable, complacent, composed, imperturbable, patient **2.** delicate, hypersensitive, sensitive, skittish, tender, thin-skinned

irritate *v.* **1.** aggravate, burn, chafe, fester, hurt, inflame, itch, redden, rub, scrape, scratch, sensitize, sting, swell *Antonyms:* appease, mollify, salve, soothe **2.** agitate, anger, annoy, badger, bait, bedevil, beleaguer, bother, bug *(Nonformal)*, confuse, discomfort, disquiet, distress, disturb, embarrass, embitter, exasperate, fret, gall, gnaw, goad, grate, harass, harry, hector, incense, infuriate, irk, madden, nag, needle, nettle, offend, pain, peeve, perturb, pester, pique, plague, prod, provoke, rankle, rattle, rile, rub, ruffle, spur, taunt, tease, torment, trouble, try, upset, vex, worry *Nonformal:* hassle, miff, ride, rub the wrong way *Antonyms:* calm, comfort, placate

irritating *adj.* abrasive, aggravating, annoying, bothersome, damnable, darn, displeasing, disturbing, galling, infernal, nagging, pesky, sharp, thorny, troublesome, trying, upsetting, vexatious, worrisome *Antonyms:* pleasant, pleasing, soothing

irritation *n.* **1.** bother, irritant, menace, nuisance, pest, plague, tease, trouble *Antonyms:* joy, pleasure, satisfaction **2.** blister, boil, bruise, burn, canker, chancre, cut, infection, inflammation, itch, pain, pimple, scrape, scratch, sore, soreness, tenderness, ulcer, welt **3.** aggravation, annoyance, crossness, displeasure, exasperation, fury, impatience, indignation, irritability, provocation, vexation, wrath

Islam *n.* Islamism *Branches of Islam:* Black Muslim, Ismailian, Shiite, Sufi, Sunni, Wahabi

island *n.* cay, holm, isle, islet, key *Kinds of island:* archipelago, atoll, continental, coral, deserted, iceberg, ice floe, oceanic, plateau, reef, volcanic – *v.* detach, divide, isolate, part, separate, set apart, sever

isolate *v.* **1.** alienate, block *or* close *or* cut off, confine, detach, exclude, garrison, ghettoize, insulate, keep apart, quarantine, remove, segregate, sequester *Antonyms:* assimilate, incorporate, transculturate **2.** disconnect, divide, part, separate, set apart, sever

isolated *adj.* **1.** alienated, alone, apart, confined, detached, hermitic, insular, lonely, outlying, out-of-the-way, private, reclusive, remote, secluded, segregated, single, withdrawn *Antonyms:* popular, populated **2.** blind, cloaked, concealed, cryptic, hidden, masked, secret *Antonyms:* exposed, revealed, unveiled **3.** abnormal, anomalous, atypical, exceptional, freak, freakish, random, rare, singular, special, uncommon, unique, unrelated, unusual *Antonyms:* everyday, normal, typical, usual

isolation *n.* **1.** aloneness, aloofness, introversion, monasticism, privacy, reclusiveness, seclusion, solitude, withdrawal **2.** dissociation, imprisonment, quarantine, segregation, separation

issue *n.* **1.** argument, business at hand, case, cause, concern, contention, controversy, crux, gist, heart, nub, plank, platform, point, principle, problem, question, salient point, subject matter, topic *Nonformal:* bone, hot potato **2.** bottom line, effect, end, fruit, outcome, product, result, upshot **3.** array, broadcast, collection, copy, edition, folio, garland, group, item, number, portfolio, publication, printing, series, set, version, volume **4.** brood, children, descendants, family, heirs, household, offspring, progeny, scions, seed **5.** capitalization, financing, flotation, issuance, launching, offering **6.** broadcasting, circulation, delivery, dispersement, dissemination, distribution, granting, spreading, supply **7.** discharge, efflux, emanation, emission, exudation, gush, leak, outflow, outpouring, overflow **8.** culvert, delta, egress, exit, mouth, outlet, spring, vent – *v.* **1.** come forth, course, drip, effuse, emerge, emanate, emit, erupt, extrude, exude, flood, flow, gush, leak, rain, stream, surface, surge **2.** broadcast, circulate, consign, deliver, dispatch, launch, promulgate, publish, release, send, spread, transmit **3.** appear, arise, ensue, hatch, materialize, originate, pop *or* turn up *(Nonformal)*, result, unfold **4.** allocate, allot, apportion, dispense, disperse, disseminate, distribute, divide, mete out, parcel, spread, supply **5.** announce, command, declare, demand, divulge, express, pronounce, utter

itch *n.* **1.** irritation, itchiness, prickling, rawness, scratching, tingling **2.** craving, desire, fancy, hankering, hunger, inclination, longing, penchant, wish, yearning, yen – *v.* **1.** irritate, prick, prickle, sting, tickle, tingle **2.** burn, crave, desire, fancy, hanker, hunger, long, lust, need, pine, want, yearn

item *n.* **1.** bit, component, detail, matter, part, particular, piece, specific, unit **2.** account, article, blurb, bulletin, column, dispatch, entry, feature, news, note, notice, paragraph, report, story, write-up

itemize *v.* catalogue, cite, count, detail, document, enter, enumerate, inventory, list, mention, note, number, particularize, quote, recite, record, recount, set out, specify, tally

itinerant *adj.* ambulatory, backpacking, floating, journeying, migratory, moving, nomadic, peripatetic, ranging, roaming, roving, shifting, travelling, vagrant, wandering, wayfaring *Nonformal:* footloose, jet-setting, road-bound *Antonyms:* rooted, settled, stationary – *n.* explorer, gadabout, nomad, pilgrim, tourist, traveller, vagabond, wanderer *Nonformal:* backpacker, hobo, tripster

itinerary *n.* **1.** agenda, battle plan *(Nonformal)*, guide, guidebook, outline, plan, program, schedule, timetable, travel plan **2.** beat, circuit, course, journey, line, path, route, run, tour, way

ivory tower *n.* a room of one's own, asylum, escape, haven, hideaway, intellectual *or* mental retreat, protection, refuge, retreat, safe harbour, sanctuary, sanctum, shelter, university

jab *n.* blow, crack, cuff, hit, knock, smite, stab, thrust, whack *Nonformal:* belt, clobber, haymaker, sallywinder, short left – *v.* **1.** buck, bump, bunt, dig, hit, jog, knock, lunge, nudge, poke, prod, punch, push, smack, stab, strike, tap, thrust *Antonyms:* rebound, recoil, spring back **2.** impale, penetrate, perforate, pierce, prick, puncture, run through, skewer, spike, stab, stick, wound

jabber *n.* blabber, jargon, nonsense, palaver, rant, rubbish, twaddle *Nonformal:* bull, gobbledygook, jazz – *v.* babble, blather, chatter, drivel, effervesce, effuse, enthuse, gab, gabble, gibber, gush, prate, prattle, ramble, rave, run on, stammer, talk, twiddle, utter *Nonformal:* gas, jaw, kvetch spout, yackety-yak, yak, yap

jack *n.* **1.** booster, crane, hoist, hydraulic *or* pneumatic lift, lift, raise **2.** emblem, flag, national colours, signal, standard, symbol **3.** connector, electricity, hydro, outlet, plug **4.** cash, currency, lucre, money, silver *Nonformal:* bread, coin, dough, moolah, wampum – *v.* boost, elevate, escalate, heave, heft, hike, hoist, increase, levitate, lift, raise

jacket *n.* **1.** anorak, blazer, coat, lumberjack *or* Kenora dinner jacket *(Nonformal)*, parka, sportscoat, windbreaker *See also:* **coat** **2.** case, casing, cover, covering, encasement, envelope, folder, hull, husk, layer, sheath, shell, skin, wrap, wrapping – *v.* cover, envelop, protect, shield, surround, wrap

jackpot *n.* award, bonanza, first prize, kitty, loot, pool, pot, prize, reward, winnings

jade *n.* birth *or* precious stone, gemstone, jadeite, nephrite – *v.* burn out, enervate, exhaust, fatigue, frazzle, overtax, overuse, overwork, run down, tire, wear down *or* out, weary, wilt, wind

jaded *adj.* **1.** exhausted, fatigued, sick, spent, tired, tired-out, wearied, weary, worn, worn-down, worn-out *Antonyms:* eager, fresh, keen **2.** blasé, bored, cool, dulled, fed up *(Nonformal)*, indifferent, inured, overindulged, sated, satiated, surfeited

jag *n.* **1.** barb, cleft, crag, notch, point, projection, protrusion, snag, spur, tooth **2.** bacchanalia, binge, bout, fit, frolic, indulgence, spell, spree *Nonformal:* bender, booze up – *v.* cut, indent, notch, score

jagged *adj.* angular, barbed, broken, cleft, craggy, indented, irregular, notched, pointed, ragged, ridged, rough, rugged, scabrous, serrated, sharp, snaggy, spiked, toothed, uneven *Antonyms:* glassy, level, rounded, sleek, smooth

jail *n.* bastille, brig, cage, cell, confinement, concentration *or* internment *or* labour camp, detention centre, dungeon, gaol *(British)*, incarceration, jailhouse, keep, limbo, oubliette, penal institution, penitentiary, prison, reformatory *Nonformal:* big house, brig, clink, hoosegow, inside, joint, jug, Kingston, lockup, pen, pokey, skookum-house, slammer, stir – *v.* book, cage, confine, constrain, detain, hold, impound, imprison, incarcerate, lock up, put away, sentence

Jainism *n.* religion *Factions of Jainism:* Digambaras, Shvetambaras, Sthanakavasi *Principles of Jainism:* Ahimsa, Apharigraha, Asteya, Brahmacharya, Satya

jalopy *n.* automobile, car, vehicle *Nonformal:* beater, bomb, bucket of bolts, canoe, clunker, crate, eyesore, heap, hot rod, junk, lemon, tub, wheels, wreck

jam *n.* **1.** bind, box, corner, difficulty, dilemma, fix, hole, plight, predicament, problem, quandary, scrape, situation, spot, strait, trouble *Nonformal:* how-do-you-do, pickle **2.** block, bottleneck, clog, congestion, crowd, crush, delay, gridlock, hold-up, impediment, impasse, logjam, obstacle, obstruction, throng **3.** compote, confiture, conserve, jelly, marmalade, preserve, spread, syrup – *v.* **1.** compress, cram, crowd, crush, elbow, force, jam-pack *(Nonformal)*, jostle, pack, press, push, ram, squash, squeeze, stuff, wedge **2.** catch, fasten, fix, hold together, lodge, secure **3.** bind, block, clog, congest, delay, disrupt, halt, hamper, hinder, interfere, obstruct **4.** ad lib, improvise, invent, perform, play, rag *(Nonformal)*, swing, syncopate

jamboree *n.* banquet, carnival, celebration, convention, feast, festival, fête, frolic, gathering, get-together, hoe-down, jubilee, party, pleasure garden *(Historical)*, potlatch, rally, soiree, spree *Nonformal:* bash, clambake, hoodang, shindig

jammed *adj.* **1.** blocked, clogged, closed, congested, delayed, locked, obstructed, plugged, stopped, stuck *Antonyms:* clear, flowing, open **2.** crammed, forced, packed, pressed, sandwiched *(Nonformal)*, serried, squished, stuffed, wedged

jangle *n.* cacophony, clang, clangour, clash, din, dissonance, distortion, hubbub, hullabaloo, pandemonium, racket, rattle, reverberation, roar, tumult, uproar *Antonyms:* calm, peace, silence – *v.* altercate, argue, bicker, contend, disagree, dispute, fall out, fight, quarrel, spat, squabble, wrangle

janitor *n.* **1.** caretaker, cleaner, custodian, handyperson, sanitary engineer, superintendent *or* super *(Nonformal)* **2.** concierge, doorkeeper, guardian, porter, valet, watchperson

jar *n.* **1.** amphora, basin, bottle, can, canister, carafe, chalice, container, crock, cruet, decanter, ewer, flagon, flask, jug, pitcher, pot, receptacle, urn, vase, vat, vessel **2.** blow, bombshell, jolt, shock, surprise *Nonformal:* eye-opener, kicker, stunner **3** cacophony, clangour, clamour, din, discord, katzenjammer, noise – *v.* **1.** bang, bounce, bump, collide, concuss, convulse, crash, hit, jerk, jiggle, jolt, jounce, quake, rattle, rock, shake, shock, slam, thump, vibrate **2** agitate, annoy, bother, chafe, disturb, grate, grind, hassle *(Nonformal)*, irk, irritate, needle, nettle, outrage, perturb, rankle, shock *Antonyms:* calm, mollify, soothe **3** bicker, clash, conflict, contend, disagree, fight, oppose, quarrel, wrangle *Antonyms:* agree, concur, harmonize

jargon *n.* **1.** babble, chatter, gabble, gibberish, gobbledygook *(Nonformal)*, jabber, nonsense, prattle, verbiage **2.** argot, cant, lingo, patois, patter, phraseology, pidgin, shoptalk, slang, vernacular *Nonformal:* jive, bunkum, lingo *Kinds of jargon:* Academese, bêche-de-mer, businessese, Chinook, computerese, doublespeak, economese, Franglais, journalese, legalese, mediaspeak, medicalese, policyspeak, psychobabble, technobabble, winespeak – *v.* babble, chatter, gabble, gibber, jabber, prattle

jaundice *n.* **1.** cirrhosis, hepatitis, icterus, liver disease **2.** anger, animosity, bigotry, bile, bitterness, contempt, cynicism, envy, intolerance, jealousy, peevishness, resentment – *v.* affect, alter, bend, bias, colour, distort, influence, mould, prejudice, shape, skew, sway, taint, twist, warp

jaundiced *adj.* **1.** biased, coloured, distorted, intolerant, one-sided, partial, partisan, prejudiced, tainted, tendentious, unfair, warped **2.** antagonistic, bitter, cynical, disagreeable, disapproving, distasteful, envious, grudging, hostile, jealous, peevish, pessimistic, resentful, sceptical, spiteful, splenetic, suspicious, unpleasant *Antonyms:* buoyant, elated, jubilant, optimistic

jaunt *n.* adventure, excursion, journey, junket, outing, picnic, pilgrimage, road trip, stroll, tour, tramp, trip, vacation, weekend away – *v.* drive, hike, journey, travel, voyage

jaunty *adj.* **1.** airy, animated, breezy, brisk, buoyant, carefree, cheerful, cocky, flippant, fresh, frisky, frolicsome, high-spirited, hilarious, impetuous, impish, jovial, lively nervy, perky, playful, prankish, spirited, sporty, sprightly, swaggering, venturesome, vivacious *Antonyms:* dull, lifeless, sedate, serious, staid **2.** dapper, debonair, dashing, fine, handsome, pretty, natty, smart, spruce, stately, trim

aw *n.* **1.** bone, chin, hinge, jowl, mandible, maxilla, maw, mouth, muzzle **2.** fangs, hooks, teeth *Nonformal:* chompers, chops **3.** aperture, entrance, entryway, opening, orifice **4.** bind, clamp, compress, fastener, girder, grasp, grip, hold, support **5.** communication, discourse, discussion, gab *or* rap session *(Nonformal)*, palaver, parlay, talk – *v.* **1.** banter, chat, communicate, converse, discourse, discuss, exchange, jabber, prate, speak, talk **2.** abuse, baste, berate, blame, censure, criticize, deride, denigrate, deprecate, flay, rail, rate, revile, scold, tongue-lash, upbraid, vituperate *Antonyms:* exalt, extol, praise

azz *n.* **1.** improvisation, music *Kinds of jazz music:* acid, avant-garde, big band, boogie *or* boogie-woogie, bebop, bop, cool, Cuban, Dixieland, East Coast, free, freestyle, fusion, hard bop, hot, jazz orchestra, jazz rock, jive, Latin, mainstream, modern, New Orleans, progressive, ragtime, samba, stride, swing, traditional, West Coast *See also:* **music** **2.** bragging, fanfaronade, jactation, nonsense, prattle, rodomontade *Nonformal:* bull, crap, gobbledygook, jive **3.** animation, drive, élan, gusto, liveliness, pep, spirit, verve, vivacity, zest *Nonformal:* chutzpah, moxie, pizzazz, zip – *v.* adorn, beautify, bedeck, brighten, deck, decorate, dress, enliven, embellish, fix up, ornament, trim *Nonformal:* pretty *or* spruce up, style

azzy *adj.* animated, exciting, exuberant, fancy, flashy, gaudy, lively, salacious, sexy, smart, spirited, vivacious, wild *Nonformal:* cool, crazy, crazy-cat, flippy, funky, snappy, snazzy, trippy, wacky, wigged-out

ealous *adj.* **1.** covetous, desirous, emulous, envious, green *(Nonformal)*, hankering, solicitous, yearning **2.** anxious, apprehensive, crazy *(Nonformal)*, distrustful, fearful, mistrustful, suspicious, uneasy *Antonyms:* assured, confident, self-possessed **3.** antagonistic, begrudging, bitter, hostile, invidious, jaundiced, malevolent, malicious, offensive, vengeful, rancorous, resentful, spiteful, venomous, vexatious, vindictive *Antonyms:* benevolent, good-natured, kind **4.** burdensome, demanding, exacting, imposing, onerous, oppressive, requiring, taxing, tolling *Antonyms:* easy, light, simple

jealousy *n.* **1.** covetousness, desire, envy, rivalry **2.** bitterness, discontent, ill-will, invidiousness, jaundice, resentment, spite **3.** distrust, mistrust, scepticism, suspicion, uncertainty

jeer *n.* abuse, affrontery, derision, dig, discourtesy, insolence, insult, mockery, offence *Nonformal:* Bronx cheer, raspberry – *v.* abuse, affront, belittle, deride, disparage, flout, gibe, heckle, hector, humiliate, insult, jest, laugh at, mock, mortify, offend, pique, poke fun, quip, ridicule, scoff, sneer, taunt *Nonformal:* dis, dump on, knock, put down, razz, slam *Antonyms:* acclaim, applaud, cheer, clap, praise

jell *v.* **1.** clot, coagulate, congeal, crystallize, freeze, harden, set, solidify, stiffen, thicken **2.** construct, fashion, form, materialize, mould, shape

jellied *adj.* clotted, coagulated, congealed, gelatinous, glutenous, grumous, inspissated, sticky, thick, viscous *Antonyms:* fluid, liquid, solvent, watery

jelly *n.* aspic, confection, confiture, conserves, gelatin, jam, marmalade, preserves, spread, syrup

jeopardize *v.* compromise, endanger, expose, gamble, hazard, imperil, risk, stake, threaten *Antonyms:* defend, protect, safeguard, shield, watch over

jeopardy *n.* danger, exposure, hazard, insecurity, liability, peril, precariousness, risk, susceptibility, threat, uncertainty, vulnerability *Antonyms:* insurance, safety, security

jerk *n.* **1.** fool, idiot, jackass, nincompoop, ninny, pain *Nonformal:* bumbler, butthead, creep, crumb, hoser, loser, piece of work, turkey, twit **2.** attack, contraction, convulsion, fit, spasm, twitch – *v.* **1.** grab, pull, snag, snatch, thrust, tug, twist, wrench, wrest **2.** contract, convulse, jostle, jounce, lurch, quake, quiver, shake, spasm, twitch, writhe **3.** age, cure, dry, preserve, salt, season, spice, smoke

jerky *adj.* **1.** bumpy, jarring, jolting, rough **2.** convulsive, jumpy, paroxysmal, palsied, shaky, spasmodic, tremulous, twitchy **3.** abrupt, choppy, discontinuous, disjunctive, episodic, fragmented, irregular, non-uniform, patchy

jest *n.* **1.** antic, bon mot, crack, gag, joke, laugh, one-liner, prank, pun, quip, ridicule, spoof, trick, wisecrack, witticism *Nonformal:* hokum, wheeze **2.** diversion, frolic, fun, gaiety, humorousness, lark, leisure, levity, merriness, mischief, playfulness, pleasantry, silliness – *v.* **1.** banter, chaff, deride, flout, fool, gibe, gird, jape, jeer, jive, joke, mock, quip, tease *Nonformal:* jolly, josh, kid, needle, rag, razz, rib, roast **2.** cut capers *(Nonformal)*, dally, frolic, idle, play, trifle

jester *n.* actor, antic, banterer, buffoon, clown, comedian, comic, fool, humorist, joker, practical joker, prankster, trickster, wag, wisecracker, wit *Nonformal:* cutup, madcap

jet *adj.* black, coal, dark, ebony, inky, obsidian, raven, sable, sloe, sooty, tar – *n.* **1.** aircraft, airplane, fighter, jetliner, jumbo jet, plane, ramjet, supersonic *or* supersonic transport, turbo **2.** column, fountain, geyser, nozzle, shower head, spout, spray, spring, sprinkle – *v.* **1.** burst, erupt, flow, gush, issue, pour, roll, rush, shoot, spew, spout, spill, spit, spritz, spurt, squirt, stream, surge **2.** fly, glide, go, leave, soar, take flight, travel

jettison *n.* debris, flotsam, garbage, jetsam, refuse – *v.* abandon, abdicate, cast, cast off, chuck, deep six *(Nonformal)*, discard, discharge, dump, eject, expel, heave, hurl, scrap, slough, throw away *or* overboard, unload

jetty *n.* barrier, breakwater, bulkhead, buttress, dock, embankment, harbour, harbourside, landing, marina, mole, pier, pierside, quay, retaining wall, seawall, wharf

jewel *n.* **1.** stone, bauble, bead, bijou, birthstone, gem, gemstone, ornament, sparkle *(Nonformal)*, trinket **2.** masterpiece, nonpareil, opus, paragon, pearl, prize, rarity, specialty, treasure, wonder – *v.* adorn, bedeck, deck, decorate, embellish, enhance, furnish, ornament, set

jewellery *n.* adornment, gems, jewel *Kinds of jewellery:* anklet, band, bangle, bauble, beads, bracelet, brooch, cameo, chain, charm, choker, cross, crown, cufflinks, earring, gem, locket, necklace, pendant, pin, ring, solitaire, tiara

jibe *v.* accord, agree, concur, correspond, dovetail, fit, harmonize, match, meet, square, tally

jig *n.* **1.** dance, hoe-down, jitterbug, shuffle *See also:* **dance 2.** artifice, deceit, deception, ruse – *v.* **1.** bob, bounce, clog, dance, fling, jerk, jiggle, hop, leap, shake, shuffle, spring, twitch, reel, waltz, wiggle, wriggle *Nonformal:* boogie, cut a rug **2** angle, deceive, entice, fish, lure, snare, spoon

jilt *v.* abandon, betray, break *or* cast off, disappoint, discard, ditch, drop, dump, forsake, leave, refuse, reject, scorn, spurn, turn down *Antonyms:* accept, acknowledge, admit, welcome

jingle *n.* **1.** chink, clink, ding, ding-a-ling, dingle, jangle, ping, ring, ting, ting-a-ling, tinkle **2.** advertisement, blurb, commercial, spot, tune **3.** alliteration, assonance, consonance, onomatopoeia, rhyme, rhythm – *v.* chink, clink, ding, ping, ring, sound, ting, tinkle

jingoism *n.* chauvinism, bias, devotion, flag-waving, nationalism, patriotism, superpatriotism, ultranationalism

jinx *n.* cantrip, charm, curse, evil eye *(Nonformal)*, hex, jinker *(Newfoundland)*, malocchio *(Italian)*, plague, spell, voodoo, whammy – *v.* bedevil, bewitch, charm, curse, damn, enchant, hex, spook

jitters *n. pl.* anxiety, excitement, nerves, nervousness, restlessness, shakes, shivers, tension *Nonformal:* creeps, heebie-jeebies jumps, willies *Antonyms:* assuredness, confidence, cool

job *n.* **1.** activity, affair, appointment, assignment, burden, care, charge, chore, commission, concern, contribution, deed, duty, effort, enterprise, errand, function, mission, obligation, onus, project, pursuit, responsibility, role, task, undertaking, venture **2.** business, calling, career, craft, employment, livelihood, métier, occupation, office, operation, position, post, profession, trade, vocation, work **3.** burglary, crime, larceny, robbery, theft *Nonformal:* caper, heist, holdup, stickup, stunt – *v.* contract, farm *or* freelance *or* source out

jockey *n.* equestrian, horseback rider, horse racer, rider, steeplechaser – *v.* **1.** adjust, cajole, coax, contrive, induce, influence, manage, manoeuvre, manipulate, negotiate **2.** beguile, betray, cheat, deceive, defraud, delude, dupe, mislead, swindle, trick **3.** bestride, direct, guide, lead, manage, race, ride

jocular *adj.* amusing, blithe, camp, campy, comical, daffy, droll, facetious, flaky, funny, humorous, jesting, jocose, joking, laughable, ludicrous, mischievous, roguish, sportive, teasing, waggish, whimsical, witty *Nonformal:* joshing, wacky *Antonyms:* humourless, serious, solemn, stern

jocund *adj.* blissful, bright, carefree, cheerful, delightful, gay, glad, gleeful, happy, jaunty, jolly, jovial, joyful, lighthearted, lively, merry, mirthful, playful, pleasant, rapturous *Antonyms:* depressing, melancholy, mournful, sad

jog *n.* angle, bend, crook, dogleg, jag, swerve, turn – *v.* **1.** exercise, practice, train, work out **2.** canter, dash, gallop, lope, pace, progress, race, run, sprint, trot *Antonyms:* amble, saunter, stagger, stroll, walk **3.** activate, agitate, arouse, jar, kindle, nudge, poke, press, prod, prompt, push, remind, start, stimulate, stir, suggest, tap **4.** bounce, bump, dislodge, jerk, jolt, jostle, move, shake

joie de vivre *n.* animation, ardour, contentment, *douceur de vivre (French)*, élan, enthusiasm, fire, joy, life, liveliness, spirit, sprightliness, verve, vivacity

join *v.* **1.** adhere, attach, coalesce, conjoin, connect, fasten, glue, link, meet, pair *Antonyms:* detach, divide, separate, sever **2.** bind, cement, combine, couple, engage, fetter, fuse, incorporate, marry, mate, unite, wed, weld **3.** affiliate, align, ally, associate with, come aboard, consort, cooperate, enrol, enter, pair with, plug into *(Nonformal)*, register, side with, sign on *or* up, subscribe *Antonyms:* leave, quit, resign **4.** affix, blend, clamp, clip, entwine, interlace, splice, suture, weave

joint *adj.* bilateral, bipartisan, collective, combined, communal, concerted, consolidated, cooperative, mutual, shared, united – *n.* **1.** abutment, articulation, bend, bond, bridge, confluence, connection, coupling, hinge, interconnection, intersection, junction, juncture, knot, link, nexus, seam, splice, tie, union *Kinds of joints:* ankle, dovetail, elbow, hinge, hip, knee, neck, pivot, rabbet, scarf, shoulder, wrist **2.** after-hours club, bar, beer parlour, beverage room, *brasserie (Quebec)*, brew pub, club, den, draft house, haunt, hotel, lair, nightclub, nightspot, pub, speakeasy *(Historical)*, taproom, tavern *Nonformal:* booze can, crib, dive, dump, hole, honky-tonk **3.** marijuana cigarette *Nonformal:* doobie, fatty, jay, reefer, smoke, spliff, toke

joke *n.* **1.** antic, bon mot, buffoonery, burlesque, farce, frolic, fun, gag, game, horseplay, hokum, humour, jest, lark, laugh, mischief, one-liner, parody, play, prank, pun, quip, raillery, repartee, rib, sally, stunt, wisecrack, witticism *Nonformal:* tall tale, wheeze, yarn **2.** frivolity, dalliance, passing fancy, trifle, whim **3.** butt, clown, fool, victim *Nonformal:* sucker, stooge – *v.* banter, chaff, deride, frolic, gambol, jest, laugh, make merry, mock, play, pun, quip, rag, ridicule, quip, spoof, sport, taunt, tease, trick, wisecrack *Nonformal:* horse, jive, josh, kid, needle, rib, ride, roast

joker *n.* buffoon, butt, clown, comedian, comic, fool, humorist, jester, kidder, prankster, punster, quipster, stand-up comic, stooge, straight man, teaser, trickster, wag, wisecracker, wit *Nonformal:* card, cutup, kibitzer

jollity *n.* buoyancy, celebration, conviviality,

elation, frivolity, gaiety, glee, good *or* high spirits, hilarity, jocularity, jocundity, jolliness, joviality, joyfulness, jubilancy, levity, merriment, mirth, playfulness, revelry *Antonyms:* despair, melancholy, misery, sadness, sorrow

jolly *adj.* blithe, bouncy, carefree, cheerful, chipper, convivial, delightful, enjoyable, entertaining, festive, frolicsome, funny, gay, gleeful, happy, hilarious, jocund, joyful, joyous, jubilant, laughing, lighthearted, merry, mirthful, playful, pleasant *Antonyms:* doleful, grave, lugubrious miserable, solemn

jolt *n.* **1.** blow, bump, clash, collision, concussion, impaction, jar, jerk, jounce, lurch **2.** astonishment, disturbance, shock, start, surprise, upset – *v.* **1.** bump, impact, jog, jostle, knock, shove, strike **2.** astonish, astound, daze, disturb, electrify, perturb, shake up, shock, stagger, startle, stir, stun, surprise, upset *Nonformal:* bowl over, floor

jolting *n.* amazing, astonishing, astounding, awakening, charging, electrifying, exciting, impassioning, shocking, startling, stimulating, stirring, stunning, surprising

jostle *v.* bump, crash, crowd, elbow, hustle, jab, jog, joggle, manoeuvre, nudge, position, press, push, scramble, shake, shoulder, shove, squeeze, thrust

jot *n.* bit, dab, fleck, iota, mote, particle, smidgen, speck – *v.* annotate, doodle, enter, indicate, note, pencil in, post, record, scribble, write

journal *n.* account, periodical, publication, magazine, serial, record *Common journals:* academic, almanac, annals, annual, calendar, chronicle, daily, daybook, diary, dossier, gazette, Hansard *(Parliament)*, historical, ledger, literary, log, magazine, medical, memoir, minutes, monthly, newspaper, notebook, quarterly, registry, review, scientific, ship's log, tabloid, weekly, yearbook

journalism *n.* **1.** broadcasting, coverage, editing, news, reportage, publishing, writing **2.** press corps, the fourth estate, the press, print *or* television media *Kinds of journalism:* broadcast, electronic, print, radio, sensational, tabloid, television, yellow *(Nonformal)*

journalist *n.* interviewer, newsman, newswoman, newswriter, paparazzi, photographer, reporter *Nonformal:* newshawk, newshound, scoop *Kinds of journalist:* broadcaster, city editor, columnist, commentator, copy editor, correspondent, cub reporter, editorial writer, feature writer, feature editor, finance, foreign correspondent, foreign editor, independent, managing editor, newspaperman, newspaperwoman, photographer, photojournalist, politics, radio, sports editor, staff writer, stringer, sub-editor, television, wire service

journey *n.* adventure, campaign, circuit, constitutional, course, drive, excursion, expedition, exploration, hike, jaunt, junket, march, migration, odyssey, outing, passage, patrol, peregrination, pilgrimage, promenade, quest, road trip, safari, saunter, stroll, survey, tour, transit, travel, trek, trip, venture, visit, voyage, walkabout, wayfaring – *v.* cruise, fly, hie, hop, jet, pass, proceed, process, push on, ramble, range, repair, roam, rove, tour, traverse, trek, wander, wend

joust *n.* combat, *concours (French)*, contest, encounter, engagement, match, meeting, rally, test, tilt, tournament, tourney trial – *v.* battle, clash, contend, engage fight, jostle, take up arms

jovial *adj.* affable, amiable, animated, blithe, bouncy, buoyant, cheery, companionable, convivial, cordial, delightful, enjoyable, festive, glad, gleeful, good-natured, happy, hilarious, humorous, jocund, jolly, jubilant, larksome, lighthearted, merry, mirthful, pleasant, sociable *Antonyms:* antisocial, depressed, grumpy, morose, surly

joy *n.* **1.** animation, bliss, charm, cheer, comfort, delectation, delight, ecstasy, elation, exaltation, exultation, felicity, festivity, gaiety, glee, gratification, happiness, hilarity, humour, indulgence, jubilance, mirth, pleasure, pride, rapture, transport, treasure, wonder *Antonyms:* despair, grief, misery, sorrow, tribulation **2.** amusement, dalliance, distraction, diversion, enjoyment, frolic, pastime, recreation, sport, trifle

joyful *adj.* **1.** cheerful, cheery, delighted, ecstatic, effervescent, elated, enraptured, festive, glad, gratified, happy, jolly, jovial, jubilant, lighthearted, merry, overjoyed, pleased, rapturous, satisfied, sunny, transported, upbeat *Antonyms:* miserable, pained, unhappy **2.** enjoyable, fulfilling, heartening, intoxicating, lovely, satisfying

joyless *adj.* **1.** black, bleak, cheerless, dejected, depressed, doleful, downcast, dragged, dreary, droopy, dull, gloomy, heavy, lifeless, low, melancholy, mournful, neurasthenic, sad, sombre, unhappy **2.** depressing, dismal, dispiriting, dreadful, frightful, miserable, terrible *Antonyms:* humorous, jocular, joyous

jubilant *adj.* celebratory, elated, enraptured, euphoric, excited, exuberant, exulted, flying *(Nonformal)*, glad, gleeful, happy, joyous, overjoyed, rejoicing, rhapsodic, thrilled, triumphal, triumphant *Antonyms:* despondent, downcast, sad, sombre

jubilation *n.* blissfulness, cheerfulness, delight, elatedness, elation, excitement, exhilaration, exultation, glee, high spirits, jollity, joy, light-heartedness, merriment, mirth, pleasure, rejoicing, revelry *Nonformal:* hoopla, whoopee

jubilee *n.* anniversary, bicentennial, birthday, carnival, celebration, centennial, charivari, commemoration, event, festival, festivity, holiday, jamboree, merrymaking, party *Nonformal:* bash, blowout, shindig, windup, wingding

Judaism *n.* Jewish religion *Forms of Judaism:* Conservative, Hasidism, Orthodox, Reform

judge *n.* adjudicator, administrator, appraiser, arbiter, arbitrator, assessor, authority, chancellor, conciliator, evaluator, intermediary, interpreter, justice, magistrate, moderator, negotiator, ombudsperson, referee, umpire, warden – *v.* **1.** adjudicate, arbitrate, conclude, condemn, criticize, decide, decree, derive, find, pass sentence, referee, rule, sit, test, try **2.** appraise, appreciate, approximate, ascertain, assess, consider, determine, discern, distinguish, estimate, evaluate, examine, gather, hear, mediate, preside, rate, review, size up, suppose, value

judgment *n.* **1.** analysis, appraisal, arbitration, assessment, conclusion, conviction, decision, deduction, determination, estimation, evaluation, finding, observation, opinion, order, probing, reckoning, reconnaissance, regard, report, result, review, ruling, scrutiny, sentence, summary, verdict, view **2.** acumen, acuteness, astuteness, awareness, brains, capacity, cleverness, comprehension, discernment, discretion, discrimination, experience, genius, grasp, incisiveness, ingenuity, insight, intelligence, intuition, keenness, knowledge, mentality, perception, perspicacity, prudence, quickness, range, rationality, reasoning, sagacity, sanity, sense, sharpness, shrewdness, sophistication, soundness, taste, understanding, wisdom, wit *Antonyms:* dullness, indiscretion, slow-wittedness, stupidity **3.** affliction, castigation, chastisement, correction, doom, infliction, fate, misfortune, punishment, retribution

judicial *adj.* **1.** administrative, authoritative, judicatory, judiciary, juristic, lawful, legal, magisterial, official, statutory **2.** acute, astute, aware, critical, discerning, discriminating, keen, rational, sagacious, sharp, shrewd, sophisticated, wise *Antonyms:* dim-witted, slow **3.** detached, dispassionate, evenhanded, impartial, just, neutral, objective, unbiased **4.** adjudicated, commanded, decided, decreed, determined, dictated, enforced, ordained, ordered, proclaimed, pronounced, sanctioned, settled **5.** daunting, formal, grave, intimidating, officious, serious, solemn *Antonyms:* inconsequential, light, superficial

judicious *adj.* **1.** accurate, astute, clear-sighted, considerate, enlightened, far-sighted, informed, keen, perceptive, perspicacious, profound, quick-witted, sagacious, sage, sapient, sharp, shrewd, skilful, sophisticated, wise, worldly-wise *Antonyms:* dumb, foolish, silly **2.** calculating, careful, cautious, circumspect, considered, diplomatic, discerning, discreet, discriminating, efficacious, expedient, judicial, politic, prudent, rational, reasonable, seasonable, seemly, sensible, sober, sound, thorough, thoughtful, wary, well-advised

Antonyms: imprudent, indiscreet, tactless, thoughtless

jug *n.* amphora, beaker, bottle, canteen, carafe, container, crock, cruet, decanter, ewer, flagon, flask, jar, pitcher, pot, receptacle, tub, urn, vase, vessel

juggle *v.* **1.** deal, handle, manoeuvre, manage, multitask, negotiate **2.** alter, change, deceive, defraud, doctor *(Nonformal),* fix, hustle, manipulate, modify, shuffle

juice *n.* **1.** alcohol, *aqua vitae (Latin),* distillation, drink, essence, extract, fluid, liquid, liquor, nectar, sap, secretion **2.** spirit, strength, vigour, vitality *Nonformal:* moxie, spunk

juicy *adj.* **1.** dewy, dripping, humid, liquid, luscious, lush, moist, oozy, pulpy, sappy, slippery, slushy, soaked, sodden, succulent, syrupy, viscid, watery, wet *Antonyms*: dehydrated, desiccated, dry **2.** colourful, exciting, fascinating, interesting, intimate, intriguing, lively, piquant, provocative, racy, risque, sensational, spicy, suggestive, tantalizing, vivid *Antonyms:* boring, dull, insipid

jumble *n.* **1.** assortment, blend, combination, gallimaufry, hodgepodge, medley, mélange, miscellany, mixture, patchwork, potpourri **2.** chaos, clutter, confusion, disarrangement, disarray, disorder, litter, mess, muddle, tangle – *v.* **1.** clutter, confuse, dishevel, disorder, disturb, entangle, foul *or* mess up, muddle, muss *(Nonformal),* strew, tangle **2.** blend, bunch, combine, cram, heap, litter, mix, pile, shuffle, throw *or* toss together *Antonyms:* array, organize, sort, tidy

jumbo *adj.* Brobdingnagian, elephantine, enormous, gargantuan, gigantic, huge, hulking, imposing, large, macro, mammoth, monstrous, tall, unwieldy, whopping *(Nonformal) Antonyms:* micro, small, tiny, wee – *n.* beast, behemoth, giant, leviathan, whale, whopper *(Nonformal)*

jump *n.* **1.** bob, bounce, bound, dance, dive, drop, fall, gambol, hop, hurdle, lurch, pounce, skip, spring, vault **2.** bar, barricade, barrier, fence, gap, hurdle, impediment, interval, obstacle, opening, rail, stretch **3.** advance, ascent, augmentation, boost, increase, increment, inflation, rise, upsurge, upturn **4.** advantage, handicap, head start, upper hand **5.** brink, buffalo jump *(Prairies historical),* cliff, drop, fall, leap, overhang, precipice – *v.* **1.** bound, clear, hop, hurtle, jounce, leap, leapfrog, lunge, somersault, spring, vault **2.** bounce, carom, flinch, jerk, rebound, recoil, ricochet, start, startle, surge **3.** accelerate, advance, augment, boost, elevate, escalate, hike, increase, jack *(Nonformal),* raise *Antonyms:* drop, fall, lower **4.** avoid, bypass, go *or* work around, leave out, neglect, omit, pass over, skip **5.** abduct, assail, assault, attack, beset, mug, pounce on, storm *Nonformal:* bushwhack, goon **6.** bail out, descend, dive, fall, parachute, plummet, plunge, skydive **7.** board, enlist enter, get on, join, subscribe **8.** abandon bail out, bolt, forsake, leave, quit

jumpy *adj.* alarmed, anxious, apprehensive, edgy, fidgety, fluctuating, fluttery, itchy, jittery, nervous, nervy, restless, shaky, skittish, skittery, tense, troubled, turbulent, twitching, uneasy, vacillating, wavering *Antonyms:* calm, peaceful, unruffled

junction *n.* **1.** alliance, assemblage, coalition, consolidation, convergence, coupling, dovetail, hinge, hookup, juncture, link, mortise, node, pivot, reunion, splice, tie-in, tie-up, union, weld **2.** crossing, crossroads, hamlet, intersection, juncture, terminal, whistle stop

juncture *n.* **1.** attachment, bond, coherence, combination, confluence, connection, joint, seam **2.** circumstance, condition, crisis, moment, occasion, point, position, state, time

jungle *n.* **1.** boondocks *(Nonformal)* brush, bush, bushveld, chaparral, foliage, forest, growth, primeval *or* rain *or* tropical forest, tangle, timberland, undergrowth, wilderness, wilds, woods **2.** disarray, jumble, maelstrom, pandemonium, turmoil, untidiness, uproar *Nonformal:* rat's nest, rumpus, snake pit **3.** asphalt *or* concrete *or* urban jungle, downtown, ghetto, inner city, megalopolis, metropolis, sprawl *Nonformal:* big smoke, mean streets

unior *adj.* **1.** inferior, lesser, secondary, subordinate, younger *Antonyms:* chief, ranking, superior **2.** beginning, apprentice, assistant, rookie, student – *n.* child, juvenile, kid *(Nonformal)*, minor, youngster

unk *n.* clutter, debris, detritus, dregs, dross, filth, flotsam, garbage, hogwash, jetsam, litter, miscellany, offal, refuse, rubbish, rubble, rummage, scrap, trash, waste – *v.* abandon, deep-six *(Nonformal)*, discard, dismiss, reject, scrap, throw out, trash *Antonyms:* keep, salvage, save

unkie *n.* addict, dope *or* drug addict, habitué, user *Nonformal:* crackhead, dopehead, druggie, mainliner, pothead, space cadet, speed-freak, stoner

unta *n.* assembly, bloc, cabal, cadre, camarilla, clique, coalition, conclave, coterie, council, crew, faction, gang, league, party, ring, wing

urisdiction *n.* **1.** administration, arbitration, authority, command, commission, control, domination, influence, power, prerogative, right, rule, say, supervision, sway **2.** area, *arrondissement (French)*, beat, district, domain, dominion, field, kingdom, limits, province, range, reach, region, scope, sphere, territory *Nonformal:* stomping grounds, turf

ury *adj. Nautical:* auxiliary, back-up, spare, temporary – *n.* board, committee, inquest, panel, tribunal *Kinds of jury:* coroner's, grand, hung, petit, petty, trial

ust *adj.* **1.** accurate, equitable, evenhanded, exact, fair, fair-minded, impartial, nondiscriminatory, proper, right, sound, strict, true, veracious, well-grounded **2.** conscientious, dependable, faithful, good, honest, objective, reliable, tried, unbiased, uncoloured, upright *Antonyms:* corrupt, devious, dishonest, inappropriate, prejudiced **3.** approved, authorized, justified, lawful, legitimate, sanctioned **4.** appropriate, apt, befitting, correct, deserved, due, fitting, merited, proper, reasonable, rightful, suitable, well-deserved **5.** cogent, considerable, firm, solid, strong, substantial, thought-out, well-founded – *adv.* **1.** absolutely, accurately, completely, definitely, directly, entirely, exactly, expressly, perfectly, precisely, right, squarely, unmistakably **2.** almost, approximately, barely, hardly, lately, merely, nearly, only, scarcely, simply, solely

justice *n.* **1.** due process, equity, evenness, fair play *or* treatment, impartiality, neutrality, objectivity, rectitude, rightness, scrupulousness, tolerance, veracity *Antonyms:* corruption, moral turpitude **2.** account, bench, court, court of law, courtroom, hearing, trial, tribunal **3.** amends, compensation, dues, recompense, retribution *Nonformal:* an eye for an eye, just desserts **4.** administrator, arbitrator, chancellor, JAG, judge, judicial officer, magistrate

justifiable *adj.* acceptable, admissible, allowable, defensible, lawful, legitimate, logical, proper, reasonable, right, rightful, sound, suitable, tenable, understandable, valid, warranted, well-founded *Antonyms:* inexcusable, unwarranted

justification *n.* **1.** basis, defence, excuse, explanation, evidence, grounds, idea, pretext, purpose, *raison d'être (French)*, rationale, reason, support **2.** excuse, exoneration, vindication **3.** answer, argument, confirmation, reply, response

justify *v.* **1.** account for, explain, rationalize, show cause **2.** absolve, acquit, clear, exculpate, excuse, exonerate, pardon *Antonyms:* charge, convict **3.** advocate, approve, condone, confirm, contend, countenance, defend, legalize, legitimize, support, sustain, substantiate, uphold, validate, verify, warrant **4.** adjust, alter, change, move, shift, square

jut *n.* extension, overhang, projection, prominence, protrusion – *v.* bulge, cover, elongate, extend, lengthen, poke, stand *or* stick out, project, protrude, protuberate, shoot forward

juvenile *adj.* adolescent, babyish, beardless, blooming, boyish, budding, callow, childish, childlike, developing, formative, fresh, girlish, green, growing, immature, inexperienced, infant, infantile, jackanapes, jejune, junior, naive, pubescent, puerile, teenage, tender, underage, undeveloped, unfledged, unsophisticated, unweaned, vernal, young, youthful *Antonyms:* adult, mature, responsible – *n.* adolescent, boy, child, girl, hobbledehoy, minor, youngster, youth *Nonformal:* kid, punk, whippersnapper *Antonyms:* father, grown-up, mother, parent

juxtapose *v.* **1.** abut, collocate, march on, neighbour, pair, partner **2.** compare, contrast, match, place *or* put side by side

kaleidoscopic *adj.* **1.** alterable, changeable, erratic, ever-changing, fluctuating, mercurial, mobile, mutable, phantasmagoric, protean, shifting, unsteady, vacillating, variable *Antonyms:* constant, fixed, invariable, set **2.** calico, dappled, motley, multi-coloured, parti-coloured, variegated *Antonyms:* monochromatic, uniform

karma *n.* **1.** destiny, fate, fortune, kismet, lot, luck, moira, portion, predestination **2.** belief, creed, doctrine, dogma, principle, teachings, tenet

katzenjammer *n.* **1.** bedlam, brouhaha, commotion, disturbance, fracas, pandemonium, uproar *Nonformal:* foofaraw, kerfuffle, rumpus **2.** cacophony, clamour, din, crash, racket, shriek, smash **3.** alcohol poisoning, crapulence, hangover, headache, Seagram's flu *(Nonformal)*

keel *n.* barge, boat, bully *(Newfoundland)*, Cape Islander *(Atlantic Provinces)*, craft, flatboat, packet, ship, vessel, yacht – *v.* **1.** capsize, founder, overturn, pitch, plunge, topple, tumble, upset **2.** collapse, drop, faint, fall, slump, swoon, tumble

keen *adj.* **1.** astute, bright, brilliant, canny, clever, discerning, discriminating, intelligent, observant, perceptive, perspicacious, quick, refined, sagacious, sapient, sensitive, sharp, shrewd, wise *Antonyms:* dull, slow, witless **2.** agog, alert, animated, anxious, ardent, athirst, avid, devoted, eager, earnest, ebullient, enthusiastic, fervid, impassioned, impatient, intense, interested, lively, spirited, sprightly, thirsty, vehement, vivacious *Antonyms:* apathetic, halfhearted, indifferent, lukewarm **3.** acrid, acute, biting, caustic, cutting, dry, extreme, honed, incisive, penetrating, piercing, pointed, quick-witted, razor-like, razor-sharp, sardonic, satirical, strong, tart, trenchant

keep *n.* **1.** bread and butter, lifeblood, livelihood, means, medium, money, pittance, property, resource, subsistence, sustenance, wealth **2.** care, charge, custody, guardianship, superintendence, supervision *Antonyms:* dereliction, negligence, remissness **3.** building, castle, chateau, donjon, fort, fortress, stronghold, tower – *v.* **1.** amass, cache, conserve, enjoy, garner, husband, hold, own, pile, possess, reserve, retain, save, stack, stock, store **2.** arrest, avert, block, check, confine, constrain, control, curb, delay, detain, deter, hamper, hamstring, hinder, hold back, impede, imprison, inhibit, limit, obstruct, prevent, restrain, retard, shackle, stall, stop, withhold **3.** bless, celebrate, commemorate, consecrate, laud, maintain, praise, regard, respect, ritualize, sanctify, solemnize **4.** adhere to, comply with, fulfill, honour, obey, observe, perform **5.** conduct, control, direct, employ, manage, tend **6.** attend to, care for, cherish, cover, defend, harbour, preserve, protect, shelter, shield, support, watch over *Antonyms:* disregard, ignore, neglect, overlook **7.** carry *or* run on, continue, linger, persist

keepsake *n.* *aide-mémoire (French)*, favour, memento, memorabilia, memorial, relic, remembrance, reminder, souvenir, symbol, token, trophy

keg *n.* barrel, canister, cask, cistern, container, drum, firkin, hogshead, kilderkin, receptacle, tankard, tub, vat, vessel

kennel *n.* **1.** doghouse, dog pound, dog shelter, houndhouse **2.** burrow, cave, den, haunt, hiding place, hole, lair, shelter **3.**

channel, drain, eavestrough, gutter, puddle, sewer, sink, sluice, trough – *v.* billet, house, lodge, room, safeguard, shelter, store

kernel *n.* **1.** germ, grain, nucleus, nut, root, seed **2.** centre, core, crux, essence, fruit, gist, heart, hub, marrow, matter, meat, morsel, nitty-gritty *(Nonformal)*, nub, pith, substance, upshot

key *adj.* basic, chief, crucial, decisive, essential, fundamental, important, indispensable, leading, main, major, material, pivotal, primary, principal, vital *Antonyms:* minor, secondary, subsidiary, superficial – *n.* **1.** instrument, opener *Kinds of key:* car, church, clock, house, latchkey, passkey, skeleton, winder, windle *(British)* **2.** lever, mechanism, punch *Computer Key Designations:* alt, arrow, backspace, break, caps lock, character, clear, command, control, delete, end, enter, escape, function, help, home, insert, num lock, option, page down *or* up, pause, print screen, program function, return, scroll lock, shift, sys req, tab **3.** answer, blueprint, cipher, clue, code, cue, earmark, explanation, guide, index, indicator, marker, password, pointer, sign, solution, ticket *(Nonformal)* **4.** key signature, pitch, sharps and flats, timbre, tonality, tone **5.** cay, island, isle, islet, reef, sandbank – *v.* **1.** attach, close, connect, enclose, fasten, interlock, link, lock, secure, shut **2.** arouse, elevate, evoke, excite, intensify, raise, stimulate **3.** enter, file, insert, list, process, punch in *(Nonformal)*, record, reference, register, type

keyboard *n.* **1.** keypad, key punch, typewriter, word processor **2.** instrument, ivories *(Nonformal) Kinds of keyboard instrument:* analogue, cembalo, clavier, digital, harpsichord, melodeon, organ, piano, sampler, spinet, synthesizer, virginal *Trademark:* Farfisa, Moog *See also:* **instrument, piano**

keynote *n.* **1.** argument, basis, centre, core, cornerstone, crux, essence, focus, gist, heart, idea, kernel, keystone, marrow, motive, pith, premise, principle, root, source, substance, theme **2.** tonic *Kinds of keynote:* dominant, major, mediant, minor, organ point, pedal point, subdominant, submediant, subtonic, supertonic, tonic major *or* minor

keystone *n.* base, basis, bed, benchmark, cardinal *or* essential point, cornerstone, crux, footing, footstone, foundation, fundamental, ground, groundwork, linchpin, mainspring, motive, principle, quoin, reason, root, source, spring, support

kick *n.* **1.** blow, hit, jolt, punt, thrust, wallop **2.** amusement, excitement, fun, hilarity, merriment, pleasure, refreshment, rush, sensation, stimulation, thrill **3.** animation, bite, energy, force, intensity, pep *(Nonformal)*, potency, power, punch, pungency, recoil, snap, sparkle, strength, tang, verve, vigour, vim, vitality, zest – *v.* **1.** belt, drop kick, punt, smack, strike, tap, thrust *Nonformal:* boot, hoof **2.** abandon, cease, desist, discontinue, foresake, give up, quit, relinquish, renounce, squelch, stop **3.** backlash, jar, jolt, kick *or* spring back, rebound, recoil, resile, return, reverberate **4.** amble, dally, dawdle, drift, jaunt, meander, roam, straggle, traipse, wander **5.** abuse, aggrieve, assail, belittle, deprecate, deride, exploit, injure, mistreat, neglect, wrong

kickback *n.* **1.** bribe, commission, compensation, cut, fund, gift, graft, payment, payoff, percentage, recompense, remuneration, reward, salary, share *Nonformal:* boodle, payola **2.** backlash, rebound, recoil, repercussion, resile, return, reverberation

kid *adj.* immature, junior, juvenile, young, youthful – *n.* adolescent, baby, boy, child, daughter, girl, hobbledehoy, infant, juvenile, lad, little one, son, teenager, toddler, tot, urchin, whippersnapper, youngster, youth – *v.* bother, delude, dupe, fool, hoax, hoodwink, jest, joke, jolly, mock, pretend, rib, ridicule, tease, trick *Nonformal:* flim-flam, josh, rag, razz, roast, spoof

kidnap *v.* abduct, bodysnatch, capture, carry *or* spirit away, coax, entice, grab, hijack, hold, lure, pirate, remove, seize, shanghai *(Nonformal)*, skyjack, snatch, steal, waylay

kill *n.* beast, bird, booty, food, game, plunder, prey, quarry, victim – *v.* **1.** annihilate, butcher, destroy, dispatch, dispose of, execute, exterminate, extinguish, martyr, murder, slaughter, slay, smite *Nonformal:* bump *or* knock *or* pick off, croak, do in erase, fix, get, hit, ice, liquidate, nuke, off, rub *or* take *or* wipe out, settle, snuff, waste, zap **2.** cease, defeat, end, finish, forbid, halt, neutralize, nix *(Nonformal)*, prohibit, quash, quell, refuse, revoke, scotch, shut off, smother, stifle, still, stop, suppress, veto **3.** annul, blue pencil, cancel, delete, efface, eradicate, erase, expunge, extirpate, nullify, obliterate, remove, scratch **4.** dally, dawdle, daydream, fritter, idle, linger, loiter, piddle, procrastinate, shirk, slack off *(Nonformal)*, slouch, trifle, vegetate, waste

killer *adj.* alluring, attractive, awesome, bodacious *(Nonformal)*, breathtaking, enticing, remarkable, stunning – *n.* assassin, bravo, butcher, executioner, guerrilla, homicidal maniac, mass murderer, murderer, ninja, serial killer, slayer, soldier *Nonformal:* cutthroat, goon, hired gun, hit man, thug *Antonyms:* conscientious objector, pacifist, peacenik

killing *adj.* deadly, fatal, final, finishing, lethal, mortal – *n.* **1.** assassination, bloodbath, bloodshed, death, destruction, dispatch, euthanasia, execution, extermination, fatality, hit *(Nonformal)*, homicide, liquidation, massacre, murder, slaughter, slaying **2.** bonanza, booty, fortune, gain, harvest, mint, prize, profit, spoils, take, windfall, winnings

killjoy *n.* complainer, critic, cynic, damper, defeatist, grinch, grouch, malcontent, nihilist, pessimist, sceptic, spoilsport *Nonformal:* Eeyore, gloomy gus, party pooper, sourpuss, wet blanket, worrywart

kind *adj.* affectionate, altruistic, amiable, amicable, benevolent, bounteous, charitable, clement, compassionate, congenial, considerate, cordial, courteous, friendly, generous, gentle, good, goodhearted, gracious, helpful, humane, indulgent, kindhearted, kindly, lenient, merciful, mild, neighbourly, obliging, philanthropic, responsive, soft-hearted, sympathetic, tender, tender-hearted, thoughtful, tolerant, understanding, warm, warmhearted *Antonyms:* cruel, harsh, heartless, merciless, vicious – *n.* **1.** brand, breed, class, classification, denomination, designation, element, grouping, family, gender, genus, ilk, make, mark, model, persuasion, race, set, sort, species, tribe, type, variety **2.** character, complexion, essence, feather, fibre, habit, mould, nature, style, temperament, tendency

kindle *v.* **1.** blaze, burn, combust, heat, ignite, inflame, light, spark *Antonyms:* douse, extinguish, quench **2.** agitate, animate, arouse, awaken, bestir, challenge, excite, foment, induce, inspire, provoke, rally, rouse, sharpen, stimulate, stir, thrill, waken, whet

kindly *adj.* attentive, beneficial, benevolent, benign, compassionate, cordial, favourable, friendly, generous, genial, gentle, good, good-hearted, good-natured, gracious, hearty, helpful, humane, kind, kind-hearted, merciful, mild, neighbourly, pleasant, polite, sociable, sympathetic, thoughtful, warm *Antonyms:* destructive, malevolent, spiteful – *adv.* affectionately, agreeably, benevolently, benignly, carefully, charitably, compassionately, considerately, cordially, courteously, delicately, enthusiastically, generously, genially, good-naturedly, graciously, heartily, heedfully, helpfully, humanely, politely, solicitously, sympathetically, tenderly, thoughtfully, tolerantly, well *Antonyms:* cruelly, painfully

kindness *n.* **1.** affection, altruism, amiability, beneficence, benevolence, clemency, compassion, consideration, cordiality, decency, delicacy, fellow-feeling, forbearance, generosity, gentleness, goodness, good will, graciousness, heart, helpfulness, hospitality, humanity, indulgence, kindliness, mildness, patience, sweetness, sympathy, tact, tenderness, thoughtfulness, tolerance, understanding, unselfishness *Antonyms:* animosity, callousness, cruelty, heartlessness, malice **2.** accommodation, aid, alms, assistance, benediction, benefaction, blessing, boost, bounty, charity, courtesy, dispensation, favour, good intentions, help, mercy, philanthropy, relief, service, succour

kindred *adj.* affinitive, agnate, akin, cognate, connected, consanguineous, enate, familial, kin, like, parallel, related, similar – *n.* affinity, blood, clan, connection, consanguinity, extraction, family, flesh, folk, house, ilk, kin, kinfolk, kinship, kinsman, kinswoman, lineage, member, race, relation, relationship, relative, sibling, stock, tribe

kinetic *adj.* active, animated, bodily, brisk, corporal, dynamic, electric, energetic, heated, intense, lively, mobile, moving, physical, proactive, spirited, strenuous, vibrant, vigorous, vivacious, vivid *Antonyms:* cold, immobile, static

king *n.* **1.** caesar, chief, czar, emperor, kaiser, khan, lord, maharajah, majesty, mikado, mogul, monarch, overlord, pasha, potentate, prince, rajah, rex, ruler, shah, sovereign, sultan **2.** baron, boss, capitalist, captain of industry, magnate, monopolist *Nonformal:* ace, monster

kingdom *n.* **1.** commonwealth, country, county, crown, domain, dominion, dynasty, empire, field, kingship, lands, monarchy, nation, possessions, principality, province, realm, reign, rule, satrapy, sovereignty, sphere, state, suzerainty, sway, territory, throne, tract **2.** class, division, family, genus, phylum, rank, species

kingly *adj.* basilic, blue-blooded, dignified, distinguished, eminent, grand, illustrious, imperial, magnificent, majestic, monarchical, noble, opulent, palatial, princely, regal, royal, sovereign

kink *n.* **1.** bend, coil, corkscrew, crimp, crinkle, curl, curve, entanglement, frizz, knot, loop, twist, wrinkle **2.** eccentricity, fetish, foible, idiosyncrasy, peculiarity, quirk, singularity, strangeness, weirdness **3.** charley horse *(Nonformal)*, cramp, crick, knot, muscle spasm, pain, pang, pinch, stab, tweak, twinge **4.** bug, complication, defect, difficulty, flaw, gremlin *(Nonformal)*, hitch, impediment, imperfection, problem, tangle – *v.* bend, coil, contort, curl, curve, distort, form, knead, knot, shape, twine, twist, wind, wring *Antonyms:* correct, rectify, straighten

kinky *adj.* **1.** bizarre, deviant, eccentric, far-out *(Nonformal)*, licentious, odd, outlandish, *outré (French)*, peculiar, perverse, provocative, queer, quirky, strange, unconventional, unusual, weird *Antonyms:* boring, common, conforming, normal **2.** coiled, crimped, curled, curly, dreadlocked, frizzled, frizzy, knotted, matted, matty, rolled, tangled, twisted

kiosk *n.* **1.** alcove, booth, bower, concession, information stand, newsstand, stand, ticket booth **2.** arbour, gardenhouse, gazebo, greenhouse, haven, hut, lattice, lean-to, pavilion, pergola, refuge, retreat, shack, shed, shelter, summerhouse, trellis

kiss *n.* buss, caress, embrace, endearment, greeting, mush, nuzzle, peck, salutation, smacker *Nonformal:* sugar, wet one – *v.* greet, peck, smack, touch *Nonformal:* make-out, neck, pucker up, smooch

kit *n.* **1.** accoutrement, apparatus, appurtenances, articles, bits and pieces, collection, conveniences, effects, equipment, fittings, furnishings, gear, implements, material, munitions, necessaries, outfit, paraphernalia, parts, provisions, rigging, stuff *(Nonformal)*, supplies, tackle, things, tools, trappings, utensils **2.** bag, box, case, container, ditty bag, duffle bag, haversack, knapsack, luggage, purse, rucksack, school bag, sea bag, tackle box **3.** caboodle *(Nonformal)*, collection, host, pile, selection

kitchen *n.* back *or* summer kitchen, canteen, cookery, cookhouse, cuisine, galley, line, kitchenette, mess, scullery

kitschy *adj.* campy, cheap, garish, Hollywood *(Nonformal)*, *kétaine (Quebec)*, maudlin, sentimental, tasteless

kitty *n.* **1.** bank, fund, jackpot, pool, pot, slush, stakes **2.** cat, feline, kitten *See also* **cat**

klutz *n.* blunderer, botcher, bungler, fumbler, stumbler *Nonformal:* butterfingers, puzzler, stone hands, stumblebum

knack *n.* ability, adroitness, aptitude, aptness, bent, capacity, cleverness, command, deftness, dexterity, expertise, facility, faculty, flair, forte, genius, gift, handiness, head, ingenuity, know-how, mastership, mastery, propensity, quickness, readiness, skill, skilfulness, talent *Nonformal:* chutzpah, moxie, savvy *Antonyms:* awkwardness, clumsiness, ineptitude

knave *n.* bastard, blackguard, cad, fraud, hoodlum, hooligan, miscreant, rake, rapscallion, rascal, reprobate, rogue, ruffian, scalawag, scamp, scoundrel, sleeveen *(Newfoundland)*, swindler, thug, villain *Nonformal:* heel, lowlife, rat, rotter, stinker

knead *v.* blend, form, manipulate, massage, mix, ply, press, pull, shape, squeeze, thump, turn, twist, work

knee *n.* connection, hinge, joint, juncture, link, patellar region, pivot – *v.* hit, jab, poke, pound, smack, smite, strike, take out *(Nonformal)*, thrust

kneel *v.* bend, bow, curtsy, genuflect, kowtow, prostrate oneself, stoop

knell *n.* **1.** bell, chime, omen, ringing, summons, threnode, tintinnabulation, toll **2.** augury, mark, omen, sign, signal, token – *v.* announce, annunciate, call, convoke, cry, declare, proclaim, signal, summon, trumpet

knick-knack *n.* bagatelle, bauble, bibelot, bric-a-brac, conversation piece, curio, curiosity, device, frill, furbelow, gadget, gewgaw, kickshaw, miniature, novelty, *objet d'art (French)*, ornament, showpiece, souvenir, toy, trifle, trinket

knife *n.* shiv *(Nonformal)*, tool, utensil *Kinds of knife:* army, bayonet, bowie, butcher, butter, carpet, cartouche *(Historical)*, carving, chopping, dagger, felt, fillet *or* fish, grapefruit, hacking, hunting, jackknife, machete, mat, oilcloth, oyster, palette, paper, paring *or* fruit, paperhanger's, penknife, pocket, putty, saw-back, scalpel, scalping, steak, Swiss Army, switchblade, table *Inuktitut:* panak, ulu *Trademark:* Gerber, Henckel, Leatherman, Victorinox, X-acto – *v.* carve, cut, hurt, impale, jab, lacerate, lance, open up, perforate, pierce, slash, stab, stick, thrust

knight *n.* cavalier, champion, chevalier, combatant, defender, devotee, equestrian, fighter, flower of chivalry, guardian, mounted soldier, paladin, protector, soldier, warrior *Fabled knights:* Banneret, Bedivere, Bors, Don Quixote, El Cid, Gaheris, Galahad, Gareth, Gawaine, Kay, Lamorak, Lancelot, Modred, Orlando, Percival, Roland, Sir Patrick Spens, Tristram, Zifar – *v.* award, bestow, commend, compliment, confer, dignify, endow, ennoble, extol, grant, hail, honour, laud, praise, present, rank, reward, salute, thank

knit *v.* **1.** bind, cable, connect, crochet, fasten, form, interlace, intertwine, join, link, loop, mend, purl, reunite, secure, sew, shape, spin, tie, unite, weave, web **2.** contract, crease, draw, fold, furrow, purse, ruffle, rumple, shrink, wrinkle

knob *n.* **1.** anthill, barrow, bilge, blob, bow, bulge, bump, butte, clump, drumlin, dune, hill, hillock, hummock, hump, kame, knoll, lump, molehill, monadnock, monticule, mound, mountain, node, protuberance, protrusion, rise, swell, tumour **2.** door handle, grasp, grip, haft, handhold, handle, helve, hold

knock *n.* **1.** beating, blow, box, clip, cuff, hammering, hit, lick, rap, slap, smack, swat, thump, whack **2.** censure, condemnation, criticism, rebuff, rejection *Nonformal:* dissing, flak, panning, slam **3.** blemish, defeat, disparagement, failure, injury, misfortune, reversal, setback, stricture – *v.* **1.** abuse, batter, beat, bruise, buffet, clap, clout, cuff, damage, deck, drub, fell, flatten, floor, goon *(Nonformal)*, hurt, level, maltreat, maul, punch, rough up, thrash, total, wound **2.** bump, collide, crash, impact, smash **3.** bang, bash, drive, hit, move, pound, slap, smack, strike, tap, thump, thwack, wallop, whack **4.** defeat, deride, discourage, disparage, overwhelm, ridicule *Nonformal:* dis, pan *Antonyms:* encourage, favour, support **5.** decrease, deduct, discount, lessen, lower, minimize, reduce, subtract *Antonyms:* add, increase, raise

knockout *adj.* defeating, deflating, finishing, killing, overpowering, overthrowing, stunning, stupefying – *n.* **1.** blow, deathblow, finishing stroke, knock down, paralyzation, prostration *Nonformal:* coldcock, kayo, K.O., T.K.O. **2.** beauty, belle, charmer, god, goddess *Nonformal:* babe, dish, hunk, looker

knoll *n.* anthill, barrow, bulge, bump, butte, drumlin, dune, elevation, hill, hillock, hummock, hump, kame, knob, kop, kopje, molehill, monadnock, mound, protuberance, rise, sand dune, sandhill

knot *n.* **1.** bond, bow, braid, bunch, coil, connection, contortion, helix, hitch, intertwining, joint, kink, ligament, ligature, link, loop, mat, perplexity, rosette, screw, spiral, splice, tangle, tie, twirl, twist, union, warp, whirl, whorl *Common Knots:* blood, bowline, double bowknot, granny, figure-eight, fisherman's, hangman's, overhand, reef *or* square, sheepshank, slipknot, surgeon's **2.** aggregate, assemblage, assortment, cluster, enclave, gathering, group **3.** bulb, burl, gnarl, joint, knob, node, nub, protrusion, protuberance, swelling, tubercle **4.** conundrum, difficulty, dilemma, enigma, entanglement, imbroglio, labyrinth, maze, mystery, problem, puzzle, quandary, riddle, snag, snarl – *v.* bind, cord, entangle, fasten, form, knit, lop, secure, snarl, stay, tangle, tether, tie, tighten, twist, weave

knotty *adj.* **1.** bumpy, burled, coarse, contorted, cross-grained, gnarled, gnarly, knurled, knurly, lumpy, nodal, nodose, nodular, nubby, rough, torose, tubercular, tuberous, uneven **2.** arduous, backbreaking, difficult, formidable, gruelling, laborious, rigorous, strenuous, torturous, tough, trying, winding **3.** baffling, Borgesian, complex, complicated, convoluted, cryptic, enigmatic, fuzzy, garbled, intricate, jumbled, labyrinthine, mazelike, mystifying, obfuscated, perplexing, puzzling, riddling, scrambled, tangled, thorny *Antonyms:* lucid, obvious, simple

know *v.* **1.** appreciate, apprehend, comprehend, conceive, conceptualize, fathom, grasp, perceive, realize, respect, understand **2.** acknowledge, admit, recall, recognize **3.** ascertain, decide, determine, differentiate, discern, discriminate, distinguish, divide, identify, isolate, judge, separate, set apart

know-how *n.* ability, adroitness, aptitude, artistry, background, capability, command, craft, cunning, deftness, dexterity, experience, expertise, expertness, faculty, flair, ingenuity, knack, knowledge, mastery, proficiency, skill, talent *Antonyms:* incompetence, ineptitude

knowing *adj.* **1.** astute, canny, clever, con prehending, deft, experienced, informe insightful, intelligent, knowledgeabl omniscient, perceptive, percipient, persp cacious, sagacious, sensible, shrew smart, sophisticated, wise, world *Antonyms:* foolish, ignorant, naive **2** aware, cognizant, conscious, mindfu thoughtful, understanding *Antonyms:* ign rant, oblivious

knowledge *n.* **1.** apprehension, awarenes cognition, comprehension, consciousnes enlightenment, experience, familiarit insight, observation, perception, realiz tion, sense *Antonyms:* ignorance, inn cence **2.** data, facts, figures, informatio lore, news, notice, notification, statistic tidings *Nonformal:* lowdown, scoop, ski ny **3.** cleverness, intelligence, sagacity, wi dom *Nonformal:* brains, savvy, smart *Antonyms:* foolishness, silliness, stupidi **4.** education, erudition, instruction, lear ing, scholarship, schooling, understandin **5.** accomplishments, attainments, cultur humanities, philosophy, science **6.** certai ty, conviction, gospel, judgment, law, pri ciples, reality, truth, verity

knowledgeable *adj.* **1.** abreast, acquain ed, alert, appreciative, apprised, awar cognizant, conscious, conversant, discer ing, experienced, familiar, informed, know ing, omniscient, posted, prescient, priv sensible, sophisticated, understandin well-rounded *French:* au courant, au fa *Nonformal:* hip, plugged in, savvy, up t speed **2.** brainy, bright, brilliant, cleve educated, erudite, insightful, intelligen learned, lettered, quick-witted, shar smart, sagacious, scholarly, verse well-informed, wise *Antonyms:* ignoran obtuse, vacuous

known *adj.* **1.** accepted, acknowledge admitted, avowed, certified, common, co fessed, established, manifest, obviou patent, plain, proverbial **2.** celebrate familiar, famous, hackneyed, noted, notor ous, popular, recognized, well-known **3** axiomatic, conscious, down put *(Nonfo mal)*, granted, implicit, tacit, understoo *Antonyms:* concealed, hidden, secre unknown

knuckle *n.* angle, articulation, bend, carpal *or* finger *or* hinged *or* pivot joint, crook, geniculation, hook, joint, knucklebone, symphysis – *v.* chafe, hit, knead, noogie *(Nonformal)*, punch, pop, press, rub

kosher *adj.* acceptable, accepted, allowed, approved, authorized, authentic, conforming, conventional, fitting, genuine, lawful, legal, legit *(Nonformal)*, legitimate, licit, orthodox, permitted, proper, sanctioned, standard

kowtow *v.* bootlick *(Nonformal)*, bow, cringe, fawn, flatter, genuflect, grovel, kneel, pander, prostrate, stoop, toady, truckle *Antonyms:* rebel, revolt

kudos *n. pl.* acclaim, applause, credit, distinction, eminence, esteem, fame, flattery, glory, honour, plaudits, praise, preeminence, prestige, prominence, raves, renown, repute

label *n.* classification, description, identification *Kinds of label:* bookplate, brand, brand *or* trade name, colophon, docket, epithet, hallmark, identification, letterhead, logo, name, nickname, pet name, Post-it note *(Trademark)*, price tag, running head *or* title, seal, signet, sobriquet, stamp, sticker, symbol, tag, ticket, token, trademark – *v.* brand, call, characterize, classify, define, describe, designate, dub, identify, mark, name, peg, pigeonhole, specify, stamp, stereotype, stigmatize, tag, tally, typecast

laborious *adj.* **1.** arduous, backbreaking, burdensome, difficult, effortful, fatiguing, forced, hard, heavy, herculean, laboured, onerous, painstaking, ponderous, stiff, strained, strenuous, tedious, tiresome, toilsome, tough, wearing *Antonyms:* easy, effortless **2.** assiduous, careful, detailed, diligent, dogged, earnest, hardworking, indefatigable, industrious, particular, persevering, precise, thorough, tireless, unflagging, zealous *Antonyms:* careless, negligent, slipshod

labour *n.* **1.** activity, assignment, chore, daily grind, duty, employment, endeavour, errand, exercise, job, livelihood, occupation, task, undertaking, vocation, work **2.** diligence, drudgery, effort, elbow grease *(Nonformal)*, energy, pains, slogging, strain, stress, struggle, sweat, toil, travail **3.** blue-collar worker, labour force, proletariat, working class **4.** childbirth, birth, contractions, delivery, parturition – *v.* bear down, bust a gut *(Nonformal)*, drive, drudge, endeavour, exert oneself, grind, moil, plod, plug away, slave, strain, strive, struggle, sweat, tend, toil, travail, work *Antonyms:* breathe easy, relax, rest

laboured *adj.* **1.** affected, artificial, awkward, contrived, far-fetched, forced, formal, inapt, overdone, overwrought, ornate, stiff, stilted, strained *Antonyms:* artful, natural, succinct **2.** arduous, backbreaking, difficult, effortful, hard, heavy, nightmarish *(Nonformal)*, relentless, strenuous, toilsome, weighty *Antonyms:* easy, effortless, unfettered

labourer *n.* apprentice, blue- *or* pink- *or* white-collar worker, breadwinner, drone, employee, hand, help, hireling, minion, peon, worker *Nonformal:* dogsbody, drudge, field hand, flunky, hack, hired hand, lackey, lazzarone, sand hog *(Historical)*, working stiff *Antonyms:* boss, employer, manager *See also:* **worker**

labyrinth *n.* coil, complexity, complication, confusion, convolution, enigma, entanglement, Gordian knot, intricacy, jungle, maze, mesh, morass, mystery, perplexity, problem, puzzle, riddle, tangle, web *Antonyms:* answer, clue, discovery, exegesis, revelation

lace *n.* **1.** appliqué, border, crochet, edging, filigree, material, net, openwork, ornament, tatting, trim *Kinds of lace:* Alençon, Battenberg, bobbin, Breton, Brussels, Chantilly, Mechlin, mignonette, Valenciennes, Venetian **2.** band, cord, rope, shoelace, string, thread, tie **3.** dash, drop, hint, iota, jot, soupçon, trace – *v.* **1.** attach, bind, close, do up, fasten, interlace, intertwine, interweave, mix, strap, tat, thread, tie, twine *Antonyms:* separate, undo, unfix, untie **2.** add, boost, doctor *(Nonformal)*, enhance, enliven, fortify, pickle, strengthen **3.** abuse, beat, berate, castigate, lambaste read out, scold, skiver *Antonyms:* commend, glorify, praise

lacerate *v.* claw, cut, gash, harm, hurt, injure, jag, lance, maim, mangle, mutilate, pierce, puncture, rend, rip, scar, score, serrate, slash, stab, tear, torture, wound

lachrymose *adj.* blubbering *(Nonformal)*, crying, dolorous, lugubrious, mournful, sad, sniveling, sobbing, teary, wailing, watery, weeping, weepy, whimpering, woeful *Antonyms:* celebratory, chortling, laughing, smiling

lack *n.* absence, dearth, decrease, deficiency, deficit, depletion, deprivation, inadequacy, insufficiency, mediocrity, need, paucity, privation, reduction, scantiness, shortage, void, want *Antonyms:* abundance, adequacy, excess, surplus – *v.* go without, miss, need, not have, want *Antonyms:* have, own, possess

lackadaisical *adj.* absentminded, abstracted, apathetic, dilatory, distracted, enervated, fainéant, idle, indifferent, indolent, inert, languid, lethargic, listless, loafing, melancholy, mooning, musing, otiose, phlegmatic, preoccupied, slack, somnolent, soporific, spiritless, stuporous, supine, torpid, unenterprising, woolgathering *Antonyms:* active, aspiring, energized, enterprising, vigorous

lackey *n.* acolyte, attendant, back-scratcher, butler, domestic, fawner, flatterer, flunky, follower, footman, groveller, hired man, inferior, kowtower, manservant, menial, minion, pawn, peon, puppet, servant, shadow, steward, sycophant, toady, tool, underling, valet, yes-man *Nonformal:* bootlicker, brown-noser, gofer, lickspittle, sniveller

lacking *adj.* **1.** absent, away, gone, missing, negligible, nonexistent **2.** bereft, deficient, destitute, impoverished, needing, short, wanting **3.** faulty, flawed, impaired, imperfect, inadequate, incomplete, without *Antonyms:* complete, intact, whole

lacklustre *adj.* boring, colourless, dim, drab, dry, dull, flat, leaden, lifeless, muted, obscure, prosaic, unimaginative, uninspired, vapid *Nonformal*: blah, nothing, pablum *Antonyms:* animated, bright, colourful, dazzling, lively

laconic *adj.* brief, brusque, compact, concise, crisp, curt, pithy, short, succinct, taciturn, terse *Antonyms:* long-winded, loquacious, rambling, verbose

lacquer *n.* coating, cover, enamel, finish, glaze, gloss, lustre, resin, shellac, varnish, veneer – *v.* coat, cover, finish, glaze, paint, shellac, varnish

lacy *adj.* delicate, elegant, fancy, filigree, fine, frilly, gauzy, gossamer, meshy, open, ornate, patterned, sheer, thin, transparent *Antonyms:* opaque, plain, unadorned

lad *n.* boy, child, fellow, guy, juvenile, kid, man, schoolboy, son, stripling, tad, youngster, youth *Nonformal*: beansprout, hobbledehoy, nipper, punk, whippersnapper

laden *adj.* burdened, charged, encumbered, fraught, full, hampered, loaded, oppressed, taxed, weighed down *Antonyms:* empty, hollow, lightweight

lady *adj.* female, feminine, she *(Nonformal)*, woman – *n.* baroness, begum, consort, contessa, countess, czarina, dame, dowager, duchess, empress, gentlewoman, her ladyship, matron, mistress, noblewoman, maharani, princess, queen, queen bee *(Nonformal)*, ranee, sultana, viscountess, wife, woman

ladylike *adj.* civil, considerate, courteous, cultured, decorous, dignified, elegant, genteel, gracious, polite, refined, well-bred, well-mannered, womanly *Antonyms:* discourteous, ill-bred, rude, unrefined

lag *n.* delay, halt, hold-up, retardation, slowdown, wait – *v.* dally, dawdle, delay, dillydally *(Nonformal)*, ebb, fail, falter, flag, hang back, hobble, idle, inch along, limp, linger, loiter, plod, poke, saunter, shuffle, slacken, slouch, stagger, stay, straggle, tail, tarry, toddle, trail, trudge, wane *Antonyms:* hurry, progress, scurry, speed

laggard *n.* dawdler, sloth, slouch *Nonformal:* foot-dragger, lollygagger, slug, slug-a-bed, stick-in-the-mud

laid-back *adj.* calm, casual, blasé, easygoing, even-tempered, indifferent, informal, leisurely, loose, nonchalant, offhand, placid, relaxed, serene, tranquil, unceremonious, unhurried, unruffled, unflappable, unflustered, untroubled *Antonyms:* agitated, anxious, excitable, frantic, riled

lair *n.* burrow, cave, cavern, cranny, den, dugout, grotto, habitat, haven, harbour, hideaway, hideout, hollow, home, nest, nook, purlieu, recess, refuge, retreat, roost, sanctuary

laissez-faire *adj.* *dégagé (French)*, do-nothing *(Nonformal)*, indifferent, lax, loose, neutral, non-interventionist, non-restrictive, passive, permissive, relaxed *Antonyms:* controlled, intervening, regulated

lake *n.* **1.** basin, inland sea *or* water, *lac (French)*, landlocked water, loch *(Scottish)*, lough *(Irish)*, mere, mouth, *nyanza (Africa)*, pond *(Newfoundland)*, reservoir, sluice, spring *Kinds of lake:* freshwater, glacial, volcanic *Kinds of small lake:* fishpond, kettle, lagoon, millpond, oasis, oxbow, pond, pool, puddle, salt pond, slough, tarn, tidal pond *or* pool *Major Canadian Lakes:* Athabasca, Bras d'Or, Erie, Grand, Great Bear, Great Slave, Huron, Laberge, Lac Saint-Jean, Lake of the Woods, Lesser Slave, Manitoba, Nipigon, Nipissing, Ontario, Simcoe, Superior, Winnipeg, Winnipegosis **2.** camp, chalet, cottage, up north, woods

lamb *n.* **1.** animal, meat, sheep *Cuts of lamb:* breast, chop, leg, mutton, saddle, sheep's head, shoulder **2.** babe, dove, infant, ingénue, innocent

lambaste *v.* **1.** castigate, criticize, punish, reprimand, reprove, scold, upbraid *Antonyms:* coddle, reward **2.** abuse, assail, attack, baste, battle, beat, berate, censure, chide, denounce, excoriate, fulminate, lash, rebuke, scourge, slam, slap, slash, strike, thrash, trim, wallop, whip *Nonformal:* lay *or* rip into, shellac, tongue-lash

lambent *adj.* **1.** aglow, alight, candescent, flickering, flitting, fluttering, glowing, incandescent, luminescent, luminous, suffused *Antonyms:* black, dark, pitch-black **2.** clever, playful, quick, teasing, witty

lame *adj.* **1.** crippled, disabled, hamstrung, handicapped, limping, sidelined **2.** faltering, faulty, feeble, flabby, flimsy, inadequate, ineffective, inefficient, insufficient, poor, thin, unconvincing, unpersuasive, unsatisfactory, unsuitable, weak *Antonyms:* authoritative, convincing, impressive

lament *n.* complaint, dirge, elegy, grievance, grieving, jeremiad, *Kaddish (Hebrew)*, keening, lamentation, moan, mourning, requiem, sobbing, sorrow, tears, ululation, wailing, weeping – *v.* bawl, bemoan, bewail, complain, cry, deplore, grieve, howl, hurt, moan, mourn, regret, rue, sing, sob, sorrow, wail, weep *Nonformal*: blubber, boo-hoo, carry on *Antonyms:* celebrate, extol, laud, rejoice

lamentable *adj.* abject, awful, bad, calamitous, deplorable, distressing, dolorous, grievous, grim, hurting, lousy *(Nonformal)*, lugubrious, miserable, pathetic, pitiful, poor, regrettable, rotten, rueful, sad, sorrowful, tragic, unfortunate, woebegone, wretched *Antonyms:* abundant, auspicious, fortunate, lucky, praiseworthy

lamp *n.* lighting *Kinds of lamp:* arc, bedside, chandelier, desk, flashlight, flood, fluorescent, gooseneck, halogen, headlight, hooded, jacklight, kudlik, lantern, neon, night-light, searchlight, spotlight, table, Tiffany *(Trademark)*, torch *(British)*, track lighting

lampoon *n.* burlesque, caricature, invective, parody, pastiche, roast, satire, takeoff, travesty *Antonyms:* glorification, honour, praise – *v.* asperse, belittle, burlesque, caricature, defame, deride, malign, mock, parody, put on, rail, ridicule, roast, satirize, scorn, send up, vilify *Antonyms:* idolize, respect, revere, worship

land *n.* **1.** acreage, acres, area, *arpentage (French)*, common, concession, crown *or* public land, down, expanse, extent, farmland, field, flats, freehold, front, ground heath, hectarage, landholding, meadow, moor, parcel, parkland, pasturage, plain plot, private property, real estate, realty, road allowance, stretch, sweep, terrain, tillage, topography, township, tract, tundra **2.** coast, coastline, continent, dry land, land mass, mainland, shore, solid ground, terra firma **3.** demesne, district, estate, grange, holding, kingdom, parish, place in the sun, realm, region, riding, seigniory, shire, township **4.** country, fatherland, homeland, mother country, nation, principality, territory **5.** crust, dirt, earth, loam, sod, soil **6.** backcountry, boondocks, bush, outback, wilderness, wilds **7.** basic, bedrock, essentials, living, roots, rural– *v.* **1.** alight, arrive, come, come to rest *Nonformal:* blow in, turn up **2.** beach, belly flop, bring in, bring to rest, hit ground *or* the water, set *or* take down **3.** deplane, disembark, offload, put ashore, unload, unship **4.** come into, gain, get, procure, receive, secure, win, wrest

landform *n.* feature, geography, geomorphology, physical feature *Kinds of landforms:* archipelago, badlands, beach, continental shelf, drumlin, côteau, delta, dune, escarpment, fjord, highlands, hill, hillock, island, kame, lake, lowlands, moraine, mountain, ocean, peninsula, plain, plateau, river, sandbank, shore, valley, volcano, waterfall

landmark *adj.* consequential, crucial, eventful, far-reaching, historical, influential, major, monumental, momentous, precedent-setting, significant – *n.* **1.** benchmark, core, crux, milestone, turning point, watershed **2.** cairn, guide, guidepost, Inukshuk, marker, milepost, object, peg, picket, pole, post, stake

landscape *n.* **1.** aspect, countryside, outlook, panorama, scene, scenery, view, vista **2.** depiction, picture, sketch, tableau

landslide *n.* **1.** deluge, avalanche, earthslip, inundation, mudslide, slide **2.** cakewalk *(Nonformal)*, conquest, overwhelming plurality, runaway victory, triumph, victory, win *Antonyms:* defeat, loss

lane *n.* access, alley, avenue, by-lane, byway, channel, drive, driveway, entrance, entry, passage, path, road, street

language *n.* **1.** communication, conversation, discourse, exchange, expression, interchange, intercourse, speech, talk, utterance **2.** argot, cant, colloquialism, Creole, demotic, dialect, idiom, jargon, lexicon, lingo *(Nonformal)*, localism, mother tongue, patois, pidgin, provincialism, slang, tongue, vernacular *Ten most used languages:* Arabic, Bengali, Chinese, English, German, Hindi, Japanese, Portuguese, Russian, Spanish **3.** articulation, diction, locution, manner, parlance, style, technique, tone, usage, vocabulary **4.** *Kinds of computer language:* Active X, ADA, ALGOL, BASIC, C, COBOL, FORTH, FORTRAN, HTML, Java, JOVIAL, LISP, LOGO, PASCAL, PL/1, RPG, SNOBOL, Virtual BASIC, VRML

languid *adj.* apathetic, comatose *(Nonformal)*, draggy, drooping, dull, exhausted, heavy, impassive, inert, lackadaisical, languorous, lazy, leaden, lethargic, listless, sickly, slow, sluggish, spiritless, tired, unconcerned, uninterested, weak *Antonyms:* active, energetic, vigorous

languish *v.* **1.** burn out *(Nonformal)*, decline, despair, deteriorate, droop, dwindle, ebb, fade, fizzle *or* peter out, flag, repine, rot, sicken, sulk, waste, weaken, wilt, wither *Antonyms:* bloom, flourish, prosper, thrive **2.** brood, grieve, hanker, hunger, long, mope, mourn, pine, sigh, sorrow, suffer

languorous *adj.* anemic, apathetic, bored, dull, enervated, drowsy, faint, feeble, frail, half-hearted, indifferent, indolent, inert, lackadaisical, languid, lethargic, listless, passionless, passive, phlegmatic, sickly, sleepy, slothful, sluggish, spiritless, tired, torpid, uninterested *Antonyms:* alert, attentive, awake, curious, interested

lanky *adj.* angular, attenuated, bony, gangly, gaunt, lean, long-legged, rangy, scrawny, skinny, slender, spindle-shanked, spindly, tall, thin, weedy, willowy, wiry *Antonyms:* brawny, burly, plump, rotund

lantern *n.* lamp, light *Kinds of lantern:* battery-powered, carbon, Chinese, Coleman *(Trademark)*, electric post, filament, gasoline, hurricane, jacklight, jack-o'-lantern,

Japanese, kerosene, miners, oil, patio, railroad, signal

lap *n.* **1.** circle, circuit, course, distance, loop, orbit, round, tour **2.** harbour, protection, refuge, safety, security **3.** knee, frontage, seat – *v.* **1.** cover, enfold, envelop, lay, overlap, protect, shingle, swaddle, swathe, turn, twist, wrap **2.** drink, imbibe, nip, quaff, sip, sup, swig, swill, take in, tipple, tongue **3.** babble, dribble, gurgle, murmur, purl, slap, slosh, splash, ripple, trickle, trill, wash **4.** move beyond, outdistance, outrun, overtake

lapse *n.* **1.** blunder, breach, bumble, bungle, error, failure, fault, imprudence, indiscretion, miscue, misjudgment, mistake, negligence, offence, omission, oversight, peccadillo, rashness, recklessness, slip, stumble, tactlessness, thoughtlessness, transgression, violation *Nonformal:* blooper, boner, flub, foul-up, gaffe, goof, muff **2.** backsliding, declension, decline, degeneration, descent, deterioration, fall, recession, recidivism, regression, relapse **3.** break, gap, hiatus, intermission, interruption, interval, lull, pause – *v.* **1.** decline, degenerate, descend, deteriorate, recede, slip, weaken **2.** cease, die, disappear, elapse, end, expire, go by, run out, stop, terminate **3.** apostatize, backslide, return, revert, slide, slip

lapsed *adj.* abrogated, antiquated, archaic, discontinued, elapsed, ended, expired, extinct, finished, gone, invalid, late, passé, past, obsolete, outdated, out-of-date, over, run *or* worn out, superceded, unrenewed *Antonyms:* current, pertinent, renewed, topical

larceny *n.* burglary, crime, fraud, grand larceny, misappropriation, petty *or* petit larceny, pilfering, robbery, stealing, theft

larder *n.* **1.** accumulations, food cache *or* supply, groceries, hoard, provender, provision, rations, tuck *(Nonformal)* **2.** buttery, cannery, chamber, commissariat, cuddy, pantry, root cellar, scullery, storage *or* store *or* supply room, store

large *adj.* **1.** ample, considerable, copious, full, generous, goodly, great, immense, liberal, plentiful *Antonyms:* brief, inconsiderable, infinitesimal, little, minute **2.** big, booming, broad, Brobdingnagian, bulky, colossal, enormous, excessive, exorbitant, giant, hefty, huge, humongous *(Nonformal)*, jumbo, king-size, massive, monumental, mountainous, roomy, sizable, skookum *(Pacific Coast)*, spacious, stupendous, substantial, vast, voluminous, whopping, wide *Antonyms:* cramped, crowded, narrow, shallow **3.** all-out, comprehensive, exhaustive, extensive, heroic, major, sweeping, thorough, wide-ranging *Antonyms:* cursory, perfunctory, slipshod **4.** arduous, challenging, demanding, hard, tall *Antonyms:* easy, simple

largely *adv.* abundantly, broadly, chiefly, comprehensively, considerably, copiously, expansively, extensively, extravagantly, generally, generously, grandly, greatly, immoderately, lavishly, liberally, magnificently, mainly, mostly, overall, predominantly, primarily, principally, prodigiously, voluminously, widely

largesse *n.* aid, allowance, alms, altruism, benefaction, beneficence, bequest, bounteousness, bounty, charity, contribution, endowment, gift, generosity, grant, gratuity, hospitality, lagniappe, liberality, magnanimity, munificence, offering, openhandedness, perquisite, philanthropy, present, stipend, subsidy *Nonformal:* grease, handout *Antonyms:* misanthropy, parsimony, pittance

lark *n.* **1.** bird, meadowlark, skylark, songbird, songster, titlark, warbler **2.** amusement, antic, caper, escapade, festivity, fling, frolic, gaiety, gambol, hijinks, merriment, mischief, party, play, prank, revel, revelry, romp, shenanigans, spree, sport, trick *Nonformal:* field day, picnic, tom-foolery – *v.* caper, cavort, celebrate, cut loose, fool around *(Nonformal)*, frisk, frolic, gambol, party, play, relax, rollick, romp, skylark, sport *Antonyms:* battle, labour, strain, struggle, task

lascivious *adj.* bawdy, carnal, coarse, crude, erotic, fleshly, immoral, indecent, lecherous, lewd, libidinous, licentious, lustful, offensive, prurient, randy, raunchy, raw, ribald, rough, salacious, satyric, scurrilous, sensual, shameless, smutty, suggestive, vulgar, wanton *Nonformal:* adult, blue, horny, rude, X-rated *Antonyms:* modest, platonic, pure

lash *v.* **1.** baste, batter, beat, buffet, chastise, dash, drum, flagellate, flay, flog, hammer, hide, hit, horsewhip, knock, lather, pommel, pound, scourge, smack, strap, strike, thrash, whale, whip **2.** affix, attach, bind, connect, fasten, fix, hitch, join, leash, rope, secure, tie, tether

lassitude *n.* apathy, burnout, exhaustion, fainéancy, fatigue, heaviness, hebetude, languor, laziness, lethargy, listlessness, supineness, slothfulness, sluggishness, soporiferousness, stagnation, tiredness, torpor, weariness *Antonyms:* activity, alertness, energy

last *adj.* **1.** climactic, closing, concluding, crowning, departing, end, final, finishing, terminating, ultimate **2.** current, latest, most recent, newest, recent, state-of-the-art, up-to-date, utmost **3.** deciding, definitive, conclusive, terminal **4.** aftermost, behind, extreme, far-off, farthest, hindmost, remotest **5.** leftover, remaining, surviving – *adv.* after, behind, finally, in conclusion, ultimately – *n.* **1.** close, completion, conclusion, curtains *(Nonformal)*, dénouement, end, finale, finish, omega, termination **2.** archetype, model, mould, original, paradigm, pattern, prototype, standard – *v.* carry on, continue, endure, hold out *or* up, persist, persevere, remain, stand up, survive

lasting *adj.* abiding, constant, continual, continuing, deep-rooted, durable, endless, enduring, eternal, evergreen, everlasting, forever, indelible, indissoluble, inexhaustible, lifelong, longstanding, long-term, nonending, perennial, permanent, perpetual, persisting, stable, unceasing, undying, unending *Antonyms:* ephemeral, momentary, passing, transient

lastly *adv.* after, after all, at last, behind, finally, in conclusion, in the end, last, to conclude, ultimately

latch *n.* bar, bolt, buckle, catch, clamp, fastening, hasp, hook, lock, padlock – *v.* bolt, cinch, close, fasten, lock, secure

late *adj.* **1.** behind, behind time, belated, delayed, dilatory, held up, overdue, postponed, slow, tardy, unpunctual **2.** dead, deceased, defunct, departed, gone, lifeless, passed on **3.** ex *(Nonformal)*, former, old, one-time, past, previous, quondam, recent – *adv.* **1.** behind, belatedly, dilatorily, slowly, tardily, unpunctually **2.** lately, not long ago, of late, recently

lately *adv.* afresh, anew, just now, new, newly, of late, recently

latent *adj.* abeyant, concealed, contained, covert, dormant, hidden, idle, implied, inactive, inherent, intrinsic, invisible, lurking, passive, potential, secret, sleeping, suppressed, suspended, tacit, unconscious, underlying, undeveloped, unexpressed, unrealized, unseen, vestigial *Antonyms:* apparent, evident, expressed, manifest, realized

later *adj.* after, ensuing, following, next, posterior, proximate, subsequent, succeeding – *adv.* after, afterwards, by and by, down the line *or* road, in time, *mañana (Spanish)*, next, subsequently, thereafter, tomorrow

lateral *adj.* **1.** askance, bordering, edgeways, flanking, indirect, marginal, peripheral, side, sidelong, sideways, skirting *Antonyms:* central, conventional, core **2.** creative, imaginative, indirect, non-linear, non-logical, oblique, roundabout, unorthodox, unusual

latest *adj.* current, *dernier cri (French)*, fashionable, groovy *(Nonformal)*, hip, in, modern, newest, the end-all *or* ultimate, up-to-date, up-to-the-minute *Antonyms:* archaic, earliest, oldest

lather *n.* **1.** bubbles, foam, froth, head, soapsuds, spume, suds **2.** agitation, bustle, clamour, commotion, confusion, dither, fever, flap, fluster, fuss, state, stew, storm, sweat, tizzy, tumult, turbulence, turmoil *Nonformal:* hassle, kerfuffle – *v.* **1.** clean, foam, froth, shampoo, soap, wash **2.** batter, beat, castigate, chastise, flog, hit, lambaste, lash, pummel, punish, thrash, strike, thump, wallop, whip

latitude *n.* **1.** elbow room *(Nonformal)*, extent, freedom, laxity, leeway, liberty, licence, margin, play, range, reach, room, run, space, span, spread, sweep, width *Antonyms:* inflexibility, limitation, restriction **2.** area, region, section, territory, zone

latitudinarian *adj.* broad-minded, catholic, ecumenical, equitable, fair, fair-handed, freethinking, impartial, indulgent, just, lenient, liberal, open-minded, outside the box *(Nonformal)*, permissive, progressive, tolerant, unmanned *Antonyms:* harsh, prejudicial, primitive, puritan – *n.* ecumenist, free spirit, freethinker, independent, liberal, neutral, progressive *Antonyms:* conservative, reactionary

latter *adj.* closing, concluding, eventual, final, following, hindmost, last, later, latest, near the end, second, terminal

lattice *n.* filigree, frame, fretwork, grating, grid, grill, latticework, mesh, net, network, openwork, reticulation, screen, structure, tracery, trellis, web

laud *v.* acclaim, admire, adore, approve, bless, boost, build up, celebrate, commend, compliment, extol, flatter, glorify, honour, hymn, magnify, praise, revere, stroke *(Nonformal)*, venerate, worship *Antonyms:* criticize, deride, harass, ridicule, spurn

laudable *adj.* admirable, commendable, creditable, deserving, estimable, excellent, meritorious, praiseworthy, stellar, terrific, worthy *Antonyms:* contemptible, despicable, ignoble, lowly, unworthy

laudatory *adj.* acclamatory, adulatory, approving, complimentary, celebrative, eulogistic, flattering, worthy of praise *Antonyms:* contemptuous, derisive, objectionable, pejorative, scoffing

laugh *n.* **1.** cackle, chortle, chuckle, crow, giggle, guffaw, smirk, snicker, snort, titter, wheeze *Nonformal:* hoot, howl, scream **2.** amusement, gag, hilarity, jape, jest, joke, merriment, mirth, play, sport *Nonformal:* ball, gas *Antonyms:* grievance, sadness, solemnity, trial **3.** absurdity, embarrassment, farce, laughingstock, mockery, travesty – *v.* **1.** chortle, chuckle, convulse, crack up *(Nonformal)*, giggle, grin, guffaw, howl, roar, scream, shout, smile, snigger, snort, titter, whoop *Antonyms:* bawl, blubber, cry, sob, wail **2.** deride, heckle, razz run down, scoff, send up, sneer, taunt, twit

laughable *adj.* absurd, amusing, asinine bizarre, comic, comical, derisive, diverting droll, eccentric, entertaining, facetious, farcical, funny, hilarious, humorous, jocose jocular, ludicrous, mirthful, mocking, nonsensical, ridiculous, risible, sidesplitting witty *Nonformal:* joshing, rich *Antonyms* dignified, impressive, poignant, serious solemn

launch *n.* dinghy, gig, motor *or* pleasure boat, pleasure craft, runabout, skiff, tende – *v.* **1.** begin, commence, embark upon, ge things rolling *(Nonformal)*, ignite, inaugurate, initiate, instigate, institute, introduce jump, kick *or* set off, open, originate, start usher in *Antonyms:* cease, end, halt, terminate **2.** bombard, cast, catapult, discharge dispatch, drive, eject, fire, fling, heave hurl, pitch, project, propel, send forth, send off, sling, throw, toss *Antonyms:* catch return, retrieve

laureate *adj.* acclaimed, distinguished, eminent, famed, famous, glorious, honoured illustrious, notable, outstanding, praised preeminent, prominent, recognized renowned, revered, venerable, well-known *Antonyms:* insignificant, minor, unknown – *n.* award winner, eminence, genius, Nobe prize winner, paragon, person of renown poet laureate, virtuoso – *v.* crown, distinguish, honour, venerate *Antonyms:* castigate, demote, denounce

laurels *n. pl.* acclaim, accolades, awards badge, commendation, credit, crown of laurels, decoration, distinction, fame, glory kudos, praise, prestige, recognition, renown reward *Antonyms:* condemnation, criticism crown of thorns, disrespect, reproof

lavatory *n.* bathroom, latrine, ladies' *or* men's room, privy, powder *or* rest room public convenience, toilet, Turkish bath urinal, washroom, water closet *or* w.c *Nonformal:* can, dames, gents, john, loo

lavish *adj.* **1.** generous, liberal, munificent prodigal, rich, unrestrained *Antonyms* cheap, frugal, meagre, miserly, stingy **2**

abundant, bountiful, copious, exuberant, overflowing, plentiful, profuse, prolific, unsparing, unstinted **3.** effusive, excessive, extravagant, immoderate, improvident, inordinate, intemperate, overabundant, profligate, smarmy *(Nonformal)*, thriftless, unreasonable, wasteful **4.** Byzantine, costly, expensive, first-class, gorgeous, grand, impressive, lush, luxuriant, luxurious, opulent, ornate, ostentatious, plush, posh, ritzy, showy, splendid, sumptuous, swanky, top drawer – *v.* **1.** bestow, deluge, give, heap, pamper, pour, shower, spend *Antonyms:* begrudge, conserve, economize, preserve, withhold **2.** dissipate, drain, exhaust, expend, fritter, go through, squander, waste

law *adj.* binding, conclusive, deciding, definitive, final, finished *Antonyms:* debatable, open to question, up in the air – *interj.* gadzooks *(Nonformal)*, mercy, my! my!, oh no – *n.* **1.** aphorism, axiom, base, divine direction, formula, fundamental, ground, hypothesis, maxim, moral, precept, principle, rubric, rule, source, standard, tenet, theorem, truth **2.** accepted practice, bill of rights, body of rules, canon, charter, civil law, code, code of chivalry, common law, constitution, dogma, jurisprudence, Napoleonic code, rules and regulations, rules of conduct, statues, statute law, tradition **3.** act, bylaw, decree, edict, enactment, ordinance, reg *(Nonformal)*, regulation, ruling **4.** bar, bench, court, court of law, tribunal **5.** fairness, justice, lawfulness, legality, legitimacy, order **6.** *carabinieri (Italian)*, constabulary, *gendarme (French)*, police, Royal Canadian Mounted Police *or* RCMP *Nonformal:* cop, fuzz, heat, mounties, the man **7.** case, legal action, litigation, redress, remedy **8.** authority, behest, command, decree, demand – *v.* action, litigate, sue, take to court

lawful *adj.* authentic, authorized, bona fide, canonical, constitutional, decreed, duty-paid, enacted, enforced, established, genuine, judged, judicial, just, justifiable, kosher, legal, legitimate, mandated, official, ordained, permissible, proper, protected, registered, rightful, statutory, taxpaid, valid, warranted *Nonformal:* card-carrying, on the level, on the up and up, paid-up *Antonyms:* banned, forbidden, illegal, illicit, prohibited

lawless *adj.* **1.** amok, chaotic, disorderly, free, riotous, wild *Antonyms:* civilized, disciplined, orderly **2.** criminal, felonious, forbidden, illegal, illicit, prohibited, transgressive *Antonyms:* legal, legitimate, permitted **3.** contumacious, disobedient, insubordinate, insurgent, mutinous, rebellious, revolutionary, seditious, traitorous, ungovernable, unrestrained, unruly, violent *Antonyms:* compliant, demure, obedient

lawlessness *n.* anarchy, chaos, mob rule, mutiny, pandemonium, pogrom, time of terror

lawn *n.* backyard, front yard, garden, grass, grassland, green, grounds, one's own piece of heaven *(Nonformal)*, park, plot, sod, terrace, turf, yard

lawsuit *n.* accusation, action, allegation, argument, arraignment, case, cause, charge, claim, contention, contest, dispute, impeachment, indictment, litigation, proceedings, prosecution, suit, trial

lawyer *n.* advocate, attorney, barrister, counsel, counsellor, defender, jurisprudent, King's Council *or* K.C., legal advisor, Queen's Counsel *or* Q.C., solicitor

lax *adj.* **1.** easygoing, indulgent, lenient, mild, permissive, soft, tolerant, yielding *Antonyms:* authoritarian, harsh, strict **2.** broad, general, hit-or-miss, imprecise, inaccurate, inexact, undefined, vague *Antonyms:* exact, pointed, precise, regimented, tight **3.** asleep on the job, blasé, careless, casual, disorderly, easy, indifferent, indolent, messy, negligent, remiss, slipshod, sloppy, slovenly, untidy *Antonyms:* careful, meticulous, vigilant, vigorous **4.** baggy, droopy, floppy *(Nonformal)*, hanging, loose, sagging, shapeless, slack *Antonyms:* moulded, skintight, taut

laxative *n.* cathartic, dose of salts *(Nonformal)*, emetic, ipecac, physic, prune juice, purgative, purge *Trademark:* Exlax, Metamucil

laxity *n.* **1.** clemency, forgiveness, indulgence, lenience, mildness, permissiveness, softness, tolerance **2.** carelessness, disorder, disregard, inaccuracy, inexactitude, laissez-faire, nonchalance **3.** amorphousness, flaccidity, plasticity, shapelessness, slackness

lay *adj.* **1.** congregational, laic, laity, nonclerical, nonordained, nonreligious, profane, secular, temporal **2.** amateur, dilettante, inexpert, nonprofessional, nonspecialist, uncertified, unschooled – *n.* air, ballad, ditty *(Nonformal)*, lyric, melody, narrative poem, refrain, song, verse – *v.* **1.** arrange, deposit, place, plant, position, rest, set, set down, situate, stick *(Nonformal)* **2.** allocate, allot, apply, ascribe, assign, attribute, burden, charge, credit, encumber, impose, impute **3.** drop, fell, lay low, prostrate, sink **4.** concoct, contrive, design, devise, hatch, plan, plot, prepare, work out **5.** advance, allege, bring forward, lodge, posit, present, submit **6.** bear, birth, drop *(Nonformal)*, eject, generate, give birth, produce, release, spawn **7.** flatten, flush, iron, level, plane, smooth **8.** bet, gamble, game, give odds, hazard, play, risk, stake, wager *Commonly misused:* **lie**

layer *n.* **1.** band, casing, coating, covering, film, lamina, lamination, panel, ply, row, sheet, slab, stratum, thickness, tier **2.** branch, graft, runner, shoot, stem, tendril, twig

layman *n.* amateur, dilettante, laic, lay person, neophyte, nonprofessional, novice, parishioner, secular *Antonyms:* aficionado, cleric, cognoscente, pundit, specialist

layout *n.* arrangement, blueprint, chart, design, diagram, draft, footprint *(Nonformal)*, formation, map, mock-up, modus operandi, organization, outline, plan

layover *n.* break, hiatus, interruption, overnighter, stopover

laziness *n.* apathy, dilatoriness, idleness, inactivity, indolence, inertia, languidness, lethargy, slothful, slowness, sluggishness *Antonyms:* activity, alertness, business, industry

lazy *adj.* **1.** dawdling, dilly-dallying *(Nonformal)*, idle, indolent, loafing, procrastinating, shirking, slothful *Antonyms:* earnest, energetic **2.** inert, languorous, lethargic, slow, slow-moving, sluggish, somnolen torpid *Antonyms:* active, alert, awake **3** asleep on the job *(Nonformal)*, careless easygoing, lax, neglectful, slack, slopp *Antonyms:* exacting, meticulous, rigorou **4.** dilatory, lackadaisical, meandering, pok ing along *Antonyms:* fast, hurried, rushed

lead *adj.* first, front, front-running, head leading, main, premier, top – *n.* **1.** advan tage, edge, front, leadership, supremacy upper hand **2.** advice, direction, example guidance, instruction, path, route **3** celebrity, diva, headliner, hero, heroine main draw, name, principal, role, star **4** clue, evidence, hint, indication, informa tion, proof, sign, suggestion, tip, trace **5** cord, harness, leash, lunge, rein, rope, teth er **6.** graphite, mineral, ore, plumbago **7** bob, plumb, sinker, weight – *v.* **1.** antecede come before *or* first, precede **2.** accompa ny, attend, chaperon, conduct, convey escort, guide, introduce, pilot, protect safeguard, shepherd, usher **3.** captain chair, command, control, direct, govern helm, manage, marshal, preside over, rule run, spark, spearhead, steer, supervise tend *Nonformal:* call the shots, quarter back **4.** affect, cause, compel, dispose effect, impel, incline, induce, influence motivate, move, persuade, prompt, spur **5** begin, coin, found, inaugurate, introduce invent, mastermind, trail blaze **6.** beat ou *(Nonformal)*, better, cap, eclipse, excel outdo, outshine, overshadow, top, tower **7** endure, experience, have, live, liv through, suffer, undergo

leaden *adj.* **1.** bleak, dark, dingy, dismal gloomy, grey, oppressive, overcas *Antonyms:* bright, gay, sunny **2.** depressed doleful, heavy-hearted, melancholy, sad sombre **3.** burdensome, crushing, cumber some, heavy, insurmountable, massive, oner ous, ponderous, weighty *Antonyms:* buoy ant, blithe, light **4.** forced, formal, inert laboured, lacklustre, lifeless, plodding, pro saic, ramrod, stiff, stilted, turgid, wooden *Antonyms:* elegant, fluent, glib, smooth

leader *n.* **1.** boss, caesar, captain, chair chief, chieftain, commander, controller czar, czarina, dean, demagogue, despot dictator, director, emir, emperor, empress frontrunner, general, governor, guide, head imperator, king, maharaja, maharani, manager, master, mikado, monarch, pendragon, president, principal, queen, raja, rani, ruler, satrap, skipper, sovereign, sultan, sultana, superintendent, superior, tyrant *Historical:* caliph, intendant, negus *Nonformal:* big cheese *or* wheel, bigwig, brains, chief cook and bottle washer, cock of the walk, head honcho, kingpin, numero uno, poo-bah, queen bee *Antonyms:* adherent, disciple, follower, minion, supporter **2.** forerunner, ground-breaker, innovator, pioneer, trailblazer, trendsetter, vanguard **3.** band leader, cantor, conductor, maestro, music director **4.** advertised merchandise, chief commodity, feature, headliner, item, lead article, loss leader, product, special

leadership *n.* administration, authority, command, control, directorship, guidance, hegemony, influence, management, oligarchy, superintendency, supremacy

leading *adj.* **1.** arch, best, best-selling, champion, dominant, famous, first, first off, foremost, greatest, highest, key, main, noted, notorious, number one with a bullet *(Nonformal)*, paramount, preeminent, prominent, stellar, superior, tops, well-known *Antonyms:* inferior, secondary, supporting **2.** directing, dominating, commanding, controlling, governing, guiding, managing, overseeing, ruling, running, steering, supervising – *n.* control, direction, guidance, influence, leadership

leaf *n.* **1.** blade, foliage, frond, petiole, scale *Types of leaves:* acuminate, amplexicaul, binate, cordate, decussate, digitally compound, lanceolate, oblong, obtuse, ovate, pinnate, sagittate, serrate, spatulate **2.** flyleaf, folio, insert, page, sheet **3.** coat, cover, covering layer, cut, foil, lamination, layer, overlay, plate, scale, veneer – *v.* browse, flip, glance, glide over, rifle through, scan, skim *Antonyms:* peruse, scrutinize, study

league *n.* **1.** alliance, association, band, brotherhood, bunch, circle, club, coalition, compact, company, confederation, consortium, crew, enclave, federation, fellowship, fraternity, gang, group, guild, mob *(Nonformal)*, order, organization, outfit, partnership, pool, ring, society, union, unit **2.** category, circle, class, grade, grouping, level, pigeonhole, rank, status, tier – *v.* ally, amalgamate, associate, band, collaborate, combine, confederate, conjoin, consolidate, cooperate, join forces, unite *Antonyms:* cleave, divide, isolate, separate

leak *n.* **1.** aperture, chink, crack, fissure, opening, puncture **2.** discharge, drip, drop, escape, leakage, loss, oozing, seepage **3.** blabbing *(Nonformal)*, communication, disclosure, divulgence, exposure, slip, tip, tip-off **4.** informer *Nonformal:* snitch, stoolie, stool pigeon, tattletale – *v.* **1.** drip, emit, excrete, ooze, seep, trickle, weep **2.** betray, communicate, disclose, divulge, expose, gossip, inform, let slip, reveal, tell *Nonformal:* blurt out, rat, snitch, spill the beans, squeal *Antonyms:* cover up, hide, suppress, withhold

lean *adj.* **1.** angular, bare, beanpole *(Nonformal)*, bony, cadaverous, emaciated, gangling, gangly, gaunt, lanky, rangy, rawboned, scrawny, sinewy, skinny, slender, slim, spare, svelte, sylphlike, thin, twiggy, wiry *Antonyms:* ample, brawny, burly, corpulent, fat **2.** barren, deficient, impoverished, inadequate, meagre, penurious, pitiful, poor, scanty, sparse, unfruitful, unproductive – *n.* angle, aspect, bow, cant, deviation, droop, incline, pitch, slant, tilt – *v.* **1.** favour, follow, gravitate toward, incline, prefer, tend *Antonyms:* banish, cast out, dislike, rebuff, reject **2.** angle, bend, bow, cant, careen, curve, droop, list, overhang, pitch, roll, slant, tilt, turn, twist, veer *Antonyms:* flatten, level, straighten **3.** incline, lie, position, prop, rest, recline, support **4.** confide, count on, depend, rely, swear by, trust *Antonyms:* doubt, mistrust, suspect **5.** browbeat, bulldoze *(Nonformal)*, bully, coerce, hassle, hector, hound

leaning *adj.* askew, awry, crooked, lounging, recumbent, sloping, slanting, tilting *Antonyms:* level, perpendicular, straight – *n.* aptitude, avidity, bent, bias, cup of tea *(Nonformal)*, desire, inclination, liking, mind-set, partiality, penchant, predilection, prejudice, proclivity, propensity, tendency, weakness *Antonyms:* antipathy, aversion, dislike, repulsion

leap *n.* **1.** bound, hop, jump, skip, spring, surge, vault **2.** advance, ascent, change, forward motion, movement, progression, step forward **3.** area, distance, expanse, space, stretch, sweep – *v.* advance, arise, ascend, bounce, bound, clear, escalate, hop, hurdle, jump, mount, pass over, rise, rocket, skip, skyrocket, soar, speed, spring, step forward, surge, vault

learn *v.* **1.** cognize, comprehend, get, grasp, master, perceive, realize, understand **2.** acquire, catch, detect, determine, discern, discover, find out, gather, glean, hear, see, uncover, unearth, worm out *(Nonformal)* **3.** absorb, assimilate, bone up on *(Nonformal)*, cram, memorize, pore over, practice, prepare, read, review, study, train

learned *adj.* **1.** academic, accomplished, adept, bluestocking, bookish, brainy, conversant, cultivated, deep, educated, erudite, experienced, expert, intellectual, lettered, literate, philosophical, proficient, profound, scholarly, scientific, skilled, sophisticated, studied, versed, well-educated, well-informed, worldly *Antonyms:* ignorant, illiterate, uneducated **2.** conditioned, inculcated, inoculated, instilled, Pavlovian, programmed, taught

learner *n.* apprentice, beginner, disciple, freshman, initiate, neophyte, novice, probationer, protégé, pupil, recruit, rookie, scholar, student, tenderfoot, trainee *Antonyms:* expert, master, maven, virtuoso, wizard

learning *n.* culture, edification, education, enlightenment, experience, illumination, inquiry, instruction, investigation, knowledge, letters, life's lessons, lore, research, scholarship, schooling, study, tuition, wisdom

lease *n.* **1.** agreement, contract, document, legal claim **2.** leasehold, possession, rental, tenancy **3.** chance, opportunity, possibility, prospect – *v.* charter, hire, let, loan, rent, sublease, sublet

leash *n.* bridle, chain, cord, lead, lunge, rein, restraint, rope, strap, tether – *v.* bridle, check, control, curb, fasten, fetter, hamper, hobble, hog-tie *(Nonformal)*, hold, hold back, rein, restrain, secure, shackle, suppress, tether, tie, trammel *Antonyms:* free, loosen, release

least *adj.* barest, fewest, lowest, minimum, most minute, scantiest, slightest, smallest, teeniest *(Nonformal)*, tiniest *Antonyms:* greatest, largest, most

leather *n.* hide, pelt, tanned animal skin *Kinds of leather:* buckskin, buff, calf, capeskin, chamois, cordovan, deerskin, doeskin, grain, kid, morocco, patent, pigskin, rawhide, sheepskin, snakeskin, suede – *v.* beat, flog, hit, pommel, punish, skiver, tan *(Nonformal)*, whip

leathery *adj.* **1.** durable, hard, hardened, resistant, rough, rugged, sinewy, strong, weathered, wrinkled *Antonyms:* satiny, smooth, soft, velvety **2.** chewy, dry, fibrous, gristly, rubbery, stringy, tough, well-done *Antonyms:* juicy, succulent, tender

leave *n.* **1.** adieu, departure, farewell, goodbye, parting, withdrawal *Antonyms:* arrival, greetings, welcome **2.** furlough, hiatus, holiday, recess, retirement, sabbatical, suspension, time off, vacation **3.** allowance, authorization, concession, consent, dispensation, freedom, go ahead, liberty, licence, permission, sanction *Nonformal:* green-light, nod, okay *Antonyms:* prohibition, refusal, rejection – *v.* **1.** break away, clear out, decamp, depart, disappear, embark, escape, evanesce, exit, flee, fly, go, go forth, migrate, move, part, quit, retire, slip out, take off, vacate, vanish, walk out, withdraw *Nonformal:* frappe la rue, haul ass, hit the trail, scram, skedaddle, split, vamoose *Antonyms:* appear, arrive, stay **2.** abandon, abscond, back *or* bail out, desert, escape, evacuate, flee, forsake **3.** allot, apportion, assign, bequeath, bequest, cede, commit, confide, consign, entrust, give, give over, hand down, leave behind, will

leaven *n.* **1.** baking powder, barm, enzyme, ferment, leavening yeast, mother *(Nonformal)* **2.** agent, alterer, catalyst, determinant element, modifier, transformer – *v.* adjust, alter, expand, ferment, inflate, lift, lighten, mitigate, modify, raise, stimulate, temper, transform *Antonyms:* abate, assuage, flatten, reduce

lecher *n.* bounder, debaucher, dissipator, libertine, playboy, profligate, rake, seducer, wanton, whoremonger, womanizer *Nonformal:* Casanova, dirty old man, Don Juan, letch, Lothario, skirt *or* woman chaser, wolf

lecherous *adj.* carnal, corrupt, dirty, fast, horny, lascivious, lewd, libertine, libidinous, licentious, lubricous, lustful, prurient, raunchy, salacious, sensual, wanton *Antonyms:* prim, proper, prudish, virtuous

lecture *n.* **1.** address, chalk talk *(Nonformal)*, diatribe, discourse, dissertation, homily, instruction, lesson, oration, pitch, screed, speech, spiel, talk, tirade **2.** admonishment, correction, discipline, rebuke, reprimand, talking to, upbraiding, warning – *v.* **1.** address, discourse, expound, harangue, instruct, moralize, pontificate, preach, sermonize, speak, talk, teach *Nonformal:* soapbox, spout **2.** admonish, card *(P.E.I.)*, castigate, chide, criticize, discipline, punish, rebuke, reprimand, scold *Nonformal:* chew out, tongue-lash

ledge *n.* bar, jut, mantle, overhang, projection, reef, ridge, sandbank, shelf, step, tier

leer *n.* gape, glance, goggle, ogle, stare, sly look *Nonformal:* once over, the eye – *v.* check out, examine, eye, goggle, ogle, scrutinize, smirk, sneer, stare

leery *adj.* cagey, careful, cautious, chary, circumspect, distrustful, doubting, dubious, guarded, hesitant, prudent, sceptical, shy, suspicious, tentative, uncertain, undecided, unsure, wary *Antonyms:* confident, faithful, trusting

leeway *n.* breathing space, elbow room *(Nonformal)*, extent, headway, latitude, margin, room, scope, slack, space *Antonyms:* confinement, limitation, restriction

left *adj.* **1.** larboard, left-hand, left-wing, port, portside, sinister, sinistral, sinistrous **2.** assigned, bequeathed, entrusted, handed down *or* over **3.** extra, extraneous, leftover, remaining, residual, surplus **4.** decamped, gone, parted, split *(Nonformal)*, vacated, vanished, withdrawn **5.** communist, left-wing, Maoist, Marxist, progressive, radical, red, revolutionary, socialist *Antonyms:* conservative, right-wing, traditionalist

leftover *adj.* excess, extra, remaining, residual, surplus, unconsumed, uneaten, untouched, unused, unwanted – *n.* detritus, extra, parts, refuse, remains, remnants, scraps, slag, surplus, tailings, waste

leg *n.* **1.** appendage, calf, limb, member, shank, thigh **2.** brace, column, pole, portion, post, stake, stilt, support, underpinning, upright **3.** fraction, lap, part, piece, portion, section, segment, stage, stretch

legacy *n.* **1.** bequest, birthright, device, endowment, estate, gift, heirloom, inheritance, patrimony **2.** ancestry, history, heritage, past, throwback *(Nonformal)*, tradition

legal *adj.* acknowledged, allowed, authorized, card-carrying, chartered, constitutional, contractual, decreed, due, duty paid, enforceable, enjoined, fair, forensic, granted, judicial, lawful, legalized, legitimate, licit, ordained, permissible, prescribed, proper, protected, registered, rightful, sanctioned, statutory, valid, warranted *Nonformal:* kosher, legit *Antonyms:* criminal, felonious, illicit, transgressive

legality *n.* constitutionality, due process, jurisdiction, justice, lawfulness, legitimacy, licitness *Antonyms:* criminality, trespass, unlawfulness, wrongdoing

legalize *v.* allow, approve, authorize, codify, constitute, decree, decriminalize, enact, establish, formulate, launder *(Nonformal)*, legislate, legitimize, license, ordain, permit, prescribe, register, regulate, sanction, validate *Antonyms:* ban, forbid, outlaw, prohibit

legend *n.* **1.** account, adventure, allegory, drama, epic, fable, fiction, moral, myth, old wive's tale, parable, romance, saga, story, tale, tall-tale *(Nonformal)*, tradition, yarn **2.** celebrity, dignitary, household name, luminary, marvel, notable, phenomenon, prodigy, spectacle, superstar, star, sensation *Nonformal:* big name, has-been **3.** caption, cipher, code, explanation, key, rubric, table **4.** epigraph, epitaph, heading, inscription, motto

legendary *adj.* **1.** fabled, fabricated, fabulous, fanciful, fictitious, imaginary, invented, mythical, mythological, storied *Antonyms:* factual, genuine, historical **2.** celebrated, famed, famous, illustrious, renowned, well-known *Antonyms:* common, everyday, unknown **3.** age-old, ancestorial, hallowed, handed *or* passed down, immortal, oral, time-honoured, traditional, venerable *Antonyms:* nascent, new

legible *adj.* **1.** clear, coherent, decipherable, distinct, explicit, intelligible, lucid, neat, plain, readable, sharp, typed, understandable *Antonyms:* obscure, rambling, scrawled, scribbled **2.** apparent, apprehensible, comprehensible, discernible, distinguishable, intelligible, manifest, obvious, recognizable

legion *adj.* countless, many, multifarious, multitudinous, myriad, numerous, populous, several, sundry, various, voluminous *Antonyms:* few, none, scant – *n.* **1.** army, body, brigade, company, division, platoon, squadron, troop, unit **2.** crowd, flock, group, horde, host, mass, multitude, myriad, number, plenitude, profusion, throng

legislate *v.* authorize, codify, constitute, decree, enforce, establish, formalize, legalize, legitimize, litigate, normalize, ordain, pass, sanction *Antonyms:* ban, criminalize, prohibit

legislation *n.* act, bill, bylaw, charter, codification, constitution, enactment, lawmaking, laws, prescription, regulation, ruling, statute

legislative *adj.* congressional, decreeing, enacting, judicial, jurisdictive, lawgiving, lawmaking, legislatorial, ordaining, parliamentary, statute-making

legislator *n.* administrator, alderman, assemblyman, congressman, councillor, deputy, lawmaker, leader, mayor, member of parliament, parliamentarian, politician, reeve, senator, warden

legislature *n.* assembly, body, caucus, chamber, congress, council, government body, House of Assembly, lawmakers, legislative assembly, National Assembly *(Quebec)*, parliament, plenum, politburo *(Historical)*, Senate, soviet

legitimate *adj.* **1.** accepted, acknowledged, authentic, authorized, bona fide, certain, genuine, just, justifiable, logical, official, orthodox, proper, real, reasonable, recognized, rightful, sound, sensible, sure, true, valid, verifiable, warranted, well-founded *Antonyms*: bogus, crazy, fake, illogical, insensible **2.** admissible, duty paid, lawful, legal, registered, sanctioned, statutory, tax-paid *Antonyms:* bootleg, criminal, felonious, illegal

leisure *adj.* at-home, carefree, free, idle, spare, unclaimed, unoccupied *Antonyms:* busy, employed, engaged, occupied – *n.* **1.** breathing space, free time, hiatus, holiday, idle hours, intermission, opportunity, pause, quiet, recess, recreation, relaxation, repose, respite, rest, retirement, spare time, time off, vacation *Antonyms:* employment, occupation, work **2.** convenience, discretion, ease, freedom, liberty, own sweet time *(Nonformal)*, pleasure

leisurely *adj.* casual, comfortable, easy, free, laid-back, languid, lazy, relaxed, restful, slack, slow, unhurried *Antonyms:* brisk, fast, hasty, hectic, rushed – *adv.* calmly, casually, comfortably, composedly, easily, gradually, in easy stages, languorously, languidly, lazily, slowly, unhurriedly *Antonyms:* briskly, hastily, quickly, rapidly

lend *v.* advance, bestow, confer, contribute, entrust, extend, furnish, give, grant, impart, lease, let, loan, oblige, permit, present, provide, shark *(Nonformal)*, stake, supply, trust *Antonyms:* deduct, retain, withhold

length *n.* breadth, dimension, duration, expanse, extensiveness, extent, interval, limit, longitude, magnitude, measure, measurement, mileage, number of kilometres, orbit, piece, portion, protractedness, range, reach, realm, space, span, stretch

lengthen *v.* amplify, augment, dilate, distend, drag *or* draw *or* string out, elongate, expand, extend, increase, let out, prolong, protract, reach, stretch *Antonyms:* abbreviate, abridge, curtail, shorten, trim

lengthy *adj.* **1.** drawn-out, elongated, extended, lengthened, long, prolonged, protracted *Antonyms:* brief, limited, short

2. boring, humdrum, interminable, long-winded, monotonous, prolix, prosaic, repetitive, singsong, tedious, tiring, verbose *Antonyms:* concise, succinct, terse, tight

leniency *n.* benevolence, clemency, compassion, decency, forbearance, generosity, gentleness, humaneness, indulgence, kindness, laxness, mercy, mildness, pardon, patience, pity, softness, tenderness, tolerance *Antonyms:* callousness, harshness, intransigence, rigidity, severity

lenient *adj.* allowing, amiable, assuaging, big *(Nonformal)*, charitable, compassionate, complaisant, compliant, easy, easygoing, excusing, favouring, forbearing, forgiving, gentle, good-natured, humouring, indulgent, kindly, merciful, mild, obliging, pampering, pardoning, permissive, soft-hearted, sparing, spoiling, sympathetic, tender, tolerant, yielding *Antonyms:* merciless, strict, uncompromising

lens *n.* eyepiece, glass *Kinds of lens:* biconcave, biconvex, bifocal, compound, concave-convex, contact, convex-concave, crystalline, fisheye, Frenel, magnifying glass, monocle, plano-concave, plano-convex, prism, telephoto, telescopic, trifocal, wide-angle *See also:* **glasses**

lesbian *adj. & n.* gay, homophile, homosexual, liz *(Historical)*, sapphic *See also:* **gay, homosexual**

lesion *n.* abrasion, bite, blemish, bruise, burn, cut, damage, gash, harm, inflammation, injury, scrape, scratch, sore, wound

less *adj.* **1.** diminished, fewer, limited, minimal, reduced, smaller **2.** beneath, inferior, lower, minor, secondary, subordinate – *adv.* barely, decreasingly, diminishingly, little, minus, *sans (French)*, without

lesser *adj.* bottom, inferior, insignificant, lower, minor, secondary, second-string, small-fry, small-time, subordinate *Nonformal:* bush league, penny ante, piddling *Antonyms:* greater, higher, major, primary, superior

lesson *n.* **1.** assignment, curriculum, drill, exercise, homework, study, task **2.** class, coaching, education, information, instruction, schooling, session, teaching, tutoring **3.** example, experience, maxim, message, model, moral **4.** admonition, castigation, censure, chiding, deterrent, punishment, reprimand, reproach, reproof, warning **5.** homily, passage, reading, scripture, text

let *n.* block, check, hindrance, interference, net, obstruction, redo – *v.* **1.** allow, approve, authorize, enable, endorse, give leave, grant, license, permit, sanction, warrant *Antonyms:* forbid, prevent, prohibit, veto **2.** acquaint, admit, appraise, brief, charter, disclose, divulge, hire, lease, notify, publicize, rent, reveal, sublet, tell *Nonformal:* blab, blow the whistle, bring up to speed, fess up to **3.** absolve, acquit, drop, exempt, exonerate, free, loose, pardon, relinquish, unhand, vindicate **4.** assign, award, contract, delegate, give out

letdown *n.* **1.** anticlimax, collapse, comedown, disappointment, disenchantment, disillusionment, frustration, humiliation, lowpoint, setback *Nonformal:* downer, fizzle *Antonyms:* climax, highpoint, summit **2.** abatement, decline, decrease, ebb, lessening, letup, mitigation, slackening, slowing, wane

lethal *adj.* deadly, fatal, harmful, injurious, killer, killing, life-threatening, malignant, malefic, noxious, pernicious, poisonous, toxic, venomous, virulent *Antonyms:* beneficial, benevolent, healthful, healthy

lethargic *adj.* **1.** apathetic, dormant *(Nonformal)*, dull, heavy, idle, impassive, indifferent, inert, lackadaisical, laggard, languid, lazy, listless, passive, phlegmatic, slow, sluggish, salubrious, spiritless, stupefied, torpid *Antonyms:* active, animated, responsive, spirited, stimulated **2.** bone-tired, comatose, dopey, draggy, exhausted, fatigued, sleepy, somnolent, tired, weary *Nonformal:* bagged, bushed, pooped, spent *Antonyms*: alert, energetic, vigorous

lethargy *n.* apathy, dullness, idleness, impassivity, inaction, indifference, indolence, inertness, lack of interest, languor, lassitude, laziness, listlessness, passivity, slowness, sluggishness, supineness, torpor *Antonyms:* animation, life, verve, vitality, zest **2.** drowsiness, exhaustion, fatigue, narcosis, sleepiness, somnolence *Antonyms:* energy, vigour, wakefulness

letter *n.* **1.** acknowledgment, answer, communication, dispatch, epistle, line, message, missive, note, reply *Kinds of letter:* aerogram, *billet doux (French)*, chain, circular, cover, covering, credit, dead, dear John, drop, e-mail, encyclical, fan, fax, form, introduction, marque, reference, resignation, patent, testamentary, to the editor, love, market, newsletter, open, pastoral, poison-pen, round robin **2.** character, hieroglyph, initial, sign, symbol

lettered *adj.* academic, articulate, bookish, educated, encyclopedic, highbrow, intellectual, learned, profound, scholarly, studious, well-read, well-versed, wise *Antonyms:* illiterate, Philistine, unenlightened, unread

lettuce *n.* greens, rabbit food *(Nonformal)*, vegetable *Kinds of lettuce:* Bibb, Boston, butter, corn salad, cos, curly, green-leaf, iceberg, mache, mesclun, mixed, red-leaf, romaine

letup *n.* **1.** break, breather *(Nonformal)*, cessation, hiatus, intermission, interval, pause, recess, remission, respite, time out *Antonyms:* constancy, continuation, prolongation **2.** abatement, lessening, lull, mitigation, moderation, slackening, softening, weakening *Antonyms*: intensification, magnification

levee *n.* **1.** bank, barricade, barrier, bulwark, dam, dike, ditch, fence, wall, embankment, mound **2.** affair, celebration, ceremony, fête, gala, get-together, jump-up, party, reception, salon, social gathering, soiree **3.** boardwalk, dock, embankment, pier, wharf

level *adj.* **1.** aligned, balanced, equal, flush, lined up, parallel, proportionate, straight, symmetric **2.** consistent, constant, even, on the same plane, regular, stable, static, steady, unchanging, uniform, unvarying **3.** aboveboard, dispassionate, genuine, honest, just, on the up and up *(Nonformal)*, straightforward **4.** calm, collected, composed, relaxed, serene – *n.* **1.** altitude, elevation, height, position, value **2.** area, expanse, field, horizon, plane, surface **3.** class, deck, degree, echelon, floor, gradation, grade, layer, place, rank, scale, stage, standing, status, story, stratum, tier – *v.* **1.** bulldoze, demolish, destroy, devastate, hew, mow, plow up, raze, strip **2.** even out, flatten, grade, plane, straighten, smooth **3.** align, even up, harmonize, regularize, square **4.** address, aim, draw a bead on, direct, focus, sight, take aim, train **5.** be frank, clear up the air *(Nonformal)*, come clean, own up, set the record straight

level-headed *adj.* balanced, calm, collected, composed, cool, dependable, discreet, even-tempered, farsighted, judicious, practical, prudent, rational, reasonable, sane, self-possessed, sensible, steady, together *(Nonformal)*, unflappable, wise *Antonyms:* emotional, impulsive, passionate, mercurial

leverage *n.* advantage, ascendancy, authority, backing, clout, drag, edge, fix, hold, influence, lift, power, pull, purchase, rank, support, vantage, weight *Nonformal*: ace in the hole, bargaining chip, juice

levity *n.* **1.** absurdity, amusement, festivity, grins, happiness, high old times *(Nonformal)*, high spirits, hilarity, jocularity, laughs, light-heartedness, mirth, pleasantry, silliness *Antonyms:* dolour, earnestness, gravity, seriousness, solemnity **2.** airiness, buoyancy, lightness, weightlessness **3.** caprice, changeableness, ditziness *(Nonformal)*, fickleness, flightiness, flippancy, inconstancy, instability

levy *n.* **1.** assessment, demand, duty, fee, fine, payment, tariff, tax, tithe, toll **2.** call-to-arms, conscription, gathering, muster, recruitment **3.** armed forces, infantry, military, recruits, regiments, reserves, soldiers troops – *v.* **1.** burden, collect, demand exact, fine, tax **2.** activate, assemble, corral convene, mobilize, muster, rally, round up

lewd *adj.* bawdy, blue *(Nonformal)*, coarse dirty, erotic, fast, filthy, foul-mouthed gross, immodest, improper, impure, indelicate, lascivious, lecherous, libertine, libidinous, licentious, loose, lustful, naughty obscene, off-colour, pornographic, profligate, questionable, racy, rakish, ribald risqué, rude, scandalous, scurrilous, shameless, smutty, suggestive, unchaste, vile, wicked *Antonyms:* chaste, clean, polite, pure

liability *n.* **1.** accountability, debt, duty, obligation, pledge, responsibility **2.** albatross *(Nonformal)*, burden, disadvantage, drawback, hindrance, impediment, millstone, obstacle, onus, stumbling block

liable *adj.* **1.** accountable, answerable, culpable, guilty, responsible *Antonyms:* exempt, immune **2.** bound, obligated, subject, tied *Antonyms:* free, untrammelled **3.** apt, disposed, given, inclined, likely, probable, prone

liaison *n.* **1.** affair, amour, entanglement, hanky panky *(Nonformal)*, indiscretion, intrigue, romance, tryst **2.** ambassador, attaché, communication, connection, contact, go-between, interchange, interface, intermediary, link, medium, mediary, mediator, referee *(Nonformal)*

liar *n.* cheat, deceiver, deluder, equivocator, fabricator, false witness, falsifier, fibber, fraud, misleader, perjurer, prevaricator, storyteller, trickster *Nonformal:* con artist, grifter, phoney, spinner of tales

libation *n.* **1.** bracer, cocktail, cordial, draft, dram, drench, drink, drop, jolt, nip, potion, quaff, refreshment, reviver, shot, sip, spot, sup, swig, tip, tonic *Nonformal:* nightcap, pick-me-up **2.** ceremony, offering, sacrifice, tribute

libel *n.* aspersion, calumny, defamation, denigration, lie, lying, misrepresentation, slander, smear *Antonyms:* accolade, kudos, laudation, praise – *v.* asperse, belie, besmirch, blacken, defame, denigrate, detract, discredit, disgrace, dishonour, disparage, malign, put down, ridicule, slander, slur, smear, stigmatize, traduce, vilify *Nonformal:* badmouth, dis, knock, roast *Antonyms:* celebrate, commend, extol, flatter, glorify

libellous *adj.* aspersive, backbiting, contumelious, debasing, defamatory, derogatory, detracting, disparaging, false, injurious, malevolent, malicious, maligning, opprobrious, pejorative, sarcastic, scurrilous, slanderous, traducing, vilifying *Antonyms:* eulogizing, flattering, laudatory, praising

liberal *adj.* **1.** altruistic, beneficent, benevolent, charitable, generous, giving, magnanimous, munificent, philanthropic, unselfish, unsparing *Antonyms:* judgmental, mean, miserly, selfish **2.** broad-minded, flexible, humanitarian, loose, progressive, receptive, tolerant, unbiased, unprejudiced *Antonyms:* closed-minded, partial, prejudiced, rigid **3.** abundant, ample, aplenty, bounteous, copious, free, handsome, lavish, plentiful, plenty, profuse, rich *Antonyms:* inadequate, limited, skimpy **4.** broad, catholic, cultural, general, humanistic – *n.* Grit, politician *See also:* **party**

liberality *n.* **1.** abundance, bounty, extravagance, lavishness, openhandedness *Antonym:* closed-fistedness, frugality, meanness **2.** altruism, benevolence, big-heartedness, broad-mindedness, charity, compassion, largesse, latitudinarianism, leniency, magnanimity, philanthropy, prodigality, tolerance *Antonyms:* bigotry, conservatism, partiality

liberate *v.* bail out, deliver, detach, emancipate, extricate, free, free up, get out from under *(Nonformal)*, manumit, release, set free, unbind, unchain, unhook, unshackle *Antonyms:* confine, detain, fetter, imprison, incarcerate

liberty *n.* **1.** autonomy, deliverance, emancipation, freedom, independence, release, self-determination, self-government, self-rule **2.** breathing space, elbow room *(Nonformal)*, latitude, leeway, margin, opportunity, range **3.** birthright, carte blanche, licence, privilege, right **4.** dispensation, exemption, franchise, leave, permission, sanction **5.** affront, arrogance, brass, cheekiness, forwardness, impertinence, impropriety *Nonformal:* gall, nerve

libidinous *adj.* carnal, debauched, lascivious, lecherous, lewd, loose, lustful, nymphomanic, prurient, salacious, satyric, sensual, steamy, wanton *Nonformal:* horny, hot, randy *Antonyms:* chaste, cold, frigid

libido *n.* appetite, carnality, instinct, lust,

prurience, sexual drive *or* longing, sensuality, sexuality, urge, yearning

library *n.* athenaeum, bibliotheca, *bibliothèque (French)*, book collection *or* depository, catalogue, den, information *or* learning centre, manuscripts, publications, reading repository, room, stack, study *Kinds of library:* bookmobile, circulating, city, college, film, lending, municipal, private, public, record, reference, school, special, territorial, town, university

licence *n.* **1.** allowance, authorization, carte blanche, consent, leave, permission, sanction *Nonformal*: go-ahead, green-light *Antonyms:* injunction, prohibition, veto **2.** emancipation, freedom, immunity, latitude, liberty, privilege, release **3.** certificate, credential, document, paper, permit, registration, scrip **4.** audacity, boldness, cheek, forwardness, impudence, insolence, nerve *(Nonformal)*, pluck, presumption, rudeness, spirit, temerity

license *v.* accredit, allow, authorize, legalize, letters, patent, permit, rubber stamp *(Nonformal)*, sanction, validate, warrant

licentious *adj.* abandoned, amoral, corrupt, debauched, depraved, disorderly, dissolute, fast, immoral, impure, lascivious, lawless, lecherous, libertine, libidinous, loose, lustful, profligate, promiscuous, salacious, unruly, wanton *Antonyms:* celibate, lawful, moral, proper, virtuous

licit *adj.* admissible, allowable, authorized, lawful, legal, legitimate, licensed, permitted, statutory *Antonyms:* criminal, illegal, prohibited

lick *n.* **1.** bit, dab, dash, hint, mote, sample, scintilla, smack, smidgen, soupçon, speck, suggestion, taste, tinge, touch, trace, vestige, whiff **2.** chance, go, opportunity, shot *(Nonformal)*, spell, stroke, tenure, try, turn **3.** brush, flick, graze, lap, stroke, tongue, wash **4.** blow, box, buffet, cuff, hit, knock, sidewinder, thump, wallop – *v.* **1.** clean, eat, groom, lap, lap up, moisten, preen, taste, tongue, wash **2.** brush, graze, flicker, pass over, touch **3.** beat, conquer, exceed, excel, outdo, overcome, prevail over, rout, surmount, surpass, top, transcend, trounce, upset, vanquish **4.** buffet, cuff, hit, knock, punch, pummel, smack, thrash

lie *n.* **1.** aspersion, calumny, deceit, deception, defamation, dishonesty, distortion, evasion, fable, fabrication, falsehood, falsification, fib, fiction, forgery, fraudulence, inexactitude, invention, libel, mendacity, misstatement, perjury, prevarication, slander, tall story *or* tale, untruth *Nonformal:* hogwash, malarky, tarradiddle, terminological inexactitude, whopper **2.** aspect, location, position, resting place, situation – *v.* **1.** laze, lie down, loll, lounge, nap, prostrate, recline, repose, rest, retire, sleep, sprawl, stretch out **2.** deceive, dissemble, dissimulate, distort, dupe, equivocate, exaggerate, fabricate, fake, falsify, fib, frame, fudge, invent, malign, misguide, misinform, mislead, misrepresent, perjure, pervert, prevaricate *Nonformal:* con, snow, string along **3.** be found, belong, be placed *or* stationed, exist, remain **4.** cease, drop, end, lapse **5.** bide, hang about, loiter, wait *Commonly misused:* **lay**

life *n.* **1.** animal, being, body, child, creation, entity, human, humankind, individual, man, mankind, mortal being, nature, organism, person, wildlife, woman, womankind **2.** animation, breath, consciousness, essence, existence, life force, sentience, soul **3.** brio, dash, energy, enthusiasm, esprit, excitement, gaiety, get-up-and-go, heart, liveliness, soul, sparkle, spice, spirit, verve, vigour, vitality, zest *Nonformal:* oomph, spark, zing **4.** autobiography, biography, confession, diary, exposé, herstory *(Nonformal)*, history, journal, letters, memoir, past, story **5.** activity, affairs, behaviour, business, career, circumstances, conduct, experiences, lifestyle **6.** course, cycle, duration, length, lifetime, orbit, period, span

lifeless *adj.* **1.** dead, deceased, defunct, departed, gone, inanimate *Nonformal:* flatlined, passed away, stiff *Antonyms:* active, alive, living **2.** bland, colourless, dull, flat, flavourless, insipid, lacklustre, limp, spiritless, stale *Antonyms:* emotional, firey, vibrant **3.** comatose, exhausted, lethargic, listless, static, still, tired, torpid, unconscious, worn out **4.** abandoned, bare, barren, deserted, empty, sterile, uninhabited

Antonyms: crowded, fertile, populous, teeming

lifelong *adj.* chronic, constant, continuing, deep-rooted, enduring, eternal, forever, inveterate, lasting, longstanding, perennial, permanent, persistent *Antonyms:* brief, ephemeral, finite, passing, transient

lifetime *n.* age, career, course, cradle to grave, days, era, existence, generation, period, span, time

lift *n.* **1.** boost, elevation, erection, heave, hike, hoist, jack, lifting, raise **2.** aid, assistance, comfort, encouragement, energizer, hope, pick-me-up *(Nonformal)*, reassurance, relief, succour, support **3.** drive, hitch, passage, ride, transportation – *v.* **1.** elevate, heave, heft, hoist, hold up *or* aloft, jack up, rise, upraise **2.** boost, buoy, encourage, pick up, promote, raise, support **3.** aggrandize, canonize, dignify, exalt, glorify, honour, immortalize, praise **4.** appropriate, copy, pilfer, pinch, pirate, plagiarize, pocket, purloin, steal, take, thieve *Nonformal:* crib, swipe **5.** annul, cancel, remove, rescind, reverse, revoke

ligature *n.* **1.** band, bandage, binding, bond, connection, cord, fastening, ligation, link, rope, tie, thread, wire, yoke **2.** character, font, letter, notation, symbol, type

light *adj.* **1.** bright, brilliant, burnished, fluorescent, glowing, illuminate, luminous, lustrous, radiant, shining **2.** bleached, faded, faint, lightened, muted, pale, pastel, soft, soft-hued, subdued **3.** dainty, ephemeral, feathery, flimsy, frail, little, portable, sheer, weightless **4.** crumbly, friable, permeable, pervious, porous, sandy **5.** frivolous, inconsequential, insignificant, slight, trifling, trivial, unimportant **6.** airy, delicate, empty, frothy, hollow, unsubstantial **7.** easy, facile, gentle, manageable, simple, undemanding, untaxing *Nonformal:* breezy, cushy, mindless **8.** amusing, comic, fun, funny, humorous, ridiculous, silly **9.** agile, buoyant, deft, graceful, light-footed, lithe, nimble, quick, spry, swift *Antonyms:* clumsy, gauche, inept **10.** delirious, dizzy, giddy, punch-drunk, woozy **11.** digestible, healthy, low-fat, meagre, nouveau, wholesome – *adv.* **1.** deftly, easily, gently, gingerly, gracefully, lightly, smoothly, softly **2.** airily, breezily, freely, unencumbered – *n.* **1.** aurora, beacon, blaze, brightness, brilliance, bulb, candle, coruscation, dawn, daybreak, daylight, daytime, flare, flash, flirrup *(Newfoundland)*, foxfire, glare, gleam, glimmer, glint, glitter, glow, illumination, incandescence, jacklight, lamp, lantern, luminescence, luminosity, lustre, phosphorescence, radiance, radiation, ray, shine, signal, sparkle, star, sun, sunbeam, sunrise, sunshine, taper, torch **2.** awareness, comprehension, elucidation, enlightenment, epiphany, knowledge, *moksha (Hindu)*, revelation, understanding **3.** anticipation, enthusiasm, happiness, hope, vivacity **4.** angle, approach, aspect, attitude, context, interpretation, meaning, outlook, perspective, position, regard, slant, vantage point, view, viewpoint **5.** fire, flame, heat, ignition, kindling, match, spark **6.** authority, big-name *(Nonformal)*, celebrity, dignitary, leader, luminary, notable, star – *v.* **1.** burn, heat, ignite, kindle, set alight, spark, start **2.** brighten, floodlight, highlight, illuminate, illumine, lighten, light up, shine, spotlight, switch *or* turn on **3.** arrive, come *or* fly *or* get *or* set *or* touch down, deplane, detrain, disembark, drop, land, perch, rest, stop

lighten *v.* **1.** allay, alleviate, ameliorate, assuage, attenuate, decrease, dilute, diminish, ease, eradicate, free, lessen, mitigate, mollify, palliate, reduce, relieve, remove, subside, unburden, unload *Antonyms:* aggravate, heighten, intensify, worsen **2.** cheer, comfort, elate, encourage, gladden, hearten, inspire, lift, perk up *Antonyms:* burden, encumber **3.** brighten, flash, gleam, glow, illuminate, irradiate, light, shine, spark

lightheaded *adj.* empty-headed, featherbrained, fickle, flighty, flippant, foolish, frivolous, harebrained, inane, scatterbrained, shallow, silly, superficial, trifling, *Antonyms:* level-headed, logical, rational, serious **2.** delirious, dizzy, faint, giddy, hazy, punchy, reeling, rocky, vertiginous, weak, whirling, woozy *Antonyms:* healthy, fine, strong

lighthearted *adj.* blithe, bright, bubbly, buoyant, carefree, cheerful, effervescent, frolicsome, gay, gleeful, happy, happy-go-lucky *(Nonformal)*, high-spirited, joyful, lively, merry, playful, sunny, untroubled, upbeat, vivacious *Antonyms:* cheerless, dejected, gloomy, morose, sad

lightly *adv.* **1.** daintily, delicately, ethereally, faintly, gently, gingerly, mildly, moderately, quietly, slightly, softly, sparingly, sparsely, subtly, tenderly, tenuously, thinly, timidly, unsubstantially *Antonyms:* abundantly, heavily **2.** briefly, hastily, in passing, momentarily, quickly *Antonyms:* at great length, in detail, thoroughly **3.** airily, breezily, carelessly, casually, easily, effortlessly, flippantly, freely, frivolously, gleefully, happily, heedlessly, indifferently, leniently, nimbly, simply, slapdash, thoughtlessly *Antonyms:* arduously, awkwardly, ponderously

lightweight *adj.* featherweight, inconsequential, insignificant, paltry, petit, petty, pint-size, slight, trifling, trivial, unimportant *Nonformal:* Mickey Mouse, penny ante, piddling *Antonyms:* important, momentous, serious, significant, substantial – *n.* **1.** bantam, Lilliputian, midget, minikin, pipsqueak, runt, scrub, shrimp *Nonformal:* peanut, peewee **2.** dolt, fool, lamebrain, *schlemiel (Yiddish)*, stupid person *Nonformal:* bozo, doofus, dummy, yo-yo **3.** cog, flunky, junior, minion, nobody, nonentity, small fry *or* potatoes

likeable *adj.* agreeable, amiable, appealing, attractive, charming, engaging, enjoyable, friendly, genial, good, good-natured, nice, pleasant, pleasing, preferable, sweet, sweet-natured, sympathetic, winning, winsome *Antonyms:* abhorrent, churlish, disagreeable, despicable, irascible

like *adj.* **1.** analogous, approximate, close, comparable, conforming, corresponding, homogenous, homologous, near, parallel, related, similar **2.** agnate, akin, alike, allied, equivalent, identical, matching, same, self-same, twin, uniform – *n.* **1.** coequal, counterpart, equal, kin, mate, match, peer, twin **2.** breed, family, ilk, kind, sort, stamp, strain, suchlike, type, vein – *prep.* **1.** analogous to, approximating, close to, near, parallel *or* similar to **2.** *á la (French)*, along the lines of, characteristic of, indicative of, natural, representative of, typical of – *v.* **1.** choose, desire, elect, fancy, favour, go for, pick, prefer, select, vote, want **2.** admire, adore, care for, cherish, delight in, get a kick out of *(Nonformal)*, love, take pleasure from, enjoy, esteem, hold dear, prize, relish, savour

likelihood *n.* bet *(Nonformal)*, chance, hope, likeliness, odds, plausibility, possibility, probability, prospect, tendency, trend *Antonyms:* impossibility, long shot

likely *adj.* **1.** anticipated, destined, expected, favoured, liable, odds on, ostensible, possible, probable *Antonyms:* hopeless, impossible, out of the question **2.** attainable, believable, conceivable, conjecturable, credible, feasible, imaginable, plausible, rational, reasonable, supposable, thinkable, true, workable *Antonyms:* doubtful, dubious, far-fetched, implausible, remote **3.** apt, disposed, like as not *(Nonformal)*, predisposed, prone, tending **4.** acceptable, appropriate, fitting, good, meet, pleasing, promising, proper, satisfactory, seemly, suitable, well-favoured, well-setup *Antonyms:* incongruous, odd, out of step, unacceptable – *adv.* assumably, doubtless, doubtlessly, most likely, no doubt, presumably, probably, seemingly

like-minded *adj.* accordant, agreeing, akin, compatible, concurring, concordant, congenial, consistent, harmonious, similar, sychronous, synergistic, unanimous *Antonyms:* antagonistic, clashing, contrary, discordant

likeness *n.* **1.** analogy, carbon copy, clone, counterpart, Doppelgänger, double, look-alike, replica, resemblance, ringer, sameness, similarity, similitude *Nonformal:* knock-off, same again **2.** bust, copy, depiction, facsimile, image, painting, photograph, picture, portrait, portrayal, representation, reproduction, scan, sculpture **3.** appearance, guise, look, manner, mein, semblance

likewise *adv.* additionally, along with, also, as well, besides, correspondingly, further, furthermore, in addition, moreover, similarly, too

liking *n.* affection, affinity, appetite, appreciation, attachment, attraction, bent, bias, desire, devotion, fancy, fondness, inclination, love, partiality, passion, penchant, predilection, preference, propensity, sympathy, taste, tendency, weakness *Antonyms:* abhorrence, impartiality, repulsion

lilt *n.* accent, beat, b.p.m. *(Nonformal),* cadence, inflection, intonation, measure, melody, modulation, pulse, rhythm, song, swing, tempo

limb *n.* **1.** appendage, arm, extremity, leg, member, part, prosthesis, wooden leg **2.** bough, branch, extension, form, jut, offshoot, projection, protrusion, shoot, stem **3.** branch, cell, chapter, division, element, sect, section, sector, segment, unit

limber *adj.* agile, deft, elastic, flexible, graceful, lissome, lithe, loose, nimble, plastic, pliable, pliant, resilient, springy, spry, supple *Antonyms:* inflexible, rigid, stiff, wooden

limbo *adj.***1.** benched, in abeyance *or* mediation, out of work, resting *(Theatrical),* shelved, sidelined, suspended, undecided, unemployed, up in the air *Nonformal:* hanging fire, on the back burner, treading water **2.** caged, captive, confined, detained, hobbled, imprisoned, incarcerated, interned, locked up, out of action – *n.* **1.** abyss, cold storage, hell, nothingness, nowhere, oblivion, purgatory, void *Nonformal:* neither here nor there, on hold **2.** bondage, cage, captivity, confinement, detention, enclosure, imprisonment, incarceration, internment, prison

limelight *n.* celebrity, centre stage, esteem, fashion, favour, high regard, newsworthiness, notoriety, public eye, rank, renown, spotlight, stardom, note, prestige, popularity, vogue

limit *n.* **1.** ambit, border, boundary, circumference, compass, confines, edge, end, extent, margin, perimeter, periphery, rim **2.** bottom line, breaking point, cap, ceiling, deadline, limitation *Nonformal:* it, last straw, the max, wit's end – *v.* bound, bridle, cap, channel, check, circumscribe, confine, constrict, contract, cramp, curb, define, delimit, demarcate, determine, frustrate, hamper, hem in, hinder, hog-tie, inhibit, impede, lessen, narrow, prescribe, ration, reduce, restrain, restrict, set *Antonyms:* free up, loose, unbridle

limitation *n.* **1.** bar, block, check, constraint, curb, disadvantage, drawback, encumbrance, hindrance, impediment, inhibition, liability, obstruction, restraint **2.** catch, condition, control, modification, qualification, restriction, stricture *Nonformal:* hitch, snag, stumbling block

limited *adj.* **1.** bound, checked, circumscribed, confined, constrained, controlled, cramped, curbed, hampered, hemmed in, hobbled, restrained, restricted **2.** diminished, finite, fixed, inadequate, insufficient, little, low, minimal, nominal, paltry, poor, reduced, short, shortened, slight, small, straightened *Antonyms:* elaborate, extensive, far-reaching, lavish, plentiful **3.** bovine, blockish, slow, slow-witted, thickheaded, unimaginative

limiting *adj.* binding, circumscribing, confining, constraining, cramping, defining, modifying, provisional, provisory, qualifying, restricting, restrictive *Antonyms:* broadening, magnifying, expansive

limitless *adj. ad infinitum or nauseum (Latin),* bottomless, boundless, countless, endless, immeasurable, immense, incalculable, incomprehensible, indefinite, inexhaustible, infinite, innumerable, measureless, never-ending, numberless, unbounded, undefined, unending, unfathomable, unlimited, untold, vast *Antonyms:* circumscribed, finite, fixed, restricted

limp *adj.* **1.** drained, enervated, exhausted, fatigued, feeble, languid, lax, lethargic, listless, spent, tired, weak, weary, worn out **2.** drooping, flabby, flaccid, flexible, flimsy, floppy, loose, pliant, relaxed, slack, soft, supple, yielding *Antonyms:* hard, rigid, solid, stiff, taut – *n.* falter, halt, hitch, hobble, lameness – *v.* dodder, falter, flag, gimp *(Nonformal),* halt, hitch, hobble, hop, lag, scuff, shamble, shuffle, stagger, stumble, teeter, totter

limpid *adj.* **1.** articulate, bright, clear, clear-cut, coherent, comprehensible, crystal-clear, crystalline, definite, distinct, exact, intelligible, logical, lucid, obvious, perspicuous, precise **2.** diaphanous, see-through, sheer, thin, translucent, transparent, vitreous **3.** calm, halcyon, pacific, peaceful, pensive, placid, quiescent, quiet, reposeful, serene, smooth, tranquil, unruffled

line *n.* **1.** band, crease, crow's foot, furrow, groove, indentation, mark, scar, streak, stream, strip, stripe, wrinkle **2.** border, boundary, circumference, concession, demarcation, division, edge, fence, frontier, limit, margin, outline, rim, skirt, wall **3.** arrangement, chain, column, file, formation, order, procession, progression, queue, row, tier, train **4.** ancestry, breed, descent, family, forebearers, heritage, lineage, pedigree, race, sire, stock, strain **5.** commodity, goods, inventory, produce, trade, vendibles, wares **6.** card, communication, e-mail, epistle, letter, message, missive, note, word **7.** course, direction, means, mode, path, plan, route, technique, track, way **8.** agreement, alignment, concord **9.** channel, conduit, passageway, pipe, road, trench **10.** employment, field, livelihood, métier, occupation, profession, province, trade, vocation, work *Nonformal:* bag, racket **11.** cable, cord, fibre, filament, rope, strand, string, thread, wire **12.** dash, hatchmark, hyphen, slash, streak, underline, underscore, virgule **13.** measure, melody, passage, refrain, verse **14.** bridge, connection, link, span **15.** drift, orientation, style, tenor, trend **16.** appeal, pitch, plot, sales talk, scenario, story – *v.* **1.** crease, etch, furrow, hatch, inscribe, mark, notch, rule, score, trace **2.** align, march, position, queue up *(British)*, straighten, string **3.** border, edge, outline, rime, skirt, verge **4.** cram, fill, jam, load, pack, stuff **5.** cover, face, insulate, panel, paper, reinforce

lineage *n.* ancestry, birth, blood, bloodline, branch, breeding, clan, descendants, descent, dynasty, extraction, family, folk, forebearers, forefathers, genealogy, heredity, house, ilk, kin, kindred, offspring, origin, pedigree, progeny, race, sire, stock, strain, succession, tribe

linear *adj.* **1.** as the crow flies, direct, rectilinear, straight, undeviating, uniform, unswerving **2.** consecutive, lineal, serial, sequential, successive **3.** flat, narrow, one-dimensional, oversimplified, simple, thin

linger *v.* **1.** abide, bide, cling, continue, endure, hang about *or* around *or* in, last, persist, remain, stand, stay, stick around, survive, wait *Antonyms:* break, cease, desist, halt, pause **2.** crawl, dally, dawdle, delay, dilly-dally *(Nonformal)*, drift, falter, hesitate, hobble, idle, lag, loiter, loll, mope, mosey, plod, poke, *putchky (Yiddish)*, procrastinate, saunter, shuffle, slouch, stagger, stop, stroll, tarry, trail, wait *Antonyms:* hasten, hurry, hustle, rush, speed

lingo *n.* argot, cant, dialect, gibberish, idiom, jargon, language, parlance, patois, patter, phraseology, shoptalk, slang, speech, terminology, tongue, vernacular *Nonformal:* bafflegab, legalese, lingua franca, mumbo-jumbo, newspeak, psychobabble

linguist *n.* **1.** dialectician, dialectologist, etymologist, grammarian, lexicographer, paleographer, philologist, phoneticist, phonologist, semanticist **2.** bilinguist, interpreter, language-hound *(Nonformal)*, multilingual, polyglot, translator

link *n.* **1.** affiliation, affinity, association, attachment, bond, connection, coupling, intersection, relationship, tie *Antonyms:* breach, division, rupture, sunderance **2.** component, connector, constituent, hook, loop, oval, portion, ring, section – *v.* associate, attach, bind, bracket, combine, connect, couple, fasten, group, hook up, incorporate, interface, join, parallel, plug, relate, tie, unite, yoke *Antonyms:* detach, disconnect, divide, sever, split

lion *n.* **1.** beast, big cat, carnivore, feline, king of the jungle, leo *(Nonformal)* **2.** bigwig, celebrity, dignitary, idol, luminary, notable *Nonformal:* big-name, monster **3.** cavalier, champion, gallant, hero, heroine, knight, paladin, soldier, stalwart, victor *Antonyms:* coward, knave, milquetoast, weakling

lionhearted *adj.* bold, brave, chivalrous, courageous, daring, dauntless, fearless, heroic, intrepid, iron-hearted, plucky, stout, stalwart, valiant, valorous *Antonyms:* fearful, pusillanimous, timid

lionize *v.* acclaim, apotheosize, applaud, celebrate, deify, elevate, ennoble, enshrine, eulogize, exalt, extol, glorify, honour, idolize, immortalize, laud, panegyrize, raise *Antonyms:* criticize, declaim, devalue

lip *n.* **1.** border, brim, brink, edge, margin, rim, spout **2.** affront, audacity, backtalk, boldness, brazenness, cheek, derision, disdain, impudence, insolence, mouthing off *(Nonformal)*, rudeness, sass, sauce *Antonyms:* courtesy, manners, respect, politeness

liqueur *n.* after dinner drink, alcohol, apéritif, appetizer, cordial, stimulant *Nonformal:* nightcap, pick-me-up *Kinds of liqueur:* absinthe, amaretto, anisette, apricot brandy, crème de cassis, crème de menthe, grappa, ice wine, Irish cream, kir, kirsch, kümmel, Pernod, schnapps *Trademark:* B and B, Bailey's, Benedictine, Chartreuse, Cointreau, Drambuie, Frangelico, Galiano, Grande Marnier, Kahlua, Sambuca, Tia Maria *See also:* **cocktail** *Commonly misused:* **liquor**

liquid *adj.* **1.** aqueous, fluid, juicy, liquefied, moist, molten, runny, solvent, watery, wet **2.** bright, clear, crystalline, glassy, limpid, shiny **3.** dulcet, facile, flowing, fluent, free, graceful, honeyed, lithe, lyric, mellifluent, melodious, poetic **4.** available, convertible, marketable, negotiable, quick, ready, solvent, useable – *n.* beverage, broth, drink, elixir, fluid, juice, liquor, sap, secretion, slop, solution, swill

liquidate *v.* **1.** cash in, convert, dump, exchange, sell off, unload, wind up **2.** come clean *(Nonformal)*, honour, pay off *or* up, redeem, reimburse, satisfy, settle, square **3.** assassinate, destroy, eliminate, exterminate, extirpate, finish off *(Nonformal)*, kill, murder, silence, slay **4.** abolish, annul, break up, cancel, disband, dissolve, terminate

liquor *n.* alcohol, aqua vitae, beverage, booze, broth, bung-your-eye *(Newfoundland)*, elixir, extract, fluid, grog, hard *or* strong drink, inebriant, infusion, intoxicant, liquid, potable, *samshu (Chinese)*, spirits *Nonformal:* barley sandwich, bathtub gin, chain lightning, demon rum, firewater, hard stuff, hooch, John Barleycorn, joy juice, juice, liquid lunch, moonshine, poison, prairie dew, red eye, rotgut, sauce, the creature *Kinds of liquor:* aguardiente, alcool *(Quebec)*, applejack, aquavit, Armagnac, bourbon, brandy, callibogus *(Newfoundland)*, Calvados, campari, cognac, eau de vie, gin, grain alcohol, hard cider, ouzo, poteen *(Irish)*, *raki (Turkish)*, rum, rye, scotch, screech, slivovitz, tequila, vermouth, vodka, whisky *Commonly misused:* **liqueur**

list *n.* **1.** arrangement, classification, listing *Kinds of list:* account, agenda, bill, brief, bulletin, calendar, catalogue, census, checklist, contents, dictionary, directory, docket, draft, enumeration, file, gazette, index, inventory, invoice, lineup, manifest, memorandum, poll, prospectus, record, register, roll, roster, schedule, scroll, slate, syllabus, table, tabulation, tally, thesaurus, timetable **2.** cant, careen, inclination, leaning, pitch, recline, slope, tilt, veer **3.** border, edge, panel, ribbon, ridge, selvage, strip – *v.* **1.** arrange, catalogue, census, chart, chronicle, classify, detail, docket, enrol, enter, enumerate, file, index, inventory, invoice, itemize, note, particularize, peg, place, poll, post, record, register, set *or* write down, specify, spell out, tab, tabulate, tally, tick off **2.** cant, careen, heel, incline, lean, pitch, recline, slant, slope, tilt, tip

listen *v.* **1.** attend, catch, concentrate, get, hark, harken, heed, lend an ear *(Nonformal)*, pay attention, receive, tune in *Antonyms:* ignore, neglect **2.** accept, admit, adopt, entertain, mind, obey, observe, take notice *Antonyms:* defy, reject, snub **3.** audit, eavesdrop, overhear, wiretap *Nonformal:* bug, tap

listless *adj.* apathetic, bored, dreamy, drowsy, dull, heavy, impassive, indifferent, lackadaisical, lagging, languishing, leaden, lethargic, lifeless, limp, moping, passive, phlegmatic, slack, sleepy, slow, sluggish, spiritless, uninterested *Antonyms:* awake, energetic, excited, spirited

litany *n.* **1.** account, catalogue, compilation, enumeration, inventory, list, narrative, recapitulation, recital, recitation, refrain, repetition, summary, tale **2.** invocation, petition, prayer, supplication

literacy *n.* ability, articulateness, background, competence, education, erudition, knowledge, learning, proficiency, reading, scholarship, tutorship

literal *adj.* **1.** accurate, actual, authentic, bona fide, exact, factual, faithful, genuine, gospel, honest, natural, real, strict, true, unadorned, unexaggerated, unvarnished, verbatim **2.** bland, boring, colourless, dull, flat, humdrum, insipid, matter-of-fact, prosaic, tedious, tiresome, unimaginative, vapid *Antonyms:* allegorical, figurative, imaginative, metaphorical

literally *adv.* **1.** completely, directly, exactly, faithfully, precisely, sic, strictly, undeviatingly, unerringly, verbatim, word-for-word **2.** actually, certainly, honestly, indisputably, surely, truly, undeniably, veritably

literary *adj.* **1.** academic, articulate, belletristic, classical, canonical, formal, polished, refined, scholarly, writerly *Antonyms:* mass-market, popular, pulp **2.** bluestocking, bookish, cultivated, educated, erudite, learned, lettered, scholastic, well-informed, well-read, well-versed

literate *adj.* **1.** able to read and write, book-learned, cultured, educated, knowledgeable, learned, lettered, well-informed **2.** articulate, coherent, comprehensible, explicit, lucid, understandable

literature *n.* **1.** belles-lettres, body of works, canon, classics, creative writing, drama, fiction, literary work, poetry, prose, text, writing, written work *See also:* **drama, fiction, poem, writing** **2.** broadsheet, brochure, handout, pamphlet, publicity, reading material, treatise

lithe *adj.* agile, flexible, graceful, limber, lissome, loose, nimble, pliable, pliant, supple, willowy *Antonyms:* inflexible, stiff, wooden

litigate *v.* appeal, bring before the courts *or* the book, contest, dispute, file suit, law *(P.E.I.)*, press charges, prosecute, sue

litigation *n.* action, case, cause, claim, contention, contest, controversy, dispute, lawsuit, process, prosecution, suit, trial

litter *n.* **1.** debris, detritus, flotsam, garbage, jetsam, junk, muck, offal, refuse, rubbish, trash, waste **2.** chaos, clutter, confusion, disarray, disorder, jumble, jungle *(Nonformal)*, mess, muddle, pandemonium, untidiness *Antonyms:* harmony, neatness, order **3.** baby, brood, family, hatch, issue, offspring, progeny, spawn, young **4.** bier, *dodly (Japan)*, *dooli (East Indies)*, hammock, *jampan (India)*, palanquin, sling, stretcher, *tonjon (Sri Lanka)* **5.** bedding, floorcover, hay, straw – *v.* clutter, dirty, drop, jumble, mess, scatter, strew, sully, throw away *or* out, toss

little *adj.* **1.** bantam, dainty, diminutive, dwarf, elfin, embryonic, impish, Lilliputian, miniature, short, slight, small, stunted, tiny, undersized, wee *Nonformal:* bitty, itty-bitty, micro-mini, mini, teensy *or* teeny, teeny-weeny *Antonyms:* huge, large, massive **2.** brief, ephemeral, fleeting, limited, passing, short, short-lived, transient *Antonyms:* eternal, forever, long-lasting **3.** imperceptible, inappreciable, meagre, microscopic, minute, paltry, scant, skimpy *Antonyms:* excessive, generous, liberal **4.** faint, feeble, flimsy, fragile, frail, muffled, muted, powerless, slight, weak *Antonyms:* potent, powerful, strong **5.** inconsequential, inconsiderable, insignificant, nugatory, trivial *Nonformal:* dinky, piddling *Antonyms:* essential, important, material, pivotal **6.** bigoted, contemptible, insular, limited, mean, narrow-gauge *(Nonformal)*, narrow-minded, parochial, petty, prejudiced *Antonyms:* open-minded, tolerant, worldly – *adv.* barely, hardly, just, only, partially, scarcely, slightly, somewhat – *n.* bit, bite, dab, dash, drop, fragment, grain, hint, iota, jot, modicum, pinch, snippet, soupçon, speck, spot, sprinkling, tad *(Nonformal)*, taste, touch, trace, trifle, whit *Antonyms:* abundance, mass, pile

liturgy *n.* celebration, ceremony, observance, rite, ritual, sacrament, service, worship

livable *adj.* **1.** agreeable, comfortable, cozy, decent, fit, habitable, sufficient, suitable *Antonyms:* inhabitable, objectionable, unsuitable **2.** acceptable, adequate, bearable, endurable, passable, satisfactory, supportable, sustainable, tolerable *Antonyms:* insufferable, intolerable, unbearable **3.**

amenable, companionable, congenial, convivial, easygoing, friendly

live *adj.* **1.** alive, animate, aware, breathing, cognizant, conscious, existent, living, material, moving, organic, quick, vital *Antonyms:* dead, inanimate, insensible **2.** actual, face-to-face, genuine, in the flesh *(Nonformal)*, real *Antonyms:* recorded, virtual **3.** controversial, current, delicate, disputatious, essential, important, interesting, latest, necessary, pertinent, pressing, sensitive, topical, unsettled, up-to-date, useful, volatile *Nonformal:* hot, sexy *Antonyms:* boring, old hat, uninteresting **4.** abounding, fraught, full, infested, prevalent, replete, rife, swarming, teeming *Antonyms:* empty, lacking, wanting **5.** brisk, bubbly, dynamic, effervescent, energetic, forceful, lively, peppy *(Nonformal)*, spirited, vigorous, vivacious, zesty *Antonyms:* enervated, flat, vapid **6.** aflame, aglow, blazing, burning, charged, combustible, electric, explosive, fiery, fulminant, igneous, incandescent, loaded, ready, smouldering **7.** brilliant, colourful, deep, rich, textured, vivid *Antonyms:* drab, muted, subdued – *v.* **1.** breathe, draw breath, eat, exist, function **2.** continue, cope, endure, fare, feed, get along *or* by, last, maintain, make it *(Nonformal)*, persist, prevail, remain, stand, stay afloat *(Nonformal)*, subsist, support, survive **3.** dwell, habituate, haunt, hole up *(Nonformal)*, nest, occupy, reside, settle, sleep, squat **4.** abide, act, behave, comport, conduct, demean, function **5.** delight, enjoy, experience, flourish, luxuriate, prosper, recuperate, relish, savour, thrive

livelihood *n.* bread and butter *(Nonformal)*, business, calling, craft, earnings, employment, income, job, line of work, living, means of support, occupation, profession, resources, subsistence, support, sustenance, trade, vocation, work

lively *adj.* **1.** active, agile, frisky, frolicsome, nimble, quick, sprightly, vigorous *Nonformal:* hyper, non-stop *Antonyms:* calm, quiet, serene **2.** bracing, brisk, invigorating, refreshing, rousing, spirited, stimulating *Antonyms:* boring, dull, tiring **3.** animated, blithe, bouncy, buoyant, chipper, effervescent, festive, gay, keen, merry, peppy *(Nonformal)*, perky, sparkling, vivacious *Antonyms:* dour, sullen, surly **4.** driving, electric, fiery, forceful, intense, passionate, striking, vivid **5.** astir, bustling, busy, enterprising, hard at work, industrious *Nonformal:* buzzing, go-go, happening, hopping, jumping *Antonyms:* dry, quiet, sleepy

liven *v.* animate, arouse, brighten, cheer, elate, encourage, goad, hearten, incite, inspire, kindle, motivate, move, promote, rouse, spark, stimulate, waken *Nonformal:* buck *or* fire *or* pep up, jump-start, kick-start *Antonyms:* depress, weaken, weary

livid *adj.* **1.** angry, apoplectic *(Nonformal)*, boiling, enraged, fuming, furious, incensed, infuriated, irate, mad, piqued, rabid, seething, simmering, sore, storming, upset, vexed *Antonyms:* calm, collected, cool, pacified **2.** ashen, ashy, blanched, bloodless, colourless, doughy, greyish, leaden, pale, pallid, pasty, wan, waxen *Antonyms:* hale, healthy, rosy **3.** black-and-blue, bruised, contused, discoloured, purple *Commonly misused:* **lurid**

living *adj.* **1.** active, alive, animate, breathing, common, existent, operative, quick, warm **2.** conventional, continuing, customary, everyday, existing, normal, ongoing, standard, typical **3.** contemporary, current, up-to-date, valid, viable **4.** carbon-copy, exact, lifelike, real, spitting *(Nonformal)* – *n.* **1.** conduct, existence, lifestyle, manner, model behaviour, way of life **2.** calling, income, job, keep, livelihood, means, occupation, subsistence, support, sustenance, wage, work

load *n.* **1.** amount, bale, bundle, capacity, cargo, consignment, contents, freight, goods, haul, jag *(Nonformal)*, lading, mass, pack, parcel, payload, shipment **2.** assignment, duty, job, occupation, onus, responsibility, task **3.** affliction, albatross, baggage *(Nonformal)*, burden, care, charge, cross, deadweight, drag, drain, encumbrance, liability, millstone, obligation, oppression, pressure, tax, trouble, weight, worry – *v.* **1.** choke, cram, fill, flood, glut, gorge, heap, lade, mass, oversupply, pack, pile, pour in, saddle, stack, store, stow, stuff, top, top off **2.** burden, charge, encumber, hamper, oppress, pressure, saddle, swamp, task, tax, trouble, weigh down, worry

loaded *adj.* **1.** burdened, charged, encumbered, fraught, hampered, laden, saddled, swamped, weighted **2.** charged, controversial, double-edged, explosive, hot *(Nonformal)*, political, sensitive, tender, touchy, volatile **3.** affluent, moneyed, prosperous, rich, wealthy, well-off, well-to-do *Antonyms:* broke, destitute, insolvent, penniless, poor **4.** besotted, drunk, high, inebriated, intoxicated, plastered, soused, wasted *Nonformal:* bombed, feeling no pain, half in the bag, lit, pickled, smashed, tight, tipsy

loaf *n.* block, brick, cake, chunk, hunk, lump, slab – *v.* dally, daydream, drift, idle, laze, loiter, lounge, put off, relax, shirk, slack, stall, trifle, vegetate *Nonformal:* bum around, lollygag

loafer *n.* beachcomber, corner boy *(Newfoundland)*, deadbeat, *flâneur (French)*, good-for-nothing, idler, indolent, layabout, lounger, malingerer, shirker, slacker, slouch, slug, wanderer, wastrel *Nonformal:* bum, goof off, lazybones, slider *Antonyms:* busybee, over-achiever, toiler

loan *n.* advance, credit, extension, investment, mortgage, trust – *v.* advance, allow, back, bank, bankroll, credit, endow, finance, float, fund, grubstake, guarantee, lend, pay for, provide, sponsor, stake, subsidize, support, underwrite *Antonyms:* borrow, give, sell

loath *adj.* averse, counter, disinclined, hesitant, opposed, reluctant, resisting, unwilling *Antonyms:* desirous, eager, enthusiastic, keen *Commonly misused:* **loathe**

loathe *v.* abhor, abominate, despise, detest, dislike, execrate, hate, reject, repudiate, spurn *Antonyms:* adore, cherish, idolize, savour, treasure *Commonly misused:* **loath**

loathsome *adj.* abhorrent, abominable, beastly, creepy, deplorable, detestable, disgusting, execrable, gross, hateful, hideous, horrible, invidious, nasty, nauseating, odious, offensive, repellent, repugnant, repulsive, revolting, vile *Nonformal*: lousy, sleazy, slimy *Antonyms:* attractive, charming, delightful, enchanting

lobby *n.* antechamber, corridor, doorway, entrance, entryway, foyer, hall, hallway, passageway, reception *or* waiting room, vestibule – *v.* advance, affect, boost, further, induce, influence, persuade, pressure, promote, push, sell, strong-arm, sway, urge *Nonformal:* ballyhoo, hype

local *adj.* **1.** aboriginal, autochthonous, city, domestic, homespun, indigenous, municipal, national, native, neighbourhood, provincial, regional, rural, territorial *Antonyms:* exotic, foreign, international **2.** limited, narrow, parochial, restricted, small *or* small-town *(Nonformal) Antonyms:* broad, urban, worldly **3.** circumscribed, confined, fixed, localized, particular, specific *Antonyms:* general, vague, widespread – *n.* **1.** aboriginal, autochthon, denizen, indigene, inhabitant, native, resident *Antonyms:* alien, foreigner, stranger **2.** bus, metro, Red Rocket *(Toronto)*, streetcar, subway, train, transportation, trolley **3.** hangout, inn, neighbourhood bar *or* restaurant, pub, public house, tavern, watering hole

locate *v.* **1.** abide, anchor, dig in, drop anchor, dwell, establish, fix, inhabit, moor, park, place, plop down *(Nonformal)*, position, post, reside, seat, set, settle, situate, squat, station **2.** come across, discover, espy, find, see, strike, stumble upon, uncover, unearth *Antonyms:* lose, mislay, misplace

location *n.* **1.** area, *arrondissement (French)*, bearings, district, environment, environs, hood *(Nonformal)*, locality, locus, neighbourhood, point, position, post, quarter, region, residence, site, spot, station, whereabouts **2.** backdrop, locale, *mise en scène (French)*, scene, set, setting, shoot, venue

lock *n.* **1.** bar, bolt, catch, chain, clasp, closing, deadbolt, fastening, fixture, hasp, hook, latch, padlock, security device **2.** braid, curl, curlicue, flock, piece, plait, ringlet, shock, tress, tuft **3.** canal, fishway, floodgate, gate, passageway, sluice, sluice gate, throughway **4.** bearhug, clinch, clutch, embrace, grip, hold, hug, Shawinigan handshake *(Nonformal)* – *v.* **1.** bar, bolt, fasten, padlock, seal, secure, shut **2.** bond, connect, enjoin, fit, fuse, interlock join, link, piece together, set, tighten **3.** clasp, clutch, embrace, grapple, grasp, grip, hang onto, hold, hug, wrestle

lockup *n.* **1.** cage, cell, gaol, jail, jailhouse, penitentiary, police station, prison, station house, stockade *Nonformal:* can, clink, hoosegow, slammer **2.** apprehension, caging, captivity, capture, confinement, imprisonment, incarceration, penning

locomotion *n.* action, journeying, motion, movement, passage, perambulation, progress, progression, transit, travelling

lodge *n.* **1.** cabin, chalet, cottage, dwelling, gatehouse, habitation, hogan, hut, igloo, quinzhee, tent, tepee, wickiup, wigwam, *wikuom (Native Peoples)* **2.** association, branch, chapter, club, enclave, group, guild, league, order, sect, society **3.** aerie, beaver lodge, cave, den, dugout, furrow, haunt, hole, lair, nest, refuge, retreat, shelter – *v.* **1.** bed down, billet, board, bunk, dwell, habituate, house, lease, rent, room, station, stay **2.** cover, harbour, set, sheathe, shelter, shield, store, stow **3.** entrench, fix, implant, instill, place, root, safekeep, stick, wedge **4.** consign, entrust, transfer, transmit, vest

lodging *n.* abode, accommodation, address, apartment, boarding *or* rooming house, camp, castle, domicile, dorm, dwelling, flat, fraternity, habitation, home, hotel, house, inn, lodge, motel, motorhome, motor lodge, palace, *pied-à-terre (French)*, place, quarters, residence, resort, room, shelter, sorority *Nonformal:* digs, nest, pad, roost, stoop

loft *n.* **1.** attic, dormer, gallery, garret, hayloft, loggia, room, sky parlour *(Nonformal)*, storeroom **2.** angle, course, flight path, height, line, path, slope, trajectory – *v.* hit, lob, pop *(Nonformal)*, strike, swing

lofty *adj.* **1.** elevated, high, high-rise *(Nonformal)*, sky-high, skyward, tall, towering **2.** distinguished, eminent, esteemed, exalted, grand, majestic, noble, noted, rarified, venerable **3.** arrogant, conceited, condescending, disdainful, haughty, hoity-toity *(Nonformal)*, proud, snobbish, toplofty

log *n.***1**. account, black box, book, chart, daybook, diary, flight recorder, journal, listing, logbook, record, register, roster, tally **2.** block, bole, chunk, firewood, fuel, timber, stump, trunk, wood – *v.* **1**. chop, clearcut, cut, exploit, fell, harvest, hew, level, moonscape *(B.C.)*, raze, remove, strip **2.** catalogue, chart, note, record, register, report, tabulate, tally

logic *n.* **1.** analysis, critical thinking, deduction, formal logic, induction, inference, proof, reasoning, syllogism, symbolic logic, thinking **2.** argument, dialectic, hypothesis, premise, thesis, treatise **3.** association, connection, correspondence, interrelation, relationship, relevance **4.** clarity, coherence, cogency, effectiveness, force, plausibility, precision, reasonableness, sense, soundness, unity *Antonyms:* delirium, dissociation, reverie

logical *adj.* **1.** analytical, cognitive, deductive, inductive, mathematical, philosophical, rational, relevant, scientific, sensible, sound **2.** cogent, convincing, germane, on the mark, persuasive, reasonable, valid *Antonyms:* foolish, irrational, silly **3.** clear, coherent, comprehensible, consistent, intelligible, reasonable, understandable *Antonyms:* chaotic, confused, random, wild

logistics *n.* disposition *or* distribution *or* maintenance *or* movement *or* procurement *or* provisioning *or* transportation science, lodging and supply, materials management and distribution, tactics design and implementation, troop movement

logjam *n.* bar, barrier, block, bottleneck, clog, congestion, deadlock, gridlock, impasse, impediment, obstruction

logo *n.* brand, cachet, design, figure, insignia, label, mark, monogram, seal, signet, stamp, symbol, tag, token, trademark, trade name

loiter *v.* amble, dally, dawdle, delay, drag, flag, fritter away, goof off, halt, hang *or* loll about, hang back, lag, laze, linger, loaf, lounge, pause, poke, putter, ramble, saunter, shamble, shuffle, stroll, tarry, trail, traipse, wait *Antonyms:* hasten, hurry, scurry

lone *adj.* **1.** alone, individual, one, separate, single, sole, solitary, stag *(Nonformal)*, unaccompanied, unassociated, unattached, unpaired, unique *Antonyms:* coupled, paired, united **2.** deserted, godforsaken, isolated, lonely, unfrequented *Antonyms:* bustling, crowded, populated

lonely *adj.* **1.** alienated, alone, apart, companionless, estranged, single, solitary, unattended, unsocial, withdrawn **2.** cheerless, comfortless, desolate, disconsolate, down, forlorn, friendless, gloomy, homesick, melancholy, neurasthenic, uncherished **3.** deserted, isolated, reclusive, remote, secluded, sequestered **4.** abandoned, forsaken, outcast, rejected, scorned

long *adj.* **1.** elongated, enlarged, expanded, extended, extensive, great, stretching, tall, towering *Antonyms:* contracted, little, short, small **2.** ceaseless, continued, diffuse, drawn-out, endless, excessive, interminable, lasting, lengthy, limitless, long-drawn-out, long-winded, loquacious, prolix, prolonged, protracted, sustained, unending, verbose, wordy *Antonyms:* abbreviated, brief, concise, terse – *v.* aspire, covet, crave, desire, dream, fancy, hanker *or* lust after, hunger, itch, pine, relish, thirst, want, wish, yearn *Antonyms:* abhor, dislike, hate

longevity *n.* age, constancy, durability, effectiveness, endurance, lastingness, lifespan, lifetime, permanence, shelf-life *(Nonformal)*, survival *Antonyms:* brevity, ephemerality, transience

longing *adj.* coveting, craving, desirous, hankering, hungering, pining, wanting, wistful – *n.* ambition, appetite, aspiration, bent, craving, desire, fondness, hunger, leaning, liking, thirst, urge, wish, yearning, yen *(Nonformal) Antonyms:* abhorrence, antipathy, disgust, indifference, revulsion

long-suffering *adj.* abiding, accepting, enduring, forbearing, patient, persevering, resigned, stoic, surviving, tolerant, understanding

long-winded *adj.* battological, chatty, circumlocutory, digressive, garrulous, lengthy, long-drawn-out, loquacious, maundering, padded, prolixed, prolonged, protracted, rambling, redundant, reiterative, repetitive, talkative, tautological, verbose, windy, wordy *Antonyms:* pithy, precise, succinct, terse

look *n.* **1.** flash, gander, gaze, glance, glimpse, inspection, observation, once-over *(Nonformal)*, peek, review, scrutiny, sight, squint, surveillance, survey, view **2.** air, appearance, aspect, bearing, cast, complexion, countenance, demeanour, effect, expression, face, fashion, guise, manner, mien, mug *(Nonformal)*, physiognomy, presence, semblance, visage – *v.* **1.** attend, behold, consider, contemplate, examine, espy, eye, focus, gaze, glance, glimpse, notice, observe, peer, scan, scrutinize, see, spot, spy, study, survey, view, visualize *Nonformal:* check out, eyeball, ogle, rubberneck **2.** appear, display, evidence, exhibit, express, indicate, manifest, present, resemble, seem, show, sound **3.** check up on, drop *or* stop in, pop by *(Nonformal)*, visit

lookout *n.* **1.** crow's nest, fire tower, outlook, station, surveillance post, tower, watchtower **2.** guard, patrol, picket, post, scout, security guard, sentinel, sentry, spotter, vigil, ward, watch, watchman

loom *n.* weaving machine *Kinds of loom:* counterbalance, countermarch, jack *Parts of a loom:* beam, beater, bench, brake, castle, heddle, lamm, ratchet, reed, shuttle, tie-up system, treadle, warp set – *v.* **1.** appear, approach, come, emerge, figure, materialize, rear, rise, show, surface, take shape *Antonyms:* disappear, evanesce, retreat, vanish **2.** bode, hover, impend, menace, overhang, overshadow, portend, threaten

looming *adj.* **1.** approaching, brewing, close, forthcoming, imminent, impending, lurking, waiting *Antonyms:* distant, far off, remote **2.** dreadful, fateful, frightening, foreboding, menacing, ominous, overshadowing, threatening

loop *n.* **1.** bend, circle, circuit, circumference, coil, curl, curve, eyelet, hoop, kink, knot, noose, ring, spiral, twirl, twist, whorl, wreath **2.** aperture, gap, loophole, opening, window – *v.* arc, arch, bend, bow, braid, circle, coil, connect, crook, curl, curve, encircle, encompass, escape clause, fold, gird, knot, ring, roll, spiral, surround, turn, twist, wind around

loose *adj.* **1.** detached, open, unattached, unbound, unfastened, unsecured, untied *Antonyms:* clasped, fastened, secured **2.** baggy, flopping, relaxed, roomy, sagging, slack *Antonyms:* taut, tight **3.** available, at large *or* liberty, escaped, free, liberated, on the lam *(Nonformal)*, stray, unfettered, unshackled, wanted *Antonyms:* captured, imprisoned, incarcerated **4.** approximate, estimated, rough *Nonformal:* ballpark, guesstimate **5.** careless, heedless, imprudent, lax, rash, reckless, thoughtless, uncontrolled, wild *Antonyms:* controlled, politic, prudent **6.** abandoned, disreputable, dissolute, fast, immoral, lascivious, lewd, libertine, licentious, profligate, promiscuous, swinging, wanton *Antonyms:* chaste, moral, virtuous **7.** desultory, diffuse, disconnected, disordered, imprecise, inaccurate, incoherent, rambling, vague, wandering *Antonyms:* concise, pithy, pointed – *adv.* approximately, closely, in a way, loosely – *v.* **1.** emancipate, free, let go, liberate, manumit, release **2.** ease, let up, mellow, mitigate, relax, soften **3.** detach, disengage, extricate, uncouple, undo, unfasten, unfetter, unhook, untie

loosen *v.* **1.** detach, disconnect, disengage, emancipate, extricate, free, let go, liberate, loose, manumit, set free, unbind, undo, unfasten, unhook, unleash, unlock, untie, work free *Antonyms:* confine, fetter, manacle, restrain, secure **2.** diminish, ease, let up, mitigate, moderate, soften, subside, temper

loot *n.* booty, gains, goods, haul, pickings, pillage, plunder, prize, spoils, take *Nonformal:* filthy lucre, goodies, hot goods, swag – *v.* appropriate, burglarize, grab, lift, pillage, plunder, raid, ransack, ravage, rifle, rob, sack, snatch, steal, swipe, take, thieve *Nonformal:* abduct, boost, kidnap, knock over, liberate, rip off, smash-and-grab

lopsided *adj.* askew, asymmetrical, awry, cockeyed, crooked, irregular, leaning, off-balance, off-kilter, one-sided, tilting, unbalanced, *Antonyms:* even, level, parallel, straight

loquacious *adj.* babbling, chattering, circumlocutory, gabby, long-winded, motormouth *(Nonformal)*, roundabout, talkative, wordy *Antonyms:* close-mouthed, taciturn, terse

Lord *n.* Absolute *or* Divine *or* Ultimate Being, All-Knowing, All-Powerful, Almighty, Anointed, Creator, Divine Father, Emmanuel, God, Infinite, King of Kings, Most Holy One, Omniscient, Redeemer, Sovereign of the Universe *See also:* **God**

lord *n.* **1.** authority, boss, captain, chief, commander, governor, khan, king, leader, liege, magnate, master, monarch, overlord, potentate, prince, ruler, satrap, sovereign, superior **2.** archbishop, aristocrat, baron, baronet, bishop, count, don, duke, earl, gentleman, knight, marquis, nobleman, patrician, peer, suzerain, viscount *Antonyms:* follower, subject, vassal **3.** *daimyo (Japanese)*, feudal lord, laird *(Scottish)*, landholder, landlord, seigneur *(Historical)*

lore *n.* **1.** anecdote, fable, folklore, legend, mythology, myth, saga, saw, story, tale, urban myth **2.** belief, custom, maxim, superstition, tradition **3.** erudition, experience, information, knowledge, learning, letters, scholarship, science, teaching, wisdom

lose *v.* **1.** forget, mislay, misplace, neglect, omit **2.** default, forfeit, miss, sacrifice *Nonformal*: kiss good-bye, let slip **3.** deplete, dissipate, drain, squander, use up, waste **4.** fail, fall, suffer defeat, succumb, yield *Antonyms:* conquer, triumph, win **5.** avoid, dodge, duck, elude, throw off **6.** chuck *(Nonformal)*, discard, dispose of, dump, jettison, junk, throw out, trash **7.** leave behind, outdistance, outstrip, pass

loser *n.* also-ran, failure, flop, no account *Nonformal:* bomb, bum, deadbeat, dud, fall guy, hoser, washout *Antonyms:* champion, hero, paragon, victor, winner

loss *n.* **1.** damage, deprivation, destruction, disaster, harm, injury, privation, property damage, ruin *Antonyms:* advantage, benefit, boon **2.** bereavement, casualty, death, misfortune, passing, tragedy **3.** debt, debit, decrease, degeneration, depletion, deterioration, diminishment, disappearance, dissipation, dissolution, erosion, lessening, minus, reduction *Antonyms:* gain, increase, retention **4.** absence, dearth, deficiency, lack, need, paucity, shortage, want **5.** beating, conquest, defeat, drubbing, fall, setback, thrashing, upset

lost *adj.* **1.** forgotten, mislaid, misplaced, missing, neglected, omitted, past, vanished *Antonyms:* found, located **2.** baffled, bewildered, bothered, confused, dazed, discombobulated *(Nonformal)*, disoriented, helpless, muddled, nonplussed, perplexed, perturbed, put-out, puzzled, stunned, stymied, upset **3.** *Computer:* corrupted, crashed, deleted, erased, formatted, irretrievable, overwritten, trashed, unrecoverable, unsalvageable **4.** absent-minded, absorbed, bemused, charmed, distracted, dreaming, engaged, engrossed, enraptured, entranced, faraway, hypnotized, involved, moonstruck, musing, preoccupied, rapt, spellbound, transported *Nonformal:* into, taken with *Antonyms:* alert, aware, clear-headed **5.** bankrupt, consumed, depleted, dissipated, dissolved, empty, exhausted, frittered away, gone, squandered, used-up, wasted *Antonyms:* left, remaining **6.** annihilated, dead, demolished, destroyed, devastated, disintegrated, eradicated, extirpated, obliterated, perished, razed, ruined, wiped out *(Nonformal) Antonyms:* preserved, saved, thriving **7.** beaten, defeated, forfeited, outdone, overthrown, routed *Nonformal:* licked, trounced, whupped **8.** corrupt, damned, debased, degenerate, depraved, deviant, sinful, wayward **9.** adrift, errant, misdirected, off-course, off-track **10.** banished, expelled, homeless, nomadic, ostracized, wandering **11.** abandoned, cut-off, deserted, forsaken, isolated, marooned

lot *n.* **1.** allotment, allowance, bite, cut, part, percentage, piece, portion, quota, ration, share, slice **2.** accident, break, chance, decree, destiny, fate, fortune, kismet, plight, predestination **3.** acreage, area, *arpentage (French)*, block, bush, clearing, concession, division, field, frontage, land, parcel, patch, plot, property, real estate, subdivision, tract, woodlot **4.** abundance, aggregation, assortment, bunch, bundle, clump, cluster, collection, conglomeration, great deal, mass, much, myriad, pack, plenitude, plenty, quantity *Nonformal:* heaps, loads, reams – *v.* allocate, allot, apportion, assign, disperse, distribute, divide, divvy up *(Nonformal)*, dole *or* mete out, earmark, ration, slice

lotion *n.* balm, conditioner, cosmetic, cream, liniment, medicine, moisturizer, oil, ointment, palliative, pomade, preparation, rub, salve, solution, unguent, wash

lottery *n.* **1.** bingo, draw, keno, lotto, pool, raffle, sweepstakes, venture **2.** chance, crapshoot *(Nonformal)*, gamble, risk, uncertainty

loud *adj.* **1.** blaring, booming, deafening, ear-piercing, noisy, piercing, resonant, resounding, roaring, sonorous, stentorian, strident, thundering *Antonyms:* inaudible, low, quiet, soft **2.** clamorous, demanding, exacting, insistent, intense, in your face *(Nonformal)*, persistent, pressing, urgent **3.** abrasive, brash, brassy, brazen, crass, crude, flamboyant, flashy, garish, gaudy, glaring, lurid, meretricious, obnoxious, obtrusive, ostentatious, rude, showy, tasteless, tawdry, uncouth, vulgar *Antonyms:* conservative, dull, sober, sombre – *adv.* **1.** blaringly, boisterously, piercingly, stridently **2.** clamorously, persistently, pressingly, urgently **3.** blatantly, brazenly, crassly, garishly, vulgarly

lounge *n.* **1.** chaise longue, chesterfield, couch, davenport, daybed, divan, glider, hammock, Lazy Boy *(Trademark)*, loveseat, sofa, Winnipeg couch **2.** bar, beverage room, club, cocktail lounge, hotel, pub, taproom, tavern, watering hole *Nonformal:* dive, juke joint **3.** atelier, den, family *or* living *or* rec *or* sitting room, parlour **4.** anteroom, foyer, lobby, reception, smoking room, vestible, waiting room – *v.* **1.** lean, recline, relax, repose, rest, sprawl **2.** dally, hang around *or* out, idle, loaf, loiter, putter

lousy *adj.* **1.** awful, bad, cheap, chintzy *(Nonformal)*, deplorable, inferior, miserable, poor, second-rate, shoddy, terrible *Antonyms:* excellent, fair, first-rate **2.** base, contemptible, despicable, execrable, foul, horrible, low, mean, rotten, vile *Antonyms:* high-minded, honourable, praiseworthy **3.** crawling, dirty, flea-ridden, infested, mangy, vermin-ridden *Nonformal:*

grubby, grungy *Antonyms:* clean, decontaminated, fumigated

lout *n.* barbarian, boor, bumpkin, clod, clown, dolt, lubber, oaf, Philistine, vulgarian *Nonformal:* ass, boob, hoser, jerk, lummox, nutbar, yahoo, yokel

lovable *adj.* adorable, agreeable, alluring, appealing, attractive, bewitching, captivating, charming, cuddly *(Nonformal)*, delightful, desirable, enchanting, endearing, enthralling, fascinating, fetching, irresistable, likeable, lovely, pleasing, ravishing, seductive, winsome *Antonyms:* abhorrent, disgusting, hideous, loathsome, offensive, revolting

love *n.* **1.** affection, affinity, association, attachment, closeness, connection, esteem, fidelity, fondness, friendship, loyalty, regard, sentiment, warmth **2.** ardour, chemistry, crush *(Nonformal)*, desire, emotion, eros, infatuation, longing, lust, passion, rapture, yearning **3.** beau, beloved, darling, dearest, fiancé, fiancée, friend, honey, intended, lover, paramour, partner, spouse, suitor, sweetheart *Nonformal:* flame, significant other **4.** affair, amour, liaison, relationship, romance, tryst **5.** delight, enjoyment, partiality, penchant, pleasure, predilection, proclivity, taste, weakness *Nonformal:* soft spot, thing **6.** agape, altruism, benevolence, care, *caritas (Latin)*, charity, concern, generosity, giving, goodwill, humanity, selflessness, sympathy, tender-heartedness **7.** carnal knowledge, coitus, copulation, fornication, intercourse, intimacy, mating, screwing *(Nonformal)*, sex, sexual union – *v.* **1.** admire, adore, burn for *(Nonformal)*, cherish, hold dear, prize, treasure **2.** esteem, exalt, glorify, idolize, worship *Antonyms:* abhor, abominate, detest **3.** desire, fancy, favour, long *or* pine *or* thirst for, want, yearn *Antonyms:* hate, repudiate, scorn **4.** appreciate, delight in, enjoy, relish, savour

lovely *adj.* **1.** adorable, alluring, attractive, beautiful, bewitching, bittersweet, captivating, charming, comely, drop-dead gorgeous *(Nonformal)*, enchanting, exquisite, fair, good-looking, handsome, photogenic, pretty, stunning *Antonyms:* repellent, repugnant, revolting, ugly, unattractive **2.** agreeable, cute, dainty, delicate, delightful, engaging, enjoyable, fun, good, pleasant, pleasing, satisfying, sweet, winsome *Antonyms:* awful, loathsome, odious

lover *n.* **1.** beau, beloved, boyfriend, cicisbeo, courtier, darling, dear, dearest, escort, girlfriend, heartthrob, husband, inamorata, mate, mistress, paramour, suitor, swain, sweetheart, true love, valentine, wife *Nonformal:* flame, main squeeze, significant other **2.** admirer, aficionado, champion, devotee, enthusiast, fan *(Nonformal)*, follower, gallant

loving *adj.* **1.** admiring, adoring, affectionate, amatory, amorous, appreciative, ardent, *aux anges (French)*, besotted, demonstrative, enamoured, expressive, fervent, fond, impassioned, infatuated, intimate, passionate, romantic *Antonyms:* aloof, cold, detached **2.** attentive, benevolent, caring, concerned, considerate, cordial, devoted, doting, earnest, faithful, friendly, generous, kind, loyal, sentimental, solicitous, tender, thoughtful, warm *Antonyms:* contemptuous, cruel, hateful

low *adj.* **1.** knee-high, little, pipsqueak, short, small, squat, stunted, undersize *Antonyms:* gigantic, huge, leviathan **2.** faint, gentle, hushed, quiet, soft, soothing, suppressed *Antonyms:* cacophonous, ear-splitting, high, loud **3.** baritone, bass, basso profundo, contralto, deep, low-pitched, murmuring, phat *(Nonformal)*, rumbling *Antonyms:* shrill, tenor, trebly **4.** below, beneath, coastal, concave, depressed, ground-level, level, low-hanging, low-lying, low-set, nether, rock-bottom, sea level, sunken, under *Antonyms:* elevated, hilly, mountainous **5.** ailing, debilitated, feeble, frail, ill, indisposed, sick, sickly, stricken, unwell, weak *Antonyms:* healthy, hearty, robust **6.** abject, base, coarse, contemptible, crass, crude, dastardly, depraved, despicable, disgraceful, dishonourable, disreputable, gross, ignoble, ill-bred, inelegant, mean, miserable, offensive, raw, rough, rude, sordid, uncouth, undignified, unworthy, vile, villainous, vulgar, wretched *Antonyms:* admirable, eminent, honourable, laudable **7.** blue, crestfallen, dejected, depressed, despondent, disheartened, down, downcast, downhearted, forlorn, gloomy, glum, lowdown, melancholy, miserable, moody, morose, neurasthenic, sad, spiritless, unhappy *Antonyms:* cheerful, elated, happy **8.** bargain, cheap, cut, cut-rate, economical, inexpensive, marked down, reduced, second-rate, slashed *(Nonformal) Antonyms:* excessive, expensive – *adv.* **1.** faintly, gently, hushedly, noiselessly, pianissimo, quietly, softly **2.** at a bargain, at cost, cheaply, inexpensively, reasonably **3.** below, beneath, under **4.** humbly, meekly, modestly, self-effacingly, subserviently – *n.* **1.** business cycle, depression, downturn, recession, slow-down *Nonformal:* bust, slump **2.** air mass, barometric pressure, cold-front, front, low-front

lowdown *n.* facts, gossip, information, inside story, news, truth *Nonformal:* dirt, dope, info, poop, scoop, skinny, straight goods

lower *adj.* **1.** humble, inferior, junior, minor, modest, second-string *(Nonformal)*, subordinate, subservient **2.** below, decreased, diminished, less, reduced, under *Antonyms:* above, greater, higher, more **3.** buss *(Maritimes)*, frown, gloom, glower, grimace, long face, point, scowl *Antonyms:* grin, laugh, smile – *v.* **1.** bump, close, debar, declass, denote, depress, down, drop, let down, sink, squat **2.** cheapen, cut, decrease, lessen, mark down, pare, prune, reduce, shave, slash *(Nonformal) Antonyms:* hike *or* jack up, increase, raise **3.** abase, belittle, condescend, debase, degrade, demean, humble, humiliate, stoop *(Nonformal) Antonyms:* deify, exalt, raise **4.** deplete, devitalize, diminish, enervate, sap, weaken

low-key *adj.* **1.** cool, modest, pallid, played *or* toned down, quiet, relaxed, restrained, softened, subdued, subtle, understated *Antonyms:* elaborate, inflated, ornate, overdone **2.** casual, easygoing, folksy, informal, laid-back *(Nonformal)*, loose, mellow, resolved

lowlands *n. pl.* bog, champaign, downs, everglades, fen, flat, grassland, marsh, moor, meadow, mud *or* tidal flats, prairie, plain, tundra, savannah, steppe, swamp, valley, veldt, wetlands

lowly *adj.* **1.** average, base, common, commonplace, humble, inferior, low, mean, menial, modest, mundane, ordinary, plain, plebeian, poor, proletarian, simple *Antonyms:* grand, luxurious, majestic **2.** docile, dutiful, meek, mild, obedient, obsequious, reverential, servile, submissive, subordinate *Antonyms:* arrogant, lofty, pompous **3.** ground-level, low-lying, short, stubby, stumpy, unelevated – *adv.* dutifully, humbly, modestly, obsequiously, reverentially, simply, unpretentiously

loyal *adj.* allegiant, constant, dependable, dyed in the wool *(Nonformal)*, ever ready, devoted, faithful, firm, patriotic, reliable, resolute, staunch, steady, tried and true, true-blue, trusty, unwavering *Antonyms:* changeable, crooked, duplicitous, fickle, perfidious

loyalty *n.* adherence, aid, allegiance, attachment, constancy, dedication, devotion, faithfulness, fealty, fidelity, friendship, reliability, staunchness, steadfastness, trustworthiness *Antonyms:* chicanery, infidelity, treachery

lubricate *v.* anoint, butter, grease, lard, lube, oil, slick, smear, smooth, wax

lubricated *adj.* **1.** buttery, greasy, oily, oleaginous, slick, slippery, soapy, unctuous **2.** dizzy, drunk, giddy, intoxicated, tipsy, wasted *Nonformal:* all liquored-up, jiggered, plotzed *Antonyms:* sober, straight, temperate

lucid *adj.* **1.** beaming, bright, brilliant, effulgent, gleaming, luminous, lustrous, radiant, shining *Antonyms:* indistinct, muddled, unclear **2.** apprehensible, clear, clear-cut, comprehensible, crystal-clear, distinct, evident, explicit, fathomable, intelligible, obvious, plain, transparent, unambiguous, understandable *Antonyms:* ambiguous, unintelligible, vague **3.** clear-headed, *compos mentis (Latin)*, in one's right mind, normal, rational, reasonable, sane, sensible, sober, sound *Antonyms:* abstracted, confused, insane

luck *n.* **1.** accident, break, chance, destiny, fate, fluke, fortune, kismet, lucky break **2.** advantage, blessing, good fortune, good medicine *(Native Peoples)*, happiness, health, karma, opportunity, profit, prosperity, serendipity, windfall *Antonyms:* adversity, calamity, blight, predicament, trial

luckily *adv.* by chance, favourably, fortuitously, fortunately, happily, opportunely, propitiously, providentially *Antonyms:* adversely, tragically

lucky *adj.* **1.** blessed, charmed, fortuitous, fortunate, happy, prosperous, serendipitous, timely *Antonyms:* detrimental, dire, foreboding, ominous, portentous **2.** auspicious, encouraging, favourable, felicitous, golden, opportune, promising, providential, turning up trumps

lucrative *adj.* advantageous, beneficial, cost effective, favourable, fruitful, gainful, moneymaking, paying, productive, profitable, remunerative, rewarding, rich, satisfying, substantial, successful, valuable, well-paying, worthwhile *Antonyms:* fruitless, losing, unprofitable

lucre *n.* cash, currency, fortune, gold, money, profit, riches, wealth, wherewithal *Nonformal:* bread, wampum, dough, jack, loot, moolah

ludicrous *adj.* **1.** amusing, comic, crazy, entertaining, farcical, funny, humorous, laughable, silly, witty, zany *Antonyms:* grave, serious, solemn **2.** absurd, asinine, bizarre, foolish, nonsensical, odd, outlandish, preposterous, queer, ridiculous, unbelievable *Nonformal:* wacky, way-out *Antonyms:* logical, rational, reasonable

lug *n.* **1.** bumpkin, clown, dolt, lout, lubber, oaf *Nonformal:* buggerlugs, galoot, hoser, rube, yahoo, yokel **2.** bulge, bump, handle, knob, projection, protrusion, protuberance – *v.* drag, draw, haul, heave, pull, tote, tow, tug

luggage *n. pl.* accoutrements, baggage, bags, belongings, case, effects, gear, goods, kit, paraphernalia, sea trunk, tackle

lugubrious *adj.* crestfallen, dismal, dolorous, funereal, gloomy, grievous, lamentable, melancholy, morose, mournful, neurasthenic, rueful, sad, sorrowful, teary, unhappy, woeful *Antonyms:* bright, gay, jovial, merry

lukewarm *adj.* **1.** heated, milk-warm, room-temperature, tepid, warm **2.** apathetic, cool, halfhearted, hesitant, indecisive, indifferent, irresolute, phlegmatic, uncertain, uncommitted, undecided, unenthusiastic, uninterested, unresolved, unresponsive, wishy-washy *(Nonformal)* *Antonyms:* determined, enthusiastic, passionate, positive

lull *n.* **1.** abeyance, break, breather, calm, downtime, hiatus, intermission, layoff, letup, pause, recess, respite **2.** hush, peace, quiescence, quiet, serenity, silence, stillness, tranquility – *v.* **1.** abate, allay, calm, cease, compose, decrease, diminish, dwindle, ebb, lessen, mitigate, palliate, quell, subdue, subside, temper, wane *Antonyms:* aggravate, agitate, continue, persist, vex **2.** cradle, hush, pacify, quiet, rock, settle, soothe *Antonyms:* arouse, excite, wake up

lulu *n. Nonformal:* a beaut, dandy, dilly, humdinger, jim-dandy, lollapalooza, peach, pip, whopper

lumber *n.* **1.** beam, board, building, logs, planks, timber, wood **2.** baggage *(Nonformal)*, burden, deadweight, encumbrance, impediment, imposition, inconvenience, load, millstone *Antonyms:* advantage, benefit, boon **3.** bat, baton, hockey stick, slugger, stick, weapon – *v.* **1.** clearcut, cut down, fell, harvest, log, moonscape *(B.C.)*, raze **2.** clump, hobble, limp, plod, shamble, trudge, trundle, waddle *Antonyms:* float, run, skip

lumbering *adj.* **1.** awkward, blundering, bumbling, clumsy, clunking, gauche, gawky, halting, heavy-footed, inept, lead-footed, lumpish, maladroit, ungainly, unhandy, unwieldy, wooden *Nonformal:* clodhopping, klutzy *Antonyms:* adroit, agile, deft, dexterous, graceful **2.** forestry, logging, pulp and paper industry, harvesting *or* the taking of timber

luminary *n.* **1.** big *or* household name, celebrity, dignitary, eminence, leader, lion, name, notable, personage, personality, somebody, superstar *Nonformal:* bigtimer, bigwig, VIP *Antonyms:* anonymous, nobody, nonentity, unknown **2.** beacon, beam, blaze, illuminator, light, moon, star, sun

luminescent *adj.* bright, effulgent, fluorescent, glowing, luminous, phosphorescent, radiant, shining

luminous *adj.* **1.** bright, dazzling, effulgent, glowing, lit, lucid, lustrous, radiant, shining, sparkling *Antonyms:* dark, dim, lustreless **2.** apparent, apprehensible, clear, comprehensible, concise, distinct, evident, explicit, express, fathomable, obvious, overt, patent, plain, vivid *Antonyms:* convoluted, incoherent, latent **3.** brilliant, clever, gifted, intelligent, percipient, perspicacious, profound, sagacious, sharp-witted, virtuoso, wise

lump *adj.* aggregate, amassed, combined, complete, compound, entire, total, whole – *n.* **1.** block, cake, chunk, clump, mass, mound, pound, wad **2.** bruise, bulge, bump, contusion, cyst, ganglion, goose-egg *(Nonformal)*, growth, melanoma, protuberance, protrusion, swelling, tumour, welt **3.** aggregate, assortment, bunch, cluster, collection, group, handful **4.** buffoon, bumpkin, clod, dolt, fool, lummox, yahoo *Nonformal:* airhead, chump, dimwit, pinhead – *v.* amalgamate, blend, coalesce, collect, combine, compound, connect, consolidate, fuse, group, integrate, join, link, mass, mix, unite, yoke *Antonyms:* apportion, divide, divvy up, segregate

lunacy *n.* **1.** dementia, derangement, imbalance, insanity, madness, mania, psychopathy, psychosis *Antonyms:* reason, sanity **2.** absurdity, asininity, craziness, folly, foolishness, senselessness, silliness, stupidity *Antonyms:* prudence, sense, wisdom

lunatic *adj.* **1.** crazy, demented, deranged, insane, mad, maniacal, *non compos mentis (Latin)*, psycho *(Nonformal)*, psychotic, unhinged, unsound **2.** absurd, daft, foolish, idiotic, irrational, nonsensical, preposterous *Nonformal:* balmy, barmy, bananas, batty, bonkers, daffy, dippy, flaky, kooky, loony, nuts, screwy, wacko – *n.* madman, madwoman, maniac, psychotic *Nonformal:* crackpot, flake, fruitcake, loony, nutcase, sicko

lunch *n.* bite *(Nonformal)*, brunch, *déjeuner (French)*, light meal, luncheon, meal, refreshment, repast, snack – *v.* chow down *(Nonformal)*, dine, eat, feed, partake, sup

lunge *n. & v.* **1.** jab, pass, poke, stab, strike, surge, thrust **2.** bound, charge, dive, jump, leap, lurch, plunge, pounce, spring

lurch *n.* difficulty, dilemma, imbroglio, pickle *(Nonformal)*, pinch, predicament, trouble – *v.* **1.** blunder, bumble, dodge, duck, falter, flounder, jerk, slip, stagger, stumble, weave **2.** careen, keel, lean, list, pitch, reel, roll, seesaw, slant, sway, teeter, tilt, toss

lure *n.* **1.** allurement, appeal, attraction, bait, call, decoy, draw, enticement, hook, incentive, inducement, inveiglement, invitation, magnet, pull, seduction, snare, temptation, trap **2.** tackle *Kinds of fishing lure:* dry fly, feather, frog, grasshopper, leech, minnow, nymph, plastic, plug, popper, roe, shiner, sinking, spinner, wetfly, wood, worm – *v.* allure, attract, beckon, beguile, bewitch, captivate, capture, catch, charm, drag, draw, enchant, ensnare, entice, fascinate, grab, hook, inveigle, invite, lead on, net, pull, rope, seduce, steer, tempt *Antonyms:* discourage, dissuade, repulse

lurid *adj.* **1.** extreme, gory, graphic, grisly, sensational, shocking, startling, vivid **2.** anemic, ashen, blanched, colourless, pale, pallid, pasty, sallow, sickly, wan, washed-out **3.** brilliant, burning, dazzling, fiery, flaming, glaring, red, yellowish *Commonly misused:* **livid**

lurk *v.* crawl, creep, crouch, hide, prowl, skulk, slink, sneak, wait, waylay *Antonyms:* flaunt, flout, strut

luscious *adj.* ambrosial, appetizing, choice, delectable, delicious, delightful, divine, enjoyable, exquisite, filling, fine, flavoursome, heavenly, honeyed, juicy, mouth-watering, piquant, pleasing, rich, satisfying, savoury, succulent, sweet, tasty *Nonformal:* scrumptious, yummy *Antonyms:* nasty, odious, putrid, vile

lush *adj.* **1.** abundant, dense, fecund, flourishing, garish, green, overgrown, rich, thick, verdant *Antonyms:* barren, desolate, vacant **2.** deluxe, elaborate, extravagant, lavish, luxurious, opulent, palatial, plush *Nonformal:* posh, ritzy, swank **3.** delectable, delicious, delightful, heavenly, luscious, succulent, tasty

lust *n.* **1.** biological urge, carnality, concupiscence, eroticism, lasciviousness, lewdness, libido, licentiousness, nymphomania, salaciousness, satyriasis, sexual desire, sexuality, urge **2.** appetite, avarice, covetousness, craving, cupidity, desire, eros, greed, itch *(Nonformal)*, longing *Antonyms:* aversion, fear, loathing **3.** ardour, élan, energy, enthusiasm, gusto, robustness, vigour, vitality *Antonyms:* apathy, enervation – *v.* covet, crave, desire, hunger *or* pine *or* yearn for, want

lustre *n.* **1.** afterglow, brightness, brilliance, burnish, dazzle, effulgence, glaze, gleam, glitter, glow, incandescence, iridescence, luminousness, radiance, sheen, shimmer, shine, sparkle *Antonyms:* dimness, drabness **2.** coating, finish, gloss, oil, polish, resin, varnish, wax **3.** achievement, distinction, glory, kudos, renown, splendour, stardom

lustrous *adj.* **1.** bright, burnished, dazzling, effulgent, gleaming, glinting, glistening, glossy, glowing, incandescent, luminous, polished, radiant, shimmering, shining *Antonyms:* drab, dull, gloomy, lacklustre **2.** admirable, august, celebrated, glorious, illustrious, magnificent, outstanding, prominent, renowned, splendid

lusty *adj.* **1.** brawny, dynamic, energetic, hale, healthy, hearty, potent, powerful, rugged, stalwart, stout, strapping, strong, sturdy, tough, vigorous, vital *Antonyms:* feeble, frail, impotent, weak **2.** aroused, bothered, excited, horny *(Nonformal)*, hot, lascivious, lecherous, lewd, licentious, lusting, randy

luxuriant *adj.* **1.** abundant, ample, copious, dense, fertile, flourishing, fruitful, luscious, lush, overflowing, plenteous, prodigal, productive, profuse, prolific, rampant, rich, superabundant, teeming, thriving **2.** adorned, deluxe, elaborate, extravagant, fancy, intricate, involved, lavish, opulent, ostentatious, palatial, rococo *Antonyms:* basic, plain, simple *Commonly misused:* **luxurious**

luxuriate *v.* **1.** appreciate, bask, eat up *(Nonformal)*, rejoice, relish, revel, wallow **2.** bloom, flourish, grow, increase, prosper, sprout *Antonyms:* desiccate, flounder, shrivel up **3.** feast, indulge, live extravagantly, overdo, satiate, surfeit

luxurious *adj.* **1.** affluent, deluxe, elaborate, fancy, grand, imposing, magnificent, opulent, palatial, plush, princely, stately, sumptuous, upscale *Antonyms:* austere, plain, squalid **2.** epicurean, extravagant, free-living, indulgent, lavish, pampered, prodigal *Antonyms:* prudent, Spartan, stoical, temperate *Commonly misused:* **luxuriant**

luxury *n.* **1.** affluence, comfort, exorbitance, hedonism, high-living, immoderation, luxuriousness, opulence, richness, splendour, sumptuousness *Nonformal:* cakes and ale, easy living, good life, high-life *Antonyms:* destitution, hardship, penury, poverty, privation **2.** extravagance, indulgence, nonessential, superfluity, treat

lying *adj.* deceitful, deceptive, delusive, dishonest, equivocating, fabricating, false, falsifying, fibbing, inventive, mendacious, misleading, misrepresenting, perfidious, prevaricating, shifty, treacherous, unreliable, untrue, untruthful, wrong *Antonyms:* frank, honest, sincere, truthful, veracious – *n.* crookedness, deceit, dishonesty, falsity, fudging, guile, mendacity

lynch *v.* draw and quarter, execute, hang, kill, murder, put to death, stone, string up

lyric *adj.* **1.** earnest, expressive, individual, inner, personal, private, subjective **2.** ardent, burning, effusive, impassioned, intense, moving, rhapsodic *Antonyms:* aloof, cool, detached **3.** dulcet, eclogic, flexible, golden, harmonious, honeyed, idyllic, light, lilting, mellifluent, melodious, musical, sweet, tuneful, vocal – *n.* **1.** ballad, eclogue, idyll, lay, poem, rhyme, song, verse *See also:* **poem** **2.** catchphrase, chorus, hook, line, passage, phrase, word

macabre *adj.* cadaverous, deathly, dreadful, eerie, frightful, ghastly, ghoulish, grim, grisly, gruesome, hideous, horrid, morbid, scary, weird *Nonformal:* gross, spooky *Antonyms:* appealing, beautiful, charming, delightful, pleasant

Machiavellian *adj.* amoral, artful, calculating, cunning, designing, devious, expedient, guileful, opportunistic, politic, scheming, shrewd, sly, smooth, underhanded, wily, without scruples *Antonyms:* artless, innocent, naive

machinate *v.* collude, connive, conspire, contrive, design, devise, engineer, hatch, intrigue, invent, manoeuvre, mastermind, plan, plot, promote, scheme, strategize *Nonformal:* finagle, pull strings, wangle

machination *n.* artifice, brinkmanship, conspiracy, design, device, dodge, gamesmanship, intrigue, manoeuvre, plot, ploy, practice, ruse, scheme, skulduggery, stratagem, trick

machine *adj.* industrial, mechanical, mechanized, robotic – *n.* **1.** apparatus, appliance, contraption, contrivance, device, engine, gadget *(Nonformal)*, implement, instrument, mechanism, motor, tool, vehicle *Kinds of machine elements:* ball bearing, belt drive, crank motion, gears, joint, lever, link motion, toggle, universal joint, wormgear **2.** agency, camp, faction, movement, organization, party, setup, structure, system **3.** android, automaton, cog, mechanical person, robot

machinery *n.* **1.** apparatus, elements, engine, inner works, instruments, mechanisms, motor, operating *or* working parts, tools, utensils, works **2.** agency, channel, device, instrument, means, medium, system, vehicle

machismo *n.* balls *(Nonformal)*, bravado, brawn, courage, grit, macho, mannishness, ultramasculinity, virility

mad *adj.* **1.** berserk, confused, crazed, delirious, demented, deranged, distracted, frantic, frenzied, insane, irrational, lunatic, *non compos mentis (Latin)*, psychotic, rabid, raving, unhinged, unstable *Nonformal:* bananas, batty, bonkers, cuckoo, daffy, loony, mental, nutty, screwy, squirrely, wacky *Antonyms:* normal, rational, sane **2.** agitated, angered, angry, distraught, enraged, exasperated, excited, fuming, furious, incensed, infuriated, irritated, livid, raging, resentful, seeing red *(Nonformal)*, uncontrolled, wild, wrathful, upset *Antonyms:* calm, even-tempered, pleased, satisfied **3.** asinine, crazy, dumb, foolish, inane, nonsensical, preposterous, senseless, silly, zany *Antonyms:* calculated, educated, well-planned **4.** ardent, avid, crazy about, devoted, enamoured, enthusiastic, fanatical, fervent, fond, impassioned, infatuated, keen, wild, zealous *Antonyms:* apathetic, cold, indifferent **5.** careless, dangerous, daring, devil-may-care, foolhardy, hairy *(Nonformal)*, reckless, risking, unsafe *Antonyms:* careful, cautious

madcap *adj.* crazy, impulsive, rash, wild, zany *Nonformal:* loony, nutty, out-of-this-world, rattlebrained

madden *v.* anger, annoy, antagonize, bother, craze, derange, distract, drive crazy *or* insane, enrage, exasperate, incense, inflame, infuriate, ire, irritate, pester, provoke, unbalance, unhinge, upset, vex *Nonformal:* hassle, steam up *Antonyms:* palliate, placate, relax, smooth

made *adj.* **1.** concocted, crafted, created, devised, fabricated, handmade, invented, prepared **2.** accomplished, complete, finished, ready **3.** affluent, burgeoning, flourishing, prosperous, successful, thriving *Nonformal:* parking in tall cotton, sitting in clover

made-up *adj.* artificial, fabricated, false, fictional, imaginary, make-believe, mythical, specious, tall *(Nonformal)*, trumped-up, unnatural, unreal, untrue *Antonyms:* accurate, genuine, true

madhouse *n.* **1.** asylum, insane *or* lunatic asylum, mental home *or* hospital *or* institution, psychiatric hospital *or* ward, sanatorium *Nonformal:* booby hatch, crazy house, funny farm, loony bin, nuthouse **2.** bedlam, chaos, craziness, madness, pandemonium, uproar *Nonformal:* circus, jungle, zoo

madly *adv.* **1.** absurdly, crazily, deliriously, dementedly, foolishly, frantically, frenziedly, furiously, insanely, irrationally, ludicrously, nonsensically, rabidly, senselessly, stormily, tumultuously, turbulently, unreasonably, violently, wildly *Antonyms:* calmly, peacefully, reasonably **2.** deeply, devotedly, exceedingly, extremely, intensely, passionately, truly **3.** desperately, energetically, excessively, excitedly, hastily, hurriedly, rapidly, speedily, rashly, recklessly

madness *n.* **1.** craziness, dementia, disturbance, insanity, irrationality, lunacy, mental disorder, psychosis, senselessness *Antonyms:* lucidity, rationality, reasonableness **2.** absurdity, dangerousness, folly, ludicrousness, ridiculousness, silliness *Antonyms:* logicalness, soundness

maelstrom *n.* **1.** Charybdis, cyclone, eddy, vortex, whirlpool **2.** bedlam, chaos, craziness, confusion, disarray, disorder, flux, pandemonium, tumult, turbulence, upheaval *Antonyms:* calm, order, serenity

maestro *n.* **1.** artist, expert, guru, master, mentor, prodigy, sensei, virtuoso **2.** arranger, composer, conductor, *kapelmeister (German)*, performer

magazine *n.* **1.** bi-monthly, comic book, graphic novel, issue, journal, monthly, periodical, publication, quarterly, serial, weekly, yearly *Nonformal:* fanzine, glossy, mag, rag, zine **2.** ammunition dump, armoury, arsenal, cache, depository, depot, repertory, repository, reservoir, store, storehouse, storeroom, supply house, warehouse

magic *adj.* alluring, bewitching, captivating, charismatic, charming, delightful, enchanting, entrancing, entertaining, fascinating, spellbinding – *n.* **1.** abracadabra, alchemy, art, astrology, augury, conjuring, diabolism, divination, exorcism, foreboding, fortunetelling, geomancy, hocus-pocus, illusion, incantation, necromancy, occultism, prophecy, smoke and mirrors *(Nonformal)*, soothsaying, sorcery, superstition, taboo, thaumaturgy, voodoo, voodooism, witchcraft, wizardry **2.** allurement, bewitchment, charm, enchantment, entrancement, fascination, magnetism, spell **3.** deception, dishonesty, jiggery-pokery *(Nonformal)*, jugglery, legerdemain, prestidigitation, sleight of hand, trickery

magical *adj.* **1.** bewitching, charismatic, enchanting, entrancing, extraordinary, magnetic, spellbinding, wonderful *Antonyms:* bland, boring, dull **2.** conjuring, diabolic, mystic, occult, runic, sorcerous, telekinetic, witchlike, wizardly **3.** eerie, ethereal, ghostly, haunted, mystical, parapsychological, otherworldly, spectral, spiritualistic, spooky *(Nonformal)* **4.** miraculous, mysterious, out of the ordinary, strange, uncanny, unexplainable, unusual, weird *Antonyms:* common, familiar, mundane

magician *n.* **1.** charlatan, conjuror, diviner, enchanter, enchantress, fortune-teller, genie, geomancer, illusionist, mage, magic-user, medium, Merlin, mountebank, necromancer, oracle, sage, seer, soothsayer, sorcerer, sorceress, spellbinder, trickster, warlock, witch, witch doctor, wizard **2.** expert, genius, maestro, mastermind, prodigy, virtuoso, whiz *(Nonformal)*

magisterial *adj.* **1.** assertive, bossy *(Nonformal)*, controlling, dictatorial, dogmatic, domineering, highhanded, imperious, overbearing, peremptory *Antonyms:* passive, shy, timid **2.** authoritative, *ex cathedra (Latin)*, legitimate, official, sanctioned

magistrate *n.* alderman, *bailie (Scottish)*, bailiff, circuit judge, civil officer, doge, JAG, judge, justice of the peace, *mullah (Islam)*, praetor, prefect, provost, public official, reeve

magnanimity *n.* altruism, beneficence, bounty, charity, generosity, largesse, munificence, nobility, open-handedness, philanthropy, selflessness *Antonyms:* meanness, selfishness, stinginess

magnanimous *adj.* **1.** altruistic, beneficent, benevolent, bountiful, charitable, generous, giving, kind, kindly, liberal, munificent, philanthropic, selfless, unselfish *Antonyms:* miserly, paltry, selfish **2.** big-hearted, compassionate, forgiving, high-minded, humane, unbegrudging *Antonyms:* bitter, petty, vindictive

magnate *n.* baron, captain of industry, chief, entrepreneur, financier, industrialist, mogul, monopolist, nabob, robber baron, tycoon, venture capitalist *Nonformal:* big cheese, fat cat, wheeler-dealer *Commonly misused:* **magnet**

magnet *n.* **1.** attractor, bait, draw, enticement, lodestone, lure, pull *Antonyms:* impedance, repellent, resistance **2.** electromagnet, solenoid, magnetic needle *Commonly misused:* **magnate**

magnetic *adj.* **1.** attracting, drawing, irresistible, pulling **2.** alluring, appealing, arresting, attractive, bewitching, captivating, charismatic, charming, enchanting, entrancing, fascinating, inviting, seductive *Antonyms:* disagreeable, repellent, repulsive, unappealing, unattractive

magnetism *n.* **1.** magnetic field, magnetosphere, Van Allen belt **2.** allure, appeal, attraction, attractiveness, charisma, charm, draw, drawing power, enchantment, fascination, glamour, hypnotism, influence, lure, mesmerism, power, pull, seductiveness

magnification *n.* **1.** amplification, boost, enhancement, expansion, increase, inflation, intensification **2.** blowup, enlargement, zoom

magnificence *n.* brilliance, elegance, glory, grandeur, impressiveness, luxury, majesty, opulence, splendour, wonderfulness *Antonyms:* drabness, dreariness, impoverishment

magnificent *adj.* **1.** arresting, brilliant, elegant, excellent, fine, glittering, gorgeous, impressive, lavish, luxurious, opulent, outstanding, plush, radiant, resplendent, splendid, striking, sumptuous, superb, superlative, towering, wonderful *Nonformal:* posh, smashing, swanky *Antonyms:* common, ordinary, plain, usual **2.** august, chivalric, commanding, elevated, exalted, grand, grandiose, imperial, imposing, lofty, majestic, noble, palatial, pompous, princely, regal, rich, royal, stately, superior *Antonyms:* humble, lowly, modest **3.** angelic, godlike, saint-like, sublime, transcendent

magnify *v.* **1.** aggrandize, aggravate, amplify, blowup, boost, deepen, dilate, distend, enlarge, expand, extend, heighten, hike, increase, inflate, mount, multiply, raise, redouble, swell, zoom *Nonformal:* beef *or* puff *or* step up *Antonyms:* decrease, diminish, lessen, minimize, reduce **2.** colour, dramatize, embellish, embroider, emphasize, enhance, exaggerate, exalt, glorify, hyperbolize, intensify, overdo, overdraw, overemphasize, overestimate, overplay, overrate, overstate, pad *Antonyms:* belittle, deflate, deprecate, understate

magniloquent *adj.* arrogant, bombastic, euphuistic, flowery, grandiloquent, grandiose, pompous, pretentious, rhetorical, turgid, vainglorious, vaunting *Antonyms:* plain, simple, unpretentious

magnitude *n.* **1.** amount, amplitude, breadth, bulk, capacity, compass, degree, dimension, enormity, expanse, extent, greatness, hugeness, immensity, intensity, largeness, mass, measure, measurement, proportion, quantity, range, reach, scope, size, space, strength, stretch, tremendousness, vastness, volume **2.** consequence, eminence, grandeur, greatness, import, importance, mark, moment, momentousness, note, pith, significance, weight *Antonyms:* insignificance, smallness, triviality

magnum opus *n.* *chef d'oeuvre (French)*, great *or* penultimate work, masterpiece, masterwork, *pièce de résistance (French)*, principal achievement, triumph

maid *n.* **1.** abigail, char *(British)*, cleaner, domestic, *femme or fille de chambre (French)*, handmaid, nanny, scullery, scullion, servant, soubrette, tweeny *(Nonformal)*, waitress, wench, woman in waiting **2.** colleen *(Irish)*, damsel, girl, lass *or* lassie *(Scottish)*, mademoiselle, sheila *(Australia)*

maiden *adj.* beginning, earliest, first, fresh, inaugural, initial, introductory, new, original, pioneer, primary, prime, untapped, untried, unused, virgin *Antonyms:* concluding, final, last – *n.* damsel, girl, maid, virgin, young woman, youth

mail *n.* **1.** communication, correspondence, e-mail, epistle, letter, matter, message, missive, package, parcel, post, printed matter, snail mail *(Nonformal)*, writing **2.** armour, chain mail, coat, covering, defence, exoskeleton, protection, shield – *v.* air mail, dispatch, drop, e-mail, exchange, express, forward, post, send, transmit

maim *v.* **1.** castrate, cripple, disfigure, dismember, hack, hurt, injure, lame, mangle, mar, massacre, maul, mutilate, truncate, warp, wound **2.** batter, break, crush, damage, disable, disqualify, goon *(Nonformal)*, harm, impair, incapacitate, spoil *Antonyms:* doctor, fix, mend, repair

main *adj.* **1.** basic, cardinal, central, chief, core, critical, crucial, essential, first, foremost, fundamental, mainstream, major, necessary, paramount, premier, primary, principal, vital *Antonyms:* insignificant, least, marginal **2.** capital, controlling, guiding, head, leading, managing, operating, pilot, presiding, prevailing, prime, regulating, supreme *Antonyms:* auxiliary, dependent, minor, secondary **3.** conspicuous, marked, outstanding, prominent, predominant, preeminent, striking **4.** absolute, complete, downright, sheer, unmitigated, utter **5.** broad, expansive, immense, vast, wide – *n.* **1.** cable, channel, conduit, duct, line, pipe, road, sluice, trunk **2.** effort, energy, force, might, power, puissance, vigour *Antonyms:* deficiency, impotence, weakness **3.** basis, centre, core, essential element, heart, kernel, key, nucleus **4.** foamy brine *(Nonformal)*, ocean, saltchuck *(Pacific Coast)*, sea, the deep

mainly *adv.* above all, by and large, chiefly, essentially, firstly, generally, in general, largely, mostly, predominantly, primarily, principally, substantially, usually

mainspring *n.* agency, basis, cause, core, driving force, dynamo, impulse, incentive, key, motive, origin, reason, root, source, wellspring

mainstay *n.* aid, anchor, backbone, brace, bulwark, buttress, crutch, linchpin, maintainer, pillar, prop, rock *(Nonformal)*, stay, strength, support, supporter, sustainer, upholder *Antonyms:* detractor, saboteur

mainstream *adj.* accepted, acknowledged, common, conventional, current, customary, established, familiar, fashionable, main, middle of the road, mundane, normal, popular, received, regular, traditional *Antonyms:* marginal, on the edge, peripheral

maintain *v.* **1.** carry on, continue, endure, keep alive, perpetuate, prolong, sustain *Antonyms:* discontinue, finish, relinquish, suspend, terminate **2.** cultivate, encourage, foster, husband, look after, manage, mind, minister to, nourish, nurse, nurture, preserve, provide for, raise, shelter, succour, support, take care of, tend, watch over *Antonyms:* abandon, abolish, neglect **3.** back, bankroll, care, feed, finance, fortify, fund, sponsor, stake, strengthen, subsidize, supply **4.** affirm, allege, announce, argue, assert, claim, counter, declare, insist, say, state **5.** champion, hold, honour, defend, protect, safeguard, shield, uphold *Antonyms:* belittle, discredit, disparage

maintenance *n.* alimony, allowance, care, continuation, keep, livelihood, living, preservation, provision, remittance money, repair, resources, subsistence, supply, support, sustenance, upkeep, wherewithal

majestic *adj.* awesome, ceremonious, courtly, dignified, elevated, exalted, grandiose, imperial, imposing, impressive, kingly, lofty, magnificent, marvellous, monumental, noble, palatine, pompous, princely, regal, royal, sovereign, splendid, stately, stunning, sublime, sumptuous, superb *Nonformal:* mind-blowing, smashing *Antonyms:* modest, ordinary, unassuming

major *adj.* **1.** chief, critical, crucial, extreme, great, important, influential, preeminent, primary, principal, senior, significant, star, stellar, supreme, top, uppermost, vital, weighty *Nonformal:* heavyweight, major-league, serious *Antonyms:* auxiliary, inconsequential, insignificant, secondary, subordinate **2.** better, bigger, dominant, greater, higher, larger, leading, overshadowing *Antonyms:* lesser, minor, smaller – *n.* **1.** commander, commissioned *or* company *or* ranking *or* staff *or* superior officer, officer, military person, official, superior *Nonformal:* CO, top brass **2.** area, domain, expertise, field, focus, specialty **3.** major chord, major interval, major key, major scale

majority *n.* **1.** bulk, greater number *or* part, lion's share *(Nonformal)*, mass, most, plurality, preponderance, superiority *Antonyms:* least, minority, slightest **2.** adulthood, age of consent, age of discretion, drinking *or* voting age, full age, legal maturity, manhood, maturity, prime, ripe age, seniority, womanhood

make *n.* brand, composition, constitution, designation, form, gender, kind, manufacture, model, number, stamp – *v.* **1.** arrange, assemble, beget, build, compose, constitute, construct, create, draw up, effect, enact, engender, fabricate, fashion, forge, form, frame, generate, invent, manufacture, prepare, produce, shape, synthesize *Antonyms:* break, burn, destroy, dismantle **2.** begin, bring about, carry on *or* out *or* through, cause, engage in, execute, exercise, initiate, originate, sire, spawn, unleash *Antonyms:* complete, end, finish **3.** appoint, assign, bring in, decree, delegate, designate, elect, enact, legislate, name, nominate, select **4.** calculate, conclude, consider, deduce, derive, draw, entertain, estimate, formulate, gauge, infer, judge, reckon, suppose, think over, work **5.** interpret, translate, understand **6.** alter, change, convert, metamorphose, mutate, transform, transmogrify **7.** declare, express, say, utter **8.** afford, bid, proffer, provide, put forward, tender **9.** acquire, bring home *(Nonformal)*, earn, gain, garner, get, harvest, net, obtain, reap, receive, take in, win **10.** accomplish, achieve, add up *or* amount to, become **11.** coerce, compel, constrain, dragoon, drive, force, impel, induce, interfere, meddle, press, prevail upon **12.** act, behave, conduct, gesture, perform **13.** clear, cover, move over, pass, travel **14.** approach, arrive at, reach, visit **15.** attach, establish, fix, secure **16.** breed, copulate, couple, know *Nonformal:* do it, get busy *or* jiggy, shag

make-believe *adj.* **1.** dream, fantasy, imaginary, pretend, surreal **2.** artificial, fake, false, fantastic, feigned, fraudulent, made-up, mock, simulated, spurious, unreal *Antonyms:* authentic, genuine, real, unfeigned, virtual – *n.* act, charade, disguise, dream, dress up, fantasy, imagination, play-acting, sham, unreality *Antonyms:* actuality, fact, reality

make out *v.* **1.** comprehend, discern, fathom, grasp, know, perceive, realize, recognize, see, understand **2.** accomplish, cope, do, get by, pan out, show, succeed **3.** kiss, osculate *Nonformal:* fool around, neck, smooch, suck face

maker *n.* **1.** architect, artificer, artisan, builder, creator, former, founder, framer, generator, manufacturer, originator, parent, shaper **2.** giver of life, supreme being, the Almighty *or* Creator *See also:* **God**

makeshift *adj.* ad hoc, alternative, band-aid, expedient, interim, jerry-built, jury-rigged, make-do, provisional, rough-and-ready, slapdash, stopgap, substitute, temporary, thrown together *Nonformal:* jackleg, quick and dirty *Antonyms:* permanent, unalterable – *n.* contrivance, expediency, *pis aller (French)*, recourse, refuge, replacement, resort, resource, shift, stopgap, substitute, temporary solution

make-up *adj.* alternate, replacement, second, substitute – *n.* **1.** cosmetics, face paint, greasepaint, maquillage, paint, powder, war paint *(Nonformal) See also:* **cosmetics** **2.** build, cast, character, complexion, constitution, disposition, fibre, grain, guts *(Nonformal)*, humour, individuality, make, mould, nature, personality, stamp, stripe, temper, temperament, vein **3.** architecture, arrangement, assembly, composition, configuration, construction, contents, design, form, format, formation, layout, order, ordering, organization, plan, protocol, scheme, setup, shape, spread, structure, style

making *n.* **1.** beginning, birth, cause, development, growth, movement, origin **2.** composition, construction, content, form, layout, structure **3.** custom, habit, practice, way **4.** batch, bunch, cluster, collection, quantity

makings *n. pl.* **1.** components, constituents, elements, fixings, ingredients, materials, parts **2.** disposition, potential, promise

maladjusted *adj.* aberrant, abnormal, different, disturbed, mixed-up, nonconforming, on the margin, out of step, out of tune, sick, strange, troubled, unadaptable, weird *Nonformal:* out of sync, wacko *Antonyms:* normal, popular, regular

maladroit *adj.* **1.** awkward, blundering, bumbling, bungling, clumsy, floundering, gauche, halting, heavy-handed, inept, inexpert, lumbering, ungraceful, unskilful *Nonformal:* all-thumbs, klutzy, stumblebum *Antonyms:* agile, deft, graceful, nimble **2.** bad-mannered, boorish, churlish, discourteous, disrespectful, ill-mannered, impolite, impolitic, inconsiderate, indelicate, insensitive, loutish, tactless, thoughtless, undiplomatic, unmannered, unpolished *Antonyms:* civilized, courteous, cultured, mannered, polite

malady *n.* affliction, ailment, complaint, debility, disease, disorder, feebleness, handicap, illness, infirmity, sickness *Antonyms:* good health, well-being

malaise *n.* angst, anxiety, depression, discomfort, disquiet, dissatisfaction, distemper, distress, doldrums, ennui, fatigue, lassitude, megrim, melancholy, neurasthenia, restlessness, sickness, unease, *Weltschmertz (German) Antonyms:* comfort, contentedness, relaxation

malapropos *adj.* absurd, discordant, egregious, improper, inappropriate, indecorous, inexpedient, out of place, solecistical, tactless, unfit, unsuitable, untimely *Antonyms:* apt, germane, pertinent

malcontent *adj.* **1.** activist, agitator, *frondeur (French)*, muckraker, rabble-rouser, revolutionary *Antonyms:* Pollyanna, Pangloss **2.** bellyacher, complainer, grouch, grump, *kvetch (Yiddish)*, whiner *Antonyms:* optimist, romantic

male *adj.* he-man *(Nonformal)*, macho, manful, manlike, manly, masculine – *n.* bloke *(British)*, boy, chap, gentleman, guy, male person, man *Nonformal:* dude, fella, Jack, Mac, mate, stud *Male forms of address: Bwana (Swahili), don (Spanish)*, esquire, fellow, *Herr (German)*, lad, Mister, *Monsieur (French)*, Mr., *sahib (Hindu), senhor (Portuguese), señor (Spanish), signore (Italian)*, sir

malediction *n.* **1.** anathema, curse, damnation, denunciation, execration, imprecation *Nonformal:* evil eye, hex, jinx, oath *Antonyms:* benediction, blessing, grace **2.** aspersion, calumny, defamation, libel, obloquy, slander *Antonyms:* glorification, praise, worship

malefactor *n.* convict, criminal, dastard, delinquent, evildoer, felon, hooligan, lawbreaker, miscreant, offender, profligate, reprobate, scoundrel, sneak, villain *Nonformal:* con, goon

malevolent *adj.* **1.** baleful, evil, evil-minded, hateful, hostile, ill-disposed, kill-crazy *(Nonformal)*, maleficent, malicious, malignant, murderous, pernicious, poisonous, rancorous, sinister, spiteful, vengeful, vicious, vindictive, wicked *Antonyms:* amiable, benign, friendly, gracious, warmhearted **2.** calamitous, dire, ill-fated, ill-omened, ill-starred, inauspicious, ominous, star-crossed *Antonyms:* fortunate, happy, lucky

malfunction *n.* breakdown, bug, crash, defect, failure, fault, flaw, glitch, slip, snafu *(Nonformal)* – *v.* break down, fall apart, misbehave, overheat, stop *Nonformal:* blow up, die, perish, self destruct

malice *n.* acerbity, animosity, animus, antipathy, bad blood, bile, bitterness, dislike, enmity, evil, grudge, hate, hatefulness, hatred, hostility, ill will, implacability, malevolence, maliciousness, meanness, poison, rancour, resentment, spite, spleen, umbrage, vengefulness, venom, viciousness, vindictiveness *Antonyms:* amiability, cordiality, decency, kindness

malicious *adj.* baleful, beastly, bitchy, bitter, envious, evil, hateful, ill-disposed, jealous, low, malefic, malign, malignant, mean, nasty, noxious, ornery, pernicious, petty, poisonous, resentful, spiteful, treacherous, vengeful, venomous *Nonformal:* accidentally on purpose, green-eyed, pestiferous *Antonyms:* benevolent, friendly, warm-hearted

malign *adj.* antagonistic, antipathetic, bad, baleful, baneful, deleterious, destructive, evil, harmful, hostile, hurtful, inimical, injurious, maleficent, malevolent, malignant, noxious, pernicious, rancorous, sinister, vicious, wicked *Antonyms:* good, harmless, kind, unselfish – *v.* abuse, accuse, asperse, badmouth, besmirch, calumniate, curse, decry, defame, denigrate, deride, detract, disparage, harm, impugn, injure, insult, libel, misrepresent, slander, slur, sully, traduce, vilify, vituperate *Nonformal:* burn, dis, run down, trash *Antonyms:* commend, compliment, extol, praise

malignant *adj.* **1.** cancerous, deadly, deleterious, destructive, diseased, fatal, harmful, lethal, mortal, metastatic, tumorous, virulent *Antonyms:* benign, innocuous **2.** evil, horrible, malicious, mean, nasty, spiteful, vicious, virulent, wicked *Antonyms:* congenial, gracious, hospitable, pleasant

malinger *v.* avoid, circumvent, delay, dilly-dally *(Nonformal)*, dodge, evade, loaf, loiter, neglect, procrastinate, shirk, side step, shun, slack off *Antonyms:* approach, beard, confront

malingerer *n.* deserter, dodger, do-nothing, faker, idler, layabout, loafer, procrastinator, shirker, slacker, truant *Nonformal:* bum, clock-watcher, goldbricker, goof-off, stick-in-the-mud

mall *n.* **1.** bazaar, emporium, gallery, market, plaza, shopping centre *or* complex, store, stores, strip mall **2.** arcade, avenue, boardwalk, boulevard, esplanade, lane, path, promenade, quay

malleable *adj.* adaptable, ductile, flexible, manageable, mouldable, plastic, pliable, pliant, putty in one's hands *(Nonformal)*, shapable, soft, submissive, supple, tractable, tractile, transformable, workable, yielding *Antonyms:* intractable, intransigent, rock- solid, unyielding

malnutrition *n.* anorexia, emaciation, emptiness, hunger, starvation, undernourishment

malodorous *adj.* bad, decayed, decomposed, evil-smelling, fetid, foul, funky, fusty, gamy, miasmic, musty, nasty, nauseating, noisome, noxious, odorous, off *(Nonformal)*, offensive, pestilential, polluted, putrid, rancid, rank, reeking, rotten, sickening, skunky, smelly, stale, stinking, strong, tainted, vile *Antonyms:* aromatic, fresh, sweet-smelling

malpractice *n.* carelessness, clumsiness, dereliction, error in judgment, misconduct, misdeed, mismanagement, negligence, offence, transgression, violation

mammal *n.* animal, beast, creature, mammalia, vertebrate *Major groupings of mammals:* artiodactyl, carnivore, cetaceous, chiropter, frugivorous, herbivore, insectivore, lagomorph, marsupial, omnivore, perissodactyl, primate, rodent, sirenian, ungulate

mammoth *adj.* behemoth, Brobdingnagian, colossal, elephantine, enormous, gargantuan, giant, gigantic, high, huge, immense, jumbo, king size, large, leviathan, long, massive, mighty, monumental, mountainous, prodigious, stupendous, titanic, vast *Antonyms:* diminutive, little, miniature, small, trivial – *n.* extinct elephant, mammathus *Kinds of mammoth*: columbian, imperial, wooly

man *n.* **1.** being, bloke *(British)*, body, chap, character, creature, earthling, fellow, gentleman, guy, human, human being, individual, male, master, mister, mortal, person, personage, sir *Nonformal:* boss, boyo, brother, bub, buddy, buster, Charlie, chief, dude, fella, gent, governor, Jack, Mac **2.**

civilization, community, everyone, folk, Homo sapiens, humanity, humankind, inhabitants, mankind, people, populace, public, society, souls, species, terrestrials, womankind – *v.* control, crew, drive, fill, handle, manoeuvre, occupy, operate, pilot, run, staff, steer, take over, use, work

manacle *v.* bind, capture, chain, constrain, fetter, hamper, handcuff, hog-tie, inhibit, lock, pillory, restrain, secure, shackle

manage *v.* **1.** administer, arrange, coordinate, deal with, execute, finagle, fix, handle, head, legislate, manipulate, operate, organize, settle, take care of **2.** boss, captain, command, control, direct, drive, govern, guide, monitor, oversee, pilot, preside, ride herd on, run, shepherd, steer, superintend, supervise, take charge **3.** carry on, cope, continue, endure, get by, hack *(Nonformal)*, make a go of it, make do, subsist, suffer, survive, thrive

manageable *adj.* **1.** amenable, biddable, compliant, conductible, controllable, docile, governable, obedient, pliant, receptive, submissive, tameable, tractable **2.** achievable, doable, makeable, possible, practicable, sustainable, wieldy **3.** driveable, feasible, negotiable, passable

management *n.* **1.** administration, authority, board, boss, chief, chief executive officer *or* CEO, chief financial officer *or* CFO, chief operating officer *or* COO, command, directorate, directors, employers, executive, government, organization, superintendent, supervisor *Nonformal:* brass, top brass, downtown, front *or* head office, the man **2.** care, charge, conduct, control, direction, governance, guidance, handling, ingenuity, manipulation, operation, rule, skilfulness, superintendence, supervision

manager *n.* **1.** administrator, boss, captain, chief, director, comptroller, conductor, controller, executive, foreperson, governor, guide, handler, head, impresario, leader, manipulator, minister, navigator, officer, official, overseer, pilot, president, prime minister, proprietor, superintendent, supervisor **2.** agent, go-between, intermediary, middleperson, negotiator, organizer, representative

mandate *n.* **1.** behest, bylaw, charge, command, commission, contract, decree, directive, edict, imperative, injunction, instruction, obligation, order, provision, ruling, warrant **2.** authority, possession, property, responsibility, territory, trust – *v.* assign, charge, delegate, designate, dictate, direct, instruct, legislate, obligate, require, set

mandatory *adj.* binding, commanding, compelling, compulsory, *de rigueur (French)*, essential, forced, fundamental, imperative, important, indispensable, involuntary, necessary, needful, obligatory, prescriptive, required, requisite, vital *Antonyms:* discretionary, noncompulsory, optional, voluntary

mangle *v.* batter, break, bruise, butcher, carve, contort, crush, cut, damage, deface, deform, destroy, disfigure, distort, flay, hack, hash, impair, injure, lacerate, maim, mar, maul, mutilate, rend, ruin, scar, slash, slay, slice, slit, spoil, tear, wound, wreck *Antonyms:* assemble, fix, heal, patch, put together

mangy *adj.* **1.** deteriorated, dilapidated, dishevelled, filthy, foul, grody *(Nonformal)*, mean, moth-eaten, ratty, seedy, shabby, squalid, tattered, wretched *Antonyms:* clean, groomed, tidy **2.** base, contemptible, disreputable, hateful, ignominious, ill-reputed, odious **3.** buggy, flea-bitten, infested, lice-ridden, lousy

manhandle *v.* **1.** abuse, batter, beat, damage, knock about, maltreat, mangle, maul, mistreat, paw, pelt, pummel, roughhouse, rough *or* shake up, slap around, smack, strong-arm, thrash *Antonyms:* coddle, massage, rub, pat, pet **2.** budge, drag, handle, hie, manipulate, manoeuvre, move, overpower, overcome, pull, push,

mania *n.* addiction, cacoethes, compulsion, craving, craze, delirium, desire, enthusiasm, fad, fancy, fascination, fetish, fixation, frenzy, furor, hangup, hysteria, *idée fixe (French)*, infatuation, insanity, lunacy, madness, obsession, passion, preoccupation, rage, urge *Kinds of mania:* Anglomania *(England)*, Beatlemania *(The Beatles)*, bibliomania *(Books)*, egomania *(Oneself)*, Francomania *or* Gallomania *(France)*, graphomania *(Writing)*, kleptomania *(Stealing)*, monomania *(One subject)*, mythomania *(Lies)*, necromania *(Death)*, nymphomania *(Female lust)*, satyromania *(Male lust)*, theomania *(God)*, Trudeaumania *(Pierre Trudeau)*, zoomania *(Animals)*

maniac *adj.* dangerous, insane, mad, violent – *n.* **1.** fiend, lunatic, madman, madwoman, pervert, psychopath *Nonformal:* crackpot, freak, fruitcake, loony, nut, perv, psycho, schizoid, sicko, weirdo, wild man **2.** devotee, enthusiast, fan *(Nonformal)*, fanatic, obsessive, zealot *Commonly misused:* **manic**

maniacal *adj.* berserk, crazy, delirious, distraught, frantic, frenzied, furious, hysterical, insane, mad, rabid, raging, ranting, raving, uncontrollable, undone, unglued *(Nonformal)*, unhinged, upset, violent, wild *Antonyms:* calm, passive, peaceful

manic *adj.* agitated, berserk, crazed, demented, deranged, desperate, excited, insane, lunatic, maniacal, overexcited, overwrought, passionate, psychotic, rampant, unbalanced, unsound, wild *Nonformal:* freaked out, high, hopped up, over the edge *Antonyms:* balanced, cool, pacific *Commonly misused:* **maniac**

manifest *adj.* apparent, bold, clear, clear-cut, conspicuous, crystal-clear, disclosed, distinct, divulged, evident, evinced, glaring, noticeable, obvious, open, out in the open, palpable, patent, plain, prominent, revealed, shown, straightforward, unambiguous, unmistakable, visible *Antonyms:* cryptic, disguised, indistinct, masked, suppressed – *n.* account, bill, bill of landing, directory, inventory, list, log, register, roster, tally – *v.* **1.** demonstrate, display, exhibit, expose, illustrate, mark, parade, present, reveal, show, showcase *Antonyms:* conceal, cover, obscure **2.** certify, confirm, demonstrate, establish, evidence, evince, prove, substantiate *Antonyms:* deny, negate, refute

manifestation *n.* **1.** affirmation, avowal, clue, demonstration, disclosure, display, epiphany, evidence, example, exhibition, explanation, illustration, indication, instance, mark, phenomenon, proof, show, sign, symptom, token **2.** appearance, emergence, exposure, materialization, publication, revelation, showing, solidification

manifesto *n.* aim, broadsheet, bull, declaration, desideratum, encyclical, explanation, little red book *(Nonformal)*, plan, polemic, political *or* position paper, proclamation, pronunciamento, publication, statement of principles, tract, treatise

manifold *adj.* **1.** abundant, considerable, copious, diverse, many, multiple, multitudinous, numerous **2.** assorted, complex, composite, compound, different, diverse, diversified, multifarious, multifold, multiform, varied, various– *n.* carbon copy, copy, double, duplicate, facsimile, reproduction, triplicate, Xerox *(Trademark)*

manipulate *v.* **1.** contrive, control, deal with, direct, employ, engineer, exploit, form, handle, influence, lead, lobby, manage, manoeuvre, move, operate, pack, plot, ply, rig, scheme, shape, spin, tamper with, use, wield *Nonformal:* doctor, fiddle, gerrymander, pull strings **2.** coax, direct, navigate, pilot, steer, take the driver's seat

manitou *n.* daimon, deity, god, *orenda (Iroquoian)*, spirit, supernatural being, *wakanda (Siouan)*

mankind *n.* civilization, flesh, Homo sapiens, humanity, humankind, human race *or* species, *Inuit (Inuktitut)*, men, mortality, people, society, womankind, women

manly *adj.* **1.** macho, male, manlike, mannish, masculine, virile **2.** aggressive, bold, brawny, courageous, daring, dauntless, determined, driven, gallant, hard, intrepid, stalwart, stout-hearted, strong, stubborn, sturdy, tough, valiant *Antonyms:* cowardly, craven, dastardly

man-made *adj.* **1.** constructed, contrived, crafted, created, engineered, fabricated, handmade, manufactured **2.** artificial, commercial, counterfeit, ersatz, false, imitation, inferior, plastic, sham, simulated, substitute, synthetic *Antonyms:* natural, organic, unprocessed

manner *n.* **1.** appearance, bearing, behaviour, comportment, conduct, demeanour mien, tact **2.** approach, custom, etiquette, fashion, form, habit, means, method, mode, practice, procedure, process, routine, style, system, technique, tenor, tone, vein, way **3.** class, genre, ilk, kind, race, sort, type

mannered *adj.* **1.** affected, artificial, contrived, overnice, precious, pretended, pseudo, self-conscious, stagy, stilted, studied *Antonyms:* genuine, honest, natural, unaffected **2.** conforming, cultured, disciplined, educated, refined, sensitive, socialized, sophisticated, trained, well- versed

mannerism *n.* affectation, air, attribute, characteristic, eccentricity, fashion, feature, foible, habit, idiosyncrasy, mode, peculiarity, pose, quality, quirk, singularity, specialty, style, trademark, trait, way

mannerly *adj.* accommodating, affable, amenable, attentive, charitable, chivalrous, civilized, compassionate, considerate, cordial, courteous, cultured, decent, deferential, diplomatic, gallant, generous, genteel, gentle, gentlemanly, gracious, ladylike, magnanimous, nice, pleasant, polished, polite, proper, refined, respectable, right, sensitive, smooth, sociable, solicitous, tactful, thoughtful, urbane, well-behaved, well-bred, well-mannered *Antonyms:* boorish, discourteous, impertinent, impolite, rude – *adv.* affably, civilly, courteously, courtly, gentlemanly, gentlewomanly, gently, graciously, kindly, neighbourly, nicely, politely, tactfully, urbanely, with grace *or* polish

manners *n. pl.* bearing, behaviour, breeding, carriage, chivalry, civility, code, conduct, convention, cordiality, correctness, courtesy, culture, customs, decency, decorum, demeanour, deportment, etiquette, form, formality, gentility, good behaviour *or* breeding, graciousness, kindness, mores, niceties, polish, politeness, propriety, protocol, refinement, respect, rules, seemliness, social conduct *or* conventions *or* grace, solicitude, sophistication, tact *Antonyms:* gracelessness, impoliteness, unruliness

manoeuvre *n.* **1.** battle, deployment, drill, exercise, measure, mission, movement, operation, parade, plan, procedure, sally, sortie, stratagem, tactics, war games **2.** action, angle, artifice, contrivance, deke *(Nonformal)*, device, dodge, feint, gambit, gimmick, intrigue, machination, manipulation, move, play, plot, ploy, proceeding, ruse, scheme, shuffle, stratagem, stroke, stunt, subterfuge, trick, wile – *v.* **1.** captain, conduct, deploy, direct, dispense, drive, engineer, exercise, guide, handle, manage, move, navigate, negotiate, operate, pilot, ply, steer, swing, wield **2.** angle, coax, conspire, contrive, design, devise, exploit, finagle, intrigue, jockey, machinate, manipulate, plan, play, plot, rig, scheme, sham, shift, toy with, trick *Nonformal:* gerrymander, pull strings *or* wires, wangle

mansion *n.* abode, building, castle, château, dwelling, estate, hall, home, house, lodging, manor, palace, palazzo, residence, seat, villa *Nonformal:* big house, monsterhome *Antonyms:* hut, shack, shanty

manslaughter *n.* assassination, bloodshed, crime, death, foul play, homicide, killing, slaying, unpremeditated murder *Nonformal:* drive-by, hit

mantle *n.* blanket, cape, chlamys, cloak, covering, hood, mask, muumuu, pall, robe, sari, shawl, shroud, toga, tunic, veil – *v.* **1.** conceal, cover, disguise, envelop, hide, mask, wrap **2.** diffuse, disperse, disseminate, overspread, spread out, suffuse

mantra *n.* canticle, chant, hymn, intonation, om

manual *adj.* by hand, hand-operated, human, physical, practical, standard *Antonyms:* automatic, robotic – *n.* bible *(Nonformal)*, compendium, cookbook, directory, document, enchiridion, encyclopedia, guide, guidebook, handbook, how-to book, information, instructions, primer, reference book, resource, text, textbook, *vade mecum (Latin)*, workbook

manufacture *n.* assembly, casting, crafting, completion, composing, composition, construction, creation, design, doing, erection, fabrication, finishing, forging, formation, making, manufacture, preparing, production, tooling – *v.* **1.** accomplish, assemble, build, carve, cast, complete, compose, construct, craft, create, develop, execute, fashion, forge, form, frame, machine, make, mass produce, mill, mould, press, process, produce, put together, shape, synthesize, tool, turn out, work **2.** concoct, fabricate, elaborate, exaggerate, fictionalize, hyperbolize, invent, lie, romanticize, stretch

manufacturer *n.* artisan, assembler, builder, craftsperson, creator, fabricator, maker, processor, producer, shaper

manumission *n.* delivery, emancipation, liberation, release, rescue, salvation, unchaining, unfettering *Antonyms:* bondage, imprisonment, oppression

manure *n.* compost, droppings, dung, excrement, feces, fertilizer, guano, muck, *Nonformal:* buffalo chips, cow patties *or* pie, crap, dump, poo, scat

manuscript *n.* argument, article, book, copy, document, draft, essay, folio, libretto, position paper, script, scripture, scroll, thesis, treatise

many *adj.* abounding, abundant, bounteous, bountiful, copious, countless, crowded, diverse, innumerable, manifold, multifarious, multifold, multitudinous, myriad, numberless, numerous, plentiful, populous, prevalent, profuse, rife, sundry, teeming, umpteen *(Nonformal)*, uncounted, varied, various *Antonyms:* few, scant, sparse – *n.* abundance, heaps, horde, large numbers, lots, mass, multitude, piles, plenty, scads *(Nonformal)*, scores

map *n.* chart, delineation, diagram, drawing, elevation, globe, graph, grid, guide, outline, representation, sketch, survey, topo *Groupings of map projection:* Azimuthal, conical, cylindrical, miscellaneous *Kinds of maps*: animated, backpackers, dot distribution, environmental, geological survey, land-use, physical, picture, political, proportional, rainfall, relief, road, route-planning, strip, thematic, three-dimensional, topographic, vegetation, weather *Selected kinds of map projections:* conformal, equalarea, mercator, Peters, Robinsons, sinusoidal, tetrahedral – *v.* arrange, chart, delineate, depict, design, draw, graph, locate, organize, pinpoint, plan, plot, position, represent, scheme, sketch, trace

mar *v.* blemish, blight, blot, brand, break, bruise, damage, deface, deform, disfigure, harm, hurt, impair, injure, maim, mangle, mark, mutilate, ruin, scar, scratch, spoil, stain, sully, taint, tarnish, vandalize, vitiate, warp, wound, wreck *Antonyms:* adorn, ameliorate, better, improve

maraud *v.* despoil, forage, foray, harass, invade, loot, pillage, pirate, plunder, raid, ransack, rape, ravage, sack, scourge, seize

marauder *n.* bandit, berserker *(Historical)*, brigand, buccaneer, corsair, desperado, freebooter, highwayman, outlaw, pirate, plunderer, raider, ransacker, renegade, robber, ronin, sacker, viking

marbled *adj.* blotched, clouded, coloured, dappled, flecked, marked, mottled, ornamented, spangled, spattered, spotted, streaked, striped, swirled, tessellated, variegated, veined *Antonyms:* clean, clear, flawless

march *n.* **1.** caravan, column, course, movement, parade, passage, procession, retinue, track **2.** excursion, hike, journey, manoeuvre, outing, saunter, stroll, trek, trip, trudge, walk **3.** advance, development, evolution, headway, progress – *v.* **1.** advance, make headway, move, pace, pound, proceed, progress, step, stomp, stride, strut, traipse, tramp, tread, trundle, walk **2.** drill, exercise, goose step, parade, patrol, promenade

margin *n.* **1.** border, bound, boundary, brim, brink, compass, confine, edge, edging, extra, field, frame, fringe, hem, limit, lip, outline, outskirts, partition, perimeter, periphery, rim, selvage, side, skirt, trimming, verge *Antonyms:* centre, core, navel **2.** allowance, elbowroom, latitude, leeway, room, space

marginal *adj.* **1.** borderline, peripheral, rimming, verging **2.** dispensable, insignificant, low, meagre, minimal, minor, negligible, slight, small *Antonyms:* central, important, significant **3.** alienated, disenfranchised, estranged, ghettoized, neglected, separated, sidelined, trivialized *Antonyms:* accepted, established, mainstream

marginalize *v.* **1.** avoid, disregard, disrespect, forget, ignore, neglect, omit, overlook, slight, snub *Antonyms:* nurture, support, value **2.** act prejudicially, alienate, discriminate against, disenfranchise, divorce, eliminate, exclude, ghettoize, isolate, oppress, ostracize, segregate, separate, shut out, sideline *Antonyms:* incorporate, integrate, unify, welcome

marina *n.* anchorage, basin, dock, harbour, mooring, port, seaport, wharf

marine *adj.* **1.** aquatic, briny, crustaceous *(Nonformal)*, oceanic, pelagic, saltwater, salty, thalassic **2.** maritime, nautical, naval, ocean-going, seafaring – *n.* ranger, sailor, soldier, troop *Nonformal:* grunt, leatherneck

mariner *n.* hand, mate, navigator, sailor, seafarer, seaman, shipmate *Nonformal:* salt, swab, tar *Antonyms:* farmer, hangashore *(Newfoundland)*, landlubber

marital *adj.* conjugal, connubial, marriage, married, matrimonial, nuptial, spousal, wedded

maritime *adj.* **1.** coastal, seaboard, seaside, seashore, tidal **2.** marine, nautical, naval, oceanic, pelagic, saltwater, seafaring, thalassic – *n.* Atlantic region, coast *Maritime provinces:* New Brunswick, Nova Scotia, Prince Edward Island

mark *n.* **1.** adornment, blaze, blemish, blot, blotch, bruise, cut, dent, dot, gash, impression, imprint, indentation, line, nick, notch, scar, score, scratch, splotch, spot, stain, streak, stripe, stroke, welt **2.** autograph, badge, brand name, check, cross, device, emblazonment, emblem, figure, hallmark, identification, image, indication, inscription, insignia, label, logo, manifestation, motto, representation, seal, sign, signature, stamp, symbol, tag, ticket, trademark, X *U.S.:* John Hancock, John Henry **3.** clue, footprint, hint, proof, remains, scent, spoor, trace, vestige **4.** degree, fail, grade, judgment, letter, pass, percentage, rating, result, score, standing, value **5.** criterion, gauge, level, norm, proficiency, quality, scale, standard **6.** attribute, characteristic, distinction, feature, idiosyncrasy, peculiarity, symptom, token, trait **7.** aim, ambition, bull's eye *(Nonformal)*, end, destination, goal, intent, objective, purpose, quarry, target **8.** buoy, guide, inukshuk, indicator, leader, marker, milestone, pointer, signpost **9.** make, model, pattern, style, type, unit **10.** annotation, character, dash, point, punctuation *See also:* **punctuation** **11.** beginning, commencement, start, starting line **12.** attention, concern, heed, note, notice, regard – *v.* **1.** blaze, brand, check, imprint, ink, line, scar, score, slash, stamp, streak, trace **2.** bind, bound, confine, fence in, hinder, impede, limit, restrict **3.** appoint, denote, designate, destine, earmark, indicate, label, note, register, select, single out, specify **4.** discern, distinguish, identify, name, place, point out, recognize **5.** attend, behold, consider, eye, harken, heed, mind, notice, observe, perceive, regard, see, view, watch **6.** demonstrate, display, exemplify, exhibit, illustrate, manifest, show **7.** assess, evaluate, grade, judge, rank, rate **8.** chronicle, document, print, record, recount, set *or* write down

marked *adj.* apparent, arresting, clear, considerable, conspicuous, decided, distinct, evident, notable, noted, noticeable, obvious, outstanding, prominent, pronounced, remarkable, signal, singular, striking *Antonyms:* concealed, hidden, imperceptible, indistinct, vague

markedly *adv.* clearly, considerably, conspicuously, decidedly, distinctly, especially, evidently, greatly, manifestly, notably, particularly, patently, strikingly, substantially

marker *n.* **1.** mark *Kinds of marker:* benchmark, bookmark, buoy, cairn, hallmark, inukshuk, landmark, lighthouse, lobstick, mai, menhir, milestone, monument, street sign, survey stake **2.** chit *(Nonformal)*, I.O.U., note, note of hand, promissory note

market *n.* **1.** auction house, bazaar, business, emporium, fair, forum, mall, marketplace, mart, shop, store *Kinds of market:* black, farmer's, fish, flea, foreign, open, stock, trade fair *See also:* **store** **2.** brokerage, business, capitalism, commerce, dealings, enterprise, exchange, free enterprise, intercourse, trade, traffic, trust, workings

Nonformal: city *or* the street, invisible hand **3.** audience, buyers, clientele, consumers, customers, listeners, public, readers, shoppers, spectators, target population, viewers, watchers **4.** appeal, call for, demand, desire, need, potential, want – *v.* advertise, barter, display, exchange, merchandise, package, promote, retail, sell, vend, wholesale

marketable *adj.* commercial, desirable, for sale, hot *(Nonformal)*, in demand, merchandisable, popular, profitable, saleable, sellable, sought-after, sound, vendible, wanted

maroon *n.* auburn, blood, burgundy, crimson, dark, red, russet, scarlet, wine – *v.* abandon, beach, cast adrift *or* ashore, cast away, desert, forsake, isolate, leave, shipwreck, strand *Antonyms:* aid, rescue, save

marriage *n.* **1.** alliance, amalgamation, association, confederation, conjugality, connubiality, espousal, match, mating, matrimony, monogamy, sacrament, union, wedding, wedlock *Antonyms:* breakup, dissolution, divorce, parting **2.** jumping the broom, nuptials, pledging, rite, ritual, vows, wedding ceremony

married *adj.* **1.** coupled, fused, hitched, joined, matched, mated, spliced, united, wed, wedded **2.** conjugal, connubial, husbandly, nuptial, wifely

marrow *n.* **1.** core, essence, gist, heart, kernel, meat, nucleus, pith, quintessence, sap, soul, spirit, stuff, substance **2.** animation, energy, force, moxie *(Nonformal)*, power, strength, verve, vigour, vitality, will

marry *v.* ally, associate, bond, combine, conjoin, contract, espouse, join, mate, merge, pledge, promise, take vows, tie the knot *(Nonformal)*, unify, unite, wed, yoke *Antonyms:* dissolve, divorce, separate

marsh *n.* bog, bottomland, everglade, fen, lowland, maremma, mire, moor, morass, *moss (Scottish)*, mud, muskeg, peat bog, quagmire, slough, swale, swamp, swampland, wash, wetland

marshal *n.* **1.** chief, officer, official, police, sheriff **2.** arranger, director, emcee *(Nonformal)*, manager, master of ceremonies, steward, supervisor **3.** commander, field marshal, general – *v.* **1.** align, arrange, array, assemble, collect, gather, group, methodize, mobilize, muster, order, organize, rally, rank, set, systematize **2.** deploy, dispose, disseminate, distribute, space **3.** conduct, direct, escort, guide, lead, shepherd, usher *Commonly misused:* **martial**

mart *n.* centre, convenience *or* grocery *or* milk store, corner store, greengrocer, market, plaza, shop, shopping mall *See also:* **store**

martial *adj.* **1.** aggressive, antagonistic, bellicose, belligerent, combative, hawkish, hostile, militant, pugnacious, warlike *Antonyms:* peaceful, serene, tranquil **2.** brave, heroic, high-spirited, military, soldierly, spirited *Commonly misused:* **marshal**

martyrdom *n.* agony, anguish, crucifixion, death, devotion, distress, mortification, ordeal, pain, persecution, sacrifice, self-immolation, self-sacrifice, suffering, torment, torture

marvel *n.* curiosity, genius, miracle, phenomenon, portent, prodigy, sensation, wonder *Nonformal:* something else, stunner, whiz – *v.* gape, gaze, goggle, stare, wonder

marvellous *adj.* **1.** amazing, astonishing, astounding, awe-inspiring, awesome, bewildering, breathtaking, colossal, divine, dreamy *(Nonformal)*, extraordinary, fabulous, fantastic, glorious, gorgeous, implausible, improbable, inconceivable, incredible, magnificent, miraculous, outrageous, phenomenal, remarkable, singular, spectacular, staggering, striking, stunning, stupendous, surprising, unbelievable, unimaginable, unlikely, unusual, wonderful, wondrous *Antonyms:* commonplace, everyday, ordinary **2.** admirable, enjoyable, excellent, good, great, pleasant, pleasurable, satisfying, sensational, splendid, superb, terrific *Nonformal:* cool, neat, nifty, smashing *Antonyms:* awful, bad, terrible

masculine *adj.* boyish, gentlemanly, male, manlike, manly, mannish – *n.* category, classification, gender, sex

masculinity *n.* **1.** gender, machismo, manhood, manliness, sex **2.** potency, swagger, testosterone *(Nonformal)*, verve, vigour, virility

mash *n.* **1.** brew, concoction, hash, hodgepodge, mixture, stew **2.** mush, paste, pulp, slops, swill – *v.* **1.** bruise, chew, crumble, crunch, crush, grind, hash, macerate, masticate, mush up, pestle, pound, powder, press, pulp, pulverize, pummel, smash, squash, squeeze, squish **2.** brew, marinate, soak, souse, steep

mask *n.* **1.** covering, cowl, disguise, domino, face mask *or* plate *or* protection, hood, veil, visor, *yashmak (Muslim)* **2.** blind, cover, feint, red herring, screen, smoke-screen **3.** facade, false front, front, guise, mien, outward demeanour, poker *or* straight face, pretense, show, veneer **4.** cast, death mask, likeness, mould – *v.* beard, camouflage, cloak, conceal, disguise, guard, hide, obscure, protect, screen, shield, shroud *Antonyms:* broadcast, expose, play up, showcase

masked *adj.* camouflaged, cloaked, concealed, covered, deceptive, disguised, hidden, incognito, masquerading, screened, shrouded, undercover, veiled *Antonyms:* bare, exposed, naked, unveiled

masquerade *n.* **1.** *bal costumé (French)*, costume *or* masked ball, festivity, gathering, Halloween party, harlequinade, Mardi Gras, masque, mummery, pantomime **2.** cloak, cover-up, deception, disguise, façade, front, guise, impersonation, imposture, mask, pretense, put-on, sham, show, subterfuge, veil – *v.* disguise, dissemble, impersonate, mask, pass off, pose, posture, pretend, simulate

mass *adj.* **1.** all-embracing, comprehensive, extensive, general, large-scale, pandemic, popular, wholesale, widespread *Antonyms:* determinate, limited, specific **2.** assembly-line, cranked out *(Nonformal)*, generic, mechanically produced *Antonyms:* handcrafted, handmade, unique – *n.* **1.** accumulation, aggregate, assemblage, batch, block, body, bunch, chunk, collection, conglomeration, gob *(Nonformal)*, horde, host, medley **2.** bulk, gross, main body, majority, preponderance, principal **3.** cyst, growth, lump, mound, protuberance **4.** entirety, extent, size, span, sum, totality, sum, wad *(Nonformal)*, whole **5.** celebration, ceremony, eucharist, liturgy, religious service, ritual – *v.* accumulate, assemble, come together, congregate, convene, gather, group, huddle, marshal, mobilize, muster, rally *Antonyms:* disband, disperse, diverge, separate

massacre *n.* annihilation, bloodbath, bloodshed, butchery, carnage, decimation, ethnic cleansing, extermination, genocide, holocaust, mass murder, pogrom, scupper *(Nonformal)*, slaughter – *v.* annihilate, butcher, decimate, destroy, eliminate, execute, extirpate, kill, murder, put to the sword, slaughter, slay, wipe out *Nonformal:* liquidate, mow down

massage *n.* chiropractic, kneading, rubbing, rubdown – *v.* caress, finger *(Nonformal)*, knead, manipulate, pat, pound, press, push, relax, rub, rub down, soothe, stimulate, stretch, stroke

masses *n. pl.* clamjamfry, crowd, electorate, hoi polloi, majority, mob, multitude, people, proletariat, public, rabble, riffraff, throng *Nonformal:* great unwashed, ragtag and bobtail, sheep

massive *adj.* bulky, colossal, cumbersome, elephantine, enormous, extensive, gargantuan, gigantic, grand, great, gross, heavy, hefty, huge, humongous, hulking, immense, imposing, impressive, large, mammoth, mighty, monster, monumental, mountainous, ponderous, prodigious, substantial, titanic, towering, tremendous, unwieldy, vast, walloping *(Nonformal) Antonyms:* little, minute, slight, small, tiny

master *adj.* **1.** ascendant, chief, controlling, dominant, foremost, grand, great, leading, main, major, paramount, predominant, preeminent, preponderant, prevalent, prime, principal, regnant, sovereign, supreme *Antonyms:* lesser, marginal, minor **2.** adept, deft, expert, masterly, proficient, skilful, skilled *Nonformal:* ace, crack, crackerjack *Antonyms:* amateur, inexperienced, unskilled – *n.* **1.** boss, chief, controller, despot, director, *hakim (Muslim)*, leader, lord, maestro, mogul, monarch, overlord, overseer, sovereign, superior **2.** authority, guide, guru, mentor, rabbi, *sadhu (Hindu)*, sage, sensei, teacher **3.** ace, artist, artiste, connoisseur, doctor, doyen, expert, genius, professional, pundit, savant, virtuoso, wizard *Nonformal:* maven, old *or* real pro, whiz *Antonyms:* beginner, learner, neophyte, novice **4.** cast, last, matrix, mould, original, prototype, source *Antonyms:* copy, reproduction **5.** champion, conqueror, hero, heroine, subjugator, vanquisher, victor, winner – *v.* **1.** check, conquer, control, curb, defeat, overcome, overpower, prevail, quash, quell, subdue, suppress, surmount, triumph *Nonformal:* bust, lick *Antonyms:* give in, surrender, yield **2.** command, direct, dominate, govern, manage, regulate, rule, subjugate **3.** break, break in, domesticate, gentle, tame **4.** absorb, acquire, digest, grasp, learn

masterful *adj.* **1.** adept, adroit, bold, consummate, deft, dexterous, excellent, expert, exquisite, fine, first-rate, preeminent, proficient, skilful, skilled, superior, superlative *Nonformal:* crack, crackerjack *Antonyms:* amateurish, incompetent, inept, unskilled, untalented **2.** authoritative, domineering, imperious, magisterial, masterly

mastermind *n.* administrator, architect, author, authority, brains, director, engineer, executor, expert, genius, guide, idea person *(Nonformal)*, intellect, leader, manager, organizer, philosopher, planner, quarterback, strategist, virtuoso – *v.* conceive, create, design, devise, direct, engineer, manage, mould, organize, plan, pull strings *(Nonformal)*, shape, supervise, think up

masterpiece *n.* classic, gem, great work, jewel, magnum opus, masterwork, pearl, prize, showpiece, standard, touchstone, treasure, yardstick *French:* chef d'oeuvre, pièce de résistance

mastery *n.* **1.** authority, command, control, dominion, domination, jurisdiction, power, sovereignty, upper hand *(Nonformal)* **2.** ability, adeptness, adroitness, deftness, expertise, expertness, finesse, genius, handling, skilfulness, skill, virtuosity, wizardry *Antonyms:* inability, maladroitness **3.** ascendency, conquest, superiority, supremacy, triumph, victory, win **4.** attainment, capacity, cognizance, comprehension, grasp, knowledge, understanding

masticate *v.* **1.** bite, chew, crunch, gnaw, munch, nibble **2.** crumble, crush, disintegrate, grind, knead, pestle, pound, pulverize, shatter

masturbation *n.* autoeroticism, self-stimulation, stroking *Nonformal:* jacking *or* jerking *or* whacking off, pocket pool

mat *n.* carpet, covering, doormat, floorcloth, rug, tatami, welcome mat

match *n.* **1.** companion, copy, correlate, counterpart, dead ringer *(Nonformal)*, *doppelgänger (German)*, double, duplicate, equal, equivalent, facsimile, fellow, mate, parallel, peer, reflection, replica, shadow self, synthesis, twin *Antonyms:* antithesis, opposite **2.** adversary, challenger, competition, enemy, foe, nemesis, opponent, rival *Antonyms:* fellow, friend, teammate **3.** affiliation, alliance, combination, couple, duet, espousal, marriage, mating, pair, pairing, partnership, union **4.** bonspiel, bout, championship, competition, contest, engagement, event, game, heat, meet, play down, playoff, race, rivalry, sport, test, trial – *v.* **1.** ally, combine, couple, join, link, marry, mate, pair, unite, yoke **2.** accompany, accord, adapt, agree, blend, coordinate, correspond, correlate, emulate, fit, go with, harmonize, jive, suit, tally **3.** compare, compete, contend, correspond, equal, measure up to, oppose, pit against, rival, vie

matching *adj.* analogous, comparable, corresponding, duplicate, equal, equivalent, identical, like, parallel, selfsame, similar, twin *Antonyms:* different, disparate, distinct

matchless *adj.* alone, consummate, excellent, exquisite, incomparable, inimitable, *ne plus ultra (Latin)*, nonpareil, only, peerless, perfect, singular, superior, superlative, supreme, unequalled, unique, unmatched, unparalleled, unrivalled *Antonyms:* common, everyday, prosaic

mate *n.* **1.** acquaintance, alter ego, amigo associate, buddy, chum, classmate, cohort colleague, companion, compeer, comrade, confidant, confrere, co-worker, fellow, fellow worker, friend, hearty, intimate, pal, partner, peer, playmate, roommate, schoolmate, sidekick *(Nonformal) Antonyms:* competitor, enemy, nemesis, rival **2.** better half, bride, consort, groom, husband, life partner, spouse, wife *Nonformal:* old lady, old man, **3.** accompaniment, analogue, book-end, complement, concomitant, coordinate, counterpart, double, duplicate, familiar, match, reciprocal, twin **4.** assistant, crony, helper, helpmate, subordinate – *v.* **1.** associate, cohabit, consort, couple, hitch, join, marry, match, merge, pair, serve, splice, tie, unite, wed **2.** breed, copulate *Nonformal:* bed down, do the deed, shag

material *adj.* **1.** actual, animal, appreciable, bodily, concrete, corporeal, earthly, palpable, perceptible, physical, real, sensual, tangible, true *Antonyms:* ethereal, imaginary, intangible, intellectual, spiritual **2.** applicable, apropos, cardinal, consequential, considerable, essential, fundamental, germane, grave, important, indispensable, intrinsic, key, meaningful, momentous, pertinent, primary, relevant, serious, significant, substantial, vital, weighty *Antonyms:* irrelevant, trivial, unimportant – *n.* **1.** components, composition, constituents, elements, fodder, ingredients, makings, raw material, staple, stock, stuff, substance **2.** data, documentation, evidence, figures, idea, information, notes, subject matter, text **3.** bolt, cloth, dry goods, fabric, textile

materialistic *adj.* acquisitive, avaricious, grasping, greedy, mammonistic, object-oriented, possessive *Antonyms:* ascetic, generous, spiritual

materialize *v.* appear, corporealize, develop, emerge, evolve, happen, loom, manifest, metamorphose, realize, reappear, reify, rise, take form *or* shape, unfold *Antonyms:* disappear, dissolve, evanesce, vanish

maternal *adj.* caring, devoted, matriarchal, matronly, motherly, nourishing, nurturing, parental, protective, vigilant

mathematical *adj.* **1.** algebraic, algorithmic, analytical, arithmetical, computative, geometrical, left-brained, logical, measurable, numerical, rational, scientific, trigonometric **2.** accurate, calculating, definite, distinct, exact, methodical, particular, precise, rigorous, severe *Antonyms:* fuzzy, indefinite, loose

mathematics *n. pl.* figures, math, number crunching *(Nonformal)*, numbers *Major mathematics groupings:* algebra, analysis, arithmetic, calculus, geodesy, geometry, quadratics, statistics, topology, trigonometry *Nonformal:* new math, trig *Mathematical elements:* addend, algorithm, aliquot, argument, base, binomial, characteristic, coefficient, combination, complement, congruence, constant, cosecant, cosine, cotangent, cube, cube root, decimal, denominator, derivative, determinant, difference, differential, dividend, divisor, equation, exponent, exponential, factor, factorial, formula, fraction, function, haversine, increment, index, integral, logarithm, mantissa, matrix, minuend, minus sign, modulus, multiple, multiplicand, multiplicator, multiplier, norm, numerator, parameter, permutation, π *(Pi)*, polynomial, power, quadratic equation, quotient, radical, radix, reciprocal, remainder, repeating decimal, root, secant, set, sine, square, square root, subtrahend, summand, tangent, variable, vector, vulgar fraction

matrimonial *adj.* betrothed, bridal, conjugal, connubial, espoused, marital, married, nuptial, plighted, spousal, wedding

matrimony *n.* **1.** common-law, connubiality, marital rites, marriage, nuptials, spousals, wedding bells *(Nonformal)*, wedding ceremony, wedlock **2.** alliance, cohabitation, match, partnership, union

matrix *n.* **1.** cast, container, forge, form, model, mould, origin, source, womb **2.** grid, network, pattern, spreadsheet

matron *n.* **1.** dame, dowager, housekeeper, housemother, lady, matriarch, mother, wife, woman **2.** administrator, attendant, governess, guard, head mistress, mother superior, principal, superintendent, supervisor, warden

matted *adj.* dishevelled, disordered, kinky, knotted, messy, mussy *(Nonformal)*, ratty, rumpled, snarled, tangled, tousled, twisted, uncombed, unkempt, untidy *Antonyms:* brushed, kempt, sorted

matter *n.* **1.** building blocks *or* components, constituents, essentials, factors, ingredients, items, makings, material, parts, pieces, stuff **2.** fabric, form, life, mass, materials, object, physical world, proteins, protoplasm, phenomenon, rock, something, substance, tangibility, thing, tissue *Antonyms:* mind, spirit, thought **3.** business, circumstance, condition, episode, event, incident, indiscretion, occasion, occurrence, proceeding, situation, undertaking **4.** ado, bother, burden, cause, complication, concern, difficulty, distress, fuss, grievance, issue, nuisance, pain, predicament, problem, reason, trouble, upset, vexation, worry **5.** consequence, import, importance, magnitude, moment, significance, weight **6.** aim, argument, concept, content, context, focus, gist, goal, idea, meaning, pith, point, purpose, sense, subject, theme, thesis, topic, upshot **7.** aggregate, amount, entirety, extent, quantity, range, scope, sum, total, whole **8.** discharge, infection, pus, secretion, suppuration, ulceration **9.** article, copy, document, essay, item, literature, paper, print, printed matter, reading, story, work **10.** correspondence, e-mail, epistle, exchange, letter, note – *v.* denote, imply, indicate, influence, involve, mean, reveal, say, signify

matter-of-fact *adj.* calm, casual, cold, deadpan, dry, dull, emotionless, factual, impassive, impersonal, like-it-is, logical, mundane, plain, plain-spoken, practical, pragmatic, realistic, serious, sober, stoic, straight-out, unadulterated, unaffected, unembellished, unimaginative, unsentimental, unvarnished *Antonyms:* embellished, exaggerated, maudlin

mature *adj.* **1.** adult, advanced, developed, fit, fledged, full, full-blown, full-grown, fully developed *or* grown, grown-up, old, older, ripened *Antonyms:* immature, undeveloped, unripe, youthful **2.** cosmopolitan, cultivated, cultured, educated, experienced, knowing, knowledgeable, learned, sophisticated, well-mannered, wise *Antonyms:* childish, juvenile, puerile **3.** aged, full-bodied, full-flavoured, mellow, rich, ripe, savoury, seasoned, sweet **4.** complete, detailed, finished, fulfilled, perfected, polished, prepared, ready **5.** cashable, due, payable, redeemable – *v.* **1.** advance, age, arrive, blossom, culminate, cut one's teeth *(Nonformal)*, develop, evolve, fill out, grow, mellow, progress, ripen, season, settle down **2.** complete, detail, finish, perfect, polish, refine

maturity *n.* **1.** adulthood, age of consent *or* majority, full development, majority, manhood, maturation, post-pubescence, prime, prime-of-life, womanhood *Antonyms:* childishness, immaturity, prepubescence, youth **2.** ability, accomplishment, capability, competency, experience, fitness, knowledge, preparedness, proficiency, qualification, readiness, skill, understanding, wisdom **3.** close, completion, due date, finish, fruition, full bloom, fullness, perfection, ripeness, termination

maudlin *adj.* cloying, drippy, emotional, gushing, insipid, lachrymose, mawkish, mushy, overemotional, sentimental, soppy, syrupy, tearful, tear-jerking, teary, weepy *Nonformal:* cornball, Hollywood, schmaltzy, slushy, soapy *Antonyms:* matter-of-fact, stoic, unsentimental

maul *n.* **1.** heavy *or* sledge hammer, mallet **2.** brawl, melee, scrimmage, scrum, set-to – *v.* abuse, bash, batter, beat, bludgeon, buffet, claw, drub, flagellate, flail, fustigate, go over *(Nonformal)*, hit, hurt, ill-treat, knock about *or* around, lacerate, lash, maltreat, mangle, manhandle, molest, mug, muscle, paste, paw, pelt, pound, pummel, rough up, smack, thrash, trample, whip, work over

maunder *v.* **1.** babble, blather, blither, chatter, drivel, gabble, grumble, mumble, mutter, prattle, ramble **2.** dally, drag, idle, laze, mill about, mosey *(Nonformal)*, saunter, waddle

mauve *adj. & n.* colour *Mauve shades:* lavender, lilac, plum, purple, rose, violet

maverick *n.* dissenter, dissident, eccentric independently minded person, malcontent nonconformist, radical, rebel, recusant renegade *Nonformal:* loner, lone wol *Antonyms:* conformist, conservative

maw *n.* **1.** abyss, black hole, chasm, gap, gape, gulf, hypermass, opening **2.** craw, gullet, jaws, mouth, stomach, throat

mawkish *adj.* **1.** cloying, emotional, gushing, maudlin, melodramatic, namby-pamby, schmaltzy, sentimental, sloppy, teary, tiresome, vapid *Nonformal:* gooey, sappy *Antonyms:* controlled, rigorous, Spartan, stoical **2.** abhorrent, disgusting, foul, nauseating, revolting, sickening, unsavoury *Antonyms:* enticing, tasty, toothsome

maxim *n.* adage, aphorism, apothegm, axiom, battle *or* rallying *or* war cry, belief, byword, canon, catch phrase, dictum, epigram, formula, law, moral, motto, platitude, precept, principle, proverb, rule, saw, saying, sentiment, shibboleth, slogan, statement, sutra, tenet, theorem, truism, values statement, watchword, word

maximize *v.* amplify, augment, build up, enhance, enlarge, expand, extend, heighten, increase, intensify, magnify, stretch, widen *Antonyms:* decrease, minimize, reduce

maximum *adj.* biggest, extreme, greatest, highest, largest, longest, paramount, superlative, supreme, topmost, utmost, widest *Nonformal:* mostest, wicked – *n.* apex, apogee, climax, crown, high point, limit, most, peak, pinnacle, summit, top, zenith

maybe *adv.* conceivably, credible, feasible, imaginably, perchance, perhaps, possibly *Antonyms:* absolutely, certainly, definitely, surely

mayhem *n.* anarchy, bedlam, chaos, commotion, craziness, disarray, furor, insanity, madness, mania, pandemonium, uproar *Antonyms:* calm, peacefulness, serenity

maze *n.* **1.** convolution, entanglement, hodgepodge, imbroglio, intricacy, jungle, knot, labyrinth, meander, network, puzzle, tangle, tortuosity, twist, web **2.** bewilderment, confusion, perplexity, quandary, uncertainty

meadow *n.* bottoms, field, grassland, heath, lea, mead, pasturage, pasture, plain, prairie, steppe

meagre *adj.* **1.** bare, barren, deficient, exiguous, flimsy, inadequate, insubstantial, insufficient, little, mere, minimum, miniscule, miserable, paltry, piddling *(Nonformal)*, poor, puny, scant, scanty, short, skimpy, slender, slight, small, spare, sparse, subtle, tenuous, wanting, weak, withered abundant, fecund, lush **2.** emaciated, gaunt, stunted, underfed

meal *n.* **1.** banquet, bite, board, bread, chaw and glutch *(Newfoundland)*, cookery, cooking, cuisine, diet, entrée, fare, feast, food, home cooking, meat, menu, mess, nourishment, nutrition, provision, ration, refection, refreshment, repast, snack, spread, square meal, sustenance, table, tuck, victuals *Nonformal:* chow, chow time, eats, feed, grub, nosh, potatoes and point, scoff, vittles *Kinds of meal:* alfresco, all you can eat, bag *or* box lunch, barbecue, breakfast, brunch, buffet, clambake, coffee break, continental breakfast, cookout, déjeuner, dinner, fast food, high tea, lunch, luncheon, picnic, potluck, power breakfast *or* lunch, sit-down, smörgåsbord, state dinner, Sunday supper, table d'hôte, takeout, *tapas (Spanish)*, TV dinner, wiener roast *British:* takeaway, tea, tiffin **2.** barley, bran, cereal, corn, flour, grain, maize, oats, rye, wheat

mean *adj.* **1.** common, humble, inferior, insignificant, lousy *(Nonformal)*, low, lowborn, lowly, mediocre, menial, ordinary, paltry, pitiful, plebeian, poor, scrimpy, scruffy, second-class, seedy, shabby, sordid, squalid, unwashed, wretched *Antonyms:* comfortable, noble, opulent **2.** bad-tempered, base, callous, churlish, contemptible, dangerous, despicable, difficult, dirty, disagreeable, dishonourable, ignoble, ill-tempered, infamous, knavish, malicious, miserable, nasty, rotten *(Nonformal)*, rough, scurrilous, scurvy, selfish, snide, troublesome, ugly, unaccommodating, unfriendly, unpleasant, unscrupulous, vicious *Antonyms:* agreeable, gentle, good, humane **3.** avaricious, miserly, narrow, parsimonious, penny-pinching, penurious, petty, stingy, stinting, tight, tightfisted, ungenerous *Antonyms:* generous, liberal, philanthropic **4.** ashamed, distressed, embarrassed, humbled, humiliated, ill, mortified, off-balance, out of sorts, uneasy **5.** average, halfway, intermediate, medial, median, mediocre, medium, middle, normal, popular, standard – *n.* **1.** average, balance, centre, compromise, happy medium *(Nonformal)*, median, middle, middle course, midpoint, norm, par **2.** moderation, nonindulgence, self-restraint, temperance – *v.* **1.** aim, anticipate, aspire, contemplate, design, desire, expect, intend, make, plan, propose, purpose, resolve, set a course for, want, wish **2.** allude to, argue, attest, connote, convey, denote, designate, determine, express, imply, intimate, involve, name, point to, suggest, touch on **3.** augur, fate, foreshadow, foretell, herald, portend, predestine, preordain, signify, symbolize

meander *v.* change, drift, gallivant, get sidetracked, peregrinate, ramble, roam, rove, snake, stray, turn, twist, wander, wind, zigzag *Nonformal:* follow one's nose, mosey

meandering *adj.* bending, circuitous, complex, convoluted, crooked, curved, indirect, labyrinthine, rambling, snaky, tortuous, turning, twisted, wandering, winding, zigzagging *Antonyms:* easy, simple, straight

meaning *n.* **1.** aim, ambition, end, goal, intention, objective, plan, purpose, reason **2.** allusion, bearing, connotation, content, context, core, definition, denotation, drift, effect, essence, explanation, force, gist, heart, implication, import, interpretation, meat, message, nuance, pith, point, significance, spirit, stuff, subject matter, substance, tenor, thrust, understanding, upshot, use, value, worth

meaningful *adj.* big *(Nonformal)*, cogent, consequential, considerable, deep, essential, heavy, important, material, momentous, pointed, pregnant, profound, purposeful, relevant, serious, significant, substantial, suggestive, useful, valid, weighty, worthwhile *Antonyms:* inconsequential, insignificant, meaningless, useless, worthless

meaningless *adj.* absurd, aimless, bankrupt, blank, empty, futile, hollow, inconsequential, insignificant, insubstantial, nonsensical, nugatory, pointless, purposeless, senseless, trifling, trivial, unimportant, useless, vacant, vague, vain, valueless, vapid, worthless *Antonyms:* clear, coherent, comprehensive, important, significant

meanness *n.* **1.** abjectness, baseness, contemptibility, cruelty, despicableness, disgracefulness, lowness, nastiness, rottenness, sordidness, vileness *Antonyms:* kindness, sympathy, tenderness **2.** cheapness, frugality, miserliness, parsimoniousness, stinginess, tightfistedness *Antonyms:* generosity, magnanimity

means *n. pl.* **1.** agent, aid, apparatus, avenue, channel, course, instrument, mechanism, medium, method, M.O. *(Nonformal)*, mode, *modus operandi (Latin)*, tool, vehicle **2.** assets, backing, goods, income, money, property, resources, revenue, wealth, wherewithal **3.** ability, aptitude, capability, experience, faculty, organization, process, skill, technique

meanwhile *adv.* concurrently, for now *or* then, in the interim, meantime, simultaneously, till, until, when

measly *adj.* **1.** infested, lousy, maggoty, putrid, rancid, rotten, worm-eaten **2.** beggarly, contemptible, meagre, mean, miserable, paltry, pathetic, penny ante, petty, pitiful, poor, skimpy, small, stingy, trivial, worthless

measurable *adj.* **1.** assessable, calculable, computable, fathomable, perceptible, quantifiable, quantitative, significant *Antonyms:* beyond measure, countless, infinite **2.** controlled, curbed, limited, moderate, reasonable, regulated, restrained, temperate

measure *n.* **1.** barometer, bellwether, benchmark, criterion, example, gauge, instrument, meter, model, norm, pattern, rule, scale, standard, system, test, touchstone, trial, type, yardstick **2.** allotment, allowance, amount, amplitude, area, breadth, bulk, capacity, degree, depth, dimension, distance, dram, duration, extent, fix, frequency, height, magnitude, mass, part, pattern, pitch, portion, proportion, quantity, quota, range, ratio, ration, reach, scope, share, size, span, strength, sum, volume, weight **3.** act, bill, enactment, law, proposal, proposition, resolution, statute **4.** action, course, device, effort manoeuvre, means, method, procedure, resort, step, stratagem **5.** boundary, constraint, control, cure, limitation, moderation, prevention, restraint **6.** beat, cadence, division, foot, melody, rhyme, rhythm, step, stress, stroke, swing, tempo, time, tune, verse, vibration – *v.* **1.** calculate, cipher, compute, estimate, figure, gauge, quantify, reckon, rule, scale, size, sound, time, weigh **2.** adapt, adjust, align, calibrate, fix, regulate, square **3.** demarcate, determine, evaluate, limit, line, mark, mete, pace off, survey **4.** appraise, assess, check, compare, evaluate, grade, judge, juxtapose, liken, match, oppose **5.** attest, denote, indicate, read, reveal, show, yield

measured *adj.* **1.** adjusted, assessed, calculated, determined, fathomed, proportioned **2.** accentual, cadent, metrical, musical, regular, rhythmical, syncopated **3.** conscious, considered, deliberate, designed, planned, premeditated, voluntary *Antonyms:* automatic, involuntary, spontaneous, unconscious **4.** controlled, limited, moderate, regulated, restrained

measurement *n.* amount, appraisal, assay, assessment, calculation, calibration, capacity, dimension, estimation, extent, frequency, gauging, instrumentation, magnitude, measure, quantity, stocktaking, survey *Kinds of measurement tool:* bevel, caliper, carpenter's level, carpenter's square, centre punch, compass, dividers, folding rule, marking gauge, meter stick, micrometer, plumb bob, protractor, rule, ruler, scale, scriber, spirit level, square, tape measure, yardstick

meat *n.* **1.** aliment, comestible, fare, flesh, food, foodstuff, nourishment, ration, sustenance, victual *Nonformal:* eats, grub *Cuts & kinds of meat:* back *or* Canadian *or* peameal bacon, barbecue, beef, beefalo, brains, brisket, burger, butt, calf's head, bacon, chitterlings, chops, cold cuts, corned beef, cottage roll, cutlet, flank, forcemeat, gizzards, goat, ham, hamburger, hash, heart, hot dog, jerky, joint, kid, kidney, lamb, liver, loin chop, lung, marrow, mince, mincemeat, Montreal smoked meat, mountain *or* prairie oysters, mutton, oxtail, pastrami, pemmican *(Historical)*, pig's feet, pork, pork knuckle, rack, red meat, ribs, roast, saddle, salt beef *or* pork, sausage meat, scruncheons *(Atlantic Provinces)*, short ribs, shoulder chop, side *or* slab bacon, spare ribs, steak, *steamé (Quebec)*, sweetbreads, tongue, tournedos, tripe, tube steak *(Nonformal)*, veal **2.** guts, innards *(Nonformal)*, insides, viscera **3.** core, essence, gist, heart, kernel, marrow, matter, meaning, nub, nucleus, pith, point, sense, short *(Nonformal)*, substance, thrust

meaty *adj.* compact, deep, factual, full, interesting, meaningful, pithy, pointed, pregnant, profound, rich, significant, substantial, weighty *Antonyms:* airy-fairy *(Nonformal)*, light, scrawny, slender

mechanic *n.* artisan, engineer, hand labourer, machinist, operative, technician *Nonformal:* grease monkey, sparks, tools

mechanical *adj.* **1.** automated, computerized, machine-driven, programmed, robotic **2.** automatic, fixed, habitual, instinctive, involuntary, knee-jerk *(Nonformal)*, reflex, routine, standard, unconscious, unthinking **3.** austere, cold, dead, impersonal, indifferent, lifeless, perfunctory, spiritless, unfeeling, vapid *Antonym:* emotional, fervid, impassioned **4.** adroit, expert, handy, inventive, proficient, skilled, useful, versatile

mechanics *n. pl.* nuts and bolts, physics *Kinds and branches of mechanics:* abstract, aeromechanics, applied, auto, biomechanics, celestial, electromechanics, fluid, hydrodynamics, hydromechanics, mechanical arts, practical, pure, quantum, servomechanics, wave

mechanism *n.* **1.** apparatus, appliance, components, contrivance, device, gears, instrument, machine, machinery, motor, system, tool, workings, works **2.** agency, means, medium, method, operation, procedure, process, technique, vehicle

medal *n.* badge, chest hardware *(Nonformal)*, commemoration, decoration, gold, honour, laurel, medallion, reward, ribbon, wreath *Canadian medals:* Air Cross, Alberta Order of Excellence, Canadian Volunteer Service, Confederation Diamond Jubilee, Conspicuous Gallantry, Distinguished Flying Cross, Distinguished Service Order, Kebeca Liberata *(Historical)*,

Lieutenant-Governor, Medal of Military Valour, Meritorious Service Cross, National Order of Quebec, Order of British Columbia, Order of Canada, Order of Military Merit, Order of Ontario, Order of Prince Edward Island, Police Exemplary Service, Queen Elizabeth II Silver Jubilee, RCMP Long Service, Royal Red Cross, Royal Society of Canada, Saskatchewan Order of Merit, Star of Military Valour, Tyrrell, Victoria Cross *See also:* **award, decoration**

meddle *v.* barge *or* horn *or* push *or* worm in, encroach, encumber, hinder, impede, impose, infringe, inquire, interfere, interlope, intervene, intrude, invade, irritate, kibitz, monkey with *(Nonformal)*, pry, snoop, tamper, trespass *Antonyms:* disregard, ignore, neglect

meddlesome *adj.* bothersome, busy, curious, hindering, impeding, interfering, interrupting, intrusive, nosy, obstructive, officious, overcurious, prying, pushy, snoopy, tampering, troublesome

media *n.* **1.** journalists, news agency, newspaper, paparazzi, reporters, tabloids, television crew, the fourth estate *Groupings of news media:* broadcast, electronic, new, old, print, webcast *See also:* **medium 2.** attention, coverage, ink *(Nonformal)*, news, press

median *adj.* average, central, centre, equatorial, equidistant, halfway, intermediate, mean, medial, mid, middle, middlemost, midpoint, midway, par *Antonyms:* extreme, marginal – *n.* barrier, curb, divider, division, partition, wall

mediate *v.* appease, arbitrate, conciliate, deal, intercede, interfere, intermediate, interpose, intervene, make peace, moderate, negotiate, propitiate, reconcile, referee, resolve, restore harmony, settle, umpire

mediation *n.* arbitration, conciliation, intercession, interposition, intervention, involvement, negotiation, reconciliation

mediator *n.* advocate, arbiter, arbitrator, broker, conciliator, fixer, go-between, *hakim (Muslim)*, interceder, intermediary, judge, medium, middleperson, moderator, negotiator, ombudsperson, peacemaker, referee

medic *n.* doctor, field doctor *or* nurse *or* surgeon, intern, medico *(Nonformal)*, nurse, physician, surgeon

medical *adj.* corrective, curative, healing, hygienic, Hippocratic, iatric, medicinal, remedial, restorative, sanitary, salutary *Antonyms:* baneful, deleterious, harmful

medicinal *adj.* alleviating, curative, healing, homeopathic, palliative, restorative, therapeutic

medicine *n.* **1.** health care, medical practice, Medicare *(Government) Branches of medicine:* anaesthesiology, anatomy, audiology, cardiology, chiropody, dental surgery, dentistry, dermatology, embryology, endocrinology, etiology, family practice, general medicine, geriatrics, gerontology, gynecology, haematology, hygiene, immunology, internal medicine, midwifery, neurology, neurosurgery, nosology, nutrition, obstetrics, oncology, ophthalmology, optometry, orthopedics, pathology, pediatrics, podiatry, psychiatry, radiology, serology, surgery, symptomatology, toxicology, virology **2.** balm, balsam, drops, drug, elixir, injection, liniment, lotion, medicament, medication, medicinal herb, ointment, over-the-counter *(Nonformal)*, patent, physic, pill, power, salve, skin patch, syrup, tablet, tincture, tisane, treatment

medieval *adj.* ancient, antediluvian, antiquated, antique, archaic, Dark-Age, feudal, Gothic, historical, old, old-fashioned, pre-Renaissance, primitive, unenlightened *Antonyms:* contemporary, current, hip, up-to-date

mediocre *adj.* average, characterless, colourless, common, commonplace, conventional, decent, everyday, fair, humdrum, indifferent, insignificant, medium, middling, moderate, ordinary, passable, pedestrian, standard, tolerable, undistinguished unexceptional, uninspired *Nonformal:* ho hum, run-of-the-mill, so-so *Antonyms:* distinctive, superior, unrivalled, unsurpassed

meditate *v.* brood, cogitate, commune, concentrate, consider, contemplate, deliberate, design, devise, dream, figure, mull *or* puzzle over, muse, plan, ponder, pray, reflect, ruminate, scheme, speculate, study, think, view, weigh, woolgather *Nonformal:* consult the little grey cells, moon

meditation *n.* brawn study *(Nonformal),* cerebration, cogitation, concentration, contemplation, deliberation, musing, pondering, reflection, reverie, rumination, speculation, study, thought

meditative *adj.* cogitative, contemplative, deliberative, pensive, prayerful, quiet, reflective, ruminant, studious, thoughtful

medium *adj.* average, common, commonplace, fair, intermediate, mean, medial, median, mediocre, middle, midway, moderate, neutral, normal, ordinary, par, passable, standard, tolerable *Antonyms:* extraordinary, extreme, uncommon, unusual, utmost – *n.* **1.** centre, mean, medium, middle, mode **2.** ambience, atmosphere, backdrop, climate, environment, layout, milieu, *mise en scène (French),* setting, shoot, surrounding **3.** agency, agent, area, avenue, channel, conduit, factor, intermediary, instrument, mark, means, measure, mechanism, message, token, symbol, way **4.** art, form, materials, media, tool, vehicle *Kinds of artistic mediums:* dance, drama, film, mixed media, music, painting, performance art, photography, sculpture, speech, video art, writing **5.** augur, clairvoyant, crystal ball, diviner, fortuneteller, mind reader, oracle, psychic, soothsayer, telepath

medley *n.* **1.** assortment, brew, collection, combination, conglomeration, hodgepodge, jumble, mélange, miscellany, mishmash, mixed bag, mixture, pastiche, patchwork, potpourri, salmagundi, variety *Nonformal:* combo, grab bag, mixed bag **2.** *capriccio (Italian),* composition, song, tune

meek *adj.* acquiescent, compliant, deferential, gentle, mild, milquetoast *(Nonformal),* modest, passive, quiet, shy, spineless, submissive, timid, unassuming, weak, yielding *Antonyms:* arrogant, bold, bossy, spirited, wilful

meet *adj.* appropriate, apt, fair, fit, fitting, good, just, proper, right, suitable – *n.* athletic event, bonspiel, competition, conflict, contest, event, heat, match, playdown, playoff, regatta, tournament, tourney – *v.* **1.** approach, bump into, cross, find, greet, happen on, rendezvous with, run across, salute *Antonyms:* avoid, miss, shirk **2.** beard, encounter, engage, experience, face, suffer, undergo **3.** accost, affront, brush against, clash, collide, confront, contact, fight, grapple, hit, joust, light, oppose, ram, run into, strike, tussle, wrestle *Antonyms:* elude, escape, evade **4.** answer, comply, cope *or* deal with, discharge, execute, fulfill, handle, match, measure up, perform, satisfy, suffice **5.** appear, assemble, collect, come *or* get together, congregate, convene, flock, gather, join, rally, rendezvous, sit *Antonyms:* adjourn, disperse, scatter **6.** abut, adhere, adjoin, border, coincide, connect, converge, cross, intersect, join, link up, reach, touch, unite

meeting *n.* **1.** assembly, conference, gathering, get together, huddle, powwow, rally, rendezvous, sit-down, synod *Nonformal:* confab, kitchen party, one on one, Pugwash **2.** agreement, confluence, conjunction, connection, contact, convergence, intersection, joining, union

melancholy *adj.* **1.** atrabilious, blue, crestfallen, dejected, depressed, despondent, destroyed, disconsolate, dispirited, doleful, down, downcast, downhearted, droopy, funereal, glum, grim, heavy-hearted, joyless, killjoy *(Nonformal),* lachrymose, low, low-spirited, lugubrious, mirthless, moody, mournful, pensive, sorrowful, sorry, unhappy, wistful, woebegone *Antonyms:* blithe, cheerful, glad, merry **2.** depressing, dismal, dreary, gloomy, grey, miserable, overcast, rainy, woeful *Nonformal:* crummy, dirty, lousy *Antonyms:* glorious, pleasant, sunny – *n.* blues, dejection, depression, despair, despondency, doldrums, dolour, ennui, gloominess, grief, low spirits, miserableness, misery, mournfulness, neurasthenia, pensiveness, pessimism, sadness, sorrow, tedium, unhappiness, *Weltschmerz (German),* wistfulness, woe, wretchedness *Nonformal:* blahs, blue funk, downer, dumps, funk *Antonyms:* delight, gladness, happiness, joy, pleasure

mélange *n.* assortment, combination, gallimaufry, hodgepodge, jumble, medley, miscellany, mix, mixture, olla-podrida, patchwork, potpourri, salad, salmagundi, soup, stew *Nonformal:* combo, mixed bag

meld *v.* amalgamate, associate, blend, bring together, combine, compound, fold, fuse, interfuse, intermingle, join, marry, merge, mingle, mix, stir, unite *Antonyms:* disconnect, separate, sever

mêlée *n.* affray, battle, brannigan, brawl, broil, brush, clash, commotion, donnybrook, fight, fracas, fray, quarrel, riot, row, scrimmage, scuffle, skirmish, tussle *Nonformal:* battle royale, bench-clearing brawl, free-for-all, knock-down-drag-out, ruckus, rumpus, set-to, slugfest

mellifluous *adj.* dulcet, elegant, euphonic, flowing, honeyed, liquid, melodic, pleasant, schmaltzy *(Nonformal)*, silvery, smooth, soft, sonorous, soothing, sweet-sounding *Antonyms:* discordant, harsh, pounding, shrill

mellow *adj.* **1.** adult-oriented, easy-listening, gentle, light, mild, smooth, soft, West Coast *(Jazz) Antonyms:* abrasive, aggressive, loud, noisy **2.** at peace, calm, content, easy, placid, relaxed, slack, tranquil *Nonformal:* cool, laid-back *Antonyms:* agitated, anxious, hyper **3.** aged, full, full-flavoured, juicy, mature, rich, ripe, seasoned, sweet, tempered *Antonyms:* immature, young – *v.* **1.** age, ameliorate, develop, grow, grow up, improve, mature, perfect, ripen, season, settle down, soften, sweeten **2.** calm oneself, cool down, meditate, mollify, relax, subside *Nonformal:* chill, take a breather *or* pill *Antonyms:* rage, rant

melodious *adj.* **1.** accordant, agreeable, appealing, assonant, concordant, dulcet, euphonious, harmonious, in tune, lilting, lyrical, mellifluous, mellow, pleasant-sounding, resonant, silvery, smooth, soft, songful, soothing, sweet, sweet-sounding, well-tuned *Antonyms:* cacophonous, grating, noisy **2.** harmonic, melodic, musical, orchestral, symphonious, tuneful

melodramatic *adj.* artificial, bathetic, cliff-hanging, cloak-and-dagger, extravagant, histrionic, maudlin, operatic, overwrought, sensational, sentimental, spectacular, stagey, theatrical *Nonformal:* ham, hokey *Antonyms:* subdued, subtle, understated

melody *n.* **1.** harmony, inflection, musicality, resonance, timbre, tonality, tone, tunefulness **2.** air, aria, carillon, chant, chime, descant, ditty *(Nonformal)*, euphony, measure, refrain, song, strain, theme, tune

melt *v.* **1.** blend, dissipate, dissolve, flux, fuse, heat, liquefy, merge, thaw, warm *Antonyms:* congeal, freeze, harden, solidify **2.** disappear, evanesce, evaporate, exit, fade, vanish, wane *Antonyms:* appear, loom, rue **3.** alleviate, appease, disarm, forgive, give in, mitigate, mollify, relax, relent, show mercy, soften, touch, yield

member *n.* **1.** adherent, affiliate, associate, brother, cohort, comrade, fellow, joiner, registrant, representative, sister, subscriber **2.** appendage, arm, digit, extremity, leg, limb, off shoot **3.** component, constituent, element, feature, fragment, part, piece, portion, segment *Antonyms:* composite, totality, whole

membership *n.* **1.** acceptance, admittance, allegiance, belonging, inclusion, incorporation, induction, welcome **2.** associates, association, body, branch, brotherhood, chapter, club, collective, community, company, division, enrollment, grassroots, fellows, fellowship, group, organization, parish, participation, rank and file, section, sisterhood, society, unit

membrane *n.* coating, cover, epidermis, exoskeleton, film, lamina, layer, leaf, sheath, sheet, skin, surface, tissue, veneer

memento *n.* favour, keepsake, memorabilia, memorial, relic, remembrance, reminder, souvenir, token, trace, vestige

memoir *n.* account, annals, autobiography, biography, chronicle, confession, diary, dissertation, experience, history, journal, letters, monograph, notes, recollections, record, reflection, register, reminiscence, report

memorable *adj.* celebrated, critical, crucial, distinguished, enduring, eventful, extraordinary, famous, historic, illustrious, important, impressive, indelible, lasting, meaningful, momentous, notable, noteworthy, red-letter *(Nonformal)*, remarkable, signal, significant, striking, unforgettable *Antonyms:* commonplace, forgettable, insignificant, ordinary, trivial

memorandum *n.* account, *aide-mémoire (French)*, brief, directive, letter, memo, message, minute, missive, notation, note, record, reminder, statement, summary

memorial *adj.* canonizing, celebrative, commemorative, consecrating, dedicatory, in tribute, remembering – *n.* **1.** cairn, cenotaph, column, cross, gravestone, headstone, inscription, keepsake, mausoleum, memento, monolith, monument, obelisk, obituary, pillar, plaque, record, relic, remembrance, reminder, slab, souvenir, statue, tablet, testimonial, token, tombstone, trophy **2.** celebration, ceremony, mass, observance, rite, sendoff, service, solemnity, wake

memory *n.* **1.** awareness, consciousness, flashback, mind, mind's eye, recall, recollection, reflection, reminiscence, retentiveness, retrospection, samskara, *(Sanskrit)*, subconsciousness, thought *Antonyms:* forgetfulness, oblivion **2.** commemoration, memento, memorial, recognition, remembrance **3.** fame, glory, honour, name, note, renown, reputation, stature **4.** memory bank, RAM, ROM, storage medium *or* space

menace *n.* **1.** caution, danger, hazard, jeopardy, peril, plague, risk, scare, threat, trouble, warning **2.** annoyance, bother, irritation, nuisance, pest, terror *(Nonformal)*, troublemaker – *v.* alarm, bother, bully, endanger, frighten, hazard, imperil, intimidate, jeopardize, portend, risk, scare, terrorize, threaten, torment *Nonformal:* hassle, spook

menacing *adj.* **1.** alarming, dangerous, frightening, hazardous, intimidating, perilous, risky, unsafe *Antonyms:* auspicious, encouraging, promising **2.** imminent, impending, looming, ominous, overhanging, threatening, warning

mend *v.* **1.** aid, correct, darn, fix, overhaul, patch, ready, rebuild, recondition, reconstruct, redress, refit, refurbish, reinforce, remedy, renew, remodel, renovate, repair, retouch, revamp, revise, right, service, sew, stitch *Antonyms:* break, demolish, destroy, rip, tear **2.** adjust, ameliorate, better, civilize, cultivate, edify, emend, improve, increase, make over, rectify, reform, rehabilitate, socialize, uplift **3.** cure, heal, recover, recuperate, rejuvenate, restore, strengthen

mendacious *adj.* deceitful, deceptive, dishonest, duplicitous, equivocating, erroneous, false, fibbing, fraudulent, insincere, lying, prevaricating, shifty, sophistic, spurious, untrue *Antonyms:* genuine, honest, true, truthful

mendicant *adj.* begging, petitionary, scavenging, scrounging, supplicant – *n.* beachcomber, beggar, fakir, friar, hobo, panhandler, ragpicker, sannyasi, supplicant, tramp *Nonformal:* bum, mooch, sponge

menial *adj.* **1.** abject, fawning, grovelling, humble, obeisant, obsequious, servile, slavish, subservient, sycophantic *Antonyms:* bossy, domineering, noble **2.** base, common, degrading, demeaning, ignoble, ignominious, low, lowly, mean, sorry *Antonyms:* elevated, important, meaningful **3.** boring, day-to-day, drab, dull, nine-to-five *(Nonformal)*, repetitive, routine – *n.* assistant, attendant, butler, chauffeur, domestic, helper, hireling, houseboy, housekeeper, janitor, labourer, maid, nanny, scullion, servant, tweeny *(Nonformal)*, valet

menstruation *n.* catamenia, menses, menstrual discharge *or* flow *or* flux, monthlies, period *Nonformal:* a visitor, the curse, that time of month

mental *adj.* **1.** brainy, cerebral, cognitive, deep *(Nonformal)*, ideological, imaginative, inner, intellectual, philosophical, psychological, rational, reasoning, subconscious, subjective, subliminal, thoughtful *Antonyms:* corporeal, physical **2.** crazy, disordered, ill, *non compos mentis (Latin)*, psychotic, sick, unbalanced, unhinged, unsound, unstable *Nonformal:* bananas, batty, buggy, loco, loony, nuts, screwy, wacky

mentality *n.* **1.** brains, capacity, cognitive skill, comprehension, faculty, intellect, know-how, mental prowess, powers, rationality, reasoning, sense, smarts *(Nonformal)*, understanding **2.** attitude, cast, character, disposition, make-up, mind, mind-set, outlook

mentally *adv.* **1.** emotionally, intellectually, inwardly, psychologically, rationally, subjectively, temperamentally **2.** abstractly, allegorically, figuratively, metaphorically, metaphysically, symbolically

mention *n.* acknowledgment, allusion, citation, credit, indication, naming, notification, quotation, recognition, reference, referral, remark, thank you, tribute – *v.* **1.** bring up, broach, disclose, discuss, divulge, hint at, impart, intimate, remark, reveal, state, suggest, tell, touch on **2.** acknowledge, allude *or* refer to, cite, reference, thank **3.** advertise, broadcast, call attention to, inform, make known, market, notify, promote, publicize, report, throw out *(Nonformal)*

mentor *n.* advisor, coach, counsellor, educator, guide, guru, instructor, master, pedagogue, preceptor, priest, rabbi, sage, sensei, spiritual leader, teacher, trainer, tutor

menu *n.* **1.** bill of fare, board, *carte (French)*, cuisine, food, list, table, table d'hôte **2.** list of commands, options, palette, table, taskbar, title bar, toolbar

mercantile *adj.* businesslike, commercial, industrial, marketable, merchant, retail, service, trade, wholesale

mercenary *adj.* **1.** acquisitive, avaricious, covetous, grabby, grasping, greedy, miserly, money-grubbing, self-serving *Antonyms:* altruistic, benevolent, charitable, generous **2.** bribable, corrupt, unethical, unprincipled, unscrupulous, venal *Antonyms:* ethical, honest, just – *n.* adventurer, assassin, bravo, condottiere, cutthroat, fighter, gun for hire, gunslinger, hired gun, hireling, hoodlum, killer, ninja, professional soldier, samurai, soldier of fortune, thug, warrior *Nonformal:* bill collector, goon, hitman

merchandise *n.* articles, cargo, chattels, commodities, consumer goods *or* items, dry goods, durables, effects, food stuffs, gear, goods, inventory, items, line of goods, list, produce, property, stock, stock-in-trade, sundries, things, truck, wares – *v.* advertise, deal *or* traffic in, distribute, market, promote, publicize, retail, sell, trade, vend

merchant *n.* dealer, distributor, exporter, entrepreneur, fish merchant *(Newfoundland)*, franchiser, huckster, importer, jobber, marketer, merchandiser, middleman, monger, peddler, retailer, shopkeeper, storekeeper, trader, tradesman, tradeswoman, trafficker, wholesaler

merciful *adj.* all heart, beneficent, benign, caring, charitable, clement, compassionate, feeling, forbearing, forgiving, generous, gentle, gracious, humane, humanitarian, indulgent, kind, kindly, lenient, liberal, loving, mild, pardoning, pitying, soft-hearted, sparing, sympathetic, tender-hearted, tolerant *Antonyms:* cruel, inhumane, merciless, unfeeling

merciless *adj.* barbarous, callous, cold-blooded, cruel, cutthroat, fierce, flinty, grim, hard, hardhearted, harsh, heartless, implacable, inexorable, inhumane, iron-fisted, mean, pitiless, relentless, remorseless, ruthless, severe, unappeasable, unfeeling, unflinching, unforgiving, unrelenting, unsparing, unsympathetic, unyielding *Antonyms:* kind, merciful, sympathetic

mercurial *adj.* **1.** active, brisk, clever, dashing, fast, jaunty, lively, quick, spirited, zesty *Antonyms:* inactive, lackadaisical, slow **2.** capricious, changeable, ephemeral, fickle inconstant, mutable, protean, quicksilver unpredictable, unstable, volatile *Antonyms:* fixed, static, steadfast

mercy *n.* benevolence, blessing, charity clemency, commiseration, compassion favour, forbearance, forgiveness, generosity, gentleness, goodwill, grace, humanity indulgence, kindness, lenience, mildness quarter, sympathy, tolerance *Antonyms* brutality, cruelty, severity

mere *adj.* bald, bare, insignificant, little minimal, minor, nothing but, only, plain poor, pure, sheer, simple, small, stark unadorned, unadulterated, unmitigated, unmixed, utter, very

meretricious *adj.* blatant, bogus, brazen, counterfeit, flashy, garish, gaudy, glaring, insincere, insipid, loud, misleading, ornate, plastic, put-on, sham, showy, spurious, superficial, tawdry, tinsel, trashy *Nonformal:* chintzy, phoney *Antonyms:* modest, plain, simple *Commonly misused:* **meritorious**

merge *v.* absorb, amalgamate, annex, assimilate, blend, cement, coalesce, combine, compound, concatenate, conglomerate, consolidate, converge, fuse, hitch *or* hook up, incorporate, intermingle, join, marry, meld, mingle, mix, plug into, slap *or* tack on, synthesize, tie in, unite *Antonyms:* detach, diverge, divide, part, sever

merger *n.* absorption, alliance, amalgamation, buyout, coalition, combination, confederation, conflation, consolidation, federation, fusion, incorporation, marriage, organization, takeover, tie-in, unification, union *Antonyms:* dissolution, disunion, severance

merit *n.* advantage, asset, benefit, calibre, credit, dignity, excellence, goodness, honour, integrity, perfection, quality, talent, value, virtue, worth, worthiness *Antonyms:* fault, uselessness, worthlessness – *v.* deserve, earn, have coming, incur, justify, rate, receive, recognize, warrant

merited *adj.* appropriate, deserved, due, earned, entitled, fitting, justified, rightful, warranted

meritorious *adj.* admirable, boss *(Nonformal)*, choice, commendable, creditable, deserving, estimable, excellent, exemplary, golden, good, honourable, laudable, meritable, noble, praiseworthy, right, righteous, virtuous, worthy *Antonyms:* dishonourable, ignoble, undeserving, unexceptional *Commonly misused:* **meretricious**

merriment *n.* amusement, buffoonery, cheerfulness, conviviality, enjoyment, festivity, frolic, fun, gaiety, glee, happiness, hijinks, hilarity, indulgence, jocularity, joviality, joy, laughter, levity, liveliness, merrymaking, mirth, recreation, revelry, sport, tomfoolery *Nonformal:* hoopla, laughs *Antonyms:* sadness, seriousness, unhappiness

merry *adj.* amusing, blithe, carefree, cheerful, comical, enjoyable, entertaining, festive, frolicsome, fun-loving, funny, gay, glad, gleeful, happy, hilarious, humorous, jocund, jolly, joyous, jumping-good *(Nonformal)*, larking, lighthearted, lively, mad, mirthful, pleasant, riotous, rocking, rollicking, sportive, sunny, unconstrained, uproarious, vivacious, wild *Antonyms:* dejected, dismal, gloomy, miserable, unhappy

mesh *n.* **1.** cobweb, net, netting, network, plexus, reticulation, skein, toils, tracery, web, weir **2.** entanglement, knot, labyrinth, maze, snare, snarl, tangle, trap – *v.* **1.** catch, enmesh, entangle, net, snare, trap **2.** combine, come together, connect, dovetail, engage, harmonize, interface, interlock, knit, meld, merge, synchronize

mesmerize *v.* captivate, charm, control, drug, enthral, entrance, fascinate, grip, hypnotize, magnetize, numb, spellbind, stupefy

mess *n.* **1.** chaos, clutter, confusion, dirtiness, disarray, disorder, disorganization, litter, mayhem, monstrosity *(Nonformal)*, pigpen, shambles, sight, turmoil, untidiness, wreck, wreckage *Antonyms:* order, sequence, tidiness **2.** botch, difficulty, dilemma, imbroglio, mix-up, muddle, plight, predicament *Nonformal:* fix, hash, jam, kettle of fish, pickle, snafu **3.** blend, collection, combination, hodgepodge, jumble, mishmash, mixture, stew **4.** food, meal, repast, sitting – *v.* **1.** botch, bungle, destroy, disturb, interfere, meddle, muddle, ruin, spoil, wreck *Nonformal:* screw up, upset the apple cart **2.** befoul, clutter, dirty, disorganize, litter, pollute, tarnish

message *n.* **1.** announcement, bulletin, communication, communiqué, cord, directive, dispatch, e-mail, epistle, flag, flare, information, intimation, letter, memo, memorandum, missive, news, note, notice, paper, report, signal, s.o.s., telegram, tidings, transmission, voicemail, warning, word **2.** drift, gist, idea, import, importance, meaning, point, purport, sense, significance, tenor, theme

messenger *n.* agent, ambassador, carrier, courier, dispatch, emissary, envoy, harbinger, herald, letter carrier, medium, nuncio, postman, postwoman, rider, runner

messy *adj.* **1.** bedraggled, botched, chaotic, cluttered, decrepit, dingy, dirty, dishevelled, disorderly, dowdy, frumpy, grimy, grubby, littered, mangy, muddled, muddy, ragged, raunchy, rough, rumpled, rundown, seedy, shabby, shoddy, sleazy, sloppy, squalid, tacky, tattered, unkempt, untidy *Nonformal:* grungy, scuzzy *Antonyms:* clean, kempt, tidy, well-kept **2.** awkward, careless, clumsy, confused, heedless, inattentive, lazy, negligent, slack, slapdash, slipshod, slovenly **3.** acrimonious, bitter, heated, turbulent, ugly, vicious

metal *n.* **1.** metallic element, mineral, ore *Common metals:* aluminum, antimony, arsenic, barium, beryllium, bismuth, cadmium, calcium, cerium, chromium, cobalt, copper, gold, iridium, iron, lead, lithium, magnesium, manganese, mercury, molybdenum, nickel, osmium, palladium, phosphorus, platinum, potassium, radium, rhenium, silver, sodium, strontium, thorium, tin, titanium, tungsten, uranium, vanadium, zinc **2.** constituency, core, essence, kernel, marrow, nature, soul, substance

metamorphosis *n.* alteration, change, changeover, conversion, evolution, mutation, rebirth, transformation, transmogrification, transmutation

metaphor *n.* allegory, analogy, comparison, figure of speech, image, parable, simile, similitude, symbol, symbolism

metaphorical *adj.* allegorical, emblematic, figurative, indicative, parabolic, paradoxical, symbolic

metaphysical *adj.* **1.** abstract, bodiless, cosmological, epistemological, eternal, ideal, immaterial, impalpable, incorporeal, insubstantial, intangible, mystical, nonphysical, preternatural, spiritual, superhuman, supermundane, supernatural, theoretical, transcendental, unearthly, unreal *Antonyms:* concrete, earthly, physical, real **2.** abstruse, bewildering, complex, deep, difficult, esoteric, hard, incomprehensible

mete *v.* allot, apportion, dish *or* dole *or* hand *or* parcel out, dispense, disseminate, distribute, ration, share

meteor *n.* aerolite, bollide, chondrite, comet, falling star, fiery streak, fireball, meteorite, meteoroid, shooting star, siderolite, tektite *See also:* **comet**

meteoric *adj.* brilliant, dazzling, ephemeral, evanescent, explosive, fleeting, momentary, passing, quick, short-lived, swift, transient *Antonyms:* classic, eternal, timeless

meter *n.* **1.** beat, cadence, cadency, feet, lilt, music, pattern, poetry, rhythm, structure, swing, time **2.** evaluator, gauge, indicator, instrument, measure, rule, scale – *v.* assess, estimate, evaluate, gauge, measure, quantify, test, value, weigh

method *n.* approach, arrangement, channel, classification, course, custom, design, discipline, fashion, form, formula, habit, manner, means, mode, *modus operandi (Latin)*, operating plan, order, organization, pattern, plan, practice, procedure, process, protocol, recipe, ritual, routine, rule, schema, scheme, structure, style, system, technique, way

methodical *adj.* analytical, calculating, careful, deliberate, disciplined, efficient, exact, fixed, logical, methodized, meticulous, neat, ordered, orderly, organized, planned, precise, regular, structured, systematic, thought out, well-regulated *Antonyms:* casual, chaotic, disorderly, improvised, irregular

meticulous *adj.* accurate, cautious, conscientious, detailed, exact, fastidious, fussy, microscopic (*Nonformal*), nitpicking painstaking, particular, pettifogging, precise, punctilious, scrupulous, strict, thorough *Antonyms:* careless, haphazard imprecise, inexact, negligent

métier *n.* avocation, bag *(Nonformal)*, business, calling, craft, employment, forte, job line, occupation, profession, pursuit, specialty, trade, vocation, work

metropolis *n.* capital, city, downtown greater metropolitan area, megacity, mothe city *(Historical)*, urban centre *Nonformal:* big smoke, concrete jungle, mean streets

ettle *n.* bravery, character, constitution, courage, daring, dauntlessness, pluck, rigour, spirit, spunk, strength, verve, vigour, vivacity *Nonformal:* cajones, chutzpah, guts, moxie, starch

iasma *n.* effluvium, emanation, gas, cloud, mephitis, reek, smell, smog, steam, stink, swamp gas, vapour

iasmal *adj.* bilious, deleterious, fetid, foul, malodorous, mephitic, noxious, pestilent, polluted, putrid, reeking, sickly, stinking, toxic

icrobe *n.* bacillus, bacteria, bacterium, coccus, germ, microorganism, pathogen, spore, virus

icroscopic *adj.* diminutive, imperceptible, infinitesimal, invisible, little, minuscule, minute, negligible, tiny, undetectable *Antonyms:* enormous, gigantic, huge, immense, macroscopic

iddle *adj.* **1.** between, central, centre, centremost, equidistant, halfway, inner, inside, intermediate, mean, medial, median, medium, mesne, *mezzo (Italian)*, mid, midmost **2.** average, mainstream, moderate, modest, ordinary, unassuming, unpretentious *Nonformal:* just right, middle-of-the-road – *n.* **1.** centre, core, deep, focus, halfway, halfway point, heart, inside, mean, media, midpoint, midst *Antonyms:* border, edge, margin, periphery **2.** belly, diaphragm, gut *(Nonformal)*, midriff, midsection, paunch, stomach, waist

iddle-class *adj.* bourgeois, common, conventional, everyday, main street, middling, suburban, white-collar *Antonyms:* aristocratic, proletarian, upper-class, working-class, working poor

iddleman *n.* agent, broker, connection, distributor, emissary, fixer, go-between, intercessor, intermediary, intermediate, intermediator, liaison, matchmaker, mediator, middlewoman, negotiator, representative, retailer, salesperson, *schadchen (Yiddish)*, wholesaler

middling *adj.* adequate, average, central, common, conventional, enough, fair, good, indifferent, intermediate, mediocre, medium, moderate, modest, ordinary, passable, respectable, tolerable, undistinguished, unexceptional, unremarkable *Nonformal:* all right, not bad, okay, run-of-the-mill, so-so *Antonyms:* exceptional, extraordinary, great – *adv.* fairly, moderately, passably, rather, somewhat, tolerably

midget *adj.* baby, bantam, diminutive, dwarfish, junior, knee-high, Lilliputian, miniature, pint-sized, pocket, pygmy, short, small, teeny, tiny *Antonyms:* elephantine, enormous, gigantic, monstrous

midst *n.* bosom, centre, core, deep, depths, epicentre, eye, halfway, heart, hub, interior, mean, medium, middle, midpoint, nucleus

mien *n.* act, affectation, air, appearance, aspect, aura, bearing, behaviour, carriage, countenance, demeanour, deportment, expression, front, guise, image, look, manner, mannerism, port, pose, presence, set, style

miffed *adj.* aggrieved, annoyed, bewildered, bothered, displeased, hurt, irked, irritated, nettled, offended, pestered, piqued, provoked, resentful, upset, vexed *Nonformal:* hassled, pissed, put out *Antonyms:* appeased, calmed, mollified, pacified, soothed

might *n.* ability, adequacy, authority, capability, capacity, clout, command, competence, control, dominance, efficacy, energy, force, forcibleness, influence, mastery, muscle, potency, power, powerfulness, prowess, punch, sinew, steam, strength, strenuousness, strings *(Nonformal)*, sway, tenacity, valour, vigorousness, vigour *Antonyms:* feebleness, timidity, weakness

mightily *adv.* **1.** decidedly, exceedingly, extremely, greatly, highly, hugely, intensely, much, notably, surpassingly, very much **2.** arduously, energetically, forcefully, forcibly, hardy, laboriously, lustily, manfully, powerfully, strenuously, strongly, vigorously

mighty *adj.* **1.** doughty, forceful, hardy, indomitable, lusty, muscular, omnipotent,

potent, powerful, puissant, robust, stalwart, stout, strapping, strong, sturdy, vigorous, wieldy *Antonyms:* feeble, impotent, weak **2.** bulky, colossal, considerable, dynamic, enormous, extensive, gargantuan, gigantic, huge, immense, impressive, large, massive, monstrous, monumental, prodigious, titanic, towering, tremendous, vast *Antonyms:* minute, small, tiny **3.** august, eminent, extraordinary, fabulous, fantastic, grand, great, heroic, illustrious, imposing, irresistible, magnificent, majestic, notable, renowned, stupendous, wonderful *Antonyms:* boring, tedious, tiresome

migrant *adj.* casual, changing, drifting, emigrating, immigrant, impermanent, itinerant, migratory, mobile, moving, nomadic, peripatetic, ranging, roving, seasonal, shifting, temporary, transient, travelling, unsettled, vagrant, wandering *Antonyms:* homebound, stationary – *n.* drifter, emigrant, émigré, evacuee, expatriate, *flâneur (French)*, foreigner, gypsy, immigrant, itinerant, mover, nomad, rover, tinker, transient, traveller, vagrant, wanderer *Antonyms:* homesteader, local, native

migrate *v.* drift, emigrate, immigrate, journey, move, range, roam, rove, scull *(Newfoundland)*, shift, travel, trek, voyage, wander

mild *adj.* **1.** balmy, calm, choice, clear, clement, halcyon, moderate, pacific, peaceful, placid, pleasant, sunny, temperate, warm *Antonyms:* cold, dirty *(Newfoundland)*, frigid, frosty, northern **2.** amiable, benign, compassionate, complaisant, deferential, docile, easy, equable, forbearing, forgiving, gentle, good-humoured, good-natured, good-tempered, humane, indulgent, kind, lenient, mellow, merciful, mild-mannered, obliging, patient, peaceable, serene, subdued, tame, tender, tranquil, unassuming *Antonyms:* belligerent, rancorous, spiteful, volcanic **3.** benign, bland, dainty, delicate, emollient, faint, fine, genial, lenitive, mollifying, non-irritating, smooth, soft, soothing *Antonyms:* caustic, corrosive, harsh, severe **4.** cool, flat, light, limited, lukewarm, tempered, tepid, weak *Antonyms:* enthusiastic, fervid, impassioned

milestone *n.* **1.** accomplishment, achievement, breakthrough, classic, climax, highlight, monument **2.** cairn, gauge, inukshuk, key, landmark, marker, milepost, pillar, post, touchstone, yardstick

milieu *n.* area, arena, beat, district, environment, habitat, locale, *mise en scène (French)*, neighbourhood, precinct, region, scene, set, surroundings, sphere, stage, vicinity *Nonformal:* hood, stomping grounds, turf

militant *adj.* **1.** aggressive, bellicose, belligerent, combative, contentious, fighting, hawkish, militaristic, offensive, pushy, quarrelsome, truculent, warlike *Antonyms:* pacifistic, passive, peaceful **2.** active, assertive, forceful, positive, resolute, self-assertive – *n.* activist, belligerent, combatant, demonstrator, fighter, firebrand, objector, partisan, protester, warrior *Antonyms:* pacifist, peacemaker, peacenik *(Nonformal)*

militarize *v.* activate, assemble, call to arms, conscript, draft, enlist, equip, marshal, mobilize, muster, prepare, rally, train

military *adj.* armed, combatant, fighting, martial, service, soldierly, warlike – *n.* air force, armed forces, army, marines, militia, navy, reserves, servicemen, servicewomen, soldiery, troops *Canadian military rankings in order:* General, Lieutenant-General, Major-General, Brigadier, Colonel, Lieutenant-Colonel, Major, Captain, Lieutenant, Second Lieutenant, Officer Cadet, Chief Warrant Officer, Master Warrant Officer, Sergeant, Mast Corporal, Corporal, Private

milk *n.* cow juice *(Nonformal)*, dairy product, fluid, food, nourishment, secretion, sustenance *Kinds of milk:* beestings, bonnyclabber, buttermilk, colostrum, condensed, cow's, cream, dry, eggnog, evaporated, goat's, homogenized, lowfat, mother's, nonfat, 1%, pasteurized, raw, skim, 2%, unpasteurized, whole – *v.* **1.** bleed, drain, draw out, extract, pump, sap, siphon, tap **2.** abuse, blackmail, dupe, exploit, misuse *Nonformal:* con, shakedown, squeeze

milky *adj.* **1.** cloudy, frosted, milk-white, opalescent, opaque, pasty, pearly, white whitish **2.** bland, dull, flavourless, mild, plain, spiritless, tempered *Antonyms:* bitter, exciting, intense, sharp, spicy

mill *n.* **1.** building, factory, foundry, manufactory, plant, sawmill, shop, windmill, works **2.** crusher, grinder, quern, roller **3.** boxing bout *or* contest, fist fight, fisticuffs, prizefight, slugfest, sparring – *v.* **1.** comminute, crush, granulate, grate, grind, pound, powder, pulp, pulverize, roll, shape, triturate **2.** meander, mosey *(Nonformal)*, move, shuffle, straggle, wander

millstone *n.* albatross, affliction, baggage *(Nonformal)*, bane, burden, cross, curse, duty, load, obligation, oppression, responsibility, weight

mimic *n.* actor, caricaturist, chameleon, clown, comedian, copycat, imitator, impersonator, impressionist, mime, mummer, parodist, performer, player, Thespian, trouper, wag – *v.* act, ape, burlesque, caricature, copy, enact, fake, imitate, impersonate, make-believe, mime, mock, pantomime, parody, parrot, perform, play, ridicule, sham, simulate, take off

mince *v.* **1.** chop, cut up, dice, divide, hash, separate, slice **2.** diminish, euphemize, lessen, minimize, moderate, soften, spare, temper, tone down, weaken **3.** flounce, pose, posture, prance, sashay *(Nonformal)*, strut

mincing *adj.* affected, coxcombic, dandified, delicate, foppish, mannered, niminy-piminy, *précieuse (French)*, precious, studied

mind *n.* **1.** brain, brains, capacity, cognizance, consciousness, faculty, head, imagination, instinct, intellect, intelligence, intuition, observation, perception, psyche, reasoning, sense, soundness, spirit, thought, understanding **2.** genius, intellectual, master, philosopher, rocket scientist *(Nonformal)*, talent, thinker, wit **3.** memory, recall, recollection, remembrance, retention, storage space **4.** attitude, belief, bent, conviction, desire, disposition, fancy, feeling, impulse, inclination, intention, leaning, liking, notion, opinion, outlook, sentiment, temper, temperament, tendency, wish **5.** judgment, lucidity, mentality, rationality, reason, sanity, soundness, wits **6.** attention, awareness, care, concentration, consideration, mindfulness, observation, regard *Antonyms:* heedlessness, neglect – *v.* **1.** adhere to, attend, behave, comply, follow, heed, honour, listen, obey, observe, regard, respect, watch **2.** babysit, care for, govern, guard, look after, mark, notice, nurse, oversee, see, sit, superintend, supervise, take care, tend, watch out for *or* over **3.** bethink, cite, perceive, recall, recollect, remember, remind, reminisce, retain, retrospect, revive

mindful *adj.* **1.** alert, alive to, apprehensive, attentive, aware, careful, cautious, cognizant, conscious, heedful, leery, observant, observing, prudent, regardful, sensible, sharp, vigilant, wary, watchful, wide awake *Antonyms:* heedless, inattentive, oblivious, unaware **2.** compliant, conscientious, dutiful, knowing, respectful, thoughtful

mindless *adj.* **1.** addlepated *(Nonformal)*, asinine, cuckoo, fatuous, foolish, idiotic, imbecilic, moronic, nonsensical, rattlebrained, senseless, silly, simple, stupid, thoughtless, witless *Antonyms:* attentive, aware, rational, sagacious, sane **2.** careless, daydreaming, distracted, *distrait (French)*, heedless, inattentive, miles away, neglectful, negligent, oblivious, rash, unaware, unmindful, woolgathering *Nonformal:* out, out to lunch

mine *n.* **1.** colliery, deposit, excavation, lode, moose pasture *(Nonformal)*, pit, quarry, shaft, trench **2.** abundance, bonanza, fount, fountain, fund, hoard, plethora, reserve, source, spring, stock, store, supply, treasury, wealth, well, wellspring **3.** antipersonnel device, bomb, depth charge, explosive, landmine – *v.* burrow, delve, dig, drill, excavate, exploit, extract, hew, pan, play out *(Nonformal)*, quarry, scoop, shovel, unearth

mineral *n.* chemical, compound, element, inorganic matter *or* material, ore, raw material, resource *Antonyms:* animal, vegetable

mingle *v.* **1.** alloy, blend, coalesce, commingle, compound, consolidate, intermingle, intermix, interweave, join, marry, meld, merge, mix, pool, unite *Antonyms:* avoid, detach, divide, part **2.** associate, circulate, consort, fraternize, hobnob, network, pool, rub shoulders, socialize, tie in *Nonformal:* hang out, interface, keep in the loop, work the room

miniature *adj.* baby, diminutive, dwarf, Lilliputian, mini *(Nonformal)*, minute, pint-sized, reduced, scaled-down, small, small-scale, tiny, toy, wee *Antonyms:* big, enlarged, enormous – *n.* model, painting, portrait, portrayal, replica, representation

minimal *adj.* insignificant, little, minimum, minuscule, minute, nominal, perfunctory, short, slight, skimpy, tiny, token

minimize *v.* **1.** abbreviate, attenuate, condense, curtail, cut, decrease, depreciate, diminish, discount, downplay, lessen, prune, put down, reduce, shrink *Antonyms:* enlarge, expand, increase, magnify, maximize **2.** belittle, detract, downgrade, marginalize, slight, underestimate, underrate *Antonyms:* elevate, exalt, praise

minimum *adj.* least, least possible, littlest, lowest, merest, minimal, narrowest, shortest, slightest, slimmest, smallest, tiniest *Antonyms:* greatest, highest, largest, maximum, most – *n.* **1.** atom, dab, dot, gleam, grain, hair, iota, jot, modicum, molecule, mote, particle, pittance, scintilla, smidgen, soupçon, spark, speck, trace, trifle, whit **2.** base, bottom, depth, nadir

minion *n.* agent, assistant, backscratcher, flunky, henchman, kowtower, lackey, pet, shave, slave, sycophant, toady, underling *Nonformal:* bootlicker, brownnose, goon, stooge, tool

minister *n.* **1.** administrator, ambassador, cabinet member, *chargé d'affaires (French)*, consul, diplomat, legate, official, plenipotentiary, political leader, premier, prime minister, provost, statesman, vizier **2.** abbot, archbishop, archdeacon, bishop, canon, chaplain, churchman, churchwoman, clergyman, clergywoman, cleric, clerical, confessor, curate, *curé (French)*, deacon, dean, father, missionary, monk, padre, *papas (Greek)*, parson, pastor, preacher, prelate, priest, rabbi, rector, reverend, servant of God, *Tzaddik (Judaism)*, vicar **3.** agent, aide, delegate, deputy, emissary, liaison, proxy, secretary, subordinate, surrogate – *v.* accommodate, administer, aid, answer, apply, attend, care for, cater to, comfort, contribute, do for, foster, furnish, help, nurse, pander, relieve, remedy, serve, succour, tend, treat, wait on, watch over

ministry *n.* **1.** administration, agency, body, bureau, cabinet, council, department, executive, office **2.** clergy, holy orders, pastorate, priesthood, sacred calling, the cloth, vicarage

minor *adj.* **1.** accessory, inconsequential, inconsiderable, inferior, insignificant, lightweight, low, negligible, not up to snuff, paltry, petty, piddling, secondary, slight, smaller, trifling, trivial, unimportant *Nonformal:* beeswax, bush league, mickey mouse, minor league, two-bit *Antonyms:* considerable, grand, important, major, momentous, profound **2.** dirgeful, dolorous, elegiac, mournful, plaintive, sad, unhappy – *n.* **1.** adolescent, baby, boy, child, cub, girl, infant, junior, kid, lad, little one, schoolboy, schoolgirl, stripling, teenager, youngster, youth *Nonformal:* juve, whippersnapper, young'un *Antonyms:* adult, grown-up **2.** bench warmer, dependant, lesser light, subordinate, subsidiary *Nonformal:* second-string, small-fry, small potatoes

minority *n.* breakaway *or* splinter group, caucus, contingent, division, enclave, faction, handful, offshoot, schism, section, sector, side, smaller part, the few *(Nonformal)*, wing *Antonyms:* bulk, majority, mass

minstrel *n.* balladeer, bard, gleeman, jongleur, mariachi, minnesinger, musician, performer, poet, rhymer, skald, singer, troubadour

minuscule *adj.* diminutive, fine, infinitesimal, Lilliputian, little, microscopic, miniature, minute, small, tiny

minute *adj.* **1.** atomic, diminutive, infinitesimal, invisible, itsy-bitsy *(Nonformal)* light, little, microscopic, miniature, minimal, minuscule, slight, subatomic, tiny, wee

Antonyms: enormous, generous, great, huge, immense **2.** careful, circumstantial, clock-like, close, critical, detailed, elaborate, exact, exhaustive, fine, itemized, meticulous, painstaking, particular, precise, scrupulous, specialized, thorough **3.** immaterial, inconsiderable, insignificant, minor, negligible, nonessential, paltry, petty, slight, small, trifling, trivial, unimportant *Antonyms:* major, significant, tremendous – *n.* flash, instant, moment, second, short time, 60 seconds, second, trice, twinkling *Nonformal:* bit, breath, jiff, jiffy, New York minute, nothing flat, sec, tick

minutiae *n. pl.* details, finer points, intricacies, particulars, small print, subtleties, trifles, trivialities

miracle *n.* God's work, marvel, phenomenon, rarity, revelation, sensation, stunner *(Nonformal)*, supernatural occurrence, surprise, wonder

miraculous *adj.* amazing, astonishing, astounding, awesome, extraordinary, fabulous, incredible, inexplicable, magical, marvellous, out of this world *(Nonformal)*, overwhelming, phenomenal, prodigious, spectacular, staggering, strange, stupefying, stupendous, superior, supernatural, unbelievable, unreal, wonderful, wondrous *Antonyms:* common, everyday, normal, ordinary, unremarkable

mirage *n.* delusion, fantasy, fata morgana, hallucination, illusion, image, optical illusion, phantasm, vision, will-o'-the-wisp

mire *n.* bog, dirt, fen, marsh, morass, muck, mud, muskeg, mussel mud *(Maritimes)*, ooze, quagmire, quicksand, slime, slush, swamp *Nonformal:* goo, gunk, loblolly – *v.* **1.** bog down, delay, embroil, enmesh, ensnare, entangle, entrap, flounder, retard, set back, sink, slow down, snare, tangle, trap **2.** debase, defile, dirty, foul, pollute, sully, taint, tarnish, vandalize *Antonyms:* care for, clean, wash

mirror *n.* glass, looking-glass, spectrum *Kinds of mirror:* cheval glass, concave, convex, driver's, hand glass, pier glass, rear-view, shaving glass, smoked, two-way, wall – *v.* ape, copy, depict, double, echo, emulate, follow, illustrate, imitate, make like *(Nonformal)*, mock, parody, personify, reflect, simulate, take off

mirth *n.* amusement, cheer, cheerfulness, entertainment, festivity, frivolity, frolic, fun, gaiety, gladness, glee, grins, happiness, hilarity, hysterics, jocularity, jollity, joviality, joy, laughs *(Nonformal)*, laughter, levity, lightheartedness, merriment, pleasure, revelry, sport *Antonyms:* grief, misery, sorrow

misadventure *n.* accident, adversity, bad break *or* luck, bad medicine *(Native Peoples)*, blunder, calamity, casualty, cataclysm, catastrophe, debacle, disaster, error, failure, fall, *faux pas (French)*, ill fortune, lapse, mischance, misfortune, mishap, reverse, setback, tragedy, woe, wrong move *Nonformal:* blooper, boner, howler

misanthropic *adj.* antisocial, *farouche (French)*, misogynistic, people-hating, reclusive, solitary, standoffish, unfriendly, unsociable *Antonyms:* friendly, gregarious, sociable – *n.* hermit, loner, lone wolf, recluse

misapprehend *v.* blunder, confuse, err, get it wrong *(Nonformal)*, misconstrue, misinterpret, misread, miss, mistake, misunderstand

misappropriate *v.* **1.** defalcate, defraud, embezzle, line one's pockets *(Nonformal)*, mulct, plunder, pocket, rob, skim, steal, swindle **2.** abuse, misapply, misspend, misuse, pervert, squander

misbegotten *adj.* **1.** contemptible, disreputable, ignominious, illegal, illicit, scandalous, shameful, unlawful **2.** adulterine, baseborn, bastard, born on the wrong side of the blanket *(Nonformal)*, illegitimate, moonlight *(Newfoundland)*

misbehave *v.* act up, disobey, go astray, offend, rebel, roughhouse, sin, transgress, violate *Nonformal:* cut up rough, sow one's wild oats

misbehaviour *n.* delinquency, disorderly conduct, fit, fuss, hijinks, impropriety, lapse, mischief, misconduct, naughtiness, row, rowdyism scene, tantrum, transgression, uproar, upset, wrongdoing *Nonformal:* goings on, monkey business

miscalculate *v.* blow, blunder, err, mess up, misconstrue, misinterpret, misjudge, misread, misunderstand, overestimate, overlook, overrate, overvalue, screw up *(Nonformal)*, stumble, underestimate, underrate, undervalue

miscarriage *n.* **1.** premature delivery, still birth **2.** abortion, botch, breakdown, defeat, disaster, error, failure, fiasco, flop, frustration, malfunction, misadventure, mistake, mockery, parody, perversion, travesty

miscellaneous *adj.* assorted, disparate, diverse, heterogeneous, jumbled, many-sided, motley, multifarious, polymorphic, scrambled, sundry, varied, variegated, various

miscellany *n.* ana, assortment, brew, collection, combination, compilation, conglomeration, diversity, farrago, hash, hodgepodge, medley, melange, mishmash, mix, mixture, mosaic, olio, patchwork, salmagundi, smörgåsbord, stew, variety

mischief *n.* **1.** damage, detriment, disturbance, harm, hurt, injury, misdemeanour, misdoing, petty crime, sabotage, trouble, vandalism **2.** capers, deviltry, hijinks, hooliganism, juvenile *or* sophomoric behaviour, prank, roguery, shenanigans, silliness, trick, waggery *Nonformal:* hanky-panky, monkey business

mischievous *adj.* **1.** annoying, bad, bothersome, disobedient, fractious, fresh, headstrong, ill-behaved, insubordinate, misbehaved, naughty, obstreperous, terrible, troublesome, unmanageable, unruly, vexatious *Antonyms:* obedient, submissive **2.** arch, devilish, devil-may-care *(Nonformal)*, elfin, fiendish, foxy, impish, playful, puckish, rascally, roguish, saucy, teasing, waggish **3.** bullying, cruel, harmful, hurtful, mean, unkind

misconception *n.* delusion, error, false idea, misapprehension, misconstruction, mistaken belief, misunderstanding, wrong interpretation

misconduct *n.* delinquency, dereliction, immorality, impropriety, larceny, malfeasance, malpractice, misbehaviour, mischief, misdemeanour, misdoing, mismanagement, naughtiness, wrongdoing – *v.* backslide, slip, stray, transgress, trip *Nonformal:* bollix up, muff, step over the line

misconstrue *v.* distort, exaggerate, garble, go off on the wrong track *(Nonformal)*, misapprehend, misconceive, misinterpret, misjudge, misread, misrepresent, mistake, misunderstand, skew

miscreant *adj.* corrupt, criminal, degenerate, depraved, evil, immoral, infamous, iniquitous, nefarious, perverse, rascally, reprehensible, reprobate, unprincipled, vicious, villainous, wicked – *n.* blackguard, bully, convict, criminal, culprit, delinquent, evildoer, felon, hoodlum, knave, malefactor, ne'er-do-well, outlaw, pickpocket, racketeer, rascal, reprobate, rogue, rowdy, ruffian, scamp, scoundrel, scapegrace, sinner, thug, tough, varlet, villain, wrongdoer *Nonformal:* highbinder, scalawag *Antonyms:* angel, good samaritan, non pareil

misdemeanour *n.* crime, fault, faux pas, infringement, malefaction, misbehaviour, misconduct, misstep, offence, peccadillo, petty crime, sin, slip, transgression, trespass, villainy, violation, wrong *Nonformal:* dirty deed *or* pool

miser *n.* chuff, churl, hoarder, Midas, penny-pincher, tightwad *Nonformal:* cheapskate, moneygrubber, nickel-nurser, piker, Scrooge, skinflint *Antonyms:* liberal, spendthrift, wastrel

miserable *adj.* **1.** afflicted, agonized, ailing, anguished, brokenhearted, crestfallen, dejected, depressed, desolate, despairing, despondent, destroyed, discomforting, disconsolate, discontented, distressed, dolorous, downcast, forlorn, gloomy, heartbroken, hopeless, hurting, ill, lamentable melancholy, mournful, neurasthenic pained, pitiable, racked, rueful, sad, sick sorrowful, suffering, tormented, tortured tragic, troubled, unhappy, woebegone *Antonyms:* cheerful, comfortable, happy **2** bad, contemptible, despicable, detestable disgraceful, disreputable, scrofulous shameful, sordid, vile, worthless, wretched *Antonyms:* admirable, good, healthy **3.** abject, decrepit, deplorable, destitute, flea-bitten *(Nonformal)*, heartrending, impoverished, inferior, low, mangy, meagre, mean, needy, paltry, pathetic, penniless, piteous, poor, poverty-stricken, scurvy, shabby, skimpy, squalid *Antonyms:* extravagant, rich, wealthy

miserly *adj.* avaricious, close-fisted, grasping, greedy, penny-pinching, penny-wise, penurious, stingy, stinting *Nonformal:* cheap, tight *Antonyms:* altruistic, generous, philanthropic

misery *n.* **1.** ache, agony, anguish, anxiety, bad news *(Nonformal)*, blues, burden, depression, desolation, despair, despondency, discomfort, distress, gloom, grief, hardship, headache, heartache, hurting, melancholy, neurasthenia, pain, pang, passion, sadness, sorrow, suffering, throe, torment, torture, twinge, unhappiness, woe, worry, wretchedness *Antonyms:* contentment, ease, happiness, joy, pleasure **2.** affliction, calamity, catastrophe, curse, difficulty, disaster, dystopia, misfortune, ordeal, problem, time of trouble, trial, tribulation, trouble **3.** adversity, destitution, need, penury, poverty, privation, squalor, want

misfit *n.* Bohemian, dissenter, eccentric, loner, maverick, nonconformist, outcast, rogue *Nonformal:* deadhead, freak, oddball, odd duck, square peg in a round hole, strange bird, weirdo

misfortune *n.* accident, adversity, affliction, bad *or* hard *or* tough luck, bad medicine *(Native Peoples)*, blow, burden, calamity, casualty, cataclysm, catastrophe, contretemps, cross, debacle, disadvantage, disappointment, disaster, discomfort, failure, hardship, loss, misadventure, misery, mishap, nuisance, reverse, setback, tragedy, trial, tribulation, trouble *Antonyms:* fortune, good luck, relief

misgiving *n.* anxiety, apprehension, apprehensiveness, compunction, disquiet, distrust, doubt, fear, foreboding, hesitation, mistrust, premonition, qualm, reservation, scruple, suspicion, uncertainty, unease, worry *Nonformal:* nerves, the willies

misguided *adj.* **1.** deceived, deluded, distorted, fallacious, misconstrued, misdirected, misinformed, misinstructed, misled, mistaught, off base, wide of the mark **2.** confused, erroneous, foolish, ill-advised, imprudent, inane, injudicious, reckless, silly, unsound, unwise

mishandle *v.* **1.** abuse, beat, damage, hurt, ill-treat, manhandle, maul, mistreat, misuse, pervert, violate *Antonyms:* preserve, protect **2.** botch, damage, destroy, drop, fumble, misjudge, mismanage, screw up *(Nonformal)*, spoil, wreck

mishap *n.* accident, calamity, disaster, hazard, incident, misadventure, misfortune, slip

misinform *v.* con *(Nonformal)*, cover up, deceive, doublespeak, double-talk, hoodwink, lead astray, lie, misdirect, misguide, mislead, put on, steer wrong

misinterpret *v.* confuse, distort, garble, misapprehend, misconstrue, misread, mistake, misunderstand, mix up

misjudge *v.* be off *or* out, err, jump to the wrong conclusion, misapprehend, miscalculate, misconceive, mistake, overestimate, overrate, overvalue, prejudge, presume, presuppose, stumble, suppose, trip up, underestimate, underrate, undervalue

mislead *v.* bait, beguile, betray, bilk, bluff, cheat, deceive, defraud, delude, double-cross, dupe, ensnare, fool, hoax, hoodwink, lead astray, lie, lure, misdirect, misguide, misinform, misrepresent, put on, tempt, trick, victimize *Nonformal:* bamboozle, con, scam

misleading *adj.* ambiguous, bewildering, confounding, confusing, deceiving, deceptive, delusionary, delusive, distracting, evasive, false, inaccurate, perplexing, puzzling, specious, spurious, tricky, wrong *Antonyms:* candid, clear, direct, explicit, frank

mishmash *n.* confusion, farrago, hash, hodgepodge, miscellany, mixture, motley, potpourri

mismanage *v.* botch, fail, foul *or* screw up

(Nonformal), make sad work of, mishandle, mistreat, misuse, muddle

misogynist *n.* male chauvinist, male chauvinist pig *(Nonformal)*, misanthrope, sexist, woman hater

misquote *v.* distort, exaggerate, falsify, fudge, misinterpret, misreport, misstate, skew, twist

misrepresent *v.* adulterate, belie, cloak, colour, confuse, cover up, disguise, distort, dress, embellish, embroider, equivocate, exaggerate, falsify, fudge, garble, lie, mask, misreport, pervert, prevaricate, skew, slander, stretch, traduce, twist, warp *Nonformal:* con, doctor, put a spin on

miss *n.* **1.** absence, blunder, defect, error, failure, fault, loss, mistake, omission, oversight, slip **2.** damsel, demoiselle, female, *Fräulein (German)*, gal, girl, lass, lassie, ma'am, madam, mademoiselle, maid, maiden, mem-sahib *(Historical)*, missy, mistress, Ms., young lady *See also:* **female** – *v.* **1.** blow, blunder, disregard, fail, fan on *(Hockey)*, flub, foul, fumble, miscarry, misfire, muff, screw up *(Nonformal)*, slip **2.** confuse, misread, mistake, misunderstand **3.** cut, dismiss, disregard, forget, ignore, neglect, omit, overlook, pass over, skip, snub *Antonyms:* heed, notice **4.** lose, mislay, misplace **5.** desire, grieve *or* pine *or* yearn for, lack, languish, need, require, want **6.** avoid, bypass, detour, dodge, elude, escape, evade, shirk, skirt *Antonyms:* accept, face, welcome

misshapen *adj.* abnormal, bent, burled, contorted, crooked, deformed, distorted, gnarled, ill-shaped, knotted, snaggy, twisted, warped

missile *n.* **1.** arrow, bolt, bullet, dart, pellet, projectile, trajectile **2.** bomb, rocket *Kinds of missile:* air-to-air, air-to-surface, anti-aircraft, anti-missile, ballistic, cruise, fléchette *(Historical)*, heat-seeking, intercontinental ballistic *or* ICBM, nuclear, Patriot *(Trademark)*, Scud, surface-to-air *(SAM)*

missing *adj.* absent, astray, away, disappeared, gone, lacking, left behind *or* out, lost, marooned, mislaid, misplaced, not present, omitted, out and about, removed, short, stray, unaccounted for, vanished *Nonformal:* AWOL, walked off *Antonyms:* available, here, present, there

mission *n.* **1.** delegation, diplomat, embassy, envoy, task force **2.** assignment, charge, commission, errand, mandate, obligation, operation, responsibility, service, sortie, task, trust, undertaking **3.** business, job, métier, office, profession, trade, work **4.** area, beat, community, conclave, congregation, district, domain, embassy, fellowship, flock, locality, parish, realm, region, territory **5.** church, friendship centre, hostel, Salvation Army, shelter, soup kitchen *Nonformal:* flophouse, Sally Ann **6.** aim, avocation, calling, duty, goal, lifework, objective, purpose, pursuit, quest, vocation

missionary *n.* apostle, chaplain, clergyman, clergywoman, curate, *curé (French)*, evangelist, minister, padre, parson, pastor, preacher, propagandist, proselytizer, revivalist, teacher

missive *n.* communication, dispatch, document, e-mail, epistle, letter, line, mail, memo, memorandum, message, note, report, word

misspent *adj.* blown, diddled, dissipated, idle, imprudent, misapplied, prodigal, profitless, profligate, squandered, thrown away, wasted *Antonyms:* industrious, meaningful, profitable, useful, worthwhile

misstep *n.* blooper, blunder, boner, bungle, error, failure, indiscretion, lapse, miscue, miss, mistake, slip, stumble, trip

mist *n.* **1.** condensation, dew, drizzle, film, moisture, spray **2.** cloud, fog, haze, pea soup *(Nonformal)*, rain, smog, steam, vapour – *v.* **1.** drizzle, precipitate, rain, shower, sprinkle **2.** blur, cloud, cover, dim, fog, haze, murk, obscure, overcast, overcloud, steam *Antonyms:* clarify, clear

mistake *n.* blunder, bungle, confusion, erratum, error, failure, fault, *faux pas (French)*, flaw, gaucherie, impropriety, inaccuracy, indecorum, indiscretion, lapse, miscalculation, misconception, misprint, misstep, misunderstanding, negligence, omission, overestimation, oversight, slight, slip-up, solecism, underestimation *Nonformal:* blooper, boner, boo-boo, flub, fluff, gaffe, goof, howler, trip, typo – *v.* blunder, botch, bungle, confound, confuse, err, goof up *(Nonformal)*, lapse, misconstrue, miscount, misinterpret, misjudge, miss, omit, overcount, overcorrect, overestimate, overlook, slip up, underestimate

mistaken *adj.* confounded, confused, deceived, deluded, duped, erroneous, fallacious, false, faulty, ill-advised, inaccurate, incorrect, misguided, misinformed, misinterpreted, misjudged, misled, misunderstood, tricked, unsound, untrue, wrong *Nonformal:* all wet, blowing smoke *Antonyms:* accurate, correct, right, sound, true

mistimed *adj.* inapt, inconvenient, inexpedient, inopportune, late, malapropos, off, out-of-place, premature, tactless, tardy, too late *Antonyms:* opportune, tactful, timely

mistreat *v.* **1.** abuse, brutalize, bully, cut up, harm, injure, kick *or* knock *or* push around, maltreat, manhandle, maul, molest, roughhouse, rough *or* shake up, wound *Nonformal*: bash, dump on, mess up, rip, total, trash *Antonyms:* baby, pamper, spoil **2.** discredit, malign, persecute, revile, slander, slight, smear, snub

mistress *n.* **1.** lady, ma'am, madam, mademoiselle, miss, Mrs., Ms., woman **2.** chatelaine, dame, dowager, doyenne, governess, hostess, housemother, housewife, lady of the house, landlady, matriarch, matron, mother superior, proprietress, schoolmarm **3.** bedmate, concubine, courtesan, doxy, fling *(Nonformal)*, girlfriend, hetaera, inamorata, ladylove, other woman, paramour, sweetheart **4.** authority, expert, pundit, scholar, specialist

mistrust *n.* apprehension, chariness, concern, distrust, doubt, doubtfulness, fear, foreboding, leeriness, misgiving, qualm, scepticism, scruple, suspicion, uncertainty, wariness, wonder – *v.* disbelieve, distrust, doubt, fear, question, suspect *Antonyms:* believe, credit, trust

misty *adj.* **1.** damp, dewy, filmy, rainy, vaporous, wet *Antonyms:* arid, dry, parched **2.** bleary, blurred, closed in, clouded, cloudy, darkened, dimmed, enveloped, foggy, fuzzy, hazy, indistinct, murky, nebulous, obscured, opaque, overcast, shrouded, soupy *(Nonformal)*, unclear, vague *Antonyms:* bright, clear, distinct, lucid, obvious

misunderstand *v.* bewilder, confound, confuse, get wrong, misapprehend, misconstrue, misinterpret, misjudge, misread, miss the point, mistake *Antonyms:* comprehend, understand

misunderstanding *n.* **1.** confusion, delusion, error, false impression, *malentendu (French)*, misconstruction, misjudgment, mix-up, wrong idea **2.** argument, conflict, difference of opinion, disagreement, dispute, falling out, fight, imbroglio, problem, quarrel, spat, squabble, tiff

misuse *n.* abuse, corruption, cruel treatment, desecration, harm, injury, misapplication, mistreatment, perversion, rough handling, waste – *v.* **1.** abuse, brutalize, corrupt, cut up, desecrate, exploit, ill-treat, maltreat, manhandle, maul, mistreat, molest, profane, prostitute *Nonformal:* bung *or* mess up **2.** diddle away, dissipate, fribble, run through, squander, use up, waste *Antonyms:* appreciate, cherish, prize, respect, treasure

mitigate *v.* abate, allay, alleviate, appease, assuage, calm, diminish, ease, lessen, lighten, moderate, mollify, palliate, placate, quiet, reduce, relieve, soften, subdue *Antonyms:* aggravate, augment, enhance, increase, strengthen

mix *n.* **1.** blend, combination, compound, fusion, hodgepodge, jumble, medley, scramble, stew **2.** bewilderment, confusion, daze, mess, muddle, mystification, perplexity, pickle *(Nonformal)* **3.** cur, half-breed, hybrid, mongrel *Nonformal:* Heinz 57, mutt – *v.* **1.** add, admix, adulterate, alloy, amalgamate, attach, blend, blunge, braid, brew, combine, compound, fold in, fuse, incorporate, infiltrate, infuse, instill, intermingle, interweave, join, jumble, link, merge, put together, saturate, stir, synthesize, tangle, transfuse, unite, weave *Antonyms:* diverge, refine, separate **2.**

associate, come together, connect, consort, fraternize, hobnob, join, mingle, network, press the flesh *(Nonformal)*, socialize **3.** crossbreed, cross-fertilize, cross-pollinate, hybridize, interbreed, intermix

mixed *adj.* **1.** alloyed, amalgamated, assimilated, assorted, blended, brewed, combined, composite, compound, conglomerate, crossed, diversified, fused, heterogeneous, hybrid, incorporated, infused, interbred, interdenominational, joint, linked, married, merged, mingled, miscellaneous, mongrel, motley, multifarious, tied, transfused, united, varied, woven *Antonyms:* homogeneous, isolated, pure, straight, unmixed **2.** cluttered, confused, disarrayed, disordered, jumbled, muddled

mixture *n.* alloy, amalgam, amalgamation, blend, combination, composite, compound, conglomeration, cross, fusion, hodgepodge, hybrid, incorporation, interfusion, jumble, mash, medley, mélange, miscellany, mosaic, olio, pastiche, patchwork, potpourri, transfusion, variety *Nonformal:* dog's breakfast, grab bag

mix-up *n.* **1.** chaos, commotion, confusion, disorder, hash, jumble, mess, muddle, shambles, tangle, turmoil *Nonformal:* rat's nest, screw-up **2.** altercation, brawl, dispute, fight, fracas, showdown, tangle, tussle *Nonformal:* bench clearing brawl, donnybrook, punch up, set-to, slugfest

moan *n.* **1.** cry, lamentation, sigh, sob, ululation, wail **2.** complaint, groan, grumble, whine – *v.* **1.** grieve, keen, lament, mourn, sigh, sob, sorrow, suffer, wail, whimper **2.** bemoan, bewail, carp, complain, deplore, groan, grumble, rue, whine *Nonformal:* beef, gripe, grouse, kvetch

mob *n.* **1.** assemblage, body, cabal, circle, collection, company, crowd, flock, gang, gathering, group, herd, hoi polloi, horde, lot, mass, multitude, populace, posse, proletariat, rabble, riffraff, scrum, set, swarm, throng, troop **2.** cosa nostra, crime syndicate, gang, mafia, organized crime, *Yakuza (Japanese)* – *v.* attack, cram, crowd, fill, hustle, jam, jostle, molest, overrun, pack, riot, set upon, surround, swarm

mobile *adj.* adaptable, ambulatory, changeable, flowing, fluid, free, itinerant, loose, migratory, movable, moving, open, peripatetic, portable, transient, travelling, versatile, wandering *Antonyms:* fixed, stationary

mobilization *n.* activation, assembly, call to arms *or* to the colours, call-up, conscription, draft, levy, muster, organization, rally, recruitment

mobilize *v.* activate, animate, assemble, call up, catalyze, drive, gather, get ready, impel, make ready, marshal, move, muster, organize, prepare, press, propel, rally, ready, set off

mock *adj.* artificial, bogus, counterfeit, dummy, ersatz, fake, false, feigned, forged, fraudulent, imitation, make-believe, mimic, phoney *(Nonformal)*, pretended, pseudo, sham, simulated, so-called, spurious, substitute, unreal *Antonyms:* authentic, genuine, natural, real, true – *v.* **1.** chaff, deride, dis *(Nonformal)*, jeer, knock, ridicule, taunt, tease **2.** affect, ape, assume, burlesque, caricature, fake, feign, imitate, lampoon, mime, mimic, mirror, parody, roast, satirize, send up, simulate, travesty **3.** beguile, belie, betray, cheat, deceive, delude, disappoint, double-cross, dupe, elude, foil, fool, juggle, mislead **4.** beard, challenge, confront, defy, disobey, disregard, face, flout

mockery *n.* burlesque, butt, caricature, deception, derision, farce, insult, jeer, jest, joke, lampoon, laughingstock, parody, pretense, ridicule, scoffing, sham, travesty *Antonyms:* apology, exultation, laudation

mode *n.* **1.** approach, behaviour, channel, condition, course, custom, form, manner, mechanism, method, plan, posture, practice, procedure, process, quality, rule, shape, situation, state, status, system, tone, vein, way **2.** chic, convention, fad, fashion, style, trend, vogue **3.** tonal arrangement *Kinds of musical mode:* Aeolian, authentic, Dorian, ecclesiastical, Gregorian, Hindu, Indian, Ionian, Locrian, Lydian, major, medieval, minor, Phrygian, plagal, raga

model *adj.* **1.** archetypal, classic, illustrative, paradigmatic, prototypical, quintessential, representative, standard, typical **2.** commendable, exemplary, flawless, ideal, impeccable, perfect – *n.* **1.** cast, clone, copy, copycat, dummy, duplicate, effigy, facsimile, illustration, image, imitation, look-alike, miniature, mockup, picture, print, replica, representation, sketch, tracing *Nonformal:* dead ringer, knock-off **2.** archetype, benchmark, configuration, embodiment, epitome, essence, forerunner, gauge, ideal, original, paradigm, paragon, quintessence, standard, touchstone, yardstick **3.** chart, design, example, guide, form, mode, mould, pattern, prototype, sample, style **4.** brand, kind, make, mark, type, variety, version, year **5.** mannequin, nude, poser, sitter, specimen, subject – *v.* **1.** display, parade, pose, represent, sit, sport, wear **2.** base, carve, cast, create, design, draw, fashion, form, make, mould, pattern, plan, sculpt, shape, sketch

moderate *adj.* **1.** balanced, bearable, calm, careful, cautious, conservative, controlled, deliberate, disciplined, equable, even, judicious, limited, low-key, measured, neutral, nonpartisan, peaceable, reasonable, steady, tame, temperate, tolerable, tranquil *Antonyms:* intemperate, ruffled, unreasonable, wild **2.** average, bland, fair, intermediate, mainstream, mediocre, medium, middle-of-the-road, middling, ordinary, passable, unexceptional *Nonformal:* fantastic, great, wonderful – *n.* centrist, liberal, progressive *Antonyms:* extremist, radical – *v.* **1.** abate, allay, alleviate, appease, assuage, calm, chasten, check, constrain, control, cool, curb, decrease, diminish, lessen, let up, mitigate, modify, mollify, pacify, palliate, qualify, quiet, regulate, restrain, soften, subdue, subside, temper, tone down *Antonyms:* amplify, excite, rouse **2.** arbitrate, chair, judge, make peace, mediate, preside over, referee

moderately *adv.* a little, averagely, enough, fairly, gently, in moderation, passably, quite, reasonably, somewhat, sort of, so-so, temperately, tolerably, within limits, within reason *Antonyms:* excessively, intemperately

moderation *n.* balance, calmness, composure, continence, equanimity, fairness, middle course, prudence, relaxation, restraint, sedateness, sobersidedness, sobriety, temperance, toleration

moderator *n.* **1.** arbiter, arbitrator, judge, mediator, ref *(Nonformal)*, referee, umpire **2.** anchorperson, chair, chairperson, coordinator, emcee, facilitator, master *or* mistress of ceremonies, presiding officer, toastmaster

modern *adj.* avant-garde, contemporary, current, cutting *or* leading edge, dernier cri, fresh, late, latest, latter-day, modernistic, modish, neoteric, new, newfangled, present, present-day, prevailing, prevalent, recent, up-to-date, up-to-the-minute *Antonyms:* ancient, antiquated, old, past

modernize *v.* adapt, automate, bring to code, computerize, downsize *(Nonformal)*, make efficient, mechanize, redesign, redo, re-engineer, reequip, reform, remake, remodel, renew, renovate, reshape, restore, retool, revamp, revise, streamline, update, upgrade

modest *adj.* **1.** affordable, economical, humble, inexpensive, middling, moderate, ordinary, plain, reasonable, simple, small, unadorned, unexceptional, unpretentious **2.** bashful, blushing, chaste, coy, demure, diffident, discreet, humble, meek, nice, proper, quiet, reserved, reticent, retiring, seemly, self-conscious, self-effacing, sheepish, shy, silent, temperate, timid, unassertive, unassuming, unobtrusive, withdrawn *Antonyms:* brazen, flagrant, impudent, shameless

modesty *n.* bashfulness, constraint, coyness, decency, decorum, delicacy, demureness, diffidence, discretion, humility, inhibition, innocence, meekness, moderation, propriety, purity, quietness, reserve, reticence, self-effacement, shyness, simplicity, timidity, unobtrusiveness, unpretentiousness, virtue *Antonyms:* arrogance, conceit, egotism, vanity

modicum *n.* atom, bit, crumb, dash, drop, fraction, fragment, grain, inch, iota, jot, little, milligram, minim, mite, molecule, *morceau (French)*, morsel, ounce, particle, pinch, scrap, semblance, shred, smidgen, soupçon, speck, tad *(Nonformal)*, tinge, touch, trifle, whit

modification *n.* **1.** adjustment, alteration, change, conversion, metamorphosis, mutation, revision, transformation **2.** condition, limitation, provision, qualification, restraint, restriction, restrictive clause

modify *v.* **1.** change, customize, improve, modernize, recalibrate, recast, re-engineer, reform, remodel, retool, revamp, rework, update *Nonformal:* doctor, shift gears, supe-up, tweak **2.** abate, curb, decrease, lessen, limit, lower, mitigate, moderate, reduce, restrain, restrict, slacken, soften, temper, tone down

modish *adj.* chic, contemporary, current, dashing, exclusive, faddish, fashionable, smart, stylish, swank, trendy, up-to-date *Nonformal:* cool, funky, gear, groovy *Antonyms:* antique, fusty, hackneyed, passé

modulate *v.* **1.** adjust, alter, calibrate, change, fine tune, season, temper, vary **2.** attune, balance, harmonize, inflect, modify, regulate, soften, tune

moist *adj.* **1.** clammy, damp, dank, dewy, dripping, drizzly, humid, muggy, oozy, rainy, soggy, watery, wet *Antonyms:* arid, dehydrated, parched, torrid **2.** blubbery, crying, lachrymose, sad, tearful, teary, weeping

moisten *v.* **1.** bathe, bedew, dampen, dip, drench, humidify, irrigate, lick, mist, moisturize, rain on, rinse, saturate, shower, soak, sop, sparge, splash, splatter, spray, sprinkle, squirt, steam, steep, wash, water, water down, waterlog, wet *Antonyms:* cure, desiccate, dry **2.** bawl, blubber, cry, shed tears, sob, tear, weep

moisture *n.* damp, dankness, dew, drizzle, fog, humidity, liquid, mist, perspiration, precipitation, rain, sleet, snow, sweat, tears, water, wateriness, wet, wetness *Antonyms:* aridity, desiccation, dryness

mole *n.* **1.** beauty mark, birthmark, blemish, fleck, freckle, melanism, nevus, protuberance, spot **2.** double *or* secret agent, infiltrator, informant, operative, plant, spy *Nonformal:* narc, snitch, spook **3.** anchorage, barricade, barrier, breakwater, dik embankment, jetty, pier, wharf

molecule *n.* atom, bit, electron, fragmen ion, iota, jot, milligram, minim, mite, mo icum, *morceau (French)*, mote, ounc part, particle, ray, speck

molest *v.* **1.** abuse, accost, assail, assaul attack, encroach, harm, hinder, hurt, il treat, injure, maltreat, manhandle, misus rape, sexually assault, violate, ravish *No formal:* grope, paw *Antonyms:* care fo comfort **2.** annoy, beleaguer, bother, di turb, harass, hassle *(Nonformal)*, interfe *or* meddle with, irritate, needle, torme *Antonyms:* aid, assist, help

mollify *v.* abate, allay, alleviate, ameliorat appease, assuage, blunt, calm, compos conciliate, cushion, decrease, diminis ease, lessen, lighten, lull, mellow, mitigat moderate, pacify, palliate, placate, propit ate, quell, quiet, reduce, relieve, salve, sof en, soothe, sweeten, take the sting ou *(Nonformal)*, temper, tranquilize *Ant nyms:* agitate, excite, incite, induce

mollusc *n.* invertebrate *Groupings of mo luscs:* bivalve, shellfish *Kinds of mollus* abalone, clam, cockle, coral, cowrie, cuttl fish, mussel, nautilus, octopus, oyster, per winkle, quahog, scallop, slug, snail, squi whelk, winkle

mollycoddle *v.* baby, cotton-wool *(Nonfor mal)*, humour, overprotect, pamper, pa der, placate, protect, smooth, smothe spoil *Antonyms:* disregard, ignore, neglect

moment *n.* **1.** bit, date, flash, hour, instan juncture, minute, second, split secon trice, twinkle, twinkling *Nonformal:* crack jiff, jiffy, mo', New York minute, nothin flat, no time, sec, three winks, tick, tw shakes **2.** avail, concern, consequence, dis tinction, gravity, import, importance, mag nitude, note, pith, profit, seriousness, sig nificance, substance, use, value, weigh worth *Antonyms:* inconsequence, triviality

momentarily *adv.* **1.** briefly, for a shor while, temporarily **2.** any minute now before long, forthwith, in a while, in goo time, instantly, on the double, shortly, soon straight away *Nonformal:* lickety-split , toot suite

momentary *adj.* brief, cursory, ephemeral, evanescent, fleeting, flying, fugitive, hasty, impulsive, instantaneous, meteoric, passing, quick, shifting, short, short-lived, spasmodic, sudden, temporary, transient, transitory, vanishing, volatile *Nonformal:* fly-by-night, stolen *Antonyms:* lasting, lengthy, permanent, timeless

momentous *adj.* big, consequential, considerable, critical, crucial, decisive, distinctive, eventful, far-reaching, grave, heavy, historic, important, material, meaningful, memorable, notable, outstanding, pivotal, serious, significant, substantial, vital, weighty *Nonformal:* earthshaking, earthshattering *Antonyms:* inconsequential, insignificant, trifling, trivial, unimportant

momentum *n.* drive, energy, force, impetus, impulse, inertia, power, propulsion, push, strength, thrust

monarch *n.* autocrat, chief, chieftain, crowned head, despot, emperor, empress, king, majesty, potentate, prince, princess, queen, regent, royal, ruler, shah, sovereign, sultan, suzerain, tetrarch *Antonyms:* commoner, peasant, subject

monastery *n.* abbey, cloister, convent, friary, house, lamasery, nunnery, priory, religious community *or* home, vihara, wat

monastic *adj.* **1.** ascetic, austere, bleak, celibate, claustral, cloistral, disciplined, harsh, Spartan, stern *Antonyms:* hedonistic, Mammonistic **2.** communal, dedicated, ecclesiastical, godly, holy, monkish, pious, religious, reverent, spiritual *Antonyms:* irreverent, profane, sacrilegious

monetary *adj.* budgetary, capital, cash, commercial, financial, fiscal, pecuniary, pocket *(Nonformal)*

money *n.* banknote, bankroll, capital, cash, coin, coinage, currency, finances, funds, gold, hard cash, legal tender, property, reserves, resources, riches, salary, scrip, shinplaster *(Historical)*, specie, sterling, wampum, wealth *Nonformal:* bills, bread, bucks, dead presidents *(U.S.)*, dough, filthy lucre, greenback, jack, kitty, moolah, simoleons

moneyed *adj.* affluent, independent, prosperous, rich, solvent, wealthy, well-off *Nonformal:* filthy *or* stinking rich, flush, in the pink, loaded, on easy street, rolling in clover *Antonyms:* down-and-out, impoverished, poor, poverty-stricken

mongrel *adj.* crossed, heterogeneous, hybrid, interbred, mixed *Antonyms:* pedigree, purebred – *n.* crossbreed, cur, dog, hound, hybrid, lurcher, mix *Nonformal:* Heinz 57, mutt

moniker *n.* agnomen, alias, allonym, appellation, cognomen, designation, handle *(Nonformal)*, name, nickname, pen name, pseudonym, signature, sobriquet, title *French:* nom de guerre, nom de plume

monitor *n.* advisor, auditor, counsellor, director, eavesdropper, floorwalker, guard, guide, informant, invigilator, listener, overseer, proctor, referee, spy, supervisor, watchdog, watcher – *v.* audit, check, control, counsel, filter, follow, listen, observe, oversee, record, referee, scan, screen, supervise, survey, track, watch *Antonyms:* disregard, ignore, neglect

monk *n.* abbot, ascetic, brother, caloyer, cenobite, friar, hegumen, hermit, lama, marabout, monastic, nun, priest, recluse, religious, *sadhu (Hindu)*, solitary

monolithic *adj.* **1.** colossal, elephantine, enormous, gargantuan, giant, gigantic, huge, monstrous, monumental *Antonyms:* miniscule, tiny, wee **2.** constant, homogeneous, single, solitary, undivided, uniform, unvariable *Antonyms:* diverse, multifarious, multitudinous

monologue *n.* harangue, homily, lecture, sermon, soliloquy, speech, talk *Nonformal:* bit, spiel *Antonyms:* chorus, conversation, dialogue

monopolize *v.* **1.** command, control, copyright, corner, corral, dominate, own, possess, take over *Nonformal:* hog, lock up

Antonyms: give, share, split **2.** consume, engross, enthrall, hypnotize, mesmerize

monopoly *n.* cartel, complete *or* exclusive *or* utter control, consortium, corner, dominance, exclusive ownership *or* possession, oligarchy

monotonous *adj.* colourless, drab, dreary, droning, dull, familiar, flat, humdrum, mechanical, pedestrian, plodding, prosaic, recurrent, repetitive, routine, sleep-inducing, soporific, tedious, tiresome, unchanging, uniform, uninteresting, unvaried, wearisome *Antonyms:* animated, different, entertaining, exciting, stimulating

monotony *n.* banality, boredom, constancy, invariability, repetitiveness, routine, uniformity *Nonformal:* groove, rut *Antonyms:* discontinuity, variableness

monster *adj.* hulking, humongous, king-size, jumbo *Nonformal:* big wheels, lumbering – *n.* **1.** anomaly, creature, curiosity, deviant, freak, miscreation, monstrosity, mutant, oddity, *Kinds of monsters:* Abominable Snowman, Bahamut, basilisk, Big Foot, bocan *(P.E.I.)*, bogeyman, Boo *(Newfoundland)*, bugbear, centaur, chimera, cockatrice, cyclops, demon, devil, Dracula, dragon, familiar, *Fenrir (Norse)*, Frankenstein's, ghoul, giant, goblin, golem, Gorgon, Gougou, gremlin, Grendel, gryphon, harpy, hellhound, hydra, kobold, *kraken (Norwegian)*, lamia, Leviathan, Loch Ness, *Loup Garou (French)*, manticore, Medusa, Memphri, mermaid, Minotaur, Mr. Hyde, Ogopogo *(Pacific Coast)*, *Oni (Japanese)*, Phoenix, Polyphemus, Sasquatch, satyr, Scylla, siren, sphinx, Tiamat *(Babylonian)*, thing from outer space, troll, undead, vampire, *wendigo (Native Peoples)*, werewolf, *Yeti (Tibetan)*, zombie **2.** barbarian, beast, brute, cannibal, criminal, fiend, killer, murderer, savage, villain **3.** *enfant terrible (French)*, hellion, irritation, nuisance, pain, pest *Nonformal:* holy terror, nightmare, terror **4.** behemoth, colossus, dinosaur, Gargantua, Goliath, hulk *(Nonformal)*, mammoth, ogre, titan

monstrous *adj.* **1.** colossal, elephantine, enormous, fantastic, gargantuan, giant, gigantic, grandiose, great, huge, immense, large, magnificent, mammoth, massive, monumental, prodigious, stupendous, titanic, towering, tremendous, vast *Antonyms:* diminutive, Lilliputian, pint-sized **2.** atrocious, cruel, desperate, diabolical, dreadful, egregious, evil, fiendish, foul, freakish, frightful, gruesome, heinous, hellish, hideous, horrendous, horrifying, infamous, inhuman, intolerable, loathsome, macabre, morbid, obscene, odious, terrible, terrifying, unconsionable, vicious, villainous **3.** absurd, despicable, disgraceful, grotesque, outrageous, preposterous, ridiculous, scandalous, shocking, slanderous, unfounded **4.** aberrant, abnormal, bizarre, irregular, strange, teratogenic, weird

monument *n.* **1.** cairn, column, herma, indicator, inukshuk, landmark, marker, memento, monolith, obelisk, pile, pillar, plaque, record, reminder, sign, statue, stone, tablet, testament, token **2.** cenotaph, commemoration, cross, footstone, gravestone, headstone, mausoleum, memorial, remembrance, shrine, tomb, tombstone

monumental *adj.* **1.** awe-inspiring, fantastic, grand, great, imposing, impressive, lofty, majestic, outstanding, overwhelming, prodigious, prominent, stupendous, tremendous *Antonyms:* insignificant, slight **2.** classic, enduring, historic, immortal, important, lasting, memorable, notable, significant, substantive, unforgettable *Antonyms:* ephemeral, fleeting, transitory **3.** enormous, gigantic, huge, immense, large, mammoth, massive, towering

mood *n.* **1.** attitude, bent, character, condition, disposition, feeling, frame of mind, humour, mind-set, state, temper, temperament **2.** air, atmosphere, aura, colour, emotion, spirit, tone **3.** form, mode *Divisions of grammatical mood:* imperative, indicative, subjunctive

moody *adj.* **1.** brooding, cantankerous, crotchety, dour, down in the dumps *(Nonformal)*, glum, ill-humoured, lugubrious, melancholy, miserable, moping, morose, pensive, saturnine, sullen, temperamental **2.** bipolar, fickle, fitful, inconstant, manic-depressive, mercurial, unpredictable, unstable, up-and-down *(Nonformal)*, volatile *Antonyms:* constant, stable, steady

moon *n.* celestial body, globe, *lune (French)*, orb, satellite *Phases and shapes of the moon:* crescent, full, gibbous, half, harvest, hunter's, new, old, waning, waxing – *v.* **1.** daydream, dream, idle, languish, mope, muse, ponder, stare, wander, waste time **2.** bare, drop one's drawers, expose, uncover

moor *n.* bog, fen, heath, marsh, morass, peat-bog, wasteland – *v.* anchor, berth, dock, fasten, fix, make fast *(Nonformal)*, secure, tie, tie up *Antonyms:* cast off, weigh anchor

moot *adj.* **1.** arguable, conjectural, contentious, contestable, controversial, debatable, discussible, questionable, refutable, suspicious, undecided, unresolved, up in the air **2.** insignificant, minor, trivial **3.** academic, conjecture, hypothetical, impractical, polemical, suppositional, theoretical *Antonyms:* actual, factual, real – *v.* argue, debate, polemicize, propound, put forward, query, question, squabble, submit

mop *n.* duster, dust mop, rag, sponge, squeegee, swab – *v.* clean, dust, rub, scrub, soak, sponge, swab, sweep, wash, whisk, wipe

mope *n.* complainer, grouch, pessimist, whiner *Nonformal:* skeleton at the banquet, sourpuss, stick-in-the-mud, wet blanket – *v.* ache, bleed, brood, chafe, despair, droop, fret, grieve, grumble, idle, kvetch *(Nonformal)*, lament, languish, pine, pout, regret, stew, sulk, yearn

moral *adj.* aboveboard, blameless, chaste, conscientious, correct, courteous, decorous, dutiful, ethical, exemplary, good, high-minded, honest, honourable, incorruptible, just, laudable, noble, principled, proper, pure, respectable, righteous, scrupulous, seemly, square, straight, trustworthy, truthful, upstanding, virtuous *Antonyms:* corrupt, dishonest, improper, unethical, venial – *n.* adage, aphorism, apothegm, axiom, dictum, epigram, lesson, maxim, message, motto, point, proverb, saw, saying, sermon *Commonly misused:* **morale**

morale *n.* assurance, attitude, confidence, disposition, drive, enthusiasm, esprit, heart, humour, mettle, mood, outlook, resolve, self-confidence, self-esteem, self-possession, spirit, state, temperament *Commonly misused:* **moral**

morality *n.* **1.** chastity, decency, good conduct, goodness, honour, ideals, incorruptibility, integrity, justice, probity, purity, rectitude, rightness, standards, virtue **2.** conscience, ethics, moral code, mores, principles, scruples

morals *n. pl.* behaviour, beliefs, conduct, customs, ethics, habits, ideals, integrity, manners, mores, policies, principles, rules, scruples, standards

morass *n.* **1.** bog, fen, heath, loblolly, marshland, quagmire, quicksand, slough, swamp **2.** chaos, confusion, jam, jungle, knot, labyrinth, logjam, maze, mesh, mess, muddle, snarl, tangle, trap

moratorium *n.* **1.** armistice, break, cessation, discontinuance, end, halt, stop, suspension, truce **2.** break, cease-fire, continuance *(Law)*, interlude, interval, pause, recess, respite

morbid *adj.* **1.** aberrant, abnormal, disturbing, odd, sick, strange, weird, worrysome *Antonyms:* everyday, normal, run-of-the-mill, usual **2.** black, dolorous, dreary, funereal, gloomy, lugubrious, morose, pessimistic *Antonyms:* happy-go-lucky, optimistic, upbeat **3.** bloody, disgusting, dreadful, frightful, ghastly, ghoulish, grim, grisly, grotesque, gruesome, hideous, horrid, kafkaesque, macabre, nasty, nightmarish, upsetting *Antonyms:* cozy, pleasant, welcoming **4.** diseased, malignant, pathological, polluted, unhealthy, unwholesome *Antonyms:* nourishing, nutritious, salubrious

mordant *adj.* acerbic, astringent, biting, caustic, corrosive, cutting, incisive, irascible, keen, mocking, penetrating, pointed, pungent, sarcastic, sardonic, scathing, sharp, trenchant, vitriolic, withering *Antonyms:* amiable, polite, pleasant, soothing

more *adj.* **1.** farther, greater, heavier, higher, larger, wider **2.** added, additional, aggrandized, amassed, another, augmented, bounteous, enhanced, exceeding, expanded, extended, extra, greater, increased, longer, massed, new, numerous, other, second, spare, supplementary, surplus – *adv.* additionally, also, as well, besides, better, beyond, further, furthermore, in addition, likewise, moreover, over, too, withal

moreover *adv.* additionally, also, as well, besides, further, furthermore, in addition, likewise, more, too, withal, yet

moribund *adj.* approaching extinction, comatose, diminishing, disappearing, dwindling, dying, dying out, ebbing, expiring, *in extremis (Latin)*, languishing, on the downward spiral *(Nonformal)*, stagnant, terminal, vanishing, waning, wasting away, weak *Antonyms:* developing, growing, healing, in the pink *(Nonformal)*, recuperating, reviving

morning *n.* after midnight, AM, ante meridian, before lunch, before noon, breakfast, brunch, cockcrow, dawn, daybreak, daylight, light, sunrise, sunup, wee hours

moron *n.* blockhead, dolt, dullard, dunce, fool, halfwit, idiot, ignoramus, imbecile, lamebrain, simpleton, *staumrel (Scottish) Nonformal:* bonehead, boob, dimwit, dingbat, dummy, hoser, loony *Antonyms:* genius, scholar

moronic *adj.* asinine, brainless, credulous, dopey *(Nonformal)*, dumb, foolish, idiotic, imbecilic, inane, mindless, senseless, silly, stupid, witless *Antonyms:* clever, intelligent, quick-witted

morose *adj.* blue, crestfallen, depressed, dolorous, dour, down, frowning, gloomy, glum, grouchy, gruff, ill-humoured, irritable, low, melancholy, moody, moping, mournful, neurasthenic, pessimistic, sad, sour, sulky, sullen, taciturn, troubled, upset *Antonyms:* blithe, cheerful, gay, happy, pleasant

morsel *n.* bit, bite, crumb, drop, fraction, fragment, iota, jot, mote, nibble, piece, sample, scrap, segment, smithereen, soupçon, taste, tidbit

mortal *adj.* **1.** corporeal, earthly, ephemeral, fleeting, human, impermanent, momentary, passing, perishable, temporal, transitory, vulnerable, worldly **2.** deadly, destructive, fatal, final, killing, lethal, murderous, poisonous, terminal, toxic **3.** baleful, dire, extreme, grave, harrowing, terrible, tragic **4.** adamant, implacable, unappeasable, unforgiving – *n.* being, biped, body, character, creature, earthling, human, individual, living soul, man, number *(Nonformal)*, party, person, personage, soul, woman *Antonyms:* angel, deity, ghost, spirit

mortality *n.* **1.** bloodshed, butchery, carnage, death, dying, extinction, fatality, killing, loss, massacre, slaughter **2.** being, creation, flesh, Homo sapiens, humanity, humankind, human race, man, mankind, woman, womankind **3.** ephemerality, evanescence, humanness, impermanence, perishability, transience, vulnerability

mortified *adj.* abashed, chagrined, crushed, deflated, degraded, disappointed, discomfited, disgraced, distressed, embarrassed, humbled, humiliated, red-faced *(Nonformal)*, shamed, upset *Antonyms:* blissful, joyous, rapturous

mortify *v.* **1.** abase, abash, affront, belittle, chagrin, chasten, crush, deny, deprecate, discipline, disgrace, displease, embarrass, humble, humiliate, punish, ridicule, shame, subdue *Nonformal:* put down, shred, take down **2.** annoy, bother, confound, discomfit, harass, upset, vex, worry *Nonformal:* dis, hassle, razz

mosaic *adj.* checkered, multicoloured, multihued, variegated – *n.* arrangement, assemblage, collage, conglomeration, design, pastiche, pattern, picture

most *adj.* **1.** biggest, greater, greatest, highest, largest, maximum **2.** best, better, finest, leading, peak, peerless, penultimate, top, ultimate, unequaled, utmost – *adv.* **1.** about, all but, almost, close, nearly, nearly all, nigh, practically, well-nigh **2.** eminently, exceedingly, extremely, mightily, remarkably, surpassingly, very – *n.* big end, bulk, lion's share, majority, preponderance, weight

mostly *adv.* chiefly, customarily, essentially, frequently, generally, largely, mainly, most often, particularly, primarily, principally, regularly, usually

motel *n.* *auberge (French)*, cabin, hotel, inn, lodge, motor court *or* inn, resort, roadhouse, rooms

moth-eaten *adj.* ancient, decrepit, dilapidated, dishevelled, frayed, musty, neglected, old, ragged, shabby, shredded, stringy, tattered, threadbare, tired, worn-out *Antonyms:* new, pristine, unused

mother *adj.* ancestral, father, home, maternal, native, original – *n.* **1.** adoptive mother, birth mother, foster mother, *madre (Spanish)*, mater *(British)*, matriarch, stepmother *Nonformal:* ma, mamma, maw, mom, mommy, mum **2.** caregiver, guardian, nurturer, parent, protector, supporter **3.** author, creator, fountainhead, genesis, origin, source, wellspring – *v.* **1.** beget, bring forth, create, engender, issue, originate, procreate, produce, spawn **2.** care for, foster, guard, mind, nourish, nurture, parent, protect, raise, rear, shelter, support, watch over

motherly *adj.* affectionate, caretaking, caring, comforting, devoted, fond, gentle, kind, loving, maternal, nurturing, protecting, protective, sheltering, supporting, sympathetic, tender, warm, watchful

motif *n.* **1.** decoration, design, device, figure, insignia, logo, mark, pattern, symbol **2.** concept, focus, leitmotif, refrain, subject, theme, topic, trope

motion *n.* **1.** act, action, agitation, ambulation, change, drift, dynamics, flow, kinesics, locomotion, mobility, movement, oscillation, stirring, sway **2.** gesture, inclination, move, sign, signal, sweep, swing, wave **3.** plan, proposal, proposition, recommendation, submission, suggestion **4.** desire, impulse, inclination, itch, urge – *v.* beckon, direct, flag, gesticulate, gesture, guide, invite, move, nod, shake, sign, signal, wave

motionless *adj.* **1.** at rest, becalmed, calm, dead, firm, frozen, halted, immobile, inanimate, inert, lifeless, numb, paralyzed, petrified, stagnant, static, stationary, stock-still, torpid, transfixed, unmoving *Antonyms:* active, animated, lively, mobile, restless **2.** at point non plus, deadlocked, fixed, jammed, locked, stalemated, stalled, stuck *Antonyms:* operative, progressing, underway

motivate *v.* abet, activate, agitate, arouse, budge, cause, compel, disturb, drive, egg on *(Nonformal)*, encourage, excite, fire up, foment, goad, impel, impress, incite, induce, inflame, influence, inspire, instigate, interest, kindle, lead, move, persuade, pique, prevail upon, prod, prompt, propel, provoke, push, raise, rouse, spark, spur, start, stimulate, stir, sway, trigger, urge, whet, whip up

motivation *n.* actuation, ambition, aspiration, carrot *(Nonformal)*, desideratum, encouragement, fire, impetus, impulse, impulsion, incitation, inducement, inspiration, motive, objective, persuasion, predetermination, predisposition, provocation, push, spur, stimulus

motive *n.* aim, ambition, basis, catalyst, cause, design, desire, drive, emotion, end, feeling, grounds, hunger, idea, incentive, intention, interest, motivation, need, object, occasion, purpose, rationale, reason, root, thinking, wish

motley *adj.* **1.** assorted, conglomerate, different, discrepant, disparate, dissimilar, diversified, heterogeneous, indiscriminate, miscellaneous, mixed, ragtag, unlike, varied *Antonyms:* homogeneous, similar, uniform **2.** dappled, harlequin, kaleidoscopic, mosaic, mottled, multicoloured, multiform, multihued, opalescent, parti-coloured, plaid, polychromatic, prismatic, rainbow, spectral, varicoloured *Antonyms:* monochromatic, monotone – *n.* collection, conglomeration, gallimaufry, hodgepodge, mixed bag, mixture

motor *adj.* ambulatory, mobile, moving, muscular – *n.* drive, dynamo, engine, generator, machine, power plant, turbine *Kinds of motor:* diesel, electric, four stroke, fuel cell, gas, inboard, internal combustion, outboard, propane, steam, two-stroke, V-8, wankel – *v.* cruise *(Nonformal)*, drive, ride, taxi, tour, travel

mottled *adj.* blotched, checkered, dappled, flecked, marble, motley, piebald, plaid, speckled, spotted, streaked, tabby, variegated *Antonyms:* clear, pure, unclouded

motto *n.* adage, catchphrase, catchword, dictum, epigram, maxim, precept, prefix, principle, rule *Canadian mottos:* From many peoples strength *(Saskatchewan)*, From sea to sea *(Canada)*, Glorious and free *(Manitoba)*, Hope restored *(New Brunswick)*, *Je me souviens (Quebec)*, Loyal she began and loyal she remains *(Ontario)*, One defends and the other conquers *(Nova Scotia)*, Our land, your land *(Nunavut)*, Seek ye first the kingdom of God *(Newfoundland)*, Splendour without diminishment *(B.C.)*, Strong and free *(Alberta)*, The small under the protection of the great *(P.E.I.)*

mould *n.* **1.** bacteria, blight, corruption, decay, dry *or* growth rot, fungus, grunge, mildew, mustiness, scum *Nonformal:* goo, guck, muck **2.** cast, container, figure, form, format, frame, last, matrix, model, pattern, shape, template, vessel **3.** character, disposition, fashion, manner, nature, style – *v.* **1.** build, cast, construct, design, develop, devise, direct, erect, fashion, forge, form, frame, make, model, pat, plan, plant, plot, put together, round, scheme, whittle **2.** affect, coach, educate, groom, guide, inculcate, indoctrinate, impress, influence, instruct, shape, teach

mouldy *adj.* decaying, fusty, green, musty, old, putrid, rotten, spoiled, stale

mound *n.* **1.** anthill, dunghill, heap, midden, mogul, pile, rick, stack **2.** bank, barrow, côteau, drift, drumlin, dune, earthworks, elevation, embankment, hill, hillock, hummock, knoll, rise, swell **3.** bump, cyst, growth, lump, mass, protuberance – *v.* bank, build, heap, pile up, stack, stook

mount *n.* **1.** base, bed, brace, foundation, frame, prop, support, truss **2.** gelding, horse, hunter, lift *(Nonformal)*, mare, palfey, pony, riding horse, stallion, steed **3.** height, mountain, peak, precipice – *v.* **1.** ascend, board, clamber *or* climb onto, embark, get astride *or* on, hop in *or* on, scale, scramp up, vault *Antonyms:* climb down, dismount, fall off **2.** affix, elevate, emplace, enshrine, fit, frame, furnish, hoist up, illuminate, install, lift, parade, place, position, prepare, set up, show, stage **3.** accumulate, build, develop, enhance, escalate, expand, grow, heighten, increase, intensify, multiply, rise, swell, upsurge *Antonyms:* contract, diminish, drop, fall, shrink

mountain *n.* **1.** alp, bulge, butte, elevation, height, high terrain, hill, *jebel (Arabic)*, mound, *nunatak (Inuit)*, peak, pile, plateau, precipice, promontory, ridge, rise *World mountains:* Annapurna, Ararat, Badham, Ben Nevis, Cook, Cotopaxi, Elbrus, Etna, Everest, Fuji, Helicon, Jungfrau, Kanchenjunga, Kenya, Kilimanjaro, Kosciusko, K2, Lhotse, Logan, Matterhorn, McKinley, Mont Blanc, Saint Helens, Olympus, Popocatépetl, Pumori, Rainier, Revelstoke, Robson, Roraima, Royal, Slide, Snowdon, Tirich Mir, Tremblant, Saint Anne, Vesuvius, Wilhelm, Zion *World Mountain Ranges:* Adirondacks, Alps, Andes, Appalachians, Atlas, Cantabrian, Carpathian, Cascade, Caucasus, Coast, Elburz, Himalayas, Hindu Kush, Iberian, Kootenays, Kunlun, Laurentians, Long Range, Mackenzie, Maya, Pyrenees, Richardson, Rockies, Selkirk, Siahan, Sierra Madre, St. Elias, Taurus, Tetons, Ural, Zagros **2.** abundance, gross, horde, multitude, profusion, quantity

mountainous *adj.* **1.** alpine, cloud-capped, hilly, rocky, rolling, rugged, sheer, soaring, steep, tall *Antonyms:* flat, unbroken **2.** awe-inspiring, daunting, difficult, enormous, gigantic, huge, inaccessible, intimidating, mighty, monumental, powerful *Antonyms:* simple, small, trivial

mountains *n.* chain, côteau, God's country *(Nonformal)*, high country, range, ridge, sierra, snow-capped peaks, uplands

mourn *v.* ache, agonize, anguish, bemoan, bewail, bleed, complain, cry, deplore, fret, grieve, hurt, keen, lament, languish, long for, miss, moan, pine, regret, rue, sigh, sit shiva, sorrow, suffer, ululate, wail, weep, yearn *Antonyms:* celebrate, party, rejoice

mournful *adj.* brokenhearted, dejected, direful, disconsolate, doleful, downcast, funereal, gloomy, melancholy, miserable, pained, rueful, sad, sombre, sorrowful, woeful *Antonyms:* blissful, happy, joyous

mourning *n.* **1.** aching, anguish, bereavement, crying, despair, grief, grieving, keening, lamentation, languishing, loss, moaning, pining, sadness, shiva, sorrow, wailing, weeping, woe **2.** black veil, crepe, sackcloth and ashes, weeds

mousy *adj.* bashful, colourless, demure, diffident, drab, dull, plain, quiet, self-effacing, shy, timid, unassertive *Antonyms:* loud, obnoxious, striking, stunning

mouth *n.* **1.** beak, cavity, gills, jaws, lips, maw, muzzle, orifice *Nonformal:* gob, kisser, pie hole, trap, yap **2.** back talk, boasting, braggadocio, bragging, empty *or* idle talk, freshness, impudence, insolence, rodomontade, rudeness *Nonformal:* gall, gas, hot air, lip, nerve, sass, sauce **3.** aperture, doorway, entrance, entryway, gap, gate, hatch, opening, passageway, portal, window, vent – *v.* articulate, call, disseminate, enunciate, murmur, pronounce, say, speak, talk, voice

movable *adj.* accessible, adaptable, adjustable, ambulatory, conveyable, fluid, mobile, portable, removable, shiftable, transferable, transportable, unattached *Antonyms:* fixed, nailed down, rooted

move *n.* act, action, alteration, change, manoeuvre, measure, modification, motion, movement, procedure, progress, shift, step, stir, stirring, turn *Nonformal:* deke, dipsy-doodle, spinarama – *v.* **1.** decamp, depart, drive, emigrate, exit, flee, fly, get *or* go away, immigrate, migrate, relocate, shift, transfer, travel *Nonformal:* scram, skedaddle **2.** exchange, substitute, swap, switch, transpose **3.** bustle, crawl, cross, dart, drift, glide, hurry, run, scamper, scurry, stroll, taxi, transport, traverse, walk **4.** advance, leap, move forward, proceed, progress, set forth **5.** associate, fraternize, hobnob, mingle, socialize *Nonformal:* hang out, run with **6.** operate, perform, revolve, spin, turn, work **7.** act, advise, advocate, appeal, apply, propose, recommend, submit **8.** actuate, affect, arouse, budge, dislodge, disturb, force, impel, impress, influence, prompt, provoke, rouse, stir, touch, urge

movement *n.* **1.** activity, alteration, change, displacement, flow, flux, locomotion, mobility, motion, moving, shift, stir, stirring **2.** emigration, flight, immigration, journey, migration, move, passage, transfer, transit, transition, transplanting, travel, uprooting, voyage **3.** coalition, company, faction, front, grassroots movement, organization, party, popular movement, schism, sect **4.** current, genre, school, style, trend, way **5.** act, chapter, part, passage, performance, piece, section, selection **6.** beat, cadence, meter, rhythm, shift, swing, tempo **7.** defection, bowel movement, evacuation, feces, stool, void *Nonformal:* crap, dump **8.** advance, campaign, drive, exercise, manoeuvre, march, mobilization, operation, plan, retreat, sortie, tactic

movie *n.* cinema, DVD *(Trademark)*, feature, film, matinee, motion *or* moving picture, rental, show, video *Historical:* picture show, silent, talkie *Nonformal:* flick, flicker, pic *See also:* **film**

moving *adj.* **1.** advancing, changing, exercising, evolving, fluid, galloping, going, in flux *or* play, itinerant, marching, mobile, retreating, running, shifting, striding, unfixed, unstable, volitant, walking *Antonyms:* fixed, stationary, still, unmoving **2.** affecting, affective, arousing, awakening, dynamic, eloquent, emotional, gripping, impelling, influential, inspirational, meaningful, motivating, motivational, persuasive, poignant, propelling, provoking, quickening, rallying, rousing, stimulating, stirring, touching *Antonyms:* directionless, dull, insignificant, pointless, unimpressive

mow *v.* **1.** bob, clip, crop, cut, harvest, pare, prune, reap, shave, shear, snip, trim, truncate **2.** assassinate, butcher, cut down, dispatch, execute, hack, kill, maul, murder, slay

much *adj.* abundant, adequate, ample, complete, considerable, copious, countless, endless, enough, extravagant, full, galore, generous, great, immeasurable, lavish, many, plenteous, plentiful, plenty, profuse, satisfying, sizeable, substantial, sufficient, voluminous *Antonyms:* inadequate, insufficient, little, scant – *adv.* a lot, considerably, decidedly, eminently, exceedingly, exceptionally, extremely, frequently, greatly, highly, hugely, indeed, notably, often, regularly, repeatedly, surpassingly *Antonyms:* barely, hardly, infrequently – *n.* abundance, amplitude, copiousness, excess, fullness, lots, mass, mountain, multiplicity, oversupply, pile, plentifulness, plenty, plethora, profuseness, profusion, riches, sufficiency, superfluity, volume, wealth *Nonformal:* heaps, loads, scads *Antonyms:* emptiness, little, nothing

muck *n.* **1.** bilge, dirt, filth, goo *(Nonformal)*, grime, mire, mud, scum, sewage, slime, slop, sludge **2.** compost, droppings, dung, excrement, feces, fertilizer, manure **3.** confusion, disarray, jam, jumble, mess, muddle – *v.* **1.** dirty, mess up, muddy, pollute, soil, stain, sully **2.** clean out, clear, do up, remove, swab

mud *n.* **1.** adobe, clay, dirt, mire, muck, mussel mud *(Maritimes)*, ooze, silt, slush *Nonformal:* crap, gumbo, loonshit, slop, soup **2.** defamation, denigration, libel, scandal, slander, vilification

muddle *n.* chaos, cock-up *(Nonformal)*, confusion, disarray, disorder, jumble, mess, uncertainty – *v.* **1.** blunder, botch, bungle, foul, make a mess of *(Nonformal)*, mishandle, mismanage, muff, snarl, tangle **2.** addle, befuddle, bewilder, clutter, complicate, confound, confuse, disorder, disorient, disturb, entangle, fluster, fuss, jumble, mess, nonplus, perplex, rattle **3.** beat, blend, churn, intermix, mix, shake, stir, whip

muddy *adj.* **1.** dingy, dirty, feculent, filthy, grimy, grubby, marshy, messy, mucky, mud-caked, reeking, roily, slushy, sodden, soiled, sooty, spattered, swampy, turbid **2.** blurred, cloudy, confused, covered, hazy, indistinct, obscure, opaque, unclear, vague – *v.* **1.** befoul, begrime, besmear, dirty, mess, smudge, soil, stain **2.** baffle, blur, confuse, muddle, mystify, obscure, perplex, puzzle

muffin *n.* biscuit, bun, cupcake, roll, scone *Kinds of muffin:* apple, banana, blueberry, bran, carrot, chocolate chip, corn, English

muffle *v.* **1.** conceal, cover, disguise, envelop, hide, shroud, smother, swaddle, veil, wrap **2.** cushion, dampen, deaden, decrease, drown, dull, gag, hush, mute, muzzle, quiet, silence, soften, squelch, stifle, subdue, suppress, tone down

muffled *adj.* dampened, deadened, dim, dull, faint, indistinct, muted, quiet, silenced, softened, stifled, strangled, subdued, suppressed *Antonyms:* augmented, increased

mug *n.* **1.** cup, flask, goblet, jar, jug, schooner, sleeve, stein, tankard, toby **2.** countenance, face, visage *Nonformal:* clock, pan, phiz, puss **3.** goon *(Nonformal)*, hoodlum, punk, ruffian, thug – *v.* **1.** assault, attack, hold *or* rough *or* stick up, pounce on, rip off, rob, roll, set upon **2.** frown, grimace, make a face, pout, scowl, smirk, sneer,

muggy *adj.* clammy, close, damp, dank, humid, moist, oppressive, soggy, steamy, sticky, stuffy, sultry *Antonyms:* arid, dry, parched

mulish *adj.* bullheaded, firm, fixed, headstrong, intractable, obdurate, obstinate, pigheaded, set, steadfast, stubborn *Antonyms:* flexible, level-headed, reasonable

mull *v.* cogitate, consider, contemplate, deliberate, examine, figure, meditate, moon *(Nonformal)*, muse on, ponder, reflect, review, revolve, ruminate, study, sweat *or* turn over, think about *or* over, weigh, woolgather

multicoloured *adj.* dappled, iridescent, kaleidoscopic, marbled, motley, multicolour, opalescent, particoloured, polychrome, prismatic, speckled, spotted, varicoloured, veined

multicultural *adj.* ethnically diverse, heterogeneous, mosaic, multiethnic, varied

multimedia *adj.* **1.** communicative, interactive, reciprocal, responsive, two-way **2.** interdisciplinary, intermedia, mixed media, multidisciplinary – *n.* digital media, hypermedia, new media

multiple *adj.* **1.** assorted, collective, conglomerate, different, diverse, diversified, indiscriminate, legionary, manifold, many, miscellaneous, mixed, motley, multifarious, multiform, multiplex, multitudinous, myriad, numerous, populous, several, sundry, varied, variegated, various, voluminous **2.** doubled, duplicated, repeated, tripled, triplicated

multiply *v.* **1.** aggregate, augment, boost, compound, enlarge, expand, extend, generate, heighten, increase, magnify, raise, repeat, reproduce, rise, spread, square *Antonyms:* abate, decline, decrease, diminish, reduce **2.** breed, populate, procreate, produce, proliferate, propagate

multitude *n.* **1.** aggregation, army, assemblage, assembly, collection, company, concatenation, congregation, crowd, crush *(Nonformal)*, drove, group, horde, host, legion, majority, mass, myriad, number, ocean, oodles *(Nonformal)*, plenitude, plurality, quantity, score, sea, slew, swarm, throng, turnout **2.** commoners, hoi polloi, masses, populace, proletariat, public, rabble, ragtag

multitudinous *adj.* abounding, abundant, beyond measure, boku *(Nonformal)*, considerable, copious, countless, great, immeasurable, innumerable, manifold, many, multifarious, numerous, populous, profuse, teeming, uncountable, untold, various, voluminous *Antonyms:* few, fixed, limited, numbered

mumble *v.* grumble, murmur, mutter, patter, rumble, speak inarticulately, sputter, swallow one's words, talk incoherently *Antonyms:* articulate, enunciate, shout – *n.* grumble, hum, low rumble, murmur

mumbo jumbo *n.* **1.** abracadabra, cantrip, chant, formula, hocus-pocus, incantation, invocation, magic charm *or* spell, rigmarole **2.** balderdash, claptrap, dribble, foolishness, froth, gibberish, hot air, nonsense *Nonformal:* baloney, bunkum, crap, double talk, garbage, gobbledygook, jazz, psychobabble, rubbish, tommyrot, tripe

munch *v.* bite, chew, chomp, crunch, eat, masticate, gnaw, gobble *(Nonformal)*, nibble, nosh, snack

mundane *adj.* banal, banausic, commonplace, day-to-day, dullsville *(Nonformal)*, earthly, everyday, humdrum, normal, of this world, ordinary, routine, utilitarian, workaday *Antonyms:* exciting, extraordinary, imaginative, novel, special

municipal *adj.* borough, city, civic, community, district, local, metropolitan, neighbourhood, town, urban, village *Antonyms:* cosmopolitan, continental, global, national, provincial

munificent *adj.* beneficent, benevolent, big, big-hearted, bounteous, bountiful, charitable, free, generous, giving, handsome, lavish, liberal, magnanimous, open-handed, philanthropic, princely, royal, sumptuous, unsparing, unstinting *Antonyms:* cheap, mean, miserly, stingy

mural *n.* decoration, fresco, painting, picture, wall painting, *Wandgemälde (German)*

murder *n.* **1.** annihilation, assassination, bloodshed, butchery, carnage, death, deicide, destruction, foul play, fratricide, homicide, infanticide, killing, knifing, liquidation, lynching, manslaughter, massacre, matricide, non-capital murder *(Historical)*, parricide, patricide, regicide, shooting, slaying, sororicide, uxoricide *Nonformal:* big chill, contract, hit **2.** difficulty, hardship, hazard, ordeal, predicament, trial, tribulation – *v.* **1.** abolish, asphyxiate, assassinate, behead, decapitate, decimate, disembowel, electrocute, eliminate, eradicate, execute, exterminate, extinguish, garrote, guillotine, hang, hit, kill, knife, liquidate, lynch, massacre, shoot, slaughter, slay, smother, strangle *Nonformal:* bump off, chill, dispatch, do in, ice, knock off, off, put away, rub *or* take out, snuff, waste **2.** abuse, blunder, botch, butcher, damage, harm, hurt, impair, mangle, mar, misuse, mutilate, ruin, spoil **3.** annihilate, beat, defeat, destroy, obliterate, overcome, overpower, ravage, surpass, trounce, vanquish *Antonyms:* lose, succumb, suffer, yield

murderer *n.* assassin, bravo, butcher, criminal, cutthroat, enforcer, executioner, gunperson, killer, slaughterer, slayer, sniper, strangler

murky *adj.* **1.** cheerless, cloudy, dark, darkened, dense, dim, dingy, dirty, dismal, drab, dreary, dull, dun, dusk, dusky, filthy, foul, gloomy, glowering, grey, lightless, lowering, misty, muddy, overcast, shadowy, shady, sombre, unlit, veiled *Antonyms:* bright, cheerful, clear, distinct, sunny **2.** abstruse, blurred, faint, fuzzy, hidden, impenetrable, indistinct, nebulous, obfuscated, obscure, stygian, unclear, unknown **3.** clandestine, illicit, open to doubt, questionable, shady, unethical

murmur *n.* **1.** babble, buzz, drone, hum, humming, purr, rumble, undertone **2.** complaint, gripe *(Nonformal)*, grumble, mumble, mutter, muttering, whisper, whispering – *v.* **1.** babble, burble, buzz, flow, gurgle, hum, ripple, tinkle, trickle **2.** mouth, purr, susurrate, verbalize, vocalize, voice, whisper **3.** complain, gripe *(Nonformal)*, grumble, mumble, mutter, utter

muscle *n.* **1.** flesh, sinew, tendon, tissue **2.** brawn, clout, energy, force, forcefulness, might, potency, power, stamina, strength, sturdiness, weight

muscular *adj.* able-bodied, athletic, beefy, brawny, bruising, burly, fibrous, hefty, herculean, hulky, husky, lusty, mighty, powerful, pumped up, robust, sinewy, strapping, strong, tough, wiry *Nonformal:* built, hunky

muse *n.* daimon, fury, genius, influence, inspiration, motivation, power, spirit, stimulus *Greek muses:* Calliope *(Epic poetry)*, Clio *(History)*, Erato *(Love poetry)*, Euterpe *(Music)*, Melpomene *(Tragedy)*, Polyhymnia *(Song)*, Terpsichore *(Dance)*, Thalia *(Comedy)*, Urania *(Astronomy)* – *v.* brood, cogitate, consider, contemplate, deliberate, dream, meditate, moon, mull *or* turn over, percolate, ponder, reflect, revolve, roll, ruminate, speculate, think, weigh

museum *n.* archive, depository, exhibition, foundation, gallery, hall, institution, library, menagerie, *musée (French)*, reliquary, repository, salon, showplace, showroom, storehouse, studio, treasury, vault

mush *interj.* come on, faster, get along, go, hit it *(Nonformal)*, marche, move, run – *n.* **1.** burgoo, goop *(Nonformal)*, oatmeal, muck, Pablum *(Trademark)*, porridge, sludge **2.** bathos, corniness, maudlinism, mawkishness, melodrama, romantic drivel, sappiness, sentimentality

mushroom *n.* champignon, fungus, meadow muffin *(Nonformal)*, toadstool, truffle *Kinds of mushroom and fungus:* black button, chanterelle, edgehog, enoki, field, magic, morel, oyster, porcini, portabello, psilocybin, puffball, shiitake, tree ear *Mushroom parts:* gill, mycelia, pileus, stipe, velum – *v.* balloon, burgeon, burst forth, expand, explode, flourish, increase, proliferate, shoot up, sprout, swell *Antonyms:* diminish, recede, wither

mushy *adj.* **1.** gelatinous, muddy, pappy, paste-like, pulpy, semi-liquid, semi-solid, slushy, soft, spongy, squashy, squishy *Antonyms:* hard, solid, springy **2.** corny, effusive, emotional, hackneyed, maudlin, mawkish, romantic, saccharine, sentimental, sloppy, sugary, sweet, weepy *Nonformal:* cornball, Hollywood, lovey-dovey, schmaltzy, tear-jerking, too too sweet

music *n.* beat, harmony, melody, rhythm, sound, strain, tune *Kinds of music:* acid rock, adult contemporary, alternative, aleatoric, ambient, aria, art *or* auteur rock, ballad, ballet, baroque, bebop, bluegrass, blues, bossanova, bubblegum, Cajun, calypso, chamber, Chicago blues, choral, Christian rock, classic rock, concert, corporate rock, country, country-and-western, dance, dancehall, delta blues, disco, easy listening, elevator, ensemble, film score, folk, folk rock, funk, fusion, gospel, grunge, hard rock, heavy metal, hillbilly, hip-hop, hymn, indie, industrial, instrumental, jazz, jingle, Latin, lounge, Mersey Beat, military, minstrel, Motown, Muzak *(Trademark)*, Nashville, new age, new country, new wave, New York punk, old time, opera, orchestral, orchestral pop, parlour, polka, polyphonic, pop, progressive *or* prog rock, protest, psychedelic, punk, raga, rap, reggae, rhythm and blues, rock, rockabilly, rock 'n' roll, rococo, romantic, sacred, salon, salsa, saraband, scat, ska, socca, soul, soundtrack, string band, suite, surf, swing, symphonic, techno, top 40, vocal, zydeco *See also:* **jazz** *Classical patrons of music:* Apollo, Erato,

Euterpe, Orpheus, Polyhymnia, St. Cecilia, the Muses, the Nine

musical *adj.* agreeable, blending, chiming, choral, consonant, dulcet, euphonious, golden, harmonic, harmonious, lilting, lyrical, mellifluous, mellow, melodic, melodious, orchestral, pleasing, rhythmic, silvery, songful, sweet, sweet-sounding, tuneful, vocal *Antonyms:* discordant, grating, harsh *Kinds of musical composition:* air, aquarelle, bagatelle, concerto, étude, fantasia, fugue, intermezzo, overture, passion, pasticcio, rhapsody, serenade, sonata, sonatina, song, suite, symphony, toccato *Selected musical terms:* accent, acciaccato, accidentals, alto, arabesque, arpeggio, bar, bass, baton, brevis, cadence, cedanza, chord, clef, coda, consonnace, counterpoint, decibel, discord, dissonance, downbeat, echo, enharmonics, finale, flat, glissando, improvisation, interval, intonation, libretto, maestoso, measure, meter, modulation, mute, natural, octave, opus, pitch, refrain, reprise, rest, score, sharp, signature, stanza, syncopation, transpose, tremolo, trill

musician *n.* artist, instrumentalist, interpreter, minstrel, music maker, performer, player, troubadour *Kinds of musician:* accompanist, arranger, backup, bandsman, bassist, brass, bugler, celloist, clarinettist, composer, conductor, cymbalist, drummer, electro-acoustician, fiddler, flautist, guitarist, hurdy-gurdy man, jazz, lyricist, mariachi, oboist, orchestral, orchestrator, organist, percussionist, pianist, reed, rhythm, saxophonist, scorer, singer, solo, songwriter, string, strummer, swing, symphonist, trombonist, trumpeter, violinist, violist, vocalist, wind *Performing musicians:* band, chamber, diva, duet, octet, orchestra, quartet, quintet, rock band, septet, sextet, soloists, symphony

muss *n.* chaos, confusion, disorder, kerfuffle *(Nonformal)*, mess, mess-up, muddle, shambles, state, turmoil, untidiness – *v.* clutter, disarray, dishevel, disorder, disorganize, disrupt, ruffle, rumple, tangle, tousle, upset

must *n.* **1.** decay, dust, mildew, mould, rot **2.** basic, duty, essential, fundamental, necessity, need, requirement, requisite, *sine qua non (Latin)*

mustache *n.* mustachio, whiskers *Nonformal:* bird's-nest, cookie-duster, handlebars, milk mustache, peach fuzz, soup-strainer, stash, tickler

muster *n.* **1.** aggregation, assembly, call-up, collection, company, congress, convocation, draft, gathering, group, head count, meeting, pow wow, rally **2.** list, register, roll, roster – *v.* assemble, collect, congregate, congress, convene, convoke, gather, group, herd, marshal, mobilize, organize, raise, rally, roundup, summon

musty *adj.* **1.** close, dark, decayed, frowsty *(Nonformal)*, fusty, malodorous, mildewed, mouldy, noisome, rotten, smelly, spoiled, stagnant, stale, stuffy **2.** aged, ancient, antediluvian, antique, archaic, moss-backed, obsolete, old, out-of-fate, passé, tired *Antonyms:* chic, hot *(Nonformal)*, new **3.** apathetic, atrabilious, depressed, disaffected, lifeless, melancholy, vigourless *Antonyms:* alive, brisk, energetic, robust, vibrant

mutable *adj* **1.** adjustable, alterable, changeable, convertable, flexible, malleable, metamorphic, modifiable, protean, transformable, variable *Antonyms:* cast in stone, irrevocable, permanent **2.** capricious, fickle, fluctuating, impermanent, mercurial, transmutable, unstable, vacillating, wavering *Antonyms:* constant, stable, steadfast

mutation *n.* **1.** alteration, change, evolution, metamorphosis, modification, transformation, transition, transmogrification, variation, vicissitude **2.** aberration, anomaly, deviation, freak, malformation, mutant, teratism

mute *adj.* **1.** inarticulate, muffled, mum, quiet, reserved, reticent, speechless, taciturn, tongue-tied, uncommunicative, voiceless, wordless *Antonyms:* loquacious, verbose **2.** silent, unexpressed, unpronounced, unspoken – *v.* dampen, deaden, gag, hush, lower, moderate, muffle, muzzle, reduce, silence, soften, subdue, suppress, tone *or* turn down

mutilate *v.* **1.** amputate, batter, butcher, cripple, crush, disable, disembowel, dismember, lacerate, lame, maim, mangle, ravage **2.** damage, deface, disfigure, hurt, injure, mar, ruin, scar, scratch, spoil, vandalize **3.** alter, bowdlerize, change, delete, distort, edit, excise, garble, hack, truncate

mutiny *n.* defiance, disobedience, insubordination, insurrection, resistance, revolt, revolution, riot, strike, uprising – *v.* defy, disobey, kick over the traces *(Nonformal)*, rebel, resist, revolt, rise against *or* up, strike back

mutter *v.* complain, groan, grumble, grunt, mumble, murmur, whisper *Nonformal:* gripe, kvetch

mutual *adj.* **1.** bilateral, collective, correspondent, equivalent, interactive, interchangeable, reciprocal **2.** associated, codependent, common, communal, connected, correlative, interdependent, joint, public, related, requited, respective, returned, shared, two-sided, united

mutually *adv.* by agreement, commonly, conjunctively, cooperatively, in collaboration *or* combination, jointly, reciprocally, together, two-way

muzzle *n.* **1.** face, jaws, mouth, mug *(Nonformal)*, nose, snout **2.** cover, covering, gag, guard, restraint, sheath, wrap – *v.* bottle up, censor, check, curb, gag, hush, muffle, prevent, quiet, quell, quieten, repress, restrain, restrict, shush, silence, squash, squelch, stifle, still, stop, suppress, tongue-tie, trammel

myopic *adj.* **1.** nearsighted, shortsighted, visually impaired **2.** closed-minded, narrow gauged *(Nonformal)*, narrow-minded, obtuse, prejudiced, stubborn

myriad *adj.* countless, endless, immeasurable, incalculable, infinite, innumerable, multiple, multitudinous, numberless, uncounted – *n.* flood, gross, heap, loads, lot, millions, multitude, piles, scores, stacks, ten thousand *Nonformal:* raft, scads, skid, slew

mysterious *adj.* **1.** baffling, confusing, cryptic, curious, enigmatic, incomprehensible, inexplicable, inscrutable, mystifying, puzzling, secretive, strange, unexplained, unknown, unnatural, unusual, weird **2.** abstruse, arcane, concealed, covert, dark, esoteric, furtive, hidden, obscure, occult, recondite, secret, stealthy, veiled *Antonyms:* apparent, clear, manifest, plain

mystery *adj.* hidden, screened, secret, shrouded, undisclosed – *n.* **1.** arcanum, conundrum, enigma, perplexity, problem, puzzle, question, riddle, rune, secret *Nonformal:* brainteaser, poser, stickler, stumper **2.** ambiguity, doubt, inscrutability, obscurity, uncertainty **3.** great unknown, limits of human understanding, *terra incognita (Latin)*, unexplored frontiers *or* territory **4.** awesomeness, majesty, miraculousness, phenomenon, wondrousness **5.** celebration, ceremony, rite, ritual, sacrament **6.** cloak and dagger, furtiveness, intrigue, stealth, surreptitiousness **7.** chiller, cliffhanger, crime fiction *or* novel, detective fiction *or* novel, murder mystery, thriller *Nonformal:* grabber, whodunit

mystic *adj.* anagogic, arcane, cabalistic, cryptic, enigmatic, impenetrable, inscrutable, occult *See also:* **mystical** – *n.* diviner, guru, *Hasid (Judaism)*, holy man *or* woman, initiate, necromancer, oracle priest, priestess, *puoin (Native Peoples)*, sage, shaman, *swami (Hindu)*, witchdoctor, wizard

mystical *adj.* abstruse, allegorical, cryptic, enigmatic, epiphanic, esoteric, hidden, ineffable, inscrutable, metaphysical, occult, otherworldly, paranormal, preternatural, supernatural, symbolic, transcendental, unrevealed *Commonly misused:* **mythical**

mystify *v.* baffle, bamboozle *(Nonformal)*, beat, bewilder, complicate, confound, confuse, elude, escape, flummox, perplex, puzzle, stump, throw, trick, vex

mystique *n.* allure, appeal, attraction, aura, charm, fascination, glamour, magic, mystery, nature, spell

myth *n.* **1.** allegory, creation, fable, fairy tale, fancy, fantasy, fiction, folk story *or* tale, folklore, legend, lore, narrative, parable, saga, story, superstition, tale, tradition

2. delusion, fabrication, fallacy, figment of the imagination, illusion, invention, lie, tall story, untruth

mythical *adj.* **1.** chimerical, fabled, fabricated, fabulous, fanciful, fantasy, fictitious, imaginary, invented, made-up, mythological, pretended, storied, traditional, unreal, whimsical *Nonformal:* tall, wild *Antonyms:* actual, historical, verifiable **2.** celebrated, famous, immortal, legendary, renowned *Commonly misused:* **mystical**

mythology *n.* **1.** belief, fable, folk story *or* tale, folklore, legend, lore, stories, superstition, tales, tradition **2.** beginnings, birth, commencement, evolution, genesis, history, inception, origins, rise

nab *v.* **1.** catch, clutch, grab, secure, seize, snare, snatch *Antonyms:* free, release **2.** apprehend, arrest, capture, take into captivity *or* custody *Nonformal:* collar, nail

nadir *n.* base, bed, bottom, depths, foot, floor, low point *Nonformal:* belly, rock bottom, the pits *Antonyms:* acme, apex, peak, pinnacle, zenith

nag *n.* **1.** gelding, horse, mare, pony, stallion *Nonformal:* bag of bones, bangtail, broomtail, cayuse, crowbait, dobbin **2.** grouch, pain, pest, shrew *Nonformal:* codger, grump – *v.* **1.** complain, criticize, fuss, grumble, whine *Nonformal:* beef, bellyache, bitch, carp, gripe, grouse, squawk **2.** annoy, badger, bother, harass, hector, henpeck, irritate, pester, plague, rile, scold, stress, torment, worry *Nonformal:* bug, work on **3.** concern, gnaw at, haunt, preoccupy, prey on, worry

nail *n.* **1.** peg, pin, rivet, screw, spike, stud, tack *Kinds of nails:* boot, casing, common, door, finishing, galvanized, hobnail, horseshoe, lath, roofing, shoe, tree, upholstery, wire **2.** claw, fingernail, hook, talon, toenail – *v.* **1.** fasten, hammer, join, pin, secure, spike, tack, whack *(Nonformal)* **2.** batten down, burglar *or* storm proof, close, close up, seal, secure, shut *Antonyms:* expose, open **3.** acquire, capture, complete, ensure, finalize, firm up, net, settle, snag, win **4.** apprehend, arrest, catch, intercept, nab, seize *Nonformal:* bag, collar, pinch **5.** box, check, drive, hit, kick, poke, pound, pummel, punch, slam *Nonformal:* clock, deck, paste

naive *adj.* **1.** artless, candid, childlike, forthright, frank, fresh, guileless, harmless, ingenuous, innocent, innocuous, jejune, natural, original, plain, simple, simpleminded, sincere, square *(Nonformal)*, unaffected, unpretentious, unsophisticated, wide-eyed *Antonyms:* artful, experienced, sophisticated, urbane, worldly **2.** accepting, biddable, born yesterday, credulous, gullible, open, trusting, uncritical, unsuspicious *Antonyms:* cautious, trenchant **3** callow, ignorant, illiterate, inexperienced, unlettered, unread, unschooled, untaught, untrained, untutored *Nonformal:* green, new to the game, rookie *Antonyms:* erudite, experienced, studied

naiveté *n.* artlessness, callowness, candour, childishness, credulity, frankness, guilelessness, gullibility, inexperience, ingenuousness, innocence, naturalness, openness, simplicity *Antonyms:* sophistication, urbanity

naked *adj.* **1.** *au natural (French)* bare, nude, unclothed, undressed *Nonformal:* in the altogether *or* buff, starkers, the full monty, without a stitch *Antonyms:* clothed, draped, dressed, garbed **2.** candid, direct, forthright, matter-of-fact, plain, plain-spoken, stark, unadorned, unedited, unembellished *Antonyms:* embellished, embroidered, enhanced **3.** blatant, boldfaced, evident, manifest, obvious, out and out, out-in-the-open, palpable, patent, plain to see, unconcealed, undisguised, unmistakable *Antonyms:* camouflaged, masked, suppressed, unseen **4.** defenseless, exposed, helpless, open, unprotected, vulnerable *Antonyms:* secure, sheltered, shielded **5.** barren, dead, desolate, devastated, devoid of life, empty, featureless, lifeless, stripped, treeless, waste *Antonyms:* green, lush, verdant

name *n.* **1.** alias, appellation, cognomen, denomination, designation, epithet, eponym, flag, heading, label, matronymic, monogram, nickname, nomen *(Historical)*, patronymic, pseudonym, rubric, sign, signature, sobriquet, style, surname, tag, term, title *French:* nom de guerre, nom de plume *Nonformal:* handle, John Doe, John Henry, moniker **2.** celebrity, entertainer, headliner, hero, lion, luminary, notable, personality, star, superstar *Nonformal:* big name, draw, glitterati, somebody **3.** credit, distinction, eminence, esteem, fame, honour, note, praise, renown, reputation, repute – *v.* **1.** baptize, call, christen, classify, define, denominate, designate, dub, entitle, identify, label, nickname, tag, term, title **2.** cite, classify, credit, index, list, mention, recognize, reference **3.** denote, finger *(Nonformal)*, identify, make, mark, peg, point *or* single out **4.** announce, decide, declare, decree, establish, fix, settle, specify **5.** appoint, choose, commission, delegate, designate, elect, nominate, select

nameless *adj.* **1.** anon, anonymous, inconspicuous, obscure, unmarked, unsung *Antonyms:* famous, notorious, renowned **2.** appalling, awful, blasphemous, disturbing, dreadful, frightful, heinous, horrible, indescribable, inexpressible, shocking, stomach-turning, unmentionable, unspeakable, unutterable, vile, wretched **3.** equivocal, generic, unacknowledged, uncategorized, unknown, unlabelled, unmentioned, unreported

namely *adv.* especially, expressly, particularly, specifically, that is to say, to wit, viz.

nanny *n.* au pair, baby sitter, caregiver, governess, housekeeper, nurse, nursemaid

nap *n.* **1.** catnap, doze, interlude, intermission, nod, pause, respite, rest, siesta, sleep *Nonformal:* 40 winks, power nap, shuteye, snooze **2.** down, fibre, grain, grit, pile, roughness, shag, smoothness, surface, tooth, wale, warp, weave, weft, woof – *v.* catnap, doze, drop *or* nod off, drowse, relax, rest, sleep *Nonformal:* catch some zzz's, cop a nod, grab some shut-eye, snooze

narcissistic *adj.* conceited, egocentric, egotistic, egotistical, self-absorbed, self- centered, self-loving, self-satisfied, vain *Nonformal:* full of oneself, puffed-up *Antonyms:* charitable, open-hearted, selfless

narcotic *adj.* analgesic, anesthetic, calming, deadening, dulling, hypnotic, numbing, opiate, painkilling, palliative, sedative, somnolent, soporific, stupefying – *n.* analgesic, anesthetic, anodyne, controlled substance, drug, lenitive, nepenthe, opiate, painkiller, sedative, somnifacient, soporific, stupefacient, tranquilizer *Nonformal:* dope, dose, fix, gear, goods, junk, stuff *See also:* **drug, tranquilizer**

narrate *v.* **1.** delineate, describe, detail, explain, fictionalize, mythologize, recite, recount, relate, report, retell, spin *(Nonformal)*, tell

narrative *adj.* anecdotal, associative, chronological, disjointed, dramatic, fictional, fictive, historical, story-like *Antonyms:* dissociative, surreal, unrelated – *n.* **1.** account, anecdote, book, chronicle, chronology, description, detail, fiction, history, line, recital, report, statement, story, tale, version *Nonformal:* potboiler, yarn **2.** disclosing, narration, play-by-play, reciting, recounting, relating, retelling, talking

narrow *adj.* **1.** attenuated, compressed, constricted, shrunken, slender, slim, small, tapering, thin, thread-like *Antonyms:* big, broad, generous, open, wide **2.** circumscribed, confined, fixed, limited, restricted *Antonyms:* broad, expansive, vast **3.** biased, bigoted, hidebound, illiberal, inflexible, intolerant, mean, narrow-minded, parochial, prejudiced, reactionary, small-minded, stupid, ungenerous *Antonyms:* broad-minded, generous **4.** close, near, precarious, slippery, ticklish, touch-and-go *(Nonformal) Antonyms:* reliable, safe **5.** exiguous, impoverished, meagre, pinched, scant, spare, straitened, tight **6.** careful, detailed, exacting, minute, painstaking, precise, rigorous *Antonyms:* clumsy, heedless, sloppy **7.** exclusive, restricted, select, snobbish, snotty *(Nonformal) Antonyms:* democratic, public – *n.* cut, fjord, gut, inlet, passage, seaway, sound, strait – *v.* attenuate, constrict, contract, diminish, limit, reduce, simplify, taper, tighten *Antonyms:* amplify, enlarge, expand, magnify

narrow-minded *adj.* biased, bigoted, conservative, hidebound, insular, intolerant, one-sided, opinionated, parochial, provincial, puritanical, reactionary, small-minded *Antonyms:* broad-minded, permissive, tolerant

nascent *adj.* beginning, bubbling, budding, developing, embryonic, evolving, germinal, growing, initiative, rising, seminal

nasty *adj.* **1.** disgusting, foul, malodorous, nauseating, noisome, noxious, objectionable, odious, polluted, putrid, repugnant, revolting, rotten, sickening, stinking, stomach-turning, unappetizing *Antonyms:* appealing, aromatic, fragrant **2.** coarse, dirty, gross, indecent, indelicate, obscene, rude, uncivil, uncouth, vulgar *Antonyms:* clean, conventional, polite **3.** awful, bad, damnable, disagreeable, disturbing, dreadful, horrible, lousy *(Nonformal)*, unattractive, unpleasant *Antonyms:* excellent, fine, great **4.** abusive, bad-tempered, beastly, cruel, despicable, distasteful, evil, fell, hateful, ill-natured, malevolent, malicious, malignant, mean, ornery, owly *(Nonformal)*, murderous, ruthless, sarcastic, scrofulous, scurvy, sordid, spiteful, squalid, unkind, vicious *Antonyms:* affable, decent, friendly, kind **5.** crippling, damaging, deadly, debilitating, excruciating, fierce, harrowing, hellish *(Nonformal)*, injurious, painful, serious, severe *Antonyms:* superficial, trivial **6.** bawdy, filthy, lascivious, lewd, licentious, off-colour, offensive, pornographic, prurient, rude, wanton, X-rated *Nonformal:* adult, blue *Antonyms:* family-oriented, G-rated, wholesome

nation *n.* **1.** city-state, commonwealth, confederation, country, dominion, federation, geopolitical entity, kingdom, land, nation-state, *pays (French)*, republic, sovereignty, state, union **2.** body, citizens, community, culture, distinct society, ethnic group, inhabitants, people, race, society, tribe

nationalism *n.* **1.** chauvinism, devotion, flag-waving, jingoism, partisanship, patriotism, regionalism, zealotry **2.** autonomy, cleavage, disassociation, disbanding, disunion, division, independence, revolution, self-determination, separation, separatism, sovereignty **3.** economic quarantine, embargoism, isolationism, protectionism, tariff *or* trade sanction *(Nonformal) Antonyms:* free trade, invisible hand, laissez faire

nationality *n.* ancestry, birthplace, citizenship, country, nation, native land, place of origin, political home, society

native *adj.* **1.** domestic, inland, inshore, internal, local, national, provincial *Antonyms:* alien, foreign **2.** built-in, congenital, hereditary, inborn, ingrained, inherent, inherited, innate, natal, natural **3.** ancestral, father, home, mother, original *Antonyms:* adopted, chosen **4.** aboriginal, autochthonous, endemic, indigenous **5.** basic, constitutional, essential, fundamental, necessary, requisite *Antonyms:* insignificant, irrelevant **6.** bucolic, country, crude, home-grown, homespun, primitive, rural, rustic, simple *Antonyms:* polished, refined **7.** authentic, genuine, pure, unsullied, untarnished *Antonyms:* adulterated, altered – *n.* **1.** citizen, habitant, inhabitant, landsman, local, patriot, resident, subject, yokel *(Nonformal)* **2.** aboriginal, aborigine, First Nations, First *or* Native Peoples, original *See also:* **First Peoples**

natural *adj.* **1.** additive *or* chemical free, authentic, genuine, original, pure, real, unadulterated, unprocessed, unrefined, unsimulated **2.** pristine, uncorrupted, undamaged, unspoiled, unsullied, untarnished, untouched, virgin *Antonyms:* defiled, polluted, violated **3.** customary, normal, ordinary, regular, standard, typical, usual *Antonyms:* abnormal, erratic, irregular **4.** adept, born, deft, endowed, gifted, skilful, skilled *Antonyms:* incapable, incompetent **5.** inborn, inbred, ingrained, innate, native *Antonyms:* learned, schooled, trained **6.** feral, raw, uncivilized, uncultivated, uncultured, undisciplined, undomesticated, untutored, wild **7.** earthy, easy, folksy, graceful, guileless, simple, unaffected, unforced, unpretentious **8.** biological, carbon-based, cellular, living, organic, protoplasmic **9.** inalienable, indefeasible, inherent, inviolable, nonnegotiable **10.** birth, blood, consanguine, family, genetic, kin, kindred **11.** credible, logical, rational, reasonable, sensible, sound *Antonyms:* contradictory, inconsistent **12.** analogous, faithful, lifelike, realistic, resemblant, similar, true-to-life **13.** actual, material, physical, solid, substantial, tangible *Antonyms:* ethereal, immaterial, incorporeal – *n.* adept, crackerjack *(Nonformal)*, expert, genius, master, prodigy, virtuoso, wizard, *wunderkind (German)*

naturalize *v.* **1.** confer citizenship, empower, endow, enfranchise, include, invest, swear in **2.** acclimatize, acculturate, accustom *or* acquaint oneself, adapt, adopt, Anglicize, assimilate, Canadianize, familiarize, Frenchify, transculturate **3.** bring in, establish, import, insert, introduce *Antonyms:* cancel, eliminate, remove

naturally *adv.* **1.** candidly, casually, characteristically, commonly, consistently, customarily, easily, normally, ordinarily, simply, typically, uniformly, usually **2.** habitually, impulsively, innocently, instinctively, spontaneously, unaffectedly **3.** absolutely, assuredly, certainly, freely, genuinely, of course, readily, surely

nature *n.* **1.** complexion, composition, constitution, crux, essence, makeup, matter, meaning, quality, structure, substance, value *Nonformal:* meat, stuff **2.** cosmos, creation, Earth, ecosphere, ecosystem, environment, life, macrocosm, Terra, universe, world **3.** character, disposition, heart, humour, individuality, mood, personality, psyche, singularity, soul, spirit, temper, temperament **4.** a priori knowledge *or* understanding, instinct, intuition, proclivity **5.** arrangement, brand, category, class, designation, extraction, genus, grouping, ilk, kind, name, order, ordination, shape, sort, species, stripe *(Nonformal)*, type, variety **6.** naturalness, normality, order, regularity, typicality **7.** primitiveness, primordialism, wildness

naughty *adj.* **1.** bad, disobedient, ill-behaved, impolite, improper, mischievous, unseemly *Antonyms:* polite, proper, seemly, well-behaved **2.** bawdy, dirty, fast, lewd, loose, off-colour, ribald, risqué, salty *(Nonformal)*

nausea *n.* **1.** airsickness, carsickness, motion sickness, nauseousness, qualms, queasiness, seasickness, sickness, squeamishness, upset stomach, vomiting **2.** abhorrence, aversion, disgust, distaste, dread, loathing, revulsion

nauseate *v.* bother, disgust, disturb, horrify, irritate, offend, repel, repulse, revolt, sicken, upset *Antonyms:* attract, appeal, interest, tempt

nauseous *adj.* **1.** airsick, carsick, nauseated, queasy, seasick, sick, squeamish, upset **2.** disgusting, nasty, nauseating, offensive, revolting, rocky *(Nonformal)*, sickening, upsetting

nautical *adj.* Atlantic, lake, marine, maritime, naval, oceanic, Pacific, salt-water, sea, seafaring, seagoing, transatlantic, transpacific *Nonformal:* crustaceous, salty

navel *n.* **1.** bellybutton *(Nonformal)*, depression, hub, middle, nave, pit, umbilicus **2.** centre, core, focus, ganglion, heart, middle *Antonyms:* fringe, periphery

navigate *v.* **1.** cruise, paddle, roll, sail, steam *(Nonformal)*, voyage, yacht **2.** march, progress, strut, travel, tread **3.** aviate, fly, glide, jet, plane, soar, take wing **4.** cross, get past *or* through, negotiate, pass, portage, traverse, weave through, wend along **5.** captain, guide, pilot, skipper, steer **6.** direct oneself, manoeuvre, orient oneself, plot a course

navigation *n.* **1.** adventure, coasting, crossing, cruise, exploration, passage, sailing, seafaring, voyage **2.** channelling, directorship, guidance, handling, helmsmanship, piloting, maneuvering, seamanship, steering **3.** bearing, celestial interpretation, compress reading, course, direction, measurement, plot

navigator *n.* **1.** airman, airwoman, aviator, captain, chief, flyer, pilot, skipper **2.** boater, coxswain, doryman, fisherman, helmsman, mariner, sailor, seafarer, seaman, skipper, steersman, submariner, yachtsman *Nonformal:* gob, salt, sea dog, tar

navy *n.* argosy, armada, coast guard, fleet, flotilla, merchant marine, naval forces, warships

near *adj.* **1.** abutting, adjacent, adjoining, beside, bordering, contiguous, neighbouring, proximate *Antonyms:* distant, remote, removed **2.** advancing, approaching, arriving, imminent, looming, nearing **3.** approximate, close, narrow, tight **4.** akin, blood, connected, consanguineous, familiar, kindred, related **5.** amicable, chummy *(Nonformal)*, congenial, dear, friendly, intimate *Antonyms:* belligerent, hostile **6.** direct, immediate, lineal, short, straight, undeviating **7.** cheap, churlish, frugal, mean, miserly, parsimonious, petty, selfish, stingy, tightfisted, ungenerous *Antonyms:* generous, liberal, philanthropic **8.** accessible, at hand, available, convenient, handy, ready – *adv.* **1.** about, around, around the corner, close by, nearby, nigh, within reach *or* walking distance **2.** almost, approximately, closely, just about, nearly **3.** congenially, friendly, intimately, lovingly, warmly **4.** cheap, economically, frugally, miserly – *prep.* beside, bordering on, close by *or* to, neighbouring on, next to, with, within reach – *v.* advance, approach, come, creep, gain on, impend, loom, progress, verge upon

nearing *adj.* advancing, approaching, approximating, coming, forthcoming, imminent, impending, looming, oncoming, threatening, upcoming

nearly *adv.* **1.** about, almost, in effect, just about, practically, virtually **2.** approximately, around, roughly, roundly, well-nigh

nearsighted *adj.* **1.** myopic, poor-sighted, short-sighted, squint eyed *(Nonformal)* **2.** chauvinistic, close-minded, fixed, insular, narrow-minded, parochial, provincial, sectarian, small-minded *Antonyms:* broadminded, catholic, receptive

neat *adj.* **1.** bright, clean, free of dirt, fresh, hygienic, immaculate, laundered, natty, orderly, prim, proper, pure, sanitary, shining, shipshape, slick, sparkling, spotless, stainless, straight, tidy, trim, unblemished, uncluttered, unpolluted, unstained, unsullied, untarnished, washed, well-arranged, well-kept *Nonformal:* apple-pie, spick-and-span *Antonyms:* cluttered, disorderly, disorganized, messy **2.** clear, exact, fastidious, finicky, flawless, meticulous, precise, scrupulous *Antonyms:* imprecise, muddled, off the mark **3.** able, adept, adroit, agile, apt, artful, clever, deft, dexterous, efficient, elegant, expert, finished, graceful, handy, practiced, precise, proficient, ready, skilful, well-judged *Antonyms:* clumsy, incompetent, inefficient **4.** brilliant, capital, excellent, fantastic, fine, grand, great, marvellous, wonderful *Nonformal:* A-OK, awesome, bad, cool, fab, far-out, funky, gear, groovy, jim dandy, keen, marvy, peachy, right on **5.** straight, straight-up *(Nonformal)*, unblended, uncut, undiluted, unmixed

nebula *n.* celestial body, dust *or* gas cloud, cluster, galaxy, interstellar mass, spiral, system *Kinds of nebula:* dark, emission, planetary, reflection *Selected nebulae:* Crab, Eagle, Great, Helix, Horsehead, Lagoon, Orion, Ring, Trifid

nebulous *adj.* **1.** ambiguous, amorphous, confused, dim, imprecise, indefinite, indeterminate, indistinct, murky, shadowy, shapeless, uncertain, unclear, unformed, vague *Antonyms:* clear, defined, sharp **2.** cloudlike, cloudy, foggy, hazy, misty **3.** astral, astrological, celestial, cosmic, heavenly, starry

necessarily *adv.* accordingly, automatically, axiomatically, cardinally, certainly, compulsorily, consequently, exigently, fundamentally, incontrovertibly, indubitably, ineluctably, inescapably, inevitably, inexorably, irresistibly, naturally, perforce, positively, pressingly, significantly, undoubtedly, unquestionably, vitally, without a doubt

necessary *adj.* **1.** basic, cardinal, chief, core, elementary, essential, fundamental, indispensible, prime, principal, quintessential, required, specified *Antonyms:* addendum, extra, extraneous, supplementary **2.** all-important, crucial, decisive, expedient, imperative, important, momentous, paramount, pressing, significant, urgent, vital *Antonyms:* insignificant, minor, of no account, trifling **3.** certain, imminent, ineluctable, inescapable, inevitable, inexorable, sure, unavoidable, unescapable *Antonyms:* avoidable, evadable **4.** binding, compelling, compulsory, *de rigueur (French)*, exigent, mandatory, obligatory, prerequisite **5.** clear, incontestable, incontrovertible, irrefutable, obvious, patent, undeniable, unquestionable

necessitate *v.* call for, cause, command, compel, constrain, demand, drive, force, impel, need, oblige, require

necessity *n.* **1.** essential, fundamental, indispensable, prerequisite, principal, requirement *Nonformal:* nitty-gritty, nuts-and-bolts **2.** demand, desire, hunger, impetus, must, need, proclivity, want, will **3.** exigency, impoverishment, lack, marginalization, paucity, penury, poverty, privation, shortage **4.** coercion, duress, force, impulsion, obligation, prescription **5.** certainty, inevitability, irrevocability, unavoidableness

neck *n.* **1.** cervix, *cou (French)*, nape, scruff **2.** cape, isthmus, passage, throat, tongue **3.** arm, canal, channel, creek, narrows, sluice, straight – *v.* caress, kiss, pet, snuggle, stroke *Nonformal:* make out, smooch

necromancy *n.* alchemy, astrology, black magic, demonology, deviltry, diabolism, divination, sorcery, voodoo, witchcraft, witchery, wizardry

need *n.* **1.** demand, desire, fancy, hankering, hunger, longing, want, wish *Nonformal:* itch, yen **2.** essential, fundamental, imperative, necessity, prerequisite, requirement, requisite, *sine qua non (Latin)* **3.** charge, commitment, committal, compulsion, duty, exigency, obligation, right, urgency **4.** danger, deficiency, deprivation, destitution, distress, extremity, hardship, impecuniousness, impoverishment, inadequacy, indigence, insufficiency, lack, paucity, pennilessness, penury, poorness, poverty, privation, shortage, want – *v.* **1.** covet, crave, demand, desire, hanker *or* hunger for, long, lust, suffer, thirst, want, yearn **2.** be compelled *or* obliged *or* ordered *or* summoned, have to, required,

needle *n.* indicator, piercer, pin, pointer, stylus *Kinds of needle:* awl, bodkin, compass, darning, engraving, etching, hypodermic, probe, quilting, sailcloth, sewing, sewing-machine, straight, surgical, syringe, tattoo, trocar – *v.* **1.** goad, nag, press, prod, spur, stimulate **2.** annoy, disturb, exasperate, hassle *(Nonformal)*, irk, pester, pick on, rile, tease, vex *Antonyms:* calm, mollify, quell, soothe **3.** crotchet, darn, fix, interlace, mend, repair, sew, stitch

needless *adj.* dispensable, excessive, expendable, gratuitous, groundless, nonessential, pointless, redundant, senseless, superfluous, uncalled for, undesired, unnecessary, unwanted, useless *Antonyms:* beneficial, essential, obligatory, required, useful

needy *adj.* bankrupt, destitute, down and out, impoverished, indigent, insolvent, lacking, mendicant, necessitous, pauperized, penniless, penurious, pinched, poor, poverty-stricken, reduced, squeezed, straitened, strapped, underdeveloped, wanting *Nonformal:* broke, busted, dirt poor, down-at-the-heels, flat *Antonyms:* affluent, monied, prosperous, rich, wealthy

ne'er-do-well *adj.* ineffective, insignificant, lazy, no-good, shiftless, unreliable, useless, worthless – *n.* delinquent, idler, knave, layabout, loafer, malingerer, rascal, reprobate, rogue, scalawag, shirker, sluggard, wastrel *Nonformal:* bum, good-for-nothing, hoser, lazybones, no-account, slacker

nefarious *adj.* abominable, atrocious, base, criminal, evil, fell, foul, gross, heinous, horrible, monstrous, odious, shameful, treacherous, vicious, vile, villainous, wicked *Antonyms:* honest, noble, praiseworthy, upright, virtuous

negate *v.* **1.** abrogate, annul, cancel, disapprove, invalidate, nix, nullify, repeal, rescind, retract, revoke, turn down, void *Nonformal:* bump, dump, kill, scratch *Antonyms:* approve, avouch, ratify **2.** contradict, controvert, cross, decline, deny, dismiss, frustrate, invalidate, neutralize, overturn, rebuff, rebut, refute, reject, repudiate, reverse, undo, vitiate *Antonyms:* affirm, assert, avow, confirm

negation *n.* **1.** antithesis, antonym, contradiction, contrary, converse, opposite, reverse **2.** abnegation, denial, disavowal, disclaimer, nullification, refusal to recognize, refutation, repudiation, veto **3.** absence, blank, emptiness, negative, nothing, nullity, vacuum, void

negative *adj.* **1.** invalidating, nullifying, refusal, rescinding, voiding **2.** antithetical, contradictory, contrary, counter, opposing, opposite, reverse **3.** below budget *or* expectation *or* zero, deficient, in the red *(Nonformal)*, less than zero, under par *(Golf)* **4.** argumentative, disagreeable, disapproving, down at the mouth, nay-saying, pessimistic, truculent – *interj.* certainly not, incorrect, nay, *nein (German)*, no, not *(Nonformal)*, not so *or* true, no way, *nyet (Russian)*, wrong – *n.* **1.** denial, disapproval, negation, refusal, rejection, turndown, veto *Nonformal:* no-go, thumbs down *Antonyms:* acceptance, authorization, blessing **2.** confutation, contradiction, gainsay, opposition, repudiation *Antonyms:* adoption, embrace, endorsement

neglect *n.* **1.** carelessness, delinquency, dereliction, disregard, failure, heedlessness, inattention, indifference, laxity, laxness, negligence, omission, oversight, slackness, thoughtlessness *Antonyms:* attention, care, consideration, notice, regard **2.** collapse, decay, degradation, disarray, disorder, disrepair, limbo, ruin, rust – *v.* **1.** discount, dismiss, disregard, evade, fail, forget, ignore, marginalize, miss, omit, overlook, postpone, procrastinate, reject, shirk, suspend *Nonformal:* let slide, pay no mind, slough over *Antonyms:* notice, observe, regard, value **2.** abandon, desert, leave, spurn

negligence *n.* carelessness, dereliction, disregard, forgetfulness, indifference, lack of attention, laxity, omission, oversight, recklessness, sloppiness, thoughtlessness

negligible *adj.* imperceptible, inconsequential, insignificant, minor, minute, not worth considering, paltry, petty, remote, slender, slight, slim, small, trace, trifling, trivial, unimportant *Nonformal:*beans, chump change *Antonyms:* important, momentous, noteworthy, significant

negotiate *v.* **1.** bargain, barter, deal, debate, dicker, discuss, haggle, horse trade *(Nonformal)*, peddle, truck **2.** accomplish, agree, arrange, conclude, contract, finalize, make terms, nail down *(Nonformal)*, seal, settle, sign, work out **3.** assign, exchange, flip *(Nonformal)*, sell, shift, transact, transfer, turn over **4.** clear, climb, cope, cross, execute, hurdle, leap, manage, manoeuvre through, pass, scramble, surmount, traverse, vault

negotiation *n.* **1.** arbitration, back and forth *(Nonformal)*, bargaining, give and take, intervention, mediation, transaction **2.** concave, conference, consultation, debate, discussion, meeting, palaver, talk

negotiator *n.* ambassador, arbitrator, bargainer, broker, controller, delegate, fixer *(Nonformal)*, go-between, intermediary, judge, mediator, moderator, ombudsperson

neighbour *n.* backyard acquaintance, over the fence friend, local, nearest house *or* person, seatmate – *v.* abut, adjoin, border, butt against, conjoin, connect, join, run along, touch, verge

neighbourhood *n.* **1.** area, *arrondissement (French)*, block, community, confines, district, environment, environs, ghetto, locale, parish, part, precinct, purlieus, quarter, region, section, slum, street, suburb, surroundings, territory *Nonformal:* beat, hood, jungle, stomping ground, turf **2.** adjacency, closeness, contiguity, immediacy, locality, nearness, proximity, vicinity

neighbourly *adj.* amiable, civil, companionable, considerate, cooperative, cordial, friendly, genial, gracious, harmonious, helpful, hospitable, kind, obliging, sociable, well-disposed *Antonyms:* distant, remote

nemesis *n.* adversary, antagonist, antithesis, competitor, contender, disputant, enemy, equal, evil twin, foe, Moriarty *(Nonformal)*, opponent, opposite, rival, shadow self *Antonyms:* assistant, friend

neophyte *n.* amateur, apprentice, beginner, convert, entrant, fledgling, freshman, intern, learner, novice, novitiate, probationer, recruit, rookie, student, tenderfoot, trainee, virgin *Nonformal:* cub, first-timer, greenhorn, new guy, new kid on the block, tyro *Antonyms:* authority, expert, professional, veteran

nepotism *n.* bias, favouritism, inequity, partiality, partisanship, patronage, preferential treatment *Antonyms:* equality, fairness, impartiality

nerd *n.* bookworm *Nonformal:* brainiac,

dork, drip, egghead, four-eyes, geek, keener, poindexter *Antonyms:* bully, jock

nerve *n.* **1.** assurance, backbone, boldness, confidence, courage, daring, determination, fortitude, gameness, grit, gumption, mettle, perspicacity, pluck, resolve, temerity *Nonformal:* chutzpah, grit, guts, intestinal fortitude, moxie, spunk, starch **2.** arrogance, audacity, brashness, brazenness, effrontery, forwardness, impudence, insolence, presumption, shamelessness *Nonformal:* cheek, gall **3.** bundle, fibre, ganglion – *v.* **1.** bolster, brace, cheer, embolden, encourage, fortify, hearten

nerveless *adj.* **1.** cowardly, craven, fearful, feeble, pusillanimous, timorous, weak **2.** calm, collected, composed, controlled, cool, impassive, imperturbable, intrepid, patient, self-possessed, tranquil, unemotional *Antonyms:* emotional, impatient, perturbed, wild

nerve-racking *adj.* **1.** annoying, bothersome, irksome, irritating, shrill, trying, vexing *Antonyms:* calming, mollifying, soothing **2.** disturbing, frightening, hair-raising, harrowing, horrendous, spine-tingling, terrifying *Antonyms:* appreciated, gratifying, pleasant

nervous *adj.* **1.** agitated, anxious, apprehensive, bothered, concerned, distressed, disturbed, edgy, excitable, fearful, fidgety, fitful, flustered, fretful, hesitant, high-strung, hysterical, irritable, jittery, jumpy, nervy, neurotic, on edge, overwrought, ruffled, shaky, shy, skittish, taut, tense, troubled, twitchy, uneasy, upset, worried *Nonformal:* spooked, uptight, white-knuckled, wired *Antonyms:* calm, cool, confident, relaxed **2.** cerebral, neural, neurological

nervousness *n.* agitation, anxiousness, discomfiture, disquiet, dithers, excitability, feverishness, impatience, jitters, quivers, shakes, stress, tension, touchiness, tremulousness, uneasiness, worry *Nonformal:* cold sweat, fidgets, goose bumps, heebie-jeebies, jimjams, jumps, pins and needles, stage fright, the creeps *or* willies *Antonyms:* aplomb, assurance, confidence

nervy *adj.* **1.** arrogant, brash, brazen, cheeky, cocky, forward, impudent, insolent, sassy, shameless *Nonformal:* flip, in your face **2.** charged, excitable, high-strung, jumpy, nervous, sensitive, skittish, wired *(Nonformal)*

nest *n.* **1.** aerie, den, hive, home, hutch, lair, perch, roost **2.** brood, colony, covey, flock, gaggle, herd, pack, school, swarm, team, troop *See also:* **group** **3.** haven, hermitage, hideaway, refuge, retreat, sanctuary, shelter, snuggery **4.** bordello, crackhouse, den of iniquity, hangout, haunt – *v.* bed down, flop, land, make a house, reside, settle *Nonformal:* set stakes, take root

nest egg *n.* cache, insurance, reserve, retirement fund, RRSP, savings, security *See also:* **investment**

nestle *v.* **1.** bundle, burrow, cuddle, curl up, huddle, lie against *or* close, nuzzle, snuggle **2.** lodge, rest, roost, settle down, take shelter

net *adj.* **1.** irreducible, leftover, remaining, spare, surplus *Nonformal:* after-tax, take-home **2.** conclusive, decisive, definitive, final, last, ultimate – *n.* **1.** bottom line, earnings, gain, income, proceeds, profit, take **2.** cheesecloth, lace, mesh, meshwork, netting, screen, sieve, tracery, web **3.** dragnet, gill net, noose, purse net, seine, snare, trap, trawl, weir **4.** goal, goalie net *Parts of a hockey net:* crease, crossbar, pipes, post, webbing – *v.* **1.** catch, enmesh, ensnare, ensnarl, entrap, hook, land, tangle, trap **2.** accumulate, bring *or* take in, clear, earn, gain, make, profit, realize, reap *Nonformal:* bag, pocket

nettle *v.* anger, annoy, badger, bother, chafe, exasperate, excite, infuriate, irk, irritate, madden, needle *(Nonformal)*, pique, rile, vex *Antonyms:* calm, pacify, soothe

network *n.* **1.** arrangement, chain, channels, checkerboard, circuitry, complex, connections, crisscross, grid, interconnection, labyrinth, maze, nexus, patchwork, reticulation, structure, system, track, web, wiring *Kinds of computer network:* bulletin board, Internet, intranet, local area network *or* LAN, Usenet, wide area network *or* WAN, World Wide Web **2.** fabric, grill, lattice, matting, mesh, netting, trellis **3.** affiliation, alliance, association, brotherhood, chain, coalition, consortium, cooperative, federation, fellowship, franchise, guild, organization, outfit, ring, sisterhood, society, syndicate, union – *v.* communicate, interface, make connections, socialize *Nonformal:* do lunch, glad hand, swap cards, work the crowd

neural *adj.* central, cerebral, cortical, nerve, nervous, neurochemical, neurogenic, neurological

neurosis *n.* aberration, abnormality, affliction, anxiety, breakdown, cenethesia, depression, derangement, disorder, disturbance, hypochondria, hysteria, insanity, insomnia, instability, maladjustment, mental illness, neurasthenia, phobia, psychological disorder, psychoneurosis

neurotic *adj.* compulsive, deviant, disordered, disoriented, distraught, disturbed, erratic, hysteric, manic, nervous, neurasthenic, obsessive, overwrought, sensitive, sick, unstable, upset *Nonformal:* hung up, spooked, strung out, superanxious, uptight, warped, wired – *n.* compulsive, hypochondriac, obsessive *Nonformal:* freak, sicko, weirdo

neuter *adj.* asexual, genderless, indefinite, middling, neutral, passive – *v.* alter, castrate, change, de-sex, emasculate, fix, geld, make barren *or* infertile, spay, sterilize

neutral *adj.* **1.** abstaining, impartial, nonaligned, non-interfering, noncommittal, nonpartisan, prejudice-free, unbiased **2.** demilitarized, demobilized, inactive, noncombatant, pacifistic, passive *Antonyms:* active, belligerent, hostile **3.** asexual, indefinite, indeterminate, intermediate, middling, neuter *Antonyms:* feminine, masculine **4.** colourless, drab, hueless, inconspicuous, indiscernible, indistinguishable, monochromatic, unexceptional, unremarkable *Antonyms:* bright, vivid – *n.* free agent, independent, nonpartisan

neutralize *v.* **1.** abrogate, annul, cancel out, invalidate, negate, nullify, overturn, reject **2.** exclude, exempt, omit **3.** counteract, counterbalance, dampen, offset, soften, suppress **4.** annihilate, destroy, eradicate, exterminate, extinguish, kill, liquidate, massacre, slaughter *Nonformal:* erase, wipe out

never *adv.* at no time, not at all, on no account, under no circumstances *Nonformal:* when hell freezes over, when pigs fly

new *adj.* **1.** contemporary, current, modern, recent, ultramodern *Antonyms:* ancient, antique, historical **2.** *au courant (French)*, avant-garde, break, chic, cutting-edge *(Nonformal)*, fashionable, latest, newfangled, nouveau, original, revolutionary, trendy, up-to-date, vanguard *Nonformal:* funky, groovy, hip, just out *Antonyms:* old-fashioned, outmoded, passé, through **3.** blooming, budding, burgeoning, dawning, developing, flourishing, growing, immature, nascent, sprouting, waxing, young, youthful *Antonyms:* dying, faltering, setting **4.** alien, foreign, novel, strange, undiscovered, unfamiliar, unheard of, unknown **5.** altered, changed, improved, modernized, redesigned, redone, reengineered, refreshed, regenerated, renewed, restored, revived, updated *Antonyms:* hackneyed, old, stale, trite **6.** dewy, fresh, green, pristine, unblemished, uncontaminated, undamaged, unspoiled, untouched, untrodden, unused, virgin *Antonyms:* broken, damaged, preowned, spoiled, used **7.** callow, green *(Nonformal)*, inexperienced, juvenile, unfledged, unseasoned, untrained *Antonyms:* experienced, trained, veteran **8.** additional, doubled, escalating, increased, reiterated, renewed, repeated **9.** energized, invigorated, recharged, refreshed, regenerated, rejuvenated

newcomer *n.* **1.** cheechako, foreigner, immigrant, new arrival, newborn, new Canadian, outsider, settler, stranger **2.** beginner, first-year, fledgling, freshman, learner, neophyte, novice, novitiate, rookie *Nonformal:* greenhorn, tenderfoot

newfangled *adj.* contemporary, current, faddish, fashionable, modern, popular, recent, state-of-the-art, trendy, up-to-date *Nonformal:* latest-kick, space-aged *Antonyms:* antediluvian, antiquated, archaic, old, outdated

newly *adv.* anew, freshly, just, lately, latterly, new, of late, recently

news *n. pl.* **1.** announcement, article, broadcast, bulletin, cable, communiqué, copy, exposé, headline, narration, news flash *or* wire, release, report, story, telecast, webcast **2.** communication, data, information, knowledge, message, notification, tidings, word **3.** gossip, hearsay, rumour, scandal *Nonformal:* buzz, dirt, goods, info, lowdown, scoop, skinny **4.** disclosure, discovery, enlightenment, revelation

newsgroup *n.* bulletin board, discussion group, forum, listserv, usenet

next *adj.* **1.** after, consequent, ensuing, following, later, subsequent, succeeding **2.** abutting, adjacent, adjoining, attached, beside, close, closest, conterminous, contiguous, immediate, nearest, neighbouring, touching – *adv.* after, afterwards, hereon, immediately, later, subsequently, successively – *prep.* abreast, alongside, close by, closest *or* nearest to, nearby, side-by-side

nibble *n.* bite, crumb, morsel, snack, soupçon, taste, tidbit – *v.* bite, eat, graze, munch, nip, nosh *(Nonformal)*, pick at, snack *Antonyms:* devour, gobble, stuff

nice *adj.* **1.** admirable, attentive, chivalrous, commendable, considerate, decorous, gallant, good, gracious, helpful, thoughtful *Antonyms:* base, cruel, vile **2.** attractive, becoming, charming, delightful, lovely, pleasing, winning, winsome *Antonyms:* heinous, hideous, ugly **3.** amiable, friendly, inviting, kind, likeable, obliging, pleasant, polite, welcoming *Nonformal:* ducky, swell *Antonyms:* aloof, distant, gruff **4.** accurate, choosy, conscientious, detailed, exact, fastidious, meticulous, persnickety *(Nonformal)*, precise, rigorous, scientific, scrupulous *Antonyms:* careless, lax, slipshod **5.** civilized, cultured, dainty, delicate, fine, smooth, subtle

nicety *n.* **1.** detail, element, facet, feature, fine point, item, particular, point **2.** appointment, bonus, comfort, delicacy, furnishing, grace, luxury, pleasure, refinement **3.** accuracy, exactness, fastidiousness, fussiness, meticulousness, precision, rigour, scrupulousness

niche *n.* alcove, corner, cove, cranny, cubbyhole, hole, nook, recess, snuggery, space

nick *n.* depression, gouge, groove, incision, mark, notch, scrape, scratch, slit – *v.* **1.** chip, cut, damage, dent, indentation, jag, knock, mark, notch, scar, scratch, slit **2.** appropriate, cheat, defraud, extort, filch, pilfer, purloin, rob, steal, swindle, swipe *(Nonformal)*, thieve

nickname *n.* appellation, cognomen, diminutive, epithet, familiar name, label, pet name, sobriquet, tag *Nonformal:* handle, moniker – *v.* baptize, call, christen, designate, dub, label, name, tag

nifty *adj.* chic, clever, enjoyable, excellent, grand, great, marvellous, pleasing, sharp, smart, stylish, super, swell, terrific *Nonformal:* cool, dandy, funky, groovy, keen, neat, peachy keen, sweet

night *n.* **1.** bedtime, dusk, evening, eventide, midnight, midnight hour, nightfall, nighttime, sleepy time *(Nonformal)*, sunset, twilight, witching hour *Antonyms:* daybreak, morning, sunrise **2.** black, blackness, dark, darkness, dim, duskiness *Antonyms:* brightness, light **3.** agony, angst, anguish, confusion, despair, dread, foreboding, gloom, misery, worry, wretchedness *Antonyms:* calm, peacefulness, serenity

nightclub *n.* bar, barroom, cabaret, casino, club, cocktail lounge, disco, discothèque, drinking establishment, lounge, speakeasy, supper club *Nonformal:* after-hours club, dive, gin mill, grog shop, honky-tonk, hot spot, joint, 19th hole, spot, watering hole

nightfall *n.* dark, dim, dusk, eve, evening, eventide, gloaming, sundown, sunset, twilight, vespers *Antonyms:* dawn, daybreak, morning

nightly *adj.* **1.** late-night, night, nighttime, nocturnal **2.** each evening, every night, recurrent, regularly, repetitious *Antonyms:* breakfast, daily, morning – *adv.* after dark, by night, nights, nocturnally

nightmare *n.* **1.** bad dream, dream, fancy, fantasy, hallucination, illusion, night terror, phantasmagoria, vision **2.** abhorrence, abomination, horror, ordeal, problem, torment, trial, tribulation **3.** demon, ghost, incubus, monster, phantasm, poltergeist, spirit

nihilism *n.* **1.** anarchy, chaos, destruction, disorder, lawlessness, revolution, terror, violence **2.** cynicism, negativity, nonbelief, pessimism, rejection, renunciation, repudiation

nil *n.* love *(Tennis)*, naught, none, nothing, zero *Nonformal:* diddly squat, goose egg, nada, nix, zilch, zip

nimble *adj.* **1.** active, adroit, agile, brisk, deft, dexterous, handy, light, lightsome, lissome, lively, spry, zippy *(Nonformal) Antonyms:* awkward, heavy, inactive, indolent, lethargic **2.** alert, bright, clever, intelligent, keen, quick, quick-witted, witty *Antonyms:* dim-witted, dull, slow

nincompoop *n.* blockhead, blunderer, clod, dolt, dunce, fool, idiot, lout, moron, nitwit, oaf, simpleton *Nonformal:* hoser, klutz

nip *n.* **1.** bite, dram, drop, morsel, mouthful, nibble, pinch, portion, sip, snifter, soupçon, swallow, taste **2.** chill, cold, freeze, frigidity, frost, gelidity, iciness, rawness **3.** caustic *or* cutting remark, crack, gibe, insult, low blow *(Nonformal)*, scoff, sneer, taunt, wisecrack **4.** fierceness, ginger, kick, punch, relish, spice, tang, zest – *v.* **1.** bite, chomp, eat, pinch, tweak **2.** arrest, blight, check, dash, frustrate, stop, stymie, thwart **3.** annex, appropriate, catch, pilfer, pirate, pocket, purloin, rob, snatch, steal, take, thieve, usurp *Nonformal:* nab, nick, swipe **4.** chip, chop, cut, cut-short, prune, remove, shear, snip, sunder, truncate **5.** benumb, chill, freeze, penetrate, pierce

nirvana *n.* **1.** absolute bliss, ecstasy, exaltation, felicity, joy, perfection, rapture **2.** ataraxia, enlightenment, freedom, liberty, *moksha (Hindu)*, oblivion, peace, serenity, thoughtlessness, tranquility **3.** afterlife, Elysium, happy hunting grounds *(Nonformal)*, heaven, paradise, spiritual unity, the hereafter, *Valhalla (Norse)*

nit-pick *v.* carp, cavil, criticize, fuss, nag, pettifog, quibble, split hairs *Antonyms:* commend, laud, praise

nitwit *n.* dimwit, dunce, fool, half-wit, idiot, ignoramus, imbecile, moron, nincompoop, ninny, numbskull, simpleton *Nonformal:* birdbrain, cement-head, chucklehead, dolt, dork, dummy, hoser, lamebrain *Antonyms:* highbrow, intellectual, scholar, sage, thinker

nitty-gritty *n.* ABC's, base, basics, bottom, core, crux, details, essence, essential, gist, heart, kernel, marrow, meat, nub, pith, root, *sine qua non (Latin)*, spirit, substance

nobility *n.* **1.** aristocracy, elite, gentry, high society, patricians, peerage, royalty, ruling *or* upper class *Antonyms:* proletariat, rabble **2.** dignity, distinction, eminence, glory, grandeur, loftiness, majesty **3.** benevolence, chivalry, errantry, high-mindedness, integrity, magnanimity, righteousness

noble *adj.* **1.** aristocratic, blue-blooded, gentle, highborn, imperial, kingly, lordly, nobiliary, patrician, princely, titled *Antonyms:* base, humble, lowborn **2.** august, courtly, cultivated, distinguished, elevated, eminent, great, lofty, preeminent, refined **3.** beneficent, benevolent, generous, gracious, high-minded, magnanimous, meritorious, righteous, upright, virtuous, worthy **4.** excellent, extraordinary, grandiose, magnificent, remarkable, splendid, striking, stunning, supreme – *n.* aristocrat, gentleman, gentlewoman, lady, lord, nobleman, noblewoman, patrician, peer *Antonyms:* commoner, peasant, serf

nobody *n.* **1.** menial, nonentity, parvenu, unimportant person *Nonformal:* lightweight, little guy, pipsqueak, wimp **2.** nary a one, none, no one, no person, not a soul

nocturnal *adj.* crepuscular, evening, late, late-night, moonlit, nightly, nighttime, twilight, vespertine

nod *n.* **1.** acknowledgment, beck, bow, dip, gesture, greeting, inclination, indication, salute, sign, signal, tip o' the hat *(Nonformal)* **2.** acceptance, affirmation, permission, yes *Nonformal:* go-ahead, green light, okay – *v.* **1.** acknowledge, beck, beckon, bend, bob, consent, curtsy, duck, gesture, greet, indicate, recognize, respond, salaam, salute, signal **2.** acquiesce, agree, approve, assent, give away *or* in, step aside **3.** doze, drift, drift off, drowse, fall asleep, nap, sleep **4.** bow, dip, droop, hang down, sag, sink, slump

node *n.* **1.** bud, bulge, bump, burl, ganglion, growth, knob, knot, lump, nodule, polyp, protuberance, swelling, tumour **2.** connection, joint, juncture, link

noise *n.* **1.** bang, blare, blast, boom, clamour, clang, clatter, crash, eruption, explosion, peal, ring, sound, thud **2.** cacophony, caterwauling, commotion, din, discord, fanfare, fireworks, fracas, hubbub, outcry, racket, row, shouting, squawking, uproar, yelling **3.** buzzing, drumming, hissing, hum, ringing **4.** atmospherics, buzz, feedback, hiss, interference, reception, static, white noise **5.** gossip, hearsay, newsmongering, rumour, scandal, scuttlebutt *(Nonformal)*, slander, talebearing – *v.* broadcast, clatter, gossip, report, sound, spread rumours, tattle

noiseless *adj.* hushed, inaudible, mute, muted, pacific, peaceful, quiet, serene, silent, soundless, speechless, still, tranquil, voiceless, wordless *Antonyms:* blaring, loud, noisy

noisome *adj.* **1.** bad, deleterious, disgusting, fetid, foul, horrid, loathsome, malodorous, nauseating, offensive, putrid, rank, reeking, repulsive, sickening, sickly, smelly, stinking, vile *Antonyms:* appealing, balmy, perfumed, pleasant **2.** baneful, dangerous, deadly, harmful, hurtful, injurious, noxious, pernicious, pestiferous, pestilential, poisonous, unhealthy, unwholesome *Antonyms:* healthy, life-giving, wholesome *Commonly misused:* **noisy**

noisy *adj.* **1.** blatant, booming, cacophonous, chattering, clamorous, clangorous, clattery, deafening, ear-popping, earsplitting, loud, piercing, screaming, strident, turned up, unharmonious, vociferous *Antonyms:* hushed, quiet, silent **2.** blusterous, boisterous, carried away *(Nonformal)*, disorderly, obnoxious, obstreperous, rackety, rambunctious, riotous, rowdy, tumultuous, turbulent, uproarious *Antonyms:* still, subdued, tranquil *Commonly misused:* **noisome, nosy**

nomad *n.* drifter, hobo, hunter and gatherer, itinerant, migrant, pilgrim, rambler, rover, sundowner, vagabond, wanderer

nomadic *adj.* **1.** drifting, itinerant, migrant, migratory, perambulatory, peripatetic, roaming, roving, travelling, wandering, wayfaring **2.** footloose, gadabout *(Nonformal)*, gallivanting, traipsing

nom de plume *n.* alias, assumed name, *nom de guerre (French)*, pen *or* professional *or* stage name, pseudonym

nomenclature *n.* **1.** calling, categorizing, codification, listing, naming, taxonomy **2.** classification, code, cognomen, denomination, designation, name, terminology, vocabulary

nominal *adj.* **1.** inconsiderable, insignificant, low, meaningless, minimal, small, trifling, trivial *Antonyms:* great, important, of major import, significant **2.** alleged, cognominal, ostensible, pretended, professed, purported, seeming, self-professed, so-called, supposed, symbolic, theoretical, token *Antonyms:* actual, genuine, real, true **3.** formal, given, honorary, titular

nominate *v.* **1.** appoint, choose, elect, induct, name, ordain, select, tab *(Nonformal)*, vote in **2.** call, choose, designate, draft, offer, present, proffer, propose, recommend, select, vote for

nomination *n.* **1.** appointment, choice, designation, naming, selection **2.** proposal, recommendation, suggestion, supposition

nominee *n.* appointee, assignee, candidate, contestant, deputy, entrant, runner, selectee

nonchalant *adj.* **1.** calm, casual, composed, cool, easygoing, impassive, imperturbable, lackadaisical, laid-back *(Nonformal)*, mellow, relaxed, smooth, unruffled, untroubled *Antonyms:* anxious, excited, nervous **2.** aloof, apathetic, detached, indifferent, neutral, unconcerned, unmoved *Antonyms:* concerned, connected, worried

noncommittal *adj.* **1.** cautious, elusive, evasive, hesitant, prevaricating, waffling *(Nonformal) Antonyms:* determined, firm, resolute **2.** middle-of-the-road, neutral, noncommitted, nonpartisan, uninvolved

noncompliant *adj.* **1.** differing, disagreeing, dissenting, dissident, divergent, nonconforming, nonobservant, protesting, rejecting, unorthodox *Antonyms:* accommodating, agreeing, complying **2.** balky, contrary, contumacious, disobedient, insubordinate, lawless, rambunctious, rebellious, recalcitrant, ungovernable, unruly *Antonyms:* dutiful, obedient, pliant

non compos mentis *adj.* demented, deranged, insane, irresponsible, mad, mentally ill, sick, unsound *Nonformal:* crazy, dippy, loopy, mental, nutty, out to lunch

nonconformist *adj.* **1.** anarchistic, dissident, rebellious, schismatic, sectarian, unwilling **2.** eccentric, maverick, offbeat, original, unorthodox, weird *Nonformal:* kinky, oddball – *n.* **1.** anarchist, deviant, dissenter, dissident, iconoclast, malcontent, protester, rebel, schismatic *Antonyms:* conventionalist, traditionalist **2.** eccentric, freak, individualist, maverick, one of a kind, radical *Nonformal:* different breed, oddball, weirdo

nonconformity *n.* **1.** disagreement, discordance, dissent, nonacceptance, noncompliance, objection, opposition, protest **2.** contumaciousness, disobedience, insubordination, lawlessness, mutiny, recalcitrance **3.** eccentricity, exception, originality, unconventionality, uniqueness **4.** condemnation, disapprobation, disapproval, hearsay, heterodoxy, iconoclasm, nonacceptance, rejection

nondescript *adj.* **1.** amorphous, formless, inchoate, indefinite, indescribable, nebulous, shapeless **2.** achromatic, bland, boring, dull, uninteresting, unremarkable, vanilla *(Nonformal)*

none *adv.* by no means, no, not at all, to no extent – *pron.* nary a soul, nobody, no one, no person, not a hint *or* thing *or* trace, not any

nonentity *n.* **1.** common man, Jane *or* John Doe, lightweight, little person, no one, nobody, nothing **2.** abstraction, apparition, chimera, delusion, dream, fantasy, hallucination, illusion, mirage, phantasmagoria, phantom **3.** emptiness, empty space, negation, nihilism, nonexistence, non-reality, nothingness, nullity, vacancy

nonessential *adj.* dispensable, excessive, expendable, extraneous, insignificant, needless, peripheral, petty, redundant, superfluous, tautological, trivial, unimportant, unnecessary, unneeded *Antonyms:* essential, important, vital – *n.* deadwood *(Nonformal)*, extra, garbage, junk, redundancy, superfluity, tautology, triviality

nonexistent *adj.* **1.** absent, blank, defunct, departed, extinguished, gone, lost, missing, perished, void *Antonyms:* alive, here, present **2.** chimerical, ethereal, fictional, illusory, imaginary, imagined, legendary, mythical, shadowy, vaporous *Antonyms:* absolute, genuine, real **3.** baseless, empty, formless, foundationless, groundless *Antonyms:* true, verifiable, veritable

non-flammable *adj.* fireproof, fire-resistant, flame-retardant, noncombustible, unignitable *Antonyms:* flammable, inflammable

nonpareil *adj.* ace, best, champion, excellent, first-class, incomparable, peerless, prize-winning, top, unbeatable, unequalled, unmatched, unrivaled – *n.* ace, acme, best, elite, first, gem, jewel, marvel, miracle, *ne plus ultra (French)*, nonesuch, one of a kind, paragon, rarity, wonder

nonpartisan *adj.* **1.** detached, equitable, impartial, indifferent, just, neutral, nondiscriminatory, objective, unaffected, unbiased, uncoloured, uninvolved, unprejudiced *Antonyms:* biased, judgmental **2.** free-wheeling, independent, mugwumpian, nonaligned, unaffiliated

nonplus *v.* astonish, astound, baffle, balk, bewilder, boggle, confound, confuse, daze, discomfit, disconcert, discountenance, dismay, dumfound, embarrass, faze, flurry, fluster, frustrate, muddle, mystify, overcome, perplex, puzzle, rattle, stun, stymie

Nonformal: beat, buffalo, discombobulate, floor, flummox, stagger, stick, stump, throw *Antonyms:* calm, ease, soothe

nonprofit *adj.* bleeding-heart *(Nonformal)*, charitable, contributory, donative, eleemosynary, not for profit, philanthropic *Antonyms:* lucrative, profitable, remunerative

nonsense *n.* **1.** absurdity, asininity, craziness, fatuity, illogicality, inanity, irrationality, ludicrousness, madness, meaninglessness, senselessness *Antonyms:* logic, rationality, sense **2.** abracadabra, babble, balderdash, bunkum, froth, gibberish, hocus-pocus *Nonformal:* baloney, bull, eyewash, gobbledygook, hogwash, hooey, jazz, mumbo jumbo, poppycock *Antonyms:* fact, truth, wisdom **3.** bombast, claptrap, dribble, empty-talk, fustian, palaver, pretense, rodomontade *Nonformal:* gas, hot air **4.** antics, clowning, folly, fun, games, hijinks, imprudence, jest, joke, monkey business, pranks, tomfoolery **5.** baubles, frippery, frivolities, nonessentials, rubbish, stuff, trash, trifles, trinkets

nonstop *adj. ad infinitum (Latin)*, ceaseless, constant, continuous, endless, incessant, interminable, never-ending, ongoing, perpetual, recurrent, relentless, steady, unbroken, unceasing, unending, uninterrupted, unrelenting, unremitting *Antonyms:* broken, inconstant, intermittent – *adv.* around the clock, ceaselessly, constantly, continuity, day-in and day-out, endlessly, interminably, persistent, relentlessly, unremittingly

nonviolent *adj.* pacifist, passive, peaceable, peaceful, quiet, resistant *Antonyms:* bellicose, belligerent, warlike

noodle *n.* **1.** dried dough, pasta *Kinds of noodles:* buckwheat, chow mein, egg, fried, glass, lo mein, macaroni, rice, Ramen, Shanghai, *soba (Japanese) See also:* **pasta** **2.** clod, dolt, dunce, fool, harebrain, nincompoop, ninny, nitwit, oaf, simpleton *Nonformal:* dingbat, flake, hoser, nut, pinhead, puzzler **3.** cranium, crown, head, skull *Nonformal:* brain, noggin – *v.* dally, dawdle, fool *or* goof around, piddle, play, putter, tinker, trifle

nook *n.* alcove, compartment, corner, cranny, crevice, cubbyhole, hideout, hole, inglenook, niche, recess, retreat, space

noon *n.* **1.** high noon, lunchtime, meridian, midday, noonday, noontide, noontime, twelve noon, twelve o'clock **2.** apex, crown, heyday, peak, pinnacle, prime, zenith

norm *n.* **1.** average, mean, median, medium, par, rule **2.** barometer, benchmark, criterion, gauge, measure, model, pattern, scale, standard, touchstone, type, yardstick

normal *adj.* **1.** characteristic, commonplace, consistent, constant, daily, expected, familiar, habitual, natural, quotidian, regular, routine, typical, usual *Antonyms:* atypical, infrequent, rare **2.** accepted, acknowledged, common, conventional, customary, established, popular, prevailing, prevalent, sanctioned, time-honoured, traditional, universal, widespread **3.** average, mean, medium, middle, ordinary, representative, standard, unexceptional **4.** *compos mentis (Latin)*, mentally fit, rational, reasonable, sane, sound, well-adjusted, whole **5.** perpendicular, straight, upright, vertical – *n.* **1.** convention, norm, paradigm, rule, standard, tradition **2.** benchmark, gauge, mean, model, prototype, standard **3.** axis, perpendicular, straight line, tangent

normalize *v.* adjust, calibrate, codify, correct, formalize, order, regulate, standardize

normally *adv.* commonly, habitually, ordinarily, regularly, typically, usually

north *adj.* arctic, boreal, hyperborean, northern, northward, polar, septentrional, upisland – *adv.* nor', northerly, northward, norward – *n.* **1.** Arctic, Far North, Great Lone Land, high north, Land of the Little Sticks, Land of the Midnight Sun, *Nord (French)*, northland, subarctic **2.** bush, cottage country, game country, getaway country, the lake *(Nonformal)*, wilderness, woods

nose *n.* **1.** organ, proboscis *Nonformal:* beak, bill, honker, nozzle, schnoz, sniffer, snoot, snout **2.** foredeck, front, point, prow, stem, tip **3.** aroma, bouquet, odour, perfume, redolence, scent, smell **4.** ability, capability, eye *(Nonformal)*, feel, insight, perception, percipience, skill – *v.* **1.** detect, examine, ferret *or* sniff out, inspect, scent, smell, uncover **2.** nuzzle, sniff, snuggle, touch **3.** meddle, pry, search, snoop **4.** inch along, move forward, push, shove

nostalgia *n.* **1.** homesickness, longing, *mal du pays (French)*, pensiveness, pining, regret, reminiscence, rue, sentimentality, wistfulness, yearning *Nonformal:* mush, schmaltz **2.** kitch, memorabilia, remembrance, relic, souvenir, token

nostalgic *adj.* homesick, maudlin, melancholy, pensive, reminiscent, romantic, sentimental, wistful *Nonformal:* sappy, syrupy

nosy *adj.* bothersome, curious, eavesdropping, inquisitive, interested, interfering, meddlesome, prying, snooping *Commonly misused:* **noisy**

notable *adj.* **1.** conspicuous, evident, manifest, marked, noticeable, observable, pronounced, striking, uncommon, unusual *Antonyms:* concealed, hidden, imperceptible **2.** celebrated, distinguished, eminent, extraordinary, famed, famous, great, heavy, illustrious, important, noteworthy, notorious, outstanding, preeminent, prominent, remarkable, renowned, serious, well-known *Nonformal:* bankable, high-profile, major-league, top-drawer *Antonyms:* anonymous, obscure, unknown **3.** eventful, memorable, momentous, rare, red-letter *(Nonformal)* – *n.* celebrity, hero, idol, literati, luminary, name, star, superstar, worthy *Nonformal:* glitterati, VIP

notably *adv.* conspicuously, distinctly, especially, exceedingly, exceptionally, extremely, greatly, highly, hugely, markedly, noticeably, outstandingly, particularly, prominently, remarkably, reputably, strikingly, very

notarize *v.* accredit, approve, attest to, authenticate, certify, legalize, legitimize, officiate, record, swear to, verify, warrant, witness

notation *n.* **1.** accent, character, code, diacritic, figures, ligature, mark, script, short hand, sign, signature, symbol, system **2.** comment, elucidation, gloss, marginalia, memo, memorandum, note, record

notch *n.* **1.** groove, hollow, indent, indentation, mark, rabbet, rut **2.** cut, gash, gouge, incision, nick, score, scratch **3.** channel, cleft, gap, passage, ridge **4.** degree, gradation, increment, level, measurement, peg, rung, step – *v.* **1.** crenellate, crimp, gash, jag, mill, perforate, pink, prick, punch, scallop **2.** chisel, cut, dent, gash, incise, mark, nick, score, scratch

note *n.* **1.** account, entry, observation, record, summary, view **2.** character, degree, figure, flat, indication, interval, key, lick, mark, natural, pitch, representation, scale, sharp, sign, step, symbol, token, tone **3.** communication, correspondence, dispatch, e-mail, epistle, letter, line *(Nonformal)*, memo, memorandum, message, missive, telegram **4.** draft, jotting, reminder, rough note, scribble, sketch **5.** annotation, comment, commentary, endnote, explanation, explication, exposition, footnote, gloss, marginalia, notation **6.** bank note, bill, cash, coupon, I.O.U. *(Nonformal)*, legal tender, money, paper money, promissory note, treasury note **7.** distinction, esteem, force, importance, mark, noteworthiness, power, regard, reputation, sway, weight **8.** care, concern, heed, mention, notice, observation, regard, solicitude, thought **9.** dash, hint, inkling, soupçon, sprinkling, taste, tinge, touch, trace, whiff *(Nonformal)* – *v.* **1.** catch, descry, discern, heed, notice, observe, perceive, spot, take in, view **2.** catalogue, enter, jot *or* put *or* set down, log, record, register, transcribe, write **3.** allude, credit, mention, remark, state, touch upon **4.** annotate, comment on, explain, footnote, gloss **5.** designate, disclose, indicate, point out, reveal

notebook *n.* account, album, blotter, calendar, cashbook, daytimer, diary, journal, ledger, log, logbook, memo *or* scratch *or* steno pad, pocketbook, record, roster, scrapbook, tablet

noted *adj.* **1.** acclaimed, celebrated, conspicuous, distinguished, eminent, famous, illustrious, leading, notable, notorious, popular, preeminent, prominent, recognized, renowned, star, well-known *Antonyms:* obscure, undistinguished, unknown **2.** chronicled, heeded, observed, preserved, recorded, registered **3.** acknowledged alluded to, cited, expressed, mentioned, noticed, said, stated, touched upon

noteworthy *adj.* exceptional, extraordinary, important, meaningful, memorable, notable, outstanding, preeminent, prominent, remarkable, serious, significant, terrific, unique, unusual *Nonformal:* heavy, major-league *Antonyms:* commonplace, insignificant, normal, ordinary, pedestrian

nothing *n.* **1.** cipher, naught, nil, none, not anything, zero *Nonformal:* beans, diddly squat, nada, zilch, zip **2.** insignificance, minor details, technicality, trifle, triviality, unimportance **3.** hollow man, nobody, nonentity, no one *Nonformal:* jerk-off, nebbish, small fry **4.** annihilation, blank, emptiness, nonexistence, nothingness, obliteration, oblivion, void

nothingness *n.* **1.** black hole, emptiness, nonexistence, oblivion, space, vacuum, void **2.** insignificance, meaninglessness, petty matter, trifle, worthlessness **3.** death, senselessness, unconsciousness

notice *n.* **1.** attention, cognizance, ear, grasp, heed, mark, mind, note, observance, observation, regard, remark, thought, understanding *Antonyms:* ignorance, neglect, omission, oversight **2.** admonition, advice, caution, caveat, clue, heads up *(Nonformal)*, instruction, warning **3.** advertisement, announcement, broadcast, broadsheet, bulletin, circular, communication, flyer, handbill, manifesto, memo, news, newsletter, pamphlet, poster, newsletter, publication, tidings **4.** declaration, directive, final demand, notification, order, summons, word **5.** article, comment, commentary, critique, piece, review, story, write-up – *v.* **1.** ascertain, behold, consider, detect, discover, distinguish, espy, heed, make out, mark, mind, observe, perceive, regard, see, spot, take in *(Nonformal)*, take note **2.** acknowledge, allude, cite, mention, point to, put down, record, remark on, signify, touch upon

noticeable *adj.* **1.** apparent, clear, conspicuous, discernible, distinct, evident, manifest, notable, observable, obvious, palpable, patent, perceptible, plain, pointed, salient, signal, unmistakable *Antonyms:* hidden, obscure, veiled **2.** arresting, eye-catching, marked, noteworthy, outstanding, prominent, remarkable, sensational, spectacular, striking, unmistakable, vivid *Antonyms:* insignificant, of no import, ordinary

notify *v.* **1.** acquaint, advise, alert, apprise, brief, bring up to date, clue in, convey, cue, disclose, enlighten, inform, post, report, reveal, tell, tip off *(Nonformal)* **2.** announce, assert, blazon, broadcast, circulate, declare, disseminate, divulge, herald, make known, mention, proclaim, promulgate, publish, sing, spread, state, write

notion *n.* **1.** conception, feeling, hazy idea, hint, hunch *(Nonformal)*, impression, inkling, sense, suspicion **2.** abstraction, belief, conceit, conjecture, idea, observation, opinion, reflection, theory, thought, view **3.** caprice, desire, fancy, flash *(Nonformal)*, humour, impulse, inclination, intention, whim, wish, yen

notoriety *n.* **1.** disgrace, dishonour, disrepute, infamy, obloquy, opprobrium, scandal **2.** celebrity, fame, popularity, publicity, renown *Nonformal:* ink, spotlight

notorious *adj.* **1.** blatant, dishonourable, disreputable, flagrant, glaring, ill-famed, infamous, naughty, of ill repute, opprobrious, questionable, scandalous, shady, shameful, villainous, wicked *Antonyms:* moral, pious, righteous **2.** acclaimed, distinguished, familiar, famous, highly-touted *(Nonformal)*, legendary, noted, popular, public, renowned, well-known, widely recognized *Antonyms:* anonymous, unknown

notwithstanding *prep.* against, albeit, all the same, despite, even though, however, in spite of, nevertheless, regardless, still, yet

nourish *v.* **1.** aid, attend, care, cherish, comfort, feed, help, maintain, nurse, nurture, provide, supply, sustain, tend *Antonyms:* neglect, starve **2.** cultivate, encourage, foster, further, patronize, promote, support *Antonyms:* hinder, obstruct

nourishing *adj.* **1.** beneficial, good-for-you *(Nonformal)*, healthful, health-giving, healthy, nutritious, wholesome *Antonyms:* injurious, toxic, unhealthy **2.** caring, cherishing, enriching, fostering, helpful, maternal, parental, promoting, supportive *Antonyms:* disavowing, disowning, ignoring

nourishment *n.* **1.** alimentation, diet, fodder, food, foodstuffs, nutriment, provender, rations, sustenance, victuals *Nonformal:* chow, eats, grub, home cooking, vittles **2.** aid, encouragement, help, maintenance, ministration, patronage, promotion, succour, support, TLC *(Nonformal)*

nouveau *adj.* fresh, modern, new, recent, stylish, up-to-date, young *Nonformal:* cool, funky, groovy, hip, now, with it *Antonyms:* antiquated, old, passé

nouveau riche *n.* arriviste, lottery winner, new money, new *or* newly rich, parvenu *Nonformal:* instant millionaire, johnny-come-lately, mushroom, pig in clover, upstart

novel *adj.* avant-garde, curious, different, exotic, foreign, fresh, innovative, modern, new, odd, offbeat, original, peculiar, rare, singular, strange, unconventional, unfamiliar, unheard of, unique, unusual *Nonformal:* hot off the press, newfangled *Antonyms:* common, customary, familiar, traditional – *n.* account, book, chronicle, fiction, narrative, story, tale, yarn *Kinds of novel:* best-seller, bodice-ripper, cliff-hanger, comic, detective, dime, epistolary, fantasy, genre, gothic, graphic, historical fiction, horror, intrigue, light fiction, literary, mass-market, mystery, novella, paperback, penny dreadful, picaresque, pocket, police procedural, potboiler, pulp fiction, regency, research, Roman á clef, romance, science *or* speculative fiction, serial, SF, spy, suspense, thriller, trashy, true crime, western, whodunit, young adult *or* YA *German:* bildungsroman, kunstleroman *See also:* **book**

novelty *n.* **1.** freshness, inventiveness, modernity, newness, originality, uniqueness **2.** fad, innovation, neoism *Nonformal:* gizmo, latest wrinkle, newfangled, contraption **3.** bagatelle, bauble, bibelot, conversation piece, curio, curiosity, gadget, gewgaw, gimcrack, gimmick, item, knick-knack, *objet d'art (French)*, oddity, souvenir, trifle, trinket

novice *n.* amateur, apprentice, beginner, fledgling, freshman, learner, neophyte, newcomer, novitiate, postulant, probationer, recruit, rookie, starter, student, trainee, tyro, undergraduate *Nonformal:* greenhorn, tenderfoot *Antonyms:* doyen, grandmaster, maestro, professional, veteran

now *adj.* chic, fresh, in, new, nouveau, trendy, up-to-date *Nonformal:* hip, hot, just out – *adv.* **1.** at once, directly, double time, first off, forthwith, immediately, instantly, promptly, right away, straightaway *Nonformal:* instanter, like now, pronto **2.** nowadays, presently, these days, this day, today **3.** just *or* right now, just past, lately, recently – *n.* current, here and now, present, today

nowadays *adv.* currently, in the present, now, presently, these days, today

noxious *adj.* **1.** baneful, dangerous, deadly, deleterious, destructive, detrimental, harmful, hurtful, injurious, killing, pestilential, poisonous, toxic, unhealthy, unwholesome, venomous, virulent *Antonyms:* innocuous, nontoxic, safe **2.** disgusting, fetid, foul, noisome, offensive, pernicious, putrid, rotten, sickly, spoiled, stinking, unpleasant *Antonyms:* fragrant, inoffensive, pleasing

nozzle *n.* **1.** shower *or* sprinkler head, socket, spout, sprayer **2.** nose, proboscis, *Nonformal:* beak, bill, muzzle, schnoz, schnozzola, sniffer

nuance *n.* dash, degree, fine distinction, gradation, nicety, shade, shadow, soupçon, subtlety, tinge, touch, trace, variation

nub *n.* **1.** bulge, bump, knob, knot, lump, node, protuberance, swelling **2.** basic, core, crux, essence, gist, gravamen, heart, kernel, meat, pith, point, substance *Nonformal:* bottom line, nitty-gritty **3.** bit, chunk, fragment, gob *(Nonformal)*, hunk, morsel, piece, scrap, shard

nubile *adj.* appealing, attractive, beautiful, fertile, lithesome, marriageable, photogenic, provocative, pubescent, stunning, voluptuous *Nonformal:* hot, luscious, sexy *Antonyms:* aged, barren, elderly, senescent

nuclear *adj.* **1.** atomic, fusion, nucleal, nucleate, nucleolate *See also:* **atom 2.** basic, central, core, focal, pivotal, principal, rudimentary

nucleus *n.* **1.** basis, centre, core, crux, focus, foundation, ganglion, heart, matter, nub *(Nonformal)*, pivot, premise, principle *Antonyms:* brim, circumference, edge, periphery **2.** bud, embryo, germ, kernel, seed, spark

nude *adj.* **1.** *au naturel (French)*, bare-skinned, disrobed, divested, naked, starkers *(Nonformal)*, stark-naked, stripped, uncovered, undressed *Antonyms:* attired, clothed, covered, dressed **2.** bald, bare, blank, plain, unadorned, unarrayed, undecorated, unembellished, unfurnished, ungarnished, unornamented – *n.* figure, portrait, representation, study

nudge *n. & v.* bump, dig, elbow, jab, jog, poke, prod, punch, push, shove, tap, touch

nugget *n.* **1.** chunk, clump, hunk, ingot, lump, mass, piece, wad **2.** diamond, find, gem, gold, jewel, pearl, treasure

nuisance *n.* **1.** aggravation, annoyance, bother, irritant, irritation, *nudnik (Yiddish)*, pismire *(P.E.I)*, trouble, vexation, worry *Nonformal:* downer, drag, hassle, headache, pain *Antonyms:* benefit, blessing, delight, joy, pleasure **2.** bully, *enfant terrible (French)*, holy terror *(Nonformal)*, mischief-maker, pest, troublemaker *Antonyms:* angel, darling, dear

null *adj.* **1.** absent, empty, hollow, negative, nonexistent, nothing, vacant, vacuous **2.** futile, inane, ineffectual, inefficacious, inoperative, pointless, useless, vain, valueless, worthless **3.** invalid, not binding, repealed, rescinded, revoked, struck down, unsanctioned, void **4.** bland, characterless, generic, indistinct, insipid, neutral *Nonformal:* beige, grey, vanilla

nullify *v.* **1.** annul, cancel, invalidate, quash, rescind, revoke, scrub, set aside, squash, trash, veto, vitiate, void *Nonformal:* axe, ice, kill, scratch *Antonyms:* authorize, confirm, endorse, ratify, validate **2.** bring to naught, counterbalance, negate, neutralize, offset

numb *adj.* **1.** aloof, apathetic, detached, disinterested, feelingless, incurious, indifferent, insensible, insensitive, listless, phlegmatic, unfeeling *Antonyms:* alert, aware, keen, observant **2.** anaesthetized, benumbed, dead to the world *(Nonformal)*, frozen, immobilized, numbed, paralyzed, stunned – *v.* anaesthetize, blunt, chill, deaden, desensitize, drug, dull, freeze, immobilize, stun, stupefy

number *n.* **1.** cipher, digit, figure, integer, numeral, statistic *Kinds of number:* abstract, cardinal, complex, composite, even, finite, fraction, googol, imaginary, imperfect, irrational, literal, mixed, natural, negative, odd, ordinal, perfect, positive, prime, rational, real, Roman numeral, round, serial, signed, transcendental, whole **2.** abundance, bunch, collection, company, crowd, host, many, multitude, throng, volume *Nonformal:* boodle, caboodle, oodles, scads **3.** aggregate, amount, estimate, quantity, sum, total, totality, whole **4.** act, bit *(Nonformal)*, ditty, piece, play, routine, scene, song, tune **5.** book, copy, edition, folio, issue, printing, run, series, volume **6.** beat, feet, lilt, measure, metrics, movement, prosody, rhythm, swing, verse **7.** artifice, chicanery, deception, hoax, racket, scheme, trick *Nonformal:* graft, snow job, song and dance **8.** bet, chance, gamble, game, lottery, numbers game *or* pool **9.** identification, ID tag *(Nonformal)*, password, PIN, serial number, SIN – *v.* **1.** account, add, add up, amount, calculate, compute, count, estimate, figure out, include, numerate, reckon, tally, total **2.** categorize, classify, enumerate, group, itemize, order, organize, take stock

numberless *adj.* **1.** countless, endless, incalculable, inexhaustible, infinite, innumerable, many, multitudinous, myriad, numerous, uncountable, untold *Nonformal:* gazillion, jillion, umpteen, zillion **2.** uncounted, unknown, unmeasured, unnumbered, untallied

numeral *n.* character, cipher, digit, figure, integer, math symbol, number

numeric *adj.* arithmetic, arithmetical, binary, mathematical, numerical, statistical

numerous *adj.* abundant, *beaucoup (French)*, copious, diverse, great, infinite, large, legion, many, multifarious, multitudinous, plentiful, populous, profuse, rife, several, various, voluminous *Nonformal:* heaps, oodles, scads *Antonyms:* few, not many, scarcely any

nun *n.* abbess, anchorite, canoness, cenobite, clergywoman, cleric, hermit, mother superior, postulant, prioress, sister, vestal

nuptial *adj.* bridal, conjugal, connubial, marital, marriage, married, matrimonial, spousal, wedded, wedding

nurse *n.* **1.** caregiver, health care worker, midwife, Registered Nurse *or* R.N., Registered Practical Nurse *or* R.P.N., therapist, Victorian Order of Nurses *or* V.O.N. **2.** amah, au pair, baby sitter, duenna, governess, nanny, nursemaid, wet nurse – *v.* **1.** breast-feed, feed, lactate, nourish, nurture, suckle, wet-nurse **2.** aid, attend, care for, cherish, feed, minister to, pamper, serve, succour, support, tend, watch out for *or* over **3.** advance, cultivate, encourage, forward, foster, further, harbour, promote

nursery *n.* **1.** baby's *or* children's *or* rumpus room, creche, daycare centre, kindergarten, preschool, school **2.** conservatory, garden centre, greenhouse, indoor garden, solarium

nurture *n.* **1.** food, nourishment, nutriment, subsistence, sustenance, victuals **2.** care, education, encouragement, fathering, fostering, guidance, instruction, mothering, patronage, support, tutelage, upbringing – *v.* **1.** baby, bring up, care for, caress, cater to, cherish, coddle, cosset, father, favour, feed, foster, help, house, humour, indulge, lodge, mind, minister to, mother, nourish, nurse, oblige, pet, protect, provide, serve, shelter, shepherd, spoil, spoon-feed, suckle, sustain, take under one's wing, tend, watch *Antonyms:* deprive, disregard, ignore, neglect, overlook **2.** assist, back, bear, bolster, cultivate, develop, discipline, educate, guide, harbour, instruct, lead, raise, rear, school, support, take in hand, train, uphold

nut *n.* **1.** caryopsis, kernel, seed, stone, utricle *Kinds of nut:* acorn, almond, beechnut, betel, black walnut, Brazil, butternut, candlenut, cashew, chestnut, chinquapin, filbert, hazelnut, hickory, kola, lichee, macadamia, palm, peanut, pecan, pignola, pine, pistachio, walnut **2.** fastener *Kinds of metal nut:* castle, chamfered square, hexagonal, lock, lug, slotted, square, thumb, untapped, wing **3.** crank, eccentric, lunatic, madman, maniac *Nonformal:* crackpot, fruitcake, kook, loony, screwball, weirdo **4.** aficionado, buff, cognoscenti, devotee, enthusiast, fan, fanatic, zealot *Nonformal:* freak, hockey mom **5.** bother, cross, dilemma, predicament, problem, puzzle

nutrition *n.* diet, food, menu, nourishment, subsistence, sustenance, victuals, vittles *(Nonformal)*

nutritious *adj.* balanced, beneficial, good, healthful, health-giving, healthy, invigorating, nourishing, strengthening, wholesome *Antonyms:* bad, junk *(Nonformal)*, unhealthy, unwholesome

nuts *adj.* **1.** crazy, ill, insane, lunatic, mad, maniacal, sick *Nonformal:* cuckoo, loony, off one's rocker **2.** *aux anges (French)*, besotted, devoted, enthusiastic, fanatical, overzealous, smitten, transported *Nonformal:* gone, wild about

nutty *adj.* **1.** absurd, crazy, eccentric, foolish, harebrained, irrational, keen, ridiculous *Nonformal:* bubbleheaded, cockamamie, cracked, daffy, daft, half-baked, kooky **2.** demented, deranged, lunatic, mad *Nonformal:* batty, loony, nuts, potty, touched, wacky **3.** appetizing, flavourful, full-bodied, lively, zestful

nuzzle *n.* caress, embrace, hug, pet – *v.* **1.** burrow, dig, nose, nudge, root **2.** bundle, caress, cosset, cuddle, fondle, nestle, pet, rub, snuggle

nymph *n.* **1.** dryad, fairy, goddess, kelpie, mermaid, naiad, oread, peri, sprite, sylph **2.** demoiselle, girl, ingénue, maiden, nymphet, schoolgirl, young woman

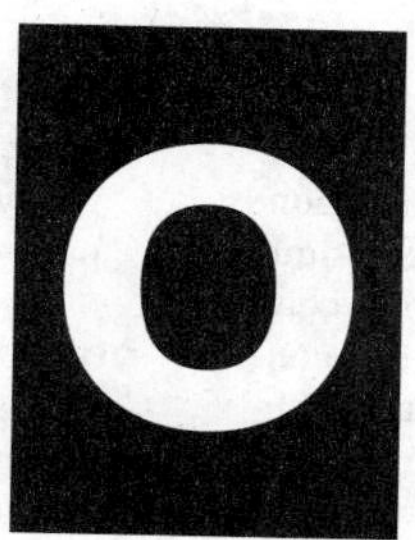

oaf *n.* blockhead, blunderer, clod, dullard, dunce, fool, half-wit, imbecile, lout, moron, nincompoop, simpleton, slob, slouch *Nonformal:* bonehead, dummy, galoot, goof, hoser, klutz, lamebrain, lummox, ox, wally *Antonyms:* genius, mastermind, virtuoso

oasis *n.* **1.** haven, refuge, resting place *or* spot, retreat, sanctuary, sanctum, Shangri-La *Antonyms:* fleapit, hellhole, inferno **2.** pond, pool, spring, watering hole

oath *n.* **1.** adjuration, affidavit, affirmation, avowal, bond, contract, deposition, pledge, profession, promise, sworn declaration *or* statement, testimony, vow, word, word of honour *Antonyms:* falsehood, lie, prevarication **2.** blasphemy, colourful *or* strong language, curse, cuss *or* four-letter word, expletive, imprecation, malediction, profanity, swearword

obdurate *adj.* **1.** adamant, callous, cruel, firm, fixed, flinty, hard, hard-hearted, heartless, impervious, incorrigible, inhumane, insensitive, iron-hearted, obstinate, pigheaded, stubborn, take no prisoner *(Nonformal)*, unyielding *Antonyms:* amenable, sensitive, soft **2.** awkward, cumbersome, inflexible, intractable, rigid, stiff, unbending, unwieldy *Antonyms:* compliant, flexible, malleable

obedience *n.* acquiescence, complaisance, compliance, conformity, deference, docility, dutifulness, good behaviour, malleability, manageability, quietness, respect, submission, subservience, tameness, tractability, willingness *Antonyms:* defiance, insubordination, obstinacy, stubbornness

obedient *adj.* acquiescent, adaptable, amenable, attentive, complaisant, compliant, conforming, controllable, deferential, docile, dutiful, governable, honouring, law-abiding, malleable, manageable, obliging, orderly, pliant, polite, respectful, submissive, subservient, tractable, well-behaved, well-mannered, willing, yielding *Antonyms:* argumentative, belligerent, intractable, recalcitrant

obese *adj.* adipose, corpulent, dumpy, fat, flabby, fleshy, full-figured, heavy, overweight, paunchy, plump, portly, pudgy, roly-poly, rotund, Rubenesque, stout, thickset, voluptuous *Nonformal:* tubby, two-ton *Antonyms:* emaciated, gaunt, lean, skeletal, slender

obey *v.* **1.** accept, accord, acquiesce, agree, assent, comply, concur, grant *Antonyms:* defy, challenge, contravene **2.** carry out, discharge, execute, fulfill, meet, perform, respond *Antonyms:* disregard, ignore, neglect **3.** act upon, adhere *or* bow to, answer, conform, embrace, follow, give in *or* way, heed, kowtow, mind, observe, serve, submit, surrender, take orders *Antonyms:* rebel, transgress, violate

obfuscate *v.* **1.** bewilder, confound, confuse, discombobulate *(Nonformal)*, discomfit, discompose, disconcert, fluster, nonplus, rattle, perplex, ruffle, upset *Antonyms:* calm, comfort, placate, soothe **2.** becloud, befog, cloak, conceal, cover, darken, eclipse, hide, obscure, screen, shadow, veil *Antonyms:* brighten, illuminate, reveal

obituary *n.* death announcement *or* notice, elegy, eulogy, memorial, necrology, obit *(Nonformal)*, testimonial, tribute

object *n.* **1.** article, commodity, entity, gadget, item, mass, matter, phenomenon, reality, something, substance, thing *Nonformal:*

gizmo, thingamabob, thingamajig, thingy, whatsit **2.** aim, desideratum, design, duty, end, function, goal, idea, intent, intention, mark, mission, motive, objective, point, purpose **3.** butt, mark *(Nonformal)*, receiver, recipient, target, victim **4.** centre, concern, focus, ground zero, issue, matter, subject, thought – *v.* **1.** argue, balk, challenge, complain, criticize, disagree, disavow, dispute, dissent, inveigh, oppose, protest, remonstrate, resist, take issue *Nonformal:* gripe, grouse *Antonyms:* accept, acquiesce, assent, endorse, support **2.** disallow, disapprove, discountenance, disfavour, dislike, eschew, negate, refuse, reject, repudiate

objection *n.* **1.** disagreement, disapproval, disfavour, dislike, rejection, thumbs-down *(Nonformal)*, veto *Antonyms:* acceptance, affirmation, agreement **2.** beef *(Nonformal)*, cavil, censure, challenge, complaint, criticism, exception, grievance, issue, protest, question, remonstrance, variance *Antonyms:* endorsement, praise, support **3.** compunction, demur, demurral, difficulty, hesitation, problem, qualm, reluctance, reservation, scruple, unwillingness **4.** argument, contention, counterstatement, defence, denial, plea, rebuttal, refutation, repudiation

objectionable *adj.* **1.** abhorrent, deplorable, distasteful, insufferable, intolerable, loathsome, lousy *(Nonformal)*, offensive, repellent, reprehensible, repugnant, repulsive, unacceptable, unpleasant *Antonyms:* fine, heroic, noble **2.** disagreeable, displeasing, ill-favoured, inadmissible, indecorous, undesirable, unfit, unseemly, unsuitable, unwanted, unwelcome *Antonyms:* acceptable, agreeable, desirable, pleasing

objective *adj.* **1.** cool, detached, dispassionate, equitable, evenhanded, fair, impartial, just, nondiscriminatory, open-minded, unbiased, uncoloured, uninvolved, unprejudiced *Antonyms:* biased, prejudiced, unfair, unjust **2.** actual, corporeal, empirical, external, extrinsic, manifest, material, patent, physical, real, substantive, tangible, true – *n.* aim, ambition, desideratum, design, desire, end, goal, intention, mark, mission, object, purpose, target

objectively *adv.* by-the-book, dispassionately, equitably, impartially, indifferently, justly, neutrally, open-mindedly, without prejudice

objectivity *n.* **1.** detachment, disinterest, dispassion, evenhandedness, fairness, impartiality, impersonality, judiciousness, neutrality, open-mindedness, toleranc *Antonyms:* bias, subjectivity **2.** exteriority, extrinsicality, materiality, physicality, substantivity, tangibility, truth

obligated *adj.* **1.** beholden, bound, committed, pledged, promised **2.** accountable, answerable, chargeable, liable, responsibl **3.** compelled, constrained, controlled, duty-bound, forced, held, obliged, required, restricted

obligation *n.* **1.** agreement, bond, commitment, compact, contract, covenant, deed, handshake *(Nonformal)*, pact, pledge, promise, transaction, understanding **2.** burden, business, charge, corvée, debt, dues, duty, IOU *(Nonformal)*, liability, onus, responsibility, task **3.** appreciation, gratitude, indebtedness, thankfulness, thanks **4** compulsion, constraint, duress, necessity, pressure

obligatory *adj.* binding, coercive, compulsory, *de rigueur (French)*, enforced, essential, imperative, involuntary, mandatory, necessary, required, requisite, unavoidabl *Antonyms:* discretionary, elective, optional, voluntary

oblige *v.* **1.** accommodate, aid, assist, bend over backwards *(Nonformal)*, contribute, favour, gratify, help, help out, indulge, please, serve *Antonyms:* bother, disrupt, inconvenience, trouble **2.** bind, dragoon, coerce, command, compel, constrain, force, impel, make, necessitate, obligate, require, strongarm

obliging *adj.* accommodating, agreeable, amiable, cheerful, civil, complaisant, considerate, cooperative, courteous, easy, easygoing, friendly, good-humoured, helpful, hospitable, kind, lenient, mild, polite, willing *Nonformal:* nice as pie, nice-guy *Antonyms:* discourteous, inconsiderate, rude, surly, uncooperative

oblique *adj.* **1.** angled, askew, awry, bent, crooked, distorted, inclining, leaning, pitching, sideways, slanted, slanting, sloping, tilted, tilting, tipped, tipping, turned, twisted, wonky *(Nonformal)* **2.** backhanded, implied, indirect, secondary, sidelong, tangential *Antonyms:* blunt, candid, direct, frank, open **3.** circumlocutory, devious, furtive, roundabout, sly, surreptitious, underhanded **4.** asymmetrical, deviating, different, diverging, nonuniform, unequal, unparallel – *n.* bevelled, diagonal, slant, transverse – *v.* bevel, deviate, lean, pitch, slant, tilt

obliterate *v.* **1.** annihilate, defeat, destroy, eliminate, expunge, exterminate, extirpate, finish, kill, level, ravage, smash, squash, torpedo *Nonformal:* ice, total, trash, waste, zap *Antonyms:* build, construct, create, establish, generate **2.** blot *or* scratch *or* wipe out, blue-pencil *(Nonformal)*, bowdlerize, cancel, censor, delete, eradicate, erase, expurgate, omit

oblivion *n.* **1.** blackness, darkness, emptiness, extinction, limbo, nirvana, nonexistence, nothing, nothingness, nowhere, nullity, void **2.** amnesia, blankness, forgetfulness *Antonyms:* awareness, consciousness, memory **3.** carelessness, disregard, inadvertence, insensibility, neglect, unconsciousness, unmindfulness *Antonyms:* realization, recognition, sensibility

oblivious *adj.* **1.** absent, absent-minded, absorbed, abstracted, day-dreaming, deaf, distracted, dreamy, forgetful, inattentive, mooning, preoccupied, rapt, woolgathering *Nonformal:* out of it, out to lunch, spacey, zoned out *Antonyms:* alert, attentive, conscious **2.** careless, disregardful, heedless, ignorant, neglectful, negligent, overlooking, unaware, unconcerned, unconscious, unknowing, unobservant, unrecognizing, unwitting *Antonyms:* heedful, mindful, observant, watchful

oblong *adj.* egg-shaped, ellipsoidal, elliptical, elongate, long, oval, ovate, rounded *Antonyms:* square, triangular

obloquy *n.* **1.** abuse, aspersion, attack, bad press, calumny, censure, criticism, defamation, diatribe, invective, opprobrium, reproach, slander, tirade, vilification *Nonformal:* hell, tongue-lashing **2.** disgrace, dishonour, downfall, fall, humiliation, ignominy, infamy, scandal, shame

obnoxious *adj.* **1.** abhorrent, abominable, awful, beastly, detestable, disagreeable, disgusting, displeasing, foul, gross, hateful, horrid, invidious, loathsome, mean, nasty, nauseating, objectionable, odious, offensive, repellent, reprehensible, repugnant, repulsive, revolting, rotten, sickening, stinking, unpleasant **2.** abrasive, annoying, boisterous, bothersome, coarse, dislikable, infernal, insufferable, irritating *Nonformal:* in your face, loud, loud-mouthed, too much *Antonyms:* amiable, charming, congenial, pleasant

obscene *adj.* **1.** coarse, crude, dirty, improper, impure, indecent, lascivious, lewd, licentious, pornographic, prurient, scatological, smutty, vulgar, wanton, X-rated *Nonformal:* adult, blue *Antonyms:* modest, pious, proper **2.** atrocious, evil, heinous, hideous, horrible, loathsome, nasty, offensive, raw, repellent, repugnant, sickening, vile, wicked *Antonyms:* alluring, captivating, respectable **3.** disgusting, filthy, foul, gross, noisome, rank, unwholesome *Antonyms:* innocuous, inoffensive, sanitized, sterilized

obscenity *n.* **1.** abomination, affront, atrocity, blight, coarseness, dirtiness, filth, foulness, grossness, immorality, impropriety, impurity, indelicacy, lewdness, licentiousness, scatology, smut, vileness, vulgarity, wrong *Antonyms:* chastity, innocence, purity **2.** curse, cuss word, dirty name, four-letter word, offence, profanity, swearword

obscure *adj.* **1.** abstruse, ambiguous, arcane, complicated, confusing, cryptic, deep *(Nonformal)*, difficult, enigmatic, esoteric, impenetrable, incomprehensible, inexplicable, mysterious, occult, recondite, unintelligible *Antonyms:* easy, simple, straightforward **2.** dim, faint, fuzzy, hazy, indefinite, indeterminate, indistinct, vague *Antonyms:* apparent, evident, obvious **3.** distant, hidden, out-of-the-way, remote, secret, sequestered **4.** anonymous, humble, inconspicuous, inglorious, little-known, minor, nameless, undistinguished, unknown, unnoted, unrecognized, unsung *Antonyms:* celebrated, notable, renowned **5.** cloudy, dark, dusky, foggy, misty, overcast, shadowy, sombre *Antonyms:* bright, clear, sunny – *v.* **1.** becloud, bedim, block, blur, camouflage, cloak, cloud, conceal, cover up, dim, disguise, eclipse, hide, mask, mist, overcloud, overshadow, screen, shroud, veil *Antonyms:* illuminate, reveal **2.** confuse, double-talk, dress-up, embroider, equivocate, misrepresent, muddy, obfuscate, pettifog *Antonyms:* clarify, elucidate, explicate

obscurity *n.* **1.** ambiguity, complexity, impenetrability, intricacy, reconditeness **2.** inconspicuousness, insignificance, lowliness, unimportance **3.** darkness, indistinctness, murkiness, shadows

obsequious *adj.* complaisant, deferential, fawning, grovelling, ingratiating, kowtowing, obeisant, oily, prostrate, servile, smarmy, submissive, subordinate, subservient, sycophantic, unctuous *Nonformal:* apple-polishing, bootlicking, brown-nosing

observable *adj.* apparent, appreciable, clear, detectable, discernible, discoverable, evident, manifest, noticeable, obvious, open, palpable, patent, perceivable, perceptible, recognizable, sensible, tangible, visible *Antonyms:* invisible, unclear, unnoticeable

observance *n.* **1.** attention, awareness, ear, examination, heed, inspection, notice, observation, scrutiny, vigilance **2.** adherence, compliance, conformity, devotion, honouring, keeping, obedience, orthodoxy, reverence **3.** celebration, ceremony, custom, fashion, form, formality, liturgy, performance, practice, rite, ritual, rule, service, tradition

observant *adj.* **1.** alert, attentive, clear-sighted, considering, contemplating, deducing, detecting, discerning, discriminating, heedful, interested, mindful, questioning, regardful, surveying, vigilant, watchful, wide-awake *Nonformal:* eagle-eyed, hawk-eyed, on the job *Antonyms:* distracted, dreamy, heedless, indifferent **2.** bright, comprehending, intelligent, keen, perceptive, quick, sharp, smart, understanding *Antonyms:* dim, dull, slow **3.** conscientious, devout, dutiful, loyal, obedient orthodox, practicing, strict, traditional

observation *n.* **1.** attention, cognizance concentration, conception, detection examination, experience, inspection, investigation, monitoring, note, notice, perception, review, scrutiny, search, study, surveillance, view, vigilance, watching **2.** comment, estimation, finding, judgment, mention, *obiter dictum (Latin)*, opinion, pronouncement, reflection, remark, saying thought, utterance *Nonformal:* two-cents two cents' worth, wisecrack

observe *v.* **1.** behold, catch, detect, discern, discover, distinguish, espy, examine inspect, mark, monitor, note, notice, perceive, recognize, regard, scrutinize, see spot, spy, survey, view, watch, witness **2** abide by, adhere, adopt, comply with, conform, follow, fulfill, heed, honour, keep mind, obey, perform, practice, respect *Antonyms:* disregard, ignore, miss, omit violate **3.** celebrate, commemorate, dedicate, hold, honour, keep, remember respect, revere, solemnize, venerate **4** announce, articulate, assert, comment on, express, opine, remark, say, state, tell, utter, verbalize, voice

obsessed *adj.* bedevilled, beset, bewitched, captivated, compelled, consumed, controlled, dominated, driven, engrossed, fixated, gripped, haunted, held, immersed in, infatuated, overpowered, plagued, possessed, preoccupied, seized tormented, troubled *Nonformal:* hooked, hung-up *Antonyms:* aloof, detached, disinterested, impassive, indifferent

obsession *n.* **1.** complex, compulsion, enthusiasm, fancy, fascination, mania, neurosis, phobia *See also:* **mania**, **phobia** **2.** attraction, craze, crush, devotion, fetish, fixation, fixed idea, *idée fixe (French)*, infatuation, passion, preoccupation, ruling passion *Nonformal:* hang-up, one-track mind, thing

obsolete *adj.* **1.** ancient, antediluvian, antiquated, antique, archaic, bygone, dated, dusty, fossilized, has-been, obsolescent, old, old-fashioned, old-time, out, outmoded, out-of-date, out-of-fashion, outworn, passé, superannuated, superseded, timeworn, unfashionable *Nonformal:* dinosaur, horse-and-buggy, moth-eaten, neanderthal, stone-age, yesterday *Antonyms:* avant-garde, fashionable, modern **2.** abandoned, discarded, disused, done for, expired, extinct, fusty, mouldy, musty, shelved *(Nonformal)* *Antonyms:* contemporary, current, new

obstacle *n.* bar, barrier, block, crimp, difficulty, drawback, encumbrance, hamper *(Nautical)*, handicap, hindrance, hurdle, impediment, interruption, obstruction, restriction, snag, stumbling block *Nonformal:* brick wall, catch, hitch *Antonyms:* advantage, aid, crutch, help

obstinate *adj.* adamant, determined, dogged, immovable, implacable, inexorable, inflexible, intractable, mulish, persevering, persistent, pertinacious, pig-headed, relentless, resolute, set, single-minded, strong-willed, stubborn, tenacious, tough, unbending, unrelenting, unyielding *Antonyms:* easygoing, flexible, yielding

obstreperous *adj.* **1.** boisterous, clamorous, disorderly, loud, noisy, out of hand, rambunctious, riotous, rowdy, swinging *(Nonformal)*, unbridled, ungoverned, unrestrained, unruly, wild *Antonyms:* calm, controlled, quiet, sedate **2.** bellicose, contumacious, defiant, feisty *(Nonformal)*, intractable, pugnacious, recalcitrant, refractory, restive, ungovernable, unmanageable *Antonyms:* disciplined, docile, gentle

obstruct *v.* **1.** circumscribe, dampen, delay, deter, forbid, foul up, frustrate, gag, hamper, hamstring, hinder, hold *or* keep back, impede, inhibit, interfere, interrupt, limit, oppose, repress, restrain, restrict, retard, slow down, stall, stay, stonewall *(Nonformal)*, stymie, suppress, suspend, thwart, trammel *Antonyms:* advance, assist, encourage, further, promote **2.** arrest, bar, barricade, block, choke, clog, close, halt, jam, occlude, pack, preclude, prevent, prohibit, sandbag, stop, terminate, throttle *Antonyms:* free up, make clear, open

obstruction *n.* bar, barricade, barrier, block, blockage, bottleneck, check, checkmate, circumvention, difficulty, embolism, gridlock, hindrance, hurdle, impediment, interference, jam, limitation, lock, logjam, mountain, obstacle, restraint, restriction, roadblock, stop, stoppage, stumbling block, trammel, trouble, wall, weir *Nonformal:* rub, snag *Antonyms:* assistance, favour, furtherance, help, support

obtain *v.* **1.** accomplish, achieve, attain, bag *(Nonformal)*, cinch, effect, reach, realize, secure, succeed, triumph *Antonyms:* give up, lose **2.** acquire, annex, buy, catch, collect, come across *or* by, cull, earn, extract, fetch, find, gain, garner, get, glean, grab, grasp, hoard, hook, inherit, procure, purchase, reap, receive, recover, retrieve, salvage, snag, take, win *Nonformal:* nab, pocket, score, scrape together *or* up, wangle *Antonyms:* forfeit, forgo **3.** capture, colonize, conquer, corral, invade, land, master, seize **4.** exist, hold, prevail, prevalent, reign, rule, stand

obtainable *adj.* achievable, acquirable, at *or* to hand, attainable, available, in stock, procurable, purchasable, realizable, securable *Nonformal:* gettable, on deck *or* tap *Antonyms:* impossible, out of reach, unattainable

obtrusive *adj.* **1.** bald-faced, blatant, brazen, clear, conspicuous, evident, flagrant, obvious, out-and-out, outright, prominent, sheer, unmitigated *Antonyms:* concealed, covert, hidden **2.** demanding, important, interfering, intrusive, invasive, meddlesome, officious, opinionated, overbearing, prying *Nonformal:* nosy, pushy, snoopy **3.** jutting *or* sticking out, overhanging, projecting, protruding *Antonyms:* depressed, hollow, level

obtuse *adj.* **1.** blind, dense, doltish, dull-witted, dumb, heedless, imperceptive, insensitive, stupid, uncomprehending, unfeeling, unintelligent, unseeing *Nonformal:* boneheaded, dim, dopey, drippy, thick *Antonyms:* aware, cognizant, perceptive **2.** abstruse, ambiguous, fuzzy, hazy, indistinct, obscure, unclear, undecipherable, vague **3.** blunt, dull, faired, rounded, smooth, unpointed *Antonyms:* edged, sharp *Commonly misused:* **abstruse**

obverse *adj.* **1.** confronting, facing, forward, frontal **2.** converse, counter, inverse – *n.* **1.** façade, face, front, surface, top **2.** alternate, complement, counterpart, equivalent, likeness, match, mate, pendant, twin

obviate *v.* avert, block, counter, counteract, deter, forestall, hinder, interfere, interpose, intervene, preclude, prevent, remove, restrain, rule out, stave *or* ward off

obvious *adj.* **1.** apparent, appreciable, bright, broad, certain, clear, clear cut, definite, discernible, distinct, evident, explicit, indisputable, legible, lucid, manifest, noticeable, observable, overt, palpable, patent, perceivable, perceptible, plain, positive, self-evident, self-explanatory, straightforward, sure, tangible, unambiguous, unconcealed, undeniable, understandable, undisguised, unmistakable *Antonyms:* ambiguous, obscure, vague **2.** barefaced, brazen, conspicuous, flagrant, glaring, heavy-handed *(Nonformal)*, open, ostensible, prominent, pronounced, public, recognizable, striking, transparent, unsubtle, visible *Antonyms:* concealed, hidden, invisible

occasion *n.* **1.** circumstance, episode, experience, happening, incident, juncture, moment, place, point, setting, situation, time **2.** affair, celebration, event, function, gala, holiday, levee, milepost, milestone, party, phenomenon *Nonformal:* do, major production **3.** break, chance, moment, occurrence, opening, opportunity, possibility, time **4.** basis, call, cause, circumstance, determinant, excuse, foundation, grounds, inducement, influence, justification, motivation, motive, necessity, obligation, pretext, provocation, purpose, reason, warrant – *v.* breed, bring about, cause, create, do, effect, elicit, engender, evoke, generate, hatch, induce, influence, inspire, move, muster, originate, persuade, produce, prompt, provoke

occasional *adj.* **1.** infrequent, intermittent, irregular, rare, scarce, seldom, specific, sporadic, unusual *Antonyms:* continual, customary, frequent, habitual **2.** casual, extra, incidental, off-and-on, part-time, seasonal **3.** celebratory, commemorative, dedicatory, memorializing, observational **4.** causal, circumstantial, conditional, determinative, formative, provisional

occasionally *adv.* every now and then, hardly ever, infrequently, intermittently, now and then, on occasion, once in a blue moon *(Nonformal)*, once in a while, periodically, seldom, sometimes, sporadically *Antonyms:* constantly, frequently, routinely

occlude *v.* **1.** block, choke, clog, close, congest, cork, jam up, obstruct, plug, seal, stopper **2.** bar, barricade, circumscribe, constrain, enclose, hedge, hinder, impede, lock out, prevent, prohibit, shut off *or* out

occult *adj.* **1.** alchemical, arcane, cabalistic, eerie, esoteric, hermetic, magic, magical, mysterious, mystic, mystical, orphic, preternatural, psychic, spectral, spooky *(Nonformal)*, supernatural, transmundane, unearthly, unexplainable, unknown, weird *Antonyms:* earthly, mundane, physical **2.** concealed, hidden, invisible, nebulous, obscure, secret, shrouded, unrevealed, veiled *Antonyms:* clear, evident, manifest, patent – *n.* alchemy, black arts *or* magic, cabalism, fortune telling, mysticism, necromancy, occultism, soothsaying, the supernatural, witchcraft

occupancy *n.* **1.** dwelling, habitation, inhabitation, location, lodging, residence, settlement, tenancy **2.** control, deed, hold, ownership, possession, proprietorship, title **3.** incumbency, length of service, reign, residency, tenure, time

occupant *n.* **1.** addressee, denizen, dweller, householder, inmate, lessee, renter, resident, resider, squatter, tenant **2.** holder, incumbent, inhabitant, occupier, owner, possessor, user

occupation *n.* **1.** activity, affair, business, calling, chosen work, craft, employment, game, job, line, livelihood, métier, post, profession, pursuit, trade, vocation, work *Nonformal:* bread and butter, daily grind **2.** habitation, holding, occupancy, ownership, possession, residence, settlement, tenancy, tenure, title, use **3.** appropriation, attack, capture, colonization, conquest, coup, invasion, rule, seizure, subjugation, takeover

occupy *v.* **1.** appropriate, capture, colonize, conquer, defeat, invade, overthrow, rule, seize, take over *or* possession, usurp *Antonyms:* abandon, depart, withdraw **2.** absorb, amuse, attend, busy, divert, employ, engage, engross, entertain, fill, interest, involve, monopolize, pass, preoccupy, take up *Antonyms:* annoy, bore **3.** dwell, inhabit, live, maintain, people, possess, remain, reside, squat, stay, tenant **4.** cover, entail, fill, hold, permeate, pervade, tie up, use, utilize

occur *v.* **1.** appear, arise, come about, develop, ensue, exist, happen, manifest, transpire **2.** come to mind, dawn on, materialize, offer *or* present *or* suggest itself

occurrence *n.* accident, adventure, affair, circumstance, episode, event, goings-on, happening, incident, juncture, materialization, mishap, occasion, proceeding, scene, situation, transaction, trip *(Nonformal)*

ocean *n.* **1.** blue water, brine, great *or* high *or* open sea, main, ocean depths, saltchuck *(Pacific Coast)*, salt water, sea, seaway, Seven Seas, tide, water *Nonformal:* big drink *or* pond, bounding main, deep blue sea, foamy brine, puddle *See also:* **sea** **2.** abundance, flood, heap, mass, multitude, plenty, profusion, slew *(Nonformal)*, volume *Antonyms:* few, modicum, speck

oceanic *adj.* **1.** abyssal, aquatic, deep-sea, marine, maritime, nautical, Neptunian, neritic, pelagic, saltwater, sea, thalassic **2.** boundless, countless, endless, enormous, extensive, huge, interminable, limitless, massive, vast

odd *adj.* **1.** aberrant, abnormal, atypical, bizarre, curious, deviant, different, eccentric, exceptional, extraordinary, freakish, idiosyncratic, neurotic, outlandish, peculiar, perverted, quaint, queer, quirky, singular, strange, uncanny, uncommon, unconventional, unnatural, unparalleled, unpredictable, unusual, weird *Nonformal:* funny, kinky, oddball, offbeat, screwy, wacko **2.** casual, erratic, irregular, occasional, part-time, sporadic, temporary **3.** detached, miscellaneous, unconnected, uneven, unmatched *Antonyms:* coupled, joined, paired **4.** additional, extra, leftover, remaining, spare, surplus **5.** alone, individual, lone, single, solitary

oddity *n.* **1.** abnormality, anomaly, curiosity, deviance, freak of nature, incongruity, irregularity, peculiarity, quirk, singularity, *Nonformal:* conversation piece, kink **2.** bizarreness, eccentricity, extraordinariness, idiosyncrasy, oddness, outlandishness, queerness, quirkiness, strangeness, unconventionality, unnaturalness, weirdness **3.** character, eccentric, individual, maverick, misfit, one of a kind, original, phenomenon, rarity *Nonformal:* case, oddball, weirdo

odds *n. pl.* **1.** advantage, allowance, edge, handicap *(Golf)*, lead **2.** balance, chances, likelihood, probability, ratio **3.** difference, discrepancy, disparity, disproportion, inequality, unevenness

ode *n.* ballad, descant, dirge, ditty, elegy, epic poem, howl, lyric, panegyric, song *See also:* **poetry**

odious *adj.* abhorrent, abominable, detestable, disgusting, egregious, execrable, hateful, horrible, horrid, loathsome, mean, obnoxious, offensive, repellent, repugnant, repulsive, revolting, sick *(Nonformal)*, vile *Antonyms:* agreeable, congenial, delightful, enchanting, winsome

odium *n.* **1.** atrociousness, evil, loathsomeness, nastiness, notoriousness, offensiveness, repulsiveness, vileness, wickedness **2.** abhorrence, animus, aversion, bitterness, condemnation, contempt, detestation, disapproval, disfavour, disgust, dislike, enmity, hatred, hostility, loathing, rancour **3.** blame, brand, castigation, censure, disgrace, dishonour, disrepute, humiliation, ignominy, infamy, obloquy, rebuke, shame, slur, spot, stain, stigma

odorous *adj.* aromatic, fragrant, heady, malodorous, odoriferous, perfumed, pungent, redolent, reeking, scented, scent-laden, smelly, stinky, strong

odour *n.* aroma, bouquet, breath, emanation, essence, fragrance, fruitiness, fustiness, mustiness, perfume, quality, redolence, savour, scent, smell, stench, stink, suggestion, touch, trace, whiff

odourless *adj.* flat, odour-free, scentless, unfragrant, unperfumed, unscented

odyssey *n.* **1.** adventure, descent, experience, journey, journeying, sojourn, travels, trip, voyage, wanderings **2.** chronicle, epic, narrative, saga, story

off *adj.* **1.** bad, decomposed, funky, gamy, high, mouldy, rancid, rotten, skunky *(Nonformal)*, sour, spoiled **2.** disappointing, inferior, irregular, poor, substandard, unsatisfactory *Nonformal:* below par, shoddy **3.** away, distant, far, further, gone, out and about, outlying, remote **4.** erroneous, inaccurate, incorrect, mistaken, off-the-mark *(Nonformal)*, wrong **5.** defunct, down, inactive, nonexistent, out of commission, void *Nonformal:* kaput, no-go, shot **6.** holidaying, idle, leisure, non-working, spare, unemployed, vacationing, weekending – *adv.* at a distance, away, distantly, far off, remotely, outside

offbeat *adj.* bizarre, different, eccentric, idiosyncratic, odd, *outré (French)*, quaint, quirky, strange, uncommon, unconventional, unusual *Nonformal:* freaky, oddball,

off-colour *adj.* **1.** green, ill, pasty, out-of-sorts, poor, queasy, run-down, sick, unwell, washed-out **2.** boorish, crude, dirty, improper, indecent, lewd, naughty, obscene, offensive, politically incorrect, raunchy, risqué, rude, tasteless, uncouth, vulgar *Antonyms:* decent, polite, politically correct

offence *n.* **1.** breach, crime, delinquency, fault, infraction, lapse, malfeasance, misdeed, misdemeanour, peccadillo, sin, transgression, trespass, violation, wrongdoing **2.** affront, atrocity, harm, hurt, indignity, injury, injustice, insult, outrage, slight, snub, wound **3.** aggression, assault, attack, battery, dragonnade *(Historical)*, forward movement, invasion, onslaught, penetration, push, raid, rush, sally, sortie **4.** displeasure, indignation, pique, resentment, umbrage

offend *v.* **1.** affront, aggrieve, anger, annoy, antagonize, disgruntle, disoblige, displease, disturb, exasperate, fret, gall, irritate, jar, miff, nettle, outrage, pique, provoke, rile, upset, vex *Antonyms:* appease, conciliate, delight, mollify, placate **2.** distress, harm, hurt, impair, insult, malign, pain, slight, slur, snub, sting, wound **3.** disgust, nauseate, repel, repulse, sicken **4.** err, lapse, sin, transgress, trespass

offensive *adj.* **1.** aggressive, assailing, assaulting, attacking, bellicose, belligerent, hostile, invading, pugnacious, truculent *Antonyms:* defensive, friendly, peaceful **2** aggravating, annoying, bothersome, crass, disagreeable, displeasing, insufferable, intolerable, irksome, irritating, obnoxious, vexatious *Antonyms:* aiding, helpful **3** abusive, biting, caustic, cutting, discourteous, disrespectful, injurious, insulting, malicious, mean, rude **4.** abhorrent, detestable, dire, dreadful, egregious, evil, foul, ghastly, grisly, heinous, hideous, horrid, loathsome, malevolent, odious, reprehensible, terrible **5.** disgusting, distasteful, fetid, gross *(Nonformal)*, nauseating, putrid, repugnant, revolting, sickening, sour, stinking, unappetizing – *n.* assault, attack, charge, forward movement, onslaught, push, rush, thrust

offer *n.* attempt, bid, endeavour, essay, overture, pitch *(Nonformal)*, presentation, proposal, proposition, submission, suggestion – *v.* **1.** award, bid, donate, extend, give, present, proffer, tender **2.** advance, pose, propose, propound, put forth *or* forward, recommend, submit, suggest **3.** bestow, pray, sacrifice, yield

offering *n.* **1.** alms, benefaction, beneficence, charity, contribution, donation **2.** gift, immolation, oblation, sacrifice

offhand *adj.* ad-lib, casual, extemporaneous, free, impromptu, improvised, informal, off the cuff *(Nonformal)*, spontaneous, spur of the moment, throwaway, unpremeditated, unprepared, unrehearsed, unstudied *Antonyms:* planned, premeditated – *adv.* carelessly, casually, extempore, informally, in passing, naturally, nonchalantly, unaffectedly, unceremoniously

office *n.* **1.** agency, building, bureau, business, centre, department, facility, suite, workplace, work station **2.** appointment, commission, occupation, place, post, position, province, role, situation, station **3.**

assignment, charge, duty, employment, function, job, mission, obligation, responsibility, work **4.** ceremony, devotion, prayer, rite, ritual, worship

officer *n.* **1.** aide-de-camp, brigadier, captain, chief of staff, colonel, commander, commanding officer, general, lieutenant, major *Nonformal:* brass, top brass *See also:* **military** **2.** administrator, agent, appointee, bailiff, chief executive officer *or* CEO, chief financial officer *or* CFO, chief operating officer *or* COO, commissioner, dignitary, executive, manciple, marshal, minister, officeholder, official, President, principle, representative, secretary, treasurer, vice president **3.** cop, Mountie, policeman, police officer, policewoman, superintendent *Nonformal:* badge, copper, fuzz, heat, narc, pig, the man *Police rankings*: captain, chief of police, constable, deputy, detective, inspector, lieutenant, patrolman, sergeant, sheriff – *v.* command, direct, lead, manage, operate, pilot, rule, steer, supervise

official *adj.* **1.** canonical, conventional, *ex cathedra (Latin)*, legal **2.** black-tie, ceremonious, formal, ornate, *pro forma (Latin)*, proper, serious, solemn – *n.* **1.** administrator, agent, apparatchik, bashaw, bureaucrat, chamberlain, commissioner, director, executive, functionary, incumbent, intendant, leader, manager, mandarin, minister, officer, pasha, Poo-Bah *(Nonformal)*, provost, reeve, representative, vizier, waldgrave **2.** arbiter, judge, line judge *(Football)*, lineman *(Hockey)*, linesman *(Tennis & Soccer)*, referee, scorekeeper, timekeeper, umpire

officiate *v.* **1.** chair, command, conduct, direct, emcee, govern, handle, lead, manage, moderate, monitor, oversee, preside, proctor, run, superintend **2.** arbitrate, judge, mediate, referee, umpire

officious *adj.* aggressive, bumptious, domineering, forward, interfering, intrusive, meddlesome, obtrusive, opinionated, overzealous, self-important *Nonformal:* bossy, pushy

offset *n.* **1.** amends, compensation, damages, indemnity, recompense, reimbursement, repayment, restitution, satisfaction **2.** antidote, balance, ballast, counteraction, counterbalance, equalizer, stabilizer **3.** angle, bend, curve, elbow – *v.* **1.** allow for, compensate, counteract, counterbalance, counterpoise, equal, equalize, even out, redress, set off **2.** cancel out, eliminate, neutralize, nullify

offshoot *n.* **1.** adjunct, by-product, consequence, derivative, descendent, development, filiation, offspring, outcome, ramification, result, spinoff **2.** appendage, branch, offset, offspring, outgrowth, shoot, sprig, sprout, sucker

offspring *n.* **1.** baby, brood, child, children, descendant, family, generation, get, hatch, heir, issue, kid, lineage, litter, posterity, progeny, scion, seed, sibling, spawn, successor, swarm, young *Antonyms:* ancestor, forebear, matriarch, sire **2.** by-product, consequence, offshoot, outcome, product, ramification, result

often *adv.* continually, frequently, generally, habitually, recurrently, regularly, repeatedly, usually *Antonyms:* hardly ever, infrequently, rarely, scarcely, seldom

ogle *n.* gape, gawk, leer, once-over *(Nonformal)*, stare – *v.* admire, examine, eye, gape, gaze, leer, lock eyes, peer, scan, scrutinize, squint, stare *Nonformal:* check out, rubberneck

ogre *n.* **1.** creature, giant, man-eater, monster, ogress, troll **2.** barbarian, beast, bruiser, brute, bully, hellion, killer, lout, oaf sadist, savage

oil *n.* **1.** crude, distillate, fossil fuel, fuel, gas, gasoline, hydrocarbon, lubricant, petrol *(British)*, petroleum **2.** animal *or* vegetable distillate, fat, grease *Kinds of cooking oil:* almond, avocado, canola, citronella, clarified butter, coconut, corn, cottonseed, Crisco *(Trademark)*, fatback, ghee, hazelnut, hydrogenated vegetable, lard, margarine, olive, rapeseed, safflower, sesame, soybean, sunflower, vegetable, walnut – *v.* **1.** anoint, coat, grease, lard, lube, lubricate, pomade, rustproof, slick, smear **2.** bribe, buy off, coax, flatter, influence, inveigle, lure, reward

oily *adj.* **1.** buttery, creamy, fatty, filmy, greasy, lubricant, lustrous, oiled, oil-soaked, polished, rich, slimy, slippery **2.** cajoling, coaxing, flattering, fulsome, obsequious, smarmy, soapy, slick, suave, unctuous

ointment *n.* balm, cream, dressing, emollient, liniment, lotion, medicine, pomade, salve, unguent

okay *adj.* **1.** acceptable, adequate, allowable, fair, fine, in good order, marginal, middling, not bad, passable, permissible, satisfactory, tolerable **2.** all right, comfortable, out of danger, resting, safe – *interj.* affirmative, agreed, aye aye, right, roger *(Nonformal)*, very good *or* well, whatever you say, yea, yes – *n.* agreement, approval, assent, authorization, consent, endorsement, green light *(Nonformal)*, permission, sanction – *v.* agree, allow, approve, authorize, consent, endorse, pass, permit, sanction

old *adj.* **1.** bygone, earlier, erstwhile, former, olden, past, preceding, previous, prior **2.** experienced, practiced, seasoned, senior, venerable, versed, veteran **3.** aged, doddering, enfeebled, exhausted, feeble, frail, grey, grizzled, impaired, infirm, wizened **4.** battered, broken-down, creaky, debilitated, deteriorated, rusty, shot *(Nonformal)*, timeworn, weathered, worn-down **5.** archaic, dated, extinct, inactive, outmoded, out-of-date, passé, retired, stale, superceded **6.** ancient, antediluvian, antiquated, antique, historic, prehistoric, primeval, primordial **7.** beloved, cherished, enduring, intimate, lasting, time-honoured, traditional, well-known – *n.* antiquity, golden age, history, past, yore

old-fashioned *adj.* **1.** antiquated, archaic, obsolescent, obsolete, outdated, outmoded, out-of-date, passé, unfashionable *Antonyms:* contemporary, current, modern **2.** dated, dowdy, fusty, moss-backed, musty, oldfangled, old-time, out, out-of-style, outworn, yesterday *Antonyms:* chic, fashionable, in

omen *n.* augury, auspice, bellwether, foreshadower, foretoken, harbinger, indication, portent, presage, sign, warning – *v.* augur, divine, forebode, foreshadow, indicate, portend, presage, signify

ominous *adj.* **1.** apocalyptic, baleful, clouded, dangerous, dark, dire, dismal, doomed, fateful, fearful, forbidding, foreboding, gloomy, grim, haunting, hostile, ill-boding, impending, inauspicious, inhospitable, malefic, menacing, perilous, portentous, sinister, threatening, unfriendly, unlucky *Antonyms:* auspicious, encouraging, favourable, promising, propitious **2.** divinatory, foreshadowing, oracular, premonitory, presaging, prognostic, prophetic

omission *n.* **1.** elimination, ellipsis, exclusion, go-by *(Nonformal)*, ignoring, inadvertency, preclusion, prohibition, repudiation, slighting, slip, withholding *Antonyms:* addition, inclusion, incorporation, insertion **2.** carelessness, failure, forgetfulness, forgetting, lapse, neglect, overlooking, oversight

omit *v.* **1.** cancel, cut, delete, edit *or* leave out, eradicate, erase, exclude, expunge **2.** disregard, eschew, except, forget, ignore, jump, miss, neglect, overlook, pass over, rule out, skip

omnipotent *adj.* all-powerful, almighty, divine, godlike, infinite, mighty, powerful, preeminent, supreme, unlimited, unrestricted

on *adj.* active, happening, humming away *(Nonformal)*, plugged-in, powered, running, working – *adv.* **1.** fast, firmly, securely, tightly **2.** *ad infinitum (Latin)*, constantly, continually, doggedly, perpetually, steadily, unceasingly, unendingly **3.** across, ahead, beyond, forward, in advance, onward, toward – *prep.* **1.** above, around, attached to, atop, covering, over, suspended from, upon **2.** adjacent, beside, close by, near, next to **3.** during, in the course of **4.** as a result of, because of, by means of, due *or* owing *or* thanks to, seeing that, upon **5.** addicted to, hooked on, using **6.** after, also, in addition to, plus **7.** about, concerning, engaged in

once *adj.* ago, bygone, erstwhile, former, late, past, preterit, previous, prior, quondam – *adv.* **1.** but once, on one occasion, onetime **2.** already, away back, back, back when, before, earlier, erstwhile, formerly, heretofore, hitherto, long ago, previously **3.**

at any time, at whatever time, ever, if ever, no matter when, whenever, whensoever – *conj.* as soon as, when, whenever – *n.* one time, single occasion *or* time

oncoming *adj.* advancing, approaching, coming, expected, forthcoming, imminent, impending, looming, nearing, onrushing, upcoming *Antonyms:* going, leaving, retreating

one *adj.* **1.** alone, individual, lone, odd, only, particular, single, singular, sole, solitary **2.** alike, compatible, complete, concordant, connected, entire, harmonious, identical, integrated, joined, joined at the hip *(Nonformal)*, kindred, like-minded, married, twin, unified, whole *Antonyms:* different, divided, separate, unique – *n.* anecdote, joke, story, tale, tall story *(Nonformal)* – *pron.* anyone, any person, a person, he, I, it, she, you

oneiric *adj.* abstract, dissociative, dream-like, fantastic, hallucinatory, imaginative, irrational, odd, strange, surreal, weird *Antonyms:* concrete, normal, realistic

onerous *adj.* arduous, back-breaking, burdensome, crushing, difficult, distressing, exhausting, fatiguing, grievous, gruelling, hard, harrowing, harsh, heavy, herculean, intolerable, irksome, laborious, nightmarish *(Nonformal)*, oppressive, strenuous, taxing, toilsome, wearing *Antonyms:* easy, light, simple

one-sided *adj.* **1.** asymmetrical, disproportionate, inharmonious, irregular, lopsided, unequal, uneven **2.** biased, close-minded, inequitable, partial, prejudiced, subjective, unfair *Antonyms:* just, neutral, objective

on-line *adj.* attached, communicating, connected, interconnected, joined, linked, plugged-in *Nonformal:* on the Net, surfing *Antonyms:* disconnected, off-line

onlooker *n.* beholder, bystander, eyewitness, looker-on, observer, sightseer, spectator, viewer, watcher, witness *Nonformal:* railbird, rubbernecker

only *adj.* alone, apart, exclusive, individual, isolated, lone, matchless, one, particular, peerless, single, singular, sole, solitary, solo, unaccompanied, unequalled, unique, unparalleled, unrivalled – *adv.* **1.** alone, apart, distinctively, exclusively, particularly, separately, solely, solitarily, solo, uniquely **2.** at most, barely, hardly, just, merely, nothing but, purely, simply – *conj.* but, except that, however, if not, nevertheless, notwithstanding, on the contrary, save

onset *n.* **1.** aggression, assault, attack, charge, encounter, offence, offensive, onrush, onslaught, seizure **2.** beginning, birth, commencement, dawn, debut, germination, inauguration, inception, incipience, kickoff, launch, opening, origin, outbreak, sendoff, start *Antonyms:* completion, end, termination

onslaught *n.* assault, attack, barrage, blitzkrieg, bombardment, broadside, cannonade, charge, *coup de main (French)*, foray, fusillade, incursion, infiltration, invasion, offensive, raid, rush, salvo, siege, storm, strike *Antonyms:* let-up, retreat, withdrawal

onus *n.* albatross, burden, cross, difficulty, duty, encumbrance, liability, millstone, obligation, oppression, responsibility, strain, task, tax, weight *Antonyms:* liberation, relief

onward *adj.* advancing, forward, moving, ongoing, proceeding, progressive – *adv.* ahead, forth, in front, in the van *(Nonformal)*

oomph *n.* **1.** animation, energy, enthusiasm, exuberance, spirit, verve, vigour, vim, vitality *Nonformal:* kick, moxie, pep, spunk, zest, zing, zip **2.** allure, appeal, attractiveness, beauty, charm, looks *(Nonformal)*, sex appeal

ooze *n.* **1.** discharge, drip, exudation, flow, leak, percolation, perspiration, sweat **2.** mire, muck, mud, slime, sludge *Nonformal:* goo, goop, guck, gunk **3.** bog, fen, marsh, morass, quagmire, quicksand, swamp – *v.* bleed, discharge, drip, drizzle, effuse, emanate, emit, escape, exude, flow, leach, percolate, release, secrete, seep, trickle, weep

opaque *adj.* **1.** clouded, dark, dim, dusky, hazy, muddy, murky, nontranslucent *Antonyms:* diaphanous, sheer, transparent **2.** baffling, blurred, concealed, cryptic, difficult, enigmatic, equivocal, impenetrable, incomprehensible, obfuscated, obscure, perplexing, tenebrous, uncertain, unclear, unfathomable, vague *Antonyms:* apparent, clear, simple **3.** drab, dull, flat, lacklustre, matte *Antonyms:* luminescent, shiny, sparkling **4.** dense, dim-witted, empty-headed, obtuse, stupid *Nonformal:* pea-brained, thick *Antonyms:* bright, brilliant, smart

open *adj.* **1.** accessible, clear, cleared, free, navigable, passable, unbarred, unbarricaded, unblocked, uncluttered, unimpeded, unobstructed *Antonyms:* barred, blocked, congested **2.** agape, ajar, gaping, unbuttoned, uncorked, unfastened, unlatched, unlocked, unplugged, unsealed **3.** holey *(Nonformal)*, honeycombed, lacey, perforated, porous **4.** apparent, avowed, blatant, clear, conspicuous, downright, evident, flagrant, manifest, noticeable, obvious, overt, plain, unconcealed, undisguised, visible, well-known *Antonyms:* closed, disguised, hidden, inaccessible, shut **5.** ambiguous, arguable, controversial, debatable, doubtful, dubious, dubitable, equivocal, indecisive, in question, moot, problematic, questionable, uncertain, undecided, unresolved, unsettled, up in the air **6.** artless, candid, frank, guileless, heartfelt, honest, ingenuous, innocent, natural, open-hearted, plain, receptive, sincere, straightforward, transparent, unreserved, up-front *Antonyms:* conniving, cunning, shrewd, sly **7.** blooming, expanding, extended, relaxed, unfolded, unfurled, unrolled **8.** in business *(Nonformal)*, manned, operative, ready, running **9.** general, inclusive, nondiscriminatory, public, tolerant, unlimited, unrestricted *Antonyms:* exclusive, intimate, private **10.** at hand, available, empty, unclaimed, unfilled, uninhabited, unoccupied, unpeopled, untaken, vacant *Antonyms:* filled, occupied, taken **11.** amenable, approachable, disinterested, easy, fair, neutral, nonpartisan, objective, unbiased, uncommitted **12.** eager, receptive, voluntary, welcoming, willing **13.** abandoned, defenceless, deserted, exposed, forsaken, helpless, insecure, penetrable, unattended, undefended, unguarded, vulnerable, weak *Antonyms:* guarded, impregnable, invincible, secure **14.** alfresco, exterior, external, outdoors, outside, roofless **15.** clement, frost-free, ice-free, mild, temperate, thawed *Antonyms:* icy, snowy, stormy – *v.* **1.** break into, jimmy, tap, unclog, unclose, uncork, uncover, unfasten, unlatch, unlock, unplug, unseal, unwrap **2.** begin, commence, embark, inaugurate, initiate, kick off *(Nonformal)*, launch, ready, start *Antonyms:* conclude, finish, terminate **3.** bloom, broaden, dilate, distend, expand, extend, spread out, unbend, unclutch, unfold, unfurl, unroll **4.** air, announce, broadcast, expose, herald, proclaim, publicize, release, uncover, unshroud, unveil

open-ended *adj.* adaptable, broad, debatable, general, indefinite, moot, undefined, undetermined, unlimited, unresolved, unrestricted, unsettled, vague

open-handed *adj.* beneficent, benevolent, bountiful, charitable, eleemosynary, freehanded, generous, giving, humanitarian, kindhearted, liberal, magnanimous, munificent, philanthropic, prodigal *Antonyms:* cheap, close-fisted, stingy

opening *adj.* beginning, commencing, initial, introductory, first, prefatory, starting, start-up – *n.* **1.** availability, break, chance, opportunity, place, possibility, run, shot, time, vacancy **2.** aperture, breach, cavity, chink, cleft, crack, cranny, crevice, cut, door, fissure, gap, hatch, hole, interstice, orifice, outlet, rent, rift, rupture, slit, slot, space, tear, vent, window **3.** beginning, birth, coming out, commencement, dawn, face-off, inauguration, inception, initiation, kickoff, launch, onset, opener, outset, start *Antonyms:* closing, completion, ending, finish **4.** introduction, foreword, preface, prologue

openly *adv.* **1.** aboveboard, artlessly, candidly, forthrightly, frankly, fully, honestly, ingenuously, naturally, plainly, simply, straightforwardly, willingly, without pretense *Antonyms:* cunningly, furtively, shrewdly, slyly **2.** blatantly, brazenly, clearly, flagrantly, in plain sight *or* view, in public, overtly, publicly, readily, shamelessly, unabashedly, unashamedly, unhesitatingly, unreservedly, wantonly *Antonyms:* covertly, privately, secretly, subtly

open-minded *adj.* approachable, broad-minded, catholic, dispassionate, enlightened, evenhanded, freethinking, impartial, just, liberal, neutral, objective, reasonable, receptive, square, tolerant

opera *n.* musical drama *Kinds of opera:* ballad, grand, light, opera ballet, *opera buffa (Italian)*, operetta, seria *French:* opéra bouffe, opéra comique

operate *v.* **1.** administer, command, conduct, control, direct, drive, govern, guide, handle, helm, keep, manage, manipulate, manoeuvre, oversee, pilot, run, steer, supervise, utilize, wield, work **2.** act, behave, function, go, perform, run, serve **3.** accomplish, achieve, bring about, effectuate, engender, engineer, evoke, illicit, produce, summon **4.** amputate, cut, excise, explore, open up, perform surgery, remove, set, transplant, treat

operation *n.* **1.** business, company, concern, corporation, enterprise, establishment, machinery, organization, outfit, plant, shop, squad, team, troop, undertaking, unit, works **2.** activity, affair, doing, effort, employment, engagement, enterprise, exercise, happening, practice, work **3.** agency, consequence, force, influence, instrumentality, manipulation **4.** agreement, bargain, deal, deed, transaction, venture **5.** procedure *Kinds of mathematical operations:* addition, approximation, differentiation, division, equation, evolution, extraction of roots, extrapolation, integration, interpolation, inversion, involution, multiplication, notation, proportion, reduction, subtraction, transformation **6.** excision, extraction, procedure, surgery

operative *adj.* **1.** active, current, effective, efficient, functioning, in force *or* practice, live, running, serviceable, standing, usable, working **2.** crucial, important, indicative, influential, key, significant **3.** blue-collar, factory, industrial, manual, mechanical – *n.* **1.** artisan, blue-collar worker, factory hand, labourer, mechanic, workperson **2.** agent, detective, private inspector *or* P.I., secret *or* undercover agent *Nonformal:* dick, gumshoe, private eye

opiate *n.* analgesic, depressant, downer *(Nonformal)*, drug, hypnotic, narcotic, sedative, soporific, tranquilizer *Antonyms:* irritant, stimulant

opinionated *adj.* adamant, assertive, believing, biased, bigoted, bossy, bullheaded, dictatorial, hard-line, inflexible, intransigent, obdurate, obstinate, overbearing, positive, set on, single-minded, stubborn, uncompromising, unyielding *Antonyms:* ambivalent, compliant, flexible

opponent *adj.* conflicting, contradictory, contrary, opposing, opposite – *n.* adversary, antagonist, assailant, challenger, competitor, contestant, entrant, foe, nemesis, opposer, opposition, player, rival *Antonyms:* accomplice, associate, colleague, helper, supporter

opportune *adj.* **1.** advantageous, appropriate, apt, auspicious, expedient, favourable, fortuitous, fortunate, helpful, lucky, propitious, suitable *Antonyms:* inappropriate, unfavourable **2.** convenient, occasional, seasonable, timely, well-timed

opportunistic *adj.* calculating, cunning, deceptive, designing, Machiavellian, manipulative, plotting, scheming, sly, wily

opportunity *n.* break, chance, circumstance, convenience, fighting chance, happening, hope, juncture, liberty, moment, move, occasion, opening, possibility, probability, run, shot, spell, turn

oppose *v.* **1.** assail, assault, attack, battle, brawl, clash, combat, fight, foray, quarrel, spar **2.** defy, hinder, neutralize, obstruct, prevent, resist, thwart, withstand *Antonyms:* quit, secede, surrender **3.** compare, contrast, liken, match, pit **4.** confront, contradict, deny, disagree, disapprove, dispute, refute *Antonyms:* accede, agree

opposed *adj.* against, antagonistic, averse, battling, clashing, combatting, confronting, contrary, counter, demurring, denying, disagreeing, disinclined, disobliging, disputing, incompatible, indisposed, inimical, irreconcilable, loath, malcontent, objecting, obstructive, opposite, protesting, rebelling, rebellious, recalcitrant, refractory, repelling, resistant, unenthusiastic, unwilling *Antonyms:* aiding, defending, supporting

opposite *adj.* **1.** adverse, antagonistic, conflicting, contradictory, contrary, diametrically opposed, different, diverse, nonconforming, oppositional, variant *Antonyms:* identical, similar **2.** facing, fronting, neighbouring, opposing – *n.* antithesis, antonym, contradiction, contrast, converse, flip side *(Nonformal)*, negative, reverse – *prep.* across, facing, in front of, toward

opposition *n.* **1.** antagonism, conflict, defiance, flak *(Nonformal)*, friction, frustration, hostility, repulsion, resistance, strife, struggle *Antonyms:* cooperation, harmony **2.** adversary, antagonist, competition, competitor, disputant, enemy, foe, loyal *or* official Opposition, opponent, rival, rivalry *Antonyms:* associate, colleague, teammate **3.** contention, criticism, debate, disagreement, disapproval, dissent, objection, recalcitrance *Antonyms:* accord, unity **4.** antithesis, antonym, counter, opposite, opposition, polar, reverse **5.** block, check, hindrance, obstacle, prevention

oppress *v.* **1.** abuse, crush, dragoon, help, hurt, ill-treat, injure, overwhelm, maltreat, misuse, persecute, scourge, squash, suppress, trample, tread upon, tyrannize, wrong *Antonyms:* ameliorate, support **2.** afflict, burden, depress, discourage, dishearten, dispirit, overload, saddle, tax, weigh down *Antonyms:* hearten, lighten, unburden

oppressed *adj.* **1.** abused, downtrodden, injured, maltreated, misused, tyrannized, victimized, wronged **2.** disenfranchised, ghettoized, marginalized, powerless *Antonyms:* authorized, potent, powerful **3.** burdened, burnt-out *(Nonformal)*, frazzled, overtaxed, overwhelmed, saddled, stressed

oppression *n.* **1.** abuse, coercion, despotism, domination, persecution, terrorism, tyranny, victimization *Antonyms:* benevolence, compassion, justice, sympathy **2.** cruelty, hardship, inequality, injustice, poverty, privation, racism, sexism **3.** dejection, depression, distress, misery, sorrow, suffering, vexation, weight

oppressive *adj.* **1.** bleak, brutal, cruel, depressive, despotic, discouraging, disheartening, dismal, gloomy, grievous, harsh, heavy-handed, inhuman, iron-fisted, mean, overbearing, overwhelming, repressive, severe, sombre, tough, troublesome, tyrannical, unjust *Antonyms:* gentle, humane, lenient, merciful, soft **2.** backbreaking, burdensome, exacting, heavy, onerous, taxing, weighty **3.** close, confined, heavy, hot, humid, muggy, overpowering, steamy, sticky, stifling, stuffy, suffocating, sultry, torrid

oppressor *n.* autocrat, bully, despot, dictator, exploiter, satrap, slave driver, slumlord, taskmaster, tyrant, warlord

opprobrious *adj.* **1.** atrocious, degraded, despicable, detestable, disgraceful, dishonourable, horrible, inglorious, shameful, vicious *Antonyms:* honourable, laudable, praiseworthy **2.** contemptuous, derogatory, detracting, libelous, malicious, pejorative, scurrilous, slanderous

opt *v.* choose, decide, elect, go for, mark, pick, prefer, select, single out, take

optimism *n.* assurance, brightness, buoyancy, certainty, cheer, cheerfulness, confidence, easiness, elation, encouragement, enthusiasm, exhilaration, good cheer, happiness, hopefulness, idealism, positivism, sanguineness, sureness, trust *Antonyms:* bleakness, cynicism, pessimism

optimist *n.* dreamer, hoper, idealist, Pangloss, Pollyanna, romantic, utopian, visionary *Antonyms:* cynic, pessimist

optimistic *adj.* assured, bright, buoyant, cheerful, confident, encouraged, expectant, happy, hopeful, hoping, idealistic, merry, Panglossian, positive, rosy, sanguine, sunny, trusting, upbeat, utopian *Antonyms:* cynical, despairing, despondent, fatalistic hopeless

optimize *v.* capitalize on, increase, make the most of *(Nonformal)*, maximize, play up

optimum *adj.* best, brightest, choice, choicest, first, greatest, highest, ideal, matchless maximum, most advantageous *or* favourable, nonpareil, optimal, peak, peerless, perfect, select, top, world class *Nonformal:* king, tops *Antonyms:* inferior, lowest, poorest, worst

option *n.* **1.** chance, discretion, freedom, opportunity, prerogative, privilege, right **2.** alternative, choice, claim, favourite, pick, preference, selection

optional *adj.* alternative, arbitrary, available, discretionary, elective, free, noncompulsory, not required, open, possible, unforced, unrestricted, voluntary *Antonyms:* compulsory, mandatory, obligatory, required

opulent *adj.* **1.** affluent, moneyed, prosperous, rich, wealthy, well-heeled, well-off, well-to-do *Nonformal:* in clover, loaded, made of money, rolling in dough *Antonyms:* destitute, down-and-out, indigent, needy, poor **2.** abundant, copious, plentiful, profuse, prolific *Antonyms:* paltry, scanty **3.** deluxe, extravagant, *(Nonformal)*, lavish, luscious, luxuriant, luxurious, ostentatious, palatial, plush, showy, sumptuous *Nonformal:* flashy, swank *Antonyms:* simple, unadorned

opus *n.* **1.** body of work, book, corpus creation, literature, manuscript, monograph, novel, production, publication, series, thesis, transcript, volume, work *See also:* **book** **2.** anthem, aria, arrangement, composition, concerto, mass, music, opera, piece, production, score, symphony

oracle *n.* **1.** augury, divination, edict, forecast, fortune, prediction, prognostication, prophecy, revelation, vision **2.** authority, elder, mandarin, master, medicine man, prophet, sage, shaman, sibyl, soothsayer, wiseman, wisewoman **3.** aphorism, axiom, canon, convention, creed, doctrine, edict, law, maxim, motto, old saw *(Nonformal)*, principle, proverb, tenet

oracular *adj.* **1.** augural, Delphic, divinatory, fatidic, forewarning, predictive, prophetic, signified, sibylline, vatic **2.** ambiguous, arcane, cryptic, enigmatic, mysterious, mystical, obscure, surrealistic, vague **3.** dire, fateful, foreboding, loaded, looming, ominous, portentous, starcrossed, threatening

oral *adj.* **1.** articulated, narrated, parol, recounted, related, said, spoken, told, uttered, verbal, vocal, voiced, word-of-mouth **2.** non-literate, pre-literate, *viva voce (Latin)* – *n.* defence, exam, examination, quiz, study, survey, test

orange *adj.* colour *Orange shades:* apricot, coral, peach, reddish-yellow, salmon, tangerine, titian – *n.* citrus *or* tropical fruit *Kinds of oranges:* blood, clementine, mandarin, navel, tangerine, Valencia

orate *v.* declaim, elocute, hold forth, lecture, pontificate, preach, rant, soliloquize, sermonize, speak, talk *Nonformal:* blather, dribble, spew

oration *n.* address, declamation, discourse, harangue, homily, lecture, pep-talk, pitch, rant, sermon, speech, spiel *(Nonformal)*, tirade

oratory *n.* **1.** address, declamation, elocution, lecturing, preaching, public speaking, sermonizing, speechifying, speechmaking **2.** eloquence, expression, smoothness, style

orb *n.* **1.** ball, circle, globe, halo, orbit, ring, sphere **2.** moon, planet, star, sun

orbit *n.* **1.** ambit, area, arena, bailiwick, boundary, circumference, department, domain, dominion, extent, field, influence, jurisdiction, limit, province, purview, radius, range, reach, realm, scope, sphere, sweep **2.** apogee, circle, circuit, course, curve, ellipse, lap, path, pattern, revolution, rotation, round, route, track, trajectory – *v.* circle, circumnavigate, revolve

orchard *n.* copse, enclosure, farm, grove, land, plantation, property, stand, vineyard

orchestrate *v.* **1.** arrange, combine, coordinate, harmonize, integrate, manage, organize, put together, set up, synthesize **2.** chart *(Nonformal)*, compose, pen, score, write

ordain *v.* **1.** decree, dictate, direct, enact, establish, order, prescribe, rule, will **2.** destine, fate, mark, predestine **3.** appoint, commission, endow, install, invest

ordeal *n.* affliction, agony, anguish, calamity, cross, difficulty, gauntlet, test, torment, trial, tribulation, trouble *Antonyms:* bliss, delight, elation, joy, pleasure

order *n.* **1.** conformity, regularity, standardization **2.** arrangement, design, disposition, distribution, form, method, pattern, plan, procedure, process, scheme, system *Antonyms:* chaos, disarray, disorganization **3.** hierarchy, ladder, procession, progression, ratio, scale, sequence, series, spectrum, structure, succession, tier **4.** cleanliness, neatness, orderliness, organization, symmetry, tidiness, uniformity *Antonyms:* messiness, sloppiness, slovenliness **5.** authorization, behest, bidding, charge, command, decree, dictate, direction, directive, establishment, injunction, instruction, law, mandate, ordinance, permission, precept, regulation, rule, stipulation, word **6.** convention, custom, fashion, manner, mode, style, usage, way **7.** condition, nature, repair, shape, state, status **8.** calm, co-existence, control, decorum, discipline, harmony, law and order, lawfulness, orderliness, peace, quiet, rightness, tranquility, unity *Antonyms:* chaos, disarray, jumble, mess, pandemonium **9.** association, brotherhood, club, community, company, cooperative, denomination, fellowship, fraternity, guild, league, lodge, organization, religious community, sect, sisterhood, society, sodality, sorority, union **10.** caste, class, economic *or* social bracket, estate, grade, hierarchy, place, position, rank, status **11.** branch, breed, classification, degree, description, family, feather, genre, genus, ilk, kind, set, sort, species, stripe, type **12.** booking, bulk, commission, goods, materials, product, purchase, purchase agreement, quantity, requisition, reservation, shipment, supplies – *v.* **1.** authorize, charge, command, dictate, establish, instruct, prescribe, request, require, tell **2.** conduct, control, direct, manage, preside over, regulate, run **3.** arrange, catalogue, class, classify, group, organize, pattern, standardize, systematize, tier *Antonyms:* clutter, confuse, disorder

orderly *adj.* **1.** clean, neat, shipshape, spick-and-span, tidy, trim, well-kept *Antonyms:* dirty, messy **2.** arranged, conventional, methodical, regular, sequential, systematic, tiered *Antonyms:* chaotic, helter-skelter *(Nonformal)* **3.** halcyon, harmonious, law-abiding, pacific, peaceful, serene, still, tranquil, untroubled *Antonyms:* stormy, tempestuous, wild

ordinance *n.* **1.** authorization, canon, code, command, decree, dictum, direction, edict, enactment, fiat, law, mandate, order, precept, prescript, regulation, ruling **2.** ceremony, custom, liturgy, rite, ritual, solemnity

ordinary *adj.* **1.** common, conventional, customary, everyday, natural, normal, normative, quotidian, typical, usual *Antonyms:* abnormal, unusual **2.** average, general, homespun, humble, middling, modest, plain *Antonyms:* eminent, extraordinary, outstanding, remarkable **3.** banal, clichéd, commonplace, hackneyed, old hat *(Nonformal)*, prevalent, threadbare, trite *Antonyms:* original, striking – *n.* average, norm, par, standard, status quo

organ *n.* **1.** component, element, gland, member, part *Human organs:* appendix, bladder, bowel, brain, ear, eye, gallbladder, heart, intestines, kidney, larynx, liver, lung, nose, ovary, pancreas, penis, spleen, stomach, tongue, uterus, vagina **2.** agency, agent, channel, device, element, forum, implement, instrument, means, medium, mouthpiece, part, process, structure, unit, way **3.** column, gazette, journal, newspaper, periodical, press, serial, sheet, tabloid, voice *(Nonformal)* **4.** barrelor, calliope, choir *or* church *or* electric *or* pedal *or* pipe organ, harmonium barrel *or* steam organ, hurdy gurdy, instrument, keyboard

organic *adj.* **1.** all-natural, chemical-free, natural, unadulterated *Antonyms:* artificial, processed, treated **2.** anatomical, biological, carbon-based, cellular, vital **3.** basal, basic, constitutional, elemental, essential, fundamental, inherent, integral, structural *Antonyms:* extraneous, irrelevant **4.** designed, fashioned, methodical, organized, patterned, systematic

organism *n.* animal, being, body, creature, entity, individual, living being *or* thing, organic matter, person, plant, structure

Classification of organisms: Animalia, Fungi, Monera, Plantae, Protista

organization *n.* **1.** affiliation, aggregation, alliance, assembly, association, band, bloc, body, brotherhood, business, cartel, circle, clique, club, coalition, combination, combine, commonwealth, company, concern, concord, confederation, consortium, cooperative, corporation, establishment, federation, fellowship, fraternity, group, institution, league, machine, order, outfit, party, profession, set, sisterhood, society, sorority, squad, syndicate, team, troupe, union *Canadian First Peoples organizations:* Assembly of First Nations, Dene Nation, Inuit Tapirisat of Canada, Native Council of Canada, Métis National Council *Historical:* Canadian Confederacy, Five Nations, Iroquois Confederacy, National Indian Brotherhood, North American Indian Brotherhood, Six Nations **2.** arrangement, composition, conformation, constitution, coordination, design, formation, grouping, management, planning **3.** aggregate, collection, gross, mass, quantity, sum, total, totality

organize *v.* **1.** associate, band, combine, cooperate, form, group, huddle, join, league, regiment, unionize **2.** arrange, catalogue, classify, codify, defragment, frame, regulate, standardize, systematize **3.** contract, enlist, marshall, muster **4.** create, establish, found, initiate, set up, start **5.** amalgamate, incorporate, merge, syndicate

orgiastic *adj.* abandoned, bacchanalian, carnal, debauched, Dionysian, dissolute, drunken, festive, frenzied, indulgent, intemperate, jocund, licentious, saturnalian, uninhibited, unrestrained, wanton, wild

orgy *n.* bacchanal, bacchanalia, carousal, debauchery, indulgence, saturnalia, spree *Nonformal:* bender, binge, jag, tear, toot

orient *v.* **1.** acclimatize, accommodate, acculturate, accustom, attune, establish, familiarize, habituate, season, transculturate **2.** adapt, adjust, change, conform, correspond, fit, modify, transform, transmute **3.** aim, align, direct oneself, shift, turn, twist, veer

orientation *n.* **1.** bearings, locale, locality, location, locus, placement, position, site, whereabouts **2.** accommodation, acculturation, adapting, adjusting, assimilation, conforming, habituation **3.** briefing, familiarization, initiation, introduction, primer, training

orifice *n.* aperture, cleft, cranny, door, fissure, gap, hole, mouth, opening, oral cavity, outlet, perforation, vent

origin *n.* **1.** beginning, birth, commencement, conception, creation, dawn, emergence, exordium, genesis, get-go *(Nonformal)*, inauguration, inception, incipience, introduction, prelude, start *Antonyms:* conclusion, death, end, termination **2.** base, foundation, fountainhead, germ, ground zero, inspiration, matrix, provenance, root, source, well, wellspring **3.** antecedent, causation, cause, determinant, influence, mainspring, motive, occasion, reason *Antonyms:* consequence, result **4.** ancestry, blood, derivation, descent, extraction, family, heritage, lineage, nativity, parentage, paternity, progenitor

original *adj.* **1.** basic, classic, earliest, early, elementary, embryonic, first, germinal, inceptive, initial, primary, pristine, rudimentary, seminal **2.** avant-garde, different, fresh, neoteric, new, newfangled *(Nonformal)*, novel, unconventional, unique, unorthodox, unprecedented *Antonyms:* clichéd, common, hackneyed **3.** brilliant, creative, fertile, imaginative, ingenious, innovative, inspired, inventive, ready, resourceful, skilful *Antonyms:* pedestrian, prosaic **4.** eccentric, idiosyncratic, individualistic, odd, strange, unusual **5.** aboriginal, autochthonous, indigenous, native *Antonyms:* alien, foreign **6.** authentic, genuine, legitimate, true *Antonyms:* fake, false, spurious – *n.* **1.** alpha, first, forerunner, precedent, precursor, primary **2.** archetype, classic, exemplar, model, mould, paradigm, prototype, standard *Antonyms:* copy, imitation, replica, reproduction **3.** artist, genius, idiot savant, master, mastermind, prodigy, talent, thinker **4.** Bohemian, deviant, eccentric, individual, maverick, misfit, nonconformist, one-of-a-kind *Nonformal:* nut, weirdo

originality *n.* **1.** boldness, brilliance, cleverness, creativeness, creativity, daring, imagination, individuality, ingenuity, inventiveness, resourcefulness, unconventionality, unorthodoxly *Antonyms:* conformity, conventionality, orthodoxy **2.** freshness, innovation, invention, newness, novelty, uniqueness *Antonyms:* imitation, plagiarism, repetition

originate *v.* **1.** cause, coin, compose, conceive, create, develop, discover, engender, evolve, father, form, formulate, found, generate, hatch, inaugurate, initiate, innovate, institute, introduce, invent, launch, make, mother, parent, pioneer, procreate, produce, sire, spark, start, think up *Antonyms:* cease, conclude, culminate **2.** arise, begin, come, come from, commence, dawn, derive, emanate, emerge, flow, issue, proceed, result, rise, spring, start, stem

ornament *n.* **1.** accessory, adornment, bauble, decoration, frill, frou-frou, furbelow, garnish, gewgaw, knickknack, trinket, superfluity, trapping, trifle *Nonformal:* doodad, tchotchke **2.** appoggiatura, arabesque, cadenza, embellishment, flight, flourish, grace *or* incidental note, motif, riff, roulade, run – *v.* adorn, array, beautify, bedeck, brighten, deck, decorate, dress up, embellish, embroider, enrich, festoon, fix up, gild, grace, gussy up *(Nonformal)*, polish, prettify, smarten, trim

ornamental *adj.* attractive, beautifying, decorative, elaborate, extravagant, fancy, flashy, luxurious, ornate, trophy *(Nonformal) Antonyms:* bare, basic, natural

ornate *adj.* **1.** adorned, bedecked, coloured, decorated, embellished, embroidered, garnished, gilded, jewelled **2.** baroque, busy, elaborate, fancy, flamboyant, flashy, flaunting, florid, fussy, gaudy, glamorous, lavish, magnificent, opulent, resplendent, rich, rococo, showy, splashy, sumptuous *Antonyms:* austere, basic, plain, severe, stark **3.** affected, exaggerated, flatulent, flowery, fulsome, grandiloquent, insufferable, orotund, pompous, pretentious, purple, rhetorical, rodomontade, stilted, turgid *Antonyms:* concise, plain, unpretentious

ornery *adj.* **1.** cantankerous, churlish, contrary, contumacious, cranky, crotchety, grouchy *(Nonformal)*, gruff, irascible, mean, obstinate, owly *(P.E.I.)*, splenetic, stubborn, surly, unmanageable *Antonyms:* gentle, kindly **2.** base, criminal, foul, low, sly *Nonformal:* dirty, no-good *Antonyms:* aboveboard, honest, straight

orphan *adj.* lone, lost, single, unloved – *n.* castaway, cast-off, foundling, guttersnipe, motherless child, mudlark, ragamuffin, stray, waif – *v.* abandon, desert, forsake, give over *or* up, let go, relinquish, renounce, surrender, yield *Antonyms:* adopt, keep, retain

orthodox *adj.* **1.** authoritative, biblical, correct, devout, doctrinal, faithful, legitimate, official, pious, proper, punctilious, received, religious, right, rightful, scriptural, solemn, sound, strict, true, zealous *Antonyms:* apocryphal, false, moot **2.** conforming, observant, practicing *Nonformal:* square, straight *Antonyms:* deviant, divergent, independent, negligent **3.** accepted, acknowledged, admitted, approved, conventional, customary, established, sanctioned, standard, traditional, well-established

oscillate *v.* **1.** fluctuate, flutter, pendulate, swing, undulate, vacillate, wag **2.** dither, equivocate, hem and haw, shilly-shally *(Nonformal)*, waffle

ostensible *adj.* a.k.a., alleged, apparent purported, quote-unquote, seeming so-called *(Nonformal)*, supposed *Antonyms:* confirmed, definite **2.** avowed declared, demonstrated, exhibited, manifest, professed

ostensibly *adv.* apparently, evidently externally, outwardly, professedly, seemingly, superficially, supposedly

ostentation *n.* **1.** affectation, boasting braggadocio, bragging, bravado, display exhibitionism, flamboyance, flash, flashiness, flaunting, flourish, garishness, grandstanding, magnificence, pageantry, parading, pomp, pomposity, pompousness, pretension, pretentiousness, shine, showiness spectacle, swagger, swank *(Nonformal* vainglory *Antonyms:* humility, modesty, reserve, simplicity

ostentatious *adj.* boastful, conspicuous, crass, exhibitionistic, extravagant, flamboyant, flashy, garish, gaudy, glittery, grandiose, loud, obtrusive, pompous, pretentious, showy, spectacular, splashy, sporty, theatrical, vainglorious, vulgar *Nonformal:* styling, swank, swanky *Antonyms:* conservative, inconspicuous, modest, reserved, simple

ostracism *n.* **1.** censure, disregard, exclusion, rejection, renunciation, repudiation *Antonyms:* acceptance, approval **2.** alienation, banishment, barring, deportation, divorce, expulsion, exile, exportation, forced removal, separation, the boot *(Nonformal) Antonyms:* open door, welcome

ostracize *v.* **1.** ban, bar, blackball, boycott, deny, disregard, exclude, neglect, omit, prohibit, reject, repudiate, shun, shut out, spurn **2.** banish, cast off, deport, drive away *or* off, drum out, eliminate, excommunicate, expatriate, expel, kick out *(Nonformal),* oust, remove, rid, separate, transport

other *adj.* **1.** different, differing, disparate, dissimilar, distinct, incongruous, separate, unlike *Antonyms:* identical, same, similar **2.** added, additional, another, extra, further, more **3.** facing, neighbouring, opposite, polar **4.** alternative, auxiliary, backup, bench, reserve, second, spare, sub, substitute, supplementary **5.** bygone, earlier, erstwhile, former, late, old, preceding, previous, prior *Antonyms:* modern, present, succeeding – *n.* addition, another, extra, something else

otherworldly *adj.* **1.** angelic, celestial, divine, glorious, heavenly, paradisiacal, seraphic **2.** ethereal, ghostly, illusory, insubstantial, intangible, phantasmal, spectral, supernatural, surreal, unearthly, vaporous *Antonyms:* corporeal, mundane **3.** distracted, faraway, impractical, ivory tower, removed, spiritual, unrealistic, unworldly, visionary *Antonyms:* earthly, secular

oust *v.* axe, banish, bounce, depose, dethrone, discharge, disinherit, displace, dispossess, divest, eject, evict, expel, fire, relegate, remove, sack, topple, transport, unseat *Nonformal:* bump, can, lose

out *adj.* **1.** absent, away, AWOL *(Nonformal),* elsewhere, lacking, missing, not here *or* present, on loan, out and about, unaccounted for, vanished *Antonyms:* at hand, attendant, available **2.** exterior, external, extraneous, outer, outside, peripheral, surface *Antonyms:* interior, middle **3.** abnormal, anomalous, atypical, bizarre, blemished, deviant, eccentric, exceptional, flawed, imperfect, irregular, nonconforming, nonuniform, queer, uneven *Antonyms:* normal, regular, typical **4.** broken, damaged, defective, disabled, down, in disrepair, inoperative, off, on the fritz *(Nonformal),* ruined, unserviced, useless, wrecked *Antonyms:* functioning, working **5.** bankrupt, impoverished, lacking, out of pocket, penniless, pinched, poor, short *Nonformal:* busted, flat, hard up, in the red, on the bum *or* nickel *Antonyms:* affluent, flush, loaded **6.** impossible, intolerable, objectionable, unacceptable, unwanted *Antonyms:* agreeable, welcome **7.** bare, evident, exposed, manifest, naked, protruding, revealed, standing out, uncovered, unveiled, visible *Antonyms:* concealed, covered, hidden **8.** amiss, erring, erroneous, in left field *(Nonformal),* inaccurate, incorrect, misinformed, misled, mistaken, off target, untrue, wrong *Antonyms:* correct, right **9.** cut, cut loose, discarded, discharged, dismissed, displaced, divested, downsized *(Nonformal),* eliminated, evicted, fired, free, released, removed, superceded, terminated *Antonyms:* employed, hired, promoted **10.** fruitless, ineffective, ineffectual, inefficient, powerless, unproductive, unprofitable, worthless *Antonyms:* potent, productive, valuable **11.** anachronistic, antiquated, bygone, dated, obsolete, outmoded, passé *Antonyms:* cutting-edge, fashionable, vogue **12.** distant, faraway, far-flung, far-off, isolated, lonely, outlying, remote, removed, secluded *Antonyms:* close, nearby **13.** blacked *or* knocked *or* passed out, comatose, dead on one's feet *(Nonformal),* horizontal, insensible, out cold, stunned, unconscious *Antonyms:* alert, awake, lucid – *adv.* **1.** aloud, clearly, distinctly, loudly, resoundingly, ringingly *Italian:* a voce alta, forte, fortissimo *Antonyms:* inaudibly, quietly, softly **2.**

away from, forth, outward, outwardly **3.** alfresco, externally, in the open air, outdoors, outside *Antonyms:* indoors, inside, internally **4.** completely, extremely, thoroughly – *interj.* away with you, flee, get out, off *Nonformal:* hit the bricks *or* road, outta here, scram, sod off *(British)*, take a hike, vamoose – *prep.* across, along, forth from, on, over, through – *n.* **1.** culvert, duct, egress, escape, escape clause, exit, faucet, hole, loophole, mouth, orifice, outlet, release, spout, vent **2.** alibi, apology, excuse, explanation, justification, rationalization

outbreak *n.* **1.** arrival, beginning, birth, commencement, dawn, surge **2.** affray, blowup, brawl, commotion, disruption, fight, flare-up, mêlée, mutiny, outburst, rebellion, revolution, sally, sortie, storm, tumult, uprising, volley **3.** break, discharge, ejection, epidemic, eruption, outpouring, paroxysm, venting

outburst *n.* **1.** attack, blow, burst, discharge, eruption, explosion, flare-up, frenzy, gust, outbreak, outpouring, paroxysm, sally, spasm, storm, surge, upheaval **2.** conniption *(Nonformal)*, display, fit, scene, show, tantrum

outcast *adj.* abandoned, deserted, discarded, forgotten, forlorn, forsaken, lost, neglected, rejected, shunned *Antonyms:* cherished, included, kept – *n.* **1.** castaway, deportee, displaced person, exile, expatriate, fugitive, refugee, unwanted **2.** bum, derelict, tramp, vagabond, vagrant, wretch **3.** leper, pariah, untouchable

outcome *n.* aftermath, bottom line *(Nonformal)*, by-product, conclusion, consequence, effect, end, event, eventuality, fallout, issue, offshoot, offspring, outgrowth, payback, payoff, product, reaction, result, score, spinoff, upshot *Antonyms:* forerunner, harbinger, precursor

outcry *n.* **1.** clamour, commotion, convulsion, cry, exclamation, howl, hullabaloo, noise, outburst, scream, screech, tumult, uproar, yell **2.** backlash, complaint, dissent, ferment, flak *(Nonformal)*, objection, protest, remonstration

outdated *adj.* anachronistic, antiquated, antique, archaic, dated, démodé, fusty, obsolete, old, old-fashioned, out, outmoded, out-of-date, out-of-style, passé, tired, unfashionable, vintage *Nonformal:* hasbeen, moth-eaten, square *Antonyms:* contemporary, fashionable, in vogue

outdo *v.* beat, best, better, blank, cap, clinch, crest, crown, defeat, eclipse, exceed, excel, finish, go above *or* beyond, leave behind, outclass, outdistance, outmaneuvre, outrival, outshine, outsmart, outstrip, overcome, pass, rise above, surmount, surpass, top, transcend *Nonformal:* blow off, bury, cook, cream, do in, leave standing, lick, lose, outfox, outgun, outjockey, shake off, snow, trash, trump

outdoor *adj.* alfresco, backyard, external, open-air, outdoorsy, outer, outside *Antonyms:* indoor, inner, inside

outer *adj.* **1.** exposed, exterior, external, extraneous, extrinsic, outermost, outside, outward *Antonyms:* central, inner, inside **2.** beyond, faraway, far-flung, lonely, marginal, outlying, peripheral, remote, removed *Antonyms:* close, nearby **3.** objective, physical, superficial, surface

outfit *n.* **1.** accoutrement, equipage, equipment, gear, kit, paraphernalia, rig, tools, trappings **2.** apparel, clothes, costume, dress, ensemble, garb, suit *Nonformal:* duds, threads, toggery **3.** business, company, corps, coterie, covey, crew, firm, gang, group, organization, platoon, squad, squadron, team, unit – *v.* accoutre, appoint, attire, equip, fit out, furnish, grubstake *(Nonformal)*, provide, supply

outgoing *adj.* **1.** departing, ebbing, leaving, migratory, outbound, outward-bound, past, receding, retiring, withdrawing *Antonyms:* arriving, entering, incoming **2.** communicative, cordial, demonstrative, extroverted, friendly, genial, gregarious, informal, kind, open, sociable, unconstrained, uninhibited, unreserved, unrestrained, warm *Antonyms:* cold, indifferent, reserved, retiring, withdrawn

outgrowth *n.* **1.** bulge, enlargement, excrescence, jutting, node, outcrop, projec tion, prolongation, prominence, protuberance, shoot, sprout, swelling **2.** aftereffect, by-product, consequence, effect, end, end result, issue, offshoot, outcome, product, result, spinoff

uthouse *n.* backhouse, latrine, outbuilding, privy, toilet *Nonformal:* closet, crapper, john

uting *n.* drive, constitutional, excursion, expedition, hike, holiday, jaunt, junket, perambulation, picnic, pleasure *or* road trip, roundabout, sally, stroll, trip, vacation, walk, weekend *Nonformal:* spin, tootle

utlandish *adj.* **1.** alien, exotic, foreign, new, novel, singular, unfamiliar, unique *Antonyms:* common, familiar, popular **2.** abnormal, asinine, bizarre, crazy, curious, eccentric, foolish, freakish, idiosyncratic, irregular, odd, outrageous, *outré (French)*, peculiar, preposterous, queer, ridiculous, silly, strange, unorthodox *Antonyms:* customary, normal, regular **3.** extravagant, fantastic, flashy, garish, gauche, gaudy, grotesque, inelegant, meretricious, ostentatious, tasteless, tawdry *Antonyms:* elegant, refined, simple **4.** distant, far-off, offshore, outlying, remote, removed *Antonyms:* adjacent, close, nearby

utlast *v.* endure, outlive, outstay, outwear, remain, survive, weather, withstand *Antonyms:* lose, succumb, yield

utlaw *n. bandido (Spanish)*, bandit, *bandito (Italian)*, brigand, criminal, crook, desperado, fugitive, gangster, gunman, hoodlum, marauder, mobster, outcast, pariah, pirate, racketeer, ronion *Nonformal:* con, goon, gunslinger, hood, hooligan, rough, thug, wanted man *or* woman – *v.* **1.** ban, banish, bar, criminalize, disallow, embargo, enjoin, forbid, prevent, prohibit, proscribe, stop, taboo *Antonyms:* allow, approve, endorse, legalize, permit **2.** condemn, exclude, excommunicate, exile, expatriate, expel, ostracize, oust

utlawed *adj.* **1.** banned, bootlegged, contraband, criminal, forbidden, illegal, illegitimate, illicit, prohibited, proscribed, smuggled, tax-free *(Nonformal)*, unapproved, unauthorized, unlicensed, unofficial *Antonyms:* approved, legal, sanctioned **2.** banished, deported, evicted, excommunicated, exiled, expatriated, transported *Nonformal:* kicked out, sent packing

outlay *n.* charge, cost, damage *(Nonformal)*, disbursement, expenditure, expense, expenses, investment, price tag, setback, spending, tab

outlet *n.* **1.** aperture, avenue, break, channel, crack, duct, egress, escape, exit, faucet, hole, nozzle, opening, orifice, porthole, release, safety valve, spout, tap, tear, vent **2.** boutique, department store, depot, discount *or* factory outlet, emporium, farmers market, mall, market, mart, retailer, specialty shop, strip mall, supermarket, superstore, trading post, wholesaler *French:* depanneur, marché **3.** catharsis, cleansing, purging, release, venting **4.** electricity, inlet, plug, power, power source

outline *n.* **1.** blueprint, diagram, draft, drawing, floor *or* general *or* ground plan, rough draft, sketch, thumbnail sketch **2.** abstract, condensation, digest, overview, précis, recapitulation, résumé, rough idea, scenario, summary, summation, synopsis, treatment *Nonformal:* gist, rundown **3.** border, contour, delineation, field, footprint, form, frame, framework, layout, limit, line, margin, perimeter, periphery, profile, shape, silhouette, skirt – *v.* **1.** boil down *(Nonformal)*, compress, concentrate, condense, describe, encapsulate, highlight, summarize **2.** chart, delineate, depict, design, diagram, draw, map out, paint, plan, rough out, sketch, trace

outlook *n.* **1.** attitude, interpretation, mind-set, notion, perspective, point of view, position, posture, read, slant, thoughts, viewpoint, vision *Nonformal:* take, twist **2.** expectation, forecast, future, likelihood, plausibility, possibility, probability, prognosis, prospect **3.** aspect, lookout, panorama, perspective, prospect, scape, scene, sight, spectacle, view, vista

outmoded *adj.* anachronistic, antediluvian, antiquated, antique, archaic, bygone, dated, démodé, extinct, moth-eaten *(Nonformal)*, obsolescent, obsolete, old, old-fashioned, old-time, out, out-of-date, out-of-style, outworn, passé, unfashionable, unusable, vintage, yesterday's news *Antonyms:* fashionable, fresh, modern, new, recent

outpouring *n.* cascade, cataclysm, current, deluge, downflow, downpour, effluence, emanation, flood, flow, flux, spate, stream, surge, tide, torrent

output *n.* **1.** achievement, amount, crop, gain, goods, harvest, product, profit, result, results, take, turnout, yield **2.** efficiency, labour, manufacture, production, productivity, work **3.** calculation, compilation, data, download, facts, feedback, figures, hard copy, information, knowledge, reckoning, statistics

outrage *n.* **1.** anger, furor, fury, hatred, rage, road-rage *(Nonformal)*, resentment, shock, vehemence, wrath **2.** abuse, affront, atrocity, barbarism, damage, desecration, evil, evildoing, harm, hurt, indignity, inhumanity, injury, offence, ravishing, violation, violence, wrongdoing – *v.* **1.** abuse, aggrieve, ill-treat, injure, insult, maltreat, mistreat, misuse, offend, persecute, scandalize, wrong **2.** assault, rape, ravage, trespass, victimize, violate **3.** agitate, anger, annoy, attack, enrage, incense, inflame, infuriate, madden, unhinge, upset *Nonformal:* drive insane, fire up

outrageous *adj.* **1.** abominable, atrocious, awful, barbaric, beastly, contemptible, contemptuous, contumelious, corrupt, criminal, egregious, fell, felonious, heinous, horrendous, horrible, ignoble, infamous, iniquitous, lawless, malevolent, malicious, monstrous, nefarious, negligent, notorious, odious, transgressive, unspeakable, villainous, violent, wicked *Antonyms:* good, law-abiding, legal, righteous, virtuous **2.** debauched, degenerate, depraved, disgraceful, inappropriate, indecent, licentious, objectionable, offensive, opprobrious, salacious, scandalous, scrofulous, shameless, shocking, wanton *Antonyms:* proper, respectable **3.** abandoned, brazen, crazy, excessive, exorbitant, extortionate, extravagant, immoderate, heedless, intemperate, over-the-top *(Nonformal)*, prodigal, profligate, unbridled, wild

outright *adj.* **1.** absolute, complete, consummate, downright, entire, out-and-out, thorough, total, unconditional, unequiv cal, utter, wholesale **2.** clear, definit undeniable, undisputed, unmitigate unquestionable – *adv.* **1.** candidly, conspi uously, frankly, freely, genuinely, honestl openly, overtly, plainly, sincerely, uncond tionally, unreservedly **2.** altogether, con pletely, entirely, thoroughly, totally, utterl wholly *Antonyms:* partly, piecemeal directly, expeditiously, forthright, hastil immediately, straight, without delay

outside *adj.* **1.** alfresco, exterior, externa extramural, extraneous, open-air, out, ou door, outdoorsy, outer, surface *Antonym* indoor, inner, inside, interior, internal alien, exotic, foreign, imported, nondome tic, offshore, overseas *Antonyms:* dome tic, inland, native **3.** extreme, farther, fa thest, maximum, outermost, outward, te minal **4.** faint, marginal, negligible, of remote, slender, slight, slim, small, unlike – *adv.* externally, extraneously, outdoor outwards, outwardly – *n.* **1.** fresh *or* ope air, outdoors, the great outdoors, street coat, cover, covering, epidermis, exoskel ton, exterior, face, fur, shell, skin appearance, affectation, display, façad front, image, shallowness, show, superf ciality

outsider *n.* **1.** alien, foreigner, income interloper, intruder, *kabloona (Inuktitut* newcomer, refugee, stranger **2.** candidat dark horse, hopeful, long shot, sleeper

outskirts *n. pl.* border, boundary, edg environs, limits, margin, periphery, purlie suburbs, vicinity

outsmart *v.* beat, best, cheat, con *(Nonfo mal)*, deceive, dupe, fool, gull, hoodwin outfox, outwit, swindle, trick

outspoken *adj.* aggressive, blunt, bol brash, candid, confident, direct, explici forthright, frank, free, open, straightfo ward, unreserved, up-front, urgent, voc *Antonyms:* diplomatic, gracious, judiciou tactful

outstanding *adj.* **1.** arresting, celebrate distinguished, dominant, eminent, exce lent, exceptional, important, leadin major, marked, memorable, notable, not worthy, preeminent, principal, prominent, remarkable, stellar, super, superior, well-known *Antonyms:* dull, inferior, mediocre, pedestrian, unimpressive **2.** appreciable, conspicuous, discernible, noticeable, obvious, plain, pronounced, salient, signal, striking, visible *Antonyms:* camouflaged, hidden **3.** attributable, due, in debt, obligatory, overdue, owed, owing, payable, pending, receivable, remaining, uncollected, unpaid, unresolved, unsettled **4.** abutting, extending, jutting, overhanging, projecting

outward *adj.* **1.** exterior, external, outer, outlying, outside *Antonyms:* inner, inside, interior, internal **2.** bodily, corporeal, fleshy, physical, sensual, somatic, substantial *Antonyms:* mental, spiritual **3.** apparent, appreciable, ascertainable, conspicuous, detectable, discernible, distinct, distinguishable, evident, manifest, marked, measurable, noticeable, observable, perceptible, visible *Antonyms:* impalpable, invisible, masked, obscure **4.** cosmetic, extrinsic, meretricious, ostensible, seemly, specious, superficial, surface – *adv.* out, outside, outwardly, without

outwardly *adv.* apparently, evidently, externally, in appearance, officially, ostensibly, seemingly, superficially

outwit *v.* baffle, beat, bewilder, cheat, circumvent, confuse, deceive, defeat, defraud, dupe, figure out, finagle, finesse, have, hoax, hoodwink, mislead, outdo, outfox, outguess, outjockey, outmaneuvre, outsmart, overreach, swindle, take in, trick *Nonformal:* bamboozle, con, hose

oval *adj.* egg-shaped, ellipsoidal, elliptic, elliptical, elongated, oblong, ovate, oviform, rounded

ovation *n.* acclaim, applause, big hand *(Nonformal)*, cheering, clapping, encore, hand, laudation, plaudits, praise, salvo, testimonial, tribute

over *adj.* **1.** completed, dead, done, ended, exhausted, finished, past **2.** abroad, across, farther, opposite, yonder **3.** exterior, external, extrinsic, outer, peripheral **4.** addition, excess, extra, leftover, remnant, surplus **5.** greater, higher, lofty, superior, upper – *adv.* **1.** additionally, again, excessively, once more **2.** above, across, aloft, on high *or* top, overhead, through **3.** completely, entirely, fully, thoroughly, wholly – *prep.* **1.** all over, here and there and everywhere, throughout **2.** by way of, en route, through, toward, via **3.** above, across, beyond, on the other side, past, on top of, upon **4.** during, in the course of, since the beginning of, through, throughout the course of, until **5.** in excess of, exceeding, more than, past

overabundance *n.* excess, exorbitance, glut, overflow, overload, oversupply, plethora, profusion, superabundance, superfluity, surfeit, surplus *Antonyms:* lack, need, want

overact *v.* embellish, embroider, emote, exaggerate, hyperbolize, overdo, overstate, strain, stretch *Nonformal:* ham, milk it

overall *adj.* all-embracing, blanket, complete, comprehensive, general, global, inclusive, long-range, long-term, sweeping, thorough, total, umbrella – *adv.* chiefly, largely, mainly, mostly, predominantly, primarily, principally, throughout *Antonyms:* incompletely, partially

overblown *adj.* bombastic, disproportionate, excessive, flatulent, flowery, fulsome, grandiloquent, hyped up *(Nonformal)*, hyperbolic, immoderate, inflated, magniloquent, oratorical, overdone, pompous, pretentious, profuse, purple, rhetorical, sonorous, superfluous, swollen, turgid, undue, verbose, windy *Antonyms:* deflated, underdone

overcast *adj.* **1.** bleak, cloudy, dark, depressing, dreary, grey, leaden, looming, lowering, murky *Antonyms:* bright, clear, sunny **2.** dismal, dull, gloomy, melancholy, sombre

overcoat *n.* cloak, coat, jacket, mackintosh, outer *or* trench coat, raglan, raincoat, slicker, topcoat *See also:* **coat**

overcome *adj.* **1.** beaten, devitalized, enervated, enfeebled, exhausted, fatigued, listless, spent, tired, washed out *(Nonformal)* **2.** affected, disturbed, *farklempt (Yiddish)*, moved, overwhelmed, overwrought, passionate, swayed, tearful – *v.* **1.** beat, conquer, defeat, drub, humble, overthrow, quash, quell, rout, scuttle, silence, subdue, subjugate, suppress, take, trounce, vanquish *Antonyms:* fall, lose, yield **2.** brave, prevail, surmount, survive, transcend, weather **3.** best, carry the day *(Nonformal)*, gain, master, succeed, triumph, win

overconfident *adj.* brash, careless, cocksure, conceited, foolhardy, half-cocked, heedless, hubristic, presumptuous, pushy, rash, reckless, riding for a fall *(Nonformal)*, sure, swaggering *Antonyms:* cautious, diffident, hesitant, uncertain

overdo *v.* **1.** ballyhoo, belabour, boast, exaggerate, ham it up *(Nonformal)*, overact, overindulge, overplay, overreach, overstate, overvalue, stretch *Antonyms:* belittle, disparage, minimize, understate **2.** exhaust, fatigue, overburden, overload, overtax, overtire, overuse, overwork, wear out **3.** burn, char, dry-out, incinerate, overcook, scorch

overdue *adj.* behind, belated, delayed, delinquent, held *or* hung up, late, outstanding, owing, past due, payable, tardy, unpaid, unpunctual, unsettled *Antonyms:* balanced, paid, up-to-date

overemotional *adj.* histrionic, lachrymose, maudlin, mawkish, melodramatic, mushy, overdone, overwrought, sensational, sentimental, teary, theatrical *Nonformal:* sappy, schmaltzy

overflow *n.* **1.** cataclysm, cataract, deluge, discharge, encroachment, flood, flooding, inundation, push, spill, spillover, submersion **2.** excess, overabundance, overcrowding, plethora, surfeit, superfluity, surplus, torrent – *v.* **1.** drench, overrun, saturate, spill over, surge, swamp, swell, wash out **2.** congest, flood the market, overload, overstock, oversupply, satiate, superabound

overhang *n.* cliff, eaves, extension, projection, protuberance, roof – *v.* **1.** bulge, dangle *or* droop over, extend, jut, project, protrude, rise *or* tower above, stand *or* stick out **2.** impend, loom, menace, portend, threaten

overhaul *v.* **1.** fix, improve, modernize rebuild, recondition, reconstruct, redo renew, renovate, repair, restore, revamp tart up *(Nonformal)* **2.** catch up, gain on intercept, overtake, pass, reach, take

overhead *adj.* aerial, atop, hanging, on high, overhanging, skyward, upper, upward *Antonyms:* below, beneath, downward underfoot, underneath – *adv.* above, aloft over – *n.* budget, costs, disbursements expenditures, expenses, operating expense, maintenance, outlay, rent upkeep, utilities

overindulgence *n.* binge, excess, gluttony, orgy, spree *Nonformal:* bender, pig out, stuffing oneself

overjoyed *adj.* delighted, deliriously happy ecstatic, elated, euphoric, joyful, jubilant rapturous, thrilled, transported *Nonformal* on cloud nine, over the moon, tickled pink *Antonyms:* crestfallen, downcast, heartbroken, unhappy, woebegone

overlap *n.* extension, extra, flap, overhang projection – *v.* **1.** coincide, conjoin, fold or lap *or* lie over, interest, overlie **2.** jut, lap overarch, overhang,

overload *v.* burden, encumber, oppress overburden, overcharge, overtax, overwhelm, saddle *(Nonformal)*, vex, weigh down

overlook *n.* **1.** inquiry, inspection, look observation, survey **2.** crow's nest, ledge lookout, tower, vista, watchtower – *v.* **1** forget, leave undone, miss, neglect, omit slip up **2.** cut *(Nonformal)*, discount, disdain, disregard, forget, ignore, slight *Antonyms:* heed, mark, note, observe **3** behold, look, observe, perceive, scan scope, see, survey, view, watch, witness **4** boss, command, control, manage, oversee superintend, supervise **5.** examine explore, inspect, investigate, review, scrutinize, study, verify **6.** bear, condone excuse, forgive, let go *or* pass *or* ride *Nonformal*: blink *or* wink at, stomach

overly *adv.* exceedingly, excessively extremely, immensely, immoderately, inordinately, over, too much, unduly, very much

overpower *v.* **1.** beat, best, better, clobber *(Nonformal)*, conquer, crush, defeat, drub, master, outdo, outstrip, overthrow, prevail *or* triumph over, put away, quell, rout, subdue, supersede, surmount, surpass, topple, total, trash, trounce, vanquish *Nonformal:* blow away, bulldoze, bury, cream *Antonyms:* lose, succumb, yield **2.** confound, floor *(Nonformal)*, nonplus, overcome, overwhelm, stagger, stun, throw

overriding *adj.* **1.** cardinal, deciding, determining, dominant, final, main, major, overruling, paramount, pivotal, predominant, prevailing, prime, ruling, supreme, ultimate **2.** quashing, smothering, suppressing, trampling

overrule *v.* **1.** annul, cancel, disallow, dismiss, invalidate, nullify, override, overturn, quash, reject, repeal, rescind, reverse, revoke, supersede, veto *Antonyms:* endorse, pass, permit **2.** conduct, control, direct, dominate, govern, influence, manage, manipulate, master, pilot, prevail over, regulate, shape, supervise, sway

overrun *n.* excess, leftovers, overstock, oversupply, surplus – *v.* **1.** infest, invade, overwhelm, plague, ravage, swarm, teem, throng **2.** assail, assault, attack, conquer, loot, pillage, plunder, raid, run amok, scourge, vandalize, violate **3.** deluge, drench, exceed, overflow, run over, spill, surge, swamp, swell **4.** expand, proliferate, radiate, spread, sweep, swell

oversee *v.* boss, captain, chaperon, command, inspect, look after, manage, overlook, shepherd, superintend, supervise, survey, watch

overseer *n.* boss, captain, commander, foreman, governor, inspector, manager, shepherd, steward, superintendent, supervisor

overshadow *v.* **1.** dominate, dwarf, eclipse, outclass, outshine, outweigh, surpass **2.** adumbrate, cloud, darken, dim, haze, obscure, overcast, overcloud, shadow, veil

oversight *n.* **1.** blank, carelessness, default, delinquency, dereliction, error, failure, goof *(Nonformal)*, inadvertency, inattention, lapse, miscue, mistake, neglect, omission, slip **2.** administration, aegis, care, charge, check, control, custody, direction, guard, guardianship, handling, inspection, keeping, maintenance, management, superintendence, supervision, surveillance, tutelage

overtake *v.* **1.** beat, better, catch, gain on, get past, leave behind, outclass, outdo, outstrip, overwhelm, pass **2.** catch off-guard, fall upon, spring up, surprise, take unawares

overthrow *n.* **1.** conquest, invasion, occupation, takeover, triumph, victory, win **2.** coup, deposal, dethronement, displacement, expulsion, insurrection, mutiny, ouster, resistance, revolution, toppling, unseating – *v.* **1.** beat, conquer, crush, defeat, destroy, eradicate, exterminate, overcome, overpower, overwhelm, subjugate, vanquish **2.** bring down, depose, dethrone, oust, overturn, purge, topple, tumble, unseat, upend, upset

overture *n.* **1.** advance, approach, invitation, offer, offering, olive branch, presentation, proposal, proposition, signal, suggestion, tender **2.** foreword, introduction, opening, preamble, preface, prelude, prologue

overturn *v.* **1.** capsize, flip *or* turn over, invert, reverse, topple, upend, upset **2.** abolish, countermand, invalidate, neutralize, nullify, rescind, revoke, veto, vitiate **3.** cripple, crush, defeat, depose, destroy, overthrow, overwhelm, topple, unseat, usurp

overweight *adj.* adipose, ample, bulky, chubby, chunky, corpulent, fat, flabby, fleshy, heavier, heavy, hefty, huge, massive, obese, outsize, overfed, overstuffed, plump, portly, pudgy, rotund, Rubenesque, stout, well-padded *(Nonformal)*, voluptuous *Antonyms:* emaciated, gaunt, lean

overwhelm *v.* **1.** bury, deluge, drown, flood, inundate, overrun, sink, smother, snow, swamp **2.** beat, clobber, conquer, cripple, crush, defeat, destroy, devastate, fell, impair, incapacitate, invade, knock *or* roll over, lambaste, massacre *(Nonformal)*, overcome, overpower, overthrow, overturn, prostrate, ruin, shatter, vanquish, whip, wreck *Nonformal:* bowl over, bulldoze, bury, floor, snow under, steamroll, torpedo **3.** debilitate, enervate, exhaust, overtire, sap, tire, wear *or* wipe out **4.** astonish, astound, bewilder, confound, confuse, daze, disturb, leave reeling, puzzle, stagger, stun

overwhelmed *adj.* **1.** buried, clobbered, defeated, in the weeds *(Nonformal)*, involved, labouring, overpowered, overrun, submerged, swamped, toiling **2.** affected, bowled over *(Nonformal)*, confused, emotional, moved **3.** exhausted, *farklempt (Yiddish)*, overburdened, overworked, sapped, tired, worn out *Nonformal:* on the edge, wiped

overwrought *adj.* **1.** affected, agitated, beside oneself, crazy, distracted, distraught, emotional, excitable, excited, exhausted, fired *or* keyed up, frantic, nervous, neurotic, on edge, overexcited, overstrung, overworked, spent, stirred, tense, tired, uneasy, upset, weary *Nonformal:* flipped *or* stressed *or* strung out, wired *Antonyms:* collected, dispassionate, emotionless, impassive, unmoved **2.** cheap, garish, loud, ornate, overdone, raffish, tacky, tawdry, vulgar

owing *adj.* **1.** behind, burdened, indebted, in arrears *or* the red, obligated **2.** due, mature, outstanding, owed, payable, redeemable, unpaid

own *adj.* endemic, individual, inherent, intrinsic, peculiar, particular, personal, private, resident, unique, very own – *v.* **1.** control, dominate, enjoy, have, hold, keep, occupy, possess, reserve, retain **2.** accede, acknowledge, acquiesce, admit, agree, allow, assent **3.** confess, declare, disclose, divulge, profess, reveal

owner *n.* buyer, consumer, landlord, manager, possessor, proprietor, proprietress, purchaser, ratepayer, titleholder *Antonyms:* leaser, renter, tenant

pace *n.* **1.** footstep, gait, motion, movement, progress, step, stride, tread **2.** clip, measure, momentum, quickness, rapidity, rapidness, rate, speed, swiftness, velocity **3.** beat, cadence, rhythm, tempo, time– *v.* **1.** canter, foot *or* hoof it *(Nonformal)*, gallop, march, patrol, step, stride, traipse, tread, troop, trot, walk **2.** count, determine, mark out, measure

pacific *adj.* **1.** calm, halcyon, motionless, peaceful, sedate, serene, settled, smooth, tranquil, unruffled *Antonyms:* rough, stormy, tempestuous **2.** clement, conciliatory, dovish, merciful, non-aggressive, nonviolent, tender-hearted *Antonyms:* angry, bellicose, belligerent, violent

pacifist *n.* conscientious objector, dissenter, dove, non-aggressor, Quaker, peacenik *(Nonformal)*, resister *Antonyms:* jingo, militarist, warmonger

pacify *v.* **1.** allay, appease, assuage, calm, compose, moderate, mollify, placate, quiet, soften, soothe, stroke, sweeten, temper *Antonyms:* excite, irritate, needle, ruffle **2.** ameliorate, conciliate, lull, make *or* negotiate peace, mitigate, propitiate, quell, relieve

pack *n.* **1.** backpack, baggage, bale, box, bundle, burden, chest, equipment, haversack, kit, knapsack, load, luggage, outfit, package, parcel, purse, ragbag, rucksack, sack, stuff *(Nonformal)*, truss **2.** barrel, bunch, collection, great deal, heap, lot, lump, mess, myriad, number, pile, press **3.** assemblage, band, bevy, brood, circle, collective, company, covey, crew, crowd, deck, drove, family, flock, gaggle, gam, gang, group, hatch, herd, horde, litter, mob, party, peck, pride, set, swarm, troop **4.** bandage, compress, dressing, gauze, plaster, poultice – *v.* **1.** arrange, bind, box, brace, bunch, bundle, collect, fasten, gather, package, ready, tie **2.** mothball, preserve, put away, reserve, stash, store, storehouse, stow **3.** compact, compress, cram, crowd, drive *or* ram *or* wedge in, fill, pile, press, push, sardine *(Nonformal)*, squeeze **4.** block, cap, check, choke, clog, dam, gag, stifle **5.** bear, carry, convey, ferry, freight, haul, journey, lug, piggyback, ride, schlep *(Nonformal)*, shoulder, tote, transport, trek, truck **6.** burden, charge, encumber, oppress, saddle, task, tax, weigh down **7.** dispatch, issue, route, send, speed, transmit **8.** decamp, depart, escape, exit, flee, leave, migrate, quit, vacate, withdraw *Nonformal:* scram, vamoose *Antonyms:* arrive, linger, stay

package *n.* **1.** assortment, bag, baggage, bale, batch, box, bunch, bundle, burden, can, carton, combination, container, crate, kit, load, lot, luggage, pack, packet, parcel, pile, sack, sheaf, stack, suitcase, tin, trunk, unit **2.** benefits, bonus, expenses, fringe, health coverage, incentive, plus, remuneration, severance *or* termination amount – *v.* assemble, bag, bottle, box, close, enclose, jar, parcel, wrap

packed *adj.* **1.** awash, brimful, brimming, compact, compressed, congested, crammed, crowded, filled, full, jammed, loaded, overflowing, overloaded, seething, serried, stuffed, swarming *Nonformal:* chock-a-block, wall-to-wall *Antonyms:* deserted, empty, uncrowded **2.** appointed, arranged, assembled, bundled, collected, filed, ordered, organized, ready **3.** dry-docked, laid up, mothballed, on the shelf *(Nonformal)*, preserved, stashed, stored, storehoused, stowed

packet *n.* **1**. bag, bundle, carton, container, envelope, file, folder, package, parcel, receptacle, wrapper, wrapping **2**. boat, freighter, ship, steamer, vessel *See also:* **boat**

pact *n.* agreement, alliance, arrangement, bargain, bond, compact, concord, concordat, contract, covenant, convention, deal, handshake, league, protocol, settlement, transaction, treaty, understanding *Antonyms:* disagreement, discord, discrepancy, dissent

pad *n.* **1.** buffer, cushion, filling, packing, protection, stuffing, wad, wadding **2.** block, jotter, memorandum, notebook, paper, scratch-pad, slips, tablet **3.** foot, hoof, paw, print **4.** abode, apartment, bachelor pad, cabin, crib, den, flat, home, house, place, refuge, room, shack *Nonformal:* hangout, lovenest, loveshack, party palace – *v.* **1.** amplify, augment, boost, bulk, embellish, embroider, elaborate, enlarge, exaggerate, expand, fudge, increase, inflate, lengthen, magnify, overstate, spin, stretch **2.** cushion, fill, fill out, line, pack, protect, shape, stuff

paddle *n.* **1.** oar, paddle wheel, pole, propeller **2.** distance, extent, gap, interval, length, kilometrage, mileage, span, spread, stretch, yardage – *v.* **1.** boat, cruise, cut water, drift, drive, navigate, oar, propel, pull, row, scull, splash, stir, sweep, thrash **2.** belt, discipline, flog, punish, spank, slap, strap, thrash

paean *n.* **1.** aria, canticle, choral, hymn, ode, oratorio, piece, psalm, requiem, song **2.** exultation, festschrift, glorification, homage, honour, laud, praise, thanks, tribute

pagan *adj.* agnostic, atheistic, heathen, heathenish, idolatrous, impious, infidel, irreligious, polytheistic, profane, unchristian – *n.* agnostic, atheist, doubter, freethinker, heathen, heretic, idolater, idolist, infidel, paganist, pantheist, polytheist, sceptic, scoffer, unbeliever *Antonyms:* believer, zealot

page *n.* **1.** endpaper, folio, leaf, paper, recto, sheet, side, signature, surface, verso **2.** attendant, bellboy, bellhop, equerry, errand boy, servant, server, squire, youth – *v.* **1.** call, ring, seek, signal, summon **2.** check, count, foliate, number, paginate

pageant *n.* **1.** celebration, ceremony, exh bition, exposition, extravaganza, fair, fête parade, procession, ritual, spectacle **2.** dis play, exhibit, float, illustration, mode panorama, tableau **3.** concert, dram entertainment, performance, play, produ tion, review, show, spectacle, theatre

pageantry *n.* ceremony, display, éclat, flai flourish, fuss, grandeur, grandness, ostent tion, pomp and circumstance, spectacl splendour, staginess, stateliness, theatrics

pail *n.* billy, bucket, can, container, cup, di per, ladle, pitcher, receptacle, vessel

pain *n.* **1.** ache, affliction, agony, burn catch, cramp, crick, discomfort, feve gripe, hurt, illness, injury, laceration, mal dy, paroxysm, shock, sickness, smartin sore, soreness, spasm, stitch, strain, suffe ing, tenderness, throb, throe, tingle twinge, wound *Antonyms:* ease, palliatio relief, remedy **2.** anguish, depressio despair, distress, grief, heartache, miser sorrow, torment, torture, wretchednes *Antonyms:* cheer, joy **3.** annoyance, bor bother, encumbrance, inconvenience, irr tation, nuisance, thorn in the side, tribula tion, trouble, vexation *Nonformal:* hassl terror *Antonyms:* delight, pleasure, thri **4.** application, attention, care, diligence effort, energy, industry, labour, rigou *Antonyms:* indifference, neglect – *v.* **1.** ai chafe, discomfit, harm, hurt, inflame injure, smart, sting, throb **2.** afflict aggrieve, agonize, cut to the quick, disqui et, distress, grieve, hurt, sadden, tormen torture, vex, worry, wound *Antonyms* alleviate, assuage, mollify

pained *adj.* **1**. brokenhearted, cut to piece *(Nonformal)*, doleful, grieving, heartbro ken, hurt, melancholy, mournful, neuras thenic, pitiable, regretful, rueful, saddene wretched *Antonyms:* carefree, content indifferent **2.** bent, bleeding, broken, dam aged, harmed, hobbled, hurt, injured, lace ated, nicked, sore, twisted, wounded

painful *adj.* **1**. aching, agonizing, biting burning, caustic, excruciating, hurting inflamed, piercing, raw, sensitive, severe sore, tender, throbbing *Antonyms:* pallia tive, remedial, soothing **2.** arduous, back breaking, difficult, hard, laborious, rigorous, taxing, tedious, tiring, torturous, troublesome, trying, unpleasant *Antonyms:* easy, fun, simple **3.** awful, dire, distressing, dreadful, grievous, harrowing, hurtful, saddening, terrible, tormenting, vexatious *Antonyms:* agreeable, enjoyable, satisfying

painkiller *n.* alleviative, analgesic, anesthetic, headache powder *(Nonformal)*, medicine, palliative, pill *Kinds of painkiller:* acetylsalicylic acid, aspirin, cocaine, ibuprofen, morphine, nitrous oxide, novocaine, whisky *Trademark:* Advil, Bufferin, Tylenol

painless *adj.* **1.** anesthetized, dull, frozen, insensitive, numb, pain-free **2.** easy, quick, simple, worry-free, unrigorous *Nonformal:* breeze, cinch, duck soup, piece of cake, snap *Antonyms:* demanding, difficult, taxing **3.** drunk, far gone, impaired, inebriated, intoxicated, tipsy *Nonformal:* boozed, canned, disguised, hammered, high, jiggered

painstaking *adj.* assiduous, careful, demanding, diligent, fastidious, finicky, industrious, meticulous, particular, punctilious, rigorous, thorough, zealous *Antonyms:* impetuous, negligent, reckless, slapdash

paint *n.* **1.** colour, colourant, colouring, dye, emulsion, pigment, shade, tincture, tint **2.** beauty-care product, cosmetics, cream, eyeliner, greasepaint, lipstick, make-up, maquillage, mascara, powder, rouge, talc, talcum powder, warpaint *(Nonformal)* **3.** acrylic, covering, enamel, flat, gloss, latex, oil, stain, varnish, veneer, wash, water colour – *v.* **1.** compose, design, draft, draw, figure, illustrate, limn, picture, portray, represent, sketch **2.** delineate, demonstrate, depict, describe, elucidate, express, show **3.** brush, coat, colour, cover, daub, decorate, ornament, shade **4.** arrange, beautify, embellish, enhance, groom, prettify, spruce up *(Nonformal)*

painter *n.* artist, colourist, craftsperson, illustrator, oil painter, old master, portrait artist, portraitist, watercolourist

painting *n.* altarpiece, art, artwork, canvas, composition, depiction, illustration, impression, interpretation, *objet d'art (French)*, picture, piece, representation, work *Kinds of painting:* abstract, acrylic, aquarelle, chiaroscuro, cityscape, collage, diorama, diptych, exterior, figurative, finger, fresco, frottage, genre, gouache, historical, icon, interior, kitsch, landscape, montage, mural, nude, oil, panorama, pastiche, pastoral, *plein-air (French)*, pointillism, portrait, still life, topographic, triptych, trompe l'oeil, votive, watercolour *Canadian painting groups:* Atlantic Magic Realists, Automatistes, Contemporary Arts Society, Group of Seven, Ontario Society of Art, Painters Eleven, Plasticiens, Prisme d'yeux, Regina Five *Schools of painting:* abstract expressionism, Art Brut, art nouveau, Barbizon, classicism, constructivism, cubism, Dadaism, de Stijl, Fauvism, futurism, German Expressionism, Impressionism, Mannerism, minimalism, Modernism, neo-classicism, neo-Gothic, neo-Impressionism, neorealism, neo-traditionalism, optical *or* op art *(Nonformal)*, outsider, photo-realism, pop art, Post-Impressionism, Pre-Raphaelite, primitivism, Renaissance, Romanticism, secessionism, social realism, Surrealism, symbolist, transavangardia

pair *n.* **1.** combo, couplet, deuce, doublet, duo, duplicates, dyad, lookalikes, twins, two-of-a-kind, twosome **2.** association, cohabitants, companions, couple, bedfellows, bedmates, friends, housemates, husband and wife, inseparables, item *(Nonformal)*, lovers, mates, pals, partners, roommates *Antonyms:* nonacquaintances, strangers **3.** complement, match, set, twin **4.** brace, combine, span, team, yoke – *v.* balance, bracket, combine, couple, join, hitch, marry, match, match up, mate, merge, pair off, put together, team, twin, unify, unite, wed, yoke *Antonyms:* divide, divorce, sever, split

pal *n.* amigo, associate, bonhomme, brother, buddy, colleague, companion, comrade, confrere, crony, friend, mate, sister *Nonformal:* bosom *or* good buddy, compadre, chum, sidekick, trout *or* old trout

palace *n.* **1.** alcazar, building, castle, chateau, dwelling, home, house, manor, mansion, official *or* royal residence, palazzo *Antonyms:* cabin, shack, shanty **2.**

arena, auditorium, chamber, concourse, conference centre *or* room, club, dome, forum, gardens, hall, rink, stadium

palatable *adj.* **1.** appetizing, delectable, delightful, delicious, flavoursome, good-tasting, mouthwatering, savoury, scrumptious, sweetened, tasteful, tasty, tempting, toothsome, yummy *(Nonformal) Antonyms:* bland, flat, stale, tasteless **2.** acceptable, admissible, agreeable, enjoyable, suitable, passable, pleasant, satisfactory *Antonyms:* obnoxious, objectionable

palate *n.* appetite, fancy, *gout (French)*, hankering, inclination, penchant, predilection, preference, relish, taste

palatial *adj.* deluxe, five-star, grand, grandiose, illustrious, imposing, impressive, lush, luxurious, magnificent, majestic, monumental, noble, opulent, plush, regal, rich, spacious, splendid, stately, sumptuous *Antonyms:* mean, ramshackle, rustic, tumble-down

palaver *n.* **1.** conference, discussion, meeting, parley, powwow, Pugwash *(Nonformal)*, round table **2.** balderdash, blarney, flattery, idle talk *Nonformal:* hogwash, malarkey, tripe – *v.* **1.** chat, chatter, consult, discuss, negotiate, talk terms **2.** cajole, flatter, humour, soft-soap, wheedle *(Nonformal)*

pale *adj.* **1.** ashen, ashy, blanched, bleached, bloodless, cadaverous, colourless, deathlike, dim, doughy, dull, faded, faint, flushed, ghastly, grey, light, pallid, pasty, sallow, wan, washed-out, waxen, waxlike, white, whitish *Antonyms:* blooming, colourful, florid, flushed, glowing, sanguine, vibrant **2.** anemic, enervated, feeble, haggard, ill, inadequate, lifeless, sapped, sick, sickly, weak *Antonyms:* fettle, fit, vigorous – *n.* bounday *or* limits *or* edge of civilization – *v.* **1.** blanch, diminish, dull, fade, lessen, lighten, lose colour *or* lustre, whiten **2.** faint, flinch, lose courage, recoil, shrink, take fright, wince *Antonyms:* beard, brave

palisade *n.* **1.** barrier, buffer, bulwark, bunker, bastion, citadel, fort, fortification, fortress, garrison, outpost, rampart, stronghold **2.** arena, corral, enclosure, fence, pen, stockade, stockyard, yard – *v.* brace, bulwark, enclose, entrench, fortify, protect, secure, strengthen, support

pall *n.* **1.** cloak, cloth, covering, coverlet, linen, mantle, shroud, spread, veil **2.** blackness, cloud, damper, darkness, dismay, drabness, ennui, gloom, gravity, melancholy, sadness, shadow, solemnity, sobreness, unhappiness

palliate *v.* **1.** alleviate, assuage, ease, heal, lighten, mitigate, moderate, mollify, relieve, soothe *Antonyms:* aggravate, heighten, inflame, intensify **2.** camouflage, cloak, conceal, cover, cover up, disguise, excuse, extenuate, gloss over, justify, mask, qualify, sugarcoat, temper, varnish, whitewash

palliative *adj.* **1.** chronic, extended, long-term, prolonged **2.** alleviative, assuasive, easing, emollient, lenitive, mitigating, soothing *Antonyms:* annoying, bothering, irritating – *n.* analgesic, antidote, balm, consolation, cure, elixir, fix, lotion, ointment, remedy, salve, solace, solution, therapeutic, treatment

palpable *adj.* **1.** concrete, material, real, sensible, solid, substantial, tactile, tangible, touchable *Antonyms:* insensible, intangible, metaphysical, surreal **2.** appreciable, clear, distinct, evident, noticeable, obvious, perceptible, visible *Antonyms:* imperceptible, undetectable

palpitate *v.* **1.** beat, flutter, oscillate, pound, pulsate, pulse, skip, throb, thump **2.** buzz, hum, quiver, shake, shimmy, shiver, tingle, tremble, vibrate, wiggle, wobble

paltry *adj.* **1.** inconsequential, insignificant, limited, meagre, minor, picayune, piddling, pitiful, poor, slight, small, trifling, trivial, unimportant, worthless *Antonyms:* considerable, essential, grand, important, major **2.** base, cheap, contemptible, ignominious, low, mean, petty, scrofulous, scurvy, sordid, vile, wretched

pamper *v.* baby, caress, cater to, coddle, cosset, fondle, gratify, humour, indulge, mollycoddle, overindulge, please, regale, satisfy, serve, spoil, tickle *Antonyms:* deny, ignore, neglect

amphlet *n.* **1.** announcement, booklet, broadside, brochure, bulletin, circular, flyer, folder, handout, insertion, leaflet, tract **2.** argument, essay, manifesto, position paper, tract, treatise

an *n.* **1.** cookware, pannikin, pot *Kinds of cooking pan:* baba, bain marie, baking dish, baking sheet, bread, cake, cookie sheet, double boiler, electric frying, frying, loaf, mould, muffin, paella, pie, pizza, poacher, roasting, saucepan, savarin, soufflé dish, steamer, stew pan, terrine, timbale, tin, wok **2.** crown, head, skull *Nonformal:* brain, melon, noggin, roof **3.** drift-ice, floe, ice, pan-ice *See also:* **ice** – *v.* **1.** follow, look, scan, search, survey, sweep, track, **2.** censure, criticize, flay *Nonformal:* dis, hammer, knock, roast, slag, slam, slate, throw bricks at **3.** separate, sift, wade for, wash

anacea *n.* cure, cure-all, elixir, magic potion, nostrum, relief, remedy, secret formula, snakeoil *(Nonformal)*, solution *Antonyms:* bane, poison, toxin

anache *n.* brio, charisma, cheek *(Nonformal)*, chic, dash, élan, energy, flair, flamboyance, flourish, ingenuity, savoir-faire, spirit, style, swagger, verve, vigour *Nonformal:* chutzpah, moxie, punch *Antonyms:* awkwardness, clumsiness

andemic *adj.* general, global, international, pestilent, universal, wholesale, widespread, worldwide *Antonyms:* particular, specific – *n.* disease, epidemic, outbreak, pestilence, plague, rash, scourge

andemonium *n.* **1.** anarchy, bedlam, chaos, commotion, craziness, hullabaloo, insurrection, mayhem, riot, ruckus, rumpus, tumult, turbulence, turmoil, uproar *Antonyms:* calm, hush, order, peace, tranquility **2.** Gehenna, Hades, hell, inferno, nether world, underworld *See also:* **hell** *Antonyms:* Elysium, heaven, paradise

ander *v.* attend, cater, cajole, cater, fawn, gratify, indulge, massage, please, satisfy, stroke, toady *Nonformal:* bootlick, brownnose, kiss ass *Antonyms:* annoy, bother, irritate, upset

panderer *n.* bawd, go-between, madam, matron, pimp, procurer, purveyor, *ruffiano (Italian)*, sleaze *(Nonformal)*, whoremaster

panegyric *n.* **1.** elegy, encomium, eulogy, glorification, memorial, requiem, testimonial **2.** acclamation, accolade, adulation, advocacy, applause, celebration, compliment, flattery, kudos, praise, recognition, tribute *Antonyms:* condemnation, criticism, disparagement

panel *n.* **1.** advisory board, board, committee, discussion group, forum, jury, newsgroup, parliamentary committee, royal commission, tribunal, usenet **2.** board, covering, pane, plate, section, sheet, strip **3.** control, device, instrument, switch

pang *n.* **1.** agony, anguish, disquiet, distress, misery, misgiving, regret, sorrow, suffering, throe, torment, torture **2.** ache, bite, discomfort, gripe, pain, prick, spasm, stab, sting, stitch, throb, twinge, wrench

panhandle *n.* arc, coast, horseshoe, landmass, region, stretch, strip, sweep – *v.* beg, canvas, petition, scrounge, solicit *Nonformal:* bum, hit up, mooch, pass the hat, sponge

panic *n.* **1.** agitation, alarm, confusion, consternation, dismay, distress, dread, fear, frenzy, fret, fright, horror, hysteria, lather *(Nonformal)*, scare, terror, trepidation, upset **2.** apprehension, caution, distrust, misgiving, qualm, scepticism, uncertainty **3.** charge, crush, dash, flight, press, run, rush, stampede – *v.* **1.** alarm, fret, frighten, scare, startle, terrify, unnerve, upset **2.** overreact *Nonformal:* crack up, flip *or* freak *or* wig out, go off halfcocked, lose it, **3.** dart, flee, flight, gallop, race, run, scatter, stampede

panic-stricken *adj.* agitated, alarmed, anxious, freaking *(Nonformal)*, frightened, frozen, nervous, overcome, overwhelmed, panicky, tormented, troubled, worried *Antonyms:* calm, peaceful, serene, tranquil

panorama *n.* **1.** environment, perspective, scenery, spectacle, survey, sweep, view, vision, vista **2.** cyclorama, diorama, landscape, picture, representation, scene

panoramic *adj.* complete, comprehensive, exhaustive, extensive, far-flung, indeterminate, sweeping, wide *Antonyms:* myopic, narrow

pant *n.* blow, breath, gasp, huff, puff – *v.* **1.** breathe, gasp, huff and puff, wheeze **2.** beat, flutter, pound, pulse, pump, throb **3.** ache, aim, aspire, covet, crave, desire, hanker, hunger, pine, sigh, thirst, want, wish, yearn

pantomime *n.* **1.** harlequinade, impersonation, imitation, mimicry, portrayal, simulation **2.** action, body *or* hand motion, expression, gesticulation, gesture, intimation, movement, mustard *(British)*, sign, signal – *v.* **1.** act, adopt, ape *(Nonformal)*, characterize, charade, imitate, mime, mimic, mirror, parody, parrot, personify, play, represent **2.** act, colour, express, gesture, indicate, motion, signify

pants *n. pl.* britches *(Nonformal)*, slacks, trousers *Kinds of pants:* bell bottoms, bloomers *(Historical)*, capri, cargo, chinos, clam diggers, cords, corduroy, denim, dungarees, flares, hip waders, jeans, jodhpurs, khakis, knickers, leisure, oilskins, overalls, pantaloons, pedal pushers, track

paper *adj.* delicate, flimsy, light, thin – *n.* **1.** card, letterhead, material, newsprint, note, notecard, onion skin, pad, page, papyrus, parchment, poster, sheet, stationery, tissue, vellum **2.** annual, bi-monthly, broadsheet, daily, gazette, journal, medium, monthly, news, newspaper, periodical, print, publication, rag *(Nonformal)*, tabloid, scandal sheet, serial, weekly **3.** analysis, argument, article, assignment, composition, critique, dissertation, essay, examination, position paper, report, script, study, theme, thesis, treatise **4.** covering, decoration, embellishment, hanging, wallpaper **5.** access, admission, admittance, entrée, free orders, ingress, ticket – *v.* cover, hang, line, paste up, plaster, wallpaper

papers *n. pl.* affidavit, archive, bill, certificate, certification, citation, contract, credentials, data, deed, diaries, diploma, document, documentation, dossier, file, identification, instrument, letters, passport, record, subpoena, summons, testimony, voucher, warrant, will, writings

par *n.* **1.** average, centre, middle, mode, norm, standard, usual **2.** balance, correspondence, equal footing, equality, equilibrium, level, parity, sameness, unity *Antonyms:* difference, disunity

parable *n.* allegory, apologue, fable, history, homily, legend, lesson, moral, narrative, parallel, speech, story, tale

parade *n.* **1.** array, cavalcade, ceremony, demonstration, display, exhibition, fanfare, march, motorcade, pageant, panapoly, procession, review, ritual, show, spectacle **2.** arcade, avenue, bicycle path, boardwalk, boulevard, circuit, course, esplanade, footpath, promenade, route, trail, walk – *v.* **1.** advertise, air, boast, brag, brandish, declare, demonstrate, disclose, display, exhibit, expose, flash, flaunt, market, peacock *(Nonformal)*, proclaim, promote, publish, reveal, show off, swagger, vaunt, wave about **2.** gallop, march, prance, stomp, stride, strut, traipse

paradise *n.* **1.** Arcadia, Canaan, Eden, El Dorado, Goshen, New Jerusalem, Shangri-la, the Promised Land, utopia, Xanadu *Nonformal:* Big Rock Candy Mountain, cloud-nine, never-never land **2.** Avalon, Elysium, Fiddler's Green, heaven, hereafter, kingdom come *See also:* **heaven 3.** bliss, cloud nine *(Nonformal)*, ecstasy, happiness, nirvana, perfection, seventh heaven, Valhalla

paradox *n.* **1.** ambiguity, anomaly, antinomy, contradiction, inconsistency, irony, nonconformity **2.** absurdity, bizarreness, impossibility, oddity, strangeness **3.** catch, conundrum, enigma, knot, mystery, pickle *(Nonformal)*, predicament, problem, quandary, riddle

paragon *n.* apotheosis, Beau Brummel *(Historical)*, blueprint, chief *(Nonformal)*, classic, crème de la crème, epitome, example, ideal, jewel, model, nonpareil, pattern, pearl, prototype, role model, superior

parallel *adj.* **1.** aligned, co-extending, equidistant, lateral, never meeting, running alongside *Antonyms:* crossing, interconnected **2.** akin, alike, analogous, comparable, complementary, conforming, consonant, corresponding, equal, identical, like, matching, resembling, similar, uniform *Antonyms:* different, divergent, unlike – *n.* **1.** analogy, complement, corollary, correlation, correspondent, counterpart, double, duplicate, equal, equivalent, homologue, kin, likeness, match, resemblance, similarity, twin *Antonyms:* difference, dissimilarity, divergence, opposite, reverse **2.** balancing, collating, comparison, contrasting, juxtaposition, matching, measuring, ranking, rating, testing – *v.* **1.** agree, collate, complement, conform, correlate, correspond, equate, keep pace *Antonyms:* differ, diverge **2.** compare, liken, match, measure, test, weigh **3.** co-extend, run abreast *or* side by side **4.** agree, chime, comport, conjoin, equal, harmonize, square *Nonformal:* jibe, see eye to eye *Antonyms:* deviate, vary

paralyze *v.* **1.** arrest, block, check, circumvent, curb, embargo, frustrate, halt, impede, interrupt, sabotage, shut down, stay, stifle, stop, suspend, thwart **2.** anesthetize, benumb, cripple, daze, deaden, demolish, disable, disarm, freeze, incapacitate, nonplus, numb, petrify, prostrate, stun, stupefy, transfix

parameter *n.* **1.** border, boundary, confine, definition, envelope, footprint *(Nonformal)*, limit, limitation, line, margin, metes and bounds, outline, pale **2.** criterion, framework, guideline, measure, model, policy, restriction, rules of play, specification, standard, stipulation, touchstone

paramount *adj.* **1.** ascendant, capital, cardinal, chief, commanding, controlling, crowning, dominant, eminent, foremost, great, headmost, important, master, overbearing, predominant, preeminent, premier, preponderant, primary, prime, principal, regnant, sovereign, superior, supreme *Antonyms:* common, inferior, plebian, secondary, subordinate **2.** exceptional, exemplary, extraordinary, fine, first, leading, main, outstanding *Antonyms:* insignificant, minor, slight – *n.* authority, chief, commander, dictator, governor, king, master, monarch, nabob, overlord, potentate, prince, princess, queen, rajah, regent, ruler, satrap, sovereign, sultan, sultana

paramour *n.* **1.** beau, boyfriend, flame, girlfriend, inamorata, inamorato, love mate, partner, sweetheart *Nonformal:* better half, gal, guy, rock, squeeze **2.** concubine, kept man *or* woman, lover, mistress, other man *or* woman

paranoia *n.* **1.** anxiety, apprehension, conspiracy syndrome *(Nonformal)*, cynicism, distrust, fear, high anxiety, nervousness, panic, suspicion, trepidation *Antonyms:* clarity, rationality, reasonableness **2.** delusion, madness, mental disease *or* illness, neurosis, obsession, psychosis *Antonyms:* health, soundness of mind

paraphernalia *n.* **1.** accoutrements, appurtenances, baggage, belongings, clutter, gear, machinery, material, merchandise, outfit, personal effects, kit, regalia, stuff, tackle, things, trappings *Nonformal:* bits and pieces, junk **2.** apparatus, equipment, impedimenta

paraphrase *n.* digest, explanation, interpretation, rendering, rendition, rephrasing, restatement, rewording, summary, translation, version – *v.* interpret, recapitulate, render, rephrase, restate, reword, summarize, transcribe, translate

parasite *n.* **1.** bedbug, bloodsucker, flea, leech, lice, louse, remora, tapeworm, tick **2.** scrounger *Nonformal:* bottom-feeder, deadbeat, deadhead, freeloader, groupie, hanger-on, lounge lizard, moocher, scab, sponge, sponger

parcel *n.* **1.** bag, box, bundle, carton, chest, container, crate, load, pack, package, packet, purse **2.** acreage, block, concession, land, lot, plot, property, square, tract, zone **3.** array, assemblage, batch, body, bunch, cluster, collection, company, covey, crew, crowd, division, group, herd, pack, selection **4.** bite, chunk, cut, division, member, moiety, part, piece, portion, section, segment, share, slice – *v.* **1.** bag, box, carton, pack, package, wrap up **2.** allot, arrange, deal, distribute, divey out *(Non-*

formal), divide, dole out, mete, sever *Antonyms:* fuse, join, keep

parch *v.* **1.** dehydrate, desiccate, dry, evaporate *Antonyms:* hydrate, moisten, wet **2.** blister, boil, broil, brown, burn, cook, crisp, fry, grill, roast, toast **3.** atrophy, flag, shrink, shrivel, waste, wilt, wither

parched *adj.* **1.** athirst, cotton-mouthed *(Nonformal)*, dehydrated, thirsty **2.** arid, baked, barren, desert, desolate, dessicated, dry, forsaken, infertile, lifeless, rainless, scorched, waterless *Antonyms:* lush, moist, verdant **3.** drooping, dried out *or* up, dying, exhausted, flagging, sagging, shrivelled, shrunken, withered, wizened

pardon *n.* **1.** allowance, benevolence, charity, clemency, compassion, conciliation, empathy, forbearance, forgiveness, generosity, good will, grace, indulgence, kindness, leniency, mercy, patience, pity, tenderness, tolerance *Antonyms:* cruelty, intolerance, ruthlessness **2.** absolution, acquittal, amnesty, commutation, discharge, dispensation, exculpation, exoneration, freeing, release, remission, reprieve, vindication *Antonyms:* penalty, punishment, retaliation, retribution, revenge – *v.* **1.** acquit, clear, discharge, exculpate, free, grant amnesty, let off, liberate, release, reprieve, rescue, spring *(Nonformal)*, suspend charges *Antonyms:* condemn, discipline, imprison, penalize **2.** absolve, exonerate, forgive, pity *Antonyms:* blame, censure, chasten, rebuke **3.** accept, allow, condone, excuse, forget, let pass, overlook, tolerate *Antonyms:* admonish, castigate, chastise

pare *v.* **1.** bark, husk, peel, scalp, scrape, shave, shear, skin, skive, uncover **2.** carve, cut, hew, knife, lop, mow, prune, slash, slit **3.** abrade, cull, decrease, diminish, dock, downsize, lessen, lower, mark, reduce, streamline, strip, thin, trim *Antonyms:* add, augment, enlarge, swell

parent *n.* **1.** begetter, dam, father, folks, foster parent, mother, procreator, sire, stepfather, step-mother *Nonformal:* dad, mom **2.** architect, author, creator, designer, founder, generator, maker, originator, producer **3.** base, beginning, cause, foundation, fountainhead, genesis, germ, origin, root, seat, seed, source, wellspring **4.** cast, forerunner, genotype, model, mould, original, pattern, precursor, predecessor, prototype – *v.* baby-sit, bring up, cultivate, educate, father, foster, husband, maintain, mother, nourish, nurture, protect, raise, rear *Antonyms:* ignore, neglect

parenthetical *adj.* bracketed, episodic, explanatory, extraneous, extrinsic, incidental, inserted, interposed, qualifying, related, secondary, subordinate *Antonyms:* central, essential, fundamental

pariah *n.* castoff, displaced person, exile, expatriot, expellee, outcast, outlaw, prodigal, undesirable, untouchable *Antonyms:* member, nonpareil, patriot

parish *n.* **1.** archdiocese, bethel, church, church district, county, demesne, diocese, district, jurisdiction, neighbourhood, precinct, region, riding, territory, vicarage, zone **2.** brothers and sisters, children, churchgoers, community, congregation, family, flock, fold, parishioners, people, religious society

parity *n.* **1.** agreement, balance, conformance, congruity, equality, equilibrium, equity, evenness, similitude, symmetry, uniformity *Antonyms:* discordance, discrepancy, diversity **2.** affinity, analogy, correspondence, identicalness, likeness, resemblance, sameness, similarity *Antonyms:* difference, variation

park *n.* **1.** conservation *or* recreation area, esplanade, estate, forest, game preserve, garden, grass, green, greenbelt, greenspace, greenway, grounds, lawn, lot, meadow, parkette, parkland, place, playground, pleasure garden *or* ground, preserve, protected greenspace *or* landscape *or* seascape *or* wilderness, refuge, reserve, square, tract, village green, wilderness reserve, woodland **2.** arena, athletic *or* playing field, ballpark, bowling green, coliseum, diamond, field, forum, friendly confines *(Nonformal)*, gardens, outdoor rink, pitch, soccer field – *v.* **1.** deposit, position, put, stash, store **2.** locate *or* seat oneself, roost, settle, sit, slump, squat

parley *n.* conference, conversation, dialogue, discussion, negotiation, palaver, powwow, Pugwash *(Nonformal)*, symposium, talk, tête-à-tête – *v.* commune, confer, consult, convene, debate, discuss, huddle, negotiate, speak, weigh terms *Nonformal:* brainstorm, chew the fat, rap

Parliament *n.* corridors of power, Ottawa *(Nonformal)*, governing body, legislature, legislative body, Parliament Hill *Parts of the Canadian Parliament:* House of Commons *or* the Commons *or* the House, Senate *Documents in the Canadian Parliament:* green paper, Hansard, Speech from the Throne *or* Throne Speech, white paper *Positions and officials in the Canadian Parliament:* backbenches, cabinet minister, frontbenches, gentleman usher of the black rod, house leader, leader of the opposition, official opposition, prime minister, senate majority leader, senate minority leader, senator, shadow cabinet, speaker, whip *See also:* **government**

parlour *n.* den, drawing *or* family *or* sitting *or* television room, front hall, reception *or* waiting area, foyer, lobby, lounge, salon, scriptorium

parochial *adj.* biased, bigoted, conservative, conventional, insular, inward-looking, limited, local, narrow, narrow-minded, petty, prejudiced, provincial, regional, restricted, sectarian, shallow, small-minded, small-town *(Nonformal) Antonyms:* broad-minded, cosmopolitan, liberal, universal

parody *n.* burlesque, caricature, cartoon, derision, farce, imitation, joke, mimicry, misrepresentation, mockery, satire, send-up, skit, spoof, takeoff, travesty – *v.* ape, burlesque, caricature, copy, deride, disparage, exaggerate, imitate, impersonate, jeer, jest, joke, lampoon, mimic, mock, ridicule, roast, send up, spoof

paroxysm *n.* **1.** agitation, anger, eruption, excitement, explosion, fit, flare-up, fuming, furor, fury, hysterics, outbreak, outburst, passion, rage, violence *Nonformal:* conniption, frenzy, frothing at the mouth **2.** attack, convulsion, seizure, spasm, spell, stroke

parrot *n.* bird *Kinds of parrot:* black-capped lorry, Blue-crowned hanging, Crimson rosella, Eclectus, fischer, Hyacinth macaw, lovebird, Rainbow lorikeet, Red-capped, Sulphur-crested cockatoo – *v.* ape, copy, copycat *(Nonformal)*, echo, imitate, iterate, mime, mimic, plagiarize, quote, recite, reiterate, repeat

parry *v.* avoid, block, bypass, circumvent, deflect, deke *(Nonformal)*, dodge, duck, elude, evade, fence, fend off, forestall, prevent, rebuff, rebuke, repel, repulse, resist, shirk, sidestep *Antonyms:* allow, further, permit – *n.* diversion, escape, evasion, machination, manoeuvre, negotiation, plan, ruse, scheme, strategy, tactic, trick

parsimonious *adj.* abstemious, careful, chary, cheap, churlish, close, close-fisted, conserving, curmudgeonly, discreet, economical, frugal, grasping, greedy, ignoble, illiberal, lean, mean, mingy *(Nonformal)*, miserly, penny-pinching, penny-wise, penurious, petty, pinchpenny, provident, prudent, saving, scrimping, selfish, skimping, sparing, stingy, thrifty, tight, tight-fisted, ungenerous *Antonyms:* extravagant, generous, lavish, spendthrift, wasteful

parsimony *n.* conservation, frugality, miserliness, penuriousness, prudence, sparingness, stinginess, thrift *Antonyms:* charity, generosity

parson *n.* abbé, chaplain, churchman, churchwoman, clergyman, clergywoman, cleric, curate, *curé (French)*, ecclesiastic, minister, padre, person of the cloth, preacher, priest, rector, saddlebag preacher *(Historical)*

part *n.* **1.** bite, chip, chunk, division, fraction, fragment, half, leaving, moiety, particle, piece, rasher, remnant, scrap, section, sector, segment, shard, side, slab, slice, sliver, splinter, subdivision, unit **2.** component, constituent, element, factor, ingredient, mechanism, member, organ, sprig, switch **3.** allotment, allowance, apportionment, bit, claim, country, cut, district, domain, helping, installment, lot, measure, neighbourhood, parcel, percentage, piece of the pie *(Nonformal)*, portion, quarter, quota, ration, section, serving, share, stake

4. chapter, clause, installment, line, page, paragraph, passage, point, sentence, stanza **5.** character, hero, heroine, lead, lines, role, supporting role **6.** line, voice *Kind of musical part:* alto, baritone, bass, canto, contralto, counter-tenor, descant, mezzo-soprano, soprano, tenor, treble **7.** assignment, business, branch, capacity, cause, charge, concern, detail, duty, function, interest, obligation, office, place, responsibility, role, share, task, work **8.** area, borough, concession, land, municipality, province, region, state, territory, township, zone – *v.* **1.** break, cleave, dismantle, divide, factor, itemize, partition, portion, rend, section, segment, split, subdivide, sunder, tear **2.** cease, close, desist, discontinue, stop, surcease, suspend, terminate **3.** disconnect, move apart, separate, unfasten, unravel, untie, unyoke **4.** administer, allocate, allot, designate, dispense, distribute, divvy *(Nonformal)*, mete, parcel, portion, ration **5.** depart, ease out, leave, pull out, say goodbye, take leave, withdraw *Nonformal:* beat it, scram, split, vamoose *Antonyms:* appear, arrive, come, gather, remain **6.** break up, call it quits *(Nonformal)*, disassociate, dissolve, disunite, divorce, go separate ways, part company, split up *Antonyms:* conjoin, marry, wed

partake *v.* **1.** consume, devour, eat, feed, ingest, receive, sample, savour, sip **2.** engage, enter into, participate, sit in, take part, try, tune in *(Nonformal)*

partial *adj.* **1.** fractional, fragmentary, half-baked *(Nonformal)*, halfway, imperfect, incomplete, lacking, limited, part, sketchy, unfinished *Antonyms:* complete, entire, full, total, whole **2.** bent, biased, coloured, compromised, disposed, inclined, influenced, interested, jaundiced, one-sided, partisan, predisposed, prejudiced, prepossessed, warped *(Nonformal) Antonyms:* impartial, objective, unbiased, unprejudiced

partiality *n.* **1.** bias, favouritism, inclination, leaning, partisanship, predilection, predisposition, prejudice, proclivity, propensity **2.** affinity, fondness, liking, love, penchant, preference, taste, tendency, weakness *Nonformal:* druthers, thing *Antonyms:* abhorrence, antipathy, aversion, dislike, revulsion **3.** bigotry, discrimination, inequality, inequitableness, injustice, oppression, racism, sexism, unfairness

partially *adv.* a little bit, by degrees or installments, fractionally, halfway, incompletely, in part, moderately, not wholly, partly, piecemeal, somewhat *Antonyms:* completely, totally

participant *adj.* active, affected, engaged, immersed, involved, participating, sharing – *n.* accomplice, actor, agent, aide, assistant, associate, attendant, colleague, co-conspirator, confrere, contributor, fellow, helper, member, partaker, participator, partner, player, sharer *Antonyms:* backbencher, spectator

participate *v.* accept, contribute, engage, enter, have a role, partake, play, share, sit in, take part *Antonyms:* avoid, pass, sit out, skip

participation *n.* aid, assistance, association, contribution, cooperation, engagement, help, inclusion, input, involvement *Antonyms:* detachment, dissociation

particle *n.* **1.** atom, bit, crumb, dot, dribble, drop, fleck, fragment, grain, iota, jot, minim, mite, modicum, molecule, morsel, piece, ray, scrap, shred, smidgen, smithereen, speck **2.** electron, meson, neutron, photon, proton, quark

particular *adj.* **1.** distinct, exclusive, individual, lone, one, peculiar, single, singular, specific, unique *Antonyms:* general, vague **2.** exceptional, notable noteworthy, remarkable, special, *sui generis (Latin)*, uncommon, unusual **3.** accurate, careful, critical, demanding, discriminating, exact, fastidious, finicky, fussy, meticulous, pettifogging, precise, scrupulous, technical, thorough *Antonyms:* casual, negligent, slack **4.** detailed, itemized, listed, marked, noted, ordered, recorded – *n.* case, circumstance, clue, detail, element, fact, feature, number, picture, point, rundown, score, speciality, specific

particularize *v.* **1.** delineate, describe, detail, itemize, list, specify, spell out **2.** differentiate, diversify, divide, order, segregate, separate

particularly *adv.* **1.** characteristically, distinctly, markedly, singularly, specifically **2.** conspicuously, especially, notably, prominently, uncommonly **3.** in detail *or* particular, minutely, part by part, piece by piece **4.** individually, personally, privately

parting *adj.* **1.** closing, departing, ending, farewell, final, goodbye, last, valedictory *Antonyms:* initial, introductory, opening **2.** breaking, cleaving, diverging, dividing, separating, shattering *Antonyms:* attaching, marrying, merging, unifying **3.** dying, fading, failing, falling, languishing, losing, shrinking, withering – *n.* **1.** departure, end, escape, exit, farewell, going, goodbye, last hurrah, leave-taking, swan song *(Nonformal)*, withdrawal *Antonyms:* introduction, meeting **2.** breakup, detachment, dismantlement, divorce, estrangement, schism, separation, severance *Antonyms:* attachment, marriage, union **3.** break, cleavage, cleft, crack, crevice, crossroads, divide, fault, fissure, fracture, gap, gully, opening, rift, rupture, split **4.** barrier, border, bulkhead, curtain, obstruction, partition, wall

partisan *adj.* **1.** biased, blind, coloured, denominational, devoted, factional, fanatical, interested, one-sided, partial, predisposed, prejudiced, sectarian, sympathetic, unjust, zealous *Antonyms:* broad-minded, impartial, objective **2.** affiliated, associated, attached, bound, connected, merged, party, related, united – *n.* **1.** accessory, accomplice, acolyte, adherent, backer, champion, cohort, defender, devotee, disciple, follower, henchman, stalwart, supporter, sycophant, sympathizer, upholder, zealot *Antonyms:* adversary, contender, critic, foe, rival **2.** guard, guerrilla, mercenary, militia man *or* woman, serviceperson, soldier, trooper, warrior

partition *n.* **1.** breakup, cleavage, curtain, detachment, divergence, division, fence, parting, segregation, section, separation, subdivision, wall **2.** fraction, fragment, half, lot, part, piece, portion, quarter, section, sector, segment, sphere, tract, zone **3.** allotment, apportionment, dole, measure, portion, ration, share – *v.* **1.** apportion, deal, disburse, dispense, disperse, distribute, divide, divvy up *(Nonformal)* **2.** breakup, section, separate, sever, split, subdivide, wall off *Antonyms:* marry, mate, unite

partly *adv.* **1.** bit by bit *(Nonformal)*, by degrees, one at a time, partially, piecemeal, **2.** carelessly, halfway, inadequately, incompletely, in part, insufficiently, not completely, not entirely, not fully, not wholly, relatively, slightly, somewhat, within limits *Antonyms:* completely, entirely, fully, totally, wholly

partner *n.* **1.** accomplice, ally, assistant, associate, bedfellow, cohort, collaborator, colleague, confederate, confrere, consort, co-owner, co-worker, crony, helper, helpmate, participant, teammate *Nonformal:* fellow victim, sidekick *Antonyms:* adversary, enemy, foe, opponent **2.** helpmate, husband, life partner, love, lover, mate, spouse, wife *Nonformal:* better half, hubbie, missus, old man *or* woman, the wife

partnership *n.* **1.** affiliation, alliance, amalgam, amalgamation, association, bloc, body, brotherhood, business, cartel, coalition, combination, combine, community, company, confederation, conglomerate, consolidation, co-op *(Nonformal)*, cooperative, corporation, coterie, crew, faction, fellowship, firm, fraternity, gang, group, joint interest, league, merger, organization, ownership, party, sisterhood, sorority, unification, union **2.** agreement, arrangement, bargain, bond, contract, covenant, deal, guarantee, handshake *(Nonformal)*, obligation, pact, pledge, promise, settlement, treaty

party *adj.* biased, interested, involved, one-sided, partial, *parti pris (French)*, partisan, political, prejudiced – *n.* **1.** affair, amusement, carousing, ceilidh, celebration, entertainment, feast, festivity, fête, get-together, good time, shivaree, social *Nonformal:* bash, bender, binge, blast, blowout, cloggaroo, do, frolic, jump-up, kitchen racket, riot, shindig, spree, time *Kinds of party:* after hours, bachelor, ball, banquet, barbecue, barn-raising, basket *or* box *or* lawn *or* pie social, beer-drinking, bush, carnival, chopping bee, clambake, dance, dinner, field, gala, Grey Cup, house, keg *or* kegger, levee, luncheon, matinée, pink tea, potlatch, prom, quilting bee, reception, shower, sleighing, soirée, stag and doe, sugaring-off, supper **2.** assembly, band, bevy, body, bunch, cluster, company, corps, covey, crew, crowd, detachment, force, gang, gathering, group, militia, mob, multitude, outfit, posse, squad, team, troop, troupe, unit **3.** alliance, association, bloc, cabal, camp, caucus, clique, coalition, combination, combine, confederacy, coterie, electorate, faction, grassroots organization, grouping, junta, league, old-line party, political group, riding association, ring, schism, sect, set, side, splinter, union *Names of political parties:* Bloc Québécois, Canadian Alliance, communist, Grits, Equality Party, Green, Liberal, New Democratic *or* NDP, Parti Québécois, Péquiste, Progressive Conservative *or* PC, Progressive, Reform, Rhinoceros, social democrat, social engineering, socialist, Tory, whig *Historical:* Block Populaire, CCF, Chateau Clique, Clear Grit, Family Compact, National Party, Parti Bleu, Parti Rouge, Social Credit *or* Socred, Union Nationale, United Farmers **4.** being, body, character, creature, head, human, individual, man, mortal, person, personage, somebody, someone, woman **5.** actor, agent, confederate, defendant, litigant, participant, plaintiff – *v.* fraternize, mingle, mix, socialize *Nonformal:* boogie, cut *or* let loose, get down, have a ball, paint the town, trip the light fantastic, turn on one's love light, wind it up

parvenu *adj.* arrogant, brash, brazen, cheeky, cocky, forward, presumptuous, pretentious – *n.* arriviste, Horatio Alger figure, imposter, johnny-come-lately *(Nonformal),* nouveau riche, status seeker, social climber, upstart

pass *n.* **1.** contingency, crisis, crossroads, crucible, dilemma, emergency, juncture, plight, predicament, situation, state, strait **2.** advance, approach, overture, play, proposition, suggestion **3.** artery, canyon, corridor, cut, entry, gap, gorge, narrows, notch, opening, passage, passageway, path, ravine, trail, valley, way **4.** admission, certificate, entrée, ingress, licence, passport, permission, permit, ticket **5.** acceptance, accreditation, acknowledgment, approval, passing grade, sanction **6.** declension, decline, refusal, rejection, veto **7.** throw, toss, transfer *Nonformal:* bomb, fling, hail Mary – *v.* **1.** accept, adopt, approve, authorize, carry, decree, enact, establish, legalize, legislate, ordain, pledge, ratify, sanction, validate, vote in, warrant *Antonyms:* ban, disallow, overrule, prohibit, veto **2.** befall, come off, develop, elapse, ensue, happen, proceed, progress, take place, transpire **3.** beat, exceed, excel, gain on, go beyond, lap, leave behind, move ahead *or* beyond, outdistance, outdo, outpace, outrun, outshine, outstrip, overhaul, overtake, overwhelm, reach, surmount, surpass, top, transcend *Antonyms:* fall behind, stagger, stumble **4.** cease, decease, depart, die, end, expire, kick-the-bucket *(Nonformal),* pass away, perish, succumb, terminate **5.** claim, declare, deliver, pronounce, state, tell, utter **6.** circulate, convey, deliver, disseminate, forward, exchange, give, hand over, transfer, transmit *Antonyms:* prohibit, refuse, reject **7.** decline, discount, disregard, fail, forget, miss, omit, pass up, refuse, relinquish, skip *Antonyms:* acknowledge, heed, note **8.** course, flood, flow, move, pour, run, rush, shuffle, stream, sweep, travel, wind **9.** announce, call, declare, decree, deliver, proclaim, pronounce, utter **10.** defecate, discharge, excrete, urinate, void **11.** cast, chuck, fling, flip, heave, hurl, launch, lob, pitch, push, shoot, throw, toss, volley, whip *Nonformal:* fire, peg **12.** achieve, breeze by *or* through *(Nonformal),* earn, obtain, succeed, win *Antonyms:* bomb, fail, lose **13.** alter, change, fluctuate, modify, mutate, oscillate, swing, transform, vacillate

passable *adj.* **1.** acceptable, adequate, admissible, allowable, average, common, fair, mediocre, moderate, ordinary, presentable, respectable, so-so *(Nonformal),* tolerable *Antonyms:* exceptional, extraordinary, outstanding **2.** accessible, attainable, beaten, clear, graded, level, navigable, open, traversable, unobstructed, well-travelled *Antonyms:* ice-bound, impervious, impregnable, washed-out

passage *n.* **1.** access, alley, alleyway, avenue, channel, corridor, course, entrance, esplanade, exit, hall, lane, opening, pass, passageway, path, pathway, road, route, slope, snye, thoroughfare, trail, tunnel, underground, walkway, way **2.** acceptance, allowance, authorization, enactment, establishment, legalization, legislation, passing, ratification **3.** citation, excerpt, extract, paragraph, piece, portion, quotation, reading, selection, sentence, text, verse **4.** bridge, chorus, coda, development, leitmotif, measure, motif, movement, ornament, part, phrase, refrain, section, stanza, strain, subject, theme, trope, variation, verse **5.** alteration, change, conversion, metamorphosis, reformation, shift, switch, transformation, transmutation **6.** adventure, campaign, expedition, jaunt, journey, junket, migration, safari, trek, trip, venture **7.** admission, berth, grant, permission **8.** authority, freedom, jurisdiction, liberty, licence, power, right

passageway *n.* aisle, corridor, hall, landing *See also:* **pass, passage**

passé *adj.* **1.** antiquated, dated, *démodé (French)*, extinct, obsolete, old-fashioned, outdated, outmoded, out-of-date, outworn, unfashionable *Nonformal:* has-been, yesterday *Antonyms:* cutting-edge, fashionable, modish, stylish **2.** disused, faded, flagged, tired, used, washed-out, weak, worn

passenger *n.* commuter, customer, drop, fare, hitchhiker, load, patron, pilgrim, rider, seat cover *(Nonformal)*, tourist, traveller, tripper, voyager

passing *adj.* **1.** departing, disappearing, fading, flitting, leaving, parting, waning *Antonyms:* burgeoning, oncoming **2.** ephemeral, faddish, fleeting, meteoric, short-lived, transient, transitory *Antonyms:* classic, timeless, universal **3.** afoot, contemporary, crossing, current, elapsing, happening, occurring, oncoming, meeting, prevalent, progressing *Antonyms:* completed, past **4.** brief, cursory, glancing, hasty, hurried, incidental, meaningless, off-hand, parting, perfunctory, quick, shallow, superficial, swift, thoughtless – *n.* **1.** death, demise, departure, eclipse, expiration, parting **2.** avenue, bridge, ford, lane, pass, passage, passageway, path, road, route, thoroughfare, trail, way

passion *n.* **1.** ardour, emotion, enthusiam, feeling, fervour, heart, love, power, sincerity, soul, spirit, verve, vivacity, zeal **2.** concupiscence, craving, desire, heat, hunger, infatuation, lust, prurience, thirst, yen *(Nonformal)* **3.** anger, furor, fury, ire, rage, tantrum, vehemence, violence, wrath **4.** interest, liking, penchant, propensity, weakness

passionate *adj.* **1.** emotional, enthusiastic, excitable, expressive, feeling, heartfelt, powerful, responsive, sincere, soulful, spirited, vivacious *Antonyms:* apathetic, indifferent, frigid, unresponsive **2.** crazy, hot-blooded, ill-tempered, irrational, irritable, quick-tempered, precipitate, rash, reckless, testy, touchy, unbridled, unmanageable, violent, volcanic, wild *Antonyms:* calm, cool, passive **3.** embroiled, excited, fierce, furious, hot, ignited, impassioned, melodramatic, tempestuous **4.** acute, ardent, blazing, burning, deep, fervent, fervid, fierce, fiery, flaming, forceful, frenzied, headlong, heated, hot, impassioned, intense, strong, vehement *Antonyms:* dim, dull, weak **5.** amorous, ardent, aroused, concupiscent, desirous, erotic, lascivious, libidinous, loving, lustful, prurient, romantic, sensual, sexy, steamy, stimulated, wanton *Antonyms:* cold, passionless, unloving **6.** affecting, dramatic, eloquent, inspiring, moving, poignant, stirring, touching

passionless *adj.* **1.** cold, frigid, frosty, impassive, insensitive, unemotional, unfeeling *Antonyms:* affectionate, ardent, zealous **2.** callous, cold-blooded, cold-hearted, hardhearted, heartless, obdurate, unmerciful, unsympathetic *Antonyms:* empathic, humane, sympathetic **3.** detached, disinterested, dispassionate, fair, impartial, judicial, neutral, nondiscriminatory, nonpartisan, objective, open-minded, unbiased *Antonyms:* bigoted, prejudiced, subjective

passive *adj.* **1.** asleep *(Nonformal)*, dormant, flat, homeostatic, idle, impassive, inactive, inanimate, latent, lifeless, motionless, quiescent, static, still, supine *Antonyms:* active, energetic, lively **2.** detached, neutral, nonaligned, nonpartisan, nonviolent, outside, uninterested, uninvolved *Antonyms:* belligerent, interested, involved, partial **3.** apathetic, impersonal, indifferent, nonchalant, stolid **4.** acquiescent, amenable, complaisant, compliant, docile, easily influenced *or* moved, malleable, nonresistant, pliable, receptive, responsive, submissive, susceptible, timid, tractable, unassertive, unresisting, yielding *Antonyms:* contrary, hostile, overbearing **5.** bearing, enduring, forbearing, longsuffering, patient, permissive, placid, tolerant

passport *n.* authorization, certification, clearance, credentials, identification, licence, papers, pass, permission, permit, safe-conduct, ticket, travel permit, visa

password *n.* identification, key, key word, open sesame *(Nonformal)*, personal identification number *or* PIN, phrase, secret word, shibboleth, signal, watchword, word

past *adj.* **1.** closed, completed, concluded, consumed, done, elapsed, ended, exhausted, extinct, finished, gone, lapsed, over, played out *(Nonformal)*, spent *Antonyms:* current, existing, ongoing **2.** ancient, antique, archaic, bygone, classic, early, forgotten, former, historical, latter-day, old, preexisting, traditional *Nonformal:* dusty, mouldy *Antonyms:* contemporary, modern **3.** aforementioned, anterior, earlier, foregoing, late, latter, preceding, previous, prior, recent *Antonyms:* future, next **4.** antecedent, emeritus, erstwhile, moth-balled *(Nonformal)*, one-time, pensioned, resigned, retired, superannuated *Antonyms:* callow, fresh, new – *n.* **1.** ages ago, antiquity, *belle époque (French)*, former times, good old days, history, long ago, olden days, old times, remote past, time gone *or* immemorial, years ago, yesterday, yesteryear, yore *Antonyms:* now, present, today, tomorrow **2.** confidence, hidden history, intimacy, mystery, secret, shame, skeleton in the closet *(Nonformal)* **3.** boyhood, carefree *or* halcyon *or* salad days, childhood, experience, girlhood, life, memory, youth *Nonformal:* misspent youth, wild times – *prep.* after, beyond, later than, subsequent to

pasta *n.* dough, noodle, paste *Kinds of pasta:* agnolotti, angel hair, cannelloni, cappeletti, conchiglie, farfel, fettuccine, fusilli, gnocchi, kreplach, lasagna, linguini, macaroni, manicotti, orzo, penne, pennette, quenelle, ravioli, rigatoni, rotelli, rotini, spaetzle, spaghetti, spaghettini, tagliatelle, tortellini, vermicelli, ziti *See also:* **noodles**

paste *n.* **1.** adhesive, cement, fastener, fixative, glue, gum, mucilage, patch, plaster, *Nonformal:* goo, gunk, stickum **2.** blend, composition, compound, dough, gruel, mixture, porridge, pulp, purée **3.** dip, hors d'oeuvre, pâté, spread **4.** counterfeit, fake, forgery, glass *or* imitation *or* junk jewellery, mock, phoney *(Nonformal)*, strass – *v.* **1.** affix, adhere, fasten, glue, secure, set, stick *Antonyms:* peel, remove, tear down **2.** beat, box, pound, pummel, punch, smack, strike, trounce *Nonformal:* deck, shellac

pastel *adj.* delicate, light, muted, pale, soft-hued, soft-toned *Antonyms:* bright, deep, rich, vibrant – *v.* **1.** crayon, chalk, pastille, pencil crayon **2.** depiction, draft, drawing, illustration, landscape, painting, picture, portrait, sketch, study **3.** blush, colour, shade, soft hue, tint, tone

pastiche *n.* **1.** approximation, copy, counterfeit, duplication, facsimile, fake, forgery, imitation, impression, replica, reproduction *Nonformal:* knock-off, rip-off **2.** burlesque, mockery, parody, satire, send-up *(Nonformal)*, travesty **3.** collage, dog's breakfast *(Nonformal)*, farrago, gallimaufry, hodgepodge, medley, mélange, mishmash, mixed bag, mixture

pastille *n.* **1.** bonbon, candy, confection, drop, lozenge, pill, tablet, troche **2.** air freshener, deodorizer, fumigant, incense, perfume

pastime *n.* amusement, avocation, distraction, diversion, divertissement, entertainment, fun, game, hobby, leisure, *passe-temps (French)*, play, pleasure, racket *(Nonformal)*, recreation, solace, sport, vice *Antonyms:* drudgery, toil, work

pastor *n.* abbé, abbot, churchman, churchwoman, clergyman, clergywoman, cleric, curate, *curé (French)*, deacon, divine, ecclesiastic, father, minister, padre, parson, preacher, priest, rector, reverend, vicar

pastoral *adj.* **1.** agrarian, bucolic, countrified, country, innocent, provincial, rural, rustic, serene, simple, sylvan, tranquil **2.** Arcadian, eclogic, Edenic, idyllic, paradisal, poetic, romantic

pastry *n.* **1.** batter, crust, dough, filo **2.** baked goods, dainty, delicacy, dessert, goody *(Nonformal)*, *patisserie (French)*, snack *Kinds of pastry:* baba au rhum, baklava, beignet, biscuit, butter tart, cake, cannoli, cookie, cornet, cream puff, crescent, croissant, crumpet, Danish, éclair, frangipani, fritter, fruit pie, madeleine, napoleon, pain au chocolate, pasty *(British)*, pâté â choux, patty, petit four, *piroshki (Russian)*, profiterole, puff, quiche, samosa, scone, *six pate (Quebec)* strudel, sweet roll, tart, turnover, vol-au-vent *See also:* **dessert, pie**

pasty *adj.* **1.** anemic, ashen, bloodless, dull, pale, pallid, sallow, sickly, unhealthy, wan, waxen, whey-faced *Antonyms:* hale, healthy **2.** doughy, gooey *(Nonformal)*, gummy, oozing, pulpy, soupy, squishy, sticky, thick, viscous

pat *adj.* **1.** clichéd, easy, facile, formulaic, glib, neat, primed, ready, rehearsed, standard, systematic, trite, typical **2.** apt, apposite, fitting, germane, meet, opportune, seasonable, suitable, timely, well-chosen *Antonyms:* malapropos, undue **3.** acceptable, adequate, fine, okay *(Nonformal)*, passable, perfect, satisfactory, sufficient *Antonyms:* incomplete, lacking – *adv.* **1.** aptly, dead on, exactly, faultlessly, fittingly, flawlessly, just right, perfectly, plumb, precisely **2.** firmly, steadfastly, strongly, stubbornly – *n.* cake, dab, lump, piece, portion, slab, slice – *v.* caress, dab, fondle, form, massage, pet, rub, stroke, tap, tip, touch

patch *n.* **1.** bandage, cover, dressing, eyepatch, pad **2**. area, field, ground, lot, meadow, pitch, plot, spot, stomping ground *(Nonformal)*, strip, tract **3.** bit, chunk, hunk, piece, remnant, scrap, section, shred **4.** band, beam, belt, ray, ribbon, streak, stream, strip, vein – *v.* **1.** attach, bandage, cover, darn, fix, mend, reinforce, repair, service, sew, stitch **2.** overhaul, rebuild, recondition, reconstruct, retread, revamp **3.** connect, hook up, put through, transfer **4.** adjust, correct, cure, improve, rectify, remedy, right, straighten-out

patchwork *n.* **1.** fabric, needlework, quilt, tapestry **2.** assemblage, collage, gallimaufry, hodgepodge, jumble, medley, miscellany, mishmash, mixture, montage, mosaic, pastiche

patchy *adj.* **1.** erratic, fitful, incongruous, irregular, random, uneven, variable, varying *Antonyms:* constant, even, regular **2.** careless, half-assed *(Nonformal)*, haphazard, heedless, lazy, shabby, sketchy, sloppy, spotty *Antonyms:* exacting, meticulous, precise, thorough

pâté *n.* dip, hors d'oeuvre, paste, purée, spread *Kinds of pâté:* chicken liver, cockaigne, *cretons (Quebec)*, pâté de foie gras, pâté de campagne, pâté en croûte, peppercorn, salmon, seafood, vegetable

patent *adj.* **1.** apparent, barefaced, blatant, clear, clear-cut, conspicuous, crystal-clear, distinct, downright, evident, flagrant, glaring, indisputable, manifest, obvious, open, palpable, plain, straightforward, transparent, unconcealed, unequivocal, unmistakable *Antonyms:* cryptic, latent, murky, obscure **2.** copyright, exclusive, guarded, licensed, owned, proprietary, trademarked *Antonyms:* common, public domain, universal **3.** blanket, broad, diffuse, dispersed, expanded, expansive, far-reaching, outstretched, sprawling, stretching, widespread – *n.* **1.** authorization, control, copyright, franchise, licence, limitation, privilege, protection **2.** badge, certificate, coupon, credential, docket, document, label, marker, notice, pass, passport, permit, receipt, tag, ticket, token, voucher – *v.* copyright, ensure, limit, protect, register, safeguard, secure, trademark

paternal *adj.* **1.** benevolent, caring, concerned, father-like, fatherly, loving, protective, solicitous, vigilant **2.** ancestral, blood, connected, family, kindred, lineal, patrilineal, related **3.** arrogant, bossy *(Nonformal)*, condescending, disdainful, haughty, lordly, overbearing, patronizing, supercilious, superior

path *n.* **1.** arcade, avenue, byway, carrying place, course, esplanade, footpath, game *or* grease trail, inn-to-inn trail, lane, passage, plaza, promenade, road, route, shortcut, thoroughfare, track, trail, walkway **2.** approach, course, manner, method, mode, process, system, way

pathetic *adj.* **1.** affecting, distressing, disturbing, heartbreaking, heartrending, lamentable, melting, moving, poignant, rueful, sad, sentimental, tender, touching, woeful *Antonyms:* amusing, droll, entertaining, funny **2.** crummy *(Nonformal)*, deplorable, feeble, inadequate, meagre, miserable, paltry, petty, piteous, pitiable, pitiful, plaintive, poor, sorry, useless, worthless, wretched *Antonyms:* exacting, skilled, virtuoso

pathos *n.* commiseration, compassion, emotion, feeling, pity, sadness, sentiment, sorrow, sympathy, tenderness

patience *n.* **1.** calm, composure, constancy, cool, diligence, equanimity, forbearance, heart, imperturbability, leniency, moderation, poise, resignation, restraint, self-control, serenity, stoicism, sufferance, tolerance, toleration *Antonyms:* agitation, excitement, impatience, nervousness, restlessness **2.** backbone, bearing, endurance, fortitude, grit, intestinal fortitude, perseverance, persistence, starch, steadfastness, toughness *Nonformal:* guts, legs, starch

patient *adj.* **1.** accommodating, calm, composed, easygoing, enduring, even-tempered, forbearing, forgiving, gentle, imperturbable, indulgent, lenient, mild, mild-tempered, quiet, resigned, self-possessed, serene, stoical, submissive, tolerant, tranquil, uncomplaining, understanding *Antonyms:* anxious, excited, intolerant **2.** determined, diligent, dogged, indefatigable, inexhaustible, persevering, persistent, steadfast, tireless, unflagging, unruffled, untiring, vigorous – *n.* case, convalescent, inmate, invalid, outpatient, shut-in, subject, sufferer, victim

patois *n.* argot, cant, colloquialism, dialect, lingo, lingua franca, idiom, jargon, slang, vernacular

patriarch *n.* **1.** alpha male, boss, chief, grand pooh-bah *(Nonformal)*, head, king, leader, president, ruler, sovereign **2.** advisor, counsellor, guide, guru, leader, master, mentor, pundit, sage, sensei, sophist, teacher **3.** ancestor, elder, father, forefather, paterfamilias, progenitor, sire *Nonformal:* dad, old man **4.** apostle, bishop, deacon, high priest, pontiff, pope, prelate

patrician *adj.* aristocratic, grand, highborn, landed, lordly, noble, royal, titled, upper-class, well-born *Antonyms:* common, servile – *n.* aristocrat, gentleman, gentlewoman, lady, noble, peer, silk stocking, socialite, thoroughbred *Antonyms:* artisan, folks, labourer, masses

patrimony *n.* **1.** background, blood, breeding, heritage, history, lineage, past, roots **2** birthright, dowry, gift, hope chest, inheritance, legacy, share

patriot *n.* chauvinist, citizen, countryman, countrywoman, flag-waver, jingoist, loyalist, nationalist, partisan, statesperson, ultranationalist, zealot *Antonyms*: malcontent, seditionary, traitor, turncoat

patrol *n.* **1.** garrison, guard, lookout, night watchman, officer, police, security guard, sentinel, watchdog, watchperson **2.** defence, policing, protection, rounds, safety, scouting, security, vigilance, watch – *v.* defend, inspect, guard, police, protect, safeguard, survey, watch

patron *n.* **1.** advocate, angel *(Nonformal)*, backer, benefactor, benefactress, booster, champion, defender, financier, guarantor, philanthropist, protector, sponsor, supporter, surety **2.** client, customer, frequenter, habitué, john *(Nonformal)*, regular

patronage *n.* **1.** advocacy, aegis, aid, assistance, auspices, backing, benefaction, encouragement, grant, guardianship, sponsorship, subsidy, support **2.** buying, consumption, purchasing, shopping, trade, traffic **3.** spoils of office *Nonformal:* boondoggle, campaign fund, logrolling, pork barrel politics, public trough, slush fund **4.** airs, condescension, disdain, haughtiness, superciliousness *Antonyms:* deference, regard, respect

patronize *v.* **1.** assist, back, foster, fund, help, maintain, promote, sponsor, subscribe to, support **2.** buy, deal *or* trade with, frequent, purchase **3.** condescend, deign, favour, indulge, overbear, stoop, talk down to

pattern *n.* **1.** decoration, design, device, motif, ornament **2.** arrangement, form, method, order, sequence, shape, sort, structure, style, type, variety **3.** blueprint, diagram, example, figure, guide, illustration, plan, representation, sample, specimen **4.** impression, matrix, model, mould, original, precedent, prototype, template **5.** archetype, beau ideal, embodiment, epitome, essence, exemplar, ideal, paradigm, paragon, standard, touchstone – *v.* **1.** copy, duplicate, emulate, follow, imitate, mirror, parrot, reflect **2.** adorn, beautify, decorate, embellish, furnish, garnish, jazz up *(Nonformal),* trim

paucity *n.* absence, bankruptcy, dearth, deficiency, famine, insufficiency, lack, meagreness, need, paltriness, poverty, scantiness, scarcity, shortage, slightness, sparseness, want *Antonyms:* bounty, opulence, wealth

paunch *n.* abdomen, belly, gut, stomach *Nonformal:* beer belly, breadbasket, love handles, Molson muscle, pot, potbelly, spare tire, swag belly

pauper *n.* almsman, beggar, dependent, destitute, guttersnipe, hobo, indigent, insolvent, loafer, mendicant, ragamuffin, supplicant, street urchin, tramp, vagrant, waif, wastrel *Nonformal:* bum, scarecrow *Antonyms:* benefactor, millionaire, philanthropist

pause *n.* **1.** abeyance, break, break-off, breather, breathing space, ceasefire, cessation, cutoff, deadlock, delay, freeze, halt, hiatus, interim, interlude, intermission, interregnum, interruption, interval, lapse, letup, lull, recess, respite, rest, rest period, standstill, stay, stop, stoppage, suspension, time out, wait **2.** doubt, hesitation, indecision, irresolution, misgiving, qualm, uncertainty, vacillation, wavering – *v.* **1.** break, call time, cease, delay, desist, discontinue, drop, halt, hesitate, hold back, interrupt, rest, sideline, stop, suspend, take five *(Nonformal),* wait *Antonyms:* begin, resume, start **2.** dawdle, deliberate, consider, linger, loiter, ponder, puzzle over, reflect, tarry, think *Antonyms:* hurry, rush, speed

pave *v.* **1.** asphalt, brick, cement, cobble, cover, flag, gravel, lay asphalt *or* concrete, resurface, surface, tar, tile **2.** break ground, break the ice, make room *or* way, open the door, pioneer, prepare, trailblaze

paw *n.* foot, hand *(Nonformal),* pad – *v.* **1.** claw, clutch, dig, feel, finger, grab, handle, hit, pat, rub, scratch, stroke **2.** cop a feel *(Nonformal),* fondle, grope, manhandle, maul, molest

pawn *n.* **1.** agent, device, dupe, henchman, implement, instrument, means, minion, peon, pigeon *(Nonformal),* servant, slave, stooge, tool, vehicle, worker **2.** captive, detainee, hostage, prisoner – *v.* deposit, hazard, hock, mortgage, pledge, risk, stake, wager

pay *n.* **1.** allowance, commission, compensation, competence, defrayment, due, earnings, emolument, fee, hire, honorarium, income, indemnity, payment, perquisite, proceeds, profit, recompensation, recompense, redress, reimbursement, remuneration, reparation, return, reward, salary, satisfaction, scale, settlement, stipend, takings, wage, wages *See also:* **payment** **2.** comeuppance *(Nonformal),* correction, discipline, just rewards, penalty, punishment, punitive measure, retribution – *v.* **1.** bequeath, bestow, compensate, confer, defray, disburse, discharge, dole out, expend, extend, give money, grant, hand over, honour, make payment, meet, offer, present, proffer, put up, recompense, reimburse, remit, remunerate, render, repay, requite, reward, satisfy, settle, spend *Nonformal:* cough up, foot *Antonyms:* keep, retain, save **2.** benefit, bring in, gain, net, produce, profit, win, yield *Antonyms:* fail, lose **3.** exact retribution, requite, retaliate, return, return the favour *(Nonformal),* square accounts, strike back, wreak vengeance

payback *n.* retaliation, retribution, return, revenge, vengeance

payment *n.* **1.** advance, alimony, annuity, award, bounty, cash, defrayment, deposit, disbursement, discharge, fee, outlay, part, payoff, pension, portion, premium, quittance, reckoning, recompense, redress, refund, reimbursement, remittance, remuneration, reparation, repayment, return, reward, salary, settlement, subsidy, sum, support, wage **2.** discipline, just desserts *(Nonformal)*, penalty, punishment, reprisal, requital, restitution, retaliation, revenge *See also:* **pay**

payoff *n.* **1.** climax, clincher, conclusion, consequence, crunch, culmination, final outcome, finale, result, upshot **2.** bribe, ransom *Nonformal:* hush money, kickback, payola **3.** pay, payment, reward, settlement **4.** punishment, reckoning, retaliation, retribution, tit for tat *(Nonformal) See also:* **pay, payment**

peace *n.* **1.** accord, agreement, amity, armistice, brotherhood, calm, calmness, composure, conciliation, concord, congeniality, contentment, equanimity, fraternalism, friendship, good will, harmony, law and order, lull, order, pax, peacefulness, placidity, quiet, reconciliation, relaxation, repose, rest, serenity, silence, stillness, tranquility, treaty, truce, union, unity *Antonyms:* bedlam, discord, disunity, war **2.** inaction, neutrality, nonparticipation, nonresistance, nonviolence, pacification, pacifism

peaceable *adj.* **1.** accommodating, amiable, amicable, conciliatory, friendly, neighbourly, nonviolent, peaceful, peace-loving, placid *Antonyms:* bellicose, hawkish, warmongering **2.** calm, gentle, mild, pacific, quiet, restful, serene, still, tranquil

peaceful *adj.* **1.** amicable, at peace, calm, collected, constant, gentle, halcyon, harmonious, mellow, placid, quiet, restful, serene, still, tranquil, untroubled *Antonyms:* loud, noisy, raucous **2.** co-existing, friendly, neutral, nonviolent, pacifistic, peace-loving *Antonyms:* antagonistic, belligerent, hostile, warlike

peacemaker *n.* ambassador, appeaser, arbitrator, conciliator, counsellor, diplomat, go-between, mediator, moderator, negotiator, pacifier, peacekeeper, reconciler *Antonyms:* agitator, belligerent, malcontent, muckraker

peak *n.* **1.** acme, apex, apogee, capstone, climax, crest, crown, culmination, cusp, height, high point, meridian, pinnacle, summit, top, zenith *Antonyms:* bottom, depression, nadir **2.** cloud-topped *or* snow-clad peak, crag, crest, horn, mountaintop, roof of the world *(Nonformal)*, spur, summit, topmost point *Antonyms:* plain, prairie, steppe, valley **3.** amplitude, breaking point, ceiling, extent, extremity, glass ceiling *(Nonformal)*, height, limit, margin, maximum, plenitude, range, reach, verge – *v.* **1.** cap, climax, crest, culminate, max out *(Nonformal)*, top **2.** burn out, devitalize, enervate, exhaust, flag, languish, sag, sicken, waste away, weaken, wither *Commonly misused:* **peek**

peaked *adj.* **1.** ailing, bilious, burned or washed out, emaciated, exhausted, ill, pale, pasty, poorly, sallow, sick, sickly, tired, wan *Antonyms:* fresh, rugged, vigorous **2.** acute, crested, jagged, pinnacled, pointed, spiked, spire-like, tapered

peal *n.* blast, carillon, chime, clamour, clang, clap, crash, resounding, reverberation, ring, ringing, rumble, sound, thunder, tintinnabulation – *v.* call, knell, resonate, resound, ring out, sound, trill, trumpet

pearly *adj.* alabaster, creamy, fair, frosted, iridescent, ivory, milky, off-white, opalescent, opaline, pearl, silver

peasant *n.* **1.** bogtrotter *(Irish)*, cottier, farmer, farm worker, *habitant (Quebec)*, *muzhik (Russian)*, ploughboy *(Nonformal)*, provincial, rustic, sharecropper *Antonyms:* bourgeois, city dweller, urbanite **2.** boor, lout, oaf, roughneck, vulgarian *Nonformal:* bumpkin, clod, cornpone, hayseed, hick, redneck, rube, yahoo, yokel

peck *n.* **1.** bite, dig, hit, jab, pick, poke, strike, stroke, tap **2.** buss, kiss, osculation, smack *Nonformal:* smooch, wet on – *v.* **1.** bite, hit, jab, poke, prick, stick, strike, tap **2.** pick up, pinch, pluck, remove **3.** kiss, osculate, smack, smooch *(Nonformal)* **4.** chew, eat, nibble, pick at

peculiar *adj.* **1.** abnormal, bizarre, curious, eccentric, exceptional, extraordinary, freakish, funny, odd, idiosyncratic, offbeat, outlandish, quaint, queer, singular, strange, surreal, uncommon, unconventional, uncustomary, unusual, weird, wonderful

Nonformal: bent, far-out, flaky, freaky, kinky, kooky, oddball, way-out, wingy *Antonyms:* commonplace, conforming, everyday, expected, familiar **2.** appropriate, belonging, characteristic, distinct, distinctive, distinguishing, endemic, exclusive, individual, intrinsic, local, particular, private, proper, quintessential, restricted, separate, specific, unique *Antonyms:* common, general, unspecific

peculiarity *n.* **1.** abnormality, bizarreness, eccentricity, foible, freakishness, kink *(Nonformal)*, oddity, odd trait, quirk, twist, unusualness **2.** attribute, characteristic, distinctiveness, feature, idiosyncrasy, mannerism, mark, particularity, property, quality, singularity, slant, specialty, trait

pecuniary *adj.* bread-and-butter *(Nonformal)*, bursarial, capital, commercial, economic, financial, fiscal, monetary, nummary

pedagogic *adj.* academic, didactic, dogmatic, edifying, educational, instructive, learned, pedantic, professorial, scholastic, sophisticating, teaching, tutorial

pedagogue *n.* academic, don, educator, guru, instructor, lecturer, master, professor, schoolteacher, sophist, swami, teacher, tutor

pedantic *adj.* **1.** academic, bluestocking, bookish, didactic, educated, erudite, intellectual, learned, pedagogic, philosophical, professorial, scholastic, studious **2.** bombastic, formal, high-flown, inflated, overblown, pompous, pretentious, sententious, stilted *Antonyms:* everyday, informal, pedestrian **3.** captious, exact, fastidious, finicky, fussy, hidebound, nit-picking, pettifogging, precise, rigid *Antonyms:* careless, heedless, slack

peddle *v.* **1.** canvass, deal, dispense, hawk, huckster, market, push, sell, solicit, trade, truck, vend **2.** advocate, market, promote, recommend

peddler *n.* butter and eggman, dealer, fruit and vegetable man, hawker, huckster, merchant, monger, pusher *(Nonformal)*, salesperson, trader, vendor

pedestal *n.* base, column, footing, foundation, pillar, podium, shaft, support

pedestrian *adj.* **1.** banal, boring, common, dull, hackneyed, humdrum, mediocre, mundane, platitudinous, prosaic, trite, unimaginative, uninspired *Nonformal:* ho-hum, run-of-the-mill, wishy-washy *Antonyms:* exciting, fascinating, interesting, remarkable **2.** civil, commonplace, demotic, everyday, ordinary, plebian, popular, proletarian, public *Antonyms:* aristocratic, high-flown, patrician **3.** ambulatory, bipedal, hiking, negotiating, perambulating, peregrine, strolling, walking – *n.* ambler, biped, hiker, jaywalker, jogger, passerby, stroller, walker

pedigree *n.* **1.** ancestry, blood, breed, clan, descent, dynasty, extraction, family, genealogy, heredity, heritage, inheritance, line, lineage, origin, parentage, race, stock **2.** blue book, family tree, genealogical register, social register

pedigreed *adj.* full-blooded, pure-blood, purebred, *purelaine (Quebec)*, thoroughbred, true-blue

peek *n.* blink, glance, glimpse, look, peep, sight *Nonformal:* gander, look-see *Antonyms:* fixate, oogle, stare – *v.* glance, glimpse, look, peep, peer, snatch, snoop, spy, squint *Commonly misused:* **peak**

peel *n.* bark, cover, covering, husk, peeling, pellicle, rind, shell, shuck, skin, zest – *v.* **1.** clean, exfoliate, flake, moult, pare, scale, shuck, skin, strip, uncover **2.** divest, expose oneself, shed, undress

peep *n.* **1.** call, chirp, cry, noise, sound, squeak **2.** aperture, crack, crevice, hole, keyhole, knothole, peephole, slit **3.** advent, beginning, crack, dawn, genesis, onset, opening, start – *v.* **1.** glimpse, look, peek, spy, squint **2.** chatter, cheep, chirrup, chuck, coo, hoot, pipe, tweet, twitter **3.** appear briefly, become visible, emerge, poke out, show partially

peer *n.* **1.** associate, coequal, colleague, companion, compeer, comrade, confrere, equal, fellow, like, match, rival **2.** aristocrat, baron, baroness, baronet, chief, dame, dignitary, duchess, duke, earl, gentleman, gentlewoman, lady, lord, marchioness, marquess, marquis, marquise, noble, nabob, peeress, rajah, seigneur, viscount – *v.* **1.** beam, eye, focus, gape, gaze, glare, inspect, look, peep, pry, scan, scrutinize, spy, squint, stare *Nonformal:* gawk, rubberneck **2.** appear, crop up, emerge, loom, occur, rise, surface, threaten

peerless *adj.* best, greatest, incomparable, matchless, nonpareil, paramount, perfect, preeminent, *sans pareil (French),* sovereign, super, superior, supreme, transcendent, unequalled, unique, unmatched, unparalleled, unrivaled, unsurpassed *Antonyms:* basest, lowest, worst

peeve *n.* annoyance, complaint, disturbance, grievance, gripe, irritation, nuisance, pet peeve – *v.* aggravate, anger, annoy, bother, disturb, exasperate, gall, get, grieve, hack, irk, irritate, miff, nettle, pique, provoke, put out, rile, roil, upset, vex *Nonformal:* bug, bum, burn, hassle, needle, steam *Antonyms:* calm, pacify, placate, smooth, soothe

peevish *adj.* **1.** acrimonious, argumentative, cantankerous, captious, censorious, cranky, cross, crotchety, crusty, difficult, fractious, ill-humoured, irritable, ornery, out-of-sorts, petulant, querulous, spiteful, sullen, surly, testy, troublesome, vexatious **2.** aggrieved, agitated, annoyed, bothered, disconcerted, discontent, fretful, inflamed, infuriated, irked, mad, maddened, malcontent, offended, taken aback, unhappy, upset

peewee *adj.* bantam, diminutive, knee-high, Lilliputian, little, miniature, minute, petite, small, tiny, wee, weeny *(Nonformal) Antonyms:* big, huge, large, massive

peg *n.* **1.** bolt, dowel, pin, stick **2.** degree, division, gradation, level, mark, notch, rank, rung, step **3.** basis, excuse, motive, pretext, rationale, reason, ulterior motive, why – *v.* **1.** attach, clinch, fasten, fix, join, make fast, secure, tighten **2.** categorize, classify, label, pigeonhole, slot, typecast **3.** circumscribe, define, delimit, delineate, designate, mark *or* mete out, stakeout **4.** cast, chuck, fling, pitch, throw, toss, sling, whip *(Nonformal)* **5.** dig, drive, labour, perform, punch away *(Nonformal),* push, strive, work

pejorative *adj.* belittling, contemptuous, debasing, degrading, deprecatory, derisive, derogatory, detracting, disparaging, insulting, irreverent, negative, rude, slighting, uncomplimentary, unpleasant *Antonyms:* complimentary, extolling, praising

pellet *n.* ammo *(Nonformal),* ammunition, ball, buckshot, bullet, shell, shot, slug

pell-mell *adj.* chaotic, confused, disordered, haphazard, higgledy-piggledy *(Nonformal),* indiscriminate, motley, ragtag, random, topsy-turvy, tumultuous – *adv.* carelessly, foolishly, hastily, headlong, heedlessly, hurriedly, impetuously, impulsively, precipitously, rashly, recklessly, slapdash, thoughtlessly, tumultuously – *n.* anarchy, chaos, clutter, confusion, disarray, disorder, ferment, helter-skelter, huddle, jumble, muddle, pandemonium, snarl, tumult, turmoil, upheaval *Nonformal:* hugger-mugger, kerfuffle

pelt *n.* coat, fell, fur, hair, hide, membrane, parfleche, pelage, pellicle, rawhide, skin, vair, wool – *v.* **1.** batter, beat, belt, drub, hammer, lambaste, pound, pummel, strike, swat, thrash, wallop **2.** assail, cast, bombard, fling, pepper, pitch, rain, shower, stone, throw, volley **3.** abuse, belittle, berate, blister, castigate, chastise, excoriate, insult, upbraid *Nonformal:* dis, smear, trash *Antonyms:* applaud, compliment, extol, honour **4.** bustle, dart, dash, flee, hurry, hustle, run, rush, scamper, scurry, speed *Nonformal:* scoot, skedaddle *Antonyms:* dawdle, linger, saunter, stroll

pen *n.* **1.** close, coop, corral, enclosure, fence, fold, hedge, hutch, sty, wall **2.** cage, jail, lockup, prison *Nonformal:* can, clink, cooler, penalty box, stir *See also:* **penitentiary** **3.** ballpoint, fountain pen, marker, nib, pencil, quill, writing tool – *v.* **1.** box, cage, case, close in, confine, coop up, corral, enclose, fence in, hedge, hem in, incarcerate, mew, shed *(Nonformal),* shut in **2.** author, autograph, compose, contrive, design, draft, draw up, engross, jot down, script, write

penal *adj.* chastening, corrective, disciplinary, penalizing, punitive, punishing, reformatory, retributive

penalize *v.* **1.** castigate, chasten, chastise, condemn, correct, discipline, punish, scold *Antonyms:* award, compensate, indemnify **2.** bench *(Nonformal)*, check, hamper, hamstring, handicap, hinder, restrain, send to the box *(Hockey)*, undermine **3.** deduct, dock, fine, mulct

penalty *n.* **1.** correction, disciplinary action, dues, infliction, judgment, penance, punishment, punitive measure, retribution, sentence **2.** compensatory damage, fine, forfeiture, payment, price **3.** breach of conduct, foul, offence *Football penalties:* clipping, delay of game, face mask, giving one the business *(Nonformal)*, holding, illegal formation, illegal motion *or* position *or* procedure, ineligible receiver downfield, kick-catching interference, more than 11 players on the field, offside, pass interference, personal foul, piling on, roughing the kicker, tripping, unnecessary roughness, unsportsmanlike conduct *Hockey penalties:* bench minor, boarding, butt ending, charging, cross checking, delay of game, delayed, elbowing, falling on the puck, fighting, game misconduct, handling the puck, high-sticking, holding, hooking, icing, interference, kneeing, man in the crease, match penalty, major *or* five-minute penalty, minor *or* two-minute penalty, misconduct, offside, penalty shot, roughing, slashing, spearing, third man in, too many men, tripping, unsportsmanlike conduct **4.** check, curb, disadvantage, discipline, handicap, hindrance, impediment

penance *n.* amends, atonement, contrition, flagellation, hair shirt, *mea culpa (Latin)*, mortification, punishment, reparation, repentance, restitution

penchant *n.* affection, affinity, attachment, bent, bias, disposition, fondness, inclination, itch, leaning, liking, lust, partiality, predilection, proclivity, propensity, taste, tendency, turn, weakness, yearning *Nonformal:* sweet tooth, yen

pendant *n.* **1.** cameo, chain, earring, lavaliere, locket, medallion, necklace, ornament, tassel **2.** analogue, correlate, correspondent, counterpart, double, match, other, parallel, reciprocal, twin *Commonly misused:* **pendent**

pendent *adj.* **1.** dangling, drooping, flagging, hanging, pendulous, suspended, swaying **2.** beetling, extending, jutting, overhanging, projecting, protruding *Commonly misused:* **pendant**

pending *adj.* **1.** at hand, awaiting, expectant, forthcoming, hanging, imminent, impending, in line, in the works, looming, next, on board, on the horizon **2.** immature, incomplete, undecided, undetermined, unfinished, unready, unresolved, unsettled, up in the air *(Nonformal) Antonyms:* completed, fulfilled, realized

pendulous *adj.* **1.** dangling, drooping, hanging, pendant, pending, suspended, swinging, undulating **2.** faltering, hesitant, indecisive, irresolute, pausing, undecided, unsettled, unsure, vacillating, waffling, wavering

penetrate *v.* **1.** bore, drill, impale, insert, jab, perforate, pierce, prick, probe, puncture, ream, spear, stab, stick **2.** barge *or* break *or* bust in *(Nonformal)*, broach, encroach, enter, go *or* filter *or* pass through, infiltrate, intrude, invade, trespass **3.** broadcast, circulate, diffuse, disseminate, impregnate, permeate, pervade, saturate, spread, suffuse **4.** comprehend, discern, fathom, grasp, perceive, register, understand **5.** affect, disturb, impress, influence, move, reach, rouse, stir, strike, sway, touch, upset

penetrating *adj.* **1.** acute, astute, bright, discerning, discriminating, incisive, intelligent, keen, penetrative, perceptive, perspicacious, profound, quick, quick-witted, sagacious, searching, sharp, sharp-witted, shrewd *Antonyms:* dull, obtuse, shallow, stupid, unperceptive **2.** biting, caustic, critical, cutting, edged, harsh, pointed, pungent, sharp, stinging, trenchant, vitriolic *Antonyms:* easy, gentle, lenient **3.** entering, forcing, infiltrating, intrusive, permeating, pervasive, piercing, puncturing

penetration *n.* **1.** entrance, infiltration, ingress, insertion, introduction, intrusion, invasion, piercing, poking, probing, stabbing **2.** diffusion, imbuement, impregnation, infusion, permeation, saturation, spreading, suffusion **3.** acumen, acuteness, awareness, cognizance, discernment, insight, keenness, perception, perspicacity, sentience, understanding **4.** deepness, depth, distance, extent, measurement, reach

penitence *n.* anguish, attrition, compunction, contrition, debasement, degradation, distress, grief, humbling, humiliation, penance, qualm, regret, remorse, repentance, ruefulness, sadness, self-castigation, self-condemnation, self-punishment, self-reproach, shame, sorrow

penitent *adj.* abject, apologetic, attritional, compunctious, conscience-stricken, contrite, penitential, regretful, remorseful, repentant, rueful, shamed, sorrowful, sorry *Antonyms:* callous, impenitent, unrepentant

penitentiary *n.* bastille, brig, correctional institution, gaol, jail, keep, penal institution, prison, reformatory, stockade *Nonformal:* big house, hoosegow, Kingston, pen, slammer, stir

pennant *n.* banner, bunting, colour, decoration, emblem, ensign, flag, gonfalon, insignia, jack, oriflamme, pennon, standard, streamer

penniless *adj.* bankrupt, destitute, impecunious, impoverished, indigent, lacking, moneyless, needy, pauperized, penurious, poor, poverty-stricken, ruined *Nonformal:* cleaned out, dead broke, dirt poor, flat, flat broke, on the bum, strapped, tapped out *Antonyms:* affluent, moneyed, rich, wealthy

pension *n.* **1.** allowance, annuity, cheque, money, payment, premium, retirement benefits *or* income, reward, social security **2.** allotment, award, contribution, endowment, fellowship, financial aid, grant, honorarium, remittance, reward, stipend, subsidy, tribute **3.** boarding house, hostel, inn, lodging, shelter

pensive *adj.* **1.** absorbed, abstracted, cogitative, contemplative, dreamy, grave, lost in thought, meditative, musing, pondering, preoccupied, reflective, ruminating, ruminative, serious, sober, solemn, speculative, thinking, thoughtful, wistful, withdrawn **2.** blue, doleful, down in the dumps *(Nonformal)*, glum, melancholy, mournful, neurasthenic, sad, saddened, sorrowful, upset, woebegone, wretched *Antonyms:* carefree, frivolous, gay, happy, joyous

penurious *adj.* **1.** begrudging, cheap, chintzy, close, close-fisted, frugal, miserly, parsimonious, prudent, stingy, tightfisted *Antonyms:* generous, open-handed, philanthropic **2.** bankrupt, bereft, broke, empty-handed, needy, penniless, poor *Antonyms:* affluent, flush, rich **3.** deficient, devoid, inadequate, insufficient, meager, scanty, scarce, shy, sparse, thin, wanting *Antonyms:* abundant, overflowing, plentiful

people *n.* **1.** bodies, boys, girls, Homo sapiens, humanity, humankind, human race, humans, individuals, *inuit (Inuktitut)*, man, mankind, men, mortals, persons, woman, womankind, women **2.** commoners, crowd, everyday people, folk, general public, grassroots, hoi polloi, horde, masses, mob, multitude, plebians, populace, proletariat, rabble, riffraff, the mundane *Nonformal:* herd, ragtag and bobtail **3.** body politic, citizens, constituency, public, the enfranchised, voters **4.** commonwealth, compatriots, countryman, denizens, dwellers, inhabitants, populace, population, residents, subjects **5.** breed, culture, distinct society, ethnic group, nation, race, society, tribe **6.** ancestors, clan, family, house, kin, kinsfolk, lineage, relations, relatives, stock **7.** collective, community, group, guild, members, party, profession, subscription, union – *v.* colonize, fill, inhabit, occupy, populate, settle, take up

pep *n.* animation, bite, buoyancy, cogency, drive, effectiveness, élan, energy, force, gusto, high spirits, impact, life, liveliness, potency, punch, spirit, verve, vigour, vim, vitality, vivacity, zest *Nonformal:* chutzpah, moxie, snap, starch, zip – *v.* animate, arouse, embolden, energize, fire up *(Nonformal)*, galvanize, imbue, inflame, inspire, invigorate, stimulate, vitalize *Antonyms:* enervate, deflate, tire, wear out

pepper *n.* **1.** black *or* white pepper, cayenne, condiment, flavouring, paprika, seasoning, spice **2.** capsicum, vegetable *Kinds of pepper:* banana, bell, chile, green, habanero, Italian, jalapeño, pickled, pimento, red, Scotch Bonnet, sweet, wax, yellow – *v.* **1.** accentuate, dash, flavour, heat, season, spice, treat **2.** discharge, fling, hurl, inundate, pelt, rain, scatter, spatter, spray, sprinkle, volley **3.** accent, dot, interject, intersperse, mark, punctuate

peppery *adj.* **1.** burning, fiery, hot, piquant, pungent, racy, seasoned, sharp, snappy, spicy, zesty *Antonyms:* bland, insipid, mild, tasteless **2.** crotchety, hasty, high-strung, irascible, irritable, peevish, quick-tempered, testy **3.** astringent, cutting, incisive, mordant, pointed, quick, sharp, stinging, strong, tart, trenchant, vitriolic

peppy *adj.* **1.** active, alert, animate, animated, bright, keen, lively, perky, rarin' to go *(Nonformal)*, sparkling, spirited, sprightly, vigorous, vivacious **2.** fast, fleet-footed, quick, rapid, speedy, spry, swift, winged *Antonyms:* listless, slow, sluggish

perceive *v.* **1.** appreciate, apprehend, comprehend, deduce, detect, digest, discern, discover, distinguish, divine, fathom, handle, gather, grasp, identify, intuit, know, learn, mark, mind, note, penetrate, read, realize, understand **2.** behold, espy, feel, makeout, notice, observe, recognize, regard, see, sense, smell, spot, spy, taste, touch

percentage *n.* **1.** allotment, allowance, bite, bonus, chunk, commission, corner, cut, discount, duty, end, fee, interest, payoff, piece, points, portion, proportion, quota, rake-off, royalty, section, slice, split, winnings *Nonformal:* juice, piece of the action, shake, squeeze **2.** division, percent, rate, ratio

perceptible *adj.* apparent, appreciable, audible, clear, cognizable, comprehensible, detectable, discernible, distinct, distinguishable, evident, legible, noticeable, observable, obvious, ostensible, palpable, perceivable, perspicuous, recognizable, salient, sensible, tangible, understandable, visible *Antonyms:* hidden, inappreciable, inconspicuous, undetectable, unnoticeable

perception *n.* **1.** feel, hearing, reception, sensation, sight, smell, taste, touch, vision **2.** apprehension, awareness, cognition, comprehension, consciousness, grasp, knowledge, realization, sense, understanding, wisdom **3.** acuteness, cleverness, discernment, discretion, discrimination, insight, penetration, perspicacity, sagacity, sharpness **4.** clairvoyance, divination, hunch, inkling, insight, instinct, intuition, premonition **5.** *aperçu (French)*, brainchild *(Nonformal)*, concept, flash, idea, image, impression, notion, observation, opinion, plan, take, view, viewpoint

perceptive *adj.* acute, alert, astute, aware, brainy, bright, bright-eyed, clever, conscious, discerning, incisive, insightful, intelligent, intuitive, keen, knowing, knowledgeable, observant, penetrating, percipient, perspicacious, quick, rational, responsive, sagacious, sage, sapient, sensitive, shrewd, understanding *Nonformal:* on the ball, quick as a whip, sharp as a tack *Antonyms:* dense, dull, insensitive, thick

perch *n.* lounge, resting-place, roost, seat, station, stoop, vantage point – *v.* alight, balance, land, light, rest, roost, set down, settle, sit atop *or* on, squat, touch down

percipience *n.* acuity, cognizance, foresight, insight, intuition, judgment, knowledge, penetration, perception, perspicacity, sagacity, sensibility, understanding

percussion *n.* **1.** beat, drumming, rhythm *Some Percussion instruments:* bells, carillon, castanets, celesta, chimes, clappers, cowbells, cymbals, drum, gamelan, glockenspiel, gong, handbell, hi-hat, maraca, marimba, metallophone, ozark harp, rattle, shaker, sleighbells, spoons, tabor, tambourine, timbrel, tam-tam, triangle, vibes *(Nonformal)*, vibraphone, xylophone *See also:* **drum**, **instrument** **2.** blow, bump, collision, contusion, impact, jar, jolt, shock

perdition *n.* **1.** abyss, damnation, Hades, hell, inferno, Tartarus, underworld *Antonyms:* Eden, heaven, paradise, utopia **2.** annihilation, devastation, downfall, extirpation, havoc, loss, obliteration, rack and ruin *(Nonformal)*, ruination, suffering, torment *See also:* **hell**

peremptory *adj.* **1.** absolute, categorical, certain, conclusive, decisive, definite, final, irrefutable, irrevocable, mandatory, obligatory, unconditional, unquestionable *Antonyms:* debatable, disputable, moot **2.** arrogant, assertive, authoritative, autocratic, bombastic, bossy *(Nonformal)*, commanding, compelling, despotic, dictatorial, domineering, emphatic, high-handed, imperative, imperious, magisterial, masterful, obstinate, officious, overbearing, pontifical, Procrustean, rigorous, severe, tyrannical *Antonyms:* lenient, tolerant, yielding

perennial *adj.* **1.** annual, every year, regular, yearlong, yearly **2.** abiding, enduring, eternal, evergreen, everlasting, immortal, immutable, imperishable, lasting, lifelong, long-lasting, long-lived, longstanding, permanent, sustained, unchanging, undying, unfailing **3.** ceaseless, chronic, constant, continual, continuing, incessant, perpetual, persistent, recurrent, unceasing, uninterrupted

perfect *adj.* **1.** absolute, complete, completed, entire, finished, full, intact, integral, plenary, pure, sound, unadulterated, unalloyed, unbroken, undamaged, unimpaired, unmitigated, whole *Antonyms:* broken, fragmented, incomplete **2.** beyond compare, blameless, exemplary, faultless, flawless, ideal, immaculate, infallible, matchless, model, spotless, stainless, sublime, supreme, unblemished, unequalled *Antonyms:* flawed, insufficient, problematic **3.** accomplished, adept, consummate, deft, experienced, expert, gifted, masterful, polished, practiced, proficient, skilful, skilled *Antonyms:* gauche, incompetent, maladroit **4.** accurate, appropriate, certain, correct, definite, exact, express, faithful, fit, precise, proper, requisite, strict, suitable, textbook, true, unerring *Antonyms:* fallacious, imprecise, unsound **5.** categorical, comprehensive, genuine, out and out, positive, rank, sheer, thorough, total, utter **6.** convincing, effective, forceful, groundbreaking, impressive, influential, persuasive, powerful, practical *Antonyms:* inadequate, useless, worthless **7.** august, capital, excellent, extraordinary, fabulous, fantastic, great, lovely, outright, remarkable, splendid, terrific *Nonformal:* cool, fab, wicked – *v.* **1.** accomplish, achieve, advance, better, carry out, complete, consummate, crown, effect, enhance, finish, fulfill, perform, realize, upgrade **2.** cultivate, develop, hone, idealize, improve, polish, refine, round, smooth *Antonym:* deface, mar, vandalize

perfection *n.* **1.** completeness, entirety, integrity, unity, wholeness **2.** exactness, excellence, exquisiteness, faultlessness, flawlessness, impeccability, infallibility, perfectness, precision *Antonyms:* defectiveness, imperfection **3.** crown, ideal, model, paragon, pinnacle, preeminence, standard, superiority, transcendence **4.** extremity, height, limit, maximum, peak *Antonyms:* base, nadir **5.** accomplishment, achievement, actualization, completion, consummation, crowning, culmination, development, end, evolution, fulfillment, maturity

perfectly *adv.* **1.** admirably, correctly, excellently, exquisitely, faultlessly, flawlessly, ideally, impeccably, infallibly, spotlessly, superbly, supremely, wonderfully **2.** absolutely, completely, entirely, fully, thoroughly, totally, utterly, wholly *Antonyms:* partially, piecemeal

perfidious *adj.* conniving, deceitful, disloyal, double-crossing *(Nonformal)*, duplicitous, faithless, false, hypocritical, insidious, seditious, traitorous, treacherous, treasonous, two-faced, unfaithful, unscrupulous

perforate *v.* bore, drill, drive, jab, penetrate, permeate, pierce, probe, punch, puncture, shish kebab *(Nonformal)*, spear, stab, stick

perform *v.* **1.** accomplish, achieve, act, behave, bring about *or* off, carry out *or* through, complete, comply, conduct, discharge, do, effect, execute, fulfill, function, labour, pull off *(Nonformal)*, transact, work **2.** act out, appear as, display, dramatize, emote, enact, entertain, exhibit, give, ham, impersonate, offer, personate, play, playact, present, produce, put on, recite, render, represent, show, sing, stage *Nonformal:* chew the scenery, tread the boards

performance *n.* **1.** act, appearance, audition, burlesque, ceremony, concert, custom, display, drama, engagement, entertainment, exhibition, extravaganza, gig *(Nonformal)*, interpretation, medley, offering, opera, pageant, play, portrayal, presentation, production, program, recital, rehearsal, representation, revue, rite, set, show, skit, special, spectacle, stunt **2.** ability, conduct, effectiveness, efficacy, efficiency, execution, exercise, functioning, operation, practice, pursuit, working **3.** accomplishment, achievement, action, deed, enterprise, exploit, initiative

performer *n.* **1.** acrobat, actor, actress, busker, clown, comedian, dancer, entertainer, headliner, impersonator, juggler, magician, mime, musician, singer, stripper *(Nonformal)*, thespian **2.** cog, doer, drudge, labourer, operator, worker **3.** faker, fraud, phoney *(Nonformal)*, poser, pretender

perfume *n.* aftershave, aroma, aromatic, attar, balm, bouquet, cologne, *eau de toilette (French)*, essence, fragrance, incense, odour, oil, sachet, scent, smell, spice, sweetness, toilet water *Kinds of perfume:* ambergris, bergamot, camomile, civet, jasmine, lavender, musk, patchouli, rose, sandalwood

perfunctory *adj.* **1.** careless, casual, cursory, haphazard, impersonal, inattentive, indifferent, involuntary, mechanical, nonchalant, routine, shallow, standard, stock, superficial *Antonyms:* ardent, attentive, careful, diligent, thorough **2.** apathetic, bland, dreary, dull, insipid, laid-back *(Nonformal)*, lifeless, listless, sluggish, soporific, torpid *Antonyms:* ebullient, enthusiastic, exuberant, vigorous

perhaps *adv.* as the case may be, conceivably, feasibly, imaginably, maybe, peradventure, perchance, plausibly, possibly, reasonably

peril *n.* danger, endangerment, exposure, foreboding, hazard, jeopardy, liability, menace, openness, risk, risky business *(Nonformal)*, threat, uncertainty, vulnerability *Antonyms:* invulnerability, safety, security – *v.* endanger, imperil, jeopardize, menace, risk, threaten *Antonym:* guard, protect, watch over

perilous *adj.* chancy, dangerous, delicate, exposed, hazardous, insecure, menacing, precarious, risky, threatening, touchy, treacherous, uncertain, unsafe, unsound, unstable, unsteady, vulnerable *Nonformal:* dicey, hairy, iffy, on thin ice, touch and go *Antonyms:* protected, safe, secure

perimeter *n.* ambit, border, borderline, boundary, bounds, brim, brink, circuit, circumference, confines, edge, fringe, hem, limit, margin, outer limits, outline, pale, periphery, skirt, verge *Antonyms:* centre, core, heart, hub

period *n.* **1.** century, course, cycle, day, decade, eon, epoch, era, instant, interval, juncture, lapse of time, millennium, moment, month, point, quarter, season, semester, session, span, spell, stage, stretch, term, time, time frame, week, year **2.** cessation, closing, conclusion, end, ending, finale, limit, omega, termination **3.** flow, menses, menstruation *Nonformal:* monthlies, the curse, time of the month **4.** dot, end *or* full stop, punctuation mark, stop

periodic *adj.* **1.** alternate, annual, centennial, cyclic, cyclical, daily, epochal, fitful, fluctuating, hourly, isochronal, monthly, orbital, perennial, periodical, recurrent, recurring, regular, repeated, rhythmic, routine, seasonal, serial, weekly, yearly **2.** desultory, infrequent, intermittent, occasional, once in a blue moon *(Nonformal)*, random, sporadic *Antonyms:* constant, steady, uniform

periodical *n.* journal, magazine, serial *Kinds of periodical:* almanac, annual, bimonthly, biweekly, daily, dossier, fortnightly, gazette, house organ, monthly, organ, quarterly, register, review, trade journal *or* magazine, weekly, yearbook, yearly *Nonformal:* e-zine, fanzine, zine

peripatetic *adj.* ambulant, itinerant, migratory, mobile, nomadic, peregrine, roadbound, roaming, roving, travelling, vagabond, vagrant, wandering, wayfaring *Antonyms:* rooted, static – *n.* drifter, *flâneur (French)*, hobo *(Nonformal)*, migrant, nomad, pilgrim, rover, transient, traveller, wayfarer

peripheral *adj.* **1.** borderline, external, outer, outermost, outside, surface, *Antonyms:* central, medial **2.** exterior, incidental, irrelevant, marginal, minor, secondary, superficial, tangential, unimportant *Antonyms:* essential, necessary – *n.* hardware *Computer peripherals:* drawing tablet, fax machine, joystick, keyboard, microphone, modem, monitor, mouse, printer, removable drive, scanner, speakers, trackball

periphery *n.* **1.** ambit, border, boundary, brim, brink, circuit, circumference, compass, covering, edge, fringe, hem, ledge, margin, outside, outskirts, pale, perimeter, rim, skirt, verge *Antonyms:* heart, hub, nucleus **2.** bark, carapace, coat, cover, crust, exoskeleton, film, fur, hide, pelage, shell, skin, surface

perish *v.* die, decease, end, expire, leave, pass *Nonformal:* buy the farm, croak, flatline, give up the ghost, kick the bucket *Antonyms:* live, survive, thrive

perishable *adj.* **1.** decayable, destructible, easily spoiled, nondurable, spoilable, temporary, transitory, unstable *Antonyms:* durable, lasting, long-lived **2.** corporeal, earthly, ephemeral, human, mortal, passing, short-lived, worldly

perjure *v.* bear false witness, deceive, delude, falsify, forswear, incriminate oneself, lie, mislead, prevaricate, trick

perk *n.* advantage, benefit, bonus, compensation, dividend, extra, fringe benefit, gratuity, lagniappe, largesse, money, pay, payment, perquisite, plus, privilege, recompense, remuneration, reward, stipend, tip *Nonformal:* gravy, points *Antonym:* downside, fine, penalty – *v.* **1.** boost, elevate, hoist, lift, raise, rear *Antonyms:* drop, lower **2.** arrange, clean, dress, groom, make one's toilet, preen, primp *Nonformal:* jazz *or* spiff *or* spruce up, trick out

perky *adj.* **1.** active, alert, animated, aware, bouncy, bright, brisk, bubbly, buoyant, cheerful, cheery, chipper *(Nonformal)*, effervescent, frisky, jaunty, lively, pert, spirited, sprightly, sunny, upbeat, vivacious *Antonyms:* doleful, dour, gloomy, woeful **2.** bold, brash, cocky, positive, secure, self assured *or* confident, sure

permanence *n.* constancy, constant, continuity, durability, endurance, entrenchment, fixedness, fixity, immovability, immutability, longevity, perpetuity, perseverance, resilience, stability, stasis

permanent *adj.* abiding, constant, continual, durable, enduring, everlasting, fixed, forever, immutable, imperishable, indestructible, lasting, long-lasting, perennial, perpetual, persistent, set, stable, steadfast, unchanging, unfading *Nonformal:* for keeps, like a rock *Antonyms:* brief, changing, ephemeral, finite, short-lived, transient – *n.* curl, curlicue, frizz, hairdo, permanent wave *Nonformal:* do, perm, wave

permeable *adj.* absorbent, absorptive, passable, penetrable, porous, soakable, sponge-like, spongy *Antonyms:* impregnable, invincible, steady

permeate *v.* diffuse, fill, filter, go through, imbue, impregnate, infiltrate, infuse, ingrain, invade, penetrate, percolate, pervade, saturate, seep, soak, spread, steep, suffuse, transfuse

permissible *adj.* acceptable, admissible, allowable, approved, authorized, endorsed, lawful, legal, legitimate, permitted, proper, sanctioned, tolerable *Antonyms:* banned, forbidden, illegal, illicit, prohibited

permission *n.* acceptance, acknowledgment, admission, admittance, agreement, allowance, approval, assent, authority, authorization, avowal, backing, carte blanche, clearance, concession, concurrence, consent, dispensation, empowerment, endorsement, freedom, imprimatur, indulgence, leave, liberty, licence, permit, privilege, promise, ratification, safe-conduct, sanction, support, tolerance, toleration, verification, visa, warrant *Nonformal:* go-ahead, green light, okay *Antonyms:* disallowance, forbiddance, rejection

permissive *adj.* agreeable, allowing, easygoing, free, indulgent, lax, lenient, liberal, open-minded, tolerant *Antonyms:* authoritarian, domineering, rigid, strict

permit *n.* **1.** allowance, approval, authorization, consent, liberty, permission, privilege, right, sanction, warrant **2.** admission, card, certificate, charter, degree, diploma, entrance, document, *laissez-passer (French)*, letter, paper, pass, passport, ticket, visa, title, voucher – *v.* **1.** abet, acquiesce, agree, allow, bless, concede, concur, condone, consent to, enable, endorse, give leave, indulge, suffer, tolerate *Nonformal:* go for, okay, rubber stamp **2.** authorize, decree, establish, franchise, grant, legalize, license, ordain, pass, privilege, sanctify, sanction, sign, validate, warrant *Antonyms:* embargo, forbid, prescribe, prohibit, veto

permutation *n.* alteration, change, conversion, metamorphosis, modification, mutation, rearrangement, reconstruction, transformation, transmogrification, vicissitude *Antonyms:* constancy, immutability, permanence

pernicious *adj.* **1.** baleful, damaging, dangerous, deadly, deleterious, destructive, detrimental, devastating, fatal, harmful, hurtful, injurious, killing, lethal, mortal, poisonous, ruinous, toxic, venomous *Antonyms:* ameliorating, beneficial, benign **2.** awful, bad, evil, dreadful, iniquitous, maleficent, malevolent, malicious, malignant, nefarious, noisome, noxious, odious, offensive, pestiferous, pestilent, pestilential, prejudicial, sinister, vile, virulent, wicked *Antonyms:* benevolent, helpful, kindly

perpendicular *adj.* erect, plumb, right-angled, sheer, standing, steep, straight, straight-up, upright, vertical *Antonyms:* horizontal, level, prostrate

perpetrate *v.* accomplish, arrange, carry through, cause, commit, consummate, effect, engineer, execute, make happen, perform

perpetual *adj.* **1.** abiding, ageless, durable, endless, enduring, eternal, everlasting, fast-frozen, firm, fixed, immortal, immutable, infinite, interminable, lasting, never-ending, perdurable, perennial, permanent, undying, unending *Antonyms:* brief, fleeting, meteoric, momentary, passing **2.** ceaseless, constant, continual, continued, continuous, incessant, never-ceasing, persistent, recurrent, regular, relentless, repeating, repetitious, steadfast, unceasing, unchanging, unfailing, unremitting *Antonyms:* irregular, now and then, occasional

perpetuate *v.* advance, attend, celebrate, champion, cherish, commemorate, consecrate, conserve, continue, cultivate, extend, keep, feed, foster, further, guard, hallow, harbour, husband, insure, keep, maintain, nurture, preserve, promote, sanctify, save, support, sustain, treasure, uphold

perplex *v.* astonish, astound, baffle, befuddle, bewilder, complicate, confound, confuse, dumfound, entangle, involve, jumble, mix up, muddle, mystify, nonplus, perturb, puzzle, rattle, ravel, snarl up, stump, surprise, tangle, thicken, thwart *Nonformal:* buffalo, discombobulate, snow *Antonyms:* clear, illuminate, set straight

perplexity *n.* **1.** bafflement, bewilderment, confoundment, confusion, discomposure, puzzlement *Antonyms:* comprehensibility, intelligibility **2.** bind, conundrum, enigma, labyrinth, maze, mystery, paradox, poser, predicament, problem, puzzle, quandary, riddle, rune *Nonformal:* stickler, stumper *Antonyms:* breeze, cinch, piece of cake *(Nonformal)*

perquisite *n.* **1.** benefit, bonus, dividend, extra, fringe benefit, gratuity, tip *Nonformal:* gravy, perk *See also:* **perk** **2.** appanage, droit, due, endowment, entitlement, liberty, privilege, provision, right *Commonly misused:* **prerequisite**

persecute *v.* **1.** abuse, afflict, aggrieve, beat, crucify, destroy, exile, expel, ill-treat, injure, kill, maim, maltreat, martyr, molest, oppress, outrage, rack, ravage, ruin, torture, victimize *Antonyms:* accommodate, calm, coddle, pamper, support **2.** annoy, badger, bait, bother, bug, distress, dog, exasperate, harass, irritate, pain, pester, plague, ride, stock, tease, torment, vex, worry *Nonformal:* hassle, hound, needle *Commonly misused:* **prosecute**

persecution *n.* **1.** abuse, affliction, agony, anguish, cruelty, distress, harassment, misery, pain, plague, sorrow, suffering, torment, torture, victimization **2.** anti-Semitism, despotism, discrimination, domination, inequality, racism, sexism, subjugation, suppression, tyranny

perseverance *n.* backbone, constancy, continuance, conviction, dedication, determination, diligence, doggedness, drive, endurance, grit, immovability, internal *or* intestinal fortitude, mettle, persistence, pluck, purposefulness, resolution, stamina, steadfastness, stubbornness, tenacity *Nonformal:* guts, spunk, stick-to-itiveness

persevere *v.* continue, endure, maintain, persist, proceed, put up with, remain, stick to it, survive *Antonyms:* dither, end, falter, hesitate, pack it in *(Nonformal)*

persistent *adj.* **1.** assiduous, determined, dogged, firm, fixed, indefatigable, insistent, obdurate, obstinate, persevering, pertinacious, resolute, steadfast, steady, sticky *(Nonformal)*, stubborn, tenacious, tireless, unflagging, unrelenting, unremitting, unshakable *Antonyms:* relenting, surrendering, yielding **2.** ceaseless, constant, continual, continuous, durable, endless, enduring, fixed, incessant, interminable, never-ending, perpetual, persisting, relentless, stable *Antonyms:* fleeting, mercurial, transitory

person *n.* **1.** being, boy, child, character, creature, girl, hominid, Homo sapien, human, human being, individual, man, mortal, personage, soul, woman **2.** bag of bones *(Nonformal)*, body, carcass, corpse, flesh and blood **3.** appearance, build, condition, constitution, form, frame, makeup, physique, repair, shape, state, style, tone **4.** common man *or* woman, commoner, face in the street, fellow, stranger *Nonformal:* chap, everyday Joe, gal, guy, Jane *or* John Doe, Joe Punchclock *or* Sixpack, lad, nobody, number, Sally Housecoat

personable *adj.* affable, agreeable, amiable, attractive, charming, easygoing, friendly, gregarious, ingratiating, likeable, nice, pleasant, pleasing, presentable, sociable, winning *Antonyms:* curmudgeonly, sullen, surly, ugly, unpleasant

personal *adj.* **1.** confidential, exclusive, intimate, nonpublic, private, privy, reserved, restricted, secret, special, specific *Antonyms:* common, open, public **2.** concealed, deep, hidden, innermost, internal, repressed **3.** characteristic, distinct, distinctive, emblematic, express, idiosyncratic, individual, particular, peculiar, unique **4.** independent, lone, separate, singular, solitary *Antonyms:* collective, social **5.** adored, esteemed, loved, precious, revered, treasured, venerated, worshiped *Antonyms:* hated, loathful, vilified **6.** abusive, abominable, disparaging, injurious, insidious, insulting, offensive, slanderous, vituperative *Antonyms:* complimentary, congratulatory, flattering **7.** corporal, cosmetic, bodily, external, physical, superficial *Commonly misused:* **personnel**

personality *n.* **1.** character, complexion, disposition, distinctiveness, emotions, humour, identity, individuality, makeup, nature, persona, psyche, selfhood, singularity, temper, temperament, traits **2.** attractiveness, charisma, charm, dynamism, likableness, lure, magnetism, pleasantness **3.** celebrity, dignitary, distinguished person, luminary, notable, personage, public figure, star, superstar, worthy *Nonformal:* glitterati, name, pop star, VIP

personally *adv.* **1.** alone, by oneself, directly, for oneself, independently, individually, in person, privately, solely, specifically *Antonyms:* communally, publically **2.** as one sees it, for one's part, if one asks me, from one's perspective, from one's vantage point, subjectively

personification *n.* **1.** metaphor, prosopopeia, symbol *National personifications:* John Bull *(Britain)*, Marianne *(France) Canada:* Janey Canuck, Johnny Canuck *Russia:* Mother Russia, the Bear *U.S.:* Brother Jonathan, Uncle Sam **2.** embodiment, epiphany, incarnation, incorporation, manifestation, reification **3.** delineation, demonstration, depiction, illustration, portrayal, realization, rendition, representation **4.** burlesque, characterization, copying, imitation, impersonation, mimicry, mocking, parody

personify *v.* **1.** contain, comprise, embody, embrace, incorporate, manifest **2.** delineate, depict, exhibit, express, illustrate, picture, portray, represent, show, sketch **3.** epitomize, exemplify, symbolize, typify **4.** act out, ape, copy, imitate, impersonate, mimic, mirror, parrot, play, repeat

personnel *n.* associates, cadre, corps, crew, employees, faculty, group, hands, helpers, human resources, members, office, organization, people, staff, task force, team, troop, workers, work force *Commonly misused:* **personal**

perspective *n.* **1.** angle, aspect, attitude, bias, context, mind set, outlook, overview, slant, stance, viewpoint *Nonformal:* end of the table, pedestal, side of the road *or* tracks **2.** horizon, landscape, panorama, scene, sweep, vantage, view, vista **3.** compass, depth, distance, length, proportion, relation, space

perspicacious *adj.* acute, alert, astute, aware, cagey, clear-sighted, clever, discerning, heady, judicious, keen, observant, penetrating, perceptive, percipient, sagacious, savvy *(Nonformal)*, sharp, sharp-witted, shrewd *Antonyms:* dense, dim-witted, slow

perspiration *n.* **1.** dampness, diaphoresis, excretion, exudation, hidrosis, lather, sweat **2.** activity, drudgery, effort, elbow grease *(Nonformal)*, exertion, industry, labour, toil, travail, work

persuade *v.* advise, affect, allure, assure, blandish, brainwash, bring around, cajole, coax, convert, convince, counsel, dragoon, draw, enlist, entice, exhort, get, impel, impress, incite, incline, induce, influence, inveigle, lead, move, prevail upon, prompt, proselytize, reason, satisfy, seduce, sell, suborn, sway, talk into, touch, urge, wheedle, win over, woo *Nonformal:* stroke, strongarm *Antonyms:* deter, discourage, dissuade

persuasion *n.* **1.** allure, blandishment, brainwashing, bribe, cajolery, enticement, exhortation, hard sell, inducement, influence, inveiglement, monetary inducement, potency, power, pull, seduction, sell *Nonformal:* boodle, carrot, snow job, soft soap, sweet talk **2.** belief, conviction, creed, faith, gospel, ideology, opinion **3.** affiliation, church, congregation, denomination, parish, religion, sect **4.** association, brotherhood, clique, club, cult, faction, fraternity, group, organization, party, sisterhood, society, sorority, syndicate

persuasive *adj.* **1.** charismatic, cogent, compelling, convincing, effective, effectual, efficacious, efficient, eloquent, emotional, emphatic, forceful, hard to ignore, impassioned, impelling, impressive, influential, inspiring, moving, potent, powerful, slick, smooth, stimulating, stringent, strong, swaying, telling, touching, weighty, well-orchestrated *(Nonformal)*, winning *Antonyms:* feeble, flimsy, unimpressive **2.** alluring, appealing, attractive, enticing, flattering, honeyed, inveigling, irresistible, luring, seductive, wheedling **3.** believable, direct, logical, rational, reasonable, sensible, sound, valid, well thought out

pert *adj.* **1.** audacious, bold, brash, brazen, breezy, cheeky, daring, disrespectful, flip, flippant, forward, fresh, impertinent, impudent, insolent, jaunty, keen, nervy, presumptuous, sassy, saucy, smart, spirited *Antonyms:* cautious, introverted, timid **2.** animated, bright, brisk, dapper, dashing, lively, perky, sprightly, vivacious

pertain *v.* affect, appertain, apply, associate, bear on, befit, belong, concern, connect, join, refer, regard, relate, touch

pertinent *adj.* admissible, *ad rem (Latin)*, applicable, appropriate, apropos, apt, befitting, connected, fit, fitting, germane, material, pertaining, proper, related, relevant, seemly, suitable *Antonyms:* discordant, foreign, immaterial, irrelevant

perturbed *adj.* **1.** agitated, alarmed, bothered, discomposed, disquieted, flustered, irritated, ruffled, troubled, unsettled, upset, vexed *Antonyms:* calm, mellow, serene **2.** chaotic, confused, convoluted, disordered, disorganized, ill-assorted, jumbled, messy, motley, muddled, ragtag *Antonyms:* clean, orderly, systematic, tidy

peruse *v.* **1.** analyze, check, consider, examine, go over, inspect, review, scrutinize, study, survey, wade through **2.** browse, dip into, eye, look *or* pore over, read, scan, skim, ripple *or* thumb through

pervade *v.* charge, diffuse, extend, fill, imbue, impregnate, infuse, penetrate, percolate, permeate, saturate, spread, steep, suffuse

pervasive *adj.* common, epidemic, extensive, general, global, inescapable, omnipresent, pandemic, permeating, pervading, prevalent, rampant, ubiquitous, universal, widespread, worldwide *Antonyms:* checked, focused, limited, local, stifled

perverse *adj.* **1.** abnormal, anomalous, atypical, bizarre, contradictory, contrary, deviant, different, divergent, freakish, irregular, marching to a different drummer *(Nonformal)*, nonconforming, strange, unconventional, unusual, weird *Antonyms:* conventional, everyday, normal **2.** balky, capricious, contumacious, delinquent, disobedient, fractious, headstrong, insubordinate, intractable, intransigent, obdurate, obstinate, oppositional, petulant, rebellious, refractory, resistant, self-willed, stubborn, unmanageable, unreasonable, unyielding, wayward, willful *Antonyms:* amiable, complaisant, cooperative, obedient **3.** cranky, crotchety, crusty, ill-humoured, peevish, petulant, quarrellous, quarrelsome, splenetic, surly, testy **4.** abandoned, blue *(Nonformal)*, corrupt, depraved, dirty, distorted, fell, grotesque, indecent, lewd, naughty, obscene, perverted, profligate, sick, twisted, vile, wanton, wicked

perversion *n.* **1.** aberration, abnormality, deviance, deviation, divergence, freakishness, irregularity, unconventionality, weirdness *Antonyms:* conformance, uniformity **2.** abuse, corruption, debauchery, depravity, dishonour, exploitation, misapplication, mistreatment, misuse, molestation, outrage, prostitution

pervert *n.* abuser, degenerate, deviant, deviate, freak, lecher, necrophile, pederast, pedophile, profligate, reprobate *Nonformal:* flasher, letch, perv, psycho, sicko, weirdo – *v.* **1.** adulterate, alter, bastardize, bend, colour, contort, distort, doctor *(Nonformal)*, fake, falsify, fudge, load, misconstrue, misinterpret, misrepresent, skew, spike, twist, warp **2.** abuse, corrupt, debase, defile, deprave, dishonour, maltreat, misapply, mistreat, misuse, molest, pollute, queer *(Nonformal)*, ruin, shame, taint, vitiate **3.** deceive, fool, hoodwink, influence, lead astray, misguide, misinform, mislead, trick

perverted *adj.* **1.** aberrant, abnormal, deviant, deviating, different, distorted, irregular, odd, off *(Nonformal)*, peculiar, strange, unusual, weird **2.** abandoned, corrupt, debased, debauched, degenerate, depraved, dissolute, evil, freakish, grotesque, immoral, indecent, monstrous, outrageous, profligate, ribald, rude, shameful, sick, twisted, unhealthy, unnatural, vicious, vile, wicked *Nonformal:* kinky, queer *Antonyms:* clean, decent **3.** abused, altered, changed, contorted, defiled, distorted, doctored *(Nonformal)*, impaired, polluted, shaped, tainted, warped **4.** lascivious, lecherous, lewd, naughty, obscene, pornographic, prurient, sexual *Nonformal:* adult, blue

pesky *adj.* annoying, bothersome, damnable, detestable, disturbing, irksome, irritating, nettlesome, pestiferous, provoking, tiresome, troublesome, unwanted, unwelcome, vexatious, vexing *Nonformal:* damn, darn, infernal *Antonyms:* calming, mitigating, soothing

pessimism *n.* cynicism, dejection, depression, despair, despondency, distrust, gloom, gloominess, glumness, grief, low spirits, melancholy, neurasthenia, sadness, unhappiness, *Weltschmerz (German)* *Antonyms:* faith, hope, optimism

pessimist *n.* complainer, cynic, defeatist, misanthrope, whiner, worrier *Nonformal:* downer, drag, drip, gloom merchant, killjoy, nay-sayer, skeleton at the banquet, sourpuss, wet blanket *Antonyms:* happy idiot, Pangloss, Pollyanna

pessimistic *adj.* bleak, cynical, dark, dejected, depressed, despairing, despondent, discouraged, distrustful, downhearted, dyspeptic, expecting the worst, fatalistic, foreboding, gloomy, glum, melancholy, misanthropic, morose, resigned *Antonyms:* assured, bright, buoyant, cheerful, optimistic

pest *n.* **1.** annoyance, bane, blight, bore, bother, curse, exasperation, headache, irritant, nag, nuisance, pain, pain in the neck *(Nonformal)*, problem, tormentor, trial, trouble, vexation *Antonyms:* balm, relief **2.** contagion, disease, epidemic, pestilence, plague, scourge, outbreak, wave

pestilence *n.* attack, blight, bug, contagion, disease, epidemic, invasion, outbreak, pandemic, plague, scourge, virus, wave *See also:* **disease**

pestilent *adj.* **1.** communicable, contagious, diseased, epidemic, infectious, pandemic, pathological, pestilential, transmittable **2.** corrupting, dangerous, deadly, destructive, detrimental, evil, fatal, harmful, injurious, lethal, malign, mortal, pernicious, ruinous, vicious *Antonyms:* constructive, palliative, safe **3.** aggravating, annoying, bothersome, damnable, detestable, distressing, disturbing, exasperating, harassing, irksome, irritating, nettlesome, tiresome, troublesome, unwelcome, upsetting, vexatious

pet *adj.* **1.** broken, docile, domesticated, gentled, housebroken, obedient, tame, trained *Antonyms:* feral, savage, wild **2.** affectionate, beloved, best, blue-eyed *(Nonformal)*, cherished, closest, darling, dearest, endearing, favoured, favourite, loved, precious, preferred – *n.* **1.** companion, domesticated *or* tame animal, friend, man's best friend *(Nonformal)*, playmate **2.** boyfriend, companion, dear, girlfriend, intimate, mate, partner, soul mate, sweetheart *Nonformal:* baby, bud, buddy, dearie, honey, love, lovey, pumpkin, sweet – *v.* baby, caress, coddle, cosset, cuddle, dandle, embrace, feel up *(Nonformal)*, fondle, grab, hug, kiss, love, pamper, pat, stroke

petite *adj.* baby, dainty, diminutive, elfin, Lilliputian, little, miniature, minute, peewee, slender, slight, slim, small, smallish, tiny, wee, weeny *(Nonformal) Antonyms:* gigantic, large, mammoth

petition *n.* address, appeal, application, entreaty, imploration, imprecation, invocation, plea, prayer, request, solicitation, supplication – *v.* appeal to, apply to, ask, beseech, entreat, implore, plead, request, requisition, solicit, urge

petrify *v.* **1.** alarm, amaze, appall, astonish, astound, benumb, chill, confound, daze, dismay, disturb, dumfound, frighten, horrify, immobilize, numb, paralyze, scare, startle, stun, stupefy, terrify, transfix *Nonformal:* floor, scare silly *or* stiff, spook *Antonyms:* calm, relieve, soothe **2.** calcify, crystallize, deaden, fossilize, harden, mineralize, set, solidify, stiffen *Antonyms:* liquefy, melt

pettifog *v.* bicker, clamour, complain, criticize, fret, fuss, moan, niggle, nitpick, quibble, whine *Nonformal:* bellyache, bitch, grouse, kvetch, raise a ruckus *or* stink *or* storm *or* the roof, split hairs

petty *adj.* **1.** cheap, frivolous, inconsequential, inconsiderable, insignificant, irrelevant, measly, negligible, niggling, paltry, picayune, piddling, slight, small, trifling, trivial *Nonformal:* dinky, peanuts, penny ante, rinky-dink, small potatoes, two-bit *Antonyms:* important, prodigious **2.** inferior, lesser, minor, subordinate, subservient, supplementary *Nonformal:* lightweight, second-fiddle, second-string *Antonyms:* main, superior **3.** biased, bigoted, dogmatic, intolerant, myopic, narrow-minded, predisposed, prejudiced, provincial, small-minded, small town *(Nonformal) Antonyms:* receptive, understanding **4.** base, contemptible, crusty, hateful, hurtful, low, malevolent, malicious, mean, rancorous, snide, spiteful, splenetic, surly, vicious, vindictive, vitriolic *Antonyms:* honest, kind, tolerant

petulant *adj.* bad-tempered, captious, caviling, complaining, crabby, cranky, cross, displeased, faultfinding, fractious, fretful, grouchy, grumbling, huffy, ill-humoured, impatient, irritable, mean, moody, peevish, perverse, querulous, snappish, sour, spoiled, sulky, tense, testy, touchy, ungracious, waspish *Nonformal:* kvetchy, uptight *Antonyms:* affable, cheerful, even-tempered, happy, smiling

phantom *adj.* ectoplasmic, ghostly, illusory, imagined, immaterial, incorporeal, intangible, surreal, unreal *Antonyms:* concrete, material, real, tangible – *n.* **1.** apparition, chimera, daydream, delusion, dream, figment, hallucination, illusion, mirage, nightmare, phantasm, presence, shade, shadow, spectre, vision, wraith **2.** banshee, bibe *(Newfoundland)*, demon, eidolon, ghost, haunting, poltergeist, revenant, *skookum (Pacific Coast)*, spirit, spook

phase *n.* **1.** chapter, epoch, era, facet, juncture, lapse, period, point, position, section, stage, state, step, stretch, time **2.** appearance, aspect, attitude, demeanour, dress, conditions, fashion, form, image, look, manifestation, manner, regard, shape, situation, status, view

phenomenal *adj.* astounding, excellent, exceptional, extraordinary, fantastic, marvellous, miraculous, outstanding, rare, remarkable, sensational, unbelievable, unique, unparalleled, unusual, wondrous *Nonformal:* cool, extreme, fab, gear, out of this world, wicked, wild *Antonyms:* common, ordinary, plain, regular

phenomenon *n.* **1.** circumstance, display, event, fact, occurrence, sight, something to see *(Nonformal)*, spectacle **2.** aberration, anomaly, departure, enigma, exception, inexplicability, oddity, puzzle, rarity, riddle, strangeness **3.** genius, maestro, marvel, master, miracle, nonpareil, phenom *(Nonformal)*, prodigy, *rara avis (Latin)*, sensation, wizard, wonder, *wunderkind (German)*

philander *v.* cheat, coquet, flirt, gallivant, lust after, make love, toy, trifle, womanize *Nonformal:* cougar hunt, fool around, play the field, skirt chase, sleep around, sow one's oats, test the waters

philanderer *n.* adulterer, dallier, debauchee, flirt, gallant, lecher, playboy, roué, womanizer, wanton *Nonformal:* Casanova, Don Juan, ladies' man, lady-killer, letch, Lothario, loverboy, ram, skirt chaser, stud, swinger, tomcat, wolf

philanthropic *adj.* altruistic, beneficent, benevolent, big-hearted, bountiful, charitable, eleemosynary, generous, giving, good, gracious, helpful, humane, humanitarian, kind, kind-hearted, liberal, magnanimous, munificent, openhanded, public-spirited *Antonyms:* avaricious, egotistic, selfish, self-seeking

philanthropy *n.* aid, almsgiving, altruism, attention, benevolence, care, charity, compassion, concern, fellow feeling, good will, help, humanity, magnanimity, succour

philistine *adj.* coarse, common, crude, demotic, dull, mediocre, prosaic, provincial, smug, uncultured, unrefined – *n.* Babbitt, boor, lout, lowbrow, roughneck, vulgarian, yahoo *Nonformal:* buttondown, square *Antonyms:* artist, radical

philosopher *n.* doctor, epistemologist, existentialist, highbrow, intellectual, logician, metaphysician, PhD, phenomenologist, philosophe, polymath, pundit, rationalist, reasoner, reckoner, sage, savant, scholar, sophist, speculator, theorist, thinker, *ulema (Muslim)*, wise man *or* woman *Nonformal:* egghead, walking encyclopedia, wise guy

philosophical *adj.* **1.** accepting, calm, collected, composed, detached, dispassionate, impassive, imperturbable, patient, resigned, serene, temperate, unruffled *Antonyms:* emotional, impulsive, rash, upset **2.** abstract, cogitative, deep, erudite, judicious, learned, logical, pensive, philosophic, profound, rational, reflective, sagacious, sapient, theoretical, thoughtful, wise *Antonyms:* illogical, irrational, mundane

philosophy *n.* **1.** knowledge, reason, truth, wisdom *Branches of philosophy:* aesthetics, axiology, cosmology, epistemology, ethics, gnosiology, logic, metaphysics, ontology, pataphysics, philosophy of art, political *Doctrines of Philosophy:* cyancism, deconstructionism, dialectical materialism, dualism, egoism, empiricism, Epicureanism, essentialism, existentialism, hedonism, humanism, idealism, individualism, linguistic philosophy, logical positivism, Marxism, materialism, monism, naturalism, nominalism, ordinary language, phenomenology, pluralism, positivism, pragmatism, rationalism, scepticism, semiotics, Stoicism, structuralism, transcendentalism, utilitarianism, vitalism *Some schools of philosophy:* Aristotelian, Augustinian, Averroist, Bergsonian, Berkeleian, Cartesian, Comtian, Epicurean, Hegelian, Heideggerian, Heraclitean, Humean, Kantian, Leibnizian, Parmenidean, Platonic,

Pythagorean, Sartrian, Socratic, Thomist, Viconian, Wittgensteinian **2.** doctrine, code, laws, method, principles, system of beliefs, tenets, way **3.** attitude, belief, conviction, ideology, interpretation, opinion, outlook, rationale, thinking, viewpoint *Nonformal:* spin, take

phglem *n.* **1.** bile, catarrh, mucus, saliva, secretion, slime, slobber, spit, spittle *Nonformal:* gob, hork, lung butter, snot **2.** apathy, indifference, lethargy, lifelessness, listlessness, sluggishness

phlegmatic *adj.* apathetic, dull, indifferent, insensitive, lackadaisical, lethargic, lifeless, listless, numb, slack, sluggish, torpid, unemotional *Antonyms:* energized, vigorous, vivacious

phobia *n.* anxiety, aversion, fear, funk *(Nonformal)*, horror, neurosis, obsession, panic, revulsion *Some kinds of phobia:* acrophobia *(High places)*, agoraphobia *(Open spaces)*, androphobia *(Men)*, arachnophobia *(Spiders)*, autophobia *(Being alone)*, chionophobia *(Snow)*, claustrophobia *(Confined places)*, demophobia *(Crowds)*, gamophobia *(Marriage)*, gynephobia *(Women)*, haptephobia *(Being touched)*, homophobia *(Homosexuals)*, pyrophobia *(Fire)*, technophobia *(Technology)*, xenophobia *(Foreigners)*, zoophobia *(Animals) Antonyms:* attraction, fondness, partiality

phoney *adj.* artificial, bogus, counterfeit, fake, false, fraudulent, imitation, make-believe, pretend, pseudo, sham, spurious, trick *Antonyms:* authentic, bona fide, original, real – *n.* **1.** cheat, copy, dummy, fabrication, falsity, forgery, fraud, hoax, substitute **2.** actor, charlatan, faker, impostor, lookalike, mountebank, pretender, trickster

phosphorescent *adj.* bright, glowing, illuminated, lucid, luminous, lustrous, radiant *Antonyms:* dark, dim, fuliginous, lack-lustre

photograph *n.* image, likeness, photo, picture, shot, take, exposure *Kinds of photograph:* aerial, black-and-white, blowup, close-up, colour, compromising, digital, enlargement, glossy, Kodachrome *or* Kodak *(Trademarks)*, matte, microfilm, montage, mugshot, negative, nude, photocopy, photogram, photomural, photostat, police portrait, positive, print, Rayograph, slide, snap *or* snapshot, solarization, still, transparency, X-ray *Historical:* daguerreotype, tintype – *v.* capture, film, picture, record, reproduce *Nonformal:* shoot, take

photographer *n.* cameraman, camerawoman, cinematograper, lensperson, paparazzo, photojournalist, shutterbug *(Nonformal)*

photographic *adj.* **1.** accurate, detailed, exact, minute, precise **2.** artistic, cinematic, faithful, filmic, genuine, graphic, lifelike, natural, pictorial, picturesque, realistic

phrase *n.* **1.** catchphrase, catchword, expression, idiom, maxim, motto, saying, shibboleth, slogan, tag, terminology **2.** announcement, articulation, locution, phrasing, remark, utterance, verbalism, vocalization **3.** clause, construction, phraseology, sentence, word group, wording, words – *v.* **1.** deliver, express, orate, pronounce, recite, remark, say, speak, talk, utter, voice **2.** adapt, carve, coach, construct, fashion, form, frame, interpret, mould, pattern, put a spin on *(Nonformal)*, shape, style, tailor

physic *n.* alleviative, cathartic, compound, cure, cure-all, elixir, medicine, ointment, powder, purge, salve, tincture – *v.* alleviate, comfort, console, cure, doctor, heal, help, palliate, relieve, remedy, restore, revive, soothe, treat

physical *adj.* **1.** bodily, brute, carnal, corporal, corporeal, fleshly, incarnate, mortal, personal, somatic, visceral *Antonyms:* ethereal, spiritual **2.** concrete, material, natural, objective, palpable, real, sensible, solid, substantial, tangible, visible *Antonyms:* cosmic, transcendent **3.** earthly, mundane, terrestrial, worldly **4.** active, aggressive, hands-on, laborious, manual, tough, violent – *n.* analysis, checkup, examination, look over, medical, probe, the rubber glove *(Nonformal)*

physician *n.* doctor, general practitioner, *hakim (Muslim)*, healer, MD, medical doctor *or* practitioner, medico, specialist *Non-*

formal: doc, medic, pill pusher, quack, sawbones

physics *n.* natural *or* physical science *Kinds of physics:* acoustics, aerophysics, applied, astrophysics, biophysics, classical, condensed-matter, cryogenics, crystallography, cytophysics, electrophysics, geophysics, high-energy, macrophysics, mechanics, microphysics, molecular, nuclear, physical chemistry, plasma, quantum, radiation, radionics, solar, solid-state, statics, theoretical, thermodynamics, zoophysics

physique *n.* anatomy, body, build, character, constitution, figure, form, frame, habit, habitus, muscles, nature, outline, power, shape, strength, structure, type

piano *n.* instrument, ivories *(Nonformal)*, keyboard, *klavier (German)*, pianoforte *Kinds of piano:* apartment, automatic, baby grand, concert grand, digital, electronic, grand, player, stage, synthesizer, upright *Historical:* clavichord, claviharpe, spinet, square *Popular brands:* Baldwin, Bechstein, Bösendorfer, Chickering, Heintzman, Kimball, Lesage, Sherlock-Manning, Steinway, Wurlitzer, Yamaha *See also:* **keyboard**

pick *n.* **1.** best, choice, cream, elect, elite, flower, preference, pride, prime, prize, select, top, tops *(Nonformal)* **2.** choosing, election, option, right, selection, vote **3.** device, implement, tool *Some kinds of pick:* cocktail, comb, icepick, pickaxe, *piolet (French)*, plectrum, tooth – *v.* **1.** choose, decide *or* fix upon, determine, draw, elect, finger, mark, name, opt for, prefer, select, slot, prefer, tab, settle on, single out, vote for *Antonyms:* cast aside, discard, dismiss, reject, turn down **2.** cut, detach, dislodge, eliminate, extract, pluck, pull, remove, shed, strip, tug at, withdraw *Antonyms:* attach, connect, insert **3.** accumulate, amass, clear, collect, cull, gather, glean, harvest, handpick, reap **4.** eat, gnaw, munch, nibble, nosh *(Nonformal)*, peck, snack **5.** drill, drive, indent, insert, penetrate, perforate, prick, probe, puncture, ream, stab, stick **6.** cavil, criticize, fuss, moan, niggle, nitpick, quibble *Nonformal:* bitch, grouse **7.** bag, filch, lift, pilfer, pinch, pirate, poach, purloin, steal, swindle **8.** break in *or* open, crack, force, invade, jimmy, open, pry, trespass **9.** improvise, perform, play, sound, strum

picket *n.* **1.** column, peg, pile, pillar, post, shaft, stake, stick, stud, upright **2.** contestant, disputant, dissenter, picketer, protester, sign *or* placard bearer, striker **3.** assurance, defender, guard, lookout, post, protector, sentinel, sentry, watch, watchperson – *v.* **1.** blockade, boycott, demonstrate, protest, strike, walk out **2.** defend, guard, look out for, mind, observe, protect, safeguard, shield, tend, view, watch

pickle *n.* **1.** chutney, compote, *confiture (French)*, condiment, jam, jelly, marmalade, preserve, spread **2.** bind, crisis, dilemma, emergency, exigency, fix, imbroglio, kettle of fish *(Nonformal)*, mess, pinch, plight, predicament, quandary, scrape, situation, spot – *v.* can, cure, keep, marinade, preserve, salt, souse, steep

pick-me-up *n.* bracer, elixir, refreshment, restorative, shot, spirits, stimulant *Nonformal:* a bit of the creature, a wee nip, hair of the dog, shot of courage, upper

picky *adj.* captious, carping, caviling, choosy, critical, dainty, fastidious, faultfinding, finicky, fussy, high maintenance *(Nonformal)*, niggling, particular, persnickety, pettifogging *Antonyms:* easygoing, inclusive, uncritical, undiscriminating

picnic *n.* **1.** barbecue, clambake, cookout, day in the country, festivity, fish fry, jamboree, meal, tailgate party, wiener roast **2.** excursion, jaunt, outing, pleasure trip **3.** insignificance, trifle, triviality *Nonformal:* bird, breeze, child's play, cinch, duck soup, joke, no-brainer, snap

pictorial *adj.* **1.** delineated, graphic, illustrated, painted, sketched, visual *Antonyms:* discursive, linguistic, rhetorical **2.** distinctive, expressive, striking, vivid – *n.* catalogue, coffee-table book, journal, picture book

picture *n.* **1.** animé, art, cartoon, collage, delineation, depiction, doodle, drawing, effigy, engraving, frontispiece, hieroglyph, icon, illustration, image, living picture, lookalike, montage, mosaic, painting, panorama, petroglyph, photo, photograph, piece, portrait, print, simulacrum, sketch, stencil, tableau, tableau vivant *See also:* **drawing, painting** **2.** account, anecdote, description, impression, narrative, outline, portrayal, recapitulation, recounting, rendition, story, tale, version **3.** case, circumstance, condition, scene, situation, state, status **4.** cinema, film, flick *(Nonformal),* motion *or* moving picture, movie, photoplay, show, television *See also:* **film** **5.** copy, duplicate, likeness, parallel, recreation, replica, representation, resemblance, similitude, twin *Nonformal:* ringer, spitting image **6.** beauty, vision *Nonformal:* babe, beefcake, dreamboat, hunk, knockout, lightning rod, looker – *v.* **1.** delineate, depict, describe, draw, illustrate, image, interpret, limn, paint, photograph, portray, render, represent, show, sketch **2.** conceive, conceptualize, create, daydream, dream, envisage, envision, fancy, fantasy, imagine, see, visualize

picturesque *adj.* **1.** alluring, arresting, attractive, beautiful, charming, comely, delightful, handsome, photogenic, pretty, quaint, scenic, striking *Antonyms:* gruesome, homely, lurid, macabre **2.** bright, colourful, distinct, graphic, illustrative, lucid, sharp, vivid

piddling *adj.* flimsy, insignificant, little, mean, measly, negligible, niggling, paltry, penny ante, petty, picayune, puny, small, superficial, trifling, trivial, unimportant, useless, worthless *Nonformal:* chump change, peanuts, small potatoes, throwaway *Antonyms:* central, considerable, important, significant, valuable

pie *n.* pastry, *pâtisserie (French),* tart, turnover *Kinds of pie:* apple, banana cream, blueberry, blueberry grunt *(Nova Scotia),* Boston cream, buttertart, bumbleberry, Cape Breton pork pie, chicken pot, coconut cream, flipper *(Newfoundland),* fruit, hare, key lime, lemon meringue, meat, mincemeat, mud, pecan, quiche, salmon, Saskatoon berry, Scotch, shepherd's, shoofly, steak and kidney, strawberry-rhubarb, sugar, *tortiére (Quebec),* turkey pot, Washington

piece *n.* **1.** bit, bite, chad, chunk, collop, component, cut, lump, member, part, particle, portion, quantity, remnant, sample, section, segment, share, slice, snippet **2.** accomplishment, arrangement, composition, creation, form, opus, score, song, work **3.** article, column, editorial, essay, interpretation, news item, op-ed *(Nonformal),* poem, review, short story, story, treatise, writing **4.** case, example, illustration, instance, item, model, occasion, representation, sample, specimen **5.** assessment, attitude, estimation, feeling, mind, opinion, perspective, point of view, say, sentiment, spin *(Nonformal)* **6.** cut *(Nonformal),* interest, involvement, measure, percentage, share **7.** armament, arms, automatic, cannon, concealed weapon, firearm, gun, handgun, hardware, pistol, rifle, weapon *Nonformal:* heat, midnight special **8.** distance, duration, interval, moment, period, phase, space, span, spell, stage, stretch, time **9.** coin, currency, dime, dollar, fifty cent piece *(Historical),* loonie, money, nickel, penny, quarter, two bits *(Nonformal),* twoonie, unit **10.** bale, bundle, fur, package, packet, parcel – *v.* add, attach, build, mend, patch, repair

piecemeal *adj.* fragmentary, gradual, partial, patchy, spotty, unsystematic – *adv.* at intervals, by degrees, fitfully, fragmentarily, gradually, intermittently, interruptively, one at a time, partially, slowly, step-by-step *Antonyms:* contiguously, entirely, *in toto (Latin)*

pier *n.* **1.** berth, dock, embarcadero, jetty, landing, levee, quay, sea wall, slip, wharf, wharfage **2.** anta, brace, buttress, column, crib, pedestal, pilaster, piling, post, pylon, shaft, stilt, support

pierce *v.* **1.** bore, broach, cleave, drill, enter, gash, gore, impale, incise, inject, jab, knife, lance, lancinate, penetrate, perforate, pike, pink, prick, probe, puncture, riddle, run through, shiv *(Nonformal),* slash, stab, stick into **2.** act, affect, alter, distress, disturb, impact, impress, influence, interest, move, pain, perturb, stir, sway, torment, touch, transfix, trouble **3.** break, crack, decipher, decode, disentangle, figure out, interpret, reckon, solve, understand, unfold, unravel

piercing *adj.* **1.** acute, agonizing, blaring, deafening, earsplitting, exquisite, fierce, high, high-pitched, loud, powerful, screaming, sharp, shattering, shrill, stentorian, treble, wailing *Antonyms:* inaudible, low-pitched, mellifluous, quiet **2.** biting, bitter, brisk, cold, crisp, freezing, glacial, numbing, severe, subzero *Antonyms:* boiling, hot, humid, warm **3.** digging, intense, penetrating, probing, searching, searing *Antonyms:* cosmetic, facile, frivolous, glib, perfunctory, superficial **4.** cleaving, cutting, deep, lacerating, lethal, mortal, shearing, stabbing, wounding

piety *n.* allegiance, application, ardour, belief, devotion, devoutness, duty, faith, fealty, fervour, fidelity, godliness, grace, holiness, loyalty, obedience, passion, piousness, religion, religiosity, reverence, sanctity, veneration, zeal *Antonyms:* iniquity, sacrilege, sinfulness

pig *n.* **1.** animal, beast, hog, piggy *(Nonformal)*, piglet, swine *Selected breeds of pig:* Berkshire, black, Cantonese, Duroc, Fengjing, Hereford, Hezuo, Iberian, Kele, Jinhua, Lacombe, Landrace, Mara Ramagnola, Meisham, Minzho, Mukota, Mulefoot, Pietrain, Potbellied, Tamsworth, white, Yorkshire **2.** boor, brute, glutton, gormandizer, guzzler, slob, vulgarian **3.** bigot, chauvinist, illiberal, intolerant, racist, sexist

pigheaded *adj.* bullheaded, intractable, intransigent, mulish, narrow-minded, obdurate, obstinate, refractory, stubborn, unyielding *Antonyms:* gracious, malleable, open, receptive

pigment *n.* colorant, colour, colouring, dye, dyestuff, oil, paint, shade, stain, tincture, tint

pigsty *n.* **1.** crib, enclosure, pen, pigpen, piggery, shed, sty **2.** mess, muss, wreck *Nonformal:* dive, dump, hellhole, rathole

pile *n.* **1.** accumulation, aggregate, assortment, collection, conglomeration, foundation, heap, mass, mound, pack, pier, piling, quantity, stack **2.** beam, column, pillar, post, stanchion, support **3.** bundle, cash, fortune, hoard, savings *Nonformal:* loot, wad **4.** loads, lots *Nonformal:* oceans, oodles, tons **5.** down, fur, fuzz, hair, pelage, shag, wool – *v.* **1.** accumulate, amass, assemble, bank, bunch, collect, gather, heap, hoard, mass, mound, stockpile, store **2.** charge, cram, crowd, jam, load, pack, rush, stream, stuff

pilfer *v.* appropriate, embezzle, filch, lift, pinch, pluck, purloin, rob, snare, steal, take, thieve *Nonformal:* bag, boost, borrow, cop, crib, knock off, liberate, moonlight, nip, palm, requisition, rip off, snatch, swipe

pilgrim *n.* **1.** crusader, hadji, palmer, *pélerin (French)*, visitant, worshipper **2.** roamer, rover, transient, traveller, wanderer, wayfarer **3.** homesteader, immigrant, newcomer, *pakeha (Maori)*, pioneer, settler, squatter

pilgrimage *n.* crusade, excursion, expedition, hadj, journey, mission, outing, sacred, tour, travel, trek, trip, walkabout

pill *n.* **1.** bollus, capsule, confection, lozenge, medicine, pastille, pellet, tablet, troche **2.** aggravation, annoyance, bother, headache, irritant, pain, pest

pillage *n.* **1.** burning, carnage, demolishing, destruction, devastation, looting, rape, ravaging, ruin, stealing, waste, wasting **2.** booty, goods, loot, lucre, prize, spoils, take, treasure, winnings – *v.* appropriate, confiscate, desecrate, despoil, destroy, devastate, devour, encroach, gut, invade, lay waste, lift, loot, maraud, plunder, purloin, raid, ransack, ravage, rifle, rob, ruin, sack, scourge, spoil, steal, strip, thieve, trespass, usurp, waste

pillar *n.* **1.** backbone, guide, leader, mainstay, rock, strength, supporter, upholder, upstanding citizen *Antonyms:* rake, reprobate, rogue **2.** caryatid, colonnade, column, mast, obelisk, pedestal, pier, pilaster, piling, post, prop, shaft, stanchion, support, telamon, tower

pilot *adj.* balloon, developmental, experimental, exploratory, preparatory, tentative, test, trial – *n.* aeronaut, airman, aviator, bush pilot, captain, conductor, driver, flier, helmsperson, kamikaze, leader, navigator, steerer *Nonformal:* ace, fly boy, top gun –

v. captain, drive, fly, guide, lead, manage, navigate, operate, oversee, skipper, steer

pimple *n.* abscess, acne, blackhead, blemish, blister, boil, bump, carbuncle, fleck, growth, hickey, inflammation, polyp, pustule, spot, swelling, whelk, whitehead, zit *(Nonformal)*

pin *n.* **1.** bolt, clasp, fastener, nail, wire *Common pins:* bodkin, bowling, clothespin, cotter, flag *(Golf)*, French, Greek, hairpin, hat, linchpin, rolling, Roman, roundhead, Russian, Scandinavian **2.** accessory, broach, cameo, embellishment, jewellery, ornament **3.** bagatelle, bauble, curio, gewgaw, insignificance, knickknack, trifle – *v.* **1.** attach, affix, bind, clasp, fasten, fix, join, nail, pinion, secure **2.** clutch, grab, grapple, hold, hold down *or* fast, immobilize, press, restrain, seize **3.** gore, jab, penetrate, pierce, pink, prick, ram, shish kebab *(Nonformal)*, stab, stick **4.** accuse, attribute, betray, blame, charge, cite, incriminate, inculpate *Nonformal:* brand, finger

pinch *n.* **1.** bit, dash, drop, jot, milligram, mite, small quantity, soupçon, speck, splash, splatter, taste **2.** charley horse *(Nonformal)*, compression, contraction, cramp, grasp, hurt, nip, pressing, pressure, tweak, twinge **3.** crisis, crucible, crunch, difficulty, dilemma, emergency, exigency, jam, predicament, pressure, situation, urgency – *v.* **1.** compress, confine, cramp, crush, grasp, hurt, nip, pain, press, squeeze, tweak, twinge **2.** crib, filch, lift, pilfer, purloin, rob, steal, take *Nonformal:* knock off, snatch, swipe **3.** economize, pinch pennies, scrape, scrimp, skimp, spare *Antonyms:* blow *(Nonformal)*, squander, waste **4.** apprehend, arrest, capture, catch, collar, grab, nab, net, reel *or* rope in, take

pine *n.* cedar, conifer, coniferous tree, evergreen, fir, timber, Tom Thomson *or* windswept pine *(Nonformal)*, tree *See also:* **tree** – *v.* **1.** ache, covet, crave, desire, hanker, long for, want, yearn **2.** decline, droop, fade, falter, flag, languish, sink, waste away, wither

pink *adj. & n.* colour *Pink shades:* blush, coral, flesh, flush, fuchsia, hot pink, peach, rose, roseate, salmon

pinpoint *v.* define, diagnose, distinguish, establish, finger, identify, label, locate, peg *(Nonformal)*, place, recognize, single out, spot

pinnacle *n.* **1.** acme, apex, crown, culmination, peak, summit, top, toppermost *(Nonformal) Antonyms:* base, bottom, nadir, root **2.** best, epitome, exemplar, finest, ideal, maximum, perfection, prime, supremacy *Antonyms:* least, worst **3.** belfry, campanile, cupola, roof, spire, spur, tower, turret

pioneer *n.* **1.** colonist, colonizer, explorer, frontiersman, guide, homesteader, immigrant, pilgrim, settler, squatter **2.** ancestor, avant-garde, developer, experimentalist, finder, forerunner, founder, innovator, inventor, leader, originator, pathbeater, pathfinder, precursor, trend-setter, trailblazer – *v.* create, develop, discover, establish, explore, found, initiate, institute, invent, launch, make way, originate, prepare, setup, spearhead, start, trailblaze

pioneering *adj.* avant-garde, cutting-edge, early, experimental, first, head, initial, innovative, introductory, lead, original, primary, prime, seminal, untried, vanguard

pious *adj.* **1.** born-again, clerical, dedicated, devoted, devout, ecclesiastical, God-fearing, godly, hallowed, holy, orthodox, prayerful, priestly, religious, reverent, righteous, sacred, saintly, spiritual *Antonyms:* impious, irreligious, irreverent, ungodly, unholy **2.** affected, high-flown, hoity-toity, holier-than-thou *(Nonformal)*, hypocritical, Pecksniffian, pharisaic, sanctimonious, self-righteous, smug, stiff, stuffy, superior

pipe *n.* **1.** aqueduct, branch, canal, capillary, conduit, core, culvert, duct, hose, line, passage, pipeline, tube, tubing, vein **2.** tobacco pipe *Kinds of pipe:* bong, briar, calabush, calumet, cherrywood, chibouk, churchwarden, clay, corncob, hookah, hubble-bubble, kalian, meerschaum, peace, water **3.** bagpipes, fife, flute, instrument, ocarina, pan flute, penny-whistle, piccolo, recorder, woodwind pipe *See also:* **instrument** **4.** call, chirp, cry, peep, sound, tweet, twitter, voice, warble, whistle – *v.* **1.** bring, carry, channel, conduct, convey, funnel, siphon, supply, transmit **2.** direct, draw, entice, escort, guide, lead, shepherd, usher **3.** alarm, call, caution, cry, shrill, signal, toot, utter, warn

piquant *adj.* **1.** appetizing, biting, delicious, flavourful, hot, peppery, pungent, savoury, seasoned, sharp, snappy, spicy, stinging, tangy, tart, well-flavoured, zestful, zesty *Antonyms:* bland, flavourless, insipid, mild **2.** absorbing, alluring, appealing, arresting, captivating, charming, compelling, engaging, engrossing, entertaining, entrancing, favourable, ingratiating, interesting, intriguing, inviting, lively, magnetic, sparkling, spirited, stimulating, stirring, tantalizing *Antonyms:* obnoxious, repulsive **3.** fresh, immodest, indecorous, naughty, provocative, racy, ribald, risqué, salty, seductive, sexy, shameless, suggestive, tempting

pique *n.* anger, annoyance, displeasure, flare-up, grudge, huff, hurt, irk, irritation, miff, offence, provocation, resentment, rise, slow burn *(Nonformal)*, sore, tiff, umbrage, vexation – *v.* **1.** arouse, excite, goad, kindle, provoke, stimulate **2.** affront, annoy, displease, incense, irk, irritate, offend, peeve, upset, vex *Antonyms:* charm, cheer, delight, gladden

pirate *n.* **1.** adventurer, buccaneer, bandit, brigand, criminal, hijacker, corsair, filibuster, freebooter, marauder, outlaw, raider, sea dog *or* rover *or* wolf **2.** copier, copyright infringer, copycat *(Nonformal)*, forger, plagiarist, thief – *v.* **1.** abscond with, commandeer, filch, freeboot, hijack, kidnap, pilfer, pillage, plunder, privateer, rob, shanghai, steal, take, trespass, wreak havoc **2.** copy, infringe, lift, mimic, parrot, plagiarize

pistol *n.* automatic, concealed gun, derringer, handgun, midnight special *(Nonformal)*, piece, protection, revolver, six-shooter, weapon *Trademark:* Colt, Beretta, Glock, Walther *See also:* **gun**

pit *n.* **1.** abyss, bowl, cavity, chasm, crater, depression, furrow, gulf, hole, hollow, moss hag *(Scottish)*, pocket, pothole, sink-hole, trench, trough, well **2.** catacomb, crypt, grave, sepulchre, tomb, vault **3.** deadfall, downfall, mantrap, pitfall, snare, tiger-trap, trap **4.** calamity, distress, grief, heartache, misfortune, pain, sorrow, stress, suffering, torment, tribulation, trouble, vexation, woe, worry *Antonyms:* glee, happiness, joy, jubilation **5.** cone, fruit, kernel, nut, pith, seed **6.** blemish, dent, dimple, impression, indentation, nick, notch, pockmark, scar **7.** arena, battle ground, enclosure, fighting *or* playing *or* trading *or* training surface, floor, ring **8.** excavation, mine, quarry, shaft – *v.* **1.** blemish, chip, dent, dig, hollow, indent, mark, nick, notch, perforate, pockmark, poke **2.** bury, conceal, ensconce, entomb, inter, sink, store, submerge **3.** confront, contrast, counter, face off, juxtapose, match, oppose, set against, vie *Antonyms:* intervene, isolate, separate

pitch *n.* **1.** frequency, harmonic key, modulation, range, rate, register, timbre, tonality, tone, tune, tuning **2.** ball, delivery, strike, throw, toss *Kinds of baseball pitch:* back door, beanball, bloop, breaking ball, change-up, circle change, curve, duster, fast ball, forkball, gopher ball, heater, hook, hummer, inside, junk, knockdown, knuckleball, knucklecurve, off-speed, palmball, purpose, roundhouse curve, screwball, sinker, slider, slurve, spitball, spitter, split-finger fastball, Uncle Charlie, wild pitch **3.** field, grounds, playing area *or* field *or* surface **4.** hard sell, line, persuasion, sales talk, sell, spiel, talk **5.** asphalt, bitumen, coating, residue, resin, sap, sealant, sealer, tar, waterproofing **6.** angle, curve, declivity, degree, descent, inclination, point, slant, slope **7.** amplitude, bound, breadth, capacity, compass, extent, extreme, extremity, magnitude, range, reach, scope, spread, sweep, volume, width – *v.* **1.** cast, chuck, fire, fling, gun, heave, hurl, launch, lob, peg, sling, throw, toss, unseat **2.** ascend, bend, bob, careen, descend, dive, drive, drop, fall, flounder, heave, lunge, lurch, pitch and roll, plunge, rise, rock, roll, seesaw, slump, stagger, tilt, topple, toss, tumble, vault, wallow, welter, yaw **3.** angle, cant, grade, incline, keel, level, list, slant, slope, tip, turn **4.** advertise, convince, hawk, induce, market, peddle, persuade, promote, sell **5.** construct, encamp, erect, establish, fix, make camp, raise tent **6.** arrange, lay out, locate, order, place, position, set, situate, station, stow

pitcher *n.* **1.** bowler *(Cricket)*, hurler *(Nonformal) Kinds of baseball pitcher:* closer, Cy Young winner, fireballer, junkballer, lefthander, long reliever, mop-up guy, relief pitcher, reliever, righthander, set-up man, short reliever, sidearmer, spitballer *(Historical)*, staff ace, starter, starting pitcher, stopper, submariner **2.** bottle, container, decanter, ewer, jar, jug, urn, vessel

piteous *adj.* affecting, beseeching, deplorable, distressing, disturbing, entreating, heartbreaking, heartrending, lamentable, melancholy, miserable, mournful, moving, pathetic, pitiful, poignant, rueful, sad, sorrowful, woeful, wretched *Antonyms:* contented, enchanted, fortunate, lucky, joyful

pitfall *n.* booby-trap, calamity, catch, Catch-22, danger, difficulty, downfall, drawback, entanglement, hazard, hook, quicksand, risk, sinkhole, snag, snare, swindle, trap, web

pith *n.* **1.** bottom line, core, crux, essence, essential, gist, heart, kernel, marrow, meaning, meat, nitty-gritty *(Nonformal)*, nub, nucleus, quintessence, reality, root, soul, spirit, substance, truth **2.** drive, energy, force, influence, might, potency, pull, strength, verve, vigour, vim, weight *Nonformal:* chutzpah, moxie

pithy *adj.* aphoristic, apothegmatic, brief, cogent, compact, concise, condensed, crisp, curt, direct, effective, epigrammatic, expressive, forceful, honed, incisive, laconic, lean, meaningful, pointed, short, significant, straightforward, succinct, summary, terse, tight, trenchant, vigorous *Antonyms:* convoluted, lengthy, long-winded, protracted, verbose

pitiful *adj.* **1.** cheerless, distressing, grievous, heartbreaking, heartrending, joyless, lamentable, miserable, mournful, pathetic, pitiable, plaintive, poor, sad, sorrowful, stirring, suffering, touching, unhappy, woeful, wretched **2.** abject, abominable, base, beggarly, contemptible, despicable, ignominious, low, mean, scrofulous, scurvy, shabby, worthless *Antonyms:* admirable, honourable, laudable, praiseworthy

pitiless *adj.* austere, barbarous, brutal, callous, cold, cold-blooded, cold-hearted, cruel, cutthroat, frigid, hardhearted, harsh, heartless, implacable, indifferent, inexorable, inhuman, inhumane, insensible, mean, merciless, obdurate, Procrustean, relentless, remorseless, ruthless, savage, soulless, stony, uncaring, uncompassionate, unconcerned, unfeeling, unmerciful, unrelenting, unsympathetic *Antonyms:* caring, compassionate, kind, merciful, responsive

pity *n.* **1.** benevolence, charity, clemency, comfort, commiseration, compassion, condolence, empathy, fellow feeling, forbearance, goodness, grace, humanity, kindliness, kindness, lenity, mercy, sadness, solace, sorrow, sympathy, understanding **2.** bad luck, crying shame *(Nonformal)*, mischance, misfortune, mishap, regret, shame – *v.* ache, bleed for, comfort, commiserate, condole, console, empathize, feel for, forgive, give quarter, identify with, pardon, show forgiveness *or* sympathy, solace, soothe, sympathize, understand, weep for

pivot *n.* **1.** axis, axle, centre, fulcrum, hinge, hub, shaft, spindle, swivel, turning point **2.** anchor, backbone, bulwark, captain, centre, chief, focal point, heart, kingpin, linchpin, mainspring, officer, quarterback – *v.* hang, hinge, pirouette, rely, revolve, rotate, spin, swivel, turn, twirl, twist, whirl

pivotal *adj.* cardinal, central, climactic, critical, crucial, decisive, determining, essential, focal, important, momentous, overriding, overruling, primary, principal, ruling, vital *Antonyms:* inconsequential, insignificant, picayune, quibbling, trifling

pixie *n.* **1.** elf, fairy, gnome, goblin, gremlin, imp, kelpie, leprechaun, peri, puck, sprite **2.** devil, *enfant terrible (French)*, holy terror *(Nonformal)*, menace, mischief-maker, nuisance, rascal, troublemaker

placard *n.* advertisement, banner, bill, billboard, broadside, bumper sticker, disclosure, display, manifesto, notice, poster, proclamation, sandwich board, sheet, sign, signpost, sticker

placate *v.* appease, assuage, calm, cheer, comfort, conciliate, cool, humour, mollify, pacify, propitiate, reconcile, soft-pedal *(Nonformal)*, soothe, sweeten, tranquilize, win over *Antonym:* agitate, annoy, antagonize, rile

place *n.* **1.** area, environment, locale, locality, location, locus, *mise en scène (French)*, point, portion, position, scene, set, setting, site, space, spot, zone **2.** address, burg, city, concession, locality, municipality, neighbourhood, postal code, province, region, rural route, territory, township, village, ville **3.** abode, accommodations, apartment, condominium, cottage, dwelling, home, house, living quarters, pad *(Nonformal)*, residence, townhouse **4.** avenue, bar, building, club, corner, court, lane, office, restaurant, square, street, tavern *Nonformal:* hangout, joint, stomping ground **5.** chapter, movement, part, passage, point, section, segment **6.** appointment, berth, capacity, connection, employment, function, job, occupation, office, position, post, profession, situation, trade **7.** class, footing, grade, pecking order *(Nonformal)*, position, post, rank, slot, standing, state, station, status **8.** alternate, backup, lieu, proxy, replacement, reserve, second, substitution **9.** affair, duty, charge, concern, duty, function, prerogative, responsibility, right, role – *v.* **1.** deposit, dwell, establish, fix, lay, locate, lodge, park, plant, plunk *(Nonformal)*, put, quarter, rest, set, settle, situate, station, store, stow **2.** allocate, allot, approximate, arrange, class, classify, group, order, position, rank, sort **3.** determine, distinguish, finger, identify, indicate, know, peg, pinpoint, recall, recognize, remember, spot **4.** appoint, assign, elect, install, invest, nominate, ordain, promote **5.** bestow, delegate, entrust, make responsible, relegate **6.** bankroll, capitalize, fund, grubstake *(Nonformal)*, infuse, invest, sink

plagiarism *n.* academic offence, appropriation, borrowing, copying, counterfeiting, cribbing, falsification, fraud, infringement, lifting, literary theft, piracy, stealing, theft

plague *n.* **1.** affliction, Black Death, blight, bubonic plague, cancer, contagion, disease, epidemic, fever, infection, infestation, influenza, invasion, outbreak, pandemic, pestilence, scourge **2.** aggravation, annoyance, bane, bother, distress, exasperation, harassment, hassle *(Nonformal)*, nuisance, pain, problem, torment, trial **3.** calamity, cataclysm, catastrophe, collapse, contretemps, disaster, evil, misfortune, mishap, tragedy *Antonyms:* advantage, benefit, blessing, boom – *v.* afflict, aggravate, annoy, bother, harass, hassle *(Nonformal)*, irritate, pester, torment

plain *adj.* **1.** average, bland, boring, common, conventional, dull, everyday, inconspicuous, modest, normal, ordinary, pedestrian, prosaic, quotidian, routine, simple, traditional, unaffected, unassuming, unpretentious, unremarkable, usual, workaday *Nonformal:* beige, garden variety, vanilla *Antonyms:* extraordinary, incredible, outstanding **2.** abrupt, artless, blunt, candid, direct, downright, forthright, frank, guileless, honest, ingenuous, open, outspoken, sincere, straightforward, unconcealed, undisguised, unfeigned *Antonyms:* bowdlerized, euphemistic, sugar-coated, tempered **3.** clear, comprehensible, discernible, intelligible, logical, lucid, understandable *Antonyms:* ambiguous, convoluted, difficult, opaque, vague **4.** austere, bare, basic, clean, modest, muted, pure, restrained, severe, simple, Spartan, stark, stripped-down, unadorned, unembellished, unvarnished *Antonyms:* Epicurean, fancy, gaudy, rococo **5.** characterless, drab, grey, inconspicuous, inelegant, mousy, plain-featured, self-effacing, unattractive *Antonyms:* attractive, beautiful, comely **6** even, flat, level, low, outstretched, prone, seamless, smooth, straight, unbroken – *n* campo, delta, downs, expanse, field, flats, grassland, heath, llano, lowland, meadow, moorland, open country, pampas, parkland, plateau, prairie, savanna, steppe, veld

plaintive *adj.* disconsolate, doloroso, grief-stricken, grievous, heartrending, lachrymose, lamenting, melancholy, mournful, pathetic, pitiful, rueful, sad, saddened, sorrowful, weeping, woeful *Antonyms:* blithe, cheerful, genial, happy, joyful

plan *n.* **1.** aim, arrangement, contrivance, deal, design, device, expedient, idea, intention, machination, means, method, mode, modus operandi, platform, plot, policy, pro cedure, program, project, proposal, proposition, purpose, scenario, scheme, stratagem, strategy, suggestion, system, tactics, treatment, undertaking, way *Nonformal:* big picture, game plan **2.** blueprint, chart, draft, drawing, elevation, footprint, floor plan, layout, mockup, model, outline, pattern, picture, rendition, sketch – *v.* **1.** arrange, concoct, conspire, construct, contrive, craft, create, design, devise, draft, engineer, form, formulate, frame, guide, hatch, invent, line up, map, mastermind, organize, outline, plot, prepare, ready, scheme, shape, sketch, survey **2.** aim, intend, mean, project, propose, reckon **3.** brainstorm, calculate, consider, contemplate, meditate, think out

plane *adj.* even, flat, flush, horizontal, level, plain, regular, smooth, straight, uniform *Antonyms:* bumpy, indented, rough – *n.* **1.** aircraft, airplane, airship, craft, jet, ship *(Nonformal)*, STOL *See also:* **aircraft** **2.** degree, grade, level, peg, phase, position, rung, stage, standing, status, step – *v.* **1.** even, flatten, grade, level, smooth out, straighten, strip, tool, trowel **2.** fly, glide, sail soar, take flight, travel, wing, zoom *(Nonformal)*

plant *n.* **1.** flower, greenery, plant kingdom, plant life, vegetable kingdom, verdure *Groupings of plants:* annual, aquatic, aromatic, berry, biennial, bulb, bush, cacti, evergreen, flora, flowering, fruit, garden flower, grain, grass, grasslike, gymnosperm, hardwood, heath, herbaceous, herbs, hothouse, insectivorous, ivy, legume, liverwort, marsh, medicinal, mosses, nut tree, perennial, plankton, reed, seaweed, sedge, shrub, softwood, tree, tuber, vegetable, vine, water, weed, wildflower *Immature plant*: cutting, seed, seedling, shoot, slip, sprout **2.** assembly line, Dickensian workhouse *(Nonformal)*, establishment, factory, foundry, industry, manufactory, mill, premises, shop, sweatshop, workshop, yard **3.** apparatus, appliances, buildings, devices, equipment, machinery, means, tools, workings **4.** artifice, chicanery, con *(Nonformal)*, deceit, deception, dodge, duplicity, fraud, hoax, swindle, trap, trick, wile **5.** agent, imposter, informant, informer, mole, operative, sleuth, source, spy, undercover agent *Nonformal:* narc, snitch, snoop, tipster – *v.* **1.** bury, cover, disseminate, grow, implant, raise, scatter, seed, sow, stock, transplant **2.** deposit, fix, imbed, insert, institute, lodge, park, position, root, set, settle, station *Nonformal:* plop, plunk **3.** build, erect, establish, found, install, institute, originate, launch **4.** hit, label, land, punch, strike *Nonformal:* sock, sucker

plantation *n.* **1.** estate, farm, field, grounds, grove, manor, nursery, orchard, parcel, ranch, vineyard, woodlot **2.** colony, community, encampment, habitation, homestead, outpost, settlement, territory

plaque *n.* award, commemoration, disc, honour, marker, medallion, memorial, ornament, plate, sign, slab, symbol, tablet, token

plaster *n.* **1.** adhesive, cement, coat, glue, gum, gypsum, lime, mortar, mucilage, paste, stucco **2.** bandage, binding, cast, compress, dressing, gauze, mould, wrap – *v.* **1.** adhere, bind, cement, coat, cover, daub, glue, gum, overlay, paste, smear, smudge, spread **2.** bandage, bind, cover, dress, swathe **3.** abuse, beat, buffet, club, drub, flog, hit, knock, plough over, pummel, punch, pound, shell, strike, thrash *Nonformal:* cream, lather, smoke, trounce, whup

plastic *adj.* **1.** bending, ductile, elastic, flexible, formable, malleable, mouldable, pliable, pliant, resilient, shapable, soft, supple, workable, yielding *Antonyms:* brittle, hard, inflexible **2.** affected, artificial, contrived, fake, feigned, ingenuine, insincere, mock, phoney *(Nonformal)*, shallow, superficial *Antonyms:* genuine, honest, straightforward – *n.* synthetic *Kinds of plastic:* acetate, acrylic, alkyd, casein, cellophane, celluloid, cellulose, epoxy, nylon, polyester, polyethylene, polypropylene, polystyrene, polyvinyl, silicone *Trademark:* Bakelite, Lucite, Formica, Mylar, Perspex, Plexiglas, Styrofoam, Teflon

plate *n.* **1.** bowl, casserole, china, cup, platter, service, trencher **2.** allotment, course, dish, distribution, helping, portion, serving **3.** armour, cover, crust, facing, film, lamina, panel, scab, sheet, shell, skin, veneer **4.** design, engraving, etching, frontispiece, illustration, impression, lithograph, picture, print, reproduction, woodcut – *v.* bronze, chrome, coat, cover, electroplate, enamel, encrust, face, foil, gild, laminate, layer, nickel, overlay, platinize, scale, stratify

plateau *n.* **1.** côteau, elevation, highland, mesa, plain, steppe, table, tableland, upland **2.** grade, level, period, phase, position, rung, stage, standing, state, step

platform *n.* **1.** board, dais, deck, flake *(Fishing)*, floor, hustings *(Historical)*, plank, podium, pulpit, rostrum, scaffold, stand, stage, staging, surface, table **2.** aim, approach, design, goal, manifesto, objective, party line, plan, policy, principle, program, promise, *raison d'état (French)*, stratagem, tenet

plating *n.* cladding, covering, plate, sheathing *Kinds of plating:* anodized aluminum, armoured, copperplate, electroplating, gold, nickel, silver

platitude *n.* **1.** banality, bromide, buzzword, catchphrase, chestnut, cliché, hackneyed saying, trite remark, truism *Nonformal:* familiar tune, old saw *or* story **2.** inanity, insipidity, monotony, staleness, triteness, triviality

platonic *adj.* chaste, ideal, idealistic, intellectual, noetic, nonphysical, nonsexual, spiritual, transcendent, utopian, visionary *Antonyms:* bacchanal, carnal, earthly, Epicurean, sexual

platoon *n.* army, array, batch, battery, bunch, clump, cluster, company, detachment, division, group, lot, military outfit, number, parcel, patrol, selection, set, squad, squadron, subdivision, team, troop, unit – *v.* alternate, change off *or* places, rotate, switch

plaudit *n.* acclamation, applause, approval, cheer, congratulations, encouragement, huzzahs, ovation, praise, standing ovation, standing O *(Nonformal) Antonyms:* censure, derision, jeering

plausible *adj.* believable, conceivable, credible, likely, logical, possible, practicable, presumable, probable, reasonable, sound, supposable, tenable, trustworthy, valid *Antonyms:* implausible, impossible, unlikely

play *n.* **1.** amusement, delight, diversion, entertainment, frolic, fun, gambol, happiness, humour, match, merrymaking, pastime, pleasure, recreation, relaxation, romp, sport **2.** action, activity, deke *(Nonformal)*, diversionary tactic, exercise, manoeuvre, motion, move, movement, operation, ruse, working **3.** dramatic *or* theatrical entertainment, pageant, performance, spectacle, stage show, theatre piece, theatrical *See also:* **drama** **4.** chance, gamble, gaming, punting, spin of the wheel, test of luck **5.** attitude, bearing, behaviour, culture, custom, decorum, fashion, form, manner, method, tact, tone, way **6.** caper, hijinks, jest, joking, pranks, shenanigans *(Nonformal)*, teasing, tomfoolery **7.** elbow room, give, latitude, leeway, margin, range, room, scope, space, sweep, swing – *v.* **1.** carouse, carry on, cavort, clown, dally, divert, entertain, frisk, frolic, gambol, horse around *(Nonformal)*, idle away, joke, make merry, rejoice, revel, romp, sport, toy, trifle **2.** act, assume, do, enact, execute, ham, imitate, impersonate, perform, personate, playact, portray, present, pretend, represent **3.** improvise, interpret, make music, perform, produce, render **4.** bet, chance, finesse, gamble, game, hazard, risk, speculate, stake, wager **5.** challenge, compete, contend, contest, engage in, participate, playdown, playoff, rival, sport, take on, take part, vie **6.** apply, employ, exercise, exploit, handle, jockey, labour, manage, manoeuvre, use, utilize, work **7.** coruscate, dance, flash, flicker, glimmer, jump, skip, twinkle

playboy *n.* philanderer, pleasure seeker, rake, roué, sport, womanizer *Nonformal:* Don Juan, ladies' man, lady-killer, Lothario, lover boy, swinger, tomcat, wolf

player *n.* **1.** actor, actress, bit player, entertainer, ham, impersonator, lead, mime, mimic, musician, performer, playactor, scene stealer, stand-in, star, Thespian, trouper **2.** agent, amateur, athlete, competitor, contestant, jock, opponent, opposition, participant, professional, scrub *(Non-*

formal), sportsman, sportswoman, team player **3.** bettor, chance *or* risk taker, gambler, gamer, punter, sport, wagerer

playful *adj.* cheerful, coltish, comical, elfish, flirtatious, frisky, frolicsome, fun-loving, funny, good-natured, happy, hilarious, humorous, impish, jaunty, jesting, jocund, joking, joyous, kittenish, lighthearted, lively, merry, mirthful, mischievous, peppy, roguish, rollicking, snappy, spirited, sportive, sprightly, teasing, vivacious, waggish, whimsical *Antonyms:* despondent, gloomy, morose, sedate

playground *n.* athletic field, field, playing field *Kinds of playground:* archery ground, badminton court, baseball field, basketball court, bowling alley, bowling green, children's, cricket field, croquet ground *or* lawn, diamond, football field, golf course, gridiron, gym, gymnasium, ice rink, links, oval, park, parkette, pitch, playroom, polo ground, racecourse, racquet *or* squash *or* tennis court, rink, soccer field, swimming pool, track

plaything *n.* **1.** amusement, ball, bauble, doll, gadget, novelty, pastime, tin soldier, toy, trifle, trinket **2.** dupe, fool, instrument, object, tool *Nonformal:* mark, patsy, pigeon, puppet, stooge, sucker

playwright *n.* author, comedian, dramatist, dramaturge, librettist, scenarist, scriptwriter, theatre writer, tragedian, writer

plea *n.* **1.** alibi, apology, defence, excuse, explanation, justification, pretext, rationalization, story, vindication **2.** accusation, allegation, appeal, argument, assertion, call, cause, charge, claim, complaint, cry, entreaty, imploration, imprecation, petition, plead, request, statement, suit, supplication

plead *v.* **1.** allege, contend, defend, state, swear **2.** appeal, ask, beg, beseech, implore, importune, petition, pray, request, supplicate

pleasant *adj.* **1.** cheerful, cheery, delectable, delightful, enchanting, enjoyable, fine, gay, lovely, mellifluous, merry, pleasing, refreshing, satisfying, welcome *Antonyms:* awful, disagreeable, offensive, repulsive **2.** affable, agreeable, amiable, amusing, charming, civilized, congenial, convivial, cordial, diplomatic, engaging, friendly, genial, genteel, gracious, jocund, jovial, kindly, likeable, obliging, polite, sociable

pleasantry *n.* anecdote, badinage, banter, bon mot, comedy, game, humour, jape, jest, jibe, jocularity, joke, levity, merriment, nicety, prank, quip, ralliery, repartee, sally, spirit, wisecrack, wit, witticism

please *v.* **1.** amuse, charm, cheer, content, delight, enchant, enrapture, entertain, exhilarate, gladden, gratify, humour, indulge, make happy, oblige, pleasure, regale, rejoice, satisfy *Nonformal:* tickle, wow *Antonyms:* annoy, depress, dissatisfy, offend, vex **2.** choose, crave, demand, desire, elect, fancy, like, prefer, require, want, will, wish, yearn

pleasing *adj.* adorable, agreeable, amiable, amusing, attractive, captivating, charming, congenial, delicious, delightful, enchanting, engaging, enjoyable, euphonious, eurythmic, favourable, good, gratifying, likeable, nice, palatable, pleasant, pleasurable, polite, satisfactory, savoury, suitable, sweet, toothsome, welcome, winning, winsome *Antonyms:* offensive, pernicious, unpleasant, vexatious

pleasure *n.* **1.** bliss, comfort, contentment, delectation, delight, ease, ecstasy, enchantment, enjoyment, gladness, glee, happiness, joy, rapture, relish, satisfaction, solace *Antonyms:* melancholy, pain, sorrow **2.** amusement, diversion, entertainment, fun, games, hijinks, indulgence, kicks *(Nonformal)*, play, recreation, sport, thrill *Antonyms:* slavery, toil, work **3.** debauchery, excess, fulfillment, gratification, hedonism, immoderation, lust, physical gratification, self-indulgence, sensuality, sex, titillation **4.** choice, command, desire, election, fancy, inclination, liking, mind, option, preference, purpose, want, will, yearning

plebeian *adj.* **1.** banal, common, conventional, demotic, everyday, humble, ignoble, low, lower-class, ordinary, pedestrian, popular, proletarian, working-class *Antonyms:* elitist, influential, monied **2.** base, coarse, lowly, mean, rough, rustic, uncultivated, unpolished, unrefined, unsophisticated, unwashed, vulgar *Antonyms:* cultured, polished, refined, socialized – *n.* citizen, commoner, common man *or* woman, everyman, man *or* woman in the street, peasant, proletarian, voter, worker *Nonformal:* Joe Schmo, plebe

pledge *n.* **1.** bail, bond, collateral, deposit, earnest, good faith, guarantee, guaranty, insurance, security, surety, token, warranty **2.** agreement, assurance, contract, covenant, duty, oath, promise, undertaking, vow, warrant, word **3.** acknowledgment, cheers, chimo, drink, salutation, salute, toast, tribute **4.** acolyte, fledgling, hopeful, initiate, neophyte, new member, novice, recruit, rookie, tyro *Nonformal:* greenhorn, new guy – *v.* **1.** bind, contract, covenant, engage, give word, guarantee, obligate, plight, promise, sign for, swear, undertake, vouch, vow **2.** bet, chance, gamble, hazard, hock *(Nonformal)*, mortgage, pawn **3.** clink *or* tip glasses, drink, drink to, honour, rejoice, toast

plenary *adj.* **1.** absolute, complete, entire, perfect, total, whole **2.** comprehensive, inclusive, open, unconditional, unlimited, unrestricted **3.** crammed, crowded, full, packed, replete, sold-out, stuffed, surfeited, teeming

plentiful *adj.* abounding, abundant, ample, appreciable, bounteous, bountiful, bumper, copious, excessive, extravagant, flowing, flush, fruitful, full, inexhaustible, infinite, large, lavish, liberal, lush, luxuriant, overflowing, plenteous, prodigal, productive, profuse, prolific, replete, ripe, sufficient, sumptuous, superabundant, superfluous, swimming, teeming, unlimited *Antonyms:* inadequate, lacking, scarce, sparing, wanting

plenty *n.* abundance, affluence, bunch, copiousness, cornucopia, deluge, excess, flood, full house, great deal, lots, luxury, mass, opulence, piles, plenitude, plethora, profuseness, profusion, prosperity, sufficiency, surfeit, surplus, wealth *Nonformal:* avalanche, heap, loads, mountain, stack, tonnes *Antonyms:* absence, dearth, lack, paucity

plethora *n.* deluge, excess, flood, glut, overabundance, overflow, overkill, plenty, profusion, redundancy, superabundance, superfluity, surfeit, surplus *Antonyms:* deficiency, scarcity, shortage

pliable *adj.* **1.** adaptable, bendable, ductile, flexible, limber, lithe, malleable, manageable, mouldable, plastic, pliant, responsive, rubbery, supple, tractable, yielding *Antonyms:* inflexible, rigid, set, stiff, unyielding **2.** amenable, biddable, compliant, docile, governable, green *(Nonformal)*, gullible, impressionable, naive, obedient, susceptible *Antonyms:* mulish, obstinate, recalcitrant, stubborn

pliers *n.* cutters, pincers, tool *Kinds of pliers:* flatnose, gas fitters, hemostats, needlenose, roundnose, snubnose, wirecutting

plight *n.* adversity, bad news, circumstance, condition, corner, difficulty, dilemma, extremity, hole, impasse, incident, misfortune, perplexity, predicament, quandary, scrape, situation, spot, state *Nonformal:* kettle of fish, pickle – *v.* betroth, engage, jump the broom, pledge, promise, swear

plod *v.* **1.** drudge, grind, labour, perform, persevere, plug, slave, slog, sweat, toil **2.** clump, drag, flounder, hike, schlep *(Nonformal)*, tramp, trample, tread, trudge, walk heavily

plot *n.* **1.** acreage, allotment, area, arpent, concession, division, ground, land, lawn, lot, parcel, patch, piece, pitch, property, real estate, yard **2.** artifice, cabal, collusion, complicity, connivance, conspiracy, contrivance, design, device, fix, frame, intrigue, machination, manoeuvre, plan, ploy, practice, ruse, scam *(Nonformal)*, scheme, setup, stratagem, trick **3.** action, development, events, incidents, movement, narrative, outline, progress, scenario, scene, story, story line, structure, subplot, thread *Plot elements:* buildup, catastrophe, climax, crisis, dénouement, discovery, irony, outcome, resolution, reversal, suspense **4.** blueprint, blues *(Nonformal)*, boundary plan, map, registered plan, sketch, survey *or* surveyor's plan, title **5.** burial ground, crypt, family plot, final resting ground, grave, gravesite, resting place, tomb – *v.* **1.** angle, brew, cabal, collude, conceive, concoct, connive, conspire, contrive, design, devise, draft, finagle, frame, hatch, imagine, intrigue, lay, machinate, manoeuvre, operate, outline, plan, project, promote, scheme, set up, sketch, wangle **2.** chart, draft, draw, delineate, map, outline, plan, rough out, sketch

plow *n.* colter, cultivator, harrow, lister, rake, rotary, rototiller, snowplow, windrower – *v.* **1.** break, break ground, cultivate, dig up, dress, farm, furrow, harrow, push, tend, till, turn *or* turn over, work **2.** bulldoze, clean, clear, remove, shove, sweep

ploy *n.* artifice, contrivance, device, dodge, feint, gambit, game, manoeuvre, move, movement, play, ruse, scheme, stratagem, subterfuge, tactic, trick, wile

pluck *n.* backbone, boldness, bravery, courage, dauntlessness, determination, drive, dynamism, energy, enthusiasm, grit, heart, mettle, nerve, spirit, spunk *Nonformal:* chutzpah, gumption, guts, intestinal fortitude, moxie *Antonyms:* cowardice, timidity – *v.* catch, clutch, collect, cull, draw, depilate, deplume, gather, grab, harvest, jerk, pick, pick at, plunk, pull at *or* out, snatch, tug, tweak, twitch, vellicate, yank

plug *n.* **1.** advertisement, blurb, marketing, mention, promotion, publicity, push, recommendation, sales pitch, write-up *Nonformal:* ballyhoo, bumph, good word, hype, puff **2.** bung, cap, check, choke, cork, curb, damper, lid, spigot, stopper, tampon, top, wadding – *v.* **1.** block, choke, clog, close, congest, cork, cover, fill, obstruct, occlude, pack, ram, seal, secure, stop, stopper, stuff **2.** advertise, boost, build up, hype *(Nonformal)*, mention, pitch, promote, publicize, push, recommend, sell **3.** endure, labour, peg away *(Nonformal)*, persevere, persist, plod, slog, strive, survive, toil, work **4.** box, drum, hammer, hit, poke, punch, rap, smite, strike *Nonformal:* bop, bust, conk, pop, sock, slug

plumb *adj.* **1.** on-line, perpendicular, straight, upright, vertical **2.** absolute, complete, full-blown, outright, perfect, sheer, stark, total, unequivocal, utter *Antonyms:* part, partial, qualified – *n.* bob, lead, plumb bob, plummet, sinker, weight – *v.* **1.** align, conform, correct, even, level, straighten **2.** mark twain, measure, sound, test **3.** delve, explore, fathom, penetrate, probe, search, unravel

plump *adj.* **1.** beefy, buxom, chubby, chunky, comfortable, corpulent, fat, fleshy, overweight, portly, pudgy, roly-poly, rotund, Rubenesque, stout, tubby, voluptuous *Antonyms:* bony, emaciated, lanky, skinny, slender **2.** brimming, bursting *(Nonformal)*, crammed, crowded, filled, flush, jammed, loaded, puffy, stuffed, swelled *Antonyms:* depleted, empty, void **3.** blunt, brusque, candid, curt, explicit, frank, matter-of-fact, straightforward *Antonyms:* hesitant, reticent, taciturn – *adv.* **1.** all of a sudden, immediately, instantly, precipitously, quickly, suddenly, swiftly, without warning *Nonformal:* bang, pop, plunk **2.** abruptly, bluntly, candidly, crassly, forthrightly, frankly, openly, plainly, straightforwardly

plunder *n.* loot, pickings, prey, prize, quarry, spoils, stolen goods, take, trappings, winnings *Nonformal:* boodle, booty, filthy lucre, hot goods, swag – *v.* appropriate, depredate, despoil, filch, freeboot, lay waste, liberate, lift, loot, maraud, pilfer, pillage, pirate, privateer, raid, ransack, ravage, rob, sack, spoil, steal, strip *Nonformal:* knock off *or* over, relieve, rip off, smash and grab, snatch

plunge *n.* **1.** bellyflop *(Nonformal)*, descent, dive, dunk, fall, header, immersion, jump, nose-dive, submersion, swoop **2.** collapse, crash, decline, depression, dip, downturn, drop, dwindling, reduction, stumble – *v.* **1.** descend, dive, fall, hurtle, nose-dive, pitch, plummet, sink, stoop, topple, tumble **2.** douse, dunk, immerse, soak, steep, submerge, wet **3.** bolt, dash, fly into, hasten, precipitate, race, run headlong, rush, tear

plurality *n.* **1.** bulk, greater number *or* part, lead, majority, mass, most, preponderance, weight **2.** abundance, greatness, horde, lot, many, multiplicity, numerousness, plethora, profusion, score, selection, variety *Nonformal:* heaps, scads, skid *Antonyms:* dearth, lack, paucity

plus *adj.* added, additional, augmented, auxiliary, extra, extraneous, more, positive, supplemental *Antonyms:* minus, negative – *n.* addition, advantage, asset, benefit, bonus, boon, credit, dividend, gain, gift, gratuity, present, prize, reward, windfall *Nonformal:* freebie, perk *Antonyms:* detriment, handicap, liability

plush *adj.* costly, deluxe, elegant, extravagant, fancy, five-star, lavish, luscious, lush, luxurious, luxury, opulent, ostentatious, palatial, rich, stylish, sumptuous, upscale *Nonformal:* cushy, fancy-schmancy, posh, ritzy *Antonyms:* cheap, inexpensive, ordinary, plain, Spartan

ply *n.* **1.** layer, leaf, sheet, strand, thickness **2.** bent, bias, disposition, fancy, inclination, interpretation, opinion, preference, proclivity, propensity, view – *v.* **1.** dispense, employ, exercise, follow, function, practice, pursue, use, utilize, wield, work at **2.** bend, carve, curve, fashion, forge, frame, mould, round shape **3.** cater to, give, minister, offer, provision, purvey, replenish, satisfy, supply, tender *Antonyms:* cut off, remove **4.** assail, beat, flail, flay, flog, hit, strike, whip **5.** carry, convey, cross, ferry, move, proceed, sail, ship, steer, transport, traverse

poach *v.* **1.** bark *(Newfoundland)*, blanch, boil, cook, heat, parboil, submerse **2.** appropriate, bag, encroach, filch, fish *or* hunt illegally, infringe upon, intrude, pilfer, plunder, rob, smuggle, snag, steal, trespass

pocket *adj.* abridged, capsulized, condensed, concealable, diminutive, itsy-bitsy *(Nonformal)*, little, midget, mini, miniature, minute, pint-sized, portable, small, tiny, wee – *n.* **1.** bag, bin, cavity, chamber, compartment, fold, hole, hollow, opening, pouch, receptacle, sack, socket **2.** bankroll, budget, capital, cash, coin, currency, finances, loot, means, money, nest-egg, savings, wealth **3.** accumulation, buildup, mine, mother lode, quantity, rich resource, stock, store, trove, vein **4.** cav
cavern, cavity, cranny, den, depressio
dimple, grotto, hole, hollow, scoop, swa
5. belt, bubble, camp, ghetto, enclosur
precinct, region, reserve, zone – *v.* **1**
appropriate, filch, misappropriate, ni
(Nonformal), pick, pilfer, purloin, seiz
snag, steal, swindle, take, thieve **2.** abid
accept, acquiesce, allow, bear, brav
endure, stomach, suffer, sustain, swallov
tolerate, weather, withstand *Antonym*
dissent, reject, spurn **3.** close off, concea
confine, enclose, hem in, hide, suppress

pod *n.* **1.** case, covering, hull, husk, sheat
sheathing, shell, shuck, skin **2.** booth, cag
carrel, chamber, compartment, cubicl
enclosure, housing, niche, nook, roon
shelter, vessel **3.** bevy, collection, cove
covey, flock, group, herd, litter, prid
school, selection *See also:* **group**

poem *n.* composition, poetry, rhyme, son
verse *Kinds of poem:* abstract, acrosti
ballad, *bhakti (Indian)*, boasting, *ca*
ligramme (French), canto, *chapka (Kor*
an), concrete, confessional, conversatio
piece, crown, dirge, doggerel, dramati
monologue, dub, eclogue, elegy, epic, ap
thalamium, epigram, epithet, found, *ghaz*
(Arabic), glosas, haiku, howl, idyll, jingl
kinetic, language, limerick, lipogram, lon
love, lyric, lyrical, nursery rhyme, occa
sional, ode, palinode, pastoral, pattern, pic
togram, prose, poster, rap, fondeau, fonde
rune, St. John's ballad, sonnet, sound, vi
lanelle, visual *Kinds of poetic devices*
accent, allegory, alliteration, alliterativ
harmony, anaphora, antiphrasis, asso
nance, bob and wheel, consonance, dic
tion, dissonance, ellipsis, enjambment, la
guage, metalepsis, metaphor, mete
metonymy, onomatopoeia, paralipsis, rep
tition, rhyme, rhythm, simile, synecdoch
tone, zeugma *Kinds of poetic structur*
couplet, line, octave, *ottava rim*
(Italian), quatrain, quintain, quintet
septet, sestet, *sestina (French)*, sextai
Spenserian stanza, stanza, *tercerill*
(Spanish), terset, verse paragraph *Kind*
of poetic verse: Alcmanic, alliterative
anacreontic, Archilochian, blank, bucolic
catalogue, chain, *changga (Korean)*, com
posite, concrete, correlative, *cossant*
(Spanish), echo, familiar, fescennine, free

gnomic, heroic, Homeric, ithyphallic, jazz, light, mosaic, narrative, occasional, Pindaric, pithiambic, rhopalic, *rhupunt (Welsh)*, sapphic, serpentine, sick, stichos, syllabic, tumbling *Japanese:* choka, tanka

poet *n.* balladmonger, bard, goliard *(Historical)*, jongleur, lyricist, lyrist, minnesinger, minstrel, oracle, poetaster, rhymer, rimester, *skald (Scandinavian)*, troubadour, *trouvère (French)*, versifier, vers-librist, visionary *Canadian poets' groups:* Blue Mountain Poets, Confederation Poets, Contact Poets, Dub Poets, First Statement Poets, Highrise Poets, McGill Poets, Poet's Corner, Preview Group, Song Fishermen, Tish

poetic *adj.* **1.** aesthetic, artistic, beautiful, elaborate, flowery, graceful, lovely, ornate, pretty, romantic, starry-eyed, well-composed *Antonyms:* commonplace, dull, prosaic **2.** dramatic, flowing, melodious, metrical, musical, poetical, rhythmic, rhythmical, songlike, tuneful, versicular **3.** bardic, bucolic, eclogic, elegiac, Homeric, idyllic, imaginative, lyric, lyrical, mystical, oracular, pastoral, runic, sublime, surrealistic, transcendental, visionary *Antonyms:* down-to-earth, reasonable, sensible **4.** bombastic, elevated, heavily embroidered, inflated, overblown, overembellished, pompous, pretentuous, purple, turgi

poetry *n.* metrical composition, poems, poesy, prosody, verse, versification *Groupings of poetry:* bucolic, civic, concrete, confessional, didactic, epic, epideictic, erotic, found, lyric, Georgian, Imagist, melic, metaphysical, nonsense, occasional, oral, pastoral, pattern, sound, slam, strict meter, topographical, underground, visual *See also:* **poem**

poignant *adj.* **1.** affecting, agonizing, distressing, disturbing, grievous, heartrending, intense, lamentable, painful, pathetic, tragic *Antonyms:* happy, joyous, lighthearted **2.** apt, biting, caustic, cutting, incisive, insightful, keen, mordant, penetrating, probing, pungent, sharp, strong, trenchant *Antonyms:* dull, flat, insipid **3.** earnest, emotional, heartfelt, moving, passionate, sentimental, sincere, touching *Antonyms:* cold, dishonest, unfeeling

point *n.* **1.** apex, cusp, end, jag, nib, pinnacle, sharp end, taper, tip **2.** antler, arrow, barb, bayonet, beak, bill, claw, cone, dagger, javelin, knife, needle, pin, prick, prong, sabre, spike, spine, spur, stick, stiletto, sword, tang, tine, tip, tooth **3.** decimal, diacritical mark, dot, full stop, mark, period, punctuation mark, stop, tittle **4.** locality, location, place, placement, position, site, situation, slot. spot **5.** cape, delta, extension, peninsula, promontory, spit, strip **6.** boundary, brim, brink, degree, end, extent, extremity, frontier, limit, maximum, reach, state, verge **7.** age, date, era, *fin de siècle (French)*, hour, minute, moment, period, second, time, turn of the century **8.** aim, argument, bottom line, cogency, core, crux, design, drift, end, essence, gist, goal, heart, idea, import, intention, main idea, marrow, matter, meaning, meat, motive, nitty-gritty *(Nonformal)*, nub, pitch, punch, purpose, reason, significance, stuff, subject, text, theme, thrust **9.** argument, case, defence, evidence, fact, idea, statement, suggestion **10.** advice, guidance, help, idea, information, instruction, pointer, teaching aid, tip **11.** aspect, attribute, characteristic, constituent, detail, element, facet, feature, item, part, particular peculiarity, property, punctilio, quality, trait **12.** *Sports:* basket *(Basketball);* conversion, rouge, safety, touchback, touchdown *(Football);* goal *(Hockey, lacrosse, soccer);* leaner, ringer *(Horseshoes);* mark, notch, run *(Baseball);* score, tally, trick *(Bridge);* try *(Rugby)* – *v.* **1.** bespeak, denote, designate, finger, hint, imply, indicate, make, name, peg, pin down, show, signify, specify, suggest, tab, tag **2.** aim, beam, cast, direct, face, guide, head, influence, lead, slant, steer, train, turn **3.** accent, accentuate, emphasize, highlight, spotlight, stress, underline, underscore **4.** file, grind to a point, hone, sharpen, shave off, taper, whet, whittle

pointed *adj.* **1.** accurate, acute, barbed, biting, cutting, incisive, insinuating, keen, mordant, penetrating, pertinent, right on *(Nonformal)*, sarcastic, sharp, straightforward, tart, telling, trenchant, uncensored **2.** cornered, edged, peaked, piked, pointy, pronged, razor-like, sharp, sharp-cornered, spiked *Antonyms:* blunt, obtuse, unedged **3.** bold, clear, emphasized, italicized, large, marked, obvious, patent, plain, underlined, visible *Antonyms:* concealed, discreet, hidden, obfuscated

pointer *n.* **1.** arrow, dial, finger, gauge, guide, hand, index, indicator, mark, needle, rod **2.** advice, caution, clue, hint, recommendation, suggestion, tip, warning

pointless *adj.* absurd, aimless, fruitless, futile, going nowhere, impotent, inane, inconsequential, ineffective, insignificant, irrelevant, meaningless, nonsensical, remote, ridiculous, senseless, silly, trivial, unavailing, uninteresting, unnecessary, unproductive, useless, vague, vain, waste of time, worthless *Antonyms:* appropriate, fitting, fruitful, meaningful, worthwhile

poise *n.* **1.** assurance, bearing, calmness, composure, coolness, dignity, diplomacy, ease, elegance, equanimity, grace, polish, presence, *savoir-faire (French)*, self-assurance, self-possession, serenity, tact, tranquility, urbanity **2.** balance, equilibrium, equipoise, firmness, stability, steadiness, support – *v.* balance, float, hang, hold, hover, stabilize, steady, support, suspend

poison *n.* bacteria, bane, blight, contagion, contamination, corruption, germ, infection, malignancy, miasma, toxicant, toxin, toxoid, venom, virus *Selected kinds of poisons:* agent orange, aldicarb, amatoxin, arsenic, belladona, bloodroot, carbolic acid, Canadian moonseed, carbon monoxide, curare, cyanide, digoxin, dioxin, dormant oil, hemlock, insecticide, jimsonweed, lead, mustard gas, nightshade, oleander, paraquat, phosgene, radiation, rat poisen, rodenticide, strychnine, venim de crapaud, venom, – *v.* **1.** contaminate, destroy, fester, harm, infect, injure, kill, pollute, taint **2.** adulterate, alter, corrupt, debase, defile, deprave, pervert, stain, subvert, undermine, vitiate, warp

poisonous *adj.* bad, baleful, baneful, corruptive, dangerous, deleterious, destructive, detrimental, evil, fatal, harmful, hurtful, infective, lethal, malicious, malignant, morbid, mortal, noisome, noxious, pernicious, pestilential, poisoned, septic, toxic, venomous, vicious, virulent *Antonyms:* benign, harmless, innocuous

poke *n.* blow, boost, butt, dig, hit, jab, nudge, prod, punch, push, shove, stab, thrust – *v.* **1.** amble, dally, dawdle, delay, drag, idle, lag, loiter, move along slowly, procrastinate, put off, tarry, trail *Nonformal:* dilly-dally, mosey, schlep **2.** arouse, awaken, dig, elbow, goose, hit, jab, jostle, nudge, prod, provoke, punch, push, ram, rouse, shoulder, shove, stab, stick, stimulate, stir, thrust **3.** butt in, kibitz, interfere, intrude, investigate, meddle, nose, peek, probe, pry, snoop, tamper **4.** bulge, extend, jut, protrude, stick out, swell

poker *n.* card game, cards, gambling *Some kinds of poker:* baseball, Caribbean stud, chase the ace, Cincinnati, death wheel, draw, five-card draw, high *or* low Chicago, iron cross, jacks or better, pass the trash, showdown, spit in the ocean, Texas hold'em, seven-card stud, wild card *Kinds of poker hands:* five of a kind, flush, four of a kind, full house, pair, royal flush, straight, straight flush, three of a kind, two of a kind, two pair

polar *adj.* **1.** antagonistic, antithetical, contradictory, contrary, counter, diametric, opposed, opposite *Antonyms:* concurrent, equivalent, homogenous, resembling, uniform **2.** arctic, antarctic, cold, extreme, freezing, frigid, frozen, glacial, icy, northern, southern, terminal **3.** axial, central, directing, guiding, leading

pole *n.* **1.** bar, beam, column, flagpole, flagstaff, leg, mast, pile, plank, post, pylon, rod, shaft, spar, staff, stake, standard, stave, stick, stilt **2.** end, extremity, farthest point, margin, nadir, terminus, ultimate

polemic *adj.* argumentative, contentious, controversial, dialectic, disputatious, quarrelsome – *n.* argument, attack, controversy, contention, debate, dispute, fight

police *n.* constable, constabulary, cop, detective, force, law, law enforcement, officer, patrolman *Nonformal:* badge, flatfoots, fuzz, heat, narc, pig, the man *Police forces: carabinièri (Italian), gendarme (French),* Interpol, Mounties *(Nonformal)*, MP *(Military)*, municipal, provincial, RCMP, Royal Canadian Mounted Police, Scotland Yard *(British)*, *Sûreté (Quebec)*, *Zaptiah*

(Turkish) Historical: Gestapo, Hepburn's Hussars, K.G.B. *U.S.:* F.B.I., Federal Bureau of Investigation – *v.* defend, enforce the law, guard, officiate, patrol, protect, regulate, safeguard, secure, serve, watch

policy *n.* **1.** action, approach, arrangement, code, course, custom, design, guideline, line, method, order, plan, practice, principle, procedure, program, protocol, regulation, rule, scheme, stratagem, strategy, tactics, tenet, theory **2.** line, party line, platform, polity, position, public policy **3.** agreement, contract, insurance, paper **4.** caution, consideration, diplomacy, discretion, judgment, judiciousness, prudence, shrewdness, wisdom *Antonyms:* impetuosity, imprudence, rashness

polish *n.* **1.** shine, brightness, brilliance, burnish, finish, glint, gloss, lustre, sheen, sparkle **2.** compound, oil, paste, rub, spit and vinegar *(Nonformal)*, spray, wax **3.** breeding, class, cultivation, culture, elegance, finesse, finish, grace, politesse, refinement, style, suavity, urbanity – *v.* **1.** amend, better, correct, cultivate, enhance, finish, improve, mature, perfect, refine, round **2.** brighten, brush, buff, burnish, clean, furbish, glaze, gloss, rub, scrub, sheen, shine, slick, smooth, wax

polite *adj.* affable, civil, cordial, courteous, courtly, cultured, deferential, elegant, diplomatic, genial, genteel, pleasing, polished, proper, refined, respectful, tactful, well-behaved, well-mannered, well-spoken *Antonyms:* boorish, brash, crude, offensive, rude, vulgar

politic *adj.* **1.** diplomatic, judicious, political, prudent, sagacious, sensible, sharp, shrewd, tactful, wise *Antonyms:* artless, guileless, naive, unsophisticated **2.** cagey, calculating, crafty, cunning, designing, Machiavellian, manipulative, scheming, sly, smooth, tricky, wily

politician *n.* candidate, favourite son, incumbent, lame duck, lawmaker, legislator, member of parliament, minister, office-holder, office seeker, parliamentarian, partisan, party member, political leader, statesman *Nonformal:* baby-kisser, bagman, flesh presser, mainstreeter, pol, politico, ward heeler, whistle-stopper, windbag

politics *n.* **1.** civics, diplomacy, government, leadership, legislature, statesmanship **2.** belief, ideology, opinions, partisanship, party line *or* philosophy, platform, policy, polity, position, program **3.** domestic affairs, foreign affairs, internal affairs, realpolitik

poll *n.* **1.** ballot, election, vote, voting **2.** count, inventory, lineup, list, registry, roll, roster, tally **3.** census, demography, enumeration, interview, opinion, questionnaire, sampling, solicitation, survey **4.** cranium, crown, head, noggin *(Nonformal)*, skull – *v.* **1.** cast one's ballot, choose, elect, select, vote **2.** analyze, canvas, collect, interview, question, record **3.** chop, clip, cut, dehorn, dock, prune, remove, shave, sheer, trim, truncate

pollute *v.* adulterate, alter, affect, besmirch, contaminate, corrupt, defile, dirty, doctor *(Nonformal)*, foul, infect, mar, poison, soil, spoil, stain, sully, taint, violate, vitiate *Antonyms:* cleanse, decontaminate, sanitize, sterilize

poltergeist *n.* banshee, ghost, manifestation, phantom, presence, shade, shadow, *skookum (Pacific Coast)*, spectre, spirit, spook *(Nonformal)*, wraith

polychromatic *adj.* colourful, gay, harlequin, kaleidoscopic, mottled, multicoloured, opalescent, prismatic, psychedelic, rich, technicoloured, varicoloured, variegated

polymorphous *adj.* alterable, changeable, mercurial, metamorphic, multiform, mutable, pleomorphic, protean, variable

pomade *n.* balm, cream, gel, greasy kid's stuff *(Nonformal)*, lotion, lubricant, oil, ointment, salve, tonic, unguent

pomp *n.* **1.** ceremony, circumstance, display, eye candy *(Nonformal)*, fanfare, flourish, formality, grandeur, pageant, rite, ritual, shine, show, solemnity, splendour, state *Antonyms:* casualness, simplicity, unpretentiousness **2.** arrogance, braggadocio, ostentation, rodomontade, self-aggrandizement, vainglory, vanity *Antonyms:* humility, modesty

pompous *adj.* **1.** affected, arrogant, conceited, dogmatic, haughty, high-brow, high-flown, pontifical, pretentious, proud, self-important, snobbish, superficial, vainglorious *Nonformal:* artsy-fartsy, snooty, snot-nosed, uppity *Antonyms:* demure, modest, retiring **2.** bombastic, embellished, flatulent, flowery, fustian, grandiloquent, inflated, ornate, overstated, poetic, rococo, stuffy *(Nonformal)*, turgid *Antonyms:* demotic, pithy, plain, prosaic, simple **3.** ceremonious, dignified, grand, impressive, lofty, magnificent, majestic, princely, solemn, splendid

ponder *v.* appraise, brood, cogitate, consider, contemplate, deliberate, dwell, evaluate, examine, meditate, mull over, muse, reason, reflect, ruminate, speculate, study, think about *or* over, turn over, use the little grey cells *(Nonformal)*, weigh

ponderous *adj.* **1.** dreary, dry, dull, laborious, laboured, lifeless, monotonous, overdone, pedantic, pedestrian, plodding, stiff, stilted, stodgy, stuffy, tedious, vapid, verbose, wooden *Antonyms:* deft, graceful, lively, nimble **2.** awkward, bulky, burdensome, cumbersome, elephantine, heavy, hefty, huge, massive, onerous, oppressive, substantial, troublesome, unmanageable, unwieldy, weighty *Antonyms:* buoyant, flimsy, light, small, weightless

pontiff *n.* abbot, archbishop, bishop, father, papa *(Nonformal)*, pontifex, pope, prelate, priest, primate

pontificate *v.* declaim, discourse, expound, harangue, lecture, orate, preach, sermonize – *n.* diocese, episcopy, papacy, popedom *(Nonformal)*, prelacy

pool *n.* **1.** basin, bath, billabong *(Australian)*, lagoon, lake, millpond, pond, puddle, splash *(Nonformal)*, swimming pool, tank, tarn, watering hole **2.** cartel, combination, conglomerate, consortium, cooperative, group, guild, hansa, shareholders, syndicate, trust **3.** ante, funds, jackpot, kitty, pot, purse, reserves, stakes – *v.* **1.** amalgamate, blend, combine, join forces, league, merge, put *or* throw in together, share, team up **2.** accumulate, collect, converge, garner, gather, glean, hoard, stockpile

poor *adj.* **1.** badly off, bankrupt, broke, deprived, destitute, dirt poor, disadvantaged, impecunious, impoverished, indigent, insolvent, mangy, moneyless, penniless, penurious, poverty-stricken, shabby, squalid, underprivileged, unfortunate *Nonformal:* hard up, pinched, skint, strapped *Antonyms:* affluent, comfortable, prosperous, rich, wealthy **2.** deficient, inadequate, incomplete, insufficient, lacking, lacklustre, meagre, measly, paltry, picayune, reduced, scanty, skimpy, slight **3.** bad, catchpenny, egregious, faulty, inferior, jerrybuilt, mean, mediocre, ordinary, rotten, second-rate, substandard, unsatisfactory *Nonformal:* crappy, lousy, shabby **4.** cursed, hapless, ill-fated, luckless, miserable, pathetic, pitiful, rueful, unfortunate, unhappy, unlucky, wretched *Antonyms:* auspicious, blessed, favoured, providential **5.** bare, barren, depleted, effete, exhausted, feeble, fruitless, impaired, imperfect, indisposed, infertile, infirm, puny, sick, sterile, unfertile, unfruitful, unproductive, weak, worthless *Antonyms:* fertile, fructuous, productive, teeming, yielding **6.** delicate, enfeebled, frail, indisposed, infirm, poorly, under the weather, unwell, valetudinary **7.** abject, base, contemptible, corrupt, disreputable, ignoble, little, low, mean, miscreant, unsavory, vile, wicked **8.** emaciated, gaunt, lanky, raw-boned, scrawny, skin and bones *(Nonformal)*, skinny, thin, undernourished

poorly *adj.* ailing, below par, ill, indisposed, low, not well, rotten, sick, sickly, unwell *Antonyms:* fit, hale, hearty, healthy, well – *adv.* **1.** amateurishly, badly, crudely, defectively, inadequately, incompetently, inexpertly, shabbily, unsatisfactorily, unsuccessfully *Antonyms:* acceptably, adequately, competently, satisfactorily, sufficiently **2.** disdainfully, disparagingly, disrespectfully, gracelessly, scornfully, tactlessly

pop *adj.* commercial, fashionable, favourite, modern, popular – *adv.* **1.** abruptly, by surprise, suddenly, unexpectedly **2.** explosively, *fortemente (Italian)*, loudly, noisily, thunderously – *n.* **1.** carbonated beverage seltzer, soda *Kinds of pop:* cherry cola, cola, cream soda, ginger ale, ginger beer, limeade, orangeade, root beer, soda *or* tonic water, spruce beer **2.** boom, detonation, discharge, explosion, fulmination, gunfire, shot **3.** bang, noise, thud, thump **4.** concert, medley, musical, performance, pop music, program **5.** da, dad, daddy, father, grandfather, pa, *père (French) Nonformal:* gramps, old man– *v.* **1.** bang, blow, boom, burst, crack, detonate, explode, go off, shoot **2.** dart, insert, jump, leap, rush, thrust **3.** bug *(Nonformal)*, bulge, dilate, goggle, protrude, stick out **4.** appear, drop by *or* in, look *or* stop in, visit

pope *n.* authority, bishop, Bishop of Rome *(Roman Catholic)*, Dalai Lama *(Buddhism)*, head, Holy Father, papa *(Nonformal)*, parish priest *(Russian Orthodox)*, patriarch, pontifex, pontiff, prelate, primate, Vicar of Christ

popinjay *n.* beau, boulevardier, clotheshorse, coxcomb, dandy, fashion plate, fop, jack-a-dandy, jackanapes, macaroni, peacock, poser *(Nonformal)*, show-off

poppycock *n.* balderdash, bombast, claptrap, drivel, exquisite, flummery, folderol, fuddle-duddle, gibberish, hot air, humbug, mumbo jumbo, nonsense, palaver, pretension, rubbish *Nonformal:* bull, crap, eyewash, gas, gobbleygook, malarkey, moonshine, tommyrot

populace *n.* citizenry, common people, demos, hoi polloi, horde, inhabitants, masses, mob, multitude, occupants, people, plebs *(Nonformal)*, proletariat, throng

popular *adj.* **1.** accepted, admired, approved, *au courant (French)*, fashionable, in, in demand *or* favour *or* vogue, praised, sought-after, stylish, trendy *Nonformal:* boffo, pop, the rage *Antonyms:* démodé, outmoded, passé **2.** conventional, customary, leading, pandemic, predominant, prevailing, prevalent, reigning, standard, stock, usual, widespread *Antonyms:* atypical, unconventional **3.** agreeable, attractive, beloved, favourite, friendly, likeable, loveable, pleasing, sociable, well-liked *Antonyms:* despised, disliked, outcast **4.** average, common, everyday, folk, homespun, normal, ordinary, quotidian, routine, workaday *Antonyms:* rare, special, unusual **5.** accessible, commercial, demotic, direct, lowest common denominator, simplified, understandable, vulgar *Antonyms:* difficult, esoteric, highbrow, highfalutin *(Nonformal)* **6.** affordable, budget, cheap, inexpensive, low-priced, moderate, reasonable *Antonyms:* exorbitant, expensive, pricey

popularity *n.* **1.** acceptance, acclaim, adoration, approval, boxoffice, celebrity, clout *(Nonformal)*, drawing power, esteem, fame, favour, idolization, lionization, recognition, regard, renown, reputation, repute *Antonyms:* denigration, deprecation, dishonour, distaste **2.** currency, fashion, fashionableness, prevalence, style, universality

popularize *v.* **1.** commercialize, coarsen, generalize, simplify *Nonformal:* doctor, dumb down, vulgarize **2.** broadcast, disseminate, familiarize, herald, propagandize, publish, spread, universalize

population *n.* citizenry, community, culture, denizens, dwellers, folk, inhabitants, mob, multitude, natives, people, populace, proletariat, public, residents, society, state

populous *adj.* crowded, dense, jampacked, overpopulated, packed, peopled, settled, swarming, teeming, thick, thronged *Antonyms:* barren, desolate, empty

porch *n.* **1.** balcony, deck, gallery, lanai, patio, stoop, sundeck, terrace, veranda **2.** covering, doorway, entryway, porte-cochere, portico, propylaeum, shelter

pore *n.* aperture, gap, hole, foramen, opening, orifice, outlet, pit, perforation, pock, stoma

pornographic *adj.* adult, bawdy, blue *(Nonformal)*, carnal, dirty, erotic, explicit, filthy, immoral, indecent, lecherous, lewd, obscene, off-colour, offensive, prurient, raunchy, ribald, risqué, salacious, sensual, sexual, smutty, steamy, X-rated

porous *adj.* **1.** absorbent, absorptive, penetrable, permeable, pervious, spongy *Antonyms:* impenetrable, impervious, solid

2. cancellous, honeycombed, perforated, poriferous, sandy, spongelike

port *adj.* larboard, left, left-side – *n.* **1.** anchorage, asylum, harbour, haven, outport *(Newfoundland)*, port-of-call, seaport, shelter **2.** door, gate, hole, window **3.** computer link, connection, socket *Computer Ports:* communications, imput/output, joystick, parallel, printer, serial **4.** air, attitude, bearing, behaviour, carriage, comport, conduct, countenance, demeanour, manner, mien, poise, posture **5.** larboard, left, left side **6.** after-dinner drink, apéritif, dessert wine, fortified wine – *v.* **1.** carry, cart, convey, haul, move, shift, portage, transfer, transport **2.** change, convert, copy, move, recode, rewrite, transfer, translate

portable *adj.* cartable, convenient, conveyable, easily carried, handy, light, lightweight, manageable, movable, transportable *Antonyms:* fixed, rooted, stationary

portage *n.* **1.** carrying place, passageway, path, route, track, trail, walkway **2.** carriage, cartage, conveyance, haulage, lugging *(Nonformal)*, moving, shipment, transporting – *v.* bear, carry, cart, convey, drag, haul, lug, move, port, pull along, schlep *(Nonformal)*, tote, transfer, transport, truck

portend *v.* augur, bespeak, betoken, bode, call, call it *(Nonformal)*, forebode, forecast, foreshadow, foretell, foretoken, forewarn, herald, hint, indicate, point to, predict, prognosticate, promise, prophesy, read, see coming, threaten, vaticinate, warn *Commonly misused:* **portent**

portent *n.* **1.** augury, boding, caution, clue, foreboding, foreshadowing, foretoken, forewarning, harbinger, hunch, indication, omen, premonition, presentiment, prognostication, sign, sinking feeling, warning **2.** concern, gravity, importance, interest, meaning, significance, urgency, weight **3.** marvel, miracle, phenomenon, prodigy, rarity, sensation, spectacle, wonder *Commonly misused:* **portend**

portentous *adj.* **1.** consequential, critical, exigent, fraught, heavy, important, landmark, momentous, noteworthy, serious, significant, substantial, vital, weighty *Antonyms:* airy, immaterial, superficial trivial **2.** doomed, foreboding, ill-omened inauspicious, menacing, ominous, sinister threatening, unfavourable *Antonyms.* hopeful, promising **3.** astonishing, astounding, breath-taking, exceptional, extraordinary, miraculous, prodigious, remarkable spectacular, wondrous

porter *n.* **1.** attendant, bearer, bellhop, caddie, carrier, coolie, cupbearer, doorkeeper gunbearer, litter-bearer, redcap, skycap stretcher-bearer **2.** cleaner, maintenance man *or* woman, sexton **3.** cerberus concierge, doorkeeper, doorman, gatekeeper, guard, ostiary, sentry, turnkey, watchman

portfolio *n.* **1.** attaché case, bag, brief bag briefcase, case, container, folder, notebook, valise **2.** bailiwick, bureau, commissariat, department, jurisdiction, ministry office, position, post **3.** credentials, documents, dossier, investments, papers, samples

portion *n.* **1.** bit, chunk, cutting, division excerpt, extract, fraction, fragment, parcel part, particle, percentile, piece, ratio, sample, scrap, section, segment **2.** allocation allotment, allowance, apportionment assignment, dole, dose, quantity, quota regale *(Historical)*, share *Nonformal:* cut fix **3.** collop, cupful, dish, handful, helping moiety, morsel, plate, platter, ration, serving, share, slice, sliver, taste **4.** bequest dot, dower, dowry, heritage, inheritance legacy – *v.* **1.** break up, divide, halve, part quarter, separate, slice, split **2.** allocate allot, assign, disperse, disseminate, distribute, divvy *or* dole out, mete **3.** bequeath endow, invest, leave

portly *adj.* **1.** ample, broad, bulky, burly corpulent, fat, fleshy, heavy, hefty, large, obese, overweight, plump, rotund, stout tubby *(Nonformal) Antonyms:* delicate lanky, slender, thin, willowy **2.** aristocratic courtly, dignified, grand, imposing, impressive, majestic, regal, stately *Antonyms.* humble, modest, plain, simple

portrait *n.* **1.** autobiography, biography characterization, depiction, description facsimile, figure, icon, illustration, image, likeness, miniature, model, painting, photograph, picture, portraiture, portrayal, profile, rendering, representation, semblance, silhouette, simulacrum, sketch, snapshot, thumbnail *(Nonformal)*, vignette **2.** account, chronicle, narrative, recounting, reproduction, story, telling, version, writing

portray *v.* **1.** draw, figure, illustrate, limn, paint, picture, profile, render, represent, silhouette, sketch **2.** bring to life, characterize, chronicle, define, depict, describe, evoke, narrate, recount, reproduce, tell, write **3.** act, assume, enact, imitate, impersonate, personify, play, recreate, simulate

pose *n.* **1.** bearing, carriage, mien, poise, position, posture, stance, stand **2.** act, affectation, air, artificiality, attitude, façade, front, guise, mannerism, masquerade, pretense, role – *v.* **1.** act, affect, fake, feign, grandstand *(Nonformal)*, impersonate, masquerade, peacock, playact, pretend, show off, strut **2.** advance, ask, extend, offer, posit, present, proffer, propose, proposition, propound, put forward, query, question, submit, suggest, tender **3.** assume a position, model, sit, sit for **4.** baffle, bewilder, confound, confuse, disconcert, muddle, perplex, puzzle *Nonformal:* stagger, stump *Antonyms:* clarify, set straight, soothe

posh *adj.* classy, deluxe, elegant, fancy, grand, grandiose, lofty, luxurious, ornate, ostentatious, port out starboard home *(Nautical)*, rich, ritzy, special, spectacular, showy, splashy, swanky *(Nonformal) Antonyms:* humble, modest, plain, unassuming

position *n.* **1.** arrangement, array, assignment, disposition, location, *mise en scène (French)*, placement, placing, order, organization, slot **2.** bearings, coign of vantage, locale, locality, *locus (Latin)*, place, setting, site, spot **3.** circumstance, condition, situation, state, status **4.** assertion, belief, contention, doctrine, hypothesis, idea, ideology, notion, proposition, tenet, theory **5.** angle, attitude, opinion, outlook, point of view, sentiment, slant, stance, take **6.** caste, class, degree, footing, level, rank, rung, social standing, standing, station **7.** benefice, duty, employment, field, function, job, occupation, office, post, profession, responsibility, role, sinecure, trade **8.** coverage, defence, goal, location, offense, place, zone **9.** consequence, dignity, distinction, esteem, gravity, honour, importance, name, prestige, reputation, weight – *v.* **1.** arrange, array, lay out, manipulate, move, order, organize, place, put, set **2.** assign, establish, locate, situate, station

positive *adj.* **1.** accordant, affirmative, agreeing, assenting, concurring, yes *Antonyms:* forbidding, negative, no **2.** assured, certain, cocksure *(Nonformal)*, confident, convinced, decided, imperious, secure, sure *Antonyms:* doubtful, dubious, unconvinced **3.** actual, authentic, bona fide, categorical, definitive, factual, genuine, patent, pukka, real, stated, the real thing *(Nonformal) Antonyms:* fake, hypothetical, pretend **4.** authoritative, express, incontestable, incontrovertible, indisputable, irrefutable, proven, reliable, undeniable, unerring, unmistakable, unquestionable *Antonyms:* controversial, debatable, moot **5.** downright, emphatic, express, forceful, imperative, plain **6.** beneficial, constructive, effective, good, helpful, healthy, practical, productive, reasonable, salubrious, sound, useful *Antonyms:* destructive, detrimental, useless **7.** affirming, auspicious, comforting, encouraging, favourable, hopeful, inspiring, optimistic, sunny *Antonyms:* dire, foreboding, ominous

positively *adv.* **1.** absolutely, assuredly, categorically, certainly, definitely, doubtless, downright, easily, emphatically, firmly, surely, totally *(Nonformal)*, undeniably, undoubtedly, unequivocally, unmistakably, unquestionably *Antonyms:* ambiguously, equivocally, speculatively, vaguely **2.** actually, *de facto (Latin)*, indeed, really, truthfully

posse *n.* band, battalion, body, brigade, carful, company, corps, covey, division, fleet, force, gang, group, lynch mob, mob, party, platoon, regiment, squad, string, team, troop, vigilantes

possess *v.* **1.** command, enjoy, fill, have, hold, monopolize, occupy, own **2.** acquire, catch, gain, get, glom *(Nonformal)*, grab, grasp, obtain, procure, seize, snatch, take

3. check, constrain, control, curb, govern, master, rein in, repress **4.** appreciate, comprehend, know, learn, master, realize, remember, retain, understand **5.** comprise, contain, embody, embrace, include, incorporate **6.** bedevil, bewitch, enchant, haunt, inhabit, manifest, spook *(Nonformal)* **7.** enslave, dominate, domineer, master, rule, subject **8.** absorb, consume, devour, engross, entrance, fascinate, obsess, preoccupy

possessed *adj.* **1.** blessed *or* endowed with, having, held, in hand *or* stock, occupying, owning **2.** calm, cool, collected, confident, poised, secure, self-assured, self-controlled, unflappable *Antonyms:* confused, disconcerted, embarrassed **3.** bedeviled, bewitched, consumed, crazed, cursed, demented, demonic, frenetic, frenzied, haunted, hooked, insane, mad, obsessed, pixilated, raving, taken over

possession *n.* **1.** control, custody, dominion, hold, mastery, occupancy, occupation, ownership, proprietorship, tenancy, tenure, title **2.** bondage, captivity, restraint, servitude, slavery, subjection, subjugation, subordination, subservience **3.** asset, capital, dowry, equity, estate, inheritance, land, money, property, real estate, resource, riches, wealth, wherewithal, worth **4.** accessory, belonging, chattel, effect, goods, junk, stock, stuff *(Nonformal)* **5.** aplomb, calm, confidence, control, ease, self-assuredness, self-possession **6.** embodiment, haunting, incarnation, manifestation

possessive *adj.* **1.** acquisitive, avaricious, covetous, envious, greedy, hoarding, materialistic, money-minded **2.** clinging, controlling, domineering, grasping, jealous, mistrustful, overbearing, overprotective

possibility *n.* chance, contingency, feasibility, hope, likelihood, odds, off chance, plausibility, potential, potentiality, probability, prospect, shot

possible *adj.* **1.** hopeful, likely, potential, probable, promising **2.** accessible, achievable, feasible, obtainable, practicable, viable, within reach, workable **3.** admissible, conceivable, credible, imaginable, reasonable, supposable, tenable, thinkable

possibly *adv.* conceivably, could be, if possible, likely, maybe, perchance, perhaps, probably *Antonyms:* doubtfully, dubiously unlikely

post *adv.* ASAP *(Nonformal)*, express, hastily, posthaste, quickly, rapidly, speedily, without delay – *n.* **1.** assignment, benefice, billet, employment, job, office, place, situation **2.** beat, locus, lookout, place, position station, whereabouts **3.** column, doorpost, leg, mast, newel, pale, palisade, panel, pedestal, picket, pile, pillar, pole, prop, rail, shaft, stake, standard, stilt, stock, stud support, upright **4.** collection, delivery, mail, postal service, post office, snail mail – *v.* **1.** paste, placard, place, poster, put *or* stick *or* tack up **2.** advertise, advise, announce, broadcast, circulate, disseminate, herald, inform, notify, publish, report, tell, trumpet, warn **3.** appoint, assign, billet, bivouac, establish, locate, position, put, situate **4.** catalogue, ledger, list, note, record, register **5.** bustle, hasten, hurry, hustle, go *(Nonformal)*, move, run, skedaddle **6.** courier, deliver, dispatch, e-mail, fax, mail, send, transmit

poster *n.* advertisement, announcement, banner, bill, billboard, broadsheet, handbill, notice, placard, public notice, sheet, sign, signboard, sticker

posterior *adj.* **1.** back, behind, dorsal, hind, hindmost, last, rear **2.** after, ensuing, following, later, latter, next, subsequent, succeeding *Antonyms:* before, preceding, precursory – *n.* anus, buttocks *Nonformal:* ass, behind, booty, bottom, bum, caboose, can, derriere, duff, fanny, gluteus maximus, rear, rump, seat, tush

posterity *n.* children, descendants, family, future generations, futurity, heirs, issue, legacy, offspring, progeny, successors, young'uns *(Nonformal) Antonyms:* ancestors, background, genealogy, lineage

posthaste *adj.* breakneck, express, fast, hasty, prompt, quick, rapid, snappy *(Nonformal)*, speedy, swift *Antonyms:* dilatory, laggard, slow, unhurried – *adv.* at once, directly, double-quick, expeditiously, hastily, instanter, promptly, quickly, rapidly, speedily, stat, straightaway, swiftly *Nonfor-*

mal: lickety-split, pronto *Antonyms:* gradually, leisurely, sluggishly – *n.* promptness, quickness, rapidity, speed, velocity *Antonyms:* deliberateness, slowness, torpidity

ost modernism *n.* deconstructionism, dialogic criticism, experimentalism, new pragmatism, non-traditionalism, po-mo *(Nonformal)*, post-colonialism, post-structuralism

ostmortem *adj.* **1.** after death, posthumous, post-obit **2.** after, following, future, later, subsequent – *n.* **1.** analysis, autopsy, coroner's *or* death report, dissection, examination, necropsy **2.** recap, regurgitation, retrospect, review, survey *Nonformal:* Monday-morning quarterbacking, picking up the pieces, rehash, replay

ostpone *v.* **1.** adjourn, defer, delay, filibuster, hold *or* put off, procrastinate, prolong, prorogue, set aside, stall, suspend, table. waive *Nonformal:* shelve, sidetrack **2.** downgrade, minimize, subordinate

ostponed *adj.* adjourned, deferred, delayed, preempted, put back on the shelf, shelved, stayed, suspended, weathered out *(North)*

ostscript *n.* addendum, addition, afterthought, afterword, appendage, attachment, codicil, epilogue, extension, P.S., sequel, update *Antonyms:* foreword, introduction, preface, prefix, prelude

ostulate *n.* **1.** assumption, axiom, adage, dictum, fundamental, maxim, position, principle, self-evident truth, supposition, truism **2.** condition, contingency, imperative, necessity, need, prerequisite, requirement, stipulation **3** antecedent, basis, foundation, grounds, premise – *v.* **1.** assert, assume, aver, claim, presuppose, presume, profess, suppose, take for granted **2.** conjecture, hypothesize, infer, posit, propose, set forth, theorize **3.** ask, beg, beseech, demand, request, require, supplicate

osture *n.* **1.** air, appearance, bearing, carriage, demeanour, deportment, mien, pose, position, presence, stance, state **2.** attitude, disposition, frame of mind, leaning, mentality, mindset, mood, outlook, point of view, view **3.** affairs, circumstance, condition, predicament, situation, status quo – *v.* adopt, affect, assume, attitudinize, pose, pretend, sashay *(Nonformal)*, show off, strut

posy *n.* bouquet, boutonniere, corsage, flowers, garland, nosegay, spray

pot *n.* **1.** flowerpot, gallipot, jardinière, pottle, vessel *Kinds of pot:* bain-marie, bean, casserole, cauldron, chafing dish, cocotte, coffeepot, cooker, crock, double boiler, Dutch oven, flagon, jug, kettle, pan, saucepan, stew, stockpot, tureen, vase, vessel **2.** ante, bank, jackpot, kitty, pool, stakes **3.** fortune, goldmine, mine, riches, treasure, wealth *Nonformal:* bundle, loads **4.** abdomen, belly, paunch, stomach *Nonformal:* Molson muscle, spare tire **5.** hemp, marijuana *Nonformal:* bud, doobie, dope, grass, joint, Mary Jane, spliff, reefer, wacky tobacco, weed

potato *n. kartoffle (German), pomme de terre (French)*, tuber *Nonformal:* lumpers, spud, tater, tattie, yam *Potato dishes:* baked, boiled, bread, chips, crisps, duchess, french-fried, fried, fries, hash browns, hush puppies, latke, mashed, pancake, *potates-frites (French)*, potato salad, poutine, roasted, scalloped, scone, skins

potbellied *adj.* adipose, ample, beefy, bloated, chubby, corpulent, fat, fleshy, heavy, large, meaty, overweight, paunchy, porky, rotund, stocky, thickset *Antonyms:* bony, diminutive, skinny, thin, tiny

potency *n.* **1.** ability, capability, capacity, effectiveness, efficacy, energy, force, hardihood, might, muscle, potential, power, puissance, strength, verve *Nonformal:* bite, go, kick, pep, punch, snap *Antonyms:* blandness, weakness **2.** authority, clout, command, control, dominion, influence, omnipotence, sovereignty, sway, weight *Antonyms:* ineffectualness, powerlessness **3.** fitness, fortitude, hot-bloodedness, lustiness, prowess, sexuality, vigour, virility, vitality *Antonyms:* emasculation, impotence, infirmity

potent *adj.* **1.** effective, energetic, full-bodied, hardy, invigorating, mighty, powerful, robust, strong, sturdy, vital **2.** authoritative, commanding, impacting, important, impressive, influential, prestigious, puissant, weighty *Antonyms:* powerless, subordinate, unimportant **3.** cogent, compelling, convincing, dynamic, effective, forceful, persuasive, trenchant, useful **4.** hot-blooded, lustful, rugged, stalwart, strapping, sexual, virile *Antonyms:* effete, infirm, weak

potential *adj.* **1.** conceivable, imaginable, implied, inherent, likely, lurking, plausible, possible, probable, promising *Antonyms:* improbable, unlikely **2.** budding, dormant, embryonic, future, hidden, latent, quiescent *Antonyms:* exhausted, spent, worn out – *n.* **1.** ability, aptitude, capacity, power, the makings *(Nonformal)*, wherewithal *Antonyms:* deficiency, impediment, incapacity **2.** chance, likelihood, odds, possibility, potentiality, prospect

potion *n.* brew, concoction, cordial, dose, draft, draught, drink, elixir, libation, liquid, liquor, medicine, mixture, philter, remedy, restorative, snake oil *(Nonformal)*, spirits, stimulant, tonic

potlatch *n.* **1.** celebration, ceremony, feast, festival, fête, gathering, holiday, observance, party, ritual, shivaree, wassail **2.** benefaction, favour, gift, offering, present

potpourri *n.* assortment, blend, collection, combination, farrago, gallimaufry, hodgepodge, jumble, medley, mélange, miscellany, mishmash, mixed bag *(Nonformal)*, mixture, olio, pastiche, patchwork, salmagundi, soup, stew

pouch *n.* **1.** bag, burse, change *or* coin purse, container, fanny pack, feed bag, gunnyside, handbag, haversack, pocketbook, poke, *(Nonformal)*, purse, receptacle, rucksack, sac, sack, satchel, sporran *(Scottish)*, wallet **2.** abdomen, belly, paunch, stomach *Nonformal*: gut, spare tire, tummy **3.** marsupium, saccule, udder **4.** craw, gizzard, ingluvies, maw

poultry *n.* capon, chicken, Cornish hen, duck, fowl, goose, grouse, guinea fowl, partridge, pheasant, pigeon, quail, rooster, squab, turkey, wild turkey

pounce *v.* **1.** ambush, attack, descend, fa upon, snatch, surprise, swoop, tak unawares **2.** bound, dart, dash, jump, lea **3.** dent, design, emboss, hammer, inden mark **4.** dust, powder, sprinkle

pound *n.* **1.** compound, confine, coop, co ral, doghouse, enclosure, kennel, pen, ru yard **2.** cell, gaol, jail, lockup, prison *No formal:* can, clink, hoosegow **3.** avo dupois, kental *(Newfoundland)*, lb, me sure, troy, unit **4.** monetary unit, mone quid *(Nonformal)*, stirling **5.** bang, blo cuff, sallywinder *(Nonformal)*, smac stroke, wallop, whack – *v.* **1.** baste, batte buffet, clobber, drum, hit, pelt, strik thrash, wallop **2.** beat, boom, palpitat pulse, throb, thump **3.** abrade, bray, crus flail, impress, mash, powder, pulveriz pummel, smash **4.** drill, hammer, impres inculcate, instill, teach **5.** confine, coop u corral, enclose, impound, restrain, she *(Nonformal)*

pour *n.* cataract, deluge, downpour, floo gullywasher *(P.E.I.)*, gush, rainstorn shower, spate, storm, torrent – *v.* **1.** di charge, disembogue, disgorge, emanat emit, expel, send forth, spew, spill **2** decant, dispernse, perform the duti *(Nonformal)*, serve, transfer **3.** cascad course, flood, flow, gush, rush out, splas spray, spurt, stream **4.** burst, drench, rai rain cats and dogs *(Nonformal)*, showe soak, storm **5.** abound, crowd, emerg move, sally, teem, throng

pout *n.* frown, glower, grimace, long *or* sa face, moue, sullen look *Antonyms:* gri smile, smirk – *v.* brood, frown, glowe grouch, mope, scowl, sulk *Antonyms:* beam, radiate, rejoice, smile

poverty *n.* **1.** bankruptcy, destitution, di straits, distress, exigency, hardship, imp cuniosity, impoverishment, indigenc insolvency, pauperism, penury, penniles ness, poorness, privation *Antonyms:* affl ence, opulence, wealth **2.** absence, barre ness, dearth, depletion, exhaustion, frui lessness, infecundity, infertility, lack, pauc ty **3.** deficiency, inadequacy, need, redu tion, scantiness, scarcity, shortage, wa *Antonyms:* multitude, profuseness

pow *interj.* bam, bang, bash, biff, boink, bonk, boom, bop, crack, crash, kaboom, kapow, pop, slam, smack, smash, whomp, zonk *(Nonformal)*

powder *n.* **1.** crumb, dust, grain, granule, grit, meal, iota, particle, pounce **2.** ammunition, cordite, dynamite, explosive, gunpowder, TNT **3.** cosmetic, face powder, make-up, talc – *v.* **1.** comminute, crumble, crush, disintegrate, hammer, mortar, pestle, pulverize, pummel, smash **2.** coat, cover, dab, dabble, dredge, dust, flour, sprinkle

powdery *adj.* chalky, crumbly, dry, dusty, fine, floury, friable, grainy, granular, gravelly, gritty, mealy, pulverized, sandy

power *n.* **1.** ascendancy, authority, clout, command, control, distinction, dominance, eminence, grassroots support, influence, leadership, leverage, omnipotence, rank, reputation, sovereignty, superiority, supremacy, sway, votes, weight *Antonyms:* subjugation, subordination, subservience **2.** ability, aptitude, capability, capacity, competence, competency, effectiveness, efficacy, éminence grise, endowment, equipment, faculty, gift, know-how, potential, potentiality, qualifications, skill, smarts *(Nonformal)*, tools *Antonyms:* inability, incapability, incapacity, incompetence **3.** beef, brawn, endurance, fortitude, hardiness, heft, main, might, muscle, musculature, pep, potency, puissance, ruggedness, size, stamina, strength, toughness, verve, vigour, vim, virility, vitality *Nonformal:* moxie, oomph, pizazz *Antonyms:* enervation, feebleness, impotence, listlessness, weakness **4.** dint, drive, dynamism, force, impetus, intensity, momentum *Nonformal:* guts, steam **5.** energy *Kinds of physical power:* atomic, electric, geothermal, horsepower, hydro, hydroelectric, jet, manpower, nuclear, rocket, solar, steam, thermonuclear, water – *v.* drive, impel, initiate, make go *or* run, move, propel, push, thrust

powerbroker *n.* boss, capitalist, captain of industry, chief, financier, kingmaker, magnate, mogul, money-baron, tycoon *Nonformal:* big cheese, wheeler-dealer

powerful *adj.* **1.** dynamic, energetic, forcible, intense, stimulating, vehement, vigorous, vital *Nonformal:* punchy, take charge, type A, zappy **2.** authoritative, commanding, dominant, great, important, impregnable, influential, omnipotent, paramount, supreme, unassailable, weighty **3.** cogent, compelling, convincing, eloquent, forceful, impressive, major-league, moving, persuasive, striking, touching **4.** burly, hale, hardy, mighty, muscular, potent, robust, rugged, stalwart, strapping, strong, sturdy *Nonformal:* buff, kick-ass *Antonyms:* feeble, infirm, puny, weak **5.** damaging, dangerous, life-threatening, potent, severe

powerfully *adv.* authoritatively, commandingly, effectively, energetically, forcefully, forcibly, intensely, mightily, passionately, strongly, vigorously, zealously *Antonyms:* feebly, ineptly, unconvincingly, weakly, wearily

powerless *adj.* **1.** crippled, debilitated, disabled, feeble, frail, hobbled, *hors de combat (French)*, impuissant, incapable, incapacitated, infirm, laid up, prostrate, shackled, tapped out **2.** forceless, harmless, impotent, ineffective, ineffectual, inept, tenuous, unable, unfit, useless, weak **3.** conquerable, defenceless, helpless, insecure, on the ropes *(Nonformal)*, open to attack, penetrable, precarious, pregnable, resourceless, unarmed, unguarded, unprotected, unsafe, vincible, vulnerable

powwow *n.* **1.** blessing, celebration, ceremony, rite, ritual, service **2.** assembly, colloquium, conference, consultation, forum, huddle, listserv, meeting, parley, Pugwash, symposium, talk, tête à tête, usenet – *v.* confer, consult, convene, converse, deliberate, discuss, meet, palaver

practicable *adj.* **1.** achievable, doable, feasible, likely, possible, probable, realizable, reasonable, viable, workable **2.** functional, operable, usable, utilitarian *Commonly misused:* **practical**

practical *adj.* **1.** applicable, appropriate, banausic, commonsensical, constructive, doable, down-to-earth, factual, feasible, functional, helpful, operable, practicable, pragmatic, rational, realistic, realizable, reasonable, sane, sensible, serviceable, solid, sound, usable, useful, utilitarian, valuable, workable, worthwhile *Nonformal:* blue sky, ivory tower *Antonyms:* idealistic, insane, off the wall, purely, speculative, theoretical, weird **2.** applied, empirical, experiential, learned *Nonformal:* hands-on, on-the-job *Commonly misused:* **practicable**

practically *adv.* **1.** commonsensically, matter-of-factly, pragmatically, rationally, realistically, sensibly, unsentimentally **2.** about, almost, approximately, basically, close to, essentially, fundamentally, in effect *or* essence, nearly, virtually

practice *n.* **1.** convention, custom, fashion, form, habit, manner, method, mode, modus operandi, praxis, procedure, proceeding, process, routine, rule, system, tradition, usage, use, utility, way **2.** action, assignment, discipline, drill, drilling, exercise, homework, preparation, recitation, rehearsal, repetition, seasoning, study **3.** business, calling, career, job, profession, pursuit, vocation, work – *v.* **1.** drill, go over, hone, polish, prepare, rehearse, repeat, run *or* walk through, sharpen, train, try out, tune *or* warm up **2.** act, apply, carry out, execute, observe, work

pragmatic *adj.* applied, bottom line, businesslike, commonplace, commonsensical, concrete, cut and dried, down-to-earth, effective, efficient, factual, logical, matter-of-fact, practical, rational, realistic, sensible, utilitarian, valuable, worthwhile *Antonyms:* impractical, theoretical, unrealistic

prairie *n.* grassland, land, llano, pampas, plain, range, savanna, steppe, veld

praise *n.* **1.** acclaim, accolade, applause, approval, bravos, commendation, compliment, congratulations, esteem, eulogy, flattery, kudos, ovation, panegyric, recognition, recommendation, thanks *Nonformal:* hurrahs, raves *Antonyms:* aspersion, criticism, reproach **2.** adoration, beatification, benediction, canonization, glorification, glory, homage, honour, hosanna, reverence, tribute, worship *Antonyms:* defamation, profanity – *v.* **1.** acclaim, admire, adulate, aggrandize, applaud, appreciate, approve, boost *(Nonformal)*, celebrate, cheer, cite, commend, compliment, congratulate, eulogize, extol, flatter, hail, laud, panegyrize, pay tribute, proclaim, recommend *Antonyms:* castigate, declaim, decry, slander **2.** beatify, bless, canonize, consecrate, deify, dignify, elevate, ennoble, exalt, glorify, honour, revere, sanctify, sanction, worship

praiseworthy *adj.* admirable, commendable, creditable, deserving, estimable, excellent, exemplary, fine, honourable, laudable, meritorious, select, worthy *Antonyms:* debased, reproachful, vile

prance *n.* caper, frolic, gambol, parade – *v.* bound, caper, cavort, dance, flounce, frisk, jump, leap, parade, romp, sashay, skip, spring, step, strut, swagger, swank *Antonyms:* crawl, creep, dawdle, trudge

prank *n.* antic, caper, escapade, fancy, foolishness, frolic, gag, hijinks, horseplay, joke, lark, levity, lightness, mischief, monkey business, play, practical joke, shenanigans, sport, tomfoolery, trick – *v.* **1.** frolic, gambol, jest, joke, play, romp, skylark, sport, trick **2.** adorn, bedeck, bespangle, decorate, dress *or* spruce up, embellish, guild

prattle *n.* *bavardage (French)*, blather, chatter, drivel, gibbering, gossip, rambling, ranting, twaddle *Nonformal:* baloney, flapdoodle, gas, hooey, jabberwocky, yackety yack, yadda yadda – *v.* babble, blather, chatter, dribble, gabble, jabber, mutter, palaver, prate, ramble, rant, spout *(Nonformal)*, twaddle, utter

pray *v.* **1.** appeal, ask, beg, beseech, entreat, implore, invoke, petition, plead, request, solicit, supplicate **2.** celebrate, exalt, extol, glorify, honour, laud, praise, revere, venerate, worship **3.** chant, contemplate, meditate, muse, ponder, study

prayer *n.* **1.** appeal, begging, beseeching, entreaty, imploration, invocation, petition, plea, request, suit, supplication **2.** affirmation, anthem, Ave Maria, benediction, blessing, celebration, chant, collect, communion, devotion, doxology, grace, Hail Mary, homage, honouring, hosanna, hymn, *Kaddish (Judaism)*, Kyrie, litany, liturgy, motet, novena, orison, paean, paternoster praise, psalm, *puja (Hindu)*, reverence, service, song, thanks, thanksgiving, veneration, versicle, worship **3.** chant, contemplation, mantra, meditation, musing, reiteration, study

preach *v.* **1.** advocate, discourse, enlighten, indoctrinate, inform, orate, press, recommend, teach **2.** declare, disseminate, evangelize, expound, minister, proclaim, sermonize **3.** admonish, advise, chastise, harangue, lecture, moralize, reprimand

preacher *n.* churchman, churchwoman, clergyman, clergywoman, cleric, curate, *curé (French)*, deacon, divine, ecclesiastic, evangelist, father, man *or* woman of the cloth, minister, missionary, padre, parson, pastor, priest, reverend, revivalist, sermonizer, teacher, vicar *Nonformal:* Bible thumper, sky pilot, tub-thumper

precarious *adj.* **1.** dangerous, delicate, flimsy, hazardous, insecure, perilous, risky, rocky, shaky, treacherous, tricky, unprotected, vulnerable *Nonformal:* dicey, iffy, out on a limb *Antonyms:* reliable, safe, secure, sound **2.** changeable, erratic, tenuous, touch-and-go, uncertain, unpredictable *Antonyms:* decided, definite, sure **3.** arguable, debatable, groundless, moot, unfounded, unsound, unsupportable, untenable, without basis *Antonyms:* documented, grounded, valid

precede *v.* **1.** antecede, anticipate, come *or* go before, come first, forerun, foreshadow, harbinger, herald, introduce, lead, pioneer, predate, preexist, preface, presage, take precedence *Antonyms:* follow, succeed *Commonly misused:* **proceed**

precedence *n.* **1.** preeminence, preference, primacy, priority, privilege, rank, seniority, superiority **2.** antecedence, first place, lead, preexistence *Commonly misused:* **precedent**

precedent *adj.* antecedent, before, earlier, former, preceding – *n.* archetype, barometer, basis, example, exemplar, guide, model, paradigm, prototype, standard, yardstick *Commonly misused:* **precedence**

preceding *adj.* above-mentioned, aforementioned, aforesaid, antecedent, before, earlier, foregoing, forerunning, leading, preliminary, preparatory, previous, prior

precept *n.* **1.** adage, axiom, convention, lesson, maxim, moral, motto, platitude, standard, tenet, tradition, truism **2.** canon, code, command, *corpus juris (Latin)*, decree, direction, edict, guideline, injunction, mitzvah, regulation, rule, statute

precinct *n.* **1.** borough, county, district, environs, neighbourhood, province, riding, subdivision, territory, ward **2.** arena, *arrondissement (French)*, bailiwick, beat *(Nonformal)*, department, domain, field, jurisdiction, realm, sphere **3.** cage, cloister, close, confine, coop, enclave, enclosure, pen, yard

precious *adj.* **1.** choice, costly, dear, expensive, fancy, fine, high-priced, invaluable, priceless, prized, valuable *Antonyms:* cheap, paltry, shoddy, worthless **2.** adored, beloved, cherished, darling, dear, dearest, favourite, idolized, inestimable, loved, treasured, valued *Nonformal:* blue-eyed, fair-haired, pet *Antonyms:* contemptible, disliked, disparaged **3.** adorned, affected, artificial, cutesy *(Nonformal)*, dainty, finicky, flowery, meticulous, nice, overwrought, poetic, purple *Antonyms:* minimal, prosaic, simple

precipice *n.* **1.** bluff, cliff, crag, escarpment, face, height, hill, palisades, peak, ridge, tor **2.** danger, dilemma, hazard, peril, plight, predicament, risk *Nonformal:* hot water, kettle of fish, pickle

precipitate *adj.* **1.** expeditious, fleet, hasty, hurried, prompt, quick, rushing, speedy, swift **2.** abrupt, immediate, instantaneous, sudden, unexpected **3.** adventurous, breakneck, daredevil, headlong, impudent, incautious, madcap, premature, rash, reckless – *v.* **1.** accelerate, advance, expedite, hasten, hurry, incite, move, press on, rush, speed, trigger **2.** discharge, fling, heave, hurl, launch, lob, pitch, project, propel, shoot, throw, toss **3.** descend, dive, down, drop, fall, plummet, plunge, pour, rain *Commonly misused:* **precipitous**

precipitation *n.* condensation, fog, hail, mist, moisture, rain, rainfall, sleet, snow, weather, wetness

precipitous *adj.* **1.** abrupt, bluff, cliff-like, craggy, mountainous, perpendicular, plunging, steep, sudden *Antonyms:* calibrated, gentle, gradual **2.** breakneck, fast, frantic, hasty, headlong, hot-footed *(Nonformal)*, hurried, precipitate, prompt, quick, rapid, rash, rushing, swift *Commonly misused:* **precipitate**

précis *n.* abridgment, abstract, compendium, condensation, digest, epitome, outline, prospectus, résumé, rundown, sketch, summary, survey, syllabus, synopsis, thumbnail *(Nonformal)*

precise *adj.* **1.** accurate, actual, authentic, correct, exact, factual, faithful, faultless, flawless, literal, on the mark *(Nonformal)*, right, true, unerring, verbatim *Antonyms:* embellished, erroneous, wrong **2.** absolute, categorical, circumscribed, clear, definite, distinct, explicit, express, fixed, obvious, plain, specific, strict, unambiguous *Antonyms:* ambiguous, murky, vague **3.** careful, choosy, conscientious, fastidious, finicky, fussy, meticulous, particular, picky, point-device, punctilious, rigorous, scrupulous, stickling, strict *Antonyms:* careless, perfunctory, relaxed

precisely *adv.* **1.** accurately, correctly, definitely, expressly, literally, specifically, strictly **2.** absolutely, categorically, exactly, indeed, quite so, sure, yes

preclude *v.* **1.** avert, contravene, counter, cross, deter, foil, forestall, frustrate, hamper, hinder, impede, inhibit, obstruct, retard, stave off, thwart *Antonyms:* advance, further, generate, precipitate, progress **2.** ban, blackball, eliminate, exclude, forbid, keep *or* rule out, omit, prohibit, veto *Antonyms:* admit, allow, include

precocious *adj.* **1.** advanced, ahead, brainy, bright, clever, forward, gifted, intelligent, mature, quick *(Nonformal)*, smart **2.** budding, early, early-bird *(Nonformal)*, premature

preconception *n.* assumption, bias, min set, notion, preconceived idea, predispos tion, prejudice, presumption *Antonym* disinterest, impartiality, objectivity

precondition *n.* essential, must, necessi prerequisite, provision, qualificatio requirement, requisite, stipulation

precursor *n.* **1.** ancestor, antecedent, for bear, forefather, original, parent, predece sor **2.** bellwether, forerunner, founde groundbreaker, harbinger, herald, messe ger, originator, pioneer, prototype, ushe vanguard, trailblazer

predatory *adj.* **1.** bestial, bloodthirsty, ca nivorous, dangerous, dog eat dog *(Nonfo mal)*, fierce, lupine, predacious, rapaciou raptorical, savage, wolfish, vulturine **2.** loo ing, marauding, pilfering, pillaging, piratin plundering, robbing, stealing, thieving

predecessor *n.* ancestor, antecedent, for bear, forefather, forerunner, mother, pr cursor, progenitor *Antonyms:* followe future, successor

predetermined *adj.* **1.** agreed, arrange cut-and-dried, established, fixed, foregon resolved, set-up, settled **2.** biased, close influenced, predecided, predisposed, prej diced, set-up, wired *(Nonformal)* **3.** calc lated, deliberate, intentional, mean planned, premeditated, preplanned, stu ied, thought-out **4.** destined, doomed, fata karmic, predestined, preordained *Nonfo mal:* in the cards, on the books

predicament *n.* bind, Catch-22, corner, cr sis, deadlock, dilemma, emergency, ex gency, fix, hardship, hole, imbrogli impasse, jam, juncture, mess, muddle, pe plexity, pinch, plight, position, problen puzzle, quagmire, quandary, situatio strait, trouble *Nonformal:* deep *or* h water, how-do-you-do, kettle of fish, pickl nightmare, rub, scrape, snafu, tight spot

predicate *v.* **1.** affirm, allege, announc assert, aver, avow, declare, postulate, pr claim, profess, pronounce, state **2.** co note, hint, imply, indicate, intimate, pu port, represent, signify, suggest **3.** bas establish, found, ground, root

predict *v.* **1.** augur, divine, dope out *(Nonformal),* forecast, foresee, foretell, guess, prognosticate, prophesy, soothsay, speculate, theorize, vaticinate **2.** anticipate, bode, forebode, foreshadow, foretoken, herald, hint at, indicate, portend, presage, suggest, telegraph

predictable *adj.* anticipated, calculable, certain, expected, foreseeable, foreseen, liable, likely, sure *Nonformal:* odds-on, sure-fire *Antonyms:* surprising, out of the blue, serendipitous, unexpected, unforeseen, unlikely

prediction *n.* augury, conjecture, divination, forecast, foresight, fortunetelling, guess, hunch, indication, omen, portent, presage, prognosis, prophecy, soothsaying, surmising

predictive *adj.* Delphic, divinatory, fatidic, mantic, mediumistic, oracular, prognostic, prophetic, psychic, sibylline, vatic, vaticinal, visionary

predilection *n.* bent, bias, fancy, fondness, inclination, leaning, liking, love, mindset, partiality, penchant, predisposition, preference, proclivity, proneness, propensity, taste, tendency, weakness *Nonformal:* druthers, groove *Antonyms:* antipathy, aversion, distaste, repulsion

predispose *v.* affect, bend, bias, incline, indoctrinate, induce, influence, inspire, lay the groundwork *or* foundation, lead, make liable *or* susceptible, prejudice, prompt, set-up, sway, teach, urge

predisposition *n.* bent, bias, inclination, leaning, likelihood, liking, partiality, penchant, predilection, preference, proclivity, propensity, susceptibility, tendency, vulnerability, weakness

predominant *adj.* absolute, all-powerful, almighty, ascendant, authoritative, capital, chief, controlling, directing, dominating, governing, imperious, influential, leading, main, master, mighty, official, omnipotent, overbearing, overpowering, paramount, potent, preeminent, preponderate, prepotent, prevailing, primary, prime, principal, prominent, reigning, ruling, sovereign, superior, supervisory, supreme, transcendent, weighty, widespread *Antonyms:* inferior, minor, secondary, subordinate

predominate *v.* **1.** command, dictate, dominate, govern, influence, manage, preponderate, prevail, reign, rule **2.** better, eclipse, exceed, excel, outdo, outshine, outstrip, outweigh, overshadow, surpass, tower, transcend, trump

preeminent *adj.* capital, chief, consummate, distinguished, excellent, foremost, incomparable, leading, main, major, matchless, number one *(Nonformal),* outstanding, paramount, peerless, predominant, prestigious, principal, renowned, stellar, superior, supreme, surpassing, towering, transcendent, ultimate, unequalled, unrivaled, unsurpassed *Antonyms:* mediocre, ordinary, second-rate, unknown

preempt *v.* acquire, annex, appropriate, arrogate, assume, bump *(Nonformal),* claim, commandeer, confiscate, co-opt, expropriate, obtain, occupy, preclude, seize, sequester, squat on, take, usurp *Antonyms:* extradite, give back, restore, return

preen *v.* **1.** adorn, beautify, bedeck, dress, embellish, fettle, groom, manicure, primp, prink, scrub *Nonformal:* doll *or* spiff *or* spruce up *Antonyms:* defile, dirty, muddy, sully **2.** bask *or* glory *or* exalt *or* take pride in

preface *n.* beginning, exordium, explanation, foreword, front matter, introduction, overture, preamble, preliminaries, prelude, proem, prologue – *v.* begin, commence, introduce, launch, lead, open, precede, prefix, usher *Antonyms:* appendix, conclusion, epilogue

prefect *n.* administrator, boss, chief, commander, dean, governor, head, head boy, legate, magistrate, official, pooh-bah *(Nonformal),* senior monitor

prefer *v.* **1.** choose, cull, desire, elect, esteem, fancy, favour, pick, select, single out, want, wish for **2.** advance, advocate, elevate, endorse, espouse, further, promote, raise **3.** present, proffer, propose, propound, submit, suggest, tender

preference *n.* **1.** choice, desire, favourite, option, pick, selection *Antonyms:* castoff, reject **2.** bias, inclination, liking, favouritism, partiality, predilection, predisposition, prejudice *Antonyms:* abhorrence, disinclination **3.** advantage, precedence, priority, upper hand *Antonyms:* handicap, liability

pregnancy *n.* gestation, gravidity, impregnation, incubation, the family way *(Nonformal)*

pregnant *adj.* **1.** anticipating, carrying, due, big *or* great *or* heavy with child, *enceinte (French)*, expectant, expecting, gestating, gravid, with child *or* young *Nonformal:* expecting, in the family way, knocked up, preggers *Antonyms:* barren, celibate, childless **2.** abundant, brimming, fecund, filled, flush, fraught, fruitful, full, loaded, plenary, plentiful, productive, prolific, replete, rich, seminal, teeming *Antonyms:* arid, depleted, exhausted, scanty, wanting **3.** charged, consequential, critical, important, meaningful, momentous, significant, substantial, symbolic, weighty *Antonyms:* inconsequential, insignificant, minor, trivial

prehistoric *adj.* **1.** preglacial, primal, primeval *Prehistoric Periods and time (all dates in millions of years ago):* Cambrian (570-510), Carboniferous (363-290), Cretaceious (144-65), Devonian (409-363), Jurassic (206-144), Ordovician (510-439), Permian (290-249), Quarternary (2.5 to present), Silurian (439-409), Sturtian (800-690), Tertiary (65-2.5), Triassic (249-206), Vendian (610-570) **2.** aged, antediluvian, antiquated, archaic, fossilized, fustian, obsolete, primitive *Antonyms:* contemporary, current, fresh, modern

prejudice *n.* **1.** ageism, animosity, anti-Semitism, apartheid, aversion, bigotry, chauvinism, classism, discrimination, dislike, enmity, hatred, homophobia, intolerance, misanthropy, misogyny, racism, revulsion, sexism, xenophobia *Antonyms:* broadmindedness, openness, tolerance **2.** bias, jaundice, one-sidedness, partiality, preconception, predisposition, prejudgment, proclivity, slant, twist, unfairness, warp *Antonyms:* neutrality, nonpartisanship, objectivity – *v.* **1.** bias, colour, dispose, distort, indoctrinate, jaundice, poison, predispose, prejudge, prepossess, skew, slant, spoil, sway, twist, warp **2** damage, harm, hinder, hurt, impair, injure, mar, scar, upset, wound

prejudicial *adj.* biased, bigoted, damaging, deleterious, detrimental, discriminatory, harmful, hurtful, injurious, mischievous, undermining, unfavourable, unjust

preliminary *adj.* basic, early, elementary, exploratory, first, fundamental, initial, introductory, opening, pilot, preparatory, primary, qualifying, rudimentary, test, trial – *n.* **1.** basic training, briefing, first round, foundation, groundwork, initial *or* introductory step, initiation, spadework *Nonformal:* homework, prep **2.** curtain raiser, introductory event, opening number, overture, *pourparler (French)*, prelim *(Nonformal)* **3.** forward, front matter, introduction, preamble, preface, prelude, proem, prologue, opening

prelude *n.* **1.** curtain raiser, musical introduction, opener *(Nonformal)*, opening, overture, vorspiel **2.** beginning, frontispiece, introduction, preamble, preface, preliminaries, proem, prologue *Antonyms:* appendage, conclusion, epilogue

premature *adj.* **1.** early, forward, hasty, ill-considered, impulsive, inopportune, overhasty, precipitate, rash, inopportune, untimely *Nonformal:* half-baked, half-cocked *Antonyms:* reasoned, studied, tempered **2.** embryonic, green, immature, imperfect, inchoate, incomplete, undeveloped, unripe, vestigial *Antonyms:* aged, full-grown, ripened

premeditated *adj.* aforethought, calculated, conscious, considered, contrived, deliberate, designed, fixed, intentional, laid out, planned, practiced, purposed, rehearsed, rigged *(Nonformal)*, set up, studied, thought-out, voluntary *Antonyms:* automatic, impromptu, impulsive, instinctual, spontaneous

premier *adj.* **1.** arch, champion, chief, foremost, head, highest, leading, main, predominant, preeminent, prime, principa

Antonyms: minor, secondary **2.** beginning, first, inaugural, initial, opening, original *Antonyms:* closing, last, latest, ultimate – *n.* chief, first minister, head, leader, numero uno *(Nonformal)*, prime minister, ruler *Commonly misused:* **premiere**

premiere *n.* **1.** debut, first night *or* performance *or* showing, opening, opening night, original **2.** diva, lead, leading lady *or* man prima donna, star – *v.* debut, launch, open, present, produce, showcase, stage *Commonly misued:* **premier**

premise *n.* argument, assertion, assumption, basis, ground, hypothesis, presumption, presupposition, proposition, supposition, thesis – *v.* **1.** assume, hypothesize, posit, predicate, presume, presuppose, suppose **2.** announce, begin, commence, prefix, start

premises *n. pl.* **1.** bounds, establishment, grounds, home, house, land, layout, limits, office, property, real estate, scene, site, spot, zone **2.** basis, data, facts, grounds, information, proof, statements

premium *adj.* crackerjack *(Nonformal)*, excellent, exceptional, first-rate, number one, prime, select, superior, supreme *Antonyms:* inferior, lowly, second rate – *n.* **1.** cut, deduction, discount, rebate, recompense, refund, rollback *(Nonformal)* **2.** benefit, bonus, bounty, extra, gratuity, incentive, lagniappe, lure, perquisite, price, reward, tip *Nonformal:* freebie, gravy, perk **3.** amount, cost, fee, installment, payment, price **4.** esteem, regard, reputation, respect, stock, store, value

premonition *n.* **1.** apprehension, dream, feeling, foreboding, funny feeling *(Nonformal)*, hunch, idea, intuition, misgiving, presage, presentiment, suspicion **2.** forewarning, omen, portent, preindication, sign, warning

preoccupied *adj.* **1.** absent-minded, abstracted, bugged, daydreaming, distracted, faraway, forgetful, heedless, hung up, inattentive, lost, mooning, oblivious, out of it *(Nonformal)*, unaware **2.** absorbed, brooding, contemplative, busy, engaged, engrossed, fascinated, focused, immersed, intent, meditative, musing, pensive, thoughtful **3.** claimed, filled, gone, in use, spoken for, taken

preordain *v.* **1.** decree, determine, foredoom, foreordain, predestine, predetermine **2.** allocate, allot, assign, dedicate, designate, earmark, mark, set, tag

preparation *n.* **1.** arranging, equipping, furnishing, organizing, outfitting, priming, readying **2.** formation, foundation, groundwork, homework *(Nonformal)*, layout, measures, outline, plan, practice, provision, rehearsal sketch, spadework, studying **3.** apprenticeship, briefing, education, experience, fitness, grooming, instruction, learning, preparedness, readiness, study, teaching, training, tutelage **4.** blend, brew, compound, concoction, confection, decoction, medicine, mixture, potion, tincture **5.** devotion, meditation, prayer, service, worship

preparatory *adj.* before, elementary, inaugural, inductive, introductory, opening, precautionary, precursory, prefatory, preliminary, previous, primary, prior *Antonyms:* closing, conclusive, final, terminal

prepare *v.* **1.** arrange, fix *or* set up, get ready, order, organize *Nonformal:* batten down the hatches, get psyched, square-away **2.** bone up on *(Nonformal)*, brief, coach, educate, familiarize, groom, instruct, practice, prime, qualify, ready, rehearse, study, teach, train **3.** accoutre, array, equip, furnish, gear, outfit, provide, supply **4.** bake, cook, fix, make *Nonformal:* throw together, whomp up **5.** assemble, construct, create, fashion, manufacture, produce, write up

prepared *adj.* **1.** armed, fit, in gear *(Nonformal)*, in shape, prepped, ready, set, warmed up **2.** blanched, fastfood, frozen, instant, precooked, ready-to-serve

preponderance *n.* **1.** advantage, ascendancy, command, dominance, dominion, favour, force, greatness, influence, lead, power, prestige, primacy, sovereignty, superiority, supremacy, sway, upper hand *(Nonformal)*, weight **2.** bulk, lion's share *(Nonformal)*, majority, mass, most

prepossessing *adj.* alluring, attractive, appealing, beautiful, bewitching, captivating, charismatic, charming, comely, delightful, disarming, enchanting, engaging, enticing, exquisite, fair, fascinating, handsome, intriguing, magnetic, photogenic, pleasing, pulchritudinous, ravishing, spellbinding, striking, tantalizing, winsome *Antonyms:* blemished, homely, repulsive, repugnant, unsightly

preposterous *adj.* absurd, asinine, bizarre, crazy, excessive, extreme, fantastic, foolish, harebrained, impossible, incredible, insane, irrational, laughable, ludicrous, nonsensical, outlandish, outrageous, ridiculous, senseless, shocking, silly, unbelievable, unusual *Nonformal:* crackpot, loony, nutty, wild *Antonyms:* credible, logical, reasonable, sound

prerequisite *adj.* called for, essential, expedient, imperative, important, indispensable, mandatory, necessary, needful, obligatory, required, requisite, *sine qua non (Latin)*, vital *Antonyms:* optional, unsolicited, voluntary – *n.* condition, essential, imperative, must, necessity, obligation, postulate, precondition, qualification, requirement, requisite, stipulation *Nonformal:* catch, rub *Antonyms:* choice, elective, option *Commonly misused:* **perquisite**

prerogative *n.* authority, birthright, dispensation, droit, due, franchise, freedom, inalienable right, legitimacy, liberty, mandate, power, precedence, preeminence, privilege, right, right-of-way, superiority, upper hand *(Nonformal)*

presage *n.* **1.** augury, forecast, foreshadowing, foretoken, forewarning, harbinger, indication, omen, portent, prediction, prophecy, sign, warning **2.** apprehensiveness, bad vibes *(Nonformal)*, dread, feeling, foreboding, hunch, inkling, intimation, intuition, misgiving, premonition, presentiment, suspicion – *v.* **1.** announce, augur, betoken, bode, forebode, foreshadow, foretoken, harbinger, herald, point to, promise, warn **2.** feel, foresee, intuit, sense **3.** divine, forecast, foretell, forewarn, portent, predict, prognosticate, prophesy, vaticinate

prescient *adj.* clairvoyant, divinatory, divining, extrasensory, foreknowing, foreseeing, foresighted, forward-looking, keen-sighted, knowing, perceptive, perspicacious, prophetic, psychic, sapient, sensitive, telepathic

prescribe *v.* **1.** administer, authorize, command, decree, demand, dictate, enjoin, impose, institute, lay *or* set down, legislate, medicate, ordain, order, proclaim, pronounce **2.** advise, advocate, counsel, direct, guide, instruct, propose, recommend, suggest *Commonly misused:* **proscribe**

prescription *n.* **1.** compound, concoction, drug, elixir, medicine, meds *(Nonformal)*, mixture, pills, potion, preparation, tincture **2.** directions, formula, how-to *(Nonformal)*, instructions, recipe **3.** decree, edict, ordinance, prescript, regulation, rule **4.** adage, convention, custom, maxim, mores, practice, precept, principle, tradition

presence *n.* **1.** attendance, company, existence, inhabitance, occupancy **2.** closeness, close quarters, immediacy, nearness, neighbourhood, proximity, short range *(Nonformal)*, surroundings, vicinity, whereabouts **3.** air, appearance, aspect, aura, bearing, behaviour, carriage, character, charisma, composure, comportment, countenance, demeanour, deportment, dignity, ease, look, majesty, mien, personality, poise, self-assurance, self-possession, stateliness **4.** apparition, entity, ghost, manifestation, poltergeist, spectre, spirit, spook *(Nonformal)*, supernatural being, wraith

present *adj.* **1.** accounted for, at hand, attendant, available, here, here today, in attendance *or* view, near, nearby, on hand, on-the-spot *(Nonformal)*, ready, there, within reach **2.** *au courant (French)*, contemporary, current, fashionable, hip *(Nonformal)*, immediate, modern, present-day, topical, trendy, up-to-date **3.** *ad hoc (Latin)*, already, begun, commenced, contemporaneous, existing, going on, in duration, in process, started, today, under consideration – *n.* **1.** benefaction, alms, baksheesh, benevolence, bonus, boon, bounty, donation, endowment, favour, gift, giveaway, grant, gratuity, handout, largesse offering, poureboire, tip, treat *(Nonformal)*, windfall **2.** just *or* right now, now, nowadays, present moment, today – *v.* **1.** award, bestow, confer, donate, entrust, furnish, give, grant, offer, proffer **2.** acquaint, debut, display, exhibit, introduce, mount **3.** advance, allege, cite, declare, submit

present-day *adj. au courant (French)*, contemporary, current, existing, fashionable, hip *(Nonformal)*, modern, now, progressive, right now, stylish, this minute, topical, trendy, up-to-date *Antonyms:* aged, antiquated, archaic, out of step

presentable *adj.* acceptable, decent, fit, good enough, okay *(Nonformal)*, passable, respectable, satisfactory, suitable, tolerable *Antonyms:* poor, unacceptable, unsatisfactory

presentation *n.* **1.** award, bestowal, boon, donation, gift, gratuity, offer, present **2.** appearance, coming out, debut, introduction, launch **3.** display, exhibition, performance, portrayal, production, representation, show, staging, tableau **4.** arrangement, design, form, make-up, order, set-up, style

presentiment *n.* apprehension, discomposure, disquietude, disturbance, fear, foreboding, hunch, intuition, misgiving, perturbation, premonition, presage, qualm, sense *Nonformal:* funny feeling, vibes

presently *adv.* **1.** anon, before long, shortly, soon **2.** at present, currently, directly, immediately, now, nowadays, these days

preserve *n.* **1.** chutney, compote, confection, *confiture (French)*, conserve, jam, jelly, marmalade, spread **2.** conservation area, park, reserve, sanctuary – *v.* **1.** defend, ensure, extend, guard, husband, keep intact, lengthen, maintain, protect, retain, safeguard, screen, shield, uphold **2.** bank, conserve, economize, put aside, save, shelve, stockpile **3.** brine, cure, dry, freeze, jerk, pickle, salt, smoke

preside *v.* administer, advise, chair, conduct, control, direct, govern, handle, head, head up, lead, manage, officiate, operate, ordain, oversee, rule, run, supervise

president *n.* boss, captain, chair, chancellor, chief, chief executive officer, chief of staff, commander, commander-in-chief, dean, director, *el presidente (Spanish)*, head, leader, manager, master, officer, principal, provost, ruler *Nonformal:* big cheese, C.E.O., head honcho, leader of the free world, prez, the man

press *n.* **1.** dailies, fleet Street *(British)*, fourth estate, journalism, magazines, media, newspapers, periodicals, print, television, the news, weeklies **2.** broadcasters, columnists, commentators, correspondents, journalists, paparazzi, photographers, photojournalists, reporters, reviewers **3.** air time, coverage, ink *(Nonformal)*, play, publicity, space **4.** bookbinder, house, imprint, manufacturer, printer, publisher, publishing company *or* house **5.** bunch, crowd, crush, drove, flock, group, herd, host, mob, multitude, pack, swarm, throng **6.** compactor, compressor, constrictor, crusher, extractor, pincher, squeezer, wringer **7.** demand, exigency, insistence, necessity, pressure, stress, urgency **8.** ado, bustle, confusion, flurry, hurry, rush, storm – *v.* **1.** compress, concentrate, condense, constrict, crush, extract, pinch, squeeze, wring, wring out **2.** flatten, iron, plane, shape, smooth, steam, straighten **3.** caress, clasp, cuddle, embrace, fondle, hold, hug, snuggle **4.** drive, force, galvanize, goad, impel, incite, induce, motivate, persuade, provoke, spur, urge **5.** annoy, assail, burden, depress, distress, grieve, harass, irk, repress, torment, vex, weigh upon **6.** appeal, beg, bid, entreat, implore, importune, nag, supplicate **7.** compel, demand, enforce, insist on, necessitate, oblige, pressure, require **8.** advance, continue, march, progress, push forward **9.** dash, hasten, hurry, hustle, rush, scamper, speed **10.** converge, cram, crowd, herd, jam, meet, mill, scurry, swarm, throng **11.** emphasize, impress, reiterate, stress, underline **12.** conscript, draft, enlist, kidnap, recruit, shanghai, sign on *or* up

pressing *adj.* acute, burning, clamorous, compelling, constraining, critical, crucial, crying, demanding, dire, distressing, exacting, exigent, high-priority, hot *(Nonformal)*, immediate, imperative, important, insistent, obliging, serious, urgent, vital

Antonyms: dispensable, unimportant, unnecessary

pressure *n.* **1.** compression, force, gravity, heaviness, load, mass, tension, weight **2.** adversity, affliction, albatross, burden, cross, difficulty, hardship, millstone **3.** crunch, demand, exigency, necessity, pinch, stress, urgency **4.** coercion, constraint, duress, forcing, harassment, influence, intimidation, railroading *Nonformal:* arm-twisting, the squeeze – *v.* browbeat, bully, coerce, compel, cow, demand, drive, force, influence, intimidate, make, oblige, press, tyrannize, urge *Nonformal:* lean on, squeeze, strong-arm *Antonyms:* coddle, indulge

prestige *n.* authority, celebrity, consequence, control, credit, dignity, distinction, draw *(Nonformal)*, eminence, esteem, fame, illustriousness, importance, influence, position, power, preeminence, prominence, rank, regard, renown, reputation, repute, standing, starpower, state, stature, status, sway, weight *Antonyms:* anonymity, insignificance, unimportance

prestigious *adj.* acclaimed, celebrated, distinguished, eminent, esteemed, exalted, famed, famous, great, illustrious, important, imposing, impressive, influential, legendary, notable, preeminent, prominent, renowned, reputable, respected, well-known *Antonyms:* minor, obscure, unimportant, unknown

presumably *adv.* apparently, assumably, doubtlessly, indubitably, likely, probably, reasonably, seemingly, supposedly, surely, unquestionably

presume *v.* **1.** assume, believe, conclude, gather, guess, imagine, infer, judge, posit, suppose, surmise, suspect, take for granted, think, understand **2.** dare, impose, infringe, intrude, overstep, take liberty, undertake, venture

presumption *n.* **1.** arrogance, audacity, boldness, brashness, brass, cheek, chutzpah *(Nonformal)*, confidence, daring, effrontery, gall, impudence, insolence, nerve, rudeness, temerity *Antonyms:* caution, discretion, graciousness, prudence, solicitude **2.** basis, evidence, foundation, grounds, premise, reason, root **3.** assumption, belief, conjecture, guess, hypothesis, idea, inference, notion, opinion, speculation, surmise, suspicion, theory, thought

presumptuous *adj.* arrogant, audacious, bold, confident, forward, fresh, insolent, obnoxious, overconfident, overfamiliar, pompous, precocious, presuming, rash, rude, self-assertive, self-assured *Nonformal:* cheeky, in your face, pushy, uppity *Antonyms:* bashful, humble, modest, timid, unassuming

pretend *v.* **1.** affect, beguile, bluff, cheat, deceive, delude, dissemble, dupe, falsify, feign, fool, profess *Nonformal:* boondoggle, fake it, fudge **2.** create, fabricate, fantasize, imagine, invent, make-believe, play, playact **3.** allege, assert, claim, presume, purport, put forward, suppose, venture

pretended *adj.* **1.** affected, artificial, bogus, counterfeit, ersatz, fake, false, feigned, fictitious, imaginary, insincere, make-believe, mock, phoney *(Nonformal)*, specious *Antonyms:* genuine, real **2.** alleged, avowed, ostensible, professed, pseudo, purported, so-called, supposed

pretense *n.* **1.** artifice, charade, deceit, deception, façade, false colours, falsehood, feint, guise, hoax, humbug, imposture, lie, mask, ruse, sham, stratagem, subterfuge, trick, trickery, wile *Antonyms:* artlessness, frankness, honesty, openess **2.** affectation, boasting, braggadocio, egotism, fanfaronade, pomposity, pose, posing, posture, ostentation, rodomontade, self-grandiosity *Antonyms:* humility, modesty **3.** fabrication, fantasy, fib, fiction, invention, make-believe *Antonyms:* reality, truth, verity **4.** allegation, assertion, claim, excuse, pretext, profession *Commonly misued:* **pretext**

pretension *n.* **1.** allegation, assumption claim, declaration, demand, pretext, profession **2.** affectation, airs, bluster, charade, conceit, disguise, gasconade hypocrisy, ostentation, pomposity, self importance, show, snobbery, snobbishness splash, vainglory, vanity *Nonformal:* big talk, false front *Antonyms:* authenticity genuiness, pukka, sincerity **3.** audacity assertion, boldness, effrontery, gall, presumption *Nonformal:* brass, cheek, chutzpah

pretentious *adj.* **1.** affected, exaggerated, extravagant, flagrant, flamboyant, flashy, flaunting, florid, flowery, gaudy, grandiloquent, grandiose, high-flown, imposing, inflated, magniloquent, ornate, ostentatious, *outré (French),* overblown, overmuch, purple, recherché. showy, splashy, vainglorious *Nonformal:* big city, highfalutin, posh, swank, too too much *Antonyms:* modest, natural, plain, simple **2.** conceited, hoity-toity, pompous, snobbish, snobby, uppity *Nonformal:* artsy-fartsy, la-di-da, stuck-up, toplofty

preternatural *adj.* **1.** ghostly, inexplicable, miraculous, mysterious, otherworldly, out of this world, paranormal, superhuman, supernatural, transcendental, unaccountable, uncanny, unearthly, unnatural *Antonyms:* bodily, corporeal, earthly, material **2.** anomalous, atypical, curious, odd, peculiar, rare, remarkable, singular, strange, surreal, uncommon, unheard-of, unusual, weird *Antonyms:* common, everyday, typical

pretext *n.* alibi, camouflage, cloak, cover, device, disguise, excuse, front, guise, justification, mask, masquerade, ploy, rationale, reason, ruse *Nonformal:* red herring, stalking horse *Commonly misued:* **pretense**

prettify *v.* adorn, beautify, bedeck, decorate, ornament, preen, primp, prink, prune, titivate, trim *Nonformal:* gussy *or* jazz *or* spruce up, whup with the pretty stick

pretty *adj.* **1.** appealing, attractive, beautiful, becoming, *belle (French),* bonny, comely, cute, delicate, fetching, fair, lovely, photogenic, pleasing, pulchritudinous, well-favoured, winsome *Nonformal:* dishy, dreamy *Antonyms:* hideous, homely, ill-favoured, ugly **2.** catchy, melodious, musical, smooth, sweet-sounding, tuneful, velvety *Antonyms:* cacophonic, grating, shrill **3.** considerable, decent, good, large, sufficient – *adv.* adequately, decently, fairly, moderately, rather, somewhat, tolerably

prevail *v.* **1.** best, command, conquer, control, defeat, dominate, overcome, predominate, preponderate, reign, rule, succeed, triumph, win **2.** abide, bear, continue, endure, hold on, persist, remain, sustain, withstand *Antonyms:* give in, quit, succumb, yield **3.** coax, dispose, exhort, induce, influence, motivate, persuade, prompt, sway, urge

prevailing *adj.* **1.** accepted, common, current, customary, established, familiar, fashionable, mainstream, popular, predominate, prevalent, standard, traditional, widespread *Antonyms:* avant-garde, unconventional, unorthodox **2.** convincing, efficacious, dominant, forceful, influential, potent, powerful, ruling, vigorous *Antonyms:* impuissant, ineffective

prevalent *adj.* **1.** accepted, accustomed, common, current, customary, established, everyday, extensive, frequent, general, habitual, popular, regular, typical, universal, usual, widespread *Antonyms:* infrequent, localized, uncommon, unusual **2.** ascendant, paramount, predominant, rife, successful, superior *Antonyms:* inferior, negligible, paltry, trifling **3.** compelling, dominant, effective, efficacious, forceful, governing, potent, powerful, regnant, useful

prevaricate *v.* **1.** deceive, distort, exaggerate, fabricate, falsify, fib, invent, lie, make up, misrepresent, stretch *(Nonformal),* tergiversate **2.** dipsy-doodle *(Nonformal),* dodge, equivocate, evade, hedge, palter, shift, shuffle

prevarication *n.* deception, distortion, evasion, exaggeration, fabrication, falsehood, falsification, fib, fiction, invention, lie, misrepresentation, perjury, untruth *Nonformal:* megillah, shaggy dog, story, tall tale, whopper, yarn *Antonyms:* fact, fidelity, reality, truth

prevent *v.* avert, bar, block, check, counter, counteract, defend against, deflect, foil, forbid, forestall, frustrate, hamper, hinder, hold back, impede, inhibit, intercept, interrupt, obstruct, obviate, parry, preclude, preempt, prohibit, repress, restrain, restrict, retard, stave off, stop, thwart *Antonyms:* allow, encourage, facilitate, help, permit

prevention *n.* **1.** arrest, avoidance, ban, block, forestalling, frustration, hindrance, impediment, injunction, interference, obstruction, obtrusion, prohibition, proscription, retardation, veto **2.** deterrent, insurance, precaution, preventative measure, safeguard, shield

preview *n.* advance screening *or* showing *or* viewing, clip, dry run, exclusive, foretaste, glimpse, shot, sneak peak *(Nonformal)*, teaser, trailer – *v.* check out, run through, sample, screen

previous *adj.* above, aforementioned, antecedent, before, earlier, erstwhile, foregoing, former, one-time, past, precedent, preceding, precursory, prior, quondam, said *Antonyms:* consequent, following, later, subsequent, succeeding

previously *adv.* ahead, already, ante, antecedently, away back, back when, before, beforehand, earlier, erstwhile, fore, formerly, heretofore, hitherto, long ago, once, then, until now *Antonyms:* afterwards, subsequently, thereafter, thereupon, therewith

prey *n.* dupe, game, hunted, kill, quarry, quest, spoil, target, victim *Nonformal:* fall guy, mark, mug *Antonyms:* captor, predator – *v.* **1.** consume, devour, feed upon, hunt, pursue, ravage, stalk **2.** bother, burden, encumber, oppress, tax, upset, vex, worry *Nonformal:* hassle, stress **3.** cheat, deceive, defraud, fleece, mulct, swindle, victimize *Nonformal:* boondoggle, con, hornswoggle, scam

price *n.* **1.** amount, bill, charge, cost, expenditure, expense, fare, fee, outlay, rate, tab *Nonformal:* damage, tab, tune **2.** appraisal, evaluation, merit, valuation, value, worth **3.** consequence, dues, fine, forfeiture, penalty, reckoning, sacrifice, toll **4.** blackmail, blood *or* hush money *(Nonformal)*, bounty, bribe, compensation, expiation, payment, payoff, ransom, reward – *v.* appraise, assess, calculate, cost, determine, evaluate, reckon

priceless *adj.* cherished, incalculable, incomparable, inestimable, invaluable, irreplaceable, precious, prized, rare, treasured *Antonyms:* cheap, common, worthless

prick *n.* **1.** dot, hole, mark, nick, notch, perforation, pock, puncture **2.** hurt, pain, pang, sensation, smart, sting, tingling, urtication **3.** barb, needle, point, projection, prong, spike, spur, tip, tooth – *v.* **1.** bore, gash, jab, perforate, pierce, puncture, stab, wound **2.** affect, afflict, cut, injure, pain, prickle, smart, sting, tingle **3.** activate, exhort, foment, goad, incite, inflame, instigate, kindle, motivate, prompt, urge *Nonformal:* egg on, whip up

prickly *adj.* **1.** bad-tempered, cantankerous, contentious, edgy, fractious, fretful, grouchy, grumpy, irritable, nettlesome, peevish, petulant, snappish, splenetic, touchy, waspish *Antonyms:* civil, courteous, easygoing, gracious, obliging, polite, unperturbed **2.** complicated, dangerous, dicey *(Nonformal)*, difficult, sticky, ticklish, tricky **3.** barbed, brambly, briery, bristly, sharp, thorny **4.** hurting, itchy, scratchy, smarting, sore, stinging, tingling

pride *n.* **1.** arrogance, big head *(Nonformal)*, braggadocio, conceit, egotism, haughtiness, hubris, overconfidence, self-importance, smugness, vainglory, vanity *Antonyms:* diffidence, humility, modesty **2.** *amour propre (French)*, confidence, dignity, ego, self-esteem, self-respect **3.** best, boast, choice, cream, elite, flower, gem, glory, jewel, pick, prime, prize, top, treasure *Antonyms:* bottom of the barrel, dregs **4.** assemblage, company, congregation, drove, family, flock, gathering, group, herd, pack

priest *n.* abbess, abbot, bishop, churchman, churchwoman, clergyman, clergywoman, cleric, confessor, curate, deacon, dean, devotee, divine, dominie, druid, ecclesiastic, elder, evangelist, father, friar, guru, holy man *or* woman, *imam (Muslim)*, lama, man *or* woman of the cloth, mendicant, minister, missionary, monk, nun, padre, *papas (Greek)*, parson, pastor, pontiff, preacher, presbyter, priestess, prior, *puoin (Native Peoples)*, rabbi, rector, reverend, sermonizer, shaman, spiritual guide, swami, talapoin *(Buddhist)*, vicar, worshipper, yogi *French:* abbé, curé *Hindu* Brahman, pundit, sadhu *Nonformal:* bible-thumper, sky pilot

prig *n.* carper, high-brow, nitpicker, pedant, puritan, priss *Nonformal:* bluenose, fusspot, goody-goody, stuffed shirt, tight-ass *Antonyms:* boor, slob

prim *adj.* **1.** exact, formal, neat, nice, orderly, particular, pat, precise, rigid, shipshape, spruce, tidy, uncluttered, well-groomed *Antonyms:* cluttered, messy, untidy **2.** coy, demure, diffident, meek, missish, modest, reserved, retiring, shrinking, shy *Antonyms:* arrogant, assertive, proud **3.** correct, fastidious, fussy, prissy, proper, prudish, stiff, strait-laced, stuffy, Victorian *Nonformal:* stuck-up, uptight *Antonyms:* casual, laid-back, relaxed

primal *adj.* **1.** aboriginal, autochthonous, first, indigene, initial, primordial, original **2.** embryonic, germinal, incipient, nascent, primitive **3.** basic, cardinal, central, chief, critical, crucial, essential, fundamental, greatest, highest, main, paramount, primary, principal, vital

primarily *adv.* **1.** above all, basically, chiefly, especially, essentially, first and foremost, fundamentally, generally, largely, mainly, mostly, on the whole, overall, predominantly, principally **2.** at first, from the get-go *(Nonformal)*, in the beginning, initially, originally

primary *adj.* **1.** basic, beginning, central, elemental, essential, foundational, fundamental, introductory, original, rudimentary, simple, underlying *Antonyms:* following, later, subsequent, succeeding **2.** best, capital, cardinal, chief, dominant, excellent, greatest, highest, leading, main, paramount, prestigious, prime, principal, world-class *Antonyms:* inferior, lesser, lowest, unimportant **3.** direct, firsthand, firstperson, immediate, original *Antonyms:* hearsay, once removed, secondary **4.** aboriginal, autochthonous, earliest, first, initial, maiden, pioneer, primal, prime, primeval, primordial, pristine *Antonyms:* ensuing, following, later

primate *n.* **1.** animal, beast, mammal *Kinds of primate:* ape, baboon, chimpanzee, galago, gibbon, gorilla, Homo sapien, human being, indra, langur, lemur, mandrill, marmset, monkey, orangutan, potto, simian, tarsier, tree shrew, white-headed saki **2.** archbishop, bishop, cardinal, ecclesiastic, hierarch, high priest, pontiff, pope, prelate

prime *adj.* **1.** best, excellent, exceptional, first-rate, great, matchless, noteworthy, outstanding, perfect, select, supreme, top *Nonformal:* ace, crack, topnotch, wicked **2.** cardinal, central, chief, dominant, foremost, leading, main, master, maximum, paramount, principal **3.** aboriginal, autochthonous, first, incipient, initial, original, primeval **4.** blooming, flowering, in the pink *(Nonformal)*, mature, vigorous – *n.* **1.** beginning, creation, dawn, genesis, inception, inchoation, nascence, onset, origin, spring **2.** adulthood, apex, bloom, climax, flower, height, heyday, maturity, peak, perfection, summit, top, zenith **3.** best, beaut *(Nonformal)*, choice, chosen, cream, elite, nonpareil, nonesuch, optimum, pick, quintessence, select, superlative – *v.* **1.** arrange, charge, cock, fix, load, prep *(Nonformal)*, prepare, ready, set **2.** apprise, brief, fill in *(Nonformal)*, inform, notify, prompt, tell **3.** coat, cover, dab, paint, undercoat

prime minister *n.* boss, chief, elected official, first minister, head, leader, minister, PM, ruler

primeval *adj.* ancient, earliest, early, first, old, original, prehistoric, primal, primary, primitive, primordial *Antonyms:* modern, new

primitive *adj.* **1.** autochthous, earliest, early, elementary, essential, first, fundamental, indigene, native, original, primal, primary, primeval, primordial *Antonyms:* advanced, later, modern **2.** austere, basic, naive, plain, quaint, simple, Spartan, straightforward, uncomplicated, unsophisticated *Antonyms:* abstract, complex, difficult **3.** banausic, coarse, crude, rough, rudimentary, uncultivated, undeveloped, unformed, unpolished, unrefined, untaught, untutored **4.** ancient, antiquated, archaic, obsolete, old, old-fashioned, outdated, outmoded, stone-age – *n.* **1.** prehistoric man *or* woman, troglodyte **2.** antique, fossil, petroglyph, prehistory

primordial *adj.* atavistic, basic, earliest, early, elemental, embryonic, first, fundamental, original, prehistoric, primal, primary, prime, primeval, primitive, pristine, seminal – *n.* base, basis, cornerstone, fundamental, premise, principle, tradition

primp *v.* adorn, array, beautify, clothe, decorate, dress, embellish, ornament, preen, outfit, titivate *Nonformal:* gussy, spruce up

prince *n.* aristocrat, atheling, blueblood, elector, heir apparent, landgrave, leader, noble, potentate, princeling, royal, ruler

princely *adj.* **1.** aristocratic, august, blue-blooded, courtly, dignified, gracious, grand, imperial, imposing, lofty, majestic, noble, opulent, regal, royal, sovereign, stately, venerable *Antonyms:* common, humble, lowly, mean, plain **2.** generous, lavish, magnificent, rich, splendid, sumptuous *Antonyms:* chintzy, impoverished, mingy, paltry

princess *n.* aristocrat, blueblood, heir apparent, infanta, noble, rani, royal

principal *adj.* arch, capital, cardinal, chief, crowning, dominant, first, foremost, head, highest, important, key, leading, main, major, paramount, predominant, preeminent, premier, prevailing, primary, prime, prominent, starring, superior, supreme *Antonyms:* auxiliary, inferior, minor, subsidiary – *n.* **1.** captain, chief, director, head, lead, ringleader *Nonformal:* big cheese, C.E.O., head honcho, kingpin, top dog **2.** chancellor, dean, director, headmaster, master, superintendent *Commonly misused:* **principle**

principally *adv.* above all, basically, cardinally, chiefly, dominantly, eminently, especially, essentially, fundamentally, generally, importantly, largely, mainly, mostly, notably, particularly, predominantly, preeminently, prevailingly, prevalently, primarily, substantially

principle *n.* **1.** axiom, dogma, hypothesis, maxim, postulate, theory, thesis, truism, truth **2.** belief, canon, code, convention, creed, directive, formula, guideline, law, mandate, mitzvah, model, moral, more, order, policy, practice, program, regulation, routine, rubric, standard, system, tenet, way **3.** basis, characteristic, constituent, element, essence, fundamental, germ, rudiment, seed **4.** conscience, ethic, ethos, fidelity, honesty, honour, integrity, morality, probity, rectitude, righteousness, trustworthiness **5.** cause, foundation, origin, root, source, wellspring *Commonly misused:* **principal**

principled *adj.* conscientious, decent, ethical, fair, high-minded, honest, just, moral, righteous, reputable, scrupulous, trustworthy, upright *Antonyms:* corrupt, crooked, unsavoury

print *adj.* journalistic, magazine, media, newspaper, press, printed, published – *n.* **1.** fingerprint, footprint, hoofprint, impress, impression, imprint, indent, indentation, mark, paw print, seal, spoor, stamp, trace, track **2.** character, font, lettering, typeface, typescript **3.** broadside, brochure, chapbook, comic, flyer, handbill, journal, magazine, newspaper, pamphlet, paper, periodical, publication *See also:* **publication** **4.** glossy, lithograph, mimeograph, offset, photograph, picture, poster, proof **5.** carbon, copy, facsimile, production, replica, reproduction, scan **6.** decoration, design, fabric, pattern, stencil – *v.* **1.** emboss, engrave, impress, imprint, indent, press, stamp **2.** copy, issue, output, produce, reprint, reproduce, run off, set, typeset

printer *n.* **1.** machine *Kinds of computer printer:* band, bubble-jet, daisy-wheel, dot-matrix, inkjet, laser, line, serial, thermal, thimble **2.** journeyman, pressman, printer's devil, typesetter, typographer **3.** bookbinder, house, manufacturer, press, publisher

prior *adj.* above-mentioned, aforementioned, ancestorial, antecedent, anterior, earlier, foregoing, former, past, preceding, preexistent, previous *Antonyms:* after, ensuing, subsequent, succeeding – *n.* abbess, abbot, brother, cleric, ecclesiastic lama, monk, monastic, mother superior, nun, priest, prioress, sister, vicar

priority *adj.* critical, first class, hot *(Nonformal)*, important, rush – *n.* **1.** code blue *or* red, consequence, importance, precedence, primacy, rank, seniority, supremacy tenure, urgency, weight **2.** antecedence antedating, anteriority, predating, preexistence

prison *n.* **1.** bastille, brig, cage, camp, cell, concentration *or* internment camp, coop, correctional facility, detention centre, dungeon, enclosure, guardhouse, gulag, house of detention, jail, jailhouse, keep, lockup, oubliette, pen, penal institution, penitentiary, pound, reformatory, remand centre, stockade *Nonformal:* big house, can, clink, cooler, hole, hoosegow, joint, jug, poky, skookum-house, slammer, stir, tank **2.** caging, captivity, confinement, custody, detention, imprisonment, incarceration, internment, penning

prisoner *n.* captive, convict, criminal, defendant, detainee, hostage, inmate, internee, kapo, trusty *Nonformal:* con, jailbird, lag, lifer, POW, punk

prissy *adj.* effeminate, fastidious, finicky, fussy, niggling, particular, persnickety, picky, precious, prim, proper, prudish, squeamish, stickler, strait-laced, stuffy, tight-laced, uptight *(Nonformal)*, Victorian *Antonyms:* casual, easygoing, laid-back – *n.* prig, prude *Nonformal:* fussbudget, fusspot, goody two-shoes, puritan

pristine *adj.* **1.** clean, natural, plain, pure, simple, spotless, undefiled, unmarred, unspoiled, unsullied, virginal *Antonyms:* blemished, corrupted, defiled, fallen, tarnished **2.** early, first, incipient, initial, native, original, primitive, primordial

privacy *n.* **1.** isolation, monasticism, reclusion, retreat, retirement, room of one's own, seclusion, separation, solitude, space, withdrawal *Antonyms:* company, fellowship **2.** concealment, confidentiality, covertness, mysteriousness, secrecy, secretiveness, silence, surreptitiousness *Antonyms:* openness, overtness, publicity

private *adj.* **1.** alone, insular, isolated, reclusive, remote, retiring, secluded, sequestered, solitary, withdrawn **2.** clandestine, closet, concealed, confidential, covert, furtive, hidden, hushed, off-the-record, secret, *sub rosa (Latin) Nonformal:* hugger-mugger, hush-hush, on the Q.T. **3.** closed, exclusive, limited, nonpublic, reserved **4.** individual, inner, intimate, particular, personal **5.** distinctive, esoteric, peculiar, special – *n.* enlisted man, first class, foot soldier, infantryman, private soldier, Pte, soldier *U.S.:* GI, Pfc *Nonformal:* G.I. Joe, grunt, tommy

privation *n.* depletion, depravation, destitution, distress, hardship, impoverishment, indigence, loss, misery, need, neediness, pauperism, pennilessness, penury, poverty, want *Antonyms:* abundance, luxuriance, opulence, profit, wealth

privilege *n.* **1.** advantage, benefit, birthright, claim, *droit du seigneur (French)*, due, entitlement, prerogative, right **2.** authorization, dispensation, exemption, freedom, immunity, indulgence, leave, liberty, licence

privileged *adj.* **1.** advantaged, elite, entitled, favoured, honoured, indulged, powerful, rich, ruling, special, wealthy *Antonyms:* afflicted, deprived, destitute, impoverished, needy **2.** authorized, chartered, empowered, enfranchised, exempt, immune, licensed, protected, sanctioned **3.** confidential, exceptional, hush-hush *(Nonformal)*, inside, privy, secret, special, top secret *Antonyms:* disclosed, known, manifest, open, revealed

privy *adj.* **1.** acquainted, apprised, aware, cognizant, conscious, familiar, informed *Nonformal:* in on, in the know, wise to **2.** concealed, confidential, covert, hidden, obscured, personal, private, secret, separate, shrouded, ulterior *Antonyms:* broached, disclosed, known, open, unveiled – *n.* backhouse, bathroom, lavatory, outhouse, toilet, washroom, water closet *Nonformal:* Blue Moon gob, Café, jane, john, W.C.

prize *adj.* award-winning, best, blue-ribbon, champion, choice, cream, elite, first-rate, outstanding, prime, topnotch, winning *Antonyms:* average, inferior, mediocre, minor, second-rate – *n.* **1.** accolade, award, citation, crown, cup, decoration, distinction, glory, guerdon, honour, kudos *(Nonformal)*, laurels, medal, reward, ribbon, title, trophy, tribute *See also:* **award, medal 2.** jackpot, lottery, purse, raffle, recompense, stakes, windfall, winnings **3.** angel, cream, gem, honey, godsend, jewel, lollapalooza *(Nonformal)*, sweetheart, treasure **4.** aim, ambition, aspiration, brass ring *(Nonformal)*, desire, end, goal, intention, object, mark, target, wish **5.** booty, capture, find, haul, loot, plunder, property, spoils, swag *(Nonformal)* – *v.* appreciate, cherish, enshrine, esteem, estimate, hold dear, rate, regard highly, treasure, value *Antonyms:* despise, disparage, underrate

probability *n.* **1.** chance, conceivability, expectation, feasibility, hope, likelihood, plausibility, possibility, prospect, odds, outlook, viability **2.** favourite, frontrunner, pick, preference, preferred

probable *adj.* apparent, apt, believable, credible, feasible, likely, odds-on, ostensible, plausible, possible, potential, presumable, presumed, rational, reasonable, sound, tenable, viable *Antonyms:* doubtful, remote, unlikely

probably *adv.* apparently, assumably, believably, doubtless, expediently, feasibly, imaginably, likely, maybe, most likely, no doubt, perchance, perhaps, plausibly, possibly, practicably, presumably, reasonably, seemingly, viably

probation *n.* apprenticeship, audition, dry run, experiment, hearing, ordeal, pilot, supervision, test, trial, trial period, try, tryout

probe *n.* **1.** delving, examination, exploration, inquest, inquiry, inquisition, investigation, research, scrutiny, study *Nonformal:* fishing expedition, third degree **2.** explorer, feeler, instrument, needle, sounder – *v.* **1.** inquire, interrogate, investigate, plumb, prospect, query, question, quiz, research, scrutinize, search, sift, sound-out, study, test **2.** check, examine, explore, feel, needle, prod, touch *Nonformal:* check out, poke around

problem *adj.* delinquent, difficult, disturbed, incorrigible, intractable, maladjusted, obstreperous, renegade, uncontrollable, unmanageable, unruly *Antonyms:* amenable, angelic, compliant, well-behaved – *n.* **1.** brain-teaser, conundrum, dilemma, enigma, labyrinth, maze, mystery, *pons asinrum (Latin)*, puzzle, question, riddle, stickler, teaser *Nonformal:* mind-boggler, stumper **2.** annoyance, bother, complication, difficulty, disagreement, dispute, headache, imbroglio, irritant, issue, mess, muddle, nuisance, obstacle, predicament, quagmire, quandary, question, trouble *Nonformal:* hassle, hot water, pickle, scrape, snafu, stew *Antonyms:* advantage, benefit **3.** catch, drawback, fault, flaw, hitch, issue, objection, obstacle, snag *Nonformal:* fly in the ointment, monkey wrench

problematic *adj.* **1.** chancy, dangerous, hazardous, iffy *(Nonformal)*, insecure, parlous, perilous, precarious, risky, rocky, shaky, slippery, touch-and-go, tricky **2.** ambiguous, arguable, borderline, debatable, dicey, disputable, doubtful, dubious, enigmatic, equivocal, indecisive, moot, puzzling, questionable, suspect, uncertain, unreliable, unsettled, unsure *Antonyms:* absolute, certain, clear, definite, settled

procedure *n.* **1.** action, approach, course, methodology, plan, strategy **2.** custom, fashion, form, method, mode, *modus operandi (Latin)*, operation, policy, polity, practice, program, routine, standard operating procedure system, tradition, way *Nonformal:* drill, grind, M.O., red tape, S.O.P., the book

proceed *v.* **1.** advance, continue, endure, forge ahead, go *or* carry *or* press on, make headway, move, move out, progress **2.** act, begin, behave, commence, do, execute, function, get going, perform, undertake **3.** course, derive, emerge, flow, issue, originate, run, stem, stream *Commonly misused:* **precede**

proceeding *n.* action, circumstance, course, deed, exercise, happening, incident, manoeuvre, measure, movement, occurrence, operation, performance, procedure, process, step, transaction, undertaking, venture

proceedings *n. pl.* **1.** affairs, business, dealings, doings, goings-on, matters, transactions **2.** account, annals, archives, documents, Hansard *(Parliament)*, minutes, records, report **3.** case, lawsuit, legal action, litigation, process, suit, trial

proceeds *n. pl.* earnings, gain, gate, income, interest, produce, product, profit, receipts, result, returns, revenue, reward, split *(Nonformal)*, take, till, yield *Antonyms:* costs, debts, losses

process *n.* **1.** action, approach, method, mode, *modus operandi (Latin)*, operation, practice, procedure, routine, rule, system, technique, way *Nonformal:* M.O., motions **2.** course, development, evolution, growth, middle, midst, movement, unfolding – *v.* **1.** analyze, arrange, compute, examine, execute, load, organize, problem solve, select, set-up, sort, systematize, translate **2.** alter, break down, change, convert, cure, distill, manipulate, modify, prepare, preserve, smelt, treat **3.** communicate, deal with, handle, interface, operate, transact, work **4.** blend, chop, liquefy, mix, mulch, purée

processed *adj.* cured, dried, fermented, freeze-dried, frozen, made, manufactured, prepared, ready-made, smoked, sun-dried, treated

processing *adj.* analyzing, arranging, communicating, competing, computing, converting, downloading, examining, executing, handling, loading, manipulating, modifying, preparing, preserving, organizing, problem solving, selecting, setting up, sorting, translating, uploading, working

procession *n.* **1.** advance, autocade, cavalcade, column, cortège, entourage, march, motorcade, movement, parade, **2.** chain, concaternation, course, cycle, file, order, process, run, sequence, series, string, succession, train

proclaim *v.* **1.** advertise, affirm, announce, blaze, broadcast, bruit, call, circulate, declare, demonstrate, disseminate, herald, make known, profess, promulgate, publish, shout out, sound off, trumpet, utter, vent *(Nonformal)*, ventilate, voice *Antonyms:* conceal, hush up, suppress, withhold **2.** characterize, illustrate, indicate, manifest, present, show **3.** accuse, brand, charge, denounce

proclamation *n.* advertisement, announcement, ban, banns, broadcast, bull, declaration, decree, edict, manifesto, notice, notification, promulgation, pronouncement, public disclaimer, publication, statement

proclivity *n.* bent, bias, disposition, facility, inclination, leaning, penchant, predilection, predisposition, prejudice, proneness, propensity, tendency, weakness

procrastinate *v.* dally, dawdle, defer, delay, gain time, hang fire, hesitate, lag, linger, pause, postpone, prolong, protract, put off, stall, suspend, tarry, wait *Nonformal:* scrimshank, shilly-shally, slack *Antonyms:* advance, expedite, hasten, proceed

procrastination *n.* abeyance, dalliance, dawdling, deferral, delay, filabuster, hesitation, idling, postponement, protraction, prolongation, stalling, suspension, vacillation *Nonformal:* dilly-dallying, foot-dragging *Antonyms:* advancement, expediency, progression, punctuality, timeliness

procreate *v.* create, beget, breed, conceive, engender, father, generate, get, hatch, impregnate, make, make babies *(Nonformal)*, mother, multiply, originate, parent, produce, proliferate, propagate, reproduce, sire, spawn

procure *v.* **1.** acquire, appropriate, buy, earn, gain, garner, get, grab, harvest, hire, obtain, secure *Nonformal:* bag, net *Antonyms:* give away, hawk, lose **2.** accomplish, actuate, bring about, cause, concoct, contrive, effect, engender, generate, manipulate, plot, scheme, wangle *(Nonformal)* **3.** hustle, pander, pimp, prostitute, solicit

prod *n.* **1.** goad, pointer, poker, rowel, spur, stick, twig **2.** dig, jab, joggle, nudge, poke, push, shake, shove, thrust *Nonformal:* boost, goose **3.** cue, hint, jog *(Nonformal)*, prompting, reminder – *v.* **1.** dig, elbow, finger, goose *(Nonformal)*, jab, jog, needle, nudge, poke at, press, prick, probe, punch, push, shove, thrust **2.** arouse, egg on *(Nonformal)*, foment, goad, ignite, incite, motivate, prompt, propel, provoke, rouse, spur, stimulate, urge

prodigal *adj.* **1.** dissipated, excessive, extravagant, immoderate, improvident, intemperate, profligate, reckless, spendthrift, squandering, wanton, wasteful *Antonyms:* careful, frugal, miserly, prudent **2.** abundant, bottomless, bounteous, bountiful, copious, exuberant, flush, lavish, lush, luxuriant, luxurious, munificent, opulent, plentiful, profuse, superabundant, teeming *Antonyms:* deficient, lacking, meagre – *n.* profligate, spender, spendthrift, squanderer, wastrel

prodigious *adj.* **1.** Brobdingnagian, colossal, enormous, giant, gigantic, gross, herculean, huge, immeasurable, immense, king-size, large, mammoth, massive, mighty, monstrous, monumental, towering, vast *Nonformal:* ginormous, humongous *Antonyms:* minuscule, negligible, puny, small, tiny **2.** amazing, astonishing, astounding, exceptional, extraordinary, fabulous, fantastic, impressive, inordinate, marvellous, phenomenal, remarkable, stupendous, surreal, thumping *(Nonformal)*, tremendous, wonderful *Antonyms:* normal, usual, ordinary, unexciting

prodigy *n.* **1.** genius, intellect, mastermind, natural, portent, talent, wizard, *wunderkind (German)*, virtuoso *Nonformal:* boy *or* girl wonder, brain, crackerjack, whiz, whiz kid **2.** idiot savant, marvel, miracle, phenomenon, rarity, sensation, wonder **3.** aberration, abnormality, anomaly, curiosity, freak of nature, monster, monstrosity, oddity, peculiarity

produce *n.* crop, fruits and vegetables, harvest, proceeds, product, return, yield – *v.* **1.** bear, beget, breed, bring forth, conceive, deliver, fructify, hatch, generate, grow, propagate, reproduce, spawn, yield **2.** build, compose, create, design, draft, frame, imagine, invent, make, manufacture, originate, perform, render, shape, write **3.** bring about, cause, effect, engender, induce, initiate, muster, occasion, provoke, secure, spark **4.** bring to light, disclose, manifest, reveal, show **5.** display, exhibit, mount, present, put on, stage

product *n.* **1.** artifact, creation, crop, goods, harvest, issue, merchandise, output, returns, stock, work, yield **2.** consequence, by-product, effect, fallout, outcome, repercussion, result, spin-off, upshot

production *n.* **1.** assembly, construction, creation, fabrication, making, manufacturing, origination, preparation, rendering **2.** article, brainchild, by-product, commodity, exhibition, goods, invention, inventory, item, line, merchandise, *oeuvre (French)*, output, result, return, ware, work, yield **3.** concert, drama, event, film, movie, musical, opera, operetta, performance, picture, play, show **4.** display, *mise en scène (French)*, presentation, set, setting, staging

productive *adj.* **1.** bounteous, bountiful, creative, fecund, fertile, fruitful, generative, germinal, inventive, progenitive, prolific, resourceful, rich, teeming **2.** advantageous, beneficial, fat *(Nonformal)*, gainful, profitable, remunerative, rewarding, useful, valuable, worthwhile

profane *adj.* **1.** blasphemous, disrespectful, faithless, godless, heathen, heretical, impious, irreligious, irreverent, sacrilegious *Antonyms:* godly, pious, religious **2.** laic, lay, mundane, nonclerical, nonreligious, nonsacred, secular, temporal, unhallowed, unholy, unsanctified *Antonyms:* cosmic, spiritual, transcendent **3.** base, bawdy, coarse, common, crude, cursing, dirty, filthy, foul, indecent, lewd, maledictive, obscene, off-colour, ribald, smutty, swearing, vile, vulgar *Antonyms:* decorous, good, proper – *v.* abuse, blaspheme, curse, cuss *(Nonformal)*, debase, defile, degrade, desecrate, despoil, misuse, pervert, pollute, prostitute, violate, vitiate

profanity *n.* **1.** blasphemy, execration, desecration, fuddle-duddle *(Nonformal)*, impiety, imprecation, irreverence, malediction, sacrilege *Antonyms:* piety, reverence, righteousness **2.** curse, cursing, dirty language *or* word, oath, obscenity, swearing, swearword *Nonformal:* cuss, four-letter word

profess *v.* **1.** acknowledge, affirm, announce, assert, aver, avow, claim, confess, declare, express, proclaim, proffer, pronounce, propound, say, state, tell, utter **2.** allege, fake, feign, lay claim to, pretend, purport, simulate

profession *n.* **1.** business, calling, career, chosen work, concern, craft, employment, engagement, field, game *(Nonformal)*, handicraft, lifework, line, livelihood, métier, occupation, office, position, post, pursuit, role, service, situation, specialty, sphere, trade, undertaking, vocation, work **2.** affirmation, assertion, avowal, claim, declaration, proclamation, pronouncement, statement, word

professional *adj.* **1.** businesslike, competent, conscientious, diligent, efficient, finished, formal, matter-of-fact, no-nonsense, polished, thorough **2.** able, card-carrying *(Nonformal)*, certified, experienced, expert, knowledgeable, licensed, practised, proficient, qualified, seasoned, trained – *n.* **1.** authority, expert, specialist *Nonformal:* mavin, pro **2.** ace, maestro, talent, virtuoso *Nonformal:* crackerjack, whiz

professor *n.* doctor, don, educator, faculty member, fellow, guru, instructor, lecturer, mentor, pedagogue, philosopher, polymath, prof *(Nonformal)*, pundit, scholar, schoolteacher, scientist, sensei, teacher, tutor, *ulema (Muslim)*

proffer *n.* idea, motion, proposal, proposition, recommendation, submission, suggestion – *v.* extend, give, offer, pose, present, propose, proposition, propound, submit, suggest, tender, volunteer *Antonyms:* check, restrain, withhold

proficiency *n.* ability, accomplishment, aptitude, competence, dexterity, efficiency, expertise, facility, green thumb, knowledge, learning, mastery, skilfulness, skill, talent, virtuosity *Nonformal:* knack, know-how, makings, meal ticket, right stuff, the goods *Antonyms:* clumsiness, feebleness, inexperience, maladroitness

proficient *adj.* able, accomplished, adept, capable, clever, competent, consummate, conversant, deft, effective, efficient, experienced, expert, finished, gifted, masterful, professional, qualified, sharp, skilful, skilled, slick, talented, trained, versed *Nonformal:* ace, crack, crackerjack, pro, savvy, with it *Antonyms:* incapable, incompetent, inept, unaccomplished, unskilled – *n.* ace, authority, expert, maestro, prodigy, wizard *Nonformal:* crackerjack, dab hand, shark

profile *n.* **1.** cameo, cast, contour, delineation, drawing, elevation, figuration, figure, form, illustration, outline, portrait, shadow, shape, side view, silhouette, sketch **2.** analysis, biography, breakdown, characterization, cross section, description, review, sketch, study, summary, survey, thumbnail *(Nonformal)*, vignette

profit *n.* **1.** gain, harvest, income, interest, receipt, return, revenue, remuneration, surplus, take, windfall, winnings *(Nonformal)*, yield **2.** advantage, aid, avail, benefit, betterment, furtherance, help, improvement, service – *v.* **1.** capitalize, earn, gain, prosper, realize, recover *Nonformal:* clean up, clear, make a killing **2.** advance, aid, avail, benefit, better, contribute, further, help, improve, promote, serve, work for *(Nonformal)*

profiteering *n.* blackmail, exploitation, extortion, fleecing, price gouging, racketeering, swindling *Nonformal:* bleeding, highway robbery, shakedown

profligate *adj.* **1.** base, corrupt, debauched, degenerate, depraved, dissolute, easy, immoral, lewd, libertine, licentious, loose, perverted, promiscuous, reckless, reprobate, shameless, unprincipled, vile, wanton, wicked, wild *Antonyms:* decent, principled, virtuous **2.** extravagant, immoderate, improvident, lavish, spendthrift, squandering, wasteful *Antonyms:* economical, frugal, thrifty – *n.* **1.** debauchee, degenerate, good-for-nothing, libertine, playboy, rake, reprobate, roué, sport *(Nonformal)*, swinger **2.** big spender, prodigal, spendthrift, squanderer, wastrel

profound *adj.* **1.** astute, erudite, informed, insightful, intellectual, knowledgeable, learned, noetic, penetrating, philosophical, sagacious, scholarly, wise **2.** acute, deep, extreme, heartfelt, heartrending, intense, keen, moving, overpowering, penetrating, piercing, poignant **3.** abstract, abstruse, arcane, complex, complicated, difficult, impenetrable, inscrutable, intricate, mysterious, recondite, tough, unfathomable **4.** absolute, complete, consummate, decided, exhaustive, out-and-out, pronounced, thorough, utter **5.** abysmal, bottomless, buried, cavernous, deep, fathomless, subterranean, yawning

profuse *adj.* **1.** excessive, extravagant, extreme, immoderate, intemperate, lavish, prodigal, wasteful **2.** abundant, ample, bountiful, copious, fruitful, limitless, lush, multitudinous, overflowing, overgrowing, plentiful, prolific, rife, swarming, teeming, yielding *Nonformal:* bumper, crawling with **3.** bounteous, free, generous, liberal, magnanimous, munificent, open-handed, unselfish

progeny *n.* breed, brood, children, descendants, family, heirs, issue, lineage, litter, offspring, spawn, stock, young *Nonformal:* get, kids, sprigs

prognosis *n.* diagnosis, forecast, foretelling, likelihood, possibility, prediction, projection, prophecy, speculation, surmisal

prognosticate *v.* augur, betoken, divine, forebode, forecast, foresee, foretell, portend, predict, presage, prophesy, read, soothsay

program *n.* **1.** broadcast, performance, presentation, production, show, simulcast, telecast **2.** agenda, announcement, bill, *dramatis personae (Latin)*, guide, index, lineup, listing, schedule, slate, syllabus, table of contents, timetable **3.** design, instructions, method, plan, procedure, protocol, routine, scheme, system **4.** course, curriculum, department, field, major, section **5.** application, firmware, game, software, spreadsheet, word processor, Trojan Horse, utility, virus *See also:* **software** **6.** introduction, opening remarks, preamble, preface, proem, statement – *v.* **1.** arrange, book, compile, line up, list, organize, schedule **2.** calculate, contrive, design, devise, engineer, formulate, plan *or* work out, prepare, process **3.** brainwash, control, direct, instruct, manipulate, train **4.** enter, input, record, write

programmer *n.* code jockey *(Nonformal)*, designer, developer, engineer, graphic designer, hacker, planner, specialist, tester, user, writer

progress *n.* **1.** ascension, ascent, betterment, climb, development, enhancement, evolution, furtherance, graduation, growth, improvement, promotion, rise **2.** advancement, breakthrough, gain, headway, innovation, movement, stride – *v.* **1.** advance, continue, forge ahead, inch along *(Nonformal)*, make headway, mount, move forward, proceed, scale, strive **2.** better, develop, enrich, evolve, grow, improve, mature, ripen, upgrade **3.** come around, convalesce, get better, recover, recuperate, revive

progressive *adj.* **1.** avant-garde, broad-minded, Bull Moose *(Historical)*, forward-looking, left of centre, open-minded, unconventional **2.** advancing, continuing, flowing, moving forward **3.** calibrated, consecutive, gradational, gradual, hierarchical, sequential, step-by-step, successive **4.** contagious, increasing, intensifying, malignant, spreading – *n.* forward thinker, left-winger, liberal, muckraker, radical, reformer, revisionist

prohibit *v.* **1.** ban, deny, disallow, forbid, freeze, interdict, nix *(Nonformal)*, outlaw, proscribe, quash, veto *Antonyms:* allow, consent, let, permit **2.** block, bottle *or* hold up, constrain, frustrate, halt, hinder, impede, inhibit, obstruct, restrain, restrict, retard, rule out, stop *Antonyms:* advance, further, progress

prohibited *adj.* **1.** criminal, forbidden, illegal, not allowed, proscribed, taboo, unsanctioned *Nonformal:* out-of-bounds, wildcat *Antonyms:* allowed, authorized, licensed, permitted **2.** banished, barred, blackballed, checked, excluded, ostracized, refused, suspended

prohibition *n.* **1.** ban, disallowance, embargo, enjoinder, excommunication, injunction, interdiction, proscription, taboo, veto *Antonyms:* assent, consent, permission, sanction **2.** check, curb, hindrance, impediment, interference, obstruction, prevention, restriction, suppression

prohibitive *adj.* **1.** confining, constraining, forbidding, limiting, preventing, restraining, restrictive *Antonyms:* emancipating, encouraging, fostering, inspiring, supportive **2.** beyond one's means, costly, exorbitant, expensive, high-priced, sky-high, steep, unafforable, unreasonable *Nonformal:* highway robbery, over the moon *Antonyms:* bargain, cheap, reduced

project *n.* **1.** activity, assignment, chore, commitment, enterprise, homework, job, obligation, task, undertaking, venture, work **2.** aim, blueprint, design, game plan *(Nonformal)*, goal, objective, outline, plan, program, scheme, strategy – *v.* **1.** balloon, billow, bulge, distend, jut, obtrude, overhang, protrude, stand out **2.** aim, conceive, concoct, design, determine, devise, intend, invent, plan, plot, present, propose, scheme *Nonformal:* cook up, hatch **3.** cast, fire, fling, hurl, launch, propel, throw, toss **4.** ballpark *(Nonformal)*, calculate, draft, estimate, figure, foreordain, predetermine, predict **5.** actualize, externalize, impart, objectify, transfer, visualize **6.** beam, flash, put on, screen, show

projection *n.* **1.** bulge, cantilever, cordillera, crenation, extension, flange, jut, knob, ledge, overhang, point, prominence, promontory, protrusion, quill, ridge, rim, shelf, sill, spike, spine, spur, step, swelling **2.** calculation, computation, estimate, estimation, extrapolation, forecast, guess, guesstimation *(Nonformal)*, prediction, prognostication, reckoning **3.** externalization, objectification, transference **4.** design, goal, intention, plan, plot, project, proposal, scheme **5.** blueprint, delineation, drawing, elevation, layout, map, outline, prospectus, sketch

proletariat *n.* commoners, hoi polloi, labour, peasants, rabble, ragtag and bobtail *(Nonformal)*, riff-raff, silent majority, the masses *or* multitude *or* populace, third estate, workers, working class *Antonyms:* aristocracy, gentry, nobility

proliferate *v.* **1.** breed, engender, make babies *(Nonformal)*, multiply, procreate, propagate, reproduce **2.** boom, burgeon, enlarge, flourish, grow, increase, inflate, skyrocket, spread, thrive *Nonformal:* mushroom, snowball *Antonyms:* diminish, evaporate, wane

prolific *adj.* **1.** abounding, abundant, bountiful, copious, profuse, spawning, swarming, teeming, yielding **2.** fecund, fertile, fruitful, generative, productive, rank, regenerative, rich *Antonyms:* barren, fruitless, infertile, sterile, unproductive

prolix *adj.* bombastic, circuitous, circumlocutory, euphemistic, detailed, digressive, discursive, grandiloquent, indirect, lengthy, long-winded, maundering, motor-mouthed *(Nonformal)*, prosaic, protracted, rambling, redundant, roundabout, spun-out, tautological, tedious, turgid, verbose, wordy *Antonyms:* abbreviated, concise, laconic, pithy, succinct

prologue *n.* exordium, exposition, foreword, introduction, opening remarks, preamble, preface, prefix, preliminaries, prelude, proem *Antonyms:* addendum, conclusion, epilogue, postscript, suffix

prolong *v.* carry on, continue, drag out, extend, keep going, lengthen, maintain, pad *(Nonformal)*, persist, protract, stretch *or* string out, sustain *Antonyms:* cut off, discontinue, prorogue, stop, terminate

promenade *n.* **1.** airing, constitutional, outing, peregrination, ramble, stroll, saunter, walk **2.** arcade, boardwalk, boulevard, esplanade, footpath, path, sidewalk – *v.* **1.** flaunt, parade, peacock, prance, sally, sashay, strut, swagger, swashbuckle *Antonyms:* cower, crawl, creep **2.** amble, meander, perambulate, roam, saunter, stroll, walk, wander *Nonformal:* boogie, toddle

prominence *n.* **1.** celebrity, distinction, drawing power, eminence, fame, greatness, illustriousness, importance, influence, name, notability, notoriety, precedence, preeminence, prestige, rank, renown, reputation, salience, standing, stardom, weight *Antonyms:* anonymity, inconspicuousness, obscurity, umimportance **2.** bulge, bump, cliff, crag, crest, headland, height, high point, hill, jut, mound, peak, pinnacle, projection, protuberance, rise, swell

prominent *adj.* **1.** celebrated, chief, distinguished, eminent, famed, famous, foremost, great, important, leading, main, notable, noted, outstanding, popular, preeminent, prestigious, renowned, respected, top, well-known *Nonformal:* big-league, big-name, high-profile, hot-shot, top drawer *Antonyms:* insignificant, minor, secondary, unimportant, unknown **2.** bulging, extended, hilly, jutting, projecting, protruding, raised **3.** conspicuous, flashy, marked, noticeable, obvious, pronounced, remarkable, salient, striking, unmistakable *Antonyms:* faint, inconspicuous, insignificant, negligable

promiscuous *adj.* **1.** abandoned, dissipated, dissolute, fast, immoral, libertine, licentious, loose, profligate, unrestrained, wanton, wild *Nonformal:* easy, horny, swinging *Antonyms:* chaste, decent, modest, pure, undefiled **2.** chaotic, confused, disorganized, helter-skelter *(Nonformal)*, jumbled, miscellaneous, motley, ragtag, scrambled, mixed **3.** careless, casual, cursory, haphazard, heedless, perfunctory, indiscriminate, irregular

promise *n.* **1.** affirmation, agreement, assurance, avowal, betrothal, bond, commitment, compact, contract, covenant, deed, guarantee, hand *(Nonformal)*, insurance, oath, obligation, pact, pledge, profession, stipulation, swearing, troth, undertaking, vow, warranty, word *Antonyms:* denial, negation, refusal, renunciation **2.** ability, capability, capacity, expectation, flair, makings, possibility, potential, prospect, talent *Antonyms:* inaptness, ineptitude, weakness – *v.* **1.** affiance, affirm, agree, answer for, assent, betroth, bind, commit, compact, consent, declare, engage, ensure, guarantee, insure, obligate, pledge, secure, stipulate, subscribe, swear, undertake, underwrite, vouch, vow, warrant *Antonyms:* disclaim, reject, rescind, revoke, veto **2.** augur, betoken, bode, foreshadow, hint, indicate, portend, presage, suggest

promising *adj.* auspicious, bright, encouraging, favourable, happy, hopeful, likely, propitious, reassuring, roseate, rosy *Antonyms:* discouraging, portentous, unfavourable

promote *v.* **1.** aid, assist, back, boost, cultivate, encourage, facilitate, foster, further, help, minister, nurture, patronize, succour, support *Antonyms:* hinder, ignore, neglect **2.** advance, elevate, graduate, move up, pass *Antonyms:* demote, diminish, fail **3.** advocate, champion, espouse, present, propose, recommend **4.** advertise, blazon, broadcast, placard, popularize, publish, trumpet *Nonformal:* ballyhoo, beat the drum, hype, plug

promotion *n.* **1.** advancement, development, elevation, furtherance, hike, jump, raise, rise, upgrade *Antonyms:* abdication, demotion, discharge, dismissal **2.** aid, assistance, backing, boost, encouragement, help, nourishment, nurturing, patronage, succour, support **3.** bargain, deal, loss leader, proposal, propisition, special offer, submission *Nonformal:* buy, price **4.** advertising, blitz, campaign, blurb, build up, press, notice, pitch, plug, propaganda, publicity, public relations *Nonformal:* hard sell, hoopla, hype

prompt *adj.* **1.** early, expeditious, instant, on time, punctual, quick, rapid, seasonable, speedy, swift, timely *Antonyms:* late, remiss, tardy **2.** alert, disposed, eager, game *(Nonformal)*, inclined, prone, ready, willing – *n.* **1.** cue, help, hint, jog, jolt, mnemonic, reminder *Antonyms:* hindrance, impediment, mental block, repression, suppression **2.** dare, goad, incitement, inducement, motive, prod, provocation, spur, stimulus, taunt – *v.* **1.** animate, arouse, cause, coax, egg on *(Nonformal)*, induce, inveigle, exhort, foment, hearten, incite, instigate, kindle, rally, persuade, stimulate, urge, vivify **2.** aid, assist, cue, feed lines, help, hint, jog, refresh, remind, suggest **3.** awaken, bring about, elicit, evoke, give rise to, inspire, occasion

promptly *adv.* at once, directly, expeditiously, fast, hastily, immediately, instantly, posthaste, pronto, punctually, quickly, rapidly, right away, sharp, sharply, speedily, straightaway, swiftly, unhesitatingly *Nonformal:* flat-out, lickety-split *Antonyms:* belatedly, dilatorily, languidly, leisurely

promulgate *v.* advertise, announce, broadcast, circulate, clarion, communicate, declare, disseminate, make public, notify, pass the word, proclaim, promote, publish, sound, speak out, spread, trumpet *Antonyms:* conceal, neglect, stifle, suppress

prone *adj.* **1.** face down, flat, horizontal, lying down, procumbent, prostrate, reclining, recumbent, supine *Antonyms:* upright, vertical **2.** apt, disposed, given, inclined, leaning, liable, likely, predisposed, subject, susceptible, tending, willing *Antonyms:*

averse, disinclined, unlikely **3.** leaning, oblique, slanting, sloping, tilted

pronounce *v.* **1.** affirm, announce, assert, broadcast, call, declare, decree, deliver, make known, proclaim, profess, trumpet *Antonyms:* muffle, silence, stifle **2.** articulate, enunciate, say, sound, speak, stress, utter, verbalize, vocalize, voice *Antonyms:* clam up, mispronounce, mumble, mutter

pronounced *adj.* bold, broad, clear, clear-cut, conspicuous, decided, definite, distinct, evident, manifest, marked, notable, noticeable, obvious, outstanding, striking, strong, unmistakable *Antonyms:* concealed, hidden, inconspicuous, unnoticeable, vague

pronouncement *n.* **1.** assertion, declaration, decree, edict, fiat, judgment, manifesto, notification, ordinance, proclamation, publication, report, statement **2.** comment, finding, observation, opinion, reflection, ruling, take *(Nonformal)*, verdict, view

pronounciation *n.* accent, accentuation, articulation, diction, enunciation, expression, inflection, orthoepy, speech,

proof *adj.* firm, impenetrable, impervious, invulnerable, locked, resistant, safe, sealed, secure, steadfast, strong, sturdy, tight – *n.* **1.** affidavit, authentication, certainty, certification, confirmation, documentation, evidence, facts, grounds, information, substantiation, support, testimony, validation, verification *Nonformal:* backup, paper trail, smoking gun, the goods **2.** exam, examination, test, trial, tryout **3.** impenetrability, invincibility, invulnerability, soundness, strength, sturdiness, toughness **4.** illustration, impression, imprint, output, print-out *Printer's proofs:* bluelines, blues *(Nonformal)*, brownlines, galley, page, vandykes – *v.* audit, check, copy-edit, correct, double-check, edit, examine, fine-tune *(Nonformal)*, inspect, monitor, review, revise, scan, scrutinize, study, verify *Antonyms:* gloss over, overlook, pass by

prop *n.* **1.** brace, buttress, column, mainstay, post, shore, stanchion, stay, strut, support, truss, underpinning **2.** backer, benefactor, financier, patron, subsidizer, supporter **3.** implement, item, object, property, set dressing, tool, utensil – *v.* **1.** bear *or* hold up, bolster, brace, buoy, buttress, carry, maintain, stay, strengthen, truss, uphold **2.** back, foster, nourish, nurse, nurture, support, sustain **3.** lean, place, rest, stand

propaganda *n.* **1.** agitprop, disinformation, doctrine, evangelism, ideology, inculcation, indoctrination, proselytism *Nonformal:* hype, newspeak **2.** advertising, bumpf *(Nonformal)*, infomercial, promotion, promulgation, publication, publicity

propagate *v.* **1.** bear, beget, breed, engender, father, generate, hatch, impregnate, inseminate, mother, originate, parent, procreate, produce, raise, reproduce, sire **2.** grow, increase, multiply, proliferate, spread **3.** broadcast, circulate, diffuse, disperse, disseminate, distribute, proclaim, promulgate, publicize, radiate, scatter, spread, strew, transmit *Antonyms:* cover up, hide, stifle, suppress

propel *v.* actuate, drive, force, impel, move, press, push, release, send, set going, shove, thrust *Antonyms:* check, halt, hamper, impede, retard **2.** catapult, chuck *(Nonformal)*, discharge, eject, fire, hurl, launch, shoot

propensity *n.* **1.** ability, aptitude, bent *(Nonformal)*, capability, competence, disposition, mindset, predilection, talent, temper **2.** affinity, appetence, appetite, attraction, bias, desire, favour, hankering, inclination, leaning, liking, partiality, passion, penchant, preference, relish, susceptibility, weakness, yen *(Nonformal)*, zeal *Antonyms:* aversion, objection, resistance

proper *adj.* **1.** applicable, appropriate, apropos, apt, becoming, befitting, *comme il faut (French)*, felicitous, fitting, just, meet, right, right as rain *(Nonformal)*, suitable *Antonyms:* inappropriate, out of place, wrong **2.** courteous, decent, decorous, dignified, formal, genteel, polite, mannerly, refined, seemly, tasteful, well-bred *Antonyms:* coarse, vile, vulgar **3.** characteristic, distinctive, idiosyncratic, individual, own, particular, peculiar, personal, private, respective *Antonyms:* common, general, generic, universal **4.** accurate, correct, customary, exact, literal, precise, specific, usual

property *n.* **1.** acreage, assets, belongings, bits and pieces *(Nonformal)*, building, capital, chattels, claim, dominion, effects, equity, estate, farm, freehold, goods, holding, home, house, inheritance, land, means, ownership, plot, possession, premises, proprietorship, real estate, realty, resources, riches, substance, title, tract, wealth, wherewithal, worth **2.** attribute, characteristic, feature, hallmark, idiosyncrasy, mark, peculiarity, quality, quirk, trait, virtue

prophecy *n.* **1.** forecast, oracle, omen, portent, prediction, presage, prognostication, revelation **2.** augury, divination, clairvoyance, E.S.P., extrasensory perception, prescience, second sight, vision *Commonly misused:* **prophesy**

prophesy *v.* augur, bode, divine, forecast, foresee, foretell, forewarn, make book *(Nonformal)*, portend, predict, presage, prognosticate, soothsay, vaticinate, warn *Commonly misused:* **prophecy**

prophet *n.* **1.** astrologer, augur, Cassandra, clairvoyant, diviner, druid, forecaster, fortuneteller, medium, oracle, palmist, predictor, prophesier, prophetess, reader, seer, sibyl, soothsayer, sorcerer, vaticinator, visionary **2.** magus, religious leader *Old Testament prophets:* Abraham, Amos, Daniel, Ezekiel, Habakkuk, Haggai, Hosea, Isaac, Isaiah, Jacob, Jeremiah, Joel, Jonah, Joseph, Joshua, Malachi, Micah, Moses, Nahum, Obadiah, Samuel, Zechariah, Zephaniah

prophetic *adj.* auspicious, bodeful, Delphic, divinatory, fatidic, mantic, mediumistic, occult, oracular, predictive, presaging, psychic, sibyllic, sibylline, vatic, vaticinal, visionary

prophylactic *adj.* hygienic, neutralizing, precautionary, preventive, protective, sanitary, shielding *Antonyms:* unguarded, unprotected, vulnerable – *n.* **1.** antidote, barrier, guard, preventive, remedy, safeguard, serum, shield *Antonyms:* contaminant, miasma, pollutant, toxin, virus **2.** birth control, condom, contraceptive, sheath *Nonformal:* protection, rubber

propinquity *n.* **1.** adjacency, approximation, closeness, nearness, neighbourhood, proximity, vicinity *Antonyms:* distance, farness, remoteness **2.** blood relative, family ties, kin, relation *Antonyms:* inconnu *(Nonformal)*, outsider, stranger **3.** affinity, compatibility, empathy, fellowship, good vibe *(Nonformal)*, likemindedness, rapport, sympathy, unity *Antonyms:* conflict, discord, disharmony, dissidence, incongruity

propitious *adj.* **1.** advantageous, auspicious, beneficial, encouraging, favourable, fortunate, good, lucky, opportune, promising, seasonable, timely, useful, well-timed *Antonyms:* baneful, detrimental, inopportune, noxious, threatening **2.** agreeable, benevolent, friendly, gracious, kind, nice, well-disposed *Antonyms:* cruel, harsh, malicious, pernicious, rancorous

proponent *n.* advocate, backer, champion, defender, enthusiast, expounder, friend, partisan, patron, protector, spokesperson, subscriber, supporter, upholder *Antonyms:* antagonist, critic, dissident, opponent

proportion *n.* **1.** comparison, correlation, correspondence, ratio, relationship **2.** allotment, allowance, bit, chunk, cut *(Nonformal)*, dole, fraction, helping, part, percentage, portion, quota, ration, segment, share, slice **3.** agreement, arrangement, balance, concord, harmony, symmetry *Antonyms:* incongruity, inequality, unevenness **4.** breadth, dimension, expanse, extent, magnitude, measurement, scope, size, volume – *v.* adjust, arrange, balance, conform, coordinate, equalize, fit, harmonize, modify, order, regulate, set, shape, square, synchronize, tailor

proportionate *adj.* balanced, commensurate, comparable, corresponding, equal, equitable, even, just, proportional, relative, symmetrical, uniform *Antonyms:* different, discordant, inconsistent, unequal – *v.* balance, equalize, handicap *(Sports)*, harmonize, level, match, square

proposal *n.* **1.** design, game plan *(Nonformal)*, idea, outline, plan, program, recommendation, scenario, scheme, submission, suggestion **2.** bid, counter-offer, invitation, motion, offer, pitch, proposition, suit, tender, terms

propose *v.* **1.** advance, ask, court, offer, proffer, put forth, recommend, request, solicit, suggest, tender, urge, woo **2.** choose, commend, designate, introduce, name, nominate, present, submit **3.** aim, design, intend, plan, purport, scheme

proposition *n.* **1.** motion, proposal, recommendation, suggestion, suit **2.** design, hypothesis, idea, outline, plan, program, scheme **3.** assertion, axiom, belief, hypothesis, premise, statement, supposition, theory, view **4.** advance, invitation, overture *Nonformal:* come-on, move, pass – *v.* accost, approach, ask, pose, propose, solicit *Nonformal:* come on to, hit up, make a move on

proprietary *adj.* certified, copyrighted, exclusive, held, house brand *or* imprint, owned, patented, private, protected, registered, trademarked

proprietor *n.* freeholder, holder of record, innkeeper, laird, landlady, landlord, landowner, owner, person on title, possessor, proprietress, titleholder *Antonyms:* lodger, renter, sharecropper, squatter, tenant

propriety *n.* accordance, appropriateness, aptness, correctness, decorum, delicacy, dignity, etiquette, fitness, grace, manners, morality, order, pleasantness, protocol, rectitude, respectability, rightness, seemliness, suitability *Antonyms:* indelicacy, rudeness, vulgarity

prosaic *adj.* **1.** austere, candid, colourless, direct, dry, flat, inornate, nonpoetic, plain, prosy, simple, unadorned, unadulterated *Antonyms:* affected, poetic, purple **2.** banal, boring, common, commonplace, dead *(Nonformal)*, drab, dull, everyday, hackneyed, insipid, lacklustre, lifeless, monotonous, mundane, ordinary, routine, stale, tedious, trite, unexceptional, unimaginative, vapid *Antonyms:* entertaining, exciting, interesting

proscribe *v.* **1.** ban, boycott, censure, condemn, denounce, disallow, embargo, forbid, interdict, outlaw, prohibit, reject, restrict, taboo **2.** banish, exclude, excommunicate, exile, expel, ostracize *Commonly misused:* **prescribe**

prose *n.* discourse, style, text, writing *Kinds of prose:* descriptive, essay, expository, expressive, fiction, lyrical, narrative, nonfiction, poetic, prose poem, purple , stream of consciousness *Antonyms:* poetry, verse

prosecute *v.* **1.** arraign, bring action *or* suit, charge, contest, indict, law *(P.E.I.)*, litigate, seek redress, sue, summon, try **2.** carry on *or* through, complete, execute, finish, persevere, pursue **3.** conduct, do *(Nonformal)*, engage in, manage, perform, practice, work at *Commonly misused:* **persecute**

prospect *n.* **1.** chance, expectation, hope, likelihood, odds, possibility, potential, probability **2.** landscape, panorama, scape *(Nonformal)*, scene, spectacle, view, vision, vista **3.** angle, direction, exposure, outlook, position, viewpoint **4.** buyer, client, customer, lead, mark *(Nonformal)*, patron, shopper – *v.* delve, dig, explore, go after *or* into, hunt for *or* out, inquire, investigate, look, look for, mine, probe, search, seek, sift, survey

prospective *adj.* anticipated, approaching, awaited, coming, destined, eventual, expected, forthcoming, future, hoped-for, imminent, impending, intended, likely, looked-for, planned, possible, potential, promised, proposed, soon-to-be

prospectus *n.* blurb *(Nonformal)*, brief, draft, outline, plan, program, project, proposal, sketch, summary, syllabus, synopsis

prosper *v.* benefit, blossom, burgeon, fare well, flourish, flower, gain, get on, grow rich, multiply, mushroom, profit, progress, rise, succeed, thrive *Nonformal:* get fat, go places, make good, make it, score

prosperity *n.* accomplishment, affluence, boom, boomlet *(Nonformal)*, ease, expansion, fortune, good fortune *or* times, growth, increase, luxury, opulence, plenty, riches, success, victory, wealth, well-being *Antonyms:* bust, depression, privation, ruin

prosperous *adj.* **1.** booming, burgeoning, flourishing, lush, multiplying, plentiful, prolific, thriving *Antonyms:* dissipating, failing, wilting **2.** moneyed, opulent, rich, successful, wealthy, well-to-do *Nonformal:* fat, flush, in clover, on easy street, parking in tall cotton *Antonyms:* down-and-out, impoverished, poor **3.** advantageous, auspicious, favourable, fortunate, good, helpful, promising, propitious, rosy, timely *Antonyms:* bleak, ominous, unpromising

prostitute *n.* concubine, courtesan, escort, geisha, gigolo, harlot, hustler, slattern, street-walker, strumpet, tramp, trollop, whore *Nonformal:* call girl, hooker, hotsy-potatsy, moll, professional, tart, working girl – *v.* abuse, besmirch, cheapen, corrupt, debase, debauch, demean, devalue, pervert, profane, sell out *(Nonformal)*

prostrate *adj.* **1.** face down, flat, horizontal, procumbent, prone, reclining, recumbent, supine *Antonyms:* perpendicular, standing, straight, upright, vertical **2.** dejected, drained, exhausted, immobilized, incapacitated, overcome, paralyzed, tired, wearied, worn out *Nonformal:* all in, beat, fagged, pooped, spent, tuckered, wiped *Antonyms:* dynamic, energetic, perky, vibrant, vigorous **3.** depressed, desolate, despairing, down-in-the-dumps *(Nonformal)*, forlorn, heartbroken, heartsick, melancholy, neurasthenic, weary, world-weary **4.** beaten, defenceless, disarmed, helpless, impotent, overpowered, overwhelmed, powerless, reduced, weak *Antonyms:* capable, cogent, empowered, virile – *v.* **1.** bow down, crawl, grovel, kowtow, snivel, stoop *Nonformal:* bellycrawl, bow and scrape **2.** bring down, bowl over *(Nonformal)*, capture, crush, disarm, fell, flatten, floor, humble, overcome, overpower, overthrow, overwhelm

protagonist *n.* **1.** central *or* lead character, hero, heroine, lead, principal, title role **2.** advocate, champion, combatant, exemplar, idol, mainstay, paladin, standard-bearer, supporter, warrior *Antonyms:* antagonist, villain

protean *adj.* **1.** alterable, chameleon, changeable, ever-changing, metamorphic, mutable, shape-shifting, transformative, variable, variform **2.** deft, flexible, manifold, multiform, resourceful, skilful, skilled, versatile, well-rounded

protect *v.* **1.** cover, defend, guard, harbour, haven, hide, screen, shelter, shield, watch out for *or* over **2.** conserve, look after, maintain, mind, preserve, safeguard, save, shepherd, tend, watch

protection *adj.* blackmail, bribe, extortion – *n.* **1.** care, conservation, preservation, safekeeping, safety, security, vigil **2.** amulet, armour, barrier, buffer, bulwark, cloak, cover, guard, insurance, screen, shelter, shield, talisman **3.** aegis, custody, guardianship, husbandry, ministry, patronage, support, tutelage, wardship **4.** bodyguard, security *Nonformal:* backup, bouncer, heat, muscle

protective *adj.* **1.** defensive, guarding, insulating, safeguarding, securing, sheltering, shielding *Antonyms:* dangerous, hazardous, risky **2.** careful, custodial, maternal, paternal, vigilant, watchful

protégé *n.* acolyte, assistant, charge, dependent, pupil, student, ward *Antonyms:* guide, mentor, teacher

protest *n.* **1.** challenge, complaint, disagreement, disapproval, dissent, grievance, objection, outcry, protestation, resistance *Nonformal:* beef, problem *Antonyms:* acceptance, assent, compliance, endorsement, sanction **2.** demonstration, march, picketing, rally, remonstration, revolt, riot, sit-in, strike *See also:* **strike** – *v.* **1.** affirm, assert, asseverate, attest, avouch, avow, contend, demur **2.** argue against, beard, blast, buck *(Nonformal)*, challenge, combat, complain, denounce, disagree, disapprove, expostulate, fight, fight back, holler, howl, kick, object, oppose, resist, scream, take exception, yell *Antonyms:* approve, concede, endorse, grant, yield **3.** demonstrate, picket, rally, revolt, riot, strike

protocol *n.* **1.** code, conduct, convention, courtesy, custom, decorum, etiquette, formality, good form, manners, obligation, propriety, rules **2.** contract, covenant, deal, document, pact, treaty

prototype *n.* **1.** archetype, benchmark, epitome, exemplar, ideal, model, norm, original, paradigm, standard, touchstone, yardstick **2.** example, instance, pattern, pilot, representative, sample, template

protract *v.* continue, delay, drag *or* draw out, elongate, extend, filibuster, lengthen, prolong, spin out *(Nonformal)*, stall, stretch, sustain *Antonyms:* abridge, capsulize, condense, summarize

protrude *v.* balloon, billow, bulge, distend, extend, jut, overhang, project, shoot *or* stand *or* stick out, swell *Antonyms:* depress, indent

protuberance *n.* bulge, bump, growth, jut, knob, lump, outgrowth, pimple, polyp, projection, prominence, protrusion, swelling

proud *adj.* **1.** contented, elated, gratified, happy, honoured, pleased, satisfied, tickled pink *(Nonformal) Antonyms:* angered, displeased, vexed **2.** arrogant, conceited, condescending, derisive, disdainful, egocentric, haughty, inflated, insolent, narcissistic, overbearing, presuming, scornful, self-important, smug, snobbish, swollen, swell-headed, vain, vainglorious *Nonformal:* bigheaded, hoity-toity, puffed-up, snooty, toplofty *Antonyms:* empathetic, fair, humble, modest, self-effacing, sympathetic, tolerant **3.** bold, dauntless, dignified, distinguished, eminent, fearless, honoured, illustrious, lofty, noteworthy, respected, revered, time-honoured, venerated, worthy, **4.** august, fancy, glorious, grand, impressive, magnificent, majestic, regal, royal, splendid, stately *Nonformal:* posh, swank

prove *v.* **1.** affirm, authenticate, back, certify, check out *(Nonformal)*, confirm, corroborate, document, double check, evidence, justify, substantiate, validate, verify **2.** analyze, check into, demonstrate, examine, show, test, try, undergo **3.** end up, happen, manifest, pan *or* turn out, result

provenance *n.* base, beginning, birthplace, derivation, fountainhead, genesis, history, inception, origin, root, source, wellspring

proverb *n.* adage, aphorism, apothegm, axiom, catchphrase, cliché, dictum, epigram, epithet, folk wisdom, maxim, moral, platitude, saw, saying, sutra, truism, witticism

proverbial *adj.* **1.** accepted, acknowledged, archetypal, cliché, common, conventional, customary, famed, notorious, time-tested, traditional, unquestioned, well-known *Antonyms:* novel, original, unknown **2.** aphoristic, apothegmatic, axiomatic, bromidic, hackneyed, oft-repeated, platitudinous, trite

provide *v.* **1.** accommodate, accoutre, cater, equip, fit, furnish, outfit, plenish, supply **2.** accord, afford, bestow, confer, contribute, donate, endow, give, grant, impart, lend, mete out, present, produce, proffer, yield *Nonformal:* fork out, hand over **3.** arrange, get set, prepare, procure, ready, stock up **4.** demand, qualify, set terms, specify, state, stipulate

Providence *n.* destiny, divine intervention, fate, fortune, God's will, Karma, kismet, predetermination, serendipity, Wheel of Fortune

providence *n.* care, caution, conservation, discretion, economy, farsightedness, foresight, frugality, husbandry, judgment, preparation, presence of mind, prudence, thriftiness, saving *Antonyms:* heedlessness, impulsiveness, recklessness

provident *adj.* canny, careful, cautious, chary, discreet, economical, expedient, frugal, judicious, penny-pinching, prudent, sagacious, saving, shrewd, thrifty, vigilant, wise *Antonyms:* heedless, imprudent, negligent, spendthrift, wasteful

province *n.* **1.** borough, country, demesne, district, division, neighbourhood, parish, precinct, quarter, region, state, territory, ward, zone *Canadian provinces and territories:* Alberta, British Columbia, Manitoba, New Brunswick, Newfoundland, Northwest Territories, Nova Scotia, Nunavut, Ontario, Prince Edward Island, Quebec, Saskatchewan, Yukon *Names for residents of Canadian provinces and territories:* Albertan, British Columbian, Inuit, Labradorian,

Manitoban, New Brunswicker, Newfoundlander, Northerner, Nova Scotian, Nunavummiut, Ontarian, Prince Edward Islander, Quebecker, Québécois, Saskatchewaner, Yukoner *Nonformal names for residents of Canadian provinces and territories:* Bluenose *(Nova Scotian)*, herring choker *(New Brunswicker)*, Habitant *(Québécois)*, Spud Islander *(P.E.I.)* *Newfoundland:* livyer, Newfie, Newfoundlander *Nonformal names for Canadian provinces:* Breadbasket *(Saskatchewan)*, Canada's Ocean Playground *(Nova Scotia)*, Keystone Province *(Manitoba)*, La Belle Province *(Quebec)*, Picture Province *(New Brunswick)*, the Rock *(Newfoundland)*, Upper Canada *(Ontario)*, Wild Rose Country *(Alberta)* *British Columbia:* Left Coast, Lotusland *Prince Edward Island:* Abegweit, Million Acre Farm, Minago, the Island **2.** arena, *arrondissement (French)*, bailiwick, beat *(Nonformal)*, billet, charge, concern, department, jurisdiction, orbit, place, sphere, station **3.** business, calling, discipline, employment, field, forte, job, metier, office, profession, role, speciality, trade

provincial *adj.* **1.** Arcadian, bucolic, country, homespun, jerkwater *(Nonformal)*, pastoral, rural, rustic **2.** backwater, banausic, close-minded, illiberal, inward-looking, limited, narrow, parochial, simple, small-minded, uncultured, unsophisticated *Nonformal:* hick, rube **3.** local, regional, sectional, territorial

provision *n.* **1.** arrangements, calculation, deliberation, plans, prearrangement, preparation, steps **2.** accumulation, cache, collection, horde, rationing, reserve, serving, stock, stockpile, supply **3.** agreement, clause, condition, demand, exception, fine print, limitation, prerequisite, proviso, qualification, requirement, reservation, restriction, rider, specification, stipulation, string *(Nonformal)*, term

provisional *adj.* **1.** bridge, interim, makeshift, *pro tempore (Latin)*, stopgap, temporary, tideover, transitional **2.** conditional, contingent, limited, restricted, stipulated

provisions *n.* edibles, foodstuffs, groceries, muckamuck *(Native peoples)*, provender, rations, sea stocks, staples, stores, supplies, tucker *(Australian)*, viands, victuals *Nonformal:* eats, grub

provocative *adj.* **1.** alluring, arousing, heady *(Nonformal)*, intoxicating, inviting, ravishing, seductive, sensual, sexy, suggestive, tantalizing, tempting **2.** affronting, aggravating, angering, bothersome, confrontational, enraging, galling, in your face *(Nonformal)*, infuriating, irksome, irritating, maddening, vexatious *Antonyms:* calming, placating, soothing

provoke *v.* **1.** affront, agitate, aggravate, anger, annoy, bother, chafe, enrage, exasperate, fret, gall, incense, inflame, infuriate, irk, irritate, madden, nettle, rile, ruffle, torment, upset *Nonformal:* bug, get, pique *Antonyms:* mollify, pacify, quiet **2.** animate, arouse, compel, electrify, enflame, foment, galvanize, goad, impassion, incite, inspire, instigate, invigorate, make waves *(Nonformal)*, motivate, rouse, seduce, shake *or* stir up, stimulate, tempt, vivify, waken **3.** bring about, cause, draw forth, elicit, induce, occasion, produce, start

prowess *n.* **1.** ability, accomplishment, adeptness, adroitness, aptitude, command, deftness, dexterity, excellence, expertise, facility, genius, know-how *(Nonformal)*, mastery, skill, talent, virtuosity *Antonyms:* clumsiness, inability, incapability, incompetence, ineptitude **2.** backbone, bodaciousness *(Nonformal)*, bravery, bravura, chivalry, courage, daring, fortitude, gallantry, heroism, intrepidity, nerve, pluck, strength, valiance, valour *Nonformal:* grit, moxie *Antonyms:* cowardice, fear, timidity

prowl *adj.* panda *(Nonformal)*, patrol, squad – *n.* hunt, lookout, search, stalk, track – *v* creep, cruise, lie in wait, pace, patrol, range roam, rove, skulk, slink, sneak, wander *Nonformal:* gumshoe, nose around, pussyfoot tiptoe

proximity *n.* adjacency, closeness, concurrence, contiguity, contiguousness, immediacy, juxtaposition, nearness, propinquity vicinity

proxy *n.* **1.** agent, alternate, deputy, double fill-in, delegate, *locum tenens (Latin)*, representative, ringer, stand-in, surrogate, substitute, understudy **2.** authorization, clearance go-ahead *(Nonformal)*, jurisdiction, licence, permission, permit, right, sanction, warrant

prude *n.* bluenose, prig, priss, puritan, Victorian *Nonformal:* goody-goody, goody two-shoes, mouldy fig, Mrs. Grundy, nice-nelly, square

prudent *adj.* **1.** careful, cautious, chary, circumspect, heedful, meticulous, vigilant **2.** discerning, discriminating, farsighted, judicious, level-headed, reasonable, reflective, sagacious, sapient, sound, thoughtful, wise **3.** canny, frugal, practical, pragmatic, sensible, shrewd, thrifty **4.** decorous, diplomatic, discreet, guarded, politic, tactful

prudish *adj.* demure, fastidious, finicky, over-nice, priggish, prim, prissy, proper, puritanical, rigid, starchy, stern, stiff, stilted, straitlaced, strict, stuffy *Nonformal:* square, uptight *Antonyms:* broad-minded, liberal, loose, permissive

prune *v.* **1.** chop, clip, cut, lop off, pare, shape, shave, shear, thin out, trim **2.** abbreviate, bowdlerize, condense, curtail, edit, gut *(Nonformal)*, reduce, truncate

prurient *adj.* **1.** carnal, concupiscent, debauched, dissolute, erotic, fleshly, lascivious, lewd, libidinous, licentious, salacious, sexual, wanton **2.** bawdy, blue *(Nonformal)*, coarse, crude, dirty, indecent, lurid, obscene, offensive, pornographic, profligate, ribald, smutty

pry *v.* **1.** examine, explore, inquire, inspect, interfere, interlope, interrogate, intrude, investigate, meddle, probe, question, root, scan, scrutinize, search, spy *Nonformal:* ferret out, horn in, nose *or* poke around, snoop **2.** crank, crowbar, detach, jack, jimmy, lever, lift, prize, pull apart *or* open, raise, wedge **3.** exert, extract, force, wrench, wrest, wring

psalm *n.* canticle, celebration, chant, chorale, doxology, eulogy, hallelujah, hymn, lyric, paean, praise, prayer, song, verse

pseudo *adj.* artificial, assumed, bogus, counterfeit, ersatz, fake, false, imitation, make-believe, not kosher, phoney *(Nonformal)*, pirate, pretended, sham, spurious *Antonyms:* actual, authentic, genuine

pseudonym *n.* a.k.a. *(Nonformal)*, alias, anonym, assumed name, pen *or* professional *or* stage name, sobriquet *French:* nom de guerre, nom de plume

psyche *n.* **1.** animus, essential nature, intellect, intelligence, life force, mind, psychic apparatus, soul, spirit, subconscious, true being, unconscious **2.** character, ego, identity, individuality, personality, self

psychedelic *adj.* **1.** consciousness-expanding, hallucinogenic, mind-altering, mind-expanding, psychochemical, psychopharmaceutical, psychotomimetic **2.** abstract, bizarre, hallucinatory, illusory, strange, weird *Nonformal:* far-out, groovy, trippy

psychiatrist *n.* alienist, analyst, clinician, doctor, psychoanalyst, psychotherapist, therapist *Nonformal:* couch doctor, head-shrinker, shrink

psychic *adj.* **1.** clairvoyant, extrasensory, fey, mystic, occult, otherworldly, preternatural, spectral, supernatural, surrealistic, telekinetic, telepathic, vatic **2.** cerebral, cognitive, intellectual, mental, metaphysical, noetic, spiritual *Antonyms:* bodily, material, physical – *n.* clairvoyant, diviner, medium, mystic, necromancer, occultist, oracle, prophet, seer, sibyl, sorcerer, spiritualist, thaumaturgist

psychological *adj.* **1.** cerebral, internal, mental, psychiatrical, subconscious, subjective, subliminal *Kinds of psychological test:* alpha, apperception, aptitude, association, Binet, Binet-Simon, inkblot, intelligence quotient, IQ, Lüscher colour, Minnesota multiphasic personality inventory *or* MMPI, Rorschach, thematic apperception, word association **2.** all in the mind *(Nonformal)*, illusory, imaginary, phantom, psychosomatic, unreal

psychologist *n.* alienist, analyst, counsellor, psychoanalyst, psychotherapist, shrink *(Nonformal)*, therapist

psychology *n.* **1.** science of human behaviour, study of the mind *Kinds of psychology:* abnormal, analytic, animal, applied, association, child, clinical, cognitive, criminal, developmental, dynamic, educational, existential, experimental, group, individual, industrial, neuropharmacology, neuropsychology, parapsychology, popular, psychobiology, psychodynamics, psychohistory, psycholinguistics, psychopathology, psychopharmacology, psychosociology, psychosomatics, psychotherapeutics, psychotherapy, social **2.** attitude, behaviour, mentality, psyche, reasoning, thinking

psychopath *n.* deranged *or* insane person, lunatic, madman, madwoman, maniac, psychotic, sociopath *Nonformal:* head *or* mental case, perv, psycho, schizoid, sicko, weirdo

psychotic *adj.* demented, deranged, disturbed, insane, lunatic, mad, psychopathic, sick, unbalanced *Nonformal:* crazy, mad, mental, nuts, psycho – *n.* bedlamite, paranoiac, schizophrenic *See also:* **psychopath**

puberty *n.* adolescence, early teens, juvenescence, pubescence, young adulthood, youth *Antonyms:* childhood, infancy

public *adj.* **1.** civic, collective, common, communal, general, popular, social **2.** free, open-door, shared, societal, unrestricted, without charge **3.** blatant, conspicuous, egregious, manifest, notorious, open, out *(Nonformal)*, overt, patent, plain, **4.** famous, eminent, prominent, recognized, visible, well-known **5.** council *(British)*, funded, government, subsidized – *n.* **1.** citizenry, community, electorate, great unwashed *(Nonformal)*, hoi polloi, masses, multitude, nation, people, populace, society **2.** audience, buyers, clientele, fans, following, patrons, regulars, subscribers, supporters, ticket holders

publication *n.* **1.** edition, impression, imprint, issue *Kinds of publication:* annual, bibliography, bimonthly, biweekly, book, booklet, broadside, brochure, bulletin, catalogue, CD-ROM, chapbook, circular, comic book, composition, daily, digest, digital, electronic, gazette, handbill, journal, leaflet, magazine, manual, monthly, multimedia, news, newsletter, newspaper, pamphlet, paper, periodical, photograph, press, print, quarterly, record, review, samizdat, stamp, tabloid, tidings, trade, Web page *or* posting *or* site, webcast, weekly *Nonformal:* e-zine, fanzine, mag, organ, pulp, rag, scandal sheet, zine **2.** advertisement, announcement, appearance, broadcast, communication, declaration, disclosure, discovery, dissemination, information, issuance, notification, printing, proclamation, promulgation, publicity, publishing, release, reporting, revelation, statement

publicity *n.* **1.** advertising, airing, announcement, broadcasting, information, news, promulgation, report **2.** fame, 15 minutes *(Nonformal)*, limelight, notoriety, spotlight **3.** attention, billing, fanfare, interest, press, promotion, write-up *Nonformal:* hoopla, hype, ink, noise, photos

publicize *v.* advertise, air, announce, broadcast, extol, headline, hype, immortalize, promote, promulgate, push, spotlight, spread, tout, trumpet *Nonformal:* ballyhoo, beat the drum, plug, puff, put on the map *Antonyms:* conceal, contain, smother, suppress

public-spirited *adj.* altruistic, beneficent, benevolent, big-hearted, charitable, generous, humanitarian, liberal, munificent, philanthropic, princely *Antonyms:* greedy, miserly, misanthropic, self-serving, selfish

publisher *n.* imprint, press, publishing house *Kinds of publisher:* book, branch plant, children's, comic book, commercial, corporate, educational, government, independent, literary, magazine, micropress, music, newspaper, not-for-profit, poetry, scholarly, small, technical, trade, vanity press

pucker *n.* crease, crinkle, crumple, fold, furrow, plait, wrinkle – *v.* compress, condense, contract, crease, crinkle, crumple, fold, furrow, gather, knit, pleat, purse, ruck, ruffle, squeeze, tighten, wrinkle *Antonyms:* iron, level, plane, smooth, straighten

puckish *adj.* cheeky, elfin, fey, frolicsome, impish, high-spirited, impudent, mischievous, naughty, playful, prankish, roguish, saucy, scampish, teasing, waggish, whimsical *Antonyms:* reserved, solemn, somber, staid

pudding *n.* cloutie, custard, dessert, duff, flan, mousse, sausage *Kinds of pudding:* black, blancmange, blood, bread, butterscotch, chocolate, *chomeur (Quebec)*, Christmas, cooked, figgy duff, instant, milk, rice, steamed, tapioca, vanilla, Yorkshire

pudgy *adj.* big, chubby, chunky, dumpy, fat, hefty, plump, roly-poly, rotund, round, stocky, stout, stumpy, thick-bodied, tubby, zaftig *(Nonformal) Antonyms:* lanky, slender, svelte, wiry

puerile *adj.* **1.** adolescent, babyish, boyish, callow, childish, fledgling, girlish, green, immature, inexperienced, infantile, undeveloped, unfledged, unsophisticated, young *Antonyms:* adult, grown-up, mature **2.** asinine, foolish, frivolous, ridiculous, silly, sophomoric, trivial, unimportant, weak

puffy *adj.* **1.** bloated, bulbous, bulging, dilated, distended, enlarged, expanded, full, inflated, swollen, tumid **2.** big-headed, boastful, bombastic, bragging, conceited, fustian, narcissistic, orotund, pompous, pretentious, purple, rodomontade, self-important, vain **3.** blowing, blustery, breezy, gusty, windy **4.** asthmatic, breathless, gasping, panting, wheezy, winded

pugnacious *adj.* aggressive, antagonistic, argumentative, bellicose, belligerent, cantankerous, choleric, combative, contentious, contumacious, disputatious, hot-tempered, irascible, irritable, militant, pushy, quarrelsome, rebellious, truculent, warlike *Nonformal:* salty, scrappy *Antonyms:* calm, gentle, peaceable, placid, quiet

pull *n.* **1.** haul, heave, jerk, tweak, twinge, twitch, tow, tug, yank **2.** clout *(Nonformal)*, force, hold, importance, influence, leverage, muscle, power, significance, strength, sway, weight **3.** appeal, attraction, charisma, charm, lure, magnetism, seductiveness *Nonformal:* chemistry, draw **4.** effort, energy, exertion, might, strain **5.** breath, drag *(Nonformal)*, inhalation, puff **6.** crank, handle, hold, grip, knob, lever, shaft – *v.* **1.** draw, exact, extract, pluck, tug, tweak, uproot, vellicate, weed, wrench, yank **2.** drag, haul, heave, lug, tow, transport **3.** rend, rip, sprain, strain, stretch **4.** breathe, inhale, inspire, puff, suck in

pulp *n.* **1.** flesh, fruit, heart, inside, marrow, pith **2.** mash, mush, pap, paste, pomace, purée, slush **3.** magazine, novel, periodical, publication, sensationalism, tabloid, thriller – *v.* bruise, crush, mash, pulverize, squash, triturate

pulsate *v.* **1.** beat, drum, hammer, palpitate, pound, pulsation, pump, throb, thud, thump, tick **2.** fluctuate, flutter, quaver, quiver, shiver, shudder, twitch, vibrate

pulse *n.* beat, beating, cadence, oscillation, pulsation, rhythm, pitapation *(Nonformal)*, sphygmus, stroke, throb, throbbing, vibration – *v.* beat, palpitate, pound, pulsate, throb, thump, tick, vibrate

pulverize *v.* **1.** comminute, crumble, disintegrate, fragment, granulate, grind, mill, mince, pound, powder, shatter, triturate **2.** annihilate, crush, demolish, devastate, lick *(Nonformal)*, ravage, raze, ruin, smash, trounce, wreck

pump *n.* compressor, extractor, piston, plunger – *v.* **1.** drain, draw, empty, remove, siphon, suck, suction **2.** bilge, bloat, dilate, enlarge, expand, extend, increase, inflate, swell **3.** deliver, drive, force, pulsate, pulse, push, send **4.** cross-examination, drill, examine, inquire, interrogate, query, question, quiz, test *Nonformal:* give the third degree, grill

pun *n.* bon mot, double entendre, joke, play on words, quip, witticism

punch *n.* **1.** blow, hit, jab, roundhouse, smack, smash, swat, thwack, uppercut, wallop *Nonformal:* knuckle sandwich, manual compliment, one-two, sallywinder *(Prince Edward Island)* **2.** beverage, concoction, drink, juice, libation, mixture **3.** awl, drill, puncheon – *v.* **1.** bash, belt, biff, blow, bop, box, buffet, clip, cuff, hit, jab, knock, plug *(Nonformal)*, pummel, rap, shot, slam, slap, slug, smack, smash, sock, strike, thump, wallop, zap **2.** bore, cut, drill, jab, perforate, pierce, poke, prick, puncture, stab, stamp

punchline *n.* climax, conclusion, kicker, Parthian shot, point, zinger *(Nonformal)*

punchy *adj.* **1.** befuddled, confused, dazed, exhausted, far gone, groggy, punch-drunk, stupefied, unsteady, wobbly, woozy *Nonformal:* baffed, bagged, goofed, out of it *Antonyms:* alert, astute, clearheaded, perceptive **2.** aggressive, animated, dynamic, forceful, incisive, lively, powerful, spirited, vigorous *Antonyms:* docile, gentle, meek

punctilious *adj.* ceremonious, conscientious, correct, exact, fastidious, formal, meticulous, particular, precise, proper, rigid, rigorous, starchy, stiff, stiff-necked *(Nonformal)*, strict *Antonyms:* carefree, informal, laid-back, offhand

punctual *adj.* **1.** expeditious, immediate, instant, on time, precise, prompt, quick, ready, speedy, swift **2.** cyclic, dependable, habitual, quotidian, regular, steady

punctuate *v.* **1.** break, insert, interject, interpolate, interrupt, intersperse, interweave, pepper, sprinkle **2.** accent, emphasize, headline, mark, play *or* point up, spotlight, stress, underline

punctuation *n.* mark, point, sign *Kinds of punctuation marks:* angle brackets *(<>)*, apostrophe *(')*, colon *(:)*, comma *(,)*, curly brackets *({})*, dash *(–)*, ellipsis *(...)*, exclamation point *(!)*, hyphen *(-)*, matilda (~), parentheses *(())*, period *(.)*, question mark *(?)*, quotation marks *(“”)*, semicolon *(;)*, single quotation mark *(‘’)*, square brackets *([])*, underscore (_), virgule *or* solidus *or* slash mark *(/)*

puncture *n.* break, cut, hole, jab, leak, nick, opening, perforation, pit, prick, rupture, stab – *v.* **1.** bore, cut, deflate, drill, knife, lacerate, lance, nick, open, penetrate, perforate, pierce, poke, prick, punch, riddle, rip, rupture, shish kebob *(Nonformal)*, stab **2.** dash, deflate, discourage, discredit, disillusion, disprove, explode, flatten, humble, shoot

pundit *n.* authority, cognoscenti, connoisseur, expert, genius, guru, intellectual, philosopher, polymath, savant, scholar, sensei, *swami (Hindu)*, teacher, thinker, *ulema (Muslim) Nonformal:* brain, maven, whiz *Antonyms:* fledgling, novice, pupil

pungent *adj.* **1.** acid, astringent, peppery, piquant, potent, savoury, seasoned, sour, spicy, tangy, tart **2.** funky, harsh, high, odoriferous, rank, redolent, smelly, stinky, strong **3.** acerbic, biting, caustic, cutting, incisive, keen, mordant, sardonic, scathing, severe, stringent, trenchant **4.** penetrating, piercing, pointed, pronged, sharp **5.** acute, agonizing, brutal, crushing, distressful, dreadful, harrowing, intense, painful, racking, smarting

punish *v.* **1.** bench, blacklist, castigate, chastise, confine, correct, defrock, disbar, discipline, excommunicate, exile, expel, fine, imprison, incarcerate, mulct, penalize, reprove, scold, sentence, suspend **2.** abuse, batter, beat up *(Nonformal)*, cuff, flog, harm, hurt, injure, lace, lash, manhandle, paddle, spank, thrash, trounce, whip *Historical:* keelhaul, rack **3.** consume, deplete, drain, empty, exhaust, impoverish, reduce, spend, use up

punishment *n.* **1.** castigation, correction, discipline, fine, gauntlet, imprisonment, lettre de cachet, penalty, retribution, sentence *Nonformal:* comeuppance, just desserts **2.** abuse, beating, cat *(Historical)*, flagellation, flogging, hardship, hiding, infliction, lacing, lashing, lumps *(Nonformal)*, maltreatment, paddling, pain, self-mortification, spanking, suffering, thrashing, trial, unhappiness, whipping

punitive *adj.* castigating, correctional, disciplinary, penal, punishing, retaliative, revengeful, vindictive *Antonyms:* atoning, compensatory, indulgent, reparative, restitutive

punk *adj.* awful, bad, lousy, rotten, worthless – *n. enfant terrible (French)*, hoodlum, hooligan, rascal, ruffian, sleeveen *(Newfoundland)*, thug, upstart, vandal *Nonformal:* goon, scrub, skinhead

puny *adj.* **1.** diminutive, frail, half-pint *(Nonformal)*, little, peewee, pint-sized, scrawny, small, stunted, tiny, underdeveloped, undersized, wee *Antonyms:* huge, large, massive **2.** inconsequential, inferior, insignificant, measly, minor, niggling, nothing, nugatory, paltry, penny ante, petty, piddling, trifling, trivial, unsubstantial, weak *Antonyms:* important, material, superior

pupil *n.* **1.** *élève (French)*, scholar, schoolboy, schoolgirl, student, undergraduate **2.** apprentice, beginner, greenhorn *(Nonformal)*, initiate, learner, neophyte, novice, postulant, probationer, trainee **3.** adherent, devotee, disciple, fan, follower, proselyte, protégé

puppet *n.* **1.** doll, dummy, *fantòccio (Italian)*, marionette, toy **2.** dupe, hireling, instrument, lackey, pawn, tool *Nonformal:* henchman, mouthpiece, patsy, stooge, straw man

purchase *n.* **1.** acquisition, asset, bargain, buy, gain, investment, possession, procurement, property **2.** advantage, clout, edge, influence, leverage, vantage **3.** clutch, footing, grasp, grip, hold, traction – *v.* **1.** acquire, buy, cop *(Nonformal)*, gain, obtain, pay for, pick up, procure, redeem, secure *Antonyms:* retail, sell, vend **2.** achieve, attain, come by *(Nonformal)*, earn, realize, win

pure *adj.* **1.** blameless, celibate, chaste, clean, decent, exemplary, good, guileless, honest, immaculate, innocent, irreproachable, modest, righteous, sinless, spotless, stainless, unblemished, uncorrupted, undefiled, unspotted, unstained, unsullied, upright, virginal, virtuous *Antonyms:* corrupt, defiled, immodest, immoral, sinful **2.** bright, clear, flawless, natural, neat, pellucid, perfect, plain, simple, straight, unadulterated, unclouded, uncut, undiluted *Antonyms:* adulterated, contaminated, dirty, filthy, foul **3.** absolute, authentic, complete, genuine, out-and-out, purebred, *pure laine (Quebec)*, real, pukka, sheer, solid, thorough, thoroughbred, true, 24-carat, unalloyed, unmitigated, unqualified, utter **4.** abstract, conceptual, hypothetical, philosophical, speculative, tentative, theoretical, unproved *Antonyms:* applied, practical

purée *n.* mash, mixture, mush, Pablum *(Trademark)*, pap, paste, pulp, slush *Nonformal:* glop, goo, guck – *v.* blend, chop, grind, mix, mulch, process

purely *adv.* **1.** blamelessly, chastely, faultlessly, flawlessly, immaculately, righteously, virtuously **2.** absolutely, all, altogether, completely, entirely, *in toto (Latin)*, perfectly, totally, wholly **3.** barely, just, merely, only, simply

purge *n.* **1.** ablution, cleansing, cleanout, detoxication, disinfection, purification, sanitation, scrub, sterilization, washing **2.** elimination, evacuation, expulsion, voidance **3.** clearance, disposal, eradication, ethnic cleansing, extirpation, holocaust, liquidation, pogrom, removal, riddance **4.** bowdlerization, censor, clean-up, edit, expurgation **5.** catharsis, deliverance, emancipation, release, respite – *v.* **1.** clean, cleanse, detoxify, disinfect, purify, sanitize, sterilize **2.** eliminate, exterminate, extirpate, kill, massacre, remove from this earth, rid, slaughter, wipe out **3.** bowdlerize, censor, edit, expurgate, remove **4.** drain, excrete, expel, release, void, vomit

purgatory *adj.* cleansing, expiating, purgatorial, purifying – *n.* abyss, God's waiting room *(Nonformal)*, limbo, netherworld, perdition, punishment, Tartarus, torment, underworld *Antonyms:* heaven, paradise, utopia *See also:* **hell**

purification *n.* **1.** bathing, cleansing, disinfection, purifying, washing *Antonyms:* contamination, defilement, dirtiness **2.** distillation, filtration, refinement, sieving, sifting, straining **3.** absolution, beatification, consecration, lustration, redemption, sanctification

purify *v.* **1.** bathe, clarify, clean, deodorize, filter, freshen, lave, refine, sanitize, wash *Antonyms:* pollute, sully, taint **2.** absolve, baptize, beatify, forgive, hallow, redeem, sanctify, vindicate

purist *n.* bluenose, elitist, extremist, fanatic, formalist, highbrow, pedant, stickler, zealot *Nonformal:* diehard, hardnose

puritanical *adj.* austere, calvinistic, fastidious, firm, moralistic, pious, prudish, rigid, spartan, straitlaced, strict *Nonformal:* square, straight, stuffy, uptight *Antonyms:* carefree, immoderate, indulgent, lenient, unrestrained

purlieu *n.* **1.** arena, forum, hangout, haunt, local, milieu, place, setting, site, stomping ground *(Nonformal)* **2.** border, fringe, margin, outskirts, pale, perimeter, periphery, suburbs

purloin *v.* extort, filch, misappropriate, pilfer, rob, shoplift, steal, take, thieve *Nonformal:* lift, palm, pinch, pocket, shake down, snitch, swipe

purple *adj.* **1.** colour *Purple shades:* lavender, lilac, livid, mauve, mulberry, orchid, plum, royal, Tyrian **2.** affected, elevated, flowery, grandiose, hyperbolic, ornate, orotund, poetic, pompous, pretentious, rhetorical, showy, turgid *Antonyms:* matter-of-fact, pithy, prosaic **3.** aristocratic, imperial, lofty, majestic, noble, princely, regal, sovereign, sublime – *n.* aristocracy, dignity, eminence, importance, majesty, nobility, power, significance

purport *n.* **1.** core, drift, essence, gist, heart, idea, meaning, meat, message, pith, point, rub, significance **2.** aim, design, intention, object, plan, purpose – *v.* **1.** betoken, denote, imply, import, infer, mean, signify, suggest **2.** allege, announce, assert, claim, declare, express, proclaim, profess

purpose *n.* **1.** aim, desideratum, design, ideal, intention, objective, plan **2.** ambition, aspiration, desire, destination, goal, mark, motivation, target, vision, wish **3.** constancy, determination, diligence, doggedness, drive, faith, firmness, persistence, resolution, resolve, single-mindedness, steadfastness, tenacity, will, volition **4.** advantage, avail, benefit, consequence, gain, good, outcome, profit, result, return, use, utility **5.** essence, gist, heart, intent, keynote, meaning, purport **6.** affair, business, concern, issue, proposal, proposition, question, scheme – *v.* aim, aspire to, design, intend, mean, purport, seek

purposeful *adj.* **1.** bent, bound, decided, determined, firm, fixed, intent, obstinate, persistent, positive, resolute, resolved, settled, stalwart, staunch, steady, stubborn, tenacious, undeviating, unfaltering, unwavering *Antonyms:* aimless, shiftless, undecided, vacillating **2.** calculated, decisive, deliberate, envisaged, intentional, premeditated, planned, thought-out, voluntary

purposeless *adj.* **1.** aimless, day-to-day *(Nonformal)*, desultory, drifting, random undirected, visionless **2.** futile, gratuitous meaningless, needless, pointless, senseless throw-away *(Nonformal)*, unnecessary useless, vain

purse *n.* **1.** accessory, bag, billfold, carryall clutch, handbag, money belt, money clip pocketbook, poke, pouch, sporran, tote wallet **2.** ante, booty, kitty *(Nonformal)* money, pot, prize, stake, winning **3.** assets capital, finances, funds, means, nest eg treasure, treasury *Nonformal:* dough ready, scratch, shekels – *v.* close, com press, contract, crease, fold, press, pucke wrinkle *Antonyms:* flatten, smooth straighten, uncurl

pursue *v.* **1.** badger, chase, dog, follow harass, haunt, hound, hunt, oppres plague, prowl after, search for *or* out, sha ow, stalk, tail, track, vex, worry **2.** aim fo aspire to, attempt, seek, tackle, take o *(Nonformal)*, undertake, work for towards **3.** adhere to, carry on, continu endure, follow up, keep going, persever persist, see through **4.** court, date, kee company *(Nonformal)*, romance, serenad woo

pursuit *n.* **1.** aim, end, goal, grail, intentio quest, target **2.** chase, coursing, followir hounding, hunt, persecution, stalking, ta ing, tracking **3.** activity, calling, care employment, field, hobby, lifework, pa time, profession, vacation

push *n.* **1.** butt, jog, jolt, jostle, shov thrust **2.** ambition, drive, dynamism, en gy, enterprise, initiative, vigour, vim, vita ty, zeal *Nonformal:* get-up-and-go, gum tion, pep, pluck, spunk **3.** force, goa impetus, incentive, inducement, inspi tion, momentum, motivation, propulsi spur, stimulation **4.** difficulty, dire strai exigency, extremity, need, plight, requi ment, trouble, urgency – *v.* **1.** budg bump, butt, elbow, force, jog, jolt, jos move, nudge, poke, propel, shove, thrust egg on *(Nonformal)*, goad, impel, indu influence, make, motivate, prompt, rou spur, urge **3.** badger, browbeat, coerce, compel, constrain, hound, nag, press, pressure *Nonformal:* hassle, railroad **4.** burden, extend, force, overextend, strain, tax **5.** advertise, boost, promote, publicize, sell *Nonformal:* ballyhoo, hype, plug

pushover *n.* **1.** milquetoast, stooge, victim *Nonformal:* chump, easy mark, mug, patsy, sap, soft-touch, sucker, wimp **2.** sinecure, snap, sure thing *Nonformal:* breeze, child's play, cinch, duck soup, no-brainer, picnic, piece of cake

pushy *adj.* aggressive, assertive, bold, bossy *(Nonformal)*, brash, bumptious, forceful, obnoxious, obtrusive, offensive, presumptuous, self-assertive *Antonyms:* diffident, inoffensive, meek

pusillanimous *adj.* afraid, cowardly, craven, dastardly, fainthearted, fearful, frightened, recreant, spineless, spiritless, timid, timorous *Nonformal:* candy-assed, chicken, gutless, lily-livered, yellow, yellow-bellied *Antonyms:* bold, courageous, intrepid

pussyfoot *v.* **1.** creep, glide, gumshoe *(Nonformal)*, lurk, prowl, skulk, slide, slink, steal, tiptoe **2.** dodge, equivocate, evade, hedge, hem and haw *(Nonformal)*, parry, prevaricate, sidestep

put *adj.* fastened, firm, fixed, positioned, rooted, secured, settled, stationary, still – *n.* cast, heave, hurl, shot – *v.* **1.** apply, attach, fit, fix, lay, move to, place, plant, position, set, settle, situate, stick *Nonformal:* park, plop *or* plunk down **2.** catapult, chuck, fling, launch, lob, pitch, throw, toss **3.** express, formulate, frame, phrase, posit, pronounce, say, state, utter **4.** advance, offer, present, propose, submit, tender **5.** ascribe, assign, attribute, blame, charge, impose **6.** bet, play, risk, stake, wager **7.** assess, estimate, evaluate, figure, guess, interpret, reckon *Nonformal:* ballpark, guesstimate **8.** attain, condemn, convict, damn, doom, sentence, subject **9.** coax, induce, influence, motivate, move, pressure, prod, prompt, urge **10.** go, move, proceed, shove off

putative *adj.* alleged, assumed, believed, given, imputed, presumed, reported, reputed, so-called, supposed

put-down *n.* criticism, disparagement, humiliation, indignity, insult, jibe, quip, rebuff, sarcasm, slight, sneer, snub *Nonformal:* crack, cut, dig, knock *Antonyms:* applause, compliment, glory, honour

putrid *adj.* **1.** decaying, decomposed, fetid, fusty, high, malodorous, noisome, off, rancid, rank, reeking, rotten, smelly, spoiled, stinky, strong, tainted **2.** abominable, base, contemptible, corrupt, depraved, evil, loathsome, low, malefic, mean, odious, shameful, unpleasant, vile, wicked *Antonyms:* moral, noble, righteous

putter *n.* golf club, flatstick – *v.* dawdle, doodle, fiddle, fritter, loiter, poke, potter, shuffle around, tinker *Nonformal:* dilly-dally, lallygag, mess about, shilly-shally *Antonyms:* dash, drive, hustle, rush, scamper

puzzle *n.* **1.** acronym, brain-teaser, conundrum, enigma, labyrinth, maze, mystery, paradox, problem, riddle *Nonformal:* mind-boggler, poser **2.** bafflement, bewilderment, confusion, difficulty, dilemma, perplexity, problem, quandary, tangle, uncertainty *Nonformal:* kettle of fish, pickle, soup, stew – *v.* **1.** addle, amaze, baffle, bamboozle, beat, befog, befuddle, bewilder, confound, confuse, disconcert, distract, disturb, dumfound, flabbergast, flummox, foil, frustrate, nonplus, perplex, rattle *Nonformal:* discombobulate, floor, psych-out, stump, throw **2.** ask oneself, brood, cudgel, marvel, mull *or* think over, muse, ponder, study, think, wonder *Antonyms:* crack, decode, excogitate, solve, untangle

pygmy *adj.* baby, diminutive, dwarf, elfin, Lilliputian, midget, miniature, pint-sized, pocket, small, stunted, teeny, tiny, toy, undersized *Nonformal:* half-pint, wee *Antonyms:* colossal, enormous, huge, massive

pyjamas *n. pl.* jim-jams *(British)*, loungewear, nightclothes, night dress, nightgown, trousers *Nonformal:* baby dolls, jammies, nighttrou, nightie, PJs, sleepers

quack *adj.* counterfeit, dishonest, fake, false, fraudulent, phoney *(Nonformal)*, pretended, sham, unprincipled *Antonyms:* authentic, certified, genuine, verified – *n.* charlatan, forger, hawker *(Nonformal)*, imposter, masquerader, medicine monger, mountebank, pretender, sham, snake oil salesman, spoiler, trickster

quaff *n.* draft, drink, gulp, lap, sip, slurp, sup, swallow, swig, swill – *v.* booze *(Nonformal)*, carouse, chug, down, drain, drink, gulp, guzzle, imbibe, knock back, swallow, swill, toss off, wash down *Antonyms:* abstain, renounce, sober-up

quagmire *n.* **1.** bog, fen, marsh, marshland, mire, morass, quicksand, slough, swamp **2.** box, corner, difficulty, dilemma, entanglement, fix, hole, imbroglio, impasse, involvement, jam, mess, muddle, pass, perplexity, pinch, plight, predicament, quandary, scrape, situation, trouble *Nonformal:* kettle of fish, pickle, sticky wicket

quaint *adj.* **1.** affected, artful, attractive, bizarre, captivating, charming, curious, droll, eccentric, enchanting, fanciful, fantastic, freakish, funny, idiosyncratic, laughable, odd, off-beat, outlandish, peculiar, queer, singular, special, strange, unfamiliar, unusual, weird, whimsical *Antonyms:* dull, normal, ordinary **2.** ancient, antiquated, antique, archaic, baroque, colonial, gothic, old-fashioned, old hat *(Nonformal)*, old-world, picturesque *Antonyms:* avant-garde, fashionable, modern, new

quake *n.* agitation, earthquake, oscillation, palpitation, pulsation, seismic convulsion, shake, trembler, tremor, vibration – *v.* bob, bobble, convulse, dodder, flutter, heave, jar, jolt, move, pulsate, quail, quaver, quiver, rock, shake, shimmy, shiver, shudder, totter, tremble, twitter, vibrate, waver, wobble

qualification *n.* **1.** allowance, caveat, condition, contingency, criterion, essential, exception, exemption, limitation, mitigation, modification, need, objection, postulation, prerequisite, provision, proviso, requirement, requisite, reservation, restriction, stipulation **2.** ability, accomplishment, adequacy, aptitude, attainment, attribute, capability, capacity, competence, eligibility, endowment, experience, fitness, quality, skill, suitability *Nonformal:* goods, makings, right stuff, stuff

qualified *adj.* **1.** able, accomplished, adept, adequate, all around, *au fait (French)*, capable, catechized, certified, competent, disciplined, efficient, equipped, experienced, expert, fit, fitted, knowledgeable, licensed, practised, professional, proficient, proved, skilful, tested, trained, up to speed *(Nonformal) Antonyms:* green, incompetent, inept, raw, unfit **2.** bound, circumscribed, conditional, contingent, determined, equivocal, guarded, limited, modified, partial, provisional, reserved, restricted *Antonyms:* categorical, outright, unconditional, unequivocal, wholehearted

qualify *v.* **1.** authorize, capacitate, certify, check out, commission, condition, empower, enable, endow, entitle, equip, ground, make ready, pass, permit, prepare, ready, sanction, suit, train *Antonyms:* ban, debar, disqualify, forbid, preclude **2.** circumscribe, confine, delineate, limit, modify, outline, prescribe, regulate, restrict **3.** counsel, direct, educate, instruct, raise, school, teach, tutor **4.** ascribe, assign, attribute, characterize, describe, designate, distinguish, mark, name **5.** adapt, alter, assuage, diminish, ease, lessen, mitigate, moderate, palliate, restrain, soften, temper **6.** graduate, make the grade, meet, measure up, pass, succeed, win

quality *n.* **1.** aspect, attribute, characteristic, element, factor, feature, individuality, mark, nature, sign, trait, virtue **2.** character, condition, description, essence, feature, kind, make, property, sort **3.** excellence, goodness, merit, morals, perfection, superbness, value **4.** calibre, capacity, class, distinction, grade, level, place, rank, standing, state, station, stature, status, worth **5.** inflection, modulation, phrasing, pitch, range, resonance, timbre, tone, volume

qualm *n.* **1.** anxiety, boggle, compunction, diffidence, disquiet, doubt, misgiving, objection, pang, pause, premonition, regret, reluctance, remorse, reserve, scruple, second thought, twinge of conscience, uncertainty, uneasiness, worry *Antonyms:* certitude, remorselessness **2.** alarm, apprehension, fear, foreboding, heebie jeebies *(Nonformal)*, terror, timidity, trepidation *Antonyms:* confidence, security **3.** ache, discomfort, nausea, pain, sickness *Antonyms:* comfort, wellness

quandary *n.* bewilderment, bind, box, Catch-22, clutch, conundrum, corner, difficulty, dilemma, doubt, embarrassment, impasse, mire, paradox, perplexity, plight, point non plus, predicament, puzzle, situation, spot, strait, uncertainty *Nonformal:* double trouble, kettle of fish, pickle

quantify *v.* calculate, calibrate, compute, count, define, determine, enumerate, figure, gauge, measure, number, quantize, rate, size up *(Nonformal)*, tally, titrate, weigh

quantity *n.* **1.** allotment, amount, batch, body, case, dash, handful, iota, kilo, length, load, mass, measure, measurement, number, ounce, pinch, pitcher, portion, pound, quota, scoop, smidgen *(Nonformal)*, splash, sum *Antonyms:* none, nothing, zero **2.** abundance, aggregate, amplitude, armload, bagful, bargeload, barrel, basket, bin, box, bucket, bulk, bunch, carton, caselot, crate, cup, expanse, extent, flock, good deal, glass, greatness, host, keg, lot, magnitude, mouthful, multitude, pile, pocketful, pot, profusion, sack, scoop, shot, shovel, spoonful, tank, tankerload, thimbleful, tub, variety, volume *Nonformal:* passel, slew *See also:* **animal**, **group**

quarantine *n.* blockade, circumscription, confinement, *cordon sanitaire (French)*, enclosure, isolation, privacy, sanitary confinement, seclusion, separation *Antonyms:* affiliation, compound, integration – *v.* alienate, circumscribe, cordon off, enclose, exile, isolate, restrict, seclude, segregate, separate, sequester *Antonyms:* bind, commune, fuse, integrate

quarrel *n.* altercation, argument, battle royal *(Nonformal)*, bickering, conflict, contention, controversy, difference, difficulty, disagreement, discord, dispute, dissension, disturbance, dustup, feud, fight, fracas, fray, misunderstanding, objection, ruction, run-in, scrap, set-to, spat, squabble, strife, struggle, tiff, tumult, vendetta, wrangle *Nonformal:* fireworks, rhubarb *Antonyms:* accord, agreement, concord, harmony, peace – *v.* argue, bicker, carp, cavil, clash, contend, debate, differ, disagree, dispute, fall out, fight, have words, quibble, scold, spar, spat, squabble, wrangle *Antonyms:* accede, agree, concur, harmonize

quarrelsome *adj.* antagonistic, argumentative, bellicose, belligerent, brawling, cantankerous, chippy *(Nonformal)*, choleric, churlish, combative, contentious, contrary, cranky, cross, discordant, dissentious, fractious, grouchy, hawkish, hostile, hot-headed, irascible, litigious, peevish, peppery, petulant, pugnacious, quick-tempered, testy, truculent, turbulent *Antonyms:* calm, cool, peaceful, placid

quarry *n.* **1.** aim, desire, game, goal, intention, object, objective, prey, prize, target, victim **2.** dig, excavation, mine, pit – *v.* dig, excavate, extract, mine

quarter *n.* **1.** fourth, one-fourth, quadrant **2.** division, fifteen minutes, interval, moment, part, period, semester, session, span, term, three months, trimester **3.** area, bailiwick, barrio, beat *(Nonformal)*, block, direction, district, environs, locality, location, neighbourhood, place, point, portion, position, precinct, province, quartier, region, section, spot, square, station, subdivision, territory, turf *(Nonformal)*, vicinity *French: arrondissement, faubourg* **4.** clemency, compassion, favour, forgiveness, grace, leniency, lenity, mercy, pity, sympathy – *v.* **1.** accommodate, billet, board, harbour, house, lodge, post, put up, shelter, station **2.** chop, cleave, cut, dismember, divide, fragment, hack, segment, separate, sever, slice, sunder

quarters *n.* abode, accommodations, barracks, billet, casern, chambers, domicile, dwelling, home, housing, living place *or* space, lodgings, residence, rooms, shelter *Nonformal:* digs, pad

quash *v.* **1.** abrogate, annul, cancel, discharge, dissolve, invalidate, kill, negate, nullify, overrule, reject, repeal, rescind, reverse, revoke, scuttle, undo, veto, vitiate, void *Antonyms:* grant, reinstate, restore, sanction, vindicate **2.** block, crush, overthrow, put down *(Nonformal)*, quell, quench, squelch, subdue, suppress

quasi *adj.* apparent, artificial, fake, kind *or* sort of, mock, near, partial, phoney *(Nonformal)*, pretend, pseudo, seeming, sham, so-called, synthetic, virtual *Antonyms:* genuine, real, true – *adv.* almost, apparently, nearly, partly, seemingly, virtually

quaver *n.* falter, flicker, jerk, jiggle, jog, joggle, palpitation, quake, quiver, quivering, shakiness, shaking, shivering, shock, shudder, trembling, tremolo, tremor, twitch, twitter, vacillation, vibration, vibrato, warble, wavering, wobble – *v.* bob, bobble, falter, fluctuate, flutter, jactitate, jar, jostle, jounce, jump, oscillate, palpitate, quail, quake, quiver, shake, shiver, shock, shudder, tremble, trill, twitter, vacillate, vibrate, waver, wobble

quay *n.* boardwalk, dock, embankment, embarcadero, harbour, jetty, landing, levee, pier, wharf

queasy *adj.* **1.** bilious, dizzy, faint, groggy, hungover, ill, light-headed, nauseated, nauseous, queer, restless, rocky, sick, sickly, unwell, upset *Antonyms:* healthy, well **2.** anxious, apprehensive, averse, excited, nervous, squeamish, tense, uneasy, worried **3.** dainty, delicate, easily disgusted, fastidious, finicky, fussy, particular, prissy

queen *n.* **1.** czarina, empress, grand duchess, highness, infanta, maharanee, majesty, monarch, queen dowager *or* mother, regina, ruler, sovereign, sultana *Antonyms:* commoner, peasant, riffraff **2.** beauty, belle, champion, choice, diva, elect, elite, *grande dame (French)*, icon, idol, model, movie queen, nobility, nonpareil, paragon, pick, prima donna, prime, prize, quintessence, select, star, the best *(Nonformal)*

queer *adj.* **1.** abnormal, anomalous, atypical, bizarre, counterfeit, crazy, curious, droll, eccentric, erratic, extraordinary, funny, idiosyncratic, irrational, irregular, odd, outlandish, *outré (French)*, peculiar, puzzling, quaint, singular, strange, uncanny, uncommon, unconventional, unnatural, unorthodox, unusual *Nonformal:* flaky, freaky, funny-peculiar, kooky, oddball, wacky *Antonyms:* conventional, normal, ordinary, regular **2.** ambiguous, disputable, doubtful, dubious, mysterious, questionable, suspect, suspicious *Nonformal:* fishy, shady **3.** dizzy, faint, giddy, ill, lightheaded, nauseous, poorly, queasy, sick, unwell – *v.* botch, bungle, cripple, destroy, foil, hurt, jeopardize, louse *or* screw up *(Nonformal)*, ruin, sabotage, spoil, tarnish, thwart, undermine, upset, weaken

quell *v.* **1.** annihilate, conquer, crush, defeat, destroy, extinguish, kill, overcome, overpower, put down, quash, repress, scuttle, shut down, silence, squash, squelch, subdue, subjugate, torpedo, vanquish **2.** allay, alleviate, appease, assuage, blunt, calm, check, compose, deaden, dull, ease, hush, mitigate, moderate, mollify, pacify, palliate, quiet, soothe, still *Antonyms:* agitate, discompose, excite

quench *v.* **1.** alleviate, assuage, content, cool, fill, glut, gorge, gratify, mitigate, refresh, rehydrate, relieve, sate, satiate, satisfy, settle, slake *Antonyms:* dehydrate, desiccate, dry **2.** douse, extinguish, hose down, put out, quell, stamp out, water **3.** arrest, block, check, choke, curb, end, finish, freeze, gag, halt, quash, repress, smother, stay, stifle, stop, suppress, suspend

querulous *adj.* annoyed, bearish, cantankerous, captious, carping, censorious, complaining, critical, cross, crotchety, demanding, discontented, dissatisfied, dour, dyspeptic, edgy, faultfinding, finicky, fractious, fretful, grouchy, grumbling, grumbly, irascible, irritable, moody, morose, Pecksniffian, peevish, perverse, petulant, quarrelsome, scrappy, snappy, sour, splenetic, sulky, testy, tetchy, touchy, wailing, waspish, whining *Nonformal:* griping, grousing, huffy, uptight *Antonyms:* contented, placid, quiescent, satisfied, tranquil

query *n.* **1.** examination, exploration, feeler, hearing, inquest, inquiry, interrogation, probe, search **2.** concern, doubt, hesitation, issue, problem, question, reservation, scepticism, scruple, uncertainty *Nonformal:* grill, pump, scrutinize, sound out– *v.* **1.** ask, enquire, examine, hit up *(Nonformal)*, inquire, interrogate, pry, question, quiz, search **2.** challenge, disbelieve, dispute, distrust, doubt, mistrust, object, protest, suspect

quest *n.* **1.** adventure, crusade, enterprise, expedition, exploration, feat, hunt, inquisition, investigation, journey, mission, pilgrimage, probe, pursuit, research, search **2.** aim, ambition, aspiration, desideratum, design, direction, end, goal, holy grail *(Nonformal)*, intention, purpose, quarry, target – *v.* chase, explore, follow, hunt, inquire, investigate, search, seek, track

question *n.* **1.** challenge, demand, inquiry, poll, probe, query, request, search *Antonyms:* answer, confirmation, reply, response **2.** argument, confusion, conundrum, contention, controversy, debate, difficulty, dilemma, disagreement, dispute, enigma, mystery, poser, problem, puzzle, riddle **3.** issue, matter, motion, point, proposition, subject, submission, suggestion **4.** doubt, misgiving, objection, pang, protest, qualm, regret, reluctance, scruple, suspicion, twinge, uncertainty, unease *Antonyms:* assurance, certainty, certitude – *v.* **1.** ask, beg, canvass, catechize, consult, cross-examine, debrief, demand, enquire, entreat, essay, evaluate, examine, hunt for, inquire, interrogate, interview, investigate, measure, petition, probe, pry into, query, quiz, search, seek, solicit *Nonformal:* go *or* work over, grill, pump, roast, sound out, sweat, give the third-degree *Antonyms:* answer, reply, respond **2.** challenge, confront, contradict, controvert, demur, deny, disbelieve, dispute, doubt, mistrust, object, oppose, suspect *Antonyms:* accept, believe, trust

questionable *adj.* **1.** ambiguous, apocryphal, arguable, controversial, counterfeit, cryptic, debatable, disputable, doubtful, dubious, enigmatic, equivocal, fake, false, fictitious, iffy *(Nonformal)*, inaccurate, indecisive, indefinite, moot, mysterious, mythical, obscure, paradoxical, polemical, problematic, suspect, uncertain, unconfirmed, undefined, unproven, unreliable, unsettled, unsubstantiated, vague *Antonyms:* absolute, certain, incontrovertible, indisputable, unequivocal **2.** base, corrupt, crooked, dishonest, disreputable, disrespectable, mean, miserable, perfidious, scrofulous, shameless, shifty, sinister, tricky, unethical, unprincipled, wily *Nonformal:* fly-by-night, shady *Antonyms:* esteemed, respectable, trustworthy

questionnaire *n.* census form, check list, examination, form, opinion poll, quiz, survey, test

queue *n.* **1.** column, file, line, order, progression, rank, row, sequence, series, string, succession, tier **2.** braid, dreadlock, lock, pigtail, ponytail, ringlet – *v.* arrange, get in line, group, line up, order *Antonyms:* disperse, dissipate, scatter *Commonly misused:* **cue**

quibble *n.* cavil, complaint, criticism, evasion, nicety, objection, protest, quiddity, trifle *Nonformal:* beef, nitpicking – *v.* **1.** argue, bicker, carp, cavil, criticize, fight, haggle, split hairs *Nonformal:* grouse, kvetch, nitpick, pettifog **2.** dipsy-doodle *(Nonformal)*, dodge, double-talk, elude, equivocate, fudge, palter, prevaricate, waffle

quick *adj.* **1.** accelerated, breakneck, brisk, energetic, expeditious, express, fast, fleet, flying, headlong, immediate, impetuous, instantaneous, lively, mercurial, nimble, prompt, rapid, red-lined *(Nonformal)*, snappy, speedy, spirited, spry, sudden, swift, winged *Antonyms:* deliberate, drawn out, gradual, slow **2.** abrupt, brief, hasty, hurried, perfunctory, precipitate, summary **3.** able, active, adept, adroit, agile, capable, competent, deft, dexterous, effective, effectual, handy *(Nonformal)*, ready, slick *Antonyms:* awkward, clumsy, inept **4.** acute, alert, astute, bright, canny, clever, discerning, intelligent, keen, knowing, nimble-witted, perceptive, perspicacious, quick-witted, receptive, sharp, shrewd, smart *Nonformal:* hep, savvy *Antonyms:* dim, dull, lazy, slow **5.** ephemeral, evanescent, fleeting, impermanent, passing, short-lived, temporary, transient *Antonyms:* immutable, permanent **6.** bracing, life-affirming, invigorating, refreshing, restorative, tonic *Antonyms:* enervating, exhausting – *interj:* at once, now, this minute, *tout de suite (French) Nonformal:* lickety-split, pretty darn quick *or* PDQ – *n.* core, crux, essence, heart, pith, soul

quicken *v.* **1.** accelerate, dispatch, expedite, hasten, hurry, increase, move, precipitate, speed, spur, step up *Antonyms:* retard, slacken, slow **2.** activate, actuate, animate, arouse, awaken, energize, excite, grow, impel, incite, inspire, invigorate, kindle, liven, motivate, propel, restore, revitalize, revive, rouse, stimulate, stir, strengthen, urge *Antonyms:* blunt, brake, deaden, drop anchor

quickly *adv.* abruptly, briskly, expeditiously, express, fast, hastily, hurriedly, immediately, instantaneously, instantly, posthaste, promptly, rapidly, soon, speedily, stat. *or* statim *(Latin)*, suddenly, swiftly, without delay *Nonformal:* ASAP, chop-chop, double-time, lickety-split, pronto, yesterday *Antonyms:* leisurely, slowly

quickness *n.* **1.** acceleration, briskness, dispatch, flight, haste, motion, rapidity, speed, swiftness, velocity *Nonformal:* jam, jets, revs, rpms, wheels, wings *Antonyms:* slowness, sluggishness **2.** acumen, acuteness, adaptability, flexibility, insight, intelligence, perceptiveness, resourcefulness, savvy *(Nonformal)*, skill, versatility, wit *Antonyms:* density, dullness

quicksilver *adj.* **1.** capricious, changeable, fickle, flighty, inconstant, mercurial, skittish, undependable, unpredictable, unreliable, vacillating, whimsical *Antonyms:* predictable, staid, steadfast **2.** active, animate brisk, chipper, energetic, full of life, livel peppy, quick, spirited, spry, swift *Antonym* lethargic, listless, slack

quick-tempered *adj.* abrupt, bellicose, ch leric, excitable, fiery, high-strung, hothea ed, hot-tempered, impatient, irascibl ornery, passionate, peppery, sensitive, spl netic, temperamental, tempestuous, test touchy, volatile, waspish *Nonformal:* shor fused, thin-skinned *Antonyms:* cool, phle matic, placid, tolerant

quick-witted *adj.* acute, adaptable, agil alert, astute, brainy, bright, brilliant, cann clever, humorous, intelligent, keen, knov ing, nimble-minded, perceptive, perspic cious, sharp, shrewd, slick, smart, wit *Nonformal:* on the ball, savvy, sharp as tack *Antonyms:* dull, obtuse, slow, slow-wi ted, stupid

quiescent *adj.* abeyant, becalmed, caln dormant, down *(Nonformal)*, hushed, ina tive, inert, in repose, motionless, pacifi passive, placid, peaceful, quiet, resting, se tled, serene, silent, sleepy, still, suspende tranquil, subsiding, waiting *Antonym* active, clamorous, raging, tumultuous, wild

quiet *adj.* **1.** hushed, inaudible, low-pitche low-sounding, muffled, mum, muted, nois less, silent, soundless, without a peep c sound *Antonyms:* cacaphonous, loud, nois strident **2.** calm, halcyon, motionless, paci ic, smooth, still, tranquil *Antonyms:* ragin stormy, turbulent, wild **3.** off the beate path, out-of-the-way, private, remot retired, secluded, undiscovered *Antonym* mainstream, popular, public, well-travelle **4.** indolent, lackadaisical, languid, laz lethargic, relaxing, reposeful, restfu restorative *Antonyms:* acrimonious, stres ful **5.** gentle, mild, pensive, philosophica placid, reserved, reticent, retiring, sedat serene, sober, subdued, taciturn, temperat thoughtful *Antonyms:* belligerent, contum cious, pugnacious **6.** homely, low key, mo est, restrained, unassuming, unobtrusiv unpretentious *Antonyms:* flashy, gaud loud, ostentatious **7.** at a standstill, do mant, in abeyance, inactive, inert, motio less, postponed, sleeping, sluggish, somn lent, stagnant, stationary, stock-still *(Nor* *formal)*, suspended, torpid *Antonyms:* active, booming, busy, buzzing **8.** at an end, dark, dead, done with, over *Antonyms:* beginning, bright, opening **9.** secret, undisclosed, unrevealed, unsaid *Antonyms:* manifest, out in the open, publicized – *interj.* be still, enough, hush, knock it off, shut up *Nonformal:* can it, hold it down – *n.* **1.** abatement, break, cessation, dead air, eye, lull, pause **2.** peace, serenity, stillness, tranquility – *v.* **1.** allay, appease, assuage, calm, pacify, soothe **2.** blunt, deaden, diminish, dull, lesson, moderate **3.** cut off *or* short, gag, mute, muzzle, shuffle, silence

quill *n.* bristle, calamus, feather, needle, pen, pinion, reed, spike, spine, stem, thorn

quilt *n.* bed covering, comforter, counterpane, cover, coverlet, duvet, eiderdown, puff *Kinds of quilts:* Amish, Amish diamond, bear paw, bow tie, crazy, Jacob's Ladder, log cabin, Mennonite, patchwork, rail fence, Robbing Peter, Roman stripes, scrap, shoo-fly, Texas Star, tumbling blocks, wedding ring – *v.* line, pad, secure, sew, stitch, work

quintessence *n.* **1.** basis, building block, core, DNA, distillation, elixir, essence, gist, heart, kernel, lifeblood, marrow, pith, quiddity, soul, spirit, stuff *(Nonformal)*, substance, sum and substance **2.** apotheosis, beau ideal, epitome, model, paragon, pattern, perfect example, personification, prototype, ultimate

quintessential *adj.* archetypal, consummate, *crème de la crème (French)*, definitive, distinguishing, embodiment, essential, exemplary, ideal, inherent, intrinsical, model, prototypical, ultimate

quip *n.* **1.** badinage, banter, bon mot, drollery, gibe, jest, joke, mockery, one-liner, pun, raillery, satire, spoof, witticism *Nonformal:* crack, gag, wisecrack **2.** epigram, rejoinder, remark, repartee, reply, retort, riposte, sally **3.** cavil, distinction, evasion, niggling, quibble – *v.* banter, crack wise *(Nonformal)*, jest, joke, mock, retort, tease

quirk *n.* **1.** aberration, characteristic, eccentricity, fetish, foible, habit, idiosyncrasy, irregularity, kink, knack, mannerism, oddity, peculiarity, perversion, singularity, trait **2.** caprice, crotchet, fancy, vagary, whim **3.** bend, dodge, evasion, feint, quibble, shift, subterfuge, turn, twist

quit *adj.* clear, discharged, exempt, free, let off, released, relieved, rid, unburdened – *v.* **1.** abandon, abdicate, beat it *(Nonformal)*, decamp, depart, desert, exit, flee, forsake, go, leave, secede, separate, sever, surrender, vacate, withdraw, yield **2.** break off, cease, conclude, desist, discontinue, end, halt, leave off, stop, suspend, terminate *Antonyms:* continue, persist, resume **3.** give notice, give up, relinquish, renounce, resign, retire, step down

quite *adv.* **1.** absolutely, actually, altogether, completely, considerably, entirely, fully, indubitably, in fact, in reality, *in toto (Latin)*, in truth, just, largely, noticeably, perfectly, positively, precisely, purely, really, surely, thoroughly, totally, truly, unreservedly, utterly, well, wholly **2.** considerably, fairly, far, moderately, pretty, rather, reasonably, relatively, significantly, somewhat, to an extent, very

quiver *n.* convulsion, fillibration, jerk, jump, quaver, shake, shiver, shudder, tremble, twitch, waver, wobble – *v.* agitate, beat, convulse, jitter, oscillate, palpitate, pulsate, pulse, quake, quail, quaver, shake, shiver, shudder, throb, tremble, twitter, vibrate *Antonyms:* calm, compose, relax, smooth

quixotic *adj.* absurd, chimerical, chivalrous, extravagant, fanciful, foolhardy, idealistic, impractical, rash, reckless, romantic, sentimental, starry-eyed, storybook, utopian, visionary, whimsical *Antonyms:* cynical, material, practical, pragmatic, realistic

quiz *n.* check, exam, examination, investigation, pop quiz, query, questioning, questionnaire, skill-tester, test – *v.* ask, check, cross-examine, examine, grill, inquire, interrogate, investigate, pump, query, question, test

quizzical *adj.* **1.** amusing, bantering, chaffing, comical, droll, entertaining, funny, humorous **2.** bizarre, confusing, curious, eccentric, peculiar, odd, off-beat, queer, quirky, strange, weird *Antonyms:* commonplace, customary, normative, ordinary, usual **3.** examining, inquisitive, perplexed, probing, puzzled, questioning, searching

quota *n.* allocation, allotment, allowance, apportionment, assignment, bite, chunk, cut, division, end, lot, measure, part, percentage, piece, proportion, quantum, ration, share, slice, split, total, whack

quotation *n.* **1.** citation, epigraph, excerpt, extract, passage, quote, recitation, reference, saying, selection, sentence **2.** charge, cost, estimate, price, quote, rate, sta price, tender

quote *v.* **1.** adduce, cite, detail, ec excerpt, extract, mention, name, pa phrase, parrot, proclaim, recall, reci recollect, reference, refer to, repeat, re **2.** bid, cost, price, rate, tender, value

quotidian *adj.* **1.** daily, evening, morni recurrent, regular, routine, usual **2.** av age, commonplace, everyday, munda nothing new *(Nonformal)*, ordinary, run-the-mill, trite, trivial, unremarkable

rabble *n.* canaille, commonalty, commoners, crowd, herd, hoi polloi, horde, lower classes, masses, mob, peasantry, plebs, populace, proletariat, riffraff, rout, swarm, throng *Nonformal:* army, bleacher bums *or* creatures, ragtag and bobtail, trash, vermin *Antonyms:* aristocracy, elite, ruling class

rabble-rouser *n.* demagogue, firebrand, fomenter, incendiary, inciter, inflamer, instigator, insurgent, malcontent, muckraker, protester, *provocateur (French)*, radical, revolutionary, ringleader, rouser, seditionary, seditionist, troublemaker

rabid *adj.* berserk, bigoted, crazed, crazy, delirious, deranged, extreme, fanatical, fervent, frantic, frenetic, frenzied, furious, hot, infuriated, insane, intemperate, intolerant, irrational, keen, mad, maniacal, obsessed, raging, revolutionary, sick, violent, virulent, wild, zealous *Nonformal:* bitten, bugged, flipped, foaming at the mouth, freaked out, mad-dog, over-the-top, wigged out *Antonyms:* lackadaisical, moderate, temperate

race *n.* **1.** blood, breed, category, clan, classification, cultural *or* ethnic group, culture, division, family, folk, lineage, nationality, people, stock, strain, subdivision, type **2.** clash, competition, contest, course, dash, derby, engagement, event, footchase, foot race, heat, marathon, match, meet, motocross, pursuit, regatta, rivalry, running, showdown, sprint, steeplechase **3.** branch, brook, creek, duct, raceway, river, rivulet, run, runnel, sluice, stream – *v.* bolt, bustle, career, chase, compete, dart, drag *(Nonformal)*, fly, gallop, hasten, hurry, run, rush, scamper, scramble, scud, scurry, scuttle, speed, sprint, spurt, swoop, whisk, whiz, wing, zip, zoom *Antonyms:* crawl, meander, stroll

racial *adj.* **1.** ancestral, cultural, ethnic, ethnological, folk, genealogical, genetic, hereditary, national **2.** bigoted, discriminatory, hateful, hostile, inappropriate, injurious, insensitive, offensive, prejudicial, racist *Antonyms:* fair, liberal, open-minded

racism *n.* alienation, apartheid, bias, bigotry, discrimination, exclusionism, fear, ghettoization, hatred, intolerance, Jim Crowism *(U.S.)*, marginalization, narrow-mindedness, prejudice, racialism, sectarianism, segregation, xenophobia

rack *n.* **1.** bracket, counter, frame, framework, grate, holder, receptacle, shelf, stand, trestle **2.** adversity, affliction, agony, anguish, difficulty, grief, hardship, misery, misfortune, ordeal, pain, sorrow, suffering, torment, trouble, woe *Antonyms:* comfort, ease, leisure **3.** damage, demolition, devastation, havoc, loss, mayhem, ruination, shambles, wreckage – *v.* **1.** cripple, crucify, martyr, punish, stretch, tear, torment, torture, wrench **2.** agonize, exert, exhaust, extend, labour, strain, stress, strive, struggle, tax, work

racket *n.* **1.** agitation, battle, blare, brawl, brouhaha, clamour, clangour, clash, clatter, commotion, din, disturbance, fight, fracas, fuss, hubbub, jangle, mêlée, noise, outcry, pandemonium, riot, roar, row, ruction, rumpus, shouting, squabble, squall, stir, tumult, turbulence, turmoil, uproar *Nonformal:* ruckus, to-do **2.** cheat, chicanery, confidence game *or* trick, conspiracy, corruption, crime, dishonesty, dodge, extortion, fraud, illegality, intrigue, machination, plot, scheme, swindle, theft, trick *Nonformal:* con, scam, shakedown **3.** hoop, paddle *Common rackets:* badminton, ping-pong *or* table tennis, racketball, squash, tennis **4.** business, calling, career, craft, employment, job, line, livelihood, living, means, métier, occupation, profession, pursuit, trade, vocation, work *Nonformal:* bread and butter, game

racy *adj.* **1.** bawdy, blue *(Nonformal)*, erotic, immodest, indecent, indelicate, lewd, lurid, naughty, off-colour, ribald, risqué, shady, shameless, smutty, suggestive, titillating *Antonyms:* chaste, prim, proper, virtuous **2.** animated, bright, buoyant, energetic, exciting, exhilarating, forceful, heady, keen, lively, quickening, sparkling, spirited, sprightly, stimulating, vigorous, vivacious, zestful **3.** fiery, fragrant, gingery, piquant, pungent, rich, salty, saucy, sharp, snappy, spicy, strong, tangy, tart, tasty, zesty *Antonyms:* bland, dull, insipid

radiance *n.* brightness, brilliance, dazzle, effulgence, energy, glare, gleam, glitter, heat, incandescence, inner glow, iridescence, luminescence, lustre, serenity, shimmer, shine, splendour, warmth *Antonyms:* darkness, gloom, opacity

radiant *adj.* **1.** beaming, bright, brilliant, gleaming, glittering, glowing, incandescent, luminous, lustrous, resplendent, shining, sparkling *Antonyms:* black, dull, lacklustre **2.** beatific, blissful, cheerful, cheery, delighted, ecstatic, enraptured, festive, glad, glorious, happy, joyful, joyous, jubilant, magnificent, rapturous, sunny, transported, vivacious, wonderful *Antonyms:* dolorous, joyless, miserable, sad, sombre, sorrowful

radiate *v.* **1.** beam, burn, emanate, emit, illumine, shed, shine, transmit *Antonyms:* darken, eclipse, obscure, shade **2.** branch out, broadcast, circulate, diffuse, disperse, disseminate, distribute, expand, scatter, sprinkle, strew

radical *adj.* **1.** basic, cardinal, constitutional, deep-seated, essential, foundational, fundamental, inherent, innate, inner, intrinsic, native, natural, original, primary, primitive, profound, rudimentary, thoroughgoing, underlying, vital *Antonyms:* insignificant, minor, token, trivial **2.** absolute, all-out, complete, exhaustive, full-blown, outright, perfect, positive, sweeping, thorough, total, ultra, unabridged, uncompromising, unrestricted, utter *Antonyms:* half-hearted, incomplete, partial **3.** anarchistic, excessive, extreme, fanatical, freethinking, immoderate, insubordinate, insurrectionary, left-wing, militant, reactionary, rebellious, recalcitrant, revolutionary, right-wing, riotous, seditious, uncompromising, violent, zealous *Antonyms:* conservative, mainstream, moderate, orthodox – *n.* agitator, anarchist, Bolshevist, crusader, extremist, fanatic, fascist, freedom fighter, iconoclast, immoderate, Jacobite, leftist, Luddite, nihilist, rebel, reformer, revolutionary, right-winger, secessionist *Antonyms:* company man, conformist, traditionalist

radio *n.* radiotelegraphy, radiotelephony *Kinds of radio:* AM, amateur, AM-FM, battery, boom-box *(Nonformal)*, broadband, car, CB, citizens' band, FM, ham, phone, pocket, portable, radio beacon, radiophonograph, radiophone, receiver, relay, scanner, ship-to-shore, shortwave, standby, stereo, three-way, transceiver, transistor, tuner, two-way, VHF-FM, walkie-talkie, Walkman *(Trademark)*, weather, wireless *(British)* – *v.* communicate, dispatch, forward, send, transfer, transmit

radioactive *adj.* charged, irradiated, isotopic, radioactivated, unstable *Radioactive elements:* actinium, americium, astatine, berkelium, californium, curium, einsteinium, fermium, francium, mendelevium, neptunium, nobelium, plutonium, polonium, promethium, protactinium, radium, radon, technetium, thorium, uranium

radiotherapy *n.* radiation therapy, radiology *Radio therapeutic pictures and graphs:* CAT scan, computer-assisted tomography, ECG, EEG, EKG, electrocardiogram, electroencephalogram, encephalogram, encephalograph, magnetic resonance imaging, MRI, MR scan, PET scan, positron emission tomography, radiogram, radiograph, ultrasound, X-ray

radius *n.* ambit, boundary, compass, distance, expanse, extent, limit, orbit, purview, range, reach, realm, space, span, stretch, sweep

raffish *adj.* **1.** flashy, garish, gaudy, glaring, Hollywood *(Nonformal)*, maudlin, ostentatious, tasteless, tawdry, vulgar *Antonyms:*

refined, simple, understated **2.** bad, base, contemptible, disgraceful, dishonourable, disreputable, ignominious, immoral, indecent, infamous, obliquitous, odious, opprobrious, scandalous, scurvy, shameful, vicious *Antonyms:* decent, honourable, virtuous

raffle *n.* bet, draw, gambling, gaming, long shot *(Nonformal)*, lottery, numbers game, stake, sweeps, sweepstake, wager – *v.* auction off, bid off, offer, provide, sacrifice

rag *n.* cloth, remnant, ribbon, scrap, strip, tatter, towel, washcloth – *v.* **1.** annoy, bother, harass, harry, hassle *(Nonformal)*, hector, irritate, nag, nettle, peeve, pester **2.** chaff, jest, lampoon, mock, poke fun, ridicule, tease *Nonformal:* give one the business, razz **3.** *Hockey:* dally, deke, delay, dipsy-doodle, run the clock down, stickhandle, waste time

ragamuffin *n.* guttersnipe, squeegee kid, street urchin, tatterdemalion, tramp, waif

rage *n.* **1.** acrimony, agitation, anger, animosity, apoplexy, asperity, bitterness, bluster, choler, convulsion, eruption, exasperation, excitement, explosion, ferment, ferocity, frenzy, furor, fury, gall, heat, hemorrhage, huff, hysterics, indignation, ire, irritation, madness, mania, obsession, outburst, paroxysm, passion, resentment, spasm, spleen, tantrum, temper, umbrage, uproar, upset, vehemence, violence, wrath *Nonformal:* blowup, conniption fit, fireworks *Antonyms:* acceptance, calmness, gladness, joy, pleasure **2.** ardour, desire, determination, drive, eagerness, enthusiasm, heart, hunger, pluck, resolution, will, zeal *Antonyms:* doubt, indifference, passivity **3.** craze, *dernier cri (French)*, fad, fancy, fashion, in thing *(Nonformal)*, look, passing fancy, trend – *v.* **1.** erupt, fulminate, fume, rampage, rant, rave, roar, scathe, scream, seethe, storm, yell *Nonformal:* blow up, boil over, go berserk, look daggers, rail against *or* at *Antonyms:* accept, relax, submit **2.** advance, burn, conflagrate, consume, engulf, escalate, extend, intensify, mushroom, spread

ragged *adj.* battered, broken, crude, dilapidated, dingy, disorganized, fragmented, frayed, frazzled, irregular, jagged, moth-eaten, notched, patched, poor, rent, rough, rugged, scraggy, seedy, shabby, shaggy, shoddy, shredded, sketchy, tattered, threadbare, torn, uneven, unfinished, unkempt, unpressed, wrinkled, worn-out *Antonyms:* new, smart, unused

raging *adj.* angry, blustering, enraged, frenzied, fuming, furious, incensed, infuriated, irate, mad, out of control, rabid, raving, seething, stormy, tempestuous, turbulent, violent, wild *Nonformal:* bent, beside oneself, boiling mad *or* over, red-hot *Antonyms:* aloof, collected, cool, indifferent

rags *n.* apparel, attire, clothes, dress, finery, garments, glad rags, outfit, raiment, suit, vestment, wardrobe *Nonformal:* duds, Sunday best, threads, toggery

ragtag *adj.* **1.** disorganized, ill-assorted, mixed-up, motley, scraggly **2.** dirty, shabby, tousled, unkempt – *n.* commoners, hoi polloi, masses, people, proletariat, rabble, riffraff, ruck

raid *n.* **1.** assault, attack, blitz, charge, foray, incursion, invasion, irruption, offensive, onslaught, rush, sortie **2.** despoliation, looting, marauding, pillage, plundering, ransacking, rapine, ravaging, spoilation **3.** arrest, capture, collar, dragnet, grab, pickup, seizure, snare *Nonformal:* bust, shakedown – *v.* assail, bomb, despoil, devastate, encroach, gut, intrude, invade, loot, pillage, plunder, ransack, sack, scourge, smash and grab *(Nonformal)*, steal, storm, trespass, usurp

raider *n.* adventurer, aggressor, assailant, attacker, bandit, brigand, buccaneer, burglar, corsair, desperado, highwayman, imperialist, invader, picaroon, pirate, riever *(Scottish)*, robber, rogue, thief, trespasser, usurper, viking

railing *n.* balustrade, banister, bar, barrier, fence, rails

raillery *n.* banter, comeback, derision, dig, disparagement, fun, humour, irony, jape, jest, jesting, jibe, jocularity, joke, joking, mockery, quip, retort, ridicule, satire, teasing, witticism

railway *n. chemin de fer (French)*, iron horse *(Nonformal)*, line, rail, rail line, railroad, steel, steel rail, track *Kinds of railway:* branch, cable, cog, consolidated, electric, elevated, fork, funicular, gravity, independent, industrial, miniature, mining, monorail, narrow-gauge, nationalized, northern, private, provincial, subsidiary, subway, tram, tramline, tramway, transcontinental, transnational, trunk, trunk line

rain *n.* CBC sunshine *(Historical)*, cloudburst, condensation, deluge, downpour, monsoon, precipitation, rainfall, rainstorm, sheets, showering, sprinkling, stream, sun shower, thunderstorm, torrential rain *Nonformal:* buckets, cats and dogs – *v.* drizzle, fall, hail, mist, mizzle, patter, piss *(Nonformal)*, pour, precipitate, shower, sprinkle, storm, teem

rainbow *adj.* banded, harlequin, iridescent, kaleidoscopic, multicoloured, multihued, opalescent, pearly, prismatic, rainbow-like, spectral, streaked, striped, varicoloured, variegated – *n.* arc, curve, iridescence, prism, spectrum, sundog

raise *n.* addition, advance, augmentation, boost, bump, hike, increase, increment, move, promotion, rise *Antonyms:* cut, decrease, reduction – *v.* **1.** elevate, heave, heighten, hoist, hold up, jack, leaven, lift, lift *or* stand up, mount, set upright, pump, upheave, uplift, upraise *Antonyms:* drop, lower, sink **2.** build, construct, engineer, erect, establish, fabricate, found, frame, make, produce, set up **3.** advance, amplify, augment, boost, enhance, enlarge, escalate, exaggerate, improve, increase, inflate, intensify, magnify, promote *Antonyms:* curtail, cut, tax **4.** beatify, build *or* move up, canonize, dignify, honour, promote, sanctify, upgrade **5.** breed, cultivate, farm, garden, grow, husband, manage, oversee, plant, produce, seed, sow, till, work **6.** beget, bring up, care *or* provide for, develop, discipline, educate, father, feed, foster, instruct, mother, nourish, nurse, nurture, parent, produce, propagate, rear, support, teach, train, wean **7.** assemble, bring together, collect, congregate, form, gather, levy, mass, mobilize, muster, obtain **8.** bring about, cause, elicit, evoke, induce, instigate, occasion, originate, precipitate *Antonyms:* curb, quell, repress, suppress **9.** activate, animate, arouse, awaken, excite, foment, incite, kindle, motivate, provoke, stir, waken *Antonyms:* dampen, mute, restrain, smother, stifle **10.** broach, initiate, introduce, present, propose, put forward, submit, suggest, table, tender

rake *n.* **1.** garden tool, implement *Kinds of rake:* broom, clam, fan, garden, lawn, refuse **2.** debauchee, lecher, libertine, philanderer, playboy, profligate, roué, seducer, sensualist, womanizer *Nonformal:* Casanova, Don Juan, Lothario, skirt-chaser, swinger, tomcat, wolf – *v.* **1.** clean up, clear, collect, gather, remove, smooth, sweep *Antonyms:* disperse, scatter, strew **2.** check, comb, examine, explore, ferret out, inspect, scan, scour, screen, scrutinize, search, sift **3.** enfilade, fire, gun down, mow down *(Nonformal)*, pelt, pepper, riddle, shell, shoot, spray, strafe, volley **4.** carve, claw, dig, grate, lacerate, rasp, rip, score, scrape, scratch **5.** cant, incline, keel, lean, list, pitch, slant, tilt, tip

rakish *adj.* **1.** abandoned, debauched, depraved, dissolute, fast, immoral, lecherous, lewd, licentious, loose, prodigal, prurient, raffish, sinful, wanton, wild *Antonyms:* chaste, prim, proper, virtuous **2.** chic, dapper, dashing, debonair, devil-may-care, fashionable, flashy, gay, high-stepping, jaunty, natty, sassy, saucy, tony *(Nonformal)*, trendy

rally *n.* **1.** comeback, improvement, miracle *(Nonformal)*, recovery, recuperation, renaissance, renewal, resurgence, victory *Antonyms:* collapse, loss, relapse **2.** assembly, celebration, congregation, convention, convocation, event, gathering, get-together, jamboree, mass meeting, meet, party, pep rally, protest, revival session, social **3.** challenge, competition, *concours (French)*, concourse, contest, derby, race, run – *v.* **1.** assemble, collect, convene, gather, marshal, mobilize, muster, organize, reassemble, redouble, re-form, regroup, reorganize, round up, unite *Antonyms:* disband, disperse, separate **2.** arouse, awaken, bestir, encourage, fire, inspirit, kindle, revive, rouse, wake, waken, whet *Antonyms:* bore, discourage, dissuade **3.** come around, comeback, enliven, grow stronger, improve, invigorate, recover, recuperate, refresh, regain rejuvenate, renew, restore, resurrect, resuscitate, strengthen, revive, surge, turn around *Antonyms:* choke, fail, worsen **4.** aggravate, bother, bug, chafe, mock, needle, pester, ride *(Nonformal)*, taunt, tease

ram *n.* **1.** Aries, male sheep, tup, wether **2.** battering ram, beam, hammer, log, pile, rammer – *v.* **1.** batter, beat, butt, collide with, crash, dash, drive, force, hammer, hit, pile into, plunge, pound, run, sink, slam, smash, strike, thrust **2.** compress, cram, crowd, squeeze, stuff, wedge

ramble *n.* constitutional, excursion, hike, journey, perambulation, roam, romp, roving, saunter, stroll, tour, traipse, trek, trip, turn, venture, walk, walkabout – *v.* **1.** amble, bum around *(Nonformal)*, clamber, dawdle, drift, gallivant, knock about *or* around, meander, perambulate, peregrinate, promenade, range, roam, rove, saunter, scramble, straggle, stray, stroll, trail, traipse, travel, walk **2.** blather, branch off, chatter, depart, digress, diverge, get sidetracked, jabber, maunder, natter, prattle, spew, sprawl, turn, twist, wander, wind

rambler *n.* beachcomber, gadabout, globetrotter, hobo, jetsetter, nomad, peregrinator, pilgrim, roamer, rover, sundowner, tourist, trekker, tripper, tumbleweed *(Nonformal)*, vagabond, vagrant, wanderer, wayfarer *Antonyms:* homebody, homesteader, settler

rambling *adj.* **1.** bumbling, circuitous, confused, diffuse, digressive, disconnected, discursive, disjointed, incoherent, irregular, random, scattered, sprawling, straggling, unplanned *Antonyms:* coherent, concise, direct, pithy **2.** garrulous, long-winded, loquacious, prolix, talkative, verbose, voluble, wordy *Antonyms:* reticent, quiet, silent

rambunctious *adj.* boisterous, brawling, clamorous, defiant, disobedient, disorderly, hyperactive, loud, obstreperous, rampageous, rebellious, recalcitrant, riotous, robust, rollicking, rough, rowdy, rude, uncontrollable, unruly, wild *Antonyms:* calm, placid, obedient, staid, sedate

ramification *n.* aftermath, backlash, consequence, development, effect, extension, fruit, issue, offshoot, outcome, product, result, sequel, upshot, wake

ramp *n.* **1.** entrance, on-ramp, passageway, roadway, stairway, wheelchair entrance **2.** grade, gradient, hill, inclination, incline, pitch, rise, ski-jump, slope

rampage *n.* ado, anger, commotion, craziness, disturbance, excitement, fracas, frenzy, furor, fury, hubbub, killing, looting, mayhem, mêlée, passion, racket, rage, riot, spree, temper, tempest, turmoil, tumult, uproar, upset, violence, wildness *Nonformal:* foofaraw, ruckus, shindy, stir, tear – *v.* burn, cripple, kill, loot, maim, rage, rant, rave, riot, run amok *or* riot *or* wild, storm, tear, tear down *Nonformal:* go berserk *or* crazy, lose it

rampant *adj.* **1.** aggressive, boisterous, clamorous, fanatical, flagrant, furious, impetuous, impulsive, outrageous, raging, riotous, turbulent, ungovernable, unrestrained, violent, wanton, wild *Antonyms:* curbed, passive, quelled, trifling **2.** diffuse, dominant, epidemic, excessive, growing, pandemic, predominant, prevalent, profuse, rife, spreading, sweeping, ubiquitous, unchecked, uncontrolled, universal, widespread *Antonyms:* contained, limited, localized

rampart *n.* barricade, barrier, bastion, breastwork, bulwark, defence, earthwork, elevation, embankment, fence, fort, fortification, guard, hill, mound, parapet, protection, ridge, security, stronghold, support, wall

ramshackle *adj.* broken-down, condemned, crumbling, decayed, decrepit, derelict, dilapidated, flimsy, jerrybuilt, neglected, poor, rickety, shabby, shaky, tottering, tumbledown, unsafe, unsteady *Antonyms:* solid, stable, steady, well-built

ranch *n.* croft, farm, grange, hacienda, homestead, plantation, station – *v.* breed, drive, husband, manage, punch, raise, rear, shepherd, work

rancid *adj.* bad, contaminated, curdled, decomposed, dodgy *(Nonformal)*, disagreeable, disgusting, evil-smelling, feculent, fetid, foul, funky, fusty, gamy, high, impure, loathsome, malodorous, mouldy, musty, nasty, noisome, noxious, off, offensive, polluted, putrefied, putrescent, putrid, rank, reeking, repulsive, rotten, sharp, smelly, sour, soured, stale, stinking, strong, tainted, turned, unhealthy *Antonyms:* fresh, pleasant, pure

rancour *n.* acerbity, acrimony, animosity, animus, antagonism, antipathy, aversion, bad blood, bile, bitterness, enmity, grudge, harshness, hate, hatred, hostility, ill feeling *or* will, malevolence, malice, malignity, pique, resentment, spite, spleen, umbrage, uncharitableness, unfriendliness, vengefulness, venom, vindictiveness *Antonyms:* benevolence, empathy, friendship, goodwill, sympathy

random *adj.* **1.** aimless, arbitrary, casual, desultory, haphazard, hit-and-miss, indiscriminate, purposeless, slapdash, unplanned, unpremeditated *Antonyms:* deliberate, intended, planned, premeditated **2.** accidental, aleatoric, chance, contingent, fluky, fortuitous, incidental, irregular, odd, serendipitous, stray

range *n.* **1.** ambit, area, biosphere, borders, boundaries, bounds, circle, compass, confines, domain, ecosphere, expanse, field, frontier, habitat, jurisdiction, ken, limits, neighbourhood, orbit, province, purview, realm, run, sphere, surface, sweep, territory, vicinity **2.** amplitude, diapason, dimension, distance, edge, extent, gamut, latitude, length, limit, magnitude, maximum, parameter, radius, reach, scope, span, spectrum, spread, stretch, sweep, verge, width **3.** back forty *(Nonformal)*, estate, farm, grassland, grazing ground *or* land, heath, homestead, meadowland, pasturage, pasture, plain, shieling *(Scottish)* **4.** chain, cordillera, mountains, sierra **5.** assortment, class, classification, collection, group, line, lot, order, rank, row, selection, sequence, series, string, tier, variation, variety **6.** Aga *(Trademark)*, cooker, cookstove, stove *See also:* **stove** – *v.* **1.** align, arrange, array, assort, bracket, catalogue, categorize, class, classify, file, grade, group, line up, order, rank, slot, stream **2.** cover, cross, cruise, drift, explore, gallivant, globetrot, journey, knock about *(Nonformal)*, meander, ramble, roam, rove, search, sort, spread, straggle, stray, stroll, sweep, traipse, tramp, travel, traverse, trek, voyage, wander

ranger *n.* caretaker, conservationist, forester, forest *or* park ranger, game warden, guardian, keeper, officer, police, preservationist, preserver, warden *Nonformal:* smokey, yogi

rangy *adj.* gangling, gawky, lanky, lean, leggy, lithe, long, long-legged, long-limbed, reedy, skinny, slender, spindly, tall, thin, weedy *Antonyms:* adipose, pudgy, stout

rank *adj.* **1.** dank, disagreeable, disgusting, evil-smelling, feculent, fetid, foul, funky, fusty, gamy, gross *(Nonformal)*, high, loathsome, malodorous, mephitic, mouldy, musty, nasty, nauseating, noisome, noxious, obnoxious, off, offensive, pungent, putrescent, putrid, rancid, reeking, repulsive, revolting, smelly, sour, stale, stinking, strong, tainted, turned *Antonyms:* ambrosial, aromatic, fragrant, perfumed **2.** atrocious, base, coarse, crass, dirty, filthy, indecent, mean, miserable, monstrous, obscene, outrageous, raunchy, scrofulous, scurrilous, shocking, smutty, uncouth, vicious, vulgar, wicked *Antonyms:* benevolent, gentle, good, kind **3.** absolute, complete, consummate, downright, sheer, stark, total, unmitigated, unqualified, utter, wholesale **4.** excessive, extreme, grievous, iniquitous, unjust **5.** abundant, dense, exuberant, fecund, fertile, flourishing, grown, high-growing, lush, overabundant, overgrown, profuse, prolific, rampant, verdant, vigorous, wild *Antonyms:* barren, depleted, desolate, fruitless, meagre – *n.* **1.** authority, control, dominance, influence, paramountcy, power, primacy, seniority, superiority, supremacy, sway **2.** consequence, degree, dignity, distinction, esteem, honour, prestige, reputation **3.** caste, circumstance, class, estate, family, grade, nobility, pecking order *(Nonformal)*, pedigree, place, position, privilege, quality, rung, situation, standing, station, stature, status, stock, stratum **4.** column, echelon, file, formation, group, line, queue, range, row, sequence, series, string, tier – *v.* **1.** align, arrange, array, assign, assort class, classify, establish, estimate, evaluate, fix, grade, include, judge, line up, list, locate, order, peg, pigeonhole, place, position, range, rate, regard, settle, size up, sort, value **2.** command, head, lead, outrank, reign supreme, rule, stand above, star **3.** antecede, come first, forerun, go before, precede

rank and file *n.* **1.** army, detail, forces, legion, men, military, regiment, soldiery, troops **2.** body politic, citizenry, community, electorate, folk, grassroots, hoi polloi, people, plebs, population, proletariat, public, silent majority, voters, workers

ranked *adj.* arranged, arrayed, catalogued, classified, graded, grouped, hierarchic, indexed, marshalled, methodized, ordered, organized, ranged, regulated, sorted, split, stratified, streamed, systematized *Antonyms:* chaotic, confused, haphazard, jumbled, muddled

ranking *adj.* authority, cardinal, chief, commanding, controlling, dominant, governing, head, highest, leading, managing, master, paramount, predominant, principal, senior, superior, topmost, uppermost *Antonyms:* inferior, insignificant, subordinate – *n.* arrangement, categorization, classification, gradation, grading, grouping, hierarchy, placement, position, rating, sorting, stratification, structure, taxonomy

rankle *v.* aggravate, anger, annoy, bother, bristle, chafe, embitter, exasperate, fester, incense, infuriate, irritate, madden, nettle, peeve, provoke, rile, roil, ruffle, suppurate, vex *Antonyms:* alleviate, mollify, placate, relieve, soothe

ransack *v.* **1.** depredate, despoil, destroy, freeboot, gut, loot, maraud, plunder, raid, rake, ravage, rob, sack, spoil, steal, thieve **2.** comb, forage, foray, hunt, look for, rifle through, rummage, scour, search, shake down *(Nonformal)*

ransom *n.* blackmail, blood money, bribe, compensation, deliverance, expiation, liberation, money, payment, payoff, price, redemption, release, rescue, wergeld – *v.* buy out, deliver, emancipate, extricate, free, liberate, manumit, recover, redeem, regain, release, reprieve, rescue, save, set free

rant *n.* bluster, bombast, demonstration, diatribe, oration, philippic, raving, rhetoric, tantrum, tirade, vociferation, yelling – *v.* bellow, clamour, cry, declaim, fume, harangue, howl, huff, objurgate, rage, rail, rave, roar, scold, scream, shout, sizzle *(Nonformal)*, soapbox, spout, storm, stump, utter, vociferate, yell

rap *n.* **1.** accusation, censure, charge, condemnation, conviction, denunciation, indictment, punishment, recrimination **2.** belt, box, drumming, knock, manual compliment *(Nonformal)*, poke, pop, punch, slap, slash **3.** banter, chat, chit-chat, colloquy, comment, communication, communion, confab, confabulation, conference, conversation, dialogue, discourse, discussion, exchange, gab *(Nonformal)*, palaver, session, spiel, talk, *tête-à-tête (French)*, verbal exchange, words – *v.* **1.** accuse, blame, castigate, censure, condemn, criticize, denounce, denunciate, reprehend, reprimand, reprobate, scold, vilify *Nonformal:* dis, knock, pan, slam, trash *Antonyms:* extol, glorify, laud, praise **2.** beat, blow, crack, fustigate, hit, knock, strike, swat, swipe, tap *Nonformal:* bust, conk, whack **3.** chat, converse, discourse, exchange, exclaim, express, interface, parley, speak, utter, yak *(Nonformal)* **4.** improvise, lyricise, perform, phrase, recite, rhyme, verse, versify

rapacious *adj.* avaricious, gluttonous, grasping, greedy, hungry, insatiable, lupine, marauding, predatory, raptorial, ravenous, voracious, wolfish *Antonyms:* full, sated, satiated, satisfied

rape *n.* criminal attack, defilement, forcible violation, molestation, outrage, perversion, ravishment, sexual assault, statutory offence, victimization, violation, violence – *v.* **1.** abuse, assault, attack, debauch, defile, dishonour, force, maltreat, molest, ravish, violate **2.** burn, clear-cut, denude, destroy, exploit, fleece, invade, lay waste, loot, pillage, plunder, ransack, ravage, raze, rob, sack, steal, strip, waste

rapid *adj.* accelerated, active, agile, breakneck, brisk, express, fast, fleet, flying, hasty, hell-bent *(Nonformal)*, hurried, light-footed, lively, mercurial, nimble, precipitate, prompt, quick, quickened, quick-fire, ready, speedy, spry, swift, winged *Antonyms:* gradual, languid, slow, unhurried

rapidity *n.* acceleration, alacrity, briskness, celerity, dispatch, expedition, fleetness, haste, hurry, precipitateness, promptitude, promptness, quickness, rapidness, speed, speediness, swiftness *Antonyms:* inertia, slowness, sluggishness

rapidly *adv.* briskly, fast, fast and furious, flat out, hastily, hurriedly, immediately, in haste, posthaste, promptly, quickly, speedily, swiftly *Nonformal:* full tilt, lickety-split *Antonyms:* gradually, slowly, unhurriedly

rapids *n. pl. chaudiere (French)*, chute, dells, falls, portage, riffle, sault, white water

rapport *n.* affinity, agreement, bond, compatibility, concord, empathy, harmony, link, relationship, soul, sympathy, togetherness, understanding, unity *Antonyms:* animosity, enmity, hostility

rapscallion *n.* devil, elf, *enfant terrible (French)*, hoodlum, hooligan, imp, knave, menace, minx, miscreant, prankster, rascal, reprobate, rogue, rowdy, ruffian, scamp, scoundrel, sleeveen *(Newfoundland)*, spalpeen, terror *(Nonformal) Antonyms:* angel, darling, saint

rapt *adj.* **1.** beguiled, bewitched, captivated, charmed, enamoured, enraptured, enthralled, entranced, fascinated, overwhelmed, spellbound, taken, transported *Antonyms:* bored, unaffected, uninterested, unmoved **2.** absent-minded, absorbed, abstracted, busy, daydreaming, dreaming, employed, engaged, engrossed, focused, gripped, held, hypnotized, immersed, intent, involved, lost, oblivious, occupied, preoccupied

rapture *n.* bliss, buoyancy, cheer, cloud nine *(Nonformal)*, contentment, delectation, delight, ecstasy, enchantment, enthusiasm, euphoria, exaltation, exhilaration, felicity, gaiety, gladness, gratification, happiness, heaven, inspiration, joy, jubilation, nirvana, passion, pleasure, rhapsody, transport, well-being *Antonyms:* agony, misery, pain, suffering, woe

rapturous *adj.* aux anges *(Nonformal)*, blissful, delighted, ecstatic, euphoric, exhilarated, exultant, happy, high, inspired, joyful, joyous, pleased *Antonyms:* depressed, melancholy, morose

rare *adj.* **1.** admirable, choice, dainty, delicate, elegant, excellent, exquisite, extreme, fine, incomparable, invaluable, notable, outstanding, precious, priceless, *rara avis (Latin)*, recherché, rich, select, superb, superlative, unique *Antonyms:* common, everyday, regular **2.** exceptional, few, infrequent, isolated, limited, occasional, scant, scarce, scattered, seldom, sparse, sporadic, uncommon, unlikely, unusual *Antonyms:* abundant, bountiful, plentiful **3.** bloody, blue, half-cooked, red, underdone *Antonyms:* burnt, charred, well-done

rarely *adv.* almost never, hardly ever, infrequently, little, not often, occasionally, scarcely, seldom *Antonyms:* commonly, frequently, often, usually

rarified *adj.* **1.** airy, attenuated, diaphanous, ethereal, fine, flimsy, gaseous, gauzy, gossamer, insubstantial, papery, slight, thin, unsubstantial, vaporous *Antonyms:* heavy, solid, sound, substantial **2.** august, elevated, grand, great, lofty, majestic, princely, sublime, supreme

rascal *n.* blackguard, bully, cad, charlatan, cheat, delinquent, disgrace, felon, fraud, good-for-nothing, grafter, hooligan, idler, imp, knave, liar, *Loki (Norse)*, mischief-maker, miscreant, mountebank, opportunist, pretender, profligate, rake, rapscallion, raven *(Native peoples)*, reprobate, rogue, rowdy, ruffian, scalawag, scamp, scaramouch, scoundrel, sleeveen *(Newfoundland)*, sneak, swindler, trickster, villain, wastrel *Nonformal:* bastard, holy terror, ugly customer, varmint

rash *adj.* abrupt, adventurous, bold, brash, dangerous, foolhardy, harum-scarum, hasty, heedless, hotheaded, ill-advised, impatient, impetuous, impulsive, incautious, madcap, off the cuff, precipitate reckless, scatterbrain, spontaneous, temerarious, thoughtless, unrestrained *Antonyms:* cautious, chary, planned, prudent – *n.* **1.** blight, breakout, epidemic, eruption, flood, outbreak, plague, profusion, series, succession, spate **2.** blister, eczema, efflorescence, hives, inflammation, itch, psoriasis, ringworm, skin eruption

rasp *n.* file, grater, tool – *v.* **1.** abrade, file *or* rub down, grate, grind, rub, sand, scour, scrape, scratch, wear **2.** aggravate, annoy, beleaguer, bother, chafe, discomfort, fret, inflame, irk, irritate, needle, nettle, peeve, tax, try *Antonyms:* assuage, comfort, soothe

rasping *adj.* **1.** creaky, croaking, deep, grating, gravelly, harsh, hoarse, husky, raspy, rough, scratchy, throaty, whisky *(Nonformal) Antonyms:* harmonious, smooth, soothing **2.** annoying, awful, bothersome, damnable, disconcerting, discordant, disquieting, disturbing, irritating, nerve-wracking, unsettling, upsetting *Nonformal:* blasted, damn, darn, infernal *Antonyms:* calming, comforting, pacifying

rat *n.* **1.** pest, rodent, vermin *Nonformal:* critter, varmint **2.** betrayer, coward, dastard, deserter, hypocrite, informer, liar, rascal, sleeveen *(Newfoundland) Nonformal:* Benedict Arnold, bum, creep, double-dealer, Judas, louse, scumbag, snitch, squealer, stool pigeon, two-face – *v.* betray, inform *or* tell on, turn in *Nonformal:* blab, fink, sing, squeal

rate *n.* **1.** allowance, charge, cost, damage *(Nonformal)*, dues, duty, estimate, fee, figure, hire, money, premium, price, quotation, scale, stumpage *(Forestry)*, tab, tariff, tax, toll, value **2.** amount, calibre, comparison, degree, estimate, percentage, proportion, quota, ratio, relation, standard, valuation, weight, worth **3.** acceleration, clip, flow, gait, klicks *(Nonformal)*, measure, pace, rpms, speed, tempo, time, velocity **4.** class, condition, echelon, footing, grade, level, position, place, standing, station, status – *v.* **1.** adjudge, appraise, assess, calculate, classify, compare, consider, count, deem, determine, esteem, estimate, evaluate, gauge, judge, measure, size up, survey, value, weigh **2.** categorize, classify, peg, position, rank, score, stack, stream

ratification *n.* approval, authorization, backing, confirmation, consent, endorsement, sanction, support, validation *Nonformal:* go-ahead, green light, thumbs up *Antonyms:* censure, decertification, disapproval

rather *adv.* **1.** alternately, by choice *or* preference, first, instead, preferably, sooner **2.** *comme ci comme ça (French)*, comparatively, fairly, moderately, passably, quite, reasonably, relatively, slightly, somewhat, so-so, tolerably

ratify *v.* affirm, approve, authenticate, authorize, bless, certify, commission, confirm, consent, corroborate, endorse, license, rubber-stamp *(Nonformal)*, sanction, sign, substantiate, uphold, validate *Antonyms:* abrogate, annul, cancel, reject, revoke

ratio *n.* arrangement, correlation, correspondence, degree, equation, fraction, percentage, proportion, proportionality, quota, quotient, rate, relation, relationship, scale

ration *n.* allocation, allotment, allowance, apportionment, assignment, batch, bit, chunk, clutch, collop, consignment, cut *(Nonformal)*, distribution, division, dole, helping, measure, modicum, moiety, part, percentage, piece, portion, provision, quota, rasher, regale *(Historical)*, share, slice, stock, store, supply – *v.* allocate, allot, apportion, assign, budget, disperse, distribute, divide, divvy up *(Nonformal)*, issue, limit, mete out, share, split

rational *adj.* analytical, Apollonian, astute, balanced, calm, cerebral, circumspect, cognitive, collected, deductive, deliberate, discerning, discriminating, enlightened, far-sighted, impartial, intelligent, judicious, just, knowing, level-headed, logical, lucid, mental, noetic, objective, philosophic, prudent, realistic, reasonable, reasoning, reflective, sagacious, sane, sensible, sober, sound, stable, thinking, thoughtful, well-advised, wise *Antonyms:* insane, irrational, unreasonable, unsound *Commonly misused:* **rationale**

rationale *n.* **1.** aim, cause, goal, grounds, impulse, motivation, motive, principle, *raison d'être (French)*, reason, thesis, why **2.**

account, defence, excuse, explanation, justification, logic, philosophy, pretense, rationalization, story, the why and wherefore *(Nonformal)*, theory *Commonly misused:* **rational**

rationality *n.* **1.** comprehension, genius, grey cells *or* matter *(Nonformal)*, intellect, intelligence, keenness, logic, mental capacity *or* grasp, mind, ratiocination, reasoning, understanding, wit *Antonyms:* emotion, impulse, instinct, intuition **2.** grounding, level-headedness, lucidity, matter-of-factness, practicality, pragmatism, realism, reasonableness, sanity, sense, sensibleness, sober-mindedness, soundness *Antonyms:* fantasy, foolishness, idealism, romanticism

rationalize *v.* **1.** back, defend, explain, extenuate, ground, justify **2.** clarify, clean up, elucidate, enlighten, harmonize, match up, organize, reconcile, regularize, resolve, settle, systematize **3.** apply logic, cogitate, contemplate, deduce, figure, know, infer, intellectualize, logic, philosophize, ponder, reckon, reflect, suppose, think, understand

rattle *n.* **1.** clank, clatter, din, jangle, noise, racket, vibration **2.** gourd, instrument, noisemaker, plaything, rainstick, shaker, toy – *v.* **1.** bang, bounce, clack, jar, jiggle, jolt, jounce, knock, shake, shatter, vibrate **2.** addle, baffle, bewilder, confuse, disarm, discompose, disconcert, distract, disturb, dumfound, faze, fluster, nonplus, perplex, puzzle, stun, upset *Nonformal:* discombobulate, floor, flummox, fouster *(P.E.I.)* *Antonyms:* calm, soothe, unruffle **3.** blab, blather, chatter, gab, go on and on, prattle, rap, spew, talk

rattlebrained *adj.* addled, bewildered, confused, dazed, flighty, foggy, foolish, giddy, harebrained, inane, muddled, punch-drunk, punchy, scatterbrained, silly *Nonformal:* batty, dippy, dizzy, ditzy, dopey, stunned *Antonyms:* alert, keen, quick-witted, thoughtful

ratty *adj.* **1.** battered, beaten, decrepit, dilapidated, dowdy, frayed, frazzled, moth-eaten, ragged, raggedy, ripped, run-down, scruffy, seedy, shabby, shoddy, shredded, tattered, tatty, torn *Antonyms:* mint, shipshape, unused **2.** cheap, disgraceful, despicable, disreputable, ignominious, infamous, lowly, odious, scandalous, scurvy, shadowy, shameful, shoddy, sordid, vicious *Antonyms:* proper, reformed, respectable

raucous *adj.* **1.** atonal, blaring, braying, cacophonous, discordant, dissonant, ear-piercing, grating, grinding, gruff, harsh, hoarse, inharmonious, jarring, loud, noisy, piercing, rasping, rough, sharp, squawking, strident, whisky-voiced *Antonyms:* dulcet, mellifluous, quiet, smooth, sweet **2.** boisterous, disorderly, riotous, rocking, rollicking, rowdy, tumultuous, unruly, uproarious, wild *Antonyms:* boring, placid, sedate

raunchy *adj.* coarse, dirty, gross, impolite, ithyphallic, lewd, lascivious, lurid, obscene, offensive, pornographic, prurient, Rabelaisian, ribald, salacious, smutty, vile, vulgar, X-rated *Nonformal:* adult, blue *Antonyms:* clean, family-oriented, wholesome

ravage *n.* annihilation, catastrophe, collapse, demolition, desolation, destruction, devastation, disaster, havoc, mutilation, rubble, ruin, ruination, scorched earth, usurpation, war, wreckage – *v.* assault, bomb, consume, crush, damage, demolish, desecrate, despoil, destroy, devastate, dismantle, exterminate, extinguish, gut, impair, lay waste, loot, maraud, overwhelm, pillage, pirate, plunder, prey, raid, ransack, rape, raze, ruin, sack, scourge, shatter, sink, spoil, strip, victimize, waste, wreak havoc, wreck *Nonformal:* nuke, trash *Antonyms:* foster, mend, nurture

rave *adj.* approving, complimentary, enthusiastic, ecstatic, flattering, glowing, happy, kind, positive, solid – *n.* **1.** agitation, excitement, frenzy, fury, outburst, passion, storm **2.** dance, event, fête, happening, party *Nonformal:* all-nighter, bash, barnburner, kegger, love-in – *v.* **1.** babble, drivel, drool, foam, maunder, ramble **2.** bluster, declaim, erupt, explode, harangue, rage, rant, roar, storm, thunder, vent, yell **3.** boost, champion, enthuse, extol, glorify, laud, praise, promote, rhapsodize, talk wildly about, trumpet *Nonformal:* gush, hype *Antonyms:* criticize, degrade, lambaste

ravel *v.* **1.** disentangle, free, loosen, tidy, unravel, unscramble, unsnarl, untangle, untie, untwine, untwist, unweave, unwind **2.** clarify, crack, decode, deduce, elucidate, explain, illustrate, interpret, simplify, spell out, solve *Antonyms:* blur, confuse, muddle, tangle

raven *adj.* black, charcoal, ebony, inky, jet, pitch-black, sloe – *n.* **1.** blackbird, carrion *or* flesh eater, crow, omnivore, rook **2.** cosmic joker *(Nonformal)*, mischief-maker, nuisance, prankster, troublemaker *See also:* **trickster**

ravenous *adj.* **1.** avaricious, covetous, desirous, devouring, gluttonous, grasping, greedy, insatiable, predatory, voracious, wolfish **2.** famished, half-starved, hungry, starving, underfed *Antonyms:* content, full, sated, satisfied

ravine *n.* abyss, *arroyo (Spanish)*, canyon, chasm, cirque, coulee, crevice, dell, dingle, ditch, draw, droke *(Newfoundland)*, fissure, flume, gap, gorge, gulch, gulf, gully, kloof, nullah, pass, rift, valley, wadi

raving *adj.* **1.** berserk, crazed, crazy, delirious, deranged, frantic, frenzied, furious, hysterical, incoherent, insane, irate, irrational, mad, maniacal, manic, possessed, rabid, raging, unhinged, violent *Nonformal:* batty, bonkers, off one's nut *Antonyms:* rational, reasonable, sane **2.** breathtaking comely, dazzling, gorgeous, handsome, lovely, ravishing, striking, stunning *Nonformal:* car-stopping, drop-dead *Antonyms:* blowzy, frightening, scary

ravish *v.* **1.** allure, attract, bewitch, captivate, charm, delight, draw, enchant, enrapture, enthral, entrance, fascinate, hold, hypnotize, magnetize, mesmerize, overjoy, please, spellbind, transport *Antonyms:* deter, repel, repulse, revolt **2.** abduct, abuse, assault, defile, deflower, despoil, force, outrage, rape, seduce, victimize, violate

ravishing *adj.* alluring, appealing, attractive, beautiful, beguiling, bewitching, breathtaking, captivating, charismatic, charming, enchanting, enticing, entrancing, fascinating, fetching, gorgeous, hypnotic, intoxicating, intriguing, mesmerizing, pulchritudinous, seductive, sexy, spellbinding, striking *Antonyms:* dowdy, homely, plain, unattractive

raw *adj.* **1.** natural, organic, pure, unfinished, unprocessed, unrefined, unstained, untreated, virgin *Antonyms:* aged, finished, matured, mellowed, ripe **2.** callow, fresh, green, ignorant, immature, inexperienced, new, nonconversant, unpracticed, unripe, unskilled, untaught, untrained, untried, young *Antonyms:* experienced, practiced, professional, seasoned, skilled **3.** abraded, bruised, chafed, cut, exposed, grazed, naked, nude, open, pared, peeled, scraped, scratched, sensitive, skinned, sore, tender, uncovered, wounded **4.** arctic, biting, bitter, bleak, breezy, chilly, cold, damp, dirty *(Nonformal)*, freezing, harsh, northern, piercing, unpleasant, wet, windy *Antonyms:* balmy, gentle, mild, temperate **5.** coarse, crass, crude, dirty, filthy, foul, gross, indecent, inelegant, nasty, obscene, pornographic, rank, rough, rude, smutty, unscrupulous, vulgar *Antonyms:* genteel, nice, refined **6.** bloody, blue, rare, red, unbaked, uncooked, underdone **7.** cruel, fell, hard, harsh, heartless, mean, ruthless, tyrannical, unfair *Antonyms:* kind, merciful, sympathetic

ray *n.* **1.** bar, beam, blaze, blink, column, emanation, flash, flicker, gleam, glimmer, glint, glitter, hint, moonbeam, patch, shine, sparkle, streak, stream **2.** cosmic ray bombardment, electron shower, energy, radiation, wavelength *Kinds of ray:* actinic, alpha, anode, Becquerel, canal, cathode, cosmic, gamma, nuclear, positive, roentgen, X-ray

raze *v.* bulldoze, clear-cut, decimate, delete, demolish, destroy, dynamite, erase, extinguish, fell, flatten, level, moonscape *(Pacific Coast)*, obliterate, overturn, rape, ravage, reduce, ruin, scatter, smash, topple, total *(Nonformal)*, wreck

reach *n.* **1.** ambit, breadth, compass, depth, diapason, distance, gap, height, interval, latitude, length, measure, radius, range, scope, space, span, spectrum, stretch **2.** authority, charge, command, control, dominion, hold, importance, influence, jurisdiction, network, power, pull, rule **3.** ability, capacity, comprehension, experience, grasp, knowledge, potential, skill level, understanding – *v.* **1.** approach, communicate, call, contact, get, interface, phone, speak to, touch base, visit **2.** accomplish, achieve, amount to, arrive at, attain, climb, gain, make, realize, rise, score, win **3.** affect, get through *or* to, impress, influence, move, stimulate, sway, touch

react *v.* **1.** act, behave, deal with, manage, respond **2.** answer, counter, reciprocate, rejoin, requite, retaliate, retort, return **3.** blanch, flinch, jerk, recoil, shy, start, wince

reaction *n.* **1.** answer, backtalk, comeback, echo, rejoinder, reply, response, retort **2.** regression, retroaction, retrogression, return, reversion **3.** conclusion, consequence, effect, outcome, reflex, result, upshot **4.** backlash, counterattack, just rewards *(Nonformal)*, kickback, payback, reprisal, requital, retaliation

reactionary *adj.* obstructionist, old-line, orthodox, regressive, rigid, traditional, unyielding *Antonyms:* liberal, progressive, rebellious – *n.* counter-revolutionary, diehard, extremist, fundamentalist, intransigent, mossback *(Nonformal)*, opponent, ultraconservative *Antonyms:* reformer, reformist, revolutionary

reactor *n.* atomic *or* reactor pile, chain-reacting pile, chain reactor, nuclear reactor *Kinds of nuclear reactor:* boiling water, breeder, CANDU, Canada deuterium oxide-uranium reactor, gas-cooled, heterogeneous, homogeneous, plutonium, power-breeder, power, pressurized-water, stellator, uranium

read *v.* **1.** apprehend, busy oneself *(Nonformal)*, comprehend, examine, judge, look over, peruse, review, scan, view **2.** announce, exclaim, express, narrate, pronounce, report, tell **3.** concentrate *or* focus on, devour, learn, memorize, practice, prepare, research, specialize in, study **4.** gauge, indicate, mark, point to, register, represent, show, specify **5.** appraise, estimate, interpret, judge, size up, take one's measure

readable *adj.* **1.** easy, engaging, engrossing, enjoyable, entertaining, enthralling, exciting, fascinating, graphic, gratifying, gripping, interesting, inviting, pleasant, pleasurable, stimulating, well-written *Antonyms:* boring, confusing, dull, incomprehensible **2.** clear, coherent, comprehensible, decipherable, distinct, explicit, flowing, fluent, intelligible, legible, lucid, orderly, plain, simple, smooth, straightforward, understandable *Antonyms:* illegible, indecipherable, obscure

reader *n.* **1.** bibliophile, bluestocking, booklover, bookworm, intellectual, lector, literate, peruser, scholar, student, subscriber **2.** anthology, bible *(Nonformal)*, book, course kit, Festschrift, *florilegium (Latin)*, hornbook, manual, primer, text, textbook

readily *adv.* **1.** cheerfully, eagerly, easily, effortlessly, freely, gladly, lightly, smoothly, willingly, without difficulty *Nonformal:* hands down, like nothing, no sweat, swimmingly **2.** at once, facilely, immediately, promptly, quickly, right away, speedily, straight away, unhesitatingly, without delay *or* hesitation

readiness *n.* **1.** alacrity, dispatch, haste, promptness, punctuality, quickness, swiftness *Antonyms:* delay, hesitation, sluggishness **2.** cheer, compliance, consent, cooperation, desire, enthusiasm, gladness, goodwill, happiness, willingness *Antonyms:* rebellion, recalcitrance, reluctance **3.** ability, aptitude, capability, competence, experience, facility, knack, knowledge, proficiency, skill *Antonyms:* incompetence, ineptitude **4.** bent, bias, inclination, leaning, proclivity, tendency, vulnerability **5.** maturity, preparedness, ripeness

reading *n.* **1.** address, discourse, discussion, lecture, narration, oration, performance, presentation, recital, rendering, speech, talk **2.** education, erudition, knowledge, research, scholarship, schooling, study, understanding **3.** book, chapter, citation, entry, excerpt, extract, journal, manuscript, matter, paper, passage, phrase, piece, position paper, psalm, quotation, section, selection, text, verse, work **4.** interpretation, judgment, observation, rendering, view *Nonformal:* spin, take

ready *adj.* **1.** able, conditioned, equipped, fit, prepared, set, waiting *Antonyms:* caught napping *(Nonformal)*, unorganized, unprepared **2.** agreeable, ardent, disposed, eager, enthusiastic, fain, happy, inclined, keen, willing, zealous *Nonformal:* game, psyched, wired *Antonyms:* disinclined, hesitant, loath, reluctant, unwilling **3.** destined, expected, fated, liable, likely, odds-on *(Nonformal)*, predisposed, probable, prone, tending **4.** expeditious, fleet, immediate, instantaneous, nimble, prompt, quick, rapid, responsive, speedy, swift, timely, winged *Antonyms:* ponderous, sleepy, slow **5.** accessible, at hand, available, close, convenient, handy, near **6.** active, acute, adept, adroit, alert, apt, astute, bright, brilliant, clever, deft, dexterous, dynamic, expert, facile, intelligent, keen, masterly, perceptive, proficient, quick-witted, resourceful, sharp, skilful, smart **7.** mature, old enough, of age, ripe, seasoned – *interj.* attention, fire in the hole *(Blasting)*, get set, on your mark *Nonformal:* buck up, this is it – *v.* arrange, brace, brief, equip, fill in, fit, fix, fortify, gear up, get ready, make ready, order, organize, outfit, post, prep, prepare, strengthen, study

ready-made *adj.* **1.** factory-made, fast-frozen, mass-produced, microwaveable, off-the-rack, off-the-shelf, precooked, prefabricated, prepared, *prêt-à-porter (French)*, ready-to-wear, store-bought *Antonyms:* customized, custom-made, personalized **2.** banal, borrowed, clichéd, common, exhausted, hackneyed, overused, pedestrian, regular, shopworn, stale, stock, threadbare, tired, trite *Nonformal:* dusty, old-hat *Antonyms:* cutting-edge, novel, original

real *adj.* **1.** absolute, actual, authentic, bona fide, certain, *de facto (Latin)*, echt, essential, factual, genuine, honest-to-goodness *(Nonformal)*, indubitable, irrefutable, legitimate, original, positive, pukka, rightful, simon-pure, true, undeniable, undoubted, valid, veritable *Antonyms:* counterfeit, fake, false **2.** appreciable, bodily, concrete, corporeal, embodied, evident, existent, existing, extant, firm, incarnate, live, material, obvious, palpable, perceptible, physical, solid, sound, stable, substantive, tangible *Antonyms:* fantastic, imaginary, immaterial **3.** artless, childlike, honest, pure, simple, sincere, straightforward, unaffected, unpretentious, up front *Antonyms:* feigned, insincere, shallow, specious

realism *n.* actuality, authenticity, fidelity, genuineness, lifelikeness, literalness, naturalism, truthfulness, verisimilitude, verism *Antonyms:* fantasy, idealism, romanticism

realistic *adj.* **1.** astute, businesslike, common-sense, down-to-earth, earthy, hard, hard-boiled *(Nonformal)*, level-headed, matter-of-fact, practical, pragmatic, prudent, rational, real, reasonable, sane, sensible, shrewd, sober, sound, unromantic, utilitarian *Antonyms:* idealistic, impractical, utopian **2.** authentic, faithful, genuine, graphic, lifelike, natural, original, representational, representative, true-to-life, truthful, virtual *Antonyms:* false, fanciful, imaginary

reality *n.* absolute truth, actuality, authenticity, certainty, concreteness, existence, facts, genuineness, matter, perceptibility, phenomenon, sensibility, solidity, sooth *(Historical)*, substance, substantiality, tangibility, truth, validity, verisimilitude *Antonyms:* fiction, falsehood, lies, make-believe

realizable *adj.* achievable, attainable, feasible, obtainable, operable, plausible, possible, practical, reachable, surmountable, viable, within the realm of possibility, workable *Antonyms:* absurd, impossible, improbable, ridiculous

realization *n.* **1.** accomplishment, achievement, closure, completion, consummation, culmination, effectuation, execution, *fait accompli (French)*, fruition, fulfilment, performance, success *Antonyms:* disaster, failure, loss **2.** appreciation, awareness, cognizance, comprehension, consciousness, discernment, identification, knowledge, recognition, understanding

realize *v.* **1.** earn, accomplish, achieve, acquire, attain, bring in, clear, gain, get, make, merit, net, obtain, pick up, produce, rack up *(Nonformal)*, reach, receive, score, take in, win **2.** appreciate, apprehend, become aware, comprehend, conceive, discover, envision, feature, grasp, imagine, know, learn, recognize, think, understand, visualize *Nonformal:* catch, dig, tumble to

really *adv.* absolutely, actually, admittedly, assuredly, authentically, beyond doubt, categorically, certainly, *de facto (Latin)*, easily, for all practical purposes, genuinely, in essence, indubitably, in fact, legitimately, positively, seriously, truly, undoubtedly, verily – *interj.* are you serious, come on, is that so, no fooling, well, I declare, I'll be, you're kidding

realm *n.* area, arena, bailiwick, circle, demesne, department, discipline, district, division, domain, dominion, field, habitat, jurisdiction, kingdom, land, milieu, monarchy, neighbourhood, orb, orbit, palatinate, principality, province, region, scope, section, space, sphere, state, territory, zone *Nonformal:* beat, neck of the woods, turf

reap *v.* acquire, bring in, collect, crop, cull, cut, derive, draw, gain, garner, gather, get, glean, harvest, mow, obtain, pick, pick up, pluck, procure, produce, profit, realize, receive, recover, retrieve, score, secure, take in, win *Antonyms:* distribute, lose, scatter, sow

rear *adj.* aft, after, astern, back, behind, dorsal, following, hind, hindmost, last, rearmost, rearward, reverse, stern, tail *Antonyms:* foremost, forward, front, leading – *n.* **1.** back, back door, back end, back part, butt, butt-end, end, end part, heel, hind end, hind part, rear end, reverse, stern, tail end, tailpiece *Antonyms:* bow, front, nose, stem **2.** backside, behind, bottom, buttocks, *derrière (French)*, gluteus maximus, hindquarters, posterior, rump, seat, tail *Nonformal:* arse, bum, buns, caboose, duff, fanny, keister, patootie – *v.* **1.** elevate, hoist, lift, raise, set upright **2.** assemble, build, construct, engineer, erect, fabricate, fashion, forge, frame, produce, shape **3.** breed, bring up, care for, cultivate, educate, father, foster, grow, look after, mother, nurture, parent, school, support, take in hand, tend, train **4.** buck, jump *or* rise up, paw the air **5.** arise, emerge, loom, tower, overshadow, take shape

rearrange *v.* adjust, alter, change, fix, modify, morph *(Nonformal)*, reconfigure, reengineer, refit, reform, rejig, reorder, reorganize, reshape, retool, revamp *Antonyms:* accept, stet, tolerate

reason *n.* **1.** antecedent, basis, cause, determinant, foundation, ground, impetus, incentive, motive, purpose, root, spring, why **2.** argument, defence, excuse, explanation, justification, proof, rationale, vindication **3.** apprehension, awareness, cognition, comprehension, consideration, deduction, induction, inference, intellect, intuition, judgment, logic, lucidity, mentality, mind, ratiocination, rationality, reasoning, sanity, sense, thought, understanding **4.** acumen, brains, common sense, discernment, good judgment, moderation, practicality, pragmatism, sagacity, sensibility, shrewdness, wisdom – *v.* **1.** analyze, cogitate, conclude, contemplate, deduce, deliberate, establish, examine, expostulate, gather, infer, intellectualize, justify, presume, rationalize, reckon, reflect, resolve, solve, speculate, study, suppose, think **2.** argue, contend, debate, demonstrate, discourse, discuss, dispute, remonstrate, syllogize **3.** bring around, convert, dissuade, guide, induce, influence, move, persuade, prejudice, prompt, push, urge, win over

reasonable *adj.* **1.** common-sensical, equitable, fair, honourable, honest, impartial, judicious, just, level-headed, moderate, practical, sensible, sober, sound, temperate, thoughtful, tolerant, unbiased, unprejudiced, wise *Antonyms:* biased, cruel, fell, partisan **2.** believable, condonable, credible, justifiable, legitimate, plausible, politic, proper, sound, tenable, understandable, valid, warrantable *Antonyms:* indefensible, inexcusable, unacceptable **3.** accessible, affordable, budget, cheap, cut-rate, economical, inexpensive, mid-range, modest, reduced, thrifty *Antonyms:* dear, outrageous, pricey, stiff **4.** acceptable, admissible, allowable, average, common, feasible, passable, satisfactory, sufficient, tolerable *Nonformal:* okay, so-so *Antonyms:* intolerable, ludicrous, ridiculous **5.** analytical, cerebral, cognitive, conscious, deductive, enlightened, inductive, intelligent, logical, lucid, perceiving, rational, reasoned, reasoning, reflective, sane, sapient, thinking

reasoning *n.* acumen, analysis, argument, case, cogitation, conclusion, corollary, deduction, dialectics, exposition, generalization, hypothesis, induction, inference, interpretation, logic, premise, proof, proposition, ratiocination, rationale, rationalizing, sophistry, thinking, thought

reassure *v.* aid, assure, bolster, brace *or* buoy up, cheer, comfort, console, encourage, fortify, give confidence, guarantee, hearten, inspire, praise, rally, relieve, restore *Antonyms:* deflate, disconcert, humble

rebate *n.* allowance, bonus, cashback, cutback, discount, kickback, reduction, refund, reimbursement, remittance, repayment

rebel *adj.* insubordinate, insurgent, insurrectionary, mutinous, noncompliant, rebellious, recalcitrant, refractory, resistant, revolutionary, schismatic – *n.* anarchist, antagonist, dissenter, dissident, fifth column, guerrilla, heretic, iconoclast, independent, individualist, innovator, Luddite, malcontent, maverick, mutineer, nihilist, nonconformist, renegade, resister, revolutionary, rioter, saboteur, secessionist, separatist, traitor, underground agent – *v.* counter, criticize, defy, denounce, disobey, dissent, fight, make waves *(Nonformal)*, mutiny, oppose, overthrow, overturn, refuse, renounce, resist, revolt, riot, rise up, run amok, secede, undermine, upset *Antonyms:* accept, concede, obey, respect, tolerate

rebellion *n.* apostasy, civil unrest, coup, *coup d'état (French)*, defiance, disobedience, dissent, heresy, insubordination, insurgency, insurrection, nonconformity, overthrow, revolt, revolution, sit-in, uprising *Historical Canadian rebellions:* Lower Canada, Northwest, Red River, Upper Canada

rebellious *adj.* anarchical, anarchistic, balky, bellicose, contrary, contumacious, defiant, difficult, disloyal, disobedient, disorderly, dissident, dissentious, fractious, iconoclastic, incorrigible, insurgent, intractable, mutinous, quarrelsome, radical, recalcitrant, refractory, resistant, riotous, seditious, threatening, treasonous, turbulent, ungovernable, unruly, warring *Antonyms:* dutiful, loyal, patriotic, subordinate, subservient

rebirth *n.* **1.** reformation, regeneration, rejuvenation, renaissance, renewal, resurgence, resurrection, resuscitation, revival **2.** baptism, catharsis, cleansing, conversion, purification, religious experience **3.** metempsychosis, palingenesis, reincarnation, transmigration

rebound *n.* carom, comeback, deflection, echo, kick *(Nonformal)*, resonance, recoil, reflection, repercussion, return, reverberation, ricochet – *v.* **1.** backfire, boomerang, bounce, deflect, echo, react, recoil, reflect, repercuss, respond, reverberate, ricochet **2.** bounce back, convalesce, heal, improve, overcome, regain, rejuvenate, restore, revive *Antonyms:* decay, deteriorate, worsen

rebuff *n.* brush-off *(Nonformal)*, defeat, denial, opposition, rebuke, refusal, rejection, snub *Antonyms:* acceptance, welcome – *v.* beat *or* fend *or* ward off, check, chide, cut, decline, deny, disallow, discourage, dismiss, disregard, ignore, neglect, oppose, rebuke, refuse, reject, repel, reprove, repudiate, repulse, resist, scoff, slight, snub, spurn, turn away *or* down *Antonyms:* encourage, entice, lead on, submit

rebuild *v.* fix, overhaul, reassemble, recondition, reconstruct, recreate, redo, refashion, remake, remodel, renovate, repair, restore, restructure, retool *Antonyms:* demolish, destroy, junk

rebuke *n.* admonishment, admonition, berating, castigation, censure, chastisement, condemnation, correction, criticism, disapproval, expostulation, objurgation, punishment, rating, rebuff, refusal, remonstrance, reprehension, reproach, reproof, repulse, scolding, snub, upbraiding *Nonformal:* bawling *or* chewing out, comeuppance, earful, put down, talking-to, tongue-lashing *Antonyms:* commendation, compliment, praise – *v.* admonish, berate, blame, card *(P.E.I.)*, castigate, chide, criticize, deride, hector, lay into, lecture, oppose, punish, rake, reprehend, reprimand, reprove, rip into *(Nonformal)*, scold, upbraid *Antonyms:* applaud, approve, congratulate

rebuttal *n.* **1.** answer, argument, comeback, counter, counterargument, counterstatement, parry, rejoinder, response, retaliation, retort, return, riposte **2.** confutation, contradiction, denial, invalidation, negation, opposition, refutation, subversion

recalcitrant *adj.* contrary, contumacious, defiant, discontent, disobedient, dissenting, fractious, headstrong, insubordinate, insurgent, mutinous, noncompliant, nonconforming, obstinate, obstreperous, ornery, rebellious, recusant, refractory, resistant, stubborn, undisciplined, unruly, wayward, willful *Antonyms:* acquiescent, mild, obedient, submissive – *n.* dissident, insurgent, malcontent, maverick, nonconformist, protester, rebel, renegade, resister

recall *n.* **1.** memory, nostalgia, recognition, recollection, remembrance, reminiscence, retrospect, retrospection *Antonyms:* amnesia, forgetfulness, obliviousness **2.** annulment, cancellation, nullification, retraction, revocation – *v.* **1.** arouse, awaken, bethink, bring *or* flash *or* harken *or* look back, cite, elicit, evoke, extract, kindle, recollect, recognize, reestablish, reintroduce, remember, remind, reminisce, renew, revive, rouse, stir, summon, think of, waken **2.** annul, call back, cancel, countermand, dismiss, disqualify, forswear, nullify, repeal, rescind, retract, reverse, revoke, withdraw

recant *v.* abjure, abnegate, abrogate, annul, back down *or* off *or* out, backtrack, countermand, deny, dial back *(Nonformal)*, disavow, forswear, nullify, renege, renounce, repeal, repudiate, rescind, retract, revoke, take back, withdraw *Antonyms:* maintain, reaffirm, reiterate, repeat, restate

recapitulate *v.* enumerate, iterate, recap, recount, reexamine, rehash, repeat, rephrase, replay, rerun, restate, review, revisit, reword, summarize, sum up

recede *v.* abate, decline, decrease, diminish, dwindle, ebb, lapse, lessen, reduce, regress, retire, retreat, return, revert, shrink, subside, wane, withdraw *Antonyms:* advance, proceed, progress, wax

receipt *n.* **1.** acknowledgment, bill, certificate, check, chit, proof of payment, quittance, stub, tab, voucher **2.** cash, draw earnings, gain, gross, income, money, payment, pickings, remittance, remuneration returns, revenue, reward, spoils, take **3.** acceptance, acknowledgment, admission avowal, confirmation **4.** acquisition, control, possession, reception, retention

receive *v.* **1.** accept, acquire, appropriate arrogate, assume, collect, come by *or* into derive, earn, gain, gather, get, grab, inherit make, obtain, pocket, procure, pull, reap redeem, secure, seize, snag, take in, wi[n] *Nonformal:* catch, cop *Antonyms:* bestow give away, relinquish **2.** bear, carry encounter, endure, experience, feel, shoulder, suffer, sustain, tolerate, undergo, withstand, witness **3.** comprise, contain embrace, hold **4.** accommodate, comfort entertain, greet, harbour, host, house, induct initiate, install, introduce, invite, meet, permit, shelter, show *or* take *or* usher in, welcome **5.** apprehend, comprehend, know perceive, 10-4 *(Nonformal)*, understand

recent *adj.* contemporary, current, fashionable, fresh, in, in vogue, just out, latter-day modern, modish, new, newfangled, novel present-day, the latest, trendy, up-to-date *Antonyms:* ancient, antiquated, dated

recently *adv.* afresh, anew, currently, freshly, just now, lately, latterly, new, newly, of late

receptacle *n.* **1.** ashtray, bag, barrel, basket, bowl, box, can, container, flask, glass hamper, hanaper, holder, hopper, jar, mickey, ossuary, pail, reliquary, repository, silent butler, tote, trashcan, urn, vessel **2.** electric outlet, hydro, power *(Nonformal)*, socket

reception *n.* **1.** assembly, celebration, do *(Nonformal)*, durbar *(Historical)*, fête formal, gathering, get-together, launch levee, party, reunion, social, soirée **2.** acceptance, acknowledgment, admission reaction, receipt, response **3.** encounter greeting, introduction, meeting, salutation welcome

receptive *adj.* **1.** amenable, favourable impressionable, inclined, influenceable interested, malleable, open, open-minded, ready, suggestible, susceptible, swayable *Antonyms:* biased, narrowminded, prejudiced **2.** accepting, accessible, amiable, approachable, friendly, hospitable, sympathetic, welcoming, well-disposed *Antonyms:* cold, intolerant, unneighbourly **3.** alert, attentive, observant, perceptive, responsive, sensitive

recess *n.* **1.** break, breather, breathing spell, cessation, closure, cutoff, halt, hiatus, holiday, interlude, intermission, interregnum, interval, letup, lull, pause, remission, respite, rest, statutory holiday, stop, suspension, time-out, vacation **2.** alcove, apse, bay, cell, closet, corner, cove, cranny, cubbyhole, cubicle, cutout, hidey-hole *(Nonformal)*, hiding place, hole, hollow, indentation, niche, nook, oriel – *v.* adjourn, break, call time, desist, discontinue, dissolve, interrupt, prorogue, rise, stop, suspend, terminate *Nonformal:* knock off, take five *or* ten *Antonyms:* continue, endure, persevere, persist

recession *n.* bad times, bear market, collapse, decline, deflation, downturn, miniregression *or* minislump, reversal, slide, slump, stagnation, withdrawal *Antonyms:* boom, bull market, growth, upturn

recherché *adj.* **1.** choice, elegant, exceptional, exemplary, exquisite, extraordinary, fine, individual, one-of-a-kind, polished, rare, refined, remarkable, singular, special, *sui generis (Latin)*, tasteful *Antonyms:* common, everyday, household, plain **2.** bizarre, crazy, fantastic, incredible, kooky *(Nonformal)*, outlandish, outrageous, queer, strange, wild **3.** abstruse, alien, arcane, exotic, far-fetched, foreign, little-known, obscure, recondite, unfamiliar

recipe *n.* directions, formula, ingredients, instructions, list, makings, method, prescription, procedure, process, program, Rx, technique

reciprocal *adj.* **1.** common, dependent, exchanged, interdependent, mutual, shared, two-way *Antonyms:* one-sided, unilateral **2.** alternate, changeable, companion, complementary, convertible, coordinate, correlative, corresponding, double, duplicate, equivalent, exchangeable, interchangeable, matching, similar *Antonyms:* divergent, opposite

reciprocate *v.* **1.** alternate, exchange, flip, interchange, platoon, rotate, share, substitute, swap, switch, take turns **2.** bandy, counter, give back, requite, respond, retaliate, return *Nonformal:* eye for an eye, tit for tat **3.** complement, correlate, correspond, match, mirror, reflect

recital *n.* **1.** account, address, delivery, description, detailing, discourse, enumeration, lecture, monologue, narration, oration, portrayal, reading, recitation, recounting, relating, rendering, repetition, report, soliloquy, statement, story, tale, telling **2.** concert, musical, musicale, performance, presentation, rehearsal, selection, show, solo

recite *v.* **1.** declaim, deliver, describe, discourse, dramatize, expatiate, explain, hold forth, impart, mention, narrate, parrot, perform, quote, read, recount, reel off, rehearse, relate, render, repeat, reply, report, retell, soliloquize, speak, state, tell, utter *Nonformal:* spiel, spout **2.** catalogue, delineate, detail, enumerate, itemize, recapitulate

reckless *adj.* adventurous, audacious, brash, breakneck, careless, daredevil, daring, death-defying, devil-may-care, disorderly, feckless, foolhardy, foolish, haphazard, harebrained, heedless, ill-advised, imprudent, impulsive, incautious, inconsiderate, indiscreet, irresponsible, madcap, negligent, out of control, pell-mell, precipitate, rash, runaway, silly, thoughtless, tumultuous, uncontrolled, venturesome, wild *Nonformal:* cowboy, fast-and-loose, insane *Antonyms:* careful, cautious, heedful, mindful, wary

recklessness *n.* audacity, boldness, desperation, foolhardiness, foolishness, haste, heedlessness, insanity, madness, rashness, temerity, wildness *Antonyms:* circumspection, wariness

reckon *v.* **1.** appraise, calculate, compute, count, count noses *(Nonformal)*, figure, score, tally, tot *or* tote up **2.** believe, consider, expect, gather, guess, hope, imagine, interpret, opine, presume, regard, suppose, surmise, suspect, think, view

reckoning *n.* **1.** addition, arithmetic, calculation, ciphering, computation, count, estimate, estimation, figuring, statement, sum, tabulation, total **2.** account, bill, charge, cost, damage *(Nonformal)*, debt, due, fee, invoice, IOU, score, settlement, tab **3.** atonement, judgment, payment, recompense

reclaim *v.* bring *or* take *or* win back, redeem, regain, repatriate, retrieve, recover, recondition, reform, rescue, restore, salvage

recline *v.* cant, heel, keel, lay down, lean, lie, lie down, list, loll, lounge, repose, rest, slant, slope, slouch, slump, sprawl, stretch, stretch out, tilt, tip *Antonyms:* rise, stand

recluse *adj.* alienated, cloistered, estranged, immured, isolated, lonely, retiring, secluded, sequestered, solitary – *n.* anchorite, ascetic, eremite, hermit, holy person, introvert, isolationist, loner, monk, opt-out *(Nonformal)*, solitudinarian, troglodyte

reclusive *adj.* antisocial, ascetic, cloistered, hermetic, isolated, misanthropic, monastic, reserved, retiring, secluded, sequestered, solitary, standoffish, unsociable, withdrawn *Antonyms:* friendly, gregarious, outgoing, sociable

recognition *n.* **1.** apprehension, awareness, cognizance, comprehension, consciousness, detection, discernment, discovery, double-take, identification, memory, notice, perception, realization, recall, recollection, remembrance, sensibility, understanding **2.** appreciation, credit, due, gratitude, honour, pat on the back, respect, thanks *Antonyms:* neglect, rejection, veto **3.** acceptance, admission, allowance, approval, certification, endorsement, exequatur, okay *(Nonformal)*, sanction **4.** acknowledgment, attention, avowal, esteem, greeting, hello, nod, salutation, salute, tribute, welcome *Antonyms:* slight, snub, spurn

recognize *v.* **1.** accept, acknowledge, admit, agree, allow, approve, assent, avow, concede, confess, grant, honour, respec *Antonyms:* forget, ignore, neglect, over look **2.** appreciate, comprehend, discern follow, grasp, know, realize, tumble t *(Nonformal)*, understand **3.** distinguish finger, identify, know again, pinpoint place, recall, recollect, remember, verif *Nonformal:* make, nail, peg, tab, tag **4** apprehend, espy, note, notice, observe, per ceive, see, sight, spot

recoil *n.* backlash, counteraction, kic *(Nonformal)*, rebound – *v.* **1.** balk, cringe dodge, draw back, duck, falter, flinch, hesi tate, quail, quake, react, shrink, tremble waver, withdraw **2.** backfire, bounce carom, kick, rebound, ricochet, sprin back

recollect *v.* awaken, bethink, call to mind cite, evoke, kindle, recall, recognize reflect, remember, reminisce, retrospect revive, rouse, stir

recommend *v.* **1.** applaud, approve, back celebrate, commend, compliment, confirm endorse, esteem, exalt, extol, favour, laud mention in dispatches *(Historical)*, plug praise, sanction, second, select, support uphold *Antonyms:* blacklist, censure, dis approve **2.** advance, advise, advocate counsel, enjoin, exhort, prescribe, propose put forward, suggest, urge

recommendation *n.* **1.** advice, counse criticism, guidance, instruction, judgment proposal, say-so *(Nonformal)*, suggestion tip, urging, wisdom **2.** advocacy, approval blessing, character reference, commenda tion, endorsement, esteem, favourabl mention, good word, plug, praise, refer ence, sanction, support, testimonial

recompense *n.* **1.** allowance, amends atonement, awards, commission, compen sation, due, indemnity, just reward, pay payment, redress, remittance, remunera tion, requital, restitution, salary, stipend wage **2.** amends, atonement, blood money indemnity, quittance, redress, requital restitution, retribution, wergild – *v.* **1** award, compensate, pay, reimburse, remu nerate, repay, requite, reward **2.** atone, bal ance, compensate, fix, make amends, rem edy, right, return, square

reconcile *v.* **1.** bury the hatchet, come together, conciliate, make peace *or* up, mend, mend fences, patch up *(Nonformal)*, placate, propitiate, reestablish relations, reunite, settle one's differences **2.** accept, capitulate, cede, give in, make the best of, resign, resolve, roll with the punches *(Nonformal)*, submit, succumb, yield **3.** arbitrate, bridge the gap *(Nonformal)*, bring around *or* to terms, intercede, intervene, mediate **4.** accommodate, adjust, arrange, conform, correspond, harmonize, make compatible, settle *or* square up *(Nonformal)*, tally

reconciliation *n.* adjustment, agreement, appeasement, compromise, conciliation, détente, harmony, mediation, pax, peace, *rapprochement (French)*, resolution, reunion, settlement, truce *Antonyms:* battle, divorce, enmity, estrangement, separation

recondite *adj.* abstruse, academic, arcane, cabalistic, concealed, cryptic, dark, deep, difficult, erudite, esoteric, hermetic, hidden, learned, little-known, mysterious, obscure, profound, secret *Antonyms:* common, simple, straightforward

recondition *v.* doctor *(Nonformal)*, fix, make over, mend, overhaul, patch, rectify, redo, refurbish, remodel, renew, renovate, repair, restore, retrofit, revamp *Antonyms:* demolish, destroy, junk

reconfigure *v.* rearrange, reengineer, reform, rejig, reorder, reorganize, reset, reshape, restructure, retool, streamline

reconnaissance *n.* analysis, espionage, examination, exploration, inspection, investigation, once-over *(Nonformal)*, patrol, perusal, preview, probe, scrutiny, study, surveillance, survey, walkaround

reconnoitre *v.* check, check out, examine, investigate, monitor, observe, peep, peruse, preview, probe, scan, scout, scout out, scrutinize, size up, spy, study, survey, view, watch *Nonformal:* get the lay of the land, recce, see what's happening, walk the course

reconsider *v.* amend, brush up, correct, emend, have another look, reassess, reevaluate, reexamine, replan, rethink, retrace, review, revise, reweigh, rework, take under advisement, think better of, think twice

reconstruct *v.* **1.** make over, reassemble, rebuild, recast, recondition, reconstitute, recreate, refashion, replace, restore, rework **2.** copy, piece together, redo, repeat, replicate, reproduce

record *adj.* best, biggest, capital, champion, chief, finest, first, greatest, leading, paramount, top, unequalled, unparalleled – *n.* **1.** account, almanac, annals, archives, black box, catalogue, chronicle, copy, diary, directory, document, entry, evidence, file, Hansard *(Parliament)*, information, inventory, journal, legend, list, little black book *(Nonformal)*, log, manuscript, memo, memorandum, minutes, muster roll, note, paper trail, *procès-verbal (French)*, register, remnant, report, roll, script, scroll, story, testimony, transcription, witness, written material **2.** background, biography, case history, conduct, curriculum vitae, dossier, experience, history, past behaviour, performance, résumé, track record, work *Medical:* anamnesis, catamnesis **3.** accomplishment, achievement, goal, mark, milestone, success, touchstone, triumph, watermark **4.** album, canned music, compact disc, CD, disc, EP, 45, LP, music, platter *(Nonformal)*, recording, release, 78, single, take, twelve inch vinyl, wax, wax cylinder – *v.* book, catalogue, chronicle, copy, document, dub, enroll, enter, enumerate, file, indicate, jot down, list, log, mark, note, preserve, register, report, show, tape, transcribe, videotape, write

recount *v.* articulate, catalogue, chronicle, communicate, depict, describe, detail, elucidate, enumerate, fictionalize, impart, narrate, orate, outline, portray, recite, relate, render, repeat, report, retell, sketch, summarize, tell, write

recoup *v.* **1.** get *or* win back, reacquire, recapture, recover, redeem, regain, reobtain, repossess, retrieve, salvage **2.** compensate, indemnify, recompense, refund, reimburse, repay, requite, satisfy

recourse *n.* **1.** appeal, application, claim, plea, request, supplication **2.** aid, asylum, comfort, cover, haven, help, patronage, refuge, relief, resort, rescue, shelter **3.** alternative, choice, escape clause *or* route, last resort, option, road, way

recover *v.* **1.** convalesce, gain, get better, grow, heal, improve, increase, mend, overcome, pull through *(Nonformal)*, rally, rebound, recuperate, refresh, renew, restore, revive *Antonyms:* deteriorate, relapse, weaken, worsen **2.** acquire, reacquire, recapture, reclaim, regain **3.** cover, defray, redeem, repair, replevin, rescue, restore, salvage, win back

recovery *n.* **1.** advancement, amelioration, betterment, comeback, convalescence, improvement, melioration, mending, progress, rally, recuperation, rehabilitation, restoration, resurgence, revival, survival *Antonyms:* decline, moribundity, turn **2.** drawing, exploitation, extraction, mining, reclamation, removal, retrieval

recreation *n.* amusement, break, distraction, diversion, ease, enjoyment, entertainment, exercise, festivity, field day, frolic, fun, game, hobby, holiday, jollity, leisure activity, occupation, pastime, picnic, play, pleasure, refreshment, relaxation, relief, sport, sports, vacation *Nonformal:* laughs, R and R, rec *Antonyms:* drudgery, labour, toil, work

recrimination *n.* accusation, avengement, counterattack, counterblow, countercharge, payment in kind, redress, repayment, reprisal, retaliation, retribution, return, revenge, vengeance

recruit *n.* **1.** beginner, convert, greenhorn, learner, neophyte, newcomer, novice, novitiate, rookie, tenderfoot, trainee, tyro **2.** combatant, draftee, enlisted person, serviceperson, soldier, volunteer – *v.* **1.** deliver, draft, engage, enlist, enroll, gather, impress, induct, levy, mobilize, muster, obtain, procure, proselytize, raise, retrieve, select, supply **2.** better, improve, reanimate, recover, recuperate, refresh, regain, renew, repair, replenish, repossess, restore, revive, strengthen

rectify *v.* adapt, adjust, align, ameliorate, amend, answer, atone, compensate, correct, emend, fit, fix, improve, indemnify, level, meet, mend, pay, put *or* set right, recompense, reconcile, redress, reform, remedy, remunerate, repair, repay, requite, revise, reward, right, satisfy, settle, square, suit, tailor *Antonyms:* aggravate, exacerbate, intensify

rectitude *n.* **1.** chastity, credibility, decency, godliness, honour, innocence, integrity, modesty, morality, probity, respectability, righteousness, unimpeachability, uprightness, virtue *Antonyms:* carnality, corruption, sinfulness **2.** accuracy, correctness, exactness, faultlessness, impeccability, point device, precision, scrupulousness, veracity

recuperate *v.* bounce back, convalesce, gain, heal, improve, mend, pull through, rally, recover, regain, renew, restore *Antonyms:* deteriorate, wane, worsen

recur *v.* **1.** come back, continue, happen again, persist, reiterate, reoccur, repeat, return, revert, turn back **2.** badger, bedevil, bother, harass, harrow, harry, haunt, hector, infest, torment, vex, visit, worry

recurrent *adj.* alternate, chain, continued, cyclical, frequent, habitual, intermittent, isochronal, nagging, periodic, regular, reoccurring, repeated, repetitive, unrelenting *Antonyms:* isolated, lone, random, single, sole

recycle *v.* blue box *(Nonformal)*, convert, reclaim, reuse, return, use over again

red *adj. & n.* colour, hue, shade *Red shades:* auburn, blood, bloody, blush, brick, burgundy, cardinal, carmine, cerise, cherry, chestnut, claret, copper, coral, crimson, dahlia, damask, flaming, florid, flushed, fuchsia, garnet, magenta, maroon, pink, puce, rose, roseate, rosy, rubicund, ruby, ruddy, russet, rust, salmon, sanguine, scarlet, terra cotta, titian, vermeil, vermilion, wine

red-blooded *adj.* dynamic, energetic, hale hearty, lusty, mighty, potent, pulsating, robust, spirited, staunch, strong, vigorous virile, vital, vivid *Antonyms:* feeble, frail impotent

edecorate *v.* modernize, overhaul, redo, refurnish, remodel, renovate, revamp, update, wallpaper *Nonformal:* do, switch the furniture around

edeem *v.* **1.** buy back, pay off, reclaim, recover, regain, repossess, retrieve, salvage *Antonyms:* hock *(Nonformal)*, lose, pawn, pledge **2.** deliver, emancipate, extricate, free, liberate, loose, manumit, ransom, release, rescue, save, unbind, unchain *Antonyms:* enslave, incarcerate, oppress **3.** cash *or* turn in, change, collect, convert, exchange **4.** answer, carry through, complete, consummate, fulfill, meet, perform, realize, satisfy **5.** atone *or* compensate for, balance, even, recompense, repay, requite, restore to favour, vouchsafe

edemption *n.* **1.** reclamation, recovery, repurchase, restitution, restoration, return **2.** amends, atonement, compensation, propitiation, redress, satisfaction *Antonyms:* delinquency, neglect **3.** conversion, forgiveness, pardon, rebirth, rehabilitation, rescue, salvation *Antonyms:* censure, condemnation, damnation

ed-faced *adj.* abashed, ashamed, blushing, chagrined, crestfallen, crushed, embarrassed, hangdog *(Nonformal)*, humbled, humiliated, mortified, shamed *Antonyms:* carefree, immodest, shameless

edolent *adj.* **1.** ambrosial, aromatic, fragrant, odoriferous, odorous, perfumed, scented, sweet, sweet-smelling *Antonyms:* malodorous, reeking, stinky **2.** evocative, haunting, indicative, reminiscent, suggestive

edress *n.* **1.** appeasement, atonement, compensation, payment, recompense, remuneration, reparation, satisfaction, transfer payment, wergeld **2.** advance, betterment, correction, development, improvement, progress, recovery, revision *Antonyms:* neglect, oversight – *v.* **1.** balance, even, set right, square, wipe clean *(Nonformal)* **2.** assuage, ease, fix, heal, help, rectify *Antonyms:* harm, hurt, pain **3.** avenge, punish, reprove, retaliate

educe *v.* **1.** abbreviate, abridge, attenuate, boil down, blue-pencil, chop, clip, collapse, compress, contract, crop, curtail, cut down, decrease, diet, diminish, downsize, edit, lessen, minimize, pare, retrench, scale down, shave, shorten, shrink, slash, streamline, subtract, taper, truncate *Antonyms:* augment, elevate, enlarge, increase, maximize **2.** abase, belittle, cheapen, debase, declass, decry, deflate, degrade, demerit, demote, depreciate, depress, devalue, discount, downgrade, humble, humiliate, lower *Nonformal:* bump, bust *Antonyms:* defend, elevate, enhance, exalt, promote **3.** bankrupt, break, bust *(Nonformal)*, impoverish, ruin, sink **4.** alleviate, ameliorate, assuage, dampen, ease, lessen, mellow, mitigate, moderate, muffle, mute, palliate, relax, relieve, soften, temper, tone down *Antonyms:* aggravate, incite, inflame, worsen **5.** conquer, crush, overpower, subdue, vanquish **6.** cut, dilute, thin, water down, weaken

reduction *n.* **1.** abbreviation, abstraction, compression, condensation, contraction, curtailment, cutback, decline, decrease, decrement, diminution, limitation, loss, minimalization, narrowing, restriction, rollback, shortening, shrinkage, subtraction *Antonyms:* augmentation, expansion, extension, growth **2.** cut, deduction, depreciation, devaluation, discount, refund, reimbursement, sale, write-downs, write-off *Antonyms:* appreciation, increase, mark-up **3.** alleviation, amelioration, easing, mitigation, moderation, muting, quieting, relaxation, relief, remission, softening, tempering *Antonyms:* heightening, intensification **4.** copy, maquette, miniature, replica, representation, scale model

redundancy *n.* **1.** affluence, deluge, excess, fat, flood, glut, inundation, lavishness, overabundance, overplenty, oversupply, plethora, prodigality, saturation, superfluity, superflux, surfeit, surplus *Antonyms:* impoverishment, insufficiency, shortage, want **2.** loquacity, pleonasm, prolixity, repetitiousness, tautology, verbosity, wordiness *Antonyms:* conciseness, succinctness, terseness **3.** dismissal, firing, superannuation, termination

redundant *adj.* **1.** diffuse, excessive, extra, inordinate, padded, spare, superfluous, surplus, unnecessary, unwanted **2.** battological, bombastic, long-winded, loquacious, prolix, repetitious, tautological, verbose, wordy *Antonyms:* laconic, succinct, terse

reef *n.* atoll, bank, bar, cay, coral island *or* reef, mud flat, shoal, skerry *(Newfoundland)*

reek *n.* effluvium, miasma, odour, smell, stench, stink – *v.* emit, fume, smell, smoke, steam, stink

reel *n.* **1.** bobbin, spool, wheel *Common fishing reels:* bait-casting, close-faced, fly-fishing, light-action, open-faced, saltwater **2.** dance, ditty, jig, song, tune – *v.* bob, careen, falter, lurch, pitch, revolve, rock, roll, shake, spin, stagger, stumble, sway, swirl, totter, turn, twirl, waver, wheel, whirl, wobble

refer *v.* **1.** commune, confer, consult, have recourse *or* reference to, look up, repair, resort, turn **2.** commit, consign, deliver, direct, guide, hand in *or* over, introduce, pass on, relegate, send, submit, transfer **3.** bear upon, belong, comprise, concern, connect, cover, deal with, encompass, hold, include, incorporate, involve, pertain, regard, relate, speak about, touch **4.** accredit, advert, allude, ascribe, assign, associate, attribute, cite, credit, direct attention, hint, impute, make allusion *or* reference, mention, name, notice, point out, recommend, speak of, specify

referee *n.* advisor, adjudicator, assessor, convener, examiner, intermediary, judge, mediator, moderator, umpire *Nonformal:* go-between, ref, zebra – *v.* advise, adjudge, adjudicate, arbitrate, assess, examine, interpose, intervene, mediate, moderate, monitor, negotiate, settle

reference *n.* **1.** affirmation, certificate, credentials, endorsement, letter, recommendation, testimonial, tribute, witness **2.** reference book *or* piece *or* work, sourcebook *Kinds of reference book:* almanac, atlas, bibliography, calendar, casebook, catalogue, concordance, cyclopedia, dictionary, directory, encyclopedia, gazetteer, glossary, guide, guidebook, index, journal, lexicon, listing, record, register, studbook, telephone book *or* directory, thesaurus, voca[bulary], workbook **3.** attribution, citatio[n], credit, cross-reference, endnote, footno[te], indication, mention, note, quotatio[n], resource, source, statement, work cited [**4.**] association, connection, corresponden[ce], pertinence, relation, relevance **5.** allusio[n], hint, implication, innuendo, insinuatio[n], remark **6.** benchmark, goal, line, mark[er], milestone, point, watermark

refine *v.* **1.** alter, cleanse, distill, filte[r], process, purify, rarefy, strain *Antonym[s]:* dirty, pollute **2.** better, civilize, cultivat[e], elevate, hone, improve, perfect, polis[h], sharpen *Antonyms:* debase, defile, sully [**3.**] clarify, distinguish, elaborate, explain, si[m]plify *Antonyms:* confuse, muddle

refined *adj.* **1.** civilized, courteous, court[ly], cultivated, cultured, enlightened, gente[el], gentlemanly, gracious, highbro[w], high-minded, ladylike, nice, polite, restrai[n]ed, sensitive, sophisticated, suave, sublim[e], subtle, urbane, well-bred, well-manner[ed] *Antonyms:* boorish, common, inelega[nt], uncultured **2.** delicate, elegant, finespu[n], polished, restrained, simple, stylish, tast[e]ful, upscale *Nonformal:* classy, snazz[y], spiffy, swanky, uptown **3.** aesthetic, di[s]cerning, discriminating, exacting, fastic[idi]ous, fine, hairsplitting, precise, punctilio[us] **4.** boiled down, clarified, cleaned, distille[d], expurgated, filtered, processed, purifie[d], rarefied, strained *Antonyms:* defiled, di[rt]ied, sullied

refinement *n.* **1.** civility, courtesy, court[li]ness, cultivation, dignity, elegance, enligh[t]enment, erudition, finesse, fine tuning, fi[n]ish, gentility, gentleness, good breeding [or] manners, grace, graciousness, knowledg[e], polish, politeness, politesse, sophisticatio[n], style, suavity, tact, taste, urbanity **2.** delic[a]cy, discrimination, fastidiousness, fuss[i]ness, meticulousness, precision, punct[il]iousness **3.** fine point, nicety, nuance, su[b]tlety, touch **4.** clarification, cleansin[g], decontamination, distillation, filtering, pr[o]cessing, purification, rarefaction

refit *v.* alter, change, improve, modif[y], rebuild, recast, rejig, renew, repair, restor[e], retrofit, revamp, update

eflect *v.* **1.** brood, cogitate, consider, contemplate, deliberate, dwell on, meditate, mull over, muse, ponder, reason, recall, remember, ruminate, speculate, study, think, weigh, wonder **2.** cast, mirror, rebound, repeat, reproduce, resonate, resound, return, reverberate, reverse, shine *or* throw back **3.** copy, duplicate, follow, imitate, match, mimic **4.** display, evince, exhibit, express, manifest, mean, represent, reveal, show, suggest

eflection *n.* **1.** brown study *(Nonformal)*, cogitation, consideration, contemplation, deliberation, imagination, meditation, musing, observation, pensiveness, pondering, reverie, rumination, speculation, study, thinking, thought **2.** appearance, image, impression, picture **3.** counterpart, double, duplicate, echo, mirror image, representation, reproduction **4.** mirroring, rebounding, recasting, resounding, reverberation

eflective *adj.* **1.** brooding, cerebral, contemplative, deliberate, intellectual, ivory towered *(Nonformal)*, meditative, pensive, philosophical, pondering, reasoning, ruminative, speculative, studious, thoughtful, withdrawn *Antonyms:* headstrong, impulsive, reckless **2.** flat, glassy, glossy, mirror-like, smooth

eflex *adj.* **1.** automatic, conditioned, immediate, impulsive, instinctual, involuntary, knee-jerk, mechanical, reactive, reflexive, unconscious, unthinking *Antonyms:* deliberate, planned, premeditated **2.** arched, bent, crooked, curved, flexed, shaped *Antonyms:* linear, straight – *n.* answer, backlash, impulse, jerk, kick *(Nonformal)*, movement, reaction, reply, response, return, visceral reaction

eform *n.* **1.** advancement, betterment, change, correction, elevation, improvement, progress, reconfiguration, reconstruction, rectification, restoration, revision, urban renewal *Nonformal:* clean sweep, housecleaning, shake-up **2.** act, amendment, bill, deal, justice, measure, plan, procedure, statute – *v.* **1.** ameliorate, amend, better, correct, cure, emend, improve, mend, mould, rebuild, reclaim, reconfigure, reconstitute, rectify, regenerate, remake, remedy, remodel, renew, renovate, reorganize, repair, reshape, resolve, restore, revise, revolutionize, rework, set to rights, standardize, transform **2.** clean up, convert, dry *or* shape up, go sober *or* straight, rehabilitate, see the light *(Nonformal)*, start anew, take the pledge *(Historical)*

reformer *n.* activist, agent, extremist, liberal, meliorist, moral improver, muckraker, progressive, radical, reformist, revisionist, revolutionary, social activist, transformer

refractory *adj.* contrary, contumacious, defiant, difficult, disobedient, high-maintenance *(Nonformal)*, mulish, nonconforming, obstinate, pig-headed, rebellious, recalcitrant, resistant, uncooperative, unmanageable, unruly, willful *Antonyms:* amenable, controllable, tractable

refrain *n.* chorus, derry *(Historical)*, interval, melody, music, phrase, recurring lines *or* phrase, saying, song, strain, theme, tune – *v.* abstain, avoid, cease, desist, eschew, forbear, go without, halt, inhibit, interrupt, pass, quit, resist, restrain, stop, withhold *Antonyms:* continue, indulge

refresh *v.* **1.** energize, freshen, invigorate, regenerate, resuscitate, revitalize, revive **2.** air out, bleach, clean, deodorize, disinfect, freshen, sanitize, wash **3.** awaken, inflame, jar, jog, kindle, reawaken, shake, stimulate **4.** fill, replenish, restock, re-supply **5.** fix, modernize, rebuild, recondition, reform, regenerate, reinitialize, reload, renew, repair, restore, retool, retrofit, touch up, update, upgrade

refreshing *adj.* **1.** bracing, cool, invigorating, life-affirming, quenching, rejuvenating, replenishing, restorative, revitalizing, reviving **2.** amusing, different, engaging, fresh, new, novel, original, stimulating, unique, unusual *Antonyms:* hackneyed, overworked, trite

refreshment *n.* **1.** drink, edibles, energy, food, liquid, nourishment, pickup, provender, provisions, repast, replenishment, restorative, snack, sustenance, tonic, victuals *Nonformal:* munchies, pick-me-up, vittles **2.** cheer, inspiration, lift, renewal, restorative, resuscitation, revitalization, revival, something new *(Nonformal)*, stimulation, strengthen

refrigerate *v.* air-condition, chill, cool, freeze, ice, keep, preserve

refuge *n.* **1.** anchorage, ark, asylum, bivouac, cover, escape, fortress, harbour, haven, hideaway, hideout, hiding place, home, oasis, port, protection, retreat, safe place, sanctuary, security, shelter, stronghold **2.** aid, comfort, mainstay, rock *(Nonformal)*, shield, solace, support

refugee *n.* alien, boat person, castaway, defector, deserter, displaced person, DP *(Nonformal)*, émigré, escapee, evacuee, exile, expatriate, expellee, foreigner, fugitive, homeless person, maroon, outcast, renegade, runaway, stateless person, stray

refund *n.* allowance, cashback, compensation, discount, money back, payment, rebate, reimbursement, repayment, restitution, settlement – *v.* adjust, compensate, make amends, pour back, recompense, recoup, reimburse, remit, repay, return, reward, square

refurbish *v.* brighten, fix *or* polish *or* spruce up, freshen, mend, modernize, recondition, refit, rehabilitate, rejuvenate, remodel, renew, renovate, repair, restore, retool, retread, revamp, update

refusal *n.* **1.** denial, negation, objection, prohibition, rebuff, rejection, repudiation, snub, veto *Nonformal:* pass, thumbs down **2.** balk, defiance, noncompliance, opposition, recusance, unwillingness **3.** choice, election, option, volition, vote, will

refuse *n.* **1.** dross, flotsam, garbage, litter, offal, swill, trash, waste **2.** castoffs, debris, detritus, discard, dregs, leavings, leftovers, rejects, remainder, remnants, scraps, scourings, scree, slag, tailings – *v.* **1.** abnegate, decline, demur, desist, pass up, rebuff, send regrets, spurn *Nonformal:* brush off, take the fifth **2.** deny, disallow, disapprove, forbid, nix *(Nonformal)*, prohibit, reject, rule against, veto *Antonyms:* allow, approve, sanction

refute *v.* argue against, belie, confute, co[n]tend, contradict, contravene, counte[r], debate, disclaim, discredit, disprove, di[s]pute, gainsay, invalidate, negate, oppos[e], quash, rebut, reply to, repudiate, silenc[e] *Nonformal:* debunk, shoot down, squelc[h] *Antonyms:* confirm, prove, substantiate

regain *v.* **1.** achieve, attain, get back, rea[c]quire, reattain, recapture, reclaim, recou[p], recover, retake, retrieve, salvage, take *o*[ver], win back **2.** gain, make, reach, return to

regal *adj.* **1.** imperial, kingly, magisteria[l], monarchical, noble, princely, queenl[y], royal, sovereign **2.** august, awesome, exal[t]ed, glorious, grand, imposing, impressiv[e], Junoesque, lofty, majestic, resplenden[t], stately, striking

regale *v.* **1.** amuse, charm, crack up *(Nonformal)*, delight, divert, entertain, enthral[l], fascinate, gladden, humour, interest, pleas[e] **2.** banquet, celebrate, dine, feast, gratif[y], indulge, party *(Nonformal)*, refresh

regard *n.* **1.** attention, care, concentratio[n], concern, heedfulness, interest, mindfu[l]ness, observation, scrutiny, study, vigilanc[e] **2.** admiration, appreciation, approbatio[n], approval, deference, devotion, esteem, favour, homage, veneration **3.** applicabilit[y], connection, correlation, reference, relatio[n] **4.** aspect, characteristic, detail, featur[e], hallmark, quality, trait – *v.* **1.** attend, co[n]template, heed, judge, mind, notice **2.** co[n]sider, deem, fancy, imagine, maintain, rec[k]on, think **3.** bear *or* touch upon, concer[n], encompass, involve, pertain *or* relate to **4.** eye, gaze, glance, goggle, inspect, loo[k], observe, oogle, scan, scrutinize, stare, su[r]vey, view, watch **5.** appreciate, cherish, esteem, extol, honour, prize, respect, revere, treasure, value, venerate

regardful *adj.* **1.** alert, aware, carefu[l], chary, mindful, observant, vigilant, watc[h]ful *Antonyms:* absent-minded, distracte[d], forgetful **2.** attentive, caring, considerat[e], courteous, deferential, punctilious, respec[t]ful, reverential, thoughtful

regarding *prep.* about, apropos, as for *o*[r] to, concerning, in connection to *or* with, i[n] reference to, in relation to, on the subje[ct] of, pertaining to, re *(Nonformal)*, respecting, touching, *vis-a-vis (French)*

regardless *adj.* blind, careless, harum-scarum *(Nonformal)*, heedless, inattentive, inconsiderate, indifferent, insensitive, mindless, neglectful, negligent, remiss, unheeding, uninterested *Antonyms:* heedful, mindful, regardful, slack – *adv.* anyhow, anyway, in spite of everything, nevertheless, nonetheless, notwithstanding, one way or another

regards *n. pl.* best *or* good wishes, commendations, compliments, devoirs, greetings, hello, remembrances, respects, salutations, welcome, wishes

regenerate *adj.* **1.** born-again, converted, reborn, redeemed, salvaged, saved *Antonyms:* fallen, lost **2.** animated, refreshed, rejuvenated, renewed, restored, revitalized – *v.* **1.** convert, edify, reclaim, redeem, reform, rehabilitate, salvage, transform **2.** mend, reconstruct, redo, refashion, remake, reshape, rework **3.** breed, develop, form, grow, multiply, procreate, proliferate, recreate, reproduce

regeneration *n.* **1.** conversion, rebirth, reclaimation, redemption, reformation, rehabilitation, renascence, salvation **2.** development, growth, progress, reestablishment, reforestation, regrowth, rejuvenation, reproduction, revitalization **3.** gentrification, improvement, mending, modernization, rebuilding, reconstruction, reform, renewal, repair, transformation, urban renewal

regime *n.* **1.** administration, apparatus, command, control, direction, dominion, dynasty, era, establishment, government, house *(Historical)*, leadership, management, party, reign, rule, system, tenure **2.** diet, exercise, habits, lifestyle, pattern, regimen, routine, schedule, way of life

region *n.* **1.** area, belt, continent, culture, ecosphere, ecosystem, ecotype, ecozone, feature, habitat, landform, landmass, landscape, province, scope, terrain, territory, tropic, zone *Canada's major landform regions:* Appalachians, Great Lakes/St. Lawrence Lowlands, Hudson Bay Lowlands, Interior Plains, Northern Mountains and Lowlands, Precambrian Shield, Western Cordillera *Canada's natural vegetation regions:* Boreal Forest, Deciduous Forest, Grassland, Mixed Forest, Mountain, Tundra, West Coast Forest **2.** *arrondissement (French)*, barrio, district, division, locale, location, neighbourhood, quarter, section, vicinity *Nonformal:* stomping ground, turf **3.** arena, authority, bailiwick, bounds, field, jurisdiction, range, responsibility, rule, sphere

regional *adj.* **1.** city, district, geographic, municipal, provincial, sectional, territorial, topographic **2.** circumscribed, confined, independent, insular, limited, local, narrow-minded, parochial, restricted, small-minded – *n.* bonspiel, championship, cup, districts, final, playdown, playoff, provincials, showdown, tournament

regionalism *n.* **1.** localism, nationalism, provincialism, territorialism *Antonyms:* centralism, globalism, internationalism **2.** defensiveness, garrison mentality, introversion, isolationism, protectionism, secessionism, separatism **3.** custom, dialect, idiom, lingo, local speak *(Nonformal)*, patois, peculiarity, vernacular

register *n.* **1.** annals, archives, blue book, book, cadastre, catalogue, chronicle, Debretts *(Trademark)*, diary, entry, file, ledger, list, log, muster roll, record, registry, roll, roster, schedule, scroll, who's who **2.** archivist, bookkeeper, chronicler, chronologer, recorder, registrar **3.** compass, diapason, gamut, range, scale, scope, sweep **4.** cashbox, cash drawer *or* register, till – *v.* **1.** catalogue, chronicle, codify, enter, file, inscribe, list, note, record, schedule, set *or* write down **2.** check in, enlist, enroll, join, sign up, subscribe, weigh in *(Nonformal)* **3.** bespeak, display, exhibit, express, manifest, mark, point, reveal, say **4.** indicate, read, reflect, represent, show, signify **5.** affect, impress, penetrate, reach, strike, sway, touch *Nonformal:* dawn on, hit

registrar *n.* **1.** annalist, archivist, chronicler, genealogist, historian, prothonotary, recorder **2.** administrator, agent, bureaucrat, clerk, official, secretary

registry *n.* account book, almanac, annals, catalogue, chronicle, chronology, daybook, diary, enrollment, filing, guest book, history, index, inventory, itemization, journal, ledger, list, listing, log, logbook, muster off *(Historical)*, record book, register, registration, roster, rota *(British)*, scroll, table, tabulation, tax roll, time sheet, voter list

regress *v.* **1.** backslide *(Nonformal)*, degenerate, deteriorate, fall, lapse, recidivate, relapse, revert **2.** ebb, recede, retreat, return, rollback, wane, withdraw *Antonyms:* advance, progress, wax

regret *n.* anguish, concern, conscience, contrition, discomfort, grief, heartbreak, misgiving, pang, penitence, qualm, remorse, repentance, shame, sorrow, uneasiness, worry *Antonyms:* contentment, pleasure, satisfaction – *v.* apologize, bemoan, bewail, deplore, grieve, lament, miss, mourn, repent, rue, weep *Antonyms:* accept, celebrate, rejoice

regretful *adj.* apologetic, ashamed, compunctious, conscious-stricken, contrite, mournful, penitent, remorseful, repentant, rueful, shameful, sorrowful, sorry *Commonly misused:* **regrettable**

regrettable *adj.* a shame *(Nonformal)*, awful, calamitous, deplorable, disappointing, disheartening, distressing, grievous, lamentable, pitiful, sad, unfortunate, unhappy, woeful, wrong *Commonly misused:* **regretful**

regular *adj.* **1.** common, conventional, customary, established, everyday, normal, ordinary, routine, typical, standard, stock **2.** controlled, cyclic, daily, diastolic, fixed, measured, methodical, orderly, periodic, regulated, rhythmic, steady, systematic *Antonyms:* arrhythmic, random, stray, unpredictable **3.** bona fide, kosher, legal, legitimate, recognized **4.** dependable, easygoing, genuine, likeable, nice, real, unassuming **5.** absolute, complete, consummate, downright, out and out *(Nonformal)*, pure, sheer, thorough, unmitigated, unqualified, utter **6.** aligned, balanced, equal, even, harmonious, level, plumb, symmetrical, uniform *Antonyms:* askew, out of whack *(Nonformal)*, discordant, off kilter – *n.* **1.** conscript, enlistee, man-at-arms, private, recruit, serviceman *or* servicewoman, soldier, troops **2.** convert, fixture, loyalist, stalwart, staunch supporter, wheelhorse **3.** barfly *(Nonformal)*, client, customer, denizen, habitué, patron

regulate *v.* **1.** administer, boss, captain, command, conduct, control, direct, drive, govern, guide, head, lead, manage, officiate, order, oversee, preside over, rule, run, steer, supervise **2.** accommodate, adjust, arrange, bring in line, equalize, fit, handicap *(Sports)*, make uniform, reconcile, set, synchronize, tailor, tune **3.** catalogue, categorize, codify, normalize, order, set straight, standardize, straighten out, systematize

regulation *adj.* basic, customary, conventional, established, standard, stock, wanted – *n.* **1.** canon, code, commandment, decree, dictate, edict, law, order, ordinance, precept, procedure, rule, standard operating practice *or* s.o.p., standing order, statute **2.** administration, authority, control, direction, governance, guidance, management, regimentation, superintendence, supervision **3.** adjustment, alignment, balance, coordination, reconciliation, squaring, fine tuning

regurgitate *v.* **1.** disgorge, retch, spew, throw up, vomit *Nonformal:* barf, hurl, lose one's lunch, puke, ralph, upchuck **2.** copy, ditto, duplicate, echo, imitate, memorize, parrot, quote, recant, recite, rehash, reissue, repeat, reproduce, restate **3.** ebb, flow *or* surge back, resurge

rehabilitate *v.* **1.** amend, fix up, gentrify, mend, modernize, rebuild, recondition, refurbish, remedy, renovate, repair, restore, retrofit **2.** ameliorate, better, convert, correct, edify, improve, redeem, re-educate, reform, save, transform, uplift **3.** bring back, reinstall, reinstate, renew, revive

rehash *n.* cut and paste job *(Nonformal)*, regurgitation, reiteration, repetition, restatement – *v.* paraphrase, recapitulate, regurgitate, reiterate, repeat, rephrase, restate, reuse, reword, rework, rewrite

rehearsal *n.* call, drill, practice, preparation, reading, test, test flight, trial balloon *or* performance, tryout, workout *Nonformal:* dry run, going-over, run-through

ehearse *v.* **1.** drill, experiment, go through *(Nonformal)*, hone, practice, prepare, ready, review, study, test, train, tune up, walk through, warm up **2.** chronicle, convey, depict, describe, impart, narrate, portray, recite, recount, relate, render, state

eify *v.* actualize, concretize, embody, hypostatize, incarnate, make real, materialize, solidify *Antonyms:* attenuate, rarefy, spiritualize

eign *n.* administration, command, control, domination, dynasty, hegemony, incumbency, power, regime, rule, sovereignty, supremacy – *v.* boss, command, govern, hold power, influence, manage, master, occupy, predominate, prevail, rule

eimburse *v.* compensate, equalize, fix *(Nonformal)*, indemnify, make amends *or* good, offset, pay back, reciprocate, recompense, recoup, recover, refund, remunerate, repay, return, reward, satisfy, square

ein *n.* **1.** bit, bridle, halter, harness, strap **2.** check, control, cramp, deterrence, governor, limitation, restraint, restrictions – *v.* **1.** circumscribe, confine, curb, hold back, impede, limit, restrain, retard, stifle, subdue, trammel **2.** direct, govern, guide, manage, rule, steer

eincarnation *n.* avatar, metempsychosis, palingenesis, rebirth, samsara, transanimation, transmigration

einforce *v.* **1.** add to, augment, bolster, brace, buttress, enlarge, fortify, increase, prop up, stiffen, strengthen, support, sustain, thicken, toughen *Nonformal:* beef *or* heat *or* soup up **2.** accent, emphasize, heighten, highlight, stress, underline *Nonformal:* headline, press home

einforcement *n.* **1.** addition, augmentation, enlargement, increase, strengthening, supplementation **2.** aid, assistance, auxiliaries, backup, help, relief, reserves **3.** brace, buttress, prop, stay, support

reinstate *v.* bring *or* put back, reelect, reestablish, rehabilitate, rehire, reintroduce, reinvest, rejig, renew, restore, return, revive, undo *(Computer) Antonyms:* impeach, recall, turf *(Nonformal)*

reiterate *v.* ditto *(Nonformal)*, harp on, play back, recapitulate, redo, regurgitate, rehash, replay, repeat, reprise, restate, retell, summarize

reject *v.* **1.** decline, deny, disallow, disavow, forbid, forswear, proscribe, refuse, renounce, turn down, veto *Antonyms:* accord, allow, permit **2.** disregard, rebuff, repel, repulse, scoff, scorn, shun, slight, spurn **3.** cast off, discard, jettison, toss *or* throw away *Nonformal:* junk, shed, scrap, trash *Antonyms:* keep, maintain, preserve **4.** challenge, contravene, disagree, disbelieve, discredit, dispute, gainsay, oppose, protest, rebel, repudiate *Antonyms:* accept, agree, concede **5.** eject, expel, vomit *Nonformal:* hurl, puke, ralph, upchuck

rejection *n.* **1.** abnegation, denial, interdiction, refusal, thumbs down *(Nonformal)*, veto **2.** brush-off *(Nonformal)*, disdain, eschewal, repulsion, shunning, snub, spurning **3.** disagreement, disapproval, disfavour, negating, opposition, protest **4.** abandonment, disposal, elimination, expulsion, removal **5.** ejection, throwing up, vomiting

rejoice *v.* bask, celebrate, delight, enchant, enjoy, exult, feel happy, glory, party *(Nonformal)*, revel, triumph, wallow *Antonyms:* grieve, lament, mourn

rejuvenate *v.* breathe new life into, exhilarate, fix, gentrify, improve, make new, modernize, reanimate, rebuild, reclaim, refresh, regenerate, reinvigorate, renew, restore, revamp, revitalize, take back *(Nonformal)*

rekindle *v.* activate, arouse, awaken, reanimate, refresh, reinspire, relight, renew, restore, resurrect, resuscitate, revitalize, revive *Antonyms:* dampen, deaden, destroy, ruin

relapse *n.* **1.** backsliding, fall, lapse, recidivism, regression, retrogression, reversion

Antonyms: improvement, rally, recovery **2.** deterioration, recurrence, return, setback, weakening, turn for the worse – *v.* **1.** backslide, degenerate, fail, regress, retrogress, revert, slip **2.** deteriorate, fade, lapse, suffer, weaken, worsen *Antonyms:* improve, recover

relate *v.* **1.** articulate, broadcast, communicate, delineate, describe, express, impart, mention, narrate, recount, say, speak, tell, utter **2.** affect, appertain, apply, bear *or* touch upon, compare, concern, coordinate, correspond *or* refer to, involve, pertain **3.** associate, bind, connect, correlate, couple, join, link, marry, match up *(Nonformal)*, meet, tie, unite, yoke

related *adj.* **1.** accompanying, affiliated, agnate, alike, analogous, associated, complementary, congenial, connected, correspondent, dependent, germane, homogeneous, interchangeable, interconnected, interdependent, intertwined, interwoven, joint, like, linked, matching, mutual, parallel, pertinent, reciprocal, relevant, similar *Antonyms:* separate, unconnected, unrelated **2.** akin, biological, birth, cognate, consanguineous, fraternal, genetic, kindred, married, maternal, natural, paired, sororal, wedded **3.** chronicled, detailed, documented, expressed, narrated, offered, published, said, spoken, told, uttered, written

relation *n.* **1.** brother, cousin, daughter, elder, father, kin, kindred, kinship, kinsman, kinswoman, kissing cousin *(Nonformal)*, mother, relative, sibling, sister, son *See also:* **relative 2.** accord, affiliation, affinity, alliance, association, attachment, bond, connection, link, marriage, nexus, partnership, rapport, reference, relationship, relevance, tie, tie-in, union

relationship *n.* accord, affair, affiliation, affinity, alliance, analogy, appositeness, association, bond, communication, communion, conjunction, connection, consanguinity, consociation, contact, contingency, correlation, dependence, dependency, exchange, friendship, homogeneity, hookup, interconnection, interrelation, interrelationship, kinship, liaison, likeness, link, nearness, network, parallel, pertinence, pertinency, proportion, rapport, relation, relativity, relevance, similarity, tie, tie-i tie-up *See also:* **relation**

relative *adj.* **1.** applicable, appropriat appurtenant, apropos, fitting, german important, material, meaningful, pertai ing, pertinent, related, relevant, suitable **2** associated, commensurate, connected, co relative, corresponding, parallel, propo tionate, reciprocal, respective **3.** conditio al, contingent, dependent, provisional – *n* agnate, aunt, blood, brother, clansma cognate, connection, cousin, daughte family, father, folks, husband, in-law, ki kinsman, kinswoman, mother, parent, rel tion, sibling, sister, son, uncle, wife *Nonfor mal:* bro, cuz, dad, kissing cousin, m mom, old lady, old man, pa, pop, sis

relatively *adv.* almost, alright, approximat ly, comparably, comparatively, nearly, pr portionately, rather, somewhat

relax *v.* **1.** idle, laze, loaf, lounge, reclin repose, rest, slump, unwind *Nonforma* chill, hang, kick back, veg **2.** halt, intermi pause, retard, stop, take a breather *(Non formal)*, wait **3.** abate, assuage, ease, calm lighten, mitigate, moderate, mollify, reduc relieve, soften *Antonyms:* aggravat heighten, increase **4.** downplay, free up loosen, release, set free, slacken, untighte **5.** attenuate, diminish, dwindle, ease of ease *or* let up, ebb, flag, lessen, lull, quel recede, subside, wane

relaxation *n.* **1.** amusement, diversion enjoyment, fun, leisure, pleasure, recre ation, refreshment *Antonyms:* drudgery labour, toil **2.** break, calm, détente, ease holiday, leisure, peace, quietude, recess remission, repose, respite, rest, time off tranquility, vacation *Nonformal:* breathe R & R **3.** abatement, decline, decrease flagging, lowering, recession, waning **4** assuagement, lightening, loosening, lettin up *(Nonformal)*, mitigation, reduction slackening, softening *Antonyms:* intensifi cation, tightening

relay *n.* **1.** alteration, change, exchange replacement, shift, stint, substitution, tur **2.** cache, collection, hoard, holdings pantry, reserve, reservoir, stockpile, store supply *Nonformal:* loot, stash **3.** competi tion, contest, dash, heat, race, run **4.** communication, dispatch, message, transmission – *v.* broadcast, carry, communicate, deliver, import, pass on, spread, transfer, transmit

release *n.* **1.** absolution, acquittal, deliverance, delivery, discharge, emancipation, exemption, exoneration, liberation, liberty, manumission, quietus, quittance, remission *Antonyms:* detention, imprisonment, incarceration, internment **2.** detachment, disconnection, disentanglement, extrication, loosening, unbinding, unfastening, unfettering, unyoking **3.** announcement, bulletin, handout, issue, news, notice, proclamation, propaganda, publication, publicity, story *Nonformal:* bumph, flash, hype, promo, scoop – *v.* **1.** absolve, acquit, clear, commute, deliver, discharge, disengage, emancipate, exculpate, excuse, exempt, exonerate, extricate, free, liberate, manumit, quit claim, remit, spring *(Nonformal)*, turn loose *Antonyms:* detain, fasten, engage, hold, imprison **2.** detach, disconnect, loosen, unbind, unchain, unfetter, unshackle, untie **3.** advertise, air, announce, broadcast, dispense, display, exhibit, print, promulgate, publish, televise, webcast

relegate *v.* **1.** assign, authorize, commission, commit, delegate, entrust **2.** consign, dispatch, send, ship, transfer **3.** accredit, arrogate, attribute, credit, impute, refer **4.** banish, deport, dismiss, displace, eject, exile, expatriate, expel, ostracize, remove, throw out, transport

relent *v.* **1.** acquiesce, bend, capitulate, collapse, concede, defer, succumb, surrender, yield *Nonformal:* cave, crumble, give in *Antonyms:* challenge, face, withstand **2.** drop, ease, ease off, ebb, fall, mitigate, moderate, relax, slacken, soften, subside, temper, wane *Antonyms:* increase, intensify, strengthen

relentless *adj.* **1.** adamant, bound, bullheaded, cruel, ferocious, fierce, grim, hard, harsh, hell-bent *(Nonformal)*, implacable, inexorable, inflexible, insistent, mulish, obdurate, obstinate, pigheaded, pitiless, remorseless, resolute, rigid, ruthless, strict, stubborn, unbending, uncompromising, unflinching, unforgiving, unyielding, vindictive *Antonyms:* compassionate, forgiving, merciful, submissive, yielding **2.** continuous, incessant, interminable, nonstop, persistent, sustained, unabated, unbroken, unfaltering, unflagging, unrelieved, unremitting, unstoppable *Latin:* ad infinitum, ad nauseam

relevance *n.* applicability, appropriateness, appurtenance, aptness, association, bearing, comparability, compatibility, congruence, connection, correspondence, fitness, meaning, pertinence, relatedness, relation, suitability, timeliness *Antonyms:* incongruity, infelicity, irrelevance, unrelatedness

relevant *adj.* admissible, *ad rem (Latin)*, allowable, applicable, appropriate, apropos, apt, becoming, cognate, compatible, congruent, consistent, correlative, correspondent, fitting, germane, harmonious, important, material, meaningful, on target *(Nonformal)*, pertinent, proper, related, suitable, timely *Antonyms:* inapplicable, irrelevant, jejune, unrelated

reliable *adj.* **1.** careful, conscientious, constant, decent, dependable, devoted, faithful, good, high-principled, honest, loyal, predictable, reputable, respectable, responsible, righteous, sincere, solid, sound, stable, staunch, steadfast, steady, sterling, trustworthy, upright, veracious *Antonyms:* capricious, fickle, flighty, irresponsible **2.** assured, certain, credible, definite, guaranteed, reputable, risk-free, safe, secure, sound, substantiated, sure, true, watertight *(Nonformal)*

reliance *n.* assurance, belief, confidence, credence, credit, dependence, faith, hope, stock, trust

relic *n.* **1.** artifact, antique, fetish, heirloom, keepsake, memento, remembrance, reminder, souvenir, token, trophy **2.** evidence, fragment, leftover, remains, shard, vestige **3.** old man, old person, old woman, senior citizen, veteran *Nonformal:* ancient one, blue hair, boat anchor, foggy, fossil, golden ager, gramps, granny, old coot, oldster, old timer

relief *n.* **1.** abatement, alleviation, amelioration, appeasement, assuagement, comfort, ease, lightening, mitigation, solace *Antonyms:* aggravation, intensification **2.** deliverance, liberation, freedom, manumission, quittance, release, rescue, salvation *Antonyms:* bondage, ensnarement **3.** aid, alms, assistance, benefaction, charity, help, support, welfare **4.** break, breather *(Nonformal)*, letup, lull, recess, refreshment, relaxation, respite, rest **5.** backup, replacement, stand-in, substitute, understudy **6.** balm, cure, medicine, pharmaceutical, pill, remedy, therapy, tonic, treatment

relieve *v.* **1.** disburden, disencumber, extricate, exempt, free, liberate, release, unburden, unload **2.** abate, alleviate, appease, assuage, calm, comfort, ease, heal, lay off, let up, lessen, mitigate, palliate, quell, reduce, remedy, soothe *Antonyms:* exacerbate, intensify, worsen **3.** aid, assist, help, succour, support, sustain **4.** break, divert, modify, relax, slacken, vary

religion *n.* **1.** belief, creed, culture, doctrine, dogma, faith, guide, law, persuasion, principles, rules, system, tenet, theology, way *World religions:* Baha'ism, Buddhism, Christianity, Confucianism, Hinduism, Islam, Jainism, Judaism, Shintoism, Sikhism, Taoism **2.** fixation, infatuation, life, love, obsession, passion *Nonformal:* everything, reason for living

religious *adj.* **1.** devotional, divine, doctrinal, ecclesiastic, holy, ministerial, orthodox, pontifical, sacerdotal, sacrosanct, scriptural, spiritual, theological *Antonyms:* lay, secular **2.** believing, born-again *(Nonformal)*, church-going, conscientious, devout, faithful, God-fearing, loyal, moral, pious, reverent, righteous, zealous *Antonyms:* atheistic, godless, heathen, infidel, pagan

relinquish *v.* **1.** abdicate, forgo, forswear. cede, give up, recuse, renounce, surrender, waive, yield **2.** abandon, cast off, ditch *(Nonformal)*, desert, discard, dump, forsake **3.** cut loose, emancipate, free, let go, liberate, release, unchain, untie

relish *n.* **1.** appetite, appreciation, enjoyment, enthusiasm, fancy, fondness, liking, love, penchant, pleasure, propensity *Antonyms:* dislike, distaste, loathing **2.** bite, excitement, flavour, punch, spice, tang, taste, zest *Nonformal:* zing, pizzazz **3.** chili, chow-chow, chutney, condiment, green seasoning *(West Indian)*, piccalilli, pickle, salsa, sauce, spread, topping – *v.* adore, appreciate, bask *or* delight *or* revel *or* wallow in, enjoy, like, savour

reluctant *adj.* **1.** careful, cautious, chary, hesitant, indisposed, leery, slow, suspicious, uncertain, unenthusiastic *Antonyms:* eager, keen, willing **2.** averse, balky, contrary, disapproving, disinclined, dissenting, hostile, loath, obstinate, opposed, rebellious, recalcitrant, unwilling *Commonly misused:* **reticent**

rely *v.* await, believe in, build *or* gamble *or* lean on, calculate, count, depend, entrust, expect, have hope, look to, swear by, trust *Nonformal:* bank, bet

remain *v.* **1.** dwell, linger, reside, rest, roost, stay, sit tight *(Nonformal)*, tarry, wait **2.** abide, continue, endure, keep on, last, outlast, persist, prevail, survive *Nonformal:* hang in, keep the faith, stand pat

remainder *n.* **1.** balance, excess, leftover, profit, remains, remnant, residue, surplus, trace, vestige **2.** detritus, dregs, flotsam, jetsam, junk, refuse, scrap **3.** bequest, claim, estate, inheritance, property, title

remark *n.* **1.** assertion, bon mot, comment, declaration, observation, opinion, Parthian shot, reflection, statement, thought, utterance, word **2.** acknowledgment, attention, consideration, heed, mention, notice, observation, recognition, regard – *v.* **1.** assert, communicate, declare, enunciate, express, mention, respond, say, speak, talk, utter **2.** note, observe, perceive, see, take note, watch

remarkable *adj.* **1.** astonishing, awesome, exceptional, extraordinary, impressive, miraculous, momentous, noteworthy, outstanding, phenomenal, rare, signal, singular, smashing *(Nonformal)*, striking, super, terrific, uncommon, unique, wonderful wondrous, world-class *Antonyms:* common, insignificant, usual **2.** apparent, clear conspicuous, distinguished, distinct, evident, marked, manifest, notable, noticeable, obvious, patent, prominent

emedial *adj.* alleviative, antidotal, corrective, curative, healing, healthful, invigorating, medicinal, purifying, recuperative, reformative, repairing, restorative, soothing, therapeutic, tonic, treating, wholesome *Antonyms:* aggravating, exacerbating, nettling

emedy *n.* **1.** aid, assistance, corrective, cure, cure-all, drug, elixir, fix-all, improvement, nostrum, panacea, pharmaceutical, physic, pill, prescription, redress, relief, restorative, solution, succour, support, therapy, treatment **2.** antidote, counteraction, countermeasure, counterstep, counterstroke – *v.* **1.** amend, ameliorate, change, correct, fix, help, improve, put right, rectify, redress, repair, restore, right, straighten out **2.** alleviate, assuage, attend to, cure, doctor, ease, heal, medicate, mend, relieve, soothe, treat **3.** annul, counteract, neutralize, overcome, remove, reverse, undo

emember *v.* **1.** recall, recognize, recollect **2.** call up, jog, reminisce, retrospect, review, summon, think back **3.** absorb, hold, keep, memorize, retain, safe keep **4.** acknowledge, cite, compensate, credit, notice, reward, thank *Antonyms:* forget, neglect, snub

emembrance *n.* **1.** anamnesis, flashback, memory, nostalgia, recall, recollection, reminder, reminiscence, retrospection **2.** commemoration, gift, keepsake, memento, memorial, relic, shrine, souvenir, token

emind *v.* advise, call up, mention, note, nudge, point out, prod, prompt, recall, recollect, refresh, rekindle, remember, reminisce, rethink, revive

eminder *n.* **1.** *aide-mémoire (French),* cue, hint, intimation, memo, memorandum, note, sign, suggestion **2.** keepsake, memento, memorial, relic, remembrance, souvenir, token, trinket, trophy

eminisce *v.* call up, hark *or* think back, mind, muse, recall, recollect, remember, remind, rethink, retrospect, review,

eminiscent *adj.* **1.** evocative, indicative, redolent, suggestive **2.** corny, emotional, maudlin, mushy, nostalgic, sentimental *Nonformal:* sappy, schmaltzy

remiss *adj.* **1.** absent-minded, asleep at the switch *or* wheel *(Nonformal),* culpable, delinquent, derelict, dilatory, forgetful, irresponsible, negligent, perfunctory, tardy *Antonyms:* dutiful, punctual, scrupulous **2.** apathetic, careless, cursory, fainéant, heedless, inattentive, indifferent, laggard, lax, lazy, loose, shiftless, slack, sloppy, slothful, thoughtless, unenterprising *Antonyms:* careful, heedful, meticulous

remission *n.* **1.** acquittal, absolution, amnesty, discharge, excuse, exoneration, forgiveness, mercy, pardon, release, vindication **2.** abatement, abeyance, break, cessation, ebb, halt, hiatus, interruption, lapse, letup, lull, pause, recess, relaxation, respite, suspension **3.** alleviation, amelioration, decline, decrease, lessening, mitigation, palliation, reduction, temperance

remit *v.* **1.** dispatch, forward, pay, recompense, remunerate, send, settle, transmit **2.** absolve, condone, excuse, exempt, exonerate, forbear, forgive, free, let off *(Nonformal),* pardon, release, spare, vindicate **3.** abate, decline, decrease, diminish, lessen, mitigate, modify, reduce, relax, slacken, still, subside, temper **4.** correct, give back, rectify, redress, remand, replace, restore, return **5.** defer, delay, intermit, postpone, procrastinate, put off, shelve *(Nonformal),* stall, suspend

remittance *n.* cash, compensation, installment, pay, recompense, repayment *See also:* **remuneration**

remnant *adj.* extant, leftover, remaining, spare, superfluous, surviving – *n.* **1.** discards, excess, leftovers, oddments, rejectamenta, remains, residue, residuum, surplus **2.** bit, hint, fragment, piece, scrap, semblance, shard, trace, vestige

remonstrate *v.* challenge, combat, criticize, decry, denounce, deprecate, disapprove, disparage, dispute, dissent, expostulate, fight, find fault, inveigh, nag, object, oppose, protest, resist, take issue

remonstrative *adj.* agonistic, disagreeing, disputatious, dissenting, expostulative, expostulatory, objecting, opposing, polemic, protesting, remonstrant

remorse *n.* angst, anguish, anxiety, attrition, compunction, contrition, grief, guilt, penance, penitence, pity, regret, remorsefulness, repentance, rue, self-reproach, shame, sorrow, woe, worry

remorseful *adj.* apologetic, ashamed, chastened, compunctious, conscience-stricken, contrite, embarrassed, guilt-ridden, guilty, mournful, penitent, regretful, repentant, rueful, sad, shamefaced, sorry *Antonyms:* brazen, shameless, unabashed

remorseless *adj.* callous, cruel, fierce, forbidding, hard, hard-hearted, harsh, icy *(Nonformal)*, impenitent, implacable, inexorable, inhumane, insensitive, merciless, obdurate, pitiless, ruthless, sanguinary, shameless, tough, tyrannical, uncompassionate, unforgiving, unmerciful, unregenerate, unrelenting, unremitting, unrepentant, unyielding, vindictive *Antonyms:* kind, sympathetic, thoughtful

remote *adj.* **1.** backwoods, beyond the pale, distant, far, faraway, far-flung, far-off, inaccessible, isolated, jerkwater *(Nonformal)*, outlying, out-of-the-way, removed, secluded, undiscovered, unpopulated *Antonyms:* central, close, near, neighbouring **2.** extraneous, extrinsic, immaterial, inappropriate, indirect, irrelevant, non-germane, pointless **3.** abstracted, aloof, cold, cool, detached, disinterested, incurious, indifferent, introspective, introverted, reserved, standoffish, unapproachable, uncommunicative, unconcerned, uninterested, uninvolved, withdrawn *Antonyms:* attentive, interested, involved **4.** blue sky *(Nonformal)*, doubtful, dubious, far-fetched, implausible, improbable, inconsiderable, meagre, negligible, off, outside, poor, slender, slight, slim, small, unlikely *Antonyms:* considerable, good, likely, strong

remove *n.* degree, distance, interval, measure, notch, peg, reach, rung, space, step – *v.* **1.** divest, disrobe, doff, shed, strip, take off, unclothe, uncover, undress **2.** abolish, ban, banish, deep six *(Nonformal)*, dc away with, dump, eliminate, exclude, rid throw out, trash **3.** abbreviate, amputate curtail, detach, diminish, excise, lessen prune, shorten, trim, truncate **4.** black o cross *or* scrub out, blue pencil, bowdlerize delete, edit, erase, expunge, rub out **5.** annihilate, assassinate, destroy, exterminate, extirpate, kill, liquidate, massacre murder, slaughter, slay, wipe out **6.** depose dislodge, dismiss, displace, eject, oust, overthrow, topple, unseat *Nonformal:* boot, bump, can, downsize, fire, ice, kick out, sack **7.** extract, pluck *or* take *or* wipe out, shave, wax, yank **8.** decamp, depart evacuate, exit, move, relocate, retire, retreat, transfer, transplant, transpose, uproot, vacate, withdraw *Nonformal:* beat it, skedaddle *Antonyms:* persist, remain, stay **9.** clarify, filter, filtrate, purify, screen, sieve, strain

remunerate *v.* award, compensate, grant, indemnify, pay, pay off *or* up, recompense redress, reimburse, remit, repay, reward, vouchsafe *Nonformal:* cough up, shell out, spring for

remuneration *n.* allowance, cash, cheque, compensation, fee, honorarium, money, pay, paycheque, remittance, reward, salary stipend, wages *Nonformal:* bacon, dough, loot, moolah, scratch

remunerative *adj.* advantageous, compensative, fat *(Nonformal)*, fruitful, gainful, lucrative, paying, productive, profitable, reparative, retributory, rewarding, satisfying, well-paying, worthwhile

renaissance *n.* flowering, new birth, renascence, reawakening, rebirth, reemergence, reestablishment, regeneration, rejuvenation, restoration, resurgence, revival *Antonyms:* atavism, reversion

renascent *adj.* awakened, born again *(Nonformal)*, reappearing, reborn, redivivus, rejuvenated, renewed, restored, resurgent, resuscitated, revitalized, revived

rend *v.* **1.** cleave, disjoin, divide, fracture, part, separate, sever, split, sunder *Antonyms:* connect, join, unite **2.** crack, mangle, rip up, rupture, shatter, shred, smash, splinter, tear **3.** afflict, bother, distress, disturb, harrow, haunt, hurt, pain, trouble, vex, worry, wound *Antonyms:* cheer, gladden, remedy

render *v.* **1.** cede, deliver, hand over, pay, present, proffer, remit, submit, surrender, tender **2.** contribute, furnish, give, impart, provide, supply **3.** accomplish, act, do, enact, execute, perform **4.** depict, display, illustrate, manifest, portray, represent, show **5.** elucidate, explain, explicate, express, interpret, rephrase, reword, transcribe, translate **6.** cause, create, effect, make, produce **7.** clarify, liquefy, melt, refine

rendezvous *n.* **1.** appointment, assignation, date, engagement, meeting, tryst **2.** hangout, haunt, hideaway, local *(Nonformal)*, meeting place, retreat, venue – *v.* assemble, come together, congregate, congress, converge, gather, join up, meet, muster, rally

rendition *n.* **1.** decoding, delineation, exegesis, interpretation, paraphrase, redoing, rewording, translation, transcription **2.** conception, cover, depiction, performance, portrayal, *rendu (French)*, representation, reproduction, take *(Nonformal)*, variation, version, understanding

renegade *adj.* disloyal, dissident, mutinous, outlaw, perfidious, radical, reactionary, rebel, rebellious, revolutionary, runaway, traitorous, unfaithful *Antonyms:* dependable, loyal, true – *n.* **1.** backslider, betrayer, cowboy *(Nonformal)*, defector, deserter, dissident, double-crosser, fugitive, insurgent, mutineer, outlaw, quisling, rebel, refugee, runaway, schismatic, traitor, turncoat **2.** apostate, atheist, heathen, idolater, infidel, nonbeliever, pagan

renege *v.* abandon, abjure, abrogate, annul, back-pedal, default, disown, forswear, recant, renounce, repeal, repudiate, rescind, retract, void, withdraw

renew *v.* **1.** fix, freshen, modernize, recondition, refurbish, refurnish, remodel, renovate, repair, restore *Nonformal:* gussy *or* jazz *or* spruce up **2.** begin *or* start again, continue, keep going, recommence, resume, start again **3.** recapitulate, recount, reiterate, repeat, restate **4.** reclaim, recoup, recover, regain, take back **5.** extend, keep up, maintain, prolong, sustain **6.** refresh, replenish, replace, restock, restore, stock up **7.** reestablish, resurrect, resuscitate, revitalize

renewal *n.* **1.** cleanup, face lift, gentrification, modernization, redevelopment, renovation, repair, restoration, revitalization, update, urban renewal **2.** instauration, rebirth, recreation, reinstatement, renaissance, resurrection, return, revival

renounce *v.* **1.** abstain, abandon, abnegate, avoid, cease, desert, eschew, forgo, forsake, forswear, give up, quit, spurn *Nonformal:* swear off, take the pledge **2.** abjure, deny, disavow, disclaim, disinherit, disown, dump *(Nonformal)*, recant, reject, repudiate, retract **3.** abdicate, cede, hand over, relinquish, resign, step down, surrender

renovate *v.* **1.** fix, modernize, overhaul, recondition, recreate, redesign, refashion, refit, refurbish, refurnish, rehabilitate, rejig, remake, remodel, repair, restore, resurrect, retrofit, revamp, update **2.** invigorate, liven up, recharge, refresh, reinvigorate, renew, revivify

renown *n.* acclaim, celebrity, distinction, eminence, esteem, fame, glory, honour, illustriousness, laurels, lustre, mark, note, notoriety, popularity, preeminence, prestige, prominence, report, reputation, standing, stardom, weight *Antonyms:* insignificance, obscurity, unknown

rent *n.* **1.** *cens (Historical)*, compensation, cost, fee, hire, lease, payment, price, rate, remuneration, rental, tariff **2.** breach, break, division, fissure, rift, schism, separation, split **3.** chasm, crack, fissure, gap, gash, hole, incision, opening, rip, slash, slit, tear – *v.* borrow, charter, contract, engage, hire, lease, lend, let, loan, sublet, tenant

renunciation *n.* **1.** abstention, forbearance, restraint, sacrifice, self-control, self-denial **2.** abjuration, denouncement, disclaimer, disavowal, rebuff, recantation, refusal, rejection, repudiation, veto **3.** abandonment, abdication, abnegation, desertion, disowning, forsaking, recusal, relinquishment, resignation, surrender, withdrawal

reorganize *n.* downsize, realign, rearrange, recombine, redistribute, redivide, reengineer, refashion, reform, regroup, rejig, remodel, remodify, renew, reorder, restructure, rethink, revise

repair *n.* **1.** condition, fettle, form, health, order, position, shape, state, status **2.** adjustment, fixing, improvement, instauration, overhaul, reconstruction, reformation, rehabilitation, renewal, reparation, replacement, restoration, revitalization – *v.* **1.** darn, doctor *(Nonformal)*, emend, fix, improve, mend, overhaul, patch, rebuild, recondition, recover, redo, reform, refresh, refurbish, renovate, revamp, revive, touch up, update *Antonyms:* damage, destroy, ruin, wreck **2.** atone, compensate, correct, indemnify, make amends *or* up, pay up, rectify, redeem, redress, reimburse, remedy, right, square **3.** go, leave, journey, mosey *(Nonformal)*, move, pass, remove, retire, saunter, stroll, travel, turn, wend, withdraw

reparation *n.* **1.** adjustment, betterment, correction, improvement, instauration, renovation, repair, restoration **2.** absolution, amends, apology, atonement, compensation, contrition, dues, expiation, indemnity, payment, penalty, penance, recompense, redress, remittance, remuneration, restitution, settlement

repartee *n.* **1.** answer, bon mot, comeback, quip, retort, riposte, wisecrack, witticism, zinger *(Nonformal)* **2.** badinage, banter, conversation, exchange, raillery, volley *(Nonformal)*, wordplay

repay *v.* **1.** accord, award, balance, compensate, give back, indemnify, make amends *or* restitution, pay back, recompense, refund, reimburse, remunerate, restore, return, reward, settle up, square **2.** avenge, get even, reciprocate, requite, retaliate, revenge *Nonformal:* settle the score, square accounts

repeal *n.* abrogation, annulment, cancellation, invalidation, nullification, rescission, revocation, withdrawal *Antonyms:* confirmation, ratification, reaffirmation, validation – *v.* abolish, abrogate, annul, back *or* call off, cancel, countermand, declare void, invalidate, nullify, overturn, quash, rescind, retract, reverse, revoke, void, withdraw *Antonyms:* confirm, pass, ratify, reaffirm, validate

repeat *n.* **1.** anaphora, dittography, echo, leitmotif, pleonasm, recapitulation, redundancy, refrain, rehash, reiteration, repetition, reprise, retelling, tautology **2.** rebroadcast, recast, replay, rerun **3.** copy, duplication, facsimile, imitation, likeness, parody, reproduction, sham, substitute – *v.* **1.** do over, echo, parrot, recapitulate, recount, regurgitate, reiterate, rephrase, restate, reword, say again **2.** ditto, duplicate, geminate, imitate, recreate, remake, replicate, reproduce **3.** broadcast, bruit, communicate, divulge, promulgate, publish, relate, spill the beans *(Nonformal)*, spread the word, tell **4.** continue, endure, haunt, linger, persist, reappear, recur, reoccur, return

repeatedly *adv.* again, again and again, continually, continuously, frequently, habitually, many times, oft, often, over and over, regularly *Antonyms:* occasionally, rarely, sometimes

repel *v.* **1.** beat *or* drive back, chase away, cross, fight *or* force back, forfend, frustrate, oppose, parry, rebuff, resist, stare *or* ward off **2.** deny, refuse, reject, slight, snub, spurn *Nonformal:* brush off, cold shoulder *Antonyms:* accept, back, welcome **3.** appall, disgust, make sick, nauseate, offend, repulse, revolt, sicken, turn off, *Nonformal:* creep *or* gross out *Antonyms:* attract, charm, fascinate

repent *v.* apologize, atone, be contrite *or* sorry, deplore, expiate, feel remorse, have qualms, kneel, lament, redress, reform, regret, reproach oneself, rue, seek forgiveness, show penitence, sorrow

repentance *n.* attrition, compunction, contrition, grief, guilt, penitence, regret, remorse, rue, self-reproach, sorriness, sorrow

repentant *adj.* abject, apologetic, ashamed, atoning, compensatory, conscience-stricken, contrite, expiatory, humbled, penitent, propitiatory, redemptive, remorseful, reparative, restitutive, rueful, shamefaced, sheepish *(Nonformal)*, sorry *Antonyms:* callous, remorseless, shameless, unrepentant

repercussion *n.* **1.** aftereffect, aftermath, backlash, chain reaction, consequence, effect, fallout, feedback, follow-up, impact, influence, outcome, reaction, result, side effect, spin-off **2.** echo, kick *(Nonformal)*, rebound, recoil, reflex, reverberation, shock wave

repertory *n.* **1.** amassment, cache, collection, depot, inventory, pile, reservoir, stock, stockpile, store, storehouse, warehouse **2.** actors, company, players, theatre, troupe

repetition *n.* **1.** anaphora, dittography, paraphrase, pleonasm, recapitulation, recurrence, redundancy, repeat, restatement, retelling, tautology **2.** copy, ditto, duplicate, imitation, replication, reproduction **3.** chant, echo, encore, leitmotif, refrain, reprise, rhythm

repetitious *adj.* anaphoric, battological, flatulent, long-winded, pleonastic, prolix, redundant, reiterative, resonant, tautological, tedious, verbose, windy, wordy

replace *v.* **1.** put back, refill, restock, restore, return **2.** fill *or* stand in, follow, subrogate, substitute, succeed, supercede, supplant **3.** compensate, pay back, refund, reimburse, remit, remunerate, repay, restitute

replenish *v.* fill, furnish, provide, provision, refill, refresh, refuel, reload, renew, replace, restock, restore, stock *or* top up *Antonyms:* consume, drain, exhaust

replete *adj.* **1.** abounding, abundant, alive, awash, brimming, charged, chock-full, complete, crammed, crowded, filled, jammed, jam-packed, lavish, loaded, luxurious, overflowing, packed, plenteous, rife, swarming, teeming, well-provided, well-stocked *Antonyms:* bare, empty, lacking **2.** cloyed, full, glutted, gorged, overfed, sated, satiated, stuffed *Antonyms:* famished, hungry, wanting *Commonly misused:* **complete**

replica *n.* clone, copy, ditto, duplicate, facsimile, fake, forgery, imitation, likeness, look-alike, mimic, model, repeat, reproduction, scan, take-off, Xerox *(Trademark)* *Nonformal:* fax, rip-off *Antonym:* genuine, original, real McCoy

reply *n.* **1.** acknowledgment, answer, communication, counterstatement, interaction, Parthian shot, R.S.V.P., reaction, rebuttal, rejoinder, repost, response, retort, return **2.** echo, repercussion, reverberation, wave – *v.* acknowledge, communicate, exchange, interact, justify, react, rebut, respond, retort

report *n.* **1.** account, address, announcement, article, brief, broadcast, cable, chronicle, communication, communiqué, declaration, description, dispatch, information, message, narration, news, note, opinion, outline, précis, proclamation, pronouncement, record, statement, summary, version, write-up **2.** gossip, hearsay, rumour, story *Nonformal:* dirt, info, lowdown, scoop, scuttlebutt **3.** character, distinction, esteem, fame, regard, renown, reputation **4.** bang, blast, boom, clap, crash, explosion, noise, rumble, shot, sound – *v.* **1.** advise, air, announce, broadcast, circulate, communicate, cover, debrief, declare, describe, detail, disclose, document, impart, inform, make along *or* known *or* public, mention, narrate, notify, pass on, present, proclaim, publish, recite, recount, relate, relay, reveal, set forth, spread, state, summarize, tell, trumpet, webcast, wire, write up **2.** betray, blab, complain, reveal, tattle, tell on, tip off *Nonformal:* rat *or* squeal on, snitch **3.** bruit, dish the dirt *(Nonformal)*, prate, prattle, gossip, spread rumours *or* the word, whisper **4.** appear, arrive, clock in *(Nonformal)*, come, get to, present, reach, show, show *or* turn up

reporter *n.* critic, intelligencer, journalist, messenger, news reader *or* writer, pressperson, talking head, writer *Nonformal:* hack, newshound, scribe *Kinds of reporter:* anchorperson, announcer, columnist, court, crime, interviewer, investigative, newscaster, newsperson, paparazzo, photojournalist, reviewer, sportswriter, stenographer, stringer, videographer *See also:* **journalist**

repose *n.* **1.** breather *(Nonformal)*, calm, ease, inaction, inactivity, leisure, peace, quiet, quietude, refreshment, relaxation, renewal, respite, rest, restfulness, sleep, slumber, stillness, tranquility *Antonyms:* drudgery, labour, toil, work **2.** assurance, composure, dignity, ease, grace, poise, self-possession, serenity – *v.* **1.** lie *or* settle down, loaf, lounge, pause, recline, relax, rest, sleep, slumber, unwind *Nonformal:* hang out, slack off, vegetate **2.** deposit, lay, live, lodge, place, put *or* set down, reposit, reside, settle, store

repository *n.* **1.** armoury, depository, depot, grain elevator, larder, pantry, store, storehouse, treasurehouse, warehouse **2.** archive, collection, dictionary, gallery, library, museum, thesaurus, treasury **3.** bin, box, case, compartment, container, file, hold, receptacle, reservoir **4.** burial case, casket, catacomb, coffin, crypt, mausoleum, ossuary, pine suit *(Nonformal)*, reliquary, sarcophagus, sepulchre, tomb, vault

reprehend *v.* berate, card *(Prince Edward Island)*, castigate, chastise, chide, criticize, remonstrate, reprimand, reprove, scold, upbraid *Nonformal:* bawl out, kick butt, lambaste *Antonyms:* encourage, spur, support

reprehensible *adj.* bad, blamable, censurable, condemnable, delinquent, disgraceful, egregious, errant, evil, flagrant, heinous, ignoble, nefarious, objectionable, opprobrious, remiss, shameful, sinful, unworthy, wicked *Antonyms:* acceptable, admirable, laudable

represent *v.* **1.** characterize, embody, epitomize, exemplify, personify, symbolize, typify **2.** act *or* negotiate *or* work for, function as, manage, replace, serve, stand in **3.** chronicle, describe, explain, express, narrate, recount, record, state **4.** depict, illustrate, limn, paint, picture, render, reproduce, trace **5.** burlesque, imitate, impersonate, mirror, parody, simulate **6.** display, enact, exhibit, present, produce, put on, stage

representation *n.* **1.** bust, carving, chart, copy, depiction, diagram, drawing, effigy, facsimile, figure, icon, image, map, model, photograph, picture, plan, reflection, reprint, reproduction, sculpture, semblance, similitude, sketch, statue, treatment **2.** account, commentary, description, detailing, elaboration, exposition, history, interpretation, rendering, rendition, statement, version **3.** burlesque, drama, imitation, impersonation, parody, performance, personification, play, skit **4.** commission, delegation, deputy, embassy, envoy, proxy, representative **5.** embodiment, epitome, example, figure, manifestation, personification, symbolization, typification **6.** appearance, display, exhibition, manifestation, materialization, presentation, showing

representative *adj.* **1.** archetypal, characteristic, descriptive, emblematic, evocative, illustrative, indicative, model, normal, prototypical, quintessential, stereotypical, symbolic, typical *Antonyms:* atypical, extraordinary, uncharacteristic **2.** ambassadorial, backup, cross-section, delegated, deputy, proxy, substitute, surrogate – *n.* **1.** archetype, epitome, example, exemplification, illustration, model, poster child *(Nonformal)*, random sample **2.** agent, alderperson, assemblyperson, ambassador, attaché, attorney, broker, burgess, commissioner, congressperson *(U.S.)*, councillor, delegate, deputy, diplomat, errand boy *(Nonformal)*, factotum, Governor General, lawyer, legate, legislator, Member of Legislative Assembly *or* MLA, Member of Parliament *or* MP, Member of Provincial Parliament *or* MPP, messenger, nuncio, ombudsperson, proxy, senator, spokesperson, stand-in, syndic, trustee

repress *v.* **1.** control, curb, deter, discontinue, fetter, hamper, harness, hog-tie *(Nonformal)*, inhibit, rein, restrain, restrict **2** block out, bottle up, censor, mute, silence smother, stifle *Nonformal:* cork, squelch swallow **3.** conquer, defeat, dominate, master, overcome, overpower, quash, quell scotch, stamp out, subdue, subvert, suppress, vanquish

repressive *adj.* absolute, authoritarian autocratic, coercive, despotic, dictatorial domineering, forbidding, harsh, high-hand ed, inhibitive, iron-handed, oppressive, overbearing, prohibitive, severe, smothering, stifling, suffocating, tough, tyrannical *Antonyms:* indulgent, lax, lenient, weak

reprieve *n.* **1.** abeyance, deferral, extension, postponement, protraction, stay, suspension **2.** abatement, breather *(Nonformal)*, hiatus, relief, remission, respite

reprimand *n.* admonishment, admonition, calling down, castigation, censure, chiding, lecture, punishment, rebuke, scolding *Nonformal:* bawling out, comeuppance, dressing-down, going over, talking-to, tongue-lashing *Antonyms:* commendation, compliment, congratulations, praise – *v.* admonish, blame, castigate, chastise, chide, criticize, denounce, lecture, punish, rebuke, reprehend, reproach, reprove, scold, upbraid *Nonformal:* bawl *or* chew out, call *or* dress down, light into, tell off *Antonyms:* applaud, commend, compliment, congratulate, praise

reprisal *n.* counterblow, counterstroke, pay back, requital, retaliation, retribution, revenge, vendetta, vengeance *Latin:* quid pro quo, lex talionis *Nonformal:* eye for an eye, tit for tat *Antonyms:* forbearance, forgiveness, pardon

reproach *n.* **1.** admonition, censure, chiding, condemnation, contempt, criticism, disapproval, obloquy, rebuke, reproof, scorn, slight *Antonyms:* acclaim, applause, kudos, praise **2.** discredit, disgrace, dishonour, disrepute, ignominy, indignity, opprobrium, reprehension, shame, slur, stain, stigma *Antonyms:* admiration, approval, honour – *v.* admonish, blame, castigate, condemn, criticize, disparage, rake, rebuke, reprimand, reprove, scold, upbraid *Nonformal:* dress down, light into, trash

reprobate *adj.* abandoned, bad, base, callous, corrupt, criminal, crooked, debased, deceitful, degenerate, dishonest, dishonourable, dissolute, evil, flagrant, hardened, immoral, iniquitous, miscreant, notorious, profligate, shameless, sinful, unprincipled, unscrupulous, vile, vitiated, wicked – *n.* bad egg *(Nonformal)*, blackguard, degenerate, knave, malefactor, miscreant, ne'er-do-well, profligate, scapegrace, sinner, wrongdoer *Antonyms:* exemplar, good George *(Nonformal)*, hero, ideal, paragon – *v.* bash *(Nonformal)*, blame, censure, condemn, damn, denounce, disapprove, impugn, reprehend, vilify

reproduce *v.* **1.** clone, copy, counterfeit, duplicate, ditto, fake, fax *(Nonformal)*, forge, photocopy, plagiarize, replicate, scan **2.** ape, emulate, follow, impersonate, mirror, model, parody, parrot, pattern, simulate, take on **3.** give birth, bear, beget, breed, engender, father, fecundate, generate, hatch, impregnate, mother, multiply, procreate, produce, proliferate, propagate, repopulate, sire, spawn **4.** bring back, evoke, imagine, recall, recollect, recreate, remember, visualize

reproduction *n.* **1.** clone, copy, duplication, figure, imitation, illustration, likeness, picture, print, replica, revival, snapshot, Xerox *(Trademark) Nonformal:* carbon, dead-ringer **2.** counterfeit, fake, forgery, rip-off, sham **3.** birth, breeding, generation, parturition, procreation, proliferation, propagation, rearing

reptile *n.* **1.** cold-blooded vertebrate *Groupings of reptiles:* crocodilian, dinosaur, lizard, snake, tortoise, turtle, tuatara, worm lizard *See also:* **dinosaur, snake** **2.** fawner, groveller, schemer, sycophant, wheedler *Nonformal:* bootlicker, piece of work, sleaze, sleazeball, toady, yes man

repudiate *v.* **1.** abjure, contradict, contravene, decline, deny, disavow, disdain, dismiss, disprove, gainsay, object, oppose, refuse, refute **2.** abandon, banish, cast off, discard, disinherit, disown, dump *(Nonformal)*, forsake, oust, spurn **3.** crap out *(Nonformal)*, default, dishonour, dodge, not pay, shirk

repugnant *adj.* **1.** abhorrent, abominable, disagreeable, disgusting, distasteful, foul, hateful, horrid, loathsome, nauseating, noxious, objectionable, obnoxious, odious, offensive, repellent, revolting, sickening, vile *Antonyms:* agreeable, attractive, compatible, pleasant **2.** adversarial, adverse, antagonistic, anti *(Nonformal)*, clashing, combative, conflicting, confrontational, contentious, contrary, disputatious, hostile, inimical, negative, opposed, oppositional, ornery, quarrelsome, resisting, surly *Antonyms:* congenial, friendly, well-disposed

repulse *n.* **1.** check, denial, rebuff, refusal, rejection, snub, spurning, turn down *Nonformal:* brush-off, cold shoulder, go-by, lumps **2.** defeat, drive off, overthrow, rout, success, win *Antonyms:* failure, full, loss – *v.* **1.** beat *or* fend *or* fight off, chase out, check, defeat, drive *or* push back, frustrate, oppose, repel, stymie **2.** rebuff, reject, snub, spurn *Nonformal:* brush off, put *or* shoot down **3.** disgust, nauseate, revolt, sicken *Antonyms:* attract, entice, seduce

repulsion *n.* **1.** abhorrence, animus, antipathy, aversion, detestation, disgust, distaste, enmity, hatred, loathing, malice, repugnance, resentment, revulsion *Antonyms:* allure, attraction, draw, temptation **2.** blockage, check, curb, defeat, defence, denial, opposition, rejection, repelling, repulse, resistance

repulsive *adj.* detestable, disgraceful, disgusting, distasteful, fetid, filthy, foul, hateful, heinous, hideous, horrid, loathsome, nauseating, objectionable, obnoxious, odious, offensive, rank, revolting, shocking, sickening, terrible, unpleasant, unsavoury, vile *Antonyms:* appealing, attractive, delightful, lovely, pleasant

reputable *adj.* **1.** conscientious, constant, creditable, dependable, established, estimable, excellent, fair, faithful, good, high-principled, honest, honourable, just, reliable, respectable, righteous, sincere, steady, straightforward, trustworthy, truthful, upfront, upright, well-thought-of, worthy *Antonyms:* backroom *(Nonformal)*, disreputable, fly-by-night, unreliable, untrustworthy **2.** acclaimed, celebrated, distinguished, eminent, esteemed, famed, famous, favoured, high-ranking, honoured, illustrious, notable, popular, prominent, renowned *Antonyms:* obscure, undefined

reputation *n.* **1.** name, place, position, rank, regard, repute, standing **2.** authority, distinction, esteem, estimation, good name, honour, influence, prestige, prominence, reliability, renown, stature, trustworthiness, virtue, weight **3.** bad name, disesteem, ignominy, ill repute, infamy, notoriety, villainy, wickedness

reputed *adj.* alleged, also known as *or* a.k.a., assumed, believed, considered, deemed, held, putative, quote unquote *(Nonformal)*, reckoned, regarded, reported, rumoured, said, self-styled, supposed *Antonyms:* actual, confirmed, real, verified

request *n.* appeal, application, approach, beseechment, call, claim, entreaty, imploration, importunity, imprecation, inquiry, intercession, invitation, offer, overture, petition, plea, prayer, proposal, proposition, question, requisition, solicitation, suggestion, suit, supplication, want, wish – *v.* abjure, address, appeal or apply to, ask, beg, beseech, besiege, bespeak, bid, call to *or* upon, canvass, demand, desire, entreat, implore, importune, inquire, invoke, plead, pray, propose, seek, solicit, suggest, supplicate

requiem *n.* *coronach (Irish)*, death song, dirge, elegy, epicedium, funeral mass, hymn, knell, lament, monody, threnody

require *v.* **1.** burn *or* hurt for *(Nonformal)*, desire, lack, miss, need, want **2.** command, demand, dictate, exact, insist upon, oblige, press for **3.** call for, entail, involve, necessitate, take *(Nonformal)*

requirement *n.* **1.** charge, demand, direction, exigency, imperative, mandate, must, need, obligation **2.** causa sine quanon *(Latin)*, condition, necessity, precondition, proviso, qualification, requisite, stipulation *Nonformal:* catch, string

requisite *adj.* basic, compulsory, essential, imperative, indispensable, mandatory, necessary, needed, obligatory, required, vital *Antonyms:* dispensable, elective, optional

requisition *n.* **1.** call, demand, mandate, request, summons **2.** application, chit, docket, form, purchase order *or* P.O., ticket, voucher – *v.* bid, call, command, compel, demand, direct, require, order, summon

requite *v.* **1.** compensate, indemnify, make amends, pay, recompense, redeem, redress, reimburse, remit, remunerate, repay, satisfy, settle **2.** exchange, give back, reciprocate, respond, return

rescind *v.* abrogate, annul, cancel, countermand, delete, invalidate, negate, nullify, quash, recall, recant, relinquish, renege, repeal, retract, reverse, revoke, suspend, veto, void, waive, withdraw *Antonyms:* accept, maintain, see through

rescue *n.* **1.** aid, assistance, help, intervention, ministration, relief, succour **2.** deliverance, extrication, freeing, liberation, manumission, salvation, saving – *v.* **1.** deliver, disentangle, emancipate, extricate, free, liberate, manumit, ransom, release, retrieve, save, set free, spring *(Nonformal)*, unleash *Antonyms:* abandon, desert, leave, lose **2.** recover, redeem, rehabilitate, retrieve, salvage *Antonyms:* dump, scrap

rescuer *n.* benefactor, deliverer, draegerman, good samaritan, helping hand, liberator, ministering angel, redeemer, SAR Tech, savior, white knight *(Nonformal)*

research *n.* analysis, examination, exploration, fact-finding, groundwork, inquest, inquiry, investigation, quest, scrutiny, study *Nonformal:* fishing expedition, legwork, research and development *or* R and D – *v.* analyze, dig into *(Nonformal)*, discover, examine, experiment, explore, find, inquire, investigate, learn, probe, scrutinize, sift through, turn up, uncover, unearth

resemblance *n.* affinity, analogy, coincidence, conformity, correspondence, kinship, likeness, parallel, parity, sameness, semblance, similarity, similitude *Antonyms:* difference, disparity, variation

resemble *v.* appear *or* seem *or* sound like, approach, approximate, coincide, come near, correspond, double, duplicate, echo, follow, match, mirror, parallel, pass for, simulate, smack of *(Nonformal)*, take after, tally

resent *v.* begrudge, despise, dislike, envy, grudge, hate, object to, take offence *or* umbrage *Antonyms:* accept, approve, like, welcome

resentment *n.* acerbity, acrimony, animosity, animus, annoyance, antagonism, bitterness, choler, cynicism, dislike, displeasure, envy, fury, grudge, hate, hurt, indignation, ire, irritation, offence, outrage, passion, pique, rancour, spleen, umbrage, vexation, wrath *Antonyms:* acceptance, cheer, contentment, goodwill

reservation *n.* **1.** appointment, booking, dibs *(Nonformal)*, place, room, seat, table **2.** condition, limitation, provision, proviso, qualification, restriction, stipulation *Nonformal:* kicker, string **3.** conservation area, crown forest *or* land, enclave, forest *or* game reserve, habitat, park, preserve, refuge, sanctuary **4.** doubt, hesitancy, nervousness, objection, qualm, scruple, second thought

reserve *n.* **1.** assets, cache, capital, fund, insurance, inventory, provisions, reservoir, resources, savings, stock, store, supply, wealth *Nonformal:* nest egg, stash *Antonyms:* debit, expenditure, expense **2.** aloofness, caution, coldness, constraint, formality, inhibition, restraint, reticence, self-restraint, silence, taciturnity, uncommunicativeness, unresponsiveness *Antonyms:* gregariousness, passion, warmth **3.** enclave, habitat, homeland, land, rez *(Nonformal)*, reservation, sanctuary, territory, tract **4.** army, auxiliaries, backup, reinforcement, reserve forces, second line, soldiers, troops – *v.* **1.** accumulate, amass, hoard, salt *or* squirrel away *(Nonformal)*, save, stash, stockpile, store up **2.** hang onto *(Nonformal)*, hold back, keep, maintain, preserve, retain, withhold **3.** book, charter, earmark, engage, guarantee, secure, set aside, tag

reserved *adj.* **1.** aloof, cautious, ceremonious, cold, collected, composed, conventional, cool, distant, formal, noncommittal, quiet, reclusive, restrained, retiring, self-contained, silent, solitary, standoffish, taciturn, unapproachable, uncommunicative, undemonstrative, unresponsive, withdrawn *Antonyms:* demonstrative, forward, open, uninhibited, warm **2.** appropriated, booked, claimed, engaged, held, kept, laid away, limited, private, restricted, retained, roped off, set apart *or* aside, spoken for, taken

reservoir *n.* **1.** basin, cistern, dam, lake, pool, source, spring, tank, well **2.** accumulation, cache, reserve, stash *(Nonformal)*, stockpile, store, supply **3.** bowl, box, chamber, container, font, keg, receptacle, repository, vat

reside *v.* abide, belong, bide, bunk, dwell, exist, homestead, inhabit, live, locate, lodge, nest, occupy, park, perch, remain, roost, settle, sleep, sojourn, squat *(Nonformal)*, stay, tenant

residence *n.* **1.** abode, address, domicile, dwelling, home, household, living place *or* quarters, lodging, place, seat, spot *Nonformal:* digs, nest, pad, stoop **2.** inhabitancy, internship, occupancy, office, prefecture, sojourn

resident *adj.* aboriginal, ethnic, indigenous, local, native, naturalized – *n.* **1.** citizen, denizen, dweller, inhabitant, livyer *(Newfoundland)*, occupant, resider, settler, tenant **2.** agent, ambassador, diplomat, emissary, governor, legate, minister, plenipotentiary **3.** doctor, house physician, intern, MD, medical practitioner, physician, registrar *(British)*

residual *adj.* additional, continuing, enduring, extra, leftover, lingering, net, remaining, resultant, surplus, surviving, unconsumed, unused, vestigial – *n.* difference, net, product, result *See also:* **residue**

residue *n.* **1.** excess, extra, leftover, remainder, surplus, trace element *Antonyms:* core, essence, nucleus **2.** clinker, debris, detritus, dregs, junk, leavings, parings, remains, remnant, residual, residuum, scouring, scraps, scum, shavings, silt, slag, slash *(Forestry)*, slurry, tailings, trash

resign *v.* **1.** abandon, abdicate, bail *or* bow out, give up, leave, quit, relinquish, renounce, retire, secede, sign off, stand down, surrender, terminate, vacate, walk, walk out **2.** accept, acquiesce, admit, capitulate, cede, fold, relent, yield *Nonformal:* cave, crumble

resignation *n.* **1.** abdication, departure, leaving, notice, quitting, relinquishment, retirement, surrender, termination, vacating, walking papers *(Nonformal)*, withdrawal **2.** acceptance, acquiescence, compliance, conformity, deference, docility, endurance, forbearance, nonresistance, passivity, patience, submission, sufferance *Antonyms:* defiance, dissent, protest, resistance

resigned *adj.* acquiescent, adapted, adjusted, agreeable, amenable, biddable, calm, compliant, enduring, passive, patient, ready, reconciled, satisfied, stoical, submissive, tolerant, used to, well-disposed, willing, yielding *Antonyms:* rebellious, recalcitrant, reticent

resilient *adj.* **1.** bendable, elastic, flexible, malleable, pliable, recovering, rubbery, springy, stretchy, supple, tensile **2.** bouncy, buoyant, breezy, chipper *(Nonformal)*, effervescent, irrepressible, lighthearted, perky, pert, sunny, unflappable

resist *v.* **1.** block, counter, foil, frustrate, hinder, oppose, preclude, prevent, rebuff, stop, stymie, thwart **2.** defeat, hold *or* bear up *(Nonformal)*, repel, repulse, weather, withstand **3.** abnegate, abstain, avoid, desist, forgo, eschew, refrain from, renounce, swear off *(Nonformal) Antonyms:* enjoy, indulge, surrender to

resistance *n.* **1.** blockage, check, clot, hindrance, impediment, obstacle, obstruction, occlusion, restriction **2.** contravention, defiance, intransigence, mutiny, non-compliance, opposition, parry, protest, refusal, rejection, sit-down, slowdown, strike, unwillingness, work-to-rule **3.** battle, conflict, fighting, friction, hostilities, insurrection, rebellion, revolt, riot, uprising

resolute *adj.* **1.** adamant, decided, determined, dogged, fast, firm, fixed, indefatigable, inflexible, intent, iron-willed, obstinate, persistent, purposeful, relentless, set, single-minded, staunch, steadfast, stubborn, sure, tenacious, unflagging, unflinching, unshakable, unwavering *Antonyms:* doubtful, undecided, unsteady **2.** bold, courageous, daring, dauntless, doughty, game *(Nonformal)*, intrepid, plucky, stalwart, valiant *Antonyms:* afraid, cowering, fearful, timid

resolution *n.* **1.** aim, ambition, aspiration, determination, end, goal, intent, objective, plan, point, purpose, target **2.** boldness, courage, dauntlessness, fixidity, fortitude, spirit, staunchness, steadfastness, tenacity, will *Nonformal:* backbone, grit, gumption, guts **3.** assertion, decree, decision, declaration, finding, judgment, motion, ruling, settlement, verdict **4.** advice, prospectus, proposition, proposal, recommendation, solution, suggestion **5.** close, conclusion, denouement, end, finish, outcome, point, reconciliation, result, settlement, termination, wind-up *See also:* **result**

resolve *n.* **1.** dedication, determination, fortitude, indomitability, iron-will, nerve, single-mindedness, strength, tenacity *Nonformal:* grit, staying-power **2.** answer, conclusion, resolution, solution – *v.* **1.** agree, conclude, decide, decree, determine, rule, settle **2.** chose, elect, opt for, pick, vote **3.** amend, correct, fix, heal, end, patch up, rectify, remedy, solve, square, straighten out **4.** aim, design, endeavour, plum, project, propose **5.** alter, channel, convert, deflect, divert, guide, transform, transmute **6.** analyze, anatomize, break down *or* up, dissect, divide, itemize, reduce, unravel, unscramble **7.** banish, dismiss, dispel, remove

resonance *n.* **1.** amplification, deepness, fullness, plangency, richness, sonorousness, sonority, tremolo **2.** echo, oscillation, rebound, return, reverberation, tremulousness

resonant *adj.* **1.** booming, deep, enhanced, fat *(Nonformal)*, full, heightened, intensified, loud, orotund, plangent, powerful, rich, roaring, round, sonorant, sonorous, stentorian, thunderous *Antonyms:* faint, low, muffled, muted, weak **2.** echoing, pulsating, pulsing, resounding, reverberant, reverberating, throbbing

resort *n.* **1.** camp, cottage country, holiday spot, haunt, haven, hideaway, hotel, hot *or* mineral spring, inn, lodge, motel, motor lodge, retreat, spa, tourist centre, tourist trap *(Nonformal)* **2.** aid, alternative, choice, option, possibility, recourse, resource *Nonformal:* escape clause *or* route, out – *v.* **1.** convene, frequent, gather, haunt, head for, patronize, repair to **2.** apply, employ, turn to, use, utilize

resounding *adj.* **1.** booming, deafening, ear-splitting, echoing, loud, piercing, plangent, noisy, ringing, rumbling, stentorian, thundering **2.** celebrated, distinguished, extolled, famed, illustrious, notable, prestigious, remarkable, renowned, widespread

resource *n.* **1.** aid, assistance, backing, backup, help, recourse, support **2.** ability, capability, faculty, know-how, knowledge, means, qualifications, savoir-faire, skill, talent **3.** gumption *(Nonformal)*, imagination, ingenuity, initiative, inventiveness

resourceful *adj.* able, bright, capable, clever, creative, enterprising, experienced, imaginative, ingenious, intelligent, inventive, original, quick-witted, sharp, shrewd, skilful, talented, venturesome *Antonyms:* incompetent, unimaginative, uninventive

resources *n. pl.* **1.** assets, backing, bankroll, belongings, bucks *(Nonformal)*, budget, capital, collateral, effects, funds, holdings, income, possessions, property, reserves, revenue, riches, savings, supplies, wealth **2.** ability, background, basics, capacity, equipment, experience, know-how, makings, means, plant, people, power, raw materials, skills, tools, wherewithal *Nonformal:* smarts, set-up

respect *n.* **1.** admiration, appreciation, esteem, favour, homage, recognition, veneration, worship **2.** attentiveness, civility, courtesy, etiquette, manners, politeness **3.** acquiescence, adherence, compliance, conformity, deference, observation, solicitude, submission **4.** aspect, characteristic, detail, feature, light, particular, point, reference, regard – *v.* **1.** adore, admire, appreciate, commend, extol, honour, idolize, laud, prize, revere, value, venerate **2.** abide by, adhere to, comply with, follow, heed, obey, observe, uphold **3.** bear on, concern, involve, regard, relate *or* pertain to

respectable *adj.* **1.** ample, appreciable, considerable, decent, goodly, sizable, substantial *Antonyms:* paltry, poor, small **2.** above-board, admirable, commendable, credible, deserving, esteemed, highly touted, laudable, reputable, respected, upright, valued, venerable, virtuous, worthy **3.** appropriate, becoming, befitting, conventional, correct, decent, decorous, polite, proper, refined, well-bred *Antonyms:* impolite, rude, vulgar **4.** adequate, all right, average, fair, mediocre, middling, ordinary, passable, reasonable, satisfactory, tolerable *Nonformal:* okay, so-so **5.** clean, neat, ordered, presentable, scrubbed, shipshape, spruce *(Nonformal)*, tidy, trim *Antonyms:* messy, shabby, untidy

respectful *adj.* civil, courtly, deferential, dutiful, filial, gracious, humble, mannerly, polite, self-effacing, solicitous *Antonyms:* cheeky, rude, saucy *Commonly misused:* **respective**

respective *adj.* corresponding, each, individual, own, particular, personal, private, relevant, separate, several, special, specific, various *Commonly misused:* **respectful**

respects *n. pl.* best wishes, commendations, compliments, courtesies, greetings, kind wishes, regards, salutations, warmthoughts, wishes

respite *n.* **1.** break, breather *(Nonformal)*, hiatus, holiday, intermission, interval, letup, lull, pause, recess, rest **2.** acquittal, deferment, delay, discharge, exculpation, immunity, postponement, release, reprieve, stay, suspension

resplendent *adj.* beaming, beautiful, bedazzling, blinding, bright, brilliant, dazzling, effulgent, flamboyant, fulgent, glaring, glittering, glorious, gorgeous, iridescent, luminous, radiant, splendid, sublime, vivid *Antonyms:* dark, dim, gloomy, murky

respond *v.* acknowledge, answer, counter, parry, R.S.V.P., react, rejoin, reply, retort, return *Antonyms:* ignore, neglect, snub

response *n.* **1.** acknowledgment, answer, comeback, counter, feedback, reaction, rejoinder, reply, retort, return, riposte **2.** communication, confirmation, e-mail, letter, memo, message

responsibility *n.* **1.** conscientiousness, dependability, dependableness, faithfulness, firmness, honesty, levelheadedness, maturity, rationality, reliability, stability, steadfastness, trustworthiness, uprightness *Antonyms:* instability, perfidy, treachery **2.** accountability, answerability, culpability, liability **3.** burden, care, charge, debt, mill stone *(Nonformal)*, obligation, onus, pledge, trouble, trust, weight, worry **4.** affair, business, concern, duty, engagement, function, incumbency, job, jurisdiction, matter, project, role, task, work

responsible *adj.* **1.** accountable, answerable, bonded, bound, contracted, chargeable, culpable, in charge *or* control, obligated, pledged, running the show *(Nonformal)*, subject, sworn to **2.** adult, dedicated, dependable, efficient, ethical, faithful, firm, levelheaded, loyal, mature, qualified, rational, reliable, sensible, sober, sound, stable, steadfast, steady, tried, true, trusty, trustworthy, upright, virtuous *Antonyms:* fly-by-night, shady, shifty, slick

rest *n.* **1.** ease, holiday, idleness, leave, leisure, long weekend, lull, mental health day *(Nonformal)*, recreation, relaxation, sabbatical, time off, vacation *Antonyms:* drudgery, toil, work **2.** break, caesura, down time *(Nonformal)*, gap, halt, interruption, interval, pause, recess, respite, stay, stop **3.** calm, hush, inertia, peace, quiet, serenity, stillness, tranquility **4.** cat nap, nap, repose, siesta, sleep, slumber *Nonformal:* forty winks, power nap, shut-eye, snooze **5.** death, decease, demise, departure, end, expiration, final resting place, grave, heaven **6.** bedrock, cornerstone, foundation, ground, mainstay, pillar, prop, stand, stay, support, trestle **7.** abode, *auberge (French)*, bivouac, haven, hotel, inn, motor inn *or* lodge, lodging *or* stopping place, motel, pension, refuge, shelter **8.** balance, change, excess, leftover, net, remainder, remains, remnant, residue, superfluity, surplus – *v.* **1.** languish, loll, lounge, refresh, retire, unwind *Nonformal:* laze, take five, vegetate **2.** doze, drowse, hibernate, lie down, recline, retire *Nonformal:* crash, hit the hay *or* sheets, nod off, saw logs **3.** base, depend *or* hang on, found, hinge, rely, sit **4.** anchor, continue, dwell, hang *(Nonformal)*, inhabit, linger, lodge, persist, remain, sojourn stay, stop, tarry

restaurant *n.* beanery, bistro, *brasserie (Quebec)*, buffet, café, cafeteria, canteen, carvery, chophouse, coffeehouse, coffee shop, deli, delicatessen, diner, dining room, drive-in, eatery, grill, grillroom, hot-dog stand, hotel, inn, lunch wagon, lunch counter, luncheonette, mess hall, osteria, pizzeria, pub, rathskeller, ristorante, roadhouse, rotisserie, smörgåsbord, snack bar, steakhouse, tavern, tearoom, trattoria *Nonformal:* all-you-can-eat, dump, greasy spoon, hamburger joint, hash house, noshery

restitution *n.* amends, blood money *(Nonformal)*, compensation, indemnification, payment, recompense, redress, reimbursement, remuneration, reparation, repayment, replacement, replevin, requital, restoration, return, satisfaction, wergeld

restive *adj.* **1.** agitated, anxious, avid, brusque, choleric, curt, edgy, fidgety, irascible, jittery, jumpy, nervy, on edge, on pins and needles *(Nonformal)*, peevish, splenetic, tense, testy *Antonyms:* calm, laid-back, peaceful, relaxed **2.** contumacious, difficult, discontent, disobedient, fractious, noncompliant, rambunctious, rebellious, uncontrollable, unhappy, unmanageable, unruly

restless *adj.* **1.** active, alive, bustling, busy, energetic, lively, moving, vibrant **2.** agitated, anxious, discontented, distressed, disturbed, edgy, excited, fretful, fidgety, jittery, jumpy, nervous, on tenterhooks, ruffled, skittish, squirrely, tense, troubled, uneasy, worried *Nonformal:* antsy, stressed, strung out, wired **3.** capricious, changeable, fickle, inconstant, irresolute, mercurial, roguish, unstable, wandering *Antonyms:* comfortable, content, satisfied **4.** alert, insomniac, sleepless, vigilant, wakeful, wide-awake *Antonyms:* asleep, dead *(Nonformal)*, unconscious

restlessness *n.* **1.** agitation, anxiety, cabin fever, discontent, disquietude, disturbance, edginess, excitability, fitfulness, fretfulness, fuss, inquietude, insomnia, jitters, jumpiness, nervousness, pother, restiveness, tension, turbulence, turmoil, uneasiness, unrest, wanderlust *Nonformal:* butterflies, fidgets, heebie-jeebies *Antonyms:* calm, contentment, peacefulness **2.** activity, ado, bustle, commotion, hurry, hustle, movement

restoration *n.* **1.** conversion, gentrification, improvement, instauration, modernization, rebirth, reconstruction, reestablishment, rehabilitation, renaissance, renewal, renovation, repair, revival, update, urban renewal **2.** compensation, recovery, replacement, requital, restitution, return

restore *v.* **1.** fix, improve, make over, modernize, patch, rebuild, recondition, reconstruct, recreate, remodel, repair, update **2.** correct, energize, heal, nurse, mend, rehabilitate, rejuvenate, remedy, resuscitate, revitalize, vivify **3.** reconnect, reerect, reestablish, reinstate, reissue, reintroduce, reinvest, undo *(Computer)*, **4.** compensate, give back, reimburse, remit, replace, return

restrain *v.* **1.** bridle, check, curb, curtail, harness, hold back, inhibit, muzzle, rein in, repress, stem, subdue, suppress **2.** contain, demarcate, limit, restrict **3.** hamper, handicap, hog-tie *(Nonformal)*, impede, pinion, prevent, retard, stop **4.** confine, detain, impound, imprison, incarcerate, jail, lock up

restrained *adj.* **1.** calm, cool, controlled, mild, moderate, plain, quiet, reasonable, reserved, subdued *Antonyms:* outrageous, over-the-top, wanton, wild **2.** business-like, conservative, considered, formal, repressed, uptight, withdrawn **3.** bound, caged, chained, confined, constrained, darbies, fettered, gagged, hobbled, imprisoned, incarcerated, limited, muffled, muzzled, shackled, suppressed, under wraps *(Nonformal)*

restraint *n.* **1.** check, cramp, curb, hindrance, hitch *(Nonformal)*, impediment, limitation, obstacle, obstruction, restriction, snag **2.** arrest, bondage, captivity, confinement, duress, imprisonment, incarceration **3.** bars, bilboes, bridle, chains, fetters, handcuffs, harness, irons, leash, manacles, muzzle, pillory, shackles, stocks, strait jacket, tether *Nonformal:* bracelets, cuffs **4.** aplomb, constraint, equanimity, poise, reserve, self-control, self-possession, will power

restrict *v.* bind, check, confine, constrict, contain, cramp, curb, decrease, define, delimit, demarcate, diminish, hamper, handicap, hem in, impede, inhibit, limit, moderate, qualify, reduce, regulate, restrain, surround, temper, tether, tie *Nonformal:* ground, hog-tie, sit on *Antonyms:* broaden, encourage, foster, free, promote

restricted *adj.* **1.** bound, boxed or hemmed in, confined, contained, cramped, hampered, inhibited, limited, modified, prescribed, reduced, straitened *Antonyms:* at liberty, free, uncurbed **2.** closed, gated, off-limits, out-of-bounds, posted *(Nonformal)*, private, protected **3.** buttoned up *(Nonformal)*, classified, confidential, eyes only, highest security clearance, hush-hush, top secret **4.** discriminatory, exclusive, lily-white, members-only, segregated **5.** blinkered, hide-bound, narrow-minded, one-track

restriction *n.* brake, catch, check, condition, curb, governor, inhibitor, limitation, qualification, regulation, reservation, rule, snag, stipulation, structure, stumbling block *Nonformal:* glitch, kicker, string

result *n.* **1.** aftereffect, aftermath, backlash, backwash. by-product, conclusion, consequence, dénouement, development, effect, eventuality, fallout, issue, outcome, repercussion, upshot, wake *Antonyms:* cause, origin, root, source **2.** decision, decree, determination, finding, judgment, resolution, verdict **3.** balance, bottom line, loss, net, proceeds, product, profit, returns, take – *v.* **1.** accrue, appear, arise, attend, come about *or* forth *or* from *or* out, derive, develop, effect, emanate, emerge, ensue, grow, happen, issue, lead to, occur, proceed, rise, spring, stem, turn *or* work out **2.** close, conclude, culminate, end, finish, terminate

resume *inter:* as you were, keep going, onward *Nonformal:* giddy-up, mush – *v.* assume *or* begin *or* start again, carry on, continue, proceed, recommence, reconvene, reembark, renew, reopen, restart

résumé *n.* abstract, bio *(Nonformal)*, biography, curriculum vitae, c.v., digest, history, outline, personal *or* work history, portfolio, précis, recapitulation, summary, summation, synopsis, vita

resurgence *n.* comeback, phoenix, rally, recovery, reanimation, reappearance, reawakening, rebirth, regeneration, rejuvenation, renaissance, renascence, renewal, restoration, resurrection, resuscitation, return, revival, revivification, risorgimento

resurrect *v.* bring back, dust off *(Nonformal)*, exhume, raise from the dead, reanimate, reestablish, rejuvenate, renew, restore, resuscitate, revive, save

resuscitate *v.* breathe new life into, imbue, inspirit, quicken, reanimate, reawaken, reinvigorate, renew, rescue, restore, resurrect, revitalize, revive, revivify, save, snatch from the jaws of death *(Nonformal)*, stimulate

retain *v.* **1.** clench, clutch, grasp, grip, harbour, secure *Antonyms:* give away, let go, release **2.** hoard, hold, keep, maintain, preserve, save **3.** commission, contract, employ, engage, hire, pay, put under contract *Antonyms:* fire, let go, release **4.** absorb, assimilate, learn, memorize, recall, recollect, remember *Antonyms:* forget, repress, suppress

retaliate *v.* counter, exact reprisals *or* retribution, get even, pay, pay *or* strike back, reciprocate, repay, requite, return, revenge, square accounts, take revenge, turn upon, wreak vengeance *Nonformal:* get, like for like, return the complement, settle the score *Antonyms:* accept, admit, forgive

retaliation *n.* reciprocation, redress, repayment, reprisal, requital, retribution, revenge, vengeance *Antonyms*: acceptance, forgiveness, *lex talionis (Latin)*, submission

retard *v.* arrest, block, brake, check, crimp, delay, detain, encumber, fetter, hamper, handicap, hinder, hold back *or* up, impede, limit, mire, obstruct, slow down, stall, stifle *Antonyms:* accelerate, advance, expedite, hasten, stimulate

reticent *adj.* **1.** moderate, quiet, reserved, restrained, shy, subdued, taciturn, unobtrusive, wallflower **2.** circumspect, secretive, silent, tight-lipped, uncommunicative, unforthcoming *Commonly misused:* **reluctant**

retire *v.* **1.** abdicate, call it a day *or* quits *(Nonformal)*, depart, hang up one's jersey, leave, resign, secede, stop working, take the golden handshake **2.** decommission, mothball, pension off, put out to pasture, remove from service, superannuate, take off the payroll **3.** cloister *or* sequester oneself, estivate, hibernate, hit the hay *or* sack *(Nonformal)*, rusticate, sleep, turn in, withdraw **4.** break ranks, decamp, fall back, flee, quit the field, recede, retreat *Nonformal:* skedaddle, take a powder

retirement *n.* **1.** golden *or* pension *or* waning years *Nonformal:* freedom, R & R, the life of Riley **2.** abdication, countermarch, flight, relinquishment, removal, resignation **3.** dismissal, pensioning off, redundancy, termination, **4.** isolation, obscurity, privacy, reclusion, seclusion, solitude *Antonyms:* exposure, limelight, publicity, spotlight **5.** asylum, cloister, covert, harbour, haunt, haven, hermitage, hideaway, hiding place, sanctuary *See also:* **retreat**

retiring *adj.* bashful, coy, demure, diffident, humble, introverted, meek, modest, mousy, quiet, reserved, restrained, reticent, self-effacing, shrinking, shy, timid, unassertive, unassuming, unsociable, withdrawn *Antonyms:* audacious, forward, gregarious, outgoing, sociable

retool *v.* adapt, doctor *(Nonformal)*, keep competitive *or* pace, modernize, overhaul, recondition, reconfigure, redo, reengineer, refurbish, refurnish, reprogram, revamp, update *See also:* **recondition**

retract *v.* **1.** abjure, back down *or* off, back pedal, cancel, countermand, disavow, disclaim, disown, eat one's words *(Nonformal)*, eliminate, forswear, recall, recant, recede, renege, renounce, repeal, repudiate, rescind, reverse, revoke, suspend, take back, unsay, withdraw *Antonyms:* advance, continue, maintain **2.** cover, draw back *or* in, hide, retreat, sheathe

retreat *n.* **1.** asylum, clinic, detox centre, hospital, sanatorium, shelter **2.** ashram, cloister, commune, convent, haunt, haven, hermitage, hideaway, monastery, nunnery, refuge, sanctuary, sanctorum, sanctum **3.** exile, isolation, privacy, recess, respite, rest, retirement, sabbatical, vacation, walkabout, withdrawal **4.** abdication, decamping, departure, escape, evacuation, exodus, flight **5.** ebbing, receding, reflux, retrogression, reversal

retribution *n.* **1.** counterblow, getting back, justice, nemesis, payback, pound of flesh, *quid pro quo (Latin)*, reprisal, revenge, vengeance, vindication *Nonformal:* an eye for an eye, just desserts **2.** atonement, compensation, recompense, redress, repayment, requital, restitution, reward

retrieve *v.* **1.** get *or* win back, reclaim, recoup, recover, regain, repair, salvage, save **2.** animate, enliven, resuscitate, refresh, rehabilitate, restore, revive, revivify, save **3.** atone, correct, make up for, rectify, redeem, remedy **4.** bring *or* draw out, recall, recollect, remember, retain **5.** bring back, fetch, find, get, hunt **6.** cull, extract, glean, obtain, procure

retrograde *adj.* **1.** declining, degenerate, deteriorating, failing, falling, on the downward slide, sinking, slipping, warning **2.** backward, contrary, counterclockwise, inverse, inverted, posterior, reversed, reactionary, rearward, transposed – *v.* **1.** recede, reverse, revert **2.** decay, decline, degenerate, deteriorate, fall, lapse, sink, worsen

retrogress *v.* backslide, decay, decline, degenerate, deteriorate, ebb, fall, recede, recidivate, regress, relapse, retreat, retrograde, revert, sink, wane, weaken, worsen *Antonyms:* advance, flourish, improve, progress, recuperate

retrospect *n.* afterthought, analysis, hindsight, memory, recollection, reconsideration, re-examination, remembering, reminiscence, review, revision, study *Antonyms:* anticipation, foresight

retrospective *adj.* *ex post facto (Latin)*, historical, recollected, remembered, reminiscent, restored, revived, sentimental, suggestive *Antonyms:* avant-garde, forward-looking, future, progressive – *n.* demonstration, display, exhibit, exhibition, exposition, look back, presentation, production, review, show

return *n.* **1.** accrual, advantage, benefit, compensation, earnings, gain, guerdon, income, interest, payout, proceeds, profit, results, revenue, reward, take, yield **2.** cashback, indemnity, *quid pro quo (Latin)*, rebate, reciprocation, recompense, redress, refund, reimbursement, remittance, reparation, repayment **3.** answer, comeback, reappearance, recurrence, repartee, response, resurrection, retort, riposte, volley **4.** advent, approach, arrival, homecoming, reentry **5.** go-round, recapitulation, reiteration, repetition, restatement **6.** account, analysis, document, list, report, statement – *v.* **1.** boomerang, come back, reappear, rebound, recoil, recur, revolve **2.** backslide, lapse, recidivate, retrogress, retrovert, reverse, revert **3.** answer, exchange, react, rejoin, reply, respond, retort **4.** reconstitute, reestablish, reinstall, reinstate, reinvest, repatriate, replace, restore **5.** compensate, indemnify, recompense, refund, remit, requite **6.** benefit, pay, profit, produce, recoup, reward, yield **7.** counter, punish, redress, repay, retaliate, revenge, settle the score *(Nonformal)*, vindicate **8.** bounce back, echo, reflect, reverberate

reunion *n.* coming together, festivity, gathering, get-together, homecoming *(U.S.)*, meeting, party, shindig *(Nonformal)*, social, soiree

reveal *v.* **1.** admit, announce, betray, broadcast, confess, declare, disclose, divulge, impart, inform, publicize, state, tell *Nonformal:* blab, give away, leak, rat, squeal **2.** bare, display, exhibit, expose, moon *(Nonformal)*, open, show, unclothe, uncover, unearth, unmask, unveil *Antonyms:* conceal, cover up, hide

revel *n.* bacchanalia, celebration, fête, feast, gala, hijinks, holiday, lark, merrymaking, party, revelry, romp, spree, wassail *Nonformal:* bender, shindig, wingding – *v.* **1.** carouse, celebrate, cut loose *(Nonformal)*, frolic, gamble, indulge, make merry, party, rejoice, riot, rollick, romp, skylark **2.** bask, delight, enjoy, luxuriate, relish, roll, savour, wallow

revelation *n.* **1.** announcement, communication, communiqué, disclosure, divulgence, exposé, leak, news, proclamation, publication, slip **2.** brainstorm, discovery, flash, shock, surprise, uncovering, unearthing, unveiling *Nonformal:* bomb, eye-opener, stunner **3.** afflatus, direct intuition, divination, epiphany, inspiration, prophecy, satori, theophany

revenge *n.* comeuppance, counterblow, counterplay, getting even, payback, rancour, repayment, reprisal, requital, retaliation, retribution, return, spitefulness, vengeance, vindictiveness, whats coming to her/him *(Nonformal) Antonyms:* amnesty, clemency, forgiveness, mercy – *v.* avenge, defend, fight back, fix, get, get even, hit back, punish, reciprocate, repay, redress, requite, retaliate, retort, return, settle up *or* with, square, vindicate *Antonyms:* absolve, forgive, pardon

revenue *n.* annuity, bottom line, cash flow, credit, dividend, earnings, fruit, gain, gate*(Nonformal)*, income, interest, net, proceeds, profit, receipt, resources, return, reward, salary, take, tax *(Government)*, wages, wealth, yield *Antonyms:* expenditures, expenses, losses

reverberate *v.* **1.** boom, echo, resound, rumble, thunder, vibrate **2.** boomerang, bounce *or* bound *or* spring back, rebound, recoil, resile, ricochet

revere *v.* admire, adore, appreciate, cherish, deify, enjoy, esteem, exalt, honour, love, prize, respect, treasure, value, venerate, worship *Antonyms:* deride, despise, scorn

reverence *n.* **1.** admiration, adoration, awe, devotion, esteem, fealty, fear, homage, honour, love, loyalty, praise, respect, veneration, worship *Antonyms:* contempt, derision, disdain, scorn **2.** genuflection, obeisance, observance, prayer, sacrifice

reverent *adj.* **1.** believing, devout, faithful, God-fearing, godly, pious, religious, reverential, righteous, theistic, worshipful *Antonyms:* blasphemous, fallen, lapsed, sacrilegious **2.** ceremonious, decorous, deferential, grave, humble, obedient, obeisant, proper, regardful, respectful, serious, solemn, submissive *Antonyms:* brazen, defiant, insubordinate, proud, saucy

reverie *n.* absent-mindedness, absorption, abstraction, brown study, contemplation, daydreaming, dreaming, fantasy, meditation, musing, pensiveness, preoccupation, trance *Nonformal:* dreamland, pipe dream *Antonyms:* alertness, attentiveness, vigilance

reversal *n.* **1.** about-face, backtracking, palinode, recantation, renunciation, retraction, second thought, switch, tergiversation, turn-about, volte-face *Nonformal:* a 360, flip-flop **2.** bath *(Nonformal)*, disappointment, hard knock, loss, setback **3.** annulment, cancellation, nullification, rejection, repeal, revocation

reverse *adj.* **1.** antipodal, antithetical, counter, opposite, polar **2.** backward, inverted, mirrored, transposed, wrong sided – *n.* **1.** antipode, antithesis, contra, contrariety, converse, opposite **2.** back, converse, hind, rear, tail *Nonformal:* b-side, flipside **3.** about-face, backing up, change, reversal, turnabout, u-turn *(Nonformal)* **4.** adversity, blow, calamity, catastrophe, downfall, hardship, misfortune, setback, sorrow, tragedy, upset, vicissitude – *v.* **1.** convert, flip *(Nonformal)*, invert, transpose **2.** abrogate, annul, call back, countermand, invalidate, negate, nullify, rescind, revoke, undo, veto, void **3.** backtrack, backpedal, back up, contradict, recant, renege, retract *Nonformal:* dipsy-doodle, flip-flop

revert *v.* backslide, change, lapse, recidivate, regress, relapse, retrogress, return

review *n.* **1.** analysis, appraisal, audit, evaluation, examination, inspection, investigation, scrutiny, study **2.** cram-session *(Nonformal)*, exercise, lesson, practice, preparation, recapitulation, recitation, session **3.** catalogue, retrospective, survey, synthesis **4.** article, commentary, critique, discussion, editorial, report, summary, write-up **5.** gazette, journal, magazine, paper, periodical, publication, serial, zine *(Nonformal)* **6.** correction, edit, improvement, overhaul, redraft, revision, rewrite, second draft or try – *v.* **1.** analyze, assess, critique, discuss, evaluate, examine, explore, inspect, interpret, peruse, probe, scan, scrutinize, survey **2.** consider, go over, reexamine, rehash, restudy, rethink, reevaluate, take under advisement, **3.** bring back, call to mind, contemplate, meditate, ponder, recall, recollect, reflect, relive, remember, reminisce, retrace, retrospect, think **4.** absorb, commit to memory, digest, get by rote, learn by heart, master, memorize, study *Nonformal:* cram, pull an all-nighter

revile *v.* abuse, admonish, asperse, assail, attack, berate, blacken, calumniate, curse, defame, defile, denigrate, execrate, fulminate, imprecate, insult, libel, malign, rail, ridicule, slander, slur, sully, traduce, vilify, vituperate *Nonformal:* bad-mouth, bash, dis, tongue-lash, trash *Antonyms:* compliment, flatter, praise

revise *v.* alter, amend, change, correct, edit, overhaul, perfect, polish, recast, reconsider, rectify, redo, redraft, redraw, reexamine, rehash, rejig, restyle, rethink, retool, retrofit, revamp, review, rework, transform, upgrade

revision *n.* amended copy, change, correction, improvement, modification, newest edition *or* draft, reorganization, restructuring, rewrite, update

revival *n.* **1.** awakening, newlife, quickening, reanimation, rebirth, recovery, rejuvenation, rekindling, renaissance, renascence, renewal, restoration, revitalization **2.** celebration, devotions, meeting, prayer meeting, prayerfest *(Nonformal)*, service

revive *v.* **1.** animate, arouse, awaken, bring *or* come around, cheer, encourage, energize, enliven, exhilarate, gladden, inspirit, invigorate, quicken, rally, reanimate, refresh, rejuvenate, rekindle, renew, resuscitate, revivify, rouse, wake up *Antonyms:* exhaust, fatigue, tire **2.** activate, bring back, reactivate, reestablish, reinstall, reinstate, restore, return

revoke *v.* **1.** abolish, abrogate, annul, cancel, invalidate, negate, nullify, quash, repeal, rescind, reverse, void *Antonyms:* confirm, endorse, implement **2.** abjure, call off, deny, disclaim, dismantle, dismiss, dump, erase, forswear, lift, obliterate, recall, recant, remove, renounce, repudiate, rescind, retract, scrap, scrub, take back, withdraw

revolt *n.* **1.** *coup d'état (French),* insurgency, insurrection, mutiny, protest, rebellion, revolution, sedition, uprising **2.** abhorrence, aversion, discontent, disgust, dislike, horror, loathing, repugnance, repulsion, revulsion – *v.* **1.** defect, defy, insurrect, kick out *(Nonformal),* oppose, overthrow, overturn, rebel, riot, rise up, strike, topple, turn against **2.** disgust, gross out *(Nonformal),* nauseate, offend, repel, repulse, shock, sicken *Antonyms:* allure, attract, entice, tempt

revolting *adj.* **1.** abhorrent, abominable, appalling, awful, crude, degrading, disgusting, distasteful, disturbing, foul, frightful, ghastly, grisly, gross *(Nonformal),* grotesque, hideous, horrible, horrid, loathsome, nasty, nauseating, noisome, obnoxious, obscene, odious, offensive, repellent, repugnant, repulsive, rotten, shocking, sickening, vile, vulgar *Nonformal:* beyond belief, icky, skunky, yucky *Antonyms:* agreeable, attractive, delightful, pleasant

revolution *n.* **1.** 360 *(Nonformal),* circle, circuit, circumvolution, cycle, gyration, gyre, lap, orbit, pirouette, reel, revolving, roll, rotation, round, spin, swirl, turn, turning, twirl, wheel, whirl **2.** anarchy, bloodshed, civic unrest, civil disobedience, coup, *coup d'état (French),* debacle, destruction, disorder, foment, guerrilla warfare, insubordination, insurgency, mutiny, outbreak, overthrow, plot, rebellion, reversal, revolt, strike, turbulence, turmoil, underground activity, unrest, upheaval, uprising, uproar, upset, violence *Major Revolutions:* American *(1775-83),* Chinese *(1911-12),* Cuban *(1959),* English *(1642-89),* French *(1789-99),* Mexican *(1911-17),* Quebec's Quiet *(1960-1966),* Russian *(1917-22)* **3.** dramatic shift, major *or* radical change, metamorphosis, realignment, reordering, reformation, shift, transformation, turnabout

revolutionary *adj.* **1.** avant-garde, countercultural, cutting-edge, drastic, experimental, extreme, fundamental, innovative, original, progressive, radical, sweeping, underground *Antonyms:* clichéd, conservative, staid, stale **2.** disobedient, factious, fractious, insubordinate, insurgent, mutinous, perfidious, rebellious, seditious, subversive, traitorous, treasonable *Antonyms:* dutiful, lawful, loyal **3.** gyrating, orbiting, revolving, rotating, spinning, turning, whirling – *n.* anarchist, extremist, fanatic, insurgent, Jacobite, left-winger, mutineer, radical, rebel, right-winger, sans-culotte, seditionist, subversive, ultraist, zealot *Antonyms:* conservative, moderate, reactionary

revolve *v.* **1.** centre, circle, gyrate, orbit, roll, rotate, spin, turn, twist, wheel, whirl **2.** brood, dwell on, consider, ponder, muse, reflect, ruminate, think, weigh

revulsion *n.* abhorrence, abomination, aversion, detestation, disgust, dislike, distaste, hatred, horror, loathing, repugnance, repulsion *Antonyms:* attraction, desire, fascination, pleasure

reward *n.* **1.** acknowledgement, award, carrot *(Nonformal),* gift, gratuity, honours, incentive, present, prize, tip, tribute **2.** compensation, earnings, fruit, income, indemnity, money, payment, recompense, redress, remittance, remuneration, return, salary, take home *(Nonformal),* wages – *v.* compensate, pay, recompense, redress, reimburse, remit, remunerate, requite

rewarding *adj.* **1.** advantageous, beneficial, edifying, fat *(Nonformal),* fruitful, gainful, productive, profitable, valuable, worthwhile *Antonyms:* detrimental, hurtful, injurious, negative **2.** delightful, enjoyable, entertaining, fulfilling, fun, glad, gratifying, happy, joyous, pleasing, satisfying, welcome *Antonyms:* disturbing, frightening, horrible

rhapsodic *adj.* **1.** *aux anges (French),* blissful, delighted, delirious, ecstatic, elated, enthusiastic, excited, exhilarated, intoxicated, joyful, over the moon *(Nonformal),* overcome, overjoyed, rapturous, thrilled, transported *Antonyms:* aloof, bored, indifferent **2.** broken, disjointed, erratic, irregular, sporadic, syncopated, unconnected

rhetoric *n.* **1.** balderdash, bombast, flowery language, grandiloquence, hyperbole, oratory, pomposity, rodomontade *Nonformal:* big talk, bull, bullshit, crap, garbage, hot air **2.** diction, discourse, language, terminology, wording, words, vocabulary **3.** articulation, cogency, elocution, eloquence, fluency, forcefulness, form, study, style, technique **4.** address, declamation, delivery, lecture, oration, sermon, speech

rhetorical *adj.* **1.** bombastic, flamboyant, flashy, flatulent, grandiloquent, hyperbolic, inflated, magniloquent, ornate, pompous, pretentious, purple, silver- tongued *(Nonformal)*, sonorous, swollen, tumescent, turgid, verbose, windy, wordy *Antonyms:* plain, simple, straightforward, unadorned **2.** articulate, Ciceronian, cogent, eloquent, expressive, facile, fluent, persuasive, styled, well-spoken

rhyme *n.* alliteration, chime, consonance, correspondence, ditty *(Nonformal)*, jingle, literary device, poem, repetition, song, verse, versification *Kinds of rhyme:* end, eye, feminine, forced, imperfect, internal, masculine, near, partial, perfect, slant, terminal

rhythm *n.* **1.** beat, beats per minute *or* B.P.M., cadence, pulsation, pulse, regularity, tempo, time, undulation **2.** balance, euphony, flow, harmony, lilt, movement, proportion, swing **3.** accent, emphasis, foot, measure, metre, stress, syllable **4.** poetry, poetics, prosody, rhyme, verse

ribald *adj.* bawdy, blue *(Nonformal)*, coarse, indecorous, lascivious, lewd, libidinous, naughty, not for polite company, off-colour, racy, raunchy, risqué, salacious, salty, scabrous, scurrilous, wanton *Antonyms:* chaste, genteel, polite, proper

ribbon *n.* **1.** band, cincture, collar, cordon, cummerbund, fillet, girdle, riband, sash, strip **2.** award, distinction, honour, laurel, medal, prize, recognition

rich *adj.* **1.** affluent, flush, monied, prosperous, wealthy, well-to-do *Nonformal:* loaded, stinking-rich, well-heeled **2.** creamy, delicious, flavourful, full-bodied, heavy, highly flavoured, satisfying, savoury, succulent, sustaining, tasty *Antonyms:* bland, tasteless **3.** abounding, abundant, ample, copious, full, luxuriant, overflowing, plentiful, replete, rife, teeming **4.** fecund, fertile, fruitful, generative, productive, yielding *Antonyms:* barren, sterile **5.** deep, eloquent, expressive, important, meaningful, pregnant, profound, significant, telling *Antonyms:* hollow, shallow, trivial **6.** fancy, lavish, luxurious, palatial, plush, opulent, ornate, resplendent, sumptuous *Nonformal:* posh, swank **7.** bright, brilliant, intense, strong, vibrant, vivid, warm **8.** deep, dulcet, mellifluous, mellow, melodic, resonant, silvery, sonorous, strong **9.** amusing, comical, diverting, droll, entertaining, farcical, foolish, funny, hilarious, humorous, laughable, ludicrous, preposterous, ridiculous, risible, sidesplitting *Antonyms:* boring, dull, insipid

rickety *adj.* **1.** broken-down, decrepit, derelict, dilapidated, jerry-built, ramshackle, rattletrap, tumbledown, unreliable, unsound **2.** flimsy, insecure, precarious, rocky, shaky, tottering, unsafe, unsteady, wobbly **3.** ailing, delicate, dotty *(Nonformal)*, enervated, feeble, fragile, infirm, weak *Antonyms:* healthy, robust, sound

rid *v.* abolish, clear, disburden, disencumber, dump, eject, eliminate, eradicate, expel, exterminate, extinguish, free, junk, purge, release, relieve, remove, scrap, shed, throw away, trash, unburden, unload, uproot *Nonformal:* deep six, ditch, kiss goodbye *or* off *Antonyms:* acquire, keep, retain

riddle *n.* anomaly, complexity, conundrum, enigma, knot, koan, labyrinth, maze, mystery, paradox, perplexity, poser, problem, puzzle, quandary, question, teaser *Nonformal:* brain-teaser, mind-boggler, stumper – *v.* bore, honeycomb, perforate, pierce, puncture

ride *n.* **1.** commute, drive, excursion, expedition, jaunt, journey, joy-ride *(Nonformal)*, outing, peregrination, road trip, run, spin, tour, trip, turn, whirl **2.** favour, hitch, lift, pick-up, transportation – *v.* **1.** cruise, motor, move, roll, travel **2.** guide, handle, lead, manage, maneuver, mount, skipper **3.** badger, bother, bully, dragoon, harass, harry, hector, intimidate, irritate, nag, nettle, pester, plague, poke fun, ridicule, tease

ridge *n.* **1.** arête, chine, cordillera, elevation, escarpment, esker, hogback, horst, hummock, kame, ledge, mountain range, razorback, reef, till, watershed, windrow **2.** excrescence, knob, knurl, projection, protuberance **3.** back, backbone, spine, vertebrae **4.** apex, brim, crest, pinnacle, point, tip, top, summit

ridicule *n.* badinage, buffoonery, burlesque, caricature, contempt, crack, derision, disdain, disparagement, farce, foolery, gibe, irony, jeer, laughter, mockery, parody, raillery, sarcasm, sardonicism, satire, send-up, sneer, swipe, taunting, teasing, travesty *Nonformal:* Bronx cheer, dig, put down, put-on, raspberry, razz, rib, roast, slam *Antonyms:* eulogy, panegyric, tribute – *v.* belittle, cartoon, chaff, condemn, criticize, decry, defame, deflate, denigrate, depreciate, deride, derogate, despise, detract, diminish, discount, disparage, discredit, disdain, expose, flout, gibe, harass, haze, humiliate, insult, jeer, jibe, josh, lampoon, laugh at, make fun *or* sport of, mimic, mock, parody, pillory, reject, revile, satirize, scoff, scorn, send *or* show up, sneer, taunt, tease *Nonformal:* bash, boo, dis, josh, kid, knock, needle, pan, pooh-pooh, put *or* run down, put on, rag, razz, rib, ride, roast, trash *Antonyms:* applaud, compliment, praise

ridiculous *adj.* **1.** absurd, bizarre, comical, droll, farcical, foolish, funny, hilarious, laughable, ludicrous, madcap, nonsensical, risible, silly, stupid *Nonformal*: daffy, kooky, wacky, zany *Antonyms:* intelligent, rational, reasonable **2.** impossible, intolerable, not to be borne, out of line, outrageous, preposterous, unbelievable, unconscionable, unreasonable

rife *adj.* **1.** abundant, aplenty, bounteous, bursting, copious, innumerable, many, multitudinous, numerous, overflowing, plentiful, profuse, rampant, replete, swarming, teeming, thick *Antonyms:* meagre, scanty, scarce **2.** common, current, extensive, pandemic, popular, prevalent, ubiquitous, universal, widespread *Antonyms:* limited, rare, unconventional

riffraff *n.* **1.** canaille, commoners, crowd, hoi polloi, masses, multitude, peasantry, people, populace, proletariat, rabble, *Nonformal:* great unwashed, ragtag and bobtail **2.** debris, dregs, garbage, leavings, litter, refuse, rubbish, trash, waste

rifle *n.* 22, firearm, gun, M-1, M-14, weapon *Trademark:* Enfield, Garand, Spencer, Springfield, Winchester – *v.* plunder, ransack, rummage, search, scour, turn inside out

rift *n.* **1.** break, chink, cleavage, cleft, crack, cranny, crevice, fault, fissure, flaw, fracture, gap, interruption, interval, opening, parting, rent **2.** alienation, breach, clash, difference, disagreement, divergence, division, divorce, estrangement, falling out, misunderstanding, quarrel, rupture, schism, separation, split *Antonyms:* affinity, connection, unity – *v.* break *or* burst, open, rend, rupture, separate, sever, split open, sunder, tear

rig *n.* **1.** apparatus, equipment, fixtures, gear, material, paraphernalia, provisions, stuff, supplies, tackle **2.** big rig *(Nonformal)*, buckboard, 18-wheeler, horse and wagon, lorry *(British)*, semi, shay, tractor-trailer, transport, truck **3.** accoutrement, costume, dress, ensemble, garb, livery, outfit, raiment, regalia, wardrobe *Nonformal:* get-up, threads, togs **4.** rigging, rope-work, service, ship's chandlery, trimming – *v.* **1.** arm, array, attire, clothe, equip, fit, furnish, gear, kit, outfit, provision, set up, supply **2.** arrange, corrupt, doctor *(Nonformal)*, engineer, fake, falsify, finagle, fix, gerrymander, juggle, manipulate, tamper with, trump up

right *adj.* **1.** accurate, correct, factual, indubitable, precise, sure, truthful, valid, unerring, unmistaken *Antonyms:* fallacious, fictitious, phony **2.** appropriate, apt, becoming, due, fit, justifiable, merited, proper, seemly, suitable *Antonyms:* unnecessary, unwanted **3.** advantageous, auspicious, beneficial, desirable, favourable, felicitous, preferable, propitious *Antonyms:* detrimental, harmful **4.** aboveboard, equitable, ethical, fair, good, high-minded, honest, just, moral, principled, righteous, scrupulous *Antonyms:* shady, shifty, villainous **5.** aligned, direct, linear, orderly, straight *Antonyms:* circuitous, curved, forked **6.** all there *(Nonformal)*, balanced, competent, *compos mentis (Latin)*, fine, fit, hale, healthy, lucid, normal, sane, sound, well *Antonyms:* sick, unhealthy, unsound **7.** conservative, mossbacked *(Nonformal)*, old-line, orthodox, reactionary, right-wing, Tory *Antonyms:* leftist, Marxist, socialist **8.** actual, authentic, lawful, legal, legitimate, real, rightful *Antonyms:* illicit, illegitimate, unauthorized – *adv.* **1.** correctly, factually, infallibly, truthfully **2.** ethically, legally, legitimately, morally, rightfully **3.** absolutely, altogether, entirely, fully, thoroughly, totally, utterly, very **4.** appropriately, aptly, befittingly, properly, suitably **5.** exactly, immediately, instantly, just, precisely, promptly, quickly – *n.* **1.** fairness, goodness, honesty, honour, integrity, justice, morality, nobleness, right-mindedness, virtue **2.** birthright, claim, droit, due, holding, licence, prerogative, privilege, title – *v.* **1.** normalize, plumb, position, set upright, stand up, straighten **2.** adjust, correct, edit, fix, mend, modify, overhaul, patch, recompense, repair, touch up **3.** assuage, cure, heal, mollify, reconcile, rectify, redress, satisfy, soothe **4.** pay back, requite, retaliate, revenge, settle, square, vindicate

righteous *adj.* blameless, charitable, commendable, conscientious, deserving, devoted, dutiful, equitable, ethical, exemplary, fair, faithful, good, honest, honourable, impartial, incorruptible, innocent, just, law-abiding, meritorious, moral, noble, pious, pure, reverent, right-minded, saintly, scrupulous, sterling, trustworthy, upright, virtuous, without sin, worthy *Antonyms:* corrupt, dishonest, immoral, wicked

rightful *adj.* **1.** approved, authorized, bona fide, decreed, lawful, legal, legitimate, ordained, prescribed, proper, sanctioned *Antonyms:* illegitimate, unlawful **2.** equitable, ethical, evenhanded, fair, honest, impartial, just, proper, scrupulous, square *(Nonformal)*, upright *Antonyms:* corrupt, criminal, underhand **3.** appropriate, befitting, deserved, due, earned, meet, merited, suitable

rigid *adj.* **1.** changeless, fast-frozen, fixed, hard, immovable, inflexible, locked in place, static, stiff, taut, tense, tight, unyielding *Antonyms:* elastic, plastic, pliant **2.** austere, firm, harsh, severe, Spartan, stark, strict, stern, strait-laced, tough, uncompromising *Antonyms:* lax, lenient, loose **3.** adamant, bullheaded, determined, dogged, resolute, single-minded, steadfast, steel-willed, stubborn, tenacious, unrelenting *Antonyms:* flexible, obliging, soft **4.** demanding, exacting, rigorous, stringent, *Antonyms:* easy, piece-of-cake *(Nonformal)*, simple **5.** according to schedule, by the book *(Nonformal)*, formal, ironclad, programmed, structured *Antonyms:* laid-back, open, relaxed

rigmarole *n.* **1.** babble, balderdash, blabber, blather, drivel, falderal, flummery, gabble, galimatias, gibberish, jabber, jargon, nonsense, palaver, prattle, rubbish, trash, trumpery *Nonformal:* baloney, b.s., bull, bunk, claptrap, fustian, gammon, malarkey, mumbo-jumbo, tommyrot, **2.** annoyance, bother, bureaucracy, ceremony, pain, pomposity, procedure, protocol *Nonformal:* hassle, red tape

rigour *n.* **1.** inflexibility, rigidity, stiffness, strictness, toughness, unyieldingness **2.** accuracy, carefulness, conscientiousness, exactitude, fastidiousness, meticulousness, precision, stringency **3.** bitterness, cold, harshness, inclemency, storminess **4.** affliction, austerity, hardship, lack, privation, suffering, want

rigorous *adj.* **1.** draconian, firm, fixed, harsh, inflexible, obdurate, relentless, set, severe, Spartan, strict, stringent, tough, uncompromising, unyielding **2.** accurate, arduous, correct, demanding, difficult, exact, laborious, literal, precise, punctilious, rigid, strenuous, trying **3.** arctic, bad, blustery, chilly, cold, freezing, frigid, inclement, raw, severe, stormy, windy *Antonyms:* balmy, topical, warm

rile *v.* **1.** aggravate, anger, annoy, chafe, disquiet, disturb, exasperate, get under one's skin, incense, irk, irritate, miff *(Nonformal)*, nettle, peeve, perturb, pester, pique, roil, ruffle, vex *Antonyms:* assuage, placate, quieten, relieve, soothe **2.** agitate, becloud, cloud, dirty, muddy, silt up, unsettle

rim *n.* ambit, border, brim, brink, circumference, edge, fringe, lip, margin, outskirt, pale, periphery, skirt *Antonyms:* centre, core, heart, middle, nucleus

ring *n.* **1.** accessory, annulet, band, coil, enclosure, ferrule, hoop, jewellery, loop **2.** aureole, brim, circle, circlet, corona, coronet, diadem, disc, girdle, halo, nimbus, spiral **3.** amphitheatre, arena, circuit, circus, course, pit, pitch, playing field, rink, squared circle *(Nonformal)*, stadium, stage, track, turf **4.** bell, buzz, call, chime, clangour, clank, jangle, jingle, knell, peal, reverberation, tinkle, toll, vibration **5.** association, band, bloc, cabal, cartel, circle, coalition, combo, confederacy, coterie, crew, faction, group, junta, mob, monopoly, operation, organization, party, pool, racket, syndicate, troop – *v.* **1.** belt, circle, circumscribe, confine, cordon *or* seal off, encircle, enclose, encompass, gird, girdle, rim, round, surround **2.** coil, curl, eddy, loop over, spiral, wind **3.** buzz, chime, clang, clank, jangle, jingle, knell, peal, resound, reverberate, tinkle, toll, vibrate **4.** call, connect with, network, phone, talk to, touch base *Nonformal:* chat up, schmooze **5.** commemorate, herald, proclaim, signal, summon, trumpet, usher

ringing *n.* buzz, chime, chiming, jangle, jingle, jingling, peal, pealing, ring, tinkle, tinnitus, tintinabulation, toll

rink *n.* **1.** arena, barn *(Nonformal)*, centre, coliseum, dome, forum, garden, gardens, ice palace, spectrum, stadium **2.** dance floor *(Nonformal)*, ice, pad, playing surface *Common outdoor rinks:* backyard, city, lake, local, marshland, neighbourhood, park, pond, river, schoolyard

riot *n.* **1.** anarchy, brawl, civil unrest, commotion, confusion, disorder, disturbance, donnybrook, fray, free-for-all, lawlessness, mêlée, pandemonium, revolt, ruckus, storm, to-do, trouble, tumult, turbulence, turmoil, uprising, uproar *Nonformal:* rumble, shindig *Antonyms:* accord, harmony, peace **2.** boisterousness, compotation, festivity, frolic, fun, hijinks, hilarity, jollification, lark, merrymaking, revelry, romp *Nonformal:* gas, high old time **3.** debauchery, dissipation, excess, incontinence, indulgence, licentiousness, loose living, profligacy, wildness **4.** brilliancy, extravaganza, flourish, kaleidoscope, panoply, rainbow, show, splash – *v.* **1.** fight, go berserk, loot, protest, rampage, raise hell *(Nonformal)*, rise up, run amok *or* riot **2.** carouse, celebrate, drink, feast, make merry, revel, wassail *Nonformal:* cut loose, party, rock, tie one on

riotous *adj.* **1.** bench-clearing *(Nonformal)*, chaotic, factious, insubordinate, insurgent, mutinous, rebellious, revolutionary, rowdy, seditious, tumultuous, turbulent, uncontrollable, unruly, wild *Antonyms:* law-abiding, orderly, restrained **2.** boisterous, hilarious, rambunctious, rip-roaring, roisterous, rollicking, side-splitting, uproarious *Antonyms:* boring, sedate, solemn **3.** abandoned, debauched, dissipated, dissolute, licentious, loose, profligate, wanton, wild *Antonyms:* chaste, modest, proper

rip *n.* **1.** cut, division, gash, hole, laceration, opening, rent, slash, slit, split, tear **2.** cheat, chicanery, exploitation, swindle trickery, underhandedness *Nonformal:* bamboozle, con job, flim-flam, rip-off – *v.* **1.** burst, cleave, cut, fray, gash, hack, lacerate, lance, penetrate, rend, rive, score, shred, slash, wound *Antonyms:* mend, patch, repair **2.** cheat, deceive, dupe, fleece, hoodwink, swindle, trick *Nonformal:* bamboozle, con, have, hornswaggle, rook, take **3.** clip, fly, hasten, hurry, hustle, scamper, scurry, scuttle, speed, tear *Nonformal:* zoom, zip

ripe *adj.* **1.** advanced, aged, finished, full-grown, in full bloom, mature, mellow **2.** accomplished, experienced, learned, seasoned, skilled, sophisticated, veteran, well-versed **3.** conditioned, prepared, primed, ready, set **4.** auspicious, favourable, ideal, opportune, right, suitable, timely *Antonyms:* inappropriate, unfavourable, unfitting, untimely

rip-off *n.* **1.** cheat, fraud, larceny, purloining, racket, rip, robbery, swindle, theft, thievery, trick *Nonformal:* bamboozle, con, flim-flam, pinch, scam, shakedown, sting **2.** exploitation, extortion, famine pricing *(Nonformal)*, overcharging, price gouging, King's ransom **3.** clone, copy, counterfeit, fake, forgery, imitation, paste, reproduction

riposte *n.* comeback, Parthian shot, reaction, reply, retort, return, thrust, volley, wisecrack, witticism *Nonformal:* barb, shot, zinger – *v.* answer, exchange, quip, reply, respond, retaliate, return

ripple *n.* babble, bubble, burble, coo, gurgle, lap, murmur, popple, purl, purr, swish, trill undulation, wavelet – *v.* crimp, crumple, curl, dimple, pucker, wrinkle

rise *n.* **1.** acclivity, ascent, climb, height, highland, hill, hillock, incline, knoll, mount, slope, upgrade, upslope *Antonyms:* descent, fall **2.** acceleration, accession, accretion, addition, advance, advancement, aggrandizement, augmentation, boost, distension, doubling, enlargement, growth, heightening, hike, improvement, increase, increment, inflation, intensification, multiplication, progress, promotion, raise, surge, swell, upsurge, upswing, upturn *Antonyms:* decline, decrease, downturn, drop, fall **3.** beginning, fountain, genesis, head, origin, source, spring, start, wellspring **4.** appearance, arising, emergence, manifestation, materialization **5.** answer, reaction, reply, response – *v.* **1.** ascend, climb, levitate, loom above, mount, spiral, soar, tower **2.** arise, awake, get up, hit the deck *(Nonformal)*, roll *or* turn out, waken **3.** advance, better, flourish, go places *(Nonformal)*, improve, progress, prosper, succeed, thrive **4.** accrue, balloon, crescendo, distend, enlarge, expand, fatten, grow, increase, intensify, mushroom, snowball, spread, swell **5.** disobey, insurrect, mutiny, overthrow, rebel, resist, revolt, riot, rise up, run wild, strike **6.** befall, ensue, eventuate, happen, occur, pass **7.** begin, commence, dawn, initiate, issue, originate, spring *or* flow from, start **8.** appear, emerge, enter, manifest, materialize, pop up *(Nonformal)*

rising *adj.* advancing, ascending, climbing, crescent, dilating, emerging, expanding, growing, increasing, inflating, maturing, mounting, progressing, soaring, swelling, waxing *Antonyms:* descending, dropping, lowering – *n.* **1.** coming together, gathering, insurrection, mutiny, outbreak, revolt **2.** eminence, hill, mound, projection, prominence, swelling

risk *n.* accident, brinkmanship, chance, danger, exposure, fortune, hazard, jeopardy, liability, luck, peril, possibility, prospect, speculation, uncertainty, vulnerability *Nonformal:* flyer, header, plunge *Antonyms:* assurance, certainty, safety – *v.* adventure, attempt, brave, confront, dare, defy, endeavour, face, gamble, guess, jeopardize, plunge, punt *(Nonformal)*, speculate, stake, submit, try, undertake, venture, volunteer, wager

risky *adj.* chancy, dangerous, delicate, dicey, difficult, hazardous, insecure, perilous, precarious, problematic, rocky, shaky, speculative, touchy, treacherous, tricky, uncertain, unhealthy, unpredictable, unsafe, unsound, venturesome *Nonformal:* crazy, hairy, iffy, wide open, wild *Antonyms:* certain, reliable, safe, secure

risqué *adj.* bawdy, blue *(Nonformal)*, daring, improper, indecent, indecorous, indelicate, naughty, off-colour, provocative, racy, ribald, salty, spicy, suggestive *Antonyms:* chaste, decent, proper, virtuous

ritual *n.* **1.** act, act of worship, celebration, ceremony, communion, custom, eucharist, form, formality, holy rite, litany, liturgy, oblation, observance, occasion, ordinance, practice, prayer, procedure, protocol, rite, ritual, sacrament, sacrifice, *samskara (Hindu)*, service, solemnity **2.** convention, custom, formality, habit, procedure, routine, tradition, usage

rival *adj.* battling, combatant, competing, competitive, conflicting, contending, contesting, disputing, emulative, opposing, opposite, vying *Antonyms:* helping, supporting, sympathetic – *n.* **1.** adversary, antagonist, challenger, competitor, contender, contestant, entrant, foe, opponent, opposite number *Antonyms:* advocate, ally, partner, supporter **2.** compeer, counterpart, parallel, equal, equivalent, fellow, match, peer – *v.* **1.** battle, combat, compete, contend, contest, counter, fight, go after *or* for, jockey, oppose, pit, play off, race, scramble for, strive, tie, touch, vie *Antonyms:* aid, back, help, support **2.** approximate, compare with, correspond, emulate, equal, match, meet, near, resemble

rivalry *n.* **1.** antagonism, antipathy, bad blood, competitiveness, conflict, contention, enmity, opposition *Antonyms:* cooperation, harmony, support **2.** challenge, clashing, competition, contest, duel, faceoff, game, jousting, meet, one on one, playoff, race, showdown, vying

river *n.* brook, channel, course, creek, estuary, *fleuve (French)*, flow, route, rivulet, sluice, stream, tributary, waterway

rivulet *n.* brooklet, freshet, *kill (Dutch)*, millstream, race, rill, runnel, streamlet *Scottish:* burn, ghyll

road *n.* **1.** access road, arterial highway, artery, *autobahn (German)*, autoroute, *autostrada (Italian)*, back road, beltway, carriageway *(British)*, causeway, concession road, corduroy road *(Historical)*, expressway, freeway, grid road, ice road, line, main, main drag *(Nonformal)*, motorway *or* M *(British)*, parkway, pike, right-of-way, ring, roadway, *rue (French)*, sideroad, snowroute, speedway, street, strip, superhighway, tarmac, toll route, turnpike **2.** approach, course, direction, means, method, path, route, way

roadhouse *n.* bar, beanery, *brasserie (Quebec)*, café, cafeteria, coffee shop, diner, dining lounge, draft house, eatery, eating-house, grill, grillroom, hospice, hostel, hotel, inn, motel, pub, public house, restaurant, steak-house, taproom, tavern *Nonformal:* burger joint, dump, greasy spoon, juke joint

roam *v.* drift, follow one's fancy, gallivant, hike, meander, peregrinate, ramble, rove, saunter, stroll, traipse, trek, wander

roar *n.* barrage, bellow, blast, boom, clamour, cry, din, explosion, outcry, rumble, shout, yell – *v.* **1.** bark, bawl, bay, bluster, bray, growl, holler, rebound, resound, reverberate, rumble, shout, sound, thunder, trumpet, yell **2.** convulse, guffaw, howl, laugh, scream, whoop

roast *n.* **1.** course, dinner, dish, entree, meal, meat, Sunday dinner, supper **2.** celebration, ceremony, farewell, salute, tribute – *v.* **1.** barbecue, broil, brown, cook, grill, sear, torrefy **2.** assail, attack, banter, caricature, castigate, chaff, criticize, deride, jape, jest, joke, jolly, lampoon, rib, ride, ridicule, scathe, scoff, scorn, tease, trounce *Nonformal:* fustigate, razz *Antonyms:* compliment, praise, rhapsodize

rob *v.* abscond, appropriate, burglarize, cheat, defraud, deprive, despoil, divest, embezzle, extort, filch, hijack, lift, loot, pilfer, pillage, plunder, purloin, raid, ransack, requisition, sack, steal, swindle, take, thieve *Nonformal:* boost, cop, knock off *or* over, liberate, relieve, rip off, roll, sack, smash-and-grab, snitch, strip, swipe

robber *n.* bandit, brigand, burglar, cat burglar, cheat, confidence trickster, con man, dacoit, footpad, *gonif (Yiddish)*, grafter, highwayman, housebreaker, looter, marauder, mugger, pickpocket, pilferer, pillager, pirate, plunderer, raider, reiver, rip-off artist, rustler, safe-cracker, shoplifter, stealer, swindler, thief *Nonformal:* holdup *or* second-story man *or* stickup man

robot *n.* **1.** android, automaton, bionic man *or* woman, cyborg, droid, golem, mechanical being **2.** cat's-paw *(Nonformal)*, drudge, figurehead, myrmidon, pawn, puppet

robust *adj.* **1.** able-bodied, athletic, beefy, brawny, built, fit, hale, hardy, healthy, hearty, hefty, husky, lusty, muscular, potent, powerful, rugged, sound, strapping, strong, sturdy, substantial, vigorous, well *Antonyms:* delicate, feeble, refined, sickly, unhealthy **2.** flavourful, full-bodied, hearty, pungent, rich **3.** coarse, loud, obnoxious, rambunctious, raw, rough, rude, uncontrollable, unmannerly, unruly, violent, vulgar

rock *n.* **1.** stone, bedrock, boulder, cobblestone, gangue, gravel, metal, mineral, ore, pebble, *roches moutonnées (French)*, rubble, slab, veinstone *Groupings of rocks:* igneous, metamorphic, sedimentary *Kinds of rock:* basalt, burrstone, chalk, dolomite, flint, gneiss, geode, granite, gypsum, hardpan, hematite, ironstone, lava, limestone, marble, obsidian, pumice, quartzite, sandstone, schist, scoria, serpentine, shale, slate, soapstone, stalactite, stalagmite, steatite, travertine, volcanic rock **2.** *Kinds of rock music:* acid, alternative, contemporary, country, devil's music *(Nonformal)*, folk, fusion, guitar, hard, heavy metal, indie, mainstream, new country, pop *or* popular, progressive, punk, rockabilly, top 40 *See also:* **music** **3.** anchor, base, cornerstone, foundation, mainstay, pillar, support **4.** asylum, citadel, defence, fortress, Gibraltar *(Nonformal)*, haven, refuge, stronghold, tower **5.** oscillation, roll, seesaw, sway, swing – *v.* **1.** move, reel, roll, sway, swing, swivel, undulate, wobble **2.** amaze, disturb, floor *(Nonformal)*, jar, shake, shock, stagger, stun, stupefy, upset

rocky *adj.* **1.** craggy, jagged, lithic, petrified, rugged, solid, stony **2.** callous, cold, cruel, flinty, grim, hard, hard-hearted, indifferent, inflexible, joyless, merciless, unfeeling **3.** at risk, dangerous, doubtful, dubious, financially unsound, on the edge, precarious, risky, shaky, teetering, tricky, uncertain, undependable, unreliable *Antonyms:* bankable, feasible, realistic, sound, steady **4.** dizzy, feeble, ill, nauseous, tottering, unsteady, weak, woozy *(Nonformal)*

rococo *adj.* bedecked, embellished, extravagant, fancy, flamboyant, florid, flowery, frilly, fussy, gonzo *(Nonformal)*, laboured, lavish, luxuriant, ornate, ostentatious, overblown, overwrought, rich,

rod *n.* **1.** alpenstock, bar, baton, caduceus, cane, crook, crosspiece, cylinder, dowel, mace, pike, pole, scourge, shaft, spike, staff, stave, stick, strip, switch, wand **2.** chastisement, correction, discipline, punishment, reproof, **3.** authority, command, control, dominion, hold, jurisdiction, mastery, power, rule, sway

rodent *n.* gnawing mammal *Some common North American rodents:* beaver, chipmunk, flying squirrel, gerbil, groundhog, ground squirrel, guinea pig, harvest mouse, jumping mouse, kangaroo rat, lemming, marmot, meadow mouse, mouse, muskrat, pack rat, pocket gopher, pocket mouse, porcupine, prairie dog, rat, squirrel, tree squirrel, vole, water rat, white-footed mouse, woodchuck, woodrat

rodomontade *adj.* boastful, bragging, conceited, fustian, narcissistic, pretentious, self-important, self-indulgent, turgid, vain – *n.* arrogance, boastfulness, bombast, braggadocio, bravado, claptrap, conceit, fanfaronade, fustian, gasconade, pretension, puffery, self-praise, vainglory, vanity *Nonformal* gas, hot air – *v.* bluff, bluster, boast, brag, crow, gasconade, puff, roister, swagger, trumpet, vaunt *Antonyms:* retire, shrink, shy away

rogue *n.* blackguard, bounder, charlatan, cheat, cheater, criminal, deceiver, defrauder, fraud, hooligan, knave, mountebank, ne'er-do-well, outlaw, rascal, reprobate, scalawag, scoundrel, sleeveen *(Newfoundland)*, swindler, trickster, villain *Nonformal:* black sheep, fourflusher, hairball, lowlife, rotter, scapegrace, scumbag *Antonyms:* model citizen, nonpareil, paragon

roisterous *adj.* **1.** boisterous, disorderly, merry, obstreperous, rambunctious *(Nonformal)*, rampageous, riotous, rollicking, rough, rowdy, unbridled, unruly, uproarious, wild *Antonyms:* orderly, peaceful, quiet, sedate **2.** blustering, boasting, bragging, blustery, swaggering, swashbuckling

role *n.* **1.** act, bit, character, impersonation, part, performance, piece, portrayal, presentation, representation, show, spiel, stint *Kinds of role:* buffoon, cameo, character, comic, deus ex machina, extra, heavy, ingenue, lead, narrator, offstage, soubrette, straightman, supporting title, villain, walk-on **2.** business, capacity, duty, execution, function, job, mandate, office, position, post, purpose, responsibility, status, stint, task *Nonformal:* game, schtick

roll *n.* **1.** annals, catalogue, census, chronicle, directory, index, inventory, list, register, roster, schedule **2.** barrel, bobbin, coil, cone, cylinder, fold, loop, reel, spiral, spool, trundle, wheel, whorl **3.** bread, biscuit, bun, dinner roll, kaiser, scone **4.** boom, resonance, reverberation, roar, rumble, sound, thunder, tremor, vibration **5.** billow, ripple, swell, undulation, wave **6.** bankroll, bundle, cash, dollars, fund, legal tender, money, resources *Nonformal:* dough, stash, wad – *v.* **1.** careen, circle, gyrate, lurch, pirouette, pitch, pivot, revolve, rock, rotate, spin, spiral, sway, swivel, toss, trundle, turn, twirl **2.** cart, coast, convey, drive, glide, move, propel, pull, push, transport **3.** bellow, boom, peal, quiver, ramble, resonate, resound, roar, thunder, reverberate, vibrate **4.** flow, surge, sway, swell, undulate, wave **5.** coil, curl, encircle, enfold, entwine, enwrap, fold, furl, loop, swathe, twist, wind, wrap **6.** even off, flatten, grade, level, press, smooth

rollicking *adj.* boisterous, carefree, cavorting, cheerful, exuberant, frisky, frolicsome, fun, gay, happy, hearty, jaunty, jovial, joyous, lighthearted, lively, merry, playful, rip-roaring *(Nonformal)*, rollicksome, romping, spirited, sportive, sprightly, uproarious *Antonyms:* cheerless, despondent, dull, gloomy

rolling *adj.* **1.** alpine, hilly, knobby, mountainous, uneven *Antonyms:* flat, level, plain **2.** billowing, heaving, rippling, surging, undulating, waving **3.** lurching, pitching, pivoting, reeling, rotating, swirling, turning **4.** rattling, resounding, resonant, resounding, reverberating, thunderous, trilled, vibrating **5.** accelerating, advancing, coming, developing, elapsing, happening, moving, passing, proceeding, progressing

romance *n.* **1.** affair, amour, attachment, chemistry, courtship, fling, flirtation, hanky-panky *(Nonformal)*, infatuation, intimacy, liaison, love affair, passion, relationship, seduction, tryst **2.** allegory, fable, fairy *or* folk tale, fantasy, legend, myth, narrative, novel, parable, story, tale **3.** concoction, fabrication, falsehood, fib, invention, lie, prevarication *Nonformal:* tall tale, yarn **4.** adventure, allure, appeal, charm, enchantment, glamour, idealism – *v.* charm, court, date, pursue, seduce, serenade, wine and dine *(Nonformal)*, woo

romantic *adj.* **1.** abstract, fantastic, idealistic, impractical, ivory-towered, starry-eyed *(Nonformal)*, unrealistic, utopian, visionary **2.** beautiful, charming, colourful, glamourous, picturesque, pretty, quaint, scenic, wonderful **3.** fanciful, fictitious, legendary, made-up, mythical, preposterous, quixotic, unreal **4.** amorous, loving, maudlin, passionate, sentimental, tender *Nonformal:* hearts and flowers, lovey-dovey, mushy, sappy, schmaltzy, syrupy – *n.* daydreamer, Don Quixote *(Nonformal)*, dreamer, idealist, stargazer, visionary

romp *n.* antic, caper, celebration, compotation, dance, escapade, frisk, frolic, fun, hop, lark, leap, play, rollick, saturnalia, skip, sport, tear *(Nonformal)* **2.** conquest, rout, sweep, triumph, trouncing, victory, win *Nonformal:* bird, breeze, cakewalk, cinch – *v.* carouse, cavort, celebrate, frisk, frolic, gallivant, gambol, have fun, lark, let loose, make merry, play, prance, revel, roister, rollick, skip, skylark, sport *Antonyms:* grieve, labour, toil

roof *n.* **1.** awning, bigtop, canopy, capital, covering, cupola, dome, housetop, rooftop, top *Roof styles:* butterfly, flat, gable, gambrel, hip, mansard, shed **2.** cosmic space, empyrean, firmament, heavens, sky, the blue *(Nonformal)* **3.** abode, accommodations, domicile, dwelling, home, house, lodging, place, residence, stoop *(Nonformal)*

rookie *n.* apprentice, beginner, debutante, entrant, fledgling, freshman, greenhorn, inductee, learner, neophyte, nestling, newcomer, novice, novitiate, probationer, recruit, tenderfoot, trainee, tyro *Nonformal* deb, greenie *Antonyms:* authority, chief, elder, master, veteran

room *n.* **1.** alcove, antechamber, anteroom, apartment, atelier, atrium, attic, auditorium, bachelor, bachelorette, back kitchen *(Prairies)*, ballroom, banquet hall, basement, bathroom, bedroom, boudoir, buttery, catacomb, cave, cavern, cell, cellar, chamber, chancellery, chapel, checkroom, closet, coatroom, conservatory, crib, crypt, cubbyhole, cubicle, cyclone cellar, den, dining room, drawing room, dressing room, fallout shelter, family room, foyer, furnace room, garage, garret, guest room, hall, keep, kitchen, landing, larder, laundry room, library, living room, lobby, lodging, loft, master bedroom, niche, nursery, office, pantry, parlour, playroom, powder room, refectory, restroom, root cellar, rotunda, rumpus room, salon, saloon, scriptorium, scullery, sitting room, solarium, stoop, storeroom, storm cellar, studio, study, suite, sunroom, television room, tomb, utility room, vault, vestibule, water closet, wine cellar, winter garden, workroom, workshop **2.** area, breathing space *(Nonformal)*, clearance, compass, elbowroom, expanse, extent, latitude, leeway, margin, range, reach, scope, space, vastness **3.** emptiness, capacity, occupancy, vacancy, vacuum, void **4.** chance, occasion, opening, opportunity, probability

roomy *adj.* ample, broad, capacious, commodious, extensive, generous, large, sizable, spacious, wide *Antonyms:* confined, cramped, small, tiny

root *n.* **1.** bulb, rhizome, rootlet, tuber **2.** beginning, cause, commencement, conception, essence, fountainhead, genesis, nucleus, origin, provenance, source, start, wellspring **3.** base, bedrock, bottom, footing, foundation, seat, substratum, underpinning – *v.* **1.** embed, fasten, fix, graft, lodge, settle, situate **2.** burrow, delve, dig, ferret, forage, hunt, nose *or* poke around, rummage, search **3.** applaud, bolster, cheer, egg on *(Nonformal)*, hail, support, urge on

roots *n.* ancestry, background, birthplace, bloodline, descent, extraction, family, genealogy, heritage, home, house, lineage, origins, pedigree, stock

rope *n.* belt, braiding, cable, cord, cordage, guy, hawser, lace, lanyard, lariat, lasso, leash, line, lunge, painter, prolonge, painter, rein, strand, string, tape, thread, twine – *v.* **1.** attach, bind, check, curb, fasten, harness, hitch, moor, restrain, secure, tether, tie *Antonyms:* emancipate, free, loosen **2.** deceive, dupe, ensnare, entrap, gull, hook, inveigle, lure, rook, take in, tempt, victimize, waylay

roster *n.* agenda, attendance sheet, index, inventory, line-up, listing, program, record, register, roll, rota *(British)*, schedule, scroll, table

rosy *adj.* **1.** ablush, blooming, blushing, coloured, glowing, healthy-looking, high-coloured, roseate, ruddy, sanguine **2.** coral, deep-pink, pale-red, peach, pink, red, reddish, rose-coloured **3.** alluring, auspicious, bright, cheerful, encouraging, favourable, glowing, hopeful, likely, optimistic, promising, sunny *Antonyms:* cheerless, depressing, discouraging

rot *n.* **1.** blight, corrosion, decay, decomposition, deterioration, foulness, mortification, putrefaction, putrescence, rancidity, rankness, rottenness, spoilage **2.** contamination, corruption, debasement, degradation, evil, perversion, wickedness **3.** balderdash, claptrap, drivel, foolishness, nonsense, rubbish, silliness *Nonformal:* b.s., bull, bunkum, crap, eyewash, garbage, guff, hogwash, hooey, poppycock, tommyrot – *v.* **1.** break down, corrode, crumble, decay, decompose, degenerate, deteriorate, disintegrate, dissolve, fester, putrefy, spoil, worsen **2.** corrupt, debase, degrade, pervert, violate, worsen

rotary *adj.* encircling, gyratory, revolving, rotating, spinning, turning, vertiginous, whirling – *n.* carousel, *circulaire (French)*, roundabout, traffic circle

rotate *v.* bump and grind *(Nonformal)*, circle, gyrate, move, pirouette, pivot, reel, revolve, roll, spin, swivel, troll, trundle, turn, twirl, twist, whirl

rotten *adj.* **1.** bad, corroded, crumbling, decayed, decaying, disgusting, disintegrating, festering, fetid, foul, infected, loathsome, mephitic, mouldy, noisome, noxious, offensive, polluted, pustular, putrid, rancid, rank, rotting, soiled, sour, spoiled, stale, stinking, tainted *Nonformal:* dodgy, high *Antonyms:* fresh, good, pure, wholesome **2.** corrupt, crooked, deceitful, deplorable, despicable, dishonourable, evil, immoral, loathsome, mean, nasty, nefarious, perverse, venal, vile, wicked **3.** ailing, feeble, frail, ill, impaired, miserable, poorly, sick, under the weather, unwell *Nonformal:* crummy, lousy **4.** cheap, defective, flimsy, inferior, second-rate, substandard, unsound *Nonformal:* cheesy, crap, Mickey Mouse

rotund *adj.* **1.** discoid, elliptical, globular, oval, round, spherical **2.** chubby, corpulent, fat, fleshy, heavy, mammoth, obese, plump, portly, pudgy, Rubenesque, stout, vast *Nonformal* roly-poly, tubby *Antonyms:* angular, gaunt, slim, thin, willowy **2.** full-toned, mellow, orotund, resonant, rich, sonorous, vibrant *Antonyms:* ear-piercing, shrill, thin, tremulous, weak

rough *adj.* **1.** broken, corrugated, irregular, jagged, lumpy, ridged, rocky, serrated, stony, uneven **2.** bedraggled, dirty, dishevelled, disorderly, down-and-out, messy, ragged, shabby, sloppy, slovenly, tousled, uncombed, unkempt, unshaven, wrinkled **3.** bristling, coarse, flaky, irritating, itchy, uncomfortable **4.** bloody, brutal, competitive, dangerous, fierce, physical, savage, violent **5.** boorish, callous, coarse, crass, impolite, insensitive, loatish, oafish, obnoxious, raw, rude, tough, uncivil **6.** blustery, buffeting, choppy, dirty *(Nonformal)*, foul, harsh, inclement, raging, riotous, rugged, squally, stormy, tempestuous, tumultuous, turbulent, wild *Antonyms:* balmy, calm, clement, still **7.** basic, crude, early, imperfect, incomplete, rough-hewn, rudimentary, sketchy, uncompleted, unfinished, unpolished, unrefined **8.** cacophonous, grating, inharmonious, jarring, strident **9.** arduous, debilitating, demanding, difficult, enervating, exhausting, extreme, hard, hardscrabble, nightmarish *(Nonformal)*, sapping, Spartan, tiring, unpleasant **10.** amorphous, approximate, ballpark *(Nonformal)*, estimated, foggy, general, guesstimated, hazy, imprecise, inexact, proximate, sketchy, uncertain, vague *Antonyms:* exact, perfected, specific – *adv.* brutally, coarsely, harshly, savagely, urgently, violently – *n.* **1.** brute, hoodlum, hooligan, knave, rapscallion, rowdy, ruffian, scoundrel, thug, tough, wretch *Nonformal:* goon, hood, plug-ugly **2.** design, draft, layout, outline, plan, sketch – *prep.* **1.** around, close to, encircling, near, surrounding **2.** about, all over, everywhere, on all sides

rough-and-ready *adj.* **1.** adequate, improvised, interim, makeshift, provisional, stopgap, temporary, usable, workable *Antonyms:* fixed, permanent **2.** approximate, crude, cursory, inexact, preliminary, rough-hewn, rudimentary, sketchy, unrefined *Antonyms:* cultivated, exact, precise, polished

roughcast *adj.* coarse, crude, embryonic, half-baked *(Nonformal)*, immature, inchoate, preliminary, rough, rude, rudimentary, simplistic, uncultivated, undeveloped, unfinished, unformed, unpolished, unrefined *Antonyms:* developed, matured, ripened

round *adj.* **1.** arced, arched, ball-shaped, bent, bowed, bulbous, circular, coiled, curled, curved, curvilinear, cylindrical, disc-shaped, egg-shaped, ellipsoidal, elliptical, globular, looped, oval, ringed, rotund, rounded, spherical, spheroid, spiral *Antonyms:* rectangular, square **2.** ample, chubby, corpulent, expansive, fat, fleshy, full, generous, large, liberal, plump, rotund, rounded, tubby *Antonyms:* gaunt, slight, wiry **3.** accomplished, complete, done, entire, finished, full, integral, solid, sound, total, unbroken, undivided, whole *Antonyms:* broken, divided, interrupted **4.** blunt, candid, direct, frank, free, honest, outspoken, plain, straightforward, unmodified, vocal **5.** aboveboard, decent, good, honest, honourable, just, principled, square, upright, upstanding **6.** consonant, full, mellifluous, orotund, plangent, resonant, resounding, rich, ringing, sonorous, vibrant – *adv.* completely, everywhere, thoroughly, throughout, totally – *n.* **1.** arc, arch, ball, band, bend, bow, circle, circlet, curvature, curve, disc, equator, eye, globe, gyre, hoop, loop, orb, orbit, ring, ringlet, sphere, wheel **2.** ammunition, bullet, cartridge, charge, discharge, load, shell, shot **3.** pirouette, pivot, revolution, rotation, spin, twirl **4.** ambit, circuit, course, lap, perimeter, route, run **5.** chain, progression, sequence, session, spell **6.** period, phase, segment, stage, step, stretch, term **7.** collection, distribution, grouping, selection, set – *v.* **1.** circle around, circulate, circumnavigate, compass, gyrate, pivot, revolve, roll, rotate, spin, turn, wheel, whirl **2.** circumscribe, encircle, encompass, flank, gird, girdle, hem, ring, skirt, surround **3.** arch, bend, bow, coil, convolute, crook, curl, curve, form, loop **4.** complete, finish, mould, perfect, polish, refine, shape, smooth

roundabout *adj.* ambagious, circuitous, circular, circumlocutory, collateral, deviating, discursive, evasive, indirect, loose *(Nonformal)*, meandering, oblique, periphrastic, prolix, tortuous *Antonyms:* direct, straight, straightforward *See also:* **rotary** – *n.* carousel, *circulaire (French)*, rotary, traffic circle

rouse *v.* **1.** agitate, aggravate, anger, challenge, disturb, foment, galvanize, incite, inflame, instigate, move, pique, provoke, rile, startle, trigger, work up *Nonformal:* bug, craze, fire up, needle *Antonyms:* dampen, quiet, soothe **2.** animate, arouse, awaken, bestir, call, enliven, excite, exhilarate, heighten, intensify, kindle, magnify, quicken, raise, rally, stimulate, stir, urge, waken

rout *n.* **1.** beating, clobbering, comedown, conquest, debacle, defeat, disaster, drubbing, embarrassment, letdown, overthrow, sweep, thrashing, trouncing, upset, whipping *Nonformal:* licking, shellacking, trashing **2.** canaille, crowd, group, hoi polloi, horde, mass, masses, mob, multitude, people, rabble, rank and file, riff-raff, throng – *v.* **1.** bash, beat, bury, clobber, conquer, crush, destroy, dispel, drive off, drub, expel, finish, lambaste, overpower, overthrow, quash, repulse, scuttle, subdue, thrash, trounce, vanquish, wallop, whip, wipe out *Nonformal:* bulldoze, cream, lick, shellac, skunk, swamp, trash **2.** forage, hunt, poke around, ransack, rummage, search, sift through **3.** drive *or* force out, roust

route *n.* **1.** artery, avenue, boulevard, drive, highway, passage, path, pavement, pike, road, roadway, street, toll road, track, trail **2.** agency, course, direction, means, medium, method, practice, system, tack, way **3.** beat, circuit, itinerary, range, rounds – *v.* address, consign, convey, direct, dispatch, forward, point and click *(Computer)*, remit, send, ship, transmit

routine *adj.* accepted, accustomed, annual, automatic, chronic, conventional, customary, daily, everyday, familiar, general, habitual, normal, ordinary, quotidian, regular, standard, typical, unthinking, usual, weekly, workaday *Antonyms:* abnormal, different, exceptional, irregular, special, unusual – *n.* **1.** convention, custom, drill, formula, grind, groove, habit, line, method, pace, pattern, practice, procedure, regimen, rote, rule, system, technique, usage, way *Nonformal:* beaten path, daily grind, donkey work, rat race **2.** act, number, performance, program, schtick *(Nonformal)*

rove *v.* amble, circumambulate, cruise, drift, gad, gallivant, jaunt, meander, perambulate, peregrinate, prowl, ramble, range, roam, saunter, stray, stroll, traipse, travel, traverse, wander *Nonformal:* bum around, follow one's nose

row *n.* **1.** bank, chain, column, echelon, file, line, order, progression, queue, range, rank, sequence, series, string, succession, tier **2.** altercation, bickering, brawl, brouhaha, commotion, controversy, dispute, disturbance, falling-out, fight, fracas, fray, fuss, incident, mêlée, quarrel, racket, scrap, shouting match, squabble, tiff, wrangle *Nonformal:* dust up, punch up, run-in, set-to, shindig *Antonyms:* accord, harmony, peace – *v.* **1.** argue, berate, bicker, brawl, dispute, feud, scold, scrap, spat, squabble, tiff, wrangle *Antonyms:* accord, cooperate, get along **2.** drive, paddle, propel, pull, punt, scull

rowdy *adj.* abandoned, boisterous, disorderly, loud, mischievous, noisy, rambunctious, unrestrained, unruly, uproarious, wild *Antonyms:* calm, restrained, sedate – *n.* brawler, bully, hellion, hoodlum, hooligan, lout, ruffian, terror, troublemaker, yahoo *Nonformal:* cowboy, goon, hellcat, holy terror, punk, tough

royal *adj.* **1.** aristocratic, baronial, imperial, kingly, monarchical, noble, patrician, queenly, regnant, reigning, sovereign **2.** august, commanding, dignified, eminent, grand, highbrow, lofty, magnificent, majestic, regal **3.** best, chief, excellent, exquisite, extraordinary, fine, prime, prize, select, sublime, superior, supreme, top

rub *n.* **1.** bar, catch, difficulty, dilemma, drawback, glitch *(Nonformal)*, hindrance, hitch, hurdle, impediment, obstacle, problem, snag, stumbling block, trouble **2.** caressing, fondling, friction, massage, stroking **3.** cut, derision, hurt, insult, jab, poke, sarcasm, slight, sneer, taunt, wound **4.** abrasion, chafing, irritation, roughness – *v.* **1.** caress, fondle, knead, massage, pet, stroke **2.** buff, burnish, polish, scrub, shine **3.** abrade, chafe, erode, fray, grate, irritate, itch, scrape

rubbish *n.* **1.** debris, dreck, dross, jetsam, garbage, landfill, litter, refuse, riffraff, scrap, waste *Antonyms:* essentials, treasures **2.** amphigory, balderdash, bombast, claptrap, drivel, folly, foolishness, froth, gibberish, idle talk, nonsense, poppycock, rant, rigmarole, rodomontade, trumpery, twaddle *Nonformal:* b.s., baloney, bosh, bunk, crap, flapdoodle, gobbledygook, malarkey

ruckus *n.* ado, ballyhoo, bother, brawl, broil, brouhaha, caterwauling, commotion, donnybrook, disturbance, embroilment, foofaraw, fracas, fuss, hassle, horseplay, hubbub, hullabaloo, mêlée, racket, rampage, rough-housing, row, rumpus, scramble, stir, to-do, trouble, tumult, turmoil, uproar *Antonyms:* calm, peace, serenity

ruddy *adj.* blooming, blushing, crimson, florid, flushed, glowing, healthy, red, roseate, rosy, ruby, sanguine, scarlet *Antonyms:* ashen, colourless, pale, pallid, wan

rude *adj.* **1.** abrupt, bad-mannered, blunt, brusque, caustic, churlish, curt, discourteous, disrespectful, graceless, gruff, impolite, inconsiderate, indecorous, indelicate, insulting, mean-spirited, sharp, tactless, thoughtless, uncivil *Antonyms:* considerate, cordial, polite, well-bred **2.** coarse, countrified, gauche, plebian, provincial, rustic, uncivilized, uncouth, uncultivated, unschooled, untaught, untrained, vulgar **3.** crude, makeshift, primitive, rough-hewn, rudimentary, simple, undeveloped, unfinished, unprocessed, unrefined **4.** barbarous, ferocious, fierce, frenzied, harsh, savage **5.** blustering, inclement, severe, stormy, tempestuous, tumultuous, wild **6.** brawny, hale, hearty, robust, strapping, strong, sturdy, vigorous

rudimentary *adj.* **1.** basic, elemental, essential, fundamental, germinal **2.** embryonic, formative, immature, imperfect, inchoate, incomplete, initial, undeveloped, vestigial

rueful *adj.* abashed, abject, apologetic, ashamed, conscience-stricken, contrite, doleful, dolorous, grievous, penitent, piteous, plaintive, red-faced, regretful, remorseful, repentant, repining, sad, self-accusing, self-reproaching, shameful, sheepish, sorrowful, sorry, woebegone, wretched *Antonyms:* cheery, happy, proud

ruffian *n.* buffoon, bully, desperado, henchman, hoodlum, hooligan, rogue, rowdy, tough *Nonformal*: bill collector, flatnose, goon, gorilla, gun thug, hood, plug-ugly, strong-arm

ruffle *n.* **1.** edging, fillet, flounce, frill, furbelow, goffer, jabot, pleat, tucking, wimple **2.** disturbance, flutter, ripple, undulation **3.** anxiety, chagrin, discomfiture, discomposure, disquiet, disquietude, fluster, fret, tizzy *(Nonformal)* – *v.* **1.** annoy, confuse, bother, disturb, irk, madden, nettle, provoke, unsettle, vex *Antonyms:* calm, placate, smooth, straighten **2.** crease, crimp, crinkle, crush, fold, gather, pucker, purse, rumple, scrunch up *(Nonformal)*, wrinkle **3.** disarrange, dishevel, disorder, mess up, shuffle, tousle

rugged *adj.* **1.** bumpy, craggy, hilly, impassible, impenetrable, jagged, mountainous, overgrown, precipitous, rock strewn, rough, scraggy, uneven **2.** furrowed, leathery, ragged, rugate, rugose, seamed, weathered, wrinkled **3.** austere, demanding, difficult, hard-line *(Nonformal)*, harsh, ironbound, ironhanded, obstinate, severe, stark, steely, strict, stringent, unbending, unyielding **4.** ill-bred, loud, obnoxious, rough-and-tumble, rude, uncouth, uncultured, unrefined, vulgar **5.** cacophonous, dissonant, ear-piercing, ear-splitting, grating, jarring, loud, noisy, raucous, strident **6.** beefy, big, brawny, bulky, burly, energetic, hale, healthy, hearty, indefatigable, robust, sturdy, tough, unflagging, vigorous, well-built *Antonyms:* delicate, feeble, fragile, soft **7.** blizzardly, choppy, dirty *(Nonformal)*, fierce, foul, gusty, inclement, squally, stormy, tempestuous, violent, wild, windy

ruin *n.* **1.** annihilation, calamity, debacle, demolishment, destruction, disaster, dissolution, havoc, obliteration, ruination, woe, wrack **2.** atrophy, breakdown, corruption, death, decay, decline, degeneration, deterioration, putrefaction, rot, wasting **3.** collapse, defeat, downfall, fall, loss, toppling, undoing, unseating, Waterloo **4.** abasement, debasement, degradtion, demoralization, disgrace, dishonour, humiliation, indignity, shame, vitiation **5.** bankruptcy, destitution, dire *or* sorry straits *(Nonformal)*, hardship, impoverishment, indigence, loss, mendicancy, misfortune, penury, poverty, privation, **6.** Achilles' heel, bane, bête noire, cross, curse, nemesis, plague **7.** remains, rubble, trace, vestige, wasteland, wreckage – *v.* **1.** bulldoze, clear-cut, demolish, destroy, despoil, destroy, extinguish, flatten, lay waste, level, moonscape *(B.C.)*, raze, smash, torpedo, wreck *Nonformal:* cream, total *Antonyms:* build, construct, repair, restore **2.** bankrupt, bust *(Nonformal)*, impoverish, pauperize, sink **3.** debauch, defile, ravish, seduce, sully, violate

ruined *adj.* **1.** clear-cut, demolished, depleted, destroyed, devastated, gutted, ravaged, razed, wasted **2.** bankrupt, cleaned out *(Nonformal)*, destitute, impoverished, insolvent, needy, out on the street, penniless, penurious, poor, wrecked **3.** crumbling, decayed, dilapidated, run-down, shabby, threadbare, tumbledown, weatherworn

ruinous *adj.* adverse, bad, baleful, calamitous, cataclysmic, catastrophic, destructive, devastating, dire, disastrous, malevolent, negative, shattering *Nonformal:* deadly, scorched earth, suicidal

rule *n.* **1.** aphorism, axiom, canon, command, commandment, criterion, decree, dictum, edict, formula, fundamental, keystone, law, mandate, maxim, model, order, ordinance, precept, principle, regulation, standard, statute, tenet **2.** convention, course, custom, formula, habit, method, normality, policy, practice, procedure, routine, way **3.** administration, authority, command, control, direction, government, influence, leadership, management, reign, sovereignty, supremacy, sway, tenure – *v.* **1.** command, conduct, direct, dominate, govern, head, lead, manage, oversee, reign, run, run the show *(Nonformal)* **2.** decide, decree, deem, dictate, judge, order, settle **3.** bridle, check, control, curb, inhibit, rein in, restrain, suppress **4.** continue, endure, last, persist, predominate, prevail, survive

ruler *n.* **1.** autocrat, caesar, chieftain, *commissar (Russian)*, crowned head, czar, despot, dictator, emir, emperor, empress, governor, kaiser, khan, king, lord, master, mogul, monarch, potentate, queen, rajah, regent, satrap, sovereign, sultan, tyrant, *vizier (Muslim) Antonyms:* chattel, peasant, subject, subordinate, underling, vassal **2.** boss, captain, chief, commander, controller, head, leader, manager, overseer, skipper, superior, supervisor **3.** folding rule, gauge, measure, straightedge, T-square, tape measure, try square, yardstick

ruling *adj.* **1.** cardinal, central, chief, current, dominant, guiding, leading, main, pivotal, popular, predominant, preeminent, preponderant, prevailing, prevalent, principal, supreme *Antonyms:* auxiliary, inferior, minor, secondary, trivial **2.** administrating, commanding, conducting, directing, managing, presiding, regulating, reigning – *n.* adjudication, decision, decree, directive, edict, finding, judgment, law, order, precept, pronouncement, resolution, rule, verdict

rum *n.* alcohol, bung-your-eye *(Newfoundland)*, demon rum, drink, grog, intoxicant, liquor, screech, sea ration *(Historical)*, spirit, stimulant *Nonformal:* booze, John Barleycorn, the captain

ruminate *v.* **1.** brainstorm, brood, cogitate, consider, contemplate, deliberate, dwell on, figure, meditate, mull over, muse, ponder, rack one's brains, reckon, reflect, revolve, think, weigh **2.** chew, eat, masticate, munch *(Nonformal)*

rummage *n.* **1.** exploration, forage, hunt, probe, pursuit, quest, ransacking, searching **2.** bazaar, boot *or* garage *or* white elephant sale, flea-market – *v.* **1.** beat the bushes, comb, delve, dig *or* ferret out, examine, explore, fish about *(Nonformal)*, forage, grub, hunt, poke, rake, ransack, root, scour, search, seek **2.** disarrange, disarray, disorder, disorganize, disrupt, disturb, muss

rumour *n.* canard, fabrication, falsehood, fiction, gossip, hearsay, innuendo, repute, scandal, story, suggestion, supposition, tale, word *Nonformal:* back-fence talk, breeze, buzz, dirt, low-down, scuttlebutt *Antonyms:* actuality, truth, verity – *v.* bruit, circulate, gossip, insinuate, pass around, report, talk, whisper *Nonformal:* blab, slug

rump *n.* back, backside, behind, bottom, buttocks, *derrière (French)*, haunches, hind end, hindquarters, posterior, rear *or* rear end, seat *Nonformal:* arse, ass, bum, buns, butt, caboose, can, duff, fanny, keister, moon, tail

rumple *n.* crease, fold, gather, pleat, pucker, ridge, wrinkle – *v.* bedraggle, crease, crimp, crinkle, crumple, crush, derange, dishevel, disorder, fold, pucker, ruffle, scrunch, tousle, wreathe, wrinkle *Antonyms:* iron, smooth, straighten

run *adj.* **1.** liquefied, melted, molten, runny, thawed, watery **2.** black-market, bootleg, contraband, illegal, illicit, prohibited, smuggled, trafficked, unlawful – *n.* **1.** competition, concours, contest, event, footrace, heat, marathon, meet, race, relay, sprint **2.** clip, form, gait, gallop, lope, movement, pace, rate, speed, trot, velocity **3.** bolt, break *(Nonformal)*, decampment, departure, disappearance, escape, flight, getaway, jailbreak **4.** drive, excursion, jaunt, journey, perambulation, outing, ride, sally, trip, visit **5.** avenue, course, laneway, passage, pathway, route, track, trail, walk, way **6.** access, blank cheque, carte blanche, clearance, free hand *or* reign, liberty, licence, permission, privledge, use **7.** distance, duration, interval, period, season, spell, stint, stretch, tenure, term, time **8.** chain, concatenation, continuum, progression, sequence, series, string **9.** direction, drift, fashion, flow, penchant, swing, tendency, trend, turn, vogue **10.** breed, category, class, classification, ilk, model, order, sort, species, type **11.** batch, number, output, portion, quantity, sum **12.** gash, hole, rip, slit, snag, tear **13.** current, deluge, drip, efflux, flood, flux, gush, leak, oozing, rush, spate, spurt **14.** brook, burn *(Scottish)*, creek, river, stream, streamlet **15.** crowd, gang, gathering, group, knot, migration, pack, party, pool, school, selection, spawn, unit **16.** coop, corral, enclosure, fold, pen, pound **17.** brandish, flourish, riff, roulade, show, sweep, swish – *v.* **1.** administer, boss, control, coordinate, direct, head, keep, lead, manage, mastermind, operate, oversee, regulate, superintend, supervise **2.** abscond, amble, barrel, beat it, bolt, bound, canter, dart, dash, escape, flee, fly, gallop, hasten, hurry, hustle, lope, race, rush, scamper, scramble, scurry, scud, scuttle, skip, speed, sprint, take flight, tear, trot *Nonformal:* cut-out, hotfoot, make tracks, skedaddle *Antonyms:* crawl, creep, dawdle **3.** challenge, compete, contend, contest, oppose, stand **4.** cascade, empty, flood, flow, gush, issue forth, jet, seep, spill, spout, spurt, stream, surge, trickle **5.** discharge, emit, leak, ooze, secrete, suppurate **6.** gad, journey, meander, migrate, move, proceed, roam, sojourn, travel, traverse, trek, wander **7.** dissolve, fuse, liquefy, melt, thaw **8.** disintegrate, rip, shred, snag, tear, unravel, unwind **9.** drive, function, go, handle, operate, perform, work **10.** climb, creep, encompass, extend, reach, span, spread, surround **11.** bootleg, convey, ship, smuggle, sneak in, transport

runaway *adj.* **1.** at large, escaped, fled, fugitive, loose, on the lam *(Nonformal)*, stray, wanted **2.** clear, decisive, easy, effortless, obvious, one-sided – *n.* absconder, delinquent, deserter, escapee, fugitive, lawbreaker, offender, truant

rundown *adj.* **1.** enfeebled, exhausted, worn out *Nonformal:* bushed, whacked **2.** beat up, decayed, dilapidated, ramshackle, rickety, seedy shabby, tumbledown *Nonformal:* crappy old, lousy – *n.* analysis, brief, outline, précis, recap, recapitulation, report, résumé, review, run-through, sketch, summary, synopsis *Nonformal:* lowdown, thumbnail

runt *n.* bantam, dwarf, manikin, scrub *Nonformal:* half-pint, Lilliputian, peewee, pipsqueak, shrimp, titman

rupture *n.* **1.** break, burst, cleavage, cleft, crack, division, fissure, fracture, gash, opening, rent, split, tear **2.** breach, discord, dispute, disunion, divergence, estrangement, feud, parting, schism – *v.* breach, burst, cleave, crack, disrupt, divide, fracture, open, part, rend, rive, separate, sever, shatter, split, sunder, tear *Antonyms:* connect, join, mend, patch

rural *adj.* **1.** agrarian, agricultural, agronomic, arable, farming, geoponic, georgic **2.** Arcadian, bucolic, countrified, country, natural, pastoral, provincial, rustic, sylvan *Antonyms:* built-up, developed, urban

ruse *n.* angle, artifice, deceit, device, dodge, feint, gambit, hoax, manoeuvre, ploy, stratagem, stunt, subterfuge, trick, twist, wile *Nonformal:* con *or* snow job, curveball, racket

rush *n.* **1.** celerity, dispatch, expedition, haste, precipitancy, promptness, quickness, rapidity, speed, swiftness, velocity **2.** exigency, gravity, importance, necessity, need, pressure, seriousness, urgency **3.** deluge, flood, flow, flux, gush, inundation, onslaught, outpouring, press, race, run, spate, stream, surge, torrent **4.** excitement, exhilaration, high, sensation, stimulation, thrill, tingle *Nonformal:* charge, jollies, kick – *v.* **1.** attack, besiege, blitz, charge, descend *or* pounce upon **2.** accelerate, dash, fly, hasten, hurry, hustle, quicken, race, run, scamper, scramble, scurry, sprint **3.** course, deluge, flood, flow, gush, issue, pour, surge

rust *n.* blight, corrosion, corruption, decay, decomposition, dilapidation, fungus, oxidation, perforation, tarnish – *v.* corrode, decay, deteriorate, oxidize, tarnish

rustic *adj.* **1.** agrarian, Arcadian, bucolic, country, farm, pastoral, provincial, rural **2.** artless, coarse, homely, natural, plain, simple, Spartan, stark, unadorned, unaffected, unvarnished **3.** awkward, boorish, graceless, maladroit, rude, uncouth, uncultured, unrefined, unsophisticated *Antonyms:* cosmopolitan, sophisticated, urban – *n.* backwoodsman, bumpkin, country boy *or* girl, farmer, hillbilly, mountaineer, peasant, provincial, yokel *Nonformal:* cornpone, country cousin, hayseed, hick, plough jockey, robe, slack-jawed yokel

rustle *n.* crackle, crinkling, friction, murmur, noise, patter, sound, stir, swish, whisper – *v.* **1.** crinkle, sibilate, swish, whish, whoosh **2.** appropriate, filch, pilfer, poach, purloin, rob, steal, take *Nonformal:* annex, lift, rip off, swipe

rusty *adj.* **1.** corroded, decayed, oxidized, rust-covered, rusted **2.** impaired, inactive, out of practice *or* shape, sluggish, soft, stale, unpracticed, unused, weak *Antonyms:* prepared, primed, ready, fit

rut *n.* **1.** furrow, gouge, groove, hollow, indentation, pothole, rabbet, score, track, trench, trough **2.** habit, pace, pattern, practice, procedure, rote, round, routine, usage, wont *Nonformal:* daily grind, hole, treadmill *Antonyms:* change, vacation **3.** estrus, heat, mating season – *v.* carve, chisel, cut, furrow, gouge, groove, gully, score, scratch

ruthless *adj.* barbarous, brutal, callous, cold-blooded, cruel, cutthroat, ferocious, flinty, grim, hard, hardhearted, harsh, heartless, inhuman, iron-fisted, malevolent, mean, merciless, obdurate, pitiless, sadistic, savage, severe, stern, stony, take no prisoners *(Nonformal)*, unfeeling, unsympathetic, unyielding, vicious, vindictive *Antonyms:* compassionate, forgiving, gentle

sable *adj.* black, coal-black, dark, ebony, inky, jet, midnight, pitch-black, raven, zibeline

sabotage *n.* damage, destruction, disruption, ecotage, injury, Luddism, subversion, subversiveness, treachery, vandalism – *v.* attack, block, cripple, destroy, disable, disrupt, frustrate, hamper, hinder, incapacitate, obstruct, scuttle, subvert, torpedo, undermine, vandalize, wreck *Antonyms:* aid, assist, help

saccharine *adj.* **1.** candied, honeyed, nectarous, sugary, sweet, toothsome *Antonyms:* bitter, sour, tart **2.** cloying, corny, mawkish, maudlin, mushy, overdone, rich, romanticized, sentimental, syrupy *Nonformal:* Hollywood, sappy, schmaltzy, sugarcoated *Antonyms:* genuine, honest, real

sack *n.* bag, carryall, container, grip, gunny, knapsack, package, pocket, poke, pouch, purse, tote, trail bag – *v.* **1.** demolish, depredate, desecrate, desolate, despoil, destroy, devour, fleece, lay waste, level, loot, maraud, pillage, plunder, raid, ravage, rifle, rob, ruin, spoil, strip, waste **2.** cashier, discharge, dismiss, fire, lay off, terminate *Nonformal:* cut loose, downsize, give the boot *or* heave-ho to, pink-slip *Antonyms:* employ, hire

sacrament *n.* holy mysteries, rite *Christian sacraments:* baptism, bread and wine, communion, confirmation, extreme unction, holy orders, last rites, matrimony, penance, the Eucharist

sacred *adj.* **1.** blessed, cherished, consecrated, dedicated, divine, enshrined, godly, hallowed, holy, numinous, pure, religious, revered, sacramental, sanctified, solemn, spiritual, venerable *Antonyms:* lay, profane, secular, temporal, worldly **2.** blameless, immune, impregnable, inexpugnable, inviolable, inviolate, invulnerable, irreproachable, sacrosanct, unimpeachable, untouchable

sacrifice *n.* **1.** appeasement, bestowal, bestowment, burnt offering, corban, donation, gift, libation, oblation, offering, present **2.** abandonment, ceding, loss, pyrrhic victory, relinquishment, suffering, yielding – *v.* **1.** burn, kill, martyr, offer, slaughter **2.** abandon, cede, cut loose, drop, eschew, forgo, give up *or* over, lose, quit, relinquish, surrender, waive, yield

sacrilege *n.* blasphemy, crime, curse, desecration, heresy, impiety, irreverence, mockery, offence, pollution, profanation, profanity, scandal, sin, violation *Antonyms:* piety, respect, reverence

sacrilegious *adj.* blasphemous, defiling, desecrating, disobedient, disrespectful, evil, godless, immoral, impious, irreverent, nefarious, nonconforming, profane, scandalous, sinful, unholy, wicked *Antonyms:* divine, pious, reverent, righteous

sacrosanct *adj.* **1.** blessed, consecrated, divine, hallowed, holy, immutable, inviolable, inviolate, sacred *Antonyms:* filthy, impure, sinful **2.** above it all *(Nonformal)*, dignified, elevated, eminent, exalted, honoured, lofty, respected, revered *Antonyms:* common, lowly, mean

sad *adj.* **1.** bereaved, blue, cheerless, dejected, depressed, despairing, despondent, disconsolate, distressed, doleful, down, downhearted, downcast, forlorn, gloomy, glum, grief-stricken, grieved, heartbroken, heartsick, heavy-hearted, hurt, in the dumps *(Nonformal)*, languishing, low, lugubrious, melancholy, miserable, morose, mournful, neurasthenic, pensive, sombre, sorrowful, tearful, troubled, unhappy, weeping, woebegone, wretched *Antonyms:* blithe, cheerful, glad, joyous, merry **2.** agonizing, depressing, disconcerting, discouraging, disheartening, dismal, distressing, grievous, heartrending, lamentable, pitiful, poignant, regrettable, tear-jerker *(Nonformal)*, tragic, unfortunate *Antonyms:* encouraging, inspiring, uplifting **3.** awful, bad, contemptible, deplorable, dreadful, inadequate, paltry, pathetic, poor, shabby, sorry *Nonformal:* crummy, half-assed, lousy

sadden *v.* bereave, bring *or* drag down, crush, dampen, darken, dash, deject, depress, disconcert, discourage, dishearten, dispirit, distress, lower, oppress, trouble, upset *Antonyms:* cheer, embolden, encourage, relieve

saddle *n.* chair, cushion, harness, pad, pillion, seat *Parts of a saddle:* back *or* front cinch, cantle, horn, pommel, saddle strings, stirrup, tapadera – *v.* **1.** equip, furnish, gear, load, outfit, prepare, ready, supply **2.** burden, encumber, fetter, load, oppress, tax, weigh down *Antonyms:* free, liberate, lighten

sadistic *adj.* algolagnic, barbarous, brutal, cruel, fiendish, inhumane, odious, perverse, ruthless, savage, vicious, tyrannical, unfeeling *Antonyms:* civil, humane, kind

sadness *n.* anguish, bleakness, cheerlessness, dejection, depression, despondency, disconsolation, dispiritedness, distress, dolefulness, dolour, dysphoria, forlornness, gloom, grief, heartache, heartbreak, heavy-heartedness, hopelessness, melancholy, misery, mopes, mourning, neurasthenia, sorrow, unhappiness, vale of tears, *Weltschmerz (German)*, woe *Nonformal:* blahs, blue funk *Antonyms:* bliss, contentment, happiness, joy

safe *adj.* **1.** airtight, bulletproof, defended, guarded, fortified, hermetically sealed, impervious, impregnable, insulated, inviolable, invulnerable, locked, preserved, protected, safeguarded, secure, sheltered, shielded, snug, tended, unassailable, watched *Antonyms:* susceptible, vulnerable **2.** intact, okay *(Nonformal)*, sound, undamaged, unharmed, unhurt, uninjured, unscathed *Antonyms:* broken, mangled, ruined **3.** drinkable, edible, harmless, innocuous, inoffensive, noncontaminated, nonpoisonous, nontoxic, tame, wholesome *Antonyms:* deadly, noxious, pernicious **4.** all clear *or* right, calm, defused, pacified, peaceful, quiet *Antonyms:* dangerous, hazardous, life-threatening **5.** careful, cautious, chary, circumspect, dependable, discreet, prudent, reliable, true, trustworthy *Antonyms:* crooked, questionable, risky, shady **6.** certain, easy, foolproof, realistic, realizable, reliable, risk-free, sound, sure *Antonyms:* chancy, dicey – *n.* bank, repository, safety-deposit box, strongbox, vault

safeguard *n.* armour, buffer, bulwark, countermeasure, defence, device, escape clause *or* hatch, outrider, palladium, poison pill, postilion, precaution, prevention, prophylactic, protection, security – *v.* cover, defend, escort, guard, harbour, oversee, protect, secure, shield, shelter, ward off, watch *Antonyms:* ignore, neglect

safety *adj.* advisory, precautionary, protective, security – *n.* asylum, cover, defence, freedom, harbour, haven, immunity, impregnability, protection, refuge, sanctuary, security, shelter

sag *n.* **1.** basin, depression, dip, drop, droop, fall off, hollow, pit, settling, sink, sinkhole, slant, tilt *Antonyms:* apex, peak, point, summit **2.** bust, decline, downswing, downtrend, downturn, slip, slump *Antonyms:* boom, rise, upturn – *v.* **1.** bend, bow, cave, curve, dangle, dip, droop, fail, fall, flag, flap, flop, hang, lean, settle, sink, slide, slip, slump, swag **2.** decline, drop, languish, soften, weaken, wilt *Antonyms:* harden, stiffen, strengthen

saga *n.* account, adventure, ballad, chronicle, epic, history, journey, legend, myth, narrative, odyssey, ordeal, romance, story, tale, wanderings, yarn

sagacious *adj.* acute, apt, astute, brilliant, cagey, canny, clear-sighted, clever, discerning, discriminating, farsighted, foxy, gnostic, heady, insightful, intelligent, judicious, keen, knowing, knowledgeable, learned, perceptive, perspicacious, profound, prudent, quick, rational, sage, sapient, sensible, sharp, shrewd, smart, wise, witty *Nonformal:* hip, savvy *Antonyms:* blunt, slow, torpid

sage *adj.* astute, canny, discerning, far-seeing, intelligent, knowing, knowledgeable, learned, perceptive, profound, prudent, quick, sagacious, sensible, smart, wise – *n.* authority, counsellor, elder, expert, greybeard, guru, *kinap (Native Peoples)*, maharishi, mahatmu, master, *mullah (Islamic)*, oracle, philosopher, priest, pundit, rabbi, rishi, savant, scholar, sensei, Solon, teacher, Tzaddik *(Judaism)*, wiseman *Hindu:* sadhu, swami *Antonyms:* fool, stooge

sail *n.* **1.** canvas, sailcloth, sheet *Sails of full-rigged ship:* flying jib, fore royal, fore skysail, fore royal studdingsail, foresail, foretopmast staysail, foretopmast studdingsail, foretopgallant sail, foretopgallant studding sail, jib, lower maintopsail, lower mizzen topsail, lower studdingsail, main royal, main royal studdingsail, main skysail, main staysail, mainsail, maintopgallant, maintopgallant studdingsail, maintopmast staysail, maintopmast studdingsail, mizzen royal, mizzen royal staysail, mizzen sail, mizzen skysail, mizzen staysail, mizzen topgallant sail, mizzen topgallant staysail, mizzen topmast staysail, spanker, upper foretopsail, uppermaintopsail, upper mizzen topsail **2.** adventure, cruise, expedition, exploration, journey, passage, ride, trip – *v.* **1.** cross, cruise, drift, scud, travel, voyage, weigh anchor **2.** captain, control, manage, navigate, pilot, skipper, steer **3.** float, flutter, fly, glide, soar, take flight *or* wing

sailor *n.* able-bodied seaman, barrelman *(Newfoundland)*, boatman, buccaneer, cadet, deck hand, highliner, lascar, marine, mariner, midshipman, navigator, pilot, pirate, Seabee *(U.S.)*, seafarer, seaman, shipmate, yachtsman *Nonformal:* bluejacket, gob, hearty, limey, jacktar, salt, salty *or* water dog, seadog, swabber, tar

saintly *adj.* angelic, beatific, blameless, blessed, devout, divine, God-fearing, godly, good, holy, pious, pure, religious, righteous, sainted, saint-like, seraphic, sinless, upright, upstanding, virtuous, worthy *Antonyms:* devilish, diabolical, nefarious, sinful

sake *n.* **1.** account, advantage, behalf, benefit, consideration, good, interest, purpose, regard, respect, welfare, well-being **2.** aim, cause, consequence, end, motive, objective, principle, reason

salacious *adj.* **1.** bawdy, carnal, dirty, lascivious, lecherous, lewd, libidinous, licentious, obscene, pornographic, prurient, raunchy, ribald, steamy, wanton *Nonformal:* adult, blue, raw *Antonyms:* innocent, pure, wholesome **2.** aroused, bothered, hot, lustful, lusty *Nonformal:* horny, hot to trot, randy *Antonyms:* bored, cold, indifferent, jaded

salad *n.* **1.** greens *Nonformal:* rabbit food, veggies *Common salads:* bean, Caesar, chicken, Cobb, cole slaw, crab, egg, fruit, Greek, house, julienne, lobster, macaroni, mandarin, marshmallow, *niçoise (French)*, pasta, potato, salmon, salmagundi, spinach, *tabbouleh (Lebanese)*, tuna, turkey, village, Waldorf **2.** assortment, gallimaufry, hodgepodge, jumble, medley, mixed bag, mixture, pastiche, stew

salary *n.* compensation, earnings, emolument, fee, honorarium, income, gross, pay, recompense, remuneration, scale, stipend, wage *Nonformal:* bacon, bread, salt, take home

sale *n.* **1.** barter, business, commerce, enterprise, exchange, negotiation, purchase, trade, transaction, transfer, unloading, vending **2.** bargain, clearance, closeout, deal, discount, markdown, reduction *Kinds of discount sale:* back-to-school, bankruptcy, blowout, boxing day, estate, fire, garage, happy hour, liquidation, police auction, red tag, rummage, unclaimed freight, white elephant, yard, year-end **3.** aggregate, amount, earning, gross, register, reward, sum, take, total

salesperson *n.* agent, clerk, floorwalker, hawker, huckster, monger, peddler, representative, sales associate, salesman, saleswoman, seller, shop assistant, vendor *Nonformal:* drummer, scalper, snake-oil salesman

salient *adj.* **1.** arresting, conspicuous, extraordinary, famous, important, impressive, marked, meaningful, moving, notable, noticeable, obvious, outstanding, pertinent, prominent, pronounced, remarkable, signal, significant, striking, weighty *Antonyms:* buried, concealed, cryptic, masked, secret **2.** extending, jutting, obtrusive, overhanging, projecting, protuberant, swollen, thrusting

sallow *adj.* anemic, ashen, ashy, bilious, dull, greenish-yellow, jaundiced, olive, pale, pallid, pasty, sickly, unhealthy, wan, waxy, yellowish *Antonyms:* glowing, rosy, ruddy

sally *n.* **1.** attack, blitz, blitzkrieg, burst, charge, effort, incursion, influx, invasion, offensive, outburst, rush, sortie, storming, try **2.** constitutional, excursion, journey, perambulation, ramble, saunter, stroll, venture, walk, walkabout **3.** banter, bon mot, comeback, Parthian shot, quip, remark, return, witticism, wordplay *Nonformal:* crack, cut, jab, poke, shot, wisecrack, zinger – *v.* **1.** embark, foray, leave, set forth *or* sail, set *or* strike *or* venture out, take flight *or* off, weigh anchor **2.** assault, attack, launch, raid, storm, strike

salon *n.* **1.** apartment, drawing *or* sitting room, lounge, parlour, reception room **2.** centre, exhibition, gallery, hall, museum, showroom **3.** assembly, dinner party, function, gathering, levee, meeting, party, reception, soiree

saloon *n.* alehouse, *auberge (French)*, bar, beer hall *or* parlour, beverage room, *brasserie (Quebec)*, drafthouse, freehouse, grill, hall, hotel, inn, legion hall, pub, public house *(British)*, rathskeller, roadhouse, taproom, tavern *Nonformal:* beer *or* juke joint, brass rail

salt *n.* **1.** brine, flavouring, seasoning, sodium chloride, spice, taste, zest **2.** Attic salt , banter, dry wit, fun, humour, jest, jocularity, repartee, sarcasm, wit – *v.* cure, flavour, jerk, marinade, prepare, preserve, season

saltchuck *n.* depths, high sea, ocean, salt water, sea, surf, swell *Nonformal:* big pond, drink, the briny deep, the deep *See also:* **sea**

salty *adj.* **1.** briny, highly flavoured, saline, salt, salted **2.** bawdy, coarse, filthy, indecent, obscene, rude, vulgar *Antonyms:* clean, upright, wholesome **3.** biting, caustic, humorous, lively, piquant, pungent, racy, risqué, sarcastic, sardonic, sharp, snappy, spicy, tangy, tart, witty, zestful

salubrious *adj.* beneficial, bracing, good, healthful, healthy, helpful, hygienic, invigorating, nutritious, profitable, salutary, tonic, wholesome *Antonyms:* detrimental, harmful, ruinous

salute *n.* acknowledgment, address, bow, curtsy, greeting, hello, kiss, nod, obeisance, recognition, salaam, *salut (French)*, salutation, tribute, welcome *Nonformal:* high five, tip o' the hat – *v.* acknowledge, congratulate, greet, hail, honour, nod, pay homage *or* respects *or* tribute, receive, recognize, wave, welcome

salvage *n.* **1.** clean-up, preservation, reclamation, recovery, renewal, rescue operation, restoration, revitalization **2.** flotsam, garbage, jetsam, junk, leftovers, refuse, remains, scrap, shmunza *(Nonformal)*, stuff – *v.* deliver, glean, reclaim, recondition, recover, recuperate, redeem, regain, rescue, restore, retrieve, save *Antonyms:* abandon, desert, leave

salvation *n.* **1.** deliverance, delivery, emancipation, escape, exemption, extrication, liberation, pardon, redemption, release, relief, reprieve, rescue, saving *Antonyms:* doom, loss, ruin **2.** care, conservancy, conservation, custody, keeping, maintenance, preservation, protection, restoration, safekeeping

salve *n.* appeasement, balm, cream, dressing, emollient, liniment, local anesthetic, lotion, medication, medicine, mollification, ointment, painkiller, palliative, pomade, remedy, solace, soother, tonic, unction, unguent – *v.* alleviate, appease, assuage, calm, ease, heal, mollify, palliate, relieve

same *adj.* **1.** alike, carbon, clonal, comparable, compatible, corresponding, double, duplicate, echoing, equal, equivalent, identical, indistinguishable, interchangeable, like, look-alike, related, selfsame, similar, synonymous, twin *Antonyms:* different, divergent, unalike **2.** homogeneous, monotonous, regular, uniform, unvaried *Antonyms:* altered, different, variable **3.** changeless, consistent, constant, invariable, recurrent, repetitive, stable, steadfast, steady, unaltered, unbroken, unchanging, unfailing, unvarying **4.** aforementioned, aforesaid, former, named, said

sameness *n.* **1.** commonality, equivalence, identicalness, parity, similarity, standardization, uniformity, unison, unity *Antonyms:* diversity, multiplicity, variety **2.** boredom, dullness, monotony, predictability, redundancy, repetition, tedium *Antonyms:* change, freshness, novelty

sample *n.* biopsy, cross-section, example, handout, part, pattern, piece, portion, representation, specimen, swatch – *v.* **1.** analyze, examine, experiment, inspect, poll, test, try **2.** drink, eat, experience, partake, savour, sip, taste

sanctify *v.* **1.** anoint, beatify, bless, canonize, consecrate, dedicate, deify, devote, enshrine, glorify, hallow, worship *Antonyms:* debase, degrade, pollute **2.** absolve, cleanse, free from sin, purify, shrive

sanctimonious *adj.* holier-than-thou *(Nonformal)*, hypocritical, insincere, Pecksniffian, pious, preachy, pretentious, self-important, self-righteous, self-satisfied, smug, unctuous *Antonyms:* humble, modest, self-deprecating

sanction *n.* **1.** accreditation, approval, assent, authority, cause, command, commission, confirmation, decree, endorsement, go ahead *(Nonformal)*, imprimatur, justification, licence, permission, ratification, validation, warrant, writ **2.** ban, boycott, coercive measure, embargo, injunction, penalty, punishment, punitive measure – *v.* allow, approve, authorize, confirm, homologate, legalize, ratify, validate, warrant *Antonyms:* forbid, prohibit, quash, veto

sanctity *n.* devotion, godliness, grace, holiness, piety, purity, religiousness, reverence, sacredness, saintliness, solemnity, spirituality, virtue, zeal *Antonyms:* amorality, impiety

sanctuary *n.* **1.** adytum, altar, bethel, chancel, church, holy place, mosque, sanctum, shrine, tabernacle, temple **2.** asylum, citadel, cover, fortress, harbour, haven, hideaway, hideout, ivory tower *(Nonformal)*, oasis, port, protection, refuge, resort, retreat, safe house, shelter, shield **3.** conservation area, enclosure, game refuge, harbourage, national *or* provincial park, nature preserve, reserve, wildlife shelter, zoo

sand *n.* backfill, beach, fill, grain, granule, gravel, grit, pebble – *v.* abrade, buff, file, finish, grind, polish, rough up, scour, scrape, smooth

sandwich *n.* food, grub *(Nonformal)*, lunch, meal, snack *Kinds of sandwich:* bacon, BLT *(Nonformal)*, cheese, cheese dream, chicken, chicken salad, club, Coney Island, corned beef, croquette monsieur, cucumber, dagwood, egg salad, footlong, grilled cheese, ham, ham and cheese, hero, hoagie, Monte Cristo, pastrami, po-boy, reuben, smoked meat, sub, submarine, tomato, torpedo, tuna salad, turkey, turkey salad, western, wrap – *v.* compact, compress, crush, jam, press, squeeze, squish

sane *adj.* **1.** balanced, *compos mentis (Latin)*, fit, healthy, lucid, normal, oriented, rational, reasonable, right-minded, sound, stable *Nonformal:* all there, together *Antonyms:* crazy, deranged, ill, insane **2.** discerning, levelheaded, logical, moderate, prudent, sagacious, self-possessed, sensible, sober, steady

sang-froid *n.* aplomb, assurance, calm, composure, confidence, control, cool, countenance, equanimity, fortitude, levelheadedness, nerve, phlegm, poise, quiet, self-assurance, stability *Antonyms:* anxiety, fear, nervousness

sanguine *adj.* **1.** assured, buoyant, cheerful, confident, enthusiastic, expectant, happy, hopeful, lively, optimistic, secure, self-assured, self-confident, spirited, upbeat *Antonyms:* despondent, dispirited, down, gloomy, pessimistic **2.** florid, flushed, glowing, healthy, red, reddish, robust, rubicund, ruddy *Antonyms:* ashen, pale, pallid, sallow

sanitary *adj.* antibacterial, antiseptic, aseptic, clean, disinfected, germ-free, germicidal, healthful, hygienic, immaculate, impeccable, pasteurized, pure, purified, spotless, stainless, sterile, taintless, unadulterated, unblemished, uncontaminated, uninfected, unpolluted, unsoiled, unspotted, unstained, untainted *Antonyms:* dirty, filthy, infectious, polluted

sanity *n.* **1.** acumen, balance, clear *or* right *or* sound mind, common sense, comprehension, good judgment, lucidity, lucidness, mental health, normality, rationality, reason, reasonableness, sense, soundness, stability, understanding *Antonyms:* dementia, illness, insanity, lunacy, madness **2.** intelligence, judiciousness, levelheadedness, prudence, sagacity

sap *n.* **1.** extract, fluid, juice, liquid, pith, milk, syrup **2.** lifeblood, potency, strength, substance, vigour, vitality **3.** dupe, fool, idiot, simpleton, twit *Nonformal:* chump, dolt, drip, dupe, goof, hoser, jerk, loser, mark, nincompoop, ninny, nitwit, sucker – *v.* attenuate, bleed, blunt, cripple, debilitate, deplete, destroy, devitalize, disable, drain, enervate, enfeeble, erode, exhaust, impair, prostrate, reduce, rob, ruin, squeeze, subvert, undermine, weaken, wear down, wreck *Antonyms:* invigorate, rejuvenate, revitalize, strengthen

sappy *adj.* absurd, cloying, crazy, foolish, idiotic, immature, insufferable, maudlin, mawkish, mushy, preposterous, romantic, saccharine, sentimental, silly, soppy, stupid, sugary, tear jerking *Nonformal:* drippy, Hollywood, schmaltzy *Antonyms:* down-to-earth, realistic, serious

sarcasm *n.* **1.** acrimony, aspersion, bitterness, censure, contempt, corrosiveness, criticism, cynicism, derision, disparagement, invective, mordancy, rancour, sardonicism, scorn, sharpness, sneering, superciliousness **2.** burlesque, flouting, jeering, lampooning, mockery, raillery, ridicule, satire, scoffing, wisecracking *(Nonformal)*

sarcastic *adj.* acerbic, acidic, acrid, biting, bitter, carping, caustic, chaffing, contemptuous, corrosive, cutting, cynical, derisive, disparaging, disrespectful, flouting, harsh, invective, ironic, jeering, malicious, mocking, mordant, offensive, pungent, ridiculing, sardonic, satiric, satirical, scoffing, scornful, smart-alecky *(Nonformal)*, sneering, stinging, taunting, trenchant, vitriolic *Antonyms:* earnest, serious, solemn

Satan *n.* Abaddon, Arch Fiend, Beelzebub, Belial, Cloot *(Scottish)*, Devil, diablo, evil one, Father of Lies, Great Adversary, Lucifer, Prince of Darkness, Tempter *Nonformal:* Old Harry, the Deuce, the dickens *See also:* **devil**

satanic *adj.* awful, demonic, devilish, diabolical, evil, fell, heartless, heinous, horrible, infernal, inhuman, malevolent, nefarious, odious, pernicious, possessed, sadistic, savage, sulphurous, terrible, vicious, villainous, wicked *Antonyms:* godly, moral, virtuous

satellite *adj.* attendant, auxiliary, dependent, peripheral, reliant, secondary, sister, subordinate – *n.* **1.** capsule, communications array *Kinds of communications satellite:* Anik, global positioning, military, observation, relay, sputnik, spy, weather **2.** comet, moon, orb, spacecraft, space station **3.** assistant, follower, hanger-on, lackey, shadow, sidekick *(Nonformal)*, sycophant, toady, underling **4.** auxiliary, branch plant, colony, domain, off-shoot, possession, puppet regime, region, territory

satiate *v.* allay, content, fill, glut, gorge, gratify, indulge, quench, sate, satisfy, slake, stuff, surfeit *Antonyms:* deny, deprive, starve, suppress

satire *n.* banter, burlesque, caricature, chafe, derision, folly, irony, lampoon, mockery, parody, pasquinade, put-on, raillery, ridicule, sarcasm, send-up, skit, spoof, takeoff, travesty, witticism *Antonyms:* homage, tribute

satirical *adj.* abusive, biting, burlesque, caustic, censorious, cutting, cynical, farcical, ironic, mocking, parodic, pungent, ridiculing, sarcastic, satiric, taunting

satisfaction *n.* **1.** amusement, bliss, cheerfulness, comfort, contentedness, contentment, delight, ease, enjoyment, gladness, gratification, happiness, indulgence, joy, prosperity, refreshment, relief, serenity, that warm and fuzzy feeling *(Nonformal)* *Antonyms:* chagrin, malaise, sorrow, woe **2.** achievement, accomplishment, attainment, completion, culmination, fulfillment, perfection, pride, success, triumph *Antonyms:* failure, loss, ruin **3.** amends, atonement, blood money *(Nonformal)*, compensation, conciliation, indemnification, justice, recompense, reimbursement, reparation, resolution, vindication, wergeld

satisfactory *adj.* **1.** ample, appeasing, assuaging, comfortable, fulfilling, gratifying, pleasing, satisfying, suitable, tolerable *Antonyms:* disappointing, inadequate, upsetting **2.** acceptable, adequate, allowable, average, competent, decent, fair, good, jake *(Nonformal)*, passable, reasonable, solid, sound, sufficient, sufficing *Antonyms:* bad, insufficient, poor

satisfy *v.* **1.** appease, content, fill, gratify, indulge, quench, satiate, slake, surfeit *Antonyms:* deny, disappoint, stint **2.** amuse, assuage, assure, calm, convince, dispel doubt, humour, inveigle, mollify, persuade, placate, quiet, reassure, sway, win over *Antonyms:* annoy, displease, frustrate **3.** absolve, atone, compensate, expiate, furnish, make good, meet, pay, requite, square *Antonyms:* default, ignore, neglect **4.** accomplish, answer, complete, conform to, fulfill, measure up, observe, pass *Antonyms:* fail, flop, flounder

saturate *v.* bathe, douche, douse, drench, flood, imbue, immerse, impregnate, infuse, overfill, penetrate, percolate, permeate, pervade, soak, sop, souse, steep, suffuse, surfeit, wash, waterlog, wet *Antonyms:* bake, dehydrate, desiccate, dry, sap

sauce *n.* **1.** condiment, dressing, garnish, gravy, relish *Common sauces:* aioli, allemande, applesauce, barbecue, Béarnaise, béchamel, Bercy, Bordelaise, brown, chasseur, chili, coady *(Newfoundland)*, cranberry, cream, curry, diablo, espagnole, hoisin, horseradish, hollandaise, hot, ketchup, marinara, mole, Mornay, mushroom, mustard, oyster, pesto, poutine, ravigote, red-eye, rémoulade, salsa, satay, soubise, soy, spaghetti, suprême, sweet-and-sour, tahini, tartar, tomato, velouté, white *Trademark:* A-1, HP, Tabasco *See also:* **condiment**, **dressing** **2.** audacity, brazenness, impertinence, impudence, insolence *Nonformal:* back talk, cheek, gall, sass **3.** alcohol, bung-your-eye *(Newfoundland)*, liquor, rum, spirits, whiskey *Nonformal:* booze, hooch, juice

saucy *adj.* audacious, bold, brash, brazen, disrespectful, flippant, fresh, impertinent, impudent, insolent, pert, precocious, presumptuous, shameless *Nonformal:* cheeky, sassy *Antonyms:* discreet, polite, reserved

saunter *n.* airing, constitutional, ramble, stroll, turn, walk – *v.* amble, canter, dally, drift, meander, promenade, roam, rove, stroll, stump, tarry, toddle, traipse, wander *Nonformal:* mosey, sashay

saturnine *adj.* blue, depressed, dour, dull, gloomy, glum, grave, heavy, melancholy, morose, neurasthenic, sad, sulky, sullen, surly, taciturn, touchy, unhappy, upset *Antonyms:* happy, jovial, joyous

savage *adj.* **1.** feral, undomesticated, untamed, wild *Antonyms:* broken, tame, trained **2.** atrocious, barbaric, barbarous, beastly, bestial, bloodthirsty, bloody, brutal, brutish, crazed, cruel, demoniac, destructive, devilish, diabolical, fell, ferocious, fierce, furious, grim, harsh, heartless, hellish, infernal, inhuman, inhumane, malevolent, malicious, merciless, murderous, pitiless, rabid, raging, rapacious, ravening, relentless, remorseless, ruthless, sadistic, truculent, unrelenting, vicious, violent, wolfish *Antonyms:* gentle, humane, kind, merciful, mild **3.** boorish, coarse, crude, natural, primitive, raw, rough, rude, rugged, uncivilized, uncouth, uncultivated, uncultured, unrefined *Antonyms:* civilized, cultured, genteel, polished, suave – *n.* barbarian, beast, boor, brute, clod, ignoramus, monster, oaf, Philistine, vulgarian – *v.* abuse, attack, assail, bite, buffet, maul, ravage, victimize

save *v.* **1.** accumulate, amass, bank, cache, collect, conserve, deposit, economize, garner, gather, hide, hoard, hold, husband, invest, lay *or* put *or* salt away, reserve, scrimp, set aside, shepherd, skimp, spare, squirrel away, stash, stockpile, store, treasure, warehouse *Antonyms:* fritter away, squander, waste **2.** bail one out, deliver, emancipate, free, liberate, manumit, ransom, redeem, release, spring *(Nonformal) Antonyms:* enslave, impound, incarcerate **3.** extricate, recapture, reclaim, recover, rescue, salvage **4.** conserve, defend, harbour, nurture, preserve, protect, safeguard, shelter, support *Antonyms:* destroy, end, ruin

savings *n. pl.* account, accumulation, bankroll, cache, capital, cash, funds, investment, kitty *(Nonformal)*, means, money, property, provision, Registered Education Savings Plan *or* RESP, Registered Retirement Income Fund *or* RRIF, Registered Retirement Savings Plan *or* RRSP, reserves, resources, Retirement Savings Plan *or* RSP, riches, stake, stockpile *Nonformal:* nest egg, sock, stash

saviour *n.* angel, defender, deliverer, Good Samaritan *(Nonformal)*, guardian, guardian angel, hero, knight, liberator, preserver, protector, redeemer, rescuer, white knight *Antonyms:* enemy, nemesis, threat

savoir-faire *n.* adroitness, aplomb, class, cultivation, culture, deftness, diplomacy, elegance, grace, manner, poise, refinement, sagacity, self-assurance, sophistication, skilfulness, skill, style, tact, urbanity, worldliness *Antonyms:* awkwardness, naiveté

savour *n.* **1.** aroma, essence, flavour, fragrance, odour, perfume, smack *(Nonformal)*, smell, spice, tang, taste **2.** appeal, flair, panache, piquancy, relish, verve, zest *Nonformal:* pep, pizzazz, shine, zip – *v.* **1.** appreciate, cherish, delight *or* luxuriate in, enjoy, experience, feel, know, like, prize, relish, value *Antonyms:* disdain, reject **2.** enhance, flavour, jerk, kick up *(Nonformal)*, marinate, pepper, season, spice

savoury *adj.* **1.** agreeable, ambrosial, appetizing, aromatic, delectable, delicious, exquisite, fragrant, full-flavoured, mouthwatering, palatable, perfumed, piquant, pleasing, pungent, redolent, rich, sapid, scrumptious *(Nonformal)*, spicy, splendid, sweet, tangy, tasty, tempting, toothsome *Antonyms:* disgusting, putrid, unpleasant **2.** decent, ethical, honest, reliable, reputable, respectable, responsible, square-dealing, straight, trustworthy, upright, virtuous *Antonyms:* corrupt, crooked, untrustworthy

saw *n.* **1.** tool *Kinds of saw:* band, bench, buck, buzz, chainsaw, circular, compass, coping, crosscut, dovetail, dry wall, hacksaw, jigsaw, mitre, power, radial arm, sabre, surgical, table, tenon, whipsaw **2.** apothegm, banality, byword, cliché, dictum, epigram, maxim, motto, proverb, saying – *v.* cut, divide, rend, sever, slice, separate

say *n.* **1.** comment, expression, interpretation, last word, observation, pronouncement, remark, speech, statement, testimonial, voice, word *Nonformal:* spin, take, two cents' worth **2.** authority, clout *(Nonformal)*, influence, leverage, power, prestige, pull, sway **3.** consent, endorsement, favour, licence, permission, permit, sanction, tribute **4.** choice, decision, election, free will, judgment, opinion, option, vote – *v.* **1.** add, affirm, allege, announce, answer, articulate, assert, claim, communicate, convey, declare, deliver, disclose, divulge, enunciate, express, give voice, impart, imply, let out, maintain, make known, mention, mumble, mutter, opine, orate, present, pronounce, read, recite, relate, remark, repeat, reply, report, respond, reveal, speak, state, suggest, tell, utter, verbalize, voice, whisper, word **2.** assume, believe, conjecture, estimate, judge, predict, reckon, speculate, suppose, think

saying *v.* adage, aphorism, apothegm, axiom, byword, dictum, epigram, maxim, motto, precept, proverb, saw, truism

scalawag *n.* brute, cad, hooligan, knave, rapscallion, rascal, rogue, ruffian, scamp, scoundrel, sleeveen *(Newfoundland)*, thug, tough *Nonformal:* goon, hood, louse, ugly customer

scale *n.* **1.** calibration, classification, compass, computation, degree, extent, gamut, gradation, hierarchy, ladder, order, progression, proportion, range, ranking, rate, ratio, reach, register, rule, scope, sequence, series, spectrum, spread, steps, system, way *Kinds of musical scale:* chromatic, diatonic, harmonic *or* melodic *or* natural minor, major, minor, octave, pentatonic, tetrachordal, tone cluster, tone row, twelve-tone, whole-tone **2.** covering, crust, dandruff, flake, hoary plate, incrustation, lamina, layer, membrane, outgrowth, scab, scote, scurf, skin **3.** balance, caliper, compass, ruler, tapemeasure, yardstick – *v.* **1.** adjust, balance, calibrate, compare, compute, estimate, gauge, graduate, measure, prorate, regulate, size **2.** ascend, climb, escalate, mount, overcome, surmount *Antonyms:* descend, drop, fall **3.** abrade, clean, flake, prepare, scrape, shave

scam *n.* confidence game, deal, deception, fraud, scheme, swindle, theft, trick, trickery *Nonformal:* fleece job, grift, con, rip-off, rook, shakedown, sting – *v.* cheat, defraud, swindle, trick *Nonformal:* con, fleece, grift, rip-off, screw, shaft, take

scamper *v.* bolt, dart, dash, flee, fly, hasten, hurry, hustle, make off, race, romp, run, rush, scoot, scud, scurry, scuttle, speed, sprint, tear, trot *Nonformal:* floor *or* hotfoot it, light out, rip *Antonyms:* dally, meander, saunter, stroll

scan *n.* bmp, digital photograph, gif, image, jpeg, png, picture, tif – *v.* **1.** analyze, check, examine, inquire, investigate, read, scrutinize, study, survey **2.** browse, glance, look over, peruse, regard, rifle through, search, skim, surf *(Nonformal)*, sweep **3.** computerize, copy, digitize, input

scandal *n.* **1.** aspersion, character assassination, defamation, disparagement, gossip, hearsay, slander, smear, sully *Nonformal:* dirt, mud, talk **2.** discredit, disgrace, disrepute, embarrassment, guilt, humiliation, ignominy, indignity, infamy, odium, shame *Antonyms:* favour, grace **3.** admonition, castigation, censure, condemnation, disapproval, disdain, reproach *Antonyms:* acceptance, approval, forgiveness **4.** crime, improper conduct, indiscretion, offence, opprobrium, sin, trespass, turpitude, wrongdoing

scandalous *adj.* **1.** abominable, atrocious, disgraceful, dishonourable, disreputable, heinous, immodest, improper, indecent, infamous, monstrous, odious, opprobrious, outrageous, shameful, shocking *Antonyms:* decent, proper, respectable, seemly **2.** calumnious, contumelious, defamatory, derogatory, detracting, disparaging, gossipy, injurious, libelous, malignant, slanderous, untrue, vilifying, vituperative *Antonyms:* complimentary, laudatory, praising

scanty *adj.* **1.** bare, deficient, exiguous, impoverished, inadequate, insufficient, meagre, mean, scarce, skimpy, slight, slim, sparing, sparse *Antonyms:* abundant, ample, profuse **2.** close, claustrophobic, cramped, narrow, slender, small, stuffy, thin, tight, tiny *Antonyms:* expansive, large, wide

scapegoat *n.* dupe, sacrifice, substitute, target, victim, whipping boy *Nonformal:* fall guy, goat, mark, patsy, stooge, sucker

scar *n.* **1.** blemish, brand, cicatrix, defect, discoloration, disfigurement, flaw, injury, lesion, mark, pockmark, scab, wound **2.** channel, crater, furrow, indentation, scrape, seam, track, trench, trough, valley **3.** aftereffects, baggage *(Nonformal)*, damage, history, nightmare, ordeal, shock, stigma, trauma, upset – *v.* blemish, brand, cut, damage, disfigure, flaw, hurt, injure, maim, mar, mark, pinch, score, scratch, slash, stab, traumatize

scarce *adj.* **1.** hard-to-find, infrequent, occasional, rare, scanty, uncommon, unusual *Antonyms:* common, frequent, numerous **2.** deficient, few, insufficient, lacking, limited, paltry, poor, shy, sparse *Antonyms:* abundant, plentiful, sufficient

scarcely *adv.* barely, hardly, imperceptibly, infrequently, occasionally, rarely, scantily, seldom, slightly, sometimes

scare *n.* agitation, alarm, dismay, fright, heart attack *(Nonformal)*, hysteria, panic, shock, terror – *v.* alarm, awe, chill, daunt, dismay, freeze, frighten, intimidate, panic, paralyze, petrify, shock, startle, terrify, terrorize, unnerve, upset *Nonformal:* scarify, spook *Antonyms:* calm, mollify, pacify, placate

scared *adj.* afraid, aghast, agitated, alarmed, anxious, appalled, cowering, dismayed, fearful, frightened, nervous, panicked, petrified, shaken, startled, terrified, terror-stricken, unnerved, upset, worried *Nonformal:* freaked, spooked *Antonyms:* carefree, placid, unmoved, unruffled

scary *adj.* **1.** alarming, bloodcurdling, chilling, frightening, hair-raising, hairy, horrendous, horrifying, intimidating, shocking, spine-chilling, spooky, terrifying, unnerving, upsetting *Antonyms:* boring, dull, hackneyed, tedious **2.** bizarre, creepy, freakish, freaky, strange, weird *Antonyms:* normal, ordinary, regular

scathing *adj.* acrimonious, belittling, biting, brutal, burning, caustic, critical, cruel, cutting, damaging, harsh, humbling, nasty, painful, sarcastic, scalding, scorching, searing, severe, sulphurous, trenchant, vitriolic *Antonyms:* complimentary, laudatory, praising, uplifting

scatter *v.* **1.** broadcast, cast, diffuse, dispel, disperse, disseminate, distribute, fling, intersperse, litter, pour, set, shed, shower, sow, spam *(Nonformal)*, spray, spread, sprinkle, strew **2.** disband, disintegrate, dissipate, divide, migrate, part, separate, split up, sunder *Antonyms:* assemble, collect, gather

scatterbrain *n.* dolt, harebrain *Nonformal:* airhead, boob, dip, ditz, dummy, flake, rubberhead, space cadet, wing nut

scatterbrained *adj.* careless, disorganized, empty-headed, fatuous, flighty, forgetful, frivolous, giddy, harebrained, illogical, inattentive, irrational, irresponsible, madcap, silly, stupid, thoughtless, unthinking, vacuous *Nonformal:* dippy, ditzy, dizzy, featherbrained, flaky *Antonyms:* careful, focused, sharp

scavenger *n.* beachcomber, forager, junk dealer, garbage *or* rag picker, salvage operator, scrounger, vulture *Nonformal:* bottom-feeder, buzzard

scenario *n.* outline, plan, plot, rundown, scheme, script, sequence, situation, sketch, story line, summary, syllabus, synopsis, treatment

scene *n.* **1.** area, arena, compass, environment, field, locality, milieu, setting, sphere, surroundings **2.** backdrop, cityscape, diorama, exterior, interior, landscape, locale, *mise en scène (French)*, picture, seascape, set, skyscape, tableau, view, vista **3.** act, bit, episode, incident, number, part, performance, piece, routine, schtick *(Nonformal)*, show, sketch, skit, spot **4.** commotion, confusion, display, disturbance, exhibition, fuss, histrionics, outburst, tantrum, trouble, tumult *Nonformal:* Cheltenham tragedy, to-do

scenic *adj.* awesome, beautiful, breathtaking, dramatic, graphic, impressive, panoramic, picturesque, spectacular, striking, vivid, wonderful *Antonyms:* drab, dreary, gloomy

scent *n.* **1.** aroma, aura, balm, bouquet, essence, extract, fragrance, incense, odour, perfume, redolence, smell, spice, tang **2.** clue, hint, spoor, suggestion, trace, track, trail, whiff

scented *adj.* ambrosial, aromatic, balmy, fragrant, incensed, perfumed, pleasing, redolent, sweet-smelling

sceptic *n.* agnostic, atheist, cynic, disbeliever, dissenter, doubter, doubting Thomas, freethinker, heathen, heretic, infidel, nihilist, pessimist, questioner, scoffer, unbeliever *Antonyms:* adherent, believer, zealot

sceptical *adj.* agnostic, cynical, disbelieving, dissenting, dubious, freethinking, hesitant, incredulous, leery, mistrustful, questioning, quizzical, scoffing, suspicious, unconvinced *Antonyms:* positive, sure, trusting

schedule *n.* agenda, appointments, calendar, catalogue, chart, docket, inventory, itinerary, line-up, list, plan, program, record, roster, syllabus, timetable – *v.* appoint, arrange, book, engage, fix, line up, organize, pencil in, register, reserve, set, slate

scheme *n.* **1.** arrangement, contrivance, design, device, expedient, game plan *(Nonformal)*, layout, order, pattern, plan, program, project, scenario, schedule, schema, strategy, system, tactics, theory **2.** blueprint, chart, diagram, draft, outline, pitch, proposal, proposition, sketch, story, suggestion, synopsis, treatment **3.** deception, intrigue, machination, manoeuvre, plot, ploy, ruse, stratagem, subterfuge, tactic, trick, twist *Nonformal:* con, grift, scam – *v.* **1.** contrive, design, devise, frame, imagine, plan, project, work out **2.** collude, conspire, intrigue, machinate, manoeuvre, plot, wheel and deal *(Nonformal)*

scheming *adj.* artful, calculating, conniving, crafty, cunning, deceitful, designing, duplicitous, foxy, Machiavellian, slippery, sly, tricky, underhanded, wily *Antonyms:* artless, guileless, honest, ingenuous, straightforward

schmooze *v.* chat up, converse, mingle, network, talk, work the room *(Nonformal)*

scholar *n.* academic, advisor, authority, bluestocking, critic, disciple, doctor, educator, expert, guru, intellectual, learned person, maven *(Nonformal)*, pedant, PhD, philosopher, polymath, professor, pundit, pupil, sage, savant, scholastic, scientist, sensei, sophist, specialist, student, *swami (Hindu)*, teacher, wise man *or* woman *Muslim:* mullah, ulema

scholarly *adj.* academic, bookish, cultured, educated, erudite, intellectual, learned, lettered, literate, profound, scholastic, schooled, studious, taught, trained, well-read *Antonyms:* ignorant, uneducated, untutored

scholarship *n.* **1.** culture, erudition, intellectuality, knowledge, learnedness, literacy, mastery, study, understanding **2.** award, bursary, grant, honourarium, maintenance, stipend

school *n.* **1.** academy, faculty, institute, institution *Kinds of school:* adult-education, alternative, arts, bible, boarding, business college, CEGEP *(Quebec)*, cheder, church, college, commerce, community college, composite *(Alberta)*, continuing education, convent, correspondence, day, dojo, elementary, finishing, grade, high, lyceum, *juku (Japanese)*, junior college, junior high, kindergarten, medical, military academy, night, open-classroom, parish, parochial, playschool, polytechnical, prep *or* preparatory, primary, private, public, reform, religious, residential, rural, secondary, seminary, senior high, separate, summer, Sunday, Talmud, Torah, technical, theological seminary, trade, university, vocational, yeshiva **2.** adherents, circle, class, clique, denomination, devotees, disciples, faction, followers, following, group, party, pupils, scholars, sect, set **3.** belief, doctrine, faith, movement, outlook, persuasion, philosophy **4.** brood, bunch, cluster, gathering, group, myriad, pool, shoal – *v.* coach, discipline, drill, edify, educate, indoctrinate, instruct, prepare, prime, socialize, train, tutor, uplift, verse

science *n.* **1.** area *or* branch *or* field of study, department of knowledge, discipline, specialty, sphere, study **2.** application, approach, fashion, laws, manner, mode, norms, process, rules, system, technique, way **3.** deduction, disinterest, logic, objectivity, reasoning, rigour **4.** erudition, expertise, knowledge, learning, mastery, skill, understanding, wisdom

scientific *adj.* **1.** accurate, applied, clear, controlled, deductive, exact, experimental, logical, mathematical, precise, sound, systematic **2.** analytical, cold, detached, disinterested, impartial, impersonal, mechanical, neutral, objective, unfeeling *Antonyms:* biased, prejudiced

scintillating *adj.* **1.** dazzling, flashing, glimmering, glinting, glittering, shining, sparkling, twinkling **2.** animated, bright, brilliant, clever, ebullient, exciting, lively, stimulating, witty *Antonyms:* boring, dull

scion *n.* child, descendant, heir, issue, junior, offshoot, offspring, progeny, seed, successor

scoff *v.* abuse, belittle, deride, disdain, dismiss, flout, gibe, heckle, insult, jeer, mock, rail, revile, ridicule, scorn, taunt, tease *Nonformal:* burn, dis, pan, trash *Antonyms:* compliment, honour, praise

scold *v.* admonish, berate, blame, card *(Nonformal)*, castigate, censure, chastise, chide, clapper-claw *(P.E.I.)*, discipline, excoriate, flay, lecture, punish, rate, rebuke, renounce, reprimand, reproach, upbraid, vituperate *Antonyms:* commend, exalt, salute

scoop *n.* **1.** dipper, ladle, shovel, spoon, spork *(Nonformal)* **2.** confidential, dirt *(Nonformal)*, exclusive, exposé, gossip, inside story, news, revelation, sensation – *v.* bail, clean *or* sweep up, dig *or* pick *or* take up, dig, excavate, gather, gouge, grub, hollow, ladle, lift, remove, shovel, spoon

scope *n.* **1.** breadth, capacity, elbow room, freedom, latitude, leeway, liberty, margin, opportunity, room, space **2.** ambit, amplitude, area, compass, comprehensiveness, extension, extent, diapason, field, fullness, gamut, orbit, purview, radius, range, reach, run, span, sphere, width **3.** attitude, bearing, bias, disposition, outlook, perspective, point of view

scorch *v.* bake, blacken, blister, boil, brown, burn, char, cook, heat, melt, roast, scald, sear, singe, sizzle, sunburn, tan, toast, torrefy

score *n.* **1.** account, aggregate, amount, average, bottom line *(Nonformal)*, final count, grade, mark, number, outcome, points, spread, rate, rating, reckoning, record, result, stock, sum, summary, summation, tab, tally, total **2.** gash, groove, indentation, marking, nick, notch **3.** army, crowd, drove, flock, group, host, hundred, legion, lot, mass, multitude, myriad, swarm, throng **4.** arrangement, chart *(Nonformal)*, composition, draft, libretto, music, notation, orchestration, sheet music, songbook, theme, transcription, version **5.** debt, grievance, grudge, vengeance, vindication – *v.* **1.** cleave, cross-hatch, cut, deface, furrow, gash, gouge, graze, groove, indent, key, line, mar, mark, nick, notch, scar, scrape, scratch, serrate, slash, slit **2.** add, calculate, chalk up, count, enumerate, rack up, reckon, record, register, summate, tally, total **3.** evaluate, examine, grade, judge, rank, rate **4.** adapt, arrange, compose, orchestrate, set, write **5.** achieve, make it *(Nonformal)*, succeed, triumph, win

scorn *n.* contempt, contumely, derision, disdain, disparagement, disregard, loathing, mockery, ridicule, sarcasm, scoffing, slight, sneer, sport, taunting *Antonyms:* admiration, affection, esteem, respect, tolerance – *v.* abhor, defy, deride, despise, disdain, dislike, disregard, flout, gibe, hate, ignore, jeer, misprize, mock, refuse, refute, reject, renounce, repudiate, ridicule, shun, slight, sneer, spurn, taunt, trash *(Nonformal)* *Antonyms:* accept, admire, revere, venerate, worship

scoundrel *n.* cad, caitiff, cheat, crook, dastard, hooligan, knave, miscreant, rapscallion, rascal, reprobate, rogue, ruffian, scalawag, scamp, scaramouch, sleeveen *(Newfoundland)*, vagabond, vermin, villain, wretch *Nonformal:* heel, lowlife, rotter, scumbag, sleaze, slime, ugly customer, weasel

scour *v.* **1.** abrade, buff, brighten, burnish, clean, clear, polish, purge, remove, rub, sand, scrape, scrub, wash, wipe **2.** beat, comb, ferret out, find, forage, grub, hunt, inquire, look for, rake, ransack, rummage, search, seek, track down

scourge *n.* **1.** contagion, disease, epidemic, outbreak **2.** albatross, bane, bête noir, burden, curse, encumbrance, millstone, nuisance, pest *Antonyms:* benefit, boon, gift **3.** abuse, beating, discipline, punishment, torture, what-for *(Nonformal)*

scout *n.* advance, adventurer, detective, emissary, escort, explorer, guard, guide, investigator, outpost, outrider, patrol, point, searcher, sleuth, spotter, spy, vanguard – *v.* case *(Nonformal)*, examine, explore, inspect, investigate, observe, probe, reconnoitre, search, seek, survey, watch

scowl *n.* dirty look, evil eye, frown, glare, glower, grimace, hairy eyeball *(Nonformal)*, moue – *v.* knit brows, menace, threaten

scramble *n.* **1.** bumble, hike, scale, shuffle, stumble, tumble **2.** commotion, competition, imbroglio, mix-up, struggle, tussle **3.** clutter, confusion, jumble, jungle, litter, muddle, upset – *v.* **1.** clamber, climb, crawl, hasten, hustle, look alive *(Nonformal)*, move, push, race, run, rush, scurry, trek **2.** argue, contend, fight, jostle, quarrel, tussle, vie **3.** blend, combine, intermingle, jumble, merge, mix, muddle, shuffle **4.** alter, confuse, corrupt, distort, encode, garble, obfuscate **5.** avoid, dodge, elude, escape, evade, swerve, veer *Nonformal:* deke, dipsy-doodle, rag

scrap *n.* **1.** atom, bite, chip, chunk, crumb, cutting, end, fragment, grain, hunk, iota, jot, mite, morsel, mote, part, particle, piece, shred, sliver, snippet, speck, trace **2.** castoff, discard, flotsam, garbage, jetsam, junk, leavings, leftovers, litter, refuse *Nonformal:* crap, shmunza **3.** altercation, contention, disagreement, donnybrook, exchange, fight, fisticuffs, fustigation, pugilism, punch-up *(Nonformal)*, quarrel, spat, tiff – *v.* **1.** abandon, cashier, cast, chuck, discard, dismiss, dispense with, ditch, drop, forsake, jettison, junk, reject, shed, slough, throw away, write off **2.** brawl, clash, disagree, drop the gloves *(Nonformal)*, fight, grapple, quarrel, scuffle, spar, squabble, wrangle, wrestle

scrape *n.* awkward *or* bad situation, box, corner, difficulty, dilemma, discomfiture, distress, embarrassment, hole, jam, mess, plight, predicament, spot, tight spot, trouble *Nonformal:* fix, hot water, kettle of fish, pickle – *v.* abrade, chafe, clean, erase, file, grate, graze, grind, irritate, pare, peel, rasp, remove, rub, sand, scour, scratch, scuff, shave, skin, thin

scratch *n.* abrasion, blemish, cut, gash, hurt, incision, injury, laceration, mark, scrape, wound – *v.* **1.** chafe, claw, cut, damage, grate, graze, lacerate, mar, prick, rasp, rip, scar, scarify, scrob, tear **2.** dig, etch, groove, incise, key, mark, score **3.** alleviate, ease, itch, mollify, relieve, rub **4.** doodle, draw, illustrate, scrawl, scribble, sign, write **5.** annul, blue pencil, cancel, delete, edit, eliminate, erase, excise, pull, remove, scotch, scrub, strike, withdraw

scrawl *v.* doodle, draw, inscribe, pen, scrabble, scratch, scribble, squiggle, write

scrawny *adj.* angular, bony, gaunt, lank, lanky, lean, malnourished, rawboned, scraggy, slender, skeletal, skin-and-bones *(Nonformal)*, skinny, spare, spindly, thin, undernourished, underweight *Antonyms:* heavy-set, stocky, thick

scream *n.* **1.** cry, holler, howl, outcry, screech, shriek, wail, yell, yelp **2.** fun, joke, jollity, laugh *Nonformal:* barrel of monkeys, hoot, killer, gas, kick in the pants, riot, thigh-slapper, trip – *v.* bawl, bellow, blare, caterwaul, cry out, holler, howl, roar, screech, shout, shriek, shrill, sing out, squeal, voice, wail, yell, yip, yowl *Antonyms:* mutter, whimper, whisper

screen *n.* **1.** curtain, divider, mantle, partition, shield, shoji *(Japanese)* **2.** awning, canopy, cover, covering, net, protection, shade, top, umbrella **3.** artifice, camouflage, deceit, disguise, ploy, ruse, scheme, strategy, tactic, trick **4.** cheese-cloth, colander, filter, sieve, sifter, strainer *Mining:* rocker, sluice box – *v.* **1.** block *or* shut out, ensconce, obstruct, shadow, shelter, shield, shroud, veil **2.** blind, bury, cache, camouflage, cloak, conceal, cover, disguise, guard, hide, obscure, protect, safeguard, seclude, secure, stash **3.** choose, cull, eliminate, evaluate, examine, extract, filter, gauge, grade, process, scan, select, separate, sieve, sift, sort, winnow **4.** exhibit, premiere, present, project, show

screw *n.* fastener *Kinds of construction screw:* brass, collar, fillister, gyproc, lag, metal, Phillips, Robertson, saw, shoulder, slotted, skein, standard, tag, thumbscrew, wood – *v.* **1.** affix, attach, fasten, fix, tighten **2.** bilk, cheat, coerce, constrain, defraud, exact, extort, extract, force, oppress, pinch, pressure, wrench, wrest *Nonformal:* bleed, con, flim flam, grift, shaft, shakedown, squeeze **3.** copulate, fornicate, have sex, know *Nonformal:* ball, do, get busy *or* jiggy, hump, nail, shag **4.** contort, contract, crimp, crinkle, crumple, pucker, spiral, turn, twist, wind

scrimp *v.* conserve, curtail, economize, limit, pinch, restrict, save, skimp, spare *Antonyms:* spend, squander

script *n.* **1.** alphabet, calligraphy, characters, fist *(Nonformal)*, font, hand, handwriting, letters, longhand, penmanship, printing, type, writing **2.** book, copy, draft, manuscript, play, story, text, treatment – *v.* compose, create, draft, pen, write

scripture *n.* holy book *or* writings, passage

text *Kinds of scripture:* Bible, Koran, New Testament, Sutras, Torah, Upanishads, Vedas *See also:* **bible**

scrub *n.* back forty *(Nonformal)*, brushwood, bush, mangrove, tangle, thicket, woods – *v.* **1.** brighten, buff, burnish, clean, cleanse, polish, rinse, rub, scrape, sponge, squeegee, wash, wipe *Antonyms:* dirty, mess, soil **2.** abandon, abolish, abort, cancel, delete, desert, discontinue, ditch, drop, dump, forget about, give up, quit, scratch

scruffy *adj.* dirty, dishevelled, mangy, messy, ragged, rough, rugged, shabby, slatternly, slovenly, squalid, tattered, tawdry, unkempt, untidy *Nonformal:* grungy, ratty, scuzzy *Antonyms:* dapper, prim, spruce, tidy

scrumptious *adj.* ambrosial, appetizing, delectable, delightful, delicious, elegant, exquisite, fine, heavenly, inviting, luscious, magnificent, mouth-watering, rich, savoury, splendid, succulent, tasty, yummy *(Nonformal) Antonyms:* disgusting, nauseating, sickening

scruples *n. pl.* **1.** attention, heed, notice, observance, regard, respect *Antonyms:* contempt, indifference **2.** apprehension, doubt, fear, qualms, hesitation, misgivings, uncertainty *Antonyms:* assurance, confidence, faith

scrutinize *v.* analyze, appraise, assess, check, comb, consider, contemplate, dissect, estimate, evaluate, examine, explore, inspect, investigate, measure, observe, oversee, peruse, probe, prospect, rate, read, research, review, scan, scope, search, sift, size, study, summarize, survey, value, view, watch, weigh *Nonformal:* case, eyeball

scuffle *n.* brawl, commotion, disturbance, exchange, fight, fisticuffs, fracas, fray, free-for-all, fuss, punch-up *(Nonformal)*, quarrel, row, scrap, set-to, struggle – *v.* clash, contend, donnybrook, fight, grapple, jostle, quarrel, skirmish, struggle, tussle, wrestle

sculptor *n.* artisan, artist, carver, craftsperson, creator, maker, modeller, moulder, Myron, Pygmalion

sculpture *n.* art, artwork, bust, bronze, cast, carving, cutting, figure, glyph, head, marble, model, piece, relief, representation, round, soapstone, statue, stonecutting, terra cotta, totem pole *or* post, wood, work – *v.* adorn, carve, cast, chisel, cut, embellish, engrave, fashion, form, hew, model, mould, represent, sculpt, shape, whittle

scum *n.* **1.** algae, crust, film, froth, impurity, residue **2.** dirt, dross, dregs, garbage, junk, litter, rubbish, refuse, sweepings, trash, waste **3.** hoi polloi, horde, masses, mob, rabble, riffraff, swarm, vermin *Nonformal:* lumpen, ragtag and bobtail, sheep

scurrilous *adj.* abusive, coarse, contumelious, defamatory, dirty, filthy, foul, gross, indecent, insulting, low, nasty, obscene, offending, offensive, profane, scandalous, scrofulous, shameless *Antonyms:* civilized, decent, proper, refined, respectful

scurry *v.* bustle, dart, dash, fly, hasten, hurry, hustle, race, run, rush, scamper, scoot, scud, scutter, scuttle, shoot, skim, sprint, tear, whirl, whisk *Nonformal:* hotfoot, rip, vamoose

sea *n.* blue water, depths, expanse, great *or* high *or* open sea, main, ocean, saltchuck *(Pacific Coast)*, salt sea *or* water, surf, swell *Nonformal:* big pond, bounding main, drink, foamy brine, the briny *or* deep *Seven Seas:* Antarctic Ocean, Arctic Ocean, Indian Ocean, North Atlantic, North Pacific, South Atlantic, South Pacific

seafaring *adj.* aquatic, maritime, nautical, naval, ocean-going, oceanic, sailing, salty *(Nonformal)*, seagoing, transatlantic, trans-Pacific

seal *n.* **1.** cartouche, emblem, impression, imprint, insignia, logo, mark, marking, signet, stamp, sticker, trademark **2.** acceptance, approval, assurance, authentication, confirmation, guarantee, pledge, promise **3.** adhesive, fastening, glue, gum, tape, wax – *v.* **1.** clinch, conclude, confirm, consummate, establish, finalize, settle **2.** approve, authenticate, authorize, certify, legalize, ratify, sanction, stamp, validate, warrant **3.** close, cork, enclose, fasten, gum, immure, paste, plug, secure, shut, stop, vacuum-pack, waterproof

seam *n.* **1.** bond, cicatrix, closure, connection, coupling, joint, juncture, link, scar, suture, union, weld **2.** break, crack, divergence, division, divorce, fissure, opening, pressure crack *or* ridge, rupture, schism, separation **3.** esker, line, rib, ridge, streak, windrow **4.** deposit, layer, lode, pay dirt *(Nonformal)*, stratum **5.** border, crease, hem, pleat, purl – *v.* **1.** close, connect, fuse, join, merge, unite **2.** break, crack, disjoin, disunite, diverge, open, part, rupture, separate, sever, split, sunder

sear *v.* **1.** brand, broil, brown, burn, cauterize, scald, scorch, singe **2.** dehydrate, desiccate, dry up, exsiccate, parch, wilt, wither **3.** blunt, callous, desensitize, dull, harden, inure, season, steel, toughen

search *n.* chase, examination, exploration, fishing expedition *(Nonformal)*, hunt, inquest, inquiry, inspection, interrogation, investigation, pursuance, quest, rummage, scrutiny, seeking – *v.* chase after, check, comb, examine, explore, ferret, forage, fossick *(Australian)*, go through, grub, hunt, inquire, inspect, investigate, look for, pan, penetrate, poke into, probe, prospect, pry, pursue, query, quest, rake, ransack, research, rifle through, root, rummage, scan, scour, scrutinize, seek, sift, study, track down *Nonformal:* beat *or* cast about, surf

seashore *n.* bayfront, bayside, beach, coast, coastland, littoral, oceanfront, oceanside, seabank, seaboard, seacoast, seafront, seaside, shore, shorefront, tideland, tidewater

season *n.* **1.** autumn, equinox, fall, spring, summer, time of year, winter **2.** cycle, division, interval, period, span, spell, stretch, term, time **3.** chance, juncture, moment, occasion, opportunity, shot, turn – *v.* **1.** flavour, kick *or* pep up *(Nonformal)*, lace, pepper, salt, spice **2.** acclimate, acclimatize, accustom, discipline, habituate, harden, inure, mature, prepare, school, steel, toughen, train **3.** age, develop, dry, mature, mellow, ripen **4.** cushion, ease, moderate, modify, mollify, mitigate, soften, temper

seasonable *adj.* appropriate, apropos, apt, auspicious, convenient, expedient, favourable, fit, opportune, pertinent, propitious, providential, relevant, suitable, timely, welcome, well-timed

seasoning *n.* condiment, dressing, flavouring, herb, pep, pepper, pungency, relish, salt, sauce, spice, zest, zing *See also:* **spice**

seat *n.* **1.** bench, chesterfield, couch, davenport, howdah, Muskoka chair, pew, settee, settle, sofa, stool **2.** base, basis, bed, bottom, footing, foundation, ground, groundwork, rest, seating, support **3.** backside, buttocks, bottom *Nonformal:* arse, back porch, behind, bum, caboose, can, derrière, duff, fanny, gluteus maximus, heinie, keister, tail, tush **4.** abode, chateau, demesne, estate, domain, home, house, mansion, palace, residence, rural seat, villa **5.** authority, chair, position, privilege, rule **6.** cause, location, matrix, origin, point, region, root, site, source – *v.* **1.** lounge, nestle, perch, settle, sit, squat **2.** centre, deposit, fix, locate, place, position, situate **3.** accommodate, contain, encompass, hold

secede *v.* abdicate, break away *or* with, leave, pull away, quit, retract, retreat, separate, split, withdraw *Antonyms:* confederate, join, unite

seclude *v.* **1.** confine, enclose, ghettoize, isolate, quarantine, segregate, separate, sequester, stream **2.** closet, conceal, hide, screen *or* shut off, veil *Antonyms:* expose, reveal

secluded *adj.* **1.** closeted, concealed, covert, curtained, hidden, private, screened, secret, sheltered *Antonyms:* overt, public **2.** cloistered, hermetic, insular, isolated, monastic, quiet, reclusive, solitary, withdrawn **3.** blockaded, confined, cordoned off, gated, off-limits, quarantined, segregated, separated *Antonyms:* free, open **4.** abandoned, backwater, deserted, forsaken, jerkwater, out-of-the-way, remote, uninhabited *Antonyms:* accessible, busy, frequented

seclusion *n.* **1.** aloneness, hibernation, isolation, reclusiveness, retirement, retreat, solitude, withdrawal *Antonyms:* association, participation **2.** apartheid, blockade, concealment, confinement, *cordon sanitaire (French)*, quarantine, segregation, separation **3.** asylum, cloister, haven, hermitage, hideout, sanctuary, shelter

second *adj.* **1.** following, next, subsequent, succeeding *Antonyms:* front, lead **2.** inferior, lesser, lower, secondary, subordinate, unimportant *Antonyms:* superior, top, ultimate **3.** alternative, double, duplicate, extra, fill-in, other, twin – *n.* **1.** eyewink, flash, instant, minute, moment, nanosecond, split second, trice *Nonformal:* jiff, New York minute, nothing flat, shake *or* two shakes, tick, twinkling, wink **2.** assistant, backer, exponent, helper, support, supporter, twin **3.** alternate, clone, counterpart, corollary, double, duplicate, other **4.** loser, placer, runner-up, silver medalist – *v.* advance, aid, approve, assist, back, champion, encourage, endorse, forward, further, promote, stand behind, support, uphold *Antonyms:* undermine, veto

secondary *adj.* **1.** inferior, insignificant, lesser, minor, petty, second-rate, subordinate, subservient *Antonyms:* head, primary **2.** accessory, alternative, auxiliary, backup, contingent, dependent, extra, relief, reserve, spare, substitute **3.** collateral, concomitant, consequent, following, next, resultant, subsequent

second-class *adj.* **1.** cheap, common, commonplace, cut-rate, inferior, jerry-built, low-grade, low-quality, mean, mediocre, poor, second-rate, shaganappi, shoddy, slapdash, substandard, tacky, tawdry *Antonyms:* excellent, superior **2.** alienated, disenfranchised, marginalized oppressed, persecuted, tyrannized, victimized

secrecy *n.* **1.** clandestineness, confidentiality, covertness, darkness, espionage, furtiveness, hugger-mugger *(Nonformal)*, mystery, reticence, secretness, silence, stealth, subterfuge *Antonyms:* disclosure, divulgence **2.** concealment, camouflage, cover, disguise *Antonyms:* exposure, openness **3.** behind closed doors *(Nonformal)*, isolation, privacy, quiet, refuge, retirement, retreat, seclusion, shelter, solitude *Antonyms:* attention, hype, publicity

secret *adj.* **1.** backdoor, clandestine, closet, concealed covert, disguised, furtive, hidden, incognito, *sub rosa (Latin)*, surreptitious, undercover, underhanded, underground, unseen *Antonyms:* aboveboard, open **2.** close-mouthed, guarded, quiet, reticent, silent, taciturn, tight-lipped, uncommunicative *Antonyms:* loquacious, loud, obnoxious, talkative **3.** classified, confidential, hush-hush *(Nonformal)*, personal, private, unavowed, unknown, unrevealed *Antonyms:* communal, open, public **4.** abstruse, arcane, cryptic, mysterious, mystic, obscure, occult, recondite, shrouded *Antonyms:* accessible, comprehensible **5.** backwater, deserted, jerkwater, isolated, out-of-the-way, remote, secluded *Antonyms:* central, overpopulated, well-known – *n.* **1.** classified *or* confidential *or* privileged information *Nonformal:* dirt, doozy, nugget, scoop **2.** answer, code, instructions, key, password, solution **3.** arcanum, enigma, knot, mystery, puzzle, riddle, sphinx, unknown

secretary *n.* amanuensis, clerk, desk *(Nonformal)*, administrative *or* executive *or* office assistant, stenographer, typist

secrete *v.* **1.** discharge, emanate, emit, excrete, extrude, exude, perspire, produce, sweat **2.** bury, cache, conceal, cover, disguise, ensconce, harbour, hide, secure, shroud, squirrel *or* stash away, stow, veil *Antonyms:* bare, display, exhibit, reveal, show

secretive *adj.* cagey, close-mouthed, evasive, furtive, reserved, reticent, silent, taciturn, tight-lipped, uncommunicative *Nonformal:* buttoned-up, clammed-up *Antonyms:* gossipy, loud, prolix

secretly *adv.* by stealth, clandestinely, confidentially, covertly, furtively, in secret, insidiously, obscurely, privately, quietly, slyly, *sub rosa (Latin)*, surreptitiously *Nonformal:* hush-hush, off the record, on the qt, under the table *Antonyms:* openly, publicly

sect *n.* camp, church, communion, creed, crew, cult, denomination, division, faction, faith, following, group, order, party, persuasion, religion, schism, splinter group

sectarian *adj.* **1.** biased, bigoted, dogmatic, fanatical, hidebound, narrow-minded, parochial, prejudiced, rigid *Antonyms:* catholic, liberal, tolerant **2.** clannish, cliquish, cultish, denominational, exclusive, factional, insular, limited, partisan – *n.* **1.** bigot, extremist, fanatic, radical, reactionary, redneck *(Nonformal)*, zealot **2.** dissenter, dissident, nonconformist, rebel, revolutionary, separatist

section *n.* 640 acres *(U.S.)*, area, arrondissement *(French)*, belt, bite, branch, category, chunk, classification, component, concession, cross-section, department, district, division, end, field, fraction, fragment, installment, locality, lot, lump, member, moiety, parcel, part, passage, piece, portion, precinct, quarter, region, sample, sector, segment, separation, share, slice, sphere, strip, subdivision, tier, tract, unit, vicinity, zone – *v.* **1.** carve, chop, cut, divide, remove, separate, sever *Antonyms:* marry, merge, unite **2.** allocate, allot, assign, divvy *(Nonformal)*, halve, portion off, quarter, share

secular *adj.* **1.** corporeal, earthly, material, mundane, physical, temporal, terrestrial, worldly *Antonyms:* metaphysical, spectral, spiritual **2.** brief, ephemeral, evanescent, fleeting, momentary, passing, short-lived, transient *Antonyms:* ageless, endless, permanent **3.** civil, lay, nonreligious, nonspiritual, profane *Antonyms:* clerical, ecclesiastical, priestly

secure *adj.* **1.** anchored, bound, fast, fastened, firm, fixed, immovable, imprisoned, locked, nailed, set, tight, under lock and key *Antonyms:* adrift, free, loose, on the lam *(Nonformal)* **2.** airtight, solid, sound, stable, steady, strong, stout, sturdy, substantial, unbreakable, watertight *Antonyms:* creaky, rickety, untrustworthy, weak **3.** defended, fortified, guarded, impregnable, immune, protected, safe, shielded *Antonyms:* assailable, naked, vulnerable **4.** absolute, certain, definite, established, guaranteed, reliable, settled, sure, surefire *(Nonformal) Antonyms:* dubious, questionable, risky **5.** assured, confident, dauntless, determined, fearless, positive, self-assured, unafraid, valiant *Antonyms:* craven, intimidated, scared, worried – *v.* **1.** anchor, attach, bind, bolt, catch, cement, chain, clamp, clinch, close, fasten, fix, lash, lock *or* lock up, make fast, moor, nail down, padlock, pinion, rivet, tie down *or* up, tighten *Antonyms:* loosen, free, untie **2.** barricade, defend, guard, protect, safeguard, shield **3.** confirm, ensure, guarantee, pledge, post bail, underwrite, validate, verify **4.** achieve, acquire, gain, get, harvest, obtain, possess, procure, reap

security *n.* **1.** immunity, imperviousness, impregnability, invulnerability, safety, unassailability *Antonyms:* exposure, susceptibility **2.** armour, cover, defence, deterrent, electronic surveillance, fortification, home security, protection, shield, weaponry **3.** backup, bodyguard, chaperon, guard, hired thug *or* tough, officer, patrolperson, police, RCMP, *Sûreté (Quebec)*, sentry, watchdog **4.** certainty, certitude, confidence, contentedness, conviction, faith, freedom, hope, peace of mind, satisfaction, self-confidence *Antonyms:* anxiety, discontent, unhappiness **5.** assurance, guarantee, promise, safeguard, warranty **6.** assets, bail, bond, capital, collateral, debenture, earnings, escrow, insurance, investment, money, pledge, property, stocks, surety, wadset *(Scottish)*

sedate *adj.* calm, collected, composed, cool, decorous, deliberate, dignified, dispassionate, earnest, imperturbable, lackadaisical, laid-back *(Nonformal)*, placid, proper, quiet, relaxed, seemly, serene, serious, sober, solemn, sombre, staid, steady, tranquil, unflappable, unhurried, unruffled *Antonyms:* agitated, edgy, excitable, impassioned, nervous – *v.* anesthetize, drug, put to sleep *or* under, render unconscious, tranquilize

sedative *adj.* calming, lenitive, relaxing, sleep-inducing, soothing, soporific, tranquilizing – *n.* anaesthetic, analgesic, anodyne, barbiturate, calmative, depressant, drug, hypnotic, medication, narcotic, nerve medicine, opiate, pacifier, painkiller, pain pill, relaxant, sleeping pill, soother, soporific, tranquilizer *Nonformal:* downer, knockout pill *See also:* **depressant**

sedentary *adj.* couch-bound, desk-bound, dormant, idle, inactive, lazy, listless motionless, quiescent, seated, sedate, settled, sitting, slack, sluggish, slumped, stationary, still, torpid *Antonyms:* active, energetic, mobile

sediment *n.* debris, deposit, dregs, dross, grounds, gunk *(Nonformal)*, lees, matter, particulate, powder, precipitate, precipitation, residue, settling, silt, slag, solids, trash, waste

sedition *n.* **1.** civil action, defiance, discontent, dissension, dissent, disobedience, perfidy, protest, rebellion, resistance, revolt, revolution, treachery, treason *Antonyms:* conformance, loyalty, submission **2.** bedlam, chaos, craziness, ferment, havoc, mayhem, pandemonium, riot, tumult, turbulence, unrest *Antonyms:* order, peace, quietude

seduce *v.* **1.** allure, attract, bait, beguile, bribe, captivate, charm, corrupt, debauch, defile, deflower, deprave, draw, ensnare, entice, entrance, entrap, hook, induce, inveigle, invite, lure, overwhelm, pervert, ravish, tease, tempt, vamp *(Nonformal)*, violate **2.** coax, con *(Nonformal)*, deceive, decoy, delude, dupe, fool, hoax, hoodwink, mislead, trick

seductive *adj.* alluring, attracting, attractive, beguiling, bewitching, captivating, charming, come-hither, desirable, drawing, enchanting, enticing, fascinating, flirtatious, inviting, irresistible, magnetic, provocative, ravishing, sexy, specious, tempting *Antonyms:* disgusting, frightening, revolting

see *v.* **1.** apprehend, behold, contemplate, notice, observe, perceive, picture, scan, survey, view **2.** comprehend, conceive, experience, get, grasp, learn, know, master, realize, recognize, understand **3.** conjure *or* dream up, consider, envisage, fancy, fathom, imagine, ponder, think, visualize **4.** ascertain, determine, discern, discover, distinguish, find out, formulate, identify, investigate, make out, specify **5.** assure, ensure, guarantee, make certain, mark, mind, note, take care that *Antonyms:* ignore, neglect **6.** encounter, greet, receive, rendezvous, visit, welcome *Antonyms:* avoid, evade, shirk **7.** attend, look on, make, spectate, witness **8.** accompany, chaperon, direct, escort, follow, guard, guide, lead, show **9.** ask, inquire, request, search, seek, solicit **10.** equal, keep pace, match, meet

seed *n.* **1.** bud, egg, embryo, germ, kernel, ovule, roe, spawn, spore **2.** milt, pollen, semen, seminal fluid, sperm, spermatozoa **3.** brood, children, descendants, family, generation, grandchildren, heirs, heritage, issue, kin, offspring, people, posterity, progeny, race, scions, successors **4.** beginning, birth, cause, conception, cradle, fount, fountainhead, origin, provenance, root, seedbed, source – *v.* **1.** broadcast, disseminate, plant, scatter, sow **2.** align, appraise, categorize, classify, divide, evaluate, grade, handicap, number, order, process, rank, stream, value

seedy *adj.* abhorrent, dank, dark, degraded, dirty, disagreeable, disgusting, disreputable, grimy, infamous, low, mean, nasty, poor, ragged, rough, seamy, shabby, shady, sleazy, sordid, squalid *Nonformal:* ratty, scuzzy *Antonyms:* clean, respectable, upstanding

seek *v.* **1.** cast about, chase, comb, explore, ferret *or* root out, follow, forage, hunt, investigate, look about *or* around, nose, probe, prowl *or* root around, pursue, search, sniff out, track down **2.** ask, beg, beseech, demand, entreat, implore, inquire, request, solicit **3.** aim, aspire, attempt, endeavour, essay, strive, struggle, try, undertake, vie

seem *v.* **1.** feel, impress *or* strike one, look, sound **2.** echo, mirror, parrot, pretend, reflect, resemble **3.** appear, exhibit, manifest, show

seeming *adj.* **1.** apparent, evident, exterior, outward, superficial, surface, visible **2.** artificial, assumed, bogus, deceptive, fake, feigned, fictitious, illusory, make-believe, mock, quasi, quote unquote *(Nonformal)*, sham, spurious, unreal **3.** conceivable, likely, ostensible, plausible, possible, presumable, probable, supposable

seemly *adj.* appropriate, becoming, befitting, compatible, conforming, congenial, congruous, consistent, correct, decent, decorous, fitting, meet, nice, pleasing, proper, suitable, suited, timely *Antonyms:* improper, unseemly, unsuitable

seep *v.* bleed, bubble, discharge, drain, drip, drop, emanate, emerge, emit, escape, exude, filter, filtrate, flow, issue, leach, leak, ooze, overflow, pass, percolate, permeate, perspire, proceed, release, rise, saturate, soak, spill, spurt, sweat, transfuse, transpire, trickle, vent, weep

seepage *n.* discharge, drainage, dripping, emission, escape, exudation, flooding, flow, leaching, leakage, loss, oozing, overflow, waste, weeping

seer *n.* **1.** eyewitness, observer, onlooker, spectator, viewer, watcher, witness **2.** augur, diviner, fortuneteller, medium, mystic, oracle, prognosticator, prophet, psychic, pythoness, soothsayer, visionary

seesaw *adj.* ambiguous, fluctuating, hesitant, irresolute, oscillating, shifting, tottering, uncertain, up-and-down, vacillating *Antonyms:* determined, firm, steady – *n.* ambiguity, doubt, hesitation, indecision, equivocalness, irresolution, prevarication, uncertainty *Antonyms:* commitment, decision, resolution – *v.* alternate, change, flip-flop, fluctuate, shilly-shally, tergiversate, vacillate, vary, waffle, waver *Nonformal:* blow hot and cold, dipsy-doodle

seethe *v.* **1.** burn, fume, rage, rant, simmer, sizzle, smoulder **2.** boil, coddle, cook, heat, parboil, poach, scald, warm **3.** douse, drench, immerse, marinate, soak, steep, wet *Antonyms:* dehydrate, desiccate, dry **4.** assemble, bunch, congregate, huddle, mass, mill, scrum, surge, swarm, swell, throng *Antonyms:* disband, disperse, dissipate

segment *n.* allotment, bit, chunk, compartment, constituent, cut, division, fraction, lot, member, moiety, parcel, part, piece, portion, section, sector, share, slice, subdivision, wedge *Antonyms:* complex, totality, whole

segregate *adj.* **1.** detached, divided, partitioned, sectional, separate, solitary **2.** discriminatory, exclusionary, racist, restrictive, seclusionist, segregated, white-bread *(Nonformal) U.S.:* Jim Crow, lily-white *Antonyms:* inclusive, multicultural, open – *v.* **1.** disconnect, dissociate, divide, insulate, island, isolate, quarantine, separate, sequester, set apart, single out, split up, stream *Antonyms:* amalgamate, combine, merge, unite **2.** alienate, discriminate, disenfranchise, exclude, ghettoize, marginalize, oppress, persecute, victimize, wrong *Antonyms:* cherish, respect, value

segregation *n.* **1.** apartheid, displacement, dispossession, eviction, forced removal, Jim-Crowism *(U.S.) Canadian historical* evacuation *(Japanese)*, expulsion *(Acadian)*, relocation *(Aboriginal)* **2.** discrimination, exclusionism, extirpation, marginalization, oppression, persecution, racism, victimization **3.** disunion, division, internment, isolation, partitioning, quarantine, segmentation, separation, sequesteration *Antonyms:* association, unification

seize *v.* **1.** catch, clench, clutch, grab, grapple, grasp, grip, handle, pick up, pluck, snag, snatch, squeeze, throttle *Antonyms:* bobble, drop, spill **2.** apprehend, arrest, bag, capture, collar, cuff, detain, fetter, impound, imprison, incarcerate, jail, nab, subdue *Nonformal:* bust, nail, pinch *Antonyms:* emancipate, free, release **3.** brace, connect, couple, fasten, hitch, hold fast, hook, link, marry, secure, tie **4.** compass, comprehend, embrace, recognize, understand *Nonformal:* capiche, catch the drift, get the picture, savvy *Antonyms:* confuse, misunderstand **5.** cease, freeze up, halt, jam, quit, stall, stem, stop *Antonyms:* continue, keep going, run **6.** abduct, appropriate, assume, commandeer, confiscate, expropriate, kidnap, requisition *(Nonformal)*, shanghai, spirit away, take **7.** attack, overcome, overpower, overwhelm, strike

seizure *n.* **1.** clasp, clutch, control, grasp, grip, hold, possession **2.** apprehension, arrest, bust *(Nonformal)*, capture, collar, incarceration, jailing *Antonyms:* discharge, liberation, release **3.** abduction, assumption, confiscation, recovery, removal, retrieval, usurpation *Antonyms:* bestowal, present, return **4.** attack, convulsion, fit, illness, paroxysm, spasm, spell, stroke, throe, turn **5.** breakdown, cessation, collapse, failure, interruption, malfunction stalling, stoppage *Antonyms:* continuance, resumption

seldom *adv.* hardly, hardly ever, infrequently, irregularly, little, not often, occasionally, rarely, scarcely, sometimes, sporadically, uncommonly, unusually *Antonyms:* frequently, much, often

select *adj.* **1.** best, choice, chosen, cream, elect, elite, excellent, exquisite, favoured, picked, preferable, preferred, prime, rare, screened, seeded, special, superior, tops, ultimate, winner, world-class **2.** circumscribed, closed, exclusionary, exclusive, limited, members-only, narrow, private, privileged, restrictive, selective **3.** choosy, conscientious, discerning, discriminating, esoteric, fastidious, finicky, fussy, meticulous, particular *Antonyms:* indifferent, impartial – *v.* **1.** choose, cull, decide, elect, finger *(Nonformal)*, make, mark, name, opt for, peg, pick, pick *or* single *or* sort out, slot, tab, tag, winnow *Antonyms:* neglect, omit, pass over, reject **2.** appreciate, consider, desire, endorse, fancy, favour, lean toward, like, patronize, prefer, value *Antonyms:* abhor, censor, prohibit

selection *n.* **1.** decision, decision making, draft, election, freedom of choice, judgement **2.** alternative, choice, draft pick, nomination, option, pick, preference, take, vote **3.** assemblage, assortment, bunch, collection, cross-section, diversity, grouping, hash, medley, miscellany, mixed bag, mixture, mosaic, myriad, variegation, variety

selective *adj.* careful, critical, demanding, discerning, discriminatory, fussy, judgmental, meticulous, particular, persnickety, picky, scrupulous, select *Antonyms:* careless, desultory, indiscriminate

self *n.* being, character, ego, human, I, individual, man, me, mortal, person, personage, soul, woman

self-assured *adj.* certain, cocksure, cocky *(Nonformal)*, confident, fearless, knowing, positive, sanguine, self-confident, sure, swaggering *Antonyms:* bashful, self-doubting, shy

self-centred *adj.* egocentric, egotistical, narcissistic, navel-gazing *(Nonformal)*, self- absorbed, self-indulgent, self-interested, self-involved, selfish, self-seeking, self-serving *Antonyms:* caring, considerate, helpful

self-confidence *n.* aplomb, assurance, assuredness, certainty, certitude, cockiness *(Nonformal)*, conviction, positiveness, sureness *Antonyms:* diffidence, doubt, timidity

self-confident *adj.* arrogant, assured, cocky *(Nonformal)*, fearless, poised, sanguine, secure, self-assured, swaggering, unafraid *Antonyms:* anxious, doubtful, hesitant, nervous

self-conscious *adj.* **1.** anxious, awkward, bashful, discomfited, embarrassed, insecure, nervous, self-reflexive, shamefaced, sheepish, shy, uncertain, uncomfortable, uneasy, unsure *Antonyms:* easy, graceful, natural **2.** affected, artificial, fabricated, mannered, overdone, stiff, stilted, studied, wooden *Antonyms:* convincing, genuine, realistic

self-control *n.* balance, calm, command, composure, cool, discipline, equanimity, levelheadedness, possession, restraint, sang-froid, self-command, self-possession, stability, temperance, will power *Antonyms:* abandon, excitability, incontinence, inflammability

self-denial *n.* abnegation, abstinence, asceticism, forebearance, puritanism, restraint, sacrifice, stoicism *Antonyms:* debauchery, dissipation, sybaritism

self-deprecating *adj.* apologetic, demurring, diffident, humble, modest, self-abasing, self-critical, self-effacing *Antonyms:* big-mouthed *(Nonformal)*, brazen, proud, self-satisfied

self-determination *n.* **1.** autarky, autonomy, democracy, home-rule, independence, secession, self-government, self-rule, separation, sovereignty *Antonyms:* colonialism, dependence, subjection **2.** choice, election, freedom, free will, liberty, option, selection *Antonyms:* bondage, constraint, tyranny

self-esteem *n. amour-propre (French)*, confidence, dignity, pride, self-assurance, self-regard, self-respect, self-worth

self-evident *adj.* apparent, axiomatic, blatant, clear, obvious, patent, plain, *prima facie (Latin)*, self-explanatory, true, unambiguous, unequivocal, unmistakable *Antonyms:* cryptic, obscure, puzzling

self-government *n.* autarchy, autonomy, freedom, home-rule, independence, self-determination, self-rule

self-important *adj.* arrogant, conceited, haughty, lordly, overblown, patronizing, pompous, pretentious, proud, self-assured, self-confident, supercilious *Nonformal:* cocky, hoity-toity, snooty, stuck-up *Antonyms:* humble, self-effacing, unassuming

self-indulgent *adj.* **1.** egocentric, greedy, self-interested, selfish, self-serving *Antonyms:* altruistic, charitable, generous **2.** excessive, hedonistic, immoderate, intemperate, unbridled, undisciplined, uninhibited, weak *Antonyms:* abstinent, ascetic, puritanical

self-interest *n.* **1.** advantage, benefit, betterment, comfort, convenience, gain, improvement, profit, wealth, welfare *Antonyms:* detriment, drawback, loss **2.** acquisitiveness, avarice, cupidity, desire, egotism, greed, narcissism, self-love, self-seeking *Antonyms:* charity, giving, philanthropy

selfish *adj.* **1.** avaricious, close-fisted, grasping, greedy, miserly, parsimonious, stingy, tight-fisted, ungenerous *Antonyms:* liberal, selfless, unstinting **2.** cruel, disobliging, hard, miserable, mean, nasty, petty, self-serving, small, stepmotherly *(Nonformal)*, unkind, unsympathetic, vicious, wicked *Antonyms:* considerate, gracious, thoughtful

selfless *adj.* altruistic, benevolent, big-hearted, generous, giving, magnanimous, philanthropic, sacrificing, self-sacrificing, unselfish *Antonyms:* avaricious, greedy, selfish

self-possessed *adj.* balanced, calm, collected, composed, cool, disciplined, dispassionate, equanimous, even, poised, self-composed, serene, temperate, unflinching, unruffled *Antonyms:* excited, perplexed, perturbed

self-reliant *adj.* autarkik, autocephalous, autonomous, independent, free, republican, self-determining, self-employed, self-ruling, self-sufficient, self-supporting, self-sustained, unconnected *Antonyms:* contingent, dependent, helpless

self-righteous *adj.* affected, canting, complacent, egotistical, holier-than-thou *(Nonformal)*, pharisaic, pious, preachy, sanctimonious, self-satisfied, smug, superior *Antonyms:* diffident, modest, unobtrusive

self-satisfaction *n.* arrogance, cockiness *(Nonformal)*, complacency, hubris, immodesty, overconfidence, self-delight, self-righteousness, smugness, vainglory, vanity *Antonyms:* anxiety, disappointment, misgiving

self-satisfied *adj.* complacent, conceited, content, pleased, proud, puffed up, self-congratulatory, self-important, smirking, smug, toffee-nosed *(Nonformal)*, triumphant, vain, vainglorious *Antonyms:* disinterested, dejected, displeased

sell *v.* **1.** auction, bargain, barter, contract, deal, deliver, dispose, exchange, merchandise, move, trade, transfer, traffic, unload, vend **2.** advertise, boost, hawk, hustle, market, peddle, pitch, plug, promote *Nonformal:* flog, hype, push **3.** carry, deal in, handle, retail, store, wholesale **4.** affect, bias, bribe, cajole, coax, influence, lead, manipulate, persuade, prejudice, seduce, shape, sway **5.** betray, break faith, deceive *Nonformal:* double-cross, finger, rat *or* squeal *or* fink *or* inform *or* snitch on

seller *n.* agent, auctioneer, businessperson, dealer, hawker, jobber, marketer, merchant, middleman, monger, peddler, representative, retailer, sales associate, salesman, saleswoman, shopkeeper, storekeeper, tradesperson, vendor

semblance *adj.* **1.** appearance, aspect, complexion, countenance, feature, look **2.** cloak, cover, display, façade, front, guise, mask, pretense, shadow, surface, veil, veneer, verisimilitude **3.** approximation, copy, forgery, imitation, likeness, mimicry, reflection, resemblance, similarity, simulation

seminal *adj.* **1.** germinal, inceptive, productive, propagative **2.** breakthrough, influential, innovative, landmark, milestone, monumental, pivotal, prototypical, signal, significant *Antonyms:* hackneyed, meaningless, trivial **3.** beginning, callow, crude, embryonic, green, half-baked *(Nonformal)*, inchoate, premature, rudimentary, undeveloped, unfinished, unrealized, unripe *Antonyms:* complete, mature, perfect

seminary *n.* academy, Bible college, college, divinity school, institution, rabbinical school, *séminaire (Quebec)*, theological college, training ground, university

send *v.* **1.** address, courier, deliver, direct, dispatch, e-mail, expedite, fax, freight, mail, point and click, post, remit, route, ship, transport **2.** broadcast, cast, convey, disseminate, forward, relay, transfer, transmit **3.** advance, hit, knock, propel, punch, shoot, shove **4.** discharge, eject, emit, gush forth, issue, leak, ooze **5.** assign, authorize, choose, commission, consign, delegate, designate, entrust, name, nominate, select **6.** bequest, bestow, bless, confer, favour, grant, hand *or* shower down, impart, offer **7.** arouse, beguile, bewitch, charm, delight, elate, entertain, enthral, please, stimulate, thrill, tickle *(Nonformal) Antonyms:* disgust, offend, sicken

sendoff *n.* **1.** beginning, commencement, embarkation, kickoff, launch, parting, setting out, start, undertaking *Antonyms:* homecoming, return **2.** celebration, feast, festival, fête, gala, party, remembrance, rite, shivaree, soiree, wake *Nonformal:* bash, blowout, do **3.** backing, cheer, encouragement, farewell, goodbye, good wishes, inspiration, reassurance, support, urging

senile *adj.* aged, ancient, decrepit, doddering, doting, enfeebled, failing, feeble, infirm, old, senescent, sick, sliding, weak *Antonyms:* strong, virile, young

senility *n.* caducity, debility, deterioration, decline, dotage, infirmity, old age, retrogression, senescence, weakness

senior *adj.* **1.** elder, first-born, older, oldest, venerable *Antonyms:* junior, younger **2.** chief, commanding, directing, eminent, higher, leading, major, preeminent, ranking, superior, upper-level *Antonyms:* inferior, lesser, lower, minor, subordinate **3.** accomplished, advanced, developed, educated, experienced, expert, mature, qualified, seasoned, skilful *Antonyms:* callow, green, inexperienced – *n.* **1.** elderly *or* retired person, old man *or* woman, pensioner, senior citizen, veteran *Nonformal:* blue-hair, geezer, golden-ager, oldster **2.** captain, chief, dean, doyen, doyenne, elder statesman, guide, head, leader, manager, patriarch, ranking official *or* head *or* officer *Native Peoples:* sachem, saqamaw

seniority *n.* **1.** advantage, precedence, preference, priority, rank, ranking, standing, station, superiority, time on the job **2.** age, education, experience, knowledge, maturity, wisdom, worldliness

sensation *n.* **1.** awareness, cognizance, consciousness, perception, response, realization, responsiveness, sensibility, sensitivity, susceptibility, understanding **2.** emotion, feeling, impression, intimation, intuition, portent, premonition, sense, tingling, thought *Nonformal:* hunch, vibe **3.** ado, agitation, commotion, confusion, excitement, furor, fuss, scandal, stir, thrill, titillation, uproar *Nonformal:* buzz, hoopla, hubbub, to-do **4.** accomplishment, achievement, feat, hit, marvel, miracle, phenomenon, success, surprise, triumph, victory *Nonformal:* barnburner, killer, stunner *Antonyms:* bomb, bust, failure

sensational *adj.* **1.** amazing, arresting, astonishing, astounding, bracing, breathtaking, classic, electrifying, emotional, exceptional, exciting, fabulous, glorious, great, impressive, incredible, mind-boggling, outstanding, poignant, pointed, remarkable, sharp, signal, spectacular, staggering, stimulating, stirring, stunning, surprising, terrific, thrilling, wonderful **2.** gratuitous, lurid, melodramatic, over-the-top, salacious, shock, shocking *Nonformal:* Hollywood, juicy, yellow

sense *n.* **1.** awareness, cognizance, comprehension, consciousness, feeling, impression, kinesthesia, muscle sense, perception, realization, recognition, sensation, sensibility, sensitivity, understanding *The five senses:* hearing, sight, smell, taste, touch **2.** cleverness, common sense, discrimination, insight, intellect, intelligence, knowledge, logic, mentality, prudence, rationalization, reason, reasoning, sagacity, sanity, wisdom *Nonformal:* brains, gumption, know-how, savvy, smarts, street smarts **3.** admiration, appreciation, capacity, discernment, feel, imagination, instinct, intuition, judgment, regard, respect, taste **4.** clarity, coherence, comprehensibility, decipherability, intelligibility, lucidity **5.** implication, import, meaning, message, purport, significance, thrust, value, weight, worth **6.** definition, drift, gist, heart, meat, nub, point, spirit, stuff, substance **7.** assessment, belief, conclusion, consensus, opinion, view – *v.* anticipate, appreciate, comprehend, discern, divine, feel, grasp, know, notice, observe, perceive, realize, savvy *(Nonformal)*, suspect, think, understand

senseless *adj.* **1.** absurd, asinine, crazy, daft, fatuous, foolish, gratuitous, idiotic, illogical, imbecilic, inane, irrational, ludicrous, mad, meaningless, mindless, moronic, nonsensical, pointless, purposeless, ridiculous, silly, simple, stupid, trivial, unimportant, unintelligent, unreasonable, unsound, unwise *Antonyms:* meaningful, sensible, useful, worthwhile **2.** barbaric, brutal, callous, cold-hearted, cruel, disturbing, harrowing, nefarious, savage, unsympathetic, vicious, wicked *Antonyms:* charitable, humane, kind **3.** impervious, insensate, insensitive, numb, oblivious, unconscious, unfeeling

sensibility *n.* **1.** awareness, emotion, feeling, insight, intuition, keenness, perceptiveness, responsiveness, sensation, sense, sensitivity *Antonyms:* insensibility, numbness, unresponsiveness **2.** acumen, discernment, discrimination, insight, intelligence, judgment, knowledge, logic, rationality, reasoning, shrewdness, wisdom **3.** delicacy, soreness, susceptibility, tenderness, vulnerability, weakness **4.** admiration, affection, appreciation, regard, taste, understanding

sensible *adj.* **1.** astute, bright, canny, commonsensical, conversant, discerning, discreet, discriminating, farsighted, informed, intelligent, judicious, knowing, logical, perceptive, practical, prudent, rational, realistic, sagacious, sage, sane, shrewd, smart, sober, thought-out, well-reasoned, wise *Nonformal:* down-to-earth, matter-of-fact *Antonyms:* blind, foolish, irrational, senseless, unwise **2.** agreeable, cogent, convincing, credible, impelling, impressive, influential, likely, persuasive, plausible, reasonable, sound, valid *Antonyms:* dubious, improbable, silly **3.** apparent, appreciable, concrete, corporeal, evident, material, obvious, palpable, perceptible, physical, real, substantial, tangible, touchable *Antonyms:* abstract, ethereal, spiritual **4.** alert, alive, attentive, awake, aware, cognizant, conscious, reactive, sentient *Nonformal:* all there, together *Antonyms:* dead, insentient, oblivious

sensitive *adj.* **1.** choleric, easily affected, emotional, excitable, feeling, high-strung, hypersensitive, impressible, irritable, passionate, petulant, susceptible, touchy *Antonyms:* apathetic, dilatory, phlegmatic **2.** aware, cognizant, conscious, knowing, perceptive, reactive, receptive, reflexive, responsive, sensory, sentient *Antonyms:* insensible, unresponsive **3.** benevolent, caring, clement, compassionate, considerate, decent, feeling, humane, kind, sympathetic, tender-hearted, thoughtful, understanding *Antonyms:* callous, hard, uncaring **4.** bruised, chafed, fragile, nicked *(Nonformal)*, painful, raw, smarting, sore, swollen, tender **5.** classified, confidential, hush-hush *(Nonformal)*, intimate, private, secret *Antonyms:* free, open, public **6.** accurate, delicate, exacting, fine, precise, subtle, supersensitive *Antonyms:* crude, simple, unrefined

sensitivity *n.* **1.** excitability, impatience, intolerance, irritability, nervousness, petulance, susceptibility, temperament, touchiness, volatility *Antonyms:* calm, composure, cool **2.** awareness, cognizance, consciousness, reactivity, receptiveness, responsiveness, sense, sensitiveness **3.** affection, caring, feeling, kindliness, sweetness, sympathy, tender-heartedness, understanding, warmth *Antonyms:* apathy, ca lousness, indifference **4.** ache, bruise, cut, discomfort, hurt, inflammation, irritation, lesion, nick, pain, rawness, sore, soreness, tenderness **5.** confidence, confidentiality, delicacy, intimacy, privacy, secrecy **6.** accuracy, correctness, faithfulness, fidelity, precision, refinement, subtlety

sensual *adj.* **1.** bawdy, concupiscent, lascivious, lewd, intimate, sexual, sexy, venereal *Nonformal:* adult, blue, dirty, smutty **2.** bodily, carnal, corporeal, fleshly, physical, tactile, material, tangible *Commonly misused:* **sensuous**

sensuous *adj.* **1.** delightful, luscious, gratifying, luxurious, pleasurable, rich, sumptuous, voluptuous, wonderful **2.** epicurean, hedonistic, pleasure-loving, pleasure-seeking, self-indulgent, sybaritic *Antonyms:* ascetic, platonic, spiritual **3.** perceptual, receptive, responsive, sensory *Commonly misused:* **sensual**

sentence *n.* **1.** clause, comment, declaration, exclamation, expression, line, note, opinion, phrase, proposition, question, quip, remark, statement *Sentence structures:* complex, compound, compound-complex, simple **2.** command, decision, determination, dictum, edict, judgment, order, pronouncement, verdict **3.** captivity, censure, condemnation, confinement, penalty, period of incarceration, punishment, stretch, term, time – *v.* condemn, confine, convict, denounce, doom, impound, imprison, incarcerate, jail, judge, lock up, mete out, pass judgment, penalize, proscribe, punish, put away, send up river *(Nonformal)*, trammel *Antonyms:* exonerate, free, liberate

sententious *adj.* **1.** aphoristic, axiomatic, brief, concise, curt, epigrammatic, laconic, pithy, short and sweet *(Nonformal)*, succinct, terse *Antonyms:* loquacious, prolix, verbose **2.** bombastic, flatulent, florid, pompous, purple, stilted, swollen, turgid **3.** high-flown, moral, preachy, sanctimonious, self-righteous, smug, superior *Antonyms:* humble, meek, self-effacing

sentiment *n.* **1.** assessment, attitude, belief, conception, consideration, conviction, judgment, mind, opinion, position, posture, slant, stance, take *(Nonformal)*, thought, view, viewpoint **2.** appreciation, attachment, bias, closeness, connection, liking, love, loyalty, partiality, passion, penchant, predilection, propensity, soft spot *(Nonformal) Antonyms:* aversion, hate, hostility **3.** awareness, emotion, feeling, inclination, sensation, sense, sensibility

sentimental *adj.* **1.** affectionate, loving, passionate, romantic, soft-hearted, tender, touching *Antonyms:* disinterested, dispassionate, unkind **2.** effusive, emotional, gushing, insipid, lachrymose, maudlin, mawkish, mushy, nostalgic, over-emotional, saccharine, silly, simpering, vapid, weepy *Nonformal:* corny, dewy-eyed, drippy, sappy, schmaltzy, slushy, tear-jerking *Antonyms:* earthy, iconoclastic, realistic

separate *adj.* **1.** different, discrete, distinct, individual, lone, only, particular, peculiar, rare, single, strange, unique *Antonyms:* identical, parallel, similar **2.** abstracted, alone, apportioned, asunder, detached, disassociated, disconnected, disembodied, disjointed, disunited, divided, divorced, loose, parted, partitioned, severed *Antonyms:* connected, fused, joined, married, merged, welded **3.** distant, desolate, deserted, far-off, godforsaken, isolated, lonely, secluded, solitary *Antonyms:* accessible, at hand, linked **4.** autonomous, free, independent, self-determining, self-governing, sovereign, unattached *Antonyms:* puppet, satellite, subject, subordinate – *v.* **1.** cast asunder, cleave, detach, disconnect, disjoin, dissect, disunite, divide, sever, uncouple, undo, unlink *Antonyms:* attach, connect, link **2.** isolate, partition, quarantine, remove, seclude, segregate **3.** annul, break up, divorce, leave, part company *or* paths, split up **4.** depart, diverge, drift, leave, stray **5.** assign, categorize, classify, compartmentalize, group, order, sort, stream **6.** break *(Boxing)*, come between, disentangle, interfere, intervene, push apart **7.** clarify, clear, distill, extract, filter, purify, refine, screen, sieve, sift, strain **8.** differentiate, discern, distinguish between, discriminate, single out

separately *adv.* alone, apart, differently, distinctly, independently, individually, personally, singly *Antonyms:* collectively, jointly, socially, together

separation *n.* **1.** break, cleavage, departure, detachment, disconnection, disjunction, division, rift, rupture **2.** partition, boundary, barrier, demarcation line, divide, fence, line, screen, separator, septum, wall **3.** annulment, breakup, dissolution, divorce, falling apart, parting, trial separation *Antonyms:* betrothal, engagement, marriage **4.** desertion, disavowal, dissension, relinquishment, repudiation, schism, secession, withdrawal *Antonyms:* confederation, convergence, unification **5.** alienation, discrimination, dissociation, exclusion, ghettoization, marginalization, segregation *Antonyms:* harmony, integration, unity

separatist *n.* **1.** Federalist *(U.S.)*, nationalist, *Péquiste (Quebec)*, republican, sovereignist **2.** apostate, dissenter, dissident, protestant, radical, revolutionary, schismatic, sectarian

sepulchral *adj.* **1.** bleak, cheerless, cold, creepy, dark, death-like, depressing, dismal, forlorn, funereal, ghostly, gloomy, grave, lugubrious, melancholy, miserable, morbid, mournful, saturnine *Antonyms:* bright, happy, lively **2.** baritone, bass, deep, echoing, hollow, low, phat *(Nonformal)*, resonant, sonorous *Antonyms:* alto, high-pitched, shrill

sepulchre *n.* barrow, burial mound *or* place, cairn, catacomb, cold storage *(Nonformal)*, crypt, grave, mausoleum, mound, ossuary, repository, resting place, tomb, vault

sequel *n.* **1.** chain, continuation, continuity, order, progression, row, sequence, series, succession **2.** addition, epilogue, follow-up, part two, spin-off, trailer **3.** aftereffect, aftermath, backlash, blowback *(Politics)*, by-product, conclusion, consequence, dénouement, development, effect, end result, fallout, inheritance, legacy, outcome, payoff, rebound, remnant, result, subsequence, upshot, wake

sequence *n.* **1.** chain, concatenation, consecutiveness, continuance, continuity, course, cycle, perpetuation, row, run, series, string, succession, track, train **2.** arrangement, array, classification, distribution, graduation, grouping, hierarchy, ladder, order, ordering, progression, rank, stairway, train

sequester *v.* **1.** cloister, close off, insulate, isolate, quarantine, seclude, segregate, separate **2.** disappear, hide, lay low, retire, withdraw *Nonformal:* go underground, opt-out **3.** assume, commandeer, confiscate, claim, impound, remove, take

sequestered *adj.* **1.** confined, divided, hidden, isolated, secluded, segregated, separated **2.** hermotic, retired, retreated, seceded, severed, withdrawn **3.** claimed, confiscated, expropriated, removed, repossessed, taken

seraphic *adj.* angelic, astral, celestial, divine, ethereal, heavenly, saintly, spiritual, supernatural

serendipity *n.* **1.** accident, chance, coincidence, dumb luck, fate, good fortune *or* luck, happenstance **2.** bonanza, casual discovery, felicity, find, fluke, jackpot, lucky strike, windfall

serene *adj.* **1.** calm, clear, clement, fair, halcyon, mild, moderate, pacific, peaceful, placid, quiet, smooth, still, subsided, temperate, tranquil, undisturbed *Antonyms:* extreme, tempestuous, wild **2.** at peace, collected, comfortable, composed, content, cool, easygoing, gentle, patient, poised, quiescent, quiet, reconciled, restful, resting, satisfied, sedate, self-possessed, unruffled *Antonyms:* agitated, anxious, troubled

serenity *n.* **1.** calm, calmness, composure, cool, patience, peace, peacefulness, placidity, quietude, tranquility *Antonyms:* disquiet, disturbance, panic **2.** clearness, clemency, eye, hush, stillness, still waters, windlessness *Antonyms:* inclemency, storm, turmoil

serf *n.* bondman, bondwoman, chattel, helot, peon, servant, slave, subject, thrall, vassal, villein *Antonyms:* lord, master, owner

serial *adj.* **1.** consistent, continual, continued, continuing **2.** consequent, ensuing following, resultant, sequent, succeeding **3.** consecutive, ordered, sequential, seriate, successive **4.** annual, bi-weekly, cyclic, monthly, periodic, rhythmic, seasonal, tidal, weekly, yearly – *n.* **1.** annual, daily, gazette, journal, magazine, monthly, paper, publication, quarterly, weekly **2.** broadcast, series, show, situation comedy, soap opera, story, television series *Nonformal:* sitcom, soap

series *n.* **1.** arrangement, array, category, catena, chain, classification, column, continuity, course, file, gradation, group, line, list, litany, order, procession, progression, range, row, run, sequence, set, streak, string, succession, suit, suite, tier, train **2.** bonspeil, championship, competition, event, final, heat, playdown, playoff, regatta, round robin, showdown, tournament

serious *adj.* **1.** austere, businesslike, determined, grave, grim, humourless, portentous, severe, sober, staid, stern *Nonformal:* deep-dish, hard-bitten, no-nonsense *Antonyms:* gay, jolly, silly **2.** earnest, genuine, honest, intent, resolute, sincere *Antonyms:* deceitful, deceptive, mischievous **3.** contemplative, introverted, meditative, pensive, ponderous, reflective, ruminant, thoughtful **4.** consequential, crucial, deep, great, important, life and death *(Nonformal)*, magnificent, major, meaningful, momentous, monumental, pressing, significant, urgent, weighty, worrying *Antonyms:* insignificant, secondary, trivial **5.** dangerous, difficult, dreadful, formidable, grievous, hazardous, horrible, life-threatening, menacing, mortal, severe, threatening **6.** arduous, backbreaking *(Nonformal)*, difficult, exhausting, hard, heavy, laborious, painful, sobering, strenuous, tough *Antonyms:* easy, light, simple **7.** arranged, considered, controlled, deliberate, intentional, marshalled, orchestrated, organized, planned, predetermined, rehearsed, set, studied *Antonyms:* accidental, chance, fortuitous, serendipitous

seriously *adv.* **1.** decidedly, determinedly, earnestly, fervently, intently, purposefully, resolutely, sedately, sincerely, soberly, solemnly, sternly, thoughtfully **2.** acutely, badly, critically, dangerously, deplorably, distressingly, gravely, grievously, harmfully, intensely, menacingly, perilously, precariously, severely, threateningly

sermon *n.* **1.** address, discourse, doctrine, homily, lecture, lesson, moral, preaching, speech, talk **2.** castigation, diatribe, exhortation, harangue, invective, opprobrium, reproof, tirade *Nonformal:* tongue-lashing, what for

serpent *n.* **1.** adder, asp, cockatrice, constrictor, hydra, ophidian, python, reptile, snake, viper *See also:* **snake** **2.** adulterer, adulteress, cheat, cheater, deceiver, fake, jilter *Nonformal:* bastard, snake-in-the-grass, two-timer **3.** apostate, quisling, traitor, turncoat *Nonformal:* back-stabber, Benedict Arnold, Judas, rat **4.** Abaddon, devil, Lucifer, Satan *See also:* **devil**

serpentine *adj.* **1.** lithe, long, sinuous, skinny, slender, slim, slinky, willowy *Antonyms:* corpulent, fat, round **2.** convoluted, crooked, indirect, labyrinthine, tortuous, winding *Antonyms:* linear, straight **3.** clever, cunning, deceptive, ingenious, oily, shifty, slick, subtle, tricky, wily *Nonformal:* slimy, slippery *Antonyms:* frank, honest, straightforward

serrated *adj.* indented, jagged, notched, ragged, saw-toothed, scored, serrate, serried, serriform, sharp, sharp-toothed, toothed

servant *n.* **1.** assistant, attendant, batman, butler, chauffeur, domestic, drudge, employee, factotum, famulus, gillie, help, helper, hired help, hireling, Jeeves *(Nonformal)*, maid, manservant, major-domo, menial, retainer, scullion, seneschal, steward, waiter, worker **2.** bondsman, bondswoman, indentured servant, peon, serf, slave, subject **3.** administrator, apparatchik, bureaucrat, civil servant, mandarin, parliamentarian, public servant, professional bureaucrat, white-collar worker *Nonformal:* desk jockey, pencil pusher, silly servant

serve *n.* at bat, attempt, effort, essay, go, offering, service, shift, try, turn – *v.* **1.** attend to, care for, keep, help, look after, mind, minister to, oblige, perform duties, service, wait on, work for **2.** advance, aid, assist, avail, benefit, booster, endorse, foster, help, patronize, plug, promote, publicize, push, sponsor, support *Antonyms:* sabotage, undermine **3.** carry on *or* out, complete, execute, fulfill, meet, satisfy **4.** celebrate, glorify, grovel before, obey, observe, pay homage, praise, respect, revere, venerate, worship *Antonyms:* denounce, profane, vilify **5.** convey, deal, deliver, discharge, distribute, give, hand over, offer, present, remit, set forth, transfer **6.** handle, manage, manipulate, operate, ply, tend, use, utilize, work **7.** belt, buffet, hit, send, strike, throw *Nonformal:* crank, hammer, smash, sock **8.** accoutre, equip, furnish, outfit, provide, provision, supply

service *n.* **1.** aid, assistance, attention, avail, backing, benefit, charity, comfort, consideration, contribution, giving, help, indulgence, kindness, support **2.** effectiveness, functionality, practicality, purpose, serviceability, significance, usefulness, utility, value, worth **3.** charge, commission, contract, craft, employ, hire, ministry, trade **4.** allegiance, deference, dutifulness, fealty, loyalty **5.** administration, arrangement, delivery, distribution, network, organization, supply system **6.** care, installation, maintenance, repair, restoration, upkeep **7.** agency, arm, branch, bureau, chapter, department, detachment, division, office, section, unit, ward, wing **8.** air force, Armed Forces, armed service, army, marines, military, navy, reserves **9.** adoration, devotion, genuflection, glorification, veneration, worship **10.** ceremony, communion, exercise, formality, liturgy, mass, observance, rite, ritual, sermon, solemnity – *v.* check, fix, maintain, overhaul, repair, tune, tuneup, upkeep

serviceable *adj.* **1.** advantageous, beneficial, convenient, effectual, functional, handy, helpful, invaluable, of aid, operative, practical, profitable, usable, useful, valuable **2.** dependable, durable, efficient, hard-wearing, rugged, sturdy, utilitarian *Antonyms:* impractical, inefficient, useless, worn-out

servile *adj.* abject, attendant, base, beggarly, craven, cringing, despicable, fawning, grovelling, humble, ignoble, low, mean, obedient, obsequious, passive, pusillanimous, sequacious, slavish, submissive, subservient, sycophantic, toadying, unctuous *Antonyms:* dominant, overbearing, superior

servitude *n.* **1.** bondage, bonds, captivity, chains, enslavement, peonage, serfdom, slavery, subjection, subjugation, thralldom, vassalage *Antonyms:* freedom, liberty, manumission **2.** acquiescence, compliance, cowardice, humility, obedience, servility, slavishness, submission, subservience, timidity *Antonyms:* dissent, recalcitrance, revolt

session *n.* affair, appointment, assembly, bout *(Nonformal)*, briefing, concourse, confab, conference, convention, court, discussion, gathering, hearing, meeting, sitting

set *adj.* **1.** appointed, certain, confirmed, definite, prearranged, pre-determined, prescribed, scheduled, specified, stipulated, strict *Antonyms:* ad hoc, impromptu, improvised **2.** customary, conventional, established, habitual, normal, regular, usual **3.** arranged, contrived, deliberate, designed, formal, ordered, organized, managed, rehearsed, studied *Antonyms:* impulsive, inadvertent **4.** anchored, entrenched, fast, firm, fixed, hardened, immovable, jelled, motionless, rigid, rooted, settled, solid, stable, static, stiff *Antonyms:* active, mobile, moving **5.** bent, decided, determined, inflexible, mulish, obstinate, pigheaded, resistant, resolved, resolute, steadfast, stubborn, unmoving, unyielding *Antonyms:* agreeable, flexible, malleable **6.** early, expectant, on call, prepared, primed, ready, vigilant, waiting, willing *Nonformal:* cocked, teed up – *n.* **1.** alliance, band, circle, class, clique, club, company, contingent, coterie, crew, crowd, division, faction, family, genus, grade, group, ilk, league, order, organization, outfit, pack, party, school, sect, society **2.** assemblage, assortment, batch, body bunch, collection, host, lot, medley, selection, sort **3.** arrangement, array, chain classification, line, parade, progression run, sequence, series, string, succession suite, train **4.** background, locale, *mise en scène (French)*, scene, setting, site, stage **5.** air, appearance, attitude, bearing, carriage, comportment, demeanour, deport ment, fit, form, frame, inclination, look, mien, posture, presence **6.** dangle, drape, hang, lilt, look **7.** decrease, drooping, fading, falling, shrinking, sinking, subsiding, wane **8.** course, direction, drift, motion **9.** cohesion, firmness, fixity, hardness, solidification, stability, stiffness – *v.* **1.** arrange, lay, place, put, position, rest, situate, stand **2.** affix, anchor, apply, embed, fasten, fix, lock, lodge, plant, secure, station, weld **3.** allot, appoint, assign, authorize, choose, confirm, delegate, designate, establish, install, post, prescribe, specify, station **4.** appraise, assess, calculate, estimate, evaluate, gauge, rank, rate, value **5.** adjust, coordinate, harmonize, regulate, standardize, synchronize, true, tune **6.** cake, cement, clot, coagulate, condense, congeal, crystallize, fix, freeze, gel, gelatinize, harden, jell, solidify, stiffen, thicken **7.** display, give, make, offer, perform, present **8.** decline, descend, dip, fall, sink, subside, wane **9.** make ready, mobilize, prepare, stand-by **10.** arrange, author, compose, contrive, forge, pen, score, script, write **11.** block, concoct, create, depict, describe, limn, manufacture, paint **12.** aim, cast, direct, flow, head, lean, make, move, stream, tend, train **13.** agree, iron out *(Nonformal)*, rectify, resolve, settle, solve, straighten out, untangle **14.** arouse, encourage, foment, incite, instigate, provoke **15.** begin, commence, execute, initiate, introduce, originate, raise, start

setback *n.* **1.** blow, defeat, disappointment, loss, misfortune, rebuff, regression, relapse, reverse, upset **2.** bottleneck, delay, difficulty, glitch, hindrance, hitch, holdup, impediment, obstacle, slowdown, snag, stumbling block, trouble

setting *adj.* creeping, descending, drooping, falling, plummeting, sinking, subsiding, waning – *n.* **1.** backdrop, background, decor, *mise en scène (French)*, ornamentation, shoot, stage **2.** arena, circumstance, era, environment, frame, locale, location, period, place, region, site, situation, surroundings, time and place, zone

settle *v.* **1.** adjust, amend, correct, fix, harmonize, reconcile, repair, right, straighten **2.** arbitrate, compromise, decide, determine, judge, negotiate, rule **3.** complete, conclude, dispose of, end, finish, kill off *(Nonformal)*, terminate **4.** allay, assuage, calm, compose, lull, pacify, quell, quiet, reassure, relax **5.** arrest, check, dampen, halt, stem, stop **6.** collapse, decline, descend, fall, flop, gravitate, plop, plunge, precipitate, set, sink, submerge, subside **7.** clarify, clear, refine **8.** clear up, make restitution, pay off *or* up, satisfy, square accounts, vindicate **9.** colonize, dwell, inhabit, live, locate, lodge, occupy, people, populate, reside, roost, take root **10.** cement, compact, firm up, harden, solidify **11.** alight, anchor, establish, land, perch, repose, rest, roost, seat, sit, slump

settlement *n.* **1.** adjustment, agreement, arrangement, bargain, compact, contract, covenant, deal, mise, promise **2.** completion, conclusion, decision, determination, resolution **3.** area, block, camp, commune, community, colony, factory *(Historical)*, fort, hamlet, house, kibbutz, outpost, post, subdivision, town, village **4.** colonization, founding, peopling, placement, populating **5.** compensation, dot, dower, dowry, package, payment, recompense, reimbursement, satisfaction, wergild **6.** covenant house, friendship centre, home, institute, refuge, school, shelter, social settlement, welfare institute

settler *n.* colonist, colonizer, farmer, habitant, homesteader, immigrant, inhabitant, pioneer, resident, squatter

setup *n.* arrangement, construction, design, format, layout, organization, package, pattern, plan, scheme, system *Nonformal:* deal, lay of the land, story

sever *v.* **1.** bisect, break apart, carve, chop, cleave, cut, dissect, divide, guillotine, lop off, rend, slice, split, sunder, tear **2.** alienate, detach, disconnect, separate *Antonyms:* join, merge, unite **3.** break up, dissolve, divorce, estrange, part company *Antonyms:* engage, marry, wed

several *adj.* **1.** assorted, diverse, few, moderate, plural, some, sundry, various **2.** individual, lone, one, private, separate, single, solitary **3.** different, distinct, particular, peculiar, unique

severe *adj.* **1.** demanding, exacting, hard, inflexible, onerous, pitiless, rough, stern, unbending, unsparing *Antonyms:* flexible, lenient, tolerant **2.** agonizing, arduous, backbreaking, difficult, excruciating, extreme, laborious, painful, sobering, strenuous, taxing, torturous, unbearable *Antonyms:* easy, simple, painless **3.** bitter, bleak, blustery, brutal, cold, harsh, inclement, penetrating, piercing, raging, stormy, tempestuous, unrelenting *Antonyms:* calm, light, moderate, pacific **4.** austere, bare, lean, mean, plain, simple, Spartan, stark, stripped, unadorned **5.** accurate, conforming, exact, fastidious, meticulous, rigid, strict *Antonyms:* loose, remiss

severely *adv.* **1.** acutely, badly, critically, dangerously, extremely, fatally, gravely, mortally, seriously **2.** firmly, harshly, painfully, rigorously, roughly, sharply, sternly, strictly, vigorously

severity *n.* **1.** accuracy, attention, conformity, exactness, diligence, discipline, fastidiousness, inflexibility, observance, orthodoxy, rigour, seriousness, strictness, stringency *Antonyms:* carelessness, indifference, negligence **2.** dourness, formality, graveness, gravity, gruffness, heaviness, staidness, sternness, solemnity *Antonyms:* levity, flippancy, silliness **3.** callousness, coldness, cruelty, hardness, harshness, heartlessness, meanness, pitilessness *Antonyms:* grace, kindness **4.** barbarity, bloodshed, brutality, brute force, ferocity, malevolence, murderous intent, rage, vehemence, viciousness *Antonyms:* aid, help, succour **5.** asceticism, austerity, bareness, bleakness, economy, emptiness, plainness, simplicity, spareness, Spartanism, starkness *Antonyms:* complexity, decoration, embellishment

sew *v.* baste, bind, darn, embroider, fasten, make, mend, piece, quilt, repair, seam, stitch, tack, tailor, work

sex *n.* **1.** carnal knowledge, coitus, conjugation, consummation, copulation, fornication, intercourse, intimacy, lovemaking, reproduction, sensuality, sexual relations *Nonformal:* balling, boffing, bouncy-bouncy, humping, it, nookie, quickie, roll in the hay, shagging **2.** category, classification, designation, gender, kind, persuasion, sort

sexism *n.* chauvinism, discrimination, gender discrimination, misanthropy, misogyny, prejudice, women hatred

sexual *adj.* carnal, erogenous, erotic, explicit, fleshly, intimate, loving, passionate, procreative, reproductive, sensual, sexy, venereal, wanton

sexy *adj.* **1.** alluring, arousing, attractive, captivating, charming, provocative, seductive, sensual, sensuous, slinky, suggestive, titillating, voluptuous **2.** erotic, explicit, libidinous, naughty, pornographic, racy, X-rated *Nonformal:* adult, blue, steamy

shabby *adj.* **1.** abandoned, bedraggled, broken-down, crumbling, decayed, decrepit, derelict, deteriorating, dilapidated, dingy, faded, frayed, frowzy, mangy, messy, miserable, moth-eaten, neglected, poor, ragged, ramshackle, rickety, ruined, rundown, scruffy, seedy, shoddy, sleazy, slovenly, sorry, squalid, tattered, tatty, threadbare, tired, torn, unkempt, untended, untidy, worn, wretched *Nonformal:* grubby, grungy, ratty, scummy, scuzzy *Antonyms:* neat, smart, spruce **2.** contemptible, despicable, dirty, disgraceful, disgusting, dishonourable, disreputable, ignominious, low, lowdown, rotten, shady, shameful, sordid *Antonyms:* heroic, honourable, praiseworthy **3.** avaricious, close, close-fisted, meagre, mean, miserly, paltry, parsimonious, pitiful, scanty, sparing, stingy, tight-fisted *Antonyms:* bountiful, generous, liberal

shack *n.* building, bush camp, cabin, cabin à sucre, hovel, hut, ice hut, lean-to, outbuilding, shanty, shed, shelter, sugar shack

shackle *n.* **1.** bilboes *(Historical)*, bracelet, chain, clasp, darbies *(British)*, fasteners, fetters, handcuffs, ring, yoke **2.** brake, deterrent, encumbrance, hindrance, impediment, millstone, obstacle, restraint, restriction – *v.* bind, chain, confine, cuff, fetter, hamper, hobble, impede, manacle, restrain, tie, trammel

shade *n.* **1.** cast, colour, hue, stain, tinge, tint, tone **2.** awning, blind, canopy, cover, covering, curtain, hood, parasol, protection, screen, shelter, sun-screen, umbrella, veil, visor **3.** cloud, darkness, dusk, dimness gloom, murkiness, obscurity, shadow **4.** degree, fraction, hint, iota, minutiae, modicum, nuance, pinch, trace, touch **5.** apparition, bibe *(Newfoundland)*, eidolon, ghost, phantom, spectre, spook *(Nonformal)* – *v.* **1.** adumbrate, becloud, blur, cloud, darken, dim, eclipse, obfuscate, obscure, overcast **2.** blind, camouflage, cloak, conceal, cover, curtain, disguise, protect, screen, shelter, veil, veneer

shadow *n.* **1.** image, outline, silhouette **2.** adumbration, cloudiness, darkness, dimness, duskiness, loom, murk, murkiness, obfuscation, obscurity, twilight, umbrage **3.** dejection, despair, gloom, grief, melancholy, misery, mournfulness, neurasthenia, pall, sadness, sorrow, unhappiness **4.** appearance, bluff, façade, feint, pose, pretense, semblance, simulation **5.** degree, flicker, glimmer, hint, modicum, nuance, ray, remains, remnant, scrap, speck, trace, vestige **6.** bibe *(Newfoundland)*, eidolon, fetch, ghost, phantom, presence, shape, spectre, spirit, vision *Nonformal:* haunt, spook **7.** detective, PI, private investigator, pursuer, spy *Nonformal:* gumshoe, narc, sherlock, tail **8.** bosom buddy, brother, follower, friend, intimate, sister, twin *Nonformal:* alter-ego, appendage, hanger-on, sidekick, stooge – *v.* **1.** dog, follow, hound, pursue, snoop on *(Nonformal)*, spy on, stalk, tag, tail, track, trail, watch **2.** blackout, conceal, cover, darken, dim, eclipse, hide, obscure, overspread, shade **3.** betoken, forebode, foreshadow, foretoken, predict, presage, portend **4.** dampen, depress, discourage, dishearten, dismay, dispirit, sadden, upset *Antonyms:* gladden, inspire, please

shadowy *adj.* **1.** cool, dark, overcast, protected, shady, tenebrous *Antonyms:* bright, scorching, sunny **2.** ambiguous, blurry, confusing, hazy, indefinite, indistinct, murky, mystifying, nebulous, obscure, puzzling, unclear, vague *Antonyms:* lucid, obvious, unequivocal **3.** cobwebbed, creepy, dream-like, eerie, ethereal, ghostly, illusory, incorporeal, spectral, surreal

shady *adj.* **1.** adumbrative, cloudy, covered, dark, dim, dusky, leafy, screened, shaded, shadowed, sheltered *Antonyms:* bright, exposed, sunny **2.** hidden, peaceful, private, quiet, remote, secluded, silent, tranquil *Antonyms:* crowded, loud, rowdy **3.** crooked, disgraceful, dishonest, dishonourable, disreputable, dubious, fishy *(Nonformal)*, fly-by-night, ignominious, infamous, notorious, questionable, scandalous, scrofulous, shameful, shifty, shoddy, sketchy, slippery, sneaky, suspect, suspicious, unethical, untrustworthy *Nonformal: Antonyms:* ethical, honourable, straight, trustworthy, upright

shaft *n.* **1.** cave, excavation, mine, opening, passage, tube, tunnel **2.** arm, bar, baton, cane, grip, handle, hilt, pole, rod, staff, stem, stick **3.** column, cylinder, pier, pile, pillar, post, support **4.** arrow, bola, dart, missile, projectile, spear **5.** cheat, deception, extortion, fraud, hoax, scam, trick *Nonformal:* con, short end – *v.* cheat, defraud, fleece, hoodwink, shortchange, swindle *Nonformal:* chisel, rip off, screw

shaggy *adj.* **1.** bristly, furry, fuzzy, hairy, hirsute, long-haired, setaceous, setiferous, unshaved, unshorn, woolly **2.** dishevelled, disordered, frowzy, ragged, rough, ruffled, rugged, scuzzy *(Nonformal)*, sloppy, slovenly, tousled, uncombed, ungroomed, unkempt, wrinkled *Antonyms:* dapper, neat, spruce

shake *n.* **1.** agitation, concussion, convulsion, disturbance, jolt, movement, pulsation, quaking, quiver, shiver, shock, tremble, vibration **2.** instant, minute, moment, second *Nonformal:* crack, flash, jiffy, sec, wink – *v.* **1.** churn, convulse, flap, flicker, flitter, flutter, jiggle, jostle, jounce, move, oscillate, palpitate, quail, quiver, shimmy, shiver, shudder, stir, swing, tremble, twitter, vibrate, waggle, wave, wiggle **2.** reel, rock, stagger, stumble, sway, totter, wobble **3.** discompose, disturb, floor *(Nonformal)*, jolt, perturb, rattle, rock, shock, unsettle, upset, weaken *Antonyms:* assuage, calm, comfort **4.** agitate, animate, arouse, awaken, challenge, foment, incite, inflame, stimulate, stir up **5.** deke out, dodge, elude, escape, evade, lose **6.** extricate, free, liberate, remove, rid, slough off *(Nonformal)*, throw off

shakeup *n.* radical change, rearrangement, reordering, reorganization, restructuring, revamping, revolution, shuffle, transformation, upheaval

shaky *adj.* **1.** aquiver, fidgety, jelly-like *(Nonformal)*, jittery, nervous, quaking, quavery, skittish, timorous **2.** altering, fluctuating, trembling, tremulant, tremulous, vacillating, wavering, weak *Antonyms:* calm, possessed, strong **3.** dangerous, flimsy, hazardous, insecure, jerry-built, precarious, rickety, tottery, tumble-down, unsound, unstable, unsteady, unsubstantial *Antonyms:* firm, secure, strong **4.** borderline, disputable, doubtful, dubious, problematic, questionable, rocky, tenuous, undependable, unreliable, unsupported *Nonformal:* full of holes, iffy, on the bubble *Antonyms:* authoritative, certain, reliable, true

shallow *adj.* **1.** ankle-deep, flat, impassable *(Nautical)*, surface, thin **2.** all hat and no cattle *(Nonformal)*, bankrupt, cursory, empty, flimsy, frivolous, hollow, insignificant, meaningless, simple, slight, superficial, trifling, trivial, vacuous, vapid *Antonyms:* deep, meaningful, profound **3.** egotistic, inconsiderate, mean, one-dimensional, petty, self-centered, self-serving, small, vain *Antonyms:* outward-looking, worldly – *n.* atoll, bank, bar, ledge, reef, ridge, sandbar, shallows, shoal, surface water

sham *adj.* artificial, bogus, counterfeit, ersatz, fake, false, feigned, forged, fraudulent, imitation, lying, make-believe, misleading, mock, phoney *(Nonformal)*, pretend, simulated, so-called, spurious, synthetic *Antonyms:* legitimate, natural, real, true, veritable – *n.* **1.** cheat, counterfeit, cover-up, deceit, deception, façade, fake, farce, feint, forgery, fraud, hoax, imitation, mock, mockery, pretense, pretext, ruse, spoof, trick, whitewash *Nonformal:* put-on, snow job **2.** carpetbagger, con artist, confidence trickster, criminal, defrauder, diddler, pretender, scoundrel, shammer, sophist, swindler, trickster *Nonformal:* bamboozler, grifter, shark, snake oil salesman – *v.* bluff, counterfeit, deceive, delude, feign, hoax, lie, mislead, pretend, put on, trick *Nonformal:* con, fleece, hoodwink, jive, play possum, scam, screw, shaft, sucker, rip off

shaman *n. angakok (Inuktitut)*, doctor, exorcist, holy man *or* woman, kahuna, magician, medicine man *or* woman, mystic, oracle, priest, *puoin (Native Peoples)*, sorcerer, sorceress, witch doctor, wizard

shambles *n. pl.* **1.** anarchy, bedlam, chaos, confusion, havoc, insanity, madness, mayhem, maelstrom, turmoil, wildness *Antonyms:* order, organization, peace **2.** clutter, disarray, disorder, dump *(Nonformal)*, litter, mess, muddle, pigsty **3.** abattoir, glue factory *(Nonformal)*, killing floor, slaughterhouse

shame *n.* **1.** agony, chagrin, contrition, disgrace, embarrassment, guilt, humiliation, mortification, pain, regret, remorse, repentance, sorrow *Antonyms:* contentedness, satisfaction **2.** degradation, derision, discredit, dishonour, disrepute, ignominy, ill-repute, infamy, obloquy, odium, opprobrium, reproach, scandal, stigma **3.** appropriateness, bashfulness, decency, decorum, dignity, humility, innocence, modesty, virtue – *v.* **1.** abase, abash, debauch, defile, degrade, demean, demoralize, disgrace, dishonour, embarrass, humble, humiliate, mortify, perturb, ridicule, smear, stain, stigmatize, take down, undermine, vitiate, warp, weaken *Nonformal:* dis, put down *Antonyms:* credit, honour, praise **2.** beat, defeat, eclipse, master, outclass, outdo, overcome, overwhelm, pass, rout, vanquish, win *Nonformal:* annihilate, clobber, cream, pummel, squelch, trounce, whip

shameful *adj.* atrocious, bad, base, contemptible, corrupt, dastardly, debauched, degrading, diabolical, disgraceful, dishonourable, disreputable, dreadful, flagrant, frightful, heinous, humiliating, ignominious, immodest, impure, indecent, infamous, lascivious, lecherous, lewd, low, mean, mortifying, notorious, opprobrious, outrageous, profligate, reprehensible, reprobate, scandalous, shocking, sinful, unholy, vile, vulgar, wicked *Antonyms:* admirable, laudable, right, virtuous

shameless *adj.* **1.** audacious, barefaced blatant, blunt, bold, brash, brassy, brazen candid, cheeky, defiant, flagrant, forward frank, glaring, impertinent, impudent incorrigible, insolent, naked, nervy, obvious, open, outrageous, transparent unabashed, unafraid, unashamed, unblush ing *Antonyms:* bashful, sheepish, shy **2.** abandoned, debauched, dissolute, immodest, improper, inappropriate, indecent, intemperate, lascivious, lecherous, lewd, obnoxious, off-colour, shocking, tasteless, unbecoming, unfit, wanton *Antonyms:* acceptable, proper, respectable

hape *n.* **1.** architecture, body, build, character, chassis, configuration, conformation, construction, contour, cut, definition, figure, form, lineation, lines, outline, pattern, profile, relief, shadow, silhouette, structure **2.** appearance, aspect, façade, front, guise, image, likeness, look, pretense, representation, semblance, show **3.** existence, expression, formulation, manifestation, materialization, materiality, practice, reality, realization **4.** condition, constitution, disposition, fettle, fitness, health, order, repair, situation, state, trim, well-being **5.** cast, frame, matrix, model, mould, negative, prototype, template **6.** being, bibe *(Nonformal)*, eidolon, ghost, image, phantom, shade, shadow, wraith – *v.* **1.** build, carve, cast, chisel, construct, craft, create, cut, fabricate, fashion, form, hew, knead, make, manufacture, mint, model, mould, pattern, sculpture, sketch, stamp, turn, whittle **2.** arrange, concoct, contrive, devise, frame, hatch, machinate, plan, prepare, produce, scheme **3.** accommodate, adapt, adjust, change, fix, modify, perfect, streamline, tailor **4.** affect, alter, brainwash, direct, impact, influence, lead, manipulate, move, sway **5.** articulate, define, express, say, utter, verbalize

hapeless *adj.* **1.** amorphous, anomalous, asymmetrical, characterless, formless, indefinite, protean, undeveloped, unformed, unstructured, variform **2.** cloudy, dim, hazy, indistinct, imprecise, loose, nebulous, obscure, undefinable, unspecific, vague *Antonyms:* definite, distinct, precise **3.** abnormal, different, eccentric, ill-defined, ill-fitting, ill-formed, imperfect, irregular, strange, weird

hapely *adj.* **1.** balanced, curved, elegant, graceful, neat, pleasing, proportioned, rounded, sightly, symmetrical, trim, well-formed, well-proportioned, well-rounded, well-turned **2.** alluring, attractive, beautiful, buxom, callipygian, curvaceous, curvy, leggy, slinky, taut *Nonformal:* bodacious, buff, built, pumped, stacked

share *n.* allotment, allowance, apportionment, claim, commission, contribution, cut, dividend, division, due, fraction, helping, issue, lot, margin, measure, parcel, part, percentage, piece, portion, proportion, quota, ration, serving, slice, split, stake, stint *Nonformal:* action, rake-off – *v.* **1.** accord, administer, allot, apportion, assign, bestow, deal, dispense, disseminate, distribute, divide, divvy up *(Nonformal)*, give, part, redistribute, split *Antonyms:* horde, keep, steal **2.** enjoy, hold common, participate *or* revel in, take pleasure

sharp *adj.* **1.** acute, edged, honed, jagged, keen-edged, knife-edged, needle-like, peaked, pointed, prickly, pronged, razor-sharp, rusty, serrated, sharp-edged, sharpened, spiked, tapered, thorny, tined, tipped, whetted *Antonyms:* blunt, dull, edgeless, rounded **2.** alert, astute, brainy *(Nonformal)*, bright, brilliant, canny, clever, discerning, discriminating, ingenious, intelligent, knowing, observant, original, penetrating, perceptive, quick-witted, resourceful, smart, subtle *Antonyms:* dim, dull-witted, obtuse, slow, stupid **3.** agonizing, distressing, disturbing, harrowing, heartbreaking, heart-rending, painful, poignant, sorrowful, stabbing, tear-jerking, tortuous **4.** arctic, blinding, bone-chilling, intense, nippy, numbing, penetrating, piercing, pinching, polar, raw, wicked *(Nonformal)* *Antonyms:* balmy, pleasant, warm **5.** chic, classy, dashing, distinctive, dressy, excellent, fashionable, fine, first-class, in style, natty, smart, stylish, trendy *Nonformal:* cool, snappy, snazzy, spiffy, swank, swish, tony **6.** artful, cagey, conniving, crafty, cunning, deceitful, designing, dishonest, foxy, Machiavellian, oily, shady, shifty, shrewd, slick, slippery, sly, smooth, tricky, unscrupulous, wily *Antonyms:* honest, trustworthy, upright **7.** acidic, acrimonious, angry, barbed, biting, bitter, caustic, critical, cutting, harsh, hurtful, incisive, inconsiderate, offensive, sarcastic, scathing, severe, stinging, trenchant, ungracious, vitriolic *Antonyms:* amicable, courteous, friendly, gentle **8.** clear, coherent, crystalline, distinct, explicit, focused, legible, lucid, plain, precise, pure *Antonyms:*

muddled, obscure, vague **9.** discordant, ear-piercing, ear-splitting, grating, horrible, jangly, metallic, screeching, shrill, strident, thin, tinny, wailing **10.** acrid, astringent, eye-watering, fiery, hot, lemony, piquant, pungent, sour, spicy, strong, tangy, tart, vinegary **11.** ambitious, animated, ardent, avid, eager, enthusiastic, fervent, impassioned, impetuous, keen, lively, spirited, unbridled, unrestrained, vigorous, zealous *Antonyms:* apathetic, cold, distant **12.** abrupt, angular, extreme, precipitous, rapid, sheer, steep, sudden, vertical – *adv.* **1.** accurately, exactly, just, on time, precisely, promptly, punctually, right, squarely *Nonformal:* bang on, smack-dab **2.** abruptly, directly, instantly, suddenly, unanticipatedly, unexpectedly, without warning

sharpen *v.* dress, edge, file, grind, hone, prepare, strop, taper, whet

sharp-tongued *adj.* abusive, acrimonious, acerbic, bitter, caustic, contemptuous, crass, critical, insulting, mocking, obnoxious, offensive, rude, sarcastic, scornful, shrill, trenchant, vitriolic *Antonyms:* civil, courteous, polite

shatter *v.* **1.** break, bust *(Nonformal)*, crack, demolish, disintegrate, explode, fracture, fragment, pulverize, rupture, smash, splinter, trash, wreck **2.** crush, damage, destroy, devastate, disturb, hurt, rattle, ruin, scar, traumatize, upset

shave *n.* **1.** bit, chopping, finger, hunk, part, piece, remnant, scrap, section, shard, shaving, skiver, slab, slice, sliver, snippet, splinter, strip, wedge, whittling **2.** close thing *(Nonformal)*, escape, narrow, near miss – *v.* **1.** clip, crop, cut, excise, groom, mow, trim **2.** ax, carve, cleave, fragment, julienne, pare, prune, shear, shred, skive, slice, whittle **3.** contact, glance off, graze, kiss, nick, scrape, skim, skin, touch **4.** decrease, devalue, discount, lessen, lower, mark down, reduce

sheaf *n.* bale, bunch, bundle, cluster, collection, group, pack, selection, shock, stack, stook

shed *n.* barn, building, covering, hangar, hut, kiosk, lean-to, outbuilding, outhouse, shack, shanty, shelter, stall, storehouse – *v* **1.** diffuse, drip, drop, effuse, emanate emit, exude, ooze, radiate, rain, secrete spill, splash **2.** bead away, check, hold *o* keep off, rebuff, reject, repulse, resist withstand **3.** divest, peel off, remove, strip undress **4.** cast off, disburden, disencum ber, discard, drop, dump, jettison, junk throw away *or* out, toss, unload

sheen *n.* brightness, burnish, finish, flash glaze, gleam, glint, glisten, glitz *(Nonfor mal)*, gloss, light, luminosity, lustre, patina polish, radiance, reflection, shimmer shine, sparkle *Antonyms:* dullness, flat ness, matte

sheepish *adj.* **1.** abashed, ashamed, cha grined, conscience-stricken, contrite embarrassed, foolish, guilty, mortified, red faced, regretful, remorseful, repentant shamefaced *Antonyms:* confident, intract able, unapologetic **2.** awkward, diffident introverted, mousy, nervous, retiring self-conscious, shy, timid, timorous, uncer tain, uncomfortable *Antonyms:* assertive bold, brash, brazen

sheer *adj.* **1.** abrupt, angled, ascending breakneck, declivitous, dizzying, elevated erect, extreme, falling, high, obliquitous precipitous, raised, rising, sharp, sloping steep, upright *Antonyms:* gentle, gradual horizontal, moderate **2.** absolute, com plete, downright, pure, rank, refined, stark thorough, total, unadulterated, uncondi tional, unmitigated, untainted, utter *Anto nyms:* extenuated, moderated, tempered **3** airy, chiffon, clear, cobwebby, delicate diaphanous, filmy, fine, flimsy, fragile gauzy, gossamer, lacy, limpid, pellucid see-through, slight, thin, translucent, trans parent *Antonyms:* coarse, heavy, thick – *v* curve, deviate, diverge, shift, swerve, turn vary, veer

sheet *n.* **1.** bedclothes, bedding, bedspread counterpane, linen, sheeting **2.** cut, pane panel, plate, ply, rectangle, roll, slab square **3.** folio, leaf, page, piece, recto spread, verso **4.** coat, cover, film, finish foil, lamina, layer, membrane, overlay veneer **5.** area, blanket, expanse, extent field, flat, sea, stratum, stretch, surface sweep **6.** advertisement, broadsheet, flyer gazette, journal, newspaper, paper, periodical, rag *(Nonformal)*, serial, tabloid, trade paper **7.** canvas, jib, muslin, rigging *See also:* **sail**

shelf *n.* **1.** board, case, ledge, mantle, platform, projection, slab, step **2.** arrangement, assortment, cluster, collection, group, quantity, number, selection, stack, stock, store **3.** atoll, bar, flat, reef, ridge, sandbar, shallow, shoal

shell *n.* **1.** armour, carapace, case, casing, conch, covering, cowry, crust, exoskeleton, exterior, frame, hull, husk, lid, lorica, peel, plate, pod, protection, rind, scute, seashell, sheath, shelter, shield, shuck, skin, surface **2.** anatomy, body, carriage, chassis, form, framework, shape, skeleton, structure **3.** ammunition, bullet, cap, cartouche, cartridge, cassette, cylinder, missile, projectile, shot **4.** relic, remainder, reminder, remnant, semblance, sign, token, trace, vestige, wreck – *v.* **1.** bark, expose, hull, husk, peel, pod, shuck, skin, unfold, unwrap **2.** attack, barrage, batter, beset, blitz, bomb, fire upon, gun down, hit, mortar, pepper, pound, shellac *(Nonformal)*, shoot, strafe, torpedo

shelter *n.* **1.** accommodation, address, apartment, barracks, cabana, camboose, camp, condo, cote, croft, domicile, duplex, dwelling, fireside, flat, habitat, hermitage, home, hut, igloo, lean-to, lodge, quarters, quinzhee, Quonset hut, residence, roof, roost, shack, shanty, shieling, snug, teepee, tent, trailer, wigwam *Nonformal:* nest, pad *See also:* **house** **2.** asylum, cover, harbour, haven, hideaway, oasis, port, protection, refuge, resort, retreat, safety, sanctuary, screen, snuggery **3.** armed guard, bodyguard, chaperone, convoy, escort, guardian, hired thug *(Nonformal)*, protector, security – *v.* conceal, cover, defend, enclose, guard, hide, house, lodge, protect, safeguard, screen, secure, shield, surround, watch over *Antonyms:* endanger, expose, hazard, imperil, risk

shelve *v.* **1.** carry, display, lay in, load up, market, offer, replenish, retail, sell, stack, stock, stockpile, store, supply, vend, wholesale, warehouse **2.** cool, defer, delay, dismiss, drop, freeze, hold off *or* up, postpone, scrub, stay, suspend, waive **3.** discharge, dismiss, fire, layoff, retire, superannuate *Nonformal:* ax, boot, can, downsize, pink slip, sack, send packing, streamline

shenanigans *n. pl.* antics, buffoonery, capers, dalliances, deviltry, escapades, folly, foxiness, frivolity, fun, hijinks, jest, jocularity, mischief, nonsense, practical jokes, pranks, silliness, sport, stunts, tomfoolery *Nonformal:* hanky-panky, horseplay, kibitzing, no good, monkey business, monkeyshines

shepherd *n.* **1.** custodian, defender, guardian, keeper, herder, herdsman, patron, protector, provider, safeguard, shepherdess **2.** church man *or* woman, clergyman, clergywoman, curate, deacon, elder, evangelist, father, guide, guru, leader, minister, missionary, padre, parson, person of God, person of the cloth, preacher, priest, proselytizer, rabbi, reverend – *v.* conduct, convey, direct, escort, guard, herd, look after, marshal, mind, pilot, protect, shelter, shield, steer, support, sustain, tend, usher, watch over

shield *n.* **1.** aegis, armament, armour, buckler, deflector, mail, pavis, scutum, target *Hockey:* cage, mask, visor **2.** buffer, bulwark, bumper, coat, covering, curtain, defence, fortification, guard, protection, rampart, roof, safeguard, screen, security, sheath, shelter, strategic defence initiative *or* Star Wars, veil, wall **3.** badge, ceremonial badge, coat of arms, crest, emblem, escutcheon, flag, heraldry, identification, label, lozenge, scutcheon, sign – *v.* bulwark, cover, defend, deflect, fend off, give cover, guard, harbour, plate, protect, safeguard, safe-house

shift *n.* **1.** changeover, exchange, relay, replacement, substitution, switch over, transference **2.** change, deviation, divergence, fluctuation, swerve, variation, veering **3.** artifice, contrivance, craft, device, dodge, equivocation, expediency, gambit, makeshift, manoeuvre, move, ploy, recourse, ruse, stratagem, strategy, trick, wile **4.** bout, go, period, span, spell, stint, stretch, time, tour, turn – *v.* **1.** change, depart from, deviate, dial back *(Nonformal)*, diverge, move, swerve, swing, tack, twist, turn, vary, veer **2.** alter, exchange, flip, morph *(Nonformal)*, relay, replace, shuffle, substitute, swap, switch, transmogrify, transfer, transpose, turn over **3.** avoid, bypass, circumvent, confound, dodge, equivocate, escape, flip-flop, evade, fluctuate, hedge, shilly-shally, vacillate, waffle *Nonformal:* deke out, dipsy-doodle

shiftless *adj.* apathetic, careless, delinquent, derelict, idle, inactive, indifferent, indolent, inefficient, lackadaisical, lazy, listless, negligent, remiss, slack, slothful, unambitious, undependable, unenterprising, unreliable, worthless *Antonyms:* ambitious, energetic, industrious

shifty *adj.* cagey, conniving, contriving, crafty, crooked, cunning, deceitful, devious, dishonest, dodging, duplicitous, elusive, equivocating, evasive, foxy, fraudulent, furtive, insidious, lubricous, lying, mendacious, scheming, shady, sketchy, slippery, sly, sneaky, tricky, underhanded, unscrupulous, untrustworthy, untruthful, wily *Antonyms:* dependable, guileless, honest, open, reliable

shilly-shally *v.* **1.** fluctuate, hem and haw, hesitate, pause, seesaw, vacillate, wax and wane *Nonformal:* blow hot and cold, fence-sit **2.** dawdle, delay, idle, linger, loiter, ponder, procrastinate, stall, tarry, wait, waste time, trifle *Nonformal:* dilly-dally, fool *or* screw around

shimmer *n.* coruscation, diffused light, flash, flicker, foxfire, gleam, glimmer, glistening, glitter, gloss, glow, incandescence, iridescence, lustre, phosphorescence, scintillation, sheen, trace – *v.* blaze, coruscate, dance, flare, flash, flicker, gleam, glint, glisten, glow, phosphoresce, scintillate, shine, sparkle, twinkle

shindig *n.* affair, ball, barn dance, bash, blowout *(Nonformal)*, ceilidh, celebration, *champêtre (Quebec)*, clambake, dance, dinner dance, fancy-dress ball, festivity, fête, fiesta, gala, hop, levee, masquerade, party, prom, revelry, shivaree, soiree *See also:* **party**

shine *n.* **1.** brightness, brilliance, glow, illumination, lustre, radiance, refulgence, sheen, shimmer, splendour **2.** clemency, cloudlessness, fairweather, high skies, heat, light, summer, sunshine *Antonyms:* cloud cover, gloom, overcast **3.** attraction, craving, fancy, fondness, hankering, liking, partiality, predilection, soft spot *(Nonformal)*, yearning – *v.* **1.** brush, buff, burnish, finish, furbish, glaze, gloss, lacquer, polish, rub, scour, shine, sleek, varnish, wax **2.** beam, bedazzle, blaze, blink, burn, dazzle, deflect, flare, flash, flicker, glare, gleam, glimmer, glisten, glitter, glow, illuminate, light up, luminesce, mirror, radiate, reflect, scintillate, shimmer, sparkle, twinkle **3.** cap, come through, excel, outclass, outdo, outperform, outshine, outstrip, predominate, top *Antonyms:* choke, crumble, fail, stumble

shiny *adj.* **1.** aglow, brilliant, burnished, glistening, glossy, glowing, lustrous, polished, reflective, shining, sparkling *Antonyms:* dull, flat, matte **2.** blazing, bright, cloudless, fair, light, radiant, sunny, unshaded *Antonyms:* dark, cloudy, overcast

ship *n.* argosy, boat, caravel, craft, vehicle, vessel *Nonformal:* saltie, tub *Kinds of ships:* aircraft carrier, barge, bark, barkentine, battleship, bean-cod, brigantine, caravel, cargo, chasse-marée, clipper, container, corsair, corvette, cruise, cutter, decoy, destroyer, dinghy, dogger, dredge, felucca, fishing boat, freighter, frigate, galleon, galliot, gig, jolly, ketch, launch, liner, lugger, man-of-war, merchantman, ocean liner, oceanographic research vessel, oil tanker, paddle boat *or* steamer *or* wheeler, polacca, roll-on roll-off, ro-ro, sack, schooner, side-wheeler, ship of the line, sloop, square rigger, steamship, sternwheeler, submarine, supertanker, tall, tanker, three-master, trawler, tugboat, war ship, whaler, windjammer, xebec *See also:* **boat** – *v.* **1.** address, cart, consign, convey, courier, deliver, direct, dispatch, export, forward, freight, haul, issue, mail, move, package, post, remit, route, send, smuggle, transfer, transmit, transport **2.** board, depart, embark, emigrate, escape, flee, go, leave, migrate, set sail, weigh anchor

shirk *v.* avoid, cheat, deke out *(Nonformal)*, dodge, duck, elude, eschew, evade, parry quit, shun, sidestep, sneak out *Antonyms:* confront, face, fulfill

shirker *n.* dodger, floater, good-for-nothing, idler, malingerer, slacker *Nonformal:* bum, clock-watcher, clog, couch potato, deadwood, dog, goldbricker, goof-off, lazybones, slider, slug

shirt *n.* clothing, garment, outerwear *Kinds of shirt:* basque, blouse, body, button-down, camisole, collarless, dashiki, dinner jacket *(Nonformal)*, doublet, dress, evening, flannel, fleece, golf, hair, halter, Hawaiian, jean, Kenora, lumberjack, middy blouse, mohair, overblouse, polo, polyester, shift, shirt coat, shirtwaist, short-sleeved, silk, sleeveless, smock, sport, sweatshirt, tank top, tee-shirt, turtleneck, undershirt, V-neck, workshirt

shiver *n.* flutter, frisson, goosebumps, gooseflesh, goose pimples, palpitation, shaking, trembling – *v.* flutter, palpitate, pulsate, quake, quaver, quiver, shake, shudder, tremble, tremor, twitter, vibrate

shoal *n.* **1.** atoll, bank, bar, ledge, reef, ridge, sandbank, sandbar, shallow **2.** assemblage, bevy, body, flock, herd, host, huddle, league, mass, multitude, myriad, school, scrum, swarm, throng

shock *n.* **1.** fright, jolt, scare, shocker, surprise *Nonformal:* bomb, eye-opener, thunderbolt, wake-up call **2.** bad news, blow, calamity, catastrophe, disappointment, disaster, disillusionment, distress, disturbance, letdown, loss, misfortune, pain, setback, sorrow, tragedy, turn **3.** battle fatigue, breakdown, catalepsy, collapse, daze, illness, paralysis, seizure, sickness, spasm, stroke, trauma **4.** bump, clash, concussion, crash, head-on, impact, jarring, smash **5.** aftershock, earthquake, oscillation, pulsation, quake, seismic convulsion *or* disturbance, tremor, undulation, vibration **6.** bunch, cluster, knot, tangle – *v.* **1.** appall, astound, awe, confound, daze, disturb, frighten, horrify, jar, jolt, numb, offend, outrage, repulse, revolt, scandalize, sicken, stagger, startle, stun, stupefy, surprise, traumatize, unruffle *Nonformal:* bowl *or* knock over, flabbergast, floor, scarify *Antonyms:* pacify, quiet, soothe **2.** agitate, convulse, jiggle, oscillate, quake, shake, undulate, vibrate *Antonyms:* arrest, check, stabilize, stop **3.** charge, electrify *Nonformal:* fry, juice, plug in, zap

shocking *adj.* **1.** abominable, appalling, atrocious, awful, detestable, disgraceful, disgusting, disquieting, distressing, dreadful, egregious, foul, frightful, ghastly, glaring, gruesome, hateful, heinous, hideous, horrible, horrific, loathsome, lurid, monstrous, nauseating, obnoxious, odious, offensive, outrageous, repulsive, revolting, scandalous, shameful, sickening, terrible, ugly, unspeakable *Antonyms:* attractive, beautiful, wholesome **2.** astonishing, amazing, extraordinary, eye-popping *(Nonformal)*, jarring, mind-boggling, staggering, startling, striking, stupefying, surprising, unprecedented *Antonyms:* boring, dull, everyday

shoddy *adj.* **1.** base, below the mark, cheap, common, crappy *(Nonformal)*, cut-rate, inferior, jerry-built, junky, makeshift, mean, poor, ramshackle, second-rate, shabby, shaganappi, slipshod, ticky-tacky, trashy *Antonyms:* choice, first-class, quality, superior **2.** artificial, bogus, counterfeit, fake, false, fraudulent, imitation, mock, phoney *(Nonformal)*, sham, simulated *Antonyms:* authentic, real, veritable

shoe *n.* boot, footwear, sandal, slipper, sneaker *(Nonformal) Kinds of shoe:* aerobic, athletic, ballet slippers, basketball, boat, bowling, brogan, brogue, buskin, button, cleats, clodhopper, clog, crampon, Cuban heel, docksider, dress, duck, espadrille, flat, flip-flop, gaiter, galoshes, golf, gym, high heel, huarache, jogging, larrigan, leather, loafer, moccan *(Atlantic Provinces)*, moccasin, Oxford, patent leather, platforms, plimsoll, ruby slipper, Roman sandal, running, saddle, sandal, seaboot, shoepack, slip-on, snowshoe, spectator pumps, spike *or* stiletto heel, thong, toe rubbers, track, wing-tipped, wooden, work *See also:* **boot**

shoot *n.* **1.** branch, bud, growth, offshoot, runner, scion, slip, stem, stock, sucker, tendril, twig **2.** chase, competition, fox hunt, hunting party, match, outing, pursuit, safari, stalk, war game **3.** cinematography, filming, filmmaking, photography, production, session – *v.* **1.** cripple, damage, dispatch, execute, gun down, hit, injure, kill, maim, pick off, wound *Nonformal:* bump off, chill, dust, erase, ice, liquidate, neutralize, off, plug, pop, smoke, snuff, waste, wipe out **2.** barrage, blast, bombard, cast, catapult, discharge, expel, explode, fire, fling, gun, launch, open fire, project, propel, pump, send, shell, slap, strafe, throw, torpedo **3.** bolt, dart, gallop, hurry, hurtle, run, rush, scoot, speed, spurt, streak, tear, whiz *(Nonformal)* **4.** chase, hunt, pursue, stalk, tail *(Nonformal)*, track, trail **5.** capture, chronicle, document, film, photograph, record, snap *(Nonformal)*, tape, videotape **6.** navigate, negotiate, pass *or* plunge *or* sail *or* skip over, skim across **7.** emit, exude, give off, radiate, send forth, spill, vomit **8.** begin, burgeon, evolve, germinate, grow, mushroom, root, sprout, take

shop *n.* **1.** bazaar, boutique, business, bodega, convenience *or* department store, deli, *dépanneur (Quebec)*, e-business, emporium, firm, groceteria, mall, market, mom-and-pop *(Nonformal)*, outlet, retailer, stall, stand, store, supermarket **2.** craftshop, Dickensian workhouse *(Nonformal)*, factory, foundry, garage, manufactory, mill, sweatshop, studio, works, workshop – *v.* browse, buy, check out, get, hunt *or* look for, obtain, purchase, web *or* window shop

shopkeeper *n.* dealer, distributor, grocer, merchant, middleman, middleperson, monger, provisioner, retailer, salesperson, victualer, storekeeper, tradesperson

shopworn *adj.* **1.** damaged, dilapidated, dirty, dogeared, faded, frayed, handled, ill-used, soiled, sullied, tarnished, worn *Antonyms:* mint, new, tip-top **2.** banal, clichéd, everyday, hackneyed, old, overused, routine, stale, stereotypical, threadbare, tired, trite *Antonyms:* fresh, novel

shore *adj.* aquatic, coastal, limicoline, littoral, marine, sea, water – *n.* bank, beach, beachfront, border, brim, brink, coast, coastland, earth, embankment, inshore, lakeshore, landwash *(Newfoundland)*, lido, mud flat, panhandle, *playa (Spanish)*, riverbank, riverside, riviera, sand, seaboard, seacoast, seashore, strand, waterfront, waterside *French:* côte, plage – *v.* bear up, bolster, brace, bulwark, buttress, carry, hold, prop, reinforce, shield, strengthen, support, sustain, underpin

short *adj.* **1.** compact, diminutive, dumpy, dwarfish, Lilliputian, little, low, midget, petite, runty, skimpy, slight, small, squat, stubby, stunted, tiny, undersized, wee *Nonformal:* pint-sized, pocket-sized, sawed-off *Antonyms:* high, lanky, lofty, tall **2.** abbreviated, abridged, compressed, concentrated, concise, condensed, laconic, pithy, pointed, precise, succinct, summarized, terse *Antonyms:* diffused, extended, long **3.** brief, ephemeral, evanescent, fleeting, momentary, passing, short-lived, temporary, transient, transitory *Antonyms:* ageless, permanent, stable **4.** bankrupt, behind, broke, busted *(Nonformal)*, destitute, down-and-out, failing, in the red, indigent, needy, poor, wanting, without *Antonyms:* flush, loaded, rich **5.** deficient, inadequate, insufficient, lacking, meagre, scant, scanty, scarce, shy, sparse *Antonyms:* abundant, plentiful **6.** abrupt, blunt, brusque, cross, curt, gruff, irascible, petulant, short-tempered, snappy, snippy, testy, unceremonious *Antonyms:* civil, courteous, polite **7.** insular, limited, myopic, narrow, parochial, provincial, restricted, shallow, short-sighted *Antonyms:* eclectic, liberal, worldly **8.** breakable, brittle, crisp, crumbly, flaky, frangible, friable *Antonyms:* elastic, flexible, resilient – *adv.* **1.** bad temperedly, brusquely, crossly, curtly, tersely, sharply **2.** inadequately, incompletely, insufficiently, partially, partly – *n.* **1.** cinema, documentary, film, motion picture, movie, music video, narrative, newsreel, preview, trailer, vignette **2.** centre, core, essence, gist, heart, marrow, meaning, pith

shortage *n.* dearth, deficiency, deficit, inadequacy, insufficiency, lack, leanness, limitation, need, paucity, pinch, poverty, scantiness, scarcity, shortfall, tightness, want *Antonyms:* abundance, excess, plethora, profusion, surplus

shortcoming *n.* blemish, defect, deficiency drawback, failing, fault, flaw, imperfection lapse, sin, weakness *Nonformal:* bug, catch *Antonyms:* advantage, merit, strength virtue

shorten *v.* **1.** abbreviate, abridge, abstract, boil down *(Nonformal)*, compress, concentrate, condense, contract, deduct, digest, edit, limit, minimize, subtract, summarize, truncate *Antonyms:* append, expand, extend, protract, stretch **2.** chop, crop, curtail, cut, decrease, diminish, dock, lessen, lop, pare, prune, reduce, shear, slash, snip, trim

short-lived *adj.* brief, disappearing, ephemeral, evanescent, fleeting, impermanent, meteoric, momentary, passing, short-haul, short-run, short-term, temporary, transient, transitory *Antonyms:* durable, enduring, eternal, lasting, permanent

shortly *adv.* **1.** anon, before long, by and by, directly, forthwith, presently, promptly, quickly, right off, soon *Antonyms:* later, never **2.** briefly, concisely, pointedly, succinctly, tersely **3.** abrasively, abruptly, brusquely, curtly, gruffly, nastily, rudely, sharply, testily

short-sighted *adj.* **1.** careless, dimwitted, dumb, foolish, ill-considered, imperceptive, improvident, imprudent, injudicious, rash, senseless, silly, stupid, thoughtless, unthinking, unwise *Antonyms:* farsighted, prudent, sagacious **2.** dim-sighted, myopic, near-sighted, vision-impaired

short-tempered *adj.* abrupt, acrimonious, bearish, biting, brusque, cantankerous, caustic, choleric, crabby, cranky, crusty, curt, cutting, discourteous, edgy, explosive, fiery, grouchy, gruff, impatient, impolite, irascible, mordant, peevish, petulant, rude, sarcastic, sharp, shirty, short-fused, sour, splenetic, stern, sullen, surly, tart, testy, thorny, touchy, trenchant, volatile, volcanic, waspish *Antonyms:* calm, gracious, polite

shot *adj.* **1.** beat, broken, done, exhausted, fatigued, finished, spent, tired, wearied, worn-out *Nonformal:* burnt, bushed, dead, dog-tired, down-for-the-count, fagged, fried, played out, pooped, ruined, toast, whacked **2.** down *(Nonformal)*, hit, hurt, injured, pierced, wounded – *n.* **1.** ammunition, B.B., ball, birdshot, buckshot, bullet, cartridge, dart, discharge, lead, missile, pellet, projectile, slug **2.** blow, clap, cuff, forearm shiver, hit, jab, punch, sallywinder, slug, stroke, thwack *(Nonformal) Kinds of hockey shot:* backhand, cannonading drive *(Nonformal)*, deflection, flip, one-timer, slapshot, snap, sweep, wrist **3.** bang, blast, boom, detonation, discharge, explosion, fusillade, peal **4.** attempt, chance, effort, endeavour, go, hope, occasion, opening, opportunity, stab, turn, try *Nonformal:* break, crack, fling, whack **5.** assumption, conjecture, estimate, guess, guesstimate *(Nonformal)*, hypothesis, opinion, prediction, supposition, thought, view **6.** image, keepsake, memory, photo, photograph, picture, record, snap, snapshot, still **7.** bracer, drink, guzzle, jigger, nip, pull, sip, sup, spot, swallow, taste, tot *Nonformal:* courage, eye-opener, finger or two, gargle, hair of the dog, jolt, pick-me-up, slug, snort, swig **8.** booster, fix *(Nonformal)*, hypodermic, injection, inoculation, needle, vaccine **9.** *artigliere (Italian)*, crack shot *(Nonformal)*, gunman, hunter, marksman, rifleman, sharpshooter, sniper **10.** cheap shot, comment, crack, dig, disparagement, insult, jab, Parthian shot, poke, quip, remark, return, wisecrack, witticism, zinger *(Nonformal)*

shoulder *n.* **1.** abutment, brace, buttress, lodge, projection, protrusion, shelf, support **2.** ball and socket, blade, bone, deltoid muscle, joint, scapula **3.** berm, ditch, edge, margin, shore, side, verge – *v.* **1.** accept, assume, back, bear, carry, embrace, sustain, tolerate, tote, undertake, withstand *Antonyms:* escape, forgo, pass **2.** bolster, brace, hold, prop, reinforce, strengthen, support **3.** clear away, elbow, hit, hustle, jostle, knock, nudge, press, push, push aside, shove, thrust

shout *n.* bark, call, cheer, clamour, cry, howl, hue, outcry, scream, shriek, squawk, uproar, vociferation, yawp *Antonyms:* murmur, susurrus, whisper – *v.* audibilize *(Football)*, bawl, bay, bellow, call *or* cry out, exclaim, holler, roar, screech, squall, vociferate, whoop, yammer, yap, yell *Antonyms:* mumble, mutter

shove *n.* jostling, nudge, prod, propulsion, push, thrust – *v.* bulldoze *(Nonformal)*, cram, crowd, dig, dragoon, drive, elbow, goad, hustle, impel, jab, jostle, nudge, press, prod, propel, push, shoulder, thrust

shovel *n.* backhoe, Bobcat *(Trademark)*, bulldozer, digger *(Nonformal)*, excavator, plow, scoop, spade, spudbar, trowel – *v.* dig up, dredge, excavate, exhume, furrow, gouge, groove, heap, ladle, load, move, scoop, shift, spade, spoon, spud, toss, trench

show *n.* **1.** act, burlesque, carnival, cinema, comedy, contest, demonstration, drama, entertainment, exhibition, expo, exposition, fair, harlequinade, masque, motion picture, movie, pageant, pantomime, performance, picture, play, presentation, production, reading, showboat, spectacle, theatre, viewing **2.** appearance, disclosure, emergence, epiphany, flash, manifestation, materialization, revelation, unveiling **3.** affectation, air, cloak, cover, display, fake, false face *or* front, guise, impression, pretense, veneer **4.** all hat and no cattle *(Nonformal)*, eye candy, fanfare, flamboyance, foppery, garishness, magnificence, ostentation, pomp, pretentiousness, vainglory **5.** hint, indication, inkling, promise, semblance, sign, sprinkling, touch, trace, vestige – *v.* **1.** appear, arise, display, emerge, expose, loom, manifest, materialize *Antonyms:* cover, disappear, hide **2.** ballyhoo, champion, endorse, exhibit, flaunt, introduce, market, present, promote, publicize, sell, showcase, unveil, vaunt **3.** delineate, demarcate, denote, gauge, indicate, mark, measure, point to, read, represent, state **4.** arrive, attend, call, come, pop *or* show *or* turn up, surface, visit **5.** accord, afford, bestow, confer, forward, furnish, give, grant, permit, proffer, render, set forth **6.** clarify, edify, elucidate, explain, explicate, illustrate, inform, instruct, reveal, spell out, teach, tell **7.** argue, authenticate, certify, confirm, convince, demonstrate, establish, influence, persuade, plead, prove, settle, substantiate, sway, validate, verify *Antonyms:* contradict, discredit, negate **8.** accompany, chaperon, conduct, escort, guide, lead, pilot, safeguard, steer, usher

showdown *n.* battle, clash, climax, competition, confrontation, crisis, face-off, finale, game seven, overtime *Nonformal:* breaking point, rubber match, sudden death

shower *n.* **1.** cloudburst, downpour, drizzle, hail, misting, precipitation, rainfall, sleet, spattering, spitting, sprinkling, sun shower, torrent **2.** avalanche, barrage, bombardment, deluge, flood, fusillade, gushing, inundation, overflow, pouring, salvo, spate, spray, stream, volley **3.** ablution *(Nonformal)*, bath, cleaning, cleansing, clean-up, douche, hosing, rinsing, wash **4.** abundance, bounty, copiousness, excess, extravagance, oversupply, plenty, plethora, profusion, superabundance, superfluity, surfeit, surplus, wealth *Antonyms:* absence, dearth, deficiency, lack **5.** baby *or* bridal shower, celebration, ceremony, exchange, farewell, fête, gathering, get-together, gift-giving, party, shivaree *Nonformal:* jack and jill, stagette **6.** nozzle, pipe, showerhead, sprayer, sprinkler, stall – *v.* **1.** descend, deluge, dribble, drizzle, drown, fall, flood, gush, hail, piss *(Nonformal)*, rain, snow, spatter, spit, spray, sprinkle, trickle **2.** bathe, clean, cleanse, douche, douse, refresh, rinse, sanitize, scrub, shampoo, soap-up, spruce up *(Nonformal)*, swab, wash, wet **3.** attack, bomb, bombard, fire upon, launch, pelt, pepper, pound, shell, storm, strafe, volley **4.** bestow, give, inundate, lavish, overwhelm, pamper, provide, spoil *Antonyms:* ignore, neglect, spurn

showoff *n.* boaster, braggadocio, braggart, dandy, egotist, exhibitionist, maw-mouth *(Newfoundland)*, swaggerer *Nonformal:* big mouth, blowhard, cock of the walk, grandstander, hot dog, hot shot, showboat

showy *adj.* **1.** flamboyant, flashy, garish, gaudy, loud, meretricious, ornate, overdone, tawdry *Nonformal:* obnoxious, screaming *Antonyms:* muted, restrained **2.** affected, artificial, flowery, grandiloquent, high-flown, ostentatious, pompous, pretentious, specious, theatrical *Nonformal:* all hat and no cattle, hammy *Antonyms:* modest, plain, simple

shred *n.* atom, bit, crumb, fragment, grain, iota, jot, modicum, ounce, part, particle, piece, remnant, scintilla, scrap, shard, sliver, smidgen, snippet, speck, tatter, trace, whit – *v.* **1.** cut, demolish, destroy, fray, frazzle, reduce, shave, skive, sliver, strip, tatter, tear **2.** abuse, attack, chastise, chide, criticize, deflate, degrade, demean, diminish, humiliate, lambaste, ridicule, scorn *Nonformal:* burn, dis, knock, pan, slam, trash *Antonyms:* compliment, encourage, support

shrew *n.* fury, hag, harridan, nag, scold, termagant, virago, vixen, witch *Nonformal:* ball-and-chain, battle-axe

shrewd *adj.* **1.** astute, bright, clever, discerning, discriminating, farsighted, ingenious, intelligent, judicious, keen, knowing, penetrating, perceptive, perspicacious, sagacious, sensible, sharp, smart, wise *Antonyms:* artless, dull, gullible, imprudent, ingenuous **2.** artful, cagey, calculating, canny, crafty, cunning, designing, foxy, Machiavellian, political, scheming, slick, slippery, sly, smooth, subtle, tricky, wily *Antonyms:* foolish, innocent, naive

shrewish *adj.* abusive, awful, bilious, bitter, cantankerous, captious, choleric, cranky, crotchety, frightful, ill-humoured, impossible, irritable, miserable, nagging, offensive, petulant, scolding, sharp, shrill, snarling, sour, splenetic, ugly, vitriolic *Antonyms:* ingratiating, lovely, pleasant

shriek *n. & v.* blare, cry, howl, scream, screech, shout, squawk, squeal, wail, whoop, yell

shrill *adj.* **1.** acute, blaring, blatant, cacophonous, clanging, clangorous, deafening, discordant, dissonant, ear-piercing, harsh, high-pitched, jangly, metallic, noisy, penetrating, piercing, piping, raucous, screeching, sharp, strident, thin, treble *Antonyms:* deep, dulcet, mellifluous, silver-tongued, soft **2.** delirious, distraught, emotional, excited, frenetic, hysterical, over the top *(Nonformal)*, panicky, unreasoning, unrestrained *Antonyms:* calm, impassive, thoughtful

shrine *n.* **1.** altar, basilica, cathedral, chapel, church, house of God, temple *Buddhist:* kaaba, stupa, tope **2.** crypt, grave, hallowed *or* holy *or* sacred place, mausoleum, memorial, reliquary, sanctum, sepulchre **3.** exemplar, ideal, jewel, monument, touchstone, treasure

shrink *v.* **1.** abate, abbreviate, attenuate, bind, compact, compress, constrict, contract, cramp, curtail, decrease, diminish, lessen, recede, reduce, retract, shorten, shrivel, squeeze, thin *Antonyms:* bulge, expand, swell **2.** cower, cringe, crouch, draw back, flinch, jump, quail, quiver, recoil, retire, retreat, shy away, wince, withdraw, wither *Antonyms:* challenge, confront, welcome

shrinkage *n.* abbreviation, attenuation, compression, contraction, curtailment, decrease, deflation, deprecation, diminishing, edit, lessening, loss, reduction, shortening, squeezing, theft *Antonyms:* dilation, expansion, growth

shrivel *v.* burn, dehydrate, desiccate, dry up, mummify, parch, scorch, shrink, wilt, wither, wizen, wrinkle

shroud *n.* **1.** burial cloth, cerecloth, pall, sheet, winding sheet, wrapper **2.** blanket, cloak, covering, garment, mantle, poncho, screen, shield, veil – *v.* **1.** clothe, cover, drape, enshroud, ensconce, envelop, enwrap, invest, jacket, sheathe, sheet, surround, wrap **2.** camouflage, cloak, conceal, cover, disguise, encrypt, hide, protect, screen, shade, shield, veil *Antonyms:* exhibit, expose, reveal

shrouded *adj.* arcane, camouflaged, coded, cryptic, dark, disguised, ensconced, hidden, masked, mysterious, obscure, surrounded, unclear, veiled, wrapped *Antonyms:* clear, exposed, open, patent

shrub *n.* bush, bramble, brier, brush, perennial, plant, scrub, shrubbery, topiary *See also:* **plant**

shrunken *adj.* **1.** abbreviated, compressed, contracted, cut, decreased, reduced, short, squeezed *Antonyms:* bloated, diluted, swelled **2.** atrophied, cadaverous, dehydrated, desiccated, deteriorated, diseased, dried, faded, gaunt, shrivelled, withered

shudder *n.* convulsion, flutter, frisson, palpitation, quaking, quiver, shake, shiver, tremor – *v.* convulse, gyrate, jitter, quake, quiver, shake, shimmy, shiver, tremble *Commonly misused:* **shutter**

shuffle *n.* **1.** alteration, change, mix-up, switch, transition, transposition, variation **2.** artifice, camouflage, device, dodge, escape, evasiveness, feint, fib, pretext, prevarication, quibble, ruse, scheme, stratagem, trick, wile **3.** dragging, hobbling, sauntering, scuffling, shambling, trudging, walk – *v.* **1.** limp, bumble, mosey *(Nonformal)*, muddle, pad, saunter, scrape, scuff, shamble, straggle, stroll, stumble, trail **2.** change, disarrange, disarray, dislocate, disorder, disorganize, disrupt, disturb, interlace, intermix, intersperse, jumble, mix, rearrange, reorganize, shift **3.** elude, evade, hedge, hide, lie, prevaricate *Nonformal:* deke out, waffle

shun *v.* **1.** avoid, balk, circumvent, cold-shoulder *(Nonformal)*, cut, demur, despise, dodge, elude, evade, ignore, neglect, repudiate, scorn, shake, shy, sidestep, snub *Antonyms:* befriend, embrace, welcome **2.** abstain, decline, eschew, forbear, forgo, pass, refrain, refuse, reject *Antonyms:* accept, allow, indulge

shut *adj.* bolted, bound, closed, fast, fastened, locked, secure *Antonyms:* ajar, open – *v.* **1.** bolt, close, fasten, fold, latch, lock, padlock, secure, seal **2.** arrest, bar, barricade, block, check, exclude, halt, impede, obstruct, occlude, stay, stifle, stop, stymie **3.** cage, corral, circumscribe, confine, constrain, fence in, hog-tie *(Nonformal)*, imprison, incarcerate, jail, pen *Antonyms:* discharge, free, liberate **4.** conceal, cover, hide, obscure, screen, shroud, veil

shutdown *n.* **1.** closure, conclusion, end, expiration, finish, termination **2.** boycott, cessation, labour unrest, lockout, revolt, strike, work stoppage *See also:* **strike**

shutter *n.* blind, cover, covering, jalousie, louvre, panel, roll-up, screen, slats, veil, venetian blind *Commonly misused:* **shudder**

shuttle *n.* **1.** boat, bus, car, ferry, jitney, plane, taxi, transport, van, vehicle **2.** rocket ship, spacecraft, spaceship, starship – *v.* carry, convey, deliver, express, ferry, move, portage, run, taxi, transfer, transport

shy *adj.* **1.** afraid, anxious, fearful, frightened, jumpy, nervous, skittish, timid, timorous, uneasy *Antonyms:* forward, impudent, outgoing **2.** awkward, bashful, coy, demure, diffident, embarrassed, humble, introverted, modest, mousy, quiet, reserved, reticent, retiring, self-conscious, self-effacing, tentative, unassertive, unassuming *Antonyms:* bold, brazen, confident **3.** apprehensive, cautious, chary, circumspect, distrustful, guarded, hesitant, suspicious, wary, watchful *Antonyms:* lax, negligent, trusting **4.** elusive, evasive, foxy, illusory, slippery *(Nonformal)*, subtle, unattainable, unreachable **5.** broke, deficient, lacking, low, scant, scarce, short, wanting, without *Nonformal:* busted, hard-up, *Antonyms:* flush, moneyed, rich – *v.* **1.** balk, buck, draw back, flinch, jerk, jump, leap, quail, rear, recoil, start, swerve, take flight, wince **2.** chuck, deliver, fling, flip, heave, pitch, propel, sling, throw, toss, whip, wing *(Nonformal)*

shyness *n.* bashfulness, diffidence, doubt, embarrassment, fearfulness, hesitancy, insecurity, lack of confidence, meekness, reserve, reticence, self-doubt, sheepishness, skittishness, timidity *Antonyms:* confidence, courage, strength

sic *adv.* exactly, so, thus – *v.* attack, bite, buffet, claw, lacerate, mangle, maul, molest

sick *adj.* **1.** ailing, bedridden, confined, debilitated, delicate, diseased, dying, feeble, feverish, frail, ill, impaired, indisposed, infected, infirm, invalid, laid-up, unhealthy, unwell, valetudinarian, weak *Nonformal:* lousy, rotten *Antonyms:* fit, healthy, robust **2.** carsick, green, motionsick, nauseous, off, queasy, seasick, squeamish, upset, vomiting *Nonformal:* pukey, sick as a dog **3.** disgusted, displeased, offended, repelled, revolted, shocked *Nonformal:* grossed-out, turned-off **4.** crazy, deranged, deviant, insane, *non compos mentis (Latin)*, psychotic, unbalanced, unsound, unstable **5.** cold-blooded, cruel, ghoulish, gross, gruesome, heartless, horrific, inhumane, macabre, monstrous, morbid, perverted, sadistic, senseless, twisted **6.** desirous, hankering, heartsick, homesick, languishing, longing, nostalgic, pining, wistful, yearning **7.** blasé, depressed, down, melancholy, neurasthenic, sad, sorrowful, suicidal, tired, troubled, world-weary **8.** fatigued, fed up, jaded, satiated, sick and tired, surfeited, weary *Nonformal:* bored to death *or* tears

sicken *v.* **1.** disgust, disturb, gross out *(Nonformal)*, offend, put off, repel, repulse, unhinge, unsettle, upset *Antonyms:* delight, enchant, please **2.** afflict, ail, cripple, damage, debilitate, enervate, enfeeble, harm, ill-treat, infect, injure, nauseate, poison, traumatize, wound *Antonyms:* aid, heal, help, palliate

sickening *adj.* **1.** awful, contemptible, despicable, disgusting, distasteful, disturbing, foul, frightening, gross, horrible, loathsome, nasty, nauseating, offensive, repugnant, repulsive, revolting, rotten, stomach-turning *Antonyms:* marvellous, pleasant, salutary **2.** dangerous, deleterious, detrimental, harmful, noisome, noxious, pernicious, poisonous, putrid, tainted

sickly *adj.* **1.** ailing, bilious, colourless, delicate, diseased, disordered, down, dragging, failing, faint, feeble, hurt, indisposed, infirm, injured, low, maimed, pale, pallid, peaked, poorly, problematic, unhealthy, wan, weak *Antonyms:* hale, healthy, well **2.** cloying, disgusting, fulsome, nauseating, noisome, offensive, revolting, vile *Antonyms:* acceptable, agreeable, wholesome **3.** bathetic, insipid, maudlin, mawkish, melodramatic, mushy, saccharine, sentimental, sugary, syrupy *Nonformal:* sappy, schmaltzy *Antonyms:* objective, realistic, scientific

sickness *n.* **1.** ailment, bug *(Nonformal)*, cancer, complaint, condition, debility, disease, disorder, dose, illness, indisposition, infirmity, malady, pox, syndrome, trouble *Antonyms:* haleness, health, healthiness, welfare, wholeness **2.** derangement, *folie (French)*, insanity, madness, neurosis, perversion, psychosis

side *adj.* **1.** bordering, edging, flanking, lateral, peripheral, skirting **2.** askew, awry, crooked, indirect, oblique, sidelong **3.** ancillary, incidental, minor, secondary, subordinate, subsidiary – *n.* **1.** border, boundary, brim, brink, edge, frame, frontier, limit, margin, perimeter, rim, shore, skirt, surface, verge **2.** body, cabal, cabinet, camp, caucus, circle, committee, division, faction, group, party, sect, team, wing **3.** angle, aspect, attitude, belief, opinion, position, posture, stance, standpoint, viewpoint *Nonformal:* spin, slant, take **4.** community, district, end, hood *(Nonformal)*, neighbourhood, part, quarter, section **5.** ancestry, background, clan, consanguinity, family, genealogy, house, lineage, tribe – *v.* back, boost, champion, endorse, join, second, support, sympathize

sidekick *n.* amigo, associate, buddy, chum, cohort, colleague, compadre, companion, comrade, friend, pal, partner *Nonformal:* hombre, Watson

sideline *n.* **1.** border, boundary, edge, extent, frame, limit, margin, outskirts, perimeter, periphery **2.** amusement, by-line, hobby, indulgence, moonlight position *(Nonformal)*, part-time employment, pursuit, second job – *v.* **1.** cripple, cut down, injure, knock out, maim *Nonformal:* goon, put on ice, rub out **2.** bench, cross off, pencil *or* take out, remove, scratch, sit *Nonformal:* give one the hook, yank out

sidesplitting *adj.* absurd, amusing, comical, crazy, droll, funny, hearty, hilarious, humorous, jocular, laughable, outrageous, ridiculous, riotous, silly, uproarious, wacky *(Nonformal)*, wild

sidestep *v.* **1.** edge, sidle, skew, veer **2.** avoid, bypass, circumvent, dodge, duck, elude, equivocate, escape, evade, hedge, hem and haw, prevaricate, pussyfoot, quibble, shift, shuffle, shun, skip, skirt, steer clear of *Nonformal:* deke out, dipsy-doodle, waffle, weasel *Antonyms:* confront, face, meet

sidetrack *v.* amuse, confuse, deflect, distract, divert, entertain, mislead, preoccupy, stall

sideways *adv.* askance, askew, aslant, crabwise, edgewise, indirectly, laterally, obliquely, sidelong, sidewise

siege *n.* **1.** attack, beleaguerment, besiegement, blockade, encirclement, envelopment **2.** bout, length, period, session, spell, stretch, term, time – *v.* attack, beleaguer, besiege, blockade, box in, circumscribe, circumvent, confine, contain, corner, encircle, encompass, surround

sieve *n.* cheesecloth, colander, filter, screen, strainer – *v.* clarify, clean, filter, purify, separate, sift, strain

sift *v.* clarify, clean, exclude, filter, purify, rack, riddle, screen, separate, sieve, sort out, strain, winnow

sigh *n.* breath, exhalation, gasp, gulp, respiration, suspiration – *v.* **1.** blow, breathe out, exhale, gasp, pant, respire, wheeze, whisper **2.** ache, bemoan, crave, desire, hanker, lament, languish, long, pine, thirst, want, yearn

sight *n.* **1.** eyesight, faculty, pathway of light, seeing, sense, vision, visual activity **2.** cityscape, landscape, panorama, scape, scene, seascape, vista, view **3.** estimation, impression, interpretation, judgment, observation, opinion, perspective, point of view, thought **4.** distance, extent, eyeshot, field of vision, limit, picture, range, reach, scope, spectrum, total visibility **5.** aim, goal, intention, purpose, target **6.** amazement, curiosity, marvel, phenomenon, rarity, specimen, spectacle, wonder *Nonformal:* eye-popper, something else **7.** abortion, eyesore, fright, mess, monstrosity, shocker – *v.* **1.** behold, eyeball *(Nonformal)*, glance, glimpse, look, observe, peek, peep, regard, survey, view **2.** calibrate, calculate, gauge, mark, measure, read **3.** aim, direct, draw a bead on, level, pinpoint, point, train *Commonly misused:* **cite, site**

sightseer *n.* day-tripper, excursionist, globe-trotter, out-of-towner, stranger, tourist, traveller, vacationer, visitor, voyager *Nonformal:* gawker, Sunday driver, tripster

sign *n.* **1.** advertisement, billboard, board, broadsheet, bulletin, placard, poster, sandwich board, signpost **2.** cipher, code, hieroglyphic, mark, monogram, notation, slogan, symbol, token **3.** badge, crest, emblem, flag, insignia, label, logo, shield, standard, trademark **4.** clue, evidence, hint, indication, manifestation, proof, scent, shadow, symptom, trace, vestige **5.** augury, delineation, foreboding, foretoken, forewarning, omen, portent, premonition, presage **6.** acknowledgement, action, cue, gesture, motion, movement, nod, signal – *v.* **1.** authorize, autograph, express, initial, ink, inscribe, notarize, rubber-stamp *(Nonformal)*, witness, write **2.** beckon, communicate, express, flag, gesticulate, gesture, indicate, motion, nod, signal, wave **3.** book, contract, employ, engage, enlist, hire, recruit, retain, take on *(Nonformal)*

signal *adj.* arresting, bright, brilliant, conspicuous, distinguished, eminent, exceptional, extraordinary, historic, illustrious, landmark, marked, memorable, momentous, notable, noteworthy, outstanding, prominent, remarkable, salient, striking, significant, stellar, unparalleled *Antonyms:* common, nondescript, ordinary – *n.* **1.** action, body English *(Nonformal)*, body language, communication, gesticulation, gesture, motion, representation **2.** call, charge, code, command, dictum, direction, instruction, mandate, order **3.** alarm, alert, beacon, caution, flare, flirrup *(Newfoundland)*, indicator, klaxon, light, siren, tocsin, torch, warning **4.** foreshadowing, harbinger, hint, omen, precursor **5.** clue, indication, message, reminder, sign, suggestion, token – *v.* **1.** communicate, convey, correspond, express, gesticulate, indicate, motion, notify, send, show, sign, signalize, signify, tell, transmit, word **2.** acknowledge, beckon, bid, call, flag, greet, hail, nod, salute, summon, tip the hat, wave, wink **3.** advise, alert, caution, tip off, warn

signature *adj.* best, choice, designer, distinguished, excellent, fine, grade A *(Nonformal)*, top, well-chosen – *n.* **1.** autograph, hand, mark, monogram, name, seal, sign, stamp *Nonformal:* John Hancock, John Henry, X **2.** approval, authorization, backing, blessing, consent, endorsement, okay *(Nonformal)*, permission, support *Antonyms:* forbiddance, veto

significance *n.* **1.** bottom line *(Nonformal)*, drift, gist, heart, matter, meaning, meat, pith, purport, sense **2.** consequence, gravity, implication, import, importance, influence, magnitude, relevance, value, weight

significant *adj.* **1.** consequential, considerable, critical, heavy, important, material, meaningful, momentous, notable, noteworthy, powerful, relevant, serious, substantial, valid, vital, weighty, worthy *Antonyms:* inconsequential, paltry, superficial, trivial, unimportant, worthless **2.** expressive, loaded, ominous, pointed, portentous, pregnant, revealing, suggestive, symbolic, telling

signify *v.* **1.** announce, bespeak, broadcast, communicate, convey, disclose, express, impart, proclaim, pronounce, speak, tell, transmit, utter **2.** augur, betoken, connote, denote, foretell, imply, import, indicate, omen, portend, presage, purport, represent, suggest, symbolize **3.** affect, amount to, concern, count, influence, involve, matter, mean

silence *n.* **1.** inarticulation, inexpression, muteness, speechlessness, uncommunicativeness **2.** calm, dead air, hush, noiselessness, peace, quiet, quietude, repose, rest, serenity, stillness, tranquility *Antonyms:* chaos, mayhem, uproar **3.** blackout, censorship, concealment, court order, curfew, obliteration, oppression, prohibition, publication ban, repression, secrecy, suppression *Antonyms:* dissemination, promotion, publicity **4.** camouflage, concealment, confidence, covertness, furtiveness, mystery, privacy, reticence, stealth **5.** black hole *(Nonformal)*, darkness, oblivion, obscurity, void – *v.* **1.** appease, calm, hush, pacify, placate, quiet, soothe **2.** censor, disable, gag, keep under wraps *(Nonformal)*, inhibit, muffle, mute, muzzle, prevent, prohibit, quell, repress, restrict, smother, squash, stifle, suppress

silent *adj.* **1.** inarticulate, mum, mute, noiseless, quiet, soundless, speechless, still, voiceless *Antonyms:* deafening, loud, resounding **2.** buttoned-up, closed-up, close-mouthed, reserved, retiring, shy, taciturn, tight-lipped, tongue-tied, uncommunicative *Antonyms:* chatty, loquacious, verbose **3.** dormant, idle, inactive, pacific, peaceful, placid, quiet, motionless, reposeful, sedate, still, subsiding, tranquil *Antonyms:* bellicose, boisterous, wild **4.** implicit, implied, inarticulated, nonvocal, signified, tacit, understood, unexpressed, unpronounced, unspoken, unvoiced, wordless *Antonyms:* declared, explicit, expressed

silhouette *n.* contour, delineation, form, line, lineation, outline, profile, shade, shadow, shape

silky *adj.* cottony, delicate, fleecy, glossy, luxurious, satiny, sericeous, silken, sleek, smooth, soft, velvety *Antonyms:* coarse, crude, rough

silly *adj.* **1.** absurd, asinine, ass-backwards, *(Nonformal)*, confused, illogical, inane, irrational, ludicrous, meaningless, mixed-up, muddled, nonsensical, preposterous, ridiculous, senseless *Antonyms:* meaningful, sane, sensible **2.** brainless, dumb, empty-headed, fatuous, flighty, foolish, idiotic, moronic, stupid, vacuous, witless *Nonformal:* bananas, barmy, batty, bird-brained, bonkers, chuckle-headed, crackers, daffy, daft, ditzy, dizzy, dopey, flighty, gormless, kooky, looney, punchy **3.** amusing, comical, droll, funny, hilarious, humorous, sidesplitting *Antonyms:* annoying, irritating, upsetting

silt *n.* alluvium, deposit, detritus, dregs, drift, loess, particles, particulate matter, scree, sediment, sinter, sullage

silver *adj.* **1.** colour *Silver shades:* argent, chrome, grey, greyish-white, pearly, salt-and-pepper *(Nonformal)*, sterling, white **2.** chromium, lustrous, metallic, plated, shiny, silvered, silvery **3.** clear, dulcet, mellifluous, mellow, melodious, musical, rich, smooth, soft, sonorous **4.** cogent, compelling, eloquent, fluent, forceful, impassioned, impelling, persuasive, powerful, spellbinding, silver-tongued – *n.* cash, change, coin, currency, mad money *(Nonformal)*, money, pocket change, spending money

silver-tongued *adj.* alluring, articulate, compelling, convincing, effective, eloquent, fluent, forceful, impassioned, mellifluent, moving, oratorical, persuasive, powerful, rhetorical, smooth, well-spoken

silverware *n. pl.* cutlery, dinnerware, flatware, forks, kitchenware, knives, silver, spoons, tableware, utensils, ware

silviculture *n.* conservation, forest management, forest maintenance *or* tending, forest regeneration, forest sustainability, forestry, resource management, tree harvesting, tree planting

similar *adj.* agnate, akin, alike, allied, analogous, coinciding, corresponding, equivalent, homogeneous, kindred, like, matching, parallel, related, resembling, same, twin, uniform *Antonyms:* different, disparate, opposite

similarity *n.* affinity, agreement, alikeness, analogy, approximation, association, closeness, coincidence, comparability, comparison, concordance, concurrence, conformity, congruity, connection, correlation, correspondence, facsimile, harmony, homogeneity, interrelation, kinship, likeness, parallelism, parity, relation, relationship, resemblance, sameness, semblance, simile, similitude *Antonyms:* clashing, contradiction, divergence

simmer *v.* **1.** boil, bubble, cook, parboil, poach, stew, warm **2.** brood, churn, ferment, foam, fume, mope, rage, seethe, sizzle, smoulder, stew

simpatico *adj.* agreeable, amicable, brotherly, charming, compatible, congenial, friendly, likeable, neighbourly, pleasant, sisterly, sociable, sympathetic *Antonyms:* abrasive, annoying, irritating, obnoxious

simpering *adj.* coy, grinning, smiling, smirking, snickering, sniggering, tittering *Antonyms:* frowning, glum, grimacing

simple *adj.* **1.** casual, folksy, homey, informal, modest, unceremonious, unpretentious *Nonformal:* come-as-you-are, down-home, meat-and-potatoes, shirt-sleeved, *Antonyms:* black-tie, formal **2.** basic, easy, elementary, facile, light, painless, self-explanatory, straightforward, uncomplicated, understandable *Nonformal:* cushy, hassle-free *Antonyms:* challenging, complex, difficult **3.** Attic, ascetic, austere, plain, Spartan, stark, unadorned, uncluttered, understated, unembellished *Antonyms:* busy, cluttered, fussy **4.** aboveboard, artless, candid, genuine, guileless, honest, ingenuous, naive, natural, open, rustic, sincere, unaffected, unstudied *Antonyms:* canny, conniving, wily **5.** clueless, dense, dim-witted, dull, dumb, feeble, ignorant, silly, simple-minded, thick-skulled, unintelligent, unsophisticated, witless *Antonyms:* astute, brilliant, intelligent **6.** average, common, garden-variety, humble, lowly, mean, middling, modest, ordinary, plebian *Antonyms:* aristocratic, haughty, upper-class **7.** inconsequential, insignificant, minor, negligible, paltry, secondary, superficial, trifling, trivial, unimportant *Antonyms:* important, landmark, momentous **8.** homogenous, monolithic, unalloyed, uncombined, uniform, unmingled, unmixed *Antonyms:* composite, heterogeneous, mixed **9.** complete, entire, mere, other, pure, sheer, single, sole, straight *Antonyms:* partial, selected, well-tempered

simple-minded *adj.* **1.** artless, genuine, innocent, plain, pure, rustic, sincere, straightforward, unaffected, uncontrived, unsophisticated, unstudied *Antonyms:* complex, expert, worldly **2.** asinine, dense, dumb, fatuous, foolish, idiotic, ignorant, inane, ludicrous, moronic, ridiculous, senseless, silly, stupid, witless *Nonformal:* cockamamie, goofy, gormless, half-baked *Antonyms:* intelligent, smart, wise *See also:* **simple**

simpleton *n.* dim-wit, dunce, fool, idiot, moron, nincompoop, ninny, noodle *Nonformal:* airhead, arse, birdbrain, blockhead, boob, chucklehead, goof, hoser, jackass, jarhead, jerk, Moe, rubberhead, turkey, twit, Wally, wombat

simplicity *n.* **1.** clarity, clearness, distinctness, explicitness, intelligibility, lucidity, obviousness, salience, straightforwardness *Antonyms:* complexity, incomprehensibility, perplexity **2.** Atticism, austerity, bareness, modesty, plainness, rusticity, severity, sparseness, starkness, unadornment *Antonyms:* gaudiness, ornation, showiness **3.** artlessness, candour, directness, frankness, ingenuousness, naiveté, naturalness, sincerity, unaffectedness *Antonyms:* craftiness, evasiveness, shrewdness **4.** dimwittedness, dullness, dumbness, feeblemindedness, foolishness, idiocy, imbecility, simple-mindedness, stupidity, vacuity *Antonyms:* intelligence, wisdom, wit

simplify *v.* **1.** boil *or* break *or* narrow down, clear up, disentangle, explicate, interpret, make clear *or* easy, reduce, separate, streamline, unravel, unscramble, untangle *Antonyms:* complicate, confuse, muddle **2.** clarify, demonstrate, elaborate, elucidate, enlighten, explain, illuminate, spell out, teach, tell, translate

simply *adv.* **1.** clearly, directly, evidently, intelligibly, lucidly, matter-of-factly, obviously **2.** artlessly, candidly, guilelessly, modestly, naturally, openly, plainly, quietly, unassumingly, unpretentiously **3.** carelessly, foolishly, heedlessly, imprudently, mindlessly, senselessly, thoughtlessly, unwisely **4.** exclusively, merely, only, purely, singly **5.** absolutely, altogether, categorically, completely, fully, totally, unreservedly, utterly, wholly

simulate *v.* **1.** copy, counterfeit, deceive, dissemble, fake, feign, pose, sham, trick **2.** ape, burlesque, imitate, mimic, mirror, mock, parody, parrot, pretend, satirize, send up *(Nonformal)*

simultaneous *adj.* accompanying, agreeing, coexistent, coinciding, concurrent, contemporaneous, parallel, synchronic, synchronous *Antonyms:* earlier, different, later

sin *n.* **1.** evil, fall, immorality, impiety, iniquity, transgression, vice, wickedness, wrongdoing *Seven Deadly Sins:* anger, covetousness, envy, gluttony, lust, pride, sloth **2.** breach, crime, error, fault, infraction, misdeed, misdemeanour, offence, slip *(Nonformal)*, trespassing, violation, wrong – *v.* backslide, deviate, err, fall, go astray, lapse, misbehave, profane, stray, sully, transgress, trespass, wander

sincere *adj.* **1.** aboveboard, artless, candid, earnest, faithful, forthright, frank, guileless, honest, ingenuous, natural, open, straightforward, unpretentious *Nonformal:* no-nonsense, upfront *Antonyms:* affected, deceptive, dishonest **2.** actual, bona fide, genuine, heartfelt, meant, real, simon-pure, true, unfeigned, wholehearted *Antonyms:* artificial, counterfeit, false

sincerely *adv.* deeply, earnestly, genuinely, honestly, openly, really, truly, truthfully, wholeheartedly, without equivocation *or* reservation

sincerity *n.* candour, earnestness, frankness, genuineness, guilelessness, heart, honesty, probity, reliability, seriousness, sincereness, straightforwardness, truth, truthfulness, veracity, wholeheartedness *Antonyms:* duplicity, falseness, hypocrisy

sinecure *n.* patronage, pay-off, political plum *Nonformal:* cushy job, easy money, easy street, free ride, gravy train, nine-to-fiver

sinewy *adj.* **1.** athletic, brawny, lusty, mighty, muscular, strapping, strong, virile, vital, wiry *Nonformal:* buffed, toned **2** chewy, elastic, fibrous, gristly, leathery, ropy, stringy, tough **3.** bracing, driving, effective, emphatic, forceful, gripping, incisive, intense, powerful, rousing, stimulating, vigorous *Antonyms:* feeble, ineffective, weak

sinful *adj.* bad, censurable, corrupt, criminal, damnable, depraved, detestable, disgraceful, evil, godless, illegal, immoral, impious, infernal, iniquitous, irreligious, odious, outrageous, reprehensible, shameful, transgressive, unlawful, unregenerate, vicious, vile, wicked, wrong *Antonyms:* good, moral, virtuous

sing *v.* **1.** belt out *(Nonformal)*, carol, chant, chirp, chorus, croon, descant, harmonize, hum, hymn, intone, lilt, lullaby, perform, serenade, trill, troll, twitter, warble, yodel **2.** amuse, entertain, enthral, regale, stage **3.** betray, confess, divulge, inform *Nonformal:* finger, fink, narc, rat, sell out, snitch, squeal, tattle, turn informant

singe *n.* burn, brand, scald, scorching, sunburn – *v.* barbecue *(Nonformal)*, blacken, blister, brown, burn, char, grill, lick, roast, scald, scorch, sear, torrefy

singer *n.* accompanist, alto, artist, artiste, balladeer, baritone, bass, cantatrice, cantor, caroler, castrato, chanter, chorister, coloratura, crooner, diva, entertainer, hymner, intoner, jongleur, melodist, mezzo-soprano, minstrel, musician, serenader, soloist, songster, soprano, tenor, thrush troubadour, vocalist, yodeller *French:* chanteur, chanteuse *Nonformal:* canary, nightingale, songbird, warbler

single *adj.* **1.** free, mateless, solo *(Nonformal)*, spouseless, unfettered, unmarried, unwed *Antonyms:* hitched, married, wed **2.** alone, companionless, estranged, forsaken, isolated, lonely, unattended *Antonyms:* matched, paired, teamed **3.** distinct, individual, lone, one, separate, singular, solitary, unique *Antonyms:* connected, together, united **4.** elementary, homogeneous, indivisible, pure, simple, unalloyed, uncompounded, uncut, undivided, unmingled, unmixed *Antonyms:* heterogeneous, mixed, motley – *n.* **1.** bachelor, bachelorette, loner, spinster, swinger *(Nonformal)* **2.** base hit, beat-out, bleeder, infield hit, one bagger, safety, seeing-eye single, Texas leaguer **3.** chart topper, hit, melody, record, recording, song, tune *Common types of singles:* cassette, CD, 7 inch, 12 inch

single-handed *adj.* individual, one-man, one-woman, singular, solitary, solo, unaccompanied, unaided, unassisted, unchaperoned, unguided *Antonyms:* collective, social, team

single-minded *adj.* dedicated, determined, devoted, dogged, firm, fixated, fixed, focused, hell-bent *(Nonformal)*, inflexible, intense, obsessed, persevering, persistent, relentless, resolved, staunch, steadfast, stubborn, tenacious, tireless, undeviating, unflinching, unswerving, untiring, unwavering, zealous *Antonyms:* hesitant, irresolute, vacillating

singular *adj.* **1.** different, exclusive, individual, one, particular, separate, sole, solitary, specific, unique *Antonyms:* multifarious, multiple, sundry **2.** abnormal, atypical, bizarre, curious, eccentric, esoteric, freakish, odd, outlandish, peculiar, quaint, strange, unconventional, way out *(Nonformal)*, weird *Antonyms:* everyday, hackneyed, trite **3.** amazing, distinctive, exceptional, extraordinary, fantastic, great, leading, matchless, nonpareil, noteworthy, peerless, preeminent, rare, remarkable, signal, special, striking, uncommon, unmistakable, unparalleled, unprecedented, unrivalled, wild, wonderful, wondrous *Antonyms:* banal, mediocre, ordinary

singularity *n.* **1.** character, extent, grandeur, greatness, immensity, prominence, reach, scale, strength, wonder **2.** conspicuousness, distinctiveness, far-fetchedness, freakiness, idiosyncrasy, originality, outlandishness, peculiarity, specialty, uniqueness, weirdness, wildness *Antonyms:* commonness, interchangeability, typicalness

sinister *adj.* **1.** corrupt, crooked, dishonest, fly-by-night, illegitimate, insidious, questionable, scrofulous, shady *(Nonformal)*, shifty, slippery, suspicious, treacherous, tricky, underhanded, unsavoury, unscrupulous *Antonyms:* lawful, principled, straight **2.** atrocious, devilish, evil, heinous, horrific, iniquitous, invidious, malefic, malevolent, malicious, malign, nefarious, odious, perverse, satanic, sinful, vile, villainous, wicked *Antonyms:* just, moral, virtuous **3.** adverse, bad, baleful, dark, deleterious, foreboding, gloomy, ill-boding, inauspicious, menacing, ominous, portentous, star-crossed, threatening, unfavourable, unlucky, unpropitious *Antonyms:* fortuitous, lucky, serendipitous

sink *n.* **1.** basin, receptacle, tub, washbasin, washbowl, washtub **2.** bog, cavity, crater, depression, excavation, hollow, laigh, marsh, pit, pothole, sinkhole, sluice, swamp **3.** cesspool, cistern, cloaca, gutter, reservoir, sewer, sump **4.** bordello, brothel, crackhouse, den of iniquity, dive, hellhole *(Nonformal)*, opium den, redlight district, rookery, skid row, slums, tenderloin – *v.* **1.** attack, capsize, destroy, founder, overturn, ruin, scuttle, shipwreck, torpedo **2.** annihilate, conquer, crush, defeat, demolish, devastate, kill, overcome, subdue, subject, vanquish, whipsaw **3.** cascade, descend, disappear, dive, drop, drown, fall, pass, plummet, plunge, precipitate, settle, submerge **4.** backslide, degenerate, degrade, regress, relapse, spiral **5.** decline, deteriorate, fade, fail, falter, languish, shrink, wane, waste, weaken, wither, worsen **6.** abate, decrease, diminish, ease, ebb, lessen, moderate, reduce, restrain, slacken, soften, subside, temper **7.** buckle under, cave in, collapse, fall, give way **8.** cant, dip, list, lower, slope, tilt **9.** bury, censor, conceal, cover up, deep-six *(Nonformal)*, hide, omit, shroud, smother, stifle, suppress, whitewash **10.** bore, dig, drill, excavate, mine **11.** fill, percolate, permeate, saturate, soak in **12.**

back, bankroll, capitalize, invest, risk, speculate, support

sinless *adj.* angelic, blameless, clear, crimeless, faultless, godly, guiltless, immaculate, impeccable, innocent, irreproachable, pure, saintly, spotless, unpolluted, unsullied, untainted *Antonyms:* damned, hellbound, wicked

sinner *n.* blasphemer, lawbreaker, malefactor, malfeasant, offender, recidivist, transgressor, trespasser, wrongdoer *Antonyms:* angel, innocent, saint

sinuous *adj.* anfractuous, bending, coiled, complex, convoluted, curled, curving, flowing, kinky, labyrinthine, meandering, serpentine, snaky, spiral, tortuous, turning, twisted, undulating, winding *Antonyms:* direct, linear, straight

sip *n.* bit, dram, drop, nip, nipperkin, ounce, snort, swallow, swig, taste, trifle – *v.* absorb, consume, drink, imbibe, partake, quaff, sample, savour, taste, tipple, try

siren *adj.* alluring, attractive, bewitching, enchanting, enticing, fascinating, irresistible, magnetic, seductive, spellbinding, tempting *Antonyms:* offensive, repugnant, repulsive – *n.* **1.** beauty, charmer, Circe, enchantress, femme fatale, Lorelei, nymph, seductress, temptress, vamp *Nonformal:* cougar, man-eater, trouble **2.** alarm, electric mule *(Nonformal)*, horn, signal, warning, whistle

sissy *adj.* cowardly, craven, cringing, shrinking, soft, timid, weak *Nonformal:* gutless, lily-livered, spineless, yellow – *n.* coward, milksop, milquetoast, weakling *Nonformal:* chicken, crybaby, fraidy-cat, jellyfish, lightweight, pantywaist, powder puff, softy, spineless wonder, suck, teacher's pet, wimp, yellow-belly

sister *n.* **1.** kin, relation, relative, sibling, sis *(Nonformal)* **2.** chum, colleague, companion, crony, friend, girlfriend, intimate, kindred spirit, mate, partner, sister-in-arms *Nonformal:* bud, buddy, pal **3.** abbess, nun, prioress, *religeuse (French)* clergywoman

sisterhood *n.* association, club, collective, commonality, community, cooperation, group, society, sorority

sit *v.* **1.** crouch, hunker down, kick back *(Nonformal)*, lounge, perch, rest, ride, seat, slump, squat, straddle **2.** deposit, dwell, exist, fix, inhabit, install, locate, lodge, occupy, park *(Nonformal)*, place, position, reside, ride the pine *(Team sports)*, settle, situate, tenant **3.** chair, officiate, oversee, preside, reign, serve, superintend **4.** assemble, congregate, convene, convoke, do business, gather, huddle *(Nonformal)*, meet, unite **5.** abide, accept, bear, carry, endure, face, permit, persevere, stand, stomach, swallow, suffer, take, tolerate, weather, withstand **6.** babysit, chaperon, guard, look after, mind, supervise, tend, watch over

site *n.* area, arena, battleground, district, environment, field, ground, locale, location, lot, milieu, place, plot, position, purlieu, quarter, region, scene, setting, spot, station, territory, theatre, venue, vicinity, whereabouts, zone *United Nations World Heritage Sites in Canada:* Canadian Rocky Mountain Parks *(Alberta, B.C.)*, Glacier International Peace Park *(Alberta, Montana U.S.)*, Historic District of Quebec City *(Quebec)*, Kluane National Park / Tatshenshini-Alsek Park *(B.C., Yukon)*, Nahanni National Park *(Northwest Territories)*, Old Town Lunenburg *(Nova Scotia)*, SGaang Gwaii *(B.C.)*, Wood Buffalo National Park *(Alberta, Northwest Territories) Alberta:* Dinosaur Provincial Park, Head-Smashed-In Buffalo Jump *Newfoundland:* Gros Morne National Park, L'Anse aux Meadows *Commonly misused:* **cite, sight**

sit-in *n.* challenge, civil disobedience, demonstration, non-violent protest, occupation, protest, rally, resistance, sit-down *See also:* **strike**

situate *v.* deposit, dump, fix, install, lay, locate, place, position, put, set, station *Nonformal:* park, plunk, stick

situation *n.* **1.** bearings, coordinates, lie *(Golf)*, locale, location, orientation, place, position, site, spot, whereabouts **2.** condition, circumstance, matter, repair, scenario, shape, state **3.** boiling point, Catch-22, climax, conundrum, crisis, danger, dilemma, emergency, face-off, imbroglio, plight, predicament, problem, trauma, trouble *Nonformal:* hot water, how-do-you-do, kettle of fish, pickle, pinch **4.** background, class, footing, influence, position, rank, reach, standing, station, status **5.** appointment, billet, capacity, employment, job, office, post, profession, trade

sizable *adj.* ample, big, comfortable, commodious, considerable, extensive, goodly, great, gross, hefty, king-size, large, major, massive, spacious, strapping, substantial, voluminous, whopping *(Nonformal) Antonyms:* little, minor, small

size *n.* **1.** amount, breadth, degree, diameter, dimension, extent, height, immensity, length, magnitude, mass, measurement, number, proportion, quantity, range, scope, strength, volume, width **2.** clout *(Nonformal)*, greatness, importance, influence, might, power, prestige, pull, significance, standing, weight, worth – *v.* **1.** arrange, array, classify, grade, group, range, rank, sort, space **2.** assess, calculate, estimate, evaluate, judge, measure, reckon, weigh *Nonformal:* ballpark, guesstimate **3.** cut, figure, fit, form, mould, shape **4.** coat, glaze, glue, stiffen, treat, wax

skeleton *adj.* abbreviated, abridged, barebones, brief, downsized, incomplete, minimal, minimum, pared-down, reduced, slashed, small-scale *Antonyms:* complete, full, total – *n.* **1.** anatomy, bones, Mr. Bones *(Nonformal)*, *osteon (Greek) Parts of the human skeleton:* carpus, cervical vertebrae, clavicle, coccyx, cranium, femur, fibula, humerus, ilium, ischium, lumbar vertebrae, mandible, metacarpus, metatarsus, olecranon, patella, phalanges, pubis, radius, ribs, sacrum, scapula, sternum, tarsus, thoracic vertebrae, tibia, ulna **2.** abbreviation, blueprint, brief, design, digest, draft, essentials, layout, outline, plan, proposal, rundown, sketch **3.** chassis, frame, rafters, scaffold, hull, shell, steel, structure, support **4.** anorexic, emaciated person, shadow, skin and bones, wisp *Nonformal:* beanpole, cadaver, scarecrow, stick, twiggy

sketch *n.* **1.** cartoon, composition, delineation, diagram, doodling, drawing, figuration, illustration, picture, preliminary, rough, study **2.** abbreviation, abstract, brief, digest, draft, epitome, impression, outline, plan, précis, résumé, skeleton, summary, synopsis **3.** act, burlesque, lampoon, pantomime, parody, pasquinade, play, presentation, satire, scene, short, show, skit, vignette *See also:* **skit** – *v.* **1.** doodle, draft, draw, limn, line, portray, trace **2.** characterize, describe, outline, summarize

sketchy *adj.* **1.** brief, crude, cursory, embryonic, inchoate, incomplete, imperfect, initial, introductory, perfunctory, preliminary, preparatory, rough, rudimentary *Antonyms:* complete, detailed, full, thorough **2.** deficient, disappointing, imperfect, inadequate, lacking, short, slipshod, sloppy, superficial, unsatisfactory, wanting *Nonformal:* crappy, crummy, garbage, lousy **3.** arcane, hazy, mysterious, obscure, unknown, vague

skew *adj.* **1.** cockeyed *(Nonformal)*, leaning, listing, lopsided, oblique, pitching, slanting, tilting **2.** asymmetrical, disparate, disproportionate, irregular, uneven – *n.* **1.** angle, bend, curve, deviation, incline, slant, slope, tilt **2.** bias, deceit, deception. distortion, doctoring *(Nonformal)*, lie, misrepresentation, prevarication, sophistry – *v.* **1.** bias, distort, change, colour, doctor *(Nonformal)*, falsify, fudge, exaggerate, lie, misconstrue, misrender, misrepresent, misstate, pervert, shape, twist, warp **2.** angle, contort, deviate, diverge, lean, swerve, tilt, twist, veer, zigzag

skid *n.* **1.** base, pallet, plank, roller, support **2.** braking, skidding, slide, stopping **3.** dive, downslide, downturn, fall, funk *(Nonformal)*, losing streak, plunge, spiral, tumble **4.** curtailment, delay, standstill, stoppage – *v.* **1.** drift, glide, glissade, skate, skim, slide **2.** lose control, reel, sheer, slip, swerve, veer **3.** arrest, brake, lock `em up *(Nonformal)*, slow, stop **4.** decline, err, fall, lose ground *or* position, plummet, plunge

skiing *n.* snow sport *Some skiing terms:* acrobatic, aerial, Alpine, backcountry, ballet, binding, chairlift, christie, cable car, cross-country, downhill, edging, *en canard (French)*, extreme, fall line, free-style, giant slalom, gondola, heli, herringbone, hotdogging, j bar, machine-groomed, mogul, montée, Nordic, parallel, pole, poma lift, powder, rope tow, schuss, sideslip, sidestep, sitzmark, ski-jumping, slalom, snowplow, speed, super g, t-bar, telemark, traverse, wedeln

skilful *adj.* **1.** able, accomplished, adept, adroit, apt, clever, competent, crack *(Nonformal)*, deft, dexterous, experienced, expert, good, handy, learned, masterful, masterly, practiced, prepared, primed, professional, proficient, quick, ready, seasoned, sharp, skilled, smart, swift, talented, trained, versed, veteran, well-versed *Antonyms:* amateurish, bungling, clumsy, incompetent, inept **2.** alive on all fronts *(Nonformal)*, adaptable, alert, aware, changeable, cunning, ingenious, smooth, wily *Antonyms:* blind, ignorant, unaware

skill *n.* **1.** ability, accomplishment, adroitness, aptitude, artistry, cleverness, command, competence, cunning, deftness, dexterity, expertise, expertness, facility, finesse, handiness, ingenuity, knack, know-how, mastery, proficiency, prowess, quickness, readiness, *savoir-faire (French)*, skilfulness, talent, technique *Nonformal:* makings, savvy, smarts, the goods, the right stuff *Antonyms:* awkwardness, clumsiness, gaucheness, inability, inexperience **2.** art, bag *(Nonformal)*, craft, forte, métier, profession, trade, vocation

skim *v.* **1.** browse, cast an eye over *(Nonformal)*, examine, flip *or* leaf *or* rifle *or* skip *or* thumb through, glance, peruse, read, scan **2.** cream, dip, ladle, ream, scoop, separate, shave **3.** brush, graze, kiss, ricochet, skip off **4.** dart, glide over, sail, scud, skate, skip, skitter, slide, slip

skimp *v.* curb, curtail, cut back, decrease, economize, lessen, limit, lower, pare, penny-pinch, prune, ration, reduce, restrain, save, scrape, scrimp, shave, slash, spare, struggle, trim, withhold *Nonformal:* cut corners, skrimshank *Antonyms:* blow, lavish, splurge, squander

skimpy *adj.* **1.** deficient, disappointing, inadequate, insubstantial, insufficient, meager, paltry, small, thin, unsatisfactory, wanting *Antonyms:* abundant, ample, substantial **2.** careful, cheap, economical, frugal, miserly, parsimonious, pennywise, stingy, tight *Antonyms:* generous, lavish, liberal

skin *n.* bark, carapace, case, casing, coating, covering, crust, epidermis, film, fur, hide, hull, husk, integument, *maktaaq (Inuktitut)*, membrane, outside, pelt, rind, sheath, sheathing, shell, surface, tissue, vair, vellum *Common skin afflictions:* acne, athlete's foot, cancer, dermatitis, cellulitis, diaper rash, eczema, heat rash, herpes, hives, jack itch, melanoma, nettle rash, prickly heat, psoriasis, shingles – *v.* abrade, bare, bark, flay, lay bare, pare, peel, pull off, remove, scale, scrape, shave, shed, shuck, slough, strip, trim

skin-deep *adj.* empty, hollow, insignificant, meaningless, minor, shallow, slight, superficial, surface, unimportant *Antonyms:* critical, deep, serious

skinflint *n.* cheapskate, churl, hoarder, miser, money-grubber, penny-pincher *Nonformal:* Scrooge, tightwad *Antonyms:* big spender, philanthropist, spendthrift

skinny *adj.* **1.** angular, attenuated, lanky, lean, slender, slight, slim, spare, svelte, thin, trim, weedy, willowy *Antonyms:* beefy, chubby, corpulent, fat, stout **2.** anorexic, bony, emaciated, gaunt, malnourished, rawboned, scraggy, scrawny, skeletal, undernourished, underweight – *n.* data, facts, gossip, information, knowledge, lore, news *Nonformal:* dirt, goods, lowdown

skip *v.* **1.** cut, ditch *(Nonformal)*, dodge, duck, go AWOL, miss **2.** alight, bolt, depart, desert, escape, flee, leave, run away, skip out on *Nonformal:* dine and dash, go on the lam, scram, split, vamoose **3.** avoid, disregard, eschew, leave out, neglect, omit, pass over, scorn, shun, sidestep, spurn **4.** bob, bound, caper, hop, jump, leap, prance, spring, step, trip **5.** bounce over, carom, glance, glissade, graze, ricochet, skate, skim

skirmish *n.* action, affray, altercation, argument, battle, bench-clearing *(Hockey)*, bout, brawl, brouhaha, brush, combat, conflict, confrontation, dispute, disturbance, donnybrook, dustup, encounter, engagement, fight, fracas, fray, free-for-all, incident, meeting, mêlée, quarrel, rhubarb *(Nonformal)*, row, run-in, scrap, scrimmage, showdown, spat, squabble, struggle, tiff, tussle, uproar

skirt *n.* **1.** clothing, garment, vestment *Kinds of skirt:* A-line, culottes, dirndl, dress, gored, hoop, kilt, midi, mini, petticoat, sarong, tutu **2.** border, brim, brink, edge, fringe, hem, margin, outskirts, perimeter, periphery, rim, skirting, verge *Antonyms:* centre, core, heart, hub – *v.* **1.** avoid, bypass, circumnavigate, circumvent, detour, dodge, duck, elude, equivocate, escape, evade, hedge, ignore, sidestep, skip *Antonyms:* face, confront, meet **2.** border, bound, edge, flank, fringe, hem, margin, rim, surround, verge

skit *n.* act, burlesque, jest, lampoon, pantomime, parody, pasquinade, play, presentation, satire, scene, send-up, sketch, spoof, take-off *See also:* **sketch**

skittish *adj.* **1.** edgy, excitable, fidgety, high-strung, jittery, jumpy, nervous, on edge, on pins and needles *(Nonformal)*, restive, restless, ruffled *Antonyms:* calm, collected, cool **2.** capricious, changeable, fickle, harebrained, mercurial, unpredictable, unreliable, whimsical *Antonyms:* sober, staid **3.** cagey, conniving, crafty, cunning, deceitful, foxy, sharp, shrewd, slippery, slinking, tricky, wily *Antonyms:* candid, open, straightforward **4.** apprehensive, coy, demur, diffident, fearful, hesitant, meek, modest, reticent, retiring, scared, shy, timid, timorous *Antonyms:* gregarious, outgoing, sociable

skookum *adj.* big, brave, fearless, great, mighty, powerful, puissant, strong *Antonyms:* cowardly, small, weak – *n.* bibe *(Newfoundland)*, ghost, phantom, presence, spirit, spook *(Nonformal)*

skulk *v.* **1.** creep, crouch, follow, gumshoe *(Nonformal)*, hide, lurk, prowl, slink, sneak, stalk **2.** avoid, circumvent, duck, evade, malinger, shirk *Nonformal:* goldbrick, goof *or* slack off

sky *n.* **1.** atmosphere, heaven, mackerel sky, upper atmosphere, vault, welkin *Nonformal:* the blue, wild blue yonder **2.** empyrean, firmament, heaven, kingdom come, paradise, promised land, the hereafter

slab *n.* bit, chip, chunk, cut, hunk, ingot, lump, mass, part, piece, portion, slice, stave, strip, wedge

slack *adj.* **1.** baggy, dangling, drooping, hanging, loose, pensile, sagging, suspended **2.** flabby, flaccid, flimsy, limp, listless, soft *Antonyms:* taut, tense, tight **3.** dull, easy, lazy, leisurely, offseason, quiet, slow, sluggish, unhurried **4.** calm, dormant, idle, inactive, inert, stagnant, unperturbed **5.** careless, delinquent, dilatory, heedless, inattentive, lackadaisical, languid, lax, lethargic, negligent, perfunctory, relaxed, remiss, slapdash, slipshod, slovenly *Antonyms:* careful, conscientious, meticulous – *adv.* easily, flimsily, half-heartedly, loosely – *n.* excess, give, latitude, leeway, looseness, margin, play, room, space – *v.* **1.** abate, decrease, diminish, drop off, dwindle, ease, ease off, lessen, let up, reduce, relax, slow down, taper off **2.** billow, droop, hang, loosen, release, sag **3.** avoid, neglect, rest, shirk, skip, take it easy *(Nonformal)*

slacker *n.* dodger, *flâneur (French)*, idler, malingerer, shirker *Nonformal:* boondoggler, bum, clock watcher, deadbeat, deadwood, goldbrick, goof off, loafer *Antonyms:* hustler, Type A, workaholic, workhorse

slacks *n.* breeches, cords, culottes, dress pants, grey flannels, jeans, khakis, pantaloons, pants, trousers *See also:* **pants**

slake *v.* **1.** abate, appease, assuage, gratify, quench, relieve, satiate, satisfy **2.** brace, freshen, moisten, refresh, restore, revivify, water **3.** calm, lessen, minimize, mitigate, moderate, pacify, palliate, quell, temper

slam *n.* **1.** bang, blast, crack, crash, pound, smack, smash, whack **2.** abuse, animadversion, aspersion, criticism, obloquy, reproof, slur, stricture *Nonformal:* burn, crack, dig, dis, fling, jab, potshot, rap, slap, swipe *Antonyms:* approval, commendation, praise – *v.* **1.** bat, batter, beat, belt, blast, clobber, cream *(Nonformal)*, cudgel, dash, fling, hammer, hit, hurl, knock, pound, slap, slug, smash, strike, swat, thump, thwack, wallop **2.** bang, close, crash, seal, secure, shut **3.** attack, castigate, censure, criticize, excoriate, flay, lambaste, scathe, scourge, vilify *Nonformal:* burn, dig, dis, jab, pan, trash

slander *n.* aspersion, attack, belittlement, blemish, calumny, character assassination, damage, defamation, denigration, detraction, disparagement, falsehood, lie, misrepresentation, muckraking, scandal, smear, smear campaign, stain, stigma, taint *Nonformal:* backbiting, black eye *Antonyms:* acclaim, approval, praise, tribute – *v.* assail, asperse, attack, badmouth, belittle, besmirch, calumniate, damage, decry, defame, defile, denigrate, depreciate, detract, dishonour, disparage, disrespect, hurt, injure, malign, revile, scandalize, slur, smear, sully, tarnish, vilify *Nonformal:* backbite, blacken the name of, blot, burn, dis, rip, roast, trash *Antonyms:* compliment, eulogize, praise

slanderous *adj.* abusive, calumnious, degrading, derogatory, detracting, disparaging, false, injurious, insulting, offensive, pejorative, unsubstantiated *Antonyms:* complimentary, congratulatory, honorific

slang *n.* **1.** colloquialism, demotic, dialect, idiom, lingo, localism, patois, provincialism, regionalism, vernacular, vulgarism **2.** argot, cant, jargon, palaver, shoptalk *Nonformal:* gobbledygook, mumbo-jumbo

slant *adj.* canted, descending, inclining, listing, oblique, sloping, tilted – *n.* **1.** bent, bias, leaning, partiality, predilection, prejudice, proclivity **2.** angle, attitude, interpretation, outlook, point-of-view, position, standpoint, understanding, viewpoint *Nonformal:* spin, take **3.** acclivity, cant, declivity, grade, gradient, inclination, lean, lilt, pitch, slope – *v.* **1.** colour, contour, distort, fabricate, falsify, fudge, misshape, misconstrue, pervert, prejudice, shape, shift, skew, twist, warp *Nonformal:* doctor, spin **2.** bevel, cant, decline, descend, incline, grade, heel, lean, level, list, slope, swerve, tilt, tip, veer

slanting *adj.* angled, askew, bent, bevelled, diagonal, falling-off, inclined, leaning, listing, off kilter *(Nonformal)*, sloped, tilted, veering *Antonyms:* flat, level, straight

slap *adv.* abruptly, directly, immediately, instantly, right, suddenly, unexpectedly, without warning – *n. & v.* **1.** bang, bash, blow, box, buffet, chop, clap, clout, crack, cuff, hit, poke, punch, slam, smack, sock, spank, strike, swat, wallop, whack **2.** gibe, insult, jeer, rebuff, rebuke, taunt

slapdash *adj.* careless, casual, clumsy, cursory, disorderly, half-assed *(Nonformal)*, haphazard, hasty, hit-and-miss, hurried, irresponsible, last-minute, lax, messy, negligent, off the cuff, offhand, passing, perfunctory, rash, remiss, slack, slipshod, sloppy, slovenly, snap, speedy, superficial, thoughtless, unmindful, unthinking, untidy *Antonyms:* fastidious, meticulous, precise, punctilious – *adv.* carelessly, casually, flippantly, negligently, perfunctorily, shoddily, thoughtlessly

slaphappy *adj.* **1.** absurd, asinine, foolish, idiotic, silly, thoughtless, uncaring *Antonyms:* careful, considerate, deliberate **2.** dazed, dizzy, giddy, punchy, stupefied, tipsy *Nonformal:* punch-drunk, stunned

slash *n.* **1.** cut, flesh wound, gaping wound, gash, incision, laceration, lesion, nick, puncture, rent, rip, scratch, slice, slit, wound **2.** aperture, break, clearance, gap, hole, opening, pass **3.** cheapening, curtailment, cutback, discount, lowering, markdown, price-cut, reduction, sale **4.** *Forestry:* debris, detritus, organic litter, remains – *v.* **1.** carve, cut, gash, gut, hack, incise, injure, knife, lacerate, lance, pierce, rend, rip, score, sever, slice, slit, split, stab, tear, wound **2.** flagellate, flail, horsewhip, lash, scourge, strike, whip **3.** attack, belittle, castigate, censure, criticize, disparage, excoriate, fustigate, skin alive *(Nonformal)*, trounce **4.** cheapen, curtail, cut, drop, lower, reduce **5.** chain saw, chop, clear, clear-cut, destroy, exploit, moonscape *(B.C.)*, rape, ravage, raze

slate *n.* **1.** blackboard, board, chalkboard, laminate, shingle, tablet **2.** agenda, ballot, bill, bill of fare, calendar, card, docket, lineup, menu, playbill, program, roster, schedule, ticket – *v.* **1.** arrange, bill, book, program, reserve, schedule **2.** appoint, assign, classify, designate, empower, name, nominate, specify

slatternly *adj.* **1.** cheap, dirty, dissolute, easy, fallen, indiscriminate, lewd, loose, profligate, promiscuous, shameless, wanton, wild *Nonformal:* sleazy, slutty *Antonyms:* inhibited, prudish, puritanical **2.** bedraggled, blowzy, dishevelled, dowdy, filthy, frowzy, messy, rumpled, slobbish, sloppy, slovenly, stained, tattered, ungroomed, unkempt, untidy *Nonformal:* grubby, grungy, scuzzy *Antonyms:* clean, neat, tidy, well-groomed

slaughter *n.* annihilation, bloodbath, bloodshed, butchery, carnage, destruction, ethnic cleansing, extermination, holocaust, killing, liquidation, massacre, murder, pogrom, slaying – *v.* **1.** butcher, decimate, destroy, devastate, exterminate, extirpate, finish, kill, liquidate, massacre, murder, ravage, ruin, slay, waste, wipe-out **2.** beat, conquer, crush, defeat, overcome, overwhelm, trounce, vanquish

slave *n.* **1.** bondsman, bondswoman, chattel, churl, helot, indentured servant, instrument, peon, retainer, serf, servant, subject, thrall, tool, vassal **2.** cog, drudge, grub, hack, labourer, plodder, toiler, worker, workhorse **3.** addict, alcoholic, habitué, user *Nonformal:* cokehead, crackhead, fiend, freak, junkie, pothead – *v.* drudge, hammer *or* pound away, moil, slog, toil, work *Nonformal:* grind, plug along, sweat

slavery *n.* **1.** bondage, captivity, chains, constraint, enslavement, exploitation, oppression, restraint, serfdom, servility, servitude, subjugation, vassalage, thralldom *Antonyms:* emancipation, freedom, liberty **2.** drudgery, exertion, grind, grunt *or* hard work, labour, moil, toil, strain, struggle, sweat and blood *(Nonformal)*

slavish *adj.* **1.** abject, base, bootlicking *(Nonformal)*, contemptible, deferential, lowly, mean, meek, obsequious, pusillanimous, servile, submissive, subservient, sycophantic, unctuous *Antonyms:* defiant, proud, rebellious **2.** arduous, backbreaking, brutal, difficult, exhausting, fatiguing, hellish *(Nonformal)*, laborious, punishing, strenuous, taxing, toiling, torturous *Antonyms:* easy, painless, simple

slay *v.* annihilate, assassinate, butcher, destroy, dispatch, eliminate, erase, execute, exterminate, finish, kill, liquidate, massacre, murder, slaughter, smite, terminate *Nonformal:* bump *or* knock off, chill, croak, dust, neutralize, rub out, snuff, waste

sleazy *adj.* **1.** cheap, chintzy, cut-rate, flimsy, gimcrack, inferior, jerrybuilt, junky, makeshift, poor, poorly made, second-rate, shoddy, trashy *Nonformal:* cheesy, crappy, crummy, dimestore *Antonyms:* choice, deluxe, fine **2.** dilapidated, dingy, filthy, grimy, mean, rough, run-down, scuzzy *(Nonformal)*, seedy, squalid, tumble-down *Antonyms:* classy, refined, elegant **3.** contemptible, corrupt, creepy, despicable, disreputable, seamy *Nonformal:* greasy, oily, shady

sled *n.* sledge, sleigh *Kinds of sled:* berline, bobsled, box-sleigh, catamaran *(Newfoundland)*, cat train, crazy carpet, dogsled, flying saucer, kibitka, luge, pung, ski-bob, snowmobile, stoneboat, toboggan, tom, travois *North:* carriole, komatik, qamutiik, tabansk – *v.* convey, glide, ride, slide, slip along, transport, travel

sleek *adj.* **1.** clean, dapper, natty *(Nonformal)*, neat, scrubbed, shipshape, smart, *soigné (French)*, spruce, tidy, trim, washed, well-groomed *Antonyms:* dirty, dishevelled, filthy **2.** burnished, lubricated, polished, oily, satiny, shiny, silken, slick, slippery, velvety, waxed **3.** courtly, diplomatic, disarming, facile, flattering, fulsome, ingratiating, polite, smooth, suave, sweet-talking, urbane *Antonyms:* obnoxious, rude, vulgar **4.** aerodynamic, efficient, fast, space-age, streamlined, wedge-like, wind-piercing *Antonyms:* boxy, bulky, cumbersome **5.** chic, chichi *(Nonformal)*, contemporary, elegant, fashionable, modern, new-wave, stylish *Antonyms:* outworn, passé, tired

sleep *n.* **1.** doze, nap, narcosis, siesta, slumber, somnolence, unconsciousness *Nonformal:* catnap, power nap, shut-eye **2.** dormancy, hibernation, inactivity, idleness, leisure, lethargy, peace, quiet, relaxation, repose, rest, slumpage *(Nonformal)*, torpor

– *v.* **1.** bed down, doze, drowse, lie down, nap, nod, retire, slumber *Nonformal:* bag some z's, catch forty winks, conk *or* flake *or* zonk out, crash, drop off, saw logs, snooze **2.** hibernate, idle, loaf, lounge, relax, unwind, vegetate *(Nonformal)*

sleepless *adj.* alert, astir, awake, disturbed, insomniac, nervous, restless, tossing and turning *(Nonformal)*, vigilant, wakeful, wide awake

sleepy *adj.* **1.** dozy, draggy, drowsy, exhausted, groggy, heavy, heavy-lidded, slumberous, tired, worn out *Nonformal:* burnt, fried, wasted, wiped *Antonyms:* alert, animated, wakeful **2.** calming, hypnotizing, narcotic, numbing, opiate, sleep-inducing, somnolent, soporific, tiring, tranquilizing, wearisome *Antonyms:* motivating, rousing, stimulating **3.** dull, inactive, languid, lazy, lethargic, listless, peaceful, quiet, restful, slow, sluggish, torpid, unhurried, yawning *Antonyms:* active, busy, boisterous

sleight *n.* **1.** ability, adroitness, aptitude, command, competence, control, dexterity, expertise, handiness, knack, mastery, quickness, skill, talent, technique **2.** artistry, craft, cunning, deceit, deception, duplicity, foxiness, guile, magic, shrewdness, sleight of hand, subterfuge, trickery, wiliness

slender *adj.* **1.** attenuated, fine, lean, lithe, narrow, reedy, skeletal, skinny, slight, slim, stalky, svelte, sylphlike, thin, threadlike, trim, twiggy *(Nonformal)*, willowy **2.** delicate, feeble, flimsy, fragile, frail, weak **3.** doubtful, dubious, flawed, questionable, shaky, shallow, sketchy, teetering, tenuous, unstable *Antonyms:* solid, strong, sturdy **4.** distant, doubtful, far fetched, improbable, limited, minimal, outside, questionable, remote, unlikely *Antonyms:* certain, sure, sure-fire **5.** dim, faded, faint, gentle, light, low, muted, quiet *Antonyms:* deafening, loud, resounding **6.** humble, inadequate, inconsiderable, insubstantial, insufficient, little, meagre, moderate, picayune, poor, scant, scanty, short, shy, small, wanting *Antonyms:* ample, considerable, fat, generous

sleuth *n.* bloodhound, detective, PI, private eye *or* investigator, sleuthhound, spy, undercover agent *Nonformal:* dick, flatfoot, gumshoe, shamus, sherlock – *v.* follow, inspect, investigate, probe, pry, shadow, stalk, track, trail

slice *n.* allotment, allowance, bite, chop, collop, cut, dividend, helping, lot, part, percentage, piece, portion, quota, rasher, section, segment, share, sliver, triangle, wedge – *v.* **1.** apportion, divide, divvy up *(Nonformal)*, part, segment, separate, sever, split, split up, subdivide **2.** carve, cleave, cut, cut through, knife, pare, peel, shave, skive, sunder, whittle

slick *adj.* **1.** glazed, glossy, greasy, icy, lubricious, oily, polished, shiny, sleek, slippery, slithery, soapy **2.** flattering, glib, obsequious, smooth, smooth-tongued, suave, unctuous **3.** adroit, artful, cunning, foxy, manipulative, shrewd, sly, sophisticated, specious, street-smart *(Nonformal)*, streetwise, tricky, wily **4.** bright, cagey, canny, clever, deft, expert, handy, ingenious, inventive, professional, quick, resourceful, sharp, smart, talented, wise **5.** appropriate, exact, excellent, fitting, good, perfect, proper, suitable, wonderful – *n.* blanket, coating, cover, covering, film, layer, surface – *v.* furbish, glaze, gloss, oil, polish, rub, shine, wax

slide *n.* **1.** avalanche, cascade, fall, landslide, mudslide **2.** channel, chute, flume, shaft, tube – *v.* **1.** coast, drift, drop, glide, glissade, sail, skate, ski, skid, skim, sled, slither, stream, toboggan, veer **2.** advance, continue, move, proceed, progress, snowball **3.** attend to itself, go, lapse, pass, run its course **4.** fall, plummet, slip, stumble, take a header *(Nonformal)*, trip, tumble

slight *adj.* **1.** insignificant, minor, petty, shallow, superficial, trifling, trivial, unessential, unimportant *Antonyms:* critical, great, important, meaningful **2.** diminutive, inconsiderable, insubstantial, meagre, modest, paltry, scanty, small, sparse **3.** attenuated, dainty, delicate, feeble, flimsy, fragile, frail, light, reedy, skinny, slender, slim, small, thin, tiny *Antonyms:* husky, muscular, solid, sturdy **4.** faint, improbable, limited, outside, remote, unlikely – *n.*

affront, contempt, cut, discourtesy, disdain, disregard, disrespect, inattention, indifference, insult, neglect, omission, rebuff, rejection, snub *Nonformal:* brush off, cold shoulder, go-by, put-down – *v.* **1.** contemn, cut, discount, discredit, disdain, disparage, disregard, insult, offend, reject, scoff, scorn, slur, snub, upstage *Nonformal:* brush off, chill, cut dead, dis, high-hat, pooh-pooh **2.** avoid, dodge, ignore, neglect, omit, shirk, sidestep, skip *Antonyms:* assume, confront, take up

slighting *adj.* **1.** abusive, caustic, defamatory, disparaging, hurtful, insulting, offensive, rude, vitriolic, vituperative *Antonyms:* complimentary, encouraging, supportive **2.** aloof, arrogant, cold, disdainful, haughty, omissive, peremptory, supercilious, superior, unfriendly *Antonyms:* open-armed, warm, welcome

slightly *adv.* a little, barely, marginally, negligibly, partially, scantily, somewhat, to some degree *or* extent

slim *adj.* **1.** gracile, lanky, lean, lithe, reedy, skinny, slender, slight, slinky, spare, svelte, sylphlike, thin, thready, trim, willowy *Antonyms:* broad, bulky, fat, obese, wide **2.** inadequate, insufficient, meagre, negligible, paltry, poor, puny, small, trifling **3.** cut-rate, flimsy, inferior, lousy *(Nonformal)*, pathetic, pitiful, second-rate, sorry, unacceptable, unsatisfactory, unsuitable *Antonyms:* adequate, admirable, first-class, good, satisfactory **4.** doubtful, dubious, farfetched, improbable, limited, tall, weak – *v.* diet, fast, lose weight, pare down, trim

slime *n.* earth, ectoplasm, fungus, gelatin, mire, muck, mucous, mud, myxomycete, ooze, refuse, residue, scum, sewage, silt, slop, sludge, substance, teleplasm, waste *Nonformal:* glop, goo, guck, gunk, mush

slimy *adj.* **1.** ectoplasmic, glutinous, gelatinous, greasy, mucky, muddy, oily, oozy, scummy, slippery, sludge-like, sticky, viscous *Nonformal:* gooey, mushy **2.** contemptible, disgusting, foul, gross, loathsome, nauseating, noxious, offensive, repulsive, sickening, wretched *Antonyms:* alluring, appealing, attractive **3.** conniving, corrupt, crooked, deceitful, dishonest, perfidious, scrofulous, shady *(Nonformal)*, sinister, tricky, unctuous, underhanded

sling *n.* **1.** catapult, mortar, slingshot **2.** band, bandage, brace, loop, parbuckle, strap, support – *v.* **1.** cast, chuck, fire, fling, heave, hurl, launch, lob, peg, pitch, send, shoot, throw, toss **2.** hang, hoist, hold, raise, suspend, swing

slink *v.* cower, creep, glide, lurk, prowl, sidle, skitter, skulk, slide, slip, slither, sneak, stalk, steal along

slinky *adj.* **1.** clandestine, covert, creeping, furtive, secretive, skulking, sly, sneaking, stealthy *Antonyms:* conspicuous, open **2.** easy, elegant, feline, flowing, fluid, graceful, seductive, serpentine, sexy, sinuous, smooth

slip *n.* **1.** fall, header *(Nonformal)*, skid, slide, spill, stumble, trip **2.** accident, blooper, blunder, boner, bungle, error, faux pas, fumble, gaffe, malapropism, mistake, parapraxis, spoonerism *Latin: lapsus, lapsus calami, lapsus linguae, lapsus memoriae Nonformal:* boo-boo, flub, fluff, goof, muff, screw-up **3.** breach, crime, fault, impropriety, indiscretion, lapse, offence, relapse, sin, trespass, wrong **4.** bill, cheque, chit, label, leaf, memorandum, note, page, paper, receipt, record, sheet, strip, tab, tag, ticket, voucher **5.** anchorage, berth, dock, harbour, landing, landing place, mooring, parking spot, pier **6.** camisole, knickers, lingerie, undergarment, underskirt, underwear *Nonformal:* skivvies, undies **7.** branch, cutting, runner, scion, shoot, sprig, sprout, tendril **8.** avoidance, deke *(Nonformal)*, elusion, escape, evasion, runaround, shift, sidestep – *v.* **1.** flow, glide, glissade, sail, skate, skid, slide **2.** abandon, avoid, bypass, disregard, ditch, dodge, dump, forget, neglect, omit, overlook, pass, scorn, shake, shirk, shun, slight, snub *Nonformal:* deke, deke out **3.** err, fall, lapse, misbehave, sin, sink, stray, transgress, trespass **4.** blunder, drop, fumble, let fall *or* go, miscalculate *Nonformal:* flub, goof up, muff **5.** abandon, break free, clear out, creep off, escape, flee, free oneself, slink away, steal out **6.** free, liberate, loosen, release, shed, undo, unfasten, unfetter, unhitch, unleash, untie **7.** fall, stumble, topple, trip, tumble

Nonformal: go ass over tea kettle, take a header **8.** betray, blab *(Nonformal)*, convey, disclose, divulge, give away, leak, let slip, reveal, spill, tell

slippery *adj.* **1.** glassy, glazed, glistening, greasy, icy, lustrous, oily, polished, satiny, silky, sleek, slick, slippy *(Nonformal)*, smooth, wet *Antonyms:* coarse, dry, rough **2.** cagey, crafty, cunning, devious, dishonest, duplicitous, elusive, evasive, false, lubricious, shifty, slithery, sneaky, treacherous, tricky, untrustworthy *Antonyms:* honest, responsible, trustworthy **3.** critical, dangerous, delicate, knotty, nasty, risky, ticklish, unpredictable, unreliable, unsafe, unsteady *Antonyms:* safe, sound, stable

slipshod *adj.* **1.** careless, casual, hurried, last-minute, lazy, loose, messy, negligent, offhand, remiss, slack, sloppy, slovenly, thoughtless, uncaring, untidy *Antonyms:* careful, exact, fastidious **2.** bedraggled, dilapidated, dirty, down-and-out, ragged, rough, rundown, shabby, squalid, tawdry, tumble-down, well-used, worn *Nonformal:* ratty, scuzzy, waterfront *Antonyms:* chic, classy, elegant, mint

slit *n.* aperture, breach, cleavage, cleft, crack, crevice, cut, fissure, gash, hole, incision, kerf, opening, rent, split, tear – *v.* cut, gash, incise, lance, open, pierce, rend, slash, slice, sunder

slither *v.* crawl, creep, glide, skulk, slide, slink, slip, snake, undulate *Antonyms:* stomp, tread

sliver *n.* bit, flake, fragment, iota, jot, paring, part, piece, portion, section, shaving, shred, skiver, slice, slip, snip, snippet, splinter, whittling

slob *n.* boor, lout, oaf, philistine, slattern, sloven *Nonformal:* bum, hog, lummox, pig, swine

slobber *v.* **1.** dirty, drip, drivel, drool, foul, mess, muck up, ooze, salivate, slaver, spill, stain, wet **2.** bootlick, fawn over, gush, palaver, sentimentalize

slog *v.* drudge, endure, lumber, persist, plod, scut, slave, toil, tramp, trudge, work *Nonformal:* hoof it, keep at it, press the bricks, schlep

slogan *n.* byword, catch phrase, catchword, expression, idiom, jingle, logo, mission statement, motto, phrase, proverb, rallying cry, saying, shibboleth, trademark

slop *n.* garbage, gruel, mire, muck, mulch, mud, purée, quagmire, rubbish, sewage, slime, slough, sludge, slush, swill, trash, waste *Nonformal:* glop, goo, guck, mush – *v.* dirty, foul, slosh, spatter, spill, splash, splatter, spray, waste

slope *n.* **1.** bank, bluff, brae, cliff, coteau, escarpment, hill, hillside, mountainside, palisades *(U.S)*, precipice, rise, steep, wall **2.** abruptness, acclivity, angle, bend, bevel, camber, cant, declination, declivity, degree, descent, diagonal, dip, downgrade, drop, fall, grade, gradient, height, incline, leaning, level, list, obliqueness, pitch, point, ramp, slant, slide, steepness, tilt – *v.* angle, ascend, cant, descend, dip, drop, fall, incline, lean, list, pitch, recline, rise, shelve, skew, slant, tilt

sloppy *adj.* **1.** marshy, oozy, pulpy, slimy, slippery, slippy, sloshy, sludgy, slushy, sodden, soggy, swampy, watery, wet *Nonformal:* gooey, gucky, mussy *Antonyms:* dry, firm, hard **2.** soiled, spattered, splashed, splattered, spotted, spotty, stained **3.** bedraggled, dirty, dishevelled, disorderly, dowdy, down-at-the-heels, filthy, frowzy, frumpy, grimy, grubby, grungy, messy, piggish, rundown, scruffy, shabby, slatternly, sleazy, slovenly, tangled, unclean, uncombed, unkempt, untidy *Antonyms:* clean, neat, spiffy, tidy **4.** amateurish, careless, clumsy, haphazard, hasty, hit-or-miss, inattentive, lazy, loose, offhand, slack, slapdash, slipshod, wretched *Nonformal:* crappy, lousy *Antonyms:* attentive, careful, focussed, orderly **5.** cloying, gushing, gushy, maudlin, mawkish, saccharine, sentimental, soppy, sugary *Nonformal:* Hollywood, mushy, schmaltzy *Antonyms:* genuine, realistic, serious

slot *n.* **1.** aperture, cavity, channel, compartment, cut, groove, hole, niche, opening, pigeonhole, recess, slit, socket **2.** place, position, space, vacancy – *v.* categorize, place, position, rank, seed

sloth *n.* **1.** acedia, dormancy, homeostasis, idleness, inactivity, indolence, inertia, languidness, laziness, lethargy, listlessness, passivity, slackness, sluggishness, stagnation, torpor *Antonyms:* activity, exertion, haste, speed **2.** laggard, lazybones, slouch, sluggard *Nonformal:* slugabed, stick-in-the-mud

slothful *adj.* drowsy, idle, indifferent, indolent, insouciant, lackadaisical, laggard, languid, languorous, lazy, lethargic, listless, phlegmatic, shiftless, slack, sleepy, sluggish, supine, torpid, unambitious, unenterprising, unindustrious, uninterested *Antonyms:* diligent, energetic, hard-working, high octane, industrious, Type A

slouch *n.* **1.** clod, dolt, fool, imbecile, klutz, lout, oaf *Nonformal:* bumbler, doofus, hoser, puzzler **2.** avoider, idler, shirker *Nonformal:* bum, couch potato, goldbricker, goof-off, lazybones – *v.* bend, bow, crouch, droop, hunch, lean, loll, lounge, sag, slump, stoop, tilt, wilt

slovenly *adj.* **1.** dirty, dishevelled, draggletailed, filthy, messy, ragged, rough, rumpled, seedy, slatternly, tousled, unclean, unhealthy, unkempt, untidy *Antonyms:* neat, smart, tidy, trim **2.** careless, casual, devil-may-care, disorderly, lackadaisical, lax, lazy, negligent, slapdash, slipshod *Antonyms:* methodical, meticulous, precise

slow *adj.* **1.** crab-like, crawling, creeping, dilatory, gradual, lingering, plodding, sluggish, snail-like, unhurried *Antonyms:* brisk, hurried **2.** behind, belated, delayed, detained, dilatory, laggard, late, negligent, overdue, prolonged, protracted, tardy *Antonyms:* prompt, punctual **3.** dense, dim, dim-witted, dull, dumb, gormless *(British)*, obtuse, simple, thick, unresponsive *Antonyms:* perceptive, quick **4.** dawdling, dreamy, drowsy, indolent, lackadaisical, lazy, leisurely, lethargic, procrastinating, sleepy, spiritless, torpid *Antonyms:* animated, driven, excited **5.** dormant, down, idle, inactive, quiet, slack *Antonyms:* active, busy, hectic **6.** boring, drawn, exhausting, insipid, lengthy, long, sapping, soporific, tedious, tiring, wearying *Nonformal:* crickets, dead, tumbleweeds **7.** careful, considered, deliberate, exacting, measured, studied, thorough, unhurried – *v.* brake, check, choke, curb, curtail, decelerate, decrease, delay, detain, diminish, ease off, govern, handicap, hinder, hold back, impede, lag, lessen, relax, retard, slacken, stall, stunt, temper, wind down *Antonyms:* accelerate, advance, boost

slowdown *n.* **1.** backup, blockage, bottleneck, clog, delay, holdup, inactivity, logjam, slow-up, snag, snarl, stoppage *Antonyms:* acceleration, peaking, rise, speed-up **2.** braking, check, deceleration **3.** decline, decrease, drop, fall-off, shrinkage **4.** job action, labour unrest, protest, revolt, sit-down strike, work stoppage, work-to-rule

slowly *adv.* adagio, all in good time, at one's own pace, calmly, carefully, cautiously, eventually, gradually, in the fullness of time *(Nonformal)*, inch by inch, largo, leisurely, steadily, unhurriedly *Antonyms:* avante, quickly, speedily, swiftly

sludge *n.* dregs, ectoplasm, mire, muck, mucous, mud, ooze, quagmire, refuse, residue, scum, sediment, sewage, silt, slime, slop, slosh, slough, slush, swill, waste *Nonformal:* glop, goo, goop, guck, gunk, mush

slug *n.* **1.** ammunition, bullet, musket ball, projectile, round, shot **2.** dallier, dawdler, *flâneur (French)*, idler, laggard, plodder, saunter, sluggard, straggler *Nonformal:* crab, ne'er-do-well, slowpoke, snail **3.** bash, blow, box, hit, jab, knock, pop, poke, punch, roundhouse, smack, uppercut, whack *Nonformal:* haymaker, knuckle sandwich **4.** bung-your-eye *(Newfoundland)*, bracer, dose, draught, drink, jigger, nip, pick-me-up, sample, sip, snort *(Nonformal)*, swallow, swig, taste – *v.* bash, bat, batter, beat, belt, clobber, clout, hit, jab, pound, punch, smack, smite, sock, strike, thump, whack *Nonformal:* bust, mash

sluggish *adj.* **1.** dormant, dull, heavy, homeostatic, inactive, inert, leaden, slack, slow, stagnant **2.** apathetic, draggy, indolent, lackadaisical, languid, languorous, lazy, lethargic, lifeless, listless, phlegmatic, sleepy, slothful, slow-moving, sluggard, slumberous, sullen, torpid, unresponsive

Antonyms: animated, brisk, dynamic, energetic, fast

slum *n.* bustee, ghetto, projects *(Nonformal)*, rookery, shack town, shantytown, skid row, squalor

slumber *n.* **1.** doze, drowse, nap, repose, rest, shut-eye *(Nonformal)*, sleep, somnolescence, unconsciousness **2.** dormancy, hibernation, homeostasis, idleness, immobility, inactivity, inertia, languor, lethargy, motionlessness, stagnation, stoppage, stupor, torpor – *v.* doze, drowse, nap, repose, rest, sleep *Nonformal:* saw logs, snooze

slump *n.* blight, collapse, decline, depression, downswing, downward spiral, drop, failure, fall, low, recession, reverse, rut, slide, slip, stagnation *Antonyms:* advance, boost, development, expansion, rise – *v.* **1.** descend, fall, plummet, plunge, sink, tumble **2.** collapse, decay, decline, deteriorate, fail, fall off, founder, lose *or* lose ground, slide, slip, topple *Antonyms:* boom, develop, expand, flourish, grow **3.** bend, crouch, dangle, droop, hunch, keel, lean, sag, settle, slouch, stoop

slur *n.* accusation, affront, aspersion, calumny, denigration, detraction, discredit, innuendo, insinuation, insult, obloquy, odium, reproach, smear, stain, stigma, stricture *Nonformal:* black eye, brickbat, burn, dig, dis, knock, put-down, rap, slam, zinger – *v.* **1.** blacken, blemish, blister, blot, brand, calumniate, contaminate, defame, denigrate, depreciate, detract, discredit, disgrace, disparage, insinuate, insult, libel, malign, offend, slander, slight, smear, snub, soil, spatter, stain, tear down, traduce, vilify *Nonformal:* cut up, dump on, kick around, put down, roast, scorch, slam **2.** elide, butcher *(Nonformal)*, garble, mispronounce, mumble *Antonyms:* articulate, enunciate **3.** conceal, cover up, disguise, gloss *or* pass over, marginalize, minimize, whitewash

slush *n.* **1.** frazil, muck, slop, wet snow **2.** bathos, cloyingness, drivel, mawkishness, sentimentality, sugar *Nonformal:* mush, sap, schmaltz, sop

sly *adj.* arch, artful, cagey, calculating, clever, conniving, crafty, cunning, deceitful, deft, designing, devious, dextrous, dissembling, dissimulative, evasive, foxy, Machiavellian, mischievous, on the watch *(Nonformal)*, roguish, secretive, sharp, shifty, shrewd, skilful, smart, snaky, subtle, tricky, underhanded, unscrupulous, wise *Antonyms:* artless, direct, honest, guileless

smack *n.* **1.** bang, blow, box, buffet, chop, clout, crack, cuff, hit, punch, roundhouse, slap, slug, snap, sock, spank, strike, whap **2.** heroin *Nonformal:* dope, drugs, horse, Mr. Brownstone **3.** bit, dab, dash, hint, smattering, sprinkling, taste, tinge, touch, trace – *v.* **1.** box, buffet, clap, cuff, hit, punch, slap, slug, sock, spank, strike, tap **2.** buss, greet, kiss, osculate *Nonformal:* peck, smooch

small *adj.* **1.** baby, bantam, diminutive, Lilliputian, little, microscopic, mignon, miniature, minute, petite, puny, tiny, wee, young *Nonformal:* mini, peewee, teensy *Antonyms:* big, enormous, large **2.** deficient, inadequate, lacking, meagre, scant, short, shy, slight, wanting *Antonyms:* ample, plentiful, sufficient **3.** bit, inconsequential, immaterial, irrelevant, lesser, marginal, minor, negligible, paltry, picayune, slight, unimportant *Antonyms:* critical, leading, major, significant **4.** humble, limited, modest, nameless, obscure, of little note, undistinguished, unheralded, unnoticed, unrenowned, unsung *Antonyms:* famous, popular, prominent **5.** childish, greedy, grudging, ignoble, immature, mean, narrow, narrow-minded, nasty, parsimonious, petty, selfish, stingy **6.** fine, gentle, low, mild, quiet, slender, soft, subdued

small-minded *adj.* bigoted, confined, envious, grudging, hidebound, ignoble, insular, intolerant, limited, mean, narrow-minded, parochial, petty, provincial, rigid, ungenerous *Antonyms:* broad-minded, far-sighted, liberal, open-minded, tolerant

smart *adj.* **1.** acute, adaptable, alert, apt, astute, brainy, bright, brilliant, canny, clever, crafty, effective, imaginative, ingenious, intelligent, inventive, keen, knowledgeable, perspicacious, pointed, quick, resourceful, sapient, sharp, shrewd, street-smart *(Nonformal)*, streetwise, wise, worldly-wise *Antonyms:* dense, dull, thick

2. bold, brash, brazen, cheeky, cocky, disrespectful, forward, fresh, impertinent, impudent, nervy, pert, sassy, saucy, witty *Nonformal:* smart-alecky, smart-assed *Antonyms:* courteous, obedient, timid **3.** active, agile, brisk, emphatic, energetic, jaunty, lively, scintillating, spirited, sprightly, vigorous *Antonyms:* crawling, inactive, slow **4.** biting, burning, caustic, irritating, piercing, pungent, sharp, stinging, vitriolic **5.** chic, dapper, dashing, elegant, exclusive, fashionable, fine, glamorous, latest, modish, natty, neat, showy, snappy, spruce, stylish, trendy, trim *Nonformal:* dressed to kill, hip, slick, swank, swish, tony, with-it *Antonyms:* dated, old, passé, tired – *v.* ache, bite, burn, hurt, irritate, pain, prick, sting, suffer, throb, tingle *Antonyms:* alleviate, ease, mitigate

smash *interj.* bam, bang, bash, boom, crash, kaboom, pop, pow, slam, smack, whack, wham – *n.* **1.** accident, bash, breakage, breakup, collapse, collision, crackup, crash, destruction, fender-bender, pileup, shattering, smash-up **2.** achievement, bestseller, hit, overnight *or* runaway sensation, success, top ten, triumph – *v.* **1.** bash, break, crash, demolish, destroy, flatten, raze, ruin, shatter, total, trash, wreck **2.** annihilate, crush, decimate, defeat, devastate, lay waste, overpower, overturn, overwhelm, smite, topple, undo, wipe out **3.** crack, hit, knock, poke, pop, punch, serve, strike

smear *n.* **1.** blemish, smudge, spot, stain **2.** representation, sample, sampling, swatch **3.** aspersion, calumny, character assassination, defamation, libel, opprobrium, slander, smear campaign, vilification – *v.* **1.** apply, bedaub, blur, coat, cover, dab, layer, overlay, overspread, plaster, rub on, slop, spatter, spray, spread, sprinkle, stipple **2.** asperse, attack, befoul, besmirch, blacken, calumniate, decry, defame, defile, denigrate, dirty, discolour, dishonour, malign, slander, slur, smudge, soil, sully, taint, tar, tarnish, traduce, vilify **3.** annihilate, beat, conquer, defeat, destroy, master, overpower, trounce, vanquish

smell *n.* **1.** aroma, bouquet, emanation, essence, flavour, fragrance, hum *(P.E.I.)*, incense, odour, perfume, redolence, savour, scent, spice, stench, stink, tang **2.** clue, hint, indicator, intimation, reminder, sign, suggestion, suspicion, trail, trace, warning – *v.* **1.** breathe, detect, discover, find, identify, inhale, nose, perceive, scent, sniff, snuff, whiff **2.** fart, foul up, offend, reek, smell bad, stink, stink out *or* up

smelly *adj.* evil-smelling, fetid, foul, foul-smelling, high, humming *(P.E.I.)*, malodorous, mephitic, noisome, obnoxious, odoriferous, odorous, P.U. *(Nonformal)*, putrid, rancid, rank, redolent, reeking, stinking, stinky, strong, strong-smelling, sweaty *Antonyms:* aromatic, fragrant, pungent, sweet-smelling

smidgen *n.* dab, dash, drop, iota, jot, little *or* tiny bit, mote, particle, pinch, soupçon, teaspoonful, touch

smile *n.* cheer, expression, grin, happiness, look, simper, smirk – *v.* beam, crack, crack a grin *(Nonformal)*, gleam, glow, grin, laugh, shine, simper, smirk *Antonyms:* frown, grimace, scowl, sneer

smirk *n. & v.* grimace, grin, leer, simper, smile, sneer

smite *v.* **1.** bash, beat, belt, biff *(Nonformal)*, bludgeon, bop, box, buffet, cane, clout, club, conk, crown, cudgel, cuff, ding, flail, flog, fustigate, hammer, hit, knock, lambaste, lash, lay into, pelt, plug, pound, pummel, punch, slap, slug, smack, sock, spank, strap, strike **2.** afflict, annihilate, assail, attack, batter, beleaguer, besiege, beset, blast, blow up, bombard, break, cast down, decimate, demolish, desolate, destroy, devastate, fell, gut, pulverize, raze, ruin, scourge, shatter, smash, tear down, total, wipe out, wreck **3.** allure, bewitch, captivate, charm, enamour, enchant, enrapture, enthrall, fascinate, infatuate, sweep off one's feet *(Nonformal) Antonyms:* bore, disgust, repel

smitten *adj.* **1.** afflicted, beset, bothered, burdened, crushed, distressed, galled, grieved, harassed, haunted, hounded, irked, laid low, overburdened, plagued, roiled, stricken, troubled, vexed, worried **2.** allured, attracted, *aux anges (French)*, bewitched, captivated, charmed, enamoured, enchanted, enraptured, enthralled, fascinated, infatuated, sweet on, taken with *Nonformal:* bowled *or* cuckoo over, crazy, gaga, head over heels, hooked

smoke *n.* **1.** carbon, cloud, coke, effluvium, exhalation, exhaust, film, fog, fume, fumes, gas, haze, mist, pollution, reek, smog, smokiness, smudge, smut, soot, suspended particles **2.** cheroot, cigar, cigarette, fag *(British)*, pipeful, stogie *Nonformal:* butt, cancer stick, cig, coffin nail, rollie, roll your own, root, stinker, weed – *v.* **1.** befog, cloud, emit, exhaust, fog, fume, give off, mist, smoulder, steam, vaporize, reek, vent **2.** blow, drag, draw, exhale, inhale, light up, puff, pull, suck, toke **3.** cure, dry, flavour, preserve, season, smoke-dry **4.** hurry, race, sail, speed, sprint, tear, travel, whisk along **5.** beat, box, buffet, defeat, pulverize, pummel, smite, strike, thrash, thump, trounce

smoky *adj.* **1.** cloudy, foggy, hazy, misty, polluted, smelly, sooty, soupy *(Nonformal)*, thick, unhealthy **2.** begrimed, blackened, coal-stained, coke-stained, dark, dirty, discoloured, dusty, filthy, fuliginous, grey, grimy, stained

smooth *adj.* **1.** constant, creamy, even, flat, flawless, flowing, flush, glabrous, level, paved, plane, regular, stable, steady, unbroken, undeviating, uniform, unwrinkled *Antonyms:* bumpy, coarse, corduroy, irregular **2.** buffed, glassy, glazed, polished, shaved, shiny, silky, sleek, slippery, varnished, velvety, waterworn **3.** agreeable, appealing, fresh, mild, pleasant **4.** calm, clement, halcyon, mellow, moderate, peaceful, quiet, subdued, tame, tranquil, unagitated, unruffled, untroubled *Antonyms:* choppy, rough, wild **5.** beguiling, cajoling, fawning, flattering, glib, greasy, guileful, obsequious, oily, suave, sycophantic, unctuous, wheedling *Nonformal:* fast-talking, smarmy *Antonyms:* awkward, clumsy, guileless **6.** cagey, calculating, clever, crafty, deceitful, devious, guileful, Machiavellian, plotting, political, scheming, slick, streetwise, treacherous *Antonyms:* angelic, innocent, naive **7.** *dégagé (French)*, easy, effortless, facile, manageable, painless, simple, straightforward, uncomplicated – *v.* **1.** clear, even, flatten, flush, level, plane, press, sand **2.** allay, alleviate, appease, assuage, calm, comfort, mellow, mitigate, mollify, palliate, soften *Antonyms:* aggravate, exacerbate, hamper, hinder **3.** clear *or* pave the way, ease, expedite, facilitate, hasten, introduce, lubricate, quicken

smother *v.* **1.** asphyxiate, burke, choke, garrote, kill, stifle, strangle, suffocate, throttle **2.** beat down, control, damp, deaden, douse, envelop, extinguish, pot *or* snuff out, quell, quench, squelch, stamp out, stifle **3.** conceal, cover, hide, muffle, obscure, repress, shield, shroud, suppress, veil, wrap **4.** baby, coddle, cosset, dote on, inundate, overindulge, overwhelm, pamper, protect, shower, spoil

smoulder *v.* **1.** burn, flicker, kindle, sizzle, smoke, smudge *Antonyms:* erupt, ignite, flame up **2.** boil, burn, fester, fume, rage, seethe, simmer, stew

smudge *n.* **1.** blot, dirt, grime, mark, smear, spot, stain, streak **2.** burn-off, cloud, fog, fume, mist, smog, smoke, smokiness – *v.* begrime, blacken, blotch, blur, daub, defile, dirty, foul, grime, mark, slop, smirch, soil, spatter, stain, sully, taint, tarnish *Antonyms:* clean, cleanse, sanitize

smug *adj.* complacent, conceited, hoity-toity, pleased, priggish, sanctimonious, self-contented, self-righteous, self-satisfied, snobbish, snot-nosed *(Nonformal)*, stuffy, supercilious, superior, triumphant, unctuous, vainglorious *Antonyms:* humble, self-effacing

smuggle *v.* bootleg, conceal, deal, pirate, push, run contraband, sneak, transfer

smuggler *n.* buccaneer, contrabandist, courier, dealer, freebooter, pirate, rum-runner, trafficker *Nonformal:* coyote, deliveryman, mule, runner

smutty *adj.* bawdy, coarse, crude, dirty, filthy, foul, immoral, improper, indecent, indelicate, lascivious, lecherous, lewd, nasty, obscene, off-colour, perverted, pornographic, prurient, racy, raunchy, raw, risqué, salacious, salty, scatological, suggestive, vulgar, X-rated *Nonformal:* adult, blue, flaming *(Computer)* *Antonyms:* clean, decent, puritanical, strait-laced

snack *n.* appetizers, bar food, bite, candy, cocktail, finger food, hors d'oeuvre, jerky, light meal, lunch, midnight snack, morsel, nourishment, ration, refreshment, samosa, sandwich, tapas, tidbit – *v.* eat, nibble, nosh, peck, taste

snag *n.* **1.** barrier, blockade, bottleneck, Catch-22, complication, difficulty, fault, glitch, hitch, hurdle, impediment, logjam, obstacle, obstruction, problem, scrape, spot, stumbling block, tight spot *Nonformal:* kettle of fish, pickle **2.** bramble, branch, projection, root, spike, spur, thorn, tooth – *v.* **1.** catch, hook, rip, run into, tear **2.** acquire, attain, assume, capture, get, grab, procure, purchase, retrieve, snatch, steal *Nonformal:* finagle, nail

snake *n.* **1.** reptile, serpent, viper *Common snakes:* adder, anaconda, boa constrictor, bull snake, cobra, copperhead, coral, cottonmouth, diamondback, garter, glossy, grass, greensnake, ground, hognose, king snake, massasauga rattler, milk, puff adder, python, queen, racer, rainbow, rat, rattlesnake, red-bellied, ribbon, ringneck, scarlet, tiger, water **2.** apostate, conspirator, deserter, double-crosser, Judas, mutineer, quisling, schemer, sneak, traitor, turncoat

snap *adj.* easy, effortless, facile, fast, light, offhand, painless, quick, simple, undemanding *Antonyms:* hard, laborious, intricate – *adv.* easily, effortlessly, quickly, readily, simply, smoothly, swimmingly – *n.* **1.** cinch, easy job *Nonformal:* bird, breeze, cakewalk, can of corn, child's play, duck soup, no-brainer, picnic *Antonyms:* challenge, difficulty, problem **2.** button, catch, clasp, fastener, hold, hook **3.** drive, *élan vital (French)*, energy, force, pep, pizzazz *(Nonformal)*, pluck, spirit, verve, vigour, vitality, zeal, zip **4.** cycle, interlude, interval, moment, period, span, spell, turn **5.** instant, minute, breath, second, wink *Nonformal:* heartbeat, two shakes – *v.* **1.** bark, flare, growl, grumble, grunt, lash out, retort, roar, snarl, snort, vent, yell **2.** break, cleave, damage, divide, fracture, fragment, pop, rupture, separate, splinter **3.** explode, go mad, lose control *Nonformal:* blow a fuse *or* gasket, blow one's top, blowup, come unglued *or* unhinged, fly off the handle, freak, get one's undies in a knot, go crazy *or* insane *or* nuts, hit the ceiling, lose a grip, lose it, wig out

snappy *adj.* **1.** breakneck, expeditious, fast, fleet, hasty, immediate, instant, quick, rapid, speedy, sudden, swift *Antonyms:* languid, lazy, slow, torpid **2.** abrupt, brusque, choleric, cranky, cross, curt, disagreeable, edgy, flippant, fractious, gruff, huffy, ill-tempered, irritable, nasty, petulant, quick-tempered, rude, short-tempered, snappish, snarky *(Nonformal)*, testy, touchy, waspish *Antonyms:* courteous, pleasant, sweet-tempered **3.** chic, classy, dapper, dashing, debonair, fashionable, modish, natty, sharp, smart, stylish, trendy *Nonformal:* swank, swish, tony

snare *n.* **1.** bait, catch, come-on, decoy, enticement, entrapment, inveiglement, lure, seduction, temptation **2.** gin, net, noose, trap, wire – *v.* capture, catch, decoy, ensnare, entice, entrap, inveigle, lure, net, noose, seduce, take, tempt, trap

snarl *n.* **1.** clutter, confusion, disarray, disorder, gallimaufry, jam, jungle, knot, maze, mess, mishmash, muddle, tangle, web **2.** catch, complexity, complication, difficulty, dilemma, entanglement, intricacy, intricateness, obstacle, problem **3.** growl, grumble, threat, utterance, warning – *v.* **1.** complicate, confuse, convolute, embroil, enmesh, ensnare, entangle, entwine, muddle, perplex, tangle **2.** bark, bluster, bully, complain, gnarl, grumble, murmur, mutter, quarrel, snap, threaten, thunder, warn, yelp

snatch *n.* bit, fragment, part, phrase, piece, portion, sample, section, smattering, smidgen, snippet – *v.* abduct, abscond, catch, clutch, collar, gain, glom onto *(Nonformal)*, grab, grapple, grasp, grip, jerk, kidnap, nab, nail, pluck, pull, rescue, seize, shanghai, snag, spirit away, steal, take, win, wrench, wrest, yank

sneak *n.* coward, crook, dastard, lowlife, meanie *(Nonformal)*, rascal, reprobate, scoundrel, sleeveen *(Newfoundland)*, snake – *v.* **1.** cower, crawl, delude, evade, glide, lurk, pad, pass, pussyfoot *(Nonformal)*, sidle, skulk, slide, slink, slip, slither, snake **2.** burgle, cheat, deceive, filch, lift, purloin, raid, ransack, rob, steal, take, thieve

sneaky *adj.* **1.** base, contemptible, cowardly, guileful, low, malicious, mean, nasty, shifty, slippery, sly, unreliable, unscrupulous, untrustworthy, yellow *(Nonformal)* **2.** back-stabbing, clandestine, covert, crafty, deceitful, devious, dishonest, disingenuous, double-dealing, duplicitous, furtive, indirect, secretive, stealthy, *sub rosa (Latin)*, surreptitious, tricky, underhanded, veiled

sneer *n.* **1.** sardonic grin, smirk, snicker, snigger **2.** derision, disdain, insult, jeer, gibe, mockery, offence, ridicule, scoff, scorn, slap, slight, taunt *Nonformal:* brickbat, burn, dig, dis – *v.* **1.** grin, laugh, leer, smirk, snicker, snigger **2.** belittle, condemn, cut, deride, despise, disdain, jeer, jibe, knock, mock, offend, revile, ridicule, scoff, scorn, taunt, tease *Nonformal:* pan, ride, roast *Antonyms:* applaud, commend, praise

snicker *v.* chortle, chuckle, giggle, guffaw, laugh, mock, smirk, titter

snide *adj.* cynical, derogatory, disparaging, hateful, hurtful, insinuating, malicious, mean, mocking, nasty, sarcastic, sardonic, scornful, sneering, spiteful, unkind

sniff *v.* breathe in, detect, humpf, inhale, scent, smell, snort, snuff, snuffle

snip *v.* chop *or* cut *or* lop off, crop, cut, cut back, dock, gash, hack, incise, nick, prune, remove, shave, shear, skive, slash, slit, trim

snippet *n.* bit, chad, cutting, dab, dot, fleck, fragment, grain, granule, iota, jot, mite, morsel, part, particle, piece, portion, remnant, sample, sampling, scrap, share, shred, skiver, slice, smidgen, snatch, speck, tatter, touch, trailing, trifle

snippy *adj.* abrupt, brusque, choleric, condescending, cranky, cross, curt, disagreeable, edgy, flippant, forward, fractious, gruff, huffy, ill-mannered, ill-tempered, impertinent, impolite, impudent, insolent, irritable, lippy, nasty, patronizing, petulant, quick-tempered, rude, sassy, saucy, sharp, short-tempered, snappish, snappy, sharp, testy, touchy, uncivil, waspish *Nonformal:* shirty, smart-alecky, snarky, snotty *Antonyms:* deferential, mannerly, polite, respectful

snitch *n.* informant, informer, spy, tattletale *Nonformal:* canary, fink, narc, rat, songbird, source, stoolie, stool pigeon, weasel, whistle-blower – *v.* **1.** blab, divulge, inform, spy, squeal, tattle, tell, turn informant *Nonformal:* rat, sing **2.** filch, lift, pilfer, purloin, rob, shoplift, steal, take, thieve *Nonformal:* cop, swipe

snivel *v.* **1.** bemoan, blubber, boohoo, cry, mewl, sniffle, sob, weep, whimper **2.** carp, cavil, complain, fret, fuss, grumble, moan, mutter, whine *Nonformal:* bitch, grouse, kvetch, squawk

snob *n.* braggart, maw-mouth *(Newfoundland)*, name-dropper, showoff, swaggerer *Nonformal:* blowhard, Miss Prissy

snobbish *adj.* arrogant, boastful, bragging, complacent, conceited, condescending, contemptuous, crowing, disdainful, egotistical, haughty, hoity-toity, inflated, lofty, lordly, narcissistic, overbearing, patronizing, peacockish, pompous, pretentious, prideful, proud, puffy, scornful, self-admiring, self-centered, self-important, self-satisfied, smug, sniffy, snobby, stuffy, supercilious, superior, uppity, vain, vainglorious *Nonformal:* bigheaded, full of oneself, high and mighty, highfalutin, snooty, snotty, stuck-up, toffee-nosed, top-lofty *Antonyms:* humble, modest, unpretentious

snoop *n.* busybody, butt-in, investigator, kibitzer, meddler, pry, spy *Nonformal:* buttinsky, nosy parker – *v.* interfere, intrude, meddle, nose around, peek, peep, peer, poke, pry, spy

snooze *n.* **1.** nap, repose, rest, siesta, sleep *Nonformal:* forty-winks, power nap, shut-eye **2.** bore *Nonformal:* bummer, downer, headache, yawn – *v.* doze, nap, sleep, slumber, turn in *Nonformal:* catch some z's, crash, saw logs, zonk out

snout *n.* beak, bill, muzzle, nose, proboscis, sniffer, trunk *Nonformal:* honker, schnozz, schnozzola

snow *n.* **1.** crystals, flakes, ice, precipitation *Kinds of snow:* artificial, black, corn, drift, firm, granular, lake, névé, packing, powder, red, skiff *(Prairies)*, slush, spring, streamer, wet *Inuktitut:* aniu, aniugie, aput, aquilluqaq, pukagag, tiaiuqaq **2.** bad reception *(Nonformal)*, interference, picture noise, static – *v.* **1.** blow, drift, drop, fall, flurry, pile up, precipitate, squall, stick *(Nonformal)*, storm **2.** deceive, trick *Nonformal:* bamboozle, con, hoodwink, scam, sting, take

snowmobile *n.* sled, snow coach, snowcat, snowsled *French:* auto neige, moto neige *Trademarks:* Arctic Cat, Bombardier, Ski-Doo *Nonformal:* bomb, engine, motor – *v.* fly *(Nonformal)*, move, ride, ski, transport, travel, trip

snowstorm *n.* blizzard, drop, heavy snow, snow dwy *(Newfoundland)*, squall, storm, streamer, *tempête de neige (French)*, whiteout, winter blast *or* storm

snowy *adj.* blinding, blizzard-like, blowing, fluffy, frosty, powdery, snow-blown, snow-capped, snow-covered, snow-drifted, snow-peaked, snow-topped, white, wintery

snub *n.* affront, contempt, cut, disdain, disrespect, insult, omission, rejection, sidestep, slight *Nonformal:* cold shoulder, go-by – *v.* censure, cut, disdain, disregard, duck, humble, humiliate, ignore, mortify, neglect, offend, ostracize, rebuff, rebuke, scold, scorn, shun, spurn, upstage *Nonformal:* brush off, cool, cut dead

snug *adj.* **1.** close-fitting, elastic, fast, neat, skintight, tight, trim *Antonyms:* baggy, loose, saggy **2.** close, comfortable, compact, cozy, cushy, homey, intimate, private, warm **3.** covered, guarded, protected, safe, secure, sheltered

snuggle *v.* bundle, caress, cleave, clutch, cuddle, curl up, embrace, hold, huddle, hug, nestle, nuzzle

soak *v.* **1.** absorb, bathe, damp, dip, drench, drown, dunk, flood, imbue, immerse, impregnate, infiltrate, infuse, macerate, marinate, moisten, penetrate, percolate, permeate, pour into *or* on, saturate, seethe, soften, sop, souse, steep, submerge, wash, water, waterlog, wet *Antonyms:* dehydrate, dry, parch, scorch **2.** bleed, cheat, defraud, fleece, mulct, overcharge, rook, swindle *Nonformal:* hose, rip off, screw, shaft

soaked *adj.* doused, drenched, dripping, flooded, immersed, moist, saturated, sodden, soggy, sopping, waterlogged, wet *Antonyms:* arid, desiccated, dry

soap *n.* **1.** abstergent, cleanser, cleansing agent, detergent, lotion, rinse, shampoo **2.** broadcast, drama, melodrama, one's stories *(Nonformal)*, serial, show, soap opera – *v.* bathe, clean, lather, scrub, swab, wash

soapy *adj.* **1.** bubbly, foamy, frothy, lathery, saponaceous, sudsy **2.** greasy, oily, oleaginous, slippery, slithery, unctuous

soar *v.* ascend, climb, escalate, fly, glide, lift, mount, rise, rocket, sail, shoot up, skyrocket, top, tower, wing *Antonyms:* descend, dive, fall, plummet, plunge

sob *n.* convulsion, cry, scream, wail, weeping – *v.* bawl, bewail, blubber, boohoo *(Nonformal)*, cry, grieve, keen, lament, mourn, shed tears, ululate, wail, weep *Antonyms:* chortle, giggle, laugh

sober *adj.* **1.** abstemious, abstinent, alcohol-free, clean, clear, continent, dried out, drug-free, dry, moderate, nonindulgent, restrained, sedate, steady, temperate *Nonformal:* on the wagon, stone cold sober *Antonyms:* drunk, hammered, inebriated, loaded **2.** calm, collected, composed, constrained, controlled, cool, disciplined, dispassionate, earnest, grave, imperturbable, judicious, levelheaded, no-nonsense *(Nonformal)*, practical, rational, realistic, reserved, restrained, sedate, serene, serious, solemn, staid, steady, well-balanced, wise, unexcited, unruffled *Antonyms:* rash, reckless, wild **3.** drab, modest, muted, plain, quiet, simple, soft, subdued, tempered, unpretentious *Antonyms:* excessive, flashy, garish

soccer *n.* football *(British)*, recreation, sport *Divisions of soccer field:* centre circle, corner area, corner flag, crossbar, goal, goal line, goalpost, halfway line, penalty area, pitch, soccer pitch, touch line *Kinds of soccer equipment:* ball, cleats, knee socks, shin guards, shorts, uniform *Scoring and procedure in soccer:* foul, free kick, goal kick, goal, overtime, penalty, penalty kick, period, point, quarter, shootout, tackle, throw-in, tiebreaker

sociability *n.* affability, bonhomie, camaraderie, clubability *(Nonformal)*, congeniality, companionability, fellowship, friendliness, geniality, good-fellowship, gregariousness, warmth *Antonyms:* boorishness, coldness, formality, introversion, stiffness

social *adj.* **1.** accessible, affable, amusing, approachable, bonhomous, close, clubby, communicative, companionable, conversable, convivial, cordial, entertaining, familiar, friendly, genial, good-natured, gracious, gregarious, hospitable, mannerly, neighbourly, nice, outgoing, phatic, pleasant, polished, polite, welcoming *Antonyms:* antisocial, boorish, cold, formal, solitary, unfriendly **2.** civil, collective, common, communal, general, group, organized, popular, public, societal, team *Antonyms:* independent, personal, private – *n.* affair, assembly, gathering, get-together, meeting, party, reception, shower, soiree

socialite *n.* celebrity, clubber, dandy, darling, dignitary, fop, man *or* woman about town, sensation, trendsetter *Nonformal:* somebody, VIP

socialize *v.* **1.** associate, chum with, consort, entertain, fraternize, get around, go out, hang around *or* out *(Nonformal)*, hobnob, join, keep company, mingle, mix, network, party **2.** collectivize, communize, nationalize, regulate, unionize *Antonyms:* deregulate, privatize

society *n.* **1.** alliance, association, auxiliary, brotherhood, circle, class, clique, club, commonality, commonwealth, community, company, corporation, fellowship, fraternity, gang, group, guild, institute, league, neighbourhood, organization, outfit, rung, sisterhood, sorority, syndicate, union **2.** body politic, citizenry, civilization, distinct society *(Constitutional)*, electorate, ethnic group, folk, inhabitants, linguistic community, nation, populace, population, public, race **3.** Homo sapiens, human race, humanity, man, mankind, people, the world **4.** aristocracy, elite, family compact, fashion-setters, gentry, polite society, upper class, who's who *French:* beau *or* haute monde *Nonformal:* beautiful people, country set, glitterati, high society, jet set, smart set, upper crust *Antonyms:* dregs, hoi polloi, rabble **5.** camaraderie, companionship, comradeship, fellowship, togetherness **6.** culture, laws, rules, social order

sock *n.* anklet, footie, hose, knee-high, leg warmer, mukluk, stocking *Types of socks:* argyle, bobby, hockey, knee, pit, slipper, sweat, tennis, work – *v.* beat, belt, bop, buffet, chop, clout, cuff, ding, hit, nail, paste, punch, slap, smack, smash, whack

sod *n.* field, glebe, grass, grassland, green, greenbelt, green space, grounds, lawn, mall, meadow, park, parkette, parkland, pasture, steppe, turf, veldt

sodden *adj.* **1.** clammy, damp, dank, drenched, dripping, drowned, flooded, imbrued, infused, marinated, marshy, moist, muddy, muggy, permeated, saturated, soaked, sopping, steeped, swampy, sweaty, waterlogged, wet *Antonyms:* arid, dry, parched **2.** doughy, fat, flabby, flaccid, fleshy, glutinous, mushy, out-of-shape, pasty, soft, spongy *Antonyms:* firm, hard, trim **3.** bland, boring, dead *(Nonformal)*, dull, humdrum, insipid, monotonous, ponderous, spiritless, stale, tedious, tiresome, tiring, uninteresting, vapid *Antonyms:* energetic, effervescent, interesting, intriguing

sofa *n.* chaise, chaise longue, chesterfield, couch, davenport, daybed, divan, futon, lounge, love seat, settee

soft *adj.* **1.** bendable, ductile, elastic, flexible, malleable, manageable, plastic, pliant, putty, yielding *Antonyms:* hard, inflexible, rigid, unyielding **2.** comfortable, cushiony, downy, feathery, plush, silky, smooth, velvety *Antonyms:* jagged, rough, sharp **3.** faint, gentle, hushed, low, light, muffled, murmured, muted, subtle, whispered *Antonyms:* blaring, ear-piercing, loud **4.** concordant, dulcet, mellifluous, melodious, pleasing, quiet *Antonyms:* discordant, dissonant, jarring **5.** benign, bland, dull, flat, tasteless, thin **6.** moderate, mellow, mild, pastel, shaded, subdued, toned down, understated *Antonyms:* flamboyant, garish, gaudy **7.** affectionate, amiable, compassionate, conciliatory, courteous, easygoing, gracious, indulgent, kind, kindly, lax, lenient, merciful, permissive, pitying, sympathetic, tender, tender-hearted *Antonyms:* austere, harsh, stern, strict **8.** delicate, emotional, open, sensitive, tender, vulnerable **9.** cowardly, craven, fainthearted, spineless, unmanly, unwomanly, weak, yellow *(Nonformal)* **10.** doughy, fat, flabby, fleshy, gelatinous, limp, mushy, overindulged, pampered, sodden *Antonyms:* firm, hard, strong **11.** cushy, easy, effortless, facile, painless, uncomplicated, undemanding *Antonyms:* difficult, intensive

soften *v.* **1.** allay, alleviate, assuage, cushion, dampen, deaden, diminish, ease, extenuate, lessen, mitigate, moderate, muffle, palliate, relieve, temper *Antonyms:* aggravate, heighten, increase **2.** affect, butter *(Nonformal)*, disarm, influence, move, persuade, touch **3.** heat, loosen, make pliable *or* workable, massage, melt, relax, warm up

softhearted *adj.* benevolent, compassionate, considerate, forgiving, generous, gentle, giving, humane, indulgent, kindly, merciful, sensitive, sparing, sympathetic, tender, tolerant, warm *Antonyms:* callous, cruel, heartless, insensitive, unkind

software *n.* application, program, utility *Common software:* animation, anti-virus, bundled, browser, common, courseware, cracked, database, desktop publishing, diagnostic, file management, file transfer protocol, firmware, freeware, ftp, graphics, groupware, network, operating system, pirate, ripped, screensaver, search engine, shareware, spreadsheet, system, telesoftware, unbundled, user-friendly, vaccine, vapourware, Web browser, word processor *See also:* **program**

soggy *adj.* clammy, damp, dank, dripping, heavy, humid, moist, mucky, muggy, mushy, pasty, pulpy, saturated, soaked, soaking, sodden, soft, sopping, spongy, sticky, waterlogged *Antonyms:* arid, desiccated, dry

soil *n.* **1.** country, fatherland, home, homeland, mother country, motherland, nation, place of origin, province, region, state **2.** clay, dirt, dry land, dust, earth, grime, ground, gumbo *(Nonformal)*, hardpan, land, loam, muskeg, sand, soot, terra firma – *v.* **1.** bedraggle, befoul, begrime, blacken, blemish, contaminate, dirty, discolour, foul, grime, ink, mess, muck, muddy, muss *(Nonformal)*, pollute, smear, smudge, spatter, spoil, spot, stain *Antonyms:* clean, disinfect, whiten **2.** besmirch, blot, darken, defame, defile, dim, disgrace, dishonour, embarrass, humiliate, stigmatize, sully, taint, tarnish

sojourn *n.* abode, *auberge (French)*, bed, bed and breakfast, dwelling, inn, kip, lodging, motel, motor lodge, pension, overnighter *(Nonformal)*, room, shelter, stay, stopover, stopping place – *v.* abide, billet, bunk, crash *(Nonformal)*, dwell, hang out, inhabit, linger, lodge, nest, perch, reside, rest, roost, sleep, squat, stay, vacation, visit

solace *n.* aid, alleviation, comfort, condolence, consolation, ease, help, mollification, peace, pity, relief, succour – *v.* assuage, buck up *(Nonformal)*, cheer, comfort, console, diminish, ease, lessen, mollify, palliate, soften, soothe *Antonyms:* aggravate, badger, exasperate

soldier *n.* **1.** airman, cadet, cavalryman, centurion, commando, common soldier, conscript, corporal, crewman, draftee, enlisted person, fighter, foot soldier, GI, Green Beret *(U.S.)*, grenadier, guard, guerrilla, gunner, gurkha, infantryman, legionnaire, marine, mercenary, military man *or* woman, musketeer, NCM, NCO, officer, paratrooper, private, recruit, rifle, scout, sentry, sepoy, sergeant, serviceman, servicewoman, soldier of fortune, Tommy *(British)*, trooper, veteran, volunteer *Nonformal:* dogface, GI Joe, grunt, merc, non-com, Van Doo **2.** gangster, goon *(Nonformal)*, hireling, lackey, minion, thug, underling

sole *adj.* **1.** alone, individual, one, separate, single, solitary, solo *Antonyms:* lots, many, several **2.** abiding, last, lone, only, remaining, surviving **3.** absolute, exclusionary, exclusive, limited, particular, private, singular, unique *Antonyms:* divided, joint, shared

solecism *n.* anacoluthon, bad grammar, barbarism, blooper, blunder, boner *(Nonformal)*, breach, corruption, error, fault, faux pas, gaffe, goof, impropriety, incongruity, lapse, *lapsus linguae (Latin)*, malapropism, misconstruction, miscue, mistake, misusage, oversight, spoonerism, violation

solely *adv.* alone, completely, entirely, exclusively, individually, merely, only, purely, simply, single-handedly, singly, singularly, totally, wholly

solemn *adj.* **1.** absolute, awe-inspiring, deep, grand, great, important, imposing, impressive, magnificent, majestic, mighty, momentous, overwhelming, powerful, profound, stately, sublime **2.** austere, earnest, funereal, glum, grave, quiet, serious, sober, sombre *Antonyms:* bright, cheerful, frivolous **3.** ceremonial, conventional, devotional, dignified, formal, hallowed, holy, procedural, religious, reverential, ritualistic, sacred, sanctified, venerable

solemnities *n. pl.* celebration, ceremonies, formalities, mysteries, obsequies, observances, pomp, proceedings, rites, rites of passage, rituals

solicit *v.* **1.** apply, approach, ask, beg, beseech, bum *(Nonformal)*, call, canvass, claim, entreat, hustle, implore, importune, petition, proposition, request, requisition, seek, sell, supplicate **2.** attract, charm, coax, induce, lure, persuade, seduce, tempt *Commonly misused:* **elicit**

solicitor *n.* **1.** campaigner, canvasser, door-to-door salesperson, drummer, hawker, hustler, monger, peddler, phone canvasser, salesperson, seller, suitor, telemarketer, travelling salesman **2.** advisor, attorney, barrister, counsellor *(U.S.)*, Crown attorney *or* counsel *or* prosecutor, King's Counsel (K.C.), lawyer, Queen's Counsel (Q.C.) *Nonformal:* ambulance chaser, mouthpiece

solicitous *adj.* anxious, ardent, athirst, attentive, avid, concerned, eager, enthusiastic, expectant, fervent, hot *(Nonformal)*, impassioned, impatient, interested, waiting, willing

solicitude *n.* anxiety, attention, attentiveness, care, concern, consideration, diligence, heed, regard, vigilance, watchfulness

solid *adj.* **1.** dimensional, figured, formed, geometric, shaped, three-dimensional *Antonyms:* fluid, formless, shapeless **2.** close, compact, concentrated, crammed, crowded, dense, filled, full, massed, packed, stuffed, thick *Nonformal:* chock-a-block, sardine-like *Antonyms:* empty, hollow, vacant **3.** hard, inflexible, rigid, rock, steely, sturdy, unbending, unmalleable, unyielding *Antonyms:* mouldable, pliant, soft **4.** barrel-chested, beefy, burly, heavy, hefty, husky, muscular, pudgy, stalwart, stout, strapping, thickset, well-built *Antonyms:* skinny, willowy **5.** actual, concrete, corporeal, material, phenomenal, physical, real, sensible, substantial, tangible, touchable, visible *Antonyms:* amorphous, hypothetical, intangible **6.** anchored, bound, established, fast, firm, immobile, locked, rooted, secure, settled, set, stable, unshakeable **7.** common, consistent, harmonious, like-minded, shared, single, unanimous, united **8.** comfortable, flush, independent, moneyed, prosperous, rich, solvent, wealthy, well-to-do *Nonformal:* okay, sitting pretty **9.** flawless, genuine, pure, straight, unadulterated, unalloyed, unchanged, uncut, unmitigated, unmixed, utter, whole *Antonyms:* impure, mixed, polluted **10.** authoritative, cogent, forceful, indisputable, influential, moving, persuasive, potent, sure, tight, unquestionable, valid *Antonyms:* dubious, flawed, specious, spurious, unsound **11.** constant, credible, dependable, faithful, reliable, serious, sober, steadfast, trustworthy *Antonyms:* deceitful, mercurial, wavering **12.** conscientious, ethical, exemplary, good, honourable, law-abiding, patriotic, righteous, true, upright, upstanding *Antonyms:* corrupt, deviant, mutinous, seditious **13.** ageless, durable, enduring, eternal, lasting, permanent, perpetual, persistent, rock-like, timeless *Antonyms:* ephemeral, fleeting, transient **14.** concatenate, contiguous, continued, continuous, regular, stable, steady, unbroken, undivided, uniform, uninterrupted **15.** assured, bound, certain, certified, confirmed, guaranteed, pledged, reliable, sure-fire *(Nonformal)*, warranted **16.** acceptable, fair, good, gratifying, passable, pleasing, satisfactory, sensible, tolerable *Antonyms:* embarrassing, laughable, poor, unacceptable

solidarity *n.* accord, association, bond, brotherhood, camaraderie, cohesion, community of interests, concord, concordance, consolidation, *esprit de corps (French)*, fellowship, fraternity, friendship, harmony, mutuality, sisterhood, *Solidarnosc (Polish)*, sorority, support, team spirit, togetherness, unanimity, unification, union, unity *Antonyms:* discord, division, separateness

solidify *v.* **1.** bond, cake, cement, compact, concrete, congeal, crystallize, firm, freeze, harden, jell *(Nonformal)*, steel, stiffen, strengthen, thicken *Antonyms:* dissolve, liquefy, melt **2.** assemble, centralize, combine, consolidate, federate, fuse, group, harmonize, join, match, merge, partner, renew, repledge, unify, unite *Antonyms:* cleave, scatter, separate

solitary *adj.* **1.** alone, individual, lone, only, separate, single, singular, sole, solo *Antonyms:* collection, group **2.** celibate, companionless, fellowless, matchless, mateless, spouseless, unaccompanied, unattended, unwed *Antonyms:* married, paired, taken *(Nonformal)*, wed **3.** abandoned, avoided, deprived, deserted, excluded, friendless, forlorn, lonely, lonesome, orphaned, shunned, unwanted **4.** alienated, aloof, antisocial, cloistered, disconnected, estranged, hermit-like, introverted, misanthropic, offish, quarantined, reclusive, removed, reserved, retired, separated, sequestered, standoffish, unsocial, withdrawn *Antonyms:* gregarious, outgoing, social **5.** desolate, distant, forsaken, hidden, isolated, out-of-the-way, remote, secluded, unfrequented *Antonyms:* central, downtown, popular

solitude *n.* **1.** aloneness, detachment, isolation, loneliness, privacy, retreat, retirement, seclusion, separateness, solitariness, withdrawal *Antonyms:* company, society, togetherness **2.** calm, harmony, peace, quiet, relaxation, repose, rest **3.** cell, confinement, jail, quarantine *Nonformal:* cage, can, cooler, drunk tank, hoosegow, lockup, stir

solution *n.* **1.** answer, clarification, explanation, explication, fix, key, panacea, resolution **2.** blend, compound, elixir, emulsion, extract, fluid, juice, lotion, mixture, snake oil *(Nonformal)*, solvent, tincture, tonic

solve *v.* answer, break, clarify, clear up, construe, crack, decide, decipher, decode, determine, disentangle, do, elucidate, enlighten, explain, expound, fathom, figure *or* find *or* puzzle *or* reason *or* think *or* work out, fix, get, hit upon, illuminate, interpret, ravel, resolve, settle, unfold, unlock, unravel, untangle *Nonformal:* beat, dope *or* iron *or* make out, lick

solvent *adj.* credit-worthy, debt-free, financially responsible, reliable, solid, sound *Nonformal:* in the black, on an even keel, out of the hole *or* red *Antonyms:* bankrupt, broke, indebted – *n.* alkahest, cleaner, dissolvent, dissolving agent, liquefier, lotion, menstruum, resolvent, thinner *Kinds of solvent:* acetone, alcohol, aqua regia, benzene, benzine, carbolic acid, carbon disulphide, carbon tetrachloride, chloroform, ether, gasoline, naphtha, phenol, toluene, turpentine, water

somatic *adj.* biological, bodily, carnal, cellular, corporal, corporeal, fleshly, genetic, mortal, organic, physical *Antonyms:* incorporeal, spiritual

sombre *adj.* **1.** black, bleak, cloudy, dark, dim, dismal, dusky, gloomy, murky, overcast, shadowy, shady, tenebrous *Antonyms:* bright, sunny **2.** depressing, dispiriting, doleful, down, drab, dreary, dull, foreboding, funereal, grim, joyless, lugubrious, melancholy, momentous, mournful, oppressive, sad, sepulchral, serious, sober, solemn, staid, upsetting, weighty *Antonyms:* cheerful, effusive, pleasant

somebody *n.* celebrity, dignitary, household name, luminary, notable, personage, public figure, socialite, star, supermodel, superstar *Nonformal:* bigwig, heavyweight, someone, swell, VIP *Antonyms:* lightweight, nobody, nonentity – *pron.* anybody, anyone, someone, you, you there

somehow *adv.* anyhow, anyway, by any means *Nonformal:* by hook or by crook, in the long run, one way or another

sometimes *adv.* frequently, from time to time, intermittently, now and then, occasionally, once in a while, on occasion, once in a while, periodically, sporadically *Antonyms:* always, constantly, eternally, everlastingly, forever

somewhat *adv.* adequately, a little, considerably, fairly, in part, insignificantly, kind of, moderately, partially, pretty, quite, rather, significantly, slightly, tolerably, to some extent, well enough

song *n.* **1.** air, anthem, aria, ballad, blues, canticle, carol, chant, chorale, chorus, death song *(Native Peoples)*, dirge, ditty, golden oldie *(Nonformal)*, hymn, lay, lullaby, lyric, melody, monody, number, poem, psalm, refrain, round, shanty, strain, threnody, tune, verse, vocal **2.** line, spiel *(Nonformal)*, story

sonorous *adj.* **1.** amplified, baritone, bass, booming, clangorous, deep, echoing, fat *(Nonformal)*, full, loud, low, powerful, pulsating, resonant, resounding, reverberant, rich, ringing, round, thunderous, vibrant *Antonyms:* thin, tinny, trebly, tremulous, weak **2.** bloated, bombastic, elevated, extravagant, flamboyant, flatulent, fustian, grandiloquent, grandiose, inflated, lofty, magniloquent, orotund, ostentatious, pompous, pretentious, purple, sesquipedalian, swollen, turgid *Anto-nyms:* plain, prosaic, unadorned

soon *adv.* before long, directly, expeditiously, forthwith, instanter, instantly, in time *or* a while, posthaste, presently, promptly, quickly, shortly, speedily

soothe *v.* **1.** appease, calm, compose, hush, pacify, placate, quiet, sedate, settle, still, subdue, tranquilize *Antonyms:* aggravate, annoy, badger, disturb **2.** allay, alleviate, assuage, cushion, ease, lighten, mitigate, mollify, palliate, relieve, soften, temper *Antonyms:* exacerbate, irritate

soothing *adj.* **1.** balmy, calming, dulcet, gentle, hushed, hypnotic, pacifying, peaceful, quieting, relaxing, restful, settling, soft, tranquilizing *Antonyms:* aggravating, agitating, disquieting, disturbing, worrying **2.** assuasive, cathartic, curative, emollient, healing, lenitive, medicinal, palliative, relieving, therapeutic

soothsayer *n.* augur, clairvoyant, fortuneteller, diviner, haruspex *(Historical)*, medium, oracle, palmist, palm reader, prophet, psychic, seer, sibyl, spiritualist

sooty *adj.* **1.** blackened, dirty, dusty, filthy, fuliginous, grimy, grungy, oily, smeared, smudged, soiled, stained **2.** black, blackish, charcoal, coal, ebony, inky, jet, onyx, pitch-black, raven, sable, slate

sophist *n.* **1.** authority, expert, guru, intellectual, master, philosopher, pundit, sage, savant, scholar, student, thinker *Nonformal:* egghead, longhair, weenie **2.** casuist, charlatan, deceiver, dissembler, equivocator, evader, paralogist, prevaricator, quibbler, trickster, vacillator, waffler

sophisticated *adj.* **1.** adult *(Nonformal)*, civilized, cosmopolitan, cultivated, cultured, discriminating, experienced, knowing, knowledgeable, mannered, mature, practiced, refined, schooled, seasoned, sharp, smooth, studied, suave, urbane, well-bred, worldly *Antonyms:* boorish, provincial, vulgar **2.** cerebral, conceptual, highbrow, intellectual, mental, philosophical, scholastic, scientific *Antonyms:* carnal, physical **3.** advanced, Borgesian, complex, complicated, delicate, elaborate, highly-developed, intricate, involved, knotty, labyrinthine, maze-like, modern, multifaceted, space-aged *(Nonformal)*, subtle *Antonyms:* basic, plain, simple

sophistication *n.* breeding, charm, class, culture, education, elegance, erudition, finesse, grace, knowledge, poise, refinement, savoir-faire, social grace, style, tact, wisdom *Antonyms:* ignorance, innocence, loutishness, vulgarity

sophistry *n.* casuistry, chicanery, deception, fallacy, false reasoning, paralogism, sophism, speciousness

sophomoric *adj.* adolescent, childish, foolish, immature, inane, infantile, juvenile, pubescent, puerile, reckless, shallow, silly, thoughtless, youthful *Antonyms:* humourless, mature, serious

soporific *adj.* **1.** bland, boring, deadly *(Nonformal)*, dull, flat, monotonous, tedious, tiresome, uninspired, vapid, wearisome *Antonyms:* animated, entertaining, lively **2.** anesthetic, calming, hypnotic, mesmerizing, narcotic, numbing, opiate, sedative, sleep-inducing, soothing, tranquilizing *Antonyms:* bracing, invigorating, stimulating **3.** dozy, drowsy, exhausted, heavy, sleepy, slumberous, tired, tuckered, weary *Nonformal:* beat, pooped, snoozy, toast, wiped, zonked

soppy *adj.* **1.** cloying, emotional, foolish maudlin, mawkish, mushy, overdone, purple, romantic, saccharine, sentimental, sickening, silly *Nonformal:* Hollywood, sappy, schmaltzy **2.** dripping, damp, moist, saturated, soaked, sodden, soggy, waterlogged, wet, wringing-wet *Antonyms:* arid, dry, parched

sorcerer *n.* conjurer, diviner, enchanter, exorcist, geomancer, mage, magician, Merlin, necromancer, occultist, seer, shaman, soothsayer, warlock, witch doctor, wizard *See also:* **magician**

sorceress *n.* bewitcher, Circe, enchantress, Lorelei, magician, siren, witch *See also:* **enchantress**

sorcery *n.* **1.** abracadabra, alchemy, black art, black magic, conjuring, deviltry, divination, enchantment, geomancy, hocus-pocus, magic, mumbo-jumbo, necromancy, sortilege, thaumaturgy, voodoo, witchcraft, witchery, wizardry **2.** bewitchery, cantrip, charm, diabolism, evil eye, hex, hoodoo, incantation, influence, jinx, rune, spell

sordid *adj.* **1.** dirty, dowdy, filthy, foul, miserable, noxious, seedy, shabby, squalid, tumble-down *Antonyms:* clean, orderly, spotless **2.** abject, bad, base, corrupt, crude, debauched, degenerate, degraded, deviant, ignoble, immoral, impure, mean, offensive, perverted, rude, shameful, sleazy, vicious, vile *Antonyms:* respectable, upright, upstanding **3.** avaricious, calculating, grasping, greedy, grubby, mercenary, miserly, rapacious, self-interested, selfish, self-seeking *Antonyms:* altruistic, magnanimous, self-sacrificing

sore *adj.* **1.** abscessed, aching, acute, afflicted, bruised, burning, chafed, distressing, hurt, inflamed, irritated, painful, raw, sensitive, sharp, smarting, tender, ulcerated, uncomfortable, unpleasant, vexatious **2.** agitated, angry, fuming, furious, incensed, infuriated, irate, livid, mad, raging, upset, vexed *Nonformal:* bent, cheesed, pissed, steaming – *n.* **1.** blemish, blister, boil, bruise, burn, canker, chancre, chilblain, cut, inflammation, injury, laceration, lesion, nick, scrape, scratch, slash, smart, sting, welt, wound **2.** bête noir, blight, bother, bug, bugaboo, bugbear, curse, hassle *(Nonformal)*, irritation, nuisance, pain, plague, problem, scourge, thorn, trouble *Antonyms:* aid, pleasure, relief

sorrow *n.* **1.** agony, anguish, blues, dejection, depression, distress, dolour, gloom, grief, heartache, hopelessness, melancholy, misery, pain, ribbon of darkness, sadness, suffering, unhappiness, *Weltschmerz (German)*, woe, worry, wretchedness *Antonyms:* ecstasy, glee, happiness, joy **2.** adversity, affliction, bane, blow, catastrophe, death, difficulty, disease, evil, fountain of sorrow, hardship, heartbreak, ill, injury, malady, misfortune, pestilence, plague, regret, remorse, repentance, rue, ruin, scourge, setback, stress, upset, wound *Antonyms:* good luck, providence, success – *v.* agonize, bemoan, bewail, deplore, grieve, groan, keen, lament, moan, mourn, regret, sob, weep *Antonyms:* celebrate, delight, rejoice

sorrowful *adj.* **1.** bereaved, blue, cheerless, depressed, dismal, despondent, doleful, down, grievous, grief-stricken, heartbroken, hopeless, lugubrious, melancholic, miserable, mournful, neurasthenic, sad, troubled, upset, vexed, wretched *Antonyms:* elated, high, pleased **2.** crushing, dismal, distressing, disturbing, frightening, heartbreaking, heart-rending, moving, painful, plaintive, pathetic, touching, tragic, traumatic, upsetting *Antonyms:* cheering, heart-warming, uplifting **3.** crying, grieving, lamenting, mourning, sobbing, tearful, wailing, weeping

sorry *adj.* **1.** apologetic, contrite, disconsolate, distressed, guilt-ridden, guilty, penitent, regretful, remorseful, repentant, rueful, shamed *Antonyms:* cocksure, impenitent, pleased, proud **2.** disconsolate, distressed, grieved, heartbroken, heavy-hearted, mournful, pained, sad, saddened, sorrowful, unhappy, wretched **3.** dismal, dispiriting, distressing, grievous, heart-rending, moving, painful, pathetic, piteous, pitiable, pitiful, plaintive, touching *Antonyms:* delightful, heartwarming, pleasurable **4.** abject, bad, base, beggarly, cheap, contemptible, deplorable, despicable, disgraceful, mean, poor, scruffy, scummy, scurvy, shabby, shoddy, vile *Nonformal:* cheesy, scuzzy *Antonyms:* compassionate, gracious, noble **5.** inadequate, insignificant, paltry, small, trifling, trivial, unimportant, worthless *Antonyms:* important, momentous, valuable

sort *n.* **1.** array, batch, battery, body, category, class, clutch, denomination, family, genus, group, ilk, kind, number, order, parcel, race, set, species, suit *See also:* **group** **2.** breed, description, feather, like, make, stamp, stripe, type, variety **3.** character, fashion, manner, mode, nature, quality, style, way – *v.* arrange, catalogue, categorize, choose, class, classify, coordinate, distribute, file, grade, group, label, order, organize, peg, pigeonhole, rank, screen, select, sift, stream, systematize, triage

sortie *n.* **1.** assault, attack, charge, counterattack, countercharge, drive, foray, incursion, offensive, onslaught, raid, rush, sally **2.** constitutional, excursion, hike, jaunt, journey, perambulation, promenade, ramble, saunter, tour, traipse, tramp, walk

so-so *adj.* acceptable, adequate, admissible, all right, average, bland, *comme ci comme ça (French),* commonplace, dull, fair, flat, indifferent, insipid, mediocre, medium, middling, moderate, neutral, ordinary, passable, presentable, respectable, satisfactory, second-rate, tolerable, undistinguished, unexceptional, uninspired, unnotable, vapid *Nonformal:* ho-hum, nothing special *or* to write home about, okay *Antonyms:* distinguished, exceptional, extraordinary, incredible, memorable – *adv.* indifferently, moderately, not bad, well enough

soul *n.* **1.** anima, *atman (Hindu),* breath of life, flame, genius, heart, *ka (Egyptian),* life force, living force, mana, pneuma, psyche, self, spirit, spiritual self **2.** being, body, character, child, creature, entity, fellow, Homo sapien, human being, individual, living soul, man, mortal, person, personage, woman *Nonformal:* head, number pilgrim **3.** ardour, craving, desire, drive, eagerness, emotion, *esprit de corps (French),* fervour, force, fortitude, heartiness, might, passion, pluck, vitality, zeal **4.** basis, centre, core, crux, essence, foundation, gist, kernel, marrow, meaning, meat, nucleus, seat **5.** agent, agitator, animator, captain, dynamo, general, inspiration, leader, motivator, organizer, point, prime mover, principal, spearhead **6.** embodiment, incarnation, manifestation, personification, proof, representation, symbol **7.** apparition, ghost, haunt, spectre, spook, the dead *(Nonformal),* wraith

soulful *adj.* **1.** deep, emotional, expressive, felt, fervid, heartfelt, impassioned, passionate, spiritual *Antonyms:* cold, passive, reserved **2.** inspiring, invigorating, meaningful, motivating, moving, poignant, powerful, profound, strong, uplifting *Antonyms:* dull, heartless, vapid

soulless *adj.* **1.** brutal, callous, cold-hearted, cruel, heartless, inhumane, merciless, ruthless, savage, senseless, uncaring, unmerciful, vicious, villainous **2.** cold, dispassionate, indifferent, lifeless, listless, plain, spiritless, starched, stiff, unemotional, vapid *Nonformal:* blah, vanilla *Antonyms:* impassioned, spirited, zealous

sound *adj.* **1.** able-bodied, fit, hale, healthy, hearty, robust, stalwart, strong, trim, vigorous, well, wholesome *Antonyms:* ailing, diseased, sick **2.** complete, entire, intact, integral, perfect, total, whole **3.** defect-free, faultless, flawless, impeccable, inviolate, mint, quality, unbroken, undamaged, unmarred **4.** accepted, established, legal, orthodox, recognized, sanctioned, valid **5.** accurate, correct, good, precise, proper, right, true **6.** commonsensical, fair, judicious, just, level-headed, logical, lucid, prudent, rational, realistic, reasonable, sane, sensible, sober, well-advised, well-founded, wise **7.** authoritative, cogent, convincing, impressive, influential, informative, instructive, persuasive, telling, well-grounded **8.** constant, firm, solid, stable, steady, strong, sturdy, substantial **9.** assured, certain, harmless, proven, risk-free, safe, secure, tame, unhazardous **10.** deep, peaceful, restful, smooth, unbroken, undisturbed, uninterrupted **11.** debt-free, financially secure, flush, loaded, moneyed, rich, solvent *Nonformal:* blue chip, rock-solid **12.** cruel, extreme, hard, harsh, heavy-handed, intense, rough, savage, severe, thorough, violent **13.** credible, decent, dependable, faithful, honest, honourable, loyal, reliable, reputable, responsible, trustworthy – *n.* **1.** din, babble, bang, banging, blast, boom, clamour, intonation, loudness, modulation, music, noise, note, outcry, peal, pitch, racket, report, resonance, reverberation, ringing, sonance, stridency, tintinnabulation, tone, vibration, uproar, vociferation, voice **2.** accent, cast, character, colour, complexion, manner, nature, overtone, quality, strain, style, vein **3.** compass, distance, earshot, hearing *or* striking distance, range, reach **4.** arm of the sea, bay, belt, bight, channel, fjord, inlet, narrows, strait – *v.* **1.** chime, clang, clank, jangle, jingle, knell, peal, reverberate, ring, thunder, toll, trumpet **2.** articulate, enunciate, express, pronounce, speak, talk, tell, utter, verbalize, vocalize, voice **3.** alert, call, celebrate, communicate, herald, signal, warn **4.** fathom, mark twain, measure, plumb, probe, search, test **5.** ascertain, check, determine, explore, investigate, penetrate, query, quiz

soup *n.* **1.** broth, stew *Kinds of soup:* alphabet, bird's-nest, bisque, borscht, bouillabaisse, bouillon, cabbage, caldo verde, chicken noodle, chowder, cock-a-leekie, consommé, cream, egg drop, gazpacho, gumbo, hot and sour, madrilène, matzo ball, menudo, minestrone, miso, mulligatawny, mushroom, onion, oxtail, pea, pepper pot, potage, rubaboo, Scotch broth, shark's fin, *shchi (Russian)*, tomato, turtle, vegetable, vichyssoise, wonton **2.** blend, jumble, mélange, mess, mix

soupçon *n.* bit, clue, dash, drop, hint, jot, modicum, pinch, shade, smidgen, suggestion, suspicion, tad, taint, taste, tinge, touch, trifle, vestige, whiff

sour *adj.* **1.** acid, acidulated, astringent, bad, bad-tasting, biting, bitter, briny, curdled, green, off, pungent, rancid, sharp, skunky, soured, stinging, tart, turned, unripe, unsavoury, vinegary *Antonyms:* mild, sugary, sweet **2.** acrid, acrimonious, angry, caustic, churlish, crabby, cranky, cynical, discontented, embittered, grouchy, grudging, ill-natured, ill-tempered, irritable, jaundiced, misanthropic, morose, peevish, resentful, rotten, unhappy, unpleasant, waspish *Antonyms:* charming, cordial, ingratiating, warm **3.** bad, disagreeable, displeasing, horrible, unpleasant – *v.* bring down, curdle, disappoint, disenchant, disgruntle, embitter, foil, frustrate, irritate, ruin, spoil, upset *Antonyms:* encourage, enhance, improve

source *n.* **1.** ancestor, architect, artist, author, begetter, creator, designer, father, framer, initiator, inventor, mother, originator, principle, producer, seed **2.** antecedent, beginning, centre, embryo, epicentre, fount, fountainhead, germ, headwater, mainspring, origin, provenance, rise, root, spring, start, supply, well, wellhead **3.** basis, cause, genesis, guiding light, influence, inspiration, lodestar, motive, reason **4.** advisor, authority, consultant, elder, example, expert, guide, guru, instructor, master, professional, sage, specialist, teacher **5.** informant, informer, reference, supergrass *(British)*, tipster, witness *Nonformal:* fink, narc, pigeon, rat, snake, snitch, stoolie **6.** archive, bank, bible, database, depository, library, primary document *or* material, reservoir, storehouse, warehouse – *v.* **1.** bargain, bind, contract, engage, freelance, outsource, send out, sign out **2.** cite, credit, document, identify, itemize, list, name, note, reference

souse *n.* alcoholic, dipsomaniac, drunk, drunkard, heavy drinker, imbiber, inebriate, problem drinker *Nonformal:* alky, barfly, boozehound, boozer, bum, lush rummy, wino – *v.* **1.** bathe, dip, drench, drown, dunk, immerse, moisten, waterlog, wet *Antonyms:* desiccate, dry **2.** bottle, brine, keep, marinate, pickle, preserve **3.** binge, drink, get liquored, imbibe, indulge, quaff, swill, tipple *Nonformal:* booze, get hammered *or* high *or* jiggered *or* loaded, hit the bottle *or* sauce, juice, pub crawl, tank up, wet one's whistle

souvenir *n.* gift, keepsake, memento, memorial, relic, remembrance, reminder, token, trophy

sovereign *adj.* **1.** chief, commanding, controlling, executive, functioning, governing, managing, regulatory, ruling, suzerain **2.** autonomous, democratic, free, independent, liberated, republican, self-governing, self-regulating **3.** divinely sanctioned, imperial, kingly, lordly, monarchical, princely, queenly, regal, reigning, royal **4.** august, capital, excellent, extraordinary, good, great, impressive, magnificent, majestic, stately, supreme **5.** effective, effectual, efficacious, efficient, extra-strength, full-strength, high-powered, potent, powerful, strong – *n.* autocrat, chief, controller, czar, czarina, dynast, emperor, empress, head, king, lord, majesty, monarch, pharaoh, potentate, prince, princess, queen, rajah, rani, royal, ruler, shah, shogun, sultan, supreme ruler, suzerain, tetrarch

sovereignist *n.* dissenter, nationalist, *Péquiste (Quebec)*, radical, rebel, revolutionary, secessionist, separatist *Antonyms:* centralist, federalist, traditionalist

sovereignty *n.* **1.** autonomy, democracy, freedom, home-rule, independence, independent status, liberty, self-determination, self-government, self-rule **2.** country, domain, dominion, government, independent nation, nation, region, republic, state, territory *Antonyms:* colony, puppet regime, satellite **3.** ascendancy, control, directorship, dominion, hegemony, leadership, power, superiority, supremacy, supreme authority

sow *n.* boar, peccary, pig, piglet, swine – *v.* broadcast, cast, cover, fling, pitch, plant, scatter, seed, send, shed, sprinkle, strew, toss

space *n.* **1.** area, capacity, compass, distance, elbow room, expanse, extent, room, scope, sweep **2.** field, lot, place, region, section, spot, territory, zone **3.** age, bit, duration, epoch, era, generation, interval, period, season, span, spell, stretch, term, time, while **4.** cleavage, cleft, crack, cranny, crevice, cut, divide, fissure, fracture, gap, interstice, rent, separation, slit, split **5.** abeyance, break, hesitation, hiatus, intermission, interruption, lacuna, lull, pause, stoppage, suspension **6.** air, blank, cavity, emptiness, hollow, nothingness, vacuum, void **7.** beyond *(Nonformal)*, cosmos, galaxy, heavens, infinity, intergalactic *or* interplanetary *or* interstellar *or* outer space, nebula, stars, universe **8.** chance, occasion, opening, opportunity, possibility, slot, window **9.** desk, employment, job, office, place, position, vacancy **10.** booking, reservation, seat, spot – *v.* adjust, align, arrange, divide, order, separate, set

spacious *adj.* ample, big, boundless, broad, capacious, cavernous, comfortable, commodious, endless, enormous, expansive, extensive, generous, great, huge, immense, infinite, large, limitless, roomy, sizable, uncrowded, vast, voluminous, wide *Antonyms:* close, confined, cramped, limited

span *n.* **1.** amount, compass, distance, extent, gap, length, measure, range, reach, space, spread, stretch, width **2.** course, duration, interval, run, session, spell, stand, tenure, term, time, tour – *v.* arch, bridge, connect, cover, cross, extend, ford, link, range, reach, stretch, traverse, vault

spank *v.* **1.** belt, cane, clobber, flog, hit, lash, paddle, slap, smack, thrash, trim, wallop, whip *Nonformal:* lick, tan, whale **2.** castigate, correct, discipline, punish, reprove, train

spar *n.* boom, gaff, mast, pole, prop, sprit, support, yard – *v.* **1.** box, combat, duel, duke it out *(Nonformal)*, exchange *or* trade blows, fight, pummel, scrap, scrimmage, skirmish **2.** argue, bandy words, bicker, clash, disagree, dispute, feud, quarrel, spat, wrangle *Nonformal:* butt heads, cross swords

spare *adj.* **1.** disposable, expendable, redundant, replaceable, superfluous, unnecessary

2. additional, excess, extra, reserve, stored, supplementary, surplus **3.** accessible, available, free, on hand *or* tap **4.** angular, bony, gaunt, lank, lean, rangy, rawboned, scrawny, skeletal, skinny, slender, slight, slim, thin, twiggy, wiry *Antonyms:* corpulent, fat, flabby, plump **5.** barren, exiguous, modest, poor, scant, scanty, sparse **6.** chary, economical, frugal, meagre, mean, parsimonious, skimpy, sparing, strict – *n.* **1.** alternate, bench warmer *(Nonformal)*, clone, double, duplicate, extra, facsimile, replacement, replica, second, stand-in, substitute, understudy **2.** break, free *or* off period, study break *or* hall *or* period – *v.* **1.** dispense, dispose, donate, fork over *(Nonformal)*, give, let go, lose, part, relinquish, share, yield **2.** abstain, cease, forbear, give quarter, halt, stop *Antonyms:* beat, kill, punish, torture **3.** deliver, emancipate, liberate, manumit, pardon, redeem, release, rescue, set free, spring *(Nonformal)*, unfasten, untie *Antonyms:* enslave, incarcerate, impound, imprison **4.** keep, preserve, put aside, salt *or* squirrel away, shelve, store **5.** economize, save, scrimp, skimp **6.** blue box *(Nonformal)*, recycle, reuse

sparing *adj.* **1.** careful, cheap, close, cost-conscious, economical, frugal, miserly, parsimonious, penurious, prudent, stingy, thrifty, tight *Antonyms:* extravagant, lavish, liberal **2.** abstinent, constrained, controlled, forbearing, limited, measured, moderate, restrained, sober, temperate *Antonyms:* devil-may-care, impulsive, reckless

spark *n.* **1.** beam, fire, flare, flash, flicker, gleam, glint, glitter, glow, light, particle, ray, scintilla, sparkle **2.** clue, evidence, indication, inkling, intimation, notice, proof, reminder, sign, signal, tip, token, trace **3.** catalyst, dynamo, incitement, inspiration, motivation, source, stimulation **4.** animation, animus, dash, drive, energy, liveliness, mettle, pep, spirit, spunk *(Nonformal)*, verve, zest – *v.* **1.** flame, flare, flicker, glitter, light, scintillate, sparkle **2.** animate, energize, excite, ignite, inspire, kindle, motivate, stimulate, whip up *(Nonformal)* *Antonyms:* demoralize, discourage, restrain **3.** activate, cause, enflame, goad, incite, initiate, instigate, precipitate, provoke, rouse, set *or* touch off, start, stir, trigger *Antonyms:* extinguish, halt, inhibit

sparkle *n.* **1.** brilliance, coruscation, dazzle, flash, flickering, gleaming, glimmering, glittering, radiance, scintillation, shimmering, spark **2.** alacrity, animation, gaiety, life, liveliness, sizzle, spirit, vitality, vivacity **3.** bubbling, carbonation, effervescence, fizz, tickle *(Nonformal)* – *v.* **1.** beam, coruscate, dance, effervesce, flash, flicker, gleam, glimmer, glint, glisten, glitter, glow, scintillate, shimmer, shine, spark, twinkle, wink **2.** amuse, animate, beam, entertain, grin, laugh, smile

sparse *adj.* **1.** bare, diffused, dispersed, infrequent, occasional, scarce, scattered, sketchy, sporadic, spotty, spread out, uncrowded *Antonyms:* close, cluttered, dense, populous **2.** exiguous, hardscrabble, inadequate, insufficient, meagre, miserable, paltry, poor, scanty, skimpy, spare *Antonyms:* abundant, ample, generous

Spartan *adj.* **1.** abstemious, ascetic, austere, disciplined, rigorous, self-denying, severe, strict, stoic, stringent *Antonyms:* hedonistic, indulgent, lax, soft **2.** bare-bones, functional, inornate, laconic, meagre, minimal, modest, plain, simple, spare, sparse, stripped-down *Antonyms:* flashy, gaudy, ostentatious, showy

spasm *n.* **1.** attack, clonus, contraction, convulsion, fit, jerking, pain, seizure, stringhalt *(Horses)*, throe, tonus, twitch **2.** burst, eruption, explosion, frenzy, fulmination, outburst, paroxysm, rush, spate, upheaval

spasmodic *adj.* choppy, discontinuous, erratic, fitful, intermittent, irregular, mercurial, scattered, sporadic, uneven, wild *Nonformal:* crazy, herky-jerky *Antonyms:* constant, regular, steady, uniform

spat *n.* altercation, argument, bout, contretemps, controversy, disagreement, dispute, encounter, exchange, fight, fracas, *mano-a-mano (Spanish)*, row, ruckus, scrap, tiff, wrangling *Nonformal:* blowup, face-off, fallout, go, rhubarb, war, words – *v.* argue, bicker, contend, debate, feud, have words, struggle *Nonformal:* butt heads, cross swords, lock horns

spate *n.* avalanche, current, emission, eruption, explosion, flowing, gushing, outburst, overflow, river, stream, torrent

spatter *v.* **1.** bespatter, bestrew, cast, dash, daub, disperse, dribble, scatter, slop, splash, spray, strew, wet **2.** dot, mottle, polka-dot, spangle, speckle, spot, stipple **3.** drizzle, drop, fall, rain, shower, spit, sprinkle **4.** besmirch, defame, dirty, slander, soil, stain

spawn *n.* **1.** caviar, eggs, hatch, roe, seed **2.** bait, fish, fry, minnows **3.** children, fruit, offspring, progeny, youngsters **4.** aftermath, conclusion, effect, end, fallout, outcome, product, result, sequel, spin-off, yield – *v.* bring forth, create, father, generate, hatch, issue, make, mother, originate, parent, procreate, produce, reproduce, sire

speak *v.* **1.** bark, cry, enunciate, mouth, noise, sound, utter, verbalize, vocalize, voice **2.** communicate, converse, discourse, exchange, share, talk *Nonformal:* bend one's ear, chew the fat *or* rag, chin, gab, gas, jaw, shoot the breeze, yak **3.** air, announce, articulate, blurt, convey, exclaim, express, have one's say, proclaim, pronounce, relate, say, state, tell, transmit, vent *Nonformal:* mouth *or* sound *or* spout off, natter, pour one's heart out, rattle away **4.** address, deliver, harangue, hold forth, lecture, perorate, pitch, pontificate, preach, sermonize *Nonformal:* soapbox, speechify, spiel, take the floor **5.** attest, assert, declaim, declare, maintain **6.** acknowledge, cite, disclose, divulge, enlighten, mention, name, note, reference, refer to, report **7.** admonish, advise, bawl out *(Nonformal)*, chide, notify, punish, rebuke, reprimand, reprove, scold, scream at, warn **8.** comprehend, grasp, know, understand, use

speaker *n.* **1.** keynoter, lecturer, orator, master of ceremonies, M.C., preacher, professor, reader, salesperson, spokesperson, talker, toastmaster *Nonformal:* emcee, pitcher **2.** amplifier, bullhorn, loudspeaker, megaphone, PA system, system

spear *n.* arrow, assagai, bolt, dart, eelspear, fishgig, gig, harpoon, lance, javelin, jereed, leister, pike, pointed stick, spontoon, trident – *v.* gore, gouge, hook, impale, jab, knife, lance, penetrate, perforate, pierce, poke, shish kebab *(Nonformal)*, skewer, spike, stab, stick, thrust

spearhead *n.* **1.** avant garde, cutting *or* leading edge, forefront, forerunner, leader, pioneer, point, revolutionary, vanguard **2.** assault, attack, initiative, movement, sortie – *v.* advance, begin, commence, drive, initiate, introduce, kick off *(Nonformal)*, launch, lead, pioneer, start, usher in

special *adj.* **1.** characteristic, determining, different, distinctive, especial, extraordinary, indicative, individual, odd, out-of-the-ordinary, particular, peculiar, rare, singular, strange, uncommon, unique, unusual *Antonyms:* common, everyday, generic, normal, ordinary, widespread **2.** appropriate, certain, designated, distinct, express, limited, marked, specific *Antonyms:* general, multipurpose, universal **3.** best, chief, choice, excellent, exceptional, fabulous, famous, fantastic, feature, great, magnificent, memorable, nonpareil, remarkable, wonderful *Nonformal:* killer, red-letter, smashing, sweet, world-class *Antonyms:* atrocious, awful, bad, criminal, poor **4.** consequential, eventful, important, impressive, landmark, major, meaningful, momentous, significant, watershed, weighty **5.** accessory, added, additional, bonus, extra, fringe, gift, supplementary **6.** beloved, bosom, cherished, close, dear, esteemed, fast, faithful, fond, intimate, loving, warm

specialist *n.* adept, authority, expert, guru, master, maven, pro, professional, sage, savant, virtuoso *Antonyms:* amateur, generalist

specialize *v.* concentrate, confine, devote, focus, major, practice, study

specially *adv.* distinctively, especially, expressly, *in specie (Latin)*, particularly, specifically, uniquely

specialty *n.* **1.** art, calling, career, craft, field, field of knowledge *or* study, forte, major, metier, occupation, practice, profession, province, pursuit, skill, study, vocation *Nonformal:* bag, game **2.** characteristic, difference, distinguishing mark, eccentricity, feature, idiosyncrasy, particularity, peculiarity, singularity, trademark *(Nonformal)*, uniqueness

species *n.* breed, category, class, classification, collection, description, division, feather, genre, group, kind, ilk, likes, lot, number, order, sort, stripe, type, variety

specific *adj.* **1.** absolute, categorical, clear, clear-cut, defined, definite, determinate, exact, explicit, express, precise, right on *(Nonformal)*, unequivocal *Antonyms:* imprecise, unclear, vague **2.** characteristic, different, distinct, distinguished, individual, inimitable, limited, particular, peculiar, personal, singular, special, *sui generis (Latin)*, uncommon, unique

specifically *adv.* accurately, categorically, characteristically, clearly, concretely, correctly, definitely, distinctively, exactly, explicitly, expressly, *in specie (Latin)*, particularly, pointedly, precisely, specially

specification *n.* **1.** blueprint, description, designation, detail, fact, information, item, key, lowdown *(Nonformal)*, map, outline, overview, particular, profile, report, statistic, summary **2.** condition, limitation, qualification, requirement, reservation, restriction, rule, stipulation, string, term

specify *v.* **1.** cite, denote, designate, identify, label, mention, name, point out, tag **2.** decide, elect, establish, fix, select, settle, stipulate **3.** arrange, catalogue, chart, chronicle, classify, detail, index, itemize, lay out, list, particularize, record **4.** bind, circumscribe, confine, define, determine, delimit, demarcate, limit, qualify, restrict, set **5.** clarify, delineate, demonstrate, elucidate, explain, explicate, illuminate, outline, reveal, spell out *(Nonformal)*, translate, unravel

specimen *n.* case, copy, cross section, embodiment, example, exemplar, exemplification, exhibit, holotype, illustration, model, part, pattern, proof, representation, representative, sample, sampling, sort, species, type, unit, variety

specious *adj.* **1.** casuistic, deceptive, delusive, empty, erroneous, fallacious, idle, inaccurate, incorrect, mendacious, misleading, nugatory, sophistic, spurious, unsound, wrong *Antonyms:* conclusive, valid, undeniable **2.** apparent, likely, ostensible, plausible, presumptive, probable, seeming, tenable

speck *n.* **1.** blemish, blot, defect, dot, fault, flaw, mark, splotch, spot, stain **2.** atom, bit, crumb, fleck, grain, iota, jot, mite, modicum, molecule, mote, particle, point, scintilla, shred, smidgen, spark, speckle, trace, whit

speckled *adj.* brindled, dappled, dotted, flecked, freckled, lentiginose, motley, mottled, patchy, peppered, polka-dotted, spotted, spotty, sprinkled, stippled, studded, variegated

spectacle *n.* **1.** attraction, carnival, celebration, ceremony, circus, concert, demonstration, display, drama, event, exhibit, expo, exposition, extravaganza, gala, game, games, match, pageant, parade, performance, production, representation, scene, show, spectacular, tamasha, tournament *Nonformal:* lollapalooza, to-do **2.** disgrace, dishonour, embarrassment, humiliation, ignominy, improbity, indecorum, scandal **3.** buffoon, butt, clown, fool, idiot, imbecile, joke, laughingstock *Nonformal:* arse, ass, piece of work, turkey

spectacular *adj.* **1.** amazing, astonishing, astounding, breathtaking, daring, dazzling, dramatic, fabulous, fantastic, impressive, magnificent, marked, marvellous, miraculous, remarkable, sensational, splendid, striking, stunning, stupendous, thrilling, wonderful, wondrous *Antonyms:* boring, dull, soporific **2.** consequential, conspicuous, copious, enormous, gargantuan, great, huge, immense, large, marked, momentous, obvious, prodigious, sizeable, staggering, substantial *Antonyms:* insignificant, minor, small, trivial – *n.* event, demonstration, feature, film, movie, play, performance, presentation, spectacle, theatrical

spectator *n.* beholder, booster, bystander, eyewitness, fan, kibitzer, moviegoer, observer, onlooker, standee, supporter, surveyor, viewer, watcher, witness *Nonformal:* couch potato, sidewalk superintendent

spectral *adj.* creepy, dreadful, eerie, ethereal, frightening, ghostly, haunting, incorporeal, insubstantial, ominous, otherworldly, scary, shadowy, spooky *(Nonformal)*, supernatural, unearthly

spectre *n.* **1.** apparition, banshee, bibe *(Newfoundland)*, bocan *(P.E.I.)*, bugaboo, demon, eidolon, fetch, ghost, ghoul, goblin, haunting, hobgoblin, nightmare, phantasm, phantom, poltergeist, presence, shade, soul, spirit, spook *(Nonformal)*, wraith **2.** chimera, delusion, dream, fantasy, figment, hallucination, illusion, mirage, vision **3.** black cloud, danger, doom, gloom, presentiment, menace, ominousness, pall, shadow, sword of Damocles, threat

spectrum *n.* band, chain, compass, diapason, distribution, gamut, line, progression, range, reach, run, scope, sequence, series, suite, sweep, system

speculate *v.* **1.** ballpark *(Nonformal)*, conjecture, consider, contemplate, deliberate, figure, guess, hypothesize, meditate, muse, reason, reckon, reflect, review, ruminate, scheme, study, suppose, surmise, theorize **2.** dare, gamble, hazard, play the market, plunge, punt, raid *(Nonformal)*, risk, sell short, trade, trade on margin, venture

speculation *n.* **1.** cogitation, contemplation, deliberation, mediation, rationalization, reasoning, reflection, rumination, thought, weighing **2.** assumption, belief, conclusion, conjecture, deduction, guess, hunch, hypothesis, idea, impulse, induction, inference, judgment, opinion, prediction, resolution, result, supposition, surmise, theory, windshield appraisal *(Nonformal)* **3.** bet, gamble, investment, hazard, plunge, profit-taking, risk, shot, smart money, speculative enterprise, stab, stake, venture, wager *Nonformal:* flier, plunge

speculative *adj.* **1.** academic, assumed, conjectural, experimental, hypothetical, philosophical, postulated, presupposed, supposed, theoretical *Antonyms:* applied, certain, incontrovertible, proven, scientific **2.** adventurous, dangerous, delicate, dicey *(Nonformal)*, doubtful, dubious, hazardous, precarious, rash, risky, shaky, unsound, venturesome *Antonyms:* risk-free, safe, secure

speech *n.* **1.** address, allocution, appeal, commentary, diatribe, dissertation, elocution, eulogy, exhortation, harangue, homily, keynote, lecture, oration, pitch, salutation, sermon, soapbox oration, spiel, tirade **2.** communication, conversation, dialogue, discourse, discussion, interchange, intercourse, palaver **3.** expression, remark, saying, talk, utterance, verbalization, vocalization **4.** colloquialism, dialect, diction, idiom, jargon, language, lexicon, lingo, localism, mother tongue, patois, slang, tongue, vernacular **5.** accent, articulation, brogue, cant, delivery, eloquence, enunciation, inflection, intonation, locution, oratory, parlance, phraseology, presentation, pronunciation, style, tone

speechless *adj.* **1.** aghast, amazed, astounded, choked-up, dumfounded *(Nonformal)*, dumbstruck, shocked, thunderstruck **2.** buttoned *or* clammed *or* dried up, close-mouthed, dumb, inarticulate, mum, mute, silent, tight-lipped, tongue-tied, voiceless, wordless *Antonyms:* loquacious, talkative, voluble **3.** reserved, reticent, shy, taciturn, uncommunicative

speed *n.* **1.** alacrity, briskness, celerity, dispatch, flight, haste, hastiness, hurriedness, promptitude, promptness, quickness, rapidity, swiftness, urgency *Nonformal:* steam, wheels **2.** acceleration, clip, gait, momentum, movement, pace, rate, rpm, rps, thrust, time, velocity *Nonformal:* klicks, revs – *v.* **1.** charge, dart, flee, fly, gallop, gather momentum *or* steam, go, hie, move, rush, scramble, sprint, streak, surge, tear *Nonformal:* barrel forward, bomb ahead, burn rubber, giddy-up, put pedal to the metal, whiz *Antonyms:* crawl, creep, dawdle, tarry **2.** advance, aid, assist, expedite, facilitate, further, hasten, hurry, promote, push, quicken, shove along, urge *Nonformal:* grease the wheels, railroad

speedy *adj.* accelerated, agile, alacritous, breakneck, brisk, expeditious, express, fast, fleet, fleet afoot, hasty, headlong, hurried, immediate, lively, precipitate, prompt, quick, quick-fire, rapid, ready, responsive, snappy, summary, supersonic, swift, winged *Antonyms:* dilatory, leisurely, lingering

spell *n.* **1.** bewitchment, charm, enchantment, evil eye, hex, hocus-pocus, incantation, jinx, magic, mumbo jumbo, sorcery, witchcraft, wizardry **2.** attraction, captivation, control, fascination, hold, hypnotism, influence, persuasion, possession, sway **3.** course, duration, extent, interlude, intermission, interval, patch, period, season, span, stint, streak, term, tide, time, while **4.** duty, go, hitch, session, shift, take, tour, turn **5.** bit, distance, gap, leap, reach, short drive *or* walk, stretch *Nonformal:* klick, piece **6.** affliction, ailment, attack, bout, complaint, debility, disease, disorder, fit, illness, jag *(Nonformal)*, lapse, malediction, seizure, spasm, stroke, throe – *v.* **1.** compose, form, make up, name, sign, report, write **2.** augur, connote, denote, herald, imply, import, indicate, insinuate, mean, portend, presage, promise, show, signal, signify, specify, suggest, symbolize

spellbound *adj.* agape, amazed, bemused, bewitched, breathless, captivated, charmed, enchanted, enthralled, entranced, fascinated, gripped, held, hooked, hypnotized, mesmerized, possessed, rapt, transfixed, transported *Antonyms:* bored, disinterested, tired

spend *v.* **1.** disperse, expend, hand *or* lay *or* shell out, invest, lavish, outlay, pay, spring for *(Nonformal)*, squander *Antonyms:* conserve, hoard, keep, save, store **2.** apply, bestow, contribute, devote, donate, employ, give, sacrifice **3.** consume, devour, eat *or* use up, exhaust, take, waste **4.** discharge, drop, eject, emit, secrete, shed, spill

spendthrift *adj.* excessive, extravagant, generous, intemperate, lavish, prodigal, squandering, wasteful *Antonyms:* miserly, protective, tight – *n.* profligate, spender, squanderer, waster, wastrel *Nonformal:* high roller, shopaholic, sieve *Antonyms:* miser, Scrooge, skinflint

spent *adj.* **1.** completed, consumed, depleted, dissipated, empty, expended, finished, gone, used up *Nonformal:* blown, shot **2.** bleary, drained, effete, enervated, exhausted, limp, played *or* tired *or* tuckered *or* washed *or* worn out, used, weakened, wearied, weary *Nonformal:* beat, burnt, dead, dog-tired, done, fagged out, fried, had, pooped, toast, wasted, whacked, wiped

spew *v.* **1.** get sick, heave, regurgitate, retch, throw up, vomit *Nonformal:* barf, beulah, blow chunks, gag, hurl, puke, ralph, ride the porcelain bus, toss one's cookies, upchuck **2.** blow, discharge, disgorge, displace, eject, emit, erupt, expel, gush, let loose, shoot, spill, spit, spout, spray, stream, surge, vent

sphere *n.* **1.** ball, circle, globe, orb, round **2.** asteroid, celestial body, comet, earth, heavenly body, moon, planet, star, sun **3.** ambit, bailiwick, bounds, department, dominion, environs, field, jurisdiction, pale, precinct, province, range, realm, scope, terrain, territory **4.** firmament, heavens, infinity, sky, space, stars, the unknown **5.** art, business, capacity, craft, employment, expertise, function, profession, skill, specialization, specialty **6.** caste, class, level, place, position, rank, relation, rung, station, step, stratum

spherical *adj.* annular, circular, cylindrical, discoid, disc-shaped, elliptical, global, globular, orblike, oval, rolled, rotund, round

spice *n.* **1.** condiment, flavour, flavouring, seasoning *Kinds of spice:* allspice, anise, black pepper, cacao, caraway, cardamom, cayenne, celery salt, chili powder, cinnamon, cloves, coriander, cumin, curry powder, fenugreek, garam masala, garlic salt, ginger, green peppercorn, juniper berry, mustard, nutmeg, paprika, peppercorn, rasel-hanoot, red pepper, saffron, salt, sesame, turmeric, white pepper *See also:* **herb** **2.** *gout (French)*, gusto, heat, kick, pep, piquancy, relish, savour, tang, zest, zip **3.** adventure, appeal, energy, enjoyment, entertainment, excitement, fun, interest, pleasure, sport, stimulation, verve *Nonformal:* electricity, pizzazz, rush – *v.* enhance, enliven, enrich, flavour, kick *or* pep up *(Nonformal)*, pepper, salt, savour, season

spicy *adj.* **1.** appetizing, aromatic, distinctive, fiery, flavourful, flavoursome, fragrant, hot, peppery, peppy, perfumed, piquant, powerful, pungent, seasoned, snappy, spirited, strong, sweet, tangy, tasty, zesty, zippy **2.** arousing, bawdy, earthy, exotic, improper, racy, raunchy, ribald, risqué, salacious, sexy, titillating, unseemly

Nonformal: adult, blue *Antonyms:* proper, prudish, unobjectionable

spike *n.* barbule, nail, needle, peg, pin, piton, point, skewer, spear, spicule, spine, stake – *v.* **1.** fasten, fix, make fast, nail down *or* on, pin, secure **2.** gouge, impale, lance, perforate, pierce, prick, punctuate, run through, skewer, spear, stab, stick, wound **3.** adulterate, alter, contaminate, doctor *(Nonformal)*, drug, fortify, lace **4.** arrest, bar, block, check, curb, halt, obstruct, prevent, scotch, stifle, stop, thwart

spill *n.* **1.** accident, dive, fall, header *(Nonformal)*, plunge, slip, trip, wipeout **2.** environmental disaster, leak, oil spill, slick, spillage, spread – *v.* **1.** dribble, drip, drop, empty, flow out, lose, overfill, overflow, overrun, overturn, pour, pour out *or* over, run, slop, spew, splash, splatter, spray, sprinkle, spurt, squirt, stream, upset, waste **2.** crash, flip, plummet, slip, spin, spin *or* wipe out, topple, tumble, upturn **3.** donate, give, offer, sacrifice **4.** clear out, discharge, disgorge, drain, empty, evacuate, leave, scatter, vacate, void **5.** communicate, disclose, disseminate, divulge, expose, inform, leak, reveal, spread, tell *Nonformal:* fink, rat, sing, snitch, squeal

spin *n.* **1.** circle, gyration, revolution, roll, rotation, spinning, twisting, whirling **2.** drive, excursion, jaunt, journey, joy ride *(Nonformal)*, pleasure trip, ride, road trip, romp, tour – *v.* **1.** gyrate, oscillate, pirouette, reel, revolve, rotate, turn, twirl, twist, whirl **2.** conceive, concoct, conjure *or* dream up, construct, craft, develop, fashion, make, originate, produce, tell, weave, write

spine *n.* **1.** backbone, chine, ridge, spinal column, vertebrae, vertebral column **2.** conviction, courage, daring, determination, firmness, fortitude, grit, mettle, pluck, resolution *Nonformal:* balls, cojones, chutzpah, gumption, guts, moxie, spunk

spineless *adj.* cowardly, craven, fainthearted, fearful, feeble, frightened, gutless, impotent, inadequate, ineffective, ineffectual, irresolute, nerveless, soft, spiritless, squeamish, submissive, timid, vacillating, weak, weak-kneed, weak-willed *Nonformal:* chicken, lily-livered, milquetoast, sissy, wimpy, wussy, yellow, yellow-bellied *Antonyms:* bold, brave, courageous, foolhardy, strong

spiral *adj.* circling, circular, coiled, corkscrew, curling, helical, radial, rolled, screw-shaped, scrolled, whorled, winding, wound – *n.* coil, corkscrew, curl, curlicue, curve, flourish, gyration, gyre, helix, loop, quirk, screw, volute, whorl – *v.* coil, corkscrew, curl, curve, gyrate, loop, whirl

spire *n.* **1.** belfry, campanile, chimney, finial, flèche, minaret, needle, obelisk, shaft, steeple, tower, turret **2.** acme, apex, cap, cone, crest, crown, extremity, head, nib, peak, pinnacle, point, summit, tip, top, vertex, zenith

spirit *n.* **1.** animus, *atman (Hindu)*, breath of life, *élan vital (French)*, essence, genius, heart, *ka (Egyptian)*, life, life force, soul, true being **2.** being, consciousness, ego, intellect, intelligence, mind, persona, personality, psyche, reason, self, self-awareness **3.** basis, content, drift, implication, import, intent, meaning, object, pertinence, purport, sense, significance, substance, truth **4.** immateriality, impalpability, incorporeality, intangibility, nothingness, otherworldliness *Antonyms:* materiality, matter, substance **5.** deity, escort, God, guardian, guide, Holy Ghost, Holy Spirit, keeper, light, lord, manitou *(Native Peoples)*, master, overseer, protector, saint, saviour, shepherd **6.** angel, apparition, bibe *(Newfoundland)*, bocan *(P.E.I.)*, daimon, demon, duppy *(Jamaican)*, elf, fairy, genii, ghost, phantasm, phantom, poltergeist, presence, shade, shadow, skookum *(Pacific Coast)*, spectre, spook *(Nonformal)*, sprite, wraith **7.** advocate, captain, champion, leader, model, pillar of society, role model, spokesperson, voice **8.** animation, dash, drive, eagerness, élan, energy, enterprise, enthusiasm, initiative, motivation, nerve, pep, verve, vigour, vim, vitality, vivacity, zeal, zip *Antonyms:* impassivity, laziness, phlegm **9.** affinity, allegiance, attachment, care, concern, dedication, devotion, emotion, feeling, fondness, loyalty, passion, regard, sympathy *Antonyms:* apathy, detachment, indifference **10.** backbone, courage, daring, dauntlessness, determination, fortitude, grit, hardihood, mettle, nerve, pluck, resolution, valour, will *Nonformal:* cojones, chutzpah, gumption, guts, moxie, spunk *Antonyms:* cowardice, fearfulness, timidity **11.** attitude, bent, bias, character, climate, colour, complexion, current, disposition, humour, inclination, mood, nature, pulse, quality, slant, state, temper, tendency, tenor, timbre

spirited *adj.* **1.** animate, animated, ardent, avid, bouncy, bright, burning, effervescent, energetic, enthusiastic, fiery, game, gingery, high-spirited, keen, passionate, snappy, sparkling, vivacious, zealous *Nonformal:* chipper, chirpy, gutbucket *Antonyms:* apathetic, calm, dispirited, indifferent, lifeless **2.** audacious, bold, brave, courageous, daring, dauntless, fearless, feisty, gritty, gutsy *(Nonformal)*, intrepid, mettlesome, nervy, plucky, valiant *Antonyms:* craven, shrinking, timid **3.** active, brisk, bustling, busy, conspirito, fast, jumping, lively, peppery, sprightly, stirring, vigorous *Antonyms:* dull, leisurely, measured, slow

spiritless *adj.* **1.** apathetic, depressed, despondent, disconsolate, dispirited, dopey *(Nonformal)*, down, downcast, downhearted, draggy, droopy, emotionless, exanimate, half-hearted, indifferent, lackadaisical, lacklustre, languid, languorous, lethargic, lifeless, limp, listless, low, melancholy, neurasthenic, subdued, torpid, unconcerned, unenthusiastic *Antonyms:* dynamic, energetic, spirited **2.** boring, dead *(Nonformal)*, dry, dull, flat, monotone, monotonous, soulless, stale, tedious, tiresome, wearisome *Antonyms:* entertaining, inspiring, lively

spirits *n.* alcohol, alcoholic beverages, bung-your-eye *(Newfoundland)*, hard liquor, pulque *Nonformal:* blue ruin, booze, demon rum, firewater, hard stuff, hootch, John Barleycorn, juice, moonshine, mountain dew, red-eye, rot-gut, sauce, sneaky pete, the creature, white lightning *See also:* **liquor**

spiritual *adj.* **1.** devotional, devout, divine, ecclesiastical, godly, hallowed, heavenly, holy, pious, pure, religious, sacred, sacramental, saintly *Antonyms:* lay, profane, temporal **2.** airy, celestial, ethereal, extramundane, immaterial, impalpable, incorporeal, insubstantial, intangible, metaphysical, mystical, nonphysical, shadowy, supernatural, transcendent *Antonyms:* concrete, material, physical, solid **3.** eerie, ghostly, haunted, mysterious, otherworldly, spectral, spooky *(Nonformal)*, wraithlike **4.** analytical, bookish, cerebral, highbrow, intellectual, mental, noetic, philosophic, platonic, rational, scholarly

spit *n.* **1.** drool, expectoration, saliva, spittle *Nonformal:* gob, goober, horker, loogie **2.** arm, atoll, cape, finger, jetty, peninsula, point, promontory, strip **3.** brochette, rotisserie, skewer, spear, stick – *v.* **1.** cough up, expectorate, hack *Nonformal:* gob, hork, let fly **2.** discharge, eject, emit, expel, jet, shoot, spew, spout, spray, vomit **3.** drizzle, drop, precipitate, rain, shower, sprinkle, weather *(Nonformal)* **4.** blaspheme, curse, damn, fulminate, imprecate, profane, swear, *Nonformal:* cuss, thunder, turn the air blue

spite *n.* **1.** animosity, antagonism, antipathy, bad blood, bile, bitterness, contempt, enmity, gall, grudge, hate, hatred, ill will, jealousy, malice, rancour, resentment, spitefulness, spleen, umbrage, venom, vindictiveness *Antonyms:* charity, compassion, kindness, love **2.** abuse, hostility, malicious intent, punishment, reprisal, retaliation, retribution, revenge, vengeance, vindication, violence, wrath – *v.* annoy, crab *(Nonformal)*, discomfit, gall, harass, harm, hurt, injure, needle, nettle, offend, peeve, pique, provoke, sting, thwart, vex *Antonyms:* aid, benefit, encourage, support

spiteful *adj.* acidic, angry, barbed, bitchy *(Nonformal)*, caustic, cruel, evil, hate-filled, hateful, hurtful, ill-disposed, ill-natured, malevolent, malicious, malign, malignant, mean, nasty, ornery, rancorous, snide, spleenful, splenetic, venomous, vicious, villainous, vindictive, vitriolic, waspish, wicked *Antonyms:* affectionate, altruistic, considerate, kind, loving

splash *n.* **1.** displacement, fume, gush, jet, ripple, spume, wave **2.** display, effect, image, impact, impression, scene, sensation, show, something to remember, spectacle, stir *Nonformal:* ballyhoo, buzz, headline, hype, wave **3.** bit, dash, daub, hint, jot, patch, spot, squeeze, squirt, taste, tinge, tincture, touch, whisper – *v.* **1.** begrime, bespatter, dirty, mark, smear, soil, spatter, stain, streak, tarnish **2.** dampen, deluge, douse, drench, moisten, saturate, shower, soak, sop, squirt, wash, waterlog, wet

spleen *n.* acrimony, anger, animosity, animus, bile, bitterness, crankiness, hatred, ill-humour, ill-temper, ill will, irascibility, jealousy, malevolence, malice, malignity, petulance, resentment, sourness, spite, spitefulness, venom, viciousness *Antonyms:* charity, good will, patience, tolerance

splendid *adj.* **1.** admirable, celebrated, distinguished, divine, eminent, excellent, exceptional, exquisite, fantastic, fine, first-class, first-rate, glorious, gorgeous, grand, great, heroic, illustrious, imposing, impressive, joyous, magnificent, marvellous, matchless, outstanding, peerless, premium, proud, rare, remarkable, royal, splendiferous *(Nonformal)*, splendorous, sterling, sublime, superb, superlative, supreme, transcendent, unparalleled, unsurpassed, wonderful *Antonyms:* drab, insipid, lacklustre, plain **2.** beaming, bright, brilliant, dazzling, glittering, glowing, luminous, radiant, resplendent, scintillating, shining, sparkling *Antonyms:* dull, flat, matte

splendour *n.* **1.** beauty, ceremony, display, glory, gorgeousness, grandeur, magnificence, majesty, pageantry, pomp, richness, show, solemnity, spectacle, stateliness, sumptuousness **2.** brightness, brilliance, dazzle, effulgence, lustre, radiance, refulgence, resplendence, shine *Antonyms:* dullness, flatness, grayness

splenetic *adj.* acrimonious, argumentative, base, bilious, cantankerous, caustic, choleric, churlish, contentious, crabby, cranky, cross, curt, difficult, disagreeable, fractious, grouchy, grumpy, ill-natured, ill-tempered, irascible, irritable, malevolent, malicious, mean, miserable, mordant, ornery, peevish, petulant, quarrelsome, rancorous, rude, sharp, spiteful, surly, tense, testy, touchy, ugly, uncivil, unfriendly, venomous, vexatious, vindictive, vicious, vitriolic *Nonformal:* bitchy, owly *Antonyms:* agreeable, easy-going, friendly

splinter *adj.* breakaway, disjoined, distinct, factional, individual, schismatic, separated – *n.* bit, chip, cutting, flake, fragment, kindling, needle, paring, piece, scrap, segment, shaving, shive, shiver, sliver, spall, splits *(Newfoundland)* – *v.* atomize, axe, bisect, break, break up, chip, chop, cleave, crack, crumble, cut, disintegrate, divide, fragment, halve, hew, part, pulverize, rive, segment, separate, shatter, shiver, snap, spall, split

splice *v.* braid, fasten, graft, hitch, interlace, intertwine, intertwist, interweave, join, knit, mesh, overlap, tie, unite, weave, wed *Antonyms:* cut, detach, separate

split *adj.* **1.** disconnected, disunited, divergent, divided, divorced, fractured, fragmented, estranged, open, segmented, separated, severed, slivered, torn *Antonyms:* unified, united, whole **2.** broken, damaged, defective, impaired, injured, mangled, ruined, ruptured – *n.* **1.** breach, break, chasm, chink, cleft, crack, disruption, divide, division, fissure, fracture, gap, opening, rent, rift, rip, rupture, slash, tear, vent **2.** dichotomy, disunification, divergence, division, offshoot, parting, schism, splinter group **3.** contrast, difference, discord, discrepancy, disharmony, disparity, dissension, incompatibility, nonconformity, opposition, variance *Antonyms:* synergy, unity **4.** annulment, breakup, dissolution, disunion, divorce, estrangement, falling out, trial separation **5.** deadlock, draw, evenness, stalemate, tie – *v.* **1.** axe, chop, cut, flake, hack, hew, lacerate, slash **2.** break, cleave, crack, diverge, divide, fork, halve, open, rend, rip, rive, sever, splinter, sunder **3.** allot, apportion, assign, distribute, divide up, divvy up *(Nonformal)*, ration, share *Antonyms:* gather, hoard **4.** break off *or* up, disband, disjoin, dissolve, disunite, divorce, part, part ways, separate **5.** alienate, detach, isolate, remove, quarantine, segregate, stream **6.** bolt, depart, escape, exit, flee, go, leave, move on, run, vacate, vanish *Nonformal:* beat it, go AWOL, skedaddle, vamoose *Antonyms:* continue, remain, stay

spoil *v.* **1.** damage, destroy, disfigure, harm, hurt, injure, mangle, mutilate, ruin, smash, wreck, vandalize *Antonyms:* improve, restore, save **2.** devastate, undo, upset *Nonformal:* blow, bugger *or* foul *or* louse *or* mess *or* muck *or* screw *or* snarl up, play merry hell with, rain on one's parade *or* picnic, shoot down, sink, total, upset the apple cart, wet **3.** besmirch, blacken, blemish, diminish, mar, smear, stain, sully, tarnish, undermine **4.** baby, cater to, coddle, cosset, favour, humour, indulge, mollycoddle, oblige, pamper, spoon-feed *Antonyms:* deprive, ignore, neglect **5.** blight, curdle, decay, decompose, deteriorate, mildew, moulder, putrefy, rot, turn, waste

spoils *n. pl.* **1.** booty, filthy lucre *(Nonformal)*, goods, loot, pickings, pillage, plunder, possessions, prey, swag **2.** cut, gain, graft, pie, prize, profit, receipts, share, take, winnings

spoilsport *n.* malcontent, pessimist, prude *Nonformal:* bummer, cry baby, drag, drip, killjoy, party-pooper, skeleton at the banquet, sourpuss, stick-in-the-mud, wet blanket

spoken *adj.* announced, articulated, aural, communicated, expressed, lingual, mentioned, oral, said, told, uttered, verbal, voiced *Antonyms:* implied, silent, unarticulated, unsaid, unuttered

spokesperson *n.* advocate, agent, ambassador, attaché, champion, communicator, delegate, deputy, diplomat, mediator, mouthpiece *(Nonformal)*, negotiator, promoter, representative, salesperson, speaker, spokesman, spokeswoman, talker

sponge *n.* **1.** absorbent cloth, loofah, pad **2.** bum, cadger, deadbeat, freeloader, leech, parasite, scrounge, scrounger, sponger *Nonformal:* chiseller, mooch, scab – *v.* **1.** absorb, clean, cleanse, mop, swab, wash, wipe, wipe down **2.** bum, cadge, freeload, live off of, scrounge *Nonformal:* chisel, mooch

spongy *adj.* **1.** compressible, cushiony, elastic, light, resilient, rubbery, soft, springy, yielding *Antonyms:* compact, hard, unyielding **2.** drenched, dripping, drippy, marshy, moist, mushy, pulpy, saturated, soaked, soaken, sodden, sopping, squishy, waterlogged, wringing-wet *Antonyms:* dry, dehydrated **3.** absorbent, airy, permeable, pervious, porous *Antonyms:* impervious, solid

sponsor *n.* advertiser, advocate, backer, benefactor, defender, financier, guarantor, patron, promoter, supporter, sustainer, underwriter *Nonformal:* angel, meal ticket – *v.* advocate, back, bankroll, champion, endorse, finance, fund, grubstake *(Nonformal)*, guarantee, help, patronize, pledge, promote, stake, subsidize, support

spontaneous *adj.* ad-lib, automatic, casual, extemporaneous, extempore, free-spirited, impetuous, impromptu, improvised, impulsive, instinctive, involuntary, natural, offhand, simple, unbidden, uncompelled, unconscious, unconstrained, uncontrived, uncontrolled, unforced, unintentional, unplanned, unpremeditated, unstudied *Nonformal:* improv, knee-jerk, off the cuff *Antonyms:* arranged, calculated, contrived, forced, premeditated

spontaneously *adv.* ad-lib, automatically, extemporaneously, freely, from the hip *(Nonformal)*, impulsively, instinctively, intuitively, involuntarily, naturally, thoughtlessly

spoof *n.* burlesque, caricature, comedy, farce, imitation, jest, joke, lampoon, mockery, parody, prank, put-on, satire, send-up, skit, take-off, travesty – *v.* **1.** imitate, lampoon, mimic, mock, poke fun at, ridicule, satirize, scoff, scorn, send-up *Nonformal:* nail, roast **2.** cheat, deceive, defraud, delude, dupe, fleece, fool, gull, hoodwink, lie, mislead, swindle *Nonformal:* chisel, con, scam, screw

spooky *adj.* bloodcurdling, chilling, creepy, disturbing, eerie, eldritch, frightening, ghastly, ghostly, hair-raising, mysterious, ominous, preternatural, scary, spine-chilling, spine-tingling, strange, supernatural, uncanny, unearthly, unnerving, unsettling, upsetting, weird *Antonyms:* delightful, humorous, light

spool *n.* bobbin, cylinder, reel, tackle, wheel, winch, windlass

spoon-fed *adj.* babied, coddled, cosseted, mollycoddled, mothered, over-humoured, overindulged, overprotected, pampered, smothered, spoiled, wrapped in cotton-wool *(Nonformal)*

sporadic *adj.* aleatoric, desultory, dispersed, fitful, infrequent, intermittent, irregular, isolated, occasional, random, rare, scarce, scattered, spasmodic, uncommon *Antonyms:* constant, continuous, incessant,

sport *n.* **1.** athletics, battle, bonspiel, championship, clash, competition, contest, event, game, games, meet, Olympics, playdown, playoff, race, regatta, rivalry, round robin, showdown, struggle, tournament **2.** amusement, distraction, diversion, entertainment, exercise, fun, leisure, pastime, play, pleasure, recreation **3.** celebrant, cutup *(Nonformal)*, gamboller, gamer, goer, good fellow, indulger, joker, merrymaker, one of the boys, one of the girls, party girl, playboy, player, reveller, trooper **4.** buffoon, butt, fall guy, jest, joke, laughingstock, plaything, target, victim *Nonformal:* mark, patsy, pigeon, sucker **5.** antics, badinage, banter, derision, drollery, escapade, frolic, hijinks, horseplay, jesting, joking, jollification, jollity, kibitzing *(Nonformal)*, kidding, laughter, merriment, mirth, mockery, nonsense, pleasantry, practical joking, raillery, teasing, trifling – *v.* **1.** assume, demonstrate, display, don, exhibit, manifest, show, show off, wear **2.** compete, contend, frolic, gambol, participate, play, revel, romp, run

sporting *adj.* **1.** acrobatic, active, athletic, gymnastic, physical, sportive **2.** combative, competitive, head-to-head, sudden-death *(Nonformal)*, winner-take-all **3.** considerate, generous, gentlemanly, good, handsome, just, kind, lavish, liberal, neighbourly, square *(Nonformal)*, thoughtful **4.** fair, good, moderate, plausible, probable, real, reasonable

spot *n.* **1.** blemish, blot, blotch, daub, discoloration, flaw, freckle, jot, lentigo, macula, mark, pimple, speck, stain, taint **2.** area, locale, locality, locus, neighborhood, place, region, scene, site, station, territory, vicinity **3.** appointment, berth, capacity, desk *(Nonformal)*, job, office, opening, place, position, post, responsibility, slot, station, work **4.** Catch-22, corner, crisis, difficulty, dilemma, fix, hole, jam, mess, plight, predicament, quandary, scrape, trouble *Nonformal:* box, kettle of fish, pickle **5.** bit, dab, dash, dram, drop, modicum, nip, portion, sample, share, smidgen, swallow, taste, trace, trickle – *v.* **1.** besmirch, bespatter, blot, blotch, dapple, dirty, dot, fleck, marble, mark, mottle, soil, spatter, speck, speckle, splash, splotch, spray, stain, sully, tarnish **2.** catch, detect, discern, discover, espy, find, finger, identify, locate, note, notice, observe, perceive, pick out, pinpoint, place, recognize, see, sight, trace, watch **3.** fix, park, place, position, set, situate **4.** advance, bankroll, credit, extend, finance, float, fund, grubstake *(Nonformal)*, lend, loan

spotless *adj.* **1.** clean, immaculate, pristine, scrubbed, snow-white, stainless, sterile, swept, tidied, tidy, washed, uninfected, unpolluted *Antonyms:* dirty, filthy, polluted **2.** above reproach, angelic, blameless, chaste, crimeless, exemplary, faultless, honourable, impeccable, innocent, just, pure, right, righteous, sinless, uncorrupted, unimpeachable, unsullied, untainted, upright, virtuous, virginal, without sin *Antonyms:* corrupt, disgraceful, guilty

spotlight *n.* centre of attention *or* publicity, centre stage, downstage, fame, glare, limelight, notoriety, public attention *or* interest *Nonformal:* hot news, media bait – *v.* accentuate, advertise, draw attention, elevate, feature, focus, headline, highlight, illuminate, italicize, magnify, point up, promote, publicize, push *Nonformal:* hype, plug

spotty *adj.* **1.** Appaloosa, blotchy, dappled, freckled, mottled, polka-dotted, stippled **2.** discontinuous, episodic, erratic, fickle, fitful, inconstant, intermittent, irregular, jerky, patchy, quirky, random, sketchy, spasmodic, sporadic, uneven, unsteady *Antonyms:* constant, even, methodical, reliable

spouse *n.* bride, common-law companion, consort, groom, helpmate, husband, life partner, mate, partner, soulmate, wife *Nonformal:* ball and chain, better half, breadwinner, hubby, missus, my man, old lady, old man, the wife, yokemate

spout *n.* **1.** channel, chute, conduit, course, drain, duct, egress, faucet, floodgate, gate, gargoyle, hole, lip, mouth, nozzle, outlet, pipe, sluice, spile, tap, trough, tube, vent, waterspout **2.** column, fountain, geyser, jet, spray, spurt, stream – *v.* **1.** belch, discharge, eject, erupt, exude, flow, gush, issue, jet, pour, shoot, spew, spit, spray, spurt, squirt, stream, surge, vent, vomit, well **2.** babble, bluster, declaim, exhort, harangue, orate, pontificate, preach, ramble, rant, rave, spiel, utter *Nonformal:* run on, speechify

sprawl *n.* **1.** development, dilation, expansion, growth, spread, swell **2.** municipal growth, suburbanization, urban sprawl, urbanism – *v.* drape, extend, flop, lie, loll, lounge, recline, sit, slouch, slump, spread, spread eagle *(Nonformal)*, spread out

spray *n.* **1.** atomization, drizzle, droplets, dusting, fog, mist, rain, spindrift, spoondrift, sprinkling, wash, vapour **2.** aerosol, atomizer, douche, propellant, spray can, sprinkler, syringe **3.** arrangement, bough, branch, bunch, corsage, decoration, festoon, garland, nosegay, sprig, shoot, wreath – *v.* atomize, diffuse, drizzle, dust, scatter, shoot, shower, spatter, splash, sprinkle, squirt

spread *n.* **1.** advance, advancement, broadening, development, diffusion, dispersion, enlargement, escalation, expansion, extension, growth, hike *(Nonformal)*, increase, multiplication, profusion, proliferation, radiation, rise, scattering, sprawl, stretch, widening *Antonyms:* curtailment, limitation, restriction **2.** advertisement, announcement, broadcast, communication, disclosure, dissemination, ink *(Nonformal)*, popularization, print, proclamation, promotion, promulgation, publication, report, revelation **3.** breadth, compass, coverage, distance, duration, expanse, extent, interval, limit, period, range, reach, scope, size, space, span, stretch, stint, sweep, term, width **4.** contrast, deviation, difference, disparity, divergence, margin, separation, variation **5.** array, banquet, brunch, buffet, dinner, fare, feast, feed *(Nonformal)*, hot table, lunch, meal, menu, repast, smörgåsbord, table **6.** butter, condiment, cream cheese, frosting, garnish, icing, jam, jelly, margarine, paste, pâté, peanut butter, preserve, purée, topping *See also:* **condiment** **7.** bedding, bedspread, blanket, buffalo robe, cover, duvet, Hudson's Bay Blanket *(Trademark)*, layer, linen, robe, rug, sheet, throw **8.** demesne, domain, estate, farm, home, homestead, land, plot, premises, property, ranch, title, tract **9.** centrefold, gatefold, layout, page, presentation, pullout – *v.* **1.** lay out, open, unfold, unfurl, unroll, unwind **2.** extend, outstretch, splay out, sprawl, spread out, stretch **3.** amplify, broaden, dilate, expand, inflate, magnify, radiate, wax, widen **4.** breed, develop, enlarge, grow, increase, multiply, mushroom, procreate, proliferate, propagate, reproduce **5.** advertise, blazon, broadcast, circulate, declare, diffuse, disseminate, distribute, make known *or* public, proclaim, promote, promulgate, propagate, publicize, publish, report, reveal, show, tell *Antonyms:* conceal, hide **6.** cast, disperse, fling, pour, scatter, shower, sow, sprinkle, strew **7.** apply, blanket, carpet, coat, cover, daub on, glaze, gloss, lacquer, overlay, paint, roll on, shellac, smear, tar, varnish *Antonyms:* remove, strip **8.** break up, cleave, detach, divide, force apart, isolate, part, segregate, separate, split *Antonyms:* attach, connect, join, link **9.** adjust, arrange, array, group, line up, order, organize, place, range

spree *n.* **1.** bacchanalia, binge, carousal, carousing, celebration, debauchery, frolic, indulgence, orgy, revel, saturnalia, *Nonformal:* bash, bender, blowout, drunk jag, pub crawl, rip, tear, toot, lost weekend **2.** bout, fit, flourish, frenzy, rampage, spell, splurge, spurt

sprig *n.* **1.** bow, branch, scion, shoot, slip, sprout **2.** adolescent, boy, *enfant (French)*, girl, juvenile, lad, urchin, whippersnapper, youngster, youth *Nonformal:* half-pint, pintsize, squirt, wee one, young'un

sprightly *adj.* active, agile, airy, alert, animated, blithe, bouncy, breezy, bright, brisk, cheerful, clever, dashing, energetic, fun, gay, jaunty, jocund, joyous, keen, light, lively, nimble, perky, playful, quick, smart, snappy, spirited, sportive, spry, vivacious

Nonformal: chipper, chirpy, full of piss and vinegar, peppy, swinging *Antonyms:* dull, lethargic, torpid

spring *n.* **1.** coil, cushion, elastic, helix *Common springs:* compression coil, double spiral, extension coil, hinge, leaf **2.** bounciness, elasticity, flexibility, recoil, resilience, return, stretch **3.** bob, bound, hop, jump, leap, lurch, skip, vault **4.** blossom time, breakup, Eastertide, Maytime, planting season, springtide, springtime, the melt *(Nonformal)*, vernal season **5.** beginning, birth, dawn, dayspring, introduction, opening, preface, prelude, start, threshold, youth **6.** antecedent, basis, cause, fount, genesis, origin, root, source, wellspring **7.** goad, impetus, impulse, incentive, inducement, motive, stimulus, spur **8.** bath, fountain, geyser, hot spring, hydro, spa, thermal spring, watering place, well **9.** breach, break, cut, fissure, gash, hole, leak, opening, rent, rift – *v.* **1.** bolt, bounce, bound, dart, hop, hurdle, jump, leap, lope, rise, rouse, skip, start, surge, trip, vault **2.** kick, react, rebound, recoil, return **3.** appear, arise, arrive, ascend, begin, burgeon, come, commence, dawn, derive, develop, emanate, emerge, flow, grow, hatch, issue, loom, originate, precede, rise, spread from, start, stem **4.** bend, buckle, crack, fracture, leak, rupture, split **5.** arrange, fix, prepare, ready, set **6.** clamp, close, shut, slam, snap **7.** bail out, deliver, escape, free, liberate, manumit, parole, post bail, rescue, release, save **8.** communicate, disclose, divulge, expose, inform, make known, reveal, unload *(Nonformal)*

springy *adj.* bouncy, coiled, elastic, flexible, marshy, pliant, resilient, rubbery, soft, stretchy, yielding *Antonyms:* brittle, hard

sprinkle *n.* **1.** distribution, dusting, sprinkling, trickle **2.** hint, pinch, soupçon, taste, touch, trifle, whisper – *v.* **1.** dampen, drip, drizzle, hail, mist, patter, piss *(Nonformal)*, pour, powder, precipitate, rain, shed, shower, snow, spatter spray, spritz, squirt **2.** broadcast, cast, disseminate, dust, fling, scatter, sow, spread, strew

sprinkling *n.* admixture, dash, dusting, handful, hint, lick, mixture, powdering, scattering, smattering, taste, tinge, touch, trace *Antonyms:* deluge, downpour, excess, surfeit

sprint *n.* **1.** dash, hustle, hurry, race, run, rush **2.** competition, contest, event, face-off, foot race, heat, showdown – *v.* dart, dash, flee, gallop, go, race, run, rush, scamper, scoot, scud, scurry, shoot, tear *Nonformal:* explode, hotfoot it *Antonyms:* crawl, creep, mosey, saunter, stroll, walk

sprite *n.* apparition, bocan *(P.E.I.)*, brownie, daimon, demon, elf, fairy, familiar, gnome, goblin, gremlin, hobgoblin, imp, kelpie, kobold, leprechaun, mischief-maker, naiad, nuisance, nymph, peri, pixie, puck, spirit, trickster, troublemaker *Newfoundland:* bibe, jinker

sprout *n.* branch, ratoon, runner, scion, sprig, stem, stock, tendril – *v.* begin, bud, burgeon, burst forth, commence, develop, flourish, germinate, grow, pullulate, rise, shoot, spring

spruce *adj.* chic, clean, dapper, elegant, fashionable, fastidious, natty, neat, prepped, smart, stylish, tidy, trim, well-groomed *Nonformal:* decked out, gussied up, nifty, snazzy, spiffy *Antonyms:* bedraggled, frowzy, messy, unkempt – *n.* conifer, fir, evergreen, pine *Common Native Canadian Spruce:* Black, Douglas Fir, Engelmann, Red, Rocky Mountain, Sitka, White – *v.* clean, comb, doll *or* swab up *(Nonformal)*, groom, neaten, order, prep, prettify, primp, ready, shave, smooth down, straighten, tidy, trim *Antonyms:* disarrange, mess up

spry *adj.* active, agile, alert, brisk, energetic, feeling one's oats *(Nonformal)*, fleet, lithe, nimble, prompt, quick, ready, spirited, sprightly, supple, vigorous, vivacious *Antonyms:* awkward, doddering, inactive, sluggish, stiff

spunk *n.* backbone, bravado, courage, daring, doggedness, feistiness, fire, fortitude, game, grit, guts, heart, mettle, nerve, panache, pluck, *skookum tumtum (Pacific Coast)*, spirit, toughness *Nonformal:* balls, chutzpah, gumption, guts, moxie, starch *Antonyms:* cowardice, fear

spunky *adj.* courageous, feisty, fiery, game, gritty, gutsy *(Nonformal)*, high-spirited, mettlesome, peppery, plucky, tough *Antonyms:* craven, pusillanimous, weak-willed

spur *adj.* ancillary, branch, connecting, secondary, side – *n.* **1.** agent, booster, catalyst, goad, impetus, incentive, incitement, inducement, instigation, motive, needle, prick, stimulus, trigger, urge **2.** cliff, crag, escarpment, outcrop, projection, ridge, spine – *v.* accelerate, activate, animate, arouse, awaken, drive, egg on *(Nonformal)*, goad, impel, incite, instigate, key up, kick, press, prick, prod, prompt, propel, push, rouse, spark, stimulate, stir, trigger, urge

spurious *adj.* **1.** affected, artificial, assumed, bogus, contrived, counterfeit, deceitful, ersatz, fake, false, feigned, fictitious, forged, fraudulent, mock, phoney *(Nonformal)*, sham, so-called, specious *Antonyms:* authentic, genuine, legitimate **2.** banned, black market, forbidden, illegal, illegitimate, illicit, prohibited, unauthorized, unlicensed *Antonyms:* sanctioned, valid, warranted

spurn *n.* denial, refusal, rejection, renunciation, repudiation, turndown *Nonformal:* brush-off, dis, cold shoulder, slam – *v.* condemn, cut, decline, deny, despise, disapprove, disdain, dismiss, disregard, drop, dump, ignore, neglect, omit, rebuff, refuse, reject, repudiate, repulse, scoff, scorn, slight, sneer, snub, turn away *or* down *Nonformal:* burn, dis, dump, flush, leave waiting at the alter, nix *Antonyms:* embrace, seize, welcome

spurt *n.* **1.** discharge, ejection, eruption, fountain, geyser, gusher, jet, spring, spume **2.** attack, burst, commotion, explosion, fit, flash, flourish, flurry, outburst, rush, spree, squirt, stream, surge, tear **3.** interval, moment, period, spate, stretch – *v.* discharge, eject, emit, erupt, gush, jet, spew, spout, spray, squirt, vomit

sputter *v.* **1.** discharge, eject, emit, expectorate, shower, spatter, spit, splatter, spray, spurt **2.** babble, drivel, gab, jabber, mumble, prattle, rant, rave, run-on *(Nonformal)*, say, shout, slur, spout, stammer **3.** cough, gag, hesitate, jerk, misfire, stop and start, struggle, wheeze

spy *n.* agent, detective, emissary, espionage *or* foreign *or* secret *or* undercover agent, fifth columnist, informant, informer, intelligence, investigator, lookout, mole, observer, operative, plant, scout, sleuth, snoop, spook *(Nonformal)* – *v.* case *(Nonformal)*, check *or* stake out, delve into, eavesdrop, eyeball, glimpse, observe, peep, pry, reconnoitre, scout, scrutinize, search, shadow, sleuth, snoop, spot, study, trail, watch

squabble *n.* altercation, argument, brawl, clash, conflict, difference of opinion, difficulty, disagreement, dispute, disturbance, encounter, exchange, fight, flareup, fracas, fray, feud, imbroglio, incident, quarrel, row, rumpus, scrap, spat, tiff – *v.* argue, bicker, brawl, clash, contend, duel, feud, fight, quarrel, scuffle, spar, tussle, wrangle

squad *n.* band, battalion, cadre, company, covey, crew, division, escadrille, force, gang, group, regiment, squadron, team, troop

squalid *adj.* abject, abominable, base, broken-down, decayed, despicable, dingy, dirty, disgusting, dishevelled, fetid, filthy, foul, grimy, grubby, gruesome, horrible, impure, low, lowdown, mean, malodorous, mouldy, muddy, musty, nasty, offensive, poor, poverty-stricken, ramshackle, reeking, repellent, repulsive, rundown, scurvy, seedy, shabby, shoddy, slatternly, sleazy, slimy, sloppy, slovenly, smutty, soiled, sordid, tumble-down, ugly, unclean, unkempt, vile, wretched *Nonformal:* cruddy, crummy, scuzzy *Antonyms:* attractive, clean, hygienic, tidy

squall *n.* **1.** blizzard, cyclone, gale, hurricane, rain, snow, storm, streamer, tempest, *tempête de neige (French)*, typhoon, turbulence, whiteout, wind, windstorm **2.** chaos, confusion, commotion, disturbance, furor, fuss, pandemonium, racket, to-do *(Nonformal)*, tumult **3.** bawling, howl, outcry, scream, shriek, shrieking, wail – *v.* **1.** blast, blow, bluster, flurry, gust, rage, surge **2.** bawl, bellow, bewail, cry, holler, screech, shout, shriek, squawk, yawp, yell

squalor *n.* decay, degradation, depression, filth, foulness, meanness, misery, neglect, poverty, rot, shabbiness, sordidness, vileness, wretchedness *Antonyms:* comfort, extravagance, luxury, splendour

squander *v.* blow *(Nonformal)*, consume, deplete, diddle *or* frivol *or* throw away, dissipate, exhaust, expend, fribble, fritter, lavish, misspend, misuse, trifle, use up, waste *Antonyms:* economize, keep, put aside, save, store

square *adj.* **1.** boxlike, boxy, equal-sided, equilateral, four-sided, foursquare, quadrangular, quadrate, quadratic, rectilinear, right-angled, symmetrical *Antonyms:* circular, round **2.** decent, direct, equitable, ethical, fair, forthright, genuine, honest, impartial, just, nonpartisan, objective, sporting, straight, unbiased, unprejudiced, upfront, upright *Antonyms:* biased, partial, prejudiced **3.** bourgeois, button-down, conservative, conventional, middle-of-the-road, mossbacked *(Nonformal)*, old-fashioned, orthodox, staid, straight, straitlaced, stuffy *Antonyms:* cool, hip, trendy, up-to-date **4.** absolute, accurate, complete, conforming, exact, definite, in agreement, perfect, precise, unequivocal **5.** adjusted, balanced, equalized, even, matched, on par, parallel, settled, tied – *n.* **1.** block, box, cube, parallelogram **2.** centre, circle, common, concession, green, park, parkette, *piazza (Italian)*, *place (French)*, plaza, quad, space, village green **3.** conformist, conventionalist, prude *Nonformal:* company man, nerd, yes man – *v.* **1.** adapt, adjust, agree, balance, coincide, conform, correspond, dovetail, equalize, even, fit, harmonize, jibe *(Nonformal)*, match, reconcile, straighten, tally **2.** balance, clear, pay up *or* off, remit, requite, satisfy, settle

squash *n.* cucurbit, gourd, vegetable *Common squash:* acorn, butternut, Hubbard, pumpkin, spaghetti, summer, winter, yellow, zucchini – *v.* **1.** beat, compress, crush, flatten, jam, macerate, mash, mush up, pound, press, pulp, smash, smush *(Nonformal)*, squeeze, squish, trample **2.** ban, block, censor, curb, defeat, extinguish, forbid, kill, quell, ruin, scotch, scud, silence, sink, squelch, stifle, suppress, thwart, wreck *Nonformal:* put the kibosh on, torpedo *Antonyms:* aid, expedite, help, nurture, support

squat *adj.* **1.** broad, chunky, compact, dumpy, fat, heavy, heavyset, scrub, short, stocky, stout, stubby, thick, thick-bodied, thickset **2.** balled up, crouched, lowered, sitting, slumped – *v.* **1.** bow, cower, crouch, hunch, hunker down, lower, perch, roost, settle, sit, stoop **2.** dwell, homestead, inhabit, lodge, reside, roost, settle, tenant **3.** assume, arrogate, claim, expropriate, seize, take over, usurp

squawk *n.* **1.** caterwaul, complaint, criticism, grievance, grumbling, lament, protestation, remonstrance, whine **2.** chirp, holler, honk, howl, scream, shriek, squall, yawl, yell – *v.* **1.** cackle, caw, crow, cry, hoot, screech, squeal, yap, yawp, yelp **2.** beef, complain, fuss, gripe, grumble, protest *Nonformal:* bellyache, bitch, crab, gripe, grouse, kvetch, raise Cain, yammer

squeak *v.* cheep, chirp, creak, grate, peep, pipe, shrill, sing, sound, squeal

squeal *n.* bawl, bleat, cry, howl, outcry, scream, screech, shout, shriek, squawk, wail, whine, wimper, yell, yelp, yip, yowl – *v.* **1.** bawl, bleat, cry, howl, protest, scream, screech, shout, shriek, squawk, wail, whine, wimper, yell, yelp, yip, yowl **2.** betray, inform, talk, tattle, tell *Nonformal:* blab, rat on *or* out, sing, snitch, spill the beans

squeamish *adj.* **1.** delicate, dizzy, fainthearted, frail, green around the gills *(Nonformal)*, qualmish, queasy, queer, sensitive, shaky, touchy, unsettled, upset, weak, weak-stomached *Antonyms:* bold, strong, unshakable **2.** captious, exacting, fastidious, finicky, fussy, hypercritical, particular, persnickety, scrupulous *Antonyms:* careless, indifferent, sloppy **3.** overmodest, priggish, prim, prissy, proper, prudish, puritanical, strait-laced, stuffy *(Nonformal)*

squeeze *n.* **1.** compression, concentration, pressure, squashing, squishing **2.** bearhug, clasp, clinch, embrace, handclasp, handshake, headlock, hold, hug, snuggle **3.** bunching, congestion, crowd, crush, overcrowding, packed house *(Nonformal)*, traffic, volume *Antonyms:* elbow room, space **4.** bind, crisis, crunch, tight spot – *v.* **1.** compress, crunch, crush, mash, press, scrunch, squash, squish, thrust **2.** draw, express, extract, force out, juice, procure, pulp, wring, yield **3.** clutch, cuddle, embrace, enfold, hold, hug, lock, snuggle, wrap **4.** cram, crowd, elbow *or* force *or* ram *or* thrust *or* wedge in, jam, pack, push, sardine *(Nonformal)*, stuff **5.** blackmail, coerce, extort, gouge, lean on, oppress, pinch, pressure, wrench, wrest, wring *Nonformal:* bleed, milk, shakedown

squelch *v.* beat, black out, censure, check, crush, dust *(Nonformal)*, extinguish, kill, muffle, oppress, quash, quench, pulverize, put-down, repress, restrain, shut out, silence, smother, squash, stifle, strangle, subdue, suppress, thwart, veto *Antonyms:* aid, assist, help

squint *v.* blink, look, look askance *or* cross-eyed, peek, peep, scrunch up, squinch, strain

squire *n.* armourbearer, attendant, beau, cavalier, date, fellow, gallant, guy *(Nonformal)*, fellow, landowner, mate, partner, suitor, swain – *v.* accompany, chaperone, direct, guide, lead, shepherd

squirm *v.* agonize, fidget, shift, sweat bullets *(Nonformal)*, toss, twist, wiggle, wriggle, writhe

squirt *n.* **1.** column, flow, fountain, jet, stream **2.** adolescent, boy, child, girl, juvenile, tot, urchin, whippersnapper, youngster, youth *Nonformal:* kid, punk, pup, rug rat, shaver, small fry, tyke, young'un – *v.* **1.** bespatter, drench, hose, moisten, pour, rinse, spatter, spritz, water, wet **2.** discharge, eject, emit, erupt, expectorate, expel, fire, flow, jet, shoot, spew, spit, splash, spout, spray, spurt, stream, vomit

squishy *adj.* damp, marshy, muddy, mushy, oozing, pasty, pulpy, slushy, soft, spongy, squashy, wet, yielding *Antonyms:* compact, dry, hard

stab *n.* **1.** gash, laceration, leak, lesion, nick, opening, penetration, rent, rip, slash, tear, wound **2.** attempt, chance, crack *(Nonformal)*, effort, endeavour, essay, gamble, shot, try, turn, venture – *v.* bayonet, brand, carve, chop, cleave, cut, dirk, eviscerate, gore, gouge, hurt, impale, injure, jab, knife, lacerate, lance, open up, penetrate, pierce, plunge, prick, prong, puncture, ram, run through, skewer, slice, spear, spike, stick, transfix, wound *Nonformal:* shish kebab, shiv

stabbing *adj.* aching, acute, cutting, extreme, intense, painful, piercing, pricking, sharp, twinging, violent *Antonyms:* minor, mild, unnoticeable

stability *n.* **1.** constancy, durability, endurance, fixedness, homeostasis, immovability, immutability, permanence, rootedness *Antonyms:* brevity, ephemeralness, transience **2.** balance, cohesion, dependability, evenness, firmness, solidity, solidness, soundness, stableness, steadiness, strength, sturdiness, substantiality, toughness *Antonyms:* delicacy, flimsiness, weakness **3.** adherence, backbone, commitment, dedication, determination, devotion, doggedness, perseverance, loyalty, resolution, stick-to-it-iveness *(Nonformal)*, tenacity, will

stabilize *v.* balance, ballast, bolt, brace, buttress, counterbalance, equalize, fasten, firm, fix, maintain, preserve, prop, secure, set, settle, steady, stiffen, strengthen, support, sustain, uphold *Antonyms:* disable, enfeeble, weaken

stable *adj.* **1.** anchored, braced, established, fast, firm, fixed, secure, solid, strong, sturdy, well grounded *or* rooted *Antonyms:* rickety, shaky, unsteady **2.** abiding, ageless, durable, enduring, fast-frozen, invariable, lasting, permanent, resilient, timeless *Antonyms:* ephemeral, evanescent, temporary **3.** dedicated, devoted, focused, persevering, purposeful, resolute, single-minded, stalwart, staunch steadfast, steady, unfaltering, unwavering *Antonyms:* fickle, mercurial, wavering **4** balanced, calm, equable, even, healthy level-headed, lucid, normal, poised, rational, sane, sensible, sound *Antonyms:* ill unstable, unwell – *n.* barn, coop, cote dovecote, house, mews, outbuilding, shelter, shieling, stall

stack *n.* **1.** arrangement, assemblage, bank, bundle, cock, drift, group, heap, hoard, load, lot, mass, mound, mountain, pack, pile, pyramid, rick, row, selection, sheaf, stock, stook, store **2.** abundance, copiousness, heaps, host, lots, myriad, plenitude, plenty, *Nonformal:* acres, oodles, scads, slew, tons *Antonyms:* dearth, deficit, lack **3.** chimney, chute, flue, funnel, smokestack – *v.* accumulate, amass, arrange, collect, gather, glean, heap, hill, hoard, load, mound, pile, stockpile

stadium *n.* amphitheatre, arena, athletic field, bowl, centre, coliseum, course, dome, diamond, field, forum, friendly confines *(Nonformal)*, gardens, gymnasium, hall, hippodrome, park, pit, ring, rink, track

staff *n.* **1.** agents, assistants, associates, cadre, cast, council, crew, deputies, employees, executives, faculty, force, help, hirelings, management, members, officers, operatives, organization, peons, personnel, retinue, servants, team, workers, work force **2.** baton, caduceus, cane, crook, crozier, crutch, cudgel, mace, pole, rod, sceptre, shillelagh *(Irish)*, stave, stick, *tetsubo (Japanese)*, wand, weapon

stage *n.* **1.** date, degree, division, footing, grade, juncture, lap, leg, length, level, moment, node, notch, period, phase, point, portion, position, rung, section, standing, status, step **2.** dais, deck, echelon, floor, frame, landing, layer, level, plate, platform, rostrum, scaffold, shelf, staging, structure **3.** drama, footlights, limelight, play, show business, spotlight, theatre *U.S.:* Broadway, off-Broadway, off-off-Broadway *Nonformal:* Stratford, showbiz **4.** arena, backdrop, field, locale, location, *mise en scène (French)*, plot, scene, scenery, set, setting – *v.* **1.** arrange, carry on, conduct, execute, give, mount, open, orchestrate, organize, perform, play, present, produce, put on, show **2.** concoct, fabricate, fake, feign, rig, sham

staged *adj.* **1.** artificial, concocted, contrived, forced, manipulated, organized, planned, premeditated, unnatural *Antonyms:* ad-lib, improvised, spontaneous **2.** fabricated, fake, feigned, mock, phoney *(Nonformal)*, rigged, schemed, sham, specious, spurious *Antonyms:* genuine, honest

stagger *v.* **1.** careen, lurch, pitch, reel, stumble **2.** balk, dilly-dally, dipsy-doodle *(Nonformal)*, hesitate, prevaricate, shift, wamble, waver **3.** amaze, astonish, astound, bewilder, boggle, confound, confuse, consternate, devastate, dumfound, nonplus, overwhelm, paralyze, perplex, puzzle, shake, shatter, shock, startle, stump, stun, stupefy, surprise, take aback, throw off *Nonformal:* bowl *or* knock over, flabbergast, floor, strike dumb **4.** alter, alternate, jumble, rearrange, reorder, reorganize, shift, shuffle, switch, transpose

stagnant *adj.* **1.** brackish, dirty, foul, mucky, nasty, putrid, rank, smelly, stale, stinking, stinky, swampy *Antonyms:* clean, clear, fresh **2.** dead, dormant, dull, idle, immobile, inactive, inert, lifeless, listless, moribund, motionless, passive, sluggish, standing, static, stationary, still, unmoving *Antonyms:* brisk, fast, quick, running

stagnate *v.* **1.** decay, decline, decompose, deteriorate, fester, putrefy, rot, spoil, stink, waste **2.** cease, delay, halt, hibernate, idle, languish, lie fallow, pause, rest, sit, slump, stall, stand, vegetate

staid *adj.* **1.** calm, collected, composed, cool, decorous, demure, dignified, earnest, formal, grave, no-nonsense, quiet, reserved, restrained, sedate, self-restrained, serious, settled, sober, solemn, sombre, steady *Antonyms:* adventurous, exuberant, giddy, rowdy, wild **2.** established, fixed, frozen, immutable, permanent, rooted, steadfast, unchanging *Antonyms:* ephemeral, fleeting, transient

stain *n.* **1.** blemish, blot, blotch, dirt, discolourization, grime, mark, muck, smudge, speck, splotch, spot **2.** brand, defilement, discredit, odium, pollution, reproach, shame, slur, smirch, stigma **3.** coating, colour, paint, pigment, preserver, tint, varnish, wash – *v.* **1.** begrime, bespatter, discolour, ensanguine, mark, muck up, muddy, ruin, smudge, soil, splatter **2.** besmirch, blemish, corrupt, debase, dis *(Nonformal)*, stigmatize, sully, taint, tarnish, undermine

stairs *n. pl.* companionway, escalator, fire escape, flight, Montreal staircase, perron, staircase, stairway, steps

stake *n.* **1.** marker, pale, picket, pile, pole, post, shaft, stick, strut, support **2.** assets, capital, cash, collateral, fortune, funds, goods, kitty *(Nonformal)*, money, principal, property, resources, riches, stock, wealth, worth **3.** concern, interest, investment, involvement, part, participation, piece, portion, share **4.** ante, bet, hazard, pledge, risk, speculation, venture, wager – *v.* **1.** anchor, fasten, fix, hold, root, secure, support, tether, tie **2.** back, bankroll, capitalize, finance, grubstake *(Nonformal)*, pledge **3.** bet, chance, gamble, game, hazard, place, play, punt, risk, speculate, venture, wager **4.** claim, earmark, establish, mark, mark out, put dibs on *(Nonformal)*, reserve

stale *adj.* **1.** decayed, dried, dry, faded, fetid, flat, fusty, hard, insipid, malodorous, musty, noisome, old, parched, rank, reeking, smelly, sour, spoiled, tasteless, warmed over, weak *Antonyms:* crisp, fresh **2.** antiquated, banal, boring, clichéd, commonplace, corny, flat, hackneyed, insipid, mawkish, out-of-date, overused, passé, platitudinous, shopworn, stereotyped, threadbare, timeworn, tired, trite, unoriginal, used, worn, worn-out *Nonformal:* dead, dusty, moth-eaten, old-hat, yesterday *Antonyms:* imaginative, new, novel **3.** dilatory, dull, idle, inactive, slow, sluggish, stagnant, torpid *Antonyms:* active, brisk, quick

stalemate *n.* blockage, cessation, dead end, deadlock, draw, gridlock, halt, impasse, Mexican standoff, point non plus, standoff, standstill, stoppage, tie

stalk *n.* axis, beanstalk, funiculus, pedicel, reed, shaft, spike, spire, stem, support, trunk, twig, upright – *v.* **1.** approach, chase, follow, flush out, follow, hunt, pursue, sneak up on, tail, track, trail **2.** badger, beleaguer, bother, harass, harry, hassle *(Nonformal)*, menace, persecute, pester, plague, torment, trouble, victimize **3.** haunt, loom, portend, shadow, threaten, tower over

stall *n.* **1.** barn, coop, lodging, outbuilding, pen, quarters, shed, shelter, stable, sty **2.** booth, carrel, cell, compartment, cubicle, hut, hutch, kiosk, space, stand **3.** device, dodge, evasion, ploy, prevarication, procrastination, ruse, stratagem, tactic, trickery – *v.* **1.** block, check, dawdle, delay, drag out, filibuster, further, halt, hamper, hedge, hinder, impede, interfere, obstruct, paralyze, postpone, prevaricate, prevent, procrastinate, prolong, put off, slow, stay, stonewall, suspend, temporize, tarry *Antonyms:* complete, hurry, speed **2.** conk out *(Nonformal)*, die, falter, flood, lose power, sputter, stop

stalwart *adj.* **1.** beefy, brawny, forceful, hefty, husky, muscular, powerful, robust, rugged, sinewy, solid, stout, strapping, strong, sturdy, substantial, vigorous *Antonyms:* puny, skinny, weak **2.** bold, brave, courageous, dauntless, fearless, gritty, gutsy *(Nonformal)*, heroic, intrepid, mettlesome, nervy, redoubtable, spirited, spunky, stout-hearted, tough, undaunted, valiant *Antonyms:* cowardly, craven, timid **3.** determined, dogged, fixed, obstinate, resolute, stubborn, steady, tenacious, uncompromising, unwavering

stamina *n.* backbone, capacity, endurance, energy, force, fortitude, grit, heart, indefatigability, lustiness, perseverance, power, resilience, resistance, strength, tolerance, vigour, vim, vitality *Nonformal:* legs, stick-to-it-iveness, wind

stammer *v.* falter, halt, hesitate, jabber, pause, repeat, splutter, sputter, stop, stumble, stutter, wobble

stamp *n.* **1.** breed, cast, character, cut, description, fashion, form, ilk, kind, lot, mould, quality, sort, stripe, type **2.** brand, chop, design, earmark, emblem, hallmark, impress, impression, imprint, insignia, label, logo, mark, print, seal, sign, signature, sticker, symbol, trademark – *v.* **1.** stomp, tramp, trample, tread, tromp *(Nonformal)* **2.** beat, break, crumble, crunch, crush, grind, mash, mill, pound, powder, press, pulp, pulverize, triturate **3.** accept, approve, authorize, bless, certify, empower, endorse, entitle, license, okay *(Nonformal)*, ratify, rubber stamp, sanction, seal sign, validate, warrant **4.** cast, engrave, etch, hammer, impress, imprint, inscribe, label, letter, mark, mould, print **5.** bookmark *(Nonformal)*, brand, categorize, class, classify, demarcate, distinguish, order, pigeonhole, stereotype, stigmatize, typecast

stampede *n.* **1.** charge, dash, flight, panic, run, rush, sprint, surge **2.** celebration, competition, event, exhibition, exposition, fair, festival, performance, rodeo, showcase, spectacle – *v.* charge, chase, crash, crowd, crush forward, dash, flee, fly, gallop, hurry, panic, run, rush, surge, tear off, trample

stance *n.* **1.** arrangement, bearing, composure, countenance, deportment, gesture, poise, positioning, posture **2.** attitude, interpretation, leaning, opinion, outlook, position, sentiment, slant, stand, standpoint, viewpoint *Nonformal:* spin, take

stand *n.* **1.** dais, floor, platform, rostrum, scaffold, stage **2.** ambo, bema, box, lectern, podium, pulpit, witness box **3.** anvil, bench, bookcase, cabinet, console, desk, jardiniere, ledge, rack, shelf, shelves, table **4.** booth, chip wagon, counter, cubicle, display unit, exhibit, hotdog stand, hutch, kiosk, nook, pavilion, stall **5.** base, bracket, footing, foundation, frame, pedestal, pillar, plate, post, support **6.** attitude, belief, determination, notion, opinion, outlook, policy, position, sentiment, slant, stance, standpoint, view **7.** brave front, confutation, counteraction, defense, objection, opposition, prevention, rebuff, resistance, struggle **8.** cessation, deadlock, freeze, halt, impasse, pause, stalemate, standoff, standstill, stoppage **9.** affair, engagement, matinee, meeting, one-night stand, rendezvous, thing *(Nonformal)*, tryst **10.** homestand *(Sports)*, layover, sojourn, stayover, stop, stop-off, stopover **11.** bluff, bunch, chicot *(Fire damaged)*, clump, cluster, collection, conglomeration, copse, deer yard, group, growth, lot, selection, thicket, sugarbush – *v.* **1.** arise, get up, lift, raise, rise **2.** abide, accept, allow, brook, continue, cope, endure, experience, handle, last, stomach, suffer, sustain, swallow, take, tolerate, undergo, weather, withstand **3.** be, belong, dwell, exist, lie, live, occupy, remain, reside, settle, sit, situate, stay **4.** halt, hesitate, hold, idle, pause, rest, stagnate, stop **5.** afford, bear, buy, carry, purchase, spare **6.** gauge, measure, place, rank, rate, weigh **7.** battle, defend, fight, parry, resist **8.** embody, personify, represent, signify, symbolize, typify **9.** aim, go, move, point, run, slide, travel **10.** campaign, run for office, seek election, toss one's hat in the ring *(Nonformal)*

stand-in *n.* alternate, assistant, back-up, body-double, deputy, double, fill-in, locum tenens *(Latin)*, pinch hitter, proxy, relief, replacement, reserve, second, secondary, stand-by, stuntman *or* stuntwoman, sub, substitute, succedaneum, surrogate, understudy

standard *adj.* **1.** average, common, everyday, garden-variety *(Nonformal)*, mediocre, medium, middling, moderate, normal, ordinary, regular, typical, usual *Antonyms:* exceptional, extraordinary, remarkable, unusual **2.** accepted, adopted, approved, basic, boilerplate, conventional, current, customary, demotic, embraced, established, familiar, general, orthodox, popular, prevailing, prevalent, rampant, recognized, regulation, set, staple, stock, ubiquitous, universal, widespread *Antonyms:* different, strange, weird **3.** authoritative, classic, complete, comprehensive, conclusive, consummate, definitive, reliable – *n.* **1.** average, centre, mean, medium, midpoint, norm, par, usual **2.** archetype, axiom, cast, example, exemplar, ideal, mirror, model, paradigm, pattern, sample **3.** bar, barometer, benchmark, criterion, degree, gauge, grade, height, level, mark, measure, quality, ruler, touchstone, value, yardstick **4.** belief, canon, code, dogma, ethic, fundamental, guideline, ideal, law, moral, principal, requirement, rule **5.** banner, colours, emblem, device, figure, flag, gonfalon, image, insignia, jack, oriflamme, pennant, pennon, shield, streamer, symbol, *vexillum (Latin)* **6.** classic, diamond, favourite, jewel, masterpiece *Nonformal:* chestnut, golden oldie

standardize *v.* adapt, adjust, assimilate, bring to code, conform, fashion, homogenize, institute, normalize, order, regiment, regulate, square, systematize

standards *n. pl.* codes of conduct, ethics, honour, integrity, morals, mores, nosims, principles, scruples, self-respect, values, virtues

standing *adj.* **1.** erect, on one's feet, raised, sheer, straight, upright, upstanding, vertical *Antonyms:* flat, horizontal, prostrate **2.** established, existing, fixed, permanent, regular, stable **3.** idle, immobile, inactive, inert, motionless, stagnant, static, stationary *Antonyms:* lively, moving, running – *n.* **1.** consequence, echelon, eminence, esteem, experience, grade, honour, level, order, place, position, preeminence, prestige, rank, reputation, repute, seniority, situation, state, station, stature, status **2.** continuance, duration, extent, length, period, span, spell, stretch, term, time

standoff *n.* **1.** dead heat, deadlock, détente, draw, impasse, Mexican standoff, stalemate, stand, tie **2.** challenge, competition, conflict, confrontation, contest, contest of wills, crisis, encounter, engagement, match, playdown, playoff, scrum, showdown, test

standoffish *adj.* aloof, antisocial, cold, cool, detached, distant, frosty, haughty, indifferent, introverted, misanthropic, Olympian, reclusive, remote, reserved, snobbish, uncompanionable, unsociable, withdrawn *Antonyms:* approachable, cordial, friendly, gregarious

standpoint *n.* angle, attitude, bias, determination, impression, interpretation, judgment, opinion, outlook, point of view, policy, position, slant, stance, understanding, view *Nonformal:* spin, take

stands *n. pl.* benches, bleachers, chairs, dog pound *(U.S.)*, end zone, gallery, isles, rows, seats, wings *Nonformal:* gods, greys, nosebleeds

standstill *n.* **1.** arrest, braking, cessation, dead stop, discontinuance, halt, stop **2.** check, checkmate, deadlock, delay, gridlock, holdup, impasse, interruption, jam, pause, snag, stalemate, stall, standoff, tie-up

staple *adj.* **1.** cardinal, chief, foremost, leading, main, predominant, primary, premier, principal, standard **2.** basic, crucial, essential, fundamental, important, indispensible, integral, key, necessary, needed, required, vital – *n.* **1.** basic, component, fundamental, necessity, prerequisite, requirement *Antonyms:* extra, luxury, nonessential, option **2.** article, commodity, food, good, inventory, merchandise, perishable, product, raw material, resource, stock item, supply, vendible – *v.* adhere, attach, bind, clip, connect, fasten, fix, pin

star *adj.* **1.** bright, brilliant, capital, celebrated, chief, dominant, famous, glittering, high-profile, illustrious, leading, luminous, main, major, marquee, notorious, outstanding, paramount, predominant, preeminent, principal, prominent, talented, virtuoso, well-known *Nonformal:* bankable, box-office **2.** astral, celestial, heavenly, sidereal, stellar – *n.* **1.** celestial body, heavenly body, orb, sun *Principal navigational stars:* Acherman, Acrux, Aldebaron, Alpheratz, Altair, Antares, Arcturus, Betelgeuse, Canopus, Capella, Deneb, Fomalhaut, Peacock, Polaris, Pollux, Procyon, Regulus, Rigel, Rigil Kentaurus, Sirius, Spica, Vega **2.** actor, actress, celebrity, diva, draw, famous person, favourite, headliner, hero, idol, lead, leading lady *or* man, luminary, starlet, superstar *Nonformal:* face, glitterati, name – *v.* **1.** act, appear, feature, headline, perform, play **2.** dominate, excel, overshadow, shine, stand out, tower above **3.** asterisk, indicate, mark, note

star-crossed *adj.* accursed, afflicted, cursed, doomed, fated, ill-fated, persecuted, unfortunate, unlucky, wretched *Nonformal:* jinxed, snakebit *Antonyms:* blessed, fortunate, lucky

stare *n.* examination, glance, inspection, look, review, scrutiny *Nonformal:* look-see, once-over – *v.* beam, bore, check out, eye, focus, gape, gaze, glare, glower, look fixedly, ogle, peer, rivet, survey, take in, watch *Nonformal:* gawk, goggle, rubberneck

stargaze *v.* daydream, fantasize, muse, pipe dream, romanticize, search the heavens, woolgather

stark *adj.* **1.** austere, bald, bare, barren bleak, desolate, empty, naked, plain, raw severe, simple, Spartan, stripped, unadorned, unornamented, vacant, vacuous, void *Antonyms:* busy, decorous, ornamented **2.** grim, harsh, inflexible, intractable, stern, stiff, strict, surly, truculent, unyielding *Antonyms:* easygoing, pliant, yielding **3.** absolute, complete, consummate, downright, entire, flagrant, gross, out-and-out, pure, rank, sheer, total, unmitigated, utter

starry-eyed *adj.* fanciful, idealistic, impractical, ivory-towered, moonstruck, naive, Panglossian, quixotic, romanticized, unrealistic, Utopian *Antonyms:* disillusioned, down-to-earth, jaded, realistic

start *n.* **1.** departure, embarkation, first step, leaving, onset, outset, take off **2.** beginning, commencement, face-off, first inning, first period, first quarter, get-go, inauguration, kickoff, opening, tip off *Antonyms:* completion, end, finish **3.** birth, creation, dawn, dawning, emergence, foundation, genesis, inception, initiation, introduction, rise **4.** basis, cause, motive, origin, reason, source, well **5.** convulsion, flinch, flinching, jar, jerk, jump, recoil, scare, shock, shrinking, spasm, startle, turn, twitch, wincing **6.** advantage, allowance, break, chance, edge, handicap, head start, lead, opportunity, shot *(Nonformal)*, vantage **7.** application, attempt, bid, effort, endeavour, essay, gamble, sally, try, venture *Nonformal:* fling, go **8.** breach, crack, crevice, fissure, fracture, leak, opening, rent, rift – *v.* **1.** advance, begin, commence, depart, embark, light *or* set out *Antonyms:* arrive, land **2.** imitate, inaugurate, initiate, introduce, kick off *(Nonformal)*, launch, open, unveil, usher in **3.** activate, encourage, get going, goad, impel, incite, instigate, motivate, prod, rouse, stimulate, stir, turn on *Antonyms:* discourage, turn off **4.** beget, cause, create, design, develop, devise, engender, generate, invent, originate, pioneer, produce, spawn *Antonyms:* destroy, eradicate, kill **5.** appear, arise, dawn, develop, emerge, rise, show, unfold, unfurl *Antonyms:* disappear, evanesce, vanish **6.** build, construct, erect, establish, form, found, institute, organize, raise, set up, undertake **7.** bug out *(Nonformal)*, bulge, extrude, pop *or* stick out, project, protrude **8.** blanch, draw back, flinch, jerk, jump, leap, quail, recoil, rise, shy, spring, startle, twitch, wince **9.** alarm, arouse, frighten, scare, spook *(Nonformal)*, startle, terrify *Antonyms:* calm, ease, help, relax

startle *v.* agitate, alarm, amaze, astonish, astound, awe, frighten, scare, shake up, shock, stagger, start, stun, surprise, take aback, terrify, terrorize *Nonformal:* blow away, floor, rock, spook

startling *adj.* alarming, amazing, astonishing, astounding, awesome, disconcerting, jolting, shocking, staggering, surprising, unnerving, upsetting *Antonyms:* assuaging, calming, soothing

starve *v.* **1.** go hungry, hanker, hunger, long for, need, pine, require, suffer, thirst **2.** decease, decline, die, expire, fall, perish, relinquish life *Nonformal:* bite it, buy the farm, check out, croak, kick the bucket **3.** bleed, deprive, choke, cut off, embargo, keep from, punish

starvation *n.* anorexia, depletion, deprivation, destitution, dire straits, emptiness, famine, inanition, lack, malnourishment, need, paucity, poverty, scarcity, want *Antonyms:* fullness, satiety, satisfaction

starving *adj.* craving, deprived, drawn, dying, emaciated, empty, faint, famished, haggard, hungry, longing, malnourished, peaked, peckish, perishing, ravenous, skin and bones, underfed, undernourished, weak *Antonyms:* full, replete, stuffed

stash *n.* booty, cache, contraband, effects, gear, goods, stuff, supply *Nonformal:* dope, goodies, shmunza, swag – *v.* bury, conceal, hide, protect, safekeep, salt *or* squirrel *or* stow away, stockpile, store

state *adj.* **1.** civil, governmental, federal, legislative, municipal, national, nation-wide, official, parliamentary, provincial, public, state-wide **2.** august, ceremonial, dignified, elegant, formal, grand, ritualistic, solemn, staid, stately *Antonyms:* everyday, low-key – *n.* **1.** circumstance, condition, environment, nature, repair, shape, situation **2.** attitude, countenance, disposition, frame of mind, mindset, mood, temper **3.** category, grade, position, post, rank, standing, station, stature, status **4.** commonwealth, community, country, domain, dominion, federation, geo-political entity, independent, kingdom, land, nation, nation-state, people, political community, political entity, province, republic, sovereignty, territory, union **5.** authority, bureaucrats, big brother *(Nonformal)*, body politic, government, legislature, officials, parliament, political unit **6.** ceremony, dignity, display, glory, grandeur, majesty, pomp, splendour, style – *v.* affirm, announce, articulate, assert, asseverate, aver, communicate, declare, describe, elucidate, enunciate, explain, expound, express, narrate, pitch *(Nonformal)*, posit, postulate, present, pronounce, propound, recite, recount, relate, report, speak, utter, vent, ventilate, voice

stately *adj.* august, ceremonious, dignified, distinguished, elegant, formal, glorious, grand, imperial, impressive, lofty, magnificent, majestic, noble, proud, regal, royal, solemn, splendid, state, stiff-necked *(Nonformal) Antonyms:* casual, informal, relaxed

statement *n.* **1.** acknowledgment, affirmation, allegation, announcement, articulation, assertion, assurance, avowal, comment, communication, communiqué, declaration, description, dictum, explanation, manifesto, mention, narrative, observation, presentation, proclamation, profession, protestation, recitation, remark, rundown, testimony, utterance, vent, verbalization, vocalization, voice, word **2.** account, affidavit, audit, bill, charge, reckoning, record, report, score, tab *(Nonformal)*

static *adj.* **1.** at rest, dormant, inactive, passive, quiescent, resting, supine, unchanging, unmoving *Antonyms:* active, energetic **2.** fixed, set, stable, statical, stationary, steady – *n.* **1.** background, buzz, distortion, disturbance, fuzz, interference, noise, snow, waves, white noise **2.** aggravation, anguish, bother, criticism, distress, grief, pain, trouble, vexation, woe, worry *Nonformal:* hassle, headache *Antonyms:* aid, assistance

station *n.* **1.** base, depot, headquarters, house, main office, stop, studio, terminal **2.** area, locale, location, place, point, position, post, seat, site, spot, territory **3.** caste, condition, grade, grouping, level, order, rank, rung, situation, slot, social sphere, standing, state, status **4.** affair, appointment, berth, business, capacity, duty, function, job, jurisdiction, mandate, mission, objective, occupation, office, role, task, work – *v.* allot, appoint, assign, base, commission, establish, fix, garrison, install, lodge, park *(Nonformal)*, place, plant, post, put, set

stationary *adj.* anchored, beached, fixed, grounded, idle, immobile, immovable, inert, locked, moored, motionless, parked, pat, passive, permanent, settled, stable, stagnant, standing, static, unchanging, unmoving *Antonyms:* nomadic, shifting, volatile *Commonly misused:* **stationery**

stationery *n.* envelopes, letterhead, office supplies, paper, pens, stock, supplies, writing paper *Commonly misused:* **stationary**

statistic *adj.* calculative, computative, enumerative, mathematical, numerative, numerical, quantified – *n.* constant, datum, detail, element, evidence, fact, factor, fodder, function, information, ingredient, input, item, number, part, particular, variable

statue *n.* bronze, bust, cast, colossus, effigy, figure, glyph, icon, image, likeness, maquette, marble, memorial, mould, piece, representation, sculpture, stabile, statuary, statuette, stone, terra cotta, torso, work

statuesque *adj.* **1.** beautiful, comely, classy *(Nonformal)*, dignified, elegant, graceful, handsome, impressive, refined, striking *Antonyms:* deformed, hideous, ugly **2.** full-bodied, imposing, Junoesque, large, looming, rangy, shapely, soaring, tall, towering *Antonyms:* diminutive, short, small

stature *n.* **1.** calibre, expanse, extent, height, length, measurement, reach **2.** advancement, capacity, competence, condition, development, evolution, growth, maturation, progress, state **3.** authority, consequence, dignity, elevation, eminence, importance, merit, position, prestige, prominence, quality, rank, reputation, significance, standing, station, status, value, virtue, worth

status *n.* **1.** cachet, calibre, caste, category, class, condition, consequence, degree, dignity, distinction, economic standing, eminence, fitness, footing, form, grade, health, importance, merit, mode, place, portent, position, prestige, prominence, quality, rank, rating, renown, repair, reputation, rung, situation, social condition *or* status, stage, standing, state, state of affairs, station, stature, value, weight, worth

statute *n.* act, assize, bill, canon, declaration, decree, edict, enactment, law, measure, ordinance, precept, regulation, rule

staunch *adj.* **1.** best, bosom, constant, dependable, devout, dutiful, faithful, loyal, reliable, steadfast, true, trustworthy, unfailing *Antonyms:* deceitful, treacherous **2.** airtight, firm, fit, ready, seaworthy, secure, sound, stout, strong, trim, watertight – *v.* arrest, bandage, bind, cauterize, check, clot, curb, dam up, halt, restrain, stem, stop

stay *n.* **1.** break, holiday, layover, rest, sojourn, stopover, vacation, visit **2.** cessation, deferment, delay, halt, hold, interruption, pause, postponement, recess, remission, respite, reprieve, rest, standstill, stop, suspension **3.** doggedness, durability, endurance, grit, longevity, mettle, perseverance, persistence, resilience, stamina, staying power, tenacity, tolerance *Nonformal:* legs, wind **4.** brace, buttress, column, guy wire, hold, prop, reinforcement, rope, shore, shoring, stanchion, support, truss, underpinning, underpropping – *v.* **1.** abide, billet, bunk, dwell, holiday, inhabit, live, lodge, overnight, reside, rest, sleep, sojourn, vacation *Nonformal:* crash, hole up, slump, squat **2.** dally, dilly-dally *(Nonformal)*, linger, loiter, pause, remain, tarry, wait *Antonyms:* continue, go, hurry, make tracks *(Nonformal)* **3.** brave, brook, endure, hold the fort *(Nonformal)*, keep up, last, outlast, persevere, persist, remain, stay up, survive, withstand *Antonyms:* surrender, yield **4.** delay, hamper, hinder, impede, postpone, procrastinate, shelve, stall **5.** arrest, brake, cease, check, curb, discontinue, halt, hold, hold back, interrupt, obstruct, prevent, stop **6.** appease, assuage, mitigate, mollify, quiet, satisfy, soothe *Antonyms:* harass, irritate, upset **7.** back, bolster, brace, bulwark, buttress, prop up, reinforce, strengthen, support, underpin, uphold *Antonyms:* cripple, topple, undermine, weaken

steadfast *adj.* **1.** abiding, allegiant, ardent, bound, dedicated, dependable, faithful, loyal, never-failing, reliable, staunch, sure, true *Antonyms:* back-stabbing, deceitful, duplicitous **2.** adamant, changeless, constant, enduring, established, fast, firm, fixed, immobile, inflexible, intent, persevering, relentless, resolute, single-minded, stable, steady, stubborn, unwavering *Antonyms:* capricious, fickle, flighty, inconstant, irresolute, unreliable

steady *adj.* **1.** anchored, balanced, firm, fixed, immovable, moored, rooted, secure, set, settled, solid, stable, supported *Antonyms:* rocking, tottering, wavering **2.** abiding, ceaseless, certain, consistent, constant, continual, continuous, direct, even, flat, habitual, incessant, nonstop, patterned, recurrent, regular, relentless, unbroken, uniform, uninterrupted, unvarying *Antonyms:* broken, irregular, odd **3.** calm, cool, equable, imperturbable, level-headed, poised, rational, sedate, self-possessed, sensible, serene, sober, tranquil, unperturbed, unruffled *Antonyms:* excitable, high-strung, nervous, restless **4.** allegiant, dependable, durable, enduring, faithful, industrious, loyal, persistent, reliable, resolute, steadfast, unfaltering, unswerving *Antonyms:* confused, distracted, diverted – *n.* **1.** boyfriend, girlfriend *Nonformal:* honey, main squeeze, regular, sweetie **2.** *Newfoundland:* pool, pond, still water – *v.* balance, brace, fix, make fast, secure, set, stabilize, support, tighten *Antonyms:* loosen, upset, unbalance

steak *n.* chop, cut, portion, slice *Kinds of beefsteak:* blade, chateaubriand, chuck, club, cube, Delmonico, fillet mignon, flank, New York, pepper, porterhouse, rib, rib eye, round, rump, saddle, Salisbury, shank, short loin, shoulder, sirloin, skirt, steakette, striploin, T-bone, tenderloin, wing

steal *n.* bargain, buy, deal, find – *v.* **1.** abduct, appropriate, burglarize, carry off, cheat, defalcate, defraud, despoil, divert, embezzle, filch, hold up, kidnap, lift, loot, make off with, misappropriate, mug, peculate, pilfer, pillage, pirate, plagiarize, plunder, poach, purloin, ransack, remove, rob, rustle, shanghai, shoplift, spirit away, strip, swindle, take, thieve *Nonformal:* bag, crib, fleece, heist, nick, pinch, rip off, sack, snaffle, stick up, swipe *Antonyms:* give, return, take back **2.** flit, glide, lurk, pass quietly, skulk, slide, slink, slip away

stealth *n.* camouflage, concealment, covertness, deceit, dirty dealing *(Nonformal)*, furtiveness, secrecy, sneakiness, surreptitiousness, undercover activity

stealthy *adj.* clandestine, covert, enigmatic, furtive, hush-hush *(Nonformal)*, private, quiet, secret, secretive, shifty, silent, skulking, sly, sneaky, *sub rosa (Latin)*, surreptitious, undercover, underhanded, wily

steam *n.* aqueous *or* water vapour, cloud, condensation, evaporation, fog, gas, haze, mist – *v.* **1.** coddle, cook, heat, moisten, parboil, poach, soften **2.** advance, continue, move, proceed, progress **3.** anger, boil, churn, erupt, fume, hit the ceiling *(Nonformal)*, lose one's temper, rage, rant, seethe

steamy *adj.* **1.** clammy, cloudy, foggy, hazy, humid, misty, muggy, soaked, soaken, vaporous, wet *Antonyms:* dry, parched **2.** bawdy, carnal, erotic, earthy, lascivious, lecherous, lewd, lusty, mature, passionate, salacious, sensual, sexy, spicy, stimulating, suggestive, titillating, X-rated *Nonformal:* adult, blue, hot *Antonyms:* family-oriented, G-rated, wholesome

steel *adj.* cold, firm, metallic, shiny, strong – *n.* **1.** alloy, compound, material, metal, tempered iron **2.** determination, endurance, firmness, fortitude, grit, hardness, resolve, steadfastness, strength, tenacity *Nonformal:* cojones, chutzpah, guts, moxie **3.** branchline, *chemin de fer (French)*, line, rails, railway track, rods, steel rails, track, trunkline **4.** blade, bayonet, cutlass, edge, foil, knife, lance, machete, razor, sabre, sword *Nonformal:* shank, shiv

steely *adj.* callous, cold, cold-blooded, cold-hearted, cruel, cutthroat, firm, harsh, implacable, iron-fisted, merciless, obstinate, pitiless, ruthless, savage, severe, stern, unfeeling, vicious *Antonyms:* caring, sympathetic, warm

steep *adj.* **1.** angled, bevelled, declivitous, extreme, high, precipitous, sharp, sheer, sloping, vertical **2.** abrupt, brisk, fast, instantaneous, quick, rapid, speedy, swift *Antonyms:* glacial, gradual, slow **3.** dear, excessive, exorbitant, expensive, extortionate, inordinate, outlandish, outrageous, overpriced, prohibitive, undue, unreasonable *Antonyms:* fair, moderate, reasonable – *n.* bluff, cliff, decline, drop, escarpment, falloff, hill, incline, precipice, wall – *v.* bathe, blanch, damp, drench, imbue, immerse, impregnate, infuse, let soak, macerate, marinate, moisten, permeate, pervade, saturate, soak, sodden, sop, souse, submerge, suffuse, waterlog, wet

steer *n.* beef, dogie, ox – *v.* **1.** captain, conduct, control, direct, drive, govern, guide, lead, manage, operate, pilot, run, sail, shepherd, skipper, take over **2.** aim, face, follow, head toward, make for, navigate, point, track, train

stellar *adj.* **1.** astral, celestial, heavenly, galactic, interstellar, luminescent, sidereal, starry *Antonyms:* earthly, mundane, terrestrial **2.** brilliant, chief, dazzling, distinguished, eminent, extraordinary, extravagant, fantastic, first-rate, great, outstanding, prominent, resplendent, shining, sparkling, superior, wonderful, world-class *(Nonformal) Antonyms:* common, dull, flat **3.** all-star, celebrity, gala, star-studded

stem *n.* **1.** axis, body, branch, leafstalk, pedicel, petiole, stalk, tendril, twig **2.** cylinder, handle, pipe, shaft, support, trunk, tube **3.** ancestry, bloodline, descent, extraction, family, family tree, heritage, house, line, parentage, pedigree, race, stock, strain – *v.* **1.** arise, come, derive, descend, emanate, emerge, flow, issue, originate, proceed, spring **2.** arrest, back up, bar, check, clog, control, dam up, hold, plug, prevent, staunch, stop *Antonyms:* open, release

stench *n.* bad smell, body odour *or* b.o., fetidness, fetor, foul *or* offensive odour, foulness, funk, fustiness, malodorousness, mouldiness, mustiness, rancidness, rankness, reek, smell, smelliness, stink

step *n.* **1.** footstep, metre, motion, movement, pace, stride, yard **2.** gait, gallop, jaunt, march, saunter, shamble, stroll, strut, tread, walk **3.** age, distance, frame, gap, interval, period, range, space, span, spread, stretch, term **4.** beat, bpm, feel, rate, speed, tempo, velocity **5.** evidence, footprint, impression, mark, spoor, trace, trail, tread mark **6.** deck, doorstep, landing, layer, rest, riser, rung, stair, stoop, tread board **7.** degree, grade, level, notch, rank, scale, stage, standing, stratum, tier **8.** advancement, development, evolution, gain, growth, headway, momentum, movement, progression, promotion **9.** act, attempt, effort, endeavour, essay, means, strategy, work – *v.* **1.** amble, march, mosey *(Nonformal)*, move, pace, prance, quickstep, saunter, skip, slog, step, stride, stroll, strut, tiptoe, traipse, tread, trek, troop, trot, walk **2.** advance, forge *or* move ahead, gain ground, journey, make strides, proceed, progress, travel

stereotype *n.* cast, cliché, mould, preconceived notion, preconception, simplification, typification – *v.* catalogue, categorize, conventionalize, define, dub, formalize, institutionalize, methodize, pigeonhole, regulate, standardize, systemize, typecast

stereotyped *adj.* banal, clichéd, commonplace, conventional, corny *(Nonformal)*, dull, formulaic, hackneyed, ordinary, overused, platitudinous, played out, shopworn, stale, standard, standardized, stock, threadbare, tired, trite, unoriginal, worn, worn-out, worn thin *Antonyms:* fresh, new, novel

sterile *adj.* **1.** barren, fallow, fruitless, infertile, unproductive *Antonyms:* fecund, productive **2.** clean, decontaminated, disinfected, germ-free, hygienic, pasteurized, purified, sanitary, sterilized, uninfected *Antonyms:* contaminated, polluted, septic **3.** arid, bootless, futile, empty, hollow, ineffectual, lacking, lifeless, nugatory, superficial, unavailing, uninspired, unoriginal, useless, vain, wanting, worthless *Antonyms:* influential, meaning, pregnant, significant

sterilize *v.* **1.** antisepticize, autoclave, clean, decontaminate, disinfect, fumigate, pasteurize, purify, sanitize, steam clean, treat *Antonyms:* dirty, infect, sully **2.** asexualize, castrate, emasculate, fix, geld, spay, tie one's tubes *(Nonformal)*

sterling *adj.* **1.** authentic, bona fide, genuine, pukka, pure, real, true, unadulterated *Antonyms:* fake, forged, imitation **2.** admired, cherished, dear, dependable, esteemed, faithful, honest, honourable, reliable, staunch, true, trustworthy, unfailing, valuable **3.** excellent, exemplary, fabulous, fantastic, fine, first-class, first-rate, great, ideal, remarkable, splendid, superlative *Nonformal:* smashing, unreal, wild, world-class *Antonyms:* cut-rate, frightful, horrible

stern *adj.* ascetic, astringent, austere, authoritarian, cruel, disciplinary, flinty, grim, hard, hard-boiled, hard-nosed, harsh, implacable, inexorable, inflexible, mean, relentless, resolute, rigid, rough, serious, severe, Spartan, steely, stiff-necked, strict, stubborn, tough, unrelenting, unsparing, unyielding *Antonyms:* flexible, lenient, permissive, soft, tolerant – *n.* aft, back, butt, end, heel, hindquarters, poop, rump, tail, tailpiece, transom *Antonyms:* bow, front, nose

stew *n.* **1.** *bouillabaisse (French)*, brew, goulash, soup *(Nonformal)* slumgullion *Common stews:* bean, beef, blanquette de veal, boeuf bourguignon, brewis, Brunswick, burgoo, callaloo, chili, cholent, curry, daube, fish and brewis, fisherman's, fricassee, gumbo, Hasenpfeffer, Irish, Jigg's dinner, lamb, lobster, matelote, mulligan, oyster, ragout, rubaboo, sagamite **2.** assortment, gallimaufry, hash, jumble, medley, melange, miscellany, mishmash, mixture, potpourri, salmagundi **3.** agony, despair, fret, sweat *(Nonformal)*, torment, worry – *v.* **1.** boil, bubble, brew, cook, crock, simmer, steep **2.** bake, broil, fry, roast, overheat, perspire, sizzle, steam, sweat, swelter **3.** agonize, brood, chafe, despair, fret, fume, fuss, seethe, worry

steward *n.* **1.** administrator, agent, controller, custodian, director, executive, executrix, executor, foreperson, governor, manager, manciple, official, overseer, sacristan, superintendent, supervisor, trustee **2.** attendant, butler, flight attendant, host, hostess, major-domo, purser, seneschal, servant, sommelier, stewardess, waiter, waitress

stick *n.* **1.** bough, branch, offshoot, shoot, stalk, stem, switch, tendril, twig **2.** board, forest fuel, kindling, log, lumber, stump, timber, wood **3.** bat, baton, billy club, cane, cudgel, hockey stick, lacrosse stick, pole, post, prod, rod, shillelagh, spare, staff, swizzle stick, truncheon, wand **4.** chunk, fragment, measure, piece, portion, section, share, slice, sliver, splinter **5.** control knob, gearshift, joystick *(Nonformal)*, lever, manual shift, shaft, shifter, stickshift – *v.* **1.** impale, insert, jab, needle, penetrate, perforate, pierce, prod, run through, stab, shish kebab *(Nonformal)*, skewer, thrust, transfix **2.** carve, cut, damage, disable, eviscerate, gut, hurt, injure, knife, lacerate, open up, slash *Antonyms:* close, sew, stitch **3.** adhere, affix, attach, cling, cohere, connect, couple, fasten, glue, join, nail, paste, pin, rivet, screw, secure, staple, unite, weld *Antonyms:* separate, sever **4.** anchor, deposit, fix, moor, park, place, plunk *(Nonformal)*, position, put, situate **5.** beard, brook, endure, hang on, hold, maintain, persist, remain, resist, stay, survive, tolerate *Antonyms:* give in, surrender, yield **6.** cheat, defraud, rob, swindle, take, trick, victimize *Nonformal:* bamboozle, finagle, fleece, hoodwink, screw, sucker

sticker *n.* adhesive, bumper sticker, decal, decalcomania, label, price tag, sign, stamp, tag

stick-in-the-mud *n.* **1.** damper, kill-joy, prude, spoilsport *Nonformal:* fuddy-duddy, grinch, party pooper, skeleton at the banquet, wet blanket **2.** conservative, traditionalist *Nonformal:* diehard, mossback, old fart *or* fogey, square *Antonyms:* progressive, radical, revolutionary

stickler *n.* **1.** fanatic, martinet, one for details, perfectionist, precisian, quibbler *Nonformal:* fuss-budget, fusspot, stinker **2.** brain-teaser, conundrum, enigma, knot, mystery, poser, problem, puzzle, riddle, stumper, teaser

sticks *n. pl.* backwater, backwoods, country, countryside, fur country, outskirts, provinces, rural area *Nonformal:* back-forty, beyond the pale, boondocks, boonies, no man's land, Timbuktu, the middle of nowhere *Antonyms:* city, downtown, Main Street

sticky *adj.* **1.** adhesive, clinging, gluey, glutinous, gooey, gummy, slimy, syrupy, tacky, tenacious, viscous *Antonyms:* oily, slippery **2.** clammy, close, dank, humid, muggy, oppressive, soggy, sultry, sweltering *Antonyms:* arctic, cold, dry **3.** complicated, challenging, demanding, difficult, gruelling, hard, intricate, knotty, painful, perplexing, problematic, puzzling, thorny, ticklish *Antonyms:* easy, simple, straightforward

stiff *adj.* **1.** cemented, fixed, hardened, inelastic, inflexible, petrified, resistant, rigid, set, solid, solidified, unbending, unyielding *Antonyms:* elastic, flexible, pliant **2.** austere, cold, constrained, distant, forced, formal, guarded, inhibited, mannered, prim, proper, prudish, reserved, square *(Nonformal)*, starchy, stilted, wooden *Antonyms:* casual, easygoing, informal, warm **3.** awkward, blundering, bumbling, bungling, clumsy, graceless, laboured, maladroit, ungainly *Nonformal:* Clouseau-esque, klutzy, stone-handed **4.** aching, achy, creaky, knotty, painful, pinched, rusty *(Nonformal)*, sore, tender, tense **5.** congealed, jelled *(Nonformal)*, gooey, hard, syrupy, thick, thickened, viscous *Antonyms:* runny, thin, watery **6.** firm, frozen *(Nonformal)*, starched, stretched, taut, tight *Antonyms:* loose, slack **7.** forceful, fresh, intense, sharp, spirited, steady, strong, vigorous **8.** bull-headed, headstrong, mulish, narrow-minded, obdurate, obstinate, pig-headed, resolute, strict, stringent, stubborn, tenacious **9.** burdensome, drastic, exacting, extreme, harsh, heavy, oppressive, severe **10.** arduous, difficult, exhausting, fatiguing, laborious, rigorous, strenuous, taxing, tiring *Antonyms:* invigorating, relaxing **11.** costly, dear, excessive, exorbitant, expensive, extravagant, high, immoderate, inordinate, prohibitive *Antonyms:* affordable, cheap, inexpensive **12.** alcoholic, fermented, fortified, inebriating, potent, powerful *Nonformal:* boozy, real – *n.* **1.** body, cadaver, carcass, corpse, *corpus delicti (Latin)*, remains **2.** annoyance, bore, bother, nuisance, pain, pest *Nonformal:* bug, bummer, drag, drip, headache, stick-in-the-mud, wet blanket, yawn **3.** employee, hand, help, helper, manual labourer, suit, worker, workman *Nonformal:* chump, jack, joe punchclock *or* six-pack, nine-to-fiver, ordinary joe, pencil pusher, sally housecoat, schmuck, slave, working-class stiff *Antonyms:* king, queen, royal – *v.* **1.** cheat defraud, fleece, overcharge, swindle *Nonformal:* rip-off, scam, screw, soak **2.** default, dine and dash *(Nonformal)*, dishonour, short change, underpay

stiffen *v.* **1.** anneal, cement, coagulate, condense, congeal, crystallize, firm, freeze, jell *(Nonformal)*, harden, petrify, set, solidify, starch, tauten, tense, thicken *Antonyms:* defrost, melt, thaw **2.** bolster, brace, buttress, fix, reinforce, stabilize, support, truss

stiff-necked *adj.* adamant, bull-headed, inflexible, intractable, intransigent, mulish, obdurate, obstinate, opinionated, ornery, pigheaded, refractory, single-minded, stubborn, unbending, unyielding, wilful *Antonyms:* compliant, flexible, reasonable, yielding

stifle *v.* **1.** asphyxiate, black out, choke, extinguish, gag, muffle, muzzle, smother, strangle, suffocate **2.** arrest, block, check, curb, halt, hush, obstruct, prevent, repress, restrain, scotch, silence, squelch, stop, suppress

stifling *adj.* **1.** blazing, blistering, boiling, broiling, hot, humid, roasting, scalding, scorching, sizzling, stuffy, sweltering *Antonyms:* cool, moderate, refreshing **2.** excruciating, exhausting, insufferable, intolerable, painful, oppressive, overwhelming, smothering, suffocating, unbearable, unendurable

stigma *n.* black eye *(Nonformal)*, blemish, brand, disgrace, dishonour, flaw, mark, reproach, scar, shame, slur, smirch, smudge, splotch, spot, stain, taint, tarnish

stigmatize *v.* besmirch, blemish, brand, characterize, dirty, discredit, disgrace, dishonour, label, mark, scar, shame, slur, stain, sully, tarnish, vilify *Nonformal:* badmouth, burn, dis, trash *Antonyms:* honour, praise

still *adj.* **1.** close-mouthed, dumb, mum, mute, noiseless, quiet, silent, soundless *Antonyms:* blaring, loud, noisy, raucous **2.** hushed, low, moderated, muffled, muted, reduced, soft, subdued, tempered **3.** calm, gentle, halcyon, harmonious, pacific, peaceful, placid, restful, serene, tranquil, undisturbed, unruffled, untroubled *Antonyms:* chaotic, rocky, stormy **4.** dead, fixed, frozen, idle, inanimate, lifeless, motionless, numb, resting, stable, standing, stagnant, stalled, static, stationary, unmoving *Antonyms:* active, alacritous, busy – *n.* **1.** calm, harmony, inactivity, motionlessness, noiselessness, peace, quiet, quietness, quietude, relaxation, silence, soundlessness, still, stillness, tranquility *Antonyms:* bustle, clamour, noise **2.** image, photo, photograph, picture, scan, single shot **3.** boiler, distillery, poteen pot *(Irish)*, vaporizer – *v.* **1.** abate, allay, alleviate, appease, becalm, calm, compose, hush, muzzle, pacify, quiet, silence, slack, smooth, soothe, tranquilize *Antonyms:* aggravate, exacerbate, rouse, stir up **2.** arrest, douse, extinguish, halt, put down, quell, squash, squelch, suppress, stall, stop, subdue, subside, suppress

stillness *n.* calm, harmony, inactivity, motionlessness, noiselessness, peace, quiet, quietude, relaxation, rest, silence, soundlessness, still, tranquility *Antonyms:* activity, bustle, noise

stilted *adj.* **1.** bloated, flatulent, fustian, pompous, pretentious, purple, rhetorical, stuffy, turgid *Antonyms:* everyday, plain, simple **2.** artificial, awkward, forced, formal, laboured, mannered, pedantic, rigid, stiff, unnatural, wooden *Antonyms:* flowing, fluid, free, natural

stimulant *n.* **1.** adrenaline, amphetamine, analeptic, bracer, caffeine, drug, energizer, pep pill, pick-me-up, restorative, reviver, tonic, upper **2.** activator, agent, catalyst, impetus, incitement, kick *(Nonformal)*, motivation, motivator, prod, push, reason, spur, stimulus

stimulate *v.* **1.** activate, agitate, animate, arouse, elate, encourage, energize, enliven, excite, exhilarate, fire, galvanize, goad, grab, hook, impel, improve, incite, inflame, inspire, instigate, motivate, move, nudge, occasion, pique, poke, prick, prod, prompt, provoke, quicken, rouse, spark, spur, urge, vitalize, work up *Antonyms:* demoralize, dishearten, restrain **2.** educe, elicit, engender, evince, generate, induce, produce, whet

stimulating *adj.* activating, animating, arousing, awakening, compelling, electrifying, energizing, enlivening, exciting, exhilarating, fortifying, galvanic, galvanizing, inspiring, intriguing, motivating, provocative, refreshing, rousing, stirring, thought-provoking, thrilling, titillating *Antonyms:* boring, discouraging, dull, uninteresting

stimulus *n.* boost, catalyst, charge, encouragement, fillip, goad, impetus, impulse, incentive, incitement, inducement, instigation, motive, needle, nudge, poke, prick, prod, propellant, provocation, push, shove, spur, stimulant *Nonformal:* kick in the pants, shot in the arm

sting *n.* **1.** bite, bump, irritation, itch, lesion, pain, pricking, smarting, swelling, wound **2.** appeal, cogency, effectiveness, force, point, potency, power, punch, pungency, strength, vigour, vitality **3.** covert operation, crime, deception, embezzlement, racket, robbery, swindle, theft *Nonformal:* con, dirty dealings, scam – *v.* **1.** bite, hurt, injure, irritate, nettle, pain, pierce, poke, prick, prickle, smart, tingle, trouble, wound **2.** bilk, cheat, defalcate, defraud, dupe, embezzle, rook, take, victimize *Nonformal:* bamboozle, con, fleece, soak, sucker

stinging *adj.* **1.** abusive, acidic, annoying, biting, brutal, caustic, disturbing, harsh, insulting, offensive, provoking, sharp, venomous, vitriolic, wounding *Antonyms:* assuaging, comforting, mollifying, pacifying, soothing **2.** needling, nettling, penetrating, piercing, pricking, stabbing

stingy *adj.* **1.** cheap, cheeseparing, close-fisted, economical, frugal, grasping, miserly, parsimonious, penny-pinching, penurious, sparing, tight, tightfisted, thrifty, ungenerous, ungiving *Antonyms:* charitable, generous, philanthropic **2.** inadequate, insubstantial, insufficient, lacking, lean, meagre, mean, modest, negligible, paltry, poor, scant, scrimpy, skimpy, slender, small, sparse, thin, wanting *Antonyms:* abundant, ample, bountiful, profuse

stink *n.* **1.** body odour *or* b.o., fetor, foulness, malodour, noisomeness, odour, smell, stench **2.** agitation, bustle, clamour, commotion, confusion, excitement, fuss, panic, stir *Nonformal:* buzz, deal, flap, hubbub, to-do **3.** argument, complaint, criticism, gripe *(Nonformal)*, objection, opposition, outcry, protestation, revolt, riot – *v.* offend the nostrils *(Nonformal)*, reek, smell, smell up

stinking *adj.* **1.** awful, bad, base, cheap, contemptible, despicable, hideous, horrible, loathsome, mean, miserable, offensive, rotten, scurvy, terrible, vile, vicious *Nonformal:* crappy, cruddy, crummy, lousy, mangy, no good, poor **2.** foul, malodorous, reeking, smelly, stinky *(Nonformal)* – *adv.* excessively, extremely, immoderately, intemperately, outrageously, overly, really, unreasonably, very

stint *n.* assignment, bit, chore, duty, hitch, job, participation, responsibility, share, shift, spell, stretch, task, term, time, tour, turn, work – *v.* budget, economize, limit, pinch, restrict, save, scrimp, spare

stipend *n.* allowance, annuity, emolument, fee, grant, honorarium, indemnity, pay, payment, pension, remittance, remuneration, salary, scholarship, sum, take, take home *(Nonformal)*, wage

stipulate *v.* **1.** designate, detail, indicate, peg, pin down, specify, spell out, state **2.** claim, command, demand, dictate, impose, insist upon, necessitate, oblige, order, press, require, rule **3.** certify, contract, covenant, guarantee, pledge, promise, swear, vouch, vow, warrant

stipulation *n.* agreement, arrangement, clause, condition, contract, limit, obligation, precondition, prerequisite, promise, provision, proviso, qualification, requirement, reservation, restriction, rider, settlement, *sine qua non (Latin)*, specification, string, term, terms

stir *n.* **1.** activity, agitation, animation, bustle, commotion, reaction *Nonformal:* buzz, hubbub, to-do **2.** motion, move, movement, rustling, stirring – *v.* **1.** beat, blend, froth, mix, swizzle, whip up, whisk **2.** budge, bump, dislodge, nudge, poke, prod, touch **3.** animate, arouse, electrify, energize, excite, inspire, kindle, motivate, prompt, rally, rouse, spark, stimulate, urge *Antonyms:* ignore, neglect **4.** agitate, anger, annoy, bother, challenge, harass, incite, inflame, irritate, pester, provoke, rile, roil, upset *Nonformal:* bug, hassle **5.** affect, impress, influence, hit home *(Nonformal)*, melt, move, penetrate, pierce, resonate, soften, strike *or* touch a chord, thrill **6.** awaken, get up, hit the deck *(Nonformal)*, raise, rise, rout, turn out, waken *Antonyms:* rest, sleep, slumber

stirring *adj.* animated, bouncy, brisk, dramatic, exciting, exhilarating, impassioned, inspiring, intoxicating, lively, moving, provocative, rousing, spirited, stimulating, thrilling, vigorous *Antonyms:* flat, stagnant, sterile

stock *adj.* **1.** basic, common, conventional, customary, established, formal, normal, off the shelf, ordinary, prêt-à-porter, ready-made, ready-to-wear, regular, routine, standard, staple, traditional, typical, usual *Antonyms:* custom, made-to-order, tailor-made **2.** banal, clichéd, commonplace, dull, hackneyed, overused, shopworn, stale, stereotyped, superficial, threadbare, trite, warmed-over, worn – *n.* **1.** articles, chattel, commodities, goods, inventory, merchandise, produce, provisions, reserve, saleables, stockpile, store, supply, vendibles, wares **2.** accumulation, amount, array, bunch, hoard, kental *(Newfoundland)*, kilo, load, lot, mass, number, pile, portion, pound, quantity, reservoir, selection, skid, sum, ton, volume **3.** animals, beasts, cattle, chicken, cows, domestic farm animals, flock, fowl, goats, herd, hogs, horses, livestock, pigs, sheep **4.** assets, bonds, capital, certificate, capital, finances, funds, investments, portfolio, security, share, wealth **5.** axis, caudex, stem, stump, trunk **6.** category, classification, genre, genus, group, kind, order, race, species, type **7.** ancestry, background, bloodline, breed, caste, clan, descent, extraction, family, folk, forebears, house, kin, kindred, line, lineage, parentage, pedigree, strain, tribe, type **8.** ancestor, forebear, forefather, parent, progenitor, root, sire, source **9.** basics, components, constituents, elements, ingredients, material, parts, pieces, raw material, resources, staples, stuff **10.** arm, base, butt, end, grip, gunstock, shaft, spindle, support **11.** base, bouillon, broth, consommé, foundation, gravy, juice, liquid, medium, reduction, soup **12.** assurance, belief, confidence, credence, dependence, faith, hope, optimism, promise, trust – *v.* **1.** equip, fill, furnish, outfit, provide, provision, supply **2.** carry, deal in, distribute, handle, have, hawk *(Nonformal)*, market, sell, trade **3.** accumulate, amass, gather, hoard, keep, lay in, put away, reserve, safekeep, save, shelve, stockpile, store, stow away

stockade *n.* barricade, enclosure, fort, fortification, palisade, zareba

stocky *adj.* chunky, corpulent, dumpy, fat, heavyset, lumpish, mesomorphic, overweight, plump, portly, pudgy, short, solid, squat, stout, stubby, stumpy, sturdy, thick, thickset, tubby *Antonyms:* bony, gaunt, lanky, skinny, slender, willowy

stodgy *adj.* **1.** conservative, conventional, dated, hidebound, old, old-fashioned, straitlaced, stuffy, tired, traditional, uptight *Nonformal:* fuddy-duddy, horse-and-buggy, square *Antonyms:* liberal, progressive **2.** awful, boring, dim, dreary, dull, humdrum, monotonous, pedestrian, plodding, ponderous, slow, tedious, unexciting, unimaginative, uninspiring, uninteresting, vapid *Antonyms:* arousing, exciting, exhilarating **3.** doughy, filling, glutinous, gooey *(Nonformal)*, heavy, porridgy, starchy, thick, viscous *Antonyms:* thin, watery

stoic *adj.* aloof, cool, detached, dispassionate, enduring, impassive, imperturbable, indifferent, indomitable, long-suffering, patient, philosophic, phlegmatic, resigned, self-controlled, sober, Spartan, stoical, stolid, unconcerned, unemotional, unflappable, unmoved *Antonyms:* anxious, excitable, sensitive, volatile

stoicism *n.* acceptance, apathy, calmness, composure, cool, dispassion, forbearance, impassivity, imperturbability, patience, philosophical attitude, resignation, phlegm, self-control, sufferance

stoke *v.* **1.** feed, fire, fuel, kindle, stir up, supply, sustain, tend *Antonyms:* douse, extinguish, put out **2.** encourage, excite, goad, instigate, incite, provoke, spark, spur, stimulate *Antonyms:* daunt, discourage, dishearten

stolid *adj.* bovine, dispassionate, dull, impassive, obtuse, passive, phlegmatic, thick, torpid, unemotional, unexcitable, wooden *Antonyms:* feeling, intelligent, perceptive

stomach *n.* **1.** abdomen, alimentary canal, belly, bowels, digestive cavity, gut, maw, middle, midriff, midsection, rumen, viscera *Nonformal:* beer *or* pot *or* swag belly, breadbasket, Molson muscle, paunch, pot, spare tire, tummy **2.** appetite, craving, desire, fondness, inclination, mind, penchant, relish, taste, zest – *v.* **1.** abide, bear, beard, brook, endure, face, stand, suffer, take, tolerate, withstand **2.** absorb, consume, digest, eat, hold down, swallow

stomp *n.* clog, dance, jig, reel, two-step *See also:* **dance** – *v.* clomp, clonk, clump, dance, hobble, march, pace, peg, stamp, step, thud, thump, tramp, trample, tread

stone *adv.* absolutely, completely, entirely, fully, thoroughly, totally, utterly, wholly – *n.* **1.** block, boulder, erratic, fieldstone, glacial debris *or* deposit, gravel, pebble, rock, rubble, slab, stone *See also:* **rock** **2.** diamond *(Nonformal)*, gem, jewel, mineral, precious metal, semi-precious metal *See also:* **gemstone** **3.** centre, core, endocarp, heart, kernel, pit, pith, seed, seedcase – *v.* **1.** assail, bombard, clobber, pelt, pepper, pound, rain, shower **2.** dispatch, execute, kill, lapidate, punish, purge, put to death

stonewall *v.* block, check, delay, filibuster, hinder, hold off, obstruct, prevent, rebuff, resist, scotch, stall

stony *adj.* **1.** craggy, cobbled, gravely, jagged, pebbly, rocky, rough, scraggy, sharp **2.** adamant, brutal, callous, cold, cold-blooded, cruel, firm, flinty, hard, hard-boiled, hardened, heartless, indifferent, inflexible, merciless, obdurate, relentless, remorseless, rough, ruthless, stubborn, tough, uncompassionate, unfeeling, unsympathetic, unyielding *Antonyms:* forgiving, kind, soft, tolerant **3.** blank, deadpan, emotionless, expressionless, flat, poker-faced, vacant *Antonyms:* demonstrative, expressive, pregnant, revealing

stool *n.* **1.** bench, campstool, footrest, footstool, hassock, milking stool, ottoman, seat **2.** defecation, excrement, fecal matter, feces, feculence, soil, waste *Nonformal:* crap, dump, number two, poop

stoop *n.* **1.** balcony, deck, entrance, gallery, lanai, platform, porch, terrace, veranda **2.** bad posture, droop, rounded shoulders, sag, slouch, slump – *v.* **1.** condescend, cringe, deign, demean, descend, grovel, humble *or* lower oneself, sink, submit **2.** bend, bow, crouch, dip, drop, fall, flag, kneel, lean, slant, squat

stop *n.* **1.** abeyance, adjournment, break, breather, hesitation, intermission, interruption, interval, layoff, letup, lull, pause, postponement, recess, rest, shutdown, stay, suspension *Antonyms:* beginning, continuance, prelude, start **2.** abandonment, abstinence, cessation, curtailment, discontinuance, forbearance, quitting, relinquishment, renunciation **3.** arrest, check, constraint, control, determent, delay, freeze, interdiction, interference, prevention **4.** barricade, blockade, blockage, bottleneck, disruption, gridlock, halt, hindrance, impasse, impediment, obstacle, obstruction, roadblock, snag, standstill, stoppage *Antonyms:* aperture, gap, hole, opening **5.** bung, cap, clog, cork, diaphragm, partition, plug, stopgap, stopper, valve, wall **6.** bus shelter, depot, station, subway stop, terminal, terminus **7.** closure, completion, conclusion, culmination, ending, epilogue, finale, finish, resolution, result, termination – *v.* **1.** brake, fix, freeze, halt, hold, stand **2.** arrest, check, control, cut short, disrupt, impede, interrupt, kill *(Nonformal)*, obstruct, prevent, repress, restrain **3.** bar, barricade, block, bottle up, cork, cut-off, gag, muffle, muzzle, occlude, staunch, stem **4.** choke, deny, hold back, starve, withhold **5.** delay, hesitate, linger, pause, rest, stall, suspend, tarry, wait **6.** abstain, cease, chuck *(Non-*

formal), desist, discard, discontinue, drop, eschew, forbear, forsake, quit, refrain **7.** cap off, close, complete, conclude, culminate, end, finish, fulfill, terminate, wrap up **8.** annihilate, beat, best, clobber, defeat, destroy, humble, lambaste, master, overcome, trounce, upset *Nonformal:* dust, lick, smoke, whip, whop *Antonyms:* give up, surrender, yield **9.** defend, fend off, foil, frustrate, save *(Baseball)*, stymie, thwart, ward off *Hockey:* block, blocker, catch, kick out, stack the pads **10.** billet, check in, dwell, holiday, lodge, overnight, quarter, rest, shelter, sleep, sojourn, stay, vacation *Antonyms:* journey, travel, wander

stopgap *adj.* ad hoc, convenient, improvised, interim, makeshift, practical, provisional, short-term, stand-in, substitute, surrogate, temporary *Antonyms:* fixed, full-time, permanent – *n.* **1.** bung, cap, cork, patch, plug, stopper, valve **2.** device, expedient, improvisation, instrument, means, medium, solution, tactic

stoppage *n.* blockage, cessation, check, end, finish, full stop, interruption, halt, shutdown, standstill, stay, stop *See also:* **stop**

storage *n.* **1.** arsenal, bank, depository, depot, dry storage, freezer, fridge, hold, inventory, pantry, refrigerator, repository, reservoir, safe, shelter, stockroom, store, storehouse, stowage, supply room, treasury, vault, warehouse **2.** archive, buffer, cache, memory, RAM, ROM

store *n.* **1.** business, mart, shop *Common stores:* baker's, bazaar, big box *(Nonformal)*, bookstore, booth, boutique, butcher's, chain, cigar, clothing, concession, convenience, co-op, corner, dairy *(Cape Breton)*, deli, delicatessen, depanneur, department, discount, dollar, drugstore, exchange, exposition, factory *(Historical)*, fair, five-and-dime *or* -ten, fish market, flea market, franchise, general, grocery, groceteria, health food, kiosk, mall, market, megastore, mom-and-pop, outlet, pawnshop, retail, salon, shopping centre *or* mall *or* plaza, showroom, specialty, stall, stand, street market, strip mall, supermarket, thrift, trading post, variety **2.** arsenal, bank, cache, chandlery, depot, lazaretto, magazine, pantry, repository, stockroom, storage, supply room, treasury, warehouse **3.** commodities, goods, inventory, merchandise, produce, saleables, staples, stock, truck, wares **4.** abundance, accumulation, backlog, collection, heap, hoard, host, load, mine, myriad, plenty, plethora, provision, quantity, selection, stack, stockpile, treasure, wealth, well – *v.* **1.** accumulate, amass, bank, bury, cache, deposit, garner, hide, hoard, husband, keep, mothball, pack, put away, reserve, save, squirrel away, stash, stock, stockpile, warehouse **2.** exchange, furnish, hawk *(Nonformal)*, market, provide, push, sell, supply, trade

storehouse *n.* arsenal, bank, depository, depot, magazine, pantry, repository, reservoir, stockroom, storage, storeroom, supply house *or* room, treasury, vault, warehouse

storey *n.* division, echelon, floor, layer, level, row, separation, stratum, tier

storied *adj.* acclaimed, celebrated, fabled, famous, historic, illustrious, legendary, renowned

storm *n.* **1.** August gale, black blizzard, blast, blizzard, cloudburst, cockeye bob, cyclone, downpour, drift storm, dust devil, gale, glitter storm, gridley grinder, hail storm, hurricane, ice storm, lake streamer, monsoon, nor'wester, robin storm, sheep storm *(Atlantic Provinces)*, smelt storm, snowstorm, squall, tempest, *tempête de neige (French)*, tornado, twister, whirlwind, whiteout, windstorm *Nonformal:* big blow, blow, dirty weather **2.** assault, barrage, bombardment, burst, cannonade, discharge, fusillade, salvo, shower, sally, spattering, spray, torrent, volley **3.** eruption, explosion, fit, flareup, frenzy, fury, outbreak, outburst, outpouring **4.** ado, commotion, disruption, disturbance, flap *(Nonformal)*, furor, insurgence, insurrection, rebellion, revolt, revolution, riot, ruckus, turbulence, turmoil, upheaval, uprising – *v.* **1.** blow, bluster, gale, gust, hail, pour, rage, rain, snow, teem, thunder **2.** erupt, fulminate, fume, harangue, rage, rant, rave, roar, shout, yell *Nonformal:* blow a gasket, hit the ceiling, steam **3.** ambush, assail, attack, beset, blitz, bombard, capture, charge, invade, penetrate, rush, sack, strike, surge, take

stormy *adj.* **1.** bitter, blowy, blustery, gusty, howling, menacing, pouring, raging, riproaring *(Nonformal)*, rough, tempestuous, threatening, torrid, turbulent, violent, wet, wild, windy *Antonyms:* pacific, pleasant, sunny **2.** chaotic, crazy, emotional, frantic, frenzied, furious, lawless, mad, rabid, reckless, untamed, violent, wild *Antonyms:* calm, mild, tranquil

story *n.* **1.** account, adventure, allegory, anecdote, apologue, autobiography, biography, chronicle, comedy, description, drama, epic, episode, fable, fairy tale, fantasy, fiction, herstory, history, interpretation, legend, memoir, megilla, myth, narration, nonfiction, novel, parable, recital, rendition, romance, saga, sea story, sequel, serial, short story, sketch, song, tale, tragedy, translation **2.** architecture, blueprint, design, narrative, plan, plot, scheme, storyline, structure, subject, subplot, theme, topic **3.** article, feature, headline, item, lead, news, report, review **4.** distortion, exaggeration, fabrication, falsehood, fib, figment, fish story *(Nonformal)*, gossip, hearsay, invention, lie, slander, tall story *or* tale, untruth , yarn **5.** alibi, allegation, assertion, declaration, defence, excuse, statement

storyteller *n.* **1.** anecdotist, artist, author, bard, biographer, chronicler, fabulist, hagiographer, journalist, narrator, novelist, poet, raconteur, writer **2.** deceiver, fibber, liar, master of deception, prevaricator *Nonformal:* bullshit artist, jive turkey

stout *adj.* **1.** big, big-boned, bulky, burly, corpulent, fat, fleshy, heavy, mesomorphic, obese, overweight, plump, porcine, portly, rotund, substantial, thick-bodied, thickset, tubby *Antonyms:* lean, puny, slight **2.** firm, hard, hardy, reliable, rigid, solid, sound, stable, strong, sturdy, thick *Antonyms:* flimsy, fragile, weak **3.** brave, courageous, determined, gallant, indomitable, invincible, proud, resolute, robust, stalwart, stubborn, tenacious, undaunted, vigorous – *n.* beer beverage, draught, drink *Nonformal:* brew, brewski, cold one, pint *or* pint of dark, wobbly pop

stout-hearted *adj.* audacious, bold, brave, courageous, dauntless, determined, fearless, gallant, hardy, heroic, indomitable, intrepid, invincible, lionhearted, proud, resolute, robust, spirited, stalwart, stubborn, tenacious, undaunted, unflinching, valiant *Nonformal:* gutsy, spunky *Antonyms:* apprehensive, fearful, gutless, spineless, timorous

stove *n.* airtight, appliance, barbecue, cooker, furnace, grill, heater, oven, range *Common stoves:* camp, coal, cook, electric, Franklin, gas, incinerator, kerosene, kiln, portable, pot-bellied, propane, oil, Quebec heater, wood *Trademark:* Aga, Coleman, Primus

stow *v.* box, bundle, cram, deposit, fill, load, pack, place, put away, safekeep, squeeze, stash, store, stuff

strafe *v.* attack, blast, bomb, bombard, gun down, mortar, open fire, pelt, pepper, punish, rake, riddle, shell, shoot

straggle *v.* **1.** dally, dawdle, lag, loiter, maunder, meander, poke around, stray, trail, wander *Nonformal:* dilly-dally, goof off **2.** drift, mosey *(Nonformal)*, ramble, range, roam, rove

straggler *n.* dawdler, *flâneur (French)*, floater, idler, laggard, lingerer, loafer, loiterer, slowpoke *(Nonformal)*

straggly *adj.* dishevelled, disordered, disorganized, jumbled, loose, ragged, scraggly, scattered, unkempt, untidy, wild *Antonyms:* neat, ordered, systematic

straight *adj.* **1.** direct, linear, rectilinear, true, unbent, undeviating, uniform, unswerving, unvarying, unwavering *Antonyms:* circuitous, indirect, crooked, curved, winding **2.** even, flat, horizontal, level, plane **3.** erect, perpendicular, plumb, sheer, upright, vertical **4.** continuous, successive, unbroken, uncut, uninterrupted *Antonyms:* broken, choppy, irregular **5.** arranged, neat, orderly, organized, shipshape, sorted, symmetrical, tidy *Antonyms:* confused, jumbled, muddled **6.** concentrated, neat, pure, unadulterated, uncomplicated, undiluted, unmodified *Antonyms:* impure, mixed, watered-down **7.** aboveboard, decent, equitable, fair, good, honest, just, reliable, right, straight-shooting *(Nonformal)*, trustworthy, truthful, virtuous *Antonyms:* dishonest, shady, unreliable **8.** blunt, brusque, candid, concise, explicit, forthright, frank, no-nonsense, outright, point-blank, straightforward, summary **9.** absolute, accurate, authentic, clear, exact, genuine, plain, unambiguous, understood, unequivocal, unmitigated, unqualified **10.** abstemious, abstinent, clean, clean and sober, continent, drug-free, nonindulgent, sober *Antonyms:* drunk, high, indulgent **11.** conforming, conservative, conventional, law-abiding, moral, prim, proper, prudish, puritanical, respectable, serious, straitlaced, traditional, Victorian *Nonformal:* mossbacked, nerdy, square *Antonyms:* defiant, devious, rebellious – *adv.* **1.** as the crow flies *(Nonformal)*, directly, linearly, undeviatingly **2.** accurately, candidly, exactly, frankly, honestly, perfectly, point-device, precisely, truthfully **3.** at once, forthwith, immediately, instantly, now, quickly, right away, straightaway, without delay – *n.* beeline, dragstrip, line, plane, road, run, straightaway, stretch, tangent

straightaway *adv.* ASAP, at once, directly, fast, immediately, instanter, instantly, now, on the double, promptly, quickly, right away, stat, straight off, swiftly, this minute *Nonformal:* lickety-split, toot sweet *Antonyms:* by and by, eventually, sooner or later – *n.* straight road *or* section, stretch, strip *See also:* **straight**

straighten *v.* **1.** align, even, iron, level, press, unbend, uncoil, uncurl, unfold, unfurl, unravel, unsnarl, untie, unwind *Antonyms:* bend, crease, fold, gather **2.** arrange, compose, dust, neaten, order, organize, pick up, reorder, spruce up *(Nonformal)*, sweep, tidy, vacuum *Antonyms:* dirty, mess, muddle

straightforward *adj.* **1.** aboveboard, candid, forthright, frank, genuine, guileless, honest, honourable, just, open, plain-dealing, sincere, straight-shooting, truthful, unequivocal, upfront, upright, upstanding, veracious *Antonyms:* lying, mendacious, untruthful **2.** apparent, clear, clear-cut, distinct, easy, elementary, evident, manifest, patent, plain, routine, simple, unambiguous, uncomplicated, undemanding *Antonyms:* complex, complicated, confusing **3.** direct, level, linear, rectilinear, steady, straight, true, unwavering *Antonyms:* bending, curving, winding

strain *n.* **1.** force, pressure, tautness, tension, tightness **2.** burden, demand, encumbrance, load, responsibility, tax, weight **3.** anxiety, concern, distress, fatigue, nervousness, stress, trouble, unease, worry *Antonyms:* comfort, ease, relaxation **4.** effort, endeavour, exertion, labour, overextension, pain, struggle, sweat *(Nonformal)* **5.** constriction, crimp, hyperextension, injury, pull, tear, wrench **6.** ancestry, blood, bloodline, breed, descent, extraction, family, lineage, pedigree, race, species, stock **7.** class, gender, genus, kind, set, sex, sort, type, variety **8.** element, factor, feature, hint, sign, streak, trace, trace element, trait **9.** character, manner, mood, quality, spirit, style, tendency, tone **10.** air, descant, measure, melody, part, passage, piece, snatch, song, spell, tune, warble – *v.* **1.** drive, endeavour, exert, extend, hustle, labour, push, strive, struggle, sweat *(Nonformal)*, toil, try, work *Antonyms:* relax, rest, take it easy **2.** enervate, exhaust, expend, fry *(Nonformal)*, overburden, overdo, overexert, overextend, overload, overtax, overuse, overwork, tire, wear out **3.** haul, jerk, lug, pull, stretch, tauten, tighten, tow, tug, yank **4.** buckle, distend, impair, injure, sprain, tear, twist, wrench **5.** clarify, clear, filter, percolate, purify, rack, refine, remove, separate, sieve, sift **6.** alter, bend, contort, distort, exaggerate, fudge, manipulate, misrepresent, skew, slant, stretch, warp

strained *adj.* **1.** affected, artificial, awkward, forced, insincere, laboured, mannered, phoney *(Nonformal)*, pretentious, stiff, stilted, unnatural, unrelaxed, wooden *Antonyms:* easy, plain, simple **2.** constrained, difficult, tense, uncomfortable, uneasy, unfriendly *Antonyms:* loose, relaxed **3.** aching, aggravated, hurt, injured, pulled, sore, sprained, stretched, taut, tight, wrenched

strainer *n.* cheesecloth, colander, filter, screen, separator, sieve, sifter, winnow

strait *n.* **1.** water, channel, inlet, narrows, sound, tickle *(Newfoundland)*, **2.** bind, crisis, crossroad, dilemma, difficulty, dire straits, distress, emergency, exigency, hardship, hole, mess, perplexity, plight, predicament, squeeze, trouble, turning point *Nonformal:* fix, hot water, jam, kettle of fish

straitlaced *adj.* correct, Grundyish, moral, prim, proper, prudish, puritanical, rigid, stern, stiff, strict, stuffy, tight-laced, uptight *(Nonformal)*, Victorian *Antonyms:* casual, laidback, relaxed

strand *n.* **1.** bank, beach, coast, *plage (French)*, *playa (Spanish)*, shore, waterfront **2.** cable, fibre, hair, piece, length, rope, skiver, stretch, string, strip, thread, vein, wire, wisp – *v.* **1.** abandon, desert, forsake, leave, maroon *Nonformal:* bail on, ditch, split **2.** beach, run aground *or* ashore, shipwreck

stranded *adj.* **1.** abandoned, adrift, alone, cast away, deserted, disowned, godforsaken, helpless, homeless, marooned, orphaned, rejected, separated, solitary **2.** aground, ashore, beached, fast, fixed, grounded, high and dry, run aground, shipwrecked, sidelined *(Nonformal)*, stuck, wrecked

strange *adj.* **1.** new, novel, uncharted, unencountered, unexplored, unfamiliar, unheard-of, unidentified, unknown, unseen *Antonyms:* common, familiar, old **2.** aberrant, abnormal, atypical, bizarre, deviant, different, eccentric, exceptional, extraordinary, fantastic, far-fetched, far-out *(Nonformal)*, funny, idiosyncratic, irregular, mystifying, odd, offbeat, original, outlandish, peculiar, perplexing, queer, rare, remarkable, unaccountable, unusual, weird *Antonyms:* normal, regular, usual **3.** alien, exotic, extraterrestrial, foreign *Antonyms:* local, native **4.** apprehensive, awkward, bashful, cautious, demure, faraway, hesitant, introverted, nervous, quiet, remote, reserved, reticent, shy, skittish, timid *Antonyms:* bold, brazen, loud, obnoxious

stranger *n.* alien, drifter, foreigner, immigrant, incomer, itinerant, migrant, new arrival, newcomer, outlander, outsider, *pakeha (Maori)*, pilgrim, *Qallunaaq (Inuktitut)*, transient, unknown, wanderer *Antonyms:* indigene, local, native

strangle *v.* **1.** asphyxiate, burke, choke, smore *(Scottish)*, suffocate, throttle, wring **2.** block, censor, check, gag, halt, mute, obstruct, retard, scotch, silence, smother, snuff, stifle, stop, suppress

strap *n.* band, belt, crupper, handgrip, handle, harness, lash, leash, loop, rope, suspender, thong, tie, whip – *v.* **1.** bind, buckle *or* strap *or* tie down, bundle, fasten, lash, restrain **2.** abuse, beat, correct, discipline, flail, flog, lash, punish, thrash, whip

strapped *adj.* broke, derelict, destitute, dirt-poor, down-and-out, flat, impoverished, indignant, needy, penniless, penurious, poor, poverty-stricken *Nonformal:* flat *or* stone broke, hard up *Antonyms:* flush, loaded, rich

strapping *adj.* beefy, brawny, built *(Nonformal)*, burly, hefty, hulking, husky, large, muscle-bound, muscled, muscular, powerful, pumped, robust, stalwart, stout, strong, sturdy, vigorous, virile, well-built *Antonyms:* bony, feeble, lanky, weak, wimpy

stratagem *n.* angle, artifice, blind, brainchild, deception, deke, device, dodge, feint, gambit, game, gimmick, intrigue, manoeuvre, method, play, plot, ploy, pretext, ruse, scenario, scheme, setup, shift, subterfuge, trick, twist, wile *Nonformal:* con, jig, scam

strategic *adj.* **1.** cardinal, chief, consequential, critical, crucial, decisive, essential, fundamental, imperative, important, key, necessary, principal, requisite, vital *Antonyms:* frivolous, meaningless, superficial **2.** calculated, clever, contrived, cunning, deliberate, designed, diplomatic, Machiavellian, mapped-out, planned, plotted, politic, premeditated, tricky *Antonyms:* ad-lib, improvised

strategy *n.* action, angle, approach, artifice, blueprint, brainchild, craft, cunning, design, game, game plan, layout, method, plan, planning, policy, procedure, program, project, proposition, racket, scenario, scene, scheme, setup, slant, system, tactic

stratum *n.* **1.** bed, layer, seam, sheet, slab, table, thickness, vein **2.** class, degree, grade, level, status, tier

stray *adj.* **1.** abandoned, astray, escaped, fugitive, homeless, lost, missing, rambling, roaming, transient, vagrant, vanished, wandering *Antonyms:* found, landed, settled **2.** deviating, errant, missed, off-line, off-target, off-track, *Antonyms:* centred, true **3.** accidental, chance, haphazard, irregular, occasional, random, rare, singular, unrelated – *n.* **1.** bolter *(Nonformal)*, deserter, dodger, escapee, fugitive, outlaw, renegade, runaway **2.** bum *(Nonformal)*, drifter, *flâneur (French)*, hobo, itinerant, roamer, tramp, transient, vagabond, waif, wanderer – *v.* **1.** drift, gad about, meander, ramble, range, roam, rove, straggle, trek, wander **2.** break off, depart, deviate, digress, diverge, separate, split, swerve **3.** backslide, err, fall, go astray, lapse, offend, slip, sin, trespass

streak *n.* **1.** bar, beam, layer, line, shaft, strip, stripe **2.** bolt, burst, crack, flame, flare, flash, ray, shot, stream **3.** dirt, discoloration, marring, residue, runoff, smear, smudge, stain, streaking **4.** dash, element, hint, intimation, pinch, shade, strain, suggestion, suspicion, touch, trace, trait, vein **5.** character, constitution, disposition, humour, makeup, mood, nature, personality, quality, spirit, temper, tone **6.** duration, interval, length, run, series, span, spell, stint, stretch, sweep, term – *v.* **1.** dapple, daub, fleck, line, marble, smear, spot, striate, stripe, variegate, vein **2.** barrel, bound, dart, dash, flee, fly, gallop, run, rush, scoot, skip, sprint, tear *Nonformal:* hightail *or* hotfoot it, whiz *Antonyms:* crawl, linger, loiter

stream *n.* **1.** branch, brook, burn, channel, course, creek, freshet, race, rill, river, rivulet, run, runlet, runnel, sluice, snye, streamlet, tributary, watercourse, waterway **2.** current, deluge, discharge, flow, flux, gushing, movement, outpouring, spate, tide, torrent, wave **3.** beam, blaze, laser, patch, ray, ribbon, shaft **4.** idiom, school, style, tradition – *v.* **1.** cascade, course, emanate, emerge, emit, exude, flood, flow, gush, issue, pour *or* pour forth, roll, run, shed, sluice, spew, spill, spout, spritz, spurt, surge *Antonyms:* dribble, drip **2.** blow, dance, flap, float, flutter, fly, wave **3.** categorize, classify, organize, pigeonhole, segregate, separate, stereotype, streamline *Antonyms:* desegregate, destream

streamer *n.* **1.** blizzard, lake snow, snowstorm, squall, storm, tempest, *tempête de neige (French)*, whiteout **2.** banderole, banner, bunting, colours, ensign, flag, jack, oriflamme, pennant, pennon, ribbon, standard **3.** banner, heading, headline, hook *(Nonformal)*

streamlined *adj.* **1.** aerodynamic, fast, fluid, sharp, sleek, slim, smooth, trim, wedge-like, wind resistant **2.** competitive, cost effective, downsized, efficient, modern, profitable, up-to-date *Nonformal:* mean, tight *Antonyms:* backward, bureaucratic, wasteful

street *n.* alley, alleyway, avenue, blind alley, boulevard, chase, court, crescent, cul-de-sac, dead end, drag *(Nonformal)*, drive, lane, one-way street, passageway, place, public way, road, roadway, route, row, square, trail, walk, way *British:* close, mews *French: chemin, rue*

strength *n.* **1.** brawn, brawniness, energy, force, health, lustiness, might, muscle, power, robustness, sinew, stoutness, vigour, vim, vitality *Antonyms:* feebleness, frailty, impotence, powerlessness **2.** backbone, courage, determination, fortitude, hardiness, mettle, nerve, pluck, spirit, stalwartness, steadiness, substance, tenacity, verve *Nonformal:* chutzpah, guts, moxie **3.** durability, elasticity, endurance, firmness, resilience, resistance, ruggedness, solidity, soundness, stamina, sturdiness, toughness *Antonyms:* frailty, weakness **4.** amplitude, calibre, concentration, degree, depth, grade, intensity, kick *(Nonformal)*, level, magnitude, potency, proof **5.** cogency, effectiveness, efficacy, importance, influence, persuasiveness, pith, punch *(Nonformal)*, significance, weight **6.** advantage, flair, forte, gift, strong point, talent *Antonyms:* defect, failing, flaw

strengthen *v.* **1.** bolster, brace, buttress, fortify, harden, intensify, reinforce, steel, stiffen, support, temper, toughen *Antonyms:* debilitate, undermine, weaken **2.** assist, embolden, empower, hearten, rally, spur **3.** energize, feed, invigorate, nourish, refresh, rejuvenate, restore, revitalize, sustain **4.** add, beef up *(Nonformal)*, boost, build up, consolidate, develop, enhance, expand, flourish, grow, increase, prosper, rise, thrive *Antonyms:* decrease, shrink **5.** affirm, authenticate, back up, corroborate, endorse, forward, substantiate, uphold, validate, verify

strenuous *adj.* **1.** challenging, demanding, difficult, draining, exhausting, fatiguing, gruelling, hard, intense, laborious, onerous, severe, taxing, tiring, tough *Antonyms:* easy, relaxed, simple **2.** active, aggressive, ardent, bold, determined, dynamic, eager, earnest, energetic, enterprising, industrious, lusty, persistent, resolute, spirited, strong, tireless, vigorous, zealous *Antonyms:* apathetic, indifferent, lazy

stress *n.* **1.** accentuation, emphasis, force, intensity, priority, urgency, weight **2.** demand, duress, dynamism, energy, exertion, force, power, pressure, pull, push, shear, strain, tension **3.** affliction, agitation, anxiety, concern, disquiet, distress, grief, hassle *(Nonformal)*, nervousness, pain, perturbation, pressure, sleepless nights, suffering, trepidation, trial, weight, worry – *v.* **1.** accentuate, belabour, emphasize, impress, play *or* point up, press, push, repeat **2.** accent, bold, feature, headline, highlight, italicize, underline, underscore **3.** burn out, enervate, exhaust, labour, oppress, overextend, overload, overwork, strain, tax

stretch *adj.* elastic, flexible, rubber, self-adjusting, spring, yielding – *n.* **1.** bit, awhile, compass, course, distance, duration, expanse, extent, hitch *(Nonformal)*, length, period, piece, radius, range, reach, run, scope, sentence, space, span, spell, spread, stint, sweep, term, time, while **2.** bounce, elasticity, flexibility, give, rebound, resilience, spring, tensility **3.** chute, line, road, runaway, straight, straightaway, track – *v.* **1.** draw out, elongate, enlarge, extend, lengthen, protract, spread, widen *Antonyms:* curtail, cut, edit, shrink **2.** balloon, bloat, bulge, dilate, distend, expand, inflate, swell *Antonyms:* attenuate, deflate, reduce **3.** bridge, connect, contact, join, cross, ford, join, link, marry, meet, reach, span, touch **4.** hold *or* thrust out, offer, present, reach **5.** colour, distort, embellish, embroider, enhance, exaggerate, hype *(Nonformal)*, pad, romanticize **6.** exert, drudge, labour, strain, strive, struggle, sweat, tax, work **7.** exercise, flex, limber up, loosen *or* warm up, prepare, work out **8.** budget, cope, economize, get along, make do, manage, prolong, scrape by

strew *v.* broadcast, cast, diffuse, disperse, disseminate, distribute, fling, litter, overspread, scatter, shower, spread, sprinkle, throw, toss

stricken *adj.* **1.** affected, disturbed, floored *(Nonformal)*, impressed, moved, overcome, overwhelmed, touched *Antonyms:* cold, disaffected, indifferent **2.** anguished, crestfallen, crushed, depressed, distressed, grief-stricken, heartbroken, melancholy, mournful, rueful, suffering, tormented, tortured, wretched *Antonyms:* ecstatic, happy, pleased **3.** afflicted, blighted, disabled, diseased, harmed, hit, hurt, ill, incapacitated, infected, injured, plagued, sick, struck, wounded *Antonyms:* fine, healed, healthy, untouched

strict *adj.* **1.** austere, authoritarian, disciplinary, draconian, firm, forbidding, harsh, oppressive, puritanical, rigid, severe, Spartan, unsparing, Victorian *Nonformal:* iron-fisted, no-nonsense, uptight *Antonyms:* easygoing, flexible, lax, open **2.** accurate, attentive, careful, correct, doctrinal, faithful, heedful, meticulous, observant, orthodox, point-device, precise, punctilious, regardful *Antonyms:* carefree, heedless, indifferent **3.** administered, enforced, enjoined, implemented, maintained, observed, pressed, reinforced **4.** absolute, complete, entire, full-fledged, thorough, total, undivided, utter *Antonyms:* incomplete, partial

stricture *n.* **1.** abuse, animadversion, aspersion, censure, criticism, disapproval, disparagement, dispersion, imputation, ridicule, scorn, vituperation *Nonformal:* burn, cut, dis, flak, knock, rap, shot, trashing *Antonyms:* commendation, compliment, flattering, praise **2.** ceiling, check, constraint, cramp, glass ceiling, governance, hindrance, limitation, restraint, restriction *Antonyms:* aid, benefit, spur, support

stride *n.* **1.** gait, gallop, march, pace, step, trot **2.** breadth, distance, extent, gap, interval, length, measure, span, stretch **3.** achievement, accomplishment, advancement, development, forward motion, furtherance, gain, headway, movement, progression, promotion, push – *v.* clump, gallop, hike, hoof it *(Nonformal)*, leg it, march, pace, parade, perambulate, pound, stamp, strut, traipse, tramp, trek, tromp, trot, trudge, walk

strident *adj.* boisterous, cacophonous, clamorous, clashing, discordant, grating, harsh, jangling, jarring, loud, noisy, obstreperous, rasping, raucous, screeching, shrill, stentorian, stridulous, urgent *Antonyms:* dulcet, gentle, harmonious, mellow, sweet

strife *n.* altercation, argument, battle, bickering, brawl, clash, combat, competition, conflict, contention, contest, controversy, difference, disagreement, discord, dispute, dissension, dissent, dissidence, donnybrook, factionalism, fighting, flap, fracas, fray, friction, fuss, quarrel, rivalry, row, rumpus, run-in, spat, squabbling, struggle, tug-of-war, variance, warfare, words, wrangle *Nonformal:* blowup, hassle, rhubarb *Antonyms:* calm, peace, tranquility

strike *n.* **1.** bang, bash, blow, box, carom, cuff, hit, punch, roundhouse, shot, slap, smack, upper-cut, wallop, whack, whap *Nonformal:* bonk, forearm shiver **2.** aggression, assault, attack, blitzkrieg, charge, drive, invasion, offensive, onslaught, sortie, storming, thrust **3.** job action, labour action *or* struggle *or* unrest, organized objection, picketing, protest, revolt, work refusal *or* stoppage *Kinds of strike:* boycott, bread and butter *(Nonformal)*, general, hunger, lock-out, outlaw, sit-down, sit-in, slowdown, sympathy, wildcat, work-to-rule **4.** acquisition, detection, discovery, location, unearthing **5.** accomplishment, achievement, advance, breakthrough, gain, success, stroke of luck – *v.* **1.** bang, bash, beat, box, bust *(Nonformal)*, clobber, drive, hammer, hit, impel, knock, lash, nail, pound, pummel, punch, smack, thrust, thump, wallop, whack **2.** assail assault, beset, blitz, bomb, charge, demolish, devastate, invade, obliterate, pulverize, raid, storm, strafe, waylay **3.** bang into, bump, collide, contact, crash, meet head-on, pile into, ram, run into, smash *Antonyms:* avoid, bypass **4.** bat, crack, knock, launch, propel, send, shoot, swat **5.** blue pencil, cut, delete, drop, erase, exclude, expunge, omit, remove, strike *or* wipe out *Antonyms:* add, append, annex **6.** afflict, alter, change, disturb, modify, shape, transform **7.** affect, appeal to, arouse, grab *(Nonformal)*, influence, impress, move, register, stimulate, stir, sway, tickle, touch *Antonyms:* alienate, disaffect **8.** encroach, enter, insert, penetrate, perforate, pierce, punctuate, ream, spear, stab **9.** achieve, accomplish, attain, clinch, consummate, land, produce, reach, score, secure, settle **10.** accept, approve, authorize, confirm, consent, endorse, sanction, sign *Antonyms:* condemn, disapprove **11.** arrive at, chance *or* happen *or* hit *or* light upon, come across *or* upon, detect, dig *or* turn up, discover, encounter, exhume, expose, find, identify, lay bare, locate, notice, spot, stumble across *or* upon, uncover, unearth **12.** boycott, demonstrate, fight, march, mutiny, object, picket, protest, rally, rebel, revolt, rise up, walk **13.** burn, ignite, kindle, light, start **14.** adopt, affect, assume, display, show, take up, vogue *(Nonformal)* **15.** brand, imprint, mint, press, print, stamp **16.** bite, catch, gnaw, grip, nip, pinch, seize, snatch at, sting, wound

striking *adj.* **1.** attractive, beautiful, becoming, breathtaking, charming, good-looking, gorgeous, handsome, lovely, sexy, stunning *Nonformal:* car-stopping, dreamy, eye-popping, head-turning, hot, intoxicating, wild *Antonyms:* frightful, repugnant, scary **2.** arresting, awesome, bodacious *(Nonformal)*, exceptional, extraordinary, impressive, incredible, magnificent, memorable, noteworthy, outstanding, phenomenal, remarkable, unique, wonderful *Antonyms:* average, undistinguished, unexceptional **3.** conspicuous, distinguished, marked, noticeable, obvious, prominent, pronounced, salient *Antonyms:* faint, hidden, obscure

string *n.* **1.** catgut, cord, fibre, filament, rope, strand, strip, twine, twist, wire **2.** chain, echelon, file, line, order, procession, queue, rank, row, sequel, sequence, series, succession, tier **3.** choker, leash, loop, necklace, tie – *v.* **1.** drape, festoon, hang, loop, suspend **2.** bead, connect, join, link, tie **3.** deceive, dissemble, fool, lie to, mislead, pretend

stringent *adj.* **1.** demanding, draconian, exacting, hard, harsh, inflexible, rigid, rigorous, rough, set, severe, Spartan, stiff, strict, tough *Antonyms:* flexible, loose, relaxed **2.** binding, close, confining, constraining, hampering, limiting, obstructive, oppressive, repressive, restrictive, tight **3.** affective, believable, cogent, compelling, convincing, credible, forceful, influential, plausible, persuasive, telling, tenable

strings *n. pl.* conditions, contingencies, limitations, obligations, prerequisites, provisions, qualifications, requirements, restrictions, special terms, stipulations, terms

stringy *adj.* **1.** fibrous, gristly, muscular, sinewy, tough *Antonyms:* mushy, soft, tender **2.** bony, gangly, lank, long, reedy, ropy, spindly, tall, thin, wiry *Antonyms:* plump, round, stout

strip *n.* **1.** bit, collup, cut, length, fillet, measure, part, piece, portion, rasher, scrap, section, segment, shred, slice, slip, stick, stripe **2.** band, bar, beach, belt, drag *(Nonformal)*, ribbon, road, spit, strait, strand, stretch, tongue – *v.* **1.** bare, disrobe, doff, expose oneself, peel *(Nonformal)*, take off, unclothe, uncover, undress **2.** denude, exfoliate, lay bare, peel, remove, scale, shed, shell, shuck **3.** burglarize, filch, lift, loot, pillage, pinch, purloin, rob, smash and grab *(Nonformal)*, spoil, steal **4.** confiscate, debar, deprive, disinherit, dispossess, divest, expropriate, remove

stripe *n.* **1.** band, bar, border, layer, line, pinstripe, streak, striation, strip, stroke **2.** badge, chevron, emblem, insignia, marking, symbol **3.** attribute, breed, character, class, ilk, kind, nature, persuasion, sort, strain, type, variety

striped *adj.* banded, brindled, layered, lined, marked, streaked, streaky, striated, variegated, veined *Antonyms:* monochromatic, polka-dot, spotted

strive *v.* **1.** aspire, attempt, endeavour, essay, exert, grind away, labour, strain, struggle, sweat *(Nonformal)*, toil, try, work *Antonyms:* fail, languish, surrender **2.** argue, bandy, battle, bicker, clash, contend, dispute, fight, grapple, quarrel, tussle, war, wrestle

stroke *n.* **1.** blow, *coup de main (French)*, cut, hit, impact, lash, poke, pop *(Nonformal)*, punch, slash, slice, smash, swing, swipe, thwack, wallop, whack, whap **2.** breath, *coup d'oeil (French)*, eyewink *or* wink, flash, instant, moment, second, shake, snap, trice *Nonformal:* jiff, sec **3.** act, circumstance, episode, event, happening, incident, occurrence **4.** coup, *coup de maître (French)*, feat, manoeuvre, masterstroke, plan, stratagem, scheme, stunt, tactic **5.** aneurysm, apoplexy, attack, fit, hemorrhage, paralysis, seizure, spasm, thrombosis **6.** bang, chime, clang, clap, peal, sound, striking, tintinnabulation **7.** beat, flutter, palpitation, pulsation, pump, throb **8.** dash, hyphen, line, mark, streak, sweep **9.** caress, feel, fondling, massage, pet, rub, touch – *v.* **1.** brush, comb, feel, fondle, handle, massage, paw, pat, rub, smooth, soothe **2.** crack, crank, hit, knock, project, send, shoot, strike, swing

stroll *n.* constitutional, excursion, perambulation, saunter, turn, walk – *v.* amble, cruise, drift, gallivant, meander, mosey, perambulate, promenade, ramble, roam, sashay *(Nonformal)*, saunter, stravage *(Irish)*, toddle, traipse, tramp, walk, wander

strong *adj.* **1.** athletic, beefy, brawny, burly, energetic, forceful, husky, lusty, mighty, muscular, powerful, rugged, sinewy, stout, strapping, vigorous, virile *Antonyms:* weak, wimpy **2.** durable, heavy-duty, reinforced, resilient, solid, sound, steady, sturdy, substantial, tough, trustworthy, well-built, well-made *Antonyms:* flimsy, fragile, jerrybuilt **3.** aggressive, assertive, dedicated, determined, dogged, firm, fixed, formidable, obdurate, obstinate, plucky, resolute, stalwart, staunch, steadfast, strong-willed, stubborn, tenacious, tough, unbending, uncompromising, unshakable, unyielding *Antonyms:* timid, weak-willed, wishy-washy **4.** bold, brave, brazen, courageous, fearless, gallant, gutsy, spirited *Antonyms:* cowardly, fearful **5.** able-bodied, fit, hale, hardy, healthy, hearty, robust, sound

Antonyms: debilitated, ill, sickly **6.** able, accomplished, adept, capable, competent, deft, expert, good, practiced, proficient, qualified, resourceful, skilful, skilled, talented *Antonyms:* gauche, incompetent, inept **7.** cogent, compelling, convincing, effective, influential, meaningful, persuasive, potent, telling, trenchant, weighty, well-founded *Antonyms:* light, slight, thin **8.** alcoholic, concentrated, fortified, heady, intoxicating, stiff, undiluted *Nonformal:* boozy, forty-proof **9.** aromatic, foul, malodorous, noisome, pungent, putrid, rank, smelly, stinking, stinky, strong-smelling, unpleasant, wretched **10.** draconian, drastic, extreme, intense, severe, sharp, strict **11.** absolute, confident, decided, emphatic, explicit, express, firm, positive, resolute, urgent, vehement **12.** booming, deafening, full, heavy, loud, resonant, resounding, stentorian, thundering **13.** ardent, burning, eager, earnest, enthusiastic, fervent, fervid, great, keen, sincere, spirited, zealous **14.** clear, conspicuous, definite, distinct, flagrant, marked, noticeable, prominent, pronounced, striking, vivid **15.** blustery, bracing, brisk, fierce, fresh, tempestuous, violent

strong-arm *v.* bully, coerce, compel, dragoon, force, harass, hector, intimidate, lean on, muscle, oblige, pressure, terrorize, threaten *Antonyms:* beg, plead, rollover

strongbox *n.* bank, box, case, chest, footlocker, locker, safe, safety-deposit box, vault

stronghold *n.* bastion, beachhead, bridgehead, bulwark, bunker, castle, citadel, fieldwork, fort, fortification, fortress, garrison, keep, outwork, pillbox, post, redoubt

strong-willed *adj.* assertive, determined, firm, hard-headed, headstrong, mulish, obdurate, obstinate, pig-headed, resolute, staunch, stubborn, tenacious, wilful *Antonyms:* soft, weak, wishy-washy

structure *n.* **1.** anatomy, architecture, arrangement, build, configuration, corpus, design, distribution, fabric, fabrication, form, format, frame, framework, interrelation, layout, morphology, network, order, organization, pattern, plan, positioning, skeleton, system *Nonformal:* bare bones, bricks and mortar **2.** building, complex, construction, creation, edifice, erection, establishment, product, wattle – *v.* build, construct, design, form, frame, organize, lay out, pattern, plan, position, systematize

struggle *n.* **1.** endeavour, essay, exertion, labour, pains, strain, strife, striving, suffering, toil, trial, undertaking, work *Nonformal:* daily grind, long haul, rat race, sweat **2.** altercation, battle, brawl, clash, combat, conflict, contest, donnybrook, encounter, fight, quarrel, tiff, tussle, war – *v.* **1.** attempt, exert oneself, labour, strain, strive, tackle, toil, try, undertake, work *Nonformal:* plug away, sweat **2.** brawl, compete, contend, fight, grapple, joust, roughhouse, row, scrap, scuffle, tangle, tussle, wrestle *Nonformal:* bump heads, cross swords, lock horns

strut *v.* flounce, grandstand, parade, peacock, prance, promenade, show-off, stride, swagger *Nonformal:* boogie, hotdog, sashay *Antonyms:* limp, stagger, totter

stub *n.* **1.** butt, end, remainder, remnant, root, short end, stump, tail, tail end **2.** bill, cheque, chit, note, proof, receipt, tab, ticket, voucher – *v.* break, bump, damage, hit, hurt, injure, knock, sprain, strike

stubborn *adj.* **1.** adamant, balky, bullheaded, contrary, contumacious, determined, dogged, hard, headstrong, implacable, inflexible, insistent, intractable, mulish, obdurate, obstinate, ornery, pigheaded, recalcitrant, resolved, rigid, self-willed, steadfast, strong-minded, strong willed, tenacious, thick-skinned, tough, uncompromising, unshakable, unyielding, wilful *Antonyms:* compliant, easy, flexible, pliable, tractable, wavering, weak-willed **2.** anchored, fastened, fixed, frozen, grounded, rooted, stuck *Antonyms:* free, loose, uprooted

stubby *adj.* chubby, chunky, corpulent, dumpy, fat, heavyset, portly, squat, stocky, stout, stumpy, thick, thick-bodied, thickset *Antonyms:* lanky, slender, tall, svelte, willowy

stuck *adj.* **1.** caught, cemented, frozen, glued, grounded, held, high-and-dry, jammed, rusted, seized, wedged *Antonyms:* free, loose, maneuverable **2.** abandoned, alone, deserted, left, marooned, stranded, without funds *or* means **3.** baffled, bewildered, confused, flummoxed *(Nonformal)*, mystified, nonplussed, puzzled, stymied, thrown, troubled

stuck-up *adj.* aloof, arrogant, conceited, contemptuous, haughty, indifferent, inflated, presumptuous, pretentious, proud, prudish, self-centered, self-important, snobbish, supercilious, superior, vain *Nonformal:* hoity-toity, snooty, snotty , toplofty, *Antonyms:* grovelling, humble, self-effacing

student *n.* **1.** apprentice, co-ed, *élève (French)*, graduand, intellectual, learner, observer, postgrad, postgraduate, pupil, registrant, scholar, schoolboy, schoolgirl, undergrad, undergraduate *Antonyms:* master, sensei, teacher **2.** aficionado, buff, devotee, disciple, enthusiast, fan, fanatic, follower *Nonformal:* freak, groupie, junkie

studied *adj.* **1.** advised, calculated, considered, contrived, deliberate, designed, intentional, meditated, organized, planned, plotted, premeditated, prepared, purposeful, thoughtful, thought-out *Antonyms:* impulsive, offhand, spontaneous, unplanned **2.** affected, artificial, assumed, fake, false, forced, laboured, mannered, phoney *(Nonformal)*, plastic, self-conscious, stiff, stilted, strained, synthetic, unnatural, wooden *Antonyms:* genuine, natural, plain, simple

studio *n.* **1.** atelier, den, gallery, library, room, scriptorium, study, workroom, workshop **2.** broadcasting studio, recording studio, sound stage, TV stage

studious *adj.* **1.** academic, bookish, cerebral, contemplative, erudite, intellectual, learned, lettered, meditative, philosophical, reflective, rhetorical, scholarly, thoughtful, well-informed, well-read *Nonformal:* egg-headed, long-haired, nerdy **2.** assiduous, attentive, devoted, diligent, eager, earnest, genuine, industrious, serious, sincere, unflagging *Antonyms:* careless, frivolous, inattentive, negligent **3.** deliberate, intentional, painstaking, planned, premeditated, studied

study *n.* **1.** absorption, analysis, bookwork, cogitation, concentration, consideration, contemplation, examination, inquiry, inspection, investigation, learning, meditation, memorization, questioning, reading, reflection, research, scrutiny, understanding **2.** analysis, argument, article, book, deconstruction, diagnosis, essay, Green Paper, interpretation, lesson, monograph, piece, presentation, report, spin *(Nonformal)*, take, theory, thesis, treatise, treatment, White Paper **3.** art, branch of knowledge, concern, course, discipline, field, field of expertise, knowledge, realm, science, specialty, sphere, subject, territory **4.** art, composition, draft, drawing, nude, piece, sketch, still life, work **5.** atelier, den, hall, library, office, refuge, retreat, room of one's own, sanctum, scriptorium, space, studio – *v.* **1.** absorb, dissect, examine, figure out, glean, inquire, inspect, investigate, learn, memorize, read, refresh, research, review, scrutinize, search into, survey *Nonformal:* bone up, case, cram **2.** analyze, cogitate, consider, contemplate, meditate, mull over, muse, ponder, reflect, think, weigh, understand **3.** apply oneself, concentrate, focus, endeavour, lucubrate, strain, strive, try, work at

stuff *n.* **1.** belongings, chattels, effects, equipment, gear, goods, impedimenta, movables, objects, paraphernalia, possessions, trappings *Nonformal:* bits and pieces, dope, loot, shmunza **2.** clutter, crap *(Nonformal)*, filth, garbage, junk, rubbish, scrap, trash, waste **3.** basics, building blocks, cloth, DNA *(Biology)*, elements, essence, essentials, fabric, fundamentals, material, matter, stuff of life, substance **4.** ability, expertise, ingenuity, knack, makings, skill, talent, touch *Nonformal:* goods, magic – *v.* **1.** compress, congest, cram, crowd, fill, force, jam, jam-pack, overfill, overload, pack, pad, push, ram, squeeze, stow, swell *Antonyms:* empty, release, remove **2.** devour, glut, gluttonize, gorge, gourmandize, overindulge, sate, satiate, satisfy *Nonformal:* inhale, pig out, wolf down **3.** block, cap, choke, choke *or* clog stop *or* up, cork, obstruct, plug, seal

stuffed *adj.* **1.** chock-a-block, chock-full, choked, complete, congested, crammed, crowded, filled, full up to the gunnels

(Nonformal), loaded, packed, rammed, rife *Antonyms:* empty, hollow, void **2.** bulging, glutted, gorged, satiated, satisfied, surfeited *Antonyms:* famished, hungry, starved

stuffy *adj.* **1.** boring, dreary, dull, humourless, musty, narrow-minded, old, old-fashioned, priggish, prim, prudish, staid, stodgy, straitlaced, tired, Victorian *Nonformal:* mossbacked, square, uptight **2.** arrogant, conceited, egocentric, haughty, narcissistic, pedantic, pompous, proud, snobbish, stuck-up, supercilious, superior *Antonyms:* humble, lowly **3.** airless, breathless, close, confined, fusty, heavy, humid, muggy, oppressive, stagnant, stale, stifling, suffocating, sultry, thick, unventilated *Antonyms:* airy, breezy, drafty, fresh

stultify *v.* **1.** annul, balk, cancel, disable, frustrate, hamstring, impair, impede, inhibit, invalidate, muzzle, negate, neutralize, nullify, repress, scotch, smother, stifle, strangle, suffocate, suppress, thwart, vitiate *Antonyms:* authorize, empower, enable **2.** astound, flabbergast, leave speechless, nonplus, stop in one's tracks, strike dumb

stumble *v.* **1.** hesitate, lurch, misstep, pitch, reel, stagger, stutter, take a header *or* spill, topple, totter, trip **2.** blunder, botch, bungle, falter, flounder, hash *or* mess up, **3.** err, fall, go astray, sin, slip, transgress, trespass, violate **4.** chance, come *or* run across, discover, encounter, find, happen *or* light upon, hit, meet, turn up

stumbling block *n.* barrier, catch, check, crimp, hindrance, hurdle, impediment, interference, obstacle, obstruction, roadblock, snag *Nonformal:* fly in the ointment, monkey wrench

stump *n.* butt, end, end piece, projection, rump, stub, tail end, tip – *v.* baffle, bamboozle *(Nonformal)*, bedevilled, befog, bewilder, confound, confuse, disconcert, dumfound, foil, mystify, nonplus, perplex, perturb, puzzle, stymie

stumped *adj.* at a loss, baffled, blank, confounded, confused, mystified, nonplussed, puzzled, stuck, stymied *Nonformal:* discombobulated, flummoxed, jiggered

stun *v.* **1.** amaze, astonish, astound, bemuse, bewilder, confound, confuse, daze, dumfound, flabbergast, muddle, overwhelm, rock, shake up, shock, stagger, strike dumb, surprise *Nonformal:* blow away, bowl over, floor **2.** daze, freeze, knock out *or* over *or* unconscious, numb, paralyze, stupefy

stung *adj.* **1.** cut, harmed, hurt, injured, lacerated, pierced, punctured, stabbed, wounded **2.** afflicted, aggrieved, beset, distressed, grieved, saddened, scorned, tortured, wronged *Antonyms:* comforted, consoled, soothed

stunning *adj.* **1.** amazing, astonishing, astounding, awesome, beyond belief, brilliant, excellent, exquisite, fine, grand, impressive, inspiring, marvellous, moving, numbing, remarkable, shocking, spectacular, startling, stupefying, touching, wonderful *Antonyms:* average, boring, expected, mediocre, mundane, plain **2.** attractive, beautiful, comely, gorgeous, handsome, lovely, ravishing, sexy, striking *Nonformal:* exciting, eye-popping, head-turning, traffic-stopping

stunt *n.* achievement, act, antic, caper, deed, exploit, feat, hijinks, performance, shocker *(Nonformal)*, show, trick – *v.* arrest, atrophy, check, cramp, curb, curtail, delimit, hamper, hinder, impede, limit, restrain, restrict, slow, stifle, stop, stultify, suppress *Antonyms:* boost, encourage, nurture

stunted *adj.* dwarf, half-pint *(Nonformal)*, little, measly, scrub, short, shrunken, small, tiny, undergrown, undersized, wee *Antonyms:* big, gigantic, huge, immense, vast

stupefaction *n.* **1.** coma, daze, numbness, stupor, torpor, trance, unconsciousness **2.** amazement, astonishment, awe, bewilderment, confusion, perplexity, puzzlement, wonder

stupefied *adj.* **1.** amazed, astonished, awestruck, bewildered, confused, dazed, dumfounded, flabbergasted, floored *(Nonformal)*, overwhelmed, shocked, speechless, staggered, startled, stunned, surprised, thunderstruck *Antonyms:* calm, composed, indifferent **2.** comatose, dazed, deadened, numb, out cold, senseless, unconscious

stupendous *adj.* **1.** amazing, astonishing, astounding, awesome, extraordinary, fabulous, incredible, impressive, marvellous, miraculous, moving, stunning, surprising, terrific, unusual, wonderful *Nonformal:* cool, far out, unreal, wicked, wild *Antonyms:* bland, common, ordinary **2.** big, colossal, enormous, giant, gigantic, huge, humongous *(Nonformal)*, immense, large, mammoth, massive, monumental, phenomenal, prodigious, tremendous, vast *Antonyms:* diminutive, minuscule, small, tiny, wee

stupid *adj.* **1.** asinine, brainless, dazed, dense, dim, doltish, dull, dumb, empty-headed, foolish, half-baked, half-witted, idiotic, imbecilic, imprudent, inane, insensate, irrational, irresponsible, laughable, ludicrous, mindless, moronic, muddleheaded, nonsensical, obtuse, outrageous, puerile, reckless, ridiculous, senseless, short-sighted, silly, simple-minded, slow, sluggish, sophomoric, thick, thickheaded, unintelligent, unreasonable, unthinking, witless *British Nonformal:* daft, gormless *Nonformal:* ass-backward, boneheaded, chuckleheaded, cockamamie, cuckoo, goofy, spinny, stunned *Antonyms:* astute, brainy, bright, smart, wise **2.** fruitless, futile, hopeless, impractical, irrelevant, lousy *(Nonformal)*, meaningless, nonsensical, pointless, purposeless, trivial, useless, vain, worthless *Antonyms:* important, meaningful, significant **3.** banal, bland, boring, dreary, dull, monotonous, soporific, stultifying, tedious, tiresome, wearisome *Antonyms:* inspiring, invigorating, stimulating

stupidity *n.* absurdity, denseness, doltishness, empty-headedness, fatuity, folly, foolishness, idiocy, imbecility, inanity, irrationality, insanity, meaninglessness, nonsense, obtuseness, pointlessness, ridiculousness, simple-mindedness *Antonyms:* brilliance, intelligence, logic

stupor *n.* anaesthesia, catatonia, coma, daze, hypnosis, inertia, inertness, insensibility, languor, lassitude, lethargy, narcosis, sleep, slumber, somnolence, stupefaction, swoon, torpor, trance, unconsciousness

sturdy *adj.* **1.** durable, firm, hard, rigid, secure, solid, sound, steady, stiff, strong, substantial, tough, unyielding, well-built, well-made *Antonyms:* flimsy, jerrybuilt, sorry, untrustworthy **2.** able-bodied, athletic, beefy, brawny, bulky, hardy, hearty, hefty, husky, muscular, powerful, robust, rugged, sinewy, stout, strapping *Antonyms:* feeble, frail, niminy-piminy *(Nonformal)*, skinny, weak **3.** determined. firm, formidable, persistent, resolute, staunch, steadfast, stubborn, tenacious, vigorous

stutter *n.* broken speech, glitch, halting, hesitation, speech impediment, stammering – *v.* falter, hesitate, splutter, sputter, stammer, stumble

style *n.* **1.** approach, behaviour, character, cut, design, form, genre, habit, kind, line, look, manner, method, mode, shape, sort, strain **2.** craze, fad, fashion, in thing *(Nonformal)*, rage, trend, vogue **3.** class, cosmopolitanism, dash, delicacy, ease, élan, elegance, flair, grace, grandeur, panache, polish, refinement, savoir-faire, sophistication, spirit, stylishness, taste, urbanity **4.** code, custom, habit, house style, law, practice, rule, usage **5.** diction, expression, language, phraseology, phrasing, wording – *v.* **1.** arrange, construct, create, cut, design, fashion, form, model, mould, pattern, present, shape, treat **2.** address, call, denominate, designate, entitle, label, name, tag, term, title

stylish *adj.* chic, classy, dapper, dashing, dressy, fashionable, in vogue, jaunty, modernistic, natty, new, polished, rakish, sharp, sleek, slick, smart, tony, trendy, upscale, up-to-date, urbane, voguish *Nonformal:* chi-chi, hip, in, nifty, ritzy, sassy, snappy, snazzy, swank, swell, swishy, with-it *Antonyms:* old-fashioned, outmoded, seedy

stymie *v.* block, check, confound, flummox *(Nonformal)*, frustrate, hamstring, hinder, hold, impede, obstruct, prevent, snooker, stall, stonewall, stump, thwart

suave *adj.* affable, agreeable, charming, civilized, cordial, courteous, courtly, cultivated, debonair, diplomatic, flattering, glib, gracious, ingratiating, pleasant, polished, politic, professional, refined, slick, smooth, sophisticated, urbane *Antonyms:* boorish, rude, tactless, vulgar

subconscious *adj.* **1.** automatic, intuitive, subliminal, unintentional, unprompted, visceral *Antonyms:* cogitated, considered, thought-out **2.** deep-rooted, deep-seated, hidden, inner, innermost, latent, psychological, repressed, suppressed – *n.* essence, id, inner thought, mind, psyche, soul, subconsciousness, subliminal self, submerged mind *Antonyms:* consciousness, ego

subdivision *n.* **1.** area, *arrondissement (French)*, bedroom *or* gated community, borough, build-up, burb *(Nonformal)*, community, development, housing development *or* tract, neighbourhood, region, sprawl, suburb **2.** block, concession, homestead, land, lot, parcel, plot, property, real estate, tract **3.** allotment, division, part, piece, portion, section, share **4.** branch, class, family, feather, genus, group, species, subclass, subsidiary, variety

subdue *v.* **1.** beat, best, conquer, crush, drub, overpower, overwhelm, put down, quell, smash, subjugate, vanquish *Nonformal:* cream, hammer, lick, pound **2.** check, choke, constrain, contain, curb, harness, keep a lid on *(Nonformal)*, limit, quash, repress, restrain, squelch, stifle, stop, strait-jacket, suppress *Antonyms:* free, liberate, release **3.** break, browbeat, control, domesticate, domineer, enslave, govern, guide, handle, influence, manage, manipulate, master, rule, tame, train **4.** calm, dampen, deaden, lessen, lighten, lower, mellow, mitigate, moderate, muffle, mute, reduce, soften, temper, tone down *Antonyms:* accentuate, heighten, increase

subdued *adj.* **1.** beaten, castigated, chastened, controlled, crushed, mastered, overwhelmed, vanquished, whipped, whupped *(Nonformal)* **2.** bridled, checked, constrained, controlled, curbed, hamstrung, limited, muzzled, repressed, restrained, silenced, stifled, tied-up **3.** crestfallen, dejected, depressed, down, downcast, grave, repentant, sad, serious, sober, solemn, sombre **4.** calm, hushed, low-key, mellow, moderate, moderated, muted, neutral, quiet, pacific, placid, quiet, reserved, soft, softened, subtle, tame, tempered, toned down *Antonyms:* garish, loud, obnoxious

subject *adj.* dependent, inferior, puppet, satellite, subordinate – *n.* **1.** element, gist, idea, item, leitmotif, material, matter, meat, motif, object, point, subject matter, text, theme, theorem, theory, thesis, thought, topic **2.** area, arena, art, branch, concern, course, discipline, field, realm, science, speciality **3.** captive, cat's paw, pawn, peon, puppet, serf, slave, tool, dupe, vassal **4.** case, client, focus of investigation, guinea pig *(Nonformal)*, patient, study, victim **5.** citizen, civilian, countryman, habitant, inhabitant, national, native, ratepayer, resident, taxpayer **6.** cause, determinant, grounds, inspiration, instigating factor, motive, rationale, reason, root, stimulus – *v.* **1.** conquer, dominate, enslave, enthrall, humble, keep-down, reduce, subjugate, subordinate **2.** allow, expose to, lay open, put to

subjection *n.* **1.** command, domination, mastery, subjugation, tyranny **2.** bondage, captivity, servitude, slavery, thralldom, vassalage **3.** acquiescence, deference, humility, resignation, servility, submission, subservience, surrender, yielding

subjective *adj.* **1.** biased, coloured, distorted, egocentric, fanciful, influenced, manipulated, misconceived, partial, prejudiced, self-serving, skewed, strained, tainted, unobjective, warped *Antonyms:* impartial, objective **2.** cerebral, emotional, individual, intellectual, internal, introspective, intuitive, mental, noetic, personal

subjugate *v.* beat, break, bring to heel *(Nonformal)*, coerce, compel, conquer, control, crush, defeat, drub, enslave, enthrall, force, hold sway, leash, master, overpower, overthrow, quell, reduce, rule over, subdue, suppress, tame *Antonyms:* acquit, free, liberate, release, spare

sublimate *v.* **1.** channel, deflect, divert, funnel, guide, redirect, sidetrack, transfer **2.** alter, change, convert, metamorphose, morph *(Nonformal)*, transform, transmute **3.** purify, rarefy, refine, vaporize

sublime *adj.* **1.** divine, exalted, grand, great, high-minded, lofty, majestic, mighty, noble, sanctified, serious, solemn, spiritual *Antonyms:* corrupt, debased, diminished **2.** awesome, brilliant, emotional, exquisite, heavenly, inspiring, intense, moving, passionate, remarkable, splendid, superb, wonderful *Antonyms:* banal, ordinary, mawkish **3.** all powerful, be-all and end-all *(Nonformal)*, superior, supreme, utmost

subliminal *adj.* **1.** automatic, preconscious, subconscious, unconscious, unprompted **2.** buried, camouflaged, deep-rooted, deep-seated, hidden, invisible, secret, shrouded, veiled

submarine *adj.* subaquatic, undersea, underwater – *n.* bathysphere, submersible, underwater boat *or* ship *or* vessel *Submarine terms:* ballast, periscope, run silent, snorkel *Nonformal:* boomer, con

submerge *v.* **1.** deluge, dip, douse, drench, drown, engulf, flood, immerse, inundate, overflow, overwhelm, souse, submerse, subside, swamp, waterlog, wet **2.** descend, dive, drop, duck, dunk, fall, plummet, plunge, sink **3.** camouflage, cloak, conceal, cover, hide, repress, seclude, suppress *Antonyms:* disclose, reveal, uncover

submerged *adj.* **1.** drowned, flooded, immersed, soaked, submersed, sunken, underwater, waterlogged, watery, wet **2.** buried, camouflaged, concealed, dark, hidden, lost, murky, secret, shadowy, shrouded, unknown, veiled

submission *n.* **1.** deference, diffidence, docility, meekness, obedience, passivity, servility, slavishness, subservience **2.** acquiescence, assent, capitulation, caving in, ceding, consent, quitting, resignation, subsiding, succumbing, surrender, yielding *Antonyms:* insurgence, rebelliousness **3.** advance, bid, motion, offer, proffer, proposal, quote, remittance, tender

submissive *adj.* abject, accommodating, acquiescent, amenable, compliant, conforming, deferential, docile, dutiful, henpecked *(Nonformal)*, humble, ingratiating, malleable, menial, nonresistant, obedient, obeisant, obsequious, passive, pliable, resigned, servile, slavish, subdued, sycophantic, tame, tractable, uncomplaining, unresisting, yielding *Antonyms:* difficult, headstrong, intractable, obstinate

submit *v.* **1.** accede, acknowledge, acquiesce, agree, appease, bend, bow, buckle, capitulate, cave, cede, comply, concede, defer, fold, give ground *or* in *or* way, obey, quit, relent, relinquish, resign oneself, succumb, surrender, toady, truckle, yield *Nonformal:* cry *or* say uncle, eat crow *or* dirt, knuckle under, kowtow, play the game **2.** abide, bear, brook, countenance, stand, stomach, suffer, tolerate, withstand **3.** affirm, argue, assert, claim, commit, contend, move, offer, propose, proposition, propound, refer, suggest **4.** deliver, give, hand in *or* over, present, proffer, put forward, supply, tender, transfer, transmit, volunteer

subordinate *adj.* **1.** apprentice, inferior, lesser, lower, minor, secondary, second-class *or* -rate *Antonyms:* dominant, primary, superior **2.** accessory, adjunct, ancillary, associate, auxiliary, contributory, dependent, subsidiary, supplementary, tributory – *n.* adjutant, adjuvant, aide, apparatchik, apprentice, assistant, attendant, employee, equerry, flunky *(Nonformal)*, hand, help, hireling, lackey, minion, myrmidon, second fiddle, subaltern, subject, underling, vassal – *v.* **1.** annex, dominate, master, subdue, subject **2.** diminish, humble, lessen, lower, reduce

subordination *n.* deference, docility, humility, prostration, servility, subjection, submission *Antonyms:* dominance, leadership, mastery, preeminence, supremacy

subscribe *v.* **1.** advocate, agree, approve, assent, endorse, sanction, support **2.** contribute, donate, enlist, enrol, enter, give, grant, offer, pay up, pledge, promise, register, sign on *or* up

subscription *n.* **1.** agreement, approval, backing, confirmation, consent, endorsement, favour, ratification, sanction, signature **2.** contract, membership fee, obligation, pledge, purchase agreement **3.** aggregate, number, readership, sum, support, total

subsequent *adj.* coming, consecutive, consequent, ensuing, following, later, next, resultant, succeeding, successive *Antonyms:* earlier, previous, prior

subsequently *adv.* **1.** after, afterwards, by and by, eventually, following, later, next, sometime in the future, thereafter **2.** accordingly, consequently, ergo, hence, therefore, thus

subservient *adj.* **1.** accessory, ancillary, appurtenant, auxiliary, conducive, contributory, secondary, subordinate, subsidiary, supplemental, useful **2.** abject, acquiescent, at one's beck and call *(Nonformal)*, compliant, deferential, fawning, menial, obeisant, obsequious, servile, slavish, submissive, sycophantic, toadying, truckling, under one's thumb *Antonyms:* disobedient, domineering, overbearing, rebellious, superior

subside *v.* **1.** abate, calm, decrease, diminish, dwindle, ease, ebb, lessen, let up, level off, melt away, moderate, quieten, recede, shrink, slacken, wane **2.** descend, drop, fall, sag, settle, sink

subsidiary *adj.* **1.** accessory, adjuvant, ancillary, appurtenant, auxiliary, backup, branch, lesser, minor, secondary, subject, subordinate, supplemental, supplementary, tributary *Antonyms:* central, head, key, primary, principal **2.** aiding, assisting, contributory, helpful, serviceable, useful – *n.* adjunct, affiliate, branch plant, department, division, sector, sister corporation, wing

subsidize *v.* aid, back, bankroll, capitalize, contribute, endow, finance, fund, grant, invest, promote, sponsor, stake, support, underwrite *Nonformal:* grubstake, put up the dough *or* funds

subsidy *n.* aid, alimony, allowance, assistance, bounty, bursary, contribution, endowment, fellowship, financial aid, gift, grant, help, investment, payment, pension, premium, remittance, remuneration, reward, scholarship, subsidization, subvention, support, tribute

subsist *v.* abide, be, breathe, cling to life, continue, cope, eke out *(Nonformal)*, endure, exist, get along *or* by, hang in *or* on *or* tough, last, live, make it, manage, persevere, remain, ride out, scrape by, stick to it, survive, sustain

subsistence *n.* **1.** aliment, basics, daily bread, basic earnings, income, keep, maintenance, means, minimum wage, money, necessities, nourishment, provisions, rations, resources, room and board, salary, staples, substance, support, sustenance, upkeep, wages **2.** circumstances, existence, life, livelihood, living, mortality, reality, survival, way

substance *n.* **1.** actuality, body, bulk, concreteness, density, force, mass, material, matter, physicality, reality, solidity, tangibility, texture, volume, weight **2.** ABCs, basics, building blocks, constituents, elements, essentials, nitty-gritty, objects, staples, stuff, thing **3.** import, importance, meaning, pith, power, purport, significance, strength **4.** basis, centre, core, crux, drift, essence, focus, gist, guts, heart, kernel, point, sense, soul, subject, tenor, theme, thrust, upshot, viscera **5.** assets, estate, fortune, inheritance, means, money, property, resources, riches, wealth

substantial *adj.* **1.** bulky, durable, firm, heavyweight, hefty, rugged, solid, sound, stable, steady, stout, strong, sturdy, well-built *Antonyms:* flimsy, jerrybuilt, weak **2.** concrete, corporeal, definable, marked, material, measurable, obvious, physical, real, tangible, touchable *Antonyms:* incorporeal, metaphysical, spiritual **3.** consequential, important, key, meaningful, momentous, serious, significant, valuable, weighty, worthwhile *Nonformal:* heavy, major league **4.** affluent, comfortable, easy, landed *(Historical)*, moneyed, prosperous, rich, wealthy, well-off, well-to-do *Nonformal:* loaded, stinking, well-heeled *Antonyms:* impoverished, needy, poor **5.** abundant, ample, considerable, generous, goodly, large, massive, plentiful, sizable, spacious, vast *Antonyms:* inadequate, insignificant, meagre

substantially *adv.* considerably, essentially, extensively, heavily, in essence *or* fact *or* reality, largely, mainly, materially, really

substantiate *v.* affirm, alibi, attest, authenticate, back up, bear out, confirm, corroborate, demonstrate, document, establish, justify, objectify, prove, ratify, realize, support, test, validate, verify *Antonyms:* confute, contradict, controvert, debunk

substitute *adj.* **1.** acting, alternative, another, back-up, makeshift, provisional, proxy, replacement, reserve, second, stopgap, surrogate, temporary **2.** artificial, counterfeit, dummy, ersatz, false, imitation, phoney *(Nonformal)*, pseudo, simulated, spurious *Antonyms:* authentic, genuine, original – *n.* agent, alternate, alternative, auxiliary, back-up, delegate, deputy, double, equivalent, fill-in, proxy, relief, stand-by, stand-in, sub, supply, surrogate, temporary, understudy *Nonformal:* benchwarmer, pinch-hitter – *v.* change, exchange, interchange, pinch hit, platoon, rearrange, relieve, replace, stand in for, swap, switch, take over, trade

substitution *n.* change, changeover, deputation, exchange, interchange, replacement, supplanting, subrogation, swap *(Nonformal)*, switch, trade

subterranean *adj.* **1.** buried, chthonian, deep, hypogeal, hypogenous, subterraneous, sunken, underground, underlying **2.** clandestine, cloaked, concealed, covert, dark, disguised, invisible, private, secret, shrouded, veiled *Antonyms:* detectable, exposed, obvious, open

subterfuge *n.* artifice, chicanery, deceit, deception, deviousness, dodge, duplicity, evasion, excuse, game-playing, guile, imposture, intrigue, machination, manoeuvre, ploy, pretense, pretext, ruse, scheme, stall, stratagem, trick, wile *Antonyms:* honesty, openness, straightforwardness

subtle *adj.* **1.** adroit, artful, crafty, cunning, designing, devious, foxy, guileful, indirect, insidious, Machiavellian, scheming, shrewd, sly, wily *Antonyms:* honest, guileless, open **2.** apt, astute, clever, deft, dexterous, diplomatic, expert, intelligent, keen, penetrating, perceptive, sharp, skilful, smart, wise **3.** careful, discriminating, exacting, fastidious, hairsplitting, judicious, meticulous, selective *Antonyms:* clumsy, slapdash **4.** abstruse, arcane, complex, complicated, deep, detailed, illusive, intricate, labyrinthine, obtuse, profound, perplexing, sophisticated *Antonyms:* blunt, direct, simple **5.** dainty, delicate, elusive, faint, fine, finespun, gentle, refined, tenuous, thin, understated

subtlety *n.* **1.** artfulness, artifice, chicanery, craft, cunning, deceit, guile, shrewdness, trickery, wiliness **2.** ability, acumen, artistry, cleverness, dexterity, expertise, finesse, ingenuity, intelligence, sagacity, skill, talent **3.** carefulness, consideration, discrimination, fastidiousness, precision, selectivity **4.** complexity, complication, convolution, elaboration, intricacy, involvement, profundity, sophistication *Antonyms:* ease, simplicity **5.** charm, delicacy, elegance, gentleness, grace, refinement *Antonyms:* awkwardness, boorishness, oafishness

subtract *v.* cut, decrease, deduct, delete, detract, diminish, discount, erase, lop, remove, take, take away *or* out, withdraw, withhold *Antonyms:* add, append, increase

suburbia *n.* bedroom community, commuter belt *or* shed, environs, exurb, exurbia, fringe, greenbelt, hamlet, neighbourhood, outlying area, outskirts, precinct, purlieu, residential area, suburban sprawl, suburbs *Nonformal:* burbs, crabgrass frontier *Antonyms:* city, downtown, urban core

subversion *n.* **1.** *coup d'état (French)*, crime against the state, dissent, insubordination, mutiny, overthrow, rebellion, revolution, sedition, treason, upheaval, violence **2.** corruption, crippling, destabilization, destruction, disruption, perversion, pollution, ruination, spoilage, undermining, vitiation, weakening

subversive *adj.* corruptive, counterproductive, destructive, deviant, incendiary, inflammatory, insurrectionary, insurgent, perversive, reactionary, rebel, rebellious, revolutionary, riotous, seditious, traitorous, treasonous, underground *Antonyms:* apolitical, harmless, supportive – *n.* anarchist, counter-revolutionary, dissident, fifth columnist, freedom fighter, guerrilla, incendiary, insurgent, insurrectionist, muckraker, mutineer, reactionary, rebel, revolutionary, saboteur, secessionist, seditionist, sympathizer, terrorist

subvert *v.* **1.** annihilate, capsize, crush, defeat, demolish, depress, destroy, eliminate, erase, invert, level, overthrow, raze, ruin, sabotage, topple, undermine, upset, violate, wreck **2.** corrupt, debase, pervert, poison, spoil, sully, vitiate, warp

subway *n.* **1.** A train *(Historical)*, Eidan *(Tokyo)*, Metro *(Montreal, Paris)*, public transit, rail line, train, transit, transit system, TTC *(Toronto) London:* tube, underground *New York:* BMT, IND, IRT **2.** passage, tunnel, underpass

sub-zero *adj.* arctic, cold, cutting, freezing, frigid, frosty, gelid, glacial, ice-cold, icy, numbing, polar, sharp, wintry *Antonyms:* boiling, hot, steaming, sultry, warm

succeed *v.* **1.** accomplish, achieve, advance, arrive, conquer, do well, earn, flourish, fulfill, gain, get ahead, graduate, make good *or* it, master, obtain, outdistance, outwit, overcome, pass, prevail, profit, progress, prosper, pull off, qualify, realize, reap, receive, rise, score, secure, surmount, thrive, triumph, vanquish, win *Nonformal:* ace, go places, make the grade *Antonyms:* collapse, fail, lose **2.** come next, ensue, follow, postdate, trail **3.** come after, displace, inherit, replace, supersede, supplant, take over *Antonyms:* come before, precede

succeeding *adj.* coming, consequent, ensuing, following, future, impending, later, next, subsequent, successive *Nonformal:* next in line for *or* off *or* up, on deck *Antonyms:* antecedent, earlier, former, previous, prior

success *n.* **1.** accomplishment, achievement, advance, arrival, ascendancy, attainment, benefit, consummation, *éclat (French)*, fruition, gain, hit, mastery, progress, realization, sensation, smash, strike, triumph, victory, win, winner *Nonformal:* bang, bellringer, knockout, flying colours, grand slam, killing, knockout, walkaway, walkover *Antonyms:* collapse, disaster, downfall, failure, misfortune **2.** eminence, fame, fortune, glamour, luxury, notoriety, profit, prosperity, riches, successfulness, wealth, windfall *Nonformal:* Easy Street, gravy train

successful *adj.* **1.** champion, conquering, crowned, triumphant, unbeaten, undefeated, victorious, winning *Antonyms:* failing, last-place, losing **2.** blooming, booming, flourishing, fruitful, lucrative, paying, profitable, prosperous, rewarding, rich, strong, thriving, wealthy, well-endowed, well-known, well-to-do *Nonformal:* fat, loaded *Antonyms:* bankrupt, dormant, down and out, dwindling, dying, poor, stagnant **3.** acclaimed, affluent, distinguished, elevated, eminent, famous, important, leading, moneyed, noteworthy, preeminent, vaunted, well-touted *Antonyms:* anonymous, little-known, taken for granted, unknown, unsung

succession *n.* **1.** consecution, continuation, progression, run **2.** chain, concatenation, series, sequence **3.** entail, inheritance, legacy **4.** children, descendants, dynasty, family, flesh and blood, issue, lineage, offspring, progeny, seed **5.** accession, assumption, promotion, rise

successive *adj.* **1.** consecutive, ensuing, following, next, sequential, serial, seriate, successional **2.** constant, continuous, nonstop, recurrent, regular, systematic, unbroken, uninterrupted *Antonyms:* desultory, erratic, sporatic

successor *n.* beneficiary, child, children, daughter, heir, heiress, next in line, progeny, recipient, replacement, sole survivor, son, substitute

succinct *adj.* bare bones *(Nonformal)*, boiled down, brief, compact, compendious, concise, condensed, laconic, pithy, short, summary, terse *Antonyms:* circuitous, discursive, prolix, verbose, wordy

succour *n.* aid, assistance, comfort, help, maintenance, relief, remedy, support, sustenance – *v.* aid, assist, befriend, comfort, encourage, foster, help, lend a hand, minister, nurse, nurture, palliate, protect, relieve, rescue, shield, support, sustain, take care of *Antonyms:* harm, hinder, injure, undermine

succulent *adj.* **1.** appetizing, delicious, juicy, luscious, lush, moist, mouthwatering, palatable, rich, tasty, yummy *(Nonformal)*

Antonyms: awful, bland, dry **2.** alluring, desirable, enticing, inviting, irresistible

succumb *v.* **1.** accede, buckle, capitulate, crumble, fold, give in *or* into *or* up, submit, surrender, yield *Nonformal:* cave, toss in the towel *Antonyms:* beat, conquer, master, overcome **2.** depart, die, expire, pass, pass away, perish *Nonformal:* buy it, croak, drop dead, give up the ghost, kick the bucket

suck *n.* complainer, coward, weakling, whiner *Maritimes:* sook, sooky baby *Nonformal:* big baby *or* wiener, chicken, crybaby, drag, drip, jellyfish, party pooper, sissy, sore loser, spineless wonder, stick-in-the-mud, suckhole, weenie, wet blanket, wimp – *v.* absorb, consume, drain, draw, drink, eat, imbibe, ingest, inhale, quaff, sip, take in, vacuum *Antonyms:* bite, chew, crunch

sucker *n.* dupe, fool, victim *Nonformal:* boob, butt, chump, fall guy, fish, mark, mug, patsy, pigeon, pushover, sap, schlemiel, sitting duck, stooge, target, tool, turkey

sudden *adj.* abrupt, accelerated, breakneck, expeditious, fast, hasty, headlong, hurried, immediate, impromptu, impulsive, precipitate, precipitous, premature, quick, rapid, rash, reckless, rushing, surprising, sweeping, swift, unanticipated, unexpected, unforeseen *Antonyms:* destined, dilatory, eventual, long-awaited, slow

suddenly *adv.* abruptly, all at once, fast, forthwith, hurriedly, quickly, rashly, surprisingly, swiftly, unexpectedly, unknowingly, without warning *Nonformal:* flash, lickety-split *Antonyms:* calmly, slowly, sluggishly

sue *v.* **1.** accuse, charge, claim, claim damages, contest, demand, file suit, indict, litigate, petition, proceed against, prosecute *Nonformal:* haul into court, law **2.** appeal, beg, beseech, entreat, implore, importune, persuade, petition, plead, request, solicit, supplicate, urge

suffer *v.* **1.** ache, agonize, ail, bleed, deteriorate, droop, flag, grieve, hurt, languish, sicken, smart, writhe *Antonyms:* flourish, prosper, thrive **2.** abide, bear, brook, endure, experience, feel, go through, receive, stand, stomach, submit, sustain, swallow, take, tolerate, undergo, yield **3.** allow, authorize, concede, countenance, indulge, permit, sanction, support

sufferance *n.* **1.** approval, consent, leave, liberty, licence, permission, sanction **2.** endurance, fortitude, patience, resilience, stamina, strength, tolerance *Antonyms:* frailty, weakness **3.** affliction, agony, anguish, distress, hardship, heartache, injury, misery, pain, suffering, torment, wretchedness

suffering *n.* **1.** adversity, affliction, agony, anguish, difficulty, discomfort, distress, gethsemane, hardship, heartache, horror, injury, melancholy, misery, misfortune, neurasthenia, pain, sadness, squalor, torment, torture, trouble, *Weltschmerz (German)*, woe, wretchedness **2.** endurance, forbearance, long-suffering, patience, resignation, stoicism, tolerance *Antonyms:* protest, rebellion, revolution

suffice *v.* answer, avail, content, do, meet the need *or* requirement, sate, satisfy, serve, suit

sufficient *adj.* **1.** acceptable, adequate, allowable, ample, enough, good, okay *(Nonformal)*, permissible, plenty, proportionate, satisfactory, suitable, tolerable *Antonyms:* deficient, inadequate, meagre, poor, scant **2.** able, capable, competent, effective, efficient, fit, proficient, qualified, serviceable

suffocate *v.* **1.** asphyxiate, burke, choke, garrote, smore *(Scottish)*, strangle, throttle **2.** check, curb, dampen, drown, extinguish, gag, prohibit, quell, repress, smother, snuff out, stifle, suppress

suffrage *n.* ballot, choice, democracy, enfranchisement, franchise, representation, voice, vote

suffuse *v.* bathe, cover, fill, flood, imbue, immerse, impregnate, infiltrate, infuse, overspread, permeate, saturate, soak, sop, spread, steep, transfuse, waterlog, wet

sugar *n.* carbohydrate, saccharin, sweetener *Groupings of sugar:* fructose, glucose, lactose *Kinds of sugar:* barley, beet, brown, cane, caramel, castor, confectioner's, cube, fruit, granulated, icing, maple, maltose, *panocha (Mexican)*, powdered, raw, spun – *v.* candy, coat, dulcify, glaze, sweeten

sugary *adj.* **1.** candied, honeyed, saccharine, sweet, sweetened, syrupy *Antonyms:* acidic, bitter, tart **2.** cloying, insincere, maudlin, mawkish, mushy, nostalgic, overdone, romantic, sentimental, sickeningly sweet *Antonyms:* cold, harsh, trenchant, unemotional

suggest *v.* **1.** advocate, bring up, introduce, opine, proffer, propose, put forward, recommend, submit, tender, volunteer **2.** allude, connote, convey, denote, evoke, hint, imply, indicate, infer, insinuate, intimate, point, refer, remind, represent, signify, symbolize

suggestion *n.* **1.** advice, exhortation, idea, impulse, invitation, notion, offering, opinion, plan, presentation, proffering, proposal, proposition, recommendation, reminder, scheme, solution, submission, submittal, tip **2.** allusion, clue, cue, hint, implication, indication, inkling, innuendo, insinuation, suspicion, symbol, thought, tinge, trace, undertone, whisper

suggestive *adj.* **1.** compelling, evocative, intriguing, provocative, stimulating, thought-provoking **2.** expressive, indicative, meaningful, pointed, pregnant, redolent, relevant, reminiscent, signifying, symbolic, weighty **3.** bawdy, erotic, immodest, lascivious, lecherous, lewd, obscene, off-colour, prurient, racy, ribald, risqué, salty, spicy, steamy *(Nonformal)*, titillating *Antonyms:* family-oriented, prim, proper

suicidal *adj.* **1.** dejected, depressed, desperate, despondent, dispirited, dissatisfied, low, melancholy, self-destructive, sick, so very tired *(Nonformal)*, troubled, unbalanced, world-weary *Antonyms:* buoyant, happy, satisfied **2.** chancy, dangerous, deadly, disastrous, extreme, fatal, hazardous, lethal, perilous, precarious, rash, reckless, risky, treacherous *Nonformal:* crazy, last ditch *Antonyms:* risk-free, safe, sound

suicide *n.* **1.** autocide, death, doctor-assisted death, felo de se, immolation, self-destruction, self-murder *Japanese:* hara-kiri, kamikaze, seppuku **2.** absurdity, craziness, foolishness, insanity, ludicrousness, madness

suit *n.* **1.** clothing, costume, dress, ensemble, garb, garment, get-up *(Nonformal)*, livery, outfit, threads, wardrobe *Common suits:* bodysuit, boiler, business, camouflage, casual, catsuit, double-breasted, formal, jump, leisure, lounge, one-piece, pantsuit, playsuit, rainsuit, scuba, seersucker, separates, single-breasted, ski, snowmobile, snowsuit, spacesuit, summer, Sunday, swimsuit, tails, three-piece, track, tuxedo, two-piece, work, zoot *Nonformal:* birthday, fox, penguin **2.** order, progression, selection, sequence, series, set, succession, train **3.** case, cause, lawsuit, legal action, litigation, proceeding, prosecution, trial **4.** address, appeal, application, asking, entreaty, imprecation, invocation, petition, plea, pursuit, request, woo – *v.* **1.** accord, agree, befit, conform, correspond, fill, fit, fulfill, harmonize, jibe, match, satisfy, square, suffice, tally **2.** amuse, entertain, flatter, gratify, please, satisfy, serve **3.** accommodate, adapt, adjust, fashion, modify, proportion, readjust, reconcile, tailor **4.** array, attire, clothe, costume, decorate, dress, equip, furnish, garb, prepare, ready, robe, vest *Antonyms:* change, disrobe, undress

suitable *adj.* acceptable, advisable, applicable, apposite, appropriate, apt, becoming, befitting, *comme il faut (French)*, commodious, compatible, convenient, correct, due, expedient, felicitous, fit, fitting, good, handy, happy, in keeping, just, meet, merited, nice, opportune, pertinent, politic, presentable, proper, propitious, reasonable, relevant, requisite, right, righteous, rightful, satisfactory, seemly, sufficient, suited, useful *Antonyms:* incongruous, malapropos, wrong

suite *n.* **1.** collection, composition, concatenation, line, progression, row, selection, sequel, sequence, series, set, string, succession, suit, train **2.** apartment, bridal *or* presidential *or* royal suite, penthouse, garret *Nonformal:* flat, pad, stoop **3.** attendants, crew, entourage, followers, groupies, hangers-on, henchmen, retainers, retinue, troupe

suitor *n.* **1.** admirer, beau, boyfriend, cavalier, cicisbeo, date, gallant, love interest, lover, paramour, supplicant, swain, white knight *(Nonformal)*, wooer **2.** accuser, aggrieved party, claimant, complainant, litigant, petitioner, plaintiff

sulk *n.* bad humour, depression, grimace, melancholy, frown, mood, moue, pout, snit, state, temper *Nonformal:* blue funk, condition, – *v.* brood, gloom, glower, gripe, grouse, huff, lower, moon, mope, pout, scowl

sulky *adj.* aloof, bitter, cantankerous, choleric, churlish, cranky, cross, disgruntled, huffy, ill-humoured, irascible, melancholy, miserable, moody, morose, petulant, resentful, unhappy, vexed *Antonyms:* amiable, cheerful, good-humoured, good-natured

sullen *adj.* **1.** bad-tempered, brooding, crabbed, crabby, cranky, cross, cynical, dour, farouche, fretful, glowering, glum, gruff, hostile, irritable, malign, mean, melancholy, moody, morose, neurasthenic, obstinate, ornery, peevish, pessimistic, petulant, resentful, silent, sombre, sour, surly, unforgiving, unsociable, upset *Nonformal:* beetle-browed, uptight *Antonyms:* amiable, bright, cheerful **2.** black, bleak, cheerless, cloudy, dark, dismal, dreary, funereal, gloomy, grey, overcast, tenebrous, threatening *Antonyms:* pleasant, sunny, warm **3.** lazy, listless, measured, phlegmatic, plodding, slack, slow, sluggish, torpid *Antonyms:* fast, rapid, swift

sully *v.* **1.** besmirch, cheapen, corrupt, debase, defile, disgrace, drag in the dirt *(Nonformal)*, hurt, muddy, pervert, savage, shame, spoil, taint, undermine, violate, vitiate *Antonyms:* enhance, honour, respect, uphold **2.** begrime, dirty, foul, mar, mark, smear, smudge, soil, stain, tarnish *Antonyms:* clean, polish, scrub

sultry *adj.* **1.** close, hot, humid, moist, muggy, oppressive, sticky, stifling, still, stuffy, sweltering *Antonyms:* cool, fresh, invigorating **2.** alluring, attractive, compelling, erotic, provocative, seductive, sensuous, sexy, titillating, voluptuous *Nonformal:* hot, steamy

sum *n.* **1.** bottom line, conclusion, consequence, outcome, product, reckoning, result, score, solution **2.** agglomerate, amount, bunch, collection, gathering, group, heap, mass, number, pile, quantity, selection, volume **3.** aggregate, all, body, bulk, entirety, grand *or* sum total, gross, integral, tally, totality, value, volume, the whole ball of wax *or* enchilada *or* megillah *or* shebang *or* schmear *(Nonformal)*, whole, worth **4.** essence, gist, heart, matter, nitty-gritty *(Nonformal)*, pith, substance, summary – *v.* **1.** abbreviate, abridge, condense, digest, encapsulate, outline, recapitulate, reiterate, summarize, sum up **2.** add up, calculate, compute, count, figure, figure out, reckon, total

summarily *adv.* **1.** briefly, concisely, cursorily, curtly, neatly, pointedly, succinctly **2.** expeditiously, fast, forthwith, immediately, instanter, instantly, peremptorily, precipitately, promptly, quickly, readily, speedily, swiftly, without delay *Antonyms:* dilatorily, slowly, unhurriedly

summarize *v.* abridge, abstract, boil *or* cut down, conclude, condense, digest, encapsulate, outline, pare, précis, prune, recap *(Nonformal)*, recapitulate, rehash, review, shorten, skim, sum up

summary *adj.* **1.** brief, compacted, compendious, concise, condensed, cursory, laconic, pithy, precise, succinct *Antonyms:* ponderous, slow, studied **2.** fast, flippant, extemporaneous, impromptu, informal, instant, offhand, quick, rapid, short, swift, unceremonious *Antonyms:* drawn-out, long, tedious – *n.* abbreviation, abridgment, abstract, analysis, brief, compendium, condensation, digest, extract, outline, précis, recapitulation, rehash, résumé, review, rundown, sketch, statement, summa, summing-up, synopsis, thumbnail *(Nonformal)*, wrap-up

summer *n.* *été (French)*, festival *or* growing season, halcyon days, summertide, summertime *Nonformal:* dog *or* lazy days – *v.* cottage, break, holiday, rest, vacation

summerhouse *n.* **1.** cabin, cottage, fishing camp, gazebo, getaway, lodge, mountain retreat, place up north *(Nonformal)*, second *or* vacation home **2.** arbour, belvedere, bower, conservatory, gazebo, greenhouse, pergola

summit *n.* **1.** acme, apex, apogee, climax, crest, crown, culmination, head, peak, pinnacle, point, prime, spire, tip, top, vertex, zenith *Antonyms:* abyss, base, bottom, nadir **2.** extent, height, limit, maximum, range, reach, total, utmost **3.** assembly, confabulation, conference, convergence, council, dialogue, discussion, exchange, forum, gathering, meeting, meeting of heads, round table, talks *Nonformal:* powwow, Pugwash

summon *v.* **1.** ask for, beckon, beep, bid, call, compel, invite, order, petition, procure, request, send for, signal, subpoena **2.** amass, assemble, collect, convene, corral, evoke, gather, marshal, muster, unite **3.** conjure up, convoke, invoke, raise, resurrect **4.** activate, arouse, awaken, embolden, encourage, excite, influence, inspire, kindle, motivate, move, pep up *(Nonformal)*, provoke, rally, stimulate

summons *n.* **1.** *azan (Muslim)*, bench warrant, command, decree, demand, dictate, instruction, mandate, notification, order, request, requirement, subpoena, ticket *(Nonformal)*, warrant **2.** alarm, alert, beacon, indication, sign, signal, warning

sumptuous *adj.* **1.** costly, dear, exorbitant, expensive, extortionate, high-priced *Nonformal:* pricey, steep, stiff *Antonyms:* bargain, cheap, cut-rate, frugal **2.** commodious, deluxe, elaborate, extravagant, fancy, five star, grand, lavish, luxurious, magnificent, opulent, plush, regal, rich, spectacular, splendid, stunning, top-of-the-line *Nonformal:* posh, ritzy, swanky, topnotch *Antonyms:* mean, seedy, shabby, wretched

sun *n.* **1.** daystar, energy source, fireball, Helios, life *or* light source, orb, orb of day, red ball, sol, star **2.** brilliance, daylight, energy, heat, light, radiance, radiant light, radiation, rays, solar energy, sunshine, ultraviolet light – *v.* bask, bronze, brown, fry *(Nonformal)*, soak in, sunbathe, suntan, tan *Nonformal:* catch some rays, fry

sunburned *adj.* blistered, burned, burnt, peeling, red, scalded, scorched, sunburnt *Nonformal:* done, fried, overcooked, toasted

sunder *v.* break, cleave, cut, detach, disconnect, disjoin, disunite, divide, divorce, hack, halve, part, rupture, separate, sever, uncouple *Antonyms:* attach, join, link, unite, wed

sundries *n.* etceteras, fine points, miscellaneous matter, notions, other stuff *(Nonformal)*

sundry *adj.* assorted, different, dissimilar, diverse, heterogeneous, manifold, many, miscellaneous, motley, multifarious, myriad, numerous, several, varied, various

sunken *adj.* **1.** buried, drowned, hidden, immersed, lost, submerged, underwater **2.** capsized, foundered, scuttled, sunk, torpedoed **3.** concave, cupped, depressed, dimpled, hollow, indented, inset, recessed *Antonyms:* bulging, convex, raised

sunless *adj.* **1.** black, cloudy, dark, grey, lightless, murky, overcast, pitch, shadowy, tenebrous, unlit *Antonyms:* bright, brilliant, sunny **2.** bleak, cheerless, depressing, disappointing, doleful, drab, dreary, gloomy, grim, melancholy, morbid, morose, mournful, sombre *Antonyms:* glad, happy, joyous

sunny *adj.* **1.** bright, brilliant, clear, cloudless, fine, light, luminous, radiant, shimmering, shining, summery, sunlit, unclouded *Antonyms:* cloudy, dark, overcast **2.** beaming, blithe, bonhomous, buoyant, cheery, chirpy, ebullient, genial, happy, joyful, lighthearted, Panglossian, optimistic, pleasant, rosy, smiling *Antonyms:* depressing, doleful, dreary, morbid

sunrise *n.* aurora, bright, cockcrow, dawn, dawning, daybreak, daylight, dayspring, morning, sun-up

sunset *n.* **1.** dusk, eve, evening, eventide, nightfall, nighttime, sundown, twilight **2.** close, decline, end, epilogue, finale, waning years

super *adj.* excellent, exceptional, fabulous, fantastic, first-rate, glorious, grand, great, incomparable, magnificent, marvellous, matchless, nonpareil, outstanding, peerless, remarkable, sensational, splendid, stupendous, superb, terrific, topnotch, unrivalled, wonderful *Nonformal:* cool, fantabulous, far-out, smashing, supercool, superduper, tickety-boo *Antonyms:* disappointing, inferior, unimpressive

superabundant *adj.* dizzying *(Nonformal)*, excessive, extra, extravagant, immoderate, inordinate, lavish, overabundant, overflowing, plethoric, profuse, superfluous, surplus, swarming, teeming *Antonyms:* deficient, insufficient, meagre, scarce, sparse

superb *adj.* **1.** beautiful, breathtaking, choice, divine, elevated, excellent, exquisite, fine, glorious, gorgeous, grand, imposing, impressive, letter-perfect, lofty, magnificent, majestic, marvellous, matchless, nonpareil, outstanding, peerless, resplendent, solid, splendid, striking, stunning, sublime, super, superlative, topnotch, unrivalled, wonderful **2.** costly, deluxe, elaborate, elegant, expensive, grandiose, high-priced, luxurious, rich *Nonformal:* out of sight, pricey, steep, unreal *Antonyms:* bargain, cheap, reasonable

supercilious *adj.* arrogant, condescending, contemptuous, disdainful, haughty, high and imperious, insolent, overbearing, patronizing, pompous, presumptuous, prideful, proud, self-important, snobbish, vainglorious *Nonformal:* hoity-toity, know-it-all, la-di-da, high and mighty, snooty, stuck-up, uppity *Antonyms:* humble, meek, modest, retiring, shy, unassuming

superficial *adj.* **1.** cosmetic, exterior, external, outward, surface *Antonyms:* inside, internal, visceral **2.** empty, facile, hollow, insincere, pasted-on *(Nonformal)*, shallow, skin-deep *Antonyms:* deep, pertinent, significant **3.** casual, cursory, half-assed *(Nonformal)*, hasty, insufficient, marginal, nodding, partial, passing, perfunctory, peripheral, sketchy, slapdash *Antonyms:* complete, comprehensive, detailed **4.** boring, common, jejune, ordinary, prosaic, stolid, tiring, vapid, wooden *Antonyms:* fresh, interesting **5.** barren, empty, fatuous, frivolous, inconsequential, insignificant, lightweight *(Nonformal)*, negligible, petty, trivial, unimportant, vacuous **6.** alleged, apparent, assumed, evident, ostensible, purported, seeming

superficially *adv.* casually, cosmetically, frivolously, hastily, insignificantly, lightly, outwardly, partially, partly, perfunctorily, quickly

superfluity *n.* **1.** deluge, excess, exorbitance, extravagance, flood, lavishness, overabundance, overflow, oversupply, plenitude, profuseness, slew *(Nonformal)*, superabundance, surfeit, surplus, wash *Antonyms:* dearth, deficiency, lack, scarcity, shortage **2.** duplication, fat, needlessness, redundancy, uselessness

superfluous *adj.* **1.** excessive, exorbitant, extravagant, extreme, immoderate, inordinate, outrageous, overflowing, profuse **2.** extra, leftover, remaining, spare, surplus **3.** *de trop (French)*, dispensable, expendable, gratuitous, irrelevant, needless, nonessential, redundant, uncalled-for, unnecessary, unneeded, unwanted, useless *Antonyms:* critical, crucial, necessary

superhuman *adj.* **1.** amazing, extraordinary, inexplicable, miraculous, otherworldly, paranormal, phenomenal, supermundane, supernatural, unaccountable, unearthly, unreal *Antonyms:* commonplace, mundane, natural, ordinary, terrestrial **2.** enormous, forceful, gargantuan, herculean, huge, immense, mammoth, monstrous, powerful, strong *Antonyms:* puny, weak **3.** brave, courageous, daring, death-defying, fearless, heroic, valiant

superintend *v.* administer, captain, command, control, direct, guide, handle, inspect, lead, look after, manage, oversee, regard, referee, regulate, rule, run, steer, supervise, watch *Antonyms:* disregard, ignore, neglect

superintendent *n.* **1.** administrator, boss, chief, conductor, controller, director, executive officer, foreman, governor, guardian, head, inspector, manager, overseer, proctor, supervisor, warden **2.** caretaker, cleaner, custodian, janitor, maintenance person, sexton, super *(Nonformal)*

superior *adj.* **1.** best, better, bigger, choice, elevated, estimable, exceeding, fitter, greater, higher, head, larger, leading, loftier, major, more advanced, notable, paramount, predominant, preeminent, preferable, preferred, premium, pukka, state-of-the-art, supreme, surpassing, top, towering, upper, worthy *Antonyms:* insignificant, least, secondary **2.** excellent, extraordinary, fabulous, fantastic, great, important, noticeable, outstanding, peerless, prominent, significant, sterling, ultimate, wonderful, worthwhile *Antonyms:* inferior, ordinary, poor, substandard **3.** authoritative, commanding, controlling, managing, presiding, ranking, regulating, ruling, supervising **4.** arrogant, disdainful, domineering, haughty, patronizing, self-important, supercilious *Nonformal:* bossy, stuck-up, uppity *Antonyms:* approachable, down-to-earth, friendly **5.** detached, disaffected, disinterested, impervious, indifferent, removed, unaffected, uncorrupted, unimpressable, unmovable, unshakable, untouchable – *n.* boss, chairman, chairperson, chief, commander, director, foreman, higher-up *(Nonformal)*, manager, master, office manager, official, president, principal, ruler, senior, superintendent, supervisor *Nonformal:* top banana *or* dog, head honcho, suit

superiority *n.* **1.** ascendancy, eminence, excellence, nobility, position, predominance, preeminence, prestige, prevalence, rank, supremacy *Antonyms:* inferiority, insignificance, lowliness **2.** authority, control, dominance, domination, influence, management, mastery, power, sway , upper hand *Antonyms:* dependency, insignificance, subordination

superlative *adj.* best, capital, choice, consummate, finest, first-class, greatest, highest, matchless, peerless, primary, principal, supreme, topmost, transcendent, ultimate, unexcelled, unparalleled, unrivalled, unsurpassed, ultimate, utmost *Nonformal:* ace, top drawer, tops – *n.* best, cream, elite, nonpareil, prime, principal, prize, quintessence, select

supernatural *adj.* **1.** abnormal, bizarre, crazy *(Nonformal)*, incomprehensible, irregular, strange, unaccountable, unbelievable, unknowable, unnatural, unusual, weird *Antonyms:* everyday, normal, standard **2.** dreamlike, eerie, ghostly, immaterial, incorporeal, haunted, metaphysical, mysterious, occult, phantom, phenomenal, preternatural, spectral, spooky, supermundane, surreal, surrealistic, unearthly *Antonyms:* comprehensible, mundane, terrestrial **3.** awesome, fabulous, fantastic, herculean, incredible, legendary, mythological, superhuman, storied, unbelievable **4.** blessed, celestial, divine, godly, heavenly, holy, infinite, miraculous, mystical, sacred, spiritual, sublime, transcendental

supersede *v.* **1.** displace, replace, substitute, succeed, supplant, take over, usurp **2.** annul, discard, oust, override, overrule, reject, remove, squash, suspend

superstition *n.* **1.** belief, impression, interpretation, notion, opinion **2.** deception, delusion, fallacy, fantasy, fear, foolishness, neurosis, phobia **3.** folklore, legend, lore, mythology, old wives' tale, tradition, urban legend

superstitious *adj.* **1.** fearful, nervous, neurotic, obsessive, phobic, skittish, timid **2.** credulous, deluded, foolish, gullible, ingenuous, irrational, silly, simple, unreasonable *Antonyms:* logical, rational, sensible

supervise *v.* administer, command, conduct, control, direct, govern, guide, handle, inspect, look after, manage, organize, oversee, preside over, referee, regulate, run, superintend, watch *Nonformal:* call the shots, ride herd on, run things *Antonyms:* ignore, neglect, overlook

supervision *n.* administration, babysitting, care, charge, control, direction, government, guidance, handling, instruction, intendance, management, operation, organization, stewardship, superintendence, superintendency, surveillance

supervisor *n.* administrator, boss, bull of the woods *(Pacific Coast)*, captain, caretaker, chief, conductor, counsellor, curator, custodian, director, executive, floor walker, foreperson, head, inspector, instructor, major-domo, manager, marshal, master, overseer, referee, seigneur *(Historical)*, seneschal, steward, superintendent, top dog *(Nonformal)*

supine *adj.* **1.** flat, horizontal, plane, prostrate, sprawled-out, spread, spread-eagled *Antonyms:* erect, upright, vertical **2.** apathetic, careless, dull, inactive, indifferent, indolent, inert, lethargic, listless, sluggish, spiritless, torpid *Antonyms:* energetic, enthusiastic, zealous

supplant *v.* cast out, change, bump *(Nonformal)*, displace, eject, exchange, expel, force out, oust, overthrow, replace, succeed, supersede, take over, topple, transfer, unseat, uproot, usurp *Antonyms:* back, keep, reinforce, strengthen

supple *adj.* **1.** bendable, ductile, elastic, flexible, limber, lissome, lithe, lithesome, malleable, mouldable, plastic, pliable, pliant, resilient, rubbery, springy, stretchy, svelte, willowy, wiry *Antonyms:* hard, rigid, stiff **2.** adaptable, all-round, clever, deft, many-sided, multi-purpose, multi-talented, multi-tasking *(Computer)*, quick, smart, versatile *Antonyms:* limited, one-dimensional, one-sided **3.** accommodating, acquiescent, compliant, fawning, grovelling, ingratiating, obliging, obsequious, servile, slavish, subservient, sycophantic, unctuous, yielding *Antonyms:* fractious, rebellious, rude

supplement *n.* addendum, addition, adjunct, aid, amendment, annex, appendix, aside, attachment, augmentation, bonus, codicil, complement, corollary, cost of living allowance, extension, extra, guide, insert, postscript, pullout, rider, sequel, special – *v.* add, augment, build up, buttress, complement, complete, contribute, enhance, enrich, extend, fill out *or* up, fortify, improve, increase, pad, reinforce, strengthen, supply *Nonformal:* beef *or* bump up

supplementary *adj.* accompanying, additional, added, associated, attached, attendant, auxiliary, bonus, complementary, contributory, extra, peripheral, secondary

supplicate *v.* appeal, ask, beg, beseech, bid, entreat, go down on bended knee, implore, importune, petition, plead, pray, press, request, seek, solicit, urge

supplication *n.* address, appeal, application, begging, beseechment, entreaty, imploration, imprecation, invocation, orison, petition, plea, pleading, prayer, request, solicitation, suit

supplies *n. pl.* accompaniments, accoutrements, equipment, étape, food, foodstuff, gear, goods, items, kit, material, necessities, outfit, provender, provisions, rations, raw materials, replenishment, rigging, stock, stores, stuff, victuals, vittles *(Nonformal)*

supply *adj.* backup, fill-in, stand-in, substitute – *n.* **1.** accumulation, amount, backlog, cache, hoard, inventory, load, lot, measure, number, quantity, reserve, size, source, stock, stockpile, store, sum **2.** equipment, goods, material, necessities, provisions, stash *(Nonformal)*, stuff, supplies, victuals **3.** assistance, coverage, disbursement, funds, maintenance, money, pay, support – *v.* **1.** cater, contribute, deliver, dispense, endow, equip, feed, fix *or* put up, furnish, give, grant, hand over, outfit, produce, provide, provision, purvey, put out, satisfy, stake, stock, store, transfer, yield *Nonformal:* kick in, pony up **2.** compensate, cover, fill in, offset, pinch-hit, relieve, replace, replenish, sub *or* substitute, take over

support *n.* **1.** aid, assistance, backing, funds, grant, money, patronage, sponsorship, subsidy **2.** alimony, allowance, care, finances, keep, livelihood, living, maintenance, means, money, necessities, payment, provision, remittance, resources, subsidy, subsistence, sustenance, upkeep, welfare **3.** advocacy, approval, assent, blessing, championship, furtherance **4.** comfort, consolation, encouragement, friendship, hand, help, lift, protection, relief, solace, succour *Antonyms:* difficulty, discouragement, trouble **5.** adherent, advocate, ally, angel, backer, benefactor, champion, cohort, comforter, confederate, defender, endorser, espouser, exponent, friend, helper, patron, patroness, promoter, proponent, sponsor, supporter, sustainer, sympathizer, upholder, well-wisher *Antonyms:* adversary, antagonist, enemy, foe **6.** anchor, back, base, beam, bed, block, brace, buttress, cable, collar, column, cornerstone, crutch, device, footing, fortification, foundation, girder, groundwork, guywire, hold, joist, line, pier, pillar, platform, pole, post, prop, rampart, reinforcement, rest, rod, shore, spine, stake, stanchion, stave, stay, substratum, substructure, timber, truss, underpinning, wall – *v.* **1.** bear, carry, cradle, hold, keep up, stand, sustain **2.** bolster, brace, buck up *(Nonformal)*, buttress, prop, reinforce, shore up, stay, strengthen *Antonyms:* damage, undermine, weaken **3.** accept, adopt, approve, authenticate, confirm, corroborate, prove, ratify, sanction, substantiate, validate, verify **4.** advocate, assist, back, beat the drum for, champion, commend, defend, embrace, endorse, espouse, forward, promote, stand behind, take up, uphold **5.** aid, finance, fund, help, maintain, preserve, subsidize, supply, sustain **6.** assuage, calm, cheer, comfort, console, ease, encourage, reassure, relieve, smooth, soothe, succour, sympathize *Antonyms:* ignore, neglect, upset **7.** abide, bear, brook, countenance, endure, face, handle, stand, stomach, submit, suffer, swallow, take, tolerate, undergo

supporter *n.* abettor, adherent, admirer, advocate, ally, backer, benefactor, champion, comforter, confederate, defender, devotee, endorser, exponent, fan, friend, helper, mainstay, partisan, patron, promoter, proponent, rock *(Nonformal)*, sponsor, standby, support, sympathizer, teammate, well-wisher *Antonyms:* enemy, opponent, rival

supportive *adj.* bolstering, caring, comforting, cooperative, encouraging, friendly, helpful, kind, protective, reassuring, stalwart, supporting, sympathetic, understanding *Antonyms:* discouraging, indifferent, unsympathetic

suppose *v.* accept, assume, calculate, conjecture, divine, dream, estimate, expect, fancy, figure, grant, guess, hypothesize, imagine, intuit, predicate, presume, presuppose, reckon, speculate, surmise, suspect, take, theorize, think, understand

supposed *adj.* a.k.a., alleged, assumed, believed, claimed, hypothetical, imaginary, presumed, professed, purported, putative, quote-unquote *(Nonformal)*, reputed, rumoured, said, so-called, supposable *Antonyms:* confirmed, established, proven, substantiated, verified

supposition *n.* assumption, attitude, belief, consideration, deduction, guess, hunch, hypothesis, idea, inference, notion, opinion, postulation, premise, presumption, presupposition, speculation, surmisal, theory, thesis, thought, view *Nonformal:* shot-in-the-dark, spin

suppress *v.* **1.** arrest, check, cut, end, halt, hinder, hold, prevent, restrain, stop *Antonyms:* encourage, foster, further **2.** abolish, ban, blacklist, censor, forbid, outlaw, prohibit, restrict, scotch, stymie *Antonyms:* allow, legalize, sanction **3.** bottle up, contain, cork, curb, hold back *or* down *or* in, inhibit, keep in, repress, stifle, swallow **4.** bury, camouflage, cloak, conceal, cover up, disguise, hide, keep secret, mask, muffle, muzzle, shush, silence, sit on, smother, veil, withhold *Antonyms:* disclose, expose, publish **5.** annihilate, conquer, crush, defeat, devastate, quell, subjugate, vanquish

suppression *n.* **1.** arrest, blocking, check, freeze, hindrance, prevention, restraint, stoppage **2.** block, bottling up, corking, hold, inhibition, repression, retention, stifling **3.** abolition, blockage, censorship, control, crackdown, disallowance, forbiddance, interdiction, prohibition, restriction **4.** concealment, conspiracy, cover-up, curtain, hush-up job, secrecy, subterfuge, veil **5.** annihilation, beating, conquest, defeat, destruction, devastation, extermination, wreckage

suppurate *v.* discharge, drain, excrete, fester, leak, ooze, pus, run, weep

supremacy *n.* **1.** authority, command, control, dominance, domination, dominion, power, preponderance, rule, sovereignty, superiority, sway, ultimacy, upper hand **2.**

ascendancy, excellence, greatness, inimitability, matchlessness, perfection, preeminence, superiority, superlativeness, transcendence, untouchability

supreme *adj.* **1.** commanding, controlling, dominant, governing, leading, managing, omnipotent, predominant, presiding, prevailing, regulating, reigning, ruling **2.** best, cardinal, chief, excellent, first, foremost, grandest, greatest, highest, incomparable, maximum, paramount, peerless, preeminent, prime, principal, superlative, top, transcendent, unparalleled, unsurpassed, ultimate, utmost *Antonyms:* last, least, lowest **3.** absolute, closing, conclusive, culminating, crowning, deciding, ending, final, last, terminal

sure *adj.* **1.** cocksure, confident, positive, secure, self-assured, self-confident, self-possessed, steadfast, staunch *Antonyms:* edgy, nervous, uncertain **2.** accurate, apodictic, certain, clear, convincing, decided, definite, evident, final, incontestable, incontrovertible, indisputable, indubitable, irrefutable, proven, solid, sound, unassailable, undeniable, undoubted, unequivocal, unquestionable *Nonformal:* airtight, watertight *Antonyms:* curious, problematic, questionable **3.** abiding, fast, firm, fixed, immutable, moored, rooted, set, stable, steady, unchanging, unfailing, unshakable, unwavering *Antonyms:* loose, rocky, shaky, wobbly **4.** assured, expected, fated, forthcoming, guaranteed, ineluctable, inescapable, inevitable, ironclad, unavoidable, unstoppable **5.** fail-safe, infallible, invincible, never-failing, risk-free, safe, trouble-free *Nonformal:* sure-fire, idiot-proof **6.** dependable, reliable, steady, trust *Antonyms:* precarious, unpredictable, up for grabs *(Nonformal)* **7.** deserving, fit, proper, suitable, worthy – *interj.* all right, indeed, most certainly, of course *Nonformal:* okay, right on, Roger, ten-four, wilco, yes, you bet

surely *adv.* absolutely, assuredly, by all means, certainly, completely, definitely, doubtlessly, emphatically, firmly, indubitably, inevitably, inexorably, infallibly, positively, truly, undoubtedly, unquestionably, without doubt

surety *n.* **1.** backer, co-signer, guarantor, insurer, sponsor, underwriter, warrantor **2.** assurance, bail, bond, collateral, deposit, down payment, guaranty, insurance, money, pledge, security, stake, warranty **3.** belief, certainty, certitude, confidence, conviction, doubtlessness, indisputability, secureness, sureness, unquestionableness *Antonyms:* ambiguity, indecision, irresolution, uncertainty

surf *n.* breaker, comber, foam, roller, swell, wave – *v.* **1.** catch a wave *(Nonformal)*, coast, crest, glide, ride, windsurf **2.** browse, cruise, examine, explore, peruse, research, scan, search, skim

surface *adj.* **1.** covering, exposed, exterior, external, facial, facing, outer, outlying, outside, outward, surficial, *Antonyms:* core, internal, inside **2.** apparent, cosmetic, skin-deep, superficial, visible – *n.* **1.** cladding, cover, covering, epidermis, exterior, façade, face, outside, periphery, plane, skin, top, veneer *Antonyms:* centre, guts, middle **2.** asphalt, Astroturf *(Trademark)*, clay, glebe, sod, tar, turf – *v.* **1.** asphalt, cover, laminate, paint, pave, resurface, tar, top, veneer **2.** appear, arise, come *or* crop *or* pop *or* show up, emerge, materialize, reveal oneself, rise

surfeit *n.* **1.** avalanche, deluge, excess, fullness, glut, outpouring, overabundance, overflow, overindulgence, overkill, overload, overplus, oversupply, plenitude, plethora, pouring, profusion, redundancy, repletion, saturation, superabundance, superfluity, surplus *Antonyms:* dearth, deficiency, insufficiency, lack, shortage **2.** bloating, cloyingness, fullness, gluttony, overindulgence, satiety, satisfaction *Nonformal:* bellyful, snootful – *v.* **1.** choke, drown, fill, flood, glut, inundate, overload, overwhelm, saturate, swamp **2.** clog, cram, glut, gorge, overeat, overdo, overindulge, pig out *(Nonformal)*, satiate, satisfy, stuff

surge *n.* **1.** burst, deluge, flood, flow, gushing, onset, outpouring, push, rush **2.** billow, breaker, comber, riser, roller, swell, undulation, wave – *v.* **1.** cascade, heave, roll, swell, undulate **2.** advance, crowd, drive, forge ahead, move, progress, push, rush, shove, steam, stream *Antonyms:* rest, slow, stop **3.** accelerate, climb, mount, rise, rocket, skyrocket, soar, tower

surgery *n.* operation, medical procedure, surgical intervention *or* treatment

surly *adj.* bearish, boorish, brusque, churlish, crabbed, crabby, cross, crusty, curmudgeonly, discourteous, dour, foul, fractious, glum, grouchy, gruff, ill-mannered, ill-natured, irritable, miserable, morose, obstinate, rude, severe, sour, stern, sulky, sullen, testy, uncivil, ungracious *Antonyms:* agreeable, cheerful, pleasant

surmise *n.* concept, conclusion, deduction, explanation, guess, hypothesis, idea, inference, opinion, possibility, supposition, suspicion, theory, thought – *v.* assume, conclude, conjecture, consider, deduce, fancy, guess, hypothesize, imagine, infer, opine, presume, reckon, regard, speculate, suppose, suspect, theorize, think

surmount *v.* **1.** beat, conquer, defeat, master, outclass, outshine, overcome, prevail, rise above, subdue, succeed, survive, withstand *Antonyms:* give in, surrender, yield **2.** bestride, climb, cross, get *or* scramble over, mount, scale

surmountable *adj.* accessible, achievable, attainable, beatable, conquerable, doable, feasible, negotiable, realizable *Antonyms:* invincible, unconquerable, undefeatable

surpass *v.* beat, best, better, cap, eclipse, exceed, excel, outclass, outdo, outmatch, outpace, outperform, outrival, outshine, outstrip, pass, smash *(Nonformal)*, surmount, top, transcend *Antonyms:* choke, fail, fumble

surpassing *adj.* exceeding, exceptional, extraordinary, incomparable, matchless, outstanding, peerless, phenomenal, rare, superior, supreme, transcendent, ultimate, unmatched, unparalleled, unrivalled, unsurpassed *Antonyms:* bad, everyday, poor

surplus *adj. de trop (French)*, excess, extra, leftover, redundant, remaining, residual, spare, superfluous, supernumerary, unused *Antonyms:* deficient, inadequate, scarce – *n.* balance, excess, extra, overabundance, overflow, overplus, overrun, overstock, oversupply, plethora, plus, remainder, remains, residue, superabundance, surfeit, superfluity *Antonyms:* dearth, deficit, lack, paucity, shortage

surprise *adj.* flying *(Nonformal)*, spontaneous, sudden, unannounced, unexpected, unforeseen, unheralded, unpredicted – *n.* **1.** amazement, astonishment, bewilderment, incredulity, stupefaction, wonder **2.** eye-opener, shock, start, upset *Nonformal:* bombshell, dark horse, jolt, kick in the head, sleeper, thunderbolt, whammy **3.** door number three *(Nonformal)*, gift, mystery, present, prize, secret – *v.* **1.** amaze, astonish, astound, awe, bewilder, confound, confuse, daze, dazzle, discomfit, disconcert, dumfound, electrify, flabbergast, jar, jolt, overwhelm, perplex, petrify, rattle, rock, shake up, shock, stagger, startle, strike dumb, stun, stupefy, unsettle, upset *Nonformal:* blow away, bowl over, floor **2.** ambush, attack, blitz, bushwhack, catch napping *or* off guard, jump, waylay

surprised *adj.* awestruck, bewildered, dazed, discomfited, embarrassed, fazed, flabbergasted, numb, open-mouthed, shaking, shocked, speechless, startled, stunned, wonder-struck, upset *Nonformal:* floored, in a tizzy *Antonyms:* calm, collected, composed

surprising *adj.* amazing, anomalous, astonishing, astounding, bewildering, bizarre, discombobulating *(Nonformal)*, disturbing, electrifying, extraordinary, incredible, marvellous, remarkable, shocking, staggering, startling, strange, stunning, unaccountable, uncommon, unexpected, unusual, wonderful, upsetting *Antonyms:* everyday, routine, usual

surreal *adj.* **1.** baffling, bizarre, enigmatic, fantastic, freakish, grotesque, Kafkaesque, marvellous, odd, peculiar, perplexing, puzzling, queer, remarkable, strange, uncommon, unconventional, unexpected, unreal, unusual, weird, wonderful *Antonyms:* conventional, normal, ordinary **2.** dissociative, dreamlike, illogical, illusory, incongruous, irrational, oneiric, phantasmagoric, preternatural, supernatural, surrealistic *Antonyms:* connected, rational, sensible

surrender *n.* abandonment, abdication, acquiescence, appeasement, capitulation, cessation, delivery, quitting, release, relinquishment, resignation, submission, transfer, yielding – *v.* **1.** abandon, cede, drop, give up, leave, let go, part with, quit, release, relinquish, resign, waive, yield *Antonyms:* beard, confront, fight **2.** deliver, give, hand over, submit, transfer *Antonyms:* hold, keep, retain **3.** abdicate, consign, relegate, renounce, retire, stand *or* step down, vacate **4.** capitulate, cave in, give in *or* way, roll over *Nonformal:* say uncle, throw in the towel

surreptitious *adj.* artful, backstair *(Nonformal)*, clandestine, covert, crafty, discreet, fraudulent, furtive, hidden, hush-hush, private, secret, secretive, skulking, slinking, sly, sneaky, stealthy, *sub rosa (Latin)*, undercover, underhanded, under wraps, veiled *Antonyms:* aboveboard, blatant, conspicuous, genuine, honest, obvious, open, overt

surrogate *n.* agent, alternate, backup, delegate, double, fill-in, pinch-hitter *(Nonformal)*, proxy, recourse, representative, stand-in, substitute, understudy *Commonly misused:* **advocate**

surround *v.* **1.** border, bound, circle, circumscribe, circumvent, close around *or* in, compass, confine, edge, encircle, enclose, encompass, envelop, environ, fence *or* hem *or* shut in, fringe, gird, girdle, limit, loop, margin, outline, rim, ring, round, skirt, verge **2.** beleaguer, beset, besiege, blockade, box in, cut off, invest

surrounding *adj.* adjacent, adjoining, attached, bordering, encircling, enclosing, encompassing, enfolding, enveloping, girdling, nearby, neighbouring, regional, vicinal *Antonyms:* distant, faraway, foreign

surroundings *n. pl.* ambience, environment, habitat, locale, location, milieu, *mise en scène (French)*, neighbourhood, outskirts, region, setting, stomping ground *(Nonformal)*, zone

surveillance *n.* **1.** detection, examination, following, inspection, observation, pursuit, scrutiny, spying, stakeout, survey, tail, vigilance, watch **2.** care, charge, control, direction, management, supervision

survey *n.* **1.** analysis, appraisal, audit, check, consideration, critique, examination, exploration, inquiry, inspection, investigation, perusal, scrutiny, search, sifting, surveillance **2.** interview, market analysis, poll, query, questioning, quiz, sample, test **3.** book, compendium, discussion, essay, history, monolith, narrative, overview, paper, précis, review, sketch, study, syllabus, synthesis, text, tome, treatise – *v.* **1.** analyze, appraise, assess, consider, contemplate, examine, investigate, look over, research, review, scrutinize, size up **2.** canvas, interrogate, interview, poll, query, question, quiz **3.** check out, inspect, look, observe, peer, regard, scan, see, study, view, watch *Nonformal:* eyeball, scope *or* scope out **4.** chain *or* mark off, delimit, delineate, determine, estimate, gauge, map out, measure, triangulate

survive *v.* **1.** breathe, continue, exist, keep, live, live and breathe, subsist, sustain *Antonyms:* die, end, finish, pass away **2.** abide, bear, beard, brook, carry on, endure, get along, handle, last, make out, persevere, persist, suffer, tolerate, weather, withstand *Antonyms:* give up, surrender, yield **3.** outlast, outlive, outwear, pull through, recover, remain, rise *Antonyms:* decline, deteriorate, sink, worsen

surviving *adj.* abiding, breathing, clinging, continuing, enduring, lasting, living, persisting, remaining, standing, subsisting, suffering

susceptibility *n.* **1.** liability, openness, predisposition, proclivity, proneness, propensity, sensitivity, softness, tendency, vulnerability, weakness *Antonyms:* imperviousness, insensibility, insensitiveness **2.** amenability, impressionability, influenceability, malleability, plasticity, pliancy, receptiveness, suggestibility **3.** credulity, deceiveability, dupability, naiveté, simpleness, simplicity, stupidity

susceptible *adj.* **1.** at risk, defenceless, exposed, liable, open, prone, vulnerable, wide open *Antonyms:* immune, invulnerable, protected **2.** easily affected, impressionable, influenceable, movable, persuadable, plastic, pliant, receptive, responsive, sensitive, suggestible, swayable, touchable **3.** artless, callow, childlike, credulous, easy *(Nonformal)*, fresh, gullible, ignorant, innocent, naive, natural, trusting, unsophisticated, unsuspecting *Antonyms:* hardened, jaded, seasoned

suspect *adj.* debatable, discreditable, doubtful, dubious, fishy *(Nonformal)*, improbable, incredible, problematic, questionable, shaky, suspicious, unbelievable, uncertain, unclear, unlikely *Antonyms:* proven, reliable, trustworthy – *n.* accused, defendant, likely one, possibility – *v.* **1.** assume, believe, conjecture, consider, expect, feel, gather, guess, hold, imagine, ponder, presume, reckon, speculate, suppose, surmise, think, understand, wonder **2.** challenge, disbelieve, distrust, doubt, fear, mistrust, question

suspense *n.* **1.** anticipation, anxiety, apprehension, disquiet, dread, edginess, excitement, expectation, fear, nervousness, stress, tension **2.** cliff-hanger *(Nonformal)*, expectancy, pendency, suspension, waiting

suspend *v.* **1.** bar, bench, bounce, debar, dismiss, eject, exclude, expel, gate, kick out *(Nonformal)*, lay off, let go, oust, reject, remove **2.** arrest, cease, check, freeze, halt, hold, prevent, stop, withhold *Antonyms:* continue, extend, maintain **3.** adjourn, break, call off, cut short, discontinue, postpone, recess **4.** commute, discharge, pretermit, prorogue, remit, waive **5.** dangle, droop, flag, float, hang, hover, swing, wave

suspended *adj.* **1.** dangling, drooping, flagging, floating, hanging, hovering, in the air *(Nonformal)*, looming, pendulous, pensile, swinging, waving **2.** adjourned, arrested, checked, deferred, discontinued, halted, moth-balled, paused, postponed, recessed, shelved, stopped **3.** blackballed *(Nonformal)*, banished, barred, excluded, exiled, expelled, ousted, removed, stripped of rank, terminated

suspenders *n. pl.* braces, gaitors, galluses, straps

suspension *n.* **1.** abeyance, adjournment, break, breather, cessation, deferment, delay, discontinuance, dormancy, downtime, halt, inactivity, intermission, interruption, interval, letup, moratorium, pause, postponement, recess, remission, respite, stoppage, surcease, time out **2.** drooping, hanging, looming, pendency, pensility, suspense, wavering **3.** discharge, dismissal, elimination, eviction, expulsion, firing, ousting, removal

suspicion *n.* **1.** concern, disbelief, distrust, doubt, dubiety, incredulity, indecision, misgivings, qualm, scepticism, uncertainty **2.** awareness, belief, feeling, hunch, idea, intuition, notion, sensation, tingling **3.** dash, flavour, hint, indication, pinch, shade, soupçon, tinge, touch, whisper

suspicious *adj.* **1.** apprehensive, cagey, careful, cautious, distrustful, incredulous, leery, mistrustful, questioning, quizzical, sceptical, suspect, unbelieving, unsure, uptight *(Nonformal)*, wary, watchful, wondering *Antonyms:* gullible, open, trusting **2.** borderline, debatable, doubtful, dubious, far-fetched, fishy *(Nonformal)*, funny, irregular, peculiar, problematic, queer, questionable, shaky, specious, suspect, unusual *Antonyms:* cogent, forceful, true

sustain *v.* **1.** abide, bear, brook, endure, persevere, stomach, take, tolerate, withstand *Antonyms:* quit, surrender, yield **2.** beard, encounter, experience, face, feel, realize, suffer, undergo *Antonyms:* avoid, dodge, flee **3.** feed, nourish, nurse, nurture, preserve, save, strengthen **4.** aid, bolster, buoy, cheer, comfort, console, gladden, hearten, help, reassure, succour *Antonyms:* sadden, upset **5.** advocate, back, bolster, brace, buttress, champion, defend, foster, maintain, promote, preserve, strengthen, support, uphold *Antonyms:* weaken, undermine **6.** authenticate, certify, confirm, corroborate, endorse, ratify, sanction, substantiate, validate, vindicate

sustenance *n.* **1.** bread, edibles, food, groceries, necessities, nourishment, nutrition, provisions, rations, refreshment, staples, victuals, water, wine **2.** competence, keep, livelihood, maintenance, means, remittance, subsistence, support, welfare, wherewithal

svelte *adj.* elegant, graceful, lean, lissome, lithe, slender, slim, slinky, sylphlike, supple, thin, willowy *Antonyms:* chubby, plump, stocky

swaddle *v.* bandage, bind, bundle, clothe, cover, diaper, drape, envelop, enwrap, straitjacket, swathe, wrap

swagger *n.* affectation, arrogance, boastfulness, boasting, braggadocio, grandstanding, fanfaronade, loftiness, machismo, ostentation – *v.* **1.** bluster, boast, brag, brandish, flourish, gloat, grandstand, hector, show off, swashbuckle, vaunt *Nonformal:* hot dog, puff up **2.** lord, parade, peacock, prance, preen, saunter, strut *Nonformal:* sashay, style

swaggerer *n.* blusterer, boaster, braggart, grandstander, maw-mouth *(Newfoundland)*, peacock, show-off *Nonformal:* blowhard, cockalorum, hot dog, loudmouth, pompous ass, windbag

swallow *n.* belt, dram, drink, mouthful, nip, quaff, taste – *v.* **1.** absorb, consume, devour, down, drink, eat, gulp, imbibe, pack *or* put away, quaff, sip, slurp, soak *or* sop up, swig, swill, wash down **2.** bear, endure, stomach, suffer, take, tolerate **3.** accept, believe, buy, fall for, lap up *(Nonformal)*, trust

swamp *n.* bog, bogan, bottoms, everglade, fen, glade, marsh, marshland, mire, moor, morass, mud, muskeg, peat bog, quagmire, slough, swampland, wetland – *v.* beset, besiege, bury, crowd, deluge, drench, drown, engulf, flood, inundate, overburden, overflow, overwhelm, saturate, submerge, submerse, suffocate, wash, waterlog

swampy *adj.* boggy, fenny, marshy, moory, mosquito-infested, mucky, muddy, mushy, quaggy, sludgy, soaking, sponge-like, squashy, waterlogged, watery, wet

swanky *adj.* classy, deluxe, exclusive, expensive, fancy, fashionable, flamboyant, flashy, glamorous, grand, lavish, luxurious, ostentatious, plush, pretentious, rich, sharp, showy, smart, snappy, stylish, sumptuous, trendy *Nonformal:* chic, chichi, posh, ritzy, splashy, swank, swish, tony *Antonyms:* discreet, humble, modest, unassuming, unpretentious

swap *v.* bandy, bargain, barter, dicker, exchange, give and take, interchange, peddle, substitute, switch, trade, traffic

swarm *n.* army, bevy, concourse, covey, crowd, crush, drove, flock, herd, horde, host, mass, mob, multitude, myriad, pack, press, push, school, scrum, throng, troop – *v.* abound, cluster, congregate, crowd, flock, flow, gather, jam, mass, multiply, stream

swarthy *adj.* brown, dark, dark-complexioned *or* -hued *or* -skinned, dusky, tan, olive, sunburned, sun-kissed *(Nonformal)*, swart, tanned, tawny

swashbuckling *adj.* adventurous, audacious, bold, bodacious *(Nonformal)*, daring, dashing, dauntless, devil-may-care, fearless, flamboyant, gallant, mettlesome, reckless, roisterous, spirited, swaggering, valiant, venturesome *Antonyms:* fainthearted, sheepish, timid

swat *n.* blow, buffet, clout, punch, smack *Nonformal:* belt, sallywinder – *v.* beat, belt, box, buffet, clobber, clout, cuff, hit, knock, punch, slap, slug, smack, smash, strike, swipe, wallop, whack, whap

sway *n.* ascendancy, authority, clout, command, control, dominion, force, influence, jurisdiction, mastery, might, power, predominance, reach, reign, rule, scope – *v.* **1.** lurch, oscillate, pulsate, rock, roll, stagger, swagger, swing, undulate, vibrate, wave, waver, weave, wobble **2.** angle, bend, careen, incline, keel, lean, list, slope, tilt, veer **3.** affect, alter, bias, brainwash, change, crack *(Nonformal)*, direct, guide, impact *or* work on, impress, induce, influence, inspire, persuade, sell, touch, win over *Antonyms:* disgust, offend, turn off

swear *v.* **1.** blaspheme, curse, damn, execrate, imprecate, profane *Nonformal:* cuss, talk dirty **2.** covenant, guarantee, pledge, plight, promise, vouch, vow, warrant **3.** affirm, assert, attest, avow, declare, depose, give witness, maintain, state, testify

swearing *n.* blasphemy, cursing, dirty language, execration, expletive, foul *or* indecent language, four-letter words, profanity, swear words *Nonformal:* blue streak, cussing

sweat *n.* **1.** body fluids, droplets, moisture, perspiration, sudor **2.** agony, anxiety, distress, impatience, nervousness, stress, suspense, torment, torture, trepidation, trouble, unease, worry **3.** drudgery, effort, exertion, grind, labour, moil, slavery, toil, travail, work – *v.* **1.** lather, perspire, swelter **2.** bleed, drip, eject, exude, leak, ooze, pour, run, secrete, seep, stream, trickle **3.** drudge, endeavour, essay, exert oneself, grind, labour, slave, strain, struggle, toil, work **4.** agonize, chafe, despair, fear, fret, fuss, stew, sweat bullets *(Nonformal)*, worry, writhe **5.** abide, bear, brook, endure, stand, stomach, suffer, take, tolerate

sweater *n.* bolero, cardigan, crewneck, fair isle, guernsey, hockey jersey, pull-on, pullover, slipover, V-neck, turtleneck, sweatshirt

sweaty *adj.* bathed, clammy, damp, drenched, drippy, feverish, glowing, hot, moist, perspiring, soaked, sticky, stinky, wet *Antonyms:* cold, dry

sweep *n.* **1.** gesture, motion, move, movement, pass, stroke **2.** cleansing, elimination, ejection, purge, removal **3.** area, compass, extent, field, gamut, horizon, ken, measure, panorama, purview, range, reach, scope, span, spectrum, stretch, string **4.** arc, bend, bow, crook, curve, horseshoe, panhandle, round, swerve, swing – *v.* **1.** broom, brush *or* brush off, clean, clear *or* clear up, collect, dust, mop, remove, scrub, tidy, vacuum, whisk **2.** careen, flit, fly, glance, glide, graze, pass over, sail, skim, touch **3.** carry, drive, force, move, propel, push, ram, thrust

sweeping *adj.* across-the-board, all-around, all-embracing, all-encompassing, all-inclusive, all-out, blanket, broad, catholic, complete, comprehensive, entire, exhaustive, extensive, full, general, global, inclusive, indiscriminate, overall, radical, thorough, thoroughgoing, total, unquantified, vast, wholesale, wide *or* wide-ranging *Nonformal:* out-and-out, wall-to-wall, whole-hog *Antonyms:* focused, limited, narrow, restricted

sweet *adj.* **1.** candied, candy-coated, cloying, delicious, honeyed, luscious, saccharine, sugar-coated, sugary, syrupy, toothsome *Antonyms:* bitter, sharp, sour, tart **2.** acceptable, agreeable, appealing, attractive, delightful, enjoyable, happy, pleasant, pleasing, satisfying *Antonyms:* dreadful, horrible, sickening **3.** beloved, cherished, darling, dear, dearest, good, honourable, loved, trustworthy **4.** affectionate, amiable, bonhomous, charming, companionable, considerate, endearing, engaging, friendly, generous, gentle, good-humoured, good-natured, kind, lovable, mild, patient, sweet-tempered, tender, treasured, unselfish, winning, winsome *Antonyms:* cantankerous, cynical, mean **5.** dulcet, euphonious, harmonious, mellifluous, mellow, melodic, melodious, musical, rich, rotund, silver-tongued, silvery, smooth, soft, sonorous, soothing, sweet-sounding, tuneful *Antonyms:* cacophonous, discordant, grating **6.** ambrosial, aromatic, balmy, clean, fragrant, fresh, new, nice-smelling, perfumed, pure, redolent, savoury, scented, spicy, sweet-smelling, wholesome *Antonyms:* loathsome, nasty, rank, stinking – *n.* **1.** bonbon, candy, candy kiss, chocolate, confection, confectionery, delight, dessert, honey, jam, maple candy, maple sugar, pastry, preserve, snack, sugar, syrup, tart **2.** darling, dear, loved one, lover, *ma coeur (French)*, sweetheart *Nonformal:* baby, gal, guy, honeybun, main squeeze, lovie, sweetie

sweeten *v.* **1.** candy, candy-coat, honey, powder, sugar, sugar-coat *Antonyms:* pepper, salt, spice **2.** alleviate, appease, assuage, conciliate, mitigate, mollify, pacify, placate, solace, soften up, soothe *Antonyms:* anger, bother, irritate, upset

sweetener *n.* **1.** sugar substitute *Kinds of sweetener:* artificial, aspartame, casareep, corn syrup, fructose, honey, maple syrup, molasses, saccharin, sorbitol, sugar, treacle *Trademark:* Nutrasweet, Sweet and Low **2.** bribe, carrot, gratuity, incentive, inducement, lure, reward

sweetheart *n.* admirer, beau, beloved, boy, boyfriend, darling, girl, girlfriend, happiness, honey, honeybun, inamorata, lady love, love, lover, paramour, partner, significant other, soulmate, swain, sweet, valentine *Nonformal:* armpiece, baby, old lady *or* man, one and only, squeeze, sugar, sweetie, toots

swell *adj.* deluxe, excellent, fantastic, fine, first, grand, great, keen, lovely, splendid, super, terrific, wonderful *Nonformal:* dreamy, spiffy, wicked, wowy-zowy – *n.* **1.** amplification, augmentation, bloating, broadening, crescendo, dilation, distension, enlargement, expansion, growth, increase, inflation, welling, widening **2.** bulge, bump, growth, lump, nodule, outgrowth, prominence, protrusion, protuberance, tuberosity **3.** billow, breaker, rise, roller, sea, surf, surge, undulation, uprise, wave **4.** dandy, exquisite, fob, marcaroni, nonpareil *Nonformal:* gentleman, toff – *v.* **1.** balloon, bloat, bulge, dilate, distend, enlarge, expand, extend, fatten, inflate, plump, protrude, puff up *Antonyms:* decrease, deflate, lessen, reduce, shrink **2.** accumulate, amplify, billow, grow, heighten, increase, rise, surge, well up **3.** boast, brag, crow, grandstand, hotdog *(Nonformal)*, preen, puff, show off, strut, swagger

swelling *n.* **1.** abscess, blister, boil, bruise, bulge, bump, bunion, chilblain, contusion, carbuncle, inflammation, injury, lesion, lump, nodule, pimple, protuberance, puffiness, sore, tumour, weal, welt **2.** augmentation, dilation, distension, enlargement, expansion, growth, increase, inflation, rise *Antonyms:* decrease, shrinkage, slump

sweltering *adj.* baking, broiling, burning, close, fiery, hot, humid, oppressive, overpowering, scalding, scorching, sizzling, stewing, sticky, stifling, stuffy, sultry, torrid *Antonyms:* arctic, cold, frigid

swerve *v.* bend, deflect, depart, deviate, dip, diverge, lurch, move, sheer, shift, sideslip, sidestep, skew, skid, slue, stray, swing, tack, train off, turn aside, veer, wander, wind

swift *adj.* **1.** abrupt, alacritous, barrelling *(Nonformal)*, breakneck, expeditious, express, fleet, fleet-footed, hasty, headlong, hurried, precipitate, quick, rapid, snappy, speedy, supersonic, winged *Antonyms:* plodding, ponderous, slow, sluggish **2.** alert, eager, efficient, prompt, punctual, ready, responsive, smart, timely, vigilant *Antonyms:* dilatory, slack, tardy **3.** ephemeral, evanescent, fleeting, mercurial, momentary, passing, short-lived, sudden, temporary, transitory *Antonyms:* endless, timeless

swiftly *adv.* **1.** apace, double-time, flat-out, fleetly, full tilt, hastily, hurriedly, immediately, posthaste, promptly, quick, quickly, rapidly, speedily, stat **2.** suddenly, unexpectedly, unforeseeably, unpredictably, without warning

swiftness *n.* acceleration, alacrity, celerity, dispatch, efficiency, fastness, fleetness, haste, promptitude, quickness, rapidity, readiness, responsiveness, speed

swill *n.* dregs, garbage, hogwash, leavings, mash, mush, refuse, scourings, scraps, slop, waste – *v.* drain, drink, gulp, guzzle, imbibe, quaff, swallow *Nonformal:* belt down, chugalug, knock back, scream, slurp, swig, tank up

swim *n.* dip, dunk, plunge, refresher, wash – *v.* bathe, float, glide, paddle, race, skinny-dip, submerge, wade *Common swim strokes:* backstroke, breaststroke, butterfly, dog paddle, freestyle, front crawl, sidestroke

swindle *n.* blackmail, bunco, cheating, chicanery, chouse, con *or* confidence trick, cozenage, deceit, deception, double-dealing, extortion, fake, frame-up, fraud, hoax, knavery, racket, roguery, shady deal, subterfuge, trickery *Nonformal:* dirty dealings *or* pool, fast one, grift, heist, hustle, monkey business, rip-off, scam, shakedown, sham, sharp practice, sting – *v.* bilk, deceive, cheat, cozen, defraud, double cross, dupe, extort, fleece, fool, frame, gouge, hoodwink, overcharge, rook, steal, trick, victimize *Nonformal:* bamboozle, chisel, con, hornswoggle, hose, screw, set up, shaft, soak, stiff, sting, sucker

swindler *n.* absconder, bunco artist, charlatan, cheat, cheater, chouse, confidence trickster, con artist, counterfeiter, crook, deceiver, defrauder, dodger, double-dealer, forger, fraud, impostor, knave, mountebank, operator, rascal, rogue, scoundrel, shark, sharper, thief, trickster *Nonformal:* chiseller, grifter, highwinder

swine *n.* **1.** boar, domestic animal, hog, peccary, pig, piglet, porker, sow **2.** brute, reprobate, savage, scoundrel, sleeveen *(Newfoundland)*, vermin, villain *Nonformal:* dog, creep, louse, lowlife, miserable *or* vicious bastard, rat, rotter, sleaze, sleazeball, slimeball, slime bucket, stinker

swing *n.* **1.** ebb and flow, fluctuation, motion, movement, oscillation, pendulation, rocking, swaying, undulation, waggle **2.** beat, cadence, flow, grace, lilt, meter, rhythm, style, time **3.** compass, distance, extent, length, limit, margin, period, range, reach, room, run, scope, space, span, streak, sweep **4.** attitude, condition, current, humour, mood, state, tenor, trend **5.** haymaker *(Nonformal)*, jab, poke, roundhouse, punch, stroke, throw, thrust, uppercut – *v.* **1.** flap, lurch, oscillate, pendulate, sway, undulate, vibrate, wag **2.** dangle, drape, drop, flag, hang, hover, suspend **3.** gyrate, pivot, reel, revolve, rotate, shift, spin, swerve, swivel, turn, twirl, whirl **4.** blow hot and cold *(Nonformal)*, change, equivocate, flip-flop, flounder, fluctuate, seesaw, vacillate, waver

swipe *n.* blow, clip, cuff, hit, jab, knock, lick, manual compliment *(Nonformal)*, punch, rap, roundhouse, smack, swing, thrust – *v.* **1.** bash, bust *(Nonformal)*, clout, hit, lash out, punch, slap, smack, sock, strike, swat, thwack, wallop **2.** appropriate, heist, lift, pilfer, purloin, steal *Nonformal:* cop, filch, nick, pinch, sneak, snitch

swirl *n.* **1**. circling, eddy, maelstrom, revolution, rotation, spinning, swirling, whirlpool **2.** coil, curl, curlicue, spiral, twist, wave **3.** chaos, commotion, confusion, disorder, disturbance – *v.* churn, curl, revolve, roil, roll, rotate, snake, spin, spiral, surge, swoosh *(Nonformal)*, twirl, twist, whirl, whorl

switch *n.* **1.** button, breaker, connection, flicker *(Nonformal)*, handle, power **2.** alteration, change, changeover, conversion, exchange, reversal, shift, substitution, swap, the ol' switcheroo *(Nonformal)*, transfer, transformation **3.** adjustment, break, deviation, difference, divergence, move, variation – *v.* **1.** deflect, deviate, divert, turn, turnabout, turn aside, veer **2.** change, convert, exchange, interchange, platoon *(Nonformal)*, rearrange, replace, shift, substitute, swap, trade, transfer,

swivel *n.* coupling, link, pivot, ring, rotation, spindle – *v.* hinge, pirouette, pivot, revolve, roll, rotate, spin, swing, turn, whirl

swollen *adj.* **1.** bloated, bulging, dilated, distended, enlarged, expanded, inflated, puffy, swelled, tumescent, tumid **2.** bombastic, extravagant, flatulent, grandiose, highfalutin *(Nonformal)*, overblown, overinflated, pompous, pretentious, showy, stilted, turgid *Antonyms:* plain, simple, unadorned

swoon *n.* insensibility, oblivion, stupor, syncope, unconsciousness – *v.* black out, collapse, drop, faint, lose consciousness, pass out

swoop *v.* descend, dip, drop, fall, nose-dive, plop, plummet, pounce

sword *n.* blade, broadsword, claymore, cutlass, Durendal, épée, Excalibur, foil, *katana (Japanese)*, machete, rapier, sabre, scimitar, steel, weapon

sybarite *n.* epicurean, gourmand, hedonist, libertine, party girl, playboy, pleasure-seeker, self-indulger, sensualist, voluptuary

sybaritic *adj.* Bacchanalian, Dionysian, epicurean, hedonistic, pleasure-loving, pleasure-seeking, self-indulgent *Antonyms:* Apollonian, Spartan, stoic

sycophant *n.* flunky, lackey, lickspittle, minion, slave, toady *Nonformal:* bootlicker, brownie, brown-noser, company man, doormat, fan, groupie, stooge, suckhole, tool, yes-man

sycophantic *adj.* acquiescent, compliant, cringing, deferential, fawning, flattering, grovelling, ingratiating, obsequious, servile, slavish, subservient, toadying, truckling, unctuous, wheedling *Nonformal:* apple-polishing, bootlicking, brown-nosing *Antonyms:* disrespectful, insolent, insulting

syllabus *n.* abridgment, abstract, brief, calender, catalogue, course of study, curriculum, digest, outline, recapitulation, résumé, rundown, sketch, synopsis, summary

sylvan *adj.* arboreous, Arcadian, bucolic, bushy, ecologic, forested, forest-like, idyllic, leafy, scenic, timbered, uncultivated, wild, wooded *Antonyms:* paved, suburban, urban

symbiotic *adj.* collaborative, common, companionable, complementary, interconnected, interdependent, interlinked, mutual, reciprocal, synergistic *Antonyms:* autonomous, independent, self-reliant

symbol *n.* **1.** attribute, badge, brand, chevron, crest, design, device, emblem, figure, flag, image, mark, model, motif, oriflamme, pattern, representation, seal, sign, stripe, token, totem, type *Phonetic and ideographical symbols:* character, cuneiform, hieroglyphic, ideogram, logogram, phonogram, pictograph, rune **2.** allegory, allusion, figure of speech, leitmotif, metaphor, simile, symbolism, symbolization, trope

symbolic *adj.* **1.** characteristic, emblematic, indicative, referential, representative, token, typical **2.** allegorical, allusive, figurative, metaphorical, suggestive

symbolize *v.* act *or* appear *or* serve as, connote, correspond to, delineate, denote, designate, embody, epitomize, equate, exemplify, exhibit, express, illustrate, imitate, indicate, mean, mirror, personify, portray, represent, reproduce, show, signify, speak *or* stand for, substitute, suggest, typify

symmetrical *adj.* balanced, biradial, commensurate, congruent, consistent, equal, even, isometric, orderly, proportional, regular, rounded, stable, uniform, well-proportioned *Antonyms:* asymmetrical, off, unbalanced, unequal

symmetry *n.* **1.** agreement, balance, conformity, congruity, consistency, correspondence, equality, equilibrium, evenness, form, orderliness, parallelism, parity, proportion, proportionality, regularity, shapeliness, similarity, similitude, uniformity *Antonyms:* clashing, distortion, irregularity **2.** art, beauty, charm, clarity, elegance, finish, grace, orderliness, poise, precision, propriety, refinement, simplicity **3.** accord, amity, calm, concord, equanimity, harmony, order, peace, repose, tranquility, unanimity *Antonyms:* disorder, friction, strife

sympathetic *adj.* **1.** affectionate, amenable, appreciative, attuned, caring, commiserating, compassionate, concerned, congenial, considerate, cooperative, encouraging, favourably disposed, feeling, friendly, interested, kind, kindly, loving, open, responsive, sensitive, supportive, tender, thoughtful, understanding, warm, well-disposed, well-intentioned *Antonyms:* apathetic, callous, cold-hearted, indifferent, insensitive **2.** agreeable, appropriate, compatible, congruent, consistent, fitting, harmonious, matching, simpatico, suitable *Antonyms:* improper, inexpedient, unfit

sympathize *v.* **1.** aid, cheer, comfort, commiserate, condole, console, empathize, feel for, identify with, pick up on *(Nonformal)*, pity, solace **2.** affirm, agree, applaud, approve, back, champion, concur, countenance, endorse, subscribe, support

sympathizer *n.* **1.** advocate, aid, ally, assistant, backer, booster, champion, collaborator, comrade, partisan, promoter, subscriber **2.** aid, comforter, commiserator, condoler, helper, helping hand, soother, supporter, well-wisher

sympathy *n.* **1.** aid, cheer, comfort, commiseration, compassion, condolence, consolation, encouragement, feelings, fellow feeling, heart, kindness, pity, responsiveness, rue, sensitivity, solace, tenderness, thoughtfulness, understanding, warmth *Antonyms:* coldness, disdain, indifference **2.** accord, affinity, agreement, alliance, congeniality, connection, harmony, rapport, shared feeling, unity *Antonyms:* antagonism, hostility, opposition *Commonly misused:* **empathy**

symphonious *adj.* concordant, euphonious, harmonious, melodious, musical, symphonic *Antonyms:* cacophonous, discordant, dissonant, shrill

symphony *n.* **1.** arrangement, classical *or* concert music, composition, masterpiece, movements, ode, offering, opus, piece, presentation **2.** group, music society, orchestra, philharmonic, troupe *Standard symphony seating plan:* conductor, drums and battery, tuba, 2 harps, 3 trumpets, 4 bassoons, 4 clarinets, 4 flutes, 4 oboes, 4 piccolos, 4 trombones, 5 french horns, 10 bass fiddles, 12 cellos, 14 violas, 16 second violins, 18 first violins **3.** accord, agreement, concert, concord, congruence, congruity, consensus, harmony *Antonyms:* discord, friction, incompatibility

symposium *n.* assembly, caucus, colloquy, conference, congregation, congress, convention, convocation, forum, meeting, panel, round table, session, synod *Nonformal:* clambake, powwow, Pugwash

symptom *n.* characteristic, earmark, evidence, hint, indication, manifestation, offshoot, representation, sign, signal, syndrome, token, trait, warning

symptomatic *adj.* emblematic, exemplary, expressive, indicative, patterned, representative, suggestive, symbolic, token

syndicate *n.* **1.** agency, alliance, association, cartel, combine, conglomerate, consortium, cooperative, enclave, federation, group, guild, hanse, incorporation, multinational, organization, pool, senate, society, trust, union **2.** Black Hand, Camorra, gang, Mafia, mob, organized crime, rogues' gallery, secret society, *Yakuza (Japanese)* – *v.* affiliate, ally, amalgamate, bind, centralize, combine, consolidate, federalize, form, league, marry, merge, pool, unify, unite, wed *Antonyms:* break, dissolve, split

syndrome *n.* affliction, ailment, complaint, complex, complication, condition, disease, disorder, illness, infirmity, malady, problem, sickness

synergy *n.* collaberation, concurrence, cooperation, correlation, union

synergistic *adj.* accomodating, collective, concerted, helpful, joint, mutual, team

synonymous *adj.* alike, coexistent, compatible, corresponding, equal, equivalent, interchangeable, like, matching, parallel, similar, tantamount *Antonyms:* antithetical, at odds, incongruous

synopsis *n.* abridgment, abstract, analysis, brief, capsule, compendium, condensation, digest, epitome, outline, overview, précis, recap *(Nonformal)*, résumé, review, rundown, run-through, sketch, summary, syllabus, update

synthesis *n.* **1.** amalgamation, coalescence, combining, forming, fusion, gathering, incorporation, integration, melding, mixing, unification, welding **2.** aggregate, alloy, amalgam, association, blend, combination, composite, compound, conglomerate, construction, mixture, organization, polymer, structure, union

synthesize *v.* amalgamate, arrange, blend, coalesce, combine, fuse, gather, group, harmonize, incorporate, integrate, manufacture, marry, merge, mix, organize, unify, unite, weld *Antonyms:* detach, divorce, separate

synthetic *adj.* artificial, constructed, contrived, counterfeit, ersatz, fake, false, imitation, man-made, manufactured, phoney *(Nonformal)*, plastic, unnatural, unreal *Antonyms:* authentic, genuine, natural, organic

syrupy *adj.* **1.** candied, cloying, gooey *(Nonformal)*, honeyed, powdered, saccharine, sticky, sugary, sweet, thick **2.** maudlin, mawkish, melodramatic, nauseating, sentimental, sickening, sweet *Nonformal:* sappy, schmaltzy

system *n.* **1.** arrangement, classification, combination, complex, integral, network, organism, setup, structure, totality, whole **2.** approach, custom, design, fashion, ideology, logical order *or* process, manner, method, mode, modus operandi, MO, operation, order, pattern, philosophy, plan, policy, practice, procedure, scheme, strategy, technique, way **3.** coordination, discipline, orderliness, organization, regularity, routine, rule **4.** cosmos, creation, ecosystem, galaxy, nebula, universe, world **5.** bureaucracy

Nonformal: establishment, proper channels, red tape

systematic *adj.* analytical, arranged, businesslike, efficient, logical, methodical, ordered, orderly, organized, precise, regular, standardized, systematized, thoroughgoing, well-ordered *Antonyms:* arbitrary, haphazard, indiscriminate, random

systematize *v.* arrange, array, contrive, design, devise, establish, frame, institute, marshal, methodize, order, organize, plan, project, pull together, put in order, rationalize, regulate, schematize, shape *or* straighten *or* tighten up, standardize

tab *n.* **1.** appendage, flap, handle, loop, projection, strip, tongue **2.** indicator, label, mark, marker, sticker, tag, ticket **3.** account, bill, cheque, chit, cost, expense, price, score, total *Nonformal:* damage, price tag

tabernacle *n.* church, dwelling, house, recess, sanctuary, shelter, temple, tent

table *n.* **1.** desk, furniture, stand *Common tables:* bar, bedside, card, coffee, counter, desk, dining, drafting, end, folding, gaming, *go (Japanese)*, harvest, kitchen, light, operating, pedestal, picnic, reading, teapoy, work **2.** agenda, blueprint, chart, diagram, graph, illustration, outline, plan, schedule, schema, statistics, tablet **3.** appendix, canon, catalogue, collection, compendium, digest, index, inventory, list, record, register, roll, summary, synopsis, tabulation **4.** *coteau (French)*, flat, flatland, mesa, plain, plateau, steppe, tableland, upland – *v.* **1.** advance, bring or put forth, offer, pose, present, proffer, suggest, tender **2.** defer, delay, hang fire, hold off, mothball, postpone, put aside *or* off, shelve, suspend

tableau *n.* diorama, illustration, painting, panorama, picture, portrayal, representation, scene, scenery, spectacle, view

tablet *n.* **1.** board, notebook, pad, paper, scribbler, slate **2.** capsule, dose, lozenge, medicine, pastille, pellet, pill, troche **3.** headstone, marker, memorial, slab, stone, tombstone

tabloid *adj.* **1.** abridged, brief, compact, compressed, concise, condensed, laconic, shortened, succinct, terse **2.** cheap, exaggerated, maudlin, mawkish, melodramatic, overblown, sensational, sentimental, trashy *Nonformal:* Hollywood, hyped, yellow – *n.* magazine, newspaper, periodical, serial *Nonformal:* rag, scandal sheet

taboo *adj.* banned, blackballed, disapproved, forbidden, frowned on, illegal, off limits, outlawed, prohibited, proscribed, reserved, restricted, ruled out, unacceptable, unmentionable, unthinkable *Antonyms:* allowed, permitted, sanctioned – *n.* anathema, ban, disapproval, exclusion, forbiddance, inhibition, law, limitation, no-no *(Nonformal)*, prohibition, proscription, religious *or* social interdict, restraint, restriction, sanction, stricture

tabulate *v.* add, alphabetize, arrange, calculate, categorize, classify, codify, count, enumerate, figure, formulate, index, itemize, list, order, range, reckon, record, register, sum, systematize

tacit *adj.* **1.** implicit, implied, inferred, taken for granted, understood, unsaid, unspoken *Antonyms:* declared, expressed, stated, voiced **2.** hushed, inaudible, noiseless, quiet, silent, soundless, still *Antonyms:* deafening, loud, roaring, thunderous

taciturn *adj.* aloof, antisocial, close-mouthed, distant, dour, laconic, mute, quiet, reserved, reticent, saturnine, secretive, silent, terse, tight-lipped, uncommunicative, unexpressive, unforthcoming, untalkative, withdrawn *Antonyms:* chatty, forthcoming, loquacious, talkative, verbose

tack *n.* **1.** cleat, nail, pin, point, push pin, staple, thumbtack **2.** aim, alteration, approach, bearing, course, direction, heading, line, method, movement, path, plan, set, tactic, tangent **3.** deflection, deviation, oblique course, shift, swerve, switch, turn, yaw, zigzag **4.** bit, bridle, equipment, gear, halter, harness, outfit, tackle, trappings **5.** edibles, fare, food, nutriment, provisions, rations, sustenance, victuals – *v.* **1.** add, affix, annex, append, attach, baste, fasten, fix, glue, mount, nail, paste, pin, secure, sew, staple, stitch, tag, tie **2.** alter *or* change course, come about, deviate, sheer, swerve, veer

tackle *n.* **1.** apparatus, duffel, equipment, gear, kit, paraphernalia, rig, rigging, supplies *Common fishing tackle:* backing, bobber, dry flies, hook, jigs, leader, line, lure, net, pliers, plugs, popping bug, reel, rod, tackle box, spinners, spoons, vest, waders, weight, wet flies **2.** block and tackle, capstan, hoist, pulley, winch, windlass – *v.* **1.** bring *or* throw down, catch, confront, grapple, grasp, halt, intercept, nail *(Nonformal)*, seize, topple **2.** apply oneself, attack, attempt, begin, deal with, dig *or* pitch *or* plunge into, embark upon, engage in, essay, get going, launch, set about, take on *or* up, try, undertake, work at *or* on *Antonyms:* avoid, evade, shun, turn tail *(Nonformal)*

tacky *adj.* **1.** cheap, crude, gaudy, inelegant, nasty, outdated, showy, sleazy, tasteless, tawdry, unbecoming, unfashionable, unsuitable, vulgar *Antonyms:* attractive, classy, elegant, tasteful **2.** dingy, dowdy, faded, frumpy, mangy, messy, ratty, neglected, scuzzy *(Nonformal)*, seedy, shabby, shaganappi, shoddy, sloppy, slovenly, threadbare, unkempt, untidy **3.** clinging, gluey, gummy, pasty, sticky, tarry

tact *n.* **1.** acumen, adroitness, aptness, care, circumspection, common sense, consideration, courtesy, delicacy, diplomacy, discretion, discrimination, finesse, intuition, perspicacity, savoir-faíre, sensitivity, subtlety, thoughtfulness, understanding *Antonyms:* awkwardness, clumsiness, indiscretion **2.** feeling, perception, sense, touch

tactful *adj.* adroit, careful, cautious, civil, considerate, courteous, delicate, diplomatic, discreet, discriminating, gentle, judicious, observant, perceptive, poised, polished, polite, politic, prudent, sensitive, skilful, solicitous, statesmanlike, suave, subtle, sympathetic, thoughtful, understanding, urbane, wise *Antonyms:* clumsy, gauche, inconsiderate, tasteless, unsubtle

tactic *n.* approach, campaign, channels, course, defence, device, gambit, game plan, line, manoeuvre, means, method, move, plan, plot, ploy, policy, procedure, ruse, scenario, scheme, stratagem, strategy, system, tack, technique, trick, way

tactical *adj.* adroit, artful, calculated, clever, cunning, deft, diplomatic, judicious, Machiavellian, planned, political, skilled, strategic, surgical

tactician *n.* campaign manager, coach, commander, coordinator, director, engineer, expert, general, mastermind, orchestrator, planner, politician, schemer, strategist *Nonformal:* puppeteer, quarterback

tactics *n.* battle, game plan, logistics, machinations, management, maneuverings, military operation, *ruse de guerre (French)*, strategy

tactless *adj.* blundering, boorish, bungling, careless, clumsy, coarse, crude, discourteous, foolish, gauche, gruff, hasty, imprudent, inconsiderate, indelicate, indiscreet, insensitive, maladroit, misunderstanding, negligent, rash, rough, rude, senseless, thoughtless, unfeeling, unkind, unperceptive, unpolished, unwise, vulgar, without thought *Antonyms:* considerate, diplomatic, discreet, polite, subtle

tag *n.* **1.** aiguillette, badge, card, emblem, flag, flap, marker, note, stamp, sticker, strip, stub, tab, tally, ticket **2.** appellation, identification, inscription, label, logo, mark, moniker *(Nonformal)*, name, nickname, title **3.** end, leaving, rag, remnant, tail, tatter **4.** blurb, catch phrase, hook, line, proverb, quotation, refrain, saying, slogan – *v.* **1.** adorn, affix, append, attach, christen, designate, dub, earmark, fit, identify, label, mark, name, nickname, supply, term, ticket, title **2.** accompany, attend, chase, follow, heel, hunt, pursue, shadow, tail, trace, track, track down, trail **3.** contact, hit, overtake, smack, touch

tail *adj.* hindmost, posterior, rear, rearmost – *n.* **1.** appendage, braid, extension, extremity, pigtail, stub, tailpiece, tip **2.** arse *(British)*, ass, backside, behind, buttocks, haunches, hind end *or* part, posterior, rear-end, rump, train *Nonformal:* bum, butt, caboose, duff, fanny, keister **3.** close, completion, conclusion, end, finale, last part, resolution **4.** course, path, route, track, trail, wake – *v.* chase, follow, hound, pursue, shadow, stalk, tag, track, trail

tailor *n.* bushelman *(Nonformal)*, clothier, costumier, couturier, dressmaker, garment maker, haberdasher, needleworker, outfitter, sartor, seamster, seamstress, sewer – *v.* accommodate, adapt, adjust, alter, conform, convert, custom-make, cut, dovetail, fashion, fit, form, modify, mold, reconcile, sew, shape, square, style, suit, tailor-make

taint *n.* black mark, blemish, blot, contagion, contamination, corruption, defect, disgrace, dishonour, fault, flaw, infection, pollution, shame, smear, spot, stain, stigma – *v.* adulterate, besmirch, blacken, blemish, blight, blot, brand, contaminate, corrupt, damage, debase, decay, defile, deprave, dirty, discolour, discredit, disgrace, dishonour, foul, harm, hurt, infect, muddy, poison, pollute, putrefy, ruin, shame, smear, soil, spoil, stain, stigmatize, sully, tar, tarnish, vitiate *Antonyms:* clean, cleanse, decontaminate, disinfect, purify

take *n.* **1.** acquisition, appropriation, catch, obtainment, procurement, seizure **2.** booty, gains, haul, ill-gotten gains, loot, lucre, plunder, proceeds, profits, receipts, share, spoils, winnings *Nonformal:* boodle, gate **3.** documentation, filming, recording, session, shooting, taping **4.** feeling, interpretation, perception, reading, understanding, version, viewpoint, – *v.* **1.** acquire, clasp, collect, gather, get, grasp, grip, obtain, pick up, pluck, salvage **2.** abduct, annex, appropriate, capture, carry off, catch, collar, commandeer, confiscate, ensnare, entrap, expropriate, grab, misappropriate, pilfer, pinch, pocket, possess, purloin, seize, snag, snare, snatch, steal, swipe *Nonformal:* bag, boost, cop, haul in, nick, rip off **3.** choose, desire, elect, engage, favour, opt for, pick, prefer, select, want *Antonyms:* ignore, neglect, overlook, pass **4.** accept, accommodate, acknowledge, admit, adopt, assume, include, receive, welcome *Antonyms:* avoid, dismiss, dodge, refuse, reject **5.** bear, brave, brook, contend *or* deal with, endure, tolerate, weather, withstand **6.** apprehend, believe, comprehend, conceive, consider, discover, experience, feel, imagine, interpret, know, look upon, observe, opine, perceive, presume, reckon, regard, sense, suppose, suspect, understand *Antonyms:* misconceive, misconstrue, misunderstand **7.** deduct, discount, draw back, eliminate, knock off, remove, subtract, take away *or* off *or* out *Antonyms:* add, amplify, enlarge, increase **8.** consume, devour, down, drink, eat, feed, imbibe, ingest, inhale, partake of, swallow, wolf down **9.** beat, bilk, cheat, deceive, defraud, dupe, hoodwink, swindle, trick *Nonformal:* bamboozle, con, flim-flam, hornswoggle **10.** book, buy, charter, hire, lease, procure, rent, reserve **11.** accompany, bring, carry, conduct, convey, escort, ferry, fetch, guide, haul, lead, move, pack, piggyback, pilot, ride, shoulder, steer, transport, tote, tour, trek, truck **12.** catch, come down with, contract, develop **13.** affect, allure, attract, bewitch, captivate, charm, delight, draw, enchant, entertain, fascinate, magnetize, please, wile **14.** beat, crush *(Nonformal)*, defeat, overwhelm, vanquish, win **15.** call for, demand, necessitate, need, require **16.** aim, direct, document, film, focus, point, shoot, tape

takeoff *n.* **1.** burlesque, caricature, cartoon, comedy, imitation, lampoon, mockery, parody, ridicule, satire, send-up, spoof, travesty **2.** ascent, beginning, blast-off, commencement, departure, liftoff, outset, start

takeover *n.* absorption, adoption, amalgamation, annexation, appropriation, assumption, buyout, coalition, confiscation, conquest, coup, coup d'état, incursion, invasion, merger, occupation, raid, seizure, subsumption, usurpation

taking *adj.* alluring, appealing, attractive, beautiful, beguiling, bewitching, captivating, charming, compelling, desirable, distracting, enchanting, engaging, entrancing, fascinating, head-turning, lovely, luring, pleasing, striking, tantalizing *Antonyms:* forbidding, scary, unattractive

tale *n.* **1.** account, allegory, anecdote, ballad, chronicle, ditty, epic, fable, fabliau, legend, myth, narrative, parable, recital, report, saga, story *Nonformal:* fish story, invention, megillah, stretch, tall tale, whopper, yarn **2.** allegation, canard, defamation, exaggeration, fabrication, falsehood, falsification, falsity, fib, fiction, gossip, hearsay, invention, lie, misrepresentation, prevarication, rumour, scandal, slander

talent *n.* ability, aptitude, art, artistry, bent, capability, capacity, craft, deftness, endowment, expertise, facility, faculty, flair, forte, genius, gift, intelligence, inventiveness, knack, power, skill *Nonformal:* know-how, nose, savvy, smarts, the formula, the goods, the stuff *Antonyms:* inability, incompetence, ineptitude

talisman *n.* Aladdin's lamp, amulet, charm, good-luck charm, fetish, horseshoe, lucky penny *or* stone, rabbit's-foot, scarab, security blanket

talk *n.* **1.** argument, chat, chit-chat, colloquy, conclave, conference, communication, consultation, conversation, deliberation, dialogue, discourse, discussion, exchange, huddle, interlocution, interview, meeting, negotiation, palaver, small talk, speaking, symposium, tête-à-tête, utterance, verbalization, visit, vocalization *Nonformal:* bull session, confab, gabfest, Pugwash, yak, yawp **2.** address, discourse, dissertation, epilogue, harangue, homily, lecture, monologue, oration, peroration, rap, recitation, seminar, sermon, speech, spiel *(Nonformal)* **3.** gossip, hearsay, report, rumour, scandal *Nonformal:* buzz, dirt, dope, scuttlebutt, skinny, word on the street **4.** central idea *or* point, keynote, subject, theme, topic **5.** banter, chatter, galimatias, gibberish, jabbering, nattering *(British)*, prattle, yammering *(Nonformal)* **6.** blather, bluster, flatulence, garrulity, hot-air *(Nonformal)*, long-windedness, verbiage, verbosity, windiness, wordiness **7.** argot, cant, dialect, jargon, language, lingo, patois, slang, vernacular – *v.* **1.** articulate, communicate, converse, declaim, drawl, elaborate, enunciate, expatiate, express, go on *(Nonformal)*, intone, pronounce, rail, rap, rave, say, scold, speak, spiel, spout, talk, utter, verbalize, voice **2.** address, deliver, discourse, harangue, lecture, orate, rhapsodize, sermonize, soapbox, speechify, state, tell **3.** babble, blabber, blather, buzz, carry on, chat, chatter, chin, chitchat, digress, drift, drivel, drone, fume, gab, gabble, gush, jabber, jaw, maunder, palaver, patter, prate, prattle, rabbit, ramble, rant, splutter, stray, vent, wander *Nonformal:* yak, yammer, yap **4.** argue, collogue, commune, confab, confabulate, confer, confide, consult, contact, deliberate, dialogue, discuss, exchange, huddle *(Nonformal)*, interact, interview, negotiate, network, parley, powwow **5.** confess, divulge, gossip, inform, reveal, tattle *Nonformal:* rat, sing, spill the beans, squeal **6.** advise, convince, influence, persuade, sway, touch

talkative *adj.* chattering, chatty, discursive, effusive, garrulous, gossipy, loquacious, mouthy, overtalkative, prolix, rattling, verbose, vocal, voluble, wordy *Nonformal:* barkative, big-mouthed, blabby, gabby, long-winded, loose-lipped, motor-mouthed, windy *Antonyms:* quiet, reserved, reticent, silent, taciturn

tall *adj.* **1.** colossal, elevated, giant, great, high, high-reaching, lanky, leggy, lofty, rangy, soaring, stretched, towering *Nonformal:* alpine, bean-pole, highpockets, sky-high, stringbean *Antonyms:* short, small, squat, stumpy, tiny **2.** boastful, embellished, extravagant, fantastic, far-fetched, grandiloquent, inordinate, outrageous, overblown, overdone, remarkable, unbelievable *Antonyms:* modest, plausible, reasonable, true – *adv.* assuredly, confidently, handsomely, proud, self-assuredly

tally *n.* **1.** account, bill, census, cheque, count, inventory, list, mark, muster, poll, receipt, reckoning, record, register, roster, running total, score, sum, summation, tab, total **2.** clone, copy, counterpart, duplicate **3.** docket, label, stamp, sticker, tag, ticket – *v.* **1.** check, mark, record, register, score **2.** add up, calculate, catalogue, compute, count, enumerate, estimate, itemize, keep score, number, numerate, reckon, sum, take inventory, total **3.** agree, coincide, concur, conform, correspond, harmonize, match, square

tame *adj.* **1.** broke, civilized, compliant, cultivated, docile, domesticated, gentle, harnessed, manageable, mastered, obedient, pliable, schooled, trained *Antonyms:* feral, unruly, wild **2.** amenable, harmless, mild, moderate, pliant, subdued, subjugated, submissive, tractable *Antonyms:* aggressive, argumentative, bombastic **3.** bland, dull, flat, tedious, tiresome, toned-down, spiritless, uninspired – *v.* **1.** accustom, break *or* break in, bridle, check, curb, discipline, domesticate, gentle, housebreak, humble, master, moderate, pacify, restrain, soften, temper, train **2.** conquer, defeat, overpower, quell, subdue, subjugate, suppress, vanquish

tamper *v.* **1.** alter, change, damage, destroy, fiddle, interfere, intrude, manipulate, meddle, modify, plot, rejig, scheme, tinker *Nonformal:* doctor, grease, monkey **2.** bribe, buy off, corrupt, falsify, fix, have, influence, lubricate, oil *(Nonformal)*

tan *adj. & n.* colour, shade *Tan shades:* beige, bronze, brown, buff, burnt umber, coffee, cream, ecru, gold, khaki, leather, light brown, natural, olive, saddle, sand, suntan, tawny, umber – *v.* **1.** cure, prepare, process, treat **2.** bask, brown, burn, sunbathe *Nonformal:* catch some rays, cook, fry **3.** discipline, flog, lash, lick, punish, spank, thrash, wallop, welt

tang *n.* **1.** aroma, bite, flavour, edge, guts *(Nonformal)*, kick, nip, piquancy, pungency, relish, savour, scent, smack, smell, spiciness, tartness, thrill, twang, zap, zest **2.** hint, soupçon, taste, tingle, touch, trace

tangible *adj.* actual, concrete, corporeal, definite, detectable, discernible, distinct, embodied, evident, factual, incarnate, manifest, material, objective, observable, obvious, palpable, patent, perceptible, physical, plain, real, solid, stable, substantial, tactile, touchable, verifiable, visible *Antonyms:* abstract, impalpable, theoretical

tangle *n.* coil, complexity, complication, confusion, entanglement, Gordian knot, hodgepodge, imbroglio, jam, jumble, jungle, kink, knot, labyrinth, mass, mat, maze, mesh, mess, mix-up, morass, muddle, rummage, skein, snag, snarl, twist, web *Nonformal:* can of worms, rat's nest – *v.* **1.** coil, interlace, interlock, intertwist, interweave, knot, mesh, muck up *(Nonformal)*, perplex, ravel, scramble, snarl, twist **2.** catch, embroil, enmesh, ensnare, trap, **3.** contest, disagree, fight, lock horns *(Nonformal)*, wrangle **4.** complicate, confuse, discompose, disorganize, unbalance, upset the apple cart *(Nonformal)*

tank *n.* **1.** aquarium, basin, cistern, container, hold, livewell, pond, pool, receptacle, reservoir, swimming pool, vat, vessel **2.** armoured car *or* personnel carrier, combat vehicle, tank-car – *v. Nonformal:* blow it, go bankrupt or belly up, outrun the banker

tantalize *v.* **1.** allure, attract, beguile, bewitch, captivate, entice, entrance, fascinate, hypnotize, interest, intrigue, pique, seduce, tempt, titillate **2.** bait, bedevil, bother, frustrate, tease, torment, torture *Antonyms:* gratify, satiate, satisfy

tantamount *adj.* alike, analogous, as good as, commensurate, comparable, equivalent, identical, like, parallel, reciprocal, same, selfsame, synonymous *Antonyms:* different, dissimilar, incongruous

tantrum *n.* blowup, dander, eruption, explosion, fit, flare-up, hemorrhage, huff, hysterics, outburst, rage, rant, storm, temper *Nonformal:* conniption, hissyfit *Antonyms:* calm, peace, tranquility

tap *n.* **1.** faucet, spigot, spile, spout, valve **2.** beat, borrow, knock, pat, rap, tattoo, touch *Nonformal:* hit on, touch – *v.* **1.** bleed, draft, drain, draw forth *or* off *or* out, empty, extract, milk, mine, pump, siphon **2.** bore, broach, drill, lance, open, penetrate, perforate, pierce **3.** employ, exploit, manipulate, use, utilize **4.** bug *(Nonformal)*, eavesdrop, listen in, wiretap **5.** beat, drum, knock, pat, percuss, rap, rat-a-tat-tat *(Nonformal)*, strike, tag, thud, thump, tip

tape *n.* **1.** adhesive, band, edging, strip **2.** end, finish line, ribbon– *v.* **1.** copy, document, film, record, register, tape-record, video, videotape **2.** bandage, bind, fasten, seal, secure, swathe, tie up, truss, wrap

taper *n.* candle, light, light source, torch, wick – *v.* **1.** abate, decrease, diminish, dwindle, ebb, fade, fall away *or* off, recede, reduce, subside, thin out, wane, weaken *Antonyms:* grow, increase, intensify **2.** come down, contact, contract, converge, narrow, shrink *Antonyms:* balloon, dilate, swell

tapestry *n.* **1.** embroidery, mosaic, needlework, ornament, tapis, wall hanging, weave **2.** kaleidoscope, myriad, range

tar *n.* **1.** asphalt, bitumen, maltha, paving material, pitch, resin, tarmac **2.** black, charcoal, coal, ebony – *v.* asphalt, blacktop, coat, cover, resurface, slather, spread

tardy *adj.* **1.** behindhand, belated, delayed, delinquent, detained, held *or* hung *or* jammed up, last-minute, late, overdue *Antonyms:* early, prompt, punctual **2.** dawdling, dilatory, laggard, loitering, procrastinating, slack, slow, sluggish,

target *n.* **1.** aim, ambition, bull's-eye, destination, end, function, goal, intention, mark, object, objective, point, purpose, spot **2.** butt, dupe, fall guy *(Nonformal)*, laughingstock, mark, prey, quarry, scapegoat, sport, victim

tariff *n.* assessment, charge, cost, customs, duty, excise, fee, levy, penalty, price, rate, tab, tax, toll

tarnish *n.* blot, eyesore, mark, smear, smudge, stain, taint – *v.* **1.** blacken, blemish, corrode, darken, discolour, dim, fade, mark, pollute, soil, stain, taint *Antonyms:* brighten, clean, polish, purify **2.** besmirch, corrupt, defile, defame, degrade, devalue, disgrace, dishonour, shame, slander, smear, smudge, stigmatize, sully, vilify *Antonyms:* aggrandize, crown, exalt

tarry *v.* abide, bide, dally, dawdle, delay, drag one's heels *(Nonformal)*, hang *or* stick around, lag, linger, loiter, pause, poke, procrastinate, rest, sojourn, stall, stay, wait *Antonyms:* hasten, hurry, rush

tart *adj.* **1.** acid, acidulous, acrid, bitter, dry, piquant, pungent, sharp, snappy, sour, tangy, vinegary *Antonyms:* honeyed, sugary, sweet **2.** acerbic, biting, caustic, cutting, derisive, harsh, sarcastic, severe, spiteful, trenchant, venomous, vitriolic – *n.* **1.** butter tart, pastry, patty, pie, quiche, sweet, tartlet, *tourtière (Quebec)*, turnover **2.** harlot, hooker, hussy, prostitute, streetwalker, strumpet, trollop, whore *Nonformal:* chippy, floozy, hotsy-potatsie

task *n.* **1.** assignment, business, calling, charge, commission, duty, effort, employment, enterprise, errand, exercise, function, gig *(Nonformal)*, job, labour, load, mission, occupation, office, onus, project, province, responsibility, stint, undertaking, vocation, work **2.** bother, burden, chore, nuisance, strain, toil, trouble *Nonformal:* deadweight, grindstone, headache, millstone, pain – *v.* **1.** assign, charge, entrust, lade, load, saddle **2.** burden, encumber, oppress, overload, overtax, push, strain, tax, test **3.** blame, censure, condemn, criticize, judge, punish, reprimand, reproof , upbraid *Antonyms:* exalt, extol, glorify, praise

taste *n.* **1.** bite, flavour, jolt, kick, oomph *(Nonformal)*, piquancy, relish, savour, smack, tang, zest, zing, zip **2.** appetizer, bit, dash, drop, fragment, hint, morsel, mouthful, nip, pinch, sample, sampling, sip, soupçon, spoonful, sprinkling, suggestion, swallow, tincture, tinge, touch, trifle, whiff **3.** appetite, appreciation, aptitude, bent, desire, disposition, fancy, flash, fondness, gustation, inclination, leaning, liking, palate, partiality, penchant, predilection, preference, proclivity, susceptibility, tendency, weakness, zest *Nonformal:* druthers, heart, soft spot, stomach **4.** correctness, cultivation, culture, decorum, delicacy, elegance, etiquette, finesse, grace, nicety, polish, politeness, propriety, refinement, restraint, style, tact *Antonyms:* boorishness, indecency, vulgarity **5.** acumen, acuteness, discernment, discretion, discrimination, feeling, judgement, perception, sagacity – *v.* **1.** bite, eat, nibble, partake, relish, sample, savour, sip, test, try **2.** encounter, experience, feel, know, meet with, perceive, sense, try out, undergo

tasteful *adj.* **1.** aesthetic, artistic, beautiful, charming, classy, delicate, elegant, exquisite, fine, graceful, gratifying, handsome, harmonious, in good taste, nice, pleasing, pretty, simple, smart, snazzy, spiffy, stylish, subdued, uptown *(Nonformal)* *Antonyms:*

garish, showy, tacky, tasteless **2.** cultivated, cultured, correct, discriminating, fastidious, polished, refined, restrained, **3.** delectable, delicious, enticing, flavourful, savoury *Antonyms:* off *(Nonformal)*, overdone, rancid, rotten

tasteless *adj.* **1.** blah *(Nonformal)*, bland, boring, dull, flat, flavourless, insipid, mild, savourless, stale, thin, unappetizing, uninspired, vapid, watered-down, watery, weak *Antonyms:* appetizing, delicious, flavoursome, savoury **2.** artificial, cheap, flashy, foolish, garish, gaudy, graceless, gross, hideous, indecorous, inelegant, infelicitous, ostentatious, pretentious, showy, tacky, tawdry **3.** coarse, crass, crude, dirty, distasteful, improper, indelicate, indiscreet, low, off-colour, raunchy, rough, rude, uncouth, vulgar

tasty *adj.* appetizing, delectable, delicious, divine, flavourful, flavoursome, good-tasting, gourmet, heavenly, luscious, mellow, palatable, piquant, pleasant, pungent, sapid, savoury, scrumptious, spicy, sugar-coated, sweetened, toothsome, yummy *(Nonformal)*, zestful *Antonyms:* bland, flavourless, repulsive, unappetizing

tattered *adj.* frayed, ragged, raggedy, ripped, scraggly, scruffy, shabby, shopworn, shredded, threadbare, torn, weathered, worn-out *Antonyms:* neat, shipshape, tidy

tattle *v.* **1.** babble, blabber, blather, chatter, gossip, prate, prattle, rumour, run off at the mouth *(Nonformal)* **2.** blab, divulge, inform, leak, tell on *Nonformal:* blow the whistle, fink, rat, snitch, spill the beans, squeal

tattletale *n.* big-mouth, informer, stool-pigeon, whistle-blower *Nonformal:* blab, fink, narc, rat, ratfink, snitch, squealer

tattoo *n.* **1.** call, display, drumming, exercise, entertainment, fête, marching, signal, summons **2.** beat, pulse, rhythm, tap **3.** brand, design, mark, print, scarification – *v.* brand, embellish, illustrate, ink, mark, prick, scar, score

taunt *n.* affront, barb, comeback, derision, gibe, indignity, insult, jab, jeer, provocation, put-down, reproach, sarcasm, swipe *Nonformal:* dig, raspberry, Salmon Arm Salute, zinger – *v.* affront, insult, jeer, mock, needle, offend, outrage, provoke, rebuke, revile, ridicule, scoff, scorn, sneer, tantalize, tease, torment, upbraid *Nonformal:* bug, hassle, ride, roast

taut *adj.* **1.** close, firm, flexed, rigid, snug, stiff, strained, stressed, stretched, tense, tight, trim, unyielding *Antonyms:* flaccid, loose, slack **2.** arranged, clean, kempt, neat, orderly, organized, shipshape, tidy *Antonyms:* chaotic, dishevelled, disorganized, unkempt

tavern *n.* alehouse, bar, beer parlour, beverage room, draft *or* public house, hostelry, hotel, inn, rathskeller, saloon, taproom *Nonformal:* beer *or* corner joint, local watering hole

tawdry *adj.* brazen, cheap, common, crude, dirty, flashy, garish, gaudy, gimcrack, glaring, glittering, junky, loud, meretricious, offensive, plastic, poor, raffish, screaming, showy, sleazy, tasteless, vulgar *Nonformal:* chintzy, Hollywood, tacky, Tinseltown *Antonyms:* elegant, graceful, refined, tasteful

tax *n.* **1.** assessment, bite *(Nonformal)*, contribution, cost, customs, death duties, dues, duty, excise, expense, fine, levy, obligation, payment, poll, price, rate, tariff, taxation, tithe, toll, value-added *or* VST *Canadian taxes:* Goods and Services Tax *or* GST, Harmonized Sales Tax *or* HST, income tax, inheritance, Provincial Sales Tax *or* PST, QST *or* Quebec sales tax *Historical:* head tax, scot **2.** albatross, burden, charge, demand, drain, imposition, load, millstone, onus, overexertion, pressure, strain, task, weight – *v.* **1.** assess, demand, exact, impose, levy, penalize, require, tithe **2.** burden, charge, encumber, exhaust, load, oppress, overburden, overuse, overwork, pressure, push, saddle, strain, stress, weaken **3.** accuse, arraign, blame, censure, charge, impeach, impugn, impute, incriminate, inculpate, indict, reproach, reprove *Antonyms:* acquit, clear, exculpate, exonerate, vindicate

teach *v.* advance, advise, brainwash, brief, catechize, coach, communicate, control, demonstrate, develop, direct, discipline, drill, drum into, edify, educate, enlighten, explain, expound, form, ground, guide, illustrate, imbue, impart, inculcate, indoctrinate, inform, instruct, lead, lecture, prepare, profess, ready, school, train, tutor, update

teacher *n.* advisor, coach, don, educator, faculty member, fellow, governess, guide, guru, *imam (Islam)*, instructor, *lama (Buddhism)*, lecturer, master, mentor, mistress, pedagogue, preceptor, preceptress, professor, pundit, rabbi, scholar, schoolmaster, schoolmistress, schoolteacher, sage, sensei, supervisor, T.A., teaching assistant, trainer, tutor, *Tzaddik (Judaism) Hinduism: sadhu, swami*

teaching *n.* belief, doctrine, dogma, lesson, maxim, moral, precept, proverb, tenet, theory, thesis

team *n.* aggregation, band, bench *(Hockey)*, body, bunch, cadre, company, contingent, crew, eleven *(Football)*, faction, first *or* second *or* third string, five *(Basketball)*, gang, group, inner circle, lineup, nine *(Baseball)*, organization, outfit, party, roster, set, side, squad, string, troop, unit, workers – *v.* assemble, couple, gather, harness, group, match, pair, yoke

tear *n.* **1.** breach, break, cut, damage, fissure, gash, hole, impairment, imperfection, laceration, mutilation, rent, rip, run, rupture, scratch, split, tatter **2.** bead, drop, droplet, saline discharge, teardrop **3.** bacchanalia, bender, binge, carousal, carouse, drunk, revelry, spree *Nonformal:* booze-up, lost weekend **4.** burst, convulsion, eruption, outburst, spasm, tantrum, tremor – *v.* **1.** claw, cleave, damage, divide, fray, frazzle, gash, impair, incise, injure, lacerate, mangle, mutilate, pull apart, rend, ribbon, rift, rip, rive, run, rupture, scratch, separate, sever, shred, slash, slit, split, sunder, **2.** extract, grab, pluck, pull, seize, snatch, wrench, wrest, yank **3.** dash, fly, gallop, hurry, race, run, rush, speed, sprint, zoom **4.** blubber, cry, secrete, sob, wail, water, weep

tearful *adj.* bawling, blubbery, crying, dolorous, grief-stricken, grieved, lachrymose, mournful, plaintive, rueful, sad, sentimental, sobbing, sorrowful, teary, upset, weeping, weepy, whimpering, woeful *Antonyms:* gleeful, happy, joyful, laughing

tease *n.* beguiler, coquette, deceiver, joker, tormentor *Nonformal:* heartbreaker, leg-puller – *v.* **1.** annoy, bait, bother, chaff, disturb, goad, harass, haze, heckle, jest, joke, needle, pester, pique, provoke, razz, torment, vex *Nonformal:* bug, pick on, rag **2.** arouse, enflame, excite, impassion, seduce, stimulate, stir up, toy with, whet **3.** backcomb, card, comb, pull apart, shred, tear, work

technical *adj.* **1.** complex, hard, hi-tech *(Nonformal)*, complicated, detailed, difficult, elaborate, exact, intricate, involved, precise *Antonyms:* easy, simple, straightforward **2.** industrial, mechanical, professional, scientific, specialized, technological, vocational

technicality *n.* **1.** insignificancy, nullity, *rien du tout (French)*, quibble, trifle, triviality **2.** fine print *(Nonformal)*, law, measure, point, procedure, rule, stipulation

technician *n.* artisan, expert, mechanic, professional, programmer, skilled hand, specialist, techie *(Nonformal)*

technique *n.* **1.** ability, art, artistry, capability, cleverness, craft, device, experience, expertise, knack, know-how, knowledge, proficiency, skill, touch, **2.** approach, course, delivery, execution, fashion, manner, means, method, mode, performance, procedure, routine, style, system, way

tedious *adj.* annoying, banal, bland, bloodless, boring, bromidic, conventional, dreary, dull, exhausting, feeble, humdrum *(Nonformal)*, insipid, laborious, lifeless, mediocre, monotonous, prosaic, repetitious, routine, soporific, spiritless, tame, tiresome, tiring, unexciting, uninteresting, unvarying, vapid, weak, wearisome *Antonyms:* enjoyable, enthralling, exhilarating, imaginative, stimulating

tedium *n.* banality, boredom, doldrums, dreariness, drudgery, dullness, ennui, infinite progression, lifelessness, monotony, repetitiousness, routine, sameness *Nonformal:* crickets, humdrum, the drabs, tumbleweed *Antonyms:* challenge, excitement, fascination, interest, liveliness

teem *v.* abound, brim, burst, crowd, flow, grow, jam, overflow, overrun, pack, pour, prosper, rain, superabound, swarm, swell *Nonformal:* come down in buckets, rain cats and dogs

teeming *adj.* abundant, alive, brimful, brimming, bursting, chock-full, crammed, crawling, crowded, filled, fruitful, full, infested, multitudinous, numerous, overflowing, packed, plentiful, populous, pregnant, productive, prolific, replete, rife, saturated, superabundant, swarming, thick, thronged *Antonyms:* deficient, lacking, short, wanting

teeter *v.* **1.** alternate, balance, fluctuate, lurch, oscillate, pivot, seesaw, totter, vacillate, waver **2.** stagger, stumble, sway, wobble

telegram *n.* cable, message, report, signal, telegraph, teletype, telex, wire – *v.* communicate, dispatch, send, telegraph, transmit, wire

telepathy *n.* clairvoyance, E.S.P., insight, mind-reading, parapsychology, premonition, psionics, sixth sense, telepathic transmission, thought transference

telephone *n.* cellular, payphone, phone *Nonformal:* horn, blower – *v.* buzz, call, call *or* dial *or* ring up, communicate, contact, dial, give a ring *or* buzz *(Nonformal)*, phone, ring, ring up

telescope *n.* refractorscope, spyglass *Kinds of Telescope:* achromatic, apochromatic, compound, Dobsonian, Maksutov-Cassegrain, Newtonian, reflector, refractor, Schmidt-Cassegrain – *v.* abbreviate, abridge, compress, condense, reduce, shorten, truncate

television *n.* small screen, telly *(British)*, TV *Nonformal:* box, boob tube, goggle *or* idiot box, the tube *Kinds of television show:* broadcast news, cartoon, children's, closed-circuit, cooking, daytime serial, direct *or* live broadcast, docudrama, documentary, drama, dramatic series, game, infomercial, infotainment, lifestyle, miniseries, music video, newscast, pilot, play, prime-time, quiz, real, rerun, serial, shock, simulcast, situation comedy *or* sitcom, soap, soap opera, sports, talk, taped, teleplay, trash, variety

tell *v.* **1.** acquaint, advise, announce, apprise, articulate, communicate, confess, declare, explain, express, give, give out, impart, inform, let know, make known, mention, narrate, notify, proclaim, recite, recount, relate, report, say, speak, state, utter, verbalize, voice *Nonformal:* cough *or* fess up, level, spout **2.** betray, blab, disclose, divulge, gossip, jabber, reveal, tattle *Nonformal:* blow the whistle, let slip, pull the plug, rat, snitch, spill, squeal **3.** ascertain, clinch, comprehend, compute, decide, deduce, determine, differentiate, discern, discover, discriminate, distinguish, divine, figure *or* find out, identify, know, learn, perceive, recognize, see, understand *Antonyms:* confuse, misunderstand, mix up **4.** bid, charge, coerce, command, compel, demand, dictate, direct, instruct, order **5.** evidence, indicate, point to, prove, reveal, show, suggest

telling *adj.* cogent, considerable, conspicuous, convincing, crucial, decisive, devastating, effective, effectual, eloquent, evidential, forceful, forcible, important, impressive, influential, marked, notable, potent, powerful, pregnant, satisfactory, satisfying, significant, solid, sound, striking, trenchant, valid, weighty *Antonyms:* insignificant, minor, negligible, slight, trivial

temerity *n.* audacity, brashness, brazenness, boldness, foolhardiness, heedlessness, nerve, rashness, recklessness *Nonformal:* balls, cheek, chutzpah, gall, guts, moxie *Antonyms:* caution, timidity, wariness

temper *n.* **1.** anger, fury, hotheadedness, ill-humour, irascibility, irritability, moodiness, passion, petulance, rage, surliness, volatility **2.** conniption, dander, hissy fit *(Nonformal)*, miff, paddywhack *(British)*, pet, spleen, stew, tizzy **3.** calm, composure, equanimity, poise, self-command, self-control **4.** attitude, character, climate, condition, disposition, mind, mood, nature, orientation, outlook, pulse, spirit, state, state of mind, strain, temperament – *v.* **1.** abate, adjust, allay, alleviate, assuage, calm, curb, ease, lessen, make reasonable, mitigate, moderate, modulate, mollify, pacify, relieve, restrain, soften, soft-pedal, soothe, tame, tone down, weaken *Antonyms:* aggravate, arouse, excite, provoke, stir **2.** bake, dry, harden, mould, petrify, set, solidify, steel, stiffen, strengthen, toughen **3.** adjust, align, harmonize, set, synchronize, tune, tweak *(Nonformal)*

temperament *n.* attitude, bent, capacity, cast, character, complexion, constitution, disposition, distinctiveness, ego, emotions, humour, idiosyncrasy, inclination, individuality, inner nature, intellect, kind, makeup, mentality, mettle, mood, nature, outlook, peculiarity, personality, quality, soul, spirit, stamp, temper, tendency, turn, type, way

temperamental *adj.* **1.** delicate, easily upset, emotional, high-strung, hyper, hypersensitive, moody, neurotic, sensitive, susceptible, tender, thin-skinned, touchy *Antonyms:* callous, hard, thick-skinned **2.** angry, cranky, excitable, explosive, fiery, hasty, hotheaded, impatient, inflammable, irascible, irritable, mean, ornery, passionate, petulant, scrappy, splenetic, surly, tetchy *(Nonformal)*, testy, unpredictable, violent, volatile, volcanic *Antonyms:* calm, controlled, cool **3.** capricious, changeable, erratic, fickle, inconsistent, mercurial, undependable, unpredictable, unreliable, unstable, wayward *Antonyms:* constant, dependable, reliable, stable, steady

temperance *n.* abstinence, control, discretion, forbearance, measure, moderation, prudence, restraint, sedateness, self-control, sobriety, teetotalism, virtue *Antonyms:* excess, extreme, overindulgence

temperate *adj.* **1.** calm, collected, composed, controlled, cool, even-tempered, levelheaded, not given to extremes, peaceful, placid, quiet, regulated, restrained, sedate, self-controlled, sober, stable, steady, subdued, unperturbed, *Antonyms:* hotheaded, unpredictable, volatile, volcanic **2.** abstemious, celibate, chaste, continent, curbed, dry, forbearing, teetotaling *Antonyms:* dissipated, excessive, indulgent **3.** agreeable, balmy, clement, equable, even, fair, gentle, mild, moderate, modest, nice, pleasant, reasonable, summery, warm *Antonyms:* inclement, tempestuous, stormy, wild

temperature *n.* condition, degree, degrees Celsius *or* centigrade *or* Fahrenheit, fever, heat, hotness, thermal reading, warmth

tempest *n.* **1.** blizzard, cyclone, dust devil, ferment, gale, hurricane, snowstorm, squall, storm, streamer, tornado, turbulence, typhoon, windstorm **2.** agitation, chaos, commotion, disturbance, furor, tumult, upheaval, uproar, wildness *Nonformal:* brouhaha, hoo-ha, to-do, whoop-de-do *Antonyms:* calm, peacefulness, placidity, serenity

tempestuous *adj.* **1.** agitated, boisterous, crazy, emotional, excited, feverish, furious, heated, passionate, tumultuous, unpredictable, wild *Antonyms:* calm, peaceful, tranquil **2.** blustery, dirty *(Newfoundland)*, gusty, raging, rough, rugged, squally, stormy, turbulent, violent, windy *Antonyms:* clement, fine, pleasant

template *n.* cast, die, gauge, guide, model, mould, pattern, shape

temple *n.* amen corner *(Nonformal)*, cathedral, chapel, church, fane, *gurdwara (Sikh)*, holy place, house *or* place of worship, monastery, mosque, pagoda, oracle, pantheon, sanctuary, shrine, shul *(Yiddish)*, synagogue, tabernacle *Buddhist: stupa, tope, wat*

tempo *n.* **1.** beat, beats per minute *or* B.P.M., measure, pulsation, rhythm, time, timing **2.** cadence, current, drift, meter, movement, pace, rate, speed, tenor, way

temporal *adj.* **1.** carnal, earthy, fleshly, lay, material, materialistic, mortal, mundane, nonclerical, nonspiritual, physical, profane, secular, sensual, subcelestial, terrestrial, worldly **2.** evanescent, fleeting, impermanent, momentary, short-lived, temporary, transient *Antonyms:* enduring, permanent, solid

temporary *adj.* **1.** brief, changeable, ephemeral, fleeting, fugitive, here today–gone tomorrow *(Nonformal)*,limited, meteoric, momentary, passing, perishable, shifting, short-lived, summary, transient, transitory, unreliable, unstable, volatile *Antonyms:* durable, everlasting, long-term, permanent **2.** acting, ad hoc, make-do, makeshift, *pro tempore (Latin)*, provisional, slapdash, stopgap, substitute, supply *Nonformal:* band aid, jackleg, pro tem, quick and dirty

temporize *v.* **1.** avoid, delay, dipsy-doodle *(Nonformal)*, equivocate, filibuster, hesitate, loiter, play for time, procrastinate, protract, put off, stall *Antonyms:* expedite, hasten, quicken **2.** accommodate, accord, acquiesce, agree, comply, compromise, submit

tempt *v.* **1.** allure, appeal to, attract, captivate, charm, coax, draw, entice, entrap, fascinate, hook, induce, influence, intrigue, inveigle, invite, lure, motivate, move, persuade, seduce, stimulate, whet *Antonyms:* deter, discourage, dissuade, hinder, inhibit, repel **2.** bait, court, dare, incite, provoke, rouse, solicit, wheedle

temptation *n.* allurement, appeal, attraction, bait, draw, enticement, fancy, fascination, inducement, invitation, lure, persuasion, provocation, seduction *Nonformal:* come-on, hook

tempting *adj.* alluring, appealing, appetizing, attractive, charming, delish *(Nonformal)*, desirable, enticing, fascinating, fetching, heavenly, intriguing, inviting, irresistible, luring, magnetic, mouth-watering, rousing, scrumptious, seductive, tantalizing *Antonyms:* offensive, repugnant, repulsive, unattractive

tenable *adj.* acceptable, arguable, believable, cogent, condonable, credible, defendable, defensible, excusable, impregnable, justifiable, maintainable, plausible, practicable, rational, reasonable, reliable, secure, sound, strong, supportable, trustworthy, viable, vindicable, warrantable, workable *Antonyms:* indefensible, insupportable, precarious, unjustifiable, untenable

tenacious *adj.* **1.** adamant, bound, determined, dogged, fast, firm, inflexible, intransigent, obdurate, obstinate, persevering, persistent, pertinacious, possessive, purposeful, relentless, resolute, set, stalwart, staunch, steadfast, stout, strong, strong-willed, stubborn, sturdy, sure, tough, true, unshakable, unswerving *Antonyms:* changeable, fickle, flexible, plastic, pliable **2.** adherent, adhesive, cohesive, gluey, gummy, sticky, tacky, viscous

tenacity *n.* determination, diligence, doggedness, firmness, intransigence, nerve, obduracy, obstinacy, perseverance, persistence, resolution, resolve, staunchness, steadfastness, stubbornness, toughness, willpower *Nonformal:* backbone, grit, intestinal fortitude, stick-to-it-iveness, *Antonyms:* feebleness, irresolution, weakness

tenant *n.* addressee, boarder, crofter, dweller, habitant *(Historical)*, holder, householder, indweller, inhabitant, leaseholder, lessee, lodger, occupant, possessor, renter, rent payer, resident, roomer, squatter *Anto-nyms:* landlord, lessor, owner

tend *v.* **1.** administer, attend, babysit, cater to, cherish, defend, feed, foster, guard, handle, look after, minister, nurse, nurture, oversee, protect, safeguard, serve, service, shepherd, superintend, supervise, wait on, watch, watch over *Antonyms:* disregard, ignore, neglect, overlook, shirk **2.** aim, bear, bend, drift, go, head, make for, move toward, point, turn, verge **3.** conduce, dispose, contribute to, favour, gravitate, incline, lead to

tendency *n.* aptitude, bearing, bent, bias, course, current, curve, direction, disposition, drift, drive, habit, heading, inclination, leaning, mind-set, movement, partiality, penchant, predilection, predisposition, preference, proclivity, proneness, propensity, purport, shift, slant, susceptibility, temper, tenor, trend, type, way, weakness *Nonformal:* bag, groove

tender *adj.* **1.** delicate, feeble, fragile, frail, infirm, meek, sickly, thin, vulnerable, weak *Antonyms:* hard, rough, strong, thick **2.** callow, green, immature, impressionable, inexperienced, new, raw, sensitive, unripe, vernal, young, youthful *Antonyms:* experienced, mature, seasoned, sophisticated **3.** affectionate, amorous, benevolent, careful, caring, charitable, compassionate, considerate, demonstrative, devoted, emotional, fond, forgiving, gentle, humane, kind, lenient, loving, merciful, mild, responsive, sensitive, soft, soft-hearted, solicitous, sympathetic, tender-hearted, thoughtful, tolerant, warm, warmhearted, yielding *Antonyms:* insensitive, tough, uncaring, unsympathetic **4.** affecting, emotive, evocative, heart-moving *or* rending *or* warming, moving, poignant, sentimental, stimulating, tear-jerking, touching **5.** aching, acute, bruised, hypersensitive, inflamed, irritated, painful, smarting, sore, ticklish, touchy – *n.* **1.** bid, estimate, offer, pitch, proposal, submission, suggestion **2.** currency, medium, money, payment, specie – *v.* extend, give, hand in, offer, pay, present, proffer, propose, proposition, put forward, submit, suggest, surrender, volunteer

tenderhearted *adj.* affectionate, compassionate, empathetic, good, gracious, kind, kind-hearted, loving, pitying, responsive, soft, sympathetic, warm *Antonyms:* callous, cold, harsh, malicious, ruthless, vicious

tenderness *n.* **1.** caring, compassion, delicacy, feeling, gentleness, humanity, mercy, pity, sensitivity, softness, sympathy, tender, thing *(Nonformal)*, warmth *Antonyms:* belligerence, truculence, vitriol **2.** ache, bruise, ding *(Nonformal)*, discomfort, pain, smart, soft spot, soreness

tenement *n.* abode, apartment, building, flat, housing, lodgings, rental, rookery, rooming house, slum, warren *Nonformal:* fleabag, firetrap, project

tenet *n.* axiom, belief, canon, conviction, credo, creed, doctrine, dogma, ideology, opinion, position, practice, precept, principle, rule, teaching, truth, view

tennis *n.* competition, game, recreation, sport *Kinds of tennis:* Canadian doubles, court, doubles, indoor, lawn, mixed doubles, outdoor, real, royal, singles, table *Kinds of tennis stroke:* backhand, backhand drive, chop, drive, drop shot, forehand, forehand drive, ground stroke, half-volley, lob, lob volley, overhead, passing shot, serve, slice, service, smash, two-handed backhand, volley *Scoring and procedure in tennis:* ace, advantage, break point, deuce, double-fault, drive, fault, fifteen, forty, game point, love, match point, point, return, serve, service ace, service break, set point, thirty, tiebreaker, unforced error, volley

tenor *n.* **1.** heroic *or* Irish *or* lyric tenor, musician, singer, vocalist, vocal stylist **2.** intent, meaning, purport, purpose, sense, stuff, substance, theme **3.** character, disposition, mood, nature, personality, spirit, temper, tendency, tone **4.** aim, course, current, design, direction, drift, inclination, path, tendency, trend, way

tense *adj.* **1.** close, firm, rigid, stiff, strained, stretched, taut, tight *Antonyms:* composed, loose, relaxed **2.** anxious, distraught, edgy, fretful, jittery, restless, skittish, troubled, uneasy, uptight, worried *Nonformal:* antsy, on pins and needles, strung out, wound up *Antonyms:* calm, carefree, laid-back *(Nonformal)* **3.** disquieting, fraught, heavy *(Nonformal)*, intense, nerve-racking, stressful, worrisome, worrying – *n.* verb form *Divisions of grammatical tense:* aorist, future, future perfect, historical present, imperfect, past, perfect, pluperfect, present, present perfect, preterit, progressive – *v.* brace, go taut, pull, stiffen, straighten, strain, tighten

tension *n.* **1.** balance, constriction, force, overextension, pressure, rigidity, stiffness, strain, stress, stretching, tautness, tenseness, tightness **2.** agitation, annoyance, anxiety, apprehension, crisis, discomfort, disquiet, edginess, friction, jitters, jumps, nerves, pressure, restlessness, shakes, strain, stress, suspense, unease, urgency, worry *Antonyms:* relaxation, serenity, tranquility

tent *n.* canopy, dwelling, hut, shelter *Common tents:* beer, big top, camper, canvas, circus, corporate, dome, kitchen, lean-to, marquee, mess, nylon, pup, teepee, tupik, umbrella, wall, wigwam, *wikuom (Native Peoples)*, yurt

tentative *adj.* **1.** acting, conditional, conjectural, contingent, dependent, experimental, indefinite, interim, makeshift, probationary, provisional, provisionary, provisory, speculative, temporary, test, trial, unconfirmed, undecided, unsettled *Latin: ad interim, pro tempore Nonformal:* iffy, pro tem *Antonyms:* definite, final, fixed, resolved, settled **2.** cautious, diffident, disinclined, doubtful, faltering, half-hearted, halting, hesitant, indecisive, indefinite, irresolute, reluctant, slow, timid, uncertain, undecided, unsure, vacillating, wobbly *Antonyms:* assured, bold, certain, confident, unhesitating

tenuous *adj.* **1.** attenuate, delicate, fine, fragile, gossamer, insignificant, insubstantial, light, rarefied, reedy, slender, slight, thin, unsubstantial *Antonyms:* coarse, heavy, meaty, thick **2.** doubtful, far-fetched, flimsy, implausible, questionable, shaky, shallow, sketchy, slim, weak *Nonformal:* lame, wonky *Antonyms:* cogent, solid, sound

tenure *n.* **1.** habitation, landholding, lease, occupancy, possession, property, tenancy **2.** appointment, dynasty, engagement, office, period, regime, reign, spell, stint, stretch, term, time **3.** duration, freehold, *in perpetuum (Latin)*, permanency, perpetuity, position for life

tepid *adj.* **1.** languid, mild, moderate, temperate, warm, warmish **2.** apathetic, cool, half-hearted, indifferent, neither here nor there *(Nonformal)*, neutral, unenthusiastic

term *n.* **1.** appellation, caption, conception, denomination, description, designation, expression, indication, language, moniker *(Nonformal)*, name, phrase, terminology, title, word **2.** course, cycle, duration, hitch, incumbency, interval, period, phase, quarter, season, semester, session, space, span, spell, standing, stretch, tenure, time, tour, turn, while **3.** article, clause, condition, provision, proviso, qualification *See also:* **terms** – *v.* baptize, call, christen, denominate, describe, designate, dub, entitle, label, name, style, subtitle, tag, title

terminal *adj.* **1.** deadly, done for *(Nonformal)*, dying, extreme, fatal, fixed, hopeless, incurable, killing, lethal, limiting, mortal **2.** closing, concluding, conclusive, crowning, ending, finishing, ultimate *Antonyms:* beginning, opening – *n.* **1.** connection, depot, destination, end, extremity, junction, juncture, limit, platform, station, terminus **2.** conductor, connection, connector, coupler, coupling, outlet, plug **3.** computer screen, CRT, display, input device, monitor, screen, VDT, video display

terminate *v.* **1.** abolish, abort, adjourn, annul, axe, can *(Nonformal)*, cancel, cashier, cease, close, complete, conclude, desist, discontinue, dismiss, dissolve, drop, eliminate, end, expire, extinguish, finish, fire, halt, kill, make redundant, scratch, scrub, stop, wrap up *Antonyms:* begin, inaugurate, initiate **2.** bound, circumscribe, define, delimit, demarcate, edge, limit, restrict

termination *n.* **1.** cessation, close, completion, conclusion, cut-off, discontinuation, end, ending, expiry, finale, *finis (French)*, finish, kill fee *(Nonformal)*, severance, stop, wind-up *Antonyms:* beginning, commencement, inauguration, initiation **2.** outcome, result, upshot

terminology *n.* argot, cant, dialect, jargon, language, lexicon, nomenclature, shoptalk, vocabulary, wording *Nonformal:* bafflegab, legalese, lingo, officialese, psychospeak

terminus *n.* destination, end, end of the line *or* road, finish, goal, stop, stopping place, station, terminal

terms *n. pl.* **1.** agreement, charge, circumstances, conclusion, conditions, details, fee, items, particulars, payment, points, premise, price, provisions, proviso, qualifications, rate, remuneration, specifications, stipulations, treaty, understanding *Nonformal:* fine *or* small print, kicker, nitty-gritty, size of it, strings **2.** balance, equality, equivalence, footing, par, parity, position, relation, standing, status

terrain *n.* area, battleground, country, domain, down, earth, field, geography, ground, land, landscape, province, range, region, soil, sphere, *straná (Russian)*, *terra firma (Latin)*, territory, topography *Nonformal:* beat, turf

terrestrial *adj.* corporeal, earthly, fleshly, material, mundane, telluric, temporal, terrene, worldly *Antonyms:* celestial, cosmic, heavenly – *n.* earthling, earthperson, human, mortal

terrible *adj.* **1.** abhorrent, appalling, atrocious, beastly, dangerous, desperate, dire, disastrous, disturbing, dreaded, dreadful, frightful, ghastly, gross *(Nonformal)*, gruesome, harrowing, hateful, hideous, horrendous, horrible, horrid, loathsome, monstrous, obnoxious, odious, offensive, repulsive, revolting, rotten, shocking, ugly, unnerving, unpleasant *Antonyms:* admirable, delightful, great, pleasant, remarkable **2.** awful, bad, base, inferior, jejune, mean, miserable, poor, off-base, second-rate *Nonformal:* crappy, crummy, flea-bitten, lousy, waste of effort *or* money *or* time **3.** drastic, excessive, extreme, intense, overwhelming, severe **4.** awesome, fearsome, formidable, petrifying, redoubtable **5.** ashamed, contrite, regretful, remorseful, sorry, wretched **6.** bilious, hungover, ill, nauseous, sick, unwell

terribly *adv.* **1.** discouragingly, disturbingly, dreadfully, fearfully, frightfully, gravely, hideously, horribly, unhappily, unpleasantly **2.** decidedly, drastically, exceedingly, extremely, greatly, highly, intensely, markedly, mightily, remarkably, seriously, staggeringly, thoroughly, unbelievably, very **3.** awfully, badly, desperately, miserably, poorly, wretchedly

terrific *adj.* **1.** amazing, awesome, breathtaking, divine, excellent, fabulous, fantastic, fine, glorious, great, keen, magnificent, marvellous, outstanding, remarkable, sensational, smashing, stupendous, super, superb, wonderful *Antonyms:* awful, bad, dreadful, hideous **2.** colossal, deafening, disquieting, enormous, excessive, extreme, fierce, formidable, gigantic, great, harsh, huge, immense, intense, large, monstrous, severe, shocking, terrible, tremendous

terrify *v.* alarm, appal, awe, chill, dismay, floor *(Nonformal)*, frighten, horrify, intimidate, paralyze, petrify, scare, scare stiff, shock, spook, startle, stun, terrorize *Antonyms:* calm, ease, pacify, placate, soothe

territorial *adj.* **1.** geographical, locational, jurisdictional, regional, sectional, zonal **2.** custodial, defensive, possessive, protective

territory *n.* bailiwick, district, domain, jurisdiction, land, *lebensraum (German)*, neighbourhood, precinct, province, range, region, space, sphere, tract, turf *Nonformal:* patch, stomping ground *Canadian territories:* Northwest Territories, Nunavut, Yukon *See also:* **province**

terror *n.* **1.** alarm, anxiety, awe, consternation, dismay, dread, fear, fearfulness, fright, horror, intimidation, panic, *schrecklichkeit (German)*, shock, trepidation **2.** brat, delinquent, devil, *enfant terrible (French)*, evildoer, fiend, hellion, mischief-maker, monster, nuisance, pest, scourge *Nonformal:* holy terror, menace,

terrorism *n.* atrocity, blackmail, coercion, destruction, extortion, extremism, fanaticism, intimidation, violence, zealotry

terrorist *n.* anarchist, arsonist, bomber, guerrilla, hostage-taker, insurgent, kidnapper, revolutionary, subversive

terrorize *v.* alarm, browbeat, bully, coerce, domineer, frighten, harass, intimidate, menace, petrify, scare, terrify, threaten, torment

terse *adj.* **1.** abbreviated, aphoristic, boiled down, brief, clear-cut, clipped, close, compact, compendious, concise, crisp, elliptical, epigrammatic, exact, gnomic, incisive, laconic, lean, neat, pithy, pointed, polished, precise, refined, sententious, snappy, succinct, summary, taut, trenchant *Antonyms:* ambiguous, circumlocutory, confused, discursive, lengthy prolix **2.** abrupt, blunt, brusque, curt, gruff, laconic, short

test *n.* **1.** analysis, assay, assessment, check, evaluation, examination, experiment, experimentation, inquest, inquiry, inspection, investigation, *pons asinorum (Latin)*, probing, scrutiny, study, trial *Nonformal:* cruise, dry run, shakedown **2.** attempt, audition, contest, countdown effort, endeavour, run, shot, stab, tryout undertaking, venture *Nonformal:* go whack **3.** exam, final, multiple choice, oral questionnaire, query, quiz **4.** bar, bench mark, criterion, gauge, law, line, rule, standard, touchstone – *v.* **1.** analyze, appraise, assess, check, confirm, demonstrate, evaluate, examine, experiment, inquire, inspect, interrogate, investigate, *pree (Scottish)*, prove, quiz, sample, scrutinize, taste, try, validate, verify, weigh **2.** assay, clarify, distill, expurgate, purify, rarefy, refine

testament *n.* affirmation, attestation, avowal, confirmation, covenant, declaration, demonstration, dispensation, evidence, proof, record, reference, ROE *or* record of employment, testimony, tribute, will, witness

testify *v.* **1.** argue, attest, authenticate, aver, back up, bear witness, confirm, corroborate, evidence, present evidence, prove, state, substantiate, swear to, vouchsafe, *Antonyms:* belie, contradict, controvert, disprove **2.** affirm, assert, certify, guarantee, pledge, promise, swear, warrant **3.** announce, declare, demonstrate, display, manifest, proclaim, publicize, reflect, show

testimonial *n.* **1.** attestation, certificate, character reference, commendation, confirmation, credential, endorsement, evidence *or* reference, good word, letter of introduction *or* recommendation, manifestation, memorial, plug, proof, recommendation, reference, statement, voucher, witness **2.** acknowledgement, appreciation, celebration, homage, honour, recognition, salutation, token, tribute

testimony *n.* affidavit, affirmation, attestation, avowal, backing, confirmation, corroboration, declaration, demonstration, deposition, documentation, evidence, facts, illustration, proof, statement, substantiation, support, testament, verification

testy *adj.* annoyed, bad-tempered, bitchy, cantankerous, captious, choleric, crabby, cranky, cross, crotchety, exasperated, grouchy, grumpy, impatient, irascible, irritable, mean, ornery, owly *(Nonformal)*, peevish, peppery, petulant, quarrelsome, quick-tempered, ratty, short-tempered, snappy, splenetic, touchy, uptight, waspish *Antonyms:* good-natured, kind, pleasant

tête-à-tête *n.* causerie, chat, conversation, coze, dialogue, discourse, discussion, heart-to-heart, meeting, one-on-one, talk *Nonformal:* confab, sit-down

tether *n.* binding, bond, chain, fastening, halter, harness, line, lead, leash, lunge, restraint, rope, shackle – *v.* bind, chain, confine, fasten, fetter, leash, manacle, moor, restrain, rope, secure, shackle, stabilize, tie

text *n.* **1.** body, citation, clause, copy, discourse, extract, line, lines, main passage, narrative, paragraph, passage, quotation, script, scripture, sentence, verse, words **2.** document, folio, manuscript, material, matter, print, treatment **3.** content, contents, focus, import, meaning, subject, theme, topic **4.** adaptation, composition, edition, paraphrase, revision, translation, vocabulary, wording, writing **5.** book, handbook, manual, primer, publication, reference, required reading, source, syllabus, textbook

textbook *n.* casebook, course binder *or* kit, exercise book, instruction manual, primer, reader, reference book, schoolbook, workbook

texture *n.* **1.** coarseness, consistency, fabric, feel, fibre, fineness, grain, nap, roughness, smoothness, stiffness, surface, touch, warp, weave, web, woof **2.** arrangement, character, composition, essence, makeup, nature, pattern, pith, quality, structure

thank *v.* acknowledge, appreciate, attribute, bless, credit, express gratitude, oblige, praise, recognize, requite, repay, reward, salute, smile on *Antonyms:* deride, discredit, jeer, mock, ridicule

thankful *adj.* appreciative, beholden, content, grateful, gratified, indebted, obliged, overwhelmed, pleased, relieved, satisfied *Antonyms:* grudging, unappreciative, ungrateful

thankless *adj.* **1.** disagreeable, distasteful, fruitless, futile, losing, miserable, unacknowledged, unappreciated, unpleasant, unprofitable, unrecognized, unrewarding, vain, wretched *Antonyms:* productive, profitable, rewarding **2.** heedless, inconsiderate, insolent, rude, unappreciative, ungracious, ungrateful, unmindful

thanks *n. pl.* acknowledgment, appreciation, benediction, blessing, credit, grace, gratefulness, gratitude, praise, recognition, thanksgiving

thaw *n.* breakup, chinook, snow-eater *(Nonformal)*, spring *or* springtime – *v.* breakup, defrost, dissolve, flow, fuse, liquefy, loosen, melt, relax, soften, unfreeze, warm, warm up *Antonyms:* chill, congeal, freeze, harden, solidify

theatre *n.* **1.** amphitheatre, arena, assembly *or* concert *or* lecture *or* show hall, auditorium, cinema, coliseum, drive-in, footlights, hall, hippodrome, house, locale, lyceum, *mise en scène (French)*, movie *or* opera house, playhouse, room, scene, site, stage, *Nonformal:* barn, boards **2.** comedy, drama, entertainment, motion picture, movie, musical, opera, play, satire, tableau, tragedy *See also:* **drama**

theatrical *adj.* **1.** affected, artificial, campy, ceremonious, exaggerated, histrionic, mannered, melodramatic, ostentatious, outrageous, pompous, schmaltzy, showy, stagy, stilted, superficial, unnatural, unreal *Nonformal:* Hollywood, over-the-top *Antonyms:* natural, simple, unaffected, unexaggerated **2.** amateur, comic, dramatic, dramaturgic, operatic, Thespian, tragic, vaudeville – n. performance, production, show, staging

theft *n.* **1.** appropriation, embezzlement, five-finger discount *(Nonformal)*, graft, heist, larceny, looting, misappropriation of funds, mugging, pilferage, pillage, piracy, plunder, purloining, robbery, shoplifting, stealing, thievery, vandalism **2.** cheat, chicanery, extortion, fraud, highway robbery *(Nonformal)*, price gouging, rip-off, scam, scandal, subterfuge, swindle, trickery

theme *n.* **1.** aim, angle, aspect, attitude, concept, conception, idea, ideal, image, intention, keynote, leitmotif, line, motif, notion, object, opinion, outlook, perspective, point, premise, question, style, subject, theory, thought, topic, view **2.** craze, dream, fad, fantasy, fetish, fixation **3.** argument, article, composition, description, dissertation, essay, exercise, manuscript, paper, report, statement, thesis **4.** anthem, composition, ditty, melody, song, tune

then *adj.* coincident, contemporaneous, erstwhile, former, previous – *adv.* **1.** afterwards, again, before long, immediately *or* soon after, later, next, soon, suddenly, when **2.** accordingly, after all, consequently, ergo, hence, in that case, so, subsequently, thence, therefore, thereupon, thus, whence **3.** additionally, also, besides, as well, in addition, moreover, yet **4.** at that time, before, formerly, years ago

theological *adj.* apostolic, canonical, churchly, deistic, divine, doctrinal, ecclesiastical, metaphysical, religious, scriptural, theistic

theorem *n.* axiom, belief, deduction, dictum, doctrine, formula, fundamental, hypothesis, law, lemma, postulate, premise, principle, proposition, rule, statement, theory, thesis, truth

theoretical *adj.* abstract, academic, analytical, conjectural, hypothetical, ideological, impractical, logical, metaphysical, philosophical, presumed, speculative, suppositional, tentative, unproved, unsubstantiated *Nonformal:* blue sky, ivory-towered *Antonyms:* applied, empirical, experiential, practical

theorize *v.* ballpark *(Nonformal)*, conjecture, guess, hypothesize, project, propose, propound, reason, speculate, submit, suggest, suppose, think

theory *n.* assumption, belief, conjecture, doctrine, explanation, generalization, guesswork, hypothesis, idea, inference, opinion, presumption, speculation, supposition, surmise *Antonyms:* practice, proof

therapeutic *adj.* beneficial, corrective, curative, healing, health-giving, helpful, palliative, remedial, restorative, salubrious, salutary, wholesome *Antonyms:* adverse, harmful, hurtful

therapy *n.* aid, corrective action, cure, healing, help, medical care *or* treatment, medication, medicine, remedial procedure, remedy, therapeutics, treatment *Common therapies:* acupressure, acupuncture, aromatherapy, chemotherapy, counseling, craniosacral, ECT, electroconvulsive, group, heat, homeopathy, hydrotherapy, hypnotherapy, massage, occupational, osteopathy, pharmaceutical, physiotherapy, physio *(Nonformal)*, psychotherapy, reflexology, reiki, shock, speech, thermal, twelve step

therefore *adv.* accordingly, as a result, consequently, ergo, hence, in consequence, since, so, then, thence, thereupon, thus

thesis *n.* argument, composition, contention, discourse, dissertation, essay, hypothesis, paper, premise, proposition, subject, supposition, theme, treatise

thick *adj.* **1.** caked, clotted, coagulated, concentrated, condensed, congealed, consolidated, curdled, firm, gelatinous, globby, gooey, gummy, jelled, opaque, ropy, set, solid, solidified, syrupy, thickened, turbid, viscous, vitrified *Antonyms:* clear, diluted, runny, watery, weak **2.** abundant, brimming, bristling, bursting, chock-a-block *(Nonformal)*, close, compact, compressed, concentrated, condensed, covered, crammed, crawling, crowded, deep, dense, heaped, multitudinous, packed, populous, swarming, teeming, tight *Antonyms:* narrow, sparse, thin **3.** cloudy, foggy, impenetrable, indistinct, muddy, obscure, pea soup, soupy **4.** blockheaded, dense, dim-witted, doltish, dopey, dull, dumb, ignorant, insensitive, obtuse, possessing obsolete intellectual equipment *(Nonformal)*, slow, slow-witted, stupid *Antonyms:* articulate, brainy, clever, needle-witted, sharp **5.** broad, bulky, burly, chunky, fat, firm, great, heavy, massive, pudgy, rotund, solid, stocky, substantial, thickset *Antonyms:* slight, slim **6.** gravelly, gruff, guttural, hoarse, husky, muffled, raspy, raucous, scratching, throaty **7.** bosom, chummy, close, confidential, cordial, devoted, familiar, fraternal, friendly, inseparable, intimate, sisterly *Antonyms:* antagonistic, cool, distant – *n.* centre, core, eye, heart, middle, midst

thicken *v.* **1.** clabber, clot, coagulate, condense, congeal, expand, freeze, gel, gelatinize, harden, increase, reduce *(cooking)*, set, solidify, stiffen *Antonyms:* dilute, thin, water down **2.** amplify, augment, broaden, deepen, elevate, heighten, intensify, peak, quicken, rise, strengthen *Antonyms:* decline, languish, wane, weaken

thicket *n.* bush, coppice, covert, copse, droke *(Newfoundland)*, grove, scrub, shrubbery, sugarbush, underbrush, undergrowth

thief *n.* **1.** bandit, burglar, cat burglar, cattle rustler, con artist, criminal, cutpurse, embezzler, footpad *(Historical)*, freebooter, *ganef (Yiddish)*, grafter, grave robber, highwayman, hijacker, housebreaker, kleptomaniac, ladrone, mugger, nightrider, picaroon, pickpocket, pilferer, pirate, plunderer, poacher, prowler, purse snatcher, robber, shoplifter, swindler, white-collar criminal *Nonformal:* booster, crook, holdup *or* rip-off artist, second-story man **2.** copyright infringer, plagiarist, plagiary

thieve *v.* burglarize, car-jack, cheat, copy, embezzle, fleece, filch, finger, heist, hijack, hustle, lift, misappropriate, mug, pickpocket, pilfer, plagiarize, plunder, poach, purloin, rob, rustle, shoplift, smuggle, steal, swindle, take, victimize *Nonformal:* borrow, make away with

thieving *adj.* criminal, crooked, cunning, dishonest, fraudulent, furtive, larcenous, pilfering, plunderous, predatory, rapacious *Nonformal:* light-fingered, sticky-fingered – *n.* burglary, embezzlement, larceny, pilfering, plundering, poaching, robbery, stealing, theft

thin *adj.* **1.** anorexic, bare, bony, cadaverous, emaciated, flat, gangly, gaunt, lank, lean, narrow, reedy, scrawny, skeletal, skinny, slender, slim, spindly, stalky, starved, twiggy, undernourished, underweight, wan, *Antonyms:* corpulent, deep, fat, thick **2.** rare, rarefied, refined, scant, scarce, sparse *Antonyms:* abundant, adequate, plentiful, profuse **3.** diffused, diluted, dispersed, insubstantial, meagre, runny, scattered, unsubstantial, watery, weak **4.** deficient, feeble, inadequate, insufficient, lacking, lame, poor, shallow, tenuous, untenable, **5.** high-pitched, metallic, piercing, sharp, shrill, treble, warbling *Antonyms:* baritone, bass, heavy, resonant **6.** attenuated, delicate, diaphanous, fine, flimsy, fragile, gossamer, light, paper-thin, see-through, sheer, skimpy, slight, slinky, superficial, translucent, transparent, wafer-thin, wispy – *v.* **1.** cull, cut, cut back, decrease, delete, diminish, edit, emaciate, prune, rarefy, refine, shave, shrink, subtract, trim, weaken, weed **2.** attenuate, dilute, disperse, dissipate, doctor *(Nonformal)*, spread, water down *Antonyms:* fortify, strengthen, thicken

thing *n.* **1.** article, device, entity, gadget, implement, item, object, particular, possession *Nonformal:* doohickey, whatchmacallit **2.** act, affair, concern, deed, development, problem, situation, transaction **3.** comment, criticism, expression, feeling, idea, notion, opinion, remark, statement, utterance **4.** attribute, characteristic, feature, property, quality, quirk, trademark, trait, virtue **5.** aberration, abnormality, creature, deviant, entity, freak, monster, oddity, peculiarity, phenomenon, UFO

things *n. pl.* **1.** apparel, attire, clothes, clothing, duds, habiliments, raiment **2.** belongings, bits and pieces *(Nonformal)*, chattels, gear, goods, impediments, luggage, paraphernalia, personal effects, personals, possessions, property, stuff, trappings

think *v.* **1.** analyze, appraise, appreciate, cogitate, comprehend, consider, contemplate, deliberate, estimate, evaluate, examine, figure *or* sort out, meditate, mull over, muse, ponder, reflect, resolve, ruminate, study, weigh **2.** brainstorm, come up with, conceive, find, invent, make up, produce **3.** anticipate, assume, believe, conceive, deduce, expect, fancy, imagine, infer, rationalize, reason, reckon, speculate, suppose **4.** identify, place, recall, recognize, recollect, remember, reminisce *Antonyms:* lose, forget, pass over **5.** have in mind, intend, mean, purpose

thinkable *adj.* believable, comprehensible, conceivable, convincing, feasible, imaginable, likely, plausible, possible, practical, presumable, reasonable, supposable, sustainable *Antonyms:* absurd, impossible, unlikely

thinking *adj.* analytical, cerebral, contemplative, deliberative, ivory-tower, meditative, mental, philosophical, pondering, rational, reasoning, reflective, thoughtful – *n.* cogitation, deduction, hypothesis, idea, induction, inference, postulation, premise, reason, reasoning, rumination, theorem, thesis, thought process

thirst *n.* **1.** aridity, dehydration, drought, dryness **2.** appetite, craving, desire, determination, eagerness, fire, hankering, hunger, keenness, longing, passion, will, yearning, yen *Antonyms:* apathy, aversion, disinclination – *v.* ache, crave, desire, hunger, long, parch, want, yearn

thirsty *adj.* **1.** arid, athirst, bone-dry, dehydrated, desiccated, dry, parched *Nonformal:* dry as dust, running on empty **2.** aching, anxious, ardent, avid, burning, craving, desirous, eager, greedy, hankering, impatient, inclined, itching, keen, longing, needing, yearning

thorn *n.* **1.** barb, bramble, briar, burr, point, prickle, snag, spike, spine **2.** affliction, annoyance, bane, *bête noir (French)*, curse, grievance, irritation, millstone, nuisance, pain, plague, scourge, torment, trouble, vexation *Antonyms:* aid, balm, comfort

thorny *adj.* **1.** barbed, bristly, pointed, prickly, sharp, spiked, spinous, spiny, stinging, thistly **2.** annoying, arduous, complex, complicated, difficult, intricate, involved, irksome, ticklish, troublesome, trying, vexatious *Antonyms:* comforting, easy, simple

thorough *adj.* **1.** accurate, assiduous, careful, complete, comprehensive, detailed, diligent, efficient, exact, exhaustive, meticulous, painstaking, scrupulous *Antonyms:* cursory, haphazard, partial, superficial **2.** absolute, all-embracing, all-inclusive, all-out, in-depth, intensive, itemized, minute, particular, sweeping, tough *Nonformal:* royal, slambang, whole hog

thoroughbred *adj.* **1.** blood, bloodstock, full-blooded, graded, papered *(Nonformal)*, pedigreed, pure, purebred, registered **2.** aristocratic, cultivated, cultured, elegant, first-class, genteel, refined, sophisticated, upper-crust

thoroughfare *n.* avenue, bi-way, boulevard, canal, channel, concourse, corridor, expressway, freeway, highway, parkway, passage, river, road, route, seaway, strait, street, strip, turnpike, way

thoroughly *adv.* assiduously, carefully, completely, comprehensively, conscientiously, diligently, earnestly, efficiently, exceedingly, exceptionally, extremely, fully, highly, in detail, intensely, intensively, meticulously, notably, painstakingly, perfectly, remarkably, scrupulously, strikingly, sweepingly, throughout, totally, unremittingly, very, wholly *Nonformal:* hugely, from A to Z *or* top to bottom *or* soup to nuts *Antonyms:* carelessly, clumsily, imperfectly, partly, slapdash, with a lick and a polish

though *adv.* but, however, nevertheless, yet – *conj.* albeit, all the same, although, however, in any case, nevertheless, notwithstanding, still, yet

thought *n.* **1.** cogito, cogitation, contemplation, deduction, deliberation, induction, inference, introspection, meditation, musing, perception, reasoning, reflection, rumination, theorization **2.** brainstorm, concept, design, idea, plan, scheme, supposition, theory, thesis *Nonformal:* brain child or wave, flash **3.** attention, care, concern, consideration, examination, regard, scrutiny, speculation, study **4.** assessment, assumption, belief, judgment, opinion, position, understanding, view **5.** anticipation, aspiration, expectation, hope, prospect, vision

thoughtful *adj.* **1.** attentive, cautious, considerate, cool *(Nonformal)*, diplomatic, discreet, heedful, indulgent, mindful, observant, regardful, sensitive, tactful, *Antonyms:* inconsiderate, insensitive **2.** caring, charitable, courteous, earnest, gracious, helpful, kind, kindly, neighbourly, obliging, polite, prudent, responsive, unselfish, well-bred *Antonyms:* brash, impolite, **3.** analytical, astute, brainy, calculating, cerebral, cogitative, deep *(Nonformal)*, deliberative, discerning, dispassionate, intellectual, judicious, keen, levelheaded, logical, meditative, objective, philosophic, rational, reasonable, sagacious, serious, sober, studious, wise *Antonyms:* flippant, shallow **3.** absorbed, contemplative, engrossed, intent, introspective, musing, on cloud nine *(Nonformal)*, pensive, pondering, preoccupied, rapt, reasoning, ruminative, reflecting, thinking

thoughtless *adj.* **1.** blind, boorish, brash, careless, discourteous, hasty, heedless, hotheaded, ill-advised, impolite, imprudent, impulsive, inconsiderate, indiscreet, indiscriminate, injudicious, insensitive, madcap, neglectful, negligent, rash, reckless, rude, self-centred, selfish, tactless, uncaring, ungracious, unkind, unmindful *Antonyms:* attentive, considerate, diplomatic, prudent, tactful **2.** absent-minded, confused, dumb, empty-headed, foolish, ignorant, inattentive, inept, mindless, obtuse, puerile, remiss, senseless, sophomoric, stupid, thick, unwise, vacuous, witless *Antonyms:* intelligent, smart, well-advised, wise

thrash *v.* **1.** batter, beat, belt, birch, buffet, cane, chastise, clobber, drub, flail, flog, hammer, horsewhip, lambaste, larrup, maul, pelt, pitch, pound, pummel, punish, rout, spank, strike, tan, thwack, trim, trounce, wallop, whack, whale, whip *Antonyms:* hug, massage, pet, rub **2.** bury, conquer, crush, defeat, overthrow, overwhelm, pulverize, vanquish *Nonformal:* lick, shellac, whup **3.** gyrate, jerk, pitch, rock, roll, shake, spasm, sway, throe, twitch **4.** make way, move, separate, thresh, work to windward

thread *n.* **1.** babiche, cable, cord, filament, fibre, hair, inkle, row, strand, string, suture, tendril, twine, wire *Common threads:* cotton, flax, floss, hemp, linen, nylon, polyester, Polyfibre, raffia, rayon, sewing, silk, wool, yarn **2.** beam, flash, ray, seam, shaft, stream, vein **3.** gist, keynote, motif, subject, theme, thesis – *v.* **1.** bead, braid, loop, meander, screw, string, twist, wind **2.** connect, imbue, interlace, permeate, pervade, string together, suffuse, weave

threadbare *adj.* **1.** dilapidated, dog-eared, down-at-the-heels, faded, frayed, frowzy, moth-eaten *(Nonformal)*, old, ragged, ratty, rundown, scruffy, seedy, shabby, shopworn, tacky, tattered, tatty, timeworn, used, well-worn, worn, worn-out *Antonyms:* new, pristine, smart, well-preserved **2.** banal, clichéd, common, commonplace, conventional, corny, dull, everyday, familiar, hackneyed, imitative, overused, stale, stereotyped, stock, tedious, trite *Antonyms:* different, fresh, novel, original

threat *n.* blackmail, bluff, danger, extortion, fix *(Nonformal)*, foreboding, foreshadowing, hazard, intimidation, menace, omen, peril, portent, presage, risk, warning

threaten *v.* **1.** abuse, admonish, blackmail, browbeat, bulldoze, bully, endanger, enforce, extort, frighten, growl, hazard, imperil, intimidate, jeopardize, peril, press, push around, risk, scare, scowl, snarl, spook, terrorize, torment *Nonformal:* chill, muscle, lean on, shakedown *Antonyms:* defend, guard, protect, shelter **2.** augur, caution, expose, forebode, foreshadow, forewarn, loom, portend, presage, warn

threatening *adj.* **1.** alarming, apocalyptic, blustery, cautionary, dangerous, dire, fateful, frought, impending, inclement, looming, lowering, ominous, overhanging, portentous, sinister, stormy *Antonyms:* auspicious, bright, encouraging, reassuring **2.** bullying, comminatory, endangering, frightening, menacing, minatory, terrorizing

threshold *n.* **1.** door, doorsill, doorstep, doorway, entrance, entryway, foyer, gate, limen, mouth, opening, sill, vestibule **2.** beginning, brink, cusp, dawn, verge

thrift *n.* austerity, conservation, economy, frugality, husbandry, making do with less, miserliness, parsimony, preservation, prudence, recycling, saving, wisdom *Antonyms:* carelessness, profligacy, waste

thrifty *adj.* **1.** canny, careful, chary, close, close-fisted, conserving, economical, frugal, parsimonious, penny-pinching, penny-wise, preserving, provident, prudent, saving, scrimpy, skimping, sparing, stingy, tight *Antonyms:* extravagant, free-spending, generous, profligate **2.** flourishing, fruitful, growing, lucrative, profitable, prosperous, successful, thriving *Antonyms:* failing, on the way out *(Nonformal)*, shrinking

thrill *n.* adventure, excitement, fireworks, frisson, fun, pleasure, pulsation, sensation, stimulation, titillation, tremor, turn-on *Nonformal:* blast, buzz, charge, flash, kick, rush *Antonyms:* boredom, dullness, ennui, monotony, tedium – *v.* animate, arouse, delight, electrify, enchant, enthuse, excite, flutter, glow, impress, inspire, move, palpitate, quicken, quiver, rally, rouse, score, shake, stimulate, stir, tickle, tingle, titillate, tremble *Nonformal:* blow away, send, slay, wow *Antonyms:* bore, exhaust, tire, weary

thrilling *adj.* breathtaking, electrifying, enchanting, exciting, exhausting, exquisite, gripping, magnificent, miraculous, pulsing, riveting, rousing, sensational, spine-tingling, stimulating, stirring, trembling, wondrous *Nonformal:* mind-blowing, out of this world, to die for *Antonyms:* dreary, dull, monotonous, staid

thrive *v.* advance, bear fruit, bloom, blossom, boom, burgeon, develop, expand, flourish, get ahead, grow fat *or* rich, increase, mushroom, progress, prosper, radiate, rise, shine, succeed, wax *Nonformal:* make it, score, *Antonyms:* decline, languish, stagnate, wane, wilt, wither

thriving *adj.* advancing, blooming, booming, burgeoning, developing, expanding, flourishing, going strong, growing, healthy, moving ahead, productive, progressing, prolific, prospering, prosperous, roaring, robust, rolling, successful, wealthy *Nonformal:* cooking, filthy rich, growing by leaps and bounds, home free, really cooking, sitting pretty *Antonyms:* ailing, bankrupt, failing, spiraling downhill

throat *n.* gorge, gullet, neck *Parts of the throat:* Adam's apple *(Nonformal)*, epiglottis, esophagus, larynx, nasal cavity, palate, pharynx, thyroid cartilage, tongue, tonsils, trachea, uvula, vocal chords

throaty *adj.* dry, gruff, guttural, harsh, hoarse, husky, sultry, thick, whisky-voiced *(Nonformal) Antonyms:* piercing, shrill, trebly

throb *n.* beat, drumming, flutter, palpitation, pounding, pulsation, pulse, tick, thrum, trembling – *v.* beat, boom *(Nonformal)*, flutter, palpitate, pound, pulsate, pulse, resonate, thrill, thump, tingle, tremble, vibrate

throe *n.* agony, anguish, chaos, confusion, convulsion, distress, grief, pain, pang, seizure, spasm, stress, struggle, suffering, torture, travail

throng *n.* assemblage, bunch, collection, congregation, crowd, crush, drove, everybody, flock, gathering, horde, host, mass, mob, multitude, pack, press, swarm – *v.* cluster, collect, congregate, crowd, flock, gather, jam, mass, surge, surround, swarm *Antonyms:* disperse, dissipate, separate

throttle *n.* **1.** accelerator, choke, lever, pedal, switch **2.** grasp, grip, hold, Shawinigan handshake *(Nonformal)* – *v.* burke, choke, control, gag, garrote, inhibit, seize, silence, smother, stifle, strangle, suffocate, suppress

through *adj.* **1.** constant, direct, free, nonstop, one-way, opened, rapid, regular, straight, straightforward, unbroken, unhindered, uninterrupted **2.** done, ended, finis, finished, fired, terminated *Nonformal:* kaput, out, out of here – *prep.* because, by means of, during, over, via

throughout *adv. & prep.* all over the place *(Nonformal)*, around, completely, during, everywhere, over, overall, right through, round

throw *v.* **1.** bandy, barrage, bombard, bunt, butt, cant, cast, catapult, chuck, chunk *(Nonformal)*, deliver, direct, discharge, drive, eject, fire, flick, fling, flip, heave, hurl, impel, lapidate, launch, let fly, let go, lift, lob, peg, pelt, pepper, pitch, precipitate, project, propel, push, punt, put, scatter, send, shower, shy, sling, splatter, spray, sprinkle, start, stone, strew, thrust, toss, tumble, volley, waft **2.** buck, bump *(Nonformal)*, dislodge, displace, fling off, overturn, unseat

thrust *n.* **1.** acceleration, advance, attack, blitz, boost, drive, forward movement, impetus, impulsion, jump, lunge, momentum, onset, onslaught, poke, prod, propulsion, punch, push, shove, stab **2.** burden, pressure, strain, stress **3.** core, effect, gist, meaning, meat, pith, point, purport, sense, short, substance, theme, upshot – *v.* **1.** advance, assail, assault, attack, bear down, boost, buck, bulldoze, butt, crowd, dig, drive, elbow, exert, force, heave, hump, impel, jab, jam, jostle, lob, lunge, obtrude, plunge, press, prod, propel, punch, push, push forward, railroad, ram, shove, stab, whack, wham **2.** edge *or* put in, implant, interject, interpose, insert, introduce, remark

thud *n. & v.* bang, beat, blow, clout, clump, clunk, crash, fall, flutter, hammer, hit, knock, poke, pound, rap, slap, smack, strike, throb, thump, thwack, wallop, whack

thug *n.* **1.** assassin, bandit, bravo, bully, cutthroat, hired gun, hit man, hoodlum, hooligan, killer, muscle, ruffian, strikebreaker, tough *Nonformal:* goon, hired help, hood, plug-ugly, roughneck, skinhead **2.** blockhead, boor, brute, clod, dolt, dunce, lout, nincompoop, numbnuts *(Nonformal)*, numskull, oaf

thunder *n.* barrage, blast, booming, clap, cannonade, crack, crashing, detonation, din, discharge, drumfire, explosion, noise, outburst, peal, reverberation, roar, rumble, thunderbolt, uproar – *v.* bark, bellow, boom, curse, declaim, denounce, explode, fulminate, gnarl, growl, proclaim, rail, rant, roar, shout, snarl, threaten, yell

thunderous *adj.* booming, deafening, earsplitting, earthshaking, explosive, loud, roaring, rolling, rumbling *Antonyms:* mousy, quiet, silent

thunderstruck *adj.* agape, aghast, amazed, astonished, confounded, confused, dazed, dumfounded, flabbergasted, floored, nonplussed, overwhelmed, paralyzed, petrified, shocked, stunned *Nonformal:* gobsmacked, knocked for a loop

thus *adv.* accordingly, ergo, for instance, for that reason, hence, in this manner *or* way, on that account, sic, similarly, so, thence, therefore

thwack *n. & v.* backhand, bash, blow, clout, cuff, hit, slap, smack, thrash, thump, wallop, whack

thwart *v.* baffle, balk, beat, bilk, check, circumvent, confuse, counter, cramp, crimp, curb, defeat, disappoint, dodge, foil, foul up, frustrate, hinder, impede, obstruct, outwit, prevent, restrain, scotch, stymie, trammel, upset *Antonyms:* assist, encourage, hasten, help, support

tic *n.* contraction, fit, jerk, nerves, quiver, seizure, shake, spasm, tremor, twitch

tick *n.* **1.** beat, blow, clack, click, pulsation, pulse, rap, shake, tap, throb, ticktock **2.** flash, instant, minute, moment, second, twinkling **3.** check, checkmark, cross, dash, dot, flick, indication, line, mark, stroke **4.** bloodsucker, louse, parasite – *v.* **1.** beat, clack, click, pulsate, pulse, rap, tap, throb **2.** agitate, aggravate, annoy, get to, irritate

ticket *n.* **1.** admission, ballot, certificate, coupon, licence, pass, stub, summons, token, voucher **2.** chit, label, marker, parking tag *(Nonformal)*, price tag, tab, tag – *v.* brand, label, mark, stamp, tab, tag

tickle *n.* **1.** aggravation, annoyance, irritant itch, **2.** frisson, stimulation, thrill, tingling, titillation **3.** *Newfoundland:* channel, narrow, passage, strait – *v.* amuse, attract, brush, caress, convulse, delight, divert, enchant, entertain, excite, gratify, interest, itch, pat, pet, please, scratch, stimulate, stroke, tease, thrill, tingle, titillate, touch

ticklish *adj.* **1.** awkward, complex, delicate, difficult, fragile, precarious, prickly, risky, touch and go *(Nonformal)*, unstable, wobbly **2.** cranky, grumpy, irritable, moody, sensitive, temperamental, tender, testy, touchy

tidbit *n.* appetizer, bit, bite, dash, delicacy, goody *(Nonformal)*, iota, jot, morsel, mouthful, portion, snack, snippet, soupçon, teaser, trailer, treat

tide *n.* **1.** course, current, direction, drag, drift, eddy, flow, flux, flux and reflux, tendency, tidal current *or* flow *or* flood *or* stream, tidewater, trend, undercurrent, undertow *Kinds of tide:* ebb, high, low, neap, rip, riptide, spring **2.** period, season, time – *v.* **1.** assist, buoy, carry, ebb, float, flow, help **2.** come through, endure, persevere, survive

tidings *n. pl.* bulletin, communication, good wishes, greetings, information, intelligence, message, news, notification, release, report, story, word *Nonformal:* low-down, scoop, scuttlebutt, skinny

tidy *adj.* **1.** apple-pie order *(Nonformal)*, clean, compact, fit, methodical, natty, neat, nice, ordered, orderly, shipshape, slick, smart, snug, spick-and-span, spruce, trim, uncluttered, well-groomed, well-kept, well-ordered *Antonyms:* careless, dirty, dishevelled, messy, scruffy **2.** ample, considerable, fair, generous, good, handsome, healthy, large, largish, respectable, sizable, substantial, vast *Antonyms:* inconsiderable, insignificant, little, tiny – *v.* clean, dust, groom, neaten, order, organize, redd, spruce up *(Nonformal)*, straighten, sweep

tie *n.* **1.** attachment, bandage, bolo, brace, connection, cord, fastening, fetter, knot, lace, ligature, link, necktie, rope, shoelace, strap, string, yoke **2.** dead heat *or* level, deadlock, draw, exact, photo finish, stalemate, standoff **3.** affiliation, allegiance, association, bond, commitment, connection, duty, fidelity, hookup, kinship, liaison, network, nexus, obligation, outfit, relationship, tie-in – *v.* **1.** anchor, attach, band, cinch, clinch, connect, do up *(Nonformal)*, fasten, gird, interlace, join, knot, make fast, marry, moor, rivet, rope, secure, splice, tether, tie up, truss, unite, wed *Antonyms:* loosen, undo, untie **2.** bind, commit, confine, constrict, obligate, require, restrain, restrict *Antonyms:* free, liberate, release **3.** balance, draw, equal, match, meet, parallel, rival

tier *n.* bank, category, class, course, echelon, file, grade, group, grouping, layer, level, order, range, rank, row, section, series

tiff *n.* altercation, argument, disagreement, dispute, falling-out, fight, huff, imbroglio, quarrel, scrap *(Nonformal)*, spat, squabble, tantrum

tight *adj.* **1.** close, close-fitting, constricted, cramped, crowded, dense, narrow, packed, rigid, skintight, snug, stiff, strained, stretched, taut *Antonyms:* limp, loose, slack **2.** airtight, cohesive, enduring, firm, hermetic, impenetrable, impermeable, impervious, resistant, secure, sealed, solid, stable, steady, sturdy, strong, sound, tenacious, watertight *Antonyms:* full of holes *(Nonformal)*, leaky, weak **3.** demanding, exacting, harsh, rigorous, rough, severe, stern, strict, stringent, tough **4.** difficult, pesky, *(Nonformal)*, troublesome, vexatious, worrisome **5.** avaricious, cheap, closefisted, miserly, parsimonious, stingy **6.** addled, blasted, drunk, flying, happy, high, inebriated, intoxicated, loaded, lubricated, mellow, merry, sloshed, stewed, woozy *Nonformal:* lit, in the bag, ripped, tanked, wasted, wet, *Antonyms:* on the wagon *(Nonformal)*, sober, straight – *adv.* densely, firmly, securely

tighten *v.* bind, clench, close, compress, condense, constrict, contract, cramp, crush, fasten, fix, grip, harden, lengthen, narrow, pinch, restrain, secure, squeeze, stiffen, stretch, tauten, tense *Antonyms:* free, loosen, undo, untie

tightfisted *adj.* careful, cheap, frugal, mean, miserly, parsimonious, penny-wise, pinch penny, prudent, stingy, thrifty

tightlipped *adj.* laconic, quiet, reserved, reticent, secretive, shy, silent, taciturn, uncommunicative *Antonyms:* forward, garrulous, loud, obnoxious

till *n.* cashbox, compartment, depository, cash drawer *or* register, safe, tray – *prep.* before, earlier *or* sooner than, until, up to – *v.* cultivate, dig, dress, farm, grow, harrow, hoe, labour, mulch, plant, plough, plow, prepare, sow, tend, turn, work

tilt *n.* **1.** angle, cant, inclination, lean, list, slant, slope **2.** competition, dispute, encounter, jousting, quarrel, tournament – *v.* **1.** bend, careen, dip, heel, incline, lean, list, lurch, pitch, rake, recline, seesaw, shift, slant, slope, slouch, swag, sway, tip, turn, yaw **2.** aim, attack, charge, engage, joust, lance, overthrow, thrust

timber *n.* **1.** beam, boards, deal, forest, hardwood, lumber, pole, softwood, spar, wood, woodland, woodlot **2.** ability, capability, capacity, character, potential, talent, worth

timbre *n.* colour, formant, mode, resonance, pitch, quality, resonance, sound, tonality, tone, voicing

time *n.* **1.** chronology, continuum, duration, progression **2.** age, eon, epoch, interval, period, span, stage, term, while *Some time measurements:* bite, century, day, decade, eternity, fortnight, future, generation, instant, life span, hour, millennium, minute, moment, month, nanosecond, past, present, season, score, second, semester, twelvemonth, week, wink, year *Canadian Standard Time Zones:* Atlantic, Eastern, Central, Mountain, Newfoundland, Pacific **3.** bout, extent, hitch, patch, shift, spell, spot *(Nonformal)*, stint, stretch, tenure, tour, watch **4.** bit, date, experience, instance, juncture, occasion, point **5.** convenience, ease, leisure, suitable moment **6.** circumstances, conditions, events, life **7.** beat, beats per minute *or* bpm, cadence, measure, meter, rate, rhythm, speed, tempo **8.** interruption, pause, stoppage, time out **9.** date, death, delivery, end **10.** celebration, festivity, gathering, jollity, shivaree **11.** imprisonment, incarceration, jail – *v.* arrange, clock, count, fix, mark, measure, organize, record, regulate, set

timeless *adj.* ageless, classic, continual, endless, enduring, eternal, everlasting, immemorial, infinite, lasting, perpetual, undying, unending *Antonyms:* ephemeral, finite, fleeting, transient

timely *adj.* appropriate, auspicious, convenient, favourable, fit, fitting, judicious, likely, meet, modern, now, pat, promising, prompt, proper, propitious, prosperous, punctual, suitable, up-to-date, well-timed, with it *(Nonformal) Antonyms:* inconvenient, late, unsuitable – *adv.* early, in the nick of time, opportunely, seasonably

timeworn *adj.* **1.** aged, bedraggled, crumbling, dilapidated, dog-eared, moth-eaten, old, shabby, shopworn, the worse for wear *(Nonformal)*, threadbare, time-scarred, worn *Antonyms:* fresh, new, shiny **2.** clichéd, hackneyed, overused, trite, unoriginal, worn thin *Antonyms:* cutting-edge, novel, original

timid *adj.* **1.** afraid, apprehensive, browbeaten, bullied, cowardly, cowed, cowering, craven, fainthearted, fearful, frightened, intimidated, nervous, spineless, spiritless, submissive, timorous, trembling, unnerved, wavering, weak *Nonformal:* yellow, yellow-bellied *Antonyms:* adventurous, aggressive, bold, daring **2.** bashful, coy, demure, diffident, gentle, humble, mild, modest, mousy, prim, reserved, retiring, shrinking, shy, unassertive *Antonyms:* abrasive, arrogant, in your face *(Nonformal)*, obnoxious, proactive, shameless

timorous *adj.* afraid, cowardly, fainthearted, milksop, pusillanimous, quavery, tremulous *Nonformal:* lily-livered, weak-kneed *Antonyms:* brave, carefree, reckless

tincture *n.* **1.** composition, mixture, solution **2.** dash, hint, infusion, inkling, seasoning, shade, spice, suggestion, taint, tinge, touch, trace, vestige – *v.* add, breathe, combine, imbue, impart, instill, leave, mix, permeate, saturate, scent, season, suffuse

tinge *n.* **1.** bit, dash, drop, hint, implication, intimation, iota, jot, pinch, shade, smattering, soupçon, sprinkling, strain, streak, suggestion, taste, touch, trace **2.** cast, colour, coloration, dye, dyestuff, hue, pigment, shade, stain, tincture, tint, tone, wash – *v.* colour, dye, highlight, imbue, impart, impregnate, infiltrate, influence, infuse, saturate, shade, stain, streak, suffuse, tint

tingle *n.* buzz, frisson, goose bumps *or* pimples, heebie-jeebies *(Nonformal)*, pins and needles, prickling sensation, shiver, thrill, twinkle – *v.* itch, prickle, scratch, shiver, smart, sting, twinge

tinker *v.* dabble, dawdle, doodle, fiddle, fidget, fool with, play around with, potter, pry, putter, repair, take apart, tamper *or* trifle with *Nonformal:* doctor, futz, mess about *or* with, monkey with, muck about *or* around, putter, putz

tinsel *adj.* artificial, cheap, false, gaudy, gilded, Hollywood *(Nonformal)*, ostentatious, showy, sparkling, superficial, tawdry *Antonyms:* authentic, bona fide, genuine – *n.* **1.** dummy, fake, imitation, paste **2.** adornment, decoration, embellishment, finery, garnish, icicles, ornamentation, spangle

tint *n.* cast, chromaticity, coloration, colour, complexion, dash, dye, flush, glow, highlight, hint, hue, luminosity, pigmentation, rinse, shade, stain, suggestion, taint, tinct, tincture, tinge, tone, touch, trace, wash – *v.* affect, colour, complexion, dye, highlight, influence, rinse, shade, stain, streak, taint, tinge, touch, wash

tiny *adj.* diminutive, dwarf, infinitesimal, insignificant, Lilliputian, little, microscopic, miniature, minuscule, minute, negligible, peewee, petite, pocket-size, puny, pygmy, slight, small, trifling, wee *Nonformal:* bitsy, bitty, teeny *Antonyms:* colossal, enormous, giant, gigantic, momentous

tip *n.* **1.** advice, buzz, clue, confidential *or* inside *or* private *or* privileged *or* secret information, forecast, help, hint, inclination, inkling, knowledge, news, pointer, prompt, suggestion, tipoff, warning, whisper, word *Nonformal:* bug, hot tip, inside dope, pipeline, the lowdown **2.** gift, gratuity, handout, largesse, money, perk *(Nonformal)*, perquisite, *pourboire (French)*, reward **3.** end, extremity, limit, peak, point, summit, top – *v.* **1.** bend, cant, capsize, careen, dump, flip, heel, incline, knock *or* turn over, list, overset, overturn, recline, shift, slant, slope, spill, tilt, topple, unload, upend, upset, upturn **2.** advise, caution, clue, cue, forewarn, hint, inform, prompt, reveal, squeal, steer, suggest, tip off, warn

tipsy *adj.* flying, happy, high, inebriated, intoxicated, loaded, lubricated, mellow, merry *Nonformal:* bleary-eyed, lit, ripped, stewed, tanked, tippy, wasted *Antonyms:* sober, straight

tirade *n.* abuse, anger, berating, bollocking *(Nonformal)*, castigation, censure, condemnation, denunciation, diatribe, fulmination, harangue, invective, jeremiad, lecture, malediction, outburst, rant, revilement, screed, sermon, tongue-lashing, vituperation

tire *n.* disc, rubber, tread, wheel – *v.* bore, collapse, debilitate, dishearten, dispirit, distress, drain, droop, drop, enervate, enfeeble, exhaust, faint, fatigue, fray, grow weary, incapacitate, overburden, overtrain, overtax, overwork, pall, strain, use up, weaken, wear, wear out *or* down, weary, wilt *Nonformal:* peter *or* poop *or* tucker out *Antonyms:* exhilarate, invigorate, refresh, revive

tired *adj.* beat, broken-down, burned out, in a state of collapse, consumed, drained, drooping, drowsy, exhausted, fatigued, finished, flagging, jaded, overtaxed, overworked, rundown, sleepy, spent, wasted, weary, worn out *Nonformal:* all in, baffed, burnt, bushed, dog-tired, fagged, fried, knackered, played out, pooped, whipped *Antonyms:* energetic, enthusiastic, keen, lively, raring to go *(Nonformal)*, rested

tireless *adj.* active, ceaseless, constant, determined, eager, energetic, enthusiastic, ever-ready *(Nonformal)*, hardworking, hyper, keen, indefatigable, industrious, jumping, perky, persevering, relentless, resolute, steadfast, strenuous, unflagging, unrelenting, unwavering, vigorous *Antonyms:* drained, exhausted, fatigued, worn out

tiresome *adj.* aggravating, annoying, boring, damnable, dull, exhausting, insipid, irksome, irritating, pesky, tedious, too much *(Nonformal)*, troublesome, troubling, wearisome, vexing *Antonyms:* appealing, entertaining, interesting

tissue *n.* **1.** fabric, frame, make-up, network, organization, pattern, shape, structure, texture, weave **2.** gauze, material, textile **3.** handkerchief, hanky *(Nonformal)*, Kleenex *(Trademark)*, towel

titanic *adj.* astronomical, Brobdingnagian, colossal, elephantine, enormous, gargantuan, gigantic, great, huge, immense, larger than life, mammoth, massive, monumental, tremendous, vast *Antonyms:* Lilliputian, miniature, small, wee

titillate *v.* amuse, arouse, delight, entertain, excite, heat up *(Nonformal)*, palpate, pet, provoke, stimulate, stroke, tantalize, tease, thrill, tickle *Antonyms:* abrade, bore, tire, wear

title *n.* **1.** appellation, banner, brand, caption, denomination, designation, description, epithet, heading, headline, honorific, inscription, label, name, pseudonym, rubric, salutation, sign, sobriquet, style, tab, tag, term *Nonformal:* handle, moniker **2.** authority, claim, class, commission, deed, degree, due, entitlement, estate, holding, justification, licence, ownership, possession, privilege, proof, right **3.** championship, crown, laurel, medal, merit, prize – *v.* baptize, call, caption, christen, denominate, designate, dub, entitle, label, name, style, term

tittle-tattle *n.* blather, chit-chat, gossip, hearsay, jabber, prattle, small talk, story, tale – *v.* blab, blather, chat, gossip, jabber, palaver, prattle, rumour, squeal, talk

toady *n.* fawner, flatterer, flunky, lackey, puppet, stooge, sycophant, tartufe, tool *Nonformal:* bootlicker, brown-noser, yes-man *Antonyms:* boss, chief, guru, master

toast *n.* **1.** bread, rusk **2.** acknowledgment, celebration, ceremony, commemoration, drink, honour, pledge, salutation, salute, tribute, wassail *Selected toasts: A sua saude (Portuguese)*, chimo, *Furah (Swahili)*, *L'Chaim (Hebrew/Israel)*, *Kamau (Hawaiian)*, *Kamjab raho (Punjabi)*, *Kan pai (Japanese)*, *Lechyd Da (Welsh)*, *Nazdrovia (Russian)*, prosit, prost, *salud (Spanish/Mexican)*, *Serefinize (Turkey)*, skoal, *Slainte (Irish)*, *Sto lat (Polish)*, your health *Italian: Cin-Cin, salute* – *v.* **1.** brown, cook, crisp, dry, grill, heat, parch, roast, warm **2.** acclaim, exalt, glorify, honour, praise, salute *Antonyms:* deride, jeer, mock, ridicule

tobacco *n.* smoke, the weed *(Nonformal)* *Common tobaccos:* broadleaf, burley, chewing, cigar, cigarette, Cuban, fire-cured, flue-cured, kinnikinnick *(Native Peoples)*, Latakia, leaf, pipe, plug, pouch, right, Russian, Turkish, Virginia

toboggan *n.* conveyance, komatik, runner, ski-bob, sled, sledge, sleigh – *v.* coast, glide, ride, scream down *(Nonformal)*, sled, sleigh, slide

together *adj.* balanced, collected, composed, cool *(Nonformal)*, level-headed, poised, sane – *adv.* **1.** attached, combined, connected, joined, linked, mixed, united **2.** consecutively, continually, continuously, running, successively, without interruption **3.** all for one and one for all *(Nonformal)*, as a group, closely, coincidentally, collectively, commonly, concertedly, concurrently, conjointly, contemporaneously, en masse, in concert *or* cooperation *or* sync *or* unison, jointly, mutually, one, simultaneously, synchronously, unanimously, unitedly *Antonyms:* alone, apart, independently, individually, separately

toil *n.* application, drudgery, effort, exertion, grind, industry, labour, moil, pains, strife, struggle, travail, work *Nonformal:* donkeywork, elbow grease, gruntwork, scutwork *Antonyms:* amusement, recreation, relaxation – *v.* drudge, exert, hammer away, labour, travail, work *Nonformal:* slog, sweat *Antonyms:* lounge, relax, snooze

toilet *n.* bathroom, bedpan, chamber pot, commode, ladies' *or* mens' room, latrine, lavatory, outhouse, porta-potty, potty, restroom, stall, urinal, washroom, water closet *or* W.C. *Nonformal:* can, jakes, john, johnny on the spot, loo *(British)*, pisser

token *adj.* earnest, nominal, perfunctory, representative, symbolic – *n.* **1.** cens *(Historical)*, clue, demonstration, emblem, evidence, expression, favour, index, indication, manifestation, note, omen, pawn, pledge, presage, proof, relic, representation, sample, security, sign, significant, symbol, symptom, warning **2.** gift, keepsake, memento, memorial, remembrance, reminder, souvenir, trophy **3.** characteristic, idiosyncrasy, mark, quality **4.** badge, card, I.D., licence, passport, warrant **5.** check, counter, coupon, currency, scrip, tag, ticket

tolerable *adj.* **1.** acceptable, adequate, all right, average, bearable, decent, endurable, fair, fairly good, good enough, goodish, indifferent, livable, mediocre, middling, not bad, okay *(Nonformal)*, ordinary, passable, presentable, respectable, satisfactory, so-so, sufferable, sufficient, tidy *Antonyms:* insufferable, intolerable, too much, unbearable, unendurable **2.** allowable, permissible, supportable, sustainable *Antonyms:* ludicrous, unacceptable

tolerance *n.* **1.** broad-mindedness, charity, clemency, compassion, concession, endurance, forbearance, forgiveness, freedom, good will, grace, humanity, indulgence, kindness, latitude, lenience, liberalism, licence, magnanimity, mercifulness, mercy, open-mindedness, patience, permissiveness, sensitivity, sympathy, understanding *Antonyms:* bigotry, discrimination, intolerance, narrow-mindedness, prejudice **2.** endurance, fortitude, grit, guts, hardiness, resilience, resistance, stamina, staying power, steadfastness, steadiness, strength, toughness, vigour *Antonyms:* incapacity, susceptibility, weakness

tolerant *adj.* benevolent, big *(Nonformal)*, broad, catholic, charitable, clement, complaisant, condoning, considerate, easygoing, easy on *or* with, excusing, fair, forbearing, forgiving, humane, indulgent, kind-hearted, lenient, liberal, long-suffering, magnanimous, merciful, objective, open-minded, patient, permissive, receptive, soft, sympathetic, understanding, unprejudiced *Antonyms:* biased, partial, prejudiced, subjective

tolerate *v.* abide, accept, admit, allow, authorize, bear, brook, condone, countenance, endure, forbear, humour, indulge, permit, pocket, receive, sanction, stand, stomach, suffer, sustain, swallow, take, undergo, wait *Antonyms:* disapprove, forbid, prohibit

toll *n.* assessment, charge, cost, customs, demand, due, duty, expense, fee, impost, levy, payment, price, rate, tariff, tax, tribute – *v.* chime, knell, peal, ring, sound

tomb *n.* box *(Nonformal)*, burial chamber *or* place, catacomb, coffin, crypt, grave, mausoleum, memorial, monument, resting place, sarcophagus, sepulchre, vault

tome *n.* book, doorstop *(Nonformal)*, massive work, masterpiece, opus, reference, volume, work

tomfoolery *n.* banter, buffoonery, capers, clowning, clownishness, foolishness, frippery, highjinks, horseplay, jocularity, monkey business *or* shines, nonsense, rough housing, shenanigans, silliness

tone *n.* **1.** accent, emphasis, force, inflection, intonation, mode, modulation, pitch, resonance, sound, strength, stress, timbre, tonality, volume **2.** blend, cast, colour, hue, shade, tinge, tint, value **3.** air, approach, aspect, attitude, character, condition, current, drift, effect, expression, fashion, feel, frame, humour, manner, mode, mood, movement, nature, note, quality, spirit, strain, style, temper, tenor, trend, vein **4.** condition, elasticity, health, healthiness, resiliency, strength, tonicity, vigour

tongue *n.* **1.** dialect, language, lingo *(Nonformal)*, lingua franca, parlance, patois, speech, vernacular **2.** mouth, organ, palate, stinger *(Nonformal)*, taste bud **3.** articulation, power of speech, utterance, vocalization **4.** cape, peninsula, promontory, spit

tonic *n.* analeptic, boost, bracer, conditioner, cordial, drink, drug, energizer, fillip, invigorator, livener, medicine, pick-me-up *(Nonformal)*, refresher, restorative, stimulant, strengthener *Antonyms:* poison, toxin

too *adv.* **1.** additionally, along with, also, as well, besides, further, furthermore, in addition, likewise, more, moreover, to boot *(Nonformal)* **2.** awfully, beyond, ever, exceptionally, excessively, exorbitantly, extremely, greatly, highly, immensely, in excess, inordinately, notably, over, overly, remarkably, strikingly, unduly, unreasonably, very

tool *n.* apparatus, appliance, contraption, contrivance, device, gadget, implement, instrument, machine, utensil *Common household tools:* crowbar, drill, file, hammer, knife, level, paint brush *or* roller, pincers, plane, pliers, saw, screwdriver, shovel, spade, trowel, vise, wrench **2.** agent, clerk, employee, factor, front-man, means, mouthpiece *(Nonformal)*, official, organ, pawn, puppet, secretary, slave, steward, vehicle – *v.* carve, cut, engrave, fashion, inscribe, mark, ornament, score

tooth *n.* denticle, fang, tusk *Kinds of tooth:* baby, bicuspid, canine, ceramic, crown, eye-tooth, gold, grinder, incisor, molar, wisdom

top *adj.* best, chief, first, greatest, highest, leading, nonpareil, topnotch, unsurpassed, upper, uppermost, utmost *Nonformal:* bestest, toppermost – *n.* **1.** best, capital, choice, cream, elite, first place *or* rate, flower, head, leader, master, number one, numero uno *(Nonformal)*, pick, pride, prime, prize, summit *Antonyms:* bottom, foot, nadir, underneath **2.** cap, cover, lid, roof, stopper – *v.* **1.** best, cap, outbid, outfox, outmaneuver, raise **2.** cloak, cover, crown, face, finish, garnish, protect, reinforce, roof **3.** ascend, climb, crest, scale **4.** amputate, cream, crop, curtail, cut off, decapitate, guillotine, hang, pare, prune, remove, shear, shorten, trim **5.** bury, clobber, cream, drub, shellac, trounce, vanquish

topic *n.* affair, business, case, discourse, division, field, issue, material, matter, motif, motion, point, problem, proposition, question, resolution, subject, text, theme, theorem, thesis, treatise

topical *adj.* **1.** insular, limited, local, parochial, particular, regional, restricted, sectional *Antonyms:* limitless, universal, worldly **2.** *au courant (French)*, contemporary, current, fashionable, modern, newsworthy, popular, thematic, trendy, up-to-date *Antonyms:* antiquated, outmoded, unfashionable

topple *v.* **1.** capsize, collapse, fall, falter, founder, lurch, nose-dive, pitch, plunge, slump, stagger, stumble, teeter, totter, tumble **2.** bring down, oust, overthrow, overturn, unhorse, unseat, upset *Antonyms:* advocate, aid, support

torah *n.* **1.** commandment, counsel, guidance, instruction, law **2.** Bible, five books of Moses, Pentateuch, the Law

torch *n.* **1.** blowtorch, Bunsen burner, burner, butane torch, candle, flame, flamethrower, flashlight, lamp, light, lighter, taper **2.** flare, flirrup *(Newfoundland)*, signal **3.** fireman *(Nonformal)*, safecracker, welder – *v.* burn, conflagrate, cook, enflame, enkindle, ignite, kindle, light *Antonyms:* douse, extinguish, put out

torment *n.* **1.** agony, anguish, distress, hair shirt, hell, misery, nuisance, pain, punishment, rack, scourge, suffering, torture, trouble, worry *Antonyms:* bliss, comfort, ease, ecstasy, happiness **2.** annoyance, bane, bother, harassment, irritation, nag, persecution, pest, plague, provocation, vexation – *v.* abuse, afflict, annoy, bedevil, break, browbeat, crucify, devil, distress, harass, harrow, harry, heckle, henpeck, hound, hurt, molest, pain, persecute, pester, plague, provoke, punish, smite, tease, torture, trouble, try, upset, vex, wring *Nonformal:* bug, drive bananas *or* crazy *or* nuts *or* round the bend, hassle *Antonyms:* delight, ease, put at ease, reassure, sooth

torn *adj.* **1.** broken, burst, bust *(Nonformal)*, cleft, cracked, damaged, divided, fractured, gashed, lacerated, mangled, rent assunder, ripped, ruptured, severed, sliced, slit, snapped, split, wrenched **2.** affected, alienated, betwixt and between *(Nonformal)*, divided, irresolute, uncertain, undecided, unsure, vacillating, wavering **3.** disintegrating, in tatters *or* threads, ragged, shabby

tornado *n.* cockeye bob *(Australian)*, cyclone, dust devil, gale, hurricane, maelstrom, squall, storm, tempest, thunderstorm, twister, typhoon, vortex, whirlwind, windstorm

torpedo *n.* dart, missile, projectile, weapon – *v.* attack, blowup, damage, destroy, knock out, sabotage, scuttle, shoot, sink, snake *(Nonformal)*, undo, wreck

torpid *adj.* apathetic, comatose, dopey, dormant, drowsy, dull, heavy, idle, inactive, indifferent, indolent, inert, languorous, lazy, leaden, lethargic, motionless, numb, passive, slack, slothful, slow, sluggish, slumberous, somnolent, stagnant, stuporous *Antonyms:* active, enthusiastic, passionate

torpor *n.* apathy, immobility, indifference, indolence, inertia, languor, lethargy, sloth, sluggishness, stagnation, stasis, stupor *Antonyms:* excitement, hyperactivity

torrent *n.* **1.** cascade, cataract, cloudburst, deluge, downpour, flood, flooding, flow, gush, raining cats and dogs *(Nonformal)*, shower, spate, waterfall **2.** cataclysm, effusion, eruption, flux, inundation, outburst, overflow, rush, speed, tumult

torrential *adj.* abundant, effusive, overpowering, overwhelming, rapid, tumultuous, voluminous

torrid *adj.* ardent, blazing, blistering, boiling, broiling, burning, charged, fiery, flaming, hot, hot and heavy *(Nonformal)*, parched, scalding, sizzling, smouldering, steamy, stifling, sultry, sweltering, tropical

tortuous *adj.* ambiguous, complex, complicated, convoluted, deceptive, delicate, devious, difficult, indirect, intricate, involved, knotty, labyrinthine, misleading, perplexing, perverse, precarious, problematic, quirky, risky, rocky, roundabout, sensitive, serpentine, slippery, sticky, thorny, ticklish, touchy, tricky, warped, winding *Antonyms:* direct, simplistic, straightforward, upright

torture *n.* ache, affliction, agony, anguish, crucifixion, distress, hell, martyrdom, misery, pain, pang, persecution, punishment, purgatory, suffering, torment, tribulation, twinge *Selected methods of torture:* bamboo shoots, bastinado, boot, hot poker, iron maiden, keelhauling, noise, pilliwink, rack, screw, sleeplessness, strap posts, thumbscrew, water, wheel, whip – *v.* abuse, afflict, agonize, beat, crucify, distort, distress, disturb, excruciate, grill, harrow, hurt, impale, injure, lacerate, maim, mangle, martyr, mutilate, oppress, pain, persecute, punish, rack, smite, torment, try, upset, whip, wound, wring *Antonyms:* alleviate, comfort, ease, relieve, soothe

tortured *adj.* agonized, bloodied, clawed, convulsed, crucified, distorted, eaten up by *(Nonformal)*, excoriated, harrowed, impaled, lacerated, mutilated, on the rack, pained, racked, ripped, savaged, wrung

toss *n.* fling, flip, heave, lob, pitch, throw – *v.* **1.** cast, chuck, chunk, fire, fling, flip, heave, hurl, launch, lob, peg, project, propel, sling, throw, twirl **2.** agitate, bob, buffet, disturb, flounder, jiggle, joggle, jolt, lurch, move restlessly, oscillate, pitch, rock, roll, shake, squirm, stir, sway, swing, thrash, tumble, undulate, wallow, wave, wobble, wriggle, writhe **3.** bandy, converse, debate, shoot the breeze *(Nonformal)*, talk over

total *adj.* absolute, accomplished, aggregate, all-encompassing, complete, comprehensive, consummate, entire, every, exhaustive, final, fixed, full, full-blown, full-length, full-scale, gross, inclusive, integral, outright, overall, perfect, plenary, positive, rounded, sheer, sweeping, thorough, totalitarian, unabbreviated, unabridged, unconditional, uncut, undivided, universal, unlimited, unrestricted, utter, whole *Antonyms:* conditional, fragmentary, incomplete, limited, partial – *n.* aggregate, all, amount, body, budget, bulk, entirety, full amount, gross, jackpot, mass, quantity, quantum, result, score, sum, sum total, totality, whole *Nonformal:* kit and caboodle, the works, whole enchilada *or* nine yards *or* shebang *or* shooting match – *v.* **1.** add, amount *or* come to, ascertain, calculate, cast, comprise, compute, consist of, count, equal, figure, number, sum up, summate, tabulate, tote *Antonyms:* deduct, subtract **2.** crash, crush, damage, demolish, destroy, smash, sink, wreck

totalitarian *adj.* absolute, Animal Farm *(Nonformal)*, authoritarian, autocratic, despotic, dictatorial, fascist, monolithic, monopolistic, one-party, oppressive, tyrannical, undemocratic *Antonyms:* autonomous, democratic, egalitarian, popular, self-governing

totality *n.* aggregation, all inclusive, entirety, everyone, everything, fullness, sum, *tout le monde (French)*, unity, universality, universe, whole *Antonyms:* alienation, partiality, segmentation

totally *adv.* absolutely, all, altogether, collectively, completely, comprehensively, consummately, en masse, entirely, exclusively, flat out, full blast, fully, in toto, perfectly, quite, thoroughly, unconditionally, unmitigatedly, utterly, wholeheartedly, wholly *Antonyms:* incompletely, partially, partly, somewhat

tote *n.* bag, box, carton, case, container, gaylord, knapsack – *v.* bear, carry, haul, transport *Nonformal:* lug, schlep

totem *n.* cipher, emblem, figure, guardian, icon, image, representation, symbol, token, totem pole

totter *v.* blunder, careen, collapse, falter, flounder, hesitate, lurch, quake, quiver, reel, rock, roll, seesaw, shake, shimmy, slide, slip, stagger, stammer, stumble, sway, teeter, toit *(British)*, topple, tremble, trip, tumble, waver, weave, wobble *Antonyms:* brace, buttress, steady

touch *n.* **1.** brush, caress, contact, cuddle, embrace, feel, fondle, handle, hug, junction, kiss, nudge, pat, peck, pet, rub, scratch, sense, stroke, taste **2.** blow, hit, poke, push, smack, stroke, swat, tap, whack **3.** effect, hand, influence, manipulation **4.** ability, adroitness, artistry, deftness, facility, familiarity, flair, handiwork, knack, method, skill, style, talent, technique, trademark *(Nonformal)* **5.** bit, dash, detail, drop, hint, implication, inkling, intimation, iota, jot, pinch, smack, small amount, smattering, speck, spot, streak, suggestion, suspicion, taste, tincture, tinge, trace, whiff – *v.* **1.** brush, caress, examine, feel, feel up, finger, fondle, frisk, grope, handle, inspect, massage, palpate, pat, paw, pet, probe, rub, stroke, thumb, tickle, **2.** graze, hit, push, strike, tag, tap **3.** abut, adjoin, border, butt on, come together, converge, contact, join, meet, neighbour **4.** correspond, equal, match, parallel, reach, rival **5.** brush, dab, delineate, line, mark, modify, retouch **6.** colour, dye, paint, shade, taint, tinge, tint **7.** affect, arouse, disturb, excite, grab, impress, influence, inspire, interest, manipulate, melt, move, stimulate, stir, strike, sway, upset **8.** allude *or* refer *or* relate to, centre upon, concern, cover, deal with, discuss, involve, mention, pertain, speak of, treat **9.** appropriate, fool about or around, meddle *or* mess with, mishandle

touched *adj.* **1.** affected, disturbed, emotional, grabbed, impressed, influenced, moved, softened, stirred, swayed, upset **2.** crazy, daft, eccentric, fanatic, insane, neurotic, odd, peculiar *Nonformal:* barmy, batty, bonkers, cuckoo, flighty, nuts, nutty, screwy

touching *adj.* **1.** affecting, appealing, compassionate, emotive, heartbreaking, heartrending, heart-warming, impressive, moving, pathetic, poignant, stirring, tender **2.** brushing, caressing, contiguous, feeling, fingering, handling, nudging, rubbing, tangent

3. abutting, adjoining, bordering, contiguous, intersecting, neighbouring, tangent – *prep.* associated with, concerning, in reference to, with regard or respect to

touchstone *n.* archetype, bellwether, benchmark, criterion, gauge, guide, measure, pattern, precedent, proof, ruler, standard, test, test case, trial, yardstick

touchy *adj.* **1.** bad-tempered, bitchy, cantankerous, captious, choleric, crabby, cranky, cross, excitable, fussy, grouchy, grumpy, hypersensitive, irascible, irritable, jumpy, offended, ornery, oversensitive, peevish, perturbable, petulant, querulous, quick-tempered, sensitive, splenetic, surly, temperamental, testy, thin-skinned, ticklish, uptight, wound up *Antonyms:* affable, cheerful, easygoing, sunny, sweet **2.** delicate, dicey, explosive, hazardous, problematic, precarious, risky, unpredictable, unsafe, volatile *Nonformal:* heavy, touch and go,

tough *adj.* **1.** brawny, conditioned, dense, durable, firm, flinty, hard-bitten, hardened, hardy, healthy, inflexible, leathery, mighty, resilient, resistant, rigid, robust, rugged, seasoned, solid, stalwart, stiff, stout, strapping, strong, sturdy, tenacious, tense, tight, unbreakable, unyielding, vigorous, withstanding *Antonyms:* delicate, fragile, meek, weak **2.** adamant, bold, firm, fixed, hard-line, hard-nosed, hard-shell, headstrong, immutable, inflexible, intractable, obdurate, obstinate, persistent, resolute, steadfast, stern, stiff, strict, stubborn, unbending, uncompromising, unforgiving, unyielding *Antonyms:* accommodating, compassionate, considerate, flexible **3.** disreputable, hard-boiled, harsh, merciless, pugnacious, rough, ruthless, unpleasant, unruly, vicious, vulgar **4.** difficult, exacting, hard, laborious, rigorous, severe – *n.* bruiser, brute, bully, combatant, criminal, gangster, hoodlum, hooligan, punk, rough, roughneck, rowdy, ruffian, thug, villain, yahoo *Nonformal:* goon, hood, plug-ugly

toughen *v.* acclimatize, anneal, harden, inure, season, steel, strengthen, temper *Antonyms:* enervate, undermine, weaken

toughness *n.* courage, durability, endurance, grit, hardiness, pluck, resilience, resistance, strength, strictness, tenacity *Nonformal:* bottom, guts *Antonyms:* feebleness, fragility, vulnerability, weakness

tour *n.* **1.** ambit, circle, circuit, course, cruise, excursion, expedition, getaway, go, hop, jaunt, journey, junket, outing, overnight, peregrination, roundabout, round trip, stint, swing, travel, trek, trip, voyage, weekend **2.** hitch, shift, stint, stretch *(Nonformal)*, tenure, term, tour of duty – *v.* cruise, explore, globe-trot, holiday, hop, jaunt, jet, journey, sightsee, swing, travel, trip, vacation, visit, voyage

tourist *n.* day-tripper, excursionist, foreigner, globetrotter, jetsetter, journeyer, sightseer, stranger, traveller, vacationist, visitor, voyager, wayfarer *Antonyms:* local, native

tournament *n.* bonspiel, clash, competition, contest, duel, event, fight, games, joust, match, meet, meeting, pageant, round robin, series, sport, test, tilt, tourney

tousled *adj.* beat-up, dirty, disarranged, disarrayed, dishevelled, disordered, grubby, messed-up, messy, mussy *(Nonformal)*, ruffled, rumpled, sloppy, tangled, uncombed, unkempt, wrinkled *Antonyms:* neat, ordered, prim and proper

tout – *v.* **1.** appeal to, beg, importune, plead, press, request, seek, solicit **2.** acclaim, advocate, ballyhoo, boast, commend, extol, hype, laud, praise, promote, publicize, recommend, speak highly of, support

tow *v.* convey, drag, draw, ferry, haul, lug, propel, pull, push, trail, trawl, truck *(Nonformal)*, tug, yank

toward *prep.* **1.** almost, approaching, close to, en route, facing, for, fronting, headed for, moving, near, nearing, proceeding **2.** apropos, as for, as to, concerning, for, in re, re, regarding, towards

tower *n.* barbican, bastion, belfry, bell, broch, buttress, castle, chimney, citadel, CN Tower, column, communications tower, donjon, fortress, high rise, keep, lookout, Martello, mast, minaret, monolith, obelisk, observation platform, pagoda, post, pillar, refuge, skyscraper, spire, steeple, stronghold, stupa, turret, watchtower, ziggurat – *v.* dominate, exceed, extend *or* rise above, loom, mount, overlook, overtop, rear, soar, surmount, surpass, top, transcend *Antonyms:* fall, falter, stumble

towering *adj.* aerial, airy, colossal, elevated, eminent, excessive, extraordinary, extravagant, extreme, fantastic, gigantic, great, high, huge, humongous *(Nonformal)*, impressive, intense, lofty, magnificent, massive, mighty, monumental, outstanding, paramount, preeminent, soaring, stately, stupendous, superior, supreme, surpassing, tall, tremendous, ultimate *Antonyms:* average, insignificant, lowly

town *n.* borough, burg, boom *or* company town, corners, county, district, hamlet, municipality, parish, service centre, settlement, *shtetl (Yiddish)*, township, village, ville *Nonformal:* jerkwater, jumping-off place, one-horse town, whistle-stop

toxic *adj.* dangerous, deadly, fatal, harmful, inimical, lethal, noxious, pernicious, pestilential, poison, poisonous, septic, toxicant, venomous, virulent *Antonyms:* harmless, non-poisonous, nontoxic, safe, salubrious, wholesome

toy *adj.* diminutive, miniature, pint-sized – *n.* amusement, bauble, doll, gewgaw, gimcrack, novelty, ornament, plaything, plush, sport, trifle, trinket – *v.* amuse oneself, cosset, dally, dawdle, dilly-dally, fiddle, flirt, fool, jest, lead on, nibble, pet, play, play games *or* with, putter, sport, string along, tease, tinker, trifle

trace *n.* **1.** clue, evidence, footmark, footprint, hint, indication, intimation, mark, nuance, odour, path, proof, remains, remnant, shadow, sign, smell, suspicion, track, trail, tread, whiff **2.** bit, crumb, dash, fragment, image, iota, jot, mote, scintilla, shred, smidgen, snippet, soupçon, spark, speck, spot, sprinkling, streak, suggestion, taste, tincture, tinge, token, touch, trifle, vestige, whisper – *v.* **1.** ascertain, detect, determine, discern, discover, ferret *or* smell out, find, follow, hunt, investigate, perceive, pursue, run down, search for, seek, shadow, smell out, spot, stalk, track, trail, unearth **2.** copy, delineate, draw, duplicate, imprint, mark, outline, record, reproduce, sketch

track *n.* **1.** clue, fingerprint, footprint, groove, hint, impression, imprint, indication, mark, record, remains, remnant, rooster tail, rut, scent, sign, slot, spoor, step, symbol, token, trace, tract, trail, trajectory, tread, vestige, wake **2.** alley, artery, avenue, beaten path, boulevard, clearing, course, footpath, highway, lane, line, passage, path, pathway, railroad, route, street, thoroughfare, towpath, trajectory, walk, way **3.** track and field *Multi track and field events:* decathlon, pentathlon, triathlon *Individual track and field events:* 100-metre dash, 100-metre hurdles, 200-metre run, 400-metre run, 800-metre run, discus throw, hammer throw, high jump, javelin throw, long jump, marathon, middle-distance race, mile race, pole vault, relay race, shot put, triple jump – *v.* chase, discover, expose, ferret *or* smell *or* sniff out, find, follow, go after, hunt, pursue, run to earth, run *or* track down, scout, shadow, stalk, tail, trace, trail, travel, traverse

tract *n.* **1.** area, block, concession, demesne, expanse, land, lot, parcel, patch, plot, quadrant, real estate, section, square, zone **2.** booklet, broadside, brochure, circular, discourse, dissertation, flyer, handout, leaflet, pamphlet, sermon, study, treatise, treatment

tractable *adj.* acquiescent, amenable, biddable, complaisant, compliant, conformable, controllable, docile, flexible, game, governable, malleable, manageable, meek, obedient, persuadable, pliable, pliant, subdued, submissive, tame, willing, workable, yielding *Antonyms:* defiant, headstrong, obstinate, obstreperous, stubborn, unruly

traction *n.* adhesion, drag, friction, grip, propulsion, pull, purchase, resistance

trade *adj.* business, commercial, occupational, professional – *n.* **1.** art, business, calling, career, commerce, craft, employment, game *(Nonformal)*, handicraft, job, line, livelihood, living, métier, occupation, position, profession, pursuit, skill, vocation, work **2.** back and forth *(Nonformal)*, bargaining, barter, business, buying and selling, clientele, commerce, contract, customers, dealing, deal-making, doing business, enterprise, exchange, industry, market, merchandising, patronage, retailing, sales, wheeler-dealing, wholesaling – *v.* bargain, barter, buy, deal, dicker, exchange, haggle, interchange, peddle, sell, traffic, transact, truck, shop, swap, switch

trademark *adj.* characteristic, distinctive, habitual, individual, noteworthy, proprietary, usual – *n.* **1.** brand, brand name, crest, design, emblem, identification, initials, label, logo, logotype, mark, motto, stamp, symbol, tag, trade name **2.** attribute, characteristic, distinction, feature, hallmark, insignia, property, quality, style, trait

trader *n.* barterer, broker, buyer, dealer, merchant, peddler, salesperson, seller *Nonformal:* fence wheeler-dealer *Historical*: comanchero, coureur de bois, factor, fur trader, voyageur, whisky trader

tradition *n.* attitude, belief, birthright, convention, culture, custom, doctrine, ethics, fable, folklore, form, habit, heritage, history, inheritance, institution, knowledge, law, legend, lore, mores, myth, mythology, practice, praxis, religion, ritual, Sunna *(Muslim)*, superstition, unwritten law, usage, wisdom

traditional *adj.* acceptable, accustomed, acknowledged, ancestral, classic, classical, common, consuetudinary, conventional, customary, doctrinal, established, fixed, folk, habitual, historical, legendary, long-established, mythological, old, oral, orthodox, prescribed, rooted, sanctioned, time-honoured, transmitted, universal, unwritten, widespread *Antonyms:* avant-garde, contemporary, modern, new, unusual

traffic *n.* **1.** barter, business, commerce, custom, dealings, doings, exchange, industry, interchange, intercourse, patronage, peddling, soliciting, trade, transaction, truck **2.** flux, congestion, movement, passengers, rush hour, transit, transportation, travel, vehicles *Nonformal:* snarl-up, volume **3.** cartage, freight, shipment, transport – *v.* bargain, barter, black-market, bootleg, buy and sell, connect *or* transact with, contact, deal, dicker, exchange, fence, handle, horse trade, interact, interface, market, negotiate, network, peddle, pimp, push, relate, shove, swap, trade

tragedy *n.* **1.** adversity, blow, calamity, cataclysm, catastrophe, curse, disaster, failure, hardship, humiliation, misadventure, misfortune, mishap, reversal *Nonformal:* bummer, downer *Antonyms:* glory, triumph **2.** buskin, cothurnus, drama, melodrama, play *Antonyms:* comedy, farce, satire

tragic *adj.* **1.** adverse, appalling, awful, bad, calamitous, cataclysmic, catastrophic, crushing, deplorable, desolate, destructive, dire, disastrous, dreadful, fatal, forlorn, grievous, grim, hapless, harrowing, heartbreaking, heart-rending, horrid, ill-fated, ill-starred, lamentable, miserable, mournful, painful, pathetic, pitiful, ruinous, sad, shocking, terrible, unfortunate, unhappy, woeful, wretched *Antonyms:* cheerful, comic, happy, lucky **2.** anguished, dramatic, histrionic, melodramatic, operatic, theatrical *Antonyms:* comic, farcical

trail *n.* **1.** beaten track, byway, course, footpath, line, marking, path, pathway, road, route, rut, track, trapline, walk, way **2.** indication, scent, spoor, trace, trajectory, vestige, wake, wash – *v.* **1.** dangle, drag, draw *or* string along, extend, haul, pull, stream, tow, truck **2.** chase, dog, follow, hunt, pursue, shadow, stalk, tail, trace, track **3.** dally, dawdle, delay, fall back *or* behind, hang back, lag, linger, loiter, plod, straggle, traipse *(Nonformal)*, trudge

trailer *n.* **1.** camper, flatbed, float, mobile home **2.** advertisement, coming attraction, preview, promo *(Nonformal)*, teaser

train *n.* **1.** choo-choo *(Nonformal)*, locomotive, railroad, railway, rolling stock *Kinds of train:* bullet, circus, day-coach, el, electric, elevated, express, flier, freight, funicular, GO, high-speed, limited, local, *metro (French)*, milk run, monorail, narrow gauge, Newfie bullet *(Historical)*, passenger, snow, special, steam, subway, *TGV (French)*, transcontinental *British:* tram, underground **2.** chain, column, concatenation, file, line, order, procession, progression, row, sequence, series, string, succession **3.** caravan, coffle, entourage, extension, party, retinue, suite, tier, trail – *v.* **1.** accustom, brainwash, break in, coach, condition, cultivate, develop, discipline, drill, educate, enlighten, equip, gentle, ground, guide, harden, hone, improve, initiate, instruct, inure, prepare, prime, qualify, rehearse, school, study, tame, teach, tutor, update **2.** aim, beam, cast, cock, direct, focus, head, line up, point, zero in

trainee *n.* apprentice, jackeroo, learner, novice, rookie, student, tenderfoot

training *n.* apprenticeship, background, coaching, conditioning, discipline, education, guidance, instruction, practice, preparation, rehearsal, schooling, teaching, upbringing

trait *n.* attribute, cast, character, characteristic, custom, distinction, feature, habit, hallmark, idiosyncrasy, insignia, mannerism, mark, nature, oddity, particularity, peculiarity, property, quality, quirk, sign, signature, singularity, style, trademark *(Nonformal)*

traitor *n.* apostate, backslider, betrayer, collaborator, conspirator, deceiver, defector, deserter, double-crosser, informer, quisling, renegade, sneak, snitch, spy, treasonist, turncoat *Nonformal:* backstabber, fifth columnist, fink, rat, snitch, squealer, stool pigeon *Antonyms:* defender, loyalist, patriot, supporter

trajectory *n.* angle, course, flight, line, path, plane, route, track, trail

tramp *n.* **1.** beachcomber, bum, derelict, down-and-out drifter, *flâneur (French)*, hobo, pilgrim, roamer, rover, runagate, sundowner *(Nonformal)*, vagabond, vagrant, wanderer *Antonyms:* homesteader, settler **2.** footfall, footstep, march, pound, stomp, tread **3.** cruise, excursion, expedition, hike, jaunt, journey, perambulation, ramble, saunter, stroll, tour, traipse *(Nonformal)*, trek, turn, walk – *v.* **1.** amble, dally, meander, ramble, range, roam, rove, saunter, straggle, stroll, tour, traipse *(Nonformal)*, trek, trip, walk, wander **2.** gallop, hike, hoof it, hop, march, plod, pound, slog, stamp, stodge, stomp, thud, toil, trample, tread, tromp, trudge

trample *v.* bruise, crush, flatten, grind, hurt, infringe, injure, override, overwhelm, pound, run over, squash, stamp, stomp, tread, tromp, violate

trance *n.* **1.** abstraction, catalepsy, daze, dream, ecstasy, exaltation, fugue, glaze, hypnosis, muse *(Archaic)*, rapture, reverie, sleepwalking, spell, stupor **2.** *Music:* disco, dub, electronica, jungle, techno, trip-hop

tranquil *adj.* agreeable, amicable, at ease *or* peace, balmy, calm, collected, comforting, composed, cool, easy, easygoing, even, even-tempered, gentle, halcyon, hushed, lenient, measured, mellow, mild, moderate, pacific, pastoral, patient, peaceful, placid, poised, quiet, reasonable, restful, sedate, serene, smooth, sober, soft, soothing, stable, still, tame, temperate, undisturbed, unexcitable, unflappable, unruffled, untroubled, whispering *Antonyms:* agitated, frantic, frenzied, hectic, troubled

tranquility *n.* calm, composure, coolness, equanimity, imperturbability, kef, mellowness, moderation, order, peace, placidness, quiescence, quiet, repose, rest, restfulness, sedateness, serenity, silence, stillness *Antonyms:* agitation, commotion, disturbance, frenzy, turmoil

tranquilizer *n.* calming agent, depressant, downer *(Nonformal)*, drug, medication, narcotic, sedative *See also:* **depressant**

transact *v.* accomplish, carry out, close, complete, conclude, conduct, discharge, do, enact, execute, fish or cut bait *(Nonformal)*, negotiate, operate, perform, prosecute, settle, trade

transaction *n.* act, action, activity, agreement, arrangement, business, compact, contract, covenant, deal, goings-on, negotiation, occurrence, pact, proceeding, purchase, sale, trade, undertaking

transcend *v.* better, eclipse, exceed, excel, go or move beyond, outshine, overstep, rise *or* tower above, surmount, surpass, top

transcendent *adj.* **1.** absolute, accomplished, boundless, consummate, entire, exceeding, extraordinary, ideal, incomparable, matchless, nonpareil, peerless, perfect, preeminent, remarkable, superior, supreme, unequalled, unique, unrivaled, unsurpassed *Antonyms:* circumscribed, finite, limited, mediocre **2.** abstract, divine, hypothetical, metaphysical, miraculous, spiritual

transcribe *v.* copy *or* write out, duplicate, interpret, note, record, render, reprint, reproduce, rewrite, make a record of, take down, tape, tape-record, transfer, translate, transliterate

transcript *n.* black box, carbon, copy, duplicate, facsimile, fax, photostat, record, recording, reproduction

transfer *n.* change, deportation, displacement, devolution, move, relegation, relocation, removal, shift, substitution, variation – *v.* **1.** assign, bequeath, cede, change, consign, convert, deed, delegate, devise, disturb, give, hand *or* sign *or* turn over, pass on *or* to, post, provide, relegate, sell, supply *Antonyms:* hold, keep, maintain **2.** bear, bring, carry, cart, convey, deliver, dispatch, dispense, express, ferry, find, forward, haul, lug, mail, move, send, ship, taxi, tote, transmit, transplant **3.** dislocate, displace, emigrate, immigrate, migrate, move house *(Nonformal)*, relocate, remove, shift, transplant, transport, transpose, uproot

transfix *v.* **1.** fix, impale, lance, nail *or* pin down, penetrate, pierce, puncture, run through, skewer, skiver, spear, spike, spit, stick **2.** bewitch, captivate, enchant, engross, fascinate, hold, hypnotize, mesmerize, paralyze, rivet, root, spellbind, stun, transport *Antonyms:* bore, fatigue, tire, weary

transform *v.* alter, become, change, convert, metamorphose, modify, mutate, render, renovate, revamp, transfigure, transmogrify, transmute *Nonformal:* morph, turn over a new leaf *Antonyms:* conserve, maintain, preserve

transformation *n.* about-face, alteration, change, conversion, evolution, flip-flop, metamorphosis, metastasis, modification, mutation, reversal, revolution, transfiguration, transmutation, volte-face *See also:* **change**

transgression *n.* breach, contravention, crime, defiance, disobedience, error, fault, felony, infraction, infringement, lapse, misbehaviour, misdeed, misdemeanour, offence, sin, slip, trespass, violation, wrong, wrongdoing

transient *adj.* brief, changeable, ephemeral, evanescent, flash, fleeting, fly-by-night *(Nonformal)*, flying, fugitive, impermanent, insubstantial, meteoric, migrating, momentary, moving, passing, provisional, short, short-lived, short-term, temporal, temporary, transitory, unstable, volatile *Antonyms:* constant, durable, enduring, long-lasting, perpetual – *n.* boarder, bum, guest, hobo, lodger, migrant worker, nomad, pilgrim, sojourner, street urchin, sundowner, traveller, vagabond, vagrant, wanderer

transistor *n.* rectifier, semiconductor *Common transistors:* base, collector, conductivity-modulation, diffusion, emitter, field-effect, germanium, phototransistor, point-contact, point-junction, power, spacistor, tandem, unijunction, unipolar

transit *n.* **1.** carrying, crossing, haul, migration, motion, movement, passage, permeation, route, shift, transfer, travel, traverse **2.** bus, cab, carriage, conveyance, ferry, freightage, haulage, jitney, public transit, Red Rocket *(Toronto)*, snow coach, streetcar, subway, taxi, transportation, trolley, wagon

transition *n.* alteration, change-over, conversion, development, growth, metamorphosis, passage, progress, saltation, segue, shift, transference, transformation *Antonyms:* constant, permanent, stasis

transitional *adj.* developing, formative, growing, intermediate, passing, *pro tempore (Latin)*, provisional, shifting, transformative

transitory *adj.* ephemeral, evanescent, fleeting, meteoric, momentary, passing, pro tem *(Nonformal)*, temporary, transient *Antonyms:* durable, lasting, permanent, static

translate *v.* alter, construe, convert, change, decipher, decode, deconstruct, deliver, elucidate, explain, explicate, gloss, interpret, paraphrase, put, reword, simplify, spell out, transcribe, transform, transliterate, transpose, turn

translation *n.* adaptation, decoding, elucidation, explanation, gloss, interpretation, key, metaphrase, paraphrase, reading, rendering, rendition, rephrasing, restatement, simplification, transcription, transliteration *Nonformal:* spin, take

translucent *adj.* clear, clear-cut, crystal, crystalline, diaphanous, glassy, limpid, lucid, pellucid, see-through, semi-opaque, semi-transparent *Antonyms:* blurred, clouded, dense, opaque

transmission *n.* broadcast, communique, communication, dissemination, program, signal, S.O.S. transference, transmittal

transmit *v.* **1.** carry, conduct, convey, forward, hand on, mail, pass along, post, relay, route, send, ship, tender, transfer **2.** broadcast, communicate, disseminate, evidence, get across *(Nonformal)*, impart, instill, telegraph, televise **3.** allow, bear, deliver, pass through, pipe **4.** bequeath, cede, devise, endow, grant

transparency *n.* **1.** clarity, clearness, explicitness, lucidity, obviousness, perceptibility, translucence *Antonyms:* ambiguity, obscurity **2.** candor, forthrightness, frankness, genuineness, honesty, openness *Antonyms:* deceitfulness, evasiveness **3.** film, overhead, photograph, picture, slide

transparent *adj.* **1.** cellophane, clear, crystalline, diaphanous, filmy, gauzy, gossamer, hyalite, lucent, pellucid, pervious, plain, see-through, sheer, translucent, vitreous *Antonyms:* muddy, murky, solid **2.** direct, easy, evident, explicit, lucid, manifest, naked, obvious, open, plain, recognizable, unequivocal, unmistakable, visible *Antonyms:* ambiguous, deceptive, mysterious, turbid, unclear **3.** artless, candid, frank, guileless, honest, ingenuous, straightforward, up front *(Nonformal)*

transpire *v.* arise, befall, come *or* go down *(Nonformal)*, come to pass, develop, emerge, ensue, eventuate, evolve, happen, materialize, occur, result, take place, turn out, unfold

transplant *n.* operation, organ exchange, procedure, surgery – *v.* displace, emigrate, graft, immigrate, migrate, move, parachute *(Nonformal)*, relocate, remove, reorient, resettle, shift, transfer, uproot

transport *n.* **1.** carriage, carrier, cartage, conveyance, float, lift, merchantman, mover, passage, shipment, shipping, transfer, transit, transportation, troopship, vehicle **2.** ardour, bliss, delight, ecstasy, enchantment, enthusiasm, euphoria, excitement, fervour, happiness, heaven, passion, rapture *Antonyms:* depression, despondency, doldrums, melancholy – *v.* **1.** back, bear, bring, carry, conduct, convey, cross-dock, ferry, fetch, haul, move, pack, piggyback, remove, ride, run, ship, shoulder, take, tote, transfer, tranship, truck *Nonformal:* hump, schlep **2.** agitate, captivate, delight, electrify, elevate, enchant, enrapture, entrance, excite, fascinate, inflame, move, provoke, quicken, spellbind, stimulate, stir, thrill **3.** banish, cast out, condemn, deport, displace, expel, exile, oust, relegate, sentence

transportation *n.* **1.** conveyance, haulage, movement, portage, ride, shipment, transfer, **2.** aircraft, ATV, automobile, bicycle, bus, car, cart, carriage, horse and buggy, plane, ship, snowmobile, train, truck, vehicle, wagon, *Nonformal:* shank's mare, wheels

transpose *v.* alternate, change, commute, convert, depose, exchange, interchange, invert, rotate, substitute, switch, transfer, turn *Nonformal:* flip-flop, platoon

transverse *adj.* across, athwart, cater-cornered, crosswise, diagonal, kitty-corner, oblique, slant

trap *n.* **1.** catch, deadfall, dragnet, hook, net, noose, pitfall, seine, snare, trawl, weir **2.** ambush, booby trap, conspiracy, deception, machination, ploy, ruse, stratagem, subterfuge, trick, web, wile **3.** hazard, hindrance, hurdle, impediment, obstacle, obstruction, stumbling block **4.** jaw, lips, mouth, orifice *Nonformal:* gob, yap – *v.* ambush, bag, beguile, catch, collar, corner, deceive, decoy, dupe, enmesh, ensnare, entangle, entrap, fool, grab, hook, inveigle, land, nab, nail, net, obstruct, rope *or* suck in, seduce, snare, surprise, take, tangle, trammel, tree, trick, trip up

trapped *adj.* ambushed, caged, captured, caught, cornered, corralled, ensnared, held, impounded, imprisoned, incarcerated, locked up, stuck *Nonformal:* backed to the wall, in a corner, nailed, up a tree

trappings *n. pl.* accoutrements, adornments, apparel, appointments, belongings, decorations, dress, duds, embellishment, equipment, finery, fittings, fixtures, furnishing, gear, livery, ornamentation, panoply, paraphernalia, personal effects, raiment, rigging, things, trimming, wardrobe *Nonformal:* bits and pieces, fixings, threads

trash *n.* **1.** chaff, debris, dross, flotsam, garbage, jetsam, junk, leftovers, litter, offal, refuse, rejects, riffraff, rubbish, scrap, sullage, waste *Antonyms:* essentials, necessities, rudiments **2.** balderdash, foolishness, gibberish, hogwash, nonsense, silliness, tripe *Nonformal:* eyewash, bilge, flummery, gammon, tommyrot – *v.* **1.** bust up, damage, destroy, ransack, ruin, smash, wreck **2.** berate, criticize, defame, denounce, deride, insult, jeer, malign, mock, revile, ridicule, scandalize, slander, vilify *Nonformal:* badmouth, dis, knock

trashy *adj.* cheap, frivolous, garrish, inferior, kitschy, meretricious, piddling, shabby, shoddy, silly, tawdry, useless, without merit, worthless *Nonformal:* catch penny, chump change, crappy, schlock, two-bit

trauma *n.* **1.** anguish, blow, calamity, combat fatigue, jolt, loss, misfortune, ordeal, shell shock, shock **2.** abrasion, cut, damage, hurt, injury, lesion, wound **3.** crisis, disaster, disturbance, emergency

traumatic *adj.* agonizing, confusing, disturbing, frightening, harrowing, hurtful, jolting, painful, scarring, shocking, stressful, unpleasant, upsetting *Antonyms:* palliative, relieving, restorative

travel *n.* excursion, expedition, globetrotting, hop, journey, junket, movement, navigation, odyssey, passage, peregrination, pilgrimage, ramble, ride, swing, tour, transit, trek, trip, voyage, walk, wayfaring – *v.* **1.** cover, cruise, drive, explore, fly, jet, journey, knock around, migrate, motor, move, mush *(Nonformal)*, overnight, pitch, ramble, ride, roam, rove, sail, scour, set out, sightsee, sojourn, tour, traverse, trek, vacation, visit, voyage, walk, wander, wend *Nonformal:* do, schlep **2.** advance, cross, proceed, make tracks *(Nonformal)*, progress, set forth *Antonyms*: rest, stay put, stop **3.** disperse, disseminate, pass, refract, spread, transmit

traveller *n.* adventurer, day-tripper, drifter, expeditionist, explorer, globetrotter, Gypsy, itinerant, jetsetter, journeyer, migrant, navigator, nomad, rambler, roamer, Romany, rover, seafarer, sightseer, snowbird *(Nonformal)*, tinker, tourist, trekker, tripper, trouper, vagabond, voyager, wanderer, wayfarer

traverse *v.* bridge, cover, crisscross, cross, ford, intersect, pass over *or* through, perambulate, peregrinate, ply, roam, span, track, travel, tread, walk, wander, wend

travesty *n.* burlesque, caricature, distortion, exaggeration, farce, imitation, lampoon, mimicry, mockery, parody, perversion, ridicule, satire, sham, spoof, takeoff – *v.* ape, burlesque, caricature, distort, exaggerate, imitate, knock *(Nonformal)*, lampoon, mimic, misrepresent, mock, parody, pervert, play *or* put on, ridicule, satirize, send up, sham, spoof

treacherous *adj.* **1.** betraying, catchy, deceitful, deceptive, dishonest, disloyal, double-crossing, double-dealing, duplicitous, faithless, false, false-hearted, insidious, misleading, nefarious, perfidious, shifty, slippery, specious, subversive, traitorous, two-faced, undependable, unfaithful, unreliable, untrustworthy *Nonformal:* back-stabbing, fork-tongued, two-timing *Antonyms:* dependable, faithful, loyal, reliable, staunch **2.** dangerous, hazardous, jeopardizing, perilous, precarious, risky, touch and go *(Nonformal)*, unsafe *Antonyms:* secure, solid

treachery *n.* betrayal, chicanery, corruption, dishonesty, disloyalty, double-cross, double-dealing, duplicity, faithlessness, falseness, hypocrisy, infidelity, perfidy, put-on, racket, sellout, treason, unfaithfulness *Nonformal:* dirty-dealing, scam *Antonyms:* allegiance, dependability, fealty, loyalty

tread *n.* footstep, gait, march, pace, step, stride, trace, track, tramp, walk – *v.* bear down, crush, foot, hike, march, pace, plod, stamp, step, step on, stride, tramp, trample, troop, trudge, walk *Nonformal:* hoof it, traipse

treadmill *n.* drudgery, monotony, routine, rut, sweat, tedium, well-worn groove, work *Nonformal:* grind, rat race *Antonyms:* ascent, fast-track, move

treason *n.* apostasy, betrayal, crime, deceit, deception, dishonesty, disloyalty, disobedience, duplicity, lese-majesty, mutiny, perfidy, regicide, revolt, sedition, subversion, traitorousness, treachery *Antonyms:* allegiance, loyalty, patriotism

treasure *n.* **1.** bounty, capital, cash, fortune, funds, gold, money, possessions, riches, valuables, wealth **2.** abundance, accumulation, cache, collection, hoard, gathering, nest-egg *(Nonformal)*, pile **3.** asset, commodity, gem, jewel, prize – *v.* **1.** accumulate, cache, collect, gather, hoard, reserve, retain, store *Antonyms:* squander, use, waste **2.** adore, appreciate, cherish, conserve, dote on, esteem, guard, hold dear, idolize, love, prize, revere, value, venerate, worship *Antonyms:* loathe, scorn, spurn

treasurer *n.* accountant, auditor, bookkeeper, bursar, cashier, C.F.O., chief financial officer, comptroller, controller, financial officer, paymaster, purser, steward, trustee

treasury *n.* **1.** archive, bank, bursar, bursary, cache, chest, coffer, depository, exchange, exchequer, Fort Knox *(U.S.)*, gallery, hoard, museum, piggy bank, pot *(Nonformal)*, register, repository, reserve, safe, storage, store, storehouse, strongbox, stronghouse, till, treasure house, vault **2.** capital, cash, funds, means, money, revenue, wealth

treat *n.* amusement, bonbon, celebration, delicacy, delight, enjoyment, entertainment, feast, frivolity, fun, gift, goody, gratification, joy, party, pleasure, refreshment, surprise, thrill, trifle – *v.* **1.** buy, entertain, escort, feast, gift, give, indulge, pick up the tab *(Nonformal)*, play host, provide, regale, satisfy, stand **2.** administer, attend, care for, cure, doctor, dose, dress, heal, medicate, minister to, nurse, operate, prescribe, prepare, remedy

treatise *n.* account, article, composition, critique, discourse, dissertation, essay, exposition, investigation, monograph, paper, screed, study, thesis, tract, work, writing

treatment *n.* **1.** analysis, care, cure, diet, doctoring, healing, hospitalization, medical care, medication, medicine, operation, prescription, prophylaxis, remedy, surgery, therapeutics, therapy **2.** action, angle, approach, bedside manner *(Nonformal)*, behaviour, conduct, custom, dealing, employment, execution, habit, handling, line, management, manipulation, manner, method, mode, modus operandi, practice, procedure, proceeding, processing, reception, strategy **3.** blueprint, draft, screenplay, script, sketch

treaty *n.* accord, agreement, alliance, arrangement, bargain, bond, cartel, charter, compact, concord, concordat, contract, convention, covenant, deal, entente, league, negotiation, pact, reconciliation, sanction, settlement, understanding

treble *adj.* **1.** high, high-pitched, high-sounding, shrill, sopranino, soprano, warble **2.** threefold, three-ply, triple, triplicate – *n.* castrato, coloratura, countertenor, falsetto, mezzo-soprano, soprano

tree *n.* *arbre (French)*, *baum (German)*, chicot, sapling, timber, woodland, ygdrasil *(Norse)* *Kinds of trees:* acacia, alder, almond, apple, apricot, ash, aspen, avocado, balsa, balsam fir, banana, banyan, baobab, basswood, bay, Bebb's willow, beech, birch, black cherry, black locust, black maple, black walnut, boxwood, Brazil nut, brazil-wood, breadfruit, buckeye, bull pine *(Nonformal)*, butternut, cacao, camphor, Canada plum, carob, cascara, cashew, cassia, catalpa, cedar, cherry, chestnut, chinaberry, cinnamon, coconut, conifer, cottonwood, cypress, date palm, dogwood, Douglas fir, eastern hemlock, ebony, elm, eucalyptus, evergreen, ficus, fig, fir, frankincense, Gary oak, ginkgo, grapefruit, ground hemlock, guava, gum, hackberry, hackmatack, hardwood, hazel, hemlock, hickory, honey locust, horse chestnut, ironwood, jacaranda, jack pine, Judas tree, jujube, junior, kumquat, laburnum, larch, lemon, liard, lignum vitae, lilac, linden, locust, mahogany, mango, maple, mesquite, mimosa, monkeypuzzle, mulberry, Norfolk *or* Norfolk Island *or* Norway pine, oak, oak, olive, orange, palm, palmetto, papaw, papaya, peach, pear, pecan, persimmon, pine, pistachio, pitch pine, plane, plum, pomegranate, poplar, quebracho, quince, raffia palm, red maple, red *or* white pine, redwood, rock elm, rock maple, rosewood, royal poinciana, rubber, sandalwood, sassafras, senna, sequoia, silverberry, softwood, soursop, spruce, star apple, sugar maple, sweet gum, sycamore, tamarack, tamarind, tangerine, teak, thorn apple, tulip tree, tupelo, walnut, wattle, sandbar *or* sandbasket *or* silverband *or* weeping *or* wolf willow, wire birch, yew *Immature trees:* sapling, shoot *Provincial trees:* balsam fir *(New Brunswick)*, black spruce *(Newfoundland)*, eastern white pine *(Ontario)*, lodgepole pine *(Alberta)*, northern red oak *(P.E.I.)*, red spruce *(Nova Scotia)*, western red cedar *(B.C.)*, white birch *(Saskatchewan)*, white spruce *(Manitoba)*, yellow birch *(Quebec)*

trek *n.* exodus, expedition, hike, journey, long haul, march, migration, odyssey, peregrination, pilgrimage, slog, tramp, travel, trip, voyage – *v.* hike, journey, march, migrate, plod, range, roam, rove, slog, tramp, travel, trudge, walk, wander *Nonformal:* schlep, traipse

tremble *n.* jerk, quake, quiver, shake, shiver, shudder, spasm, tremor – *v.* flutter, jar, jitter, oscillate, palpitate, quake, quaver, quiver, rock, shake, shimmy, shiver, shudder, teeter, throb, totter, vibrate

trembling *adj.* **1.** herky-jerky *(Nonformal)*, jerking, quivering, shaking, shivering, spasmodic, tremulant, twitching **2.** agitated, angry, anxious, emotional, fearful, frenzied, frightened, nervous, shaken, upset

tremendous *adj.* **1.** Brobdingnagian, colossal, enormous, formidable, gargantuan, gigantic, great, huge, humongous *(Nonformal)*, immense, jumbo, king-size, large, mammoth, massive, titanic, vast, whopping *Antonyms:* diminutive, little, minuscule, minute, small **2.** amazing, astounding, awesome, exceptional, extraordinary, fabulous, fantastic, monumental, overwhelming, prodigious, splendiferous *(Nonformal)*, stupendous, superb, terrific, unusual, wonderful *Antonyms:* appalling, dreadful, dull, trite

tremor *n.* agitation, earthquake, flutter, frisson, jerk, jolt, quake, quaver, quiver, ripple, shake, shiver, shock, spasm, trembling, vibration, wobble

tremulous *adj.* agitated, anxious, fearful, fidgety, jittery, jumpy, mousy, nervous, shaky, shivery, shrinking, shy, skittish, squirrely *(Nonformal)*, timid, undulating , vacillating, weak-kneed *Antonyms:* bold, dauntless, intrepid

trench *n.* canal, channel, conduit, coulee, course, crack, cut, ditch, duct, excavation, furrow, gutter, moat, passage, ravine, trough, valley, wash – *v.* channel, cut, dig, ditch, dredge, excavate, fortify, groove

trenchant *adj.* **1.** acerbic, acid, acidulous, acrimonious, acute, astringent, biting, caustic, critical, crushing, cutting, hurtful, mordant, piquant, pointed, razor-sharp, salty, sarcastic, scathing, sententious, severe, sharp, tart, true-to-life, unsparing *Antonyms:* appeasing, mollifying, soothing **2.** crisp, distinct, incisive, intense, keen, salient, significant, unequivocal, well-defined **3.** driving, forceful, forcible, impressive, potent, powerful, pungent, strong, vigorous, weighty *Antonyms:* impotent, powerless, weak

trend *n.* **1.** aim, bearing, bent, bias, course, current, direction, drift, flow, inclination, leaning, movement, orientation, penchant, progression, run, swing, tendency, tenor, wind **2.** craze, fad, fashion, furor, look, mode, style, vogue *Nonformal:* flavour of the month, in-thing, kick, latest thing, newest wrinkle, rage

trendy *adj.* au courant, contemporary, fashionable, hot *(Nonformal)*, in, in vogue, latest, modish, now, popular, stylish, with-it *Antonyms:* dated, demodé, hackneyed, tired

trepidation *n.* agitation, alarm, anxiety, apprehension, cold sweat *(Nonformal)*, consternation, creeps, dismay, disquiet, disturbance, dread, emotion, excitement, fear, fright, horror, jitters, nervousness, palpitation, panic, perturbation, shock, terror, uneasiness, worry *Nonformal:* blue funk, butterflies, goose bumps, heebie-jeebies , shakes *Antonyms:* aplomb, composure, confidence, equanimity, self-assurance

trespass *n.* fall, infringement, intrusion, invasion, misdemeanour, offence, sin, transgression, violation, wrongdoing, wrongful entry – *v.* disturb, encroach, impinge infringe, intrude, invade, meddle, obtrude, overstep, poach, pry, transgress, violate *Nonformal:* butt *or* chisel *or* horn in, crash

trial *adj.* experimental, exploratory, investigative, pilot, preliminary, probationary, provisional, tentative, test – *n.* **1.** action, arraignment, assize, case, citation, claim, contest, court action, court martial, cross-examination, crucible, examination, experiment, hearing, impeachment, investigation, kangaroo court, lawsuit, litigation, proceeding, prosecution, suit, tribunal **2.** dry run, stab, tryout, whack, workout **3.** adversity, albatross, anguish, annoyance, bane, bother, burden, complication, crucible, difficulty, distress, drag, experience, grief, handful, hardship, heartbreak, misery, misfortune, nuisance, ordeal, pest, plague, rigour, suffering, tribulation, trouble, trying time, vexation, vicissitude, woe, wretchedness *Nonformal:* botheration, hassle, pain in the neck, worriment *Antonyms:* delight, joy, pleasure, rapture

tribe *n.* blood, caste, clan, class, division, dynasty, family, group, ilk, kin, kind, lineage, people, phyle, race, stirps, stock, type *See also:* **First Peoples**

tribulation *n.* adversity, affliction, bad luck, blow, curse, difficulty, distress, grief, hard knocks *(Nonformal)*, hardship, headache, heartache, misery, misfortune, ordeal, pain, reverse, sorrow, suffering, trial, trouble, unhappiness, vexation, woe, worry, wretchedness *Antonyms:* blessing, bliss, ease, happiness, rest

tribunal *n.* adjudication, court, hearing, inquiry, inquisition, investigation, kangaroo court, royal commission, Sanhedrin, Star Chamber, trial

tribute *n.* **1.** accolade, acknowledgment, admiration, applause, appreciation, celebration, *cens et rentes (Quebec Historical)*, citation, commendation, compliment, esteem, eulogy, gift, gratitude, honour, hurrahs, huzzas, laurels, memorial, offering, praise, recognition, recommendation, respect, salutation, standing ovation, testimonial *Antonyms:* condemnation, criticism, disapproval, reproach, reproof **2.** customs, duty excise, fee, payment, tax, tithe, toll

trick *n.* **1.** artifice, bluff, chicanery, deceit, deception, decoy, device, disguise, distortion, dodge, duplicity, feint, forgery, fraud, hoax, invention, machination, manoeuvre, ploy, rip-off, ruse, snare, subterfuge, swindle, trap, treachery, wile *Nonformal:* con, deke, flimflam **2.** antic, caper, catch, escapade, frolic, gag, jest, joke, lark, practical joke, prank, put-on, shenanigan, sport, stunt **3.** characteristic, custom, foible, habit, habitude, idiosyncrasy, manner, mannerism, peculiarity, praxis, quirk, trait, way **4.** ability, art, command, craft, expertise, facility, gift, hang, knack, method, secret, skill, style, swing, technique **5.** hocus-pocus, illusion, legerdemain, magic, sleight of hand – *v.* cheat, deceive, defraud, delude, dupe, fool, hoax, mislead, outwit, shaft, swindle, trap, victimize *Nonformal:* bamboozle, con, deke, gull, rook, scam, snow, take

trickery *n.* artifice, cheat, cheating, chicanery, deceit, deception, dishonesty, dodge, fraud, guile, knavery, quackery, shenanigans, skulduggery, sting, stratagem, stunt, underhandedness, wiles *Nonformal:* con, hanky-panky, jiggery-pokery, monkey business, rip-off, scam

trickle *n.* dribble, flow, leak, leakage, seepage – *v.* crawl, creep, distill, dribble, drip, drop, exude, flow, issue, leak, ooze, percolate, seep, stream, weep *Antonyms:* cascade, gush, spew

trickster *n.* **1.** devil, *Eshu (African)*, flimflam man, fox, *kitsune (Japanese)*, *Loki (Norse)*, *Maui (Polynesian)*, mischief-maker, monkey, *Monkey King (Chinese)*, nuisance, Puck, Sisyphus, troublemaker *Native Peoples:* coyote, Glooscap, Nanabush, raven **2.** cheat, con artist, confidence trickster, fraud, impostor, slyboots *(Nonformal)*, swindler

tricky *adj.* artful, cagey, catchy, clever, crafty, cunning, deceitful, deceptive, devious, difficult, dishonest, foxy, guileful, misleading, scheming, shady, sharp, shifty, slick, slippery, sly, sneaky, streetwise, treacherous, wily *Antonyms:* artless, direct, genuine, sincere, truthful

tried *adj.* approved, certified, constant, demonstrated, dependable, faithful, practiced, proved, reliable, secure, staunch, steadfast, tested, time-tested, trustworthy, trusty, used *Antonyms:* newfangled *(Nonformal)*, unreliable, untested

trifle *n.* **1.** bagatelle, bauble, bibelot, curio, gewgaw, kickshaw, knick-knack, novelty, *objet d'art (French)*, plaything, toy, trinket, triviality **2.** bit, dash, drop, fraction, hint, iota, jot, particle, piece, pinch, shade, soupçon, speck, spot, suggestion, suspicion, touch, trace, trivia *Nonformal:* beans, diddly-squat, fiddle-faddle, tad – *v.* dabble, dally, dawdle, fidget, flirt, fool, fritter, idle, indulge, lead on, lollygag, lounge, palter, philander, play, potter, putter, squander, string along, toy, waste time

trifling *adj.* **1.** extravagant, frivolous, playful, profligate, silly **2.** banal, empty, hollow, inane, inconsequential, inconsiderable, insignificant, insipid, negligible, niggling, nugatory, paltry, penny ante, petty, piddling, shallow, slight, small, tiny, trivial, unimportant, valueless, vapid, worthless *Nonformal:* chump change, dinky, no-account *Antonyms:* crucial, important, major, momentous, serious, vital

trigger *n.* button, catalyst, catch, device, lever, release, switch – *v.* activate, bring about, cause, elicit, generate, initiate, kindle, launch, precipitate, produce, prompt, provoke, set off, spark, start *Antonyms:* close, extinguish, put out

trill *n.* flutter, music, quaver, tremolo, vibrato – *v.* lilt, play, quaver, shake, sing, twitter, warble

trim *adj.* chic, clean, fine, fit, graceful, jaunty, neat, nice, polished, pretty, shapely, shipshape, sleek, slender, slick, slim, streamlined, svelte, tidy, well-balanced, well-proportioned, willowy *Nonformal:* in fine fettle *or* apple-pie order, spruce– *n.* **1.** condition, disposition, dress, fettle, fitness, form, health, kilter, order, repair, shape, situation, state, style **2.** adornment, bauble, border, decoration, display, dressing, edging, embellishment, fanciness, flashiness, frill, fringe, frippery, fussiness, garnish, gaudiness, gingerbread, jigaree *(Newfoundland)*, knick-knack, nonsense, ornament, piping, toy, trinket – *v.* **1.** abbreviate, adjust, boil down, clip, crop, curtail, cut, cut back *or* down, dock, even up, lop, mow, pare, pare down, plane, prune, shave, shear, shorten, slice off, snip, tidy, truncate *Antonyms:* add, adjoin, append, attach **2.** adorn, arrange, bedeck, decorate, dress, embellish, enhance, garnish, ornament

trinket *n.* bagatelle, bibelot, bauble, charm, curio, gadget, gewgaw, good luck piece, jewellery, junk, keepsake, knickknack, momento, novelty, *objet d'art (French)*, ornament, plaything, souvenir, token, toy, trifle

trio *n.* three, three-piece, threesome, trey, triad, triangle, trilogy, trinity, triple, triplet, triplicate, triptych, triumvirate, triune, troika

trip *n.* **1.** cruise, errand, excursion, expedition, flight, flying visit, foray, hop, jaunt, journey, junket, outing, overnight, peregrination, ramble, run, swing, tour, travel, trek, voyage, weekender **2.** blunder, booboo *(Nonformal)*, bungle, error, misdeed, misstep, mistake, stumble – *v.* **1.** buck, bungle, canter, confuse, disconcert, err, fall, fall over, founder, lapse, lurch, miscalculate, misstep, plunge, skip, slide, sprawl, spring, stumble, topple, tumble, unsettle **2.** dance, hasten, hurry, scurry, slip

triple *adj.* ternary, ternate, three, threefold, three-ply, treble, triplicate – *n.* hat trick, three-bagger *(Nonformal)*, trey, triad, trinity, triplex, troika – *v.* increase, multiply, treble, triplicate

trite *adj.* banal, clichéd, common, commonplace, drained, dull, everyday, exhausted, flat, hackneyed, mildewed, moth-eaten *(Nonformal)*, ordinary, overdone, pedestrian, routine, shopworn, silly, stale, stereotyped, stock, threadbare, timeworn, tired, trivial, uninspired, unoriginal, used-up, vapid, warmed-over *Antonyms:* exciting, fresh, interesting, novel, original

triumph *n.* **1.** celebration, elation, exultation, festivity, happiness, joy, jubilation, merriment, pride, rejoicing **2.** achievement, accomplishment, ascendancy, attainment, coup, feat, gain, hit, mastery, score, sensation, success, surmounting, takeover, victory, win *Nonformal:* big win, clinch conquest, clean sweep, grand slam, homer, kill, killing, paydirt, pushover, shoo-in, smash, smash hit, splash, the bacon, the gold, walkover *Antonyms:* catastrophe, disaster, failure, fiasco, flop – *v.* **1.** achieve, conquer, defeat, dominate, flourish, master, overcome, overwhelm, prevail, prosper, subdue, succeed, sweep, thrive, trounce, vanquish, win, win out *Nonformal:* best, blow away, lick **2.** celebrate, cheer, crow, delight, exult, gloat, glory, jubilate, rejoice

triumphant *adj.* successful, celebratory, champion, conquering, dominant, elated, exultant, glorious, happy, jubilant, numero uno *(Nonformal)*, on top, out front, prize-winning, proud, rejoicing, unbeaten, undefeated, victorious, winning *Antonyms:* defeated, humbled, shamed, unsuccessful

trivia *n.* bagatelle, details, ephemera, fine points, frivolities, incidentals, minutiae, niceties, nonessentials, trifles, trivialities *Nonformal:* small change *or* potatoes

trivial *adj.* commonplace, diminutive, dismissible, everyday, flimsy, frivolous, immaterial, inappreciable, incidental, inconsequential, inconsiderable, inferior, insignificant, irrelevant, little, meagre, mean, meaningless, measly, microscopic, minor, minute, momentary, negligible, nonessential, paltry, petty, picayune, piddling, puny, quibbling, scanty, small, superficial, trifling, trite, unimportant, valueless, worthless *Nonformal:* bupkes, chickenfeed, Mickey Mouse, peanuts *Antonyms:* considerable, earthshattering, essential, important, momentous, profound

trivialize *v.* belittle, deprecate, depreciate, deride, devalue, dismiss, downplay, jeer, minimize, mock, underestimate, undervalue

troll *n.* cave dweller, creature, giant, monster, ogre, troglodyte – *v.* angle, drag, draw, fish, pull, trawl

troop *n.* army, assembly, band, bevy, body, cavalry, combatants, company, contingent, corps, crew, crowd, delegation, flock, force, gaggle, gathering, group, herd, horde, host, infantry, legion, military, multitude, number, outfit, pack, party, patrol, personnel, servicemen, shoal, soldiers, squad, swarm, team, throng, unit – *v.* march, parade, stride, tramp, walk

trophy *adj.* decorative, display, ornamental, prize, show, token – *n.* award, badge, booty, citation, cup, decoration, gold, keepsake, laurels, memento, memorial, ornamentation, pennant, prize, ribbon, souvenir, spoils, statue, symbol *See also:* **award**, **championship**

tropic *n.* latitude, parallel, Tropic of Cancer, Tropic of Capricorn, Torrid Zone

tropical *adj.* close, equatorial, hot, humid, lush, steamy, sticky, stifling, sultry, sweltering, torrid, warm *Antonyms:* arctic, chilly, cold, cool, freezing, frigid, frosty

trot *n.* bearing, gait, pace, stride, walk – *v.* amble, canter, go, hurry, jog, lope, pad, ride, run, saunter, scamper, step lively

troubadour *n.* bard, busker, gleeman, jongleuer, *Meistersinger (German)*, minstrel, minnesinger, street performer, wandering singer

trouble *n.* **1.** adversity, affliction, agitation, annoyance, anxiety, bad news, bind, bother, commotion, concern, confusion, danger, difficulty, dilemma, dire straits, discontent, discord, disorder, disquiet, dissatisfaction, distress, disturbance, grief, heartache, hindrance, impediment, imposition, inconvenience, irritation, jam, mess, misfortune, nuisance, pain, pest, pickle, predicament, problem, puzzle, row, scrape, sorrow, spot, strain, stress, strife, struggle, suffering, task, torment, tribulation, tumult, unrest, upset, vexation, woe, worry *Kinds of trouble codes:* black *(Bomb threat)*, blue *(Cardiac arrest)*, red *(Fire)*, white *(Violent patient)* *Nonformal:* behind the eight ball, botheration, come-a-cropper, crash 99, crisis mode, fix, hassle, hot water, pickle, pretty pass, red alert, tight spot *Antonyms:* comfort, contentment, happiness, peace, tranquility **2.** ailment, bad health, complaint, defect, disability, disease, failure, illness, malady, malfunction, sickness *Antonyms:* health, vigour, well-being – *v.* agitate, annoy, beset, bother, discommode, distress, disturb, harass, irritate, pester, pother, torment, upset, vex, worry *Nonformal:* bug, hassle, pick on *Antonyms:* mollify, placate

troublemaker *n.* agitator, devil, firebrand, hellion, holy terror, incendiary, inciter, inflamer, instigator, jinker *(Newfoundland)*, mischief-maker, nuisance, pest, problem, punk, rascal, rogue, sleeveen *(Newfoundland)*, smart aleck, sprite, trickster, wise guy *French:* agent provocateur, enfant terrible *Nonformal:* bad actor, bull in a china shop, loose cannon, punk, rabble-rouser

troublesome *adj.* adverse, annoying, bothersome, burdensome, damnable, difficult, hindering, inconvenient, irksome, irritating, laborious, oppressive, pesky, trying, vexatious, worrisome *Nonformal:* damn, darn, infernal, no picnic, sticky wicket *Antonyms:* easygoing, pleasant

trough *n.* **1.** aqueduct, canal, channel, chute, conduit, depression, dike, ditch, duct, flume, furrow, gully, gutter, moat, trench, watercourse **2.** feed box, manger, mow

trounce *v.* beat, best, conquer, crush, defeat, drub, lambaste, outdo, overcome, overpower, overwhelm, pummel, punish, subdue, thrash, top, trim, upend, vanquish, wallop, whip *Nonformal:* blow away, bury, cap, clobber, cream, lick, shellac, slaughter, smother, snow under, swamp, total, trash, walk over, waste, whup

troupe *n.* band, cast, company, ensemble, group, set

truce *n.* accord, agreement, amnesty, armistice, cease-fire, cessation, de-escalation, entente, halt, intermission, interval, lull, moratorium, pause, pax, peace, reconciliation, reprieve, respite, rest, stand-down, stay, suspension, terms, treaty *Nonformal:* let-up, olive branch, white flag

truck *n.* **1.** carryall, lorry *(British)*, wagon *Kinds of truck:* delivery, dump, 18-wheeler, flatbed, four-wheel drive, half-ton, ice cream, milk, monster, moving van, panel, pickup, quarter-ton, refrigerated, rig, sandwich, semi, SUV, tow, van **2.** commodities, goods, merchandise, stock, stuff, trade, traffic, wares – *v.* **1.** carry, ferry, float, haul, lift, motor, move, roll, schlep *(Nonformal)*, transport, tug, wheel **2.** bargain, barter, buy, deal, exchange, handle, negotiate, peddle, retail, sell, swap, trade, traffic, transact

truculent *adj.* abusive, aggressive, antagonistic, bad-tempered, barbarous, bellicose, belligerent, brutal, bullying, caustic, chippy *(Nonformal)*, combative, contentious, contumelious, cross, cruel, defiant, farouche, ferocious, fierce, frightening, gruff, harsh, hateful, hostile, inhumane, intimidating, mean, militant, mordacious, mordant, obstreperous, opprobrious, ornery, pugnacious, quarrelsome, rude, savage, scathing, scrappy, scurrilous, sharp, sullen, terrifying, violent, vitriolic, vituperative *Antonyms:* agreeable, amiable, civil, gentle

trudge *v.* clump, drag, hike, keep on going, lumber, march, plod, plug along, slog, step, stumble, tramp, tread, trek, wade, walk *Nonformal:* schlep, traipse

true *adj.* **1.** accurate, actual, certain, confirmed, constant, correct, exact, factual, indubitable, precise, right, truthful, undeniable, unerring, unquestionable, valid, veracious, veritable *Antonyms:* counterfeit, fake, fictional, inaccurate, incorrect **2.** authentic, bona fide, genuine, lawful, legal, legitimate, natural, proper, pukka, pure, real, unfeigned, **3.** conscientious, dedicated, dependable, devoted, dutiful, faithful, high-principled, honest, honourable, just, loyal, reliable, resolute, right-minded, scrupulous, sincere, staunch, steadfast, trustworthy, unaffected, unswerving, upright, wholehearted *Antonyms:* deceitful, disloyal, faithless, treacherous **4.** aligned, even, level, straight – *adv.* accurately, candidly, correctly, honestly, on target, perfectly, point-device, precisely, properly, rightly, truthfully, unerringly, veritably – *v.* align, even, level, make *or* set true, straighten

truly *adv.* absolutely, accurately, actually, authentically, certainly, constantly, correctly, definitely, devotedly, doubtlessly, exactly so, factually, faithfully, firmly, genuinely, honestly, honourably, legitimately, loyally, positively, precisely, really, reliably, righteously, rightly, sincerely, staunchly, steadily, surely, totally *(Nonformal)*, truthfully, unequivocally, verily, veritably *Antonyms:* doubtfully, falsely, fraudulently

trumpet *n.* **1.** brass, coronet, bugle, clarion, horn, tooter *(Nonformal)* **2.** blare, blast, fanfare, flourish, honk – *v.* **1.** blare, blast, bugle, fanfaron, honk, pipe, shriek **2.** acclaim, commend, dignify, exalt, glorify, laud, praise **3.** advertise, announce, ballyhoo, declare, proclaim, promulgate, summon

truncate *v.* abbreviate, abridge, curtail, cut, cut off *or* short, decollate, lop, pare, prune, shear, shorten, trim *Antonyms:* append, extend, lengthen, prolong

trunk *n.* **1.** block, body, bole, butt, column, core, log, stalk, stem, stock, thorax, torso **2.** bag, baggage, bin, box, case, chest, coffer, coffin, compartment, container, crate, foot locker, kist (Scottish), locker, luggage, portmanteau, sample case, sea-chart, suitcase, wanigan, wardrobe **3.** nose, proboscis, snout

truss *n.* bar, beam, brace, support, tie *Common trusses:* bowstring, collar, deck, dome, hammer-beam, Mansard, Pegrem, Warren – *v.* bind, bind up, brace, bundle, cinch, fasten, gird, lash, rope, secure, swaddle, tie, tie up, tighten, wrap

trust *n.* **1.** assurance, belief, certainty, certitude, confidence, conviction, credence, credit, dependence, entrustment, expectation, faith, gospel, hope, positiveness, reliance, stock, store, sureness *Antonyms:* distrust, doubt, fear, mistrust, uncertainty **2.** account, blind *or* frozen trust, care, charge, custody, duty, guard, guardianship, keeping, liability, moment, obligation, protection, responsibility, safekeeping, trusteeship, ward **3.** association, business, cartel, chain, combine, company, conglomerate, corner, corporation, estate, group, holding company, institution, investment company *or* trust, monopoly, multinational, mutual fund, organization, outfit, pool, ring, syndicate, transitional, trust company – *v.* accept, accredit, assume, bank *or* bet *or* build *or* calculate *or* count *or* depend *or* gamble on, believe, confide in, entrust, expect, hope, imagine, look to, presume, rely upon, suppose, surmise, swear by, take, think likely

trusting *adj.* believing, blind, careless, credulous, foolish, ingenuous, innocent, naive, gullible, simple, sure, trustful, unquestioning, unsuspecting *Antonyms:* cautious, distrustful, suspicious, unsure

trustworthy *adj.* accurate, all right, authentic, authoritative, believable, convincing, credible, dependable, ethical, exact, honest, honourable, level-headed, mature, open, plausible, principled, realistic, reliable, reputable, responsible, righteous, rock-solid, secure, sensible, square, steadfast, there *(Nonformal)*, tried, true, trusty, truthful, unfailing, valid *Antonyms:* deceitful, dishonest, irresponsible, unethical, untrustworthy

truth *n.* **1.** accuracy, actuality, authenticity, axiom, certainty, correctness, exactitude, exactness, fact, genuineness, infallibility, law, legitimacy, maxim, precision, reality, rectitude, rightness, truism, validity, veracity, verity, verisimilitude *Nonformal:* gospel, straight goods *Antonyms:* deceit, deception, delusion, fabrication, invention **2.** candour, constancy, dedication, devotion, dutifulness, faith, fidelity, frankness, honesty, integrity, loyalty, openness, sincerity, steadfastness *Antonyms:* dishonesty, infidelity, treachery

truthful *adj.* **1.** candid, faithful, forthright, frank, guileless, honest, ingenuous, open, outspoken, plain-spoken, reliable, righteous, scrupulous, sincere, straightforward, straight-shooting, trustworthy *Antonyms:* deceptive, dishonest, lying, treacherous **2.** accurate, believable, correct, credible, exact, factual, literal, precise, real, realistic, unfeigned, veracious, veritable

try *n.* attempt, crack, effort, endeavour, experiment, test, trial – *v.* **1.** approximate, aspire, attempt, compete, contend, contest, dabble, drive for, endeavour, essay, go after, propose, risk, seek, seize, shoot for *(Nonformal)*, speculate, strive, struggle, tackle, undertake, venture, vie, work, wrangle **2.** analyze, assess, consider, decide, examine, hear, inspect, judge, referee, sample, taste, test **3.** drain, exert, irk, sap, strain, tax, tire, torment, weary

trying *adj.* annoying, bothersome, damnable, demanding, difficult, disagreeable, distressing, disturbing, exacting, exasperating, heavy, irksome, irritating, laborious, nagging, onerous, provoking, rough, severe, stressful, taxing, tiresome, tormenting, troublesome, unendurable, ungovernable, unpleasant, unruly, upsetting, vexing, wearisome, worrisome *Nonformal:* damn, darn, infernal *Antonyms:* calming, easy, painless, simple, undemanding

tryst *n.* appointment, assignation, date, engagement, love affair, meet, meeting, one-night stand, rendezvous, union

tub *n.* basin, bath, bucket, cask, firkin, keg, tureen, vat, vessel, washbasin, washtub

tube *n.* **1.** conduit, connector, cylinder, duct, hose, line, monitor, pathway, pipe, pipette, roll, viaduct, vein **2.** electric *or* radio *or* test tube, vacuum

tuck *n.* food, snackers *(Nonformal)*, sweets, treats – *v.* **1.** draw *or* fold together *or* in, enfold, envelop, gather, insert, pinch, pleat, swaddle, turn in, wrap **2.** bury, cram, hide, pack, seclude, stash, stow, thrust **3.** bend, crouch, curl, tighten

tuft *n.* bunch, clump, cluster, collection, group, growth, hair, knot, plumage, ruff, shock, tussock

tug *n.* **1.** attraction, exertion, pull **2.** alligator, deep-sea tug, log tug, ocean-going tug, towboat, tugboat, steam warping tug – *v.* drag, draw, haul, heave, jerk, lug, pull, strain, struggle, toil, tow, wrench, yank

tuition *n.* **1.** admission *or* entrance fee, charge, cost, entrance, expense, fee, payment, price **2.** education, instruction, lessons, schooling, teaching, training, tutelage

tumble *n.* collapse, descent, fall, flounder, jumble, nose dive, upset *Nonformal:* gainer, header, toss – *v.* descend, dip, disturb, down, drop, fall, flatten, pitch, plummet, plunge, roll, sag, skid, slip, slump, somersault, spill, stumble, topple, trip, unsettle,

tumble-down *adj.* battered, broken-down, decrepit, derelict, dilapidated, ramshackle, rickety, run-down, seedy, tottery, weathered *Antonyms:* pristine, solid, well-kept

tumour *n.* bump, cancer, carcinoma, cyst, growth, lump, metastasis, neoplasm, sarcoma, swelling, tumefaction

tumult *n.* ado, affray, agitation, altercation, bedlam, brawl, brouhaha, cacophony, clamour, commotion, confusion, convulsion, din, disorder, disturbance, dither, donnybrook, excitement, ferment, fracas, fuss, hubbub, hue and cry, hullabaloo, maelstrom, noise, outbreak, outcry, pandemonium, quarrel, racket, riot, row, stir, strife, turbulence, turmoil, unrest, unsettlement, upheaval, uproar, violence *Nonformal:* brannigan, dust-up, flap, lather, mill, rhubarb, stew, to-do *Antonyms:* calm, hassle, peace, quiet, repose, silence

tumultuous *adj.* agitated, boisterous, clamorous, confused, disturbed, earth-shattering, excited, fierce, hectic, irregular, lawless, noisy, obstreperous, raging, rambunctious, raucous, restless, riotous, rowdy, stormy, tempestuous, turbulent, unrestrained, unruly, uproarious, violent, vociferous, volatile, volcanic, wild *Antonyms:* hushed, restful, serene, still, tranquil

tune *n.* **1.** air, aria, carol, chorus, composition, descant, diapason, ditty, jingle, measure, melody, motif, motive, music, number, piece, riff, song, strain, theme **2.** accord, agreement, concord, concordance, consonance, sympathy, unison *Antonyms:* contention, discordance, disharmony, disunity, friction – *v.* adapt, adjust, align, attune, blend, chord, harmonize, regulate

tunnel *n.* burrow, channel, crawl space, crawlway, crosscut, drift, flue, gallery, hole, mine, passage, passageway, shaft, subway, tube, underpass – *v.* burrow, dig, excavate, exhume, mine, penetrate, scoop out

turbid *adj.* **1.** cloudy, dense, foggy, hazy, murky, opaque, polluted, soupy, thick, unclear **2.** confused, deranged, disoriented, incoherent, jumbled, muddled, troubled

turbulent *adj.* **1.** agitated, blustery, boisterous, choppy, coarse, confused, destructive, disordered, disturbed, excited, fierce, foaming, furious, howling, inclement, noisy, raging, rebellious, roaring, roily, rough, rugged, stormy, swirling, tempestuous, tumultuous, unpredictable, unsettled, unstable, violent, volcanic, wild *Antonyms:* calm, pacific, peaceful **2.** insubordinate, insurgent, mutinous, rebellious, refractory, riotous, seditious

turgid *adj.* battological, bloated, bombastic, distended, flatulent, full *(Nonformal)*, grandiloquent, inflated, ostentatious, overblown, plethoric, pompous, pretentious, swollen *Antonyms:* laconic, no-nonsense, simple, terse

turmoil *n.* **1.** agitation, bedlam, brouhaha, bustle, chaos, commotion, confusion, disorder, disturbance, flurry, fuss, hubbub, jumble, mix-up, pandemonium, riot, row, stir, strife, trouble, tumult, turbulence, unrest, uproar, violence *Nonformal:* rhubarb, stew, to-do *Antonyms:* peace, quiet, rest, serenity, stillness **2.** anxiety, disquiet, distress, dither, ferment, flap

turn *n.* **1.** circle, circuit, circulation, cycle, gyration, gyre, pirouette, pivot, revolution, roll, rotation, spin, spinarama *(Nonformal)*, spiral, turnabout, twirl, twist, wheel, whirl, winding, yaw **2.** alteration, change, deflection, deviation, difference, reversal, swerve, variation, veer **3.** arch, bend, bow, crescent, curve **4.** bout, chance, crack, opportunity, period, round, shot, spell, stint **5.** bent, direction, inclination, movement, proclivity, tendency **6.** act, courtesy, deed, favour, gesture, kindness, service – *v.* **1.** circle, circulate, gyrate, orbit, oscillate, pirouette, pivot, revolve, rotate, spin, swivel, twirl, wheel, whirl, **2.** adapt, alter, change, convert, fashion, fit, form, metamorphose, modify, morph *(Nonformal)*, mould, recast, refashion, rejig, remake, remodel, render, retool, revert, shape, transfigure, transform, translate, vary **3.** loosen, screw, tighten, undo, unhinge, wrench **4.** contort, dislocate, hurt, rupture, sprain, strain **5.** aim, direct, focus, head, incline, lead, point, steer **6.** about face, flip-flop, invert, reverse, switch, turn-turtle *(Nonformal)*, upend, volte-face **7.** acidify, curdle, decay, decompose, ferment, go off *(Nonformal)*, putrefy, rot, sour, spoil, taint **8.** deflect, detour, deviate, divert, double back, rechannel, redirect, repel, sidetrack, turn away **9.** disgust, nauseate, repulse, revolt, sicken, unsettle, upset

turnout *n.* **1.** aggregate, GNP, gross national product, output, product, production, productivity, quota, throughput, turnover, volume, yield **2.** assemblage, assembly, attendance, audience, congregation, crowd, gate, gathering, meeting, number **3.** field, grazing area, paddock, pasture, range

turpitude *n.* baseness, corruption, degeneracy, depravity, dissoluteness, immortality, vileness, villainy, wickedness *Antonyms:* rectitude, uprightness, virtue

turret *n.* bartizan, minaret, mirador, pinnacle, tourelle, tower

tutor *n.* docent, crammer, educator, guide, guru, helper, instructor, lecturer, mentor, preceptor, rabbi, sensei, supervisor, T.A., teacher – *v.* assist, coach, discipline, educate, guide, instruct, lecture, school, teach, train

twice *adj.* again, double, pair, repeat, two, two times, twofold

twiddle *v.* adjust, fiddle, piddle *(Nonformal)*, play, putter, putz *(Yiddish)*, tinker, twirl

twig *n.* scion, shoot, withe – *v.* catch on, get *(Nonformal)*, perceive, recognize, understand

twilight *n.* **1.** afterglow, dimness, dusk, early evening, evening, eventide, foredawn, gloaming, half-light, late afternoon, night, nightfall, owl-light, sundown, sunset *Antonyms:* dawn, daybreak, morning **2.** autumn, decline, ebb, end, fall, *Götterdämmerung (German)*, later years, recession, wane, weakening *Antonyms:* beginning, commencement, rise, start

twin *adj.* accompanying, copied, corresponding, double, dual, duplicate, fraternal, geminate, identical, joint, like, matched, matching, paired, parallel, second, selfsame, similar, twofold – *n.* clone, counterpart, *Doppelgänger (German)*, double, duplicate, equivalent, freemartin, image, likeness, look-alike, mate, ringer, shadow, Siamese twin, spitting image *(Nonformal)*

twine *n.* braid, coil, cord, cordage, rope, shaganappi, string, thread, twist, yarn – *v.* bend, braid, coil, corkscrew, curl, encircle, enmesh, entangle, entwine, interlace, interweave, knit, loop, plait, spiral, splice, tangle, twist, weave, wind, wrap, wreathe

twinge *n.* ache, bite, gripe, misery, pain, pang, pinch, prick, shiver, smart, spasm, stab, stitch, throb, throe, tic, tweak, twist, twitch

twinkle *n.* flash, instant, moment – *v.* coruscate, flicker, gleam, glimmer, glint, glisten, glitter, glow, illuminate, light, scintillate, shine, sparkle, wink

twinkling *adj.* blinking, bright, dazzling, flashing, fulgent, fulgurant, gleaming, glistening, glittering, resplendent, shimmering, sparkling

twirl *v.* **1.** circle, gyrate, pirouette, pivot, purl, revolve, rotate, spin, swirl, turn, twist, wheel, whirl **2.** coil, corkscrew, curl, round, twine, wind

twist *n.* **1.** aberration, idiosyncrasy, kink, oddity, peculiarity, quirk **2.** bend, change, turn, variation **3.** complication, development, revelation, slant, surprise, wrinkle *(Nonformal)* – *v.* **1.** braid, coil, corkscrew, curl, encircle, entwine, intertwine, rotate, screw, spin, spiral, swivel, tighten, turn, twine, twirl, warp, weave, wind, wrap, wreathe, wring **2.** contort, dance, shake, squirm, swing, wiggle, wriggle, writhe *Nonformal:* boogie, twist and shout **3.** alter, belie, change, colour, contort, corrupt, deform, distort, falsify, garble, misrepresent, misstate, pervert, put a spin on *(Nonformal)*, warp **4.** baffle, bewilder, confuse, mislead, mystify, perplex, puzzle **5.** break, hurt, injure, sprain, strain, wrench **6.** bend, curve, meander, snake, veer, worm, zigzag

twisted *adj.* **1.** bent, depraved, morally warped, perverted, venal **2.** aberrant, abnormal, contorted, distorted, deviant, misshapen, perverse, tortuous **3.** convoluted, intricate, labyrinthine, tangled *Antonyms:* conventional, easy, simplistic , straightforward **4.** coiled, curled, furled, rolled, rotated, tortile, wound *Antonyms:* linear, straight

twitch *n & v.* blink, fidget, flutter, jerk, jiggle, jump, kick, lug, lurch, pluck, shiver, shudder, snap, spasm, squirm, tic, tremble, tug, twinge, yank

tycoon *n.* baron, billionaire, boss, businessman, capitalist, captain of industry, entrepreneur, executive, financier, industrialist, investor, magnate, merchant prince, millionaire, mogul, potentate, prince, robber baron

type *n.* **1.** brand, breed, cast, category, character, class, classification, cut, example, family, form, gender, genre, group, ilk, kind, lot, model, nature, number, persuasion, preference, sort, species, standard, strain, variety **2.** case, characters, emblem, face, figure, font, mark, print, printing, sign, stamp, symbol *Selected type fonts:* aerial, bookman, courier, elite, garamond, gothic, helvetica, ITC Century Book, prestige, script, symbol, times, Times Roman, universe, zaph dingbats *Selected type styles:* bold, italics, narrow, regular, sans serif, serif – *v.* **1.** copy, print, record, represent, teletype, touch-type, transcribe, typewrite, write **2.** arrange, categorize, class, classify, peg, pigeonhole, sort, standardize, stereotype, typecast

typhoon *n.* cyclone, hurricane, monsoon, squall, storm, tempest, tidal wave, tornado, tsunami, twister, whirlwind

typical *adj.* archetypal, average, characteristic, classic, classical, common, commonplace, conventional, emblematic, essential, everyday, exemplary, expected, general, habitual, ideal, illustrative, in character *or* keeping, indicative, matter-of-course, model, natural, normal, ordinary, orthodox, paradigmatic, patterned, prevalent, regular, representative, run of the mill, standard, stock, suggestive, symbolic, unexceptional, usual *Antonyms:* atypical, exceptional, rare, singular, unique, unrepresentative

typify *v.* adumbrate, characterize, constitute, describe, embody, epitomize, exemplify, illustrate, incarnate, mean, mirror, model, personify, represent, signify, stand for, sum up, symbolize

tyrannical *adj.* autocratic, authoritarian, brutal, cruel, despotic, dictatorial, domineering, fascist, harsh, implacable, inhuman, merciless, oppressive, overbearing, pharaonic, pitiless, ruthless, savage, severe, strict *Antonyms:* benevolent, generous, kind

tyranny *n.* **1.** absolutism, authoritarianism, autocracy, despotism, dictatorship, domination, fascism, force, imperiousness, monocracy, oppression, satrapy, subjection, terrorism, totalitarianism **2.** coercion, cruelty, harshness, roughness, ruthlessness, severity, *Antonyms:* laxity, leniency, mercy, understanding

tyrant *n.* absolute ruler, absolutist, authoritarian, autocrat, bully, Caesar. czar, despot, dictator, fascist, fuhrer, kaiser, khan, king, martinet, oppressor, satrap, suzerain, *Nonformal:* slave driver, strong man

ubiquitous *adj.* all-encompassing, all-over, catholic, established, ever-present, everywhere, global, legion, omnipresent, pervasive, universal, wall-to-wall *(Nonformal)* *Antonyms:* hard-to-find, rare, sparse, specific

UFO *n.* alien, extraterrestrial craft, flying saucer, spaceship, unidentified flying object *Nonformal:* the greys, visitors

ugly *adj.* **1.** appalling, awful, bad-looking, beastly, foul, frightful, grisly, grotesque, grungy, haglike, horrid, ill-favoured, loathsome, monstrous, repelling, repugnant, repulsive, revolting, uninviting, unprepossessing, unsightly *Antonyms:* attractive, friendly, handsome **2.** base, despicable, dirty, disagreeable, disgusting, distasteful, evil, filthy, foul, frightful, hideous, horrid, ignoble, low, mean, messy, monstrous, nasty, objectionable, odious, offensive, repellent, repulsive, revolting, scandalous, shocking, sickening, sordid, sorry, terrible, troublesome, vile, wicked, wretched *Antonyms:* glorious, heavenly, lovely, unblemished, uplifting **3.** cantankerous, dangerous, disagreeable, forbidding, malevolent, menacing, nasty, ornery, sinister, threatening, treacherous, vicious, violent *Antonyms:* good-natured, placid, pleasant, serene

ulcer *n.* **1.** abscess, blister, canker, carbuncle, chancre, cold sore, eruption, lesion, sore, suppuration, welt **2.** bane, corruption, evil, pestilence, plague, scourge

ulcerated *adj.* **1.** corrupted, erupted, festering, gangrenous, mortified, polluted, septic, tainted **2.** corroded, destroyed, eaten up, eroded, gnawn away

ulterior *adj.* **1.** buried, concealed, covert, cryptic, enigmatic, hidden, secret, shrouded, under wraps *(Nonformal)*, undisclosed, undivulged, unrevealed, unsaid, unseen *Antonyms:* declared, manifest, obvious, open, overt **2.** ancillary, auxiliary, secondary *Antonyms:* central, crucial, vital **3.** in the future, later in time, remote, removed *Antonyms:* at the beset, basic, central, vital **4.** beyond the boundary *or* pale, distant, far away, outside, over the edge *Antonyms:* close, nearby, next to

ultimate *adj.* **1.** best, extreme, greatest, highest, incomparable, maximum, paramount, preeminent, superlative, supreme, topmost, utmost **2.** absolute, basic, categorical, elemental, fundamental, primary, transcendental **3.** closing, concluding, end, eventual, extreme, final, hindmost, last, latest, latter, lattermost – *n.* climax, epitome, granddaddy *(Nonformal)*, pinnacle, summit, zenith *Antonyms:* nadir, rock bottom

ultimately *adv.* after all, at last, conclusively, eventually, finally, fundamentally, indubitably, inevitably, in the end, lastly, sooner or later, unquestionably *Antonyms:* at this time, instantly, next, now

ultimatum *n.* demand, final offer, last proposal, stand, terms *Nonformal:* crunch, sticking point *Antonyms:* draft, overture, proposal, tender

ulu *n.* blade, carving *or* chopping *or* utility knife, cutlery, cutter, knife, whittle

ululate *v.* bawl, bewail, cry, groan, holler *(Nonformal)*, hoot, howl, lament, moan, mourn, shed tears, sob, wail, weep, yell

umbrage *n.* anger, annoyance, chagrin, displeasure, exasperation, fury, grudge, indignation, injury, ire, irritation, miff, offence, pique, rage, resentment, vexation, wrath

Antonyms: amity, cordiality, harmony, pleasure, understanding

umbrella *n.* **1.** brolly *(British)*, parasol, sunscreen, sunshade **2.** canopy, cordon, cover, safeguard, shield

umpire *n.* adjudicator, arbitrator, assessor, judge, mediator, moderator, negotiator, peacemaker, referee, ump *(Nonformal)* – *v.* adjudicate, pass judgment, referee, set the rules *(Nonformal)*, settle

unabashed *adj.* bold, brazen, confident, flagrant, forward, full of oneself, in your face *(Nonformal)*, rash, shameless, unashamed, uncowed, unembarrassed, upfront *Antonyms:* cowed, retiring, shy

unable *adj.* **1.** clumsy, helpless, impotent, inadequate, incapable, incompetent, ineffectual, inefficient, inept, inoperative, not able, powerless, sidelined, unfitted, unqualified, unskilled, weak *Antonyms:* able, adept, adequate, capable, effective **2.** idiotic, imbecilic, incapacitated, insane, out to lunch *(Nonformal)*, zany, zonked *Antonyms:* cognizant, competent, on target, sane

unabridged *adj.* aggregate, all, complete, comprehensive, corpus, encyclopedic, entire, everything, full-length, original, total, uncondensed, uncut, unexpurgated, voluminous, whole *Antonyms:* abbreviated, bowdlerized, contracted, digested, shortened

unacceptable *adj.* **1.** below par, damaged, inadequate, flawed, not up to snuff *(Nonformal)*, sub par, substandard *Antonyms:* admirable, excellent, penultimate, perfect **2.** disagreeable, displeasing, distasteful, improper, inadmissible, insupportable, lousy *(Nonformal)*, objectionable, obnoxious, offensive, repugnant, uninviting, unpleasant, unwanted, unwelcome *Antonyms:* agreeable, delightful, pleasant, urbane

unaccompanied *adj.* abandoned, a cappella *(Music)*, alone, apart, by oneself, detached, individual, isolated, lone, loner, odd, rejected, removed, single, solitary, solo, unattended, unescorted *Nonformal:* stag, travelling light *Antonyms:* guided, chaperoned, escorted

unaccountable *adj.* **1.** astonishing, bizarre, extraordinary, inconceivable, incredible, indecipherable, inexplicable, miraculous, mysterious, puzzling, remarkable, surreal, unfathomable, weird *Antonyms:* defined, described, explained, understood **2.** excused, exempt, free, immune, in the clear, not responsible, unanswerable *Antonym:* liable **3.** capricious, fly-by-night, irresponsible, reckless, wayward *Antonyms:* accustomed, predictable, regimented

unaccustomed *adj.* **1.** alien, bizarre, different, eccentric, exceptional, exotic, foreign, imported, new, novel, outlandish, remarkable, special, strange, surprising, uncommon, unconventional, unexpected, unknown, unorthodox, unprecedented, unusual, variant *Antonyms:* everyday, normal, regular **2.** green, ignorant, incompetent, inexperienced, new, novice, unacquainted, unfamiliar with, uninformed, unpracticed, unskilled *Antonyms:* habituated, seasoned, used to, well-versed

unacknowledged *adj.* **1.** anonymous, bastard, nameless, unknown **2.** ignored, neglected, omitted, slighted, snubbed, uncredited, unrecognized, unrewarded *Antonyms:* credited, legitimatized, sanctioned, validated, warranted

unadorned *adj.* ascetic, austere, bare, basic, natural, plain, pure, simple, Spartan, stark, unembellished, unvarnished *Antonyms:* decorated, festooned, emblazoned, equipped

unadulterated *adj.* pollution-free, pristine, pure, unspoiled, untainted, untouched, virgin *Antonyms:* corrupt, diluted, impure, poisoned

unaffected *adj.* **1.** artless, candid, direct, folksy, forthright, frank, genuine, guileless, honest, ingenuous, modest, naive, natural, plain, simple, sincere, single, spontaneous, straightforward, true, unassuming, unpretentious, up-front *Antonyms:* affected, devious, mannered, sophisticated **2.** calm, cool, impassive, impervious, stoic, thick-skinned, unemotional, unimpressed, unmoved *Antonyms:* disquieted, disturbed, moved, ruffled, touched

unalterable *adj.* adamant, constant, fixed, immutable, lasting, permanent, rigid, rooted, steadfast, stubborn, unbending, unchangeable, unyielding *Antonyms:* adjustable, changeable, modifiable, mutable, vacillating

unanimity *n.* accord, agreement, chorus, concert, concordance, concurrence, consensus, harmony, meeting of minds, rapport, togetherness, uniformity, union, unison, unity *Antonyms:* contention, discord, dispute

unanimous *adj.* collective, concordant, harmonious, in agreement *or* harmony, like-minded, single, universal, uncontested, undisputed, unquestioned, with one voice

unappetizing *adj.* distasteful, flat, flavourless, off-putting, rancid, rank, rotten, tasteless, unappealing, unpalatable, unpleasant, vapid *Nonformal:* grody, gross, icky, yucky *Antonyms:* delectable, delicious, palatable, satisfying, succulent

unapproachable *adj.* **1.** aloof, chilly, cold, cool, difficult, frigid, haughty, reserved, standoffish, uncommunicative, unfriendly, unsociable, withdrawn *Antonyms:* affable, approachable, cordial, friendly, sociable **2.** distant, forsaken, inaccessible, hard to reach, out of the way, remote *Antonyms:* adjacent, close, nearby, neighbouring

unarmed *adj.* declawed, defenceless, exposed, helpless, open, open to attack, unequipped, unfurnished, unprotected, vulnerable, weaponless *Antonyms:* decked out, equipped, furnished

unashamed *adj.* **1.** bold, brazen, exhibitionistic, flagrant, immodest, impudent, notorious, shameless *Antonyms:* disgraced, embarrassed, mortified **2.** accepting, comfortable, familiar, proud, satisfied *Antonyms:* contrite, guilt-ridden, regretful, remorseful, shy

unasked *adj.* **1.** free, gratuitous, impromptu, off the cuff *(Nonformal)*, spontaneous, voluntary, willing, without cause *Antonyms:* laid-out, ordered, planned, scheduled **2.** presumptuous, unbidden, unsolicited *Antonyms:* invited, requested, welcome

unassailable *adj.* **1.** immune, incontrovertible, indisputable, inviolable, irrefutable, perfect, watertight **2.** bulletproof, impregnable, impenetrable, insuperable, invincible, secure, unconquerable *Antonyms:* breachable, poorly manned, vulnerable

unassisted *adj.* alone, individually, single-handed, solitary, solo, unabetted, unaided, unsupported, without help *Antonyms:* collectively, supported by, together with

unassuming *adj.* bashful, diffident, humble, low-key, meek, modest, quiet, reserved, restrained, retiring, self-effacing, shy, simple, unobtrusive, unpretentious *Antonyms:* aggressive, audacious, bombastic, conceited, presumptuous

unattached *adj.* **1.** at large *or* liberty, autonomous, free, independent, self-reliant *Nonformal:* cruising, fancy-free, footloose *Antonyms:* associated, bound, linked **2.** available, single, unengaged, unfettered, unmarried *Nonformal:* on the loose, trolling *Antonyms:* coupled, engaged, married, tied

unattended *adj.* **1.** alone, by oneself, solo, unaccompanied, unescorted *Antonyms:* chaperoned, escorted **2.** forgotten, ignored, left out, neglected, omitted, passed over, put aside, undone *Antonyms:* accomplished, cherished, looked-after, nourished

unauthorized *adj.* **1.** not permitted, off base *or* limits, out of bounds, unofficial, unsanctioned **2.** bootleg *(Nonformal)*, illegal, illegitimate, pirated, unlawful, unlicensed, wildcat *Antonyms:* copyrighted, lawful, legal, licensed, official, sanctioned,

unavoidable *adj.* **1.** certain, destined, fated, inescapable, inevitable, inexorable, ordained, sure, unpreventible, unstoppable *Antonyms:* escapable, evadable **2.** cast in stone *(Nonformal)*, certified, irrevocable, undeniable *Antonyms:* cancelable, changeable, voidable

unaware *adj.* **1.** blind, caught napping *(Nonformal)*, forgetful, ignorant, negligent, uninformed, unsuspecting, unwitting *Antonyms:* attentive, conscious, informed, knowing, mindful **2.** careless, daydreaming, dopey, heedless, inattentive, mooning, oblivious, out of touch, out to lunch *(Nonformal)*, **3.** asleep, resting, sleeping, unconscious, unresponsive *Nonformal:* dead to the world, napping, zonked out

unawares *adv.* **1.** aback, abruptly, inadvertently, off-guard, short, sudden, suddenly, unexpectedly, unprepared, without warning **2.** accidentally, by accident *or* chance *or* happenstance *or* mistake *or* surprise, carelessly, ignorantly, mistakenly, surprisingly, unconsciously, unintentionally, unknowingly *Antonyms:* by design, calculated, devised, planned

unbalanced *adj.* **1.** askew, asymmetrical, disproportionate, irregular, lopsided, off-balance, shaky, top-heavy, unequal, uneven, unsteady, unsymmetrical, wobbly *Nonformal:* cock-eyed, off-kilter *Antonyms:* balanced, equal, even, symmetrical **2.** crazy, demented, deranged, disturbed, eccentric, erratic, insane, irrational, lunatic, mad, psychotic, troubled, unhinged, unsound, unstable *Nonformal:* batty, daft, kooky, nobody home, nutty, unglued, wacky *Antonyms:* level-headed, rational, sane

unbearable *adj.* agonizing, excruciating, heavy-handed, insufferable, insupportable, intolerable, oppressive, painful, unacceptable, unendurable *Nonformal:* the last straw, too much *Antonyms:* acceptable, supportable, tolerable

unbeatable *adj.* formidable, indestructible, indomitable, invincible, overpowering, overwhelming, unconquerable *Nonformal:* no win, tough proposition *Antonyms:* helpless, indefensible, powerless, weak

unbecoming *adj.* **1.** cheap, flashy, garish, gaudy, ill-fitting, inappropriate, loud, ostentatious, poorly-sized, tawdry, unattractive, vulgar *Antonyms:* complimentary, flattering, well-tailored **2.** affected, arrogant, asinine, awkward, boorish, clumsy, discreditable, embarrassing, false, gauche, ill-mannered, improper, in poor taste, incongruous, indecent, maladroit, obnoxious, pretentious, tacky, unbefitting *Antonyms:* civil, diplomatic, exquisite, practiced, respectful, reverential, suave, urbane

unbeknown *adj.* buried, clandestine, concealed, hidden, secreted, unapparent, undiscovered, unrevealed, unsuspected *Antonyms:* comprehended, fathomed, grasped, manifest

unbelievable *adj.* **1.** astonishing, beyond belief, fantastic, impossible, inconceivable, incredible, kooky *(Nonformal)*, mind-boggling, otherworldly, staggering, strange, surreal, unthinkable, weird *Antonyms:* authentic, credible, likely, possible, trustworthy **2.** absurd, doubtful, dubious, flimsy, improbable, outlandish, preposterous, questionable, suspect, thin, unsubstantiated, weak *Nonformal:* cockamamie, phoney, thick, thin

unbeliever *n.* agnostic, atheist, disbeliever, doubter, heathen, infidel, nihilist, nonbeliever, sceptic, scoffer *Antonyms:* converted, faithful, follower, pilgrim, supporter

unbend *v.* **1.** ease *or* free *or* let up, give way, let loose, loosen, relax, relent, slacken, soften, yield *Antonyms:* stiffen, tense, tighten **2.** rectify, smooth, straighten, uncurl, unkink *Antonyms:* loop, tangle, twine, twist **3.** come down, sit back, take a breather, unwind *Nonformal:* chill out, crash, hang out *or* loose

unbending *adj.* crisp, firm, inflexible, intransigent, obstinate, rigid, set in one's ways *(Nonformal)*, severe, stiff, stubborn *Antonyms:* approachable, elastic, flexible, yielding

unbiased *adj.* dispassionate, equitable, fair, impartial, just, neutral, nondiscriminatory, objective, open-minded, without prejudice *Antonyms:* bigoted, partial, slanted, subjective, swayed, unfair, unjust

unbidden *adj.* **1.** gratuitous, spontaneous, unannounced, unasked, uninvited *Nonformal:* ad-lib, off the cuff

unblemished *adj.* chaste, clean, faultless, flawless, immaculate, intact, perfect, pristine, pure, spotless, stainless, undamaged, virginal, whole *Antonyms:* dirty, flawed, marred, sullied, tarnished

unblinking *adj.* **1.** alert, attentive, awake, vigilant, wakeful, watchful *Antonyms:* daydreaming, negligent **2.** firm, stalwart, steadfast, steady, undaunted, unflinching, unshrinking *Antonyms:* scared, unnerved **3.** blasé, cool, nonchalant, stolid, unimpressed *Antonyms:* astounded, awed, blown away *(Nonformal)*

unbounded *adj.* **1.** endless, great, immeasurable, immense, infinite, limitless, unlimited, vast **2.** excessive, extravagant, free, intemperate, lavish, loose, profligate, rampant, unchecked, uncurbed, unmeasured, wild *Antonyms:* curbed, reserved, restricted

unbowed *adj.* **1.** doughty, indomitable, proud, proud-spirited, undaunted, unwavering, valiant *Antonyms:* broken, cowed, crushed, defeated **2.** flat, level, linear, plumb, straight, true *Antonyms:* bent, warped

unbreakable *adj.* fortified, fractureproof, indestructible, reinforced, shatterproof, solid, strong *Nonformal:* cast iron, rock-solid *Antonyms:* delicate, flimsy, jerry-built, ramshackle

unbridled *adj.* **1.** on the loose, unchecked, uncurbed, unrestrained *Antonyms:* confined, harnessed, reined in **2.** excessive, immoderate, intemperate, lawless, profligate, uninhibited, unruly *Antonyms:* ascetic, cautious, puritan

unbroken *adj.* **1.** ceaseless, constant, continual, continuous, endless, perpetual, recurrent, uninterrupted *Antonyms:* erratic, fitful, intermittent, occasional **2.** complete, entire, unexpurgated, whole *Antonyms:* incomplete, in pieces, piecemeal **3.** as-the-crow-flies *(Nonformal)*, direct, straight, unswerving *Antonyms:* meandering, roundabout, veering, wayward **4.** even, flat, regular, seamless, smooth, uniform *Antonyms:* bumpy, coarse, rocky, rough **5.** pure, undamaged, untouched, unviolated, virgin *Antonyms:* soiled, spoiled, ravished, tarnished **6.** firm, stalwart, staunch, steady, strong *Antonyms:* cringing, vacillating, weak **7.** feral, green *(Nonformal)*, novice, rookie, unschooled, untrained, wild **8.** nonpareil, peerless, unequalled, unmatched, unrivaled, unsurpassed *Antonyms:* beaten, bested, defeated

unbuckle *v.* detach, disengage, free, loose, loosen, release, unbind, unchain, undo, unfasten, unlace, unlatch, unstrap, untie *Antonyms:* attach, clasp, latch, lock

unburden *v.* **1.** assuage, ease, lighten, relieve, set at ease, subside *Antonyms:* bother, tax, worry **2.** confess, confide, disclose, divulge, fess up *(Nonformal) Antonyms:* conceal, hold in, keep secret, stifle, suppress **3.** clear, discharge, empty, unload *Antonyms:* fill, pack, stow, stuff

uncanny *adj.* astonishing, astounding, bizarre, creepy, devilish, eerie, exceptional, extraordinary, fantastic, ghostly, incredible, inspired, magical, miraculous, mysterious, mystifying, out of this world *(Nonformal)*, paranormal, preternatural, remarkable, scary, singular, strange, supernatural, surreal, unearthly, unexplainable, unheard-of, unnatural, unusual, very strange, weird, wonderful *Antonyms:* average, down-to-earth, pedestrian, regular

unceasing *adj.* constant, continuous, endless, eternal, incessant, interminable, never-ending, non-stop, persistent, recurrent, relentless, time after time, unrelenting *Antonyms:* casual, desultory, intermittent, periodic

uncensored *adj.* complete, raw, uncut, unedited, unexpurgated, unmodified, unvarnished, whole *Nonformal:* as is, naked *Antonyms:* bowdlerized, edited, refined, reworked

uncertain *adj.* **1.** chary, distrustful, doubtful, dubious, leery, questionable, sceptical, speculative, suspicious, wary *Antonyms:* sure, trusting **2.** ambivalent, equivocal, faltering, hesitant, iffy *(Nonformal)*, indecisive, irresolute, of two minds, undecided, unsure, up in the air, vacillating, wavering *Antonyms:* confident, resolute **3.** capricious, changeable, fickle, inconsistent, mercurial, mutable, precarious, transient, unstable, variable, volatile *Nonformal:* chancy, dicey *Antonyms:* dependable, fixed **4.** ambiguous, arcane, cloudy, fuzzy, hazy, imprecise, indeterminate, indistinct, nebulous, obscure, vague *Antonyms:* manifest, precise

uncertainty *n.* **1.** chanciness, gamble, guesswork, riskiness, unforeseeability, unpredictability *Antonyms:* incontrovertibility, truth **2.** ambivalence, anxiety, apprehension, concern, disbelief, doubt, dubiousness, leeriness, misgiving, qualm, scepticism *Antonyms:* assurance, conviction, definitiveness, positiveness **3.** ambiguity, bewilderment, bother, confusion, fogginess, fuzziness, haziness, indistinctness, inexactitude, perplexity, perturbation, vagueness *Nonformal:* discombobulation, muddle-headedness *Antonyms:* clarity, exactitude, sharpness, vividness

unchangeable *adj.* **1.** cast in stone *(Nonformal)*, enduring, everlasting, firm, fixed, inalterable, inevitable, irrevocable, permanent, resolute, stable, steadfast, steady, strong, stubborn, unyielding *Antonyms:* ad hoc, ephemeral, temporary **2.** consistent, homogeneous, invariable, monolithic *Antonyms:* assorted, irregular, jumbled, variegated

unchanging *adj.* abiding, constant, continuing, equable, even, immutable, lasting, perpetual, rigid, same, stable, static, steady, unfailing *Antonyms:* capricious, unpredictable, wayward

uncharitable *adj.* cold-blooded, hard-hearted, harsh, insensitive, iron-fisted, mean-spirited, pitiless, remorseless, selfish, unaccommodating, unfeeling, unforgiving, unkind, unsparing, unsympathetic *Nonformal:* hard-boiled, immune *Antonyms:* benevolent, generous, magnanimous

uncharted *adj.* new, unconquered, undiscovered, unexplored, unknown, untouched, untravelled, untrodden, virgin *Antonyms:* familiar, known

uncivil *adj.* abrupt, boorish, brash, discourteous, ill-bred, impolite, inconsiderate, insolent, insulting, misbehaved, rude, saucy, sullen, surly, tactless, uncouth, ungracious *Nonformal:* chippy, snippy *Antonyms:* courteous, mannerly, polite

unclear *adj.* ambiguous, buried, cloudy, dim, dubious, hidden, indistinct, murky, obscure, suspect, unknown *Antonyms:* apparent, obvious, overt, transparent, unmistakable

uncomfortable *adj.* **1.** awkward, deplorable, distasteful, embarrassing, hard, irritating, messy *(Nonformal)*, nasty, regrettable, unpleasant, vexatious *Antonyms:* agreeable, amiable, congenial, pleasant **2.** cheerless, distressed, impecunious, impoverished, indignant, miserable, wretched *Antonyms:* affluent, rich, successful, wealthy **3.** aching, on tenterhooks *(Nonformal)*, painful, smarting, sore, stiff, suffering **4.** disquieted, disturbed, restless, self-conscious, troubled, uneasy *Antonyms:* at ease, content, pleased, satisfied

uncommitted *adj.* available, free, neutral, nonaligned, nonpartisan, unaffiliated, unattached, uninvolved *Antonyms:* engaged, involved, vested

uncommon *adj.* **1.** bizarre, different, distinctive, exceptional, exotic, extraordinary, fantastic, notable, noteworthy, novel, odd, original, outlandish, outstanding, singular, special, startling, strange, surprising, unconventional, unimaginable, unprecedented, wonderful *Nonformal:* off the wall, zany *Antonyms:* conventional, stock, typical, usual **2.** few-and-far-between, infrequent, one-of-a-kind, rare, scarce, seldom seen, *sui generis (Latin) Antonyms:* commonplace, everyday, familiar, recurring

uncommonly *adv.* exceptionally, hardly ever, infrequently, irregularly, occasionally, on occasion, rarely, scarcely ever, seldom, sporadically, unusually *Antonyms:* always, incessantly, often, repeatedly

uncommunicative *adj.* aloof, clammed up *(Nonformal)*, close, close-mouthed, curt, distant, evasive, guarded, quiet, reserved, reticent, retiring, secretive, short, shy, silent, taciturn, tight-lipped, unapproachable, unresponsive, unsociable, withdrawn *Antonyms:* chatty, forthcoming, garrulous, talkative, voluble

uncompromising *adj.* decided, determined, firm, inexorable, inflexible, intransigent, locked, obdurate, obstinate, resolute, rigid, single-minded, steadfast, strict, strong, stubborn, tough, unbending, uncompliant, unyielding *Nonformal:* hard-core, hard-line, stiff-necked *Antonyms:* biddable, compliant, flexible, pliant, tractable

unconcerned *adj.* **1.** blithe, carefree, free-spirited, insouciant, untroubled *Antonyms:* fidgety, harried, stressed out, tense **2.** apart, cool-headed, detached, dispassionate, distant, impassive, indifferent, neutral, nonchalant, objective, separate, uninterested *Antonyms:* ardent, committed, intense, passionate, vehement

unconditional *adj.* absolute, certain, complete, conclusive, decided, decisive, definitive, emphatic, fixed, incontestable, incontrovertible, indisputable, indubitable, outright, positive, pronounced, sure, thorough, total, unreserved, unrestricted *Nonformal:* flat out, no bones about it, straight out *Antonyms:* limited, probational, provisional, tentative

unconscionable *adj.* **1.** amoral, barbaric, corrupt, criminal, dishonest, evil, heinous, immoral, villainous, wicked **2.** excessive, exorbitant, extortionate, extravagant, extreme, immoderate, outlandish, outrageous, preposterous, unethical, unjustified, unprincipled, unreasonable, wanton

unconscious *adj.* **1.** asleep, comatose, inanimate, inert, insensible, senseless *Nonformal:* dead-to-the-world, out, out of it *Antonyms:* alive, awake, responsible, sensible **2.** abstracted, blind, dazed, deaf, heedless, ignorant, inattentive, not-with-it, oblivious, unaware, unperceiving *Nonformal:* out-to-lunch, stunned *Antonyms:* alert, attentive, aware, cognizant, sharp-eyed **3.** deep-rooted, dormant, latent, subliminal, unrecognized *Antonyms:* exterior, manifest, superficial, surface **4.** automatic, gut *(Nonformal)*, instinctive, involuntary, reflex, surrealistic, unthinking, unwitting *Antonyms:* deliberate, learned, practiced, studied **5.** accidental, inadvertent, uncalculated, unintentional, unmeant *Antonyms:* determined, premeditated, purposeful – *n.* id, mind, psyche, soul

unconventional *adj.* atypical, avant-garde, bizarre, bohemian, different, eccentric, funny, idiosyncratic, irregular, nonconformist, oddball, offbeat, original, strange, uncommon, unique, unorthodox, unusual, weird *Nonformal:* kooky, way-out *Antonyms:* normal, ordinary, orthodox, proper, typical

unconvincing *adj.* beyond belief, doubtful, dubious, feeble, flimsy, implausible, inconclusive, lame, open to attack, questionable, unbelievable, unlikely, weak *Nonformal:* fishy, iffy *Antonyms:* believable, credible, plausible, tenable

uncooperative *adj.* balky, fractious, headstrong, intractable, non-compliant, obstinate, rebellious, recalcitrant, refractory, unwilling *Antonyms:* eager, enthusiastic

uncouth *adj.* **1.** boorish, coarse, crass, crude, ill-bred, infelicitous, loutish, oafish, obnoxious, raunchy, rough, tasteless, unseemly, vulgar *Antonyms:* charming, courteous, elegant, polite, seemly **2.** all thumbs *(Nonformal)*, awkward, clumsy, gauche, gawky, graceless, inept, ungainly *Antonyms:* agile, deft, facile, smooth, suave **3.** countrified, lumpen *(Nonformal)*, uncultivated, unrefined, unsophisticated *Antonyms:* cultivated, enlightened, urbane

uncover *v.* bring to light, disclose, discover, divulge, exhume, expose, lay bare *or* open, reveal, turn up, unmask *Nonformal:* blow the lid off, crack *Antonyms:* bury, hide, suppress

uncritical *adj.* casual, cursory, imprecise, indiscriminate, naive, off-hand, perfunctory, shallow, superficial, undiscerning, undiscriminating, unexacting *Antonyms:* exacting, fastidious, stringent

unctuous *adj.* **1.** buttery, greasy, lubricated, oily, sebaceous, slippery, slithery, smooth, soapy **2.** dissembling, fawning, flattering, ingratiating, hypocritical, obsequious, oily-tongued *(Nonformal)*, sanctimonious, servile, sycophantic *Nonformal:* plummy, smarmy *Antonyms:* authentic, down-to-earth, genuine, sincere

undaunted *adj.* audacious, bold, brave, courageous, daring, doughty, firm, game, gritty, hardy, heroic, indefatigable, indomitable, intrepid, plucky, resolute, spunky, stalwart, steadfast, tenacious, persevering, persistent, undeterred, undismayed, unflagging, unflinching, unswerving, valorous, valiant *Antonyms:* discouraged, disheartened, intimidated

undecided *adj.* **1.** ambivalent, dithering, dubious, equivocal, hedging, hesitant, indecisive, irresolute, tentative, torn, uncommitted, vacillating, waffling, wavering *Nonformal:* back and forth, iffy, fence-sitting, on the fence, wishy-washy *Antonyms:* confident, convinced, positive **2.** debatable, doubtful, indefinite, open, pending, uncertain, unclear, undetermined, unsettled, unsure, vague *Nonformal:* hanging fire, up for grabs *Antonyms:* clear, established, final, incontrovertible, resolved

undefined *adj.* **1.** arcane, blurred, clouded, dim, hazy, indistinct, inexact, mysterious, nebulous, obscure, shadowy, tenuous, uncertain, unclear, unexplained, vague, veiled *Antonyms:* clear-cut, concrete, specific **2.** boundless, endless, eternal, infinite, limitless, timeless

undeniable *adj.* **1.** categorical, conclusive, correct, definitive, incontestable, indisputable, irrefutable, obviously, patent, true, unimpeachable, without question *Antonyms:* indeterminate, shaky, suspect, uncertain **2.** absolute, excellent, infallible, matchless, superb, superlative, unrivaled, without peer *Antonyms:* commonplace, mediocre, second-rate, so-so

undependable *adj.* **1.** capricious, changeable, erratic, fickle, inconsistent, irresponsible, loose, mercurial, shilly-shallying, unpredictable, variable *Antonyms:* conscientious, level-headed **2.** hazardous, insecure, precarious, risky, shaky, uncertain, unsafe, unsound, unstable *Antonyms:* safe, solid, secure **3.** back-stabbing, deceitful, disloyal, double-crossing, perfidious, tricky, treacherous, turncoat, untrustworthy *Antonyms:* faithful, staunch, steadfast

under *adj.* **1.** lesser, lower, nether, secondary, subjacent, subordinate, subsidiary **2.** deficient, in short supply, insufficient, lacking, not enough, short **3.** held down, in check *or* restraint, subjugated – *adv.* below, below deck, beneath, downstairs **2.** below the mark, bottom of the heap, less, low ebb, sub *or* under par – *prep.* at the base *or* bottom *or* foot of, beneath

undercover *adj.* clandestine, closet, concealed, confidential, covert, furtive, hidden, incognito, private, stealthy, surreptitious *Nonformal:* hush-hush, on the q.t., under wraps *Antonyms:* manifest, open, plain, unconcealed, visible **2.** cloak and dagger, intelligence, spy, surveillance, underground – *adv. à couvert (French)*, behind the scenes, secretly, up one's sleeve

undercurrent *n.* **1.** counterforce, drift, eddy, flow, riptide, undertow **2.** disguised *or* hidden tendency, groundswell, hint, implication, murmur, suggestion

undercut *n.* cleft, incision, nick, notch – *v.* **1.** destroy, discredit, disprove, sabotage, subvert, undermine **2.** sacrifice, slash, underprice, undersell

underdog *n.* casualty, dark horse, downtrodden, failure, loser, victim *Nonformal:* little guy, low man *Antonyms:* favourite, preferred, top pick, victor

underestimate *v.* belittle, deprecate, disparage, minimize, slight, underrate, undervalue *Nonformal:* low ball, put down, sell short *Antonyms:* exaggerate, inflate, overdo, overrate, overstate

undergo *v.* **1.** accept, accommodate, brook, encounter, experience, know, live *or* pass through, meet with, share, support, taste, tolerate, welcome **2.** bear up, endure, suffer, survive, weather, withstand

underground *adj.* **1.** beneath the surface, buried, earth-covered, substrative, subsurface, subterranean *Antonyms:* aloft, atop, in the air, sky-high **2.** back *or* side door, clandestine, concealed, covert, hush-hush, secret, surreptitious, under the table *Antonyms:* aboveboard, manifest, out-in-the-open **3.** avant-garde, counter-culture, cutting edge, experimental *Antonyms:* conservative, hide-bound, reactionary – *n.* **1.**

metro, subterranean railway, subway, tube *(Nonformal)* **2.** fifth column, guerrillas, insurrectionists, radicals, resistance, revolutionaries, subversives

underhanded *adj.* crafty, crooked, deceitful, deceptive, devious, dirty-dealing *(Nonformal)*, dishonourable, double-crossing, duplicitous, fraudulent, furtive, guileful, indirect, invidious, oblique, secret, shady, shifty, slippery, sly, sneaking, sneaky, stealthy, treacherous, tricky, unethical, unfair, unjust, unscrupulous, wily *Antonyms:* frank, honest, honourable, legal, scrupulous

underline *v.* accentuate, bracket, caption, check off, emphasize, feature, highlight, indicate, italicize, mark, play *or* point up, rule, stress, underscore *Antonyms:* bury, diminish, downplay

underling *n.* flunky, inferior, junior, menial, peon, serf, servant, slave, subaltern, subordinate, toady, vassal *Nonformal:* gofer, second banana

underlying *adj.* **1.** basal, basic, cardinal, elementary, essential, fundamental, intrinsic, primary, root, vital *Nonformal:* meat and potatoes, nub, nuts and bolts *Antonyms:* gratuitous, nonessential, superfluous, useless **2.** concealed, hidden, latent, lurking, obscured *Antonyms:* apparent, obvious, open, palpable

undermine *v.* **1.** burrow, dig, dig *or* hollow *or* scoop out, excavate, tunnel under, undercut *Antonyms:* augment, backfill, fill in, heap up, supplement **2.** corrode, cripple, debilitate, derail, disable, eat away, enfeeble, erode, foil, frustrate, hurt, impair, ruin, sabotage, sap, subvert, thwart, torpedo, weaken, wear *or* whittle away, wreck *Nonformal:* knock the bottom out of, sandbag *Antonyms:* bolster, buttress, strengthen, support

underneath *prep.* **1.** at the foot *or* base of, below, beneath, on the bottom of, under **2.** reporting to, subordinate to

underprivileged *adj.* deprived, destitute, hard-up, impoverished, indigent, in need, poor, poverty-stricken, under-developed

underscore *v.* accent, bring to the fore, emphasize, headline, highlight, point out, punctuate, spotlight, underline *Antonyms:* bury, de-emphasize, downgrade, minimize

understand *v.* **1.** comprehend, consider, fathom, grasp *Nonformal:* capiche, copy, get, get the picture, hear you, read, savvy, see the light, twig *Antonyms:* lose, miss the point **2.** accept, come to grips with, realize, recognize *Antonyms:* evade, ignore, neglect **3.** conclude, construe, deduce, figure, infer, interpret, reckon, translate **4.** absorb, appreciate, assimilate, digest, follow, soak up, take in, track *Antonyms:* discard, eschew, ignore, reject **5.** empathize, mesh with, relate, sympathize *Nonformal:* get close *or* next to, hear, tune into *Antonyms:* be at loggerheads *or* out of synch **6.** believe, daresay, opine, presume, suggest, suppose, venture **7.** discover, find out, gather, get wind *or* word of

understanding *adj.* **1.** astute, bright, comprehending, discerning, intelligent, knowing, mindful, perceptive, rational, sagacious, sensible, wise **2.** accepting, considerate, forbearing, patient, reasonable, tolerant **3.** charitable, compassionate, empathetic, generous, humane, sensitive, sympathetic, tender-hearted, warmhearted – *n.* **1.** accommodation, accord, compact, compromise, concurrence, consensus, deal, entente, pact, settlement **2.** comprehension, intellect, knowledge, judgment, mind, perception, perspicacity, rationality, reason, sense *Nonformal:* brains, savvy, smarts **3.** address, competence, know-how, proficiency, savoir-faire, skilfulness **4.** arrangement, commitment, covenant, engagement

understood *adj.* **1.** accepted, acknowledged, agreed, assumed, axiomatic, clear, implicit, intimated, *prima facie (Latin)*, self-evident, tacit, unexpressed, universal, wordless **2.** customary, established, hallowed, long-standing, unrecorded, venerable *Antonyms:* extemporaneous, modern, nouveau, untried

undertaking *n.* **1.** adventure, affair, assignment, attempt, business, campaign, enterprise, *gescheft (German)*, operation, program, project, quest, search, task, venture

Nonformal: beeswax, biz, goings-on **2.** agreement, betrothal, bond, commitment, pledge, promise, treaty, word of honour

undertone *n.* **1.** aside, mumble, murmuration, *sotto voce (Italian)*, whisper **2.** flavour, hint, implication, suggestion, tinge, touch, trace **3.** atmosphere, aura, current, feel, milieu, sense, vibe

underwear *n.* intimate apparel, lingerie, shorts, skivvies, underclothes, undergarments, underthings, undies *(Nonformal)*, unmentionables *Kinds of underwear:* all-in-one, bikini, bloomers, bodystocking, boxer shorts, bra, brassiere, breechclout, briefs, bustle, cami-nickers, camisole, chemise, combination, corset, crinoline, diapers, drawers, foundation, gotchies *(Nonformal)*, leotard, lingerie, loincloth, long johns, nappies, panties, pants, pantyhose, petticoat, scanties, shift, shorts, singlet, slip, smock, teddy, thermal, underpants, undershirt, woolies *Trademark:* BVDs, Jockey Shorts

underweight *adj.* anorexic, emaciated, gaunt, hollow-cheeked, malnourished, puny, scrawny, skeletal, skinny, spindle-shanked *(Nonformal)*, starved, thin, undernourished

underworld *n.* **1.** abode of the dead, Aidoneus, Anubis, Avernus, Charon, Dis, grave, Hades, Hel, hell, nether region, Orcus, Pluto, River Styx, Sheol **2.** Black Hand, Cosa Nostra, criminals, gangsters, Mafia, organized crime, racket, syndicate, the mob *(Nonformal)*, *Yakuza (Japanese)*

underwrite *v.* **1.** assume the risk, back, bankroll, endorse, execute and deliver, guarantee, protect, secure, sponsor, stake, subscribe, subsidize, support, warrant **2.** authorize, certify, confirm, ratify, sign, validate

undesirable *adj.* **1.** abominable, annoying, bothersome, damnable, detrimental, disagreeable, disliked, displeasing, distasteful, inconvenient, inexpedient, injurious, insufferable, loathed, objectionable, obnoxious, offensive, repellent, repugnant, troublesome, unattractive, unlikeable, unpleasing, unsatisfactory, unsavoury, unsought, unsuitable, unwanted, useless *Nonformal:* damn, darn, infernal *Antonyms:* acceptable, agreeable, attractive, inviting **2.** black-balled, inadmissable, inappropriate, out of place, rejected, scorned, shunned, unacceptable, unwelcome – *n.* bad example, exile, leper, outcast, outlaw, pariah, *persona non grata (Latin)*, sleazeball *(Nonformal)*, untouchable

undetectable *adj.* **1.** infinitesimal, microscopic, miniscule, minute, small, tiny, trace *Nonformal:* itsy-bitsy, teeny, wee, weeny *Antonyms:* humongous, prodigious, titanic **2.** buried, camouflaged, hidden, imperceptible, invisible, lost, out of sight *Antonyms:* conspicuous, obvious, visible **3.** fathomless, infinite, undeterminable, unknown, unmeasurable *Antonyms:* comprehended, known, predetermined, recognized

undeveloped *adj.* **1.** callow, immature, inchoate, incomplete, primitive, rudimentary, unfinished *Antonyms:* comprehensive, complete, sophisticated **2.** open, untouched, unused, vacant, virgin *Antonyms:* converted, enhanced, enriched, improved **3.** developing, emerging, evolving, growing, maturing *Antonyms:* declining, quiescent, stagnant, static

undirected *adj.* aimless, desultory, discursive, haphazard, indiscriminate, meandering, purposeless, random, unguided, wandering

undisciplined *adj.* **1.** free-range, green, raw, unpracticed, unprepared, unschooled, untrained, untutored *Antonyms:* drilled, experienced, hardened, seasoned, veteran **2.** all over the place *(Nonformal)*, disorganized, ramshackle, undependable, unreliable, unsteady *Antonyms:* constant, steady **3.** disobedient, lawless, obstreperous, pain in the arse *(Nonformal)*, unrestrained, unruly, wild *Antonyms:* docile, tractable

undiscovered *adj.* foreign, new, trackless, unbeknown, uncharted, unexplored, unheard of, unknown, unseen, virgin *Antonyms:* cliché, common, familiar, stock, well-known

undisputed *adj.* accepted, acknowledged, admitted, assured, authoritative, certain, conclusive, decided, final, recognized, sure, unchallenged, uncontested, undeniable, undoubted *Antonyms:* deniable, doubtful, inconclusive

undisturbed *adj.* **1.** calm, halcyon, pacific, peaceful, placid, relaxed, restful, serene, tranquil *Antonyms:* stormy, tempestuous, turbulent **2.** collected, equable, imperturbable, unaffected, unclouded, unruffled, untouched, well insulated *(Nonformal)*, worry-free *Antonyms:* animated, fervid, impassioned, overzealous, vivacious

undivided *adj.* **1.** aggregate, complete, concentrated, contained, entire, exclusive, full, total **2.** in one piece, intact, one, solid, together, unanimous, whole-hearted

undo *v.* **1.** invalidate, negate, overturn, put an end to, quash, rescind, retract, reverse, terminate *Antonyms:* consummate, decide, pledge **2.** loose, open, separate, spring, take apart, unbolt, unbutton, unfasten, unhitch, unlock, untie *Antonyms:* bind, close, lock, seal, secure **3.** annihilate, break, bring down, demolish, destroy, overthrow, raze, ruin, wipe out, wreck *Antonyms:* build-up, create, foster, found, establish, institute **4.** upset *Nonformal:* bug, discombobulate, flip *or* psyche out, get to, rattle, snooker, stir up, stymie *Antonyms:* help, maintain, settle, soothe, sustain

undoing *n.* **1.** collapse, *coup de grace (French)*, defeat, destruction, downfall, ruination, Waterloo *Antonyms:* finest hour, supreme moment, victory **2.** breakup, disassembly, disintegration, dismantling, dismemberment, divestiture, downsizing, taking apart *or* down, tearing down *Antonyms:* annexation, consolidation, expansion **3.** annulment, cancellation, divorce, neutralization, nullification

undone *adj.* **1.** forgotten, ignored, incomplete, missed, neglected, omitted, overlooked, postponed, shelved, skipped, unfinished *Antonyms:* accomplished, complete, concluded, polished off **2.** bankrupt, broken, crippled, destroyed, disabled, ravaged, ruined *Nonformal:* toast, washed up **3.** crestfallen, dejected, depressed, discouraged, downcast, heartsick *Nonformal:* rattled, shot to pieces *Antonyms:* ebullient, effervescent, overjoyed, sparkling **4.** loosed, opened, released, unfastened, unfurled, untied, unzipped

undoubtedly *adv.* absolutely, certainment *(Nonformal)*, indubitably, most assuredly, of course, positively, undeniably, without question *Antonyms:* dubiously, problematically, questionably

undress *v.* **1.** cast aside, disrobe, divest, shed, slip out of, strip, take *or* throw off *Nonformal:* doff, peel, shuck **2.** bring to light, expose, lay naked, reveal, unmask, unveil **3.** bluff, fake out, hoax *Nonformal:* deke, leave looking

undue *adj.* **1.** disproportionate, excessive, exorbitant, extravagant, extreme, fulsome, outrageous, overmuch, superfluous *Nonformal:* overmuch, too great *Antonyms:* chary, grudging, parsimonious, sparing **2.** ill-fitting, ill-timed, immoderate, improper, inappropriate, indiscreet, uncalled for, unwarranted *Antonyms:* pleasing, refreshing, welcome **3.** illegal, underhanded, unjust, wrong *Antonyms:* by the book, legitimate, licit, permissible

undulate *v.* billow, fluctuate, heave, pulsate, ripple, roll, surge, swell, wave, weave *Antonyms:* smooth, still, straighten

undying *adj.* abiding, amaranthine, constant, continuing, deathless, enduring, eternal, everlasting, immortal, indefatigable, indestructible, infinite, perennial, permanent, unceasing, undiminished, unfading, unremitting, unwavering *Antonyms:* ephemeral, finite, fleeting, momentary

unearth *v.* **1.** dig *or* dredge up, disinter, excavate, exhume, uproot *Antonyms:* bury, entomb, lay to rest **2.** come across, discover, expose, find, reveal, turn up *Nonformal:* ferret out, hit *or* stumble upon, strike *Antonyms:* conceal, cover up, hide, secrete, stow away

unearthly *adj.* **1.** astral, chimerical, ethereal, heavenly, immaterial, otherworldly, spiritual, sublime *Antonyms:* corporeal, incarnate, material, physical **2.** eerie, ghostly, haunting, macabre, out of this world, phantasmagoric, spectral, spooky *(Nonformal)*, strange, supernatural, terrifying, uncanny, unnatural, weird *Antonyms:* banal, commonplace **3.** extraordinary, inconvenient, odd, preposterous, ridiculous, unconventional, unreasonable *Antonyms:* habitual, regular, routine *Commonly misused:* **unworldly**

uneasy *adj.* agitated, anxious, apprehensive, bothered, concerned, distressed, disturbed, edgy, feverish, fidgety, flustered, fretful, ill-fitting, jittery, jumpy, nervous, on edge, overwrought, painful, peevish, perturbed, queasy, rattled, restive, ruffled, shifting, skittish, tense, troubled, uncomfortable, unnerved, unsettled, unstable, upset, uptight, vexed, withdrawn, worried *Nonformal:* antsy, a twitter, in a dither, on tenterhooks *Antonyms:* at ease, calm, comfortable, relaxed, tranquil

uneducated *adj.* benighted, empty-headed, ignorant, illiterate, inexperienced, lowbrow, philistine, uncultured, unlearned, unlettered, unread, unschooled, untaught, untutored *Nonformal:* ignoramus, know-nothing *Antonyms:* informed, lettered, literate, schooled, skilled

unemotional *adj.* apathetic, callous, chilly, cold, cold-hearted, cool, deadpan, dispassionate, flat, frigid, glacial, hard-boiled, hardhearted, heartless, impassive, indifferent, insensitive, laid-back *(Nonformal)*, listless, passionless, quiet, reserved, reticent, undemonstrative, unresponsive *Antonyms:* excitable, maudlin, passionate, responsive, sensitive

unemployed *adj.* **1.** fired, free, jobless, laid-off, resting *(Theatrical)*, workless *Nonformal:* at liberty, between engagements, freelancing, on the beach *or* street, scuffling **2.** disengaged, down, idle, inactive, inoperative, unoccupied **3.** uninvested, unrealized, untapped, unused, wasted

unending *adj.* ceaseless, continuous, endless, incessant, interminable, never-ending, perpetual, recurrent, regular, steady, unbroken, unceasing, uninterrupted *Antonyms:* fitful, irregular, punctuated

unequal *adj.* **1.** asymmetrical, different, discordant, incompatible, incongruous, inharmonious, variant, unalike *Antonyms:* complementary, congruent, homogeneous, uniform **2.** bottom-heavy, disparate, disproportionate, irregular, lop-sided, mismatched, one-sided, outmatched, poles apart *(Nonformal)*, skewed, top-heavy, unbalanced, uneven, unsymmetrical *Antonyms:* balanced, even **3.** insufficient, lacking, not enough, short, unsuitable, wanting *Antonyms:* ample, enough, suitable **4.** biased, inequitable, partisan, prejudiced, unfair, unjust *Antonyms:* dispassionate, even-handed, fair, impartial

unerring *adj.* accurate, certain, exact, faultless, flawless, impeccable, infallible, invariable, just, on the beam *(Nonformal)*, perfect, precise, reliable, sure, true, true to life, trustworthy, unfailing *Antonyms:* miles off *(Nonformal)*, below par, off-key, poor

unethical *adj.* bent, cheating, corrupt, crooked, dirty, dishonest, disreputable, double-crossing, illegal, immoral, improper, lowdown, sharp, slippery, sneaky, two-faced, underhanded, unfair, unprofessional, unscrupulous, wrong *Nonformal:* fishy, fly-by-night, shady, two-timing *Antonyms:* honest, legal, moral, scrupulous, upright

uneven *adj.* **1.** bumpy, coarse, pitted, potholed, rocky, rough, rutted, textured *Antonyms:* flat, level, smooth **2.** imperfect, incomplete, partial, patchy, sketchy, unfinished *Antonyms:* expert, first-rate, proficient, well-executed **3.** asymmetrical, nonparallel, odd, off kilter *Antonyms:* aligned, coequal, corresponding, matched **4.** erratic, fitful, irregular, spasmodic, unbalanced, unpredictable, unsteady *Antonyms:* constant, established, regulated, set

uneventful *adj.* boring, commonplace, dull, humdrum, monotonous, ordinary, prosaic, quiet, routine, tedious, unexceptional, unremarkable *Antonyms:* exceptional, exciting, momentous, remarkable

unexpected *adj.* **1.** abrupt, accidental, chance, fortuitous, impetuous, impulsive, instantaneous, out of left field *(Nonformal)*, startling, stunning, sudden, swift, unanticipated, unforeseen, unheralded *Antonyms:* awaited, expected, predicted **2.** amazing, astonishing, electrifying, eye-opening, surprising, unusual, wowie-zowie *(Nonformal)*, wonderful *Antonyms:* mundane, ordinary, prosaic

unfair *adj.* **1.** arbitrary, bigoted, partial, prejudiced, subjective, warped *Antonyms:* detached, objective, open-minded **2.** crooked, dishonest, fraudulent, unscrupulous *Nonformal:* below the belt, dirty pool *Antonyms:* conscientious, ethical, honest, straightforward **3.** drastic, excessive, grievous, uncalled for, unjustifiable, unreasonable, unwarranted *Antonyms:* defensible, legitimate, rightful, legitimate

unfaithful *adj.* **1.** deceitful, disloyal, double-crossing, faithless, false-hearted, perfidious, traitorous, treacherous *Antonyms:* incorruptible, loyal, steadfast, true **2.** erring, erroneous, faulty, imprecise, inaccurate, incorrect, inexact, untrue, wrong *Antonyms:* authentic, correct, literal, meticulous, precise **3.** adulterous, cheating, philandering, straying, unchaste *Nonformal:* fooling around, moonlighting, stepping out, two-timing *Antonyms:* ardent, besotted, devoted, single-minded **4.** abjuring, apostate, recidivistic, recreant, unbelieving *Antonyms:* devout, pious, zealous

unfaltering *adj.* bound, enduring, firm, indefatigable, resolute, steadfast, steady, sure, tireless, unquestioning, unwavering *Nonformal:* bound and determined, hellbent *Antonyms:* doubtful, hesitant, uncertain, wobbly

unfamiliar *adj.* **1.** alien, anomalous, bizarre, curious, different, exotic, extraordinary, fantastic, foreign, little-known, obscure, original, outlandish, out-of-the-way, peculiar, remarkable, remote, strange, unaccustomed, uncommon, unexpected, unusual *Antonyms:* common, normal, popular, regular, well-known **2.** green, ignorant, inexperienced, not cognizant, novice, unaccustomed, uninitiated, unschooled, wet behind the ears *(Nonformal)* *Antonyms:* skilled, trained, well-versed **3.** new, uncharted, unexplored, unknown, uninvestigated, virgin *Antonyms:* defined, delineated, mapped-out, well-trodden

unfashionable *adj.* **1.** old hat *(Nonformal)*, outdated, outmoded, out of date, outworn, passé, tired *Antonyms:* faddy, in vogue, latest thing, the rage **2.** eccentric, heretical, unconventional, unorthodox *Antonyms:* accepted, popular, predominant, prevalent

unfathomable *adj.* **1.** baffling, deep, difficult, enigmatic, esoteric, heavy, impenetrable, incomprehensible, indecipherable, inexplicable, nebulous, obscure, profound, unintelligible *Antonyms:* comprehended, explained, known, understood **2.** bottomless, boundless, deep, eternal, immeasurable, infinite, soundless, unending, unmeasurable, unplumbed

unfavourable *adj.* **1.** adverse, antagonistic, disapproving, hostile, negative, opposing *Antonyms:* accepting, positive, supportive, sympathetic **2.** forbidding, ill-fated, inauspicious, menacing, ominous, threatening, unpromising *Antonyms:* bright, encouraging, rosy **3.** ill-advised, inappropriate, inconvenient, infelicitous, inopportune, unfortunate, unhappy, unlucky, untimely *Antonyms:* beneficial, propitious, right, suitable

unfeeling *adj.* **1.** brutal, callous, cold, cold-blooded, cold-hearted, hard, hard-hearted, harsh, heartless, insensitive, thick-skinned, unsympathetic *Antonyms:* benevolent, caring, concerned, gentle, kind **2.** anesthetized, benumbed, dead, deadened, drugged, inanimate, insensate, in shock, numb, unconscious *Antonyms:* active, lively, robust, vibrant

unfinished *adj.* **1.** fragmentary, half-baked *(Nonformal)*, half done, inchoate, incomplete, makeshift, partial, under construction *Antonyms:* complete, comprehensive, extensive **2.** amateurish, deficient, faulty, imperfect, wanting *Antonyms:* flawless, impeccable, perfect **3.** missed, neglected, overlooked, postponed, shelved, unassembled, unattended, undone, unrealized *Antonyms:* accomplished, achieved, concluded, done **4.** bare, green, natural, plain, rough, roughhewn, raw, unbleached, untreated *Antonyms:* dyed, lacquered, painted, stained, varnished

unfit *adj.* **1.** ill-suited, improper, inappropriate, inapt, infelicitous, inopportune, objectionable, uncalled-for, unhappy, unseemly *Antonyms:* befitting, germane, meet, pertinent, to the point **2.** bush league, inadequate, incapable, incompetent, unprepared, unqualified, untrained *Nonformal:* bumblefingered, lame-brained, not cut out for *Antonyms:* able, experienced, on the ball, practiced, qualified **3.** below par, debilitated, ill, in poor condition, out of commission *or* shape, run down, unsound *Antonyms:* healthy, hearty, robust

unflagging *adj.* constant, diligent, fixed, focused, immune, inexhaustible, persevering, steadfast, steady, tireless, unceasing, unfailing, unrelenting, unremitting *Antonyms:* drained, exhausted, fatigued, indolent, lazy

unflappable *adj.* calm, collected, composed, cool, easy, impassive, laid-back *(Nonformal)*, nonchalant, relaxed, self-possessed, unruffled *Antonyms:* excitable, hotheaded, nervous, volatile

unfold *v.* **1.** expand, extend, open, open up, spread out, uncoil, unfurl, unroll, unwind *Antonyms:* close, curl up, droop, shrink, shut **2.** bloom, blossom, develop, evolve, flower, germinate, grow, mature, ripen, sprout, take shape *Antonyms:* deteriorate, die, fade, fail, pass away **3.** bring to light, clarify, disclose, divulge, elucidate, expose, present to view *Antonyms:* conceal, muddy, obfuscate

unforeseen *adj.* abrupt, accidental, chance, startling, sudden, surprise, unanticipated, unexpected, unlooked-for, unpredicted *Antonyms:* planned, projected, purposeful

unforgettable *adj.* celebrated, exceptional, extraordinary, historic, indelible, memorable, meteoric, momentous, notable, remarkable, special, striking *Antonyms:* insignificant, negligible, of no import

unforgivable *adj.* **1.** indefensible, inexcusable, unjustifiable, unpardonable, untenable, too much *(Nonformal)* **2.** abject, abominable, atrocious, awful, contemptible, deplorable, despicable, disgraceful, evil, ghastly, heinous, horrible, horrific, odious, outrageous, reprehensible, scandalous, terrible, vile, villainous

unfortunate *adj.* **1.** bummed *(Nonformal)*, doomed, down on one's luck, hapless, jinxed, luckless, unlucky, unsuccessful *Antonyms:* booming, burgeoning, flourishing, prosperous, successful **2.** ill-considered, inappropriate, lamentable, poorly planned, unbecoming, unsuitable, untoward *Antonyms:* expedient, proper, seemly **3.** awful, calamitous, catastrophic, disastrous, grievous, horrific, ruinous, shattering, terrible

unfounded *adj.* baseless, fabricated, false, fallacious, groundless, idle, illogical, misleading, spurious, trumped up, unjustified, unproven, unsubstantiated, untrue, unwarranted, without basis *Antonyms:* attested, confirmed, factual, justified

unfriendly *adj.* **1.** antagonistic, belligerent, combative, disaffected, disposed, inimical, pugilistic, quarrelsome, warlike *Antonyms:* affable, amiable, cordial, courteous, gracious **2.** inauspicious, menacing, portentous, sinister, unfavourable, unpromising *Antonyms:* advantageous, encouraging, reassuring **3.** alien, barbarian, foreign, hostile, inhospitable *Antonyms:* benign, familiar, welcoming **4.** aloof, chilly, cold, frosty, remote, standoffish, unapproachable, unsympathetic *Antonyms:* affectionate, compassionate, caring, supportive

ungainly *adj.* awkward, boorish, clumsy, gangling, gauche, klutzy *(Nonformal)*, loutish, lumbering, oafish *Antonyms:* decorous, delicate, graceful, suave

ungodly *adj.* **1.** blasphemous, godless, immoral, impious, improper, irreligious, profane, sinful *Antonyms:* religious, spiritual **2.** atrocious, barbarous, depraved, dreadful, evil, fiendish, horrendous, unconscionable, vile, villainous, wicked *Antonyms:* angelic, godly, heavenly

ungrateful *adj.* demanding, dissatisfied, faultfinding, forgetful, grasping, grumbling, heedless, ingrate, insensible, oblivious, self-centred, selfish, unappreciative, unmindful, unnatural *Antonyms:* appreciative, beholden, indebted, mindful, thankful

unguarded *adj.* **1.** artless, candid, casual, downright, forthright, frank, impulsive, informal, ingenuous, offhand, off the cuff *(Nonformal)*, spontaneous, straightforward *Antonyms:* orchestrated, prepared, rehearsed, staged, taped **2.** brash, careless, imprudent, indiscreet, injudicious, tactless *Antonyms:* diplomatic, discreet, sensitive, wary **3.** alone, open to attack, unattended, unchaperoned, unprotected, vulnerable *Antonyms:* monitored, under surveillance, watched

unhappy *adj.* **1.** bleak, blue, crestfallen, dejected, depressed, dismal, down, downcast, down-hearted, lugubrious, melancholy, miserable, morose, mournful, neurasthenic, sad, saddened, sorrowful, upset *Nonformal:* hurting, in the pits, long-faced *Antonyms:* celebratory, exhilarated, gleeful, joyous **2.** bedeviled, bewitched, doomed, star-crossed, troubled, unlucky *Antonyms:* blessed, endowed, favoured **3.** clumsy, foolish, inappropriate, out-of-place, poorly-chosen, tactless, unbecoming *Antonyms:* apt, fitting, proper, prudent, well-timed

unharmed *adj.* home-free *(Nonformal)*, intact, out of danger, safe, undamaged, unhurt, uninjured, unscathed, unscratched *Antonyms:* accosted, hurt, injured, molested, violated

unhealthy *adj.* **1.** ailing, debilitated, feeble, frail, infirm, pale, shaky, sickly, unsound *Nonformal:* laid low, rundown *Antonyms:* healthy, sound, sturdy **2.** detrimental, dirty, foul, insalubrious, noxious, rotten, toxic, unclean *Antonyms:* beneficial, hygienic, nutritious **3.** corrupt, degenerate, degrading, depraved, impure, licentious, morally unsound, sinful, suborned, unwholesome, vile *Antonyms:* elevating, enriching, inspiring, uplifting **4.** chancy, dangerous, life-threatening, perilous, risky, treacherous, unsafe *Antonyms:* dependable, innocuous, safe, secure

unhinged *adj.* **1.** detached, disconnected, disengaged, dislocated, separated *Antonyms:* affixed, conjoined, coupled, fastened, united **2.** chaotic, crazed, discomposed, disconcerted, maddened, unsettled *Nonformal:* off one's nut, overboard, over the edge, round the bend, unglued

unholy *adj.* **1.** godless, irreligious, irreverent, profane, sacrilegious, sinful, unrighteous, unsanctified *Antonyms:* godfearing, pious, religious **2.** appalling, atrocious, dire, dreadful, fearful, fiendish, frightful, ghastly, outrageous, terrifying *Antonyms:* exquisite, fabulous, marvelous

unidentified *adj.* **1.** anon, anonymous, faceless, incognito, pseudonymous, unknown, unmarked, unnamed, unspecified, unsung *Antonyms:* celebrated, familiar, known, recognized **2.** disguised, hidden, inexplicable, mysterious, out of view, perplexing, puzzling, secret, unseen *Antonyms:* evident, manifest, ostensible, obvious, plain

unification *n.* affinity, alliance, coalescence, coalition, combination, concurrence, confederation, conjoining, connection, consolidation, coupling, federation, fusion, interlocking, joining, linkage, melding, merger, uniting *Antonyms:* crumbling, decomposition, disintegration, dispersal, erosion

uniform *adj.* **1.** alike, analogous, comparable, consistent, equal, homogeneous, identical, like, selfsame *Nonformal:* carbon copy, spitting image *Antonyms:* discordant, dissimilar, diverse, lone, one of a kind, unique **2.** measured, methodical, ordered, patterned, regimented, systematic *Antonyms:* chaotic, haphazard, random **3.** continuous, never-ending, recurrent, relentless, repeated, repetitious, uninterrupted *Antonyms:* arrhythmic, brief, short, spasmodic **4.** colourless, one-toned, monochromatic, monotone *Antonyms:* iridescent, kaleidoscopic, prismatical – *n.* attire, dress, garb, gown, habit, livery, outfit, regalia, suit *Nonformal:* get-up, monkey suit *Kinds of uniform:* apron, blues, coveralls, dress blues, dress whites, fatigues, full dress, khaki, mufti, olive drab, regimentals, robe, stripes *(Prison)*, tuxedo, whites

unify *v.* amalgamate, blend, bring together, combine, confederate, consolidate, federate, fuse, integrate, join, link, marry, meld, merge, unite, wed *Antonyms:* divide, separate

unimaginable *adj.* beyond belief, exceptional, extraordinary, fantastic, impossible, improbable, incomprehensible, inconceivable, incredible, indescribable, rare, singular, unbelievable, uncommon, unheard-of, unique, unthinkable, unwonted *Nonformal:* mind-boggling, out of the question *Antonyms:* feasible, plausible, possible

unimaginative *adj.* banal, boring, bromidic, dry, dull, flat, hackneyed, ho-hum, lifeless, ordinary, pedestrian, predictable, prosaic, routine, tame, tiresome, trite, unoriginal, well-worn *Antonyms:* creative, exciting, fresh, innovative, inventive

unimportant *adj.* casual, fleeting, frivolous, humble, immaterial, inconsequential, inconsiderable, indifferent, insignificant, irrelevant, little, low-priority, low-ranking, marginal, nonessential, nothing, nugatory, paltry, piddling, secondary, slight, trifling, trivial, unnecessary, useless, worthless *Nonformal:* big zero, diddly-squat, no big thing, no matter, pennyante, small potatoes, zippo *Antonyms:* essential, grave, important, vital, weighty

unimpeded *adj.* **1.** clean, clear, unblocked, unobstructed, wide open **2.** burden-free, footloose, free, free-wheeling, unchecked, unhampered

uninhibited *adj.* **1.** candid, easy-going, frank, free, informal, liberated, natural, open, relaxed, spontaneous, unbridled, unrepressed, unselfconscious, up-front *Antonyms:* bashful, careful, constrained, modest, uptight **2.** abandoned, immoderate, intemperate, lax, loose, rampant, wanton, wayward, wild

uninspired *adj.* commonplace, corny, everyday, heavy-handed, humdrum, indifferent, old hat *(Nonformal)*, ordinary, pedestrian, ponderous, prosaic, stale, sterile, stock, unexciting, unoriginal *Antonyms:* brilliant, different, inspired, original, outstanding

unintelligible *adj.* **1.** inarticulate, incoherent, incomprehensible, indecipherable, meaningless, murmuring, muttering, unreadable *Nonformal:* breaking-up, mumbo-jumbo *Antonyms:* audible, clear, coherent, legible, readable **2.** ambiguous, clear as mud *(Nonformal)*, enigmatical, equivocal, impenetrable, indistinct, inscrutable, mysterious, obscure, opaque, tenebrous, uncertain, unfathomable, vague *Antonyms:* certain, exact, known, proven, understandable

unintentional *adj.* accidental, casual, chance, extemporaneous, fortuitous, haphazard, inadvertent, involuntary, luck, random, serendipitous, unexpected, unforeseen, unplanned, unpremeditated, unthinking, unwitting *Antonyms:* conscious, deliberate, preplanned, scheduled

uninterested *adj.* apathetic, blasé, bored stiff, clock-watching, emotionless, impassive, incurious, indifferent, passionless, perfunctory, weary *Nonformal:* fed up, turned off *Antonyms:* alert, curious, enthusiastic, keen, responsive *Commonly misused:* **disinterested**

uninteresting *adj.* characterless, dismal, drab, dreary, dry, insipid, irksome, jejune, lifeless, monotonous, prosy, soporific, tedious, tired, tiresome, vapid *Nonformal:* beige, blah, depressing *Antonyms:* absorbing, compelling, exciting, inspiring, stimulating

uninterrupted *adj.* **1.** ceaseless, constant, continual, continuous, endless, interminable, never-ending, nonstop, perpetual, unbroken, unremitting *Nonformal:* day in and day out, round the clock *Antonyms:* alternating, cyclic, discontinuous, intermittent **2.** peaceful, restful, sound, tranquil, unbroken, undisturbed *Antonyms:* fitful, restive, unquiet

union *n.* **1.** alliance, bloc, cabal, cartel, coalition, combination, confederation, consortium, cooperative, federation, league **2.** coming together, confluence, convergence, junction, meeting *Antonyms:* divergence, division, fork **3.** accord, agreement, concurrence, harmony, mutual understanding *Antonyms:* alienation, estrangement **4.** brotherhood, craft *or* labour *or* trade association, club, congress, fraternity, guild, syndicate, team **5.** coupling, marriage, matrimony, partnership, wedlock **6.** fusing, hook up, melding, seam, welding

unique *adj.* **1.** different, exceptional, matchless, new, nonpareil, original, out of the ordinary, peerless, second to none, strange, unfamiliar, unparalleled, unusual, without equal *Antonyms:* mediocre, modest, regular **2.** individual, lone, one of a kind, one-off *(British)*, only begotten *(Nonformal)*, single, sole, solitary, *Antonyms:* commonplace, everyday, many, unexceptional, various **3.** few and far between *(Nonformal)*, infrequent, rare, *sui generis (Latin)*, uncommon *Antonyms:* frequent, habitual, recurring, repeated **4.** characterizing, distinctive, idiosyncratic, innate, inherent, particular, specific *Antonyms:* collective, mutual, shared, vernacular

unison *n.* accord, agreement, assonance, concert, concordance, consonance, cooperation, fellowship, harmony, league, unanimity *Antonyms:* discord, dissension, dissonance

unit *n.* **1.** arm, block, component, constituent, detail, digit, element, factor, feature, fraction, ingredient, integer, item, joint, layer, length, link, member, module, one, part, piece, portion, section, segment **2.** assembly, battalion, brigade, clan, complement, contingent, corps, crew, crowd, detachment, entirety, entity, family, gang, group, mob, outfit, regiment, section, squadron, system, total, totality, whole

unite *v.* **1.** amalgamate, blend, combine, fold into, homogenize, integrate, intermix, lump together *(Nonformal)*, mix *Antonyms:* classify, separate, sort, subdivide **2.** become one, coalesce, converge, meet, merge *Antonyms:* bifurcate, diverge, fork, radiate **3.** attach, bind, bond, connect, fasten, fuse, glue, hitch together *or* up, join, link *Antonyms:* cleave, detach, loose, sever, split, sunder **4.** affiliate, ally, associate, band together, hook *or* take up with *(Nonformal)*, marry, pool, wed *Antonyms:* break-up, disassociate, disband, disengage, divorce **5.** consolidate, fortify, reinforce, solidify, strengthen *Antonyms:* alienate, isolate, weaken

united *adj.* **1.** allied, collaborative, collective, conjuncture, cooperative, joint, massed, mutual, shared, synergetic *Antonyms:* individual, lone, separate, single, solitary **2.** agreed, concordant, harmonious, like-minded, unanimous *Antonyms:* breakaway, divisive, schismatic, separatist

unity *n.* **1.** aggregation, individuality, oneness, singularity, soleness, uniqueness, wholeness *Antonyms:* heterogeneousness, multifarious, multiform, multiplex **2.** accord, affinity, consensus, consistency, consonance, continuity *Antonyms:* abhorrence, abomination, antipathy, disinclination, loathing

universal *adj.* accepted, across-the-board, all, all-embracing, all-inclusive, broad, catholic, comprehensive, extensive, galactic, generic, global, intergalactic, interplanetary, omnipresent, planetary, preponderant, prevailing, sweeping, total, ubiquitous, unlimited, unrestricted, widespread, worldwide *Antonyms:* local, provincial, parochial, small-town

universe *n.* **1.** all creation, cosmos, firmament, galaxy, macrocosm, the whole enchilada *(Nonformal)* **2.** humanity, humankind, human race, mankind, peoples, populace, womankind, world-at-large **3.** earth, ecosystem, global village, globe, world **4.** bailiwick, beat, circle, domain, element, environment, milieu, neighbourhood, orbit, surroundings

university *adj.* advanced, graduate, higher, post-secondary, undergraduate – *n.* academe, academia, alma mater, halls of academe, college, institute of higher learning, institution, polytechnical, school *Nonformal:* diploma factory, ivory tower, think-tank

unjust *adj.* **1.** biased, fixed *(Nonformal)*, illegitimate, jaundiced, one-sided, partisan, prejudicial, unreasonable, warped, wrongful *Antonyms:* equitable, even-handed, objective **2.** excessive, gratuitous, groundless, out-of-line, uncalled-for, undeserved, undue, unnecessary, unwarranted *Nonformal:* below the belt, cheap, dirty pool *Antonyms:* defensible, legitimate, reasonable, sound

unkempt *adj.* **1.** bedraggled, dishevelled, mussy *(Nonformal)*, scraggly, shaggy, tangled, tousled, windblown *Antonyms:* coiffed, dressed, groomed **2.** dirty, grubby, messy, rumpled, slatternly, slovenly, soiled, stained, sullied, untidy *Nonformal:* grungy, scuzzy *Antonyms:* immaculate, scrubbed, wholesome **3.** crass, crude, insensitive, rough, uncouth, unpolished, vulgar *Antonyms:* cultivated, fastidious, genteel, refined

unkind *adj.* barbarous, brutal, callous, cold-blooded, cold-hearted, cruel, disobliging, evil, harsh, heartless, inconsiderate, inhumane, insensitive, mean, nasty, sadistic, savage, spiteful, uncharitable, unfriendly, unsparing, vengeful, villainous, vindictive *Antonyms:* benevolent, caring, charitable, forbearing, merciful

unknown *adj.* **1.** alien, distant, exotic, far-off, foreign, remote, strange, unfamiliar **2.** concealed, cryptic, dark, hidden, mysterious, obscure **3.** foreign, new, trackless, uncharted, undiscovered, unexplored, unmapped, untamed, untold, virgin **4.** anon, anonymous, incognito, *inconnu (French)*, nameless, unnamed *Nonformal:* incog, Jane *or* John Doe **5.** humble, person-on-the-street, uncelebrated, undistinguished, unrenowned, unsung – *n.* beyond land's end, cosmos, future, new territory, uncharted lands *or* seas, universe, virgin soil

unlawful *adj.* **1.** actionable, criminal, crooked, felonious, forbidden, illicit, larcenous, prohibited, under-the-counter, unlicensed *Antonyms:* authorized, legal, sanctioned **2.** baseborn, bastard, illegitimate, misbegotten, natural, out of wedlock, spurious, unsanctioned *Antonyms:* acknowledged, deeded, legitimate, rightful, true

unlike *adj.* **1.** conflicting, contrary, different, discordant, disparate, dissimilar, incongruous, mismatched, opposite, unconnected, unrelated *Nonformal:* apples and oranges, night and day, poles part *Antonyms:* identical, synonymous **2.** aberrant, abnormal, atypical, uncharacteristic *Antonyms:* accustomed, conventional, expected, normal, usual

unlikely *adj.* **1.** absurd, doomed, doubtful, dubious, implausible, improbable, outside, questionable, rare, remote, slight, strange, unbelievable, unimaginable *Antonyms:* believable, probable, tenable **2.** foolish, impetuous, reckless, wrong-headed *Antonyms:* calculated, planned, predetermined, select

unlimited *adj.* **1.** absolute, boundless, extensive, full, great, illimitable, inexhaustible, infinite, total, unchecked, unconditional, undefined, unhampered, unqualified, unrestrained, unrestricted *Nonformal:* no holds barred, no strings, wide-open *Antonyms:* bound, confined, hindered, hobbled, restricted **2.** countless, immeasurable, immense, incalculable, indeterminate, never-ending, unending, uninterrupted, vast *Antonyms:* calibrated, computed, determined, measured

unload *v.* **1.** cast out, dispose of, discharge, disencumber, disgorge, empty, get off one's chest *(Nonformal)*, jettison, lighten, off-load, relieve, remove, unburden, unpack **2.** get rid of, markdown, remainder, sacrifice, sell *Nonformal:* dump, fire-sale *Antonyms:* gouge, mark-up, overprice

unlucky *adj.* **1.** cursed, damned, hapless, hexed, jinxed, plagued, star-crossed, unfortunate *Nonformal:* behind the eight ball, hoodooed *Antonyms:* blessed, charmed, favoured, fortuitous **2.** calamitous, catastrophic, dire, disastrous, pitiable, tragic, wretched *Antonyms:* flourishing, promising, successful **3.** badly judged, careless, ill-advised, impudent, incautious, injudicious, misguided, unwise *Antonyms:* circumspect, considered, provident, thought-out

unmanageable *adj.* **1.** balky, contrary, contumacious, difficult, fractious, intractable, perverse, rebellious, recalcitrant, resistant, stubborn, uncooperative, unruly, wild, wilful *Antonyms:* controllable, receptive, tractable **2.** awkward, bulky, cumbersome, difficult, heavy, large, inconvenient, unwieldy *Antonyms:* compact, light, small

unmanned *adj.* automatic, computer-controlled, computerized, robotic, self-regulating

unmerciful *adj.* **1.** barbarous, brutal, brutish, cold-hearted, cruel, evil, flinty, hard, heartless, implacable, inexorable, inhumane, monstrous, pitiless, relentless, remorseless, ruthless, savage, uncaring, unfeeling, unforgiving, unsparing, unyielding, vengeful, villainous, vindictive *Antonyms:* beneficent, caring, feeling, humane **2.** excessive, exorbitant, extreme, immoderate, inexorable, inflexible, outrageous

unmistakable *adj.* apparent, blatant, categorical, certain, clear, clear-cut, conspicuous, distinct, evident, explicit, exposed, glaring, indubitable, manifest, obvious, patent, plain, positive, prominent, pronounced, recognized, specific, stark, striking, sure, undisputed, unequivocal, utter, vivid *Nonformal:* dead-to-rights, for sure *Antonyms:* confusing, doubtful, obscure, unsure, vague

unmitigated *adj.* **1.** absolute, complete, consummate, downright, out-and-out, perfect, professional, rank, straight out, thoroughgoing, veritable *Antonyms:* amateur, occasional, part-time **2.** relentless, remorseless, unabated, unbroken, unbridled, uncontrolled, unremorseful, unrestrained, untempered *Antonyms:* checked, controlled, curbed, restrained

unnatural *adj.* **1.** astounding, bizarre, extraordinary, out of this world, unbelievable, uncanny, uncommon, unreal *Antonyms:* inconsequential, insignificant, undistinguished, unimpressive **2.** affected, artificial, contrived, fabricated, false, forced, insincere, laboured, mannered, phoney *(Nonformal)*, simulated, stilted, strained, studied, synthetic, theatrical *Antonyms:* candid, frank, genuine, heartfelt, sincere **3.** aberrant, abnormal, amoral, bent, bestial, degenerate, depraved, deviant, horrific, irregular, kinky *(Nonformal)*, strange, uncharacteristic, warped *Antonyms:* expected, habitual, normal, routine, standard

unnecessary *adj.* **1.** deadwood *(Nonformal)*, *de trop (French)*, disposable, expendable, extraneous, in the way, needless, nonessential, uncalled-for, unneeded, unwanted *Antonyms:* indispensible, required, vital **2.** abundant, augmented, excess, extra, superfluous, surplus, too much *Antonyms:* correct, enough, full measure, right, sufficient

unnerve *v.* alarm, buffalo *(Nonformal)*, confound, daunt, demoralize, disconcert, dismay, enervate, fluster, needle, perturb, rattle, shake, undermine, unhinge, unman, unsettle, upset, weaken *Nonformal:* faze, rock, throw off balance *Antonyms:* bolster, brace, encourage, support

unnoticed *adj.* disregarded, glossed over, hidden, ignored, neglected, overlooked, passed by, pushed aside, unconsidered, unheeded, unobserved, unrecognized *Antonyms:* discovered, noted, observed, recognized, recorded, remarked

unobtrusive *adj.* demure, discreet, humble, inconspicuous, low-key, low-profile, modest, quiet, reserved, reticent, retiring, wallflower *Antonyms:* assertive, blatant, bold

unoccupied *adj.* **1.** available, deserted, empty, uninhabited, unused, up for grabs *(Nonformal)*, vacant *Antonyms:* leased, spoken for, taken **2.** at leisure, dormant, free, idle, open, out of work, resting, unemployed *Antonyms:* active, busy, engaged

unofficial *adj.* **1.** background, confidential, *entre nous (French)*, not verified, off the record, unauthorized, unconfirmed *Antonyms:* accredited, authenticated, documented, recorded **2.** casual, informal, private, unceremonious *Antonyms:* ceremonial, formal, public

unorganized *adj.* chaotic, disarrayed, disjointed, disordered, haphazard, scrambled, slapdash, unkempt, unsystematic *Nonformal:* all over the place, hugger-mugger, willy-nilly *Antonyms:* arranged, classified, neat, orderly, well-run

unorthodox *adj.* aberrant, abnormal, anomalous, beatnik, different, dissident, eccentric, heretical, irregular, nonconformist, unconventional, unusual, weird *Nonformal:* bohemian, crazy, quirky *Antonyms:* canonical, conservative, conventional, customary, established,

unpaid *adj.* **1.** donated, free, gratuitous, honourary, unsalaried, voluntary, volunteer **2.** due, outstanding, overdue, outstanding, unsettled

unpleasant *adj.* abhorrent, bad, disagreeable, displeasing, distasteful, irksome, lousy, nasty, objectionable, obnoxious, repulsive, rotten, sour, troublesome, unacceptable, unattractive, undesirable, unlikeable, unpalatable *Antonyms:* agreeable, congenial, delicious, lovely, nice

unpopular *adj.* **1.** condemned, despised, detested, disliked, hated, loathed, ostracized, rebuffed, rejected, scorned, shunned, unloved, unwanted, unwelcome *Antonyms:* desirable, favoured, liked, loved, welcome **2.** lonely, obscure, out of the way, unknown, unrenowned

unprecedented *adj.* atypical, distinctive, extraordinary, new, novel, one-of-a-kind, prototypical, rare, recherché, singular, special, uncommon, unfamiliar, unheard of, unique, unparalleled, unusual *Antonyms:* common, everyday, run-of-the-mill

unpredictable *adj.* capricious, changeable, dicey, doubtful, erratic, fickle, fluctuating, incalculable, inconstant, random, touchy, uncertain, unreliable, unstable, variable, whimsical *Nonformal:* fluky, iffy, touchy *Antonyms:* certain, constant, dependable, reliable, stable

unprejudiced *adj.* balanced, detached, dispassionate, equitable, fair, fair-minded, impartial, just, nondiscriminatory, nonpartisan, objective, open-minded, unbiased, uninfluenced *Antonyms:* biased, bigoted, influenced, unfair, unjust

unprepared *adj.* **1.** green, ignorant, ill-prepared, inexperienced, naive, new, raw, unpracticed, unqualified, unready, unskilled, untrained *Antonyms:* expert, seasoned, trained **2.** extemporaneous, ill-considered, impromptu, improvised, not thought out *Nonformal:* ad-lib, from the hip, off the cuff, thrown together *Antonyms:* blocked out, rehearsed, repeated, stock **3.** disconcerted, flabbergasted, shocked, surprised, taken aback *Nonformal:* caught flatfooted *or* napping **4.** half-baked *(Nonformal)*, inchoate, messy, undeveloped, undone, unfinished, unmade

unpretentious *adj.* **1.** artless, guileless, honest, humble, lowly, modest, plain, prosaic, simple, straightforward, unaffected, unassuming *Antonyms:* arrogant, conceited, grandiloquent, ostentatious, pompous **2.** easygoing, folksy, self-effacing *Nonformal:* down-home, laid-back

unprincipled *adj.* abandoned, bent, cheating, conscienceless, corrupt, crooked, deceitful, devious, dishonest, dissolute, double-crossing, double-dealing, licentious, profligate, reprobate, sly, suborned, tricky, two-faced, unconscionable, unethical, unprofessional, unscrupulous, venal *Nonformal*: dirty-dealing, two-timing *Antonyms:* ethical, honest, moral, scrupulous, virtuous

unproductive *adj.* **1.** barren, childless, dry, fallow, impotent, issueless, sterile *Antonyms:* fecund, potent, prolific **2.** fruitless, futile, to no avail, unrewarding, unsuccessful, wasted *Antonyms:* lucrative, profitable, triumphant, worthwhile

unprofessional *adj.* **1.** base, crooked, improper, unbefitting, unbusinesslike, unethical, unseemly, unsuitable, unworthy *Antonyms:* correct, efficient, formal, impersonal, polished **2.** amateurish, bungling, bush league, corner, inadequate, incompetent, lax, negligent, not up to par *or* snuff, second-rate, shoddy, slipshod *Antonyms:* cracker-jack, excellent, masterful

unpromising *adj.* adverse, dire, discouraging, dreary, gloomy, inauspicious, looming, menacing, ominous, portentous, threatening, unfavourable, unlikely *Antonyms:* encouraging, favourable, rosy, sunny

unprotected *adj.* assailable, defenceless, exposed, helpless, liable, naked, open, susceptible, unattended, uncovered, undefended, unfenced, unguarded, unscreened, unsecured, unsheltered, unshielded, vulnerable, wide-open *Antonyms:* defended, guarded, immune, protected, secure

unqualified *adj.* **1.** amateur, ill-equipped, inadequate, incapable, incompetent, ineligible, inexperienced, uncertified, unequal, unfitted, unlicensed, unprepared, unschooled, without papers **2.** absolute, categorical, complete, enduring, outright, perfect, positive, steadfast, steady, sure, thorough, unconditional, unmitigated, unreserved, utter, wholehearted *Nonformal:* flat, out-and-out

unquestionable *adj.* absolute, certain, charming likely *(Newfoundland)*, clear, definitive, inherent, indubitable, irrefutable, obvious, posolutely *(Nonformal)*, sure, true, undeniable *Antonyms:* ambiguous, cryptic, vague

unravel *v.* **1.** break, crack, decipher, decode, define, dope out *(Nonformal)*, elucidate, explain, fathom, figure, interpret, pierce, plumb, simplify, solve, translate, unriddle *Antonyms:* confuse, encode, obscure **2.** card, comb out, part, separate, straighten, unbind, uncoil, undo, unknit, unknot, unscramble, unsew, unsnarl, untie, unweave, unwind *Antonyms:* snarl, knot, twist

unreal *adj.* **1.** chimerical, ethereal, fabled, fanciful, fictitious, hallucinatory, hypothetical, ideal, illusive, illusory, intangible, mythical, nebulous, shadowy, suppositional, theoretical *Antonyms:* applied, useful, workable **2.** artificial, fake, false, fraudulent, insincere, mock, pretend, sham, spurious *Nonformal:* ersatz, phoney, pseudo

unrealistic *adj.* impossible, impractical, improbable, nonsensical, quixotic, romantic, theoretical, unbelievable, unreal *Nonformal:* ivory-towered, starry-eyed *Antonyms:* down to earth, practical, pragmatic, probable, sensible

unreasonable *adj.* **1.** brainless, foolish, idiotic, illogical, incoherent, insane, irrational, mindless, preposterous, senseless, silly *Nonformal:* far-out, harebrained *Antonyms:* logical, rational, sane, sensible **2.** arbitrary, capricious, erratic, intemperate, temperamental, unwarranted, whimsical **3.** extreme, fanatical, headstrong, impossible, inflexible, intransigent, opinionated, steadfast, stubborn, untenable *Antonyms:* flexible, pliable

unrefined *adj.* **1.** coarse, crude, natural, raw, unfinished, unprocessed, untreated *Antonyms:* distilled, pasteurized, pure **2.** boorish, churlish, cloddish, ill-bred, ill-mannered, inelegant, obnoxious, philistine, uncivilized, uncouth, uncultured, unpolished, unsophisticated, vulgar *Nonformal:* cheap, loud-mouthed, raunchy *Antonyms:* cultivated, delicate, mannered, polite, suave

unrelenting *adj.* **1.** implacable, indomitable, merciless, persevering, remorseless, ruthless, steadfast, stubborn, unsparing, unyielding *Nonformal:* bound and determined, hang tough, hard-nosed *Antonyms:* docile, malleable, passive, submissive **2.** ceaseless, constant, continuous, endless, nonstop, recurrent, unabated, unbroken *Antonyms:* seldom, sporadic, spotty

unreliable *adj.* **1.** dubious, erroneous, false, inaccurate, suspect, tricky, unsound, untrustworthy *Nonformal:* bent, fair-weather, fly-by-night *Antonyms:* aboveboard, honourable, reputable, responsible **2.** all-over-the-place, capricious, fickle, inconsistent, unpredictable, unstable, unsteady, vacillating, wavering *Antonyms:* committed, steadfast, steady, unswerving

unrequited *adj.* denied, neglected, rejected, repulsed, scorned, snubbed, spurned, thankless, unreturned, unrewarded, unwelcome *Antonyms:* appreciated, reciprocated, sought

unreserved *adj.* **1.** blunt, bold, candid, direct, forthright, frank, honest, on the level, open, plain-speaking, straightforward, truthful, uninhibited, up-front *Nonformal:* from the hip, in your face, off the cuff *Antonyms:* chary, guarded, secretive **2.** absolute, all *or* flat-out, complete, entire, full, total, unconditional, unlimited, unrestricted *Antonyms:* contained, restricted, tentative

unresolved *adj.* debatable, doubtful, hesitant, hesitating, in play, incomplete, indecisive, irresolute, moot, pending, problematical, unanswered, uncertain, undecided, undetermined, unsettled, up in the air, vague *Antonyms:* achieved, clinched, consummated, finished

unrest *n.* **1.** angst, anxiety, concern, disquiet, fidgets, jitters, malaise, nervousness, restlessness, unease *Antonyms:* bliss, contentment, satisfaction **2.** anarchy, chaos, commotion, discord, pandemonium, rebellion, strife, trouble, turbulence, turmoil, uprising *Antonyms:* cease-fire, peace, tranquility

unrestrained *adj.* **1.** boisterous, immoderate, on the loose, spirited, uncontrolled, unfettered, unhampered, uproarious, wild *Nonformal:* in the fast lane, on a tear *Antonyms:* prohibited, repressed, shackled, tied-up **2.** abrasive, artless, brash, loose-lipped, motor-mouth *(Nonformal)*, obnoxious, pushy, unmuzzled *Antonyms:* gagged, muffled, silenced

unrestricted *n.* **1.** free, freewheeling, laissez-faire, limitless, open, unchecked, unhindered, ungoverned, unregulated *Nonformal:* bare knuckle, gloves off, no-holds-barred, out of bounds *Antonyms:* conditional, forbidden, prescribed, under wraps **2.** absolute, complete, entire, full, sheer, total *Antonyms:* mitigated, qualified, mitigated, tempered

unruffled *adj.* **1.** balanced, calm, collected, composed, controlled, cool, laid-back, level-headed, peaceful, placid, poised, sedate, serene, steady, stoical, tranquil, unflappable, unperturbed *Antonyms:* agitated, disconcerted, rattled, **2.** combed, ironed, kempt, ordered, pressed, smooth, straight, uncreased, uniform *Antonyms:* crumpled, uneven, wrinkled

unruly *adj.* breachy *(P.E.I.)*, disobedient, disorderly, fractious, headstrong, insubordinate, intractable, lawless, mutinous, obnoxious, ornery, out-of-hand, out-of-order, rambunctious, rampant, recalcitrant, restive, riotous, rowdy, stormy, turbulent, undisciplined, unmanageable, violent, wild *Antonyms:* disciplined, orderly, under control

unsafe *adj.* **1.** dangerous, hazardous, hot *(Nonformal)*, life-threatening, menacing, ominous, perilous, threatening, treacherous *Antonyms:* benevolent, friendly, hospitable **2.** contaminated, deadly, noxious, poisonous, polluted, tainted, unhealthy, virulent *Antonyms:* bacteria-free, benign, harmless, pure, wholesome **3.** on slippery ground, uncertain, unstable, unsteady *Nonformal:* chancy, dicey, hairy, iffy, ticklish, touch and go *Antonyms:* stable, sure-footed **4.** decrepit, flimsy, precarious, rickety, shaky, tottering, unsound, untrustworthy, wobbling *Nonformal:* hanging by a thread, on its last legs **5.** defenceless, exposed, insecure, open to attack, penetrable, pregnable, susceptible, unprotected, vulnerable *Antonyms:* fortified, impregnable, reinforced, secure

unsaid *adj.* implicit, implied, inferred, suppressed, tacit, undeclared, understood, unexpressed, unmentioned, unspoken, unstated, unuttered, unvoiced, wordless

unsatisfactory *adj.* **1.** disturbing, inappropriate, offensive, troublesome, uncooperative *Antonyms:* commendable, helpful, obliging, synergetic **2.** damaged, defective, flawed, inferior, not up to par *or* snuff, substandard *Nonformal:* no good, sleazy *Antonyms:* acceptable, award-winning, first-rate **3.** deficient, inadequate, inchoate, incomplete, lacking, unfinished, wanting *Antonyms:* enough, plenty, sufficient

unsavoury *adj.* acid, bitter, bland, disagreeable, distasteful, dull, insipid, lousy, nasty, nauseating, objectionable, obnoxious, offensive, rank, raunchy, repellent, repugnant, repulsive, revolting, rough, sad, *(Nonformal)*, shady, sharp, shifty, sickening, slimy, sneaky, sour, stinking, stinky, tart, tasteless, tough, unappetizing, unpalatable, unpleasant, wrong *Antonyms:* appetizing, palatable, pleasant, savoury, tasty

unscathed *adj.* safe, sound, unharmed, unhurt, uninjured, unmarked, unscarred, untouched, unwounded, whole *Nonformal:* home *or* scot free, in one piece *Antonyms:* crippled, maimed, wounded

unscrupulous *adj.* base, corrupt, crafty, crooked, deceitful, disgraceful, dishonest, illegal, immoral, improper, knavish, low-down, mercenary, petty, questionable, ruthless, scandalous, scheming, selfish, shady, shameless, shifty, sinister, slippery, sly, unconscionable, unethical, unprincipled, wicked, wrongful *Antonyms:* ethical, honourable, moral, principled, upright

unseasonable *adj.* **1.** abnormal, bizarre, different, extraordinary, out of season, strange, uncommon, unusual, weird *Antonyms:* customary, expected, normal **2.**

inexpedient, inopportune, malapropos, poorly timed, unfortunate, unlucky, unpropitious *Antonyms:* fortunate, ripe, timely

unseemly *adj.* cheap, coarse, crude, discreditable, disreputable, embarrassing, improper, inappropriate, incorrect, indecorous, indelicate, inelegant, inept, poor, scuzzy *(Nonformal)*, tawdry, unbefitting, unsuitable, vulgar, wrong *Antonyms:* acceptable, appropriate, becoming, fitting, suitable

unseen *adj.* **1.** background, inconspicuous, undetected, undiscovered, unheeded, unnoticed, unobserved *Antonyms:* blatant, obvious, unmistakable **2.** concealed, covered, hidden, invisible, masked, obscured, out of sight, shrouded, veiled *Antonyms:* on display, showing, visible **3.** fabled, imaginary, imagined, mysterious, mythological *Antonyms:* actual, corporeal, real

unselfish *adj.* altruistic, benevolent, charitable, chivalrous, devoted, generous, giving, humanitarian, kind, loving, magnanimous, philanthropic, self-effacing, selfless, self-sacrificing *Antonyms:* avaricious, mean, rapacious, stingy

unsettled *adj.* **1.** agitated, discomposed, disordered, disquieted, disturbed, flustered, jumpy, restless *Nonformal:* antsy, fussed, on edge, rattled, thrown **2.** changeable, debatable, moot, open to doubt, of two minds, problematic, uncertain, undecided, undetermined, unfinished, unresolved, up in the air *Antonyms:* concluded, decided, finished **3.** dangerous, stormy, turbulent, unpredictable, violent, volatile *Antonyms:* calm, halcyon, serene, tranquil **4.** abandoned, barren, desolate, empty, uninhabited, vacant *Antonyms:* colonized, lived on, occupied, populated **5.** deranged, disordered, insane, irrational, mad, manic, out of whack, unstable *Antonyms:* healthy, lucid, rational, sound **6.** due, outstanding, overdue, pending, unpaid *Antonyms:* discharged, liquidated, paid, reconciled

unsightly *adj.* disagreeable, hideous, horrid, not pretty, off-putting, repulsive, revolting, slatternly, slovenly, squalid, ugly, unattractive, unpleasant *Nonformal:* blowzy, cruddy, gross, hard on the eyes *Antonyms:* attractive, beautiful, handsome, pleasing, pretty

unskilled *adj.* amateur, bumbling, clumsy, fumbling, gauche, incapable, incompetent, inept, inexperienced, inexpert, manual, menial, unqualified, unskilful, untaught, untrained *Nonformal:* all-thumbs, butter-fingered, klutzy *Antonyms:* proficient, talented, trained

unsociable *adj.* aloof, antisocial, cool, distant, hostile, misanthropic, reclusive, reticent, retiring, secretive, shy, solitary, standoffish, unapproachable, withdrawn *Antonyms:* congenial, easygoing, gregarious, neighbourly

unsolicited *adj.* free, gratuitous, spontaneous, unasked *or* unlooked for, uninvited, unwelcome, voluntary, volunteered *Antonyms:* demanded, petitioned, requested

unsophisticated *adj.* **1.** artless, callow, green, guileless, inexperienced, innocent, naive, unaffected, unworldly, wet behind the ears *(Nonformal) Antonyms:* knowledgeable, seasoned, veteran, worldly **2.** down-home, homespun, homey, minimalist, modest, plain, simple, unassuming, unpretentious *Antonyms:* baroque, flashy, garish, ostentatious **3.** crude, primitive, rough, roughcast, rudimentary, unpolished *Antonyms:* cosmopolitan, debonair, elegant

unsound *adj.* **1.** crumbling, dilapidated, jerrybuilt, jury-rigged, poorly constructed, ramshackle, rickety, shoddy, slipshod, unsupported *Antonyms:* durable, strong, sturdy, well-built **2.** certifiable, crazy, demented, deranged, insane, irrational, mad, psychotic, unbalanced, unhinged *Nonformal:* bonkers, nuts *Antonyms:* level-headed, prudent, rational, sane **3.** ailing, diseased, frail, in poor health, sickly, unwell *Antonyms:* hale and hearty, healthy, vigorous **4.** defective, erroneous, fallacious, flawed, illogical, incorrect, specious, unreal *Antonyms:* ethical, factual, faultless, judicious **5.** disturbed, fitful, fractured, light, restless, uneasy *Antonyms:* deep, heavy, profound, undisturbed

unspeakable *adj.* **1.** awe-inspiring, beyond words, extraordinary, impressive, indescribable, inexpressible, phenomenal, stupendous, unequalled, unparalleled, unutterable *Antonyms:* average, commonplace, everyday, pedestrian **2.** appalling, beastly, calamitous, disgusting, frightening, frightful, grisly, gruesome, heinous, horrendous, horrible, horrific, loathsome, sickening, terrifying, upsetting *Antonyms:* refreshing, salubrious, wholesome **3.** abusive, degrading, humiliating, insolent, insulting, reprehensible, scurrilous *Antonyms:* courteous, mannerly, polite, well-behaved

unstable *adj.* **1.** dubious, faltering, insecure, hazardous, insecure, listing, off-balance, perilous, precarious, rickety, rocky, shaky, teetering, tippy, top-heavy, tottering, unsafe *Antonyms:* deep-rooted, established, rock-solid, steady **2.** capricious, erratic, faithless, fickle, flighty, giddy, inconstant, mercurial, mutable, unreliable *Antonyms:* dependable, persistent, relentless, unswerving **3.** dangerous, explosive, ill-tempered, irritable, moody, testy, touchy, volatile, volcanic, wild *Antonyms:* even-tempered, placid, self-possessed **4.** crazed, deranged, ill, illogical, insane, irrational, mad, schizoid, sick, unhealthy, unwell *Nonformal:* loony, nuts, screwed in the head

unstoppable *adj.* **1.** hell-bent *(Nonformal)*, indomitable, inescapable, inevitable, inexorable, relentless, unceasing, unpreventible, unrelenting **2.** breakaway, careening, on the loose, out of control, runaway

unsuccessful *adj.* **1.** abortive, failed, fruitless, futile, ineffectual, unproductive, unprofitable, useless, vain *Antonyms:* rewarding, triumphant, victorious **2.** beaten, cursed, down on one's luck, hapless, luckless, star-crossed, unfortunate, unlucky, washed-up *(Nonformal) Antonyms:* blessed, lucky, prosperous, thriving

unsuitable *adj.* **1.** garish, improper, inappropriate, incompatible, incongruous, indecorous, out-of-keeping, unbefitting, unseemly *Antonyms:* correct, expected, fitting, meet, proper **2.** disagreeable, distasteful, indecent, intolerable, off-colour *(Nonformal)*, unacceptable, uncalled for, unsupportable *Antonyms:* acceptable, admirable, laudable, praiseworthy **3.** flawed, inadequate, ineffectual, unsatisfactory, useless, wanting *Antonyms:* effective, practical, serviceable

unsung *adj.* anonymous, forgotten, insignificant, little-known, minor, nameless, unheard of, unheralded, unidentified, unknown *Antonyms:* celebrated, famous, prominent

unsure *adj.* distrustful, doubtful, dubious, hesitant, indecisive, insecure, irresolute, mistrustful, sceptical, suspicious, tentative, uncertain, undecided, wishy-washy *(Nonformal) Antonyms:* convinced, determined, firm

unsuspecting *adj.* **1.** credulous, deceived, easy *(Nonformal)*, gullible, inexperienced, innocent, naive, simple, trusting, wide-eyed *Antonyms:* cynical, sceptical, suspicious **2.** asleep, heedless, inattentive, napping, off-guard, resting, unaware *Antonyms:* alert, vigilant

unsympathetic *adj.* aloof, antipathetic, apathetic, averse, callous, cold, cold-blooded, cool, cruel, disinterested, frigid, hard, harsh, heartless, icy, indifferent, insensitive, mean, obdurate, pitiless, stony, tough, uncompassionate, unconcerned, unfeeling, unmoved, unresponsive *Antonyms:* caring, compassionate, kind, generous, sensitive

untangle *v.* clear up, disentangle, explain, extricate, solve, straighten out, unravel, unscramble, unsnarl, untwist *Antonyms:* complicate, jumble, tie-up

untenable *adj.* **1.** baseless, contestable, debatable, faulty, flawed, illogical, insupportable, questionable, refutable, specious, unfounded, unsound, unsustainable, weak *Antonyms:* faultless, strong **2.** defenceless, helpless, pregnable, unfortified, unprotected, violable, vulnerable *Antonyms:* fortified, invincible, protected

unthinkable *adj.* **1.** absurd, beyond belief *or* possibility, illogical, impossible, improbable, inconceivable, ludicrous, outlandish, out of the question, preposterous, unbelievable, unlikely **2.** exceptional, extraordinary, incredible, mind-boggling, rare, singular, uncommon, unimaginable, unique, unusual

untidy *adj.* bedraggled, careless, chaotic, cluttered, disarranged, disarrayed, dishevelled, disorderly, grubby, jumbled, littered, messy, mixed up, muddled, rumpled, slapdash, slipshod, sloppy, slovenly, snarled, tangled, topsy-turvy, tousled, uncombed, unkempt, unsettled, upset *Nonformal:* scruffy, scuzzy *Antonyms:* methodical, neat, orderly, presentable, tidy

untimely *adj.* **1.** awkward, ill-timed, inappropriate, inconvenient, inopportune, intrusive, unfortunate, unseasonable, wrong *Antonyms:* auspicious, opportune, right **2.** bright and early *(Nonformal)*, early, premature, too early *or* soon **3.** belated, late, overdue, tardy

untiring *adj.* constant, continuing, dedicated, determined, devoted, dogged, firm, hyper, incessant, indefatigable, indomitable, inexhaustible, patient, persevering, persistent, pertinacious, plodding, plugging, relentless, resolute, staunch, steady, strong, tenacious, tireless, unceasing, undeterred, unfailing, unfaltering, unflagging, unflinching, unremitting, unstinted, unswerving, unwavering, unwearied *Antonyms:* indolent, lackadaisical, laggard, slothful, sluggish, sporadic

untold *adj.* **1.** beyond measure, countless, enormous, gigantic, huge, immense, incalculable, innumerable, manifold, many, measureless, mighty, monstrous, multiple, multitudinous, myriad, numberless, prodigious, staggering, titanic, uncounted, undreamed of, unimaginable, vast **2.** hidden, private, unexpressed, unknown, unpublished, unreported

untouched *adj.* **1.** chaste, entire, flawless, fresh, immaculate, intact, natural, new, pure, sanitary, spotless, unblemished, uncorrupted, unspoiled, unsullied, untarnished, virginal *Antonyms:* blighted, debased, raped, violated **2.** home *or* scott free *(Nonformal)*, safe, safe and sound, secure, undamaged, unharmed, unhurt, uninjured, unscathed, whole *Antonyms:* injured, maimed, mangled, wounded **3.** callous, hard, impenitent, unemotional, unmoved, unrepentant *Antonyms:* conscience-stricken, contrite, remorseful **4.** left, left over, uneaten, unsampled, untasted, untried, unused *Antonyms:* consumed, finished **5.** uncharted, undiscovered, unexplored, virgin *Antonyms:* familiar, populous, well-trodden **6.** ignored, neglected, omitted, overlooked, passed over *Antonyms:* exposed, featured, highlighted

untoward *adj.* **1.** impolite, improper, inappropriate, indecent, indelicate, out-of-bounds, rough, tactless, unbecoming, uncouth, undiplomatic, unfitting, ungodly, unseemly, unsuitable **2.** adverse, menacing, ominous, portentous, sinister, unfriendly, unpropitious

untroubled *adj.* calm, composed, halcyon, hushed, laid-back *(Nonformal)*, mellow, peaceful, philosophical, placid, quiet, serene, steady, still, tranquil, unconcerned, unperturbed, unruffled *Antonyms:* agitated, disturbed, flustered, worried

untrue *adj.* **1.** conjured-up, erroneous, fallacious, false, fantasy, fictitious, fraudulent, misleading, spurious *Nonformal:* bogus, crock, hogwash, horse feathers, phoney *Antonyms:* confirmed, factual, genuine, real **2.** apostate, deceitful, dishonest, disloyal, prevaricating, straying, suborned, traitorous, treacherous, two-faced, two-timing, unfaithful, untrustworthy *Nonformal:* cheating, moonlighting, sneaking around *Antonyms:* dependable, loving, reliable, uncorruptible **3.** imprecise, inaccurate, incorrect, inexact, invalid, substandard *Nonformal:* off, out

untrustworthy *adj.* **1.** cheating, conniving, crooked, devious, dishonest, lying, mendacious, shady, sharp, shifty, shifty-eyed, sneaky, thieving, two-faced, underhanded **2.** capricious, erratic, flighty, fly-by-night, impulsive, irresponsible, undependable, unpredictable, unreliable **3.** accident-prone, dangerous, perilous, questionable, rickety, shaky, tottering, unsafe, unsupported, weak

unused *adj.* **1.** fresh, intact, mint, new, pristine, unopened, untouched **2.** abandoned, derelict, empty, free, idle, suspended, vacant *Antonyms:* engaged, occupied, tenanted **3.** extra, leftover, remaining, remnant, reserve, saved, set aside, surplus **4.** inexperienced, innocent, naive, unaccustomed, unfamiliar, unskilled, untrained

unusual *adj.* abnormal, amazing, astonishing, atypical, awe-inspiring, awesome, bizarre, conspicuous, curious, different, eccentric, exceptional, extraordinary, incredible, memorable, noteworthy, odd, outstanding, phenomenal, prodigious, prominent, quirky, radical, rare, refreshing, remarkable, significant, singular, special, strange, surprising, surreal, uncommon, unconventional, unexpected, unfamiliar, unique, unparalleled, weird *Nonformal:* bent, far out, funky, kinky, off the wall, something else, unbelievable *Antonyms:* average, conventional, everyday, routine, typical

unusually *adv.* almighty *(Nonformal)*, awful, awfully, curiously, especially, extra, extraordinarily, extremely, mighty, odd, peculiarly, plenty, powerful, rarely, real, really, remarkably, so much, strangely, surprisingly, terribly, terrifically, too much, uncommonly, unutterable, very

unveil *v.* bare, betray, bring to light, disclose, discover, display, divulge, exhume, expose, illuminate, open, open up, present, reveal, show, spring, tell, tip one's hand *(Nonformal)*, unbosom, uncover, unroll *Antonyms:* cloak, cover, disguise, obscure, mask

unwarranted *adj.* baseless, gratuitous, groundless, indefensible, inexcusable, uncalled-for, unconscionable, undue, unfair, unfounded, unjustifiable, unprovoked, unreasonable *Antonyms:* authorized, defensible, requested

unwavering *adj.* abiding, consistent, dedicated, determined, enduring, firm, fixed, never-failing, regular, resolute, set, single-minded, solid, staunch, steadfast, steady, sure, unchanging, undeviating, unfaltering, unflagging, unshakable, unswerving *Nonformal:* brick-wall, concretized, rock-solid, rooted

unwelcome *adj.* **1.** black-balled, cold-shouldered, excluded, neglected, not admitted, omitted, rejected, shut-out *Nonformal:* given the old heave-ho, left out in the cold **2.** objectionable, opposed, unacceptable, undesirable, uninvited, unwanted, unwished for **3.** disagreeable, distasteful, lousy *(Nonformal)*, obnoxious, repellent, thankless, unpleasant

unwholesome *adj.* **1.** contaminated, corrupt, deleterious, foul, infected, insalubrious, morbid, noisome, noxious, putrid, rotten, sullied, tarnished, toxic, unsanitary *Antonyms:* antiseptic, fresh, healthy, invigorating, nourishing **2.** dirty, filthy, lascivious, lewd, pornographic, X-rated *Nonformal:* adult, blue

unwieldy *adj.* awkward, bulky, burdensome, clumsy, cumbersome, cumbrous, gross, heavy, hefty, inconvenient, massive, onerous, ponderous, uncontrollable, ungainly, unhandy, unmanageable, unmanoeuvrable, weighty *Antonyms:* compact, streamlined, compact

unwilling *adj.* **1.** against, at odds, averse, balky, coerced, contrary, disinclined, grudging, indisposed, loath, obstinate, opposed, perverse, recalcitrant, reluctant, stubborn, uncooperative *Antonyms:* biddable, eager, keen **2.** automatic, involuntary, reflexive, spontaneous, unconscious *Commonly misused:* **unwitting**

unwind *v.* **1.** disentangle, free, loose, loosen, separate, slacken, uncoil, undo, unfurl, unravel, untangle, unwrap **2.** calm down, crash *(Nonformal)*, ease off, let go, loosen up, quieten, recline, relax, rest, sit back, take a break *or* breather

unwise *adj.* asinine, careless, childish, empty-headed, fatuous, foolhardy, foolish, ill-advised, ill-considered, immature, impetuous, impolite, improvident, imprudent, inadvisable, inane, inappropriate, indiscreet, inept, injudicious, irresponsible, misguided, naive, rash, reckless, senseless, silly, stupid, thoughtless, unfortunate, unintelligent, witless *Antonyms:* discreet, politic, prudent, sagacious, sensible, shrewd

unwitting *adj.* accidental, chance, ignorant, innocent, random, unaware, unconscious, uninformed, unintentional, unknowing, unplanned, unthinking *Antonyms:* conscious, deliberate, designed *Commonly misused:* **unwilling**

unworldly *adj.* **1.** ascetic, devout, idealistic, religious, spiritually-minded **2.** celestial, ethereal, heavenly, immaterial, metaphysical, not of this earth, spiritual, transcendental **3.** country, green, inexperienced, innocent, naive, natural, raw, simple, unsophisticated, wide-eyed *Nonformal:* corn-fed, wet behind the ears *Commonly misused:* **unearthly**

unworthy *adj.* **1.** ill-equipped, ineligible, not good enough, undeserving, unmerited, unprepared, unready, wrong *Antonyms:* due, just, meet, meritorious, proper **2.** contemptible, disgraceful, dishonourable, ignoble, improper, inexcusable, reprehensible, shameful, wretched *Antonyms:* blameless, sterling, unimpeachable

unyielding *adj.* adamant, determined, firm, fixed, headstrong, immovable, implacable, inexorable, inflexible, intransigent, obdurate, pertinacious, relentless, resolute, rigid, ruthless, solid, staunch, steadfast, steady, stiff, strong, stubborn, tough, unbending, uncompromising, unwavering *Nonformal:* hard-nosed, stiff-necked *Antonyms:* adaptable, compromising, cooperative, flexible

up *adj.* **1.** alert, awake, cognizant, conscious, stirring, wide-awake **2.** anticipating, eager, energetic, enthusiastic, excited, impatient, restless, willing *Antonyms:* adverse, loath, reluctant – *adv.* **1.** aloft, heavenward, in the air, in the clouds, overhead, skywards, towards the ceiling **2.** north, uphill, up-island, up north, upstairs, uptown, upstream **3.** erectly, on end, on one's feet, vertically – *v.* boost, broaden, enlarge, expand, hike, increase, inflate, magnify, raise, widen *Antonyms:* decrease, deflate, depress, falter

upbeat *adj.* buoyant, cheerful, cheery, encouraging, favourable, happy, heartening, hopeful, lively, optimistic, pleasant, positive, swinging, uptempo *Nonformal:* funky, groovy *Antonyms:* melancholy, plaintive, sad, slow

upbraid *v.* admonish, berate, castigate, censure, chide, dress down, rebuke, reprimand, reproach, scold *Prince Edward Island:* card, growl, skivver *Nonformal:* bawl *or* chew *or* ream out, rake over the coals *Antonyms:* commend, laud, praise, puff up

upbringing *n.* education, fostering, moulding, nurture, preparation, raising, rearing, training, tutelage

upcoming *adj.* approaching, forthcoming, future, imminent, impending, looming

upchuck *v.* heave, vomit *Nonformal:* barf, beulah, hurl, lose it, puke, toss one's cookies

upcountry *adj.* backcountry, backwoods, bush, inland, interior, wilderness

update *n.* breaking story, flash, latest news, recent events *Nonformal:* dirt, goods, lowdown, poop, scoop, the latest – *v.* **1.** amend, brief, bring up to par *or* speed, refresh, revise **2.** modernize, remodel, streamline, upgrade

up-front *adj.* aboveboard, blunt, brusque, brutal, frank, from the hip *(Nonformal)*, genuine, honest, open, straightforward *Antonyms:* mendacious, sycophantic

upgrade *n.* **1.** addition, advancement, bump *(Nonformal)*, enhancement, improvement, move *or* step up **2.** acclivity, assent, incline, climb, rise, slope – *v.* better, develop, enhance, enrich, fix up, improve, modernize, refurbish, rejuvenate, renew, renovate, restore, spruce up *(Nonformal)*, update *Antonyms:* debase, demean, reduce

upheaval *n.* **1.** blowout, cataclysm, convulsion, earthquake, eruption, explosion, groundswell, outburst, quake, tidal wave, tsunami **2.** anarchy, breakdown, chaos, confusion, craziness, debacle, disorder, furor, madness, overthrow, pandemonium, revolt, revolution

uphill *adj.* **1.** ascending, climbing, going up, mounting, rising, skyward, sloping, upward *Antonyms:* descending, downhill, lowering **2.** arduous, backbreaking, difficult, gruelling, laborous, punishing, tough *Antonyms:* a cinch, duck soup, effortless

uphold *v.* **1.** aid, back, bear out, bolster, buttress, confirm, corroborate, defend, endorse, ensure, fortify, maintain, prop, protect, shore up, reinforce, sanction, strengthen, substantiate, sustain *Antonyms:* reject, renounce, repudiate, sabotage, subvert, undermine **2.** advocate, boost, champion, hoist, promote *Antonyms:* attack, criticize, denounce, deride

up-island *adj.* distant, far-away, isolated, northern, out of the way, remote, secluded, unpopulated – *adv.* into the woods *(Nonformal)*, north, northward, upcountry, up north

upkeep *n.* **1.** budget, costs, expenditure, expenses, keep, operating funds, outlay, overhead, running costs, subsistence, support, sustenance **2.** conservation, maintenance, preservation, repair

uplift *n.* **1.** betterment, cultivation, edification, education, enhancement, enlightenment, enrichment, improvement, modification, update, upgrade *Antonyms:* degradation, oppression **2.** elevation, erection, upthrust – *v.* **1.** boost, elevate, erect, heave, hoist, jack, lift, raise, rear **2.** better, enhance, enrich, exalt, foster, further, improve, modify, promote, restore *Antonyms:* debase, disparage

upper *adj.* above, elevated, elite, eminent, greater, high, higher, important, loftier, nose-bleed *(Nonformal)*, overhead, superior, top, topmost, uppermost, upward *Antonyms:* bottom, inferior, junior, low, lower

uppermost *adj.* best, biggest, chief, dominant, executive, foremost, greatest, highest up, leading, main, paramount, predominant, preeminent, primary, principal, prominent, supreme, tops *(Nonformal)*, ultimate, winner, world-class *Antonyms:* bottom, least, lowest, slightest, smallest

upright *adj.* **1.** aboveboard, blameless, circumspect, conscientious, correct, equitable, ethical, exemplary, fair, faithful, good, high-minded, honest, honourable, impartial, incorruptible, just, moral, noble, principled, punctilious, pure, righteous, true, trustworthy, unimpeachable, virtuous *Nonformal:* straight arrow, true-blue *Antonyms:* corrupt, devious, dishonest, unethical, unjust **2.** cocked, erect, perpendicular, plumb, raised, sheer, standing, steep, stiff, straight, straight-up, upended, upstanding, upward, vertical *Antonyms:* flat, horizontal, prone, prostrate, supine

uprising *n.* coup d'etat, disturbance, insurgence, insurrection, mutiny, outbreak, Putsch, rebellion, revolt, revolution, riot, upheaval

uproar *n.* agitation, attack, barrage, bedlam, bombardment, broadside, bustle, chaos, clamour, clatter, commotion, confusion, craziness, debacle, din, disturbance, excitement, ferment, flutter, fracas, furor, fusillade, fuss, hassle, hysteria, madness, mayhem, mêlée, noise, onslaught, pandemonium, passion, riot, scene, squall, stir, storm, strife, tempest, tumult, turbulence, upheaval, upset, violence, whirl, whirlwind *Nonformal:* ado, brouhaha, din, dust-up, flap, free-for-all, hoo-ha, hubbub, kerfuffle, lather, racket, rhubarb, rumpus, whoop-de-do

uproarious *adj.* **1.** boisterous, clamorous, noisy, rip-roaring *(Nonformal)*, rowdy, turbulent **2.** entertaining, funny, hilarious, humorous, hysterical, screamingly funny *Nonformal:* a gas, a riot, gut-busting, side-splitting, too much

uproot *v.* **1.** dig out *or* up, exhume, grub *or* tear out, pluck, pull out *or* up, remove, weed **2.** displace, emigrate, evacuate, immigrate, move, relocate, take away, transfer, transplant **3.** demolish, destroy, eliminate, eradicate, extirpate, snuff *or* stamp out

upset *adj.* **1.** agitated, angry, anguished, apprehensive, bewildered, bothered, confused, crestfallen, depressed, disconcerted, disordered, distressed, disturbed, flustered, frightened, heartsick, horrified, jumbled, melancholy, morose, nervous, off-balance, overwrought, perturbed, restless, sad, saddened, sorrowful, startled, terrified, traumatized, troubled, unnerved, worried *Nonformal:* antsy, beside oneself, fussed, rattled, shook up, shot to pieces, thrown, unglued **2.** gaseous, ill, nauseous, queasy, rumbling, sick, unsettled **3.** capsized, inverted, overturned, tipped over, topsy-turvy, upended – *n.* **1.** agitation, bother, difficulty, disorder *Nonformal:* flustration, mishmash, stew, tizzy, to-do **2.** comeback, defeat, overthrow, reverse, rout, shake-up, unseating, victory **3.** ache, ailment, complaint, distress, malady, pain, problem, soreness, worry – *v.* **1.** afflict, aggravate, aggrieve, agonize, alarm, anger, appal, bother, burden, confuse, consternate, debilitate, depress, distress, embitter, enrage, exasperate, frighten, gall, grieve, harass, harry, horrify, hurt, impair, incense, inflame, infuriate, irk, irritate, madden, nag, nonplus, oppress, pain, peeve, perplex, perturb, rankle, rattle, rile, roil, ruffle, sadden, scare, shock, startle, stir, stress, terrify, torment, torture, trouble, try, unhinge, unnerve, vex, weaken, wear, weigh, work up, worry, wound *Nonformal:* flummox, hassle, miff **2.** capsize, change, derange, disarray, disorder, disorganize, disturb, invert, jumble, keel *or* knock *or* tip over, mix up, overset, overturn, pitch, reverse, spill, subvert, tilt, topple, turn, turn turtle, unsettle, upend, upturn **3.** beat, conquer, defeat, overcome, overpower, overthrow, unhelm, unhorse, vanquish, win *Nonformal:* hammer, trash, trounce

upshot *n.* aftereffect, aftermath, bottom line *(Nonformal)*, conclusion, consequence, culmination, effect, end, eventuality, finish, gist, issue, outcome, payoff, result, sequel, thrust

upstage *v.* cast in the shade, eclipse, outmanoeuvre, outshine, outstrip, overshadow, steal the scene *or* show **2.** cold shoulder, rebuff, snub

upstanding *adj.* decent, ethical, good, honest, honourable, incorruptible, kind, moral, principled, straightforward, trustworthy, upright *Antonyms:* bad, corrupt, dishonest, false, suborned

upstart *adj.* audacious, brash, brazen, cheeky, common, forward, presumptuous – *n.* arriviste, firebrand, nouveau riche, pretender, social climber, status seeker *Nonformal:* jackanapes, johnny-come-lately, new money, parvenu

uptake *n.* acuity, comprehension, grasp, insight, perception, perspicacity, sharpness, understanding

uptight *adj.* **1.** anxious, impatient, insecure, nervous, taut, tense, uneasy, worked up, wound up *Antonyms:* easygoing, loose, nonchalant, relaxed **2.** close-minded, hidebound, narrow-minded, prim, proper, rigid, straitlaced, tight-laced, ultra-conservative, Victorian *Nonformal:* anal-retentive, finicky, programmed

up-to-date *adj.* **1.** advanced, contemporary, current, hot *(Nonformal)*, hot off the press, late, latebreaking, latest, modern, newest, recent, up-to-the-minute **2.** avant-garde, cutting *or* leading edge, fashionable, modish, newfangled, state-of-the-art, stylish, trendy, *Nonformal:* funky, groovy, tony **3.** abreast, *au courant (French)*, aware, briefed, informed, in the know, primed, with it *(Nonformal)*

upturn *n.* ascent, boost, bull market, improvement, increase, jump, recovery, revival, rise, surge, upswing *Antonyms:* decline, lapse, slide

upward *adj.* ascending, climbing, mounting, on the rise, rising, skyrocketing, soaring – *adv.* aloft, bound for the stars, into the blue, into the great wide open, into the heavens, into the wild blue yonder, skyward, straight up, uphill

urban *adj.* citified, civic, cosmopolitan, downtown, metropolitan, midtown, municipal, oppidan, uptown *Antonyms:* agricultural, rural, sylvan *Commonly misused:* **urbane**

urbane *adj.* affable, balanced, bland, civilized, cosmopolitan, courteous, cultivated, cultured, debonair, diplomatic, elegant, gracious, mannerly, polished, polite, refined, sophisticated, suave, well-bred, well-mannered, worldly *Antonyms:* boorish, gauche, rude, uncultured *Commonly misused:* **urban**

urchin *n.* brat, child, *enfant terrible (French)*, gamin, guttersnipe, imp, mischief-maker, mudlark, nuisance, puck, scamp, stray, whelp *Nonformal:* holy terror, little monkey, menace, whippersnapper

urge *n.* compulsion, craving, desire, drive, hankering, impetus, impulse, longing, motivation, pressure, thirst, yearning *Nonformal:* itch, yen – *v.* **1.** compel, drive, force, goad, hasten, impel, prod, pull, push, spur *Nonformal:* egg on, hound *Antonyms:*

check, counsel, deter, prevent, stop **2.** beg, beseech, blandish, coax, encourage, entreat, exhort, importune, incite, induce, influence, persuade, plead, press, prevail upon, wheedle *Nonformal:* twist one's arm, work on *Antonyms:* caution, discourage, dissuade, remonstrate **3.** advance, advise, advocate, defend, forward, further, persist, promote *Antonyms:* dismiss, walk away, write off

urgent *adj.* **1.** compelling, critical, crucial, exigent, grave, high-priority, immediate, imperative, important, pressing *Nonformal:* code red, life and death, red alert , S.O.S. *Antonyms:* insignificant, marginal, trivial, unimportant **2.** demanding, dogged, energetic, insistent, pertinacious, tenacious *Antonyms:* half-hearted, indifferent, lackadaisical **3.** ardent, eloquent, earnest, fervent, fiery, impassioned, passionate, stirring *Antonyms:* clumsy, pedestrian, uninspired **4.** fast, hasty, hurried, instant, quick, rapid, speedy *Antonyms:* drawn out, prolonged, protracted – *interj.* high *or* top priority, hot rush *(Nonformal)*, now, right now, on the double, rush, stat

urinate *v.* make *or* pass water, relieve oneself, void, wet *Nonformal:* pee, piss, squirt, see a man about a dog, take a leak *or* whizz, tinkle

urine *n.* water *Nonformal:* pee, piddle, piss, wee-wee, yellow water

urn *n.* container, ewer, jar, ossuary, pitcher, pot, samovar, vase, vessel

usable *adj.* accessible, adaptable, advantageous, applicable, at one's disposal *or* hand, available, beneficial, consumable, convenient, employable, fit, helpful, instrumental, operative, ready, running, serviceable, useful, valuable, wieldable, working

usage *n.* **1.** common practice, convention, custom, habit, practice, routine, standard, tradition, way, wont **2.** application, employment, handling, manipulation, operation, treatment **3.** dialect, expression, idiom, jargon, language, manner of speaking, parlance, patois, phraseology, speech, talk, turn of phrase, vernacular, wording

use *n.* **1.** application, employment, function, practice, purpose **2.** advantage, avail, basis, need, object, point, profit, purpose, reason **3.** common practice, custom, habit, operation, tradition, working **4.** benefit, enjoyment, satisfaction, service **5.** liberty, licence, power, prerogative, right – *v.* **1.** access, adapt, apply, bring on board, call upon, employ, exercise, exert, make use of, operate, practice, press into service, put into operation, run, wield, work **2.** appropriate, capitalize, exploit, mine, manipulate, play upon, profit from, take advantage of, turn to account **3.** act *or* behave towards, deal with, do by, handle, treat **4.** chew up *(Nonformal)*, consume, drink, eat, exhaust, expand, ingest, spend

used *adj.* **1.** cast-off, hand-me-down, leftover, old, pre-loved, pre-owned, previously owned, recycled, second-hand, worn **2.** dirty, filthy, soiled, shopworn, stained, sullied, tarnished **3.** blown *(Nonformal)*, consumed, depleted, dissipated, exhausted, frittered away **4.** acclimatized, accustomed, adjusted, conditioned, hardened, inured, familiar with

useful *adj.* available, advantageous, beneficial, fruitful, functional, handy, helpful, instrumental, of assistance *or* service *or* use, operational, productive, propitious, serviceable, suitable, valuable, worthwhile *Antonyms:* counterproductive, deleterious, harmful, superfluous

useless *adj.* **1.** broken, defunct, malfunctioning, out of order *or* service, scrap, unserviceable, unusable, unworkable *Nonformal:* busted, had it, kaput, on the blink *or* fritz, out of commission *Antonyms:* functioning, working **2.** abortive, counterproductive, frivolous, futile, impractical, inane, ineffective, in vain, meaningless, pointless, superfluous, unprofitable, unrewarding, wasted *Antonyms:* effective, important, meaningful, successful **3.** good-for-nothing, hopeless, impotent, incapable, incompetent, ineffectual, inept, worthless *Nonformal:* disaster, dud, garbage *Antonyms:* central, crucial, intrinsic, paramount

user *n.* **1.** consumer, demographic, employer, market, owner, target audience **2.** calculator, Machiavelli, manoeuverer, manipulator, operator, schemer *Nonformal:* piece of work, puller of strings, slyboots **3.** abuser, addict, alcoholic, junkie, tripper *(Nonformal)*

user-friendly *adj.* accessible, approachable, comprehensible, easy to understand, intelligible, practical, simple, usable *Antonyms:* complicated, intricate, undecipherable

usher *n.* attendant, conductor, doorkeeper, doorman, escort, guide, lead, leader, page, pilot – *v.* accompany, bring in, chaperone, conduct, direct, escort, guide, herald, initiate, introduce, launch, lead, marshal, pilot, precede, receive, shepherd, show around, squire, steer

usual *adj.* **1.** chronic, common, frequent, oft-repeated, recurring *Antonyms:* rare, singular, unique **2.** average, commonplace, demotic, hackneyed, middling, run of the mill, so-so, unexceptional, unremarkable *Antonyms:* formidable, magnificent, outstanding, remarkable **3.** customary, everyday, expected, familiar, natural, normal, regular, unaffected *Antonyms:* aberrant, deviant, different – *n.* familiar, favourite, norm *(Nonformal)*, regular

usually *adv.* **1.** broadly, chiefly, consistently, extensively, frequently, for the most part, in general, largely, mainly, most often, mostly, on average, principally, predominantly, primarily, regularly, universally, widely *Antonyms:* infrequently, never, seldom **2.** commonly, conventionally, customarily, habitually, routinely, traditionally, typically *Antonyms:* erratically, out of character, randomly, unexpected

usurp *v.* **1.** annex, commandeer, encroach, expropriate, relieve, seize, steal, supplant, swipe, take, take over *or* possession of, wrest *Nonformal:* glom onto, hijack, shanghai *Antonyms:* abandon, give back, resign, return **2.** barge *or* butt *or* elbow *or* muscle *or* squeeze *or* worm in on, bump *(Nonformal)*, dispossess, infringe, invade, trespass *Antonyms:* avoid, shun, steer clear of

utensil *n.* apparatus, appliance, device, equipment, gadget, implement, instrument, tool *Nonformal:* dingus, doohickey, dojigger, gizmo, thingamajig, whatchamacallit *Kinds of cooking utensil:* apple corer, baster, biscuit cutter, blender, brush, cleaver, cookie cutter, cutlery, egg beater, frying pan, funnel, garlic press, grader, grapefruit knife *or* spoon, ice pick, kitchen shears, knife, ladle, potato masher, measuring cup *or* spoon, melon baller, meat thermometer, mixing bowl, mortar and pestle, nutcracker, oyster knife, pan, paring knife, pastry brush, peeler, pepper mill, pizza cutter, pot, poultry shears, ricer, scoop, sharpening steel, skimmer, spatula, steamer, steamer basket, strainer, trussing needle, vegetable parer, whisk, wooden spoon, zester

utilitarian *adj.* commonsensical, down-to-earth, effective, efficient, functional, hard-headed, practical, pragmatic, realistic, sensible, serviceable, unromantic, useful, workable *Antonyms:* fanciful, impractical, ineffective, sentimental, unworldly

utility *adj.* alternate, backup, reserve, spare, substitute – *n.* advantage, applicability, benefit, efficacy, expediency, fitness, function, helpfulness, practicality, productiveness, serviceability, usefulness

utilize *v.* access, control, drive, employ, exploit, make use of, manage, manoeuvre, manipulate, operate, program, use, wield, work

utmost *adj.* absolute, chief, complete, entire, exhaustive, extreme, farthest, final, full, furthermost, greatest, highest, last, maximal, maximum, most, most distant, outermost, outside, paramount, remotest, sheer, supreme, thorough, thoroughgoing, topmost, total, ultimate, unconditional, undiminished, unlimited, unmitigated, unqualified, unreserved, uttermost, whole

utopia *n.* bliss, cakes and ale, cloud-cuckoo-land, cloudland, cloud nine, Elysium, Erewhon, Garden of Eden, heaven, New Atlantis, nirvana, nowheresville, paradise, perfection, seventh heaven, Shangri-La, Valhalla *Nonformal:* la-la land, never never land *Antonyms:* dystopia, hades, hell, purgatory

utopian *adj.* abstract, airy, ambitious chimerical, dream, fanciful, fantasy grandiose, hopeful, ideal, illusory, imaginary, impractical, lofty, quixotic, romantic, theoretical, unfeasible, unrealistic, visionary *Nonformal:* ivory-towered, pie-in-the-sky *Antonyms:* applied, employable, practical, ready – *n.* Don Quixote, dreamer, idealist, romantic, seer, tilter of windmills, visionary, wishful thinker *Antonyms:* cynic, gloomster, pessimist

utter *adj.* **1.** absolute, categorical, complete, consummate, downright, extreme, outright, overwhelming, perfect, positive, quintessential, sheer, thorough, total **2.** final, unconditional, unequivocal, unmitigated, unqualified, wholesale *Antonyms:* contingent, provisional – *v.* articulate, breathe, declare, enunciate, express, mouth off *(Nonformal)*, mumble, murmur, mutter, pronounce, reply, retort, say, shout, sound, speak, swear, talk, tell, verbalize, vocalize, voice, yell

utterance *n.* **1.** announcement, assertion, asseveration, declaration, delivery, discourse, expression, opinion, oration, pronouncement, rant, recitation, remark, reply, response, saying, sentence, speech, spiel *(Nonformal)*, statement, talk, tongue, vent, verbalization, vocalization, word, words **2.** articulation, bark, bawl, bellow, blare, blubbering, boom, braying, buzz, cackle, chant, chirp, cooing, crowing, drawl, ejaculation, exclamation, flute, gasp, growl, grunt, hiss, keening, lilt, mumble, murmur, mutter, noise, panting, piping, roar, rumble, scream, screech, shriek, sigh, singing, snap, snarl, snort, sob, squall, squawk, squeak, squeal, thunder, trumpet, twang, vociferation, voicing, wail, warble, whine, whisper, yap, yawp, yell, yelp

utterly *adv.* absolutely, all, altogether, completely, entirely, exactly, extremely, fully, *in toto (Latin)*, just, perfectly, plumb *(Nonformal)*, purely, quite, thoroughly, totally, well, wholly

U-turn *n.* **1.** driving infraction, illegal turn, turnaround *Nonformal:* a 180, spinorama **2.** about-face, change, dipsy-doodle *(Nonformal)*, reversal, reversion, turnabout, volte-face

uxorious *adj.* **1.** attached, devoted, doting, enamoured, enchanted, fond, ga-ga *(Nonformal)*, infatuated, love lost, smitten *Antonyms:* bored, jaded, regretful **2.** browbeaten, bullied, dominated, emasculated, enslaved, henpecked, scared, subjugated, submissive, subservient, timid, whipped *(Nonformal)*

vacancy *n.* **1.** availability, empty space, rental, room *or* space for rent **2.** job opening, opportunity, position, posting, situation, slot **3.** break, cavity, chasm, crater, crevice, emptiness, gap, hole, pore, vacuity, vacuum, void

vacant *adj.* **1.** bare, devoid of contents, empty, hollow, stark *Antonyms:* full, loaded, teeming **2.** free, idle, resting, unemployed, unencumbered, unengaged *Antonyms:* at work, employed, industrious **3.** blank, deadpan, expressionless, poker-faced *(Nonformal)*, vague *Antonyms:* apparent, emotional, revealing **4.** carefree, dumb, empty-headed, fatuous, foolish, inane, out to lunch *(Nonformal)*, silly, stupid, thoughtless, unintelligent, vacuous *Antonyms:* erudite, learned, wise **5.** *à louer (French)*, for rent, uninhabited, unoccupied, untenanted, without incumbent *Antonyms:* held, occupied, leased, rented, tenanted **6.** abandoned, barren, deserted, destitute, exhausted, unclaimed *Antonyms:* cherished, cultivated, developed

vacate *v.* **1.** abandon, clear, depart, desert, empty, evacuate, go away, leave, move out, surrender, withdraw, yield *Nonformal:* beat it, *frappe la rue (French)*, get lost, scram, take off *Antonyms:* crowd, fill, occupy **2.** abdicate, cede, deliver, give up, part with, quit, renounce, resign *Antonyms:* confront, face, stay **3.** quash, repudiate, reverse, revoke, set aside, void

vacation *n.* **1.** break, fiesta, furlough, hiatus, holiday, intermission, leave, liberty, long weekend, March break, R and R, recess, recreation, recuperation, respite, rest, rest and relaxation, sabbatical, spell, time off **2.** drive, excursion, expedition, jaunt, journey, tour, trip, visit – *v.* **1.** cottage, drive, explore, holiday, journey, sightsee, tour, travel, visit **2.** recover, recuperate, relax, rest

vaccinate *v.* immunize, inoculate, prevent, protect, treat

vacillate *v.* alternate, dither, equivocate, fluctuate, hedge, hesitate, oscillate, sway, swing, tergiversate, totter, waffle, waver *Nonformal:* flip-flop, hem and haw, fence-sit, pussyfoot, seesaw, shilly-shally *Antonyms:* decide, determine

vacillation *n.* **1.** fluctuation, oscillation, rocking, rolling, swaying, swinging, undulation, vibration, wavering, wobbling *Antonyms:* stability, steadiness **2.** ambivalence, caprice, erraticism, fickleness, hesitation, indecision, indecisiveness, irresolution, variability, whimsy *Antonyms:* resolve, steadfastness, stubbornness

vacuity *n.* **1.** barrenness, emptiness, meaninglessness, nothingness, sparsity, vacancy, vacuum, void **2.** boredom, ease, ennui, idleness, laxity, monotony, rest, tedium **3.** asininity, dullness, empty-headedness, idiocy, inanity, fatuity, foolishness, silliness, stupidity, vapidity *Antonyms:* seriousness, sobriety

vacuous *adj.* **1.** austere, bare, blank, clear, drained, emptied, empty, hollow, minimal, shallow, stark, vacant, void *Antonyms:* crammed, crowded, full, **2.** dumb, empty-headed, foolish, inane, irrational, silly, superficial, unintelligent, unreasonable *Nonformal:* birdbrain, half-baked, lamebrain *Antonyms:* rational, reasonable, sensible

vacuum *n.* black hole, emptiness, exhaustion, free space, gap, nothing, nothingness, rarefaction, space, vacuity, void – *v.* clean, mop up *(Nonformal)*, suck, sweep, syphon, tidy

vagabond *adj.* aimless, bohemian, drifting, footloose, gadabout, gypsy, homeless, itinerant, journeying, migratory, moving, nomadic, peripatetic, roaming, rootless, roving, runaway, transient, travelling, unsettled, uprooted, wandering, wayfaring, wayward *Antonyms:* established, fixed, rooted, stationary – *n.* bohemian, *flâneur (French)*, migrant worker, minstrel, nomad, peddler, pilgrim, roamer, rover, sundowner, vagrant, wanderer *Antonyms:* agoraphobic, homebody, shut-in

vagary *n.* brain wave, caprice, eccentricity, fancy, humour, idea, notion, quirk, temper, whim, whimsy

vagrant *adj.* destitute, homeless, roving, wandering, wayfaring *Nonformal:* of no fixed address, on the streets – *n.* bohemian, bum *(Nonformal)*, drifter, hobo, homeless *or* street person, roamer, squeegee kid, tramp, transient, vagabond, wanderer

vague *adj.* **1.** equivocal, generalized, ill-defined, imprecise, indeterminate, indirect, indistinct, inexact, nonspecific *Antonyms:* direct, explicit, marked, precise, specific **2.** faraway, garbled, inaudible, low, muffled, mumbled, unclear, unintelligible, weak, whispered *Antonyms:* articulate, clear, distinct, enunciated **3.** amorphous, blurred, cloudy, dim, hazy, indistinct, murky, nebulous, shadowy *Antonyms:* illuminated, recognizable, vivid **4.** ambiguous, borderline, curious, difficult, dubious, elusive, enigmatic, obscure, obtuse, puzzling, questionable *Antonyms:* backed, secured, sound, valid, well-grounded

vain *adj.* **1.** abortive, barren, delusive, empty, frivolous, fruitless, futile, hollow, idle, insignificant, misleading, paltry, petty, pointless, profitless, senseless, slight, sterile, time-wasting, trifling, trivial, unavailing, unimportant, unproductive, unprofitable, unsuccessful, useless, valueless, void, worthless *Antonyms:* fruitful, profitable, useful, worthwhile **2.** arrogant, cocksure, cocky, conceited, egocentric, haughty, high-flown, high-and-mighty *(Nonformal)*, impertinent, inflated, officious, pompous, prejudiced, proud, self-important, self-centred, snobbish, stuck-up, superior, ungenerous, uppity, vainglorious *Antonyms:* bashful, humble, meek, modest, self-deprecating **3.** affected, egotistical, grandiloquent, ostentatious, pretentious, showy

valedictory *adj.* departing, ending, farewell, final, goodbye, last, parting *Antonyms:* initial, introductory – *n.* address, diatribe, graduation speech, lecture, oration, summation, talk

valet *n.* butler, chauffeur, concierge, dresser, driver, flunky *(Nonformal)*, groom, personal servant, servant, steward, *valet de chambre (French)*

valetudinarian *adj.* bed-ridden, crippled, debilitated, decrepit, enfeebled, feeble, frail, ill, infirm, paralyzed, prostrate, sick, sickly, supine, unhealthy, unwell – *n.* convalescent, invalid, patient, shut-in

valiant *adj.* **1.** adventurous, assertive, audacious, bodacious *(Nonformal)*, bold, brave, courageous, daring, dauntless, fearless, game, gutsy, high-minded, intrepid, manly, plucky, polite, powerful, reckless, *skookum (Pacific Coast)*, spirited, strong, unafraid, undaunted *Antonyms:* fearful, shrinking, spineless, timid, weak **2.** chivalrous, courtly, gallant, heroic, honourable, knightly, lofty, magnanimous, noble-minded, quixotic, true, valorous *Antonyms:* dastardly, depraved, villainous

valid *adj.* **1.** acceptable, cogent, compelling, convincing, efficacious, grounded, just, persuasive, potent, powerful, rational, reasonable, solid, sound, strong, substantial, thought-out, weighty, well-founded *Antonyms:* deceptive, specious **2.** accurate, authentic, authoritative, bona fide, genuine, irrefutable, original, pure, real, unadulterated, uncorrupted *Antonyms:* fake, false, substituted **3.** binding, confirmed, current, effective, good, in force, lawful, legal, legally binding, legit *(Nonformal)*, legitimate, official, warranted *Antonyms:* expired, invalid, unlawful **4.** applied, correlated, derived, determinative, logical, proven, telling, tested *Antonyms:* tangential, unproven, vectoring

validate *v.* **1.** approve, ascertain, attest, authenticate, authorize, bear out, certify, circumstantiate, confirm, corroborate, document, empower, enable, endorse, justify, legalize, legitimize, license, permit, prove, ratify, sanction, substantiate, verify *Antonyms:* disprove, refute **2.** check, mark, notarize, stamp, warrant

validity *n.* authority, cogency, effectiveness, efficacy, force, foundation, genuineness, gravity, grounds, lawfulness, legality, legitimacy, point, potency, power, punch, right, soundness, strength, substance, validness, weight

valley *n.* basin, bottom, canyon, channel, coulee, dale, dell, depression, droke *(Newfoundland)*, flume, glen, gorge, hollow, intervale, lowland, notch, nullah, plain, ravine, trough, vale

valour *n.* boldness, brashness, bravado, bravery, courage, daring, dauntlessness, élan, fearlessness, gallantry, gumption, heroism, intrepidness, mettle, pluck, prowess, recklessness, spirit, steadfastness, strength, valiance, verve *Nonformal:* backbone, bodaciousness, chutzpah, guts, moxie *Antonyms:* cowardice, cravenness, timidity

valuable *adj.* **1.** admired, appreciated, cherished, dear, esteemed, important, precious, respected, treasured, welcome, worthwhile, worthy *Antonyms:* superfluous, worthless **2.** advantageous, aiding, assisting, beneficial, effective, handy, helpful, relevant, serviceable, significant, usable, useful *Antonyms:* petty, trivial, useless **3.** collectible, costly, expensive, high-priced, hot, in demand, inestimable, invaluable, priceless, prized, profitable, scarce *Nonformal:* pricey, steep, stiff *Antonyms:* cheap, inexpensive – *n.* antique, asset, benefit, collectible, commodity, gem, heirloom, nugget, plum, possession, prize, treasure *Antonyms:* trifle, triviality

value *n.* **1.** advantage, benefit, desirability, good, importance, merit, quality, serviceableness, use, utility *Antonyms:* uselessness, worthlessness **2.** account, market price *or* value, price, retail, selling price, stumpage *(Forestry)*, worth *Nonformal:* bottom line, ticket **3.** bargain, deal, sale item *Nonformal:* knockdown, steal **4.** calibre, distinction, eminence, esteem, regard, reputation, repute, respect, stature *Antonyms:* disregard, disrepute, disrespect **5.** denotation, force, implication, import, meaning, purpose, sense, significance *Antonyms:* foolishness, gibberish, meaninglessness **6.** grade, magnitude, number, quantity, rank – *v.* **1.** admire, cherish, enjoy, esteem, relish, respect, revere, treasure *Antonyms:* despise, loathe, scorn **2.** appraise, assess, calculate, determine, evaluate, mark down, price, set

valued *adj.* **1.** admired, adored, cherished, eminent, esteemed, highly regarded, idolized, loved, popular, prized, preeminent, prominent, relished, respected, revered, treasured, venerated, well-respected, worshiped *Antonyms:* abhorred, despised, hated **2.** functional, many-sided, specific, specified, tooled, useful

values *n. pl.* beliefs, creed, credo, doctrines, dogma, ethics, guides, ideals, ideologies, moral precepts, morals, mores, norms, principles, standards, tenets, theories, traditions, virtues

valve *n.* cork, faucet, flap, gate, hydrant, lid, pipe, plug, spigot, stopcock, stopper, tap

vampire *n.* bat, blood-sucker, *chupacabra (Mexican)*, creature, Dracula, fiend, ghoul, leech, monster, Nosferatu, pain in the neck *(Nonformal)*, revenant, undead

vandal *n.* barbarian, despoiler, destroyer, hoodlum, hooligan, looter, pillager, pirate, plunderer, raider, ravager, ruffian

vandalize *v.* damage, deface, demolish, despoil, destroy, mar, mark, pillage, rape, ravage, ruin, savage *Antonyms:* fix, paint, repair, service

vanguard *n.* advance guard, avant-garde, beginning, cutting edge, forefront, foremost, forerunner, herald, leader, pioneer, precursor, scout, trailblazer, trendsetter, van, vaunt-courier *Antonyms:* conservative, laggard

vanilla *adj.* bland, boring, dull, normal, ordinary, plain, plain-vanilla, regular, safe, simple, unadventurous, unexciting, uninteresting, usual, vapid *Antonyms:* different, extraordinary, wonderful – *n.* extract, flavouring, substance

vanish *v.* **1.** dematerialize, depart, die out, disappear, dissipate, dissolve, evanesce, evaporate, exit, fade, fade *or* go *or* melt away, leave, melt, vacate, vaporize, withdraw *Nonformal:* clear out, hightail it, scram, split, vamoose *Antonyms:* appear, arrive, materialize

vanity *n.* **1.** affectation, arrogance, bluster, boasting, braggadocio, bragging, bravado, complacency, conceit, egocentrism, egoism, excess, gall, gloating, haughtiness, hubris, narcissism, pride, rodomontade, self worship, smugness, swagger, vainglory *Antonyms:* humility, self-abasement, self-doubt **2.** display, fanfaronade, glitter, hype *(Nonformal)*, immodesty, ostentation, pageantry, pretension, show **3.** emptiness, fruitlessness, insubstantialness, unsubstantiality, uselessness, vacuity, worthlessness **4.** compact, cosmetic bag *or* case, dressing *or* make up table

vanquish *v.* beat, best, confute, conquer, crush, defeat, destroy, devastate, foil, master, overcome, overpower, overthrow, overturn, overwhelm, put down, quell, rout, smash, subdue, subjugate, suppress, surmount, thwart, trample, triumph over, trounce, whip *Antonyms:* give in, surrender, yield

vapid *adj.* banal, bland, boring, dull, empty, flaccid, flat, heartless, insipid, jejune, lifeless, limp, maudlin, plain-vanilla, sentimental, soft, spiritless, weak, wishy-washy *Nonformal:* gutless, soppy *Antonyms:* mordant, trenchant, vigorous

vaporize *v.* aerate, boil, disintegrate, dissipate, distill, evanesce, evaporate, gasify, steam *Antonyms:* freeze, solidify

vapour *n.* breath, cloud, condensation, dampness, dew, effluvium, exhalation, fog, fume, gas, haze, miasma, mist, moisture, smog, smoke, steam

variable *adj.* **1.** adjustable, alterable, changeable, convertible, metamorphic, modifiable, mutable, permutable, protean, transformable, transmutable, variform *Antonyms:* immutable, set, solid **2.** capricious, fickle, fluctuating, inconsistent, inconstant, mercurial, undependable, unreliable, unstable, unsteady, wavering *Antonyms:* constant, fixed, steadfast, steady **3.** different, irregular, nonuniform, odd, unusual *Antonyms:* normal, regular – *n.* condition, factor, issue, quantity, subject, symbol

variance *n.* **1.** departure, difference, discrepancy, disparity, diversity, heterogeneity, incongruity *Antonyms:* likeness, similitude, uniformity **2.** altercation, conflict, contention, controversy, debate, disagreement, discord, discordance, dispute, dissension, dissent, inconsonance, schism, strife *Antonyms:* accord, consonance, harmony

variant *adj.* **1.** another, alternate, changing, differing, discrepant, divergent *Antonyms:* equivalent, same, similar **2.** capricious, ever-changing, fickle, inconsistent, manic, mercurial, moody, reckless, shifting, unreliable – *n.* alternate, alternative, branch, copy, derivative, exception, imitation, irregularity, knock-off *(Nonformal)*, modification, offprint, spinoff, substitute, variation, version

variation *n.* **1.** alteration, change, conversion, diversity, metamorphosis, modification, modulation, mutation, permutation, switch *(Nonformal)*, transformation, transmogrification, transposition **2.** change of pace *(Nonformal)*, departure, deviation, difference, reversal, revolution, transition

varied *adj.* assorted, dissimilar, diverse, diversified, heterogeneous, incongruous, jumbled, manifold, miscellaneous, mixed, motley, patchwork, ragtag *Antonyms:* consistent, homogenous, uniform

variegated *adj.* blotched, brindled, calico, colourful, dappled, marble, mottled, multicoloured, multi-hued, plaid, polychromatic, rainbow, spectral, spotted, stippled, streaked, tabby, varicoloured, veined *Antonyms:* black, monochromatic, white

variety *n.* **1.** brand, breed, category, character, class, classification, description, family, gender, genus, grade, kind, make, nature, order, quality, race, rank, sex, sort, species, strain, stripe, type **2.** assortment, collection, conglomeration, diversity, gallimaufry, hash, hodge-podge, medley, mélange, miscellany, mixed bag, mixture, multifariousness, multiplicity, selection, stew *Antonyms:* homogeneity, singularity, uniformity

various *adj.* **1.** assorted, countless, legion, many, multiple, myriad, numerous, several, sundry *Antonyms:* lone, one, solitary **2.** different, disparate, dissimilar, diverse, heterogeneous, manifold, miscellaneous, motley, multifarious, unlike *Antonyms:* alike, similar

varnish *n.* coating, covering, enamel, finish, glaze, gum, lacquer, linseed, oil, paint, polish, preserver, resin, sealer, shellac, urethane, wax – *v.* colour, cover, finish, glaze, gloss, oil, paint, polish, preserve, seal, shine, smooth, waterproof, wax *Antonyms:* remove, strip

vary *v.* **1.** adjust, alter, alternate, calibrate, change, convert, differentiate, diversify, metamorphose, modify, modulate, mutate, refit, reform, remould, reshape, transform, transmogrify, transmute, tweak **2.** change course, depart, deviate, differ, digress, diverge, separate, shift, swerve, veer

vase *n.* amphora, bottle, carafe, chinoiserie, container, jug, pitcher, pottery, receptacle, urn, vessel

vassal *n.* bondman, *daimyo (Japanese)*, dependent, homager, landholder, liegeman, peon, retainer, serf, servant, sharecropper, slave, tenant, thrall, varlet *Antonyms:* lord, seigneur

vast *adj.* **1.** ample, astronomical, broad, capacious, colossal, enormous, full-scale, galactic, giant, gigantic, great, huge, immense, intergalactic, interplanetary, massive, monstrous, monumental, planetary, spacious, super, titanic, tremendous, universal, whopping *(Nonformal) Antonyms:* small, small-scale, tiny **2.** all-inclusive, comprehensive, detailed, extensive, prodigious, voluminous **3.** boundless, endless, eternal, far-reaching, immeasurable, infinite, measureless, sweeping, unbounded, unlimited, widespread

vat *n.* barrel, basin, bucket, cask, cauldron, container, firkin, hogshead, holder, keg, pot, receptacle, tank, tub, vessel

vatic *adj.* augural, Delphic, divinatory, fatidic, fortunetelling, mantic, mediumistic, occult, oracular, prophetic, psychic, sibylline, surrealistic, vaticinal

vault *n.* **1.** burial chamber, crypt, grave, mausoleum, sarcophagus, sepulchre, tomb **2.** basement, bomb *or* fall-out shelter, cavity, cellar, chamber, cavern, crib, dungeon, storm *or* wine cellar **3.** bank, box, cash *or* safety deposit box, chest, coffer, depository, repository, safe, strongroom – *v.* bound, clear, hurdle, jump, leap, mount, soar over, spring, surmount

vaunt *v.* aggrandize, bluster, boast, brag, celebrate, crow, exaggerate, flaunt, parade, trumpet *(Nonformal) Antonyms:* deprecate, depreciate, disparage

vaunted *adj.* **1.** celebrated, fabled, famous, flaunted, glorious, highly praised, infamous, lauded, legendary, notorious, praised, renowned, touted *Antonyms:* hidden, latent, unknown **2.** aggrandized, bombastic, exaggerated, inflated, overblown, swollen, turgid

veer *v.* angle off, avert, bear, bend, change course, curve, deflect, deviate, digress, dip, diverge, divert, drift, pivot, shift, skew, skid, spin, swerve, swing, swivel, tack, turn, twist, wheel, whip, whirl

vegetable *n.* **1.** green groceries, legume, produce, veggie *(Nonformal)*, verdure *Groupings of vegetables:* greens, legumes, tubers, root *Common vegetables:* alfalfa sprout, artichoke, arugula, asparagus, aubergine, bamboo shoot, bean, bean sprout, beet, bok choy, broccoli, cabbage, cactus, cardoon, carrot, cassava, cauliflower, celeriac, celery, chard, chayote, chicory, collard greens, corn, courgette, cress, cucumber, daikon, dandelion greens, eggplant, endive, escarole, fiddlehead, kale, kohlrabi, leek, lettuce, manioc, mushroom, mustard greens, okra, onion, oyster plant, parsnip, pea, pepper, potato, pumpkin, radicchio, radish, rhubarb, rutabaga, seaweed, sorrel, spinach, squash, taro root, turnip, water chestnut, watercress, yam, zucchini **2.** lazybones, slacker, walking dead, zombie *Nonformal:* blob, bum, couch-potato

vegetarian *adj.* meatless, organic, vegetable, veggie *(Nonformal)* – *n.* fruitarian, herbivore, phytophagan, vegan, vegetist *Antonyms:* carnivore, meat-eater

vegetate *v.* **1.** bloom, develop, germinate, grow, spread, sprout **2.** exist, hibernate, idle, languish, loaf, lounge around, relax, rest, stagnate *Nonformal:* hang out, veg, zone out *Antonyms:* act, move, perform

vehement *adj.* **1.** ardent, blazing, burning, earnest, energetic, enthusiastic, fervent, feverish, fiery, heated, impassioned, impetuous, interested, keen, passionate, spirited, zealous *Antonyms:* bored, dispassionate, stagnant, tired **2.** acrimonious, angry, bilious, bitter, choleric, forceful, furious, hot-blooded, ill-tempered, irascible, raging, savage, steaming, stormy, turbulent, violent, volcanic *Antonyms:* cool, placid, unemotional, unflappable

vehicle *n.* **1.** carrier, contrivance, conveyance, machine, motor vehicle, transit, transportation *Kinds of vehicle:* aircraft, airplane, all-terrain *or* ATV, automobile, berline, bicycle, boat, buggy, bus, cab, calèche, canoe, car, cariole, chariot, cube van, ferry, freighter, go-cart, helicopter, hovercraft, jeep, jet, kayak, limousine, motorcycle, Red River cart, ship, Sky-Train *(BC)*, sled, sleigh, snowmobile, snowplough, sport utility *or* SUV, stoneboat, streetcar, subway, taxi, tractor, transport, truck, van, wagon, watercraft *Trademark:* Caterpillar, Jet Ski, Sea-Doo, Ski-Doo, Zamboni **2.** agency, agent, channel, conduit, excipient, implement, instrument, means, mechanism, medium, ministry, organ, tool, way

veil *n.* **1.** *chador (Muslim)*, kerchief, *mantilla (Spanish)*, *purdah (Iranian)*, scarf, *yashmak (Turkish)* **2.** cloak, cover, curtain, hanging drapery, mantle, shield, shroud **3.** artifice, deception, disguise, façade, pretext, ruse, smoke screen, subterfuge, trickery, veneer – *v.* camouflage, cloak, conceal, cover, disguise, hide, mask, muffle, obscure, protect, screen, shield, shroud *Antonyms:* display, expose, highlight, manifest, reveal

vein *n.* **1.** blood vessel, capillary, conduit, conveyance, duct, nervure, tube, venule **2.** bed, cavity, cleft, deposit, filling, fissure, lode, mine, seam, stratum **3.** attitude, bent, characteristic, countenance, demeanour, disposition, faculty, fashion, hint, humour, inclination, manner, mind, mode, mood, note, spirit, strain, style, suggestion, temper, temperament, tendency, tenor, tinge, tone, way **4.** channel, course, crevice, stream, tunnel, watercourse **5.** furrow, line, marbling, streak, string, stripe, thread

velocity *n.* acceleration, celerity, dispatch, expedition, fleetness, gait, haste, headway, hustle, impetus, kph, momentum, mph, pace, quickness, rapidity, rapidness, rate of speed *or* rpm, speed, swiftness, tempo

velvety *adj.* cottony, deep, downy, fleecy, furry, luxurious, plush, satiny, silky, smooth, soft, sumptuous, thick, velveteen *Antonyms:* abrasive, coarse, rough, sandpapery

venal *adj.* avaricious, bribable, corrupt, corruptible, dishonourable, grasping, greedy, mercenary, rapacious, shady, unprincipled, unscrupulous *Nonformal:* bad, bent, crooked *Antonyms:* honest, straight forward, uncorruptible, upright *Commonly misused:* **venial**

vend *v.* auction, barter, deal, hawk, market, offer, peddle, pitch, retail, sell, trade, transfer *Nonformal:* push, unload

vendetta *n.* blood feud, campaign, conflict, crusade, feud, jihad, quarrel, rivalry, war, warfare

vendor *n.* dealer, hawker, huckster, merchant, monger, peddler, pitchman, pusher, salesman, salesperson, saleswomen, seller, trader

veneer *n.* **1.** cladding, coating, cover, covering, exterior, façade, face, facing, finish, front, gloss, lamina, lacquer, sheath, shellac, surface, urethane **2.** appearance, disguise, guise, mask, pretense, show, window dressing – *v.* coat, cover, finish, lacquer, laminate, paint, urethane, varnish

venerable *adj.* **1.** august, beatified, eminent, esteemed, hallowed, honoured, illustrious, respected, revered, sacred, worshiped *Antonyms:* derided, despised, disrespected, mocked **2.** aged, ancient, antique, experienced, grey, hoary, old, sagacious, white-haired, wise *Antonyms:* adolescent, callow, green, immature, youthful

venerate *v.* admire, adore, apotheosize, celebrate, cherish, deify, esteem, exalt, extol, favour, glorify, hallow, honour, idolize, praise, regard, respect, revere, treasure, value, vaunt, worship *Antonyms:* condemn, despise, ridicule, scorn

vengeance *n.* avengement, counterblow, punishment, *quid pro quo (Latin)*, reprisal, requital, retaliation, retribution, *revanche (French)*, revenge, settlement, vindication, wrath *Antonyms:* amnesty, exoneration, forgiveness, pardon, remission

vengeful *adj.* hateful, heartless, hostile, implacable, merciless, on the warpath *(Nonformal)*, punitive, rancorous, relentless, retaliatory, revengeful, spiteful, unforgiving, villainous, vindictive, wrathful *Antonyms:* benevolent, clement, forgiving

venial *adj.* excusable, forgivable, trifling, minor, pardonable *Commonly misused:* **venal**

venom *n.* **1.** bane, neurotoxin, poison, snake poison, toxin, virus **2.** acrimony, animosity, bile, bitterness, hatred, dislike, enmity, hate, hatred, ill-will, malevolence, malice, malignity, rancour, spite, spleen, vindictiveness *Antonyms:* benevolence, compassion, mercy

venomous *adj.* **1.** baneful, deadly, fatal, harmful, lethal, noxious, poisonous, toxic, virulent **2.** astringent, biting, caustic, destructive, hurtful, hurting, injurious, malicious, noxious, savage, spiteful, vicious, viperish, vitriolic *Antonyms:* affectionate, benevolent, compassionate, kind

vent *n.* air *or* hole passage, aperture, avenue, blow hole, chimney, drain, duct, escape, exhaust, exit, flue, opening, orifice, outlet, pipe, porthole, release, split, spout, ventilation, window – *v.* **1.** blow *or* let out, discharge, eject, emit, erupt, explode, extrude, release, spit, spray, vomit **2.** air, announce, declaim, divulge, express, proclaim, say, state, utter, verbalize, voice

ventilate *v.* aerate, air condition *or* air out, circulate, deodorize, freshen, open up, refresh, winnow

venture *n.* **1.** adventure, enterprise, expedition, initiative, mission, operation, opportunity, trek, undertaking **2.** arbitrage, gamble, hazard, long shot, plunge, risk, speculation – *v.* **1.** bet, dare, expose, gamble, hazard, jeopardize, plunge, risk, stake, wager *Nonformal:* lay it on the line, shoot the works **2.** advance, express, hypothesize, put forward, speculate, suggest, tender

venturesome *adj.* **1.** adventurous, aggressive, audacious, bold, brave, courageous, daring, enterprising, fearless, foolhardy, foolish, game, heroic, intrepid, plucky, pushy, rash, reckless, spirited, stout, sturdy, undaunted, valiant, valorous, venturous *Antonyms:* shy, timid **2.** chancy, dangerous, difficult, hazardous, insecure, perilous, precarious, risky, shaky, slippery, uncertain, unsafe *Antonyms:* safe, secure, sound

venue *n.* amphitheatre, arena, building, club, coliseum, Colosseum, forum, gardens, locale, location, place, site, stadium, theatre

veracious *adj.* **1.** credible, dependable, ethical, faithful, frank, genuine, high-principled, honest, just, reliable, straightforward, true blue, trustworthy, truthful, veridical *Antonyms:* lying, mendacious **2.** accurate, direct, factual, realistic, right, strict, true, valid *Antonyms:* false, incredible

veracity *n.* **1.** candour, credibility, fairness, fidelity, frankness, genuineness, honesty, honour, impartiality, integrity, morality, openness, rightness, sincerity, straightforwardness, truthfulness, uprightness, *Antonyms:* dishonesty, fraudulence, hypocrisy **2.** accuracy, actuality, authenticity, correctness, exactitude, exactness, precision, realism, reality, rectitude, validity **3.** certainty, fact, fundamental, law, rule, truth, verity

veranda *n.* balcony, deck, gallery, lanai, patio, porch, stoop, sun parlour *or* porch

verbal *adj.* **1.** articulated, dialectic, expressed, lexical, linguistic, mouthed, mumbled, muttered, oral, rhetorical, said, spoken, stated, told, unwritten, uttered, vocal, word-of-mouth *Antonyms:* bookish, written **2.** accurate, close, exact, faithful, letter-for-letter, literal, precise, reliable, verbatim *Antonyms:* inaccurate, suspect

verbatim *adv.* accurately, closely, directly, exactly, faithfully, literally, precisely, reliably, word for word *Antonyms:* approximated, paraphrased

verbiage *n.* circumlocution, expansiveness, floridness, long-windedness, loquacity, periphrasis, prolixity, redundancy, repetition, tautology, verbosity, wordiness *Antonyms:* curtness, pithiness, succinctness, terseness

verbose *adj.* babbling, blathering, bombastic, circuitous, circumlocutory, diffuse, discursive, flatulent, fustian, garrulous, grandiloquent, involved, long-winded, loquacious, magniloquent, overblown, periphrastic, purple, prolix, redundant, repeating, repetitious, repetitive, rhetorical, swollen, talkative, tautological, tedious, tortuous, turgid, wandering, wordy *Nonformal:* gabby, motor-mouth, windy *Antonyms:* compact, concise, terse

verdant *adj.* **1.** blooming, flourishing, fresh, grassy, green, leafy, lush **2.** artless, callow, guileless, naive, plain, simple, unsophisticated *Antonyms:* learned, suave, sophisticated

verdict *n.* adjudication, answer, conclusion, decision, deduction, determination, edict, finding, judgment, opinion, ruling, sentence

verdure *n.* flora, foliage, grass, grasslands, greenery, herbage, meadow, pasture, vegetation

verge *n.* border, borderline, boundary, brim, brink, edge, extreme, extremity, fringe, hem, limit, lip, margin, outskirts, pole, rim, selvage, skirt, terminus, threshold *Antonyms:* centre, core, middle

verification *n.* agreement, assurance, authentication, certification, confirmation, corroboration, endorsement, evidence, guarantee, proof, substantiation, surety, testimony, validation

verify *v.* add *or* hold *or* size up, attest, authenticate, certify, check, check out *or* up, confirm, corroborate, demonstrate, document, double-check, establish, find out, justify, prove, settle, substantiate, support, test, try, validate *Antonyms:* debunk, discount, discredit, dispute, invalidate, nullify

verisimilitude *n.* actuality, authenticity, credibility, genuineness, likelihood, likeliness, literalness, naturalism, plausibility, probability, realism, similarity, truth, verism

veritable *adj.* accurate, actual, authentic, bona fide, factual, genuine, indubitable, legitimate, real, true, true to life, undoubted, unquestionable, without a doubt *Nonformal:* for real, true blue

verity *n.* **1.** actuality, authenticity, factuality, genuineness, plausibility, realism, reality, soundness, validity, veracity, veridicality, verism, verismo, verité, verisimilitude *Antonyms:* fallacy, falsehood, lie **2.** certainty, certitude, dogma, fact, law, principle, rule, tenet, truism, truth

vermin *n. pl.* **1.** cockroaches, fleas, lice, maggots, mice, parasites, rats, worms **2.** dregs, hoi polloi, lumpen proletariat, rabble, the masses, trash *Nonformal:* cattle, sheep, swine **3.** brute, dog, lowlife, reprobate, rotter, scalawag, scum, scumbag *(Nonformal)*, sleeveen *(Newfoundland)*, vulgarian

vernacular *adj.* colloquial, common, demotic, domesticated, everyday, familiar, idiomatic, indigenous, informal, inherent, local, native, natural, nonformal, ordinary, popular, slang, vulgar *Antonyms:* affected, bombastic, forced – *n.* argot, cant, dialect, idiom, jargon, jive talk *(Nonformal)*, language, lingo, mother tongue, parlance, patois, patter, phraseology, slang, speech, street talk, tongue

versatile *adj.* **1.** adaptable, adjustable, handy, many-sided, multifaceted, multipurpose, multi-tasking, useful, variable *Antonyms:* one-dimensional, rigid **2.** able, clever, deft, flexible, quick on one's feet *(Nonformal)*, resourceful, skilful, skilled, talented **3.** changeable, inconstant, mutable, protean, unstable, unsteady

verse *n.* ballad, composition, epigram, free verse, haiku, lyric, metre, poem, poetry, prose, prosody, rhyme, rhythm, song, sonnet, stanza, *vers libre (French) See also:* **poem**

versed *adj.* abreast, accomplished, acquainted, *au courant (French)*, briefed, competent, conversant, deft, enlightened, experienced, familiar, informed, knowledgeable, learned, literate, practised, professional, proficient, qualified, seasoned, skilful, skilled, sophisticated, trained, veteran, well-informed, well-read, well-trained *Nonformal:* in the know, up to speed *Antonyms:* callow, inexperienced, new, raw, unacquainted

version *n.* **1.** account, adaptation, arrangement, chronicle, depiction, description, enactment, interpretation, number, portrayal, production, rendering, rendition, report, rewording, story, translation, variation **2.** copy, edition, form, pressing, printing, reproduction, type, update, variant

versus *prep.* against, confronting, facing, opposing, v., vs.

vertex *n.* acme, apex, apogee, cap, crest, crown, culmination, head, peak, pinnacle, point, spire, summit, tip, top, zenith *Antonyms:* base, bottom, nadir, perigee

vertical *adj.* cocked, erect, heightwise, lengthwise, perpendicular, plumb, sheer, steep, straight, upright, upward *Antonyms:* flat, horizontal, widthwise

verve *n.* ardour, brio, élan, energy, enthusiasm, esprit, exuberance, feeling, fervour, force, gusto, life, passion, pluck, spice, spirit, swagger, vigour, vim, vivacity *Nonformal:* chutzpah, moxie, pizzazz *Antonyms:* apathy, indifference, languor, lassitude

very *adj.* **1.** actual, authentic, bona fide, correct, exact, genuine, identical, perfect, precise, real, right, selfsame, true, veritable **2.** absolute, complete, express, sheer, total, utter – *adv.* **1.** astonishingly, awfully, exceedingly, exceptionally, excessively, extraordinarily, extremely, incredibly, particularly, prodigiously, profoundly, remarkably, surprisingly, terribly, uncommonly, unusually, wonderfully **2.** absolutely, acutely, certainly, considerably, dearly, decidedly, deeply, eminently, emphatically, extensively, largely, notably, really, substantially, truly, vastly

vessel *n.* **1.** amphora, barrel, basin, beaker, bottle, box, bowl, bucket, can, canister, carafe, carboy, cask, cauldron, chalice, container, cup, decanter, dish, firkin, flagon, flask, glass, goblet, jar, jug, keg, kettle, ladle, mickey, mug, pail, pitcher, plate, pot, receptacle, stein, tank, tankard, test tube, tub, tumbler, urn, utensil, vase, vat, vial **2.** barge, boat, caravel, clipper, corsair, craft, destroyer, frigate, icebreaker, liner, saltie *(Nonformal)*, schooner, ship, steamer, submarine, tall ship, tanker, tug *See also:* **boat**, **ship**

vested *adj.* **1.** complete, constant, decided, earned out, established, fixed, held, permanent, set, stable, steady *Antonyms:* ephemeral, passing **2.** attired, clothed, draped, dressed, fully-dressed, garbed, kitted out *(Nonformal)*, outfitted, robed

vestibule *n.* antechamber, anteroom, doorway, entrance, entrance hall, entry, entryway, foyer, gateway, hall, hallway, lobby, lounge, mud room, parlour, passage, porch, portal, portico, room

vestige *n.* evidence, glimmer, hint, indication, print, relic, remainder, remains, remnant, residue, scrap, shadow, sign, suspicion, token, trace, track

vestment *n.* alb, apparel, article, attire, chasuble, clothes, clothing, covering, drapery, dress, finery, frock, garment, gown, outfit, raiment, robe, tunicle, vesture, wear

veteran *adj.* able, adept, adroit, battle-scarred, deft, disciplined, exercised, experienced, expert, hardened, initiated, inured, knowledgeable, longtime, mature, old, old-hand, old-time, practiced, prepared, proficient, seasoned, senior, skilled, sophisticated, strengthened, toughened, trained, versed, weathered, wise – *n.* authority, expert, guide, master, maven, old soldier, sensei, specialist *Nonformal:* old warhorse, vet *Antonyms:* apprentice, beginner, freshman

veterinarian *n.* animal doctor, vet *(Nonformal)*, veterinary, veterinary surgeon

veto *n.* ban, blackball, check, disapproval, embargo, prohibition, refusal, rejection *Antonyms:* approval, endorsement – *v.* ban, blackball, decline, defeat, deny, disallow, disapprove, forbid, interdict, kill, negate, pass, prohibit, put down, quell, refuse, reject, rule out, throw out, turn down *Antonyms:* approve, endorse, pass, ratify

vex *v.* abrade, afflict, agitate, anger, annoy, bother, chafe, displease, disturb, exasperate, excite, gall, harass, hassle *(Nonformal)*, hector, incense, infuriate, irk, irritate, madden, nettle, peeve, persecute, perturb, pester, pique, plague, prod, provoke, rankle, rattle, rile, ruffle, shake, taunt, tease, torment, trouble, upset *Antonyms:* calm, mollify, pacify, subside

vexatious *adj.* aggravating, annoying, bothersome, damnable, disconcerting, disquieting, distressing, disturbing, enraging, exacerbating, harassing, infuriating, irksome, irritating, maddening, nagging, perturbing, rankling, troublesome, troubling, upsetting *Nonformal:* damn, darn, infernal, pesky *Antonyms:* calming, palliative, relaxing, soothing

viable *adj.* applicable, capable, doable, feasible, manageable, negotiable, operable, performable, possible, practicable, practical, reasonable, serviceable, usable, workable *Antonyms:* hopeless, impossible, unthinkable, unworkable

viaduct *n.* bridge, crossing, flyover *(British)*, overpass, railway, road, roadway, span, trestle, way

vial *n.* beaker, bottle, carafe, container, decanter, flask, phial, receptacle, test tube, tube, vessel

vibrant *adj.* **1.** bright, brilliant, colourful, dynamic, electrifying, resonant, rich, sparkling, striking, vivid *Antonyms:* drab, dull **2.** alive, animated, brisk, cheerful, chipper *(Nonformal)*, effervescent, energetic, enthusiastic, lively, peppy, pulsing, spirited, throbbing, vivacious *Antonyms:* lifeless, serious, sombre, staid, torpid

vibrate *v.* beat, echo, fluctuate, flutter, oscillate, pulsate, pulse, quake, quaver, quiver, reel, resonate, resound, reverberate, ripple, shake, shiver, sway, swing, teeter, throb, tremble, tremor, undulate, wave, waver, wobble

vibration *n.* **1.** excitation, fluctuation, frisson, oscillation, quake, quiver, quivering, shake, shaking, shimmy, sway, swinging, trembling, tremor, undulation, vacillation, wavering **2.** beating, noise burst, palpitation, pulsation, pulse, resonance, reverberation, throb **3.** atmosphere, feeling, juju, sensation, vibe

vicar *n.* **1.** churchman, churchwoman, clergyman, clergywoman, cleric, deacon, ecclesiastic, incumbent, minister, padre *(Nonformal)*, parson, pastor, priest, rector, reverend **2.** agent, deputy, representative, substitute, vicegerent

vicarious *adj.* **1.** commissioned, delegated, deputed, substituted, substitutional, surrogate *Antonyms:* direct, first-hand, original, primary **2.** empathetic, eventual, imagined, indirect, pretended, secondary, second-hand, sympathetic

vice *n.* **1.** bad habit, carnality, corruption, debasement, debauchery, degeneracy, degradation, error, evil, evildoing, ill, immorality, indecency, lapse, maleficence, misdeed, offence, perversion, sin, transgression, trespass, violation, wickedness, wrong *Antonyms:* honour, morality, virtue **2.** blemish, defect, demerit, failing, fault, flaw, foible, frailty, imperfection, mar, mark, scar, shortcoming, taint, weakness, weak point

viceroy *n.* authority, deputy, governor, Governor General, intendant, leader, lieutenant-governor, manager, nabob, official, *pasha (Turkish)*, proconsul, representative, ruler, vicegerent, vice-regent, vicereine, vizier

vicinity *n.* **1.** area, *arrondissement (French)*, environment, environs, hood *(Nonformal)*, neighbourhood, precinct, quarter, region, scene, section, setting, surroundings, vicinage **2.** adjacency, closeness, close quarters, nearness, propinquity, proximity *Antonyms:* distance, remoteness

vicious *adj.* **1.** atrocious, bad, bitchy *(Nonformal)*, cruel, cutting, defamatory, evil, foul, hateful, heinous, hellish, horrid, hurtful, indecent, malevolent, malicious, mean, nasty, slanderous, spiteful, venomous, vile, wicked **2.** barbarous, beastly, bloodthirsty, brutal, dangerous, deadly, ferocious, fiendish, fierce, frightful, furious, iniquitous, monstrous, murderous, nefarious, refractory, savage, sinful, unpredictable, vehement, violent *Antonyms:* docile, friendly, gentle, kind, tame **3.** abandoned, abhorrent, base, contaminated, corrupt, debased, debauched, degenerate, degraded, demoralized, depraved, immoral, infamous, lewd, licentious, miserable, perverse, rough, ruthless, sinful, unprincipled, villainous, vindictive **4.** extreme, grim, hard, harsh, heavy, intense, relentless, severe, sudden, terrible, unrelenting *Antonyms:* light, moderate

vicissitude *n.* **1.** alteration, change, fluctuation, inconstancy, instability, mutation, rotation, shift, torn, ups and downs, vacillation, variation, wheel of fortune *Antonyms:* constancy, continuation **2.** adversity, affliction, difficulties, hardship, misfortune, suffering

victim *n.* **1.** body, corpse, dead *or* injured person, injured, stiff *(Nonformal)*, sufferer **2.** hunted, prey, quarry **3.** martyr, offering, sacrifice, sacrificial lamb, scapegoat *Nonformal:* easy mark, fall guy, patsy

victimize *v.* cheat, clip, deceive, defraud, dupe, exploit, fool, hoax, hoodwink, immolate, persecute, pick *or* prey on, set up, sucker, swindle, trick, use *Nonformal:* bamboozle, con, fleece, rope in, scam, screw, snow, stick, stiff, sting

victor *adj.* dominant, victorious, winning – *n.* champion, conquering hero, conqueror, gold medallist, hero, king, last one left, master, medallist, prizewinner, subjugator, survivor, title holder, vanquisher, white knight *(Nonformal)*, winner *Antonyms:* failure, fall guy, loser, scapegoat, victim

Victorian *adj.* **1.** moral, prim, priggish, prissy, prudish, puritanical, stern, stiff, strait-laced, strict, stuffy, tight-laced, uptight *(Nonformal)* **2.** conservative, conventional, courtly, decorous, formal, genteel, mannered, old-fashioned, old-world, traditional

victorious *adj.* blue-ribbon, champion, conquering, masterful, prize-winning, successful, triumphant, vanquishing, winning *Antonyms:* beaten, conquered, defeated, overcome, vanquished

victory *n.* accomplishment, achievement, ascendancy, conquest, control, dominion, gain, laurels, mastery, overthrow, prize, subjugation, success, superiority, supremacy, sweep, triumph, upper hand, win, winning *Nonformal:* bull's-eye, clean sweep, grand slam, smash, killing, pay dirt, slam, the bacon *or* gold *Antonyms:* defeat, failure, loss

victuals *n. pl.* consumables, eatables, edibles, fare, food, groceries, nourishment, nutriment, provisions, rations, refreshments, sustenance *Nonformal:* eats, grub, tuck, vittles

video *n.* cassette, DVD, film, movie, recording, rental *(Nonformal)*, tape, video cassette, videodisc, videotape *Trademark:* Betamax, VHS – *v.* document, film, record, tape, videotape

vie *v.* buck, challenge, compete, contend, contest, counter, endeavour, fight, go for *or* up against, match, oppose, pit, play, play off, push, rival, scramble for, strive, struggle, sweat

view *n.* **1.** analysis, audit, check, contemplation, examination, inspection, look-see *(Nonformal)*, observation, review, scan, scrutiny, study, survey **2.** landscape, outlook, panorama, prospect, scene, seascape, sight, tableau, vision, vista **3.** attitude, belief, conception, conviction, credo, creed, deed, doctrine, dogma, principle, tenet **4.** determination, estimation, judgment, opinion, perspective, premise, standpoint, supposition, theory, understanding **5.** aim, design, end, intention, objective, purpose – *v.* **1.** behold, check out *or* over, discern, distinguish, espy, examine, explore, eye, glance over, notice, observe, perceive, regard, rubberneck *(Nonformal)*, scan, scope, scrutinize, see, spot, spy, squint, stare, survey, take in, watch, witness **2.** believe, consider, interpret, opine, read

viewer *n.* **1.** audience member, moviegoer, observer, spectator, voyeur, watcher *Nonformal:* couch-potato, sidewalk superintendent **2.** bystander, eye-witness, on-looker, passerby, witness *Nonformal:* peeping Tom, railbird, rubbernecker

viewpoint *n.* angle, aspect, attitude, direction, estimation, outlook, perspective, posture, prospect, sentiment, side, slant, stand, standpoint, thinking, twist, vantage, view

vigil *n.* candlelight service, commemoration, demonstration, mourning, observance, occasion, prayer session, remembrance, wake, watch

vigilance *n.* attention, care, carefulness, caution, circumspection, diligence, discretion, foresight, forethought, guardedness, lookout, observance, precaution, preventative *or* safety measure, provision, prudence, regard, surveillance, wariness, watch, watchfulness *Antonyms:* disregard, heedlessness, neglect

vigilant *adj.* alert, attentive, avid, careful, cautious, chary, circumspect, eagle-eyed, heedful, keen, observant, prepared, prudent, ready, wary, watchful, wide-awake *Antonyms:* careless, heedless, inattentive, lax, spaced out *(Nonformal)*

vigilante *n.* death squad, lynch mob, posse, punisher

vignette *n.* **1.** account, anecdote, cameo, depiction, description, episode, essay, portrayal, profile, short, sketch **2.** design, drawing, engraving, etching, frontispiece, headshot, mugshot, illustration, photograph, picture, portrait, print

vigorous *adj.* active, athletic, bouncing, brisk, dashing, driving, dynamic, ebullient, energetic, enterprising, exuberant, flourishing, forceful, forcible, hale, hard-driving, hardy, healthy, hearty, intense, lively, lusty, masterful, peppy, persuasive, potent, powerful, red-blooded, robust, rugged, snappy, sound, spirited, strenuous, sturdy, vital *Nonformal:* loaded for bear, take-charge *Antonyms:* apathetic, frail, inactive, lethargic, torpid

vigour *n.* ability, activity, agility, alertness, ardour, capability, capacity, dash, determination, drive, dynamism, eagerness, ebullience, élan, endurance, energy, enterprise, enthusiasm, fire, force, hardiness, intensity, liveliness, might, pith, potency, power, push, soundness, strength, urgency, vehemence, verve, vim, virility, vitality *Nonformal:* bounce, chutzpah, kick, moxie, pep, piss and vinegar, punch, starch, steam, zing *Antonyms:* apathy, feebleness, impotence, lethargy, sluggishness

vile *adj.* **1.** abject, bad, base, blasphemous, coarse, contemptible, corrupt, debased, degenerate, depraved, disgraceful, evil, fiendish, ignoble, ignominious, immoral, impure, iniquitous, low, nefarious, obscene, shameful, sinful, sordid, villainous, vulgar, wicked *Antonyms:* angelic, benevolent, saintly **2.** appalling, despicable, disagreeable, disgusting, filthy, foul, fulsome, horrid, loathsome, mean, miserable, nasty, nauseating, noxious, offensive, repellent, repugnant, repulsive, revolting, shameless, shocking, sickening, stinking, ugly, unpleasant, vicious, wretched *Antonyms:* agreeable, delicate, genteel, lovely, marvellous

vilify *v.* abuse, attack, berate, blister, calumniate, castigate, censure, criticize, damn, debase, decry, defame, degrade, denigrate, denounce, disparage, fulminate, fume, inveigh, libel, malign, mistreat, objurgate, rail *or* rant against, revile, slander, slur, upbraid *Nonformal:* badmouth, burn, dis, knock, pan, smear, tongue-lash *Antonyms:* commend, exalt, glorify, revere, venerate

villa *n.* bungalow, chalet, *château (French)*, cottage, *dacha (Russian)*, estate, farmhouse, hacienda, home, house, lodge, manor, mansion, ranch, residence, resort, retreat, summer cottage *or* house

village *n.* borough, burg, community, crossroads, hamlet, neighbourhood, outport *(Newfoundland)*, post, settlement, *shtetl (Yiddish)*, town, ville, whistle-stop *(Nonformal)*

villain *n.* **1.** antagonist, assassin, bad guy, blackguard, bully, brute, cad, criminal, cur, dastard, devil, evildoer, evil person, felon, fiend, knave, malefactor, miscreant, monster, murderer, offender, outlaw, rascal, reprobate, rogue, scoundrel, scumbag *(Nonformal)*, sleeveen *(Newfoundland)*, snake, thug, viper, wretch *Antonyms:* hero, heroine, protagonist **2.** Benedict Arnold *(U.S.)*, betrayer, informer, Judas, quisling, renegade, snake in the grass *(Nonformal)*, traitor, turncoat

villainous *adj.* abominable, atrocious, bad, backstabbing, corrupt, criminal, crooked, cruel, dastardly, degenerate, demonic, depraved, devilish, diabolical, dishonourable, dissolute, double-crossing, double-dealing, evil, felonious, fiendish, foul, hateful, heinous, hellish, horrible, ignominious, immoral, infamous, iniquitous, mean, malevolent, monstrous, nefarious, notorious, odious, opprobrious, profligate, reprehensible, satanic, sinful, spiteful, traitorous, treacherous, unpleasant, unprincipled, unscrupulous, vile, wicked *Antonyms:* heroic, moral, upstanding

vindicate *v.* **1.** absolve, acquit, bear out, clear, confirm, corroborate, establish, exculpate, exonerate, justify, prove, substantiate, support, uphold *Antonyms:* accuse, blame, condemn **2.** advocate, assert, champion, claim, contend, defend, guard, maintain, plead for, protect, rationalize, second,

vindictive *adj.* avenging, cruel, grim, hurtful, malicious, malignant, merciless, rancorous, resentful, retaliatory, revengeful, ruthless, spiteful, unforgiving, unrelenting, vengeful, venomous *Antonyms:* forgiving, generous, magnanimous, merciful, relenting

vine *n.* clematis, climber, creeper, grapevine, ivy, kudzu, liana, peduncle, petiole, root, stalk, stem, tendril, twine

vintage *adj.* best, choice, classic, excellent, mature, old, prime, rare, select, superior, venerable *Antonyms:* fresh, new, ripe – *n.* collection, crop, epoch, era, generation, grapes, harvest, origin, wine, year, yield

vineyard *n.* farm, grapery, orchard, plantation, vinery, vintager, winery

violate *v.* **1.** breach, break, contravene, defy, disobey, disregard, disrupt, encroach, err, gate-crash *(Nonformal)*, infract, infringe, meddle, misbehave, offend, oppose, outrage, resist, sin, transgress, trespass *Antonyms:* honour, obey, respect **2.** abuse, assault, blaspheme, contaminate, debauch, defile, desecrate, dishonour, force, invade, molest, pillage, plunder, pollute, profane, rape, ravage, ravish, ruin, spoil, swarm *(Nonformal)*, vandalize *Antonyms:* defend, protect, revere

violation *n.* **1.** breach, break, contravention, defacement, desecration, destruction, dishonour, encroachment, infringement, invasion, mistreatment, illegality, offence, rupture, swarming *(Nonformal)*, trespass, vandalism **2.** abuse, assault, attack, brutalization, damage, injury, molestation, mugging, outrage, rape, ravishment, sexual assault **3.** blasphemy, fall, sin, transgression, wrong, wrongdoing **4.** *faux pas (French)*, infraction, misbehaviour, misdemeanour, misstep, slip, solecism

violence *n.* **1.** abuse, aggression, brutality, cruelty, damage, desecration, destruction, devastation, harm, injury, molestation, outrage, profanation, rage, rape, violation **2.** brannigan, donnybrook, dustup *(Nonformal)*, fighting, fisticuffs, free-for-all, mêlée, rampage, riot **3.** anger, barbarity, ferocity, force, frenzy, fury, harshness, hysteria, intensity, madness, rage, roughness, savagery, severity, vehemence

violent *adj.* **1.** barbaric, brutal, cruel, forceful, harmful, hurtful, physical, rough, savage **2.** angry, berserk, crazy, dangerous, deranged, enraged, explosive, fierce, fiery, frantic, frenetic, frenzied, furious, homicidal, impassioned, impetuous, killing, maniacal, murderous, out of control, over the edge, psychopathic, raging, seething, unrestrained, vehement, vicious, volcanic, wild *Nonformal:* ballistic, rabid, medieval **3.** catastrophic, desperate, destructive, devastating, disastrous, extreme, harsh, intense, potent, powerful, ruinous, severe, stormy, strong, tumultuous, turbulent *Antonyms:* calm, gentle, halcyon, mild, peaceful, serene **4.** bloody, disturbing, gruesome, horrible, painful, sadistic, shocking, terrible, upsetting

virgin *adj.* **1.** celibate, chaste, immaculate, maidenly, vestal, virginal, virtuous **2.** callow, green, inexperienced, innocent, naive, protected, sheltered, uninitiated **3.** clean, fresh, intact, natural, new, original, pristine, pure, spotless, tractless, uncorrupted, undefiled, undisturbed, unexplored, unspoiled, unsullied, untouched, untried, untrodden, wilderness

virile *adj.* brave, driving, energetic, forceful, fertile, generative, intrepid, lusty, macho, male, manly, masculine, potent, reproductive, robust, sound, strong, sturdy, vigorous, vital *Nonformal:* he-man, red-blooded *Antonyms:* impotent, sterile

virtual *adj.* **1.** artificial, ersatz, fake, feigned, imaginary, non-existent, perceived, phoney *(Nonformal)*, simulated, substitute, synthetic *Antonyms:* actual, genuine, real **2.** effective, fundamental, near, practical, total

virtually *adv.* almost, around, basically, clearly, effectively, effectually, essentially, fundamentally, implicitly, in effect *or* essence *or* substance, just about, nearly, not quite, practically, very nearly

virtue *n.* **1.** charity, faithfulness, fortitude, generosity, high-mindedness, honour, incorruptibility, integrity, morality, probity, prudence, rectitude, respectability, righteousness, uprightness, worthiness *Antonyms:* corruption, debauchery, depravity, dishonesty, immorality **2.** advantage, asset, benefit, boon, consideration, credit, feature, hope, ideal, merit, practice, quality, trait, value, worth **3.** abstinence, chastity, innocence, purity, virginity

virtuosity *n.* ability, artistry, brilliance, chop *(Nonformal)*, craftsmanship, deftness, éclat, excellence, expertise, facility, finesse, genius, mastery, musicianship, polish, preeminence, prowess, skilfulness, skill, talent, wizardry

virtuoso *n.* ace, adept, champ, champion, expert, genius, maestro, magician, master, pro, prodigy, professional, specialist, star, talent, wizard *Nonformal:* black belt, crackerjack, maven, shark, whiz

virtuous *adj.* aboveboard, beneficent, blameless, celibate, chaste, clean-living, commendable, decent, effective, ethical, excellent, exemplary, fair, faithful, good, guiltless, high-principled, honest, honourable, immaculate, incorruptible, innocent, just, laudable, moral, noble, praiseworthy, pure, righteous, saintly, salt of the earth *(Nonformal)*, scrupulous, unspoiled, unsullied, untarnished, upright, wholesome, worthy *Antonyms:* corrupt, debauched, depraved, fallen, sinful, wicked

virulent *adj.* **1.** acerbic, acrimonious, aggressive, antagonistic, bitter, caustic, cutting, hateful, hostile, malevolent, malicious, mordant, petulant, rancorous, resentful, scathing, sharp, sour, spiteful, splenetic, stabbing, surly, unfriendly, vicious, vindictive, vitriolic *Antonyms:* amiable, compassionate, kind **2.** baneful, cancerous, deadly, deleterious, destructive, fatal, harmful, hurtful, infectious, infective, injurious, lethal, malignant, noxious, pernicious, poison, poisonous, septic, toxic, venomous *Antonyms:* benign, harmless, innocuous

virus *n.* **1.** aerobe, anaerobe, bacillus, bacteria, bacterium, bug *(Nonformal)*, coccus, germ, microbe, microorganism, retrovirus, streptococcus **2.** cold, condition, contagion, contamination, disease, epidemic, flu, grip, grippe, illness, infection, influenza, intruder, syndrome, taint

visage *n.* appearance, aspect, brow, cast, composure, countenance, demeanor, face, features, look, mien, physiognomy *Nonformal:* clock, mug, kisser, pan, phiz, puss

visceral *adj.* automatic, emotional, instinctive, intuitive, spontaneous, subconscious, surrealistic, unconscious *Nonformal:* gut, knee-jerk

viscous *adj.* adhesive, clammy, clotted, gelatinous, gluey, glutinous, gooey, gummy, lumpy, mucilaginous, ropy, slimy, sticky, stiff, syrupy, tenacious, thick, tough, viscid *Antonyms:* thin, runny, watery

visible *adj.* **1.** apparent, bold, clear, detectable, discernible, discoverable, distinguishable, evident, inescapable, in sight *or* view, manifest, marked, noticeable, obtrusive, obvious, ocular, out in the open, palpable, patent, perceivable, perceptible, plain, pointed, revealed, salient, seeable, seen, signal, viewable, visual *Antonyms:* concealed, cryptic, hidden, imperceptible, obscured **2.** arresting, big as life *(Nonformal)*, bizarre, conspicuous, distinct, flagrant, outlandish, outstanding, prominent, pronounced, show-stopping, striking, unmistakable

vision *n.* **1.** eyes, eyesight, optics, perceiving, perception, seeing, sight, view **2.** clairvoyance, conception, discernment, expectation, foresight, insight, intuition, perspicacity, sagacity, second sight, wisdom **3.** apparition, banshee, bibe *(Newfoundland)*, chimera, delusion, dream, ecstasy, fantasy, ghost, hallucination, illusion, mirage, nightmare, oracle, phantasm, phantom, phenomenon, presence, prophecy, revelation, spectre, trance, wraith *Nonformal:* mind trip, pipe dream, trip **4.** angel, dazzler, eyeful *Nonformal:* dreamboat, stunner

visionary *adj.* **1.** delusory, dreamy, fanciful, fantastic, idealistic, illusory, imaginary, imaginative, impractical, insensible, irrational, ivory-towered, romantic, quixotic, starry-eyed, unfeasible, unrealistic, utopian *Antonyms:* down-to-earth, pragmatic, sensible **2.** clairvoyant, Delphic, foreshadowing, oracular, prophetic, sibylline, surrealistic, vatic, vaticinal – *n.* Cassandra, daydreamer, Don Quixote, dreamer, enthusiast, futurist, idealist, mystic, oracle, prophet, romantic, seer, utopian, zealot *Antonyms:* pragmatist, realist

visit *n.* **1.** appointment, call, conversation, coze, evening, exchange, gabfest *(Nonformal)*, gossip, holiday, interview, meeting, personal *or* social call, sojourn, stay, stop, stopover, talk, time, vacation, visitation, weekend **2.** check, examination, inspection, perusal, review, scrutiny, search – *v.* **1.** call on, chat, converse, drop by *or* in *or* over, dwell, frequent, inspect, leave one's card, play, see, sojourn, stay at *or* with, stop in, take in, talk, tour, travel to *Nonformal:* crash, cruise, hit **2.** afflict, assail, attack, befall, harrow, inflict, overtake, punish, scourge, sic, smite, torture

visitation *n.* **1.** call, meeting, social exercise, sojourn, stay, stop, stopover, vacation **2.** check, examination, inspection, perusal, review, scrutiny, search **3.** event, happening, episode, incident, occasion, occurrence **4.** bane, blight, calamity, catastrophe, disaster, famine, plague, trial, tribulation **5.** appearance, haunting, manifestation, materialization, presence, spooking *(Nonformal)*

visitor *n.* alien, caller, company, foreigner, gate-crasher, guest, habitué, invader, invitee, out-of-towner, patron, tourist, transient, traveller, trespasser

vista *n.* cityscape, cloudscape, landscape, lookout, outlook, panorama, perspective, prospect, scape, scene, scenery, seascape, sight, sweep, view

visual *adj.* discernible, graphic, imaged, manifest, observable, observed, obvious, optical, perceptible, seeable, seen, sight, viewed, visible *Antonyms:* hidden, imperceptible, invisible, obscured, screened – *n.* chart, display, film, graph, graphics, map, model, overhead, picture, slide, tool, visual aid

visualize *v.* anticipate, apprehend, conceive, conjure up, create, depict, envision, fancy, feature, foresee, imagine, map out, picture, see, view

vital *adj.* **1.** basic, cardinal, central, core, critical, crucial, decisive, essential, fundamental, imperative, important, indispensable, integral, key, necessary, needed, prerequisite, required, requisite, significant, urgent *Nonformal:* heavy, meat and potatoes, nitty-gritty *Antonyms:* ancillary, dispensable, sideline, trifling, unnecessary **2.**

alive, animate, animated, breathing, generative, life-giving, live, living, quickening *Antonyms:* dead, dying, flatlining *(Nonformal)*, inanimate, moribund **3.** dynamic, energetic, enthusiastic, forceful, lively, lusty, red-blooded, spirited, strenuous, vibrant, vigorous, virile, vivacious, *Antonyms:* apathetic, listless, uninvolved **4.** dangerous, fatal, grave, life *or* death, serious

vitality *n.* animation, ardour, audacity, bang, being, bloom, bounce, brio, drive, endurance, élan, energy, existence, exuberance, fervour, force, intensity, life, liveliness, power, pulse, punch, robustness, snap, sparkle, spirit, spunk, stamina, starch, steam, strength, stuff, verve, vigour, vim, vivacity, zest *Antonyms:* apathy, inertia, lethargy, sluggishness, weakness

vitamin *n.* **1.** organic nutrient *Kinds of vitamin: Fat-soluble:* A (retonol), D (ergocaliciferol), E (tocopheral), K (philloqione, hytonadoine), K2 (menaquinone), K3 (menadione); *Water-soluble:* B (thiamine), B2 (roboflavin), B3 (niacin), B6 (pyridoxine, pyridoximine), B12 (cyanocobalamin), biotin, C (ascorbic acid, calcium ascorbate), sodium ascorbatefolic acid, pontothenic acid **2.** capsule, lozenge, medication, medicine, pastille, pill, supplement, tablet, troche

vitiate *v.* **1.** abolish, annul, cancel, delete, deny, invalidate, negate, nullify, quash, recant, revoke, scuttle, spoil, undermine, undo *Antonyms:* advocate, prove, support **2.** besmirch, blemish, blight, contaminate, corrupt, debase, defile, deprave, harm, hurt, impair, mar, muddy, pervert, poison, pollute, stain, stigmatize, sully, taint, tarnish, violate *Antonyms:* cleanse, purify, sterilize

vitriolic *adj.* acerbic, acid, acrid, acrimonious, astringent, barbed, biting, bitter, burning, caustic, cutting, harsh, hateful, hostile, hurtful, invidious, malicious, mordant, offensive, pointed, scathing, severe, slashing, spiteful, trenchant, venomous, vicious *Antonyms:* amiable, congenial, friendly

vituperate *v.* abuse, accuse, asperse, badmouth, belittle, berate, blame, calumniate, castigate, censure, condemn, contemn, criticize, curse, damn, denounce, disparage, execrate, growl, inculpate, injure, insult, lambaste, lash, malign, objurgate, rail, rebuke, reprimand, reproach, revile, scold, scorn, smear, tear into, traduce, upbraid, vilify *Prince Edward Island:* card, clapperclaw, read *Nonformal:* burn, dis, rip into, run down, tongue-lash *Antonyms:* applaud, compliment, encourage

vivacious *adj.* active, alert, animate, animated, blithe, bouncy, brash, breezy, bubbling, buoyant, cheerful, ebullient, effervescent, exuberant, flirtatious, frolicsome, gay, high-spirited, jaunty, keen, lively, playful, scintillating, sparkling, spirited, sprightly, swinging, upbeat, vibrant, vital, zesty *Antonyms:* dull, languid, listless, melancholy, spiritless

vivid *adj.* **1.** bright, brilliant, colourful, dazzling, dynamic, fresh, intense, radiant, resplendent, rich, sharp, shining, striking *Antonyms:* colourless, drab, dull, ordinary, pale **2.** dramatic, eloquent, emotional, expressive, imaginative, memorable, powerful, stirring, strong, theatrical **3.** clear, definite, distinct, graphic, lifelike, picturesque, real, realistic, telling, visible **4.** active, animated, energetic, lively, spirited, vigorous, vivacious *Antonyms:* lazy, lethargic

vocabulary *n.* argot, classification, dialect, dictionary, glossary, jargon, language, lexicon, lexis, lingo, nomenclature, palaver, phraseology, terminology, vernacular, words, word stock

vocal *adj.* **1.** articulated, expressed, oral, pronounced, said, spoken, uttered, verbalized, voiced *Antonyms:* mute, silent **2.** insistent, loud, loud-mouthed, noisy, obnoxious, raucous, strident, vehement, vociferous

vocalist *n.* bard, busker, canary, cantor, caroler, chantress, chanteuse, crooner, diva, hymner, melodist, minstrel, nightingale, opera *or* pop singer, performer, prima donna, scatter *(Jazz)*, singer, songbird, stylist, troubadour *Antonyms:* instrumentalist, mime

vocalize *v.* chant, chirp, communicate, convey, croon, enunciate, express, groan, holler, impart, moan, orate, pronounce, say, screech, scream, shout, sing, sound, speak, talk, utter, vent, verbalize, voice, warble, whisper, yell, yodel *Nonformal:* belt *or* give out, crank up, let flow

vocation *n.* art, business, calling, career, craft, duty, employment, field, forte, game, handicraft, job, lifework, line, livelihood, living, métier, mission, occupation, office, post, profession, pursuit, role, specialty, trade, undertaking, work *Nonformal:* bag, racket, thing

vociferous *adj.* boisterous, clamorous, deafening, distracting, in your face *(Nonformal)*, insistent, loud, loud-mouthed, noisy, obnoxious, obstreperous, ranting, shouting, shrill, stentorian, strident, uproarious, vehement, vocal *Antonyms:* hushed, muted, noiseless, quiet, silent

vogue *n.* chic, craze, currency, custom, *dernier cri (French)*, fad, fashion, fashionableness, favour, popularity, practice, prevalence, rage, style, stylishness, trend, usage, use, way *Nonformal:* last word, latest thing – *v.* model, mug *(Nonformal)*, pose, posture, sashay, strut

voice *n.* **1.** articulation, call, cry, delivery, exclamation, expression, inflection, intonation, language, modulation, sound, speech, timbre, tone, tongue, utterance, vent, vocalization **2.** approval, choice, decision, expression, opinion, option, part, participation, preference, representation, say, say-so *(Nonformal)*, suffrage, vent, view, vote, *vox populi (Latin)*, will, wish **3.** agent, ambassador, champion, congressman, council, lawyer, mouthpiece, M.L.A., M.P., M.P.P., ombudsperson, proxy, representative, speaker, stand-in – *v.* **1.** air, announce, articulate, assert, communicate, cry, declare, discharge, disclose, divulge, enunciate, express, issue, let out, make known, narrate, orate, proclaim, pronounce, release, say, shout, speak, state, talk, tell, unleash, utter, vent, ventilate, verbalize, vocalize, yell *Antonyms:* suppress, stifle **2.** advertise, broadcast, circulate, disseminate, hype *(Nonformal)*, make public, publicize, spread

voiceless *adj.* **1.** close-mouthed, inarticulate, mum, mute, quiet, silent, speechless, taciturn, tongue-tied, wordless *Antonyms:* chatty, loquacious, verbose **2.** alienated, censored, disenfranchised, marginalized, oppressed, silenced

void *adj.* **1.** abnegated, annulled, cancelled, checked, curbed, ineffectual, invalid, negated, nugatory, null, nullified, stopped, useless, voided, worthless *Antonyms:* consequential, useful **2.** bare, barren, bereft, deprived, devoid, drained, emptied, empty, fruitless, hollow, lacking, meaningless, scant, short, shy, unfilled, vacuous *Antonyms:* filled, occupied, replete **3.** abandoned, destitute, tenantless, uninhabited, unoccupied, vacant – *n.* black hole, blankness, cavity, emptiness, gap, hole, hollow, lack, nothingness, nullity, opening, space, starkness, vacuity, vacuum – *v.* **1.** abnegate, abrogate, annul, cancel, check, curb, dissolve, invalidate, negate, nullify, quash, rescind, rub, sanitize, snip, squash, squelch, stop, veto *Nonformal:* nix, rub out, shoot down, torpedo **2.** clear, defecate, deplete, discharge, dispose, drain, eject, eliminate, emit, empty, evacuate, expunge, flow, let go, pour, purge, release, relieve oneself, remove, urinate, vacate *Nonformal:* crap, dump, pee, poo, piss

volatile *adj.* **1.** capricious, changeable, erratic, fickle, impulsive, inconsistent, inconstant, mercurial, moody, protean, temperamental, undependable, unpredictable, unsettled, unstable, unsteady, variable, whimsical *Antonyms:* fixed, set, solid **2.** ephemeral, evanescent, fleeting, impermanent, momentary, passing, short-lived, transient, transitory *Antonyms:* classic, timeless **3.** charged, controversial, dangerous, eruptive, explosive, hot, loaded, tense, unpredictable, wired *(Nonformal)*

volcanic *adj.* ardent, bursting, combustible, detonating, explosive, eruptive, fiery, fulminating, hot-headed, hot-tempered, impassioned, inflamed, steaming, violent *Antonyms:* calm, collected

volition *n.* accord, choice, choosing, desire, determination, decision, discretion, election, free will, option, preference, purpose, resolution, selection, will, willingness, will power, wish *Antonyms:* coercion, compulsion, determinism

volley *n.* assault, barrage, broadside, burst, cannonade, deluge, discharge, enfilade, exchange, fire, fusillade, return, sally, salvo, shelling, shower

voluble *adj.* bombastic, chatty, discursive, effusive, flatulent, fluent, garrulous, glib, long-winded, loquacious, talkative, verbose, vocal *Nonformal:* gabby, motormouthed *Antonyms:* curt, laconic, quiet, reticent, silent

volume *n.* **1.** anthology, book, collection, copy, edition, opus, piece, publication, tome, work **2.** amplification, degree, intensity, loudness, power, sonority, strength **3.** aggregate, amount, body, bulk, capacity, content, cubic content, dimensions, extent, kental *(Newfoundland)*, mass, measure, measurement, number, object, quantity, size, space, total *Volume measurements:* barrel, bushel, centilitre, cord, cubic foot *or* metre *or* yard, cup, decalitre, decastere, decilitre, dry pint *or* quart, fifth, finger, fluid dram *or* ounce, gallon, gill, hectolitre, hogshead, jeroboam, jigger, kilolitre, liquid pint *or* quart, litre, magnum, millilitre, minim, peck, pint, pony, quart, stumpage, tablespoon, teaspoon

voluminous *adj.* **1.** abundant, ample, big, broad, capacious, cavernous, colossal, commodious, enormous, expansive, extensive, gigantic, great, huge, immense, large, massive, monster *(Nonformal)*, monstrous, numerous, roomy, spacious, tremendous, vast, wide, widespread *Antonyms:* insufficient, scanty, skimpy, slight, tiny **2.** billowing, bountiful, copious, flowing, full, inexhaustible, loose, overflowing, plenteous, productive, profuse, prolific

voluntarily *adv.* agreeably, by choice *or* preference, cheerfully, compliantly, deliberately, freely, gladly, happily, intentionally, optionally, preferentially, spontaneously, willingly, with pleasure *Antonyms:* reluctantly, unwillingly

voluntary *adj.* autonomous, chosen, deliberate, elected, free, gratuitous, independent, intended, intentional, spontaneous, unasked, unbidden, unconstrained, unsolicited, volitional, volunteer, willing *Antonyms:* coerced, conscripted, forced

volunteer *adj.* by choice, optional, self-determined, unforced, unprompted – *v.* advance, bring, come forward, enlist, enroll, initiate, offer, offer one's services, present, proffer, propose, put *or* step forward, sign up, suggest

voluptuous *adj.* **1.** alluring, enticing, epicurean, erotic, exciting, hedonistic, luscious, luxurious, provocative, rapturous, seductive, sensual, sensuous, sexual, sexy **2.** attractive, beautiful, curvaceous, full, handsome, lovely, shapely, striking, stunning, well-shaped *Nonformal:* buff, busty, pumped, stacked

vomit *v.* beulah *(P.E.I.)*, bring *or* throw up, disgorge, eject, emit, expel, gag, heave, nauseate, regurgitate, retch, spew *Nonformal:* barf, hurl, puke, ralph, ride the porcelain bus, toss one's cookies, upchuck, yak

voracious *adj.* avid, barracuda *(Nonformal)*, covetous, desirous, desperate, devouring, esurient, gluttonous, grasping, greedy, hungry, immoderate, insatiable, prodigious, rabid, rapacious, ravenous, starved, starving, uncontrollable, unquenchable *Antonyms:* moderate, temperate

vortex *n.* black hole, Charybdis, cyclone, dust devil, eddy, hypermass, maelstrom, spiral, tornado, twister, typhoon, whirlwind, whirlpool

vote *n.* **1.** ballot, choice, say, tally, ticket **2.** election, franchise, majority, plebiscite, poll, referendum, selection – *v.* cast a ballot, choose, declare, determine, effect, elect, exercise the franchise, judge, opt, pronounce, propose, select

vouch *v.* affirm, answer for, assert, asseverate, assure, attest to, avert, avow, back, certify, confirm, contend, corroborate, declare, get behind, guarantee, maintain, predicate, profess, prove, put forth, recommend, say so, sign for, sponsor, substantiate, support, swear to, testify, uphold, verify, vow, warrant, witness *Nonformal:* go to bat for, rubber-stamp *Antonyms:* deny, pass, reject

voucher *n.* **1.** acknowledgment, bill, bill of sale, bond, chit, guarantee, note, paper, proof, receipt, slip, stub, ticket, token, warranty **2.** backer, guarantor, insurer, supporter, underwriter, vouchee, witness

vow *n.* affiance, affirmation, agreement, assertion, assurance, avowal, betrothal, bond, contract, engagement, oath, pledge, profession, promise, solemnity, testimony, troth, word – *v.* affirm, assure, consecrate, covenant, declare, dedicate, devote, pledge, profess, promise, swear, testify, vouch, warrant

voyage *n.* circumnavigation, course, crossing, cruise, day-trip, enterprise, excursion, expedition, holiday, jaunt, journey, odyssey, passage, peregrination, project, road-trip, safari, swing, tour, travel, travels, trek, trip, vacation, wanderings – *v.* circumnavigate, cross, cruise, explore, fly, globe-trot, jet, journey, ramble, roam, sail, sightsee, tour, travel, wander

voyageur *n.* adventurer, boatsman, explorer, fur trader, Hudson's Bay person, trader, trapper, woodsman *Historical:* coureur de bois, *mangeur de lard (French)*, porkeater

voyeur *n.* peeping Tom, pervert, viewer, watcher *Nonformal:* freak, perv, sicko, weirdo

vulgar *adj.* **1.** barbarous, base, blatant, boorish, brassy, cheap, coarse, common, crass, crude, discourteous, disgusting, filthy, flashy, garish, gaudy, graceless, gross, ignorant, ill-bred, ill-mannered, impolite, improper, indelicate, inelegant, lewd, loud-mouthed, loutish, low, lowbred, obnoxious, obscene, odious, offensive, profane, raunchy, raw, rough, rude, saucy, scatological, shameless, slatternly, slovenly, smutty, tacky, tasteless, tawdry, uncivil, uncouth uncultured, unmannerly, unrefined *Antonyms:* civil, refined **2.** colloquial, conversational, demotic, everyday, familiar, general, native, ordinary, plastic, plebeian, popular, patois, public, vernacular, vulgate *Antonyms:* academic, aristocratic, high-flown, pompous

vulgarity *n.* **1.** barbarity, boorishness, coarseness, crassness, crudeness, ignorance, impropriety, indecency, inelegance, lewdness, obnoxiousness, offensiveness, ribaldry, roughness, rudeness, sauciness, shamelessness, sordidness, tawdriness *Antonyms:* decency, grace, propriety **2.** curse, cuss *(Nonformal)*, dirt, dirty word, expletive, filth, obscenity, profanity, smut, swearword, vulgarism

vulnerable *adj.* **1.** accessible, assailable, attackable, declawed, defenceless, exposed, helpless, impotent, invadable, liable, naked, penetrable, powerless, pregnable, susceptible, uncovered, unguarded, unprotected, unsafe, unshielded, weak *Nonformal:* sitting duck, wide open *Antonyms:* guarded, immune, impervious, invulnerable **2.** innocent, naive, sensitive, tender, thin-skinned *Antonyms:* thick-skinned, tough

vulture *n.* **1.** buzzard, condor, lammergeier, scavenger **2.** extortionist, harpy, opportunist, predator, profiteer, rack-renter, shark

wacky *adj.* bizarre, crazy, curious, daft *(British)*, eccentric, erratic, flighty, irrational, ludicrous, nutty, odd, offbeat, outlandish, peculiar, silly, strange, unpredictable, unusual, weird, wild, wing-nut *Nonformal:* daffy, kooky, loony, out there, screwball, screwy, way out, whacked, wonky *Antonyms:* conventional, formulaic, ordinary, staid, typical

wad *n.* **1.** bale, bundle, chunk, clump, hunk, lump, mound **2.** abundance, bounty, bulk, cartload, hoard, mass, oodles, plug, profusion, scads, stockpile, store, tons **3.** bankroll, cash, money, spending money, stash *Nonformal:* cash, coin, loot, moolah – *v.* crumple, fold, pack, plug, press, roll, stuff

wadding *n.* batting, bung, carded cotton, cotton batten *or* batting, filling, filler, plug, stopper, stuffing, tampon

waddle *v.* bob, bumble, duck-walk, lumber, lunge, paddle, stagger, sway, swing, toddle, totter, waggle, wiggle, wobble *Antonyms:* march, prance, sashay, strut

wade *v.* **1.** cross, ford, move, navigate, negotiate, pass, traverse, walk **2.** bathe, dip, paddle, splash, swim, wallow **3.** drudge, hammer *or* toil away, labour, muck *or* plough through, plod, pour over, slog, study, toil, trudge *Antonyms:* breeze *or* flip through, glide over, scan, skim

wafer *n.* biscuit, chip, cookie, cracker, crisp *(British)*, disc, Eucharist, host, saltine, slice

waffle *n.* blather, drivel, gibberish, hot air *(Nonformal)*, palaver, prattle, talk, verbiage, verbosity – *v.* **1.** dodge, duck, evade, equivocate, hedge, hesitate, hover, parry, prevaricate, pussyfoot, quibble, shuffle, sidestep, straddle the fence, vacillate, waver *Nonformal:* deke, dipsy-doodle, fence-sit, hem and haw *Antonyms:* decide, determine **2.** blather, chatter, jabber, natter, prate, prattle, yak *(Nonformal)*

wag *n.* clown, comedian, comic, farceur, funnyman, funny person, funnywoman, gawmoge *(Newfoundland)*, humorist, jester, joker, prankster, punster, quipster, trickster, wit *Nonformal:* card, cutup, kidder, wisecracker – *v.* bob, flap, flutter, nod, oscillate, quiver, rock, shake, stir, sway, swing, twitter, vibrate, waggle, wave, wiggle

wage *n.* allowance, compensation, cut, earnings, emolument, fee, hire, honorarium, pay, payment, price, receipts, recompense, remuneration, requital, return, returns, reward, salary, share, stipend, take *(Nonformal)*– *v.* carry on *or* out, conduct, engage in, maintain, pursue, undertake

wager *n.* action, ante, bet, challenge, flier, gamble, game, handle, hazard, hunch, odds, risk, shot, stake, toss-up, venture – *v.* bet, chance, gamble, hazard, hedge, lay *or* lay odds, play, pledge, plunge, punt *(Nonformal)*, put on *or* up, risk, roll the dice, shoot, speculate, stake, venture

waggish *adj.* amusing, capersome, clowning, comical, diverting, droll, entertaining, facetious, frolicsome, funny, humorous, impish, jesting, jocose, jocular, joking, merry, mischievous, playful, prankish, puckish, rompish, silly, sportive, teasing, tongue in cheek, tricky, whimsical, witty *Antonyms:* demure, grave, serious, staid, wearisome

wagon *n.* cart, truck, van, vehicle *Kinds of wagon:* Black Maria, buggy, caisson, camion, carriage, chariot, chuck, coaster,

Conestoga, dray, freight, hay, milk, paddy, runabout, spring, station, tea, tipcart, trolley, tumbrel, wagonette *See also:* **cart**

waif *n.* castaway, castoff, derelict, foundling, hobo, homeless person, mudlark, orphan, outcast, ragamuffin, squeegee-kid, stray, street kid *or* urchin, vagabond, vagrant,

wail *n.* complaint, cry, grief, howl, keening *(Irish)*, lamentation, moan, mourning, ululation, weeping, whimper, whine, yowl *Antonyms:* hilarity, laughter, rejoicing – *v.* bawl, beat one's breast, blubber, carry on *(Nonformal)*, caterwaul, complain, cry, grieve, howl, keen, lament, moan, mourn, shriek, sob, ululate, weep, whimper, whine, yowl *Antonyms:* cheer, exult, revel

wailing *n.* bawling, bemoaning, blubbering, boohooing *(Nonformal)*, caterwauling, complaining, crying, grieving, howling, lamentation, moaning, mourns, sniveling, sobbing, tearfulness, ululation, weeping, whimpering, yammering, yowling *Antonyms:* jubilation, thanks

waist *n.* abdomen, belt, circumference, middle, midriff, mid-section, narrowing, waistband, waistline

wait *n.* **1.** break, continuance, dalliance, delay, downtime, gap, halt, holdup, pause, recess, rest, stoppage *Antonyms:* advancement, headway, progress **2.** age *(Nonformal)*, duration, interim, interval, period, respite, stage, stop, time, while – *v.* **1.** abide, await, bide, hang about *or* around, linger, loiter, remain, stay, tarry *Antonyms:* depart, go, leave **2.** halt, hold, lag, pause, rest, sit tight *(Nonformal)*, slow down, stop **3.** anticipate, expect, hope, pine, yearn **4.** dally, dawdle, defer, delay, dilly-dally *(Nonformal)*, mark time, neglect, postpone, procrastinate, put aside, shelve **5.** attend, perform, satisfy, serve, supply, waiter, waitress

waitstaff *n. pl.* attendants, barmaids, barmen, bartenders, footmen, hostesses, hosts, restaurant staff, servers, sommeliers, victuallers, waiters, waitpersons, waitresses *Nonformal:* carhops, soup jockeys

waive *v.* **1.** abandon, cede, decline, defer, disclaim, disown, dispense with, forgo, give up, grant, hand over, leave, let go, reject, relinquish, remit, remove, renege, renounce, reserve, resign, sign away, surrender, turn over, yield *Antonyms:* claim, keep, pursue **2.** delay, neglect, postpone, procrastinate, put off, set aside, shelve, stall, suspend, table

wake *n.* **1.** aftermath, backwash, feather, furrow, path, rooster tail *(Nonformal)*, track, trail, train, wash, wave **2.** celebration, deathwatch, dedication, funeral service, obsequies, rites, vigil, watch – *v.* activate, animate, arise, arouse, awaken, challenge, come to, enliven, excite, freshen, galvanize, kindle, nudge, provoke, quicken, rally, renew, rise, rouse, shake, stimulate, stir, stir *or* wake up, turn out, waken *Antonyms:* doze, lull, retire, slumber

wakeful *adj.* **1.** alert, alive, astir, attentive, careful, heedful, observant, on guard, vigilant, waiting, wary, watchful *Antonyms:* dilatory, inattentive, neglectful, remiss **2.** anxious, awake, insomniac, insomnious, restless, wide-eyed *Antonyms:* asleep, out, somnambulant, unconscious

walk *n.* **1.** constitutional, hike, jaunt, march, parade, perambulation, peregrination, portage, promenade, ramble, saunter, stroll, tour, traipse, tramp, walkabout *Nonformal:* sashay, schlep **2.** gait, pace, step, stride, tread **3.** aisle, alley, avenue, boardwalk, boulevard, bricks, by-path, byway, carrying place, catwalk, close, course, court, crossing, esplanade, footpath, footway, gangway, lane, mall, passage, path, pathway, pavement, pier, platform, Plus-15 *(Calgary)*, promenade, road, route, sidewalk, street, track, trail **4.** area, arena, bailiwick, course, domain, dominion, field, province, sphere, terrain, territory *Nonformal:* beat, turf **5.** calling, career, discipline, line, métier, profession, trade, vocation, walk of life – *v.* **1.** advance, amble, go, hike, jog, knock about, march, meander, mince, pace, parade, patrol, perambulate, plod, prance, promenade, rove, run, sashay, shuffle, slog, stalk, step, stride, stroll, strut, tour, traipse, tramp, traverse, tread, trek, trudge, wander *Antonyms:* idle, rest, sit **2.** accompany, chaperone, escort, exercise, guide, lead, protect, shepherd, tail **3.** abandon, break away *or* out, decamp, depart, desert, egress, exit, flee, forsake, leave, quit, retire, terminate *Nonformal:* scram, skedaddle, take a powder **4.** protest, rebel, revolt, shut down, stop *or* stop work, strike, walk out

walkout *n.* boycott, day of action, dissent, job action, outlaw strike, protest, revolt, shutdown, solidarity, strike, uprising, wildcat strike, work stoppage *See also:* **strike**

wall *n.* **1.** bailey, bank, boards, bulkhead, clerestory, dam, divider, division, embankment, enclosure, façade, fence, levee, outer layer, panel, panelling, parapet, partition, retainer, screen, side, surface **2.** bar, barricade, barrier, block, blockade, bulwark, fortification, hindrance, hurdle, impediment, limitation, obstruction, protection, rampart, restriction, roadblock, stockade, stop

wallet *n.* bag, billfold, card case, case, change purse, fanny pack, handbag, money belt, money clip, pocketbook, purse

wallop *n.* **1.** bash, belt, blow, bop, bump, clash, collision, hit, jar, punch, slam, slug, smack, smash, thump, thwack, roundhouse, whack *Nonformal:* grooming, haymaker, manual compliment, sallywinder **2.** backlash, charge, heft, impact, jolt, kick, might, power, recoil, shock – *v.* **1.** beat, best, clobber, defeat, drub, lick, rout, trim, trounce, vanquish, whip **2.** bash, batter, belt, blast, bop, buffet, bushwhack, clobber, drub, hide, hit, lambaste, paste, pelt, plant one, pound, pummel, punch, slam, slog, slug, smack, smash, sock, strike, swat, take out, tan, thrash, thump, thwack, whack

wallow *n.* bog, depression, hollow, moss hag, mudhole, pool, puddle, sink, slough, swamp, trough – *v.* **1.** bask, delight, enjoy, glory, grovel, humour *or* pamper oneself, indulge, luxuriate, relish, revel, rollick, take pleasure *Antonyms:* abstain, avoid, eschew, forgo, refrain **2.** bob, falter, flounder, keel, lie, lurch, pitch, roll, sprawl, stagger, stumble, teeter, waddle, waiver, wobble

wan *adj.* **1.** anemic, ashen, ashy, bilious, blanched, bleached, bloodless, cadaverous, colourless, dim, discoloured, faint, ghastly, livid, pale, pallid, pasty, peaked, sickly, washed-out, waxen, white *Antonyms:* blooming, bright, rosy, rubicund, ruddy **2.** exhausted, feeble, forceless, frail, haggard, impotent, ineffective, ineffectual, tired, weak, weary, worn *Antonyms:* forceful, strong, vibrant

wand *n.* **1.** Aaron's rod, baton, Black Rod *(Parliament)*, caduceus, cane, crook, cross staff, divining *or* dowsing rod, herald's wand, mace, magic *or* magician's wand, rod, sceptre, staff, truncheon **2.** bough, branch, osier, shoot, stem, stick, switch, tendril, twig, vine

wander *v.* **1.** drift, journey, migrate, peregrinate, prowl, ramble, roam, rove, travel, trek, trip, wend *Nonformal:* follow the sun, mosey **2.** amble, dally, dawdle, daydream, idle, linger, meander, mill *or* shuffle about, putter, saunter, stroll, traipse, walk *Nonformal:* dilly-dally, woolgather **3.** cross the line, depart, deviate, divagate, diverge, err, go adrift *or* astray, stray, swerve, veer *Antonyms:* concentrate, focus **4.** babble, bluster, chatter, digress, drone *or* run on, gab, prattle *Nonformal:* jaw, yak – *n.* constitutional, excursion, journey, pilgrimage, rambling, roaming, roving, stroll, survey, trek, walk, walkabout *Antonyms:* homeostasis, inactivity, inertia, motionlessness

wanderer *n.* adventurer, bohemian, day-tripper, drifter, *flâneur (French)*, floater, gadabout, globetrotter, gypsy, hobo, itinerant, journeyer, meanderer, migrant, nomad, peregrinator, pilgrim, rambler, ranger, roamer, rover, sight-seer, straggler, stray, tinker, tramp, transient, tripper *(North)*, vagabond, vagrant *Nonformal:* rolling stone, saddle tramp *Antonyms:* homebody, homesteader, settler

wandering *adj.* **1.** aimless, circuitous, circumlocutory, desultory, digressive, discursive, drifting, indirect, itinerant, meandering, peripatetic, rambling, roaming, roundabout, roving, straggling, wending, winding, zigzagging *Antonyms:* direct, straight **2.** journeying, migrant, migratory, nomadic, travelling, wayfaring

wane *n.* abatement, decline, degeneration, degradation, deterioration, dwindling, fading, failure, regression, slump, weakening –

v. abate, age, decrease, diminish, drift away, dwindle, ebb, fade, lapse, lessen, lull, peter out, recede, retract, retreat, retire, shrink, sink, subside, taper off, weaken, wind down, withdraw *Antonyms:* intensify, strengthen, swell, wax

wangle *v.* angle, connive, contrive, elicit, engineer, exact, exploit, extort, fake, induce, intrigue, jockey, manoeuvre, manipulate, obtain, persuade, plot, procure, pull strings, scheme *Nonformal:* doctor, finagle, weasel

want *n.* **1.** appetency, appetite, concupiscence, craving, demand, desire, fancy, hankering, hunger, itch, longing, lust, need, passion, pining, propensity, thirst, urge, yearning, yen *(Nonformal) Antonyms:* apathy, aversion, distaste, indifference **2.** absence, barrenness, dearth, deficiency, exigency, inadequacy, insufficiency, lack, meagreness, paucity, scantiness, scarcity, shortage, skimpiness *Antonyms:* abundance, adequacy, sufficiency, surplus **3.** beggary, destitution, impoverishment, indigence, pauperism, penury, poorness, poverty, privation *Antonyms:* affluence, riches, wealth – *v.* **1.** ache, aspire, covet, crave, desire, expect, fancy, hanker, hunger, long, lust, pine, thirst, wish, yearn **2.** choose, cull, elect, favour, finger, mark, opt, prefer, select *Antonyms:* eschew, reject, spurn **3.** demand, lack, miss, need, require

wanting *adj.* **1.** damaged, defective, deficient, disappointing, failing, faulty, impaired, imperfect, inadequate, incomplete, inferior, not up to par *or* scratch *(Nonformal)*, patchy, poor, scanty, sketchy, substandard, unfulfilled, unsatisfactory *Antonyms:* adequate, complete, flawless, intact, satisfactory **2.** absent, bankrupt, bereft, deprived, devoid, empty, lacking, less, minus, missing, needy, scarce, short, shy *Antonyms:* adequate, complete, fulfilled

wanton *adj.* **1.** bacchanalian, carnal, cheap, concupiscent, Dionysian, dissolute, drunken, fast, hedonistic, immoral, lax, lecherous, lewd, libertine, libidinous, licentious, loose, lustful, promiscuous, prurient, raunchy, raw, rough, salty, satyric, sensuous, shameless, swinging, unscrupulous, wayward *Antonyms:* chaste, pure, wholesome **2.** arbitrary, capricious, careless, gratuitous, groundless, heedless, random, senseless, unasked, uncalled-for, unfair, unjust, unjustified, unprovoked, wilful *Antonyms:* fair, just, merited, sensible, warranted **3.** acrimonious, belligerent, contrary, cruel, fell, hostile, ill-disposed, malevolent, malicious, ornery, rancorous, spiteful, surly, venomous, vitriolic *Antonyms:* benevolent, compassionate, humane **4.** abandoned, excessive, exorbitant, extravagant, extreme, overboard, over-the-top, sprawling, sweeping, unrestrained *Antonyms:* moderate, modest, temperate **5.** abundant, flourishing, luxuriant, profuse, prolific, rampant, rank, vigorous *Antonyms:* limited, sparse, stifled

war *n.* aggression, atrocity, attack, battle, campaign, civil war, combat, conflict, contest, death, enmity, fighting, hell *(Nonformal)*, hostility, hostilities, slaughter, state of war, theatre of operation, total war, virtual war, warfare, warring, war zone *Major wars:* Afghanistan *(1979-89)*, American Revolution *(1775-1783)*, Balkan *(1912-1913; 1913)*, Boer *(1899-1902)*, Crimean *(1854-56)*, Crusades *(1096-1291)*, English Civil *(1642-46)*, Falkland Islands *(1982)*, France-Prussian *(1870-71)*, French and Indian *(1755-63)*, Greco-Persian *(499-478 B.C.)*, Greek War of Independence *(1821-29)*, Hundred Years' *(1338-1453)*, Korean *(1950-1952)*, Mexican *(1846-1848)*, Napoleonic *(1796-1815)*, Norman Conquest *(1066)*, Opium *(1839-1842)*, Peloponnesian *(431-404 B.C.)*, Persian Gulf *(1991)*, Punic *(264-241 B.C.; 218-201 B.C.; 149-146 B.C.)*, Russo-Japanese *(1904-1905)*, Second Great Northern *(1700-1721)*, Seven Years' *(1756-1763)*, Spanish-American *(1898)*, Spanish Armada *(1588)*, Spanish Civil *(1936-1939)*, Thirty Years' *(1618-1648)*, U.S. Civil *(1861-1865)*, Vietnam *(1961-1975)*, War of 1812 *(1812-1815)*, War of the Austrian Succession *(1740-1748)*, Wars of the Roses *(1455-1485)*, War of the Spanish Succession *(1701-1714)*, World War I *(1914-1918)*, World War II *(1939-1945)*, Yom Kippur *(1973) Antonyms:* accord, armistice, cease-fire, peace, truce – *v.* attack, battle, bombard, challenge, clash, combat, contend, contest, differ, disagree, fight, kill, meet, oppose, shell, shoot, strive, struggle, take on, take up arms, wage war *Antonyms:* concur, cooperate, harmonize, mediate

ward *n.* **1.** cell, chamber, room, suite, wing **2.** *arrondissement (French)*, barrio, block, borough, city, constituency, county, district, division, electoral district, electorate, neighbourhood, parish, quarter, section, zone **3.** adopted child, child, client, dependent, foster child, godchild, minor, orphan, pensioner, protégé, pupil **4.** care, charge, confinement, custody, guardianship, protection, supervision, trust **5.** manager, officer, overseer, supervisor, warden *See also:* **warden** – *v.* check, repel, repulse, scotch, turn aside

warden *n.* attendant, caretaker, concierge, curator, custodian, doorkeeper, doorperson, executive, gatekeeper, governor, guard, guardian, head, jailer, janitor, key master, patrol, porter, public official, reeve, sentinel, sexton, steward, turnkey, warder, watchperson

wardrobe *n.* **1.** accoutrements, apparel, array, attire, clothes, clothing, costume, garb, garments, gear, kit, outfit, raiments *Nonformal:* duds, get-up, rig, threads, toggery, weeds **2.** bureau, cabinet, chiffonier, chifforobe *(U.S.)*, cloakroom, closet, cupboard, dresser, furnishing, furniture **3.** collection, fashion, line, mode, style, trend, variety

warehouse *n.* barn, bin, depository, retail *or* wholesale depot, distribution centre, entrepôt, establishment, godown, repository, shed, stockpile, stockroom, storage, storehouse – *v.* accumulate, amass, deposit, hoard, pile, stock, stockpile, store

wares *n. pl.* articles, commodities, goods, line, manufactures, material, merchandise, products, range, stock, stuff *(Nonformal)*

warlike *adj.* aggressive, attacking, battling, bellicose, belligerent, bloodthirsty, bombastic, combative, confrontational, contentious, contrary, dangerous, gladiatorial, hawkish, hostile, martial, militant, militaristic, offensive, pugnacious, quarrelsome, threatening, unfriendly, warmongering, warring *Antonyms:* conciliatory, cooperative, friendly, peaceful, placid

warlock *n.* conjurer, demon, diviner, enchanter, fortuneteller, magician, magus, Merlin, necromancer, palmist, shaman, soothsayer, sorcerer, witch, witch doctor, wizard, wonderworker

warlord *n.* conquistador, daimio, military commander *or* leader, tuchun

warm *adj.* **1.** balmy, clement, cozy, lukewarm, mild, pleasant, summery, sunny, temperate, tepid, toasty, warmish *Antonyms:* chilly, cold, freezing, icy **2.** affable, affectionate, amiable, amorous, cheerful, compassionate, cordial, empathetic, friendly, genial, gracious, happy, heartfelt, hearty, hospitable, kind, kind-hearted, kindly, loving, pleasant, responsive, sincere, soft-hearted, sympathetic, tender, warmhearted, wholehearted *Antonyms:* aloof, apathetic, phlegmatic, remote, standoffish **3.** amorous, animated, ardent, earnest, effusive, emotional, enthusiastic, excited, fervent, fervid, glowing, heated, hot, intense, keen, lively, passionate, spirited, vigorous, zealous – *v.* bake, cook, defrost, heat, melt, microwave, nuke *(Nonformal)*, prepare, reheat, thaw, toast

warmth *n.* **1.** fieriness, fire, heat, sun, swelter, warmness *Antonyms:* cold, iciness **2.** affability, amiability, cordiality, earnestness, friendliness, geniality, genuineness, heartiness, hospitableness, open-heartedness, receptiveness, sincerity *Antonyms:* aloofness, coldness, detachment, standoffishness **3.** amorousness, ardour, desire, ebullience, enthusiasm, excitement, fervidity, fervour, love, passion, spirit, vigour, zeal, zest *Antonyms:* apathy, indifference

warn *v.* **1.** acquaint, address, advise, advocate, alert, apprise, clue in, counsel, forewarn, give notice *or* warning, hint, inform, instruct, notify, prepare, prompt, recommend, remind, signal, suggest, teach, tip off **2.** admonish, caution, deprecate, direct, disapprove, dissuade, enjoin, exhort, forbid, guide, order, remonstrate, reprove, threaten, urge

warning *adj.* admonishing, cautionary, exemplary, exhortatory, looming, ominous, threatening – *interj.* amscray *(Nonformal)*, beat it, fire in the hole *(Blasting)*, fore, heads up, look out, watch it – *n.* **1.** admonition, caution, caveat, counsel, threat **2.** advice, example, guidance, hint, information, injunction, lesson, notice, notification, recommendation, suggestion, tip, tipoff **3.** augury, flirrup *(Newfoundland)*, foreshadowing, foretoken, indication, intimation, omen, portent, premonition, presage, prophesy, sign, word **4.** alarm, alert, distress signal, flare, forewarning, foghorn, light, lighthouse, signal, siren,

warp *n.* **1.** angle, bend, crook, curve, deviation, distraction, hook, kink, turn, twist **2.** aberration, bent, bias, fetish, idiosyncrasy, oddity, partiality, peculiarity, perversion, prejudice, quirk **3.** cable, cord, rope, tether, towline, towrope, yarn – *v.* **1**. bend, contort, curve, deviate, misshape, slant, stretch, swerve, turn, twist **2.** colour, corrupt, distort, falsify, misquote, misrender, misrepresent, pervert, put a spin on *(Nonformal)* **3.** bias, influence, predispose, prejudice, sway, taint

warrant *n.* **1.** approval, authorization, carte blanche, entitlement, letters patent, licence, permission, right, sanction, vouchsafement **2.** assurance, guarantee, pledge, security, verification, warranty **3.** affidavit, document, fiat, order, paper, permit, subpoena, voucher, waiver, writ **4.** authority, basis, evidence, grounds, justification, reason – *v.* **1.** assure, attest, bank *(Nonformal)*, guarantee, promise, secure **2.** defend, explain, excuse, justify, rationalize **3.** allow, approve, authorize, certify, commission, empower, invest, notarize, ordain, permit, sanction, validate, verify

warranty *n.* **1.** assurance, bond, certificate, contract, covenant, guarantee, pledge, promise, waiver, writ, written promise **2.** authorization, green light *(Nonformal)*, liberty, licence, permission, sanction

warrior *n.* archer, barbarian, berserker, brave, cavalier, champion, combatant, conscript, dragonslayer, fighter, guerrilla, Gurkka, knight, man-at-arms, man-of-war, marine, martial artist, mercenary, ninja, paladin, partisan, pikeman, rebel, ronin, samurai, serviceman, soldier, swordsman, trooper *Nonformal:* cannon fodder, doughboy, G.I., grunt *Antonyms:* dove, pacifist, peacenik

warship *n.* aircraft carrier, battle cruiser, battleship, corvette, destroyer, frigate, galleon, man-o'-war, mine sweeper, sloop, war vessel *See also:* **ship**

wary *adj.* **1.** alert, attentive, careful, cautious, chary, guarded, heedful, prudent, suspicious, vigilant, watchful *Nonformal:* awake, eagle-eyed *Antonyms:* bumbling, clumsy, inattentive **2.** artful, astute, cagey *(Nonformal)*, canny, clever, cunning, deft, sharp, shrewd, sly, wily *Antonyms:* dumb, slow, stupid

wash *n.* **1.** ablution, bath, bathing, cleansing, lathering, laundering, lavation, rinse, scrub, shampoo, shower, soaping **2.** dirty clothes, housework, laundry, load **3.** antiseptic, cleanser, disinfectant, eyewash, liniment, mouthwash **4.** dregs, garbage, gobbledygook *(Nonformal)*, hogwash, slosh, swill, waste **5.** backwash, break, eddy, flow, rooster tail *(Nonformal)*, swell, surf, swish, trail, undulation, wake, wave **6.** disappearance, dissipation, erosion, landslide, wearing away **7.** coating, colour, dye, film, glaze, layer, stain **8.** bayou, bog, everglade, fen, marsh, morass, quagmire, swamp **9.** arroyo, donga *(African)*, dry bed, gulch, gully, winterbourne – *v.* **1.** bathe, clean, cleanse, douche, flush, freshen up, hose down, launder, mop, scour, scrub, shampoo, shower, soap, sponge, swab, wipe *Antonyms:* dirty, soil, sully **2.** clarify, distill, filter, purify, refine, strain **3.** drench, immerse, soak, submerge, waterlog, wet *Antonyms:* desiccate, dry **4.** flow, lap, rinse, slosh, splash, surge, swell **5.** abrade, denude, disintegrate, erode, wear away **6.** brush, coat, cover, glaze, paint, stain, suffuse

washer *n.* **1.** cleaner, dishwasher, launderer, laundress, laundryperson, pot-walloper *(Nonformal)*, scullion, washerwoman **2.** dishpan, sink, washbasin, washbowl, washing machine, washpot, washstand, washtub

washout *n.* **1.** botch, bungle, collapse, cataclysm, catastrophe, debacle, disappointment, disaster, dud *(Nonformal)*, failure, fiasco, flop, loss, meltdown, total loss *Antonyms:* accomplishment, success, triumph **2.** erosion, gulch, gully, ravine, watershed

washroom *n.* bathroom, comfort station, gents' *or* mens' room, ladies' *or* womens' room, latrine, lavatory, little boys' *or* girls' room, loo, outhouse, powder room, privy, restroom, toilet, urinal, water closet, W.C. *Nonformal:* blue moon cafe, bog, can, john, throne

waspish *adj.* cantankerous, crabby, cross, crusty, curmudgeonly, grouchy, grumpy, huffish, ill-humoured, irascible, irritable, mean, ornery, peevish, petulant, prickly, querulous, resentful, sour, spiteful, splenetic, testy, touchy *Antonyms:* cordial, kind, sunny

waste *adj.* **1.** excess, extra, leftover, remnant, superfluous, unused **2.** arid, barren, desolate, fallen, unfruitful, unproductive, untilled, wild **3.** futile, pointless, unprofitable, useless, worthless *Nonformal:* crap, howling – *n.* **1.** debris, dregs, dross, filth, flotsam, garbage, hogwash, jetsam, junk, leavings, leftovers, litter, mullock, offal, refuse, remainder, rubbish, rubble, scrap, scum, sediment, sewage, shavings, slag, slop, sweepings, swill, trash **2.** defecation, discharge, dung, excrement, feces, urine *Nonformal:* caca, crap, pee, piss, poo, whizz **3.** annihilation, demolition, desolation, destruction, devastation, eradication, exhaustion, obliteration, ravage, ruin **4.** dissipation, excessiveness, extravagance, improvidence, indulgence, lavishness, misuse, overspending, prodigality, profligacy, squandering, wastefulness **5.** decay, decline, degeneration, dilapidation, fall, impairment, neglect, weakening, wear – *v.* **1.** desecrate, desolate, destroy, devastate, pillage, ravage, raze, reduce, ruin, sack, scourge, spoil *Antonyms:* build, conserve, defend **2.** fribble, fritter, lavish, spend, splurge, squander *Nonformal:* blow, burn, run through, throw away **3.** atrophy, decline, deteriorate, droop, emaciate, languish, macerate, regress, slip, weaken, wilt, wither, worsen **4.** abate, decrease, diminish, disintegrate, dwindle, erode, evanesce, shrink, subside, wear away **5.** assassinate, dispose of, do away with, kill, murder *Nonformal:* ice, rub out, snuff

wasteful *adj.* careless, cavalier, extravagant, immoderate, improvident, incontinent, overindulgent, penny-wise and pound-foolish *(Nonformal)*, prodigal, profligate, reckless, spendthrift, squandering, uneconomical, unthrifty *Antonyms:* economical, frugal, money-saving, parsimonious

wasteland *n.* backwoods, badlands, barrens, brush, desert, dust bowl, hinterlands, moose pasture, outback, plain, the bush *(Nonformal)*, veld

wastrel *n.* **1.** derelict, good-for-nothing, hobo, idler, loafer, ne'er-do-well *(Nonformal)*, rascal, ronion, schnorrer *(Yiddish)*, sleeveen *(Newfoundland)*, tramp, vagabond, vagrant **2.** foundling, mudlark, raga muffin, stray, urchin, waif **3.** consumer, prodigal, spendthrift, squanderer *Nonformal:* big time spender, good-time Charlie

watch *n.* **1.** attentiveness, inspection, observation, scrutiny, study, surveillance, vigil, wake **2.** chronometer, devil's mill *(Historical)*, hourglass, *montre (French)*, pocket *or* wrist watch, quartz *(Nonformal)*, stopwatch, sundial, timepiece *Trademark:* Rolex, Swatch, Timex **3.** guard, lookout, patrol, picket, scout, security, sentinel, watchdog – *v.* **1.** check out *(Nonformal)*, contemplate, espy, examine, gaze, inspect, look, notice, observe, reconnoitre, regard, scan, scout, scrutinize, see, stare, study, survey, view *Nonformal:* kibitz, rubberneck *Antonyms:* miss, neglect, overlook **2.** attend, baby-sit, guard, husband, keep an eye out, look after *or* out for, monitor, patrol, ride shotgun *(Nonformal)*, safeguard, secure, vigilate **3.** heed, mark, take care *or* note *or* precautions

watchdog *n.* Cerberus, concierge, custodian, garrison, gatekeeper, guard, inspector, lookout, monitor, patroller, scout, scrutineer, sentinel, vigilante, watchmen

watchful *adj.* alert, apprehensive, attentive, careful, cautious, chary, circumspect, distrustful, guarded, mindful, observant, prudent, sharp-eyed, suspicious, vigilant, wary, weather-eyed *Antonyms:* careless, distracted, heedless, inattentive, oblivious

watchtower *n.* beacon, citadel, crow's-nest, fire tower, landmark, lighthouse, lookout, mark, milepost, minaret, observation point *or* post, observatory, rampart, Texas tower

watchword *n.* abracadabra *(Nonformal),* battle cry, bugle call, buzzword, byword, catchword, clarion, countersign, exhortation, magic word, maxim, motto, password, rallying cry, shibboleth, signal, slogan, tagline

water *n.* **1.** *agua (Spanish),* aqua, drink, *eau (French),* elixir, fluid, H_2O, liquid **2.** creek, crick *(Nonformal),* lagoon, lake, ocean, pond, river, saltchuck *(Pacific Coast),* sea, stream, tarn **3.** condensation, dampness, dew, irrigation, moisture, perspiration, rain, splash, sweat, tears, waterworks, wetness – *v.* **1.** bathe, dampen, douse, drench, drown, flood, hose, inundate, irrigate, moisten, rinse, saturate, shower, soak, sodden, souse, spray, sprinkle, submerge, swamp, wash, waterlog, wet **2.** adulterate, alter, censor, change, dilute, thin, weaken *Nonformal:* cut, doctor, water down **3.** cry, discharge, drool, exude, leak, ooze, perspire, secrete, transude, weep

water nymph *n.* kelpie, naiad, nerveid, ondine, sea nymph, sprite, Thetis, undine

waterfall *n.* cascade, cataract, chute, falls, Niagara *(Nonformal),* sault

waterfront *n.* bank, beach, coastline, docks, embankment, foreshore, harbourfront, lakefront, lakeshore, quay, riverside, shoreline

waterlogged *adj.* dripping, drenched, drowned, flooded, inundated, irrigated, marshy, moist, permeated, saturated, soaked, soaking, sodden, soggy, sopping, soused, submerged, swampy, wet, wringing *Antonyms:* arid, dry, parched

waterman *n.* bargee *(Nonformal),* bargeman, boatman, crabber, ferryman, fisherman, gondolier, oarsman, punter, sculler

watermark *n.* **1.** insignia, line, mark, seal, sign, stamp **2.** flood *or* tide mark, indication, indicator, plimsoll line *or* mark, waterline

waterproof *adj.* close, hermetic, impenetrable, leakproof, rainproof, raintight, resistant, sealed, seaworthy, tight, weatherproof, water-repellent, water-resistant, watertight *Antonyms:* leaky, permeable, pervious

watershed *n.* **1.** Continental *or* Great Divide, crestline, division, height of land, ridge, separation, water parting **2.** basin, drainage basin, harbour, supply, valley, wellspring **3.** change, crisis, crucial moment, cusp, hinge, reversal, transition, turning point

waterway *n.* aqueduct, brook, canal, channel, creek, crick *(Nonformal),* culvert, fairway, gulch, gully, narrows, oceanlane, passageway, river, rivulet, run, runlet, sealane, seaway, sewer, ship route, sluice, spillway, stream, watercourse, watergate

watery *adj.* **1.** aqueous, fluid, liquid, serous, soupy, thin **2.** boggy, damp, dank, dewy, drenched, marshy, moist, saturated, seeping, soaked, sodden, soggy, waterlogged, wet *Antonyms:* arid, dry, parched **3.** adulterated, altered, anemic, bland, diluted, runny, tasteless, thin, watered-down, weak *Nonformal:* cut, doctored *Antonyms:* concentrated, fortified, strong **4.** lachrymose, rheumy, tearful, teary, weeping, wishy-washy

wave *n.* **1.** backwash, billow, bore, breaker, chop, comber, crest, groundswell, ripple, surf, tsunami, whitecap **2.** flood, gush, inundation, stream, surge, swell **3.** curl, curve, frizz, frizzies, hairdo, ringlet, twist **4.** greeting, hail, hello, salutation, salute **5.** bob, careen, lean, lilt, pitch, rock, sway, undulation **6.** condition, emotion, influence, occurrence, period – *v.* **1.** beat, flap, fluctuate, flutter, nod, oscillate, pulsate, ripple, rock, ruffle, sway **2.** gesture, greet, hail, indicate, salute, signal, sweep **3.** brandish, shake, swing, wag, waggle

waver *v.* **1.** equivocate, fluctuate, oscillate, tergiversate, vacillate, waffle *Nonformal:* hem and haw, shilly-shally **2.** beat, flap, flutter, ripple, sway, undulate **3.** dither, fall back, falter, pause, stumble, totter, wobble **4.** dance, flicker, gleam, glimmer, play, quiver, shine, sputter, twinkle **5.** flinch, quake, quaver, shake, shiver, shudder, tremble, twitter

wavering *adj.* **1.** capricious, equivocal, faltering, fickle, fluctuating, hedging, hesitant, indecisive, irresolute, oscillating, shrinking, uncertain, uncommitted, unsure, vacillating, wishy-washy *Antonyms:* constant, firm, relentless, staunch, tenacious **2.** flapping, fluttering, reeling, rocking, pitching, swaying, tottering, twitching, twittering, undulating, unsteady

wax *n.* beeswax, carnauba, cerate, cerumen, earwax, hydrocarbon, lipid, ozocerite, paraffin, polish, secretion, spermaceti – *v.* **1.** augment, build, develop, enlarge, expand, grow, heighten, increase, magnify, mount, multiply, mushroom, rise, run, swell, upsurge *Antonyms:* contract, dwindle, ebb, narrow, shrink, wane **2.** buff, coat, cover, polish, shine, treat

waxen *adj.* achromatic, anemic, ashen, blanched, bloodless, colourless, deathly, dull, etiolated, faint, flat, ghostly, hueless, lurid, pale, pallid, pasty, sallow, toneless, translucent, wan, washed-out *Antonyms:* flushed, healthy, rosy, sanguine

way *n.* **1.** access, channel, course, direction, passage, path, route, track, turn **2.** apiece, bit, distance, space, step *Nonformal:* stone's throw, tidy step **3.** advance, ground, headway, progress, range, **4.** business, convention, custom, means, method, mode, *modus operandi (Latin)*, policy, practice, procedure, rule, SOP (Standard Operating Procedure), system, tradition **5.** approach, character, habit, idiosyncrasy, manner, nature, particularity, personality, quirk, style, thing *(Nonformal)*, trait **6.** aspect, circumstance, detail, feature, particular

wayfaring *adj.* drifting, footloose, gadabout, globetrotting, jet-setting, journeying, nomadic, perambulatory, peripatetic, rambling, roving, transient, travelling, voyaging, walking, wandering *Antonyms:* inhabiting, loitering, motionless

wayward *adj.* **1.** bull-headed, contrary, contumacious, disagreeable, disobedient, dogged, forward, fractious, head-strong, incorrigible, intractable, mulish, obstinate, self-indulgent, spoiled, stubborn, ungovernable *Antonyms:* agreeable, complaisant, compliant **2.** arbitrary, capricious, changeable, drifting, erratic, fickle, flighty, inconstant, mercurial, unstable, unsteady, variable *Antonyms:* constant, steadfast, unwavering **3.** surprise, unanticipated, unexpected, unforeseen, unplanned for, unpredictable *Antonyms:* anticipated, planned, predetermined

weak *adj.* **1.** anemic, debilitated, delicate, effete, enervated, exhausted, faint, feeble, forceless, fragile, frail, impotent, impuissant, infirm, limp, powerless, prostrate, puny, rotten, senile, sickly, sluggish, spent, tired, wasted, worn out *Nonformal:* burnt, fried *Antonyms:* able, hardy, healthy, strong, tough **2.** capricious, changeable, fickle, inconstant, indecisive, mercurial, pliable, shilly-shallying, undependable, unreliable, unstable, vacillating, wavering, whimsical *Antonyms:* determined, dogged, steadfast **3.** deficient, forceless, hollow, inadequate, ineffectual, lacking, lame, off the mark *(Nonformal)*, poor, thin, unconvincing, unimpressive *Antonyms:* effective, forceful, potent **4.** cowardly, craven, gutless *(Nonformal)*, pusillanimous, spineless **5.** cobbled-together *(Nonformal)*, jerrybuilt, ramshackle, rickety, shaky, substandard, unsound, unstable, unsteady, wobbly **6.** adulterated, altered, diluted, doctored *(Nonformal)*, insipid, runny, tasteless, watery *Antonyms:* bracing, concentrated, exhilarating, intense, stimulating **7.** dim, distant, dull, faded, gentle, imperceptible, inaudible, indistinct, low, muffled, pale, poor, quiet, reedy, slight, small, soft, stifled, unaccented, unstressed, whispered *Antonyms:* bright, loud, powerful **8.** assailable, declawed, defenceless, exposed, helpless, undefended, unguarded, unprotected, unsafe, untenable, vulnerable, wide open, woundable *Antonyms:* safe, solid, well-defended

weaken *v.* **1.** adulterate, alter, cut, dilute, doctor *(Nonformal)*, minimize, mitigate, moderate, temper, thin, water down **2.** abate, diminish, dwindle, ease up, lessen, reduce, subside, wane **3.** belittle, debilitate, devitalize, emasculate, enervate, enfeeble, impair, invalidate, sap, undermine **4.** droop, exhaust, fade *(Nonformal)*, fatigue, flag, slow down, strain, tire, waste, wear out **5.** accede, acquiesce, concur, consent, give in, relent, soften, surrender, yield *Nonformal:* call uncle, crack, throw in the towel *Antonyms:* beard, confront, face, fight

weakling *n.* coward, crybaby, featherweight, hangashore *(Newfoundland)*, milksop, milquetoast, pushover, sooky baby *(Maritimes) Nonformal:* baby, chicken, cream puff, mama's boy, namby-pamby, nerd, pussy, sissy, wimp *Antonyms:* bruiser, bull, ox, strongman

weakly *adj.* ailing, anemic, ashen, doddering, enervate, feeble, frail, gaunt, haggard, ill, infirm, invalid, sickly, susceptible, unhealthy, unwell, vulnerable, *Antonyms:* hardy, healthy, hearty, robust, rugged, sound

weakness *n.* **1.** Achilles' heel, blemish, defect, failing, fault, flaw, imperfection, loophole, shortcoming, vice **2.** appetite, appreciation, fancy, fondness, inclination, liking, penchant, predilection, proclivity, taste, soft spot **3.** debility, decrepitude, delicacy, enervation, feebleness, fragility, frailty, impairment, impotence, powerlessness, valetudinarianism, vulnerability

wealth *n.* **1.** affluence, assets, belongings, bounty, cache, capital, cash, commodities, estate, fortune, funds, goods, holdings, mammon, means, money, pelf, possessions, property, resources, revenue, riches, security, substance, treasure, wherewithal, worth *Nonformal:* booty, clover *Antonyms:* destitution, indigence, need, paucity **2.** abundance, cornucopia, load, mass, myriad, pile, plenitude, profusion *Nonformal:* bonanza, bumper, scads, ton *Antonyms:* dearth, insufficiency, lack

wealthy *adj.* **1.** affluent, booming, easy, flourishing, independent, moneyed, propertied, prospering, prosperous, rich, successful, upscale, well-off, well-to-do *Nonformal:* comfortable, fat, filthy *or* stinking rich, flush, in clover, loaded, sitting pretty, well-heeled *Antonyms:* deprived, impoverished, penniless, poor **2.** abounding, ample, plenty, profuse, replete, swimming *(Nonformal)*, teeming

wear *n.* **1.** apparel, attire, clothes, dress, duds *(Nonformal)*, garb, toggery **2.** abrasion, attrition, corrosion, damage, depreciation, deterioration, dilapidation, friction, loss, rent, tear, waste *Antonyms:* conservation, maintenance, preservation, repair, upkeep – *v.* **1.** abrade, chafe, consume, corrode, decay, deteriorate, dwindle, erode, fray, grind, impair, overuse, overwork, rub, weather *Antonyms:* keep, maintain, preserve, protect, save **2.** annoy, bother, exasperate, exhaust, gall, harass, hassle *(Nonformal)*, irk, irritate, pester, provoke, tax, undermine, vex, weaken, weary *Antonyms:* nourish, relieve, succour, support, sustain **3.** assume, carry, display, don, put on, show, sport **4.** bear, endure, last, stand up, survive, withstand

weariness *n.* boredom, burnout, enervation, ennui, exhaustion, fatigue, heaviness, jadedness, languor, lassitude, lethargy, sluggishness, tedium, tiredness, *Weltschmerz (German) Antonyms:* ardour, fervour, passion, zeal

wearisome *adj.* **1.** bland, boring, dreary, dull, flat, humdrum, insipid, leaden, monotonous, protracted, repetitious, routine, spiritless, stale, soporific, tedious, unvaried *Nonformal:* blah, ho-hum, yawny *Antonyms*: amusing, exciting, marvelous, wondrous **2.** burdensome, difficult, dismal, exhausting, fatiguing, grinding, heavy, interminable, onerous, oppressive, Sisyphean, tiring, trying, wearing, weighty

weary *adj.* **1.** battle-scarred, bone *or* dog tired, dispirited, drained, enervated, exhausted, flagging, sleepy, tired, war-weary, worn out *Nonformal:* beat, burnt, bushed, fried, pooped, spent, wiped *Antonyms:* energetic, excited, wired **2.** bored, bothered, depressed, discontented, irked, irritated, jaded, listless, taxed, vexed *Nonformal:* fed up, up-to-here **3.** annoying, boring, drawn-out, irritating, monotonous, tedious, tiring, wearisome – *v.* bore, drain, enervate, exhaust, fatigue, fizzle, peter *or* wear out, poop out *(Nonformal)*, tire

weasel *n.* **1.** ermine, ferret, mink, mousehound *(British)*, polecat, stoat **2.** backstabber, coward, quisling, spy, traitor, turncoat *Nonformal:* skunk, sleaze, snake in the grass, sneak – *v.* avoid, dodge, equivocate, evade, palter, prevaricate, quibble, sidestep, slide away

weather *n.* **1.** climate, clime, conditions, meteorology, temperature **2.** blizzard, blowing, cold, cold *or* warm front, disturbance, drought, föhn, El Niño, fog, front, hail, heat, heatwave, hurricane, La Niña, precipitation, rain, rainfall, sleet, snow, squall, storm, streamer, tempest, tornado, whiteout, wind *See also:* **storm**, **wind** **3.** ambiance, atmosphere, aura, environment, mood, tenor, tone, vibes *(Nonformal)* – *v.* **1.** acclimatize, harden, season, sharpen, strengthen, toughen **2.** bear, beard, brave, combat, confront, contest, cope, endure, face, overcome, resist, stand, suffer, surmount, survive, take, thwart, tolerate, withstand *Antonyms:* succumb, surrender, yield **3.** crumble, disintegrate, erode, fade, oxidize, rot

weave *v.* **1.** bind, braid, darn, embroider, entwine, fasten, interlace, intertwine, knit, knot, loom, loop, mat, mend, needlework, spin, seam, sew, stitch, twist *Antonyms:* undo, unravel, untwist **2.** blend, compose, construct, create, fuse, merge, mesh, unite **3.** detour, dodge, sway, swerve, tilt, veer, wend, wobble, zigzag *Nonformal:* deke, dipsy-doodle

Web *n.* Internet, Intranet, Net *(Nonformal)*, network, web site, World Wide Web, WWW

web *n.* **1.** cobweb, entrapment, mesh, net, snare, tangle, trap, weir **2.** fabric, filigree, gossamer, lace, netting, weave **3.** circuitous course, labyrinth, maze, network

wed *v.* **1.** cleave onto, couple, handfast, join, jump the broom, link, marry, mate, publish *or* post *or* put up the banns, unite, yoke *Antonyms:* annul, break up, divorce, separate **2.** amalgamate, blend, combine, commingle, comix, consolidate, fuse, homogenize, intermix, meld, merge, mix, pool, splice, synthesize *Antonyms:* divide, sever, split

wedded *adj.* attached, connected, connubial, coupled, fused, hitched, joined at the hip *(Nonformal)*, linked, married, matched, mated, merged, paired, united, yoked *Antonyms:* divided, split, sundered

wedding *n.* **1.** bridal, ceremony, confarreation *(Historical)*, espousal, handfasting, marriage, marrying, matrimony, nuptials, spousals, union, wedlock **2.** alliance, amalgamation, association, blending, bloc, combination, combining, consolidation, integration, joining, merger, mingling, unification, uniting *Antonyms:* break-up, disintegration

wedge *n.* **1.** block, chock, chunk, cleat, cut, lump, part, piece, portion, section, segment, slice **2.** coign, cotter, prong, quoin, shim, spire, taper **3.** chink, cleavage, cleft, division, fissure, separation, split – *v.* **1.** force apart *or* in, separate, split, stick **2.** compress, crowd, jam, jampack, pack, secure, squeeze, squish, tighten

weed *n.* **1.** choker, encroacher, intruder, invader, noxious *or* pernicious plant, suffocator *Some common weeds:* buttercup, cinquefoil, chess, chicory, chickweed, clover, coltsfoot, common plantain, clover, creeping Charley, couchgrass, dandelion, dock, fescue, figwort, fall hawkbit, goutweed, ground ivy, horsetail, madder, mallow, mustard, nettle, Queen Anne's Lace, ragweed, sorrel, thistle, yarrow **2.** cigar, cigarette, marijuana, tobacco – *v.* clear away, cull, cultivate, eliminate, eradicate, excise, extract, pull *or* thin out, purge, prune, refine, remove, uproot *Antonyms:* accumulate, amass, collect, hoard, stockpile

weep *v.* **1.** bawl, bewail, cry, fret, grieve, howl, keen, lament, moan, mope, mourn, pine, shed tears, snivel, snuffle, sob, tear, wail, whimper, yammer *Nonformal:* blubber, boohoo **2.** bleed, discharge, effuse, emit, excrete, exude, leak, ooze **3.** dangle, droop, hang, sag, trail

weepy *adj.* **1.** blubbery, depressing, emotional, lachrymose, mournful, sad, tearful, teary *Antonyms:* cheerful, happy, smiling, sunny **2.** exudative, leaky, oozy, permeable, porous, runny, weeping

weigh *v.* **1.** balance, counterbalance, gauge, measure, scale, stack up *(Nonformal)* **2.** analyze, cogitate, consider, contemplate, deliberate, examine, figure, kick *or* knock around *(Nonformal)*, meditate, ponder, reflect upon, sort out, study, turn over **3.** appraise, assess, estimate, evaluate, judge, rate, size up *(Nonformal)*, value **4.** bother, burden, depress, encumber, oppress, tax, trouble, try, vex

weight *n.* **1.** avoirdupois, corpulence, deadweight, gravity, heaviness, mass, measure, oppression, tonnage *Apothecaries' weight:* dram, grain, ounce, scruple *Imperial weights:* dram, grain, hundredweight, ounce, pound, quarter, short ton, stone, ton *Metric weights:* centigram, decigram, dekagram, gram, hectogram, kilogram, milligram **2.** albatross, burden, cross, encumbrance, excess baggage, millstone, misery, onus, oppression, pressure, responsibility, sorrow, strain, tribulation, trouble **3.** authority, clout, connection, consequence, consideration, credit, effectiveness, efficacy, emphasis, forcefulness, impact, import, importance, influence, magnitude, moment, persuasiveness, pith, potency, power, prestige, pull *(Nonformal)*, significance, signification, substance, sway, value *Antonyms:* frivolity, inanity, insignificance, worthlessness – *v.* **1.** add to, charge, handicap, hold down, load **2.** alter, bias, favour, influence, multiply, rig

weighty *adj.* **1.** beefy, bulky, corpulent, elephantine, enormous, fat, heavy, hefty, huge, large, mammoth, massive, obese, ponderous, prodigious, substantial **2.** consequential, critical, crucial, grave, heavy *(Nonformal)*, important, momentous, portentous, pressing *Antonyms:* immaterial, incidental, insignificant **3.** cogent, forcible, influential, moving, potent, powerful, puissant **4.** burdensome, onerous, oppressive, overwhelming, taxing, troublesome, trying, worrisome

weird *adj.* **1.** bizarre, crazy, curious, dreamlike, eccentric, enigmatic, esoteric, fabulous, fantastic, flaky *(Nonformal)*, freaky, Kafkaesque, nightmarish, odd, outlandish, peculiar, puzzling, queer, singular, strange, surreal, surrealistic, uncanny, unexplainable, unhinged, unnatural *Antonyms:* common, ordinary, typical, usual **2.** eerie, eldritch, ghostly, haunting, mysterious, occult, otherworldly, phantasmagoric, spooky *(Nonformal)*, supernatural, unearthly

welcome *adj.* **1.** agreeable, congenial, cordial, delightful, favourable, genial, good, nice, opportune, pleasant, pleasing, propitious, refreshing, satisfying *Antonyms:* disagreeable, excluded, rebuffed, rejected **2.** appreciated, cherished, esteemed, gratifying, honoured, wanted – *interj.* aloha, *bienvenido (Spanish)*, *bienvenue (French)*, hi, hello, greetings, howdy, Salaam, salutations, what's up *German: Gröss Gott, Willkommen* *Antonyms:* beat it, good riddance, it's been real, sayonara – *n.* address, admittance, greeting, high five *(Nonformal)*, reception, salutation, salute – *v.* accept, admit, embrace, entertain, espouse, flag, greet, hail, hug, receive, salute *Nonformal:* glad hand, roll out the red carpet *Antonyms:* exclude, rebuff, refuse, reject, spurn

weld *n.* bond, joint, juncture, seam – *v.* associate, attach, bind, bond, braze, cement, combine, connect, fix, fuse, join, link, meld, repair, solder, unite *Antonyms:* cleave, divide, section, split, sunder

welfare *n.* **1.** abundance, advantage, benefit, contentment, ease, good fortune, happiness, health, interest, profit, prosperity, satisfaction, success, well-being *Antonyms:* detriment, disadvantage, drawback **2.** aid, assistance, employment insurance *or* E.I., financial aid, help, social assistance, support, workfare *Nonformal:* dole, pogey

well *adj.* **1.** able-bodied, blooming, bright-eyed, chipper, fine, firm, fit, flourishing, fresh, hale, hardy, healthy, hearty, robust, sane, sound, strong, trim, vigorous, whole *Nonformal:* alive and kicking, together *Antonyms:* ailing, ill, poorly, sick, weak **2.** acceptable, admirable, okay *(Nonformal)*, respectable, right, satisfactory **3.** comfortable, flourishing, fortunate, prosperous, successful, thriving **4.** advisable, appropriate, becoming, fitting, judicious, meet, proper, prudent, recommendable, sensible, sound – *adv.* **1.** advantageously, beneficially, favourably, good, profitably, propitiously **2.** adequately, nicely, okay *(Nonformal)*, satisfactorily, sufficiently **3.** accurately, befittingly, conscientiously, correctly, fairly, justly, properly, reasonably, rightly, suitably **4.** ably, adeptly, commendably, deftly, easily, effortlessly, excellently, expertly, irreproachably, skilfully **5.** agreeably, luxuriously, prosperously, successfully, swimmingly *(Nonformal)* **6.** closely, completely, entirely, extremely, fully, intimately, soundly, thoroughly **7.** beyond, decidedly, definitely, far, far and away, obviously, quite, sizably **8.** affectionately, amiably, cordially, generously, graciously, kindly, lovingly, warmly **9.** affably, calmly, equably, good-naturedly, serenely, soberly – *n.* **1.** aquifer, cistern, fountain, lake, reservoir, spring, wellspring **2.** abyss, cavity, chasm, crevasse, gulf, hole, mine, moss hag, opening, pit, sump – *v.* emanate, flood, flow, gush, issue, ooze, overflow, pour forth, spring, surge, swell, trickle

well-being *n.* **1.** advantage, benefit, enjoyment, euphoria, felicity, fortune, good fortune, happiness, joy, pleasure, profit, satisfaction, success, weal *Antonyms:* adversity, hardship, misfortune **2.** comfort, condition, contentment, ease, fitness, health, prosperity, welfare

well-known *adj.* **1.** acclaimed, celebrated, conspicuous, eminent, famous, illustrious, important, infamous, leading, name, notable, noted, notorious, outstanding, popular, preeminent, prominent, public, recognized, renowned, reputable, star *Nonformal:* big, big-name, face, large *Antonyms:* unrenowned, unsung **2.** acknowledged, common, customary, established, everyday, familiar, known, routine, traditional, usual *Antonyms:* little-known, obscure, unknown

well-rounded *adj.* **1.** cultured, educated, erudite, learned, resourceful, sophisticated, travelled, well-informed, well-read, well-schooled, well-versed, worldly *Antonyms:* insular, provincial **2.** cogent, complete, comprehensive, persuasive, thorough, total, well-balanced, whole *Antonyms:* limited, narrow

well-spoken *adj.* articulate, clear, coherent, comprehensible, eloquent, fluent, intelligible, lucid, natural, smooth, understandable

well-timed *adj.* appropriate, auspicious, convenient, expedient, felicitous, fit, fortunate, opportune, propitious, suitable, timely *Antonyms:* ill-timed, inexpedient, untimely

welt *n.* blemish, blister, bruise, contusion, injury, laceration, lump, mark, pimple, ridge, scar, slash, sore, streak, stripe, wale, weal, wound, zit *(Nonformal)*

west *adj.* occidental, Pacific, western, westward – *n.* **1.** Pacific coast, Western hemisphere, western seaboard *Western Canadian Provinces:* British Columbia, Alberta, Manitoba, Saskatchewan **2.** Europe, Occident, the Americas

wet *adj.* **1.** aqueous, clammy, damp, drenched, dripping, moist, saturated, slimy, slippery, soaked, sodden, soggy, sopping, soused, waterlogged, watery *Antonyms:* desiccated, dried, parched **2.** dewy, drizzling, foggy, humid, misty, muggy, pouring, rainy, showery, slushy, snowy, stormy, teeming, torrential *Antonyms:* balmy, hot, sunny – *n.* clamminess, condensation, damp, drizzle, humidity, liquid, moisture, rain, water, wetness *Antonyms:* aridity, drought, dryness – *v.* bathe, damp, dampen, deluge, dip, douse, drench, drown, flood, hose down, humidify, imbue, irrigate, moisten, rinse, saturate, soak, splash, spray, sprinkle, steep, wash, water, waterlog *Antonyms:* dehydrate, desiccate, dry, parch

wet blanket *n.* bore, damper, grinch, grouch, killjoy, malcontent, nuisance, pest, spoilsport *Nonformal:* drag, party pooper, skeleton at the banquet, sourpuss, stick in the mud

wetlands *n.* bog, delta, estuary, fen, flood plain, mangrove, marsh, mire, moor, muskeg, quagmire, reedbed, salt marsh, slough, swamp, tidal flats,

whale *n.* **1.** cetacean, leviathan, Moby Dick *Common North American Whales:* Atlantic pilot, Baird's, beaked, beluga *or* white, blue, Bryde's, Cuvier's beaked, Dall's porpoise, false killer, fin, grey, harbour porpoise, humpback, killer, long-finned pilot, minke, narwhal, northern bottlenose, orca, pacific white-sided dolphin, right, sei, short-finned pilot, sperm, Stenjneger's beaked **2.** beast, behemoth, colossus, enormity, giant, mammoth, monster, titan – *v.* beat, belt, bruise, flog, injure, lambaste, thrash, thwack, whack, whip, whup *(Nonformal)*, wound

what *interj.* are you crazy *or* nuts, *bist meshugeh (Yiddish)*, come again, eh, get lost *or* out of here, give me a break, howzat, huh, no way, qué, you're joking

wheat *n.* cereal, grain *Common varieties of wheat:* Alberta Winter, Chinook, Durum, Garnet, Lee, Manitoba Hard, Manitoba Northern, Manitoba Nos. 1, 2, 3, and 4, Manitou, Marquis, Neepawa, Red Bobs, Red Fife, Red Spring, Rescue, Selkirk, Softwinter, Thatcher

wheedle *v.* beguile, blandish, cajole, charm, coax, court, draw, entice, finagle, flatter, inveigle, lure, persuade, seduce, talk into *Nonformal:* butter up, con, soft-soap, sweet-talk *Antonyms:* compel, force, press

wheel *n.* **1.** circle, disc, drum, hoop, hub, rim, ring, roll, roller, tire, trundle, **2.** circuit, circumvolution, cycle, gyration, revolution, rotation, spin, turning *Nonformal:* spinorama, wheely – *v.* about-face, circle, gyrate, move, orbit, pirouette, pivot, reel, revolve, roll, rotate, spin, spiral, swing, swivel, turn, twirl, veer, whirl

whereabouts *n.* area, environs, locale, location, neighbourhood, place, placement, position, residence, site, situation, spot, station, vicinity

wherewithal *n.* **1.** assets, backing, capital, cash flow, finances, funding, funds, means, method, money, resources, supplies, ways *Nonformal:* dough, moolah, stash, wampum **2.** ability, background, balance, capacity, competence, experience, facility, foresight, fortitude, intellectual prowess, knowledge, power, skill, talent *Nonformal:* brains, right stuff *or* stuff, smarts

whet *v.* **1.** animate, arouse, awaken, challenge, enhance, excite, fire, incite, increase, kindle, light, pique, provoke, quicken, rally, rouse, stimulate, stir, waken *Antonyms:* dampen, depress, stifle, suppress **2.** edge, file, finish, grind, hone, sharpen, strop *Antonyms:* blunt, dull

whiff *n.* **1.** aroma, odour, reek, scent, smell, stench **2.** hint, murmur, rumour, suggestion, touch, trace, undertone, waft **3.** breath, draft, inhalation, puff, pull, sniff, snuff **4.** miss, strikeout, swing – *v.* blow, exhale, inhale, puff, smell, smoke, sniff

while *adv.* as long as, at the time, during, when, whilst – *n.* bit, instant, interim, interval, meantime, moment, occasion, period, space, spell, stretch, time – *v.* fill, fritter, use, pass, putter, spend

whim *n.* caprice, desire, dream, fancy, fantasy, humour, idea, impulse, inclination, megrim, notion, quirk, urge, vagary, vision, whimsy

whimper *n.* bleat, cry, mean, mew, murmur, sob, sound, wail, whine – *v.* bawl, blubber *(Nonformal)*, complain, cry, fuss, lament, mewl, moan, mope, pine, pule, snivel, sob, tear, weep, whine

whimsical *adj.* **1.** baroque, capricious, eccentric, erratic, fey, fickle, impulsive, mercurial, quizzical, spontaneous, unconventional, wayward **2.** amusing, curious, droll, fanciful, fantastic, imaginative, odd, offbeat *(Nonformal)*, playful, waggish *Antonyms:* dull, prudent, serious, sober, staid

whine *n.* complaint, cry, gripe, lamentation, mewl, moan, mope, pule, sob, wail, whimper – *v.* ache, bleat, carp, complain, cry, fuss, grouch, grumble, kvetch, lament, mewl, moan, mope, pine, snivel, tear, weep, whimper *Nonformal:* beef, bellyache, bitch, go on about, gripe, grouse, whinge

whip *n.* belt, birch, bullwhip, cane, cat-o'-nine-tails, chabouk, cord, flail, hickory, knout, kurbash, lash, quirt, rawhide, riding crop, rod, rope, ruler, strap, switch, thong – *v.* **1.** bash, beat, cane, cudgel, flagellate, flay, flog, hide, hit, horsewhip, larrup, lash, scourge, spank, strap, strike, switch, thrash, thwack, wallop, whack *Nonformal:* tan, whale *Antonyms:* massage, pet, rub **2.** berate, castigate, chastise, correct, criticize, discipline, lambaste, punish, scold, upbraid *Antonyms:* praise, reward **3.** aerate, agitate, beat, blend, froth, mix, stir up, whisk **4.** beat, conquer, defeat, outdo, outstrip, overcome, thwart, trample, top, vanquish *Nonformal:* cream, pulverize, whup, wipe the floor with *Antonyms:* give in, succumb, surrender, yield **5.** dart, dash, deflect, dive, divert, flash, flit, fly, jerk, pivot, pull, rush, shoot, surge, turn, veer, wheel, whirl

whirl *n.* **1.** circle, circuit, eddy, gyration, maelstrom, pirouette, reel, revolution, roll, rotation, round, spin, spinorama *(Nonformal)*, spiral, surge, swirl, turn, twirl, twist, wheel, whirlpool **2.** agitation, chaos, confusion, disturbance, madness, mayhem, pandemonium, turmoil, whoop-de-do *(Nonformal)*, whirlwind *Antonyms:* calm, lassitude, order, peace, torpor – *v.* circle, eddy, gyrate, pirouette, pivot, reel, revolve, roll, rotate, spin, spiral, swirl, turn, twirl, twist, wheel, whir

whirlwind *adj.* blinding, confusing, fast, hasty, headlong, impetuous, impulsive, lightning, rapid, rash, speedy, sudden, swift *Antonyms:* calculated, cautious, considered, prudent – *n.* anticyclone, cyclone, dust devil, hurricane, spout, tornado, tourbillion, twister, typhoon, white squall

whisk *v.* **1.** aerate, agitate, beat, blend, churn, disturb, excite, foam, froth, mix, stir, whip up **2.** brush, flick, sweep, wave **3.** carry, dispatch, fly, hustle, rush, speed, transport, whiz *(Nonformal)*, wing

whiskers *n. pl.* beard, chin *or* facial hair, growth, moustache, vibrissae *Nonformal:* burnsides, muttonchops, peach fuzz, soup-strainer, stubble

whisky *n.* alcohol, bung-your-eye *(Newfoundland)*, firewater, homebrew, liquor, moonshine, spirits *Nonformal:* John Barleycorn, the creature *Kinds of whisky:* blended, bourbon, Canadian, corn, Irish, malt, mountain *or* prairie dew, poteen *(Irish)*, rye, Scotch, single malt, whisky blanc *See also:* **liquor**

whisper *n.* **1.** breath, hushed *or* muted tone, mumbling, murmur, sibilation, susurration, susurrus, undertone *Antonyms:* scream, shout, yell **2.** hint, inkling, indication, inference, insinuation, rumour, scent, shadow, soupçon, suggestion, suspicion, tad, trace, undertone, whiff – *v.* **1.** hiss, mumble, mutter, sibilate, sigh, speak, susurrate, utter **2.** advise, confide, disclose, divulge, gossip, hint, insinuate, intimate, reveal, rumour

whit *n.* atom, bit, crumb, dash, drop, fragment, grain, iota, jot, mite, modicum, mote, particle, piece, pinch, scrap, shaving, shred, smidgen, speck, spot, tinge, touch, trace

white *adj.* **1.** albino, blanched, bleached, blond, clear, colourless, light, pale, snowy *Antonyms:* black, dark, sable **2.** anemic, ashen, ashy, bloodless, pallid, pasty, sickly, wan, washed-out, waxen *Antonyms:* robust, ruddy, sanguine **3.** beyond reproach, blameless, decent, fair, faultless, guiltless, honourable, immaculate, innocent, irreproachable, pure, sinless, unsullied *Antonyms:* culpable, guilty, liable **4.** blank, fresh, new, pristine, unblemished, unmarked, unused, vacant *Antonyms:* discoloured, tainted, used **5.** ancient, frosted, grey, grizzled, hoary, mature, old, silvery, venerable, wise *Antonyms:* fresh, young – *n. White shades:* alabaster, bleach, bone, chalk, egg-shell, grey, hoary, horn, ivory, light, lily-white, marmoreal, milk-white, milky, neutral, oyster, pearl, silver, silvery, snow-white, snowy, transparent, vanilla

whiten *v.* blanch, bleach, blench, chalk, decolour, dull, etiolate, fade, frost, lighten, pale, silver, whitewash *Antonyms:* blacken, colour, darken, stain

whiteout *n.* Alberta clipper, blizzard, snow devil, snow storm, squall, storm, tempest, torrent, *tempête de neige (French)*

whitewash *v.* **1.** bury, camouflage, conceal, cover, disguise, downplay, extenuate, gloss over, hide, minimize, paint, veil, wrap *Antonyms:* expose, present, reveal **2.** blanch, bleach, clean, launder, sanitize, whiten

whiz *n.* ace, adept, connoisseur, expert, genius, maestro, marvel, master, maven *(Nonformal)*, prodigy, star, virtuoso, wizard, wonder, wunderkind *Antonyms:* dullard, fool, simpleton – *v.* buzz, hiss, hum, whir

whole *adj.* **1.** complete, entire, perfect, total, unabridged, uncut, undiminished, undivided, unexpurgated *Antonyms:* bowdlerized, fragmented, part, partial **2.** flawless, good, intact, mint, solid, sound, unscathed, untouched, virgin *Antonyms:* broken, damaged, marred **3.** better, cured, fit, hale, healed, healthy, hearty, recovered, right, robust, strong, well, wholesome – *n.* all, collective, complex, entirety, integrity, organism, package, sum, system, totality, unity *Nonformal:* caboodle, megillah, the works *Antonyms:* part, piece, portion

wholehearted *adj.* abiding, ardent, authentic, bona fide, candid, committed, complete, dedicated, determined, devoted, earnest, emphatic, enduring, enthusiastic, fervent, frank, genuine, heartfelt, impassioned, in all the way *(Nonformal)*, never-failing, passionate, real, serious, sincere, steadfast, steady, sure, true, unqualified, unquestioning, unreserved, unstinting, unwavering *Antonyms:* contingent, insincere, lukewarm, qualified, reserved, tepid

wholesale *adj.* all-inclusive, complete, comprehensive, extensive, far-reaching, full-scale, general, indiscriminate, mass, sweeping, total, wide-ranging, widespread *Antonyms:* limited, qualified, specified – *adv.* en bloc, in bulk, mutually, together

wholesome *adj.* **1.** beneficial, fit, good, hale, healthy, invigorating, nourishing, nutritious, salubrious, sound, strengthening *Antonyms:* pernicious, putrid, rancid, rotten **2.** clean, decent, edifying, ethical, exemplary, family-oriented, G-rated, proper, upright *Antonyms:* lewd, salacious, vulgar, X-rated

wholly *adv.* **1.** altogether, completely, comprehensively, entirely, from top to bottom, fully, on mass, totally, utterly, without exception *Nonformal:* lock, stock, and barrel, 100 per cent, whole hog *Antonyms:* partially, partly **2.** exclusively, explicitly, individually, only, particularly, solely, specially, specifically *Antonyms:* generally, universally

whoop *n. & v.* bark, bellow, boo, call, cheer, cry, holler *(Nonformal)*, hoot, howl, hurrah, jeer, scream, screech, shout, shriek, squawk, yell

whopping *adj.* big, Brobdingnagian, colossal, enormous, extraordinary, gargantuan, giant, gigantic, great, huge, immense, large, mammoth, massive, mighty, monstrous, mountainous, prodigious, tremendous, walloping *Nonformal:* ginormous, humungous, thumping *Antonyms:* diminutive, miniature, tiny, wee

whore *n.* call girl, hooker, hussy, paid escort, philanderer, prostitute, slag, slut, streetwalker, strumpet, tart, working girl *(Nonformal)*

wicked *adj.* **1.** abominable, base, beastly, contemptible, dastardly, despicable, egregious, evil, fiendish, foul, gross, heartless, heinous, iniquitous, loathsome, mean, nefarious, rotten, vicious, vile, villainous *Antonyms:* heroic, noble, virtuous **2.** abandoned, amoral, bad, corrupt, degenerate, depraved, dissolute, immoral, impious, profane, scandalous, shameless, sinful, wanton, wayward *Antonyms:* pious, moral, religious **3.** criminal, cunning, incorrigible, lawless, nasty, naughty, reprobate, troublesome, worthless *Antonyms:* honest, innocent, kind **4.** carnal, filthy, indecent, lewd, licentious, obscene, pornographic, prurient, raunchy *(Nonformal)*, salacious, smutty *Antonyms:* chaste, decent, pure **5.** baleful, damaging, dangerous, destructive, fatal, hurtful, lethal, malignant, noxious, pernicious, poisonous, toxic, venomous, virulent *Antonyms:* harmless, innocuous **6.** impish, mischievous, picaresque, raffish, roguish**7.** awesome, cool *(Nonformal)*, excellent, exceptional, extraordinary, great, impressive, marked, notable, outstanding, phenomenal, remarkable, striking, wonderful *Antonyms:* blasé, boring, common

wide *adj.* **1.** ample, broad, commodious, dilated, distended, expansive, far-ranging, far-reaching, full, immense, inclusive, large, large-scale, outspread, outstretched, roomy, spacious, splay, sweeping, voluminous, widespread *Antonyms:* confined, cramped, limited **2.** advanced, catholic, comprehensive, deep, encyclopedic, exhaustive, general, in-depth, liberal, open, progressive, thorough, tolerant, universal, vast *Antonyms:* myopic, narrow, specialized **3.** astray, away, deviating, distant, errant, inaccurate, off, remote

widespread *adj.* **1.** all-encompassing, all-inclusive, blanket, catholic, communicable, comprehensive, contagious, cosmic, ecumenical, encyclopedic, endemic, epidemic, exhaustive, extensive, far-flung, far-reaching, galactic, global, infectious, international, interplanetary, outspread, pandemic, planetary, rampant, rife, sweeping, thorough, total, ubiquitous, universal, unlimited, unrestricted, wholesale, wide-ranging, worldwide *Antonyms:* confined, exclusive, limited, local, sporadic **2.** common, current, demotic, diffuse, general, omnipresent, overall, pervasive, popular, prevailing, prevalent *Antonyms:* rare, sui generis, uncommon, unique

widow *n.* dowager, grieving party *(Nonformal)*, relict, sati, survivor

width *n.* **1.** amplitude, area, broadness, compass, cross measure, diameter, distance, girth, measure, thickness, wideness **2.** breadth, expanse, extent, range, reach, scope, span, stretch

wield *v.* **1.** brandish, flash, flourish, handle, hold up, shake, swing, use, utilize, wave *Antonyms:* discard, scrap **2.** control, employ, exercise, manage, manipulate, ply, touch

wife *n.* bride, common-law partner, consort, helpmate, country wife *(Historical)*, lady, life partner, mate, partner, spouse *Nonformal:* better *or* other half, little woman, missus, old lady, rib, significant other

wiggle *n. & v.* bump and grind, dance, flitter, flutter, grind, jerk, jiggle, move, quiver, shake, squirm, twist, twitch, twitter, waggle, waver, wobble, wriggle

wigwam *n.* abode, domicile, dwelling, hogan, house, jacal, lodging, place, quinzhee, residence, shelter, structure, tepee, tupik, *wikuom (Native Peoples)*, wickiup

wild *adj.* **1.** barbaric, farouche, feral, primitive, savage, uncivilized, untamed *Antonyms:* broke, civilized, domesticated **2.** lush, natural, overgrown, uninhabited, unpopulated, virgin *Antonyms:* colonized, settled **3.** autochthonous, common, indigenous, native, natural **4.** berserk, crazy, daft *(British)*, demented, deranged, eccentric, erratic, flighty, fractious, hysterical, irrational, lawless, lunatic, mad, preposterous, rabid *Antonyms:* civilized, genteel, gentle, restrained, self-controlled, tame, thoughtful, unenthusiastic, well-behaved **5.** anarchic, corybantic, chaotic, hell-bent, hell-raising, impetuous, incautious, noisy, rambunctious, rampant, rash, raucous, rebellious, reckless, seditious, tumultuous, unbridled, uncontrolled, unmanageable, unpredictable, unrestrained *Antonyms:* civilized, genteel, gentle, normal, sane stable **6.** blustering, blustery, choppy, disturbed, furious, howling, inclement, intense, raging, rough, storming, stormy, tempestuous, turbulent, violent *Antonyms:* calm, peaceful, serene, tame

wilderness *n.* back country, backwoods, badlands, barrens, bush, desert, forest, hinterland, jungle, no-man's land, outback, primeval forest, uncharted territory, wasteland, wilds *Nonformal:* back forty, back of beyond, boonies, God's Country, sticks *Antonyms:* city, metropolis, municipality, urban sprawl

wile *n.* angle, artifice, chicanery, craftiness, cunning, deceit, deception, device, dodge, feint, fraud, gambit, game, gimmick, guile, hoax, horseplay, manoeuvre, plot, ploy, racket, ruse, scheming, setup, shenanigans, stratagem, stunt, subterfuge, switch, trickery *Nonformal:* con, monkey business, scam – *v.* beguile, decoy, entice, inveigle, lure, seduce, trick

wilful *adj.* **1.** adamant, decided, determined, dogged, headstrong, inflexible, intractable, intransigent, mulish, obdurate, obstinate, persistent, pertinacious, perverse, pigheaded *(Nonformal)*, refractory, resolved, self-willed, stubborn, unyielding, volitive *Antonyms:* complacent, compromising, docile, flexible, obedient **2.** conscious, deliberate, designed, intentional, premeditated, purposeful, studied, voluntary, willing *Antonyms:* accidental, intuitive, involuntary, unplanned, unwitting

will *n.* **1.** action, choice, decision, discretion, election, free will, judgment, volition **2.** backbone, conviction, decisiveness, determination, discipline, enthusiasm, obstinacy, persistence, purpose, resolution, resolve, self-control, steadfastness, stick-to-it-iveness *(Nonformal)*, stubbornness **3.** command, desire, intention, need, pleasure, want, whim, wish **4.** bequest, bestowal, declaration, decree, directions, estate, instructions, last wishes, property, testament – *v.* **1.** choose, command, compel, decide, desire, determine, elect, force, make, opt, pick, prefer, resolve, want, wish **2.** bequeath, bequest, confer, devise, give, hand down, leave, pass on, transfer

willing *adj.* **1.** ardent, eager, earnest, enthusiastic, excited, exuberant, fervid, game *(Nonformal)*, happy, hearty, keen, ready, warm *Antonyms:* grudging, loath, reluctant **2.** accommodating, acquiescent, agreeable, amenable, compliant, consenting, disposed, favourable, inclined, well-disposed **3.** deliberate, intentional, prepared, unforced, voluntary

willingly *adv. ad libitum (Latin)*, eagerly, fain, lief *Nonformal:* at the drop of a hat, game for, lined up

willowy *adj.* agile, flexible, graceful, lanky, light, limber, lissome, lithe, nimble, slender, slight, sprightly, supple, svelte, thin, whispy *Antonyms:* heavy-set, large, Rubenesque, rotund

willpower *n.* decidedness, determination, drive, fire in the belly (Nonformal), firmness, force, fortitude, grit, mettle, pluck, resolution, resolve, self-control, self-discipline, single-mindedness, strength, tenacity *Antonyms:* apathy, docility, weakness

wilt *v.* **1.** bend, decay, droop, lean, sag, shrink, shrivel, waste, wither, wizen *Antonyms:* bloom, flourish, thrive **2.** deteriorate, disappear, dwindle, ebb, erode, fade, fall, fatigue, flag, languish, sink, slump, wane, wear down *or* out **3.** acquiesce, bow, cave, concede, defer, fail, give in, relent, succumb, surrender, throw in the towel *(Nonformal)*, yield *Antonyms:* fight, oppose, struggle

wily *adj.* arch, artful, astute, cagey, clever, crafty, crooked, cunning, deceitful, deceptive, designing, foxy, guileful, insidious, intriguing, Machiavellian, practised, sagacious, scheming, sharp, shifty, shrewd, slick, sly, smooth, sneaky, streetwise, tricky, underhanded, wise *Antonyms:* artless, candid, honest, naive, simple

wimp *n.* coward, crybaby, milquetoast, sissy, sooky baby *(Maritimes)*, weakling *Nonformal:* baby, chicken, mama's boy, nerd, pussy, sook, wuss

wimpy *adj.* afraid, cowardly, craven, fainthearted, fearful, feeble, gutless *(Nonformal)*, impotent, ineffective, ineffectual, infirm, malleable, powerless, sapless, soft, spineless, timid, timorous, weak, yielding *Nonformal:* wishy-washy, wussy *Antonyms:* courageous, daring, heroic, influential

win *n.* accomplishment, achievement, championship, conquest, cup, first, gain, score, success, sweep, triumph, victory *Nonformal:* gold *or* gold medal, kill *Antonyms:* defeat, failure, loss – *v.* **1.** beat, best, conquer, come first, overcome, overwhelm, prevail, shellac *(Nonformal)*, shut down, sink, snow, succeed, thrash, triumph, trounce, unhelm, upset, vanquish, walk over *Nonformal:* lick, whup *Antonyms:* fail, fall, forfeit, lose **2.** achieve, accomplish, acquire, attain, bag, capture, catch, collect, earn, gain, get, harvest, make *or* nail it, obtain, procure, reach, realize, score, secure, seize, take *Nonformal:* hit pay dirt, make a killing, rake it in, strike it lucky **3.** allure, attract, charm, convert, convince, disarm, draw, induce, influence, move, persuade, stir, sway, win over *Antonyms:* disgust, repel, scare

wince *n.* blink, hesitation, reaction, retreat, start – *v.* blink, cringe, dodge, duck, flinch, jerk, pull away, quail, quake, recoil, shrink, shy *Antonyms:* brave, confront, face

winch *n.* capstan, crank, gurdy *(P.E.I.)*, hoist, pulley, reel, windlass – *v.* drag, haul, hoist, move, pull, reel in, tighten

wind *n.* **1.** air, blast, blow, breeze, current, draft, flurry, puff **2.** Alberta clipper *or*

Pipeline, chinook, cyclone, dust devil, föhn, gale, gust, hurricane, mackerel breeze, mistral, mosser *(Maritimes)*, nor'wester *(Nonformal)*, simoom, sirocco, snoweater, squall, tempest, tornado, torrent, twister, whirlwind, williwaw, windstorm, zephyr **3.** allusion, clue, communication, gossip, hint, implication, inkling, insinuation, intimation, news, notice, report, rumour, suggestion, talk, tidings, warning, whisper **4.** babble, blather, chatter, humbug, idle talk, loquacity, prattle, profusiveness, rambling, twaddle, verbiage, verbosity *Nonformal:* baloney, hogwash, hot air, malarkey, rot **5.** aroma, fragrance, odour, perfume, redolence, reek, scent, smell, stink, trace, trail **6.** belch, burp, fart, flatulence, gas – *v.* **1.** coil, curl, loop, reel, rotate, spin, spiral, spool, turn, twine, twist, weave, winch, wrap, wreath **2.** angle, bend, careen, curve, pitch, snake, swerve, veer, zigzag **3.** depart, deviate, meander, ramble, roam, rove, wander

winding *adj.* **1.** bending, bent, coiling, curving, flexuous, serpentine, sinuous, snaking, spiralling, tortuous, turning, twisted, twisting, undulating, wriggly, writhing, zigzagging *Antonyms:* direct, even, level, plumb, smooth **2.** ambiguous, circuitous, convoluted, deceptive, deviating, divergent, indirect, intricate, involved, labyrinthine, mazy, meandering, misleading, puzzling, rambling, roundabout, stray *Antonyms:* simple, straightforward

windfall *n.* blessing, bonanza, bonus, boom, boon, godsend, good fortune *or* luck, gravy *(Nonformal)*, jackpot, manna, pay dirt, pot of gold, plus

window *n.* **1.** aperture, hole, sash, wall opening *Kinds of window:* bay, casement, cinquefoil, display, dormer, double hung, French, insulated, Judas hole, lancet, louvered, multi-paned, oriel, pane, peep-hole, picture, porthole, rose, skylight, sliding, stained-glass, storm, ticket **2.** break, chance, gap, occasion, opening, opportunity, possibility, prospect, space **3.** *Computer:* access, application, display, graphical interface

windy *adj.* **1.** airy, blowing, blustery, breezy, brisk, drafty, fresh, gusty, raw, squally, stormy, tempestuous, torrential, wild, windswept *Antonyms:* calm, halcyon, serene, stagnant, still **2.** bombastic, free-spoken, garrulous, long-winded, loquacious, outspoken, pompous, prolix, rambling, talkative, turgid, verbose, vocal, vociferous, voluble, wordy *Antonyms:* reserved, restrained, quiet, shy **3.** boring, drawn-out, dull, exhausting, lengthy, long, prolonged, tedious, tiresome, tiring, wearisome *Antonyms:* concise, succinct, terse

wine *n.* alcohol, mead, *vin (French)*, vino *Nonformal:* plonk, vintage *Common wines:* Beaujolais, Bordeaux, Burgundy, Cabernet, Chablis, Champagne, Chardonnay, Chenin Blanc, Chianti, claret, dessert, fortified, Frascati, fruit, Gewürztraminer, Gutturnio, hock, ice, Madeira, Marsala, Medoc, Merlot, Moselle, Muscadel, Muscat, Pinotage, Pinot Blanc, Pinot Grigio, Pinot Noir, port, Pouilly-Fumé, Pouilly-Fuissé, red, retsina, Rhine, Rhone, Riesling, rosé, sacramental, sake, Sauternes, Sauvignon, sherry, shiraz, Soave, sparkling, Spätlese, syrah, table, Tokay, Vidal, vin ordinaire, Vouvray, white, Yquem, zinfandel

wing *n.* **1.** airfoil, appendage, arm, fin, pennon, pinion *Kinds of airplane wing:* delta, fixed, straight, swept, swing **2.** bloc, branch, company, division, faction, group, offshoot, party, schism, splinter, unit **3.** addition, ala, annex, ell, extension, outwork, projection, section, sector, side – *v.* **1.** aviate, drift, fly, migrate, move, sail, shuttle, soar, travel **2.** cripple, disable, graze, hurt, injure, main, wound **3.** ad lib, concoct, extemporize, fake it, improvise, invent, play by ear

wink *n.* **1.** hint, indication, insinuation, intimation, nictitation, sign, signal, squint, warning **2.** blink, flash, instant, jiffy, minute, moment, second, shake, split second, twinkle, twinkling *Antonyms:* age, eon, eternity – *v.* **1.** bat, blink, flutter, nictitate, squinch *(Nonformal)*, squint **2.** flicker, gleam, glint, glitter, scintillate, shimmer, sparkle, twinkle **3.** express, indicate, signal **4.** ignore, let slide, overlook, turn a blind eye

winner *n.* champion, first, hero, master, medallist, prizewinner, titleholder, vanquisher, victor *Nonformal:* champ, king,

king *or* queen of the hill, numero uno, queen, top dog, top of the heap *Antonyms:* loser, runner-up, vanquished

winning *adj.* **1.** champion, conquering, leading, successful, triumphant, unbeatable, undefeated, victorious *Nonformal:* top drawer, *Antonyms:* beaten, failing, losing **2.** adorable, agreeable, alluring, amiable, attractive, bewitching, captivating, charming, comely, cute, delectable, delightful, disarming, dulcet, enchanting, endearing, engaging, fascinating, fetching, gratifying, lovable, lovely, pleasing, prepossessing, sweet, toothsome *Antonyms:* disagreeable, offensive, repellent, ugly

winnow *v.* **1.** choose, cull, divide, eliminate, extract, glean, pick, segregate, select, separate, weed out **2.** filter, filtrate, purify, refine, screen, sieve, sift, strain **3.** catalogue, categorize, classify, discriminate, distinguish, factor, group, sort **4.** beat, fan, flap, flutter, fly, vibrate, wave **5.** blow, broadcast, circulate, disperse, disseminate, distribute, scatter

winsome *adj.* agreeable, alluring, appealing, attractive, bewitching, captivating, charismatic, charming, cheerful, comely, delectable, delightful, disarming, enchanting, endearing, engaging, enthralling, enticing, exquisite, fetching, glamorous, inviting, lovely, pleasing, ravishing, spellbinding, winning *Nonformal:* babelicious, dishy *Antonyms:* homely, plain, unattractive

winter *n.* **1.** chill, cold, frost, midwinter, winter solstice, wintertide *Nonformal:* brass monkey weather, freeze-up, Jack Frost, old man winter, the freeze **2.** darkness, decline, ebb, old age, wane – *v.* **1.** hibernate, overwinter, protect, shelter, store **2.** fly south, holiday, reside, sojourn, stay, vacation

wintry *adj.* **1.** arctic, biting, bleak, bone-chilling, brumal, brutal, chilly, cold, cutting, freezing, frigid, frosty, frozen, glacial, harsh, hibernal, hiemal, hyperborean, icy, inclement, nippy, piercing, raw, shivering, snappy, snowy, three-dog-night *(Nonformal)*, white *Antonyms:* balmy, mild, pleasant, summery, warm **2.** bleak, cheerless, cool, dangerous, dark, dismal, dreary, unfriendly, unpleasant

wipe *n.* cleaner, cloth, handkerchief, paper towel, rag, tissue, towelette – *v.* **1.** blot, brush, clean, cleanse, clear, dry, dust, rub, soak up, scour, scrub, sponge, swab, sweep, swipe, tidy, wash, whisk **2.** annihilate, decimate, delete, destroy, eliminate, eradicate, erase, exterminate, extirpate, get ride of, kill, obliterate, remove, rub out

wire *n.* **1.** cable, connection, cord, line, optical fibre, rope, strand, string, thread **2.** cablegram, communication, e-mail, facsimile, fax, message, note, telegram, telegraph, telex, word **3.** close, closing, conclusion, culmination, end, finale, finish, finish line, last chance, termination – *v.* **1.** call, communicate, contact, forward, phone, radio, ring, telegraph, send, talk, touch base **2.** bind, chain, fasten, lash, leash, ring, secure, strap, tie **3.** bug *(Nonformal)*, connect, electrify, fit, install, tap, wiretap

wiry *adj.* **1.** agile, athletic, lanky, lean, light, limber, muscular, powerful, ropy, sinewy, stringy, supple, thew, thin, tough *Antonyms:* flabby, fleshy, puny, weak **2.** bristly, fibrous, prickly, rigid, stiff, stubbly

wisdom *n.* **1.** acumen, astuteness, balance, clear thinking, comprehension, discernment, discrimination, foresight, good judgment, insight, judgment, judiciousness, poise, reason, sagacity, sageness, sapience, savoir-faire, shrewdness, sophistication, understanding *Nonformal:* savvy, street smarts *Antonyms:* foolishness, idiocy, naiveté, silliness **2.** caution, circumspection, common sense, discretion, practicality, prudence *Antonyms:* carelessness, inattention, recklessness **3.** awareness, book learning *(Nonformal)*, enlightenment, erudition, intelligence, knowledge, learning, scholarship, schooling, sophistication *Antonyms:* backwardness, ignorance

wise *adj.* astute, cogitative, contemplative, discerning, experienced, foresighted, insightful, intuitive, judicious, perceptive, perspicacious, rational, reasonable, reflective, sagacious, sage, sapient, scholarly, tactful, thoughtful, understanding, well-informed, witty *Antonyms:* foolish, injudicious, rash, stupid **2.** advisable, aware, calculating,careful, clever, crafty, cunning, discreet, expedient, knowing, politic, prudent, sane, sensible, shrewd, smart, sound, tactical, wary, well-advised *Nonformal:* fly, savvy, with it *Antonyms:* careless, ingenuous, naive, rash, stupid **3.** educated, enlightened, erudite, informed, intelligent, knowledgeable, scholarly, schooled *Antonyms:* backward, uneducated **4.** arrogant, brazen, cocky, impertinent, impudent, saucy *Nonformal:* brassy, cheeky, smart-alecky

wisecrack *n.* barb, bon mot, crack, double entendre, drollery, epigram, funny, gag, gibe, jest, joke, pun, quip, repartee, retort, sally, waggery, witticism *Nonformal:* one-liner, zinger

wish *n.* ambition, choice, desire, hankering, hope, hunger, inclination, intention, liking, longing, pleasure, preference, request, thirst, urge, want, whim, will, yearning, yen *Antonyms:* aversion, disinclination, dislike, distaste, revulsion – *v.* **1.** choose, covet, crave, desire, elect, fancy, hanker, hope, hunger, itch, like, long, need, prefer, thirst, yearn, yen *(Nonformal)* **2.** command, demand, entreat, request, require, solicit, will,

wishful *adj.* anticipatory, craving, desiring, desirous, expectant, hankering, hoping, hopeful, languishing, longing, nostalgic, optimistic, pining, yearning *Antonyms:* averse, hopeless, pessimistic

wishy-washy *adj.* **1.** fence-sitting *(Nonformal)*, indecisive, ineffective, ineffectual, irresolute, tergiversating, uncertain, undecided, vacillating, wavering *Antonyms:* decisive, definite, sure **2.** characterless, cowardly, feeble, half-hearted, languid, listless, namby-pamby *(Nonformal)*, sapless, spineless, spiritless, wimpy *(Nonformal) Antonyms:* potent, powerful, vigorous **3.** banal, bland, diluted, dull, flat, flavourless, insipid, mediocre, tasteless, thin, unsubstantial, watery, weak, watered-down *Antonyms:* concentrated, full-bodied, strong

wisp *n.* bit, lock, piece, shock, shred, snippet, strand, string, thread, tuft, twist

wistful *adj.* **1.** desirous, disconsolate, longing, melancholy, mournful, plaintive, wishful, yearning **2.** contemplative, daydreaming, dreamy, idling, meditative, musing, pensive, reflective, thoughtful

wit *n.* **1.** acumen, acuity, astuteness, awareness, balance, brainpower, brains, cleverness, common sense, comprehension, discernment, discrimination, esprit, grasp, ingenuity, insight, intelligence, judgment, keenness, lucidity, mentality, mind, perception, perspicacity, practicality, prudence, rationality, reason, sagacity, sanity, sapience, sense, shrewdness, soundness, understanding, wisdom *Antonyms:* dullness, folly, ignorance, stupidity **2.** aphorist, banterer, comedian, comedienne, epigrammatist, funny person, humorist, jester, punster, quipster *Nonformal:* card, comic, cutup, joker, kibitzer, wag, wisecracker, wise guy **3.** badinage, banter, burlesque, drollery, facetiousness, fun, humour, jest, jocularity, levity, pleasantry, raillery, repartee, satire, whimsicality, wittiness, wordplay *Antonyms:* gravity, humourlessness, solemnness

witch *n.* **1.** bewitcher, charmer, Circe, enchantress, magician, magic-user, necromancer, occultist, sibyl, siren, sorceress, spellbinder *See also:* **enchantress** **2.** beldam, cailleach, crone, hag, battle-axe *(Nonformal)*, fishwife, nag, shrew, termagant, virago, vixen

witch hunt *n.* **1.** inquiry, inquisition, interrogation, investigation, probe, quest, scrutiny, search **2.** abuse of power, harassment, McCarthyism *(U.S.)*, persecution, shakedown *(Nonformal)*, torment, tyranny

witchcraft *n.* bewitchment, black art *or* magic, conjuring, demonology, devil worship, divination, enchantment, geomancy, incantation, jinx, magic, necromancy, occultism, sorcery, spell, thaumaturgy, voodoo, voodooism, witchery, wizardry *Nonformal:* abracadabra, hocus-pocus, hoodoo, mumbo- jumbo

withdraw *v.* **1.** back out, extract, remove, scratch, subtract, take back *or* out *Antonyms:* add to, deposit, enter **2.** abjure, abolish, abrogate, annul, ban, bar, call off, cancel, disavow, disengage, disclaim, draw away *or* back, ease *or* phase out, forswear, invalidate, nullify, quash, recall, recant, recede, repress, repudiate, rescind, retract, reverse, revoke, stamp out, strike, suppress, void *Antonyms:* assert, promise, swear **3.** depart, exit, forfeit, give way, go, leave, pull back, quit, retire, retreat, secede, vacate *Nonformal:* do a bunk, fly the coop, kick the habit, renege, skedaddle

withdrawal *n.* **1.** abdication, departure, disengagement, exit, exodus, hibernation, resignation, retirement, retreat, secession *Antonyms:* furtherance, headway, progress, promotion **2.** abandonment, denunciation, disavowal, disclaimer, relinquishment, renunciation, repudiation **3.** alienation, disposal, extraction, marginalization, reduction, removal *Antonyms:* addition, inclusion, subsumption **4.** cold turkey, delirium tremens *or* d.t.'s, the cure, the sweats

withdrawn *adj.* **1.** aloof, autistic, cool, detached, disinterested, distant, hesitant, indifferent, inner-directed, introverted, misanthropic, noncommunicant, quiet, reclusive, remote, reserved, restrained, reticent, silent, solitary, standoffish, taciturn, uncompanionable, undemonstrative, uninterested, unsociable *Antonyms:* boisterous, extrovert, friendly, gregarious, outgoing **2.** cloistered, exclusive, hermitic, hidden, isolated, out-of-the-way, private, reclusive, remote, removed, retreated, secluded, solitary *Antonyms:* bustling, busy, open, public

wither *v.* atrophy, collapse, decay, decline, deflate, desiccate, disappear, disintegrate, droop, dry, fade, perish, sear, sere, shrink, shrivel, waste, wilt *Antonyms:* bloom, develop, flourish, increase

withhold *v.* **1.** arrest, bridle, censor, check, control, curb, deduct, detain, deter, harness, hold, hold down *or* out, inhibit, leash, limit, muzzle, prohibit, rein in, repress, reserve, restrain, retain, screen, shroud, silence, sit on, squelch, suppress, suspend *Antonyms:* accord, bequeath, bestow, give, grant **2.** abstain, clam *or* hush up, cloak, conceal, deny, hide, mask, refrain, resist *Antonyms:* expose, reveal

without *adv.* beyond, externally, out, outdoors, out-of-doors, outside – *prep.* free from, in the absence of, lacking, not having, outside of, sans

withstand *v.* abide, bear, beard, brave, brook, challenge, combat, confront, contradict, contravene, defend, defy, dispute, endure, face fight, oppose, resist, stomach, suffer, survive, thwart, tolerate, undergo, weather *Nonformal:* hang tough, stand the gaff *Antonyms:* cave, give in, succumb, surrender, yield

witless *adj.* **1.** asinine, daft *(British)*, dense, doltish, dull, dumb, foolish, idiotic, ignorant, inept, insane, senseless, silly, stupid, thick, unintelligent, unthinking, unwise *Nonformal:* gormless, lame-brained, numskull, pea-brained *Antonyms:* acute, keen, perceptive, sagacious, sharp **2.** crazy, demented, deranged, mad, mindless, unhinged *Nonformal:* mental, nuts, screwy *Antonyms:* clearheaded, rational, sane

witness *n.* attestant, beholder, bystander, corroborator, eyewitness, gawker, observer, onlooker, proof, sidewalk superintendent *(Nonformal)*, spectator, testifier, viewer – *v.* **1.** attend, behold, eyeball *(Nonformal)*, look on, mark, note, notice, observe, perceive, pipe, read, see, sight, spot, spy, take in, view, watch **2.** affirm, attest, confirm, corroborate, prove, testify, verify **3.** authenticate, certify, co-sign, endorse, sign

witticism *n.* bon mot, hokum, jab, jest, joke, one-liner, pleasantry, quip, remark, sally, throwaway, wisecrack *Nonformal:* crack, gag, topper, wheeze, zinger

witty *adj.* amusing, bright, brilliant, clever, comedic, crazy, droll, entertaining, facetious, fanciful, funny, gay, humorous, ingenious, intelligent, jocular, lively, original, piquant, quick-witted, ridiculous, sarcastic, tongue-in-cheek, waggish, whimsical *Antonyms:* boring, dull, serious, tedious, tiresome

wizard *n.* **1.** *angakok (Inuktitut)*, astrologer, clairvoyant, conjurer, diviner, enchanter, fortuneteller, geomancer, hypnotist, illusionist, kahuna, magician, magic-user, magus, medicine man, medium, Merlin, necromancer, occultist, palmist, seer, shaman, soothsayer, sorcerer, summoner, thaumaturge, warlock, witch **2.** ace, expert, genius, guru, maestro, marvel, master, maven *(Nonformal)*, prodigy, star, virtuoso *Antonyms:* dullard, dunce, fool

wizened *adj.* desiccated, diminished, dried up, gnarled, lean, macerated, mummified, old, reduced, shrivelled, shrunken, wilted, withered, worn, wrinkled *Antonyms:* blooming, flourishing, fresh, glowing

wobble *v.* careen, falter, flounder, lean, lurch, oscillate, quake, quiver, reel, rock, roll, seesaw, shake, shimmy, stagger, stumble, sway, swing, teeter, totter, tremble, vacillate, vibrate, waver, weave *Antonyms:* rest, stay

woe *n.* adversity, affliction, agony, anguish, blues, burden, calamity, cataclysm, dejection, depression, desolation, disaster, distress, dolor, grief, hardship, headache, heartache, heartbreak, lamentation, melancholy, misadventure, misery, misfortune, pain, regret, rue, sadness, sorrow, suffering, tragedy, trial, tribulation, trouble, unhappiness, vale of tears, wretchedness *Nonformal:* bummer, heavy sledding *Antonyms:* bliss, elation, fortune, happiness, joy

woebegone *adj.* black, bleak, blue, cheerless, crestfallen, dejected, depressed, despondent, dismal, dispirited, doleful, downcast, downhearted, down-in-the-mouth *(Nonformal)*, dreary, forlorn, glum, grief-stricken, hangdog, heartsick, heavy-hearted, hurting, low, lugubrious, miserable, mournful, sad, sorrowful, troubled, unhappy, wretched *Antonyms:* blithe, cheery, elated, jubilant, sunny

woeful *adj.* **1.** afflicted, agonized, anguished, disconsolate, distressed, doleful, gloomy, breaking, heartrending, hopeless, lamentable, melancholy, miserable, mournful, plaintive, racked, sad, sorrowful, tortured, tragic, unfortunate, unhappy, wretched *Antonyms:* carefree, cheerful, contented, joyful **2.** appalling, awful, bad, calamitous, catastrophic, deplorable, disappointing, disastrous, disgraceful, dreadful, hideous, lousy, pathetic, pitiable, pitiful, poor, rotten, shocking, sorry, terrible *Nonformal:* crappy, lousy *Antonyms:* extraordinary, marvellous, outstanding **3.** deficient, feeble, inadequate, insignificant, insufficient, meagre, mean, paltry, piddling, skimpy, small, sparse *Antonyms:* abundant, generous, great

wolf *n.* **1.** canine, Canis lupus, carnivore, lobo, predator **2.** adulterer, Casanova, dallier, flirt, ladies' man, lecher, philanderer, playboy, rake, seducer, swinger, trifler, womanizer *Nonformal:* masher, Romeo, skirt chaser, stud – *v.* bolt, consume, devour, gobble, gorge, gulp, guzzle, inhale *(Nonformal)*, scarf, stuff

woman *n.* **1.** adult female, demoiselle, femme, gentlewoman, human, lady, lass, mademoiselle, madonna, maid, maiden, miss, mistress, Mrs., Ms., person, senora, she, signora *Nonformal:* biddie, bird, chick, creature, jane, skirt, tomato **2.** companion, girlfriend, helpmate, lover, partner, wife *Nonformal:* better half, squeeze **3.** abigail, chambermaid, char *(Nonformal)*, cleaning lady, domestic, housekeeper, servant *See also:* **female**

womanhood *n.* **1.** femininity, womankind, women, womenfolk, wimmin *or* womyn **2.** adulthood, age, age of majority, majority, maturity

womanizer *n.* Casanova, dallier, debauchee, Don Juan, hedonist, ladies' man, libertine, philanderer, playboy, profligate, rake, seducer, swinger *Nonformal:* good-time Charlie, lech, stud, tomcat, wolf

wonder *n.* **1.** admiration, amazement, astonishment, awe, bewilderment, fascination, incredulity, perplexity, puzzlement, reverence, shock, stupefaction, stupor, surprise, veneration, *Antonyms:* apathy, indifference, nonchalance **2.** curiosity, cynosure, freak, marvel, miracle, nonpareil, oddity, phenomenon, *rara avis (Latin)*, rarity, sensation, sight, spectacle – *v.* **1.** admire, amaze, boggle, gape, gawk, look aghast, marvel, stare **2.** cogitate, conceive, conceptualize, consider, envisage, fancy, imagine, meditate, muse, ponder, ruminate, speculate, think over, visualize

wonderful *adj.* admirable, amazing, astonishing, astounding, awe-inspiring, awesome, brilliant, charming, divine, engaging, enjoyable, excellent, extraordinary, fabulous, fantastic, great, incredible, magnificent, marvellous, miraculous, phenomenal, pleasing, prime, remarkable, sensational, staggering, startling, strange, stupendous, super, superb, surprising, terrific, tremendous *Nonformal:* boffo, cool, dynamite, wicked *Antonyms:* average, common, ordinary

wont *adj.* accepted, accustomed, common, conventional, customary, daily, demotic, established, familiar, formulaic, given, habitual, normative, ordinary, prescribed, routine, standard – *n.* convention, custom, formula, habit, norm, observance, practice, praxis, ritual, routine, rule, tradition, way *Antonyms:* change, deviation, divergence

woo *v.* **1.** ask out, chase, court, date, make advances, propose, pursue, serenade, trail **2.** beg, beseech, cajole, coax, entreat, implore, importune, plead, wheedle **3.** allure, attract, charm, entice, influence, invite, lead, lure, seduce, solicit, win

wood *n.* **1.** board, building material, firewood, hardwood, kindling, lumber, softwood, timber, xylem *Selected wood measurements:* board foot, bush cord or cord, cubit, face cord, deal, standard *See also:* **tree** **2.** arbor, coppice, copse, dell, forest, grove, growth, jungle, stand, sugarbush, thicket, timber, timberland, trees, weald *(British)*, woodlot, woods

wooden *adj.* **1.** awkward, clumsy, cumbersome, heavy, mechanical, ponderous, rigid, robotic, stiff, stilted, ungainly **2.** dense, dim-witted, doltish, dumb, inane, obtuse, slow, stodgy, stupid, thick, wooden-headed *(Nonformal)*, vacant, vacuous **3.** apathetic, dull, lethargic, lifeless, sluggish, spiritless, torpid **4.** blank, deadpan, devoid, expressionless, glassy, inexpressive, oaken, poker-faced, sphinx-like, void

woods *n.* back country, boscage, brush, bush, bushveld, copse, forest, frontier, grove, growth, hinterland, jungle, rainforest, scrub, scrubland, shrubland, stand, thicket, timber, timberlands, trees, wilderness, wilds, woodland, woodlot *See also:* **wood**

woodwind *n.* bassoon, clarinet, fife, flute, hornpipe, krummhorn, oboe, ocarina, panpipes, piccolo, pipe, recorder, reed pipe, saxophone, shepherd's pipe, whistle *See also:* **instrument**

wool *n.* coat, down, fibre, fleece, fluff, fur, hair, nap, pashm, pelt, pile, qiviut, shag, under-fur, yarn

woolgathering *n.* absent-mindedness, abstraction, brown study, distraction, daydreaming, dreaming, drifting, idleness, inattention, pondering, reverie, stargazing, wandering *Antonyms:* attention, focus

woolly *adj.* **1.** bushy, downy, feathery, fleecy, fluffy, furry, hairy, hirsute, lanate, laniferous, nappy, pilose, shaggy, soft, tufty, velvety, villous, wooden *Antonyms:* firm, hard, rigid, stiff **2.** blurred, confounded, confused, disorganized, fuzzy, ill-defined, indistinct, jumbled, muddled, nebulous, unclear **3.** boisterous, chaotic, crazy, exciting, frantic, frenetic, frenzied, hectic, lawless, restless, rough and ready, tempestuous, turbulent, unsettled *Antonyms:* calm, pacific, peaceful

word *n.* **1.** antonym, character, concept, designation, free *or* linguistic form, homonym, idiom, lexicon, locution, monosyllable, morpheme, name, *parole (French)*, polysyllable, representation, sound, syllable, synonym, term, unit, usage, utterance, vocabulary **2.** chit-chat, communication, conversation, coze, discourse, interchange, parley, talk, tête-à-tête **3.** comment, hint, message, remark, suggestion **4.** adage, aphorism, byword, declaration, expression, maxim, motto, proverb, quote, saw, saying, scripture **5.** command, dictate, direction, directive, edict, instruction, law, rule, statute **6.** alert, gesture, notice, sign, signal, warning **7.** access, code word, entry, password, secret word, shibboleth, watchword *Nonformal:* abracadabra, open sesame **8.** affirmation, assurance, commitment, construct, guarantee, oath, parole, pledge, plight, promise, undertaking, vow, warranty **9.** account, gossip, information, intelligence, lowdown, announcement, bulletin, news, report, rumour, story, tidings, update *Nonformal:* scuttlebutt, skinny – *v.* communicate, delineate, disclose, explain, expound, express, phrase, say, spell out, style

wording *n.* arrangement, diction, expression, language, locution, manner, mode, organization, phraseology, phrasing, presentation, style, terminology, usage, verbiage, words

words *n.* **1.** altercation, argument, bickering, clash, contention, debate, disagreement, dispute, fight, fracas, logomachy, quarrel, row, spat, squabble, tiff *Antonyms:* agreement, concord, harmony **2.** chat, communication, confab *(Nonformal)*, confabulation, conversation, discourse, elocution, gab, palaver, parole, prattle, talk **3.** dialect, language, lexicon, patois, speech, verbiage, vernacular, vocabulary **4.** book, dialogue, libretto, lyrics, script, text, wording

wordy *adj.* battological, bombastic, chatty, diffuse, discursive, flatulent, garrulous, inflated, lengthy, long-winded, loquacious, palaverous, pleonastic, prolix, rambling, redundant, rhetorical, talkative, tautological, tedious, turgid, verbose, voluble, windy *Antonyms:* brief, concise, laconic, pithy

work *n.* **1.** act, activity, effort, endeavour, enterprise, exertion, labour, movement, muscle, performance **2.** drudgery, grindstone, pains, servitude, slavery, striving, struggle, toil, travail, trial, trouble *Nonformal:* daily grind, donkeywork, elbow grease, grind, gruntwork, rat race, salt mines, scutwork *Antonyms:* ease, leisure, relaxation **3.** art, business, calling, career, employment, job, line, livelihood, métier, occupation, office, practice, profession, pursuit, responsibility, specialization, vocation, walk *Nonformal:* gig, racket **4.** assignment, chore, contract, duty, operation, stint, task, undertaking **5.** accomplishment, achievement, corpus, exploit, feat, output, performance, throughput **6.** artistry, care, craft, diligence, expertise, know-how, knowledge, proficiency, skill, talent, technique, workmanship **7.** article, commodity, concoction, construction, creation, end, fabrication, goods, handiwork, manufacture, masterpiece, merchandise, oeuvre, opus notes, piece, *pièce de résistance (French)*, presentation, product, production, result, script, sketch, text, ware **8.** energy, force, motion, potency, power, strength – *v.* **1.** drudge, hustle, labour, moil, slave, strive, sweat, toil, undertake *Nonformal:* bust a gut, scratch **2.** act, behave, function, go, perform, progress, react, run **3.** do, earn a living, occupy oneself, pay the bills *(Nonformal)*, ply, practise, serve **4.** control, direct, drive, handle, manage, manoeuvre, manipulate, operate, use, wield **5.** fashion, form, knead, make, mould, mix, process, shape **6.** accomplish, achieve, become, reach, realize, succeed **7.** bring about, carry out, cause, effect, execute, implement, occasion **8.** associate, gladhand, interact, mix, network, schmooze *(Nonformal)*, sell oneself, socialize **9.** affect, impress, induce, influence, move, persuade, sway, touch **10.** care for, cultivate, dig, farm, garden, harvest, plant, plow, ranch, seed, sow, tend, till *Antonyms:* disregard, neglect

workable *adj.* **1.** applicable, exploitable, feasible, functional, no sweat *(Nonformal)*, plausible, possible, practicable, practical, producible, usable, useful, viable *Antonyms:* hopeless, impossible, unattainable **2.** ductile, formable, malleable, mouldable, plastic, pliant, shapable, soft, tractable, yielding *Antonyms:* breakable, rigid, stiff

worker *n.* agent, artisan, author, blue-collar worker, breadwinner, craftsman, day labourer, employee, executor, floater, functionary, hand, help, jobber, labourer, lead hand, mechanic, migrant worker, operative, operator, performer, pieceworker, practitioner, producer, proletarian, roustabout, stevedore, wage earner, white-collar worker, workhorse, workman, workwoman, wright *Nonformal:* drone, drudge, flunky, hand, lackey, stiff, temp, worky joe

working *adj.* **1.** busy, earning, employed, engaged, gainfully employed, hired, labouring, under contract *Antonyms:* available, looking, unemployed **2.** active, alive, dynamic, effective, functioning, going, live, moving, okay *(Nonformal)*, operative, practical, running, useful, viable *Antonyms:* broken, damaged, defective, faulty

workmanship *n.* ability, art, artistry, attention, command, craft, craftsmanship, detail, expertise, genius, knowledge, mastery, polish, pride, skill, talent, technique

workout *n.* **1.** aerobics, aquatics, athletics, calisthenics, conditioning, constitutional, dancercize, exercise, gym class, isometrics, jazzercize, jogging, warmup, weight training **2.** dress rehearsal, drill, practice, preparation, rehearsal, run-through, session, test, training, trial, tryout

world *n.* **1.** biosphere, earth, ecosystem, firmament, four corners, globe, global village, land and sea, macrocosm, mortal coil, mother earth, planet, terra firma **2.** cosmos, creation, galaxy, heavens, system, universe **3.** everybody, everyone, humanity, humankind, human race, man, mankind, nation, people, race, woman, womankind **4.** circumstance, dust to dust, ephemerality, evanescence, existence, impermanence, life, mortality, temporariness, transience **5.** area, arena, class, department, division, domain, field, kingdom, part, province, realm, sector, sphere **6.** business *or* community *or* social life, clan, crowd, public, real *or* working world, society, streets *(Nonformal)*, tribe **7.** abundance, flood, heap, ocean, pile, profusion, quantity, sackful, sea, spate, stack

worldly *adj.* **1.** carnal, earthly, material, mundane, natural, physical, profane, secular, tangible, temporal, terrestrial, unsacred *Antonyms:* ethereal, immaterial, metaphysical, spiritual **2.** broad-minded, cosmopolitan, experienced, knowledgeable, knowing, mature, sagacious, streetwise, smart, sophisticated, suave, travelled, urbane, wise *Nonformal:* hip, street-smart, with it

worm *n.* **1.** grub, helminth, invertebrate, larva *Common worms:* annelid, armyworm, dewworm, earthworm, flatworm, fluke, glowworm, hookworm, inchworm, leech, marine, nightcrawler, pinworm, roundworm, silkworm, tapeworm, trichna, tubeworm, woodworm **2.** groveller, sneak, weasel *Nonformal:* flea, jerk, louse, maggot, rat, scum, sleaze, slime, sniveller, stinker, vermin – *v.* **1.** crawl, creep, inch along, insinuate, pussyfoot, sidle, slink, sneak, wriggle, writhe *Antonyms:* lumber, lunge, run, stomp **2.** cajole, elicit, extract, extricate, inveigle, wheedle, wring

worn *adj.* **1.** hand-me-down, old, preloved *(Nonformal)*, preused, preworn, second-hand, tried, used *Antonyms:* fresh, mint, new, pristine **2.** deteriorated, frayed, holey, kaput *(Nonformal)*, ragged, ruined, seedy, shabby, shot, tattered, threadbare, time-worn, weathered, well-worn **3.** battle-scarred, beat, depleted, dispirited, drained, drawn, effete, exhausted, fatigued, haggard, overworked, spent, tired, used up, war-weary, wearied, worn-down, worn-out *Nonformal:* burned *or* wiped out, burnt, bushed, destroyed, drained, fried, pooped, totalled, zapped **4.** banal, clichéd, corny, hackneyed, overused, trite

worry *n.* affliction, anguish, annoyance, anxiety, apprehension, care, concern, disquiet, distress, doubt, fear, headache, misery, misgiving, perplexity, pest, plague, presentiment, problem, responsibility, torment, torture, trial, trouble, uncertainty, uneasiness, vexation, woe *Antonyms:* calm, comfort, solace – *v.* **1.** agonize, bleed, despair, feel, fret, grieve, pain, sigh, stew *(Nonformal)*, suffer, weep, wince, writhe *Antonyms:* enjoy, rejoice, relax **2.** afflict, aggrieve, annoy, attack, beleaguer, beset, bother, disturb, goad, harass, harry, hassle *(Nonformal)*, hector, importune, irk, irritate, nag, needle, nettle, oppress, peeve, persecute, perturb, pester, plague, tantalize, tear, tease, test, torment, torture, trouble, try, unsettle, upset, vex, wrong *Antonyms:* cheer, console, reassure, soothe

worsen *v.* **1.** aggravate, corrode, damage, depress, exacerbate, impair, irritate *Antonyms:* better, improve, rally **2.** corrode, decay, decline, degenerate, descend, deteriorate, diminish, drop, ebb, fall, increase, intensify, lapse, lower, regress, retrogress, rot, slide, slip, sink, wane

worship *n.* **1.** adoration, awe, beatification, *bhakti (Hindu)*, deification, devotion, exaltation, genuflection, glorification, glory, hagiolatry, homage, honouring, idolatry, idolization, invocation, laudation, love, mantra, meditation, regard, reverence, supplication, veneration *Antonyms:* contempt, disdain, scorn **2.** benediction, blessing, chapel, church service, liturgy, mass, mystery, oblation, observance, offering, prayer, *puja (Hindu)*, rite, ritual, sacrifice, service, vespers – *v.* adore, adulate, bow down, canonize, celebrate, chant, deify, esteem, exalt, extol, glorify, honour, idolize, laud, magnify, praise, pray to, respect, revere, sanctify, sing, venerate *Antonyms:* blaspheme, dishonour, flout, revile, scoff

worst *adj.* atrocious, awful, bad, dangerous, dreadful, deplorable, evil, harmful, hideous, horrid, horrible, outrageous, pitiful, shameful, terrible, wretched – *v.* beat, best, defeat, drub, outclass, outdistance, outdo, outshine, overcome, surpass, trounce, vanquish *Nonformal:* clobber, cream, lick, slaughter, trash, wallop, whip, whomp, whup

worth *n.* **1.** benefit, character, desirability, goodness, importance, meaning, merit, preciousness, quality, significance, superiority **2.** amount, appraisal, assessment, cost, equity, expense, figure, list, market price, monetary value, net, outlay, price, retail, usefulness, value **3.** affluence, assets, capital, circumstances, effects, estate, fortune, funds, holdings, land, means, money, position, possessions, property, resources, riches, store, valuables, wampum *(Nonformal)*

worthless *adj.* **1.** cheap, inconsequential, insignificant, nothing, paltry, profitless, unavailing, unprofitable, unrewarding, unusable, valueless *Nonformal:* nickel and dime, pissant, two-bit *Antonyms:* costly, expensive, priceless **2.** barren, bootless, empty, futile, good-for-nothing, ineffectual, sterile, unproductive, useless, vacant, waste *Antonyms:* fecund, fruitful, productive **3.** awful, bad, dreadful, garbage, ghastly, hideous, horrible, horrific, sad, sorry, terrible, worst, wretched *Nonformal:* cheesy, crappy, lousy *Antonyms:* beautiful, great, fantastic, wonderful **4.** bogus, counterfeit, ersatz, fake, forged, imitation, mock, paste, phoney *(Nonformal)*, spurious *Antonyms:* authentic, genuine, original **5.** contemptible, despicable, disgraceful, dishonourable, ignoble, no-account *(Nonformal)*, scrofulous, shameful, sneaky

worthwhile *adj.* advantageous, beneficial, constructive, estimable, excellent, gainful, good, helpful, important, invaluable, justifiable, lucrative, meritorious, moneymaking, paying, productive, profitable, remunerative, rewarding, salubrious, useful, valuable, worthy *Antonyms:* inconsequential, pointless, trivial, useless, vain

worthy *adj.* **1.** admirable, best, blue-chip, choice, commendable, creditable, decent, dependable, deserving, desirable, estimable, excellent, exemplary, first class, first-rate, gilt-edged, invaluable, laudable, meritorious, model, pleasing, praiseworthy, precious, priceless, reliable, reputable, respectable, satisfying, sterling, top-drawer, topnotch, trustworthy, valuable, winning, worthwhile *Antonyms:* disreputable, dubious, undeserving, unproductive, useless **2.** angelic, blameless, divine, ethical, good, honest, honourable, moral, noble, pure, righteous, right-minded, true, uncorrupt, upright, upstanding, virtuous *Antonyms:* devilish, evil, villainous – *n.* dignitary, eminence, lion, luminary, notable, official, personage *Nonformal:* bigwig, hot shot, pooh-bah

wound *n.* **1.** abrasion, battle scar, booboo *(Nonformal)*, bruise, bump, contusion, cut, damage, gash, harm, hurt, injury, laceration, lesion, pain, puncture, scar, scrape, scratch, slash, sore, stab, tear, trauma, war wound, welt **2.** anguish, blow, distress, embarrassment, grief, hardship, heartbreak, insult, memory, misery, pang, scandal, shock, slander, sorrow, torment, torture – *v.* **1.** bruise, carve, clip, contuse, cut, damage, gash, harm, hit, hurt, injure, irritate, knife, lacerate, nick, open, pierce, rough up, scrape, scratch, shoot, slash, slice, stab, stick, wing *(Nonformal) Antonyms:* cure, doctor, heal, remedy, repair **2.** abuse, aggrieve, bother, distress, disturb, do in, dump on *(Nonformal)*, get, grieve, hurt, kick around, mortify, offend, outrage, pain, put down, shake up, shock, slander, sting, traumatize, trouble, upset, vilify, wrong *Antonyms:* comfort, ease, soothe

wow *interj.* amazing, awesome, fabulous, fantastic, great, incredible, marvellous, spectacular, splendid, stupendous, thrilling, wonderful *Nonformal:* cool, crazy, criminy, cripes, fab, fantabulous, far out, gear, golly, gosh, holy cow *or* mackerel *or* mackinaw, jeepers, splendiferous, too much, zounds, zowie – *v.* amaze, amuse, beguile, captivate, charm, delight, enchant, enliven, enrapture, entertain, enthrall, fascinate, refresh, regale, thrill, tickle, titillate, transport *Nonformal:* gobsmack, knock out, slay *Antonyms:* annoy, bother, irritate

wraith *n.* apparition, banshee, bibe *(Newfoundland)*, double, fetch, ghost, haunting, nightmare, phantom, poltergeist, presence, revenant, shade, shadow, spectre, spirit, spook *(Nonformal)*, sprite, vision

wrangle *n.* altercation, argument, bickering, brawl, clash, contest, controversy, disagreement, dispute, disruption, donnybrook, exchange, falling-out, fight, flap, fracas, hassle *(Nonformal)*, quarrel, row, ruction, rumble, rumpus, set-to, squabble, tiff *Antonyms:* accord, agreement, amity, consensus – *v.* **1.** argue, bicker, clash, contend, disagree, dispute, fight, quarrel, quibble, scrap, squabble, spat, take on, tangle *Nonformal:* bump heads, cross swords, have words, lock horns *Antonyms:* concur, cooperate, harmonize **2.** collect, corral, drive, gather, herd, rope, round up, shepherd

wrap *n.* **1.** blanket, boa, cape, cloak, clothing, coat, cover, cummerbund, ermine, fur, jacket, mantle, poncho, sarape, scarf, shawl, stole **2.** burrito, pita, roll, sandwich, tortilla – *v.* **1.** bandage, bundle up, cloak, clothe, cover, drape, dress, encase, encircle, enclose, enfold, envelop, fold, muffle, sheathe, shroud, surround, swaddle, swathe *Antonyms:* expose, open, uncover, unseal **2.** bind, girdle, lash, strap, tie **3.** batch, bundle, gift-wrap, pack, package, parcel, protect **4.** close or close off, complete, conclude, end, finish, terminate, wind up

wrath *n.* anger, choler, ferocity, fit, furor, fury, indignation, ire, madness, passion, rage, raving, resentment, righteous indignation, punishment, storm, temper, vengeance, *Antonyms:* calm, control, quiet

wrathful *adj.* angry, antagonistic, boiling, choleric, enraged, explosive, ferocious, fiery, frenetic, frenzied, fuming, furious, incensed, indignant, infuriated, irate, mad, raging, seething, steaming, storming, tempestuous, torrential, vehement, violent, volcanic *Nonformal:* fit to be tied, on the warpath *Antonyms:* contented, happy, peaceful, satisfied

wreath *n.* **1.** band, bay, bouquet, chaplet, circle, circlet, corona, crown, diadem, festoon, garland, laurels, lei, loop, ring, ringlet **2.** coil, curl, spiral, twist, whorl

wreck *n.* **1.** bits and pieces, debris, derelict, detritus, flotsam, jetsam, leftovers, parts, pieces, remains, remnants, ruin, salvage, shipwreck, wrack, wreckage, write-off *Nonformal:* carcass, sunken treasure **2.** adversity, blow, blowdown *(Forestry)*, cataclysm, catastrophe, collapse, collision, crackup, crash, debacle, destruction, devastation, disaster, mess, misfortune, mishap, shock, smash, wreckage *Nonformal:* pile-up, smash up *Antonyms:* good fortune, luck, prosperity – *v.* **1.** bash, beach, break, capsize, crash, cream *(Nonformal)*, decimate, destroy, devastate, dilapidate, founder, mangle, mar, ravage, ruin, run aground, shatter, shipwreck, sink, smash, total, trash **2.** cripple, disable, impair, injure, kneecap, ruin, sabotage, scuttle, spoil, subvert, take out, torpedo, undermine **3.** bulldoze, demolish, dismantle, dynamite, eliminate, flatten, gut *(Nonformal)*, knock *or* pull *or* tear down, raze, scrap, steamroll

wrecked *adj.* busted, finished, finito, gone, kaput, shot, sunk, totalled *Nonformal:* down the tube, dusted

wrench *n.* **1.** tool *Kinds of wrench:* adjustable, Allen, alligator, bicycle, crescent, monkey, off-set, open-end, pipe, plumbers, ratchet, S-wrench, socket, spanner, Stillson, tappet, tire iron, valve **2.** ache, agony, anguish, bereavement, despair, distress, grief, heartache, heartbreak, melancholy, pang, pain, sadness, sorrow, throe, woe **3.** jerk, jolt, pull, spin, tug, turn, twist, yank **4.** cramp, crimp, injury, spasm, sprain, strain – *v.* **1.** extract, force, grab, jerk, jolt, pluck, pry, pull, rip, snatch, spin, tug, turn, twist, wrest, yank **2.** aggravate, damage, dash, hurt, injure, rend, strain, tear, tweak **3.** afflict, agonize, break, distress, harrow, pain, rack, torment, torture **4.** alter, bend, bias, change, colour, distort, fudge, misrepresent, mutate, pervert, skew

wrestle *v.* **1.** battle, combat, contend, fight, grapple, scuffle, tangle, tussle, wrassle *(Nonformal) Kinds of wrestling:* freestyle,

Greco Roman, sambo, sumo *Selected wrestling terms:* Boston crab, bridge position, bye, clinch, contact red, cross ankle tilt, exposure, fall, forearm shiver, full nelson, flying mare, grand amplitude, gut wrench, hold, par terre, passivity call, pile driver, reversal, salto, sleeper, suplay, take down, throw **2.** endeavour, essay, exert, labour, strain, strive, struggle, toil, travail, trouble, try, work

wretched *adj.* **1.** afflicted, dejected, depressed, despondent, disconsolate, dispirited, dolorous, down, downcast, forlorn, grieved, hapless, heartbroken, hopeless, inconsolable, languishing away, melancholy, miserable, pitiful, sad, sorrowful, sorry, unfortunate, unhappy, woeful *Antonyms:* carefree, cheerful, contented **2.** distressing, harrowing, heart-wrenching, horrible, pathetic, piteous, pitiable, tear-jerking, tragic **3.** deplorable, destitute, dilapidated, distressed, impoverished, indigent, neglected, penurious, poverty-stricken, slum, squalid, tumbledown **4.** appalling, atrocious, awful, bad, disgusting, dreadful, horrid, rotten, terrible, unfortunate, worthless **5.** abject, base, coarse, contemptible, despicable, detestable, low, lowdown, nefarious, scrofulous, scurvy, shady, shameful, shifty, sordid, vulgar, vile *Antonyms:* aboveboard, decent, upstanding

wriggle *n.* crawl, fidget, fuss, jiggle, shimmy, slink, slither, snake, squiggle, squirm, turn, twist, waggle, wiggle, wobble, writhe, zigzag – *v.* avoid, dodge, escape, flee, sidestep, slip away *Nonformal:* deke, dipsy-doodle, worm,

wring *v.* **1.** choke, compress, contort, pinch, screw, squeeze, strain, strangle, throttle, turn, twist, wrench **2.** blackmail, coerce, exact, extort, extract, force, gouge, shake down, threaten **3.** aggrieve, agonize, distress, hurt, pain, rack, torment, torture, wound

wrinkle *n.* **1.** contraction, corrugation, crease, crinkle, crow's foot, crumple, depression, fold, furrow, gather, line, pleat, pucker, ridge, tuck **2.** device, gimmick, gizmo *(Nonformal)*, idea, method, scheme, situation, spin, strategy, stunt, technique, trick – *v.* compress, contract, corrugate, crease, crumple, fold, furrow, gather, pleat, press, pucker, rumple, seam, shrivel, tuck, twist *Antonyms:* flatten, iron, press, smooth

writ *n.* charge, command, court order, decree, document, habeas corpus, law citation, licence, mandate, permit, precept, scire facias, subpoena, summons, warrant

write *v.* **1.** inscribe, keyboard, key in, letter, mark, note, pen, pencil, print, score, scratch, scrawl, scribble, scribe, scroll, sign, spell, trace, transcribe, type **2.** commit, copy, delineate, describe, detail, document, expand on, flesh *or* spell out, narrate, outline, paint, record, report, represent, rewrite, set down *or* forth, sketch, tell, transcribe, write down *or* up **3.** communicate, contact, convey, correspond, e-mail, fax, mail, relate, send **4.** author, compose, concoct, create, draft, formulate, ghost, pen, produce, score, wax

write-off *n.* **1.** ruin, smash-up, wreck *Nonformal:* goner, pile of junk, toast **2.** disappointment, disaster, dud, failure, fiasco, flop, loss, mess, misfortune, screw-up *(Nonformal)*, shambles, washout **3.** cancellation, discount, dismissal, eradication, nullification, obliteration, tax credit, voidance

writer *n.* author, biographer, collaborator, columnist, copywriter, creator, critic, diarist, dramatist, dramaturgist, editor, encyclopedist, essayist, ghostwriter, hack, journalist, lexicographer, newspaperperson, novelist, pamphleteer, penman, playwright, poet, reporter, scholar, screenwriter, scribbler, scribe, scriptwriter, scrivener, stringer, wordsmith *Nonformal:* pencil pusher, scribbler, word-slinger *See also:* **author, poet**

writhe *v.* **1.** bend, contort, convulse, distort, jerk, squirm, struggle, thrash, twist, wiggle, worm, wriggle **2.** ache, anguish, grieve, hurt, lament, mourn, pain, smart, sorrow, suffer, torment

writing *n.* **1.** autograph, calligraphy, chirography, hand, handwriting, hieroglyphics, holograph, lettering, longhand, penmanship, print, printing, scrawl, scribbling, shorthand, signature *Nonformal:* chicken scratch, fist **2.** argument, article, autobiography, *belles-lettres (French)*, biography, book, collection, commentary, composition, creation, critique, dialogue, discourse, discussion, dissertation, document, drama, editorial, essay, exposition, fiction, history, journal, letter, libretto, lines, literature, magazine, manifesto, manual, manuscript, memoir, music, newspaper, non-fiction, notes, novel, opus, pamphlet, paper, piece, play, poem, poetry, position paper, production, prose, publication, record, review, script, story, study, text, theme, thesis, tome, tract, treatise, volume, words, work *See also:* **drama, fiction, poetry** **3.** art, craft, expression, form, manner, mode, pen, phraseology, quality, readability, style, wording

wrong *adj.* **1.** erroneous, fallacious, false, imprecise, inaccurate, inexact, incongruous, incorrect, misinformed, mistaken, untrue *Nonformal:* blowing smoke, bum, full of beans, off the mark, out in left field, out to lunch *Antonyms:* correct, okay *(Nonformal)*, right **2.** disproportionate, gauche, ill-advised, ill-considered, improper, inappropriate, inapt, incompatible, malapropos, misplaced, unacceptable, unsatisfactory, unsuitable *Antonyms:* appropriate, apt, becoming, fitting **3.** amoral, bad, base, blasphemous, censurable, corrupt, criminal, crooked, debauched, depraved, dishonest, dissipated, evil, felonious, illegal, illicit, immoral, indecent, lowdown, naughty, nefarious, odious, profane, profligate, reprehensible, reprobate, risqué, rotten, rude, sacrilegious, salacious, shameful, sinful, smutty, terrible, unethical, unfair, unjust, unlawful, vicious, villainous, wicked *Antonyms:* ethical, moral, praiseworthy **4.** amiss, awkward, curious, different, eccentric, flawed, funny *(Nonformal)*, odd, off-balance, opposite, out of order, peculiar, perverted, queer, reversed, strange, unaccountable, unusual – *adv.* askew, astray, awry, badly, erroneously, imperfectly, improperly, inaccurately, incorrectly, mistakenly, unfairly, unfavourably, unjustly *Antonyms:* accurately, correctly, exactly – *n.* abuse, blunder, breach, crime, damage, delinquency, disservice, error, evil, faux pas, foul play, grievance, harm, hurt, imposition, indecency, infraction, injury, injustice, insult, invasion, libel, mischief, misdeed, misdemeanour, miscarriage, mistake, offence, persecution, prejudice, sin, slander, slight, transgression, trespass, villainy, violation, wickedness *Antonyms:* decency, favour, goodness, kindness, service – *v.* **1.** abuse, aggrieve, cheat, crush, damage, destroy, harm, hurt, ill-treat, injure, maltreat, mistreat, offend, oppress, outrage, persecute, torment, violate *Antonyms:* aid, help, support **2.** besmirch, defame, discredit, dishonour, malign, misrepresent, slander, smear, stain, sully **3.** deviate, disobey, encroach, fall, infringe, profane, sin, slide, slip, trespass

wrongdoer *n.* criminal, culprit, delinquent, deviant, evildoer, felon, guilty party, lawbreaker, malefactor, malfeasant, miscreant, offender, perpetrator, reprobate, scoundrel, sinner, transgressor, trespasser, vandal, villain *Nonformal:* crook

wrought *adj.* assembled, built, constructed, crafted, created, defined, fashioned, forged, formed, hammered, made, manufactured, moulded, ornate, polished, produced, shaped, worked

wry *adj.* **1.** askew, aslant, awry, bevelled, contorted, crooked, lopsided, oblique, off-centre, tilted, twisted, uneven, warped *Antonyms:* aligned, level, smooth, straight **2.** aberrant, deformed, deviant, distorted, perverted, skewed **3.** amusing, biting, bitter, caustic, cynical, droll, dry, ironic, mocking, perverse, sarcastic, sardonic, self-depreciating, trenchant, vitriolic

x *n.* **1.** autograph, fist *(Nonformal)*, hand, inscription, John Hancock, John Henry, signature **2.** conundrum, mystery, puzzle, question, riddle, variable, unknown factor *or* quantity

xanthous *adj.* blond, golden, honey, jaundiced, luteous, saffron, sallow, topaz, tope, yellow, yellowish

xenophobia *n.* bigotry, ethnocentrism, discrimination, fear of foreigners, hatred, jingoism, myopia, narrowness, parochialism, provincialism, racism, regionalism

xenophobic *adj.* chauvinistic, ethnocentric, extremist, insular, isolationist, jingoistic, limited, myopic, narrow, narrow-minded, nationalistic, parochial, prejudiced, provincial, racist, right-wing

x-out *v.* annul, blue pencil, cancel, cross *or* wipe out, delete, eliminate, erase, purge, strike, void

X-rated *adj.* carnal, erotic, indecent, lewd, obscene, pornographic, raunchy, raw, sensual, sensuous, sexual, sexy *Nonformal:* adult, blue, dirty, hot, naughty, smutty, xxx *Antonyms:* clean, family-oriented, G-rated

x-ray *n.* **1.** cathode ray, electromagnetic radiation, radioactivity, Roentgen ray **2.** film, hard copy, image, photograph, picture, radiogram, radiograph, screening, tomogram – *v.* appraise, check, confirm, examine, explore, inspect, look, probe, read, scan, scope, search, see, uncover, verify, view

yacht *n.* boat, cabin-cruiser, cruiser, racer, sailboat, ship, sloop, vessel, windjammer *(Nonformal) See also:* **boat, ship** – *v.* cruise, escape, journey, race, sail, travel, venture

yahoo *n.* barbarian, boor, brute, clown, lout, low-brow, philistine, ruffian, savage, thug, vulgarian, yokel *Nonformal:* ass, boob, bozo, bumpkin, hoser, knucklehead, piece of work, rube, slob, ugly customer, wally *Antonyms:* exemplar, longhair, paragon

yak *v.* babble, blather, chatter, chitchat, converse, gab, jabber, palaver, prate, prattle, ramble, rattle, speak, spiel on *(Nonformal)*, talk

yammer *v.* blubber, complain, cry, groan, grumble, howl, moan, nag, snivel, squawk, wail, whine *Nonformal:* bellyache, bitch, gripe, grouse, yada yada yada *Antonyms:* exult, glory, rejoice

yank *v.* draw, extract, hitch, jerk, lug, pluck, pull, snap, snatch, tear, tug, twitch, wrench

yard *n.* backyard, barnyard, close, compound, coop, corral, courtyard, enclosure, exercise ground, fold, garden, graveyard, grounds, lawn, lot, millyard, patch, patio, pen, playground, plot, quadrangle, railyard, shipyard, stockyard, terrace

yardstick *n.* benchmark, criteria, example. exemplar, formula, gauge, guide, model, paradigm, pattern, rule of thumb, ruler, scale, standard, touchstone

yarn *n.* **1.** fibre, hank, skein, strand, string, thread, twist, wool **2.** account, anecdote, chronicle, cock-and-bull story, discourse, epic, fabrication, falsehood, farrago, fiction, invention, megillah, narration, narrative, saga, tale, whopper *(Nonformal)*

yawning *adj.* broad, cavernous, gaping, great, inviting, open, wide, widespread *Antonyms:* closed, shut, tight – *n.* chasm, cleavage, cleft, divide, gape, gulf, mouth, opening, parting, rift, spread

yearly *adj.* annual, annually, cyclical, once a year, per annum, perennial, predictable, recurrent, regular, repetitive, rhythmical, yearlong

yearn *v.* ache, burn, covet, crave, desire, dream, fume, hanker, hunger, long, pine, relish, smoulder, thirst, want, yen *(Nonformal)*

yeast *n.* **1.** catalyst, enzyme, fungi, leavening agent, mould, pepsin **2.** bubbles, foam, froth, fuzz, head, lather, spume, suds **3.** agitation, anxiety, commotion, confusion, discontent, disquiet, fuss, tension, tumult, turmoil, uneasiness, unrest – *v.* agitate, boil, bubble, ferment, foam, froth, leaven, rise

yeasty *adj.* **1.** agitated, anxious, brewing, distraught, excited, frantic, frenzied, hysterical, mad, restless, ruffled, unsettled, wild **2.** flimsy, frivolous, insignificant, light, paltry, petty, superficial, trifling *Antonyms:* critical, significant, substantial, weighty **3.** bubbly, effervescent, foamy, frothy

yell *n. & v.* bawl, bellow, call, cheer, complain, cry, holler, hoot, howl, lament, let loose *(Nonformal)*, roar, scream, screech, shout, shriek, shrill, squawk, squeal, wail, weep, whoop, yap, yelp *Antonyms:* murmur, mutter, whisper

yellow *adj.* **1.** afraid, chicken, cowardly, craven, daunted, deceitful, dishonourable, frightened, gutless, lily-livered, low, mean, mousy, pusillanimous, scared, shaking in one's boots *(Nonformal)*, sneaking, timid, timorous, untrustworthy **2.** bilious, jaundiced, sallow, sick, sickly, wan, waxy **3.** blatant, cheap, excessive, flagrant, histrionic, muckraking, sensational, tabloid, tacky, trashy – *n.* colour *Yellow shades:* amber, bisque, blond, buff, banana, cadmium, canary, chrome, citron, cream, daffodil, dirty blond, ecru, flaxen, fulvous, gold, khaki, lemon, mustard, ochre, primrose, saffron, sallow, sand, straw, sun, tawny, topaz, tope, vitelline, xanthous

yelp *n. & v.* bark, caterwaul, cry, hoot, howl, kyoodle, screech, yap, yip, yowl

yen *n.* craving, desire, hankering, hunger, itch, longing, lust, passion, thirst, urge, yearning

yes *interj.* absolutely, affirmative, all right, amen, assuredly, as *or* whatever you say, aye, certainly, definitely, exactly, gladly, indubitably, just so, *li (Inuktitut)*, most assuredly, naturally, of course, *oui (French)*, positively, precisely, really, roger, sure, surely, sure thing, truly, undoubtedly, unquestionably, willingly, without fail, yea *Nonformal:* fine, okay, roger, yeah, yep, yup – *n.* acceptance, acquiescence, affirmation, agreement, approval, assent, consent, endorsement, go-ahead, permission, ratification, sanction, warrant *Nonformal:* A Okay, clear track, go-ahead, green light *Antonyms:* denial, prohibition, veto

yes-person *n.* conformist, disciple, fawner, flatterer, groveler, henchman, kowtower, lackey, minion, puppet, sycophant, toady *Nonformal:* brown-noser, sidekick, stooge, tool *Antonyms:* leader, maverick, rebel

yet *adv.* **1.** earlier, hitherto, prior to, so far, until now **2.** after all, although, anyhow, besides, but, despite, even though, however, nevertheless, nonetheless, notwithstanding, regardless, still and all, though **3.** additionally, along, also, as well, ditto, further, furthermore, likewise, moreover, still, to boot *(Nonformal)*

yield *n.* crop, earnings, gain, harvest, income, net, output, produce, production, profit, receipt, return, revenue, take *or* takings, turnout *Nonformal:* bottom line, gate *Antonyms:* consumption, input, loss – *v.* **1.** accrue, admit, afford, bear, bring forth, discharge, earn, furnish, generate, give, offer, pay, produce, provide, render, return, sell for, supply, tender, turn out *Antonyms:* hold, keep, maintain **2.** abandon, abdicate, admit defeat, back *or* step down, bend, capitulate, cave in, cede, collapse, crumble, crumple, defer, fold, give in, leave the field, let go, relax, relent, relinquish, resign, submit, succumb, surrender *Antonyms:* fight, protect, resist **3.** accede, accept, accord, acknowledge, acquiesce, admit, agree, allow, assent, award, bow *(Nonformal)*, comply, concede, consent, defer, grant, pay homage, permit, waive

yielding *adj.* **1.** accommodating, acquiescent, compliant, docile, easy, nonresistant, obedient, passive, pliable, pliant, resigned, submissive, tractable *Antonyms:* headstrong, mulish, obstinate, stubborn, tenacious **2.** elastic, flexible, malleable, mushy, pliable, pulpy, resilient, soft, spongy, springy, squishy, supple *Antonyms:* hard, impassive, solid **3.** bounteous, fecund, fertile, fruitful, lush, luxuriant, productive, profitable, prolific, willowy *Antonyms:* barren, farrow, infertile, sterile

yoke *n.* **1.** bond, clamp, coupling, harness, strap **2.** bondage, burden, domination, enslavement, exploitation, impoverishment, misery, oppression, serfdom, servility, servitude, slavery, subjection, subjugation, subordination, thraldom, tyranny, weight *Antonyms:* deliverance, freedom, independence – *v.* associate, attach, bracket, combine, conjoin, connect, couple, harness, hitch, join, link, strap, tack, tie, unite, wed *Antonyms:* divide, separate, sever

yokel *n.* boor, bucolic, bumpkin, rustic *Nonformal:* clodhopper, country cousin, hayseed, hick, hillbilly, hoser, rube, yahoo

young *adj.* **1.** adolescent, boyish, boy-like, childish, childlike, girlish, girl-like, infant, junior, juvenile, little, newborn, puerile, unfledged **2.** callow, crude, fledgling, green *(Nonformal)*, ignorant, immature, inexperienced, raw, tender, undisciplined, unlearned, unripe, unseasoned, untried, unversed **3.** blooming, blossoming, budding, burgeoning, dawning, developing, dewy, early, fresh, growing, modern, new, pubescent, recent, undeveloped, unfinished, vernal, youthful *Antonyms:* advanced, closing, late **4.** active, dynamic, energetic, hale, healthy, lively, strong, vigorous **5.** extreme, fanatical, militant, progressive, radical, rebellious, revolutionary, seditious, zealous *Antonyms:* conservative, conventional, orthodox – *n.* babies, brood, children, family, issue, kids, litter, little ones, offspring, progeny

youngster *n.* boy, child, fledgling, girl, junior, lad, lass, minor, offspring, pupil, sapling, stripling, student, teenager, urchin, young adult, young person, youth *Nonformal:* boyo, brat, cub, imp, little guy *or* kid *or* shaver, moppet, nipper, peewee, punk, pup, puppy, rinkrat, rugrat, shaver, small fry, sonny, squirt, tad, teenybopper, whelp, whippersnapper

youth *n.* **1.** adolescence, awkward age, boyhood, childhood, early period, girlhood, golden age, halcyon days, hormone years *(Nonformal)*, immaturity, inexperience, innocence, juvenescence, prime, puberty, salad days, teens, younger generation, youthfulness *Youth organizations:* Beavers, Boys and Girls Club of Canada, Boy Scouts, Brownies, Cubs, 4-H Club, Girl Guides, YMCA, YWCA *Antonyms:* adulthood, autumn years, later life, maturity, old age

youthful *adj.* active, adolescent, boyish, budding, buoyant, callow, childish, childlike, enthusiastic, fresh, girlish, green *(Nonformal)*, immature, inexperienced, infantile, innocent, juvenile, keen, new, pubescent, puerile, sophomoric, tender, underage, vernal, vigorous, virginal, young *Antonyms:* adult, aged, ancient, elderly, old *See also:* **young**

yummy *adj.* appetizing, delectable, delicious, flavourful, flavoursome, mouthwatering, savory, scrumptious, tasty, toothsome

Zamboni *(Trademark) n.* flooder, ice cleaner, ice resurfacing machine, ice scraping vehicle, scraper, tractor *(Nonformal)*

zany *adj.* amusing, camp, clownish, comical, crazy, eccentric, foolish, funny, gay, hilarious, inane, jocund, jolly, ludicrous, madcap, merry, mirthful, odd, outlandish, playful, silly *Nonformal:* goofy, kooky, loony, nutty, out there, wacky – *n.* bozo *(Nonformal),* buffoon, clown, comedian, cut-up, fool, gawmoge *(Newfoundland),* jester, simpleton, stooge

zap *v.* **1.** add pizzazz, freshen, invigorate, make lively, revitalize, spice up **2.** channel-hop *(Nonformal),* dart, fast-forward, flash, move, rewind **3.** destroy, erase, kill

zeal *n.* alacrity, ardour, bustle, determination, devotion, diligence, dispatch, drive, eagerness, earnestness, enterprise, enthusiasm, fanaticism, fervour, fierceness, fire, inclination, intensity, mania, passion, perseverance, push, readiness, sincerity, spirit, urgency, vehemence *Antonyms:* indifference, passivity, stoicism

zealot *n.* **1.** aficionado, buff, champion, disciple, enthusiast, extremist, fan, fanatic, maniac, militant, sectarian *Nonformal:* hockey mom, junky, nut **2.** counter-revolutionary, militiaman, partisan, reactionary, revolutionary

zealous *adj.* afire, ardent, avid, burning, dedicated, determined, devoted, earnest, enthusiastic, fanatical, fervent, fervid, frenetic, hot, impassioned, inspired, keen, obsessed, passionate, possessed, rabid, spirited, uncompromising *Nonformal:* card-carrying, fired-up, gung ho *Antonyms*: apathetic, indifferent, lackadaisical, listless, torpid

zenith *n.* **1.** acme, apogee, cap, crown, culmination, height, high point, *ne plus ultra (Latin),* peak, pinnacle, summit, top, vertex *Antonyms:* depths, lowest point, nadir **2.** best, crowning glory, jewel, pearl, perfection, pride, tops *French:* crème de la crème, pièce de résistance

zero *n.* **1.** aught, black hole, blank, cipher, love *(Tennis),* naught, nil, nonentity, nothing, nought, nullity, oblivion, ought, scratch, shutout, void *Nonformal:* big zero, goose egg, nada, nix, zilch, zip **2.** base, bottom, depths, ground zero, lowest point, nadir, rock bottom, seat

zest *n.* **1.** bite, body, charm, flavour, flavouring, ginger, interest, kick, nip, piquancy, pizzazz *(Nonformal),* punch, pungency, relish, salt, savour, seasoning, smack, snap, spice, tang, taste, zap, zip *Antonyms:* tastelessness, vapidity **2.** animation, elation, élan, enjoyment, excitement, exuberance, gusto, heart, *joi de vivre (French),* life, soul, spirit, vitality, vivacity *Antonyms:* enervation, indifference, sangfroid

zesty *adj.* **1.** hot, peppery, peppy, pungent, savory, snippy, spicy, tasty *Antonyms:* bland, boring, tasteless **2.** animated, energetic, frisky, invigorated, lively, vivacious

zing *n.* **1.** energy, liveliness, vigour, vitality, zest **2.** buzz, drill, hum, ping, shrill

zinger *n.* **1.** derision, insult, jeering, mocking *Nonformal:* burn, dis **2.** joke, Parthian shot, punch line, quip, witticism

zither *n.* cithara, cittern, musical strings, stringed instrument *Kinds of zither:* hammered dulcimer, psaltery, switzerharp

zodiac *n.* astrology, charts, horoscope, moonsign, sign, starsign, sunsign *Signs of the Zodiac:* Aquarius (Water bearer), Aries (Ram), Cancer (Crab), Capricorn (Goat), Gemini (Twins), Leo (Lion), Libra (Scales), Pisces (Fish), Sagittarius (Archer), Scorpio (Scorpion), Taurus (Bull), Virgo (Virgin)

zombie *n. duppy (Jamaican),* flesh eater, ghost, ghoul, living *or* walking dead, monster, skeleton, spirit, undead, wraith

zone *n.* area, barrio, belt, community, department, district, division, domain, dominion, field, province, purlieu, quarter, region, section, terrain, territory, tract *Terrestrial Zones:* Antarctic Frigid, Arctic Frigid, North Temperate, South Temperate, Torrid

zonk *interj.* bam, bang, bash, biff, boff, boink, bonk, boom, crack, crash, kaboom, kapow, pop, pow, slam, smack, smash, thwack, whap, whomp, zap

zoo *n.* **1.** animal display *or* exhibit *or* garden, menagerie, park, safari, zoological park **2.** bedlam, chaos, circus, confusion, disarray, fracas, madhouse, pandemonium *Nonformal:* freak show, free-for-all

zoom *v.* **1.** accelerate, bolt, bound, dart, dash, flit, fly, go fast, hasten, hurry, hurtle, make haste, race, run, rush, scramble, scurry, shoot, soar, speed, sprint *Antonyms:* dally, dawdle, meander, piddle **2.** blowup, close in, enlarge, increase, intensify, magnify

Greek and Latin Elements in English

The following list contains a selection of English words, listed alphabetically, each of which is shown with a corresponding combining form, prefix, or suffix of Greek or Latin derivation. The list will prove of great assistance in word study and the enrichment of one's vocabulary, and will give some insight into the origins and general range of meaning of new and unfamiliar words.

COMBINING FORMS

abdomen Gk. coelo-, gastro-; L. ventro-.
agriculture Gk. agro-.
air Gk. aero-; L. aeri-. *See also* BREATH, WIND.
aircraft Gk. aero-.
all Gk. pan-, panto-; L. omni-. *See also* WHOLE.
ancient Gk. archeo-, paleo-.
angle Gk. -gon, gonlo-.
animal Gk. zoo-.
appearance Gk. -opsis.
arm Gk. brachio-.
art Gk. techno-.
artery Gk. arterio-.
back Gk. noto-; L. dorsi-, dorso-.
bad Gk. caco-, dys-; L. mal-. *See also* DIFFICULT.
bag Gk. asco-. *See also* BLADDER, VESSEL.
bare Gk. gymno-; L. nudi-.
beautiful Gk. calli-.
bearing L. -fer, -ferous, -gerous, -parous. *See also* PRODUCING.
bent Gk. ankylo-; L. flexi-. *See also* CURVED.
berry L. bacci-.
berry-shaped Gk. & L. cocci-, -coccus.
big *See* GREAT.
bile Gk. chole-, cholo-.
bird Gk. ornitho-; L. avi-.
birth Gk. toco-; L. nati-. *See also* CHILD.
bitter Gk. picro-.
black Gk. melano-; L. nigri-.
bladder Gk. cysto-; L. vesico-. *See also* BAG, VESSEL.
blind Gk. typhlo-.
blood Gk. -emia (condition or disease), hema-, hemato-; L. sangui-.
bluish Gk. cyano-, glauco-.
body Gk. somato-, -soma, -some.
bone Gk. osteo-; L. ossi-.
book Gk. biblio-.
both Gk. amphi-; L. ambi-.
brain Gk. encephalo-, phreno-; L. cerebro-. *See also* MIND.
brass *See* COPPER.
breast Gk. masto-.
breath Gk. pneumato-; L. Spiro-. *See also* AIR, WIND.
bristle L. seti-.
broad Gk. eury-; L. lati-. *See also* FLAT.
bronze *See* COPPER.
bud Gk. blasto-, -blast; L. gemmi-.
burning *See* FIRE.
carbon L. carbo-, carboni-.
carrying *See* BEARING.
cartilage Gk. chondro-.
carved, carving Gk. glypto-, -glyph.
cattle Gk. tauro-; L. bovi-.
cave Gk. & L. speleo-.
cavity Gk. -cele.
cell Gk. cyto-, -plast.
centre Gk. centro-; L. centri-.
chemical Gk. chemo-.
chest Gk. stetho-.
chief Gk. arch-, archi-.
child Gk. pedo-, toco-.
Chinese L. Sino-.
chlorine Gk. chloro-.
circle Gk. cyclo-, gyro-, -cyclic.
class *See* NATION, ORDER, SPECIES, TYPE.

clear	*See* VISIBLE.
climate	Gk. climato-.
closed	Gk. cleisto-.
cloud	Gk. nepho-.
cold	Gk. cyro-, psychro-.
colon	Gk. colo.-
colour	Gk. chromato-, chromo-, -chrome; L. colori-.
comb	Gk. cteno-.
common	Gk. ceno-.
complete	*See* FINAL.
cone	Gk. cono-.
copper	Gk. chalco-; L. cupro-.
cornea	Gk. kerato-.
corpse	Gk. necro-.
correct	Gk. ortho-.
country	Gk. choro-.
covered	*See* HIDDEN.
craving	Gk. -mania, -maniac.
crest	Gk. lopho-.
cross	Gk. stauro-; L. cruci-.
crystal	Gk. crystallo-.
cup	Gk. scypho-; L. scyphi-.
curly	L. cirro-.
current	Gk. rheo-.
curved	L. curvi-.
custom	Gk. nomo-.
cut	Gk. tomo-, -tomy; L. -sect, -section. *See also* KNIFE, SPLIT.
cyanogen	Gk. cyano-.
cyst	Gk. cysto-.
dance	Gk. choreo-, choro-.
darkness	Gk. scoto-.
death	Gk. thanato-. *See also* CORPSE.
decompose	Gk. sapro-.
deep, depth	Gk. batho-, bathy-.
diaphragm	Gk. phreno-.
different	Gk. hetero-; L. vari-, vario-. *See also* FOREIGN, OTHER.
difficult	Gk. dys-.
disease	Gk. noso-, patho-, -iasis, -osis, -pathy. *See also* PAIN.
dissolving	Gk. lyo-, lysi-, -lysis, -lyte.
divide	*See* CUT, SPLIT.
divining	Gk. -mancy, -mantic.
double	Gk. diplo-.
dream	Gk. oneiro-.
drug	Gk. pharmaco-.
dry	Gk. xero-.
dung	Gk. copro-, scato-; L. sterco-, stercori-.
duodenum	L. duodeno-.
dust	Gk. conio-.
ear	Gk. oto-.
early, earliest	Gk. eo-. *See also* ANCIENT, FIRST, PRIMITIVE.
earth	Gk. geo-; L. terri-.
earthquake	Gk. seismo-.
eat	Gk. phago-, -phage, -phagous, -phagy; L. -vorous. *See also* FOOD, NOURISHMENT.
egg	Gk. oo-; L. ovi-, ovo-.
eight	Gk. & L. octa-, octo-.
electric	Gk. & L. electro-. *See also* CURRENT.
embryo	Gk. embryo-.
end	*See* FINAL.
English	L. Anglo-.
equal	Gk. iso-; L. equi-, pari-. *See also* LIKE, SAME.
existence	Gk. onto-.
external	Gk. ecto-, exo-; L. extra-.
extremity	*See* TIP.
eye	Gk. ophthalmo-, -opia; L. oculo-. *See also* SIGHT.
eyelid	Gk. blepharo-.
false	Gk. pseudo-.
far	Gk. tele-, telo-.
fat, fatty	Gk. lipo-; L. sebi-, sebo-.
father	L. patri-.
fear	Gk. -phobia.
feather	*See* WING.
feed	*See* EAT, NOURISHMENT
female	*See* WOMAN.
fermentation	Gk. zymo-.
fever	L. febri-.
few	Gk. oligo-.
fibrous	L. fibro-.
field	*See* AGRICULTURE.
fight	Gk. -machy.
filament	*See* THREAD.
fin	L. pinni-.
final	Gk. teleo-, telo-.
finger	Gk. dactylo-; L. digiti-.
fire	Gk. pyro-; L. igni-.
first	Gk. proto-; L. primi-.
fish	Gk. ichthyo-; L. pisci-.
five	Gk. penta-; L. quinque-.
flat	Gk. platy-; L. plano-.
flee	L. -fugal, -fuge.
flesh	Gk. sarco-.
flow	Gk. -rrhea, -rrhagia,

	-rrhagic. *See also* CURRENT.
flower	Gk. antho-; L. -florous.
fluorescence	L. fluo-, fluoro-.
fluorine	L. fluo-, fluoro-.
food	Gk. sito-. *See also* EAT, NOURISHMENT.
foot	Gk. -pod, -podous; L. pedi-, -ped, -pede.
fond of	*See* LOVE.
force	*See* POWER.
foreign	Gk. xeno-. *See also* DIFFERENT, OTHER.
foretelling	*See* DIVINING.
form	Gk. morpho-, -morphic, -morphous. *See also* APPEARANCE, IMAGE, LIKE.
four	Gk. tetra-; L. quadri-, quadru-.
French	L. Gallo-.
front, frontal	L. fronto-.
fruit	Gk. carpo-, -carpous.
fungus	Gk. myco-, -mycete; L. fungi-.
gamete	Gk. gameto-.
ganglion	Gk. ganglio-.
gas	Gk. aero-.
genital	L. genito-.
gigantic	Gk. giganto-.
gills	Gk. branchio-, -branch.
gland	Gk. adeno-.
glass	Gk. hyalo-; L. vitri-.
god	Gk. theo-.
gold	Gk. chryso-.
good	Gk. eu-.
govern	Gk. -archy, -cracy, -crat.
grain	L. grani-.
great	Gk. mega-, megalo-; L. magni-. *See also* LARGE, LONG.
Greek	L. Greco-.
green	Gk. chloro-.
grey matter	Gk. polio-.
groin	L. inguino-.
growth	Gk. -plasia; -plasis. *See also* BUD, TUMOR.
hair	Gk. chaeto-, tricho-.
half	Gk. hemi-; L. demi-, semi-.
hand	Gk. chiro-.
hard	Gk. sclero-. *See also* SOLID.
hate	Gk. miso-.
head	Gk. cephalo-, -cephalic, -cephalous. *See also* SKULL.
healing	*See* MEDICINE.
hear	Gk. acous-; L. audio-.
heart	Gk. cardio-.
heat	Gk. thermo-. *See* FIRE.
the heavens	Gk. urano-.
hernia	Gk. -cele; L. hernio-.
hidden	Gk. crypto-.
high, height	Gk. hypso-; L. alti-, alto-.
hollow	*See* CAVITY.
holy	*See* SACRED.
horn	Gk. kerato-.
horse	Gk. hippo-.
hundred	Gk. hecto-; L. centi-.
hysteria	Gk. hystero-.
idea	Gk. ideo-.
ileum	L. ileo-.
image	Gk. icono-.
individual	Gk. idio-.
inflammation	Gk. -itis.
inhabiting	L. -colous.
insect	Gk. entomo-.
interior	Gk. endo-, ento-; L. intra-, intro-.
intestine	Gk. entero-. *See also* COLON, DUODENUM, ILEUM, RECTUM, VISCERA.
iodine	Gk. iodo-.
iris (of eye)	Gk. irido-.
iron	Gk. sidero-; L. ferro-, ferri-.
jaw	Gk. gnatho-, -gnathous.
joint	Gk. arthro-.
kidney	Gk. nephro-; L. reni-.
kill	L. -cidal, -cide.
knife	Gk. -tome.
knowledge of	Gk. -gnomy, -gnosis, -sophy.
large	Gk. macro-. *See also* GREAT, LONG.
larynx	Gk. laryngo-.
law	Gk. nomo-.
lead (metal)	L. plumbo-.
leading	Gk. –agog, -agogue.
leaf, leafy	Gk. phyllo-, -phyllous; L. -folious.
left	L. levo-.
level	*See* FLAT.
life	Gk. bio-, -biosis.
light	Gk. photo-; L. luci-, lumini-; Gk. action- (light ray).
like	Gk. homeo-, homoio-, -oid, -ode; L. quasi-. *See also* APPEARANCE, EQUAL, FORM, SAME.

lime	L. calci-.
lip	Gk. chilo-; L. labio-.
list	Gk. -logy.
little	*See* SMALL.
liver	Gk. hepato-.
lizard	Gk. sauro-.
long	Gk. macro-; L. longi-.
love	Gk. philo-, -phile; -philia, -phily (morbid love).
lung	Gk. pneumo-; L. pulmo-.
lymph	L. lympho-, lymphato-.
magnet	L. magneto-.
making	Gk. -plastic, -poietic. *See also* PRODUCING.
man	Gk. andro-, anthropo-, -androus.
manifestation	Gk. -phany.
many	Gk. poly-, myria- (very many); L. multi-.
marriage	Gk. -gamy.
material, matter	Gk. hylo-, -plasm.
measure	Gk. metro-, -meter, -metry.
medicine	Gk. iatro-, -iatrics, -iatry; L. medico-.
membrane	Gk. hymeno-.
middle	Gk. meso-; L. medio-.
milk	Gk. galacto-; L. lacto-.
mind	Gk. phreno-, psycho-. *See also* SPIRIT.
monster	Gk. terato-.
moon	Gk. seleno-; L. luni-.
mother	L. matri-.
motion pictures	Gk. cine-.
mountain	Gk. oro-.
mouth	Gk. stomato-, -stome, -stomous; L. oro-.
movement	Gk. kinesi-, kineto-, -kinesis.
mucus	L. muco-, muci-. See also SLIMY.
much	*See* MANY.
muscle	Gk. myo-.
myth	Gk. mytho-.
naked	*See* BARE.
narrow	Gk. steno-.
nation	Gk. ethno-. *See also* SPECIES.
nature	Gk. physio-.
near	Gk. para-; L. juxta-.
neck	L. cervico-.
needle	*See* POINT.
nerve	Gk. neuro-.
new	Gk. neo-.
night	Gk. nycto-; L. nocti-.
nine	Gk. ennea-.
nitrogen	Gk. aso-; L. nitro-.
nose	Gk. rhino-; L. naso-.
nourishment	Gk. tropho-, -trophy. *See also* EAT, FOOD.
nucleus	Gk. karyo-; L. nucleo-.
observation	Gk. -scope, -scopy.
oil	L. oleo-.
old age	Gk. geronto-.
one	Gk. mono-; L. uni-.
opening	Gk. -stomy (surgical).
orchid	Gk. orchido-.
order	Gk. -taxis, -taxy.
organ, organic	Gk. organo-.
other	Gk. allo-. *See also* DIFFERENT, FOREIGN.
outside	Gk. ecto-, exo-; L. extra-.
ovary	Gk. gyno-.
oxygen	Gk. oxy-.
pain	Gk. algia, -odynia. *See also* DISEASE, SUFFERING.
pair	Gk. zygo-. *See also* DOUBLE, TWO.
palm	L. palmi-.
paralysis	Gk. -plegia.
part	Gk. mero-, -mere, -merous.
path	*See* WAY.
pelvis	Gk. pyelo-; L. pelvi-.
people	Gk. demo-. *See also* NATION.
perpendicular	*See* UPRIGHT.
pharynx	Gk. pharyngo-.
photography	Gk. photo-.
physics	Gk. physico-.
pillar	Gk. stylo-.
pistil	*See* OVARY.
place	Gk. topo-.
plant	Gk. phyto-, -phyte.
plate	*See* SCALE.
pleura	Gk. pleuro-.
point	L. acu-. *See also* SPINY.
poison	Gk. toxico-.
position	Gk. stato-.
power	Gk. dyna-, dynamo-.
pressure	Gk. piezo-, baro- (atmospheric pressure)
primitive	Gk. archi-.
producing	Gk. –gen, -genous, -geny, -gony. *See also* BEARING, MAKING.
pulse	Gk. sphygmo-.

pus Gk. pyo-.
race *See* NATION, SPECIES.
radiant energy L. radio-.
radiate Gk. actino-.
radio L. radio-.
radioactive L. radio-.
rain Gk. hyeto-, ombro-; L. pluvio-.
ray *See* LIGHT.
recent Gk. -cene (geology and anthropology).
rectum Gk. procto-; L. recto-.
red Gk. erythro-.
region *See* COUNTRY, PLACE.
reproduction Gk. gono-.
rib L. costo-.
right L. dextro-.
river L. fluvio-.
rock *See* STONE.
root Gk. rhizo-.
rot *See* DECOMPOSE.
rough Gk. trachy-.
row Gk. stichous.
rule *See* GOVERN.
run Gk. -drome, -dromous.
sacred Gk. hagio-, hiero-.
sacrum L. sacro-.
salt Gk. halo-.
same Gk. homo-, tauto-. *See also* EQUAL, LIKE.
scale Gk. lepido-; L. lamelli-.
science of Gk. -logy, -logical, -nomy.
sea Gk. halo-, thalasso-.
seaweed Gk. phyco-.
second (adj.) Gk. deutero-.
seed Gk. spermato-, -gonium, -sperm, -spermous. *See also* SPORE.
seizure Gk. -lepsy.
self Gk. auto-.
serum L. sero-.
seven Gk. hepta-; L. septi-.
sewing Gk. -rrhaphy (surgical).
sexual union Gk. gamo-.
sharp Gk. oxy-.
short Gk. brachy-; L. brevi-.
side Gk. pleuro-, -hedral, -hedron (geometry).
sight Gk. -opia, -opsia.
silicon L. silico-.
simple Gk. haplo-; L. simplici-.
single Gk. haplo-.
six Gk. hexa-; L. sex-.
skin Gk. dermato-, dermo-, -derm.
skull Gk. cranio-.
sleep Gk. hypno-; L. somni-.
slender Gk. lepto-.
slimy Gk. myxo-.
slope Gk. clino-, -cline (geology).
slow Gk. brady-.
small Gk. micro-. *See also* FEW.
snake Gk. ophio-.
society L. socio-.
soft Gk. malaco-.
solid Gk. stereo-.
sound Gk. phono-, -phone, -phony.
speech Gk. logo-, -phasia (defective).
species Gk. phylo-.
spectrum L. spectro-.
spermatozoa Gk. spermato-.
sphere Gk. -sphere.
spinal cord Gk. myelo-.
spiny Gk. acantho-, echino-; L. spini-.
spiral Gk. helico-, spiro-.
spirit Gk. pneumato-, psycho-. *See also* MIND.
spleen Gk. speno-.
split Gk. schisto-, schizo-; L. fissi-, -fid.
spore Gk. sporo-, -sporous.
sprout *See* BUD.
stamen Gk. andro-; L. stamini-.
star Gk. aster-, astro-; L. sidero- stelli-.
starch Gk. amylo-.
stomach Gk. gastero-, gastro-.
stone Gk. litho-, petro-, -lith.
stop Gk. -stat.
straight Gk. ortho-; L. recti-.
strange *See* FOREIGN.
style Gk. stylo- (biology).
substitute L. vice-.
suffering Gk. patho-, -pathy.
sugar Gk. saccharo-.
sulfur Gk. thio-; L. sulfa-, sulfo-.
sun Gk. helio-.
sweet Gk. glyco-.
swift Gk. tachy-.
sword Gk. xiphi-.
tail Gk. uro-.
technical Gk. techno-.
ten Gk. deca-.

a tenth	L. deci-.
terrible	Gk. dino-.
testicle	Gk. orchio-.
thick	Gk. pachy-.
thorax	Gk. thoraco-.
thorny	*See* SPINY.
thousand, thousandth	L. milli-.
thread	Gk. nemato-.
three	L. ter-, tri-.
throat	*See* LARYNX, PHARYNX, TRACHEA.
thyroid	Gk. thyro-.
time	Gk. chrono-.
tip	Gk. acro-.
tissue	Gk. histo-.
toe	*See* FINGER.
tone	Gk. tono-.
tongue	Gk. glosso-.
tooth	Gk. odonto-, -odont; L. denti-.
top	*See* TIP.
torpor	Gk. narco-.
trachea	Gk. broncho-, traeheo-.
tree	Gk. dendro-, -dendron; L. arbori-.
tribe	*See* SPECIES.
tumour	Gk. -cele, -oma.
turned	Gk. -tropous, -tropy.
twelve	Gk. dodeca-.
two	Gk. dl-; L. bi-, duo-.
type	Gk. typo-.
united	Gk. gamo-.
universe	Gk. cosmo-.
upright	Gk. ortho-.
urethra	Gk. urethro-.
urine	Gk. uro-, -uria; L. urino-.
uterus	Gk. hystero-, metro-; L. utero-.
vagina	L. vagino-.
vapour	Gk. atmo-; L. vapori-.
vein	Gk. phlebo-; L. veni-.
vessel	Gk. angio-; L. vaso-. *See also* BAG, BLADDER, CUP.
viscera	Gk. splanchno-.
visible	Gk. phanero-.
voice	*See* SOUND.
walking	L. -grade.
water	Gk. hydro-; L. aqui-.
wave	Gk. cymo-.
wax	Gk. cero-.
way	Gk. hodo-, odo-, -ode.
web	L. pinni-.
wealth	Gk. pluto-.
wedge	Gk. spheno-.
weight	Gk. baro-.
wet	Gk. hygro-.
white	Gk. leuko-.
whole	Gk. holo-; L. toti-.
wide	*See* BROAD.
wind	Gk. anemo-. *See also* AIR, BREATH.
wine	L. vini-.
wing	Gk. ptero-, -pterous; L. -pennate.
woman	Gk. gyneco-, gyno-.
(a) wonder	Gk. thaumato-.
wood	Gk. xylo-; L. ligni-.
word	Gk. logo-.
work	Gk. ergo-.
world	*See* UNIVERSE.
worm	L. vermi-.
write	Gk. grapho-, -gram, -graph, -graphy.
yellow	Gk. xantho-.
yoke	Gk. zygo-.

PREFIXES

about	*See* AROUND.
above	Gk. hyper-; L. super-, supra-. *See also* ON.
across	L. trans-. *See also* THROUGH.
after	Gk. meta-; L. post-.
again	Gk. ana-; L. re-. *See also* BACK.
against	Gk. anti-; L. contra-, in- (il-, im-, ir-), ob- (oc-, of-, op-).
among	*See* BETWEEN, WITHIN.
apart	L. dis- (di-), se-. *See also* AWAY, FROM.
around	Gk. peri-; L. circum-.
at	*See* BESIDE, NEAR, TO.
away	Gk. apo-. *See also* APART, FROM.
back	L. retro-. *See also* AGAIN.
badly	L. mal-, mis-.
before	Gk. pro-; L. ante-, pre-.
behind	*See* AFTER.
beside	Gk. para-; L. juxta-.
between	L. inter-.
beyond	Gk. meta-; L. preter-, ultra
changed	Gk. meta-.
down	Gk. cata- (cath-); L. de-.
excessively	*See* ABOVE.
for	L. pro-.